SHORT STORY INDEX

1984–1988

PERMANENT CUMULATIONS

1900–1949
1950–1954
1955–1958
1959–1963
1964–1968
1969–1973
1974–1978
1979–1983

SHORT STORY INDEX

1984–1988

AN INDEX TO STORIES IN
COLLECTIONS AND PERIODICALS

Edited by

JULIETTE YAAKOV

NEW YORK
THE H.W. WILSON COMPANY
1989

Copyright © 1989 by The H. W. Wilson Company. All rights reserved. No part of this work may be reproduced or copied in any form or by any means, including but not restricted to graphic, electronic, or mechanical—for example, photocopying, recording, taping, or information storage and retrieval systems—without the express written permission of the Publisher.

ISSN 0360-9774

Library of Congress Catalog Card Number 75-649762

Printed in the United States of America

016.808831
S559
1984-88

PREFACE

This cumulation of *Short Story Index* covers short stories published in collections and selected periodicals from 1984–1988. Short stories in periodicals included in this volume are indexed in two other Wilson publications: *Readers' Guide to Periodical Literature* and *Humanities Index*.

Over the past four years there has been a marked resurgence in short story publishing which is reflected in the increased number of collections analyzed. The present volume indexes 22,431 stories; of these, 19,579 stories appeared in 1,221 collections and 2,852 appeared in 84 periodicals. Beginning with this cumulation, authors' names are entered according to AACR2 practice. As in previous volumes, the arrangement is alphabetical by author, title, and subject. The author entry, which mentions the collection or periodical where the story can be found, is the most complete entry. The stories in periodicals are indexed only by author and title. A List of Collections Indexed, a Directory of Publishers and Distributors, and a Directory of Periodicals complete the volume. This index is published annually and a cumulative volume is issued every five years.

The H. W. Wilson Company is grateful to those publishers who provided copies of their books for indexing.

CONTENTS

Preface v

Directions for Use viii

Part I. Index to Short Stories 1

Part II. List of Collections Indexed 1083

Part III. Directory of Publishers and Distributors 1183

Part IV. Directory of Periodicals 1193

DIRECTIONS FOR USE

Part I, Index to Short Stories, is arranged in dictionary form with author, title, and subject entries in one alphabet. Part II is a List of Collections Indexed. Part III is a Directory of Publishers and Distributors. Part IV is a Directory of Periodicals. The following directions apply to Part I:

Author entry. This entry gives the name of the author and title of the story. For stories found in collections, information provided includes title and editor of the collected work. For stories found in periodicals the periodical title, volume number, pagination, and date are included.

Sample entry from a collection:

> **Lessing, Doris May, 1919-**
> The habit of loving
> The Art of the tale; ed. by D. Halpern

The above example shows that the story by Doris May Lessing, "The habit of loving," appears in the collection *The Art of the tale,* which is edited by D. Halpern. For fuller information about the book consult the List of Collections Indexed.

Sample entry from a periodical:

> **Tyler, Anne, 1941-**
> Rerun
> *The New Yorker* 64:20-32 Jl 4 '88

The above entry indicates that the story by Anne Tyler, "Rerun," appears in *The New Yorker,* volume 64, pages 20-32 in the July 4, 1988 issue. For fuller information about the periodical consult the Directory of Periodicals.

Title entry. This entry is used to identify the author under whose name the source of the story will be found. The first word (not an article) of each title is in boldface type.

Sample entries:

> The **habit** of loving. Lessing, D. M.
> **Rerun.** Tyler, A.

Subject entry. Stories found in collections, which deal in whole or in part with a particular subject, are listed under that subject. Such entries are in capital letters, in boldface type. Consult the author entry for the title of the story collection.

Sample entry:

> **MARRIAGE PROBLEMS**
> Lessing, D. M. The habit of loving

SHORT STORY INDEX, 1984–1988

PART 1

Author, Title, and Subject Index

.240, lifetime. Hildebidle, J.
1/3, 1/3, 1/3. Brautigan, R.
$1.98. Porges, A.
1 to 999. Asimov, I.
5 1/2 Charlotte Mews. Livia, A.
The 23 brown paper bags. Ritchie, J.
25 August 1983. Borges, J. L.
37 years. Franzen, B.
A 50-50 marriage. Abbott, K.
99.6. West, J.
$100 and nothing! Cooper, J. C.
110 West Sixty-First Street. Barthelme, D.
400 boys. Laidlaw, M.
The 545 pound boy. Millman, L.
1,000 unknown facts about country music. Porterfield, N.
1-800-YOUR BOY. Dickinson, C.
1928 story. Agee, J.
1934. Phillips, J. A.
1954: days of the roomers. Stead, C.
A 1957 Ford. Abbott, K.
1975 has come and gone. Drake, R.
2020 A.D. Wolfe, T.
2066: Election Day. Shaara, M.
2072 days. Nowakowski, M.
3,000 years among the microbes. Twain, M.
The $5,000 getaway. Ritchie, J.
The $2,000,000 defense. Masur, H. Q.
197903042100 (Sunday). Bradley, D.

A

A, B, C, D, E, F, G, H, I, J, K, L, M, N, O, P, Q, R, S, T, U, V, W, X, Y, Z. Bail, M.
A la carte. Archer, J.
An a posteriori ghost. Piñera, V.
A. V. Laider. Beerbohm, M.
Aaron makes a match. Stern, S.

ABANDONED CHILDREN
  See also Orphans
DeMarinis, R. Your story
Godshalk, C. S. Wonderland
Goyen, W. Pore Perrie
Keillor, G. David and Agnes, a romance
Takahashi, T. A happy home
The abandoned path. Nagibin, ÍŨ. M.

ABANDONED TOWNS *See* Cities and towns, Ruined, extinct, etc.
ABANDONMENT OF FAMILY *See* Desertion and nonsupport
Abaza, Sarwat
Swimming in the sand
  Egyptian tales and short stories of the 1970s and 1980s
Abbasi, Talat
Going to Baltistan
  The Massachusetts Review 29:633-6 Wint '88/'89
ABBESSES *See* Nuns
Abbey, Edward, 1927-
Black sun [excerpt]
  The Interior country; ed. by A. Blackburn
ABBEYS
  See also Cathedrals; Churches; Convent life; Monasticism and religious orders
ABBOTT, GREGORY
                   Flatland
Rucker, R. von B. Message found in a copy of Flatland
Abbott, Keith
A 50-50 marriage
  Abbott, K. Harum scarum
A 1957 Ford
  Abbott, K. The first thing coming
Back to nature
  Abbott, K. Harum scarum
Blood, binoculars, and a blizzard
  Abbott, K. The first thing coming
A can of smoked oysters
  Abbott, K. The first thing coming
The commercial break
  Abbott, K. The first thing coming
Crème de la crème
  Abbott, K. The first thing coming
The first thing coming
  Abbott, K. The first thing coming
The fort
  Abbott, K. The first thing coming
The ghost of the senior banquet
  Abbott, K. The first thing coming
Harum scarum
  Abbott, K. Harum scarum

Abbott, Keith—*Continued*
He was reaching for a shovel
  Abbott, K. The first thing coming
Jesus Christ and the plaster squirrels
  Abbott, K. The first thing coming
Like you used to do
  Abbott, K. The first thing coming
A little surprise
  Abbott, K. The first thing coming
Logger Linkhorn's 1928 Buick
  Abbott, K. Harum scarum
Mary Lou and the perfect husband
  Abbott, K. The first thing coming
Out on the res
  Abbott, K. The first thing coming
Over and under
  Abbott, K. The first thing coming
Rick's first visit to the A & W
  Abbott, K. The first thing coming
The sea lion
  Abbott, K. The first thing coming
The second Pete
  Abbott, K. The first thing coming
Spanish Castle
  Abbott, K. The first thing coming
Tell the truth
  Abbott, K. The first thing coming
We have another ape
  Abbott, K. The first thing coming
When this van is rockin' don't bother knockin'
  Abbott, K. Harum scarum
Yellow rock
  Abbott, K. The first thing coming
You can't miss it
  Abbott, K. Harum scarum

Abbott, Lee K.
Be free, die young
  Abbott, L. K. Love is the crooked thing
The beauties of drink: an essay
  Abbott, L. K. Strangers in paradise
Category Z
  Abbott, L. K. Strangers in paradise
  The Atlantic 256:68-72 D '85
Dreams of distant lives
  The Best American short stories, 1987
  Harper's 273:66-8 N '86
Driving his Buick home
  The North American Review 273:25-9 Mr '88
The eldest of things
  Abbott, L. K. Love is the crooked thing
The end of grief
  Abbott, L. K. Strangers in paradise
  The Atlantic 256:69-74 Ag '85
The final proof of fate and circumstance
  Abbott, L. K. Love is the crooked thing
  The Best American short stories, 1984
  The Georgia Review 40:9-18 Spr '86
  Necessary fictions; ed. by S. W. Lindberg and S. Corey
Having the human thing of joy
  Abbott, L. K. Love is the crooked thing

Here in time and not
  The Georgia Review 42:569-80 Fall '88
I'm glad you asked
  Abbott, L. K. Strangers in paradise
Living alone in Iota
  Abbott, L. K. Strangers in paradise
  Prize stories, 1984
Love is the crooked thing
  Abbott, L. K. Love is the crooked thing
Martians [Variant title: The other world I see]
  Abbott, L. K. Love is the crooked thing
A modern story of Woe and Lovecraft
  A Collection of classic Southern humor; ed. by G. W. Koon
Notes I made on the man I was
  Abbott, L. K. Strangers in paradise
Once upon a time
  The Georgia Review 41:385-93 Summ '87
The other world I see
  The North American Review 270:41-3 Mr '85
The purpose of this creature man
  Abbott, L. K. Love is the crooked thing
Revolutionaries
  The Atlantic 259:62-8 F '87
Rolling thunder
  Abbott, L. K. Strangers in paradise
Stand in a row and learn
  Abbott, L. K. Love is the crooked thing
Time and fear and somehow love
  Abbott, L. K. Strangers in paradise
  The Editors' choice v3; ed. by G. E. Murphy, Jr.
  The Georgia Review 39:7-22 Spr '85
The unfinished business of childhood
  Abbott, L. K. Love is the crooked thing
The valley of sin
  Abbott, L. K. Strangers in paradise
The view of me from Mars
  Harper's 276:63-6 Je '88
We get smashed and our endings are swift
  Abbott, L. K. Love is the crooked thing
When our dream world finds us, and these hard times are gone
  Abbott, L. K. Love is the crooked thing
Where is Garland Steeples now?
  Abbott, L. K. Strangers in paradise
The world is almost rotten
  Abbott, L. K. Strangers in paradise
The world of apples
  Abbott, L. K. Strangers in paradise
X
  Abbott, L. K. Strangers in paradise
  The Georgia Review 39:785-805 Wint '85
  The Pushcart prize XI
Youth on Mars
  Abbott, L. K. Strangers in paradise
ABC. Maheux-Forcier, L.
ABC. Proulx, M.
Abd al-Salam al-Ujayli *See* Al-Ujayli, Abd al-Salam

ABDUCTION *See* Kidnapping
The **abduction**. Oates, J. C.
Abdullah and Mariam. Thomas, M.
Abe, Akira, 1934-
Friends
The Shōwa anthology 2
Abe, Kōbō, 1924-
The dream soldier
Murder in Japan; ed. by J. L. Apostolou and M. H. Greenberg
The flood
A Late chrysanthemum; tr. by L. Dunlop
The magic chalk
The Shōwa anthology 1
The red cocoon
Harper's 274:34-5 Ja '87
A Late chrysanthemum; tr. by L. Dunlop
Song of a dead girl
The Mother of dreams, and other short stories; ed. by M. Ueda
The stick
A Late chrysanthemum; tr. by L. Dunlop
Abernathy, Robert
Heirs apparent
Beyond Armageddon; ed. by W. M. Miller and M. H. Greenberg
Abid, Abdullah
Our fighting cock
Modern Syrian short stories; ed. by M. G. Azrak
Abish, Walter
Happiness
New directions in prose and poetry 50
Able, Baker, Charlie, Dog. Vaughn, S.
The **ablution**. al-Rahib, H.
ABNORMALITIES AND DEFORMITIES
See Deformities; Dwarfs; Face—Abnormalities and deformities; Monsters
A:B:O.. De la Mare, W.
Aboard the cart. Palma, C.
ABOLITIONISTS
See also Slavery
ABORIGINES, AUSTRALIAN *See* Australian aborigines
ABORTION
Baykurt, F. Jeyfo
Colette. Gribiche
Crabtree, L. V. Holy Spirit
Dorr, L. Two hundred yards past Wordsworth's house
Dubus, A. Miranda over the valley
Ferguson, P. The products of conception
Finger, A. Abortion
Floyd, P. L. The voice in the whirlwind
Hemingway, E. Hills like white elephants
Hempel, A. Beg, sl tog, inc, cont, rep
Kim, S.-O. Operation
Marshall, O. Don't blame yourself at all
Moyer, K. Ruth's daughter
O'Hara, J. Zero

Sandel, C. Thank you, doctor
Spivack, K. Terms
Tremain, R. Words with Marigold
Verma, N. The difference
Viramontes, H. M. Birthday
Walker, A. The abortion
West, J. The day of the hawk
Wicomb, Z. You can't get lost in Cape Town
Zahn, T. The final report on the lifeline experiment
Abortion. Finger, A.
The **abortion**. Walker, A.
About all kinds of ships. Twain, M.
About Boston. Just, W. S.
About fame. Gullard, P.
About love and money; or, Love's lore and money's myth. Cooper, J. C.
About the house. Stead, C.
About the sea. Rose, D. A.
Abraham Lincoln's clue. Queen, E.
Abrahams, Lionel
Invisible worm
Echad 2: South African Jewish voices
Knowledge
Echad 2: South African Jewish voices
The moment
Echad 2: South African Jewish voices
Abrahams, Peter
Crackling day
Somehow tenderness survives; ed. by H. Rochman
Lonesome
The Penguin book of Southern African stories
Abramov, Fyodor, 1920-1983
Olesha's cabin
The Barsukov Triangle, The two-toned blond & other stories; ed. by C. R. Proffer & E. Proffer
Abramowitsch, Solomon Jacob *See* Mendele Mokher Seforim, 1835?-1917
Abrams, Linsey
Secrets men keep
The Editors' choice v3; ed. by G. E. Murphy, Jr.
Mademoiselle 91:144+ Ag '85
Abrams, Rachel
School days
Commentary 86:44-8 Jl '88
Abroad. Gordimer, N.
Abromowitz, S. I. *See* Mendele Mokher Seforim, 1835?-1917
Abrons, Richard
The best of both worlds
The North American Review 271:37-41 D '86
The **abrupt** edge. Lynch, L.
Absence and echo. Josipovici, G.
An **absence** of cousins. Segal, L. G.
Absence of mercy. Stone, R.
Absent friends. Sladek, J. T.
The **absent** toy. McLaughlin, L.

The **absolutely** ordinary family. Taylor, A.
Absolution. Callaghan, M.
An **abstract** concept. Landolfi, T.
Abundance. Dickinson, C.
ABUSED WIVES *See* Wife abuse
The **abyss**. Andreyev, L.
ABYSSINIA *See* Ethiopia
The **academy**. Ely, D.
The **accent**. Maupassant, G. de
The **accent** of a coming foot. Williams, T.
Accents. Stead, C.
Accepted wisdom. McGraw, E.
An **accident**. Martone, M.
Accident. Oates, J. C.
Accident. Shannon, D.
An **accident**. See Shiga, N. An incident
Accident. Whitaker, M.
An **accident** at "The Palace of Happiness".
al-Siba'i, F.
ACCIDENTAL DEATH *See* Accidents
The **accidental** trip to Jamaica. Osborn, C.
ACCIDENTS
  See also Airplane accidents; Drowning; Fires; Hunting accidents; Industrial accidents; Mine accidents; Railroad accidents; Shipwrecks and castaways; Traffic accidents
al-Siba'i, F. An accident at "The Palace of Happiness"
Atwood, M. Two stories about Emma: The whirlpool rapids
Atwood, M. The whirlpool rapids
Banks, R. Success story
Barstow, S. The pity of it all
Bates, H. E. Summer in Salandar
Bausch, R. Wise men at their end
Biggs, M. The other Catherine Irene
Bitov, A. The leg
Böll, H. Lohengrin's death
Bonner, M. The whipping
Bowles, P. Rumor and a ladder
Brender à Brandis, M. To grow into a man
Cameron, E. The last visit
Campbell, E. Piranesi's dream
Cinca, S. The wedding
Conroy, J. Down in Happy Hollow
Corrington, J. W. Heroic measures/vital signs
Davis, L. The bone
Dixon, S. The rescuer
Fairman, P. W. The cosmic frame
Fleming, B. Happy New Year, Mr. Ganaway
García Márquez, G. Nabo: the black man who made the angels wait
Gardam, J. Benevolence
Gardner, J. Redemption
Gilchrist, E. Miss Crystal's maid name Traceleen, she's talking, she's telling everything she knows
Gordon, C. The brilliant leaves
Greenberg, A. Closed Mondays

Greene, G. The basement room
Greene, G. A shocking accident
Hartley, L. P. Paradise Paddock
Hartley, L. P. Someone in the lift
Haslam, G. W. Trophies
Hood, M. Moths
Hospital, J. T. Golden girl
Houbein, L. The basement of happiness
Hughes, J. An open house
Humphrey, W. Man with a family
Kawabata, Y. Glass
Kessler, J. F. A Theban ostrakon
Kinsella, W. P. Panache
Körner, W. Bleep, crash, zap, wow: accidents in the Ruhr
Le Guin, U. K. Buffalo gals, won't you come out tonight
Lee, H. Down the hole
Lieber, T. Country things
Maupassant, G. de. A costly outing
Nimmo, D. The healing
O'Hara, J. Flight
Olmstead, R. In this life
Osborn, C. The accidental trip to Jamaica
Pascoe, B. Splitter
Power, V. An eye for an eye
Quiroga, H. The dead man
Reynolds, M. Prone
Rifaat, A. Mansoura
Rose, D. A. About the sea
Sallis, J. Miranda-Escobedo
Sandberg, P. L. Gabe's fall
Sanders, S. R. Fetching the dead
Sanford, W. M. Luck
Schinto, J. The motorcycle riders
Shiga, N. An incident
Silvis, R. Trash man
Skrzynecki, P. The chainsaw incident
St. Pierre, P. H. Dry storm
Strand, M. Two stories
Su Ye. Scatterbrain
Terry, W. S. The bottomless well
Thomas, J. Talma Levy is falling
Tinkham, B. Doppelganger
Tuohy, F. Fingers in the door
Vizyēnos, G. M. My mother's sin
Warner, S. T. The mahogany table
Whitaker, M. Accident
Wilson, A. Paul's eyes
Wilson, B. Disaster
Wright, D. L. The hawk
Yamamoto, M. Powers
Ziem, J. Payday
ACCIDENTS, INDUSTRIAL *See* Industrial accidents
Accidents. La Chapelle, M.
Accidents. Thompson, J.
Accidents will happen. McWey, M.
Accommodation vacant. Fremlin, C.
The **accompanist**. Colette
Accompanists. Davie, E.
According to scientific data. Bakhnov, V.
The **accordion** player. Berger, J.

ACCORDIONISTS
Taylor, R. Lady of Spain
The **accountant**. Sheckley, R.

ACCOUNTANTS
Austin, D. And now he was beginning to feel uneasy about the weather
Barker, C. Confessions of a (pornographer's) shroud
Block, L. The books always balance
Ch'en, Y.-C. One day in the life of a white-collar worker
Friedman, B. J. The tax man
Gilbert, M. Audited and found correct
Gilliatt, P. Suspense item
Highsmith, P. The button
Maupassant, G. de. A little walk
Sheckley, R. The accountant
The **accounting**. Schwartz, L. S.
Accounts receivable: I am Brian. Bailey, R.

ACCULTURATION
See also Race relations
Prichard, K. S. Flight
The **accursed** bread. Maupassant, G. de
The **accuser** and the accused. Singer, I. B.
Ace. Oates, J. C.
Ace in the hole. Cameron, E.
Ace in the hole. Pronzini, B.

Achebe, Chinua, 1930-
Civil peace
African short stories; ed. by C. Achebe and C. L. Innes
African short stories in English; ed. by J. de Grandsaigne
The sacrificial egg
The Art of the tale; ed. by D. Halpern
Acheron. Pacheco, J. E.
Acid rain. Claiborne, S.

Aćin-Kosta, Miloš
Arbeit macht Frei
Aćin-Kosta, M. Tales of socialist Yugoslavia
Boulevard of the revolution
Aćin-Kosta, M. Tales of socialist Yugoslavia
Dam on crutches
Aćin-Kosta, M. Tales of socialist Yugoslavia
In the spirit of socialism
Aćin-Kosta, M. Tales of socialist Yugoslavia
The privileged class
Aćin-Kosta, M. Tales of socialist Yugoslavia
A psychological warrior
Aćin-Kosta, M. Tales of socialist Yugoslavia
The rape
Aćin-Kosta, M. Tales of socialist Yugoslavia
Rassim
Aćin-Kosta, M. Tales of socialist Yugoslavia

The red bread
Aćin-Kosta, M. Tales of socialist Yugoslavia
Spring flower
Aćin-Kosta, M. Tales of socialist Yugoslavia
Yugoslavia revisited
Aćin-Kosta, M. Tales of socialist Yugoslavia

Acker, Kathy, 1948-
Male
Between C & D; ed. by J. Rose and C. Texier
Ackerman, Felicia
The forecasting game
Commentary 86:49-56 D '88
Ackerman, Joanne Leedom- *See* Leedom-Ackerman, Joanne, 1948-
Acolytes. Woods, C.
Acorns. McQueen, J.
Acosta, Luis Alberto
A color television
Américas 39:47-9 Jl/Ag '87
Acquainted with the night. Schwartz, L. S.
Acquiring point of view. Taylor, P. E.

ACROBATS
See also Stunt men
Clifford, F. Turn and turn about
Colette. Moments of stress
Garrett, G. P. An evening performance
The **acrobat's** grave. Livesey, M.
Across a crowded room. Pym, B.
Across from the Motoheads. Whisnant, L.
Across the bridge. Böll, H.
Across the bridge. Greene, G.
Across the street. MacLaverty, B.
Across those endless skies. Frazier, R.
Act of faith. Shaw, I.
Act of honor. Morrill, G. P.
An **act** of pity. Blais, M.-C.
Act of rage. Hayes, J. A.
The **Actæon** case. Piñera, V.
The **actes** and monuments. Corrington, J. W.
Action will be taken. Böll, H.

ACTIONS AND DEFENSES
Ciment, J. Small claims
Activity time. Dickens, M.
The **actor**. Bergner, H.
The **actor**. Ruta, S.

ACTORS
See also Motion picture actors and actresses; Theater life
Bergner, H. The actor
Bishop, M. Saving face
Bloch, R. In the cards
Bloch, R. The movie people
Bloch, R. The play's the thing
Bloch, R. Show biz
Bloch, R. The show must go on
Bloch, R. Sock finish
Bloch, R. Underground
Bloch, R. Untouchable
Botwinik, B. Jake

ACTORS—*Continued*
  Boyd, W. Not yet Jayette
  Breen, J. L. Starstruck
  Brown, F. Good night, good knight
  Colette. The starveling
  Coriolan, J. Interview in the number two
      dressing-room
  Crane, S. Manacled
  Davis, D. S. Sweet William
  Doyle, Sir A. C. The tragedians
  Ellison, H. All the sounds of fear
  Forsh, O. Ham's wife
  Fraser, A. On the battlements
  Gallant, M. Baum, Gabriel, 1935-( )
  Galsworthy, J. The broken boot
  Garrett, G. P. What's the matter with
      Mary Jane?
  Halligan, M. The porch of Paradise
  Highsmith, P. Chris's last party
  Kees, W. Do you like the mountains?
  Monreal, D. N. Faces
  Mrożek, S. Tiny
  Murphy, P. The Santa class test
  Petrakis, H. M. The castle
  Queen, E. The death of Don Juan
  Raphael, F. You don't remember me
  Reaves, J. M. Werewind
  Robinson, K. S. The disguise
  Ruta, S. The actor
  Soukup, M. Dress rehearsal
  Tabucchi, A. Theatre
  Taylor, R. Billy Gashade and glory
  Taylor, R. The James boys ride again
  Tremain, R. My love affair with James
      I
  Updike, J. One more interview
  Washburn, L. J. On the prod
  Williams, T. The vine
  Wolfe, T. In the park
  Wolfe, T. The winter of our discontent
  Yourcenar, M. A lovely morning

ACTRESSES
        See also Motion picture actors and
      actresses; Theater life
  Alcott, L. M. A double tragedy. An actor's
      story
  Ardizzone, T. The transplant
  Baumbach, J. The errant melancholy of
      twilight
  Bloch, R. Betsy Blake will live forever
  Bloch, R. Terror over Hollywood
  Bloch, R. The unpardonable crime
  Cather, W. Coming, Aphrodite!
  Cohen, M. At the Empress Hotel
  Coleman, W. A war of eyes
  Colette. The victim
  Dawson, F. Mary will be good for Warren
  Etchison, D., and Johnson, M. The spot
  Garrett, G. P. What's the matter with
      Mary Jane?
  Gilbert, W. S. Comedy and tragedy
  Gilliatt, P. Dame of the British Empire,
      BBC

  Henderson, M. R. Dream house
  Henry, O. The memento
  Henry, O. The rathskeller and the rose
  Hoffmann, E. T. A. Don Juan
  James, H. Nona Vincent
  Kawabata, Y. Faces
  Kress, N. With the original cast
  Maupassant, G. de. An honest deal
  Moore, G. Under the fan
  Mori, Y. Spring storm
  Mortimer, J. C. Rumpole and the show-
      folk
  O'Hara, J. Can I stay here?
  Osborn, C. Dreamer when last seen
  Rhys, J. Before the deluge
  Rhys, J. Overture and beginners please
  Stone, R. Not for love
  Turgenev, I. S. Clara Militch
  Valenzuela, L. Fourth version
  Warren, J. The Corn Dolly
  Wolfe, G. Seven American nights
Acts of love. Nelson, K.
Acts of merit. Gohorry, J.
Adada the idiot. Kye, Y.-M.
Adagio. Longyear, B. B.
ADAM (BIBLICAL FIGURE)
                   About
  Tournier, M. The Adam family
Adam. See Böll, H. And where were you,
      Adam?
The **Adam** family. Tournier, M.
Adam Link's vengeance. Binder, E.
Adam, one afternoon. Calvino, I.
Adamidou, Irena Ioannidou *See* Ioannidou
      Adamidou, Irena
Adams, Alice, 1926-
  Against all odds
    Redbook 165:52+ Ag '85
  Alaska
    Adams, A. Return trips
    The Editors' choice: new American
      stories v1
    Prize stories, 1984
    Shenandoah: an anthology; ed. by J.
      Boatwright
  Barcelona
    Adams, A. Return trips
    The New Yorker 60:42-3 F 27 '84
  The drinking club
    The New Yorker 63:28-34 Ag 31 '87
  Elizabeth
    Adams, A. Return trips
  A legendary lover
    McCall's 112:90 N '84
  Mexican dust
    Adams, A. Return trips
  Molly's dog
    Adams, A. Return trips
    Prize stories, 1986
    The Pushcart prize XI
  My first and only house
    Adams, A. Return trips

Adams, Alice, 1926—— *Continued*
New best friends
  Adams, A. Return trips
The oasis
  The Best of the West; ed. by J. Thomas
  The Graywolf annual 2
Ocracoke Island
  The Paris Review 29:136-48 Spr '87
  Prize stories, 1988
A public pool
  Adams, A. Return trips
Return trips
  Adams, A. Return trips
  The New Yorker 59:26-35 Ja 2 '84
La Señora
  Adams, A. Return trips
Separate planes
  Adams, A. Return trips
  The New Yorker 60:40-2 O 8 '84
Sintra
  Adams, A. Return trips
  New American short stories; ed. by G.
    Norris
Tide pools
  The New Yorker 61:38-46 D 16 '85
  Prize stories, 1987
Time alone
  The New Yorker 62:28-36 Ag 4 '86
Time in Santa Fe
  Adams, A. Return trips
  The Graywolf annual [1]
Waiting for Stella
  Adams, A. Return trips
You are what you own: a notebook
  Adams, A. Return trips
Adams, Cleve Franklin, 1895-1949
Flowers for Violet
  Hard-boiled dames; ed. by B. A. Drew
Adams, Gail Galloway
Alice remembers
  Adams, G. G. The purchase of order
Bow wow and good-bye
  Adams, G. G. The purchase of order
The Christmas house
  Adams, G. G. The purchase of order
Doing yoga
  Adams, G. G. The purchase of order
Houdini's wife
  Adams, G. G. The purchase of order
Inside dope
  Adams, G. G. The purchase of order
  The Editors' choice v4; ed. by G. E.
    Murphy, Jr.
  The North American Review 271:17-21
    S '86
Marva Jean Howard confesses
  Adams, G. G. The purchase of order
La plume de ma tante
  Adams, G. G. The purchase of order
The purchase of order
  Adams, G. G. The purchase of order
A small hotel
  Adams, G. G. The purchase of order

A teller's tale
  Adams, G. G. The purchase of order
  The Georgia Review 39:563-70 Fall '85
Adams, Glenda, 1939-
Coral dance
  Room to move; ed. by S. Falkiner
The voyage of their life
  Home and away; ed. by R. Creswell
Adams, John Coleman
Midshipman, the cat
  Roger Caras' Treasury of great cat
    stories
Adam's bride. Jolley, E.
Adcock, Thomas Larry, 1947-
Thrown-away child
  The Year's best mystery and suspense
    stories, 1987
Addendum to the first fleet journals. Windsor, G.
Addio. Gilliatt, P.
Addison, Joseph, 1672-1719
A story of an heir
  The Treasury of English short stories;
    ed. by N. Sullivan
The **addition** to Aunt Ella's house. Heise, K.
Ade, George, 1866-1944
The Alfalfa European Hotel
  Ade, G. The best of George Ade
Artie Blanchard
  Ade, G. The best of George Ade
The Buell cherry
  Ade, G. The best of George Ade
Dubley, '89
  Ade, G. The best of George Ade
Effie Whittlesy
  Ade, G. The best of George Ade
The fable of how the fool-killer backed out
    of a contract
  Ade, G. The best of George Ade
The fable of Lutie, the false alarm, and
    how she finished about the time that
    she started
  Ade, G. The best of George Ade
The fable of sister Mae, who did as well
    as could be expected
  Ade, G. The best of George Ade
The fable of the grass widow and the mes-
    meree and the six dollars
  Ade, G. The best of George Ade
The fable of the honest money-maker and
    the partner of his joys, such as they
    were
  Ade, G. The best of George Ade
The fable of the lawyer who brought in
    a minority report
  Ade, G. The best of George Ade
The fable of the man who was going to
    retire
  Ade, G. The best of George Ade
The fable of the two mandolin players and
    the willing performer
  Ade, G. The best of George Ade

Ade, George, 1866-1944—*Continued*
The fable of what happened the night the
men came to the women's club
Ade, G. The best of George Ade
How "Pink" was reformed
Ade, G. The best of George Ade
In the roof garden
Ade, G. The best of George Ade
The intellectual awakening in Burton's
Row
Ade, G. The best of George Ade
Il janitoro
Ade, G. The best of George Ade
The judge's son
Ade, G. The best of George Ade
Mr. Payson's satirical Christmas
Ade, G. The best of George Ade
The mystery of the back-roomer
Ade, G. The best of George Ade
Olof Lindstrom goes fishing
Ade, G. The best of George Ade
Our private romance
Ade, G. The best of George Ade
Sophie's Sunday afternoon
Ade, G. The best of George Ade
What they had laid out for their vacation
Ade, G. The best of George Ade
When father meets father
Ade, G. The best of George Ade
ADELAIDE (AUSTRALIA) *See* Australia—
Adelaide
Adelaide. Oliveira, L. L. de
Adeste fideles. Pohl, F.
Adios, Mr. Moxley. Jacobsen, J.
ADIRONDACK MOUNTAINS (N.Y.)
Thompson, J. Applause, applause
Adisa, Opal Palmer, 1954-
Bake-Face
Adisa, O. P. Bake-Face, and other guava
stories
Duppy get her
Adisa, O. P. Bake-Face, and other guava
stories
The Pushcart prize XII
Me man Angel
Adisa, O. P. Bake-Face, and other guava
stories
Widows' walk
Adisa, O. P. Bake-Face, and other guava
stories
ADJ, Inc. Vega, A. L.
An **adjustment** of nature. Henry, O.
Adler, Warren
The angel of mercy
Full measure; ed. by D. Sennett
The **Admiral** and the nuns. Tuohy, F.
Admirals. Chabon, M.
The **admission** ticket. Ornstien, E.
ADOLESCENCE
See also Boys; Girls; Youth
Abbott, K. Harum scarum
Abbott, K. Logger Linkhorn's 1928 Buick
Abbott, K. Out on the res

Abbott, K. Tell the truth
Agee, J. 1928 story
Andres, K. Things to draw
Antoni, R. W. Two-head Fred and Tree-
foot Frieda
Ardizzone, T. The daughter and the trades-
man
Ardizzone, T. Idling
Barich, B. Hard to be good
Barrett, L. Inventory
Barrett, L. Moon walk
Barton, M. Jacob's angel
Bates, H. E. Nina
Bender, H. La Paloma; or, The food of
love
Benét, S. V. Too early spring
Bird, C. One with the lot
Blaise, C. A North American education
Bloch, R. The gloating place
Böll, H. In the Valley of the Thundering
Hoofs
Boyle, T. C. Greasy Lake
Briskin, M. Theresa McCann and Joe
Brodkey, H. The state of grace
Brown, S. The lesson
Bumpus, J. Plenty of time
Burt, S. Hiding
Burt, S. I just kept on smiling
Burt, S. Wh'appen?
Busch, F. The settlement of Mars
Calisher, H. Gargantua
Calvino, I. Adam, one afternoon
Cameron, E. The girl on the beach
Cameron, M. R. And the hunter home
from the hill
Cameron, P. Homework
Canin, E. American Beauty
Cárdenas, M. But what if I liked the
Panchos, not the Beatles
Carlson, R. At the hop
Carver, R. Nobody said anything
Choyce, L. Breakage
Choyce, L. The paper route
Clark, G. Lunar frisson
Clark, G. Mister Period
Clayton, J. J. Bodies of the rich
Cohen, M. Death of a guppy
Coleman, W. Chuck and the boss man's
wife
Colette. Green sealing wax
Colette. The tender shoot
Collins, S. R. A day at Hot Creek
Colter, C. A man in the house
Connelly, J. Teamwork
Cook, H. A Canadian education
Coombs, M. Nothing happened
Cross, R. A. The forever summer
Crowell, D. Says Velma
Dadswell, M. Mr. Macnamee
Dawson, F. Kid stuff
De Haven, T. He's all mine
De Haven, T. Where we'll never grow old
Deaver, P. F. Arcola girls

ADOLESCENCE—*Continued*

Dixon, M. Red leaves

Dorr, L. The wedding anniversary

Doubiago, S. Ramon/Ramona

Doubiago, S. Raquel

Drake, R. Mrs. Picture Show Green

Drake, R. Remember the Errol-mo!

Driskell, L. V. Martha Jean

Dumas, H. Ark of bones

Dumas, H. A boll of roses

Dybek, S. Blight

Eighner, L. Park

Eisenberg, D. What it was like, seeing Chris

Eisenstein, S. Moray eel

Eisenstein, S. A place of refuge

Eldridge, M. Aubade

Eldridge, M. Cream sponge on Sunday

Eldridge, M. The ringbarker's daughter

Faik, S. Coming of age on Kasikadasi

Federspiel, J. Prospects for an expedition

Ferron, J. Martine

Finney, E. J. Birds landing

Flaherty, G. Filthy the man

Flanagan, J. Chinook

Flanagan, R. Close dancing

Floyd, P. L. The silver DeSoto

Ford, R. Children

Ford, R. Great Falls

Fox, J. The superhero

Frame, J. The bull calf

Franklin, P. Stale beer and roses

Franzen, B. The ways we surfed

Fremlin, C. Don't be frightened

Garber, E. K. The lover

Gardner, J. Nimram

Gault, C. A shame

Geras, A. Don't sing love songs . . .

Geras, A. Monday

Gilchrist, E. The expansion of the universe

Gilchrist, E. Music

Gingher, M. Aurora Island

Gingher, M. The magic circle

Gingher, M. Teen angel

Gingher, M. Toy Paris

Gingher, M. Wearing glasses

Glasser, P. The last game

Gordon, M. Temporary shelter

Hall, R. W. The Purple Prince

Hankla, C. The moped massacre

Hannah, B. Horning in--A

Heise, K. Long pants day at last

Hemingway, E. The capital of the world

Hemingway, E. Fathers and sons

Hemley, R. Riding The Whip

Hemley, R. What's that in your ear?

Hempel, A. The most girl part of you

Henley, P. Victory

Holmes, C. Metropolitan

Hood, M. Something good for Ginnie

Huddle, D. Summer of the magic show

Huggan, I. Getting out of Garten

Hull, H. R. Alley ways

Hull, H. R. Groping

Hulme, K. Kaibutsu-san

Hulme, K. Te Kaihau: the windeater

Interollo, L. The quickening

Jeffrey, T. Habits of contact

Jordan, N. Night in Tunisia

Kalpakian, L. Sonata in G minor

Kaniuk, Y. The parched earth

Kauffman, J. Patriotic

Kidman, F. Flower man

Kinsella, W. P. The further adventures of Slugger McBatt

Kinsella, W. P. K Mart

Klass, P. Bloomingdale's

Klass, P. Two New Jersey stories: Hudson Towers

Klass, P. Two New Jersey stories: Stealing

Klíma, I. My country

Kranes, D. The phantom Mercury of Nevada

Kunstler, J. H. The rise, fall, and redemption of Mooski Toffski Offski

La Puma, S. The boys of Bensonhurst

La Puma, S. The gangster's ghost

La Puma, S. Gravesend Bay

La Puma, S. Guys under their fedoras

La Puma, S. The jilted groom

Lispector, C. The message

Long, D. Alex's fire

Lurie, M. A social life

Macinnes, P. View from Kwaj

Marshall, O. The paper parcel

McCullers, C. Like that

McElroy, C. J. A house full of Maude

McGarry, J. Margery's prom

McGarry, J. They meet a boy

McKinley, J. Alastair and Jeremy

Miller, S. The birds and the bees

Miller, S. The quality of life

Millhauser, S. In the penny arcade

Millhauser, S. The sledding party

Millman, L. Prudence

Minot, S. Lust

Minot, S. The seawall

Moyer, K. The compass of the heart

Moyer, K. Life jackets

Munro, A. The moon in the Orange Street Skating Rink

Murphy, Y. Rough seas

Ndebele, N. The test

Ndebele, N. Uncle

Neville, K. Overture

Nicolai, D. Day out

Oates, J. C. Sharpshooting

Oates, J. C. Where are you going, where have you been?

O'Brien, E. Courtship

O'Connor, F. A Temple of the Holy Ghost

O'Hara, J. Winter dance

Orphée, E. The silken whale

Pacheco, J. E. August afternoon

Pacheco, J. E. Battles in the desert

Pacheco, J. E. The pleasure principle

ADOLESCENCE—*Continued*
Panshin, A. Down to the worlds of men
Pavese, C. The beggars
Phillips, J. A. Blue moon
Pollack, E. The vanity of small differences
Power, V. No cigarettes, no matches, no lights allowed
Power, V. The threshold
Pugmire, W. H., and Salmonson, J. A. "Pale trembling youth"
Rasputin, V. G. Rudolfio
Rasputin, V. G. You live and love
Rees, D. Plums
Ríos, A. The secret lion
Ross, V. Whistling
Schoemperlen, D. Clues
Schulman, H. In God's country
Schulman, H. Pushing the point
Schwartz, S. Slow-motion
Shaik, F. Climbing Monkey Hill
Shaw, J. B. Inventing the kiss
Silverberg, R. Push no more
Slesinger, T. White on black
Somers, A. The tunnel
Sorrells, R. T. Talking to the boy
Spark, D. Summer of the Dead Frogs
Steele, M. Ah love! Ah me!
Stewart, J. I. M. André
Summers, M. Ronnie so long at the fair
Swados, H. My Coney Island uncle
Swift, G. The tunnel
Taylor, P. H. Promise of rain
Taylor, R. Lady of Spain
Thomas, D. Extraordinary little cough
Thompson, J. Little Face
Thompson, K. Some things I won't do
Thompson, R. Under the swaying curtain
Tuohy, F. The license
Tuohy, F. The Palladian Bridge
Updike, D. The end of the reign
Updike, D. Summer
Viramontes, H. M. Growing
Viramontes, H. M. The moths
Warner, S. T. The proper circumstances
Watmough, D. In the mood
Watmough, D. Return of the native
Watmough, D. Sacred & secular
Watmough, D. Seduction
West, J. Crimson Ramblers of the world, farewell
Wetherell, W. D. The bass, the river, and Sheila Mant
White, E. A man of the world
Williams, J. Health
Wilson, B. Miss Venezuela
Winton, T. No memory comes
Wolff, T. Coming attractions
Wolff, T. Smorgasbord
Wyndham, F. Mrs. Henderson
Yasuoka, S. Bad company
Yasuoka, S. Thick the new leaves
Zigal, T. Curios

ADOLESCENTS *See* Adolescence
Adolph Menjou's tryout camp. Klinkowitz, J.
ADOPTED CHILDREN *See* Adoption; Foster children
ADOPTION
          See also Foster children
Jahnn, H. H. The slave's story
McGuane, T. The millionaire
Robison, J. Home
Shi Tiesheng. One winter's evening
Sholem Aleichem. It doesn't pay to be good
Stewart, J. I. M. Tom Dick and Harry
Swift, G. The son
Timperley, R. Harry
Tiptree, J. Morality meat
Wilson, L. A. The raising
Adoration. Gilchrist, E.
Adore her. Robison, M.
Adult art. Gurganus, A.
Adult education. Eldridge, M.
The **adulterous** woman. Camus, A.
ADULTERY *See* Marriage problems
Adultery. Banks, R.
Adultery. Dubus, A.
Adultress. Oates, J. C.
Advanced beginners. Taylor-Hall, M. A.
ADVENTURE
          See also Buried treasure; Escapes; International intrigue; Manhunts; Pirates; Science fiction; Sea stories; Soldiers of fortune; Spies; Underwater exploration; Voyages and travels; Western stories
Anaya, R. A. B. Traven is alive and well in Cuernavaca
Buzzati, D. Barnabo of the mountains
Curwood, J. O. Back to God's country
Davidson, A. Sleep well of nights
Grandbois, A. The thirteenth
London, J. A hyperborean brew [excerpt]
Lupoff, R. A. God of the Naked Unicorn
MacLean, A. St. George and the dragon
Panshin, A. Down to the worlds of men
Poe, E. A. The narrative of Arthur Gordon Pym of Nantucket
Speer, H. Shawm of the stars
Tremblay, M. The eye of the idol
Weinbaum, S. G. Dawn of flame
An **adventure.** Maupassant, G. de
An **adventure** from a work in progress. Thomas, D.
The **adventure** of a bather. Calvino, I.
The **adventure** of a clerk. Calvino, I.
The **adventure** of a nearsighted man. Calvino, I.
The **adventure** of a photographer. Calvino, I.
The **adventure** of a poet. Calvino, I.
The **adventure** of a reader. Calvino, I.
The **adventure** of a soldier. Calvino, I.
The **adventure** of a traveler. Calvino, I.

The **adventure** of Abraham Lincoln's clue. See Queen, E. Abraham Lincoln's clue

The **adventure** of Johnnie Waverly. Christie, A.

The **adventure** of Silver Blaze. See Doyle, Sir A. C. Silver Blaze

The **adventure** of the bearded lady. Queen, E.

The **adventure** of the Beryl Coronet. Doyle, Sir A. C.

The **adventure** of the blue carbuncle. Doyle, Sir A. C.

The **adventure** of the Bruce-Partington plans. Doyle, Sir A. C.

The **adventure** of the cheap flat. Christie, A.

The **adventure** of the Clapham cook. Christie, A.

The **adventure** of the copper beeches. Doyle, Sir A. C.

The **adventure** of the Dauphin's doll. See Queen, E. The Dauphin's doll

The **adventure** of the devil's foot. Doyle, Sir A. C.

The **adventure** of the Egyptian tomb. Christie, A.

The **adventure** of the engineer's thumb. Doyle, Sir A. C.

The **adventure** of the extraterrestrial. Reynolds, M.

The **adventure** of the German student. Irving, W.

The **adventure** of the glass-domed clock. See Queen, E. The glass-domed clock

The **adventure** of the global traveler. Lear, A.

The **adventure** of the Gowanus abduction. Harrington, J.

The **adventure** of the hanging acrobat. Queen, E.

The **adventure** of the Italian nobleman. Christie, A.

The **adventure** of the mad tea-party. See Queen, E. The mad tea-party

Adventure of the metal murderer. Saberhagen, F.

The **adventure** of the misplaced hound. Anderson, P., and Dickson, G. R.

The **adventure** of the noble bachelor. Doyle, Sir A. C.

The **adventure** of the oval window. Dirckx, J. H.

The **adventure** of the perpetual husbands. Dearmore, E.

The **adventure** of the persistent marksman. De la Torre, L.

The **adventure** of the speckled band. Doyle, Sir A. C.

The **adventure** of the spurious Tamerlane. Derleth, A. W.

The **adventure** of the unique Holmes. Breen, J. L.

The **adventure** of "The Western Star". Christie, A.

An **adventure** with a dog. Muir, J.

An **adventure** with a dog and a glacier. See Muir, J. An adventure with a dog

Adventurer. Asscher-Pinkhof, C.

The **adventurer**. Friedman, B. J.

Adventures in the skin trade: A fine beginning. Thomas, D.

Adventures in the skin trade: Four lost souls. Thomas, D.

Adventures in the skin trade: Plenty of furniture. Thomas, D.

Adventures of a haversack. Böll, H.

Adventures of a novelist. Crane, S.

The **adventures** of Strike-out Stratton. Shannon, J.

ADVERTISING
    See also Publicity
  Bloch, R. The weird doom of Floyd Scrilch
  Bonnie, F. Name the general
  Brondoli, M. Sixty-three questions
  Calisher, H. The tenth child
  Davis, S. The circus advance agent
The **advice**. Colette
Advice. Singer, I. B.
Advice from a sensible young man. Taher, B.
Aeaea. Kessler, J. F.
Æpyornis Island. Wells, H. G.
AERONAUTICS
    See also Air pilots; Airships; Flight
  Doyle, Sir A. C. The horror of the heights
  Gardner, J. Nimram
  Wells, H. G. The Argonauts of the air
  Wells, H. G. Filmer
            Flights
    See Air travel
AERONAUTICS, COMMERCIAL
    See also Airlines
AERONAUTICS, MILITARY
    See also World War, 1914-1918—Aerial operations; World War, 1939-1945—Aerial operations
AESTHETICS
  Chekhov, A. P. Beauties
  Hawthorne, N. The artist of the beautiful
  Henry, O. Art and the bronco
  Wells, H. G. A misunderstood artist
The **affair**. Silverberg, R.
The **affair**. Weinheber, J.
The **affair** at the bungalow. Christie, A.
The **affair** at the victory ball. Christie, A.
An **affair**, edited. Gaitskill, M.
An **affair** of heart. Fineman, M.
An **affair** of state. Maupassant, G. de
The **affair** of the arabesque inlay. Ishikawa, T.
The **affair** of the 'Avalanche Bicycle and Tyre Co., Limited'. Morrison, A.
The **affair** of the clasps. Gorky, M.
Affairs of amputees. Piñera, V.
Affection. Barthelme, D.

AFGHANISTAN
Ahern, T. Unsophar and Onsopur
Afoot in a field of men. Taylor, P. E.
AFRICA
> See also East Africa; North Africa;
> West Africa

Anthony, P. Small mouth, bad taste
Boyd, W. Killing lizards
Gordimer, N. At the rendezvous of victory
Grin, A. Gatt, Witt and Redott
Grin, A. The heart of the wilderness
Hemingway, E. An African story
Hemingway, E. The short happy life of
     Francis Macomber
Hemingway, E. The snows of Kilimanjaro
Honwana, L. B. Papa, snake & I
Hoyt, M. S. Small suns
Kirk, R. The peculiar demesne of Arch-
     vicar Gerontion
Marechera, D. Protista
Mortimer, J. C. Rumpole and the golden
     thread
Mphahlele, E. The coffee-cart girl
Owoyele, D. The will of Allah
Saidi, W. The nightmare
Thomas, M. Abdullah and Mariam
Thomas, M. Jim Chance
Thomas, M. Mama Angelina's
Thomas, M. Neighbors
Thomas, M. A thief in my house
> **Marriage customs**
> See Marriage customs—Africa
> **Native peoples**
> See also Masai (African people);
> Xhosa (African people); Zulus (African
> people)

Balogun, O. The apprentice
Bloch, R. The funnel of God
Conrad, J. An outpost of progress
Gordimer, N. A hunting accident
Gordimer, N. Oral history
Head, B. Snapshots of a wedding
Meiring, J. Bird of my voice
Ogot, G. The green leaves
Russo, A. The universe of Mama Malkia
Sodowsky, R. E. Landlady
Wright, R. Man, God ain't like that. . .

> **Politics**
> See Politics—Africa
> **Prisoners and prisons**
> See Prisoners and prisons—Africa
> **Race relations**

Kibera, L. The spider's web
AFRICA, EAST See East Africa
AFRICA, GERMAN EAST See East Africa
AFRICA, NORTH See North Africa
AFRICA, SOUTH See South Africa
AFRICA, WEST See West Africa
Africa wall. Lurie, M.
An African river. Coskran, K.
African story. Davis, G. P.
An African story. Hemingway, E.

The African tree-beavers. Gilbert, M.
AFRICAN TRIBES See Africa—Native
     peoples
AFRICANS
> **United States**

Swanwick, M. The feast of Saint Janis
AFRIKANERS
Bosman, H. C. The Rooinek
Havemann, E. The going home of Ntambo
Smith, P. The schoolmaster
AFRO-AMERICANS See Blacks
Afrodite. Kessler, J. F.
After. Maupassant, G. de
After all these years. Kennedy, D.
After death. Maupassant, G. de
After eight. Asscher-Pinkhof, C.
After Emily. Lipman, E.
After Flaubert. Sladek, J. T.
After hours. Burns, M.
After I won the lottery. Franzen, B.
After I'm gone. Westlake, D. E.
After-images. Edwards, M.
After King Kong fell. Farmer, P. J.
After Lazarus. Coover, R.
After long absence. Hospital, J. T.
After midnight. Colette
After Moore. Hood, M.
After Noumea. Drewe, R.
After the ball. Colter, C.
After the denim. Carver, R.
After the fair. Thomas, D.
After the fall. Hospital, J. T.
After the game. Dubus, A.
After the storm. Harrison, H.
After the storm. Hemingway, E.
After the wedding. Lawler, P.
After the yarn is spun. Swartz, J.
After Titian's Susannah and the elders. War-
     ner, M.
After twenty years. Henry, O.
The afterlife. Updike, J.
The aftermath. Ransom, W. M.
Aftermath. Thurm, M.
Aftermath of a duel. Sagan, F.
Afternoon at Schrafft's. Dozois, G. R., and
     others
Afternoon in the country. Fleming, B.
An afternoon in the woods. O'Connor, F.
An afternoon miracle. Henry, O.
The afternoon of the poetess. Thompson, J.
Afterward. Wharton, E.
Again, again, again. Robison, M.
Again the Antilles. Rhys, J.
Against a crooked stile. Kress, N.
Against all odds. Adams, A.
Against Babylon. Silverberg, R.
Against the wall. Anderson, J.
Agathe. Keeling, N.
Agawam. Updike, D.
Age. Desaulniers, J.
The age of analysis. Schwartz, L. S.
The age of anxiety. Feinberg, D. B.
The age of desire. Barker, C.

The **age** of fish. Stoll, P.
The **age** of grief. Smiley, J.
The **age** of unreason. Harvor, E.
The **age-old** problem of who. Cassity, K.
AGED *See* Elderly; Old age
Agee, James, 1909-1955
  1928 story
    Stories of the modern South; ed. by B. Forkner and P. Samway
Agee, Jonis
  Stiller's pond
    Stiller's pond; ed. by J. Agee; R. Blakely and S. Welch
Agency. Connelly, J.
The **agent** in travelling. Jolley, E.
AGENTS, SECRET *See* Spies
AGING
  Amis, M. The time disease
  Ballantyne, S. Key Largo
  Bissoondath, N. Veins visible
  Eisenstein, S. Hear anything from Bakersfield?
  Eisenstein, S. Post coitus tristus
  Eliade, M. Youth without youth
  Floyd, P. L. Uncle Tom's daybook
  Gill, B. M. Murder most kind
  Hamilton, R. C. Da Vinci is dead
  Henderson, D. Broken treaty
  Henry, O. The Indian Summer of Dry Valley Johnson
  Hirsch, G. The housing correspondence of prisoner number 100293/8
  Keeling, N. George's eyes & the red ball
  Keillor, G. High rise
  Keillor, G. Out in the cold
  Keillor, G. Truckstop
  Kundera, M. Let the old dead make room for the young dead
  McCluskey, J. The best teacher in Georgia
  Nichols, J. T. The Milagro beanfield war [excerpt]
  Robbins, T. The hair of the beast
  Russ, J. The little dirty girl
  Sandel, C. The sisters
  Thompson, K. A blunt affair
  Thompson, K. Green things
  Updike, J. Killing
  Updike, J. The wallet
  Viramontes, H. M. Snapshots
  Wong, M. V. When I see Hui Lan again
Agnes. Gordon, M.
Agnes and the cobwebs. Rooke, L.
Agnon, Shmuel Yosef, 1888-1970
  The kerchief
    The Nobel reader; ed. by J. Eisen and S. Troy
Agony. Lish, G.
Agra outwits two pirate ships. Reade, C.
AGRICULTURAL LABORERS *See* Farm workers
Agriculture. Kittredge, W.
Agua prieta. Ebon, W.

Aguinis, Marcos
  Short story contest
    Winter's tales, new ser. v4
Ah love! Ah me! Steele, M.
Ahern, Tom
  The anatomist of Petrus Borel
    Ahern, T. Hecatombs of lake
  Chenken and Nartzarzen in several days on the town
    Ahern, T. Hecatombs of lake
  The discontent of Franz Boas
    Ahern, T. Hecatombs of lake
  Dr. Zifhart leaves for Atlantic City
    Ahern, T. Hecatombs of lake
  The Habbitson stories
    Ahern, T. Hecatombs of lake
  An implied acquaintance
    Ahern, T. Hecatombs of lake
  Monsters
    Ahern, T. Hecatombs of lake
  My summer scenes
    Ahern, T. Hecatombs of lake
  The new life
    Ahern, T. Hecatombs of lake
  Unsophar and Onsopur
    Ahern, T. Hecatombs of lake
Ahlswede, Ann
  The promise of the fruit
    She won the West; ed. by M. Muller and B. Pronzini
    Westward the women; ed. by V. Piekarski
Ahmed, Fathelbari
  The wicked city
    Short story international 60
Ahoy, sailor boy! Coppard, A. E.
Aichinger, Ilse
  The bound man
    The Art of the tale; ed. by D. Halpern
  Story in a mirror
    The Slaying of the dragon; ed. by F. Rottensteiner
Aickman, Robert, 1914-1981
  Bind your hair
    Aickman, R. The wine-dark sea
  The Cicerones
    The Oxford book of English ghost stories
  The fetch
    Aickman, R. The wine-dark sea
    The Architecture of fear; ed. by K. Cramer and P. D. Pautz
  Growing boys
    Aickman, R. The wine-dark sea
  Hand in glove
    The Best horror stories from the Magazine of fantasy and science fiction
  The hospice
    The Dark descent; ed. by D. G. Hartwell
    Masterpieces of terror and the supernatural; ed. by M. Kaye and S. Kaye

Aickman, Robert, 1914-1981—*Continued*
The inner room
    Aickman, R. The wine-dark sea
Into the wood
    Aickman, R. The wine-dark sea
Larger than oneself
    The Dark descent; ed. by D. G. Hart-
    well
Never visit Venice
    Aickman, R. The wine-dark sea
The next glade
    Aickman, R. The wine-dark sea
Pages from a young girl's journal
    Vampires; ed. by A. Ryan
The same dog
    Lost souls; ed. by J. Sullivan
The stains
    Aickman, R. The wine-dark sea
The swords
    The Dark descent; ed. by D. G. Hart-
    well
The trains
    Aickman, R. The wine-dark sea
The wine-dark sea
    Aickman, R. The wine-dark sea
Your tiny hand is frozen
    Aickman, R. The wine-dark sea
Aidoo, Christina Ama Ata
Certain winds from the south
    African short stories; ed. by C. Achebe
    and C. L. Innes
    Short story international 68
In the cutting of a drink
    African short stories in English; ed. by
    J. de Grandsaigne
AIDS (DISEASE)
Davis, C. The boys in the bars
Innaurato, A. Solidarity
Mordden, E. The dinner party
Sontag, S. The way we live now
Aiken, Conrad, 1889-1973
Mr. Arcularis
    Full measure; ed. by D. Sennett
    Haunted New England; ed. by C. G.
    Waugh; M. H. Greenberg and F. D.
    McSherry
Silent snow, secret snow
    Look who's talking; ed. by B. Weber
    The Norton book of American short
    stories
Aiken, Joan, 1924-
The black cliffs
    Ellery Queen's Prime crimes
The cat who lived in a drainpipe
    Roger Caras' Treasury of great cat
    stories
The jealous apprentice
    John Creasey's Crime collection, 1984
Lodging for the night
    Spirits, spooks, and other sinister crea-
    tures; ed. by H. Hoke

The moon's revenge
    The Year's best fantasy, first annual
    collection
Smell
    Venomous tales of villainy and
    vengeance; ed. by H. Hoke
Sonata for harp and bicycle
    The Penguin book of ghost stories
Time to laugh
    John Creasey's Crime collection, 1985
Aikin, Jim
Dance for the king
    Omni (New York, N.Y.) 7:66+ N '84
My life in the jungle
    Beyond Armageddon; ed. by W. M. Mil-
    ler and M. H. Greenberg
Air. Carlson, R.
Air. Wilner, H.
AIR CRASHES *See* Airplane accidents
AIR PILOTS
Austin, D. The past is a doomed
    parachutist
Ballard, J. G. Memories of the Space Age
Barber, D. W. Wings of the hunter
Barrett, N., Jr. Sallie C.
Barrett, W. E. The destroyer
Bates, H. E. Sergeant Carmichael
Bishop, M. Cold war orphans
Boyd, W. Extracts from the journal of
    Flying Officer J
Boyd, W. On the Yankee station
Burke, J. L. The pilot
Carpentier, A. Birdy's flight
DeGrazia, E. The mask
Doyle, Sir A. C. The horror of the heights
Hannah, B. Even Greenland
Hannah, B. Testimony of pilot
Kittredge, W. Agriculture
Markham, B. Appointment in Khartoum
Plant, R. Cecil grounded
Pritchett, M. Flying lessons
Wells, H. G. Little mother up the Mörder-
    berg
Woolrich, C. Jane Brown's body
AIR RAID SHELTERS
Oates, J. C. Shelter
AIR SHIPS *See* Airships
AIR TRAVEL
Broinowski, A. Holy mackerel
Gilliatt, P. Autumn of a dormouse
Greene, G. The over-night bag
Lish, G. Last descent to earth
Morris, W. Glimpse into another country
AIR WARFARE *See* World War, 1914-
    1918—Aerial operations; World War,
    1939-1945—Aerial operations
AIRLINES
    See also Airports
Lutz, J. Discount fare
        Flight attendants
    See Flight attendants
AIRMEN *See* Air pilots
Airmen. Poole, F. F.

AIRPLANE ACCIDENTS
  Atwood, M. A travel piece
  Bates, H. E. It's just the way it is
  Bates, H. E. Sergeant Carmichael
  Grau, S. A. Hunter
  Hannah, B. Even Greenland
  Long, D. Clearance
  Markham, B. Your heart will tell you
  Onopa, R. The man who swam through
    jellyfish, through men-of-war
  Rothman, C. The transformation
  Tiptree, J. The women men don't see
  Ullmann, A. Those in peril in the air
The **airplane** ticket. Baykurt, F.
AIRPLANES
  Lipsyte, R. Red carpet treatment
  Munro, A. Eskimo
  Raphael, F. Welcome aboard
  Van de Wetering, J. A great sight
  Vreuls, D. Meeting you
  Wells, H. G. My first aeroplane
  Wilding, M. Sex in Australia from the
    man's point of view
                Accidents
        See Airplane accidents
                Pilots
        See Air pilots
AIRPLANES, MILITARY
  Redd, D. On the deck of the Flying Bomb
  Regent, P. Schoolboy war
The **airport,** the pizzeria, the motel, the ren-
    ted car, and the mysteries of life.
    Moorhouse, F.
AIRPORTS
        See also Airlines
  Austin, D. A pear
  Beattie, A. When can I see you again?
  Mazel, D. Homage
AIRSHIPS
  Clarke, A. C. A meeting with Medusa
  Leiber, F. Catch that zeppelin!
  Redd, D. On the deck of the Flying Bomb
Aithal, S. K., and Rothfork, John
  Moksha
    Short story international 57
Akanishi Kakita. Shiga, N.
Akhnilo. Salter, J.
Akins, Ellen
  George Bailey fishing
    New stories from the South: the year's
    best, 1988
    Southwest Review 72:110-18 Wint '87
  Her book
    The Georgia Review 40:972-85 Wint '86
  Near November
    Southwest Review 69:250-7 Summ '84
  Something you won't understand
    The Southern Review (Baton Rouge, La.)
    21:162-7 Ja '85
Aksenov, Vasilii Pavlovich, 1932-
  Destruction of Pompeii (a story for Bella)
    Aksenov, V. P. Surplussed barrelware

Little whale, varnisher of reality [Variant
    title: Little whale, the painter of
    reality]
    The Art of the tale; ed. by D. Halpern
  A poem of ecstasy
    Aksenov, V. P. Surplussed barrelware
  Rendezvous
    Aksenov, V. P. Surplussed barrelware
  Super-deluxe
    Aksenov, V. P. Surplussed barrelware
  Surplussed barrelware
    Aksenov, V. P. Surplussed barrelware
Aksyonov, Vassily See Aksenov, Vasilii Pav-
    lovich, 1932-
Akutagawa, Ryunosuke, 1892-1927
  'Autumn Mountain'
    Black water; ed. by A. Manguel
  Cogwheels
    Akutagawa, R. Hell screen, Cogwheels,
    A fool's life
  A fool's life
    Akutagawa, R. Hell screen, Cogwheels,
    A fool's life
  Hell screen
    Akutagawa, R. Hell screen, Cogwheels,
    A fool's life
  In a grove
    Murder in Japan; ed. by J. L. Apostolou
    and M. H. Greenberg
Al-Idlibi, Ulfat
  The women's baths
    Modern Syrian short stories; ed. by M.
    G. Azrak
Al-Kouni, Ibrahim
  The drumming sands
    Arabic short stories; tr. by D. Johnson-
    Davies
Al Magid, Ibrahim Abd
  Over there
    Egyptian tales and short stories of the
    1970s and 1980s
Al-Mak, Ali
  Forty-one minarets
    Short story international 63
Al Makhzangy, Mohammed
  Just a touch
    Egyptian tales and short stories of the
    1970s and 1980s
Al-Qa'id, Yusuf
  Three meaningless tales
    Egyptian tales and short stories of the
    1970s and 1980s
Al-Rahib, Hani
  The ablution
    Modern Syrian short stories; ed. by M.
    G. Azrak
Al Shaikh, Ahmed
  The heir
    Egyptian tales and short stories of the
    1970s and 1980s

Al Sharuni, Ya'qub
  Guha the judge
    Egyptian tales and short stories of the
      1970s and 1980s
Al-Shayib, Fu'ad
  East is east
    Modern Syrian short stories; ed. by M.
      G. Azrak
Al-Shaykh, Hanan
  The Persian carpet
    Arabic short stories; tr. by D. Johnson-
      Davies
Al-Siba'i, Fadil
  An accident at "The Palace of Happiness"
    Modern Syrian short stories; ed. by M.
      G. Azrak
Al-Ujayli, Abd al-Salam
  Madness
    Modern Syrian short stories; ed. by M.
      G. Azrak
Al-Wardani, Mahmoud
  The kerosene stove
    Arabic short stories; tr. by D. Johnson-
      Davies
ALABAMA
  Anderson Imbert, E. Murder
  Barr, J. G. John Bealle's accident—or,
    How the widow Dudu treated insanity
  Bierce, A. An occurrence at Owl Creek
    Bridge
  Brown, M. W. The cure
  Hall, T. T. An early spring morning
    remembered and understood
  Rud, A. M. Ooze
            Selma
  Hays, D. The Dixie Association [excerpt]
Alaindelon de la patrie. Ribeiro, J. U.
ALAMO (SAN ANTONIO, TEX.)
            Siege, 1836
  Hoch, E. D. Who rides with Santa Anna?
Alan, A. J.
  My adventure in Norfolk
    The Penguin book of ghost stories
Alan. Benson, P.
Alarcón, Pedro Antonio de, 1833-1891
  The tall woman
    Black water; ed. by A. Manguel
The **alarm** system. Murphy, P.
Alas, all thinking. Bates, H.
Alas, poor Maling. Greene, G.
ALASKA
  Apple, M. Eskimo love
  Cassity, K. The age-old problem of who
  London, J. For the love of a man
  London, J. Negore, the Coward
  London, J. The one thousand dozen
  Muir, J. An adventure with a dog
  O'Brien, D. Seals
  Schwartz, S. In Alaska
  Whelan, G. Sympathy notes
Alaska. Adams, A.
Alastair and Jeremy. McKinley, J.

ALBANIA
  Eisenstein, S. From in Albania
Albarelli, Dean
  Honeymoon
    20 under 30; ed. by D. Spark
  Infatuated
    The Virginia Quarterly Review 60:688-
      701 Aut '84
Albatross. Gault, C.
Albergo terminal. Corbluth, J.
ALBERTA *See* Canada—Alberta
Alberta. Sandel, C.
Alberts, Laurie
  Veterans
    The New generation; ed. by A. Kaufman
ALBINONI, TOMASO, 1671-1750
            About
  Aiken, J. The cat who lived in a drainpipe
ALBINOS
  Maupassant, G. de. A night in
    Whitechapel
The **album**. Piñera, V.
The **album**. Teleky, R.
ALBUQUERQUE (N.M.) *See* New Mex-
    ico—Albuquerque
ALCATRAZ ISLAND (CALIF.)
  Ritchie, J. The $5,000 getaway
ALCHEMY
  Kuttner, H. The portal in the picture
  Lee, T. Into gold
  Poe, E. A. Von Kempelen and his
    discovery
  Waldrop, H. ". . . the world, as we
    know't."
An **alcoholic** case. Fitzgerald, F. S.
ALCOHOLICS *See* Alcoholism; Drunkards
ALCOHOLISM
    See also Drunkards
  Abbott, L. K. The beauties of drink: an
    essay
  Abbott, L. K. Time and fear and somehow
    love
  Abbott, L. K. The world of apples
  Allen, P. G. Tough love
  Austin, D. Milton Freabe
  Barich, B. October
  Barthelme, S. Zorro
  Bausch, R. All the way in Flagstaff,
    Arizona
  Baxter, C. The eleventh floor
  Bellow, S. Leaving the yellow house
  Benedict, P. All the dead
  Bloch, R. Lucy comes to stay
  Bonnie, F. A settlement of wages
  Bourjaily, V. The Duchess
  Callaghan, M. Absolution
  Campbell, R. The hands
  Carver, R. Careful
  Carver, R. One more thing
  Carver, R. Where I'm calling from
  Cather, W. On the divide
  Chavez, A. Wake for Don Corsinio

ALCOHOLISM—*Continued*

Cullen, E. J. I try to look out for my family

Cullen, E. J. Mayberry

Dadswell, M. Crockfoot Lilli

Duff, G. Fire ants

Dundas, R. The respecter of persons

Fitzgerald, F. S. Babylon, revisited

Flanagan, R. Local anaesthetic

Flynn, R. Place

Friedman, B. J. A different ball game

Gilchrist, E. Traceleen at dawn

Goyen, W. Where's Esther?

Halligan, M. A cage of gold

Heller, S. The man who drank a thousand beers

Heller, S. The rainbow syndrome

Hemingway, E. The three-day blow

Keillor, G. Christmas dinner

Klinkowitz, J. Hot dogs and the Sox

Lawson, H. Telling Mrs. Baker

Lish, G. Resurrection

Lynch, L. At a bar II: In the morning

MacLaverty, B. The beginnings of a sin

Matthews, J. A marriage of solipsists

Maupassant, G. de. The little cask

McGrath, P. Lush triumphant

McIlroy, C. All my relations

McKinley, J. Each new springtime, each new summer

McKinley, J. Praying for a Fickleman

Minot, S. The navigator

Moore, G. Parted

Morris, M. Conquering space

Mortimer, J. C. Rumpole and the spirit of Christmas

O'Brien, D. Final touches

Osborn, C. Stalking strangers

Pynchon, T. The secret integration

Rasputin, V. G. I can't sta-and it . . .

Roberts, N. The bruise

Roberts, N. Water babies

Rossi, A. Meetings

Runciman, J. The lost skipper

Sams, F. Fubar

Sandel, C. Mother

Sears, V. L. Sticktalk

Shea, M. The horror on the #33

Spark, M. 'A sad tale's best for winter'

St. Clair, M. The goddess on the street corner

Stephens, M. Everlast

Stone, R. Helping

Warner, S. T. The three cats

Weaver, G. Whiskey, whiskey, gin, gin, gin

Whelan, G. The dogs in Renoir's garden

Williams, J. Escapes

Williams, T. Three players of a summer game

Windsor, G. The life of a man's man

Working, R. Shooting

Young, R. F. A drink of darkness

Ziem, J. Clarifications

Alcott, Louisa May, 1832-1888

Ariel. A legend of the lighthouse
Alcott, L. M. A double life

The brothers
Civil War women; ed. by F. McSherry; C. G. Waugh and M. Greenberg

A double tragedy. An actor's story
Alcott, L. M. A double life

The fate of the Forrests
Alcott, L. M. A double life

A March Christmas
"May your days be merry and bright" and other Christmas stories by women; ed. by S. Koppelman

A pair of eyes; or, Modern magic
Alcott, L. M. A double life

Taming a Tartar
Alcott, L. M. A double life

Aldani, Lino

Quo vadis, Francisco?
The Penguin world omnibus of science fiction

S is for snake
Tales from the planet Earth

Alden, Paulette Bates, 1947-

All the way to East Texas
Alden, P. B. Feeding the eagles

At the beach
Alden, P. B. Feeding the eagles

The Batsons of Brown and Batson
Alden, P. B. Feeding the eagles

Blue mountains
Alden, P. B. Feeding the eagles

Feeding the eagles
Alden, P. B. Feeding the eagles

In a piney wood
Alden, P. B. Feeding the eagles

Ladies' luncheon
Alden, P. B. Feeding the eagles

Legacies
Alden, P. B. Feeding the eagles

A member of the family
Alden, P. B. Feeding the eagles

The reunion
Alden, P. B. Feeding the eagles

Two women
Alden, P. B. Feeding the eagles

Alderson, Tom

At salt river
Alderson, T. Michelson in the desert

The auction
Alderson, T. Michelson in the desert

FTX; Fort Irwin
Alderson, T. Michelson in the desert

Michelson in the desert
Alderson, T. Michelson in the desert

Tim's back home
Alderson, T. Michelson in the desert

Vigil
Alderson, T. Michelson in the desert

Aldiss, Brian Wilson, 1925-

The blue background
Aldiss, B. W. Seasons in flight

Aldiss, Brian Wilson, 1925-—*Continued*
Consolations of age
Aldiss, B. W. Seasons in flight
The girl who sang
Aldiss, B. W. Seasons in flight
The gods in flight
Aldiss, B. W. Seasons in flight
Hothouse
Robert Silverberg's Worlds of wonder
Igur and the mountain
Aldiss, B. W. Seasons in flight
Incident in a far country
Aldiss, B. W. Seasons in flight
Infestation
Tales from the planet Earth
My country 'tis not only of thee
In the field of fire; ed. by J. Van B.
Dann and J. Dann
The O in José
Aldiss, B. W. Seasons in flight
The other side of the lake
Aldiss, B. W. Seasons in flight
The plain, the endless plain
Aldiss, B. W. Seasons in flight
Poor little warrior!
The Best horror stories from the
Magazine of fantasy and science fiction
A romance of the equator
Aldiss, B. W. Seasons in flight
Aldrich, Thomas Bailey, 1836-1907
Out of his head
Death locked in; ed. by D. G. Greene
and R. C. S. Adey
The white feather
A Treasury of Civil War stories; ed. by
M. H. Greenberg and B. Pronzini
Aldridge, Ray
Click
L. Ron Hubbard presents Writers of the
future v2
Alegría, Claribel
Granny and the golden bridge
The Massachusetts Review 27:503-5 Fall/
Wint '86
Aleichem, Sholem *See* Sholem Aleichem,
1859-1916
The **Aleph**. Borges, J. L.
Alēthia. Johnson, C. R.
Alewives. Morris, M.
Alex Fairburn. Welch, D.
Alexan, John
The locusts
Modern Syrian short stories; ed. by M.
G. Azrak
Alexander, David, 1907-1973
The man who went to Taltavul's
Murder and mystery in Boston; ed. by
C. L. R. Waugh; F. D. McSherry and
M. H. Greenberg
ALEXANDRIA (EGYPT) *See* Egypt—Alex-
andria

Alexin, Anatoly
The class photograph
Short story international 50
Alex's fire. Long, D.
The **Alfalfa** European Hotel. Ade, G.
Alford, Edna
Half past eight
Alberta bound; ed. by F. Stenson
The late date
The Old dance; ed. by B. Burnard
Mid-May's eldest child
The Oxford book of Canadian short
stories in English
ALGERIA
Bowles, P. He of the assembly
Bowles, P. The time of friendship
ALGONQUIAN INDIANS
See also Menominee Indians
Garner, H. One-two-three little Indians
Algren, Nelson, 1909-1981
A bottle of milk for mother
Algren, N. The neon wilderness
The brothers' house
Algren, N. The neon wilderness
The captain has bad dreams
Algren, N. The neon wilderness
The children
Algren, N. The neon wilderness
Depend on Aunt Elly
Algren, N. The neon wilderness
Design for departure
Algren, N. The neon wilderness
The face on the barroom floor
Algren, N. The neon wilderness
He couldn't boogie-woogie worth a damn
Algren, N. The neon wilderness
He swung and he missed
Algren, N. The neon wilderness
The heroes
Algren, N. The neon wilderness
How the Devil came down Division Street
Algren, N. The neon wilderness
Is your name Joe?
Algren, N. The neon wilderness
Katz
Algren, N. The neon wilderness
Kingdom City to Cairo
Algren, N. The neon wilderness
A lot you got to holler
Algren, N. The neon wilderness
Million-dollar brainstorm
Algren, N. The neon wilderness
No man's laughter
Algren, N. The neon wilderness
Pero venceremos
Algren, N. The neon wilderness
Please don't talk about me when I'm gone
Algren, N. The neon wilderness
Poor man's pennies
Algren, N. The neon wilderness
El presidente de Méjico
Algren, N. The neon wilderness

Algren, Nelson, 1909-1981—*Continued*
  So help me
    Algren, N. The neon wilderness
  Stickman's laughter
    Algren, N. The neon wilderness
  That's the way it's always been
    Algren, N. The neon wilderness

ALIBIS
  Asimov, I. Never out of sight
  Matsumoto, S. The secret alibi

Alice. Geras, A.
Alice Long's dachshunds. Spark, M.
The **Alice** P. Gamboe strip. Vreuls, D.
Alice remembers. Adams, G. G.
Alice's brother. Meinke, P.
Alice's last adventure. Ligotti, T.
Alice's snazzy pajamas. Tyler, S. G.
Alien graffiti. Bishop, M.
The **alien** mind. Dick, P. K.
The **alien** rulers. Anthony, P.
The **alien** secret. Berdnyk, O.
Alien stones. Wolfe, G.

ALIENATION (SOCIAL PSYCHOLOGY)
    See also Social isolation
  Bissoondath, N. There are a lot of ways
    to die
  Federspiel, J. Prospects for an expedition
  Handke, P. The lesson of Mont Sainte-
    Victoire
  Handke, P. The long way around
  Malamud, B. My son the murderer

Alienation. Ribeyro, J. R.

ALIENS, ILLEGAL *See* Undocumented
  aliens

ALIENS, UNDOCUMENTED *See* Undocumented aliens

The **aliens**. Jhabvala, R. P.
Aliens. Leavitt, D.
The **aliens**. McCullers, C.
The **aliens** who knew, I mean, everything.
  Effinger, G. A.
Alive and real. West, J.
Alix's refusal. Colette
All about suicide. Valenzuela, L.
The **all-American's** wife. Finney, E. J.
All at sea. Watmough, D.
All avoidable talk. Narayan, R. K.
The **all-bad** hat. Keating, H. R. F.
All business. Lutz, J.
All for the love of David. Lambert, N.
The **all-girl** football team. Nordan, L.
All Gold Cañon. See London, J. All Gold
  Canyon
All Gold Canyon. London, J.
All in a lifetime. Traba, M.
All kinds of flowers. Hunnicutt, E.
All little colored children should play the
  harmonica. Patchett, A.
All living things. Colvin, C.
All mixed up. Batistich, A.
All my darling daughters. Willis, C.
All my darlings. Michaelson, L. W.
All my relations. McIlroy, C.

All my sad captains. Jewett, S. O.
All on a golden afternoon. Bloch, R.
All over. Maupassant, G. de
ALL SAINTS' DAY
  Stead, C. La Toussaint (All Saints' Day,
    November 1)
All set about with fever trees. Durban, P.
All shook up. Boyle, T. C.
All sorts of impossible things. McGahern, J.
All Souls'. Wharton, E.
All-star team. Breen, J. L.
All that counts. Brender à Brandis, M.
All that mattered. Hensley, J. L.
All the dead. Benedict, P.
All the girls had gone. Flook, M.
All the hues of hell. Wolfe, G.
All the livelong night. Clemence, B.
All the long years. Pronzini, B.
All the men are called McCabe. Carter, E.
All the men she loved and lost. Solwitz, S.
All the monkeys. Eisenstein, S.
All the names of Baby Hag. MacLachlan,
  P.
All the old harkening faces at the rail. Han-
  nah, B.
All the roses. Campos, J.
All the sounds of fear. Ellison, H.
All the storms and sun-sets. Lewitt, M.
All the things you are. Sheckley, R.
All the troubles of the world. Asimov, I.
All the way in Flagstaff, Arizona. Bausch,
  R.
All the way to East Texas. Alden, P. B.
All the way to the moon. Wheeler, H. C.
All this and heaven too. Tiptree, J.
The **all-time** master grand-master of solitaire.
  Sorrells, R. T.
All to scale. Durrell, L.
All you can eat. Baumgart, D.
All you can eat. Hemley, R.
Allal. Bowles, P.

Allan, Bryan
  Confession of a catamite
    P.E.N. new fiction I

Allan, J. N.
  The aquarist
    The Penguin book of horror stories

Allan, John B.
    *For works written by this author under
    other names see* Westlake, Donald
    E.

Allan Bloom. Navarre, Y.

Allbeury, Ted, 1917-
  The party of the second part
    Winter's crimes 16
  Time spent in reconnaissance
    John Creasey's Crime collection, 1986

Allegiance. Taylor, P. H.

ALLEGORIES
    See also Fantasies; Good and evil;
    Parables; Symbolism
  Aichinger, I. The bound man

ALLEGORIES—*Continued*

Aksenov, V. P. Destruction of Pompeii (a story for Bella)

Aksenov, V. P. Surplussed barrelware

Aldiss, B. W. Incident in a far country

Aldiss, B. W. The other side of the lake

Aldiss, B. W. The plain, the endless plain

Auster, P. In the country of last things [excerpt]

Benson, R. H. The watcher

Boulaich, A. Cowardice

Calisher, H. The summer rebellion

Chamisso, A. von. The strange story of Peter Schlemihl

Chavez, A. The lean years

Chesterton, G. K. The roots of the world

Chesterton, G. K. The sword of wood

Chesterton, G. K. The tree of pride

Clifford, L. L. The new mother

Colette. A fable: the tendrils of the vine

Davis, L. Once a very stupid man

Eliade, M. The cape

Ellison, H. The silver corridor

Ely, D. The running man

Feng Jicai. The hornets' nest

Feng Jicai. Winding brook way

Ferber, E. No room at the inn

Gardner, M. The Devil and the trombone

Gide, A. The return of the prodigal son

Gilbert, W. S. The wicked world

Granit, A. I went to the market place to see the world! Oy, Mama, oy!

Hawthorne, N. The Celestial rail-road

Hawthorne, N. The Christmas banquet

Hawthorne, N. Earth's holocaust

Hawthorne, N. The man of Adamant

Hawthorne, N. The May-Pole of Merry Mount

Hemingway, E. The faithful bull

Hemingway, E. The good lion

Huang Qingyun. Annals of a fossil

Josipovici, G. The bird cage

Kōda, R. Encounter with a skull

Lagerkvist, P. The myth of mankind

Le Guin, U. K. The ones who walk away from Omelas

Lutz, J. Mortal combat

Marechera, D. Protista

Martin, G. R. R. In the lost lands

Mazel, D. Our Zaideh

Mazel, D. The well

McConnell, J. V. Learning theory

McGrath, P. The angel

Mrożek, S. The ugupu bird

Nakagami, K. The immortal

Ng'maryo, E. S. Ivory bangles

Pil'niāk, B. A dog's life

Poe, E. A. Silence—a fable

Poe, E. A. Siope (Silence)

Pontoppidan, H. Eagle's flight

Rölvaag, O. E. Whitebear and Graybear: an Indian legend

Sciascia, L. The American aunt

Stockton, F. The Bee-man of Orn

Tamer, Z. Hasan as a king

Tamer, Z. Sun for the young

Tamer, Z. Tigers on the tenth day

Tamer, Z. The water's crime

Tiptree, J. All this and heaven too

Tremblay, M. The devil and the mushroom

Wells, H. G. The pearl of love

Wolfe, T. The train and the city

Allen, Grant, 1848-1899

The episode of the Mexican seer

Isaac Asimov presents the best crime stories of the 19th century

Allen, Henry W., 1912-

For works by this author under other names see Fisher, Clay, 1912-; Henry, Will, 1912-

Allen, Joyce C.

Houseraising

The Hudson Review 38:401-14 Aut '85

Allen, Paula Gunn

Tough love

Earth power coming; ed. by S. J. Ortiz

Allen, Richard

A Carol Christmas

'Teen 31:32+ D '87

The peanut girl

'Teen 29:28+ N '85

Allen, Roberta, 1945-

The woman in the shadows

Between C & D; ed. by J. Rose and C. Texier

Allen, Woody

Count Dracula

Great ghost stories; ed. by B. A. Schwartz

ALLENDE, HORTENSIA

About

Ruta, S. Hortensia

Allende, Isabel

Rosa the beautiful

Women's fiction from Latin America; ed. by E. P. Garfield

Allergic. Bonnie, F.

ALLERGY

Jeppson, J. O. Seasonal special

Maupassant, G. de. Mohammed Fripouli

The **alley** man. Farmer, P. J.

Alley ways. Hull, H. R.

Alleywalk. Wexler, J.

Allie. Sandel, C.

Allie. Sanford, W. M.

Alligator love. Hilbert, B.

The **Alligator** Report—with questions for discussion. Kinsella, W. P.

Allison's hair. Wood, M.

Allowance. Minot, S.

Allyn, Doug

The puddle diver

The Year's best mystery and suspense stories, 1987

Alma redeemed. Malamud, B.

The **almond** torte equilibrium. Klass, P.
Almos' a man. Wright, R.
Almost graceful like a dancer. Sproat, R.
Almost heaven. Kilworth, G.
Almost human. Bloch, R.
Almost magnificence. Barber, P.
Almost the real thing. Cherry, K.
Aloe: part three: the making of "Aloe".
　Boylan, J.
Aloha, farewell to thee. West, J.
Alone in Africa. Rush, N.
Alone or with others. Pulaski, J.
Along came a stranger. Rogers, J.
Along the mountain ridge. Morio, K.
Alopecia. Weldon, F.
Alpha. Woiwode, L.
The **alphabet** murders. Ritchie, J.
An **Alpine** idyll. Hemingway, E.
ALPS
　Berger, J. Boris is buying horses
　Berger, J. The time of the cosmonauts
　Helprin, M. The Schreuderspitze
　Maupassant, G. de. The inn
ALSACE (FRANCE) *See* France—Alsace
Altamirano, César Enrique
　The world upside down
　　Américas 40:61-3 Mr/Ap '88
Altar boy. Fante, J.
Altarpiece. Hoffman, W.
Alter, Robert Edmond
　Bummer's roost
　　A Treasury of Civil War stories; ed. by
　　　M. H. Greenberg and B. Pronzini
　The centennial comment
　　A Treasury of Civil War stories; ed. by
　　　M. H. Greenberg and B. Pronzini
　The exile
　　A Treasury of World War II stories; ed.
　　　by B. Pronzini and M. H. Greenberg
　"I," said the fly
　　The Wickedest show on earth; ed. by
　　　M. Muller and B. Pronzini
　A killer in the dark
　　The Black Lizard anthology of crime fic-
　　　tion; ed. by E. Gorman
　To catch a big one
　　Alfred Hitchcock's Grave suspicions
Alter ego. Correa, H.
The **alteration.** Hamilton, D.
Alther, Lisa
　The art of dying well
　　A Collection of classic Southern humor;
　　　ed. by G. W. Koon
　Termites
　　Homewords: a book of Tennessee
　　　writers; ed. by D. Paschall
Altsheler, Joseph
　At the twelfth hour
　　A Treasury of Civil War stories; ed. by
　　　M. H. Greenberg and B. Pronzini
ALUMINUM CANS
　Cowan, P. The tins
Aluminum house. Barthelme, F.

ALUMNI, COLLEGE *See* College alumni
Alumni fund. Reed, K.
Álvarez Gardeazábal, Gustavo
　Donaldo Arrieta
　　Anthology of contemporary Latin Ameri-
　　　can literature, 1960-1984
Alvira, Lettie, and Pip. Schell, J.
The **Alvordton** Spa and Sweat Shop. Kauff-
　man, J.
Always room for one more. Dubus, E. N.
Alzheimer's. Cherry, K.
Am I Blue? Walker, A.
Am I insane. Maupassant, G. de
Amado, Jorge, 1912-
　The lights of the carrousel
　　Short story international 61
Amahl and the Night Visitors: a guide to
　the tenor of love. Moore, L.
AMALFI (ITALY) *See* Italy—Amalfi
Amanda and the alien. Silverberg, R.
Amandine; or, The two gardens. Tournier,
　M.
The **amaryllis.** Brown, M. W.
Amaryllis & the telephone. Summers, H. S.
An **amateur's** guide to the night. Robison,
　M.
Amazing Grace. Hospital, J. T.
Amazing powers. Martin, D.
AMAZON RIVER VALLEY
　Ballard, J. G. A question of re-entry
AMBASSADORS *See* Diplomatic life
The **amber** frog. Smith, S. A.
The **amber** gods. Spofford, H. E. P.
The **amber-trader.** Schwob, M.
Ambience. Klinkowitz, J.
AMBITION
　　See also Self-made men
　Archer, J. Not the real thing
　Asimov, I. Lest we remember
　Bloch, R. His and hearse
　Bonnie, F. Take a seat, not a solo
　Clarke, A. C. Death and the senator
　Dub, O. The rebel wolf and Petrina
　Floyd, P. L. Dream rocket
　Gordon, M. Eileen
　Liyong, T. lo. Lexicographicide
　Masefield, J. Ambitious Jimmy Hicks
　Naipaul, S. The political education of
　　Clarissa Forbes
　Nestor, T. G. Ulick's Island
　Whittier, G. Turning out
The **ambitious** guest. Hawthorne, N.
Ambitious Jimmy Hicks. Masefield, J.
Ambler, Eric, 1909-
　The blood bargain
　　The Mammoth book of modern crime
　　　stories; ed. by G. Hardinge
　The case of the emerald sky
　　The Ethnic detectives; ed. by B. Pronzini
　　　and M. H. Greenberg
　　Masterpieces of mystery and suspense;
　　　ed. by M. H. Greenberg

Ambler, Eric, 1909-—*Continued*
Case of the gentlemen poet
John Creasey's Crime collection, 1984
Ambrose Syme. McGrath, P.
AMBULANCES
Stuart, J. Competition at Slush Creek
The **Amelia** Barons. Camoin, F. A.
Amen. Hogan, L.
AMERICA
See also Central America; South
America
America. Card, O. S.
America. Schnitzler, A.
America competes. Gurganus, A.
America first. Auchincloss, L.
America is one long bloody fight. Sanders,
S. R.
America, the beautiful. Stefaniak, M. H.
America you have gone and left me.
Solomon, B. P.
The **American** aunt. Sciascia, L.
The **American** bakery. Apple, M.
American Beauty. Canin, E.
The **American** Book of the Dead. Scott, J.
AMERICAN CIVIL WAR, 1861-1865 *See*
United States—Civil War, 1861-1865
American express. Salter, J.
American Gothic. Russell, R.
American Horse. Erdrich, L.
An **American** in Paris. Chernin, K.
An **American** presence. Blei, N.
The **American** queen. Laser, M.
American shoes. Lurie, M.
AMERICAN SOLDIERS *See* Soldiers—
United States
AMERICAN SPANISH WAR, 1898 *See*
United States—War of 1898
AMERICANS

Africa
Garfield, B. Trust Charlie
Thomas, M. Jim Chance
Thomas, M. A thief in my house

Australia
Clark, M. A diet of bananas and Nietzsche
Morrison, J. Sailors belong ships

Barbados
Meriwether, L. A happening in Barbados
Shacochis, B. Lord Short Shoe wants the
monkey

Belgium
Peterson, L. S. The gift
Williams, S. And say good-bye to yourself

Belize
Gilchrist, E. Belize

Botswana
Rush, N. Alone in Africa
Rush, N. Instruments of seduction
Rush, N. Official Americans

Canada
Blaise, C. North
Eisenberg, D. Transactions in a foreign
currency

Horvitz, L. A. The fishing village of
Roebush
Thomas, A. C. Elevation

Caribbean region
Morris, M. Death apples
Pritchard, M. Taking hold of Renee
Shacochis, B. Dead reckoning

Chile
Silverberg, R. How they pass the time in
Pelpel

China
Paley, G. Somewhere else

Colombia
Bowles, P. The echo

Costa Rica
Pritchard, M. In foreign country

Cuba
Hemingway, E. One trip across
Herbst, J. The enemy
Loos, A. Liquor makes you smart
O'Brien, T. Underground tests

Denmark
Barthelme, D. A few moments of sleeping
and waking

Eastern Europe
Tuohy, F. The candidate

Egypt
Holding, J. The grave robber
Nevai, L. The Nile

El Salvador
Shepard, L. Salvador

England
Busch, F. Time is money
Dorr, L. Two hundred yards past Word-
sworth's house
Doyle, Sir A. C. The American's tale
Doyle, Sir A. C. The last resource
Fisher, M. F. K. The lost, strayed, stolen
Flanagan, M. Wild garlic
Gilliatt, P. When are you going back?
Givner, J. Conversation pieces
Hazzard, S. Weekend
Hoch, E. D. A flash of red
Hornung, E. W. A trap to catch a cracks-
man
Jakes, J. Dr. Sweetkill
James, H. The author of Beltraffio
James, H. An international episode
James, H. Lady Barberina
Janowitz, T. Fondue
Kalpakian, L. Youth in Asia
King, S. Crouch end
Lurie, M. A fool in winter
Mcauley, P. J. The king of the hill
McGrath, P. The Arnold Crombeck story
Mordden, E. The woggle
Sambrot, W. Black night, white night; or,
The battle of Dingle on the Dangle
Sanders, S. R. The recovery of vision
Seabrooke, D. Secrets
Tallent, E. Faux pas
Tallent, E. The forgiveness trick
Tallent, E. Time with children

AMERICANS—England—*Continued*
Taylor, P. H. Allegiance
Thomas, R. New men, old ways
Updike, J. The afterlife
Warren, J. Anny's men
Westall, R. The Big Rock Candy Mountain
Wetherell, W. D. Spitfire autumn
Wilde, O. The Canterville ghost
Wolfe, T. 'E: a recollection
Wolfe, T. The house of the far and lost

Ethiopia
Thomas, M. Why the sky is so far away

Europe
Barthelme, D. Overnight to many distant cities
Block, L. As good as a rest
Carver, R. The compartment
James, H. Daisy Miller
Just, W. S. I'm worried about you
Leach, A. R. A captain out of Etruria
Morris, M. The typewriter
Raphael, F. Welcome aboard
Shaw, I. Then we were three
Wharton, E. Souls belated
Yates, R. A compassionate leave

France
Algren, N. He couldn't boogie-woogie worth a damn
Bovey, J. The overlap
Christmas, R. A. Another angel
Davis, L. The bone
Faust, I. Gary Dis-Donc
Fink, I. Night of surrender
Fisher, M. F. K. The oldest man
Fisher, M. F. K. The second time around
Fitzgerald, F. S. Babylon, revisited
Garrett, G. P. Don't take no for an answer
Gold, H. Annique
Gold, H. Paris and Cleveland are voyages
Gold, H. Young man, old days
Jaffe, H. Mussel
James, H. A bundle of letters
Jespersen, R. Yport
Kercheval, J. L. Underground women
Kessler, J. F. Hermes
Lopatin, J. The death of Joe Dassin
Lopatin, J. Nuit blanche
Maxwell, W. The Pilgrimage
Meinke, P. Winter term
Moss, R. The shopping trip
Osborn, C. Other people's mail
Pierce, C. Manosque
Rhys, J. Tout Montparnasse and a lady
Russ, J. This afternoon
Shaw, I. The man who married a French wife
Smith, R. The Continental
Spivack, K. The honeymoon
Stead, C. Lost American
Steele, M. Color the daydream yellow
Steele, M. Forget the geraniums
Swados, H. The peacocks of Avignon

Swados, H. Year of grace
Wharton, E. The last asset
Wolfe, T. The sun and the rain

Germany
Davis, L. Mr. Burdoff's visit to Germany
Eisenstein, S. The Kassel ballet
Gusewelle, C. W. Horst Wessel
Ingalls, R. On ice
Oates, J. C. Ich bin ein Berliner
Oates, J. C. Master race
Stoker, B. The squaw
Weaver, G. Flowers: memento mori
Wilson, B. Walking on the moon
Wolfe, T. Dark in the forest, strange as time
Wolfe, T. The dark messiah
Wolfe, T. The Spanish letter

Greece
Hayman, R. Urchins
McCourt, J. I go back to the mais oui
Thomas, J. Half frame
Thomas, J. Santorini gray
Whelan, G. A lesson in the classics

Guam
Bishop, M. Patriots
Pritchard, M. Dead finish

Guatemala
Ruta, S. The bus

Haiti
Gold, H. Child of embassy
Gold, H. A Haitian gentleman
Gold, H. Paternity
Gold, H. Ti-Moune
Working, R. Resurrectionists

Honduras
Morris, M. The watermelon people
Shepard, L. Aymara

Hungary
Oates, J. C. Old Budapest

India
Bloch, R. Untouchable
Hospital, J. T. Waiting
Johnson, H. Victoria
Narayan, R. K. A horse and two goats
Ray, D. Ram Ram
Sharat Chandra, G. S. Bhat's return

Iran
Farnsworth, K. A. Counterpoint

Ireland
Power, V. Night
Tremayne, P. Tavesher

Israel
Mazel, D. Karen
Mazel, D. A story of hope
Mazel, D. The wall
Schafler, N. The social hour
Silverberg, R. A thousand paces along the Via Dolorosa
Thomas, J. Talma Levy is falling

Italy
Ahern, T. An implied acquaintance
Barich, B. Caravaggio
Barich, B. Giorgio's mother

AMERICANS—Italy—*Continued*
Briskin, M. Marshall in Rome
Brodkey, H. Verona: a young woman speaks
Calvino, I. Dollars and the demimondaine
Cassiday, B. Deep-sleep
Day, R. C. Annunciation
Day, R. C. First love
Day, R. C. Grace
Day, R. C. Idiots
Day, R. C. Memory
Day, R. C. Two paces east
Day, R. C. The violation
Ellin, S. The twelfth statue
Goyen, W. The Texas principessa
Hartley, L. P. Mrs. Carteret receives
Hartley, L. P. Simonetta Perkins
Hemingway, E. Cat in the rain
Hemingway, E. Mr. and Mrs. Elliot
Kalpakian, L. Fair Augusto
Parise, G. Freedom
Picano, F. The most golden Bulgari
Pritchard, M. Disturbing no one
Sisk, F. The fly swatter
Spencer, E. The cousins
Swados, H. Something a little special
Trevor, W. Cocktails at Doney's
Updike, D. Due cappuccini
Williams, T. Das Wasser ist kalt
Wilson, B. Il circo delle donne
Woolson, C. F. At the château of Corinne
Woolson, C. F. "Miss Grief"
Woolson, C. F. The street of the Hyacinth
Jamaica
Bowles, P. Pages from Cold Point
Greene, G. Cheap in August
Katz, S. The stolen stories
Osborn, C. The accidental trip to Jamaica
Shacochis, B. The pelican
Japan
Dubus, A. Over the hill
Eisenstein, S. All the monkeys
Kaikō, T. A certain voice
Mailer, N. The paper house
Starr, V. A Japanese play
Tuohy, F. The broken bridge
Whitehouse, A. Savoias out of Sapporo
Woolrich, C. Tokyo, 1941
Korea
Kim, Y. The cuckoo
Sexson, L. Ice cream birth
Majorca
Hall, R. W. A rose in Murcia
Malaysia
Clarke, T. Apai
Clarke, T. The champion
Clarke, T. The day nothing happened
Clarke, T. The king
Clarke, T. The lost D.O.
Clarke, T. A posthumous gift
Clarke, T. The red
Clarke, T. A rite of passion
Clarke, T. The truth

Clarke, T. The wee manok
Clarke, T. The well
Clarke, T. The Wo family
Mexico
Adams, A. Mexican dust
Adams, A. Separate planes
Boswell, R. Flipflops
Bowles, P. Tapiama
Bradbury, R. The candy skull
Crane, S. The five white mice
Crane, S. Horses—one dash
Crane, S. One dash—horses
Crane, S. The wise men: a detail of American life in Mexico
Curley, D. Revenge
Gébler, C. Puerto Vallarta
Highsmith, P. A shot from nowhere
Matthiessen, P. The wolves of Aguila
Ruta, S. At the border
Swados, H. The balcony
Swados, H. The tree of life
Whelan, G. The mummies of Guanajuato
Williams, T. The night of the Iguana
ZoBell, B. Avenida revolucion
Middle East
Wilmot, T. The finger of suspicion
Morocco
Haldeman, J. W. Lindsay and the red city blues
Netherlands
Mazel, D. A longing to live
Nigeria
Meinke, P. The bracelet
Meinke, P. The water-tree
Thomas, M. Summer opportunity
Pakistan
Thompson, B. Crossing
Peru
Miller, S. Travel
Morris, M. Shining path
Philippines
Roberts, N. A second wife
Poland
Meinke, P. The twisted river
Oates, J. C. My Warszawa: 1980
Portugal
Adams, A. Sintra
Rhodes
Ingalls, R. Early morning sightseer
Ingalls, R. Something to write home about
Ingalls, R. St. George and the nightclub
Lurie, M. Home is
Scotland
Kalpakian, L. The last dream before waking
Sanders, S. R. The recovery of vision
Thomas, A. C. Relics
Senegal
McKnight, R. How I met Idi at the Bassi Dakaru restaurant
McKnight, R. Mali is very dangerous
Sicily
Sciascia, L. The American aunt

AMERICANS—*Continued*
Soviet Union
Cullen, E. J. Tolstoy's son
Haylock, J. Traveling towards Boris
Patron, J. F. Miss Bell
Watson, I. Returning home
Spain
Adams, A. Barcelona
Boylan, C. Villa Marta
Campbell, E. In the Rambla de Cataluña
Delbanco, N. At the Prado: a short story
Hemingway, E. The denunciation
Hemingway, E. Hills like white elephants
Hemingway, E. Night before battle
Morris, W. In another country
Raphael, F. On the black list
Sanders, S. R. The cry
Shepard, L. A Spanish lesson
Thomas, J. Christmas in Calpe
Sri Lanka
Bowles, P. In the red room
Switzerland
James, H. The Pension Beaurepas
Shaw, I. The inhabitants of Venus
Taiwan
Ch'en, Y.-C. Night freight
Tanzania
Thomas, M. The Texan
Thailand
Bowles, P. You have left your lotus pods
    on the bus
Turkey
Brondoli, M. The death of the vice consul
Brondoli, M. The love letter hack
Disch, T. M. The Asian shore
Leaton, A. Destiny
Venezuela
Peterson, J. Yellow dust
Vietnam
Loewald, U. Prosperity
Wales
Rossiter, S. Tea party
West Africa
Thomas, M. Come to Africa and save
    your marriage
West Indies
Shacochis, B. Easy in the islands
Zaire
Durban, P. All set about with fever trees
The **American's** tale. Doyle, Sir A. C.
The **amethyst** fly. Decrest, J.
The **amiable** assassin. Crispin, A. C.
Amichai, Yehuda
The Bar Mitzvah party
    Amichai, Y. The world is a room, and
    other stories
Battle for the hill
    Amichai, Y. The world is a room, and
    other stories
Dicky's death
    Amichai, Y. The world is a room, and
    other stories

Love in reverse
    Amichai, Y. The world is a room, and
    other stories
Nina of Ashkelon
    Amichai, Y. The world is a room, and
    other stories
The orgy
    Amichai, Y. The world is a room, and
    other stories
The snow
    Amichai, Y. The world is a room, and
    other stories
Terrible spring
    Amichai, Y. The world is a room, and
    other stories
The times my father died
    Amichai, Y. The world is a room, and
    other stories
The world is a room
    Amichai, Y. The world is a room, and
    other stories
Amihai, Yehuda *See* Amichai, Yehuda
Amis, Kingsley, 1922-
My enemy's enemy
    The Penguin book of modern British
    short stories
Amis, Martin
Bujak and the strong force; or, God's dice
    Amis, M. Einstein's monsters
The immortals
    Amis, M. Einstein's monsters
Insight at Flame Lake
    Amis, M. Einstein's monsters
Let me count the times
    The Penguin book of modern British
    short stories
The little puppy that could
    Amis, M. Einstein's monsters
The time disease
    Amis, M. Einstein's monsters
The **Amish** farmer. Bourjaily, V.
Amita. Pilcher, R.
AMNESIA
Bloch, R. Ego trip
Godfrey, P. And turn the hour
Lovecraft, H. P. The shadow out of time
Matthews, J. The amnesia ballet
Norris, H. The singing well
Stephens, M. Everlast
Symons, J. Has anybody here seen me?
Vinge, J. D. Phoenix in the ashes
Yarbro, C. Q. Do I dare to eat a peach?
The **amnesia** ballet. Matthews, J.
Amnesia's child. Osborn, C.
Among the pictures are these. Campbell, R.
Among thieves. Anderson, P.
El **amor** no tiene orgullo. Kolankiewicz, S.
    J.
The **amoralists.** Colter, C.
Amos. Hunnicutt, E.
Amos Bond, the gunsmith. Matthews, J.
Amphiskios. MacDonald, J. D.
The **ampulla.** Landolfi, T.

AMPUTATION
Maupassant, G. de. At sea
AMPUTEES
Böll, H. My expensive leg
Hulme, K. Hooks and feelers
La Chapelle, M. Homer
McCormack, E. P. The one-legged men
Morrow, W. C. His unconquerable enemy
O'Connor, F. Good country people
Power, V. The operation
AMSTERDAM (NETHERLANDS) *See* Netherlands—Amsterdam
The **amusement-doctor**. Lenz, S.
The **amusement** park. Pacheco, J. E.
AMUSEMENT PARKS
Bell, M. Decatur
Bloch, R. The animal fair
Bloch, R. Double whammy
Boyd, W. Bat-girl!
Conroy, J. The high divers
Dick, P. K. A game of unchance
Dickinson, C. Black Bart
Harris, M. The fun dome
Hemley, R. Riding The Whip
Hoch, E. D. Too long at the fair
Howard, C. Spook house
Jahnn, H. H. A boy weeps
Lynch, L. Pleasure Park
Matthew, J. R. Sweet Letty
Pacheco, J. E. The amusement park
Amy Rose, 1947. Matthew, J. R.
An, Su-Gil
The green chrysanthemum
The Unenlightened, and other Korean short stories
An-Ski, S. *See* Ansky, S., 1863-1920
Analysis of the vessel and its contents. Caponegro, M.
ANALYSTS *See* Psychoanalysts
ANARCHISM AND ANARCHISTS
Austin, D. The relaxed anarchist
Barr, R. The chemistry of anarchy
Ferguson, W. A summer at Estabrook
Sayles, J. At the anarchists' convention
Wells, H. G. The thumbmark
ANARCHISTS *See* Anarchism and anarchists
The **anatomist** of Petrus Borel. Ahern, T.
ANATOMY, HUMAN
See also Arm; Eye; Nose; Teeth
The **anatomy** lesson. Sanders, S. R.
The **anatomy** of desire. L'Heureux, J.
The **anatomy** of loneliness. Wolfe, T.
The **anatomy** of the brain. Klass, P.
Anaya, Rudolfo A.
B. Traven is alive and well in Cuernavaca
Cuentos Chicanos; ed. by R. A. Anaya and A. Márquez
Bless me, Ultima [excerpt]
Writers of the purple sage; ed. by R. Martin and M. Barasch

The silence of the llano
The Interior country; ed. by A. Blackburn
Ancestors. Woolf, V.
The **anchor.** Snow, J.
ANCHOR PERSONS *See* Television announcing
Anchovy trees. Thorman, C.
Ancient airs, voices. Oates, J. C.
The **ancient** gate. Tamer, Z.
Ancient gentility. Williams, W. C.
Ancient history. Bausch, R.
Ancient history. Osborn, C.
Ancient voices. Mooney, M.
And come from miles around. Willis, C.
And cordiality. Judson, J.
And departing leave behind us. Kalpakian, L.
And give you peace. Treadway, J.
". . . .and he chose a mule". Levinson, B.
And he not busy being born . . . Stableford, B. M.
And here in Chicago it's 78°. Gans, B. M.
And I alone am escaped to tell thee. Zelazny, R.
And I only am escaped to tell thee. See Zelazny, R. And I alone am escaped to tell thee
"**And** if he wills, we must die". Crane, S.
And Judith, daughter of Ester, raised the sword above her head. Krysl, M.
—**And** murder makes four! Gault, W. C.
And now he was beginning to feel uneasy about the weather. Austin, D.
And one to dream on. Bates, M.
And say good-bye to yourself. Williams, S.
And seven times never kill man. Martin, G. R. R.
And so died Riabouchinska. Bradbury, R.
And so to bed. Turtledove, H.
And the four animals. Watson, S.
And the green grass grew all around. Blythe, R.
And the hunter home from the hill. Cameron, M. R.
And the marlin spoke. Bishop, M.
And the monsters walk. Jakes, J.
And there was Bert. Campos-De Metro, J.
And there was the evening and the morning . . . Böll, H.
And through the woods. O'Connor, K.
And turn the hour. Godfrey, P.
And Venus is blue. Hood, M.
And where were you, Adam? Böll, H.
And with advantages. Delbanco, N.
"**And** women must weep". Richardson, H. H.
Andax and Odi. Cox, E.
Anderman, Janusz, 1949-
Bitter red star
Anderman, J. Poland under black light
Breathless
Anderman, J. Poland under black light

Anderman, Janusz, 1949——*Continued*
Chain of pure hearts
  Anderman, J. The edge of the world
Czarnoleka: Black Meadow
  Anderman, J. Poland under black light
Day of mist and cloud
  Anderman, J. Poland under black light
Empty . . . sort of
  Anderman, J. The edge of the world
  Anderman, J. Poland under black light
Journey
  Anderman, J. Poland under black light
The National Theatre's burning down
  Anderman, J. The edge of the world
Night shift in emergency
  Anderman, J. Poland under black light
No sound of footsteps in the treetops
  Anderman, J. Poland under black light
Poland still?
  Anderman, J. The edge of the world
Prison sickness
  Anderman, J. Poland under black light
Return visit
  Anderman, J. Poland under black light
A sense of
  Anderman, J. The edge of the world
Shabby lodgings
  Anderman, J. Poland under black light
Sinking wells
  Anderman, J. Poland under black light
The three kings
  Anderman, J. The edge of the world
Topical subject
  Anderman, J. Poland under black light
Turkish baths
  Anderman, J. Poland under black light
VICTO . . .
  Anderman, J. The edge of the world
White night
  Anderman, J. Poland under black light
World of worlds
  Anderman, J. The edge of the world
Andersen, Benny
The phone call
  Editor's choice II; ed. by M. Sklar and
    M. Biggs
Andersen, Hans Christian, 1805-1875
The traveling companion
  Black water; ed. by A. Manguel
Anderson, Charles R.
Saipan the shoeshine man
  The Virginia Quarterly Review 60:661-74
    Aut '84
Anderson, Jane McDill
Choices
  The Virginia Quarterly Review 61:117-29
    Wint '85
Anderson, Jessica
Against the wall
  Anderson, J. Stories from the warm zone
    and Sydney stories

The appearance of things
  Anderson, J. Stories from the warm zone
    and Sydney stories
The aviator
  Anderson, J. Stories from the warm zone
    and Sydney stories
The late sunlight
  Anderson, J. Stories from the warm zone
    and Sydney stories
The milk
  Anderson, J. Stories from the warm zone
    and Sydney stories
Outdoor friends
  Anderson, J. Stories from the warm zone
    and Sydney stories
Under the house
  Anderson, J. Stories from the warm zone
    and Sydney stories
The way to Budjerra Heights
  Anderson, J. Stories from the warm zone
    and Sydney stories
Anderson, Kathy Elaine
Louisiana shade
  The Southern Review (Baton Rouge, La.)
    21:672-81 Jl '85
Anderson, Kevin J., and Fortier, Ron
Skeleton in the closet
  Bringing down the moon; ed. by J. An-
    derson
Anderson, Lars
The Domino Lady doubles back
  Hard-boiled dames; ed. by B. A. Drew
Anderson, Poul, 1926-
Among thieves
  Robert Adams' Book of soldiers
Delenda est
  Alternative histories; ed. by C. G.
    Waugh and M. H. Greenberg
  Time wars; ed. by C. Waugh and M.
    H. Greenberg
The discovery of the past
  Anderson, P. Past times
Eutopia
  Anderson, P. Past times
Eve times four
  Fantastic stories; ed. by M. H. Green-
    berg and P. L. Price
Flight to forever
  Anderson, P. Past times
The forest
  Moonsinger's friends; ed by S. Shwartz
The Gate of the Flying Knives
  Baker's dozen: 13 short fantasy novels
Honorable enemies
  Intergalactic empires; ed. by I. Asimov;
    M. H. Greenberg and C. G. Waugh
Hunter's moon
  The Hugo winners v4
  Medea: Harlan's world; ed. by H. Ellison
The light
  Anderson, P. Past times
The little monster
  Anderson, P. Past times

Anderson, Poul, 1926——*Continued*
The Nest
  Anderson, P. Past times
No truce with kings
  Space wars; created by P. Anderson
Operation afreet
  Masterpieces of fantasy and enchantment; ed. by D. G. Hartwell
Operation salamander
  Witches; ed. by I. Asimov; M. H. Greenberg and C. G. Waugh
Rachaela
  Devils & demons; ed. by M. Kaye and S. Kaye
Requiem for a universe
  The Universe; ed. by B. Preiss
Sam Hall
  Machines that think; ed. by I. Asimov; P. S. Warrick and M. H. Greenberg
The Saturn game
  The Hugo winners v5
Third stage
  Amazing stories: visions of other worlds
Tomorrow's children
  Beyond Armageddon; ed. by W. M. Miller and M. H. Greenberg
Vulcan's forge
  The Year's best science fiction, first annual collection
Welcome
  Anderson, P. Past times
Wildcat
  Anderson, P. Past times
Anderson, Poul, 1926-, and Dickson, Gordon R.
The adventure of the misplaced hound
  Sherlock Holmes through time and space
Anderson, Sherwood, 1876-1941
Death in the woods
  The Norton book of American short stories
Milk bottles
  Inspired by drink; ed. by Joan Digby and John Digby
Unlighted lamps
  Family: stories from the interior; ed. by G. G. Chavis
The **Anderson** boy. Hansen, J.
Anderson Imbert, Enrique, 1910-
Murder
  A Matter of crime v1
ANDES
Valenzuela, L. City of the unknown
Valenzuela, L. Up among the eagles
André. Stewart, J. I. M.
Andres, Katharine
Things to draw
  The New generation; ed. by A. Kaufman
  The New Yorker 59:34-42 Ja 9 '84
Andrews, Cecily Isabel Fairfield *See* West, Dame Rebecca, 1892-1983

Andrews, Raymond
Appalachee Red [excerpt]
  The New writers of the South; ed. by C. East
Andreyev, Leonid, 1871-1919
The abyss
  Andreyev, L. Visions
At the station
  Andreyev, L. Visions
Darkness
  Andreyev, L. Visions
Lazarus
  Masterpieces of terror and the supernatural; ed. by M. Kaye and S. Kaye
The seven who were hanged [Variant title: The seven that were hanged]
  Andreyev, L. Visions
The thief
  Andreyev, L. Visions
The thought
  Andreyev, L. Visions
Andrézel, Pierre, 1885-1962
  For works written by this author under other names see Dinesen, Isak, 1885-1962
Andrić, Ivo, 1892-1975
Thirst
  The Nobel reader; ed. by J. Eisen and S. Troy
  The World of the short story; ed. by C. Fadiman
Words
  Antaeus 60:66-71 Spr '88
Andrina. Brown, G. M.
ANDROS, SIR EDMUND, 1637-1714
                    About
Hawthorne, N. The gray champion
Anecdote. Oates, J. C.
Anecdote concerning the lowering of productivity. Böll, H.
Anecdote from the last Prussian war. Kleist, H. von
Anecdotes of Chairman Maimaiti. Wang Meng
Angel, Albalucía
The guerrillero
  Other fires; ed. by A. Manguel
Angel, George
The bridge
  Southwest Review 73:546-52 Aut '88
Angel. Cadigan, P.
The **angel.** McGrath, P.
Angel. Shelnutt, E.
The **angel.** Skelton, R.
Angel baby. Pollack, R.
The **angel-child.** Crane, S.
The **angel** from hell. Sonderlund, N. O.
The **angel** in the alcove. Williams, T.
The **Angel** of Death. Shea, M.
The **angel** of mercy. Adler, W.
The **angel** of the bridge. Cheever, J.
The **Angel** of the Odd. Poe, E. A.
The **angel** of the tar sands. Wiebe, R. H.

An **angel** on the porch. Wolfe, T.
Angel rolling the heavens together. Metz, J.
Angela. Gilbert, W. S.
Angela. Mukherjee, B.
Angelica. Yolen, J.
Angeline; or, The haunted house. Zola, É.
Ângelo, Ivan
    Little girl
      The Massachusetts Review 27:565-9 Fall/
      Wint '86
ANGELS
    Chavez, A. The fiddler and the Angelito
    Coville, B. The box
    Crouch, C. The wicked season
    Daviau, D.-M. Under the bell jar
    Donaldson, S. R. Unworthy of the angel
    Ferron, J. The archangel of the suburb
    Mazel, D. The angel's overcoat
    McGrath, P. The angel
    Poe, E. A. The Angel of the Odd
    Pollack, R. Angel baby
    Reynolds, M. Your soul comes C.O.D.
    Salmonson, J. A. Angel's exchange
    Sexson, L. Starlings, mute swans, a goose,
      an impossible angel, evening grosbeaks,
      an ostrich, some ducks, and a sparrow
    Spark, M. The Seraph and the Zambesi
    Stern, S. Aaron makes a match
    Wiebe, R. H. The angel of the tar sands
    Williams, O. The angel's gift
    Yolen, J. Angelica
    Zalygin, S. The night of the angels
Angel's exchange. Salmonson, J. A.
The **angel's** gift. Williams, O.
Angels in the snow. Vogan, S.
Angel's last conquest. Orphée, E.
The **angel's** new wings. Chavez, A.
The **angel's** overcoat. Mazel, D.
ANGER
    Coleman, W. A war of eyes
    Connelly, J. Agency
    Dadswell, M. "Hello?"
    Lispector, C. The solution
    Phillips, J. A. How Mickey made it
ANGIOLIERI, CECCO
            About
    Schwob, M. Cecco Angiolieri, malevolent
    poet
ANGLICAN AND EPISCOPAL CLERGY
    See Clergy, Anglican and Episcopal
ANGLICANS
    Watmough, D. False start
The **Anglo-Saxons** of Auxierville. Stuart, J.
An **angry** man. Tamer, Z.
The **angry** street. Chesterton, G. K.
The **anhinga**. White, W. M.
The **animal**. Rey Rosa, R.
ANIMAL ABUSE *See* Animals—Treatment
ANIMAL COMMUNICATION
    Gearhart, S. M. Roxie raccoon
    Jarvis, M. C. Collaboration
    Sargent, P. Out of place
    Vance, J. The gift of gab

The **animal** fair. Bloch, R.
ANIMAL INTELLIGENCE
    Vance, J. The gift of gab
ANIMAL LANGUAGE *See* Animal commu-
    nication
Animal lover. Donaldson, S. R.
The **animal** lover. Havemann, E.
Animal magic. Barrett, A.
Animal prison. Kerr, R.
Animal stew. Liederman, E.
Animal woods. Calvino, I.
ANIMALS
        See also Extinct animals; Mythical
        animals; Taxidermy; also names of in-
        dividual animals
    Arnason, E. The ivory comb
    Böll, H. Unexpected guests
    Boylan, C. L'amour
    Carroll, J. Friend's best man
    Donaldson, S. R. Animal lover
    Harris, J. C. The wonderful Tar-Baby story
    Hemingway, E. Old man at the bridge
    Hoyle, F. Blackmail
    Johnson, C. R. Menagerie, a child's fable
    Le Guin, U. K. Buffalo gals, won't you
      come out tonight
    Lewitt, S. The shaman flute
    MacLeod, A. Second spring
    Martin, V. Elegy for dead animals
    Norton, A. Swamp dweller
    Rendell, R. Loopy
    Updike, D. Indian summer
    Virgo, S. Through the eyes of a cat
    Woolf, V. Nurse Lugton's curtain
            Training
    Kennedy, L. Her furry face
            Treatment
      See also Cockfighting; Dogfighting
    Cockrell, C. In praise of creeping things
    Everett, P. L. Last fair deal
    Highsmith, P. Djemal's revenge
    Howard, C. Animals
    Olmstead, R. River dogs
    Ptacek, K. Dead possums
    Sarton, M. The donkey
    Spark, M. Alice Long's dachshunds
    Walker, A. Am I Blue?
    Wheatcroft, J. The shadow of a bear
    Winton, T. Secrets
ANIMALS, MYTHICAL *See* Mythical
    animals
Animals. Howard, C.
Anis del mono. Monzó, Q.
Anita's dance. Engel, M.
Aniwaya, Anikawa, and the killer teen-agers.
    Salisbury, R.
Ankle. Law-Yone, W.
ANN ARBOR (MICH.) *See* Michigan—Ann
    Arbor
Ann Marie's advice. Lester, D.
Anna. Dubus, A.
Anna and the Ripper of Siam. Somtow, S.
    P.

Anna Dillon. Welch, D.
Anna in a small town. La Chapelle, M.
Anna, Part 1. Gilchrist, E.
Anna, soror . . . Yourcenar, M.
Annals of a fossil. Huang Qingyun
Annamalai. Narayan, R. K.

Annan, Kwabena

Ding dong bell
   African short stories in English; ed. by
      J. de Grandsaigne
Anne. Friedenkraft, G.

**ANNE BOLEYN, QUEEN, CONSORT OF
   HENRY VIII, KING OF ENGLAND,
   1507-1536**

About
Rooke, L. The history of England, part
   four
Anne Marie. Greeley, A. M.
Anne Rey. Kaplan, D. M.
Annemarie singing. Brodkey, H.
Annie Bardwell gets back her cutlery. Mill-
   man, L.
Annie Gray: a tale. Dall, C. W. H.
Annique. Gold, H.

ANNIVERSARIES, WEDDING *See* Wed-
   ding anniversaries
The **anniversary.** Frucht, A.
Anniversary. Smith, E. C.
Anniversary. Starkman, E. M.
The **anniversary** party. Lashuay, N.
Annoyances. Spivack, K.
Annunciation. Day, R. C.
Anny's men. Warren, J.
The **anobiid.** Leask, I. G.
Anodyne. MacLaverty, B.
Another angel. Christmas, R. A.
Another blue-eyed quarterback. Girion, B.
Another burnt-out case. Pronzini, B., and
   Malzberg, B. N.
Another community. Narayan, R. K.
Another dark and stormy night. Hall, T. T.
Another Eve. Kang, S.-J.
Another evening at the club. Rifaat, A.
Another hard winter. Huraniyyah, S.
Another holiday for the Prince. Jolley, E.
Another kind of nostalgia. Haake, K.
Another love story. Fisher, M. F. K.
Another love story. Steele, M.
Another man's room. Choe, I.-H.
Another marvelous thing. Colwin, L.
Another me. Olson, D.
Another moon. Evans, E.
Another pair of hands. Spark, M.
Another party. Carey, J.
Another savage day in the belly of the
   whale. Johnson, D.
Another Sunday morning. Thornton, V.
Another Sunday story. McGarry, J.
Another time. O'Brien, E.
Another's memory. Bulychev, K.

Ansky, S., 1863-1920
Behind a mask
   A Shtetl, and other Yiddish novellas; ed.
      by R. R. Wisse
Anstey, F., 1856-1934
The curse of the catafalques
   Christmas ghosts; ed. by K. Cramer and
      D. G. Hartwell
Answer. Brown, F.
The **answer.** Juarez, H.
Answer in the affirmative. Fisher, M. F. K.
Answer to prayer. Clark, D.
Answer to prayer. Wells, H. G.
The **answer** tree. Boyett, S. R.
Answering the inquisitor. Taylor, P. E.
Answers. Sladek, J. T.
The **answers** they have. Murphy, T. M.
Antaeus. Deal, B.
ANTARCTIC REGIONS
      See also Arctic regions
   Campbell, J. W., Jr. Who goes there?
ANTELOPES
   Austin, M. H. The last antelope
   Swift, G. Hoffmeier's Antelope
ANTHONY, THE ABBOT, SAINT *See* An-
   tony, the Abbot, Saint
Anthony, Piers
The alien rulers
   Space wars; created by P. Anderson
Beak by beak
   Anthony, P. Anthonology
The bridge
   Anthony, P. Anthonology
Encounter
   Anthony, P. Anthonology
Getting through University
   Anthony, P. Anthonology
   The Science fictional Olympics; ed. by
      I. Asimov; M. H. Greenberg and C.
      G. Waugh
The ghost galaxies
   Anthony, P. Anthonology
Gone to the dogs
   Anthony, P. Anthonology
Hard sell
   Anthony, P. Anthonology
Hurdle
   Anthony, P. Anthonology
In the barn
   Anthony, P. Anthonology
In the jaws of danger
   Anthony, P. Anthonology
   Young extraterrestrials; ed. by I. Asimov;
      M. H. Greenberg and C. G. Waugh
The life of the stripe
   Anthony, P. Anthonology
On the uses of torture
   Anthony, P. Anthonology
Phog
   Anthony, P. Anthonology
Possible to rue
   Anthony, P. Anthonology

Anthony, Piers—*Continued*
Quinquepedalian
Amazing stories: visions of other worlds
Anthony, P. Anthonology
Small mouth, bad taste
Anthony, P. Anthonology
The toaster
Anthony, P. Anthonology
Up Schist Crick
Anthony, P. Anthonology
The whole truth
Anthony, P. Anthonology
Within the cloud
Anthony, P. Anthonology
Wood you?
Anthony, P. Anthonology
Anthony's wives. Crump, R.
ANTHROPOLOGISTS
Kaplan, D. M. A Mexican tale
Loukakis, A. Islands
McKnight, R. How I met Idi at the Bassi Dakaru restaurant
McKnight, R. Mali is very dangerous
Nimmo, H. A. Lim
Shefner, E. Royal bones
The **antichrist**. Terry, M.
Anticipation. Dai Qing
Anticipatory grief. Willett, J.
The **anticlerical** pup. Leonard, H.
The **antidote**. Narayan, R. K.
Antieau, Kim
Cycles
Shadows 8
Sanctuary
Shadows 9
Antigone. Watson, S.
ANTIGRAVITY
See also Gravitation
Antimony. Sciascia, L.
Antiphus on Tmolus. Parotti, P.
Antique. Eldridge, M.
ANTIQUE DEALERS
See also Art dealers
Dundas, R. The respecter of persons
Finney, E. J. The divine dealer
Finney, E. J. Lot no. 17
Gerber, M. J. The mistress of Goldman's Antiques
Kotzwinkle, W. Fading tattoo
Millard, P. The diamond
Pritchard, M. Rocking on water, floating in glass
Purdy, J. Mr. Evening
Sampson, R. Far eyes
Spark, M. Miss Pinkerton's apocalypse
Warner, S. T. A pair of duelling pistols
Warner, S. T. A saint (unknown) with two donors
Warner, S. T. Sopwith Hall
Warner, S. T. The three cats
ANTIQUES
See also Antiquities
Gordimer, N. Native country

Halligan, M. The marble angel
Hartley, L. P. The price of the absolute
Kilworth, G. Lord of the dance
Pritchett, V. S. The Camberwell beauty
ANTIQUITIES
See also Archeology
De la Mare, W. A:B:O.
Hornung, E. W. A Jubilee present
Sladek, J. T. The island of Dr. Circe
Antiquities. Crowley, J.
ANTISEMITISM
See also Holocaust, Jewish (1933-1945)
Komie, L. B. Mentoring
Schwartz, S. To Leningrad in winter
Shaw, I. Act of faith
Terry, M. The antichrist
Waldrop, H. Horror, we got
Yates, R. Oh, Joseph, I'm so tired
Antoni, Robert William
Frogchild on the day of Corpus Christi
Hot type; ed. by J. Miller
Two-head Fred and Tree-foot Frieda
The Editors' choice: new American stories v2
Antônio, João
Babylon Johnny
The Literary Review (Madison, N.J.) 27:414-29 Summ '84
ANTONY, THE ABBOT, SAINT
About
Barthelme, D. The temptation of St. Anthony
ANTS
Calvino, I. The Argentine ant
Fast, H. The large ant
Haydar, H. The ants and the qat
Moravia, A. There's a neutron bomb for ants too
Stephenson, C. Leiningen versus the ants
Wells, H. G. The empire of the ants
Ants. Hoffman, N. K.
The **ants**. Vilela, L.
The **ants** and the qat. Haydar, H.
Anukazi's daughter. Gentle, M.
Anvil, Christopher
Babel II
From mind to mind: tales of communication from Analog
A rose by other name . . .
Election Day 2084; ed. by I. Asimov and M. H. Greenberg
Two-way communication
From mind to mind: tales of communication from Analog
The **anvil** of the times. Elman, R.
ANXIETY *See* Fear
Anxiety. Paley, G.
Any minute Mom should come blasting through the door. Ordan, D.
Any more at home like you? Oliver, C.
Anyhow in a corner. McCormack, E. P.
Anyone else would learn. Burt, S.

Anyone for murder? Ritchie, J.
Anyplace but here. Conroy, J.
Anything is possible. Monreal, D. N.
Anything you want. Coe, C.
Apache. Huddle, D.
APACHE INDIANS
  Austin, M. H. The man who lied about a woman
  Austin, M. H. Stewed beans
  Haycox, E. Stage to Lordsburg
Apai. Clarke, T.
APARTHEID *See* South Africa—Race relations
APARTMENT HOUSES
  Bell, M. S. Irene
  Bell, M. S. The lie detector
  Brulotte, G. The elevator messengers
  Carrier, R. The room
  Cheever, J. The enormous radio
  Colette. The find
  Gallant, M. The assembly
  Gallant, M. Overhead in a balloon
  Gilliatt, P. As we have learnt from Freud, there are no jokes
  Grant, C. L. Out there
  Martin, G. R. R. The Pear-shaped Man
  McCullers, C. Court in the West eighties
  Rossi, A. Winter rentals
  Standiford, L. Guerin and the presidential revue
APARTMENTS *See* Apartment houses
The **Apelles** mark. Pasternak, B. L.
Aperitif. Raphael, F.
APES
      See also Gorillas
  Bloch, R. The animal fair
  Del Rey, L. The faithful
  Helprin, M. Letters from the Samantha
  Moffett, J. Surviving
Aphrodissia, the widow. Yourcenar, M.
Apocalypse. Holt, T. E.
The **apocalypse** of Mary the unbeliever. Sexson, L.
Apocalyptic flirtation. Molinaro, U.
Apollinaire, Guillaume, 1880-1918
  Arthur, the once and future king
    Apollinaire, G. The poet assassinated, and other stories
  The blue eye
    Apollinaire, G. The poet assassinated, and other stories
  The case of the masked corporal, that is, the poet resuscitated
    Apollinaire, G. The poet assassinated, and other stories
  The deified invalid
    Apollinaire, G. The poet assassinated, and other stories
  The departure of the shadow
    Apollinaire, G. The poet assassinated, and other stories

The eagle hunt
    Apollinaire, G. The poet assassinated, and other stories
The favorite
    Apollinaire, G. The poet assassinated, and other stories
Giovanni Moroni
    Apollinaire, G. The poet assassinated, and other stories
Little recipes from modern magic
    Apollinaire, G. The poet assassinated, and other stories
The meeting at the mixed club
    Apollinaire, G. The poet assassinated, and other stories
The moon king
    Apollinaire, G. The poet assassinated, and other stories
Our friend Méritarte
    Apollinaire, G. The poet assassinated, and other stories
The poet assassinated
    Apollinaire, G. The poet assassinated, and other stories
The posthumous fiance
    Apollinaire, G. The poet assassinated, and other stories
Saint Adorata
    Apollinaire, G. The poet assassinated, and other stories
The talking memories
    Apollinaire, G. The poet assassinated, and other stories
                    About
Davenport, G. The Haile Selassie Funeral Train
Apollo's thing. Izgü, M.
The **apology.** Dadswell, M.
Apondé, the Magnificent times two. Glynn, T.
The **apostle** of immortality, a tale of the unprecedented. Berdnyk, O.
APOTHECARIES *See* Pharmacists
The **apotheosis** of Isaac Rosen. Dann, J., and Dann, J. V. B.
Appalachee Red. Andrews, R.
APPALACHIAN HIGHLANDERS
  O'Connor, F. The life you save may be your own
  O'Connor, F. A stroke of good fortune
  Still, J. The moving
APPALACHIAN REGION
  Crabtree, L. V. Holy Spirit
  Crabtree, L. V. Homer-snake
  Crabtree, L. V. The Jake Pond
  Crabtree, L. V. Little Jesus
  Crabtree, L. V. The miracle in Sweet Hollow
  Crabtree, L. V. Prices' bewitched cow
  Crabtree, L. V. Wildcat John
The **Appaloosa** house. Stark, S. S.
The **apparition.** Sisskind, M.

An **apparition** in the Engineers' Castle. Leskov, N. S.

The **apparition** of Mrs. Veal. Defoe, D.

Apparitions. Walters, A. L.

The **appeal**. Wheatcroft, J.

The **appearance** of things. Anderson, J.

APPENDICITIS
Updike, J. The city

Appetites. King, F. H.

Applause, applause. Thompson, J.

Apple, Max
The American bakery [Variant title: My love affair with English]
Apple, M. Free agents
Blood relatives
Apple, M. Free agents
Bridging
Apple, M. Free agents
The Atlantic 253:93-6 Ap '84
New stories from the South: the year's best, 1986
The Norton book of American short stories
Short story international 54
Business talk
Apple, M. Free agents
Carbo-loading
Apple, M. Free agents
Child's play
Apple, M. Free agents
The eighth day
Apple, M. Free agents
The Ploughshares reader: new fiction for the eighties
Eskimo love
Apple, M. Free agents
Esquire 101:216-18+ Ap '84
The Esquire fiction reader v1
The four Apples
Apple, M. Free agents
Free agents
Apple, M. Free agents
Heart attack
Sudden fiction; ed. by R. Shapard and J. Thomas
Help
Apple, M. Free agents
Kitty partners
Apple, M. Free agents
Momma's boy
Apple, M. Free agents
My real estate
The Georgia Review 40:19-31 Spr '86
Necessary fictions; ed. by S. W. Lindberg and S. Corey
The national debt
Apple, M. Free agents
An offering
Apple, M. Free agents
Pizza time
Apple, M. Free agents
Post-modernism
Apple, M. Free agents

Harper's 269:31-2 S '84
Research
Harper's 274:66-71 Ja '87
Small island republics
Apple, M. Free agents
Short story international 62
Stepdaughters
Esquire 102:286-7+ S '84
Stranger at the table [Variant title: Keeping kosher]
Apple, M. Free agents
Walt and Will [Variant title: Disneyad]
Apple, M. Free agents

The **apple**. Novakovich, J.

The **apple**. Wells, H. G.

An **apple** for the preacher. Rees, D.

Apple peels and knives. Lane, P.

The **apple-tree** table; or, Original spiritual manifestations. Melville, H.

APPLE TREES
Keillor, G. How the crab apple grew

The **apple** war. Doyle, B.

Apples. Berry, R. M.

Apples. Campbell, R.

Apples. Hartley, L. P.

Apples. Updike, D.

Apples and pears: Het Erewhonisch schetsboek: Messidor-Vendémiaire 1981. Davenport, G.

The **apples** of paradise. Barstow, S.

The **apples** of the Hesperides. Christie, A.

Application for a small life. Ty-Casper, L.

The **appointment**. Murphy, P.

Appointment at Princess Gate. Morrison, J.

Appointment in Khartoum. Markham, B.

The **apprentice**. Balogun, O.

The **apprentice**. Whitaker, M.

The **apprentice** sorcerer. Rynas, S.

APPRENTICES
Balogun, O. The apprentice
Conroy, J. Freight car repair yard pranks
Dinesen, I. The cloak
Gallacher, T. A friend of Dosser Farr
Gallacher, T. Lord Sweatrag
Gallacher, T. Portrait of Isa Mulvenny
Gallacher, T. Store quarter
Gardner, C. S. A malady of magicks
Gimbel, A. Hardwood
Johnson, C. R. The sorcerer's apprentice
Linaweaver, B. Shadow quest
Shiga, N. The shopboy's god
Van de Wetering, J. The new disciple

Approaching substance. Murphy, P.

Appropriate affect. Miller, S.

Approximations. Simpson, M.

April. Campbell, A.

April. Colette

April. Oates, J. C.

April in peril. Gault, W. C.

April, late April. Wolfe, T.

The **April** witch. Bradbury, R.

Aprille. Keillor, G.

The **aquarist**. Allan, J. N.

AQUARIUMS
Allan, J. N. The aquarist
Haas, B. The green life
Kant, H. A bit of the South Sea
Aquin, Hubert, 1929-1977
Back on April eleventh
The Oxford book of French-Canadian short stories
Aquino, J.
We've been invited to a party
A Matter of crime v2
ARAB-JEWISH RELATIONS *See* Jewish-Arab relations
Arabella. Hall, J.
Arabella's answer. Lovesey, P.
Arabesque—the mouse. Coppard, A. E.
ARABIA *See* Arabian Peninsula
ARABIAN NIGHTS
A Dream
Parodies, travesties, etc.
Poe, E. A. The thousand-and-second tale of Scheherazade
Thériault, M.-J. The thirty-first bird
ARABIAN PENINSULA
Kilworth, G. The dissemblers
ARABS
See also Bedouins; Jewish-Arab relations; Palestinian Arabs
Al-Wardani, M. The kerosene stove
Aslan, I. The little girl in green
Barrada, M. Life by instalments
Camus, A. The adulterous woman
Chukri, M. Flower Crazy
Colette. The rendezvous
Dunsany, E. J. M. D. P., Baron. A story of land and sea
El-Bisatie, M. My brother
Gurnah, A. Bossy
Ibrahim, I. The gap in Kaltouma's fence
Idris, Y. The chair carrier
Kassem, A.-H. The trial of the small black woman
Khudayyir, M. Clocks like horses
Kotzwinkle, W. Fana
Razzak, A. I. A. Voices from near and far
Selmi, H. Distant seas
Sharouni, Y. Glimpses from the life of Maugoud Abdul Maugoud and two postscripts
Taher, B. Advice from a sensible young man
France
Rhys, J. The Sidi
Arachne. Mason, L.
Arachné. Schwob, M.
The **Arandora** Star. MacLean, A.
Arbeit macht Frei. Aćin-Kosta, M.
Arbre de décision. Bowering, G.
Arcadia. Dickinson, C.
Arcadia. Greenwood, R.
The **Arcadian** Deer. Christie, A.
Arcadus Arcane. Pimple, D. J.

The **archangel** of the suburb. Ferron, J.
The **archbishop;** or, The lady. Windsor, G.
ARCHEOLOGICAL SPECIMENS *See* Antiquities
ARCHEOLOGISTS
Clee, M. A. Dust
Holding, J. The Treasure of Pachacamac
Howes, C. The resurrection man
Kessler, J. F. Maya
Meinke, P. The bracelet
Narayan, R. K. The Roman image
Piper, H. B. Omnilingual
Rizkalla, J. The black figurine
Shannon, D. Need-fire
Simak, C. D. Grotto of the dancing deer
Strugatskiĭ, B. N., and Strugatskiĭ, A. N. The visitors
Thomas, J. Talma Levy is falling
ARCHEOLOGY
See also Antiquities; Man, Prehistoric
Taylor, C. Leanderthal lady
Archeology. Cameron, P.
Archer, Jeffrey, 1940-
A la carte
Archer, J. A twist in the tale
A chapter of accidents
Archer, J. A twist in the tale
Checkmate
Archer, J. A twist in the tale
Christina Rosenthal
Archer, J. A twist in the tale
Clean sweep Ignatius
Archer, J. A twist in the tale
Colonel Bullfrog
Archer, J. A twist in the tale
Honor among thieves
Archer, J. A twist in the tale
Just good friends
Archer, J. A twist in the tale
The loophole
Archer, J. A twist in the tale
Not the real thing
Archer, J. A twist in the tale
The perfect murder
Archer, J. A twist in the tale
The steal
Archer, J. A twist in the tale
Archetypes. Greenwood, R.
ARCHITECTS
Boyle, K. The meeting of the stones
Colette. The rendezvous
Delbanco, N. The consolation of philosophy
Disch, T. M. The Asian shore
Finney, J. Where the Cluetts are
Houbein, L. Green marmalade
Robison, J. Set off
Architecture. Barthelme, F.
Architecture. Lurie, M.
Arcola girls. Deaver, P. F.

ARCTIC REGIONS
> *See also* Alaska; Antarctic regions; Greenland

Burns, M. The circle
Handke, P. The long way around
Kinsella, W. P. The Indian Nation Cultural Exchange Program
London, J. A hyperborean brew [excerpt]
London, J. Love of life
London, J. The white silence
Murphy, G. R. War
White, T. H. The troll

Arden, William, 1924-
> *For works written by this author under other names see* Collins, Michael, 1924-; Lynds, Dennis, 1924-; Sadler, Mark, 1924-

Homecoming
  Uncollected crimes; ed. by B. Pronzini and M. H. Greenberg
Hot night homicide
  Murder California style; ed. by J. L. Breen and J. Ball
The **ardent** commandant. Chavez, A.

Ardizzone, Tony
The daughter and the tradesman
  Ardizzone, T. The evening news
The evening news
  Ardizzone, T. The evening news
The eyes of children
  Ardizzone, T. The evening news
Idling
  Ardizzone, T. The evening news
The intersection
  Ardizzone, T. The evening news
Larabi's ox
  Prairie Schooner 62:39-50 Fall '88
My father's laugh
  Ardizzone, T. The evening news
My mother's stories
  Ardizzone, T. The evening news
Nonna
  Ardizzone, T. The evening news
The transplant
  Ardizzone, T. The evening news
The walk-on
  Ardizzone, T. The evening news
World without end
  Ardizzone, T. The evening news
Are the trees green? Yoshiyuki, J.
Are these actual miles? Carver, R.
Are we leaving tomorrow? O'Hara, J.
Are you stone-cold, Santa Claus? Ferreira, R.

ARGENTINA
> *See also* Patagonia (Argentina and Chile)

Orphée, E. Angel's last conquest [excerpt]
Orphée, E. The silken whale
Silvis, R. The luckiest man in the world
Traba, M. Mothers and shadows [excerpt]

Peasant life
> *See* Peasant life—Argentina

Rural life
Quiroga, H. The dead man
Buenos Aires
Cortázar, J. Return trip tango
The **Argentine** ant. Calvino, I.
ARGENTINE REPUBLIC *See* Argentina
ARGENTINES
New York (N.Y.)
Codrescu, A. Samba de los agentes
ARGENTINIANS *See* Argentines
The **Argonauts** of the air. Wells, H. G.
Argument against the free-standing bathtub. Piñera, V.
Argument with my father. Glück, T.
Ariail, Jacqueline
The mother next door
  Redbook 168:46-8+ F '87
Arias, Ron, 1941-
Lupe
  Cuentos Chicanos; ed. by R. A. Anaya and A. Márquez
Ariel. A legend of the lighthouse. Alcott, L. M.
The **Ariel** defeats the Alacrity. Cooper, J. F.
ARISTOCRACY
> *See also* Courts and courtiers

Chesterton, G. K. Dukes
Davidson, A. Duke Pasquale's ring
Mathews, P. S. Well met in Ithkar
Roth, J. The bust of the emperor
Watmough, D. Connecticut countess
Williams, T. The inventory at Fontana Bella
Wolfenstein, M. Chayah
Austria
Morris, W. Here is Einbaum
Sagan, F. Aftermath of a duel
Denmark
Gathorne-Hardy, J. Peiter and Paulina
England
Hornung, E. W. To catch a thief
James, H. An international episode
James, H. Lady Barberina
Maugham, W. S. Lord Mountdrago
Raphael, F. Private views
Raphael, F. Sleeps six
Thomas, D. The end of the river
Tremain, R. The stately roller coaster
France
Sagan, F. A country outing
Sagan, F. The distant cousin
Tournier, M. The Woodcock
Germany
Becher, U. A very Baltic story
Dickens, C. The Baron of Grogzwig
Gilbert, W. S. The triumph of vice
Mitchell, E. P. An uncommon sort of spectre
Italy
King, F. H. Unmaking
Sagan, F. "La Futura"

ARISTOCRACY—*Continued*
Soviet Union
Alcott, L. M. Taming a Tartar
Gogol', N. V. The coach
Aristotelian logic. Škvorecký, J.
ARITHMETIC
Crane, S. A ghoul's accountant
Ariyoshi, Sawako, 1931-
The Tomoshibi
  The Mother of dreams, and other short
  stories; ed. by M. Ueda
ARIZONA
Camoin, F. A. The Amelia Barons
Carr, P. M. Indian burial
Hauptman, W. The desert
Ríos, A. La boda
Frontier and pioneer life
  See Frontier and pioneer life—
  Arizona
Phoenix
St. Clair, M. An egg a month from all
  over
Wilson, B. Take Louise Nevelson
Ark. Dumas, H.
The **ark.** McAllister, B.
The **ark.** Sheehan, R.
The **ark.** Zhang Jie
Ark of bones. Dumas, H.
ARKANSAS
Jones, D. C. Halloween and other sacred
  events
Jones, D. C. In pastures green
Jones, D. C. Knights of the Flaming Circle
Jones, D. C. The last fastball
Jones, D. C. The Law
Jones, D. C. Once a year
Jones, D. C. Raised in the wilderness
Jones, D. C. The saga of Slaven Budd
Jones, D. C. The trombone and the lady
Jones, D. C. Trusty
Nordan, L. Storyteller
Read, O. An Arkansas hanging
Read, O. Big Bill and Little Bill
Thanet, O. Sist' Chaney's black silk
Thorpe, T. B. The big bear of Arkansas
Little Rock
Ebon, W. Little girl from Little Rock
Leedom-Ackerman, J. History lesson
An **Arkansas** hanging. Read, O.
ARLES (FRANCE) *See* France—Arles
ARM
Kawabata, Y. One arm
The **arm.** Grin, A.
The **arm-chair** of Tustenuggee. Simms, W.
  G.
ARMADA, 1588
Robinson, K. S. Black air
Armadillo. Hendrie, L.
Armageddon. Brown, F.
Armageddon. Ferron, J.
Armaja das. Haldeman, J. W.

ARMAMENTS
  See also Munitions
Armande. Colette
Armas, José
El tonto del Barrio
  Cuentos Chicanos; ed. by R. A. Anaya
  and A. Márquez
ARMENIANS
Chekhov, A. P. Beauties
Saroyan, W. How to choose a wife
Saroyan, W. Mystic games
United States
Kalpakian, L. The land of lucky strike
Saroyan, W. The beautiful white horse
Saroyan, W. Madness in the family
Armer, Karl Michael
BCO equipment
  The Penguin world omnibus of science
  fiction
On the inside track
  Tales from the planet Earth
Armistice Day. Liben, M.
Armitage, Robert
Lost time
  The Literary Review (Madison, N.J.)
  32:91-103 Fall '88
ARMS AND ARMOR
  See also Munitions; Swords
Herbert, F. Committee of the whole
Kersh, G. Comrade death
Pronzini, B. Toy
Arms of the flame goddess. James, F.
Armstrong, Charlotte, 1905-1969
The enemy
  Hound dunnit; ed. by I. Asimov; M. H.
  Greenberg and C. L. R. Waugh
The hedge between
  Child's ploy; ed. by M. Muller and B.
  Pronzini
The other shoe
  Ellery Queen's Memorable characters
The splintered Monday
  Masterpieces of mystery and suspense;
  ed. by M. H. Greenberg
Army-chaplain Schmelzle's journey to Flätz.
  Jean Paul
ARMY HOSPITALS *See* Hospitals and
  sanatoriums
ARMY OFFICERS *See* France—Army—Of-
  ficers;   Germany—Army—Officers;
  Great Britain. Army—Officers; New
  Zealand. Army—Officers; Poland—
  Army—Officers; Soviet Union. Red
  Army—Officers;   United States.
  Army—Officers
Arnason, E.
The ivory comb
  Stiller's pond; ed. by J. Agee; R. Blakely
  and S. Welch
Arnaud's nixie. Walker, W.

Arnim, Ludwig Achim, Freiherr von, 1781-1831
The madman of Fort Ratonneau
German romantic stories; ed. by F. G. Ryder
Arno. Hofmann, G.
Arnold, H. F.
The night wire
Masterpieces of terror and the supernatural; ed. by M. Kaye and S. Kaye
Arnold, Margot
The girl in the mirror
Ready or not; ed. by J. Kahn
Arnold, Marianne
The old woman
Stories and poems from close to home; ed. by F. Salas
Arnold, Mark
Pilgrims to the cathedral
Silver scream; ed. by D. J. Schow
The **Arnold** Crombeck story. McGrath, P.
Arnold Pentland. Wolfe, T.
Arnow, Harriette Louisa Simpson, 1908-1986
Fra Lippi and me
The Georgia Review 40:32-9 Spr '86
Necessary fictions; ed. by S. W. Lindberg and S. Corey
Around the crate. Papaellinas, G.
The **arrangement.** Saiki, J.
An **arrangement** of shadows. Bissoondath, N.
The **arrangements** of Françoise Dumoutier. Villefranche, A.-M.
Arredondo, Inés
The shunammite
Other fires; ed. by A. Manguel
Arreola, Juan José
The switchman
Anthology of contemporary Latin American literature, 1960-1984
ARRESTS
Coleman, W. Stashed
Grace, P. The hills
Jhabvala, R. P. On bail
Nowakowski, M. Judas in the square
Willson, H. Loyalty erosion
Working, R. On freedom
Arriki. Dabbs, D. E.
Arrival and rehearsal. Colette
Arrival of the picture brides. Saiki, J.
Ars poetica. Sorrentino, F.
ARSON
Drewe, R. The silver medallist
Ellin, S. The nine-to-five man
Faulkner, W. Barn burning
Ferguson, P. The dry familiar plains
Givner, J. A climate of extremes
Haake, K. Burning the lost country
Howard, C. Animals
Hyon, C.-G. Fire
Nevai, L. Hooked
Regent, P. Schoolboy war
Saroyan, W. Fire
Schwob, M. Herostratos, incendiary

Van Derveer, M. The quiet investigation
Wilson, R., Jr. Payment in kind
ART
Barthelme, D. Letters to the editore
Cohen, A. Hans Cassebeer and the virgin's rose
Cohen, A. Malenov's revenge
Disch, T. M. Canned goods
Eisenstein, S. Straight razor
Ellison, H. With Virgil Oddum at the East Pole
Feng Jicai. Plum blossoms in the snow
Soukup, M. Frenchmen and plumbers
Spark, M. The Playhouse called Remarkable
Taylor, C. Grom's story: naked lady
Exhibitions
Gallant, M. Speck's idea
Ozick, C. The suitcase
Wady, T. The madman
Art. Mrożek, S.
Art and Mr. Mahoney. McCullers, C.
Art and the bronco. Henry, O.
ART COLLECTORS
Auchincloss, L. The reckoning
Bowles, P. Rumor and a ladder
Fish, R. L. The wager
Futrelle, J. The stolen Rubens
Goyen, W. The Texas principessa
Janowitz, T. Turkey talk
Silverberg, R. Not our brother
Art colony. Boyle, K.
ART CRITICS
Farmer, P. J. Riders of the purple wage
Mathers, P. Picking a loser
Woolson, C. F. The street of the Hyacinth
ART DEALERS
See also Antique dealers
Ellin, S. Kindly dig your grave
Hoch, E. D. The melting man
Lurie, M. Repository
Lurie, M. Two artists
Masur, H. Q. Framed for murder
Soldatow, S. Hass story
ART EXHIBITIONS *See* Art—Exhibitions
ART FORGERIES *See* Forgery of works of art
ART GALLERIES AND MUSEUMS
Clark, M. At the exhibition
Davie, E. Security
Gallant, M. Speck's idea
Krysl, M. And Judith, daughter of Ester, raised the sword above her head
Lurie, M. Camille Pissaro 1830-1903
Mathers, P. Picking a loser
Art in the war zone. Murphy, P.
Art is lost. Mattison, A.
ART OBJECTS
See also Antiques
Maupassant, G. de. Bric-à-brac
The **art** of cartography. Marcus, J. S.
The **art** of dying well. Alther, L.
The **art** of murder. Sandel, C.

The **art** of seeing with one's own eyes. Doubiago, S.

The **art** of surviving November. Gustafsson, L.

The **art** of the knock. Graham, P.

The **art** of Vietnam. Wiebe, D. E.

ART PATRONAGE
Williams, T. Man bring this up road

ARTHUR, KING

About

Apollinaire, G. Arthur, the once and future king

Sir Galahad and the Holy Grail

Arthur, Robert, d. 1969
The haunted trailer
  Great ghost stories; ed. by B. A. Schwartz
The wonderful day
  Young witches & warlocks; ed. by I. Asimov; M. H. Greenberg and C. G. Waugh

Arthur & Alwyn. Mathers, P.

Arthur Bond. Goyen, W.

Arthur, the once and future king. Apollinaire, G.

The **artichoke.** Krysl, M.

Artie Blanchard. Ade, G.

An **artifice.** Maupassant, G. de

The **artificial** family. Tyler, A.

ARTIFICIAL INTELLIGENCE
Kelly, J. P. The prisoner of Chillon
Maddox, T. Snake-eyes
Van Vogt, A. E. Fulfillment

The **artificial** liar. Brittain, W.

ARTIFICIAL LIFE
Bester, A. Galatea Galante
Bilenkin, D. The genius house
Blumlein, M. Tissue ablation and variant regeneration: a case report
Bulychev, K. Another's memory
Cadigan, P. Pretty boy crossover
Cogswell, T. R. Deal with the D.E.V.I.L.
Gunn, J. E. Out of my head
Haldeman, J. W. Blood sisters
Halligan, M. Mozart is best
Leiber, F. Yesterday house
Sheckley, R. Restricted area
Sheffield, C. Dies irae
Shirley, J. Triggering
Sykes, S. C. Rockabye Baby
Temple, W. F. The four-sided triangle
Watson, I. The rooms of paradise

The **artificial** moonlight. Justice, D. R.

The **artificial** nigger. O'Connor, F.

Artificial roses. García Márquez, G.

ARTIFICIAL SATELLITES
Clarke, A. C. Dial F for Frankenstein
Silverberg, R. Blindsight
Vincent, H. Rex

ARTISANS
Crace, J. Sins and virtues
García Márquez, G. Balthazar's marvelous afternoon

Jackson, G. The fly-screen
MacLaverty, B. Words the happy say
Rasulov, M.-R. The eve of love
Wady, T. The madman
Wier, A. Campbell Oakley's gospel sun shines on Roy Singing Grass

The **artist.** Austin, D.

The **artist.** Maupassant, G. de

The **artist.** Silva, B.

The **artist.** Winters, J.

ARTIST COLONIES
Nevai, L. Diamond twill
Summers, H. S. The vireo's nest

The **artist** (Inez). Mohr, N.

ARTIST LIFE
Aksenov, V. P. Super-deluxe
Allen, R. The woman in the shadows
Boyle, K. Art colony
Crane, S. Stories told by an artist
Faulkner, W. A portrait of Elmer
Glickfeld, C. L. Out of the lion's belly
Henry, O. A service of love
Hoffmann, E. T. A. Don Juan
Humphrey, W. The fauve
Janowitz, T. Kurt and Natasha, a relationship
Janowitz, T. Spells
Skiles, D. The loft
Tuohy, F. A young girl
Williams, T. In memory of an aristocrat
Woolson, C. F. The street of the Hyacinth

The **artist** of the beautiful. Hawthorne, N.

The **artistic** career of Corky. Wodehouse, P. G.

The **artistic** temperament. Crowley, A.

The **artistic** touch. Watson, I.

ARTISTS

    See also Artist life; Illustrators; Painters; Sculptors; Women artists

Abe, K. The magic chalk
Alcott, L. M. A pair of eyes; or, Modern magic
Auchincloss, L. Portrait of the artist by another
Austin, D. The artist
Barich, B. Caravaggio
Barthelme, D. Engineer-private Paul Klee misplaces an aircraft between Milbertshofen and Cambrai, March 1916
Barthelme, D. Great days
Baxter, C. Cataract
Beattie, A. Skeletons
Bellow, S. Zetland: by a character witness
Bissoondath, N. A short visit to a failed artist
Borden, J. The shoes of death
Campbell, R. The other woman
Carr, J. Blind spot
Carrington, L. Pigeon, fly!
Conner, M. Vamp
Conroy, F. Roses

ARTISTS—*Continued*

Covino, M. The passion of the artist is nothing compared to the passion of the businessman

Crane, S. The third violet

DeMarinis, R. The swimmer in hard light

Ellin, S. Kindly dig your grave

Everett, P. L. A good home for Hachita

Feng Jicai. Winding brook way

Forsh, O. The little mermaid Rotozeyechka

Gardner, M. At the feet of Karl Klodhopper

Garfield, B. Scrimshaw

Greening, J. Pleasure trips

Harrington, J. Birdbrain

Hemley, R. Installations

Henry, O. An adjustment of nature

Highsmith, P. A shot from nowhere

Hospital, J. T. After the fall

Janowitz, T. Conviction

Janowitz, T. In and out of the cat bag

Janowitz, T. Life in the pre-Cambrian era

Janowitz, T. On and off the African veldt

Janowitz, T. Physics

Janowitz, T. Snowball

Johnston, G. Requiem mass

Juarez, H. The answer

Kawabata, Y. Samurai descendant

Kilworth, G. Scarlet fever

Kress, N. Ten thousand pictures, one word

Lee, T. Elle est trois, (la mort)

Lurie, M. Two artists

MacLaverty, B. The drapery man

Mazel, D. Lily's Deli

McDevitt, J. In the tower

McGrath, P. Lush triumphant

Moravia, A. The sign of the operation

Morrell, D. Orange is for anguish, blue for insanity

Morris, K. The eyeless dragons: a Chinese story

Murphy, P. Art in the war zone

Oates, J. C. Further confessions

Prose, F. Criminals

Ruta, S. At the border

Ruta, S. In Fiona's country

Sandel, C. Thank you, doctor

Schwartz, L. S. The infidel

Sheil, G. Of gumleaves and clove-scented cigarettes

Shepard, L. The man who painted the dragon Griaule

Steele, M. Forget the geraniums

Stewart, J. I. M. Melencolia I

Swados, H. The balcony

Swados, H. The tree of life

Swanwick, M. The man who met Picasso

Thorman, C. God giving Lithuania to the world

Thorman, C. Persecution is for you

Upward, E. The procession

Van de Wetering, J. The jughead file

Vogan, S. China across the bay

Williams, T. The angel in the alcove

Artist's Christmas. Sandel, C.

ARTISTS' MODELS

Atwood, M. The sunrise

Baxter, C. The model

Chambers, R. W. The yellow sign

Conroy, F. Roses

Leiber, F. The girl with the hungry eyes

Malamud, B. The model

Maupassant, G. de. The artist's wife

Oates, J. C. Photographer's model

O'Donnell, P. Salamander Four

Pain, B. Rose Rose

Pritchard, M. La Bête: a figure study

Regent, P. Feet of clay

Rhys, J. Till September Petronella

Sandel, C. Lola

Vanderhaeghe, G. Going to Russia

The **artist's** wife. Maupassant, G. de

Arturo and Eve. Rose, D. A.

Aryan papers. Fink, I.

As above, so below. Ford, J. M.

As birds bring forth the sun. MacLeod, A.

"As drink the dead . . . ". Carr, J. D.

As far as Abashiri. Shiga, N.

As good as a rest. Block, L.

As good as gold. Watt, N.

As is. Gilliatt, P.

As is. Silverberg, R.

As luck would have it. Henley, P.

As small as your shadow. Dundas, R.

As they rode along the edge. Carrington, L.

As we have learnt from Freud, there are no jokes. Gilliatt, P.

As ye sow—. Fisher, D. C.

As you'd like it. Coriolan, J.

ASEXUAL REPRODUCTION *See* Reproduction, Asexual

Ash, Paul

Minds meet

From mind to mind: tales of communication from Analog

The **ash** heel's tendon. Hemingway, E.

Ash on my sleeve. Wicomb, Z.

The **ash-tree.** James, M. R.

Asher, Helen W.

Three happy Japanese

Room to move; ed. by S. Falkiner

Ashes. Thompson, S.

Ashes for an urn. Sisk, F.

Ashes to ashes. Hospital, J. T.

Ashiepattle. Walker, W.

Ashley, Franklin

"Listen buddy, we don't throw gutter balls here"

A Collection of classic Southern humor; ed. by G. W. Koon

Ashley, Mary Anne

Gracefully afraid

When I am an old woman I shall wear purple; ed. by S. K. Martz

Ashour, Linda
  Stories I'd rather not tell
    The Paris Review 26:60-70 Summ '84
ASHRAMS
  Glover, D. H. The seeker, the snake and
    the baba
Ashwood-Collins, Anna
  Film at eleven
    The Womansleuth anthology; ed. by I.
    Zahava
ASIA
      See also East Asia
The **Asian** shore. Disch, T. M.
ASIANS
           England
  Wells, H. G. The Lord of the Dynamos
         United States
  Wetherell, W. D. Why I love America
Asilomarian lecture (The dirmal life of the
  inhabitats). Shannon, B. T.
Asimov, Isaac, 1920-
  1 to 999
    Mathenauts: tales of mathematical won-
    der; ed. by R. Rucker
  All the troubles of the world
    Asimov, I. The best science fiction of
    Isaac Asimov
  Belief
    Asimov, I. The edge of tomorrow
  Belief (first version)
    Asimov, I. The alternate Asimovs
  Belief (published version)
    Asimov, I. The alternate Asimovs
  The Bicentennial Man
    The Hugo winners v4
    Machines that think; ed. by I. Asimov;
    P. S. Warrick and M. H. Greenberg
  The billiard ball
    Asimov, I. The edge of tomorrow
    Asimov, I. Robot dreams
  Blind alley
    Intergalactic empires; ed. by I. Asimov;
    M. H. Greenberg and C. G. Waugh
  The brazen locked room
    Devils & demons; ed. by M. Kaye and
    S. Kaye
  "Breeds there a man . . .?"
    [Analog]: Writers' choice v2
    Asimov, I. The edge of tomorrow
    Asimov, I. Robot dreams
  C-chute
    Asimov, I. Other worlds of Isaac
    Asimov
  Can you prove it?
    Asimov, I. Banquets of the Black
    Widowers
    Asimov, I. The best mysteries of Isaac
    Asimov
  The Cross of Lorraine
    Asimov, I. The best mysteries of Isaac
    Asimov
    Masterpieces of mystery and suspense;
    ed. by M. H. Greenberg

The dead past
  Asimov, I. The best science fiction of
  Isaac Asimov
  Asimov, I. The edge of tomorrow
  Asimov, I. Other worlds of Isaac
  Asimov
Death of a Foy
  Asimov, I. The best science fiction of
  Isaac Asimov
Does a bee care?
  Asimov, I. Robot dreams
Dollars and cents
  Asimov, I. The best mysteries of Isaac
  Asimov
Dreaming is a private thing
  Asimov, I. The best science fiction of
  Isaac Asimov
Dreamworld
  Asimov, I. The best science fiction of
  Isaac Asimov
The driver
  Asimov, I. Banquets of the Black
  Widowers
The end of eternity
  Asimov, I. The alternate Asimovs
Evidence
  Election Day 2084; ed. by I. Asimov
  and M. H. Greenberg
  Machines that think; ed. by I. Asimov;
  P. S. Warrick and M. H. Greenberg
The evitable conflict
  Machines that think; ed. by I. Asimov;
  P. S. Warrick and M. H. Greenberg
Eyes do more than see
  Asimov, I. The best science fiction of
  Isaac Asimov
  Asimov, I. Robot dreams
The feeling of power
  Asimov, I. The best science fiction of
  Isaac Asimov
  Asimov, I. The edge of tomorrow
  Asimov, I. Robot dreams
  Mathenauts: tales of mathematical won-
  der; ed. by R. Rucker
  Science Digest 92:70-3 Mr '84
Flies
  Asimov, I. The best science fiction of
  Isaac Asimov
  Masterpieces of terror and the super-
  natural; ed. by M. Kaye and S. Kaye
Found!
  Asimov, I. The best science fiction of
  Isaac Asimov
  Asimov, I. The edge of tomorrow
  Omni book of science fiction 1
Franchise
  Asimov, I. The best science fiction of
  Isaac Asimov
  Asimov, I. Robot dreams
  Election Day 2084; ed. by I. Asimov
  and M. H. Greenberg

Asimov, Isaac, 1920-—_Continued_

The fun they had
  Asimov, I. The best science fiction of Isaac Asimov

Getting the combination
  Asimov, I. The best mysteries of Isaac Asimov

The Good Samaritan
  Asimov, I. Banquets of the Black Widowers
  Asimov, I. The best mysteries of Isaac Asimov
  Manhattan mysteries; ed. by B. Pronzini; C. L. R. Waugh and M. H. Greenberg

Grow old along with me
  Asimov, I. The alternate Asimovs

Halloween
  Asimov, I. The best mysteries of Isaac Asimov

He wasn't there
  Asimov, I. The best mysteries of Isaac Asimov

Hide and seek
  Asimov, I. The best mysteries of Isaac Asimov

Hostess
  Asimov, I. Other worlds of Isaac Asimov
  Asimov, I. Robot dreams

How it happened
  Asimov, I. The best science fiction of Isaac Asimov

I'm in Marsport without Hilda
  Asimov, I. The best science fiction of Isaac Asimov

The Immortal Bard
  Asimov, I. The best science fiction of Isaac Asimov

"In a good cause--"
  Asimov, I. Other worlds of Isaac Asimov

The intrusion
  Asimov, I. Banquets of the Black Widowers

It's such a beautiful day
  Asimov, I. The best science fiction of Isaac Asimov

Jokester
  Asimov, I. The best science fiction of Isaac Asimov
  Asimov, I. Robot dreams

The key
  Asimov, I. The best mysteries of Isaac Asimov
  Asimov, I. Other worlds of Isaac Asimov

The key word
  Asimov, I. The best mysteries of Isaac Asimov

The last answer
  Asimov, I. The best science fiction of Isaac Asimov
  Asimov, I. Robot dreams

The last question
  Asimov, I. The best science fiction of Isaac Asimov
  Asimov, I. The edge of tomorrow
  Asimov, I. Robot dreams

Lest we remember
  Asimov, I. Other worlds of Isaac Asimov
  Asimov, I. Robot dreams

The library book
  Asimov, I. The best mysteries of Isaac Asimov

Light verse
  Asimov, I. Robot dreams

Little lost robot
  Asimov, I. Robot dreams

The little things
  Asimov, I. The best mysteries of Isaac Asimov

A loint of paw
  Asimov, I. The best science fiction of Isaac Asimov

The machine that won the war
  Asimov, I. Robot dreams

The magic umbrella
  Asimov, I. The best mysteries of Isaac Asimov

The Martian way
  Asimov, I. Other worlds of Isaac Asimov
  Asimov, I. Robot dreams

Middle name
  Asimov, I. The best mysteries of Isaac Asimov

A Monday in April
  Asimov, I. Banquets of the Black Widowers

My son, the physicist
  Asimov, I. The best science fiction of Isaac Asimov

Neither brute nor human
  Asimov, I. Banquets of the Black Widowers

Never out of sight
  Asimov, I. The best mysteries of Isaac Asimov

The next day
  Asimov, I. The best mysteries of Isaac Asimov

Nightfall
  Asimov, I. The edge of tomorrow
  Asimov, I. Other worlds of Isaac Asimov

Nothing might happen
  Asimov, I. The best mysteries of Isaac Asimov

Obituary
  Asimov, I. The best science fiction of Isaac Asimov

The obvious factor
  Asimov, I. The best mysteries of Isaac Asimov

Asimov, Isaac, 1920——*Continued*
The one and only east
  Asimov, I. The best mysteries of Isaac
    Asimov
Out of sight
  Asimov, I. The best mysteries of Isaac
    Asimov
Paté de foie gras
  Asimov, I. The edge of tomorrow
The Phoenician bauble
  Asimov, I. Banquets of the Black
    Widowers
The pointing finger
  Asimov, I. The best mysteries of Isaac
    Asimov
Potential
  Tales from Isaac Asimov's science fiction
    magazine: short stories for young
    adults
A problem of numbers
  Asimov, I. The best mysteries of Isaac
    Asimov
Profession
  Asimov, I. Other worlds of Isaac
    Asimov
  Baker's dozen: 13 short science fiction
    novels
Quicker than the eye
  Asimov, I. The best mysteries of Isaac
    Asimov
Reason
  Isaac Asimov presents the best science
    fiction firsts
The redhead
  Asimov, I. Banquets of the Black
    Widowers
  Asimov, I. The best mysteries of Isaac
    Asimov
Robbie
  Machines that think; ed. by I. Asimov;
    P. S. Warrick and M. H. Greenberg
Robot AL-76 goes astray
  Amazing science fiction anthology: The
    war years, 1936-1945; ed. by M. H.
    Greenberg
Robot dreams
  Asimov, I. Robot dreams
  Nebula awards 22
Runaround
  Machines that think; ed. by I. Asimov;
    P. S. Warrick and M. H. Greenberg
Sally
  Asimov, I. Robot dreams
Satisfaction guaranteed
  Amazing science fiction anthology: The
    wild years, 1946-1955; ed. by M. H.
    Greenberg
The sign
  Asimov, I. The best mysteries of Isaac
    Asimov

Sixty million trillion combinations
  Asimov, I. Banquets of the Black
    Widowers
  Asimov, I. The best mysteries of Isaac
    Asimov
The speck
  Asimov, I. The best mysteries of Isaac
    Asimov
Spell my name with an S
  Asimov, I. The best science fiction of
    Isaac Asimov
  Asimov, I. Robot dreams
The stamp
  The Year's best mystery and suspense
    stories, 1988
Strikebreaker
  Asimov, I. The best science fiction of
    Isaac Asimov
  Asimov, I. Robot dreams
Sucker bait
  Asimov, I. Other worlds of Isaac
    Asimov
Sure thing
  Asimov, I. The best science fiction of
    Isaac Asimov
The ten-second election
  Omni (New York, N.Y.) 7:112 N '84
The thirteenth day of Christmas
  Asimov, I. The best mysteries of Isaac
    Asimov
The three numbers
  Asimov, I. The best mysteries of Isaac
    Asimov
True love
  Asimov, I. Robot dreams
The ugly little boy
  Asimov, I. The best science fiction of
    Isaac Asimov
  Asimov, I. The edge of tomorrow
  Asimov, I. Other worlds of Isaac
    Asimov
  Asimov, I. Robot dreams
The ultimate crime
  Sherlock Holmes through time and space
Unique is where you find it
  Asimov, I. The edge of tomorrow
Unto the fourth generation
  Asimov, I. The best science fiction of
    Isaac Asimov
What if . . .
  Fantastic stories; ed. by M. H. Green-
    berg and P. L. Price
What is this thing called love? [Variant
    title: Playboy and the slime god]
  Amazing stories: 60 years of the best
    science fiction
What time is it?
  Asimov, I. The best mysteries of Isaac
    Asimov
The winds of change
  Asimov, I. The edge of tomorrow

Asimov, Isaac, 1920----*Continued*
The winnowing
Great science fiction; ed. by I. Asimov;
M. H. Greenberg and C. G. Waugh
The woman in the bar
Asimov, I. Banquets of the Black
Widowers
The wrong house
Asimov, I. Banquets of the Black
Widowers
Yankee Doodle went to town
Asimov, I. The best mysteries of Isaac
Asimov
The year of the action
Asimov, I. Banquets of the Black
Widowers
Youth
Asimov, I. Other worlds of Isaac
Asimov
Askounis, Christina
The blessed legacy
Redbook 171:78+ My '88
Aslan, Ibrahim
The little girl in green
Arabic short stories; tr. by D. Johnson-
Davies
The **assassin**. Gummerman, J.
The **assassin**. Maupassant, G. de
ASSASSINATION
Abbott, L. K. We get smashed and our
endings are swift
Apollinaire, G. The poet assassinated
Ballard, J. G. The object of the attack
Brennan, D. The trouble shooters
Carr, J. D. The black cabinet
De la Torre Bueno, T. The murder of the
governor
Dickson, G. R. The faithful wilf
Greenwood, R. Like Lucifer
Hoch, E. D. I'd know you anywhere
Kaiser, H. D. Just a poor working girl
Malzberg, B. N. On the campaign trail
Russo, A. Murder of an African prince
Van Greenaway, P. Cadenza
Wiebe, D. E. Narodny Rasprava
Windsor, G. Memories of the assassination
attempt
ASSAULT AND BATTERY
Frucht, A. The anniversary
Kiely, B. Through the fields in gloves
Michaels, L. The deal
Oates, J. C. The quarrel
O'Connor, F. Revelation
Taylor, C. Wince's story
Thompson, K. Getting saved
Tufel, A. A name for herself
Asscher-Pinkhof, Clara
Adventurer
Asscher-Pinkhof, C. Star children
After eight
Asscher-Pinkhof, C. Star children
Baby in the basket
Asscher-Pinkhof, C. Star children

Back and forth
Asscher-Pinkhof, C. Star children
Bath
Asscher-Pinkhof, C. Star children
Bogeyman
Asscher-Pinkhof, C. Star children
Breakdown
Asscher-Pinkhof, C. Star children
Caravan
Asscher-Pinkhof, C. Star children
Celebrations
Asscher-Pinkhof, C. Star children
The chosen
Asscher-Pinkhof, C. Star children
Comforting milk
Asscher-Pinkhof, C. Star children
The curtain falls
Asscher-Pinkhof, C. Star children
Dance
Asscher-Pinkhof, C. Star children
Dawn
Asscher-Pinkhof, C. Star children
Disaster
Asscher-Pinkhof, C. Star children
Expensive purchase
Asscher-Pinkhof, C. Star children
First worry
Asscher-Pinkhof, C. Star children
Flap of wings
Asscher-Pinkhof, C. Star children
Free afternoon
Asscher-Pinkhof, C. Star children
French
Asscher-Pinkhof, C. Star children
Game of dice
Asscher-Pinkhof, C. Star children
Gift
Asscher-Pinkhof, C. Star children
Good luck songs
Asscher-Pinkhof, C. Star children
Good night—good morning
Asscher-Pinkhof, C. Star children
Grandson
Asscher-Pinkhof, C. Star children
Harmonica
Asscher-Pinkhof, C. Star children
Hora
Asscher-Pinkhof, C. Star children
Hospital barrack
Asscher-Pinkhof, C. Star children
Housekeeping
Asscher-Pinkhof, C. Star children
How can Herod bear the light
Asscher-Pinkhof, C. Star children
Hunger
Asscher-Pinkhof, C. Star children
Island
Asscher-Pinkhof, C. Star children
A laundry basket full
Asscher-Pinkhof, C. Star children
Little white bundle
Asscher-Pinkhof, C. Star children

Asscher-Pinkhof, Clara—*Continued*
Madonna
  Asscher-Pinkhof, C. Star children
Market woman
  Asscher-Pinkhof, C. Star children
Merry child
  Asscher-Pinkhof, C. Star children
Missed chance
  Asscher-Pinkhof, C. Star children
Must
  Asscher-Pinkhof, C. Star children
Neighbor below
  Asscher-Pinkhof, C. Star children
New mother
  Asscher-Pinkhof, C. Star children
Nights
  Asscher-Pinkhof, C. Star children
Nursery
  Asscher-Pinkhof, C. Star children
Old tales
  Asscher-Pinkhof, C. Star children
Operation
  Asscher-Pinkhof, C. Star children
Packages
  Asscher-Pinkhof, C. Star children
Passage to Heaven
  Asscher-Pinkhof, C. Star children
Passage to Hell
  Asscher-Pinkhof, C. Star children
Peddling in the dark
  Asscher-Pinkhof, C. Star children
Pied piper of Hamelin
  Asscher-Pinkhof, C. Star children
Promenade
  Asscher-Pinkhof, C. Star children
Return
  Asscher-Pinkhof, C. Star children
Roll call
  Asscher-Pinkhof, C. Star children
Safety
  Asscher-Pinkhof, C. Star children
Secret
  Asscher-Pinkhof, C. Star children
See again
  Asscher-Pinkhof, C. Star children
Shopping
  Asscher-Pinkhof, C. Star children
Star dance
  Asscher-Pinkhof, C. Star children
Star wife
  Asscher-Pinkhof, C. Star children
They put their heads together
  Asscher-Pinkhof, C. Star children
Transfer
  Asscher-Pinkhof, C. Star children
Transport night
  Asscher-Pinkhof, C. Star children
Trust
  Asscher-Pinkhof, C. Star children
Tucking in
  Asscher-Pinkhof, C. Star children
Unloading
  Asscher-Pinkhof, C. Star children

White lie
  Asscher-Pinkhof, C. Star children
Women's talk
  Asscher-Pinkhof, C. Star children
The younger
  Asscher-Pinkhof, C. Star children
The **assembly**. Gallant, M.
ASSES AND MULES
  Caldwell, E. Meddlesome Jack
  Carter, A. The donkey prince
  Clark, W. V. T. The Indian well
  Farmer, B. Milk
  Gordon, C. Hear the nightingale sing
  Grey, Z. Tappan's burro
  O'Flaherty, L. The stolen ass
  Sarton, M. The donkey
  Smith, P. The schoolmaster
  Spivack, K. The donkey
  Stuart, J. Coming down the mountain
  Stuart, J. Hot-collared mule
The **assignation**. Oates, J. C.
The **assignation**. Poe, E. A.
Assignment: love. Carlson, J.
ASTEROIDS *See* Planets, Minor
ASTHMA
  Curtiss, U. R. Change of climate
Astley, Thea
  The scenery never changes
    Room to move; ed. by S. Falkiner
  Seeing Mrs. Landers
    The Australian short story; ed. by L.
      Hergenhan
Astral travel. Painter, P.
Astray in the suburbs. Parini, J.
ASTROLOGERS
  Latham, P. Jeannette's hands
  Smith, C. A. The last hieroglyph
The **Astrologer's** prediction
  The Penguin book of horror stories
ASTROLOGY
  Asimov, I. The sign
  Gilliatt, P. The position of the planets
  Narayan, R. K. All avoidable talk
  Winterson, J. Orion
ASTRONAUTS
    See also Women astronauts
  Anderson, P. Third stage
  Ballard, J. G. The dead astronaut
  Ballard, J. G. The man who walked on
    the moon
  Ballard, J. G. My dream of flying to Wake
    Island
  Ballard, J. G. News from the sun
  Ballard, J. G. A question of re-entry
  Berdnyk, O. The alien secret
  Biggle, L. Orphan of the void
  Blish, J. Common time
  Clarke, A. C. Breaking strain
  Dick, P. K. A little something for us tem-
    punauts
  Dick, P. K. Rautavaara's case
  Haldeman, J. W. The pilot
  Miller, W. M. Memento homo

ASTRONAUTS—*Continued*
Niven, L. Neutron star
Sabah, V. An imaginary journey to the moon
Silverberg, R. The feast of St. Dionysus
Steele, M. The death of a chimp
Tiptree, J. Houston, Houston, do you read?
Vance, J. Sail 25
ASTRONOMERS
Clarke, A. C. Dog Star
Latham, P. Jeannette's hands
Wells, H. G. The star
Astronomer's wife. Boyle, K.
ASTRONOMICAL OBSERVATORIES
Asimov, I. Nightfall
Wells, H. G. In the Avu observatory
ASTRONOMY
    See also Outer space; Stars; Telescope; also names of individual planets
Berriault, G. The island of Ven
Ellison, H. The sky is burning
Astronomy. Ciment, J.
ASTROPHYSICISTS
Clark, J. D. Minus planet
Astypalaian knife. Johnston, G.
At 21st Street. Rees, D.
At a bar I: The Jersey dyke. Lynch, L.
At a bar II: In the morning. Lynch, L.
At a bar III: Sally the bartender goes on jury duty. Lynch, L.
At a bar IV: White wine. Lynch, L.
At a bar V: Summer storm. Lynch, L.
At a bar VI: Winter sun. Lynch, L.
At a bar VII: The florist shop. Lynch, L.
At a bar VIII: The long slow-burning fuse. Lynch, L.
At a bar IX: Halloween. Lynch, L.
At a bar X: How they got together. Lynch, L.
At a certain angle. Dorr, L.
At a country house. Chekhov, A. P.
At a woman's house. Wali, M. A. A.
At Abu Ali. Moore, A.
At Aunt Charlotte's. Havird, A. M.
At Aunt Sophia's. Porter, H.
At D'Ambrosia's. Johnson, J. A.
At dusk / just when / the light is filled with birds. Gault, C.
At first it looks like nothing. Kauffman, J.
At Fumicaro. Ozick, C.
At home. Chekhov, A. P.
At home I would be a princess. Bernstein, L. S.
At home with the Colonel. Tuohy, F.
At Kinosaki. Shiga, N.
At least they'll have candlelight. See Garrett, G. P. The insects are winning: At least they'll have candlelight
At long last. Cooper, J. C.
At Lowry's. Clark, G.
At Manoli's sheepfold. Regent, P.

At mercy. Gallagher, T.
At middle age. Chen Rong
At midnight, in the month of June. Bradbury, R.
At odds. Kauffman, J.
At Paso Rojo. Bowles, P.
At salt river. Alderson, T.
At sea. Maupassant, G. de
At sea. Welch, D.
At St. Croix. Dubus, A.
At St. Theresa's College for Women. Hunnicutt, E.
At Swan Gates. Blythe, R.
At that time; or, The history of a joke. Paley, G.
At the airport. Farmer, B.
At the altar. Taylor, P. E.
At the anarchists' convention. Sayles, J.
At the bay. Mansfield, K.
At the beach. Alden, P. B.
At the beach. Mullen, R.
At the border. Böll, H.
At the border. Ruta, S.
At the bridge. Böll, H.
At the bureau. Tem, S. R.
At the Center for Younger Mothers. Collins, L.
At the château of Corinne. Woolson, C. F.
At the conglomeroid cocktail party. Silverberg, R.
At the cross-time jaunters' ball. Jablokov, A.
At the depot. Bergelson, D.
At the dig. Domini, J.
At the double solstice. Benford, G.
At the Embassy Club. Lynn, E. A.
At the Empress Hotel. Cohen, M.
At the end of the world. Son, S.-H.
At the exhibition. Clark, M.
At the feet of Karl Klodhopper. Gardner, M.
At the fence. Gerber, M. J.
At the Ferry Inn. Upward, E.
At the flood. Shelley, R.
At the hop. Carlson, R.
At the human limit. Williamson, J.
At the Lulu-Bar Motel. Dexter, C.
At the market. Thomas, N.
At the old swimming hole. Paretsky, S.
At the pawnshop. Kawabata, Y.
At the portal. Narayan, R. K.
At the post office. Zeiss, T. R.
At the Prado: a short story. Delbanco, N.
At the railroad track. Nałkowska, Z.
At the rainbow's end. London, J.
At the rendezvous of victory. Gordimer, N.
At the Rotonde. Wiebe, D. E.
At the Rue Hamelin (a hitherto unpublished account). Gekiere, M.
At the Signora's. Eldridge, M.
At the station. Andreyev, L.
At the time of the jasmine. Rifaat, A.
At the Tolstoy Museum. Barthelme, D.
At the turn of the road. Moore, G.

At the tutor's. Mountzoures, H. L.
At the twelfth hour. Altsheler, J.
At the Villa d'Or. Rhys, J.
At the walls of Jericho. Hawkes, G. W.
At thirteen. Curtis, J.
At this very instant. Sukenick, R.
At war with Amy. Hood, A.
The **Athanasia** League. Hoch, E. D.
The **atheist**. Chatto, J.
Atheling, William, Jr. *See* Blish, James, 1921-1975
ATHENS (GREECE) *See* Greece—Athens
Atherton, Gertrude Franklin Horn, 1857-1948
  The bell in the fog
    Haunted women; ed. by A. Bendixen
  The conquest of Doña Jacoba
    She won the West; ed. by M. Muller and B. Pronzini
  The foghorn
    Haunting women; ed. by A. Ryan
  The striding place
    Witches' brew; ed. by M. Muller and B. Pronzini
  The wash-tub mail
    Westward the women; ed. by V. Piekarski
ATHLETES
      See also Olympic Games
  Bonosky, P. Hank
  Broun, H. Slow grounder
  Girion, B. Trophy
  Kotzwinkle, W. Victory at North Antor
  Wilner, H. The quarterback speaks to his god
Athletes and artists. Rossi, A.
Atkey, Philip *See* Perowne, Barry, 1908-
Atkins, Jack *See* Harris, Mark, 1922-
ATLANTA (GA.) *See* Georgia—Atlanta
ATLANTIC CITY (N.J.) *See* New Jersey—Atlantic City
ATOMIC BOMB
  Benét, S. V. By the waters of Babylon
  Bloch, R. Daybroke
  Butler, O. E. Speech sounds
  Gardner, M. The stranger
  Hara, T. Summer flower
  Ibuse, M. The crazy iris
  Inoue, M. The House of Hands
  Kornbluth, C. M. Two dooms
  Macinnes, P. View from Kwaj
  Oda, K. Human ashes
  Ota, Y. Fireflies
  Robinson, K. S. The lucky strike
  Sata, I. The colorless paintings
  Spinrad, N. The big flash
  Williams, T. The knightly guest
  Willis, C. A letter from the Cleary's
ATOMIC ENERGY *See* Nuclear energy
ATOMIC POWER *See* Nuclear energy
Atomic tourism. Shepard, J.
ATOMIC WARFARE *See* Nuclear warfare
ATONEMENT
  Eisenstein, S. The sacrifice

  Smith, P. The schoolmaster
  Williams, T. Desire and the black masseur
ATONEMENT, DAY OF *See* Yom Kippur
ATROCITIES
      See also Holocaust, Jewish (1933-1945); Massacres; Torture
  L'Heureux, J. The anatomy of desire
  Yarbro, C. Q. Do I dare to eat a peach?
The **attack** by yoghurt. Izgü, M.
The **attack** on San Clemente. Bumpus, J.
The **attainment** of knowledge. Valenzuela, L.
Attaway, William
  Blood on the forge [excerpt]
    Mississippi writers v1: Fiction; ed. by D. Abbott
ATTEMPTED MURDER *See* Murder stories
ATTEMPTED SUICIDE *See* Suicide
The **attendant**. Nordan, L.
Atthis. Gilkison, A.
Attia, Naim
  Games
    Egyptian tales and short stories of the 1970s and 1980s
Attila. Narayan, R. K.
ATTITUDE (PSYCHOLOGY)
      See also Prejudices
The **attorney**. Goethe, J. W. von
ATTORNEYS *See* Law and lawyers
Atwood, Margaret, 1939-
  Bluebeard's egg
    Atwood, M. Bluebeard's egg, and other stories
    Don't bet on the prince; ed. by J. Zipes
    The North American Review 269:31-40 D '84
  Dancing girls
    Short story international 64
  Giving birth
    Love, struggle & change; ed. by I. Zahava
  Hair jewellery
    The Art of the tale; ed. by D. Halpern
  Happy endings
    Ms. 15:58+ F '87
  Hurricane Hazel
    Atwood, M. Bluebeard's egg, and other stories
  In search of the rattlesnake plantain
    Atwood, M. Bluebeard's egg, and other stories
    Harper's 273:68-72 Ag '86
  Loulou; or, The domestic life of the language
    Atwood, M. Bluebeard's egg, and other stories
  The man from Mars
    The World of the short story; ed. by C. Fadiman
  Rape fantasies
    The Treasury of English short stories; ed. by N. Sullivan

Atwood, Margaret, 1939——_Continued_
The salt garden
  Atwood, M. Bluebeard's egg, and other
    stories
  The Editors' choice: new American
    stories v2
  _Ms._ 13:70-1+ S '84
Scarlet ibis
  Atwood, M. Bluebeard's egg, and other
    stories
Significant moments in the life of my
  mother
  Atwood, M. Bluebeard's egg, and other
    stories
Simmering
  The Graywolf annual [1]
The sin eater
  The Oxford book of Canadian short
    stories in English
Spring song of the frogs
  Atwood, M. Bluebeard's egg, and other
    stories
The sunrise
  Atwood, M. Bluebeard's egg, and other
    stories
Theology
  Harper's 277:36-7 S '88
A travel piece
  Short story international 57
Two stories about Emma: The whirlpool
  rapids
  Atwood, M. Bluebeard's egg, and other
    stories
Two stories about Emma: Walking on
  water
  Atwood, M. Bluebeard's egg, and other
    stories
Uglypuss
  Atwood, M. Bluebeard's egg, and other
    stories
Unearthing suite
  Atwood, M. Bluebeard's egg, and other
    stories
When it happens
  The Editors' choice: new American
    stories v1
The whirlpool rapids
  The Editors' choice v4; ed. by G. E.
    Murphy, Jr.
  Redbook 168:51-2+ N '86
Au pair. Weldon, F.
The **au** pair girl. Harrington, J.
Aubade. Eldershaw, M. B.
Aubade. Eldridge, M.
Aucamp, Hennie
Soup for the sick
  The Penguin book of Southern African
    stories
Auchincloss, Louis
America first
  Auchincloss, L. Skinny island
The cup of coffee
  Short story international 69

A diary of old New York
  Auchincloss, L. Skinny island
Equitable awards
  Short story international 52
The Fabbri tape
  Short story international 45
The "fulfillment" of Grace Eliot
  Auchincloss, L. Skinny island
Greg's peg
  The Best Maine stories; ed. by S. Phip-
    pen; C. Waugh and M. Greenberg
Marcus: a Gothic tale
  Auchincloss, L. Skinny island
No friend like a new friend
  Auchincloss, L. Skinny island
Portrait of the artist by another
  Auchincloss, L. Skinny island
The reckoning
  Auchincloss, L. Skinny island
The seagull
  Short story international 61
The senior partner's ethics
  Auchincloss, L. Skinny island
The shells of Horace
  Auchincloss, L. Skinny island
The Stations of the Cross
  Auchincloss, L. Skinny island
Suttee
  Full measure; ed. by D. Sennett
The takeover
  Auchincloss, L. Skinny island
The wedding guest
  Auchincloss, L. Skinny island
AUCKLAND (N.Z.) _See_ New Zealand—
  Auckland
The **auction**. Alderson, T.
The **auction**. Morgan, B.
AUCTIONS
  Lurie, M. Rappaport lays an egg
  Markham, B. The splendid outcast
  St. Pierre, P. H. Sale of one small ranch
Audited and found correct. Gilbert, M.
Audition. Tenney, E. M.
The **Augean** stables. Christie, A.
August 25, 1983. Borges, J. L.
August afternoon. Caldwell, E.
August afternoon. Pacheco, J. E.
August angst. Jeppson, J. O.
August Eschenburg. Millhauser, S.
August evening. Oates, J. C.
August heat. Tauscher, D.
August Saturday. Trevor, W.
Augusta Brennan I: The coat. Lynch, L.
Augusta Brennan II: The tracks. Lynch, L.
**AUGUSTINE, SAINT, BISHOP OF
  HIPPO**
                  About
  Bishop, M. For thus do I remember Car-
    thage
Augustus Esborn's marriage. Grin, A.
Aunt Agatha. Buck, D. P.
Aunt Agatha takes the count. Wodehouse, P.
  G.

Aunt Agnes. Wodhams, J.

The **aunt** and the sluggard. Wodehouse, P.
G.

Aunt Ella and my first communion. Heise,
K.

Aunt Ella gits it. Heise, K.

Aunt Ella's funeral. Heise, K.

Aunt Ella's taxes. Heise, K.

Aunt Leah. Mazel, D.

Aunt Mable's love story. Pindar, S.

Aunt Mara. Dovlatov, S.

Aunt Michelina. Pirandello, L.

Aunt Norah. Durrell, L.

Aunt Rosana's rocker (Zoraida). Mohr, N.

AUNTS

   See also Nieces

   Adams, G. G. La plume de ma tante

   Asimov, I. Dreamworld

   Bell, C. G. The married land [excerpt]

   Blythe, R. The common soldiery

   Blythe, R. A wedding in the family

   Blythe, R. The windfall

   Böll, H. Christmas not just once a year

   Brady, M. Novena

   Brown, A. Natalie Blayne

   Buck, D. P. Aunt Agatha

   Claiborne, S. Rubble

   Clark, M. A long time ago

   Curley, D. Visiting the dead

   Davie, E. In the train

   De la Mare, W. Seaton's aunt

   Duff, G. Fire ants

   Durrell, L. Aunt Norah

   Engberg, S. Soliloquy

   Federspiel, J. Infirtaris inoaknoneis

   Galloway, F. Vida's child

   Garber, E. K. The lover

   Gogol', N. V. Ivan Fiodorovich Shponka
      and his aunt

   Gold, H. A ninety-six-year-old big sister

   Gordon, M. The thorn

   Greenburg, J. Certain distant suns

   Grenville, K. A summer aunt

   Haake, K. Bear and other pale giants

   Hall, M. L. Just a little sore throat

   Halligan, M. Family album

   Head, B. Snapshots of a wedding

   Heise, K. The addition to Aunt Ella's
      house

   Heise, K. Aunt Ella gits it

   Heise, K. Aunt Ella's taxes

   Heise, K. Children's crusade

   Heise, K. "Don't pick any apples for your
      Aunt Ella"

   Heise, K. Eating out

   Heise, K. The little boy who was left
      behind

   Heise, K. My Aunt Ella

   Heise, K. Shazam

   Heise, K. The Woodward Avenue streetcar

   Jennings, G. Tom cat

   Johnson, D. M. Lost sister

   Jolley, E. The jarrah thieves

   Jolley, E. One Christmas knitting

   Le Guin, U. K. Small change

   Lish, G. Imp among aunts

   Lum, D. H. Y. Yahk fahn, Auntie

   Lynch, L. The LoPresto Traveling Magic
      Show

   MacLaverty, B. Secrets

   MacLeod, J. L. The Jesus Flag

   Mattison, A. A date with Dmitri

   Mattison, A. Exactments

   Mattison, A. The knitting

   Mazel, D. Aunt Leah

   McDonald, S. Falling

   Morris, W. Real losses, imaginary gains

   Paley, G. In this country, but in another
      language, my aunt refuses to marry
      the men everyone wants her to

   Pierce, C. What I did for Aunt Berthe

   Pindar, S. Aunt Mable's love story

   Porter, H. At Aunt Sophia's

   Rand, P. The nephew

   Rifaat, A. The flat in Nakshabandi Street

   Robertson, M. E. The baptism

   Sandor, M. Still life

   Stead, C. An iced cake with cherries

   Taylor, P. H. Allegiance

   Taylor, P. H. A friend and protector

   Theroux, P. Yard sale

   Thompson, J. The birch tree

   Turgenev, I. S. Clara Militch

   Vanderhaeghe, G. The watcher

   Warren, J. Anny's men

   Watmough, D. Sacred & secular

   Weaver, G. The two sides of things

   Wells, J. Two willow chairs

   West, J. Mother's Day

   Wheeler, H. C. Little boy lost

   Whitaker, M. Time for chapel

   Wicomb, Z. A trip to the Gifberge

   Williams, T. Completed

   Wilson, B. How to fix a roof

   Wodehouse, P. G. The go-getter

Aura. Fuentes, C.

Aurora. Morand, P.

Aurora Island. Gingher, M.

Auslander. Herman, M.

Auspicious occasion. Mistry, R.

AUSTEN, JANE, 1775-1817

                  Parodies, travesties, etc.

   Hill, R. Poor Emma

Auster, Paul, 1947-

In the country of last things
   The Paris Review 27:204-25 Summ '85
   The Pushcart prize XI

Austin, Don, 1946-

And now he was beginning to feel uneasy
   about the weather
   Austin, D. The portable city

The artist
   Austin, D. The portable city

The bishop
   Austin, D. The portable city

Austin, Don, 1946——*Continued*
Cortez
  Austin, D. The portable city
The detective
  Austin, D. The portable city
The dictator
  Austin, D. The portable city
Empires of the air
  Austin, D. The portable city
The great man
  Austin, D. The portable city
He was there when they came across the
    bridge on their bicycles
  Austin, D. The portable city
He won't go down to the park with me
    today
  Austin, D. The portable city
The hypnotic mailbox
  Austin, D. The portable city
I am an employee
  Austin, D. The portable city
It's the same old story
  Austin, D. The portable city
Men without women
  Austin, D. The portable city
Milton Freabe
  Austin, D. The portable city
The other room
  Austin, D. The portable city
The past is a doomed parachutist
  Austin, D. The portable city
A pear
  Austin, D. The portable city
A perfect crime
  Austin, D. The portable city
The poet
  Austin, D. The portable city
Portable cities
  Austin, D. The portable city
Pray for China
  Austin, D. The portable city
The relaxed anarchist
  Austin, D. The portable city
She fell asleep sunbathing on the grass
    outside her apartment building
  Austin, D. The portable city
Something similar would be a boarding
    house
  Austin, D. The portable city
Austin, Mary Hunter, 1868-1934
The basket maker
  Austin, M. H. Western trails
The Basket Woman: first story
  Austin, M. H. Western trails
The Basket Woman: second story
  Austin, M. H. Western trails
Bitterness of women
  Austin, M. H. Western trails
Blue roses
  Austin, M. H. Western trails
A case of conscience
  Austin, M. H. Western trails

The Castro baby
  Austin, M. H. Western trails
The Coyote-Spirit and the Weaving
    Woman
  Austin, M. H. Western trails
The divorcing of Sina
  Austin, M. H. Western trails
The fakir
  Austin, M. H. Western trails
Frustrate
  Austin, M. H. Western trails
The House of offence
  Austin, M. H. Western trails
How the corn came
  Austin, M. H. Western trails
Kate Bixby's queerness
  Austin, M. H. Western trails
The land
  Austin, M. H. Western trails
The last antelope
  Austin, M. H. Western trails
  Westward the women; ed. by V. Piekar-
    ski
The lost mine of Fisherman's Peak
  Austin, M. H. Western trails
Mahala Joe
  Austin, M. H. Western trails
The man who lied about a woman
  Austin, M. H. Western trails
The man who was loved by women
  Austin, M. H. Western trails
The medicine of Bow-Returning
  Austin, M. H. Western trails
Old Spanish gardens
  Austin, M. H. Western trails
Papago wedding
  Austin, M. H. Western trails
  The Other woman; ed. by S. Koppelman
The portrait
  Austin, M. H. Western trails
The return of Mr. Wills
  Austin, M. H. Western trails
The secret of the holy places
  Austin, M. H. Western trails
Stewed beans
  Austin, M. H. Western trails
The Walking Woman
  Austin, M. H. Western trails
  She won the West; ed. by M. Muller
    and B. Pronzini
White wisdom
  Austin, M. H. Western trails
The Woman at the Eighteen-Mile
  Austin, M. H. Western trails
AUSTIN (TEX.) *See* Texas—Austin
AUSTRALIA
  See also Tasmania (Australia)
Carter, R. Cityman
Chandler, A. B. Kelly country
Lawson, H. The iron-bark chip
Lawson, H. The loaded dog
Lawson, H. Mitchell: a character sketch
Lawson, H. An old mate of your father's

AUSTRALIA—*Continued*
Lawson, H. Our pipes
Lawson, H. Shooting the moon
Lawson, H. 'Some day'
London, J. Burning off
London, J. Lilies
London, J. New Year
P.G.M. The monster mine
Skrzynecki, P. Lilies
Skrzynecki, P. The wild dogs
20th century
Adams, G. The voyage of their life
Anderson, J. Against the wall
Anderson, J. The appearance of things
Anderson, J. The aviator
Anderson, J. Under the house
Anderson, J. The way to Budjerra Heights
Bail, M. The drover's wife
Baranay, I. The saddest pleasure
Beckett, R. Forty Susan Sangsters stride
    out at the Wellington Boot
Casey, G. Short-shift Saturday
Collins, A. The trouble with Felix
Cowan, P. Escape
Cowan, P. The tractor
Cowan, P. A window in Mrs X's place
Drewe, R. After Noumea
Drewe, R. The bodysurfers
Drewe, R. Eighty per cent humidity
Drewe, R. The manageress and the mirage
Drewe, R. Shark logic
Drewe, R. The silver medallist
Drewe, R. Sweetlip
Eldridge, M. Solitaire
Eldridge, M. Walking the dog
Farmer, B. At the airport
Farmer, B. Inheritance
Farmer, B. Ismini
Farmer, B. Melpo
Forshaw, T. The mateship syndrome
Grey, Z. Strange partners of Two-Fold Bay
Hospital, J. T. After long absence
Keesing, N. Garden Island people
Loukakis, A. Being here now
Loukakis, A. Billy and the birds
Loukakis, A. The cheerfulness of the bush
Loukakis, A. Hooray for Haralambos
Loukakis, A. I told mama not to come
Loukakis, A. Islands
Loukakis, A. The jigsaw puzzle
Loukakis, A. My neighbour's death
Loukakis, A. Only in the truth
Loukakis, A. Our own business
Loukakis, A. Partying on parquet
Loukakis, A. Perfect holiday sounds
Loukakis, A. Single lens reflex
Loukakis, A. This wizened creature
Loukakis, A. To Mrs. Starkey
Loukakis, A. Velodrome
Lurie, M. American shoes
Prichard, K. S. Bad debts
Prichard, K. S. Communists are always
    young

Prichard, K. S. Flight
Prichard, K. S. The galah
Prichard, K. S. Genieve
Prichard, K. S. Jimble
Prichard, K. S. The old track
Prichard, K. S. A young comrade
Scott, R. Diary of a woman
Sheil, G. Dogs, in Denpasar
Sheil, G. Mad like Lasseter
Soldatow, S. Details, before the event
Stone, K. Summer of a stick man
Tennant, K. Lady Weare and the Bodhisat-
    tva
Titcher, M. Someone-else
White, P. Down at the dump
Womersley, J. The year granpa won the
    Melbourne Cup
Yamamoto, M. Betty-san
Yamamoto, M. Powers
College life
    See College life—Australia
Communism
    See Communism—Australia
Farm life
    See Farm life—Australia
Frontier and pioneer life
    See Frontier and pioneer life—Aus-
tralia
Native peoples
    See Australian aborigines
Politics
    See Politics—Australia
Prisoners and prisons
    See Prisoners and prisons—Australia
Rural life
Carter, R. A generous man
Dadswell, M. Backtracking
Dadswell, M. An interval of time
Disher, G. The bamboo flute
Hospital, J. T. You gave me hyacinths
Jackson, G. The decline of Western Hill
Jackson, G. Fly in the ointment
Jackson, G. The fly-screen
Jackson, G. Holing out
Jackson, G. Pyjamas
Jackson, G. Structural unemployment
Jackson, G. Sweet things
Pascoe, B. Thylacine
Prichard, K. S. The curse
Prichard, K. S. The frogs of Quirra-Quirra
Prichard, K. S. The grey horse
Prichard, K. S. Hero of the mines
Prichard, K. S. Josephina Anna Maria
Prichard, K. S. Naninja and Janey
Prichard, K. S. N'goola
Prichard, K. S. Painted finches
Prichard, K. S. The rabbit trapper's wife
Prichard, K. S. The siren of Sandy Gap
Prichard, K. S. Yoirimba
Scott, G. F. The bunyip dies
Skrzynecki, P. The biggest bonfire of all
Skrzynecki, P. The chainsaw incident
Skrzynecki, P. Hoeing

AUSTRALIA—Rural life—*Continued*
Skrzynecki, P. The peewit's nest
Skrzynecki, P. Pick-and-shovel hero
Stead, C. The milk run
Adelaide
Bail, M. Healing
Canberra
Eldridge, M. Adult education
Hungerford
Lawson, H. Hungerford
Melbourne
Farmer, B. Sally's birthday
Farmer, B. Summer on ice
Hornung, E. W. Le premier pas
Liberman, S. Two years in exile
Lurie, M. Outrageous behaviour
Lurie, M. Popov
Lurie, M. Rappaport lays an egg
Lurie, M. Running nicely
Turner, G. In a Petri dish upstairs
New South Wales
Drewe, R. Baby oil
Sydney
Anderson, J. The late sunlight
Anderson, J. The milk
Anderson, J. Outdoor friends
Brooks, B. Summer in Sydney
Johnston, H. The shadow falls
Loukakis, A. Velodrome
AUSTRALIAN ABORIGINES
Bryning, F. Place of the throwing-stick
Eldershaw, M. B. Aubade
Houbein, L. Having it both ways
Page, F. The spear thrower
Pascoe, B. Black velvet night
Pascoe, B. Flour for your grave
Prichard, K. S. The cooboo
Prichard, K. S. Flight
Prichard, K. S. Jimble
Prichard, K. S. Naninja and Janey
Prichard, K. S. N'goola
AUSTRALIAN SOLDIERS *See* Soldiers—
    Australia
AUSTRALIANS
Belgium
Malouf, D. The sun in winter
Canada
Rule, J. Joy
China
Hungerford, T. A. G. Green grow the
    rushes
Cyprus
Clift, C. The small animus
England
Lurie, M. Russian boxes
Morrison, J. The incense-burner
Europe
Graham, J. Two tales of a trip
France
Grenville, K. Meeting the folks
Halligan, M. The living hothouse
Halligan, M. Trespassers or guests?

Germany
Haig, M. Eighteen hours in Frankfurt
Greece
Bewley, G. Blood and wine
Farmer, B. Pumpkin
Farmer, B. Saint Kay's day
Grenville, K. Having a wonderful time
Maniaty, T. 'Who was that masked man?'
India
Clark, M. A democrat on the Ganges
Israel
Lurie, M. Tell me what you want
Italy
Blair, R. McBride's list
Eldridge, M. At the Signora's
Taylor, A. The absolutely ordinary family
Laos
London, J. Travelling
Morocco
Lurie, M. Swallows
Netherlands
Falkiner, S. The killing of a hedgehog
Poland
Clark, M. Still hope for God
Singapore
Clark, M. The love of Christ
Tahiti
Farmer, B. Darling Odile
United States
Drewe, R. Looking for Malibu
Farmer, B. Summer on ice
Lawson, S. PASTA MOMA
Shapcott, T. W. Telephones
Skrzynecki, P. "Is your wife here, honey?"
AUSTRIA
Doyle, Sir A. C. A pastoral horror
Gordon, G. Hans Pfeifer
Maupassant, G. de. A deer park in the
    provinces
Roth, J. Fallmerayer the stationmaster
Spark, M. The ormolu clock
Aristocracy
See Aristocracy—Austria
Vienna
Apollinaire, G. The eagle hunt
Maupassant, G. de. A fashionable woman
Morand, P. Hungarian night
Rhys, J. Vienne
AUSTRIAN ALPS *See* Alps
AUSTRIANS
United States
Morris, W. The safe place
Pronzini, B. The same old grind
Auswaks, Alex
The dowry
    Short story international 64
The familiar
    Short story international 55
Mrs. Halprin and the lottery
    Short story international 46
The priest
    P.E.N. new fiction I
Auteur. Heller, S.

Auteur theory. Hill, R.
The author of Beltraffio. James, H.
The author of Caryatids. See Dennison, G.
     Interview with the author of Caryatids
"The author of the acacia seeds" and other
     extracts from the Journal of the
     Association of Therolinguistics. Le
     Guin, U. K.
The authoress. Hall, M. L.
AUTHORITARIANISM See Totalitarianism
AUTHORS
          See also Art critics; Authorship;
     Dramatists; Poets; Women authors;
     also names of individual authors,
     dramatists, poets, etc.
Abbott, K. Over and under
Anaya, R. A. B. Traven is alive and well
     in Cuernavaca
Anderman, J. Topical subject
Anderson, P. Rachaela
Asimov, I. The next day
Asimov, I. The stamp
Bankier, W. A hint of danger
Barich, B. Where the mountains are
Barnes, J. One of a kind
Baumbach, J. The dinner party
Baumbach, J. The errant melancholy of
     twilight
Bayles, M. The "New Yorker" story
Beaulieu, V. L. Monsieur Melville [excerpt]
Bellow, S. What kind of day did you
     have?
Bernard, K. Question and answer
Berriault, G. Works of the imagination
Blaise, C. Translation
Blaise, C. The voice of unhousement
Bloch, R. Crime in rhyme
Bloch, R. Method for murder
Bloch, R. Reaper
Bloch, R. The shadow from the steeple
Block, L. The dangerous business
Block, L. One thousand dollars a word
Block, L. With a smile for the ending
Böll, H. In search of the reader
Borges, J. L. August 25, 1983
Borges, J. L. Shakespeare's memory
Bradbury, R. Banshee
Bradbury, R. A careful man dies
Bradbury, R. Lafayette, farewell
Brautigan, R. 1/3, 1/3, 1/3
Bruce-Novoa. The manuscript
Bumpus, J. K
Busch, F. Making change
Byatt, A. S. The changeling
Camoin, F. A. Diehl: the wandering years
Campbell, E. The ghost of an apprehension
Campbell, R. Next time you'll know me
Carroll, L. E. Without wings
Carver, R. Errand
Carver, R. Put yourself in my shoes
Chambers, G. March 11
Charbonneau-Tissot, C. Compulsion
Codrescu, A. The babysitter

Codrescu, A. Samba de los agentes
Cohen, M. Café Le Dog
Coleman, W. Word monkey
Colette. The half-crazy
Colette. Literature
Conroy, F. Gossip
Conroy, F. The mysterious case of R
Coriolan, J. As you'd like it
Creveling, W. Thinking the unthinkable
Crispin, E. We know you're busy writing,
     but we thought you wouldn't mind if
     we just dropped in for a minute
Cullen, E. J. Trying to grow up American
Curtiss, U. R. Snowball
Davis, L. Sketches for a life of Wassilly
Dawson, F. Mary will be good for Warren
Dazai, O. Chiyojo
Dixon, S. The book review
Dixon, S. The ringer
Dixon, S. The second part
Dixon, S. Self-portrait
Dixon, S. Will's book
Doctorow, E. L. Lives of the poets
Eldridge, M. Adult education
Eliade, M. Nineteen roses
Ellis, J. One step to murder
Etchison, D. The blood kiss
Etchison, D. Talking in the dark
Faik, S. First letter from a reader
Fante, J. The dreamer
Federman, R. Report from the World
     Federation of Displaced Writers
Finney, J. Hey, look at me!
Fitzgerald, M. J. The fire eater
Fraser, A. Have a nice death
Friedman, B. J. An ironic Yetta Montana
Friedman, B. J. Living together
Friedman, P. The family
Friedman, P. A period of grace
Gallant, M. A flying start
Gallant, M. Grippes and Poche
Gallant, M. Irina
Galsworthy, J. The consummation
Gilbert, W. S. Maxwell and I
Gilden, M. Deadline
Gold, H. A death on the East Side
Gold, H. A karmic lover
Goulart, R. Groucho
Greene, G. May we borrow your husband?
Greene, G. A visit to Morin
Haldeman, J. W. No future in it
Haldeman, J. W. Seven and the stars
Hall, T. T. The gate
Halligan, M. Down to earth
Hankla, C. Skeleton
Happy, E. A collection of letters
Hartley, L. P. The corner cupboard
Hartley, L. P. A rewarding experience
Hartley, L. P. W.S.
Haylock, J. The worries of Laurence Rid-
     ley
Hébert, L.-P. A text concerning strawber-
     ries

AUTHORS—*Continued*

Hemensley, K. The book (Chez Claude Mauriac)

Hemingway, E. The snows of Kilimanjaro

Henry, R. Subject: Petri Ganton

Heyrman, P. Funeral for a friend

Hoch, E. D. The great American novel

Hoch, E. D. Murder at the Bouchercon

Hughes, F. 'Dear ghost . . .'

James, H. The author of Beltraffio

James, H. The death of the lion

James, H. The figure in the carpet

James, H. John Delavoy

James, H. The lesson of the master

James, H. The middle years

James, H. The next time

James, P. D. The murder of Santa Claus

Jeppson, J. O. The mysterious cure

Johnson, C. R. Moving pictures

Jolley, E. Woman in a lampshade

Josipovici, G. The bitter end

Josipovici, G. A changeable report

Josipovici, G. Volume IV, pp. 167-9

Kaikō, T. The crushed pellet

Kanai, M. Platonic love

Kant, U. A letter to comrade Ernst L.

Katz, S. The stolen stories

Kessler, J. F. The bird cage

King, F. H. A scent of mimosa

King, S. The ballad of the flexible bullet

Klein, T. E. D. Black man with a horn

Klíma, I. Tuesday morning: a sentimental story

Klíma, I. Wednesday morning: a Christmas conspiracy tale

Konwicki, T. A minor apocalypse [excerpt]

Kress, N. Casey's empire

Landolfi, T. Personaphilological-dramatic conference with implications

Lee, T. The gorgon

Levine, N. We all begin in a little magazine

Liben, M. Change of heart

Liggett, B. The Cat Man

Lish, G. For Jerome—with love and kisses

Lish, G. For Rupert—with no promises

Lish, G. History; or, The four pictures of Vludka

Lish, G. Imagination

Liyong, T. lo. Lexicographicide

Lodge, D. Hotel des Boobs

Longyear, B. B. Where do you get your ideas?

Lowry, M. Strange comfort afforded by the profession

Lurie, M. Africa wall

Lurie, M. French toothpaste

Lurie, M. Losing things

MacLaverty, B. A pornographer woos

Malamud, B. The last Mohican

Martin, C. The gift

Martin, G. R. R. Portraits of his children

Matheson, R. C. Sentences

Matsumoto, S. The woman who took the local paper

Mazel, D. Old folks

Mazel, D. The storekeeper

McCormack, E. P. Anyhow in a corner

McCullers, C. Who has seen the wind?

Meinke, P. The piano tuner

Meinke, P. The starlings of Leicester Square

Mrożek, S. Art

Mrożek, S. The trial

Nesin, A. The first woman who understood me

Oakes, P. You're in my story

Oates, J. C. The bingo master

Oates, J. C. Blackmail

O'Connor, F. The enduring chill

Onions, O. The beckoning fair one

Ota, Y. Fireflies

Ozick, C. Levitation

Parry, H. T. The punchboards

Pavel, T. G. The Persian mirror

Pritchett, M. The Venus tree

Pritchett, V. S. The Spanish bed

Pronzini, B. A craving for originality

Pronzini, B., and Malzberg, B. N. Prose Bowl

Purdy, J. On the rebound

Reed, K. A unique service

Rendell, R. The green road to Quephanda

Revill, P. Book review

Rosenfeld, I. The hand that fed me

Rossi, A. Winter rentals

Rule, J. Dulce

Ruta, S. Soldier's rest

Schulberg, B. The barracudas

Schwartz, L. S. The accounting

Schwartz, S. A program for writers

Schwob, M. Petronius, novelist

Shapcott, T. W. Telephones

Sheckley, R. Miss Mouse and the fourth dimension

Sheckley, R. The shaggy average American man story

Singer, I. B. The bond

Singer, I. B. Confused

Singer, I. B. Remnants

Singer, I. B. Why Heisherik was born

Smith, C. A. The city of the singing flame

Sorrentino, F. Ars poetica

Spark, M. The fathers' daughters

Stafford, J. Woden's day

Stead, C. UNO 1945

Steele, M. Where she brushed her hair

Stern, S. Bruno's metamorphosis

Stern, S. The ghost and Saul Bozoff

Stevens, J. A. The sacrifice

Stewart, J. I. M. Two strings to his bow

Stone, R. In a Mexican garden

Strieber, W. Pain

Sturgeon, T. The traveling Crag

Summers, H. S. Diving

Summers, H. S. The vireo's nest

AUTHORS—*Continued*
Swados, H. Claudine's book
Swados, H. The hack
Swados, H. The man in the toolhouse
Symons, J. The flaw
Tabucchi, A. The little Gatsby
Taylor, P. E. Acquiring point of view
Thompson, J. Applause, applause
Tremain, R. A shooting season
Trevanian. The sacking of Miss Plimsoll
Tuohy, F. A ghost garden
Van Greenaway, P. The immortal coil
Vanderhaeghe, G. Sam, Soren, and Ed
Varshavsky, I. The secrets of the genre
Wagner, K. E. Neither brute nor human
Wang Meng. Eye of the night
Waten, J. Well, what do you say to my boy?
Watmough, D. Closeted
Welch, D. The diamond badge
Welch, D. Ghosts
Wells, H. G. The wild asses of the devil
Wendt, A. Birthdays
West, J. Breach of promise
Wiebe, D. E. Night flight to Stockholm
Williams, T. Rubio y Morena
Williamson, J. N. Wordsong
Wilson, Sir A. More friend than lodger
Wilson, B. The Hulk
Wolfe, T. The return of the prodigal
Wollheim, D. A. Malice aforethought
Woolf, V. Memoirs of a novelist
Woolson, C. F. "Miss Grief"
Wyndham, F. The Ground Hostess
Yates, R. The right thing
Author's notes. Bryant, E.
Author's tour. Campbell, K.
AUTHORSHIP
   See also Authors
Abrahams, L. Knowledge
Aguinis, M. Short story contest
Baumbach, J. A famous Russian poet
Baumbach, J. How you play the game
Baumbach, J. The life and times of Major Fiction
Berry, R. M. History
Bloch, R. Crook of the month
Bourjaily, V. The Amish farmer
Boylan, J. Aloe: part three: the making of "Aloe"
Buzzati, D. Confidential
Buzzati, D. An interrupted story
Dixon, S. The beginning of something
Gordon, M. A writing lesson
Littke, L. The bantam phantom
Moore, L. How to become a writer
Olson, D. Enter the stranger
Scott, G. Car wrecks and bleeding hearts
Thomas, D. Where Tawe flows
Tremain, R. My love affair with James I
Valenzuela, L. The place of its quietude
Wideman, J. E. Surfiction
Wilson, B. In the archives

Woolrich, C. The penny-a-worder
Auto erotic. Mayes, S. S.
Auto repair. Warren, R.
AUTOBIOGRAPHICAL STORIES
Ahern, T. My summer scenes
Akutagawa, R. Cogwheels
Atwood, M. In search of the rattlesnake plantain
Atwood, M. Significant moments in the life of my mother
Atwood, M. Unearthing suite
Blaise, C. Memories of unhousement
Blaise, C. The voice of unhousement
Botwinik, B. Discovered
Botwinik, B. The general strike
Brasch, C. Dunedin
Buzzati, D. Kafka's houses
Carrington, L. Little Francis
Colette. A letter
Ellison, H. Eidolons
Ellison, H. The function of dream sleep
Gold, H. A selfish story
Hall, R. W. Letter from a great-uncle
Hannah, B. Idaho
Irving, J. Trying to save Piggy Sneed
Landolfi, T. Prefigurations: Prato
Lish, G. [Entitled story]
MacLean, N. Logging and pimping and "your pal, Jim"
Maupassant, G. de. Waiter, a bock!
Mauriac, F. A Christmas tale
McCullers, C. The orphanage
Mendele Mokher Seforim. Of bygone days
Nabokov, V. V. First love
Ocampo, S. The autobiography of Irene
Ocampo, S. The punishment
Ooka, S. The mother of dreams
Sandel, C. Allie
Sandel, C. Simple memories
Sandel, C. Two cats in Paris and one in Florence
Setouchi, H. Pheasant
Singer, I. B. Confused
Thomas, D. Return journey
Williams, T. "Grand"
Wright, R. The man who went to Chicago
Yi, P.-J. The wind and landscape of Yenang
The **autobiography** of Irene. Ocampo, S.
Autobiography of my mother. Russ, J.
Autofac. Dick, P. K.
The **autograph.** Ruta, S.
AUTOMATA *See* Robots
The **automatic** exemption. Sholem Aleichem
AUTOMATION
Sheckley, R. Cost of living
AUTOMOBILE ACCIDENTS *See* Traffic accidents
AUTOMOBILE DRIVERS
   See also Chauffeurs; Hit-and-run drivers
Austin, D. A perfect crime
Bell, C. G. The married land [excerpt]

AUTOMOBILE DRIVERS—*Continued*
Cortázar, J. The southern thruway
Dann, J. Night visions
King, S. Mrs. Todd's shortcut
Lafferty, R. A. Interurban queen
Lurie, M. Happy times
Lurie, M. A king of the road
McElroy, C. J. Sister Detroit
Oates, J. C. Accident
Pohl, F. The high test
Silva, B. Happy hour
Valenzuela, L. Love of animals
Wheatcroft, J. The appeal
Wilson, B. Drive-away
AUTOMOBILE RACES
Martone, M. The third day of trials
AUTOMOBILES
Abbott, K. Back to nature
Abbott, K. Out on the res
Asimov, I. Sally
Baker, R. High-tech insolence
Barthelme, F. Driver
Bonnie, F. Too hot
Buzzati, D. The plague
Cadigan, P. Roadside rescue
Carey, P. Crabs
Casper, S. Spring fever
Finney, J. Second chance
Floyd, P. L. The silver DeSoto
Foster, A. D. Why Johnny can't speed
Fraser, A. Who's been sitting in my car?
Freeman, C. The ride
Furman, L. Eldorado
Hamilton, A. Moonlighting
Hartley, L. P. The prayer
Heise, K. The mystery of the Higgins
  coupe
Keller, D. H. The revolt of the pedestrians
Kranes, D. The phantom Mercury of
  Nevada
Lagory, M. Seaside idle
Lynch, L. That old Studebaker
MacDonald, J. D. The legend of Joe Lee
Martin, G. R. R. The exit to San Breta
Michaelson, L. W. The Ferrari
Montgomery, M. I got a gal
O'Brien, D. Eminent domain
Silva, B. The woes of a single woman and
  her car
Silverberg, R. As is
Symons, J. Love affair
Taylor, C. Wince's story
Warner, S. T. Idenborough
Williams, J. Rot
Wolfe, T. In the park
Zelazny, R. Last of the wild ones
Accidents
See Traffic accidents
Service stations
Currey, R. Waiting for trains
Gordimer, N. Good climate, friendly inhabitants
Sams, F. Fubar

Touring
Kiely, B. A journey to the seven streams
Thompson, S. Montauk
Welty, E. No place for you, my love
Trailers
Arthur, R. The haunted trailer
Campbell, R. The faces at Pine Dunes
The **autopsy**. Shea, M.
AUTRY, GENE, 1907-
About
Kinsella, W. P. Preserving fireweed for the
  White Pass and Yukon Railroad
AUTUMN
Collins, L. Going to see the leaves
Updike, J. Leaf season
Autumn. Erwin, C.
Autumn. Li Ping
Autumn crocus. Griffiths, E.
Autumn in Florida. Tremain, R.
Autumn loneliness. Böll, H.
Autumn madness. Lutz, J.
'**Autumn** Mountain'. Akutagawa, R.
Autumn note. Chu, T.-J.
Autumn of a dormouse. Gilliatt, P.
Autumn rain. Kawabata, Y.
Autumn: the garden of stubborn cats. Calvino, I.
Autumnscape. Stark, S. S.
Avalanche. Sandel, C.
Avallone, Michael, 1924-
  Walter ego
  A Matter of crime v2
AVANT GARDE STORIES *See* Experimental stories
AVARICE
  See also Misers
Asimov, I. Nothing might happen
Baxt, G. Stroke of genius
Blinkin, M. Troubles
Bloch, R. Pin-up girl
Brett, S. The nuggy bar
Davis, D. S. Sweet William
Doyle, Sir A. C. The stone of Boxman's
  Drift
Fish, R. L. Muldoon and the numbers
  game
Frazee, S. The singing sands
Garcia, J. S. The harvest
Holding, J. A padlock for Charlie Draper
Humphrey, W. The pump
Kirk, R. Fate's purse
Kornbluth, C. M. The little black bag
Lemay, P. Blood and gold
Lispector, C. The sharing of bread
Matthews, J. Amos Bond, the gunsmith
Maupassant, G. de. The little cask
Narayan, R. K. Half a rupee worth
Rice, J. The crossroads
Roth, J. Hotel Savoy
Shibaki, Y. Ripples
Stephens, W. M. The state against Sam
  Tucker

AVARICE—*Continued*
Twain, M. The man that corrupted Hadleyburg
Ave Lutie. Sanders, T. E.
The **avenger**. Maupassant, G. de
The **avenger** of death. Ellison, H.
Avenida revolucion. ZoBell, B.
Avery, Martin, 1956-
The Canadian Diaspora
Avery, M. The Singing Rabbi
The Holocaust remembrance service
Avery, M. The Singing Rabbi
Jerusalem & home
Avery, M. The Singing Rabbi
The Komedy Kabaret
Avery, M. The Singing Rabbi
Nazis, communists, Presbyterians & Jews in Norman Bethune's hometown
Avery, M. The Singing Rabbi
Promised land Newfoundland
Avery, M. The Singing Rabbi
The Singing Rabbi
Avery, M. The Singing Rabbi
Soviet jewellery
Avery, M. The Singing Rabbi
AVIATION *See* Aeronautics
The **aviator**. Anderson, J.
AVIATORS *See* Air pilots
Avid. Casey, J.
AVIGNON (FRANCE) *See* France—Avignon
Avoiding the shoals of passion. Rose, D. A.
The **awakening**. Lynch, L.
The **awakening**. Maupassant, G. de
AWARDS *See* Rewards (Prizes, etc.)
An **awareness** of angels. Wagner, K. E.
Away from the heart. Thurm, M.
Away in a manger. Littke, L.
Away out and over. Glasser, P.
The **awful** secret of Monsieur Bonneval. Gallico, P.
Awful when you think of it. Greene, G.
The **axe**. Fitzgerald, P.
The **axe**, the axe, the axe. Wilson, E. H.
Axolotl. Cortázar, J.
Axton, David, 1945-
For works written by this author under other names see Koontz, Dean, 1945-
Aya, Koda
Rain
Prairie Schooner 59:67-72 Fall '85
Ayers, Mary Alice
Change at Jamaica
The Literary Review (Madison, N.J.) 29:5-10 Fall '85
Aymara. Shepard, L.
Aymé, Marcel, 1902-1967
The state of grace
Black water; ed. by A. Manguel
Ayor. Leavitt, D.
Azabache. Ocampo, S.
The **Azhdanov** tailors. Stead, C.
Aziz Khan. Essop, A.

AZTECS
Hoch, E. D. The maiden's sacrifice

B

B-Tower west wall. Sandberg, P. L.
B. Traven is alive and well in Cuernavaca. Anaya, R. A.
Baba Yaga and the sorcerer's son. McKillip, P. A.
Babbitt, Natalie
Simple sentences
The Year's best fantasy, first annual collection
Babe and Evie I: Sunshine. Lynch, L.
Babe and Evie II: Thanksgiving. Lynch, L.
Babel', I. (Isaac), 1894-1941
My first goose
The World of the short story; ed. by C. Fadiman
Babel', Isaac *See* Babel', I. (Isaac), 1894-1941
Babel II. Anvil, C.
Babel's children. Barker, C.
Baber, Asa
The surfer
Passages to the dream shore; ed. by F. Stewart
Babes on bawd way. Effinger, G. A.
Babette. Maupassant, G. de
Babies from heaven. Ryan, A.
Babushka in the blue bus. Mackay, S.
The **baby**. Barthelme, D.
The **baby**. Campbell, W. B.
Baby. Oates, J. C.
Baby blue. O'Brien, E.
Baby Boy. Rand, P.
Baby Hood. Donohue, G.
The **baby** in mid-air. Thompson, S.
Baby in the basket. Asscher-Pinkhof, C.
The **baby** in the icebox. Cain, J. M.
Baby oil. Drewe, R.
Baby pictures. Giles, M.
The **baby-sitter**. Bache, E.
The **baby-sitter**. Brown, S. H.
A **baby-sitter** and why they're weird or turn weird. Winters, J.
BABY SITTERS
Beattie, A. High school
Brodkey, H. The state of grace
Carver, R. Fever
Codrescu, A. The babysitter
Coover, R. The babysitter
Dixon, S. Milk is very good for you
Harrington, J. The au pair girl
O'Connor, F. The river
Rossiter, S. Sinners
Schinto, J. Shadow bands
Swados, H. A question of loneliness
Tallent, E. Time with children
The **baby**, the parrot. Hankla, C.
Baby town. Birtha, B.

Baby wood. Nevai, L.
Babylon Johnny. Antônio, J.
The Babylon lottery. See Borges, J. L. The
lottery in Babylon
Babylon, revisited. Fitzgerald, F. S.
Baby's first Christmas. Lipman, E.
Baby's first Christmas. Modrack, B. A.
The babysitter. Codrescu, A.
The babysitter. Coover, R.
The babysitter. McGarry, J.
Bace, Kathleen M.
Sterile relationships
Cuentos Chicanos; ed. by R. A. Anaya
and A. Márquez
Bache, Ellyn
The baby-sitter
McCall's 145:147-9 Mr '87
Bird of passage
McCall's 113:118-19+ N '85
The lucky one
McCall's 111:96-7+ Jl '84
Pigeons
Short story international 68
Running from love
McCall's 115:178+ O '87
The bachelor. O'Brien, E.
Bachelor life. Fitzgerald, M. J.
Bachelor of Arts. Updike, D.
BACHELORS See Single men
Bachelors. Walpole, Sir H.
Bachman, Richard See King, Stephen, 1947-
Bachmann, Ingeborg, 1926-1973
Everything
The Art of the tale; ed. by D. Halpern
Back. Straight, S.
Back and forth. Asscher-Pinkhof, C.
Back country. Oates, J. C.
The back door of America. Wilson, B.
Back in the days. Rossi, A.
Back on April eleventh. Aquin, H.
Back on my feet again. Goulart, R.
The back-seat talker. Mardeusz, S.
Back to God's country. Curwood, J. O.
Back to Kentucky. Ferron, J.
Back to nature. Abbott, K.
Back to normal. Lipman, E.
Back to the drawing boards. Ellison, H.
Back to Val-d'Or. Ferron, J.
The back way to Fantasyland. Brown, A.
Backbone of the nation. Hall, T. T.
The background to an era. Mrożek, S.
Backman, Brian
The plane in the woods
Encounter (London, England) 70:11-15 Ja
'88
BACKPACKING
Shaw, J. B. In high country
The backroom. Little, B.
The backslider. Fisher, R.
Backtracking. Dadswell, M.

Backus, Jean L.
Ludmila
Child's ploy; ed. by M. Muller and B.
Pronzini
Backward, turn backward. Davis, D. S.
Backward, turn backward. Tiptree, J.
Backwards. Hall, R. W.
The backwards game. Tabucchi, A.
BACTERIOLOGISTS
Wells, H. G. The stolen bacillus
Bad blood. Doyle, D., and Macdonald, J. D.
The bad boy. Doherty, B.
Bad company. De la Mare, W.
Bad company. Gallagher, T.
Bad company. Yasuoka, S.
Bad debts. Prichard, K. S.
Bad dreams. Taylor, P. H.
A bad error. Maupassant, G. de
Bad habits. Oates, J. C.
Bad medicine. Dann, J.
A bad memory block. Moravia, A.
A bad morning. Colette
A bad night. Hornung, E. W.
Bad pictures. Hoctel, P.
Badby. Kim, S.-H.
The baddest, baddest days. Cullen, E. J.
Badger. Conley, R. J.
Badriyya and her husband. Rifaat, A.
BAG LADIES See Homeless
Bagasse. Ferreira, R.
Bagley's progress. Sage, V.
The bagman's story. Dickens, C.
The bagpiping people. Dunn, D.
BAHAMAS
Antoni, R. W. Two-head Fred and Tree-
foot Frieda
BAHIA ISLANDS (HONDURAS)
Murphy, P. In the islands
Bahiyya's eyes. Rifaat, A.
Bail, Murray, 1941-
A, B, C, D, E, F, G, H, I, J, K, L, M,
N, O, P, Q, R, S, T, U, V, W, X,
Y, Z
Bail, M. The drover's wife, and other
stories
Cul-de-sac (uncompleted)
Bail, M. The drover's wife, and other
stories
The drover's wife
Bail, M. The drover's wife, and other
stories
Healing
Bail, M. The drover's wife, and other
stories
Home ownership
Bail, M. The drover's wife, and other
stories
Huebler
Bail, M. The drover's wife, and other
stories
Life of the party
Bail, M. The drover's wife, and other
stories

Bail, Murray, 1941---_Continued_
Ore
　The Australian short story; ed. by L. Hergenhan
　Bail, M. The drover's wife, and other stories
Paradise
　Bail, M. The drover's wife, and other stories
The partitions
　Bail, M. The drover's wife, and other stories
Portrait of electricity
　Bail, M. The drover's wife, and other stories
The silence
　Bail, M. The drover's wife, and other stories
Zoellner's definition
　Bail, M. The drover's wife, and other stories
BAIL
Jhabvala, R. P. On bail
Bailey, Hilary
The fall of Frenchy Steiner
　Hitler victorious; ed. by G. Benford and M. H. Greenberg
Bailey, Richard
Accounts receivable: I am Brian
　Chicago Review 34:26-36 Summ '84
Baillie, Allan, 1943-
Snap
　Home and away; ed. by R. Creswell
Bain, C. J.
Dream walker
　'Teen 32:24+ My '88
Bainbridge, Beryl, 1933-
Clap hands, here comes Charlie
　The Penguin book of modern British short stories
Bake-Face. Adisa, O. P.
Baker, Christina
From whence the rivers come
　The Yale Review 76:285-94 Wint '87
Baker, Nicholson
Pants on fire
　The New Yorker 62:28-9 Je 2 '86
Baker, Russell, 1925-
High-tech insolence
　Devils & demons; ed. by M. Kaye and S. Kaye
Baker, Scott
Nesting instinct
　The Architecture of fear; ed. by K. Cramer and P. D. Pautz
Sea change
　The Year's best science fiction, fourth annual collection
The sins of the fathers
　Ripper! Ed. by G. Dozois and S. Casper
BAKERIES AND BAKERS
Carver, R. A small, good thing
Gorky, M. Twenty-six men and a girl

Mazel, D. Mr. Tessler
The **baker's** daughter or A tale of Holy Russia. Bocock, M.
Bakhnov, Vladen
According to scientific data
　Aliens, travelers, and other strangers; by B. and A. Strugatsky and others
The fifth on the left
　Aliens, travelers, and other strangers; by B. and A. Strugatsky and others
A remark concerning a little something about the devil
　Aliens, travelers, and other strangers; by B. and A. Strugatsky and others
Balancing water. Kittredge, W.
The **balcony.** Piñera, V.
The **balcony.** Swados, H.
The **baldheaded** mirage. Bloch, R.
Baldwin, Dick
Last respects
　Masterpieces of terror and the supernatural; ed. by M. Kaye and S. Kaye
The shadow watchers
　Devils & demons; ed. by M. Kaye and S. Kaye
Baldwin, James, 1924-1987
Going to meet the man
　The Art of the tale; ed. by D. Halpern
Sonny's blues
　American short story masterpieces; ed. by R. Carver and T. Jenks
Baldwin, Joseph Glover, 1815-1864
Samuel Hele, Esq.
　The Art of fiction in the heart of Dixie; ed. by P. D. Beidler
Bale jumpers. Harper, R. B.
The **Balek** scales. Böll, H.
Balfour, Bruce J.
Some days are like that
　100 great fantasy short short stories; ed. by I. Asimov; T. Carr and M. H. Greenberg
Balfour, Conrad
To the torturor
　Stiller's pond; ed. by J. Agee; R. Blakely and S. Welch
Balgrummo's hell. Kirk, R.
Ball, Bo
Heart leaves
　Love stories for the time being; ed. by G. D. Chipps and B. Henderson
　The Pushcart prize X
It's just one Elvis
　Chicago Review 34 no4:4-25 '85
Ball, John
Good evening, Mr. Tibbs
　Murder California style; ed. by J. L. Breen and J. Ball
One for Virgil Tibbs
　The Ethnic detectives; ed. by B. Pronzini and M. H. Greenberg
The **ball.** Liben, M.
The **ball.** Piñera, V.

Ball and socket. Murphy, Y.

Ball game. Madison, C.

BALL GAMES

    See also Baseball; Basketball; Bowling; Football; Rugby football; Soccer; Softball; Tennis

  Liben, M. The ball

Ball-of-fat. Maupassant, G. de

Ball of fire. Liben, M.

Ball of tallow. See Maupassant, G. de. Ball-of-fat

Ball two. Klinkowitz, J.

Ballad. Oates, J. C.

The **ballad** of Daphne and Apollo. Petrakis, H. M.

The **ballad** of Jesse Neighbours. Humphrey, W.

The **ballad** of the flexible bullet. King, S.

The **ballad** of the sad café. McCullers, C.

The **ballad** of the Toft Boy. Heinesen, W.

Ballantyne, Sheila

  Flaubert in Miami Beach

    Ballantyne, S. Life on earth

  Key Largo

    Ballantyne, S. Life on earth

  Letter to John Lennon

    Ballantyne, S. Life on earth

  Letters to the darkness

    Ballantyne, S. Life on earth

  Life on earth

    Ballantyne, S. Life on earth

  Mourning Henry

    Ballantyne, S. Life on earth

  Pelicans in flight

    Ballantyne, S. Life on earth

  Perpetual care

    Ballantyne, S. Life on earth

  Untitled—Ink on paper

    Ballantyne, S. Life on earth

  You are here

    Ballantyne, S. Life on earth

Ballard, J. G., 1930-

  The cage of sand

    Ballard, J. G. Memories of the Space Age

  The dead astronaut

    Ballard, J. G. Memories of the Space Age

  The drowned giant

    The Slaying of the dragon; ed. by F. Rottensteiner

  The man who walked on the moon

    Ballard, J. G. Memories of the Space Age

    Interzone: the 2nd anthology; ed. by J. Clute; D. Pringle and S. Ounsley

  Memories of the Space Age

    Ballard, J. G. Memories of the Space Age

    The Penguin book of modern British short stories

  My dream of flying to Wake Island

    Ballard, J. G. Memories of the Space Age

  Myths of the near future

    Ballard, J. G. Memories of the Space Age

  News from the sun

    Ballard, J. G. Memories of the Space Age

  The object of the attack

    Interzone: the first anthology; ed. by J. Clute; C. Greenland and D. Pringle

  A question of re-entry

    Ballard, J. G. Memories of the Space Age

    Fantastic stories; ed. by M. H. Greenberg and P. L. Price

  The terminal beach

    Beyond Armageddon; ed. by W. M. Miller and M. H. Greenberg

  Time of passage

    Afterlives; ed. by P. Sargent and I. Watson

Ballard, W. T. (Willis Todhunter)

  Gamblers don't win

    Ballard, W. T. Hollywood troubleshooter

  Lights, action—killer!

    Ballard, W. T. Hollywood troubleshooter

  A little different

    Ballard, W. T. Hollywood troubleshooter

  A million-dollar tramp

    Ballard, W. T. Hollywood troubleshooter

  Scars of murder

    Ballard, W. T. Hollywood troubleshooter

Ballard, Willis Todhunter See Ballard, W. T. (Willis Todhunter)

Ballenger's people. Neville, K.

Ballerina. Oates, J. C.

BALLET

    See also Dancers

  Cameron, P. Excerpts from Swan Lake

  Evans, M. Xavier's folly

  Hecht, B. Specter of the Rose

  Huggan, I. Jack of hearts

  Johnson, W. The great Valentinova

BALLOON ASCENSIONS

  Finney, J. Home alone

  Poe, E. A. The balloon-hoax

  Poe, E. A. Hans Phaall

  Poe, E. A. Mellonta Tauta

  Poe, E. A. The unparalleled adventure of one Hans Pfaall

The **balloon-hoax**. Poe, E. A.

The **balloon** lady. Bird, C.

Balloon magic. Willson, H.

The **balloon** of William Fuerst. Komie, L. B.

The **balloonfish** and the armadillo. Wendt, A.

BALLOONS

  Bitov, A. The big balloon

  Tiptree, J. Excursion fare

  Willson, H. Balloon magic

The **ballroom** of romance. Trevor, W.
BALLS (PARTIES) *See* Parties
Balogun, Odun
  The apprentice
    African short stories; ed. by C. Achebe
      and C. L. Innes
Balthazar's marvelous afternoon. García Márquez, G.
BALTIMORE (MD.) *See* Maryland—Baltimore
Baltimore. Rheinheimer, K.
Balzac, Honoré de, 1799-1850
  La Grande Bretêche
    The Penguin book of horror stories
  A passion in the desert
    Classic European short stories; ed. by R.
      Beum
  The red inn
    Classic European short stories; ed. by R.
      Beum
              About
Ekström, M. Balzac's valet
Hofmann, G. A conversation about Balzac's horse
Balzac's valet. Ekström, M.
Balzano & Son. Lish, G.
Bambara, Toni Cade
  Christmas Eve at Johnson's Drugs N
    Goods
    Love, struggle & change; ed. by I.
      Zahava
  Gorilla, my love
    The Norton book of American short
      stories
  My man Bovanne
    New women and new fiction; ed. by S.
      Cahill
  Raymond's run
    Family: stories from the interior; ed. by
      G. G. Chavis
The **bamboo** flute. Disher, G.
Bamboo-leaf boats. Kawabata, Y.
Banal story. Hemingway, E.
Banana boats. Taylor-Hall, M. A.
The **banana** fever. Morris, M.
Banasiowa. Konopnicka, M.
The **bandit** was my neighbor. Prose, F.
BANDITS *See* Brigands and robbers
BANDS (MUSIC)
  Campos-De Metro, J. Bands
  Fisher, L. Overnight
  Hannah, B. Testimony of pilot
  Jones, D. C. The trombone and the lady
  Mrożek, S. The parson and the band
  Pulaski, J. Music story
  Robinson, K. S. Coming back to Dixieland
  Vogan, S. Sunday's no name band
  Whitaker, M. Strange music
  Woolrich, C. Dark melody of madness
Bands. Campos-De Metro, J.
Bang-bang you're dead. Spark, M.
BANGLADESH
  Saint, R. The Imam

              Revolution, 1971
  Enayetullah, A. This also happened
  Mufti, M. Good luck
  Rahman, T. Bingo
Bangs, Carol Jane, 1949-
  Existentialists
    New directions in prose and poetry 52
Bangs, John Kendrick, 1862-1922
  A midnight visitor
    Devils & demons; ed. by M. Kaye and
      S. Kaye
  The water ghost of Harrowby Hall
    Christmas ghosts; ed. by K. Cramer and
      D. G. Hartwell
BANK CLERKS *See* Clerks
Bank job. Pronzini, B.
Bank night. Young, C.
BANK ROBBERS
  Block, L. One thousand dollars a word
  Burnett, W. R. Traveling light
  Clark, N. M. No fish for the cat
  Frazee, S. The fire killer
  Gallagher, T. Desperate measures
  Gault, W. C. —And murder makes four!
  Gilbert, M. A very special relationship
  Henry, O. The hiding of Black Bill
  Henson, R. Billie loses her job
  Hornung, E. W. The chest of silver
  Hornung, E. W. Le premier pas
  Humphrey, W. The ballad of Jesse Neighbours
  Humphrey, W. A voice from the woods
  MacDonald, J. D. The homesick Buick
  Martone, M. Biograph
  McGerr, P. The day of the bookmobile
  Muheim, H. The dusty drawer
  Overholser, W. D. Smart
  Pronzini, B. Bank job
  Pronzini, B. Shell game
  Schutzman, S. The bank robbery
  Spillane, M. Tomorrow I die
  Steinbeck, J. How Mr. Hogan robbed a
    bank
The **bank** robbery. Schutzman, S.
BANKERS
  Apollinaire, G. Giovanni Moroni
  Henry, O. Friends in San Rosario
  Sturgeon, T. Microcosmic god
  Zangwill, I. Cheating the gallows
Bankier, William, 1928-
  Beliveau pays
    Ellery Queen's Prime crimes 2
  The dog who hated jazz
    Ellery Queen's Prime crimes
    Hound dunnit; ed. by I. Asimov; M. H.
      Greenberg and C. L. R. Waugh
  A hint of danger
    Ellery Queen's Crimes and punishments
  One clear sweet clue
    Ellery Queen's Memorable characters
BANKRUPTCY
  Alden, P. B. The Batsons of Brown and
    Batson

BANKRUPTCY—*Continued*
Carver, R. Are these actual miles?
Lee, H. Remme's ride
Nova, C. The prince
Olmstead, R. Onions
Phillips, J. A. 1934
Rossiter, S. Skinner
Banks, Barbara A.
Miss Esther's land
Editor's choice II; ed. by M. Sklar and M. Biggs
Banks, Carolyn
A long, long time
Erotic interludes; ed. by L. Barbach
Banks, Russell, 1940-
Adultery
Banks, R. Success stories
Captions
Banks, R. Success stories
The child screams and looks back at you
The Art of the tale; ed. by D. Halpern
Children's story
Banks, R. Success stories
Firewood
Banks, R. Success stories
The fish
American made; ed. by M. Leyner; C. White and T. Glynn
Banks, R. Success stories
The gully
Banks, R. Success stories
Hostage
Banks, R. Success stories
Esquire 105:193+ Ap '86
Indisposed
Prime number; ed. by A. L. Weir
Mistake
Banks, R. Success stories
Harper's 272:35-8 My '86
My mother's memoirs, my father's lie, and other true stories
Banks, R. Success stories
The Editors' choice v4; ed. by G. E. Murphy, Jr.
The neighbor
Sudden fiction; ed. by R. Shapard and J. Thomas
Queen for a Day
Banks, R. Success stories
Sarah Cole: a type of love story
Banks, R. Success stories
The Best American short stories, 1985
Love stories for the time being; ed. by G. D. Chipps and B. Henderson
The Pushcart prize X
Success story
Banks, R. Success stories
BANKS
See also Bankers
Archer, J. Clean sweep Ignatius
Gholson, C. Temple to the economics of love
Lopatin, J. Etiology of the new war

Bannister. Lurie, M.
The **banquet**. Gombrowicz, W.
Banquet. Neville, S.
Banshee. Bradbury, R.
The **bantam** phantom. Littke, L.
BANYAN TREE
Michaelson, L. W. An early frost
Baptie in her homeland. Schmahmann, D. R.
BAPTISM
Willis, C. Samaritan
The **baptism**. Robertson, M. E.
Baptism of desire. Smith, I.
Baptism of fire. Crapser, W.
The **baptism** of water. Manley, F.
BAPTISTS
Vanderhaeghe, G. Drummer
Bar bar bar. Faust, I.
A **bar** in Brooklyn. Codrescu, A.
BAR MITZVAH
Amichai, Y. The Bar Mitzvah party
Thurm, M. Sanctuary
The **Bar** Mitzvah party. Amichai, Y.
Bar song. Matthew, J. R.
Bar Yosef, Yehoshua
The stranger
Commentary 78:51-9 N '84
Baranay, Inez
The saddest pleasure
Room to move; ed. by S. Falkiner
Baranovich Station. Sholem Aleichem
Baranskaya, Natalya
The retirement party
The Barsukov Triangle, The two-toned blond & other stories; ed. by C. R. Proffer & E. Proffer
Barany, Michelle
Desert
The Antioch Review 42:234-46 Spr '84
Barba, Rick
Godzilla America Ballpark Products, Inc
Chicago Review 35:50-6 Aut '85
BARBADOS

Bridgetown

Kaplan, D. M. Elisabetta, Carlotta, Catherine (raising the demon)
Shacochis, B. Lord Short Shoe wants the monkey
Barbasch, Annette
Plotting Elsa
Southwest Review 73:83-5 Wint '88
The **barbecue**. Brown, M. W.
Barbecue. Thomas, J.
Barber, Daniel Wynn
Wings of the hunter
Bringing down the moon; ed. by J. Anderson
Barber, Kathleen
To remain a ripple people
'Teen 28:34+ Ap '84

Barber, Phyllis
Almost magnificence
The North American Review 269:43 Mr
'84
Silver dollars
The Kenyon Review ns10:50-7 Wint '88
The **barber**. O'Connor, F.
The **barber** of Duncow—a real ghost story.
Hogg, J.
BARBERS
Carver, R. The calm
Durrell, L. High barbary
Hall, M. L. The man who gave brother
double pneumonia
Heller, S. A matter of style
Jaffe, H. Giraffe
Lardner, R. Haircut
Lovesey, P. Curl up and dye
Mathers, P. Like a Maori prince
O'Connor, F. The barber
O'Hara, J. Good-by, Herman
Sams, F. Run with the horsemen [excerpt]
Saroyan, W. How the barber finally got
himself into a fable
Shiga, N. The razor
Sonu, H. The mirror
Thompson, K. Promises
Woodman, A. Fathers
Barbey d'Aurevilly, J., 1808-1889
A woman's vengeance
Dark arrows; ed. by A. Manguel
Barcelo, François
The man who stopped trains
Intimate strangers; ed. by M. Cohen and
W. Grady
BARCELONA (SPAIN) *See* Spain—Bar-
celona
Barcelona. Adams, A.
Barclay, Byrna
A greenhouse for Maureen
The Old dance; ed. by B. Burnard
Bardon bus. Munro, A.
Bare root season. Kalpakian, L.
Barefoot and pregnant in Des Moines.
Kinsella, W. P.
Bargain cinema. Sheckley, J.
Bargaining. Hunnicutt, E.
Barich, Bill
Caravaggio
Barich, B. Hard to be good
The New Yorker 62:35-43 Mr 24 '86
The end of the world
Barich, B. Hard to be good
Giorgio's mother
Barich, B. Hard to be good
Hard to be good
Barich, B. Hard to be good
October
Barich, B. Hard to be good
Too much electricity
Barich, B. Hard to be good
The New Yorker 60:44-52 Mr 26 '84

Where the mountains are
Barich, B. Hard to be good
Barker, Clive
The age of desire
Barker, C. The inhuman condition
Babel's children
Barker, C. In the flesh
Omni (New York, N.Y.) 9:48-50+ Mr '87
The body politic
Barker, C. The inhuman condition
The Book of Blood
Barker, C. The Books of Blood
Omni (New York, N.Y.) 8:54-6+ My '86
The Book of Blood (a postscript): on Jeru-
salem Street
Barker, C. The Books of Blood
Cabal
Barker, C. Cabal
Coming to grief
Prime evil; ed. by D. E. Winter
Confessions of a (pornographer's) shroud
Barker, C. The Books of Blood
Down, Satan!
Barker, C. The inhuman condition
Dread
Barker, C. The Books of Blood
The Dark descent; ed. by D. G. Hart-
well
The forbidden
Barker, C. In the flesh
Hell's event
Barker, C. The Books of Blood
How spoilers bleed
Barker, C. Cabal
Human remains
Barker, C. The Books of Blood
In the flesh
Barker, C. In the flesh
In the hills, the cities
Barker, C. The Books of Blood
The inhuman condition
Barker, C. The inhuman condition
Jacqueline Ess: her will and testament
Barker, C. The Books of Blood
The last illusion
Barker, C. Cabal
The life of death
Barker, C. Cabal
Lost souls
Cutting edge; ed. by D. Etchison
The madonna
Barker, C. In the flesh
The midnight meat train
Barker, C. The Books of Blood
New murders in the Rue Morgue
Barker, C. The Books of Blood
Pig blood blues
Barker, C. The Books of Blood
Rawhead Rex
Barker, C. The Books of Blood
Revelations
Barker, C. The inhuman condition

Barker, Clive—*Continued*
Scape-goats
 Barker, C. The Books of Blood
Sex, death and starshine
 Barker, C. The Books of Blood
The skins of the fathers
 Barker, C. The Books of Blood
Son of celluloid
 Barker, C. The Books of Blood
 Silver scream; ed. by D. J. Schow
Twilight at the towers
 Barker, C. Cabal
The Yattering and Jack
 Barker, C. The Books of Blood
Barker, Elsa
First notch
 She won the West; ed. by M. Muller
  and B. Pronzini
Barker, S. Omar
Outlaw trail
 The Western hall of fame; ed. by B.
  Pronzini and M. H. Greenberg
Barker, Shirley
The fog on Pemble Green
 Yankee witches; ed. by C. G. Waugh;
  M. H. Greenberg and F. D. McSherry
The **Barlip** run. Stark, S. S.
The **barn**. Welch, D.
Barn burning. Faulkner, W.
Barnabo of the mountains. Buzzati, D.
Barnard, Marjorie
The persimmon tree
 The Australian short story; ed. by L.
  Hergenhan
Barnard, Marjorie Faith, 1897-
 For works written by this author in
  collaboration with Flora Sydney
  Patricia Eldershaw see Eldershaw, M.
  Barnard
Barnard, Robert
Happy Christmas
 The Year's best mystery and suspense
  stories, 1987
Little Terror
 Masterpieces of mystery and suspense;
  ed. by M. H. Greenberg
 Winter's crimes 18
The woman in the wardrobe
 The Year's best mystery and suspense
  stories, 1988
Barnea, Lilian
My grandfather
 Echad 4: Jewish writing from down un-
  der: Australia and New Zealand
Barnes, Candyce
Bride of the thing
 The Southern Review (Baton Rouge, La.)
  22:589-99 Summ '86
Barnes, Julian
One of a kind
 The Penguin book of modern British
  short stories

Barnes, Linda
Lucky penny
 Masterpieces of mystery and suspense;
  ed. by M. H. Greenberg
 Murder and mystery in Boston; ed. by
  C. L. R. Waugh; F. D. McSherry and
  M. H. Greenberg
 The Year's best mystery & suspense
  stories, 1986
A trouble of fools [excerpt]
 A Matter of crime v2
Barnes, Yolanda
Sometimes pain waits
 Ploughshares 14 no2/3:61-8 '88
Barnett, A. N.
For three hundred years
 The Southern Review (Baton Rouge, La.)
  23:658-65 Summ '87
Barnett, Allen
Snapshot
 Men on men 2; ed. by G. Stambolian
Barnhill, Sarah
Near places, far places
 When I am an old woman I shall wear
  purple; ed. by S. K. Martz
BARNS
Anthony, P. In the barn
The **barometer**. Faik, S.
The **Baron** of Grogzwig. Dickens, C.
BARONS *See* Aristocracy
The **baroque** ensemble. Hospital, J. T.
Barr, John Gorman
John Bealle's accident—or, How the widow
  Dudu treated insanity
 The Art of fiction in the heart of Dixie;
  ed. by P. D. Beidler
Barr, Robert, 1850-1912
The chemistry of anarchy
 Isaac Asimov presents the best crime
  stories of the 19th century
The **barracudas**. Schulberg, B.
Barrada, Mohammed
Life by instalments
 Arabic short stories; tr. by D. Johnson-
  Davies
"A **barrel** of fun". Conroy, J.
The **barrel** racer. Pritchett, M.
Barrett, Andrea
Animal magic
 Prairie Schooner 61:51-9 Spr '87
Here at the Starlight Motel
 Michigan Quarterly Review 26:769-76
  Fall '87
Barrett, Lynne
Inventory
 Barrett, L. The land of go
Moon walk
 Barrett, L. The land of go
Out with the crowd
 Barrett, L. The land of go
Realty
 Barrett, L. The land of go

Barrett, Lynne—*Continued*
Wampum
   Barrett, L. The land of go
Barrett, Marvin
A kind of dying
   The New Yorker 63:40-3 O 12 '87
Barrett, Neal, Jr.
Diner
   Omni (New York, N.Y.) 10:92-4+ N '87
   The Year's best science fiction, fifth an-
     nual collection
Perpetuity blues
   The Year's best science fiction, fifth an-
     nual collection
Sallie C.
   The Year's best science fiction, fourth
     annual collection
Barrett, William E.
Dealers in doom
   Baker's dozen: 13 short espionage novels
The destroyer
   A Treasury of World War II stories; ed.
     by B. Pronzini and M. H. Greenberg
A love story
   The Saturday Evening Post 256:50-1+ S
     '84
Barrier. Boucher, A.
BARRISTERS *See* Law and lawyers
Barrus, Tim
Life sucks; or, Ernest Hemingway never
   slept here
   Men on men 2; ed. by G. Stambolian
Barry, Ben
Clemency
   Chicago Review 34:138-9 Spr '84
Barry, Lynda
The tighten up
   Mother Jones 13:25-9+ S '88
BARS *See* Hotels, taverns, etc.
Barstow, Stan, 1928-
The apples of paradise
   Barstow, S. The glad eye, and other
     stories
Foreign parts
   Barstow, S. The glad eye, and other
     stories
The glad eye
   Barstow, S. The glad eye, and other
     stories
Good
   Barstow, S. The glad eye, and other
     stories
Huby falling
   Barstow, S. The glad eye, and other
     stories
The middle of the journey
   Barstow, S. The glad eye, and other
     stories
The pity of it all
   Barstow, S. The glad eye, and other
     stories

Rue
   Barstow, S. The glad eye, and other
     stories
The running and the lame
   Barstow, S. The glad eye, and other
     stories
Work in progress
   Barstow, S. The glad eye, and other
     stories
The **Barsukov** Triangle. Katerli, N.
Bart and Helene at Annie-and-Fred's. Gold,
   H.
BARTENDERS
Ardizzone, T. The walk-on
Ariyoshi, S. The Tomoshibi
Dubus, A. The curse
Lutz, J. The explosives expert
Lynch, L. At a bar I: The Jersey dyke
Lynch, L. At a bar II: In the morning
Lynch, L. At a bar III: Sally the bartender
   goes on jury duty
Lynch, L. At a bar IV: White wine
Lynch, L. At a bar V: Summer storm
Mankiewicz, D. M. Two rolls, no coffee
Meinke, P. Even crazy old barmaids need
   love
Neff, O. The Porton Potion
BARTER
Heise, K. The addition to Aunt Ella's
   house
Heise, K. Aunt Ella and my first com-
   munion
Heise, K. Children's crusade
Barth, John
Night-sea journey
   New directions in prose and poetry 50
Water-message
   Stories of the modern South; ed. by B.
     Forkner and P. Samway
Barth, Stephen
The broken dam
   Stiller's pond; ed. by J. Agee; R. Blakely
     and S. Welch
Barthelme, Donald
110 West Sixty-First Street
   Barthelme, D. Forty stories
Affection
   Barthelme, D. Forty stories
At the Tolstoy Museum
   Barthelme, D. Forty stories
The baby
   Barthelme, D. Forty stories
Basil from her garden
   The Best American short stories, 1986
   The New Yorker 61:36-9 O 21 '85
   Prize stories, 1987
Bluebeard
   Barthelme, D. Forty stories
   The New Yorker 62:33-5 Je 16 '86
Captain Blood
   Barthelme, D. Forty stories
The catechist
   Barthelme, D. Forty stories

Barthelme, Donald—*Continued*
Chablis
    Barthelme, D. Forty stories
Concerning the bodyguard
    Barthelme, D. Forty stories
Construction
    Barthelme, D. Forty stories
    The New Yorker 61:34-6 Ap 29 '85
Conversations with Goethe
    Barthelme, D. Forty stories
Cortés and Montezuma
    The Art of the tale; ed. by D. Halpern
Departures
    Barthelme, D. Forty stories
The educational experience
    Barthelme, D. Forty stories
The emerald
    The Slaying of the dragon; ed. by F.
        Rottensteiner
Engineer-private Paul Klee misplaces an
    aircraft between Milbertshofen and
    Cambrai, March 1916
    Barthelme, D. Forty stories
The explanation
    Barthelme, D. Forty stories
A few moments of sleeping and waking
    Barthelme, D. Forty stories
The film
    Barthelme, D. Forty stories
The flight of pigeons from the palace
    Barthelme, D. Forty stories
Game
    The World of the short story; ed. by
        C. Fadiman
The genius
    Barthelme, D. Forty stories
Great days
    Barthelme, D. Forty stories
January
    Barthelme, D. Forty stories
    The New Yorker 63:40-4 Ap 6 '87
Jaws
    Barthelme, D. Forty stories
    The New Yorker 63:20-1 Ag 17 '87
The king of jazz
    Sudden fiction; ed. by R. Shapard and
        J. Thomas
Letters to the editore
    Barthelme, D. Forty stories
Lightning
    Barthelme, D. Forty stories
The new owner
    Barthelme, D. Forty stories
Not-knowing
    The Pushcart prize XI
On the deck
    Barthelme, D. Forty stories
    The New Yorker 62:27 Ja 12 '87
Opening
    Barthelme, D. Forty stories
    The New Yorker 60:41 O 22 '84
Overnight to many distant cities
    Barthelme, D. Forty stories

The palace at four A.M.
    Barthelme, D. Forty stories
Pepperoni
    Barthelme, D. Forty stories
Porcupines at the university
    Barthelme, D. Forty stories
Rif
    Barthelme, D. Forty stories
Robert Kennedy saved from drowning
    The Norton book of American short
        stories
Sakrete
    Barthelme, D. Forty stories
The school
    New directions in prose and poetry 50
Sentence
    Barthelme, D. Forty stories
Simon
    The New Yorker 60:44-5 S 24 '84
Sindbad
    Barthelme, D. Forty stories
    The New Yorker 60:30-2 Ag 27 '84
Some of us had been threatening our
    friend Colby
    Barthelme, D. Forty stories
The temptation of St. Anthony
    Barthelme, D. Forty stories
Terminus
    Barthelme, D. Forty stories
Visitors
    Barthelme, D. Forty stories
The wound
    Barthelme, D. Forty stories
Barthelme, Frederick
Aluminum house
    Barthelme, F. Chroma
Architecture
    Barthelme, F. Chroma
Black tie
    Barthelme, F. Chroma
Chroma
    Barthelme, F. Chroma
Cleo
    Barthelme, F. Chroma
    The New Yorker 61:48-53 N 18 '85
Cooker
    The New Yorker 63:22-8 Ag 10 '87
Cut glass
    Barthelme, F. Chroma
Driver
    Barthelme, F. Chroma
    The New Yorker 61:36-42 S 23 '85
Export
    The New Yorker 60:42-9 Ap 23 '84
Gila Flambé
    Mississippi writers v1: Fiction; ed. by D.
        Abbott
Law of averages
    The New Yorker 63:36-9 O 5 '87
Magic castle
    Barthelme, F. Chroma
Parents
    Barthelme, F. Chroma

Barthelme, Frederick—*Continued*
Perfect things
Barthelme, F. Chroma
Pupil
Barthelme, F. Chroma
The New Yorker 61:26-32 Ag 5 '85
Reset
Barthelme, F. Chroma
The New Yorker 62:36-42 D 1 '86
Restraint
Barthelme, F. Chroma
Sis
Barthelme, F. Chroma
Trick scenery
Barthelme, F. Chroma
War with Japan
The New Yorker 64:43-9 D 12 '88
Barthelme, Steve
Beach
Barthelme, S. And he tells the little horse the whole story
Black Jack
Barthelme, S. And he tells the little horse the whole story
Chat
Barthelme, S. And he tells the little horse the whole story
Failing all else
Barthelme, S. And he tells the little horse the whole story
The friend
Barthelme, S. And he tells the little horse the whole story
Get-together
Barthelme, S. And he tells the little horse the whole story
Here you are
Barthelme, S. And he tells the little horse the whole story
Liars
Barthelme, S. And he tells the little horse the whole story
Michael
Barthelme, S. And he tells the little horse the whole story
The Massachusetts Review 29:357-67 Summ '88
Mrs. Sims
Barthelme, S. And he tells the little horse the whole story
The Massachusetts Review 26:104-14 Spr '85
Problematical species
Barthelme, S. And he tells the little horse the whole story
Samaritan
Barthelme, S. And he tells the little horse the whole story
Stoner's lament
Barthelme, S. And he tells the little horse the whole story

That's no reason
Barthelme, S. And he tells the little horse the whole story
Their house
Barthelme, S. And he tells the little horse the whole story
Zach
Barthelme, S. And he tells the little horse the whole story
Zorro
Barthelme, S. And he tells the little horse the whole story
The Yale Review 76:557-68 Summ '87
Bartleby. See Melville, H. Bartleby the scrivener
Bartleby the scrivener. Melville, H.
Bartlett, Brian
Fearful children [excerpt]
Fatal recurrences; ed. by H. Hugh and P. O'Brien
Bartlett, Honora
Some notes on evolution
Stepping out; ed. by A. Oosthuizen
Barton, Marie
Jacob's angel
Short story international 43
Bartov, Hanoch
Son, father, judge
Commentary 81:32-9 Mr '86
BASEBALL
See also Softball
Biggle, L. Who's on first?
Blount, R. Five Ives
Boyle, T. C. The Hector Quesadilla story
Breen, J. L. All-star team
Broun, H. Slow grounder
Burke, J. L. Taking a second look
Cheever, J. The national pastime
Chowder, K. Hall of Fame
Deaver, P. F. Infield
Dubus, A. After the game
Dubus, A. The pitcher
Fante, J. In the spring
Flaherty, G. The terrible speed of mercy
Israeloff, R. City ball
Kinsella, W. P. Diehard
Kinsella, W. P. Distances
Kinsella, W. P. The Eddie Scissons syndrome
Kinsella, W. P. Frank Pierce, Iowa
Kinsella, W. P. The further adventures of Slugger McBatt
Kinsella, W. P. K Mart
Kinsella, W. P. The managers
Kinsella, W. P. Punchlines
Kinsella, W. P. Reports concerning the death of the Seattle Albatross are somewhat exaggerated
Kinsella, W. P. Searching for Freddy
Kinsella, W. P. The thrill of the grass
Kinsella, W. P. The Valley of the Schmoon

BASEBALL—*Continued*

Klinkowitz, J. Adolph Menjou's tryout camp

Klinkowitz, J. Ambience

Klinkowitz, J. Ball two

Klinkowitz, J. Baseball bingo

Klinkowitz, J. Beer night in Bettendorf

Klinkowitz, J. BP

Klinkowitz, J. Costy Pedraza's greatest pitch

Klinkowitz, J. Eddie and the niña

Klinkowitz, J. Freddie's up

Klinkowitz, J. Game time

Klinkowitz, J. Hot dogs and the Sox

Klinkowitz, J. The language game

Klinkowitz, J. Mack's stats

Klinkowitz, J. Metaphors

Klinkowitz, J. Nicknames

Klinkowitz, J. Pregame

Klinkowitz, J. Rain date

Klinkowitz, J. Release

Klinkowitz, J. Road work

Klinkowitz, J. Short season

Klinkowitz, J. The squeeze is on

Klinkowitz, J. Sweet home Chicago

Klinkowitz, J. Sweet Jayne

Klinkowitz, J. The swoon wagon

Meissner, W. The outfielder

O'Hara, J. Bread alone

Ramírez, S. The centerfielder

Ramírez, S. The perfect game

Rheinheimer, K. Umpire

Ríos, A. The iguana killer

Rosenfeld, I. The misfortunes of the Flapjacks

Sorrells, R. T. A fan of the game

Sorrells, R. T. The phone call

Spinelli, J. Gus Zernial and me

West, J. Public-address system

White, C. Metaphysics in the Midwest

Wolfe, T. Nebraska Crane

Baseball bingo. Klinkowitz, J.

The **basement**. Ocampo, S.

The **basement** of happiness. Houbein, L.

The **basement** room. Greene, G.

BASHŌ *See* Matsuo, Bashō, 1644-1694

Basic skills. Finger, A.

Basil from her garden. Barthelme, D.

Basilisk. Ellison, H.

The **Basilisk**. Gilchrist, M.

The **basket** maker. Austin, M. H.

The **Basket** Woman: first story. Austin, M. H.

The **Basket** Woman: second story. Austin, M. H.

BASKETBALL

Baumbach, J. Familiar games

Baumbach, J. How you play the game

Bonosky, P. Hank

Connelly, J. Lock

Cook, M. Parting shots

Effinger, G. A. From downtown at the buzzer

Finney, E. J. The all-American's wife

Liben, M. The record

Pronzini, B., and Malzberg, B. N. Rebound

Sorrells, R. T. Rookie

BASLE (SWITZERLAND) *See* Switzerland—Basle

Basques. Connelly, J.

Bass, Rick, 1958-

Cats and students, bubbles and abysses

    The Best American short stories, 1988

Choteau

    Gentlemen's Quarterly 58:216+ D '88

The government bears

    The Southern Review (Baton Rouge, La.) 23:645-52 Summ '87

Mexico

    Antaeus 60:122-37 Spr '88

Other

    The Southern Review (Baton Rouge, La.) 23:653-7 Summ '87

Redfish

    Esquire 110:140-2+ Ag '88

The watch

    New stories from the South: the year's best, 1988

Where the sea used to be

    The Paris Review 29:14-45 Spr '87

Wild horses

    The Paris Review 30:133-55 Summ '88

The **bass**, the river, and Sheila Mant. Wetherell, W. D.

Bassen, Lois Shapley

Flash Gordon

    The Kenyon Review ns6:29-45 Wint '84

The **bastards** of Thanos. Petrakis, H. M.

BASTARDY *See* Illegitimacy

Bastienne's child. Colette

Basu, Romen

Sambal and Putki

    Short story international 60

Bat-girl!. Boyd, W.

Bataan landing. Whitehouse, A.

Bates, Arthenia J.

A ceremony of innocence

Full measure; ed. by D. Sennett

Bates, H. E. (Herbert Ernest), 1905-1974

The butterfly

    Bates, H. E. A month by the lake & other stories

The chords of youth

    Bates, H. E. A month by the lake & other stories

Country society

    Bates, H. E. A month by the lake & other stories

The cowslip field

    Bates, H. E. A month by the lake & other stories

Death and the cherry tree

    Bates, H. E. A month by the lake & other stories

Death of a huntsman

    Bates, H. E. A party for the girls

Bates, H. E. (Herbert Ernest), 1905-1974—
Continued
The death of Uncle Silas
  Bates, H. E. My Uncle Silas
Elaine
  Bates, H. E. A month by the lake &
    other stories
The evolution of Saxby
  Bates, H. E. A month by the lake &
    other stories
Finger wet, finger dry
  Bates, H. E. My Uncle Silas
The flag
  Bates, H. E. A month by the lake &
    other stories
The flame
  Bates, H. E. A month by the lake &
    other stories
A funny thing
  Bates, H. E. My Uncle Silas
A great day for Bonzo
  Bates, H. E. A party for the girls
A happy man
  Bates, H. E. My Uncle Silas
It's just the way it is
  Bates, H. E. A month by the lake &
    other stories
The lily
  Bates, H. E. My Uncle Silas
The maker of coffins
  Bates, H. E. A month by the lake &
    other stories
The mill
  Bates, H. E. A party for the girls
A month by the lake
  Bates, H. E. A month by the lake &
    other stories
Mrs. Eglantine
  Bates, H. E. A month by the lake &
    other stories
Nina
  Early sorrow: ten stories of youth; ed.
    by C. Zolotow
A party for the girls
  Bates, H. E. A party for the girls
The race
  Bates, H. E. My Uncle Silas
The return
  Bates, H. E. My Uncle Silas
The revelation
  Bates, H. E. My Uncle Silas
Sergeant Carmichael
  Bates, H. E. A month by the lake &
    other stories
The shooting party
  Bates, H. E. My Uncle Silas
Silas and Goliath
  Bates, H. E. My Uncle Silas
A Silas idyll
  Bates, H. E. My Uncle Silas
Silas the good
  Bates, H. E. My Uncle Silas

The song of the wren
  Bates, H. E. A month by the lake &
    other stories
The sow and Silas
  Bates, H. E. My Uncle Silas
The spring hat
  The Treasury of English short stories;
    ed. by N. Sullivan
Summer in Salandar
  Bates, H. E. A party for the girls
Time
  Bates, H. E. A month by the lake &
    other stories
The wedding
  Bates, H. E. My Uncle Silas
Where the cloud breaks
  Bates, H. E. A month by the lake &
    other stories
The white wind
  Bates, H. E. A party for the girls
Bates, Harry
Alas, all thinking
  The Mammoth book of classic science
    fiction; ed. by I. Asimov; C. G.
    Waugh and M. H. Greenberg
Farewell to the master
  Machines that think; ed. by I. Asimov;
    P. S. Warrick and M. H. Greenberg
Bates, Herbert Ernest See Bates, H. E. (Her-
    bert Ernest), 1905-1974
Bates, Marian
And one to dream on
  Good Housekeeping 202:120-1 My '86
A man in a million
  Good Housekeeping 202:136-7 F '86
Where tomorrow waits
  Good Housekeeping 199:182-3 O '84
The wonder of Jenny
  Good Housekeeping 207:28+ N '88
BATH (ENGLAND) See England—Bath
Bath. Asscher-Pinkhof, C.
The **bath-chair.** Benson, E. F.
The **bathetic** fallacy. Silva, B.
The **bathroom** dance. Jolley, E.
BATHS, TURKISH See Turkish baths
BATHTUBS
  Mathers, P. Immersion
BATHYSCAPHE
  Wells, H. G. In the abyss
Batistich, Amelia, 1915-
All mixed up
  Women's work; ed. by M. McLeod and
    L. Wevers
BATON TWIRLING
  Lowry, B. Come back, Lolly Ray [excerpt]
  Martin, J. Twirler
BATS
  Willson, H. Front seat
The **Batsons** of Brown and Batson. Alden,
    P. B.
BATTERED WIVES See Wife abuse
The **battering.** Tem, S. R.
The **battle.** Piñera, V.

The **battle**. Sheckley, R.
Battle for the hill. Amichai, Y.
The **battle** in the hills. Brown, G. M.
The **battle** of boiling water. Phelan, F.
The **battle** of Bonhomme Richard and Serapis. Thomson, V.
The **battle** of Manila. Kalpakian, L.
The **battle** of Reno's Bend. Washburn, L. J.
The **battle** of Squashy Hollow. Wodehouse, P. G.
The **battle** of the suits. West, J.
Battle with the bees. Stuart, J.
Battlefield. Ellison, H.
The **battleground**. Singmaster, E.
The **battler**. Hemingway, E.
BATTLES
    See also names of individual battles
Altsheler, J. At the twelfth hour
Bishop, M. Vernalfest morning
Brown, G. M. The battle in the hills
De Forest, J. W. The brigade commander
Fitzgerald, F. S. The night before Chancellorsville
Salmonson, J. A. The prodigal daughter
Battles in the desert. Pacheco, J. E.
Baudelaire, Charles, 1821-1867
The generous gambler
    Devils & demons; ed. by M. Kaye and S. Kaye
                    About
Carter, A. Black Venus
Bauer, Douglas
Lore
    Hot type; ed. by J. Miller
Bauer-Stuchly, Judy
The man he used to be
    Redbook 168:36+ F '87
Baukin, Larry
Jar-boy
    Bringing down the moon; ed. by J. Anderson
Baum, L. Frank (Lyman Frank), 1856-1919
The dummy that lived
    Masterpieces of fantasy and enchantment; ed. by D. G. Hartwell
The glass dog
    Masterpieces of fantasy and enchantment; ed. by D. G. Hartwell
The magic bonbons
    Masterpieces of fantasy and enchantment; ed. by D. G. Hartwell
The queen of Quok
    Masterpieces of fantasy and enchantment; ed. by D. G. Hartwell
The suicide of Kiaros
    Death locked in; ed. by D. G. Greene and R. C. S. Adey
Baum, Lyman Frank *See* Baum, L. Frank (Lyman Frank), 1856-1919
Baum, Gabriel, 1935-( ). Gallant, M.

Baumbach, Jonathan, 1933-
Children of divorced parents
    Baumbach, J. The life and times of Major Fiction
The dinner party
    Baumbach, J. The life and times of Major Fiction
    Prize stories, 1988
The errant melancholy of twilight
    Baumbach, J. The life and times of Major Fiction
Familiar games
    Baumbach, J. The life and times of Major Fiction
A famous Russian poet
    Baumbach, J. The life and times of Major Fiction
From the life of the president
    Baumbach, J. The life and times of Major Fiction
The great Cape Cod shock scare
    Baumbach, J. The life and times of Major Fiction
The Honest Company
    Baumbach, J. The life and times of Major Fiction
How you play the game
    Baumbach, J. The life and times of Major Fiction
The life and times of Major Fiction
    Baumbach, J. The life and times of Major Fiction
    Prize stories, 1984
Mother and father
    Baumbach, J. The life and times of Major Fiction
Mr. and Mrs. McFeely at home and away
    Baumbach, J. The life and times of Major Fiction
Passion?
    American made; ed. by M. Leyner; C. White and T. Glynn
    Baumbach, J. The life and times of Major Fiction
Who shall escape whipping
    Baumbach, J. The life and times of Major Fiction
Baumgart, Don
All you can eat
    L. Ron Hubbard presents Writers of the future v2
Bausch, Richard, 1945-
All the way in Flagstaff, Arizona
    Bausch, R. Spirits, and other stories
Ancient history
    Bausch, R. Spirits, and other stories
Contrition
    Bausch, R. Spirits, and other stories

Bausch, Richard, 1945-—Continued
The man who knew Belle Starr
  The Atlantic 259:61-9 Ap '87
  Bausch, R. Spirits, and other stories
  The Best of the West; ed. by J. Thomas
  New stories from the South: the year's
    best, 1988
Police dreams
  The Atlantic 259:54-60 My '87
  Bausch, R. Spirits, and other stories
  The Best American short stories, 1988
Spirits
  Bausch, R. Spirits, and other stories
What feels like the world
  The Atlantic 256:58-64 O '85
  Bausch, R. Spirits, and other stories
  Prize stories, 1987
The wife's tale
  Bausch, R. Spirits, and other stories
Wise men at their end
  Bausch, R. Spirits, and other stories
Bausch, Robert
The white rooster
  The Atlantic 257:56-63 My '86
BAVARIA (GERMANY) *See* Germany—
    Bavaria
Bax, Martin
Beds
  New Directions in prose and poetry 51
Bax, Roger, 1908-
  *For works written by this author under
    other names see Garve, Andrew,
    1908-*
Baxt, George
Stroke of genius
  The Year's best mystery and suspense
    stories, 1988
The woman I envied
  Manhattan mysteries; ed. by B. Pronzini;
    C. L. R. Waugh and M. H. Greenberg
Baxter, Alida
A telephone call from David
  Ms. 13:54-6+ Je '85
Baxter, Charles
Cataract
  Baxter, C. Through the safety net
The cliff
  Baxter, C. Harmony of the world
  Sudden fiction; ed. by R. Shapard and
    J. Thomas
The crank
  Baxter, C. Harmony of the world
The eleventh floor
  Baxter, C. Through the safety net
Fenstad's mother
  The Atlantic 262:60-6 S '88
Gershwin's second prelude
  Baxter, C. Harmony of the world
Gryphon
  Baxter, C. Through the safety net
  The Best American short stories, 1986

Harmony of the world
  Baxter, C. Harmony of the world
  Love stories for the time being; ed. by
    G. D. Chipps and B. Henderson
Horace and Margaret's fifty-second
  Baxter, C. Harmony of the world
How I found my brother
  The Best American short stories, 1987
  The Graywolf annual 4
A late Sunday afternoon by the Huron
  Baxter, C. Through the safety net
  Michigan Quarterly Review 24:52-68
    Wint '85
Media event
  Baxter, C. Through the safety net
The model
  Baxter, C. Harmony of the world
Saul and Patsy are getting comfortable in
    Michigan
  Baxter, C. Through the safety net
A short course in Nietzschean ethics
  Baxter, C. Harmony of the world
Snow
  The New Yorker 64:34-9 D 19 '88
Stained glass
  Baxter, C. Through the safety net
Surprised by joy
  Baxter, C. Through the safety net
  The Editors' choice v4; ed. by G. E.
    Murphy, Jr.
Talk show
  Baxter, C. Through the safety net
Through the safety net
  Baxter, C. Through the safety net
Weights
  Baxter, C. Harmony of the world
Westland
  The Paris Review 30:12-33 Fall '88
Winter journey
  Baxter, C. Through the safety net
The would-be father
  Baxter, C. Harmony of the world
Xavier speaking
  Baxter, C. Harmony of the world
Bay of Angels. Winton, T.
Baykurt, Fakir
The airplane ticket
  Short story international 44
Jeyfo
  Short story international 69
The wolf
  Short story international 53
Bayles, Martha
The "New Yorker" story
  The Editors' choice: new American
    stories v2
  Harper's 269:69-71 Jl '84
Baynton, Barbara
The chosen vessel
  The Australian short story; ed. by L.
    Hergenhan
Bayou boy. Eighner, L.

Bayou l'Ombre: an incident of the war. King, G. E.
BCO equipment. Armer, K. M.
Be careful what you want. Kittredge, W.
Be free, die young. Abbott, L. K.
Be it ever so humble. Mori, Y.
Be lucky. Prior, A.
Beach. Barthelme, S.
The **beach.** Cowan, P.
Beach blanket mah-jongg. Mordden, E.
Beach party. Fleming, B.
The **beach** umbrella. Colter, C.
Beachboy. McPherson, M.
BEACHCOMBERS
   Williams, T. The poet
Beachworld. King, S.
Beagle, Peter S.
   Lila the werewolf
      Great American love stories; ed. by L. Rosenthal
Beak by beak. Anthony, P.
Beal, M. F.
   Veterans
      The Paris Review 27:107-22 Wint '85
Beam pirate. Smith, G. O.
Beam us home. Tiptree, J.
Bean, Amelia
   The warhorse of Spotted Tail
      She won the West; ed. by M. Muller and B. Pronzini
Beans!. Stewart, R.
The **beanstalk** analysis. Jeppson, J. O.
Bear, Greg, 1951-
   Blood music
      Nebula awards #19
      The Year's best science fiction, first annual collection
   Dead run
      Omni (New York, N.Y.) 7:90-2+ Ap '85
   Hardfought
      Nebula awards #19
      The Year's best science fiction, first annual collection
   If I die before I wake
      Dragons of light; ed. by O. S. Card
   Petra
      Mirrorshades; ed. by B. Sterling
      Omni book of science fiction 1
   Tangents
      Mathenauts: tales of mathematical wonder; ed. by R. Rucker
      Nebula awards 22
      Omni (New York, N.Y.) 8:40-2+ Ja '86
      The Year's best science fiction, fourth annual collection
   Through road no whither
      Hitler victorious; ed. by G. Benford and M. H. Greenberg
   The visitation
      Omni (New York, N.Y.) 9:54-6 Je '87
   The white horse child
      Wizards; ed. by I. Asimov; M. H. Greenberg and C. G. Waugh
Bear and other pale giants. Haake, K.

The **bear** as symbol. Everett, P. L.
A **bear** hunt. Faulkner, W.
The **bear** tamers. Woodman, A.
The **bear** went over the mountain. Kinsella, W. P.
The **bearded** lady. Queen, E.
The **Bearded** Lady. Weaver, G.
The **bearded** samurai. Kōda, R.
BEARDS
   Goyen, W. Zamour; or, A tale of inheritance
BEARS
   Bedard, B. Sweet Billy
   Burns, M. Collected bear stories
   Carrier, R. What language do bears speak?
   Crane, S. Killing his bear
   Crane, S. A tent in agony
   Everett, P. L. The bear as symbol
   Kittredge, W. We are not in this together
   Sandel, C. The polar bears
   Stuart, J. No hero
   Thorpe, T. B. The big bear of Arkansas
   Woodman, A. The bear tamers
Bears. Mattison, A.
Beasley, Conger
   Blue oraciones
      Missouri short fiction; ed. by C. Beasley
Beast. Gustafson, J.
Beast and beauty. Olesen, K.
A **beast** is born. Robbins, W. W.
The **beast** with five fingers. Harvey, W. F.
The **beasts** of Barsac. Bloch, R.
BEAT GENERATION *See* Bohemianism
The **beatings.** Hunter, E.
BEATNIKS *See* Bohemianism
Beattie, Ann
   The big outside world
      Beattie, A. Where you'll find me, and other stories
   Cards
      Beattie, A. Where you'll find me, and other stories
      Esquire 104:118-19+ Ag '85
      The Esquire fiction reader v2
      The Graywolf annual 2
   Coney Island
      Beattie, A. Where you'll find me, and other stories
   Deuce
      Gentlemen's Quarterly 58:194+ Ap '88
   Gypsy moths
      The Bread Loaf anthology of contemporary American short stories; ed. by R. Pack and J. Parini
   Heaven on a summer night
      Beattie, A. Where you'll find me, and other stories
   High school
      Beattie, A. Where you'll find me, and other stories
   Home to Marie
      The New Yorker 62:38-43 D 15 '86

Beattie, Ann—*Continued*
Honey
Prize stories, 1988
Horatio's trick
The New Yorker 63:42-50 D 28 '87
Imagine a day at the end of your life
Harper's 275:70-2 D '87
In the white night
Beattie, A. Where you'll find me, and other stories
New American short stories; ed. by G. Norris
The New Yorker 60:42-3 Je 4 '84
Prize stories, 1985
It's just another day in Big Bear City, California
New women and new fiction; ed. by S. Cahill
Jacklighting
The Art of the tale; ed. by D. Halpern
Janus
Beattie, A. Where you'll find me, and other stories
The Best American short stories, 1986
The New Yorker 61:33-5 My 27 '85
Lofty
Beattie, A. Where you'll find me, and other stories
Mermaids
The Virginia Quarterly Review 63:23-35 Wint '87
A shaggy love story
Ladies' Home Journal 101:88+ Je '84
Skeletons
Beattie, A. Where you'll find me, and other stories
The New Yorker 61:36-7 F 3 '86
Snow
Beattie, A. Where you'll find me, and other stories
Spiritus
Beattie, A. Where you'll find me, and other stories
Summer people
Beattie, A. Where you'll find me, and other stories
The New Yorker 60:46-53 S 24 '84
Sunshine and shadow
Look who's talking; ed. by B. Weber
Times
Beattie, A. Where you'll find me, and other stories
Weekend
American short story masterpieces; ed. by R. Carver and T. Jenks
The World of the short story; ed. by C. Fadiman
When can I see you again?
Beattie, A. Where you'll find me, and other stories
Where you'll find me
Beattie, A. Where you'll find me, and other stories

The New Yorker 62:32-40 Mr 3 '86
Beaulieu, Victor Lévy, 1945-
Monsieur Melville [excerpt]
Invisible fictions; ed. by G. Hancock
The rubber ball
Intimate strangers; ed. by M. Cohen and W. Grady
Beaumont, Charles, 1929-1967
Free dirt
The Best horror stories from the Magazine of fantasy and science fiction
Fritzchen
Young monsters; ed. by I. Asimov; M. H. Greenberg and C. G. Waugh
My grandmother's japonicas
Masques; ed. by J. N. Williamson
Place of meeting
Vampires; ed. by A. Ryan
Beauties. Chekhov, A. P.
The **beauties** of drink: an essay. Abbott, L. K.
Beautiful. Poverman, C. E.
The **beautiful** and the sublime. Sterling, B.
Beautiful husbands. Updike, J.
The **beautiful** intruder. Moore, S. J.
The **beautiful** journey. Marrington, P.
Beautiful my mane in the wind. Petroski, C.
Beautiful rebel. Jones, P.
The **beautiful** stranger. Jackson, S.
The **beautiful** suit. Wells, H. G.
The **beautiful** white horse. Saroyan, W.
BEAUTY *See* Aesthetics
BEAUTY, PERSONAL
Colette. The little Bouilloux girl
Cooper, J. C. Loved to death
Cooper, J. C. Sins leave scars
De Larrabeiti, M. Malagan and the Lady of Rascas
García Márquez, G. The handsomest drowned man in the world
Girion, B. The makeover of Meredith Kaplan
Houbein, L. The marriage of the beautiful lady who had a mind of her own
Poverman, C. E. Beautiful
Rooke, L. Narcissus consulted
Beauty. Greene, G.
The **beauty** contest. Naipaul, S.
BEAUTY CONTESTS
Doubiago, S. Raquel
Drake, R. Football Queen
Naipaul, S. The beauty contest
Wilson, B. Miss Venezuela
Beauty for sale. Quinliven, J. O.
BEAUTY SHOPS
Colette. A hairdresser
Honig, L. No friends, all strangers
Kauffman, J. The Alvordton Spa and Sweat Shop
Kawabata, Y. Hair
Employees
Filippi, C. L. Milagros, on Mercurio Street
Filippi, C. L. Pilar, your curls

BEAUTY SHOPS—Employees—*Continued*
O'Hara, J. The friends of Miss Julia
Bebe. Dawson, F.
Because our skins are finer. Lee, T.
Bech in Czech. Updike, J.
Becher, Ulrich, 1910-
A very Baltic story
Voices East and West: German short stories since 1945
Becker, Jillian, 1932-
The stench
Echad 2: South African Jewish voices
Becker, Leslee
Signs and wonders
The Atlantic 256:54-61 Jl '85
Beckett, Richard
Forty Susan Sangsters stride out at the Wellington Boot
Transgressions; ed. by D. Anderson
Beckett, Samuel, 1906-
The calmative
The Nobel reader; ed. by J. Eisen and S. Troy
First love
The Art of the tale; ed. by D. Halpern
Ping
The Penguin book of modern British short stories
The **beckoning** fair one. Onions, O.
Becky. Toomer, J.
Becky Henderson's other life. Rosenberg, J.
Becoming Elaine. Wood, M.
The **bed**. Dadswell, M.
The **bed**. Maupassant, G. de
The **bed**. Ocampo, S.
Bed no. 29. Maupassant, G. de
A **bed** of bauxite in Weipa. Ramírez, S.
Bed of roses. Finney, E. J.
Bedard, Brian, 1945-
Benedict's dove
Bedard, B. Hour of the beast, and other stories
Entries in a drowned man's dictionary
Bedard, B. Hour of the beast, and other stories
The fifth letter
Bedard, B. Hour of the beast, and other stories
Hour of the beast
Bedard, B. Hour of the beast, and other stories
Hubbard Squash
Bedard, B. Hour of the beast, and other stories
The ostrich
Bedard, B. Hour of the beast, and other stories
Sheer Energy
Bedard, B. Hour of the beast, and other stories
South Dakota samaritans
Bedard, B. Hour of the beast, and other stories

Stalking
Bedard, B. Hour of the beast, and other stories
Sweet Billy
Bedard, B. Hour of the beast, and other stories
Bedbugs. Sinclair, C.
Bedclothes. Wexler, J.
Bedford, Jean, 1946-
Campaign
Transgressions; ed. by D. Anderson
Through road
Home and away; ed. by R. Creswell
Bedford, William
The painter's daughter
Encounter (London, England) 65:3-6 S/O '85
Bedford-Jones, H.
Ram him, damn him!
Mississippi River tales; ed. by F. McSherry; C. G. Waugh and M. H. Greenberg
Bedlam at the Budgie. Ritchie, J.
BEDOUINS
Gorgy, N. Cairo is a small city
Oz, A. Nomad and viper
Bedrock. Proulx, A.
BEDS
Collins, W. A terribly strange bed
Wexler, J. Bedclothes
Beds. Bax, M.
A **bee** in amber. Norris, H.
The **Bee-man** of Orn. Stockton, F.
Beebee. Vreuls, D.
Beecher Island. Overholser, W. D.
Beef. Kinsella, W. P.
The **beekeeper**. Neville, S.
Beekman, E. M., 1939-
Frisian horses
New directions in prose and poetry 48
Beelzebub. Bloch, R.
The **beer** drinkers. Pachter, J.
Beer night in Bettendorf. Klinkowitz, J.
Beerbohm, Max, 1872-1956
A. V. Laider
The World of the short story; ed. by C. Fadiman
Enoch Soames
Black water; ed. by A. Manguel
BEES
Dahl, R. Royal jelly
Durrell, L. Where the bee sucks . . .
Schwartz, L. S. Killing the bees
Sonnemann, W. K. The council of drones
Stuart, J. Battle with the bees
Wynne, A. The Cyprian bees
The **beet** queen. Erdrich, L.
BEETLES
Poe, E. A. The gold-bug
Before and after Celeste. Briskin, M.
Before and after: snapshots. Schulman, H.
The **before-Christmas** present. Pilcher, R.
Before echo. Shaik, F.

Before Eden. Clarke, A. C.
Before he kills. Russell, R.
Before he went out west. Freeman, C.
Before sewing one must cut. Schinto, J.
Before she kills. Brown, F.
Before summer comes. Stratton, M.
Before the cock crows thrice. Shukshin, V. M.
Before the dawn. Haris, P.
Before the deluge. Rhys, J.
Before the law. Kafka, F.
Before the party. Maugham, W. S.
Before the rain. McLaughlin, L.
Before the rainbow. Klass, F.
Before the storm. Campbell, R.
Before the thunderstorm. Ziem, J.
Beg, sl tog, inc, cont, rep. Hempel, A.
Begamudré, Ven
   A promise we shall wake in the pink city after harvest
      The Old dance; ed. by B. Burnard
The **beggar.** Ioannidou Adamidou, I.
The **beggar** and his cat. DeWeese, G.
Beggar my neighbour. Jacobson, D.
The **beggar** on Dublin Bridge. Bradbury, R.
BEGGARS
   Bowles, P. Mejdoub
   Burrage, A. M. The sweeper
   Ferreira, R. Dream with no name
   Ferreira, R. No one looks out anymore
   Jacobson, D. Beggar my neighbour
   Kim, Y. I. The gold watch
   Lawson, H. Mitchell: a character sketch
   Narayan, R. K. The blind dog
   Narayan, R. K. The mute companions
   Walpole, Sir H. The silver mask
The **beggars.** Pavese, C.
The **beggar's** knife. Rey Rosa, R.
The **beggarwoman** of Locarno. Kleist, H. von
The **beginning.** Grau, S. A.
Beginning. Harington, D.
A **beginning.** Jones, M.
The **beginning** of science. Sulivan, J.
The **beginning** of something. Dixon, S.
The **beginning** of violence. Leedom-Ackerman, J.
Beginnings. Roth, H. H.
The **beginnings** of a sin. MacLaverty, B.
Behan, Brendan
   The confirmation suit
      The Treasury of English short stories; ed. by N. Sullivan
   The last of Mrs. Murphy
      The Best of Irish wit and wisdom; ed. by J. McCarthy
BEHAVIOR MODIFICATION
      See also Brainwashing
   Sladek, J. T. The brass monkey
Behind a mask. Ansky, S.
Behind my lace curtain. Sims, L.
Behind the Bougainvillea. Wicomb, Z.
Behind the hedge. Fink, I.

Behold the incredible revenge of the shifted P. O. V. Lish, G.
Beholder. Matheson, R. C.
Behrens, Peter, 1954-
   Vulcan
      The Atlantic 255:82-7 Je '85
Beidenbauer's flea. Ellin, S.
BEIJING (CHINA) See China—Beijing
Being a murderer myself. Williams, A.
Being ashore. Masefield, J.
Being here now. Loukakis, A.
Being occupied. Hopkins, D.
Bel. Palmer, W.
Un **bel** di. Tiempo, E.
Belben, Rosalind
   The licences to eat meat
      P.E.N. new fiction I
The **Beldame** Feng. Li, K.-T.
Belden, Wilanne Schneider
   Fenneca
      Tales of the Witch World [1]
BELFAST (NORTHERN IRELAND) See Northern Ireland—Belfast
BELGIAN CONGO See Zaire
BELGIANS
                  Canada
   Vanderhaeghe, G. What I learned from Caesar
BELGIUM
                  Liège
   Peterson, L. S. The gift
Belief. Asimov, I.
Believer in death. Murphy, Y.
Belinda's seal. Rosta, H.
Beliveau pays. Bankier, W.
Belize. Gilchrist, E.
Bell, Alison
   Hijacked heart
      'Teen 31:62+ Ag '87
Bell, Charles G.
   The married land [excerpt]
      Mississippi writers v1: Fiction; ed. by D. Abbott
Bell, Clare, 1952-
   The hunting of Lord Etsalian's daughter
      Tales of the Witch World 2
Bell, David
   You may not be an angel
      Short story international 57
Bell, J. Leslie
   The curlew's cry
      Alberta bound; ed. by F. Stenson
Bell, Madison Smartt
   Customs of the country
      Harper's 276:66-72 F '88
   The day I shot my dog
      Homewords: a book of Tennessee writers; ed. by D. Paschall
   The forgotten bridge
      Bell, M. S. Zero db, and other stories
   I [love] NY
      Bell, M. S. Zero db, and other stories

Bell, Madison Smartt—*Continued*
Irene
  Bell, M. S. Zero db, and other stories
The lie detector
  Bell, M. S. Zero db, and other stories
  The Best American short stories, 1987
Monkey Park
  Bell, M. S. Zero db, and other stories
  The Hudson Review 38:85-99 Spr '85
  The New writers of the South; ed. by
    C. East
The naked lady
  Bell, M. S. Zero db, and other stories
  The Best American short stories, 1984
  Harper's 269:36-8 O '84
The structure and meaning of dormitory
  and food services
  Bell, M. S. Zero db, and other stories
Today is a good day to die
  Bell, M. S. Zero db, and other stories
Triptych I [Variant title: Triptych 2]
  Bell, M. S. Zero db, and other stories
Triptych II
  Bell, M. S. Zero db, and other stories
Triptych 2 [Variant title: Triptych I]
  New stories from the South: the year's
    best, 1986
World without end
  The North American Review 272:93-7 S
    '87
Zero db
  Bell, M. S. Zero db, and other stories
  The Editors' choice v3; ed. by G. E.
    Murphy, Jr.
  Harper's 271:64-7 Ag '85
Bell, Martin
Brady
  Bell, M. Wolf
Conrad
  Bell, M. Wolf
Decatur
  Bell, M. Wolf
Helen
  Bell, M. Wolf
Reba
  Bell, M. Wolf
Bell, Shayne
Jacob's ladder
  L. Ron Hubbard presents Writers of the
    future v3
Bell, Vereen, 1911-1944
Brag dog
  Roger Caras' Treasury of great dog
    stories
"**Bell**". Maupassant, G. de
The **bell**. Russell, R.
The **bell** in the fog. Atherton, G. F. H.
The **bell** remembered. Wolfe, T.
BELL-RINGERS *See* Bells and bell ringers
The **bell** that sang again. Chavez, A.
The **bell-tower**. Melville, H.
Bella-Vista. Colette

Bellah, James Warner, b. 1899
Big hunt
  The Second reel West; ed. by B. Pron-
    zini and M. H. Greenberg
Command
  The Second reel West; ed. by B. Pron-
    zini and M. H. Greenberg
Day of terror
  A Treasury of World War II stories; ed.
    by B. Pronzini and M. H. Greenberg
How Stonewall came back
  A Treasury of Civil War stories; ed. by
    M. H. Greenberg and B. Pronzini
Bellamy, Joe David
Make love not war
  Prairie Schooner 58:55-61 Wint '84
Roth's deadman
  Sudden fiction; ed. by R. Shapard and
    J. Thomas
Saving the boat people
  New Directions in prose and poetry 51
Bellem, Robert Leslie, 1902-1968
Diamonds of death
  The Mammoth book of private eye
    stories; ed. by B. Pronzini and M. H.
    Greenberg
Belles Demoiselles plantation. Cable, G. W.
Belles excentriques. Pomerance, M.
Bellflower. Maupassant, G. de
Belloc, Hilaire, 1870-1953
Home
  Black water; ed. by A. Manguel
Bellow, Saul
Cousins
  Bellow, S. Him with his foot in his
    mouth, and other stories
Him with his foot in his mouth
  Bellow, S. Him with his foot in his
    mouth, and other stories
Leaving the yellow house
  Full measure; ed. by D. Sennett
A silver dish
  Bellow, S. Him with his foot in his
    mouth, and other stories
  The World of the short story; ed. by
    C. Fadiman
What kind of day did you have?
  Bellow, S. Him with his foot in his
    mouth, and other stories
Zetland: by a character witness
  Bellow, S. Him with his foot in his
    mouth, and other stories
Bells. Shamosh, A.
BELLS AND BELL RINGERS
Melville, H. The bell-tower
O'Brien, F.-J. Jubal, the Ringer
Il **bell'uomo**. Fitzgerald, M. J.
The **belly** of darkness. Walden, W.
Belly on a stick. Umbach, E.
Belonging. Durban, P.
The **beloved**. See Carrington, L. A man in
  love
Below the heavens. Davin, D.

Belsen Express. Leiber, F.
The **belt**. Moravia, A.
The **belvedere**. Stubbs, J.
Beman, Barbara
A cowboy for a madam
Westeryear; ed. by E. Gorman
Set 'em up, Joe
The Black Lizard anthology of crime fiction; ed. by E. Gorman
Ben-Hur escapes from the Astroea. Wallace, L.
Benbow, Margaret
In the midnight hour
The Antioch Review 43:445-54 Fall '85
The **bench**. Dixon, S.
The **bench**. See Jolley, E. Adam's bride
The **bench**. Rive, R.
Benchmark. Raphael, F.
Bendel, Stephanie Kay
The woman in the shadows
Distant danger; ed. by J. Van de Wetering
Bender, Hans, 1907-
La Paloma; or, The food of love
Voices East and West: German short stories since 1945
Benderson, Bruce
A visit from Mom
Between C & D; ed. by J. Rose and C. Texier
Beneath the fig trees. Whelan, G.
Benedict, Dianne, 1941-
Unknown feathers
The Best American short stories, 1984
Benedict, Elizabeth
If you ever go
McCall's 111:100-1+ My '84
Benedict, Pinckney, 1964-
All the dead
Benedict, P. Town smokes
Booze
Benedict, P. Town smokes
Dog
Benedict, P. Town smokes
Fat Tuesday
Benedict, P. Town smokes
Getting over Arnette
Hot type; ed. by J. Miller
Hackberry
Benedict, P. Town smokes
Pit
Benedict, P. Town smokes
The Sutton Pie Safe
Benedict, P. Town smokes
Town smokes
Benedict, P. Town smokes
Water witch
Benedict, P. Town smokes
Benedict, Salli
Tahotahontanekent-seratkerontakwenhakie
Earth power coming; ed. by S. J. Ortiz
Benedict's dove. Bedard, B.
A **beneficial** walk. Curtiss, U. R.

Beneficiaries. Gallagher, T.
The **beneficiaries**. Waugh, H.
Benefit of the bargain. Toner, G. R.
Bénet, Stephen Vincent, 1898-1943
The bishop's beggar
The Saturday Evening Post 257:68-72+ Mr '85
By the waters of Babylon
Beyond Armageddon; ed. by W. M. Miller and M. H. Greenberg
The curfew tolls
Alternative histories; ed. by C. G. Waugh and M. H. Greenberg
Black water; ed. by A. Manguel
The die-hard
A Treasury of Civil War stories; ed. by M. H. Greenberg and B. Pronzini
Henry and the golden mine
The Saturday Evening Post 256:46-9 Jl/Ag '84
The Saturday Evening Post 256:32+ S '84
Jack Ellyat at Gettysburg
A Treasury of Civil War stories; ed. by M. H. Greenberg and B. Pronzini
Johnny Pye and the Fool-killer
The Saturday Evening Post 259:34-8+ S '87
The Saturday Evening Post 259:42-5+ O '87
A judgment in the mountains
A Treasury of World War II stories; ed. by B. Pronzini and M. H. Greenberg
The king of the cats
Masterpieces of fantasy and enchantment; ed. by D. G. Hartwell
Roger Caras' Treasury of great cat stories
Too early spring
Child's ploy; ed. by M. Muller and B. Pronzini
Early sorrow: ten stories of youth; ed. by C. Zolotow
Benevolence. Gardam, J.
Benevolence. Moussa, S.
The **benevolent** ghost and Captain Lowrie. Sale, R.
Benford, Gregory, 1941-
At the double solstice
Terry's universe; ed. by B. Meacham
Freezeframe
Interzone: the 2nd anthology; ed. by J. Clute; D. Pringle and S. Ounsley
The future of the Jovian system
The Planets; ed. by B. Preiss
How to sound like an expert
L. Ron Hubbard presents Writers of the future v3
Immortal night
Omni (New York, N.Y.) 7:70-2+ Ap '85
Mandikini
The Universe; ed. by B. Preiss

Benford, Gregory, 1941——*Continued*
Me/days
Universe 14
Newton sleep
Nebula awards 22
Of space-time and the river
Afterlives; ed. by P. Sargent and I. Watson
Time's rub
Mathenauts: tales of mathematical wonder; ed. by R. Rucker
Titan falling
Amazing stories: visions of other worlds
Valhalla
Hitler victorious; ed. by G. Benford and M. H. Greenberg
White creatures
Great science fiction; ed. by I. Asimov; M. H. Greenberg and C. G. Waugh
Benford, Gregory, 1941-, and Carter, Paul A.
Proserpina's daughter
Synergy v3
Benford, Gregory, 1941-, and Laidlaw, Marc
A hiss of dragon
Omni book of science fiction 3
The **Bengal** tiger. Hunnicutt, E.
Benítez-Rojo, Antonio
The death of an absolutist
New England Review and Bread Loaf Quarterly 10:355-67 Spr '88
Heaven and earth
The Pushcart prize X
The man in the armchair
The Massachusetts Review 27:609-23 Fall/Wint '86
Benito Cereno. Melville, H.
Benjamin, Dorothy
Things will look brighter in the morning
Ellery Queen's Prime crimes 2
Benner, Richard
The business card
First love/last love; ed. by M. Denneny; C. Ortleb and T. Steele
Bennet, John
Flat Creek Road
The New Yorker 62:46-52 N 3 '86
Bennett, Hal, 1930-
Chewing gum
Black American Literature Forum 21:379-92 Wint '87
Bennett, James Gordon
Dependents
New stories from the South: the year's best, 1987
The Virginia Quarterly Review 62:54-69 Wint '86
Pacific theater
The Virginia Quarterly Review 64:249-61 Spr '88
Bennett, Lerone, 1928-
The convert
Mississippi writers v1: Fiction; ed. by D. Abbott

Benny's place. Forrest, K. V.
Benoist. Maupassant, G. de
Bensink, John Robert
Lake George in high August
Masques II; ed. by J. N. Williamson
The Year's best fantasy, first annual collection
Benson, Arthur Christopher, 1862-1925
The uttermost farthing
The Mammoth book of short horror novels; ed. by M. Ashley
Benson, E. F.
The bath-chair
Lost souls; ed. by J. Sullivan
The confession of Charles Linkworth
The Oxford book of English ghost stories
The man who went too far
Dark banquet; ed. by L. Child
Monkeys
Spirits, spooks, and other sinister creatures; ed. by H. Hoke
Mrs. Amworth
The Penguin book of horror stories
The room in the tower
The Penguin book of ghost stories
Vampires; ed. by A. Ryan
Benson, Peter, 1956-
Alan
Winter's tales, new ser. v4
Jude
Winter's tales, new ser. v3
Benson, Robert Hugh, 1871-1914
Father Meuron's tale
Devils & demons; ed. by M. Kaye and S. Kaye
The watcher
Lost souls; ed. by J. Sullivan
Benson Watts is dead and in Virginia. Betts, D.
Bentley, E. C. (Edmund Clerihew), 1875-1956
The unknown peer
Through a glass, darkly; ed. by B. Woelfel
Bentley, Edmund Clerihew *See* Bentley, E. C. (Edmund Clerihew), 1875-1956
Bentley, Phyllis
Mother and daughter
Family: stories from the interior; ed. by G. G. Chavis
Benton, Kenneth Carter, 1909-
Cast for murder
John Creasey's Crime collection, 1987
The **bequest.** Wexler, J.
Berard's rapture. Chiarella, T.
Berberova, Nina
Sentence commuted
The Literary Review (Madison, N.J.) 28:489-532 Summ '85
Berdnyk, Oles
The alien secret
Berdnyk, O. Apostle of immortality

Berdnyk, Oles—*Continued*
The apostle of immortality, a tale of the unprecedented
  Berdnyk, O. Apostle of immortality
A chorus of elements
  Berdnyk, O. Apostle of immortality
The constellation of green fish, a tale of the unprecedented
  Berdnyk, O. Apostle of immortality
A journey to the antiworld
  Berdnyk, O. Apostle of immortality
Two abysses
  Berdnyk, O. Apostle of immortality

BEREAVEMENT
Anaya, R. A. The silence of the llano
Bausch, R. Ancient history
Benson, P. Jude
Böll, H. Action will be taken
Carver, R. A small, good thing
Ch'en, Y.-C. My kid brother, K'ang-hsiung
Clark, G. Ice fishing
Coleman, W. In the city of sleep
Connolly, L. C. Echoes
Coskran, K. Facing Mount Kenya
Crapser, W. For Timothy Baer
Crapser, W. Land of the free, home of the brave
Deaver, P. F. The valence of common ions
Dickinson, C. Risk
Dodd, S. M. Potions
Durban, P. This heat
Fitzgerald, M. J. The game
Floyd, P. L. When Mother played Moonshine
Friedman, B. J. The mourner
Frucht, A. How to live alone
Gordon, M. The thorn
Hulme, K. Kiteflying party at Doctors' Point
Hulme, K. Unnamed islands in the unknown sea
Hunnicutt, E. Amos
Josipovici, G. He
Kawabata, Y. Canaries
La Chapelle, M. Homer
Leslie, P. Exits
Loizeaux, W. Beside the Passaic
MacDonald, D. R. Holy Annie
MacDonald, D. R. The wharf king
Mansfield, K. The canary
Mansfield, K. Six years after
McElroy, C. J. More than a notion
McElroy, C. J. Sister Detroit
McKinley, J. Each new springtime, each new summer
Moskowitz, F. Whoever finds this: I love you
Nevai, L. The sad-womb son
Neville, S. Cousins
Niatum, D. She keeps the dance turning like the earth
Prichard, K. S. Hero of the mines

Pritchard, M. Taking hold of Renee
Pritchett, M. Trinity
Raphael, F. Forgetting it
Robison, M. I am twenty-one
Robison, M. I get by
Schulman, H. Before and after: snapshots
Schulman, H. James Dean's widow
Shaw, J. B. A new life
Sholem Aleichem. Elul
Steele, M. The Tin Can
Summers, H. S. Diving
Traba, M. Mothers and shadows [excerpt]
Valle, C. Diary entry #1
Wells, H. G. The presence by the fire
Berenice. Poe, E. A.
Bergelson, David
At the depot
  A Shtetl, and other Yiddish novellas; ed. by R. R. Wisse
Berger, John, 1926-
The accordion player
  Berger, J. Once in Europa
Boris is buying horses
  Berger, J. Once in Europa
Once in Europa
  Berger, J. Once in Europa
Play me something
  Berger, J. Once in Europa
The time of the cosmonauts
  Berger, J. Once in Europa
Bergland, Martha
An embarrassment of ordinary riches
  The Pushcart prize XII
Bergner, Herz
The actor
  Echad 4: Jewish writing from down under: Australia and New Zealand
BERKELEY (CALIF.) *See* California—Berkeley
Berkie. Dodd, S. M.
Berle, Milton
Closing night at the Zebra Lounge
  Redbook 168:62+ Mr '87
A new act
  Ladies' Home Journal 104:112+ N '87
BERLIN (GERMANY) *See* Germany—Berlin
Berlin snowfall. Dische, I.
BERLIN WALL
Oates, J. C. Our wall
Berlioz & the ghetto blaster. Kelly, V.
Berman, Ruth
Professor and colonel
  Mathenauts: tales of mathematical wonder; ed. by R. Rucker
Bernard, Kenneth
Bird-watching
  Bernard, K. The Maldive chronicles
Dirty old man
  Bernard, K. The Maldive chronicles
Epistemology on the march
  Bernard, K. The Maldive chronicles
The films of R. Nixon
  Bernard, K. The Maldive chronicles

Bernard, Kenneth—*Continued*
Firm ground
  Bernard, K. The Maldive chronicles
Fox-trot and other matters
  Bernard, K. The Maldive chronicles
George Washington's birthday
  Bernard, K. The Maldive chronicles
The girl who might or might not have
    read Sartre
  Bernard, K. The Maldive chronicles
King Kong: a meditation
  Bernard, K. The Maldive chronicles
The Maldive chronicles
  Bernard, K. The Maldive chronicles
Morsels
  Bernard, K. The Maldive chronicles
Preparations
  Bernard, K. The Maldive chronicles
  Harper's 276:32+ Ja '88
Question and answer
  Bernard, K. The Maldive chronicles
Rescheduling
  Bernard, K. The Maldive chronicles
Sister Francetta and the pig baby
  Bernard, K. The Maldive chronicles
Teddy and I go Kong
  Bernard, K. The Maldive chronicles
Walking
  Bernard, K. The Maldive chronicles
The Whitman lesson
  Bernard, K. The Maldive chronicles
The woman who thought she was beautiful
  Bernard, K. The Maldive chronicles

Berne, Suzanne
Who's been sleeping in my bed?
  Mademoiselle 91:110+ D '85

Bernen, Robert
Brock
  Bernen, R. The hills: more tales from
    the Blue Stacks
The extra wether
  Bernen, R. The hills: more tales from
    the Blue Stacks
Fox
  Bernen, R. The hills: more tales from
    the Blue Stacks
A keen observer of footwear
  Bernen, R. The hills: more tales from
    the Blue Stacks
The rush
  Bernen, R. The hills: more tales from
    the Blue Stacks
Sacrament of the sick
  Bernen, R. The hills: more tales from
    the Blue Stacks
The scythe
  Bernen, R. The hills: more tales from
    the Blue Stacks
Two lives
  Bernen, R. The hills: more tales from
    the Blue Stacks

The windcharger
  Bernen, R. The hills: more tales from
    the Blue Stacks
Bernhardt. Sandel, C.
Bernstein, Leonard S.
At home I would be a princess
  Prairie Schooner 60:56-61 Wint '86
A gentleman from sole to crown
  Prairie Schooner 58:61-6 Spr '84
Berriault, Gina
The bystander
  American short story masterpieces; ed.
    by R. Carver and T. Jenks
A dream of fair women
  The Kenyon Review ns7:1-6 Wint '85
The houses of the city
  Family: stories from the interior; ed. by
    G. G. Chavis
The infinite passion of expectation
  Love stories for the time being; ed. by
    G. D. Chipps and B. Henderson
The island of Ven
  Prize stories, 1987
  The Pushcart prize XI
Works of the imagination
  The Ploughshares reader: new fiction for
    the eighties
BERRIES
Kenny, M. Yaikni
Berry, R. M.
Apples
  Berry, R. M. Plane geometry and other
    affairs of the heart
A circle is the shape of perfection
  Berry, R. M. Plane geometry and other
    affairs of the heart
A decisive refutation of Herbert Dingle's
    objection to Einstein's twin paradox;
    or, Gravitas
  Berry, R. M. Plane geometry and other
    affairs of the heart
History
  A Good deal; ed. by M. Heath and F.
    M. Robinson
  The Massachusetts Review 25:497-512
    Wint '84
Metempsychosis
  Berry, R. M. Plane geometry and other
    affairs of the heart
November 14, 1864
  Berry, R. M. Plane geometry and other
    affairs of the heart
Paradise lost
  Berry, R. M. Plane geometry and other
    affairs of the heart
Song of the geometry instructor
  Berry, R. M. Plane geometry and other
    affairs of the heart
Tractatus cantatus
  Berry, R. M. Plane geometry and other
    affairs of the heart
Berrying. Cummings, R.
The **Bert** and Ernie show. Otto, L.

Bertha. Maupassant, G. de
Berthiaume, André
  A change of air
    Intimate strangers; ed. by M. Cohen and
    W. Grady
Berthilde's holiday. Keeling, N.
Bertie changes his mind. Wodehouse, P. G.
Bertner: emergency room. Eighner, L.
Berzerk. Flanagan, R.
Beside a dead man. Maupassant, G. de
Beside still waters. Sheckley, R.
Beside the Passaic. Loizeaux, W.
Beside the railroad track. See Nałkowska, Z.
    At the railroad track
Beside the river. Böll, H.
Bess. Phillips, J. A.
BESSARABIA (SOVIET UNION) See Sovi-
    et Union—Bessarabia
Bessette, Gérard, 1920-
  The mustard plaster
    The Oxford book of French-Canadian
    short stories
Best, Elizabeth
  Sunday
    Short story international 47
The best bid. Costa, C.
The best chess player in the world. Symons,
    J.
Best foot forward. Nelson, J.
The best foot forward. Turnley, J. E.
The best-friend murder. Westlake, D. E.
Best friends and other strangers. Mills, L.
The best it could be. Thompson, J.
The best man in town. Winslow, T. S.
The best of Betty. Willett, J.
The best of both worlds. Abrons, R.
The best of everything. Yates, R.
The best of friends. Schweitzer, G.
The best place for it. Powers, R.
Best Quality Glass Company, New York.
    Stark, S. S.
The best shod. Valenzuela, L.
The best teacher in Georgia. McCluskey, J.
The best thing to do. Bird, C.
The best we have. Friedman, B. J.
Bester, Alfred, 1913-1987
  Fondly Fahrenheit
    Robert Silverberg's Worlds of wonder
  Galatea Galante
    Omni book of science fiction 3
BESTIALITY
  McLaughlin, L. In hock
  Moravia, A. The thing
Bestiary. Cortázar, J.
The bet. Chekhov, A. P.
Betancourt, John Gregory
  Vernon's dragon
    100 great fantasy short short stories; ed.
    by I. Asimov; T. Carr and M. H.
    Greenberg
La Bête: a figure study. Pritchard, M.
Betel Palm Village. Cheng, C.-W.

Bethel, J. David
  The fields
    Américas 38:50-2 S/O '86
The betrayal. Essop, A.
The betrayal of the fives. Matthews, J.
Betrayed. MacDonald, J. D.
Betraying Jilly. Rose, D. A.
Betrothal in Santo Domingo. Kleist, H. von
BETROTHALS
  Blinkin, M. Women
  Brender à Brandis, M. Foreigner in the
    family
  Carter, A. A. The fortune hunter
  Chekhov, A. P. The fiancée
  Colette. Secrets
  Crowley, A. The hearth
  Dykeman, W. Lydia McQueen
  Essop, A. Red Beard's daughter
  Freeman, M. E. W. A moral exigency
  Gee, M. The losers
  Geras, A. Love letters
  Hill, E. Marriage at noon
  Kip, L. The ghosts at Grantley
  Pouvillon, E. Duck shooting
  Rose, D. A. Avoiding the shoals of pas-
    sion
  Saroyan, W. The inscribed copy of the
    Kreutzer sonata
  Walpole, Sir H. Bachelors
  Yates, R. The best of everything
BETS See Wagers
Betsy Blake will live forever. Bloch, R.
The better bargain. Deming, R.
Better bars and garden. Cullen, E. J.
A better day to die. O'Donnell, P.
Better tomorrow. Minkhoff, R.
BETTING See Gambling
Betts, Doris, 1932-
  Benson Watts is dead and in Virginia
    A Good deal; ed. by M. Heath and F.
    M. Robinson
  The ugliest pilgrim
    Stories of the modern South; ed. by B.
    Forkner and P. Samway
Betty-san. Yamamoto, M.
Bettyann. Neville, K.
Between. Kinsella, W. P.
Between brothers. Jones, J.
Between now and then. Yarbrough, S.
Between Peiraeus and Naples. Vizyēnos, G.
    M.
Between sleep and death. Petrakis, H. M.
Between sunset and moonrise. Malden, R. H.
Between the minute and the hour. Burrage,
    A. M.
Between the sheets. Eskapa, S.
Between the windows of the sea. Dann, J.
Between trains in X. Böll, H.
Between two shores. MacLaverty, B.
Between zero and one. Gallant, M.
Beutner, Edward F.
  A wedding parable
    U.S. Catholic 50:19-22 My '85

BEVERLY HILLS (CALIF.) *See* California—Beverly Hills
Bewitched. Wharton, E.
The **bewitched** bourgeois. Buzzati, D.
A **bewitched** place. Gogol', N. V.
A **bewitched** ship. Russell, W. C.
Bewley, Geoffrey
  Blood and wine
    Home and away; ed. by R. Creswell
Beynon, John *See* Wyndham, John, 1903-1969
Beyond any measure. Wagner, K. E.
Beyond death. Kawabata, Y.
Beyond doubt. Heinlein, R. A.
Beyond loneliness. Zorrilla de Rodríguez, A. M.
Beyond New Forks. Brown, M. W.
Beyond the cleft. Reamy, T.
Beyond the dead reef. Tiptree, J.
Beyond the moving shadow problem. Murphy, P.
Beyond the pale. Trevor, W.
Beyond the wall. Tyre, N.
Beyond their reach. Stewart, D.
Bhat's return. Sharat Chandra, G. S.
Biali, Zahira el *See* El Biali, Zahira
BIBLICAL STORIES
  Chekhov, A. P. The student
  Chesterton, G. K. A fish story
  Givner, J. The testament of Leyla
  Metzger, D. The tree on the mountain
  Singer, I. B. The death of Methuselah
  Willard, N. How poetry came into the world and why God doesn't write it
The **Bicentennial** Man. Asimov, I.
Bickel, Bill
  Make it never happened
    Isaac Asimov's Tomorrow's voices
BICYCLE RACING
  Morand, P. The six-day night
The **bicycle** rider. Davenport, G.
BICYCLES AND BICYCLING
  Bail, M. Healing
  Brodkey, H. Falling and ascending bodies: four passages
  Crane, S. "Showin' off"
  Holditch, W. K. One of these mornings
  Hornung, E. W. The wrong house
  Ishikawa, J. Moon gems
  Loukakis, A. To Mrs. Starkey
  Loukakis, A. Velodrome
  Mathers, P. Getting there
  Morrison, A. The affair of the 'Avalanche Bicycle and Tyre Co., Limited'
  Saroyan, W. Lord Chugger of cheer
  Wells, H. G. A perfect gentleman on wheels
Bicycles, muscles, cigarettes. Carver, R.
Bierce, Ambrose, 1842-1914?
  The boarded window
    Great ghost stories; ed. by B. A. Schwartz
    The Penguin book of horror stories

  Chickamauga
    The Norton book of American short stories
  The damned thing
    The Dark descent; ed. by D. G. Hartwell
  The moonlit road
    The Penguin book of ghost stories
  Moxon's master
    Machines that think; ed. by I. Asimov; P. S. Warrick and M. H. Greenberg
  An occurrence at Owl Creek Bridge [Variant title: Incident at Owl Creek]
    A Treasury of Civil War stories; ed. by M. H. Greenberg and B. Pronzini
  One of the missing
    A Treasury of Civil War stories; ed. by M. H. Greenberg and B. Pronzini
  One summer night
    Masterpieces of terror and the supernatural; ed. by M. Kaye and S. Kaye
  A watcher by the dead
    Mystery in the mainstream; ed. by B. Pronzini; M. H. Greenberg and B. N. Malzberg
    The Penguin classic crime omnibus
The **big** balloon. Bitov, A.
The **big** bear of Arkansas. Thorpe, T. B.
Big Bertha stories. Mason, B. A.
Big Bill and Little Bill. Read, O.
Big Black: a Mississippi idyll. Williams, T.
Big black good man. Wright, R.
The **big** Bow mystery. Zangwill, I.
Big boy leaves home. Wright, R.
Big Boy, Little Boy. Brett, S.
Big Buck. Caldwell, E.
Big dog. Lavers, N.
Big dome. Randall, M.
Big dreams. Coleman, W.
Big Eagle, Duane
  The journey
    Earth power coming; ed. by S. J. Ortiz
A **big** fish. Deng Gang
Big fish, little fish. Calvino, I.
The **big** flash. Spinrad, N.
Big game. Crowley, A.
Big game. Lutz, J.
Big Herb. Keeling, N.
Big hunt. Bellah, J. W.
The **big** kick. Bloch, R.
Big leaguer. Fante, J.
The **big** little gang. Coleman, W.
Big Mama's funeral. García Márquez, G.
The **big** outside world. Beattie, A.
The **Big** Rock Candy Mountain. Westall, R.
Big Star woman. Sams, F.
Big Sur pig. Kamstra, J.
Big surprise. Matheson, R.
The **big** sway. Johnson, D.
Big two-hearted river: part I. Hemingway, E.
Big two-hearted river: part II. Hemingway, E.

Big wheels: a tale of the laundry game (milkman #2). King, S.
The bigamist. Potter, N. A. J.
BIGAMY
Cortázar, J. Return trip tango
De la Torre, L. Milady bigamy
Keillor, G. David and Agnes, a romance
Poniatowska, E. The night visitor
Pronzini, B. The pattern
Yang Zhenwen. Fu Da regains his wife
Bigfoot stole my wife. Carlson, R.
The biggest bonfire of all. Skrzynecki, P.
The biggest bridge in the world. Pellegrini, D., Jr.
The biggest tent in the world. Black, S.
Biggle, Lloyd, 1923-
Orphan of the void
Intergalactic empires; ed. by I. Asimov; M. H. Greenberg and C. G. Waugh
Who's on first?
Young extraterrestrials; ed. by I. Asimov; M. H. Greenberg and C. G. Waugh
Biggs, Mary
The other Catherine Irene
Here's the story: fiction with heart; ed. by M. Sklar
BIGOTRY See Prejudices
Bijou. Dybek, S.
Biker boy. Eighner, L.
Bilenkin, Dmitri
Crossing of the paths
Aliens, travelers, and other strangers; by B. and A. Strugatsky and others
The genius house
Omni book of science fiction 2
Bill Boston. Dickinson, C.
Bill Sprockett's land. Jolley, E.
Bill, the ventriloquial rooster. Lawson, H.
The billiard ball. Asimov, I.
BILLIARDS
Asimov, I. The billiard ball
Baumbach, J. Mother and father
Kelman, J. Remember young Cecil
Stegner, W. E. The blue-winged teal
Wilson, L. A. Massé
Billie loses her job. Henson, R.
Billington, Rachel
One afternoon
Winter's tales, new ser. v2
The photograph
Winter's tales, new ser. v1
Billy. Gordon, M.
Billy and the birds. Loukakis, A.
Billy Bathgate. Doctorow, E. L.
Billy Botzweiler's last dance. Choyce, L.
Billy Budd, foretopman. See Melville, H. Billy Budd, Sailor
Billy Budd, Sailor. Melville, H.
Billy Ducks among the Pharoahs. DeMarinis, R.
Billy Gashade and glory. Taylor, R.
Billy Sunday. Crapser, W.
Billy Will's song. Curley, D.

Billy's girl. Jackson, G.
Bimini kill. MacDonald, J. D.
Binchy, Maeve
An open (and closed) marriage
Redbook 164:48+ F '85
Bind your hair. Aickman, R.
Binder, Eando
Adam Link's vengeance
Amazing science fiction anthology: The war years, 1936-1945; ed. by M. H. Greenberg
I, robot
Amazing stories: 60 years of the best science fiction
Bing, Jon, 1944-
A meeting in Georgestown
The Penguin world omnibus of science fiction
The Owl of Bear Island
Tales from the planet Earth
Bingham, John, 1908-
Mr. Bulmer's golden carp
The Mammoth book of modern crime stories; ed. by G. Hardinge
Bingham, Sallie
Fear
New women and new fiction; ed. by S. Cahill
Reunion
Here's the story: fiction with heart; ed. by M. Sklar
Bingo. Kilgore, D.
Bingo. Rahman, T.
Bingo and the little woman. Wodehouse, P. G.
The bingo master. Oates, J. C.
Binkas sausage. Thorman, C.
BIOCHEMISTS
Clement, H. The mechanic
Vance, J. The gift of gab
Biograph. Martone, M.
BIOGRAPHERS See Authors
BIOLOGICAL CONTROL SYSTEMS
McKinley, J. Traveler's advisory
BIOLOGICAL RHYTHMS
Wilkerson, C. The man who watched the glaciers run
BIOLOGICAL WARFARE
Longyear, B. B. A time for terror
Pohl, F. The kindly isle
BIOLOGISTS
Cook, H. Pisces
Hamilton, E. Devolution
Leiber, F. Yesterday house
Prose, F. Everything is about animals
Scholz, C. The menagerie of Babel
BIOLOGY

Experiments
Hospital, J. T. The owl-bander
Lanier, S. E. A father's tale
BIONICS
Shirley, J., and Sterling, B. The unfolding
Wolverton, D. On my way to paradise

The **biopsy** report. Stacey, K.
Bioy Casares, Adolfo, 1914-
The first class passenger
Anthology of contemporary Latin American literature, 1960-1984
Plans for an escape to Carmelo
The New York Review of Books 33:26-8 Ap 10 '86
Venetian masks
Black water; ed. by A. Manguel
The **birch** tree. Thompson, J.
Bird, Carmel, 1940-
The balloon lady
Bird, C. Woodpecker Point & other stories
The best thing to do
Bird, C. Woodpecker Point & other stories
Boy and girl
Bird, C. Woodpecker Point & other stories
Brother Gregory
Bird, C. Woodpecker Point & other stories
Buff Orpington and the disasters of middle life
Bird, C. Woodpecker Point & other stories
Buttercup and Wendy
Bird, C. Woodpecker Point & other stories
Bye baby bunting
Bird, C. Woodpecker Point & other stories
Cave amantem
Bird, C. Woodpecker Point & other stories
Cherries jubilee; or, Whichever way you look at it
Bird, C. Woodpecker Point & other stories
The enlargement of Bethany
Bird, C. Woodpecker Point & other stories
Every home should have a cedar chest
Bird, C. Woodpecker Point & other stories
New directions in prose and poetry 52
Goczka
Bird, C. Woodpecker Point & other stories
Transgressions; ed. by D. Anderson
The hair and the teeth
Bird, C. Woodpecker Point & other stories
Higher animals
Bird, C. Woodpecker Point & other stories
In the conservatory
Bird, C. Woodpecker Point & other stories
Room to move; ed. by S. Falkiner

Introducing your friends
Bird, C. Woodpecker Point & other stories
Kay Petman's coloured pencils
Bird, C. Woodpecker Point & other stories
Ladies in the snow
Prairie Schooner 62:78-81 Wint '88/'89
Mother of the bride
Bird, C. Woodpecker Point & other stories
One with the lot
Bird, C. Woodpecker Point & other stories
The right stuff
Bird, C. Woodpecker Point & other stories
Seeking its level
Bird, C. Woodpecker Point & other stories
A taste of earth
Bird, C. Woodpecker Point & other stories
Woodpecker Point
Bird, C. Woodpecker Point & other stories
The woodpecker toy fact
Bird, C. Woodpecker Point & other stories
Bird, Michael
Churchgoing
Encounter (London, England) 67:21-4 D '86
The **bird**. Carrier, R.
The **bird** cage. Josipovici, G.
The **bird** cage. Kessler, J. F.
BIRD HUNTERS
Jewett, S. O. A white heron
O'Brien, D. The Georgia breeze
Proulx, A. Stone City
Proulx, A. The unclouded day
Bird in ambush. Molinaro, U.
A **bird** in hand. Boyle, T. C.
A **bird** in her hair. Bonosky, P.
The **bird** in the breast. Gustafsson, L.
Bird of my voice. Meiring, J.
The **bird** of paradise. Fernando, C.
Bird of paradise. Haldeman, L.
Bird of paradise. Piñón, N.
Bird of passage. Bache, E.
The **bird** of passage. O, Y.
Bird of prey. Bradley, M. Z.
Bird of prey. Collier, J.
Bird prayer and no amen. Taylor, P. E.
The **bird** that couldn't fly. Winters, J.
BIRD WATCHERS
Winton, T. Wilderness
Bird-watching. Bernard, K.
The **birdbath**. Smith, W. A.
Birdbrain. Harrington, J.
BIRDCAGES
García Márquez, G. Balthazar's marvelous afternoon

BIRDS

See also Ostriches; Owls; Parrots; Pigeons; Seagulls

Bates, H. E. The song of the wren
Boyle, T. C. A bird in hand
Boyle, T. C. Rara avis
Colette. Bella-Vista
Connolly, P. Dead flower
Du Maurier, Dame D. The birds
Endō, S. A forty-year-old man
García Márquez, G. One day after Saturday
Haldeman, L. Bird of paradise
Hood, H. The small birds
Korabelnikov, O. Tower of birds
Liu, F. Wang Hsieh; or Dark robe land
Loukakis, A. Billy and the birds
Malamud, B. The Jewbird
O'Brien, D. Winter cat
Ozaki, S. The wagtail's nest
Simon, B. The birds
Skrzynecki, P. Empty cages
Skrzynecki, P. Indian mynas
Skrzynecki, P. The peewit's nest
Stuart, R. M. The Woman's Exchange of Simpkinsville
Wodehouse, P. G. Open house
The **birds**. Du Maurier, Dame D.
The **birds**. Simon, B.
The **birds** and the bees. Miller, S.
Birds' footsteps in the sand. El-Kharrat, E.
Birds in air. Thompson, J.
Birds landing. Finney, E. J.
The **bird's** nest. Walpole, H.
Birds of a feather. Chang, T.-C.

Birdsell, Sandra, 1942-

Night travellers
  The Old dance; ed. by B. Burnard
The wild plum tree
  The Oxford book of Canadian short stories in English
Birdy's flight. Carpentier, A.
The **birth** and death of the miracle man. Wendt, A.

BIRTH CONTROL

See also Abortion; Contraceptives
Fremlin, C. Test case
The **birth** control king of the Upper Volta. Rooke, L.
Birth of a man. Gorky, M.

Birtha, Becky, 1948-

Baby town
  Birtha, B. Lovers' choice
  Hear the silence; ed. by I. Zahava
Both ways
  Birtha, B. Lovers' choice
Her ex-lover
  Birtha, B. Lovers' choice
Ice castle
  Birtha, B. Lovers' choice
In the deep heart's core
  Birtha, B. Lovers' choice
  Love, struggle & change; ed. by I. Zahava
In the life
  Birtha, B. Lovers' choice
Johnnieruth
  Birtha, B. Lovers' choice
Past halfway
  Birtha, B. Lovers' choice
Pencil sketches for a story: the gray whelk shell
  Birtha, B. Lovers' choice
Route 23: 10th and Bigler to Bethlehem Pike
  Birtha, B. Lovers' choice
The saints and sinners run
  Birtha, B. Lovers' choice
  Hear the silence; ed. by I. Zahava
Birthday. Mrożek, S.
Birthday. Ruffolo, L.
Birthday. Troy, J.
Birthday. Viramontes, H. M.
The **birthday**. Wolfe, T.
The **birthday** of Mrs. Piñeda. Ríos, A.
The **birthday** of the Infanta. Wilde, O.

BIRTHDAY PARTIES *See* Birthdays

Birthday party. Campbell, W. B.
The **birthday** party. Hall, M. L.
The **birthday** party. Thompson, S.
The **birthday** picture. Drake, R.
The **birthday** present. Lo Bosco, R.
The **birthday** present. Martínez-Serros, H.
A **birthday** remembered. Shockley, A. A.

BIRTHDAYS

Beattie, A. Jacklighting
Bernard, K. George Washington's birthday
Broun, H. No smoking
Carr, P. E. The party
Carver, R. A small, good thing
Crane, S. The angel-child
Fowler, K. J. The faithful companion at forty
Haley, R. Fog
Houbein, L. Talking to the dark
Jolley, E. 'Surprise! Surprise!' from Matron
Lurie, M. A partial portrait of my father, his birthdays, my gifts, bottled in bond
Martínez-Serros, H. The birthday present
Mazel, D. When you swing upon a star
Munro, A. White dump
Narayan, R. K. Fruition at forty
Ocampo, S. The guests
Ocampo, S. The photographs
Purdy, J. Summer tidings
Ríos, A. The birthday of Mrs. Piñeda
Taylor, P. E. Turning thirty-eight
Updike, D. Out on the marsh
Wendt, A. Birthdays
West, J. Child of the century
Birthdays. Wendt, A.
The **birthing**. Henley, P.

Birthing. Poretz, D.
The **birthmark**. Hawthorne, N.
The **birthmark**. Symons, J.
BISEXUALITY
> *See also* Homosexuality
Gault, C. The other Ellen
Hagy, A. C. Shoreline
Henley, P. Black ice
Mohr, N. Brief miracle (Virginia)
Rossi, A. Teeth and nails
Rule, J. Puzzle
Valenzuela, L. A family for Clotilde
Bishop, Elizabeth, 1911-1979
Memories of Uncle Neddy
> Selected stories from The Southern review, 1965-1985
Bishop, Michael, 1945-
Alien graffiti
> Bishop, M. Close encounters with the deity
And the marlin spoke
> Bishop, M. Close encounters with the deity
The Bob Dylan Tambourine Software & Satori Support Services Consortium, Ltd.
> Bishop, M. Close encounters with the deity
Close encounter with the deity
> Bishop, M. Close encounters with the deity
Cold war orphans
> Bishop, M. One winter in Eden
Collaborating
> Bishop, M. One winter in Eden
Diary of a dead man
> Afterlives; ed. by P. Sargent and I. Watson
> Bishop, M. Close encounters with the deity
Dogs' lives
> The Best American short stories, 1985
> Bishop, M. Close encounters with the deity
> Nebula awards 20
For thus do I remember Carthage
> The Universe; ed. by B. Preiss
> The Year's best science fiction, fifth annual collection
A gift from the GrayLanders
> Bishop, M. Close encounters with the deity
God's hour
> *Omni (New York, N.Y.)* 9:58-60 Je '87
The gospel according to Gamaliel Crucis; or, The astrogator's testimony
> Bishop, M. Close encounters with the deity
In the memory room
> The Architecture of fear; ed. by K. Cramer and P. D. Pautz

Love's heresy
> Bishop, M. Close encounters with the deity
The monkey's bride
> Bishop, M. One winter in Eden
One winter in Eden
> Bishop, M. One winter in Eden
> Dragons of light; ed. by O. S. Card
Out of the mouths of Olympus
> Bishop, M. One winter in Eden
Patriots
> Bishop, M. One winter in Eden
The quickening
> Bishop, M. One winter in Eden
Saving face
> Bishop, M. One winter in Eden
Scrimptalon's test
> Bishop, M. Close encounters with the deity
Seasons of belief
> Bishop, M. One winter in Eden
A short history of the bicycle: 401 B.C. to 2677 A.D.
> Bishop, M. Close encounters with the deity
A spy in the domain of Arnheim
> Bishop, M. Close encounters with the deity
Storming the bijou, mon amour
> Bishop, M. Close encounters with the deity
A tapestry of little murders
> Midnight; ed. by C. L. Grant
Vernalfest morning
> Bishop, M. One winter in Eden
Voices
> Bishop, M. Close encounters with the deity
Vox Olympica
> Omni book of science fiction 2
Within the walls of Tyre
> Bishop, M. One winter in Eden
> The Dark descent; ed. by D. G. Hartwell
The Yukio Mishima Cultural Association of Kudzu Valley, Georgia
> Bishop, M. One winter in Eden
The **bishop**. Austin, D.
BISHOPS
Wells, H. G. Answer to prayer
BISHOPS, ANGLICAN AND EPISCOPAL
Gilliatt, P. Splendid lives
Watson, I. Cold light
BISHOPS, CATHOLIC
Austin, D. The bishop
Leitão, L. The colonial bishop's visit
Rhys, J. The bishop's feast
Windsor, G. The archbishop; or, The lady
BISHOPS, ORTHODOX EASTERN CHURCH, RUSSIAN
Harris, F. The holy man
The **bishop's** beggar. Benét, S. V.
The **bishop's** feast. Rhys, J.

BISMARCK (BATTLESHIP)
MacLean, A. The sinking of the Bismarck
BISON
Bloch, R. Where the buffalo roam
BISSET, JACQUELINE
About
Sisskind, M. It so happens
Bissoondath, Neil, 1955-
An arrangement of shadows
Bissoondath, N. Digging up the mountains
The cage
Bissoondath, N. Digging up the mountains
Christmas lunch
Bissoondath, N. Digging up the mountains
Continental drift
Bissoondath, N. Digging up the mountains
Counting the wind
Bissoondath, N. Digging up the mountains
Dancing
Bissoondath, N. Digging up the mountains
Digging up the mountains
Bissoondath, N. Digging up the mountains
In the kingdom of the golden dust
Bissoondath, N. Digging up the mountains
Insecurity
Bissoondath, N. Digging up the mountains
Man as plaything, life as mockery
Bissoondath, N. Digging up the mountains
The revolutionary
Bissoondath, N. Digging up the mountains
A short visit to a failed artist
Bissoondath, N. Digging up the mountains
There are a lot of ways to die
Bissoondath, N. Digging up the mountains
Things best forgotten
The Literary Review (Madison, N.J.) 29:402-11 Summ '86
Veins visible
Bissoondath, N. Digging up the mountains
A **bit** of the South Sea. Kant, H.
A **bit** simple. Blythe, R.
The **bitch**. Colette
The **bitch**. Wilkinson, R.
Bite-me-not; or, Fleur de feu. Lee, T.
A **bite** of the pie. Darling, J.
The **biter** bit. Collins, W.
Bitov, Andreï
The big balloon
Bitov, A. Life in windy weather

The door
Bitov, A. Life in windy weather
The forest
Bitov, A. Life in windy weather
The garden
Bitov, A. Life in windy weather
The idler
Bitov, A. Life in windy weather
Infantiev
Bitov, A. Life in windy weather
The leg
Bitov, A. Life in windy weather
Life in windy weather
Bitov, A. Life in windy weather
Notes from the corner
Bitov, A. Life in windy weather
Penelope
Bitov, A. Life in windy weather
The soldier
Bitov, A. Life in windy weather
The taste
Bitov, A. Life in windy weather
The third story
Bitov, A. Life in windy weather
Bits & pieces. Silva, B.
The **bitter** end. Josipovici, G.
Bitter red star. Anderman, J.
The **bitter** truth. Singer, I. B.
Bitterness for three sleepwalkers. García Márquez, G.
Bitterness of women. Austin, M. H.
Bitterwater. Cummins, A.
Bittle, Camilla R.
Decision from the heart
Good Housekeeping 199:158-9+ S '84
Her secret
Redbook 169:22-4 Ag '87
Summer visit
McCall's 112:94-5+ Je '85
Bitzius, Albert See Gotthelf, Jeremias, 1797-1854
Bixby, Jerome, 1923-
The draw
Amazing science fiction anthology: The wild years, 1946-1955; ed. by M. H. Greenberg
The young one
Young monsters; ed. by I. Asimov; M. H. Greenberg and C. G. Waugh
Bizarre births. Reed, D.
Bizarre situations. Boyd, W.
Blacamán the good, vendor of miracles. García Márquez, G.
Black, Shirley
The biggest tent in the world
Alberta bound; ed. by F. Stenson
Black, Stephen
The cloud child
The Penguin book of Southern African stories
A **black** affair. Jacobs, W. W.
Black air. Robinson, K. S.
Black and white. Essop, A.

Black as ink. Lee, T.
Black ass at the cross roads. Hemingway, E.
Black Bart. Dickinson, C.
The black beast. Fink, I.
The black cabinet. Carr, J. D.
Black cargo ships of war. Ferron, J.
The black cat. Poe, E. A.
The black cat. Shimaki, K.
Black child. Sanford, W. M.
BLACK CHILDREN
  Bambara, T. C. Gorilla, my love
  Brown, M. W. Fruit of the season
  Grau, S. A. The beginning
  McElroy, C. J. Jeremy Franklin Simmons
  McElroy, C. J. Sun, wind and water
  O'Connor, F. The lame shall enter first
  Sanford, W. M. Black child
The black cliffs. Aiken, J.
Black coral. Shepard, L.
The black dahlia. Ellroy, J.
Black dirt. Vervaecke, K.
The black dog. Brown, M. W.
The black dog. Crane, S.
BLACK ENGLISH DIALECT See Dialect stories—Black English
The black ewe. Chavez, A.
The Black Farm. Watson, S.
The black figurine. Rizkalla, J.
Black for dinner. Colter, C.
Black fronts. Bonner, M.
The Black Hand of the Raj. McGrath, P.
Black heart and white heart. Haggard, H. R.
BLACK HOLES (ASTRONOMY)
  Brin, D. Bubbles
  Silverberg, R. The iron star
  Varley, J. Lollipop and the tar baby
  Willis, C. Schwarzschild radius
  Zahn, T. The energy crisis of 2215
Black holes. Tallent, E.
The black house. Highsmith, P.
BLACK HUMOR See Humor; Satire
Black ice. Henley, P.
Black in the snow. Collins, M.
Black Jack. Barthelme, S.
BLACK-JEWISH RELATIONS
  Briskin, M. Giant sequoia
  Rose, D. A. Summer heat
The black lunch box. Winters, J.
The black madonna. Skrzynecki, P.
The Black Madonna. Spark, M.
Black madonna two-wheel gypsy queen. Sproat, R.
BLACK MAGIC See Witchcraft
Black man with a horn. Klein, T. E. D.
Black market blues. Ko, H.
BLACK MARKETS
  Böll, H. The green silk shirt
  Ko, H. Black market blues
  Nowakowski, M. CPD
  So, C.-I. Home-coming
The black mate. Conrad, J.
The Black Monk. Chekhov, A. P.

Black night in Collingwood. Morrison, J.
Black night, white night; or, The battle of Dingle on the Dangle. Sambrot, W.
The black queen. Callaghan, B.
The black room. Rey Rosa, R.
Black Rose and White Rose. Pollack, R.
The black sampan. Whitfield, R.
BLACK SERVANTS
  Caldwell, E. The picture
  Caldwell, E. Squire Dinwiddy
  Crane, S. The carriage-lamps
  Faulkner, W. That evening sun
  McCorkle, J. July 7th [excerpt]
  Painter, P. Sylvia
  Smith, E. V. 'Lijah
  Taylor, P. H. Bad dreams
  Taylor, P. H. A friend and protector
  Taylor, P. H. A long fourth
  Thomas, E. Our house
  Williams, T. Mama's old stucco house
  Wright, R. Man, God ain't like that. . .
  Wright, R. Man of all work
The black shawl. Pirandello, L.
Black sheep. Böll, H.
BLACK SOLDIERS
  Algren, N. He couldn't boogie-woogie worth a damn
  Ch'en, Y.-C. Roses in June
  Crapser, W. Baptism of fire
  Kelly, C. A season for heroes
  Sambrot, W. Black night, white night; or, The battle of Dingle on the Dangle
  Wolfe, T. The child by tiger
The black stairway. Ellson, H.
Black sun. Abbey, E.
Black tie. Barthelme, F.
Black tie. Winters, J.
Black velvet night. Pascoe, B.
Black Venus. Carter, A.
The black wedding. Singer, I. B.
Black wind. Pronzini, B.
BLACK WOMEN
  Barthelme, D. Lightning
  Bonner, M. Corner store
  Bonner, M. Of Jimmy Harris
  Bonner, M. There were three
  Booth, B. Still life
  Carter, A. Black Venus
  Coleman, W. Big dreams
  Coleman, W. Buying primo time
  Coleman, W. Dream 5281
  Coleman, W. The Dufus Rufus
  Coleman, W. Fat Lena
  Coleman, W. The Friday night shift at the Taco House blues (wah-wah)
  Coleman, W. The habit
  Coleman, W. In the city of sleep
  Coleman, W. Jonesed
  Coleman, W. Ladies
  Coleman, W. The screamer
  Coleman, W. The seamstress
  Coleman, W. The stare down

BLACK WOMEN—*Continued*
Coleman, W. A war of eyes
Cooper, J. C. $100 and nothing!
Cooper, J. C. About love and money; or, Love's lore and money's myth
Cooper, J. C. Feeling for life
Cooper, J. C. The free and the caged
Cooper, J. C. Funeral plans
Cooper, J. C. A jewel for a friend
Cooper, J. C. Liberated
Cooper, J. C. The life you live (may not be your own)
Cooper, J. C. Loved to death
Cooper, J. C. Red-winged blackbirds
Cooper, J. C. Sins leave scars
Cooper, J. C. Sisters of the rain
Gomez, J. Don't explain
Gomez, J. No day too long
Hurston, Z. N. Muttsy
Lowenstein, A. F. The mother right
Maupassant, G. de. Boitelle
Paley, G. Lavinia: an old story
Shange, N. Sassafrass, Cypress & Indigo [excerpt]
Sorrells, R. T. Lovers
Walker, A. Kindred spirits
Blackberries. Miller, E. V.
Blackberries. Norris, L.
Blackberry day. Whitaker, M.
Blackberry winter. Warren, R. P.
Blackbird pie. Carver, R.
Blackburn. Friedman, P.
Blacked out. Campbell, R.
BLACKFOOT INDIANS *See* Siksika Indians
BLACKMAIL
       See also Extortion
Barker, C. Confessions of a (pornographer's) shroud
Block, L. The books always balance
Block, L. You could call it blackmail
Brown, F. Good night, good knight
Buzzati, D. The gnawing worm
Christie, A. The adventure of the Italian nobleman
Derleth, A. W. The adventure of the spurious Tamerlane
Doyle, Sir A. C. The end of Devil Hawker
Ellin, S. Kindly dig your grave
Fremlin, C. The post-graduate thesis
Gardner, E. S. Danger out of the past
Hall, T. T. A letter from home
Highsmith, P. Under a dark angel's eye
Hoffman, N. K. Lost lives
Johnson, C. R. Alēthia
Lutz, J. Big game
Lutz, J. The weapon
Moyes, P. The honest blackmailer
Pronzini, B. Here lies another blackmailer
Pronzini, B. Skeletons
Rendell, R. Bribery and corruption
Ritchie, J. Sound alibi
Rooke, L. Friendship and property
Shea, M. The pearls of the vampire queen

Slesar, H. A choice of witnesses
Tomlinson, G. Hizzoner's water supply
Treat, L. Suburban tigress
Wainwright, J. W. A peal from the past
Wilkinson, R. The ebbing tide
Wilkinson, R. The lean
Williamson, C. The personal touch
Zahn, T. Job inaction
Blackmail. Hoyle, F.
Blackmail. Oates, J. C.
Blackmailers don't shoot. Chandler, R.
Blackman, Michael
The Golden Shadows old west museum
    Prize stories, Texas Institute of Letters; ed. by M. Terry
BLACKS
       See also Black children; Black servants; Black soldiers; Black women; Mulattoes; Slavery
Ade, G. How "Pink" was reformed
Apple, M. Blood relatives
Attaway, W. Blood on the forge [excerpt]
Baldwin, J. Going to meet the man
Bambara, T. C. Christmas Eve at Johnson's Drugs N Goods
Barich, B. The end of the world
Bell, V. Brag dog
Bennett, L. The convert
Birtha, B. Her ex-lover
Birtha, B. Ice castle
Birtha, B. In the life
Birtha, B. Johnnieruth
Birtha, B. Route 23: 10th and Bigler to Bethlehem Pike
Bonner, M. Black fronts
Bonner, M. Drab rambles
Bonner, M. Hate is nothing
Bonner, M. Hongry fire
Bonner, M. The makin's
Bonner, M. Nothing new
Bonner, M. One boy's story
Bonner, M. One true love
Bonner, M. Patch quilt
Bonner, M. The prison-bound
Bonner, M. Stones for bread
Bonner, M. Tin can
Bonner, M. The whipping
Bradley, D. 197903042100 (Sunday)
Caldwell, E. Big Buck
Caldwell, E. Blue Boy
Caldwell, E. Daughter
Caldwell, E. Nine dollars' worth of mumble
Caldwell, E. The people v. Abe Lathan, colored
Caldwell, E. Runaway
Caldwell, E. Wild flowers
Chappell, F. Blue dive
Coleman, W. The buyer
Coleman, W. Eyes and teeth
Coleman, W. Gamblers
Coleman, W. Hamburgers
Coleman, W. Kelele

BLACKS—*Continued*

Coleman, W. Reba
Coleman, W. 'Shrooms
Coleman, W. The twinight of Reverend Jones
Coleman, W. Without visible means
Coleman, W. Word monkey
Conroy, J. Anyplace but here
Conroy, J. The cement king
Cooper, J. C. He was a man! (But he did himself wrong)
Cooper, J. C. Say what you Willomay!
Cooper, J. C. Too hep to be happy!
Cooper, J. C. Who are the fools?
Douglas, E. On the lake
Dove, R. Second-hand man
Dumas, H. Ark
Dumas, H. Ark of bones
Dumas, H. A boll of roses
Dumas, H. Double nigger
Dumas, H. Echo tree
Dumas, H. Fever
Dumas, H. Rain god
Dumas, H. Six days you shall labor
Dumas, H. Strike and fade
Dumas, H. Thrust counter thrust
Dumas, H. Wandering in the wilderness
Dumas, H. The white horse
Dumas, H. Will the circle be unbroken?
Farmer, P. J. The oogenesis of Bird City
Faulkner, W. A bear hunt
Gaines, E. J. Robert Louis Stevenson Banks, a.k.a. Chimley
García Márquez, G. Nabo: the black man who made the angels wait
Gordon, C. The dragon's teeth
Grahn, J. Ernesta
Grau, S. A. White girl, fine girl
Haynes, D. Taking Miss Kezee to the polls
Hemingway, E. The battler
Hemingway, E. The tradesman's return
Hillabold, J. Yellow roses
Hughes, L. Thank you, m'am
Humphrey, W. Mouth of brass
James, D. Negrophobia
Jeffrey, T. Habits of contact
Lee, A. The ride
Lowe, R. The woman in the window
Maupassant, G. de. A king's son
McElroy, C. J. A dance with a dolly with a hole in her stocking
McElroy, C. J. Exercises
McElroy, C. J. Farm day
McElroy, C. J. A house full of Maude
McElroy, C. J. More than a notion
McElroy, C. J. Take mama's picture out of the light
McElroy, C. J. Under the equinox
McKnight, R. First I look at the purse
McKnight, R. Getting to be like the studs
McKnight, R. The honey boys
McKnight, R. Peaches
McPherson, J. A. The story of a scar

Melville, H. Benito Cereno
Mrożek, S. My uncle's stories
O'Connor, F. The artificial nigger
O'Connor, F. The enduring chill
O'Connor, F. Everything that rises must converge
O'Connor, F. Judgement Day
Painter, P. Night walk
Paley, G. Zagrowsky tells
Patchett, A. All little colored children should play the harmonica
Petrakis, H. M. Zena Dawn
Price, R. The Warrior Princess Ozimba
Purdy, J. Eventide
Purdy, J. On the rebound
Rooke, L. Mama Tuddi done over
Slesinger, T. White on black
Swados, H. Bobby Shafter's gone to sea
Swados, H. A chance encounter
Thanet, O. Sist' Chaney's black silk
Thompson, J. Danny's chick
Tuohy, F. The potlatch of Esmeralda
Tyler, A. The geologist's maid
Walker, A. The abortion
Walker, A. Coming apart
Walker, A. Everyday use
Warren, R. P. Blackberry winter
Welty, E. A worn path
Wetherell, W. D. Why I love America
Williams, S. A. The lawd don't like ugly
Williams, T. Desire and the black masseur
Wolfe, T. The face of the war
Wright, R. The man who killed a shadow
Wright, R. The man who lived underground
Wright, R. The man who saw the flood
Wyndham, F. Ursula

Civil rights

Dumas, H. The marchers
Leedom-Ackerman, J. The beginning of violence

Alabama

Brown, M. W. Fruit of the season
McKnight, R. Rebirth
Murray, A. Gasoline Point, Alabama

Arkansas

Dumas, H. Goodbye, sweetwater
Jones, D. C. Knights of the Flaming Circle

Barbados

Meriwether, L. A happening in Barbados

Brazil

Camus, A. The growing stone

California

Coleman, W. The big little gang
Coleman, W. Stashed

Canada

Clarke, A. C. Griff!

Chicago (Ill.)

Colter, C. After the ball
Colter, C. The beach umbrella
Colter, C. Black for dinner
Colter, C. A chance meeting
Colter, C. A gift

BLACKS—Chicago (Ill.)—*Continued*
Colter, C. Girl friend
Colter, C. The lookout
Colter, C. Macabre
Colter, C. A man in the house
Colter, C. The march
Colter, C. Mary's convert
Colter, C. Moot
Colter, C. Overnight trip
Colter, C. Rapport
Colter, C. The rescue
Colter, C. An untold story
Johnson, C. R. Alēthia
Johnson, C. R. Exchange value
Major, C. Tattoo
Wright, R. The man who went to Chicago
Cuba
Ferreira, R. Facade
Denmark
Wright, R. Big black good man
Dominican Republic
Kleist, H. von. Betrothal in Santo Domingo
England
Spark, M. The Black Madonna
Florida
Hurston, Z. N. Isis
Hurston, Z. N. Sweat
France
Algren, N. He couldn't boogie-woogie worth a damn
Maupassant, G. de. The man with the blue eyes
Georgia
Caldwell, E. Candy-Man Beechum
Caldwell, E. The end of Christy Tucker
Illinois
Johnson, C. R. Popper's disease
Louisiana
Dubus, A. Sorrowful mysteries
Gifkins, M. Metamorphosis
Kincaid, N. Like the old wolf in all those wolf stories
McElroy, C. J. Jesus and Fat Tuesday
Shaik, F. Climbing Monkey Hill
Maryland
Leedom-Ackerman, J. The tutor
Michigan
McElroy, C. J. Sister Detroit
Mississippi
Plumpp, S. Mighty long time
Williams, T. Big Black: a Mississippi idyll
Missouri
McElroy, C. J. A brief spell by the river
McElroy, C. J. The limitations of Jason Packard
New York (N.Y.)
Baldwin, J. Sonny's blues
Bambara, T. C. My man Bovanne
Coleman, W. Watching the sunset
Dumas, H. Harlem
Dumas, H. A Harlem game
Dumas, H. The voice

Faust, I. The Dalai Lama of Harlem
Faust, I. Operation Buena Vista
Fisher, R. The backslider
Fisher, R. Blades of steel
Fisher, R. The city of refuge
Fisher, R. Common meter
Fisher, R. Ezekiel
Fisher, R. Ezekiel learns
Fisher, R. Fire by night
Fisher, R. Guardian of the law
Fisher, R. High yaller
Fisher, R. The promised land
Fisher, R. Ringtail
Fisher, R. The South lingers on
Hughes, L. Slave on the block
Hurston, Z. N. Book of Harlem
Hurston, Z. N. Muttsy
Hurston, Z. N. Story in Harlem slang
Wilmot, J. Dirt angel
New York (State)
Cooper, J. C. Happiness does not come in colors
Crane, S. The knife
Crane, S. The monster
North Carolina
Clark, M. A moment of illumination
Price, R. Uncle Grant
Paris (France)
Rhys, J. Trio
Pennsylvania
Wideman, J. E. Tommy
Poland
Nowakowski, M. The peacock
Seattle (Wash.)
Johnson, C. R. China
South Carolina
Johnson, C. R. The sorcerer's apprentice
Southern States
Bates, A. J. A ceremony of innocence
Caldwell, E. Kneel to the rising sun
Coleman, W. Chuck and the boss man's wife
Cooper, J. C. Sisters of the rain
Creekmore, H. The chain in the heart [excerpt]
Cullen, E. J. The baddest, baddest days
Dumas, H. Fon
Dumas, H. Rope of wind
Elgin, S. H. Hush my mouth
Fisher, R. Dust
Gaines, E. J. Just like a tree
Gaines, E. J. The sky is gray
Goyen, W. Had I a hundred mouths
Hairston, L. The revolt of Brud Bascomb
Hentz, C. L. Wild Jack; or, The stolen child
Holditch, W. K. One of these mornings
Hurston, Z. N. Cock Robin Beale Street
Hurston, Z. N. The gilded six-bits
Hurston, Z. N. Spunk
Matthiessen, P. On the River Styx
McKnight, R. Who Big Bob?
Morgan, B. The organ piece

BLACKS—Southern States—*Continued*
O'Connor, F. Wildcat
Phillips, T. H. The shadow of an arm
Taylor, M. D. Roll of thunder, hear my cry [excerpt]
Thibault, D. A woman like Dilsie
Walker, A. Strong horse tea
Walker, M. Jubilee [excerpt]
Wright, R. Almos' a man
Wright, R. Big boy leaves home
Wright, R. The man who was almost a man

Tennessee
Boswell, R. The darkness of love
Taylor, P. H. What you hear from 'em?
Virginia
Birtha, B. Baby town
BLACKS IN POLITICS
Perry, R. Blues for my father, my mother, and me
BLACKSMITHS
Donaldson, S. R. The Lady in White
Frost, G. Sardofa's horseshoes
Gogol', N. V. Christmas Eve
The **blacktop** champion of Ickey Honey. Sorrells, R. T.
Blackwood, Algernon, 1869-1951
The damned
The Mammoth book of short horror novels; ed. by M. Ashley
The empty house
The Oxford book of English ghost stories
A haunted island
Lost souls; ed. by J. Sullivan
The Penguin book of ghost stories
Secret worship
Devils & demons; ed. by M. Kaye and S. Kaye
The transfer
Vampires; ed. by A. Ryan
The willows
Dark company; ed. by L. Child
The Dark descent; ed. by D. G. Hartwell
Blacky. Shi Tiesheng
Blades of steel. Fisher, R.
Blaine, Edward
Whistle's complaint
The North American Review 270:23-6 D '85
Blaine, Michael
Gogol's stomach
The North American Review 272:32-4 D '87
Live souls
New England Review and Bread Loaf Quarterly 11:65-73 Aut '88
Blair, Ron
McBride's list
Transgressions; ed. by D. Anderson

Blais, Marie-Claire, 1939-
An act of pity
The Oxford book of French-Canadian short stories
Blaisdell, Anne, 1921-
For works written by this author under other names see Shannon, Dell, 1921-
Blaise, Clark
A class of new Canadians
The Oxford book of Canadian short stories in English
Grids and doglegs
Our roots grow deeper than we know; ed. by L. Gutkind
How I became a Jew
Making it new; ed. by J. Metcalf
Identity
Blaise, C. Resident alien
Man and his world
The Literary Review (Madison, N.J.) 29:412-22 Summ '86
Memories of unhousement
Blaise, C. Resident alien
North
Blaise, C. Resident alien
The New press anthology #1
A North American education
The Literary Review (Madison, N.J.) 28:337-50 Spr '85
Making it new; ed. by J. Metcalf
South
Blaise, C. Resident alien
Translation
Blaise, C. Resident alien
The voice of unhousement
Blaise, C. Resident alien
Blaisten, Isidoro
Uncle Facundo
Dark arrows; ed. by A. Manguel
Blanche the bloody. Schwob, M.
Blandine, or The father's visit. Tournier, M.
The **blank** shot. Sabatini, R.
The **blanket.** Faik, S.
Blankets. La Guma, A.
Blassingame, Wyatt
The horror at his heels
The Weirds; comp. and ed. by S. Jaffery
The tongueless horror
Selected tales of grim and grue from the horror pulps; ed. by S. Jaffery
Blast off. Grenville, K.
Blaushild, Lisa
Witness
Between C & D; ed. by J. Rose and C. Texier
Blaylock, James P.
Paper dragons
Imaginary lands; ed. by R. McKinley
Nebula awards 21
The Year's best science fiction, third annual collection
Blazer. Sternberg, A.

Bled, Rory Norton
  Marielle
    Stories and poems from close to home;
      ed. by F. Salas
Bleep, crash, zap, wow: accidents in the
    Ruhr. Körner, W.
Blei, Norbert
  An American presence
    Blei, N. The ghost of Sandburg's phiz-
      zog, and other stories
  The chair trick
    Blei, N. The ghost of Sandburg's phiz-
      zog, and other stories
  Dwelling
    Blei, N. The ghost of Sandburg's phiz-
      zog, and other stories
  The ghost of Sandburg's phizzog
    Blei, N. The ghost of Sandburg's phiz-
      zog, and other stories
    The Pushcart prize XII
  In the secret places of the stairs
    Blei, N. The ghost of Sandburg's phiz-
      zog, and other stories
  The landscaper
    Blei, N. The ghost of Sandburg's phiz-
      zog, and other stories
  Skarda
    Blei, N. The ghost of Sandburg's phiz-
      zog, and other stories
  Stars
    Blei, N. The ghost of Sandburg's phiz-
      zog, and other stories
  This horse of a body of mine
    Blei, N. The ghost of Sandburg's phiz-
      zog, and other stories
Bless me, Father, for I have sinned. Brad-
    bury, R.
Bless me, Ultima. Anaya, R. A.
Bless the child. Stewart, I.
Bless this house. Brand, C.
Blessed are the dead. Rule, J.
'**Blessed** are the geeks'. Hiles, R.
Blessed are the meek. Simenon, G.
Blessed art thou. Ingalls, R.
The **blessed** legacy. Askounis, C.
Blessing, Richard
  Song on Royal Street
    Sudden fiction; ed. by R. Shapard and
      J. Thomas
Blessings. Dubus, A.
The **Blessington** method. Ellin, S.
Blew, Mary Clearman
  Forby and the Mayan maidens
    The Georgia Review 40:40-51 Spr '86
    Necessary fictions; ed. by S. W. Lind-
      berg and S. Corey
Blight. Dybek, S.
BLIMPS *See* Airships
BLIND
  Bambara, T. C. My man Bovanne
  Bell, M. S. The structure and meaning of
    dormitory and food services
  Bloch, R. The unpardonable crime

Bradbury, R. Hell's half hour
Brooks, J. A value
Brown, F. Witness in the dark
Byatt, A. S. In the air
Cameron, E. The dark mirror
Campbell, R. Second sight
Canning, V. Lady in the dark
Carver, R. Cathedral
Cooper, J. C. Feeling for life
Ellison, H. In lonely lands
García Márquez, G. Artificial roses
García Márquez, G. The night of the cur-
    lews
Glover, D. H. Dog attempts to drown
    man in Saskatoon
Gordon, M. The magician's wife
Grin, A. Voice and eye
Hemingway, E. Get a seeing-eyed dog
Hemingway, E. A man of the world
Kipling, R. "They"
Kirk, R. The invasion of the Church of
    the Holy Ghost
Kirk-Kuwaye, C. Complete with fireworks
    above Magic Island
Lutz, J. Something for the dark
MacDonald, D. R. Of one kind
MacLaverty, B. The drapery man
Maupassant, G. de. The blind man
McLaughlin, L. A teacher of the blind
Morrison, J. The blind man's story
Norton, A. Spider silk
Perea, R. L. Miracle at Chimayo
Petrakis, H. M. The eyes of love
Price, R. The Warrior Princess Ozimba
Rey Rosa, R. The seeing eye
Reynolds, M. Optical illusion
Rifaat, A. Bahiyya's eyes
Schnitzler, A. The blind Geronimo and his
    brother
Shaw, J. B. The geese at Presque Isle
Sherman, C. H. Tapestry
Silverberg, R. Blindsight
Silverberg, R. Ship-sister, star-sister
Stevenson, J. The blind alley
Tuohy, F. The white stick
Varley, J. The persistence of vision
Watson, I. Sunstroke
Wellen, E. Scents in the dark
Wells, H. G. The country of the blind
Williamson, C. Prometheus's ghost
Yaryura-Tobías, A. The voyeur
Zahn, T. The giftie gie us
Blind alley. Asimov, I.
The **blind** alley. Stevenson, J.
Blind, blind date. Gold, H.
The **blind** dog. Narayan, R. K.
Blind euchre. DeMarinis, R.
The **blind** Geronimo and his brother. Schnit-
    zler, A.
Blind girls. Phillips, J. A.
Blind man. Hall, O. M.
The **blind** man. Maupassant, G. de
The **blind** man. Salmonson, J. A.

The **blind** man and the girl. Kawabata, Y.
The **blind** man eats many flies. Profumo, D.
Blind man's buff. Enchi, F.
Blind man's buff. Wakefield, H. R.
The **blind** man's story. Morrison, J.
Blind shemmy. Dann, J.
Blind spot. Carr, J.
Blind windows. Kilworth, G.
Blinder. Gordimer, N.
A **blinding** snowstorm. Winters, J.
Blindness. Woiwode, L.
Blindsight. Silverberg, R.
Blinkin, Meir, 1879-1915
  Card game
    Blinkin, M. Stories
  Doctor Machover
    Blinkin, M. Stories
  Family life: a chapter
    Blinkin, M. Stories
  The freethinker: a shtetl atheist
    Blinkin, M. Stories
  In a dream
    Blinkin, M. Stories
  Incomprehensible
    Blinkin, M. Stories
  The little calf
    Blinkin, M. Stories
  The mysterious secret
    Blinkin, M. Stories
  A simple life
    Blinkin, M. Stories
  Smoke
    Blinkin, M. Stories
  Troubles
    Blinkin, M. Stories
  Women
    Blinkin, M. Stories
Blish, James, 1921-1975
  Common time
    Robert Silverberg's Worlds of wonder
  A dusk of idols
    Amazing stories: visions of other worlds
  A work of art
    Afterlives; ed. by P. Sargent and I. Watson
Bliss, Corinne Demas, 1947-
  Consuming passion
    Mademoiselle 90:102+ F '84
  The dream broker
    Redbook 169:52+ Jl '87
  Forbidden waters
    The Virginia Quarterly Review 64:126-33
      Wint '88
  Headlines
    Michigan Quarterly Review 24:403-12
      Summ '85
  Margaret, are you grieving?
    Mademoiselle 90:136+ Ap '84
  Payment
    McCall's 113:125-7 Ag '86
Bliss. Mansfield, K.
The **blister**. Pohl, F.

Bliven, Naomi
  Chamber music
    The New Yorker 64:28-37 Ag 8 '88
Blixen, Karen, Baroness, 1885-1962
    *For works written by this author under
    other names see* Dinesen, Isak, 1885-
    1962
BLIZZARDS *See* Storms
Bloch, Don
  An eavesdropper's notebook
    The Kenyon Review ns9:1-27 Wint '87
  Free association
    The North American Review 272:46-7 Mr
      '87
Bloch, Robert, 1917-
  All on a golden afternoon
    Bloch, R. The selected stories of Robert
      Bloch v1
  Almost human
    Bloch, R. The selected stories of Robert
      Bloch v1
  The animal fair
    Bloch, R. The selected stories of Robert
      Bloch v3
    Masters of darkness; ed. by D. Etchison
  The baldheaded mirage
    Amazing stories: visions of other worlds
    Bloch, R. The selected stories of Robert
      Bloch v2
  The beasts of Barsac
    Bloch, R. The selected stories of Robert
      Bloch v1
  Beelzebub
    Bloch, R. The selected stories of Robert
      Bloch v3
  Betsy Blake will live forever
    Bloch, R. The selected stories of Robert
      Bloch v2
  The big kick
    Bloch, R. The selected stories of Robert
      Bloch v2
  The bogey man will get you
    Bloch, R. The selected stories of Robert
      Bloch v1
  Broomstick ride
    Bloch, R. The selected stories of Robert
      Bloch v2
  A case of the stubborns
    Bloch, R. The selected stories of Robert
      Bloch v3
  Constant reader
    Bloch, R. The selected stories of Robert
      Bloch v1
  Crime in rhyme
    Bloch, R. The selected stories of Robert
      Bloch v2
  Crime machine
    Bloch, R. The selected stories of Robert
      Bloch v3
  Crook of the month
    Bloch, R. The selected stories of Robert
      Bloch v3

Bloch, Robert, 1917-—_Continued_

The cure
  Bloch, R. The selected stories of Robert Bloch v2
Daybroke
  Bloch, R. The selected stories of Robert Bloch v2
Dead-end doctor
  Bloch, R. The selected stories of Robert Bloch v1
The deadliest art
  Bloch, R. The selected stories of Robert Bloch v2
The double whammy
  Bloch, R. The selected stories of Robert Bloch v3
  Fantastic stories; ed. by M. H. Greenberg and P. L. Price
  The Wickedest show on earth; ed. by M. Muller and B. Pronzini
Ego trip
  Bloch, R. The selected stories of Robert Bloch v3
Enoch
  Devils & demons; ed. by M. Kaye and S. Kaye
Everybody needs a little love
  Masques; ed. by J. N. Williamson
Fat chance
  Bloch, R. The selected stories of Robert Bloch v3
The final performance
  Bloch, R. The selected stories of Robert Bloch v3
  Murder California style; ed. by J. L. Breen and J. Ball
Forever and amen
  Bloch, R. The selected stories of Robert Bloch v3
Founding fathers
  Bloch, R. The selected stories of Robert Bloch v1
Freak show
  Bloch, R. The selected stories of Robert Bloch v3
Frozen fear
  Bloch, R. The selected stories of Robert Bloch v1
The funnel of God
  Bloch, R. The selected stories of Robert Bloch v2
Gather 'round the flowing bowler
  Bloch, R. Lost in time and space with Lefty Feep
The gloating place
  Bloch, R. The selected stories of Robert Bloch v2
The goddess of wisdom
  Bloch, R. The selected stories of Robert Bloch v1
The gods are not mocked
  Bloch, R. The selected stories of Robert Bloch v3

The golden opportunity of Lefty Feep
  Bloch, R. Lost in time and space with Lefty Feep
A good imagination
  Bloch, R. The selected stories of Robert Bloch v1
The head man
  Bloch, R. The selected stories of Robert Bloch v1
Heir apparent
  Tales of the Witch World [1]
His and hearse
  Bloch, R. The selected stories of Robert Bloch v3
Hobo
  Bloch, R. The selected stories of Robert Bloch v3
A home away from home
  Bloch, R. The selected stories of Robert Bloch v3
  Hitchcock in prime time; ed. by F. M. Nevins and M. H. Greenberg
How like a god
  Bloch, R. The selected stories of Robert Bloch v3
The hungry eye
  Bloch, R. The selected stories of Robert Bloch v2
The hungry house
  Masterpieces of terror and the supernatural; ed. by M. Kaye and S. Kaye
  Venomous tales of villainy and vengeance; ed. by H. Hoke
I like blondes
  Bloch, R. The selected stories of Robert Bloch v1
Impractical joker
  Bloch, R. The selected stories of Robert Bloch v3
In the cards
  Bloch, R. The selected stories of Robert Bloch v3
Jerk the giant killer
  Bloch, R. Lost in time and space with Lefty Feep
The learning maze
  Bloch, R. The selected stories of Robert Bloch v3
Life in our time
  Bloch, R. The selected stories of Robert Bloch v3
The little man who wasn't all there
  Bloch, R. Lost in time and space with Lefty Feep
The living dead
  Vampires; ed. by A. Ryan
The living end
  Bloch, R. The selected stories of Robert Bloch v3
Luck is no lady
  Bloch, R. The selected stories of Robert Bloch v2

Bloch, Robert, 1917-—*Continued*

Lucy comes to stay
  Bloch, R. The selected stories of Robert
    Bloch v1
The man who collected Poe
  Bloch, R. The selected stories of Robert
    Bloch v1
  Chapter & hearse; ed. by M. Muller and
    B. Pronzini
  Masterpieces of mystery and suspense;
    ed. by M. H. Greenberg
The man who knew women
  Bloch, R. The selected stories of Robert
    Bloch v2
  Crime of my life; ed. by B. Garfield
Man with a hobby
  Bloch, R. The selected stories of Robert
    Bloch v2
Mannikins of horror
  Bloch, R. The selected stories of Robert
    Bloch v1
The masterpiece
  Bloch, R. The selected stories of Robert
    Bloch v2
A matter of life
  Bloch, R. The selected stories of Robert
    Bloch v2
Method for murder
  Bloch, R. The selected stories of Robert
    Bloch v3
The model
  Bloch, R. The selected stories of Robert
    Bloch v3
A most unusual murder
  Spirits, spooks, and other sinister crea-
    tures; ed. by H. Hoke
The movie people
  Bloch, R. The selected stories of Robert
    Bloch v3
  Silver scream; ed. by D. J. Schow
Mr. Steinway
  The Deadly arts; ed. by B. Pronzini and
    M. Muller
The new season
  Masques II; ed. by J. N. Williamson
Night school
  Bloch, R. The selected stories of Robert
    Bloch v2
Nina
  The Best horror stories from the
    Magazine of fantasy and science fiction
  Bloch, R. The selected stories of Robert
    Bloch v3
The old college try
  Bloch, R. The selected stories of Robert
    Bloch v3
The oracle
  Bloch, R. The selected stories of Robert
    Bloch v3
The past master
  Bloch, R. The selected stories of Robert
    Bloch v1

The Pied Piper fights the Gestapo
  Bloch, R. Lost in time and space with
    Lefty Feep
The pin
  Bloch, R. The selected stories of Robert
    Bloch v1
Pin-up girl
  Bloch, R. The selected stories of Robert
    Bloch v2
The play's the thing
  Bloch, R. The selected stories of Robert
    Bloch v3
  Murder and mystery in Chicago; ed. by
    C. R. Waugh; F. D. McSherry and M.
    H. Greenberg
The plot is the thing
  Bloch, R. The selected stories of Robert
    Bloch v3
Pranks
  Halloween horrors; ed. by A. Ryan
A quiet funeral
  Bloch, R. The selected stories of Robert
    Bloch v3
The real bad friend
  Bloch, R. The selected stories of Robert
    Bloch v2
Reaper
  Cutting edge; ed. by D. Etchison
Sabbatical
  Bloch, R. The selected stories of Robert
    Bloch v2
The screaming people
  Bloch, R. The selected stories of Robert
    Bloch v2
See how they run
  Bloch, R. The selected stories of Robert
    Bloch v3
The shadow from the steeple
  Bloch, R. The selected stories of Robert
    Bloch v1
Show biz
  Bloch, R. The selected stories of Robert
    Bloch v2
The show must go on
  Bloch, R. The selected stories of Robert
    Bloch v2
The skull of the Marquis de Sade
  Bloch, R. The selected stories of Robert
    Bloch v1
A snitch in time
  Bloch, R. Lost in time and space with
    Lefty Feep
Sock finish
  Bloch, R. The selected stories of Robert
    Bloch v2
Son of a witch
  Bloch, R. Lost in time and space with
    Lefty Feep
Space-born
  Bloch, R. The selected stories of Robert
    Bloch v3

Bloch, Robert, 1917-—_Continued_
The strange flight of Richard Clayton
  Amazing stories: 60 years of the best
    science fiction
String of pearls
  Bloch, R. The selected stories of Robert
    Bloch v1
Sweets to the sweet
  Midnight; ed. by C. L. Grant
  Witches; ed. by I. Asimov; M. H.
    Greenberg and C. G. Waugh
Talent
  Bloch, R. The selected stories of Robert
    Bloch v3
Tell your fortune
  Bloch, R. The selected stories of Robert
    Bloch v1
Terror in Cut-throat Cove
  Bloch, R. The selected stories of Robert
    Bloch v2
Terror in the night
  Bloch, R. The selected stories of Robert
    Bloch v1
Terror over Hollywood
  Bloch, R. The selected stories of Robert
    Bloch v2
That old black magic
  Bloch, R. The selected stories of Robert
    Bloch v2
The thinking cap
  Bloch, R. The selected stories of Robert
    Bloch v1
'Til death do us part
  Bloch, R. The selected stories of Robert
    Bloch v2
Time wounds all heels
  Bloch, R. Lost in time and space with
    Lefty Feep
A toy for Juliette
  Bloch, R. The selected stories of Robert
    Bloch v3
The tunnel of love
  Bloch, R. The selected stories of Robert
    Bloch v1
Underground
  Bloch, R. The selected stories of Robert
    Bloch v3
The unpardonable crime
  Bloch, R. The selected stories of Robert
    Bloch v3
The unspeakable betrothal
  Bloch, R. The selected stories of Robert
    Bloch v1
Untouchable
  Bloch, R. The selected stories of Robert
    Bloch v3
The warm farewell
  Bloch, R. The selected stories of Robert
    Bloch v3
Water's edge
  Bloch, R. The selected stories of Robert
    Bloch v2

The weird doom of Floyd Scrilch
  Bloch, R. Lost in time and space with
    Lefty Feep
Welcome, stranger
  Bloch, R. The selected stories of Robert
    Bloch v2
Where the buffalo roam
  Bloch, R. The selected stories of Robert
    Bloch v1
Word of honor
  Bloch, R. The selected stories of Robert
    Bloch v2
The world-timer
  Bloch, R. The selected stories of Robert
    Bloch v3
You could be wrong
  Amazing science fiction anthology: The
    wild years, 1946-1955; ed. by M. H.
    Greenberg
You got to have brains
  Bloch, R. The selected stories of Robert
    Bloch v1
Yours truly, Jack the Ripper
  The Dark descent; ed. by D. G. Hart-
    well
  Ripper! Ed. by G. Dozois and S. Casper
Blochman, Lawrence Goldtree, 1900-1975
But the patient died
  Kill or cure; ed. by M. Muller and B.
    Pronzini
Murder walks in marble halls
  Chapter & hearse; ed. by M. Muller and
    B. Pronzini
Block, Lawrence, 1938-
As good as a rest
  The Year's best mystery and suspense
    stories, 1987
The books always balance
  Block, L. Like a lamb to slaughter
The boy who disappeared clouds
  Block, L. Like a lamb to slaughter
By the dawn's early light
  The Eyes have it; ed. by R. J. Randisi
  The Year's best mystery and suspense
    stories, 1985
Change of life
  Block, L. Like a lamb to slaughter
Click!
  Block, L. Like a lamb to slaughter
The dangerous business
  Block, L. Like a lamb to slaughter
Death of the Mallory Queen
  Block, L. Like a lamb to slaughter
The Ehrengraf appointment
  Block, L. Like a lamb to slaughter
The Ehrengraf experience
  Block, L. Like a lamb to slaughter
The Ehrengraf method
  Ellery Queen's Crimes and punishments
Hot eyes, cold eyes
  Block, L. Like a lamb to slaughter
If this be madness
  Block, L. Like a lamb to slaughter

Block, Lawrence, 1938-—_Continued_
Leo Youngdahl, R.I.P.
    Block, L. Like a lamb to slaughter
Like a bug on a windshield
    The Year's best mystery & suspense
        stories, 1986
Like a lamb to slaughter
    Block, L. Like a lamb to slaughter
Like a thief in the night
    The Year's best mystery and suspense
        stories, 1984
A little off the top
    Block, L. Like a lamb to slaughter
The most unusual snatch
    Block, L. Like a lamb to slaughter
One thousand dollars a word
    Chapter & hearse; ed. by M. Muller and
        B. Pronzini
    Masterpieces of mystery and suspense;
        ed. by M. H. Greenberg
Out of the window
    The Mammoth book of private eye
        stories; ed. by B. Pronzini and M. H.
        Greenberg
Passport in order
    Block, L. Like a lamb to slaughter
That kind of a day
    Block, L. Like a lamb to slaughter
Weekend guests
    Block, L. Like a lamb to slaughter
With a smile for the ending
    Block, L. Like a lamb to slaughter
You could call it blackmail
    Block, L. Like a lamb to slaughter
Block, Susan, 1955-
Leaving Sasha; or, The bed makes the
    man
    Erotic interludes; ed. by L. Barbach
Blond and blue. Estleman, L. D.
Blonde hairs. Phillips, M.
Blood. Flaherty, G.
Blood. Navas, D.
Blood and gold. Lemay, P.
Blood and its relationship to water. Carlson,
    R.
Blood and water. McGrath, P.
Blood and water. Winton, T.
Blood and wine. Bewley, G.
Blood Aspens. Broun, H.
Blood bait. DeGravelles, C.
The **blood** bargain. Ambler, E.
Blood, binoculars, and a blizzard. Abbott, K.
Blood blossom. Clark, G.
Blood brothers. Haldeman, J. W.
Blood disease. McGrath, P.
BLOOD DONORS
    Bewley, G. Blood and wine
    Faik, S. The test
    Flaherty, G. Blood
    Schwebel, B. A gift for Lucrecia
    Thomas, J. Blood money
Blood gothic. Holder, N.
The **blood** kiss. Etchison, D.

Blood money. Thomas, J.
Blood music. Bear, G.
Blood on the forge. Attaway, W.
Blood on the sun. Thompson, T.
Blood oranges. Metzger, D.
Blood relations. Stephen, J.
Blood relatives. Apple, M.
Blood relatives. Olson, D.
Blood sisters. Haldeman, J. W.
Blood son. See Matheson, R. Drink my
    blood
Blood, sweat, and fears. Hamilton, D. C.
Blood will tell. Bradley, M. Z.
Blood will tell. Marquis, D.
Bloodchild. Butler, O. E.
Bloodflowers. Valgardson, W. D.
Bloodless Byrne of a Monday. Kiely, B.
Bloodsong. Havemann, E.
Bloodspell. Crispin, A. C.
The **bloodstained** pavement. Christie, A.
Bloodwine, Gareth
    Three knives in Ithkar
        Magic in Ithkar 3; ed. by A. Norton and
            R. Adams
Bloodwolf. Tem, S. R.
The **bloody** countess. Pizarnik, A.
Bloody July. Estleman, L. D.
The **bloody** past, the wandering future.
    Hospital, J. T.
Blooming Violet. Dyer, S.
Bloomingdale's. Klass, P.
Bloomington, Fall 1971. Choi, Y. H.
Blount, Roy
    Five Ives
        Sudden fiction; ed. by R. Shapard and
            J. Thomas
A **blow,** a kiss. Winton, T.
Blow it. Highsmith, P.
The **blow-up** of the Mohawk. Robinson, W.
"**Blow** up with the brig". Collins, W.
Bloy, Léon, 1846-1917
    The captives of Longjumeau
        Black water; ed. by A. Manguel
Blue, Adrianne
    Transatlantic passage
        Critical Quarterly 29:37-44 Spr '87
Blue. Brickhouse, R.
Blue. Dawson, F.
The **blue** background. Aldiss, B. W.
Blue-bearded lover. Oates, J. C.
The **blue** bedroom. Pilcher, R.
The **blue** bird. Rhys, J.
The **blue** birthmark. Gardner, M.
Blue Boy. Caldwell, E.
Blue Cloud, Peter
    Coyote meets Raven
        Earth power coming; ed. by S. J. Ortiz
    Stinkbug
        Earth power coming; ed. by S. J. Ortiz
    Waterbugs
        Earth power coming; ed. by S. J. Ortiz
Blue country. Mason, B. A.
The **blue** cross. Chesterton, G. K.

Blue day. Lustig, A.
Blue dive. Chappell, F.
The blue eye. Apollinaire, G.
The blue-eyed Buddhist. Gilchrist, E.
The blue eyes. Dinesen, I.
The blue film. Greene, G.
The blue geranium. Christie, A.
Blue haired chickens. Thorman, C.
The Blue Hill Massacre. Winters, J.
The blue hotel. Crane, S.
The blue hotel. Van Wert, W. F.
The blue in the sky. Dawson, F.
The blue man. Muschg, A.
The blue man. Parkinson, T. L.
The blue men. Williams, J.
Blue milk. Tarkington, B.
Blue moon. Phillips, J. A.
Blue mountains. Alden, P. B.
Blue murder. Brown, F.
Blue news. Evans, E.
Blue oraciones. Beasley, C.
Blue Rise. Hill, R.
The blue room. Gopnik, A.
Blue rose. Straub, P.
Blue roses. Austin, M. H.
The blue skull and the dark palms. Gon-
    zalez, N. V. M.
The blue spruce. Sanford, W. M.
Blue stone. Kittredge, W.
Blue water-man. Valenzuela, L.
The blue weapon. Gad, H.
The blue-winged teal. Stegner, W. E.
Bluebeard. Barthelme, D.
Bluebeard's egg. Atwood, M.
Bluebeard's key. Fremlin, C.
Bluebeard's second wife. Schaeffer, S. F.
Blued moon. Willis, C.
Bluegill. Phillips, J. A.
Blues for my father, my mother, and me.
    Perry, R.
Blum, Jennifer Joerg
    The legacy of Frank Finklestein
        Seventeen 45:168-9+ O '86
Blumlein, Michael
    The brains of rats
        Interzone: the 2nd anthology; ed. by J.
            Clute; D. Pringle and S. Ounsley
    The domino master
        Omni (New York, N.Y.) 10:52-4+ Je '88
    Tissue ablation and variant regeneration:
        a case report
        Interzone: the first anthology; ed. by J.
            Clute; C. Greenland and D. Pringle
A blunt affair. Thompson, K.
Bly, Carol
    A committee of the whole
        TriQuarterly no73:19-30 Fall '88
    The dignity of life
        Bly, C. Backbone
    Gunnar's sword
        Bly, C. Backbone
        Full measure; ed. by D. Sennett

The last of the gold star mothers
    Bly, C. Backbone
The mouse roulette wheel
    Bly, C. Backbone
Talk of heroes
    American short story masterpieces; ed.
        by R. Carver and T. Jenks
    Bly, C. Backbone
Blythe, Ronald, 1922-
    And the green grass grew all around
        Blythe, R. The visitors
    At Swan Gates
        Blythe, R. The visitors
    A bit simple
        Blythe, R. The visitors
    Bride Michael
        Blythe, R. The visitors
    The church mouse
        Blythe, R. The visitors
    The common soldiery
        Blythe, R. The visitors
    Dear dead Pippa
        Blythe, R. The visitors
    Everything a man needs
        Blythe, R. The visitors
    Here be dragons
        Blythe, R. The visitors
    Immediate possession
        Blythe, R. The visitors
    The nature of poetry
        Blythe, R. The visitors
    The October Bagman
        Blythe, R. The visitors
    The packhorse path
        Blythe, R. The visitors
    Period return
        Blythe, R. The visitors
    The right day to kill a pike
        Blythe, R. The visitors
    The schism
        Blythe, R. The visitors
    The shadows of the living
        Blythe, R. The visitors
    Take your partners
        Blythe, R. The visitors
    A wedding in the family
        Blythe, R. The visitors
    The windfall
        Blythe, R. The visitors
Blythe, Will
    The taming power of the small
        The Best American short stories, 1988
Blyton, Carey
    The final solution
        Short story international 56
    A fine summer's day
        Short story international 50
The boarded window. Bierce, A.
The boarder. Botwinik, B.
BOARDERS See Boarding houses
Boarding. MacIntyre, T.
The boarding house. Bonnie, K. F.
The boarding house. Joyce, J.

BOARDING HOUSES
Ade, G. The mystery of the back-roomer
Ade, G. Our private romance
Apollinaire, G. The talking memories
Atwood, M. Dancing girls
Austin, D. Something similar would be a boarding house
Böll, H. Pale Anna
Brennan, J. P. Mrs. Clendon's place
Busch, F. The new honesty
Colegate, I. The girl who had lived among artists
Colette. Bella-Vista
Curtiss, U. R. Tiger by the tail
Dadswell, M. Mimi
Davie, E. Bulbs
Eldridge, M. At the Signora's
Fisher, M. F. K. The second time around
Godwin, G. Over the mountain
Granit, A. Come into the hallway, for five cents!
Granit, A. The penny is for God!
Hall, T. T. The boardinghouse ballad
Henry, O. The furnished room
Hogg, J. Sound morality
Humphrey, W. A home away from home
James, H. A bundle of letters
James, H. The Pension Beaurepas
Jolley, E. Bill Sprockett's land
Joyce, J. The boarding house
Kinsella, W. P. Gabon
Kinsella, W. P. The secret
Kinsella, W. P. The silver porcupine
Klein, R. E. Mrs. Rahlo's closet
Leaton, A. Little pictures
Leedom-Ackerman, J. Of imagination
Martin, H. R. A poet though married
Maupassant, G. de. My landlady
Metcalf, J. Single gents only
Moffatt, D. The lodger
Moore, G. Dried fruit
Morris, W. Drrdla
Naipaul, S. Lack of sleep
Painter, P. Patterns
Phelps, E. S. Number 13
Power, V. The ragged rascal ran
Pronzini, B. The dispatching of George Ferris
Rhys, J. A solid house
Rooke, L. The birth control king of the Upper Volta
Spark, D. The incorrect hour
Spark, M. The pawnbroker's wife
Stead, C. 1954: days of the roomers
Stead, C. Accents
Stead, C. The boy
Stead, C. A household
Swados, H. The hack
Trevor, W. Music
Wijenaike, P. The visitor
Williams, T. The angel in the alcove
Williams, T. The coming of something to Widow Holly
Williams, T. Something about him
Wollheim, D. A. The rag thing

BOARDING SCHOOLS *See* School life
The **boardinghouse** ballad. Hall, T. T.

BOARS
Benedict, P. Booze
The **boat**. MacLeod, A.

BOAT RACING
Helprin, M. Palais de Justice
Jacobs, W. W. Outsailed

BOATMEN
O'Kelly, S. Hike and Calcutta
O'Kelly, S. The man with the gift
O'Kelly, S. Michael and Mary

BOATS AND BOATING
Atwood, M. Two stories about Emma: The whirlpool rapids
Atwood, M. The whirlpool rapids
Bates, H. E. The white wind
Chipulina, E. G. The disaster
Clement, H. The mechanic
Durrell, L. Call of the sea
Faik, S. Searchlight operator
Fisher, M. F. K. Another love story
Gaitens, E. The sailing ship
Garrett, G. P. The rivals
Hannah, B. All the old harkening faces at the rail
Keillor, G. Pontoon boat
MacLean, A. St. George and the dragon
MacLeod, A. The boat
Maupassant, G. de. On the river
Pavese, C. The leather jacket
Pavese, C. Summer storm
Peterson, M. Coastal
Schulberg, B. The barracudas
Schwartz, L. S. The sunfish and the mermaid
Shacochis, B. Dead reckoning
Virgo, S. Horsey horsey
Boats coming ashore. Gildner, G.
Bob and the other man. Wier, A.
The **Bob** Dylan Tambourine Software & Satori Support Services Consortium, Ltd. Bishop, M.
Bob Parris's temper. Conley, R. J.
Bobbeh. Lurie, M.
Bobby. See Wideman, J. E. Tommy
Bobby Shafter's gone to sea. Swados, H.
Bobby's room. Dunn, D.
Bocock, Maclin
  The baker's daughter or A tale of Holy Russia
    The Southern Review (Baton Rouge, La.) 24:593-604 Summ '88
  Don't save your kisses
    New Directions in prose and poetry 51
    The Southern Review (Baton Rouge, La.) 22:179-90 Ja '86
La **boda**. Ríos, A.
The **Bodega** War. Lee, H.
Bodies. Russ, J.
Bodies at sea. McGraw, E.

Bodies like mouths. Clayton, J. J.
Bodies of the rich. Clayton, J. J.
Bodies piled up. Hammett, D.
Bodily secrets. Trevor, W.
Bodkin, M. McDonnell
  Murder by proxy
    Death locked in; ed. by D. G. Greene
      and R. C. S. Adey
Body count. Dundee, W. D.
The **body** mask. Carpenter, D. A.
The **body** politic. Barker, C.
Body snatchers. Schulman, H.
The **body** snatchers. Stevenson, R. L.
A **body** tends to shine. Gurganus, A.
The **body** upstairs. Woolrich, C.
BODYGUARDS
  Hoch, E. D. A flash of red
  Ingalls, R. I see a long journey
Bodyguards shoot second. Estleman, L. D.
The **bodysurfers**. Drewe, R.
Boeckman, Charles
  You can get away with murder
    Alfred Hitchcock's Crimewatch
Boehm, Lucille
  Two-bit piece
    Writing red; ed. by C. Nekola and P.
      Rabinowitz
Boerema, Ryan
  Green shoes
    The Antioch Review 43:22-35 Wint '85
BOERS *See* Afrikaners
The **Boffer**. Mordden, E.
The **bogey** man will get you. Bloch, R.
Bogeyman. Asscher-Pinkhof, C.
Bogotá. Munves, J.
The **Bohemian**. O'Brien, F.-J.
BOHEMIANISM
  Bloch, R. The big kick
  Colegate, I. The girl who had lived among
    artists
  Gold, H. Waiting for the forty-one union
  Gold, H. Young man, old days
  Rosenfeld, I. George
  Rosenfeld, I. Wolfie
The **boiler**. Symons, J.
Boiling river. Engberg, S.
Boissard, Janine
  Christmas lessons in love
    Redbook 164:73+ D '84
Boisvert, Claude
  The prophet
    Invisible fictions; ed. by G. Hancock
  A slice of nothingness
    Invisible fictions; ed. by G. Hancock
Boitelle. Maupassant, G. de
Boler, Richard
  The old flame
    The North American Review 271:37 S
      '86
Boles, Paul Darcy, 1916-1984
  The twister
    The Saturday Evening Post 257:44-7+ N
      '85

BOLEYN, ANNE *See* Anne Boleyn, Queen,
  consort of Henry VIII, King of
  England, 1507-1536
Böll, Heinrich, 1917-1985
  Across the bridge
    Böll, H. The stories of Heinrich Böll
  Action will be taken
    The Art of the tale; ed. by D. Halpern
  Adventures of a haversack
    Böll, H. The stories of Heinrich Böll
  And there was the evening and the mor-
    ning . . .
    Böll, H. The stories of Heinrich Böll
  And where were you, Adam? [Variant title:
    Adam]
    Böll, H. The stories of Heinrich Böll
  Anecdote concerning the lowering of
    productivity
    Böll, H. The stories of Heinrich Böll
  At the border
    Böll, H. The casualty
  At the bridge
    Böll, H. The stories of Heinrich Böll
  Autumn loneliness
    Böll, H. The casualty
  The Balek scales
    Böll, H. The stories of Heinrich Böll
  Beside the river
    Böll, H. The casualty
  Between trains in X
    Böll, H. The stories of Heinrich Böll
  Black sheep
    Böll, H. The stories of Heinrich Böll
  Breaking the news
    Böll, H. The stories of Heinrich Böll
  Broommakers
    Böll, H. The stories of Heinrich Böll
  Business is business
    Böll, H. The stories of Heinrich Böll
  The cage
    Böll, H. The casualty
  Candles for the Madonna
    Böll, H. The stories of Heinrich Böll
    The Substance of things hoped for; ed.
      by J. B. Breslin
  A case for Kop
    Böll, H. The stories of Heinrich Böll
  The casualty
    Böll, H. The casualty
  Cause of death: hooked nose
    Böll, H. The casualty
  Children are civilians too
    Böll, H. The stories of Heinrich Böll
  Christmas not just once a year [Variant
    title: Christmas every day]
    Böll, H. The stories of Heinrich Böll
  Contacts
    Böll, H. The casualty
  Daniel the Just
    Böll, H. The stories of Heinrich Böll
  The death of Elsa Baskoleit
    Böll, H. The stories of Heinrich Böll

Böll, Heinrich, 1917-1985—*Continued*
Drinking in Petöcki
  Böll, H. The stories of Heinrich Böll
  Inspired by drink; ed. by Joan Digby
    and John Digby
The embrace
  Böll, H. The casualty
Green are the meadows
  Böll, H. The casualty
The green silk shirt
  Böll, H. The casualty
He came as a beer-truck driver
  Böll, H. The stories of Heinrich Böll
I can't forget her
  Böll, H. The casualty
I'm not a Communist
  Böll, H. The casualty
In Friedenstadt
  Böll, H. The casualty
In search of the reader
  Böll, H. The stories of Heinrich Böll
In the darkness
  Böll, H. The stories of Heinrich Böll
In the Valley of the Thundering Hoofs
  Böll, H. The stories of Heinrich Böll
In which language is one called Schnecken-
  röder?
  Böll, H. The stories of Heinrich Böll
Jak the tout
  Böll, H. The casualty
Like a bad dream
  Böll, H. The stories of Heinrich Böll
Lohengrin's death
  Böll, H. The stories of Heinrich Böll
The man with the knives
  Böll, H. The stories of Heinrich Böll
Monologue of a waiter
  Böll, H. The stories of Heinrich Böll
The murder
  Böll, H. The casualty
Murke's collected silences
  Böll, H. The stories of Heinrich Böll
My expensive leg
  Böll, H. The stories of Heinrich Böll
My father's cough
  Böll, H. The stories of Heinrich Böll
My pal with the long hair
  Böll, H. The stories of Heinrich Böll
My sad face
  Böll, H. The stories of Heinrich Böll
  Voices East and West: German short
    stories since 1945
My Uncle Fred
  Böll, H. The stories of Heinrich Böll
No tears for Schmeck
  Böll, H. The stories of Heinrich Böll
Nostalgia; or, Grease spots
  Böll, H. The stories of Heinrich Böll
On being courteous when compelled to
  break the law
  Böll, H. The stories of Heinrich Böll
On the hook
  Böll, H. The stories of Heinrich Böll

An optimistic story
  Böll, H. The casualty
Pale Anna
  Böll, H. The stories of Heinrich Böll
  Short story international 44
Parting
  Böll, H. The stories of Heinrich Böll
A peach tree in his garden stands
  Böll, H. The stories of Heinrich Böll
The postcard
  Böll, H. The stories of Heinrich Böll
The railway station of Zimpren
  German stories; ed. by H. Steinhauer
The rain gutter
  Böll, H. The casualty
The ration runners
  Böll, H. The stories of Heinrich Böll
Recollections of a young king
  Böll, H. The stories of Heinrich Böll
Rendezvous with Margret; or, Happy en-
  ding
  Böll, H. The stories of Heinrich Böll
Reunion on the avenue
  Böll, H. The stories of Heinrich Böll
Reunion with Drüng
  Böll, H. The stories of Heinrich Böll
A soldier's legacy
  Böll, H. The stories of Heinrich Böll
The Staech affair
  Böll, H. The stories of Heinrich Böll
"Stranger, bear word to the Spartans we
  . . ."
  Böll, H. The stories of Heinrich Böll
The surfer
  Böll, H. The casualty
The taste of bread
  Böll, H. The stories of Heinrich Böll
That time we were in Odessa
  Böll, H. The stories of Heinrich Böll
This is Tibten!
  Böll, H. The stories of Heinrich Böll
The thrower-away
  Böll, H. The stories of Heinrich Böll
The tidings of Bethlehem
  Böll, H. The stories of Heinrich Böll
Till death us do part
  Böll, H. The stories of Heinrich Böll
Too many trips to Heidelberg
  Böll, H. The stories of Heinrich Böll
The train was on time [Variant title: The
  train]
  Böll, H. The stories of Heinrich Böll
Undine's mighty father
  Böll, H. The stories of Heinrich Böll
Unexpected guests
  Böll, H. The stories of Heinrich Böll
The unknown soldier
  Böll, H. The casualty
Vingt-et-un
  Böll, H. The casualty
Vive la France!
  Böll, H. The casualty

Böll, Heinrich, 1917-1985—*Continued*
  The waiting-room
    Böll, H. The casualty
  What a racket
    Böll, H. The stories of Heinrich Böll
  When the war broke out
    Böll, H. The stories of Heinrich Böll
  When the war was over
    Böll, H. The stories of Heinrich Böll
A **boll** of roses. Dumas, H.
BOLSHEVISM *See* Communism
A **bolt** of white cloth. Rooke, L.
BOMB SHELTERS *See* Air raid shelters
Bombal, María Luisa, 1910-1980
  The tree
    Short story international 53
Bombardier. Gallico, P.
BOMBAY (INDIA) *See* India—Bombay
Bombay. Jhabvala, R. P.
BOMBING MISSIONS *See* World War,
    1914-1918—Aerial operations
BOMBS
      See also Atomic bomb
  Asimov, I. Dollars and cents
  Asimov, I. The thirteenth day of Christmas
  Asscher-Pinkhof, C. Disaster
  Block, L. The books always balance
  Brooks, J. A value
  Davis, D. S. Mrs. Norris observes
  Ignatow, R. G. How?
  Pronzini, B. Perfect timing
  Saki. The Easter egg
  Sheffield, C. Skystalk
  Wickert, M. The scythe of Saturn
Bon-bon. Poe, E. A.
BONAPARTE, NAPOLEON *See* Napoleon
    I, Emperor of the French, 1769-1821
Bonaventure. Gallant, M.
Bond, Nelson
  Pilgrimage
    Amazing stories: 60 years of the best
      science fiction
Bond. Loewald, U.
The **bond.** Singer, I. B.
Bondage. Krysl, M.
The **bonds** of love. Heffernan, M. J.
Bone, Jesse Franklin, 1916-
  On the fourth planet
    Great science fiction; ed. by I. Asimov;
      M. H. Greenberg and C. G. Waugh
  Triggerman
    Machines that think; ed. by I. Asimov;
      P. S. Warrick and M. H. Greenberg
  Tween
    Young extraterrestrials; ed. by I. Asimov;
      M. H. Greenberg and C. G. Waugh
The **bone.** Davis, L.
Bone to his bone. Swain, E. G.
Bones and bouquets. Davie, E.
The **bones** of Charlemagne. Pei, M.
Bones. The April fool of Harvey's Sluice.
    Doyle, Sir A. C.

The **bones** wizard. Ryan, A.
Bonham, Frank
  Chivaree
    Wild westerns; ed. by B. Pronzini
Bonner, Marita, 1899-1971
  Black fronts
    Bonner, M. Frye Street & environs
  Corner store
    Bonner, M. Frye Street & environs
  Drab rambles
    Bonner, M. Frye Street & environs
  The hands: a story
    Bonner, M. Frye Street & environs
  Hate is nothing
    Bonner, M. Frye Street & environs
  High-stepper
    Bonner, M. Frye Street & environs
  Hongry fire
    Bonner, M. Frye Street & environs
  Light in dark places
    Bonner, M. Frye Street & environs
  The makin's
    Bonner, M. Frye Street & environs
  Nothing new
    Bonner, M. Frye Street & environs
  Of Jimmy Harris
    Bonner, M. Frye Street & environs
  On the altar
    Bonner, M. Frye Street & environs
  One boy's story
    Bonner, M. Frye Street & environs
  One true love
    Bonner, M. Frye Street & environs
  Patch quilt
    Bonner, M. Frye Street & environs
  The prison-bound
    Bonner, M. Frye Street & environs
  Reap it as you sow it
    Bonner, M. Frye Street & environs
  A sealed pod
    Bonner, M. Frye Street & environs
  Stones for bread
    Bonner, M. Frye Street & environs
  There were three
    Bonner, M. Frye Street & environs
  Tin can
    Bonner, M. Frye Street & environs
  The whipping
    Bonner, M. Frye Street & environs
    Writing red; ed. by C. Nekola and P.
      Rabinowitz
BONNET, STEDE, d. 1718
              About
  Schwob, M. Major Stede Bonnet, pirate by
    vagary
Bonnie, Fred
  Allergic
    Bonnie, F. Too hot, and other Maine
      stories
  The bulk tour
    Bonnie, F. Wide load
  In another language
    Bonnie, F. Wide load

Bonnie, Fred—*Continued*
Mistrial
  Bonnie, F. Wide load
Name the general
  Bonnie, F. Wide load
A settlement of wages
  Bonnie, F. Too hot, and other Maine
  stories
Squatter's rights
  Bonnie, F. Too hot, and other Maine
  stories
The state meet
  Bonnie, F. Too hot, and other Maine
  stories
Take a seat, not a solo
  Bonnie, F. Wide load
Too hot
  Bonnie, F. Too hot, and other Maine
  stories
Two widows
  Bonnie, F. Too hot, and other Maine
  stories
Wide load, where are you?
  Bonnie, F. Wide load
Bonnie, Kathleen Ford
The boarding house
  The Virginia Quarterly Review 61:472-82
  Summ '85
Summer of sanctity
  U.S. Catholic 51:31-6 Ap '86
Bonosky, Phillip, 1916-
A bird in her hair
  Bonosky, P. A bird in her hair, and
  other stories
The cathedral
  Bonosky, P. A bird in her hair, and
  other stories
Charity ward
  Bonosky, P. A bird in her hair, and
  other stories
The delegate
  Bonosky, P. A bird in her hair, and
  other stories
The first robin in the world
  Bonosky, P. A bird in her hair, and
  other stories
Hank
  Bonosky, P. A bird in her hair, and
  other stories
Home for supper
  Bonosky, P. A bird in her hair, and
  other stories
Johnny Cucu's record
  Bonosky, P. A bird in her hair, and
  other stories
Poor Joey
  Bonosky, P. A bird in her hair, and
  other stories
A quiet summer's day
  Bonosky, P. A bird in her hair, and
  other stories

Sin
  Bonosky, P. A bird in her hair, and
  other stories
A sweet tooth
  Bonosky, P. A bird in her hair, and
  other stories
Walk to the moon
  Bonosky, P. A bird in her hair, and
  other stories
The **bonus**. Holland, B.
The **bonus** years. Fremlin, C.
The **bony-fish** that came into my net. Cho,
  S.-H.
Boogie Man. King, T.
The **book**. Rey Rosa, R.
The **book** buyers. Kinsella, W. P.
The **book** (Chez Claude Mauriac). Hemens-
  ley, K.
The **book-healer**. Miesel, S.
Book-l'arnin' and the equalizer. Overholser,
  W. D.
**BOOK OF A THOUSAND AND ONE
  NIGHTS** *See* Arabian nights
The **book** of ands. Grossmith, R.
The **book** of blood. Barker, C.
The **Book** of Blood (a postscript): on Jerusa-
  lem Street. Barker, C.
Book of dreams. Grimm, M.
Book of Harlem. Hurston, Z. N.
The **book** of life. Sperling, L.
The **book** of Mordecai. Stern, S.
The **book** of time. Decarnin, C.
BOOK RARITIES *See* Rare books
The **book** review. Dixon, S.
Book review. Revill, P.
BOOK SHOPS *See* Booksellers and book-
  selling
The **book** that squealed. Woolrich, C.
Booker's End. Dundas, R.
The **bookman's** tale. Fleming, B.
BOOKS
      See also Books and reading;
    Manuscripts; Rare books
  Asimov, I. The fun they had
  Asimov, I. The library book
  Chambers, R. W. The yellow sign
  Heise, K. Aunt Ella and my first com-
    munion
  Kirk, R. What shadows we pursue
  Lasswitz, K. The universal library
  Lindsay, F. The people of the book
  Noyes, A. Midnight express
  Rhys, J. The day they burned the books
  Sorrentino, F. Piccirilli
  Zeldis, L. The whore of Babylon
BOOKS, RARE *See* Rare books
The **books** always balance. Block, L.
BOOKS AND READING
  Bernard, K. Rescheduling
  Faik, S. The village teacher and the herds-
    boy
  Ferguson, N. The second third of C
  Fink, I. Jean-Christophe

BOOKS AND READING—*Continued*
Hankla, C. In search of literary heroes
Harris, M. Little Eddy
Jackson, S. Seven types of ambiguity
Kinsella, W. P. The book buyers
Leedom-Ackerman, J. The tutor
MacLaverty, B. Anodyne
MacLaverty, B. Hugo
Morris, W. The character of the lover
Prebehalla, G., and Moran, D. K. Realtime
Sayers, D. L. The Dragon's head
Schwebel, B. El Señor Lector
Waugh, E. The man who liked Dickens
Williamson, B. The thing waiting outside
Winton, T. Distant lands
Woolrich, C. The book that squealed
Books by the pound. Kinsella, W. P.
BOOKSELLERS AND BOOKSELLING
Bloch, R. Night school
Brennan, J. P. Canavan's back yard
Broun, H. Ice water
Chatto, J. Tricky customers
Cozzens, J. G. Clerical error
Davis, D. S. The Devil and his due
Desaulniers, J. Age
Fetler, J. The dust of Yuri Serafimovich
Harrison, M. J. Egnaro
Kinsella, W. P. Books by the pound
McConnor, V. The house of crime
Miesel, S. The book-healer
Mitchell, K. The centre of gravity
Ryan, A. I shall not leave England now
Taylor, C. In and out of the arms of the law
Taylor, C. The new and the old, the old and the new
West, J. Tom Wolfe's my name
Williams, T. Something by Tolstoi
Winton, T. Distant lands
Boole de suif. See Maupassant, G. de. Ball-of-fat
Boom job. Sanders, H. G.
Boom town. Hauptman, W.
Boom town. Wolfe, T.
The **Boomer's** fireman's fast sooner hound. Conroy, J.
The **boon**. Olmstead, R.
Boone, Bruce
David's charm
Men on men; ed. by G. Stambolian
Booth, Bob
Still life
After midnight; ed. by C. L. Grant
BOOTH, JOHN WILKES, 1838-1865
About
Carr, J. D. The black cabinet
BOOTLEGGING *See* Liquor traffic
Boots. Fraser, A.
BOOTS AND SHOES
Aiken, J. The moon's revenge
Davie, E. Shoe in the sand
Dick, P. K. The short happy life of the brown oxford

Lish, G. Balzano & Son
Lish, G. I'm wide
Mazel, D. Shining
McGrath, P. The boot's tale
Price, R. The Warrior Princess Ozimba
Schmidt, H. J. Shoe
Soucy, J.-Y. The red boots
Turner, B. The shoes
Valenzuela, L. The best shod
The **Boots** at the Holly-Tree Inn. Dickens, C.
The **boot's** tale. McGrath, P.
Booty for a badman. L'Amour, L.
Booze. Benedict, P.
The **boozers'** home. Lawson, H.
Bop. Chernoff, M.
Boras, Helen
Fifty years of eternal vigilance
Southern Exposure (Durham, N.C.) 13:62-7 Mr/Je '85
Borchert, Wolfgang, 1921-1947
Do stay, Giraffe
The Art of the tale; ed. by D. Halpern
Stories from a first reader
Voices East and West: German short stories since 1945
The three dark kings [Variant title: The three dark Magi]
Voices East and West: German short stories since 1945
Borden, Jonathan
The shoes of death
Stiller's pond; ed. by J. Agee; R. Blakely and S. Welch
BORDEN, LIZZIE, 1860-1927
About
Carter, A. The Fall River axe murders
Border crossers. Schneider, R.
The **borderland** of Sol. Niven, L.
Borders, Andrew
Daniel's garden
Southern Exposure (Durham, N.C.) 12:54-8 Mr/Ap '84
Borealis. Morand, P.
BOREDOM
Adams, G. The voyage of their life
Gustafsson, L. The girl in the blue cap
Heller, S. A matter of style
Parise, G. Boredom
Regent, P. Memories of colonialism
Rose, D. A. Envy the dead
Tournier, M. Death and the maiden
Yi, H.-C. The sultriness of a cold evening
Boredom. Parise, G.
Boren, Terry
Sliding rock
A Very large array; ed. by M. M. Snodgrass
BORES (PERSONS)
Rooke, L. Why Agnes left
Borgen, Johan, 1902-
Song of stars
Short story international 50

Borgen, Johan, 1902-—_Continued_
The swan
Short story international 43
Borges, Jorge Luis, 1899-1986
25 August 1983
Winter's tales, new ser. v3
The Aleph
The Art of the tale; ed. by D. Halpern
August 25, 1983
Black water; ed. by A. Manguel
Borges: a dream
Harper's 268:25 My '84
The captive
On being foreign; ed. by T. J. Lewis and
R. E. Jungman
Emma Zunz
Dark arrows; ed. by A. Manguel
The lottery in Babylon [Variant title: The
Babylon lottery]
The Slaying of the dragon; ed. by F.
Rottensteiner
Paracelsus and the rose
The Antioch Review 44:133-6 Spr '86
Winter's tales, new ser. v3
Shakespeare's memory
Winter's tales, new ser. v2
Story of the warrior and the captive
On being foreign; ed. by T. J. Lewis and
R. E. Jungman
Tlön, Uqbar, Orbis Tertius
The World of the short story; ed. by
C. Fadiman
Borges: a dream. Borges, J. L.
Borgman, C. F.
A queer red spirit
Men on men; ed. by G. Stambolian
Borgman, Charles F. _See_ Borgman, C. F.
(Charles F.)
Borg's last word. Taylor, C.
Boris. Eisenstein, S.
Boris is buying horses. Berger, J.
Born and bred. Lee, L.
Born killer. Davis, D. S.
Born of man and woman. Matheson, R.
Born to ride. Killingsworth, S.
Born victims. Wellen, E.
BORNEO
Maugham, W. S. Before the party
Wells, H. G. In the Avu observatory
Borovsky's hollow woman. Duntemann, J.,
and Kress, N.
Borovsky's hollow woman. Kress, N.
Borowski, Tadeusz, 1922-1951
The supper
The World of the short story; ed. by
C. Fadiman
This way for the gas, ladies and gentlemen
The Art of the tale; ed. by D. Halpern
Borrowing. Brondoli, M.
Borthwick, Cathi
Yellow fever
'Teen 29:86-8 Je '85

BORZOI
Linehan, P. One last hunting pack
The **Boscombe** Valley mystery. Doyle, Sir A.
C.
Bosman, Herman Charles
The Rooinek
The Penguin book of Southern African
stories
BOSNIA (YUGOSLAVIA) _See_ Yugoslavia—
Bosnia
Bosniak, M. E.
A second chance
The Antioch Review 42:219-23 Spr '84
Bossboy and the wild West. Drew, E.
Bossy. Gurnah, A.
Boston, Bruce
Interview with a gentleman farmer
100 great fantasy short short stories; ed.
by I. Asimov; T. Carr and M. H.
Greenberg
BOSTON (MASS.) _See_ Massachusetts—
Boston
BOSWELL, JAMES, 1740-1795
About
De la Torre, L. Milady bigamy
Boswell, Robert, 1953-
Dancing in the movies
Boswell, R. Dancing in the movies
The darkness of love
Boswell, R. Dancing in the movies
Prize stories, 1987
Edward and Jill
The Georgia Review 40:939-49 Wint '86
New stories from the South: the year's
best, 1987
Flipflops
Boswell, R. Dancing in the movies
The good man
The New Yorker 64:36-9 O 3 '88
Kentucky
Boswell, R. Dancing in the movies
Little Bear
Boswell, R. Dancing in the movies
The right thing
Boswell, R. Dancing in the movies
Bosworth summit pound. Rolt, L. T. C.
The **Botanic** Gardens. Freeman, J.
BOTANISTS
Davie, E. A botanist's romance
Silverberg, R. How they pass the time in
Pelpel
A **botanist's** romance. Davie, E.
Both ways. Birtha, B.
Bothering. Matthews, J.
BOTSWANA
Rush, N. Alone in Africa
Rush, N. Bruns
Rush, N. Instruments of seduction
Rush, N. Near Pala
Rush, N. Official Americans
Rush, N. Thieving
The **bottle** imp. Stevenson, R. L.
The **bottle** of 1912. Raven, S.

A **bottle** of milk for mother. Algren, N.
The **bottomless** well. Chesterton, G. K.
The **bottomless** well. Terry, W. S.
Botts runs for his life. Upson, W. H.
Botwinik, Berl, 1885?-1945
  The boarder
    Botwinik, B. Lead pencil
  The Bubbe
    Botwinik, B. Lead pencil
  Death went astray
    Botwinik, B. Lead pencil
  Discovered
    Botwinik, B. Lead pencil
  Esperanto
    Botwinik, B. Lead pencil
  The general strike
    Botwinik, B. Lead pencil
  The glazier
    Botwinik, B. Lead pencil
  Israel and his children
    Botwinik, B. Lead pencil
  Jake
    Botwinik, B. Lead pencil
  The last young man
    Botwinik, B. Lead pencil
  A man
    Botwinik, B. Lead pencil
  Mendel the Tinsmith
    Botwinik, B. Lead pencil
  The mother's Yom Kippur
    Botwinik, B. Lead pencil
  The one I didn't marry
    Botwinik, B. Lead pencil
  The radicals
    Botwinik, B. Lead pencil
  Rivals
    Botwinik, B. Lead pencil
  Shabbas
    Botwinik, B. Lead pencil
  Shabbas morning
    Botwinik, B. Lead pencil
  A shoemaker for a husband
    Botwinik, B. Lead pencil
  Yankel
    Botwinik, B. Lead pencil
Boucher, Anthony, 1911-1968
  Barrier
    From mind to mind: tales of communi-
      cation from Analog
  Elsewhen
    Death locked in; ed. by D. G. Greene
      and R. C. S. Adey
  Mr. Lupescu
    Masterpieces of fantasy and enchant-
      ment; ed. by D. G. Hartwell
    QL 696.C9
    Chapter & hearse; ed. by M. Muller and
      B. Pronzini
Boucher, Sandy
  The healing
    Hear the silence; ed. by I. Zahava
  Humming
    Erotic interludes; ed. by L. Barbach

La **boucherie**. Roy, J.
The **Boudicca** killing. Price, A.
Boulaich, Abdeslam
  Cowardice
    The Art of the tale; ed. by D. Halpern
Boulanger, Daniel, 1922-
  Small change
    The Antioch Review 45:306-7 Summ '87
  The staircase
    Michigan Quarterly Review 26:515-23
      Summ '87
  The wheat in the pyramids
    The Antioch Review 45:308-9 Summ '87
The **boulevard** of broken dreams. Ellison, H.
Boulevard of the revolution. Aćin-Kosta, M.
Bouma, J. L.
  Final mission
    A Treasury of World War II stories; ed.
      by B. Pronzini and M. H. Greenberg
Bound away. Makuck, P.
The **bound** husband. Kawabata, Y.
The **bound** man. Aichinger, I.
Boundaries. El Naga, A. el M. A.
The **boundary** wall. Lu Wenfu
Boundary waters. Logue, M.
The **bounty** killers. Frazee, S.
Bouquet. Kalfus, K.
Bourbons. Davin, D.
BOURGEOISIE *See* Middle classes
Bourjaily, Vance, 1922-
  The Amish farmer
    American short story masterpieces; ed.
      by R. Carver and T. Jenks
  The Duchess
    Stand one; ed. by M. Blackburn; J.
      Silkin and L. Tracy
Bova, Ben, 1932-
  Brothers
    In the field of fire; ed. by J. Van B.
      Dann and J. Dann
  Out of time
    Omni (New York, N.Y.) 7:88-90+ N '84
  A small kindness
    [Analog]: Writers' choice v2
  To touch a star
    The Universe; ed. by B. Preiss
Bovey, John
  The calculus
    The Literary Review (Madison, N.J.)
      30:577-87 Summ '87
  In another country
    The Virginia Quarterly Review 63:452-68
      Summ '87
  The overlap
    On being foreign; ed. by T. J. Lewis and
      R. E. Jungman
  Pomfret
    The Virginia Quarterly Review 60:406-23
      Summ '84
Bow wow and good-bye. Adams, G. G.

Bowen, Elizabeth, 1899-1973
Coming home
    Family: stories from the interior; ed. by
      G. G. Chavis
Hand in glove
    Lost souls; ed. by J. Sullivan
    The Oxford book of English ghost
      stories
    The Treasury of English short stories;
      ed. by N. Sullivan
Mysterious Kor
    The Penguin book of modern British
      short stories
    The World of the short story; ed. by
      C. Fadiman
Tears, idle tears
    Classic European short stories; ed. by R.
      Beum
The visitor
    Early sorrow: ten stories of youth; ed.
      by C. Zolotow
Bowen, John, 1924-
A rabbit in the garden
    Critical Quarterly 29:9-25 Summ '87
Bowen, Marjorie, 1886-1952
The Crown Derby plate
    Christmas ghosts; ed. by K. Cramer and
      D. G. Hartwell
Bowen, Susan Petigru, 1824-1875
A marriage of persuasion
    Between mothers & daughters; ed. by S.
      Koppelman
Old maidism versus marriage
    Old maids; ed. by S. Koppelman
Bowen Island confessions. Watmough, D.
Bowen-Judd, Sara Hutton *See* Woods, Sara
Bower, B. M.
The lamb of the Flying U
    She won the West; ed. by M. Muller
      and B. Pronzini
When the cook fell ill
    Westward the women; ed. by V. Piekar-
      ski
Bowering, George, 1935-
Arbre de décision
    Bowering, G. A place to die
Carter fell
    Bowering, G. A place to die
The clam-digger
    Bowering, G. A place to die
Comparative public deaths
    Bowering, G. A place to die
Four California deaths
    Bowering, G. A place to die
Match-boxes
    Bowering, G. A place to die
Old bottles
    Bowering, G. A place to die
A short story
    Bowering, G. A place to die
    The Oxford book of Canadian short
      stories in English

Student, petty thief, TV star
    Bowering, G. A place to die
Bowers, John, 1928-
Crackers
    Homewords: a book of Tennessee
      writers; ed. by D. Paschall
Bowker, Richard
The other train phenomenon
    100 great fantasy short short stories; ed.
      by I. Asimov; T. Carr and M. H.
      Greenberg
The **bowl**. Williams, T. T.
Bowl like hole. Wicomb, Z.
Bowles, Colin
The song of the fisherman
    Short story international 52
Bowles, Jane Auer, 1917-1973
Everything is nice
    On being foreign; ed. by T. J. Lewis and
      R. E. Jungman
Señorita Córdoba
    The Graywolf annual 2
Bowles, Paul, 1910-
Allal
    Bowles, P. A distant episode
At Paso Rojo
    Bowles, P. A distant episode
Call at Corazón
    Bowles, P. A distant episode
The circular valley
    Bowles, P. A distant episode
The delicate prey
    Bowles, P. A distant episode
A distant episode
    The Art of the tale; ed. by D. Halpern
    Bowles, P. A distant episode
The echo
    Bowles, P. A distant episode
The eye
    Bowles, P. A distant episode
The frozen fields
    Bowles, P. A distant episode
He of the assembly
    Bowles, P. A distant episode
Here to learn
    Bowles, P. A distant episode
In absentia
    Bowles, P. A distant episode
In the red room
    The Best American short stories, 1984
    Bowles, P. A distant episode
An inopportune visit
    Bowles, P. A distant episode
The little house
    Bowles, P. A distant episode
Mejdoub
    Bowles, P. A distant episode
Monologue—Tangier 1975 [Variant title:
    Tangier 1975]
    Buying time; ed. by S. Walker
Pages from Cold Point
    Bowles, P. A distant episode

Bowles, Paul, 1910——*Continued*
  Pastor Dowe at Tacaté
    Bowles, P. A distant episode
    On being foreign; ed. by T. J. Lewis and
      R. E. Jungman
  Rumor and a ladder
    Bowles, P. A distant episode
  Señor Ong and Señor Ha
    Bowles, P. A distant episode
  Tangier 1975 [Variant title: Monologue--
      Tangier 1975]
    Bowles, P. A distant episode
  Tapiama
    Bowles, P. A distant episode
  The time of friendship
    Bowles, P. A distant episode
  Unwelcome words
    Bowles, P. A distant episode
  You have left your lotus pods on the bus
    On being foreign; ed. by T. J. Lewis and
      R. E. Jungman
BOWLING
  Ashley, F. "Listen buddy, we don't throw
    gutter balls here"
  Bloch, R. Gather 'round the flowing bow-
    ler
  Clark, M. Learning to bowl an out-swinger
  Hemley, R. Clues
The **bowmen** of Shu. Davenport, G.
The **box**. Coville, B.
The **box**. El Sayyed, S. A.
The **box**. Straight, S.
A **box** for dreams. Hankla, C.
Box in a box. Ritchie, J.
A **box** of books. Harcourt, P.
The **box** of contents. Thorman, R.
The **box** of fish. Brown, G. M.
Box social. Bye, C.
Boxes. Carver, R.
BOXING
  Aksenov, V. P. A poem of ecstasy
  Algren, N. Depend on Aunt Elly
  Algren, N. He swung and he missed
  Algren, N. Million-dollar brainstorm
  Flanagan, R. Smoker
  Flynn, R. Champion of the world
  Gee, M. The champion
  Granit, A. "When we produce prostitutes
    and thieves, we shall be a normal
    people!"—Jabotinsky
  Hemingway, E. The battler
  Hemingway, E. Fifty grand
  Hendry, J. F. The disinherited
  Hoch, E. D. The ring with the velvet
    ropes
  Hornung, E. W. A trap to catch a cracks-
    man
  Kiely, B. Eton Crop
  Kittredge, W. Thirty-four seasons of winter
  Lardner, R. Champion
  Monreal, D. N. The eleventh round
  Murphy, M. Lesson number one
  Oates, J. C. Golden gloves

  Salas, F. Kid victory
  Williams, T. One arm
The **boy**. Oates, J. C.
The **boy**. Stead, C.
Boy and girl. Bird, C.
A **boy** and his dog. Ellison, H.
The **boy** and the piano tuner. Fontes, S.
Boy-boy. Motsisi, C.
The **boy** friend. Oates, J. C.
The **boy** from Chillicothe. Flynn, R.
The **boy** from the woods. Savage, R.
A **boy** in search of rest. Hong, S.-W.
A **boy** like Astrid's mother. Briskin, M.
Boy on the loose! Satran, K.
The **boy** on the train. Robinson, A.
BOY SCOUTS
  James, M. R. Wailing well
  Weidman, J. Good man, bad man
  Williamson, J. Jamboree
A **boy** weeps. Jahnn, H. H.
The **boy** who came back from the dead.
    Rodgers, A.
The **boy** who disappeared clouds. Block, L.
The **boy** who drew cats. Hearn, L.
The **boy** who had no jackknife. Rölvaag, O.
    E.
The **boy** who hated girls. Vonnegut, K.
The **boy** who predicted earthquakes. St.
    Clair, M.
The **boy** who read Agatha Christie. Brittain,
    W.
The **boy** who was Astrid's mother. See
    Briskin, M. A boy like Astrid's mother
The **boy** who wouldn't say his name. Nunes,
    S.
Boy with an injured eye. Sheehan, R.
Boy with body. See Woolrich, C. The corpse
    and the kid
Boyd, Catherine
  The wildcat
    When I am an old woman I shall wear
      purple; ed. by S. K. Martz
Boyd, Susan
  Shadows
    Critical Quarterly 29:88-94 Wint '87
Boyd, William, 1952-
  Bat-girl!
    Boyd, W. On the Yankee station
  Bizarre situations
    Boyd, W. On the Yankee station
  The care and attention of swimming pools
    Boyd, W. On the Yankee station
  The coup
    Boyd, W. On the Yankee station
  Extracts from the journal of Flying Officer
    J
    Boyd, W. On the Yankee station
  Gifts
    Boyd, W. On the Yankee station
  Hardly ever
    Boyd, W. On the Yankee station
  Histoire vache
    Boyd, W. On the Yankee station

Boyd, William, 1952—— *Continued*
Killing lizards
    Boyd, W. On the Yankee station
Long story short
    Boyd, W. On the Yankee station
Love hurts
    Boyd, W. On the Yankee station
My girl in skintight jeans
    Boyd, W. On the Yankee station
Next boat from Douala
    Boyd, W. On the Yankee station
Not yet Jayette
    Boyd, W. On the Yankee station
On the Yankee station
    Boyd, W. On the Yankee station
Boyett, Steven R.
The answer tree
    Silver scream; ed. by D. J. Schow
Boyfriends and girlfriends. Dunn, D.
Boylan, Clare
L'amour
    Foreign exchange; ed. by J. Evans
Villa Marta
    P.E.N. new fiction I
Boylan, Eleanor
My daughter, the murderer
    Alfred Hitchcock's Grave suspicions
Boylan, James, 1958-
Aloe: part three: the making of "Aloe"
    Boylan, J. Remind me to murder you
    later
Bride of Frankenstein
    Boylan, J. Remind me to murder you
    later
Day to die
    Boylan, J. Remind me to murder you
    later
Dictionary art review
    Boylan, J. Remind me to murder you
    later
Elvis in space
    Boylan, J. Remind me to murder you
    later
Final exam
    Boylan, J. Remind me to murder you
    later
Fugue for violin and Three Stooges
    Boylan, J. Remind me to murder you
    later
The gissix project
    Boylan, J. Remind me to murder you
    later
Horse year
    Boylan, J. Remind me to murder you
    later
Invisible woman
    Boylan, J. Remind me to murder you
    later
Jimmy Durante lost in Antarctica
    Boylan, J. Remind me to murder you
    later

Lost in space
    Boylan, J. Remind me to murder you
    later
The love starter
    Boylan, J. Remind me to murder you
    later
Pickett's charge
    Boylan, J. Remind me to murder you
    later
Potter's field
    Boylan, J. Remind me to murder you
    later
The rescue
    Boylan, J. Remind me to murder you
    later
The string
    Boylan, J. Remind me to murder you
    later
There's the sea
    Boylan, J. Remind me to murder you
    later
Thirty-six miracles of Lyndon Johnson
    Boylan, J. Remind me to murder you
    later
Weasels
    Boylan, J. Remind me to murder you
    later
Boylan, Roger Brendan
The old guard
    The Literary Review (Madison, N.J.)
    30:595-604 Summ '87
Boyle, Kay, 1902-
Art colony
    Boyle, K. Life being the best & other
    stories
Astronomer's wife
    Boyle, K. Life being the best & other
    stories
Career
    Boyle, K. Life being the best & other
    stories
Convalescence
    Boyle, K. Life being the best & other
    stories
The first lover
    Boyle, K. Life being the best & other
    stories
His idea of a mother
    Boyle, K. Life being the best & other
    stories
I can't get drunk
    Boyle, K. Life being the best & other
    stories
Letters of a lady
    Boyle, K. Life being the best & other
    stories
Life being the best
    Boyle, K. Life being the best & other
    stories
The meeting of the stones
    Boyle, K. Life being the best & other
    stories

Boyle, Kay, 1902-—*Continued*
Men
  The World of the short story; ed. by
    C. Fadiman
On the run
  Twentieth Century Literature 34:258-60
    Fall '88
Peter Foxe
  Boyle, K. Life being the best & other
    stories
To the pure
  Boyle, K. Life being the best & other
    stories
Winter in Italy
  Boyle, K. Life being the best & other
    stories
Boyle, T. Coraghessan
All shook up
  Boyle, T. C. Greasy Lake & other
    stories
A bird in hand
  Boyle, T. C. Greasy Lake & other
    stories
Caviar
  Boyle, T. C. Greasy Lake & other
    stories
  The Pushcart prize IX
The Devil and Irv Cherniske
  The Antioch Review 46:413-27 Fall '88
Greasy Lake
  The Art of the tale; ed. by D. Halpern
  Boyle, T. C. Greasy Lake & other
    stories
The hat
  The Editors' choice v3; ed. by G. E.
    Murphy, Jr.
The Hector Quesadilla story
  Boyle, T. C. Greasy Lake & other
    stories
  The Paris Review 26:253-66 Fall '84
  The Pushcart prize X
The hit man
  Sudden fiction; ed. by R. Shapard and
    J. Thomas
I dated Jane Austen
  The Georgia Review 40:52-6 Spr '86
  Necessary fictions; ed. by S. W. Lind-
    berg and S. Corey
If the river was whiskey
  Gentlemen's Quarterly 58:161-2+ Je '88
Ike and Nina
  Boyle, T. C. Greasy Lake & other
    stories
The New Moon Party
  Boyle, T. C. Greasy Lake & other
    stories
Not a leg to stand on
  Boyle, T. C. Greasy Lake & other
    stories
On for the long haul
  Boyle, T. C. Greasy Lake & other
    stories

Esquire 103:136-42+ F '85
  The Esquire fiction reader v2
  Soldiers & civilians; ed. by T. Jenks
The overcoat II
  Boyle, T. C. Greasy Lake & other
    stories
Rara avis
  Boyle, T. C. Greasy Lake & other
    stories
Rupert Beersley and the beggar master of
    Sivani-Hoota
  The Antioch Review 43:158-74 Spr '85
  Boyle, T. C. Greasy Lake & other
    stories
Sinking house
  The Atlantic 261:53-9 F '88
Sorry fugu
  Harper's 275:50-7 O '87
Stones in my passway, hellhound on my
    trail
  Boyle, T. C. Greasy Lake & other
    stories
Two ships
  Boyle, T. C. Greasy Lake & other
    stories
Urban renewal
  Omni (New York, N.Y.) 11:98-100+ O
    '88
We are Norsemen
  New American short stories; ed. by G.
    Norris
Whales weep
  Boyle, T. C. Greasy Lake & other
    stories
BOYS
  See also Adolescence; Children;
    Youth
Anaya, R. A. Bless me, Ultima [excerpt]
Anthony, P. Wood you?
Armstrong, C. The enemy
Asimov, I. Potential
Asimov, I. The ugly little boy
Asscher-Pinkhof, C. After eight
Austin, M. H. The Basket Woman: first
    story
Austin, M. H. The Basket Woman: second
    story
Barich, B. Giorgio's mother
Barnard, R. Little Terror
Barth, J. Water-message
Baukin, L. Jar-boy
Baxter, C. The cliff
Baxter, C. Talk show
Bear, G. If I die before I wake
Benedict, P. Town smokes
Benedict, P. Water witch
Benét, S. V. The die-hard
Benson, P. Alan
Bishop, M. A gift from the GrayLanders
Bitov, A. The leg
Blei, N. Stars
Blew, M. C. Forby and the Mayan
    maidens

BOYS—*Continued*

Blythe, R. Immediate possession
Blythe, R. The packhorse path
Böll, H. Recollections of a young king
Bonosky, P. Home for supper
Bonosky, P. A sweet tooth
Bowen, E. The visitor
Boyd, W. Killing lizards
Boylan, J. Invisible woman
Boyle, K. Career
Boyle, K. His idea of a mother
Boyle, K. Life being the best
Bradbury, R. Colonel Stonesteel's genuine home-made truly Egyptian mummy
Bradbury, R. The last circus
Brooks, J. I'll fight you
Brown, G. M. The lost boy
Brown, G. M. Men and gold and bread
Bukoski, A. Great sea battles
Bukoski, A. True adventures
Burke, J. L. Losses
Buzzati, D. The bewitched bourgeois
Byatt, A. S. The July ghost
Caldwell, P. A sense of place
Calvino, I. Big fish, little fish
Calvino, I. A ship loaded with crabs
Cameron, P. Homework
Card, O. S. America
Carlson, R. Air
Chappell, F. Children of strikers
Chase, V. The search
Chavez, A. The Tesuque Pony Express
Chernoff, M. Two times two
Choyce, L. Major repairs
Clark, M. Discovery
Clark, M. A long time ago
Colter, C. The frog hunters
Connelly, J. Foreign objects
Conroy, J. Down in Happy Hollow
Cook, H. Clown
Cowan, P. A window in Mrs X's place
Crabtree, L. V. The Jake Pond
Crabtree, L. V. Little Jesus
Crane, S. The carriage-lamps
Crane, S. The city urchin and the chaste villagers
Crane, S. The fight
Crane, S. A great mistake
Crane, S. His new mittens
Crane, S. The lover and the tell-tale
Crane, S. Lynx-hunting
Crane, S. Shame
Crane, S. "Showin' off"
Crane, S. The trial, execution, and burial of Homer Phelps
Creekmore, H. The chain in the heart [excerpt]
Dahl, R. The wish
Davis, R. H. Gallegher
Deal, B. Antaeus
Dickinson, C. The fire
Dixon, M. Red leaves
DuBois, B. Final marks, final secrets

Dubus, A. Delivering
Dubus, A. Sorrowful mysteries
Dumas, H. Echo tree
Dumas, H. A Harlem game
Dumas, H. Rain god
Dumas, H. Thrust counter thrust
Dunn, D. Bobby's room
Dunn, D. Something for little Robert
Dunsany, E. J. M. D. P., Baron. The pirate of the Round Pond
Durban, P. World of women
Dybek, S. Hot ice
Eldridge, M. The sea
Elkin, S. A poetics for bullies
Ellin, S. The day of the bullet
Fairman, P. W. The dark road home
Fante, J. Altar boy
Fante, J. Big leaguer
Fante, J. First Communion
Fante, J. In the spring
Fante, J. My mother's goofy song
Fante, J. The Road to Hell
Farmer, B. Milk
Faust, I. Simon Girty go ape
Federspiel, J. Death of a foal
Fenton, E. Gun-shy
Ferreira, R. Dream with no name
Fisher, R. Ezekiel
Fisher, R. Ezekiel learns
Fox, J. Over the Pyrenees
Freeman, C. Dreaming of Africa
Furlong, M. The drum
Gaitens, E. Growing up
Gardner, M. Private Eye Oglesby
Garrett, G. P. The test
Gault, W. C. The threatening three
Gee, M. Schooldays
Giardinelli, M. Revolution on a bicycle
Gold, H. Child of embassy
González, C. A. Toño
Gooch, B. Spring
Gould, R. The child and the poet
Granberry, E. A trip to Czardis
Granit, A. Songs my mother taught me that are not in Hamlet; or, "Come into my house, Horatio! there are more things under the mattress than are dreamt of in your philosophy!"
Granit, A. Usher
Greene, G. The basement room
Greene, G. The destructor
Greene, G. I spy
Griesemer, J. Comfort stations
Gustafsson, L. Greatness strikes where it pleases
Gustafsson, L. The truly great strikes wherever it wants
Haldeman, J. C. Playing for keeps
Harington, D. Beginning
Harris, M. Little Eddy
Hawthorne, N. The gentle boy
Hemingway, E. A day's wait
Hemley, R. The mouse town

BOYS—*Continued*

Henderson, D. The test
Henderson, Z. Stevie and The Dark
Hill, B. Lizards
Holder, N. Moving night
Holditch, W. K. One of these mornings
Jahnn, H. H. A boy weeps
Kavaler, R. Depression glass
Kawabata, Y. Up in the tree
Keller, D. H. The lost language
Kiely, B. The jeweller's boy
Klíma, I. Monday morning: a black market tale
Kornblatt, J. R. Daniel
Kramer, K. Seeds of conflict
Kump, E. G. Everncere
Lavin, M. The living
Law, W. Lincoln's doctor's son's dog
Lee, A. The ride
Leedom-Ackerman, J. Sissy Mamma's wig
Leonard, H. The anticlerical pup
Liben, M. Homage to Benny Leonard
Lish, G. The death of me
Lish, G. Fish story
Lish, G. Guilt
Lispector, C. The evolution of myopia
Livesey, M. The salt course
Loesch, C. Horse story
Long, F. B. The Mississippi saucer
MacDonald, J. D. Looie follows me
MacLaverty, B. The deep end
MacLaverty, B. More than just the disease
Marshall, O. The master of big jingles
Martínez-Serros, H. The birthday present
Martínez-Serros, H. The last laugh
Martínez-Serros, H. Octavo
Martínez-Serros, H. Ricardo's war
Mathers, P. A change for the better
Maupassant, G. de. Simon's papa
Mazel, D. The angel's overcoat
Mazel, D. Choosing
Mazel, D. A crossing
Mazel, D. Jeopardies
Mazel, D. A matter of pride
Mazel, D. Sprucy wages
Mazel, D. When you swing upon a star
McCann, R. My mother's clothes: the school of beauty and shame
McCulla, J. How Esco Mize got religion
McCullers, C. Sucker
McGarry, J. Providence, 1957: an accident
McGarvey, C. Sense of wonder, sense of awe
McGrath, W. M. The evening of Mr. Boch's baloney factory
McGuane, T. A skirmish
McGuane, T. Sportsmen
McKnight, R. Getting to be like the studs
Meinke, P. The ponoes
Michaels, L. Murderers
Mills, W. To pass him out
Mordden, E. The right boy for Cosgrove
Morris, W. Good old boy [excerpt]

Morris, W. A fight between a white boy and a black boy in the dusk of a fall afternoon in Omaha, Nebraska
Mrożek, S. A confession about Bobby
Mukherjee, B. The imaginary assassin
Nagibin, IŪ. M. Winter oak
Narayan, R. K. Crime and punishment
Narayan, R. K. Dodu
Ndebele, N. The prophetess
Ndebele, N. The test
Ndebele, N. Uncle
Nérault, F. The dusty sunbeam
Nordan, L. The Sears and Roebuck catalog game
Nordan, L. Sugar among the chickens
Nordan, L. Sugar, the eunuchs, and Big G.B.
Nordan, L. The talker at the freak-show
Norris, L. Blackberries
Norris, L. Some opposites of good
Norris, L. The wind, the cold wind
Nugent, B. City of boys
O, Y. The bird of passage
Oates, J. C. Only son
O'Connor, F. An afternoon in the woods
O'Connor, F. A circle in the fire
O'Connor, F. The river
O'Connor, F. The turkey
O'Connor, F. A set of variations on a borrowed theme
Olmstead, R. River dogs
Osier, J. The ritual
Pacheco, J. E. The sunken park
Padilla, M. Papel
Parise, G. Hotel
Parise, G. Mother
Parise, G. War
Pavese, C. First love
Pavese, C. The name
Peden, W. The hatchet man in the lighthouse
Phelan, F. The battle of boiling water
Phillips, J. A. Machine dreams [excerpt]
Pilcher, R. Toby
Poole, F. F. Airmen
Povod, R. Things to do today
Powell, P. Edisto [excerpt]
Price, R. Michael Egerton
Pronzini, B. The storm tunnel
Pulaski, J. Don Juan, the senior citizen
Purdy, J. Sleep tight
Rambach, P. Home
Rice, J. The Idol of the Flies
Ríos, A. The iguana killer
Rölvaag, O. E. The boy who had no jackknife
Rosenfeld, I. The world of the ceiling
Roth, P. The conversion of the Jews
Sams, F. Run with the horsemen [excerpt]
Sandel, C. The flight to America
Saroyan, W. The beautiful white horse
Saroyan, W. Picnic time
Schwartz, S. I can't sleep anymore

BOYS—*Continued*
Selmi, H. Distant seas
Sexson, L. Turning
Shannon, D. Flash attachment
Shaw, I. Peter Two
Sheckley, R. The swamp
Skrzynecki, P. The black madonna
Skrzynecki, P. The Superman t-shirt
Smith, P. D. Forever Island [excerpt]
Soldatow, S. White noise
Spielberg, P. Prognosis
St. Clair, M. The listening child
Stead, C. A little demon
Stead, C. Trains
Stern, S. The gramophone
Stern, S. Moishe the Just
Stewart, J. I. M. Parlour 4
Stewart, J. I. M. Sweets from a stranger
Street, J. Weep no more, my lady
Strieber, W. The pool
Sturgeon, T. Shadow, shadow on the wall
Sultan, M. The butterfly collector
Tamer, Z. The enemy
Taylor, P. H. Two ladies in retirement
Thomas, A. C. Local customs
Thomas, D. The fight
Thomas, D. The followers
Thomas, D. The peaches
Thomas, D. A prospect of the sea
Tournier, M. Prikli
Tuohy, F. Live bait
Updike, D. The cushion of time
Vanderhaeghe, G. How the story ends
Vanderhaeghe, G. The watcher
Warren, J. Last Chance
Weaver, G. Some killers
Webb, S. A demon in rosewood
Wegner, H. Butcher's beguine
Welch, D. The barn
Welch, D. The coffin on the hill
Welch, D. Narcissus bay
Welch, D. A picture in the snow
Welch, D. The trout stream
Wells, H. G. The beautiful suit
Wexler, J. A small crime
Willson, H. A Christmas tale
Wolfe, G. War beneath the tree
Wolfe, T. No cure for it
Wolfe, T. Three o'clock
Woolrich, C. Fire escape
Wright, R. Big boy leaves home
Young, A. Snakes [excerpt]
Zalygin, S. The night of the angels
Boys. Gordon, P.
The **boys**. Heynen, J.
Boys and music. Vreuls, D.
The **boys** in the bars. Davis, C.
The **boys** of Bensonhurst. La Puma, S.
Boys who do the bop. Rofihe, R.
BP. Klinkowitz, J.
The **bracelet**. Colette
The **bracelet**. Meinke, P.
The **bracelet**. Sandel, C.

Bracken, Michael
Of memories dying
    Midnight; ed. by C. L. Grant
Bradbury, Malcolm, 1932-
Composition
    The Penguin book of modern British
    short stories
Bradbury, Ray, 1920-
And so died Riabouchinska
    Hitchcock in prime time; ed. by F. M.
    Nevins and M. H. Greenberg
    Masterpieces of mystery and suspense;
    ed. by M. H. Greenberg
The April witch
    The Saturday Evening Post 257:48-51
    My/Je '85
    Young witches & warlocks; ed. by I.
    Asimov; M. H. Greenberg and C. G.
    Waugh
At midnight, in the month of June
    Bradbury, R. The Toynbee convector
Banshee
    Bradbury, R. The Toynbee convector
The beggar on Dublin Bridge
    The Saturday Evening Post 257:48-51+
    Ja/F '85
Bless me, Father, for I have sinned
    Bradbury, R. The Toynbee convector
By the numbers!
    Bradbury, R. The Toynbee convector
The candy skull
    Bradbury, R. A memory of murder
A careful man dies
    Bradbury, R. A memory of murder
Chrysalis
    Amazing science fiction anthology: The
    wild years, 1946-1955; ed. by M. H.
    Greenberg
Colonel Stonesteel's genuine home-made
    truly Egyptian mummy
    Bradbury, R. The Toynbee convector
Omni book of science fiction 2
Come, and bring Constance!
    Bradbury, R. The Toynbee convector
Corpse carnival
    Bradbury, R. A memory of murder
The crowd
    The Dark descent; ed. by D. G. Hart-
    well
The dead man
    Masters of darkness; ed. by D. Etchison
Dead men rise up never
    Bradbury, R. A memory of murder
The dwarf
    The Penguin book of horror stories
The emissary
    Roger Caras' Treasury of great dog
    stories
Four-way funeral
    Bradbury, R. A memory of murder
Good-by, Grandma
    The Saturday Evening Post 260:62-3+
    Jl/Ag '88

Bradbury, Ray, 1920——_Continued_
Hail and farewell
  Young mutants; ed. by I. Asimov; M.
    H. Greenberg and C. G. Waugh
Half-pint homicide
  Bradbury, R. A memory of murder
Hell's half hour
  Bradbury, R. A memory of murder
Homecoming
  Young monsters; ed. by I. Asimov; M.
    H. Greenberg and C. G. Waugh
I, rocket
  Amazing science fiction anthology: The
    war years, 1936-1945; ed. by M. H.
    Greenberg
I see you never
  Sudden fiction; ed. by R. Shapard and
    J. Thomas
I suppose you are wondering why we are
    here?
  Bradbury, R. The Toynbee convector
  Omni (New York, N.Y.) 7:64-5+ O '84
"I'm not so dumb!"
  Bradbury, R. A memory of murder
It burns me up!
  Bradbury, R. A memory of murder
Junior
  Bradbury, R. The Toynbee convector
Lafayette, farewell
  Bradbury, R. The Toynbee convector
The lake
  Young ghosts; ed. by I. Asimov; M. H.
    Greenberg and C. G. Waugh
The last circus
  Bradbury, R. The Toynbee convector
The Laurel and Hardy love affair
  Bradbury, R. The Toynbee convector
  Reader's Digest 133:149-52 S '88
Long division
  Bradbury, R. The Toynbee convector
The long night
  Bradbury, R. A memory of murder
The long way home
  Bradbury, R. A memory of murder
The love affair
  Bradbury, R. The Toynbee convector
  The Planets; ed. by B. Preiss
On the Orient, North
  Bradbury, R. The Toynbee convector
One for his lordship, and one for the
    road!
  Bradbury, R. The Toynbee convector
One night in your life
  Bradbury, R. The Toynbee convector
The playground
  Black water; ed. by A. Manguel
  Ready or not; ed. by J. Kahn
Promises, promises
  Bradbury, R. The Toynbee convector
The screaming woman
  Reader's Digest 124:119-23 My '84

Skeleton
  Venomous tales of villainy and
    vengeance; ed. by H. Hoke
The small assassin
  Bradbury, R. A memory of murder
There will come soft rains
  Beyond Armageddon; ed. by W. M. Mil-
    ler and M. H. Greenberg
The thing at the top of the stairs
  Bradbury, R. The Toynbee convector
To the Chicago Abyss
  Beyond Armageddon; ed. by W. M. Mil-
    ler and M. H. Greenberg
The tombstone
  Bradbury, R. The Toynbee convector
A touch of petulance
  Bradbury, R. The Toynbee convector
The Toynbee convector
  Bradbury, R. The Toynbee convector
Trapdoor
  Bradbury, R. The Toynbee convector
  Omni (New York, N.Y.) 7:58-60+ Ap '85
The trunk lady
  Bradbury, R. A memory of murder
Uncle Elinar
  Masterpieces of fantasy and enchant-
    ment; ed. by D. G. Hartwell
Undersea guardians
  Mysterious sea stories; ed. by W. Pat-
    trick
Wake for the living
  Bradbury, R. A memory of murder
West of October
  Bradbury, R. The Toynbee convector
The wind
  The Penguin book of ghost stories
Yesterday I lived!
  Bradbury, R. A memory of murder
  Great detectives; ed. by D. W. McCul-
    lough
Braddon, M. E. (Mary Elizabeth), 1835-1915
Good Lady Ducayne
  Vampires; ed. by A. Ryan
The shadow in the corner
  The Oxford book of English ghost
    stories
Braddon, Mary Elizabeth _See_ Braddon, M.
    E. (Mary Elizabeth), 1835-1915
Bradfield, Scott
The dream of the wolf
  Omni (New York, N.Y.) 10:42-4+ Jl '88
The Flash! Kid
  Interzone: the first anthology; ed. by J.
    Clute; C. Greenland and D. Pringle
Unmistakably the finest
  Interzone: the 2nd anthology; ed. by J.
    Clute; D. Pringle and S. Ounsley
Bradley, David, 1950-
197903042100 (Sunday)
  Our roots grow deeper than we know;
    ed. by L. Gutkind

Bradley, Jane
Mistletoe
The Virginia Quarterly Review 62:695-705 Aut '86
Twirling
The North American Review 271:42-5 D '86
Bradley, John Ed
Tupelo nights
Esquire 109:170-2+ My '88
Bradley, Marion Zimmer
Bird of prey
Bradley, M. Z. The best of Marion Zimmer Bradley
Blood will tell
Bradley, M. Z. The best of Marion Zimmer Bradley
Centaurus changeling
Bradley, M. Z. The best of Marion Zimmer Bradley
The climbing wave
Bradley, M. Z. The best of Marion Zimmer Bradley
The day of the butterflies
Bradley, M. Z. The best of Marion Zimmer Bradley
Death between the stars
Bradley, M. Z. The best of Marion Zimmer Bradley
A dozen of everything
100 great fantasy short short stories; ed. by I. Asimov; T. Carr and M. H. Greenberg
Elbow room
Bradley, M. Z. The best of Marion Zimmer Bradley
The engine
Bradley, M. Z. The best of Marion Zimmer Bradley
Exiles of tomorrow
Bradley, M. Z. The best of Marion Zimmer Bradley
Hero's moon
Bradley, M. Z. The best of Marion Zimmer Bradley
The jewel of Arwen
Bradley, M. Z. The best of Marion Zimmer Bradley
Sea wrack
Moonsinger's friends; ed by S. Shwartz
The secret of the Blue Star
Bradley, M. Z. The best of Marion Zimmer Bradley
To keep the oath
Bradley, M. Z. The best of Marion Zimmer Bradley
Worlds apart; ed. by C. Decarnin; E. Garber and L. Paleo
Treason of the blood
Bradley, M. Z. The best of Marion Zimmer Bradley

The wild one
Bradley, M. Z. The best of Marion Zimmer Bradley
The wind people
Bradley, M. Z. The best of Marion Zimmer Bradley
Brady, Maureen
Care in the holding
Brady, M. The question she put to herself
Chiggers
Brady, M. The question she put to herself
Corsage
Brady, M. The question she put to herself
Early autumn exchange
Brady, M. The question she put to herself
The field is full of daisies and I'm afraid to pass
Brady, M. The question she put to herself
Grinning underneath
Brady, M. The question she put to herself
Novena
Brady, M. The question she put to herself
On the way to the ERA
Brady, M. The question she put to herself
The question she put to herself
Brady, M. The question she put to herself
Seneca morning
Brady, M. The question she put to herself
Strike it rich
Brady, M. The question she put to herself
Wilderness journal
Brady, M. The question she put to herself
Brady. Bell, M.
Brag dog. Bell, V.
BRAIN
Silverberg, R. In the House of Double Minds
Experiments
Dick, P. K. Rautavaara's case
Gansovsky, S. A part of the world
Surgery
Crehan, S. The operation
Gloss, M. Interlocking pieces
Stýblová, V. Scalpel, please
Brains. Givner, J.
The **brains** of rats. Blumlein, M.
BRAINWASHING
Morrow, J. Veritas
Zahn, T. Return to the fold

BRAKHAGE, STAN
About
Doubiago, S. The art of seeing with one's own eyes
Braly, David
The gallowglass
The Year's best mystery and suspense stories, 1987
Bramah, Ernest, 1868-1942
The coin of Dionysius
The Penguin classic crime omnibus
Brami's view. Muschg, A.
Brand, Christianna, 1907-
Bless this house
The Mammoth book of modern crime stories; ed. by G. Hardinge
Double cross
Ellery Queen's Prime crimes
The whispering
John Creasey's Crime collection, 1985
Brand, Max, 1892-1944
See also Faust, Frederick, 1892-1944
Cayenne Charlie
Brand, M. Max Brand's Best western stories v2
Crazy rhythm
Brand, M. Max Brand's Best western stories v3
Dark Rosaleen
Brand, M. Max Brand's Best western stories v2
Dust storm
Brand, M. Max Brand's Best western stories v3
The fear of Morgan the Fearless
Brand, M. Max Brand's Best western stories v2
The golden day
Brand, M. Max Brand's Best western stories v2
Half a partner
Brand, M. Max Brand's Best western stories v3
The laughter of Slim Malone
Wild westerns; ed. by B. Pronzini
A lucky dog
Brand, M. Max Brand's Best western stories v3
Outcast [Variant title: Outcast breed]
Brand, M. Max Brand's Best western stories v2
Reata's peril trek
Brand, M. Max Brand's Best western stories v3
The sun stood still
Brand, M. Max Brand's Best western stories v3
Westeryear; ed. by E. Gorman
The third bullet
Brand, M. Max Brand's Best western stories v3

Brandão, Ignácio de Loyola, 1936-
The man who saw the lizard eat his child
The Literary Review (Madison, N.J.) 27:440-1 Summ '84
The men who discovered forbidden chairs
The Literary Review (Madison, N.J.) 27:437-9 Summ '84
Brandis, Madzy Brender à *See* Brender à Brandis, Madzy
Brandner, Gary
The pigeon hunters
Murder California style; ed. by J. L. Breen and J. Ball
Brandt, Pamela
L.A. child
The Pushcart prize IX
Branham, R. V.
In the sickbay
L. Ron Hubbard presents Writers of the future v3
Brantingham, Juleen
Giraffe Tuesday
Universe 15
Lobotomy shoals
Omni book of science fiction 2
Brasch, Charles
Dunedin
Echad 4: Jewish writing from down under: Australia and New Zealand
Brashler, Anne
Sheets
The Literary Review (Madison, N.J.) 31:195-8 Wint '88
The brass monkey. Sladek, J. T.
Brass on the cannons. Sheiner, R.
Brat. Sturgeon, T.
Braun, Lilian Jackson
The sin of Madame Phloi
Roger Caras' Treasury of great cat stories
Braund, Mary
What's on the telly tonight?
Ellery Queen's Crimes and punishments
Brautigan, Richard
1/3, 1/3, 1/3
American short story masterpieces; ed. by R. Carver and T. Jenks
Revenge of the lawn
The Norton book of American short stories
About
Kinsella, W. P. The resurrection of Trout-fishing in America Shorty
Brave and cruel. Welch, D.
The bravest rat in Venice. Highsmith, P.
The brazen locked room. Asimov, I.
BRAZIL
Amado, J. The lights of the carrousel
Fonseca, R. The game of dead men
Lispector, C. Journey to Petrópolis
Machado, A. M. The piano
Ribeiro, J. U. Alaindelon de la Patrie
Waugh, E. The man who liked Dickens

BRAZIL—*Continued*
Wells, H. G. The empire of the ants
Plantation life
See Plantation life—Brazil
Breach of promise. West, J.
Breach of the peace. Gilbert, M.
Bread alone. O'Hara, J.
Bread and butter questions. Koch, C.
Bread and hunger. Taylor, A.
Bread from stones. Garrett, G. P.
The **break**. MacLaverty, B.
Break and enter. Rooke, L.
Break it down. Davis, L.
Break-up. Matheson, R. C.
Breakage. Choyce, L.
Breakdown. Asscher-Pinkhof, C.
Breakfast at twilight. Dick, P. K.
Breakfast, lunch, and dinner. Rossi, A.
Breakfast with the Murgatroyds. Sladek, J. T.
BREAKFASTS
Sladek, J. T. Breakfast with the Murgatroyds
Breaking off. Hood, H.
Breaking strain. Clarke, A. C.
Breaking the ice. Thomas, A. C.
Breaking the news. Böll, H.
Breaking the news to Doll. Kauffman, J.
Breaking the rules. Hegi, U.
A **breaking** wave. Warner, S. T.
Breaking with Brezhnev. Cullen, E. J.
BREAST
Radiography
See Mammography
Breath from the sky. McCullers, C.
A **breath** of air. Pirandello, L.
Breath of God. Martini, C.
A **breath** of Lucifer. Narayan, R. K.
Breathing Jesus. Hempel, A.
Breathless. Anderman, J.
Breault, Mary Elsbury
Speeding
Mademoiselle 91:146+ S '85
Breckenridge and the continuum. Silverberg, R.
"**Breeds** there a man . . . .?". Asimov, I.
Breen, Jon L., 1943-
The adventure of the unique Holmes
The New adventures of Sherlock Holmes; ed. by M. H. Greenberg and C. L. R. Waugh
All-star team
Murder California style; ed. by J. L. Breen and J. Ball
Malice at the mike
Murder and mystery in Chicago; ed. by C. R. Waugh; F. D. McSherry and M. H. Greenberg
Starstruck
Murder in Los Angeles; ed. by J. L. Breen and others
A thumb on the scales
Winter's crimes 17

Brember. Thomas, D.
Brenda. St. Clair, M.
Brender à Brandis, Madzy
All that counts
Brender à Brandis, M. The scent of spruce
Fall fair
Brender à Brandis, M. The scent of spruce
Foreigner in the family
Brender à Brandis, M. The scent of spruce
The little old Dutch church bell
Brender à Brandis, M. The scent of spruce
The living Christmas tree
Brender à Brandis, M. The scent of spruce
To grow into a man
Brender à Brandis, M. The scent of spruce
Brennan, Dan
The trouble shooters
A Matter of crime v1
Brennan, Joseph Payne, 1918-
Canavan's back yard
Yankee witches; ed. by C. G. Waugh; M. H. Greenberg and F. D. McSherry
Mrs. Clendon's place
Shadows 7
An ordinary brick house
Shadows 9
Rhea
After midnight; ed. by C. L. Grant
Road to Granville
Midnight; ed. by C. L. Grant
Brenner, Gerry, 1937-
A letter to Nick Carraway: fifty years after
Michigan Quarterly Review 23:196-206 Spr '84
Brenner's dream. Liben, M.
Brentano, Clemens, 1778-1842
The story of good Caspar and fair Annie [Variant title: The story of Honest Casper and Fair Annie]
German romantic stories; ed. by F. G. Ryder
Brethren. Keillor, G.
The **Bretnall** feud. Frazee, S.
Bretnor, Reginald
Dr. Birdmouse
Fantastic stories; ed. by M. H. Greenberg and P. L. Price
Markham
After midnight; ed. by C. L. Grant
No other gods
Midnight; ed. by C. L. Grant
Brett, Michael *See* Tripp, Miles, 1923-
Brett, Sally A.
My mother's secret life
Mademoiselle 94:89-92+ Jl '88

Brett, Simon, 1945-
Big Boy, Little Boy
  Brett, S. Tickled to death, and other
    stories of crime and suspense
Don't know much about art
  Brett, S. Tickled to death, and other
    stories of crime and suspense
  The Mammoth book of modern crime
    stories; ed. by G. Hardinge
  Winter's crimes 16
Double glazing
  Brett, S. Tickled to death, and other
    stories of crime and suspense
The girls in Villa Costas
  Brett, S. Tickled to death, and other
    stories of crime and suspense
The haunted actress
  Brett, S. Tickled to death, and other
    stories of crime and suspense
How's your mother?
  Brett, S. Tickled to death, and other
    stories of crime and suspense
Letter to his son
  Winter's crimes 18
The nuggy bar [Variant title: Metaphor for
    murder]
  Brett, S. Tickled to death, and other
    stories of crime and suspense
  Masterpieces of mystery and suspense;
    ed. by M. H. Greenberg
Parking space
  Brett, S. Tickled to death, and other
    stories of crime and suspense
Private areas
  Brett, S. Tickled to death, and other
    stories of crime and suspense
The thirteenth killer
  Brett, S. Tickled to death, and other
    stories of crime and suspense
  John Creasey's Crime collection, 1986
Tickled to death
  Brett, S. Tickled to death, and other
    stories of crime and suspense
Unwilling sleep
  Brett, S. Tickled to death, and other
    stories of crime and suspense
Breuer, Miles J.
The gostak and the doshes
  Amazing stories: 60 years of the best
    science fiction
Brewer, Gil, d. 1983
Fool's gold
  Alfred Hitchcock's Mortal errors
Brewster, Elizabeth, 1922-
Golden anniversary
  The Old dance; ed. by B. Burnard
The **Brewster** family time capsule. Franzen,
  B.
Brězan, Jurij
How Krabat lost Smjala
  Voices East and West: German short
    stories since 1945

BREZHNEV, LEONID IL'ICH, 1906-1982
About
Ferguson, N. The Monroe Doctrine
Brian. Jacobson, D.
Brian 'Squizzy' Taylor. Costello, M.
BRIBERY
Auchincloss, L. The Fabbri tape
Nowakowski, M. Little sunshine
Yang, K. Mother Goose gets married
Bribery and corruption. Rendell, R.
Bric-à-brac. Maupassant, G. de
Brickhouse, Robert
Blue
  The Virginia Quarterly Review 64:695-
    704 Aut '88
Bricklayer in the snow. Fante, J.
BRICKLAYERS
Conroy, J. The demon bricksetter from
  Williamson County
Fante, J. Bricklayer in the snow
The **bridal** party. Fitzgerald, F. S.
The **bride.** Skelton, R.
The **bride** comes to Yellow Sky. Crane, S.
Bride Michael. Blythe, R.
The **bride** of Ambrose. Freeman, C.
The **bride** of Bigfoot. Reed, K.
The **bride** of Far-away. Prichard, K. S.
Bride of Frankenstein. Boylan, J.
The **bride** of the grave. See Tieck, J. L.
  Wake not the dead
Bride of the thing. Barnes, C.
The **bride** wore red. Sethi, R. C.
The **bridegroom.** Gordimer, N.
Brides of the pleiades. Sinclair, I.
Bridge, Ann, 1889-1974
The Buick saloon
  The Penguin book of ghost stories
BRIDGE (GAME)
Ingalls, R. On ice
The **bridge.** Angel, G.
The **bridge.** Anthony, P.
The **bridge.** Dixon, S.
The **bridge.** Ferron, J.
The **bridge.** Painter, P.
Bridge of music, river of sand. Goyen, W.
The **Bridge** of Sighs. Gordon, P.
The **bridge** sings. Richards, J.
BRIDGES
Austin, D. He was there when they came
  across the bridge on their bicycles
Chekhov, A. P. New villa
Goyen, W. Bridge of music, river of sand
Marshall, O. The master of big jingles
BRIDGETOWN (BARBADOS) *See* Bar-
  bados—Bridgetown
Bridgework. Cullen, E. J.
Bridging. Apple, M.
Brief miracle (Virginia). Mohr, N.
A **brief** spell by the river. McElroy, C. J.
Briefs, E. Castendyk
'Half Chick'
  Commonweal 112:522-3 O 4 '85
The **brigade** commander. De Forest, J. W.

BRIGANDS AND ROBBERS
See also Outlaws; Robbery
Andrić, I. Thirst
Cho, H.-I. Iron masks
Hoch, E. D. The most dangerous man
O'Donnell, P. A better day to die
Prose, F. The bandit was my neighbor
Roberts, K. The Lady Margaret
Russ, J. The man who could not see devils
Simon, B. The fourth day of Christmas
Stoker, B. The burial of the rats

Brigham, Besmilr
Lopez and the Maya bull
The Southern Review (Baton Rouge, La.) 20:167-87 Ja '84
The lottery drawing
Mississippi writers v1: Fiction; ed. by D. Abbott

Bright burning tiger. Lee, T.
Bright-eyed black pony. Springer, N.
The **bright** illusion. Moore, C. L.
Bright segment. Sturgeon, T.
Brighten's sister-in-law. Lawson, H.
Brightness falls from the air. St. Clair, M.
BRIGHTON (ENGLAND) See England—Brighton
The **Brighton** Belle. King, F. H.
The **brilliant** leaves. Gordon, C.

Brin, David
Bubbles
The Universe; ed. by B. Preiss
The fourth vocation of George Gustaf
Isaac Asimov's Tomorrow's voices
Thor meets Captain America
Hitler victorious; ed. by G. Benford and M. H. Greenberg
The warm space
Great science fiction; ed. by I. Asimov; M. H. Greenberg and C. G. Waugh

Bring back the cat! Hill, R.
Bringing the news. Hunnicutt, E.
The **brink** of darkness. Winters, Y.

Brinsmead, H. F. (Hesba Fay), 1922-
The twilight road
Young ghosts; ed. by I. Asimov; M. H. Greenberg and C. G. Waugh

Brinsmead, Hesba Fay See Brinsmead, H. F. (Hesba Fay), 1922-

Brint, Steven
Notes on veritarian bookfighting
TriQuarterly no72:91-101 Spr/Summ '88

Briskin, Mae, 1924-
Before and after Celeste
Briskin, M. A boy like Astrid's mother
A boy like Astrid's mother [Variant title: The boy who was Astrid's mother]
Briskin, M. A boy like Astrid's mother
By evil and kindness
Briskin, M. A boy like Astrid's mother
Children, dogs and dying men
Briskin, M. A boy like Astrid's mother

Florence, May '86
Briskin, M. A boy like Astrid's mother
Giant sequoia
Briskin, M. A boy like Astrid's mother
The kid
Briskin, M. A boy like Astrid's mother
Marshall in Rome
Briskin, M. A boy like Astrid's mother
My father and Signor Corelli
Briskin, M. A boy like Astrid's mother
Present tense
Briskin, M. A boy like Astrid's mother
Preservation
Briskin, M. A boy like Astrid's mother
Theresa McCann and Joe
Briskin, M. A boy like Astrid's mother
Two hours in the life of Steven Malinowski
Briskin, M. A boy like Astrid's mother
Two women, one child
Briskin, M. A boy like Astrid's mother
Vincenzo and Giulia
Briskin, M. A boy like Astrid's mother

BRITISH
Afghanistan
Kipling, R. East and West
Africa
Annan, K. Ding dong bell
Boyd, W. Killing lizards
Conrad, J. An outpost of progress
Greene, G. A chance for Mr. Lever
Haggard, H. R. Black heart and white heart
Hill, R. The worst crime known to man
Jones, E. D. A man can try
Markham, B. Appointment in Khartoum
Mortimer, J. C. Rumpole and the golden thread
Rendell, R. The fever tree
Spark, M. Bang-bang you're dead
Spark, M. The go-away bird
Thomas, A. C. Degrees
Arabian Peninsula
Kilworth, G. Spiral sands
Argentina
Borges, J. L. Story of the warrior and the captive
Australia
Doyle, Sir A. C. Bones. The April fool of Harvey's Sluice
Jolley, E. Mr. Parker's valentine
London, J. First night
Loukakis, A. The jigsaw puzzle
Ribeyro, J. R. The double
Austria
Boyle, K. Peter Foxe
Clift, C. Wild Emperor
Doyle, Sir A. C. A pastoral horror
Le Fanu, J. S. Carmilla
Borneo
Maugham, W. S. Before the party
Canada
Callaghan, M. Last spring they came over

BRITISH—Canada—*Continued*
Ferron, J. Chronicle of Anse Saint-Roch
Harrison, S. F. The idyl of the island
China
Bridge, A. The Buick saloon
Maugham, W. S. The taipan
Welch, D. The coffin on the hill
Dominica
Rhys, J. Fishy waters
East Africa
Markham, B. He was a good lion
Egypt
Pynchon, T. Under the rose
France
Boyd, W. Gifts
Boyd, W. Histoire vache
Burrage, A. M. One who saw
Doyle, Sir A. C. The tragedians
Givner, J. A spectator sport
Greene, G. May we borrow your husband?
Maupassant, G. de. Jeroboam
Maupassant, G. de. Miss Harriet
Mortimer, P. The skylight
O'Brien, E. Mrs. Reinhardt
Onions, O. The cigarette case
Raphael, F. Aperitif
Rhys, J. The Chevalier of the Place Blanche
Rhys, J. Illusion
Rhys, J. Night out 1925
Singmaster, D. Stella Artois
Stein, G. A water-fall and a piano
Stoker, B. The burial of the rats
Tremain, R. La plume de mon ami
Germany
Mortimer, J. C. Rumpole and the bright seraphim
Piper, H. B. He walked around the horses
Greece
Johnston, G. Astypalaian knife
Johnston, G. The verdict
King, F. H. So hurt and humiliated
Regent, P. At Manoli's sheepfold
Regent, P. Great Pan is dead!
Rendell, R. Father's day
Spillard, A. Ionian white and gold
Thomas, A. C. Local customs
India
Blythe, R. At Swan Gates
Chipulina, E. G. Your obedient servant
Heald, T. A jumbo death
Hesse, H. Robert Aghion
Jhabvala, R. P. How I became a holy mother
Jhabvala, R. P. Passion
Jhabvala, R. P. A spiritual call
Jhabvala, R. P. Two more under the Indian sun
Kipling, R. Lispeth
Kipling, R. The return of Imray
Lee, T. Foreign skins
McGrath, P. The Black Hand of the Raj
Pilcher, R. Amita

Wells, H. G. The flying man
Ireland
Doyle, Sir A. C. The heiress of Glenmahowley
Ross, M., and Somerville, E. A. Œ. Poisson d'Avril
Tracy, H. A rest and a change
Trevor, W. Virgins
Italy
Bates, H. E. A month by the lake
Boyle, K. To the pure
Forster, E. M. The story of a panic
Fraser, A. On the battlements
Garrett, G. P. A wreath for Garibaldi
Gilbert, W. S. Angela
Grenville, K. Country pleasures
Hartley, L. P. Per far l'amore
Hartley, L. P. Three, or four, for dinner
Hartley, L. P. The white wand
King, F. H. The soutane
King, F. H. Sundays
Tremain, R. La plume de mon ami
Wells, H. G. Miss Winchelsea's heart
Jamaica
Greene, G. Cheap in August
Kelly, T. Their first American
Wells, H. G. Mr. Ledbetter's vacation
Japan
Carter, A. Flesh and the mirror
Green, E. Marginals
Haylock, J. Choice
Haylock, J. Fan mail
King, F. H. A corner of a foreign field
King, F. H. The Festival of the Dead
King, F. H. Indirect method
Tuohy, F. Nocturne with neon lights
Morocco
Dundas, R. Mr. de la Torre
Netherlands
Dundas, R. The uniform
Watmough, D. False start
New Zealand
Hill, E. Marriage at noon
Nigeria
Regent, P. Memories of colonialism
Poland
Tuohy, F. The student
Riviera (France and Italy)
Rhys, J. La Grosse Fifi
Sierra Leone
Wells, H. G. Pollock and the Porroh man
Solomon Islands
Wollaston, N. Walkabout
South Africa
Bosman, H. C. The Rooinek
Doyle, Sir A. C. The mystery of Sasassa Valley
Doyle, Sir A. C. The stone of Boxman's Drift
Havemann, E. A farm at Raraba
Havemann, E. An interview
South America
Tuohy, F. The Admiral and the nuns

BRITISH—South America—*Continued*

Tuohy, F. Showing the flag

Tuohy, F. Two private lives

Soviet Union

Haylock, J. Traveling towards Boris

Patron, J. F. The wallet

Thubron, C. The ear

Watson, I. The thousand cuts

Spain

Mortimer, J. C. Rumpole and the winter break

Switzerland

James, H. The private life

Tunisia

Jordan, N. Night in Tunisia

Turkey

Archer, J. The steal

Swift, G. Seraglio

United States

Austin, M. H. A case of conscience

Bradbury, M. Composition

Carter, A. Our Lady of the Massacre

Doyle, Sir A. C. The American's tale

Fraser, A. Have a nice death

Geras, A. Snapshots of paradise

Gilliatt, P. F.R.A.N.K.

James, H. An international episode

McEwan, I. Psychopolis

Rendell, R. The whistler

Tremain, R. Autumn in Florida

Tuohy, F. Evening in Connecticut

Tuohy, F. Windows

Warren, J. Fetters

Warren, J. Michael

Warren, J. Wedding garment

Watmough, D. Connecticut countess

Watmough, D. Who shall be the judge?

Wyndham, F. Ursula

West Africa

Boyd, W. The coup

Boyd, W. Next boat from Douala

West Indies

Rhys, J. Pioneers, oh, pioneers

BRITISH ARISTOCRACY *See* Aristocracy—England

BRITISH COLUMBIA *See* Canada—British Columbia

The **British** Museum. Hearon, S.

BRITISH SOLDIERS *See* Soldiers—Great Britain

BRITISH WEST INDIES *See* West Indies

Brittain, William, 1930-

The artificial liar

Alfred Hitchcock's Mortal errors

The boy who read Agatha Christie

Tales from Ellery Queen's Mystery Magazine: short stories for young adults

Mr. Strang and the purloined memo

Tales from Ellery Queen's Mystery Magazine: short stories for young adults

Mr. Strang picks up the pieces

Handle with care; ed. by J. Kahn

BRITTANY (FRANCE) *See* France—Brittany

The **broad** versus the narrow outlook. Sandel, C.

Brock. Bernen, R.

Broder, Gloria Kurian

Elena, unfaithful

Great American love stories; ed. by L. Rosenthal

The man who loved Detroit

Ploughshares 14 no4:83-97 '88

Broderick, Damien

I lost my love to the space shuttle 'Columbia'

Transgressions; ed. by D. Anderson

A passage in Earth

Australian science fiction; ed. by V. Ikin

Thy sting

Omni (New York, N.Y.) 9:117-18 Je '87

Broderie anglaise. Gilliatt, P.

Broder's loves. Sulkin, S.

Brodine, Karen

Here, take my words

When I am an old woman I shall wear purple; ed. by S. K. Martz

Brodkey, Harold

Annemarie singing

The New Yorker 64:22-39+ Ag 22 '88

The bullies

The New Yorker 62:27-38+ Je 30 '86

Ceil

The Art of the tale; ed. by D. Halpern

Falling and ascending bodies: four passages

The Bread Loaf anthology of contemporary American short stories; ed. by R. Pack and J. Parini

Innocence

Great American love stories; ed. by L. Rosenthal

The laugh

The New Yorker 62:31-8 F 2 '87

Nonie

The New Yorker 60:46-56+ Mr 5 '84

S.L.

The New Yorker 61:35-44+ S 9 '85

The state of grace

Early sorrow: ten stories of youth; ed. by C. Zolotow

Verona: a young woman speaks

American short story masterpieces; ed. by R. Carver and T. Jenks

Broinowski, Alison

Holy mackerel

Home and away; ed. by R. Creswell

Broken bonds. Joseph, T. Y.

The **broken** boot. Galsworthy, J.

The **broken** bridge. Tuohy, F.

The **broken** dam. Barth, J.

The **broken-down** van. Crane, S.

Broken glass. Eisenberg, D.

Broken glass. Ellison, H.

The **broken** globe. Kreisel, H.
The **broken** men. Muller, M.
Broken tool. Thomas, T. L.
Broken treaty. Henderson, D.
Broken water pipe. Erbaugh, H.
The **broken** web. Viramontes, H. M.
Brondoli, Michael
  Borrowing
    Brondoli, M. Showdown, and other stories
  Coldbeer at the Only
    Brondoli, M. Showdown, and other stories
  The death of the vice consul
    Brondoli, M. Showdown, and other stories
  I swear I always wished you were a possibility
    Brondoli, M. Showdown, and other stories
  The love letter hack
    Brondoli, M. Showdown, and other stories
  Showdown
    Brondoli, M. Showdown, and other stories
    Shenandoah: an anthology; ed. by J. Boatwright
  Sixty-three questions
    Brondoli, M. Showdown, and other stories
  What do you think about three times a day?
    Brondoli, M. Showdown, and other stories
Bronstein, Elliott
  Magic
    Here's the story: fiction with heart; ed. by M. Sklar
BRONTË FAMILY
                  About
West, J. Like visitant of air
BRONX (NEW YORK, N.Y.) *See* New York (N.Y.)—Bronx
Bronze. Tidmarsh, W. M.
The **bronze** cat. Shannon, D.
Bronze leaves and red. Davenport, G.
Brook on Iapetus. Mikhailov, V.
BROOKLYN (NEW YORK, N.Y.) *See* New York (N.Y.)—Brooklyn
Brooks, Barbara
  Summer in Sydney
    Transgressions; ed. by D. Anderson
Brooks, Ben
  Wednesday afternoon
    The Sewanee Review 96:350-68 Summ '88
Brooks, David, 1953-
  The misbehaviour of things
    Transgressions; ed. by D. Anderson

Brooks, Gwendolyn
  The young couple at home
    Family: stories from the interior; ed. by G. G. Chavis
Brooks, Jeremy
  Doing the voices
    Brooks, J. Doing the voices
  I'll fight you
    Brooks, J. Doing the voices
  A value
    Brooks, J. Doing the voices
  Wrong play
    Brooks, J. Doing the voices
Brooks, Juanita, 1898-
  The outsider
    Westward the women; ed. by V. Piekarski
Brooksmith. James, H.
Brooksmith by Henry James: a story. Stern, D.
The **broommaker** of Rychiswyl. Gotthelf, J.
Broommakers. Böll, H.
Broomstick ride. Bloch, R.
Brossard, Jacques
  The metamorfalsis
    Invisible fictions; ed. by G. Hancock
Broster, D. K. (Dorothy Kathleen), 1877-1950
  Couching at the door
    The Penguin book of horror stories
Broster, Dorothy Kathleen *See* Broster, D. K. (Dorothy Kathleen), 1877-1950
BROTHELS *See* Prostitution
Brother. Greene, G.
Brother. Morison, S.
Brother Dael's new year. Virgo, S.
Brother grasshopper. Updike, J.
Brother Gregory. Bird, C.
Brother in arms. Exley, F.
The **brother-in-law**. Davis, L.
Brother Oedipus. Watson, S.
Brother Orchid. Connell, R.
Brother Wolf. Jaffe, H.
Brotherly love. Mullen, J. A.
BROTHERS
    See also Brothers and sisters; Halfbrothers; Stepbrothers; Twins
Abbott, L. K. The end of grief
Alderson, T. Tim's back home
Apple, M. Walt and Will
Asscher-Pinkhof, C. The younger
Attaway, W. Blood on the forge [excerpt]
Baldwin, J. Sonny's blues
Baxter, C. How I found my brother
Bellah, J. W. How Stonewall came back
Berman, R. Professor and colonel
Bishop, M. Collaborating
Block, L. A little off the top
Boswell, R. Kentucky
Bradbury, R. Wake for the living
Broun, H. Phosphates
Busch, F. Rise and fall
Buzzati, D. The five brothers
Callaghan, M. Last spring they came over

BROTHERS—*Continued*

Campbell, E. Watch without time
Carter, R. Composition
Carver, R. Elephant
Cheever, J. The lowboy
Chon, S.-G. Wings that will carry us both
Clark, G. Ice fishing
Clark, G. Lunar frisson
Clark, G. Mister Period
Cohen, M. A love for the infinite
Connelly, J. Wait
Covino, M. Salient facts
Cowper, R. Brothers
Cox, A. Twentieth frame
Crane, S. The little regiment
De Bruyn, G. Someday he really will come home
Donaldson, S. R. The Lady in White
Dubus, A. Delivering
Dunn, D. Fishermen
El-Bisatie, M. My brother
Essop, A. The Hajji
Everett, P. L. Last fair deal
Frazee, S. The Bretnall feud
Freeman, J. Pretend we're French
García Márquez, G. The other side of death
Garrett, G. P. A game of catch
Gerber, M. J. Tragic lives
Gilchrist, M. The Noble Courtesan
Gingher, M. No news
Godshalk, C. S. Wonderland
Goyen, W. Precious door
Haake, K. Another kind of nostalgia
Haas, B. Dying in the goldenwest
Haley, R. Fischer's mirror
Hall, T. T. The day Jimmy killed the rabbit
Harris, H. Death at the barbecue
Hauptman, W. Good rockin' tonight
Hayes, M. The cottage in winter
Huddle, D. Summer of the magic show
Hughes, J. An open house
Hunnicutt, E. The Bengal tiger
Jahnn, H. H. Ragna and Nils
Jahnn, H. H. The slave's story
Jahnn, H. H. The story of the twins
Johnson, C. R. Exchange value
Josipovici, G. Brothers
Kees, W. The brothers
Kibera, L. A silent song
Kittredge, W. The underground river
Le Fanu, J. S. Squire Toby's will
Lish, G. For Rupert—with no promises
Long, D. The Oriental Limited
Lurie, M. Running nicely
Lurie, M. Sunday lunch
MacDonald, D. R. The wharf king
Martínez-Serros, H. Victor and David
Maupassant, G. de. At sea
Maupassant, G. de. The mountebanks
Maupassant, G. de. The white wolf
McConnell, C. R. Sidney, Seth and S.A.M.

McGuane, T. The road atlas
Menaker, D. Brothers
Miller, S. Inventing the Abbotts
Miller, S. The lover of women
Monreal, D. N. The visit
Mordden, E. I read my nephew stories
Morison, S. Brother
Munro, A. Monsieur les Deux Chapeaux
Murphy, Y. Where dead is best
Nielsen, H. The deadly Mrs. Haversham
Norris, H. The quarry
Oates, J. C. Ich bin ein Berliner
O'Hara, J. Exactly eight thousand dollars exactly
Olmstead, R. In this life
Olmstead, R. The mason
Pascoe, B. Thylacine
Penner, J. Things to be thrown away
Pirandello, L. The stuffed bird
Power, V. An eye for an eye
Pronzini, B. A cold foggy day
Raphael, F. Oxbridge blues
Ríos, A. La boda
Rulfo, J. Talpa
Schnitzler, A. The blind Geronimo and his brother
Schwartz, L. S. The sound of Velcro
Silvis, R. Prayer and old jokes
Singer, I. B. A nest egg for paradise
Sorrells, R. T. Charley Billy
Sproat, R. When the sailor was far away
Stewart, J. I. M. Tom Dick and Harry
Straub, P. Blue rose
Swift, G. Cliffedge
Takahashi, T. A happy home
Taylor, R. Charley Ford betrayed
Taylor, R. The Tennessee war of the roses
Thomas, M. Shellers
Tremain, R. Wedding night
Trevor, W. Death in Jerusalem
Tuohy, F. In the hotel
Vanderhaeghe, G. Cages
Vanderhaeghe, G. Drummer
Vizyēnos, G. M. Who was my brother's killer?
Walpole, Sir H. Bachelors
Wang Anyi. The destination
Watson, I. Slow birds
Weaver, G. My brother and the perfect people
Webb, S. The thing that goes burp in the night
Whitaker, M. Pin's fee wife
Windsor, G. Far on the ringing plains
Wolfe, T. Circus at dawn
Wolfe, T. The Company
Wolff, T. The rich brother
Woodman, A. The cruelty of chairs
Working, R. The monkey
The **brothers**. Alcott, L. M.
Brothers. Bova, B.
Brothers. Cowper, R.
Brothers. Josipovici, G.

The **brothers**. Kees, W.
Brothers. Menaker, D.
BROTHERS AND SISTERS
See also Twins
Abrams, L. Secrets men keep
Aidoo, C. A. A. In the cutting of a drink
Akins, E. George Bailey fishing
Bambara, T. C. Raymond's run
Barthelme, F. Aluminum house
Barthelme, F. Sis
Barthelme, S. Problematical species
Bausch, R. Contrition
Beattie, A. Heaven on a summer night
Beattie, A. Where you'll find me
Bennett, J. G. Dependents
Benton, K. C. Cast for murder
Bird, C. Boy and girl
Blackwood, A. The damned
Bowles, P. At Paso Rojo
Bukoski, A. Hello from Ture
Campos-De Metro, J. Evvy's brother
Canin, E. American Beauty
Cary, J. A private ghost
Chekhov, A. P. My life
Ch'en, Y.-C. My kid brother, K'ang-hsiung
Choe, I.-H. The end of the highway
Colter, C. The amoralists
Cortázar, J. House taken over
Crichton Smith, I. Timoshenko
Crowley, A. The old man of the peepul-tree
Davis, L. Sketches for a life of Wassilly
De Forest, J. W. The brigade commander
De Haven, T. Clap hands! Here comes Charley
Donaldson, S. R. Unworthy of the angel
Engel, M. Anita's dance
Erdrich, L. The beet queen
Faik, S. The neighborhood coffeehouse
Fetler, A. The third count
Field, I. Hungry lion
Floyd, P. L. Uncle Tom's daybook
Flynn, R. Place
Foley, B. The child killers
Garrett, G. P. Sweeter than the flesh of birds
Gilchrist, E. Nineteen forty-one
Gilchrist, E. Traceleen, she's still talking
Goldsmith, H. The voices of El Dorado
Grace, P. Electric city
Hall, D. Reunion
Hall, M. L. The man who gave brother double pneumonia
Harrington, J. A place of her own
Hartley, L. P. Hilda's letter
Hartley, L. P. A summons
Hemingway, E. The last good country
Hempel, A. Today will be a quiet day
Highsmith, P. The kite
Hoch, E. D. The man who came back
Humphries, J. Quincy
Janowitz, T. Conviction
Jolley, E. One bite for Christmas

Kalpakian, L. Veteran's Day
Kees, W. I should worry
Kessler, J. F. Esau
Kinsella, W. P. Indian Joe
Kirk, R. The reflex-man in Whinnymuir Close
Kittredge, W. Phantom Silver
La Chapelle, M. Superstitions
Long, D. Cooper Loftus
Long, D. The flood of '64
MacDonald, D. R. Holy Annie
Madden, D. Hidden symptoms
Matthews, J. Haunted by name our ignorant lips
Mazel, D. Surprises
McCormack, E. P. Edward and Georgina
Meinke, P. Alice's brother
Metcalfe, R. The cat
Millman, L. Annie Bardwell gets back her cutlery
Minot, S. Thorofare
Moffatt, D. When Roger got married
Morrow, B. Cutt's grace
Murphy, Y. The headdress
Niatum, D. She keeps the dance turning like the earth
Nolan, W. F. Saturday's shadow
Osborn, C. Amnesia's child
Pak, S.-J. Ten minutes to seven
Percy, W. The moviegoer [excerpt]
Perlman, H. H. Twelfth summer
Phillips, J. A. Bess
Pilcher, R. The house on the hill
Pirandello, L. The black shawl
Poe, E. A. The fall of the House of Usher
Polidori, J. W. The vampyre
Potter, N. A. J. Viewing the remains
Pritchett, M. The barrel racer
Proulx, A. Bedrock
Purdy, J. Rapture
Raphael, L. Dancing on Tishe B'av
Reaney, J. The bully
Robison, M. While home
Russo, A. The Sephardic sisters
Sarrantonio, A. Wish
Sawai, G. Hang out your washing on the Siegfried Line
Schneider, R. Border crossers
Schwob, M. Clodia, shameless matron
Sexson, L. Starlings, mute swans, a goose, an impossible angel, evening grosbeaks, an ostrich, some ducks, and a sparrow
Son, C.-S. The rainy season
Sorrells, R. T. Talking to the boy
Spark, D. Summer of the Dead Frogs
Spark, M. The dark glasses
Stark, S. S. Ode to the big school
Stark, S. S. A wrestler's tale
Steele, Sir R. The wedding of Jenny Distaff
Swick, M. Heart
Tamer, Z. Snow at the end of the night

BROTHERS AND SISTERS—*Continued*

Taylor, M. D. Roll of thunder, hear my cry [excerpt]

Taylor, R. Eddy the man

Taylor, R. Glory

Tem, S. R. Hidey hole

Thompson, J. This world, then the fireworks

Tuohy, F. A reprieve

Upward, E. The white-pinafored black cat

Van Name, M. L. My sister, my self

Vaughn, S. Kid MacArthur

West, J. Aloha, farewell to thee

West, J. Foot-shaped shoes

West, J. Probably Shakespeare

Wetherell, W. D. The lob

Willett, J. Julie in the funhouse

Williams, T. The accent of a coming foot

Williams, T. Portrait of a girl in glass

Williams, T. Resemblance between a violin case and a coffin

Wilson, A. Paul's eyes

Wilson, B. The back door of America

Wilson, B. Crater Lake

Wilson, B. Starfish

Wilson, B. Thin ice

Wilson, L. A. Country blues for Melissa

Windsor, G. Edging around the fat man

Working, R. Rendering Byzantium

Yates, R. A compassionate leave

Yourcenar, M. Anna, soror . . .

Brothers are the same. Markham, B.

The **brothers'** house. Algren, N.

Brothers in honor. LeClaire, A. D.

BROTHERS-IN-LAW

Alden, P. B. A member of the family

Barthelme, F. Sis

Davis, L. The brother-in-law

Dundas, R. Booker's End

Ferguson, W. Freedom

Gerber, M. J. Memorial service

Kinsella, W. P. The McGuffin

O'Hara, J. The gentleman in the tan suit

Raphael, F. Welcome aboard

Brothers of the tiger. DeGrazia, E.

Broughton, T. Alan (Thomas Alan), 1936-

Ceremony

The Literary Review (Madison, N.J.) 31:437-46 Summ '88

The classicist

The Georgia Review 42:811-20 Wint '88

Duck season

The Ploughshares reader: new fiction for the eighties

Lily

The Ploughshares reader: new fiction for the eighties

Spring cleaning

The Virginia Quarterly Review 63:600-16 Aut '87

Broughton, Thomas Alan *See* Broughton, T. Alan (Thomas Alan), 1936-

Broun, Hob

Blood Aspens

Broun, H. Cardinal numbers

By the numbers

Broun, H. Cardinal numbers

Cows on the drag strip

Broun, H. Cardinal numbers

Cycling posture

Broun, H. Cardinal numbers

The deep blue eastern sky

Broun, H. Cardinal numbers

Development

Broun, H. Cardinal numbers

Finding Florida

Broun, H. Cardinal numbers

Fryed cutlets

Broun, H. Cardinal numbers

Highspeed linear Main St.

Broun, H. Cardinal numbers

Ice water

Broun, H. Cardinal numbers

Is this civilization?

Broun, H. Cardinal numbers

Municipal noir

Broun, H. Cardinal numbers

No smoking

Broun, H. Cardinal numbers

Phosphates

Broun, H. Cardinal numbers

Rosella, in stages

Broun, H. Cardinal numbers

Ruby Dawn, private duty nurse

Broun, H. Cardinal numbers

Slow grounder

Broun, H. Cardinal numbers

South Sea sensations

Broun, H. Cardinal numbers

A tale of no more demands

Broun, H. Cardinal numbers

Brown, Alan

The back way to Fantasyland

New Directions in prose and poetry 51

Family tremors

Seventeen 47:188-9+ My '88

A sense of humor

New directions in prose and poetry 49

Brown, Alice

Natalie Blayne

The Other woman; ed. by S. Koppelman

The way of peace

Between mothers & daughters; ed. by S. Koppelman

Brown, Ann R.

The clockwork woman

Magic in Ithkar 4; ed. by A. Norton and R. Adams

Were-sisters

Magic in Ithkar 3; ed. by A. Norton and R. Adams

Brown, B. C.

Dancer on the edge

Seventeen 45:150-2+ Je '86

Brown, Clark
A winter's tale
The Interior country; ed. by A. Blackburn
The Pushcart prize IX
Brown, Elizabeth Inness- *See* Inness-Brown, Elizabeth, 1954-
Brown, Fredric, 1906-1972
Answer
Machines that think; ed. by I. Asimov; P. S. Warrick and M. H. Greenberg
Armageddon
Devils & demons; ed. by M. Kaye and S. Kaye
Before she kills
The Mammoth book of private eye stories; ed. by B. Pronzini and M. H. Greenberg
Blue murder
Brown, F. Carnival of crime
Cain
Brown, F. Carnival of crime
The case of the dancing sandwiches
Brown, F. Carnival of crime
Cry silence
Brown, F. Carnival of crime
The dangerous people
Brown, F. Carnival of crime
Hitchcock in prime time; ed. by F. M. Nevins and M. H. Greenberg
The Djinn murder
Brown, F. Carnival of crime
Don't look behind you
Brown, F. Carnival of crime
The four blind men
The Wickedest show on earth; ed. by M. Muller and B. Pronzini
Good night, good knight
The Deadly arts; ed. by B. Pronzini and M. Muller
Granny's birthday
Brown, F. Carnival of crime
Hobbyist
Brown, F. Carnival of crime
I'll cut your throat again, Kathleen
Brown, F. Carnival of crime
Murder and mystery in Chicago; ed. by C. R. Waugh; F. D. McSherry and M. H. Greenberg
The joke
Brown, F. Carnival of crime
Keep out
Young mutants; ed. by I. Asimov; M. H. Greenberg and C. G. Waugh
The laughing butcher
Brown, F. Carnival of crime
Little Apple Hard to Peel
Brown, F. Carnival of crime
A little white lye
Brown, F. Carnival of crime
Miss Darkness
Brown, F. Carnival of crime

Mouse
Spirits, spooks, and other sinister creatures; ed. by H. Hoke
Mr. Smith kicks the bucket
Brown, F. Carnival of crime
Murder while you wait
Brown, F. Carnival of crime
The night the world ended
Brown, F. Carnival of crime
Nightmare in yellow
Brown, F. Carnival of crime
The spherical ghoul
Death locked in; ed. by D. G. Greene and R. C. S. Adey
Town wanted
Brown, F. Carnival of crime
A voice behind him
Brown, F. Carnival of crime
Witness in the dark
Brown, F. Carnival of crime
Brown, George Mackay
Andrina
Brown, G. M. Andrina, and other stories
The Penguin book of ghost stories
The battle in the hills
Brown, G. M. Andrina, and other stories
The box of fish
Brown, G. M. Andrina, and other stories
A candle for milk and grass
Brown, G. M. Andrina, and other stories
The chamber of poetry
Brown, G. M. Andrina, and other stories
Darkness and light
Brown, G. M. Andrina, and other stories
The day of the ox
Brown, G. M. Andrina, and other stories
An epiphany tale
Brown, G. M. Andrina, and other stories
The feast at Paplay
Brown, G. M. Andrina, and other stories
Gold dust
Brown, G. M. Andrina, and other stories
King and shepherd
Brown, G. M. Andrina, and other stories
Lord of silence
Brown, G. M. Andrina, and other stories
The lost boy
Brown, G. M. Andrina, and other stories
Magi
Brown, G. M. Andrina, and other stories
Men and gold and bread
Brown, G. M. Andrina, and other stories
Michael Surfax, whaler
Brown, G. M. Andrina, and other stories
The satirist
Brown, G. M. Andrina, and other stories
The skald in the cave
Brown, G. M. Andrina, and other stories
A winter legend
Brown, G. M. Andrina, and other stories

Brown, Harry, 1917-1986
A walk in the sun
A Treasury of World War II stories; ed.
by B. Pronzini and M. H. Greenberg
Brown, J. D. (James Dale), 1948-
White Mud Lake
Southwest Review 70:114-26 Wint '85
Brown, James Dale *See* Brown, J. D. (James
Dale), 1948-
Brown, Larry
Facing the music
New stories from the South: the year's
best, 1988
Brown, Mary Ward
The amaryllis
Brown, M. W. Tongues of flame
The barbecue
Brown, M. W. Tongues of flame
Beyond New Forks
Brown, M. W. Tongues of flame
The black dog
Brown, M. W. Tongues of flame
The cure
The Best American short stories, 1984
Brown, M. W. Tongues of flame
Disturber of the peace
Brown, M. W. Tongues of flame
Fruit of the season
Brown, M. W. Tongues of flame
Good-bye, Cliff
Brown, M. W. Tongues of flame
It wasn't all dancing
Grand Street 7:36-49 Summ '88
Let him live
Brown, M. W. Tongues of flame
New dresses
Brown, M. W. Tongues of flame
One regret
Redbook 171:54+ S '88
Tongues of flame
Brown, M. W. Tongues of flame
New stories from the South: the year's
best, 1986
Prairie Schooner 58:33-44 Wint '84
Brown, Morna Doris MacTaggart, 1907-
*For works written by this author under
other names see Ferrars, E. X.,
1907-; Ferrars, Elizabeth, 1907-*
BROWN, PHYLLIS GEORGE *See* George,
Phyllis
Brown, Rita Mae
Rubyfruit jungle [excerpt]
Buying time; ed. by S. Walker
Brown, Rosellen
A good deal
The Bread Loaf anthology of contem-
porary American short stories; ed. by
R. Pack and J. Parini
A Good deal; ed. by M. Heath and F.
M. Robinson
The Massachusetts Review 26:11-25 Spr
'85

One of two
The Pushcart prize XII
Brown, Roswell
Hit the baby!
Hard-boiled dames; ed. by B. A. Drew
Brown, Sam, 1945-
The lesson
The Best Maine stories; ed. by S. Phip-
pen; C. Waugh and M. Greenberg
Brown, Suzanne Hunter
The baby-sitter
The Southern Review (Baton Rouge, La.)
23:194-205 Ja '87
Communion
New stories from the South: the year's
best, 1986
The Southern Review (Baton Rouge, La.)
20:419-28 Ap '84
In the garden
Southwest Review 71:246-50 Spr '86
The **brown** grass. Cowan, P.
Brown Wolf. London, J.
Browne, Christopher
The lesson
Shadows 9
Browne, Howard, 1908-
House call
Murder California style; ed. by J. L.
Breen and J. Ball
So dark for April
The Mammoth book of private eye
stories; ed. by B. Pronzini and M. H.
Greenberg
Murder and mystery in Chicago; ed. by
C. R. Waugh; F. D. McSherry and M.
H. Greenberg
The **Brownie** of the Black Haggs. Hogg, J.
BROWNING, ROBERT, 1812-1889
About
Byatt, A. S. Precipice-encurled
Brownlee, Frank
Dove and jackal
The Penguin book of Southern African
stories
Brownstein, Michael, 1943-
Lorenzo's collection
The Paris Review 26:71-9 Summ '84
Browsing. Dodd, S. M.
Broxon, Mildred Downey
First do no harm
Magic in Ithkar 4; ed. by A. Norton and
R. Adams
Flux of fortune
Magic in Ithkar 2; ed. by A. Norton and
R. Adams
Bruce-Novoa, 1944-
The manuscript
Cuentos Chicanos; ed. by R. A. Anaya
and A. Márquez
Bruchac, Joseph, 1942-
Turtle meat
Earth power coming; ed. by S. J. Ortiz

Bruehl, Elisabeth Young- *See* Young-Bruehl, Elisabeth

The **bruise**. Roberts, N.

Bruller, Jean *See* Vercors, 1902-

Brulotte, Gaétan
The elevator messengers
   Intimate strangers; ed. by M. Cohen and W. Grady

Brumbacher breathing. Matthews, J.

BRUNEI
Sterling, B. Green days in Brunei

Brunner, John, 1934-
Elixir for the emperor
   Fantastic stories; ed. by M. H. Greenberg and P. L. Price
The fable of the farmer and fox
   Omni (New York, N.Y.) 9:110+ Je '87
   The Year's best fantasy, first annual collection
Judas
   Machines that think; ed. by I. Asimov; P. S. Warrick and M. H. Greenberg
What friends are for
   Young mutants; ed. by I. Asimov; M. H. Greenberg and C. G. Waugh

Bruno and Rachel. Olmstead, R.

Bruno-Holley, Maria
A matter of disguise
   Ms. 13:101-2+ O '84

Bruno's metamorphosis. Stern, S.

Bruno's shadow. Laidlaw, M.

Bruns. Rush, N.

The **brushoff**. Curry, P. S.

Brust, Steven, 1955-
Csucskári
   The Year's best fantasy, first annual collection

BRUTALITY *See* Cruelty; Violence

Bryan, J. Y. (Jack Yeaman), 1907-
Frontier vigil
   Prize stories, Texas Institute of Letters; ed. by M. Terry

Bryan, Jack Yeaman *See* Bryan, J. Y. (Jack Yeaman), 1907-

Bryant, Edward
Author's notes
   The Year's best fantasy, first annual collection
The cutter
   Silver scream; ed. by D. J. Schow
Jade Blue
   Magicats! Ed. by J. Dann and G. Dozois
Jody after the war
   Beyond Armageddon; ed. by W. M. Miller and M. H. Greenberg
The man who always wanted to travel
   Omni (New York, N.Y.) 7:90-2+ Je '85
Prairie sun
   Omni book of science fiction 3
The serrated edge
   Omni (New York, N.Y.) 7:64-6+ D '84
Skin and blood
   Omni (New York, N.Y.) 10:45-6+ Ap '88

Teeth marks
   Masters of darkness; ed. by D. Etchison
The transfer
   Cutting edge; ed. by D. Etchison

Bryant, Susan Keith
Secrets
   Michigan Quarterly Review 27:172-8 Wint '88

Bryce Echenique, Alfredo
In Paracas with Jimmy
   Anthology of contemporary Latin American literature, 1960-1984

Bryning, Frank
Place of the throwing-stick
   Australian science fiction; ed. by V. Ikin

BRZESKA, HENRI GAUDIER- *See* Gaudier-Brzeska, Henri, 1891-1915

The **Bubbe**. Botwinik, B.

Bubbles. Brin, D.

Bubnoff and the Devil. Turgenev, I. S.

BUBONIC PLAGUE *See* Plague

Buch, Hans Christoph, 1944-
Epilogue
   Short story international 57

Buchan, John, 1875-1940
Fullcircle
   The Oxford book of English ghost stories

Buck, Doris Pitkin
Aunt Agatha
   100 great fantasy short short stories; ed. by I. Asimov; T. Carr and M. H. Greenberg

Buck, Pearl S. (Pearl Sydenstricker), 1892-1973
A certain star
   "May your days be merry and bright" and other Christmas stories by women; ed. by S. Koppelman
Christmas Day in the morning
   Reader's Digest 127:73-6 D '85
The enemy
   A Treasury of World War II stories; ed. by B. Pronzini and M. H. Greenberg
The good deed
   The Nobel reader; ed. by J. Eisen and S. Troy
The silver butterfly
   The Saturday Evening Post 260:50-3+ O '88

Buckley, David
Randall's band
   The Literary Review (Madison, N.J.) 30:621-35 Summ '87

Buckley, William F. (William Frank), 1925-
The Ellington affair
   TV Guide 36:26-7+ Ag 20-26 '88
   TV Guide 36:34-9 Ag 27-S 2 '88
Thumbs up, thumbs down
   Money 14:215-16+ N '85

The **buckwheat** season. Yi, H.

Bud. Watson, I.

BUDAPEST (HUNGARY) *See* Hungary—
    Budapest
Budapest dangereux. Lopatin, J.
Buddah. Straight, S.
The **Buddha** of suburbia. Kureishi, H.
BUDDHISM
        See also Buddhist priests; Temples,
        Buddhist
    Ferron, J. The Buddhist
    Kōda, R. The five-storied pagoda
    Levy, D. Proletarian Zen
    Prose, F. Tibetan time
The **Buddhist.** Ferron, J.
BUDDHIST PRIESTS
    Bowles, P. You have left your lotus pods
        on the bus
Buddy. Furman, L.
BUDGERIGARS
    Cohen, M. Death of a guppy
Budhos, Marina
    Devotions
        The Literary Review (Madison, N.J.)
        31:451-67 Summ '88
Budrys, Algis, 1931-
    The end of summer
        [Analog]: Writers' choice v2
    Never meet again
        Hitler victorious; ed. by G. Benford and
            M. H. Greenberg
    Shadow on the stars
        Space wars; created by P. Anderson
The **Buell** cherry. Ade, G.
Buenaventura Durruti's funeral. Moorhouse,
    F.
BUENOS AIRES (ARGENTINA) *See* Ar-
    gentina—Buenos Aires
Buff Orpington and the disasters of middle
    life. Bird, C.
BUFFALO, AMERICAN *See* Bison
BUFFALO (N.Y.) *See* New York (State)—
    Buffalo
Buffalo gals, won't you come out tonight.
    Le Guin, U. K.
Buffalo, sun and strawberries. Hoyt, M. S.
Bug house. Tuttle, L.
Bugs. Holmes, N.
The **Buick** saloon. Bridge, A.
Building a shell mound. Kaikō, T.
Buisson, Justine
    If I don't go now I never will
        The North American Review 269:37-9 Je
        '84
Bujak and the strong force; or, God's dice.
    Amis, M.
Bukiet, Melvin Jules
    Old words for new
        The Antioch Review 44:305-26 Summ '86
    Sincerely, yours
        The Kenyon Review ns9:36-46 Spr '87
Bukoski, Anthony
    The children of strangers
        Bukoski, A. Twelve below zero

Great sea battles
    Bukoski, A. Twelve below zero
The happiness farm
    Bukoski, A. Twelve below zero
Harry and the dancer
    Bukoski, A. Twelve below zero
Hello from Ture
    Bukoski, A. Twelve below zero
I, Lillian
    Bukoski, A. Twelve below zero
Ice days
    Bukoski, A. Twelve below zero
The kissing booth
    Bukoski, A. Twelve below zero
The Pulaski Guards
    Southern Humanities Review 22:19-31
        Wint '88
Route of the zephyrs
    Bukoski, A. Twelve below zero
A spinster's confession regarding her sor-
    rows
    Bukoski, A. Twelve below zero
Stan and Ollie
    Bukoski, A. Twelve below zero
This heat
    Bukoski, A. Twelve below zero
True adventures
    Bukoski, A. Twelve below zero
Twelve below zero
    Bukoski, A. Twelve below zero
The woman who ate cat food
    Bukoski, A. Twelve below zero
Bulbs. Davie, E.
The **bulk** tour. Bonnie, F.
The **bull** calf. Frame, J.
Bull market. Conroy, J.
The **bull** ring. Hill, R.
The **bull** with the hard hat. MacLaverty, B.
Bullard, Sara
    Refugees
        Southern Humanities Review 22:39-45
            Wint '88
Bullen, Frank T.
    The debt of the whale
        Sea captains' tales; ed. by A. Enfield
The **bullfight.** Power, V.
BULLFIGHTERS AND BULLFIGHTING
    Barthelme, D. The wound
    Campbell, E. La güera
    Hemingway, E. The capital of the world
    Hemingway, E. The mother of a queen
    Hemingway, E. The undefeated
    Lutz, J. Mortal combat
BULLFIGHTING *See* Bullfighters and bull-
    fighting
The **bullies.** Brodkey, H.
BULLS
    O'Connor, F. Greenleaf
    Olmstead, R. A pair of bulls
    Power, V. The bullfight
    Ribeiro, J. U. Alaindelon de la Patrie
    Stuart, J. To market, to market
Bullseye. Corwin, P.

The **bully**. Reaney, J.
The **bully**. Williams, D.
Bulwer-Lytton, Edward *See* Lytton, Edward
    Bulwer Lytton, Baron, 1803-1873
Bulychev, K. (Kirill)
    Another's memory
        Earth and elsewhere, by K. Bulychev
            and others
    The empty house
        Aliens, travelers, and other strangers; by
            B. and A. Strugatsky and others
Bulychev, Kirill *See* Bulychev, K. (Kirill)
Bumblebees. Mason, B. A.
Bummer's roost. Alter, R. E.
Bumpus, Jerry
    The attack on San Clemente
        Bumpus, J. Heroes and villains
    Chums
        Bumpus, J. Heroes and villains
    The dirigible
        American made; ed. by M. Leyner; C.
            White and T. Glynn
    Fable
        Bumpus, J. Heroes and villains
    Heroes and villains
        Bumpus, J. Heroes and villains
    K
        Bumpus, J. Heroes and villains
    The outdoorsman
        Bumpus, J. Heroes and villains
    Plenty of time
        Bumpus, J. Heroes and villains
    Popinjay's African notes
        Bumpus, J. Heroes and villains
    Shame
        Bumpus, J. Heroes and villains
The **bums** at sunset. Wolfe, T.
Bums on needles and pins. Rossi, A.
Bun Grady. Conroy, J.
Bunch, David R.
    A small miracle of fishhooks and straight
        pins
        Fantastic stories; ed. by M. H. Green-
            berg and P. L. Price
Bunco. Conner, M. J.
The **bundle**. Faik, S.
A **bundle** of letters. James, H.
Bundoran, Co. Donegal. Ryan, A.
Bunin, Ivan Alekseevich, 1870-1953
    Sunstroke
        Classic European short stories; ed. by R.
            Beum
Bunny Berigan in the elephants' graveyard.
    Faust, I.
BUNYAN, JOHN, 1628-1688
                About
    Waldrop, H. God's hooks!
The **bunyip** dies. Scott, G. F.
BUONARROTI, MICHEL ANGELO *See*
    Michelangelo Buonarroti, 1475-1564

Burdick, Bruce Stanley
    From time to time
        From mind to mind: tales of communi-
            cation from Analog
The **Bureau** d'Echange de Maux. Dunsany,
    E. J. M. D. P., Baron
BUREAUCRACY
        See also Civil service
    Eisenreich, H. A friend of the family
    Feng Jicai. Numbskull
    Feng Jicai. The street-sweeping show
    Greenwood, R. The last survivor of Sierra
        Flat
    Nesin, A. Regulations for meatball pedd-
        lers
    Tem, S. R. At the bureau
    Tem, S. R. The poor
Burford, Barbara
    Falling
        Stepping out; ed. by A. Oosthuizen
Burger, Knox
    The cat lover
        Magicats! Ed. by J. Dann and G. Dozois
Burgess, Fred
    Exit, stage right
        Ellery Queen's Prime crimes 2; ed. by
            E. Sullivan and K. A. Prince
Burgin, Richard
    Carlin's trio
        Southwest Review 73:529-42 Aut '88
    The victims
        The Pushcart prize XI
The **burglar**. Colette
The **burglar** alarm. Updike, J.
The **burglar** face. Michaelson, L. W.
BURGLARS *See* Thieves
The **burglar's** Christmas. Cather, W.
The **burglar's** story. Gilbert, W. S.
BURIAL *See* Funeral rites and ceremonies
BURIAL, PREMATURE *See* Premature
    burial
Burial. Huybensz, J.
The **burial**. Matthews, J.
The **burial**. Somers, A.
Burial at sea. Singer, I. B.
The **burial** of the guns. Page, T. N.
The **burial** of the rats. Stoker, B.
BURIED ALIVE *See* Premature burial
Buried lives. Mukherjee, B.
Buried talents. Matheson, R.
BURIED TREASURE
    Brown, G. M. Men and gold and bread
    Daley, R. The cannons of the Atocha
    Holding, J. The Treasure of Pachacamac
    Masefield, J. Don Alfonso's treasure hunt
    Poe, E. A. The gold-bug
    Wells, H. G. Mr. Brisher's treasure
    Wells, H. G. The treasure in the forest
    Wolfe, G. The map
Buried treasure. Lutz, J.
Buried treasure. Paolucci, A.
Buried treasure, old bones. Gee, M.

Burk, Ronnie
The housekeeper
Southwest tales; ed. by Alurista and X. Rojas-Urista
Burke, James Lee, 1936-
The convict
The Best American short stories, 1986
Burke, J. L. The convict
The Kenyon Review ns7:103-13 Summ '85
New stories from the South: the year's best, 1986
Hack
Burke, J. L. The convict
Losses
Burke, J. L. The convict
Lower me down with a golden chain
Burke, J. L. The convict
The pilot
Burke, J. L. The convict
Taking a second look
Burke, J. L. The convict
Uncle Sidney and the Mexicans
Burke, J. L. The convict
We Build Churches, Inc.
Burke, J. L. The convict
When it's Decoration Day
Burke, J. L. The convict
Burke, John, 1922-
Lucille would have known
After midnight; ed. by C. L. Grant
Burke, Jonathan, 1922-
For works written by this author under other names see Burke, John, 1922-
Burke, Meredith
Lou's corner
Stories and poems from close to home; ed. by F. Salas
Burke, Owen, 1922-
For works written by this author under other names see Burke, John, 1922-
Burke, Thomas, 1886-1945
The hands of Mr. Ottermole
Hitchcock in prime time; ed. by F. M. Nevins and M. H. Greenberg
The hollow man
The Oxford book of English ghost stories
BURKE, WILLIAM
About
Schwob, M. Burke and Hare, murderers
Burke and Hare, murderers. Schwob, M.
Burkert, Rand
The stone inscription of Caleb Pellor
20 under 30; ed. by D. Spark
The **Burkes** and the blue. LaSalle, P.
Burks, Arthur J.
Dance of the damned
Selected tales of grim and grue from the horror pulps; ed. by S. Jaffery
Burned out. Sholem Aleichem

Burnet, Dana
Fog
Haunted New England; ed. by C. G. Waugh; M. H. Greenberg and F. D. McSherry
Burnett, W. R. (William Riley), 1899-1982
Traveling light
Ellery Queen's Memorable characters
Burnett, William Riley *See* Burnett, W. R. (William Riley), 1899-1982
Burnham camp. Sligo, J.
The **burning**. Welty, E.
The **burning** baby. Thomas, D.
The **burning** bush. Michaelson, L. W.
The **burning** bush. Verma, N.
Burning chrome. Gibson, W.
Burning issues. Morris, M.
The **burning** of Melcarth. Crowley, A.
Burning off. London, J.
Burning the lost country. Haake, K.
The **burnout** kid. Eighner, L.
Burns, Christopher
How things are put together
Critical Quarterly 29:20-9 Aut '87
Burns, Ellie
My first script
American Film 10:30-5 Jl/Ag '85
Burns, George
Sometimes, when it's slow on the 2 1/2's
The Massachusetts Review 25:439-43 Aut '84
Burns, Mary
After hours
Burns, M. Suburbs of the Arctic Circle
The circle
Burns, M. Suburbs of the Arctic Circle
Collected bear stories
Burns, M. Suburbs of the Arctic Circle
Greta
Burns, M. Suburbs of the Arctic Circle
How it happened
Burns, M. Suburbs of the Arctic Circle
A joint communique
Burns, M. Suburbs of the Arctic Circle
The men on my window
Burns, M. Suburbs of the Arctic Circle
Monuments
Burns, M. Suburbs of the Arctic Circle
The Norman Fisher Memorial Ski Race
Burns, M. Suburbs of the Arctic Circle
Suburbs of the Arctic Circle
Burns, M. Suburbs of the Arctic Circle
Burns, Tex, 1908-1988
For works written by this author under other names see L'Amour, Louis, 1908-1988
BURR, AARON, 1756-1836
About
Welty, E. First love

Burrage, A. M. (Alfred McLelland), 1889-1956

Between the minute and the hour
  Charles Keeping's Classic tales of the macabre

One who saw
  The Penguin book of ghost stories

Smee
  The Oxford book of English ghost stories

The sweeper
  Charles Keeping's Book of classic ghost stories

The waxwork
  The Deadly arts; ed. by B. Pronzini and M. Muller
  Great ghost stories; ed. by B. A. Schwartz
  Masterpieces of terror and the supernatural; ed. by M. Kaye and S. Kaye
  The Penguin book of horror stories

Burrage, Alfred McLelland See Burrage, A. M. (Alfred McLelland), 1889-1956

BURROUGHS, EDGAR RICE, 1875-1950
            Parodies, travesties, etc.
Farmer, P. J. The jungle rot kid on the nod

Burroughs, William S., 1914-
The ghost lemurs of Madagascar
  Omni (New York, N.Y.) 9:48-50+ Ap '87

Twilight's last gleamings
  The Paris Review 30:12-20 Wint '88

The Valley
  Esquire 108:215-16 S '87

BURSA (TURKEY) See Turkey—Bursa

Burt, Deirdre
Sydney to Brisbane
  The Massachusetts Review 26:529-43 Wint '85

Burt, Elizabeth
No witnesses
  The Womansleuth anthology; ed. by I. Zahava

Burt, Simon
Anyone else would learn
  Burt, S. Floral Street

Fellow passengers
  Burt, S. Floral Street

Floral Street
  Burt, S. Floral Street

The General's toothache
  Burt, S. Floral Street

Good fortune
  Critical Quarterly 29:17-32 Spr '87

Hiding
  Burt, S. Floral Street

I just kept on smiling
  Burt, S. Floral Street

QB/3854/294 & 6
  Burt, S. Floral Street

The single tractor track
  Burt, S. Floral Street

Welcome
  Burt, S. Floral Street

Wh'appen?
  Burt, S. Floral Street

BURUNDI
Russo, A. Murder of an African prince

BURYING GROUNDS See Cemeteries

The **bus**. Ruta, S.

BUS DRIVERS
Klinkowitz, J. Bus trip
O'Hara, J. Now we know

"**Bus** is coming!". Caspers, N.

The **bus** of dreams. Morris, M.

Bus stop. Saiki, J.

Bus trip. Klinkowitz, J.

Busby, F. M.
Once upon a unicorn
  100 great fantasy short short stories; ed. by I. Asimov; T. Carr and M. H. Greenberg

Busch, Frederick, 1941-
Comrades
  New directions in prose and poetry 50

Critics
  Busch, F. Too late American boyhood blues

Defense
  Busch, F. Too late American boyhood blues

Dog song
  The Georgia Review 39:251-69 Summ '85
  The Graywolf annual 4

A history of small ideas
  Busch, F. Too late American boyhood blues

In foreign tongues
  New directions in prose and poetry 52

Making change
  Busch, F. Too late American boyhood blues

The new honesty
  Busch, F. Too late American boyhood blues

The news
  Busch, F. Too late American boyhood blues

Orbits
  The New Yorker 61:30-3 Ja 20 '86

Rise and fall
  Busch, F. Too late American boyhood blues

The settlement of Mars
  Busch, F. Too late American boyhood blues

Stand, and be recognized
  Busch, F. Too late American boyhood blues

Time is money
  Busch, F. Too late American boyhood blues

BUSES
        See also Trolley buses
Betts, D. The ugliest pilgrim

BUSES—*Continued*

Birtha, B. The saints and sinners run
Cheuse, A. The quest for Ambrose Bierce
Flaherty, G. The man who wore sunlight
Haake, K. The meaning of their names
Houbein, L. Round trip
Lipenga, K. The road to Migowi
McCullers, C. The aliens
Nizer, L. The zipper
Nowakowski, M. On the bus
Piñera, V. The candy
Robinson, K. S. Stone eggs
Rooke, L. Saloam frigid with time's legacy
  while Mrs. Willoughby Bight-Davies
  sits naked through the night on a tree
  stump awaiting the lizard that will
  make her loins go boom-boom
Salmonson, J. A. The blind man
Sayles, J. The Halfway Diner
Thomson, G. Pride of lions
Zhang Jie. Who knows how to live?

Accidents

See Traffic accidents

Bush, Geoffrey, 1920-

(jt. auth) See Crispin, Edmund, 1921-1978,
  and Bush, Geoffrey, 1920-

Bush, Jeffrey

The last meeting of the Butlers Club
  Last laughs; ed. by G. Mcdonald
The problem of Li T'ang
  Last laughs; ed. by G. Mcdonald
Bush tea and sympathy. Payne, N.
The **bush** undertaker. Lawson, H.
Bushfire. Morrison, J.

BUSINESS

See also Advertising; Department
  stores; Merchants
Austin, D. I am an employee
Gibson, W. New Rose Hotel
Goulart, R. Junior partner
Hood, H. Breaking off
Jakes, J. The sellers of the dream
Liben, M. Frimmell's successor
Liben, M. The perils of trade
Munro, A. Working for a living
O'Hara, J. The hardware man
Perlman, H. H. Twelfth summer
Pritchett, M. Open twenty-four hours
Rossi, A. Pollyanna

Unscrupulous methods

Böll, H. Like a bad dream
Ebon, W. Death of a lover
Griner, P. Worboys' transaction
O'Donnell, P. Salamander Four
The **business** card. Benner, R.

BUSINESS DEPRESSION, 1929

Conroy, J. Anyplace but here
Conroy, J. Bull market
Conroy, J. Hard winter
Conroy, J. High bridge
Erdrich, L. The beet queen
Floyd, P. L. Dream rocket
Goldberg, L. One more river

Hall, T. T. The day Jimmy killed the rab-
  bit
Heise, K. The chocolate Easter bunny
Lee, H. Going home
McKenney, R. Industrial valley [excerpt]
Mitchell, K. The great electrical revolution
Slesinger, T. The mouse-trap
Business is business. Böll, H.
Business is business. Friedman, B. J.
Business lunch. Dale, C.
The **business** man. Poe, E. A.
Business talk. Apple, M.
The **business** venture. Spencer, E.

BUSINESSMEN

Bail, M. The partitions
Barthelme, D. Construction
Barthelme, F. Restraint
Brett, S. The nuggy bar
Camoin, F. A. It could happen
Coleman, W. The buyer
Covino, M. Little by little they come back
  for you
Covino, M. The passion of the artist is
  nothing compared to the passion of
  the businessman
Dale, C. Business lunch
Friedman, B. J. Business is business
Friedman, B. J. The Candide of copiers
Grzimek, M. Heartstop
Gustafsson, L. Uncle Sven and the Cul-
  tural Revolution
Kaikō, T. Five thousand runaways
Kessler, J. F. Iocasta
Lenz, S. The amusement-doctor
Lutz, J. One man's manual
McGuane, T. The road atlas
McQueen, J. Acorns
Mooney, M. A civilized man
Mooney, M. Fidelity savings
Mooney, M. Married
Mooney, M. The numbers
Pascoe, B. Jimmy the dancer: necromancer
Poe, E. A. The business man
Poe, E. A. Peter Pendulum, the business
  man
Stockanes, A. E. Ladies who knit for a
  living

BUSINESSWOMEN

Apple, M. Business talk
Gallant, M. The ice wagon going down the
  street
Liben, M. Past due
Lofts, N. Debt of gratitude
Weldon, F. Alopecia
The **bust** of the emperor. Roth, J.
Busted blossoms. Kaminsky, S. M.
The **busting** of Rory O'Mahony. Morrison,
  J.
But America is far. Wegner, H.
But not the herald. Zelazny, R.
But the patient died. Blochman, L. G.
But what if I liked the Panchos, not the
  Beatles. Cárdenas, M.

The **butcher** shop. Roberts, S.
The **butcher** sultan and the musical brothers. Sharif, M. T.
The **butcher**, the baker. Lutz, J.
Butcherdom. Michaelson, L. W.
BUTCHERS
　Caldwell, E. Saturday afternoon
　Cook, H. The white rabbit
　Keillor, G. Chicken
　Koea, S. Meat
　Pascoe, B. The slaughters of the bulum-waal butcher
　Sorrentino, F. The fetid tale of Antul'in
　Thorman, C. Binkas sausage
Butcher's beguine. Wegner, H.
Butler, Ellis Parker
　Getting rid of Fluff
　　Roger Caras' Treasury of great dog stories
　Philo Gubb's greatest case
　　Mississippi River tales; ed. by F. McSherry; C. G. Waugh and M. H. Greenberg
Butler, Gwendoline
　Chicken feed
　　Winter's crimes 17
　North wind
　　The Mammoth book of modern crime stories; ed. by G. Hardinge
　The sisterhood
　　Ellery Queen's Memorable characters
Butler, Jack, 1944-
　Without any ears
　　Mississippi writers v1: Fiction; ed. by D. Abbott
Butler, Karen
　Television, trashbags and love
　　'Teen 30:20+ Jl '86
Butler, Octavia E.
　Bloodchild
　　Nebula awards 20
　　The Year's best science fiction, second annual collection
　The evening and the morning and the night
　　Omni (New York, N.Y.) 9:56-8+ My '87
　　The Year's best science fiction, fifth annual collection
　Speech sounds
　　Tales from Isaac Asimov's science fiction magazine: short stories for young adults
The **butler**. Rand, P.
BUTLERS
　Bush, J. The last meeting of the Butlers Club
　Durrell, L. Drage's divine discontent
　Greene, G. The basement room
　James, H. Brooksmith
　Queen, E. Last man to die
　Rand, P. The butler
　Trevor, W. The news from Ireland
Butter butter butter for a boat. Jolley, E.

The **butter** war in Greenfield. Rölvaag, O. E.
Buttercup and Wendy. Bird, C.
Butterflies. Grace, P.
Butterflies. Kinsella, W. P.
The **butterfly**. Bates, H. E.
The **butterfly**. Komie, L. B.
The **butterfly** and the tank. Hemingway, E.
The **butterfly** collector. Sultan, M.
Buttermilk. Pronzini, B.
The **button**. Highsmith, P.
The **buyer**. Coleman, W.
The **buyer** from Cactus City. Henry, O.
The **buyer** of souls. Knox, J. H.
Buying primo time. Coleman, W.
BUZZARDS
　West, J. Up a tree
Buzzati, Dino, 1906-1972
　Barnabo of the mountains
　　Buzzati, D. The siren
　The bewitched bourgeois
　　Buzzati, D. The siren
　Confidential
　　Buzzati, D. The siren
　A difficult evening
　　Buzzati, D. The siren
　Duelling stories
　　Buzzati, D. The siren
　The end of the world
　　The World of the short story; ed. by C. Fadiman
　The five brothers
　　Buzzati, D. The siren
　The flying carpet
　　Buzzati, D. The siren
　The gnawing worm
　　Buzzati, D. The siren
　An interrupted story
　　Buzzati, D. The siren
　Kafka's houses
　　Buzzati, D. The siren
　Personal escort
　　Buzzati, D. The siren
　The plague
　　Buzzati, D. The siren
　The prohibited word
　　Buzzati, D. The siren
　Seven floors [Variant title: Seven stories]
　　The Art of the tale; ed. by D. Halpern
　The slaying of the dragon
　　The Slaying of the dragon; ed. by F. Rottensteiner
　The time machine
　　Buzzati, D. The siren
Buzzati Traverso, Dino See Buzzati, Dino, 1906-1972
Buzzing. El Ghitany, G.
By a quiet lake. Nagibin, ÎÛ. M.
By any other name. Lavin, J.
By any other name. Robinson, S.
By child undone. Ritchie, J.
By evil and kindness. Briskin, M.
By himself. Pirandello, L.

By means unlovely. Marlowe, D. J.
By reason of darkness. Cady, J.
By the book. Herbert, F.
By the dawn's early light. Block, L.
By the fountain. Faik, S.
By the numbers! Bradbury, R.
By the numbers. Broun, H.
By the river. Hodgins, J.
By the river, Fontainebleau. Gallagher, S.
By the scruff of the soul. Davis, D. S.
By the sea. Mountzoures, H. L.
By the waters of Babylon. Benét, S. V.

Byatt, A. S. (Antonia Susan), 1936-
The changeling
  Byatt, A. S. Sugar, and other stories
  Encounter (London, England) 64:3-7 My '85
The dried witch
  Byatt, A. S. Sugar, and other stories
In the air
  Byatt, A. S. Sugar, and other stories
The July ghost
  Byatt, A. S. Sugar, and other stories
  The Penguin book of ghost stories
Loss of face
  Byatt, A. S. Sugar, and other stories
The next room
  Byatt, A. S. Sugar, and other stories
On the day that E. M. Forster died
  Byatt, A. S. Sugar, and other stories
Precipice-encurled
  Byatt, A. S. Sugar, and other stories
  Encounter (London, England) 68:21-31 Ap '87
Racine and the tablecloth
  Byatt, A. S. Sugar, and other stories
Rose-coloured teacups
  Byatt, A. S. Sugar, and other stories
Sugar
  Byatt, A. S. Sugar, and other stories
  The New Yorker 62:28-38+ Ja 12 '87
Byatt, Antonia Susan *See* Byatt, A. S. (Antonia Susan), 1936-
Bye, Cristine
Box social
  Alberta bound; ed. by F. Stenson
Bye baby bunting. Bird, C.
Bye bye Billy. Taylor, A.
Bygone spring. Colette
Byram, George
The wonder horse
  Young mutants; ed. by I. Asimov; M. H. Greenberg and C. G. Waugh
Byrd, Lee Merrill
Order and disorder
  The North American Review 269:44-8 Je '84
Byrne, John Keyes *See* Leonard, Hugh
Byrne, Leon
Guest-room in Hell
  The Weirds; ed. by S. Jaffery

Byron, George Gordon Byron, 6th Baron, 1788-1824
Fragment of a novel
  Vampires; ed. by A. Ryan
The **bystander**. Berriault, G.
The **bystander**. Oates, J. C.
Byway of the rose. Nestor, T. G.
BYZANTINE EMPIRE
  Leskov, N. S. Pamphalon the entertainer

C

C-chute. Asimov, I.
CAB DRIVERS
  Anderman, J. Empty . . . sort of
  Barnes, L. Lucky penny
  Doyle, Sir A. C. The cabman's story
  Hoyt, M. S. Park taxi
  Kinsella, W. P. A page from the marriage manual for Songhees brides
  Nowakowski, M. The taxi driver's story
  Nowakowski, M. Wastepaper
  Parise, G. Memory
Cabal. Barker, C.
The **caballero's** way. Henry, O.
The **cabbage** patch. Cogswell, T. R.
The **cabbie** wore red. Serotta, E.
Cabin 33. Yarbro, C. Q.
Cabin class to Pubjanice. Ravin, B. L.
Cabin fever. St. Pierre, P. H.
Cabin number six. Sohl, J.
A **cabin** on the coast. Wolfe, G.
The **cabinet** of Edgar Allan Poe. Carter, A.
Cable, George Washington, 1844-1925
Belles Demoiselles plantation
  The Norton book of American short stories
The **cabman's** story. Doyle, Sir A. C.
Cabrera, Lydia, 1900-
How the monkey lost the fruit of his labor
  Other fires; ed. by A. Manguel
The mire of Almendares
  Women's fiction from Latin America; ed. by E. P. Garfield
Tatabisako
  Women's fiction from Latin America; ed. by E. P. Garfield
The **Cabuliwallah**. Tagore, Sir R.
Cache and carry. Pronzini, B.
Cache reward. Reininger, C.
The **cackle** bladder. Gault, W. C.
Caddies' Day. Schinto, J.
CADDOAN INDIANS
  Humphrey, W. The last of the Caddoes
Cade, Toni
Mississippi Ham Rider
  A Good deal; ed. by M. Heath and F. M. Robinson
Cadence. Dubus, A.
Cadenza. Van Greenaway, P.

CADETS
Leskov, N. S. An apparition in the Engineers' Castle
Cadieu. Ferron, J.
Cadigan, Pat
Angel
The Year's best science fiction, fifth annual collection
The edge
Ripper! Ed. by G. Dozois and S. Casper
Heal
Omni (New York, N.Y.) 10:52+ Ap '88
Mind over matters: headset
Omni (New York, N.Y.) 10:82-5 Ja '88
Nearly departed
The Year's best science fiction, first annual collection
Patterns
Omni (New York, N.Y.) 9:68-70+ Ag '87
Pretty boy crossover
The Year's best science fiction, fourth annual collection
Roadside rescue
Omni (New York, N.Y.) 7:62-4+ Jl '85
The Year's best science fiction, third annual collection
Rock on
Mirrorshades; ed. by B. Sterling
The Year's best science fiction, second annual collection
Variation on a man
Omni (New York, N.Y.) 6:68-70+ Ja '84
Cady, Jack, 1932-
By reason of darkness
Prime evil; ed. by D. E. Winter
Caesar, Judith
A different language
The Antioch Review 45:176-84 Spr '87
CAESAR, JULIUS, 100-44 B.C.
                    About
Gardner, J. Julius Caesar and the werewolf
Café Le Dog. Cohen, M.
Cafe Martinique. Walcott, D.
CAFÉS *See* Restaurants, lunchrooms, etc.
The **cage.** Bissoondath, N.
The **cage.** Böll, H.
The **cage.** Chandler, A. B.
A **cage** of gold. Halligan, M.
The **cage** of sand. Ballard, J. G.
Cages. Vanderhaeghe, G.
Cahoon, Brad
The Millennium Garden of the New Jerusalem
The Southern Review (Baton Rouge, La.) 21:482-502 Ap '85
Cain, James M. (James Mallahan), 1892-1977
The baby in the icebox
The Norton book of American short stories

Cigarette girl
Mystery in the mainstream; ed. by B. Pronzini; M. H. Greenberg and B. N. Malzberg
Pay-off girl
Ellery Queen's Crimes and punishments
Two o'clock blonde
Uncollected crimes; ed. by B. Pronzini and M. H. Greenberg
Cain, Paul, 1902-1966
Gundown
The Black mask boys; ed. by W. F. Nolan
Cain. Brown, F.
Cain and Artyom. Gorky, M.
Cain rose up. King, S.
Cain's mark. Pronzini, B.
CAIRO (EGYPT) *See* Egypt—Cairo
Cairo is a small city. Gorgy, N.
Cake night. Mattison, A.
Cakewalk. Smith, L.
The **calash.** See Gogol', N. V. The coach
Calcagno, Anne
Something like a risk
The North American Review 272:23-7 D '87
Story of my weight
TriQuarterly no72:41-7 Spr/Summ '88
CALCULATING MACHINES *See* Calculators
CALCULATORS
Asimov, I. All the troubles of the world
Asimov, I. The feeling of power
Asimov, I. Jokester
The **calculus.** Bovey, J.
Caldecott, Sir Andrew, 1884-1951
Christmas reunion
Christmas ghosts; ed. by K. Cramer and D. G. Hartwell
Caldwell, Erskine, 1903-1987
August afternoon
Caldwell, E. The black & white stories of Erskine Caldwell
Big Buck
Caldwell, E. The black & white stories of Erskine Caldwell
Blue Boy
Caldwell, E. The black & white stories of Erskine Caldwell
Candy-Man Beechum
Caldwell, E. The black & white stories of Erskine Caldwell
The courting of Susie Brown
Caldwell, E. The black & white stories of Erskine Caldwell
Daughter
Caldwell, E. The black & white stories of Erskine Caldwell
The end of Christy Tucker
Caldwell, E. The black & white stories of Erskine Caldwell

Caldwell, Erskine, 1903-1987—*Continued*

The fly in the coffin
  Caldwell, E. The black & white stories of Erskine Caldwell
Kneel to the rising sun
  Caldwell, E. The black & white stories of Erskine Caldwell
  The Norton book of American short stories
Maud Island
  Mississippi River tales; ed. by F. McSherry; C. G. Waugh and M. H. Greeberg
Meddlesome Jack
  Caldwell, E. The black & white stories of Erskine Caldwell
The medicine man
  Inspired by drink; ed. by Joan Digby and John Digby
The Negro in the well
  Caldwell, E. The black & white stories of Erskine Caldwell
Nine dollars' worth of mumble
  Caldwell, E. The black & white stories of Erskine Caldwell
The people v. Abe Lathan, colored
  Caldwell, E. The black & white stories of Erskine Caldwell
Picking cotton
  Caldwell, E. The black & white stories of Erskine Caldwell
The picture
  Caldwell, E. The black & white stories of Erskine Caldwell
Return to Lavinia
  Caldwell, E. The black & white stories of Erskine Caldwell
Runaway
  Caldwell, E. The black & white stories of Erskine Caldwell
Saturday afternoon
  Caldwell, E. The black & white stories of Erskine Caldwell
Savannah River payday
  Caldwell, E. The black & white stories of Erskine Caldwell
Squire Dinwiddy
  Caldwell, E. The black & white stories of Erskine Caldwell
Wild flowers
  Caldwell, E. The black & white stories of Erskine Caldwell
Yellow girl
  Caldwell, E. The black & white stories of Erskine Caldwell

Caldwell, Price
A sense of place
  Mississippi writers v1: Fiction; ed. by D. Abbott
The **calendar** chest. Pribus, M.
Calendar Day. Potter, N. A. J.
CALENDARS
Baumbach, J. Who shall escape whipping

Calf Roper's bandit car. Conley, R. J.
Calf Roper's house guest. Conley, R. J.
CALGARY (ALTA.) *See* Canada—Calgary
Caliban. Silverberg, R.
Caliban's revenge. Schweitzer, D.
The **calico** dog. Eberhart, M. G.
CALIFORNIA

> *See also* Mojave Desert (Calif.); Morro Bay (Calif.); Sierra Nevada Mountains (Calif. and Nev.)

Birtha, B. In the deep heart's core
Fisher, M. F. K. Mrs. Teeters' tomato jar
Gates, E. A yellow man and a white
Schwartz, J. Day trip
Silverberg, R. Amanda and the alien
Silverberg, R. The palace at midnight

19th century
Harte, B. The idyl of Red Gulch
1846-1900
Atherton, G. F. H. The wash-tub mail
Davis, S. Miss Armstrong's homicide
Harte, B. The outcasts of Poker Flat
20th century
Ballantyne, S. Pelicans in flight
Barich, B. Hard to be good
Birtha, B. In the deep heart's core
Boyd, W. The care and attention of swimming pools
Boyd, W. Love hurts
Boyd, W. My girl in skintight jeans
Camoin, F. A. It could happen
Canin, E. Where we are now
Carpenter, L. The ebbing
Dodd, S. M. Snowbird
Doubiago, S. Ramon/Ramona
Doubiago, S. Raquel
Drewe, R. Looking for Malibu
Dubus, A. Waiting
Fante, J. The dreamer
Fontana, D. C. Cut to: murder
Gilchrist, E. The Double Happiness Bun
Gilchrist, E. Jade Buddhas, red bridges, fruits of love
Gilchrist, E. The starlight express
Greenwood, R. Charley Wales
Greenwood, R. Seed grain
Haas, B. Dying in the goldenwest
Haas, B. The green life
Haas, B. Like a cactus in a field of corn
Haas, B. Princess Gilda talks to the unborn
Haas, B. When California was an island
Haas, B. A wolf in the heart
Haas, B. You'll remember me long after
Handke, P. The long way around
Hauptman, W. Sierra wave
Hempel, A. Tonight is a favor to Holly
Kessler, J. F. The foundation
Kessler, J. F. Sphinx
L'Heureux, J. The comedian
Miriam, L. Maiden names
Monreal, D. N. In the train station

CALIFORNIA—20th century—*Continued*
Morris, W. Since when do they charge admission
Muller, M. The broken men
Pronzini, B. Smuggler's Island
Robison, J. The ecstasy of the animals
St. Clair, M. The wines of earth
Stegner, W. E. Field guide to the western birds
Steinbeck, J. The chrysanthemums
West, J. Alive and real
Wilson, B. Miss Venezuela
Wolff, T. The poor are always with us
Farm life
See Farm life—California
Gold discoveries
See California—1846-1900
Berkeley
Scholz, C. The menagerie of Babel
Beverly Hills
Gault, W. C. The Kerman kill
Simpson, M. Three maids' children
Carmel
Adams, A. Molly's dog
Hollywood
Bloch, R. His and hearse
Bloch, R. Terror over Hollywood
Breen, J. L. Starstruck
Coriolan, J. A marriage, a mantra, a massage
Fante, J. Hail Mary
Goulart, R. How come my dog don't bark?
Hanson, D. The whisper business
Henderson, M. R. Dream house
Kees, W. Do you like the mountains?
O'Hara, J. Natica Jackson
Reaves, J. M. Werewind
Russell, R. Ding-dong, the lizard's dead
Wagner, K. E. More sinned against
Los Angeles
Boucher, A. QL 696.C9
Bowers, J. Crackers
Boyd, W. Not yet Jayette
Brandt, P. L.A. child
Canin, E. Where we are now
Ciment, J. Small claims
Cooper, S. Terminal Island
DeMarinis, R. The smile of a turtle
Matheson, R. C. Dead end
McConnor, V. The house of crime
McEwan, I. Psychopolis
Nolan, W. F. Pirate's moon
Silverberg, R. Against Babylon
Silverberg, R. The pardoner's tale
Thompson, S. L.A.
Wilson, B. The Hulk
Los Gatos
Rees, D. Quiet days in Los Gatos
Monterey
Abbott, K. The second Pete
Oakland
Salas, F. Kid victory

Palm Springs
Adams, A. The oasis
San Francisco
Atherton, G. F. H. The foghorn
Barich, B. The end of the world
Berriault, G. The infinite passion of expectation
Davis, S. A fair exchange
Doubiago, S. Warriors
Fetler, J. The dust of Yuri Serafimovich
Gold, H. San Francisco petal
Gold, H. Waiting for the forty-one union
Gold, H. Winter of '73
Hauptman, W. Kozmic Blues
Kotzwinkle, W. Postcard found in a trunk
Lee, H. Lucia and old lace
Michaels, L. Toiler
Pronzini, B. The pattern
Rees, D. At 21st Street
Rees, D. In the fast lane
Ryan, N. Stavrogin
Vogan, S. China across the bay
Wolff, T. Our story begins
Santa Barbara
Camoin, F. A. Diehl: the wandering years
Santa Cruz
Connell, E. S. The fisherman from Chihuahua
Santa Monica
Williams, T. The mattress by the tomato patch
Venice
Eisenstein, S. Ecospasm
Fox, G. Return to Venice
California. Thurm, M.
The **Caliph,** cupid, and the clock. Henry, O.
Calisher, Hortense
A Christmas carillon
    Family: stories from the interior; ed. by G. G. Chavis
The Evershams' Willie
    Southwest Review 72:298-335 Summ '87
Gargantua
    Calisher, H. Saratoga, hot
Heartburn
    Haunting women; ed. by A. Ryan
The library
    Calisher, H. Saratoga, hot
The middle drawer
    Full measure; ed. by D. Sennett
The passenger
    Calisher, H. Saratoga, hot
Real impudence
    Calisher, H. Saratoga, hot
Saratoga, hot
    Calisher, H. Saratoga, hot
The sound track
    Calisher, H. Saratoga, hot
The summer rebellion
    Haunted New England; ed. by C. G. Waugh; M. H. Greenberg and F. D. McSherry

Calisher, Hortense—*Continued*
Survival techniques
  Calisher, H. Saratoga, hot
The tenth child
  Calisher, H. Saratoga, hot
The **call**. O'Brien, E.
Call at Corazón. Bowles, P.
Call first. Campbell, R.
A **call** from brotherland. Taylor, P. E.
A **call** loan. Henry, O.
The **call** of Cthulhu. Lovecraft, H. P.
The **call** of the running tide. Chard, J.
Call of the sea. Durrell, L.
The **call** of the wild: the dog-flea version.
  Watson, I.
The **Calla** Lily Cleaners & Dyers. West, J.
Callaghan, Barry
The black queen
  The Oxford book of Canadian short
    stories in English
  Sudden fiction; ed. by R. Shapard and
    J. Thomas
Callaghan, Morley
Absolution
  The Substance of things hoped for; ed.
    by J. B. Breslin
A cap for Steve
  The World of the short story; ed. by
    C. Fadiman
Last spring they came over
  The Oxford book of Canadian short
    stories in English
A wedding-dress
  The Treasury of English short stories;
    ed. by N. Sullivan
The **caller**. Liben, M.
Calling. Miller, S.
Calling all gumdrops! Sladek, J. T.
Calling card. Campbell, R.
Calling Dr. Clockwork. Goulart, R.
Calloway's climb. Sandberg, P. L.
The **calm**. Carver, R.
Calm seas and a prosperous voyage.
  Wetherell, W. D.
The **calmative**. Beckett, S.
Calvert, Mary
Deirdre
  *New England Review and Bread Loaf
    Quarterly* 11:181-90 Wint '88
Calvin—his life and death. See Warner, C.
  D. Calvin, the cat
Calvin, the cat. Warner, C. D.
Calvino, Italo
Adam, one afternoon [Variant title: One
    afternoon, Adam . . .]
  Calvino, I. Difficult loves
  The Slaying of the dragon; ed. by F.
    Rottensteiner
The adventure of a bather
  Calvino, I. Difficult loves
The adventure of a clerk
  Calvino, I. Difficult loves

The adventure of a nearsighted man
  Calvino, I. Difficult loves
The adventure of a photographer
  Calvino, I. Difficult loves
The adventure of a poet
  Calvino, I. Difficult loves
The adventure of a reader
  Calvino, I. Difficult loves
The adventure of a soldier
  Calvino, I. Difficult loves
The adventure of a traveler
  The Art of the tale; ed. by D. Halpern
  Calvino, I. Difficult loves
Animal woods
  Calvino, I. Difficult loves
The Argentine ant
  Black water; ed. by A. Manguel
Autumn: the garden of stubborn cats
    [Variant title: The garden of stubborn
    cats]
  Roger Caras' Treasury of great cat
    stories
Big fish, little fish
  Calvino, I. Difficult loves
Casanova's memoirs
  Esquire 101:104-8 F '84
The crow comes last
  Calvino, I. Difficult loves
Desire in November
  Calvino, I. Difficult loves
Dollars and the demimondaine
  Calvino, I. Difficult loves
The enchanted garden
  Calvino, I. Difficult loves
Fear on the footpath
  Calvino, I. Difficult loves
A goatherd at luncheon
  Calvino, I. Difficult loves
Going to headquarters
  Calvino, I. Difficult loves
The house of the beehives
  Calvino, I. Difficult loves
Hunger at Bévera
  Calvino, I. Difficult loves
The implosion
  The Literary Review (Madison, N.J.)
    28:215-17 Wint '85
Lazy sons
  Calvino, I. Difficult loves
Man in the wasteland
  Calvino, I. Difficult loves
Mine field
  Calvino, I. Difficult loves
One of the three is still alive
  Calvino, I. Difficult loves
A ship loaded with crabs
  Calvino, I. Difficult loves
Sleeping like dogs
  Calvino, I. Difficult loves
Theft in a pastry shop
  Calvino, I. Difficult loves
Transit bed
  Calvino, I. Difficult loves

The **Camberwell** beauty. Pritchett, V. S.
CAMBODIA
 Baillie, A. Snap
 Keeley, E. Cambodian diary
Cambodian diary. Keeley, E.
CAMBRIDGE (ENGLAND) *See* England—
 Cambridge
CAMBRIDGE (MASS.) *See* Massachusetts—
 Cambridge
Cambridge is sinking! Clayton, J. J.
CAMELS
 Highsmith, P. Djemal's revenge
Camera obscura. Daitch, S.
Cameron, Anne
 Magic in a world of magic
 Hear the silence; ed. by I. Zahava
Cameron, Eric
 Ace in the hole
 Short story international 47
 The dark mirror
 Short story international 59
 The girl on the beach
 Short story international 45
 The last visit
 Short story international 44
Cameron, Lindsley
 Private lesson
 The New Yorker 64:32-40 My 2 '88
Cameron, Michael Rink
 And the hunter home from the hill
 Editor's choice II; ed. by M. Sklar and
 M. Biggs
Cameron, Peter
 Archeology
 Cameron, P. One way or another
 Excerpts from Swan Lake
 Cameron, P. One way or another
 The Kenyon Review ns7:41-7 Spr '85
 Prize stories, 1986
 Fast forward
 Cameron, P. One way or another
 The New Yorker 60:42-7 F 4 '85
 Fear of math
 Cameron, P. One way or another
 The New Yorker 61:42-9 Mr 11 '85
 Freddie's haircut
 Cameron, P. One way or another
 The Kenyon Review ns8:56-63 Wint '86
 Grounded
 Cameron, P. One way or another
 Homework
 Cameron, P. One way or another
 The New Yorker 60:46-9 My 7 '84
 Prize stories, 1985
 Jump or dive
 Cameron, P. One way or another
 The New Yorker 61:38-44 Je 17 '85
 The last possible moment
 Cameron, P. One way or another
 Melissa & Henry—September 10, 1983
 Cameron, P. One way or another
 The New Yorker 60:40-5 Je 18 '84

 Memorial Day
 Cameron, P. One way or another
 The next best thing to happy
 Mademoiselle 91:106+ Je '85
 Nuptials & heathens
 Cameron, P. One way or another
 Odd jobs
 Cameron, P. One way or another
 The New Yorker 61:24-8 Ja 20 '86
 Practically engaged
 Mademoiselle 91:128+ Mr '85
 The secret dog
 The Kenyon Review ns9:1-7 Fall '87
 Slowly
 The New Yorker 63:28-32 Ja 18 '88
 What do people do all day?
 Cameron, P. One way or another
 Why I live where I live
 Rolling Stone p97+ Jl 16-30 '87
The **Cameronian** preacher's tale. Hogg, J.
Camille Pissaro 1830-1903. Lurie, M.
Camoin, François André, 1939-
 The Amelia Barons
 Camoin, F. A. Why men are afraid of
 women
 Cheerful wisdom
 Camoin, F. A. Why men are afraid of
 women
 Diehl: the wandering years
 Camoin, F. A. Why men are afraid of
 women
 Home is the Blue Moon Cafe
 Camoin, F. A. Why men are afraid of
 women
 A hunk of burning love
 The Best of the West; ed. by J. Thomas
 Camoin, F. A. Why men are afraid of
 women
 It could happen
 Camoin, F. A. Why men are afraid of
 women
 The Georgia Review 38:327-44 Summ '84
 Miami
 Camoin, F. A. Why men are afraid of
 women
 Peacock blue
 Camoin, F. A. Why men are afraid of
 women
 Sometimes the wrong thing is the right
 thing
 Camoin, F. A. Why men are afraid of
 women
 A special case
 Camoin, F. A. Why men are afraid of
 women
 Things I did to make it possible
 Sudden fiction; ed. by R. Shapard and
 J. Thomas
 La vida
 Camoin, F. A. Why men are afraid of
 women
CAMORRA
 Conrad, J. Il Conde

Camouflage. Gingher, M.
Camouflage. Hall, T. T.
CAMP COUNSELORS
Klass, P. Trivia
Shaw, J. B. The trail to the ledge
Camp Rose. Freeman, J.
Campaign. Bedford, J.
CAMPAIGNS, PRESIDENTIAL
United States
See Presidents—United States—Election
Campanile, Achille
Lord Brummel; or, How not to get noticed
The Literary Review (Madison, N.J.)
28:218-19 Wint '85
Campbell, Anne
April
The Old dance; ed. by B. Burnard
Campbell, Ewing
Delphinium blue
Campbell, E. Piranesi's dream
Duties and liabilities
Campbell, E. Piranesi's dream
The forty and eight
Campbell, E. Piranesi's dream
The ghost of an apprehension
Campbell, E. Piranesi's dream
La güera
Campbell, E. Piranesi's dream
In the Rambla de Cataluña
Campbell, E. Piranesi's dream
Maundy Thursday
Campbell, E. Piranesi's dream
Out of empty cisterns
Campbell, E. Piranesi's dream
Piranesi's dream
Campbell, E. Piranesi's dream
The room in the Driskill
The Kenyon Review ns8:57-60 Summ '86
September crickets
Campbell, E. Piranesi's dream
Sister love
*New England Review and Bread Loaf
Quarterly* 11:95-102 Aut '88
Squares of opposition, signs of disorder
Campbell, E. Piranesi's dream
The Kenyon Review ns7:71-83 Spr '85
They're talking about Chernobyl today
Campbell, E. Piranesi's dream
Watch without time
Campbell, E. Piranesi's dream
Campbell, John W., Jr.
Who goes there?
Baker's dozen: 13 short science fiction
novels
The Mammoth book of classic science
fiction; ed. by I. Asimov; C. G.
Waugh and M. H. Greenberg
Campbell, Katie
Author's tour
Critical Quarterly 30:23-8 Wint '88

Campbell, Laura
A sum of moments
L. Ron Hubbard presents Writers of the
future v2
Campbell, Ramsey, 1946-
Among the pictures are these
Campbell, R. Cold print
Apples
Halloween horrors; ed. by A. Ryan
Before the storm
Campbell, R. Cold print
Blacked out
Campbell, R. Cold print
Call first
After midnight; ed. by C. L. Grant
Calling card
Christmas ghosts; ed. by K. Cramer and
D. G. Hartwell
The church in High Street
Campbell, R. Cold print
Cold print
Campbell, R. Cold print
Dolls
Campbell, R. Scared stiff
The faces at Pine Dunes
Campbell, R. Cold print
The hands
Cutting edge; ed. by D. Etchison
The horror from the bridge
Campbell, R. Cold print
The inhabitant of the lake
Campbell, R. Cold print
The insects from Shaggai
Campbell, R. Cold print
The invocation
Lost souls; ed. by J. Sullivan
Lilith's
Campbell, R. Scared stiff
Loveman's comeback
Campbell, R. Scared stiff
Mackintosh Willy
The Best of Shadows; ed. by C. L.
Grant
The Dark descent; ed. by D. G. Hart-
well
Merry May
Campbell, R. Scared stiff
The moon-lens
Campbell, R. Cold print
Next time you'll know me
Prime evil; ed. by D. E. Winter
Old clothes
Midnight; ed. by C. L. Grant
The other side
The Year's best fantasy, first annual
collection
The other woman
Campbell, R. Scared stiff
The render of the veils
Campbell, R. Cold print
The room in the castle
Campbell, R. Cold print

Campbell, Ramsey, 1946—*Continued*
The scar
  Lost souls; ed. by J. Sullivan
Second sight
  Masques II; ed. by J. N. Williamson
The seductress
  Campbell, R. Scared stiff
Seeing the world
  Shadows 7
The show goes on
  Silver scream; ed. by D. J. Schow
Stages
  Campbell, R. Scared stiff
The sunshine club
  Vampires; ed. by A. Ryan
The tugging
  Campbell, R. Cold print
The voice of the beach
  Campbell, R. Cold print
Where the heart is
  The Architecture of fear; ed. by K.
    Cramer and P. D. Pautz
The will of Stanley Brooke
  Campbell, R. Cold print
The words that count
  Masters of darkness; ed. by D. Etchison
Campbell, Wanda Blynn, 1944-
The baby
  Campbell, W. B. The promise
Birthday party
  Campbell, W. B. The promise
Death is always part of dinner
  Campbell, W. B. The promise
The favour
  Campbell, W. B. The promise
Headlights
  Campbell, W. B. The promise
In season
  Campbell, W. B. The promise
Kisses
  Campbell, W. B. The promise
Moose
  Campbell, W. B. The promise
Of generations
  Campbell, W. B. The promise
Rabbit
  Campbell, W. B. The promise
Socks
  Campbell, W. B. The promise
The thaw
  Campbell, W. B. The promise
Campbell Oakley's gospel sun shines on Roy
  Singing Grass. Wier, A.
The **camper**. Sprengnether, M.
The **campers**. Winters, J.
CAMPING
        See also Wilderness survival
Blackwood, A. The willows
Crane, S. A tent in agony
Gault, C. This bright night
Haake, K. Recently I've discovered my
  mistake
Hagy, A. C. Shoreline

Logue, M. Boundary waters
Morrison, J. The man on the 'bidgee
Schulman, H. In God's country
Thomas, D. Extraordinary little cough
Wegner, R. Incident at the old tin bridge
Campion, Edith
Good morning wardrobe
  Women's work; ed. by M. McLeod and
    L. Wevers
Campos, Julieta, 1932-
All the roses
  Women's fiction from Latin America; ed.
    by E. P. Garfield
A redhead named Sabina [excerpt]
  Women's fiction from Latin America; ed.
    by E. P. Garfield
Campos-De Metro, Joseph
And there was Bert
  Campos-De Metro, J. The slugger heart
    & other stories
Bands
  Campos-De Metro, J. The slugger heart
    & other stories
Evvy's brother
  Campos-De Metro, J. The slugger heart
    & other stories
The feather
  Campos-De Metro, J. The slugger heart
    & other stories
The grape's vine, the horse's mouth
  Campos-De Metro, J. The slugger heart
    & other stories
Little mooses
  Campos-De Metro, J. The slugger heart
    & other stories
Shooting for Jupiter
  Campos-De Metro, J. The slugger heart
    & other stories
The slugger heart
  Campos-De Metro, J. The slugger heart
    & other stories
Stock
  Campos-De Metro, J. The slugger heart
    & other stories
CAMPS, SUMMER *See* Summer camps
Camps. Dann, J.
CAMPUS LIFE *See* College life
Camus, Albert, 1913-1960
The adulterous woman
  The Art of the tale; ed. by D. Halpern
The growing stone
  On being foreign; ed. by T. J. Lewis and
    R. E. Jungman
The renegade
  The Nobel reader; ed. by J. Eisen and
    S. Troy
Can a Morris Minor break the speed of
  sound? Safransky, R.
Can ball. Dickson, M.
Can-can. Vivante, A.
Can daddy come home? Dyer, S.
Can I stay here? O'Hara, J.
A **can** of smoked oysters. Abbott, K.

Can the blind lead the blind? Latham, J.
Can these bones live? Windsor, G.
Can these dry bones live? Russell, W. C.
The **can** with the diamond notch. O'Kelly, S.
Can you feel anything when I do this? Sheckley, R.
Can you prove it? Asimov, I.
Can you top this? Lish, G.
Canaan. Smith, C.
CANADA
>See also Klondike River Valley (Yukon)

Harrison, S. F. The idyl of the island
Willis, C. Daisy, in the sun
>**20th century**

Brender à Brandis, M. Foreigner in the family
Carpentier, A. Birdy's flight
Choyce, L. Major repairs
Cook, H. The white rabbit
Ferron, J. The provinces
Gallant, M. Jorinda and Jorindel
Gallant, M. Thank you for the lovely tea
Gallant, M. Up north
Harvor, E. Heart trouble
Thompson, K. A blunt affair
Thompson, K. Some things I won't do
Wiebe, R. H. Where is the voice coming from?
>**College life**
>See College life—Canada
>**Farm life**
>See Farm life—Canada
>**Frontier and pioneer life**
>See Frontier and pioneer life—Canada
>**Politics**
>See Politics—Canada
>**Rural life**

Avery, M. Nazis, communists, Presbyterians & Jews in Norman Bethune's hometown
Brender à Brandis, M. All that counts
Burns, M. Greta
Burns, M. How it happened
Burns, M. Suburbs of the Arctic Circle
Campbell, W. B. In season
Campbell, W. B. Rabbit
Carrier, R. What language do bears speak?
Choyce, L. Local heroes
Cook, H. A Canadian education
Cook, H. Clown
Cook, H. Homesickness
Cook, H. Pisces
Crawford, I. V. Extradited
Dall, C. W. H. Annie Gray: a tale
Ferron, J. The bridge
Ferron, J. The dead cow in the canyon
Ferron, J. Mélie and the bull
Ferron, J. The parrot
Ferron, J. Tiresome company
Fines, B. Neighbors

Fréchette, L. Tom Cariboo
Gault, C. This now fenceless world
Hodgins, J. By the river
Huggan, I. Getting out of Garten
Huggan, I. Into the green stillness
Huggan, I. Queen Esther
Huggan, I. Secrets
Huggan, I. Sorrows of the flesh
Kamminga, A. Moleman
Kessler, J. F. Moses
Munro, A. Fits
Munro, A. Jesse and Meribeth
Munro, A. Lichen
Munro, A. The moon in the Orange Street Skating Rink
Munro, A. A queer streak
Munro, A. Royal beatings
Munro, A. White dump
Munro, A. Who do you think you are?
Munro, A. Working for a living
Ross, S. The lamp at noon
Thomas, A. C. Kill day on the government wharf
Valgardson, W. D. Bloodflowers
Vanderhaeghe, G. Cages
Vanderhaeghe, G. What I learned from Caesar
Wilson, E. From Flores
>**Alberta**

Cook, H. First snow
Kreisel, H. The broken globe
>**British Columbia**

Brender à Brandis, M. The little old Dutch church bell
Burns, M. Collected bear stories
St. Pierre, P. H. Cabin fever
St. Pierre, P. H. A day with a deer, a bear and Norah Smith
St. Pierre, P. H. December Nilsen
St. Pierre, P. H. Dry storm
St. Pierre, P. H. The education of Phyllisteen
St. Pierre, P. H. Frenchie's wife
St. Pierre, P. H. How to run the country
St. Pierre, P. H. Ol Antoine's wooden overcoat
St. Pierre, P. H. The owner of the gang
St. Pierre, P. H. Sarah's copper
Watmough, D. Bowen Island confessions
>**Calgary**

Van Herk, A. Waiting for the rodeo
>**Gaspé Peninsula (Québec)**
>See Gaspé Peninsula (Québec)
>**Halifax**

Cook, H. Exodus
>**Klondike**
>See Klondike River Valley (Yukon)
>**Manitoba**

Roy, G. Ely! Ely! Ely!
Vanderhaeghe, G. Reunion
>**Montreal**

Bankier, W. One clear sweet clue
Blaise, C. A class of new Canadians

CANADA—Montreal—*Continued*
Blaise, C. North
Ferron, J. Back to Kentucky
Ferron, J. Back to Val-d'Or
Gallant, M. Between zero and one
Gallant, M. The chosen husband
Gallant, M. The doctor
Gallant, M. In youth is pleasure
Gallant, M. Saturday
Gallant, M. Varieties of exile
Gallant, M. Voices lost in snow
Gallant, M. With a capital T
Hood, H. Flying a red kite
Metcalf, J. Gentle as flowers make the stones
Spencer, E. Jean-Pierre
Wexler, J. The bequest
Wexler, J. For Ann
Wexler, J. Your eighteenth birthday was a long time ago

New Brunswick
Thompson, K. A local hanging
Thompson, K. Night train through the snow to Montreal

Newfoundland
MacLeod, A. The lost salt gift of blood

Nova Scotia
Brender à Brandis, M. To grow into a man
MacDonald, D. R. Eyestone
MacDonald, D. R. The flowers of Bermuda
MacDonald, D. R. Holy Annie
MacDonald, D. R. Of one kind
MacDonald, D. R. Poplars
MacDonald, D. R. Sailing
MacDonald, D. R. The wharf king
MacDonald, D. R. Work
MacLeod, A. The boat
MacLeod, A. The closing down of summer
Raddall, T. H. The wedding gift

Ontario
Bissoondath, N. A short visit to a failed artist
Gallant, M. Orphans' progress
Garner, H. One-two-three little Indians
Levine, N. A small piece of blue
MacLeod, A. Winter dog

Québec (Province)
Carrier, R. What language do bears speak?
Châtillon, P. Ghost island
Dagg, M. The second coming of Little Richard [excerpt]
Marshall, J. The old woman
Roiter, H. Only Sam knows
Scott, D. C. The Desjardins

Saskatchewan
West, J. Hunting for hoot owls

Toronto
Bissoondath, N. The cage
Bissoondath, N. Christmas lunch
Bissoondath, N. Dancing
Mukherjee, B. Isolated incidents

Watson, S. The rumble seat
Wexler, J. Two year's absence

Vancouver
Kinsella, W. P. Punchlines

Vancouver Island
See Vancouver Island (B.C.)

Victoria
Cook, H. Cracked wheat

Yukon Territory
Curwood, J. O. Back to God's country
London, J. All Gold Canyon
London, J. At the rainbow's end
London, J. A daughter of the aurora
London, J. Nam-Bok, the unveracious
London, J. Negore, the Coward
London, J. The sickness of Lone Chief
London, J. To build a fire
London, J. To the man on the trail
London, J. Which make men remember

The **Canadian** Diaspora. Avery, M.
A **Canadian** education. Cook, H.
Canadian experience. Clarke, A. C.
CANADIAN SOLDIERS *See* Soldiers—Canada

CANADIANS
Africa
Mukherjee, B. The world according to Hsü

England
Kinsella, W. P. To look at the Queen
Vanderhaeghe, G. The expatriates' party
Wexler, J. Simon goes to London

Europe
Bissoondath, N. Continental drift

France
Cohen, M. Café Le Dog
Cohen, M. Sentimental meetings
Gallant, M. Virus X
Levine, N. Something happened here

Greece
Thomas, A. C. The dance

Japan
Green, E. Peters in Shinjuku: a set of miniatures

Switzerland
Gallant, M. Bonaventure
Gallant, M. The ice wagon going down the street
Gallant, M. In the tunnel

United States
Bronstein, E. Magic
Elflandsson, G. Icarus
MacDonald, D. R. The Chinese rifle
Munro, A. Miles City, Montana

Canal Road. Oates, J. C.

CANARIES
Granit, A. Free the canaries from their cages!
Mansfield, K. The canary
Nowakowski, M. The canary
Canaries. Kawabata, Y.
Canary. Cowan, P.
The **canary.** Mansfield, K.
The **canary.** Nowakowski, M.

A **canary** for one. Hemingway, E.
Canavan's back yard. Brennan, J. P.
Canavan's knee. Weaver, G.
CANBERRA (AUSTRALIA) *See* Australia—
   Canberra
Cancelled. Matheson, R. C.
CANCER
   Cameron, P. Fast forward
   Conroy, F. Celestial events
   Dubus, A. Adultery
   Farmer, B. Inheritance
   Ferrell, A. Why people get cancer
   Flanagan, M. Death in Sussex
   Friedman, P. A period of grace
   Gerber, M. J. Straight from the deathbed
   Greene, G. Doctor Crombie
   Groff, D. Nobody's child
   Halligan, M. Remember the rug
   Harrison, M. J. The incalling
   Houbein, L. I shall live until I die
   Hunnicutt, E. A hidden thing
   Ioannides, P. The unseen aspect
   Leavitt, D. Counting months
   Leavitt, D. Radiation
   Michaelson, L. W. The rhyme in Freddy's
     face
   Moskowitz, F. In going is a drama
   Nagibin, IU. M. The peak of success
   Neville, S. Banquet
   O'Hara, J. The pig
   Potter, N. A. J. Gypsies
   Roth, H. H. This time
   Rule, J. Slogans
   Stern, R. G. Dr. Cahn's visit
   Sullivan, T. A night at the head of a
     grave
   Van Langenberg, C. An unfinished head
   Watson, I. Immune dreams
   Wilk, M. Singing with Skulnick
   Willett, J. The jaws of life
   Wilner, H. Consultations
   Wodhams, J. Aunt Agnes
Candala. Chesbro, G. C.
Candelaria, Nash, 1928-
   El patrón
     Cuentos Chicanos; ed. by R. A. Anaya
     and A. Márquez
Candelora. Pirandello, L.
The **candidate**. Tuohy, F.
The **Candide** of copiers. Friedman, B. J.
A **candle** for milk and grass. Brown, G. M.
Candle in a cosmic wind. Manzione, J.
Candlebark. Eldridge, M.
CANDLES
   Böll, H. Candles for the Madonna
   Howard, H. The dipping of the candle-
     maker
   Willson, H. A Christmas tale
Candles for the Madonna. Böll, H.
Candles in the bottom of the pool. Evans,
   M.
The **candles** of your eyes. Purdy, J.

CANDLESTICKS
   Waters, E. Cold spell
The **candy**. Piñera, V.
Candy. Ruffolo, L.
Candy-Man Beechum. Caldwell, E.
The **candy** skull. Bradbury, R.
Cane Road. Wiesinger, S.
Cane toads. Murphy, P.
Canes. Rees, D.
Canessa, Gustavo
   Notes of a condottiere
     Short story international 46
Canin, Ethan
   American Beauty
     Canin, E. Emperor of the air
   The carnival dog, the buyer of diamonds
     Canin, E. Emperor of the air
   Emperor of the air
     The Atlantic 254:88-93 D '84
     The Best American short stories, 1985
     Canin, E. Emperor of the air
   Lies
     Canin, E. Emperor of the air
   Pitch memory
     Canin, E. Emperor of the air
   Star Food
     The Best American short stories, 1986
     Canin, E. Emperor of the air
   We are nighttime travelers
     Canin, E. Emperor of the air
     Esquire 109:114-18 Ja '88
   Where we are now
     The Atlantic 258:48-53 Jl '86
     Canin, E. Emperor of the air
     The New generation; ed. by A. Kaufman
   The year of getting to know us
     The Atlantic 259:47-9+ Mr '87
     Canin, E. Emperor of the air
Canned goods. Disch, T. M.
CANNES (FRANCE) *See* France—Cannes
CANNIBALISM
   Aickman, R. Growing boys
   Anderson, P. Welcome
   Borowski, T. The supper
   Campbell, R. The hands
   Cave, H. B. Footprints in Perdu
   Dickens, C. Captain Murderer and the
     Devil's bargain
   Drake, M. The feast to end all feasts
   Dunsany, E. J. M. D. P., Baron. The two
     bottles of relish
   El Rahman, M. A. Gentlemen eating gen-
     tlemen
   Gallagher, S. By the river, Fontainebleau
   Hazel, P. Having a woman at lunch
   Household, G. Taboo
   Katz, S. Friendship
   Kessler, J. F. Perceval
   King, S. Survivor type
   Lovecraft, H. P. The picture in the house
   Lutz, J. Tough
   Matheson, R. C. Incorporation
   McGrath, P. The boot's tale

CANNIBALISM—*Continued*
Nolan, W. F. Pirate's moon
Piñera, V. A few children
Piñera, V. Meat
Pronzini, B. Thirst
Reamy, T. Beyond the cleft
West, J. A. Gladys's Gregory
Wilson, R. The thing that stared

Canning, Victor
Lady in the dark
John Creasey's Crime collection, 1986
The **cannon**. Greenwood, R.
The **cannons** of the Atocha. Daley, R.
The **canoe**. Gilbert, D.
The **canoes**. Dunn, D.

CANOES AND CANOEING
Dunn, D. The canoes
Rosa, J. G. The third bank of the river
Smith, C. Crystal River
The **canonization**. Krist, G.
The **Canterville** ghost. Wilde, O.

Canton, William
The song of the Minster
Christian short stories; ed. by M. Booth

Cantwell, Mary
First love
Ladies' Home Journal 101:88+ Je '84
The **canvasser's** tale. Twain, M.

Canzoneri, Robert
The harp of the winds
Mississippi writers v1: Fiction; ed. by D. Abbott
An introduction to opera
The Southern Review (Baton Rouge, La.) 21:168-77 Ja '85
Upstream
The Southern Review (Baton Rouge, La.) 24:924-33 Aut '88

Cao Guanlong
Three professors
Roses and thorns; ed. by P. Link
A **cap** for Steve. Callaghan, M.
The **cape**. Eliade, M.
Cape Breton is the thought control centre of Canada. Smith, R.

CAPE COD (MASS.) *See* Massachusetts—Cape Cod

CAPE TOWN (SOUTH AFRICA) *See* South Africa—Cape Town
The **capital** of the world. Hemingway, E.

CAPITAL PUNISHMENT
Chekhov, A. P. The bet
Matthews, J. Mange
Capital punishment. Oates, J. C.

CAPITALISM
Böll, H. The railway station of Zimpren
Feng Jicai. The Mao button

CAPITALISTS AND FINANCIERS
See also Bankers; Millionaires; Wealth
Evans, M. Candles in the bottom of the pool
Greenwood, R. Seed grain

Caplan, Nora
Murder in miniature
Alfred Hitchcock's Grave suspicions

Caponegro, Mary, 1956-
Analysis of the vessel and its contents
Caponegro, M. Tales from the next village
The convention
Caponegro, M. Tales from the next village
Deformity
Caponegro, M. Tales from the next village
Heart as nails
Caponegro, M. Tales from the next village
Monday
Caponegro, M. Tales from the next village
The Star Cafe
Caponegro, M. Tales from the next village
Tales from the next village
Caponegro, M. Tales from the next village

Capote, Truman, 1924-1984
Children on their birthdays
The Art of the tale; ed. by D. Halpern
A Modern Southern reader; ed. by B. Forkner and P. Samway
Stories of the modern South; ed. by B. Forkner and P. Samway
"I remember my grandpa"
Redbook 168:36-7+ D '86
Miriam
The World of the short story; ed. by C. Fadiman

CAPRI
Wells, H. G. A dream of Armageddon
Capricorn games. Silverberg, R.
The **captain**. Dubus, A.
The **captain** and his horse. Markham, B.
Captain Blackman. Williams, J. A.
Captain Blood. Barthelme, D.
The **captain** has bad dreams. Algren, N.
Captain Heimrich stumbles. Lockridge, F. L. D., and Lockridge, R.
Captain Hendrik's story. Ingalls, R.
Captain Joe. McCormack, E. P.
Captain Leopold and the ghost-killer. Hoch, E. D.
Captain Leopold goes home. Hoch, E. D.
Captain Leopold goes to the dogs. Hoch, E. D.
Captain Leopold looks for the cause. Hoch, E. D.
Captain Leopold plays a hunch. Hoch, E. D.
Captain Leopold's secret. Hoch, E. D.
Captain Murderer. See Dickens, C. Captain Murderer and the Devil's bargain
Captain Murderer and the Devil's bargain. Dickens, C.
Captain Nemo's revenge. Verne, J.

A **captain** out of Etruria. Leach, A. R.
Captain Stormfield's visit to heaven. Twain, M.
The **captain's** house. Farmer, B.
The **captain's** house. Stead, C.
CAPTAINS OF SHIPS *See* Shipmasters
Captions. Banks, R.
The **captive.** Borges, J. L.
The **captive.** Pacheco, J. E.
The **captive** outfielder. Wibberley, L.
The **captives.** Leonard, E.
The **captives** of Longjumeau. Bloy, L.
The **capture** of Cerberus. Christie, A.
The **car.** Thomas, D.
Car games. Conroy, F.
Car wrecks and bleeding hearts. Scott, G.
Caravaggio. Barich, B.
The **Caravaggio** kid. Hochstein, R.
Caravan. Asscher-Pinkhof, C.
CARAVANS
   Thomas, D. After the fair
Caraway. Kinsella, W. P.
The **carbide** lamp. Pascoe, B.
Carbo-loading. Apple, M.
The **carbon** paper poet. Dennison, G.
Carbonation. Martone, M.
Card, Orson Scott
   America
      The Year's best science fiction, fifth annual collection
   Eumenides in the fourth floor lavatory
      Masterpieces of terror and the supernatural; ed. by M. Kaye and S. Kaye
   The fringe
      Nebula awards 21
      The Year's best science fiction, third annual collection
   Hatrack River
      Terry Carr's Best science fiction and fantasy of the year #16
      The Year's best science fiction, fourth annual collection
   Salvage
      Nebula awards 22
   A sepulcher of songs
      Omni book of science fiction 2
   St. Amy's tale
      Omni book of science fiction 1
Card game. Blinkin, M.
The **card-players.** Lurie, M.
Cardal, Matías
   Yesterday's angel
      Américas 36:12-15 My/Je '84
The **cardboard** box. Doyle, Sir A. C.
The **cardboard** man. Winters, J.
Carden, Sarah
   Live performance
      McCall's 145:153-4 Mr '87
Cárdenas, Magolo
   But what if I liked the Panchos, not the Beatles
      Anthology of contemporary Latin American literature, 1960-1984

CARDIFF GIANT
   Twain, M. A ghost story
CARDINALS
   MacLaverty, B. The break
CARDS
      See also Tarot
   Coleman, W. Gamblers
   Dann, J. Blind shemmy
   Glasser, P. The last game
   Hartley, L. P. Witheling End
   Hoch, E. D. The theft of the four of spades
   Jones, D. C. Raised in the wilderness
   Lurie, M. The card-players
   McGarry, J. Providence, 1970: behind this soft eclipse
   Sorrells, R. T. The all-time master grandmaster of solitaire
Cards. Beattie, A.
The **cards** of Eldrianza. Schaub, M. H.
The **care** and attention of swimming pools. Boyd, W.
Care in the holding. Brady, M.
Career. Boyle, K.
A **career.** Narayan, R. K.
Careful. Carver, R.
A **careful** man dies. Bradbury, R.
Careful, or you might get scratched. Dash, J.
A **careless** man of the 20th century. Ignatow, R. G.
Carelessness. Chekhov, A. P.
Carey, Jacqueline
   Another party
      The New Yorker 62:46-52 N 10 '86
   Good gossip
      The New Yorker 62:30-7 Je 2 '86
Carey, Mary, 1925-
   The entrance exam
      Young witches & warlocks; ed. by I. Asimov; M. H. Greenberg and C. G. Waugh
Carey, Peter
   Crabs
      The Australian short story; ed. by L. Hergenhan
   Report on the shadow industry
      Australian science fiction; ed. by V. Ikin
Cargo. Sturgeon, T.
CARIBBEAN ISLANDS *See* West Indies
CARIBBEAN REGION
   Antoni, R. W. Frogchild on the day of Corpus Christi
   Bloch, R. Terror in Cut-throat Cove
   Elliott, L. T. Flint/steel sparks on tropic moon-night
   Jacobsen, J. The mango community
   Jaffe, H. John Crow
   Shacochis, B. Hot day on the Gold Coast
   Shacochis, B. Hunger
   Shacochis, B. Mundo's sign
   Thomas, N. At the market
The **Cariboo** Cafe. Viramontes, H. M.

Caring for Rosie. Schell, J.

Carl Herst. Ocampo, S.

Carlin, M. M.
Waiting for His Excellency
Encounter (London, England) 66:3-5 Ja '86

Carlin's trio. Burgin, R.

Carlisle, Andrea, 1944-
Don't it make you wonder
Editor's choice II; ed. by M. Sklar and M. Biggs

CARLOS I, KING OF SPAIN *See* Charles V, Holy Roman Emperor, 1500-1558

CARLSBAD CAVERNS NATIONAL PARK (N.M.)
Willson, H. Front seat

Carlson, Judy
Assignment: love
Seventeen 43:96-7+ F '84

Carlson, Ron
Air
New stories from the South: the year's best, 1986
At the hop
The Editors' choice v3; ed. by G. E. Murphy, Jr.
Bigfoot stole my wife
Carlson, R. The news of the world
Blood and its relationship to water
Carlson, R. The news of the world
Family ritual
McCall's 114:43-5 Ja '87
The Governor's Ball
Carlson, R. The news of the world
The H Street sledding record
Carlson, R. The news of the world
Half life
Carlson, R. The news of the world
I am Bigfoot
Carlson, R. The news of the world
Harper's 273:36 D '86
Life before science
Carlson, R. The news of the world
Madame Zelena finally comes clean
Carlson, R. The news of the world
Max
Carlson, R. The news of the world
Milk
The Best American short stories, 1987
Carlson, R. The news of the world
The North American Review 271:11-15 D '86
Olympus Hills
Carlson, R. The news of the world
Phenomena
The Best of the West; ed. by J. Thomas
Carlson, R. The news of the world
Reading the paper
Sudden fiction; ed. by R. Shapard and J. Thomas
Santa Monica
Carlson, R. The news of the world

The status quo
Carlson, R. The news of the world
The time I died
Carlson, R. The news of the world
The uses of videotape
Carlson, R. The news of the world

CARMEL (CALIF.) *See* California—Carmel

Carmela. Ruta, S.

Carmen and Maia. Sandel, C.

Carmen Miranda's navel. Parris, P. B.

Carmilla. Le Fanu, J. S.

The **carnation.** Maheux-Forcier, L.

Carneiro, André
Life as an ant
Tales from the planet Earth
A perfect marriage
The Penguin world omnibus of science fiction

CARNIVAL
Alter, R. E. "I," said the fly
Bloch, R. The animal fair
Bloch, R. The double whammy
Bradbury, R. Corpse carnival
Bradbury, R. The dwarf
Maniaty, T. 'Who was that masked man?'
Marlowe, S. The shill
Moravia, A. What use have I got for carnival?
Pronzini, B., and Malzberg, B. N. Another burnt-out case
Stuart, J. No hero
Tyre, N. Carnival day

Carnival. Francis, H. E.

Carnival day. Tyre, N.

The **carnival** dog, the buyer of diamonds. Canin, E.

Carnival for the gods. Swan, G.

CARNIVALS (CIRCUS) *See* Amusement parks

A **Carol** Christmas. Allen, R.

Carol Oneir's hundredth dream. Jones, D. W.

A **Carolina** Christmas carol. Daniels, C.

Caroling on command. Toner, G. R.

CAROLS
Naipaul, S. Mr. Sookhoo and the carol singers

Carousel. Derleth, A. W.

The **carp.** Li, F.-Y.

The **carp.** Masuji, I.

The **carp.** Nordin, S.

Carpenter, David
The father's love
The Old dance; ed. by B. Burnard

Carpenter, David A.
The body mask
The Southern Review (Baton Rouge, La.) 24:435-44 Spr '88

Carpenter, Helen, and Carpenter, Lorri
The disappearing diamond
The Womansleuth anthology; ed. by I. Zahava

Carpenter, Leonard
The ebbing
L. Ron Hubbard presents Writers of the future
Carpenter, Lorri
(jt. auth) See Carpenter, Helen, and Carpenter, Lorri
CARPENTERS
Engberg, S. Morgan and Joanna
Gimbel, A. Hardwood
Hammer, C. The new roof
Kōda, R. The five-storied pagoda
Mazel, D. The merry-go-round
Nagibin, ÍÙ. M. By a quiet lake
Nam, C.-H. Chaos
Norris, L. A piece of archangel
Olmstead, R. What to do first
Shukshin, V. M. Shiva dancing
Carpentier, André
Birdy's flight
Invisible fictions; ed. by G. Hancock
The seven dreams and the reality of Perrine Blanc
Intimate strangers; ed. by M. Cohen and W. Grady
CARPETS
Al-Shaykh, H. The Persian carpet
Bloch, R. Son of a witch
Gault, W. C. The Kerman kill
Carr, Carol
Tooth fairy
Omni (New York, N.Y.) 6:106-8+ S '84
(jt. auth) See Carr, Terry, 1937-1987, and Carr, Carol
Carr, Cathy
Claire de la lune
Ploughshares 14 no2/3:100-17 '88
Carr, Jayge
Blind spot
Omni book of science fiction 2
The heart in the egg
Isaac Asimov's Tomorrow's voices
The price of lightning
Moonsinger's friends; ed. by S. Shwartz
Webrider
Omni book of science fiction 3
Carr, John Dickson, 1906-1977
"As drink the dead . . . "
The Deadly arts; ed. by B. Pronzini and M. Muller
The black cabinet
Handle with care; ed. by J. Kahn
The gentleman from Paris
Manhattan mysteries; ed. by B. Pronzini; C. L. R. Waugh and M. H. Greenberg
The house in Goblin Wood
Masterpieces of terror and the supernatural; ed. by M. Kaye and S. Kaye
Invisible hands
Death locked in; ed. by D. G. Greene and R. C. S. Adey
The proverbial murder
The Penguin classic crime omnibus

Strictly diplomatic
Masterpieces of mystery and suspense; ed. by M. H. Greenberg
Carr, Pat Esslinger
The party
Selected stories from The Southern review, 1965-1985
Carr, Pat M., 1932-
Diary of a Union soldier
The Southern Review (Baton Rouge, La.) 21:534-46 Ap '85
Indian burial
Prize stories, Texas Institute of Letters; ed. by M. Terry
Night of the luminarias
Here's the story: fiction with heart; ed. by M. Sklar
Carr, Terry, 1937-1987
The Dance of the Changer and the Three
Terry's universe; ed. by B. Meacham
Thus I refute
100 great fantasy short short stories; ed. by I. Asimov; T. Carr and M. H. Greenberg
Carr, Terry, 1937-1987, and Carr, Carol
Some are born cats
Magicats! Ed. by J. Dann and G. Dozois
Roger Caras' Treasury of great cat stories
Carraud, Jypé
For piano and vocal accompaniment
Great French detective stories; ed. by T. J. Hale
Carrère, Enrique Jorge Contou- *See* Contou-Carrère, Enrique Jorge
The **carriage-lamps.** Crane, S.
CARRIAGES AND CARTS
Edwards, A. A. B. The phantom coach
Gogol', N. V. The coach
Lawson, H. A double buggy at Lahey's Creek
Carrier, Roch, 1937-
The bird
Invisible fictions; ed. by G. Hancock
The ink
Invisible fictions; ed. by G. Hancock
The room
Invisible fictions; ed. by G. Hancock
Steps
Invisible fictions; ed. by G. Hancock
The wedding
Invisible fictions; ed. by G. Hancock
What language do bears speak?
The Oxford book of French-Canadian short stories
Carrig, Joan
One husband too many
Mademoiselle 91:116+ F '85
Carrington, Leonora, 1917-
As they rode along the edge
Carrington, L. The seventh horse, and other tales

Carrington, Leonora, 1917— *Continued*

Cast down by sadness
Carrington, L. The seventh horse, and other tales

The debutante
Carrington, L. The house of fear

Et in bellicus lunarum medicalis
Carrington, L. The seventh horse, and other tales

The happy corpse story
Carrington, L. The seventh horse, and other tales

The house of fear
Carrington, L. The house of fear

How to start a pharmaceuticals business
Carrington, L. The seventh horse, and other tales

Little Francis
Carrington, L. The house of fear

A man in love [Variant title: The beloved]
Carrington, L. The house of fear

A Mexican fairy tale
Carrington, L. The seventh horse, and other tales

Monsieur Cyril de Guindre
Carrington, L. The seventh horse, and other tales

My flannel knickers
Carrington, L. The seventh horse, and other tales

My mother is a cow
Carrington, L. The seventh horse, and other tales

The neutral man
Carrington, L. The seventh horse, and other tales

The oval lady
Carrington, L. The house of fear

Pigeon, fly!
Carrington, L. The seventh horse, and other tales

The royal summons [Variant title: The royal command]
Carrington, L. The house of fear

The seventh horse
Carrington, L. The seventh horse, and other tales

The sisters
Carrington, L. The seventh horse, and other tales

The skeleton's holiday
Carrington, L. The seventh horse, and other tales

The stone door
Carrington, L. The seventh horse, and other tales

The three hunters
Carrington, L. The seventh horse, and other tales

Uncle Sam Carrington
Carrington, L. The house of fear

Waiting
Carrington, L. The seventh horse, and other tales

White rabbits
Carrington, L. The seventh horse, and other tales

Carrion comfort. Simmons, D.

Carrion crypt. Yerxa, L.

Carroll, Gladys Hasty, 1904-

Head of the line
The Best Maine stories; ed. by S. Phippen; C. Waugh and M. Greenberg

Carroll, Jonathan, 1949-

Friend's best man
The Year's best fantasy, first annual collection

Carroll, L. E.

The very last party at #13 Mallory Way
L. Ron Hubbard presents Writers of the future v3

Without wings
L. Ron Hubbard presents Writers of the future

CARROLL, LEWIS, 1832-1898

About

Bloch, R. All on a golden afternoon

CARS (AUTOMOBILES) *See* Automobiles

Cars. Finger, A.

A **Carson** poker incident. Davis, S.

Cartagena Portalatín, Aida

"Colita"
Anthology of contemporary Latin American literature, 1960-1984

Carter, Alice Ann

The fortune hunter
Old maids; ed. by S. Koppelman

Carter, Angela, 1940-

Black Venus
Carter, A. Saints and strangers

The cabinet of Edgar Allan Poe
Carter, A. Saints and strangers
Interzone: the first anthology; ed. by J. Clute; C. Greenland and D. Pringle

The courtship of Mr. Lyon
The Treasury of English short stories; ed. by N. Sullivan

The donkey prince
Don't bet on the prince; ed. by J. Zipes

The Fall River axe murders
Carter, A. Saints and strangers

Flesh and the mirror
The Penguin book of modern British short stories

The kiss
Carter, A. Saints and strangers

The kitchen child
Carter, A. Saints and strangers

Our Lady of the Massacre
Carter, A. Saints and strangers

Overture and incidental music for A midsummer night's dream
Carter, A. Saints and strangers

Carter, Angela, 1940-—*Continued*
Peter and the wolf
Carter, A. Saints and strangers

Carter, Barbara
The secrets of phylogeny, or What Jason knew
The North American Review 271:42-3 Je '86

Carter, Emily
All the men are called McCabe
Between C & D; ed. by J. Rose and C. Texier

Carter, Lin
Geydelle's protective
Magic in Ithkar 2; ed. by A. Norton and R. Adams
The goblinry of Ais
Magic in Ithkar [1]; ed. by A. Norton and R. Adams

Carter, Michelle
Teacher
20 under 30; ed. by D. Spark
The things that would never be mine
The New generation; ed. by A. Kaufman

Carter, Nicholas, 1865-1922
The mystery of room no. 11
Death locked in; ed. by D. G. Greene and R. C. S. Adey

Carter, Paul A.
(jt. auth) See Benford, Gregory, 1941-, and Carter, Paul A.

Carter, Robert, 1945-
Cityman
Carter, R. The pleasure within
Composition
Carter, R. The pleasure within
The drought
Carter, R. The pleasure within
A generous man
Carter, R. The pleasure within
Kid in a bin
Carter, R. The pleasure within
Critical Quarterly 28:31-6 Wint '86
Mal and fem
Carter, R. The pleasure within
The pleasure
Carter, R. The pleasure within
Prints in the valley
Carter, R. The pleasure within
Sixties into eighties won't go
Carter, R. The pleasure within
Tergiversator
Carter, R. The pleasure within
Within
Carter, R. The pleasure within
Carter fell. Bowering, G.
The **carter's** wench. Maupassant, G. de
CARTHAGE (ANCIENT CITY)
Anderson, P. Delenda est
Bishop, M. For thus do I remember Carthage

Cartier, Francis A.
The signals
From mind to mind: tales of communication from Analog
Cartoon. Coover, R.
The **cartoonist.** Hankla, C.
CARTOONISTS
Apple, M. Walt and Will
Drewe, R. After Noumea
Goulart, R. Out of the inkwell
Kinsella, W. P. The further adventures of Slugger McBatt
Lurie, M. My greatest ambition
Stout, R. See no evil
Cartwright, Vickie
The winner
'Teen 29:46+ Jl '85
Carunungan, Celso Al.
Hide-out for a hero
A Treasury of World War II stories; ed. by B. Pronzini and M. H. Greenberg
The **carved** table. Peterson, M.
Carver, Raymond
After the denim
Full measure; ed. by D. Sennett
Are these actual miles?
Carver, R. Where I'm calling from
Bicycles, muscles, cigarettes
Carver, R. Where I'm calling from
Blackbird pie
Carver, R. Where I'm calling from
The New Yorker 62:26-34 Jl 7 '86
Boxes
The Best American short stories, 1987
The Bread Loaf anthology of contemporary American short stories; ed. by R. Pack and J. Parini
Carver, R. Where I'm calling from
New American short stories; ed. by G. Norris
The New Yorker 62:31-7 F 24 '86
The calm
Carver, R. Where I'm calling from
Careful
Carver, R. Where I'm calling from
The Pushcart prize IX
Cathedral
Carver, R. Where I'm calling from
Look who's talking; ed. by B. Weber
Chef's house
Carver, R. Where I'm calling from
Collectors
Carver, R. Where I'm calling from
The compartment
New directions in prose and poetry 50
Distance
Carver, R. Where I'm calling from
Elephant
Carver, R. Where I'm calling from
The New Yorker 62:38-45 Je 9 '86
Errand
The Best American short stories, 1988
Carver, R. Where I'm calling from

Carver, Raymond—*Continued*
  The New Yorker 63:30-6 Je 1 '87
  Prize stories, 1988

Fat
  The Art of the tale; ed. by D. Halpern
  Carver, R. Where I'm calling from

Feathers
  Carver, R. Where I'm calling from

Fever
  American short story masterpieces; ed.
    by R. Carver and T. Jenks
  Carver, R. Where I'm calling from

Gazebo
  Buying time; ed. by S. Walker
  Carver, R. Where I'm calling from

Intimacy
  Carver, R. Where I'm calling from
  Esquire 106:58-60 Ag '86

Little things
  Carver, R. Where I'm calling from

Menudo
  Carver, R. Where I'm calling from
  The Graywolf annual 4

Neighbors
  Carver, R. Where I'm calling from

Nobody said anything
  Carver, R. Where I'm calling from

One more thing
  Carver, R. Where I'm calling from

Popular mechanics
  Sudden fiction; ed. by R. Shapard and
    J. Thomas

Put yourself in my shoes
  Carver, R. Where I'm calling from

A serious talk
  Carver, R. Where I'm calling from

A small, good thing
  Carver, R. Where I'm calling from
  The Ploughshares reader: new fiction for
    the eighties
  The World of the short story; ed. by
    C. Fadiman

So much water so close to home
  Carver, R. Where I'm calling from
  The Interior country; ed. by A. Black-
    burn

The student's wife
  Carver, R. Where I'm calling from

They're not your husband
  Carver, R. Where I'm calling from

The third thing that killed my father off
  [Variant title: Dummy]
  The Best of the West; ed. by J. Thomas
  Carver, R. Where I'm calling from

Vitamins
  Carver, R. Where I'm calling from

What do you do in San Francisco?
  Carver, R. Where I'm calling from

What we talk about when we talk about
    love
  Carver, R. Where I'm calling from
  Love stories for the time being; ed. by
    G. D. Chipps and B. Henderson
  The Norton book of American short
    stories

What's in Alaska
  Carver, R. Where I'm calling from

Where I'm calling from
  Carver, R. Where I'm calling from

Whoever was using this bed
  Carver, R. Where I'm calling from
  The New Yorker 62:33-40 Ap 28 '86

Why don't you dance?
  Carver, R. Where I'm calling from

Why, honey?
  Carver, R. Where I'm calling from

Carver, Wayne
  With voice of joy and praise
  Greening wheat: fifteen Mormon short
    stories

The **carving**. Gómez Antelo, C.

The **carving**. Taylor, A.

Cary, Alice
  An old maid's story
  Old maids; ed. by S. Koppelman

Cary, Arthur Joyce Lunel *See* Cary, Joyce,
    1888-1957

Cary, Joyce, 1888-1957
  New women
  The Treasury of English short stories;
    ed. by N. Sullivan
  A private ghost
  Ready or not; ed. by J. Kahn

CASABLANCA (MOTION PICTURE)
  Coover, R. You must remember this

CASANOVA, GIACOMO, 1725-1798
                    About
  Hofmann, G. Casanova and the extra

Casanova and the extra. Hofmann, G.

Casanova's memoirs. Calvino, I.

Casares, Adolfo Bioy *See* Bioy Casares, Adol-
    fo, 1914-

Cascade point. Zahn, T.

Case, David
  Fengriffen
  The Mammoth book of short horror
    novels; ed. by M. Ashley

The **case**. El Makk, A.

Case blue. Twohy, R.

A **case** for Kop. Böll, H.

A **case** for quiet. Jeffrey, W.

A **case** for quiet. Pronzini, B.

The **case** for the defence. Greene, G.

Case history. Durrell, L.

Case history #4: Fred. Janowitz, T.

Case history #15: Melinda. Janowitz, T.

Case history #179: Tina. Janowitz, T.

A **case** of Chivas Regal. Higgins, G. V.

A **case** of conscience. Austin, M. H.

A **case** of dementia. Kirchheimer, G. L.

A **case** of identity. Doyle, Sir A. C.

The **case** of M. Valdemar. Poe, E. A.
A **case** of maximum need. Fremlin, C.
The **case** of the caretaker. Christie, A.
The **case** of the dancing sandwiches. Brown, F.
The **case** of the emerald sky. Ambler, E.
The **case** of the frozen diplomat. Heald, T.
Case of the gentlemen poet. Ambler, E.
The **case** of the horizontal trajectory. Škvorecký, J.
The **case** of the masked corporal, that is, the poet resuscitated. Apollinaire, G.
The **case** of the missing will. Christie, A.
The **case** of the Parr children. Fraser, A.
The **case** of the perfect maid. Christie, A.
A **case** of the stubborns. Bloch, R.
Case still open. Dé, C., and Dandurand, A.
The **casebook** Casanova. Tripp, M.
Casey, Gavin
Short-shift Saturday
The Australian short story; ed. by L. Hergenhan
Casey, John, 1939-
Avid
The New Yorker 64:37-46+ Ap 18 '88
Casey and Sarah. Taylor, A.
Casey at the bat. Deford, F.
Casey's empire. Kress, N.
Cash. Young-Bruehl, E.
Cash in hand. Gilbert, M.
Cash or credit. McCandless, D. B.
The **cashier.** Colette
The **cask** of Amontillado. Poe, E. A.
Casper, Linda Ty- *See* Ty-Casper, Linda
Casper, Susan
Covenant with a dragon
In the field of fire; ed. by J. Van B. Dann and J. Dann
The haunting
Shadows 7
Spring fever
Midnight; ed. by C. L. Grant
Spring-fingered Jack
Ripper! Ed. by G. Dozois and S. Casper
Caspers, Nona
"Bus is coming!"
Stiller's pond; ed. by J. Agee; R. Blakely and S. Welch
Cassandra. Cherryh, C. J.
The **Cassandra.** Zahn, T.
Cassiday, Bruce
Deep-sleep
Baker's dozen: 13 short espionage novels
CASSINO (ITALY), BATTLE OF, 1944
Sambrot, W. The man who hated
Cassino casualty. Davin, D.
Cassirer, Nadine Gordimer *See* Gordimer, Nadine, 1923-
Cassity, Kevin
The age-old problem of who
Greening wheat: fifteen Mormon short stories

Cassutt, Michael
Stillwater, 1896
Mississippi River tales; ed. by F. McSherry; C. G. Waugh and M. H. Greenberg
Shadows 7
Cast down by sadness. Carrington, L.
Cast for murder. Benton, K. C.
CASTE
Asimov, I. Strikebreaker
Leitão, L. Dona Amalia Quadros
India
Basu, R. Sambal and Putki
Sri Lanka
Swan, A. Monsoon
Castellanos, Rosario
Death of the tiger
Other fires; ed. by A. Manguel
Castillo, Ana
Ghost talk
Cuentos Chicanos; ed. by R. A. Anaya and A. Márquez
Castillo, Rafael C.
The miracle
Southwest tales; ed. by Alurista and X. Rojas-Urista
Castle, Mort
If you take my hand, my son
Masques II; ed. by J. N. Williamson
Party time
Masques; ed. by J. N. Williamson
The **castle.** Petrakis, H. M.
Castle Nowhere. Woolson, C. F.
CASTLES
Anderson, K. J., and Fortier, R. Skeleton in the closet
Campbell, R. The room in the castle
Doyle, Sir A. C. Selecting a ghost. The ghosts of Goresthorpe Grange
Hartley, L. P. The killing bottle
Hoffmann, E. T. A. The entail
Kirk, R. Balgrummo's hell
Kleist, H. von. The beggarwoman of Locarno
Le Fanu, J. S. Carmilla
Leskov, N. S. An apparition in the Engineers' Castle
Lovecraft, H. P. The outsider
Metcalfe, J. The feasting dead
Sagan, F. The exchange
Sheckley, R. The Skag Castle
CASTRATION
Hemingway, E. God rest you merry, gentlemen
Olmstead, R. A pair of bulls
Painter, P. Winter evenings: spring night
Tournier, M. Prikli
The **Castro** baby. Austin, M. H.
CASUALTIES (WORLD WAR, 1914-1918)
See World War, 1914-1918—Casualties
CASUALTIES (WORLD WAR, 1939-1945)
See World War, 1939-1945—Casualties
The **casualty.** Böll, H.

The **Cat**. Freeman, M. E. W.
The **cat**. Metcalfe, R.
The **cat**. Shannon, D.
The **cat**. Silva, B.
The **cat**. Wolfe, G.
Cat and muse. Wolf, R.
The **cat** and the casino. Sagan, F.
The **cat** and the coffee drinkers. Steele, M.
Cat and the Other. Dunn, M.
The **cat** by the fire. Hunt, L.
Cat dance. Feuer, E.
The **cat** from hell. King, S.
The **cat-hater**. DeGrazia, E.
The **cat** in the attic. Martin, V.
The **cat** in the picture. Morris, W.
Cat in the rain. Hemingway, E.
The **cat** lover. Burger, K.
The **Cat Man**. Liggett, B.
A **cat** may look. Matthews, J.
Cat nipped. Schaefer, J. W.
The **cat** that walked by himself. Kipling, R.
The **cat** who fought the rain. Shaw, J. B.
The **cat** who lived in a drainpipe. Aiken, J.
CATACOMBS
    Doyle, Sir A. C. The new catacomb
    Poe, E. A. The cask of Amontillado
Catalan night. Morand, P.
The **catalyst**. Chipulina, E. G.
Catalyst. Kurtz, K.
Catalytic converter. Franklin, P.
Cataract. Baxter, C.
A **catastrophe**. Wells, H. G.
CATASTROPHES See Disasters
The **catbird** seat. Thurber, J.
The **catch**. Lesley, C.
Catch a tartar. Dickson, G. R.
Catch that zeppelin! Leiber, F.
Catch the sun. Longyear, B. B.
Catchers. Doyle, B.
The **catechist**. Barthelme, D.
Category Z. Abbott, L. K.
CATERERS AND CATERING
    Gilliatt, P. Catering
Catering. Gilliatt, P.
Catering. Lipman, E.
Cathay. Millhauser, S.
The **cathedral**. Bonosky, P.
Cathedral. Carver, R.
The **cathedral**. Walker, W.
CATHEDRALS
    Bear, G. Petra
    Golding, W. Miss Pulkinhorn
    James, M. R. An episode of cathedral history
Cather, Willa, 1873-1947
    The burglar's Christmas
        "May your days be merry and bright" and other Christmas stories by women; ed. by S. Koppelman
    Coming, Aphrodite!
        Great American love stories; ed. by L. Rosenthal

    On the divide
        She won the West; ed. by M. Muller and B. Pronzini
        Westward the women; ed. by V. Piekarski
    Paul's case
        Child's ploy; ed. by M. Muller and B. Pronzini
        The Norton book of American short stories
    The sentimentality of William Tavener
        Family: stories from the interior; ed. by G. G. Chavis
Catherine and Michael. Taylor, C.
Catherine Mulamphy and the man from the north. Colum, P.
CATHOLIC CHURCH See Catholic faith
CATHOLIC CLERGY See Catholic priests
CATHOLIC FAITH
    See also Bishops, Catholic; Cardinals; Catholic priests; Convent life; Inquisition; Monasticism and religious orders
    Albarelli, D. Honeymoon
    Austin, D. The bishop
    Behan, B. The confirmation suit
    Böll, H. In the Valley of the Thundering Hoofs
    Bonosky, P. The first robin in the world
    Bonosky, P. Sin
    Bradley, M. Z. Treason of the blood
    Campbell, R. The words that count
    Crowley, A. The mass of Saint Sécaire
    Daudet, A. The elixir
    Deaver, P. F. Silent retreats
    Dubus, A. A father's story
    Dubus, A. If they knew Yvonne
    Dubus, A. Voices from the moon
    Dybek, S. Hot ice
    Endō, S. A forty-year-old man
    Endō, S. Mothers
    Fante, J. Altar boy
    Fante, J. First Communion
    Fante, J. The Road to Hell
    Fante, J. The wrath of God
    Ferron, J. The provinces
    Fitzgerald, M. J. Communions
    Gardner, M. The horrible horns
    Grau, S. A. Letting go
    Greene, G. The hint of an explanation
    Greene, G. A visit to Morin
    Heise, K. Aunt Ella and my first communion
    Lavin, M. A voice from the dead (a monologue)
    Leitão, L. Jaffer's chicken
    Perea, R. L. Miracle at Chimayo
    Phelan, F. The battle of boiling water
    Spark, M. The Black Madonna
    Sutherland, M. Codling-moth
    Valenzuela, L. The son of Kermaria
    Valenzuela, L. Trial of the Virgin

CATHOLIC PRIESTS

See also Bishops, Catholic; Cardinals; Catholic faith

Aldani, L. Quo vadis, Francisco?
Avery, M. The Canadian Diaspora
Barthelme, D. The catechist
Benson, R. H. Father Meuron's tale
Bernen, R. Sacrament of the sick
Blais, M.-C. An act of pity
Bradbury, R. Bless me, Father, for I have sinned
Briskin, M. Florence, May '86
Burke, J. L. Lower me down with a golden chain
Calvino, I. Desire in November
Chesterton, G. K. The blue cross
Dangor, A. A strange romance
Day, R. C. Umbrella dance
DiFranco, A. M. The garden of redemption
Doyle, Sir A. C. The confession
Dubus, A. Adultery
Endō, S. Fuda-no-Tsuji
Endō, S. Old friends
Endō, S. Unzen
Fante, J. My father's God
García Márquez, G. One day after Saturday
García Márquez, G. Tuesday siesta
Hughes, M. G. The stuttering priest
Kirk, R. Watchers at the strait gate
Koch, C. You taught us good
Lemelin, R. The Stations of the Cross
MacLaverty, B. The beginnings of a sin
MacLaverty, B. Death of a parish priest
MacLaverty, B. St. Paul could hit the nail on the head
Martínez-Serros, H. Father Palomo
Martínez-Serros, H. "Learn! Learn!"
Maupassant, G. de. After
Maupassant, G. de. Christening
Maupassant, G. de. In the moonlight
Maupassant, G. de. Making a convert
McLaverty, M. The priest's housekeeper
Monterroso, A. The eclipse
Moore, G. A letter to Rome
Moore, G. The voice of the mountain
Mrożek, S. Siesta
O'Faoláin, S. Sinners
Paolucci, A. Rarà
Pavese, C. Festival night
Power, V. The miracle of Glendyne
Powers, J. F. The valiant woman
Powers, J. F. The warm sand
Ryan, A. Following the way
Schinto, J. Before sewing one must cut
Shaw, J. B. Love and other lessons
Silvis, R. A walk in the moonlight
Struthers, A. Gathering evidence
Thompson, R. Under the swaying curtain
Trevor, W. Death in Jerusalem
Van Greenaway, P. Indefinite article

Warner, S. T. One thing leading to another
Whelan, G. Two are better than one
Wolff, T. The missing person

CATHOLIC RELIGION *See* Catholic faith

CATHOLICS *See* Catholic faith

Catmagic. Chin, M. L.

CATS

Adams, J. C. Midshipman, the cat
Aiken, J. The cat who lived in a drainpipe
Archer, J. Just good friends
Barthelme, S. Chat
Bradley, M. Z. The wild one
Braun, L. J. The sin of Madame Phloi
Brown, F. Mouse
Burger, K. The cat lover
Calvino, I. Autumn: the garden of stubborn cats
Carr, T., and Carr, C. Some are born cats
Chin, M. L. Catmagic
Conley, R. J. Moon Face
Crowley, J. Antiquities
Curtiss, U. R. Snowball
Dabrowska, C. Huntress
Dadswell, M. The game
Dick, P. K. The alien mind
Dickson, G. R. Show me the way to go home
Dozois, G. R., and others. Afternoon at Schrafft's
Dunn, M. Cat and the Other
Durrell, L. Smoke, the embassy cat
Farjeon, E. Spooner
Ferreira, R. Guest for the weekend
Freeman, M. E. W. The Cat
Gallico, P. Jennie's lessons to Peter on how to behave like a cat
Gallico, P. "When in doubt—wash!"
Giles, M. Peril
Goulart, R. Groucho
Goyen, W. Zamour; or, A tale of inheritance
Hartley, L. P. Pains and pleasures
Hartley, L. P. Podolo
Hearn, L. The boy who drew cats
Hemingway, E. Cat in the rain
Herbert, J. Maurice and Mog
Highsmith, P. Engine horse
Highsmith, P. Ming's biggest prey
Hill, R. Bring back the cat!
Humphrey, W. Sister
Hunt, L. The cat by the fire
Jacobs, W. W. A black affair
Jacobs, W. W. The white cat
Jennings, G. Tom cat
Johnson, G. C. The man with the hoe
Keeling, N. Chasing her own tail
Keeling, N. Mine
King, S. The cat from hell
Kinsella, W. P. Syzygy
Kipling, R. The cat that walked by himself
Kurtz, K. Catalyst

CATS—*Continued*
 Le Fanu, J. S. The white cat of Drumgun-
  niol
 Le Guin, U. K. Schrödinger's cat
 Leiber, F. Space-time for springers
 Lessing, D. M. An old woman and her
  cat
 Liggett, B. The Cat Man
 Littke, L. A feline felony
 Lover, S. Ye marvelous legend of Tom
  Connor's cat
 Major, A. R. Kissmeowt and the healing
  friar
 Martin, V. The cat in the attic
 Matthews, J. A cat may look
 Maupassant, G. de. On cats
 Metcalfe, R. The cat
 Morris, W. The cat in the picture
 Morris, W. The cat's meow
 Morris, W. Drrdla
 Oates, J. C. The white cat
 Pacheco, J. E. The sunken park
 Poe, E. A. The black cat
 Pym, B. The Christmas visit
 Rey Rosa, R. A yellow cat
 Saki. The philanthropist and the happy cat
 Saki. Tobermory
 Sandel, C. Two cats in Paris and one in
  Florence
 Sandham, A. A. The conscientious cat
 Sargent, P. Out of place
 Sayers, D. L. The Cyprian cat
 Schaefer, J. W. Cat nipped
 Schmitz, J. H. Novice
 Shaw, J. B. The cat who fought the rain
 Shimaki, K. The black cat
 Silva, B. Precious
 Slesar, H. My father, the cat
 Smith, C. The crime and glory of Com-
  mander Suzdal
 Smith, C. The game of rat and dragon
 Stoker, B. The squaw
 Suckow, R. Three, counting the cat
 Tamer, Z. Sun for the young
 Tournier, M. Amandine; or, The two
  gardens
 Twain, M. Dick Baker's cat
 Warner, C. D. Calvin, the cat
 Warner, S. T. A pair of duelling pistols
 Wellman, M. W. The witch's cat
 Wheeler, H. C. The fat cat
 Williams, T. The malediction
 Wodehouse, P. G. The story of Webster
Cats. Hamerton, P. G.
Cats. Wilson, R., Jr.
Cats and students, bubbles and abysses.
  Bass, R.
Cat's eye. Valenzuela, L.
The **cat's** meow. Morris, W.
Cat's-paw. Pronzini, B.
CATTLE
 Adams, G. G. Marva Jean Howard confes-
  ses

 Blinkin, M. The little calf
 Boyle, K. His idea of a mother
 Crabtree, L. V. Prices' bewitched cow
 Crace, J. Talking Skull
 Evans, M. One-eyed sky
 Frame, J. The bull calf
 Gilgun, J. Cow
 Kauffman, J. Places in the world a woman
  could walk
 Kinsella, W. P. Beef
 MacLaverty, B. The bull with the hard hat
 Michaelson, L. W. Phocian
 Olmstead, R. A good cow
 Rose, M. Henderson
 West, J. Learn to say good-bye
The **cattle** pen. Leskov, N. S.
CATTLE THIEVES
 Mulford, C. E. Hopalong sits in
 Pronzini, B. All the long years
 Silko, L. Yellow Woman
 White, S. E. The two-gun man
Caught. Maupassant, G. de
Caught and bowled, Mrs. Craggs. Keating,
  H. R. F.
Caught in the act. Pronzini, B.
Caught in the organ draft. Silverberg, R.
Causation. Weinzweig, H.
Cause of death: hooked nose. Böll, H.
The **cause** of some recent changes. Gray, A.
The **causes.** St. Clair, M.
A **cautionary** tale. Eisenberg, D.
CAVALRY (U.S.) *See* United States. Army.
  Cavalry
Cave, Hugh B.
 Death tolls the bell
 Selected tales of grim and grue from the
  horror pulps; ed. by S. Jaffery
 Footprints in Perdu
  Whispers V
 The mission
  The Saturday Evening Post 259:42-5+ Mr
   '87
  The Saturday Evening Post 259:32+
   Ap '87
The **cave.** Han, S.-W.
Cave amantem. Bird, C.
CAVES
 Crane, S. Four men in a cave
 Hawthorne, N. The man of Adamant
 Simak, C. D. Grotto of the dancing deer
 Smith, C. A. The dweller in the gulf
Caviar. Boyle, T. C.
Cayenne Charlie. Brand, M.
Cease fire. Herbert, F.
Cecala, Kathy Petersen
 A place of our own
  McCall's 112:59-60 Mr '85
Cecco Angiolieri, malevolent poet. Schwob,
  M.
Cecil, Henry, 1902-1976
 The wanted man
  Through a glass, darkly; ed. by B. Woel-
   fel

Cecil grounded. Plant, R.
Cedering, Siv
Family album
The Georgia Review 40:57-9 Spr '86
Necessary fictions; ed. by S. W. Lindberg and S. Corey
Cehai, Cai
The distant sound of tree-felling
Short story international 51
Ceil. Brodkey, H.
The **celebrant.** Givner, J.
The **celebrated** jumping frog of Calaveras County. See Twain, M. The notorious jumping frog of Calaveras County
The **celebrated** Millard County Dramatic Stock Company. Lee, H.
Celebrating the Prophet's birthday. Roushdi, Z.
Celebration. Lawler, P.
Celebrations. Asscher-Pinkhof, C.
CELEBRITIES
Bail, M. Portrait of electricity
Daniels, C. Mrs. Eloise
Mathers, P. Lights
The **celery** munchers. Valenzuela, L.
Celestial events. Conroy, F.
The **Celestial** rail-road. Hawthorne, N.
Celia behind me. Huggan, I.
Celia is back. Hempel, A.
CELIBACY
See also Virginity
Moore, G. A letter to Rome
CELLARS
Bishop, M. A gift from the GrayLanders
Kirk, R. Lex Talionis
Ocampo, S. The basement
CELLISTS
Gilliatt, P. Staying in bed
McCullers, C. Poldi
Wilcox, J. North Gladiola [excerpt]
CELTS
De Camp, L. S., and Pratt, F. The green magician
The **cement** king. Conroy, J.
CEMETERIES
See also Tombstones
Ballantyne, S. Mourning Henry
Ballantyne, S. Perpetual care
Ballantyne, S. Untitled—Ink on paper
Barker, C. Scape-goats
Birtha, B. Baby town
Bissoondath, N. Counting the wind
Boylan, J. Potter's field
Canzoneri, R. The harp of the winds
Carr, P. M. Indian burial
Curley, D. Visiting the dead
Easton, T. A. Roll them bones
Flythe, S. Walking, walking
Fontane, T. A woman in my years
Gallagher, T. Bad company
Haas, B. A wolf in the heart
Hofmann, G. Casanova and the extra
Howes, C. The resurrection man

Kearns, R. Grave angels
Kotzwinkle, W. Letter to a swan
Kuttner, H. The graveyard rats
Lovecraft, H. P. The hound
Lovecraft, H. P. The statement of Randolph Carter
Malamud, B. A lost grave
Matthews, J. The grave at Mount Nebo
Maupassant, G. de. Graveyard sirens
Maupassant, G. de. Was it a dream?
O'Brien, F.-J. The child that loved a grave
O'Kelly, S. The weaver's grave
Stead, C. La Toussaint (All Saints' Day, November 1)
Sutter, B. You ain't dead yet
Wendt, A. Prospecting
Windsor, G. Can these bones live?
The **censors.** Valenzuela, L.
CENSORSHIP
Essop, A. Film
Harris, M. The martyred poet
Heise, K. The condemned movie
Tsutsui, Y. Standing woman
Valenzuela, L. The censors
Centaurus changeling. Bradley, M. Z.
The **centennial** comment. Alter, R. E.
The **center.** Lott, J.
The **center** of attraction. Covino, M.
The **centerfielder.** Ramírez, S.
The **centipede.** Shimaki, K.
CENTIPEDES
Donaldson, S. R. The conqueror worm
Shimaki, K. The centipede
CENTRAL AMERICA
Kessler, J. F. Maya
Mukherjee, B. The middleman
Updike, J. The ideal village
Politics
See Politics—Central America
The **centre** of gravity. Mitchell, K.
The **centre** of the universe is 18 Baedekerstrasse. Gathorne-Hardy, J.
The **centurion.** Doyle, Sir A. C.
Cephalus. Strand, M.
CERAMICS *See* Pottery
CEREBRAL PALSY
Johnston, S. Iris Holmes
CEREMONIES *See* Rites and ceremonies
Ceremony. Broughton, T. A.
The **ceremony.** Kees, W.
Ceremony. Nolan, W. F.
A **ceremony** of innocence. Bates, A. J.
A **certain** date. Wolf, C.
Certain distant suns. Greenburg, J.
A **certain** kind of people. Faik, S.
A **certain** kind of skill. Gill, B. M.
A **certain** star. Buck, P. S.
A **certain** view. Wilbur, E.
A **certain** voice. Kaikō, T.
Certain winds from the south. Aidoo, C. A. A.
CEYLON *See* Sri Lanka
Cezary Strzybisz, Necrobes. Lem, S.

"Châ". Colette

Chablis. Barthelme, D.

Chabon, Michael
Admirals
The New Yorker 63:34-8 S 14 '87
A foreign affair
Mademoiselle 93:196+ S '87
The Halloween party
The New Yorker 64:38-44 S 26 '88
The little knife
The New Yorker 64:28-30 Ap 4 '88

Chacón, Chacón. Everett, P. L.

Chadwick, Paul, 1959-
Fangs of the cobra
A Cent a story! Ed. by G. G. Roberts

Chae, Man-Sik
My idiot uncle
The Unenlightened, and other Korean
short stories

A Chagall story. Day, R. C.

Chagrin in three parts. Greene, G.

The chain in the heart. Creekmore, H.

The chain of Aforgomon. Smith, C. A.

Chain of pure hearts. Anderman, J.

Chained. Malzberg, B. N.

Chained to the fast lane in the Red Queen's
race. Ellison, H.

Chains. Mathers, P.

Chains of air, web of aether. Dick, P. K.

The chainsaw incident. Skrzynecki, P.

The chair. Davenport, G.

The chair. Longrigg, R.

The chair carrier. Idris, Y.

A chair for George. Rule, J.

Chair in the rain. Yamamoto, M.

The chair trick. Blei, N.

CHAIRS
Dickens, C. The bagman's story
Idris, Y. The chair carrier
Woodman, A. The cruelty of chairs

Châli. Maupassant, G. de

Chalice of death. Silverberg, R.

Chalk line. Sexson, L.

Chalk talk. Wellen, E.

A challenge. Pirandello, L.

The challenge. Vandercook, J. W.

The challenge. Vargas Llosa, M.

The challenge. Zahn, T.

Chamber music. Bliven, N.

The chamber of poetry. Brown, G. M.

Chambers, George
March 11
American made; ed. by M. Leyner; C.
White and T. Glynn
(jt. auth) See Greenberg, Barbara, 1940-,
and Chambers, George

**Chambers, Robert W. (Robert William),
1865-1933**
The pickets
A Treasury of Civil War stories; ed. by
M. H. Greenberg and B. Pronzini

The repairer of reputations
The Dark descent; ed. by D. G. Hart-
well
The yellow sign
Dark banquet; ed. by L. Child

Chambers, Whitman
The Duchess pulls a fast one
Hard-boiled dames; ed. by B. A. Drew

Chambers. McKinley, J.

Chambrun and the double event. Pentecost,
H.

Chambrun and the electronic ear. Pentecost,
H.

Chambrun and the melting swan. Pentecost,
H.

Chambrun and the obvious clue. Pentecost,
H.

Chambrun gets the message. Pentecost, H.

The Chameleon. Eisenberg, L.

Chamisso, Adelbert von, 1781-1838
The strange story of Peter Schlemihl
German romantic stories; ed. by F. G.
Ryder

Champagne for one. Penney, A.

The champagne party. Digby, J.

The champion. Clarke, T.

The champion. Gee, M.

Champion. Lardner, R.

The champion. Stuart, J.

Champion of the world. Flynn, R.

CHANCE
Fisk, N. Find the lady
Gardner, T. S. It's all a matter of luck
Heideman, E. M. Time and chance
Lutz, J. Close calls
Shiga, N. At Kinosaki
Wells, H. G. A catastrophe

Chance. Willis, C.

A chance encounter. Swados, H.

A chance for Mr. Lever. Greene, G.

A chance meeting. Colter, C.

Chand, Meira
The gift of Sunday
P.E.N. new fiction I

Chandler, A. Bertram, 1912-1984
The cage
The Penguin world omnibus of science
fiction
Don't knock the rock
Tales from the planet Earth
Kelly country
Australian science fiction; ed. by V. Ikin

Chandler, Raymond, 1888-1959
Blackmailers don't shoot
The Black mask boys; ed. by W. F.
Nolan
Trouble is my business
Great detectives; ed. by D. W. McCul-
lough
Wrong pigeon
The Mammoth book of private eye
stories; ed. by B. Pronzini and M. H.
Greenberg

Chandra, G. S. Sharat *See* Sharat Chandra, G. S.

Chang, Chieh *See* Zhang Jie, 1937-

Chang, Diana
Getting around
The North American Review 271:46-9 D '86

Chang, Hsi-kuo
Red boy
The Unbroken chain; ed. by J. S. M. Lau

Chang, Hsien-liang *See* Zhang Xianliang, 1936-

Chang, Ta-ch'un
Birds of a feather
The Unbroken chain; ed. by J. S. M. Lau

Chang, Yong-Hak
Poems of John the Baptist
A Respite, and other Korean short stories

Change. Dixon, S.

The **change.** Moskowitz, F.

Change at Jamaica. Ayers, M. A.

A **change** for the better. Mathers, P.

A **change** of air. Berthiaume, A.

Change of climate. Curtiss, U. R.

A **change** of heart. Glasser, L. B.

Change of heart. Kaufman, L.

Change of heart. Liben, M.

Change of heart. Pilcher, R.

Change of life. Block, L.

A **change** of ownership. Hartley, L. P.

A **changeable** report. Josipovici, G.

The **changeling.** Byatt, A. S.

The **changeling.** Silverberg, R.

The **changes.** Perkins, F.

Changes. Pronzini, B.

The **changing** of the guard. Serling, R.

Chanson d'automne. Eldridge, M.

Chaos. Nam, C.-H.

The **chaperon.** James, H.

CHAPLIN, CHARLIE, 1889-1977
About
Coover, R. Charlie in the house of rue

Chapman, Beverly
Now we are three
McCall's 113:102-3+ F '86

Chapman, Walker
For works written by this author under other names see Silverberg, Robert

Chappaquiddick. Doubiago, S.

Chappell, Fred, 1936-
Blue dive
Stories of the modern South; ed. by B. Forkner and P. Samway
Children of strikers
Sudden fiction; ed. by R. Shapard and J. Thomas
The snow that is nothing in the triangle
The Georgia Review 40:60-7 Spr '86
Necessary fictions; ed. by S. W. Lindberg and S. Corey

Chapter and verse. Marsh, Dame N.

A **chapter** of accidents. Archer, J.

The **chapter** on love. Murphy, P.

Chapters from the life of Vera Angi. Vészi, E.

The **character** of the lover. Morris, W.

CHARACTERS IN LITERATURE
Camoin, F. A. Diehl: the wandering years
Gilchrist, M. The pageant of ghosts
Shukshin, V. M. Before the cock crows thrice

Charades. Rand, P.

Charbonneau-Tissot, Claudette
Compulsion
Invisible fictions; ed. by G. Hancock

Chard, Judy
The call of the running tide
John Creasey's Crime collection, 1987

Charis. Working, R.

CHARITIES *See* Endowments

Charity begins at home. Shaik, F.

Charity dance. Robinson, R.

Charity ward. Bonosky, P.

CHARLEMAGNE, EMPEROR, 742-814
About
Pei, M. The bones of Charlemagne

CHARLES V, HOLY ROMAN EMPEROR, 1500-1558
About
Morazzoni, M. The last assignment

Charles, Franklin *See* Adams, Cleve Franklin, 1895-1949

Charles Atlas also dies. Ramírez, S.

CHARLES RIVER (MASS.)
Helprin, M. Palais de Justice

CHARLES THE GREAT *See* Charlemagne, Emperor, 742-814

CHARLESTON (S.C.) *See* South Carolina—Charleston

Charley Billy. Sorrells, R. T.

Charley Ford betrayed. Taylor, R.

Charley Wales. Greenwood, R.

Charley was our darlin'. Conroy, J.

Charlie in the house of rue. Coover, R.

Charlie-O. Kadohata, C.

Charlie Speed. Thomas, M.

Charlton, William
Hakanono
Stand one; ed. by M. Blackburn; J. Silkin and L. Tracy

The **charm** dispelled. Maupassant, G. de

Charmatz, Al
Sailing, through program management
From mind to mind: tales of communication from Analog

CHARMS
Arthur, R. The wonderful day
Bradley, M. Z. The secret of the Blue Star
Finney, J. Lunch-hour magic
Gilbert, W. S. Creatures of impulse
Gilbert, W. S. An elixir of love
Jacobs, W. W. The monkey's paw
Tamer, Z. A lone woman

Charnas, Suzy McKee
Listening to Brahms
Nebula awards 22
Omni (New York, N.Y.) 8:56-8+ S '86
A musical interlude
A Very large array; ed. by M. M. Snodgrass
Unicorn tapestry
Baker's dozen: 13 short fantasy novels
Vampires; ed. by A. Ryan
The **charnel** god. Smith, C. A.
Charney, Ann
From the outside
Ms. 12:58+ My '84
Charteris, Leslie, 1907-
The sizzling saboteur
Baker's dozen: 13 short espionage novels
The well-meaning mayor
Devils & demons; ed. by M. Kaye and S. Kaye
Chase, C.
In the Jardin des plantes
The Antioch Review 43:209-16 Spr '85
Chase, Virginia
The search
The Best Maine stories; ed. by S. Phippen; C. Waugh and M. Greenberg
The **chase**. Melville, H.
Chasek, Judith
A ticket to America
Short story international 52
CHASIDISM *See* Hasidism
Chasing her own tail. Keeling, N.
Chastain, Thomas
Directed verdict
Murder in Manhattan; ed. by B. Adler
The return of the Robins family
Redbook 164:60+ D '84
CHASTITY
Larson, L. Original sin
Chat. Barthelme, S.
CHATEAUX *See* Castles
Chatham County. Daniels, C.
Châtillon, Pierre
Ghost island
Invisible fictions; ed. by G. Hancock
Chatto, James
The atheist
Winter's tales, new ser. v1
Tricky customers
Winter's tales, new ser. v2
Chaucer, Geoffrey, d. 1400
The Reeve's tale
The Treasury of English short stories; ed. by N. Sullivan
CHAUFFEURS
Apollinaire, G. The deified invalid
Berry, R. M. November 14, 1864
Cadigan, P. Roadside rescue
Hartley, L. P. The prayer
Wilmot, T. The finger of suspicion
Chava. Sholem Aleichem

Chavez, Angelico
The angel's new wings
Chavez, A. The short stories of Fray Angelico Chavez
The ardent commandant
Chavez, A. The short stories of Fray Angelico Chavez
The bell that sang again
Chavez, A. The short stories of Fray Angelico Chavez
The black ewe
Chavez, A. The short stories of Fray Angelico Chavez
The Colonel and the santo
Chavez, A. The short stories of Fray Angelico Chavez
A desert idyll
Chavez, A. The short stories of Fray Angelico Chavez
The fiddler and the Angelito
Chavez, A. The short stories of Fray Angelico Chavez
Hunchback Madonna
Chavez, A. The short stories of Fray Angelico Chavez
The lean years
Chavez, A. The short stories of Fray Angelico Chavez
My ancestor—Don Pedro
Chavez, A. The short stories of Fray Angelico Chavez
The penitente thief
Chavez, A. The short stories of Fray Angelico Chavez
A Romeo and Juliet story in early New Mexico
Chavez, A. The short stories of Fray Angelico Chavez
The Tesuque Pony Express
Chavez, A. The short stories of Fray Angelico Chavez
Wake for Don Corsinio
Chavez, A. The short stories of Fray Angelico Chavez
Chávez, Denise
Willow game
Cuentos Chicanos; ed. by R. A. Anaya and A. Márquez
Chayah. Wolfenstein, M.
Che ti dice la patria? Hemingway, E.
Cheap day. Raphael, F.
Cheap in August. Greene, G.
Cheap seats. Klinkowitz, J.
Cheating the gallows. Zangwill, I.
Checking in. Murphy, P.
Checking out. Wolfe, G.
Checkmate. Archer, J.
The **checkup**. Kenney, S.
Cheer for me. McCollum, L.
Cheerful wisdom. Camoin, F. A.
The **cheerfulness** of the bush. Loukakis, A.

Cheever, John, 1912-1982

The angel of the bridge
Reader's Digest 130:99-103 Ap '87

The country husband
The Art of the tale; ed. by D. Halpern

The enormous radio
Look who's talking; ed. by B. Weber

The five-forty-eight
The World of the short story; ed. by
C. Fadiman

The lowboy
Christian short stories; ed. by M. Booth

The music teacher
Yankee witches; ed. by C. G. Waugh;
M. H. Greenberg and F. D. McSherry

The national pastime
Family: stories from the interior; ed. by
G. G. Chavis

The pot of gold
Great American love stories; ed. by L.
Rosenthal

Reunion
Sudden fiction; ed. by R. Shapard and
J. Thomas

The swimmer
The Norton book of American short
stories

The world of apples
Full measure; ed. by D. Sennett

The worm in the apple
Reader's Digest 125:54-7 Ag '84

Chef's house. Carver, R.

Cheiron. Kessler, J. F.

Chekhov, Anton Pavlovich, 1860-1904

At a country house
Chekhov, A. P. The fiancée, and other
stories

At home [Variant title: Home]
Classic European short stories; ed. by R.
Beum

Beauties
Chekhov, A. P. The fiancée, and other
stories

The bet
Chekhov, A. P. The fiancée, and other
stories
Mystery in the mainstream; ed. by B.
Pronzini; M. H. Greenberg and B. N.
Malzberg

The Black Monk
Chekhov, A. P. The duel, and other
stories

Carelessness
Inspired by drink; ed. by Joan Digby
and John Digby

The duel
Chekhov, A. P. The duel, and other
stories

The fiancée
Chekhov, A. P. The fiancée, and other
stories

His wife
Chekhov, A. P. The fiancée, and other
stories

The kiss
Classic European short stories; ed. by R.
Beum

Murder
Chekhov, A. P. The duel, and other
stories

My life
Chekhov, A. P. The party, and other
stories

My wife
Chekhov, A. P. The duel, and other
stories

A nervous breakdown
Chekhov, A. P. The party, and other
stories

New villa
Chekhov, A. P. The fiancée, and other
stories

On official business
Chekhov, A. P. The fiancée, and other
stories

The party
Chekhov, A. P. The party, and other
stories

Peasant women
Chekhov, A. P. The fiancée, and other
stories

The requiem
Christian short stories; ed. by M. Booth

Rothschild's fiddle
Chekhov, A. P. The fiancée, and other
stories

The student
Chekhov, A. P. The fiancée, and other
stories

Terror
Chekhov, A. P. The duel, and other
stories

Three years
Chekhov, A. P. The fiancée, and other
stories

The two Volodyas
Chekhov, A. P. The duel, and other
stories

An unpleasant business
Chekhov, A. P. The party, and other
stories

With friends
Chekhov, A. P. The fiancée, and other
stories

A woman's kingdom
Chekhov, A. P. The party, and other
stories

About

Carver, R. Errand

Chelkash. Gorky, M.

CHEMICAL WARFARE

Boylan, J. The gissix project

Michaelson, L. W. The rabbit that lost its
nose

The **chemical** works. Mathers, P.
CHEMICALS
Kersh, G. Comrade death
Mathers, P. The chemical works
Chemistry. Swift, G.
The **chemistry** of anarchy. Barr, R.
CHEMISTS
See also Medicines, patent, proprietary, etc.
Alderson, T. Michelson in the desert
Asimov, I. Unique is where you find it
Barr, R. The chemistry of anarchy
Herbert, F. Cease fire
Ch'en, Hsüan-yu
'Twixt soul and body [Variant title: The divided daughter]
Tales of the supernatural; ed. by H. C. Chang
Chen, Maiping See Wan Zhi
Ch'en, Ying-chen
The comedy of Narcissa T'ang
Ch'en, Y. Exiles at home: short stories
The country village teacher
Ch'en, Y. Exiles at home: short stories
A couple of generals
Ch'en, Y. Exiles at home: short stories
The dying
Ch'en, Y. Exiles at home: short stories
The last day of summer
Ch'en, Y. Exiles at home: short stories
My kid brother, K'ang-hsiung
Ch'en, Y. Exiles at home: short stories
Night freight
The Unbroken chain; ed. by J. S. M. Lau
One day in the life of a white-collar worker
Ch'en, Y. Exiles at home: short stories
Poor poor dumb mouths
Ch'en, Y. Exiles at home: short stories
Roses in June
Ch'en, Y. Exiles at home: short stories
Chen Rong
At middle age
Roses and thorns; ed. by P. Link
Cheng, Ch'ing-wen
Betel Palm Village
The Unbroken chain; ed. by J. S. M. Lau
Chenken and Nartzarzen in several days on the town. Ahern, T.
Cherches, Peter
Dirty windows
Between C & D; ed. by J. Rose and C. Texier
Chéri. Colette
Chernin, Kim
An American in Paris
Erotic interludes; ed. by L. Barbach
Chernoff, Maxine, 1952-
Bop
Chernoff, M. Bop

Degan dying
Chernoff, M. Bop
Don't send poems, send money
Chernoff, M. Bop
Enough
Chernoff, M. Bop
Heroes
Chernoff, M. Bop
The hills of Andorra
Chernoff, M. Bop
The North American Review 270:42-5 Je '85
Infinks
Chernoff, M. Bop
Phantom pleasure
Chernoff, M. Bop
Respect for the dead
Chernoff, M. Bop
The spirit of giving
Chernoff, M. Bop
That summer
Chernoff, M. Bop
Two times two
Chernoff, M. Bop
CHEROKEE INDIANS
Conley, R. J. Badger
Conley, R. J. Bob Parris's temper
Conley, R. J. Calf Roper's bandit car
Conley, R. J. Calf Roper's house guest
Conley, R. J. The endless dark of the night
Conley, R. J. The hanging of Mose Miller
Conley, R. J. The immortals
Conley, R. J. The Mexican tattoo
Conley, R. J. Moon Face
Conley, R. J. The name
Conley, R. J. The night George Wolfe died
Conley, R. J. Old Joe
Conley, R. J. Wesley's story
Conley, R. J. Wickliffe
Conley, R. J. Wili Woyi
Conley, R. J. The witch of Goingsnake
Conley, R. J. Yellow Bird: an imaginary autobiography
Cherries jubilee; or, Whichever way you look at it. Bird, C.
Cherry, Kelly
Almost the real thing
Mademoiselle 93:127-30+ O '87
Alzheimer's
Commentary 83:50-5 Je '87
Eternity dies
The North American Review 270:42-3 S '85
More precious than gold
Redbook 170:49-51 D '87
Rules for a normal relationship
Mademoiselle 94:146+ N '88
The train
Commentary 86:52-4 N '88
The violin of his mind
Reader's Digest 131:172-6 O '87

Cherry, Kelly—*Continued*
  Voyage of the heart
    Redbook 171:64-6+ My '88
  Where she was
    The Virginia Quarterly Review 64:417-32
      Summ '88
Cherryh, C. J.
  Cassandra
    The Hugo winners v4
  Of law and magic
    Moonsinger's friends; ed. by S. Shwartz
  To take a thief
    Magic in Ithkar [1]; ed. by A. Norton
      and R. Adams
Cherryhurst. Eighner, L.
CHESAPEAKE BAY (MD. AND VA.)
  Hoffman, W. Moorings
Chesbro, George C.
  Candala
    An Eye for justice; ed. by R. J. Randisi
  Strange prey
    Alfred Hitchcock's Grave suspicions
CHESHIRE (ENGLAND) *See* England—
  Cheshire
CHESS
  Archer, J. Checkmate
  Fitzgerald, M. J. The game
  Gardner, M. Nora says "check."
  Krivich, M., and Olgin, O. Plays and wins
  Wheatcroft, J. The forfeit
  Zelazny, R. Unicorn variations
The **chest** of silver. Hornung, E. W.
Chester's Christmas surprise. Stanton, W.
Chesterton, G. K. (Gilbert Keith), 1874-1936
  The angry street
    Chesterton, G. K. Daylight and night-
      mare
  The blue cross
    Christian short stories; ed. by M. Booth
    Masterpieces of mystery and suspense;
      ed. by M. H. Greenberg
  The bottomless well
    Chesterton, G. K. Thirteen detectives
  Chivalry begins at home
    Chesterton, G. K. Daylight and night-
      mare
  Concerning grocers as gods
    Chesterton, G. K. Daylight and night-
      mare
  The conversion of an anarchist
    Chesterton, G. K. Daylight and night-
      mare
  A crazy tale
    Chesterton, G. K. Daylight and night-
      mare
  Culture and the light
    Chesterton, G. K. Daylight and night-
      mare
  The curious Englishman
    Chesterton, G. K. Daylight and night-
      mare

The Donnington affair [Father Brown sol-
  ves]
    Chesterton, G. K. Thirteen detectives
The Donnington affair [Max Pemberton
  presents the puzzle of]
    Chesterton, G. K. Thirteen detectives
The dragon at hide-and-seek
    Chesterton, G. K. Daylight and night-
      mare
Dukes
    Chesterton, G. K. Daylight and night-
      mare
The end of wisdom
    Chesterton, G. K. Daylight and night-
      mare
The finger of stone
    Chesterton, G. K. Thirteen detectives
A fish story
    Chesterton, G. K. Daylight and night-
      mare
The garden of smoke
    Chesterton, G. K. Thirteen detectives
The giant
    Chesterton, G. K. Daylight and night-
      mare
The great amalgamation
    Chesterton, G. K. Daylight and night-
      mare
The hole in the wall
    Chesterton, G. K. Thirteen detectives
Homesick at home
    Chesterton, G. K. Daylight and night-
      mare
How I found the superman
    Chesterton, G. K. Daylight and night-
      mare
The invisible man
    Death locked in; ed. by D. G. Greene
      and R. C. S. Adey
    Great detectives; ed. by D. W. McCul-
      lough
A legend of Saint Francis
    Chesterton, G. K. Daylight and night-
      mare
The legend of the sword
    Chesterton, G. K. Daylight and night-
      mare
The long bow
    Chesterton, G. K. Daylight and night-
      mare
A nightmare
    Chesterton, G. K. Daylight and night-
      mare
On private property
    Chesterton, G. K. Daylight and night-
      mare
On secular education
    Chesterton, G. K. Daylight and night-
      mare
The paradise of human fishes
    Chesterton, G. K. Daylight and night-
      mare

Chesterton, G. K. (Gilbert Keith), 1874-1936—*Continued*
A picture of Tuesday
  Chesterton, G. K. Daylight and nightmare
A real discovery
  Chesterton, G. K. Daylight and nightmare
The roots of the world
  Chesterton, G. K. Daylight and nightmare
The second miracle
  Chesterton, G. K. Daylight and nightmare
The shadow of the shark
  Chesterton, G. K. Thirteen detectives
The singular speculation of the house agent
  Chesterton, G. K. Thirteen detectives
The sword of wood
  Chesterton, G. K. Daylight and nightmare
The taming of the nightmare
  Chesterton, G. K. Daylight and nightmare
The three dogs
  Chesterton, G. K. Daylight and nightmare
The three horsemen of the apocalypse
  Chesterton, G. K. Thirteen detectives
The tree of pride
  Chesterton, G. K. Daylight and nightmare
The tremendous adventure of Major Brown
  Chesterton, G. K. Thirteen detectives
The two taverns
  Chesterton, G. K. Daylight and nightmare
When doctors agree
  Chesterton, G. K. Thirteen detectives
The White Pillars murder
  Chesterton, G. K. Thirteen detectives
The wrong shape
  The Penguin classic crime omnibus
Chesterton, Gilbert Keith *See* Chesterton, G. K. (Gilbert Keith), 1874-1936
Chetwynd-Hayes, R., 1919-
The colored transmission
  After midnight; ed. by C. L. Grant
The fly-by-night
  Midnight; ed. by C. L. Grant
The werewolf and the vampire
  Vampires; ed. by A. Ryan
Cheuse, Alan
The quest for Ambrose Bierce
  The Graywolf annual 4
The Tennessee waltz
  Homewords: a book of Tennessee writers; ed. by D. Paschall
The **Chevalier** of the Place Blanche. Rhys, J.
Chewing gum. Bennett, H.

CHEYENNE (WYO.) *See* Wyoming—Cheyenne
CHEYENNE INDIANS
Mears, S. S. Thirty horses for your daughter
Overholser, W. D. Beecher Island
Chez les petits suisses. Pierce, C.
Chiarella, Tom
Berard's rapture
  The New Yorker 64:51-8 N 21 '88
CHICAGO (ILL.) *See* Illinois—Chicago
Chicago. Ross, B.
CHICANOS *See* Mexican Americans
CHICKAMAUGA, BATTLE OF, 1863
Bierce, A. Chickamauga
Wolfe, T. Chickamauga
Chickamauga. Bierce, A.
Chickamauga. Wolfe, T.
Chicken. Keillor, G.
Chicken Charley. Ritchie, J.
Chicken fate. Landolfi, T.
Chicken feed. Butler, G.
Chicken Little. Herrick, A.
Chicken Simon. Wilkinson, S.
Chicken skin sandwiches. Gerber, M. J.
Chicken soup. Reed, K.
CHICKENS
Bonnie, F. Allergic
Chang, T.-C. Birds of a feather
Highsmith, P. The day of reckoning
Kauffman, J. Who has lived from a child with chickens
Keillor, G. Chicken
Lagier, J. Tending the flock
Landolfi, T. Chicken fate
Lispector, C. The egg and the chicken
Lispector, C. The foreign legion
Rifaat, A. The kite
Wilkinson, S. Chicken Simon
Chickweed. Hutton, S.
Chidester, Ann
The healing touch
  Good Housekeeping 200:120-1+ Je '85
Chiggers. Brady, M.
Child, Lydia Maria Francis, 1802-1880
The quadroons
  The Other woman; ed. by S. Koppelman
The **child.** Ferron, J.
The **child.** Gare, N.
The **child.** Rïos, A.
The **child.** Sandel, C.
CHILD ABUSE
Bingham, S. Fear
Cullen, E. J. Letter to the institution
Dubus, A. Rose
Gathorne-Hardy, J. Mothers
Grenville, K. Refractions
Havemann, E. Tom and Beauty
Highsmith, P. Those awful dawns
Huggan, I. Celia behind me
Martínez-Serros, H. Killdeer
Oates, J. C. A theory of knowledge
Rhys, J. Fishy waters

CHILD ABUSE—Continued
Tem, S. R. The battering
CHILD AND PARENT See Parent and child
The **child** and the poet. Gould, R.
The **child** by tiger. Wolfe, T.
Child Ellen. Trippett, F.
A **child** in the dark, and a foreign father. Lawson, H.
Child in the leaves. Dickinson, C.
The **child** in time. McEwan, I.
The **child** killers. Foley, B.
CHILD MOLESTING
Brady, M. Chiggers
Campos-De Metro, J. Little mooses
Dadswell, M. Eighth birthday
Jolley, E. Clever and pretty
Mortimer, J. C. Rumpole and the course of true love
Schinto, J. Caddies' Day
Simpson, M. Lawns
Straub, P. The juniper tree
Child of embassy. Gold, H.
Child of my heart. Gillette, V.
Child of the century. West, J.
Child of two sisters. Houbein, L.
Child of void. St. Clair, M.
The **child** prodigy. Colette
The **child** screams and looks back at you. Banks, R.
Child story. Handke, P.
The **child** that loved a grave. O'Brien, F.-J.
The **child** who loved roads. Sandel, C.
CHILDBIRTH
Abbott, K. The second Pete
Atwood, M. Giving birth
Chekhov, A. P. The party
Cogswell, T. R. The cabbage patch
Colwin, L. Another marvelous thing
Ekström, M. Death's midwives
Eldridge, M. Maternity
Ferron, J. The grey dog
Ferron, J. La Mi-Carême
Flynn, R. Christmas in a very small place
Godwin, G. Dream children
Gorky, M. Birth of a man
Govier, K. Sociology
Hemingway, E. Indian camp
Kinsella, W. P. Penance
Kranes, D. Cordials
Levinson, B. Tokai
Mulrine, S. A cold coming
Novitski, P. Nuclear fission
Nowakowski, M. A new life
Oldfield, J. Life-sentence
Pilcher, R. The blue bedroom
Pilcher, R. The house on the hill
Pilcher, R. Miss Cameron at Christmas
Pirandello, L. In silence
Prichard, K. S. Josephina Anna Maria
Roushdi, Z. Celebrating the Prophet's birthday
Shelley, R. At the flood

Sturgeon, T. Twink
Suter, J. F. Doctor's orders
Varley, J. Manikins
Williams, W. C. A night in June
Wilmot, J. Dirt angel
Winton, T. Blood and water
Wolitzer, H. Mother
CHILDHOOD See Boys; Children; Girls
CHILDLESS MARRIAGE
Carlson, R. Life before science
Chernoff, M. Infinks
Gault, C. Dinner for two
Kilworth, G. The rose bush
Pierce, C. Manosque
Rodoreda, M. A flock of lambs in all colors
Walker, W. The contract with the beast
Willett, J. Melinda falling
Yamamoto, M. Chair in the rain
CHILDLESSNESS
See also Childless marriage
Austin, M. H. The House of offence
Grau, S. A. Home
CHILDREN
See also Abandoned children; Adolescence; Black children; Boys; Emotionally disturbed children; Foster children; Girls; Jewish children; Lost children; Mentally handicapped children; Missing children; Orphans; Physically handicapped children; War and children; Wild children
Abe, K. The stick
Anderson, J. The aviator
Anderson, J. The way to Budjerra Heights
Ardizzone, T. The eyes of children
Barrett, L. Wampum
Bates, H. E. Death and the cherry tree
Bates, H. E. A great day for Bonzo
Bates, H. E. The revelation
Belden, W. S. Fenneca
Bishop, M. Seasons of belief
Bishop, M. Vernalfest morning
Blinkin, M. The little calf
Böll, H. Lohengrin's death
Bonner, M. The makin's
Borgen, J. The swan
Boylan, J. Horse year
Bunch, D. R. A small miracle of fishhooks and straight pins
Calvino, I. The enchanted garden
Capote, T. Children on their birthdays
Caspers, N. "Bus is coming!"
Chard, J. The call of the running tide
Chávez, D. Willow game
Cogswell, T. R. The cabbage patch
Colette. Bastienne's child
Colette. The hollow nut
Colette. "If I had a daughter . . ."
Collins, A. The trouble with Felix
Crabtree, L. V. Homer-snake
Crane, S. The angel-child
Crane, S. A dark-brown dog

CHILDREN—*Continued*

Crane, S. The lover and the tell-tale
Crane, S. An ominous baby
Curtiss, U. R. A judicious half inch
Davie, E. A traveller's room
Desai, A. Games at twilight
Dickens, C. The Boots at the Holly-Tree Inn
Dickinson, D. The mythical kid
Ellison, H. Jeffty is five
Erdrich, L. American Horse
Faik, S. The Stelyanos Hrisopulos
Faulkner, W. That evening sun
Ferguson, W. Terror
Ferreira, R. No one looks out anymore
Fink, I. A spring morning
Floyd, P. L. Secrets
Forrest, K. V. The gift
Fraser, A. The night mother
Gale, Z. "Not as the world giveth": a friendship story
Gallagher, T. A pair of glasses
Gaskell, E. C. The old nurse's story
Gilbert, W. S. Little Mim
Gilchrist, E. Summer, an elegy
Gordon, C. The dragon's teeth
Grace, P. Flies
Grace, P. Kepa
Grace, P. The urupa
Greene, G. A discovery in the woods
Ha, K.-C. The white paper beard
Hall, M. M. The glass doorknob
Halligan, M. The noise of the lorries
Hankla, C. Fishing
Havazelet, E. Jillie
Henderson, Z. Come on, wagon!
Huggan, I. Celia behind me
Huggan, I. Into the green stillness
Huggan, I. Jack of hearts
Huggan, I. Sawdust
Jacobson, D. Beggar my neighbour
Johnston, B. Never the right time
Kawabata, Y. The grasshopper and the bell cricket
Keating, H. R. F. A crime child
Keillor, G. Easter
La Chapelle, M. Superstitions
Lansky, E. What she really did
Latimer, M. Gisela
Levinson, B. The night Motke Behr danced
Lewis, T. Half measures
Mahfūz, N. The conjurer made off with the dish
Mansfield, K. The doll's house
Mansfield, K. Prelude
Maupassant, G. de. Poor Andrew
Mauriac, F. A Christmas tale
Mazel, D. Children of the universe
McLean, A. Snakebite
Morrison, J. Man in the night
Murphy, Y. The summer the men landed on the moon

Nabokov, V. V. First love
Nagibin, IŪ. M. Shurik
Neville, K. From the government printing office
Nimmo, D. Rabbits
Norton, A. Outside
Oates, J. C. Baby
Ocampo, S. Leopoldina's dream
Ocampo, S. Magush
Ocampo, S. Thus were their faces
Ocampo, S. The wedding
Ozick, C. Trust [excerpt]
Paley, G. An interest in life
Paley, G. A subject of childhood
Paley, G. The used-boy raisers
Palmer, V. Josie
Parise, G. Happiness
Pavese, C. Free will
Pritchard, M. Dead finish
Pulaski, J. The merry-go-round
Rhys, J. The day they burned the books
Rhys, J. Invitation to the dance
Ríos, A. A friend, brother maybe
Ríos, A. Pato
Robertson, M. E. Locust
Robison, M. Seizing control
Rodoreda, M. A flock of lambs in all colors
Rossiter, S. Sinners
Schwob, M. The narrative of Pope Gregory IX
Schwob, M. The narrative of Pope Innocent III
Shaw, B. Small world
Shirley, J. What Cindy saw
Skrzynecki, P. Lilies
Skrzynecki, P. The peewit's nest
Sladek, J. T. Calling all gumdrops!
Stubbs, J. The belvedere
Suckow, R. The crick
Swados, H. Claudine's book
Taylor, P. H. Bad dreams
Thomas, D. The tree
Titcher, M. No fairies at the bottom of the garden
Updike, D. The cushion of time
Updike, D. First impressions
Verma, N. The world elsewhere
Viramontes, H. M. The Cariboo Cafe
Wagner, R. E. I'm going down to watch the horses come alive
Wetherell, W. D. Volpi's farewell
Whatley, W. Something to lose
Wicomb, Z. Bowl like hole
Wicomb, Z. When the train comes
Wiebe, D. E. Going to the mountain
Williams, W. C. The girl with a pimply face
Williamson, B. The thing waiting outside
Winton, T. Secrets
Wolfe, T. The child by tiger
Wong, M. V. Doubt
Zugsmith, L. Room in the world

CHILDREN—*Continued*
Adoption
See Adoption
CHILDREN, ABANDONED *See* Abandoned children
CHILDREN, ADOPTED *See* Adoption
CHILDREN, CRUELTY TO *See* Child abuse
CHILDREN, GIFTED
Colette. The child prodigy
Cullen, E. J. I try to look out for my family
Gordimer, N. Not for publication
Gould, R. The child and the poet
Humphrey, W. Report cards
Mann, T. The infant prodigy
McCullers, C. Wunderkind
Patchett, A. All little colored children should play the harmonica
Sage, V. Little Goethe
CHILDREN, JEWISH *See* Jewish children
CHILDREN, LOST *See* Lost children
CHILDREN, SICK *See* Sick children
The children. Algren, N.
Children. Ford, R.
The children. Morrison, J.
Children. Mrożek, S.
Children are bored on Sunday. Stafford, J.
Children are civilians too. Böll, H.
CHILDREN AS SLAVES *See* Slavery
Children, dogs and dying men. Briskin, M.
Children in the park. Whelan, G.
The children inside the trunk. Murphy, Y.
Children of divorced parents. Baumbach, J.
The children of night. Pohl, F.
Children of old somebody. Goyen, W.
The children of strangers. Bukoski, A.
Children of strikers. Chappell, F.
Children of the kingdom. Klein, T. E. D.
Children of the universe. Mazel, D.
Children of the wind. Levi, P.
Children on their birthdays. Capote, T.
Children with the house to themselves. Gordimer, N.
Children's crusade. Heise, K.
Children's games. Josipovici, G.
CHILDREN'S PARTIES
Drake, R. The birthday picture
Greene, G. The end of the party
Heker, L. The stolen party
Thompson, S. The birthday party
The children's room. Jones, R. F.
Children's story. Banks, R.
Children's voices. Josipovici, G.
The children's wing. Johnson, J.
Childress, Alice, 1920-
Merry Christmas, Marge!
"May your days be merry and bright" and other Christmas stories by women; ed. by S. Koppelman
A child's Christmas in Wales. Thomas, D.
A child's dream of a star. Dickens, C.
The child's garden. Ekström, M.
Child's play. Apple, M.

Child's play. Levinson, R., and Link, W.
A child's viewpoint. Kawabata, Y.
CHILE
See also Patagonia (Argentina and Chile)
Allende, I. Rosa the beautiful
Kleist, H. von. The earthquake in Chile
Trujillo, R. The illusionist
Rural life
Silverberg, R. How they pass the time in Pelpel
Chimera dreams. Keizer, G.
The chimes. Dickens, C.
CHIMNEY SWEEPS
MacLaverty, B. Umberto Verdi, chimney sweep
CHIMNEYS
Melville, H. I and my chimney
CHIMPANZEES
Murphy, P. Rachel in love
Silverberg, R. The Pope of the chimps
Chin, Frank, 1940-
The Chinatown Kid
Chin, F. The Chinaman Pacific & Frisco R.R. Co.
A Chinese lady dies
Chin, F. The Chinaman Pacific & Frisco R.R. Co.
The eat and run midnight people
Chin, F. The Chinaman Pacific & Frisco R.R. Co.
"Give the enemy sweet sissies and women to infatuate him, and jades and silks to blind him with greed"
Chin, F. The Chinaman Pacific & Frisco R.R. Co.
The only real day
Chin, F. The Chinaman Pacific & Frisco R.R. Co.
Railroad standard time
Chin, F. The Chinaman Pacific & Frisco R.R. Co.
The sons of Chan
Chin, F. The Chinaman Pacific & Frisco R.R. Co.
Yes, young daddy
Chin, F. The Chinaman Pacific & Frisco R.R. Co.
Chin, M. Lucie
Catmagic
Devils & demons; ed. by M. Kaye and S. Kaye
Lan Lung
Masterpieces of terror and the supernatural; ed. by M. Kaye and S. Kaye
CHINA
Morris, K. The eyeless dragons: a Chinese story
Ts'ai-hua, T. The feast of "Flower-Pattern" wine
To 1643
Ch'en, H.-Y. 'Twixt soul and body
Li, F.-Y. The carp

CHINA—To 1643—*Continued*
Li, F.-Y. Old Chang
Li, F.-Y. Rain-making
Li, F.-Y. The tiger
Li, K.-T. The Beldame Feng
Liu, F. Wang Hsieh; or Dark robe land
Pu, S.-L. The cricket
Pu, S.-L. The Tou lass
Pu, S.-L. Yellow pride
Pu, S.-L. Yüeh Chung
Shen, C.-C. Miss Jen

20th century
Deng Gang. A big fish
Kawabata, Y. At the pawnshop
Lu Wenfu. Graduation
Smedley, A. Shan-fei, communist
Wang Meng. The wind on the plateau

1900-1949
Pil'nīāk, B. Chinese story

1949-
Cao Guanlong. Three professors
Chen Rong. At middle age
Dai Houying. Father's milk is also blood transformed
Dai Qing. Anticipation
Dai Qing. No!
Feng Jicai. Chrysanthemums
Feng Jicai. The hornets' nest
Feng Jicai. A letter
Feng Jicai. The Mao button
Feng Jicai. Nectar
Feng Jicai. Numbskull
Feng Jicai. Plum blossoms in the snow
Feng Jicai. The street-sweeping show
Feng Jicai. The tall woman and her short husband
Feng Jicai. Winding brook way
Ge Wujue. A summer experience
Gu Hua. The log cabin overgrown with creepers
Gustafsson, L. Uncle Sven and the Cultural Revolution
Huang Qingyun. Annals of a fossil
Jia Pingwa. How much can a man bear?
Jin He. Reencounter
Lao Hong. The gap
Lee, Y.-H. The last rite
Li Chao. Spring chill
Li Ping. Autumn
Lin Jinlan. The transcript
Liu, Q. The good luck bun
Lu Wenfu. The boundary wall
Lu Wenfu. The doorbell
Lu Wenfu. The gourmet
Lu Wenfu. The man from a peddlers' family
Lu Wenfu. Tang Qiaodi
Lu Wenfu. World of dreams, a valediction
Paley, G. The expensive moment
Paley, G. Somewhere else
Petchsingh, T. The sacrifice
Qiao Shi. Providing a meal
Shen Rong. Troubled Sunday

Shi Tiesheng. Blacky
Shi Tiesheng. Lunch break
Shi Tiesheng. One winter's evening
Sun Shaoshan. Eight hundred meters below
Tang Dong. The progress of the military patrol car
Wang Meng. Anecdotes of Chairman Maimaiti
Wang Meng. Eye of the night
Wang Zhecheng, and Wen Xiaoyu. Nest egg
Yang Zhenwen. Fu Da regains his wife
Zhang Jie. The ark
Zhang Jie. Emerald
Zhang Jie. Love must not be forgotten
Zhang Jie. The time is not yet ripe
Zhang Jie. Under the hawthorn
Zhang Jie. An unfinished record
Zhang Jie. Who knows how to live?
Zhang Kangkang, and Mei Jin. The tolling of a distant bell
Zhang Xian. The widow
Zhang Xianliang. Shorblac: a driver's story
Zhang Xianliang. The story of an old man and a dog
Zhao Zhenkai. The homecoming stranger
Zhu Lin. Downpour on a leaky roof

Coal mines and mining
See Coal mines and mining—China

College life
See College life—China

Communism
See Communism—China

Kings and rulers
Walpole, H. Mi Li: a Chinese fairy tale

Marriage customs
See Marriage customs—China

Officials and employees
An Injustice revealed

Politics
See Politics—China

Rural life
Brown, G. M. The satirist
Cehai, C. The distant sound of tree-felling
Jia Pingwa. Family chronicle of a wooden bowl maker
Jia Pingwa. Shasha and the pigeons
Kong Jiesheng. On the other side of the stream
Li, Y.-P. The rain from the sun
Li Hangyu. The last angler
Liu, Q. The good luck bun
Shi Tiesheng. Blacky
Su Ye. Scatterbrain
Tong Enzheng. The middle kingdom
Wang Hongzhen, and Zhou Peisheng. Weishan Lake
Wang Jiada. Daughter of the Yellow River
Zhu Xiaoping. Chronicle of Mulberry Tree Village

Beijing
Bridge, A. The Buick saloon

CHINA—*Continued*
Hong Kong
See Hong Kong
Peking
See China—Beijing
Shanghai
Wang Anyi. The destination
Tibet
Yerxa, L. Carrion crypt
China. Creamer, E. S.
China. Dixon, S.
China. Johnson, C. R.
China across the bay. Vogan, S.
China Blue. Gates, D.
The **Chinaman's** garden. Price, A.
The **Chinatown** Kid. Chin, F.
CHINESE
Chin, F. A Chinese lady dies
Seepaul, L. A key for Dolcina
Australia
Winton, T. The oppressed
Canada
Kattan, N. The neighbour
Hawaii
London, J. Chun Ah Chun
Lum, D. H. Y. Yahk fahn, Auntie
Hong Kong
Grandbois, A. May Blossom
Japan
Ishikawa, T. The affair of the arabesque inlay
Malaysia
Clarke, T. The Wo family
Hsiu, H. The trap
New York (N.Y.)
Buck, P. S. The good deed
Philippines
Nimmo, H. A. Lim
Scotland
Greening, J. Pleasure trips
United States
Chin, F. The Chinatown Kid
Chin, F. The eat and run midnight people
Chin, F. "Give the enemy sweet sissies and women to infatuate him, and jades and silks to blind him with greed"
Chin, F. The only real day
Chin, F. Railroad standard time
Chin, F. The sons of Chan
Chin, F. Yes, young daddy
CHINESE AMERICANS
Gates, E. A yellow man and a white
Jen, G. In the American society
Jen, G. The water-faucet vision
Low, D. Winterblossom Garden
Ng, F. M. A red sweater
A **Chinese** lady dies. Chin, F.
The **Chinese** language. Liang Xiaosheng
The **Chinese** rifle. MacDonald, D. R.
Chinese story. Pil′niāk, B.
Chinoiserie. McCloy, H.
Chinook. Flanagan, J.

A **chip** of glass ruby. Gordimer, N.
The **chipko**. Gearhart, S. M.
CHIPPEWA INDIANS
Erdrich, L. Fleur
Chippy. Narayan, R. K.
Chipulina, E. G.
The catalyst
Short story international 51
Diamonds are forever
Short story international 46
The disaster
Short story international 53
The exiles
Short story international 65
Good clean fun
Short story international 43
Hazards of war
Short story international 58
A man called Lovac
Short story international 69
One of those things
Short story international 55
The procession
Short story international 48
Sirocco
Short story international 67
Square peg, round hole
Short story international 57
Your obedient servant
Short story international 64
CHIROPODISTS
Ade, G. The mystery of the back-roomer
Chishimba, Maurice
Weekend of carousal
African short stories in English; ed. by J. de Grandsaigne
Chisholm, Lee
Someone else's house
Tales from Isaac Asimov's science fiction magazine: short stories for young adults
Chittum, Ida
The monster of Poot Holler
Spirits, spooks, and other sinister creatures; ed. by H. Hoke
CHIVALRY
See also Knights and knighthood
De Camp, L. S. Divide and rule
Chivalry begins at home. Chesterton, G. K.
Chivaree. Bonham, F.
Chiyojo. Dazai, O.
Chloe Hummel of the Chicago White Sox. Schwartz, J.
Chloroform for all. Warner, S. T.
Cho, Hae-Il
Iron masks
The Road to Sampo, and other Korean short stories
Cho, Se-Hui
The bony-fish that came into my net
The Road to Sampo, and other Korean short stories

Cho, Se-Hui—*Continued*
On the overhead bridge
The Road to Sampo, and other Korean
short stories
The **chocolate** box. Christie, A.
The **chocolate** Easter bunny. Heise, K.
Chocolate footballs. Giles, M.
Choe, Chong-Hui
Hospital room 205
Hospital room 205, and other Korean
short stories
When the cricket chirrs
Hospital room 205, and other Korean
short stories
Choe, Il-Nam
The color of mugwort
Two travelers, and other Korean short
stories
Choe, In-Ho
Another man's room
The Road to Sampo, and other Korean
short stories
Choe, In-Hun
Christmas carol
One way, and other Korean short stories
The end of the highway
One way, and other Korean short stories
Ch'oe, Sanggyu
Point
Flowers of fire; ed. by P. H. Lee
Choi, Yearn Hong
Bloomington, Fall 1971
Short story international 67
Choice. Fox, J.
Choice. Haylock, J.
Choice. Pierce, J. R.
The **choice.** Sadler, M.
A **choice** of witnesses. Slesar, H.
Choices. Anderson, J. M.
Choices of the heart. McKimmey, J.
CHOIRS (MUSIC)
Naipaul, S. Mr. Sookhoo and the carol
singers
CHOLERA
Matthews, J. The burial
Schwob, M. Train 081
Chon, Kwang-Yong
Driver's assistant
A Respite, and other Korean short
stories
Kapitan Lee
Flowers of fire; ed. by P. H. Lee
A Respite, and other Korean short
stories
Chon, Sang-Guk
Wings that will carry us both
Early spring, mid-summer, and other
Korean short stories
Choobeedoo Yum-yum and the ANC.
Thomas, M.
Choosing. Mazel, D.

Chopin, Kate, 1851-1904
Her letters
Haunted women; ed. by A. Bendixen
The locket
Civil War women; ed. by F. McSherry;
C. G. Waugh and M. Greenberg
The story of an hour
The Norton book of American short
stories
Chopin in winter. Dybek, S.
The **chords** of youth. Bates, H. E.
Chorus girl's absolutely final performance.
Highsmith, P.
A **chorus** of elements. Berdnyk, O.
The **chosen.** Asscher-Pinkhof, C.
The **chosen** husband. Gallant, M.
The **chosen** vessel. Baynton, B.
Choteau. Bass, R.
Chowder, Ken
Hall of Fame
Short story international 67
In the house of glass
Commentary 81:58-65 F '86
Chowder. Dunning, S.
Choyce, Lesley, 1951-
Billy Botzweiler's last dance
Choyce, L. Billy Botzweiler's last dance,
and other stories
Breakage
Choyce, L. Billy Botzweiler's last dance,
and other stories
Dancing the night away
Choyce, L. Billy Botzweiler's last dance,
and other stories
Family protection
Choyce, L. Billy Botzweiler's last dance,
and other stories
Local heroes
Choyce, L. Billy Botzweiler's last dance,
and other stories
Major repairs
Choyce, L. Billy Botzweiler's last dance,
and other stories
The paper route
Choyce, L. Billy Botzweiler's last dance,
and other stories
Prying loose
Choyce, L. Billy Botzweiler's last dance,
and other stories
Chrisoula. Petrakis, H. M.
Chris's last party. Highsmith, P.
CHRIST *See* Jesus Christ
Christ, the Devil and the lunatic. Morrison,
J.
Christening. Maupassant, G. de
CHRISTENINGS
Hardy, T. The three strangers
Maupassant, G. de. Christening
Christensen, Kate
Temptations
Mademoiselle 94:204+ S '88
CHRISTIAN LIFE
Bell, M. Brady

CHRISTIAN LIFE—*Continued*
    Bell, M. Conrad
    Bell, M. Decatur
    Bell, M. Helen
    Bell, M. Reba
    Bellow, S. A silver dish
    Canton, W. The song of the Minster
    Clark, M. The love of Christ
    Dorr, L. Vladimir's kitchen
    Pritchett, V. S. Tea with Mrs. Bittell
    Waters, M. The Love Chapter
CHRISTIAN MARTYRS *See* Martyrs
The **Christian** roommates. Updike, J.
CHRISTIANITY
        See also Catholic faith; also names
        of Christian churches or sects
    Chavez, A. A desert idyll
    Driskell, L. V. Martha Jean
    Endō, S. The day before
    Endō, S. My belongings
    Leskov, N. S. Pamphalon the entertainer
CHRISTIANS
        See also Christians, Early
    Ferrell, A. Why people get cancer
    Garratt, P. T. If the driver vanishes. . .

                        Korea
    Kim, T. Portrait of a shaman
CHRISTIANS, EARLY
    Doyle, Sir A. C. The centurion
    Leskov, N. S. The mountain
Christie, Agatha, 1891-1976
    The adventure of Johnnie Waverly
        Christie, A. Hercule Poirot's casebook
    The adventure of the cheap flat
        Christie, A. Hercule Poirot's casebook
    The adventure of the Clapham cook
        Christie, A. Hercule Poirot's casebook
    The adventure of the Egyptian tomb
        Christie, A. Hercule Poirot's casebook
    The adventure of the Italian nobleman
        Christie, A. Hercule Poirot's casebook
    The adventure of "The Western Star"
        Christie, A. Hercule Poirot's casebook
    The affair at the bungalow
        Christie, A. Miss Marple
    The affair at the victory ball
        Christie, A. Hercule Poirot's casebook
    The apples of the Hesperides
        Christie, A. Hercule Poirot's casebook
    The Arcadian Deer
        Christie, A. Hercule Poirot's casebook
    The Augean stables
        Christie, A. Hercule Poirot's casebook
    The bloodstained pavement
        Christie, A. Miss Marple
    The blue geranium
        Christie, A. Miss Marple
    The capture of Cerberus
        Christie, A. Hercule Poirot's casebook
    The case of the caretaker
        Christie, A. Miss Marple

    The case of the missing will
        Christie, A. Hercule Poirot's casebook
    The case of the perfect maid
        Christie, A. Miss Marple
    The chocolate box
        Christie, A. Hercule Poirot's casebook
    A Christmas tragedy
        Christie, A. Miss Marple
    The companion
        Christie, A. Miss Marple
    The Cornish mystery
        Christie, A. Hercule Poirot's casebook
    The Cretan bull
        Christie, A. Hercule Poirot's casebook
    Dead man's mirror
        Christie, A. Hercule Poirot's casebook
    Death by drowning
        Christie, A. Miss Marple
    The disappearance of Mr. Davenheim
        Christie, A. Hercule Poirot's casebook
    The double clue
        Christie, A. Hercule Poirot's casebook
    Double sin
        Christie, A. Hercule Poirot's casebook
    The dream
        Christie, A. Hercule Poirot's casebook
    The dressmaker's doll
        Handle with care; ed. by J. Kahn
    The Erymanthian boar
        Christie, A. Hercule Poirot's casebook
    The flock of Geryon
        Christie, A. Hercule Poirot's casebook
    Four-and-twenty blackbirds
        Christie, A. Hercule Poirot's casebook
    The four suspects
        Christie, A. Miss Marple
    The Girdle of Hyppolita
        Christie, A. Hercule Poirot's casebook
    The girl in the train
        Great detectives; ed. by D. W. McCul-
        lough
    Greenshaw's Folly
        Christie, A. Miss Marple
    The harlequin tea set
        The Mammoth book of modern crime
        stories; ed. by G. Hardinge
    The herb of death
        Christie, A. Miss Marple
    The horses of Diomedes
        Christie, A. Hercule Poirot's casebook
    How does your garden grow?
        Christie, A. Hercule Poirot's casebook
        Ladies' Home Journal 101:50+ Ja '84
    The Idol House of Astarte
        Christie, A. Miss Marple
    The incredible theft
        Christie, A. Hercule Poirot's casebook
    Ingots of gold
        Christie, A. Miss Marple
    The jewel robbery at the Grand
        Metropolitan
        Christie, A. Hercule Poirot's casebook

Christie, Agatha, 1891-1976—Continued

The kidnapped Prime Minister
    Christie, A. Hercule Poirot's casebook
The king of clubs
    Christie, A. Hercule Poirot's casebook
The lamp
    Witches' brew; ed. by M. Muller and
      B. Pronzini
The Lemesurier inheritance
    Christie, A. Hercule Poirot's casebook
The Lernean Hydra
    Christie, A. Hercule Poirot's casebook
The lost mine
    Christie, A. Hercule Poirot's casebook
The Market Basing mystery
    Christie, A. Hercule Poirot's casebook
The million dollar bond robbery
    Christie, A. Hercule Poirot's casebook
Miss Marple tells a story
    Christie, A. Miss Marple
Motive v. opportunity
    Christie, A. Miss Marple
Murder in the mews
    Christie, A. Hercule Poirot's casebook
The mystery of Hunter's Lodge
    Christie, A. Hercule Poirot's casebook
The mystery of the Bagdad Chest
    Christie, A. Hercule Poirot's casebook
The Nemean lion
    Christie, A. Hercule Poirot's casebook
The Plymouth Express
    Christie, A. Hercule Poirot's casebook
Problem at sea
    Christie, A. Hercule Poirot's casebook
Sanctuary
    Christie, A. Miss Marple
Siren business
    Ladies' Home Journal 105:100-1+ F '88
Strange jest
    Christie, A. Miss Marple
The Stymphalean birds
    Christie, A. Hercule Poirot's casebook
The submarine plans
    Masterpieces of mystery and suspense;
      ed. by M. H. Greenberg
    The Penguin classic crime omnibus
Tape-measure murder
    Christie, A. Miss Marple
The theft of the royal ruby
    Christie, A. Hercule Poirot's casebook
The third-floor flat
    Christie, A. Hercule Poirot's casebook
The thumbmark of St. Peter
    Christie, A. Miss Marple
The tragedy at Marsdon Manor
    Christie, A. Hercule Poirot's casebook
Triangle at Rhodes
    Christie, A. Hercule Poirot's casebook
The Tuesday Night Club
    Christie, A. Miss Marple
The under dog
    Christie, A. Hercule Poirot's casebook

The veiled lady
    Christie, A. Hercule Poirot's casebook
Wasps' nest
    Christie, A. Hercule Poirot's casebook
Yellow Iris
    Christie, A. Hercule Poirot's casebook
Christina Rosenthal. Archer, J.
Christman, Kathryn
Never talk to strangers
    Redbook 170:58-9+ Mr '88
Christman, Rick
The Mai-Loan and the man who could fly
    Stiller's pond; ed. by J. Agee; R. Blakely
      and S. Welch
Christmas, R. A.
Another angel
    Greening wheat: fifteen Mormon short
      stories
Christmas. Lee, H.
Christmas 1940. Roosevelt, E.
Christmas at the line shack. Daniels, C.
The **Christmas** banquet. Hawthorne, N.
A **Christmas** carillon. Calisher, H.
Christmas carol. Choe, I.-H.
A **Christmas** carol. Dickens, C.
A **Christmas** cordial. Kalpakian, L.
Christmas Day in the morning. Buck, P. S.
Christmas dinner. Keillor, G.
Christmas Eve. Gogol', N. V.
Christmas Eve. Maupassant, G. de
Christmas Eve at Johnson's Drugs N Goods.
    Bambara, T. C.
Christmas every day. See Böll, H. Christmas
    not just once a year
Christmas for Sassafrass, Cypress & Indigo.
    Shange, N.
A **Christmas** game. Munby, A. N. L.
Christmas ghosts. Dickens, C.
The **Christmas** house. Adams, G. G.
Christmas in a very small place. Flynn, R.
Christmas in Calpe. Thomas, J.
Christmas in Dakar. Gold, H.
Christmas in Lake Wobegon. Keillor, G.
Christmas in port. Swenson, J.
Christmas in the aisles. Shannon, J.
Christmas is for cops. Hoch, E. D.
Christmas is over. Romun, I.
A **Christmas** legend. Gordon, A.
Christmas lessons in love. Boissard, J.
Christmas lunch. Bissoondath, N.
Christmas meeting. Timperley, R.
Christmas night. Walter, E.
Christmas not just once a year. Böll, H.
The **Christmas** offering. Rölvaag, O. E.
Christmas on the island. Ruhen, O.
The **Christmas** party. Komie, L. B.
The **Christmas** party. Thompson, J.
A **Christmas** promise. Mach, M.
Christmas reunion. Caldecott, Sir A.
A **Christmas** romance. Preston, M.
Christmas roses. O'Brien, E.
Christmas (Shirley Temple is a wife and
    mother). Du Fresne, Y.

CHRISTMAS STORIES

Adams, G. G. The Christmas house
Ade, G. Mr. Payson's satirical Christmas
Alcott, L. M. A March Christmas
Asimov, I. The thirteenth day of Christmas
Beattie, A. Times
Beattie, A. Where you'll find me
Bell, M. Conrad
Bissoondath, N. Christmas lunch
Böll, H. And there was the evening and the morning . . .
Borchert, W. The three dark kings
Bowles, P. The frozen fields
Bradbury, R. Bless me, Father, for I have sinned
Brender à Brandis, M. The living Christmas tree
Brown, A. A sense of humor
Brown, G. M. The lost boy
Buck, P. S. A certain star
Burns, M. After hours
Caldecott, Sir A. Christmas reunion
Calisher, H. A Christmas carillon
Carlson, R. The H Street sledding record
Cather, W. The burglar's Christmas
Chavez, A. The angel's new wings
Chekhov, A. P. A woman's kingdom
Childress, A. Merry Christmas, Marge!
Choe, I.-H. Christmas carol
Clayton, J. J. An old 3 A.M. story
Couani, A. Xmas in the bush
Crabtree, L. V. The miracle in Sweet Hollow
Daniels, C. A Carolina Christmas carol
Daniels, C. Christmas at the line shack
Dawson, F. The fourth surprise
Dawson, F. The vertical fields
Desnoues, L. The poplars
Desnoues, L. The triumph and the celery stick
Dickens, C. The chimes
Dickens, C. A Christmas carol
Dickens, C. A Christmas tree
Dickens, C. The cricket on the hearth
Drewe, R. The manageress and the mirage
Du Fresne, Y. Christmas (Shirley Temple is a wife and mother)
Ferber, E. No room at the inn
Fisher, D. C. As ye sow—
Flynn, R. Christmas in a very small place
Flynn, R. Tumbleweed Christmas
Fox, J. Choice
Freeman, M. E. W. The twelfth guest
Gale, Z. "Not as the world giveth": a friendship story
Girion, B. To Francie, with love
Gogol', N. V. Christmas Eve
Gold, H. Christmas in Dakar
Hartley, L. P. The waits
Hawthorne, N. The Christmas banquet
Hemingway, E. God rest you merry, gentlemen

Henry, O. The gift of the Magi
Highsmith, P. A clock ticks at Christmas
Hurst, F. The nth commandment
Jewett, S. O. Mrs. Parkins's Christmas Eve
Jones, D. C. In pastures green
Kalpakian, L. A Christmas cordial
Keillor, G. Exiles
Kip, L. The ghosts at Grantley
Klíma, I. Wednesday morning: a Christmas conspiracy tale
Lagerlöf, S. The peace of God
Le Braz, A. The owl
Leskov, N. S. The sealed angel
Lipman, E. Baby's first Christmas
Machen, A. A new Christmas carol
MacLaverty, B. A present for Christmas
MacLeod, A. To everything there is a season
MacLeod, A. Winter dog
Mason, B. A. Drawing names
Maupassant, G. de. Christmas Eve
Maupassant, G. de. An odd feast
Mauriac, F. A Christmas tale
McCormack, E. P. No country for old men
Murphy, P. The Santa class test
Norris, H. The Christmas wife
O'Connor, W. D. The ghost
Paley, G. The loudest voice
Patton, F. G. First principles
Peattie, E. W. Their dear little ghost
Phelps, E. S. Old Mother Goose
Plemmons, M. Noel
Prichard, K. S. Jimble
Pym, B. The Christmas visit
Roberts, K. Weihnachtsabend
Rölvaag, O. E. The Christmas offering
Rossi, A. Pollyanna
Rule, J. A migrant Christmas
Sagan, F. A dog's night
Sandel, C. Artist's Christmas
Sarrantonio, A. Wish
Schaefer, J. W. Stubby Pringle's Christmas
Shange, N. Christmas for Sassafrass, Cypress & Indigo
Shore, W. May your days be merry and bright
Simon, B. The fourth day of Christmas
Smiley, J. Long distance
Spark, M. The leaf-sweeper
Spark, M. The Seraph and the Zambesi
Spence, A. Tinsel
St. Clair, M. An old-fashioned bird Christmas
Stark, S. S. In the surprise of life
Stifter, A. Rock crystal
Thomas, A. C. Breaking the ice
Thomas, D. A child's Christmas in Wales
Timperley, R. Christmas meeting
Tournier, M. Jesu, Joy of Man's Desiring
Tournier, M. Mother Christmas
Van Den Heever, T. Outa Sem and Father Christmas

CHRISTMAS STORIES—*Continued*
Weaver, G. Neery Christmas
Willson, H. A Christmas tale
Wolfe, G. War beneath the tree
The **Christmas** story. Dickens, C.
A **Christmas** story. Stubblefield, C.
A **Christmas** tale. Mauriac, F.
A **Christmas** tale. Willson, H.
A **Christmas** tragedy. Christie, A.
A **Christmas** tree. Dickens, C.

CHRISTMAS TREES
Böll, H. Christmas not just once a year
Mazel, D. Sprucy wages
The **Christmas** visit. Pym, B.
The **Christmas** visitation. Toner, G. R.
Christmas wedding. Pilcher, R.
The **Christmas** wife. Norris, H.
Christophe and the virgin. Villefranche, A.-M.
Christos Mavromatis is a welder. Papaellinas, G.
Chroma. Barthelme, F.
The **chronicle** of a besieged city. Mrożek, S.
Chronicle of a demise. Williams, T.
Chronicle of Anse Saint-Roch. Ferron, J.
A **chronicle** of love. Francis, H. E.
Chronicle of Mulberry Tree Village. Zhu Xiaoping
Chrysalis. Bradbury, R.
Chrysalis. Liu, T.-J.
The **chrysanthemum** beetle. Tsushima, Y.

CHRYSANTHEMUMS
Pu, S.-L. Yellow pride
Chrysanthemums. Feng Jicai
The **chrysanthemums.** Steinbeck, J.

Chu, Tien-jen
Autumn note
The Unbroken chain; ed. by J. S. M. Lau

Chua, Rebecca
The morning after
Short story international 44
Second thoughts
Short story international 51
Chuck and the boss man's wife. Coleman, W.
Chudka popoy ugh cha cha. Taylor, A.

Chukri, Mohammed
Flower Crazy
Arabic short stories; tr. by D. Johnson-Davies
Chums. Bumpus, J.
Chums. Gorky, M.
Chun Ah Chun. London, J.

Chung, Li-ho
Together through thick and thin
The Unbroken chain; ed. by J. S. M. Lau

CHURCH ATTENDANCE
Dawson, F. The vertical fields
The **church** in High Street. Campbell, R.
The **church** mouse. Blythe, R.

The **church** of summer sausage. Woodman, A.

CHURCH SCHOOLS
Bonosky, P. Sin
Burke, J. L. Losses
Fante, J. Big leaguer
Gordimer, N. Not for publication
McGahern, J. The recruiting officer
Rahmann, P. Heathen ways

CHURCHES
See also Cathedrals
Aickman, R. The Cicerones
Aldiss, B. W. The blue background
Grace, P. The lamp
Hemley, R. All you can eat
Johnson, W. Heir to the realm
Lemelin, R. The Stations of the Cross
Lovecraft, H. P. The haunter of the dark
Melville, H. The two temples: Temple first
Noonan, B. Fruit drink
Ruch, T. Claire's lover's church
Sexson, L. The apocalypse of Mary the unbeliever
Sullivan, T. Whores in the pulpit
Swain, E. G. The man with the roller
Valenzuela, L. The son of Kermaria
West, J. The heavy stone
Yourcenar, M. Our-Lady-of-the-Swallows
Churchgoing. Bird, M.

Chute, Carolyn
"Ollie, oh . . ."
The Best Maine stories; ed. by S. Phippen; C. Waugh and M. Greenberg
The Ploughshares reader: new fiction for the eighties

Chute, Patricia
A room of her own
McCall's 111:98-9+ F '84
Ciao, mio tesoro. Paolucci, A.
Cicada Queen. Sterling, B.
Cicadas. Pascoe, B.
The **cicadas** of summer. Hulme, K.
The **Cicerones.** Aickman, R.
The **cigarette** boat. Milton, B.
The **cigarette** case. Onions, O.
Cigarette girl. Cain, J. M.

Ciment, Jill, 1953-
Astronomy
Ciment, J. Small claims
Genetics
Ciment, J. Small claims
Money
Ciment, J. Small claims
Self-portrait with vanishing point
Ciment, J. Small claims
Small claims
Ciment, J. Small claims

Cinca, Silvia
The voice
Short story international 45
The wedding
Short story international 53

CINCINNATI (OHIO) *See* Ohio—Cincinnati
The **Cinderella** caper. Kathenor, S.
CIPHERS
  Asimov, I. 1 to 999
  Asimov, I. The key
  Asimov, I. The key word
  Asimov, I. The three numbers
  King, R. Malice in wonderland
  Poe, E. A. The gold-bug
Circe. Rand, P.
The **circle**. Burns, M.
A **circle** in the fire. O'Connor, F.
A **circle** is the shape of perfection. Berry,
    R. M.
Circle of prayer. Munro, A.
Il **circo** delle donne. Wilson, B.
The **circuit**. Jiménez, F.
The **circuit** rider. Osborn, C.
The **circular** library of stones. Emshwiller, C.
The **circular** valley. Bowles, P.
CIRCUMCISION
  Apple, M. The eighth day
CIRCUMSTANTIAL EVIDENCE
  Tolstoy, L., graf. God sees the truth but
    waits
CIRCUS
  Aichinger, I. The bound man
  Baukin, L. Jar-boy
  Böll, H. What a racket
  Bradbury, R. The last circus
  Brooks, J. Wrong play
  Carrier, R. What language do bears speak?
  Colette. "Lola"
  Cook, H. Clown
  Davis, G. P. African story
  Ellin, S. Beidenbauer's flea
  Garrett, G. P. Lion
  Gingher, M. The kiss
  Goldberg, L. In Siberia it is very cold
  Green, J. The tallest man in the world
  Hartley, L. P. A high dive
  Highsmith, P. Chorus girl's absolutely final
    performance
  Hoch, E. D. The theft of the circus poster
  Hofmann, G. Tolstoy's head
  Hunter, E. The fallen angel
  King, S. The night of the tiger
  London, J. The Leopard Man's story
  Maupassant, G. de. Lilie Lala
  Mordden, E. The complete death of the
    clown dog
  Olesen, K. Beast and beauty
  Powell, T. Motive for murder
  Roscoe, P. The National Circus of Argen-
    tina
  Tournier, M. The red dwarf
  Wilson, B. Il circo delle donne
  Wolfe, T. Circus at dawn
  Wolfe, T. His father's earth
  Woolrich, C. If the dead could talk
The **circus**. Graham, W.
Circus. Hoch, E. D.
The **circus**. Lazarre, J.

The **circus** advance agent. Davis, S.
Circus at dawn. Wolfe, T.
The **circus** horse. Colette
Cirone, Patricia B.
  Just another working mom
    Yankee witches; ed. by C. G. Waugh;
      M. H. Greenberg and F. D. McSherry
CITIES AND TOWNS
    See also Cities and towns, Ruined,
      extinct, etc. Imaginary cities
  Austin, D. Portable cities
  Cooper, J. C. Living
  Covino, M. The hour of the ungovernable
  Covino, M. An intimacy beyond words
  Covino, M. Matinee at the Bijou
  Covino, M. The return of possibility
  Davie, E. Out of order
  Davis, L. City employment
  Faik, S. I kept grumbling
  Faik, S. The man who forgot the city
  Ferguson, W. The claims adjuster
  Gardner, M. The stranger
  Romero, N. L. The city
  Taylor, C. Borg's last word
  Taylor, C. Denver's story
  Taylor, C. Spare change
  Taylor, C. State of the streets
  Tem, S. R. Little cruelties
  Thompson, J. The best it could be
  Wang Meng. Eye of the night
  Wolfe, T. The train and the city
**CITIES AND TOWNS, RUINED, EX-
    TINCT, ETC.**
    See also Carthage (Ancient city)
  Davis, S. The hermit of Treasure Peaks
  Goldsmith, H. The voices of El Dorado
  Kinsella, W. P. Frank Pierce, Iowa
  Pritchard, M. Photograph of Luisa
A **citizen's** fate. Mrożek, S.
The **city**. Romero, N. L.
The **city**. Updike, J.
City ball. Israeloff, R.
City employment. Davis, L.
City in ashes. Tamer, Z.
City lovers. Gordimer, N.
A **city** morning and a man. Faik, S.
City of Benares. MacLean, A.
City of boys. Nugent, B.
The **city** of refuge. Fisher, R.
A **city** of the dead, a city of the living.
    Gordimer, N.
The **city** of the singing flame. Smith, C. A.
City of the unknown. Valenzuela, L.
The **city**, seen from the water, 1924. Silber,
    J.
City Sundays. Dowell, C.
The **city** urchin and the chaste villagers.
    Crane, S.
Cityman. Carter, R.
Civic pride. Hall, T. T.
Civil peace. Achebe, C.
CIVIL RIGHTS DEMONSTRATIONS *See*
    Blacks—Civil rights

CIVIL SERVICE
 Chekhov, A. P. On official business
 Clark, D. Answer to prayer
 Colette. Monsieur Maurice
 Gallant, M. Grippes and Poche
 Gogol', N. V. Diary of a madman
 Gogol', N. V. The overcoat
 Greene, G. Men at work
 Mathers, P. Immersion
 Silverberg, R. The desert of stolen dreams
 Wall, M. "They also serve . . ."
CIVIL WAR
                England
        See England—17th century
                  Spain
        See Spain—Civil War, 1936-1939
             United States
        See United States—Civil War, 1861-
 1865
Civil War. Rossiter, S.
CIVILIZATION AND TECHNOLOGY *See*
 Technology and civilization
A **civilized** man. Mooney, M.
Claeson, Eva
 Independence
  Short story international 49
Claiborne, Sybil
 Acid rain
  Claiborne, S. Loose connections
 Final words
  Claiborne, S. Loose connections
 Flotsam and Jetsam
  Claiborne, S. Loose connections
 The future of conglomerates
  Claiborne, S. Loose connections
 The gulag computer: dead souls in the ter-
  minal
  Claiborne, S. Loose connections
 The guru and his mother
  Claiborne, S. Loose connections
 Historic moments: the discovery of love
  Claiborne, S. Loose connections
 An incurable malady
  Claiborne, S. Loose connections
 Last year at Pittsburgh
  Claiborne, S. Loose connections
 Loose connections
  Claiborne, S. Loose connections
 Okinawa's wife
  Claiborne, S. Loose connections
 On vacation
  Claiborne, S. Loose connections
 A pretty fine life
  Claiborne, S. Loose connections
 Rubble
  Claiborne, S. Loose connections
 Scenes from a novel: replenishing Ava
  Claiborne, S. Loose connections
 Visions and revisions
  Claiborne, S. Loose connections
The **claims** adjuster. Ferguson, W.
Claire de la lune. Carr, C.
Claire's lover's church. Ruch, T.

CLAIRVOYANCE
 Barker, C. Lost souls
 Carlson, R. Madame Zelena finally comes
  clean
 Ellison, H. The very last day of a good
  woman
 MacLean, K. The missing man
 Moore, B. The sight
 Russ, J. Reasonable people
 Vinge, J. D. Mother & child
 Wells, H. G. The crystal egg
The **clam-digger**. Bowering, G.
The **clan** of no-name. Crane, S.
**Clanmorris, John Michael Ward Bingham,
 7th Baron** *See* Bingham, John, 1908-
CLANS
     See also Tribes
 Howard, R. E. Red nails
Clap hands! Here comes Charley. De Haven,
 T.
Clap hands, here comes Charlie. Bainbridge,
 B.
Clara and Benedict. Pinsky, R.
Clara Militch. Turgenev, I. S.
CLARE (IRELAND) *See* Ireland—Clare
Clarifications. Ziem, J.
CLARINETISTS
 Bloch, R. The Pied Piper fights the
  Gestapo
The **clarion** call. Henry, O.
Clarissa. Morand, P.
Clark, Curt
     *For works written by this author under
     other names see* Westlake, Donald
     E.
Clark, Dennis, 1927-
 Answer to prayer
  Greening wheat: fifteen Mormon short
   stories
Clark, Eleanor
 Hurry, hurry
  Writing red; ed. by C. Nekola and P.
   Rabinowitz
Clark, Geoffrey, 1940-
 At Lowry's
  Clark, G. Ruffian on the stair
 Blood blossom
  Clark, G. Ruffian on the stair
 Crazy 8's
  Clark, G. Ruffian on the stair
 Ice fishing
  Clark, G. Ruffian on the stair
 Lunar frisson
  Clark, G. Ruffian on the stair
 Mister Period
  Clark, G. Ruffian on the stair
Clark, James
 The magic carpet
  Magic in Ithkar 3; ed. by A. Norton and
   R. Adams
Clark, Joan
 Passage by water
  Alberta bound; ed. by F. Stenson

Clark, John D.
Minus planet
Isaac Asimov presents the best science
fiction firsts
Clark, Manning, 1915-
At the exhibition
Clark, M. Collected short stories
A democrat on the Ganges
Clark, M. Collected short stories
A diet of bananas and Nietzsche
Clark, M. Collected short stories
Discovery
Clark, M. Collected short stories
Disquiet
Clark, M. Collected short stories
A footnote to the Kokoda story
Clark, M. Collected short stories
Learning to bowl an out-swinger
Clark, M. Collected short stories
A long time ago
Clark, M. Collected short stories
The love of Christ
Clark, M. Collected short stories
A moment of illumination
Clark, M. Collected short stories
Monologue by a man in black
Clark, M. Collected short stories
Portrait of a freethinker
Clark, M. Collected short stories
Still hope for God
Clark, M. Collected short stories
"'Twere best not know myself"
Clark, M. Collected short stories
Clark, Mary Higgins
Lucky day
Ladies' Home Journal 103:46+ Ag '86
Murder in Manhattan; ed. by B. Adler
Weep no more, my lady
Redbook 169:70-2+ My '87
Redbook 169:38-40+ Je '87
Clark, Michael
Makeup
Our roots grow deeper than we know;
ed. by L. Gutkind
Clark, Neil M.
No fish for the cat
Alfred Hitchcock's Grave suspicions
Clark, Walter Van Tilburg, 1909-1971
The Indian well
The Interior country; ed. by A. Black-
burn
The Western hall of fame; ed. by B.
Pronzini and M. H. Greenberg
Clarke, Arthur C., 1917-
Before Eden
Amazing stories: visions of other worlds
Breaking strain
Clarke, A. C. The sentinel
Death and the senator
Election Day 2084; ed. by I. Asimov
and M. H. Greenberg

Dial F for Frankenstein
Machines that think; ed. by I. Asimov;
P. S. Warrick and M. H. Greenberg
Dog Star
Roger Caras' Treasury of great dog
stories
Guardian angel
Clarke, A. C. The sentinel
Hide and seek
Space wars; created by P. Anderson
"If I forget thee, oh Earth . . . "
Beyond Armageddon; ed. by W. M. Mil-
ler and M. H. Greenberg
Jupiter V
Clarke, A. C. The sentinel
A meeting with Medusa
Clarke, A. C. The sentinel
Moving spirit
Through a glass, darkly; ed. by B. Woel-
fel
The nine billion names of God
Science Digest 93:60-2+ F '85
On golden seas
Omni (New York, N.Y.) 9:88-90 My '87
Refugee
Clarke, A. C. The sentinel
Rescue party
Clarke, A. C. The sentinel
The sentinel
Clarke, A. C. The sentinel
Reader's Digest 131:153-7 D '87
The songs of distant Earth
Clarke, A. C. The sentinel
Transit of earth
Omni (New York, N.Y.) 6:70-3+ My '84
The wind from the sun
Clarke, A. C. The sentinel
Great science fiction; ed. by I. Asimov;
M. H. Greenberg and C. G. Waugh
The Science fictional Olympics; ed. by
I. Asimov; M. H. Greenberg and C.
G. Waugh
Clarke, Austin Chesterfield
Canadian experience
Clarke, A. C. Nine men who laughed
Coll. ss. trins. ap. toron.—a fable
Clarke, A. C. Nine men who laughed
Doing right
Clarke, A. C. Nine men who laughed
A funeral
Clarke, A. C. Nine men who laughed
Griff!
The Oxford book of Canadian short
stories in English
How he does it
Clarke, A. C. Nine men who laughed
If only: only if . . .
Clarke, A. C. Nine men who laughed
A man
Clarke, A. C. Nine men who laughed
A short acquaintance
Clarke, A. C. Nine men who laughed

Clarke, Austin Chesterfield—Continued
The smell
  Clarke, A. C. Nine men who laughed
Clarke, John
Farnarkeling: a typical report
  Transgressions; ed. by D. Anderson
Clarke, Linda
Monarchs
  The Southern Review (Baton Rouge, La.)
    24:222-8 Wint '88
Clarke, Marcus, 1846-1881
Human repetends
  Australian science fiction; ed. by V. Ikin
Clarke, Terence
Apai
  Clarke, T. The day nothing happened
The champion
  Clarke, T. The day nothing happened
The day nothing happened
  Clarke, T. The day nothing happened
The king
  Clarke, T. The day nothing happened
The lost D.O.
  Clarke, T. The day nothing happened
A posthumous gift
  Clarke, T. The day nothing happened
The red
  Clarke, T. The day nothing happened
  The Yale Review 74:538-56 Summ '85
A rite of passion
  Clarke, T. The day nothing happened
The truth
  Clarke, T. The day nothing happened
The wee manok
  Clarke, T. The day nothing happened
The well
  Clarke, T. The day nothing happened
The Wo family
  Clarke, T. The day nothing happened
Clash by night. O'Donnell, L.
CLASS DISTINCTION
      See also Middle classes; Social classes
Abbott, K. The fort
Abbott, K. Spanish Castle
Aćin-Kosta, M. The privileged class
Ardizzone, T. The daughter and the tradesman
Auchincloss, L. The shells of Horace
Barstow, S. Rue
Bioy Casares, A. The first class passenger
Bonner, M. One true love
Chekhov, A. P. At a country house
Chekhov, A. P. A woman's kingdom
Clayton, J. J. Bodies of the rich
Gardam, J. Benevolence
Grin, A. The green lamp
Hoffman, W. Moorings
Jen, G. In the American society
Kathenor, S. The Cinderella caper
Kawabata, Y. Glass
Kay, H. The fifth generation
King, F. H. The tree

Mansfield, K. The doll's house
Maupassant, G. de. The accent
Moore, G. An episode in bachelor life
Naranjo, C. Why kill the Countess?
Oates, J. C. How I contemplated the world from the Detroit House of Correction and began my life over again
Parise, G. Melancholy
Parry, H. T. The Plum Point Ladies
Silone, I. Polikushka
Simpson, M. Three maids' children
Thomas, A. C. Degrees
Tiptree, J. Backward, turn backward
Tuohy, F. Live bait
Wells, H. G. The loyalty of Esau Common
Wong, M. V. Doubt
Zhang Kangkang, and Mei Jin. The tolling of a distant bell
Class notes. Cooper, L.
A **class** of new Canadians. Blaise, C.
The **class** photograph. Alexin, A.
CLASS STRUGGLE
Naranjo, C. Why kill the Countess?
Pil'niāk, B. A dog's life
The **classicist.** Broughton, T. A.
The **classy** woman. Ziem, J.
Clastomina. Nunes, N.
Claudine's book. Swados, H.
Claudius, Eduard
How the jungle soldiers became sons of heaven
  Voices East and West: German short stories since 1945
Claws of the white hawk. Daugherty, S. R.
Clay songs. Hoyt, M. S.
Clayton, Jo
Jezeri and her beast go to the fair and find more excitement than they want
  Magic in Ithkar [1]; ed. by A. Norton and R. Adams
Team venture
  Moonsinger's friends; ed. by S. Shwartz
Clayton, John Jacob
Bodies like mouths
  Clayton, J. J. Bodies of the rich
Bodies of the rich
  Clayton, J. J. Bodies of the rich
  Prime number; ed. by A. L. Weir
Cambridge is sinking!
  Clayton, J. J. Bodies of the rich
  A Good deal; ed. by M. Heath and F. M. Robinson
Comedy of eros
  The Virginia Quarterly Review 62:115-30 Wint '86
Fantasy for a Friday afternoon
  Clayton, J. J. Bodies of the rich
An old 3 A.M. story
  Clayton, J. J. Bodies of the rich
Part-time father
  Clayton, J. J. Bodies of the rich

Clayton, John Jacob—*Continued*
Prewar quality
Clayton, J. J. Bodies of the rich
Clayton, Sara
How do you do? May I marry you?
Redbook 168:32+ Ja '87
A reluctant grandmother
Redbook 171:48+ Je '88
A **clean** house. Kercheval, J. L.
Clean sweep Ignatius. Archer, J.
The **clean-up** man. Dixon, S.
A **clean,** well-lighted place. Hemingway, E.
The **cleaner.** Murphy, P.
CLEANING WOMEN
Adams, A. Alaska
Berriault, G. The houses of the city
Grossman, L. The sleeves
Jolley, E. Five acre virgin
Jolley, E. The last crop
Jolley, E. One bite for Christmas
Jolley, E. Pear tree dance
Clearance. Long, D.
Clearfield. Freeman, J.
A **clearing** in the bush. Wicomb, Z.
Clearing in the sky. Stuart, J.
Clearing the thickets. Tsushima, Y.
Clee, Mona A.
Dust
Afterlives; ed. by P. Sargent and I. Watson
Encounter on the ladder
Universe 15
Cleeve, Brian, 1921-
The horse thieves of Ballysaggert
The Saturday Evening Post 257:62-5+ Jl/Ag '85
Clemence, Bruce
All the livelong night
Synergy v3
Clemency. Barry, B.
Clemens, Samuel Langhorne *See* Twain, Mark, 1835-1910
Clemens, Sarah
A good night's work
Ripper! Ed. by G. Dozois and S. Casper
Clement, Hal, 1922-
The mechanic
[Analog]: Writers' choice v2
Seasoning
Medea: Harlan's world; ed. by H. Ellison
Cleo. Barthelme, F.
CLEPTOMANIA *See* Kleptomania
CLERGY
See also Catholic priests; Evangelists; Rabbis
Aldiss, B. W. The other side of the lake
Archer, J. Colonel Bullfrog
Auchincloss, L. The Stations of the Cross
Benson, A. C. The uttermost farthing
Blackwood, A. Secret worship
Bly, C. The mouse roulette wheel
Bretnor, R. No other gods
Buchan, J. Fullcircle

Cary, A. An old maid's story
Chesterton, G. K. The second miracle
Coleman, W. The twinight of Reverend Jones
Cook, H. Clown
Cook, H. First snow
Coskran, K. Graven images
Crabtree, L. V. Wildcat John
Del Rey, L. For I am a jealous people!
Finney, E. J. The divine dealer
Fisher, M. F. K. The lost, strayed, stolen
Fisher, R. The South lingers on
Gingher, M. The kiss
Givner, J. The lost sheep
Goldswain, R. Oh, ye of little faith
Gray, A. The true history of Anthony Ffryar
Grizzard, L. Good men of God
Hawthorne, N. The minister's black veil
Hillmer, J. New day coming
Hoffman, W. Faces at the window
Hoffman, W. The question of rain
Hogan, D. The vicar's wife
Hogg, J. The Cameronian preacher's tale
Howard, C. The last revival
Jean Paul. Army-chaplain Schmelzle's journey to Flätz
Johnson, W. The ice fish
Jones, K. The green man
Keillor, G. A glass of Wendy
Keillor, G. New Year's
Keillor, G. Out in the cold
Keillor, G. Pontoon boat
Koch, C. Bread and butter questions
Le Fanu, J. S. Green tea
MacDonald, D. R. The flowers of Bermuda
Martin, G. R. R. The way of cross and dragon
McGarry, J. Providence, 1966: ducks and lucks
Millman, L. The laying on of hands
Mitchell, W. O. Patterns
Mrożek, S. The pastor
Naipaul, S. The dolly house
Osborn, C. The circuit rider
Payne, P. The pure in heart
Petrakis, H. M. The miracle
Preuss, P. Small bodies
Pritchard, M. The housekeeper
Rölvaag, O. E. The butter war in Greenfield
Ruch, T. Claire's lover's church
Sams, F. Judgment
Sams, F. The widow's mite
Sarton, M. The silent minister
Song, Y. Overnight at Matthew's
Spofford, H. E. P. Her story
Stevenson, R. L. Thrawn Janet
Stocks, D. Therapeutic bondage
Sturges, A. E. The last loneliness
Thanet, O. Why Abbylonia surrendered
Thomas, D. The enemies

CLERGY—*Continued*
Thorman, C. Persecution is for you
Wells, H. G. Mr. Marshall's doppelganger
Wheatcroft, J. The appeal
Whelan, G. A dwelling place for dragons
Williams, J. Taking care
Williams, T. The yellow bird
Willis, C. Samaritan

CLERGY, ANGLICAN AND EPISCOPAL
Auchincloss, L. The seagull
Blythe, R. The shadows of the living
Clark, M. Disquiet
Gordimer, N. Not for publication
Hardy, T. Old Mrs. Chundle
Kirk, R. The invasion of the Church of
the Holy Ghost
Mortimer, J. C. Rumpole and the Man of
God
Regent, P. Great Pan is dead!
Warren, J. Mrs. Rogers

CLERGY, CATHOLIC *See* Catholic priests

CLERGY, ITINERANT *See* Itinerant clergy

**CLERGY, ORTHODOX EASTERN
CHURCH**
Faik, S. Priest Effendi
Petrakis, H. M. The bastards of Thanos
Petrakis, H. M. The waves of night

**CLERGY, ORTHODOX EASTERN
CHURCH, RUSSIAN**
Johnson, W. The ice fish
Johnson, W. Prayer for the dying
Clerical error. Cozzens, J. G.

CLERKS

See also Civil service
Calvino, I. The adventure of a clerk
Coskran, K. Miss Clay County 1960
Crane, S. Mr. Binks' day off
Doyle, Sir A. C. Gentlemanly Joe
Gallant, M. Between zero and one
Hurst, F. The nth commandment
Murphy, P. Getting out
Pavese, C. The evil eye
Schinto, J. Sounds of the rude world

CLEVELAND (OHIO) *See* Ohio—Cleveland
Clever. Ziem, J.
Clever and pretty. Jolley, E.
Clever dogs. Colette
The **clever** rain tree. Oe, K.
The **cleverness** of Elsie. Walker, W.
The **clichés** from outer space. Russ, J.
Click. Aldridge, R.
Click!. Block, L.
The **cliff.** Baxter, C.
Cliff. Rees, D.
Cliff Dwellers. Martin, R.
Cliffedge. Swift, G.

Clifford, Francis, 1917-1975

Turn and turn about
The Mammoth book of modern crime
stories; ed. by G. Hardinge

Clifford, Lucy Lane, 1855?-1929
The new mother
The Dark descent; ed. by D. G. Hart-
well
Masterpieces of fantasy and enchant-
ment; ed. by D. G. Hartwell

Clift, Charmian, 1923-1969
Even the thrush has wings
Johnston, G. and Clift, C. Strong-man
from Piraeus, and other stories
The small animus
Johnston, G. and Clift, C. Strong-man
from Piraeus, and other stories
Three old men of Lerici
Johnston, G. and Clift, C. Strong-man
from Piraeus, and other stories
Wild Emperor
Johnston, G. and Clift, C. Strong-man
from Piraeus, and other stories

Clifton, Mark
Hang head, vandal!
Amazing stories: 60 years of the best
science fiction

A **climate** of extremes. Givner, J.
The **climber** on the hill. Dundas, R.
Climbing Monkey Hill. Shaik, F.
The **climbing** wave. Bradley, M. Z.
The **clincher.** Pronzini, B.
The **clinging** woman. Rendell, R.
The **cloak.** Dinesen, I.
The **cloak** and the staff. Dickson, G. R.
The **clock.** Harvey, W. F.
The **clock** house. Ocampo, S.
A **clock** in San Diego. Fahy, C.
A **clock** ticks at Christmas. Highsmith, P.

CLOCKS AND WATCHES
Aiken, J. Time to laugh
Asimov, I. What time is it?
Eldridge, M. Antique
Ellison, H. Paladin of the lost hour
Frost, G. From Hell, again
Hartley, L. P. The silver clock
Harvey, W. F. The clock
Hawthorne, N. The artist of the beautiful
Jahnn, H. H. The watchmaker
Khudayyir, M. Clocks like horses
Kiely, B. The jeweller's boy
Lee, T. When the clock strikes
Lish, G. Behold the incredible revenge of
the shifted P. O. V.
MacLean, A. The gold watch
Poe, E. A. The devil in the belfry
Rendell, R. The convolvulus clock
Sharat Chandra, G. S. The holy wristwatch
Spark, M. The ormolu clock
Swift, G. The watch

Clocks like horses. Khudayyir, M.
The **clockwork** woman. Brown, A. R.
Clodia, shameless matron. Schwob, M.
CLONES *See* Reproduction, Asexual
Clorinda. Pieyre de Mandiargues, A.
Close. Nevai, L.
Close calls. Kaplan, J.

Close calls. Lutz, J.
Close dancing. Flanagan, R.
Close encounter with the deity. Bishop, M.
Close to autumn. Schad, C. M.
Close to home. Ortalda, C.
Close-ups. Thompson, S.
Close water. Pritchett, M.
Closed Mondays. Greenberg, A.
Closeted. Watmough, D.
The **closing** down of summer. MacLeod, A.
Closing night at the Zebra Lounge. Berle, M.
Clothing. L'Heureux, J.

CLOTHING AND DRESS
See also Trousers
Anthony, P. Up Schist Crick
Behan, B. The confirmation suit
Callaghan, M. A wedding-dress
Colette. Rites
Davie, E. The free fur coat
Hurst, F. Oats for the woman
Kessler, J. F. Jacob
McCann, R. My mother's clothes: the school of beauty and shame
Moore, G. An episode in married life
Nizer, L. The zipper
Rand, P. Charades
Rhys, J. Illusion
Rothberg, A. The red dress
Shelnutt, E. Angel
Tournier, M. The fetishist
Weldon, F. Alopecia
Wells, H. G. The beautiful suit
West, J. The battle of the suits
Woolf, V. The new dress

The **cloud** child. Black, S.
A **clouded** visit with Rolling Thunder. Taylor, P. E.

CLOUDS
Anthony, P. Within the cloud

Clouk alone. Colette
Clouk's fling. Colette
The **cloven** tree. Norris, H.
Clown. Cook, H.
A **clown**. Ignatow, R. G.
The **clown**. Maupassant, G. de

CLOWNS
Muller, M. The broken men
Robison, M. For real

CLUBS
Ade, G. The fable of what happened the night the men came to the women's club
Ade, G. The intellectual awakening in Burton's Row
Asimov, I. Can you prove it?
Asimov, I. The Cross of Lorraine
Asimov, I. Dollars and cents
Asimov, I. The driver
Asimov, I. Getting the combination
Asimov, I. The Good Samaritan
Asimov, I. He wasn't there
Asimov, I. Hide and seek
Asimov, I. The intrusion
Asimov, I. The library book
Asimov, I. The magic umbrella
Asimov, I. Middle name
Asimov, I. A Monday in April
Asimov, I. Neither brute nor human
Asimov, I. Never out of sight
Asimov, I. The next day
Asimov, I. The obvious factor
Asimov, I. The one and only east
Asimov, I. Out of sight
Asimov, I. The Phoenician bauble
Asimov, I. The pointing finger
Asimov, I. Quicker than the eye
Asimov, I. The redhead
Asimov, I. The sign
Asimov, I. Sixty million trillion combinations
Asimov, I. The speck
Asimov, I. The three numbers
Asimov, I. What time is it?
Asimov, I. The woman in the bar
Asimov, I. The wrong house
Asimov, I. Yankee Doodle went to town
Asimov, I. The year of the action
Blythe, R. The schism
Doyle, Sir A. C. The end of Devil Hawker
Gault, W. C. The threatening three
Gilbert, W. S. Tom Poulton's joke
Gray, A. The Everlasting Club
Hecht, B. Miracle of the fifteen murderers
Hornung, E. W. The criminologists' club
Lutz, J. The Insomniacs Club
Suckow, R. What have I?
Thorman, C. Knights of Puntukas
Thorman, C. Society for the benefit of the Daughters of Vilnius
Wharton, E. Xingu

The **clue**. Shannon, D.
Clues. Hemley, R.
Clues. Schoemperlen, D.
Clustering round young Bingo. Wodehouse, P. G.
Clytemnestra in the suburbs. Klass, P.
The **co-operative**. Mrożek, S.
The **coach**. Gogol', N. V.

COACHING (ATHLETICS)
Kinsella, W. P. The Valley of the Schmoon
Robison, M. Again, again, again
Stark, S. S. Ode to the big school
Willson, H. Tufts and Wink

COAL MINERS *See* Coal mines and mining

COAL MINES AND MINING
Benedict, P. Hackberry
Crane, S. In the depths of a coal mine
Wegner, H. But America is far
Wegner, H. Miner's tattoo

China
Liang Xiaosheng. The jet ruler
Petchsingh, T. The sacrifice
Sun Shaoshan. Eight hundred meters below

COAL MINES AND MINING—*Continued*

England

Lawrence, D. H. Odour of chrysan-themums

Warren, J. The underground banquet

Kentucky

Stuart, J. The Anglo-Saxons of Auxierville

Missouri

Conroy, J. Down in Happy Hollow

Scotland

McCormack, E. P. The one-legged men

COAL TOWNS *See* Coal mines and mining

Coalhouse, Violet

The mask

Women's work; ed. by M. McLeod and L. Wevers

Coastal. Peterson, M.

The **coat.** See Gogol', N. V. The overcoat

Coates, Robert M. (Robert Myron), 1897-1973

The hour after Westerly

Haunted New England; ed. by C. G. Waugh; M. H. Greenberg and F. D. McSherry

Coates, Ruth Allison

Hurry up and love me

'Teen 31:42+ F '87

Coatsworth, Elizabeth Jane, 1893-1986

Witch girl

Young witches & warlocks; ed. by I. Asimov; M. H. Greenberg and C. G. Waugh

Cobb, Irvin S., 1876-1944

Fishhead

Mississippi River tales; ed. by F. McSherry; C. G. Waugh and M. H. Greenberg

Cobb, William

The stone soldier

The Art of fiction in the heart of Dixie; ed. by P. D. Beidler

Cobber: Peach Face. Pascoe, B.

Cobber: The cat men of Genoa. Pascoe, B.

Cobbold, Diana

Naming the enemy

The Sewanee Review 94:58-72 Wint '86

COBRAS

Colvin, C. Near Forelanders Kop

Lee, T. Foreign skins

Narayan, R. K. Naga

Narayan, R. K. A snake in the grass

Rifaat, A. My world of the unknown

Woolrich, C. Kiss of the cobra

The **Coca-Cola** Kid. Moorhouse, F.

COCAINE

Abbott, L. K. The eldest of things

Calisher, H. The sound track

Friedman, B. J. The adventurer

Mrabet, M. Doctor Safi

Rossi, A. Bums on needles and pins

Wolff, T. Leviathan

Cock-a-doodle-doo; or, The crowing of the noble cock beneventano. Melville, H.

A **cock** crowed. Maupassant, G. de

Cock-fighting. Song, Y.

Cock Robin Beale Street. Hurston, Z. N.

Cockfight. Yolen, J.

COCKFIGHTING

Abid, A. Our fighting cock

Ferreira, R. The well

Lawson, H. Bill, the ventriloquial rooster

Song, Y. Cock-fighting

Cockrell, Cathy, 1951-

In praise of creeping things

Through other eyes; ed. by I. Zahava

COCKROACHES

Davis, L. Cockroaches in autumn

Disch, T. M. The roaches

Highsmith, P. Notes from a respectable cockroach

Lispector, C. The fifth story

Reed, K. Sisohpromatem

Cockroaches in autumn. Davis, L.

COCKTAIL PARTIES *See* Parties

Cocktails at Doney's. Trevor, W.

Cocky olly. Pritchett, V. S.

The **cocotte.** See Maupassant, G. de. Ball-of-fat

COCTEAU, JEAN, 1889-1963

About

Lopatin, J. Fast and loose, a historical romance

Code blue! Hyde, E.

Codling-moth. Sutherland, M.

Codrescu, Andrei, 1946-

The babysitter

Codrescu, A. Monsieur Teste in America & other instances of realism

A bar in Brooklyn

Codrescu, A. Monsieur Teste in America & other instances of realism

The herald

Codrescu, A. Monsieur Teste in America & other instances of realism

Julie

Codrescu, A. Monsieur Teste in America & other instances of realism

Monsieur Teste in America

Codrescu, A. Monsieur Teste in America & other instances of realism

The old couple

Codrescu, A. Monsieur Teste in America & other instances of realism

Petra

Codrescu, A. Monsieur Teste in America & other instances of realism

Samba de los agentes

Codrescu, A. Monsieur Teste in America & other instances of realism

Cody's story. Olmstead, R.

Coe, Christopher

Anything you want

Men on men 2; ed. by G. Stambolian

Coe, Christopher—*Continued*
Easy
Harper's 273:32+ Ag '86
Coe, Tucker
For works written by this author under other names see Westlake, Donald E.
Coelostat. Dodd, S. M.
COFFEE
Vizenor, G. R. Reservation café: the origins of American Indian instant coffee
The **coffee-cart** girl. Mphahlele, E.
Coffey, Brian, 1945-
For works written by this author under other names see Koontz, Dean, 1945-
The **coffin** on the hill. Welch, D.
COFFINS
Bradbury, R. Wake for the living
Kimball, R. W. Destination
Lovecraft, H. P. In the vault
Poe, E. A. The oblong box
St. Pierre, P. H. Ol Antoine's wooden overcoat
The **coffins** of the Emperor. Gulik, R. H. van
Coffman, Bill
Incest rock
The Antioch Review 42:335-43 Summ '84
Coggeshall, Rosanne, 1946-
Peter the Rock
New stories from the South: the year's best, 1987
The Southern Review (Baton Rouge, La.) 22:191-202 Ja '86
The **Coggios.** Layfield, S.
Cogswell, Theodore R.
The cabbage patch
Young monsters; ed. by I. Asimov; M. H. Greenberg and C. G. Waugh
Deal with the D.E.V.I.L.
100 great fantasy short short stories; ed. by I. Asimov; T. Carr and M. H. Greenberg
The wall around the world
Wizards; ed. by I. Asimov; M. H. Greenberg and C. G. Waugh
Cogwheels. Akutagawa, R.
Cohen, Anthea
On her feet again
Ellery Queen's Prime crimes 2
Cohen, Arthur (Arthur Allen), 1928-1986
Hans Cassebeer and the virgin's rose
Cohen, A. Artists & enemies
Malenov's revenge
Cohen, A. Artists & enemies
The monumental sculptor
Cohen, A. Artists & enemies
Cohen, Matt, 1942-
At the Empress Hotel
Cohen, M. Life on this planet, and other stories

Café Le Dog
Cohen, M. Life on this planet, and other stories
Death of a guppy
Cohen, M. Life on this planet, and other stories
The Eiffel Tower in three parts
The Oxford book of Canadian short stories in English
Golden whore of the heartland
Cohen, M. Life on this planet, and other stories
Life on this planet
Cohen, M. Life on this planet, and other stories
A love for the infinite
Cohen, M. Life on this planet, and other stories
Sentimental meetings
Cohen, M. Life on this planet, and other stories
The sins of Tomas Benares
Cohen, M. Life on this planet, and other stories
Cohen, Robert, 1957-
Dostoevsky's whore
The Massachusetts Review 26:47-56 Spr '85
A flight of sparks
The Paris Review 30:16-39 Summ '88
The scientific method
The Editors' choice v4; ed. by G. E. Murphy, Jr.
Shamsky and other casualties
The Pushcart prize XII
Cohen, Sharron
The man on the motorcycle
McCall's 111:104-5+ Ap '84
Cohorts. Gold, H.
The **coin** collector. Finney, J.
The **coin** of Dionysius. Bramah, E.
COINS
Bramah, E. The coin of Dionysius
Greenwood, R. Archetypes
Colasanti, Marina
The house of being
The Literary Review (Madison, N.J.) 27:446-9 Summ '84
Cold bridge. Vonarburg, E.
A **cold** coming. Mulrine, S.
A **cold** foggy day. Pronzini, B.
Cold light. Wagner, K. E.
Cold light. Watson, I.
Cold money. Queen, E.
Cold print. Campbell, R.
The **cold** room. Pei, L.
Cold spell. Langford, D.
Cold spell. Waters, E.
Cold storage. Neugeboren, J.
Cold war. Neville, K.
Cold war orphans. Bishop, M.
Coldbeer at the Only. Brondoli, M.

Cole, Dana
  The wife's new automobile
    The North American Review 273:28-31
      D '88
Cole, E. B.
  Fighting Philosopher
    Intergalactic empires; ed. by I. Asimov;
      M. H. Greenberg and C. G. Waugh
**Cole, G. D. H. (George Douglas Howard),
    1889-1959, and Cole, Margaret, 1893-
    1980**
  The toys of death
    Women sleuths; ed. by M. H. Greenberg
      and B. Pronzini
Cole, Margaret, 1893-1980
  (jt. auth) See Cole, G. D. H. (George
    Douglas Howard), 1889-1959, and
    Cole, Margaret, 1893-1980
Colegate, Isabel
  Distant cousins
    Colegate, I. A glimpse of Sion's glory
  The girl who had lived among artists
    Colegate, I. A glimpse of Sion's glory
  A glimpse of Sion's glory
    Colegate, I. A glimpse of Sion's glory
Coleman, Wanda
  Big dreams
    Coleman, W. A war of eyes, and other
      stories
  The big little gang
    Coleman, W. A war of eyes, and other
      stories
  The buyer
    Coleman, W. A war of eyes, and other
      stories
  Buying primo time
    Coleman, W. A war of eyes, and other
      stories
  Chuck and the boss man's wife
    Coleman, W. A war of eyes, and other
      stories
  Dream 5281
    Coleman, W. A war of eyes, and other
      stories
  The Dufus Rufus
    Coleman, W. A war of eyes, and other
      stories
  Eyes and teeth
    Coleman, W. A war of eyes, and other
      stories
  Fat Lena
    Coleman, W. A war of eyes, and other
      stories
  The Friday night shift at the Taco House
    blues (wah-wah)
    Coleman, W. A war of eyes, and other
      stories
  Gamblers
    Coleman, W. A war of eyes, and other
      stories
  The habit
    Coleman, W. A war of eyes, and other
      stories

  Hamburgers
    Coleman, W. A war of eyes, and other
      stories
  In the city of sleep
    Coleman, W. A war of eyes, and other
      stories
  Jonesed
    Coleman, W. A war of eyes, and other
      stories
  Kelele
    Coleman, W. A war of eyes, and other
      stories
  Ladies
    Coleman, W. A war of eyes, and other
      stories
  Lickety-split
    Coleman, W. A war of eyes, and other
      stories
  Lonnie's cousin
    Coleman, W. A war of eyes, and other
      stories
  Reba
    Coleman, W. A war of eyes, and other
      stories
  The screamer
    Coleman, W. A war of eyes, and other
      stories
  The seamstress
    Coleman, W. A war of eyes, and other
      stories
  'Shrooms
    Coleman, W. A war of eyes, and other
      stories
  The stare down
    Coleman, W. A war of eyes, and other
      stories
  Stashed
    Coleman, W. A war of eyes, and other
      stories
  Take it up at the bridge
    Coleman, W. A war of eyes, and other
      stories
  The twinight of Reverend Jones
    Coleman, W. A war of eyes, and other
      stories
  A war of eyes
    Coleman, W. A war of eyes, and other
      stories
  Watching the sunset
    Coleman, W. A war of eyes, and other
      stories
  Without visible means
    Coleman, W. A war of eyes, and other
      stories
  Word monkey
    Coleman, W. A war of eyes, and other
      stories
Coleridge, Sara, 1802-1852
  Phantasmion [excerpt]
    Masterpieces of fantasy and enchant-
      ment; ed. by D. G. Hartwell

Colette, 1873-1954

The accompanist
  Colette. The collected stories of Colette
The advice
  Colette. The collected stories of Colette
After midnight
  Colette. The collected stories of Colette
Alix's refusal
  Colette. The collected stories of Colette
April
  Colette. The collected stories of Colette
Armande
  Colette. The collected stories of Colette
Arrival and rehearsal
  Colette. The collected stories of Colette
A bad morning
  Colette. The collected stories of Colette
Bastienne's child
  Colette. The collected stories of Colette
Bella-Vista
  Colette. The collected stories of Colette
The bitch
  Colette. The collected stories of Colette
The bracelet
  Classic European short stories; ed. by R.
    Beum
  Colette. The collected stories of Colette
The burglar
  Colette. The collected stories of Colette
Bygone spring
  Colette. The collected stories of Colette
The cashier
  Colette. The collected stories of Colette
"Châ"
  Colette. The collected stories of Colette
Chéri
  Colette. The collected stories of Colette
The child prodigy
  Colette. The collected stories of Colette
The circus horse
  Colette. The collected stories of Colette
Clever dogs
  Colette. The collected stories of Colette
Clouk alone
  Colette. The collected stories of Colette
Clouk's fling
  Colette. The collected stories of Colette
The cure
  Colette. The collected stories of Colette
Dawn
  Classic European short stories; ed. by R.
    Beum
  Colette. The collected stories of Colette
A dead end
  Colette. The collected stories of Colette
A fable: the tendrils of the vine
  Colette. The collected stories of Colette
"La Fenice"
  Colette. The collected stories of Colette
The find
  Colette. The collected stories of Colette
Florie
  Colette. The collected stories of Colette

The fox
  Colette. The collected stories of Colette
"Gitanette"
  Colette. The collected stories of Colette
Grape harvest
  Colette. The collected stories of Colette
Gray days
  Colette. The collected stories of Colette
Green sealing wax
  Colette. The collected stories of Colette
Gribiche
  Colette. The collected stories of Colette
Habit
  Colette. The collected stories of Colette
A hairdresser
  Colette. The collected stories of Colette
The half-crazy
  Colette. The collected stories of Colette
The halt
  Colette. The collected stories of Colette
The hand
  Colette. The collected stories of Colette
The hard worker
  Colette. The collected stories of Colette
The hidden woman
  Colette. The collected stories of Colette
The hollow nut
  Colette. The collected stories of Colette
"If I had a daughter . . ."
  Colette. The collected stories of Colette
In the boudoir
  Colette. The collected stories of Colette
In the flower of age
  Colette. The collected stories of Colette
An interview
  Colette. The collected stories of Colette
Journey's end
  Colette. The collected stories of Colette
The judge
  Colette. The collected stories of Colette
The kepi
  Colette. The collected stories of Colette
The landscape
  Colette. The collected stories of Colette
The last fire
  Colette. The collected stories of Colette
A letter
  Colette. The collected stories of Colette
Literature
  Colette. The collected stories of Colette
The little Bouilloux girl
  Classic European short stories; ed. by R.
    Beum
  Colette. The collected stories of Colette
"Lola"
  Colette. The collected stories of Colette
Love
  Colette. The collected stories of Colette
A masseuse
  Colette. The collected stories of Colette
The "master"
  Colette. The collected stories of Colette

Colette, 1873-1954—*Continued*

Matinee
  Colette. The collected stories of Colette
Mirror games [Variant title: Mirror-play]
  Colette. The collected stories of Colette
The misfit
  Colette. The collected stories of Colette
Moments of stress
  Colette. The collected stories of Colette
Monsieur Maurice
  Colette. The collected stories of Colette
Morning glories
  Colette. The collected stories of Colette
The murderer
  Colette. The collected stories of Colette
My corset maker
  Colette. The collected stories of Colette
My goddaughter
  Colette. The collected stories of Colette
Newly shorn
  Colette. The collected stories of Colette
Nostalgia
  Colette. The collected stories of Colette
October
  Colette. The collected stories of Colette
The omelette
  Colette. The collected stories of Colette
One evening
  Colette. The collected stories of Colette
The other table
  Colette. The collected stories of Colette
The other wife
  The World of the short story; ed. by
    C. Fadiman
The patriarch
  Colette. The collected stories of Colette
The pearls
  Colette. The collected stories of Colette
The photographer's wife [Variant title: The
    photographer's Missus]
  Colette. The collected stories of Colette
The portrait
  Colette. The collected stories of Colette
The quick-change artist
  Colette. The collected stories of Colette
The rainy moon
  Colette. The collected stories of Colette
The rendezvous
  Colette. The collected stories of Colette
The respite
  Colette. The collected stories of Colette
The return
  Colette. The collected stories of Colette
Rites
  Colette. The collected stories of Colette
The rivals
  Colette. The collected stories of Colette
The saleswoman
  Colette. The collected stories of Colette
The screen
  Colette. The collected stories of Colette
The seamstress
  Colette. The collected stories of Colette

Secrets
  Colette. The collected stories of Colette
The Sémiramis bar
  Colette. The collected stories of Colette
The sempstress
  Family: stories from the interior; ed. by
    G. G. Chavis
The sick child
  Colette. The collected stories of Colette
Sleepless nights
  Colette. The collected stories of Colette
The starveling
  Colette. The collected stories of Colette
"The strike, oh, Lord, the strike!"
  Colette. The collected stories of Colette
The tender shoot
  Colette. The collected stories of Colette
The tenor
  Colette. The collected stories of Colette
The victim
  Colette. The collected stories of Colette
The watchman
  Colette. The collected stories of Colette
What must we look like?
  Colette. The collected stories of Colette
The workroom
  Colette. The collected stories of Colette
"Colita". Cartagena Portalatín, A.
Coll. ss. trins. ap. toron.—a fable. Clarke,
    A. C.
Collaborating. Bishop, M.
Collaboration. Jarvis, M. C.
Collage. Martins, A. M.
Collected bear stories. Burns, M.
The **collected** works of Brown. Pfeil, F.
Collection. Keillor, G.
COLLECTION AGENCIES
  Elkin, S. I look out for Ed Wolfe
  Yuill, P. B. Hazell and the patriot
A **collection** of letters. Happy, E.
COLLECTIVE SETTLEMENTS
  Novitski, P. Nuclear fission
                California
  Greenwood, R. Arcadia
                Israel
  Eisenstein, S. The sacrifice
  Oz, A. Nomad and viper
  Shaham, N. The other side of the wall
  Shamosh, A. Bells
                United States
  Henley, P. As luck would have it
  Henley, P. The birthing
  Henley, P. Let me call you sweetheart
  Varley, J. The persistence of vision
Collector. Cowan, P.
Collectors. Carver, R.
COLLECTORS AND COLLECTING
  Barnhill, S. Near places, far places
  Bloch, R. The man who collected Poe
  Bloch, R. The skull of the Marquis de
    Sade
  Ellin, S. The orderly world of Mr. Appleby
  Mathers, P. A knight of teeth

COLLECTORS AND COLLECTING—*Continued*

Pronzini, B. The man who collected "The Shadow"

Skelton, R. Sarah

St. Clair, M. An egg a month from all over

Woolf, V. Solid objects

Collector's item. Longyear, B. B.

COLLEGE ALUMNI

Ade, G. Dubley, '89

Queen, E. The inner circle

Schulman, H. Like brothers

Steele, M. The man in the doll house

COLLEGE AND SCHOOL DRAMA

Paley, G. The loudest voice

Tuohy, F. The broken bridge

COLLEGE LIFE

See also College students; School life; Students; Teachers

Bartlett, H. Some notes on evolution

Bradbury, M. Composition

Drake, R. Tennis whites

Oates, J. C. A sentimental encounter

Pastan, R. Underground

Poe, E. A. Mystification

Poe, E. A. Von Jung, the mystific

Russ, J. The view from this window

Scott, J. The American Book of the Dead

Suckow, R. A part of the institution

Wells, H. G. A slip under the microscope

Wilson, E. H. The axe, the axe, the axe

Australia

Clark, M. Monologue by a man in black

Clark, M. Portrait of a freethinker

Canada

Blaise, C. A class of new Canadians

China

Shen Rong. Troubled Sunday

Ireland

Trevor, W. Two more gallants

Japan

Haylock, J. Tomiko

Korea

Kim, S.-O. Good bargain

Mexico

Keller, G. D. The raza who scored big in Anáhuac

Poland

Tuohy, F. The student

United States

Floyd, P. L. Second best

Glasser, P. Easily and well

Ingalls, R. People to people

Janowitz, T. The new acquaintances

Kessler, J. F. Cheiron

Kessler, J. F. Dafne

King, S. Cain rose up

Matheson, R. Old haunts

Matheson, R. C. Graduation

Simpson, M. Lawns

Updike, J. The Christian roommates

Wheatcroft, J. The lapse

Williams, T. Field of blue children

Williams, T. The important thing

College life. Paulson, A. B.

COLLEGE STUDENTS

See also College life

Abbott, L. K. A modern story of Woe and Lovecraft

Atwood, M. The man from Mars

Bell, M. Brady

Bissoondath, N. The revolutionary

Böll, H. No tears for Schmeck

Bourjaily, V. The Amish farmer

Boyd, W. Gifts

Cameron, P. Fear of math

Campbell, E. Duties and liabilities

Clarke, A. C. Coll. ss. trins. ap. toron.—a fable

Clayton, J. J. Bodies like mouths

Dixon, S. Eating the placenta

Dixon, S. Will's book

Dubus, A. Finding a girl in America

Dubus, A. Townies

Ebon, W. The doctorate

Ebon, W. The supermarket manager's daughter

Endō, S. Despicable bastard

Gardner, M. The dome of many colors

Gilliatt, P. As is

Girion, B. Another blue-eyed quarterback

Girion, B. Next of kin

Haldeman, J. C. Wet behind the ears

Hall, M. L. The visit

Halligan, M. Thrift

Irving, W. The adventure of the German student

Johnson, C. R. Alēthia

Kagan, N. Four brands of impossible

Komie, L. B. The law clerk's lament

Komie, L. B. The loves of David Freund

Li Chao. Spring chill

Metcalf, J. Single gents only

Michaels, L. Toiler

Nahin, P. J. Publish and perish

Nesin, A. The university committee's sociological study of a village

Oates, J. C. Harrow Street at Linden

Phillips, J. A. November and December: Billy, 1969

Robison, M. I am twenty-one

Rubin, D. Longing for America

Schulman, H. Having fun

Sheehan, R. Every angel is terrible

Sheehan, R. Several sweet ecstasies

Sheehan, R. Universitas

Sillitoe, L. Four walls and an empty door

Silva, B. The bathetic fallacy

Silva, B. The thesis

Simpson, M. Lawns

Sinclair, C. Bedbugs

Thompson, J. Foreigners

Thompson, J. Little Face

Thompson, S. Close-ups

Updike, D. Apples

COLLEGE STUDENTS—*Continued*
  Updike, D. Bachelor of arts
  Updike, D. Spring
  Wells, H. G. The thumbmark
  Whelan, G. The secret meeting with Mr.
    Eliot

COLLEGE TEACHERS *See* Teachers

Colless, Ted, and Kelly, David
  The lost world: signs of life
    Transgressions; ed. by D. Anderson

Collier, John, 1901-1980
  Bird of prey
    Masterpieces of fantasy and enchant-
      ment; ed. by D. G. Hartwell
  Evening primrose
    The Dark descent; ed. by D. G. Hart-
      well
  The lady on the grey
    Black water; ed. by A. Manguel

Collins, Alan, 1928-
  The trouble with Felix
    Echad 4: Jewish writing from down un-
      der: Australia and New Zealand

Collins, Carol
  Coming of age
    Michigan Quarterly Review 24:177-85 Spr
      '85

Collins, Jackie
  The rock star and the lifeguard
    Rolling Stone p66-8+ Jl 19-Ag 2 '84

Collins, Linda
  At the Center for Younger Mothers
    The Kenyon Review ns9:74-90 Fall '87
  The doctor's house
    Collins, L. Going to see the leaves
  Driving back from the funeral
    Collins, L. Going to see the leaves
    The Kenyon Review ns8:17-26 Wint '86
  Fears [Variant title: A nighttime story]
    Collins, L. Going to see the leaves
  Going to see the leaves
    Collins, L. Going to see the leaves
  Intimacy
    Collins, L. Going to see the leaves
  Meditation on play, thoughts on death
    Collins, L. Going to see the leaves
  A summer's day
    Collins, L. Going to see the leaves
  When the pipes froze
    Collins, L. Going to see the leaves
    Commentary 79:56-62 Ap '85

Collins, Max Allan
  House call
    Mean streets; ed. by R. J. Randisi
  Marble Mildred
    An Eye for justice; ed. by R. J. Randisi
  Scrap
    The Black Lizard anthology of crime fic-
      tion; ed. by E. Gorman

  The strawberry teardrop
    The Eyes have it; ed. by R. J. Randisi
    The Mammoth book of private eye
      stories; ed. by B. Pronzini and M. H.
      Greenberg

Collins, Meghan
  The green woman
    Don't bet on the prince; ed. by J. Zipes

Collins, Michael, 1924-
  *For works written by this author under
    other names see* Arden, William,
    1924-; Lynds, Dennis, 1924-; Sadler,
    Mark, 1924-
  Black in the snow
    An Eye for justice; ed. by R. J. Randisi
  Eighty million dead
    The Eyes have it; ed. by R. J. Randisi
  The motive
    A Matter of crime v2
  The oldest killer
    The Year's best mystery and suspense
      stories, 1984
  A reason to die
    The Mammoth book of private eye
      stories; ed. by B. Pronzini and M. H.
      Greenberg

Collins, Susi Robinson
  A day at Hot Creek
    Women's work; ed. by M. McLeod and
      L. Wevers

Collins, Wilkie, 1824-1899
  The biter bit
    Mystery in the mainstream; ed. by B.
      Pronzini; M. H. Greenberg and B. N.
      Malzberg
  "Blow up with the brig"
    Short stories of the sea; ed. by G. C.
      Solley and E. Steinbaugh
  The dead hand
    The Treasury of English short stories;
      ed. by N. Sullivan
  Mad Monkton
    The Book of the dead; ed. by A. K.
      Russell
  A terribly strange bed
    Death locked in; ed. by D. G. Greene
      and R. C. S. Adey
    Isaac Asimov presents the best crime
      stories of the 19th century

Collison, Elizabeth
  Ed
    The North American Review 272:35-8 Je
      '87

The colloquy of Monos and Una. Poe, E.
  A.

COLOMBIA
  Mcdonald, G. The robbery
  Silvis, R. The fatalist
        Rural life
  García Márquez, G. Big Mama's funeral
  García Márquez, G. One day after
    Saturday

COLOMBO, CRISTOFORO *See* Columbus,
Christopher
The **colonel** and his friend. Sonu, H.
The **Colonel** and the santo. Chavez, A.
Colonel Bullfrog. Archer, J.
The **colonel** says I love you. Dovlatov, S.
Colonel Stonesteel's genuine home-made truly
Egyptian mummy. Bradbury, R.
The **colonel's** child. Gallant, M.
The **colonel's** choice. Doyle, Sir A. C.
The **Colonel's** daughter. Tremain, R.
The **colonel's** ideas. Maupassant, G. de
The **colonel's** lady. Maugham, W. S.
The **colonel's** predicament. Stribling, T. S.
The **colonial** bishop's visit. Leitão, L.
COLONIAL UNITED STATES *See* United
States—To 1776
COLONIALISM *See* Imperialism
COLONIES, ARTIST *See* Artist colonies
Colony. Dick, P. K.
A **color** for that fear. Ferreira, R.
Color me real. Cooper, J. C.
The **color** of mugwort. Choe, I.-N.
A **color** television. Acosta, L. A.
Color the daydream yellow. Steele, M.
COLORADO
Fante, J. In the spring
Nayman, M. The house on Lafayette Street
Overholser, W. D. High-grade
Overholser, W. D. Winchester wedding
The **colored** transmission. Chetwynd-Hayes,
R.
The **colorful** alphabet. Mattison, A.
The **colorless** paintings. Sata, I.
Colors. Ignatow, R. G.
Colors. Watanabe, S. A.
The **colossus** of Ylourgne. Smith, C. A.
COLOSTOMY
Gordimer, N. Terminal
The **colour** out of space. Lovecraft, H. P.
Colter, Cyrus, 1910-
After the ball
Colter, C. The amoralists & other tales
The amoralists
Colter, C. The amoralists & other tales
The beach umbrella
Colter, C. The amoralists & other tales
Black for dinner
Colter, C. The amoralists & other tales
A chance meeting
Colter, C. The amoralists & other tales
The frog hunters
Colter, C. The amoralists & other tales
A gift
Colter, C. The amoralists & other tales
Girl friend
Colter, C. The amoralists & other tales
The lookout
Colter, C. The amoralists & other tales
Macabre
Colter, C. The amoralists & other tales
A man in the house
Colter, C. The amoralists & other tales

The march
Colter, C. The amoralists & other tales
Mary's convert
Colter, C. The amoralists & other tales
Moot
Colter, C. The amoralists & other tales
Overnight trip
Colter, C. The amoralists & other tales
Rapport
Colter, C. The amoralists & other tales
The rescue
Colter, C. The amoralists & other tales
An untold story
Colter, C. The amoralists & other tales
Colum, Padraic, 1881-1972
Catherine Mulamphy and the man from
the north
Colum, P. Selected short stories of
Padraic Colum
The death of the rich man
Colum, P. Selected short stories of
Padraic Colum
A Dublin day
Colum, P. Selected short stories of
Padraic Colum
Eilis: a woman's story
Colum, P. Selected short stories of
Padraic Colum
The flute player's story
Colum, P. Selected short stories of
Padraic Colum
Land hunger
Colum, P. Selected short stories of
Padraic Colum
The little pension
Colum, P. Selected short stories of
Padraic Colum
Marcus of Clooney
Colum, P. Selected short stories of
Padraic Colum
Marriage
Colum, P. Selected short stories of
Padraic Colum
The Peacocks of Baron's Hall
Colum, P. Selected short stories of
Padraic Colum
Pilgrimage home
Colum, P. Selected short stories of
Padraic Colum
The slopes of Tara
Colum, P. Selected short stories of
Padraic Colum
Three men
Colum, P. Selected short stories of
Padraic Colum
COLUMBUS, CHRISTOPHER
About
Charmatz, A. Sailing, through program
management
COLUMNISTS *See* Journalists
Colvin, Clare
All living things
Winter's tales, new ser. v2

Colvin, Clare—_Continued_
Near Forelanders Kop
  Winter's tales, new ser. v1
Colwin, Laurie
Another marvelous thing
  Colwin, L. Another marvelous thing
  The New Yorker 60:34-44 F 11 '85
A country wedding
  Colwin, L. Another marvelous thing
  The New Yorker 59:38-42 Ja 23 '84
A couple of old flames [Variant title: Old
    flames]
  Colwin, L. Another marvelous thing
Frank and Billy
  Colwin, L. Another marvelous thing
  The Editors' choice: new American
    stories v1
French movie
  Colwin, L. Another marvelous thing
A little something
  Colwin, L. Another marvelous thing
The lone pilgrim
  New women and new fiction; ed. by S.
    Cahill
My mistress
  Colwin, L. Another marvelous thing
Old flames [Variant title: A couple of old
    flames]
  The Graywolf annual 2
  The New Yorker 61:42-5 My 13 '85
Swan song
  Colwin, L. Another marvelous thing
Colyton, Henry John
The countess and the devil
  The Saturday Evening Post 259:68-71+
    Ja/F '87
  The Saturday Evening Post 259:36+
    Mr '87
COMANCHE INDIANS
Gordon, R. Pilgrims
Combinations. Rossiter, S.
Come along, Marjorie. Spark, M.
Come, and bring Constance! Bradbury, R.
Come and get me. Walter, E.
Come back, come back. Westlake, D. E.
Come back if it doesn't get better. Gilliatt,
  P.
Come back, Lolly Ray. Lowry, B.
Come closer. Russ, J.
"Come into my house, Horatio! there are
  more things under the mattress than
  are dreamt of in your philosophy!".
  See Granit, A. Songs my mother
  taught me that are not in Hamlet; or,
  "Come into my house, Horatio! there
  are more things under the mattress
  than are dreamt of in your philoso-
  phy!"
Come into the drawing-room, Doris. See
  O'Brien, E. Irish revel
Come into the hallway, for five cents!
  Granit, A.
Come live with me. Tiptree, J.

Come on a coming. Dixon, S.
Come on, wagon! Henderson, Z.
Come September. Ledbetter, E.
Come soar with me. McConnell, J.
Come stay with us. Franzen, B.
Come to Africa and save your marriage.
  Thomas, M.
Come to dust. Peters, E.
The **comedian**. L'Heureux, J.
COMEDIANS
Gilliatt, P. Fred and Arthur
Hempel, A. Three popes walk into a bar
Kunstler, J. H. The rise, fall, and redemp-
  tion of Mooski Toffski Offski
L'Heureux, J. The comedian
Morressy, J. The last Jerry Fagin Show
Pascoe, B. Funny man
Stark, S. S. Heart of the Dutch country
Waldrop, H. Save a place in the lifeboat
  for me
Comedy and tragedy. Gilbert, W. S.
Comedy entombed: 1930. Williams, W. C.
Comedy of eros. Clayton, J. J.
Comedy of Eros. Flanagan, R.
The **comedy** of Narcissa T'ang. Ch'en, Y.-C.
The **comedy** of the white dog. Gray, A.
Comes an earthquake. Gerber, M. J.
COMETS
Poe, E. A. The conversation of Eiros and
  Charmion
Twain, M. A curious pleasure excursion
Comfort, Alex, 1920-
The lemmings
  Black water; ed. by A. Manguel
Comfort. Kaplan, D. M.
Comfort and joy. Dash, J.
Comfort stations. Griesemer, J.
Comforting milk. Asscher-Pinkhof, C.
The **comforts** of home. O'Connor, F.
The **comforts** of home. Salvatore, D.
Comic dialogue. Zweibel, A.
Coming about. Peterson, M.
Coming and going. Davin, D.
Coming apart. Walker, A.
Coming, Aphrodite! Cather, W.
Coming attractions. Wolff, T.
Coming back. Nelson, V.
Coming back to Dixieland. Robinson, K. S.
Coming down the mountain. Stuart, J.
Coming home. Bowen, E.
Coming home. Thaler, S.
Coming of age. Collins, C.
Coming of age on Kasikadasi. Faik, S.
The **coming** of Lad. Terhune, A. P.
The **coming** of snow. Covino, M.
The **coming** of something to Widow Holly.
  Williams, T.
Coming of the dry season. Mungoshi, C.
The **coming** of the Goonga. Shockley, G. W.
The **coming** of the white worm. Smith, C.
  A.
Coming out Rosy! Wright, B. R.
Coming to grief. Barker, C.

The **coming** triumph of the free world. DeMarinis, R.

Coming unbalanced. Moyer, K.

COMMANCHE INDIANS *See* Comanche Indians

Command. Bellah, J. W.

The **commandment.** Essop, A.

The **commandos** go in. Glemser, B.

COMMENCEMENTS
  Gibbs, A. Father was a wit
  Keillor, G. Dale
  O'Connor, F. A late encounter with the enemy

The **commercial** break. Abbott, K.

COMMERCIAL TRAVELERS
  Aickman, R. The swords
  Anthony, P. Up Schist Crick
  Bishop, M. Within the walls of Tyre
  Campbell, R. The hands
  Covino, M. The lament of the salesman
  DeMarinis, R. The smile of a turtle
  Dickens, C. The bagman's story
  Dunsany, E. J. M. D. P., Baron. The two bottles of relish
  Fisher, M. F. K. The unswept emptiness
  Matthews, J. The story Mac told
  Munro, A. Walker Brothers cowboy
  O'Connor, F. Good country people
  Rule, J. The investment years
  Updike, J. The city
  Welty, E. Death of a traveling salesman

Commercials. Ruffolo, L.

Commings, Joseph
  The X Street murders
  Death locked in; ed. by D. G. Greene and R. C. S. Adey

A **committee** of the whole. Bly, C.

Committee of the whole. Herbert, F.

The **common** body. Shefner, E.

Common happiness. Engberg, S.

Common meter. Fisher, R.

Common sense should tell you. O'Hara, J.

The **common** soldiery. Blythe, R.

Common time. Blish, J.

COMMUNES *See* Collective settlements

Communes and Sara. Wexler, J.

COMMUNICATION
  See also Telecommunication
  Anvil, C. Two-way communication
  Ash, P. Minds meet
  Burdick, B. S. From time to time
  Le Guin, U. K. "The author of the acacia seeds" and other extracts from the Journal of the Association of Therolinguistics

COMMUNICATION OF ANIMALS *See* Animal communication

Communion. Brown, S. H.

Communion. Saiki, P. S.

Communions. Fitzgerald, M. J.

COMMUNISM
  See also Totalitarianism
  Abernathy, R. Heirs apparent

Chang, H.-kuo. Red boy

Eliade, M. The cape

Jahnn, H. H. The marmalade eaters

Mrożek, S. The chronicle of a besieged city

Mrożek, S. A citizen's fate

Mrożek, S. Letter from an old people's home

Mrożek, S. Modern life

Mrożek, S. Peer Gynt

Mrożek, S. Siesta

Sciascia, L. The death of Stalin

Australia
Prichard, K. S. Communists are always young

Prichard, K. S. A young comrade

China
Cao Guanlong. Three professors

Dai Qing. Anticipation

Feng Jicai. A letter

Feng Jicai. Plum blossoms in the snow

Kong Jiesheng. On the other side of the stream

Lin Jinlan. The transcript

Liu, Q. The good luck bun

Smedley, A. Shan-fei, communist

Wang Meng. Anecdotes of Chairman Maimaiti

Wang Meng. Eye of the night

Wang Zhecheng, and Wen Xiaoyu. Nest egg

Zhang Jie. The time is not yet ripe

France
Greene, G. Brother

Germany
Oates, J. C. Our wall

Ziem, J. Clever

Ziem, J. Uprising in East Germany

Italy
Berger, J. Play me something

Korea
O, S.-W. A respite

Poland
Mrożek, S. From the darkness

Nowakowski, M. The horn of plenty

Nowakowski, M. The mongrel

Nowakowski, M. The spring walk

Tuohy, F. In the dark years

Tuohy, F. The Palace of Culture

Tuohy, F. The student

Soviet Union
Pasternak, B. L. Without love

Pil'ñāk, B. Mahogany

Pil'ñāk, B. Mother earth

Pil'ñāk, B. The tale of the unextinguished moon

Yugoslavia
Aćin-Kosta, M. Boulevard of the revolution

Aćin-Kosta, M. Dam on crutches

Aćin-Kosta, M. In the spirit of socialism

Aćin-Kosta, M. A psychological warrior

Aćin-Kosta, M. The rape

COMMUNISM—Yugoslavia—*Continued*
Aćin-Kosta, M. Rassim
Aćin-Kosta, M. The red bread
Aćin-Kosta, M. Spring flower
Aćin-Kosta, M. Yugoslavia revisited
Communist. Ford, R.
COMMUNISTS *See* Communism
Communists are always young. Prichard, K.
S.
COMMUNITY LIFE
Apple, M. Blood relatives
Warren, J. Mr. McAlligator
COMMUTERS
Bowker, R. The other train phenomenon
Humphrey, W. The last husband
Mathers, P. Getting there
Commuters. Matheson, R. C.
Commuter's problem. Ellison, H.
The **companion**. Christie, A.
COMPANIONS
Asimov, I. Robbie
Block, L. With a smile for the ending
Braddon, M. E. Good Lady Ducayne
Nordan, L. The attendant
Rossiter, S. Civil War
Tabucchi, A. Heavenly bliss
Thurm, M. Ice
Companions. Pritchard, M.
The **Company**. Wolfe, T.
Company in the wings. Lafferty, R. A.
Comparative public deaths. Bowering, G.
The **compartment**. Carver, R.
The **compass** of the heart. Moyer, K.
Compassion. Macauley, C.
A **compassionate** leave. Yates, R.
Compensation. Long, D.
COMPETITION
Abbott, L. K. The world is almost rotten
Aldiss, B. W. Consolations of age
Anthony, P. Getting through University
Baumbach, J. Familiar games
Heinesen, W. The lucky stone
MacLeod, C. It was an awful shame
Maillet, A. Two saints
Naipaul, S. The beauty contest
Robinson, K. S. Coming back to Dixieland
Shaw, B. Dream fighter
Stark, S. S. A wrestler's tale
Sturges, A. E. Pianoforte
Vance, J. The new prime
Waldrop, H. Mary Margaret Road-Grader
Wheatcroft, J. The forfeit
Wheatcroft, J. Hero
Willson, H. Tufts and Wink
Wollheim, D. A. Malice aforethought
Zhang Jie. The time is not yet ripe
Competition at Slush Creek. Stuart, J.
Competitors. Sholem Aleichem
The **complete** death of the clown dog. Mord-
den, E.
The **complete** life of John Hopkins. Henry,
O.
Complete with fireworks above Magic Island.
Kirk-Kuwaye, C.
Completed. Williams, T.
A **complicated** nature. Trevor, W.
Complication. Maupassant, G. de
COMPOSERS
Aiken, J. The cat who lived in a drainpipe
Blish, J. A work of art
Crowley, A. The old man of the peepul-
tree
Gildner, G. Sleepy time gal
Han, M.-S. Mr. Kim, the Bohemian
minstrel
Kaplan, D. M. Elias Schneebaum
Katz, S. Death of the band
Mathers, P. Sound worm
Morazzoni, M. The dignity of Signor Da
Ponte
Morazzoni, M. The white door
Sagan, F. Incidental music
Schwartz, J. The man who knew Cary
Grant
Schwartz, J. Over the purple hills
Snodgrass, M. Requiem
Swados, H. A glance in the mirror
Composition. Bradbury, M.
Composition. Carter, R.
COMPOST
Graves, R. Earth to earth
Compset. Schwartz, H.
Compton, Jennifer
One of my families
Women's work; ed. by M. McLeod and
L. Wevers
Compulsion. Charbonneau-Tissot, C.
Compulsory figures. Thomas, A. C.
COMPULSORY MILITARY SERVICE *See*
Draft
COMPUTER CRIMES
Bing, J. A meeting in Georgestown
Grabowski, Z. A. The state of the art
COMPUTER PROGRAMMING *See* Pro-
gramming (Computers)
COMPUTERS
See also Programming (Computers)
Anderson, P. Vulcan's forge
Apple, M. Pizza time
Asimov, I. 1 to 999
Asimov, I. The feeling of power
Asimov, I. Found!
Asimov, I. Franchise
Asimov, I. The last question
Asimov, I. The machine that won the war
Benford, G. Me/days
Bing, J. The Owl of Bear Island
Bloch, R. The oracle
Brown, F. Answer
Cogswell, T. R. Deal with the D.E.V.I.L.
Dick, P. K. Holy quarrel
Dickson, G. R. Catch a tartar
Dickson, G. R. The monkey wrench
Ellison, H. I have no mouth, and I must
scream

COMPUTERS—*Continued*
Gathorne-Hardy, J. The centre of the universe is 18 Baedekerstrasse
Gibson, W. Burning chrome
Haldeman, J. W. Armaja das
Jarvis, M. C. Collaboration
King, S. Word processor of the gods
Krivich, M., and Olgin, O. Plays and wins
Leinster, M. A logic named Joe
Lem, S. Golem XIV
Pierce, J. R. Choice
Pohl, F. Schematic man
Prebehalla, G., and Moran, D. K. Realtime
Sarrantonio, A. The haunting of Y-12
Shaara, M. 2066: Election Day
Sheckley, R. Good-bye forever to Mr. Pain
Silverberg, R. The Macauley circuit
Silverberg, R. The pardoner's tale
Sladek, J. T. Answers
Sladek, J. T. The next dwarf
Swanwick, M. Trojan horse
Varley, J. Press enter
Watson, I. Jewels in an angel's wing
Zelazny, R. For a breath I tarry
Comrade Bingo. Wodehouse, P. G.
Comrade death. Kersh, G.
Comrades. Busch, F.
Comrades. Phelps, E. S.
CON MEN *See* Swindlers and swindling
Conard, Brad
Schmoozing
The Virginia Quarterly Review 63:281-99 Spr '87
CONCENTRATION CAMPS
See also Political prisoners; World War, 1939-1945—Prisoners and prisons
Aćin-Kosta, M. Arbeit macht Frei
Asscher-Pinkhof, C. Back and forth
Asscher-Pinkhof, C. Bath
Asscher-Pinkhof, C. Bogeyman
Asscher-Pinkhof, C. Celebrations
Asscher-Pinkhof, C. The chosen
Asscher-Pinkhof, C. Dance
Asscher-Pinkhof, C. Flap of wings
Asscher-Pinkhof, C. Free afternoon
Asscher-Pinkhof, C. French
Asscher-Pinkhof, C. Game of dice
Asscher-Pinkhof, C. Good luck songs
Asscher-Pinkhof, C. Good night—good morning
Asscher-Pinkhof, C. Hora
Asscher-Pinkhof, C. Hospital barrack
Asscher-Pinkhof, C. Housekeeping
Asscher-Pinkhof, C. How can Herod bear the light
Asscher-Pinkhof, C. Hunger
Asscher-Pinkhof, C. Little white bundle
Asscher-Pinkhof, C. Neighbor below
Asscher-Pinkhof, C. Nights
Asscher-Pinkhof, C. Nursery
Asscher-Pinkhof, C. Old tales
Asscher-Pinkhof, C. Packages
Asscher-Pinkhof, C. Passage to Hell

Asscher-Pinkhof, C. Pied piper of Hamelin
Asscher-Pinkhof, C. Roll call
Asscher-Pinkhof, C. See again
Asscher-Pinkhof, C. They put their heads together
Asscher-Pinkhof, C. Transport night
Asscher-Pinkhof, C. Tucking in
Borowski, T. This way for the gas, ladies and gentlemen
Burt, S. QB/3854/294 & 6
Dann, J. Camps
Eisenstein, S. Holocaust envy
Fein, Y. Rumkowsky was right
Nałkowska, Z. Rock bottom
Ozick, C. The shawl
Ryman, G. O happy day!
Concepts. Disch, T. M.
Concerning grocers as gods. Chesterton, G. K.
Concerning, I suppose my father. Summers, H. S.
Concerning the bodyguard. Barthelme, D.
The **concert.** Dadswell, M.
The **concert** party. Gallant, M.
A **concerto** for the nay. Salmawy, M.
CONCERTS
Bronstein, E. Magic
Charnas, S. M. Listening to Brahms
Davie, E. Accompanists
Jeppson, J. O. The horn of Elfland
Mazel, D. The maestro
McCullers, C. Art and Mr. Mahoney
Il **Conde.** Conrad, J.
The **condemned** librarian. West, J.
The **condemned** movie. Heise, K.
CONDEMNED PRISONERS *See* Prisoners, Condemned
Condensed milk. Shalamov, V. T.
The **condition.** Packer, M.
A **condition** of release. Hartley, L. P.
The **conduct** of John Briggs. Crowley, A.
CONDUCT OF LIFE *See* Ethics
The **conductor.** Winters, J.
CONDUCTORS (MUSIC)
Benét, S. V. The King of the Cats
Gardner, J. Nimram
Harris, M. The orphan bassoonist
The **cone.** Wells, H. G.
CONEY ISLAND (NEW YORK, N.Y.) *See* New York (N.Y.)—Coney Island
Coney Island. Beattie, A.
Coney Island revisited. Rosenfeld, I.
Coney Island's failing days. Crane, S.
A **confederacy** of dunces. Toole, J. K.
CONFEDERATE AGENTS *See* Spies
CONFEDERATE STATES OF AMERICA. ARMY
Bierce, A. One of the missing
Chambers, R. W. The pickets
East, C. A tribute to the general [excerpt]
Foote, S. Shiloh [excerpt]
Page, T. N. The burial of the guns
Williams, J. A. Captain Blackman [excerpt]

The **conference**. Singer, I. B.
CONFESSION
Burt, S. I just kept on smiling
Camoin, F. A. Cheerful wisdom
Dickens, C. A confession found in a prison in the time of Charles the Second
Finney, E. J. The divine dealer
Hensley, J. L. Paint doctor
Johnson, W. Sarajevo
Lutz, J. The butcher, the baker
Maupassant, G. de. Making a convert
Pulaski, J. Alone or with others
Rooke, L. The woman's guide to home companionship
CONFESSION (CATHOLIC)
Anaya, R. A. Bless me, Ultima [excerpt]
Böll, H. Candles for the Madonna
Bradbury, R. Bless me, Father, for I have sinned
Buzzati, D. The end of the world
Clark, M. Portrait of a freethinker
Dubus, A. If they knew Yvonne
Heise, K. My father's confession
Kirk, R. Watchers at the strait gate
Mrożek, S. A fact
Ocampo, S. The prayer
O'Faoláin, S. Sinners
The **confession**. Doyle, Sir A. C.
A **confession** about Bobby. Mrożek, S.
A **confession** found in a prison in the time of Charles the Second. Dickens, C.
Confession of a catamite. Allan, B.
The **confession** of Charles Linkworth. Benson, E. F.
The **confession** of the Finch. Vogan, S.
Confessions. Dempsey, D.
Confessions of a (pornographer's) shroud. Barker, C.
The **confidence** man. Garrett, G. P.
Confidential. Buzzati, D.
The **confidential** call. Nowakowski, M.
CONFIRMATION
Keillor, G. Aprille
Maupassant, G. de. Mme. Tellier's excursion
The **confirmation** suit. Behan, B.
The **conflict**. Piñera, V.
CONFLICT OF GENERATIONS
Bambara, T. C. My man Bovanne
Briskin, M. The kid
Gee, M. Eleventh holiday
Gilchrist, E. Music
Girion, B. A very brief season
Hayes, L. Kiss good night to the princess, frog
Keillor, G. Eloise
Kim, Y. I. The first election
Lao Hong. The gap
Liang, L. K. The pei-pa
Schwartz, L. S. Over the hill
Walton, D. One blood

CONFORMITY
Asimov, I. It's such a beautiful day
O'Connor, F. The Partridge festival
Silverberg, R. Caliban
Smith, L. Cakewalk
Valenzuela, L. The censors
Conformity. Traba, M.
Confused. Singer, I. B.
CONGO (DEMOCRATIC REPUBLIC) *See* Zaire
CONGRESS (U.S.) *See* United States. Congress
The **Congress** of Wonders. McClanahan, E.
CONGRESSES AND CONFERENCES
See also Meetings
Aickman, R. Larger than oneself
Baumbach, J. A famous Russian poet
Edwards, M. F. Roses
Friedman, B. J. The scientist
Kotzwinkle, W. Mr. Jones's convention
Sayles, J. At the anarchists' convention
Singer, I. B. The conference
Conjunction. Updike, J.
The **conjurer** made off with the dish. Maḥfūz, N.
Conley, Robert J.
Badger
Conley, R. J. The witch of Goingsnake, and other stories
Bob Parris's temper
Conley, R. J. The witch of Goingsnake, and other stories
Calf Roper's bandit car
Conley, R. J. The witch of Goingsnake, and other stories
Calf Roper's house guest
Conley, R. J. The witch of Goingsnake, and other stories
The endless dark of the night
Conley, R. J. The witch of Goingsnake, and other stories
Earth power coming; ed. by S. J. Ortiz
The hanging of Mose Miller
Conley, R. J. The witch of Goingsnake, and other stories
His grandma's wedding
Conley, R. J. The witch of Goingsnake, and other stories
The immortals
Conley, R. J. The witch of Goingsnake, and other stories
The Mexican tattoo
Conley, R. J. The witch of Goingsnake, and other stories
Moon Face
Conley, R. J. The witch of Goingsnake, and other stories
The name
Conley, R. J. The witch of Goingsnake, and other stories
The night George Wolfe died
Conley, R. J. The witch of Goingsnake, and other stories

Conley, Robert J.—*Continued*
Old Joe
  Conley, R. J. The witch of Goingsnake,
    and other stories
Wesley's story
  Conley, R. J. The witch of Goingsnake,
    and other stories
Wickliffe
  Conley, R. J. The witch of Goingsnake,
    and other stories
Wili Woyi
  Conley, R. J. The witch of Goingsnake,
    and other stories
The witch of Goingsnake
  Conley, R. J. The witch of Goingsnake,
    and other stories
Yellow Bird: an imaginary autobiography
  Conley, R. J. The witch of Goingsnake,
    and other stories
Conn, Charis W.
Two fathers
  The North American Review 272:38-9 D
    '87
CONNECTICUT
Serling, R. The changing of the guard
Tuohy, F. Evening in Connecticut
18th century
Twain, M. The facts concerning the recent
  carnival of crime in Connecticut
Connecticut countess. Watmough, D.
The **connecting** link. Ritchie, J.
Connection. Gaitskill, M.
Connell, Evan S., 1924-
The fisherman from Chihuahua
  American short story masterpieces; ed.
    by R. Carver and T. Jenks
Connell, Richard
Brother Orchid
  Murder and mystery in Chicago; ed. by
    C. R. Waugh; F. D. McSherry and M.
    H. Greenberg
Connelly, John, 1959-
Agency
  Connelly, J. Man's work
Basques
  Connelly, J. Man's work
Foreign objects
  Connelly, J. Man's work
The holidays
  Connelly, J. Man's work
Lock
  Connelly, J. Man's work
Ours
  Connelly, J. Man's work
Partner
  Connelly, J. Man's work
Sleeping together
  Connelly, J. Man's work
Teamwork
  Connelly, J. Man's work
Wait
  Connelly, J. Man's work

Conner, Marilyn Jean
Bunco
  The Ploughshares reader: new fiction for
    the eighties
Conner, Michael
Stillborn
  The Best horror stories from the
    Magazine of fantasy and science fiction
Conner, Mike
Vamp
  Kindred spirits; ed. by J. M. Elliot
Connie. Umans, R.
Connie Bronson. Robinson, M.
Connoisseur. Pronzini, B.
Connolly, Lawrence C.
Echoes
  100 great fantasy short short stories; ed.
    by I. Asimov; T. Carr and M. H.
    Greenberg
Connolly, Patricia
Dead flower
  P.E.N. new fiction I
The **Connor** girls. O'Brien, E.
Connors, Robert J.
The genius
  Road & Track 36:58-60+ Ag '85
Connor's lake. Nevai, L.
Conquering space. Morris, M.
The **conqueror** worm. Donaldson, S. R.
The **conquest** of Doña Jacoba. Atherton, G.
  F. H.
Conrad, Brad
Mrs. Pilate's duty
  The Southern Review (Baton Rouge, La.)
    24:182-201 Wint '88
Swimming
  The Yale Review 74:557-66 Summ '85
Conrad, Joseph, 1857-1924
The black mate
  Mysterious sea stories; ed. by W. Pat-
    trick
Il Conde
  The Treasury of English short stories;
    ed. by N. Sullivan
The gale
  Men at sea; ed. by B. Aymar
An outpost of progress
  On being foreign; ed. by T. J. Lewis and
    R. E. Jungman
The secret sharer
  Short stories of the sea; ed. by G. C.
    Solley and E. Steinbaugh
Typhoon
  Sea captains' tales; ed. by A. Enfield
Youth
  Short stories of the sea; ed. by G. C.
    Solley and E. Steinbaugh
Conrad. Bell, M.
Conrad and the dragon. Hartley, L. P.
Conrad's bear. Hampton, S.
Conrat!. Ramspeck, D.

Conroy, Frank, 1936-
 Car games
  Conroy, F. Midair
 Celestial events
  Conroy, F. Midair
 Gossip
  The Best American short stories, 1986
  Conroy, F. Midair
  Esquire 104:64-5+ Ag '85
  The Esquire fiction reader v2
 Midair
  American short story masterpieces; ed.
   by R. Carver and T. Jenks
  Conroy, F. Midair
  The New Yorker 60:44-53 F 27 '84
  The Norton book of American short
   stories
 The mysterious case of R
  Conroy, F. Midair
 Roses
  Conroy, F. Midair
 The sense of the meeting
  Conroy, F. Midair
 Transit
  Conroy, F. Midair
Conroy, Jack, 1899-
 Anyplace but here
  Conroy, J. The weed king & other
   stories
 "A barrel of fun"
  Conroy, J. The weed king & other
   stories
 The Boomer's fireman's fast sooner hound
  Conroy, J. The weed king & other
   stories
 Bull market
  Conroy, J. The weed king & other
   stories
 Bun Grady
  Conroy, J. The weed king & other
   stories
 The cement king
  Conroy, J. The weed king & other
   stories
 Charley was our darlin'
  Conroy, J. The weed king & other
   stories
 The demon bricksetter from Williamson
   County
  Conroy, J. The weed king & other
   stories
 Down in Happy Hollow
  Conroy, J. The weed king & other
   stories
 The fields of golden glow
  Conroy, J. The weed king & other
   stories
 Freight car repair yard pranks
  Conroy, J. The weed king & other
   stories
 Greedy-Gut Gus, the car toad
  Conroy, J. The weed king & other
   stories

Hard winter
 Conroy, J. The weed king & other
  stories
High bridge
 Conroy, J. The weed king & other
  stories
The high divers
 Conroy, J. The weed king & other
  stories
Home to Uncle Ollie's
 Conroy, J. The weed king & other
  stories
The Kimberly toughs
 Conroy, J. The weed king & other
  stories
Lute Goin's sawmill
 Conroy, J. The weed king & other
  stories
The morphadite
 Conroy, J. The weed king & other
  stories
Paving gang—on a job in Missouri
 Conroy, J. The weed king & other
  stories
Pipe line
 Conroy, J. The weed king & other
  stories
Rubber heels
 Conroy, J. The weed king & other
  stories
The siren
 Conroy, J. The weed king & other
  stories
The sissy from the Hardscrabble County
  rock quarries
 Conroy, J. The weed king & other
  stories
Slappy Hooper, world's biggest, fastest, and
  bestest sign painter
 Conroy, J. The weed king & other
  stories
That Skinner Bottoms winter
 Conroy, J. The weed king & other
  stories
The type louse
 Conroy, J. The weed king & other
  stories
Uncle Ollie finds a new market
 Conroy, J. The weed king & other
  stories
Uncle Ollie on trial
 Conroy, J. The weed king & other
  stories
Uncle Ollie's rabbit hunt
 Conroy, J. The weed king & other
  stories
Uncle Ollie's spite fence
 Conroy, J. The weed king & other
  stories
The weed king
 Conroy, J. The weed king & other
  stories

Conroy, Monika
  (jt. auth) See Curry, Ginger Simpson, and Conroy, Monika
CONSANGUINITY
  Goyen, W. The faces of blood kindred
  Neville, S. The beekeeper
CONSCIENCE
  See also Ethics; Guilt
  Poe, E. A. The imp of the perverse
  Poe, E. A. William Wilson
  Stevenson, R. L. Markheim
  Twain, M. The facts concerning the recent carnival of crime in Connecticut
  Wharton, E. The touchstone
The **conscientious** cat. Sandham, A. A.
The **consequences** of the old story. Vizyēnos, G. M.
The **conservation** of matter. Greenberg, A.
CONSERVATION OF NATURE See Nature conservation
The **conservatory**. Maupassant, G. de
Consideration. Maupassant, G. de
Consolation. McBain, E.
The **consolation** of nature. Martin, V.
The **consolation** of philosophy. Delbanco, N.
Consolations of age. Aldiss, B. W.
The **conspicuous** turtle. Gardner, M.
CONSPIRACIES
  Barker, C. Babel's children
  Francis, D. The gift
  Heinlein, R. A. Gulf
The **conspirators**. Gilbert, M.
Constance, Lady Willet. Welch, D.
Constant reader. Bloch, R.
Constantine, David
  The home boy
  Critical Quarterly 28:5-16 Aut '86
CONSTANTINOPLE See Turkey—Istanbul
A **constellation** of events. Updike, J.
The **constellation** of green fish, a tale of the unprecedented. Berdnyk, O.
Consternation and empire. Jeppson, J. O.
Construction. Barthelme, D.
CONSTRUCTION INDUSTRY
  Cinca, S. The wedding
  Conroy, J. The cement king
  Conroy, J. High bridge
  Conroy, J. Pipe line
  Easton, T. A. Roll them bones
  Klíma, I. Saturday morning: a thief's tale
  Mooney, M. A civilized man
  Mordden, E. Hardhats
  Olmstead, R. The mason
CONSULS See Diplomatic life
Consultations. Wilner, H.
Consuming passion. Bliss, C. D.
The **consummation**. Galsworthy, J.
Conta, Marcia Maher
  When the kids grow up
  Redbook 170:76+ Mr '88
Contact. Sagan, C.
Contacts. Böll, H.
Contacts of a fourth kind. Dilov, L.

CONTENTMENT
  See also Happiness
  Pascoe, B. Primary colours
The **contest**. Paley, G.
The **contest**. Sawyer, R. J.
CONTESTS
  Aguinis, M. Short story contest
  Lish, G. The death of me
  Palmer, M. Esmerelda's hands
  Sanford, W. M. The blue spruce
  Saroyan, W. There was a young lady of Perth
  Sterling, B. Sunken gardens
  West, J. A. Gladys's Gregory
The **Continental**. Smith, R.
Continental drift. Bissoondath, N.
Contingency planning. Gold, H.
Continuing care. Menaker, D.
Continuo. Starer, R.
The **contortionist**. Eisenstein, S.
Contou-Carrère, Enrique Jorge
  Pulitzer
  Américas 39:25-7 S/O '87
CONTRACEPTION See Birth control
CONTRACEPTIVES
  Van Greenaway, P. Indefinite article
The **contract** with the beast. Walker, W.
Contrition. Bausch, R.
The **contrivance**. Curley, D.
Conundrum. Shannon, D.
CONVALESCENCE
  Chung, L.-H. Together through thick and thin
  Sanders, S. R. The cry
Convalescence. Boyle, K.
Conveniences. Pearlman, E.
CONVENT LIFE
  See also Nuns
  Apollinaire, G. The blue eye
  Ferron, J. The pigeon and the parakeet
  Rummel, M. K. White-out
The **convention**. Caponegro, M.
The **conventional** wisdom. Elkin, S.
CONVENTS See Convent life
CONVENTS AND NUNNERIES See Convent life
Convergent series. Niven, L.
CONVERSATION
  Babbitt, N. Simple sentences
  Barthelme, D. Basil from her garden
  Carter, R. Sixties into eighties won't go
  Carver, R. What we talk about when we talk about love
  Costello, M. Brian 'Squizzy' Taylor
  Cowan, P. The beach
  Deaver, P. F. Rosie
  Flanagan, R. Gaming
  Gilliatt, P. Splendid lives
  Hemingway, E. The three-day blow
  Hemmerchts, K. Words
  Josipovici, G. Absence and echo
  Josipovici, G. Children's voices
  Lish, G. Spell bereavement

CONVERSATION—*Continued*
Mardeusz, S. The back-seat talker
Meinke, P. Conversation with a pole
Parotti, P. Antiphus on Tmolus
Parotti, P. Diator beyond Olympus
Parotti, P. Diomedes at Aulis
Parotti, P. Eurypylus at Dodona
Parotti, P. Heptaporos in Phrygia
Parotti, P. Keas on Ida
Parotti, P. Machaon at Tricca
Parotti, P. Medon in Thrace
Parotti, P. Meges at Dulichium
Parotti, P. Menestheus at Athens
Parotti, P. Meriones at Gortyn
Parotti, P. Merops in Mysia
Parotti, P. Nastes at Miletus
Parotti, P. Neoptolemus in Phthia
Parotti, P. Odios at Alybe
Parotti, P. Pheidippus at Cos
Parotti, P. Polydamas on the Plain
Parotti, P. Pyracchmes beneath Laurion
Parotti, P. Sinon at Elis
Parotti, P. Thersites at Mytilene
Parotti, P. Thoas at Pylene
Parotti, P. Thrasymedes at Pylos
Rodoreda, M. The sea
Silva, B. Yellow bird
Sladek, J. T. After Flaubert
Tuohy, F. Love to Patsy
Wolfe, T. Only the dead know Brooklyn
Woolf, V. Together and apart
Yunker, T. Margaritas
A **conversation**. Fink, I.
Conversation. Ioannidou Adamidou, I.
Conversation. Norris, K.
A **conversation** about Balzac's horse. Hofmann, G.
A **conversation** from the third floor. El-Bisatie, M.
The **conversation** of Eiros and Charmion. Poe, E. A.
Conversation piece. Matheson, R. C.
Conversation pieces. Givner, J.
Conversation with a pole. Meinke, P.
Conversations with Goethe. Barthelme, D.
Conversations with Ruth: the farmer's tale. Rooke, L.

CONVERSION
Gordon, M. Temporary shelter
Jackson, G. Holing out
Kipling, R. Lispeth
Leskov, N. S. Pamphalon the entertainer
Maupassant, G. de. My uncle Sosthenes
Prose, F. Electricity
The **conversion** of an anarchist. Chesterton, G. K.
The **conversion** of the Jews. Roth, P.
The **convert**. Bennett, L.
The **convict**. Burke, J. L.
Conviction. Janowitz, T.

CONVICTS *See* Crime and criminals; Ex-convicts; Prisoners and prisons

CONVICTS, ESCAPED *See* Escaped convicts
The **convolvulus** clock. Rendell, R.
The **cooboo**. Prichard, K. S.
Cook, Hugh, 1942-
A Canadian education
  Cook, H. Cracked wheat, and other stories
Clown
  Cook, H. Cracked wheat, and other stories
Cracked wheat
  Cook, H. Cracked wheat, and other stories
Easter lily
  Cook, H. Cracked wheat, and other stories
Exodus
  Cook, H. Cracked wheat, and other stories
First snow
  Cook, H. Cracked wheat, and other stories
Homesickness
  Cook, H. Cracked wheat, and other stories
A lesson in dance
  Cook, H. Cracked wheat, and other stories
Pisces
  Cook, H. Cracked wheat, and other stories
The white rabbit
  Cook, H. Cracked wheat, and other stories
Cook, Marshall
Parting shots
  Here's the story: fiction with heart; ed. by M. Sklar
Cook, Patrick, 1949-
Not the news
  Transgressions; ed. by D. Anderson
Cook-Lynn, Elizabeth
A good chance
  Earth power coming; ed. by S. J. Ortiz
The power of horses
  Earth power coming; ed. by S. J. Ortiz
Cooke, Rose Terry, 1827-1892
How Celia changed her mind
  Old maids; ed. by S. Koppelman
A woman
  Civil War women; ed. by F. McSherry; C. G. Waugh and M. Greenberg
Cooker. Barthelme, F.
COOKERY
Apollinaire, G. Our friend Méritarte
Carter, A. The kitchen child
Fisher, M. F. K. Mrs. Teeters' tomato jar
Flanagan, M. Cream sauce
Warner, S. T. One thing leading to another
Wells, H. G. A misunderstood artist
Cookie and Toni. Lynch, L.

The **cookies**. Nye, N. S.
COOKS
  Archer, J. A la carte
  Carter, A. The kitchen child
  Crane, S. Shame
  Desnoues, L. The triumph and the celery stick
  Lipman, E. Catering
  Nowotny, J. Pimpush
  Sargent, P. Originals
Cool air. Lovecraft, H. P.
A **cool** day in August. Drake, R.
Cooley, Nicole
  Ithaca
    The North American Review 269:40-1 S '84
Coombs, Margaret
  Nothing happened
  Room to move; ed. by S. Falkiner
Cooper, Bernard, 1951-
  Maps to anywhere
    Grand Street 7:74-7 Spr '88
  Utopia
    Grand Street 8:47-9 Aut '88
Cooper, Courtney Ryley
  Monarch
    The Saturday Evening Post 258:36-8+ Jl/Ag '86
Cooper, Darius
  Pestonjee's tower of silence
    The Massachusetts Review 29:666-70 Wint '88/'89
Cooper, Dennis, 1953-
  George: Wednesday, Thursday, Friday
  Between C & D; ed. by J. Rose and C. Texier
  The outsiders
  Men on men; ed. by G. Stambolian
Cooper, J. California
  $100 and nothing!
    Cooper, J. C. A piece of mine
  About love and money; or, Love's lore and money's myth
    Cooper, J. C. Some soul to keep
  At long last
    Cooper, J. C. Homemade love
  Color me real
    Cooper, J. C. A piece of mine
  Down that lonesome road
    Cooper, J. C. Homemade love
  Feeling for life
    Cooper, J. C. Some soul to keep
  The free and the caged
    Cooper, J. C. A piece of mine
  Funeral plans
    Cooper, J. C. A piece of mine
  Funny valentines
    Cooper, J. C. Homemade love
  Happiness does not come in colors
    Cooper, J. C. Homemade love
  Having fun
    Cooper, J. C. Homemade love

He was a man! (But he did himself wrong)
    Cooper, J. C. A piece of mine
    Essence 16:86-8+ S '85
A jewel for a friend
    Cooper, J. C. A piece of mine
Liberated
    Cooper, J. C. A piece of mine
The life you live (may not be your own)
    Cooper, J. C. Some soul to keep
Living
    Cooper, J. C. Homemade love
Loved to death
    Cooper, J. C. A piece of mine
The magic strength of need
    Cooper, J. C. Homemade love
Red-winged blackbirds
    Cooper, J. C. Some soul to keep
Say what you Willomay!
    Cooper, J. C. A piece of mine
Sins leave scars
    Cooper, J. C. A piece of mine
Sisters of the rain
    Cooper, J. C. Some soul to keep
Spooks
    Cooper, J. C. Homemade love
Swimming to the top of the rain
    Cooper, J. C. Homemade love
Swingers and squares
    Cooper, J. C. Homemade love
Too hep to be happy!
    Cooper, J. C. A piece of mine
The watcher
    Cooper, J. C. Homemade love
When life begins!
    Cooper, J. C. Homemade love
Who are the fools?
    Cooper, J. C. A piece of mine
Without love
    Cooper, J. C. Homemade love
Cooper, James Fenimore, 1789-1851
The Ariel defeats the Alacrity
  Men at sea; ed. by B. Aymar
Cooper, Lettice, 1897-
The heavy splash
    Critical Quarterly 29:8-15 Aut '87
Cooper, Lucas
Class notes
    The North American Review 269:40-1 Je '84
  Sudden fiction; ed. by R. Shapard and J. Thomas
Cooper, Rand Richards
Eclipse!
    The Atlantic 255:61-72 F '85
Sparkling celluloid
    Ladies' Home Journal 101:52+ O '84
Cooper, Stephen
Terminal Island
  Hot type; ed. by J. Miller
Cooper Loftus. Long, D.
COOPERATIVE SOCIETIES
  Gallacher, T. Store quarter

Coover, Robert
After Lazarus
Coover, R. A night at the movies
The babysitter
The Norton book of American short stories
Cartoon
Coover, R. A night at the movies
Charlie in the house of rue
Coover, R. A night at the movies
Gilda's dream
Coover, R. A night at the movies
Inside the frame
Coover, R. A night at the movies
Intermission
Coover, R. A night at the movies
Lap dissolves
Coover, R. A night at the movies
Milford Junction, 1939: a brief encounter
Coover, R. A night at the movies
The phantom of the movie palace
Coover, R. A night at the movies
Quenby and Ola, Swede and Carl
The Art of the tale; ed. by D. Halpern
Shootout at Gentry's Junction
Coover, R. A night at the movies
A sudden story
Sudden fiction; ed. by R. Shapard and J. Thomas
Top hat
Coover, R. A night at the movies
You must remember this
Coover, R. A night at the movies
About
Bumpus, J. The attack on San Clemente
The **cop** and the anthem. Henry, O.
Cope, Jack, 1913-
Ekaterina
The Penguin book of Southern African stories
Copeland, Ann
Portfolio
Southwest Review 70:249-61 Spr '85
Taking the discipline
Southwest Review 72:542-53 Aut '87
Copies. Morris, M.
Coping with Paul. Halliday, M.
Coplon, Jeff
What were you wearing when you met?
Mademoiselle 90:143-55 D '84
Coppard, A. E. (Alfred Edgar), 1878-1957
Ahoy, sailor boy!
The Oxford book of English ghost stories
Arabesque—the mouse
The Treasury of English short stories; ed. by N. Sullivan
Dusky Ruth
The World of the short story; ed. by C. Fadiman
Coppard, Alfred Edgar *See* Coppard, A. E. (Alfred Edgar), 1878-1957
The **copper** beeches. Doyle, Sir A. C.

The **copper** mine. Thompson, J.
The **copy** cats. Jennings, P. S.
COPYING PROCESSES
Friedman, B. J. The Candide of copiers
Liben, M. Minkin copying
Coral dance. Adams, G.
CORAL SEA
Adams, G. Coral dance
Michener, J. A. Coral Sea
Coral Sea. Michener, J. A.
Corbluth, Julian
Albergo terminal
Encounter (London, England) 68:17-24 F '87
Cordials. Kranes, D.
Cordle to onion to carrot. Sheckley, R.
Cordor, Similih M.
A farewell to the old order
Short story international 67
In the hospital
Short story international 55
Cords. O'Brien, E.
Corey, Deborah Joy
Drivin'
Ploughshares 14 no2/3:146-51 '88
CORFU ISLAND (GREECE)
Profumo, D. The blind man eats many flies
Corinne, Tee A.
The woman in love
Erotic interludes; ed. by L. Barbach
Corinne. Keillor, G.
Corinth. Kessler, J. F.
Coriolan, John
As you'd like it
Coriolan, J. Dream stud, and other stories
Counting coup
Coriolan, J. Dream stud, and other stories
Dream stud
Coriolan, J. Dream stud, and other stories
The G'issimo
Coriolan, J. Dream stud, and other stories
In the Blair's Lair
Coriolan, J. Dream stud, and other stories
Interview in the number two dressing-room
Coriolan, J. Dream stud, and other stories
Kindred
Coriolan, J. Dream stud, and other stories
A marriage, a mantra, a massage
Coriolan, J. Dream stud, and other stories
CORK (IRELAND: COUNTY) *See* Ireland—Cork (County)
A **corking** evening. Durrell, L.
The **cormorant.** Norris, H.
The **Corn** Dolly. Warren, J.

Cornell, Jennifer C.
Táim ainnis
Américas 36:40-5 N/D '84
The **corner**. Cowan, P.
The **corner** cupboard. Hartley, L. P.
A **corner** of a foreign field. King, F. H.
Corner store. Bonner, M.
The **cornfield**. Pavese, C.
Cornfield with lights. Smith, A.
The **Cornish** mystery. Christie, A.
The **cornucopia** of Julia K. Komie, L. B.
CORNWALL (ENGLAND) *See* England—
Cornwall
Corodimas, Peter
Marching to Byzantium
The North American Review 269:13-15
S '84
CORPORAL PUNISHMENT
Rees, D. Canes
Whitman, W. Death in the school-room
CORPORATIONS *See* Business
The **corpse**. Vargas, K.
The **corpse** and the kid. Woolrich, C.
Corpse carnival. Bradbury, R.
The **corpse** in the Statue of Liberty. Irish,
W.
The **corpse** laughs. Widmer, H.
Corpses on parade. Jacobson, E., and Jacobson, E.
CORPULENCE *See* Obesity
Correa, Hugo
Alter ego
The Penguin world omnibus of science
fiction
Correspondence. McCullers, C.
A **correspondence** course. Gordimer, N.
CORRESPONDENCE SCHOOLS AND COURSES
Greene, G. When Greek meets Greek
Correy, Lee
Industrial accident
Great science fiction; ed. by I. Asimov;
M. H. Greenberg and C. G. Waugh
The **corridors** of Mr. Cyril. Gilliatt, P.
Corrington, John William
The actes and monuments
Prime number; ed. by A. L. Weir
Heroic measures/vital signs
New stories from the South: the year's
best, 1987
The Southern Review (Baton Rouge, La.)
22:804-27 O '86
Pleadings
Selected stories from The Southern
review, 1965-1985
CORRUPTION (IN POLITICS)
See also Bribery
Al-Kouni, I. The drumming sands
Archer, J. Clean sweep Ignatius
Brown, F. Town wanted
Doyle, Sir A. C. The last resource
Mcdonald, G. The robbery
Norris, L. The girl from Cardigan

Overholser, W. D. Debt cancelled
Sackett, S. Hail to the chief
Corruption. Lively, P.
Corsage. Brady, M.
CORSAIRS *See* Pirates
CORSICA
Maupassant, G. de. The Corsican bandit
Maupassant, G. de. Happiness
Maupassant, G. de. Semillante
The **Corsican** bandit. Maupassant, G. de
Cortázar, Julio, 1914-1984
Axolotl
The Slaying of the dragon; ed. by F.
Rottensteiner
Bestiary
The Art of the tale; ed. by D. Halpern
House taken over
Black water; ed. by A. Manguel
The most profound caress
Omni (New York, N.Y.) 8:84-6+ N '85
No, no, and no
Harper's 272:28+ Ap '86
Return trip tango
Short story international 51
A small paradise
Harper's 268:32 My '84
The southern thruway
The World of the short story; ed. by
C. Fadiman
Stairs again
Harper's 272:30 Ap '86
Stories I tell myself
Short story international 44
CORTÉS, HERNÁN, 1485-1547
About
Barthelme, D. Cortés and Montezuma
Cortés and Montezuma. Barthelme, D.
Cortez. Austin, D.
Cortez. Ferguson, W.
Corwin, Phillip
Bullseye
Américas 40:36-9 My/Je '88
COSA NOSTRA *See* Mafia
Coskran, Kathleen
An African river
Coskran, K. The high price of everything
Disturbances
Coskran, K. The high price of everything
Facing Mount Kenya
Coskran, K. The high price of everything
Graven images
Coskran, K. The high price of everything
Handyman
Coskran, K. The high price of everything
The high price of everything
Coskran, K. The high price of everything
Miss Clay County 1960
Coskran, K. The high price of everything
Natural causes
Coskran, K. The high price of everything
The **cosmetic** factory. Haley, R.
The **cosmic** frame. Fairman, P. W.

COSSACKS
Babel', I. My first goose
Gogol', N. V. The lost letter
Gogol', N. V. A May night; or, The drowned maiden
Gogol', N. V. St. John's Eve
Gogol', N. V. Taras Bulba
Gogol', N. V. A terrible vengeance
Cost of living. Sheckley, R.
Costa, Carol
The best bid
The Womansleuth anthology; ed. by I. Zahava
Costa, Shelley
The passion of Marisol
The North American Review 272:55-63 Mr '87
COSTA BRAVA (SPAIN) *See* Spain—Costa Brava
The Costa Brava, 1959. Just, W. S.
COSTA RICA
19th century
Trollope, A. Returning home
20th century
Pritchard, M. In foreign country
COSTA RICANS
United States
Kessler, J. F. Corinth
Costello, Kevin
The immortal soul of Tommy O'
Short story international 60
Costello, Mark
Forty-hour devotion
TriQuarterly no71:86-108 Wint '88
Costello, Moya
Brian 'Squizzy' Taylor
Transgressions; ed. by D. Anderson
Coster, Graham
Spokane
The New Yorker 64:22-4 Jl 11 '88
A costly outing. Maupassant, G. de
The costume. Winters, J.
COSTUME PARTIES *See* Parties
A costume piece. Hornung, E. W.
Costy Pedraza's greatest pitch. Klinkowitz, J.
The cotillon. Hartley, L. P.
Cotillon. Wing, B.
COTSWOLDS (ENGLAND)
Buchan, J. Fullcircle
Coppard, A. E. Dusky Ruth
The cottage in winter. Hayes, M.
COTTAGES
Poe, E. A. Landor's cottage
Thompson, K. Holiday Haven
The cottages. Davis, L.
Couani, Anna
Xmas in the bush
Transgressions; ed. by D. Anderson
Couch, Arthur Thomas Quiller- *See* Quiller-Couch, Sir Arthur Thomas, 1863-1944
Couchettes. Davie, E.·
Couching at the door. Broster, D. K.
The Coulman handicap. Gilbert, M.

The council of drones. Sonnemann, W. K.
COUNSELING
Brunner, J. What friends are for
De Queiroz, D. S. Guidance
Counselman, Mary Elizabeth, 1911-
Night court
Witches' brew; ed. by M. Muller and B. Pronzini
Count Dracula. Allen, W.
Count Magnus. James, M. R.
Count the clock that tells the time. Ellison, H.
Count the ways. Greeley, A. M.
COUNTER CULTURE
Doubiago, S. The art of seeing with one's own eyes
COUNTERESPIONAGE *See* International intrigue; Spies
COUNTERFEITERS
Brown, F. Don't look behind you
Pronzini, B. The facsimile shop
Prose, F. Criminals
Counterplot. Gilbert, M.
Counterpoint. Farnsworth, K. A.
The countess and the devil. Colyton, H. J.
Countess Satan. Maupassant, G. de
Counting coup. Coriolan, J.
Counting months. Leavitt, D.
Counting the wind. Bissoondath, N.
Country blues for Melissa. Wilson, L. A.
Country carnival. Valenzuela, L.
A country excursion. Maupassant, G. de
A country girl. Hood, M.
A country home. Kenny, W.
The country house; or, Defaulted presence. Muschg, A.
The country husband. Cheever, J.
COUNTRY LIFE
See also Farm life; Mountain life; Outdoor life; Plantation life; Ranch life; Small town life
Banks, R. The neighbor
Bates, H. E. Death of a huntsman
Caldwell, E. August afternoon
Calisher, H. The summer rebellion
Chute, C. "Ollie, oh . . . "
Davis, L. The house plans
Dykeman, W. Lydia McQueen
Edwards, H. S. His defense
Engberg, S. A stay by the river
Everett, P. L. The bear as symbol
Everett, P. L. Nice white people
Everett, P. L. Turtle
Fahy, C. A clock in San Diego
Finney, E. J. Birds landing
Fleming, B. Afternoon in the country
Franzen, B. The Park Avenue Social Review visits the Drought Dinner in Eagle Grove, Iowa
Freeman, J. Camp Rose
Gass, W. H. The Sunday drive
Greenberg, A. Where do folk sayings come from?

COUNTRY LIFE—*Continued*
Hoffman, W. Indian gift
Hood, M. A country girl
Hood, M. How far she went
Hood, M. Solomon's seal
Horne, L. Taking care
Jewett, S. O. The foreigner
Kingsolver, B. Rose-Johnny
Klein, T. E. D. Petey
Matthew, J. R. Family visit
Matthew, J. R. Testimony
McGahern, J. All sorts of impossible things
Moskowitz, F. They all ran after the farmer's wife
O'Connor, F. Good country people
Peck, S. M. Pap's mules
Perkins, F. The changes
Phillips, J. A. Bess
Potter, N. A. J. Talking to trees
Proulx, A. Electric arrows
Proulx, A. On the Antler
Proulx, A. A run of bad luck
Proulx, A. Stone City
Schulman, H. Good practice
Stuart, J. From the mountains of Pike
Suckow, R. Home-coming
Tallent, E. Favor
Vines, H. The ginsing gatherers
Wolfe, T. The hollyhock sowers
Country lovers. Gordimer, N.

COUNTRY MUSIC
Cheuse, A. The Tennessee waltz
Mason, B. A. Hunktown
Proulx, A. Heart songs
Wilson, L. A. Country blues for Melissa
Country music. Morris, W.
The country of the blind. Wells, H. G.
A country outing. Sagan, F.
Country pleasures. Grenville, K.
Country society. Bates, H. E.
Country things. Lieber, T.
The country village teacher. Ch'en, Y.-C.
A country wedding. Colwin, L.
The coup. Boyd, W.
A couple of generals. Ch'en, Y.-C.
A couple of old flames. Colwin, L.
Coupon for blood. Huss, S.

COUPS D'ÉTAT
Ambler, E. The blood bargain

COURAGE
Brand, M. The third bullet
Carter, A. The donkey prince
Crane, S. The veteran
Davis, S. Mark Haverly
Faulkner, W. Turn about
Fenton, E. Gun-shy
Heise, K. Shazam
Henry, O. An afternoon miracle
Henry, O. The higher pragmatism
Humphrey, W. The shell
Ioannidou Adamidou, I. Hero
McDevitt, J. Promises to keep

Narayan, R. K. A hero
Saki. The Easter egg
The courage of Millie Baldwin. Trueblood, H.
The court case. Shukshin, V. M.
Court in the West eighties. McCullers, C.
COURT LIFE *See* Courts and courtiers
COURTESANS
           See also Prostitutes
The courting of Susie Brown. Caldwell, E.
Courtly love. Kessler, J. F.
Courtly vision. Mukherjee, B.
Courtois, Pierre Jacques
  The silent couple
    Masterpieces of terror and the supernatural; ed. by M. Kaye and S. Kaye
COURTROOM SCENES *See* Trials
COURTS AND COURTIERS
           See also names of individual kings, queens, and rulers; also subdivision Kings and rulers under names of countries
Lee, T. Prince Amilec
Millhauser, S. Cathay
COURTS-MARTIAL
Melville, H. Billy Budd, Sailor
Mortimer, J. C. Rumpole and the bright seraphim
The courts of the lord. Zwicky, F.
COURTSHIP
Abbott, L. K. A modern story of Woe and Lovecraft
Ade, G. Sophie's Sunday afternoon
Anstey, F. The curse of the catafalques
Bryant, E. Jody after the war
Caldwell, E. The courting of Susie Brown
Crane, S. The pace of youth
Crane, S. The third violet
Dove, R. Second-hand man
Doyle, Sir A. C. The heiress of Glenmahowley
Doyle, Sir A. C. Our Derby sweepstakes
Flynn, R. The midnight clear
Gallant, M. The chosen husband
Gilliatt, P. As we have learnt from Freud, there are no jokes
Gotthelf, J. The broommaker of Rychiswyl
Gotthelf, J. Elsi the unusual farm maid
Gotthelf, J. How Christen wins a bride
Gotthelf, J. How Joggeli finds a wife: a country tale
Gotthelf, J. Michel's courtship adventures
Gotthelf, J. The notary gets caught
Hamilton, M. Jenny Stairy's hat
Hamilton, N. Made for each other
Henry, O. The Indian Summer of Dry Valley Johnson
Henry, O. Schools and schools
Inoue, Y. A marriage interview
James, H. Sir Edmund Orme
Kawabata, Y. Umbrella
Keillor, G. How the crab apple grew
Latimer, M. Two in love

COURTSHIP—*Continued*
Norris, H. Water into wine
O'Connor, F. Judas
Pacheco, J. E. Acheron
Pacheco, J. E. The pleasure principle
Petrakis, H. M. The wooing of Ariadne
Poe, E. A. Why the little Frenchman wears his hand in a sling
Russ, J. "I had vacantly crumpled it into my pocket . . . but by God, Eliot, it was a photograph from life!"
Scobie, S. A marriage of convenience
Sheckley, R. The robot who looked like me
Spencer, E. First dark
Thériault, Y. Nuliak
Twain, M. The loves of Alonzo Fitz Clarence and Rosannah Ethelton
Verma, N. A room of their own
Wells, H. G. The jilting of Jane
Wells, H. G. Miss Winchelsea's heart
Wild, M. Tied in knots
Courtship. O'Brien, E.
A **courtship**. Thompson, J.
The **courtship** of Mr. Lyon. Carter, A.
Courtship of the blue widow. Petrakis, H. M.
The **courtship** of the thin girl. Shaw, J. B.
Cousin Petherick and the will. Watmough, D.

COUSINS
Abbott, K. We have another ape
Bellow, S. Cousins
Biggs, M. The other Catherine Irene
Billington, R. One afternoon
Boylan, J. The rescue
Burt, S. Hiding
Chekhov, A. P. Murder
Chernoff, M. Respect for the dead
Chin, F. Yes, young daddy
Cho, S.-H. The bony-fish that came into my net
Coleman, W. Eyes and teeth
Compton, J. One of my families
Cooper, J. C. Funny valentines
Coriolan, J. Counting coup
Drake, R. Shoot, child, what you talking about?
Drake, R. A ticket as long as your arm
Fante, J. One of us
Fink, I. A scrap of time
Fisher, R. The promised land
Franklin, P. For merit
Gallant, M. Jorinda and Jorindel
Garber, E. K. The lover
Gardiner, J. R. Game farm
Garrett, G. P. Bread from stones
Gilbert, D. The canoe
Gilbert, W. S. Little Mim
Givner, J. The celebrant
Goyen, W. The faces of blood kindred
Goyen, W. Had I a hundred mouths
Griggs, T. India

Harper, F. E. W. The two offers
Havazelet, E. Jillie
Hoffman, N. K. Lost lives
Huggan, I. Into the green stillness
James, H. Paste
La Chapelle, M. Anna in a small town
Le Fanu, J. S. Passage in the secret history of an Irish countess
Loewald, U. Cycle
MacLaverty, B. St. Paul could hit the nail on the head
Mazel, D. Friends
McCullers, C. Sucker
Minot, S. Thanksgiving Day
Munro, A. The moon in the Orange Street Skating Rink
Oates, J. C. In traction
Oates, J. C. Yarrow
Osborn, C. Reversals
Overholser, W. D. The hero
Pacheco, J. E. August afternoon
Poe, E. A. Berenice
Poe, E. A. Eleonora
Purdy, J. How I became a shadow
Rand, P. Cousins
Rhys, J. The whistling bird
Saroyan, W. The duel
Schulman, H. Good practice
Smith, L. Life on the moon
Smith, S. A. The amber frog
Spencer, E. The cousins
Spofford, H. E. P. The amber gods
Taylor, P. H. The hand of Emmagene
Villefranche, A.-M. The Italian cousin
Watmough, D. Cousin Petherick and the will
Watmough, D. Seduction
Whitaker, M. No stone for Jochebed
Williams, T. Das Wasser ist kalt
Wodehouse, P. G. Sir Roderick comes to lunch
Cousins. Bellow, S.
Cousins. Neville, S.
Cousins. Rand, P.
The **cousins**. Spencer, E.

Coutinho, Edilberto
Peace on earth, good will to men
The Literary Review (Madison, N.J.) 27:514-20 Summ '84

Coutinho, Sônia
Lucrecia's poisons
Michigan Quarterly Review 25:96-102 Wint '86
Coven. Wellman, M. W.
Covenant. Griffin, P.
Covenant of souls. Swanwick, M.
Covenant with a dragon. Casper, S.

COVERLETS
Smith, P. C. The patchwork quilt
Warner, S. T. A widow's quilt

Coville, Bruce
  The box
    Dragons and dreams; ed. by J. Yolen;
      M. H. Greenberg and C. G. Waugh
  The passing of the pack
    Werewolves; ed. by J. Yolen and M. H.
      Greenberg
Covington, Vicki
  Duty
    The New Yorker 62:22-3 Ag 18 '86
  Magnolia
    New stories from the South: the year's
      best, 1987
    The New Yorker 62:32-4 Mr 24 '86
Covino, Michael, 1950-
  The center of attraction
    Covino, M. The off-season
  The coming of snow
    Covino, M. The off-season
  Dialectical materialism
    Covino, M. The off-season
  The director of death
    Covino, M. The off-season
  The foreigners
    Covino, M. The off-season
  The hour of the ungovernable
    Covino, M. The off-season
  In winter the snow never stops
    Covino, M. The off-season
  Interruptions
    Covino, M. The off-season
  An intimacy beyond words
    Covino, M. The off-season
  The lament of the salesman
    Covino, M. The off-season
  Libel
    Covino, M. The off-season
  Little by little they come back for you
    Covino, M. The off-season
  Matinee at the Bijou
    Covino, M. The off-season
  Monologue of the movie mogul
    Covino, M. The off-season
    The Editors' choice: new American
      stories v2
    The Paris Review 26:16-37 Wint '84
  Not even the bones will be left to tell the
    story
    Covino, M. The off-season
  The passion of the artist is nothing com-
    pared to the passion of the business-
    man
    Covino, M. The off-season
  The return of possibility
    Covino, M. The off-season
  Salient facts
    Covino, M. The off-season
  You are here
    Covino, M. The off-season
Cow. Gilgun, J.
The cow. Prichard, K. S.
Cow tipping in the land of the truck farms.
  Sethi, R. C.

Cowan, Peter, 1914-
  The beach
    Cowan, P. A window in Mrs X's place
  The brown grass
    Cowan, P. A window in Mrs X's place
  Canary
    Cowan, P. A window in Mrs X's place
  Collector
    Cowan, P. A window in Mrs X's place
  The corner
    Cowan, P. A window in Mrs X's place
  Drift
    Cowan, P. A window in Mrs X's place
  Escape
    Cowan, P. A window in Mrs X's place
  The fence
    Cowan, P. A window in Mrs X's place
  Form in wood
    Cowan, P. A window in Mrs X's place
  The house
    Cowan, P. A window in Mrs X's place
  Living
    Cowan, P. A window in Mrs X's place
  Mobiles
    Cowan, P. A window in Mrs X's place
  The red-backed spiders
    Cowan, P. A window in Mrs X's place
  Requiem
    Cowan, P. A window in Mrs X's place
  Seminar
    Cowan, P. A window in Mrs X's place
  Shadow
    The Australian short story; ed. by L.
      Hergenhan
    Cowan, P. A window in Mrs X's place
  The tins
    Cowan, P. A window in Mrs X's place
  The tractor
    Cowan, P. A window in Mrs X's place
  A window in Mrs X's place
    Cowan, P. A window in Mrs X's place
COWARDICE
  Crane, S. The red badge of courage
  Ekström, M. The night between the second
    and the third
  Lish, G. Two families
  Lutz, J. Until you are dead
  Mitchell, M. E. For the honor of the com-
    pany
  Sagan, F. Aftermath of a duel
  Saroyan, W. Cowards
Cowardice. Boulaich, A.
Cowards. Saroyan, W.
A **cowboy** Christmas. Eighner, L.
A **cowboy** for a madam. Beman, B.
Cowboy on the Concord bridge. O'Brien, D.
Cowboy time. Klass, P.
COWBOYS
  Barthelme, D. Porcupines at the university
  Bedard, B. The ostrich
  Beman, B. A cowboy for a madam
  Bower, B. M. The lamb of the Flying U
  Crane, S. Twelve o'clock

COWBOYS—*Continued*
  Daniels, C. Me and Deke
  Evans, M. One-eyed sky
  Everett, P. L. Gaining the door
  Everett, P. L. Thirty-seven just to take a
    fall
  Fisher, C. Isley's stranger
  Miller, A. The misfits
  Phillips, J. A. El Paso
  Schaefer, J. W. Stubby Pringle's Christmas
  Shaw, J. B. Saturday night in Pinedale,
    Wyoming
  Waldrop, H. Der untergang des Abendlan-
    desmenschen
  Warren, D. Sunday rodeos
  Washburn, L. J. On the prod
COWHANDS *See* Cowboys
Cowley, Joy
  God loves you, Miss Rosewater
    Women's work; ed. by M. McLeod and
      L. Wevers
  The silk
    Women's work; ed. by M. McLeod and
      L. Wevers
Cowper, Richard, 1926-
  Brothers
    Cowper, R. The Tithonian Factor, and
      other stories
  The custodians
    Cowper, R. The custodians, and other
      stories
  The Hertford Manuscript
    Cowper, R. The custodians, and other
      stories
  Incident at Huacaloc
    Cowper, R. The Tithonian Factor, and
      other stories
  A message to the King of Brobdingnag
    Cowper, R. The Tithonian Factor, and
      other stories
    The Year's best science fiction, second
      annual collection
  Paradise beach
    Cowper, R. The custodians, and other
      stories
  Piper at the gates of dawn
    Cowper, R. The custodians, and other
      stories
  The scent of silverdill
    Cowper, R. The Tithonian Factor, and
      other stories
  The Tithonian Factor
    Cowper, R. The Tithonian Factor, and
      other stories
  What did the Deazies do?
    Cowper, R. The Tithonian Factor, and
      other stories
COWS *See* Cattle
Cows. James-French, D.
Cows on the drag strip. Broun, H.
The **cowslip** field. Bates, H. E.

Cox, Ailsa
  Just like Robert De Niro
    Critical Quarterly 28:35-9 Aut '86
  Twentieth frame
    Stand one; ed. by M. Blackburn; J.
      Silkin and L. Tracy
Cox, Arthur Jean
  Evergreen
    Universe 15
Cox, Elizabeth
  A sounding brass
    The Graywolf annual [1]
Cox, Erle
  Andax and Odi
    Australian science fiction; ed. by V. Ikin
Cox, Irving E., Jr.
  In the circle of nowhere
    Alternative histories; ed. by C. G.
      Waugh and M. H. Greenberg
Coxe, George Harmon, 1901-1984
  The doctor takes a case
    Kill or cure; ed. by M. Muller and B.
      Pronzini
  Seed of suspicion
    Murder and mystery in Boston; ed. by
      C. L. R. Waugh; F. D. McSherry and
      M. H. Greenberg
The **Coxon** Fund. James, H.
Coyote and Quarter Moon. Pronzini, B., and
    Wallmann, J. M.
Coyote meets Raven. Blue Cloud, P.
The **Coyote-Spirit** and the Weaving Woman.
    Austin, M. H.
COYOTES
  Evans, M. One-eyed sky
Coyotes. Mason, B. A.
Cozzens, James Gould, 1903-1978
  Clerical error
    Chapter & hearse; ed. by M. Muller and
      B. Pronzini
CPD. Nowakowski, M.
Crab Celestine. Hall, M. L.
Crabs. Carey, P.
Crabtree, Lou V.
  Holy Spirit
    Crabtree, L. V. Sweet Hollow
  Homer-snake
    Crabtree, L. V. Sweet Hollow
    Through other eyes; ed. by I. Zahava
  The Jake Pond
    Crabtree, L. V. Sweet Hollow
  Little Jesus
    Crabtree, L. V. Sweet Hollow
  The miracle in Sweet Hollow
    Crabtree, L. V. Sweet Hollow
  Prices' bewitched cow
    Crabtree, L. V. Sweet Hollow
  Wildcat John
    Crabtree, L. V. Sweet Hollow
Crace, Jim
  Cross-country
    Crace, J. Continent

Crace, Jim—*Continued*
Electricity
  Crace, J. Continent
  Encounter (London, England) 64:3-8 F
    '85
In heat
  Crace, J. Continent
The prospect from the silver hill
  Crace, J. Continent
Sins and virtues
  Crace, J. Continent
Talking Skull
  Crace, J. Continent
The world with one eye shut
  Crace, J. Continent
The **crack**. Plante, D.
Cracked wheat. Cook, H.
Crackers. Bowers, J.
Crackling day. Abrahams, P.
Cradles of light. Griffin, S.
The **craft** of death. Ross, R. T.
Craig, David, 1932-
I want to be alone
  Critical Quarterly 28:41-4 Aut '86
Craig, Jonathan, 1919-
The late unlamented
  Alfred Hitchcock's Mortal errors
This day's evil
  Alfred Hitchcock's Grave suspicions
Cram, Ralph Adams, 1863-1942
No. 252 Rue M le Prince
  Masterpieces of terror and the super-
    natural; ed. by M. Kaye and S. Kaye
Cramer, Kathryn, 1962-
Forbidden knowledge
  Mathenauts: tales of mathematical won-
    der; ed. by R. Rucker
The **cramp**. Hofmann, G.
Crampsey, Robert A. (Robert Anthony)
Felicity
  Short story international 42
Cranch, Christopher Pearse, 1813-1892
The last of the Huggermuggers: a giant
    story
  Masterpieces of fantasy and enchant-
    ment; ed. by D. G. Hartwell
Crandall, Dorothea
Dispensation
  The Sewanee Review 94:361-70 Summ
    '86
Crane, Stephen, 1871-1900
Adventures of a novelist
  Crane, S. Prose and poetry
"And if he wills, we must die"
  Crane, S. Prose and poetry
The angel-child
  Crane, S. Prose and poetry
The black dog
  Crane, S. Prose and poetry

The blue hotel
  Crane, S. Prose and poetry
  On being foreign; ed. by T. J. Lewis and
    R. E. Jungman
  The Western hall of fame; ed. by B.
    Pronzini and M. H. Greenberg
The bride comes to Yellow Sky
  Crane, S. Prose and poetry
The broken-down van
  Crane, S. Prose and poetry
The carriage-lamps
  Crane, S. Prose and poetry
The city urchin and the chaste villagers
  Crane, S. Prose and poetry
The clan of no-name
  Crane, S. Prose and poetry
Coney Island's failing days
  Crane, S. Prose and poetry
A dark-brown dog
  Crane, S. Prose and poetry
  Roger Caras' Treasury of great dog
    stories
Death and the child
  Crane, S. Prose and poetry
An eloquence of grief
  Crane, S. Prose and poetry
An episode of war
  Crane, S. Prose and poetry
An excursion ticket
  Crane, S. Prose and poetry
An experiment in luxury
  Crane, S. Prose and poetry
An experiment in misery
  Crane, S. Prose and poetry
The fight
  Crane, S. Prose and poetry
The fire
  Crane, S. Prose and poetry
A fishing village
  Crane, S. Prose and poetry
The five white mice
  Crane, S. Prose and poetry
Flanagan and his short filibustering adven-
    ture
  Crane, S. Prose and poetry
Four men in a cave
  Crane, S. Prose and poetry
George's mother
  Crane, S. Prose and poetry
A ghoul's accountant
  Crane, S. Prose and poetry
"God rest ye, merry gentlemen"
  Crane, S. Prose and poetry
A great mistake
  Crane, S. Prose and poetry
A grey sleeve
  Crane, S. Prose and poetry
His new mittens
  Crane, S. Prose and poetry
Horses—one dash [Variant title: One dash
    —horses]
  Westeryear; ed. by E. Gorman

Crane, Stephen, 1871-1900—*Continued*
  In a Park Row restaurant
    Crane, S. Prose and poetry
  In the depths of a coal mine
    Crane, S. Prose and poetry
  The Kicking Twelfth
    Crane, S. Prose and poetry
  Killing his bear
    Crane, S. Prose and poetry
  The knife
    Crane, S. Prose and poetry
  The little regiment
    Crane, S. Prose and poetry
    A Treasury of Civil War stories; ed. by
      M. H. Greenberg and B. Pronzini
  The lover and the tell-tale
    Crane, S. Prose and poetry
  Lynx-hunting
    Crane, S. Prose and poetry
  Maggie: a girl of the streets
    Crane, S. Prose and poetry
  A man and some others
    Crane, S. Prose and poetry
  Manacled
    Crane, S. Prose and poetry
  Marines signaling under fire at Guan-
      tanamo
    Crane, S. Prose and poetry
  The men in the storm
    Crane, S. Prose and poetry
  The mesmeric mountain
    Crane, S. Prose and poetry
  The monster
    Crane, S. Prose and poetry
  Moonlight on the snow
    Crane, S. Prose and poetry
  Mr. Binks' day off
    Crane, S. Prose and poetry
  A mystery of heroism: a detail of an
      American battle
    Crane, S. Prose and poetry
  The octopush [Variant title: The fishermen]
    Crane, S. Prose and poetry
  An ominous baby
    Crane, S. Prose and poetry
  One dash—horses [Variant title: Horses--
      one dash]
    Crane, S. Prose and poetry
  The open boat
    Crane, S. Prose and poetry
    Men at sea; ed. by B. Aymar
    The Norton book of American short
      stories
    Short stories of the sea; ed. by G. C.
      Solley and E. Steinbaugh
  The pace of youth
    Crane, S. Prose and poetry
  A poker game
    Crane, S. Prose and poetry
  The price of the harness
    Crane, S. Prose and poetry

  The red badge of courage
    Crane, S. Prose and poetry
    A Treasury of Civil War stories; ed. by
      M. H. Greenberg and B. Pronzini
  The revenge of the Adolphus
    Crane, S. Prose and poetry
  The second generation
    Crane, S. Prose and poetry
  Shame
    Crane, S. Prose and poetry
  "Showin' off"
    Crane, S. Prose and poetry
  The shrapnel of their friends
    Crane, S. Prose and poetry
  Stephen Crane's own story
    Crane, S. Prose and poetry
  Stories told by an artist
    Crane, S. Prose and poetry
  A tent in agony
    Crane, S. Prose and poetry
  The third violet
    Crane, S. Prose and poetry
  This majestic lie
    Crane, S. Prose and poetry
  The trial, execution, and burial of Homer
      Phelps
    Crane, S. Prose and poetry
  Twelve o'clock
    Crane, S. Prose and poetry
  The upturned face
    Crane, S. Prose and poetry
    Masterpieces of terror and the super-
      natural; ed. by M. Kaye and S. Kaye
  The veteran
    Crane, S. Prose and poetry
  Virtue in war
    Crane, S. Prose and poetry
  When man falls, a crowd gathers
    Crane, S. Prose and poetry
  The wise men: a detail of American life
      in Mexico
    Crane, S. Prose and poetry
The **crane** wife. Vogan, S.
Cranes. Hwang, S.
The **crank**. Baxter, C.
The **crank** that made the revolution. Gray,
    A.
Crapser, William, 1949-
  Baptism of fire
    Crapser, W. Remains: stories of Vietnam
  Billy Sunday
    Crapser, W. Remains: stories of Vietnam
  The descent
    Crapser, W. Remains: stories of Vietnam
  Education of a pointman
    Crapser, W. Remains: stories of Vietnam
  For Timothy Baer
    Crapser, W. Remains: stories of Vietnam
  Hungers
    Crapser, W. Remains: stories of Vietnam
  Land of the free, home of the brave
    Crapser, W. Remains: stories of Vietnam

Crapser, William, 1949-—*Continued*
Let it be
Crapser, W. Remains: stories of Vietnam
A letter home [1]
Crapser, W. Remains: stories of Vietnam
A letter home [2]
Crapser, W. Remains: stories of Vietnam
A letter home [3]
Crapser, W. Remains: stories of Vietnam
A letter home [4]
Crapser, W. Remains: stories of Vietnam
New man
Crapser, W. Remains: stories of Vietnam
Nicky Martinez
Crapser, W. Remains: stories of Vietnam
Proud
Crapser, W. Remains: stories of Vietnam
R&R
Crapser, W. Remains: stories of Vietnam
Remains
Crapser, W. Remains: stories of Vietnam
The rest
Crapser, W. Remains: stories of Vietnam
The wall: Michael Bowle
Crapser, W. Remains: stories of Vietnam
The war enters
Crapser, W. Remains: stories of Vietnam
Wild child
Crapser, W. Remains: stories of Vietnam
Crash. Warren, J.
Crater Lake. Rogers, T. N. R.
Crater Lake. Wilson, B.
CRATES, OF THEBES, 4TH CENT. B.C.
About
Schwob, M. Crates, cynic
Crates, cynic. Schwob, M.
Cravens, Gwyneth
Wedding
The New Yorker 62:32-40 F 16 '87
A **craving** for originality. Pronzini, B.
Crawford, F. Marion (Francis Marion), 1854-1909
The doll's ghost
Ready or not; ed. by J. Kahn
For the blood is the life
Vampires; ed. by A. Ryan
Man overboard!
The Book of the dead; ed. by A. K. Russell
The upper berth
Dark banquet; ed. by L. Child
The Oxford book of English ghost stories
Crawford, Francis Marion *See* Crawford, F. Marion (Francis Marion), 1854-1909
Crawford, Isabella Valancy, 1850-1887
Extradited
The Oxford book of Canadian short stories in English
Crayford, Kathleen
Duncan
Women's work; ed. by M. McLeod and L. Wevers

Crazy. Fink, I.
Crazy. Schwartz, J.
The **crazy.** Smith, P. C.
Crazy 8's. Clark, G.
Crazy, crazy, now showing everywhere. Gilchrist, E.
CRAZY HORSE, SIOUX CHIEF, ca. 1842-1877
About
Utley, S., and Waldrop, H. Custer's last jump
The **crazy** iris. Ibuse, M.
Crazy ladies. Johnson, G.
Crazy rhythm. Brand, M.
A **crazy** tale. Chesterton, G. K.
Cream sauce. Flanagan, M.
Cream sponge on Sunday. Eldridge, M.
Creamer, E. S.
China
The Antioch Review 46:257-65 Spr '88
Stung
The Antioch Review 44:424-6 Fall '86
Creases. Fitzgerald, M. J.
CREATION
Asimov, I. How it happened
Metzger, D. In the beginning there was humming
Poe, E. A. The power of words
Stein, J. Why the moon is small and dark when the sun is big and shiny
CREATION (LITERARY, ARTISTIC, ETC.)
See also Authorship
Josipovici, G. Death of the word
The **creature.** O'Brien, E.
Creature comforts. Kumin, M.
Creature comforts. Prose, F.
The **creatures.** De la Mare, W.
Creatures of impulse. Gilbert, W. S.
Creatures that once were men. Gorky, M.
CREDIBILITY *See* Truthfulness and falsehood
Credibility. Kessel, J.
Credit to Shakespeare. Symons, J.
CREE INDIANS
Wiebe, R. H. Where is the voice coming from?
Creech, Wendy Goodall
The myth
'Teen 31:40+ Je '87
Creekmore, Hubert
The chain in the heart [excerpt]
Mississippi writers v1: Fiction; ed. by D. Abbott
Crehan, Stewart
The operation
Short story international 43
CREMATION
Ballantyne, S. Perpetual care
Gerber, M. J. "I don't believe this"
Kinsella, W. P. Diehard
Minot, S. Thorofare
Thomas, D. The burning baby

CREMATORIUMS
Hospital, J. T. Ashes to ashes
Muschg, A. Reparations; or, Making good
Crème de la crème. Abbott, K.
CREOLES
Cable, G. W. Belles Demoiselles plantation
Henry, O. The renaissance at Charleroi
Shaik, F. Before echo
The **crescent**. Rambach, P.
Creswell, Rosemary
Epithalamium
Transgressions; ed. by D. Anderson
The **Cretan** bull. Christie, A.
Creveling, Wil
Thinking the unthinkable
100 great fantasy short short stories; ed.
by I. Asimov; T. Carr and M. H.
Greenberg
The **crew** of the Foraker. Frazee, S.
Crews, Harry, 1935-
A long wail
The Georgia Review 40:68-74 Spr '86
Necessary fictions; ed. by S. W. Lind-
berg and S. Corey
Crichton, Michael, 1942-
Mousetrap
Life 7:116-18+ Ja '84
Crichton, Sarah
Independence day
Seventeen 43:118-19+ D '84
Crichton Smith, Iain
A night with Kant
Encounter (London, England) 64:3-6 Ap
'85
Timoshenko
The Treasury of English short stories;
ed. by N. Sullivan
The **crick**. Suckow, R.
CRICKET
Rees, D. Canes
The **cricket**. Pu, S.-L.
The **cricket** on the hearth. Dickens, C.
CRICKETS
Kawabata, Y. The grasshopper and the bell
cricket
Pu, S.-L. The cricket
Crider, Bill
Wolf night
Westeryear; ed. by E. Gorman
CRIME AND CRIMINALS
See also Arson; Atrocities; Bank rob-
bers; Brigands and robbers; Child
abuse; Counterfeiters; Escaped convicts;
Extortion; Gangs; Gangsters; Hostages;
Juvenile delinquency; Kidnapping;
Kleptomania; Mafia; Murder stories;
Rape; Smuggling; Swindlers and swind-
ling; Thieves; Vandalism; Vigilance
committees; War criminals; Wife abuse
Algren, N. The captain has bad dreams
Algren, N. Please don't talk about me
when I'm gone
Algren, N. Poor man's pennies

Algren, N. El presidente de Méjico
Andreyev, L. The seven who were hanged
Asimov, I. All the troubles of the world
Barker, C. In the flesh
Blaushild, L. Witness
Bloch, R. Water's edge
Block, L. Change of life
Böll, H. My sad face
Boyle, T. C. The hit man
Bradbury, R. Four-way funeral
Bradbury, R. Half-pint homicide
Brett, S. Letter to his son
Brown, F. Town wanted
Calvino, I. Transit bed
Coleman, W. The big little gang
Colette. The murderer
Connell, R. Brother Orchid
Corrington, J. W. The actes and monu-
ments
Delany, S. R. Time considered as a helix
of semi-precious stones
Doyle, Sir A. C. The cabman's story
Doyle, Sir A. C. The final problem
Faust, I. The year of the hot jock
Ford, R. Rock Springs
Ford, R. Sweethearts
Gault, W. C. The threatening three
Glasser, P. Mexico
Gorky, M. Evil-doers
Harris, M. The martyred poet
Henry, O. A retrieved reformation
Keating, H. R. F. A crime child
Keating, H. R. F. An upright woman
Kelly, J. P. The prisoner of Chillon
Kipp, G. G. Lessons from a pro
Kittredge, W. The underground river
Leiber, F. Ill met in Lankhmar
Lowden, D. The old mob
Lurie, M. American shoes
Mailer, N. The killer
Maloney, J. J. The Mid-City Meat Com-
pany
Mortimer, J. C. Rumpole and the younger
generation
Oates, J. C. Fin de siècle
Prior, A. Be lucky
Pronzini, B. Cain's mark
Pronzini, B. Changes
Pronzini, B. The killing
Pronzini, B. Muggers' moon
Pronzini, B. One of those days
Pronzini, B. Retirement
Pronzini, B. Skeletons
Pronzini, B. Unchained
Pronzini, B. Waiting, waiting . . .
Pronzini, B. Words do not a book make
Runyon, D. The informal execution of
Soupbone Pew
Sandberg, P. L. B-Tower west wall
Shacochis, B. I ate her heart
Sheckley, R. Meanwhile, back at the
bromide
Silverberg, R. Blindsight

CRIME AND CRIMINALS—*Continued*
Smith, C. A planet named Shayol
Spillane, M. Everybody's watching me
Spillane, M. The gold fever tapes
Spillane, M. The pickpocket
Spillane, M. Tomorrow I die
Symons, J. The flaw
Taylor, A. The kumara plant
Welch, D. Brave and cruel
Wells, H. G. Mr. Ledbetter's vacation
The **crime** and glory of Commander Suzdal.
    Smith, C.
Crime and punishment. Narayan, R. K.
A **crime** child. Keating, H. R. F.
Crime in a girls' high school. Škvorecký, J.
Crime in Italy. Evans, E.
Crime in rhyme. Bloch, R.
Crime machine. Bloch, R.
The **crime** machine. Ritchie, J.
Crime of the century. Freeman, C.
The **crime** of the century. Hoch, E. D.

CRIME PASSIONEL
    See also Murder stories
Osborn, C. The last of it
Woolrich, C. New York blues
The **Crimean** hotel. Lively, P.

CRIMEAN WAR, 1853-1856
Doyle, Sir A. C. That veteran
Crimes of conscience. Gordimer, N.
Crimes of passion. Schoemperlen, D.

CRIMINAL INVESTIGATION
James, P. D. Great Aunt Allie's flypapers
McBain, E. Nightshade
Rampo, E. The psychological test

CRIMINALLY INSANE *See* Insane,
    Criminal and dangerous

CRIMINALS *See* Crime and criminals
Criminals. Prose, F.
The **criminologists'** club. Hornung, E. W.
Crimson markings. Kono, T.
Crimson Ramblers of the world, farewell.
    West, J.

Cripps, Arthur Shearly
Fuel of fire
    The Penguin book of Southern African
    stories
A **crisis.** Maupassant, G. de

CRISIS COUNSELING *See* Hotlines
    (Telephone counseling)

Crispin, A. C.
The amiable assassin
    Magic in Ithkar 3; ed. by A. Norton and
    R. Adams
Bloodspell
    Tales of the Witch World [1]

Crispin, Edmund, 1921-1978
The hunchback cat
    Great detectives; ed. by D. W. McCul-
    lough

We know you're busy writing, but we
    thought you wouldn't mind if we just
    dropped in for a minute
    The Mammoth book of modern crime
    stories; ed. by G. Hardinge
**Crispin, Edmund, 1921-1978, and Bush,
    Geoffrey, 1920-**
Who killed Baker?
    The Penguin classic crime omnibus
Critical decisions of early years. Matthews,
    J.
Critical theory. White, C.
Critics. Busch, F.
CRO-MAGNON MAN *See* Man, Prehistoric
Crocheting. Crone, M.
Crockfoot Lilli. Dadswell, M.
Crocodile. Wendt, A.
CROCODILES
Hedge, P. Snap dragon
Houbein, L. Not without rain
Croft, Barbara
The ragpicker's boy
    The Kenyon Review ns7:70-4 Fall '85
Croft, Michael
The pit
    Stories and poems from close to home;
    ed. by F. Salas
Crompton, Anne E.
Met by moonlight
    Werewolves; ed. by J. Yolen and M. H.
    Greenberg
Crone, Moira, 1952-
Crocheting
    American made; ed. by M. Leyner; C.
    White and T. Glynn
Oslo
    The New Yorker 60:38-40 My 28 '84
Paris leaves me cold
    Mademoiselle 91:58-9+ Ja '85
Recovery
    The Southern Review (Baton Rouge, La.)
    20:188-98 Ja '84
Crook of the month. Bloch, R.
The **crooked** man. Doyle, Sir A. C.
The **crop.** O'Connor, F.
Cropped. Drew, E.
CROQUET
Williams, T. Three players of a summer
    game
Cross, Amanda, 1926-
Tania's no where
    Distant danger; ed. by J. Van de
    Wetering
Cross, Celia
Midnight promise
    Good Housekeeping 200:108-9 Ja '85
Thoroughly modern magic
    Good Housekeeping 201:120-1 Ag '85
Cross, Ronald Anthony
The forever summer
    Tales from Isaac Asimov's science fiction
    magazine: short stories for young
    adults

Cross, Ronald Anthony—*Continued*
The heavenly blue answer
  In the field of fire; ed. by J. Van B.
    Dann and J. Dann
Hotel mind slaves
  Universe 16
Cross-country. Crace, J.
Cross-country. Finger, A.
The **cross-country** run. Watmough, D.
Cross-country snow. Hemingway, E.
The **Cross** of Lorraine. Asimov, I.
Cross purposes. Murphy, P.
Crossbones. Michaels, L.
The **crossing**. Huddle, D.
A **crossing**. Mazel, D.
Crossing. Olsen, P.
Crossing. Thompson, B.
Crossing demon. New, J.
Crossing of the paths. Bilenkin, D.
Crossing Spider Creek. O'Brien, D.
Crossman, Patricia R.
A time to remember
  Good Housekeeping 200:128-9 F '85
The **crossroads**. Rice, J.
Crossroads—an anthology. Hemingway, E.
The **crosstie**. Molnar, A. K.
The **crossways**. Hartley, L. P.
Crouch, Cl.
The wicked season
  Isaac Asimov's Tomorrow's voices
Crouch end. King, S.
Croup. Llewellyn, K.
The **crow**. Meckel, C.
The **crow** comes last. Calvino, I.
CROW INDIANS
Johnson, D. M. A man called Horse
The **Crow Woman**. Heller, S.
The **crowd**. Bradbury, R.
Crowded hour. Hill, R.
Crowder's Cove: a story of the war.
  Woolson, C. F.
CROWDS
Crane, S. When man falls, a crowd gathers
Crowe, John, 1924-
  *For works written by this author under
    other names see* Arden, William,
    1924-; Collins, Michael, 1924-;
    Lynds, Dennis, 1924-; Sadler, Mark,
    1924-
Crowell, Doug
Says Velma
  New stories from the South: the year's
    best, 1986
Work
  Prize stories, Texas Institute of Letters;
    ed. by M. Terry
Crowley, Aleister, 1875-1947
The artistic temperament
  Crowley, A. The scrutinies of Simon Iff
Big game
  Crowley, A. The scrutinies of Simon Iff
The burning of Melcarth
  Crowley, A. Golden twigs

The conduct of John Briggs
  Crowley, A. The scrutinies of Simon Iff
The god of Ibreez
  Crowley, A. Golden twigs
The hearth
  Crowley, A. Golden twigs
Ineligible
  Crowley, A. The scrutinies of Simon Iff
The king of the wood
  Crowley, A. Golden twigs
The mass of Saint Sécaire
  Crowley, A. Golden twigs
Not good enough
  Crowley, A. The scrutinies of Simon Iff
The old man of the peepul-tree
  Crowley, A. Golden twigs
The oracle of the Corycian cave
  Crowley, A. Golden twigs
Outside the bank's routine
  Crowley, A. The scrutinies of Simon Iff
The stone of Cybele
  Crowley, A. Golden twigs
Crowley, Bridget
A sudden enthusiasm
  Critical Quarterly 30:107-10 Spr '88
Crowley, John
Antiquities
  Magicats! Ed. by J. Dann and G. Dozois
Snow
  Omni (New York, N.Y.) 8:50-2+ N '85
  The Year's best science fiction, third an-
    nual collection
The **Crown** Derby plate. Bowen, M.
CROWS
Peterson, M. Crows
Crows. Peterson, M.
Crucifixus etiam. Miller, W. M.
The **cruellest** month. Highsmith, P.
CRUELTY
  See also Atrocities; Violence
Brooks, J. Doing the voices
Bukoski, A. This heat
Dennison, G. Shawno
García Márquez, G. The incredible and
  sad tale of innocent Eréndira and her
  heartless grandmother
Hébert, A. The torrent
Jackson, S. The renegade
Kojima, N. Stars
Lustig, A. Indecent dreams
MacLaverty, B. In the hills above Lugano
Monreal, D. N. Leprosy
Rice, J. The Idol of the Flies
Ríos, A. Pato
Shimaki, K. The centipede
Straub, P. Blue rose
Tem, S. R. Little cruelties
Wollheim, D. A. Give her hell
The **cruelty** of chairs. Woodman, A.
CRUELTY TO CHILDREN *See* Child abuse
Cruise control. McWey, M.
The **crumb**. Rogers, S.
The **crumbs** of one man's year. Thomas, D.

Crump, Randell
Anthony's wives
L. Ron Hubbard presents Writers of the future
Crunchy Wunchy's first case. See Gardner, M. Private Eye Oglesby
CRUSADES
See also Knights and knighthood
The **crushed** pellet. Kaikō, T.
Crusoe. Sage, V.
Crusoe visits the wreck. Defoe, D.
The **cry.** Sanders, S. R.
Cry about a nickel. Everett, P. L.
A **cry** for help. Love, J. M.
Cry havoc. Grubb, D.
Cry silence. Brown, F.
Cry wolf. Durrell, L.
CRYING
Bowen, E. Tears, idle tears
Fisher, M. F. K. Moment of wisdom
CRYONICS
Dick, P. K. Frozen journey
Dick, P. K. I hope I shall arrive soon
Hamilton, E. The stars, my brothers
Morris, W. Fiona
Cryptic. McDevitt, J.
Crystal, Serena
In the village
The Antioch Review 42:188-205 Spr '84
The **crystal** egg. Wells, H. G.
Crystal River. Smith, C.
Csiffary, Sylvia
Russian songs
Here's the story: fiction with heart; ed. by M. Sklar
Csucskári. Brust, S.
CUBA
Benítez-Rojo, A. Heaven and earth
Crane, S. The clan of no-name
Crane, S. "God rest ye, merry gentlemen"
Crane, S. Marines signaling under fire at Guantanamo
Hemingway, E. Great news from the mainland
Hemingway, E. I guess everything reminds you of something
Herbst, J. The enemy
Loos, A. Liquor makes you smart
Havana
Crane, S. This majestic lie
Figueredo, D. H. Tell the night
Hemingway, E. One trip across
Lewis, N. A weekend in Havana
Valladares, A. Reality
Cuba night. Halliday, M.
A **Cuban** girl. Glück, T.
Cubeworld. Gross, H. H.
The **cuckoo.** Kim, Y.
Cuddling. Walker, A.
CUERNAVACA (MEXICO) See Mexico—Cuernavaca
La **Cueva** Del Círculo Sin Fin. Trebelo, J.
Cuisinart. Leebron, F.

Cul-de-sac (uncompleted). Bail, M.
Cullen, E. J.
The baddest, baddest days
Cullen, E. J. Our war and how we won it
Better bars and garden
Cullen, E. J. Our war and how we won it
Breaking with Brezhnev
Cullen, E. J. Our war and how we won it
Bridgework
Cullen, E. J. Our war and how we won it
Down time Tyler, Texas
Cullen, E. J. Our war and how we won it
The first law of classical mechanics
Cullen, E. J. Our war and how we won it
First sight
Cullen, E. J. Our war and how we won it
Gorbachev's wife
Cullen, E. J. Our war and how we won it
The North American Review 271:31-2 S '86
Honesty
Cullen, E. J. Our war and how we won it
How some people feel about Jesus
Cullen, E. J. Our war and how we won it
I break into houses
Cullen, E. J. Our war and how we won it
I try to look out for my family
Cullen, E. J. Our war and how we won it
Larmer said he would be King
Cullen, E. J. Our war and how we won it
Lawn City
Cullen, E. J. Our war and how we won it
Letter to the institution
Cullen, E. J. Our war and how we won it
A life for the theater
Cullen, E. J. Our war and how we won it
Mayberry
Cullen, E. J. Our war and how we won it
Mayberry '86
The North American Review 271:34-7 Mr '86
One-eyed Jacks
Cullen, E. J. Our war and how we won it

Cullen, E. J.—*Continued*
  Our war and how we won it
    Cullen, E. J. Our war and how we won
    it
  Pleadings
    Cullen, E. J. Our war and how we won
    it
  Post cards
    Cullen, E. J. Our war and how we won
    it
  The second law of thermodynamics
    Cullen, E. J. Our war and how we won
    it
  Sleepy Hollow
    Cullen, E. J. Our war and how we won
    it
  Tolstoy's son
    Cullen, E. J. Our war and how we won
    it
  Trying to grow up American
    Cullen, E. J. Our war and how we won
    it
  What Uncle Tom did
    Cullen, E. J. Our war and how we won
    it
  What's left
    Cullen, E. J. Our war and how we won
    it
  Worrying
    Cullen, E. J. Our war and how we won
    it
Cullinan, Elizabeth, 1933-
  Life after death
    The Substance of things hoped for; ed.
    by J. B. Breslin
Culpability. Robison, M.
CULTS
  Ballard, J. G. The object of the attack
  Bloch, R. The shadow from the steeple
  Bloch, R. String of pearls
  Henley, P. The birthing
  Hoch, E. D. Sword for a sinner
  Lovecraft, H. P. The call of Cthulhu
  McKinley, J. Praying for a Fickleman
  Reed, K. The wait
  Silverberg, R. A thousand paces along the
    Via Dolorosa
  St. Clair, M. Idris' pig
  Wagner, K. E. Sticks
Culture and the light. Chesterton, G. K.
CULTURE CONFLICT
  See also East and West
  Aldiss, B. W. The other side of the lake
  Austin, M. H. The Basket Woman: first
    story
  Austin, M. H. The Basket Woman: second
    story
  Austin, M. H. The secret of the holy
    places
  Becker, J. The stench
  Bowles, P. Here to learn
  Bowles, P. Pastor Dowe at Tacaté
  Camus, A. The growing stone

  Chernoff, M. Bop
  Garro, E. The tree
  Gold, H. Ti-Moune
  Holt, J. D. The pool
  Huang, C.-M. I love Mary
  Johnson, W. The girl who would be Rus-
    sian
  Kim, Y. The cuckoo
  Kinsella, W. P. Illianna comes home
  Liberman, S. Two years in exile
  Moore, L. The deep valley
  Nimmo, H. A. Lim
  Nooteboom, C. Mokusei: a love story
  Oe, K. The clever rain tree
  Oz, A. Nomad and viper
  Pritchard, M. Ramon: souvenirs
  Schwartz, L. S. The melting pot
  Shacochis, B. The pelican
  Sharat Chandra, G. S. Bhat's return
  Silko, L. Lullaby
  Spark, M. The go-away bird
  Sproat, R. A small difference only
  Theroux, P. Yard sale
  Wu, C.-L. The doctor's mother
  Yamamoto, M. Betty-san
  Yi, H. The woman who fulled clothes
CULTURE CONTACT *See* Acculturation
Culture shocks. DeMarinis, R.
Culver, Timothy J.
    For works written by this author under
    other names see Westlake, Donald
    E.
Cummings, Rebecca
  Berrying
    The Best Maine stories; ed. by S. Phip-
    pen; C. Waugh and M. Greenberg
Cummins, Ann
  Bitterwater
    The New Yorker 64:31-6 Ap 4 '88
  Neutral zone
    The Antioch Review 43:470-9 Fall '85
  Starburst
    The New Yorker 64:36-42 My 16 '88
Cummins, Walter
  Oxfords
    The Virginia Quarterly Review 63:324-39
    Spr '87
Cunningham, Jere
  Decoys
    Shadows 7
  Fire
    Omni (New York, N.Y.) 6:54-6+ Ap '84
Cunningham, John
  Gardeners
    Critical Quarterly 29:16-19 Aut '87
Cunningham, John M.
  Yankee gold
    The Second reel West; ed. by B. Pron-
    zini and M. H. Greenberg
Cunningham, Michael, 1952-
  White angel
    The New Yorker 64:25-33 Jl 25 '88
The cup of coffee. Auchincloss, L.

A **cup** of coffee. Rudloff, S. A.
A **cup** of tea. Lavin, M.
The **cure**. Bloch, R.
The **cure**. Brown, M. W.
The **cure**. Colette
A **cure** for boredom, dumpy spirits. Sprecher, L.

CURFEW
  Nowakowski, M. Silent night, holy night
The **curfew**. Gordon, P.
The **curfew** tolls. Benét, S. V.
The **curio** shop. Kotzwinkle, W.
Curios. Zigal, T.
The **curious** computer. Lovesey, P.
The **curious** conspiracy. Gilbert, M.
The **curious** consultation. Jeppson, J. O.
The **curious** Englishman. Chesterton, G. K.
A **curious** inconsistency of the Man in Black. Goldsmith, O.
A **curious** pleasure excursion. Twain, M.
The **curious** republic of Gondour. Twain, M.
Curl up and dye. Lovesey, P.

CURLEWS
  García Márquez, G. The night of the curlews
The **curlew's** cry. Bell, J. L.

Curley, Daniel
  Billy Will's song
    Curley, D. Living with snakes
  The contrivance
    Curley, D. Living with snakes
  The first baseman
    Curley, D. Living with snakes
  The inlet
    Curley, D. Living with snakes
  Living with snakes
    Curley, D. Living with snakes
  The other two
    Curley, D. Living with snakes
  Reflections in the ice
    Curley, D. Living with snakes
  Revenge
    Curley, D. Living with snakes
  Trinity
    Curley, D. Living with snakes
  Visiting the dead
    Curley, D. Living with snakes
  Wild geese
    Curley, D. Living with snakes
Current account. Tremain, R.

Currer, Barney
  Second coming
    The Antioch Review 42:409-15 Fall '84

Currey, Richard, 1949-
  Old fires
    The North American Review 271:23-5 S '86
  Waiting for trains
    The Best American short stories, 1988
    The North American Review 272:18-21 S '87
  The war of heaven
    Prize stories, 1988

Curry, Ginger Simpson
  Sea-serpents of Domnudale
    Tales of the Witch World 2
Curry, Ginger Simpson, and Conroy, Monika
  Guardians of the secret
    Magic in Ithkar 3; ed. by A. Norton and R. Adams
Curry, Peggy Simson, 1911-1987
  The brushoff
    She won the West; ed. by M. Muller and B. Pronzini
  Geranium House
    Westward the women; ed. by V. Piekarski
The **curse**. Dubus, A.
The **curse**. Prichard, K. S.
The **curse** of Hooligan's Bar. Fritch, C. E.
The **curse** of Igamor. De Larrabeiti, M.
The **curse** of the catafalques. Anstey, F.
The **curse** of the smalls and the stars. Leiber, F.

CURSES
  Barker, C. How spoilers bleed
  Burrage, A. M. Between the minute and the hour
  Crabtree, L. V. Prices' bewitched cow
  Erdrich, L. Snares
  Haldeman, J. W. Armaja das
  Jakes, J. Storm in a bottle
  Jones, G. The snow apples
  King, S. The man who would not shake hands
  Lovecraft, H. P. The hound
  Rushdie, S. The Prophet's hair
  Tremayne, P. The pooka
  Wellman, M. W. The little black train
CURSES, FAMILY
  Anstey, F. The curse of the catafalques
  Ingalls, R. Third time lucky
  Lee, H. The Mink Creek ghost
The **curtain** blown by the breeze. Spark, M.
The **curtain** falls. Asscher-Pinkhof, C.
CURTIS, EDWARD
                  About
  Doubiago, S. The art of seeing with one's own eyes
Curtis, Jack
  At thirteen
    Encounter (London, England) 66:14-19 My '86
  Mistress Bearberry & lovers
    Encounter (London, England) 69:32+ D '87
Curtis Loach. Daniels, C.
Curtiss, Ursula Reilly, 1923-1984
  A beneficial walk
    Curtiss, U. R. The house on Plymouth Street, and other stories
  Change of climate
    Curtiss, U. R. The house on Plymouth Street, and other stories
    The Penguin classic crime omnibus

Curtiss, Ursula Reilly, 1923-1984 — *Continued*

Good neighbor
  Curtiss, U. R. The house on Plymouth Street, and other stories
The house on Plymouth Street
  Curtiss, U. R. The house on Plymouth Street, and other stories
A judicious half inch
  Curtiss, U. R. The house on Plymouth Street, and other stories
The marked man
  Curtiss, U. R. The house on Plymouth Street, and other stories
  Ellery Queen's Memorable characters
  Masterpieces of mystery and suspense; ed. by M. H. Greenberg
The old barn on the pond
  Curtiss, U. R. The house on Plymouth Street, and other stories
Point of no return
  Curtiss, U. R. The house on Plymouth Street, and other stories
The pool sharks
  Curtiss, U. R. The house on Plymouth Street, and other stories
The right perspective
  Curtiss, U. R. The house on Plymouth Street, and other stories
Snowball
  Curtiss, U. R. The house on Plymouth Street, and other stories
Something green and growing
  Curtiss, U. R. The house on Plymouth Street, and other stories
Tiger by the tail
  Curtiss, U. R. The house on Plymouth Street, and other stories

Curval, Philippe

Progenitor
  The Penguin world omnibus of science fiction

Curwood, James Oliver

Back to God's country
  The Second reel West; ed. by B. Pronzini and M. H. Greenberg

Cusack, Isabel Langis

Love song
  Good Housekeeping 204:138-9 F '87

Cushi. Woodforde, C.

The **cushion** of time. Updike, D.

Cushman, Dan

I.O.U.—one bullet
  Wild westerns; ed. by B. Pronzini

Cusie. Reynolds, S.

CUSTER, GEORGE ARMSTRONG, 1839-1876

About

Utley, S., and Waldrop, H. Custer's last jump

Custer's ghost. Howard, C.

Custer's last jump. Utley, S., and Waldrop, H.

The **custodians**. Cowper, R.

Customs of the country. Bell, M. S.

The **customs** of the country. Morris, W.

Cut glass. Barthelme, F.

Cut to: murder. Fontana, D. C.

Cuts. Wilson, F. P.

The **cutter**. Bryant, E.

Cuttings. Hoffman, W.

Cutt's grace. Morrow, B.

CV10. Flythe, M., Jr.

Cyankali. Wegner, H.

CYBERNETICS

  See also Bionics

  Dick, P. K. Service call
  MacLean, K. The missing man

CYBORGS *See* Bionics

Cycle. Loewald, U.

Cycles. Antieau, K.

Cycling posture. Broun, H.

CYPRESS

  Perry, M. C. Stumps

The **Cyprian** bees. Wynne, A.

The **Cyprian** cat. Sayers, D. L.

The **Cypriot** man. Ṣāliḥ, al-Ṭ.

CYPRUS

  Ioannides, P. The unseen aspect

Nicosia

  Ṣāliḥ, al-Ṭ. The Cypriot man

Cyrion in wax. Lee, T.

Czadek. Russell, R.

CZARIST RUSSIA *See* Soviet Union—1900-1917

Czarnoleka: Black Meadow. Anderman, J.

Czarny, Halina

Signs
  The North American Review 271:21-5 D '86

CZECHOSLOVAKIA

  Klíma, I. My country
  Klíma, I. The truth game
  Šmahelová, H. House of joy

Rural life

  Klíma, I. Sunday morning: a foolish tale
  Lurie, M. A red fox, a Polish lady, a Russian samovar

Marienbad

  Davenport, G. The chair

Prague

  Ahern, T. Chenken and Nartzarzen in several days on the town
  Buzzati, D. Kafka's houses
  Kaplický, V. Theatrum magnum
  Klíma, I. Friday morning: an orderly's tale
  Klíma, I. Monday morning: a black market tale
  Klíma, I. Saturday morning: a thief's tale
  Klíma, I. Thursday morning: an erotic tale
  Klíma, I. Tuesday morning: a sentimental story
  Klíma, I. Wednesday morning: a Christmas conspiracy tale

CZECHOSLOVAKIAN SOLDIERS *See* Soldiers—Czechoslovakia

D

D.M.Z.. Yu, H.-J.

A **D-minor** fugue. Dorr, L.

Da Costa, Flavio Moreira
Life, passion, and death of Glutton da Silva, the man who ate films
The Literary Review (Madison, N.J.) 27:483-91 Summ '84

DA PONTE, LORENZO, 1749-1838
About
Morazzoni, M. The dignity of Signor Da Ponte

DA VINCI, LEONARDO *See* Leonardo, da Vinci, 1452-1519

Da Vinci is dead. Hamilton, R. C.

Dabbs, Daniell E.
Arriki
Isaac Asimov's Tomorrow's voices

Dabrowska, Cecilia
Huntress
Short story international 62
Paradise sheldrake
Short story international 49
Red stag
Short story international 47

Dabrowska, Maria
Miss Vincent
Russian and Polish women's fiction; ed. by H. Goscilo

Dabydeen, Cyril, 1945-
Mannita's garden cove
The Literary Review (Madison, N.J.) 29:423-9 Summ '86

The **dacha.** Stewart, N.

DACHSHUNDS
Spark, M. Alice Long's dachshunds

Dad, I need you now. McWey, M.

DADD, RICHARD, 1819-1887
About
Wiebe, D. E. The fairy feller's master stroke

Daddy. Godwin, E.

Daddy Rat. Jones, C.

Daddy's baby. Franco, M.

Daddy's big girl. Le Guin, U. K.

Dadswell, Mary, 1943-
The apology
Dadswell, M. Circles of faces
Backtracking
Dadswell, M. Circles of faces
The bed
Dadswell, M. Circles of faces
The concert
Dadswell, M. Circles of faces
Crockfoot Lilli
Dadswell, M. Circles of faces
Eighth birthday
Dadswell, M. Circles of faces
The game
Dadswell, M. Circles of faces

"Hello?"
Dadswell, M. Circles of faces
An interval of time
Dadswell, M. Circles of faces
The joys of speculating
Dadswell, M. Circles of faces
Lewd and lascivious conjugations
Dadswell, M. Circles of faces
Mimi
Dadswell, M. Circles of faces
Mr. Macnamee
Dadswell, M. Circles of faces
Mrs. McGrath
Dadswell, M. Circles of faces
On the way to the Goat
Dadswell, M. Circles of faces
Postscript
Dadswell, M. Circles of faces
Retirement
Dadswell, M. Circles of faces
Self-exposure
Dadswell, M. Circles of faces
A spectre of ancient dust
Dadswell, M. Circles of faces
Supper after the show
Dadswell, M. Circles of faces
Swinging round a circle
Dadswell, M. Circles of faces
To eat or not to eat
Dadswell, M. Circles of faces
A vignette of Susannah
Dadswell, M. Circles of faces

Dafne. Kessler, J. F.

Daft Jenny. Montgomerie, W.

Dagg, Mel
The second coming of Little Richard [excerpt]
Fatal recurrences; ed. by H. Hugh and P. O'Brien

Dagon, Janet
Waiting for Carrie
'Teen 32:30+ Ag '88
When Carrie came home
'Teen 32:24+ S '88

Dahl, Roald
The landlady
The Penguin classic crime omnibus
Man from the south
The Penguin book of horror stories
Royal jelly
The Treasury of English short stories; ed. by N. Sullivan
Taste
Through a glass, darkly; ed. by B. Woelfel
The wish
Ready or not; ed. by J. Kahn

Dai Houying
Father's milk is also blood transformed
Contemporary Chinese literature; ed. by M. S. Duke

Dai Qing
Anticipation
Roses and thorns; ed. by P. Link
No!
Contemporary Chinese literature; ed. by
M. S. Duke
The **daily** Chernobyl. Frazier, R.
Daisy, in the sun. Willis, C.
Daisy Miller. James, H.
Daisy Overend. Spark, M.
Daisy's Valentine. Gaitskill, M.
Daitch, Susan
Camera obscura
Between C & D; ed. by J. Rose and
C. Texier
DAKAR (SENEGAL) *See* Senegal—Dakar
DAKOTA INDIANS
Perea, R. L. Miracle at Chimayo
The **Dalai** Lama of Harlem. Faust, I.
Dale, Celia
Business lunch
John Creasey's Crime collection, 1985
Faery tale
The Mammoth book of modern crime
stories; ed. by G. Hardinge
Good investments
John Creasey's Crime collection, 1984
Kindness
Winter's crimes 17
Dale. Keillor, G.
Daley, Robert
The cannons of the Atocha
Men at sea; ed. by B. Aymar
Dall, Caroline Wells Healey, 1822-1912
Annie Gray: a tale
Between mothers & daughters; ed. by S.
Koppelman
DALLAS (TEX.) *See* Texas—Dallas
D'Allesandro, Sam
Nothing ever just disappears
Men on men; ed. by G. Stambolian
Dalva: how it happened to me. Harrison, J.
Daly, Carroll John, 1889-1958
Not my corpse
The Mammoth book of private eye
stories; ed. by B. Pronzini and M. H.
Greenberg
Three gun Terry
The Black mask boys; ed. by W. F.
Nolan
Daly, Patricia
Our family doctors
Encounter (London, England) 63:3-8 D
'84
Dam on crutches. Aćin-Kosta, M.
Dame Inowslad. Gilchrist, M.
Dame of the British Empire, BBC. Gilliatt,
P.
The **damned**. Blackwood, A.
The **damned**. Tobin, G.
Damned funny. Kaye, M.
The **damned** thing. Bierce, A.

Damon, Philip
Davidson among the chosen
The Ploughshares reader: new fiction for
the eighties
DAMS
Ibuse, M. Kuchisuke's valley
Dan Peters and Casey Jones. Schramm, W.
L.
Danby, Mary, 1941-
Robbie
Haunting women; ed. by A. Ryan
Dance. Asscher-Pinkhof, C.
A **dance**. Mazel, D.
The **dance**. Thomas, A. C.
Dance for the king. Aikin, J.
DANCE HALLS
Abbott, K. Spanish Castle
Kees, W. Gents 50¢/Ladies 25¢
Trevor, W. The ballroom of romance
Valenzuela, L. Country carnival
Woolrich, C. The dancing detective
Dance me outside. Kinsella, W. P.
Dance of the bloodless ones. James, F.
The **Dance** of the Changer and the Three.
Carr, T.
Dance of the damned. Burks, A. J.
Dance of the dead. Matheson, R.
A **dance** with a dolly with a hole in her
stocking. McElroy, C. J.
A **dance** with Alison. Pritchard, M.
The **dancer**. Swados, H.
A **dancer** in the lake. Doucette, R. J.
Dancer on the edge. Brown, B. C.
DANCERS
Blochman, L. G. Murder walks in marble
halls
Böll, H. The death of Elsa Baskoleit
Colette. After midnight
Colette. Bastienne's child
Colette. "Châ"
Colette. The hard worker
Colette. The misfit
Colette. The quick-change artist
Cook, H. A lesson in dance
Ekwensi, C. The ivory dancer
Ferré, R. Sleeping beauty
Fisher, R. Miss Cynthie
Gordon, M. Watching the tango
Hecht, B. Specter of the Rose
Irish, W. The dancing detective
Kawabata, Y. The rooster and the dancing
girl
Kelly, J. P., and Kessel, J. Friend
Kim, I.-S. Tombstone without an inscrip-
tion
Maupassant, G. de. The dancers
Maupassant, G. de. Virtue in the ballet
McElroy, C. J. Take mama's picture out
of the light
Oates, J. C. Señorita
Phillips, J. A. El Paso
Robinson, S., and Robinson, J. Stardance
Swados, H. The dancer

DANCERS—*Continued*
  Whittier, G. Turning out
The **dancers**. Maupassant, G. de
DANCING
  Boehm, L. Two-bit piece
  Francis, H. E. A chronicle of love
  Jerome, J. K. The dancing partner
  Johnson, D. The big sway
  Kiely, B. Your left foot is crazy
  Lynch, L. Jefferson II: in and out of the
    darkness
  Mazel, D. A dance
  Peterson, M. To dance
  Thomas, A. C. The dance
  Wetherell, W. D. Spitfire autumn
  Woolrich, C. Dead on her feet
Dancing. Bissoondath, N.
Dancing. Kinsella, W. P.
Dancing bear. Vanderhaeghe, G.
The **dancing** detective. Irish, W.
The **dancing** detective. Woolrich, C.
Dancing girls. Atwood, M.
Dancing in the movies. Boswell, R.
Dancing in Trolley Square. Roberts, N.
Dancing on Tishe B'av. Raphael, L.
The **dancing** partner. Jerome, J. K.
The **dancing** party. Gordon, M.
Dancing the night away. Choyce, L.
Dancing with father. Flynt, C.
Dancing with gloom and broken noses.
    Haines, H. A.
Dancing with my sister Jane. Flook, M.
Dandelion golf. Gasner, D.
Dandurand, Anne
  (jt. auth) See Dé, Claire, and Dandurand,
    Anne
Danes, Julia Johnson
  Not marrying Martha
    Mademoiselle 90:134+ O '84
DANES
        See also Vikings
            England
  Weldon, F. Au pair
Danger out of the past. Gardner, E. S.
The **danger** zone. Gardner, E. S.
The **dangerous** business. Block, L.
Dangerous orders. Savage, L.
The **dangerous** people. Brown, F.
Dangerous sport. Fremlin, C.
Dangerous structure. Gilbert, M.
A **dangerous** thing, Mrs. Craggs. Keating, H.
    R. F.
Dangerous widows. Eberhart, M. G.
Danger's flower. Davin, D.
Dangers of the world. Herman, E.
Dangor, Achmat
  A strange romance
    The Penguin book of Southern African
    stories
Daniel. Kornblatt, J. R.
Daniel the Just. Böll, H.

Daniélou, Alain
  The game of dice
    The Penguin book of ghost stories
Daniels, Charlie, 1936-
  A Carolina Christmas carol
    Daniels, C. The devil went down to
    Georgia
  Chatham County
    Daniels, C. The devil went down to
    Georgia
  Christmas at the line shack
    Daniels, C. The devil went down to
    Georgia
  Curtis Loach
    Daniels, C. The devil went down to
    Georgia
  The devil went down to Georgia
    Daniels, C. The devil went down to
    Georgia
  Honky-Tonk Avenue
    Daniels, C. The devil went down to
    Georgia
  Lacy Mallard
    Daniels, C. The devil went down to
    Georgia
  The legend of Wooley Swamp
    Daniels, C. The devil went down to
    Georgia
  Me and Deke
    Daniels, C. The devil went down to
    Georgia
  Mrs. Effie
    Daniels, C. The devil went down to
    Georgia
  Mrs. Eloise
    Daniels, C. The devil went down to
    Georgia
  Radio Smith
    Daniels, C. The devil went down to
    Georgia
  The story of uneasy rider
    Daniels, C. The devil went down to
    Georgia
  Swami Swafford
    Daniels, C. The devil went down to
    Georgia
  Trudy
    Daniels, C. The devil went down to
    Georgia
Daniels, Les
  They're coming for you
    Cutting edge; ed. by D. Etchison
Daniel's garden. Borders, A.
Dann, Jack
  Bad medicine
    The Year's best science fiction, second
    annual collection
  Between the windows of the sea
    Shadows 8
  Blind shemmy
    Omni book of science fiction 3
    The Year's best science fiction, first an-
    nual collection

Dann, Jack—*Continued*
Camps
Masters of darkness; ed. by D. Etchison
A Treasury of World War II stories; ed.
by B. Pronzini and M. H. Greenberg
Night visions
100 great fantasy short short stories; ed.
by I. Asimov; T. Carr and M. H.
Greenberg
Tattoos
Omni (New York, N.Y.) 9:68-70+ N '86
The Year's best science fiction, fourth
annual collection
Visitors
The Architecture of fear; ed. by K.
Cramer and P. D. Pautz
Dann, Jack, and Dann, Jeanne Van Buren
The apotheosis of Isaac Rosen
Omni (New York, N.Y.) 9:113+ Je '87
Dann, Jeanne Van Buren
(jt. auth) See Dann, Jack, and Dann,
Jeanne Van Buren
Dannay, Frederic, 1905-1982
*For works written by this author in
collaboration with Manfred Lee see
Queen, Ellery*
Danny in transit. Leavitt, D.
Danny's chick. Thompson, J.
Danny's girl. Mukherjee, B.
Danse pseudomacabre. Williams, W. C.
Dantin, Louis
You're coughing?
The Oxford book of French-Canadian
short stories
DANUBE RIVER
Blackwood, A. The willows
Dark blue. Dawson, F.
A **dark** blue perfume. Rendell, R.
The **dark** boy. Derleth, A. W.
A **dark-brown** dog. Crane, S.
Dark, dark. Matthews, J.
The **dark** eidolon. Smith, C. A.
Dark eye. Petrakis, H. M.
The **dark** glasses. Spark, M.
Dark in the forest, strange as time. Wolfe,
T.
Dark melody of madness. Woolrich, C.
The **dark** men. Dubus, A.
The **dark** messiah. Wolfe, T.
The **dark** mirror. Cameron, E.
A **dark** Norwegian person. Gold, H.
The **Dark** Ones. Matheson, R. C.
The **dark** road home. Fairman, P. W.
The **dark** room. Williams, T.
Dark Rosaleen. Brand, M.
Dark secrets. Ross, V.
The **dark** shadow. Pohl, F.
The **dark** snake. Dorris, M.
Dark steps. Wallace, S. R.
The **dark** wood. Hospital, J. T.
The **dark** world. Kuttner, H.
Darkness. Andreyev, L.
Darkness and light. Brown, G. M.

The **darkness** of love. Boswell, R.
Darkness over Mirhold. Mathews, P. S.
Darlene makes a move. Keillor, G.
Darling, Jean
A bite of the pie
Ellery Queen's Prime crimes
The matchstick hut
Distant danger; ed. by J. Van de
Wetering
Darling Odile. Farmer, B.
Darwish, Ali
What happened the day of the big
meeting?
Egyptian tales and short stories of the
1970s and 1980s
Das **Wasser** ist kalt. Williams, T.
Dash, Joan
Careful, or you might get scratched
Seventeen 44:244-5+ Mr '85
Comfort and joy
Redbook 166:72+ Ap '86
The holdout
McCall's 111:86-7+ Je '84
Just before the wedding
Good Housekeeping 198:144-5 Je '84
A **dash** of murder. Morrison, J.
DASSIN, JOE, 1938-1980
About
Lopatin, J. The death of Joe Dassin
A **date** at nine. Ferreira, R.
A **date** with Dmitri. Mattison, A.
A **date** with fate. Yellin, L. N.
DATING (SOCIAL CUSTOMS)
Abbott, K. Harum scarum
Abbott, K. A little surprise
Ardizzone, T. Idling
Boyle, T. C. I dated Jane Austen
Briskin, M. Before and after Celeste
Choyce, L. Breakage
Crowell, D. Work
Drake, R. First date
Floyd, P. L. The silver DeSoto
Gold, H. Blind, blind date
Highsmith, P. The romantic
Hoctel, P. Bad pictures
Hood, H. Breaking off
Huggan, I. Getting out of Garten
Janowitz, T. Engagements
Janowitz, T. Patterns
Johnston, S. Jesse and Louise
Kirk-Kuwaye, C. Complete with fireworks
above Magic Island
Lipman, E. A daughter your age
Lipman, E. Land of the midnight sun
Lipman, E. Obit
Lipman, E. You're right, I know you're
right
McKnight, R. First I look at the purse
Murphy, P. Jester
Nordan, L. John Thomas Bird
O'Hara, J. Common sense should tell you
Okudzhava, B. S. Singular misfortunes
amidst a parade of successes

DATING (SOCIAL CUSTOMS) — *Continued*
  Petrakis, H. M. The sweet life
  Rifaat, A. Me and my sister
  Rodoreda, M. Rain
  Silva, B. Poet
  Spencer, E. A southern landscape
  Spivack, K. The hat
  Steele, M. Ah love! Ah me!
  Swados, H. A story for Teddy
  Thurm, M. Romance
  Vanderhaeghe, G. Drummer
  Wesseler, M. June's night
  West, J. The second (or perhaps third) time round
  Wetherell, W. D. The bass, the river, and Sheila Mant
Dating your mom. Frazier, I.
Daudet, Alphonse, 1840-1897
  The elixir [Variant title: The elixir of the Reverend Father Gaucher]
    Inspired by drink; ed. by Joan Digby and John Digby
  The last class
    Classic European short stories; ed. by R. Beum
Dauenhauer, Nora
  Egg boat
    Earth power coming; ed. by S. J. Ortiz
Daugherty, Leo
  Pig thieves on Ptolemy: a tale of the Tricentennial
    Omni (New York, N.Y.) 9:100-2+ O '86
Daugherty, Steven Roy
  Claws of the white hawk
    Bringing down the moon; ed. by J. Anderson
Daugherty, Tracy
  Low rider
    The New Yorker 63:40-8 N 23 '87
Daughter. Caldwell, E.
The **daughter** and the tradesman. Ardizzone, T.
Daughter of Lescale. Sparling, E. E.
Daughter of Regals. Donaldson, S. R.
A **daughter** of the aurora. London, J.
Daughter of the mango season. Wendt, A.
Daughter of the revolution. McElroy, J.
Daughter of the Yellow River. Wang Jiada
A **daughter** your age. Lipman, E.
DAUGHTERS *See* Fathers and daughters; Mothers and daughters; Stepdaughters
Daughters. Munves, J.
A **daughter's** duty. Hudson, H.
A **daughter's** heart. Engberg, S.
DAUGHTERS-IN-LAW
  Brown, M. W. New dresses
  Cohen, M. The sins of Tomas Benares
The **Dauphin's** doll. Queen, E.
D'Aurevilly, J. Barbey *See* Barbey d'Aurevilly, J., 1808-1889

Davenport, Guy
  Apples and pears: Het Erewhonisch schetsboek: Messidor-Vendémiaire 1981
    Davenport, G. Apples and pears, and other stories
  The bicycle rider
    Davenport, G. The Jules Verne steam balloon
  The bowmen of Shu
    Davenport, G. Apples and pears, and other stories
  Bronze leaves and red
    Davenport, G. The Jules Verne steam balloon
  The chair
    Davenport, G. Apples and pears, and other stories
    Harper's 269:60-1 S '84
  Les exploits de Nat Pinkerton de jour en jour: un texte de René Magritte translated and improved
    Davenport, G. The Jules Verne steam balloon
  Fifty-seven views of Fujiyama
    Davenport, G. Apples and pears, and other stories
  The Haile Selassie Funeral Train
    The Art of the tale; ed. by D. Halpern
  Jonah
    Davenport, G. The Jules Verne steam balloon
  The Jules Verne steam balloon
    Davenport, G. The Jules Verne steam balloon
  The meadow [Variant title: Wild clover]
    Davenport, G. The Jules Verne steam balloon
  Pyrrhon of Elis
    Davenport, G. The Jules Verne steam balloon
  The ringdove sign
    Davenport, G. The Jules Verne steam balloon
  We often think of Lenin at the clothespin factory
    Davenport, G. The Jules Verne steam balloon
  Wild clover [Variant title: The meadow]
    New directions in prose and poetry 50
Dave's depression. Goldman, E. S.
Daviau, Diane-Monique
  Under the bell jar
    Intimate strangers; ed. by M. Cohen and W. Grady
David and Agnes, a romance. Keillor, G.
David's charm. Boone, B.
David's song. Harlow, E.
Davidson, Avram
  Duke Pasquale's ring
    The Year's best science fiction, third annual collection

Davidson, Avram—*Continued*
Full chicken richness
  The Year's best science fiction, first annual collection
Great is Diana
  Masterpieces of fantasy and enchantment; ed. by D. G. Hartwell
The last wizard
  100 great fantasy short short stories; ed. by I. Asimov; T. Carr and M. H. Greenberg
The lord of Central Park [Variant title: Manhattan night's entertainment]
  Manhattan mysteries; ed. by B. Pronzini; C. L. R. Waugh and M. H. Greenberg
Naples
  The Best of Shadows; ed. by C. L. Grant
Sleep well of nights
  Baker's dozen: 13 short fantasy novels
The Slovo stove
  Universe 15
Davidson, Lionel
I do dwell
  Winter's crimes 16
Indian rope trick
  The Mammoth book of modern crime stories; ed. by G. Hardinge
Davidson among the chosen. Damon, P.
Davie, Elspeth
Accompanists
  Davie, E. A traveller's room
Bones and bouquets
  Davie, E. A traveller's room
A botanist's romance
  Davie, E. A traveller's room
Bulbs
  Davie, E. A traveller's room
Couchettes
  Davie, E. A traveller's room
A field in space
  Davie, E. A traveller's room
The free fur coat
  Davie, E. A traveller's room
The gift
  Davie, E. A traveller's room
Green head
  Davie, E. A traveller's room
In the train
  Davie, E. A traveller's room
Kiosk encounter
  Davie, E. A traveller's room
Lines
  Davie, E. A traveller's room
Out of order
  Davie, E. A traveller's room
The return
  Davie, E. A traveller's room
Security
  Davie, E. A traveller's room
Shoe in the sand
  Davie, E. A traveller's room

The stamp
  Davie, E. A traveller's room
Thorns and gifts
  Davie, E. A traveller's room
A traveller's room
  Davie, E. A traveller's room
Davies, Andrew
Early Bird & Smiley Face
  Encounter (London, England) 70:14-18 F [i.e. Mr] '88
Davies, Dorothy
A quiet man
  Short story international 68
Davies, Peter Ho
Mountain
  Critical Quarterly 30:55-62 Aut '88
Davies, Vaughan
A line of communication
  Critical Quarterly 30:67-71 Spr '88
Dávila, Amparo
Haute cuisine
  Other fires; ed. by A. Manguel
Davin, Dan, 1913-
Below the heavens
  Davin, D. The salamander and the fire
Bourbons
  Davin, D. The salamander and the fire
Cassino casualty
  Davin, D. The salamander and the fire
Coming and going
  Davin, D. The salamander and the fire
Danger's flower
  Davin, D. The salamander and the fire
The dog and the dead
  Davin, D. The salamander and the fire
Finders and losers
  Davin, D. The salamander and the fire
The general and the nightingale
  Davin, D. The salamander and the fire
In transit
  Davin, D. The salamander and the fire
Jaundiced
  Davin, D. The salamander and the fire
Liberation
  Davin, D. The salamander and the fire
Mortal
  Davin, D. The salamander and the fire
North of the Sangro
  Davin, D. The salamander and the fire
Not substantial things
  Davin, D. The salamander and the fire
The Persian's grave
  Davin, D. The salamander and the fire
Psychological warfare at Cassino
  Davin, D. The salamander and the fire
Under the bridge
  Davin, D. The salamander and the fire
Unwrung withers
  Davin, D. The salamander and the fire
When mum died
  Davin, D. The salamander and the fire

Davis, Christopher
The boys in the bars
  Men on men 2; ed. by G. Stambolian
Davis, Dorothy Salisbury, 1916-
Backward, turn backward
  Davis, D. S. Tales for a stormy night
  Hitchcock in prime time; ed. by F. M.
    Nevins and M. H. Greenberg
Born killer
  Davis, D. S. Tales for a stormy night
By the scruff of the soul
  Davis, D. S. Tales for a stormy night
The Devil and his due
  Davis, D. S. Tales for a stormy night
The last party
  Davis, D. S. Tales for a stormy night
Lost generation
  Davis, D. S. Tales for a stormy night
A matter of public notice
  Davis, D. S. Tales for a stormy night
Meeting at the crossroad
  Davis, D. S. Tales for a stormy night
Mrs. Norris observes
  Davis, D. S. Tales for a stormy night
The muted horn
  Davis, D. S. Tales for a stormy night
Natural causes
  Davis, D. S. Tales for a stormy night
  The Year's best mystery and suspense
    stories, 1984
Old friends
  Davis, D. S. Tales for a stormy night
The purple is everything
  The Crime of my life; ed. by B. Gar-
    field
  Davis, D. S. Tales for a stormy night
Spring fever
  Davis, D. S. Tales for a stormy night
  Ellery Queen's Memorable characters
Sweet William
  Davis, D. S. Tales for a stormy night
Till death do us part
  Murder in Manhattan; ed. by B. Adler
Davis, Frederick C., 1902-1977
Fingers of fear
  Hard-boiled dames; ed. by B. A. Drew
Mark of the Moon Man
  A Cent a story! Ed. by G. G. Roberts
The mole men want your eyes
  The Weirds; ed. by S. Jaffery
Davis, G. P.
African story
  P.E.N. new fiction I
Davis, Jessica Thorpe
The spirit sweep
  Essence 16:58-9+ Ag '85
Davis, Kiernan
Roach bait
  Homewords: a book of Tennessee
    writers; ed. by D. Paschall
Davis, Lydia
The bone
  Davis, L. Break it down

Break it down
  Davis, L. Break it down
The brother-in-law
  Davis, L. Break it down
City employment
  Davis, L. Break it down
Cockroaches in autumn
  Davis, L. Break it down
The cottages
  Davis, L. Break it down
Extracts from a life
  Davis, L. Break it down
The fears of Mrs. Orlando
  Davis, L. Break it down
A few things wrong with me
  Davis, L. Break it down
Five signs of disturbance
  Davis, L. Break it down
French lesson I: le meurtre
  Davis, L. Break it down
The house plans
  Davis, L. Break it down
The housemaid
  Davis, L. Break it down
The letter
  Davis, L. Break it down
Liminal: the little man
  Davis, L. Break it down
The mouse
  Davis, L. Break it down
Mr. Burdoff's visit to Germany
  Davis, L. Break it down
Once a very stupid man
  Davis, L. Break it down
Sketches for a life of Wassilly
  Davis, L. Break it down
The sock
  Davis, L. Break it down
  Sudden fiction; ed. by R. Shapard and
    J. Thomas
Story
  Davis, L. Break it down
  Harper's 273:32-4 S '86
Therapy
  Davis, L. Break it down
Two sisters
  Davis, L. Break it down
Visit to her husband
  Davis, L. Break it down
What an old woman will wear
  Davis, L. Break it down
Davis, Rebecca Harding, 1831-1910
An ignoble martyr
  Old maids; ed. by S. Koppelman
Davis, Richard Harding, 1864-1916
Gallegher
  Isaac Asimov presents the best crime
    stories of the 19th century
Davis, Sam, 1850-1918
A Carson poker incident
  Davis, S. A miner's Christmas carol, and
    other frontier tales

Davis, Sam, 1850-1918—*Continued*
  The circus advance agent
    Davis, S. A miner's Christmas carol, and
      other frontier tales
  A fair exchange
    Davis, S. A miner's Christmas carol, and
      other frontier tales
  The hermit of Treasure Peaks
    Davis, S. A miner's Christmas carol, and
      other frontier tales
  Mark Haverly
    Davis, S. A miner's Christmas carol, and
      other frontier tales
  A miner's Christmas carol
    Davis, S. A miner's Christmas carol, and
      other frontier tales
  Miss Armstrong's homicide
    Davis, S. A miner's Christmas carol, and
      other frontier tales
  The pocket-miner
    Davis, S. A miner's Christmas carol, and
      other frontier tales
  Schools and stocks
    Davis, S. A miner's Christmas carol, and
      other frontier tales
DAVIS, SAMMY, JR.
                              About
    Friedman, B. J. Let's hear it for a beauti-
      ful guy
Davison, Scott
  The edge of the world
    Southwest Review 69:155-67 Spr '84
Daviú, Matilde
  Ofelia's transfiguration
    Anthology of contemporary Latin Ameri-
      can literature, 1960-1984
Davol, Marguerite W.
  Flesh and blood
    Werewolves; ed. by J. Yolen and M. H.
      Greenberg
Davy Jones's gift. Masefield, J.
Dawkins, Cecil, 1927-
  The mourner
    The Art of fiction in the heart of Dixie;
      ed. by P. D. Beidler
Dawn. Asscher-Pinkhof, C.
Dawn. Colette
Dawn. Purdy, J.
Dawn attack. Forester, C. S.
The **dawn** of a new day. Sisskind, M.
Dawn of flame. Weinbaum, S. G.
Dawson, Clare
  Supergrass
    John Creasey's Crime collection, 1984
  To have and to hold
    John Creasey's Crime collection, 1985
Dawson, Fielding, 1930-
  Bebe
    Dawson, F. Will she understand?
  Blue
    Dawson, F. Will she understand?
  The blue in the sky
    Dawson, F. Will she understand?

Dark blue
  Dawson, F. Will she understand?
Dorothy
  Dawson, F. Will she understand?
Double vision—The rewrite
  Dawson, F. Will she understand?
The dream
  Dawson, F. Will she understand?
End of a dream
  Dawson, F. Will she understand?
Fan letter
  Dawson, F. Will she understand?
The fourth surprise
  Dawson, F. Will she understand?
Full circle
  Dawson, F. Will she understand?
Funny
  Dawson, F. Will she understand?
Ghost
  Dawson, F. Will she understand?
If
  Dawson, F. Will she understand?
It
  Dawson, F. Will she understand?
Kid stuff
  Dawson, F. Will she understand?
The man
  Dawson, F. Will she understand?
Mary will be good for Warren
  Dawson, F. Will she understand?
Miles
  Dawson, F. Will she understand?
Night
  Dawson, F. Will she understand?
Over there
  Dawson, F. Will she understand?
The planets
  Dawson, F. Will she understand?
The reason
  Dawson, F. Will she understand?
September in the rain
  Dawson, F. Will she understand?
Singing stars and stripes forever
  Dawson, F. Will she understand?
So
  Dawson, F. Will she understand?
The song
  Dawson, F. Will she understand?
Supreme Court defends 50 racial
    equivalence in nationwide police de-
    partments
  Dawson, F. Will she understand?
Triumph!
  Dawson, F. Will she understand?
The vertical fields
  Sudden fiction; ed. by R. Shapard and
    J. Thomas
The white
  Dawson, F. Will she understand?
Who was Ted?
  Dawson, F. Will she understand?
Yes!
  Dawson, F. Will she understand?

Day, Holman
  When Dustin "called on"
    The Best Maine stories; ed. by S. Phippen; C. Waugh and M. Greenberg
Day, Richard Cortez, 1927-
  Annunciation
    Day, R. C. When in Florence
  A Chagall story
    Day, R. C. When in Florence
  First love
    Day, R. C. When in Florence
  The fugitive
    The Kenyon Review ns6:34-47 Spr '84
  Grace
    Day, R. C. When in Florence
  Idiots
    Day, R. C. When in Florence
  Leaning man
    Day, R. C. When in Florence
  Massimo
    Day, R. C. When in Florence
  Memory
    Day, R. C. When in Florence
  Men are like children, like the beasts
    Day, R. C. When in Florence
  The pleasures of the senses
    Day, R. C. When in Florence
  Relative motion
    Day, R. C. When in Florence
  Two paces east
    Day, R. C. When in Florence
  Uccello
    Day, R. C. When in Florence
  Umbrella dance
    Day, R. C. When in Florence
  The violation
    Day, R. C. When in Florence
Day after day, like a terrible fish. McPherson, D.
The **day** after Saturday. See García Márquez, G. One day after Saturday
The **day** another Izumi Shikibu was born. Oe, K.
A **day** at Hot Creek. Collins, S. R.
Day at the beach. Emshwiller, C.
The **day** before. Endō, S.
The **day** before. Spencer, E.
Day for a picnic. Hoch, E. D.
A **day** for dying. Nuetzel, C.
The **day** Genghis Khan became angry. Tamer, Z.
The **day** I sat with Jesus on the sun deck and a wind came up and blew my kimono open and he saw my breasts. Sawai, G.
The **day** I shot my dog. Bell, M. S.
A **day** I'll never forget. Sisskind, M.
A **day** in the country. Jacobson, D.
A **day** in the country. Millhauser, S.
A **day** in the life. Ewart, C.
A **day** in the skin; or, The century we were out of them. Lee, T.
A **day** in town. Haycox, E.

The **day** Jimmy killed the rabbit. Hall, T. T.
Day million. Pohl, F.
The **day** my nose stopped growing. Rigby, R.
The **day** nothing happened. Clarke, T.
A **day** of encounters. Gilbert, A.
DAY OF JUDGMENT *See* Judgment Day
Day of mist and cloud. Anderman, J.
The **day** of reckoning. Highsmith, P.
Day of strange fortune. Severance, C.
Day of terror. Bellah, J. W.
The **day** of the bookmobile. McGerr, P.
The **day** of the bullet. Ellin, S.
The **day** of the butterflies. Bradley, M. Z.
The **day** of the execution. Slesar, H.
The **day** of the hawk. West, J.
The **day** of the ox. Brown, G. M.
The **day** of the picnic. Lutz, J.
Day out. Nicolai, D.
A **day** saved. Greene, G.
The **day** Stokowski saved the world. Kotzwinkle, W.
The **day** the bottom fell out of Yugoslavia. Lurie, M.
The **day** they burned the books. Rhys, J.
Day to die. Boylan, J.
Day trip. Schwartz, J.
The **day** we discovered we were black. Kilgore, D.
A **day** with a deer, a bear and Norah Smith. St. Pierre, P. H.
The **day** woman. Lipman, E.
Daybroke. Bloch, R.
Days. Eisenberg, D.
A **day's** journey. Petrakis, H. M.
Days of awe. Greenberg, J.
The **days** of October. Settle, M. L.
The **days** of Perky Pat. Dick, P. K.
The **days** of the Thunderbirds. Lee, A.
A **day's** wait. Hemingway, E.
Dayspring mishandled. Kipling, R.
Dazai, Osamu, 1909-1948
  Chiyojo
    A Late chrysanthemum; tr. by L. Dunlop
  The garden lantern
    A Late chrysanthemum; tr. by L. Dunlop
  A golden picture
    A Late chrysanthemum; tr. by L. Dunlop
  The lady who entertained
    The Mother of dreams, and other short stories; ed. by M. Ueda
  Magic lantern
    The Shōwa anthology 1
  Memories
    A Late chrysanthemum; tr. by L. Dunlop
Dazzled. Singer, I. B.
DDS 10752 Libra. Lutz, J., and Pachter, J.

Dé, Claire, and Dandurand, Anne
Case still open
    Invisible fictions; ed. by G. Hancock
Metamorphosis
    Invisible fictions; ed. by G. Hancock
De Alarcón, Pedro Antonio *See* Alarcón,
    Pedro Antonio de, 1833-1891
De Balzac, Honoré *See* Balzac, Honoré de,
    1799-1850
De Bruyn, Günter, 1926-
Someday he really will come home
    Voices East and West: German short
    stories since 1945
De Camp, L. Sprague (Lyon Sprague), 1907-
Divide and rule
    The Mammoth book of classic science
    fiction; ed. by I. Asimov; C. G.
    Waugh and M. H. Greenberg
The eye of Tandyla
    Wizards; ed. by I. Asimov; M. H.
    Greenberg and C. G. Waugh
Nothing in the rules
    The Science fictional Olympics; ed. by
    I. Asimov; M. H. Greenberg and C.
    G. Waugh
The wheels of if
    Alternative histories; ed. by C. G.
    Waugh and M. H. Greenberg
**De Camp, L. Sprague (Lyon Sprague), 1907-,
    and Pratt, Fletcher, 1897-1956**
The green magician
    Masterpieces of fantasy and enchant-
    ment; ed. by D. G. Hartwell
De Camp, Lyon Sprague *See* De Camp, L.
    Sprague (Lyon Sprague), 1907-
De Carteret, Guy Malet
Rainy day
    Encounter (London, England) 70:18-22 F
    '88
De Celles, Michel
Recurrence
    Invisible fictions; ed. by G. Hancock
DE' CONTI, GIOVANNI LOTARIO *See*
    Innocent III, Pope, 1160 or 61-1216
De Feo, Ronald
Solo pass
    The Hudson Review 41:289-99 Summ '88
De Forest, John William, 1826-1906
The brigade commander
    A Treasury of Civil War stories; ed. by
    M. H. Greenberg and B. Pronzini
De Haven, Tom
Clap hands! Here comes Charley
    De Haven, T. Sunburn Lake
He's all mine
    De Haven, T. Sunburn Lake
Where we'll never grow old
    De Haven, T. Sunburn Lake
De Jong, Daphne
Vagabundus Vinea
    Women's work; ed. by M. McLeod and
    L. Wevers

De la Mare, Walter, 1873-1956
A:B:O.
    Lost souls; ed. by J. Sullivan
Bad company
    Lost souls; ed. by J. Sullivan
    The Oxford book of English ghost
    stories
The creatures
    The Treasury of English short stories;
    ed. by N. Sullivan
Seaton's aunt
    Black water; ed. by A. Manguel
    Dark banquet; ed. by L. Child
    The Dark descent; ed. by D. G. Hart-
    well
De la Torre, Alfredo
Diamond eyes and pig tails
    Southwest tales; ed. by Alurista and X.
    Rojas-Urista
De la Torre, Lillian, 1902-
The adventure of the persistent marksman
    The New adventures of Sherlock
    Holmes; ed. by M. H. Greenberg and
    C. L. R. Waugh
The first locked room
    Death locked in; ed. by D. G. Greene
    and R. C. S. Adey
Milady bigamy
    The Crime of my life; ed. by B. Gar-
    field
    Masterpieces of mystery and suspense;
    ed. by M. H. Greenberg
The missing Shakespeare manuscript
    Chapter & hearse; ed. by M. Muller and
    B. Pronzini
The second sight of Dr. Sam: Johnson
    Distant danger; ed. by J. Van de
    Wetering
De la Torre Bueno, Theodore
The murder of the governor
    Ellery Queen's Prime crimes 2
De Larrabeiti, Michael
The curse of Igamor
    Imaginary lands; ed. by R. McKinley
Malagan and the Lady of Rascas
    Don't bet on the prince; ed. by J. Zipes
De Lint, Charles, 1951-
Laughter in the leaves
    Dragons and dreams; ed. by J. Yolen;
    M. H. Greenberg and C. G. Waugh
One chance
    Werewolves; ed. by J. Yolen and M. H.
    Greenberg
Uncle Dobbin's Parrot Fair
    The Year's best fantasy, first annual
    collection
The white road
    Tales of the Witch World [1]
De Metro, Joseph Campos- *See* Campos-De
    Metro, Joseph
De Oliveira, Lolio Lourenco *See* Oliveira,
    Lolio Lourenco de

De Queiroz, Dinah Silveira
  Guidance
    Other fires; ed. by A. Manguel
De Queiroz, Rachel
  Metonymy; or, The husband's revenge
    Other fires; ed. by A. Manguel
De Saint-Aubin, Horace *See* Balzac, Honoré de, 1799-1850
De Terán, Lisa St. Aubin *See* St. Aubin de Terán, Lisa, 1953-
De Walef, A. N.
  Untitled/wailing landscape
    The Kenyon Review ns8:44-6 Fall '86
DEACONS
  Chekhov, A. P. The duel
DEAD
      See also Funeral rites and ceremonies
  Andersen, H. C. The traveling companion
  Baldwin, D. Last respects
  Barker, C. Cabal
  Barker, C. Human remains
  Bradbury, R. I suppose you are wondering why we are here?
  Brennan, J. P. Road to Granville
  Buck, D. P. Aunt Agatha
  Caldwell, E. Savannah River payday
  Campbell, R. Loveman's comeback
  Carver, R. So much water so close to home
  Chekhov, A. P. The requiem
  Clark, M. Disquiet
  Collins, W. Mad Monkton
  Daniels, L. They're coming for you
  Dick, P. K. Rautavaara's case
  Dixon, S. Time to go
  Du Maurier, Dame D. Split second
  Garrett, G. P. Unmapped country
  Godwin, P. A matter of taste
  Greene, G. A little place off the Edgeware Road
  Hemingway, E. A natural history of the dead
  Jahnn, H. H. The diver
  Jahnn, H. H. Kebad Kenya
  Kawabata, Y. God's bones
  Kawabata, Y. Immortality
  Kees, W. The ceremony
  Kennedy, L. Tropism
  Kirk, R. An encounter by Mortstone pond
  Kirk, R. The invasion of the Church of the Holy Ghost
  Kirk, R. Lex Talionis
  Lavin, M. The living
  Lovecraft, H. P. Cool air
  Martin, G. R. R. Override
  Matheson, R. C., and Matheson, R. Where there's a will
  Maupassant, G. de. Was it a dream?
  Millman, L. The preserved woman
  The Monk of horror; or, The Conclave of corpses
  Mujica Láinez, M. Importance

  Nolan, W. F. Dead call
  Oates, J. C. Night-side
  Poe, E. A. The conversation of Eiros and Charmion
  Poe, E. A. The Duc de l'Omelette
  Poe, E. A. King Pest
  Poe, E. A. Shadow—a parable
  Rodgers, A. The boy who came back from the dead
  Sanford, W. M. Mr. Carmichael's room
  Schwob, M. The embalming-women
  Schwob, M. The sleeping city
  Scott, J. The American Book of the Dead
  Shacochis, B. Easy in the islands
  Shea, M. The autopsy
  Tieck, J. L. Wake not the dead
  Valenzuela, L. City of the unknown
  Wagner, K. E. Sticks
  Waldrop, H. Fair game
  Wan Zhi. Open ground
  Wells, H. G. The Plattner story
  Woolf, V. Sympathy
Dead air. Nicoll, G.
The **dead** and the dying. Verma, N.
The **dead** astronaut. Ballard, J. G.
Dead call. Nolan, W. F.
A **dead** city. Haris, P.
Dead copy. Lyons, A.
The **dead** cow in the canyon. Ferron, J.
The **dead** don't steal. Griffiths, E.
Dead drunk. Porges, A.
A **dead** end. Colette
The **dead** end. Kharal, N.
Dead end. Matheson, R. C.
Dead-end doctor. Bloch, R.
Dead eye. Disher, G.
The **dead** fiddler. Singer, I. B.
Dead finish. Pritchard, M.
Dead flower. Connolly, P.
Dead game. Masur, H. Q.
Dead giveaway. Prather, R. S.
Dead ground. Thomson, J.
The **dead** hand. Collins, W.
Dead-letter drop. Keating, H. R. F.
The **dead** man. Bradbury, R.
The **dead** man. Leiber, F.
Dead man. Lutz, J.
The **dead** man. Quiroga, H.
Dead man's mirror. Christie, A.
Dead man's spoons. Smith, I.
Dead men rise up never. Bradbury, R.
Dead on her feet. Woolrich, C.
The **dead** past. Asimov, I.
Dead possums. Ptacek, K.
Dead reckoning. Shacochis, B.
Dead ringer. Ullman, J. M.
Dead run. Bear, G.
A **dead** secret. O'Brien, F.-J.
Dead soldier. Estleman, L. D.
Dead talk. Tillman, L.
A **dead** woman's secret. Maupassant, G. de
Deadboy Donner and the Filstone Cup. Zelazny, R.

Deadhead coming down. Maron, M.
The **deadliest** art. Bloch, R.
Deadline. Gilden, M.
The **deadly** egg. Van de Wetering, J.
The **deadly** Mrs. Haversham. Nielsen, H.
The **deadly** orchid. Flynn, T. T.
Deadspace. Etchison, D.
Deadtime. Richards, J.
DEAF
   Bierce, A. Chickamauga
   Garrett, G. P. An evening performance
   Hardy, T. Old Mrs. Chundle
   Hoyt, M. S. The monastery floor
   Kees, W. I should worry
   Kim, T. Portrait of a shaman
   Maupassant, G. de. The deaf-mute
   St. Clair, M. The listening child
   Tremain, R. Wildtrack
   Turgenev, I. S. Mumú
   Umans, R. Speech
The **deaf-mute**. Maupassant, G. de
DEAFNESS *See* Deaf
Deal, Borden, 1922-1985
   Antaeus
      Mississippi writers v1: Fiction; ed. by D.
      Abbott
   The taste of melon
      The Saturday Evening Post 257:50-3+ S
      '85
The **deal**. Michaels, L.
Deal from the bottom. Ellison, H.
A **deal** in ostriches. Wells, H. G.
Deal with the D.E.V.I.L. Cogswell, T. R.
Dealers in doom. Barrett, W. E.
The **dealers'** yard. Stark, S. S.
**DEANS (CATHEDRAL AND COL-
   LEGIATE)** *See* Clergy, Anglican and
   Episcopal
Dear darling Mr. Ramage. See Rhys, J.
   Pioneers, oh, pioneers
Dear dead Pippa. Blythe, R.
Dear Dorie. Lutz, J.
'**Dear** ghost . . .'. Hughes, F.
Dear poisoner. Pronzini, B.
Dearmore, Ellen
   The adventure of the perpetual husbands
      The Womansleuth anthology; ed. by I.
      Zahava
DEATH
      See also Bereavement; Dead
   Abbott, L. K. The final proof of fate and
      circumstance
   Adams, A. La Señora
   Adams, A. Waiting for Stella
   Adams, G. G. The Christmas house
   Adisa, O. P. Me man Angel
   Agee, J. Stiller's pond
   Ahern, T. The discontent of Franz Boas
   Aichinger, I. Story in a mirror
   Al-Mak, A. Forty-one minarets
   Alcott, L. M. A double tragedy. An actor's
     story
   Alcott, L. M. The fate of the Forrests

Amichai, Y. Dicky's death
Amichai, Y. The times my father died
Andersen, B. The phone call
Anderson, S. Death in the woods
Andres, K. Things to draw
Andreyev, L. Lazarus
Andreyev, L. The seven who were hanged
Archer, J. Christina Rosenthal
Arredondo, I. The shunammite
Asscher-Pinkhof, C. Little white bundle
Asscher-Pinkhof, C. Neighbor below
Atwood, M. The sin eater
Auster, P. In the country of last things
   [excerpt]
Austin, M. H. The Castro baby
Baldwin, D. The shadow watchers
Banks, R. The child screams and looks
   back at you
Barthelme, D. 110 West Sixty-First Street
Barthelme, F. Aluminum house
Baxter, C. Cataract
Baxter, C. Surprised by joy
Baxter, C. Talk show
Beattie, A. Jacklighting
Beaumont, C. My grandmother's japonicas
Beckett, S. The calmative
Bell, D. You may not be an angel
Bell, M. S. The day I shot my dog
Bell, M. S. Triptych I
Bell, M. S. Triptych 2
Bellamy, J. D. Roth's deadman
Benedict, P. Dog
Benedict, P. Town smokes
Betts, D. Benson Watts is dead and in
   Virginia
Bierce, A. A watcher by the dead
Bird, C. A taste of earth
Bitov, A. Infantiev
Blei, N. The chair trick
Blew, M. C. Forby and the Mayan
   maidens
Bloch, R. A case of the stubborns
Bloch, R. The pin
Bloch, R. Reaper
Block, L. Leo Youngdahl, R.I.P.
Blythe, R. Dear dead Pippa
Blyton, C. The final solution
Botwinik, B. Death went astray
Bourjaily, V. The Duchess
Bowen, E. The visitor
Boyle, T. C. Stones in my passway, hell-
   hound on my trail
Brondoli, M. The death of the vice consul
Brown, R. M. Rubyfruit jungle [excerpt]
Brown, S. H. Communion
Bumpus, J. Heroes and villains
Burns, M. After hours
Burns, M. Suburbs of the Arctic Circle
Buzzati, D. The bewitched bourgeois
Byatt, A. S. The next room
Caldwell, E. Wild flowers
Calisher, H. The library
Cameron, P. Homework

DEATH—*Continued*

Campbell, E. Delphinium blue
Campbell, W. B. The favour
Campos-De Metro, J. The slugger heart
Carlson, R. The time I died
Chappell, F. The snow that is nothing in the triangle
Chernoff, M. Degan dying
Choe, C.-H. Hospital room 205
Claiborne, S. The gulag computer: dead souls in the terminal
Clarke, A. C. Death and the senator
Clee, M. A. Dust
Colum, P. The death of the rich man
Conroy, F. Celestial events
Cook, H. The white rabbit
Costello, K. The immortal soul of Tommy O'
Covino, M. The director of death
Cowan, P. The corner
Cowley, J. The silk
Crane, S. The black dog
Curley, D. Trinity
Davidson, A. Naples
Davin, D. Mortal
Day, R. C. A Chagall story
Day, R. C. Men are like children, like the beasts
De Haven, T. Where we'll never grow old
Deaver, P. F. The valence of common ions
Dick, P. K. Chains of air, web of aether
Dickens, C. A child's dream of a star
Dickson, M. M. The farmer
Dixon, S. Magna takes the calls
Dixon, S. The signing
Doctorow, E. L. The Water Works
Doctorow, E. L. The writer in the family
Dorr, L. Neither death nor life
Drewe, R. Sweetlip
Ekström, M. Left alone
Ekström, M. Perfect
Ellison, H. The avenger of death
Ellison, H. In lonely lands
Etchison, D. Deadspace
Etchison, D. Deathtracks
Eustis, H. Mister Death and the redheaded woman
Evans, E. Relics
Faik, S. By the fountain
Faik, S. Samovar
Faik, S. Tomb with an arbor
Faik, S. White gold
Fante, J. One of us
Federspiel, J. Death of a foal
Federspiel, J. The Monderau chronicle
Ferron, J. Armageddon
Ferron, J. The child
Ferron, J. How the old man died
Ferron, J. The lady from Ferme-Neuve
Ferron, J. The old heathen
Ferron, J. The sea-lion

Fisher, M. F. K. Notes on a necessary pact
Fisher, M. F. K. The weather within
Fleming, B. Happy New Year, Mr. Ganaway
Floyd, P. L. Secrets
Floyd, P. L. When Mother played Moonshine
Flythe, S. Walking, walking
Foltz-Gray, D. Departed coming back
Ford, J. H. Fishes, birds and sons of men
Franklin, P. Love under glass
Franzen, B. Hearing from Wayne
Freeman, J. The death of a Mormon elder
Friedman, P. A period of grace
García Márquez, G. Death constant beyond love
García Márquez, G. The other side of death
García Márquez, G. The third resignation
Garner, H. One-two-three little Indians
Gathorne-Hardy, J. The picnic
Geras, A. The green behind the glass
Gilbert, W. S. Little Mim
Gilbert, W. S. Tom Poulton's joke
Gilchrist, E. The blue-eyed Buddhist
Giles, M. The planter box
Giles, M. Rough translations
Gilliatt, P. Stephanie, Stephen, Steph, Steve
Gold, H. A ninety-six-year-old big sister
Grant, C. L. The old men know
Grau, S. A. Flight
Grau, S. A. Hunter
Grau, S. A. Widow's walk
Greene, G. Proof positive
Greene, G. The second death
Grin, A. Mystery on a moonlit night
Gustafsson, L. The bird in the breast
Hall, M. M. Rapture
Hall, T. T. Wet Stump
Han, M.-S. Shadow
Hannah, B. Even Greenland
Hartley, L. P. Mrs. Carteret receives
Hartley, L. P. Night fears
Hearn, L. Oshidori
Hempel, A. In the cemetery where Al Jolson is buried
Hempel, A. When it's human instead of when it's dog
Henry, O. A fog in Santone
Herbert, F. Murder will in
Highsmith, P. Chris's last party
Highsmith, P. The kite
Highsmith, P. Under a dark angel's eye
Hoffman, W. Altarpiece
Hoffman, W. Landfall
Hoffman, W. Patriot
Holleran, A. Friends at evening
Hong, S.-W. A boy in search of rest
Hood, M. The goodwife Hawkins
Hood, M. A man among men
Hood, M. Manly conclusions

DEATH—*Continued*

Huynh, Q. N. The family's secret move
Hyon, C.-G. The death of my grandmother
Johnson, W. Prayer for the dying
Johnston, G. The dying day of Francis Bainsbridge
Kaikō, T. The crushed pellet
Kaplan, D. M. Elias Schneebaum
Kauffman, J. Places in the world a woman could walk
Kawabata, Y. Death mask
Kawabata, Y. The incident of the dead face
Kearns, R. Grave angels
Keillor, G. Collection
Keizer, G. I am the burning bush
Kelman, J. The hon
Kercheval, J. L. Willy
Kessler, J. F. Xanthippe
Kilworth, G. The dissemblers
Kim, I.-S. Tombstone without an inscription
King, G. E. The story of a day
King, S. Gramma
King, S. The monkey
King, S. The reaper's image
Kirk, R. Watchers at the strait gate
Kittredge, W. Momentum is always the weapon
Klein, T. E. D. Black man with a horn
Knight, W. E. The resurrection man
Kociancich, V. Knight, death and the devil
Lafferty, R. A. Le Hot Sport
Lagerkvist, P. The myth of mankind
Landolfi, T. An abstract concept
Landolfi, T. Two wakes
Lavin, M. A voice from the dead (a monologue)
Lawrence, D. H. Odour of chrysanthemums
Le Guin, U. K. Small change
Leavitt, D. Spouse night
Lee, A. The ride
Lee, T. Elle est trois, (la mort)
Leedom-Ackerman, J. History lesson
Leedom-Ackerman, J. No marble angels
Liben, M. Frimmell's successor
Lieber, T. Country things
Lish, G. Guilt
Livesey, M. Jean and Little Aunt
Long, D. Great blue
López Heredia, J. The retiree
Loukakis, A. My neighbour's death
Lurie, M. The death of Rappaport
Lurie, M. Outrageous behaviour
MacDonald, D. R. The flowers of Bermuda
MacLaverty, B. Death of a parish priest
Mansfield, K. The fly
Martin, D. Amazing powers
Martin, R. Cliff Dwellers
Martin, V. Elegy for dead animals
Martin, V. The freeze

Mason, B. A. Blue country
Matheson, R. C. Dead end
Mathews, A. Nephritis
Matthews, J. Harry the woman killer
Matthews, J. The sound of a girl singing
Maupassant, G. de. The Devil
Mazel, D. Aunt Leah
McCormack, E. P. One picture of Trotsky
McGuane, T. Two hours to kill
Menaker, D. Brothers
Michaelson, L. W. Klitzee one—God zero
Michaelson, L. W. On my being dead
Michaelson, L. W. The rhyme in Freddy's face
Mohr, N. A time with a future (Carmela)
Monteleone, T. F. The night is freezing fast
Moore, B. The sight
Moore, G. A strange death
Morazzoni, M. The last assignment
Morazzoni, M. Order in the house
Morazzoni, M. The white door
Morris, W. Fiona
Morris, W. Real losses, imaginary gains
Morris, W. The sound tape
Morrow, B. Cutt's grace
Moyer, K. Movements of the hand
Mungoshi, C. Coming of the dry season
Murphy, Y. A good father
Murphy, Y. The slit
Murphy, Y. The summer the men landed on the moon
Murphy, Y. Where dead is best
Naipaul, S. A man of mystery
Nordan, L. The sin eater
Norris, L. The wind, the cold wind
Oates, J. C. Further confessions
Oates, J. C. Party
Oba, M. The Pale Fox
O'Brien, E. The small-town lovers
Ocampo, S. Mimoso
Ocampo, S. The photographs
O'Connor, F. The enduring chill
Ordan, D. Any minute Mom should come blasting through the door
Osborn, C. The circuit rider
Óskar, J. The man in the attic and the woman on the main floor
Paley, G. Friends
Palma, C. Mors ex vita
Palmer, V. Josie
Papaellinas, G. You told me
Pasternak, B. L. Suboctave story
Petrakis, H. M. Between sleep and death
Petrakis, H. M. Matsoukas
Pilcher, R. Gilbert
Pilcher, R. Spanish ladies
Pilcher, R. Toby
Piñera, V. The one who came to save me
Poe, E. A. The assignation
Poe, E. A. The case of M. Valdemar
Poe, E. A. The colloquy of Monos and Una

DEATH—*Continued*

Poe, E. A. The facts in the case of M. Valdemar

Poe, E. A. The facts of M. Valdemar's case

Poe, E. A. Mesmeric revelation

Poe, E. A. The visionary

Potter, N. A. J. Gypsies

Power, V. In the town of Ballymuck

Purdy, J. The candles of your eyes

Purdy, J. Short Papa

Quammen, D. Nathan's rime

Quiroga, H. The dead man

Regent, P. Pleasures of the flesh

Regent, P. The proposal

Rey Rosa, R. The release

Rey Rosa, R. A version of my death

Rhys, J. The sound of the river

Richards, J. Mencken stuff

Richler, M. The summer my grandmother was supposed to die

Roberts, N. A proper introduction

Rodoreda, M. The hen

Rodoreda, M. A white geranium petal

Russell, R. The bell

Ṣāliḥ, al-Ṭ. The Cypriot man

Salmonson, J. A. Angel's exchange

Sammān, G. Old enough to be your father . . .

Sargent, P. If ever I should leave you

Scholz, C. A draft of canto ci

Schwartz, L. S. The death of Harriet Gross

Schwartz, L. S. What I did for love

Schwob, M. The strigae

Sexson, L. Foxglove

Sheckley, R. Five minutes early

Shiga, N. At Kinosaki

Shukshin, V. M. The outsider

Silverberg, R. The Pope of the chimps

Singer, I. B. Short Friday

Singer, I. B. Strong as death is love

Skrzynecki, P. The black madonna

Skrzynecki, P. Indian mynas

Smith, C. A. The death of Malygris

Somers, A. The burial

Somers, A. The tunnel

Spofford, H. E. P. The amber gods

Sproat, R. A former security with Helen Damnation

St. Aubin de Terán, L. I never eat crabmeat now

St. Clair, M. The listening child

Stern, S. The book of Mordecai

Stern, S. Goldfinch & Son

Stern, S. Lazar Malkin enters heaven

Strand, M. Under water

Strieber, W. Pain

Sutter, B. You ain't dead yet

Swift, G. Chemistry

Swift, G. The hypochondriac

Takenishi, H. The rite

Tamer, Z. The ancient gate

Tamer, Z. An angry man

Tamer, Z. The family

Taylor, A. Bye bye Billy

Thomas, D. The visitor

Thompson, J. Lenny dying, Pacific standard time

Thompson, J. Remembering Sonny

Thompson, K. Goodbye

Tinkham, B. Doppelganger

Titcher, M. No fairies at the bottom of the garden

Tournier, M. Death and the maiden

Ty-Casper, L. Application for a small life

Updike, D. Indian summer

Upward, E. Her day

Upward, E. The white-pinafored black cat

Vanderhaeghe, G. Dancing bear

Vargas, K. The corpse

Varley, J. The persistence of vision

Vaughan, D. The death of a champion

Verma, N. Exile

Viramontes, H. M. The moths

Virgo, S. Brother Dael's new year

Virgo, S. Shan Val Mór

Wagner, R. E. I'm going down to watch the horses come alive

Wakefield, H. R. "He cometh and he passeth by!"

Warner, S. T. The mother tongue

Watson, S. Antigone

Welch, D. The coffin on the hill

Welch, D. Full circle

Welch, D. The trout stream

West, J. The day of the hawk

West, J. The wake

Wharton, E. The fullness of life

White, P. Down at the dump

Whitehead, J. Joiner [excerpt]

Whittier, G. B. Lost time accident

Wilbur, E. Safe

Williams, T. Chronicle of a demise

Williams, T. Mother Yaws

Williamson, J. N. They never even see me

Wilner, H. St. Denis

Wilner, H. Whitestone & Greenberg

Winton, T. Death belongs to the dead, his father told him, and sadness to the sad

Winton, T. A measure of eloquence

Winton, T. Wilderness

Wodhams, J. Aunt Agnes

Wolfe, G. Checking out

Wolfe, T. Death the proud brother

Woolf, V. Three pictures

Working, R. Resurrectionists

Yŏm, S. The last moment

Young, R. F. A drink of darkness

Yourcenar, M. Aphrodissia, the widow

Yourcenar, M. The end of Marko Kraljević

Yourcenar, M. The last love of Prince Genji

Ziem, J. Statement

DEATH, APPARENT

Chesbro, G. C. Strange prey

DEATH, APPARENT—*Continued*

Freeman, C. Before he went out west
Hornung, E. W. An old flame
Maupassant, G. de. The spasm
Trevor, W. A complicated nature
Death and the cherry tree. Bates, H. E.
Death and the child. Crane, S.
Death and the dancing shadows. Reasoner, J. M.
Death and the maiden. Tournier, M.
Death and the senator. Clarke, A. C.
Death apples. Morris, M.
Death at the barbecue. Harris, H.
Death at the Burlesque. Woolrich, C.
Death belongs to the dead, his father told him, and sadness to the sad. Winton, T.
Death between the stars. Bradley, M. Z.
Death by drowning. Christie, A.
Death by the waterfall. Gbadamosi, R. A.
Death constant beyond love. García Márquez, G.
Death flight. McBain, E.
Death goes to a party. Martin, V.
A **death** in a quiet town. Wegner, H.
Death in Jerusalem. Trevor, W.
A **death** in Palestine. Hanniya, A.
A **death** in Souvála. Smyth, P.
Death in Sussex. Flanagan, M.
Death in the Christmas hour. Powell, J.
Death in the harbor. Hoch, E. D.
Death in the school-room. Whitman, W.
Death in the woods. Anderson, S.
Death is always part of dinner. Campbell, W. B.
Death mask. Kawabata, Y.
The **death** master. Fleming-Roberts, G. T.
The **death** of a bum. Westlake, D. E.
The **death** of a champion. Vaughan, D.
The **death** of a chimp. Steele, M.
Death of a city. Herbert, F.
Death of a foal. Federspiel, J.
Death of a Foy. Asimov, I.
Death of a guppy. Cohen, M.
Death of a huntsman. Bates, H. E.
Death of a lover. Ebon, W.
The **death** of a Mormon elder. Freeman, J.
Death of a parish priest. MacLaverty, B.
Death of a traveling salesman. Welty, E.
The **death** of an absolutist. Benítez-Rojo, A.
Death of an old dog. Fraser, A.
Death of an otter. Hansen, J.
The **death** of Belle Starr. Taylor, R.
The **death** of Doctor Island. Wolfe, G.
The **death** of Don Juan. Queen, E.
The **death** of Elsa Baskoleit. Böll, H.
The **death** of Harriet Gross. Schwartz, L. S.
The **death** of Ilalotha. Smith, C. A.
The **death** of Joe Dassin. Lopatin, J.
The **death** of Malygris. Smith, C. A.
The **death** of Masaba. Dhlomo, R. R. R.
The **death** of me. Lish, G.
The **death** of me. Woolrich, C.

The **death** of Methuselah. Singer, I. B.
Death of Mrs. Vanderwood. Latimer, M.
The **death** of my grandmother. Hyon, C.-G.
The **death** of Odjigh. Schwob, M.
The **death** of Olivier Bécaille. Zola, É.
The **death** of Petronius. Sheehan, R.
The **death** of Rappaport. Lurie, M.
The **death** of Romelink. Grin, A.
The **death** of Sin. DeGrazia, E.
The **death** of Stalin. Sciascia, L.
The **death** of Sun. Eastlake, W.
Death of the band. Katz, S.
The **death** of the birds. Piñera, V.
Death of the black hair. Tamer, Z.
The **death** of the fat man. Layland, P.
Death of the jasmine. Tamer, Z.
The **death** of the knife-thrower's wife. See Shiga, N. Han's crime
The **death** of the lion. James, H.
Death of the Mallory Queen. Block, L.
Death of the Nation. Havemann, E.
The **death** of the rich man. Colum, P.
Death of the tiger. Castellanos, R.
The **death** of the vice consul. Brondoli, M.
Death of the word. Josipovici, G.
The **death** of Uncle Silas. Bates, H. E.
Death on Goose Hill. Penfold, N.
Death on needlepoint. Škvorecký, J.
Death on the air. Marsh, Dame N.
A **death** on the East Side. Gold, H.
Death scene. Nielsen, H.
Death sits in the dentist's chair. Woolrich, C.
Death stalks a building once it enters. Leedom-Ackerman, J.
Death the proud brother. Wolfe, T.
Death to the hunter. Pentecost, H.
Death tolls the bell. Cave, H. B.
The **death** triple. Pouvoir, J. L.
Death Valley. Oates, J. C.
Death Valley Scotty. Lee, H.
The **death** voyage. Doyle, Sir A. C.
Death watch. Gilbert, M.
Death went astray. Botwinik, B.
Deathbed. Matheson, R. C.

DEATHBED SCENES

Asscher-Pinkhof, C. Hospital barrack
Bates, H. E. The death of Uncle Silas
Bukoski, A. A spinster's confession regarding her sorrows
Carver, R. Errand
Castle, M. If you take my hand, my son
Clayton, J. J. Prewar quality
Gold, H. A death on the East Side
Josipovici, G. The bitter end
Kibera, L. A silent song
La Guma, A. Blankets
Latimer, M. Death of Mrs. Vanderwood
Loewald, U. Bond
Lytle, A. Jericho, Jericho, Jericho
Maupassant, G. de. Revenge
McGarry, J. Providence, 1954: watch
Miller, W. M. Memento homo

DEATHBED SCENES—*Continued*
  Muller, D. N. The old woman's blessing
  Oates, J. C. Stroke
  O'Hara, J. Flight
  Poe, E. A. Ligeia
  Porter, K. A. The jilting of Granny
    Weatherall
  Roberts, N. The inversion
  Salmonson, J. A. Eagle-worm
  Samarakis, A. The flesh
  Shukshin, V. M. The old man's dying
  Sontag, S. The way we live now
  Stuart, J. When mountain men make peace
  Windsor, G. The archbishop; or, The lady
  Yasuoka, S. A view by the sea
Deathlist. Randisi, R. J.
Deaths at sea. Dubus, A.
Death's midwives. Ekström, M.
Deaths of distant friends. Updike, J.
Deathtracks. Etchison, D.
Deathwatch. Pronzini, B.
Deaver, Philip F.
  Arcola girls
    Deaver, P. F. Silent retreats
    Prize stories, 1988
  Fiona's rooms
    Deaver, P. F. Silent retreats
  Geneseo
    Deaver, P. F. Silent retreats
  Infield
    Deaver, P. F. Silent retreats
  Long Pine
    Deaver, P. F. Silent retreats
  Marguerite Howe
    Deaver, P. F. Silent retreats
  Rosie
    Deaver, P. F. Silent retreats
  Silent retreats
    Deaver, P. F. Silent retreats
  The valence of common ions
    Deaver, P. F. Silent retreats
  Why I shacked up with Martha
    Deaver, P. F. Silent retreats
  Wilbur Gray falls in love with an idea
    Deaver, P. F. Silent retreats
DEBATES AND DEBATING
  Amichai, Y. The orgy
Debris. Song, P.-S.
The **debt**. Maupassant, G. de
The **debt**. Williams, J.
Debt cancelled. Overholser, W. D.
Debt of gratitude. Lofts, N.
The **debt** of the whale. Bullen, F. T.
A **debt** to Doc. Rathjen, C. H.
DEBTOR AND CREDITOR
  Elkin, S. I look out for Ed Wolfe
  Haruf, K. Private debts/public holdings
  Rooke, L. Friendship and property
  Ṣāliḥ, al-Ṭ. A handful of dates
  Sanford, W. M. Mr. Carmichael's room
  Yuill, P. B. Hazell and the patriot
DEBTS
  Ferron, J. Servitude

  Hall, M. L. Music lesson
  Hsiu, H. The trap
  Kilgore, D. Unpaid debts
  Lutz, J. High stakes
  Prichard, K. S. Bad debts
  Schwob, M. Blanche the bloody
  Sheckley, R. Cost of living
The **debutante**. Carrington, L.
DECADENCE *See* Degeneration
Decarnin, Camilla
  The book of time
    L. Ron Hubbard presents Writers of the
    future v2
Decatur. Bell, M.
December Nilsen. St. Pierre, P. H.
December roses. Shannon, J.
December's pecans. Middleton, H.
A **decent** interval. McLaughlin, L.
A **decent** life. Meinke, P.
Deceptions. Hoch, E. D.
Deceptions. Muller, M.
The **decision**. Görlich, G.
The **decision**. Hensley, J. L.
Decision from the heart. Bittle, C. R.
A **decisive** refutation of Herbert Dingle's
    objection to Einstein's twin paradox;
    or, Gravitas. Berry, R. M.
The **deck**. Griesemer, J.
Declarations of intent. Spackman, W. M.
Déclassé. Gallant, M.
The **decline** and fall of a reasonable woman.
    Givner, J.
The **decline** and fall of Howard Dawn.
    Gowan, L.
The **decline** of Western Hill. Jackson, G.
The **decoration**. Piñera, V.
DECORATIONS OF HONOR
  Maupassant, G. de. How he got the Le-
    gion of Honor
Decoys. Cunningham, J.
Decrest, Jacques
  The amethyst fly
    Great French detective stories; ed. by T.
    J. Hale
Dédé. Gallant, M.
Dede's talking, it's her turn. Gilchrist, E.
Dedicated. Leavitt, D.
The **deep** blue eastern sky. Broun, H.
The **deep** end. MacLaverty, B.
Deep-sleep. Cassiday, B.
The **deep** valley. Moore, L.
Deep water. Misitano, R. A.
Deepening dusk. Durham, E. M.
Deeper and deeper. Lutz, J.
Deer crossing. Sexson, L.
DEER HUNTING
  Bedard, B. Stalking
  Campbell, W. B. In season
  Carver, R. The calm
  Dubus, A. The captain
  Henderson, D. The test
  Kaplan, D. M. Doe season
  Littlebird, L. The hunter

DEER HUNTING—*Continued*

Teixeira, K. The last hunt

A **deer** park in the provinces. Maupassant, G. de

Deerglen Queen. Knox, B.

The **deerhide**. Rosen, S.

Defaulted presence. See Muschg, A. The country house; or, Defaulted presence

The **defeat** of the city. Henry, O.

Defect. Pronzini, B.

DEFECTORS

Butler, G. North wind

O'Donnell, P. The giggle-wrecker

Pronzini, B. Defect

Schneider, R. Border crossers

Defender of the faith. Tarr, J.

Defender of the Little Falaya. Gilchrist, E.

The **defenders**. Dick, P. K.

Defense. Busch, F.

Defoe, Daniel, 1661?-1731

The apparition of Mrs. Veal

The Treasury of English short stories; ed. by N. Sullivan

Crusoe visits the wreck

Men at sea; ed. by B. Aymar

Characters--Robinson Crusoe

Tournier, M. The end of Robinson Crusoe

Defoliation. Thompson, J.

Deford, Frank

Casey at the bat

Sports Illustrated 69:52-62+ Jl 18 '88

DeFord, Miriam Allen

Not snow nor rain

Spirits, spooks, and other sinister creatures; ed. by H. Hoke

DEFORMITIES

See also Face—Abnormalities and deformities; Monsters

Baukin, L. Jar-boy

Bernard, K. Sister Francetta and the pig baby

Böll, H. What a racket

Corrington, J. W. Pleadings

Davie, E. Green head

Faik, S. The man who doesn't know what a tooth or a toothache is

Gardner, M. The blue birthmark

Hardy, T. The withered arm

Hawthorne, N. The birthmark

Knuttel, W. Fugue

McGrath, P. Blood and water

Tinker, L. The horse

Deformity. Caponegro, M.

Degan dying. Chernoff, M.

DEGENERACY See Degeneration

DEGENERATION

Falkiner, S. The killing of a hedgehog

Faulkner, W. Wash

Flanagan, M. A parma violet room

Flanagan, M. Simple pleasures

García Márquez, G. Bitterness for three sleepwalkers

Jackson, G. The decline of Western Hill

Jhabvala, R. P. An experience of India

Leaton, A. Destiny

Rand, P. A grandson of the Golden West

Rhys, J. The Lotus

Sheckley, R. The store of the worlds

Summerville, J. Paper fires

DeGravelles, Charles

Blood bait

The Southern Review (Baton Rouge, La.) 20:212-20 Ja '84

DeGrazia, Emilio

Brothers of the tiger

DeGrazia, E. Enemy country

The cat-hater

DeGrazia, E. Enemy country

The death of Sin

DeGrazia, E. Enemy country

The enemy

DeGrazia, E. Enemy country

Enemy country

DeGrazia, E. Enemy country

The girl and two old men

DeGrazia, E. Enemy country

The light at the end of the tunnel

DeGrazia, E. Enemy country

The man who cursed and the good Lutheran boy

DeGrazia, E. Enemy country

The mask

DeGrazia, E. Enemy country

The sniper

DeGrazia, E. Enemy country

Zabel's choice

DeGrazia, E. Enemy country

Degrees. Thomas, A. C.

Degrees of death. Rifaat, A.

The **deified** invalid. Apollinaire, G.

Deirdre. Calvert, M.

Dejection. Husain, A.

Del Rey, Lester, 1915-

The faithful

Isaac Asimov presents the best science fiction firsts

Roger Caras' Treasury of great dog stories

For I am a jealous people!

Baker's dozen: 13 short science fiction novels

The still waters

Fantastic stories; ed. by M. H. Greenberg and P. L. Price

Though dreamers die

Machines that think; ed. by I. Asimov; P. S. Warrick and M. H. Greenberg

Delany, Samuel R.

The tale of dragons and dreamers

Masterpieces of fantasy and enchantment; ed. by D. G. Hartwell

Time considered as a helix of semi-precious stones

Worlds apart; ed. by C. Decarnin; E. Garber and L. Paleo

Delany, Sheila
Tree day
The Massachusetts Review 26:146-52 Spr
'85
DELAWARE
Friedman, B. J. Marching through
Delaware
The **delayed** exit of Claude and Eustace.
Wodehouse, P. G.
A **delayed** meeting. Fisher, M. F. K.
Delbanco, Nicholas
And with advantages
Michigan Quarterly Review 27:263-79 Spr
'88
At the Prado: a short story
The Bread Loaf anthology of contem-
porary American short stories; ed. by
R. Pack and J. Parini
The consolation of philosophy
Great American love stories; ed. by L.
Rosenthal
The **delegate**. Bonosky, P.
The **delegate** from Guapanga. Guin, W.
Delenda est. Anderson, P.
Delfino, Augusto Mario
The telephone
Short story international 45
DELHI (INDIA) *See* India—Delhi
Delia. Gordon, M.
A **delicate** nose. Regent, P.
The **delicate** prey. Bowles, P.
Delila. Maupassant, G. de
DeLillo, Don
Human moments in World War III
Soldiers & civilians; ed. by T. Jenks
Oswald in the Lone Star State
Esquire 110:52-4+ Jl '88
The runner
Harper's 277:61-3 S '88
Delius, Anthony
Hannie's journal
The Penguin book of Southern African
stories
Delivering. Dubus, A.
Delivery. Kruse, L.
Delivery. Smith, W. A.
Delphine. Morand, P.
Delphinium blue. Campbell, E.
Delta Sly Honey. Shepard, L.
DeLynn, Jane
Sex
First love/last love; ed. by M. Denneny;
C. Ortleb and T. Steele
DeMarinis, Rick, 1934-
Billy Ducks among the Pharoahs
DeMarinis, R. Under the wheat
Blind euchre [Variant title: A game
without children]
DeMarinis, R. Under the wheat
The coming triumph of the free world
DeMarinis, R. The coming triumph of
the free world
Harper's 276:32-3+ Je '88

Culture shocks
DeMarinis, R. The coming triumph of
the free world
Disneyland
Antaeus 60:146-67 Spr '88
DeMarinis, R. The coming triumph of
the free world
The flowers of boredom
The Antioch Review 46:37-45 Wint '88
DeMarinis, R. The coming triumph of
the free world
Gent
The Best American short stories, 1984
Good wars
DeMarinis, R. Under the wheat
The handgun
DeMarinis, R. The coming triumph of
the free world
Life between meals
DeMarinis, R. Under the wheat
Medicine man
DeMarinis, R. The coming triumph of
the free world
Mole
DeMarinis, R. The coming triumph of
the free world
Harper's 274:63-5 Mr '87
Pagans
DeMarinis, R. The coming triumph of
the free world
Harper's 276:58-60 Ja '88
Queen
DeMarinis, R. The coming triumph of
the free world
Red chair
DeMarinis, R. The coming triumph of
the free world
Romance: a prose villanelle
DeMarinis, R. The coming triumph of
the free world
The smile of a turtle
DeMarinis, R. Under the wheat
The swimmer in hard light
DeMarinis, R. The coming triumph of
the free world
Under the wheat
The Best of the West; ed. by J. Thomas
DeMarinis, R. Under the wheat
The Graywolf annual [1]
Soldiers & civilians; ed. by T. Jenks
Weeds
DeMarinis, R. Under the wheat
Writers of the purple sage; ed. by R.
Martin and M. Barasch
Your burden is lifted, love returns
DeMarinis, R. The coming triumph of
the free world
Your story
DeMarinis, R. The coming triumph of
the free world
Dembling, Arthur
The dragon of Dunloon
Dragons of light; ed. by O. S. Card

Demijohn, Thom *See* Sladek, John Thomas

Deming, Richard, 1915-1983

The better bargain
  Hitchcock in prime time; ed. by F. M.
    Nevins and M. H. Greenberg

A **democrat** on the Ganges. Clark, M.

The **demon** bricksetter from Williamson
  County. Conroy, J.

A **demon** in rosewood. Webb, S.

Demon luck. Gardner, C. S.

DEMONIAC POSSESSION

  See also Exorcism

  Barker, C. The last illusion
  Bloch, R. Enoch
  Blythe, R. Immediate possession
  Bowles, P. The circular valley
  Gilchrist, M. The Basilisk
  Gilchrist, M. Midsummer madness
  Hogg, J. The Brownie of the Black Haggs
  Kirk, R. The invasion of the Church of
    the Holy Ghost
  Lee, T. A lynx with lions
  Lovecraft, H. P. The thing on the doorstep
  Malzberg, B. N. Spree
  Maupassant, G. de. Le Horla
  Shelley, M. W. The transformation
  Shepard, L. The night of white Bhairab
  Silverberg, R. The dybbuk of Mazel Tov
    IV
  Singer, I. B. The dead fiddler
  Stevenson, R. L. Thrawn Janet
  Webb, S. A demon in rosewood
  Williamson, J. Wolves of darkness

DEMONOLOGY

  See also Demoniac possession;
    Satanism; Witchcraft

  Anderson, P. Operation salamander
  Barker, C. Lost souls
  Gilbert, W. S. The fairy's dilemma
  Gilchrist, M. The Basilisk
  Hofstadter, D. R. The tale of Happiton
  Jakes, J. And the monsters walk
  Kuttner, R. The imitation demon
  Linzner, G. The independent fiend
  Lovecraft, H. P. The call of Cthulhu
  Niven, L. Convergent series
  Sheckley, R. The demons
  Singer, I. B. The black wedding
  Vander Putten, J. Just a little thing

The **demons**. Sheckley, R.

The **demon's** gift. O'Malley, K.

Demonstration. Hoover, P.

DEMONSTRATIONS

  Ardizzone, T. The intersection
  Haake, K. The meaning of their names
  Hulme, K. Swansong
  Nowakowski, M. Hatred
  Willson, H. Ground zero

Dempsey, David

Confessions
  The Antioch Review 42:177-87 Spr '84

Denevi, Marco

A dog in Durer's etching 'The knight,
  death and the devil'
  Black water; ed. by A. Manguel

Deng Gang

A big fish
  Short story international 62

The dragon king's troops thunder past
  Short story international 67

DENMARK

  Gathorne-Hardy, J. Peiter and Paulina

  Aristocracy

    See Aristocracy—Denmark

Dennis Haggarty's wife. Thackeray, W. M.

Dennison, George, 1925-1987

The carbon paper poet
  Dennison, G. A tale of Pierrot, and
    other stories

Interview with the author of Caryatids
  [Variant title: The author of Caryatids]
  Dennison, G. A tale of Pierrot, and
    other stories

Oilers and sweepers [Variant title: Oilers
    and sweepers cantata]
  Dennison, G. A tale of Pierrot, and
    other stories

On being a son
  Dennison, G. A tale of Pierrot, and
    other stories

Shawno
  Dennison, G. A tale of Pierrot, and
    other stories

The sufficiency of everyday life: Avenue
    A and Eleventh Street, 1963 [Variant
    title: The smiles of Konarak]
  Dennison, G. A tale of Pierrot, and
    other stories

A tale of Pierrot [Variant title: Larbaud]
  Dennison, G. A tale of Pierrot, and
    other stories

Dent, Lester, 1904-1959

The tank of terror
  A Cent a story! Ed. by G. G. Roberts

DENTISTS

  Anthony, P. Getting through University
  Anthony, P. In the jaws of danger
  Cullen, E. J. Bridgework
  Dawson, F. The white
  Dé, C., and Dandurand, A. Case still open
  Dickson, G. R. A matter of technique
  García Márquez, G. One of these days
  Gilliatt, P. Teeth
  Kirk, S. Morrison's reaction
  McGarry, J. Providence, 1960: cavities
  Smiley, J. The age of grief
  Wilbur, E. A strange elation
  Woolrich, C. Death sits in the dentist's
    chair
  Woolrich, C. Hurting much?

The **denunciation**. Hemingway, E.

Denver's story. Taylor, C.

Déon, Michel
  Umbrian afternoon
    Foreign exchange; ed. by J. Evans
Departed coming back. Foltz-Gray, D.
DEPARTMENT STORES
  Banks, R. Success story
  Barrett, L. Inventory
  Collier, J. Evening primrose
  Johnson, J. A. At D'Ambrosia's
  Kees, W. So cold outside
  Loukakis, A. Hooray for Haralambos
  White, C. More crimes against the people
    of Illinois
A **departmental** case. Henry, O.
The **departure** of the shadow. Apollinaire, G.
Departures. Barthelme, D.
Departures. Rees, D.
Depend on Aunt Elly. Algren, N.
Dependents. Bennett, J. G.
DEPRESSION, 1929 *See* Business depres-
    sion, 1929
Depression glass. Kavaler, R.
DEPRESSIONS, BUSINESS *See* Business
    depression, 1929
Depth of field. Tetu, R.
DERBYSHIRE (ENGLAND) *See* England—
    Derbyshire
The **derelict.** Hodgson, W. H.
The **derelict.** Tomlinson, H. M.
Derleth, August William, 1909-1971
  The adventure of the spurious Tamerlane
    Chapter & hearse; ed. by M. Muller and
      B. Pronzini
  Carousel
    The Wickedest show on earth; ed. by
      M. Muller and B. Pronzini
  The dark boy
    Rod Serling's Night gallery reader
  The drifting snow
    Vampires; ed. by A. Ryan
  House—with ghost
    Rod Serling's Night gallery reader
  Miss Esperson
    Dark arrows; ed. by A. Manguel
  The night train to Lost Valley
    Yankee witches; ed. by C. G. Waugh;
      M. H. Greenberg and F. D. McSherry
DeRosso, H. A.
  Vigilante
    Wild westerns; ed. by B. Pronzini
Desai, Anita, 1937-
  Games at twilight
    New women and new fiction; ed. by S.
      Cahill
  Private tuition by Mr Bose
    The Literary Review (Madison, N.J.)
      29:430-5 Summ '86
Desaulniers, Janet
  Age
    Love stories for the time being; ed. by
      G. D. Chipps and B. Henderson
    The Ploughshares reader: new fiction for
      the eighties

Everyone is wearing a hat
    The New Yorker 64:38-41 O 10 '88
  Pears
    The North American Review 269:56-7 Mr
      '84
The **descent.** Crapser, W.
Descent into brotherland. Taylor, P. E.
A **descent** into the maelström. Poe, E. A.
Description (of a description). Sontag, S.
Desecration. Jhabvala, R. P.
Desert. Barany, M.
The **desert.** Hauptman, W.
Desert birds. Evans, E.
Desert breakdown, 1968. Wolff, T.
Desert couple. Wilner, H.
A **desert** idyll. Chavez, A.
The **desert** of stolen dreams. Silverberg, R.
Desert owls. Ripley, B.
Deserted cities of the heart. Shiner, L.
DESERTED HOUSES
  Aiken, J. Time to laugh
  Balzac, H. de. La Grande Bretêche
  Bryant, E. Teeth marks
  Hamilton, E. Requiem
  Kirk, R. There's a long, long trail a-
    winding
  Mortimer, P. The skylight
  Wells, H. G. The thing in No. 7
The **deserter.** Sarkadi, I.
DESERTION, MILITARY
  Davin, D. Coming and going
  Grin, A. He came and went
  Grin, A. Reno Island
  Jolley, E. Clever and pretty
  O'Brien, T. Going after Cacciato
  Sarkadi, I. The deserter
DESERTION AND NONSUPPORT
  Becher, U. A very Baltic story
  Dodd, S. M. Rue
  Ferguson, P. The dry familiar plains
  Hawthorne, N. Wakefield
  Hodgins, J. By the river
  Klass, P. Gringo city
  Nestor, T. G. The mountain top
  Paley, G. An interest in life
  Sandel, C. The flight to America
  Singer, I. B. Disguised
  Whitaker, M. Home to wagonhouses
DESERTS
    See also Mojave Desert (Calif.);
      Negev (Israel); Sahara
  Abbey, E. Black sun [excerpt]
  Al-Kouni, I. The drumming sands
  Dundas, R. As small as your shadow
  Faust, F. Wine on the desert
  Fisher, M. F. K. Mrs. Teeters' tomato jar
  Grey, Z. Tappan's burro
  Haake, K. Natural histories
  Hoyt, M. S. The wind wizard
  Kilworth, G. The dissemblers
  Milán, V. Feast of John the Baptist
  Pronzini, B. Thirst
  Silverberg, R. The desert of stolen dreams

Deserving Princess. Holloway, J.
Design. Raffel, D.
Design for a dream. Piñera, V.
Design for departure. Algren, N.
Desirable lakeside residence. Norton, A.
Desire. Oates, J. C.
Desire. O'Donnell, P.
Desire, and other topics. Murray, W. C.
Desire and the black masseur. Williams, T.
Desire call of the wild hen. Hood, M.
Desire in November. Calvino, I.
Désirs. Krysl, M.
The **Desjardins**. Scott, D. C.

Desnoues, Lucienne
  Philéas
    Short story international 48
  The poplars
    Short story international 42
  The silent treatment
    Short story international 54
  The triumph and the celery stick
    Short story international 66

DESOLATION ISLANDS *See* Kerguelen Islands

DESPAIR
  Abe, K. The red cocoon
  Andreyev, L. The thief
  Bonner, M. The prison-bound
  Faik, S. A city morning and a man
  Ferreira, R. Bagasse
  Goyen, W. In the icebound hothouse
  Ingalls, R. The man who was left behind
  Morris, W. The origin of sadness
  Wolfe, T. The house of the far and lost
Desperate measures. Gallagher, T.
Despicable bastard. Endō, S.
Despoilers of the golden empire. Garrett, R.
Destination. Kimball, R. W.
The **destination**. Wang Anyi
DESTINY *See* Fate and fatalism
Destiny. Erdrich, L.
Destiny. Leaton, A.
The **destroyer**. Barrett, W. E.
The **destroyer** of families. Sabah, M. 'l--D.
Destroying angel. Sage, V.
DESTRUCTION OF EARTH *See* Earth, Destruction of
Destruction of Pompeii (a story for Bella). Aksenov, V. P.
DESTRUCTION OF THE JEWS *See* Holocaust, Jewish (1933-1945)
The **destruction** of the world. See Poe, E. A. The conversation of Eiros and Charmion
The **destructor**. Greene, G.

Desy, Jeanne
  The princess who stood on her own two feet
    Don't bet on the prince; ed. by J. Zipes
Details, before the event. Soldatow, S.
The **detective**. Austin, D.
The **detective** of dreams. Wolfe, G.

DETECTIVES
  Alleyn, Superintendent Roderick. See stories by Marsh, Dame N.
  Amos, Walker. See stories by Estleman, L. D.
  Appleby, Sir John. See stories by Innes, M.
  Archer, Lew. See stories by Macdonald, R.
  Ark, Simon. See stories by Hoch, E. D.
  Asch, Jacob. See stories by Lyons, A.
  Banner, Senator Brooks U. See stories by Commings, J.
  Barnes, Mr. See stories by Ottolengui, R.
  Barnett, Jim. See stories by Leblanc, M.
  Beck, Paul. See stories by Bodkin, M. M.
  Behrens, Samuel. See stories by Gilbert, M.
  Blair, Mike. See stories by Searls, H.
  Blaise, Modesty. See stories by O'Donnell, P.
  Blayne, Katie. See stories by Chambers, W.
  Bohannon, Hack. See stories by Hansen, J.
  Bond, James. See stories by Fleming, I.
  Boruvka, Lieutenant. See stories by Skvorecký, J.
  Brandstetter, Dave. See stories by Hansen, J.
  Brown, Father. See stories by Chesterton, G. K.
  Burke, Inspector. See stories by Woolrich, C.
  Burma, Nestor. See stories by Malet, L.
  Cadfael, Brother. See stories by Peters, E.
  Calder, Daniel Joseph. See stories by Gilbert, M.
  Callahan, Brock. See stories by Gault, W. C.
  Cardigan, Jack. See stories by Nebel, F.
  Carella, Detective Steve. See stories by McBain, E.
  Carlton, Queen Sue. See stories by Yorke, C. B.
  Carlyle, Carlotta. See stories by Barnes, L.
  Carrados, Max. See stories by Bramah, E.
  Carter, Ken. See stories by Page, N.
  Carter, Nick. See stories by Carter, N.
  Cashin, Carrie. See stories by Tinsley, T.
  Challis, Bart. See stories by Nolan, W. F.
  Chambers, Peter. See stories by Kane, H.
  Chambrun, Pierre. See stories by Pentecost, H.
  Chaudri, Mahboob. See stories by Pachter, J.
  Chee, Corporal Jim. See stories by Hillerman, T.
  Cody. See stories by Reasoner, J. M.
  Coffee, Dr. Daniel Webster. See stories by Blochman, L. G.
  Continental Op. See stories by Hammett, D.

DETECTIVES—*Continued*

Courvoisier, Inspector. See stories by Peyrou, M.

Craggs, Mrs. See stories by Keating, H. R. F.

Craig, Detective Sergeant Peter. See stories by Brown, F.

Crumlish, Father Francis Xavier. See stories by Reach, A. S.

Culver, Grace Redsie. See stories by Brown, R.

Czissar, Dr. Jan. See stories by Ambler, E.

Dalgliesh, Commander Adam. See stories by James, P. D.

Darcy, Lord. See stories by Garrett, R.

Dare, Susan. See stories by Eberhart, M. G.

Darlan, Al. See stories by Hoch, E. D.

Davis, Milt. See stories by McBain, E.

De Gier, Detective-Sergeant. See stories by Van de Wetering, J.

Dee, Judge. See stories by Gulik, R. H. van

Delvecchio, Nick. See stories by Randisi, R. J.

Denson, John. See stories by Hoyt, R.

Dill, Daffy. See stories by Sale, R.

Donahue. See stories by Nebel, F.

Doolin, Johnny. See stories by Cain, P.

Dorrington. See stories by Morrison, A.

Drum, Chester. See stories by Marlowe, S.

Dupin, C. Auguste. See stories by Poe, E. A.

Dwyer, Jack. See stories by Gorman, E.

Ehrengraf, Martin. See stories by Block, L.

Evans, Detective Charlie. See stories by Parker, P. S.

Fell, Dr. Gideon. See stories by Carr, J. D.

Fen, Gervase. See stories by Crispin, E.

Fen, Gervase. See stories by Crispin, E., and Bush, G.

Fisher, Horne. See stories by Chesterton, G. K.

Fortune, Dan. See stories by Collins, M.

Fox, Captain Edward Allan. See stories by Davis, D. S.

Frederickson, Dr. Bob "Mongo". See stories by Chesbro, G. C.

Frost, Jerry. See stories by McCoy, H.

Gale, Gabriel. See stories by Chesterton, G. K.

Galton, Mike. See stories by Waugh, H.

Gar, Jo. See stories by Whitfield, R.

Ghote, Inspector Ganesh. See stories by Keating, H. R. F.

Gilles, Superintendent. See stories by Decrest, J.

Goodwin, Archie. See stories by Stout, R.

Gorgon, Ed. See stories by Breen, J. L.

Grant, Rupert. See stories by Chesterton, G. K.

Great Merlini. See stories by Rawson, C.

Greer, Gary. See stories by Whitfield, R.

Grijpstra, Detective-Adjutant. See stories by Van de Wetering, J.

Hallam, Lucas. See stories by Washburn, L. J.

Hammond, Wade. See stories by Chadwick, P.

Hannibal, Joe. See stories by Dundee, W. D.

Harris, Mike. See stories by Flynn, T. T.

Harrison, Chip. See stories by Block, L.

Hawthorne, Dr. Sam. See stories by Hoch, E. D.

Heimrich, Captain M. L. See stories by Lockridge, F. L. D., and Lockridge, R.

Heller, Nate. See stories by Collins, M. A.

Holmes, Sherlock. See stories by Doyle, Sir A. C.

Hyde, Dr. Adrian. See stories by Chesterton, G. K.

Iff, Simon. See stories by Crowley, A.

Jacoby, Miles. See stories by Randisi, R. J.

Jenkins, Ed. See stories by Gardner, E. S.

Johnson, Dr. Sam. See stories by De la Torre, L.

Jordan, Scott. See stories by Masur, H. Q.

Keith, Lieutenant Drummond. See stories by Chesterton, G. K.

Knowles, Libby. See stories by Hoch, E. D.

Krajewski, Bonecrack. See stories by Gores, J.

Le Roux, Rolf. See stories by Godfrey, P.

Legrand, Vivian. See stories by Thomas, E.

Lennox, Bill. See stories by Ballard, W. T.

Leopold, Captain. See stories by Hoch, E. D.

Lepicq, Prosper. See stories by Véry, P.

Levine, Detective Abraham. See stories by Westlake, D. E.

Lopez, Sergeant Vincente. See stories by Somerlott, R.

Lupin, Arsene. See stories by Leblanc, M.

Mack, Terry. See stories by Daly, C. J.

Maigret, Chief Inspector. See stories by Simenon, G.

Mallory. See stories by Chandler, R.

Malone, Dizzy. See stories by Paul, P.

Malone, John J. See stories by Rice, C.

Marlowe, Philip. See stories by Chandler, R.

Marple, Miss Jane. See stories by Christie, A.

Mastro, Lieutenant. See stories by Arden W.

McCone, Sharon. See stories by Muller, M.

McDade, Violet. See stories by Adams, C. F.

DETECTIVES—*Continued*

Mechinet, Monsieur. See stories by Gaboriau, E.

Meehan, Trixie. See stories by Flynn, T. T.

Mellor, Chief Superintendent. See stories by Ferrars, E. X.

Mendoza, Lieutenant Luis. See stories by Shannon, D.

Merrivale, Sir Henry. See stories by Carr, J. D.

Meyer, Detective Meyer. See stories by McBain, E.

Millhone, Kinsey. See stories by Grafton, S.

Mom. See stories by Yaffe, J.

Moon Man. See stories by Davis, F. C.

Murdock, Captain John. See stories by Saunders, C. M.

Noble, Nick. See stories by Boucher, A.

Nudger, Alo. See stories by Lutz, J.

Nudger, Alo. See stories by Lutz, J., and Pachter, J.

Oliverez, Elena. See stories by Muller, M.

Paige, Henry. See stories by Stodghill, D.

Paris, Charles. See stories by Brett, S.

Patrick, Ellen. See stories by Anderson, L.

Perkins, Ben. See stories by Kantner, R.

Peters, Toby. See stories by Kaminsky, S. M.

Petrella, Detective Chief Inspector Patrick. See stories by Gilbert, M.

Pine, Paul. See stories by Browne, H.

Po, Henry. See stories by Randisi, R. J.

Poirot, Hercule. See stories by Christie, A.

Pond, Mr. See stories by Chesterton, G. K.

Ponder, Harry. See stories by Hoch, E. D.

Pons, Solar. See stories by Derleth, A. W.

Puma, Joe. See stories by Gault, W. C.

Quade, Marty. See stories by Tepperman, E. C.

Quarles, Francis. See stories by Symons, J.

Queen, Ellery. See stories by Queen, E.

Quin, Harley. See stories by Christie, A.

Raffles, A. J. See stories by Hornung, E. W.

Raffles, A. J. See stories by Perowne, B.

Rason, Detective Inspector. See stories by Vickers, R.

Return, David. See stories by Wellman, M. W.

Saint, The. See stories by Charteris, L.

Saito, Inspector Matsuo. See stories by Van de Wetering, J.

Satterthwaite, Mr. See stories by Christie, A.

Scott, Shell. See stories by Prather, R. S.

Scudder, Matt. See stories by Block, L.

Shore, Jemima. See stories by Fraser, A.

Slime. See stories by Twohy, R.

Snow, Ben. See stories by Hoch, E. D.

Snowdrop, Stanislaw. See stories by Carraud, J.

Spade, Sam. See stories by Hammett, D.

Standish, Dr. See stories by Coxe, G. H.

Stonebreaker, D. See stories by Brandner, G.

Storey, Rosita. See stories by Footner, H.

Strang, Leonard. See stories by Brittain, W.

Tanner, John Marshall. See stories by Greenleaf, S.

Taylor, Mitch. See stories by Treat, L.

Thatcher, Detective Sergeant Steve. See stories by Davis, F. C.

Thinking Machine. See stories by Futrelle, J.

Thinking Machine. See stories by Futrelle, M.

Tibbs, Virgil. See stories by Ball, J.

Train, Sam. See stories by Savage, E.

Trant, Lieutenant. See stories by Wheeler, H. C.

Trask, Ivy. See stories by Pentecost, H.

Trent, Philip. See stories by Bentley, E. C.

Trooper, Sergeant. See stories by Brett, S.

Turnbuckle, Henry. See stories by Ritchie, J.

Turner, Dan. See stories by Bellem, R. L.

Turner, Milo. See stories by Nevins, F. M., Jr.

Urth, Wendell. See stories by Asimov, I.

Valentin, Aristide. See stories by Chesterton, G. K.

Van Dusen, Professor. See stories by Futrelle, J.

Velvet, Nick. See stories by Hoch, E. D.

Walker, Amos. See stories by Estleman, L. D.

Walsh, Inspector. See stories by Brett, S.

Warshawski, V. I. See stories by Paretsky, S.

Watson, Sarah. See stories by McCandless, D. B.

Wield, Inspector. See stories by Dickens, C.

Willets, Sheriff Andrew. See stories by Davis, D. S.

Williams, Race. See stories by Daly, C. J.

Wimsey, Lord Peter. See stories by Sayers, D. L.

Wolfe, Nero. See stories by Stout, R.

DETECTIVES, PRIVATE

Austin, D. The detective

Bankier, W. Beliveau pays

Barker, C. Lost souls

Brett, S. Unwilling sleep

Brown, F. Before she kills

Bush, J. The last meeting of the Butlers Club

Butler, E. P. Philo Gubb's greatest case

DETECTIVES, PRIVATE—*Continued*

Davenport, G. Les exploits de Nat Pinkerton de jour en jour: un texte de René Magritte translated and improved

Finney, E. J. The investigator

Greenwood, R. Like Lucifer

Haldeman, J. W. Blood sisters

Healey, R. M. A neat crime

Hoch, E. D. The luck of a gypsy

Howard, C. The Dublin eye

Hughes, D. B. F. The spotted pup

James, P. D. The murder of Santa Claus

Johnson, W. R. White water

Lewin, M. Z. The reluctant detective

MacLeod, C. It was an awful shame

Peirce, H. Goldfish

Pronzini, B. Ace in the hole

Pronzini, B. Cache and carry

Pronzini, B. Cat's-paw

Pronzini, B. A dip in the Poole

Pronzini, B. Incident in a neighborhood tavern

Pronzini, B. Memento mori

Pronzini, B. Sanctuary

Pronzini, B. Skeleton rattle your mouldy leg

Pronzini, B. Something wrong

Pronzini, B. Stacked deck

Pronzini, B. Thin air

Rudloff, S. A. A cup of coffee

Sheckley, R. Shootout in the toy shop

Spillane, M. Trouble . . . come and get it!

Washburn, L. J. Hallam

Wilhelm, K. Forever yours, Anna

Wilson, K. Hot as a pistol

Wolfe, G. The detective of dreams

Woolrich, C. Hot water

Yuill, P. B. Hazell and the patriot

The **detective's** dilemma. Woolrich, C.

Detective's wife. Harris, H.

Détente. Oates, J. C.

The **deterioration** of 47th Street. Kilgore, D.

DETROIT (MICH.) *See* Michigan—Detroit

Detroit Abe. Friedman, B. J.

Deuce. Beattie, A.

Development. Broun, H.

Deveson, Richard

Struth

Encounter (London, England) 69:11-14 S/O '87

DEVIL

Anderson, P. Rachaela

Asimov, I. The brazen locked room

Babbitt, N. Simple sentences

Bangs, J. K. A midnight visitor

Barker, C. The Yattering and Jack

Baudelaire, C. The generous gambler

Beerbohm, M. Enoch Soames

Bloch, R. How like a god

Brown, F. Armageddon

Castle, M. If you take my hand, my son

Chamisso, A. von. The strange story of Peter Schlemihl

Chavez, A. The ardent commandant

Daniels, C. The devil went down to Georgia

Dumas, H. Devil bird

Ellison, H. Deal from the bottom

Gaspé, P. A. de. Rose Latulipe

Godwin, P. Influencing the hell out of time and Teresa Golowitz

Gogol', N. V. A bewitched place

Gogol', N. V. Christmas Eve

Gogol', N. V. The fair at Sorochintsy

Gogol', N. V. St. John's Eve

Hawthorne, N. Ethan Brand

Hawthorne, N. Young Goodman Brown

Hogg, J. Mr. Adamson of Laverhope

Hunter, E. The fallen angel

Irving, W. The Devil and Tom Walker

James, M. R. Count Magnus

Karr, P. A. The toe

Kaye, M. Damned funny

Kessler, J. F. Gnosis

King, T. Boogie Man

Le Fanu, J. S. Sir Dominick's bargain

Lee, V. A wicked voice

Leinster, M. Devil's henchman

Leith, R. Loaded dice

Machen, A. The great god Pan

Masefield, J. Davy Jones's gift

Matheson, R. Buried talents

McCormack, F. Hell-bent

Melville, H. The lightning-rod man

Moravia, A. The devil can't save the world

Pinkwater, D. M. Devil in the drain

Poe, E. A. Bon-bon

Poe, E. A. The devil in the belfry

Poe, E. A. The Duc de l'Omelette

Poe, E. A. Never bet the devil your head

Pronzini, B., and Malzberg, B. N. Opening a vein

Russ, J. The man who could not see devils

Russ, J. This afternoon

Russell, B. The Queen of Sheba's nightmare

Russell, E. F. Displaced person

Russell, R. The bell

Schwob, M. The sabbat at Mofflaines

Sheckley, R. The battle

Sherman, C. H. Tapestry

Singer, I. B. The last demon

Summers, H. S. Fortunato & the night visitor

Thackeray, W. M. The devil's wager

Tiptree, J. Our resident djinn

Treat, L. Give the devil his due

Tremblay, M. The devil and the mushroom

Turgenev, I. S. Bubnoff and the Devil

Twain, M. Sold to Satan

Volsky, P. The tenancy of Mr. Eex

DEVIL—*Continued*
Wells, H. G. The devotee of art
Wells, H. G. The temptation of Harringay
Wells, H. G. The wild asses of the devil
Wnorowska, D. Seven come heaven?
Wollheim, D. A. Give her hell
The **Devil**. Maupassant, G. de
The **Devil** and his due. Davis, D. S.
The **Devil** and Irv Cherniske. Boyle, T. C.
The **Devil** and Sister Lena. Walters, A. L.
The **devil** and the deep sea. Kipling, R.
The **devil** and the mushroom. Tremblay, M.
The **Devil** and the trombone. Gardner, M.
The **Devil** and Tom Walker. Irving, W.
Devil bird. Dumas, H.
The **devil** can't save the world. Moravia, A.
The **devil** comes and goes. Moravia, A.
The **devil** dog. See London, J. Diable: a dog
The **devil** don't dance with strangers. Elflandsson, G.
The **Devil** finds work. Reynolds, M.
The **devil** in the belfry. Poe, E. A.
Devil in the drain. Pinkwater, D. M.
The **Devil** is not mocked. Wellman, M. W.
The **devil** went down to Georgia. Daniels, C.
DEVIL WORSHIP *See* Satanism
The **devilish** rat. Mitchell, E. P.
Devil's henchman. Leinster, M.
The **devil's** thumb. Sandberg, P. L.
The **devil's** wager. Thackeray, W. M.
Devlin's dream. Johnson, G. C.
Devolution. Hamilton, E.
DEVON (ENGLAND) *See* England—Devon
Devoted Moslem Ismail Effendi. Izgü, M.
The **devotee** of art. Wells, H. G.
Devotions. Budhos, M.
The **devotions** of Jean Blysema. Sisskind, M.
Dew, Robb Forman
  Silverfish
    The New Yorker 60:36-43 Je 11 '84
  Two girls wearing perfume in the summer
    Selected stories from The Southern review, 1965-1985
DeWeese, Gene, 1934-
  The beggar and his cat
    Magic in Ithkar 3; ed. by A. Norton and R. Adams
  Everything's going to be all right
    Shadows 8
Dexter, Colin
  At the Lulu-Bar Motel
    The Mammoth book of modern crime stories; ed. by G. Hardinge
Dey, Frederic Van Rensselaer, 1865-1922 *See* Carter, Nicholas, 1865-1922
Dhlomo, R. R. R.
  The death of Masaba
    The Penguin book of Southern African stories
Di Filippo, Paul
  Phylogenesis
    Synergy v3

Stone lives
    Mirrorshades; ed. by B. Sterling
DIABETES
  Bedford, J. Through road
  Campos-De Metro, J. The slugger heart
Diable: a dog. London, J.
Diabologic. Russell, E. F.
Diaconú, Alina
  Mamaya
    Short story international 62
Dial an alibi. Ritchie, J.
Dial F for Frankenstein. Clarke, A. C.
DIALECT STORIES
                  Black English
  Attaway, W. Blood on the forge [excerpt]
  Bambara, T. C. Gorilla, my love
  Birtha, B. In the life
  Birtha, B. The saints and sinners run
  Bradley, D. 197903042100 (Sunday)
  Cooper, J. C. Happiness does not come in colors
  Cooper, J. C. Having fun
  Cooper, J. C. Living
  Cooper, J. C. The magic strength of need
  Cooper, J. C. The watcher
  Cooper, J. C. When life begins!
  Cullen, E. J. The baddest, baddest days
  Cullen, E. J. Gorbachev's wife
  Dumas, H. Ark of bones
  Dumas, H. Strike and fade
  Fisher, R. Miss Cynthie
  Gaines, E. J. Just like a tree
  Gaines, E. J. The sky is gray
  Haldeman, J. W. The monster
  Harris, J. C. The wonderful Tar-Baby story
  Hurston, Z. N. Book of Harlem
  Hurston, Z. N. Cock Robin Beale Street
  Hurston, Z. N. The gilded six-bits
  Hurston, Z. N. Isis
  Hurston, Z. N. Muttsy
  Hurston, Z. N. Spunk
  Hurston, Z. N. Story in Harlem slang
  Hurston, Z. N. Sweat
  Jeffrey, T. Habits of contact
  Jordan, J. His own where
  Lowenstein, A. F. The mother right
  Mancuso, C. Mamie
  Matthiessen, P. Sadie
  Paley, G. Lavinia: an old story
  Read, O. An Arkansas hanging
  Thibault, D. A woman like Dilsie
  Williams, S. A. Tell Martha not to moan
  Wright, R. Almos' a man
  Wright, R. Big boy leaves home
  Wright, R. The man who was almost a man
                  English—Sussex
  Kipling, R. The wish house
                  Irish
  Le Fanu, J. S. The white cat of Drumgunniol
  Poe, E. A. Why the little Frenchman wears his hand in a sling

DIALECT STORIES—*Continued*

New England

Lovecraft, H. P. The shadow over Innsmouth

Wharton, E. Ethan Frome

Pennsylvania Dutch

Stark, S. S. Best Quality Glass Company, New York

Pidgin English

Lum, D. H. Y. The Moiliili Bag Man

Yamanaka, C. What the ironwood whispered

Scottish

Dunn, D. Mozart's Clarinet Concerto

Dunn, D. Twin-sets and pickle forks

Faulkner, W. Thrift

Hamilton, A. Moonlighting

Hogg, J. The barber of Duncow—a real ghost story

Hogg, J. The Brownie of the Black Haggs

Hogg, J. Mary Burnet

Hogg, J. Mr. Adamson of Laverhope

Hogg, J. Sound morality

Hogg, J. Tibby Hyslop's dream

Kelman, J. The hon

Leonard, T. Honest

Ollivant, A. The tailless tyke at bay

Scott, Sir W. Wandering Willie's tale

Stevenson, R. L. Thrawn Janet

Southern States

Benedict, P. All the dead

Benedict, P. Town smokes

Cobb, W. The stone soldier

Cooper, J. C. Spooks

Cooper, J. C. Swimming to the top of the rain

Crews, H. A long wail

Faulkner, W. Barn burning

Faulkner, W. Wash

Gingher, M. No news

Granberry, E. A trip to Czardis

Hairston, L. The revolt of Brud Bascomb

Hobson, G. The talking that trees does

Read, O. Big Bill and Little Bill

Still, J. A master time

Stuart, J. Battle with the bees

Stuart, J. The champion

Stuart, J. Competition at Slush Creek

Stuart, J. Fight number twenty-five

Stuart, J. Horse-trading trembles

Stuart, J. No petty thief

Stuart, J. Old Gore

Stuart, J. Testimony of trees

Stuart, J. Thirty-two votes before breakfast

Stuart, J. To market, to market

Stuart, J. When mountain men make peace

Walker, M. Jubilee [excerpt]

West Indian

Adisa, O. P. Bake-Face

Adisa, O. P. Duppy get her

Adisa, O. P. Me man Angel

Adisa, O. P. Widows' walk

Bissoondath, N. Dancing

Clarke, A. C. How he does it

Seepaul, L. Sou-Sou money

Shacochis, B. Easy in the islands

Shacochis, B. Hunger

Shacochis, B. Mundo's sign

Shacochis, B. The pelican

Shacochis, B. Redemption songs

Dialectical materialism. Covino, M.

DIALOGUE *See* Conversation

Dialogue of the greater systems. Landolfi, T.

A **dialogue** upon Mount Pentelicus. Woolf, V.

Dialogue with the mirror. García Márquez, G.

Diamond, Rickey Gard

In jeopardy

The Sewanee Review 93:372-86 Summ '85

The **diamond**. Millard, P.

The **diamond** badge. Welch, D.

Diamond eyes and pig tails. De la Torre, A.

The **diamond** lens. O'Brien, F.-J.

The **diamond** maker. Wells, H. G.

DIAMOND MINES AND MINING

Grin, A. Gatt, Witt and Redott

The **diamond** necklace. Maupassant, G. de

Diamond twill. Nevai, L.

DIAMONDS

See also Diamond mines and mining

Darling, J. The matchstick hut

Doyle, Sir A. C. The mystery of Sasassa Valley

Doyle, Sir A. C. Our midnight visitor

Doyle, Sir A. C. The stone of Boxman's Drift

Holding, J. A good kid

Hornung, E. W. A costume piece

Maupassant, G. de. The diamond necklace

Wells, H. G. A deal in ostriches

Wells, H. G. The diamond maker

Williamson, J. At the human limit

Diamonds. Gilbert, W. S.

Diamonds are forever. Chipulina, E. G.

Diamonds of death. Bellem, R. L.

DIARIES, STORIES ABOUT

Auchincloss, L. A diary of old New York

Bruce-Novoa. The manuscript

DIARIES (STORIES IN DIARY FORM)

See also Letters (Stories in letter form)

Aickman, R. Pages from a young girl's journal

Austin, D. It's the same old story

Barthelme, D. Conversations with Goethe

Benford, G. Of space-time and the river

Bird, C. Woodpecker Point

Birtha, B. Both ways

Bishop, M. Diary of a dead man

Bitov, A. Notes from the corner

Bloch, R. See how they run

Boyd, W. Extracts from the journal of Flying Officer J

Brulotte, G. The elevator messengers

DIARIES (STORIES IN DIARY FORM)
—Continued

Carrington, L. The stone door
Charnas, S. M. Listening to Brahms
Collier, J. Evening primrose
Cooper, J. C. Loved to death
Davenport, G. Apples and pears: Het
  Erewhonisch schetsboek: Messidor-
  Vendémiaire 1981
Delius, A. Hannie's journal
Doyle, Sir A. C. The parasite
Ebon, W. The supermarket manager's
  daughter
Farmer, P. J. Sketches among the ruins
  of my mind
Gilman, C. P. The yellow wallpaper
Halligan, M. A gigolo, Miss Emery?
Hankla, C. If it were dark
Jacoby, J. Diary of a polesitter
Keeley, E. Cambodian diary
Maupassant, G. de. The diary of a mad-
  man
Maupassant, G. de. Le Horla
Maupassant, G. de. My twenty-five days
McConnell, J. V. Learning theory
Michaelson, L. W. All my darlings
Nourse, A. E. Second sight
Poe, E. A. The light-house
Robinson, S. By any other name
Rostopchina, E. P., grafinīā. Rank and
  money
Schnurre, W. Diary of a dayfly
Scott, R. Diary of a woman
Sladek, J. T. The next dwarf
Smith, C. A. The city of the singing flame
Smith, C. A. Master of the asteroid
Tournier, M. Amandine; or, The two
  gardens
Turtledove, H. And so to bed
Waters, M. The Love Chapter
West, J. The day of the hawk
Wilner, H. Consultations
Wilson, R. The thing that stared
Woolf, V. The journal of Mistress Joan
  Martyn
Diary entry #1. Valle, C.
Diary entry #6. Valle, C.
Diary of a dayfly. Schnurre, W.
Diary of a dead man. Bishop, M.
Diary of a mad deity. Morrow, J.
Diary of a madman. Gogol', N. V.
The **diary** of a madman. Maupassant, G. de
Diary of a polesitter. Jacoby, J.
Diary of a Union soldier. Carr, P. M.
Diary of a woman. Scott, R.
A **diary** of old New York. Auchincloss, L.
Diator beyond Olympus. Parotti, P.

Dibble, J. Birney

To sleep, perchance to dream
  A Matter of crime v1
The **dice-box**: a fairy tale. Walpole, H.

Dick, Philip K.
The alien mind
  Dick, P. K. I hope I shall arrive soon
Autofac
  Dick, P. K. Robots, androids, and
  mechanical oddities
Breakfast at twilight
  Amazing science fiction anthology: The
  wild years, 1946-1955; ed. by M. H.
  Greenberg
Chains of air, web of aether
  Dick, P. K. I hope I shall arrive soon
Colony
  Robert Silverberg's Worlds of wonder
The days of Perky Pat
  Amazing stories: 60 years of the best
  science fiction
The defenders
  Dick, P. K. Robots, androids, and
  mechanical oddities
The electric ant
  Dick, P. K. Robots, androids, and
  mechanical oddities
  Machines that think; ed. by I. Asimov;
  P. S. Warrick and M. H. Greenberg
The exit door leads in
  Dick, P. K. I hope I shall arrive soon
  Dick, P. K. Robots, androids, and
  mechanical oddities
Explorers we
  Dick, P. K. I hope I shall arrive soon
Frozen journey
  Dick, P. K. Robots, androids, and
  mechanical oddities
A game of unchance
  Dick, P. K. Robots, androids, and
  mechanical oddities
Holy quarrel
  Dick, P. K. I hope I shall arrive soon
I hope I shall arrive soon
  Dick, P. K. I hope I shall arrive soon
If there were no Benny Cemoli
  Machines that think; ed. by I. Asimov;
  P. S. Warrick and M. H. Greenberg
Imposter
  Dick, P. K. Robots, androids, and
  mechanical oddities
The king of the elves
  Masterpieces of fantasy and enchant-
  ment; ed. by D. G. Hartwell
The last of the masters
  Dick, P. K. Robots, androids, and
  mechanical oddities
The little movement
  Dick, P. K. Robots, androids, and
  mechanical oddities
A little something for us tempunauts
  The Dark descent; ed. by D. G. Hart-
  well
Novelty act
  Fantastic stories; ed. by M. H. Green-
  berg and P. L. Price

Dick, Philip K.—*Continued*
The Preserving Machine
Dick, P. K. Robots, androids, and mechanical oddities
Rautavaara's case
Dick, P. K. I hope I shall arrive soon
Omni book of science fiction 3
Sales pitch
Dick, P. K. Robots, androids, and mechanical oddities
Second Variety
Dick, P. K. Robots, androids, and mechanical oddities
Service call
Dick, P. K. Robots, androids, and mechanical oddities
The short happy life of the brown oxford
Dick, P. K. I hope I shall arrive soon
Strange memories of death
Dick, P. K. I hope I shall arrive soon
To serve the master
Dick, P. K. Robots, androids, and mechanical oddities
War game
Dick, P. K. Robots, androids, and mechanical oddities
What'll we do with Ragland Park?
Dick, P. K. I hope I shall arrive soon
Dick Baker's cat. Twain, M.
Dickens, Charles, 1812-1870
The bagman's story
Dickens, C. The signalman & other ghost stories
The Baron of Grogzwig
Dickens, C. The signalman & other ghost stories
The Boots at the Holly-Tree Inn
The Treasury of English short stories; ed. by N. Sullivan
Captain Murderer and the Devil's bargain [Variant title: Captain Murderer]
Great ghost stories; ed. by B. A. Schwartz
A child's dream of a star
Christian short stories; ed. by M. Booth
Dickens, C. The signalman & other ghost stories
The chimes
Dickens, C. A Christmas carol, and other Christmas stories
A Christmas carol
Dickens, C. A Christmas carol, and other Christmas stories
Christmas ghosts
Dickens, C. The signalman & other ghost stories
The Christmas story
The Saturday Evening Post 256:58-9+ D '84
A Christmas tree
Christmas ghosts; ed. by K. Cramer and D. G. Hartwell

A confession found in a prison in the time of Charles the Second
Dickens, C. The signalman & other ghost stories
The cricket on the hearth
Dickens, C. A Christmas carol, and other Christmas stories
The hanged man's bride
Dickens, C. The signalman & other ghost stories
A madman's manuscript
Dickens, C. The signalman & other ghost stories
The magic fishbone
Masterpieces of fantasy and enchantment; ed. by D. G. Hartwell
Mr. Testator's visitation
Dickens, C. The signalman & other ghost stories
A pair of gloves
Mystery in the mainstream; ed. by B. Pronzini; M. H. Greenberg and B. N. Malzberg
The signalman
Black water; ed. by A. Manguel
Charles Keeping's Book of classic ghost stories
Classic European short stories; ed. by R. Beum
Dark banquet; ed. by L. Child
The Dark descent; ed. by D. G. Hartwell
Dickens, C. The signalman & other ghost stories
Sketches by Boz [excerpt]
Inspired by drink; ed. by Joan Digby and John Digby
The story of the bagman's uncle [Variant title: The ghosts of the mail: the story of the bagman's uncle; The tale of the bagman's uncle]
The Book of the dead; ed. by A. K. Russell
Dickens, C. The signalman & other ghost stories
The story of the goblins who stole a sexton
Christmas ghosts; ed. by K. Cramer and D. G. Hartwell
Dickens, C. The signalman & other ghost stories
To be read at dusk
Dickens, C. The signalman & other ghost stories
The trial for murder
Dickens, C. The signalman & other ghost stories
The wreck of the Golden Mary
Short stories of the sea; ed. by G. C. Solley and E. Steinbaugh
Parodies, travesties, etc.
Machen, A. A new Christmas carol

Dickens, Monica, 1915-
Activity time
The Penguin book of horror stories

Dickerson, Karle
The gift
'*Teen* 29:30+ Mr '85
Just my type
'*Teen* 30:40+ Ag '86
The messenger
'*Teen* 31:46-8+ Ap '87
A second impression
'*Teen* 28:38-41+ F '84

Dickinson, Charles, 1951-
1-800-YOUR BOY
The Atlantic 261:62-4+ Mr '88
Abundance
The New Yorker 63:46-53 N 9 '87
Arcadia
Dickinson, C. With or without, and
other stories
A Grand Street reader; ed. by B. Son-
nenberg
Bill Boston
Dickinson, C. With or without, and
other stories
Black Bart
Dickinson, C. With or without, and
other stories
Child in the leaves
The New Yorker 64:35-42 Mr 7 '88
The fire
Dickinson, C. With or without, and
other stories
The jinx
Dickinson, C. With or without, and
other stories
My livelihood
Dickinson, C. With or without, and
other stories
A night in the garden
Dickinson, C. With or without, and
other stories
The New Yorker 61:28-31 F 17 '86
Risk
Dickinson, C. With or without, and
other stories
Prize stories, 1984
Sofa art
Dickinson, C. With or without, and
other stories
The New Yorker 61:42-8 My 6 '85
With or without
Dickinson, C. With or without, and
other stories

Dickinson, Don
The mythical kid
The New press anthology #1

Dickinson, Peter, 1927-
Flight
Imaginary lands; ed. by R. McKinley

Dickson, Carr, 1906-1977
*For works written by this author under
other names see* Carr, John Dickson,
1906-1977

Dickson, Carter, 1906-1977
*For works written by this author under
other names see* Carr, John Dickson,
1906-1977

Dickson, Gordon R.
Catch a tartar
Dickson, G. R. Mindspan
The cloak and the staff
The Hugo winners v5
The faithful wilf
Dickson, G. R. Mindspan
Fleegl of Fleegl
Dickson, G. R. Mindspan
Jackal's meal
Space wars; created by P. Anderson
Lost Dorsai
The Hugo winners v5
A matter of technique
Dickson, G. R. Mindspan
Miss Prinks
Dickson, G. R. Mindspan
The monkey wrench
Machines that think; ed. by I. Asimov;
P. S. Warrick and M. H. Greenberg
The mortal and the monster
Baker's dozen: 13 short science fiction
novels
Operation P-Button
Dickson, G. R. Mindspan
Rex and Mr. Rejilla
Dickson, G. R. Mindspan
Show me the way to go home
Dickson, G. R. Mindspan
Sleight of wit
Dickson, G. R. Mindspan
Soupstone
Dickson, G. R. Mindspan
Warrior
Robert Adams' Book of soldiers
Who dares a Bulbur eat?
Dickson, G. R. Mindspan
A wobble in Wockii futures
Dickson, G. R. Mindspan
(jt. auth) See Anderson, Poul, 1926-, and
Dickson, Gordon R.

Dickson, Margaret
Can ball
The Antioch Review 42:93-102 Wint '84

Dickson, Marie Maziarz
The farmer
Here's the story: fiction with heart; ed.
by M. Sklar

Dicky's death. Amichai, Y.
The **dictator.** Austin, D.
DICTATORS
See also Fascism; Totalitarianism
Austin, D. The dictator
Sackett, S. Hail to the chief
Valenzuela, L. The gift of words

DICTATORS—*Continued*
  Valenzuela, L. The place of its quietude
DICTATORSHIP *See* Dictators
Dictionary art review. Boylan, J.
Did anyone see my doggie? Winters, J.
Did you say—Dad? Ferreira, R.
Did you see the window-cleaner? Edgell, J.
Did you tell Daddy? Lovesey, P.
Diddling considered as one of the exact sciences. Poe, E. A.
The **die-hard**. Benét, S. V.
Die like a dog. See Stout, R. A dog in the daytime
Diehard. Kinsella, W. P.
Diehl: the wandering years. Camoin, F. A.
Dies irae. Ferguson, W.
Dies irae. Sheffield, C.
A **diet** of bananas and Nietzsche. Clark, M.
The **dietary** exploits of Bessie. Kilgore, D.
DIETING *See* Reducing
The **difference**. Glasgow, E.
The **difference**. Swenson, K.
The **difference**. Verma, N.
A **different** ball game. Friedman, B. J.
A **different** language. Caesar, J.
A **difficult** evening. Buzzati, D.
A **difficult** hour. Mann, T.
A **difficult** undertaking. Turtledove, H.
DiFranco, Anthony Mario, 1945-
  The garden of redemption
    Prize stories, 1986
Digby, John, 1938-
  The champagne party
    Inspired by drink; ed. by Joan Digby and John Digby
  Incident at the Gaumont
    Inspired by drink; ed. by Joan Digby and John Digby
  It's a man's drink, tonic water
    Inspired by drink; ed. by Joan Digby and John Digby
  The one and only bottle
    Inspired by drink; ed. by Joan Digby and John Digby
Digging a hole. Hemley, R.
Digging up the mountains. Bissoondath, N.
The **dignity** of life. Bly, C.
The **dignity** of Signor Da Ponte. Morazzoni, M.
The **Dileas**. MacLean, A.
DILLINGER, JOHN, 1903-1934
  About
  Henson, R. Billie loses her job
Dillon, Millicent
  Monitor
    Prize stories, 1987
  Wrong stories
    Southwest Review 73:30-55 Wint '88
The **Dilmun** Exchange. Pachter, J.
Dilov, Ljuben
  Contacts of a fourth kind
    Tales from the planet Earth

  Forward, mankind!
    The Penguin world omnibus of science fiction
Dilworth, Sharon
  Independence Day
    Dilworth, S. The long white
  The lady on the plane
    Dilworth, S. The long white
  Lip service résumé
    Dilworth, S. The long white
    Michigan Quarterly Review 27:400-16 Summ '88
  The long white
    Dilworth, S. The long white
  Lunch at Archibald's
    Dilworth, S. The long white
  Mad Dog Queen
    Dilworth, S. The long white
  Miles from Coconut Grove
    Dilworth, S. The long white
  The seeney stretch
    Dilworth, S. The long white
  Winter mines
    Dilworth, S. The long white
    The North American Review 272:52-6 Je '87
Dime a dance. See Irish, W. The dancing detective
A **DimEn** is forever. Franklin, P.
Diner. Barrett, N., Jr.
Dinesen, Isak, 1885-1962
  The blue eyes
    Ladies' Home Journal 103:88+ Ap '86
  The cloak
    The Art of the tale; ed. by D. Halpern
    Haunting women; ed. by A. Ryan
  From 'Peter and Rosa'
    Black water; ed. by A. Manguel
  The sailor-boy's tale
    Handle with care; ed. by J. Kahn
Ding dong bell. Annan, K.
Ding-dong, the lizard's dead. Russell, R.
Ding Ling
  The silent speech of love
    Ms. 16:64-5+ D '87
Dingle the fool. Jolley, E.
Dinner along the Amazon. Findley, T.
Dinner for one. Tremain, R.
Dinner for two. Gault, C.
Dinner for two. Wright, D. W.
Dinner in Audoghast. Sterling, B.
DINNER PARTIES *See* Dinners
The **dinner** party. Baumbach, J.
The **dinner** party. Mordden, E.
Dinner time. Edson, R.
DINNERS
  Apollinaire, G. Our friend Méritarte
  Baumbach, J. The dinner party
  Calvino, I. A goatherd at luncheon
  Carver, R. Feathers
  Chernoff, M. Don't send poems, send money
  Colter, C. Black for dinner

DINNERS—*Continued*
Dadswell, M. To eat or not to eat
Durrell, L. Jots and tittles
Findley, T. Dinner along the Amazon
Godwin, P. A matter of taste
Grenville, K. No such thing as a free lunch
Halligan, M. The living hothouse
Haylock, J. Fan mail
Henry, O. The renaissance at Charleroi
Humphrey, W. Quail for Mr. Forester
Minot, S. Sparks
Munro, A. Labor Day dinner
O'Brien, E. The plan
Pilcher, R. An evening to remember
Pym, B. Across a crowded room
Rhys, J. Kikimora
Sagan, F. One year later
Shannon, D. They will call it insane
Stuart, J. The champion
Tallent, E. Half a mussel shell
Thomas, J. Barbecue
Dinnertime. Muschg, A.
DINOSAURS
Aldiss, B. W. Poor little warrior!
Drake, D. Time safari
Gustafson, J. Beast
Silverberg, R. Our Lady of the Sauropods
Waldrop, H. Green Brother
Dinosaurs. Williams, W. J.
Diomedes at Aulis. Parotti, P.
DIONYSUS
Silverberg, R. The feast of St. Dionysus
A **dip** in the Poole. Pronzini, B.
DIPLOMATIC LIFE
Bloch, R. The old college try
Bradley, M. Z. Centaurus changeling
Colette. "Châ"
Dickson, G. R. The faithful wilf
Dickson, G. R. Jackal's meal
Dickson, G. R. Who dares a Bulbur eat?
Dickson, G. R. A wobble in Wockii futures
Durrell, L. All to scale
Durrell, L. Call of the sea
Durrell, L. Case history
Durrell, L. A corking evening
Durrell, L. Cry wolf
Durrell, L. Drage's divine discontent
Durrell, L. For immediate release
Durrell, L. The game's the thing
Durrell, L. The ghost train
Durrell, L. High barbary
Durrell, L. If garlic be the food of love . . .
Durrell, L. The iron hand
Durrell, L. Jots and tittles
Durrell, L. The little affair in Paris
Durrell, L. 'Noblesse oblige'
Durrell, L. Sauve qui peut
Durrell, L. Seraglios and imbroglios
Durrell, L. Smoke, the embassy cat
Durrell, L. Something à la carte?

Durrell, L. Stiff upper lip
Durrell, L. The swami's secret
Durrell, L. Taking the consequences
Durrell, L. The unspeakable attaché
Durrell, L. La valise
Durrell, L. What-ho on the Rialto!
Durrell, L. Where the bee sucks . . .
Durrell, L. White man's milk
Ellison, H. Hadj
Fisher, M. F. K. Diplomatic, retired
Heald, T. The case of the frozen diplomat
Longyear, B. B. The homecoming
Oates, J. C. Old Budapest
Piper, H. B. He walked around the horses
Ruta, S. The shoe clerk
Tuohy, F. Two private lives
Diplomatic, retired. Fisher, M. F. K.
DIPLOMATS *See* Diplomatic life
The **dipping** of the candlemaker. Howard, H.
Dirckx, John H.
The adventure of the oval window
Ellery Queen's Prime crimes
Directed verdict. Chastain, T.
The **director** of death. Covino, M.
DIRECTORS, MOTION PICTURE *See* Motion picture producers and directors
The **dirigible.** Bumpus, J.
DIRIGIBLES *See* Airships
Dirt angel. Wilmot, J.
Dirty heels of the fine young children. Rooke, L.
Dirty old man. Bernard, K.
Dirty windows. Cherches, P.
The **disappearance.** Schinto, J.
The **disappearance** of Mr. Davenheim. Christie, A.
DISAPPEARANCES *See* Missing persons
Disappearing act. Moore, A.
The **disappearing** diamond. Carpenter, H., and Carpenter, L.
Disarmament. Zancanella, D.
Disarming Big Mad. Karbo, K.
Disaster. Asscher-Pinkhof, C.
The **disaster.** Chipulina, E. G.
Disaster. Wilson, B.
DISASTERS
See also Earthquakes; Epidemics; Famines; Floods; Industrial accidents; Shipwrecks and castaways
Clark, E. Hurry, hurry
McDevitt, J. Promises to keep
DISC JOCKEYS
Pak, Y.-S. Eroica Symphony
Tournier, M. Tristan Vox
Wilson, F. P. The last one mo once golden oldies revival
Disch, Thomas M.
The Asian shore
The Dark descent; ed. by D. G. Hartwell
Canned goods
Interzone: the 2nd anthology; ed. by J. Clute; D. Pringle and S. Ounsley

Disch, Thomas M.—*Continued*
Concepts
Medea: Harlan's world; ed. by H. Ellison
The **girl** with the Vita-Gel hair
Omni (New York, N.Y.) 9:68-70+ D '86
Palindrome
Omni (New York, N.Y.) 9:42-4+ S '87
Ringtime
Omni book of science fiction 3
The roaches
The Dark descent; ed. by D. G. Hartwell
Rude awakening
Omni (New York, N.Y.) 9:64-9 My '87
Dische, Irene
Berlin snowfall
The New Yorker 61:44-7 N 18 '85
Disciple pigeons. Smolens, J.
A **disciplined** life. White, C.
The **discontent** of Franz Boas. Ahern, T.
A **discontinued** knot. Yi, S.
Discontinued lines. Tuohy, F.
DISCOTHEQUES
Burt, S. Welcome
Discount fare. Lutz, J.
Discourse of a lady standing a dinner to a down-and-out friend. Rhys, J.
Discoverable laws. Wilson, B.
Discovered. Botwinik, B.
Discoveries. Nelson, K.
Discovery. Clark, M.
Discovery. Hull, H. R.
The **discovery**. Mazel, D.
A **discovery** in the woods. Greene, G.
The **discovery** of the past. Anderson, P.
DISEASES
See also Sexually transmitted diseases; Tuberculosis; Typhus fever
Boyle, T. C. A bird in hand
Butler, O. E. The evening and the morning and the night
Harrison, M. J. The new rays
Kilworth, G. Scarlet fever
McGrath, P. Blood disease
Pirandello, L. The stuffed bird
Wilson, P. F. Soft
The **disguise**. Robinson, K. S.
Disguised. Singer, I. B.
DISGUISES *See* Impersonations
A **dish** of homicide. Searls, H.
Disher, Garry
The bamboo flute
Short story international 64
Dead eye
Prairie Schooner 62:113-17 Wint '88/'89
The **disinherited**. Hendry, J. F.
DISNEY, WALT, 1901-1966
About
Apple, M. Walt and Will
Disneyad. See Apple, M. Walt and Will
DISNEYLAND (ANAHEIM, CALIF.)
Keller, G. D. Mocha in Disneyland
Disneyland. DeMarinis, R.

Disneyland. Gowdy, B.
DISORDERS OF PERSONALITY *See* Personality disorders
Disparities. Okri, B.
Dispatching Bootsie. Harrington, J.
The **dispatching** of George Ferris. Pronzini, B.
Dispensation. Crandall, D.
The **displaced** person. O'Connor, F.
Displaced person. Russell, E. F.
Displacement. Louie, D. W.
The **dispossessed**. Gifkins, M.
Disquiet. Clark, M.
The **dissemblers**. Kilworth, G.
DISSENTERS
Gilliatt, P. Splendid lives
Jhabvala, R. P. My first marriage
Nowakowski, M. The June cross
Nowakowski, M. The search
Nowakowski, M. The shadow
Nowakowski, M. The well-matched couple
DISSIDENTS *See* Dissenters
Distance. Carver, R.
Distances. Kinsella, W. P.
A **distant** bell. Enright, E.
The **distant** cousin. Sagan, F.
Distant cousins. Colegate, I.
A **distant** episode. Bowles, P.
Distant lands. Winton, T.
Distant seas. Selmi, H.
The **distant** sound of tree-felling. Cehai, C.
Distant view of a minaret. Rifaat, A.
Distillation. Martínez-Serros, H.
DISTILLERIES
Knox, B. Deerglen Queen
Wilkinson, R. The lean
DISTILLING, ILLICIT *See* Moonshiners
The **distributor**. Nowakowski, M.
The **distributors**. Dumas, H.
DISTRICT OF COLUMBIA *See* Washington (D.C.)
Disturb not my slumbering fair. Yarbro, C. Q.
Disturbance reported on a pipeline. Kotzwinkle, W.
Disturbances. Coskran, K.
Disturber of the peace. Brown, M. W.
Disturbing no one. Pritchard, M.
The **diver**. Jahnn, H. H.
Divide and rule. De Camp, L. S.
The **divided** Carla. Nesvadba, J.
The **divided** daughter. *See* Ch'en, H.-Y. 'Twixt soul and body
DIVINATION
Schwob, M. Sufrah, geomancer
The **divine** dealer. Finney, E. J.
Diving. Summers, H. S.
DIVORCE
See also Desertion and nonsupport; Divorced persons; Marriage problems
Abbott, K. Jesus Christ and the plaster squirrels
Abbott, L. K. Martians

DIVORCE—*Continued*

Al-Shaykh, H. The Persian carpet
Alderson, T. Michelson in the desert
Allbeury, T. The party of the second part
Anderson, J. The milk
Apple, M. Momma's boy
Auchincloss, L. Equitable awards
Auchincloss, L. The takeover
Austin, M. H. The divorcing of Sina
Barich, B. Giorgio's mother
Barstow, S. The glad eye
Baumbach, J. Children of divorced parents
Bird, C. Bye baby bunting
Böll, H. Till death us do part
Bradbury, R. Long division
Chernoff, M. Heroes
Chipulina, E. G. One of those things
Clayton, J. J. An old 3 A.M. story
Cohen, R. The scientific method
Colette. The find
Cooper, J. C. The life you live (may not be your own)
Curley, D. The first baseman
Curley, D. The other two
Curley, D. Trinity
Curley, D. Wild geese
Davis, L. Therapy
Finney, E. J. The investigator
Ford, R. Sweethearts
Gallagher, T. Recourse
Gardner, C. S. Walk home alone
Gilchrist, E. The lower garden district free gravity mule blight; or, Rhoda, a fable
Giles, M. Pie dance
Giles, M. What do you say?
Gold, H. Love and like
Gold, H. The smallest part
Grau, S. A. Ending
Grau, S. A. Letting go
Greene, G. Mortmain
Griesemer, J. Comfort stations
Harris, E. The world record holder
Harrison, M. J. The ice monkey
Heller, S. Postcard from Lahaina
Hood, M. Desire call of the wild hen
Hood, M. Hindsight
Hood, M. Solomon's seal
Hospital, J. T. The Dominican season
James, H. The chaperon
Johnston, B. Never the right time
Just, W. S. About Boston
Keillor, G. The royal family
Kidman, F. A strange delight
Leavitt, D. Danny in transit
Leavitt, D. Family dancing
Leavitt, D. The lost cottage
Lofts, N. The horse-leech hath two daughters
Lutz, J. Fractions
McCullers, C. The sojourner
McDonald, J. Settlement
Moore, L. The kid's guide to divorce

Mortimer, J. C. Rumpole and the married lady
Painter, P. The kidnappers
Painter, P. The visitor
Peterson, M. Mercy flights
Roberts, N. Dancing in Trolley Square
Rule, J. His nor hers
Schwartz, L. S. The subversive divorce
Shaw, J. B. In high country
Singer, I. B. The divorce
Skrzynecki, P. Hoeing
Smith, L. Life on the moon
Stafford, J. Children are bored on Sunday
Swados, H. A glance in the mirror
Swados, H. A hot day in Nuevo Laredo
Thomas, A. C. Breaking the ice
Thompson, K. A husband and a father
Treat, L. Who's innocent?
Trevor, W. A meeting in middle age
Updike, J. Deaths of distant friends
Updike, J. Here come the Maples
Updike, J. Still of some use
Updike, J. Trust me
Vanderhaeghe, G. Sam, Soren, and Ed
Walker, A. Kindred spirits
Wharton, E. The other two
Wharton, E. Souls belated
Willson, H. Moonset near Magdalena
Yi, S. A discontinued knot
The **divorce**. Singer, I. B.

DIVORCED PERSONS

Abbott, L. K. Dreams of distant lives
Abbott, L. K. The valley of sin
Alden, P. B. A member of the family
Banks, R. Sarah Cole: a type of love story
Barthelme, D. Visitors
Barthelme, S. Problematical species
Baxter, C. The crank
Beattie, A. Cards
Bellow, S. What kind of day did you have?
Blessing, R. Song on Royal Street
Bowers, J. Crackers
Boylan, J. Jimmy Durante lost in Antarctica
Bradbury, R. One night in your life
Broun, H. Ice water
Busch, F. Defense
Busch, F. The news
Busch, F. Rise and fall
Cadigan, P. The edge
Camoin, F. A. The Amelia Barons
Carter, M. Teacher
Carver, R. Chef's house
Carver, R. Intimacy
Cooper, J. C. The free and the caged
Davis, L. The letter
Davis, L. The sock
Deaver, P. F. Fiona's rooms
DeMarinis, R. Romance: a prose villanelle
Dilworth, S. Lunch at Archibald's
Dodd, S. M. Browsing
Dodd, S. M. Walls

DIVORCED PERSONS—*Continued*
Dubus, A. At St. Croix
Dubus, A. Finding a girl in America
Dubus, A. Voices from the moon
Dubus, A. The winter father
Evans, E. Locomotion
Everett, P. L. A good day for the laughing blow
Everett, P. L. A good home for Hachita
Farmer, B. At the airport
Ford, R. Sweethearts
Frucht, A. The anniversary
Gilchrist, E. The perfect stone
Gildner, G. Somewhere geese are flying
Glasser, P. What doesn't kill me
Greenberg, A. The man in the cardboard mask
Gustafsson, L. The fugitives discover that they knew nothing
Halligan, M. Hard sausage
Harvor, E. Heart trouble
Harvor, E. The students' soirée
Harvor, E. To supper in the morning and to bed at noon
Hauptman, W. Moon walking
Hemley, R. Digging a hole
Kalpakian, L. The last page
Kalpakian, L. A time change
Kavaler, R. Tigers in the wood
Kessler, J. F. Aeaea
Krist, G. Tribes of northern New Jersey
Lipsky, D. Three thousand dollars
Livesey, M. Peter and the asteroids
Lopatin, J. A phantasm, a bird—
Lott, B. This plumber
Malterre, E. Touching the buffalo
Martin, V. The freeze
Martini, C. Breath of God
Mason, B. A. Drawing names
Mason, B. A. Graveyard day
McFarland, D. Last night
Miller, S. Expensive gifts
Miller, S. Leaving home
Miller, S. Slides
Mills, W. Sweet Tickfaw run softly, till I end my song
Mooney, M. Married
Moorhouse, F. The airport, the pizzeria, the motel, the rented car, and the mysteries of life
Mukherjee, B. The tenant
Munro, A. Bardon bus
Munro, A. Labor Day dinner
Munro, A. Prue
Neugeboren, J. Don't worry about the kids
Nevai, L. Star game
Oates, J. C. August evening
Oates, J. C. Holiday
Oates, J. C. Visitation rights
Pesetsky, B. A walker's manual
Peterson, M. Coming about
Pfeil, F. The night game
Phillips, J. A. Something that happened

Prose, F. Tibetan time
Prose, F. Women and children first
Robison, M. An amateur's guide to the night
Robison, M. In the woods
Robison, M. Your errant mom
Rose, D. A. Parties and storms
Ross, J. Unfinished business
Rule, J. A perfectly nice man
Sagan, F. One year later
Salter, J. The fields at dusk
Sandel, C. A mystery
Schoemperlen, D. Crimes of passion
Schwartz, J. The last and only messenger
Schwartz, L. S. The accounting
Silva, B. Precious
Sorrells, R. T. A mature and civilized relationship
Steele, M. The girl from Carthage
Steele, M. The man in the doll house
Tallent, E. Why I love country music
Tamer, Z. The face of the moon
Thompson, S. The birthday party
Thompson, S. Memoir, cut short
Thompson, S. Notes
Thurm, M. Away from the heart
Thurm, M. Snow-child
Thurm, M. Squirrels
Thurm, M. Starlight
Thurm, M. Still life
Tremain, R. A shooting season
Tremayne, P. The Samhain Feis
Updike, J. Nevada
Welch, D. Alex Fairburn
Whelan, G. Sympathy notes
Zhang Jie. The ark
Ziem, J. His own boss

DIVORCÉES *See* Divorced persons
DIVORCÉS *See* Divorced persons
The **divorcing** of Sina. Austin, M. H.
The **Dixie** Association. Hays, D.
Dixon, Melvin, 1950-
Red leaves
   Men on men 2; ed. by G. Stambolian
Dixon, Stephen, 1936-
The beginning of something
   Dixon, S. Time to go
The bench
   Dixon, S. Time to go
The book review
   Dixon, S. The play, and other stories
The bridge
   Dixon, S. The play, and other stories
Change
   Dixon, S. The play, and other stories
China
   Southwest Review 72:247-57 Spr '87
The clean-up man
   Dixon, S. The play, and other stories
Come on a coming
   Dixon, S. Time to go
Don
   Dixon, S. Time to go

Dixon, Stephen, 1936—*Continued*
  Down the road
    Dixon, S. The play, and other stories
  Eating the placenta
    Dixon, S. Time to go
  Encountering revolution
    Dixon, S. Time to go
  End of Magna
    Dixon, S. Time to go
  For a man your age
    Dixon, S. Time to go
  Frog acts
    TriQuarterly no71:53-64 Wint '88
  Frog's break
    The Literary Review (Madison, N.J.)
      31:473-84 Summ '88
  Goodbye to goodbye
    Dixon, S. Time to go
    The Paris Review 27:14-25 Fall '85
  The last resort
    Dixon, S. The play, and other stories
  The letter
    Dixon, S. The play, and other stories
    The North American Review 271:38-9 Je
      '86
  Magna takes the calls
    Dixon, S. Time to go
  Meeting Aline
    Dixon, S. Time to go
  Milk is very good for you
    Love stories for the time being; ed. by
      G. D. Chipps and B. Henderson
  Moving on
    Dixon, S. The play, and other stories
  My life up till now
    The Literary Review (Madison, N.J.)
      29:239-49 Wint '86
  The news
    Dixon, S. The play, and other stories
  The package store
    Dixon, S. Time to go
  A parting
    Dixon, S. The play, and other stories
  The play
    Dixon, S. The play, and other stories
  Ray
    Dixon, S. The play, and other stories
  The rescuer
    Dixon, S. The play, and other stories
  Reversal
    Dixon, S. Time to go
  The ringer
    Dixon, S. The play, and other stories
  Scratch scratch
    Dixon, S. The play, and other stories
  The second part
    Dixon, S. The play, and other stories
  Self-portrait
    Dixon, S. Time to go
  The signing
    Sudden fiction; ed. by R. Shapard and
      J. Thomas
  Speak
    Dixon, S. The play, and other stories
  Takes
    Michigan Quarterly Review 26:759-68
      Fall '87
  Time to go
    Dixon, S. Time to go
  Wheels
    Dixon, S. Time to go
  Will as a boy
    Dixon, S. Time to go
  Will's book
    Dixon, S. Time to go
  Windows
    The North American Review 270:34-9 Mr
      '85
Django, Karfunkelstein, & roses. Levine, N.
Djemal's revenge. Highsmith, P.
The **Djinn** murder. Brown, F.
Dlugos, Tim
  Generation
    First love/last love; ed. by M. Denneny;
      C. Ortleb and T. Steele
Dnieprov, Anatoly
  The Maxwell equations
    Mathenauts: tales of mathematical won-
      der; ed. by R. Rucker
Do androids dream of electric love? Lieb-
  scher, W.
Do I dare to eat a peach? Yarbro, C. Q.
Do-it-yourself. Ellison, H.
Do-it-yourself S & M. Mordden, E.
Do not forsake me, O my darlin'. Yarbro,
  C. Q.
Do seek their meat from God. Roberts, C.
  G. D.
Do stay, Giraffe. Borchert, W.
Do the dead sing. See King, S. The reach
Do ye hear the children weeping? Goldsmith,
  H.
Do you know what it means to Miss New
  Orleans? Mason, B. A.
Do you like it here? O'Hara, J.
Do you like the mountains? Kees, W.
Do you want my opinion? Kerr, M. E.
Doan whispers. Raine, W. M.
Dobbs Ferry. Patten, L. B.
DOBERMAN PINSCHERS
  Reed, K. Dog days
DOCK HANDS *See* Longshore workers
Doc's story. Wideman, J. E.
The **doctor.** Gallant, M.
The **doctor** & the social worker. Luks, A.
The **doctor** afraid of blood. Harris, H.
The **doctor** and the doctor's wife. Heming-
  way, E.
Doctor Crombie. Greene, G.
Doctor Machover. Blinkin, M.
Doctor Safi. Mrabet, P.
The **doctor** takes a case. Coxe, G. H.
Doctor Zeit. Fraser, A.
The **doctorate.** Ebon, W.

Doctorow, E. L., 1931-
Billy Bathgate
Gentlemen's Quarterly 58:344-52 N '88
The foreign legation
Doctorow, E. L. Lives of the poets
The hunter
The Art of the tale; ed. by D. Halpern
Doctorow, E. L. Lives of the poets
The leather man
The Best American short stories, 1985
Doctorow, E. L. Lives of the poets
The Paris Review 26:12-21 Summ '84
Lives of the poets
Doctorow, E. L. Lives of the poets
The Water Works
Doctorow, E. L. Lives of the poets
Willi
American short story masterpieces; ed.
by R. Carver and T. Jenks
The Atlantic 253:89-92 My '84
Dark arrows; ed. by A. Manguel
Doctorow, E. L. Lives of the poets
The writer in the family
Doctorow, E. L. Lives of the poets
Early sorrow: ten stories of youth; ed.
by C. Zolotow
The Esquire fiction reader v1
Look who's talking; ed. by B. Weber
DOCTORS *See* Physicians; Surgeons; Women physicians
The **doctor's** case. King, S.
The **doctor's** house. Collins, L.
The **doctor's** mother. Wu, C.-L.
Doctor's orders. Suter, J. F.
The **doctor's** son. O'Hara, J.
DOCUMENTS *See* Manuscripts
Dodd, Susan M., 1946-
Berkie
Dodd, S. M. Old wives' tales
Browsing
Dodd, S. M. Old wives' tales
Coelostat
Dodd, S. M. Old wives' tales
Hell-bent men and their cities
The North American Review 271:56-9 S
'86
Isometropia
The North American Review 273:46-8 Mr
'88
One hundred years of solicitude: The
meditations of Ursula
Dodd, S. M. Old wives' tales
Potions
Dodd, S. M. Old wives' tales
Public appearances
Dodd, S. M. Old wives' tales
Rue
Dodd, S. M. Old wives' tales
Sinatra
The New Yorker 64:32-5 My 16 '88
Snowbird
Dodd, S. M. Old wives' tales

Walls
Dodd, S. M. Old wives' tales
Wild men of Borneo
Dodd, S. M. Old wives' tales
Doderer, Heimito von, 1896-1966
The last adventure
Southern Humanities Review 22:113-68
Spr '88
DODGSON, CHARLES LUTWIDGE *See*
Carroll, Lewis, 1832-1898
DODOS
Waldrop, H. The ugly chickens
Dodu. Narayan, R. K.
Doe season. Kaplan, D. M.
Doerr, Harriet
Picnic at Amapolas
The New Yorker 61:32-8 F 17 '86
Does a bee care? Asimov, I.
Dog. Benedict, P.
A **dog.** Fink, I.
The **dog.** Lish, G.
The **dog** and the dead. Davin, D.
Dog attempts to drown man in Saskatoon.
Glover, D. H.
Dog, Cat, and Baby. Lansdale, J. R.
Dog days. Mantel, H.
Dog days. Reed, K.
A **dog** in Durer's etching 'The knight, death
and the devil'. Denevi, M.
A **dog** in the daytime. Stout, R.
Dog life. Strand, M.
The **dog** mafia. Harris, M.
Dog man. Hensley, J. L.
Dog people. Goldman, E. S.
Dog problems. Nelson, A.
DOG RACING
Hoch, E. D. Captain Leopold goes to the
dogs
Dog song. Busch, F.
Dog Star. Clarke, A. C.
The **dog** that knew better. Flynn, R.
The **dog** who hated jazz. Bankier, W.
Dogbane. Sisk, F.
The **dogeater.** Kercheval, J. L.
Dogfight. Swanwick, M., and Gibson, W.
DOGFIGHTING
Benedict, P. Pit
Dogmaster. Haley, R.
DOGS
Abbott, L. K. Where is Garland Steeples
now?
Adams, A. Molly's dog
Aickman, R. The same dog
Amis, M. The little puppy that could
Anderson, S. Death in the woods
Anthony, P. Gone to the dogs
Armstrong, C. The enemy
Bankier, W. The dog who hated jazz
Barthelme, S. Beach
Bates, H. E. A great day for Bonzo
Bell, M. S. The day I shot my dog
Bell, V. Brag dog
Benedict, P. Dog

DOGS—*Continued*

Bernen, R. Brock
Bernen, R. A keen observer of footwear
Bishop, M. Dogs' lives
Blythe, R. Dear dead Pippa
Botwinik, B. Jake
Bradbury, R. The emissary
Brand, M. A lucky dog
Briskin, M. Children, dogs and dying men
Brown, M. W. The black dog
Butler, E. P. Getting rid of Fluff
Cameron, P. Homework
Carlson, R. Max
Christie, A. The Nemean lion
Clarke, A. C. Dog Star
Cockrell, C. In praise of creeping things
Colette. Bella-Vista
Colette. The bitch
Colette. Clever dogs
Colette. "Lola"
Conroy, J. The Boomer's fireman's fast sooner hound
Crane, S. The black dog
Crane, S. A dark-brown dog
Davin, D. The dog and the dead
DeGrazia, E. The death of Sin
Del Rey, L. The faithful
DeMarinis, R. The handgun
Dennison, G. Shawno
Dickinson, C. With or without
Dickson, G. R. Rex and Mr. Rejilla
Doyle, Sir A. C. Silver Blaze
Durrell, L. The unspeakable attaché
Edmonds, W. D. Moses
Ekström, M. The nothingness forest
Ellis, M. Mister Dog
Ellison, H. A boy and his dog
Essop, A. Mr Moonreddy
Everett, P. L. Thirty-seven just to take a fall
Faik, S. Filbert
Fairman, P. W. The dark road home
Farmer, P. J. A Scarletin study
Fenton, E. Gun-shy
Fink, I. The black beast
Fink, I. A dog
Flynn, R. The dog that knew better
Ford, C. Slipstream
Fraser, A. Death of an old dog
Freeman, J. The rake people
Gébler, C. Puerto Vallarta
Gerber, M. J. At the fence
Giardinelli, M. Revolution on a bicycle
Giles, M. Pie dance
Gilford, C. B. The forgiving ghost
Gold, H. L. A matter of form
Goulart, R. How come my dog don't bark?
Gray, A. The comedy of the white dog
Greene, G. Beauty
Grey, Z. Don
Haley, R. Dogmaster
Haley, R. Story

Harrington, J. Dispatching Bootsie
Harris, M. The dog mafia
Hartley, L. P. A rewarding experience
Hartley, L. P. The silver clock
Hempel, A. Breathing Jesus
Hempel, A. Nashville gone to ashes
Henderson, D. Broken treaty
Henderson, D. The test
Henry, O. Memoirs of a yellow dog
Hensley, J. L. Dog man
Highsmith, P. There I was, stuck with Bubsy
Hoch, E. D. Just one more
Hood, M. Manly conclusions
Huang, C.-M. I love Mary
Jackson, S. The renegade
Kaplan, D. M. Elias Schneebaum
Katz, S. Mongolian Whiskey
Kawabata, Y. A pet dog's safe birthing
Keith, D. L. When the morning comes
Kessler, J. F. Hermes
Kim, Y. I. From below the bridge
Knight, E. M. Lassie come-home
La Chapelle, M. The understanding
Law, W. Lincoln's doctor's son's dog
Lawrence, D. H. Rex
Lawson, H. The loaded dog
Leonard, H. The anticlerical pup
Lispector, C. Temptation
London, J. Brown Wolf
London, J. A daughter of the aurora
London, J. Diable: a dog
London, J. For the love of a man
London, J. That Spot
London, J. The white silence
Lutz, J. Dead man
MacLaverty, B. Where the tides meet
MacLeod, A. As birds bring forth the sun
Marquis, D. Blood will tell
Martin, V. Spats
Matthews, J. The immortal dog
Matthiessen, P. Sadie
Maupassant, G. de. Francis
Maupassant, G. de. Semillante
Maupassant, G. de. The watchdog
Mazel, D. Dragons and puppies
Mazel, D. Jeopardies
Mazel, D. Our Zaideh
McGuane, T. Dogs
McGuane, T. Flight
McGuane, T. A man in Louisiana
McGuane, T. Two hours to kill
Mordden, E. The complete death of the clown dog
Morris, W. Victrola
Muir, J. An adventure with a dog
Narayan, R. K. Attila
Narayan, R. K. The blind dog
Narayan, R. K. Chippy
Nevins, F. M., Jr. The Dogsbody case
Nordan, L. Wild dog
Norris, L. Lurchers
O'Brien, D. The Georgia breeze

DOGS—*Continued*

Ocampo, S. Mimoso

Ollivant, A. The tailless tyke at bay

Olmstead, R. How to bury a dog

Olmstead, R. River dogs

Painter, P. A man of his time

Pascoe, B. Splitter

Pascoe, B. Thylacine

Perowne, B. Raffles on the trail of the hound

Pronzini, B. On guard!

Pronzini, B., and Wallmann, J. M. Coyote and Quarter Moon

Rinehart, M. R. The splinter

Rosenbaum, K. Low tide

Rosenfeld, I. Red Wolf

Rudin, J. Sellin' some wood

Rush, N. Official Americans

Sagan, F. A dog's night

Sandel, C. Allie

Savage, E. The man who liked noise

Schwartz, L. S. Sound is second sight

Shi Tiesheng. Blacky

Sholem Aleichem. Rabchik, a Jewish dog

Sisk, F. Dogbane

Skelton, R. Finder

Stafford, J. In the zoo

Stead, C. Yac, yac

Strand, M. Dog life

Stratton, M. Before summer comes

Street, J. Weep no more, my lady

Stuart, J. Fight number twenty-five

Tarkington, B. Blue milk

Terhune, A. P. The coming of Lad

Terhune, A. P. The grudge

Thomas, J. Barbecue

Thompson, J. Ice flowers

Tuohy, F. The matchmakers

Turgenev, I. S. Mumú

Twain, M. A dog's tale

Updike, D. The end of the reign

Varley, J. Tango Charlie and Foxtrot Romeo

Wellen, E. Voiceover

Wheeler, H. C. Puzzle for Poppy

Winters, Y. The brink of darkness

Wodehouse, P. G. The mixer

Wodehouse, P. G. Open house

Wodehouse, P. G. Ukridge's dog college

Wolfe, T. Three o'clock

Woolf, V. Gipsy, the mongrel

Zhang Xianliang. The story of an old man and a dog

Training

Maupassant, G. de. The man with the dogs

Dogs. Kooser, T.

Dogs. McGuane, T.

Dogs and foreigners. Lester, C. S.

Dogs, in Denpasar. Sheil, G.

The **dogs** in Renoir's garden. Whelan, G.

A **dog's** life. Pil'niāk, B.

Dogs' lives. Bishop, M.

A **dog's** night. Sagan, F.

A **dog's** tale. Twain, M.

The **Dogsbody** case. Nevins, F. M., Jr.

Doherty, Berlie

The bad boy
Critical Quarterly 30:52-7 Summ '88

Doig, D. T.

A love song for Christmas
Good Housekeeping 205:248+ D '87

The man who married Mom
Good Housekeeping 204:182-3+ My '87

Midnight dreams
Good Housekeeping 201:202-3+ D '85

A precious memory
Good Housekeeping 203:117-18+ D '86

Doing right. Clarke, A. C.

Doing the voices. Brooks, J.

Doing this, saying that, to applause. Hood, M.

Doing yoga. Adams, G. G.

Dokey, Richard

Heartland
Southwest Review 69:148-53 Spr '84

Dolce far' niente. Humphrey, W.

Doll. Hall, M. L.

The **doll.** O'Brien, E.

The **doll.** Ocampo, S.

The **doll** queen. Fuentes, C.

Dollarhide, Louis

The gift
Mississippi writers v1: Fiction; ed. by D. Abbott

Dollars and cents. Asimov, I.

Dollars and the demimondaine. Calvino, I.

A **dollar's** worth. Valdez, O. J.

DOLLS

Bloch, R. Sweets to the sweet

Campbell, R. Lilith's

Caplan, N. Murder in miniature

Christie, A. The dressmaker's doll

Crawford, F. M. The doll's ghost

Dick, P. K. The days of Perky Pat

Ferré, R. The youngest doll

Millhauser, S. August Eschenburg

Ocampo, S. The doll

Rodoreda, M. The dolls' room

Schinto, J. Keepsake

Sheckley, R. Shootout in the toy shop

Dolls. Campbell, R.

The **doll's** ghost. Crawford, F. M.

Doll's house. Eisenstein, S.

The **doll's** house. Mansfield, K.

The **dolls'** room. Rodoreda, M.

Dolly. Essop, A.

Dolly. Summers, H. S.

The **dolly** house. Naipaul, S.

Dolores Ibarruri sheds bitter tears. Tabucchi, A.

Dolphin dreaming. LaSalle, P.

DOLPHINS

Jarvis, M. C. Collaboration

Silverberg, R. Ishmael in love

The **Dom.** Schwob, M.

The **domain** of Arnheim. Poe, E. A.
The **dome** of many colors. Gardner, M.
A **domestic** dilemma. McCullers, C.
Domestic order. James-French, D.
DOMESTIC RELATIONS *See* Family life
Domini, John, 1951-
At the dig
  The Massachusetts Review 25:445-54 Aut
  '84
Highway trade
  Southwest Review 73:180-207 Spr '88
DOMINICA
Rhys, J. Fishy waters
Dominica. Lopatin, J.
DOMINICAN REPUBLIC
                    Santo Domingo
Kleist, H. von. Betrothal in Santo
  Domingo
The **Dominican** season. Hospital, J. T.
The **Domino** Lady doubles back. Anderson,
  L.
The **domino** master. Blumlein, M.
Don. Dixon, S.
Don. Grey, Z.
The **Don.** Thompson, S.
Don Alfonso's treasure hunt. Masefield, J.
Don Giacomo. Paolucci, A.
DON JUAN (LEGENDARY CHARACTER)
Pritchett, V. S. A story of Don Juan
Don Juan. Hoffmann, E. T. A.
Don Juan, the senior citizen. Pulaski, J.
Dona Amalia Quadros. Leitão, L.
Doña baby. Truesdale, C. W.
DONAHUE (TELEVISION PROGRAM)
Gilchrist, E. First Manhattans
Donaldo Arrieta. Álvarez Gardeazábal, G.
Donaldson, Stephen R.
Animal lover
  Donaldson, S. R. Daughter of Regals,
    and other tales
The conqueror worm
  Donaldson, S. R. Daughter of Regals,
    and other tales
Daughter of Regals
  Donaldson, S. R. Daughter of Regals,
    and other tales
Gilden-Fire
  Donaldson, S. R. Daughter of Regals,
    and other tales
The Lady in White
  Donaldson, S. R. Daughter of Regals,
    and other tales
Mythological beast
  Donaldson, S. R. Daughter of Regals,
    and other tales
Ser Visal's tale
  Donaldson, S. R. Daughter of Regals,
    and other tales
Unworthy of the angel
  Donaldson, S. R. Daughter of Regals,
    and other tales
A Very large array; ed. by M. M. Snod-
  grass

DONEGAL (IRELAND: COUNTY) *See*
  Ireland—Donegal (County)
The **donkey.** Sarton, M.
The **donkey.** Spivack, K.
The **donkey** prince. Carter, A.
DONKEYS *See* Asses and mules
Donnelly, Nisa
The scavenger hunt
  Erotic interludes; ed. by L. Barbach
The **Donnington** affair. Chesterton, G. K.
Donohue, Gail
Baby Hood
  The North American Review 271:52-4 Mr
  '86
Totally nude live girls
  Chicago Review 34:37-41 Summ '84
Donor. Gunn, J. E.
The **donor.** Marlowe, D. J.
DONS *See* Teachers
Donson, Cyril
Heat wave
  John Creasey's Crime collection, 1984
Don't be frightened. Fremlin, C.
Don't blame yourself at all. Marshall, O.
Don't die. Lish, G.
Don't explain. Gomez, J.
Don't it make you wonder. Carlisle, A.
Don't knock the rock. Chandler, A. B.
Don't know much about art. Brett, S.
Don't look behind you. Brown, F.
"**Don't** pick any apples for your Aunt Ella".
  Heise, K.
Don't save your kisses. Bocock, M.
Don't send poems, send money. Chernoff, M.
Don't sing love songs . . . Geras, A.
Don't spend it all in one place. Pronzini,
  B.
Don't take no for an answer. Garrett, G. P.
Don't wash the carats. Farmer, P. J.
Don't worry about the kids. Neugeboren, J.
Doolittle, Hilda *See* H. D. (Hilda Doolittle),
  1886-1961
DOOMSDAY *See* Judgment Day
The **door.** Bitov, A.
The **door.** Valenzuela, L.
The **door.** White, E. B.
The **door** in the wall. La Farge, O.
The **door** in the wall. Wells, H. G.
The **doorbell.** Lu Wenfu
Doorstep. Laumer, K.
Doppelganger. Tinkham, B.
Doran, Jeff
That wonderful lizard of ours
  Redbook 163:174+ My '84
DORDOGNE (FRANCE) *See* France—
  Dordogne
Dorman, Sonya
The Noah heritage
  U.S. Catholic 49:18-25 Je '84
Dorme-toi, mon petit. Nisbet, R.
DORMITORIES
Coriolan, J. In the Blair's Lair
Wilson, B. Walking on the moon

Dorothy. Dawson, F.
Dorothy. Spivack, K.
Dorr, Lawrence
At a certain angle
Dorr, L. A slight momentary affliction
A D-minor fugue
Dorr, L. A slight momentary affliction
An early Christmas
Dorr, L. A slight momentary affliction
The immigrant
Dorr, L. A slight momentary affliction
Lazarus
Dorr, L. A slight momentary affliction
Neither death nor life
Dorr, L. A slight momentary affliction
The noise was heard afar off
Dorr, L. A slight momentary affliction
Old men shall dream dreams
Dorr, L. A slight momentary affliction
A slight momentary affliction
Dorr, L. A slight momentary affliction
Two hundred yards past Wordsworth's house
Dorr, L. A slight momentary affliction
Vladimir's kitchen
Dorr, L. A slight momentary affliction
The wedding anniversary
Dorr, L. A slight momentary affliction
Dorris, Michael
The dark snake
The Georgia Review 42:773-81 Wint '88
Ida
Southwest Review 72:75-93 Wint '87
DORSET (ENGLAND) See England—Dorset
DOSTOEVSKIĬ, FEDOR MIKHAĬLOVICH
See Dostoyevsky, Fyodor, 1821-1881
Dostoevsky's whore. Cohen, R.
DOSTOYEVSKY, FYODOR, 1821-1881
About
Ellison, H. Prince Myshkin, and hold the relish
A **dot** on the map. Faik, S.
Doubiago, Sharon
The art of seeing with one's own eyes
Doubiago, S. The book of seeing with one's own eyes
The Pushcart prize X
Chappaquiddick
Doubiago, S. The book of seeing with one's own eyes
Jonah
Doubiago, S. The book of seeing with one's own eyes
Joyce
Doubiago, S. The book of seeing with one's own eyes
Ramon/Ramona
Doubiago, S. The book of seeing with one's own eyes
Raquel
Doubiago, S. The book of seeing with one's own eyes

Vets
Doubiago, S. The book of seeing with one's own eyes
Warriors
Doubiago, S. The book of seeing with one's own eyes
The whore
Doubiago, S. The book of seeing with one's own eyes
The **double.** Ribeyro, J. R.
A **double** because it's snowing. Porter, H.
A **double** buggy at Lahey's Creek. Lawson, H.
The **double** clue. Christie, A.
Double cross. Brand, C.
A **double-dyed** deceiver. Henry, O.
The **double-edged** knife. Oates, J. C.
Double feature. Zinsky, C. L.
Double glazing. Brett, S.
Double-glazing. McNeill, C.
The **Double** Happiness Bun. Gilchrist, E.
Double lives. Schwartz, S.
Double nigger. Dumas, H.
The **double** pins. Maupassant, G. de
Double sin. Christie, A.
The **double** snapper. Faust, I.
Double solitaire. Oates, J. C.
A **double** tragedy. An actor's story. Alcott, L. M.
Double trouble. Sale, R.
Double vision—The rewrite. Dawson, F.
Double whammy. Bloch, R.
Doubles. Meinke, P.
Doubt. Wong, M. V.
Doubtful happiness. Maupassant, G. de
Doucette, Rita J.
A dancer in the lake
Michigan Quarterly Review 26:369-78 Spr '87
Man at low volume
The Kenyon Review ns10:44-9 Wint '88
Maria
Michigan Quarterly Review 24:208-16 Spr '85
Doug Broome, hamburger king. Fox, W. P.
Dougherty's eye-opener. Henry, O.
Douglas, Ellen
On the lake
Mississippi River tales; ed. by F. McSherry; C. G. Waugh and M. H. Greenberg
Mississippi writers v1: Fiction; ed. by D. Abbott
Dove, Rita
Second-hand man
Selected stories from The Southern review, 1965-1985
The Southern Review (Baton Rouge, La.) 21:651-7 Jl '85
Dove and jackal. Brownlee, F.
Dove shooting. Moore, S.
Doves and proverbs. Kinsella, W. P.

Dovlatov, Sergeï
  Aunt Mara
    Partisan Review 55:404-8 Summ '88
  The colonel says I love you
    The New Yorker 62:42-7 My 5 '86
  Father
    The New Yorker 63:34-6 N 30 '87
  Glasha
    Grand Street 8:7-16 Aut '88
  Uncle Aron
    The New Yorker 62:40-1 O 20 '86
  Uncle Leopold
    The New Yorker 63:25-30 Jl 13 '87
Dow, Leona
  Midnight angel
    Good Housekeeping 198:120-1 Ja '84
Dowdey, Clifford, 1904-
  Weep not for them
    A Treasury of Civil War stories; ed. by
      M. H. Greenberg and B. Pronz
Dowell, Coleman, 1925-1985
  City Sundays
    Harper's 274:34-5 Ap '87
  The surgeon
    New directions in prose and poetry 50
Dowling, Lee
  Raindrops from heaven
    Good Housekeeping 199:128-9 Jl '84
A **down-and-out** disciple meets his match.
    Shea, J.
Down and out in the year 2000. Robinson,
    K. S.
Down at the dump. White, P.
Down by the river. Moran, V. A. K.
Down by the sea near the great big rock.
    Lansdale, J. R.
Down in Florida. Shapiro, J.
Down in Happy Hollow. Conroy, J.
Down in Las Vegas. Monreal, D. N.
Down in the darkness. Koontz, D.
Down in the greenwood O. Snodgrass, R.
Down in the world. Gee, M.
Down, Satan! Barker, C.
Down Styphon! Piper, H. B.
Down that lonesome road. Cooper, J. C.
Down the hole. Lee, H.
Down the road. Dixon, S.
Down time Tyler, Texas. Cullen, E. J.
Down to earth. Halligan, M.
Down to the worlds of men. Panshin, A.
Down under. Schwartz, S.
Downpour on a leaky roof. Zhu Lin
DOWRY *See* Marriage customs
The **dowry**. Auswaks, A.
The **dowry**. Nelson, P.
The **dowry**. Russo, R.
Doyle, Sir Arthur Conan, 1859-1930
  The adventure of the Beryl Coronet
    Doyle, Sir A. C. The adventures of Sher-
      lock Holmes
  The adventure of the blue carbuncle
    Doyle, Sir A. C. The adventures of Sher-
      lock Holmes

The adventure of the Bruce-Partington
    plans
  Baker's dozen: 13 short espionage novels
The adventure of the copper beeches
    [Variant title: The copper beeches]
  Doyle, Sir A. C. The adventures of Sher-
    lock Holmes
The adventure of the devil's foot
  Sherlock Holmes through time and space
The adventure of the engineer's thumb
  Doyle, Sir A. C. The adventures of Sher-
    lock Holmes
The adventure of the noble bachelor
  Doyle, Sir A. C. The adventures of Sher-
    lock Holmes
The adventure of the speckled band
    [Variant title: The speckled band]
  Doyle, Sir A. C. The adventures of Sher-
    lock Holmes
The American's tale
  Doyle, Sir A. C. Uncollected stories
Bones. The April fool of Harvey's Sluice
  Doyle, Sir A. C. Uncollected stories
The Boscombe Valley mystery
  Doyle, Sir A. C. The adventures of Sher-
    lock Holmes
The cabman's story
  Doyle, Sir A. C. Uncollected stories
The cardboard box
  Doyle, Sir A. C. The memoirs of Sher-
    lock Holmes
A case of identity
  Doyle, Sir A. C. The adventures of Sher-
    lock Holmes
The centurion
  Doyle, Sir A. C. Uncollected stories
The colonel's choice
  Doyle, Sir A. C. Uncollected stories
The confession
  Doyle, Sir A. C. Uncollected stories
The copper beeches [Variant title: The
    adventure of the copper beeches]
  Masterpieces of mystery and suspense;
    ed. by M. H. Greenberg
  The Penguin classic crime omnibus
The crooked man
  Doyle, Sir A. C. The memoirs of Sher-
    lock Holmes
The death voyage
  Doyle, Sir A. C. Uncollected stories
The end of Devil Hawker
  Doyle, Sir A. C. Uncollected stories
An exciting Christmas Eve; or, My lecture
    on dynamite
  Doyle, Sir A. C. Uncollected stories
The fate of the Evangeline
  Doyle, Sir A. C. Uncollected stories
The final problem
  Doyle, Sir A. C. The memoirs of Sher-
    lock Holmes
The five orange pips
  Doyle, Sir A. C. The adventures of Sher-
    lock Holmes

Doyle, Sir Arthur Conan, 1859-1930—*Continued*

Gentlemanly Joe
 Doyle, Sir A. C. Uncollected stories
The Gloria Scott
 Doyle, Sir A. C. The memoirs of Sherlock Holmes
The Greek interpreter
 Doyle, Sir A. C. The memoirs of Sherlock Holmes
The heiress of Glenmahowley
 Doyle, Sir A. C. Uncollected stories
The horror of the heights
 Dark banquet; ed. by L. Child
An impression of the Regency
 Doyle, Sir A. C. Uncollected stories
J. Habakuk Jephson's statement
 Mysterious sea stories; ed. by W. Patrick
The last resource
 Doyle, Sir A. C. Uncollected stories
The lonely Hampshire cottage
 Doyle, Sir A. C. Uncollected stories
Lot no 249
 Charles Keeping's Classic tales of the macabre
The man with the twisted lip
 Doyle, Sir A. C. The adventures of Sherlock Holmes
The Musgrave ritual
 Doyle, Sir A. C. The memoirs of Sherlock Holmes
The mystery of Sasassa Valley
 Doyle, Sir A. C. Uncollected stories
The mystery of the lost special
 Death locked in; ed. by D. G. Greene and R. C. S. Adey
The naval treaty
 Doyle, Sir A. C. The memoirs of Sherlock Holmes
The new catacomb
 The Treasury of English short stories; ed. by N. Sullivan
Our Derby sweepstakes
 Doyle, Sir A. C. Uncollected stories
Our midnight visitor
 Doyle, Sir A. C. Uncollected stories
The parasite
 The Mammoth book of short horror novels; ed. by M. Ashley
The Parish Magazine
 Doyle, Sir A. C. Uncollected stories
A pastoral horror
 Doyle, Sir A. C. Uncollected stories
The recollections of Captain Wilkie
 Doyle, Sir A. C. Uncollected stories
The red-headed league
 Doyle, Sir A. C. The adventures of Sherlock Holmes
 Isaac Asimov presents the best crime stories of the 19th century
A regimental scandal
 Doyle, Sir A. C. Uncollected stories

The reigate squires
 Doyle, Sir A. C. The memoirs of Sherlock Holmes
The resident patient
 Doyle, Sir A. C. The memoirs of Sherlock Holmes
 Kill or cure; ed. by M. Muller and B. Pronzini
The retirement of Signor Lambert
 Doyle, Sir A. C. Uncollected stories
A scandal in Bohemia
 Doyle, Sir A. C. The adventures of Sherlock Holmes
Selecting a ghost. The ghosts of Goresthorpe Grange
 Doyle, Sir A. C. Uncollected stories
Silver Blaze
 Doyle, Sir A. C. The memoirs of Sherlock Holmes
 Hound dunnit; ed. by I. Asimov; M. H. Greenberg and C. L. R. Waugh
A sordid affair
 Doyle, Sir A. C. Uncollected stories
The stockbroker's clerk
 Doyle, Sir A. C. The memoirs of Sherlock Holmes
The stone of Boxman's Drift
 Doyle, Sir A. C. Uncollected stories
That veteran
 Doyle, Sir A. C. Uncollected stories
Touch and go: a midshipman's story
 Doyle, Sir A. C. Uncollected stories
The tragedians
 Doyle, Sir A. C. Uncollected stories
A true story of the tragedy of Flowery Land
 Doyle, Sir A. C. Uncollected stories
Uncle Jeremy's household
 Doyle, Sir A. C. Uncollected stories
The voice of science
 Doyle, Sir A. C. Uncollected stories
The winning shot
 Doyle, Sir A. C. Uncollected stories
The yellow face
 Doyle, Sir A. C. The memoirs of Sherlock Holmes
 The hound of the Baskervilles
Perowne, B. Raffles on the trail of the hound
 Parodies, travesties, etc.
Anderson, P., and Dickson, G. R. The adventure of the misplaced hound
Asimov, I. The ultimate crime
Boyle, T. C. Rupert Beersley and the Beggar Master of Sivani-Hoota
Breen, J. L. The adventure of the unique Holmes
De la Torre, L. The adventure of the persistent marksman
Farber, S. N. The great dormitory mystery
Farmer, P. J. The problem of the sore bridge—among others
Farmer, P. J. A Scarletin study

Doyle, Sir Arthur Conan, 1859-1930 —
Parodies, travesties, etc.—*Continued*
  Gilbert, M. The two footmen
  Harrington, J. The adventure of the Gowanus abduction
  Harrison, M. Sherlock Holmes and "The woman": an explanatory memoir by Dr. John H. Watson, MD.
  Hoch, E. D. The most dangerous man
  Hoch, E. D. The return of the speckled band
  Hughes, D. B. F. Sherlock Holmes and the muffin
  Jones, B. The shadows on the lawn: an adventure of Sherlock Holmes
  Kaminsky, S. M. The final toast
  King, S. The doctor's case
  Lanier, S. E. A father's tale
  Lear, A. The adventure of the global traveler
  Lovesey, P. The curious computer
  Lupoff, R. A. God of the Naked Unicorn
  Lutz, J. The infernal machine
  Nolan, W. F. Sungrab
  Powell, J. Death in the Christmas hour
  Reynolds, M. The adventure of the extraterrestrial
  Ruse, G. A. The phantom chamber
  Saberhagen, F. Adventure of the metal murderer
  Wellen, E. The house that Jack built
  Wellen, E. Voiceover
  Wolfe, G. Slaves of silver
Doyle, Brian
  The apple war
    U.S. Catholic 53:32-7 D '88
  Catchers
    U.S. Catholic 51:26-30 S '86
  The St. Stephen Martyr Bears
    U.S. Catholic 50:22-9 Jl '85
Doyle, Conan *See* Doyle, Sir Arthur Conan, 1859-1930
Doyle, Debra, and Macdonald, J. D. (James David), 1908-
  Bad blood
    Werewolves; ed. by J. Yolen and M. H. Greenberg
A **dozen** of everything. Bradley, M. Z.
Dozois, Gardner R.
  A dream at noonday
    In the field of fire; ed. by J. Van B. Dann and J. Dann
  Flash point
    Masters of darkness; ed. by D. Etchison
  Morning child
    Nebula awards 20
    Omni (New York, N.Y.) 6:78-80+ Ja '84
  The peacemaker
    Nebula awards #19
  The sacrifice
    100 great fantasy short short stories; ed. by I. Asimov; T. Carr and M. H. Greenberg

Dozois, Gardner R., and Haldeman, Jack C., 1941-
  Executive clemency
    Omni book of science fiction 3
Dozois, Gardner R., and others
  Afternoon at Schrafft's
    Magicats! Ed. by J. Dann and G. Dozois
  The gods of Mars
    Omni (New York, N.Y.) 7:50-2+ Mr '85
  Touring
    After midnight; ed. by C. L. Grant
Dr. Birdmouse. Bretnor, R.
Dr. Cahn's visit. Stern, R. G.
Dr. Faguet amuses himself. Villefranche, A.-M.
Dr. Hudson's secret gorilla. Waldrop, H.
Dr. John Wookey to surgery. Winters, J.
Dr. Pettigot's face. Harris, M.
Dr. Snow Maiden. Eisenberg, L.
Dr. Sweetkill. Jakes, J.
Dr. Zifhart leaves for Atlantic City. Ahern, T.
Drab rambles. Bonner, M.
Drabble, Margaret, 1939-
  The dying year
    Harper's 275:59-69 Jl '87
Dracula's daughter. See Stoker, B. Dracula's guest
Dracula's guest. Stoker, B.
DRAFT
  Böll, H. The postcard
  Candelaria, N. El patrón
  Ch'oe, S. Point
  Pancake, B. D. The honored dead
  Petchsingh, T. The two moons of Vira's world
  Phillips, J. A. November and December: Billy, 1969
  Sanders, S. R. Time and again
  Saroyan, W. Cowards
  Sholem Aleichem. The automatic exemption
DRAFT, MILITARY *See* Draft
A **draft** of canto ci. Scholz, C.
DRAFT RESISTERS *See* Draft
Drage's divine discontent. Durrell, L.
The **Dragon.** Spark, M.
The **dragon** at hide-and-seek. Chesterton, G. K.
Dragon in the sea. Herbert, F.
The **dragon** king's troops thunder past. Deng Gang
The **dragon** line. Swanwick, M.
The **dragon** of Dunloon. Dembling, A.
Dragon pax. Zahn, T.
The **dragon** seed. Wilhelm, K.
Dragon touched. Smeds, D.
Dragonrider. McCaffrey, A.
DRAGONS
  Benford, G., and Laidlaw, M. A hiss of dragon
  Bishop, M. One winter in Eden
  Blythe, R. Here be dragons

DRAGONS—*Continued*

Buzzati, D. The slaying of the dragon

Chin, M. L. Lan Lung

Delany, S. R. The tale of dragons and dreamers

Ford, J. M. As above, so below

Gardner, C. S. A drama of dragons

Hartley, L. P. Conrad and the dragon

Le Guin, U. K. The rule of names

Martin, G. R. R. The ice dragon

McCaffrey, A. Dragonrider

McDonald, S. E. Silken dragon

Morris, K. The eyeless dragons: a Chinese story

O'Faolain, J. Legend for a painting

Shepard, L. The man who painted the dragon Griaule

Smeds, D. Dragon touched

Vinge, J. D. The storm king

Yolen, J. Cockfight

Yolen, J. Great-grandfather dragon's tale

Zelazny, R. The George business

Dragons and puppies. Mazel, D.

The **Dragon's** head. Sayers, D. L.

Dragon's horn. Schutz, J. W.

Dragon's teeth. Drake, D.

The **dragon's** teeth. Gordon, C.

Drake, Benjamin

Putting a black-leg on shore

Mississippi River tales; ed. by F. McSherry; C. G. Waugh and M. H. Greenberg

Drake, David

Dragon's teeth

Robert Adams' Book of soldiers

Dreams in amber

Whispers V

Men like us

Omni book of science fiction 3

Time safari

Baker's dozen: 13 short science fiction novels

Drake, Mary, 1912-

The feast to end all feasts

Short story international 50

The prison

Short story international 69

Remembrance of things past

Short story international 63

Tea break

Short story international 59

Drake, Robert, 1930-

1975 has come and gone

Drake, R. Survivors and others

The birthday picture

Drake, R. Survivors and others

A cool day in August

Drake, R. Survivors and others

Ella Biggs

The Southern Review (Baton Rouge, La.) 24:215-21 Wint '88

Fairy tale

Drake, R. Survivors and others

First date

Drake, R. Survivors and others

The first year

Drake, R. Survivors and others

The Southern Review (Baton Rouge, La.) 20:928-33 O '84

Football Queen

Drake, R. Survivors and others

A husband and a home of her own and nice things

Drake, R. Survivors and others

I am counting with you all the way

Drake, R. Survivors and others

I don't know what he's doing now

The Christian Century 105:641-2 Jl 6-13 '88

I never have been a well woman

Drake, R. Survivors and others

If she knowed what I knowed, she never would woke

Drake, R. Survivors and others

June

Drake, R. Survivors and others

Miss Effie, the Peabody, and Father Time

Drake, R. Survivors and others

The Southern Review (Baton Rouge, La.) 22:651-7 Summ '86

The moon-fixer

Drake, R. Survivors and others

Mrs. English

Drake, R. Survivors and others

Mrs. Picture Show Green

Drake, R. Survivors and others

My sweetheart's house

The Southern Review (Baton Rouge, La.) 22:174-8 Ja '86

Now, Baby, do you know one thing?

Drake, R. Survivors and others

On the side porch

Drake, R. Survivors and others

The operetta

Drake, R. Survivors and others

Remember the Errol-mo!

Drake, R. Survivors and others

Shoot, child, what you talking about?

Drake, R. Survivors and others

Sisters

Drake, R. Survivors and others

Still swinging

Drake, R. Survivors and others

Tennis whites

Drake, R. Survivors and others

A ticket as long as your arm

Drake, R. Survivors and others

Up on the corner, on the dogleg

Drake, R. Survivors and others

The veteran

Drake, R. Survivors and others

Were you there?

Drake, R. Survivors and others

DRAMA CRITICS

Friedman, B. J. King of the Bloodies

DRAMA CRITICS—Continued
  Wells, H. G. The sad story of a dramatic
    critic
A **drama** of dragons. Gardner, C. S.
DRAMATISTS
  Curtiss, U. R. The old barn on the pond
  Dennison, G. Interview with the author of
    Caryatids
  Dennison, G. The sufficiency of everyday
    life: Avenue A and Eleventh Street,
    1963
  Dixon, S. The play
  Friedman, B. J. The adventurer
  Friedman, B. J. The best we have
  Friedman, B. J. King of the Bloodies
  Gilliatt, P. Known for her frankness
  James, H. Nona Vincent
  James, H. The private life
  Lurie, M. Russian boxes
  Michaelson, L. W. Me and Will
  O'Hara, J. Flight
  Wolfe, T. For professional appearance
The **drapery** man. MacLaverty, B.
The **draw.** Bixby, J.
Drawing names. Mason, B. A.
Drawing room B. O'Hara, J.
Drawn from life. Pierson, A.
Draycott, Manny
  Splices
    P.E.N. new fiction I
Dread. Barker, C.
Dreadsong. Zelazny, R.
A **Dream**
    Black water; ed. by A. Manguel
The **dream.** Christie, A.
The **dream.** Dawson, F.
The **dream.** Henry, O.
Dream. Parise, G.
A **dream.** Roy, J.
Dream 5281. Coleman, W.
A **dream** at noonday. Dozois, G. R.
Dream baby. McAllister, B.
The **dream** broker. Bliss, C. D.
A **dream** can never complete itself. Ignatow,
    R. G.
Dream children. Godwin, G.
The **dream** diet. Dyer, S.
Dream evolution. Murrey, M.
Dream fighter. Shaw, B.
A **dream** for tomorrow. Shyer, M. F.
Dream house. Henderson, M. R.
Dream in a bottle. Meredith, J., and Smirl,
    D. E.
The **dream** is better. Symons, J.
Dream Lady. Rooke, L.
The **dream** of a mask. Yi, C.-J.
Dream of a strange land. Greene, G.
A **dream** of Armageddon. Wells, H. G.
A **dream** of collaboration. Liben, M.
A **dream** of fair women. Berriault, G.
A **dream** of Grand Junction. McDaniel, W.
    E.
Dream of Jeannie. Kesey, K.

The **dream** of the bridge. Gauvreau, C.
The **dream** of the Emma C. Highsmith, P.
A **dream** of the future (not excluding lob-
    sters). Vonnegut, K.
The **dream** of the wolf. Bradfield, S.
Dream pirates' jewel. Linaweaver, B., and
    Linaweaver, C.
Dream rocket. Floyd, P. L.
The **dream** soldier. Abe, K.
Dream stud. Coriolan, J.
The **dream-vendor's** August. Okri, B.
Dream walker. Bain, C. J.
Dream with no name. Ferreira, R.
The **dreamer.** Fante, J.
Dreamer in a dead language. Paley, G.
Dreamer when last seen. Osborn, C.
Dreamers. Newman, K.
Dreaming. Pascoe, B.
Dreaming is a lonely thing. Hoch, E. D.
Dreaming is a private thing. Asimov, I.
Dreaming of Africa. Freeman, C.
Dreaming of Grandpa. Sanders, W.
DREAMS
  Abbott, L. K. Dreams of distant lives
  Adams, A. La Señora
  Aickman, R. Never visit Venice
  Aiken, C. Mr. Arcularis
  Aksenov, V. P. Surplussed barrelware
  Asimov, I. Dreaming is a private thing
  Asimov, I. Dreamworld
  Asimov, I. Robot dreams
  Barthelme, D. A few moments of sleeping
    and waking
  Baumbach, J. The dinner party
  Bear, G. If I die before I wake
  Betts, D. Benson Watts is dead and in
    Virginia
  Blinkin, M. In a dream
  Bloch, R. All on a golden afternoon
  Borges, J. L. 25 August 1983
  Brennan, J. P. Mrs. Clendon's place
  Bryant, E. Jade Blue
  Campbell, R. The tugging
  Card, O. S. America
  Carpentier, A. The seven dreams and the
    reality of Perrine Blanc
  Carrington, L. The stone door
  Chesterton, G. K. A nightmare
  Chesterton, G. K. The taming of the night-
    mare
  Cortázar, J. Stories I tell myself
  Curley, D. Wild geese
  Dann, J. Camps
  Davidson, A. Sleep well of nights
  Diaconú, A. Mamaya
  Dickens, C. A child's dream of a star
  Dickens, C. The hanged man's bride
  Dixon, S. Meeting Aline
  Doyle, Sir A. C. The last resource
  A Dream
  El Saadawi, N. The veil
  Faik, S. The bundle
  Fitzgerald, M. J. The game

DREAMS—*Continued*

Fitzgerald, M. J. Mystery story
Flores, C. N. Yellow flowers
Franklin, P. Splendor and black wool
Fremlin, C. A lovely day to die
García Márquez, G. Eyes of a blue dog
García Márquez, G. The incredible and sad tale of innocent Eréndira and her heartless grandmother
Gault, C. My perseus
Gogol', N. V. Nevsky Prospekt
Greene, G. Under the garden
Haggard, H. R. Only a dream
Hartley, L. P. Home, sweet home
Hartley, L. P. The pylon
Hartley, L. P. A very present help
Hawthorne, N. The Celestial rail-road
Hawthorne, N. The haunted mind
Hearn, L. Oshidori
Helprin, M. The Schreuderspitze
Hemley, R. Dropping the baby
Henry, O. The dream
Herschel, J. Geometry
Hoch, E. D. Dreaming is a lonely thing
Hogg, J. Tibby Hyslop's dream
Ignatow, R. G. Dreams for sale
James, H. The great good place
Johnson, G. C. Devlin's dream
Jones, D. W. Carol Oneir's hundredth dream
Kawabata, Y. Eggs
Kawabata, Y. The girl who approached the fire
Kawabata, Y. A saw and childbirth
Kawabata, Y. The snakes
Kawabata, Y. Toward winter
Kawabata, Y. The weaker vessel
Kinsella, W. P. Strawberry stew
Kornbluth, C. M. Two dooms
Krysl, M. We are ready
La Chapelle, M. The meadow bell
Laidlaw, M. Sneakers
Landolfi, T. Rain
LaSalle, P. Dolphin dreaming
Lessing, D. M. Two potters
Liben, M. Brenner's dream
Longyear, B. B. Dreams
Lovecraft, H. P. The shadow out of time
Lutz, J. The landscape of dreams
Mansfield, K. Taking the veil
Maugham, W. S. Lord Mountdrago
Maurois, A. The house
Mazel, D. Mr. Tessler
McAllister, B. Dream baby
McCloy, H. The other side of the curtain
McCormack, E. P. Captain Joe
Meinke, P. The ponoes
Meredith, J., and Smirl, D. E. Dream in a bottle
Moravia, A. The devil comes and goes
Moravia, A. In my dream I always hear a step on the stairs

Moravia, A. The woman in the customs officer's house
Morris, M. The bus of dreams
Newman, K. Dreamers
O'Brien, E. Number 10
O'Brien, F.-J. What was it?
Ocampo, S. Leopoldina's dream
Ooka, S. The mother of dreams
Papini, G. The sick gentleman's last visit
Parise, G. Dream
Pavese, C. Evocation
Phipps, H. J. The saintmaker's wife
Rey Rosa, R. The beggar's knife
Rey Rosa, R. The monastery
Rey Rosa, R. A prisoner
Rey Rosa, R. Recurrent dreams
Rey Rosa, R. A yellow cat
Rhys, J. Mixing cocktails
Royle, N. Irrelativity
Russ, J. How Dorothy kept away the spring
Russell, B. The Queen of Sheba's nightmare
Salmonson, J. A. Eagle-worm
Seidman, M. Perchance to dream
Sheckley, R. Fear in the night
Sheckley, R. The petrified world
Silverberg, R. The desert of stolen dreams
Silverberg, R. Gate of horn, gate of ivory
Steele, M. Color the daydream yellow
Steele, M. Where she brushed her hair
Sturgeon, T. The professor's teddy bear
Tem, S. R. Sleep
Thomas, A. C. Miss Foote
Thomas, D. The orchards
Twain, M. My platonic sweetheart
Vanderhaeghe, G. Dancing bear
Virgo, S. The hanging man
Walpole, H. The bird's nest
Watson, I. Immune dreams
Wells, H. G. The devotee of art
Wells, H. G. A dream of Armageddon
Welty, E. A memory
West, J. Night piece for Julia
West, Dame R. The gray men
Wiater, S. Moist dreams
Wolfe, G. The detective of dreams
Zebrowski, G. The idea trap

Dreams. Longyear, B. B.
Dreams & disappointments. Ignatow, R. G.
Dreams & sleep. Ross, V.
Dreams for sale. Ignatow, R. G.
Dreams in amber. Drake, D.
Dreams of a new mother. Thompson, J.
The **dreams** of all men. Ratner, D.
Dreams of distant lives. Abbott, L. K.
Dreams of leaving. Taylor, D. J.
Dreams of sleep. Humphreys, J.
Dreams of unfair women. Tuohy, F.
Dreams unwind. Hansen, K.
The **dreamsender**. Zahn, T.
Dreamworld. Asimov, I.

Drenched in light. See Hurston, Z. N. Isis
The **dress**. Thomas, D.
Dress of white silk. Matheson, R.
Dress rehearsal. Soukup, M.
Dressed like summer leaves. Dubus, A.
Dressing down. Luciano, E.
Dressing up. Payson, H. L.
DRESSMAKERS
  Bates, H. E. A Silas idyll
  Christie, A. The dressmaker's doll
  Colette. The "master"
  Colette. The seamstress
  Colette. The sempstress
  Doyle, Sir A. C. A sordid affair
  Loukakis, A. This wizened creature
  Maupassant, G. de. Bellflower
  Ocampo, S. The velvet dress
  Phelps, E. S. Number 13
  Spark, M. The Dragon
The **dressmaker's** doll. Christie, A.
Drew, Eileen
  Bossboy and the wild West
    The Antioch Review 44:88-104 Wint '86
  Cropped
    The Literary Review (Madison, N.J.)
    30:33-40 Fall '86
Drewe, Robert, 1943-
  After Noumea
    Drewe, R. The bodysurfers
  Baby oil
    Drewe, R. The bodysurfers
  The bodysurfers
    Drewe, R. The bodysurfers
  Eighty per cent humidity
    Drewe, R. The bodysurfers
  The last explorer
    Drewe, R. The bodysurfers
  Looking for Malibu
    Drewe, R. The bodysurfers
  The manageress and the mirage
    Drewe, R. The bodysurfers
  Shark logic
    Drewe, R. The bodysurfers
  The silver medallist
    Drewe, R. The bodysurfers
  Stingray
    Drewe, R. The bodysurfers
  Sweetlip
    Drewe, R. The bodysurfers
  The view from the sandhills
    Drewe, R. The bodysurfers
Drewitz, Ingeborg, 1923-1986
  The news
    New directions in prose and poetry 49
Drexel's Garage. Targan, B.
Dried fruit. Moore, G.
The **dried** witch. Byatt, A. S.
Drift. Cowan, P.
A **drift** in dream. Hulme, K.
Drifting. Liberman, S.
The **drifting** snow. Derleth, A. W.
A **drink** in the passage. Paton, A.
Drink my blood. Matheson, R.

A **drink** of darkness. Young, R. F.
Drinking. La Chapelle, M.
The **drinking** club. Adams, A.
Drinking in Petöcki. Böll, H.
Driscoll, Jack
  Wanting only to be heard
    The Georgia Review 41:665-76 Wint '87
Driskell, Leon V.
  Martha Jean
    New stories from the South: the year's
      best, 1986
    Prairie Schooner 59:83-103 Fall '85
Drive-away. Wilson, B.
A **drive** in the country. Greene, G.
The **driver**. Asimov, I.
Driver. Barthelme, F.
Driver's assistant. Chon, K.-Y.
Drivin'. Corey, D. J.
Driving. Franzen, B.
Driving back from the funeral. Collins, L.
Driving his Buick home. Abbott, L. K.
Driving into the light. Thomas, E.
Drogo. Strand, M.
Dropping dance. Grenville, K.
Dropping the baby. Hemley, R.
Drops that trickle away. Leblanc, M.
The **drought**. Carter, R.
Drought. Rabie, J.
DROUGHTS
  Benedict, P. Water witch
  Carter, R. The drought
  Humphrey, W. The rainmaker
  Jakes, J. Storm in a bottle
  Sandoz, M. The vine
The **drover's** wife. Bail, M.
The **drover's** wife. Lawson, H.
The **drowned** giant. Ballard, J. G.
The **drowned** maiden. See Gogol', N. V. A
  May night; or, The drowned maiden
The **drowned** men's inn. Simenon, G.
Drowne's wooden image. Hawthorne, N.
DROWNING
  Atwood, M. Two stories about Emma:
    Walking on water
  Barich, B. Giorgio's mother
  Bedard, B. Entries in a drowned man's
    dictionary
  Bensink, J. R. Lake George in high August
  Bird, C. Boy and girl
  Boswell, R. Flipflops
  Bradbury, R. The lake
  Burger, K. The cat lover
  Cassutt, M. Stillwater, 1896
  Chernoff, M. That summer
  Coskran, K. An African river
  Crawford, F. M. Man overboard!
  Ekström, M. The night between the second
    and the third
  Federspiel, J. The survivor
  García Márquez, G. The handsomest
    drowned man in the world
  Garrett, G. P. The test
  Hall, L. S. The ledge

DROWNING—*Continued*
Jackson, G. Billy's girl
La Chapelle, M. Accidents
Lutz, J. Deeper and deeper
Matthiessen, P. The fifth day
McDevitt, J. Tidal effects
O'Connor, F. The river
Pavese, C. Summer storm
Pronzini, B. The storm tunnel
Rogers, T. N. R. Rainfall
Silvis, R. Prayer and old jokes
Sorrells, R. T. Drowning
Stephens, W. M. Water Witch
Strand, M. Wooley
Trollope, A. Returning home
Yorke, M. The wrath of Zeus
The **drowning**. Kenneth, J.
Drowning. Sorrells, R. T.
Drrdla. Morris, W.
DRUG ABUSE
   See also Marijuana
Foley, B. The child killers
Frazier, R. Across those endless skies
Jaffe, H. Brother Wolf
O'Brien, F.-J. What was it?
Rathjen, C. H. A debt to Doc
Schulman, H. Having fun
Schulman, H. Siblings
Tiptree, J. Yanqui Doodle
Viidikas, V. A modern Snowwhite
Wilmot, J. Dirt angel
DRUG ADDICTION *See* Narcotic habit
DRUG INDUSTRY *See* Drug trade
DRUG TRADE
Coleman, W. Stashed
Gores, J. Smart guys don't snore
Harper, R. B. Bale jumpers
Post, J. No handicap
Rudloff, S. A. A cup of coffee
Williams, W. J. Video star
DRUG TRAFFIC *See* Narcotics
DRUGGISTS *See* Pharmacists
DRUGS
   See also Narcotic habit
Asimov, I. I'm in Marsport without Hilda
Austin, D. The hypnotic mailbox
Bronstein, E. Magic
Campbell, R. Stages
Cohen, M. A love for the infinite
Coleman, W. Jonesed
Coleman, W. 'Shrooms
Enayetullah, A. Enemy
Gilchrist, E. The gauzy edge of paradise
Gold, H. San Francisco petal
Hensley, J. L. Finder
Hesse, H. A man by the name of Ziegler
Machen, A. Novel of the white powder
McInerney, J. It's six a.m. do you know where you are?
Moore, W. Peacebringer
Pronzini, B., and Wallmann, J. M. Coyote and Quarter Moon
Shepard, L. Black coral

Shiner, L. Jeff Beck
Silverberg, R. Schwartz between the galaxies
Silverberg, R. A thousand paces along the Via Dolorosa
Simon, B. Monologue for Danny
St. Clair, M. The invested libido
Tomlinson, G. Hizzoner's water supply
Wagner, K. E. Lacunae
Wells, H. G. The new accelerator
Wolfe, G. Seven American nights
DRUGSTORES *See* Pharmacists
The **drum**. Furlong, M.
Drummer. Vanderhaeghe, G.
DRUMMERS
Hannah, B. Testimony of pilot
Mrożek, S. A drummer's adventure
Painter, P. The next time I meet Buddy Rich
A **drummer's** adventure. Mrożek, S.
A **drummer's** gift. Sechler, T.
The **drumming** sands. Al-Kouni, I.
Drunk with love. Gilchrist, E.
The **drunkard**. O'Connor, F.
DRUNKARDS
   See also Alcoholism
Abbott, K. When this van is rockin' don't bother knockin'
Alexander, D. The man who went to Taltavul's
Algren, N. A bottle of milk for mother
Algren, N. Design for departure
Algren, N. How the Devil came down Division Street
Bates, H. E. The sow and Silas
Baxter, C. Winter journey
Beman, B. Set 'em up, Joe
Boyle, K. I can't get drunk
Brown, M. W. Tongues of flame
Burns, M. After hours
Choyce, L. Breakage
Choyce, L. Local heroes
Conley, R. J. Calf Roper's bandit car
Crane, S. The bride comes to Yellow Sky
Crane, S. The five white mice
Crane, S. Twelve o'clock
Curley, D. Reflections in the ice
Daniels, C. Honky-Tonk Avenue
Daniels, C. Lacy Mallard
Daniels, C. Trudy
Deaver, P. F. Rosie
DeRosso, H. A. Vigilante
Dickens, C. Sketches by Boz [excerpt]
Digby, J. Incident at the Gaumont
Digby, J. The one and only bottle
Doyle, Sir A. C. A sordid affair
Dunn, D. A night out at the Club Harmonica
Eighner, L. Windsor
Faulkner, W. Pantaloon in black
Feng Jicai. Nectar
Ferguson, W. Freedom
Fitzgerald, F. S. An alcoholic case

DRUNKARDS—*Continued*

Galsworthy, J. The neighbors
Givner, J. The lost sheep
Gurley, G. H. The seventh day
Hannah, B. It spoke of exactly the things
Hannah, B. Ride, fly, penetrate, loiter
Jones, D. C. The saga of Slaven Budd
King, S. Big wheels: a tale of the laundry game (milkman #2)
Krysl, M. Something unforgivable
Lawson, H. The boozers' home
London, J. A hyperborean brew [excerpt]
MacDonald, J. D. Hangover
MacLaverty, B. A present for Christmas
Maugham, W. S. Before the party
Maupassant, G. de. An enthusiast
Maupassant, G. de. A night in Whitechapel
McLaughlin, L. The stomach
Meinke, P. Conversation with a pole
Meinke, P. The piano tuner
Meinke, P. Winter term
Millman, L. The pickling of Rewt Chaney
Narayan, R. K. The evening gift
Nowakowski, M. The vetting session
O'Connor, F. The drunkard
Palma, C. Aboard the cart
Petrakis, H. M. Dark eye
Rabelais, F. Gargantua and pantagruel [excerpt]
Rooke, L. Friendship and property
Runyon, C. Hangover
Soldatow, S. Last drink is on the house
Spencer, E. A southern landscape
Stafford, J. In the zoo
Stuart, J. Coming down the mountain
Tamer, Z. Small sun
Taylor, A. In the rubbish tin
Taylor, A. Old mates
Updike, J. More stately mansions
Van Vechten, C. Parties [excerpt]
Vanderhaeghe, G. Man descending
Vanderhaeghe, G. Reunion
Weaver, G. Canavan's knee
Welch, D. Constance, Lady Willet
Welch, D. Leaves from a young person's notebook
Welch, D. Touchett's party
Wells, H. G. Mr. Marshall's doppelganger
Williams, T. Sabbatha and solitude
Williams, T. Two on a party
Ziem, J. Payday

Drunkboat. Smith, C.

Drury, Tom

In our state
  Harper's 277:37-8 D '88
Preventing snow
  The North American Review 273:26-9 S '88

DRY CLEANING

West, J. The Calla Lily Cleaners & Dyers
The **dry** familiar plains. Ferguson, P.
The **dry** season. Lee, T.

Dry September. Faulkner, W.
Dry storm. St. Pierre, P. H.
Du, du liegst mir im herzen. Keillor, G.

Du Fresne, Yvonne

Christmas (Shirley Temple is a wife and mother)
  Women's work; ed. by M. McLeod and L. Wevers

Du Lac, Lois

"What's cooking? murder?"
  Murder California style; ed. by J. L. Breen and J. Ball

Du Maurier, Dame Daphne, 1907-1989

The birds
  Good Housekeeping 200:228-9+ My '85
  Witches' brew; ed. by M. Muller and B. Pronzini
Escort
  Charles Keeping's Book of classic ghost stories
The old man
  The Treasury of English short stories; ed. by N. Sullivan
Split second
  Black water; ed. by A. Manguel

DUAL PERSONALITY

This subject is used for novels and stories describing a condition in which one individual shows in alternation two very different characters. For tales dealing with individuals who assume or act the character of another, see the subject: Impersonations

  See also Multiple personality; Personality disorders

Boyd, W. Bizarre situations
Ellson, H. The black stairway
McCormack, E. P. Twins

Duane, Diane, 1952-

Lior and the sea
  Moonsinger's friends; ed by S. Shwartz
Uptown local
  Dragons and dreams; ed. by J. Yolen; M. H. Greenberg and C. G. Waugh

Dub, Ota

The rebel wolf and Petrina
  Short story international 53

Dubbs, Chris

A physician's log
  The Antioch Review 43:284-96 Summ '85

Dube's first day. Goldswain, R.
Dubley, '89. Ade, G.

DUBLIN (IRELAND) *See* Ireland—Dublin

A **Dublin** day. Colum, P.
The **Dublin** eye. Howard, C.

DuBois, Brendan

Final marks, final secrets
  The Year's best mystery and suspense stories, 1988

Dubus, Andre, 1936-

Adultery
  Dubus, A. Selected stories
  Dubus, A. We don't live here anymore

Dubus, Andre, 1936——*Continued*
After the game
  Dubus, A. Selected stories
  Dubus, A. The last worthless evening
  The Graywolf annual [1]
Anna
  Dubus, A. Selected stories
At St. Croix
  The Ploughshares reader: new fiction for
    the eighties
Blessings
  Prize stories, 1988
Cadence
  Dubus, A. Selected stories
The captain
  Dubus, A. Selected stories
The curse
  Dubus, A. Selected stories
The dark men
  Soldiers & civilians; ed. by T. Jenks
Deaths at sea
  Dubus, A. The last worthless evening
Delivering
  Dubus, A. Selected stories
Dressed like summer leaves
  Dubus, A. The last worthless evening
  New stories from the South: the year's
    best, 1987
  The Sewanee Review 94:541-54 Fall '86
The fat girl
  American short story masterpieces; ed.
    by R. Carver and T. Jenks
  Dubus, A. Selected stories
  Love stories for the time being; ed. by
    G. D. Chipps and B. Henderson
A father's story
  The Best American short stories, 1984
  Dubus, A. Selected stories
  The Substance of things hoped for; ed.
    by J. B. Breslin
Finding a girl in America
  Dubus, A. We don't live here anymore
Graduation
  Dubus, A. Selected stories
If they knew Yvonne
  Dubus, A. Selected stories
Killings
  Dubus, A. Selected stories
Land where my fathers died
  Dubus, A. The last worthless evening
  The Editors' choice: new American
    stories v2
Leslie in California
  Dubus, A. Selected stories
Miranda over the valley
  Dubus, A. Selected stories
Molly
  Dubus, A. The last worthless evening
Over the hill
  Stories of the modern South; ed. by B.
    Forkner and P. Samway
The pitcher
  Dubus, A. Selected stories

The pretty girl
  Dubus, A. Selected stories
  Dubus, A. We don't live here anymore
Rose
  Dubus, A. Selected stories
  Dubus, A. The last worthless evening
  The Pushcart prize XI
Sorrowful mysteries
  Dubus, A. Selected stories
They now live in Texas
  Dubus, A. Selected stories
Townies
  Dubus, A. Selected stories
Voices from the moon
  Dubus, A. Selected stories
Waiting
  Dubus, A. Selected stories
We don't live here anymore
  Dubus, A. We don't live here anymore
The winter father
  Dubus, A. Selected stories
Dubus, Elizabeth Nell
Always room for one more
  Redbook 170:48+ N '87
The sum of love
  Good Housekeeping 202:118-19+ Ap '86
Under the influence
  Redbook 162:71+ Ap '84
The **Duc** de l'Omelette. Poe, E. A.
The **Duchess**. Bourjaily, V.
The **Duchess** and the jeweller. Woolf, V.
The **Duchess** pulls a fast one. Chambers, W.
Duck hunt. Lansdale, J. R.
DUCK HUNTING
  Finney, E. J. Birds landing
  Hall, L. S. The ledge
  Lansdale, J. R. Duck hunt
  Maupassant, G. de. Love
  Nagibin, ĬŬ. M. The last hunt
  Nagibin, ĬŬ. M. The newlywed
  Pouvillon, E. Duck shooting
  Stegner, W. E. The blue-winged teal
Duck season. Broughton, T. A.
Duck shooting. Pouvillon, E.
DUCKS
  Dabrowska, C. Paradise sheldrake
  Shiner, L., and Shiner, E. Things that go
    quack in the night
  Skelton, R. Portrait of Duck
  Yamamoto, M. Father Goose
Duckwalking. Porter, J. A.
Duckworth, Marilyn
Explosions on the sun
  Critical Quarterly 30:55-63 Wint '88
**DUDEVANT, AMANTINE LUCILE
  AURORE DUPIN** *See* Sand, George,
  1804-1876
Dudley, William
A season for Idols
  Southern Humanities Review 22:263-71
    Summ '88
Due cappuccini. Updike, D.
Due process. Frazee, S.

Duecker, Kurt
  Saving the dead
    The Editors' choice: new American
      stories v2
The **duel**. Chekhov, A. P.
Duel. Eighner, L.
Duel. Kaikō, T.
The **duel**. Maupassant, G. de
The **duel**. Saroyan, W.
DUELING
  Brand, M. The fear of Morgan the Fearless
  Chekhov, A. P. The duel
  Doyle, Sir A. C. The tragedians
  Ellison, H. The silver corridor
  Johnson, G. C. Devlin's dream
  Maupassant, G. de. The duel
  Maupassant, G. de. A fashionable woman
  Poe, E. A. Mystification
  Poe, E. A. Von Jung, the mystific
  Sabatini, R. The blank shot
  Saroyan, W. The duel
  Vargas Llosa, M. The challenge
Duelling stories. Buzzati, D.
DUELS See Dueling
Duff, Gerald
  Fire ants
    The Editors' choice: new American
      stories v2
The **Dufus** Rufus. Coleman, W.
Dugan, Melanie
  Primavera
    The North American Review 271:41-6 Mr
      '86
Duke, Madelaine, 1925-
  Little knives
    John Creasey's Crime collection, 1985
  The notif
    John Creasey's Crime collection, 1987
Duke & Jill. Kolm, R.
Duke City alchemist. Willson, H.
The **Duke** of Orkney's Leonardo. Warner, S.
    T.
Duke Pasquale's ring. Davidson, A.
Dukes. Chesterton, G. K.
Dulce. Rule, J.
Dullas, Inez
  Shanti, simple, sweet and—sinister!
    Short story international 62
  X marks the spot
    Short story international 43
Dumas, Henry, 1934-1968
  Ark
    Dumas, H. Goodbye, sweetwater
  Ark of bones
    Dumas, H. Goodbye, sweetwater
  A boll of roses
    Dumas, H. Goodbye, sweetwater
  Devil bird
    Dumas, H. Goodbye, sweetwater
  The distributors
    Dumas, H. Goodbye, sweetwater
  Double nigger
    Dumas, H. Goodbye, sweetwater

  Echo tree
    Dumas, H. Goodbye, sweetwater
  Fever
    Dumas, H. Goodbye, sweetwater
  Fon
    Dumas, H. Goodbye, sweetwater
  Goodbye, sweetwater
    Dumas, H. Goodbye, sweetwater
  Harlem
    Dumas, H. Goodbye, sweetwater
  A Harlem game
    Dumas, H. Goodbye, sweetwater
  The marchers
    Dumas, H. Goodbye, sweetwater
  Rain god
    Dumas, H. Goodbye, sweetwater
  Rope of wind
    Dumas, H. Goodbye, sweetwater
  Six days you shall labor
    Dumas, H. Goodbye, sweetwater
  Strike and fade
    Dumas, H. Goodbye, sweetwater
  Thalia
    Dumas, H. Goodbye, sweetwater
  Thrust counter thrust
    Dumas, H. Goodbye, sweetwater
  The university of man
    Dumas, H. Goodbye, sweetwater
  The voice
    Dumas, H. Goodbye, sweetwater
  Wandering in the wilderness
    Dumas, H. Goodbye, sweetwater
  The white horse
    Dumas, H. Goodbye, sweetwater
  Will the circle be unbroken?
    Dumas, H. Goodbye, sweetwater
Dummy. See Carver, R. The third thing that
    killed my father off
The **dummy**. Piñera, V.
The **dummy** in the jeep. Rizkalla, J.
The **dummy** that lived. Baum, L. F.
Dumont, Fernand, 1903-1945
  The region of the heart
    The Literary Review (Madison, N.J.)
      32:43-61 Fall '88
Dumonte, Ed
  Mr. Reed goes to dinner
    Alfred Hitchcock's Grave suspicions
Dumoustier, Fernand See Dumont, Fernand,
    1903-1945
Duncan, Alex, 1925-
    See also Duke, Madelaine, 1925-
Duncan. Crayford, K.
Dundas, Robert
  As small as your shadow
    Short story international 44
  Booker's End
    Short story international 50
  The climber on the hill
    Short story international 67
  Mr. de la Torre
    Short story international 48

Dundas, Robert—*Continued*
The respecter of persons
Short story international 52
Six faces of Feridah Challoner
Short story international 57
The uniform
Short story international 54
Dundee, Wayne D.
Body count
Mean streets; ed. by R. J. Randisi
The Judas target
An Eye for justice; ed. by R. J. Randisi
Shooting match
The Black Lizard anthology of crime fiction; ed. by E. Gorman
Dunedin. Brasch, C.
Dunlap, Susan
Hit-and-run
Great modern police stories; ed. by B. Pronzini and M. H. Greenberg
Dunn, Douglas
The bagpiping people
Dunn, D. Secret villages
Bobby's room
Dunn, D. Secret villages
The New Yorker 59:38-46 Ja 16 '84
Boyfriends and girlfriends
The New Yorker 61:22-32 D 30 '85
The canoes
Dunn, D. Secret villages
Ever let the fancy roam
Dunn, D. Secret villages
Fishermen
Dunn, D. Secret villages
Getting used to it
Dunn, D. Secret villages
Kilbinnin men
Dunn, D. Secret villages
Mozart's Clarinet Concerto
Dunn, D. Secret villages
Needlework
The New Yorker 61:26-34 Ag 19 '85
A night out at the Club Harmonica
Dunn, D. Secret villages
Old women without gardens
Dunn, D. Secret villages
Orr Mount
The New Yorker 60:46-56 S 17 '84
Photographs of Stanley's grandfather
Dunn, D. Secret villages
Something for little Robert
Dunn, D. Secret villages
South America
Dunn, D. Secret villages
The New Yorker 60:32-40 Je 25 '84
The tennis court
Dunn, D. Secret villages
Twin-sets and pickle forks
Dunn, D. Secret villages
Wives in the garden
Dunn, D. Secret villages

Dunn, J. R.
Long knives
L. Ron Hubbard presents Writers of the future v3
Dunn, Marylois
Cat and the Other
Tales of the Witch World [1]
If there be magic
Magic in Ithkar 2; ed. by A. Norton and R. Adams
Dunn, Robert, 1950-
The kite man
Omni (New York, N.Y.) 7:68-70+ Ag '85
Dunning, Stephen
Chowder
Michigan Quarterly Review 27:160-6 Wint '88
Dunsany, Edward John Moreton Drax Plunkett, Baron, 1878-1957
The Bureau d'Echange de Maux
Black water; ed. by A. Manguel
In a dim room
Great ghost stories; ed. by B. A. Schwartz
The pirate of the Round Pond
Dark arrows; ed. by A. Manguel
A story of land and sea
Short stories of the sea; ed. by G. C. Solley and E. Steinbaugh
The sword of Welleran
Masterpieces of fantasy and enchantment; ed. by D. G. Hartwell
The two bottles of relish
The Penguin book of horror stories
Duntemann, Jeff, and Kress, Nancy
Borovsky's hollow woman
Omni book of science fiction 3
The **Dunwich** horror. Lovecraft, H. P.
Duplex. Foray, V.
Duppy get her. Adisa, O. P.
Durban, Pam
All set about with fever trees
Durban, P. All set about with fever trees, and other stories
The Editors' choice: new American stories v2
The Georgia Review 38:265-87 Summ '84
Belonging
New stories from the South: the year's best, 1988
In darkness
Durban, P. All set about with fever trees, and other stories
A long time coming, a long time gone
Durban, P. All set about with fever trees, and other stories
The New writers of the South; ed. by C. East
Made to last
Durban, P. All set about with fever trees, and other stories

Durban, Pam—*Continued*
Notes toward an understanding of my father's novel
Durban, P. All set about with fever trees, and other stories
This heat
Durban, P. All set about with fever trees, and other stories
The Georgia Review 40:75-94 Spr '86
Necessary fictions; ed. by S. W. Lindberg and S. Corey
World of women
Durban, P. All set about with fever trees, and other stories
Dureddu. Holme, T.
Durham, Edith Manuel
Deepening dusk
Writing red; ed. by C. Nekola and P. Rabinowitz
Durrell, Lawrence
All to scale
Durrell, L. Antrobus complete
Aunt Norah
Durrell, L. Antrobus complete
Call of the sea
Durrell, L. Antrobus complete
Case history
Durrell, L. Antrobus complete
A corking evening
Durrell, L. Antrobus complete
Cry wolf
Durrell, L. Antrobus complete
Drage's divine discontent
Durrell, L. Antrobus complete
For immediate release
Durrell, L. Antrobus complete
Frying the flag
Durrell, L. Antrobus complete
The game's the thing
Durrell, L. Antrobus complete
The ghost train
Durrell, L. Antrobus complete
High barbary
Durrell, L. Antrobus complete
If garlic be the food of love . . .
Durrell, L. Antrobus complete
The iron hand
Durrell, L. Antrobus complete
Jots and tittles
Durrell, L. Antrobus complete
The little affair in Paris
Durrell, L. Antrobus complete
'Noblesse oblige'
Durrell, L. Antrobus complete
Sauve qui peut
Durrell, L. Antrobus complete
Seraglios and imbroglios
Durrell, L. Antrobus complete
Smoke, the embassy cat
Durrell, L. Antrobus complete
Something à la carte?
Durrell, L. Antrobus complete

Stiff upper lip
Durrell, L. Antrobus complete
The swami's secret
Durrell, L. Antrobus complete
Taking the consequences
Durrell, L. Antrobus complete
The unspeakable attaché
Durrell, L. Antrobus complete
La valise
Durrell, L. Antrobus complete
What-ho on the Rialto!
Durrell, L. Antrobus complete
Where the bee sucks . . .
Durrell, L. Antrobus complete
White man's milk
Durrell, L. Antrobus complete
A **dusk** of idols. Blish, J.
Dusky Ruth. Coppard, A. E.
DÜSSELDORF (GERMANY) *See* Germany—Düsseldorf
Dust. Clee, M. A.
Dust. El Hamamssy, A.
Dust. Fisher, R.
Dust. Matheson, R. C.
The **dust** of Yuri Serafimovich. Fetler, J.
Dust storm. Brand, M.
The **dusty** drawer. Muheim, H.
The **dusty** sunbeam. Nérault, F.
DUTCH
Africa
Rush, N. Bruns
Australia
Jolley, E. The agent in travelling
Jolley, E. Outink to Uncle's place
Jolley, E. The outworks of the kingdom
Jolley, E. Uncle Bernard's proposal
Canada
Brender à Brandis, M. Fall fair
Cook, H. A Canadian education
Cook, H. Clown
Cook, H. Cracked wheat
Cook, H. Exodus
Cook, H. First snow
Cook, H. Homesickness
Cook, H. A lesson in dance
Cook, H. Pisces
Cook, H. The white rabbit
England
Rhys, J. Who knows what's up in the attic?
France
Apollinaire, G. The meeting at the mixed club
Rhys, J. Tea with an artist
Germany
Kohlhaase, W. Invention of a language
India
Jhabvala, R. P. The man with the dog
Japan
Nooteboom, C. Mokusei: a love story
United States
Salter, J. Foreign shores

Dutch and Sybil I: Eleanor Roosevelt's garden. Lynch, L.

Dutch and Sybil II: Beachfront hotel. Lynch, L.

Duties and liabilities. Campbell, E.

Dutko's story. Taylor, C.

Duty. Covington, V.

Duty. Wetjen, A. R.

The **dwarf.** Bradbury, R.

DWARFS

Bloch, R. Gather 'round the flowing bowler

Bradbury, R. The dwarf

Etchison, D. Talking in the dark

Green, J. The tallest man in the world

Kinsella, W. P. The performance

Mrożek, S. An event

Mrożek, S. Tiny

Poe, E. A. Hop-frog

Sage, V. Obscurity

Shelley, M. W. The transformation

Tournier, M. The red dwarf

Wells, H. G. Our little neighbour

Wilde, O. The birthday of the Infanta

The **dweller** in the gulf. Smith, C. A.

Dwelling. Blei, N.

A **dwelling** place for dragons. Whelan, G.

Dwyer, K. R., 1945-

For works written by this author under other names see Koontz, Dean, 1945-

Dwyer's girl. Milton, E.

DX. Haldeman, J. W.

The **dybbuk** of Mazel Tov IV. Silverberg, R.

Dybek, Stuart, 1942-

Bijou

The Ploughshares reader: new fiction for the eighties

Blight

New American short stories; ed. by G. Norris

Prize stories, 1987

Chopin in winter

The Graywolf annual 4

Hot ice

Prize stories, 1985

The Pushcart prize X

The Substance of things hoped for; ed. by J. B. Breslin

Pet Milk

The New Yorker 60:26-7 Ag 13 '84

Prize stories, 1986

Sunday at the zoo

Sudden fiction; ed. by R. Shapard and J. Thomas

Dyer, Susan

Blooming Violet

Redbook 164:48-50+ Ap '85

Can daddy come home?

Redbook 171:36+ Je '88

The dream diet

Redbook 166:48+ Ja '86

Look at Violet now!

Redbook 168:16+ Ja '87

No shrinking Violet

Redbook 166:58-60+ Mr '86

Over the river and through the woods

McCall's 113:124-5+ N '85

Two's a crowd

McCall's 114:99-100 Ag '87

The **dyer's** art. Ponsoldt, S.

The **dying.** Ch'en, Y.-C.

The **dying** day of Francis Bainsbridge. Johnston, G.

Dying in the goldenwest. Haas, B.

A **dying** man. Pritchard, M.

The **dying** year. Drabble, M.

Dykeman, Wilma

Lydia McQueen

Homewords: a book of Tennessee writers; ed. by D. Paschall

DYLAN, BOB, 1941-

About

Bishop, M. The Bob Dylan Tambourine Software & Satori Support Services Consortium, Ltd.

Dynamite. Smiley, J.

DYSLEXIA

Stewart, J. I. M. The dyslexia factor

The **dyslexia** factor. Stewart, J. I. M.

E

'**E:** a recollection. Wolfe, T.

E-ticket to Namland. Simmons, D.

Each new springtime, each new summer. McKinley, J.

The **eagle** cage. Ekström, M.

Eagle flies on Friday; greyhound runs at dawn. Hillis, R.

The **eagle** hunt. Apollinaire, G.

Eagle-worm. Salmonson, J. A.

Eagle's flight. Pontoppidan, H.

Eakins, Patricia

The hungry girls

The Literary Review (Madison, N.J.) 30:45-52 Fall '86

Yiqh-Yaqh (Ying-Yang, Y'ukq-Y'akq, Y'Shi'Yah)

Chicago Review 34:59-67 Summ '84

EAR

Butler, J. Without any ears

Yasuoka, S. The moth

The **ear.** Thubron, C.

Earle, Alice Morse, 1851-1911

The witch sheep

Yankee witches; ed. by C. G. Waugh; M. H. Greenberg and F. D. McSherry

Earle, Mary Alice Morse *See* Earle, Alice Morse, 1851-1911

Early, Patricia

The French prize

'Teen 28:32+ N '84

Early autumn exchange. Brady, M.

Early Bird & Smiley Face. Davies, A.

EARLY CHRISTIANS *See* Christians, Early

An **early** Christmas. Dorr, L.

Early deaths. Taylor, E. R.

An **early** frost. Michaelson, L. W.

Early morning, lonely ride. Packer, N. H.

Early morning sightseer. Ingalls, R.

Early spring, mid-summer. Yi, M.-Y.

An **early** spring morning remembered and understood. Hall, T. T.

Earshot. Gilliatt, P.

EARTH

DeLillo, D. Human moments in World War III

Gunn, J. E. Kindergarten

Haldeman, J. W. Tricentennial

Sheckley, R. Pilgrimage to Earth

Silverberg, R. Chalice of death

Silverberg, R. The wind and the rain

EARTH, DESTRUCTION OF

Bradfield, S. The Flash! Kid

Clarke, A. C. "If I forget thee, oh Earth . . ."

Clarke, A. C. Rescue party

Clemence, B. All the livelong night

Edwards, M. After-images

Gordon, M. The imagination of disaster

Hamilton, E. Requiem

Harness, C. L. Signals

Heinlein, R. A. Gulf

Herbert, J. Maurice and Mog

McGrath, P. The boot's tale

Sheckley, R. The last days of (parallel?) Earth

Silverberg, R. When we went to see the end of the world

Soukup, M. Frenchmen and plumbers

Tiptree, J. The Earth doth like a snake renew

Van Greenaway, P. The exhibition

Earth. Kawabata, Y.

The **Earth** doth like a snake renew. Tiptree, J.

Earth to earth. Graves, R.

Earthquake baroque. Wilson, B.

The **earthquake** in Chile. Kleist, H. von

An **earthquake** in my family. Federspiel, J.

EARTHQUAKES

See also Disasters

Clarke, A. C. Dog Star

Fante, J. The wrath of God

Federspiel, J. An earthquake in my family

Hill, E. Marriage at noon

Kleist, H. von. The earthquake in Chile

Pacheco, J. E. The captive

Silverberg, R. Waiting for the earthquake

Updike, J. Slippage

Weinbaum, S. G. Shifting seas

The **earth's** crust. Welch, D.

Earth's holocaust. Hawthorne, N.

Earthworks. Eisenstein, S.

Easily and well. Glasser, P.

East, Charles

The last person

Selected stories from The Southern review, 1965-1985

A tribute to the general

Mississippi writers v1: Fiction; ed. by D. Abbott

EAST (FAR EAST) *See* East Asia

EAST AFRICA

Coskran, K. An African river

Coskran, K. Facing Mount Kenya

Markham, B. Your heart will tell you

Watson, I. Flame and the healer

EAST AND WEST

Eisenstein, S. All the monkeys

Haylock, J. Choice

Kaikō, T. The crushed pellet

Kipling, R. East and West

Lester, C. S. Dogs and foreigners

Saint, R. The Imam

East and West. Kipling, R.

EAST ANGLIA (ENGLAND) *See* England— East Anglia

EAST ASIA

Kilworth, G. Blind windows

The **East** Beaverton monster. Ryan, A.

The **East** End Umbrella Company endowment for the arts. Kinsella, W. P.

East from Botwood. Jameison, L.

EAST INDIANS

Africa

Gordimer, N. A chip of glass ruby

Thomas, A. C. Degrees

Canada

Hospital, J. T. Happy Diwali

Mukherjee, B. Isolated incidents

Mukherjee, B. The management of grief

Mukherjee, B. Tamurlane

England

Doyle, Sir A. C. Uncle Jeremy's household

Draycott, M. Splices

Naipaul, S. The tenant

Ornstien, E. English for immigrants

Sproat, R. A small difference only

Verma, N. The world elsewhere

Kenya

Leitão, L. The son

New York (N.Y.)

Mukherjee, B. Danny's girl

Sharat Chandra, G. S. Saree of the gods

Northern Ireland

Forsyth, F. There are no snakes in Ireland

South Africa

Essop, A. Dolly

Essop, A. Gladiators

Essop, A. The Hajji

Essop, A. Mr Moonreddy

Essop, A. The notice

Essop, A. Obsession

Essop, A. The visitation

Essop, A. The yogi

Gordimer, N. A chip of glass ruby

EAST INDIANS—*Continued*
Tanzania
Thomas, M. Silver sugar from Bombay
United States
Hospital, J. T. Waiting
Mukherjee, B. Angela
Mukherjee, B. A father
Mukherjee, B. Hindus
Mukherjee, B. The imaginary assassin
Mukherjee, B. The lady from Lucknow
Mukherjee, B. Nostalgia
Mukherjee, B. The tenant
Mukherjee, B. Visitors
Mukherjee, B. A wife's story
East is east. al-Shayib, F.
East Jesus. Schulman, H.
EAST SIDE, LOWER (NEW YORK, N.Y.)
See New York (N.Y.)—Lower East
Side
EASTER
Chavez, A. The penitente thief
Heise, K. The chocolate Easter bunny
Henry, O. The red roses of Tonia
Kauffman, J. The Easter we lived in
Detroit
Lish, G. Resurrection
Saki. The Easter egg
Valenzuela, L. Blue water-man
West, J. The heavy stone
Easter. Keillor, G.
The **Easter** bunny. Winters, J.
Easter devil. Eberhart, M. G.
The **Easter** egg. Saki
Easter flowers. Kantor, M.
Easter lily. Cook, H.
The **Easter** we lived in Detroit. Kauffman,
J.
EASTERN EUROPE
Aldiss, B. W. The blue background
Roth, J. Hotel Savoy
Tuohy, F. The candidate
Wegner, H. The counter of Lvov
Wegner, H. Cyankali
Wegner, H. The huzul flute
Wegner, H. The stoning of Stanislava
Eastlake, William, 1917-
The death of Sun
The Interior country; ed. by A. Black-
burn
Easton, M. Coleman
Flarrin red-chin
Magic in Ithkar 3; ed. by A. Norton and
R. Adams
Easton, Richard
The rivalry
The Virginia Quarterly Review 63:133-48
Wint '87
Easton, Thomas A.
Roll them bones
Haunted New England; ed. by C. G.
Waugh; M. H. Greenberg and F. D.
McSherry
Eastward ho! Tenn, W.

Easy. Coe, C.
Easy in the islands. Shacochis, B.
Easy money. Tesich, N.
An **easy** score. Nussbaum, A.
The **eat** and run midnight people. Chin, F.
Eating crazy. Jen, G.
Eating out. Heise, K.
Eating the placenta. Dixon, S.
Eaton, Charles Edward, 1916-
Saint Cecilia's son
Southwest Review 69:16-30 Wint '84
The **Eatonville** anthology. Hurston, Z. N.
An **eavesdropper's** notebook. Bloch, D.
EAVESDROPPING
Butler, G. The sisterhood
Hall, M. L. Privacy
Thubron, C. The ear
The **ebbing.** Carpenter, L.
The **ebbing** tide. Wilkinson, R.
Ebejer, Francis
Mediterranean lifestyle: the parvis pry
Short story international 57
Eberhart, Mignon Good, 1899-
The calico dog
Women sleuths; ed. by M. H. Greenberg
and B. Pronzini
Dangerous widows
Ellery Queen's Crimes and punishments
Easter devil
Kill or cure; ed. by M. Muller and B.
Pronzini
Ebon, William
Agua prieta
Ebon, W. Death of a lover, and other
stories
Death of a lover
Ebon, W. Death of a lover, and other
stories
The doctorate
Ebon, W. Death of a lover, and other
stories
Little girl from Little Rock
Ebon, W. Death of a lover, and other
stories
The supermarket manager's daughter
Ebon, W. Death of a lover, and other
stories
ECCENTRICS AND ECCENTRICITIES
See also Recluses
Allende, I. Rosa the beautiful
Armas, J. El tonto del Barrio
Barthelme, F. Gila Flambé
Bass, R. The watch
Baxter, C. Gryphon
Bell, C. G. The married land [excerpt]
Blythe, R. Everything a man needs
Bonosky, P. A bird in her hair
Bukoski, A. The woman who ate cat food
Bumpus, J. The outdoorsman
Carver, R. Why don't you dance?
Chappell, F. The snow that is nothing in
the triangle
Coskran, K. Handyman

ECCENTRICS AND ECCENTRICITIES—
Continued
  Cowan, P. The tins
  Daviau, D.-M. Under the bell jar
  Drake, R. Still swinging
  Gallant, M. Kingdom come
  Gilliatt, P. On each other's time
  Givner, J. Brains
  Goyen, W. Where's Esther?
  Goyen, W. Zamour; or, A tale of inheritance
  Gray, A. The crank that made the revolution
  Grenville, K. The test is, if they drown
  Hankla, C. Skeleton
  Harrison, M. J. Running down
  Jackson, G. The fly-screen
  Janowitz, T. Case history #4: Fred
  Kamminga, A. Moleman
  Kinsella, W. P. Gabon
  Leaton, A. Little pictures
  Lurie, M. Good people in the house
  Lurie, M. Skylight in Lausanne
  MacLeod, J. L. The Jesus Flag
  Maheux-Forcier, L. The carnation
  Matthews, J. Haunted by name our ignorant lips
  Morris, W. Drrdla
  Morris, W. Magic
  Nowakowski, M. Madam Amalia Bessarabo
  Purdy, J. Mr. Evening
  Rhys, J. Illusion
  Rhys, J. Sleep it off lady
  Robison, J. The ecstasy of the animals
  Robison, J. The house sitter
  Rooke, L. In the garden
  Rooke, L. The man in the green bathrobe
  Schell, J. Alvira, Lettie, and Pip
  Sisskind, M. Mr. Tivy
  Skelton, R. The angel
  Skelton, R. The importance of being Percy
  Stead, C. A household
  Summers, H. S. Fortunato & the night visitor
  Thurm, M. Ice
  Tremain, R. The stately roller coaster
  Watson, S. The Black Farm
  Welch, D. Evergreen Seaton-Leverett
  Williams, J. The blue men
  Willson, H. Duke City alchemist
  Wolff, T. The poor are always with us
The **echo**. Bowles, P.
Echo. Nagibin, IŪ. M.
Echo tree. Dumas, H.
Echoes. Connolly, L. C.
Echoes. Matheson, R. C.
Echoes in an empty gym. Nelson, M. B.
Eckhardt at a window. McCormack, E. P.
Eckstein, Barbara
  A story of inland life
    The Georgia Review 39:345-9 Summ '85
Eclipse!. Cooper, R. R.
The **eclipse**. Landolfi, T.

The **eclipse**. Monterroso, A.
ECLIPSES
  Landolfi, T. The eclipse
  Monterroso, A. The eclipse
  Willis, C. And come from miles around
ECOLOGY
  Longyear, B. B. Catch the sun
  Martin, G. R. R. Nor the many-colored fires of a star ring
  Norton, A. Desirable lakeside residence
  O'Neil, D. Report on a broken bridge
  Silverberg, R. The wind and the rain
ECONOMISTS
  Claiborne, S. The future of conglomerates
  Gustafsson, L. The fugitives discover that they knew nothing
Ecospasm. Eisenstein, S.
The **ecstasy** of the animals. Robison, J.
ECUADOR
        See also Galapagos Islands
ECZEMA
  Thomas, J. My journal as the fishwoman
Ed. Collison, E.
Eddie. Ronk-Lifson, M.
Eddie and the monkey robberies. Highsmith, P.
Eddie and the niña. Klinkowitz, J.
Eddie Mac. McGahern, J.
The **Eddie** Scissons syndrome. Kinsella, W. P.
Eddy the boy. Taylor, R.
Eddy the man. Taylor, R.
EDEN
  Farmer, P. J. The god business
  Wells, H. G. The apple
The **edge**. Cadigan, P.
The **edge** of the world. Davison, S.
Edgell, John
  Did you see the window-cleaner?
    Venomous tales of villainy and vengeance; ed. by H. Hoke
Edgerton, Clyde, 1944-
  Raney [excerpt]
    The New writers of the South; ed. by C. East
Edging around the fat man. Windsor, G.
EDINBURGH (SCOTLAND) *See* Scotland—Edinburgh
Edisto. Powell, P.
The **editor** of A. Targan, B.
EDITORS
        See also Journalists
  Adams, G. G. La plume de ma tante
  Asimov, I. The next day
  Berry, R. M. History
  Codrescu, A. The herald
  King, S. The ballad of the flexible bullet
  Poe, E. A. 'X-ing a paragrab'
  Rhys, J. Again the Antilles
Edkins, Anthony
  What's eating you?
    P.E.N. new fiction I

Edler, Peter R.
Last dance
The Antioch Review 46:303-7 Summ '88
Edmonds, Walter Dumaux, 1903-
Moses
Roger Caras' Treasury of great dog stories
Edmundson, Mark
The peach dance
New England Review and Bread Loaf Quarterly 11:22-38 Aut '88
Edric, Robert
The mighty Titanic is sinking
Critical Quarterly 29:30-4 Aut '87
A well-spent life
Winter's tales, new ser. v4
Edson, Russell
Dinner time
Sudden fiction; ed. by R. Shapard and J. Thomas
An **educated** taste. Horsdal, M.
EDUCATION
See also Books and reading; Literacy; Teachers
Asimov, I. Profession
Barthelme, D. The educational experience
Bloch, R. The learning maze
Chesterton, G. K. On secular education
Foote, S. Jordan County [excerpt]
Gallacher, T. Store quarter
Jiménez, F. The circuit
Lafferty, R. A. Primary education of the Camiroi
Education of a pointman. Crapser, W.
The **education** of Mingo. Johnson, C. R.
The **education** of Phyllisteen. St. Pierre, P. H.
Une **éducation** sentimentale. Young-Bruehl, E.
The **educational** experience. Barthelme, D.
EDUCATORS See Teachers
Edward and Georgina. McCormack, E. P.
Edward and Jill. Boswell, R.
Edwards, Amelia Ann Blanford, 1831-1892
The phantom coach
The Oxford book of English ghost stories
Edwards, Caterina
Prima vera
Alberta bound; ed. by F. Stenson
Edwards, Dolton
Meihem in ce klasrum
From mind to mind: tales of communication from Analog
Edwards, Harry Stillwell, 1855-1938
His defense
Isaac Asimov presents the best crime stories of the 19th century
Edwards, Kim A.
In the ice house
The North American Review 271:25-31 Mr '86

Edwards, Malcolm
After-images
Interzone: the first anthology; ed. by J. Clute; C. Greenland and D. Pringle
Edwards, Margaret F.
Getting over Russell
Mademoiselle 92:128-30+ Ja '86
Roses
The Best American short stories, 1985
The Virginia Quarterly Review 60:488-506 Summ '84
Twice shy
The Virginia Quarterly Review 62:285-301 Spr '86
The **eel** man. Schinto, J.
Effie Whittlesy. Ade, G.
Effinger, George Alec
The aliens who knew, I mean, everything
Nebula awards 20
Babes on bawd way
Magic in Ithkar 2; ed. by A. Norton and R. Adams
From downtown at the buzzer
The Science fictional Olympics; ed. by I. Asimov; M. H. Greenberg and C. G. Waugh
Schrödinger's kitten
Omni (New York, N.Y.) 10:58-60+ S '88
Egan, Lesley, 1921-
For works written by this author under other names see Shannon, Dell, 1921-
An **egg** a month from all over. St. Clair, M.
The **egg** and the chicken. Lispector, C.
Egg boat. Dauenhauer, N.
The **egghead**. Roberts, R.
EGGS
Asimov, I. Paté de foie gras
London, J. The one thousand dozen
St. Clair, M. An egg a month from all over
Eggs. Kawabata, Y.
Egnaro. Harrison, M. J.
The **ego** in Arcadia. Halligan, M.
Ego trip. Bloch, R.
EGOISM
Bloch, R. Forever and amen
Mujica Láinez, M. Importance
Spofford, H. E. P. The amber gods
EGYPT
Benford, G. Of space-time and the river
To 640
Hoyt, M. S. The wind wizard
Poe, E. A. Some words with a mummy
Williams, T. The vengeance of Nitocris
19th century
Pynchon, T. Under the rose
20th century
Al Makhzangy, M. Just a touch
Al Shaikh, A. The heir
Attia, N. Games

EGYPT—20th century—*Continued*
Darwish, A. What happened the day of the big meeting?
Eid, H. The train at eleven
El Ghitany, G. Buzzing
El Hamamssy, A. Dust
El Milady, F. A. K. The night of the festival
El Naga, A. el M. A. Boundaries
El Sayyed, S. A. The box
Gad, H. The blue weapon
Higazy, F. The source of the Nile is Cairo's Muqattam Hills
Holding, J. The grave robber
Ingalls, R. Third time lucky
Maḥfūz, N. The conjurer made off with the dish
Monem, H. A. The thief
Nowaira, A. Lost and found
Ragab, M. A taste of success
Rifaat, A. Mansoura
Rifaat, A. Me and my sister
Rizkalla, J. The black figurine
Rizkalla, J. A janitor for sale
Rizkalla, J. The landlord
Rizkalla, J. The servant of the last hour
Roushdi, Z. Celebrating the Prophet's birthday
Salama, F. Friends' eyes
Tahir, B. Last night I dreamt of you
Villemaire, Y. In front of the Temple of Luxor, 31 July 1980
Wady, T. The madman
Kings and rulers
Williams, T. The vengeance of Nitocris
Prisoners and prisons
See Prisoners and prisons—Egypt
Rural life
Rifaat, A. At the time of the jasmine
Rifaat, A. An incident in the Ghobashi household
Alexandria
Leskov, N. S. The mountain
MacLean, A. McCrimmon and the blue moonstones
Cairo
Benson, E. F. Monkeys
Gorgy, N. Cairo is a small city
Idris, Y. The chair carrier
Maḥfūz, N. The time and the place
Rifaat, A. Another evening at the club
Rifaat, A. Distant view of a minaret
Rifaat, A. The flat in Nakshabandi Street
Rifaat, A. Telephone call
Rifaat, A. Thursday lunch
Sharouni, Y. Glimpses from the life of Maugoud Abdul Maugoud and two postscripts
EGYPTIANS
France
Schwob, M. The 'Papier Rouge'
Saudi Arabia
Al Magid, I. A. Over there

Ehlenbeck, Steve
In hiding
Seventeen 46:196-7+ S '87
The **Ehrengraf** appointment. Block, L.
The **Ehrengraf** experience. Block, L.
The **Ehrengraf** method. Block, L.
Ehrhart, W. D. (William Daniel), 1948-
Vietnam-Perkasie
Editor's choice II; ed. by M. Sklar and M. Biggs
Ehrhart, William Daniel *See* Ehrhart, W. D. (William Daniel), 1948-
Eichendorff, Joseph, Freiherr von, 1788-1857
Memoirs of a good-for-nothing
German romantic stories; ed. by F. G. Ryder
Eicher, Terry
Topolino
The North American Review 273:34-9 D '88
EICHMANN, ADOLF, 1906-1962
About
Zebrowski, G. The Eichmann variations
The **Eichmann** variations. Zebrowski, G.
Eid, Hussein
The train at eleven
Egyptian tales and short stories of the 1970s and 1980s
Eidolons. Ellison, H.
Eidus, Janice, 1951-
The resolution of muscle
The North American Review 269:46-7 Mr '84
Eiferman, Lee
Summer flying
Between C & D; ed. by J. Rose and C. Texier
The **Eiffel** Tower in three parts. Cohen, M.
Eighner, Lars
Bayou boy
Eighner, L. Bayou boy, and other stories
Bertner: emergency room
Eighner, L. Bayou boy, and other stories
Biker boy
Eighner, L. Bayou boy, and other stories
The burnout kid
Eighner, L. Bayou boy, and other stories
Cherryhurst
Eighner, L. Bayou boy, and other stories
A cowboy Christmas
Eighner, L. Bayou boy, and other stories
Duel
Eighner, L. Bayou boy, and other stories
Fairview
Eighner, L. Bayou boy, and other stories
Greenbriar
Eighner, L. Bayou boy, and other stories
Highway 71
Eighner, L. Bayou boy, and other stories
Montrose Boulevard
Eighner, L. Bayou boy, and other stories
Park
Eighner, L. Bayou boy, and other stories

Eighner, Lars—*Continued*
  Texarkana
    Eighner, L. Bayou boy, and other stories
  Waugh
    Eighner, L. Bayou boy, and other stories
  Westheimer
    Eighner, L. Bayou boy, and other stories
  Windsor
    Eighner, L. Bayou boy, and other stories
  Woodhead
    Eighner, L. Bayou boy, and other stories
  Yoakum: the cruising circuit
    Eighner, L. Bayou boy, and other stories
Eight hundred meters below. Sun Shaoshan
Eight Mile and Dequindre. Estleman, L. D.
Eighteen from Pereshchepena. Sholem
    Aleichem
Eighteen hours in Frankfurt. Haig, M.
Eighteen minutes. Schulze, A.
Eighth birthday. Dadswell, M.
The **eighth** day. Apple, M.
Eighty million dead. Collins, M.
Eighty per cent humidity. Drewe, R.
The **eighty-yard** run. Shaw, I.
Eileen. Gordon, M.
Eilis: a woman's story. Colum, P.
Eis, Jacqueline
  Imaginary lives
    Prairie Schooner 60:10-19 Summ '86
  The sea snake
    Prairie Schooner 60:55-63 Fall '86
Eisenberg, Deborah
  Broken glass
    Eisenberg, D. Transactions in a foreign
      currency
    The New Yorker 61:46-56+ D 2 '85
  A cautionary tale
    The New Yorker 63:32-42+ Mr 23 '87
  Days
    Eisenberg, D. Transactions in a foreign
      currency
  Flotsam
    Eisenberg, D. Transactions in a foreign
      currency
    The New Yorker 60:33-42+ S 3 '84
  A lesson in traveling light
    The Editors' choice v3; ed. by G. E.
      Murphy, Jr.
    Eisenberg, D. Transactions in a foreign
      currency
  Presents
    The New Yorker 63:25-36+ Jl 20 '87
  Rafe's coat
    Eisenberg, D. Transactions in a foreign
      currency
  Transactions in a foreign currency
    Eisenberg, D. Transactions in a foreign
      currency
    The New Yorker 60:28-38+ Ja 21 '85
    Prize stories, 1986
  What it was like, seeing Chris
    Eisenberg, D. Transactions in a foreign
      currency

    The New Yorker 61:26-36+ Jl 29 '85
Eisenberg, Larry
  The Chameleon
    Election Day 2084; ed. by I. Asimov
      and M. H. Greenberg
  Dr. Snow Maiden
    Great science fiction; ed. by I. Asimov;
      M. H. Greenberg and C. G. Waugh
**EISENHOWER, DWIGHT D. (DWIGHT
    DAVID), 1890-1969**
      About
  Boyle, T. C. Ike and Nina
  Waldrop, H. Ike at the mike
Eisenreich, Herbert
  A farewell to love
    Short story international 61
  A friend of the family
    Short story international 68
Eisenstein, Phyllis
  In the Western tradition
    Baker's dozen: 13 short science fiction
      novels
Eisenstein, Sam
  All the monkeys
    Eisenstein, S. The inner garden
  Boris
    Eisenstein, S. The inner garden
  The contortionist
    Eisenstein, S. The inner garden
  Doll's house
    Eisenstein, S. The inner garden
  Earthworks
    Eisenstein, S. The inner garden
  Ecospasm
    Eisenstein, S. The inner garden
  From in Albania
    Eisenstein, S. The inner garden
  The Greek smile
    Eisenstein, S. The inner garden
  Hear anything from Bakersfield?
    Eisenstein, S. The inner garden
  Holocaust envy
    Eisenstein, S. The inner garden
  The inner garden
    Eisenstein, S. The inner garden
  The Kassel ballet
    Eisenstein, S. The inner garden
  Michali among the roses
    Eisenstein, S. The inner garden
  Moray eel
    Eisenstein, S. The inner garden
  A place of refuge
    Eisenstein, S. The inner garden
  Post coitus tristus
    Eisenstein, S. The inner garden
  The sacrifice
    Eisenstein, S. The inner garden
  Straight razor
    Eisenstein, S. The inner garden
  The weight goes on the downhill ski
    Eisenstein, S. The inner garden
Ekaterina. Cope, J.

Ekström, Margareta, 1930-
Balzac's valet
Ekström, M. Death's midwives
The child's garden
Ekström, M. Death's midwives
Death's midwives
Ekström, M. Death's midwives
The Pushcart prize X
The eagle cage
Ekström, M. Death's midwives
Hebe laughs
Ekström, M. Death's midwives
The king is threatened
Ekström, M. Death's midwives
Left alone
Ekström, M. Death's midwives
The night between the second and the
third
Ekström, M. Death's midwives
The nothingness forest
Ekström, M. Death's midwives
Perfect
Ekström, M. Death's midwives
When we are home alone we dance all
around the house
Ekström, M. Death's midwives

Ekwensi, Cyprian, 1921-
The ivory dancer
African short stories in English; ed. by
J. de Grandsaigne

El Biali, Zahira
The glass barrier
Egyptian tales and short stories of the
1970s and 1980s

El-Bisatie, Mohamed
A conversation from the third floor
African short stories; ed. by C. Achebe
and C. L. Innes
My brother
Arabic short stories; tr. by D. Johnson-
Davies

El Ghitany, Gamal
Buzzing
Egyptian tales and short stories of the
1970s and 1980s

El Hady, Wageh Abd
Who's superstitious?
Egyptian tales and short stories of the
1970s and 1980s

El Hamamssy, Abdelal
Dust
Egyptian tales and short stories of the
1970s and 1980s

El-Kharrat, Edward
Birds' footsteps in the sand
Arabic short stories; tr. by D. Johnson-
Davies

El Makk, Ali
The case
Short story international 49

El Milady, Fawzi Abdel Kader
The night of the festival
Egyptian tales and short stories of the
1970s and 1980s

El Naga, Abu el Ma'ati Abu
Boundaries
Egyptian tales and short stories of the
1970s and 1980s

EL PASO (TEX.) *See* Texas—El Paso

El Rahman, Mahfouz Abd
Gentlemen eating gentlemen
Egyptian tales and short stories of the
1970s and 1980s

El Saadawi, Nawal
The veil
Egyptian tales and short stories of the
1970s and 1980s

EL SALVADOR
Shepard, L. Salvador

El Sayyed, Salah Abd
The box
Egyptian tales and short stories of the
1970s and 1980s

The **El** Western. McGuane, T.
Elaine. Bates, H. E.
Elba Nazario. Sepúlveda, E.
Elbow room. Bradley, M. Z.

ELDERLY
See also Old age
Alford, E. Half past eight
Briskin, M. Present tense
Conley, R. J. Old Joe
Highsmith, P. Old folks at home
Jolley, E. A new world
La Chapelle, M. The understanding
Pierce, C. Chez les petits suisses
Sandel, C. Madame
Schwartz, J. Waiting weeping
Seema, N. Helpless
Wilner, H. Desert couple

Eldershaw, Flora Sydney Patricia, 1897-
*For works written by this author in
collaboration with Marjorie Faith
Barnard see* Eldershaw, M. Barnard

Eldershaw, M. Barnard
Aubade
Australian science fiction; ed. by V. Ikin
The **eldest** of things. Abbott, L. K.
Eldorado. Furman, L.

Eldridge, Marian, 1936-
Adult education
Eldridge, M. Walking the dog, and other
stories
Antique
Eldridge, M. Walking the dog, and other
stories
At the Signora's
Transgressions; ed. by D. Anderson
Aubade
Eldridge, M. Walking the dog, and other
stories

Eldridge, Marian, 1936——*Continued*
  Candlebark
    Eldridge, M. Walking the dog, and other stories
  Chanson d'automne
    Eldridge, M. Walking the dog, and other stories
  Cream sponge on Sunday
    Eldridge, M. Walking the dog, and other stories
  A family story
    Eldridge, M. Walking the dog, and other stories
  Flight
    Eldridge, M. Walking the dog, and other stories
  Fragment
    Eldridge, M. Walking the dog, and other stories
  Interior
    Eldridge, M. Walking the dog, and other stories
  Maternity
    Eldridge, M. Walking the dog, and other stories
  Nature
    Eldridge, M. Walking the dog, and other stories
  Nuclear
    Eldridge, M. Walking the dog, and other stories
  Paterson's Flats
    Eldridge, M. Walking the dog, and other stories
  The ringbarker's daughter
    Eldridge, M. Walking the dog, and other stories
  The sea
    Eldridge, M. Walking the dog, and other stories
  Selling out
    Eldridge, M. Walking the dog, and other stories
  Solitaire
    Eldridge, M. Walking the dog, and other stories
  Together
    Eldridge, M. Walking the dog, and other stories
  Tourist
    Home and away; ed. by R. Creswell
  Walking the dog
    Eldridge, M. Walking the dog, and other stories
  Wayside
    Eldridge, M. Walking the dog, and other stories
Election day. Hansen, J.
ELECTIONS
    See also Presidents—United States—Election
  Faulkner, W. Skirmish at Sartoris
  Haynes, D. Taking Miss Kezee to the polls

  Kim, Y. I. The first election
  Moore, W. Frank Merriwell in the White House
The **electric** ant. Dick, P. K.
Electric arrows. Proulx, A.
Electric city. Grace, P.
ELECTRIC POWER FAILURES
  Klein, T. E. D. Children of the kingdom
ELECTRICITY
  Crace, J. Electricity
  Kress, N. Against a crooked stile
  Lutz, J. Understanding electricity
  Mitchell, K. The great electrical revolution
Electricity. Crace, J.
Electricity. Prose, F.
Electrico utensilio. Kinsella, W. P.
The **Electrolux** man. Kroll, J.
ELECTRONIC COMPUTERS *See* Computers
Elegy. Wiebe, D. E.
Elegy for dead animals. Martin, V.
An **element** of surprise. Murphy, W.
Elena, unfaithful. Broder, G. K.
Elena's son. Wendt, A.
Eleonora. Poe, E. A.
Elephant. Carver, R.
The **elephant**. Mrożek, S.
The **elephant**. Rodoreda, M.
ELEPHANT MAN *See* Merrick, Joseph Carey, 1862 or 3-1890
The **elephant** story (The stroke, I). Rose, D. A.
ELEPHANTS
  Goulart, R. Please stand by
  Hemingway, E. An African story
  Highsmith, P. Chorus girl's absolutely final performance
  Rodoreda, M. The elephant
  Twain, M. The stolen white elephant
Eleuthéria. Oates, J. C.
Elevation. Thomas, A. C.
The **elevator** man. Volkmer, J.
The **elevator** messengers. Brulotte, G.
ELEVATORS
  Brady, M. On the way to the ERA
  Hartley, L. P. Someone in the lift
Eleven. Robison, J.
The **eleven** dollar story. Hall, T. T.
The **eleventh** floor. Baxter, C.
Eleventh holiday. Gee, M.
The **eleventh** round. Monreal, D. N.
Elf hill. Russ, J.
Elflandsson, Galad
  The devil don't dance with strangers
    After midnight; ed. by C. L. Grant
  Icarus
    Shadows 9
  The last time I saw Harris
    Shadows 9

Elgin, Suzette Haden
For the sake of Grace
The Science fictional Olympics; ed. by
I. Asimov; M. H. Greenberg and C.
G. Waugh
Hush my mouth
Alternative histories; ed. by C. G.
Waugh and M. H. Greenberg
Modulation in all things
Great science fiction; ed. by I. Asimov;
M. H. Greenberg and C. G. Waugh
Eli, the fanatic. Roth, P.
Eliade, Mircea, 1907-1986
The cape
Eliade, M. Youth without youth, and
other novellas
Nineteen roses
Eliade, M. Youth without youth, and
other novellas
With the gypsy girls
The Slaying of the dragon; ed. by F.
Rottensteiner
Youth without youth
Eliade, M. Youth without youth, and
other novellas
Elias Schneebaum. Kaplan, D. M.
Elijah's Day. Nagibin, IŪ. M.
Elisabetta, Carlotta, Catherine (raising the
demon). Kaplan, D. M.
The **elixir**. Daudet, A.
Elixir for the emperor. Brunner, J.
An **elixir** of love. Gilbert, W. S.
The **elixir** of the Reverend Father Gaucher.
See Daudet, A. The elixir
**ELIZABETH II, QUEEN OF GREAT
BRITAIN, 1926-**
About
Kinsella, W. P. To look at the Queen
Elizabeth. Adams, A.
Elizabeth. Perez, N.
Elizabeth's things. Ford, K.
The **Elk**. See Poe, E. A. Morning on the
Wissahiccon
Elkin, Stanley, 1930-
The conventional wisdom
Buying time; ed. by S. Walker
I look out for Ed Wolfe
The Art of the tale; ed. by D. Halpern
A poetics for bullies
American short story masterpieces; ed.
by R. Carver and T. Jenks
The Norton book of American short
stories
Ella Biggs. Drake, R.
Elle est trois, (la mort). Lee, T.
Ellen, in her time. Grant, C. L.
Ellenberger, Daphne
The sewing machine
Short story international 42
Ellin, Stanley
Beidenbauer's flea
The Wickedest show on earth; ed. by
M. Muller and B. Pronzini

The Blessington method
Full measure; ed. by D. Sennett
The day of the bullet
Ellery Queen's Memorable characters
Manhattan mysteries; ed. by B. Pronzini;
C. L. R. Waugh and M. H. Greenberg
Kindly dig your grave
Last laughs; ed. by G. Mcdonald
The last bottle in the world
Through a glass, darkly; ed. by B. Woel-
fel
Mrs. Mouse
The Year's best mystery and suspense
stories, 1984
The nine-to-five man
Masterpieces of mystery and suspense;
ed. by M. H. Greenberg
The orderly world of Mr. Appleby
Hitchcock in prime time; ed. by F. M.
Nevins and M. H. Greenberg
The question [Variant title: The question
my son asked] .
The Crime of my life; ed. by B. Gar-
field
Masterpieces of terror and the super-
natural; ed. by M. Kaye and S. Kaye
The Penguin classic crime omnibus
Robert
Ready or not; ed. by J. Kahn
The twelfth statue
The Deadly arts; ed. by B. Pronzini and
M. Muller
Unacceptable procedures
The Year's best mystery & suspense
stories, 1986
Ellingson, Marnie
The wonder of Jenny
Good Housekeeping 202:108-9+ Ja '86
The **Ellington** affair. Buckley, W. F.
Elliott, Lorris T.
Flint/steel sparks on tropic moon-night
Fatal recurrences; ed. by H. Hugh and
P. O'Brien
Elliott, William *See* Bradbury, Ray, 1920-
Ellis, Jamie
One step to murder
Alfred Hitchcock's Mortal errors
Ellis, Leo R.
The great rodeo fix
Alfred Hitchcock's Mortal errors
Operation wild ass
A Treasury of World War II stories; ed.
by B. Pronzini and M. H. Greenberg
Ellis, Mel, 1912-1984
Mister Dog
Roger Caras' Treasury of great dog
stories
Ellison, Harlan
All the sounds of fear
Ellison, H. Ellison wonderland
The avenger of death
Ellison, H. Angry candy
Omni (New York, N.Y.) 10:48-50+ Ja '88

Ellison, Harlan—*Continued*
  Back to the drawing boards
    Ellison, H. Ellison wonderland
  Basilisk
    In the field of fire; ed. by J. Van B. Dann and J. Dann
  Battlefield
    Ellison, H. Ellison wonderland
  The boulevard of broken dreams
    100 great fantasy short short stories; ed. by I. Asimov; T. Carr and M. H. Greenberg
  A boy and his dog
    Beyond Armageddon; ed. by W. M. Miller and M. H. Greenberg
  Broken glass
    Ellison, H. Angry candy
  Chained to the fast lane in the Red Queen's race
    Ellison, H. Angry candy
  Commuter's problem
    Ellison, H. Ellison wonderland
  Count the clock that tells the time
    Omni book of science fiction 1
  Deal from the bottom
    Ellison, H. Ellison wonderland
  Do-it-yourself
    Ellison, H. Ellison wonderland
  Eidolons
    Ellison, H. Angry candy
  The end of the time of Leinard
    Westeryear; ed. by E. Gorman
  Escapegoat
    Ellison, H. Angry candy
  Footsteps
    Ellison, H. Angry candy
  The function of dream sleep
    Ellison, H. Angry candy
  Gnomebody
    Ellison, H. Ellison wonderland
  Hadj
    Ellison, H. Ellison wonderland
  I have no mouth, and I must scream
    Machines that think; ed. by I. Asimov; P. S. Warrick and M. H. Greenberg
  In lonely lands
    Ellison, H. Ellison wonderland
  Jeffty is five
    The Hugo winners v4
  Laugh track
    Ellison, H. Angry candy
  Mealtime
    Ellison, H. Ellison wonderland
  Nothing from my noon meal
    Ellison, H. Ellison wonderland
  On the downhill side
    The Best from Universe
  On the slab
    Ellison, H. Angry candy
    Omni book of science fiction 2
  Paladin of the lost hour
    Ellison, H. Angry candy
    Universe 15

  Prince Myshkin, and hold the relish
    Ellison, H. Angry candy
  The prowler in the city at the edge of the world
    Ripper! Ed. by G. Dozois and S. Casper
  Quicktime
    Ellison, H. Angry candy
    Omni (New York, N.Y.) 8:58-60+ O '85
  Rain, rain, go away
    Ellison, H. Ellison wonderland
  The region between
    Afterlives; ed. by P. Sargent and I. Watson
    Ellison, H. Angry candy
  The silver corridor
    Ellison, H. Ellison wonderland
  The sky is burning
    Ellison, H. Ellison wonderland
  Soft monkey
    The Black Lizard anthology of crime fiction; ed. by E. Gorman
    Ellison, H. Angry candy
    The Year's best fantasy, first annual collection
    The Year's best mystery and suspense stories, 1988
  Strange wine
    Amazing stories: visions of other worlds
  Stuffing
    Ellison, H. Angry candy
  The very last day of a good woman
    Ellison, H. Ellison wonderland
  When Auld's acquaintance is forgot
    Ellison, H. Angry candy
  The whimper of whipped dogs
    The Dark descent; ed. by D. G. Hartwell
  The wind beyond the mountains
    Ellison, H. Ellison wonderland
  With Virgil Oddum at the East Pole
    Ellison, H. Angry candy
    Medea: Harlan's world; ed. by H. Ellison
    Omni (New York, N.Y.) 7:44-6+ Ja '85
Ellroy, James
  The black dahlia [excerpt]
    A Matter of crime v1
Ellson, Hal
  The black stairway
    Manhattan mysteries; ed. by B. Pronzini; C. L. R. Waugh and M. H. Greenberg
Elman, Richard
  The anvil of the times
    Michigan Quarterly Review 26:673-6 Fall '87
  Little sharks
    Antaeus 60:87-92 Spr '88
  Turnabout
    Michigan Quarterly Review 26:677-8 Fall '87
Eloise. Keillor, G.
ELOPEMENTS
  Crane, S. The pace of youth

ELOPEMENTS—*Continued*
Doyle, Sir A. C. The fate of the Evangeline
Wells, H. G. A family elopement
An **eloquence** of grief. Crane, S.
Elric at the end of time. Moorcock, M.
Elsewhen. Boucher, A.
Elsi the unusual farm maid. Gotthelf, J.
Elul. Sholem Aleichem
Elvis in space. Boylan, J.

Ely, David
The academy
Rod Serling's Night gallery reader
The running man
Murder and mystery in Boston; ed. by C. L. R. Waugh; F. D. McSherry and M. H. Greenberg
Sound effects
The Kenyon Review ns10:63-72 Wint '88
Ely! Ely! Ely! Roy, G.
Emancipation. Klein, C.
The **emancipator.** Gilchrist, E.

EMBALMERS
Haas, B. On Mu
Ocampo, S. Mimoso
Pfeil, F. Shine on
The **embalming-women.** Schwob, M.
An **embarrassment** of ordinary riches. Bergland, M.

EMBEZZLEMENT
Baum, L. F. The suicide of Kiaros
Brown, F. Nightmare in yellow
Estleman, L. D. The used
Hall, T. T. Camouflage
Post, M. D. The sheriff of Gullmore
Pronzini, B. Bank job
Pronzini, B. A cold foggy day
Sheehan, R. Optics
The **embrace.** Böll, H.
An **embrace.** Tsushima, Y.
The **emerald.** Barthelme, D.
Emerald. Zhang Jie
The **emerald** city. Fraser, K.

EMERALDS
Smith, C. A. The weird of Avoosl Wuthoqquan
Emergency exit. Gilbert, M.
The **emergency** exit affair. Gilbert, M.
Emergency room bicentennial. Wilner, H.

Emerson, Ru
The werewolf's gift
Werewolves; ed. by J. Yolen and M. H. Greenberg
EMIGRÉS *See* Refugees
Emily's arrows. Wilson, B.
Eminent domain. O'Brien, D.
The **emir's** clock. Watson, I.
The **emissary.** Bradbury, R.
'**Emma** Bovary'. Moore, G.
Emma Zunz. Borges, J. L.
Emotion recollected in tranquillity. Penner, J.

EMOTIONALLY DISTURBED CHILDREN
Barich, B. Hard to be good
Brunner, J. What friends are for
Cortázar, J. Bestiary
Leavitt, D. Danny in transit
Levinson, R., and Link, W. Child's play
Olsen, T. I stand here ironing
Ramchandani, K. Gitley
Shimao, T. With Maya
Willett, J. Mr. Lazenbee

EMPATHY
Reamy, T. Insects in amber

EMPEDOCLES
About
Schwob, M. Empedocles, reputed god
Empedocles, reputed god. Schwob, M.
Emperor of the air. Canin, E.
Empire. Ford, R.
The **empire** of the ants. Wells, H. G.
The **empire** of the necromancers. Smith, C. A.
Empires of the air. Austin, D.
The **employ** of darkness. Piñera, V.

EMPLOYEES, DISMISSAL OF
Görlich, G. The decision
Spark, M. The Dragon
Warren, J. A special occasion

EMPLOYMENT INTERVIEWING
Draycott, M. Splices
Murphy, P. The appointment
Murphy, P. The little American executive
Murphy, P. Looking for work
Empty cages. Skrzynecki, P.
The **empty** can. Hayashi, K.
The **empty** house. Blackwood, A.
The **empty** house. Bulychev, K.
The **empty** lunch-tin. Malouf, D.
Empty . . . sort of. Anderman, J.

Emshwiller, Carol
The circular library of stones
Omni (New York, N.Y.) 9:74-6+ F '87
The Year's best fantasy, first annual collection
Day at the beach
Beyond Armageddon; ed. by W. M. Miller and M. H. Greenberg
Fledged
Omni (New York, N.Y.) 11:96-8+ D '88
Yukon
The Pushcart prize XII

Enayetullah, Anwar
Enemy
Short story international 57
This also happened
Short story international 46
The **encantadas;** or, Enchanted isles. Melville, H.
Enchanted evening. Soman, F. J.
The **enchanted** garden. Calvino, I.
The **enchanted** kiss. Henry, O.
The **enchanted** morning. Whitaker, M.
Enchantment. Merkin, D.

Enchi, Fumiko, 1905-
Blind man's buff
The Mother of dreams, and other short stories; ed. by M. Ueda
Encore. Purdy, J.
Encounter. Anthony, P.
An **encounter** by Mortstone pond. Kirk, R.
An **encounter** in the mist. Munby, A. N. L.
Encounter on the ladder. Clee, M. A.
Encounter with a skull. Kōda, R.
Encountering revolution. Dixon, S.
Encounters. Stambolian, G.
ENCYCLOPEDIAS AND DICTIONARIES
Lem, S. Vestrand's Extelopedia in 44 magnetomes
End game. Sciascia, L.
End of a dream. Dawson, F.
End of an era. Keillor, G.
The **end** of an old tom-cat. Škvorecký, J.
The **end** of Christy Tucker. Caldwell, E.
The **end** of Devil Hawker. Doyle, Sir A. C.
The **end** of eternity. Asimov, I.
The **end** of grief. Abbott, L. K.
The **end** of life as we know it. Shepard, L.
End of Magna. Dixon, S.
The **end** of Marko Kraljević. Yourcenar, M.
The **end** of Robinson Crusoe. Tournier, M.
End of season. MacLaverty, B.
The **end** of something. Hemingway, E.
The **end** of summer. Budrys, A.
The **end** of summer. Rule, J.
End of the affair. Keesing, N.
The **end** of the Axletree. Gray, A.
The **end** of the carnival. Yarbro, C. Q.
End of the day. Hoch, E. D.
The **end** of the highway. Choe, I.-H.
The **end** of the party. Greene, G.
The **end** of the queue. Whitaker, M.
The **end** of the reign. Updike, D.
The **end** of the revolution and other stories. Rooke, L.
The **end** of the river. Thomas, D.
The **end** of the story. Smith, C. A.
The **end** of the time of Leinard. Ellison, H.
The **end** of the whole mess. King, S.
END OF THE WORLD
See also Earth, Destruction of
Beaumont, C. Place of meeting
Bloch, R. Daybroke
Bloch, R. The funnel of God
Bradbury, R. There will come soft rains
Buzzati, D. The end of the world
Ellison, H. The very last day of a good woman
Manzione, J. Candle in a cosmic wind
Montgomerie, L. War and/or peace
Moss, R. The shopping trip
Oates, J. C. Nuclear holocaust
Poe, E. A. The conversation of Eiros and Charmion
Pronzini, B. The prophecy
Ryan, A. Waiting for the papers
Shelley, M. W. The last man

Silverberg, R. Waiting for the earthquake
Wells, H. G. The story of the Last Trump
Willis, C. Daisy, in the sun
Willis, C. Lost and found
The **end** of the world. Barich, B.
The **end** of the world. Buzzati, D.
End of winter. Petrakis, H. M.
The **end** of wisdom. Chesterton, G. K.
ENDECOTT, JOHN, 1588?-1665
About
Hawthorne, N. Endicott and the Red Cross
ENDICOTT, JOHN *See* Endecott, John, 1588?-1665
Endicott and the Red Cross. Hawthorne, N.
Ending. Grau, S. A.
The **endless** dark of the night. Conley, R. J.
Endless night. Wagner, K. E.
Endō, Shūsaku, 1923-
The day before
Endō, S. Stained glass elegies
The Shōwa anthology 2
Despicable bastard
Endō, S. Stained glass elegies
A forty-year-old man
Endō, S. Stained glass elegies
Fuda-no-Tsuji
Encounter (London, England) 63:3-8 Jl/Ag '84
Endō, S. Stained glass elegies
Incredible voyage
Endō, S. Stained glass elegies
A man sixty
New Directions in prose and poetry 51
Mothers
Endō, S. Stained glass elegies
The Substance of things hoped for; ed. by J. B. Breslin
My belongings
Endō, S. Stained glass elegies
Old friends
Endō, S. Stained glass elegies
Retreating figures
Endō, S. Stained glass elegies
Unzen
Endō, S. Stained glass elegies
The war generation
Endō, S. Stained glass elegies
ENDOWMENTS
James, H. The Coxon Fund
The **enduring** chill. O'Connor, F.
Enemies. Gordimer, N.
The **enemies.** Thomas, D.
The **enemy.** Armstrong, C.
The **enemy.** Buck, P. S.
The **enemy.** DeGrazia, E.
Enemy. Enayetullah, A.
The **enemy.** Herbst, J.
The **enemy.** Nowakowski, M.
The **enemy.** Singer, I. B.
The **enemy.** Tamer, Z.
Enemy country. DeGrazia, E.
Enemy mine. Longyear, B. B.

Enemy transmissions. Shippey, T.
Energy. Hunnicutt, E.
Energy. Miller, E. V.
The **energy** crisis of 2215. Zahn, T.
The **engagement.** Smith, E. C.
The **engagement** in Santo Domingo. See
    Kleist, H. von. Betrothal in Santo
    Domingo
ENGAGEMENTS *See* Betrothals
Engagements. Frucht, A.
Engagements. Janowitz, T.
Engberg, Susan, 1940-
  Boiling river
    Engberg, S. A stay by the river
  Common happiness
    Engberg, S. A stay by the river
    The Southern Review (Baton Rouge, La.)
    20:645-61 Jl '84
  A daughter's heart
    Engberg, S. A stay by the river
  Fourth brother
    Engberg, S. A stay by the river
  Household
    Engberg, S. A stay by the river
    The Ploughshares reader: new fiction for
    the eighties
  The mile run
    Engberg, S. A stay by the river
  Morgan and Joanna
    Engberg, S. A stay by the river
  Northern light
    Engberg, S. A stay by the river
  Pastorale
    Prime number; ed. by A. L. Weir
  Riffraff
    Engberg, S. A stay by the river
  Soliloquy
    Engberg, S. A stay by the river
  A stay by the river
    Engberg, S. A stay by the river
  Trio
    A Good deal; ed. by M. Heath and F.
    M. Robinson
Engel, Marian, 1933-1985
  Anita's dance
    The Oxford book of Canadian short
    stories in English
The **engine.** Bradley, M. Z.
Engine horse. Highsmith, P.
Engineer-private Paul Klee misplaces an air-
    craft between Milbertshofen and Cam-
    brai, March 1916. Barthelme, D.
ENGINEERS
  Aćin-Kosta, M. Dam on crutches
  Camus, A. The growing stone
  Clarke, T. Apai
  Clarke, T. The champion
  Clarke, T. The day nothing happened
  Clarke, T. The king
  Clarke, T. The lost D.O.
  Clarke, T. A posthumous gift
  Clarke, T. The red
  Clarke, T. A rite of passion

  Clarke, T. The truth
  Clarke, T. The wee manok
  Clarke, T. The well
  Clarke, T. The Wo family
  DeMarinis, R. The flowers of boredom
  Fitzgerald, F. S. "The sensible thing"
  Gorgy, N. Cairo is a small city
  Kingsbury, D. The moon goddess and the
    son
  Taher, B. Advice from a sensible young
    man
ENGLAND
    See also Cotswolds (England);
    Stonehenge (England)
  Rooke, L. The history of England, part
    four
      Roman period, 55 B.C.-449 A.D.
  Price, A. The Boudicca killing
        15th century
  Woolf, V. The journal of Mistress Joan
    Martyn
        17th century
  Gilchrist, M. The manuscript of Francis
    Shackerley
  Turtledove, H. And so to bed
  Waldrop, H. God's hooks!
        18th century
  Gilchrist, M. Excerpts from Witherton's
    journal: also a letter of Crystalla's
  Gilchrist, M. The writings of Althea
    Swarthmoor
        19th century
  Dickens, C. The chimes
  Dickens, C. A Christmas carol
  Dickens, C. The cricket on the hearth
  Dickens, C. The magic fishbone
  Doyle, Sir A. C. An impression of the
    Regency
  Gilbert, W. S. Diamonds
  Gilbert, W. S. Foggerty's fairy
  Gilbert, W. S. Jones' Victoria Cross
  Gilbert, W. S. Maxwell and I
  Gilbert, W. S. Tom Poulton's joke
  Gilchrist, M. The stone dragon
  Hill, R. Poor Emma
  Hogan, D. Guy 'Micko' Delaney
  James, H. The great good place
  Morrison, A. The affair of the 'Avalanche
    Bicycle and Tyre Co., Limited'
  Wells, H. G. A perfect gentleman on
    wheels
        20th century
  Barstow, S. Good
  Barstow, S. Huby falling
  Boyd, W. Bat-girl!
  Boyd, W. Extracts from the journal of
    Flying Officer J
  Boyd, W. Long story short
  Dorr, L. At a certain angle
  Doyle, Sir A. C. The recollections of Cap-
    tain Wilkie
  Edric, R. A well-spent life
  Ferreira, R. Guest for the weekend

ENGLAND—20th century—*Continued*
Francis, D. Twenty-one good men and true
Gathorne-Hardy, J. The Infant Hercules
Gathorne-Hardy, J. The man who laughed
Gilbert, M. The spoilers
Gill, B. M. Murder most kind
Harding, M. Visit
James, P. D. Great Aunt Allie's flypapers
King, F. H. The Brighton Belle
King, F. H. Hard feelings
King, F. H. Mess
King, F. H. The tree
Kipling, R. Dayspring mishandled
Lake, D. J. Re-deem the time
Lofts, N. Debt of gratitude
Lofts, N. God's own elect
Lofts, N. The horse-leech hath two
  daughters
Lofts, N. A late flowering
Lofts, N. Lord, who is my neighbour?
Lofts, N. Now you have me
Lofts, N. Saving face
Markham, B. The quitter
Markham, B. The splendid outcast
Mortimer, J. C. Rumpole and the sporting
  life
Pronzini, B. A case for quiet
Raphael, F. Oxbridge blues
Raphael, F. Private views
Raven, S. The bottle of 1912
Rees, D. In the same boat
Scarfe, E. The five o'clock train
Shannon, D. Need-fire
Spark, M. The Black Madonna
Spark, M. The Portobello Road
Sproat, R. The fascination of the vanity
Stead, C. Accents
Stead, C. A routine
Stewart, J. I. M. Pipkin Grove
Tuohy, F. The white stick
Van Greenaway, P. A western
Warner, S. T. I met a lady
Warner, S. T. A pair of duelling pistols
Warner, S. T. The proper circumstances
Warner, S. T. A saint (unknown) with two
  donors
Warner, S. T. Sopwith Hall
Warner, S. T. The three cats
Whitaker, M. The apprentice
Whitaker, M. The enchanted morning
Whitaker, M. Landlord of the Crystal
  Fountain
Whitaker, M. The mandoline
Whitaker, M. Pin's fee wife
Whitaker, M. Spring day at Slater's End
Whitaker, M. Time for chapel
Whitaker, M. The wife
Whitaker, M. X
Wyndham, F. The half brother
Wyndham, F. Obsessions
Wyndham, F. Ursula

Aristocracy
See Aristocracy—England
Civil War
See England—17th century
Coal mines and mining
See Coal mines and mining—
England
Farm life
See Farm life—England
Fascism
See Fascism—England
Invasions
Hardy, T. A tradition of eighteen hundred
and four
Politics
See Politics—England
Prisoners and prisons
See Prisoners and prisons—England
Rural life
Addison, J. A story of an heir
Auswaks, A. The familiar
Barstow, S. The middle of the journey
Bentley, P. Mother and daughter
Blackwood, A. The damned
Blythe, R. And the green grass grew all
around
Blythe, R. At Swan Gates
Blythe, R. Bride Michael
Blythe, R. The common soldiery
Blythe, R. Dear dead Pippa
Blythe, R. Immediate possession
Blythe, R. The October Bagman
Blythe, R. The packhorse path
Blythe, R. Period return
Blythe, R. The right day to kill a pike
Blythe, R. The schism
Blythe, R. The shadows of the living
Blythe, R. Take your partners
Blythe, R. A wedding in the family
Blythe, R. The windfall
Blyton, C. A fine summer's day
Bowen, M. The Crown Derby plate
Campbell, R. The church in High Street
Campbell, R. Cold print
Campbell, R. The hands
Campbell, R. The inhabitant of the lake
Campbell, R. The moon-lens
Campbell, R. The tugging
Carter, A. The kitchen child
Cole, G. D. H., and Cole, M. The toys
of death
Colvin, C. All living things
Dickens, C. The Boots at the Holly-Tree
Inn
Doyle, Sir A. C. The voice of science
Du Maurier, Dame D. The birds
Fisher, M. F. K. The lost, strayed, stolen
Fraser, A. Who would kill a cat?
Fremlin, C. The post-graduate thesis
Gash, J. The Julian Mondays
Gathorne-Hardy, J. The picnic
Gilbert, W. S. Creatures of impulse
Gilchrist, M. Dame Inowslad

ENGLAND—Rural life—*Continued*
Gilchrist, M. Midsummer madness
Givner, J. The decline and fall of a reasonable woman
Givner, J. The lost sheep
Greene, G. The innocent
Greene, G. Under the garden
Haley, R. The Polish village
Hardy, T. The withered arm
Hartley, L. P. A change of ownership
Hartley, L. P. Fall in at the double
Hartley, L. P. Feet foremost
Highsmith, P. Something the cat dragged in
Jacobs, W. W. The white cat
James, M. R. 'Oh, whistle, and I'll come to you, my lad'
Kip, L. The ghosts at Grantley
Kipling, R. Mary Postgate
Kipling, R. "They"
Knight, E. M. Lassie come-home
Langford, D. Cold spell
Lofts, N. Gateway to happiness?
Lofts, N. The natives are friendly
Moore, G. A strange death
Mortimer, J. C. Rumpole and the alternative society
Mortimer, J. C. Rumpole and the show-folk
New, J. Crossing demon
Ornstien, E. The admission ticket
Pilcher, R. The house on the hill
Raphael, F. You don't remember me
Regent, P. Schoolboy war
Rendell, R. The convolvulus clock
Rendell, R. Fen Hall
Rendell, R. The orchard walls
Rhys, J. I spy a stranger
Scott, Sir W. The tapestried chamber
Stockton, F. The great staircase at Landover Hall
Tripp, M. Form
Tuohy, F. Live bait
Tuohy, F. Love to Patsy
Tuohy, F. A war of liberation
Updike, J. The afterlife
Van Greenaway, P. Janus
Walpole, Sir H. Bachelors
Walter, E. Christmas night
Warner, S. T. A breaking wave
Warner, S. T. Narrative of events preceding the death of Queen Ermine
Warner, S. T. Some effects of a hat
Welch, D. Brave and cruel
Welch, D. Evergreen Seaton-Leverett
Wells, H. G. Mr. Marshall's doppelganger
Wharton, E. Mr. Jones
Whitaker, M. Frost in April
Whitaker, M. Home to wagonhouses
Whitaker, M. Sultan Jekker
White, T. H. Soft voices at Passenham
Wild, M. Tied in knots
Williams, D. The bully

Wodehouse, P. G. The go-getter
Wodehouse, P. G. The mixer
Wodehouse, P. G. Unpleasantness at Bludleigh Court
Wolfe, T. The house of the far and lost
Woolf, V. A simple melody
World War, 1914-1918
See World War, 1914-1918—England
World War, 1939-1945
See World War, 1939-1945—England
Bath
Colegate, I. The girl who had lived among artists
Brighton
King, F. H. I lived for you
Cambridge
O'Brien, E. In the hours of darkness
Cheshire
Crowley, J. Antiquities
Cornwall
Quiller-Couch, Sir A. T. A pair of hands
Trollope, A. Malachi's Cove
Watmough, D. In the mood
West, Dame R. The gray men
Cotswold Hills
See Cotswolds (England)
Derbyshire
Warren, J. The Corn Dolly
Warren, J. Last Chance
Warren, J. Time Lucy went
Devon
Boyd, W. Bizarre situations
Warner, S. T. Chloroform for all
Warner, S. T. A view of Exmoor
Dorset
Gilbert, W. S. An elixir of love
Hardy, T. Old Mrs. Chundle
Hardy, T. The three strangers
Hornung, E. W. Gentlemen and players
Wharton, E. Afterward
East Anglia
Cowper, R. What did the Deazies do?
Mortimer, J. C. Rumpole and the boat people
Essex
Kilworth, G. Lord of the dance
Gloucester
Campbell, R. The horror from the bridge
Gloucestershire
Lively, P. Grow old along with me, the best is yet to be
Hampshire
Doyle, Sir A. C. The lonely Hampshire cottage
Hertfordshire
Woodforde, C. Cushi
London
Allan, B. Confession of a catamite
Bloch, R. A most unusual murder
Hornung, E. W. The chest of silver
Hornung, E. W. A costume piece
Hornung, E. W. The rest cure

ENGLAND—*Continued*
          London—14th century
Poe, E. A. King Pest
          London—15th century
Kim, S.-H. Badby
          London—17th century
Turtledove, H. And so to bed
          London—18th century
De la Torre, L. The first locked room
          London—19th century
Beerbohm, M. Enoch Soames
Dickens, C. Sketches by Boz [excerpt]
Doyle, Sir A. C. The cabman's story
Doyle, Sir A. C. The end of Devil Hawker
Gilbert, W. S. The burglar's story
Gilbert, W. S. The fairy's dilemma
Gilbert, W. S. The lady in the plaid shawl
Gilbert, W. S. My maiden brief
James, H. The chaperon
Maupassant, G. de. A night in Whitechapel
Melville, H. Rich man's crumbs
Melville, H. The two temples: Temple second
Moore, G. Parted
Poe, E. A. The man of the crowd
          London—20th century
Amis, M. Bujak and the strong force; or, God's dice
Apollinaire, G. The talking memories
Ballard, J. G. The object of the attack
Bankier, W. A hint of danger
Blythe, R. The church mouse
Bowen, E. Tears, idle tears
Brooks, J. A value
Burford, B. Falling
Burt, S. Floral Street
Busch, F. Time is money
Draycott, M. Splices
Fowles, J. The enigma
Gilliatt, P. When are you going back?
Gordimer, N. Native country
Greene, G. Jubilee
Greene, G. Special duties
Grin, A. The green lamp
Harrison, M. J. The ice monkey
Hartley, L. P. A visitor from down under
Houbein, L. Every poet's pipe-dream
Kalpakian, L. A Christmas cordial
Kessler, J. F. Jacob
King, F. H. Appetites
King, F. H. Home
King, F. H. The mouse
Lessing, D. M. An old woman and her cat
Lessing, D. M. To room nineteen
Levine, N. We all begin in a little magazine
Livesey, M. A small price
Livia, A. 5 1/2 Charlotte Mews
Lurie, M. Russian boxes
Metcalf, J. Single gents only
Morand, P. Aurora
Morand, P. Clarissa
Morand, P. Delphine
Mordden, E. The woggle
Mortimer, J. C. Rumpole and the age for retirement
Mortimer, J. C. Rumpole and the blind tasting
Mortimer, J. C. Rumpole and the case of identity
Mortimer, J. C. Rumpole and the confession of guilt
Mortimer, J. C. Rumpole and the dear departed
Mortimer, J. C. Rumpole and the fascist beast
Mortimer, J. C. Rumpole and the female of the species
Mortimer, J. C. Rumpole and the genuine article
Mortimer, J. C. Rumpole and the heavy brigade
Mortimer, J. C. Rumpole and the Honourable Member
Mortimer, J. C. Rumpole and the judge's elbow
Mortimer, J. C. Rumpole and the last resort
Mortimer, J. C. Rumpole and the learned friends
Mortimer, J. C. Rumpole and the Man of God
Mortimer, J. C. Rumpole and the married lady
Mortimer, J. C. Rumpole and the official secret
Mortimer, J. C. Rumpole and the old boy net
Mortimer, J. C. Rumpole and the old, old story
Mortimer, J. C. Rumpole and the rotten apple
Mortimer, J. C. Rumpole and the spirit of Christmas
Mortimer, J. C. Rumpole and the younger generation
Mortimer, J. C. Rumpole's last case
Okri, B. Disparities
Rendell, R. Bribery and corruption
Rendell, R. The green road to Quephanda
Rhys, J. Let them call it jazz
Rhys, J. Tigers are better-looking
Rhys, J. Till September Petronella
Ryan, A. I shall not leave England now
Sheehan, R. Optics
Sproat, R. Almost graceful like a dancer
Sproat, R. Black madonna two-wheel gypsy queen
Sproat, R. Firework night isn't in it
Sproat, R. A former security with Helen Damnation
Sproat, R. Mistaken identify
Sproat, R. A small difference only
Sproat, R. Stunning the punters

ENGLAND — London—20th century — *Continued*

Sproat, R. When the sailor was far away
Stead, C. 1954: days of the roomers
Swift, G. Hoffmeier's Antelope
Swift, G. The tunnel
Taylor, B. Forget-me-not
Thomas, D. Adventures in the skin trade: A fine beginning
Thomas, D. Adventures in the skin trade: Four lost souls
Thomas, D. Adventures in the skin trade: Plenty of furniture
Tuohy, F. A life membership
Tuohy, F. The trap
Tuohy, F. Windows
Tuohy, F. A young girl
Van Greenaway, P. The immortal coil
Vanderhaeghe, G. The expatriates' party
Verma, N. The world elsewhere
Welch, D. Memories of a vanished period
Wetherell, W. D. Spitfire autumn
Wexler, J. Simon goes to London
Whitaker, M. Five for silver
Willis, C. Fire watch
Wodehouse, P. G. Comrade Bingo
Wodehouse, P. G. Open house
Wodehouse, P. G. Sir Roderick comes to lunch
Wodehouse, P. G. Uncle Fred flits by
Wodhams, J. Aunt Agnes
Wolfe, T. 'E: a recollection
Woolf, V. Mrs. Dalloway in Bond Street
Woolf, V. A society
Wyndham, F. The Ground Hostess
Zangwill, I. The big Bow mystery

Manchester

Gaskell, E. C. The three eras of Libbie Marsh

Norfolk

Gilbert, M. The African tree-beavers

Northumberland

Gilliatt, P. They sleep without dreaming

Oxford

Doyle, Sir A. C. Lot no 249
Mortimer, J. C. Rumpole and the gentle art of blackmail
Pym, B. Across a crowded room
Pym, B. So, some tempestuous morn

Somerset

Norris, L. In the west country

Staffordshire

De la Torre, L. The missing Shakespeare manuscript

Suffolk

James, M. R. The ash-tree

Surrey

Aickman, R. The same dog
Mortimer, J. C. Rumpole and the expert witness

Sussex

Benson, E. F. Mrs. Amworth
Tuohy, F. A summer pilgrim

Wiltshire

Gilliatt, P. Foreigners
Tuohy, F. A ghost garden

Yorkshire

Atherton, G. F. H. The striding place
Bentley, P. Mother and daughter
Collins, W. The dead hand
Harrison, M. J. The quarry
Whitaker, M. Blackberry day
Whitaker, M. Honeymoon
Whitaker, M. The man in black

ENGLISH CIVIL WAR *See* England—17th century

ENGLISH DIALECT *See* Dialect stories—English

English for immigrants. Ornstien, E.

ENGLISH LANGUAGE

Bedard, B. Benedict's dove
Carrier, R. What language do bears speak?
Lem, S. Reginald Gulliver, Eruntics
Nesbitt, J. D. Half the way back
Ornstien, E. English for immigrants
Wetherell, W. D. Why I love America

ENGLISH PEOPLE *See* British

The **Englishman**. Maupassant, G. de

The **enigma**. Fowles, J.

The **enigma** of arrival. Naipaul, V. S.

The **enlargement** of Bethany. Bird, C.

Enlisting. Liu, M. E.

ENNUI *See* Boredom

Enoch. Bloch, R.

ENOCH ARDEN STORIES

Maupassant, G. de. A French Enoch Arden

Enoch Soames. Beerbohm, M.

The **enormous** radio. Cheever, J.

Enough. Chernoff, M.

Enough gold. Johnson, W. R.

Enough rope. London, J.

Enough rope for two. Howard, C.

Enright, Elizabeth, 1909-1968

A distant bell
Early sorrow: ten stories of youth; ed. by C. Zolotow

Enroute. See Mrożek, S. On a journey

Ensemble. Lentricchia, M.

The **entail**. Hoffmann, E. T. A.

Enter the stranger. Olson, D.

Entering the house of the 'Lord. Taylor, P. E.

ENTERTAINERS

See also Acrobats; Actors; Actresses; Clowns; Ventriloquists

Bangs, J. K. A midnight visitor
Camoin, F. A. Sometimes the wrong thing is the right thing
Dick, P. K. Novelty act
Huddle, D. Apache
Hulme, K. He tauware kawa, he kawa tauware
Knight, D. F. The handler
O'Hara, J. Pal Joey
Regent, P. Mr. Parsley's lunchtime pursuit
Spinrad, N. The big flash

ENTERTAINING *See* Parties
An **enthusiast**. Maupassant, G. de
[**Entitled** story]. Lish, G.
ENTOMOLOGISTS
   Kiteley, B. Still life with insects
   Wells, H. G. The moth
The **entrance** exam. Carey, M.
Entrechat. Milton, E.
Entries in a drowned man's dictionary.
   Bedard, B.
Entropy. Pynchon, T.
ENVIRONMENTALISTS
   Boyle, T. C. Whales weep
ENVY *See* Jealousy
Envy. Robison, J.
Envy the dead. Rose, D. A.
EPHESUS (TURKEY) *See* Turkey—Ephesus
Ephron, Nora
   Etheleen Grossberg takes stock
     Esquire 108:215-16 N '87
   Insider trading
     Esquire 108:94-5 Jl '87
   Landscaping
     Esquire 107:102-4 Ap '87
   Love and potatoes
     Ladies' Home Journal 101:90+ Je '84
   Moral questions of our time
     Esquire 109:107-9 Ja '88
   Ms. Grossberg's legs
     Esquire 108:225-6+ S '87
   Parallel play
     Esquire 107:110-11 My '87
   Taking the road not taken
     Esquire 108:197-9 O '87
EPIDEMICS
     See also Plague
   O'Hara, J. The doctor's son
EPILEPTICS
   Blaise, C. Translation
   La Chapelle, M. Superstitions
Epilogue. Buch, H. C.
Epimanes. See Poe, E. A. Four beasts in
   one—the homo-cameleopard
Epiphany. Maupassant, G. de
An **epiphany** tale. Brown, G. M.
EPISCOPAL CLERGY *See* Clergy, Anglican
   and Episcopal
An **episode** in bachelor life. Moore, G.
An **episode** in married life. Moore, G.
An **episode** of cathedral history. James, M.
   R.
Episode of the dog McIntosh. Wodehouse,
   P. G.
The **episode** of the Mexican seer. Allen, G.
An **episode** of two. Faik, S.
An **episode** of war. Crane, S.
Epistemology on the march. Bernard, K.
Epistemology, sex, and the shedding of light.
   Schwartz, L. S.
Epitaph. O'Brien, E.
Epithalamium. Creswell, R.

Epstein, Joseph
   No Pulitzer for Pinsker
     Commentary 85:59-68 Mr '88
   Schlifkin on my books
     The Hudson Review 38:63-78 Spr '85
Epstein, Leslie
   The magic flute
     Epstein, L. Goldkorn tales
   Music of the spheres
     Epstein, L. Goldkorn tales
     The Georgia Review 38:765-823 Wint '84
   The Steinway quintet
     Epstein, L. Goldkorn tales
Equality. Quah Kung Yu
Equitable awards. Auchincloss, L.
Erbaugh, Herbert
   Broken water pipe
     'Teen 29:14+ F '85
   Parent conference
     'Teen 30:20+ Ja '86
Erbe, Pamela
   Inland
     The North American Review 272:11-18
     Mr '87
Erdrich, Louise
   American Horse
     Earth power coming; ed. by S. J. Ortiz
   The beet queen
     The Graywolf annual 2
     The Paris Review 27:10-26 Spr '85
   Destiny
     The Atlantic 255:64-8 Ja '85
   Flesh and blood
     Buying time; ed. by S. Walker
   Fleur
     Esquire 106:52-5+ Ag '86
     Prize stories, 1987
   Mister Argus
     The Georgia Review 39:379-90 Summ '85
   Saint Marie
     The Atlantic 253:78-84 Mr '84
     Prize stories, 1985
   Snares
     The Best American short stories, 1988
     Harper's 274:60-4 My '87
Eric. Finger, C. J.
Erich Auerbach leaves Istanbul. Sucher, C.
   P.
Ericson, David *See* Kelley, Leo P., 1928-
Erika. Warren, J.
Ernesta. Grahn, J.
Eroica Symphony. Pak, Y.-S.
Eros and crazy. Mooney, M.
The **e(rot)ic** potato. McGrath, P.
EROTICISM *See* Sex
Errand. Carver, R.
The **errant** melancholy of twilight. Baum-
   bach, J.
Errata. Weiner, E.
ERRORS
   Ekström, M. Hebe laughs
   Gardner, M. The loves of Lady Coldpence
   Liben, M. The pharmacist

ERRORS—*Continued*
Pilcher, R. An evening to remember
Singer, I. B. The mistake
Wilson, B. Looking for the Golden Gate
Erskine-Lindop, Audrey, 1921-
The mistaken smile
The Mammoth book of modern crime
stories; ed. by G. Hardinge
Erwin, Charles
Autumn
The Southern Review (Baton Rouge, La.)
23:483-93 Spr '87
Words
The Southern Review (Baton Rouge, La.)
22:203-9 Ja '86
The **Erymanthian** boar. Christie, A.
Esau. Kessler, J. F.
Escape. Cowan, P.
The **escape.** Murphy, Y.
Escape from Kathmandu. Robinson, K. S.
The **escape** route. Serling, R.
ESCAPED CONVICTS
Burke, J. L. The convict
Cecil, H. The wanted man
Frazee, S. My brother down there
Garrett, G. P. The victim
Hardy, T. The three strangers
Honig, D. My escaped convict
Jones, M. The fugitives
Link, W., and Levinson, R. One bad win-
ter's day
Matthiessen, P. Travelin man
Norris, H. The quarry
O'Connor, F. A good man is hard to find
Pavese, C. Gaol birds
Pronzini, B. The clincher
Pronzini, B. Strangers in the fog
Russell, J. The fourth man
Shukshin, V. M. Stefan
Tripp, M. Form
Escapegoat. Ellison, H.
ESCAPES
Cogswell, T. R. The wall around the world
Conrad, J. The secret sharer
Farley, R. M. The living mist
Fitzgerald, M. J. Eurydice
Gorky, M. Chelkash
Harrington, E. The prisoners [excerpt]
Hill, R. Exit line
Nałkowska, Z. At the railroad track
Norton, A. Wizard's world
Pavese, C. Misogyny
Prior, A. Be lucky
Rucker, R. von B. Tales of Houdini
Stoker, B. The burial of the rats
Escapes. Williams, J.
The **escargot** story (The stroke, II). Rose, D.
A.
Escort. Du Maurier, Dame D.
Eskapa, Shirley
Between the sheets
Echad 2: South African Jewish voices

White and injured
Echad 2: South African Jewish voices
Eskimo. Munro, A.
Eskimo love. Apple, M.
ESKIMOS *See* Inuit
Esmene's eyes. Mayhar, A.
Esmerelda's hands. Palmer, M.
ESP *See* Extrasensory perception
Esperanto. Botwinik, B.
Espina-Moore, LIna
Man around a maypole
Short story international 70
Espino González, Miguel A.
A hell so fearsome
Américas 37:13-15 My/Je '85
ESPIONAGE *See* International intrigue;
Spies
Esposito, Michelene
A protective fuzz
'Teen 30:74+ S '86
ESSEX (ENGLAND) *See* England—Essex
Essop, Ahmed
Aziz Khan
Essop, A. Hajji Musa and the Hindu
fire-walker
The betrayal
African short stories; ed. by C. Achebe
and C. L. Innes
Essop, A. Hajji Musa and the Hindu
fire-walker
Black and white
Essop, A. Hajji Musa and the Hindu
fire-walker
The commandment
Essop, A. Hajji Musa and the Hindu
fire-walker
Dolly
Essop, A. Hajji Musa and the Hindu
fire-walker
Father and son
Essop, A. Hajji Musa and the Hindu
fire-walker
Film
Essop, A. Hajji Musa and the Hindu
fire-walker
Gerty's brother
Essop, A. Hajji Musa and the Hindu
fire-walker
Gladiators
Essop, A. Hajji Musa and the Hindu
fire-walker
The Hajji
Essop, A. Hajji Musa and the Hindu
fire-walker
Hajji Musa and the Hindu fire-walker
Essop, A. Hajji Musa and the Hindu
fire-walker
Labyrinth
Essop, A. Hajji Musa and the Hindu
fire-walker
Mr Moonreddy
Essop, A. Hajji Musa and the Hindu
fire-walker

Essop, Ahmed—*Continued*
The notice
Essop, A. Hajji Musa and the Hindu fire-walker
Obsession
Essop, A. Hajji Musa and the Hindu fire-walker
Red Beard's daughter
Essop, A. Hajji Musa and the Hindu fire-walker
The target
Essop, A. Hajji Musa and the Hindu fire-walker
Ten years
Essop, A. Hajji Musa and the Hindu fire-walker
Two sisters
Essop, A. Hajji Musa and the Hindu fire-walker
The Penguin book of Southern African stories
The visitation
Essop, A. Hajji Musa and the Hindu fire-walker
The yogi
Essop, A. Hajji Musa and the Hindu fire-walker
Estarolly's mountain. Vreuls, D.
ESTATES *See* Houses
Esteban. Everett, P. L.
ESTHETICS *See* Aesthetics
Estleman, Loren D.
Blond and blue
Estleman, L. D. General murders
Bloody July
Estleman, L. D. General murders
The Year's best mystery & suspense stories, 1986
Bodyguards shoot second
Estleman, L. D. General murders
A Matter of crime v1
Dead soldier
Estleman, L. D. General murders
Eight Mile and Dequindre
Estleman, L. D. General murders
Fast burn
Estleman, L. D. General murders
Greektown
Estleman, L. D. General murders
The Mammoth book of private eye stories; ed. by B. Pronzini and M. H. Greenberg
I'm in the book
Estleman, L. D. General murders
Mean streets; ed. by R. J. Randisi
Mago's bride
Westeryear; ed. by E. Gorman
The prettiest dead girl in Detroit
Estleman, L. D. General murders
The Eyes have it; ed. by R. J. Randisi
Robbers' roost
Estleman, L. D. General murders

State of grace
An Eye for justice; ed. by R. J. Randisi
The tree on Execution Hill
Uncollected crimes; ed. by B. Pronzini and M. H. Greenberg
The used
The Black Lizard anthology of crime fiction; ed. by E. Gorman
Et in bellicus lunarum medicalis. Carrington, L.
Et in sempiternum pereant. Williams, C.
Etchemendy, Nancy, 1952-
The tuckahoe
Shadows 8
Etchison, Dennis, 1943-
The blood kiss
Prime evil; ed. by D. E. Winter
Deadspace
Whispers V
Deathtracks
In the field of fire; ed. by J. Van B. Dann and J. Dann
Somebody like you
Masques; ed. by J. N. Williamson
Talking in the dark
Shadows 7
You can go now
The Dark descent; ed. by D. G. Hartwell
Etchison, Dennis, 1943-, and Johnson, Mark
The spot
Midnight; ed. by C. L. Grant
Eterna. Lavin, M.
The **eternal** duffer. Temple, W.
The **eternal** province. Landolfi, T.
Eternity dies. Cherry, K.
Ethan Brand. Hawthorne, N.
Ethan Frome. Wharton, E.
Etheleen Grossberg takes stock. Ephron, N.
The **etheric** transmitter. Shepard, L.
ETHICS
See also Conscience; Honesty; Sin; Truthfulness and falsehood
Auchincloss, L. The senior partner's ethics
O'Connor, F. The lame shall enter first
Wolff, T. The poor are always with us
ETHIOPIA
Thomas, M. Second rains
Thomas, M. Why the sky is so far away
ETHNOLOGISTS
La Farge, O. The door in the wall
Etiology of the new war. Lopatin, J.
Etiquette for dying. Fremlin, C.
Eton Crop. Kiely, B.
Étude. Mogan, J.
ETYMOLOGISTS
Targan, B. The editor of A
Eubanks, Georgann
The magic hour
The North American Review 272:11-14 Je '87
Euclid alone. Orr, W. F.

Eumenides in the fourth floor lavatory. Card, O. S.

Eunson, Dale
The hero's son
Family: stories from the interior; ed. by G. G. Chavis

Eurlanda's box. Leedom-Ackerman, J.

EUROPE
See also Danube River; Eastern Europe; Rhine River

EUROPE, EASTERN See Eastern Europe

EUROPEANS
Africa
Gordimer, N. A hunting accident
Russo, A. The universe of Mama Malkia
India
Jhabvala, R. P. An experience of India
United States
Handke, P. The long way around

Eurydice. Fitzgerald, M. J.

Eurypylus at Dodona. Parotti, P.

Eustace, Robert
(jt. auth) See Meade, L. T., 1854-1914, and Eustace, Robert

Eustis, Helen
Mister Death and the redheaded woman [Variant title: The rider on the pale horse]
Westward the women; ed. by V. Piekarski

EUTHANASIA
Gorman, E. Turn away
Herbert, F. Murder will in
Matheson, R. The test

Eutopia. Anderson, P.

Eva. Hart, J.

Eva and the apple tree. Simmons, C.

Eva is inside her cat. García Márquez, G.

EVANGELISTS
Austin, D. Pray for China
Bear, G. The white horse child
Faust, I. The Dalai Lama of Harlem
Glynn, T. The world's most amazing prophet, a.k.a. Wallace Mumford Amazon Polleau
Goyen, W. Rhody's path
Kinsella, W. P. Dancing
Madden, D. The singer
Taylor, P. E. The god-chaser
Woolson, C. F. The Lady of Little Fishing

Evans, David, 1935-
Sabbatical
Critical Quarterly 30:6-18 Spr '88

Evans, Elizabeth
Another moon
Evans, E. Locomotion
Blue news
Evans, E. Locomotion
Crime in Italy
Evans, E. Locomotion
Desert birds
Evans, E. Locomotion

Honey
Evans, E. Locomotion
In spring
Evans, E. Locomotion
Locomotion
Evans, E. Locomotion
Relics
Evans, E. Locomotion
Silver Fox
Evans, E. Locomotion
The sleeping gypsy
Evans, E. Locomotion
Small acts
Evans, E. Locomotion
Will
Evans, E. Locomotion

Evans, Juliann
Purple prose
A Matter of crime v2

Evans, Lawrence Watt- See Watt-Evans, Lawrence, 1954-

Evans, Max
Candles in the bottom of the pool
Evans, M. Xavier's folly, and other stories
One-eyed sky
Evans, M. Xavier's folly, and other stories
Xavier's folly
Evans, M. Xavier's folly, and other stories

Evarts, Hal G.
The trap
A Treasury of World War II stories; ed. by B. Pronzini and M. H. Greenberg

Evdokia. Panova, V. F.

Eve. Whitaker, M.

The **eve** of love. Rasulov, M.-R.

Eve times four. Anderson, P.

Evelyn, John Michael See Underwood, Michael, 1916-

Even crazy old barmaids need love. Meinke, P.

Even Greenland. Hannah, B.

Even nice women do. Yellin, L. N.

Even the thrush has wings. Clift, C.

The **evening** and the morning and the night. Butler, O. E.

Evening bells. Harada, Y.

The **evening** gift. Narayan, R. K.

Evening in Connecticut. Tuohy, F.

The **evening** news. Ardizzone, T.

The **evening** of Mr. Boch's baloney factory. McGrath, W. M.

The **evening** of the Fourth of July. Kees, W.

The **evening** party. Woolf, V.

An **evening** performance. Garrett, G. P.

Evening primrose. Collier, J.

An **evening** to remember. Pilcher, R.

An **event.** Mrożek, S.

Eventide. Purdy, J.

Ever after. Palwick, S.

The **ever-blossoming** garden. Roshchin, M.

Ever let the fancy roam. Dunn, D.
Everett, Percival L.
The bear as symbol
  Everett, P. L. The weather and women treat me fair
Chacón, Chacón
  Everett, P. L. The weather and women treat me fair
Cry about a nickel
  Everett, P. L. The weather and women treat me fair
Esteban
  Everett, P. L. The weather and women treat me fair
Gaining the door
  Everett, P. L. The weather and women treat me fair
A good day for the laughing blow
  Everett, P. L. The weather and women treat me fair
A good home for Hachita
  Everett, P. L. The weather and women treat me fair
Hear that long train moan
  Everett, P. L. The weather and women treat me fair
Last fair deal
  Everett, P. L. The weather and women treat me fair
Nice white people
  Everett, P. L. The weather and women treat me fair
A real hard rain
  Everett, P. L. The weather and women treat me fair
Still hunting
  Everett, P. L. The weather and women treat me fair
Thirty-seven just to take a fall
  Everett, P. L. The weather and women treat me fair
Turtle
  Everett, P. L. The weather and women treat me fair
The weather and women treat me fair
  Everett, P. L. The weather and women treat me fair
Evergreen. Cox, A. J.
Evergreen Seaton-Leverett. Welch, D.
Everlast. Stephens, M.
The **Everlasting** Club. Gray, A.
Everman, Welch D., 1946-
Harry and Sylvia and Sylvia and so on
  A Grand Street reader; ed. by B. Sonnenberg
Everncere. Kump, E. G.
The **Evershams'** Willie. Calisher, H.
An **every-afternoon** affair. Green, J.
Every airborne particle. Moskowitz, F.
Every angel is terrible. Sheehan, R.
Every home should have a cedar chest. Bird, C.

Every hour that goes by grows younger. McGarry, J.
Every poet's pipe-dream. Houbein, L.
Every tale condemns me. Woods, S.
Everybody needs a little love. Bloch, R.
Everybody needs a mink. Hughes, D. B. F.
Everybody's watching me. Spillane, M.
Everyday depressions. Russ, J.
Everyday disorders. Prose, F.
An **everyday** heroism. Kafka, F.
Everyday living. Van Arkel, J.
Everyday use. Walker, A.
Everyone had a lobster. Prose, F.
Everyone is wearing a hat. Desaulniers, J.
Everyone knows somebody who's dead. Johnson, B. S.
Everything. Bachmann, I.
Everything. Wilson, M.
Everything a man needs. Blythe, R.
Everything I know. Lish, G.
Everything is about animals. Prose, F.
Everything is nice. Bowles, J. A.
Everything is real. Houbein, L.
Everything that rises must converge. O'Connor, F.
Everything's going to be all right. DeWeese, G.
Everything's up-to-date in South Roxy. Keillor, G.
Evian Steel. Yolen, J.
EVICTION
  Lynch, L. Fruitstand II: Honeydew moon
  Taylor, P. E. News from El Corazon: in the composing room
EVIDENCE, CIRCUMSTANTIAL *See* Circumstantial evidence
Evidence. Asimov, I.
Evidence. Krist, G.
Evidence is high proof. Stuart, J.
EVIL *See* Good and evil
Evil-doers. Gorky, M.
The **evil** eye. Le Guin, U. K.
The **evil** eye. Pavese, C.
The **evitable** conflict. Asimov, I.
Evocation. Pavese, C.
EVOLUTION
  Aldiss, B. W. Hothouse
  Hamilton, E. Devolution
  Oliver, C. Transfusion
  Turtledove, H. And so to bed
  Vonnegut, K. A dream of the future (not excluding lobsters)
  Williams, W. J. Dinosaurs
The **evolution** of birds of paradise. Tallent, E.
The **evolution** of myopia. Lispector, C.
The **evolution** of Saxby. Bates, H. E.
Evvy's brother. Campos-De Metro, J.
Ewart, Christopher
A day in the life
  L. Ron Hubbard presents Writers of the future v3

EX-CONVICTS
Andreyev, L. The thief
Barstow, S. The running and the lame
Brand, M. Crazy rhythm
Covino, M. Salient facts
Gardner, E. S. Danger out of the past
Hays, D. The Dixie Association [excerpt]
Hoch, E. D. Deceptions
Howard, C. Enough rope for two
Howard, C. Horn man
Howard, C. The last revival
Howard, C. New Orleans getaway
Jones, D. C. Trusty
Kirk, R. There's a long, long trail a-
    winding
Lynds, D. Yellow gal
Mansfield, K. Ole Underwood
Mundstock, K. A judgment worthy of
    Solomon
Otto, L. The Bert and Ernie show
Pavese, C. Summer storm
Rifaat, A. Badriyya and her husband
Sadler, M. The choice
EX-HUSBANDS See Divorced persons
Ex libris. Gilliatt, P.
EX-NAZIS See National socialism
Exactly eight thousand dollars exactly.
    O'Hara, J.
Exactments. Mattison, A.
Exam failure praying. Wendt, A.
EXAMINATIONS
Boylan, J. Final exam
MacLaverty, B. The miraculous candidate
Matheson, R. The test
Robison, M. I am twenty-one
Tuohy, F. The candidate
Except that they move and talk. Haley, R.
Excerpts from Sunnyview journal. Viola, A.
Excerpts from Swan Lake. Cameron, P.
Excerpts from Witherton's journal: also a let-
    ter of Crystalla's. Gilchrist, M.
The **exchange.** Sagan, F.
Exchange value. Johnson, C. R.
An **exciting** Christmas Eve; or, My lecture
    on dynamite. Doyle, Sir A. C.
Excursion fare. Tiptree, J.
An **excursion** ticket. Crane, S.
EXECUTIONS AND EXECUTIONERS
    See also Hangings
Benítez-Rojo, A. Heaven and earth
Benson, E. F. The confession of Charles
    Linkworth
Bloch, R. The head man
Carter, R. Tergiversator
Ellin, S. The question
Gautreaux, T. Just turn like a gear
Gores, J. The second coming
Humphrey, W. The ballad of Jesse Neigh-
    bours
Kafka, F. In the penal colony
Kim, S.-H. Badby
Matthews, J. Dark, dark
Maupassant, G. de. A fishing excursion

O, S.-W. A respite
Piñera, V. The conflict
Sagan, F. "La Futura"
Tamer, Z. The smile
Executive clemency. Dozois, G. R., and Hal-
    deman, J. C.
EXECUTIVES
Auchincloss, L. The cup of coffee
Austin, D. I am an employee
Slesar, H. Light fingers
The **executor.** Spark, M.
EXERCISE
Baxter, C. Weights
The **exercise.** MacLaverty, B.
Exercises. McElroy, C. J.
The **exhibition.** Van Greenaway, P.
The **exile.** Alter, R. E.
Exile. Josipovici, G.
Exile. Moss, R.
Exile. Verma, N.
The **exile,** the housekeeper, and Flora, the
    beauty of Rome. Freeman, C.
EXILES
    See also Refugees
Bellow, S. Him with his foot in his mouth
Gallant, M. Varieties of exile
Grin, A. Fire and water
Josipovici, G. Exile
Thomas, M. Silver sugar from Bombay
Thomas, M. Why the sky is so far away
Tuohy, F. A survivor in Salvador
Wolfe, T. The names of the nation
Woolson, C. F. Castle Nowhere
Woolson, C. F. St. Clair Flats
The **exiles.** Chipulina, E. G.
The **exiles.** Havemann, E.
Exiles. Keillor, G.
Exiles of tomorrow. Bradley, M. Z.
Exile's return. MacMahon, B.
Existence. Russ, J.
Existentialists. Bangs, C. J.
The **exit** door leads in. Dick, P. K.
Exit line. Hill, R.
Exit, stage right. Burgess, F.
The **exit** to San Breta. Martin, G. R. R.
Exits. Leslie, P.
Exley, Frederick
    Brother in arms
    Rolling Stone p81-2+ Jl 17-31 '86
Exodus. Cook, H.
The **exoneration** of Phineas Droogan.
    Wasylyk, S.
EXORCISM
    See also Demoniac possession
Benson, R. H. Father Meuron's tale
Singer, I. B. The dead fiddler
Sucharitkul, S. Fiddling for water buffaloes
Exorcizing Baldassare. Hyams, E.
The **expansion** of the universe. Gilchrist, E.
Expatriate. Hospital, J. T.
EXPATRIATES See Exiles
The **expatriates'** party. Vanderhaeghe, G.
The **expedition** to Hell. Hogg, J.

Expensive gifts. Miller, S.
The **expensive** moment. Paley, G.
Expensive purchase. Asscher-Pinkhof, C.
An **experience** of India. Jhabvala, R. P.
An **experiment** in luxury. Crane, S.
An **experiment** in misery. Crane, S.
Experiment with time. Fitzgerald, M. J.
EXPERIMENTAL DRUGS See Drugs
EXPERIMENTAL MEDICINE See
Medicine, Experimental
EXPERIMENTAL STORIES
    See also Surrealism
Ahern, T. The Habbitson stories
Ahern, T. My summer scenes
Ahern, T. The new life
Akutagawa, R. A fool's life
Allan, B. Confession of a catamite
Apollinaire, G. The case of the masked
    corporal, that is, the poet resuscitated
Apollinaire, G. The moon king
Apollinaire, G. The poet assassinated
Austin, D. The artist
Austin, D. Cortez
Austin, D. The dictator
Austin, D. Empires of the air
Austin, D. The great man
Austin, D. The other room
Austin, D. Portable cities
Austin, D. The relaxed anarchist
Avery, M. Jerusalem & home
Avery, M. Promised land Newfoundland
Bail, M. Cul-de-sac (uncompleted)
Bail, M. Huebler
Bail, M. Zoellner's definition
Barthelme, D. At the Tolstoy Museum
Barthelme, D. The emerald
Barthelme, D. The explanation
Barthelme, D. The flight of pigeons from
    the palace
Barthelme, D. Not-knowing
Barthelme, D. Sentence
Barthelme, D. Sindbad
Baxter, C. Media event
Belben, R. The licences to eat meat
Bernard, K. The Maldive chronicles
Berry, R. M. Apples
Berry, R. M. A decisive refutation of Her-
    bert Dingle's objection to Einstein's
    twin paradox; or, Gravitas
Berry, R. M. November 14, 1864
Berry, R. M. Paradise lost
Berry, R. M. Tractatus cantatus
Birdsell, S. The wild plum tree
Boylan, J. Day to die
Boylan, J. Dictionary art review
Boylan, J. Jimmy Durante lost in Antarcti-
    ca
Boyle, T. C. The hit man
Brossard, J. The metamorfalsis
Camoin, F. A. Things I did to make it
    possible
Caponegro, M. Analysis of the vessel and
    its contents

Caponegro, M. Tales from the next village
Cherches, P. Dirty windows
Codrescu, A. Samba de los agentes
Colless, T., and Kelly, D. The lost world:
    signs of life
Coover, R. The babysitter
Coover, R. A sudden story
Covino, M. Dialectical materialism
Covino, M. You are here
Cullen, E. J. A life for the theater
Cullen, E. J. Sleepy Hollow
Daitch, S. Camera obscura
Davenport, G. Apples and pears: Het
    Erewhonisch schetsboek: Messidor-
    Vendémiaire 1981
Davenport, G. The bicycle rider
Davenport, G. The bowmen of Shu
Davenport, G. Fifty-seven views of
    Fujiyama
Davenport, G. The Haile Selassie Funeral
    Train
Davenport, G. The Jules Verne steam bal-
    loon
Davenport, G. The meadow
Davenport, G. The ringdove sign
Davenport, G. We often think of Lenin
    at the clothespin factory
Davenport, G. Wild clover
Davis, L. Cockroaches in autumn
Davis, L. Extracts from a life
DeGrazia, E. Brothers of the tiger
Doctorow, E. L. The leather man
Federman, R. Report from the World
    Federation of Displaced Writers
Friedman, B. H. Whispers
Gault, C. Lost
Giguère, R. Miror
Gray, A. The cause of some recent
    changes
Gray, A. The crank that made the revolu-
    tion
Gray, A. The Great Bear Cult
Gray, A. Logopandocy
Gray, A. The problem
Gray, A. Prometheus
Gray, A. The spread of Ian Nicol
Grayson, R. The facts are always friendly
Haldeman, J. W. DX
Haley, R. Except that they move and talk
Hannah, B. Power and light
Henry, R. Subject: Petri Ganton
Howe, F. The Ruth tractate
Hulme, K. Stations on the way to Avalon
Hulme, K. A window drunken in the brain
Jaffe, H. John Crow
Jaffe, H. Mussel
Jaffe, H. Persian lamb
Jaffe, H. Sidewinder
James, D. Negrophobia
Katz, S. Made of wax
Katz, S. On self-knowledge
Katz, S. One on one
Katz, S. The Perfect Life

EXPERIMENTAL STORIES—*Continued*
Katz, S. Smooth
Katz, S. Three essays
Katz, S. Two essays
Katz, S. Two seaside yarns
Katz, S. The zippo stories
Kilworth, G. Sumi dreams of a paper frog
Kinsella, W. P. The Alligator Report—with questions for discussion
Kinsella, W. P. Doves and proverbs
Krysl, M. Macroscopic phenomena
Krysl, M. Mozart, Westmoreland, and me
Krysl, M. Sons
Landolfi, T. The ampulla
Landolfi, T. Gogol's wife
Landolfi, T. The test
Leyner, M. Ode to autumn
Lish, G. The dog
Lish, G. Don't die
Lish, G. [Entitled story]
Lish, G. Fleur
Lish, G. For Rupert—with no promises
Lish, G. How to write a novel
Lish, G. Imagination
Lish, G. Imp among aunts
Lish, G. Leopard in a temple
Lish, G. The merry chase
Lish, G. On the business of generating transforms
Lish, G. The psoriasis diet
Lish, G. Three
Lish, G. Two families
Lish, G. Weight
Liyong, T. lo. Lexicographicide
Lopatin, J. Modern romances
Matheson, R. C. Vampire
Millhauser, S. Cathay
Molinaro, U. Apocalyptic flirtation
Mrożek, S. Golden thoughts
Paulson, A. B. College life
Regent, P. Ziggy's last dance
Rey Rosa, R. The book
Rey Rosa, R. The heart of God
Rey Rosa, R. Nine occasions
Rey Rosa, R. The path doubles back
Rey Rosa, R. The rain and other children
Rey Rosa, R. The river bed
Rey Rosa, R. Sunrise
Rey Rosa, R. Uncertain readings
Rey Rosa, R. A version of my death
Scholz, C. Transients
Shannon, B. T. Asilomarian lecture (The dirmal life of the inhabitats)
Smith, J. Ulrike Meinhof
Sontag, S. Unguided tour
Soutter, A. S F
Sukenick, R. At this very instant
Sweeney, B. Licorice lozenges. french safety pins. and jelly snakes.
Valenzuela, L. Fourth version
Vega, A. L. ADJ, Inc.
Villemaire, Y. In front of the Temple of Luxor, 31 July 1980

Walwicz, A. House
Walwicz, A. Neons
West, P. The place in flowers where pollen rests
Whalen, T. The visitation
Whisnant, L. Wallwork
White, C. Howdy Doody is dead
White, E. B. The door
Wideman, J. E. Surfiction
The **experimenter**. Russ, J.
EXPERIMENTS, SCIENTIFIC
Asimov, I. Lest we remember
Barker, C. The age of desire
Bear, G. Blood music
Bear, G. Tangents
Bulychev, K. Another's memory
Ciment, J. Genetics
Dnieprov, A. The Maxwell equations
Eisenberg, L. The Chameleon
Eisenberg, L. Dr. Snow Maiden
Fowler, K. J. Recalling Cinderella
Hawthorne, N. The birthmark
Hobana, I. Night broadcast
Kilworth, G. God's cold lips
Klass, M. In the beginning
Kress, N. Against a crooked stile
Kress, N. Trinity
Larionova, O. A tale of kings
Leman, B. Window
Mårtensson, B. Myxomatosis forte
McConnell, J. V. Learning theory
Rao, B. S. Victims of time
Shepard, L. Mengele
Strugaťskiĭ, A. N., and Strugaťskiĭ, B. N. Six matches
Waldrop, H. Dr. Hudson's secret gorilla
Watson, I. Immune dreams
Woolrich, C. Jane Brown's body
The **expiation**. Ocampo, S.
The **explanation**. Barthelme, D.
An **explanation** for the disappearance of the moon. Sladek, J. T.
Explanations, Inc. Kress, N.
Les **exploits** de Nat Pinkerton de jour en jour: un texte de René Magritte translated and improved. Davenport, G.
EXPLORERS
Barker, C. How spoilers bleed
Drewe, R. The last explorer
Grin, A. The heart of the wilderness
Haldeman, J. W. Seasons
Keating, H. R. F. The Old Haddock
McGrath, P. The lost explorer
Poe, E. A. The journal of Julius Rodman
Wolfe, T. Polyphemus
Explorers we. Dick, P. K.
EXPLOSIONS
Chipulina, E. G. The disaster
Parise, G. Nostalgia
Explosions on the sun. Duckworth, M.
EXPLOSIVES
Doyle, Sir A. C. An exciting Christmas Eve; or, My lecture on dynamite

EXPLOSIVES—*Continued*
Lutz, J. The very best
The **explosives** expert. Lutz, J.
Export. Barthelme, F.
The **extension**. Sullivan, T.
EXTERMINATION, JEWISH *See* Holocaust, Jewish (1933-1945)
The **exterminator**. Roberts, N.
EXTINCT ANIMALS
        See also Dodos
Farmer, P. J. The king of beasts
Wells, H. G. Æpyornis Island
EXTORTION
Curtiss, U. R. Tiger by the tail
Ferrars, E. Instrument of justice
Hyne, C. J. C. The liner and the iceberg
Lejeune, A. Something on everyone
Mortimer, J. C. Rumpole and the gentle art of blackmail
Mortimer, J. C. Rumpole and the judge's elbow
Mortimer, J. C. Rumpole and the old boy net
Pronzini, B. Tiger, tiger
The **extra**. Shea, M.
The **extra** wether. Bernen, R.
Extracts from a life. Davis, L.
Extracts from the journal of Flying Officer J. Boyd, W.
Extradited. Crawford, I. V.
Extraordinary little cough. Thomas, D.
EXTRASENSORY PERCEPTION
        See also Clairvoyance; Telepathy
Anderson, P. The Saturn game
Asimov, I. The obvious factor
Asimov, I. Potential
Card, O. S. Hatrack River
Fowler, K. J. The gate of ghosts
Kress, N. Against a crooked stile
Leiber, F. Smoke ghost
Mackenzie, A. I can't help saying goodbye
Maupassant, G. de. Magnetism
Nourse, A. E. Second sight
O'Neil, D. Report on a broken bridge
Prose, F. Women and children first
Shefner, E. The common body
Silverberg, R. (Now + n, now - n)
Spencer, E. The finder
St. Clair, M. The listening child
Strete, C. The game of cat and eagle
Thurston, R. Was that house there yesterday?
West, Dame R. The gray men
Zahn, T. The Cassandra
Zahn, T. Not always to the strong
Zahn, T. The shadows of evening
EYE
        See also Vision
Apollinaire, G. The blue eye
Campbell, R. Mackintosh Willy
Hogan, L. Amen
Kaplan, D. M. The man with Picasso's eyes

Schwartz, L. S. Acquainted with the night
Diseases
McKnight, R. Uncle Moustapha's eclipse
Sanders, S. R. The recovery of vision
Sheehan, R. Boy with an injured eye
The **eye**. Bowles, P.
An **eye** for an eye. Power, V.
The **eye** of Tandyla. De Camp, L. S.
The **eye** of the idol. Tremblay, M.
Eye of the night. Wang Meng
EYEGLASSES
Calvino, I. The adventure of a nearsighted man
Gallagher, T. A pair of glasses
Poe, E. A. The spectacles
The **eyeless** dragons: a Chinese story. Morris, K.
Eyes. Grant, C. L.
Eyes and teeth. Coleman, W.
Eyes do more than see. Asimov, I.
Eyes I dare not meet in dreams. Simmons, D.
Eyes like they say the devil has. Ríos, A.
Eyes of a blue dog. García Márquez, G.
Eyes of amber. Vinge, J. D.
The **eyes** of children. Ardizzone, T.
The **eyes** of love. Petrakis, H. M.
Eyes of the seer. Inks, C., and Miller, G.
Eyestone. MacDonald, D. R.
EYEWITNESSES *See* Witnesses
Ezekiel. Fisher, R.
Ezekiel learns. Fisher, R.

F

F.R.A.N.K.. Gilliatt, P.
The **Fabbri** tape. Auchincloss, L.
Fable. Bumpus, J.
A **fable**. Fox, R.
The **fable** of how the fool-killer backed out of a contract. Ade, G.
The **fable** of Lutie, the false alarm, and how she finished about the time that she started. Ade, G.
The **fable** of sister Mae, who did as well as could be expected. Ade, G.
The **fable** of the farmer and fox. Brunner, J.
The **fable** of the grass widow and the mesmeree and the six dollars. Ade, G.
The **fable** of the honest money-maker and the partner of his joys, such as they were. Ade, G.
The **fable** of the lawyer who brought in a minority report. Ade, G.
The **fable** of the man who was going to retire. Ade, G.
The **fable** of the two mandolin players and the willing performer. Ade, G.

The **fable** of what happened the night the men came to the women's club. Ade, G.

A **fable**: the tendrils of the vine. Colette

FABLES

Al-Qa'id, Y. Three meaningless tales

Brunner, J. The fable of the farmer and fox

Bumpus, J. Fable

Chesterton, G. K. The three dogs

Federspiel, J. The promised village

Heitkamp, K. The yellow deer

Johnson, C. R. Menagerie, a child's fable

Kenyatta, J. The gentlemen of the jungle

Kipling, R. The cat that walked by himself

Manuel, J. The wizard postponed

Narayan, R. K. At the portal

Narayan, R. K. Flavour of coconut

Ozaki, S. The wagtail's nest

Paré, P. Five fables

Sladek, J. T. Fables

Taylor, A. Chudka popoy ugh cha cha

Taylor, A. He korero

Taylor, A. Nga tui

Taylor, A. Pou

Fables. Sladek, J. T.

Fabricius, Sara See Sandel, Cora, 1880-1974

Facade. Ferreira, R.

FACE

Bishop, M. Saving face

Greenberg, A. The man in the cardboard mask

Monreal, D. N. Faces

Abnormalities and deformities

Böll, H. Pale Anna

Ellison, H. Nothing from my noon meal

Garrett, G. P. Wounded soldier

McLaughlin, L. Troubled by his complexion

McPherson, J. A. The story of a scar

Olmstead, R. In this life

Piñera, V. The face

Rothman, C. The transformation

Warren, J. Michael

Wilner, H. Facial nerve

The **face**. Hartley, L. P.

Face. Oates, J. C.

The **face**. Piñera, V.

The **face** in the photo. Finney, J.

The **face-lift**. Winters, J.

FACE MASKS See Masks (for the face)

The **face** of hate. Lavin, M.

A **face** of stone. Williams, W. C.

The **face** of the moon. Tamer, Z.

The **face** of the war. Wolfe, T.

The **face** on the barroom floor. Algren, N.

The **faceless** thing. Hoch, E. D.

Faces. Kawabata, Y.

Faces. Monreal, D. N.

Faces. Winters, J.

The **faces** at Pine Dunes. Campbell, R.

Faces at the window. Hoffman, W.

The **faces** of blood kindred. Goyen, W.

Facial nerve. Wilner, H.

Facing Mount Kenya. Coskran, K.

Facing the cold. Vreuls, D.

Facing the music. Brown, L.

Facing west. Parotti, P.

The **facsimile** shop. Pronzini, B.

A **fact**. Mrozek, S.

FACTORIES

					See also Labor and laboring classes

Abe, K. Song of a dead girl

Berger, J. Once in Europa

Bonosky, P. A sweet tooth

Conroy, J. Bull market

Conroy, J. Bun Grady

Conroy, J. Rubber heels

Dennison, G. Oilers and sweepers

Dick, P. K. Autofac

Franzen, B. So what are you going to do now if you're a friend of Jim's?

Haley, R. The cosmetic factory

Helprin, M. The Pacific

Hemley, R. Looking for kin

Petrakis, H. M. The witness

Shi Tiesheng. Lunch break

Thomas, J. Last factory blues

Williams, T. The malediction

Wilson, B. Disaster

The **facts** are always friendly. Grayson, R.

The **facts** concerning the recent carnival of crime in Connecticut. Twain, M.

The **facts** in the case of M. Valdemar. Poe, E. A.

The **facts** of life. Maugham, W. S.

The **facts** of M. Valdemar's case. Poe, E. A.

FACULTY (EDUCATION) See Teachers

Fading tattoo. Kotzwinkle, W.

Faery tale. Dale, C.

Fagan, Annabel

In a bamboo garden

Women's work; ed. by M. McLeod and L. Wevers

Fahy, Christopher

A clock in San Diego

Fahy, C. One day in the short happy life of Anna Banana, and other Maine stories

The glow of copper

Fahy, C. One day in the short happy life of Anna Banana, and other Maine stories

One day in the short happy life of Anna Banana

Fahy, C. One day in the short happy life of Anna Banana, and other Maine stories

The rock

Fahy, C. One day in the short happy life of Anna Banana, and other Maine stories

Faik, Sait

The barometer

Faik, S. A dot on the map

Faik, Sait—*Continued*

The blanket
  Faik, S. A dot on the map
The bundle
  Faik, S. A dot on the map
By the fountain
  Faik, S. A dot on the map
A certain kind of people
  Faik, S. A dot on the map
A city morning and a man
  Faik, S. A dot on the map
Coming of age on Kasikadasi
  Faik, S. A dot on the map
A dot on the map
  Faik, S. A dot on the map
An episode of two
  Faik, S. A dot on the map
Fear of loving
  Faik, S. A dot on the map
Filbert
  Faik, S. A dot on the map
First letter from a reader
  Faik, S. A dot on the map
Four plus signs
  Faik, S. A dot on the map
The futile man
  Faik, S. A dot on the map
Good deeds are never forgotten
  Faik, S. A dot on the map
The head and the bottle
  Faik, S. A dot on the map
Hotel Joy
  Faik, S. A dot on the map
I kept grumbling
  Faik, S. A dot on the map
In search of a story
  Faik, S. A dot on the map
Jealousy
  Faik, S. A dot on the map
Kalinikhta [good night]
  Faik, S. A dot on the map
King Mike
  Faik, S. A dot on the map
Last birds
  Faik, S. A dot on the map
Love letter
  Faik, S. A dot on the map
A love story
  Faik, S. A dot on the map
A man and his habit
  Faik, S. A dot on the map
The man who doesn't know what a tooth
    or a toothache is
  Faik, S. A dot on the map
The man who forgot the city
  Faik, S. A dot on the map
The mirror at the beach
  Faik, S. A dot on the map
My father's second home
  Faik, S. A dot on the map
The neighborhood coffeehouse
  Faik, S. A dot on the map
The park's mornings, evenings, nights
  Faik, S. A dot on the map
Priest Effendi
  Faik, S. A dot on the map
Psst, psst!
  Faik, S. A dot on the map
Robinson
  Faik, S. A dot on the map
Samovar
  Faik, S. A dot on the map
Searchlight operator
  Faik, S. A dot on the map
A ship
  Faik, S. A dot on the map
The silk handkerchief
  Faik, S. A dot on the map
Sivriada nights
  Faik, S. A dot on the map
The statue I stole from the Louvre
  Faik, S. A dot on the map
The Stelyanos Hrisopulos
  Faik, S. A dot on the map
The test
  Faik, S. A dot on the map
There is a snake in Alemdağ
  Faik, S. A dot on the map
Tin container
  Faik, S. A dot on the map
Tomb with an arbor
  Faik, S. A dot on the map
The village teacher and the herdsboy
  Faik, S. A dot on the map
Waiting for love
  Faik, S. A dot on the map
The wedding night
  Faik, S. A dot on the map
White gold
  Faik, S. A dot on the map
Failing all else. Barthelme, S.
FAILURE
  Baxter, C. Media event
  Carver, R. Gazebo
  Colegate, I. A glimpse of Sion's glory
  Hannah, B. Getting ready
  Keller, G. D. Papi invented the automatic
    jumping bean
  West, J. Child of the century
  Yourcenar, M. The sadness of Cornelius
    Berg
  Ziem, J. Clarifications
Fainlight, Ruth
  Three ambiguous visitors
    Critical Quarterly 30:97-105 Aut '88
The **fair** at Sorochintsy. Gogol', N. V.
Fair Augusto. Kalpakian, L.
A **fair** exchange. Davis, S.
A **fair** exchange. Maupassant, G. de
A **fair** exchange. Wicomb, Z.
Fair game. Waldrop, H.
Fairfields. Jolley, E.
FAIRIES
  Carter, L. The goblinry of Ais
  De Lint, C. Laughter in the leaves

FAIRIES—*Continued*
Dickens, C. The magic fishbone
Dickens, C. The story of the goblins who stole a sexton
Ellison, H. Gnomebody
Gilbert, W. S. Creatures of impulse
Gilbert, W. S. The fairy's dilemma
Gilbert, W. S. Foggerty's fairy
Gilbert, W. S. The triumph of vice
Gilbert, W. S. The wicked world
Jahnn, H. H. The gardener
McKinley, R. The stone fey
Palwick, S. Ever after
Shen, C.-C. Miss Jen
Vinge, J. D. Tam Lin
Warner, S. T. The Duke of Orkney's Leonardo
Warner, S. T. An improbable story
Warner, S. T. Narrative of events preceding the death of Queen Ermine
Warner, S. T. Queen Mousie
Wells, H. G. Mr. Skelmersdale in Fairyland
Wolfe, G. A cabin on the coast
Yourcenar, M. The man who loved the Nereids

Fairman, Paul W.
The cosmic frame
Amazing stories: visions of other worlds
The dark road home
Hound dunnit; ed. by I. Asimov; M. H. Greenberg and C. L. R. Waugh

FAIRS
Ade, G. The fable of how the fool-killer backed out of a contract
Aickman, R. The swords
Amado, J. The lights of the carrousel
Broxon, M. D. Flux of fortune
Carter, L. Geydelle's protective
Cherryh, C. J. To take a thief
Clayton, J. Jezeri and her beast go to the fair and find more excitement than they want
Dunn, M. If there be magic
Effinger, G. A. Babes on bawd way
Gogol', N. V. The fair at Sorochintsy
Green, J. The ruby wand of Asrazel
Haldeman, L. Bird of paradise
Hardy, T. The mayor of Casterbridge [excerpt]
Hoch, E. D. The problem of the county fair
Keillor, G. State Fair
Llywelyn, M. Fletcher found
Major, A. R. Kissmeowt and the healing friar
Matheson, R. Buried talents
Nordan, L. The talker at the freak-show
Peck, C. The gentle art of making enemies
Schaub, M. H. The cards of Eldrianza
Thomas, D. After the fair
Ward, L. The marbled horn
West, J. Learn to say good-bye

Wetherell, W. D. Nickel a throw
Wolfe, T. Oktoberfest
Fair's fair. Speed, J.
Fairview. Eighner, L.
The **fairway**. Flook, M.
The **fairy** feller's master stroke. Wiebe, D. E.
Fairy tale. Drake, R.
A **fairy** tale for our time. Zipes, J. D.

FAIRY TALES *See* Fantasies
The **fairy's** dilemma. Gilbert, W. S.

FAITH
Blinkin, M. Doctor Machover
Bowles, C. The song of the fisherman
Bradfield, S. Unmistakably the finest
Coville, B. The box
Del Rey, L. For I am a jealous people!
Fetler, A. The third count
Goyen, W. Arthur Bond
Greenburg, J. Certain distant suns
Hemingway, E. Nobody ever dies
Hempel, A. Breathing Jesus
Hogg, J. On the separate existence of the soul
Jen, G. The water-faucet vision
Keillor, G. Aprille
Kibera, L. A silent song
L'Heureux, J. Clothing
MacLaverty, B. The break
Martin, G. R. R. The way of cross and dragon
Mauriac, F. A Christmas tale
McGrath, W. M. The evening of Mr. Boch's baloney factory
Melville, H. The lightning-rod man
Morrison, J. Christ, the Devil and the lunatic
O'Connor, F. Parker's back
O'Connor, F. Revelation
O'Grady, D. Say one for Leo
Pak, K.-N. A time of disbelief
Petrakis, H. M. The waves of night
Rooke, L. The problem shop
Rosenbaum, K. Low tide
Sanders, T. E. Ave Lutie
Schwob, M. The Dom
Sharat Chandra, G. S. The holy wristwatch
Singer, I. B. The pocket remembered
Updike, J. Made in heaven
Waldrop, H. God's hooks!
Faith. La Chapelle, M.
Faith. Schwartz, J.
Faith. Tindall, G.
Faith. Wilbur, E.

FAITH CURE
Essop, A. Hajji Musa and the Hindu firewalker
García Márquez, G. Blacamán the good, vendor of miracles
Ndebele, N. The prophetess
O'Connor, F. The river
Paynter, J. The miracle

FAITH HEALERS *See* Faith cure
Faith in a tree. Paley, G.
The **faithful**. Del Rey, L.
The **faithful** bull. Hemingway, E.
The **faithful** companion at forty. Fowler, K. J.
A **faithful** heart. Moore, G.
The **faithful** wilf. Dickson, G. R.
FAITHFULNESS
  Bitov, A. The door
  Brand, M. A lucky dog
  De Larrabeiti, M. Malagan and the Lady of Rascas
  Friedman, B. J. The pledges
  Henry, O. The caballero's way
The **fakir**. Austin, M. H.
Falco, Edward
  Plato at Scratch Daniels
    The Virginia Quarterly Review 62:312-25 Spr '86
  Prodigies
    The Virginia Quarterly Review 64:466-78 Summ '88
  Sir Thomas More in the Hall of Languages
    The Georgia Review 38:583-91 Fall '84
Falkiner, Suzanne, 1952-
  The killing of a hedgehog
    Home and away; ed. by R. Creswell
The **fall**. Heinesen, W.
The **fall**. Piñera, V.
Fall. Riches, B.
The **fall**. Somers, A.
Fall fair. Brender à Brandis, M.
The **fall** fling. Herrick, A. C.
Fall in at the double. Hartley, L. P.
The **fall** of an Eagle's Nest. Mrożek, S.
The **fall** of Flatbush Smith. Gardner, M.
The **fall** of Frenchy Steiner. Bailey, H.
The **fall** of Texas. Johnson, J.
The **fall** of the House of Usher. Poe, E. A.
The **Fall** River axe murders. Carter, A.
The **fallen** angel. Hunter, E.
Falling. Burford, B.
Falling. Francis, H. E.
Falling. McDonald, S.
Falling and ascending bodies: four passages. Brodkey, H.
Falling light. Škvorecký, J.
Falling sickness. Fitzgerald, M. J.
Fallmerayer the stationmaster. Roth, J.
Fallout. Krysl, M.
FALSE ACCUSATION
  Balzac, H. de. The red inn
  Benét, S. V. Too early spring
  Fairman, P. W. The cosmic frame
  Fremlin, C. The post-graduate thesis
  Jarman, M. Goose, dog, fish, stars
  Kassem, A.-H. The trial of the small black woman
  Maupassant, G. de. A piece of string
  Narayan, R. K. The evening gift
  Overholser, W. D. Debt cancelled
  Post, M. D. The forgotten witness

  Tamer, Z. A summary of what happened to Mohammed al-Mahmoudi
  Tolstoy, L., graf. God sees the truth but waits
  Woolrich, C. Murder in wax
False alarm. Maupassant, G. de
The **false** gems. Maupassant, G. de
The **false** prophet. Sembene, O.
False start. Watmough, D.
FAME
  Baxter, C. Media event
Fame and the poet. Wolfe, T.
The **fame** of price. Pfeil, F.
The **familiar**. Auswaks, A.
Familiar games. Baumbach, J.
Families. Stevens, J. A.
The **family**. Ferguson, W.
The **family**. Friedman, P.
The **family**. Latimer, M.
A **family**. Maupassant, G. de
The **family**. Pavese, C.
The **family**. Tamer, Z.
Family album. Cedering, S.
Family album. Halligan, M.
Family attractions. Freeman, J.
Family business. Saiki, J.
Family butcher. Sims, G.
Family chronicle of a wooden bowl maker. Jia Pingwa
FAMILY CHRONICLES
  See also Family life
  Burkert, R. The stone inscription of Caleb Pellor
  Byatt, A. S. Sugar
  Fein, Y. Rumkowsky was right
  Gordon, M. Now I am married
  Haake, K. Bear and other pale giants
  Haley, R. Looping the loop
  Hobson, G. The talking that trees does
  Houbein, L. Child of two sisters
  José, F. S. The heirs
  Kornblatt, J. R. Pa
  Kuznetsova, A. Storms of a cruel fate
  Le Fanu, J. S. The white cat of Drumgunniol
  Liu, T.-J. Chrysalis
  Lovecraft, H. P. The shunned house
  Quammen, D. Uriah's letter
  Sandor, M. The Gittel
  Simon, B. Our war
  Wier, A. Bob and the other man
FAMILY CURSES *See* Curses, Family
Family dancing. Leavitt, D.
A **family** elopement. Wells, H. G.
A **family** for Clotilde. Valenzuela, L.

FAMILY LIFE

See also Aunts; Brothers; Brothers and sisters; Family chronicles; Fathers; Fathers and sons; Fathers-in-law; Grandchildren; Granddaughters; Grandfathers; Grandmothers; Grandparents; Grandsons; Half-brothers; Half-sisters; Marriage; Marriage problems; Mothers and daughters; Mothers and sons; Mothers-in-law; Nephews; Nieces; Parent and child; Sisters; Stepbrothers; Stepdaughters; Stepfathers; Stepmothers; Stepsisters; Twins; Uncles

Abbott, K. The fort
Aćin-Kosta, M. The red bread
Adisa, O. P. Me man Angel
Adisa, O. P. Widows' walk
Al Makhzangy, M. Just a touch
Alden, P. B. All the way to East Texas
Alden, P. B. The Batsons of Brown and Batson
Alden, P. B. Blue mountains
Alden, P. B. Feeding the eagles
Allende, I. Rosa the beautiful
Alther, L. The art of dying well
Anderson, J. Against the wall
Anderson, J. The appearance of things
Anderson, J. The way to Budjerra Heights
Apollinaire, G. Giovanni Moroni
Apple, M. The American bakery
Apple, M. Pizza time
Ardizzone, T. My mother's stories
Ardizzone, T. World without end
Bainbridge, B. Clap hands, here comes Charlie
Baker, S. The sins of the fathers
Ballantyne, S. Flaubert in Miami Beach
Ballantyne, S. Letter to John Lennon
Barker, E. First notch
Barnhill, S. Near places, far places
Bartlett, B. Fearful children [excerpt]
Bausch, R. Police dreams
Baxter, C. Through the safety net
Beattie, A. Gypsy moths
Beattie, A. High school
Beattie, A. Times
Beattie, A. Where you'll find me
Bell, M. Reba
Bellow, S. Him with his foot in his mouth
Benedict, P. Fat Tuesday
Bird, C. The balloon lady
Bird, C. Brother Gregory
Bitov, A. Life in windy weather
Bitov, A. The soldier
Blaise, C. Identity
Blaise, C. Memories of unhousement
Blaise, C. North
Blaise, C. South
Blaisten, I. Uncle Facundo
Blei, N. The chair trick
Blinkin, M. The little calf
Bocock, M. Don't save your kisses
Böll, H. Christmas not just once a year

Bonner, M. Hongry fire
Bonnie, F. Allergic
Bonosky, P. The delegate
Bonosky, P. The first robin in the world
Bowles, P. In the red room
Broder, G. K. Elena, unfaithful
Brunner, J. What friends are for
Buck, P. S. A certain star
Bukoski, A. Great sea battles
Burt, S. Anyone else would learn
Busch, F. Critics
Busch, F. A history of small ideas
Calvino, I. Lazy sons
Cameron, E. The girl on the beach
Cameron, P. What do people do all day?
Campbell, W. B. Of generations
Campos-De Metro, J. Bands
Campos-De Metro, J. Little mooses
Campos-De Metro, J. The slugger heart
Campos-De Metro, J. Stock
Canin, E. American Beauty
Carlson, R. The H Street sledding record
Carlson, R. Milk
Carlson, R. The status quo
Carter, R. Composition
Carter, R. The drought
Cather, W. The sentimentality of William Tavener
Cedering, S. Family album
Chand, M. The gift of Sunday
Chekhov, A. P. Three years
Chon, S.-G. Wings that will carry us both
Choyce, L. Family protection
Chute, C. "Ollie, oh . . . "
Claiborne, S. On vacation
Claiborne, S. A pretty fine life
Clark, D. Answer to prayer
Cockrell, C. In praise of creeping things
Coe, C. Anything you want
Collins, L. Fears
Collins, L. Going to see the leaves
Collins, L. Intimacy
Collins, L. A summer's day
Conroy, J. Charley was our darlin'
Conroy, J. The fields of golden glow
Cook, H. Homesickness
Cook, H. Pisces
Cook-Lynn, E. The power of horses
Cooper, J. C. Funny valentines
Cooper, J. C. Swimming to the top of the rain
Cooper, J. C. Swingers and squares
Cooper, J. C. When life begins!
Cullen, E. J. Honesty
Cullen, E. J. What Uncle Tom did
Cullen, E. J. What's left
Dabbs, D. E. Arriki
Danby, M. Robbie
Dauenhauer, N. Egg boat
Dawkins, C. The mourner
Dawson, F. The man
Dawson, F. Yes!
Day, R. C. Massimo

FAMILY LIFE—*Continued*

Dazai, O. Memories
Delbanco, N. At the Prado: a short story
Dickinson, C. My livelihood
Dickinson, C. Sofa art
Dilworth, S. The lady on the plane
Disher, G. The bamboo flute
Dixon, S. Don
Dixon, S. Magna takes the calls
Doctorow, E. L. The writer in the family
Donaldson, S. R. Mythological beast
Dorr, L. Lazarus
Drewe, R. The bodysurfers
Drewe, R. Looking for Malibu
Dunn, D. Mozart's Clarinet Concerto
Durban, P. Belonging
Eldridge, M. Aubade
Eldridge, M. A family story
Eldridge, M. Nuclear
Eldridge, M. The sea
Eldridge, M. Walking the dog
Endō, S. My belongings
Engberg, S. Household
Engberg, S. The mile run
Engberg, S. Pastorale
Evans, E. In spring
Everett, P. L. A real hard rain
Fahy, C. One day in the short happy life of Anna Banana
Fante, J. Bricklayer in the snow
Fante, J. Home, sweet home
Fante, J. A wife for Dino Rossi
Farmer, B. The captain's house
Farmer, B. Ismini
Farmer, B. Milk
Farmer, B. Our lady of the beehives
Feeney, J. A married woman
Ferguson, P. The dry familiar plains
Ferguson, W. The family
Ferreira, R. The gravedigger
Ferreira, R. Juan de Dios
Ferreira, R. The well
Ferron, J. Cadieu
Ferron, J. Martine
Ferron, J. Mélie and the bull
Finger, A. Like the Hully-Gully but not so slow
Flanagan, M. Cream sauce
Flanagan, R. Father's Day
Flynn, R. Place
Ford, R. Optimists
Forrest, K. V. Mother was an alien
Franzen, B. The Brewster family time capsule
Freeman, J. Camp Rose
Freeman, J. Family attractions
Freeman, J. Pretend we're French
Freeman, M. E. W. Louisa
Friedman, B. J. Business is business
Friedman, P. An unexpected death
Gaitskill, M. Heaven
Gallagher, T. The wimp
Gallant, M. Dédé

Gallant, M. Larry
Gallant, M. Luc and his father
Gallant, M. Saturday
Gass, W. H. The Sunday drive
Gathorne-Hardy, J. The picnic
Gee, M. The hole in the window
Gee, M. Joker and wife
Gerber, M. J. Straight from the deathbed
Gerber, M. J. Tragic lives
Gerber, M. J. Witnesses
Gide, A. The return of the prodigal son
Gilliatt, P. Catering
Gilliatt, P. F.R.A.N.K.
Gilliatt, P. Foreigners
Gilliatt, P. On each other's time
Gilliatt, P. The tactics of hunger
Gilliatt, P. They sleep without dreaming
Gingher, M. Camouflage
Gingher, M. Teen angel
Gingher, M. Toy Paris
Gingher, M. Wearing glasses
Ginzburg, N. The mother
Glasser, P. Steering clear
Godwin, G. Over the mountain
Gordon, M. Delia
Gottlieb, E. The lizard
Granit, A. Come into the hallway, for five cents!
Greenwood, R. Arcadia
Groff, D. Nobody's child
Haake, K. Bear and other pale giants
Haake, K. Wait until heaven
Haley, R. Real illusions
Hall, J. Gas
Hall, T. T. A letter from home
Hall, T. T. The wooden box
Han, S.-W. The cave
Hankla, C. A box for dreams
Hankla, C. Fishing
Hankla, C. Skeleton
Harada, Y. Evening bells
Harding, M. Visit
Harris, B. Light
Harris, E. The world record holder
Harvor, E. The age of unreason
Hauptman, W. Hands across America
Hausmann, J. Offices of instruction
Havazelet, E. The only thing you've got
Havazelet, E. What everyone wants
Hemingway, E. Soldier's home
Hemley, R. What's that in your ear?
Henderson, Z. Subcommittee
Henley, P. Victory
Hill, R. Blue Rise [excerpt]
Hoffman, W. Indian gift
Hoffman, W. Moon lady
Hoffman, W. Smoke
Hollingshead, G. Rat with tangerine
Honwana, L. B. Papa, snake & I
Hood, M. And Venus is blue
Hood, M. Finding the chain
Hood, M. Inexorable progress
Hood, M. Something good for Ginnie

FAMILY LIFE—*Continued*
Horne, L. Taking care
Hughes, J. An open house
Hull, H. R. Alley ways
Hull, H. R. The fire
Hulme, K. The cicadas of summer
Hulme, K. Hooks and feelers
Hulme, K. The knife and the stone
Hulme, K. Te Kaihau: the windeater
Humphrey, W. A job of the plains
Humphrey, W. Sister
Hunnicutt, E. A hidden thing
Ignatow, R. G. Resurrection
Jackson, S. The renegade
Jen, G. In the American society
Jhabvala, R. P. Rose petals
Jhabvala, R. P. The widow
Johnson, G. Crazy ladies
Jolley, E. Another holiday for the Prince
Jolley, E. Dingle the fool
Jolley, E. Five acre virgin
Jolley, E. A gentleman's agreement
Jolley, E. One Christmas knitting
Jolley, E. 'Surprise! Surprise!' from Matron
Jolley, E. The wedding of the painted doll
Jones, E. P. Island
Kalpakian, L. And departing leave behind us
Kalpakian, L. Bare root season
Kauffman, J. How many boys?
Kavaler, R. Depression glass
Keillor, G. Hansel
Keillor, G. A trip to Grand Rapids
Kessler, J. F. Moses
Kessler, J. F. Xanthippe
Kiely, B. Your left foot is crazy
Kim, W.-I. The spirit of the darkness
King, F. H. Mess
King, F. H. Sundays
Komie, L. B. Picasso is dead
Kornblatt, J. R. Offerings
Kramer, K. Seeds of conflict
Krysl, M. Désirs
Krysl, M. Fallout
Krysl, M. Snegurochka
La Forme, A. Telephone poles
Lane, P. Apple peels and knives
Latimer, M. The family
Latimer, M. Gisela
Lawrence, D. H. Odour of chrysanthemums
Lawson, H. Brighten's sister-in-law
Lawson, H. A child in the dark, and a foreign father
Layfield, S. The Coggios
Leask, I. G. The anobiid
Leaton, A. Tracks to the cold country
Leavitt, D. Aliens
Leavitt, D. Counting months
Leavitt, D. Family dancing
Leavitt, D. The lost cottage
Leavitt, D. Radiation
Lee, Y.-H. The last rite

Liberman, S. Seeds
Liphshitz, A. A man and his house
Lish, G. Mr. Goldbaum
Lish, G. Spell bereavement
Lispector, C. Family ties
Loewald, U. Prosperity
London, J. New Year
Lovesey, P. Did you tell Daddy?
Low, D. Winterblossom Garden
Lowry, B. So far from the road, so long until morning
Lu Wenfu. Graduation
Lurie, M. Losing things
MacLeod, A. The boat
MacLeod, A. In the fall
MacLeod, A. Winter dog
Mansfield, K. An ideal family
Mansfield, K. New dresses
Mansfield, K. Prelude
March, W. Not worthy of a Wentworth
Martin, R. Cliff Dwellers
Martin, V. The consolation of nature
Martínez-Serros, H. Jitomates
Martone, M. King of safety
Mason, B. A. Big Bertha stories
Mason, B. A. Bumblebees
Mason, B. A. Drawing names
Masters, O. The Lang women
Masters, O. The rages of Mrs. Torrens
Mathers, P. A change for the better
Mathers, P. Something touchy and delicate again
Matthews, J. Five women
Maupassant, G. de. A family
Mazel, D. Lily's Deli
McCreary, L. Static discharge
McCullers, C. A domestic dilemma
McDaniel, W. E. A dream of Grand Junction
McElroy, C. J. More than a notion
McElroy, C. J. Sun, wind and water
McGarry, J. Penmanship
McGarry, J. Providence, 1934: the house at the beach
McGarry, J. Stayed back
McKinley, J. A Fickleman jogs
McPherson, D. Day after day, like a terrible fish
Meinke, P. Uncle George and Uncle Stefan
Miller, S. Appropriate affect
Miller, S. The quality of life
Millhauser, S. A protest against the sun
Millman, L. Scenes from the island
Minot, S. Hiding
Minot, S. The navigator
Minot, S. Thanksgiving Day
Monreal, D. N. Lola's return
Mooney, M. Ancient voices
Morris, M. Conquering space
Morris, W. Green grass, blue sky, white house
Morris, W. Magic
Morrison, J. Black night in Collingwood

FAMILY LIFE—*Continued*

Morrison, J. The busting of Rory O'Mahony
Moskowitz, F. Irene
Mukherjee, B. Orbiting
Mullen, R. At the beach
Munro, A. Miles City, Montana
Munro, A. The progress of love
Munro, A. A queer streak
Munro, A. Royal beatings
Munro, A. White dump
Munro, A. Working for a living
Mzamane, M. My cousin comes to Jo'burg
Narell, I. Papa's tea
Naylor, G. Kiswana Browne
Ndebele, N. The music of the violin
Nelson, K. Invisible life
Nestor, T. G. Ulick's Island
Nevai, L. Mother's Day
Ngugi wa Thiong'o. The return
Nimmo, D. Wake and call me mother
Nordan, L. The Sears and Roebuck catalog game
Norris, L. Blackberries
Novitski, P. Nuclear fission
Oates, J. C. Baby
Oates, J. C. Ballerina
Oates, J. C. The witness
O'Brien, E. My mother's mother
O'Connor, F. A good man is hard to find
O'Grady, D. Say one for Leo
Ortalda, C. Close to home
Osborn, C. House of the blue woman
Osborn, C. Stalking strangers
Pacheco, J. E. Battles in the desert
Painter, P. Suppertime
Pak, W.-S. How I kept our house while my husband was away
Panova, V. F. Evdokia
Paolucci, A. Buried treasure
Paolucci, A. Don Giacomo
Paolucci, A. Lights
Paolucci, A. A small clearing
Pascoe, B. Friday night
Pascoe, B. Primary colours
Pasternak, B. L. Zhenya Luvers' childhood
Patton, F. G. First principles
Penner, J. Things to be thrown away
Perlman, H. H. Twelfth summer
Perry, R. Blues for my father, my mother, and me
Peterson, M. The carved table
Petrakis, H. M. Homecoming
Petrakis, H. M. The witness
Phillips, J. A. 1934
Pilcher, R. The blue bedroom
Pilcher, R. Gilbert
Pilcher, R. The tree
Porter, K. A. Holiday
Potter, N. A. J. Calendar Day
Pritchard, M. A private landscape
Prose, F. Creature comforts
Prose, F. Electricity
Prose, F. Everyday disorders

Proulx, A. A run of bad luck
Pulaski, J. Minnie the Moocher's hair
Pulaski, J. Religious instruction
Pulaski, J. The romance
Rahmann, P. Heathen ways
Rand, N. No sore losers
Reed, K. Into the parlor
Ríos, A. A friend, brother maybe
Robison, J. Home
Robison, J. Nor'easter
Robison, M. Again, again, again
Robison, M. An amateur's guide to the night
Rölvaag, O. E. The boy who had no jack-knife
Rölvaag, O. E. The Christmas offering
Rose, D. A. Betraying Jilly
Rose, D. A. The escargot story (The stroke, II)
Rose, D. A. The good-bye present
Rose, D. A. Jumping from high places
Rose, D. A. Small family with rooster
Rosen, G. Growing up Bronx
Ross, V. Dreams & sleep
Rosta, H. Belinda's seal
Rule, J. A migrant Christmas
Rule, J. Seaweed and song
Rule, J. You cannot judge a pumpkin's happiness by the smile upon his face
Ryan, A. Sand
Saiki, J. Family business
Saiki, J. Hapa hapa/half and half
Sandel, C. Papen
Saroyan, W. The last word was love
Saroyan, W. Lord Chugger of cheer
Schell, J. Alvira, Lettie, and Pip
Schinto, J. The disappearance
Schwartz, L. S. Epistemology, sex, and the shedding of light
Sexson, L. The apocalypse of Mary the unbeliever
Sexson, L. When the pie was opened
Shamosh, A. A nature reserve
Sheckley, R. Good-bye forever to Mr. Pain
Shelnutt, E. Angel
Shelnutt, E. The pilot-messenger
Shelnutt, E. Voice
Shibaki, Y. Ripples
Sholem Aleichem. Tevye blows a small fortune
Sholem Aleichem. Today's children
Shōno, J. Still life
Shukshin, V. M. The microscope
Shukshin, V. M. Stefan
Silverberg, R. The mutant season
Sisskind, M. A day I'll never forget
Sladek, J. T. Breakfast with the Murgatroyds
Sladek, J. T. Calling all gumdrops!
Sligo, J. Going home
Smiley, J. Long distance
Spence, A. Tinsel
Sproat, R. Firework night isn't in it

FAMILY LIFE—*Continued*
St. Pierre, P. H. A day with a deer, a bear and Norah Smith
St. Pierre, P. H. Sale of one small ranch
Stafford, J. Woden's day
Stark, S. S. Best Quality Glass Company, New York
Stark, S. S. His color
Stead, C. About the house
Stead, C. A little demon
Stead, C. The milk run
Stead, C. Uncle Morgan at the Nats
Steele, M. The glass-brick apartment
Stern, S. The book of Mordecai
Stewart, J. I. M. Napier into Ffinch
Stewart, J. I. M. Parlour 4
Stewart, J. I. M. Pipkin Grove
Stewart, J. I. M. Tom Dick and Harry
Still, J. The moving
Strand, M. Under water
Stratton, M. Before summer comes
Su Ye. Scatterbrain
Suckow, R. Visiting
Summers, H. S. Concerning, I suppose my father
Summers, H. S. Diving
Summers, M. Song of willow
Summerville, J. Paper fires
Svendsen, L. Flight
Swados, H. Where does your music come from?
Swift, G. Chemistry
Tabucchi, A. Letter from Casablanca
Tabucchi, A. Saturday afternoons
Tallent, E. The fence party
Taylor, A. The absolutely ordinary family
Taylor, P. E. At the altar
Taylor, P. H. The scoutmaster
Theroux, P. Yard sale
Thompson, K. Getting ready to go camping down in Maine
Thompson, K. Holiday Haven
Thompson, S. Mother's Day
Thompson, S. Snow
Thurm, M. Grace
Thurm, M. Lovers
Thurm, M. Skaters
Traba, M. All in a lifetime
Tsuboi, S. Umbrella on a moonlit night
Tuohy, F. Fingers in the door
Tyler, A. The artificial family
Updike, D. The cushion of time
Updike, D. The end of the reign
Updike, J. Pigeon feathers
Updike, J. Trust me
Upward, E. Over the cliff
Valenzuela, L. A family for Clotilde
Verma, N. The dead and the dying
Verma, N. Maya Darpan
Verma, N. Under cover of darkness
Vogan, S. Scenes from the homefront
Vogan, S. The strength of steel
Wallace, W. Up home
Wang Anyi. The destination

Wang Hongzhen, and Zhou Peisheng. Weishan Lake
Wang Meng. The wind on the plateau
Warner, S. T. A breaking wave
Warner, S. T. A view of Exmoor
Warren, J. Time Lucy went
Watanabe, S. A. Colors
Weaver, G. Morality play
Weaver, G. Neery Christmas
Weaver, G. The two sides of things
Weaver, G. Whiskey, whiskey, gin, gin, gin
Wegner, H. The counter of Lvov
Wegner, H. Cyankali
Wegner, H. The huzul flute
Welty, E. Why I live at the P.O.
West, J. Grand opening
Wetherell, W. D. If a woodchuck could chuck wood
Wheatcroft, J. Letter from a stranger
Wheatcroft, J. The shadow of a bear
Whisnant, L. Across from the Motoheads
Whitaker, M. Eve
Whitaker, M. The music-box
Whitaker, M. No luggage?
Whittier, G. B. Lost time accident
Wicomb, Z. Home sweet home
Wilbur, E. Wealth
Willett, J. Julie in the funhouse
Williams, J. Taking care
Willson, H. Moonset near Magdalena
Wilson, B. The investment
Winton, T. Forest winter
Winton, T. Gravity
Winton, T. Laps
Winton, T. More
Winton, T. The strong one
Wohmann, G. The swan
Wolf, S. The legacy of Beau Kremel
Wolff, T. Coming attractions
Wolff, T. The liar
Working, R. The monkey
Yasuoka, S. A view by the sea
Yates, R. Oh, Joseph, I'm so tired
Yi, H.-C. Midnight
Yi, H.-C. Torn flesh
Yi, P. A stray bullet
Zhang Xian. The widow
Zhao Zhenkai. The homecoming stranger
Zhu Lin. Downpour on a leaky roof
Family life: a chapter. Blinkin, M.
A **family** man. Pritchett, V. S.
A **family** man. Saroff, S. S.
The **family** man. Thorman, R.
Family matters. Hyde, E.
Family men. Yarbrough, S.
Family protection. Choyce, L.
A **family** record. McConkey, J.
FAMILY REUNIONS
Alderson, T. The auction
Bowles, P. The frozen fields
Geras, A. Snapshots of paradise
Grau, S. A. Summer shore
Kawabata, Y. Hometown

FAMILY REUNIONS—*Continued*
  Neville, S. Banquet
  Ravin, B. L. Cabin class to Pubjanice
  Ruffolo, L. Holidays
  Vanderhaeghe, G. Reunion
  Yates, R. A compassionate leave
Family ritual. Carlson, R.
Family secrets. Lewis, S. E.
Family secrets. Shields, C.
Family sins. Trevor, W.
A **family** story. Eldridge, M.
A **family** supper. Ishiguro, K.
Family ties. Lispector, C.
Family tremors. Brown, A.
Family visit. Matthew, J. R.
The **family's** secret move. Huynh, Q. N.
FAMINES
  Asimov, I. The winnowing
  Chekhov, A. P. My wife
Famous people. Working, R.
A **famous** Russian poet. Baumbach, J.
Fan letter. Dawson, F.
Fan mail. Haylock, J.
A **fan** of the game. Sorrells, R. T.
Fana. Kotzwinkle, W.
FANATICISM
  Kimball, R. W. Destination
  Lansdale, J. R. The pit
  Sanders, S. R. Prophet
FANATICS *See* Fanaticism
Fancy meeting you. McConnell, J.
Fangs of the cobra. Chadwick, P.
Fanny's comfort station. Moskowitz, F.
Fans. Hannah, B.
FANTASIES

  See also Allegories; End of the
  world; Experimental stories; Future,
  Stories of the; Improbable stories;
  Science fiction; Utopias
Abe, K. The magic chalk
Aichinger, I. Story in a mirror
Aickman, R. The Cicerones
Aickman, R. The inner room
Aiken, J. The cat who lived in a drainpipe
Aiken, J. The moon's revenge
Aldiss, B. W. Hothouse
Aldiss, B. W. The O in José
Aldiss, B. W. A romance of the equator
Andersen, H. C. The traveling companion
Anderson, P. The forest
Anderson, P. The Gate of the Flying
  Knives
Anderson, P. Operation afreet
Anthony, P. In the barn
Anthony, P. Possible to rue
Anthony, P. Wood you?
Arnason, E. The ivory comb
Arnold, M. The girl in the mirror
Asimov, I. Sally
Asimov, I. Unto the fourth generation
Asimov, I. What if . . .
Austin, D. The past is a doomed
  parachutist

Bail, M. Paradise
Baker, S. Sea change
Ballard, J. G. Time of passage
Barrett, W. E. The destroyer
Barthelme, D. Captain Blood
Barthelme, D. Conversations with Goethe
Baum, L. F. The dummy that lived
Baxter, C. The cliff
Bear, G. Petra
Bear, G. The white horse child
Beaumont, C. Free dirt
Beerbohm, M. A. V. Laider
Belden, W. S. Fenneca
Bell, C. The hunting of Lord Etsalian's
  daughter
Belloc, H. Home
Benét, S. V. By the waters of Babylon
Benét, S. V. The curfew tolls
Benét, S. V. A judgment in the mountains
Benét, S. V. The King of the Cats
Benford, G. Newton sleep
Berry, R. M. A circle is the shape of
  perfection
Betancourt, J. G. Vernon's dragon
Bishop, M. For thus do I remember Car-
  thage
Bishop, M. The monkey's bride
Bishop, M. The quickening
Bitov, A. Infantiev
Bixby, J. The draw
Blaylock, J. P. Paper dragons
Bloch, R. All on a golden afternoon
Bloch, R. The funnel of God
Bloch, R. Heir apparent
Bloch, R. The movie people
Bloch, R. Mr. Steinway
Bloch, R. The pin
Bloy, L. The captives of Longjumeau
Borges, J. L. The Aleph
Borges, J. L. Tlön, Uqbar, Orbis Tertius
Boucher, A. Mr. Lupescu
Bradbury, R. And so died Riabouchinska
Bradbury, R. The April witch
Bradbury, R. The crowd
Bradbury, R. The playground
Bradbury, R. Skeleton
Bradbury, R. The small assassin
Bradley, M. Z. A dozen of everything
Bradley, M. Z. The jewel of Arwen
Bradley, M. Z. Sea wrack
Brantingham, J. Giraffe Tuesday
Brown, F. Armageddon
Brown, G. M. The chamber of poetry
Bumpus, J. Fable
Bunch, D. R. A small miracle of fishhooks
  and straight pins
Burkert, R. The stone inscription of Caleb
  Pellor
Buzzati, D. The flying carpet
Buzzati, D. The slaying of the dragon
Buzzati, D. The time machine
Cadigan, P. Nearly departed
Cadigan, P. Pretty boy crossover

FANTASIES—*Continued*

Calvino, I. Adam, one afternoon
Calvino, I. The Argentine ant
Cameron, A. Magic in a world of magic
Card, O. S. Hatrack River
Carr, J. The price of lightning
Carr, T. Thus I refute
Carrier, R. The ink
Carrier, R. The room
Carroll, J. Friend's best man
Carroll, L. E. Without wings
Carter, A. The courtship of Mr. Lyon
Carter, R. Cityman
Chamisso, A. von. The strange story of Peter Schlemihl
Cherryh, C. J. Of law and magic
Chesterton, G. K. The giant
Chesterton, G. K. The taming of the nightmare
Chin, M. L. Lan Lung
Choe, I.-H. Another man's room
Clayton, J. Jezeri and her beast go to the fair and find more excitement than they want
Clayton, J. Team venture
Clift, C. Even the thrush has wings
Cohen, M. The Eiffel Tower in three parts
Coleridge, S. Phantasmion [excerpt]
Colette. The sick child
Collier, J. Evening primrose
Comfort, A. The lemmings
Cortázar, J. The southern thruway
Crabtree, L. V. The miracle in Sweet Hollow
Crouch, C. The wicked season
Crowley, A. The burning of Melcarth
Cullen, E. J. Larmer said he would be King
Curry, G. S. Sea-serpents of Domnudale
Davidson, A. Duke Pasquale's ring
Davidson, A. Great is Diana
Davidson, A. Sleep well of nights
Delany, S. R. The tale of dragons and dreamers
Denevi, M. A dog in Durer's etching 'The knight, death and the devil'
Dick, P. K. Autofac
Dick, P. K. The king of the elves
Dickens, C. A child's dream of a star
Dinesen, I. The sailor-boy's tale
Dixon, S. Come on a coming
Dixon, S. Encountering revolution
Dixon, S. Goodbye to goodbye
Donaldson, S. R. Daughter of Regals
Donaldson, S. R. Gilden-Fire
Donaldson, S. R. The Lady in White
Dozois, G. R. The sacrifice
Drake, D. Dreams in amber
Duane, D. Lior and the sea
Dunsany, E. J. M. D. P., Baron. The Bureau d'Echange de Maux
Dunsany, E. J. M. D. P., Baron. The sword of Welleran

Eisenstein, S. The contortionist
Eisenstein, S. Ecospasm
Eisenstein, S. The inner garden
Eisenstein, S. Straight razor
Elgin, S. H. For the sake of Grace
Elgin, S. H. Hush my mouth
Eliade, M. With the gypsy girls
Ellison, H. The boulevard of broken dreams
Ellison, H. Count the clock that tells the time
Ellison, H. Eidolons
Ellison, H. The function of dream sleep
Ellison, H. Jeffty is five
Ellison, H. On the downhill side
Ellison, H. The region between
Eustis, H. Mister Death and the redheaded woman
Evans, M. Candles in the bottom of the pool
Ferguson, N. The Monroe Doctrine
Ferron, J. The flood
Ferron, J. The jailer's son
Finney, J. Lunch-hour magic
Fox, J. Garage sale
Fritch, C. E. The curse of Hooligan's Bar
Gallico, P. Jennie's lessons to Peter on how to behave like a cat
García Márquez, G. Eva is inside her cat
García Márquez, G. The handsomest drowned man in the world
García Márquez, G. A very old man with enormous wings
Gardner, C. S. Demon luck
Gardner, C. S. A drama of dragons
Gardner, C. S. A malady of magicks
Gardner, M. The stranger
Gauvreau, C. The dream of the bridge
Gauvreau, C. The prophet in the sea
Gearhart, S. M. The chipko
Gearhart, S. M. Roxie raccoon
Gibson, W. The Gernsback continuum
Gilchrist, E. The young man
Gilchrist, M. The pageant of ghosts
Gilden, M. Deadline
Godwin, E. Daddy
Goldin, S. The world where wishes worked
Gottlieb, E. The lizard
Goulart, R. Groucho
Goulart, R. Please stand by
Granit, A. With a herring in one hand and a bottle of schnapps in the other; oh! how he did dance!
Gravel, G. Old Toad
Gray, A. The end of the Axletree
Gray, A. Five letters from an eastern empire
Gray, A. The star
Gray, A. The start of the Axletree
Greene, G. Alas, poor Maling
Guin, W. The root and the ring
Gunn, J. E. Feeding time

FANTASIES—*Continued*

Haldeman, J. C. Mortimer Snodgrass Turtle

Hale, E. E. Hands off

Hamilton, E. He that hath wings

Harrison, M. J. Settling the world

Hartley, L. P. Conrad and the dragon

Hartley, L. P. The crossways

Hawthorne, N. Drowne's wooden image

Hawthorne, N. Feathertop

Hearn, L. Of a promise kept

Heinlein, R. A. Our fair city

Helfman, E. S. Voices in the wind

Henry, O. The enchanted kiss

Hesse, H. A man by the name of Ziegler

Highsmith, P. Mermaids on the golf course

Hoch, E. D. The maiden's sacrifice

Hofmann, G. A conversation about Balzac's horse

Howard, R. E. The people of the Black Circle

Howard, R. E. Red nails

Hoyle, F. Blackmail

Hutman, N. The land of the leaves

Izzo, F. E. Tank

Jackson, G. Fly in the ointment

Jakes, J. Storm in a bottle

Jeppson, J. O. The horn of Elfland

Jones, G. The snow apples

Karr, P. A. The toe

Katz, S. Death of the band

Kawabata, Y. One arm

Kearns, R. Grave angels

Kennedy, L. The silent cradle

Kessel, J. Hearts do not in eyes shine

Kessel, J. The pure product

Kessler, J. F. Gnosis

King, S. Nona

Kirk, R. Balgrummo's hell

Klein, T. E. D. Nadelman's god

Korabelnikov, O. Tower of birds

Kotzwinkle, W. The curio shop

Kotzwinkle, W. Jewel of the moon

Kraski, G. Wings of eucalyptus leaves

Kress, N. Night win

Kress, N. Ten thousand pictures, one word

Kress, N. With the original cast

Kurtz, K. Catalyst

Kusenberg, K. Who am I?

La Motte-Fouqué, F. H. K., Freiherr von. Undine

Lackey, M. Were-hunter

Lafferty, R. A. Nor limestone islands

Landolfi, T. Chicken fate

Landolfi, T. The kiss

Lansdale, J. R. Trains not taken

Le Guin, U. K. Buffalo gals, won't you come out tonight

Le Guin, U. K. Semley's necklace

Lee, T. Odds against the gods

Lee, T. The pale girl, the dark mage, and the green sea

Lee, T. The princess and her future

Lee, T. Red as blood

Lee, T. Southern lights

Leiber, F. The curse of the smalls and the stars

Leiber, F. Ill met in Lankhmar

Leiber, F. The mer she

Leiber, F. A rite of spring

Leiber, F. Sea magic

Leiber, F. Slack Lankhmar afternoon featuring Hisvet

Leiber, F. Space-time for springers

Lewitt, S. N. The judgment of Neave

Lichtenberg, J. Through the moon gate

Linaweaver, B., and Linaweaver, C. Dream pirates' jewel

Lipsyte, R. Red carpet treatment

Littke, L. A feline felony

Livesey, M. A story to be illustrated by Max Ernst

Lynn, E. A. The gods of Reorth

Lynn, E. A. The woman who loved the moon

Machen, A. The white people

MacLean, K. Perchance to dream

Major, A. R. La Verdad: the magic sword

Malamud, B. The Jewbird

Malzberg, B. N. Going down

Martin, G. R. R. The ice dragon

Martin, G. R. R. The monkey treatment

Mathews, P. S. Darkness over Mirhold

Matuszewicz, J. M. Power times one

McCaffrey, A. Dragonrider

McCaffrey, A. A flock of geese

McCormack, E. P. The hobby

McCormack, E. P. A long day in the town

McDonald, S. E. Silken dragon

McGrath, P. The e(rot)ic potato

McKillip, P. A. The old woman and the storm

McKinley, R. The stone fey

Meier, S. Peacock eyes

Miesel, S. The salt garden

Miesel, S. The shadow hart

Miller, A. The stones of Sharnon

Miller, S. To rebuild the eyrie

Moorcock, M. Elric at the end of time

Moorcock, M. The lands beyond the world

Moore, A. A hypothetical lizard

Moore, R. Getting back to before it began

Morris, J. A man and his god

Morris, K. The sapphire necklace

Mrożek, S. In the drawer

Murphy, P. In the islands

Nabokov, V. V. The visit to the museum

Nimmo, D. Rabbits

Nolan, W. F. Of time and Kathy Benedict

Nolan, W. F. Saturday's shadow

Norton, A. The long night of waiting

Norton, A. Moon mirror

Norton, A. Of the shaping of Ulm's heir

Norton, A. One spell wizard

Norton, A. Spider silk

Norton, A. The toymaker's snuffbox

Norton, A. Wizard's world

FANTASIES—*Continued*

Norton, M. Paul's tale
O'Brien, F. John Duffy's brother
O'Faolain, J. Legend for a painting
Palwick, S. Ever after
Pangborn, E. Pick-up for Olympus
Paxson, D. L. Heroes
Paxson, D. L. Sky sister
Phillips, R. Game preserve
Pierce, M. A. The woman who loved reindeer
Pieyre de Mandiargues, A. Clorinda
Poe, E. A. The island of the fay
Pohl, F. Day million
Pollack, R. Angel baby
Pollack, R. Black Rose and White Rose
Pollard, J. A. Old woman
Porges, A. $1.98
Powers, T. Night moves
Pynchon, T. Low-lands
Rampo, E. The Red Chamber
Rausch, B. Snows of yesteryear
Reed, K. Great Escape Tours Inc.
Rendell, R. The green road to Quephanda
Reynolds, M. The Devil finds work
Reynolds, M. Your soul comes C.O.D.
Roberts, K. The Lady Margaret
Robinson, K. S. Escape from Kathmandu
Rooke, L. Dream Lady
Rooke, L. The madwoman of Cherry Vale
Rudoski, A. If big brother says so
Russ, J. How Dorothy kept away the spring
Russ, J. The little dirty girl
Russ, J. Main street: 1953
Russ, J. The man who could not see devils
Russ, J. Mr. Wilde's second chance
Russ, J. Window dressing
Ryan, A. Babies from heaven
Sage, V. Crusoe
Saki. Tobermory
Sallis, J. Miranda-Escobedo
Salmonson, J. A. The prodigal daughter
Sanders, S. R. The anatomy lesson
Sargent, P. Out of place
Sawai, G. The day I sat with Jesus on the sun deck and a wind came up and blew my kimono open and he saw my breasts
Sawyer, R. J. The contest
Scarborough, E. Milk from a maiden's breast
Schaub, M. H. Night hound's moon
Schnurre, W. Diary of a dayfly
Schwartz, L. S. Plaisir d'amour
Schwartz, L. S. Sound is second sight
Severance, C. Isle of illusion
Shea, M. The horror on the #33
Sheckley, R. The accountant
Sheckley, R. The battle
Sheckley, R. Is that what people do?
Sheckley, R. Silversmith wishes
Shepard, L. The jaguar hunter

Shepard, L. The man who painted the dragon Griaule
Shepard, L. Pictures made of stones
Sherman, D. The maid on the shore
Shiner, L. Jeff Beck
Shiner, L., and Shiner, E. Things that go quack in the night
Shwartz, S. M. Rite of failure
Silverberg, R. As is
Silverberg, R. Breckenridge and the continuum
Silverberg, R. Ms. found in an abandoned time machine
Silverberg, R. Multiples
Silverberg, R. The regulars
Silverberg, R. Trips
Simmie, L. You tell me your dreams
Sisskind, M. A day I'll never forget
Sisskind, M. Grrrrr!
Sisskind, M. I'm stupid and my wife is stupid
Sisskind, M. The Playboy Rabbit
Sisskind, M. Twenty questions
Slesar, H. My father, the cat
Smeds, D. Dragon touched
Smith, C. A. The charnel god
Smith, C. A. The city of the singing flame
Smith, C. A. The colossus of Ylourgne
Smith, C. A. The coming of the white worm
Smith, C. A. The dark eidolon
Smith, C. A. The death of Ilalotha
Smith, C. A. The death of Malygris
Smith, C. A. The empire of the necromancers
Smith, C. A. The end of the story
Smith, C. A. The garden of Adompha
Smith, C. A. The holiness of Azédarac
Smith, C. A. The isle of the torturers
Smith, C. A. The last hieroglyph
Smith, C. A. The maze of Maal Dweb
Smith, C. A. Necromancy in Naat
Smith, C. A. The seven geases
Smith, C. A. The tale of Satampra Zeiros
Smith, C. A. The weird of Avoosl Wuthoqquan
Smith, C. A. Xeethra
Smith, D. W. One last dance
Smith, E. E. The good husband
Smith, E. E. Weather prediction
Snodgrass, M. Futures yet unseen
Snow, J. The anchor
Spark, M. The house of the famous poet
Spark, M. The Playhouse called Remarkable
Speer, H. Shawm of the stars
Springer, N. Bright-eyed black pony
St. Clair, M. Child of void
St. Clair, M. The man who sold rope to the Gnoles
St. Clair, M. An old-fashioned bird Christmas
Stewart, J. I. M. The dyslexia factor

FANTASIES—*Continued*

Stockton, F. The Bee-man of Orn
Stuart, K. Green in High Hallack
Sturgeon, T. Brat
Sturgeon, T. Shadow, shadow on the wall
Sturgeon, T. The silken-swift . . .
Swallow, L. S'Olcarias's sons
Swann, T. B. Where is the bird of fire?
Tarr, J. Defender of the faith
Tem, S. R. The painters are coming today
Tem, S. R. The poor
Thomas, A. C. The man with clam eyes
Thomas, A. C. One size fits all
Thomas, A. C. The princess and the zucchini
Thomas, D. An adventure from a work in progress
Thomas, D. The holy six
Thomas, D. The horse's ha
Tiptree, J. Beyond the dead reef
Tiptree, J. The Earth doth like a snake renew
Titcher, M. No fairies at the bottom of the garden
Tolkien, J. R. R. Riddles in the dark
Tournier, M. Tom Thumb runs away
Twain, M. "The great dark"
Twain, M. Sold to Satan
Utley, S., and Waldrop, H. Custer's last jump
Van Gelder, G. Santa's tenth reindeer
Vance, J. Guyal of Sfere
Vance, J. Mazirian the Magician
Vardeman, R. E. The Road of Dreams and death
Vinge, J. D., and Vinge, V. The peddler's apprentice
Vizyēnos, G. M. The only journey of his life
Vogan, S. The confession of the Finch
Walker, W. Ashiepattle
Walker, W. The cleverness of Elsie
Walker, W. The contract with the beast
Walker, W. The rescuer
Walker, W. The sea-rabbit; or, The artist of life
Walker, W. The unseen soldier
Walpole, H. The bird's nest
Walpole, H. The dice-box: a fairy tale
Walpole, H. Hieroglyphic tales
Walpole, H. The king and his three daughters
Walpole, H. Mi Li: a Chinese fairy tale
Walpole, H. The peach in brandy: a Milesian tale
Walpole, H. A true love story
Wandor, M. Judy's kiss
Watson, I. Flame and the healer
Watt-Evans, L. Paranoid fantasy #1
Wellen, E. Chalk talk
Wellman, M. W. The seeker in the fortress
Wellman, M. W. The witch's cat
Wells, H. G. The wild asses of the devil
Westall, R. The Big Rock Candy Mountain

Wilde, O. The selfish giant
Willett, J. Father of invention
Williamson, B. The thing waiting outside
Wilson, F. P. The last one mo once golden oldies revival
Wilson, L. A. The snipe hunters
Wind, D. The sentinel at the edge of the world
Winterson, J. Orion
Wodehouse, P. G. Monkey business
Wolf, R. Tall dames go walking
Wolfe, G. The cat
Wolfe, G. The detective of dreams
Wolfe, G. Game in the pope's head
Wolfe, G. Lukora
Woolf, V. Lappin and Lapinova
Wrede, P. C. The improper princess
Yano, T. The legend of the paper spaceship
Yolen, J. Angelica
Yolen, J. The foxwife
Yolen, J. The lady and the merman
Yolen, J. Words of power
Yourcenar, M. Our-Lady-of-the-Swallows
Zambreno, M. F. A way out
Zelazny, R. Tower of ice
Zelazny, R. Unicorn variations
Zindell, D. Shanidar
Zinnes, H. Wings

FANTASTIC FICTION *See* Fantasies; Science fiction

Fantasy for a Friday afternoon. Clayton, J. J.

Fante, John, 1909-1983

Altar boy
  Fante, J. The wine of youth
Big leaguer
  Fante, J. The wine of youth
Bricklayer in the snow
  Fante, J. The wine of youth
The dreamer
  Fante, J. The wine of youth
First Communion
  Fante, J. The wine of youth
Hail Mary
  Fante, J. The wine of youth
Helen, thy beauty is to me—
  Fante, J. The wine of youth
Home, sweet home
  Fante, J. The wine of youth
In the spring
  Fante, J. The wine of youth
A kidnaping in the family
  Fante, J. The wine of youth
My father's God
  Fante, J. The wine of youth
My mother's goofy song
  Fante, J. The wine of youth
A nun no more
  Fante, J. The wine of youth
The odyssey of a Wop
  Fante, J. The wine of youth

Fante, John, 1909-1983—*Continued*
  One of us
    Fante, J. The wine of youth
  One-play Oscar
    Fante, J. The wine of youth
  The Road to Hell
    Fante, J. The wine of youth
  Scoundrel
    Fante, J. The wine of youth
  A wife for Dino Rossi
    Fante, J. The wine of youth
  The wrath of God
    Fante, J. The wine of youth
The **far** and the near. Wolfe, T.
FAR EAST *See* East Asia
Far eyes. Sampson, R.
Far on the ringing plains. Windsor, G.
The **far** side of the bell-shaped curve. Silverberg, R.
Farber, Sharon N.
  The great dormitory mystery
    Sherlock Holmes through time and space
  On the edge
    Omni (New York, N.Y.) 11:70-2+ D '88
  Passing as a flower in the city of the dead
    Universe 14
  Return of the dust vampires
    Whispers V
Farber and Mr. White. O'Donnell, P.
Fard. Huxley, A.
Farewell gesture. Kipp, G. G.
Farewell party. Wilson, R.
Farewell to Frognall. Kees, W.
A **farewell** to love. Eisenreich, H.
Farewell to the master. Bates, H.
A **farewell** to the old order. Cordor, S. M.
FAREWELLS
  Aidoo, C. A. A. Certain winds from the south
  Böll, H. Autumn loneliness
  Böll, H. Parting
  Chekhov, A. P. The fiancée
  Eisenreich, H. A farewell to love
  Kees, W. Farewell to Frognall
  Wexler, J. Communes and Sara
Farid and Farida. Jhabvala, R. P.
Farjeon, Eleanor, 1881-1965
  Spooner
    Roger Caras' Treasury of great cat stories
Farley, Ralph Milne
  The living mist
    Amazing science fiction anthology: The war years, 1936-1945; ed. by M. H. Greenberg
A **farm** at Raraba. Havemann, E.
Farm day. McElroy, C. J.
FARM HANDS *See* Farm workers
FARM LIFE
    See also Peasant life
  Atwood, M. When it happens
  Benedict, D. Unknown feathers
  Bonnie, F. Allergic

  Bonnie, F. Mistrial
  Conroy, J. Pipe line
  Ferguson, W. The third voice
  Flynn, R. Champion of the world
  Flynn, R. The saviour of the bees
  Flynn, R. Seasonal rain
  Hagy, A. C. No kind of name
  Highsmith, P. The day of reckoning
  Humphrey, W. Man with a family
  Kauffman, J. Patriotic
  Kauffman, J. Who has lived from a child with chickens
  Keillor, G. Life is good
  Kittredge, W. Agriculture
  Kittredge, W. Flight
  La Chapelle, M. The meadow bell
  Lieber, T. Country things
  MacLeod, A. As birds bring forth the sun
  MacLeod, A. In the fall
  MacLeod, A. Second spring
  MacLeod, A. To everything there is a season
  Mathers, P. Something touchy and delicate again
  McDaniel, W. E. Shamrock Road
  McKinley, R. The stone fey
  McPherson, D. Day after day, like a terrible fish
  Millman, L. Midnight at the dump
  Muschg, A. Brami's view
  Nestor, T. G. Ulick's Island
  Nordan, L. Wild dog
  O'Brien, D. Strand of wire
  Olmstead, R. Bruno and Rachel
  Olmstead, R. Onions
  Pfeil, F. Holding on
  Pfeil, F. The idiocy of rural life
  Phillips, J. A. Machine dreams [excerpt]
  Proulx, A. Bedrock
  Rose, M. Henderson
  Russell, R. American Gothic
  Schwartz, L. S. Sound is second sight
  Shivers, L. Here to get my baby out of jail [excerpt]
  Silvis, R. Murphy
  Spark, D. Summer of the Dead Frogs
  Spencer, B. The small things that save us
  Suckow, R. A great Mollie
  West, J. Grand opening
  Wilson, R., Jr. Payment in kind
  Zenowich, C. On the roof

           Australia
  Carter, R. The drought
  Eldridge, M. The ringbarker's daughter
  Eldridge, M. The sea
  Eldridge, M. Selling out
  Eldridge, M. Wayside
  Houbein, L. Everything is real
  Loukakis, A. Billy and the birds
  Morrison, J. The ticket
  Prichard, K. S. The cow
  Sheil, G. The picking season

FARM LIFE—*Continued*

California
Burke, J. L. Uncle Sidney and the Mexicans

Greenwood, R. Arcadia

Viramontes, H. M. The broken web

Yamamoto, H. Seventeen syllables

Canada
Ferron, J. The dead cow in the canyon

Munro, A. The progress of love

Panneton, P. The heritage

Reaney, J. The bully

England
Cox, A. Twentieth frame

Watmough, D. Sacred & secular

Watmough, D. Seduction

France
Maupassant, G. de. The story of a farm-girl

Germany
Rinser, L. A handful of white daffodils

Seghers, A. The reed

Ireland
Bernen, R. Brock

Bernen, R. The extra wether

Bernen, R. Fox

Bernen, R. A keen observer of footwear

Bernen, R. The rush

Bernen, R. The scythe

Bernen, R. Two lives

Bernen, R. The windcharger

Moore, G. A flood

O'Brien, E. My mother's mother

O'Flaherty, L. Spring sowing

Power, V. The bullfight

Power, V. Lackendara

Trevor, W. The ballroom of romance

Virgo, S. On this good ground

Virgo, S. Through the eyes of a cat

Italy
Calvino, I. Lazy sons

Kentucky
Stuart, J. Clearing in the sky

Stuart, J. Old Gore

Kenya
Markham, B. The captain and his horse

Markham, B. Something I remember

Markham, B. The transformation

Korea
Han, S.-W. The cave

Maine
Kumin, M. West

Minnesota
Rossiter, S. Skinner

Mississippi
Sanders, S. R. Fetching the dead

Missouri
Conroy, J. "A barrel of fun"

Conroy, J. Home to Uncle Ollie's

Conroy, J. Uncle Ollie finds a new market

Conroy, J. Uncle Ollie's spite fence

Conroy, J. The weed king

Gilgun, J. Cow

Nebraska
Cather, W. On the divide

O'Brien, D. Cowboy on the Concord bridge

New England
Davis, D. S. The muted horn

Jewett, S. O. A white heron

Wharton, E. Ethan Frome

New York (State)
Henry, O. The defeat of the city

Mazel, D. Jeopardies

New Zealand
Collins, S. R. A day at Hot Creek

Ohio
Hall, J. B. Old man finds what was lost

Oklahoma
Humphrey, W. The ballad of Jesse Neighbours

Oregon
Kittredge, W. The Van Gogh field

Pennsylvania
Taube, M. The student

South Africa
Gordimer, N. Six feet of the country

Mphahlele, E. The master of Doornvlei

Southern States
Bell, M. S. Triptych I

Bell, M. S. Triptych II

Bell, M. S. Triptych 2

Daniels, C. Swami Swafford

O'Connor, F. Revelation

Switzerland
Gotthelf, J. Elsi the unusual farm maid

Gotthelf, J. How Joggeli finds a wife: a country tale

Gotthelf, J. Michel's courtship adventures

Muschg, A. The scythe hand; or, The homestead

Taiwan
Cheng, C.-W. Betel Palm Village

Lai, H. The steelyard

Tennessee
Warren, R. P. Blackberry winter

Warren, R. P. The patented gate and the mean hamburger

Texas
Benedict, P. Water witch

Porter, K. A. Holiday

Turkey
Faik, S. White gold

West Virginia
Thorman, C. Blue haired chickens

Western States
Cather, W. The sentimentality of William Tavener

DeMarinis, R. Weeds

Martin, R. Cliff Dwellers

Wisconsin
Baxter, C. Xavier speaking

Zambia
Mulikita, F. M. The tender crop

FARM TENANCY *See* Tenant farming
FARM WORKERS
  Dumas, H. A boll of roses
  Hall, T. T. An early spring morning remembered and understood
  Heller, S. The summer game
  Kittredge, W. The Van Gogh field
  Long, D. Cooper Loftus
  McKnight, R. Who Big Bob?
  Suarez, M. The migrant
Farmer, Beverley, 1941-
  At the airport
    Farmer, B. Milk
  The captain's house
    Farmer, B. Milk
  Darling Odile
    Farmer, B. Milk
  Gerontissa
    Farmer, B. Milk
  Inheritance
    Farmer, B. Milk
  Ismini
    The Australian short story; ed. by L. Hergenhan
    Farmer, B. Milk
  Maria's girl
    Farmer, B. Milk
  Melpo
    Farmer, B. Milk
  Milk
    Farmer, B. Milk
  Our lady of the beehives
    Transgressions; ed. by D. Anderson
  Pumpkin
    Farmer, B. Milk
  Saint Kay's day
    Farmer, B. Milk
    Home and away; ed. by R. Creswell
  Sally's birthday
    Farmer, B. Milk
  Snake
    Farmer, B. Milk
  Summer on ice
    Farmer, B. Milk
  Woman in a mirror
    Farmer, B. Milk
Farmer, Philip José
  After King Kong fell
    Farmer, P. J. The classic Philip José Farmer, 1964-1973
  The alley man
    Baker's dozen: 13 short science fiction novels
    Farmer, P. J. The classic Philip José Farmer, 1952-1964
  Don't wash the carats
    Farmer, P. J. The classic Philip José Farmer, 1964-1973
  The god business
    Farmer, P. J. The classic Philip José Farmer, 1952-1964

  The jungle rot kid on the nod
    Farmer, P. J. The classic Philip José Farmer, 1964-1973
  The king of beasts
    Farmer, P. J. The classic Philip José Farmer, 1952-1964
  Mother
    Farmer, P. J. The classic Philip José Farmer, 1952-1964
  My sister's brother
    Farmer, P. J. The classic Philip José Farmer, 1952-1964
  The oogenesis of Bird City
    Amazing stories: 60 years of the best science fiction
    Farmer, P. J. The classic Philip José Farmer, 1964-1973
  The problem of the sore bridge—among others
    Sherlock Holmes through time and space
  Riders of the purple wage
    Farmer, P. J. The classic Philip José Farmer, 1964-1973
  Sail on! Sail on!
    Farmer, P. J. The classic Philip José Farmer, 1952-1964
  A Scarletin study
    Sherlock Holmes through time and space
  The shadow of space
    Farmer, P. J. The classic Philip José Farmer, 1964-1973
  Sketches among the ruins of my mind
    Farmer, P. J. The classic Philip José Farmer, 1964-1973
  The sliced-crosswise only-on-Tuesday world
    Farmer, P. J. The classic Philip José Farmer, 1964-1973
  Uranus; or, UFO versus IRS
    The Planets; ed. by B. Preiss
The farmer. Dickson, M. M.
Farmer in the dell. Garrett, G. P.
Farmer on the dole. Pohl, F.
FARMERS *See* Farm life
The farmers' daughter. Nordan, L.
The farmer's wife. Maupassant, G. de
Farming on the Esso. Goldberg, L.
FARMWORKERS *See* Farm workers
Farnarkeling: a typical report. Clarke, J.
Farnsworth, Kent A.
  Counterpoint
    Greening wheat: fifteen Mormon short stories
Farr, Douglas
  Sam's conscience
    Alfred Hitchcock's Crimewatch
Farris, Jack, 1921-
  Fire enough for you
    Homewords: a book of Tennessee writers; ed. by D. Paschall

Farris, John
You can keep your razors & guns but check your loud mouths at the door
Between C & D; ed. by J. Rose and C. Texier
Farside station. Williamson, J.
Fascination. Parise, G.
The **fascination** of the pool. Woolf, V.
The **fascination** of the vanity. Sproat, R.

FASCISM
See also Communism; Dictators; National socialism; Totalitarianism
Sandel, C. The broad versus the narrow outlook
Sciascia, L. The American aunt
England
Mortimer, J. C. Rumpole and the fascist beast
Fashion in the Third World. Pritchett, M.

FASHION MODELS
Bloch, R. The model
Poverman, C. E. Beautiful
Rhys, J. Mannequin
Russ, J. Window dressing
Vogan, S. Miss Buick of 1942
Winton, T. Scission
A **fashionable** woman. Maupassant, G. de

Fast, Howard, 1914-
The large ant
Black water; ed. by A. Manguel
Fast and loose, a historical romance. Lopatin, J.
Fast burn. Estleman, L. D.
Fast forward. Cameron, P.
Fast lanes. Phillips, J. A.
Fast-Train Ike. Stuart, J.

FASTING
Botwinik, B. The mother's Yom Kippur
Clark, M. A diet of bananas and Nietzsche
Fat. Carver, R.
The **fat** cat. Wheeler, H. C.
Fat chance. Bloch, R.
Fat chance. Gilliatt, P.
Fat chance. Halligan, M.
The **fat** child. Kaschnitz, M. L.
Fat Face. Shea, M.
The **fat** girl. Dubus, A.
Fat Lena. Coleman, W.
The **fat** man. Schwob, M.
Fat Tuesday. Benedict, P.
The **fatal** flaw. MacDonald, J. D.
The **fatal** footlights. See Woolrich, C. Death at the Burlesque
The **fatalist**. Silvis, R.

FATE AND FATALISM
Fitzgerald, M. J. Phebican
Gilbert, W. S. The finger of fate
Henry, O. An adjustment of nature
Henry, O. Roads of destiny
Hospital, J. T. The owl-bander
Matheson, R. C. Sentences
Rhys, J. Kismet

Waldrop, H. Save a place in the lifeboat for me
Fate and the poet. Frucht, A.
The **fate** of Faustina. Hornung, E. W.
The **fate** of the Evangeline. Doyle, Sir A. C.
The **fate** of the Forrests. Alcott, L. M.
Fated for misfortune. Sholem Aleichem
Fate's purse. Kirk, R.
Father. Dovlatov, S.
The **father**. Maupassant, G. de
A **father**. Mukherjee, B.
Father all over again. Wallace, D.
Father and son. Essop, A.
Father Crumlish remembers his Poe. Reach, A. S.
The **father** figure. Parkinson, T. L.
Father for hire. Freund, E.
Father Goose. Yamamoto, M.
Father Meuron's tale. Benson, R. H.
Father must. Rofihe, R.
Father of invention. Willett, J.
Father of the bride. Pulaski, J.
The **father** of the bride. Willis, C.
Father Palomo. Martínez-Serros, H.
The **father**, the son and the Holy Ghost. Naipaul, S.
Father was a wit. Gibbs, A.
Fatherhood. Parise, G.
Fathering. Mukherjee, B.

FATHERS
See also Fathers and daughters; Fathers and sons; Fathers-in-law; Step-fathers
Abbott, K. The second Pete
Ade, G. When father meets father
Amichai, Y. The times my father died
Apple, M. The four Apples
Barthelme, D. Chablis
Barthelme, F. Aluminum house
Bax, M. Beds
Berry, R. M. A circle is the shape of perfection
Bitov, A. The third story
Brady, M. Strike it rich
Caldwell, E. Daughter
Crayford, K. Duncan
Curval, P. Progenitor
Dai Houying. Father's milk is also blood transformed
Dodd, S. M. Berkie
Drewe, R. The manageress and the mirage
Dubus, A. At St. Croix
Dubus, A. The winter father
Eisenstein, S. Hear anything from Bakersfield?
Fante, J. Bricklayer in the snow
Floyd, P. L. Second best
Flynn, R. Place
Heise, K. My father's confession
Hempel, A. Celia is back
Hempel, A. Today will be a quiet day
Hoffman, W. Patriot

FATHERS—*Continued*

Hood, M. A man among men
Kawabata, Y. Snow
Keillor, G. Hansel
Keillor, G. A trip to Grand Rapids
Kratz, E. Poppa
Lacy, R. The natural father
Liang, L. K. The pei-pa
Lurie, M. The card-players
Lurie, M. A king of the road
Martínez-Serros, H. Distillation
Maupassant, G. de. The father
Maupassant, G. de. Monsieur Parent
McGarry, J. The hospital: seeing him there almost dead
Nichols, J. T. The Milagro beanfield war [excerpt]
Painter, P. Suppertime
Painter, P. The visitor
Petrakis, H. M. The witness
Saroyan, W. What a world, said the bicycle rider
Schulz, B. Father's last escape
Son, S.-H. At the end of the world
Stafford, J. Woden's day
Strand, M. More life
Stuart, J. Clearing in the sky
Sturgeon, T. Twink
Swift, G. Gabor
Terry, W. S. The bottomless well
Vogan, S. No other women
Wendt, A. Birthdays
Zhao Zhenkai. The homecoming stranger
The **fathers**. Stead, C.
Fathers. Wilson, R., Jr.
Fathers. Woodman, A.

FATHERS AND DAUGHTERS

    See also Fathers and sons; Parent and child

Anaya, R. A. The silence of the llano
Anderson, S. Unlighted lamps
Andres, K. Things to draw
Apple, M. Bridging
Austin, D. He won't go down to the park with me today
Ballantyne, S. Perpetual care
Barthelme, D. Visitors
Bissoondath, N. Man as plaything, life as mockery
Bitov, A. The big balloon
Bloch, R. Sweets to the sweet
Blythe, R. Bride Michael
Bonosky, P. Walk to the moon
Botwinik, B. Rivals
Boyle, K. The meeting of the stones
Bradbury, R. Promises, promises
Brand, C. The whispering
Busch, F. Making change
Campbell, R. The words that count
Carpenter, D. The father's love
Carr, P. M. Night of the luminarias
Carver, R. Distance
Castillo, A. Ghost talk

Cehai, C. The distant sound of tree-felling
Chekhov, A. P. At a country house
Chekhov, A. P. The requiem
Chernoff, M. Degan dying
Chernoff, M. Heroes
Chetwynd-Hayes, R. The fly-by-night
Clark, M. Makeup
Colter, C. After the ball
Cook, H. A lesson in dance
Corrington, J. W. Heroic measures/vital signs
Crawford, F. M. The doll's ghost
Crews, H. A long wail
Day, R. C. First love
Day, R. C. Men are like children, like the beasts
Delfino, A. M. The telephone
Dickson, M. M. The farmer
Dodd, S. M. Snowbird
Dubus, A. A father's story
Durban, P. Notes toward an understanding of my father's novel
Eisenstein, S. Moray eel
Eisenstein, S. Post coitus tristus
Engberg, S. Morgan and Joanna
Engberg, S. Trio
Enright, E. A distant bell
Farmer, B. Sally's birthday
Ferron, J. The wedding bouquet
Fink, I. Crazy
Fitzgerald, F. S. Babylon, revisited
Flynn, R. The dog that knew better
Flynn, R. Tumbleweed Christmas
Forrest, K. V. Force majeur
Gallagher, T. The lover of horses
Gallant, M. The prodigal parent
Gallant, M. Voices lost in snow
Ge Wujue. A summer experience
Gee, M. A glorious morning, comrade
Geras, A. Love letters
Gibbs, A. Father was a wit
Gilliatt, P. Stephanie, Stephen, Steph, Steve
Glasser, P. Singing on the Titanic
Godwin, E. Daddy
Gordon, M. The thorn
Graham, J. Two tales of a trip
Haas, B. Like a cactus in a field of corn
Hall, J. Gas
Handke, P. Child story
Harada, Y. Evening bells
Harrington, J. A letter to Amy
Hartley, L. P. Per far l'amore
Hartley, L. P. Roman charity
Hauptman, W. Moon walking
Hauptman, W. Pure sex
Hawthorne, N. Rappaccini's daughter
Hemmerchts, K. The sixth of the sixth of the year nineteen sixty-six
Hendrie, L. Armadillo
Hoffman, W. Fathers and daughters
Hofmann, G. Moth
Hood, M. Nobody's fool

FATHERS AND DAUGHTERS—*Continued*
Hospital, J. T. Waiting
Houbein, L. Everything is real
Jorgensen, B. W. A song for one still voice
Kaplan, D. M. Elisabetta, Carlotta, Catherine (raising the demon)
Kaplan, D. M. In the realm of the herons
Kaplan, D. M. Magic
Kauffman, J. Breaking the news to Doll
Kawabata, Y. Goldfish on the roof
Keillor, G. Corinne
Kercheval, J. L. The dogeater
Krist, G. Layover
Lannes, R. Goodbye, dark love
Lao Hong. The gap
Latimer, M. Marriage eve
Lee, H. Christmas
Li Chao. Spring chill
Lish, G. Fear: four examples
Lynn, E. A. The island
Martin, G. R. R. Portraits of his children
Mattison, A. Art is lost
Mattison, A. Great wits
Mattison, A. In family
Maupassant, G. de. The spasm
Moffatt, D. Willie's war
Moon, S.-T. The sound of the gong
Moore, L. The deep valley
Moravia, A. My daughter is called Giulia too
Morris, W. The sound tape
Morrison, J. Appointment at Princess Gate
Mukherjee, B. A father
Mukherjee, B. Fathering
Murphy, Y. Ball and socket
Murphy, Y. A good father
Muschg, A. The scythe hand; or, The homestead
Naipaul, S. The political education of Clarissa Forbes
Narell, I. Papa's tea
Oates, J. C. Funland
Oates, J. C. Stroke
O'Brien, T. Quantum jumps
O'Connor, F. Judgement Day
Osborn, C. Reversals
Pacheco, J. E. You wouldn't understand
Paley, G. Dreamer in a dead language
Paley, G. Zagrowsky tells
Phillips, J. A. The heavenly animal
Phillips, J. A. Something that happened
Piñón, N. The new kingdom
Prichard, K. S. N'goola
Pritchett, M. Open twenty-four hours
Prosser, H. L. Summer wine
Rambach, P. When the animals leave
Rasputin, V. G. What shall I tell the crow?
Ravin, B. L. Cabin class to Pubjanice
Regent, P. Mr. Parsley's lunchtime pursuit
Rich, C. My sister's marriage
Robison, J. Set off

Rooke, L. Dirty heels of the fine young children
Rose, D. A. Arturo and Eve
Rose, D. A. The elephant story (The stroke, I)
Rosta, H. Belinda's seal
Ruffolo, L. Holidays
Saiki, J. Sisters
Sarah, R. Première arabesque
Saroyan, W. Gaston
Schulberg, B. Señor Discretion himself
Schulman, H. The heart of my heart
Schwartz, L. S. The opiate of the people
Schwartz, L. S. The wrath-bearing tree
Schwartz, S. Navajo Café
Shepard, L. Voyage South from Thousand Willows
Shimao, T. With Maya
Sholem Aleichem. Chava
Sholem Aleichem. Hodl
Sholem Aleichem. Shprintze
Simpson, M. Approximations
Simpson, M. Lawns
Slayter, E. The silver fish
Spark, M. The fathers' daughters
Sparling, E. E. Daughter of Lescale
Sproat, R. Black madonna two-wheel gypsy queen
Sproat, R. The fascination of the vanity
Stark, S. S. His color
Strachan, T. A father's love
Tagore, Sir R. The Cabuliwallah
Tallent, E. Black holes
Tallent, E. Lightly
Tallent, E. Migrants
Taube, M. The student
Tem, S. R. The giveaway
Thompson, J. The copper mine
Thorman, C. No job too small
Thurm, M. Aftermath
Thurm, M. Flying
Thurm, M. Sounds
Trevor, W. On the Zattere
Tuohy, F. At home with the Colonel
Updike, J. Killing
Updike, J. Man and daughter in the cold
Updike, J. Nevada
Vaughn, S. Able, Baker, Charlie, Dog
Verma, N. Weekend
Vogan, S. Scenes from the homefront
West, J. Live life deeply
Wharton, E. The last asset
Whelan, G. First light
Whitaker, M. Frost in April
White, C. Critical theory
Willett, J. My father, at the wheel
Williams, T. The yellow bird
Willson, H. Moonset near Magdalena
Wilson, A. J. E. The old general and the lost granddaughter
Wilson, B. Crater Lake
Wilson, B. Hearings
Wilson, R., Jr. Fathers

FATHERS AND DAUGHTERS—*Continued*
Wolfe, T. In the park
Wollheim, D. A. Give her hell
Yolen, J. The lady and the merman
Fathers and daughters. Hoffman, W.

FATHERS AND SONS
			See also Fathers and daughters;
		Parent and child
Abbott, L. K. The end of grief
Abbott, L. K. The final proof of fate and
	circumstance
Abbott, L. K. X
Aksenov, V. P. Little whale, varnisher of
	reality
Al Shaikh, A. The heir
Aldrich, T. B. The white feather
Anthony, P. Possible to rue
Archer, J. A la carte
Ardizzone, T. My father's laugh
Asimov, I. The key word
Asimov, I. The thirteenth day of Christ-
	mas
Austin, D. The past is a doomed
	parachutist
Banks, R. Firewood
Barthelme, S. Black Jack
Barthelme, S. Stoner's lament
Bass, R. The watch
Bates, H. E. The butterfly
Bausch, R. Police dreams
Baxter, C. The eleventh floor
Beattie, A. Summer people
Bellow, S. A silver dish
Benedict, P. The Sutton Pie Safe
Benson, E. F. The bath-chair
Bergner, H. The actor
Berriault, G. The bystander
Bishop, M. Cold war orphans
Bishop, M. Out of the mouths of Olympus
Bissoondath, N. Insecurity
Bitov, A. The leg
Blaise, C. A North American education
Böll, H. My father's cough
Bonosky, P. The cathedral
Bonosky, P. A quiet summer's day
Botwinik, B. Israel and his children
Bowen, E. The visitor
Bowles, P. The frozen fields
Bowles, P. Pages from Cold Point
Boylan, C. L'amour
Boylan, J. The string
Bradbury, R. By the numbers!
Bradbury, R. The playground
Briskin, M. The kid
Brondoli, M. Borrowing
Brown, G. M. The skald in the cave
Brown, R. A good deal
Bryce Echenique, A. In Paracas with
	Jimmy
Burt, S. Floral Street
Busch, F. The settlement of Mars
Callaghan, M. A cap for Steve
Calvino, I. Man in the wasteland
Camoin, F. A. The Amelia Barons

Camoin, F. A. Peacock blue
Campbell, E. Watch without time
Candelaria, N. El patrón
Canin, E. The carnival dog, the buyer of
	diamonds
Canin, E. Lies
Canin, E. The year of getting to know us
Carlson, R. Blood and its relationship to
	water
Carver, R. Bicycles, muscles, cigarettes
Carver, R. The compartment
Cheever, J. Reunion
Chekhov, A. P. At home
Chekhov, A. P. My life
Chipulina, E. G. Your obedient servant
Clark, G. Blood blossom
Clark, G. Crazy 8's
Clark, G. Ice fishing
Clark, M. A diet of bananas and Nietzsche
Clark, M. Disquiet
Clayton, J. J. Part-time father
Colum, P. Land hunger
Connelly, J. Foreign objects
Conroy, F. Midair
Conroy, F. The sense of the meeting
Cook, M. Parting shots
Cowan, P. The red-backed spiders
Crabtree, L. V. Wildcat John
Crane, S. The monster
Crane, S. The second generation
Deaver, P. F. Infield
DeMarinis, R. Disneyland
DeMarinis, R. Weeds
Deng Gang. The dragon king's troops
	thunder past
Dennison, G. On being a son
Dickinson, C. Black Bart
Dixon, S. Time to go
Dodd, S. M. Wild men of Borneo
Doyle, Sir A. C. The lonely Hampshire
	cottage
Doyle, Sir A. C. Our midnight visitor
Dozois, G. R. Morning child
Dubus, A. The captain
Dubus, A. Killings
Dubus, A. Voices from the moon
El Hamamssy, A. Dust
Ellin, S. Mrs. Mouse
Enayetullah, A. This also happened
Endō, S. Retreating figures
Engberg, S. The mile run
Essop, A. Father and son
Eunson, D. The hero's son
Everett, P. L. Cry about a nickel
Everett, P. L. A good day for the laughing
	blow
Faulkner, W. Barn burning
Faust, I. Operation Buena Vista
Ferguson, W. The third voice
Ferreira, R. Did you say—Dad?
Ferron, J. The jailer's son
Ferron, J. The old heathen
Finger, A. Cars

FATHERS AND SONS—*Continued*

Flaherty, G. The terrible speed of mercy
Flanagan, R. Local anaesthetic
Ford, R. Great Falls
Ford, R. A piece of my heart [excerpt]
Franzen, B. Something the matter with Dad
Freeman, C. Dreaming of Africa
Freeman, C. My life on the snowplow
Freeman, C. The song of Roland
Friedman, P. A period of grace
Fühmann, F. The isle of dreams
Gaitens, E. Growing up
Gallant, M. Luc and his father
Garrett, G. P. The gun and the hat
Garrett, G. P. King of the mountain
Garrett, G. P. The rivals
Gates, D. China Blue
Gee, M. A sleeping face
Giardinelli, M. Revolution on a bicycle
Gifkins, M. Living out the past
Gilliatt, P. The wind-child factor
Gingher, M. The magic circle
Glickman, G. Magic
Gold, H. Cohorts
Goldberg, L. One more river
Gordimer, N. Abroad
Gordimer, N. Letter from his father
Gordon, M. The magician's wife
Gordon, M. The only son of the doctor
Goulart, R. Junior partner
Goyen, W. Precious door
Grant, C. L. If Damon comes
Grant, C. L. Spinning tales with the dead
Greene, G. A shocking accident
Grubb, D. Cry havoc
Gustafsson, L. A water story
Ha, K.-C. Ill-fated father and son
Hagy, A. C. Stadia
Hairston, L. The revolt of Brud Bascomb
Haley, R. Grand-uncle's legs
Haley, R. Occam's electric razor
Haley, R. The Polish village
Hannah, B. Fans
Hannah, B. Horning in--A
Hartley, L. P. The pylon
Hauptman, W. The desert
Havazelet, E. Solace
Heller, S. The Crow Woman
Heller, S. The man who drank a thousand beers
Hemingway, E. I guess everything reminds you of something
Hemingway, E. My old man
Herring, R. Hub [excerpt]
Highsmith, P. I despise your life
Horne, L. Taking care
Hunnicutt, E. Energy
Huynh, Q. N. The family's secret move
Jahnn, H. H. The watchmaker
Jia Pingwa. Shasha and the pigeons
Johnson, C. R. The sorcerer's apprentice
Jolley, E. Bill Sprockett's land

Jolley, E. Two men running
Jones, M. A beginning
Josipovici, G. Death of the word
Kaplan, D. M. Summer people
Kauffman, J. At odds
Kazakov, Y. Nikishka's secrets
Keillor, G. Life is good
Keller, G. D. Mocha in Disneyland
Keller, G. D. Papi invented the automatic jumping bean
Kim, I.-S. Tombstone without an inscription
King, S. The monkey
Kittredge, W. The waterfowl tree
Klíma, I. Monday morning: a black market tale
Kreisel, H. The broken globe
Kress, N. Against a crooked stile
Krist, G. Tribes of northern New Jersey
La Chapelle, M. Accidents
La Puma, S. The gangster's ghost
Lee, R. B. Full fathom five my father lies
Lish, G. Agony
Lish, G. Balzano & Son
Lish, G. For Jerome—with love and kisses
Lish, G. For Rupert—with no promises
Lish, G. Frank Sinatra or Carleton Carpenter
Lish, G. The lesson which is sufficient unto the day thereof
Lish, G. Two families
Little, J. Wild rabbits
Livesey, M. Obituary
Longyear, B. B. Collector's item
Loukakis, A. Being here now
Lurie, M. Architecture
Lurie, M. Outrageous behaviour
Lurie, M. A partial portrait of my father, his birthdays, my gifts, bottled in bond
Lurie, M. Tell me what you want
MacDonald, D. R. The Chinese rifle
MacDonald, D. R. Sailing
MacLaverty, B. The break
MacLaverty, B. The exercise
MacLaverty, B. Some surrender
MacLaverty, B. Where the tides meet
MacLean, A. The Dileas
MacLeod, A. The lost salt gift of blood
Madden, D. No trace
Makuck, P. Filling the igloo
Malamud, B. Idiots first
Malamud, B. My son the murderer
Martínez-Serros, H. Killdeer
Martone, M. The third day of trials
Mathers, P. Arthur & Alwyn
Matheson, R. The test
Matthews, J. Mange
Matthews, J. The visionary land
Maupassant, G. de. The relics
McGuane, T. The El Western
Meinke, P. The starlings of Leicester Square

FATHERS AND SONS—*Continued*

Mérimée, P. Mateo Falcone
Metcalfe, J. The feasting dead
Mitchell, E. P. An uncommon sort of spectre
Monreal, D. N. Anything is possible
Mooney, M. The mysteries of banking
Moravia, A. Revealing thunder
Morris, M. The lure
Morris, W. The ram in the thicket
Moyer, K. The compass of the heart
Murphy, T. M. The answers they have
Nam, C.-H. Chaos
Nestor, T. G. The mountain top
Nordan, L. Sugar, the eunuchs, and Big G.B.
Nordan, L. The talker at the freak-show
Norris, H. The healing
Norris, L. The kingfisher
Norris, L. Shaving
Nowakowski, M. 2072 days
Nowakowski, M. The distributor
Nowakowski, M. Squad ready for action
O'Brien, D. The inheritance
O'Brien, D. Winter cat
O'Connor, F. The lame shall enter first
O'Connor, F. The drunkard
O'Hara, J. Bread alone
Olson, D. A voice from the leaves
Overholser, W. D. The O'Keefe luck
Ozick, C. The suitcase
Padgett, L. The piper's son
Painter, P. Winter evenings: spring night
Paolucci, A. Lights
Parise, G. Fatherhood
Parkinson, T. L. The father figure
Pascoe, B. The carbide lamp
Pasternak, B. L. Suboctave story
Peña, D. One story too many
Percy, W. The second coming [excerpt]
Peters, S. Spring concert
Petrakis, H. M. Between sleep and death
Petrakis, H. M. A hand for tomorrow
Phippen, S. Step-over toe-hold
Piñera, V. The decoration
Power, V. In the town of Ballymuck
Price, R. The names and faces of heroes
Pritchard, M. Dead finish
Prose, F. Tomatoes
Purdy, J. Dawn
Purdy, J. Short Papa
Quammen, D. Nathan's rime
Quammen, D. Uriah's letter
Quammen, D. Walking out
Ramírez, S. The perfect game
Rees, D. The year of the bulls
Regent, P. The proposal
Rey Rosa, R. Son and father
Rifaat, A. At the time of the jasmine
Ríos, A. Then they'd watch comedies
Rizkalla, J. The dummy in the jeep
Rogers, T. N. R. Rainfall
Rogers, T. N. R. You can do anything
Rosa, J. G. The third bank of the river

Rose, D. A. About the sea
Rose, D. A. Growing things at Bad Luck Pond
Rose, D. A. Katey Foster's two boys
Rose, D. A. Stranger in the house
Rossiter, S. Civil War
Sanders, S. R. Fetching the dead
Sanders, S. R. Walking to sleep
Saroyan, W. Twenty is the greatest time in any man's life
Saunders, C. R. Outsteppin' Fetchit
Scarfe, E. The five o'clock train
Schinto, J. The eel man
Schwartz, J. The last and only messenger
Schwartz, J. The man who knew Cary Grant
Schwartz, J. Over the purple hills
Schwartz, J. Waiting weeping
Shaw, J. B. In high country
Shea, M. Uncle Tuggs
Sheil, G. Mad like Lasseter
Silva, D. B. The turn of time
Simon, B. The birds
Sisskind, M. Twenty questions
Skrzynecki, P. Pick-and-shovel hero
Sonu, H. Thoughts of home
Sorrells, R. T. Charley Billy
Stegner, W. E. The blue-winged teal
Stern, S. Goldfinch & Son
Stern, S. Shimmele fly-by-night
Stern, S. The theft of Lily
Swan, G. Losing game
Taylor, P. H. The gift of the prodigal
Taylor, P. H. Porte Cochere
Taylor, P. H. Promise of rain
Teixeira, K. The last hunt
Tem, S. R. Father's Day
Tem, S. R. Little cruelties
Thompson, J. The stud
Thorman, C. Persecution is for you
Tournier, M. The Adam family
Trujillo, R. The illusionist
Tuohy, F. The license
Updike, J. Still of some use
Vanderhaeghe, G. Cages
Vanderhaeghe, G. The expatriates' party
Vanderhaeghe, G. What I learned from Caesar
Vargas Llosa, M. The challenge
Verma, N. The dead and the dying
Vivante, A. The soft core
Wallin, L. The redneck poacher's son [excerpt]
Weidman, J. My father sits in the dark
Wells, H. G. The magic shop
Wendt, A. The balloonfish and the armadillo
Wendt, A. Exam failure praying
Wetherell, W. D. Volpi's farewell
Wexler, J. Lament for a son
Wheatcroft, J. Hero
Whitaker, M. The end of the queue
Winton, T. A blow, a kiss

FATHERS AND SONS—*Continued*
Winton, T. Gravity
Winton, T. My father's axe
Wolf, S. The legacy of Beau Kremel
Wolfe, G. A cabin on the coast
Wolfe, T. The bell remembered
Wolfe, T. His father's earth
Wolff, T. The liar
Woodman, A. Fathers
Woodrell, D. Woe to live on
Woolrich, C. The corpse and the kid
Wright, D. L. The hawk
Yaryura-Tobías, A. The voyeur
Yi, H. The buckwheat season
Young, S. River house [excerpt]
Zeldis, L. The whore of Babylon
Fathers and sons. Hemingway, E.
The **fathers'** daughters. Spark, M.
Father's Day. Flanagan, R.
Father's day. Rendell, R.
Father's Day. Tem, S. R.
FATHERS-IN-LAW
Flanagan, R. Father's Day
Goyen, W. The white rooster
Grau, S. A. Letting go
Krist, G. Tribes of northern New Jersey
Liu, T.-J. Chrysalis
Ozick, C. The suitcase
Paolucci, A. Buried treasure
Pulaski, J. Father of the bride
Stern, S. Lazar Malkin enters heaven
Tallent, E. The evolution of birds of paradise
Father's last escape. Schulz, B.
The **father's** love. Carpenter, D.
A **father's** love. Strachan, T.
Father's milk is also blood transformed. Dai Houying
A **father's** story. Dubus, A.
A **father's** story. Ford, K.
A **father's** tale. Lanier, S. E.
A **father's** wish. Slater, J.
Fatimas and kisses. O'Hara, J.
Faulkner, William, 1897-1962
As I lay dying
The Mississippi Quarterly 39:369-85 Summ '86
Barn burning
Mississippi writers v1: Fiction; ed. by D. Abbott
A Modern Southern reader; ed. by B. Forkner and P. Samway
A bear hunt
Dark arrows; ed. by A. Manguel
Dry September
The Penguin book of horror stories
Hand upon the waters
Great detectives; ed. by D. W. McCullough
The Saturday Evening Post 257:70-1+ Ja/F '85
Pantaloon in black
Stories of the modern South; ed. by B. Forkner and P. Samway

A portrait of Elmer
The Georgia Review 40:95-124 Spr '86
Necessary fictions; ed. by S. W. Lindberg and S. Corey
Race at morning
The Saturday Evening Post 260:60-5+ N '88
A rose for Emily
The Dark descent; ed. by D. G. Hartwell
Skirmish at Sartoris
A Treasury of Civil War stories; ed. by M. H. Greenberg and B. Pronzini
Smoke
The Penguin classic crime omnibus
That evening sun [Variant title: That evening sun go down]
Mississippi writers v1: Fiction; ed. by D. Abbott
The World of the short story; ed. by C. Fadiman
Thrift
The Nobel reader; ed. by J. Eisen and S. Troy
Turn about
Short stories of the sea; ed. by G. C. Solley and E. Steinbaugh
Was
Look who's talking; ed. by B. Weber
Wash
The Norton book of American short stories
Parodies, travesties, etc.
Nordan, L. The farmers' daughter
Quammen, D. Uriah's letter
Fault lines. Kamenetz, R.
Faust, Frederick, 1892-1944
See also Brand, Max, 1892-1944
Wine on the desert
The Western hall of fame; ed. by B. Pronzini and M. H. Greenberg
Faust, Irvin, 1924-
Bar bar bar
Faust, I. The year of the hot jock, and other stories
Bunny Berigan in the elephants' graveyard
Faust, I. The year of the hot jock, and other stories
The Dalai Lama of Harlem
Faust, I. The year of the hot jock, and other stories
The double snapper
Faust, I. The year of the hot jock, and other stories
Gary Dis-Donc
Faust, I. The year of the hot jock, and other stories
Melanie and the purple people eaters
Faust, I. The year of the hot jock, and other stories
Operation Buena Vista
Faust, I. The year of the hot jock, and other stories

Faust, Irvin, 1924-—*Continued*
Simon Girty go ape
  Faust, I. The year of the hot jock, and
    other stories
The year of the hot jock
  Faust, I. The year of the hot jock, and
    other stories
  Prize stories, 1986
FAUST LEGEND
Bakhnov, V. A remark concerning a little
  something about the devil
Carroll, L. E. Without wings
Cogswell, T. R. Deal with the D.E.V.I.L.
Moravia, A. The devil can't save the
  world
Reynolds, M. The Devil finds work
Wells, H. G. The new Faust
The **fauve**. Humphrey, W.
Faux pas. Tallent, E.
Favor. Tallent, E.
The **favorite**. Apollinaire, G.
The **favour**. Campbell, W. B.
FBI *See* United States. Federal Bureau of
  Investigation
FEAR
Adams, A. Alaska
Atwood, M. When it happens
Bierce, A. A watcher by the dead
Bowles, P. He of the assembly
Boyle, T. C. Two ships
Bradbury, R. The wind
Buzzati, D. A difficult evening
Byatt, A. S. The changeling
Byatt, A. S. In the air
Calvino, I. Fear on the footpath
Conroy, F. Transit
Dahl, R. The wish
Davis, L. The fears of Mrs. Orlando
Dundas, R. As small as your shadow
Eisenstein, S. The Greek smile
Faulkner, W. That evening sun
Feinberg, D. B. The age of anxiety
Feng Jicai. A letter
Ferreira, R. Shark
Greene, G. The end of the party
Hemingway, E. The short happy life of
  Francis Macomber
Hempel, A. In a tub
Jenkins, W. F. Uneasy home-coming
King, S. The monkey
Kress, N. Against a crooked stile
Leedom-Ackerman, J. Death stalks a build-
  ing once it enters
London, J. Good-by, Jack
Maupassant, G. de. The duel
Maupassant, G. de. He?
Maupassant, G. de. Le Horla
Maupassant, G. de. The traveler's story
Moore, G. A strange death
Moravia, A. I've stuttered all my life
Moravia, A. Revealing thunder
Oates, J. C. Ace
Oates, J. C. The stadium

Parise, G. Fear
Phillips, J. A. Blind girls
Poe, E. A. The fall of the House of Usher
Price, R. The names and faces of heroes
Pronzini, B. Under the skin
Sansom, W. The vertical ladder
Schwartz, S. Slow-motion
Thomas, D. In the garden
Timperley, R. Hell on both sides of the
  gate
Updike, J. The wallet
Wells, H. G. The red room
Wharton, E. All Souls'
Wolfe, T. No more rivers
Wood, Mrs. H. The ghost
Wyndham, J. The wheel
Fear. Bingham, S.
Fear. Parise, G.
Fear: four examples. Lish, G.
Fear in the night. Sheckley, R.
Fear of loving. Faik, S.
Fear of math. Cameron, P.
The **fear** of Morgan the Fearless. Brand, M.
Fear of trembling. Van Wert, W. F.
Fear on the footpath. Calvino, I.
Fearful children. Bartlett, B.
Fearful symmetry. Silver, R.
Fears. Collins, L.
The **fears** of Mrs. Orlando. Davis, L.
The **feast** at Paplay. Brown, G. M.
The **feast** of "Flower-Pattern" wine. Ts'ai-
  hua, T.
Feast of John the Baptist. Milán, V.
The **feast** of Saint Janis. Swanwick, M.
The **feast** of St. Dionysus. Silverberg, R.
The **feast** to end all feasts. Drake, M.
The **feasting** dead. Metcalfe, J.
The **feather**. Campos-De Metro, J.
The **feather** pillow. Quiroga, H.
Feathers. Carver, R.
Feathers. Kinsella, W. P.
Feathertop. Hawthorne, N.
Feature presentations. Wilson, R., Jr.
Fecundity. Maupassant, G. de
FEDERAL BUREAU OF INVESTIGATION
  (U.S.) *See* United States. Federal
  Bureau of Investigation
Federici, Carlos M.
In the blink of an eye
  Tales from the planet Earth
'Oh, Lenore!' came the echo
  The Penguin world omnibus of science
  fiction
Federman, Raymond
Report from the World Federation of
  Displaced Writers
  American made; ed. by M. Leyner; C.
  White and T. Glynn
Federspiel, Jürg, 1931-
Death of a foal
  Federspiel, J. An earthquake in my
  family

Federspiel, Jürg, 1931---*Continued*
An earthquake in my family
  Federspiel, J. An earthquake in my family
Hitler's daughter
  Federspiel, J. An earthquake in my family
Infirtaris inoaknoneis
  Federspiel, J. An earthquake in my family
The man who brought happiness
  Federspiel, J. An earthquake in my family
The Monderau chronicle
  Federspiel, J. An earthquake in my family
Oranges on her windowsill
  Federspiel, J. An earthquake in my family
Paratuga will return
  Federspiel, J. An earthquake in my family
The promised village
  Federspiel, J. An earthquake in my family
Prospects for an expedition
  Federspiel, J. An earthquake in my family
The sapper: a romance
  Federspiel, J. An earthquake in my family
The survivor
  Federspiel, J. An earthquake in my family
The Turk
  Federspiel, J. An earthquake in my family
The wasps
  Federspiel, J. An earthquake in my family
The **fedora**. Texier, C.
Feeding the eagles. Alden, P. B.
Feeding time. Gunn, J. E.
The **feel** of the trigger. Westlake, D. E.
Feeling for life. Cooper, J. C.
The **feeling** of power. Asimov, I.
The **feelings** of the dead. Flynn, R.
Feeney, Jessie
A married woman
  Women's work; ed. by M. McLeod and L. Wevers
Feet foremost. Hartley, L. P.
Feet of clay. Regent, P.
Fein, Naomi
Rituals
  Chicago Review 34 no4:54-5 '85
Fein, Yvonne
Rumkowsky was right
  Echad 4: Jewish writing from down under: Australia and New Zealand
Feinberg, David B.
The age of anxiety
  Men on men 2; ed. by G. Stambolian

Feint of heart. Proulx, M.
Feldman and Goldman, barbers. Sanders, B.
Felicity. Crampsey, R. A.
A **feline** felony. Littke, L.
Felipa. Woolson, C. F.
The **fellmonger**. Jolley, E.
Fellow-creatures. Morris, W.
The **fellow** passenger. Jolley, E.
Fellow passengers. Burt, S.
FEMINISM
Asimov, I. Middle name
Cary, J. New women
Cooper, J. C. Liberated
Desy, J. The princess who stood on her own two feet
Gilman, C. P. The yellow wallpaper
Lee, T. Prince Amilec
Oosthuizen, A. A fine romance
Russ, J. Old thoughts, old presences: Daddy's girl
Scott, G. Car wrecks and bleeding hearts
Walker, A. Coming apart
Williams, J. Petronella
Wilson, B. Sense and sensitivity
The **feminist**. Wong, S. H.
Fen Hall. Rendell, R.
The **fence**. Cowan, P.
The **fence** party. Tallent, E.
Feng, Chi-ts'ai *See* Feng Jicai
Feng Jicai
Chrysanthemums
  Feng Jicai. Chrysanthemums, and other stories
The hornets' nest
  Feng Jicai. Chrysanthemums, and other stories
A letter
  Feng Jicai. Chrysanthemums, and other stories
The Mao button
  Feng Jicai. Chrysanthemums, and other stories
Nectar
  Feng Jicai. Chrysanthemums, and other stories
Numbskull
  Feng Jicai. Chrysanthemums, and other stories
Plum blossoms in the snow
  Feng Jicai. Chrysanthemums, and other stories
The street-sweeping show
  Feng Jicai. Chrysanthemums, and other stories
The tall woman and her short husband
  Short story international 70
Winding brook way
  Feng Jicai. Chrysanthemums, and other stories
Fengriffen. Case, D.
"La Fenice". Colette
Fenneca. Belden, W. S.
Fenner. Lurie, M.

Fenstad's mother. Baxter, C.
Fenton, Edward, 1917-
 Gun-shy
  Roger Caras' Treasury of great dog
  stories
FERAL CHILDREN *See* Wild children
Ferber, Edna, 1887-1968
 No room at the inn
  "May your days be merry and bright"
  and other Christmas stories by wom-
  en; ed. by S. Koppelman
Ferguson, Jean, 1940-
 Ker, the god killer
  Invisible fictions; ed. by G. Hancock
Ferguson, Neil, 1947-
 The Monroe Doctrine
  Interzone: the first anthology; ed. by J.
  Clute; C. Greenland and D. Pringle
 The second third of C
  Interzone: the 2nd anthology; ed. by J.
  Clute; D. Pringle and S. Ounsley
Ferguson, Patricia
 The dry familiar plains
  Ferguson, P. Indefinite nights, and other
  stories
 Indefinite nights
  Ferguson, P. Indefinite nights, and other
  stories
 Inside knowledge
  Ferguson, P. Indefinite nights, and other
  stories
 Patrick
  Ferguson, P. Indefinite nights, and other
  stories
 The products of conception
  Ferguson, P. Indefinite nights, and other
  stories
 The quality of mercy
  Ferguson, P. Indefinite nights, and other
  stories
 Sister Hilary
  Ferguson, P. Indefinite nights, and other
  stories
Ferguson, William, 1943-
 The claims adjuster
  Ferguson, W. Freedom, and other fic-
  tions
 Cortez
  Ferguson, W. Freedom, and other fic-
  tions
 Dies irae
  Ferguson, W. Freedom, and other fic-
  tions
 The family
  Ferguson, W. Freedom, and other fic-
  tions
 Freedom
  Ferguson, W. Freedom, and other fic-
  tions
 Morrissey
  Ferguson, W. Freedom, and other fic-
  tions

 Scherzo with TV antenna
  Ferguson, W. Freedom, and other fic-
  tions
 Space Invaders
  Ferguson, W. Freedom, and other fic-
  tions
 A summer at Estabrook
  Ferguson, W. Freedom, and other fic-
  tions
 The teacher
  Ferguson, W. Freedom, and other fic-
  tions
 Terror
  Ferguson, W. Freedom, and other fic-
  tions
 The third voice
  Ferguson, W. Freedom, and other fic-
  tions
  Harper's 268:28-9 Ap '84
Fermi and frost. Pohl, F.
Fernando, Chitra
 The bird of paradise
  Short story international 71
 Of bread and power
  Short story international 59
Ferndale fights the flies. Heise, K.
Ferndale fireworks. Heise, K.
Ferrandino, Joseph, 1948-
 Ten cents a dance
  The New generation; ed. by A. Kaufman
  The Southern Review (Baton Rouge, La.)
  23:164-76 Ja '87
Ferrara, Patricia
 Rising waters
  The Best horror stories from the
  Magazine of fantasy and science fiction
Ferrari, Hugo
 Old Ramón and the devil
  Américas 40:50-2 N/D '88
The **Ferrari**. Michaelson, L. W.
Ferrars, E. X., 1907-
  *For works written by this author under
  other names see* Ferrars, Elizabeth,
  1907-
 A very small clue
  Ellery Queen's Crimes and punishments
Ferrars, Elizabeth, 1907-
  *For works written by this author under
  other names see* Ferrars, E. X.,
  1907-
 Instrument of justice
  The Mammoth book of modern crime
  stories; ed. by G. Hardinge
Ferré, Rosario
 The glass box
  The Massachusetts Review 27:699-711
  Fall/Wint '86
 Pico Rico, mandorico
  Reclaiming Medusa; ed. by D. L. Vélez
 Sleeping beauty
  Reclaiming Medusa; ed. by D. L. Vélez
 The youngest doll
  Reclaiming Medusa; ed. by D. L. Vélez

Ferreira, Ramón
Bagasse
  Ferreira, R. The gravedigger, and other
  stories
A color for that fear
  Ferreira, R. The gravedigger, and other
  stories
A date at nine
  Ferreira, R. The gravedigger, and other
  stories
Dream with no name
  Ferreira, R. The gravedigger, and other
  stories
Facade
  Ferreira, R. The gravedigger, and other
  stories
The gold chain
  Ferreira, R. The gravedigger, and other
  stories
The gravedigger
  Ferreira, R. The gravedigger, and other
  stories
The hands of God
  Ferreira, R. The gravedigger, and other
  stories
Juan de Dios
  Ferreira, R. The gravedigger, and other
  stories
No one looks out anymore
  Ferreira, R. The gravedigger, and other
  stories
A road somewhere
  Ferreira, R. The gravedigger, and other
  stories
Shark
  Ferreira, R. The gravedigger, and other
  stories
Twilight hunt
  Ferreira, R. The gravedigger, and other
  stories
The well
  Ferreira, R. The gravedigger, and other
  stories
Ferreira, Rick
Are you stone-cold, Santa Claus?
  Short story international 59
Did you say—Dad?
  Short story international 50
Guest for the weekend
  Short story international 42
Ferrell, Anderson
Why people get cancer
  Men on men 2; ed. by G. Stambolian
FERRETS
Highsmith, P. Harry: a ferret
Saki. Sredni Vashtar
Ferriss, Lucy, 1954-
Surfacing
  The Southern Review (Baton Rouge, La.)
  23:879-87 Aut '87

Ferro, Robert, 1941-1988
Frank's party
  First love/last love; ed. by M. Denneny;
  C. Ortleb and T. Steele
Second son [excerpt]
  Men on men; ed. by G. Stambolian
Ferron, Jacques
The archangel of the suburb
  Ferron, J. Selected tales of Jacques Fer-
  ron
Armageddon
  Ferron, J. Selected tales of Jacques Fer-
  ron
Back to Kentucky
  Ferron, J. Selected tales of Jacques Fer-
  ron
Back to Val-d'Or
  Ferron, J. Selected tales of Jacques Fer-
  ron
Black cargo ships of war
  Ferron, J. Selected tales of Jacques Fer-
  ron
The bridge
  Ferron, J. Selected tales of Jacques Fer-
  ron
The Buddhist
  Ferron, J. Selected tales of Jacques Fer-
  ron
Cadieu
  Ferron, J. Selected tales of Jacques Fer-
  ron
The child
  Ferron, J. Selected tales of Jacques Fer-
  ron
Chronicle of Anse Saint-Roch
  Ferron, J. Selected tales of Jacques Fer-
  ron
The dead cow in the canyon
  Ferron, J. Selected tales of Jacques Fer-
  ron
  Invisible fictions; ed. by G. Hancock
The flood
  Ferron, J. Selected tales of Jacques Fer-
  ron
The grey dog
  Ferron, J. Selected tales of Jacques Fer-
  ron
How the old man died
  Ferron, J. Selected tales of Jacques Fer-
  ron
The jailer's son
  Ferron, J. Selected tales of Jacques Fer-
  ron
The lady from Ferme-Neuve
  Ferron, J. Selected tales of Jacques Fer-
  ron
The landscape painter
  Ferron, J. Selected tales of Jacques Fer-
  ron
Little Red Riding Hood
  Ferron, J. Selected tales of Jacques Fer-
  ron

Ferron, Jacques—*Continued*
Martine
Ferron, J. Selected tales of Jacques Ferron
Martine continued
Ferron, J. Selected tales of Jacques Ferron
Les Méchins
Ferron, J. Selected tales of Jacques Ferron
Mélie and the bull
Ferron, J. Selected tales of Jacques Ferron
The Oxford book of French-Canadian short stories
La Mi-Carême
Ferron, J. Selected tales of Jacques Ferron
The old heathen
Ferron, J. Selected tales of Jacques Ferron
The parakeet
Ferron, J. Selected tales of Jacques Ferron
The parrot
Ferron, J. Selected tales of Jacques Ferron
The pigeon and the parakeet
Ferron, J. Selected tales of Jacques Ferron
The provinces
Ferron, J. Selected tales of Jacques Ferron
The sea-lion
Ferron, J. Selected tales of Jacques Ferron
Servitude
Ferron, J. Selected tales of Jacques Ferron
The Sirens
Ferron, J. Selected tales of Jacques Ferron
Summer Lethe
Ferron, J. Selected tales of Jacques Ferron
Tiresome company
Ferron, J. Selected tales of Jacques Ferron
Ulysses
Ferron, J. Selected tales of Jacques Ferron
The wedding bouquet
Ferron, J. Selected tales of Jacques Ferron
The woman next door
Ferron, J. Selected tales of Jacques Ferron
The wool nightshirt and the horsehair tunic
Ferron, J. Selected tales of Jacques Ferron

Ferron, Madeleine, 1922-
The weaker sex
Invisible fictions; ed. by G. Hancock
Fertility doll. Tucker, E.
Festival. McCormack, E. P.
Festival night. Pavese, C.
A **festival** of parrots. Levine, D. M.
The **Festival** of the Dead. King, F. H.
FESTIVALS
Gardner, M. Old man gloom
Hawthorne, N. The May-Pole of Merry Mount
O'Connor, F. The Partridge festival
Valenzuela, L. The door
Festivities by the river. Kaikō, T.
The **fetch.** Aickman, R.
Fetching the dead. Sanders, S. R.
The **fetid** tale of Antulín. Sorrentino, F.
The **fetishist.** Tournier, M.
Fetler, Andrew
The third count
Prize stories, 1984
Fetler, James
The dust of Yuri Serafimovich
Full measure; ed. by D. Sennett
Fetters. Warren, J.
FETUS
See also Pregnancy
Halligan, M. Mozart is best
Zahn, T. The final report on the lifeline experiment
FETUS, DEATH OF THE
Bishop, M. Within the walls of Tyre
The **feud.** Webster, C.
FEUDS
Aćin-Kosta, M. The red bread
Bradley, M. Z. Bird of prey
Conroy, J. Uncle Ollie's spite fence
Frazee, S. The Bretnall feud
Kuttner, H., and Moore, C. L. Or else
MacLeod, A. Vision
Stuart, J. Land of our enemies
Trollope, A. Malachi's Cove
Webster, C. The feud
Wells, H. G. The moth
Feuer, Elizabeth
Cat dance
The Literary Review (Madison, N.J.) 31:35-8 Fall '87
Fever, Buck *See* Anderson, Sherwood, 1876-1941
FEVER
West, J. 99.6
Fever. Carver, R.
Fever. Dumas, H.
Fever in the South. Sanford, W. M.
A **fever** of dying. Madden, D.
The **fever** tree. Rendell, R.
A **few** beers. Piñera, V.
A **few** children. Piñera, V.
A **few** moments of sleeping and waking. Barthelme, D.

A **few** problems in the Day Case Unit. Hammick, G.
A **few** selected sentences. Johnson, B. S.
A **few** things wrong with me. Davis, L.
Feyrer, Gayle
  The House of the Twin Jewels
    Erotic interludes; ed. by L. Barbach
Fialkowski, Konrad
  A perfect Christmas evening
    The Penguin world omnibus of science fiction
The **fiancée**. Chekhov, A. P.
A **Fickleman** jogs. McKinley, J.
Fiction, fact and dream. See Steele, M. Where she brushed her hair
FICTITIOUS ANIMALS See Mythical animals
Fiddle and bow. Taylor, R.
The **fiddler**. Melville, H.
The **fiddler**. Taylor, R.
The **fiddler** and the Angelito. Chavez, A.
Fiddler fair. Lackey, M.
FIDDLERS See Violinists
Fiddling for water buffaloes. Sucharitkul, S.
Fidelity savings. Mooney, M.
Field, Ben
  Three sisters
    A Good deal; ed. by M. Heath and F. M. Robinson
Field, Isabel
  Hungry lion
    Alfred Hitchcock's Mortal errors
The **field**. Holden, M.
FIELD GLASSES
  Sheckley, R. Is that what people do?
Field guide to the western birds. Stegner, W. E.
A **field** in space. Davie, E.
The **field** is full of daisies and I'm afraid to pass. Brady, M.
Field of blue children. Williams, T.
The **field** of Philippi. Hornung, E. W.
The **fields**. Bethel, J. D.
The **fields** at dusk. Salter, J.
The **fields** of golden glow. Conroy, J.
The **fifth** day. Matthiessen, P.
The **fifth** generation. Kay, H.
The **fifth** grave. Ritchie, J.
The **fifth** letter. Bedard, B.
The **fifth** on the left. Bakhnov, V.
The **fifth** story. Lispector, C.
Fifty-eight cents. Paynter, J.
A **fifty-fifty** marriage. See Abbott, K. A 50-50 marriage
Fifty grand. Hemingway, E.
Fifty-seven views of Fujiyama. Davenport, G.
Fifty years of eternal vigilance. Boras, H.
Fifty years of eternal vigilance. Thorman, C.
The **fight**. Crane, S.
The **fight**. Nabokov, V. V.
The **fight**. Thomas, D.

A **fight** between a white boy and a black boy in the dusk of a fall afternoon in Omaha, Nebraska. Morris, W.
Fight number twenty-five. Stuart, J.
FIGHTING, COCK See Cockfighting
FIGHTING, DOG See Dogfighting
FIGHTING, HAND-TO-HAND See Hand-to-hand fighting
Fighting crickets. Nhuong, H. Q.
Fighting for peace. Houbein, L.
Fighting for the rebound. Mukherjee, B.
Fighting Philosopher. Cole, E. B.
Fighting the "tiger" and other speculations. Hooper, J. J.
Figueredo, D. H.
  Tell the night
    Short story international 44
The **figure** in the carpet. James, H.
A **figure** of speech. See Gallagher, T. King Death
Figure over the town. Goyen, W.
FIGURINES See Art objects
FIJI
  Drake, M. The feast to end all feasts
FIJI ISLANDS See Fiji
Filbert. Faik, S.
Fili. Goldman, F.
FILIPINOS
United States
  Dibble, J. B. To sleep, perchance to dream
  Fante, J. The dreamer
  Fante, J. Helen, thy beauty is to me—
  Mukherjee, B. Fighting for the rebound
  Wolff, T. Our story begins
Filippi, Carmen Lugo
  Milagros, on Mercurio Street
    Reclaiming Medusa; ed. by D. L. Vélez
  Pilar, your curls
    Reclaiming Medusa; ed. by D. L. Vélez
Filling the igloo. Makuck, P.
The **film**. Barthelme, D.
Film. Essop, A.
Film at eleven. Ashwood-Collins, A.
Film at eleven. Skipp, J.
Filmer. Wells, H. G.
The **films** of R. Nixon. Bernard, K.
Filthy the man. Flaherty, G.
Fin de siècle. Oates, J. C.
The **finagle** fiasco. Sakers, D.
Final exam. Boylan, J.
A **final** fling. Gifkins, M.
Final marks, final secrets. DuBois, B.
Final mission. Bouma, J. L.
Final performance. Bloch, R.
The **final** problem. Doyle, Sir A. C.
The **final** proof of fate and circumstance. Abbott, L. K.
The **final** report on the lifeline experiment. Zahn, T.
The **final** solution. Blyton, C.
The **final** stone. Nolan, W. F.
The **final** toast. Kaminsky, S. M.
Final touches. O'Brien, D.

Final tribute. Reed, K.
The **final** truth. Ritchie, J.
Final version. Morressy, J.
Final words. Claiborne, S.
FINANCE
    See also Banks; Taxation
  Sams, F. The widow's mite
FINANCIERS *See* Capitalists and financiers
Finch, Sheila
  Reichs-peace
    Hitler victorious; ed. by G. Benford and
      M. H. Greenberg
The **find**. Colette
Find the lady. Fisk, N.
Finder. Hensley, J. L.
Finder. Skelton, R.
The **finder**. Spencer, E.
Finders and losers. Davin, D.
Finding a girl in America. Dubus, A.
Finding Florida. Broun, H.
The **finding** of the Graiken. Hodgson, W. H.
Finding the chain. Hood, M.
Findley, Timothy
  Dinner along the Amazon
    The Oxford book of Canadian short
      stories in English
A **fine** beginning. See Thomas, D. Adven-
  tures in the skin trade: A fine begin-
  ning
Fine points. Lee, A.
A **fine** romance. Oosthuizen, A.
A **fine** summer's day. Blyton, C.
A **fine** zoo day. Stone, A.
Fineman, Morton
  An affair of heart
    Good Housekeeping 202:162-3+ Mr '86
Fines, Beatrice
  Neighbors
    Short story international 58
Finger, Anne
  Abortion
    Finger, A. Basic skills
  Basic skills
    Finger, A. Basic skills
  Cars
    Finger, A. Basic skills
  Cross-country
    Finger, A. Basic skills
  Like the Hully-Gully but not so slow
    Finger, A. Basic skills
  Old maids
    Finger, A. Basic skills
  A tragedy
    Finger, A. Basic skills
Finger, Charles J.
  Eric
    Arkansas in short fiction; ed. by W. M.
      Baker and E. C. Simpson
Finger exercise. Ritchie, J.
The **finger** of fate. Gilbert, W. S.
The **finger** of stone. Chesterton, G. K.
The **finger** of suspicion. Wilmot, T.
Finger wet, finger dry. Bates, H. E.

FINGERPRINTS
  Harris, H. The doctor afraid of blood
  Mortimer, J. C. Rumpole and the learned
    friends
FINGERS
  Dahl, R. Man from the south
Fingers in the door. Tuohy, F.
Fingers of fear. Davis, F. C.
Fink, Ida
  Aryan papers
    Fink, I. A scrap of time, and other
      stories
  Behind the hedge
    Fink, I. A scrap of time, and other
      stories
  The black beast
    Fink, I. A scrap of time, and other
      stories
  A conversation
    Fink, I. A scrap of time, and other
      stories
  Crazy
    Fink, I. A scrap of time, and other
      stories
  A dog
    Fink, I. A scrap of time, and other
      stories
  The garden that floated away
    Fink, I. A scrap of time, and other
      stories
  Inspector von Galoshinsky
    Fink, I. A scrap of time, and other
      stories
  Jean-Christophe
    Fink, I. A scrap of time, and other
      stories
  Jump!
    Fink, I. A scrap of time, and other
      stories
  The key game
    Fink, I. A scrap of time, and other
      stories
  Night of surrender
    Fink, I. A scrap of time, and other
      stories
  The other shore
    Fink, I. A scrap of time, and other
      stories
  The pig
    Fink, I. A scrap of time, and other
      stories
  A scrap of time
    Fink, I. A scrap of time, and other
      stories
    The New Yorker 63:32-4 My 25 '87
  The shelter
    Fink, I. A scrap of time, and other
      stories
  Splinter
    Fink, I. A scrap of time, and other
      stories

Fink, Ida—*Continued*
A spring morning
    Fink, I. A scrap of time, and other
      stories
The tenth man
    Fink, I. A scrap of time, and other
      stories
Titina
    Fink, I. A scrap of time, and other
      stories
Traces
    Fink, I. A scrap of time, and other
      stories
Finkelstein, Mark Harris *See* Harris, Mark,
    1922-
FINLAND
Helsinki
Martin, G. R. R. Under siege
Finlandia. Grzimek, M.
Finney, Ernest J.
The all-American's wife
    Finney, E. J. Birds landing
Bed of roses
    Finney, E. J. Birds landing
Birds landing
    Finney, E. J. Birds landing
The divine dealer
    Finney, E. J. Birds landing
The investigator
    Finney, E. J. Birds landing
Lot no. 17
    Finney, E. J. Birds landing
Night life
    Finney, E. J. Birds landing
Nights and days
    Finney, E. J. Birds landing
    New American short stories; ed. by G.
      Norris
    The Sewanee Review 92:512-27 Fall '84
Peacocks
    The Sewanee Review 96:1-34 Wint '88
Talus
    The Kenyon Review ns9:105-15 Summ
      '87
Finney, Jack
The coin collector
    Finney, J. About time
The face in the photo
    Finney, J. About time
Hey, look at me!
    Finney, J. About time
Home alone
    Finney, J. About time
I love Galesburg in the springtime
    Finney, J. About time
I'm scared
    Finney, J. About time
The love letter
    The Saturday Evening Post 260:44-7+
      Ja/F '88
Lunch-hour magic
    Finney, J. About time

Of missing persons
    Finney, J. About time
Second chance
    Finney, J. About time
Such interesting neighbors
    Finney, J. About time
The third level
    Finney, J. About time
    Spirits, spooks, and other sinister crea-
      tures; ed. by H. Hoke
Where the Cluetts are
    Finney, J. About time
    Haunted New England; ed. by C. G.
      Waugh; M. H. Greenberg and F. D.
      McSherry
FINNS
United States
Cummings, R. Berrying
Fiona. Morris, W.
Fiona's rooms. Deaver, P. F.
Fioretta. Vivante, A.
The **fire**. Crane, S.
Fire. Cunningham, J.
The **fire**. Dickinson, C.
The **fire**. Hull, H. R.
Fire. Hyon, C.-G.
The **fire**. Meckel, C.
Fire. Saroyan, W.
Fire. Tung, N.
Fire and water. Grin, A.
Fire ants. Duff, G.
Fire blight. Kornblatt, J. R.
Fire by night. Fisher, R.
Fire catcher. Kadrey, R.
Fire dreams. Thompson, J.
Fire drill. Glover, D. H.
The **fire** eater. Fitzgerald, M. J.
Fire enough for you. Farris, J.
Fire escape. Woolrich, C.
A **fire** in the box that could truly light the
      world. Keisling, W.
The **fire** in the wood. Welch, D.
Fire is burning on our street! Granit, A.
Fire Island. Roberts, N.
The **fire** killer. Frazee, S.
The **fire** on the other side of the glass. Hut-
      nik, I.
The **fire-pump** test. Heinesen, W.
Fire watch. Willis, C.
The **fire** woman. Sanders, S. R.
FIREARMS
Benson, R. H. The watcher
Cushman, D. I.O.U.—one bullet
Daniels, C. Me and Deke
DeMarinis, R. The handgun
Gant, P. The revolver
Kessler, J. F. Teiresias
Moravia, A. That damned gun
Piper, H. B. Gunpowder god
Shaw, I. Act of faith
Wright, R. Almos' a man
Wright, R. The man who was almost a
      man

The **firebrands**. Schwob, M.
FIREFIGHTERS
 Cassity, K. The age-old problem of who
 Heinesen, W. The fire-pump test
Fireflies. Ota, Y.
The **fireplace**. Whitehead, H. S. C.
FIRES
  See also Arson; Disasters
 Ade, G. The Alfalfa European Hotel
 Anderman, J. The National Theatre's burn-
  ing down
 Berry, R. M. November 14, 1864
 Bracken, M. Of memories dying
 Brown, M. W. Tongues of flame
 Chesterton, G. K. Culture and the light
 Crane, S. The fire
 Crane, S. Manacled
 Crane, S. The monster
 Crane, S. The veteran
 Dickinson, C. The fire
 Doyle, Sir A. C. Gentlemanly Joe
 Engberg, S. Riffraff
 Fisher, M. F. K. A delayed meeting
 Freeman, J. Clearfield
 Grin, A. Fire and water
 Gu Hua. The log cabin overgrown with
  creepers
 Hempel, A. Pool Night
 Kilgore, D. Three alarm fire
 London, J. To build a fire
 Morrison, J. Bushfire
 Morrison, J. The children
 Morrison, J. This freedom
 Ocampo, S. Voice on the telephone
 O'Connor, F. A circle in the fire
 Rule, J. Power failure
 Sanford, W. M. The forest fire
 Saroyan, W. Fire
 Singer, I. B. Henne Fire
 Waldrop, H. ". . . the world, as we
  know't."
 Watson, I. Flame and the healer
 Welty, E. The burning
FIRES (AT SEA)
 Conrad, J. Youth
Firewood. Banks, R.
Firework night isn't in it. Sproat, R.
FIREWORKS
 Heise, K. Ferndale fireworks
Fireworks. Ford, R.
Fireworks. Vinz, M.
Firm ground. Bernard, K.
The **first** baseman. Curley, D.
The **first** city. Whelan, G.
The **first** class passenger. Bioy Casares, A.
First Communion. Fante, J.
The **first** crime of Ruby Martinson. Slesar,
 H.
First dark. Spencer, E.
First date. Drake, R.
First date. Honig, D.
First day. Stevenson, M. M.
The **first** day. Vesity, A.

The **first** day of spring. Knoles, D.
First do no harm. Broxon, M. D.
The **first** election. Kim, Y. I.
A **first** encounter of the marital kind.
 Padayachee, D.
The **first** good-bye. Horan, H.
First I look at the purse. McKnight, R.
First impressions. Updike, D.
The **first** kill. Robinson, M. A.
The **first** law of classical mechanics. Cullen,
 E. J.
First letter from a reader. Faik, S.
First light. Whelan, G.
The **first** locked room. De la Torre, L.
First love. Beckett, S.
First love. Cantwell, M.
First love. Day, R. C.
First love. Givner, J.
First love. Nabokov, V. V.
First love. Pavese, C.
First love. Welty, E.
First love/last love. Rule, J.
First love, last rites. McEwan, I.
The **first** lover. Boyle, K.
First Manhattans. Gilchrist, E.
The **first** move. Shyer, M. F.
First night. London, J.
First notch. Barker, E.
The **first** portrait. Szell, T.
First principles. Patton, F. G.
The **first** robin in the world. Bonosky, P.
First sight. Cullen, E. J.
First sight. Gould, J.
First snow. Cook, H.
The **first** snowfall. Maupassant, G. de
The **first** thing coming. Abbott, K.
First time. Garber, L. J.
First union blues. McCorkle, J.
The **first** weekend. Lewis, S. E.
The **first** woman who understood me. Nesin,
 A.
First worry. Asscher-Pinkhof, C.
The **first** year. Drake, R.
The **first** year of my life. Spark, M.

Fischer, Curtis E.

 Indian poker
  A Matter of crime v2
Fischer's mirror. Haley, R.

Fish, Robert L., 1912-

 Muldoon and the numbers game
  Murder and mystery in Boston; ed. by
   C. L. R. Waugh; F. D. McSherry and
   M. H. Greenberg

 The wager
  Ellery Queen's Crimes and punishments
The **fish**. Banks, R.
Fish heads. Taylor, A.
Fish scales. Shibusawa, T.
A **fish** story. Chesterton, G. K.
Fish story. Hamilton, D.
Fish story. Lish, G.

FISH TRADE
Ross, M., and Somerville, E. A. Œ. Poisson d'Avril
West, J. A little collar for the monkey
The **fish** trap. Pirandello, L.
Fishbein's fast. Klein, E.
Fisher, Clay
For works by this author under other names see Henry, Will, 1912-
Fisher, Clay, 1912-
Isley's stranger
The Western hall of fame; ed. by B. Pronzini and M. H. Greenberg
Fisher, Dorothy Canfield, 1879-1958
As ye sow—
"May your days be merry and bright" and other Christmas stories by women; ed. by S. Koppelman
Fisher, Lou
Overnight
Shadows 9
Fisher, M. F. K. (Mary Frances Kennedy), 1908-
Another love story
Fisher, M. F. K. Sister age
Answer in the affirmative
Fisher, M. F. K. Sister age
A delayed meeting
Fisher, M. F. K. Sister age
Diplomatic, retired
Fisher, M. F. K. Sister age
A kitchen allegory
Fisher, M. F. K. Sister age
The lost, strayed, stolen
Fisher, M. F. K. Sister age
Moment of wisdom
Fisher, M. F. K. Sister age
Mrs. Teeters' tomato jar
Fisher, M. F. K. Sister age
Notes on a necessary pact
Fisher, M. F. K. Sister age
The oldest man
Fisher, M. F. K. Sister age
A question answered
Fisher, M. F. K. Sister age
The reunion
Fisher, M. F. K. Sister age
The second time around
Fisher, M. F. K. Sister age
The unswept emptiness
Fisher, M. F. K. Sister age
The weather within
Fisher, M. F. K. Sister age
Fisher, Mary Frances Kennedy *See* Fisher, M. F. K. (Mary Frances Kennedy), 1908-
Fisher, Peggy Wurtz
The pickup
The Year's best mystery and suspense stories, 1985

Fisher, Rudolph, 1897-1934
The backslider
Fisher, R. The city of refuge
Fisher, R. The short fiction of Rudolph Fisher
Blades of steel
Fisher, R. The city of refuge
Fisher, R. The short fiction of Rudolph Fisher
The city of refuge
Fisher, R. The city of refuge
Fisher, R. The short fiction of Rudolph Fisher
Common meter
Fisher, R. The city of refuge
Fisher, R. The short fiction of Rudolph Fisher
Dust
Fisher, R. The city of refuge
Fisher, R. The short fiction of Rudolph Fisher
Ezekiel
Fisher, R. The city of refuge
Fisher, R. The short fiction of Rudolph Fisher
Ezekiel learns
Fisher, R. The city of refuge
Fisher, R. The short fiction of Rudolph Fisher
Fire by night
Fisher, R. The city of refuge
Fisher, R. The short fiction of Rudolph Fisher
Guardian of the law
Fisher, R. The city of refuge
Fisher, R. The short fiction of Rudolph Fisher
High yaller
Fisher, R. The city of refuge
Fisher, R. The short fiction of Rudolph Fisher
John Archer's nose
Fisher, R. The city of refuge
Fisher, R. The short fiction of Rudolph Fisher
Miss Cynthie
Fisher, R. The city of refuge
Fisher, R. The short fiction of Rudolph Fisher
The promised land
Fisher, R. The city of refuge
Fisher, R. The short fiction of Rudolph Fisher
Ringtail
Fisher, R. The city of refuge
Fisher, R. The short fiction of Rudolph Fisher
The South lingers on
Fisher, R. The city of refuge
Fisher, R. The short fiction of Rudolph Fisher
FISHERIES
Nagibin, IÛ. M. By a quiet lake

The **fisherman**. Saiki, J.
The **fisherman**. Winters, J.
The **fisherman** and his soul. Wilde, O.
The **fisherman** from Chihuahua. Connell, E.
    S.
FISHERMEN
    See also Fishing
Blyton, C. A fine summer's day
Böll, H. Anecdote concerning the lowering
    of productivity
Boyle, T. C. Caviar
Brown, G. M. The box of fish
Carver, R. So much water so close to
    home
Covino, M. Little by little they come back
    for you
Crane, S. A fishing village
Crane, S. The octopush
Curley, D. Reflections in the ice
Deng Gang. A big fish
Faik, S. A dot on the map
Faik, S. An episode of two
Faik, S. King Mike
Faik, S. Sivriada nights
Faik, S. The Stelyanos Hrisopulos
Gorky, M. Going home
Hamilton, D. Fish story
Hannah, B. Getting ready
Heinesen, W. The fall
Herbert, F. Seed stock
Hulme, K. The knife and the stone
Jahnn, H. H. Ragna and Nils
Kaikō, T. Building a shell mound
Kaikō, T. The fishing hole (Ana)
Lesley, C. The catch
MacDonald, D. R. The flowers of Ber-
    muda
MacLeod, A. The lost salt gift of blood
Matthiessen, P. On the River Styx
Maupassant, G. de. At sea
Maupassant, G. de. Selfishness
Maupassant, G. de. The victim
Misitano, R. A. Deep water
Onopa, R. The man who swam through
    jellyfish, through men-of-war
Poe, E. A. A descent into the maelström
Pronzini, B. Deathwatch
Pronzini, B. Smuggler's Island
Proulx, A. The wer-trout
Rölvaag, O. E. When the wind is in the
    south
Ross, V. Whistling
Schinto, J. The eel man
Schwartz, S. In Alaska
Schwob, M. The amber-trader
Shacochis, B. Hunger
Shacochis, B. Mundo's sign
Thériault, Y. The whale
Thomas, A. C. Kill day on the govern-
    ment wharf
Valenzuela, L. Trial of the Virgin
Vogan, S. Hearts of a shark
Wilde, O. The fisherman and his soul

The **fishermen**. See Crane, S. The octopush
Fishermen. Dunn, D.
FISHES
    See also Aquariums
Banks, R. The fish
Chesterton, G. K. A fish story
Hogan, L. Amen
Li, F.-Y. The carp
Michaelson, L. W. The goldfish
Plomer, W. When the sardines came
Rodoreda, M. The river and the boat
Slayter, E. The silver fish
Fishes, birds and sons of men. Ford, J. H.
Fishhead. Cobb, I. S.
FISHING
    See also Fishermen; Pearl fishing;
    Salmon fishing
Ade, G. Olof Lindstrom goes fishing
Benton, K. C. Cast for murder
Blythe, R. The right day to kill a pike
Calvino, I. Big fish, little fish
Carver, R. Nobody said anything
Coover, R. Quenby and Ola, Swede and
    Carl
Daniels, C. Radio Smith
Davidson, L. Indian rope trick
Deng Gang. The dragon king's troops
    thunder past
Douglas, E. On the lake
Dunn, D. Fishermen
Ford, R. Winterkill
Frahm, L. On the turn
Friel, B. The gold in the sea
Gordon, C. Old Red
Grace, P. Kahawai
Hall, T. T. Wet Stump
Hemingway, E. Big two-hearted river: part
    I
Hemingway, E. Big two-hearted river: part
    II
Hemingway, E. The end of something
Hemingway, E. The last good country
Hemingway, E. Out of season
Hulme, K. King bait
Li Hangyu. The last angler
MacLeod, A. The boat
MacLeod, A. The road to Rankin's Point
MacLeod, A. Vision
Makuck, P. Filling the igloo
Maupassant, G. de. The hole
McKinley, J. Ozark episode
Nagibin, IŪ. M. The night guest
O'Brien, D. The inheritance
Peterson, M. Coming about
Shacochis, B. The heart's advantage
Tuohy, F. Live bait
Waldrop, H. God's hooks!
Welty, E. The wide net
Wetherell, W. D. The bass, the river, and
    Sheila Mant
Fishing. Grace, P.
Fishing. Hankla, C.
Fishing. Robinson, M. A.

The **fishing-boat** picture. Sillitoe, A.

A **fishing** excursion. Maupassant, G. de

The **fishing** hole (Ana). Kaikō, T.

Fishing season. Sheckley, R.

A **fishing** village. Crane, S.

The **fishing** village of Roebush. Horvitz, L. A.

Fishy waters. Rhys, J.

Fisk, Nicholas, 1923-
  Find the lady
    Worlds apart; ed. by C. Decarnin; E. Garber and L. Paleo

Fit for felony. Maddren, G.

Fitch, Marina
  They that go down to the sea in ships
    L. Ron Hubbard presents Writers of the future v2

Fits. Munro, A.

Fitzgerald, F. Scott (Francis Scott), 1896-1940
  An alcoholic case
    Inspired by drink; ed. by Joan Digby and John Digby
  Babylon, revisited
    The World of the short story; ed. by C. Fadiman
  The bridal party
    The Norton book of American short stories
  The night before Chancellorsville
    A Treasury of Civil War stories; ed. by M. H. Greenberg and B. Pronzini
  The rough crossing
    Short stories of the sea; ed. by G. C. Solley and E. Steinbaugh
  "The sensible thing"
    Great American love stories; ed. by L. Rosenthal

Fitzgerald, Francis Scott Key *See* Fitzgerald, F. Scott (Francis Scott), 1896-1940

Fitzgerald, M. J.
  Bachelor life
    Fitzgerald, M. J. Rope-dancer
  Il bell'uomo
    Fitzgerald, M. J. Rope-dancer
  Communions
    Fitzgerald, M. J. Rope-dancer
  Creases
    Fitzgerald, M. J. Rope-dancer
  Eurydice
    Fitzgerald, M. J. Rope-dancer
  Experiment with time
    Fitzgerald, M. J. Rope-dancer
  Falling sickness
    Fitzgerald, M. J. Rope-dancer
  The fire eater
    Fitzgerald, M. J. Rope-dancer
  The game
    Fitzgerald, M. J. Rope-dancer
  Glass
    Fitzgerald, M. J. Rope-dancer
  A landscape with walls
    Fitzgerald, M. J. Rope-dancer

  Mystery story
    Fitzgerald, M. J. Rope-dancer
  Objects
    Fitzgerald, M. J. Rope-dancer
  Perspective on the first you
    Fitzgerald, M. J. Rope-dancer
  Phebican
    Fitzgerald, M. J. Rope-dancer

Fitzgerald, Penelope
  The axe
    The Penguin book of ghost stories

Fitzgerald, Zelda, 1900-1948
  Miss Ella
    The Art of fiction in the heart of Dixie; ed. by P. D. Beidler

Fitzpatrick, J. Percy
  The outspan
    The Penguin book of Southern African stories

Five acre virgin. Jolley, E.

Five and one half Charlotte Mews. See Livia, A. 5 1/2 Charlotte Mews

Five bad hands and the wild mouse folds. Klinkowitz, J.

The **five** brothers. Buzzati, D.

Five-day forecast. Hoch, E. D.

Five fables. Paré, P.

Five for silver. Whitaker, M.

The **five-forty-eight.** Cheever, J.

The **five** forty five pound boy. See Millman, L. The 545 pound boy

Five Ives. Blount, R.

Five letters from an eastern empire. Gray, A.

Five minutes early. Sheckley, R.

The **five** o'clock train. Scarfe, E.

The **five** orange pips. Doyle, Sir A. C.

Five pears or peaches. Gibbons, R.

Five points. Munro, A.

The **five** senses of Mrs. Craggs. Keating, H. R. F.

Five signs of disturbance. Davis, L.

The **five-storied** pagoda. Kōda, R.

The **five** thousand dollar getaway. See Ritchie, J. The $5,000 getaway

Five thousand runaways. Kaikō, T.

Five-twenty. White, P.

The **five** white mice. Crane, S.

Five women. Matthews, J.

Fivesight. Robinson, S.

Fixation. Tripp, M.

Fixing it for Freddie. Wodehouse, P. G.

The **flag.** Bates, H. E.

FLAGPOLE SITTERS
  Goyen, W. Figure over the town

Flaherty, Gerald
  Blood
    Flaherty, G. Filthy the man
  Filthy the man
    Flaherty, G. Filthy the man
  The main chance
    Flaherty, G. Filthy the man

Flaherty, Gerald—*Continued*
The man who saved himself
Flaherty, G. Filthy the man
The man who wore sunlight
Flaherty, G. Filthy the man
Something to talk like a family about
Flaherty, G. Filthy the man
The terrible speed of mercy
Flaherty, G. Filthy the man
Whom God hath promised
Flaherty, G. Filthy the man
The **flambé'd** thing. Treitel, J.
The **flame**. Bates, H. E.
Flame and the healer. Watson, I.
FLAMENCO DANCERS *See* Dancers
Flames. Roberts, N.
Flaming-arrow. Lafferty, R. A.
Flaming doorway. Halliday, M.
Flanagan, Jackie
Chinook
The Old dance; ed. by B. Burnard
Flanagan, Mary
Cream sauce
Flanagan, M. Bad girls
Death in Sussex
Flanagan, M. Bad girls
Melusina
Flanagan, M. Bad girls
A parma violet room
Flanagan, M. Bad girls
Simple pleasures
Flanagan, M. Bad girls
A view of Manhattan
Flanagan, M. Bad girls
White places
Flanagan, M. Bad girls
Wild garlic
Flanagan, M. Bad girls
Flanagan, Robert
Berzerk
Flanagan, R. Naked to naked goes
Close dancing
Flanagan, R. Naked to naked goes
Comedy of Eros
Flanagan, R. Naked to naked goes
Father's Day
Flanagan, R. Naked to naked goes
Gaming
Flanagan, R. Naked to naked goes
Local anaesthetic
Flanagan, R. Naked to naked goes
Naked to naked goes
Flanagan, R. Naked to naked goes
Smoker
Flanagan, R. Naked to naked goes
Teller's ticket
Flanagan, R. Naked to naked goes
The Norton book of American short
stories
Flanagan and his short filibustering adven-
ture. Crane, S.
Flap of wings. Asscher-Pinkhof, C.
Flare time. Niven, L.

Flarrin red-chin. Easton, M. C.
Flash attachment. Shannon, D.
Flash crowd. Niven, L.
Flash Gordon. Bassen, L. S.
The **Flash!** Kid. Bradfield, S.
A **flash** of red. Hoch, E. D.
Flash point. Dozois, G. R.
Flat Creek Road. Bennet, J.
The **flat** in Nakshabandi Street. Rifaat, A.
The **flatted** saxophone. O'Hara, J.
FLAUBERT, GUSTAVE, 1821-1880
Madame Bovary
Moore, G. 'Emma Bovary'
Flaubert in Miami Beach. Ballantyne, S.
Flavour of coconut. Narayan, R. K.
The **flaw**. Symons, J.
Flawless execution. Smith, D. W.
The **flayed** hand. Maupassant, G. de
Flea circus. Gardner, L.
Flea market. Valenzuela, L.
FLEA MARKETS
Stark, S. S. The dealers' yard
FLEAS
Ellin, S. Beidenbauer's flea
Woodman, A. The lampshade vendor
Fledged. Emshwiller, C.
Fleegl of Fleegl. Dickson, G. R.
Fleming, Berry, 1899-1989
Afternoon in the country
Fleming, B. The bookman's tale, and
others
Beach party
Fleming, B. The bookman's tale, and
others
The bookman's tale
Fleming, B. The bookman's tale, and
others
Happy New Year, Mr. Ganaway
Fleming, B. The bookman's tale, and
others
War memorial
Fleming, B. The bookman's tale, and
others
Fleming, Ian, 1908-1964
Octopussy
Baker's dozen: 13 short espionage novels
Fleming, Thomas J., 1927-
Office romance
Good Housekeeping 205:152-3 N '87
Fleming-Roberts, G. T.
The death master
A Cent a story! Ed. by G. G. Roberts
Moulder of monsters
Selected tales of grim and grue from the
horror pulps; ed. by S. Jaffery
The **flesh**. Samarakis, A.
Flesh and blood. Davol, M. W.
Flesh and blood. Erdrich, L.
Flesh and the mirror. Carter, A.
Fletcher, Claudia
Luisa
Chicago Review 34 no4:80-90 '85

Fletcher, George U. *See* Pratt, Fletcher, 1897-1956
Fletcher found. Llywelyn, M.
Fleur. Erdrich, L.
Fleur. Lish, G.
Fleutiaux, Pierrette
 The house
 Michigan Quarterly Review 25:559-61 Summ '86
 In the street
 Michigan Quarterly Review 25:562-7 Summ '86
FLIERS *See* Air pilots
FLIES
 Asimov, I. Flies
 Asscher-Pinkhof, C. Nursery
 Bloch, R. Beelzebub
 Caldwell, E. The fly in the coffin
 Grace, P. Flies
 Heise, K. Ferndale fights the flies
 McGrath, P. The e(rot)ic potato
 Rice, J. The Idol of the Flies
 Shea, M. The horror on the #33
Flies. Asimov, I.
Flies. Grace, P.
Flies. McIlrath, J. H.
FLIGHT
 See also Aeronautics
 Ballard, J. G. My dream of flying to Wake Island
 Baxter, C. The cliff
 Bradbury, R. Uncle Elinar
 Hamilton, E. He that hath wings
 Jackson, G. Fly in the ointment
 Lafferty, R. A. Flaming-arrow
Flight. Dickinson, P.
Flight. Eldridge, M.
Flight. Grau, S. A.
Flight. Kittredge, W.
Flight. McGuane, T.
Flight. O'Hara, J.
Flight. Prichard, K. S.
Flight. Svendsen, L.
FLIGHT ATTENDANTS
 Haas, B. When California was an island
Flight from danger. Garve, A.
The **flight** of Andy Burns. Mattison, A.
A **flight** of geese. Norris, L.
The **flight** of pigeons from the palace. Barthelme, D.
A **flight** of sparks. Cohen, R.
The **flight** to America. Sandel, C.
Flight to forever. Anderson, P.
Flint/steel sparks on tropic moon-night. Elliott, L. T.
Flipflops. Boswell, R.
Flo. Kornblatt, J. R.
Floating. Thurm, M.
A **flock** of geese. McCaffrey, A.
The **flock** of Geryon. Christie, A.
A **flock** of lambs in all colors. Rodoreda, M.
The **flood.** Abe, K.

The **flood.** Ferron, J.
Flood. Hill, K.
A **flood.** Moore, G.
Flood. Powell, P.
The **flood** of '64. Long, D.
FLOODS
 See also Disasters
 Dollarhide, L. The gift
 Dumas, H. Ark
 Dumas, H. Fever
 Dumas, H. Wandering in the wilderness
 Dumas, H. The white horse
 Eisenstein, S. Earthworks
 Everett, P. L. A real hard rain
 Franzen, B. Getting Herbert back
 García Márquez, G. Monologue of Isabel watching it rain in Macondo
 Hempel, A. Pool Night
 Jia Pingwa. How much can a man bear?
 Klass, F. Before the rainbow
 Long, D. The flood of '64
 Moon, S.-T. The sound of the gong
 Moore, G. A flood
 O'Donnell, E. P. Jesus knew
 Pascoe, B. Harold's Trudy
 Prichard, K. S. The frogs of Quirra-Quirra
 Robinson, K. S. Venice drowned
 Stark, S. S. The Johnstown Polka
 Wilson, R., Jr. Land fishers
 Wright, R. The man who saw the flood
Flook, Maria
 All the girls had gone
 Flook, M. Dancing with my sister Jane
 Dancing with my sister Jane
 Flook, M. Dancing with my sister Jane
 The fairway
 Flook, M. Dancing with my sister Jane
 Richard's girl
 Flook, M. Dancing with my sister Jane
 A walk in the city
 Flook, M. Dancing with my sister Jane
Flora, Fletcher, 1914-1968
 A husband is missing
 Alfred Hitchcock's Crimewatch
 Where's Milo
 Alfred Hitchcock's Mortal errors
Floral Street. Burt, S.
A **floral** tribute. Tuohy, F.
FLORENCE (ITALY) *See* Italy—Florence
Florence and the new shoes. Gallegos, M.
Florence, May '86. Briskin, M.
Florentine. Maupassant, G. de
Flores, Carlos Nicolás
 Yellow flowers
 Cuentos Chicanos; ed. by R. A. Anaya and A. Márquez
FLORIDA
 Ballard, J. G. The cage of sand
 Woolson, C. F. Felipa
  20th century
 Ballantyne, S. Key Largo
 Berry, R. M. Song of the geometry instructor

FLORIDA—20th century—*Continued*
Brady, M. Strike it rich
Dilworth, S. Miles from Coconut Grove
Dorr, L. The immigrant
Dorr, L. Old men shall dream dreams
Garrett, G. P. King of the mountain
Granberry, E. A trip to Czardis
Kinsella, W. P. The Alligator Report—with questions for discussion
MacDonald, J. D. The legend of Joe Lee
Morris, M. Conquering space
Rawlings, M. K. Gal young un
Shacochis, B. The heart's advantage
Shacochis, B. Hot day on the Gold Coast
Smith, C. Crystal River
Steele, M. What to do till the postman comes
Thurm, M. Winter
Williams, J. The blue men
Woodman, A. Gulf

Politics
See Politics—Florida

Fort Lauderdale
Dann, J. Between the windows of the sea
Friedman, B. J. The adventurer
Thurm, M. Starlight

Key West
Barrus, T. Life sucks; or, Ernest Hemingway never slept here
Lee, R. B. Knight of shallows

Miami
Camoin, F. A. Miami
Walker, A. Kindred spirits
Working, R. Famous people

Saint Petersburg
Banks, R. Success story
Thompson, S. The Don

Tampa
Haldeman, J. W. No future in it

Florida. Gallant, M.
Florie. Colette
Florinto. Mares, E. A.
Flotsam. Eisenberg, D.
Flotsam and Jetsam. Claiborne, S.
The flounder. Osborn, M.
Flour for your grave. Pascoe, B.
Flow gently, sweet aspirin. West, J.
Flower Crazy. Chukri, M.
Flower man. Kidman, F.

Flowerday, Edis
Rubbish day
Stiller's pond; ed. by J. Agee; R. Blakely and S. Welch

Flowering Narcissus. Scortia, T. N.
The flowering of the strange orchid. Wells, H. G.

FLOWERS
See also Orchids
Bates, H. E. The cowslip field
Davie, E. Green head
Kidman, F. Flower man
Shiga, N. The little girl and the rapeseed flower

West, J. The heavy stone
Flowers. Troy, J.
The flowers at Anat Qesh. Hoyt, M. S.
Flowers for Violet. Adams, C. F.
Flowers in January. Healey, J.
Flowers: memento mori. Weaver, G.
The flowers of Bermuda. MacDonald, D. R.
The flowers of boredom. DeMarinis, R.
Flowers of Edo. Sterling, B.
Flowers of fire. Sonu, H.

Floyd, Patty Lou
Dream rocket
Floyd, P. L. The silver DeSoto
Second best
Floyd, P. L. The silver DeSoto
Secrets
Floyd, P. L. The silver DeSoto
The silver DeSoto
Floyd, P. L. The silver DeSoto
The summer no one was poor
Floyd, P. L. The silver DeSoto
Uncle Tom's daybook
Floyd, P. L. The silver DeSoto
The voice in the whirlwind
Floyd, P. L. The silver DeSoto
When Mother played Moonshine
Floyd, P. L. The silver DeSoto

The flute. Schwob, M.
The flute player's story. Colum, P.
FLUTISTS
Colum, P. The flute player's story
Cowper, R. Piper at the gates of dawn
Lewitt, S. The shaman flute
Flux of fortune. Broxon, M. D.
The fly. Mansfield, K.
Fly away home. Kantner, R.
The fly-by-night. Chetwynd-Hayes, R.
The fly in the coffin. Caldwell, E.
Fly in the ointment. Jackson, G.
The fly-screen. Jackson, G.
The fly swatter. Sisk, F.
Fly to fly. Purdin, S.
The flyaway heart. Kempson, J.
FLYING *See* Flight
Flying. Thurm, M.
Flying a red kite. Hood, H.
The flying ark. Mazel, D.
The flying carpet. Buzzati, D.
FLYING DUTCHMAN
Zelazny, R. And I alone am escaped to tell thee
The flying Dutchman. Michaelson, L. W.
Flying lessons. Pritchett, M.
The flying man. Wells, H. G.
Flying saucer rock & roll. Waldrop, H.
FLYING SAUCERS
Spark, M. Miss Pinkerton's apocalypse
A flying start. Gallant, M.
Flynn, Michael
The forest of time
The Year's best science fiction, fifth annual collection

Flynn, Robert, 1932-
The boy from Chillicothe
  Flynn, R. Seasonal rain, and other stories
Champion of the world
  Flynn, R. Seasonal rain, and other stories
Christmas in a very small place
  Flynn, R. Seasonal rain, and other stories
The dog that knew better
  Flynn, R. Seasonal rain, and other stories
The feelings of the dead
  Flynn, R. Seasonal rain, and other stories
The great plain
  Flynn, R. Seasonal rain, and other stories
The killer
  Flynn, R. Seasonal rain, and other stories
The midnight clear
  Flynn, R. Seasonal rain, and other stories
Pictures
  Flynn, R. Seasonal rain, and other stories
Place
  Flynn, R. Seasonal rain, and other stories
The saviour of the bees
  Flynn, R. Seasonal rain, and other stories
Seasonal rain
  Flynn, R. Seasonal rain, and other stories
Tumbleweed Christmas
  Flynn, R. Seasonal rain, and other stories
Waiting for the postman
  Flynn, R. Seasonal rain, and other stories
Flynn, T. T.
The deadly orchid
  Hard-boiled dames; ed. by B. A. Drew
Flynt, Candace, 1947-
Dancing with father
  The Atlantic 255:65-9 Je '85
Flythe, Markey, Jr.
CV10
  Ploughshares 14 no1:18-26 '88
Flythe, Starkey
Walking, walking
  The Best American short stories, 1985
FOETUS *See* Fetus
FOG
Anthony, P. Phog
King, S. The mist
Matheson, R. C. Dead end
Fog. Burnet, D.
Fog. Haley, R.
The **fog.** Kinsella, W. P.

A **fog** in Santone. Henry, O.
The **fog** on Pemble Green. Barker, S.
Foggerty's fairy. Gilbert, W. S.
The **foghorn.** Atherton, G. F. H.
Foie gras. Merwin, W. S.
Foley, Barbara, 1948-
The child killers
  Stories and poems from close to home; ed. by F. Salas
The **Folio** Club. Poe, E. A.
FOLK MEDICINE
Bessette, G. The mustard plaster
Boucher, S. The healing
DeMarinis, R. Medicine man
Walker, A. Strong horse tea
Wendt, A. Daughter of the mango season
The **followers.** Thomas, D.
Following the way. Ryan, A.
Foltz, Lynn
If I had three wishes
  'Teen 28:38 Mr '84
Foltz-Gray, Daniel
Departed coming back
  Homewords: a book of Tennessee writers; ed. by D. Paschall
Fon. Dumas, H.
Fondly Fahrenheit. Bester, A.
Fondue. Janowitz, T.
Fonseca, Rubem
The game of dead men
  Short story international 67
Happy new year
  The Literary Review (Madison, N.J.) 27:430-6 Summ '84
Fontana, D. C.
Cut to: murder
  Murder in Los Angeles; ed. by J. L. Breen and others
Fontane, Henri Théodore *See* Fontane, Theodor, 1819-1898
Fontane, Theodor, 1819-1898
A woman in my years
  German stories; ed. by H. Steinhauer
Fontes, Saavedra
The boy and the piano tuner
  Américas 36:30-1 S/O '84
FOOD
Apple, M. Stranger at the table
Bates, H. E. Finger wet, finger dry
Blei, N. This horse of a body of mine
Broinowski, A. Holy mackerel
Chatto, J. The atheist
Claiborne, S. Scenes from a novel: replenishing Ava
Conroy, J. "A barrel of fun"
Dadswell, M. Mrs. McGrath
DeMarinis, R. Life between meals
Durrell, L. Something à la carte?
Fisher, M. F. K. A kitchen allegory
Janowitz, T. Lunch involuntary
King, F. H. Appetites
Lispector, C. The sharing of bread
Lu Wenfu. The gourmet

FOOD—*Continued*
Rossi, A. Breakfast, lunch, and dinner
Sargent, P. Originals
Valenzuela, L. The celery munchers
Weinstein, J. A Jean-Marie cookbook
Wolfe, T. His father's earth
Food. Tessier, T.
A **fool** in winter. Lurie, M.
Fools. Ndebele, N.
Fools. Sanford, W. M.
FOOLS AND JESTERS
Poe, E. A. Hop-frog
Singer, I. B. Gimpel the fool
Fool's gold. Brewer, G.
A **fool's** life. Akutagawa, R.
Fool's mate. Sheckley, R.
FOOT
Camoin, F. A. La vida
Gardner, M. At the feet of Karl Klodhopper
Thomas, A. C. Compulsory figures
The **foot.** Harris, H.
The **foot.** Huneven, M.
Foot-prints on the sea-shore. Hawthorne, N.
Foot-shaped shoes. West, J.
FOOTBALL
Abbott, L. K. Love is the crooked thing
Abbott, L. K. A modern story of Woe and Lovecraft
Fante, J. One-play Oscar
Gadow, D. Football
LaSalle, P. Dolphin dreaming
Lutz, J. Autumn madness
Martin, G. R. R. Run to starlight
Morrison, J. Black night in Collingwood
Shaw, I. The eighty-yard run
Spinrad, N. The national pastime
Wilner, H. The quarterback speaks to his god
Football. Gadow, D.
Football Queen. Drake, R.
Foote, Shelby
Jordan County [excerpt]
Mississippi writers v1: Fiction; ed. by D. Abbott
Pillar of fire
A Treasury of Civil War stories; ed. by M. H. Greenberg and B. Pronzini
Shiloh [excerpt]
Mississippi writers v1: Fiction; ed. by D. Abbott
Footner, Hulbert, 1879-1944
Wolves of Monte Carlo
Hard-boiled dames; ed. by B. A. Drew
A **footnote** to the Kokoda story. Clark, M.
Footprints in a ghost town. Martin, D.
Footprints in Perdu. Cave, H. B.
Footprints of Maria. Houbein, L.
Footsteps. Ellison, H.
Footsteps in the snow. Soldati, M.
For a breath I tarry. Zelazny, R.
For a crate of lemons. Nesin, A.
For a man your age. Dixon, S.

For Ann. Wexler, J.
For art's sake. Spivack, K.
For auld lang crime. Searls, H.
For better, for worse . . . but not for lunch. Kupfer, F.
For I am a jealous people! Del Rey, L.
"**For** I will consider my cat Jeoffry". Oates, J. C.
For immediate release. Durrell, L.
For Jeromé—with love and kisses. Lish, G.
For Joannie. Raphael, F.
For love. Pronzini, B.
For lovers only. Schlobin, R. C.
For luck. Roberts, N.
For merit. Franklin, P.
For my wife's eyes only. MacLaverty, B.
For piano and vocal accompaniment. Carraud, J.
For professional appearance. Wolfe, T.
For real. Robison, M.
For Rupert—with no promises. Lish, G.
For the blood is the life. Crawford, F. M.
For the honor of the company. Mitchell, M. E.
For the love of a man. London, J.
For the love of Katie. Levi, J. H.
For the love of my sons. Kupfer, F.
For the sake of Grace. Elgin, S. H.
For these and all my sins. Morrell, D.
For three hundred years. Barnett, A. N.
For thus do I remember Carthage. Bishop, M.
For Timothy Baer. Crapser, W.
Foray, Verge
Duplex
From mind to mind: tales of communication from Analog
Forbes, Jack
Only approved Indians can play: made in USA
Earth power coming; ed. by S. J. Ortiz
The **forbidden.** Barker, C.
Forbidden fruit. Maupassant, G. de
Forbidden knowledge. Cramer, K.
Forbidden waters. Bliss, C. D.
Forby and the Mayan maidens. Blew, M. C.
FORCE AND ENERGY
Asimov, I. Eyes do more than see
Force majeur. Forrest, K. V.
Force of habit. Palmieri, A.
Forcier, Louise Maheux- *See* Maheux-Forcier, Louise, 1929-
FORD, CHARLES WILSON, 1857-1884
About
Taylor, R. Charley Ford betrayed
Ford, Corey, 1902-1969
Slipstream
Roger Caras' Treasury of great dog stories
Ford, Jesse Hill, 1928-
Fishes, birds and sons of men
Homewords: a book of Tennessee writers; ed. by D. Paschall

Ford, John
The girl with the gift
Redbook 170:58-61 N '87
Ford, John M.
As above, so below
Dragons of light; ed. by O. S. Card
Preflash
Silver scream; ed. by D. J. Schow
Street of dreams
Ripper! Ed. by G. Dozois and S. Casper
Tales from the original gothic
The Architecture of fear; ed. by K.
Cramer and P. D. Pautz
Ford, Kathleen, 1945-
Elizabeth's things
U.S. Catholic 53:35-8 Jl '88
A father's story
Ladies' Home Journal 105:90+ Jl '88
The Ryans
U.S. Catholic 52:32-7 Ag '87
Snowfall
U.S. Catholic 51:27-32 D '86
Ford, Richard, 1944-
Children
Ford, R. Rock Springs
The New Yorker 63:25-34+ Ag 3 '87
Communist
The Art of the tale; ed. by D. Halpern
The Best American short stories, 1986
Ford, R. Rock Springs
The Norton book of American short
stories
The Pushcart prize XI
Soldiers & civilians; ed. by T. Jenks
Empire
Ford, R. Rock Springs
Fireworks
The Bread Loaf anthology of contem-
porary American short stories; ed. by
R. Pack and J. Parini
Esquire 102:256-7+ O '84
The Esquire fiction reader v1
Ford, R. Rock Springs
Going to the dogs
Ford, R. Rock Springs
Great Falls
The Best of the West; ed. by J. Thomas
Ford, R. Rock Springs
The Graywolf annual 4
Optimists
Ford, R. Rock Springs
The New Yorker 63:28-36 Mr 30 '87
A piece of my heart [excerpt]
Mississippi writers v1: Fiction; ed. by D.
Abbott
Rock Springs
American short story masterpieces; ed.
by R. Carver and T. Jenks
Ford, R. Rock Springs
Look who's talking; ed. by B. Weber

Sweethearts
Esquire 106:86-90 Ag '86
Ford, R. Rock Springs
New American short stories; ed. by G.
Norris
The New writers of the South; ed. by
C. East
Winterkill
The Editors' choice: new American
stories v1
Ford, R. Rock Springs
The Graywolf annual [1]
Writers of the purple sage; ed. by R.
Martin and M. Barasch
FORD, ROBERT, 1862-1892
About
Taylor, R. The tragedy of Bob Ford
The **forecasting** game. Ackerman, F.
A **foreign** affair. Chabon, M.
The **foreign** legation. Doctorow, E. L.
The **foreign** legion. Lispector, C.
Foreign objects. Connelly, J.
Foreign parts. Barstow, S.
Foreign postcard. Woodman, A.
FOREIGN SERVICE *See* Diplomatic life
Foreign shores. Salter, J.
Foreign skins. Lee, T.
FOREIGN VISITORS *See* Visitors, Foreign
The **foreigner**. Jewett, S. O.
Foreigner. Kerslake, S.
Foreigner in the family. Brender à Brandis,
M.
The **foreigners**. Covino, M.
Foreigners. Gilliatt, P.
Foreigners. Thompson, J.
Forer, Anne U.
Thanksgiving with Trudy
Hot type; ed. by J. Miller
The **forest**. Anderson, P.
The **forest**. Bitov, A.
The **forest**. Nowakowski, M.
The **forest** fire. Sanford, W. M.
The **forest** of time. Flynn, M.
The **forest** of Zil. Neville, K.
Forest winter. Winton, T.
Forester, C. S. (Cecil Scott), 1899-1966
Dawn attack
Sea captains' tales; ed. by A. Enfield
Night stalk
Short stories of the sea; ed. by G. C.
Solley and E. Steinbaugh
The sinking of the Bismarck
Men at sea; ed. by B. Aymar
The turning of the tide
Mysterious sea stories; ed. by W. Pat-
trick
Forester, Cecil Scott *See* Forester, C. S.
(Cecil Scott), 1899-1966
A **forester** in love. Mrożek, S.
FORESTS AND FORESTRY
See also Wilderness areas
Ekström, M. The nothingness forest
Nowakowski, M. The forest

FORESTS AND FORESTRY—*Continued*
Pil'nīāk, B. Mother earth
Welch, D. The fire in the wood
Forever. Knight, D. F.
Forever. MacDuff, L.
Forever and amen. Bloch, R.
Forever Island. Smith, P. D.
The **forever** summer. Cross, R. A.
Forever with you. Thaler, S.
Forever yours, Anna. Wilhelm, K.
The **forfeit**. Wheatcroft, J.

FORGERY OF WORKS OF ART
Longyear, B. B. The portrait of Baron Negay
Mortimer, J. C. Rumpole and the genuine article
Robinson, K. S. Mercurial
Forget-me-not. Taylor, B.
Forget the geraniums. Steele, M.
Forgetting it. Raphael, F.

FORGIVENESS
Banks, R. The child screams and looks back at you
Havemann, E. Spirits do not forgive
Sams, F. Judgment
Forgiveness. Maupassant, G. de
The **forgiveness** trick. Tallent, E.
Forgiving. Hazzard, S.
The **forgiving** ghost. Gilford, C. B.
The **forgotten** bridge. Bell, M. S.
The **forgotten** witness. Post, M. D.
Form. Tripp, M.
Form in wood. Cowan, P.
A **former** security with Helen Damnation. Sproat, R.
The **formula**. Yarbrough, S.

Forrest, Felix C., 1913-1966
For works written by this author under other names see Smith, Cordwainer, 1913-1966

Forrest, Katherine V., 1939-
Benny's place
   Forrest, K. V. Dreams and swords
Force majeur
   Forrest, K. V. Dreams and swords
The gift
   Forrest, K. V. Dreams and swords
Jessie
   Forrest, K. V. Dreams and swords
Mandy Larkin
   Forrest, K. V. Dreams and swords
Mother was an alien
   Forrest, K. V. Dreams and swords
O captain, my captain
   Forrest, K. V. Dreams and swords
Survivor
   Forrest, K. V. Dreams and swords
The test
   Forrest, K. V. Dreams and swords
Xessex
   Forrest, K. V. Dreams and swords

Forsh, Olga
Ham's wife
   Russian and Polish women's fiction; ed. by H. Goscilo
The little mermaid Rotozeyechka
   Russian and Polish women's fiction; ed. by H. Goscilo

Forshaw, Thelma
The mateship syndrome
   The Australian short story; ed. by L. Hergenhan

Forster, E. M. (Edward Morgan), 1879-1970
The machine stops
   Whole Earth Review no44:40-55 D/Ja '84/'85
The story of a panic
   Black water; ed. by A. Manguel
The story of the siren
   Short stories of the sea; ed. by G. C. Solley and E. Steinbaugh

Forster, Edward Morgan *See* Forster, E. M. (Edward Morgan), 1879-1970

Forsyth, Frederick, 1938-
There are no snakes in Ireland
   Dark arrows; ed. by A. Manguel
   Masterpieces of mystery and suspense; ed. by M. H. Greenberg
The **fort**. Abbott, K.

FORT LAUDERDALE (FLA.) *See* Florida—Fort Lauderdale

Fortier, Ron
(jt. auth) See Anderson, Kevin J., and Fortier, Ron
Fortunato & the night visitor. Summers, H. S.
The **fortune** hunter. Carter, A. A.
The **fortune-teller**. Spark, M.

FORTUNE TELLING
Bloch, R. In the cards
Fish, R. L. Muldoon and the numbers game
Gallagher, S. The jigsaw girl
Gallico, P. Hurry, hurry, hurry!
Hoch, E. D. The theft of the four of spades
Lopatin, J. Budapest dangereux
Rīos, A. Eyes like they say the devil has
Schaub, M. H. The cards of Eldrianza
Spark, M. The fortune-teller
Vargas, K. The corpse

FORTUNES *See* Wealth
Fortunes and old perfumes. Ross, J.
The **forty** and eight. Campbell, E.
'Forty-eight'. Sciascia, L.
Forty-hour devotion. Costello, M.
Forty-one minarets. Al-Mak, A.
Forty Susan Sangsters stride out at the Wellington Boot. Beckett, R.
A **forty-year-old** man. Endō, S.

Forward, Robert L.
The singing diamond
   Great science fiction; ed. by I. Asimov; M. H. Greenberg and C. G. Waugh

Forward, mankind! Dilov, L.
Fosdick, C. J.
  A season of acceptance
    Seventeen 44:108-9+ D '85
FOSSILS
  Oliver, C. Transfusion
Foster, Alan Dean, 1946-
  Why Johnny can't speed
    The Science fictional Olympics; ed. by
     I. Asimov; M. H. Greenberg and C.
     G. Waugh
Foster, Melville
  The ticket
    Américas 40:31-3 Jl/Ag '88
FOSTER CHILDREN
    See also Adoption
  Biggle, L. Orphan of the void
  Cullen, E. J. Letter to the institution
  Faik, S. The bundle
  Fremlin, C. Bluebeard's key
  Harris, M. Little Eddy
  Kessler, J. F. Corinth
  O'Connor, F. A set of variations on a bor-
    rowed theme
  Phillips, J. A. Lechery
  Prichard, K. S. Josephina Anna Maria
  Swift, G. Gabor
  Vizyēnos, G. M. My mother's sin
  West, J. Hunting for hoot owls
Foster home. Oates, J. C.
Foul fowl. Russ, J.
Found!. Asimov, I.
The **foundation.** Kessler, J. F.
FOUNDATION GARMENTS
  Colette. My corset maker
FOUNDATIONS (ENDOWMENTS) *See*
  Endowments
Founding fathers. Bloch, R.
The **foundling.** Kleist, H. von
FOUNDLINGS *See* Abandoned children
The **foundry.** Robison, J.
FOUNDRYMEN
  Zimpel, L. Ovenmen
Fouqué, Friedrich Heinrich Karl La Motte-
  See La Motte-Fouqué, Friedrich Hein-
    rich Karl, Freiherr von, 1777-1843
Four and a half. Haris, P.
Four-and-twenty blackbirds. Christie, A.
The **four** Apples. Apple, M.
Four beasts in one—the homo-cameleopard.
  Poe, E. A.
The **four** blind men. Brown, F.
Four brands of impossible. Kagan, N.
Four California deaths. Bowering, G.
Four camels out of the desert. Telpaz, G.
Four hundred boys. See Laidlaw, M. 400
  boys
Four in one. Knight, D. F.
The **four** lost men. Wolfe, T.
Four lost souls. See Thomas, D. Adventures
  in the skin trade: Four lost souls
Four men in a cave. Crane, S.
Four plus signs. Faik, S.

The **four** railroads of Iserlohn. Gustafsson,
  L.
Four rupees. Narayan, R. K.
The **four-sided** triangle. Temple, W. F.
The **four** suspects. Christie, A.
Four walls and an empty door. Sillitoe, L.
Four-way funeral. Bradbury, R.
FOURIER, CHARLES *See* Fourier, François
  Marie Charles, 1772-1837
FOURIER, FRANÇOIS MARIE CHARLES,
  1772-1837
    About
  Davenport, G. Apples and pears: Het
    Erewhonisch schetsboek: Messidor-
    Vendémiaire 1981
Fourth brother. Engberg, S.
The **fourth** day of Christmas. Simon, B.
FOURTH DIMENSION
  Asimov, I. The brazen locked room
  Bear, G. Tangents
  Hobana, I. Night broadcast
  Longyear, B. B. Dreams
  Powers, T. Night moves
  Russ, J. Elf hill
  Sheckley, R. Fishing season
  Sheckley, R. Miss Mouse and the fourth
    dimension
The **fourth** man. Russell, J.
FOURTH OF JULY
  Dilworth, S. Independence Day
  Heise, K. Ferndale fireworks
  Kees, W. The evening of the Fourth of
    July
  Murphy, Y. Believer in death
  Ruffolo, L. Independence Day
  Weaver, G. Canavan's knee
Fourth of July. Tetu, R.
The **fourth** surprise. Dawson, F.
Fourth version. Valenzuela, L.
The **fourth** vocation of George Gustaf. Brin,
  D.
Fowler, Karen Joy
  The faithful companion at forty
    The Year's best science fiction, fifth an-
     nual collection
  The gate of ghosts
    The Year's best science fiction, fourth
     annual collection
  The lake was full of artificial things
    The Year's best science fiction, third an-
     nual collection
  Letters from home
    In the field of fire; ed. by J. Van B.
     Dann and J. Dann
  Recalling Cinderella
    L. Ron Hubbard presents Writers of the
     future
Fowles, John, 1926-
  The enigma
    The Penguin book of modern British
     short stories

Fox, George, 1933-
Return to Venice
  Murder in Los Angeles; ed. by J. L.
  Breen and others
Fox, Hugh
Romarias dos mutilados
  The Massachusetts Review 25:368-80 Aut
  '84
Fox, Janet
Garage sale
  100 great fantasy short short stories; ed.
  by I. Asimov; T. Carr and M. H.
  Greenberg
Intimately, with rain
  Midnight; ed. by C. L. Grant
The skins you love to touch
  Shadows 9
Fox, John, 1952-
Choice
  Men on men; ed. by G. Stambolian
Over the Pyrenees
  First love/last love; ed. by M. Denneny;
  C. Ortleb and T. Steele
The superhero
  First love/last love; ed. by M. Denneny;
  C. Ortleb and T. Steele
Fox, Paula
Travels with my father
  Seventeen 43:100-3+ Jl '84
Fox, Robert, 1943-
A fable
  Sudden fiction; ed. by R. Shapard and
  J. Thomas
Fox, William Price
Doug Broome, hamburger king
  A Collection of classic Southern humor;
  ed. by G. W. Koon
You don't smell it: you drink it
  Through a glass, darkly; ed. by B. Woel-
  fel
Fox. Bernen, R.
The **fox.** Colette
The **fox.** Ruffin, P.
The **fox** fairy. See Shen, C.-C. Miss Jen
FOX HUNTING
Caldwell, E. The Negro in the well
Jones, D. C. Once a year
Kantor, M. The voice of Bugle Ann
Fox-trot and other matters. Bernard, K.
FOXES
Bernen, R. Fox
Colette. The fox
Garnett, D. Lady into fox
Hunnicutt, E. The Bengal tiger
Shen, C.-C. Miss Jen
Yolen, J. The foxwife
Foxglove. Sexson, L.
The **foxwife.** Yolen, J.
Fra Lippi and me. Arnow, H. L. S.
Fractions. Lutz, J.
Fragment. Eldridge, M.
The **fragment.** McCormack, E. P.
A **fragment** of a life story. Welch, D.

Fragment of a novel. Byron, G. G. B., 6th
  Baron
Fragments of papyrus from the temple of the
  older gods. Kotzwinkle, W.
Frahm, Leanne
On the turn
  Shadows 9
The visitor
  Midnight; ed. by C. L. Grant
Frame, Janet
The bull calf
  Women's work; ed. by M. McLeod and
  L. Wevers
Insulation
  Women's work; ed. by M. McLeod and
  L. Wevers
Prizes
  The Treasury of English short stories;
  ed. by N. Sullivan
Frame, Ronald
Rowena Fletcher
  Winter's tales, new ser. v3
Framed. Pointon, S.
Framed for murder. Masur, H. Q.
France, Anatole, 1844-1924
The ocean Christ
  Short stories of the sea; ed. by G. C.
  Solley and E. Steinbaugh
FRANCE
      See also Corsica; Mont Sainte-
  Victoire (France); Seine River (France)
Lee, T. Three days
Maupassant, G. de. Le Horla
Schwob, M. The firebrands
Tournier, M. The Lily of the Valley rest
  area
        18th century
Arnim, L. A., Freiherr von. The madman
  of Fort Ratonneau
Gilbert, W. S. Comedy and tragedy
        1789-1799
Benét, S. V. The curfew tolls
        19th century
Maupassant, G. de. The accent
Pritchard, M. La Bête: a figure study
Schwob, M. Train 081
Smith, R. The Continental
        1848-1870
Maupassant, G. de. An affair of state
        1870-1940
Cohen, A. The monumental sculptor
        20th century
Boyd, W. Gifts
Burrage, A. M. One who saw
Cortázar, J. The southern thruway
Dennison, G. A tale of Pierrot
Desnoues, L. The poplars
Gallant, M. The assembly
Gallant, M. A flying start
Gallant, M. Grippes and Poche
Gallant, M. Luc and his father
Gallant, M. A painful affair
Highsmith, P. A clock ticks at Christmas

FRANCE—20th century—*Continued*
King, F. H. A scent of mimosa
Levine, N. Something happened here
Smith, R. The Continental
Tournier, M. Tristan Vox
Wolfe, T. The sun and the rain
    1940-1945
Boyle, K. Men
Gallant, M. A recollection
    Aristocracy
  See Aristocracy—France
    Army—Officers
Stead, C. The captain's house
    Communism
  See Communism—France
    Farm life
  See Farm life—France
  German occupation, 1940-1945
  See France—1940-1945
    Peasant life
  See Peasant life—France
    Politics
  See Politics—France
  Prisoners and prisons
  See Prisoners and prisons—France
    Rural life
Apollinaire, G. The favorite
Bovey, J. The overlap
Colette. Grape harvest
Colette. The patriarch
Davis, L. French lesson I: le meurtre
Fisher, M. F. K. The oldest man
Highsmith, P. Harry: a ferret
Highsmith, P. In the dead of truffle season
Kessler, J. F. Hermes
Maupassant, G. de. A country excursion
Maupassant, G. de. In the wood
Maupassant, G. de. The little cask
Maupassant, G. de. Mme. Tellier's excursion
Maupassant, G. de. A piece of string
Maupassant, G. de. Simon's papa
Maupassant, G. de. That pig of a Morin
Maupassant, G. de. Toine
Maupassant, G. de. Two little soldiers
Maupassant, G. de. The wooden shoes
Onions, O. The rope in the rafters
Sagan, F. A country outing
Schwob, M. Mérigot Marchès
Seabrook, W. B. The witch's vengeance
Sheehan, R. The ark
Stead, C. The captain's house
Tournier, M. Mother Christmas
Zola, É. Angeline; or, The haunted house
  World War, 1914-1918
  See World War, 1914-1918—France
    Alsace
Daudet, A. The last class
    Arles
Tournier, M. Veronica's shrouds
    Avignon
Swados, H. The peacocks of Avignon

    Brittany
Maupassant, G. de. Fecundity
O'Brien, E. Mrs. Reinhardt
Pierce, C. What I did for Aunt Berthe
Sandel, C. Simple memories
Valenzuela, L. The minstrels
Valenzuela, L. The son of Kermaria
    Cannes
Apollinaire, G. The posthumous fiance
Rhys, J. At the Villa d'Or
    Dordogne
Maxwell, W. The Pilgrimage
    Nice
Lacy, E. You can't win 'em (at) all
Sagan, F. The cat and the casino
Spark, M. The fathers' daughters
    Normandy
Maupassant, G. de. The farmer's wife
St. Aubin de Terán, L. I never eat crab-
  meat now
    Paris
Lee, T. Elle est trois, (la mort)
Maupassant, G. de. Graveyard sirens
   Paris—15th century
Stevenson, R. L. A lodging for the night
   Paris—19th century
Collins, W. A terribly strange bed
Doyle, Sir A. C. The tragedians
Gaboriau, E. The little old man of
  Batignolles
Gilbert, W. S. The lady in the plaid shawl
Hofmann, G. A conversation about Bal-
  zac's horse
Maupassant, G. de. The diamond necklace
Maupassant, G. de. The father
Maupassant, G. de. The new sensation
Maupassant, G. de. A queer night in Paris
Stoker, B. The burial of the rats
   Paris—20th century
Boylan, C. L'amour
Christmas, R. A. Another angel
Colette. The find
Colette. The fox
Ellin, S. Kindly dig your grave
Faik, S. The statue I stole from the Louv-
  re
Faulkner, W. A portrait of Elmer
Gallant, M. Luc and his father
Gallant, M. Overhead in a balloon
Geras, A. Don't sing love songs . . .
Gold, H. Annique
Gold, H. Paris and Cleveland are voyages
Gold, H. Young man, old days
Greene, G. Brother
Greene, G. Two gentle people
Halligan, M. Paris vicarious
Halligan, M. The porch of Paradise
Handke, P. Child story
Morand, P. The six-day night
Osborn, C. Other people's mail
Rhys, J. In the Rue de l'Arrivée
Sandel, C. Lola
Sandel, C. There's a war on

FRANCE—Paris—20th century—*Continued*
Shaw, I. The man who married a French wife
Simenon, G. Inspector Maigret pursues
Stead, C. La Toussaint (All Saints' Day, November 1)
Tuohy, F. The potlatch of Esmeralda
Provence
Fisher, M. F. K. The second time around
Greene, G. Beauty
Handke, P. The lesson of Mont Sainte-Victoire
Onions, O. The cigarette case
Franchise. Asimov, I.
FRANCIS, OF ASSISI, SAINT, 1182-1226
About
Chesterton, G. K. A legend of Saint Francis
Francis, Dick
The gift
The Mammoth book of modern crime stories; ed. by G. Hardinge
Twenty-one good men and true
Masterpieces of mystery and suspense; ed. by M. H. Greenberg
Francis, H. E. (Herbert Edward), 1924-
Carnival
The Literary Review (Madison, N.J.) 29:177-92 Wint '86
A chronicle of love
Love stories for the time being; ed. by G. D. Chipps and B. Henderson
Short story international 44
Falling
The Antioch Review 42:478-94 Fall '84
Her
The Georgia Review 40:125-31 Spr '86
Necessary fictions; ed. by S. W. Lindberg and S. Corey
The island
Southwest Review 69:62-77 Wint '84
Joshua
The Sewanee Review 95:199-218 Spr '87
Normal experience
The Kenyon Review ns10:76-94 Summ '88
Sitting
Sudden fiction; ed. by R. Shapard and J. Thomas
The sudden trees
The Best American short stories, 1985
Prairie Schooner 58:33-50 Spr '84
Short story international 57
Francis, Herbert Edward *See* Francis, H. E. (Herbert Edward), 1924-
Francis, Jay
Sniped at
Ellery Queen's Prime crimes
Francis, Matthew
Green winter
Encounter (London, England) 69:20-3 N '87
Francis. Maupassant, G. de

Franco, Audrey
Just for kicks
'Teen 30:36+ My '86
Franco, Marjorie
Daddy's baby
Redbook 171:32-4+ S '88
Genevieve goes back to work
Redbook 165:42+ Ag '85
Genevieve's psychic experience
Redbook 163:26-7+ Ag '84
Just not my type
Redbook 167:78 S '86
Lives of a cat
Redbook 167:38+ Jl '86
Midnight caller
Redbook 164:56+ Ap '85
No kidding!?!
Redbook 170:36+ Ja '88
Time to laugh again
Redbook 169:40+ Ag '87
A way with men
Redbook 169:30+ Je '87
What will be
Good Housekeeping 204:198-9 My '87
You by my side
Good Housekeeping 203:130-1+ O '86
FRANCO-GERMAN WAR, 1870-1871
Maupassant, G. de. Ball-of-fat
Maupassant, G. de. The duel
Maupassant, G. de. A fishing excursion
Maupassant, G. de. The horrible
Maupassant, G. de. A king's son
Maupassant, G. de. The mad woman
FRANK, ANNE, 1929-1945
About
Mazel, D. A longing to live
Frank and Billy. Colwin, L.
Frank Merriwell in the White House. Moore, W.
Frank Pierce, Iowa. Kinsella, W. P.
Frank Sinatra or Carleton Carpenter. Lish, G.
Frankie's soup. Lipman, E.
Franklin, Benjamin, 1706-1790
The speech of Polly Baker
The Norton book of American short stories
Franklin, Patrick, 1937-
Catalytic converter
Franklin, P. The uncertainty of strangers, and other stories
A DimEn is forever
Franklin, P. The uncertainty of strangers, and other stories
For merit
Franklin, P. The uncertainty of strangers, and other stories
Grease hunger
Franklin, P. The uncertainty of strangers, and other stories
A little peace
Franklin, P. The uncertainty of strangers, and other stories

Franklin, Patrick, 1937—_Continued_
  Love under glass
    Franklin, P. The uncertainty of strangers,
      and other stories
  The luck of the Irish
    Franklin, P. The uncertainty of strangers,
      and other stories
  New clothes
    Franklin, P. The uncertainty of strangers,
      and other stories
  Splendor and black wool
    Franklin, P. The uncertainty of strangers,
      and other stories
  Stale beer and roses
    Franklin, P. The uncertainty of strangers,
      and other stories
  Tzigane
    Franklin, P. The uncertainty of strangers,
      and other stories
  The uncertainty of strangers
    Franklin, P. The uncertainty of strangers,
      and other stories
Frank's party. Ferro, R.
Franzen, Bill, 1952-
  37 years
    Franzen, B. Hearing from Wayne, and
      other stories
  After I won the lottery
    Franzen, B. Hearing from Wayne, and
      other stories
  The Brewster family time capsule
    Franzen, B. Hearing from Wayne, and
      other stories
  Come stay with us
    Franzen, B. Hearing from Wayne, and
      other stories
  Driving
    Harper's 274:36 Je '87
  The Gene Norman Collection
    Franzen, B. Hearing from Wayne, and
      other stories
  Getting Herbert back
    Franzen, B. Hearing from Wayne, and
      other stories
  Hearing from Wayne
    Franzen, B. Hearing from Wayne, and
      other stories
  The long donut hole
    Franzen, B. Hearing from Wayne, and
      other stories
  Mom and Pop biz
    Franzen, B. Hearing from Wayne, and
      other stories
  The Park Avenue Social Review visits the
    Drought Dinner in Eagle Grove, Iowa
    Franzen, B. Hearing from Wayne, and
      other stories
  Peacekeeper
    Franzen, B. Hearing from Wayne, and
      other stories

  So what are you going to do now if you're
    a friend of Jim's?
    Franzen, B. Hearing from Wayne, and
      other stories
  Something the matter with Dad
    Franzen, B. Hearing from Wayne, and
      other stories
  This uncle
    Franzen, B. Hearing from Wayne, and
      other stories
  The volunteer organist
    Franzen, B. Hearing from Wayne, and
      other stories
  Wayne
    Franzen, B. Hearing from Wayne, and
      other stories
  The ways we surfed
    Franzen, B. Hearing from Wayne, and
      other stories
  What the twister did
    Franzen, B. Hearing from Wayne, and
      other stories
Fraser, Antonia, 1932-
  Boots
    Fraser, A. Jemima Shore's first case, and
      other stories
    John Creasey's Crime collection, 1985
  The case of the Parr children
    Fraser, A. Jemima Shore's first case, and
      other stories
  Death of an old dog
    Fraser, A. Jemima Shore's first case, and
      other stories
    The Mammoth book of modern crime
      stories; ed. by G. Hardinge
  Doctor Zeit
    Fraser, A. Jemima Shore's first case, and
      other stories
  The girl who wanted to see Venice
    Fraser, A. Jemima Shore's first case, and
      other stories
  Have a nice death
    Fraser, A. Jemima Shore's first case, and
      other stories
    Masterpieces of mystery and suspense;
      ed. by M. H. Greenberg
    The Year's best mystery and suspense
      stories, 1984
  House poison
    John Creasey's Crime collection, 1987
  Jemima Shore's first case
    Fraser, A. Jemima Shore's first case, and
      other stories
  The night mother
    Fraser, A. Jemima Shore's first case, and
      other stories
  On the battlements
    Fraser, A. Jemima Shore's first case, and
      other stories
  Swimming will be the death of you
    Fraser, A. Jemima Shore's first case, and
      other stories

Fraser, Antonia, 1932-—_Continued_
Who would kill a cat?
  Fraser, A. Jemima Shore's first case, and
    other stories
Who's been sitting in my car?
  Fraser, A. Jemima Shore's first case, and
    other stories
Your appointment is cancelled
  Ellery Queen's Prime crimes 2
  Fraser, A. Jemima Shore's first case, and
    other stories
Fraser, Joseph
Utopian dreams
  Australian science fiction; ed. by V. Ikin
Fraser, Keath
The emerald city
  The New press anthology #1
Healing
  The Literary Review (Madison, N.J.)
    28:361-72 Spr '85
Frate Dolcino, heretic. Schwob, M.
FRATRICIDE
Bradbury, R. Corpse carnival
Hoch, E. D. The problem of the fatal
  fireworks
Kirk, R. Fate's purse
McConnell, C. R. Sidney, Seth and S.A.M.
Smith, C. A. The return of the sorcerer
Wells, H. G. Walcote
Frau Messinger. Trevor, W.
FRAUD
      See also Tax evasion; Trials (Fraud)
Bickel, B. Make it never happened
Bitov, A. Penelope
Brown, F. Before she kills
Cain, J. M. Two o'clock blonde
Chipulina, E. G. Diamonds are forever
Ellis, L. R. The great rodeo fix
Francis, D. Twenty-one good men and true
Gates, D. China Blue
Gilbert, M. Audited and found correct
Gilchrist, E. The lower garden district free
  gravity mule blight; or, Rhoda, a fable
Gilchrist, E. The perfect stone
Hoch, E. D. The theft of the four of
  spades
Hyams, E. Exorcizing Baldassare
Keillor, G. The royal family
Lawson, H. The iron-bark chip
Marlowe, D. J. By means unlovely
Morrison, J. Christ, the Devil and the
  lunatic
Mortimer, J. C. Rumpole and the blind
  tasting
Mortimer, J. C. Rumpole and the last
  resort
Nielsen, H. Death scene
Pronzini, B. Caught in the act
Pronzini, B. A little larceny
Rizkalla, J. A janitor for sale
Sampson, R. Far eyes
Short, L. Swindle at Piute Sink
Stuart, J. Thirty-two votes before breakfast

Watt, N. As good as gold
Woolrich, C. The death of me
Frayne, Alula
Ripe plums
  _Ms._ 13:78+ Jl '84
Frazee, Steve, 1909-
The bounty killers
  Frazee, S. The best western stories of
    Steve Frazee
The Bretnall feud
  Frazee, S. The best western stories of
    Steve Frazee
The crew of the Foraker
  A Treasury of World War II stories; ed.
    by B. Pronzini and M. H. Greenberg
Due process
  Frazee, S. The best western stories of
    Steve Frazee
The fire killer
  Frazee, S. The best western stories of
    Steve Frazee
Great medicine
  Frazee, S. The best western stories of
    Steve Frazee
Learn the hard way
  Frazee, S. The best western stories of
    Steve Frazee
Luck of Riley
  Frazee, S. The best western stories of
    Steve Frazee
The man at Gantt's place
  Frazee, S. The best western stories of
    Steve Frazee
The man who made a beeline
  Frazee, S. The best western stories of
    Steve Frazee
My brother down there
  Frazee, S. The best western stories of
    Steve Frazee
The singing sands
  Frazee, S. The best western stories of
    Steve Frazee
  The Second reel West; ed. by B. Pron-
    zini and M. H. Greenberg
Frazier, Ian
Dating your mom
  Great American love stories; ed. by L.
    Rosenthal
Webbing
  The New Yorker 62:29-30 F 24 '86
Frazier, Levi, Jr.
In the presence of mine enemies
  Homewords: a book of Tennessee
    writers; ed. by D. Paschall
Frazier, Robert
Across those endless skies
  In the field of fire; ed. by J. Van B.
    Dann and J. Dann
The daily Chernobyl
  Synergy v2
Freak show. Bloch, R.
A freakish girl. Shen Rong

Fréchette, Louis
Tom Cariboo
  The Oxford book of French-Canadian short stories
Fred and Arthur. Gilliatt, P.
Freddie's haircut. Cameron, P.
Freddie's up. Klinkowitz, J.
Frede, Richard
Mr. Murdoch's ghost
  Haunted New England; ed. by C. G. Waugh; M. H. Greenberg and F. D. McSherry
The three of us
  McCall's 111:80-1+ Ja '84
Free. O'Hara, J.
Free afternoon. Asscher-Pinkhof, C.
Free agents. Apple, M.
Free and equal. Gandbhir, L.
The **free** and the caged. Cooper, J. C.
Free association. Bloch, D.
Free dirt. Beaumont, C.
Free fall (R's account). Nichols, R.
The **free** fur coat. Davie, E.
Free the canaries from their cages! Granit, A.
Free will. Pavese, C.
FREEDOM *See* Liberty
Freedom. Ferguson, W.
Freedom. Parise, G.
FREEDOM OF RELIGION *See* Religious liberty
Freeman, Anne Hobson
Hugh
  The Virginia Quarterly Review 61:277-301 Spr '85
Freeman, Castle, 1944-
Before he went out west
  Freeman, C. The bride of Ambrose, and other stories
  The Massachusetts Review 26:208-16 Summ/Aut '85
The bride of Ambrose
  Freeman, C. The bride of Ambrose, and other stories
Crime of the century
  Freeman, C. The bride of Ambrose, and other stories
Dreaming of Africa
  Freeman, C. The bride of Ambrose, and other stories
The exile, the housekeeper, and Flora, the beauty of Rome
  Freeman, C. The bride of Ambrose, and other stories
My life on the snowplow
  Freeman, C. The bride of Ambrose, and other stories
Not everyone can be a soldier
  Freeman, C. The bride of Ambrose, and other stories
The ride
  Freeman, C. The bride of Ambrose, and other stories

Seven prophecies of Egypt
  Freeman, C. The bride of Ambrose, and other stories
The song of Roland
  Freeman, C. The bride of Ambrose, and other stories
That is no country for old men
  Freeman, C. The bride of Ambrose, and other stories
Freeman, Jean Todd
Where tomorrow waits
  Good Housekeeping 206:166-7+ My '88
Freeman, Judith, 1946-
The Botanic Gardens
  Freeman, J. Family attractions
Camp Rose
  Freeman, J. Family attractions
Clearfield
  Freeman, J. Family attractions
The death of a Mormon elder
  Freeman, J. Family attractions
Family attractions
  Freeman, J. Family attractions
Going out to sea
  Freeman, J. Family attractions
It sure is cold here at night
  Freeman, J. Family attractions
The Joan Crawford letter
  Freeman, J. Family attractions
Pretend we're French
  Freeman, J. Family attractions
The rake people
  Freeman, J. Family attractions
What is this movie?
  Freeman, J. Family attractions
Freeman, Lucy
The last dream
  Murder in Manhattan; ed. by B. Adler
Freeman, Mary Eleanor Wilkins, 1852-1930
The Cat
  Roger Caras' Treasury of great cat stories
The lost ghost
  Haunted women; ed. by A. Bendixen
  The Oxford book of English ghost stories
Louisa
  Old maids; ed. by S. Koppelman
Luella Miller
  Haunted women; ed. by A. Bendixen
  The Norton book of American short stories
  Vampires; ed. by A. Ryan
A moral exigency
  The Other woman; ed. by S. Koppelman
Old Woman Magoun
  Between mothers & daughters; ed. by S. Koppelman
Silence
  Yankee witches; ed. by C. G. Waugh; M. H. Greenberg and F. D. McSherry

Freeman, Mary Eleanor Wilkins, 1852-1930
—Continued
The twelfth guest
"May your days be merry and bright"
and other Christmas stories by wom-
en; ed. by S. Koppelman
FREEMASONS
Maupassant, G. de. My uncle Sosthenes
The **freethinker**: a shtetl atheist. Blinkin, M.
Freeze. Jauss, D.
The **freeze.** Martin, V.
Freezeframe. Benford, G.
FREEZING OF HUMAN BODIES *See*
Cryonics
Freezone. Shirley, J.
Freight car repair yard pranks. Conroy, J.
FREIGHTERS *See* Ships
Fremlin, Celia
Accommodation vacant
John Creasey's Crime collection, 1984
Bluebeard's key
John Creasey's Crime collection, 1985
The bonus years
Fremlin, C. A lovely day to die, and
other stories
A case of maximum need
Fremlin, C. A lovely day to die, and
other stories
Dangerous sport
Fremlin, C. A lovely day to die, and
other stories
Don't be frightened
Tales from Ellery Queen's Mystery
Magazine: short stories for young
adults
Etiquette for dying
Fremlin, C. A lovely day to die, and
other stories
High dive
Fremlin, C. A lovely day to die, and
other stories
The holiday
Fremlin, C. A lovely day to die, and
other stories
A lovely day to die [Variant title: A lovely
morning to die]
Fremlin, C. A lovely day to die, and
other stories
The luck of the Devil
Fremlin, C. A lovely day to die, and
other stories
The miracle
Fremlin, C. A lovely day to die, and
other stories
The post-graduate thesis
Fremlin, C. A lovely day to die, and
other stories
The sensory deprivation tank
John Creasey's Crime collection, 1987
A strong shoulder to weep on
Fremlin, C. A lovely day to die, and
other stories

Test case
Fremlin, C. A lovely day to die, and
other stories
The woman who had everything
Fremlin, C. A lovely day to die, and
other stories
FRENCH
Africa
Balzac, H. de. A passion in the desert
Camus, A. The adulterous woman
Maupassant, G. de. Marroca
Brazil
Camus, A. The growing stone
England
Gallant, M. The colonel's child
Morand, P. Delphine
Germany
Balzac, H. de. The red inn
Sagan, F. The distant cousin
Iraq
Kotzwinkle, W. Disturbance reported on a
pipeline
Italy
Déon, M. Umbrian afternoon
Maupassant, G. de. An adventure
Sweden
Morand, P. Borealis
Tunisia
Colette. The pearls
United States
Briskin, M. Before and after Celeste
Hemingway, E. Wine of Wyoming
French. Asscher-Pinkhof, C.
FRENCH CANADIANS
Carrier, R. What language do bears speak?
Ferron, J. The bridge
Ferron, J. Cadieu
Ferron, J. The dead cow in the canyon
Ferron, J. The grey dog
Ferron, J. Mélie and the bull
Ferron, J. La Mi-Carême
Ferron, J. The parrot
Ferron, J. The provinces
Ferron, J. Tiresome company
Gallant, M. Saturday
Gaspé, P. A. de. Rose Latulipe
Laurence, M. The loons
London, J. Diable: a dog
Maillet, A. Two saints
Spencer, E. Jean-Pierre
A **French** Enoch Arden. Maupassant, G. de
FRENCH LANGUAGE
Davis, L. French lesson I: le meurtre
French lesson I: le meurtre. Davis, L.
French lessons. Rasputin, V. G.
French movie. Colwin, L.
The **French** prize. Early, P.
FRENCH REVOLUTION *See* France—1789-
1799
FRENCH RIVIERA *See* Riviera (France and
Italy)
French scenes. Waldrop, H.

FRENCH SOLDIERS *See* Soldiers—France
French toothpaste. Lurie, M.
Frenchie's wife. St. Pierre, P. H.
Frenchmen and plumbers. Soukup, M.
Freriks, Kester
Grand Hotel Lembang
The Massachusetts Review 27:203-15
Summ '86
Medea's kiss
The Literary Review (Madison, N.J.)
30:511-31 Summ '87
A **fresh** snow. Humphrey, W.
A **Fresno** fable. Saroyan, W.
FREUD, SIGMUND, 1856-1939
About
Sage, V. Obscurity
Soutter, A. S F
Freund, Edith
Father for hire
Redbook 164:54+ N '84
Friday morning: an orderly's tale. Klíma, I.
Friday night. Pascoe, B.
Friday night at Silver Star. Henley, P.
The **Friday** night shift at the Taco House
blues (wah-wah). Coleman, W.
Friedenkraft, Georges
Anne
Short story international 58
Friedman, B. H.
Whispers
American made; ed. by M. Leyner; C.
White and T. Glynn
Friedman, Bruce Jay, 1930-
The adventurer
Friedman, B. J. Let's hear it for a
beautiful guy, and other works of
short fiction
The best we have
Friedman, B. J. Let's hear it for a
beautiful guy, and other works of
short fiction
Business is business
Friedman, B. J. Let's hear it for a
beautiful guy, and other works of
short fiction
The Candide of copiers
Friedman, B. J. Let's hear it for a
beautiful guy, and other works of
short fiction
Detroit Abe
Friedman, B. J. Let's hear it for a
beautiful guy, and other works of
short fiction
A different ball game
Friedman, B. J. Let's hear it for a
beautiful guy, and other works of
short fiction
An ironic Yetta Montana
Friedman, B. J. Let's hear it for a
beautiful guy, and other works of
short fiction

King of the Bloodies
Friedman, B. J. Let's hear it for a
beautiful guy, and other works of
short fiction
Let's hear it for a beautiful guy
Friedman, B. J. Let's hear it for a
beautiful guy, and other works of
short fiction
Living together
Friedman, B. J. Let's hear it for a
beautiful guy, and other works of
short fiction
Marching through Delaware
Friedman, B. J. Let's hear it for a
beautiful guy, and other works of
short fiction
The mourner
Friedman, B. J. Let's hear it for a
beautiful guy, and other works of
short fiction
Our Lady of the Lockers
Friedman, B. J. Let's hear it for a
beautiful guy, and other works of
short fiction
Pitched out
Esquire 110:62-4+ Jl '88
The pledges
Friedman, B. J. Let's hear it for a
beautiful guy, and other works of
short fiction
The scientist
Friedman, B. J. Let's hear it for a
beautiful guy, and other works of
short fiction
The tax man
Friedman, B. J. Let's hear it for a
beautiful guy, and other works of
short fiction
The war criminal
Friedman, B. J. Let's hear it for a
beautiful guy, and other works of
short fiction
Friedman, Paul, 1937-
Blackburn
Friedman, P. Serious trouble
The family
Friedman, P. Serious trouble
A period of grace
Friedman, P. Serious trouble
An unexpected death
Friedman, P. Serious trouble
Friel, Brian
The gold in the sea
The Best of Irish wit and wisdom; ed.
by J. McCarthy
Friel, George
Onlookers
Streets of stone; ed. by M. Burgess and
H. Whyte
The **friend**. Barthelme, S.
Friend. Kelly, J. P., and Kessel, J.
The **friend**. Lish, G.
A **friend** and protector. Taylor, P. H.

A **friend,** brother maybe. Ríos, A.
A **friend** in need. Maugham, W. S.
A **friend** of Dosser Farr. Gallacher, T.
A **friend** of the family. Eisenreich, H.
A **friend** of the family. Wexelblatt, R.
FRIENDS *See* Friendship
FRIENDS, SOCIETY OF *See* Society of Friends
Friends. Abe, A.
The **friends.** Jacobsen, J.
Friends. Mazel, D.
The **friends.** Ocampo, S.
Friends. Paley, G.
Friends. Pavese, C.
Friends and fortunes. Hogan, L.
Friends at evening. Holleran, A.
Friend's best man. Carroll, J.
Friends' eyes. Salama, F.
Friends in San Rosario. Henry, O.
The **friends** of Miss Julia. O'Hara, J.
The **friends** of the friends. James, H.
Friends with you. Hathaway, W.
FRIENDSHIP
    See also Love
  Abbott, K. He was reaching for a shovel
  Abbott, L. K. Category Z
  Abbott, L. K. Martians
  Abe, A. Friends
  Adams, A. Elizabeth
  Adams, A. New best friends
  Adams, A. Tide pools
  Adams, A. Time in Santa Fe
  Adams, A. Waiting for Stella
  Archer, J. Colonel Bullfrog
  Ashley, M. A. Gracefully afraid
  Asimov, I. The magic umbrella
  Aucamp, H. Soup for the sick
  Auchincloss, L. No friend like a new friend
  Austin, M. H. Blue roses
  Bangs, C. J. Existentialists
  Barstow, S. The apples of paradise
  Barthelme, D. Some of us had been threatening our friend Colby
  Barthelme, S. Their house
  Baxter, C. A short course in Nietzschean ethics
  Baxter, C. Xavier speaking
  Beattie, A. Cards
  Beattie, A. Coney Island
  Beattie, A. Honey
  Bedard, B. Sheer Energy
  Bernard, K. Morsels
  Bernen, R. Two lives
  Bonnie, F. A settlement of wages
  Bonosky, P. Sin
  Boswell, R. Dancing in the movies
  Boswell, R. Little Bear
  Boswell, R. The right thing
  Bowles, P. He of the assembly
  Bowles, P. The time of friendship
  Boyle, T. C. Two ships
  Brand, M. Half a partner

  Briskin, M. Children, dogs and dying men
  Briskin, M. My father and Signor Corelli
  Brodkey, H. Falling and ascending bodies: four passages
  Brown, R. One of two
  Burgin, R. The victims
  Burke, T. The hollow man
  Burns, M. The Norman Fisher Memorial Ski Race
  Carlson, R. Santa Monica
  Carlson, R. The time I died
  Carpentier, A. Birdy's flight
  Carter, M. The things that would never be mine
  Carver, R. Cathedral
  Carver, R. Feathers
  Carver, R. What we talk about when we talk about love
  Carver, R. Where I'm calling from
  Chernoff, M. Don't send poems, send money
  Chernoff, M. The hills of Andorra
  Chipulina, E. G. One of those things
  Choyce, L. Major repairs
  Choyce, L. Prying loose
  Clayton, J. J. Prewar quality
  Cohen, R. Shamsky and other casualties
  Colette. Habit
  Colette. The portrait
  Colwin, L. A couple of old flames
  Cooper, J. C. Happiness does not come in colors
  Cooper, J. C. A jewel for a friend
  Cooper, J. C. The life you live (may not be your own)
  Cooper, J. C. Without love
  Covino, M. The passion of the artist is nothing compared to the passion of the businessman
  Crapser, W. Wild child
  Cullen, E. J. Down time Tyler, Texas
  Davie, E. Shoe in the sand
  Davis, L. The house plans
  Day, H. When Dustin "called on"
  Dickinson, C. Bill Boston
  Dickinson, C. A night in the garden
  Drake, M. Remembrance of things past
  Drake, R. 1975 has come and gone
  Drake, R. The moon-fixer
  Drake, R. On the side porch
  Drake, R. The veteran
  Dubus, A. The dark men
  Dubus, A. Deaths at sea
  Dunn, D. Getting used to it
  Dybek, S. Blight
  Dybek, S. Hot ice
  Eisenberg, D. Flotsam
  Engberg, S. Morgan and Joanna
  Everett, P. L. Turtle
  Faik, S. Coming of age on Kasikadasi
  Faik, S. A man and his habit
  Ferguson, W. Terror
  Fetler, J. The dust of Yuri Serafimovich

FRIENDSHIP—*Continued*

Flook, M. The fairway
Flook, M. A walk in the city
Flynn, R. The boy from Chillicothe
Franzen, B. Hearing from Wayne
Friedman, B. J. The best we have
Frucht, A. The habit of friendship
Frucht, A. Paradise
Gaines, C. Three o'clock and woodstream
Gaitskill, M. Connection
Gallagher, T. Girls
Gallagher, T. Recourse
Garrett, G. P. Farmer in the dell
Garrett, G. P. Love is a cold kingdom
Garrett, G. P. A record as long as your arm
Gbadamosi, R. A. Death by the waterfall
Gifkins, M. Matching the blue
Gilchrist, E. Summer, an elegy
Gilchrist, M. My friend
Gilliatt, P. Fred and Arthur
Gilliatt, P. Staying in bed
Gingher, M. My mother's confession
Girion, B. King of the hill
Girion, B. Rip-off!
Glasser, P. Marmosets
Gogol', N. V. The tale of how Ivan Ivanovich quarreled with Ivan Nikiforovich
Gold, H. Bart and Helene at Annie-and-Fred's
Gold, H. A death on the East Side
Gold, H. A karmic lover
Gold, H. A selfish story
Gooch, B. Maine
Gordon, M. Out of the fray
Gorky, M. The affair of the clasps
Gorky, M. Chums
Goyen, W. The Texas principessa
Groff, D. Nobody's child
Gurnah, A. Bossy
Haake, K. One pair red, one pair blue
Haake, K. A scrap of green silk
Hall, M. L. Lucky Lafe
Hall, R. W. The Purple Prince
Hartley, L. P. Witheling End
Havemann, E. Death of the Nation
Hemingway, E. The three-day blow
Hemley, R. The mouse town
Hempel, A. In the cemetery where Al Jolson is buried
Henry, O. After twenty years
Henry, O. Friends in San Rosario
Higgins, G. V. A case of Chivas Regal
Highsmith, P. Chris's last party
Hochstein, R. She should have died hereafter
Hogan, L. Friends and fortunes
Hornung, E. W. The last word
Ingalls, R. Early morning sightseer
An Injustice revealed
Jackson, G. Billy's girl
Janowitz, T. The slaves in New York

Jhabvala, R. P. Two more under the Indian sun
Jia Pingwa. How much can a man bear?
Johnson, B. S. Everyone knows somebody who's dead
Johnson, W. The girl who would be Russian
Johnson, W. The last song of exile
Josipovici, G. He
Kant, U. A letter to comrade Ernst L.
Kauffman, J. Harmony
Kawabata, Y. The young lady of Suruga
Keesing, N. End of the affair
Kercheval, J. L. A clean house
Kessler, J. F. Ikaros
Kilgore, D. Last summer "How I spent my summer vacation" by Diana Lancaster
Kilgore, D. Unpaid debts
King, F. H. Indirect method
Kingsolver, B. Rose-Johnny
Kinsella, W. P. The further adventures of Slugger McBatt
Kinsella, W. P. Pretend dinners
Klass, P. Cowboy time
Klass, P. Gingerbread men
Klass, P. Murderers don't cook for themselves
Klass, P. Officemate with pink feathers
Klíma, I. Saturday morning: a thief's tale
Klinkowitz, J. Release
Kornblatt, J. R. Susan
Lawson, H. An old mate of your father's
Lawson, H. Telling Mrs. Baker
Leavitt, D. Dedicated
Liben, M. Change of heart
Liben, M. One
Liben, M. The Tolstoy quotation
Liphshitz, A. Jum'a and Jamila
Liphshitz, A. Under the horses' hooves
Lipman, E. Frankie's soup
Lish, G. What is left to link us
Lispector, C. The message
Lispector, C. A sincere friendship
Lispector, C. The solution
Livesey, M. Peter and the asteroids
Lofts, N. Gateway to happiness?
London, J. Burning off
London, J. Enough rope
Longyear, B. B. Enemy mine
Lopatin, J. Krystal goes mystical
Lurie, M. The death of Rappaport
Lurie, M. Kicking on
Lynch, L. Jefferson II: in and out of the darkness
MacDonald, D. R. The Chinese rifle
MacDonald, D. R. Work
Madden, D. Hidden symptoms
Major, A. The good old days
Mares, E. A. Florinto
Martone, M. Parting
Mathers, P. The master & servant act
Mattison, A. Painting day

FRIENDSHIP—*Continued*

Maupassant, G. de. Profitable business
Mazel, D. A matter of pride
Mazel, D. The storekeeper
Mazel, D. A visit with Esta
McCorkle, J. First union blues
McGuane, T. Sportsmen
Meckel, C. The crow
Mencken, S. H. Little white girl
Millard, P. The diamond
Moore, S. Dove shooting
Moravia, A. Jewellery
Mordden, E. The dinner party
Morgan, B. The organ piece
Morris, W. To Calabria
Morris, W. Wishing you and your loved ones every happiness
Morrison, J. It opens your eyes
Mukherjee, B. Isolated incidents
Munro, A. Jesse and Meribeth
Munro, A. Monsieur les Deux Chapeaux
Murphy, Y. The children inside the trunk
Nagibin, ÍÙ. M. The outsider
Nevai, L. Star game
Norris, L. Gamblers
Norris, L. A professional man
Norris, L. Reverse for Dennis
Norris, L. Sing it again, Wordsworth
Nugent, B. Tough as a man
O'Brien, D. Final touches
O'Brien, D. Seals
O'Brien, E. Savages
Ocampo, S. The friends
Paley, G. Friends
Paley, G. Midrash on happiness
Pancake, B. D. The salvation of me
Parise, G. Memory
Pascoe, B. Neither did I
Pascoe, B. That's what friends are for
Pavese, C. The beggars
Pavese, C. The evil eye
Pavese, C. First love
Pavese, C. Friends
Pavese, C. Loyalty
Pavese, C. The name
Pavese, C. The villa on the hill
Peterson, M. Mercy flights
Petrakis, H. M. The miracle
Petrakis, H. M. The passing of the ice
Pfeil, F. The night game
Pfeil, F. The quality of light in Maine
Pilcher, R. Miss Cameron at Christmas
Pitzen, J. The village
Potter, N. A. J. Pen pals
Pritchett, M. Close water
Profumo, D. The blind man eats many flies
Pronzini, B. Under the skin
Prose, F. Other lives
Rambach, P. The crescent
Raphael, F. Sleeps six
Rasputin, V. G. Meeting
Rasputin, V. G. Rudolfio
Rile, K. Solid walls

Ríos, A. The way spaghetti feels
Roberts, N. Flames
Robinson, K. S. Ridge running
Robison, M. Mirror
Rossiter, S. Question of light
Rossiter, S. Secrets
Russ, J. Visiting
Russ, J. Visiting day
Sams, F. Fubar
Sams, F. Howdy Doody time
Sanders, S. R. Wake
Sayles, J. The Halfway Diner
Schinto, J. The friendships of girls unpopular together
Schinto, J. The ring; or, A girl confesses
Scholz, C. The menagerie of Babel
Schow, D. J. Pamela's get
Schwartz, J. Day trip
Schwartz, L. S. The death of Harriet Gross
Schwartz, S. Slow-motion
Schwartz, S. Society of Friends
Shaw, I. Act of faith
Shaw, I. Then we were three
Shaw, J. B. A new life
Simpson, M. Three maids' children
Skrzynecki, P. "Is your wife here, honey?"
Skrzynecki, P. The wild dogs
Šmahelová, H. House of joy
Smiley, J. Lily
Smiley, J. The pleasure of her company
Soldatow, S. Never blue
Soldatow, S. Pleasure
Sontag, S. The way we live now
Sorrells, R. T. Three rivers
Spark, M. The Portobello Road
Spencer, E. The business venture
Spivack, K. The guardian
Spivack, K. My friend who lives in a commune
Stephen, J. The other side of summer
Strand, M. Wooley
Summers, H. S. Herschell
Summers, H. S. A hundred paths
Swados, H. Nights in the gardens of Brooklyn
Swados, H. Where does your music come from?
Targan, B. Surviving adverse seasons
Taylor, C. Catherine and Michael
Taylor, C. These women
Thomas, J. Christmas in Calpe
Thomas, J. Last factory blues
Thompson, J. Applause, applause
Thompson, J. Lenny dying, Pacific standard time
Thurm, M. Winter
Tremain, R. La plume de mon ami
Trevor, W. Beyond the pale
Trevor, W. Virgins
Tsushima, Y. South wind
Underwood, M. The man who nursed grievances
Updike, J. Deaths of distant friends

FRIENDSHIP—*Continued*

Upward, E. At the Ferry Inn

Verma, N. Exile

Verma, N. The world elsewhere

Walpole, Sir H. The little ghost

Warren, J. Michael

Waters, M. The Love Chapter

Weaver, G. Morality play

Welch, D. Memories of a vanished period

Wexler, J. World of women

Whatley, W. Something to lose

Whelan, G. The dogs in Renoir's garden

Wilbur, E. Perfection

Williams, T. Two on a party

Willson, H. Loyalty erosion

Wilson, B. Take Louise Nevelson

Wilson, B. Walking on the moon

Winton, T. Bay of Angels

Winton, T. Holding

Winton, T. Nilsam's friend

Winton, T. The oppressed

Wolfe, T. Katamoto

Wolff, T. Hunters in the snow

Woodman, A. Life story

Woodman, A. Still points

Woods, C. The quarry

Yasuoka, S. Bad company

Zhang Jie. Under the hawthorn

Zhang Jie. Who knows how to live?

Friendship. José, F. S.

Friendship. Katz, S.

Friendship and property. Rooke, L.

The **friendships** of girls unpopular together. Schinto, J.

Fries, Wanda Haynes

Mel's back

Michigan Quarterly Review 27:167-71 Wint '88

Friesner, Esther M.

Honeycomb

Magic in Ithkar 4; ed. by A. Norton and R. Adams

A winter's night

Werewolves; ed. by J. Yolen and M. H. Greenberg

Frimmell's successor. Liben, M.

The **fringe**. Card, O. S.

Frisian horses. Beekman, E. M.

Fritch, Charles E.

The curse of Hooligan's Bar

100 great fantasy short short stories; ed. by I. Asimov; T. Carr and M. H. Greenberg

Fritzchen. Beaumont, C.

Frog acts. Dixon, S.

The **frog** hunters. Colter, C.

Frogchild on the day of Corpus Christi. Antoni, R. W.

FROGS

Antoni, R. W. Frogchild on the day of Corpus Christi

Shimaki, K. The red frog

Twain, M. The notorious jumping frog of Calaveras County

Frogs and scientists. Herbert, F.

Frog's break. Dixon, S.

The **frogs** of Quirra-Quirra. Prichard, K. S.

From a French prison. Rhys, J.

From a juror's notebook. Schinto, J.

From a novel in progress: Dusty eats out. Lynch, L.

From Bach to broccoli. Kearns, R.

From below the bridge. Kim, Y. I.

From cloud to cloud. Gallant, M.

From downtown at the buzzer. Effinger, G. A.

From Flores. Wilson, E.

From genealogies. Glantz, M.

From Hank in Nashville. Hall, T. T.

From Hell, again. Frost, G.

From in Albania. Eisenstein, S.

From noon to midnight. Vorsatz, F.

From 'Peter and Rosa'. Dinesen, I.

From Proust to Dada. Gold, H.

From the bottom up. Wilson, L. A.

From the darkness. Mrożek, S.

From the government printing office. Neville, K.

From the life of the president. Baumbach, J.

From The "London Times" of 1904. Twain, M.

From the mountains of Pike. Stuart, J.

From the outside. Charney, A.

From time to time. Burdick, B. S.

From whence the rivers come. Baker, C.

Front seat. Willson, H.

FRONTIER AND PIONEER LIFE

Card, O. S. Hatrack River

Johnson, D. M. A man called Horse

Windsor, G. Addendum to the first fleet journals

Arizona

Doyle, Sir A. C. The American's tale

Australia

Baynton, B. The chosen vessel

Doyle, Sir A. C. Bones. The April fool of Harvey's Sluice

Eldershaw, M. B. Aubade

Lawson, H. The bush undertaker

Lawson, H. A child in the dark, and a foreign father

Lawson, H. A double buggy at Lahey's Creek

Lawson, H. The drover's wife

Lawson, H. In a dry season

Lawson, H. Joe Wilson's courtship

Lawson, H. On the edge of a plain

Lawson, H. Telling Mrs. Baker

Lawson, H. 'Water them geraniums'

Murnane, G. Land deal

Pascoe, B. Flour for your grave

Prichard, K. S. The bride of Far-away

Prichard, K. S. Luck

Canada

Ferron, J. The dead cow in the canyon

FRONTIER AND PIONEER LIFE—Continued

Indiana
Kercheval, J. L. A history of Indiana

Kansas
Muller, M. The time of the wolves

Montana
Pronzini, B. Hero

Nevada
Davis, S. A Carson poker incident
Davis, S. A miner's Christmas carol

New England
Hawthorne, N. Roger Malvin's burial

New Mexico
Barker, E. First notch

Ohio
Bierce, A. The boarded window

Western States
Austin, M. H. The House of offence
Austin, M. H. Mahala Joe
Sandoz, M. The vine
Schaefer, J. W. Cat nipped

Frontier vigil. Bryan, J. Y.
Frontiers. Reed, K.

Frost, Gregory
From Hell, again
Ripper! Ed. by G. Dozois and S. Casper
Sardofa's horseshoes
Magic in Ithkar 2; ed. by A. Norton and R. Adams

Frost and thunder. Garrett, R.
Frost flies alone. McCoy, H.
Frost in April. Whitaker, M.
Frozen. Treadway, J.
Frozen fear. Bloch, R.
The **frozen** fields. Bowles, P.
Frozen journey. Dick, P. K.

Frucht, Abby
The anniversary
Frucht, A. Fruit of the month
Engagements
Frucht, A. Fruit of the month
Fate and the poet
Frucht, A. Fruit of the month
Fruit of the month
Frucht, A. Fruit of the month
The habit of friendship
Frucht, A. Fruit of the month
How to live alone
Frucht, A. Fruit of the month
Midnight
Frucht, A. Fruit of the month
Nuns in love
Frucht, A. Fruit of the month
Paradise
Frucht, A. Fruit of the month
Peace and passivity
Frucht, A. Fruit of the month
Trees at night
Frucht, A. Fruit of the month
Winter
Frucht, A. Fruit of the month

Fruit drink. Noonan, B.

Fruit of the month. Frucht, A.
Fruit of the season. Brown, M. W.
FRUIT PICKERS See Migrant labor
Fruition at forty. Narayan, R. K.
Fruits of sorrow; or, An old maid's story. Vaughan, M. C.
Fruitstand I: Oranges out of season. Lynch, L.
Fruitstand II: Honeydew moon. Lynch, L.
Frustrate. Austin, M. H.
Fryday. Summers, B.
Fryed cutlets. Broun, H.
Frying the flag. Durrell, L.
FTX; Fort Irwin. Alderson, T.
Fu Da regains his wife. Yang Zhenwen
Fubar. Sams, F.
Fuda-no-Tsuji. Endō, S.
Fuel of fire. Cripps, A. S.

Fuentes, Carlos
Aura
The Slaying of the dragon; ed. by F. Rottensteiner
The doll queen
The Art of the tale; ed. by D. Halpern
Mother and doctor
The Review of Contemporary Fiction 8:168-78 Summ '88
The two Elenas
Short story international 46

Fuentes Millán, Hugo
Just what it says
Américas 39:48-50 Ja/F '87

Fuerst, Robert E.
The plight of the dragonfly
Short story international 64

Fuga. Josipovici, G.
The **fugitive.** Day, R. C.
The **fugitive.** Morrison, J.

FUGITIVE SLAVES
Crowley, A. The king of the wood
Dall, C. W. H. Annie Gray: a tale

FUGITIVES
See also Escaped convicts; Fugitive slaves; Manhunts; Outlaws
Barker, C. Son of celluloid
Bates, H. E. A great day for Bonzo
Bloch, R. The cure
Conley, R. J. Wickliffe
Conley, R. J. Wili Woyi
Ford, R. Rock Springs
Gordimer, N. A city of the dead, a city of the living
Gordimer, N. A correspondence course
Greene, G. Across the bridge
Hood, M. Doing this, saying that, to applause
Kalpakian, L. Veteran's Day
Linehan, P. One last hunting pack
Morrison, J. The fugitive
Pascoe, B. Sirens
Stuart, J. Evidence is high proof
Valladares, A. Reality
Wright, R. Big boy leaves home

FUGITIVES—*Continued*
Wright, R. The man who lived underground
The **fugitives**. Jones, M.
The **fugitives** discover that they knew nothing. Gustafsson, L.
Fugue. Knuttel, W.
The **fugue**. McCormack, E. P.
Fugue for violin and Three Stooges. Boylan, J.
Fühmann, Franz
The isle of dreams
Short story international 63
FUJIWARA, MURASAKI *See* Murasaki Shikibu, b. 978?
Fulfillment. Sams, F.
Fulfillment. Van Vogt, A. E.
The **"fulfillment"** of Grace Eliot. Auchincloss, L.
Full chicken richness. Davidson, A.
Full circle. Dawson, F.
Full circle. Welch, D.
Full fathom five my father lies. Lee, R. B.
Fullcircle. Buchan, J.
Fuller, Robert G.
Sherman was right
A Treasury of World War II stories; ed. by B. Pronzini and M. H. Greenberg
The **fullness** of life. Wharton, E.
The **fun** dome. Harris, M.
The **fun** they had. Asimov, I.
The **function** of dream sleep. Ellison, H.
FUND RAISING
Hauptman, W. Hands across America
Wolff, T. The missing person
The **fundamentals**. Robinson, M. A.
A **funeral**. Clarke, A. C.
The **funeral**. Scarth, L.
FUNERAL DIRECTORS *See* Undertakers and undertaking
Funeral for a friend. Heyrman, P.
Funeral in a small town. Wasylyk, S.
Funeral plans. Cooper, J. C.
FUNERAL RITES AND CEREMONIES
Alden, P. B. All the way to East Texas
Bloch, R. A quiet funeral
Blythe, R. The windfall
Bradbury, R. One for his lordship, and one for the road!
Brown, S. H. Communion
Caldwell, E. The fly in the coffin
Campos-De Metro, J. The grape's vine, the horse's mouth
Chavez, A. The fiddler and the Angelito
Ch'en, Y.-C. The dying
Clark, M. Disquiet
Clarke, A. C. A funeral
Collins, L. Driving back from the funeral
Colter, C. The amoralists
Crane, S. The upturned face
Crowley, J. Snow
Daniels, C. Chatham County
Dawkins, C. The mourner

Dennison, G. On being a son
Durban, P. This heat
Friedman, B. J. The mourner
García Márquez, G. Big Mama's funeral
Gordimer, N. Six feet of the country
Grace, P. Waimarie
Hall, M. L. Joanna
Heise, K. Aunt Ella's funeral
Hemingway, E. An Alpine idyll
Hemley, R. Polish luggage
Hospital, J. T. Ashes to ashes
Hurston, Z. N. Cock Robin Beale Street
Kawabata, Y. Makeup
Krist, G. How I learned to raise the dead of Bergen County
La Puma, S. Wear it in good health
Lawson, H. The bush undertaker
Lawson, H. The union buries its dead
Leedom-Ackerman, J. The impostor
Lish, G. Mr. Goldbaum
Mason, B. A. Blue country
Matthew, J. R. Testimony
Miller, B. The lonesomes ain't no spring picnic
Murphy, P. Master of ceremonies
Nelson, P. The dowry
O'Connor, F. The drunkard
Padilla, M. Papel
Petrakis, H. M. The victim
Pritchett, M. Close water
Pritchett, M. The principles of flotation
Rifaat, A. At the time of the jasmine
Rive, R. Resurrection
Robison, M. I get by
Rooke, L. Mama Tuddi done over
Rule, J. Blessed are the dead
Scarth, L. The funeral
Schulman, H. We were of two minds
Scott, L. The house of funerals
Singer, I. B. The last gaze
Somers, A. The burial
Stern, S. Goldfinch & Son
Stern, S. The theft of Lily
Stuart, J. Land of our enemies
Thorman, C. Fifty years of eternal vigilance
Tuohy, F. A floral tribute
Wan Zhi. Open ground
West, J. The wake
Whitaker, M. No stone for Jochebed
White, P. Down at the dump
Willis, C. Service for the burial of the dead
Wilson, L. A. From the bottom up
Windsor, G. In the house of the dead
Wolfe, T. An angel on the porch
Funland. Oates, J. C.
The **funnel** of God. Bloch, R.
Funny. Dawson, F.
Funny man. Pascoe, B.
The **funny** tale of . . . Vergil, the laid-back dog. Robinson, B.
A **funny** thing. Bates, H. E.

A **funny** thing about mother. Robinson, B.
Funny valentines. Cooper, J. C.
The **fur** coat. O'Faoláin, S.
FUR GARMENTS
Davie, E. The free fur coat
Hughes, D. B. F. Everybody needs a mink
O'Faoláin, S. The fur coat
The **fur** of the bear. Krysl, M.
FUR TRADE
See also Trading posts
Furlong, Monica
The drum
Winter's tales, new ser. v2
The garden
Winter's tales, new ser. v4
Furman, Laura
Buddy
The New Yorker 60:42-9 Ap 9 '84
Eldorado
Prize stories, Texas Institute of Letters;
ed. by M. Terry
Something called San Francisco
Southwest Review 72:168-81 Spr '87
Sunny
The New Yorker 60:29-34 Ja 28 '85
The **furnished** room. Henry, O.
FURNITURE
See also Chairs; Tables
Carver, R. Why don't you dance?
Dickens, C. Mr. Testator's visitation
Maupassant, G. de. Who knows?
Poe, E. A. The philosophy of furniture
The **furniture** store. Minus, E.
The **further** adventures of Slugger McBatt.
Kinsella, W. P.
Further confessions. Oates, J. C.
Further reading in gastrotopology: a memoir
by J. J. Case. Westlake, M.
Furui, Yoshikichi
Night fragrance
The Literary Review (Madison, N.J.)
30:141-83 Wint '87
The **fury.** Ocampo, S.
The **fusing.** Hull, H. R.
The **futile** man. Faik, S.
Futrelle, Jacques, 1875-1912
The house that was
Death locked in; ed. by D. G. Greene
and R. C. S. Adey
The phantom motor
The Penguin classic crime omnibus
The scarlet thread
Murder and mystery in Boston; ed. by
C. L. R. Waugh; F. D. McSherry and
M. H. Greenberg
The stolen Rubens
The Deadly arts; ed. by B. Pronzini and
M. Muller
The superfluous finger
Kill or cure; ed. by M. Muller and B.
Pronzini

Futrelle, May
The grinning god
Death locked in; ed. by D. G. Greene
and R. C. S. Adey
"La **Futura**". Sagan, F.
FUTURE, STORIES OF THE
See also Science fiction
Abbott, L. K. Youth on Mars
Abernathy, R. Heirs apparent
Aikin, J. My life in the jungle
Aldiss, B. W. The gods in flight
Aldridge, R. Click
Amis, M. The immortals
Amis, M. The little puppy that could
Amis, M. The time disease
Anderson, P. No truce with kings
Anthony, P. Encounter
Anthony, P. Phog
Anthony, P. Small mouth, bad taste
Asimov, I. All the troubles of the world
Asimov, I. Dreaming is a private thing
Asimov, I. The end of eternity
Asimov, I. The feeling of power
Asimov, I. Franchise
Asimov, I. Grow old along with me
Asimov, I. I'm in Marsport without Hilda
Asimov, I. "In a good cause--"
Asimov, I. It's such a beautiful day
Asimov, I. The last question
Asimov, I. Profession
Asimov, I. Spell my name with an S
Asimov, I. Sure thing
Asimov, I. The ugly little boy
Asimov, I. The winnowing
Auster, P. In the country of last things
[excerpt]
Ballard, J. G. The cage of sand
Ballard, J. G. Memories of the Space Age
Ballard, J. G. Myths of the near future
Baumgart, D. All you can eat
Bear, G. Petra
Benét, S. V. By the waters of Babylon
Benford, G. The future of the Jovian sys-
tem
Benford, G. Time's rub
Benford, G. Titan falling
Benford, G. White creatures
Biggle, L. Orphan of the void
Blish, J. A work of art
Bloch, R. Broomstick ride
Bloch, R. Crime machine
Bloch, R. The learning maze
Bloch, R. Where the buffalo roam
Bond, N. Pilgrimage
Bone, J. F. Triggerman
Boucher, A. Barrier
Bova, B. A small kindness
Bova, B. To touch a star
Bradbury, R. There will come soft rains
Bradbury, R. To the Chicago Abyss
Bradbury, R. The Toynbee convector
Bradley, M. Z. The climbing wave
Bradley, M. Z. Exiles of tomorrow

FUTURE, STORIES OF THE—*Continued*

Branham, R. V. In the sickbay
Brantingham, J. Lobotomy shoals
Brin, D. The fourth vocation of George Gustaf
Brin, D. The warm space
Bryant, E. Jody after the war
Budrys, A. The end of summer
Butler, O. E. The evening and the morning and the night
Cadigan, P. Rock on
Card, O. S. Salvage
Card, O. S. St. Amy's tale
Carneiro, A. A perfect marriage
Carter, R. Mal and fem
Chambers, R. W. The repairer of reputations
Clarke, A. C. Death and the senator
Clarke, A. C. Guardian angel
Clarke, A. C. "If I forget thee, oh Earth . . ."
Clarke, A. C. The songs of distant Earth
Clement, H. The mechanic
Cogswell, T. R. The cabbage patch
Coleman, W. Buying primo time
Cowper, R. Piper at the gates of dawn
Cowper, R. The Tithonian Factor
Cox, A. J. Evergreen
Cross, R. A. Hotel mind slaves
Crowley, J. Snow
Dann, J. Blind shemmy
De Camp, L. S. Divide and rule
De Haven, T. Where we'll never grow old
Del Rey, L. The faithful
Delany, S. R. Time considered as a helix of semi-precious stones
DeLillo, D. Human moments in World War III
Di Filippo, P. Stone lives
Dick, P. K. The days of Perky Pat
Dick, P. K. The defenders
Dick, P. K. If there were no Benny Cemoli
Dick, P. K. The last of the masters
Dick, P. K. Novelty act
Dick, P. K. Sales pitch
Dick, P. K. Second Variety
Dick, P. K. To serve the master
Dick, P. K. What'll we do with Ragland Park?
Disch, T. M. Canned goods
Disch, T. M. Concepts
Donaldson, S. R. Animal lover
Donaldson, S. R. Mythological beast
Dozois, G. R. Morning child
Dozois, G. R. The peacemaker
Dozois, G. R., and Haldeman, J. C. Executive clemency
Drake, D. Men like us
Eisenstein, S. Earthworks
Eldershaw, M. B. Aubade
Elgin, S. H. Modulation in all things
Ellison, H. A boy and his dog

Ellison, H. Commuter's problem
Ellison, H. Do-it-yourself
Ellison, H. Mealtime
Emshwiller, C. Day at the beach
Endō, S. Incredible voyage
Etchison, D. Deathtracks
Ewart, C. A day in the life
Farmer, P. J. The king of beasts
Farmer, P. J. The oogenesis of Bird City
Farmer, P. J. Riders of the purple wage
Farmer, P. J. Sketches among the ruins of my mind
Farmer, P. J. The sliced-crosswise only-on-Tuesday world
Farmer, P. J. Uranus; or, UFO versus IRS
Ferguson, J. Ker, the god killer
Ferguson, N. The second third of C
Fialkowski, K. A perfect Christmas evening
Forrest, K. V. The test
Foster, A. D. Why Johnny can't speed
Fowler, K. J. The lake was full of artificial things
Gansovsky, S. A part of the world
Garrett, R. A little intelligence
Gathorne-Hardy, J. The centre of the universe is 18 Baedekerstrasse
Gerrold, D. How we saved the human race
Gibson, W. Burning chrome
Gibson, W. Johnny Mnemonic
Gibson, W. New Rose Hotel
Gloss, M. Interlocking pieces
Gold, H. L. No charge for alterations
Gunn, J. E. Donor
Haldeman, J. W. Armaja das
Haldeman, J. W. Blood sisters
Haldeman, J. W. More than the sum of his parts
Haldeman, J. W. You can never go back
Hamilton, E. The stars, my brothers
Harrison, H. After the storm
Hartmann, W. K. Handprints on the Moon
Heinlein, R. A. Gulf
Hendrix, H. V. In the smoke
Herbert, F. Dragon in the sea
Herbert, F. A matter of traces
Herbert, F. Transcript: Mercury program
Hoch, E. D. Uncle Max
Hoyt, M. S. Lyrical voices
Huston, N. Pliny's commentaries
Jafek, B. You've come a long way, Mickey Mouse
Jakes, J. The man who wanted to be in the movies
Jakes, J. Political machine
Jakes, J. The sellers of the dream
Jakes, J. There's no vinism like chauvinism
Johnston, H. The shadow falls
Kagan, N. Four brands of impossible
Kathenor, S. The Cinderella caper
Keller, D. H. The revolt of the pedestrians

FUTURE, STORIES OF THE—*Continued*

Kelly, J. P. Glass cloud
Kelly, J. P. The prisoner of Chillon
Kelly, J. P. Solstice
Killough, L., and Killough, H. P. Keeping the customer satisfied
Kilworth, G. Almost heaven
Kilworth, G. God's cold lips
Kilworth, G. Scarlet fever
King, S. The Jaunt
Kingsbury, D. The moon goddess and the son
Knight, D. F. Forever
Konas, G. What genius
Kornbluth, C. M. Two dooms
Kress, N. Shadows on the cave wall
Kuttner, H. Home is the hunter
Laidlaw, M. 400 boys
Le Guin, U. K. SQ
Lem, S. Golem XIV
Lem, S. Vestrand's Extelopedia in 44 magnetomes
Linehan, P. One last hunting pack
Longyear, B. B. The initiation
Longyear, B. B. The portrait of Baron Negay
Longyear, B. B. SHAWNA, Ltd.
Lundwall, S. J. Time everlasting
MacLean, K. The missing man
Maddox, T. Snake-eyes
Malzberg, B. N. Going down
Malzberg, B. N. Icons
Mårtensson, B. Myxomatosis forte
Martin, G. R. R. The exit to San Breta
Martin, G. R. R. The way of cross and dragon
Matheson, R. The test
Matheson, R. C. Mugger
Mayhew, A. J. In the garden
Mcauley, P. J. The king of the hill
McDevitt, J. Cryptic
McKenna, B. The old organ trail
Michaelson, L. W. Phocian
Miller, M. D. Tyson's turn
Mitchell, E. P. An uncommon sort of spectre
Morgan, C. The hitmaker
Morrow, J. Diary of a mad deity
Morrow, J. Veritas
Moudy, W. F. The survivor
Neville, K. From the government printing office
Neville, K. New apples in the garden
Neville, K. Old Man Henderson
Neville, K. The price of Simeryl
Newman, K. Patricia's profession
Niven, L. Flash crowd
Nolan, W. F. Sungrab
Norton, A. Desirable lakeside residence
Norton, A. Outside
Novitski, P. Nuclear fission
Nuetzel, C. A day for dying
P.G.M. The monster mine
Padgett, L. The piper's son

Pangborn, E. A master of Babylon
Panshin, A. Down to the worlds of men
Pearlman, D. Taking from the top
Pierce, J. R. Choice
Poe, E. A. Mellonta Tauta
Pohl, F. The blister
Pohl, F. The children of night
Pohl, F. Day million
Pohl, F. Farmer on the dole
Pohl, F. Fermi and frost
Pohl, F. The greening of Bed-Stuy
Pohl, F. Gwenanda and the Supremes
Pohl, F. In the problem pit
Pohl, F. Second-hand sky
Pohl, F. Sitting around the pool, soaking up the rays
Pohl, F. We servants of the stars
Pohl, F. When New York hit the fan
Prebehalla, G., and Moran, D. K. Realtime
Pronzini, B., and Malzberg, B. N. Prose Bowl
Rata. The invasion of Sydney
Reed, R. Treading in the afterglow
Resnick, M. The Olympians
Robinson, K. S. Coming back to Dixieland
Robinson, K. S. Down and out in the year 2000
Robinson, K. S. Venice drowned
Robinson, S. By any other name
Robinson, S., and Robinson, J. Stardance
Russ, J. Bodies
Russ, J. Elf hill
Russ, J. Nor custom stale
Russ, J. The throaways
Russ, J. What did you do during the revolution, Grandma?
Russo, A. The target
Sanders, S. R. Time and again
Sargent, P. Originals
Schmidt, S. The unreachable star
Schulze, K. Redmond
Scortia, T. N. Flowering Narcissus
Shaara, M. 2066: Election Day
Shea, M. The extra
Shea, M. Polyphemus
Sheckley, R. Cost of living
Sheckley, R. The future lost
Sheckley, R. The future of sex: speculative journalism
Sheckley, R. Good-bye forever to Mr. Pain
Sheckley, R. The language of love
Sheckley, R. The people trap
Sheckley, R. The perfect woman
Sheckley, R. The store of the worlds
Sheffield, C. Skystalk
Shelley, M. W. The last man
Shelley, R. At the flood
Shepard, L. R&r
Shepard, L. Voyage South from Thousand Willows
Shirley, J. Freezone
Silverberg, R. At the conglomeroid cocktail party

FUTURE, STORIES OF THE—*Continued*

Silverberg, R. Caliban
Silverberg, R. Capricorn games
Silverberg, R. Caught in the organ draft
Silverberg, R. Chalice of death
Silverberg, R. Gate of horn, gate of ivory
Silverberg, R. Gianni
Silverberg, R. Homefaring
Silverberg, R. In entropy's jaws
Silverberg, R. In the group
Silverberg, R. In the House of Double Minds
Silverberg, R. The palace at midnight
Silverberg, R. The pardoner's tale
Silverberg, R. Passengers
Silverberg, R. Schwartz between the galaxies
Silverberg, R. Some notes on the pre-dynastic epoch
Silverberg, R. This is the road
Silverberg, R. When we went to see the end of the world
Silverberg, R. The wind and the rain
Sladek, J. T. The brass monkey
Sladek, J. T. The last of the whaleburgers
Smith, D. W. Flawless execution
Snodgrass, M. Requiem
Soukup, M. Dress rehearsal
Soukup, M. Living in the jungle
St. Clair, M. The gardener
St. Clair, M. Short in the chest
Stableford, B. M. And he not busy being born . . .
Sterling, B. The beautiful and the sublime
Sterling, B. Cicada Queen
Sterling, B. Green days in Brunei
Sterling, B., and Shiner, L. Mozart in mirrorshades
Stokes, T. No pets
Sturgeon, T. The touch of your hand
Sucharitkul, S. Fiddling for water buffaloes
Swanwick, M. Covenant of souls
Swanwick, M. The feast of Saint Janis
Swanwick, M. Trojan horse
Swanwick, M., and Gibson, W. Dogfight
Tenn, W. Eastward ho!
Thurston, R. Was that house there yesterday?
Tiptree, J. Backward, turn backward
Tiptree, J. Morality meat
Tiptree, J. Your faces, o my sisters! Your faces filled of light!
Touzalin, R. Mudpuppies
Turner, G. In a Petri dish upstairs
Van de Wetering, J. A tale with an end
Van Greenaway, P. The exhibition
Varley, J. The persistence of vision
Varley, J. Press enter
Varley, J. Tango Charlie and Foxtrot Romeo
Vinge, J. D. Phoenix in the ashes
Vonnegut, K. A dream of the future (not excluding lobsters)
Waldrop, H. Mary Margaret Road-Grader

Watson, I. Jewels in an angel's wing
Watson, I. The legend of the seven who found the true egg of lightning
Watson, I. Slow birds
Weinbaum, S. G. Dawn of flame
Wells, H. G. The star
Wells, H. G. A story of the days to come
Whitlock, D. The million-dollar wound
Wilder, C. Something coming through
Wilhelm, P. Space invaders
Williams, W. J. Dinosaurs
Williams, W. J. Video star
Williamson, J. Jamboree
Willis, C. All my darling daughters
Willis, C. The father of the bride
Wolfe, G. The map
Wolfe, G. Seven American nights
Wolfe, G. Sonya, Crane Wessleman, and Kittee
Wolverton, D. On my way to paradise
Wyndham, J. The wheel
Yermakov, N. A glint of gold
Yount, R. Pursuit of excellence
Zahn, T. Cascade point
Zahn, T. The Cassandra
Zahn, T. The challenge
Zahn, T. The dreamsender
Zahn, T. The energy crisis of 2215
Zahn, T. The final report on the lifeline experiment
Zahn, T. The giftie gie us
Zahn, T. Job inaction
Zahn, T. Not always to the strong
Zahn, T. Return to the fold
Zahn, T. The shadows of evening
Zebrowski, G. The idea trap
Zelazny, R. Deadboy Donner and the Filstone Cup
Zelazny, R. Dreadsong
Zelazny, R. For a breath I tarry
Zelazny, R. Lucifer
Zeldis, L. The whore of Babylon

FUTURE LIFE

Asimov, I. The last answer
Benford, G. Of space-time and the river
Bishop, M. Diary of a dead man
Day, R. C. A Chagall story
Gunn, J. E. Out of my head
Rucker, R. von B. In frozen time
Scott, J. The American Book of the Dead
Stevens, J. Into that good night
Wagar, W. W. A woman's life
Waldrop, H. Fair game
Watson, I. The rooms of paradise
Wharton, E. The fullness of life
Williamson, C. Prometheus's ghost
Willis, C. Substitution trick
The **future** lost. Sheckley, R.
The **future** of conglomerates. Claiborne, S.
The **future** of sex: speculative journalism. Sheckley, R.
The **future** of the Jovian system. Benford, G.

Futures yet unseen. Snodgrass, M.

G

Gabe's fall. Sandberg, P. L.
Gable, Amanda C.
  Go get a girlfriend
    The North American Review 273:54-6 S
    '88
Gabon. Kinsella, W. P.
Gabor. Swift, G.
Gaboriau, Emile, 1823-1873
  The little old man of Batignolles
    Great French detective stories; ed. by T.
    J. Hale
Gabriel-Ernest. Saki
Gad, Hoda
  The blue weapon
    Egyptian tales and short stories of the
    1970s and 1980s
Gadow, Don
  Football
    Stiller's pond; ed. by J. Agee; R. Blakely
    and S. Welch
Gahagan, Judy
  Journey
    Critical Quarterly 30:99-101 Spr '88
Gaines, Charles
  Three o'clock and woodstream
    The Art of fiction in the heart of Dixie;
    ed. by P. D. Beidler
Gaines, Ernest J., 1933-
  Just like a tree
    A Modern Southern reader; ed. by B.
    Forkner and P. Samway
  Robert Louis Stevenson Banks, a.k.a.
    Chimley
    Necessary fictions; ed. by S. W. Lind-
    berg and S. Corey
  The sky is gray
    Family: stories from the interior; ed. by
    G. G. Chavis
    Stories of the modern South; ed. by B.
    Forkner and P. Samway
Gaining the door. Everett, P. L.
Gaitens, Edward
  Growing up
    Streets of stone; ed. by M. Burgess and
    H. Whyte
  The sailing ship
    Streets of stone; ed. by M. Burgess and
    H. Whyte
Gaitskill, Mary, 1954-
  An affair, edited
    Gaitskill, M. Bad behavior
  Connection
    Gaitskill, M. Bad behavior
  Daisy's Valentine
    Gaitskill, M. Bad behavior
  Heaven
    Gaitskill, M. Bad behavior

  Other factors
    Gaitskill, M. Bad behavior
  A romantic weekend
    Gaitskill, M. Bad behavior
  Secretary
    Gaitskill, M. Bad behavior
  Something nice
    Gaitskill, M. Bad behavior
  Trying to be
    Gaitskill, M. Bad behavior
Gal young un. Rawlings, M. K.
The **gala** cocktail party. Sorrentino, G.
The **galah**. Prichard, K. S.
GALAPAGOS ISLANDS
  Melville, H. The encantadas; or, Enchanted
    isles
  Vonnegut, K. A dream of the future (not
    excluding lobsters)
Galatea Galante. Bester, A.
GALATIANS *See* Celts
Galb's elbow. Rogers, T. N. R.
Gale, Zona, 1874-1938
  "Not as the world giveth": a friendship
    story
    "May your days be merry and bright"
    and other Christmas stories by wom-
    en; ed. by S. Koppelman
The **gale**. Conrad, J.
GALES *See* Storms
GALESBURG (ILL.) *See* Illinois—Galesburg
Galgut, Damon, 1963-
  The night the blood
    Winter's tales, new ser. v4
GALILEI, GALILEO, 1564-1642
About
  Scholz, C. Galileo complains
GALILEO *See* Galilei, Galileo, 1564-1642
Galileo complains. Scholz, C.
Gallacher, Tom
  A friend of Dosser Farr
    Gallacher, T. Apprentice
  Lord Sweatrag
    Gallacher, T. Apprentice
  Perfect pitch
    Gallacher, T. Apprentice
  Portrait of Isa Mulvenny
    Gallacher, T. Apprentice
  Store quarter
    Gallacher, T. Apprentice
Gallagher, Rachel
  The girl who loved Garbo
    Mademoiselle 94:130+ Mr '88
Gallagher, Stephen
  By the river, Fontainebleau
    The Best horror stories from the
    Magazine of fantasy and science fiction
  The jigsaw girl
    Shadows 9
  Old red shoes
    Ripper! Ed. by G. Dozois and S. Casper

Gallagher, Tess

At mercy
  Gallagher, T. The lover of horses, and other stories

Bad company
  The Best American short stories, 1986
  Gallagher, T. The lover of horses, and other stories
  The Graywolf annual 2

Beneficiaries
  Gallagher, T. The lover of horses, and other stories

Desperate measures
  Gallagher, T. The lover of horses, and other stories

Girls
  Gallagher, T. The lover of horses, and other stories

King Death [Variant title: A figure of speech]
  Gallagher, T. The lover of horses, and other stories

The leper
  The Editors' choice v3; ed. by G. E. Murphy, Jr.
  The Paris Review 27:144-52 Summ '85

The lover of horses
  American short story masterpieces; ed. by R. Carver and T. Jenks
  Gallagher, T. The lover of horses, and other stories
  The Pushcart prize XII

A pair of glasses
  Gallagher, T. The lover of horses, and other stories

Recourse
  The Editors' choice: new American stories v1
  Gallagher, T. The lover of horses, and other stories

Turpentine
  Gallagher, T. The lover of horses, and other stories

The wimp
  Gallagher, T. The lover of horses, and other stories

The woman who saved Jesse James
  Gallagher, T. The lover of horses, and other stories

Gallant, James

Home again, home again
  The Massachusetts Review 28:81-92 Spr '87

Gallant, Mavis

The assembly
  Gallant, M. Overhead in a balloon

Baum, Gabriel, 1935-( )
  Making it new; ed. by J. Metcalf

Between zero and one
  Gallant, M. Home truths

Bonaventure
  Gallant, M. Home truths

The chosen husband
  The Art of the tale; ed. by D. Halpern
  The New Yorker 61:40-9 Ap 15 '85

The colonel's child
  Gallant, M. Overhead in a balloon

The concert party
  The New Yorker 63:32-42+ Ja 25 '88

Déclassé
  Mademoiselle 93:116+ F '87

Dédé
  The Best American short stories, 1988
  The New Yorker 62:28-34 Ja 5 '87

The doctor
  Gallant, M. Home truths

Florida
  The New Yorker 61:24-7 Ag 26 '85

A flying start
  Gallant, M. Overhead in a balloon

From cloud to cloud
  The New Yorker 61:22-5 Jl 8 '85

Going ashore
  The World of the short story; ed. by C. Fadiman

Grippes and Poche
  Gallant, M. Overhead in a balloon

His mother
  Making it new; ed. by J. Metcalf

The ice wagon going down the street
  Gallant, M. Home truths
  The Oxford book of Canadian short stories in English

In the tunnel
  Gallant, M. Home truths

In youth is pleasure
  Gallant, M. Home truths

Irina
  The Graywolf annual 2
  The Literary Review (Madison, N.J.) 28:373-88 Spr '85

Jorinda and Jorindel
  Gallant, M. Home truths

Kingdom come
  The Best American short stories, 1987
  The New Yorker 62:32-5 S 8 '86

Larry
  Gallant, M. Overhead in a balloon

Leaving the party
  The New Yorker 62:30-1 Mr 3 '86

Lena
  The Best American short stories, 1984
  Gallant, M. Overhead in a balloon

Let it pass
  The New Yorker 63:38-50+ My 18 '87

Luc and his father
  Gallant, M. Overhead in a balloon
  The New press anthology #1

Orphans' progress
  Gallant, M. Home truths

Overhead in a balloon
  Gallant, M. Overhead in a balloon
  The New Yorker 60:34-44 Jl 2 '84

A painful affair
  Gallant, M. Overhead in a balloon

Gallant, Mavis—*Continued*
  The prodigal parent
    Gallant, M. Home truths
  A recollection
    Gallant, M. Overhead in a balloon
  Rue de Lille
    Gallant, M. Overhead in a balloon
  Saturday
    Gallant, M. Home truths
  Speck's idea
    Gallant, M. Overhead in a balloon
  Thank you for the lovely tea
    Gallant, M. Home truths
  Up north
    Gallant, M. Home truths
  Varieties of exile
    Gallant, M. Home truths
  Virus X
    Gallant, M. Home truths
  Voices lost in snow
    Gallant, M. Home truths
  With a capital T
    Gallant, M. Home truths
Gallegher. Davis, R. H.
Gallegos, Magdalena
  Florence and the new shoes
    Southwest tales; ed. by Alurista and X.
      Rojas-Urista
Gallico, Paul, 1897-
  The awful secret of Monsieur Bonneval
    Reader's Digest 130:143-6 My '87
  Bombardier
    A Treasury of World War II stories; ed.
      by B. Pronzini and M. H. Greenberg
  Hurry, hurry, hurry!
    The Wickedest show on earth; ed. by
      M. Muller and B. Pronzini
  "I love ya, baby"
    50 Plus 27:70-1+ Jl '87
  Jennie's lessons to Peter on how to behave
      like a cat
    Roger Caras' Treasury of great cat
      stories
  "When in doubt—wash!"
    Roger Caras' Treasury of great cat
      stories
Galloway, Freda
  Vida's child
    Room to move; ed. by S. Falkiner
The **gallowglass**. Braly, D.
The **gallows**. Willis, T.
Gallup Poll. West, J.
Galsworthy, John, 1867-1933
  The broken boot
    The Treasury of English short stories;
      ed. by N. Sullivan
  The consummation
    The Nobel reader; ed. by J. Eisen and
      S. Troy
  The neighbors
    Mystery in the mainstream; ed. by B.
      Pronzini; M. H. Greenberg and B. N.
      Malzberg

Galton and the yelling boys. Waugh, H.
Galyan, Deborah
  In the dreamhouse
    Chicago Review 36 no1:53-8 '88
  Kerouac
    The North American Review 272:98-101
      S '87
Gambit declined. Moody, H.
Gamble, James S.
  Kansas
    A Matter of crime v2
The **gambler**, the nun, and the radio.
    Hemingway, E.
GAMBLERS *See* Gambling
Gamblers. Coleman, W.
Gamblers. Norris, L.
Gamblers don't win. Ballard, W. T.
GAMBLING
    See also Lotteries; Wagers
  Algren, N. Katz
  Algren, N. Stickman's laughter
  Apollinaire, G. The favorite
  Apollinaire, G. The meeting at the mixed
    club
  Baudelaire, C. The generous gambler
  Bloch, R. Luck is no lady
  Cain, J. M. Cigarette girl
  Cain, J. M. Pay-off girl
  Chekhov, A. P. The bet
  Coleman, W. Gamblers
  Collins, W. A terribly strange bed
  Connelly, J. Basques
  Connelly, J. Lock
  Crane, S. The blue hotel
  Crane, S. The five white mice
  Crane, S. Four men in a cave
  Croft, M. The pit
  Daniélou, A. The game of dice
  Daniels, C. Trudy
  Dexter, C. At the Lulu-Bar Motel
  Doyle, Sir A. C. The end of Devil Hawker
  Doyle, Sir A. C. A regimental scandal
  Drake, B. Putting a black-leg on shore
  Dumas, H. A Harlem game
  Faust, I. The year of the hot jock
  Fish, R. L. Muldoon and the numbers
    game
  Flanagan, R. Teller's ticket
  Fonseca, R. The game of dead men
  Francis, D. The gift
  Francis, D. Twenty-one good men and true
  Fraser, A. House poison
  Frazee, S. Luck of Riley
  Gallagher, T. The lover of horses
  Gee, M. The losers
  Greene, G. Dream of a strange land
  Haake, K. Recently I've discovered my
    mistake
  Harte, B. The outcasts of Poker Flat
  Hemingway, E. The gambler, the nun, and
    the radio
  Hooper, J. J. Fighting the "tiger" and
    other speculations

GAMBLING—*Continued*

Kavaler, R. Local habitations
Lacy, E. You can't win 'em (at) all
Landolfi, T. Prize in spite of
Lawrence, D. H. The rocking-horse winner
Little, B. The backroom
London, J. Which make men remember
Lutz, J. High stakes
Mankiewicz, D. M. Two rolls, no coffee
Markham, B. The quitter
Marlowe, D. J. Give-and-take
Maugham, W. S. The facts of life
Mayer, R. The system
Monreal, D. N. Down in Las Vegas
Norris, L. Gamblers
Olmstead, R. High-low-jack
Price, A. The Boudicca killing
Pronzini, B. Words do not a book make
Rand, P. Baby Boy
Rasputin, V. G. French lessons
Ritchie, J. The $5,000 getaway
Sagan, F. The cat and the casino
Sholem Aleichem. A game of sixty-six
Swan, G. Losing game
Twain, M. The notorious jumping frog of Calaveras County
Wnorowska, D. Seven come heaven?
Womersley, J. The year granpa won the Melbourne Cup
Woolrich, C. Hot water
Game. Barthelme, D.
The **game.** Dadswell, M.
The **game.** Fitzgerald, M. J.
Game farm. Gardiner, J. R.
Game in the pope's head. Wolfe, G.
The **game** of cat and eagle. Strete, C.
A **game** of catch. Garrett, G. P.
The **game** of dead men. Fonseca, R.
Game of dice. Asscher-Pinkhof, C.
The **game** of dice. Daniélou, A.
The **game** of rat and dragon. Smith, C.
A **game** of sixty-six. Sholem Aleichem
A **game** of unchance. Dick, P. K.
Game plan. See Prince, H. Requiem for a busted flush
Game preserve. Phillips, R.
Game time. Klinkowitz, J.
A **game** without children. See DeMarinis, R. Blind euchre

GAMES

See also Ball games; Sports; Video games

Anderson Imbert, E. Murder
Burrage, A. M. Smee
Carver, R. After the denim
Dick, P. K. The days of Perky Pat
Dick, P. K. War game
Dickinson, C. Risk
Ferguson, W. Space Invaders
Gardner, M. Love and tiddlywinks
Grace, P. Kepa
Izzo, F. E. Tank
Josipovici, G. Children's games

Kilgore, D. Bingo
King, S. The monkey
Landolfi, T. The provincial night
Leiber, F. A rite of spring
Liben, M. A dream of collaboration
Liben, M. King of the Hill
Liben, M. Lady, I did it
Liben, M. You're it
Lutz, J. Games for adults
Oates, J. C. Double solitaire
Rhys, J. Invitation to the dance
Saroyan, W. Mystic games
Stewart, J. I. M. Parlour 4
Swanwick, M., and Gibson, W. Dogfight
Trifonov, ÍŬ. Games at dusk
Watson, I. Jewels in an angel's wing
Wilson, L. A. Massé
Zahn, T. The challenge
GAMES, WAR *See* War games
Games. Attia, N.
Games. Zabriskie, G.
Games at dusk. Trifonov, ÍŬ.
Games at twilight. Desai, A.
Games for adults. Lutz, J.
The **game's** the thing. Durrell, L.
Gaming. Flanagan, R.
Gandbhir, Lalita
Free and equal
The Massachusetts Review 29:733-41 Wint '88/'89
Gangemi, Kenneth, 1937-
Greenbaum, O'Reilly & Stephens The Pushcart prize X
GANGS

See also Juvenile delinquency

Calvino, I. A ship loaded with crabs
Covino, M. The hour of the ungovernable
Covino, M. An intimacy beyond words
Covino, M. Matinee at the Bijou
Covino, M. The return of possibility
Laidlaw, M. 400 boys
Oates, J. C. Ace
Rose, J. The sunshine of Paradise Alley
Zambreno, M. F. A way out
GANGSTERS

See also Mafia

Bloch, R. Crime machine
Bloch, R. Ego trip
Coriolan, J. The G'issimo
Currey, R. The war of heaven
Deming, R. The better bargain
Doyle, Sir A. C. The last resource
Ellin, S. The day of the bullet
Essop, A. Labyrinth
Essop, A. The visitation
Gibson, W. Johnny Mnemonic
Hemingway, E. The killers
Hughes, D. B. F. Everybody needs a mink
King, S. The wedding gig
Kirk, R. Uncle Isaiah
La Puma, S. Guys under their fedoras
Schulberg, B. Murder on the waterfront
Sisk, F. The fly swatter

The **gangster's** ghost. La Puma, S.

Gans, Bruce Michael
And here in Chicago it's 78°
Here's the story: fiction with heart; ed.
by M. Sklar

Gansovsky, Sever
A part of the world
Earth and elsewhere, by K. Bulychev
and others
Vincent Van Gogh
Aliens, travelers, and other strangers; by
B. and A. Strugatsky and others

Gant, Phyllis
The revolver
Women's work; ed. by M. McLeod and
L. Wevers

Ganz, Earl
While you're up
The Literary Review (Madison, N.J.)
29:197-207 Wint '86

Gaol birds. Pavese, C.
The **gap.** Lao Hong
The **gap** in Kaltouma's fence. Ibrahim, I.
Garage sale. Fox, J.

Garber, Eugene K.
The lover
Shenandoah: an anthology; ed. by J.
Boatwright
The uncle
The Kenyon Review ns8:10-23 Spr '86

Garber, Leslie J.
First time
McCall's 111:84-5+ Jl '84
Promising signs
McCall's 112:122-3+ O '84

Garcia, Julian S.
The harvest
Southwest tales; ed. by Alurista and X.
Rojas-Urista

Garcia, Lionel G.
The wedding
Cuentos Chicanos; ed. by R. A. Anaya
and A. Márquez

García Márquez, Gabriel, 1928-
Artificial roses
García Márquez, G. Collected stories
Balthazar's marvelous afternoon
García Márquez, G. Collected stories
Big Mama's funeral
García Márquez, G. Collected stories
Bitterness for three sleepwalkers
García Márquez, G. Collected stories
Blacamán the good, vendor of miracles
García Márquez, G. Collected stories
Death constant beyond love
García Márquez, G. Collected stories
The World of the short story; ed. by
C. Fadiman
Dialogue with the mirror
García Márquez, G. Collected stories

Eva is inside her cat
García Márquez, G. Collected stories
The Nobel reader; ed. by J. Eisen and
S. Troy
Eyes of a blue dog
The Art of the tale; ed. by D. Halpern
García Márquez, G. Collected stories
The handsomest drowned man in the
world
García Márquez, G. Collected stories
The incredible and sad tale of innocent
Eréndira and her heartless grand-
mother
García Márquez, G. Collected stories
The last voyage of the ghost ship
García Márquez, G. Collected stories
Monologue of Isabel watching it rain in
Macondo
García Márquez, G. Collected stories
Montiel's widow
García Márquez, G. Collected stories
Nabo: the black man who made the angels
wait
García Márquez, G. Collected stories
The night of the curlews
García Márquez, G. Collected stories
One day after Saturday [Variant title: The
day after Saturday]
García Márquez, G. Collected stories
One of these days
García Márquez, G. Collected stories
The other side of death
García Márquez, G. Collected stories
Pentecost Sunday
The New Yorker 64:24-36+ Mr 28 '88
The sea of lost time
García Márquez, G. Collected stories
Someone has been disarranging these roses
García Márquez, G. Collected stories
There are no thieves in this town
García Márquez, G. Collected stories
The third resignation
García Márquez, G. Collected stories
Tuesday siesta
García Márquez, G. Collected stories
A very old man with enormous wings
García Márquez, G. Collected stories
The woman who came at six o'clock
García Márquez, G. Collected stories

Garcia y Robertson, R.
The moon of popping trees
The Year's best science fiction, fifth an-
nual collection

Gardam, Jane
Benevolence
Winter's tales, new ser. v2
Showing the flag
Winter's tales, new ser. v3

The **garden.** Bitov, A.
The **garden.** Furlong, M.
The **garden.** Liben, M.
Garden Island people. Keesing, N.
The **garden** lantern. Dazai, O.

The **garden** of Adompha. Smith, C. A.

Garden of glass. Haas, B.

Garden of love. Pilcher, R.

The **garden** of redemption. DiFranco, A. M.

The **garden** of smoke. Chesterton, G. K.

The **garden** of stubborn cats. See Calvino, I. Autumn: the garden of stubborn cats

The **garden** of the Villa Mollini. Tremain, R.

GARDEN PARTIES *See* Parties

The **garden** party. Mansfield, K.

The **garden** that floated away. Fink, I.

The **gardener**. Godine, A.

The **gardener**. Jahnn, H. H.

The **gardener**. St. Clair, M.

Gardener. Verdery, D.

GARDENERS

Eisenstein, S. Michali among the roses

Feng Jicai. Chrysanthemums

Freeman, J. The rake people

Purdy, J. Summer tidings

Sagan, F. Third person singular

Thomas, D. The tree

Gardeners. Cunningham, J.

GARDENING *See* Gardens

GARDENS

See also Weeds

Aithal, S. K., and Rothfork, J. Moksha

Austin, M. H. Old Spanish gardens

Bird, C. In the conservatory

Blackwood, A. The transfer

Calvino, I. Autumn: the garden of stubborn cats

Chekhov, A. P. The Black Monk

Deal, B. Antaeus

Eisenstein, S. The inner garden

Engberg, S. A stay by the river

Fink, I. The garden that floated away

Garrett, G. P. September morn

Geras, A. The green behind the glass

Hankla, C. The strawberry patch

Hartley, L. P. Up the garden path

Hawthorne, N. Rappaccini's daughter

Jacobsen, J. Jack Frost

Martínez-Serros, H. Killdeer

McCormack, E. P. A train of gardens— Part II: the machine

Narayan, R. K. Annamalai

O'Brien, E. Christmas roses

Skrzynecki, P. Hoeing

Skrzynecki, P. The red-back spider

Steinbeck, J. The chrysanthemums

Thomas, D. In the garden

Tournier, M. Amandine; or, The two gardens

Tuohy, F. A ghost garden

Yang, K. Mother Goose gets married

Gardiner, John Rolfe

Game farm

New stories from the South: the year's best, 1988

The New Yorker 63:36-42 S 21 '87

Karaghala's daughter

The New Yorker 61:30-6 Je 24 '85

Our Janice

The New Yorker 60:34-7 Ag 27 '84

World after dark

The New Yorker 62:28-34 Ja 26 '87

Gardner, Craig Shaw

Demon luck

Magic in Ithkar 4; ed. by A. Norton and R. Adams

The Year's best fantasy, first annual collection

A drama of dragons

Dragons of light; ed. by O. S. Card

A malady of magicks

Masterpieces of terror and the supernatural; ed. by M. Kaye and S. Kaye

The man who loved water

Shadows 8

Overnight guest

Midnight; ed. by C. L. Grant

Three faces of the night

Halloween horrors; ed. by A. Ryan

Walk home alone

Shadows 9

Gardner, Erle Stanley, 1889-1970

Danger out of the past

Masterpieces of mystery and suspense; ed. by M. H. Greenberg

The danger zone

Baker's dozen: 13 short espionage novels

Hell's kettle

The Black mask boys; ed. by W. F. Nolan

Gardner, John, 1933-1982

Julius Caesar and the werewolf

The Editors' choice: new American stories v2

Nimram

Buying time; ed. by S. Walker

Redemption

American short story masterpieces; ed. by R. Carver and T. Jenks

Gardner, John Champlin *See* Gardner, John, 1933-1982

Gardner, Leonard

Flea circus

Stories and poems from close to home; ed. by F. Salas

Gardner, Martin, 1914-

At the feet of Karl Klodhopper

Gardner, M. The no-sided professor, and other tales of fantasy, humor, mystery, and philosophy

The blue birthmark

Gardner, M. The no-sided professor, and other tales of fantasy, humor, mystery, and philosophy

The conspicuous turtle

Gardner, M. The no-sided professor, and other tales of fantasy, humor, mystery, and philosophy

Gardner, Martin, 1914——*Continued*

The Devil and the trombone
Gardner, M. The no-sided professor, and other tales of fantasy, humor, mystery, and philosophy

The dome of many colors
Gardner, M. The no-sided professor, and other tales of fantasy, humor, mystery, and philosophy

The fall of Flatbush Smith
Gardner, M. The no-sided professor, and other tales of fantasy, humor, mystery, and philosophy

Good dancing, sailor!
Gardner, M. The no-sided professor, and other tales of fantasy, humor, mystery, and philosophy

The horrible horns
Gardner, M. The no-sided professor, and other tales of fantasy, humor, mystery, and philosophy

The horse on the escalator
Gardner, M. The no-sided professor, and other tales of fantasy, humor, mystery, and philosophy

Left or right?
Mathenauts: tales of mathematical wonder; ed. by R. Rucker

Love and tiddlywinks
Gardner, M. The no-sided professor, and other tales of fantasy, humor, mystery, and philosophy

The loves of Lady Coldpence
Gardner, M. The no-sided professor, and other tales of fantasy, humor, mystery, and philosophy

Merlina and the colored ice
Gardner, M. The no-sided professor, and other tales of fantasy, humor, mystery, and philosophy

Mysterious Smith
Gardner, M. The no-sided professor, and other tales of fantasy, humor, mystery, and philosophy

No-sided professor
Gardner, M. The no-sided professor, and other tales of fantasy, humor, mystery, and philosophy
Mathenauts: tales of mathematical wonder; ed. by R. Rucker

Nora says "check."
Gardner, M. The no-sided professor, and other tales of fantasy, humor, mystery, and philosophy

Old man gloom
Gardner, M. The no-sided professor, and other tales of fantasy, humor, mystery, and philosophy

One more martini
Gardner, M. The no-sided professor, and other tales of fantasy, humor, mystery, and philosophy

Oom
Gardner, M. The no-sided professor, and other tales of fantasy, humor, mystery, and philosophy

Private Eye Oglesby [Variant title: Crunchy Wunchy's first case]
Gardner, M. The no-sided professor, and other tales of fantasy, humor, mystery, and philosophy

Ranklin Felano Doosevelt
Gardner, M. The no-sided professor, and other tales of fantasy, humor, mystery, and philosophy

Sibyl sits in
Gardner, M. The no-sided professor, and other tales of fantasy, humor, mystery, and philosophy

The sixth ship
Gardner, M. The no-sided professor, and other tales of fantasy, humor, mystery, and philosophy

The stranger
Gardner, M. The no-sided professor, and other tales of fantasy, humor, mystery, and philosophy

Thang
Gardner, M. The no-sided professor, and other tales of fantasy, humor, mystery, and philosophy

The three cowboys
Gardner, M. The no-sided professor, and other tales of fantasy, humor, mystery, and philosophy

The virgin from Kalamazoo
Gardner, M. The no-sided professor, and other tales of fantasy, humor, mystery, and philosophy

Gardner, Tonita S.

It's all a matter of luck
Last laughs; ed. by G. Mcdonald

You could have done better
Ellery Queen's Prime crimes

Gare, Nene

The child
Room to move; ed. by S. Falkiner

Garfield, Brian

King's X
Murder California style; ed. by J. L. Breen and J. Ball
The Year's best mystery and suspense stories, 1988

Scrimshaw
The Crime of my life; ed. by B. Garfield

Trust Charlie
Ellery Queen's Crimes and punishments

The view
The Year's best mystery and suspense stories, 1984

Gargantua. Calisher, H.

Gargantua and pantagruel. Rabelais, F.

GARIBALDI, GIUSEPPE, 1807-1882
About
Garrett, G. P. A wreath for Garibaldi
Garland, Hamlin, 1860-1940
The return of a private
Westeryear; ed. by E. Gorman
Garner, Helen, 1942-
The life of art
Room to move; ed. by S. Falkiner
Postcards from surfers
Transgressions; ed. by D. Anderson
A thousand miles from the ocean
Home and away; ed. by R. Creswell
Garner, Hugh, 1913-1979
One-two-three little Indians
The Oxford book of Canadian short
stories in English
Garnett, David, 1892-1981
Lady into fox
Black water; ed. by A. Manguel
Garratt, Peter T.
If the driver vanishes. . . .
Interzone: the 2nd anthology; ed. by J.
Clute; D. Pringle and S. Ounsley
Garrett, George P., 1929-
Bread from stones
Garrett, G. P. An evening performance
The confidence man
The Georgia Review 40:137-42 Spr '86
Necessary fictions; ed. by S. W. Lind-
berg and S. Corey
Don't take no for an answer
Garrett, G. P. An evening performance
An evening performance
Garrett, G. P. An evening performance
Farmer in the dell
Garrett, G. P. An evening performance
A game of catch
Garrett, G. P. An evening performance
Good-bye, good-bye, be always kind and
true
Garrett, G. P. An evening performance
The gun and the hat
Garrett, G. P. An evening performance
The insects are winning: At least they'll
have candlelight
Garrett, G. P. An evening performance
The insects are winning: The moth
Garrett, G. P. An evening performance
King of the mountain
Garrett, G. P. An evening performance
Last of the old buffalo hunters
Garrett, G. P. An evening performance
The last of the Spanish blood
Garrett, G. P. An evening performance
Lion
Garrett, G. P. An evening performance
Love is a cold kingdom
Garrett, G. P. An evening performance
More geese than swans
Garrett, G. P. An evening performance
My picture left in Scotland
Garrett, G. P. An evening performance

Noise of strangers
Garrett, G. P. An evening performance
The old Army game
Garrett, G. P. An evening performance
Pretty birdie
Garrett, G. P. An evening performance
The rarer thing
Garrett, G. P. An evening performance
A record as long as your arm
Garrett, G. P. An evening performance
The rivals
Garrett, G. P. An evening performance
September morn
Garrett, G. P. An evening performance
The sleeping beauty
Garrett, G. P. An evening performance
Song of a drowning sailor: a fabliau
Garrett, G. P. An evening performance
The strong man
Garrett, G. P. An evening performance
Sudden fiction; ed. by R. Shapard and
J. Thomas
Sweeter than the flesh of birds
Garrett, G. P. An evening performance
The test
Garrett, G. P. An evening performance
Texarkana was a crazy town
Garrett, G. P. An evening performance
Thus the early gods
Garrett, G. P. An evening performance
Time of bitter children
Garrett, G. P. An evening performance
Stories of the modern South; ed. by B.
Forkner and P. Samway
Unmapped country
Garrett, G. P. An evening performance
The victim
Garrett, G. P. An evening performance
What's the matter with Mary Jane?
Garrett, G. P. An evening performance
What's the purpose of the bayonet?
Garrett, G. P. An evening performance
The witness
Garrett, G. P. An evening performance
Wounded soldier
Garrett, G. P. An evening performance
A wreath for Garibaldi
Garrett, G. P. An evening performance
Garrett, Randall
Despoilers of the golden empire
Robert Adams' Book of soldiers
Frost and thunder
Time wars; ed. by C. Waugh and M.
H. Greenberg
Hail to the chief
Election Day 2084; ed. by I. Asimov
and M. H. Greenberg
The highest treason
Space wars; created by P. Anderson
The Ipswich Phial
Witches; ed. by I. Asimov; M. H.
Greenberg and C. G. Waugh

Garrett, Randall—*Continued*
A little intelligence
Magicats! Ed. by J. Dann and G. Dozois
Garris, Mick
A life in the cinema
Silver scream; ed. by D. J. Schow
Garro, Elena
It's the fault of the Tlaxcaltecas
Other fires; ed. by A. Manguel
The tree
Women's fiction from Latin America; ed.
by E. P. Garfield
The **garrulous** Garrity grand scam. Nevins,
F. M., Jr.
Garton, Ray
Sinema
Silver scream; ed. by D. J. Schow
Garve, Andrew, 1908-
Flight from danger
John Creasey's Crime collection, 1986
Gary Dis-Donc. Faust, I.
Gas. Hall, J.
GASES, ASPHYXIATING AND POISONOUS See Poisonous gases
Gash, Jonathan, 1933-
The Julian Mondays
Winter's crimes 18
GASHADE, BILLY
About
Taylor, R. Billy Gashade and glory
Taylor, R. Glory
Taylor, R. The James boys ride again
Gaskell, Elizabeth Cleghorn, 1810-1865
The half-brothers
The Treasury of English short stories;
ed. by N. Sullivan
The old nurse's story
The Book of the dead; ed. by A. K.
Russell
Handle with care; ed. by J. Kahn
The Penguin book of ghost stories
The three eras of Libbie Marsh
Christian short stories; ed. by M. Booth
Gasner, Douglas
Dandelion golf
The New Yorker 62:28-9 S 1 '86
Gasoline Point, Alabama. Murray, A.
GASOLINE STATIONS See Automobiles—
Service stations
Gaspar, Melchior, Balthasar. Thomas, D.
Gaspé, Philippe Aubert de
Rose Latulipe
The Oxford book of French-Canadian
short stories
GASPÉ PENINSULA (QUÉBEC)
Ferron, J. Chronicle of Anse Saint-Roch
Ferron, J. The lady from Ferme-Neuve
Ferron, J. The landscape painter
Ferron, J. La Mi-Carême
Gass, William H., 1924-
In the heart of the heart of the country
The Norton book of American short
stories

Order of insects
The Art of the tale; ed. by D. Halpern
The Sunday drive
The Esquire fiction reader v1
Gaston. Saroyan, W.
The **gate.** Hall, T. T.
The **gate** house. La Chapelle, M.
The **gate** of ghosts. Fowler, K. J.
Gate of horn, gate of ivory. Silverberg, R.
The **Gate** of the Flying Knives. Anderson,
P.
Gates, David
China Blue
A Matter of crime v1
Gates, Eleanor
A yellow man and a white
She won the West; ed. by M. Muller
and B. Pronzini
Gates of joy. Liphshitz, A.
Gateway to happiness? Lofts, N.
Gather 'round the flowing bowler. Bloch, R.
Gathering evidence. Struthers, A.
Gathorne-Hardy, Jonathan
The centre of the universe is 18 Baedeker-
strasse
Gathorne-Hardy, J. The centre of the
universe is 18 Baedekerstrasse
The Infant Hercules
Gathorne-Hardy, J. The centre of the
universe is 18 Baedekerstrasse
The man who laughed
Gathorne-Hardy, J. The centre of the
universe is 18 Baedekerstrasse
Mothers
Gathorne-Hardy, J. The centre of the
universe is 18 Baedekerstrasse
Peiter and Paulina
Gathorne-Hardy, J. The centre of the
universe is 18 Baedekerstrasse
The picnic
Gathorne-Hardy, J. The centre of the
universe is 18 Baedekerstrasse
Gatt, Witt and Redott. Grin, A.
GAUDIER-BRZESKA, HENRI, 1891-1915
About
Davenport, G. The bowmen of Shu
Gauger, Rick
The vacuum-packed picnic
Omni book of science fiction 2
GAULS See Celts
Gault, Connie
Albatross
Gault, C. Some of Eve's daughters
At dusk / just when / the light is filled
with birds
Gault, C. Some of Eve's daughters
Dinner for two
Gault, C. Some of Eve's daughters
Lost
Gault, C. Some of Eve's daughters
Mary Beth
Gault, C. Some of Eve's daughters

Gault, Connie—*Continued*

My perseus
  Gault, C. Some of Eve's daughters
The other Ellen
  Gault, C. Some of Eve's daughters
Providence
  Gault, C. Some of Eve's daughters
A shame
  Gault, C. Some of Eve's daughters
The tables
  Gault, C. Some of Eve's daughters
This bright night
  Gault, C. Some of Eve's daughters
  The Old dance; ed. by B. Burnard
This now fenceless world
  Gault, C. Some of Eve's daughters
The trade
  Gault, C. Some of Eve's daughters
Where the apple reddens
  Gault, C. Some of Eve's daughters
Why fade these children of the spring?
  Gault, C. Some of Eve's daughters

Gault, William Campbell

—And murder makes four!
  Murder California style; ed. by J. L.
    Breen and J. Ball
April in peril
  Mean streets; ed. by R. J. Randisi
The cackle bladder
  Uncollected crimes; ed. by B. Pronzini
    and M. H. Greenberg
The Kerman kill
  Murder in Los Angeles; ed. by J. L.
    Breen and others
Night work
  Great modern police stories; ed. by B.
    Pronzini and M. H. Greenberg
Stolen star
  The Mammoth book of private eye
    stories; ed. by B. Pronzini and M. H.
    Greenberg
Take care of yourself
  The Black Lizard anthology of crime fic-
    tion; ed. by E. Gorman
The threatening three
  Child's ploy; ed. by M. Muller and B.
    Pronzini
The **Gauter** letters. Halligan, M.

Gautreaux, Tim

Just turn like a gear
  A Good deal; ed. by M. Heath and F.
    M. Robinson
  The Massachusetts Review 27:5-32 Spr
    '86

Gauvreau, Claude

The dream of the bridge
  Invisible fictions; ed. by G. Hancock
The prophet in the sea
  Invisible fictions; ed. by G. Hancock
The **gauzy** edge of paradise. Gilchrist, E.
Gay cat burglar seeks same for long-lasting
    relationship. Rees, D.
Gazebo. Carver, R.

Gbadamosi, Rasheed A.

Death by the waterfall
  African short stories in English; ed. by
    J. de Grandsaigne

Ge Wujue

A summer experience
  Short story international 43

Gearhart, Sally Miller

The chipko
  Love, struggle & change; ed. by I.
    Zahava
Roxie raccoon
  Through other eyes; ed. by I. Zahava

Gébler, Carlo, 1954-

Puerto Vallarta
  Foreign exchange; ed. by J. Evans

Gee, Maurice

Buried treasure, old bones
  Gee, M. Collected stories
The champion
  Gee, M. Collected stories
Down in the world
  Gee, M. Collected stories
Eleventh holiday
  Gee, M. Collected stories
A glorious morning, comrade
  Gee, M. Collected stories
The hole in the window
  Gee, M. Collected stories
Joker and wife
  Gee, M. Collected stories
The losers
  Gee, M. Collected stories
A retired life
  Gee, M. Collected stories
Right-hand man
  Gee, M. Collected stories
Schooldays
  Gee, M. Collected stories
A sleeping face
  Gee, M. Collected stories
The widow
  Gee, M. Collected stories
The **'Gees**. Melville, H.

GEESE

Asimov, I. Paté de foie gras
Chernoff, M. Infinks
Ford, R. Communist
Halligan, M. The living hothouse
Norris, L. A flight of geese
O'Brien, D. The wild geese
Wagoner, D. Wild goose chase
Geese. Oates, J. C.
The **geese** at Presque Isle. Shaw, J. B.

GEISHAS

Enchi, F. Blind man's buff
Hirabayashi, T. A woman to call mother
Kawabata, Y. Gleanings from snow coun-
  try
Kawabata, Y. The ring

Gekiere, Madeleine
　At the Rue Hamelin (a hitherto un-
　　published account)
　　Southwest Review 70:320-33 Summ '85
　Jewels
　　The North American Review 271:18-23
　　Mr '86
GEMS *See* Diamonds; Emeralds; Jade
Gemstone. Vinge, V.
The **Gene** Norman Collection. Franzen, B.
GENEALOGY
　Keillor, G. The royal family
　Swift, G. The watch
　Westlake, D. E. Never shake a family tree
　Wickstrom, L. Vines
Genealogy. Gildner, G.
The **general.** Strand, M.
The **general** and the nightingale. Davin, D.
General Patton did not sleep here. Muller,
　R.
The **general** strike. Botwinik, B.
GENERALS
　Davin, D. The general and the nightingale
　Gordimer, N. At the rendezvous of victory
　Kaikō, T. Monster and toothpick
　Poe, E. A. The man that was used up
　Scott, Sir W. The tapestried chamber
　Strand, M. The general
　Trebelo, J. La Cueva Del Círculo Sin Fin
The **General's** toothache. Burt, S.
Generation. Dlugos, T.
GENERATION GAP *See* Conflict of genera-
　tions
Generations. Spivack, K.
The **generous** gambler. Baudelaire, C.
Generous impediments float downriver.
　Valenzuela, L.
A **generous** man. Carter, R.
Geneseo. Deaver, P. F.
GENETIC EXPERIMENTATION *See*
　Genetics
GENETIC RESEARCH *See* Genetics
GENETICS
　Benford, G. Freezeframe
　Bilenkin, D. The genius house
　Di Filippo, P. Phylogenesis
　Donaldson, S. R. Animal lover
　Fowler, K. J. Recalling Cinderella
　Knuttel, W. Fugue
　Miller, M. D. Tyson's turn
　Shirley, J., and Sterling, B. The unfolding
　Sullivan, T. The Mickey Mouse Olympics
　Watson, I. Jean Sandwich, the sponsor and
　　I
　Wellen, E. Shapes to come
　Williamson, J. Jamboree
　Yermakov, N. A glint of gold
　Yount, R. Pursuit of excellence
　Zindell, D. Shanidar
Genetics. Ciment, J.
Genevieve goes back to work. Franco, M.
Genevieve's psychic experience. Franco, M.

Geng, Veronica
　A lot in common
　　The New Yorker 63:30-1 Ja 25 '88
GENGHIS KHAN, 1162-1227
About
　Tamer, Z. The day Genghis Khan became
　　angry
　Tamer, Z. Genghis Khan
Genghis Khan. Tamer, Z.
Genieve. Prichard, K. S.
GENIUS
　　See also Children, Gifted
　Asimov, I. Sucker bait
　Barthelme, D. The genius
　Dennison, G. A tale of Pierrot
　Heinlein, R. A. Gulf
　Hoyt, M. S. The wind wizard
　Oates, J. C. Ancient airs, voices
The **genius.** Barthelme, D.
The **genius.** Connors, R. J.
The **genius** house. Bilenkin, D.
Genius loci. Smith, C. A.
GENOA (ITALY) *See* Italy—Genoa
Gent. DeMarinis, R.
The **gentile** Jewesses. Spark, M.
Gentility. Hartmut
Gentle, Mary, 1956-
　Anukazi's daughter
　Isaac Asimov's Tomorrow's voices
The **gentle** art of making enemies. Peck, C.
Gentle as flowers make the stones. Metcalf,
　J.
The **gentle** basilisk. Stivens, D.
The **gentle** boy. Hawthorne, N.
The **gentleman** and the moon. Rodoreda, M.
The **gentleman** from Paris. Carr, J. D.
A **gentleman** from sole to crown. Bernstein,
　L. S.
The **gentleman** in the tan suit. O'Hara, J.
Gentlemanly Joe. Doyle, Sir A. C.
A **gentleman's** agreement. Jolley, E.
Gentlemen. Skipp, J., and Spector, C.
Gentlemen and players. Hornung, E. W.
Gentlemen eating gentlemen. El Rahman, M.
　A.
The **gentlemen** of the jungle. Kenyatta, J.
Gentlemen of the press. See Wolfe, T. The
　newspaper
Gentlemen of the shade. Turtledove, H.
Gents 50¢/Ladies 25¢. Kees, W.
Geography. Smith, G. B.
Geography lesson. O'Grady, D.
The **geological** spieler. Lawson, H.
GEOLOGISTS
　Handke, P. The long way around
　Hauptman, W. The desert
The **geologist's** maid. Tyler, A.
Geometry. Herschel, J.
Geometry. Troy, J.

GEORGE IV, KING OF GREAT BRITAIN, 1762-1830
About
Doyle, Sir A. C. An impression of the Regency

George, Jonathan, 1922-
For works written by this author under other names see Burke, John, 1922-

GEORGE, PHYLLIS
About
McKinley, J. Traveler's advisory

George. Rosenfeld, I.

George Bailey fishing. Akins, E.

The **George** business. Zelazny, R.

George Dobson's expedition to Hell. Hogg, J.

George Washington's birthday. Bernard, K.

George: Wednesday, Thursday, Friday. Cooper, D.

George's eyes & the red ball. Keeling, N.

George's mother. Crane, S.

GEORGIA
L'Engle, M. Poor little Saturday
19th century
Child, L. M. F. The quadroons
20th century
Bishop, M. One winter in Eden

Bishop, M. The Yukio Mishima Cultural Association of Kudzu Valley, Georgia

Durban, P. All set about with fever trees

Durban, P. This heat

Garrett, G. P. Pretty birdie

Hood, M. Finding the chain

Matthiessen, P. Sadie

McCluskey, J. The best teacher in Georgia

O'Connor, F. A good man is hard to find

O'Connor, F. Judgement Day

Sams, F. Fulfillment
Atlanta
Berry, R. M. November 14, 1864

O'Connor, F. The artificial nigger

Sams, F. Howdy Doody time

The **Georgia** breeze. O'Brien, D.

Georgia's ruling. Henry, O.

Gerald's song. O'Connor, P. F.

The **geranium.** Grace, P.

The **geranium.** O'Connor, F.

Geranium House. Curry, P. S.

Geras, Adèle
Alice
  Geras, A. Snapshots of paradise
Don't sing love songs . . .
  Geras, A. Snapshots of paradise
The green behind the glass
  Geras, A. Snapshots of paradise
Love for lunch
  Seventeen 44:130-1+ F '85
Love letters
  Geras, A. Snapshots of paradise
Monday
  Geras, A. Snapshots of paradise
Snapshots of paradise
  Geras, A. Snapshots of paradise

Tea in the Wendy House
  Geras, A. Snapshots of paradise
The whole truth
  Geras, A. Snapshots of paradise

Gerber, Merrill Joan
At the fence
  Gerber, M. J. Honeymoon
  Prime number; ed. by A. L. Weir
  The Sewanee Review 93:5-19 Wint '85
Chicken skin sandwiches
  Prairie Schooner 62:52-61 Summ '88
Comes an earthquake
  The Sewanee Review 95:528-42 Fall '87
Hold tight, my love
  Redbook 168:60+ Ap '87
Honeymoon
  Gerber, M. J. Honeymoon
  The Sewanee Review 92:4-19 Wint '84
How can she get along without me?
  Redbook 167:35-6+ Ag '86
I don't believe this
  The Atlantic 254:96-100 O '84
  Gerber, M. J. Honeymoon
  Prize stories, 1986
Memorial service
  Gerber, M. J. Honeymoon
The mistress of Goldman's Antiques
  Gerber, M. J. Honeymoon
Mozart you can't give them
  The Sewanee Review 94:352-60 Summ '86
Someone should know this story
  Gerber, M. J. Honeymoon
Straight from the deathbed
  Gerber, M. J. Honeymoon
Tragic lives
  Gerber, M. J. Honeymoon
What to do about mother
  Redbook 165:56+ My '85
What's a family for?
  Redbook 164:69-70+ N '84
Witnesses
  Gerber, M. J. Honeymoon

The **gerbil** that ate Los Angeles. Kinsella, W. P.

GERMAN EAST AFRICA *See* East Africa

GERMAN REFUGEES *See* Refugees, German

GERMAN SOLDIERS *See* Soldiers—Germany

GERMANS
Africa
Rush, N. Bruns
Argentina
Serling, R. The escape route
Australia
Sheil, G. The picking season
Austria
Wegner, H. A death in a quiet town
Canada
Haensel, R. Goldenrod
Czechoslovakia
Lustig, A. Blue day

GERMANS—*Continued*
England
Bates, H. E. The chords of youth
Watmough, D. The cross-country run
Welch, D. The hateful word
Whitaker, M. The mandoline
Finland
Grzimek, M. Finlandia
France
Boyle, K. The first lover
Gallant, M. Baum, Gabriel, 1935-( )
Greene, G. Brother
Hawkes, J. The traveler
Maupassant, G. de. A duel
Maupassant, G. de. A jolly fellow
Maupassant, G. de. Mademoiselle Fifi
Greece
Haris, P. Before the dawn
Haris, P. A dead city
Haris, P. Four and a half
Haris, P. Lights on the sea
Haris, P. Not a bird in the sky
Haris, P. Of love and darkness
Hungary
Böll, H. Between trains in X
Böll, H. Drinking in Petöcki
Ireland
Leaton, A. Gita's story
Israel
Eisenstein, S. The sacrifice
Italy
Barich, B. October
King, F. H. Unmaking
Netherlands
Hebel, J. P. Kannitverstan
Poland
Maupassant, G. de. A mésalliance
South Africa
Becker, J. The stench
Soviet Union
Böll, H. Children are civilians too
Böll, H. That time we were in Odessa
United States
Friedman, B. J. The war criminal
Garrett, G. P. Pretty birdie
Ozick, C. The suitcase
Porter, K. A. Holiday
Robison, M. For real
Spingarn, L. P. Ingermann
Wilson, B. Looking for the Golden Gate
Vietnam
Claudius, E. How the jungle soldiers became sons of heaven
Ziem, J. Something's missing

GERMANY
8th century
Pei, M. The bones of Charlemagne
16th century
Kleist, H. von. Michael Kohlhaas
18th century
Balzac, H. de. The red inn
Pasternak, B. L. Suboctave story

19th century
Jean Paul. Army-chaplain Schmelzle's journey to Flätz
Jean Paul. The life of Maria Wuz, the merry-hearted Dominie of Auenthal
20th century
Böll, H. Across the bridge
Böll, H. At the border
Böll, H. The railway station of Zimpren
Böll, H. A soldier's legacy
Budrys, A. Never meet again
Finch, S. Reichs-peace
Ziem, J. Clever
Ziem, J. His own boss
1918-1945
Bloch, R. The head man
Böll, H. "Stranger, bear word to the Spartans we . . ."
Cohen, A. Hans Cassebeer and the virgin's rose
Pierce, C. When things get back to normal
Wolfe, T. The dark messiah
Wolfe, T. The Spanish letter
1945-
Böll, H. Beside the river
Böll, H. Christmas not just once a year
Böll, H. Contacts
Böll, H. I'm not a Communist
Böll, H. In Friedenstadt
Böll, H. Murke's collected silences
Böll, H. My pal with the long hair
Böll, H. An optimistic story
Böll, H. The waiting-room
De Bruyn, G. Someday he really will come home
Eisenstein, S. The Kassel ballet
Görlich, G. The decision
Haley, R. The cosmetic factory
Heym, S. My Richard
Krisman, S. No marks for Rolf
Mundstock, K. A judgment worthy of Solomon
Schneider, R. Border crossers
Schulze, A. Eighteen minutes
Wegner, H. But America is far
Wegner, H. Butcher's beguine
Wegner, H. Miner's tattoo
Wolf, C. A certain date
American occupation, 1945-1955
See Germany—1945-
Aristocracy
See Aristocracy—Germany
Army—Officers
Lawrence, D. H. The Prussian officer
Communism
See Communism—Germany
Farm life
See Farm life—Germany
Navy
Thomason, J. Mutiny

GERMANY—*Continued*
Politics
See Politics—Germany
Rural life
Böll, H. The Balek scales
Böll, H. The Staech affair
Campbell, R. Blacked out
Jean Paul. The life of Maria Wuz, the merry-hearted Dominie of Auenthal
Kant, H. A bit of the South Sea
Stephan, M. The tub
World War, 1939-1945
See World War, 1939-1945—Germany
Bavaria
Apollinaire, G. The moon king
Helprin, M. The Schreuderspitze
Waldrop, H. Fair game
Berlin
Oates, J. C. Ich bin ein Berliner
Oates, J. C. Our wall
Ziem, J. Uprising in East Germany
Düsseldorf
Wilson, B. Walking on the moon
Munich
Wolfe, T. Oktoberfest
Würzburg
Grzimek, M. Heartstop
Germination period. McConnell, J.
GERMS *See* Microorganisms
The **Gernsback** continuum. Gibson, W.
Gerontissa. Farmer, B.
GERONTOLOGISTS *See* Physicians
Gerrold, David, 1944-
How we saved the human race
Kindred spirits; ed. by J. M. Elliot
Gershwin's second prelude. Baxter, C.
Gerty's brother. Essop, A.
GESTAPO *See* National socialism
Get a seeing-eyed dog. Hemingway, E.
Get right or get left. Williford, L.
Get-together. Barthelme, S.
Get your jive on highway five. Kerr, D.
The **getaway**. Savage, J.
Getting across. Silverberg, R.
Getting ahead. Winton, T.
Getting around. Chang, D.
Getting back to before it began. Moore, R.
Getting better. Josipovici, G.
Getting even. Povolo, G.
Getting Herbert back. Franzen, B.
Getting into the set. Updike, J.
Getting out. Murphy, P.
Getting out of Garten. Huggan, I.
Getting over Arnette. Benedict, P.
Getting over Russell. Edwards, M. F.
Getting ready. Hannah, B.
Getting ready to go camping down in Maine. Thompson, K.
Getting rid of Fluff. Butler, E. P.
Getting saved. Thompson, K.
Getting serious. Weesner, T.
Getting the combination. Asimov, I.

Getting there. Mathers, P.
Getting through University. Anthony, P.
Getting to be like the studs. McKnight, R.
Getting to know all about you. Oates, J. C.
Getting to know the weather. Painter, P.
Getting used to it. Dunn, D.
GETTYSBURG, BATTLE OF, 1863
Benét, S. V. Jack Ellyat at Gettysburg
Geydelle's protective. Carter, L.
GHANA
Aidoo, C. A. A. Certain winds from the south
Aidoo, C. A. A. In the cutting of a drink
Annan, K. Ding dong bell
Ghindi. Snow, K.
Ghitany, Gamal el *See* El Ghitany, Gamal
Gholson, Craig
Temple to the economics of love
Between C & D; ed. by J. Rose and C. Texier
Ghose, Zulfikar, 1935-
A translator's fiction
Winter's tales, new ser. v1
Ghost. Dawson, F.
The **ghost**. O'Connor, W. D.
The **ghost**. Wood, Mrs. H.
Ghost and flesh, water and dirt. Goyen, W.
The **ghost** and Saul Bozoff. Stern, S.
The **ghost** galaxies. Anthony, P.
A **ghost** garden. Tuohy, F.
The **ghost** in the Cap'n Brown House. Stowe, H. B.
Ghost island. Châtillon, P.
The **ghost** lemurs of Madagascar. Burroughs, W. S.
The **Ghost** loses her seal-hunting boats. London, J.
Ghost makers. Lester, D.
The **ghost** of an apprehension. Campbell, E.
The **ghost** of Champ McQuest. Mordden, E.
The **ghost** of Don Carlos. Tremblay, M.
The **ghost** of First Crow. Matthews, J.
The **ghost** of Sandburg's phizzog. Blei, N.
The **ghost** of the senior banquet. Abbott, K.
GHOST SHIPS
Collins, W. "Blow up with the brig"
Du Maurier, Dame D. Escort
García Márquez, G. The last voyage of the ghost ship
Hodgson, W. H. The derelict
Marryat, F. The legend of the bell rock
Norris, F. The ship that saw a ghost
Percy, H. R. Haliburton
Poe, E. A. Ms. found in a bottle
Russell, W. C. A bewitched ship
Sale, R. The benevolent ghost and Captain Lowrie
Tomlinson, H. M. The derelict
The **ghost** soldiers. O'Brien, T.
GHOST STORIES
See also Horror stories; Supernatural phenomena

GHOST STORIES—*Continued*

Abbott, K. The ghost of the senior banquet
Abe, K. Song of a dead girl
Aiken, J. The jealous apprentice
Aiken, J. Lodging for the night
Aiken, J. Sonata for harp and bicycle
Alan, A. J. My adventure in Norfolk
Anderson, K. J., and Fortier, R. Skeleton in the closet
Anstey, F. The curse of the catafalques
Arthur, R. The haunted trailer
Atherton, G. F. H. The bell in the fog
Bangs, J. K. The water ghost of Harrowby Hall
Barber, D. W. Wings of the hunter
Barker, C. Coming to grief
Barker, C. In the flesh
Barker, C. Revelations
Barker, C. The Yattering and Jack
Benson, A. C. The uttermost farthing
Benson, E. F. The bath-chair
Benson, E. F. The confession of Charles Linkworth
Benson, R. H. The watcher
Bierce, A. The moonlit road
Blackwood, A. The damned
Blackwood, A. The empty house
Blackwood, A. A haunted island
Bloch, R. The hungry house
Booth, B. Still life
Borgman, C. F. A queer red spirit
Bowen, E. Hand in glove
Bowen, M. The Crown Derby plate
Bradbury, R. I suppose you are wondering why we are here?
Bradbury, R. Lafayette, farewell
Bradbury, R. On the Orient, North
Bradbury, R. The tombstone
Braddon, M. E. The shadow in the corner
Brennan, J. P. An ordinary brick house
Brennan, J. P. Rhea
Bretnor, R. Markham
Bridge, A. The Buick saloon
Brinsmead, H. F. The twilight road
Brown, G. M. Andrina
Buchan, J. Fullcircle
Burke, J. Lucille would have known
Burke, T. The hollow man
Burnet, D. Fog
Burrage, A. M. One who saw
Burrage, A. M. Smee
Burrage, A. M. The sweeper
Byatt, A. S. The July ghost
Caldecott, Sir A. Christmas reunion
Casper, S. The haunting
Châtillon, P. Ghost island
Chetwynd-Hayes, R. The colored transmission
Chin, M. L. Lan Lung
Christie, A. The lamp
Clemens, S. A good night's work
Coppard, A. E. Ahoy, sailor boy!

Costello, K. The immortal soul of Tommy O'
Cowan, P. Form in wood
Cram, R. A. No. 252 Rue M le Prince
Crawford, F. M. The doll's ghost
Crawford, F. M. Man overboard!
Crawford, F. M. The upper berth
Daniélou, A. The game of dice
Daugherty, S. R. Claws of the white hawk
De la Mare, W. Bad company
De la Mare, W. Seaton's aunt
Defoe, D. The apparition of Mrs. Veal
Derleth, A. W. Carousel
Derleth, A. W. The dark boy
Derleth, A. W. House—with ghost
DeWeese, G. Everything's going to be all right
Dickens, C. The Baron of Grogzwig
Dickens, C. A Christmas carol
Dickens, C. Christmas ghosts
Dickens, C. The hanged man's bride
Dickens, C. The signalman
Dickens, C. The story of the bagman's uncle
Dickens, C. The trial for murder
Doyle, Sir A. C. Selecting a ghost. The ghosts of Goresthorpe Grange
Easton, T. A. Roll them bones
Edwards, A. A. B. The phantom coach
Ellison, H. On the downhill side
Farjeon, E. Spooner
Ferguson, W. The third voice
Finney, J. Hey, look at me!
Fisher, M. F. K. The lost, strayed, stolen
Fitzgerald, P. The axe
Frahm, L. The visitor
Fraser, A. The night mother
Fraser, A. Who's been sitting in my car?
Frede, R. Mr. Murdoch's ghost
Freeman, M. E. W. The lost ghost
Fremlin, C. Don't be frightened
Fuentes, C. Aura
Gallant, M. Up north
Gardner, M. The sixth ship
Garrett, G. P. Song of a drowning sailor: a fabliau
Gaskell, E. C. The old nurse's story
Gilchrist, M. The return
Gilford, C. B. The forgiving ghost
Glasgow, E. The shadowy third
Gogol', N. V. Viy
Goldsmith, H. The voices of El Dorado
Goyen, W. Ghost and flesh, water and dirt
Goyen, W. The letter in the cedarchest
Goyen, W. Pore Perrie
Grubb, D. The horsehair trunk
Harding, L. Limbo
Harrison, M. J. Small heirlooms
Hartley, L. P. A change of ownership
Hartley, L. P. The cotillon
Hartley, L. P. Fall in at the double
Hartley, L. P. Feet foremost
Hartley, L. P. Interference

GHOST STORIES—*Continued*

Hartley, L. P. Monkshood Manor
Hartley, L. P. The shadow on the wall
Hartley, L. P. Three, or four, for dinner
Hartley, L. P. A visitor from down under
Hartman, W. S. Poltergeist
Hawthorne, N. The gray champion
Heinesen, W. The silent guests
Hill, R. There are no ghosts in the Soviet Union
Hoch, E. D. Who rides with Santa Anna?
Hoffmann, E. T. A. The entail
Hogg, J. The barber of Duncow—a real ghost story
Hogg, J. The mysterious bride
Hogg, J. The unearthly witness
Hughes, F. 'Dear ghost . . .'
Hyams, E. Exorcizing Baldassare
An Injustice revealed
Jacobs, W. W. The monkey's paw
Jakes, J. I still see Sally
James, H. The friends of the friends
James, H. The jolly corner
James, H. The romance of certain old clothes
James, H. Sir Edmund Orme
James, H. The way it came
James, M. R. Count Magnus
James, M. R. Lost hearts
James, M. R. 'Oh, whistle, and I'll come to you, my lad'
James, M. R. The rose garden
James, M. R. Wailing well
Jewett, S. O. Lady Ferry
Kawabata, Y. Beyond death
King, F. H. A scent of mimosa
King, S. The reach
Kip, L. The ghosts at Grantley
Kipling, R. "They"
Kirk, R. Balgrummo's hell
Kirk, R. Sorworth Place
Kirk, R. Uncle Isaiah
Kleist, H. von. The beggarwoman of Locarno
Kosztolányi, D. The wondrous visitation of Krisztina Hrussz
La Farge, O. Haunted ground
Landon, P. Thurnley Abbey
Le Fanu, J. S. Mr. Justice Harbottle
Le Fanu, J. S. Squire Toby's will
L'Engle, M. Poor little Saturday
Leskov, N. S. An apparition in the Engineers' Castle
Li, K.-T. The Beldame Feng
Littke, L. The bantam phantom
Lytton, E. B. L., Baron. The haunted and the haunters
Malzberg, B. N. Chained
Mann, T. The wardrobe
Martin, D. Footprints in a ghost town
Martin, G. R. R. The exit to San Breta
Martin, G. R. R. Nightflyers
Matheson, R. Old haunts
Maupassant, G. de. He?

Maupassant, G. de. The specter
Maupassant, G. de. The White Lady
McGrath, P. The lost explorer
Michaelson, L. W. The flying Dutchman
Middleton, R. On the Brighton Road
Miller, G. W. Wiping the slate clean
Mitchell, E. P. An uncommon sort of spectre
Mordden, E. The ghost of Champ McQuest
Muller, M. Kindling point
Munby, A. N. L. A Christmas game
Munby, A. N. L. An encounter in the mist
Murphy, D. Roller
Narayan, R. K. Old man of the temple
Nelson, V. Coming back
Nesbit, E. John Charrington's wedding
Nesbit, E. Man-size in marble
New, J. Crossing demon
Oates, J. C. Haunted
O'Brien, F.-J. The pot of tulips
O'Connor, W. D. The ghost
Oliphant, M. The open door
Onions, O. The beckoning fair one
Onions, O. The cigarette case
Onions, O. The rope in the rafters
Pain, B. Rose Rose
Parkinson, T. L. The blue man
Peattie, E. W. Their dear little ghost
Piñera, V. An a posteriori ghost
Poe, E. A. Ligeia
Powell, T. I had a hunch, and . . .
Pritchett, V. S. A story of Don Juan
Pu, S.-L. The Tou lass
Pugmire, W. H., and Salmonson, J. A. "Pale trembling youth"
Quiller-Couch, Sir A. T. A pair of hands
Quiller-Couch, Sir A. T. The roll-call of the reef
Radcliffe, A. W. The haunted chamber
Raven, S. The bottle of 1912
Rey Rosa, R. The widow of Don Juan Manuel
Riddell, J. H., Mrs. A strange Christmas game
Rose, G. B. William Wilson
Russ, J. Come closer
Saki. The open window
Schwob, M. A skeleton
Scott, Sir W. The tapestried chamber
Scott, Sir W. Wandering Willie's tale
Serling, R. The changing of the guard
Shannon, D. The practical joke
Shea, M. Uncle Tuggs
Shepard, L. Delta Sly Honey
Silverberg, R. Push no more
Sinclair, M. The victim
Sinclair, M. The Villa Désirée
Sinclair, M. Where their fire is not quenched
Sinclair, M. J. P. Secrets
Skelton, R. Householder
Skelton, R. Raftery's ghost

GHOST STORIES—*Continued*

Sladek, J. T. Ursa Minor
Soldati, M. Footsteps in the snow
Spark, M. Another pair of hands
Spark, M. The executor
Spark, M. The leaf-sweeper
Spark, M. The Portobello Road
Springer, N. The prince out of the past
Steele, W. D. The woman at Seven Brothers
Stern, S. The ghost and Saul Bozoff
Stockton, F. The great staircase at Landover Hall
Stowe, H. B. The ghost in the Cap'n Brown House
Sulayman, N. The wrath of Shaykh Muhammad Al-Ajami
Swain, E. G. Bone to his bone
Tapahonso, L. She sits on the bridge
Taylor, B. Forget-me-not
Timperley, R. Christmas meeting
Timperley, R. Harry
Tiptree, J. In midst of life
Tremayne, P. Tavesher
Tremblay, M. The ghost of Don Carlos
Wakefield, H. R. Blind man's buff
Walpole, Sir H. The little ghost
Walter, E. Come and get me
Warner, S. T. Mr. Mackenzie's last hour
Welch, D. Ghosts
Wells, H. G. The inexperienced ghost
Wells, H. G. The moth
Wharton, E. Afterward
Wharton, E. All Souls'
Wharton, E. Bewitched
Wharton, E. Mr. Jones
Wharton, E. Pomegranate seed
Wharton, E. The triumph of night
White, E. L. The house of the nightmare
White, T. H. Soft voices at Passenham
Whitehead, H. S. C. The fireplace
Wijenaike, P. The visitor
Wilde, O. The Canterville ghost
Williamson, C. Prometheus's ghost
Williamson, J. N. Wordsong
Willis, C. Service for the burial of the dead
Wolfe, G. All the hues of hell
Wood, Mrs. H. The ghost
Woolf, V. A haunted house
Zola, É. Angeline; or, The haunted house
A **ghost** story. Twain, M.
Ghost talk. Castillo, A.
GHOST TOWNS *See* Cities and towns, Ruined, extinct, etc.
The **ghost** train. Durrell, L.
Ghostly. Ziegler, A.
Ghostly populations. Matthews, J.

GHOSTS *See* Ghost stories
Ghosts. Maupassant, G. de
Ghosts. O'Brien, E.
Ghosts. Welch, D.
The **ghosts** at Grantley. Kip, L.

The **ghosts** of the mail: the story of the bagman's uncle. See Dickens, C. The story of the bagman's uncle
A **ghoul's** accountant. Crane, S.
GHOULS AND OGRES
Yarbro, C. Q. Disturb not my slumbering fair
GI story. Queen, E.
Giammatteo, Hollis
Mrs. Pacal's bike-athon
The North American Review 269:25-8 Je '84
Gianni. Silverberg, R.
The **giant**. Chesterton, G. K.
Giant sequoia. Briskin, M.
GIANTS
Ballard, J. G. The drowned giant
Cranch, C. P. The last of the Huggermuggers: a giant story
Ellison, H. On the slab
Green, J. The tallest man in the world
Hoyt, M. S. The river giantess
Laidlaw, M. Love comes to the middleman
Wilde, O. The selfish giant
Wolfe, T. Gulliver, the story of a tall man
Giardinelli, Mempo
Revolution on a bicycle
Anthology of contemporary Latin American literature, 1960-1984
Gibbons, DeLamar
Zoofield follies
The Saturday Evening Post 256:56-9 Ap '84
Gibbons, Reginald, 1947-
Five pears or peaches
The North American Review 270:41 S '85
Mr. Walsh's mare
Southwest Review 70:470-84 Aut '85
Gibbs, Angelica
Father was a wit
Family: stories from the interior; ed. by G. G. Chavis
GIBRALTAR
Chipulina, E. G. One of those things
Gibson, Dana
An unswallowable love
Ploughshares 14 no2/3:129-37 '88
Gibson, Stephen
A hotel on Broadwalk
The Georgia Review 41:496-507 Fall '87
Gibson, William, 1948-
Burning chrome
Omni book of science fiction 1
The Gernsback continuum
Mirrorshades; ed. by B. Sterling
Johnny Mnemonic
Omni book of science fiction 2
New Rose Hotel
Nebula awards 20

Gibson, William, 1948——*Continued*
  Omni (New York, N.Y.) 6:46-7+ Jl '84
    The Year's best science fiction, second
      annual collection
  The winter market
    The Year's best science fiction, fourth
      annual collection
  (jt. auth) See Sterling, Bruce, and Gibson,
    William, 1948-
  (jt. auth) See Swanwick, Michael, and Gib-
    son, William, 1948-
Gibson, Willis
  Murnane and the Illinois
    Mississippi River tales; ed. by F.
      McSherry; C. G. Waugh and M. H.
      Greenberg
Gide, André, 1869-1951
  The return of the prodigal son
    The Nobel reader; ed. by J. Eisen and
      S. Troy
Gifkins, Michael
  The dispossessed
    Gifkins, M. Summer is the Côte d'Azur
  A final fling
    Gifkins, M. Summer is the Côte d'Azur
  Head over heels
    Gifkins, M. Summer is the Côte d'Azur
  The latter-day triumph of Graves
    Gifkins, M. Summer is the Côte d'Azur
  Living out the past
    Gifkins, M. Summer is the Côte d'Azur
  Local time
    Gifkins, M. Summer is the Côte d'Azur
  Matching the blue
    Gifkins, M. Summer is the Côte d'Azur
  Metamorphosis
    Gifkins, M. Summer is the Côte d'Azur
  Natural histories
    Gifkins, M. Summer is the Côte d'Azur
  Playing for keeps
    Gifkins, M. Summer is the Côte d'Azur
  Summer is the Côte d'Azur
    Gifkins, M. Summer is the Côte d'Azur
Gift. Asscher-Pinkhof, C.
A **gift**. Colter, C.
The **gift**. Davie, E.
The **gift**. Dickerson, K.
The **gift**. Dollarhide, L.
The **gift**. Forrest, K. V.
The **gift**. Francis, D.
The **gift**. Martin, C.
The **gift**. Peterson, L. S.
A **gift** for Lucrecia. Schwebel, B.
A **gift** from the GrayLanders. Bishop, M.
A **gift** from the past. Johnson, S. B.
Gift of an apple. Williams, T.
The **gift** of Cochise. L'Amour, L.
The **gift** of gab. Vance, J.
The **gift** of love. King, C.
The **gift** of love. Pilcher, R.
The **gift** of Sunday. Chand, M.
A **gift** of sweet mustard. Klass, P.
The **gift** of the emperor. Hornung, E. W.

The **gift** of the Magi. Henry, O.
The **gift** of the prodigal. Taylor, P. H.
The **gift** of words. Valenzuela, L.
A **gift** to the future. Greenwood, R.
Gifted and talented. Reich, T.
GIFTED CHILDREN *See* Children, Gifted
The **giftie** gie us. Zahn, T.
GIFTS
  Ade, G. Mr. Payson's satirical Christmas
  Cameron, P. Melissa & Henry—September
    10, 1983
  Chernoff, M. The spirit of giving
  Colette. The bracelet
  Davie, E. The gift
  Henry, O. The gift of the Magi
  Kawabata, Y. The grasshopper and the bell
    cricket
  Kawabata, Y. The silverberry thief
  Lo Bosco, R. The birthday present
  Sorrentino, F. In self-defense
  Twain, M. The man that corrupted Had-
    leyburg
  Windsor, G. Wedding presents for break-
    fast
Gifts. Boyd, W.
Gifts. Singer, I. B.
Gifts from the bridegroom. Yorke, M.
The **giggle-wrecker**. O'Donnell, P.
A **gigolo**, Miss Emery? Halligan, M.
GIGOLOS
  Bloch, R. The man who knew women
  Rhys, J. La Grosse Fifi
  Tuohy, F. The potlatch of Esmeralda
  Williams, T. Miss Coynte of Greene
  Williams, T. Sabbatha and solitude
Giguère, Roland, 1929-
  Miror
    Invisible fictions; ed. by G. Hancock
Gila Flambé. Barthelme, F.
Gilbert, Anthony, 1899-1973
  A day of encounters
    Ellery Queen's Memorable characters
Gilbert, Don
  The canoe
    Ellery Queen's Prime crimes 2
Gilbert, Michael, 1912-
  The African tree-beavers
    John Creasey's Crime collection, 1986
    Masterpieces of mystery and suspense;
      ed. by M. H. Greenberg
  Audited and found correct
    The Mammoth book of modern crime
      stories; ed. by G. Hardinge
  Breach of the peace
    Gilbert, M. Young Petrella
  Cash in hand
    Gilbert, M. Young Petrella
  The conspirators
    Gilbert, M. Young Petrella
  The Coulman handicap
    Gilbert, M. Young Petrella
  Counterplot
    The Penguin classic crime omnibus

Gilbert, Michael, 1912—— *Continued*
The curious conspiracy
Through a glass, darkly; ed. by B. Woelfel
Dangerous structure
Gilbert, M. Young Petrella
Death watch
Gilbert, M. Young Petrella
Emergency exit [Variant title: The emergency exit affair]
John Creasey's Crime collection, 1984
The emergency exit affair [Variant title: Emergency exit]
Hound dunnit; ed. by I. Asimov; M. H. Greenberg and C. L. R. Waugh
The happy brotherhood
Handle with care; ed. by J. Kahn
The killing of Michael Finnegan
John Creasey's Crime collection, 1985
The king in pawn
Great modern police stories; ed. by B. Pronzini and M. H. Greenberg
Lost leader
Gilbert, M. Young Petrella
The night the cat stayed out
Gilbert, M. Young Petrella
Nothing ever happens on Highside
Gilbert, M. Young Petrella
The oyster catcher
Gilbert, M. Young Petrella
Paris in summer
Gilbert, M. Young Petrella
The prophet and the bird
Gilbert, M. Young Petrella
Rough justice
Ellery Queen's Crimes and punishments
The Sark Lane Mission
Gilbert, M. Young Petrella
A sense of history
John Creasey's Crime collection, 1987
Source seven
Gilbert, M. Young Petrella
The spoilers
Baker's dozen: 13 short espionage novels
The two footmen
The New adventures of Sherlock Holmes; ed. by M. H. Greenberg and C. L. R. Waugh
The unstoppable man
Ellery Queen's Memorable characters
A very special relationship
Winter's crimes 16
Voyage into illusion
Gilbert, M. Young Petrella
Who has seen the wind?
Gilbert, M. Young Petrella
Gilbert, W. S. (William Schwenck), 1836-1911
Angela
Gilbert, W. S. The lost stories of W. S. Gilbert

The burglar's story
Gilbert, W. S. The lost stories of W. S. Gilbert
Comedy and tragedy
Gilbert, W. S. The lost stories of W. S. Gilbert
Creatures of impulse
Gilbert, W. S. The lost stories of W. S. Gilbert
Diamonds
Gilbert, W. S. The lost stories of W. S. Gilbert
An elixir of love
Gilbert, W. S. The lost stories of W. S. Gilbert
The fairy's dilemma
Gilbert, W. S. The lost stories of W. S. Gilbert
The finger of fate
Gilbert, W. S. The lost stories of W. S. Gilbert
Foggerty's fairy
Gilbert, W. S. The lost stories of W. S. Gilbert
Jones' Victoria Cross
Gilbert, W. S. The lost stories of W. S. Gilbert
The lady in the plaid shawl
Gilbert, W. S. The lost stories of W. S. Gilbert
Little Mim
Gilbert, W. S. The lost stories of W. S. Gilbert
Maxwell and I
Gilbert, W. S. The lost stories of W. S. Gilbert
My maiden brief
Gilbert, W. S. The lost stories of W. S. Gilbert
The poisoned postage stamp
Gilbert, W. S. The lost stories of W. S. Gilbert
Tom Poulton's joke
Gilbert, W. S. The lost stories of W. S. Gilbert
The triumph of vice
Gilbert, W. S. The lost stories of W. S. Gilbert
The wicked world
Gilbert, W. S. The lost stories of W. S. Gilbert
Wide awake
Gilbert, W. S. The lost stories of W. S. Gilbert
Gilbert, William Schwenck *See* Gilbert, W. S. (William Schwenck), 1836-1911
Gilbert. Pilcher, R.
Gilchrist, Ellen, 1935-
Adoration
Gilchrist, E. Drunk with love
Anna, Part 1
Gilchrist, E. Drunk with love

Gilchrist, Ellen, 1935-—*Continued*
Belize
  Gilchrist, E. Drunk with love
The blue-eyed Buddhist
  Gilchrist, E. Drunk with love
Crazy, crazy, now showing everywhere
  Gilchrist, E. Victory over Japan
Dede's talking, it's her turn
  Gilchrist, E. Victory over Japan
Defender of the Little Falaya
  Gilchrist, E. Victory over Japan
The Double Happiness Bun
  Gilchrist, E. Victory over Japan
Drunk with love
  Gilchrist, E. Drunk with love
The emancipator
  Gilchrist, E. Drunk with love
The expansion of the universe
  Gilchrist, E. Drunk with love
First Manhattans
  Gilchrist, E. Drunk with love
The gauzy edge of paradise
  Gilchrist, E. Victory over Japan
Jade Buddhas, red bridges, fruits of love
  Gilchrist, E. Victory over Japan
The last diet
  Gilchrist, E. Drunk with love
Looking over Jordan
  Gilchrist, E. Victory over Japan
The lower garden district free gravity mule
  blight; or, Rhoda, a fable
  Gilchrist, E. Victory over Japan
Memphis
  Gilchrist, E. Drunk with love
Miss Crystal's maid name Traceleen, she's
  talking, she's telling everything she
  knows
  Gilchrist, E. Victory over Japan
Music
  Gilchrist, E. Victory over Japan
Nineteen forty-one
  Gilchrist, E. Drunk with love
The perfect stone
  The Editors' choice v3; ed. by G. E.
  Murphy, Jr.
Revenge
  Mississippi writers v1: Fiction; ed. by D.
  Abbott
  Stories of the modern South; ed. by B.
  Forkner and P. Samway
The starlight express
  New American short stories; ed. by G.
  Norris
Summer, an elegy
  Love stories for the time being; ed. by
  G. D. Chipps and B. Henderson
There's a Garden of Eden
  The New writers of the South; ed. by
  C. East
Traceleen at dawn
  Gilchrist, E. Drunk with love
Traceleen, she's still talking
  Gilchrist, E. Victory over Japan

Traceleen's diary
  Gilchrist, E. Victory over Japan
Traceleen's telling a story called "A bad
  year"
  Gilchrist, E. Victory over Japan
Victory over Japan
  Gilchrist, E. Victory over Japan
  New women and new fiction; ed. by S.
  Cahill
  The Norton book of American short
  stories
The young man
  Gilchrist, E. Drunk with love
  The Graywolf annual [1]
Gilchrist, Murray, 1868-1917
The Basilisk
  Gilchrist, M. The stone dragon, and
  other stories
Dame Inowslad
  Gilchrist, M. The stone dragon, and
  other stories
Excerpts from Witherton's journal: also a
  letter of Crystalla's
  Gilchrist, M. The stone dragon, and
  other stories
The lost mistress
  Gilchrist, M. The stone dragon, and
  other stories
The manuscript of Francis Shackerley
  Gilchrist, M. The stone dragon, and
  other stories
Midsummer madness
  Gilchrist, M. The stone dragon, and
  other stories
My friend
  Gilchrist, M. The stone dragon, and
  other stories
The Noble Courtesan
  Gilchrist, M. The stone dragon, and
  other stories
The pageant of ghosts
  Gilchrist, M. The stone dragon, and
  other stories
The return
  Gilchrist, M. The stone dragon, and
  other stories
  Lost souls; ed. by J. Sullivan
Roxana runs lunatick
  Gilchrist, M. The stone dragon, and
  other stories
The stone dragon
  Gilchrist, M. The stone dragon, and
  other stories
Witch in-grain
  Gilchrist, M. The stone dragon, and
  other stories
The writings of Althea Swarthmoor
  Gilchrist, M. The stone dragon, and
  other stories
Gilda's dream. Coover, R.
The **gilded** six-bits. Hurston, Z. N.
The **gilded** youth of Los Gatos. Rees, D.

Gilden, Mel
Deadline
100 great fantasy short short stories; ed.
by I. Asimov; T. Carr and M. H.
Greenberg
Gilden-Fire. Donaldson, S. R.
Gildner, Gary
Boats coming ashore
The North American Review 270:51-3 Mr
'85
Genealogy
The North American Review 273:27-31
Je '88
Sleepy time gal
The Georgia Review 40:143-5 Spr '86
Necessary fictions; ed. by S. W. Lind-
berg and S. Corey
Sudden fiction; ed. by R. Shapard and
J. Thomas
Somewhere geese are flying
The Georgia Review 39:717-34 Wint '85
The Pushcart prize XI
A week in South Dakota
The Georgia Review 38:478-83 Fall '84
Giles, Molly
Baby pictures [Variant title: Loving pic-
tures]
Giles, M. Rough translations
Chocolate footballs
Giles, M. Rough translations
Heart and soul
Giles, M. Rough translations
How to quit smoking
Giles, M. Rough translations
A jar of emeralds
Giles, M. Rough translations
Old souls [Variant title: Night cries]
Giles, M. Rough translations
Peril
Giles, M. Rough translations
Pie dance
Giles, M. Rough translations
The planter box
Giles, M. Rough translations
Rough translations
Giles, M. Rough translations
Self-defense
The Editors' choice: new American
stories v1
Giles, M. Rough translations
What do you say?
Giles, M. Rough translations
Gilford, C. B.
The forgiving ghost
Alfred Hitchcock's Grave suspicions
Gilgun, John
Cow
Missouri short fiction; ed. by C. Beasley
Gilkison, Alex
Atthis
Streets of stone; ed. by M. Burgess and
H. Whyte

Gill, B. M.
A certain kind of skill
Winter's crimes 18
The Year's best mystery and suspense
stories, 1987
Murder most kind
A Matter of crime v1
Gillette, Jane Brown
Sins against animals
The Virginia Quarterly Review 64:599-
616 Aut '88
Gillette, Virginia
Child of my heart
Good Housekeeping 206:98-9 Je '88
Season's greetings
Good Housekeeping 207:96+ D '88
Gilliatt, Penelope
Addio
Gilliatt, P. 22 stories
Gilliatt, P. They sleep without dreaming
The New Yorker 60:26-7 Jl 30 '84
As is
Gilliatt, P. 22 stories
As we have learnt from Freud, there are
no jokes
Gilliatt, P. 22 stories
Autumn of a dormouse
Gilliatt, P. 22 stories
Broderie anglaise
Gilliatt, P. They sleep without dreaming
The New Yorker 60:44-8 N 26 '84
Catering
Gilliatt, P. 22 stories
Come back if it doesn't get better
Gilliatt, P. 22 stories
The corridors of Mr. Cyril
The New Yorker 61:28-33 Ag 26 '85
Dame of the British Empire, BBC
Gilliatt, P. 22 stories
Gilliatt, P. They sleep without dreaming
Earshot
The New Yorker 62:28-32 D 29 '86
Ex libris
The New Yorker 63:32-7 My 4 '87
F.R.A.N.K.
Gilliatt, P. 22 stories
Fat chance
The New Yorker 64:24-31 S 5 '88
Foreigners
Gilliatt, P. 22 stories
Fred and Arthur
Gilliatt, P. 22 stories
A half-life ahead
The New Yorker 62:24-32 Ag 25 '86
Hic haec hoc
The New Yorker 64:26-34 Je 27 '88
The hinge
Gilliatt, P. They sleep without dreaming
The New Yorker 60:42-9 My 28 '84
Known for her frankness
Gilliatt, P. 22 stories
Lingo
The New Yorker 63:30-5 S 7 '87

Gilliatt, Penelope—*Continued*
 Nobody's business
  Gilliatt, P. 22 stories
 The nuisance
  Gilliatt, P. They sleep without dreaming
  A Grand Street reader; ed. by B. Sonnenberg
 On each other's time
  Gilliatt, P. 22 stories
  Gilliatt, P. They sleep without dreaming
 Phone-in
  Gilliatt, P. 22 stories
 The position of the planets
  Gilliatt, P. 22 stories
 Purse
  Gilliatt, P. They sleep without dreaming
 The redhead
  Gilliatt, P. 22 stories
 Splendid lives
  Gilliatt, P. 22 stories
 Staying in bed
  Gilliatt, P. 22 stories
 Steam gives way to sail
  The New Yorker 62:39-45 S 22 '86
 Stephanie, Stephen, Steph, Steve
  Gilliatt, P. 22 stories
 Suspense item
  Gilliatt, P. They sleep without dreaming
 The tactics of hunger
  Gilliatt, P. 22 stories
 Teeth
  Gilliatt, P. 22 stories
 They sleep without dreaming
  Gilliatt, P. They sleep without dreaming
 When are you going back?
  Gilliatt, P. 22 stories
 The wind-child factor
  Gilliatt, P. They sleep without dreaming
  The New Yorker 61:43-50 Ap 22 '85
Gillie, William T.
 Motor-driven
  Short story international 47
Gilman, Carolyn, 1954-
 The language of the sea
  L. Ron Hubbard presents Writers of the future v3
Gilman, Charlotte Perkins, 1860-1935
 Turned
  The Other woman; ed. by S. Koppelman
 The yellow wallpaper
  The Dark descent; ed. by D. G. Hartwell
  Haunted women; ed. by A. Bendixen
  Haunting women; ed. by A. Ryan
  The Norton book of American short stories
  Witches' brew; ed. by M. Muller and B. Pronzini
Gimbel, Avram
 Hardwood
  Stories and poems from close to home; ed. by F. Salas
Gimpel the fool. Singer, I. B.

Ginette on the Metro. Villefranche, A.-M.
Gingerbread men. Klass, P.
Gingher, Marianne
 Aurora Island
  Gingher, M. Teen angel, and other stories of young love
 Camouflage
  Gingher, M. Teen angel, and other stories of young love
 The hummingbird kimono
  Gingher, M. Teen angel, and other stories of young love
 The kiss
  Gingher, M. Teen angel, and other stories of young love
 The magic circle
  Gingher, M. Teen angel, and other stories of young love
  McCall's 113:116-17+ Mr '86
 My mother's confession
  Gingher, M. Teen angel, and other stories of young love
  Ladies' Home Journal 105:90+ Je '88
 No news
  Gingher, M. Teen angel, and other stories of young love
 Teen angel
  Gingher, M. Teen angel, and other stories of young love
 Toy Paris
  Gingher, M. Teen angel, and other stories of young love
 Wearing glasses
  Gingher, M. Teen angel, and other stories of young love
The **ginsing** gatherers. Vines, H.
Ginzburg, Natalia
 The mother
  The Art of the tale; ed. by D. Halpern
The **Gioconda** aria. Straub, J.
The **Gioconda** smile. Huxley, A.
Giono, Jean, 1895-1970
 The man who planted trees
  Blair & Ketchum's Country Journal 12:27-32 D '85
Giorgio's mother. Barich, B.
Giovanni Moroni. Apollinaire, G.
GIPSIES *See* Gypsies
The **gipsies**. Shaw, H.
Gipsy, the mongrel. Woolf, V.
Giraffe. Jaffe, H.
The **giraffe**. Mrożek, S.
Giraffe Tuesday. Brantingham, J.
GIRAFFES
 Brantingham, J. Giraffe Tuesday
The **Girdle** of Hyppolita. Christie, A.
Girion, Barbara, 1937-
 Another blue-eyed quarterback
  Girion, B. A very brief season
 King of the hill
  Girion, B. A very brief season
 The makeover of Meredith Kaplan
  Girion, B. A very brief season

Girion, Barbara, 1937——_Continued_
   The moon cookies
      Girion, B. A very brief season
   Next of kin
      Girion, B. A very brief season
   Rip-off!
      Girion, B. A very brief season
   To Francie, with love
      Girion, B. A very brief season
   Trophy
      Girion, B. A very brief season
   A very brief season
      Girion, B. A very brief season
   With a little gold pencil
      Girion, B. A very brief season
The **girl** and the ghost. Savage, E.
The **girl** and two old men. DeGrazia, E.
The **girl** behind the hedge. Spillane, M.
Girl friend. Colter, C.
The **girl** from California. O'Hara, J.
The **girl** from Cardigan. Norris, L.
The **girl** from Carthage. Steele, M.
Girl in a turban. Morazzoni, M.
Girl in danger. Walsh, T.
The **girl** in the blue cap. Gustafsson, L.
The **girl** in the Humbert. Sandoz, M.
The **girl** in the mirror. Arnold, M.
The **girl** in the train. Christie, A.
The **girl** on the beach. Cameron, E.

GIRL SCOUTS
   Apple, M. Bridging
The **girl** who approached the fire. Kawabata, Y.
The **girl** who fell into the sky. Wilhelm, K.
The **girl** who had lived among artists. Colegate, I.
The **girl** who loved animals. McAllister, B.
The **girl** who loved Garbo. Gallagher, R.
The **girl** who loved graveyards. James, P. D.
The **girl** who might or might not have read Sartre. Bernard, K.
The **girl** who sang. Aldiss, B. W.
The **girl** who turned into cider. Valenzuela, L.
The **girl** who wanted to see Venice. Fraser, A.
The **girl** who was plugged in. Tiptree, J.
The **girl** who would be Russian. Johnson, W.
The **girl** with a pimply face. Williams, W. C.
The **girl** with the gift. Ford, J.
The **girl** with the hungry eyes. Leiber, F.
The **girl** with the scar. Lustig, A.
The **girl** with the Vita-Gel hair. Disch, T. M.

GIRLS
         See also Adolescence; Children; Youth
   Apollinaire, G. The blue eye
   Asscher-Pinkhof, C. Expensive purchase
   Backus, J. L. Ludmila

Bambara, T. C. Raymond's run
Barrett, L. Inventory
Barrett, N., Jr. Perpetuity blues
Bausch, R. The wife's tale
Bell, M. S. Triptych I
Bell, M. S. Triptych 2
Birtha, B. Baby town
Black, S. The biggest tent in the world
Bowles, P. Here to learn
Brinsmead, H. F. The twilight road
Butler, J. Without any ears
Byatt, A. S. Racine and the tablecloth
Camoin, F. A. It could happen
Campbell, A. April
Campbell, W. B. Headlights
Caplan, N. Murder in miniature
Cárdenas, M. But what if I liked the Panchos, not the Beatles
Carlisle, A. Don't it make you wonder
Carr, P. E. The party
Chappell, F. Children of strikers
Ciment, J. Astronomy
Ciment, J. Genetics
Ciment, J. Self-portrait with vanishing point
Coggeshall, R. Peter the Rock
Cook, H. Easter lily
Crowell, D. Says Velma
Deaver, P. F. Arcola girls
Doubiago, S. Raquel
Drake, R. The first year
Drake, R. I am counting with you all the way
Drake, R. The operetta
Ekström, M. The nothingness forest
Ekström, M. When we are home alone we dance all around the house
El Biali, Z. The glass barrier
Eldridge, M. Nature
Farmer, B. Ismini
Federspiel, J. Infirtaris inoaknoneis
Federspiel, J. The sapper: a romance
Ferguson, P. The dry familiar plains
Ferreira, R. The gravedigger
Finger, A. Like the Hully-Gully but not so slow
Finger, A. Old maids
Finger, A. A tragedy
Flanagan, M. White places
Fowler, K. J. The gate of ghosts
Francis, H. E. The sudden trees
Fraser, A. Boots
Freeman, M. E. W. The lost ghost
Gallant, M. Jorinda and Jorindel
Gallant, M. Orphans' progress
Gallant, M. Thank you for the lovely tea
Gallegos, M. Florence and the new shoes
Gault, C. Mary Beth
Gault, C. The other Ellen
Gault, C. Where the apple reddens
Gerber, M. J. Someone should know this story
Gilchrist, E. The expansion of the universe

GIRLS—*Continued*

Gilchrist, E. Revenge
Gilchrist, E. Victory over Japan
Gingher, M. Camouflage
Gingher, M. The kiss
Gingher, M. Teen angel
Givner, J. Brains
Givner, J. The celebrant
Gold, H. Ti-Moune
Gordon, M. The murderer guest
Grace, P. Going for the bread
Grace, P. The lamp
Grahn, J. Ernesta
Grenon, J. A new dress for Maggie
Haensel, R. Goldenrod
Hall, M. L. The peaceful eye
Hankla, C. A box for dreams
Hankla, C. Learning the mother tongue
Haynes, D. K. Thou shalt not suffer a witch . . .
Hill, R. Blue Rise [excerpt]
Hoyt, M. S. An island of curving stone
Huggan, I. Queen Esther
Huggan, I. Sorrows of the flesh
Ignatow, R. G. I have looked for Carrie
Ignatow, R. G. Stealing the bread
Interollo, L. The quickening
Jen, G. The water-faucet vision
Jewett, S. O. Lady Ferry
Jones, L. B. The whole idea of Cindy Potts
Kaplan, D. M. Doe season
Kawabata, Y. The silverberry thief
Kawabata, Y. Up in the tree
Kawabata, Y. The young lady of Suruga
Kilgore, D. Three alarm fire
King, G. E. The little convent girl
Kingsolver, B. Rose-Johnny
Krysl, M. Fallout
Krysl, M. Snegurochka
Larson, L. Original sin
Le Guin, U. K. Buffalo gals, won't you come out tonight
Leedom-Ackerman, J. Eurlanda's box
Lispector, C. The foreign legion
Lispector, C. The misfortunes of Sofia
Lispector, C. Temptation
Livesey, M. Learning by heart
Livesey, M. The salt course
London, J. First night
Luce-Kapler, R. The Rawleigh man
Lustig, A. The girl with the scar
Mackenzie, A. I can't help saying goodbye
Mansfield, K. How Pearl Button was kidnapped
Mansfield, K. New dresses
Mansfield, K. The voyage
Markham, B. He was a good lion
Marshall, D. R. Lavender blue
Matthews, J. A cat may look
Matthews, J. The grave at Mount Nebo
Matthews, J. The sound of a girl singing
McGarry, J. Providence, 1956: toy box

McGrath, P. The lost explorer
McLaughlin, L. Looking like Virginia Woolf
Miller, B. The lonesomes ain't no spring picnic
Miller, S. The birds and the bees
Miller, S. What Ernest says
Moravia, A. The devil comes and goes
Moravia, A. What use have I got for carnival?
Morris, M. Alewives
Moskowitz, F. Every airborne particle
Moskowitz, F. Fanny's comfort station
Moskowitz, F. The runaround
Moskowitz, F. Thelma
Moyer, K. In the castle
Munro, A. Jesse and Meribeth
Murphy, Y. Red, red
Murphy, Y. The slit
Murphy, Y. Stories in another language
Murphy, Y. The toys
Nevai, L. Baby wood
Oates, J. C. April
Oates, J. C. Ballerina
Oates, J. C. Haunted
Oates, J. C. Picnic
Ocampo, S. Icera
O'Connor, F. A Temple of the Holy Ghost
O'Donnell, P. A better day to die
Osborn, C. Ancient history
Paley, G. Ruthy and Edie
Parise, G. Melancholy
Pasternak, B. L. Zhenya Luvers' childhood
Petroski, C. Beautiful my mane in the wind
Phillips, J. A. Blind girls
Phillips, J. A. Lechery
Pilcher, R. Amita
Pilcher, R. The blue bedroom
Pilcher, R. Gilbert
Pritchard, M. A dance with Alison
Quiller-Couch, Sir A. T. A pair of hands
Rahmann, P. Heathen ways
Rambach, P. The crescent
Rambach, P. When the animals leave
Robison, M. Trying
Rooke, L. The only daughter
Russ, J. How Dorothy kept away the spring
Russ, J. The little dirty girl
Saiki, J. Petty larceny
Saiki, J. Plumeria days
Sandel, C. The child who loved roads
Schinto, J. Before sewing one must cut
Schinto, J. Caddies' day
Schinto, J. The friendships of girls unpopular together
Schinto, J. The ring; or, A girl confesses
Schulman, H. Good practice
Schulman, H. Like sisters
Schulman, H. Pushing the point
Shiga, N. The little girl and the rapeseed flower

GIRLS—*Continued*
  Stafford, J. The healthiest girl in town
  Stark, S. S. The Appaloosa house
  Stark, S. S. The horsehair
  Stone, K. Summer of a stick man
  Suckow, R. The little girl from town
  Sutherland, M. Codling-moth
  Tem, S. R. The battering
  Tem, S. R. The giveaway
  Thompson, J. The afternoon of the poetess
  Thompson, J. The Christmas party
  Thorman, C. Gurlas
  Tournier, M. Amandine; or, The two
      gardens
  Tremain, R. Words with Marigold
  Trevor, W. Virgins
  Tyre, N. Carnival day
  Valenzuela, L. The verb to kill
  Varley, J. The pusher
  Warren, D. Sunday rodeos
  West, J. Aloha, farewell to thee
  West, J. Probably Shakespeare
  West, J. The second (or perhaps third)
      time round
  Whitaker, M. The enchanted morning
  Whittier, G. Turning out
  Wilkinson, S. Chicken Simon
  Wilson, B. The investment
  Wilson, L. A. From the bottom up
  Wolff, T. Coming attractions
  Woolson, C. F. Felipa
  Ziem, J. Statement
Girls. Gallagher, T.
The girls. Ross, V.
The girls in Villa Costas. Brett, S.
The girls love each other. London, J.
Gisela. Latimer, J.
The G'issimo. Coriolan, J.
The gissix project. Boylan, J.
"Gitanette". Colette
Gita's story. Leaton, A.
Gitley. Ramchandani, K.
The Gittel. Sandor, M.
Give-and-take. Marlowe, D. J.
Give her hell. Wollheim, D. A.
Give him an inch . . . Harris, H.
Give it back to the Indians. Messenger, B.
Give the devil his due. Treat, L.
"Give the enemy sweet sissies and women
      to infatuate him, and jades and silks
      to blind him with greed". Chin, F.
The giveaway. Tem, S. R.
Given, Amanda
  Love's an itinerant
    Room to move; ed. by S. Falkiner
The giver. Lebar, A. B.
Giving birth. Atwood, M.
Givner, Joan. 1936-
  Brains
    Givner, J. Tentacles of unreason
  The celebrant
    Givner, J. Tentacles of unreason
  A climate of extremes
    Givner, J. Tentacles of unreason
  Conversation pieces
    Givner, J. Tentacles of unreason
  The decline and fall of a reasonable
      woman
    Givner, J. Tentacles of unreason
  First love
    Givner, J. Tentacles of unreason
  Laocoön, my father
    Givner, J. Tentacles of unreason
  The lost sheep
    Givner, J. Tentacles of unreason
  A spectator sport
    Givner, J. Tentacles of unreason
  The testament of Leyla
    Givner, J. Tentacles of unreason
  The woman who couldn't imagine men
    The North American Review 270:50-3 Je
    '85
GLACIERS
  Muir, J. An adventure with a dog
The glad eye. Barstow, S.
Gladiators. Essop, A.
GLADNESS *See* Happiness
Gladys's Gregory. West, J. A.
A glance in the mirror. Swados, H.
Glantz, Margot
  From genealogies
    Anthology of contemporary Latin Ameri-
      can literature, 1960-1984
Glasgow, Ellen
  The difference
    The Other woman; ed. by S. Koppelman
  The shadowy third
    Haunting women; ed. by A. Ryan
    Young ghosts; ed. by I. Asimov; M. H.
      Greenberg and C. G. Waugh
GLASGOW (SCOTLAND) *See* Scotland—
    Glasgow
Glasha. Dovlatov, S.
GLASS
  Waters, E. Cold spell
  Williams, T. Portrait of a girl in glass
Glass. Fitzgerald, M. J.
Glass. Havazelet, E.
Glass. Kawabata, Y.
The glass barrier. El Biali, Z.
The glass box. Ferré, R.
The glass-brick apartment. Steele, M.
Glass cloud. Kelly, J. P.
The glass dog. Baum, L. F.
The glass-domed clock. Queen, E.
The glass doorknob. Hall, M. M.
A glass of Wendy. Keillor, G.
Glasser, Leah Blatt
  A change of heart
    Redbook 164:40+ F '85
Glasser, Perry
  Away out and over
    Glasser, P. Singing on the Titanic
  Easily and well
    Glasser, P. Singing on the Titanic
  The last game
    Glasser, P. Singing on the Titanic

Glasser, Perry—*Continued*
   Ms. 13:58-60+ Ag '84
Marmosets
   Glasser, P. Singing on the Titanic
Mexico
   Glasser, P. Singing on the Titanic
Singing on the Titanic
   Glasser, P. Singing on the Titanic
Steering clear
   Glasser, P. Singing on the Titanic
   The North American Review 272:49-53
      Mr '87
Visit
   Glasser, P. Singing on the Titanic
What doesn't kill me
   Glasser, P. Singing on the Titanic
Glavin, Anthony
One for sorrow
   Short story international 51
Glaze, Eleanor
A small triumph
   Redbook 165:64+ Ag '85
Glazer, Daphne
The touch of the monkey god
   Critical Quarterly 29:3-7 Aut '87
The **glazier**. Botwinik, B.
The **gleams**. Salisbury, R.
Gleanings from snow country. Kawabata, Y.
Glemser, Bernard
The commandos go in
   A Treasury of World War II stories; ed.
      by B. Pronzini and M. H. Greenberg
Glickfeld, Carole L.
Out of the lion's belly
   When I am an old woman I shall wear
      purple; ed. by S. K. Martz
Glickman, Gary, 1959-
Magic
   Men on men 2; ed. by G. Stambolian
Glickman, James
"Leave my daughter alone!"
   Redbook 171:78+ O '88
Glidden, Frederick Dilley *See* Short, Luke,
   1908-1975
GLIDING AND SOARING
   Pohl, F. Second-hand sky
Glimm, Adele
To the rescue
   McCall's 113:114-15+ O '85
Glimpse into another country. Morris, W.
A **glimpse** of Sion's glory. Colegate, I.
Glimpses from the life of Maugoud Abdul
      Maugoud and two postscripts.
      Sharouni, Y.
A **glint** of gold. Yermakov, N.
The **gloating** place. Bloch, R.
Gloomy pleasures. Yasuoka, S.
The **Gloria** Scott. Doyle, Sir A. C.
A **glorious** morning, comrade. Gee, M.
Glory. Goulart, R.
Glory. Sherman, C. W.
Glory. Taylor, R.

Gloss, Molly
Interlocking pieces
   Universe 14
   The Year's best science fiction, second
      annual collection
GLOUCESTER (ENGLAND) *See* England—
   Gloucester
GLOUCESTERSHIRE (ENGLAND) *See*
   England—Gloucestershire
Glover, Douglas H.
Dog attempts to drown man in Saskatoon
   First fictions: Introduction 9
Fire drill
   First fictions: Introduction 9
Red
   First fictions: Introduction 9
The seeker, the snake and the baba
   First fictions: Introduction 9
GLOVES
   Bowen, E. Hand in glove
   Dawson, F. The fourth surprise
   Dickens, C. A pair of gloves
   Liben, M. No sale 1
   Slesar, H. Light fingers
   Woolf, V. Mrs. Dalloway in Bond Street
Gloves and fishes. McKinley, J.
The **glow** of copper. Fahy, C.
Glück, Robert
Sex story
   Men on men; ed. by G. Stambolian
Glück, Tereze
Argument with my father
   The Antioch Review 45:164-8 Spr '87
A Cuban girl
   The Antioch Review 45:169-75 Spr '87
Glynn, Thomas, 1935-
Apondé, the Magnificent times two
   The Paris Review 30:206-20 Spr '88
The world's most amazing prophet, a.k.a.
   Wallace Mumford Amazon Polleau
   American made; ed. by M. Leyner; C.
      White and T. Glynn
The **gnat**. Landolfi, T.
The **gnawing** worm. Buzzati, D.
Gnomebody. Ellison, H.
Gnosis. Kessler, J. F.
The **go-away** bird. Spark, M.
Go climb a tree if you don't like it. Sholem
      Aleichem
Go get a girlfriend. Gable, A. C.
The **go-getter**. Wodehouse, P. G.
Go like this. Moore, L.
The **goat**. Jonker, I.
The **goat**. King, F. H.
Goat ride. Highsmith, P.
A **goatherd** at luncheon. Calvino, I.
GOATHERDS
   Narayan, R. K. A horse and two goats
GOATS
   Highsmith, P. Goat ride
   Oates, J. C. Secret observations on the
      goat-girl
Goats. Smeds, D.

The **goblinry** of Ais. Carter, L.
Goczka. Bird, C.
GOD
Bloch, R. How like a god
Brunner, J. Judas
Elkin, S. The conventional wisdom
Ellison, H. The region between
Ellison, H. Stuffing
Harrison, M. J. Settling the world
Huston, N. Pliny's commentaries
Knight, D. F. God's nose
Kress, N. Trinity
Michaelson, L. W. The burning bush
Michaelson, L. W. Klitzee one—God zero
Morressy, J. Final version
Payne, P. The pure in heart
Poe, E. A. Mesmeric revelation
Salmonson, J. A. The prodigal daughter
Stern, S. The Lord and Morton Gruber
Swanwick, M. Trojan horse
Wells, H. G. The story of the Last Trump
Wells, H. G. A vision of judgment
The **god** business. Farmer, P. J.
The **god-chaser**. Taylor, P. E.
God giving Lithuania to the world. Thorman, C.
God is an iron. Robinson, S.
God loves you, Miss Rosewater. Cowley, J.
The **god** of Ibreez. Crowley, A.
God of the Naked Unicorn. Lupoff, R. A.
"**God** rest ye, merry gentlemen". Crane, S.
God rest you merry, gentlemen. Hemingway, E.
God sees the truth but is in no hurry to reveal it. See Tolstoy, L., graf. God sees the truth but waits
God sees the truth but waits. Tolstoy, L., graf
"**God** sent you into that Gomorrah this morning to bring up the truth". Holt, J. D.
The **goddess** of wisdom. Bloch, R.
The **goddess** on the street corner. St. Clair, M.
GODDESSES
Fitzgerald, M. J. Eurydice
Le Guin, U. K. Kore 87
Lynn, E. A. The gods of Reorth
Lynn, E. A. The red hawk
Robinson, K. S. Mother goddess of the world
St. Clair, M. The goddess on the street corner
Goddin, Nell
Hold on
The Antioch Review 45:190-3 Spr '87
Gödel's doom. Zebrowski, G.
Godfrey, Peter, 1924-
And turn the hour
John Creasey's Crime collection, 1986
The lady and the dragon
The Deadly arts; ed. by B. Pronzini and M. Muller

Out of this world
Death locked in; ed. by D. G. Greene and R. C. S. Adey
The shadow behind the face
John Creasey's Crime collection, 1984
Time out of mind
Ellery Queen's Memorable characters
Godine, Amy
The gardener
The North American Review 271:49-56 Je '86
GODMOTHERS
Colette. My goddaughter
Flanagan, M. Wild garlic
GODS
Ballard, J. G. A question of re-entry
Bishop, M. Voices
Bretnor, R. No other gods
Crowley, A. The god of Ibreez
Farmer, P. J. The god business
Ferguson, J. Ker, the god killer
Gardner, M. Oom
Gardner, M. Thang
Kotzwinkle, W. Disturbance reported on a pipeline
Li, F.-Y. Old Chang
Li, F.-Y. Rain-making
Lynn, E. A. The red hawk
Pu, S.-L. Yellow pride
Schwob, M. Empedocles, reputed god
Smith, C. A. The charnel god
St. Clair, M. The causes
Wells, H. G. Jimmy Goggles the god
The **gods** are not mocked. Bloch, R.
God's bones. Kawabata, Y.
God's cold lips. Kilworth, G.
God's hooks! Waldrop, H.
God's hour. Bishop, M.
The **gods** in flight. Aldiss, B. W.
God's nose. Knight, D. F.
The **gods** of Mars. Dozois, G. R., and others
The **gods** of Reorth. Lynn, E. A.
God's own elect. Lofts, N.
God's typhoon. Hersey, J.
Godshalk, C. S.
Wonderland
The Best American short stories, 1988
Godwin, Earl
Daddy
Devils & demons; ed. by M. Kaye and S. Kaye
Shadows 7
Godwin, Gail
Dream children
American short story masterpieces; ed. by R. Carver and T. Jenks
Over the mountain
The Bread Loaf anthology of contemporary American short stories; ed. by R. Pack and J. Parini
New American short stories; ed. by G. Norris
The Pushcart prize IX

Godwin, Gail—*Continued*
St. George
Great American love stories; ed. by L. Rosenthal
Godwin, Parke
Influencing the hell out of time and Teresa Golowitz
Devils & demons; ed. by M. Kaye and S. Kaye
A matter of taste
Shadows 7
Stroke of mercy
Masterpieces of terror and the supernatural; ed. by M. Kaye and S. Kaye
Godwin, Tom
Too soon to die
Space wars; created by P. Anderson
Godzilla America Ballpark Products, Inc. Barba, R.
GOEBBELS, JOSEPH, 1897-1945
About
Linaweaver, B. Moon of ice
GOEBBELS, PAUL JOSEPH *See* Goebbels, Joseph, 1897-1945
Goethe, Johann Wolfgang von, 1749-1832
The attorney
German stories; ed. by H. Steinhauer
About
Barthelme, D. Conversations with Goethe
Goff, Inna
A ticket to Odessa
Short story international 46
GOGH, VINCENT VAN, 1853-1890
About
Gansovsky, S. Vincent Van Gogh
Gogol', Nikolai Vasil'evich, 1809-1852
A bewitched place
Gogol', N. V. The complete tales of Nikolaĭ Gogol' v1
Christmas Eve
Gogol', N. V. The complete tales of Nikolaĭ Gogol' v1
The coach [Variant title: The calash]
Gogol', N. V. The complete tales of Nikolaĭ Gogol' v2
Diary of a madman
Gogol', N. V. The complete tales of Nikolaĭ Gogol' v1
The fair at Sorochintsy
Gogol', N. V. The complete tales of Nikolaĭ Gogol' v1
Ivan Fiodorovich Shponka and his aunt
Gogol', N. V. The complete tales of Nikolaĭ Gogol' v1
The lost letter
Gogol', N. V. The complete tales of Nikolaĭ Gogol' v1
A May night; or, The drowned maiden
Gogol', N. V. The complete tales of Nikolaĭ Gogol' v1

Nevsky Prospekt [Variant title: Nevsky Avenue]
Gogol', N. V. The complete tales of Nikolaĭ Gogol' v1
The nose
Gogol', N. V. The complete tales of Nikolaĭ Gogol' v2
Old-world landowners
Gogol', N. V. The complete tales of Nikolaĭ Gogol' v2
The overcoat [Variant title: The coat]
Gogol', N. V. The complete tales of Nikolaĭ Gogol' v2
The portrait [Variant title: The mysterious portrait]
Gogol', N. V. The complete tales of Nikolaĭ Gogol' v2
St. John's Eve
Gogol', N. V. The complete tales of Nikolaĭ Gogol' v1
The tale of how Ivan Ivanovich quarreled with Ivan Nikiforovich [Variant title: How the two Ivans guarreled]
Gogol', N. V. The complete tales of Nikolaĭ Gogol' v2
Taras Bulba
Gogol', N. V. The complete tales of Nikolaĭ Gogol' v2
A terrible vengeance [Variant title: A terrible revenge]
Gogol', N. V. The complete tales of Nikolaĭ Gogol' v1
Viy
Gogol', N. V. The complete tales of Nikolaĭ Gogol' v2
Parodies, travesties, etc.
Boyle, T. C. The overcoat II
Gogol's stomach. Blaine, M.
Gogol's wife. Landolfi, T.
Gohorry, John
Acts of merit
Encounter (London, England) 63:3-9 S/O '84
Going. Hempel, A.
Going after Cacciato. O'Brien, T.
Going ashore. Gallant, M.
Going back. McCulloch, J.
Going down. Malzberg, B. N.
Going for the bread. Grace, P.
Going home. Gorky, M.
Going home. Lee, H.
Going home. Sligo, J.
Going home. Walters, A. L.
The **going** home of Ntambo. Havemann, E.
Going into exile. Morris, W.
Going out as a ghost. Hood, H.
Going out to sea. Freeman, J.
Going to Baltistan. Abbasi, T.
Going to headquarters. Calvino, I.
Going to meet the man. Baldwin, J.
Going to Russia. Vanderhaeghe, G.
Going to school. Sanders, W.
Going to see the leaves. Collins, L.

Going to the dogs. Ford, R.
Going to the mountain. Wiebe, D. E.
Gojawiczyńska, Pola
A mother
  Russian and Polish women's fiction; ed.
  by H. Goscilo
Two women
  Russian and Polish women's fiction; ed.
  by H. Goscilo
Gold, Herbert, 1924-
Annique
  Gold, H. Lovers & cohorts
Bart and Helene at Annie-and-Fred's
  Gold, H. Lovers & cohorts
Blind, blind date
  Gold, H. Lovers & cohorts
Child of embassy
  Gold, H. Lovers & cohorts
Christmas in Dakar
  Gold, H. Lovers & cohorts
Cohorts
  Gold, H. Lovers & cohorts
Contingency planning
  Gold, H. Lovers & cohorts
A dark Norwegian person
  Gold, H. Lovers & cohorts
A death on the East Side
  Gold, H. Lovers & cohorts
From Proust to Dada
  Gold, H. Lovers & cohorts
A Haitian gentleman
  Gold, H. Lovers & cohorts
A karmic lover
  Gold, H. Lovers & cohorts
Love and like
  Gold, H. Lovers & cohorts
Max and the pacemaker
  Gold, H. Lovers & cohorts
A ninety-six-year-old big sister
  Gold, H. Lovers & cohorts
Paris and Cleveland are voyages
  Gold, H. Lovers & cohorts
Paternity
  Gold, H. Lovers & cohorts
San Francisco petal
  Gold, H. Lovers & cohorts
A selfish story
  Gold, H. Lovers & cohorts
The smallest part
  Gold, H. Lovers & cohorts
Stages
  Gold, H. Lovers & cohorts
  Stories and poems from close to home;
  ed. by F. Salas
Susanna at the beach
  Gold, H. Lovers & cohorts
Ti-Moune
  Gold, H. Lovers & cohorts
Waiting for the forty-one union
  Gold, H. Lovers & cohorts
What's become of your creature?
  Gold, H. Lovers & cohorts

Winter of '73
  Gold, H. Lovers & cohorts
Young man, old days
  Gold, H. Lovers & cohorts
Gold, Horace L.
A matter of form
  The Mammoth book of classic science
  fiction; ed. by I. Asimov; C. G.
  Waugh and M. H. Greenberg
No charge for alterations
  Amazing stories: visions of other worlds
GOLD
    See also Alchemy
Bloch, R. The golden opportunity of Lefty
  Feep
Cunningham, J. M. Yankee gold
Frazee, S. The singing sands
Johnson, W. R. Enough gold
Lafferty, R. A. Golden gate
Poe, E. A. Von Kempelen and his
  discovery
Schlobin, R. C. For lovers only
Scott, G. F. The bunyip dies
Sheil, G. Mad like Lasseter
Wolfe, T. Polyphemus
The **gold-bug**. Poe, E. A.
The **gold** chain. Ferreira, R.
Gold dust. Brown, G. M.
The **gold** fever tapes. Spillane, M.
The **gold** in the sea. Friel, B.
GOLD MINES AND MINING
Brand, M. Half a partner
Doyle, Sir A. C. Bones. The April fool
  of Harvey's Sluice
Gates, E. A yellow man and a white
Johnson, D. M. The hanging tree
London, J. All Gold Canyon
Marshall, A. Trees can speak
Prichard, K. S. Bad debts
Prichard, K. S. Genieve
Prichard, K. S. Luck
Gold rings & orange blossoms. St. Clair, J.
GOLD RUSH *See* California—1846-1900
GOLD SMUGGLING
Spillane, M. The gold fever tapes
The **gold** watch. Kim, Y. I.
The **gold** watch. MacLean, A.
Goldberg, Lester, 1924-
Farming on the Esso
  The Literary Review (Madison, N.J.)
  29:31-8 Fall '85
In Siberia it is very cold
  Here's the story: fiction with heart; ed.
  by M. Sklar
One more river
  Prime number; ed. by A. L. Weir
Golden anniversary. Brewster, E.
The **golden** day. Brand, M.
Golden gate. Lafferty, R. A.
Golden girl. Hospital, J. T.
Golden gloves. Oates, J. C.
The **golden** opportunity of Lefty Feep. Bloch,
  R.

A **golden** picture. Dazai, O.
The **Golden** Shadows old west museum. Blackman, M.
The **golden** spike. Wilkinson, A.
Golden thoughts. Mrożek, S.
Golden whore of the heartland. Cohen, M.
Goldenrod. Haensel, R.
Goldfinch & Son. Stern, S.
The **goldfish.** Michaelson, L. W.
Goldfish. Peirce, H.
Goldfish on the roof. Kawabata, Y.
Goldin, Stephen
 The world where wishes worked
  100 great fantasy short short stories; ed. by I. Asimov; T. Carr and M. H. Greenberg
Golding, William, 1911-
 Miss Pulkinhorn
  The Penguin book of modern British short stories
Goldleaf, Steven
 Used goods
  The Massachusetts Review 28:723-34 Wint '87
Goldman, E. S.
 Dave's depression
  The Atlantic 262:58-62+ O '88
 Dog people
  The Atlantic 262:47-53 Ag '88
 Way to the dump
  The Atlantic 260:81-4+ D '87
  The Best American short stories, 1988
Goldman, Francisco
 Fili
  Esquire 101:94-5+ Ja '84
  The Esquire fiction reader v1
Goldman, Lawrence
 Temporarily at liberty
  100 great fantasy short short stories; ed. by I. Asimov; T. Carr and M. H. Greenberg
Goldreich, Gloria
 A mother's good-bye
  Redbook 165:55-6 S '85
 Something to remember you by
  McCall's 111:59-61 Ag '84
 A symbol of our love
  Redbook 166:72+ D '85
 Winter courage
  Ladies' Home Journal 103:94+ F '86
Goldsmith, Howard
 Do ye hear the children weeping?
  Hitler victorious; ed. by G. Benford and M. H. Greenberg
 The voices of El Dorado
  Young ghosts; ed. by I. Asimov; M. H. Greenberg and C. G. Waugh
Goldsmith, Oliver, 1728-1774
 A curious inconsistency of the Man in Black
  Christian short stories; ed. by M. Booth

Goldswain, Ralph
 Dube's first day
  Winter's tale, new ser. v2
 Oh, ye of little faith
  Winter's tales, new ser. v3
Golem XIV. Lem, S.
GOLF
 Abbott, L. K. Category Z
 Abbott, L. K. The valley of sin
 Abbott, L. K. The world is almost rotten
 Heise, K. Children's crusade
 Jackson, G. The decline of Western Hill
 Sagan, F. Partway round the course
 Schinto, J. Caddies' Day
 Wilson, R., Jr. Fathers
Gombrowicz, Witold
 The banquet
  Partisan Review 54:549-56 Fall '87
Gomez, Jewelle
 Don't explain
  Love, struggle & change; ed. by I. Zahava
 No day too long
  Worlds apart; ed. by C. Decarnin; E. Garber and L. Paleo
Gómez Antelo, Carmen
 The carving
  Américas 40:50-2 S/O '88
GONCHAROV, IVAN ALEKSAN- DROVICH, 1812-1891
    Oblomov
 Liben, M. Ball of fire
Gone to the dogs. Anthony, P.
González, César A.
 Toño
  Southwest tales; ed. by Alurista and X. Rojas-Urista
González, Miguel A. Espino *See* Espino González, Miguel A.
Gonzalez, Nestor Vicente Madali
 The blue skull and the dark palms
  Short story international 42
Gooch, Brad, 1952-
 Maine
  Men on men; ed. by G. Stambolian
 Spring
  First love/last love; ed. by M. Denneny; C. Ortleb and T. Steele
Gooch. Kinsella, W. P.
Good. Barstow, S.
Good advice is rarer than rubies. Rushdie, S.
The **good** always comes back. Matheson, R. C.
GOOD AND EVIL
  See also Sin; Suffering
 Andersen, H. C. The traveling companion
 Andreyev, L. Darkness
 Barich, B. Hard to be good
 Barker, C. Down, Satan!
 Benson, A. C. The uttermost farthing
 Bonner, M. Reap it as you sow it
 Bonner, M. Tin can

GOOD AND EVIL—*Continued*
Brand, M. Reata's peril trek
Clifford, L. L. The new mother
De la Mare, W. Bad company
Dick, P. K. Holy quarrel
Elkin, S. The conventional wisdom
Fante, J. The Road to Hell
Hawthorne, N. Young Goodman Brown
Kirk, R. The peculiar demesne of Arch-
vicar Gerontion
Klein, T. E. D. Nadelman's god
O'Connor, F. An afternoon in the woods
O'Connor, W. D. The ghost
Pritchett, V. S. The saint
Russ, J. Souls
Sargent, P. The old darkness
Sawyer, R. J. The contest
Shepard, L. Mengele
Shiner, L. Love in vain
Singer, I. B. The Jew from Babylon
Stevenson, R. L. Markheim
Tilton, L. In the service of evil
Twain, M. The man that corrupted Had-
leyburg
Vinge, J. D. The storm king
Winters, Y. The brink of darkness
Zelazny, R. But not the herald
Zelazny, R. Tower of ice
Good bargain. Kim, S.-O.
Good-by, Grandma. Bradbury, R.
Good-by, Herman. O'Hara, J.
Good-by, Jack. London, J.
Good-by, Miss Patterson. MacLennan, P.
Good-bye, Cliff. Brown, M. W.
Good-bye, Columbus Avenue. Tippens, E.
Good-bye forever to Mr. Pain. Sheckley, R.
Good-bye, good-bye, be always kind and
true. Garrett, G. P.
Good-bye Marcus, good-bye Rose. Rhys, J.
The **good-bye** present. Rose, D. A.
Good-bye, sweetheart. Smith, L.
GOOD-BYES *See* Farewells
A **good** chance. Cook-Lynn, E.
Good clean fun. Chipulina, E. G.
Good climate, friendly inhabitants. Gordimer,
N.
Good country people. O'Connor, F.
A **good** cow. Olmstead, R.
Good dancing, sailor! Gardner, M.
A **good** day for the laughing blow. Everett,
P. L.
A **good** deal. Brown, R.
The **good** deed. Buck, P. S.
Good deeds are never forgotten. Faik, S.
Good evening, Mr. Tibbs. Ball, J.
A **good** father. Murphy, Y.
Good fortune. Burt, S.
Good gossip. Carey, J.
A **good** home for Hachita. Everett, P. L.
The **good** husband. Smith, E. E.
A **good** imagination. Bloch, R.
A **good** Indian. Humphrey, W.
Good investments. Dale, C.

A **good** kid. Holding, J.
A **good** kid in a troubled world. Rule, J.
Good Lady Ducayne. Braddon, M. E.
The **good** lion. Hemingway, E.
Good luck. Mufti, M.
The **good** luck bun. Liu, Q.
Good luck, schoolboy. See Okudzhava, B. S.
Lots of luck, kid!
Good luck songs. Asscher-Pinkhof, C.
The **good** man. Boswell, R.
Good man, bad man. Weidman, J.
A **good** man is hard to find. O'Connor, F.
Good men of God. Grizzard, L.
Good morning to you, Lieutenant.
Heinemann, L.
Good morning wardrobe. Campion, E.
Good neighbor. Curtiss, U. R.
The **good** neighbour. Williams, D.
Good news. Lipman, E.
Good news from the Vatican. Silverberg, R.
Good night, good knight. Brown, F.
Good night—good morning. Asscher-Pinkhof,
C.
A **good** night's work. Clemens, S.
Good old boy. Morris, W.
The **good** old days. Major, A.
Good people in the house. Lurie, M.
Good practice. Schulman, H.
Good reasons. Maupassant, G. de
Good rockin' tonight. Hauptman, W.
The **Good** Samaritan. Asimov, I.
The **good** Soldier Švejk. Hašek, J.
The **good** soldiers. Young-Bruehl, E.
Good wars. DeMarinis, R.
Goodbye. Thompson, K.
Goodbye and good luck. Raab, S.
Goodbye Balkan capital. Pym, B.
Goodbye, dark love. Lannes, R.
Goodbye Harold, good luck. Thomas, A. C.
Goodbye, sweetwater. Dumas, H.
Goodbye to goodbye. Dixon, S.
Goodbye to the lake. Keillor, G.
GOODBYES *See* Farewells
Goodis, David
Hawk of the Sudan
A Treasury of World War II stories; ed.
by B. Pronzini and M. H. Greenberg
Goodman, Allegra
The succession
Commentary 84:45-52 S '87
Total immersion
Commentary 84:45-53 O '87
Variant text
Commentary 81:55-63 Je '86
Wish list
Commentary 82:48-58 D '86
Young people
Commentary 83:59-65 Mr '87
Goodman, Ivy, 1953-
White boy
The Ploughshares reader: new fiction for
the eighties
Goodnight piece. Morgan, K.

The **goodwife** Hawkins. Hood, M.
Goose, dog, fish, stars. Jarman, M.
Goosebumps. Matheson, R. C.
Gopnik, Adam
The blue room
The New Yorker 63:34-8 F 23 '87
Gorbachev's wife. Cullen, E. J.
The **Gordian** knot. Herbert, Z.
Gordimer, Nadine, 1923-
Abroad
Selected stories from The Southern review, 1965-1985
At the rendezvous of victory
Gordimer, N. Something out there
The Penguin book of Southern African stories
Blinder
Gordimer, N. Something out there
The bridegroom
African short stories; ed. by C. Achebe and C. L. Innes
Children with the house to themselves
The Paris Review 28:172-86 Summ/Fall '86
A chip of glass ruby
Gordimer, N. Six feet of the country
Somehow tenderness survives; ed. by H. Rochman
City lovers [Variant title: Town lovers]
Gordimer, N. Six feet of the country
A city of the dead, a city of the living
Gordimer, N. Something out there
A correspondence course
Gordimer, N. Something out there
Country lovers
Gordimer, N. Six feet of the country
Short story international 46
Somehow tenderness survives; ed. by H. Rochman
Crimes of conscience
Gordimer, N. Something out there
Enemies
Full measure; ed. by D. Sennett
Good climate, friendly inhabitants
Gordimer, N. Six feet of the country
Home
The New Yorker 64:34-42 Ap 25 '88
A hunting accident
Echad 2: South African Jewish voices
Letter from his father
Dark arrows; ed. by A. Manguel
Gordimer, N. Something out there
The World of the short story; ed. by C. Fadiman
The life of the imagination
The Art of the tale; ed. by D. Halpern
The moment before the gun went off
Harper's 277:63-5 Ag '88
Native country
The Treasury of English short stories; ed. by N. Sullivan
Not for publication
Gordimer, N. Six feet of the country

Oral history
Gordimer, N. Six feet of the country
Rags and bones
Gordimer, N. Something out there
Sins of the third age
Gordimer, N. Something out there
Six feet of the country
Gordimer, N. Six feet of the country
Something out there
Gordimer, N. Something out there
Terminal
Gordimer, N. Something out there
Town lovers [Variant title: City lovers]
Short story international 54
Gordon, Arthur
A Christmas legend
Reader's Digest 127:77-8 D '85
Jeremy's first hunt
Reader's Digest 125:147-9 N '84
A rose for Miss Caroline
Reader's Digest 124:86-8 F '84
The sea devil
The Saturday Evening Post 260:42-5+ My/Je '88
Gordon, Caroline, 1895-1981
The brilliant leaves
Stories of the modern South; ed. by B. Forkner and P. Samway
The dragon's teeth [Variant title: One against Thebes]
Shenandoah: an anthology; ed. by J. Boatwright
Hear the nightingale sing
Civil War women; ed. by F. McSherry; C. G. Waugh and M. Greenberg
Old Red
A Modern Southern reader; ed. by B. Forkner and P. Samway
Gordon, Giles, 1940-
Hans Pfeifer
Winter's tales, new ser. v1
Mutual of Omaha
Critical Quarterly 30:40-8 Wint '88
Gordon, Mary, 1949-
Agnes
Gordon, M. Temporary shelter
Billy
Gordon, M. Temporary shelter
The dancing party
The Editors' choice v4; ed. by G. E. Murphy, Jr.
Gordon, M. Temporary shelter
Ms. 15:64-6+ Ag '86
Delia
Gordon, M. Temporary shelter
The Substance of things hoped for; ed. by J. B. Breslin
Eileen
Gordon, M. Temporary shelter
The imagination of disaster
Gordon, M. Temporary shelter
The magician's wife
Gordon, M. Temporary shelter

Gordon, Mary, 1949—_Continued_
Mrs. Cassidy's last year
  Gordon, M. Temporary shelter
The murderer guest
  Gordon, M. Temporary shelter
The neighborhood
  Gordon, M. Temporary shelter
  _Ms._ 13:70+ Jl '84
Now I am married
  Gordon, M. Temporary shelter
  Love stories for the time being; ed. by
    G. D. Chipps and B. Henderson
The only son of the doctor
  Gordon, M. Temporary shelter
The other woman
  Gordon, M. Temporary shelter
Out of the fray
  Gordon, M. Temporary shelter
  Short story international 70
Safe
  The Editors' choice: new American
    stories v1
  Gordon, M. Temporary shelter
Temporary shelter
  Gordon, M. Temporary shelter
The thorn
  Gordon, M. Temporary shelter
Violation
  Gordon, M. Temporary shelter
  Mademoiselle 93:132+ My '87
Watching the tango
  Gordon, M. Temporary shelter
A writing lesson
  Gordon, M. Temporary shelter
Gordon, Peter
Boys
  The New Yorker 61:32-5 S 23 '85
The Bridge of Sighs
  The New Yorker 62:44-7 N 17 '86
The curfew
  The New Yorker 63:38-44 O 19 '87
Honeymoon
  The New Yorker 62:34-5 My 12 '86
Gordon, Roxy
Pilgrims
  Earth power coming; ed. by S. J. Ortiz
Gores, Joe
Pahua
  Distant danger; ed. by J. Van de
    Wetering
The second coming
  The Black Lizard anthology of crime fic-
    tion; ed. by E. Gorman
Smart guys don't snore
  A Matter of crime v2
Gores, Joseph N. _See_ Gores, Joe
Gorgio. Nowakowski, M.
The **gorgon.** Lee, T.
Gorgy, Nabil
Cairo is a small city
  Arabic short stories; tr. by D. Johnson-
    Davies
Gorilla, my love. Bambara, T. C.

GORILLAS
Farmer, P. J. After King Kong fell
Waldrop, H. Dr. Hudson's secret gorilla
Gorky, Maksim, 1868-1936
The affair of the clasps
  Gorky, M. The collected short stories of
    Maxim Gorky
Birth of a man
  Gorky, M. The collected short stories of
    Maxim Gorky
Cain and Artyom
  Gorky, M. The collected short stories of
    Maxim Gorky
Chelkash
  Gorky, M. The collected short stories of
    Maxim Gorky
Chums
  Gorky, M. The collected short stories of
    Maxim Gorky
Creatures that once were men
  Gorky, M. The collected short stories of
    Maxim Gorky
Evil-doers
  Gorky, M. The collected short stories of
    Maxim Gorky
Going home
  Gorky, M. The collected short stories of
    Maxim Gorky
The hermit
  Gorky, M. The collected short stories of
    Maxim Gorky
Karamora
  Gorky, M. The collected short stories of
    Maxim Gorky
Lullaby
  Gorky, M. The collected short stories of
    Maxim Gorky
Notch
  Gorky, M. The collected short stories of
    Maxim Gorky
One autumn evening
  Gorky, M. The collected short stories of
    Maxim Gorky
Red
  Gorky, M. The collected short stories of
    Maxim Gorky
Twenty-six men and a girl
  Gorky, M. The collected short stories of
    Maxim Gorky
Gorky, Maxim _See_ Gorky, Maksim, 1868-
  1936
Görlich, Günter
The decision
  Voices East and West: German short
    stories since 1945
Gorman, Edward
Guild and the Indian woman
  Westeryear; ed. by E. Gorman
The reason why
  The Mammoth book of private eye
    stories; ed. by B. Pronzini and M. H.
    Greenberg

Gorman, Edward—*Continued*
Turn away
The Black Lizard anthology of crime fiction; ed. by E. Gorman
Gorodischer, Angélica
Man's dwelling place
Other fires; ed. by A. Manguel
Gosling, Paula
Mr. Felix
The Year's best mystery and suspense stories, 1988
The perfect alibi
Winter's crimes 17
The **gospel** according to Gamaliel Crucis; or, The astrogator's testimony. Bishop, M.
GOSSIP
Bird, C. The woodpecker toy fact
Colette. A masseuse
Covino, M. Libel
Dixon, S. The bench
Friel, G. Onlookers
Gallant, M. The assembly
Hawthorne, N. Mr. Higginbotham's catastrophe
Leedom-Ackerman, J. Sissy Mamma's wig
Leitão, L. Jaffer's chicken
O'Hara, J. Olive
Stead, C. Accents
West, J. Love, death, and the ladies' drill team
Gossip. Conroy, F.
The **gostak** and the doshes. Breuer, M. J.
GÖTEBORG (SWEDEN) *See* Sweden—Göteborg
GOTHIC ROMANCES
See also Horror stories
Gottfried, Ted
A wedding surprise
Redbook 166:36+ F '86
Gotthelf, Jeremias, 1797-1854
The broommaker of Rychiswyl
Gotthelf, J. Tales of courtship
Elsi the unusual farm maid
Gotthelf, J. Tales of courtship
How Christen wins a bride
Gotthelf, J. Tales of courtship
How Joggeli finds a wife: a country tale
Gotthelf, J. Tales of courtship
Michel's courtship adventures
Gotthelf, J. Tales of courtship
The notary gets caught
Gotthelf, J. Tales of courtship
Gottlieb, Elaine
Joker
The Southern Review (Baton Rouge, La.) 22:620-33 Summ '86
The lizard
Selected stories from The Southern review, 1965-1985
Sacrifice
The Southern Review (Baton Rouge, La.) 20:662-72 Jl '84

Goulart, Ron, 1933-
Back on my feet again
Ellery Queen's Prime crimes
Calling Dr. Clockwork
Amazing stories: 60 years of the best science fiction
Glory
The Best horror stories from the Magazine of fantasy and science fiction
Groucho
Magicats! Ed. by J. Dann and G. Dozois
How come my dog don't bark?
Hound dunnit; ed. by I. Asimov; M. H. Greenberg and C. L. R. Waugh
Junior partner
Fantastic stories; ed. by M. H. Greenberg and P. L. Price
Out of the inkwell
The Deadly arts; ed. by B. Pronzini and M. Muller
Please stand by
Wizards; ed. by I. Asimov; M. H. Greenberg and C. G. Waugh
Gould, Joan, 1927-
First sight
Ladies' Home Journal 101:91+ Je '84
Gould, Rachel
The child and the poet
Winter's tales, new ser. v1
Gourd Dance Song. Kim, Y. I.
GOURDS
Shiga, N. Seibei and his gourds
The **gourmand.** Pierce, C.
The **gourmet.** Lu Wenfu
The **gourmet** kidnaper. Ritchie, J.
GOVERNESSES
See also Housekeepers
Bird, C. The balloon lady
Doyle, Sir A. C. The adventure of the copper beeches
Doyle, Sir A. C. The copper beeches
Mansfield, K. The little governess
Taylor, P. H. The little cousins
GOVERNMENT, RESISTANCE TO
Dick, P. K. The last of the masters
Upward, E. The interview
Upward, E. The night walk
Valenzuela, L. The place of its quietude
Valenzuela, L. A story about greenery
The **government** bears. Bass, R.
Governor Warburton's right-hand man. Stuart, J.
GOVERNORS
Dodd, S. M. Public appearances
The **Governor's** Ball. Carlson, R.
Govier, Katherine, 1948-
The king of Siam
Encounter (London, England) 71:16-19 Je '88
Sociology
The Oxford book of Canadian short stories in English

Gowan, Lee
The decline and fall of Howard Dawn
The Old dance; ed. by B. Burnard
Gowdy, Barbara
Disneyland
The North American Review 273:21-5 S
'88
Goyen, William
Arthur Bond
Goyen, W. Had I a hundred mouths
Bridge of music, river of sand
Goyen, W. Had I a hundred mouths
Children of old somebody
Goyen, W. Had I a hundred mouths
The faces of blood kindred
Goyen, W. Had I a hundred mouths
Stories of the modern South; ed. by B.
Forkner and P. Samway
Figure over the town
Goyen, W. Had I a hundred mouths
Ghost and flesh, water and dirt
Goyen, W. Had I a hundred mouths
The grasshopper's burden
Goyen, W. Had I a hundred mouths
Had I a hundred mouths
Goyen, W. Had I a hundred mouths
In the icebound hothouse
Goyen, W. Had I a hundred mouths
The letter in the cedarchest
Goyen, W. Had I a hundred mouths
Old wildwood
Goyen, W. Had I a hundred mouths
Pore Perrie
Goyen, W. Had I a hundred mouths
Precious door
Goyen, W. Had I a hundred mouths
Rhody's path
Goyen, W. Had I a hundred mouths
The Texas principessa
Goyen, W. Had I a hundred mouths
Tongues of men and of angels
Goyen, W. Had I a hundred mouths
Where's Esther?
Goyen, W. Had I a hundred mouths
The white rooster
Goyen, W. Had I a hundred mouths
Zamour; or, A tale of inheritance
Goyen, W. Had I a hundred mouths
**Grabowski, Z. Anthony (Zbigniew Anthony),
1903-**
The state of the art
Tales from Ellery Queen's Mystery
Magazine: short stories for young
adults
Grabowski, Zbigniew Anthony *See*
Grabowski, Z. Anthony (Zbigniew An-
thony), 1903-
Grace, Patricia, 1937-
Butterflies
Grace, P. Electric city, and other stories
Electric city
Grace, P. Electric city, and other stories

Fishing
Grace, P. Electric city, and other stories
Flies
Grace, P. Electric city, and other stories
The geranium
Grace, P. Electric city, and other stories
Going for the bread
Grace, P. Electric city, and other stories
The hills
Grace, P. Electric city, and other stories
Hospital
Grace, P. Electric city, and other stories
Kahawai
Grace, P. Electric city, and other stories
Kepa
Women's work; ed. by M. McLeod and
L. Wevers
The lamp
Grace, P. Electric city, and other stories
Mirrors
Women's work; ed. by M. McLeod and
L. Wevers
The urupa
Grace, P. Electric city, and other stories
Waimarie
Grace, P. Electric city, and other stories
The wall
Grace, P. Electric city, and other stories
Grace. Day, R. C.
Grace. Thurm, M.
The **grace** of God. Landolfi, T.
Gracefully afraid. Ashley, M. A.
GRADUATION *See* Commencements
Graduation. Dubus, A.
Graduation. Lu Wenfu
Graduation. Matheson, R. C.
GRAFFITI
McLay, F. Headlines for Whitey
Schwartz, L. S. Mrs. Saunders writes to
the world
Sproat, R. Stunning the punters
Grafton, Sue
Murder between the sheets
Redbook 167:70+ O '86
Non Sung Smoke
An Eye for justice; ed. by R. J. Randisi
The Parker shotgun
Masterpieces of mystery and suspense;
ed. by M. H. Greenberg
Mean streets; ed. by R. J. Randisi
She didn't come home
The Mammoth book of private eye
stories; ed. by B. Pronzini and M. H.
Greenberg
Redbook 166:58+ Ap '86
The Year's best mystery and suspense
stories, 1987
Graham, Jane
Two tales of a trip
Home and away; ed. by R. Creswell
Graham, Philip, 1951-
The art of the knock
Chicago Review 35:60-8 Aut '85

Graham, Winston
The circus
  The Mammoth book of modern crime
    stories; ed. by G. Hardinge
Grahn, Judy, 1940-
Ernesta
  Hear the silence; ed. by I. Zahava
GRAIL
Sir Galahad and the Holy Grail
Gramma. King, S.
The **grammar** of love. Schwartz, A.
The **gramophone**. Stern, S.
Granberry, Edwin
A trip to Czardis
  Mississippi writers v1: Fiction; ed. by D.
    Abbott
"Grand". Williams, T.
Grand Hotel Lembang. Freriks, K.
Grand opening. West, J.
Grand staircases. Schwartz, L. S.
Grand-uncle's legs. Haley, R.
Grandbois, Alain, 1900-1975
May Blossom
  The Oxford book of French-Canadian
    short stories
The thirteenth
  Invisible fictions; ed. by G. Hancock
GRANDCHILDREN
     See also Granddaughters; Grandsons
Kelly, G. The holiday house
GRANDDAUGHTERS
Alexin, A. The class photograph
Antoni, R. W. Frogchild on the day of
  Corpus Christi
Brown, G. M. Andrina
Ferron, J. Little Red Riding Hood
Grace, P. Butterflies
Hospital, J. T. Morgan Morgan
Norris, H. The singing well
O'Connor, F. A view of the woods
Vinge, V. Gemstone
Walters, A. L. The Devil and Sister Lena
La **Grande** Bretêche. Balzac, H. de
Grandfather. Iskander, F.
GRANDFATHERS
Alexin, A. The class photograph
Asscher-Pinkhof, C. Must
Barnea, L. My grandfather
Bessette, G. The mustard plaster
Blythe, R. Take your partners
Carter, R. A generous man
Cook, H. The white rabbit
Daniels, C. A Carolina Christmas carol
Dybek, S. Chopin in winter
Everett, P. L. Hear that long train moan
Farmer, P. J. After King Kong fell
Farmer, P. J. Riders of the purple wage
Feng Jicai. The hornets' nest
Floyd, P. L. The summer no one was
  poor
Gifkins, M. Head over heels
Goyen, W. Old wildwood
Granit, A. Fire is burning on our street!

Griesemer, J. Comfort stations
Hoch, E. D. Day for a picnic
Hospital, J. T. The bloody past, the wan-
  dering future
Hospital, J. T. Morgan Morgan
Iskander, F. Grandfather
Kavaler, R. Depression glass
Kees, W. Letter from Maine
Kelly, G. The holiday house
Klein, T. E. D. Children of the kingdom
Kornblatt, J. R. Offerings
Kramer, K. Seeds of conflict
Kraski, G. Wings of eucalyptus leaves
Liberman, S. Seeds
Long, D. Great blue
Martone, M. Nein
Matthews, J. The two of them together
Maupassant, G. de. A family
Mazel, D. The angel's overcoat
Mazel, D. Late prayers
Mazel, D. The merry-go-round
Mazel, D. A story of hope
McHaney, T. L. The habits of guineas
Mitchell, K. The great electrical revolution
Mukherjee, B. The imaginary assassin
Muschg, A. Grandfather's little pleasure
Norris, H. The singing well
O'Connor, F. The artificial nigger
O'Connor, F. A late encounter with the
  enemy
O'Connor, F. A view of the woods
O'Hara, J. Over the river and through the
  wood
Paley, G. Telling
Pascoe, B. Work-horses
Pilcher, R. Spanish ladies
Pirandello, L. A breath of air
Ribeyro, J. R. Vultures without feathers
Rule, J. A chair for George
Schmidt, H. J. Shoe
Silverberg, R. Many mansions
Smith, P. D. Forever Island [excerpt]
So, K.-W. The heir
Swift, G. Chemistry
Taylor, P. H. In the Miro District
Thomas, D. A visit to grandpa's
Wetherell, W. D. If a woodchuck could
  chuck wood
Whitaker, M. Spring day at Slater's End
Wilson, A. J. E. The old general and the
  lost granddaughter
Wilson, L. A. From the bottom up
Wilson, L. A. The snipe hunters
Grandfather's little pleasure. Muschg, A.
GRANDMOTHERS
al-Idlibi, U. The women's baths
Alden, P. B. Legacies
Backus, J. L. Ludmila
Baxter, C. Talk show
Beaumont, C. My grandmother's japonicas
Blei, N. Skarda
Botwinik, B. The Bubbe
Brautigan, R. Revenge of the lawn

GRANDMOTHERS—*Continued*

Briskin, M. Two women, one child
Brodine, K. Here, take my words
Cameron, P. Excerpts from Swan Lake
Cameron, P. Grounded
Campbell, W. B. Of generations
Campos-De Metro, J. The grape's vine, the horse's mouth
Canzoneri, R. The harp of the winds
Curtiss, U. R. A judicious half inch
Durban, P. All set about with fever trees
Fahy, C. One day in the short happy life of Anna Banana
Floyd, P. L. Dream rocket
Freeman, M. E. W. Old Woman Magoun
Gallant, M. Irina
García Márquez, G. Artificial roses
García Márquez, G. The incredible and sad tale of innocent Eréndira and her heartless grandmother
Gathorne-Hardy, J. Peiter and Paulina
Gerber, M. J. Witnesses
Giles, M. Old souls
Gilliatt, P. Autumn of a dormouse
Girion, B. The moon cookies
Givner, J. Brains
Givner, J. A spectator sport
Grace, P. Butterflies
Haake, K. Wait until heaven
Hospital, J. T. Port after port, the same baggage
Hurston, Z. N. Isis
Hyon, C.-G. The death of my grandmother
Juarez, H. The answer
Kelly, G. The holiday house
Kenny, M. Yaikni
King, S. Gramma
King, S. The reach
Krist, G. The canonization
Lee, C. One Florida night
Lee, T. Wolfland
Lurie, M. Bobbeh
Lytle, A. Jericho, Jericho, Jericho
MacCall, L. Mrs. Henderson talks to God
Matthews, J. The grave at Mount Nebo
Matthews, J. Toward a distant train
Mattison, A. In family
Mazel, D. Late prayers
Mazel, D. Strawberries
Miller, B. The lonesomes ain't no spring picnic
Miller, S. Appropriate affect
Morris, M. Links
Muller, D. N. The old woman's blessing
Munro, A. White dump
Murphy, Y. The toys
Neville, S. Cousins
Norris, H. The healing
Norris, H. The love child
Nye, N. S. The cookies
O'Connor, F. A good man is hard to find
Osier, J. The ritual
Perea, R. L. Miracle at Chimayo

Pilcher, R. Toby
Pulaski, J. The romance
Richler, M. The summer my grandmother was supposed to die
Rossiter, S. Star light, star bright
Rule, J. A chair for George
Rule, J. Musical beds
Rule, J. The real world
Salloum, V. Sitty Victoria
Sandor, M. The Gittel
Spark, M. The gentile Jewesses
Stafford, J. In the zoo
Stark, S. S. In the surprise of life
Stern, S. The gramophone
Thompson, J. Birds in air
Traba, M. All in a lifetime
Updike, D. Indian summer
Vanderhaeghe, G. The watcher
Vinge, V. Gemstone
Viramontes, H. M. The moths
Walsh, T. My other grandmother
Warren, J. Ready money
Welch, D. In the vast house
Williams, J. The blue men
Williams, T. "Grand"

Grandmother's little girl. Sanford, A.
Grandpa Hopewell and his flying tractor. Schramm, W. L.

GRANDPARENTS

La Puma, S. Wear it in good health
MacLeod, A. The road to Rankin's Point
MacLeod, A. Vision
Mattison, A. Sleeping giant
Sexson, L. When the pie was opened
Willson, H. A Christmas tale

Grandpa's growth. Young, M.
Grandson. Asscher-Pinkhof, C.
A **grandson** of the Golden West. Rand, P.

GRANDSONS

Carter, R. A generous man
Chernoff, M. Degan dying
Coe, C. Anything you want
Krist, G. The canonization
Lytle, A. Jericho, Jericho, Jericho
Matthews, J. Toward a distant train
Norris, H. The love child
O'Connor, F. The artificial nigger
Papaellinas, G. A merchant's widow
Pascoe, B. Work-horses
Pollack, E. The vanity of small differences
Rand, P. A grandson of the Golden West
Ribeyro, J. R. Vultures without feathers
Rifaat, A. Degrees of death
Taylor, P. H. In the Miro District
Tsushima, Y. A sensitive season

Granit, Arthur

Come into the hallway, for five cents!
    Granit, A. I am from Brownsville
Fire is burning on our street!
    Granit, A. I am from Brownsville
Free the canaries from their cages!
    Granit, A. I am from Brownsville

Granit, Arthur—*Continued*
Hello, Lenin! Hello, Stalin! How's the revolution today?
  Granit, A. I am from Brownsville
I went to the market place to see the world! Oy, Mama, oy!
  Granit, A. I am from Brownsville
No golden tombstones for me!
  Granit, A. I am from Brownsville
The penny is for God!
  Granit, A. I am from Brownsville
Songs my mother taught me that are not in Hamlet; or, "Come into my house, Horatio! there are more things under the mattress than are dreamt of in your philosophy!"
  Granit, A. I am from Brownsville
Tessie, don't give away the raisin; without it, you're lost!
  Granit, A. I am from Brownsville
They're killing Jews on Sackman Street!
  Granit, A. I am from Brownsville
Usher
  Granit, A. I am from Brownsville
"When we produce prostitutes and thieves, we shall be a normal people!"—Jabotinsky
  Granit, A. I am from Brownsville
With a herring in one hand and a bottle of schnapps in the other; oh! how he did dance!
  Granit, A. I am from Brownsville
Granny and the golden bridge. Alegría, C.
Granny's birthday. Brown, F.
Grant, Charles L.
Ellen, in her time
  The Architecture of fear; ed. by K. Cramer and P. D. Pautz
Eyes
  Halloween horrors; ed. by A. Ryan
If Damon comes
  The Dark descent; ed. by D. G. Hartwell
Love-starved
  Vampires; ed. by A. Ryan
My shadow is the fog
  Ripper! Ed. by G. Dozois and S. Casper
The old men know
  Masques; ed. by J. N. Williamson
Out there
  Cutting edge; ed. by D. Etchison
Pride
  The Best horror stories from the Magazine of fantasy and science fiction
The sheeted dead
  In the field of fire; ed. by J. Van B. Dann and J. Dann
Spinning tales with the dead
  Prime evil; ed. by D. E. Winter
Grant, John *See* Gash, Jonathan, 1933-
Grant of easement. Tallent, E.
Grape harvest. Colette

GRAPES
Colette. Grape harvest
The **grape's** vine, the horse's mouth. Campos-De Metro, J.
Graphomania. Piñera, V.
Grass, Günter, 1927-
The left-handers
  Voices East and West: German short stories since 1945
The **grasshopper** and the bell cricket. Kawabata, Y.
Grasshoppers. Jolley, E.
The **grasshopper's** burden. Goyen, W.
Grau, Shirley Ann, 1929-
The beginning
  Grau, S. A. Nine women
Ending
  Grau, S. A. Nine women
Flight
  Grau, S. A. Nine women
Home
  Grau, S. A. Nine women
Housekeeper
  Grau, S. A. Nine women
Hunter
  Grau, S. A. Nine women
Letting go
  Grau, S. A. Nine women
Summer shore
  Grau, S. A. Nine women
The way back
  Selected stories from The Southern review, 1965-1985
White girl, fine girl
  The Art of fiction in the heart of Dixie; ed. by P. D. Beidler
Widow's walk
  Grau, S. A. Nine women
Grave angels. Kearns, R.
The **grave** at Mount Nebo. Matthews, J.
The **grave** robber. Holding, J.
GRAVE ROBBERS
Bierce, A. One summer night
Stevenson, R. L. The body snatchers
The **gravedigger.** Ferreira, R.
Gravedigger. Thrapp, D.
GRAVEDIGGERS
Bates, H. E. Silas the good
Boylan, J. Potter's field
Kearns, R. Grave angels
Sutter, B. You ain't dead yet
Gravel, Geary
Old Toad
  Tales of the Witch World 2
Graven image. O'Hara, J.
Graven images. Coskran, K.
Graves, Mrs. A. J.
Mary and Ellen Grosvenor; or, The two sisters
  Old maids; ed. by S. Koppelman
Graves, Robert, 1895-1985
Earth to earth
  The Penguin book of horror stories

Gravesend Bay. La Puma, S.
GRAVESTONES *See* Tombstones
Graveyard day. Mason, B. A.
The **graveyard** rats. Kuttner, H.
Graveyard shift. Matheson, R.
Graveyard sirens. Maupassant, G. de
GRAVEYARDS *See* Cemeteries
GRAVITATION
　　　See also Relativity (Physics); Weight-
　　lessness
　Asimov, I. The billiard ball
　Niven, L. Neutron star
GRAVITY *See* Gravitation
Gravity. Winton, T.
Gravity and levity. Pascoe, B.
Gray, Alasdair
　The cause of some recent changes
　　Gray, A. Unlikely stories, mostly
　The comedy of the white dog
　　Gray, A. Unlikely stories, mostly
　The crank that made the revolution
　　Gray, A. Unlikely stories, mostly
　　Streets of stone; ed. by M. Burgess and
　　　H. Whyte
　The end of the Axletree
　　Gray, A. Unlikely stories, mostly
　Five letters from an eastern empire
　　Gray, A. Unlikely stories, mostly
　The Great Bear Cult
　　Gray, A. Unlikely stories, mostly
　Logopandocy
　　Gray, A. Unlikely stories, mostly
　The problem
　　Gray, A. Unlikely stories, mostly
　Prometheus
　　Gray, A. Unlikely stories, mostly
　The spread of Ian Nicol
　　Gray, A. Unlikely stories, mostly
　　Streets of stone; ed. by M. Burgess and
　　　H. Whyte
　The star
　　Gray, A. Unlikely stories, mostly
　The start of the Axletree
　　Gray, A. Unlikely stories, mostly
Gray, Arthur, 1852-1940
　The Everlasting Club
　　Lost souls; ed. by J. Sullivan
　The true history of Anthony Ffryar
　　The Oxford book of English ghost
　　　stories
Gray, Malcolm, 1927-
　*For works written by this author under
　　other names see* Stuart, Ian, 1927-
Gray, Patrick Worth
　Too soon solos
　　The Georgia Review 40:146-54 Spr '86
　　Necessary fictions; ed. by S. W. Lind-
　　　berg and S. Corey
The **gray** champion. Hawthorne, N.
Gray days. Colette
The **gray** lady. Matthews, J.
The **gray** men. West, Dame R.
A **gray** moon. Shiga, N.

A **gray** pigeon. Wang Meng
Grayson, Richard
　Murder à la mode
　　John Creasey's Crime collection, 1987
Grayson, Richard, 1951-
　The facts are always friendly
　　Editor's choice II; ed. by M. Sklar and
　　　M. Biggs
Grease hunger. Franklin, P.
Greasy Lake. Boyle, T. C.
The **great** amalgamation. Chesterton, G. K.
The **great** American novel. Hoch, E. D.
Great Aunt Allie's flypapers. James, P. D.
GREAT AUNTS *See* Aunts
The **Great** Bear Cult. Gray, A.
Great blue. Long, D.
GREAT BRITAIN
　　　See also England; Northern Ireland;
　　Scotland; Wales
GREAT BRITAIN. ARMY
　Amis, K. My enemy's enemy
　Mortimer, J. C. Rumpole and the bright
　　seraphim
　　　　Officers
　Davin, D. The general and the nightingale
　Doyle, Sir A. C. The colonel's choice
　Doyle, Sir A. C. A regimental scandal
　Gilbert, W. S. Jones' Victoria Cross
GREAT BRITAIN. NAVY *See* Great Brit-
　ain. Royal Navy
GREAT BRITAIN. ROYAL NAVY
　Melville, H. Billy Budd, Sailor
　Monsarrat, N. "HMS Marlborough will
　　enter harbour"
　Watmough, D. All at sea
　　　　Officers
　Forester, C. S. Dawn attack
　Forester, C. S. Night stalk
　Woolf, V. Scenes from the life of a British
　　naval officer
Great Cain. Schmidt, A.
The **great** Cape Cod shock scare. Baumbach,
　J.
"The **great** dark". Twain, M.
A **great** day for Bonzo. Bates, H. E.
Great days. Barthelme, D.
The **great** defender. Lee, N.
The **great** dormitory mystery. Farber, S. N.
The **great** electrical revolution. Mitchell, K.
Great Escape Tours Inc. Reed, K.
Great Falls. Ford, R.
The **great** fire. Tillinghast, D.
The **Great** God Pan. Harrison, M. J.
The **great** god Pan. Machen, A.
The **great** good place. James, H.
Great-grandfather dragon's tale. Yolen, J.
Great is Diana. Davidson, A.
GREAT LAKES
　Woolson, C. F. Castle Nowhere
The **great** man. Austin, D.
Great medicine. Frazee, S.
A **great** mistake. Crane, S.
A **great** Mollie. Suckow, R.

Great mysteries explained! Sladek, J. T.
Great news from the mainland. Hemingway, E.
Great Pan is dead! Regent, P.
The **great** plain. Flynn, R.
The **Great** Profundo. MacLaverty, B.
Great Pumpkins I have known & loved. Pierce, J. P.
The **great** rodeo fix. Ellis, L. R.
Great sea battles. Bukoski, A.
The **great** sermon handicap. Wodehouse, P. G.
A **great** sight. Van de Wetering, J.
The **great** snake massacre. Millman, L.
The **great** speckled bird. Lowrey, P. H.
The **great** staircase at Landover Hall. Stockton, F.
The **great** staircase of the legislative palace. Piñera, V.
The **great** Valentinova. Johnson, W.
Great wits. Mattison, A.
Greater love than this . . . Resnicow, H.
The **greatest** cook in Christendom. Rafferty, S. S.
The **greatest** gift. Stern, P. V. D.
The **greatest** man in the world. Thurber, J.
Greatness strikes where it pleases. Gustafsson, L.
The **greats**. Osborn, C.
GREECE
        See also Corfu Island (Greece); Lesbos Island (Greece)
King, F. H. So hurt and humiliated
Yourcenar, M. Aphrodissia, the widow
Yourcenar, M. Our-Lady-of-the-Swallows
        20th century
Aickman, R. The wine-dark sea
Eisenstein, S. The Greek smile
Eisenstein, S. Michali among the roses
Farmer, B. The captain's house
Farmer, B. Maria's girl
Farmer, B. Milk
Farmer, B. Our lady of the beehives
Farmer, B. Pumpkin
Farmer, B. Saint Kay's day
Farmer, B. Snake
Farmer, B. Woman in a mirror
Hayman, R. Urchins
Lee, T. The gorgon
Marrington, P. The beautiful journey
Regent, P. At Manoli's sheepfold
Regent, P. Great Pan is dead!
Samarakis, A. The mother
        Marriage customs
        See Marriage customs—Greece
        Rural life
Dadswell, M. A spectre of ancient dust
Haris, P. Lights on the sea
        Athens
Gustafsson, L. The fugitives discover that they knew nothing
Haris, P. Before the dawn
Haris, P. A dead city

Haris, P. Four and a half
Haris, P. Not a bird in the sky
Haris, P. Of love and darkness
Haris, P. Reinforced concrete
Haris, P. The third son
Haris, P. A young man's dance
Johnston, G. The verdict
Maniaty, T. 'Who was that masked man?'
GREED *See* Avarice
Greedy-Gut Gus, the car toad. Conroy, J.
GREEK CIVIL WAR, 1944-1949 *See* Greece—20th century
The **Greek** interpreter. Doyle, Sir A. C.
The **Greek** smile. Eisenstein, S.
GREEKS
        Australia
Farmer, B. Ismini
Farmer, B. Melpo
Loukakis, A. Being here now
Loukakis, A. I told mama not to come
Loukakis, A. Only in the truth
Loukakis, A. This wizened creature
Papaellinas, G. Around the crate
Papaellinas, G. Christos Mavromatis is a welder
Papaellinas, G. In which Peter Mavromatis lives up to his name
Papaellinas, G. Into a further dimension
Papaellinas, G. Peter Mavromatis rides the tail of the donkey
Papaellinas, G. Peter's song
Papaellinas, G. You told me
        England
King, F. H. Appetites
        South Africa
Cope, J. Ekaterina
        United States
Dubus, A. Land where my fathers died
Mooney, M. Ancient voices
Petrakis, H. M. The ballad of Daphne and Apollo
Petrakis, H. M. Chrisoula
Petrakis, H. M. Courtship of the blue widow
Petrakis, H. M. Dark eye
Petrakis, H. M. A hand for tomorrow
Petrakis, H. M. The journal of a wife beater
Petrakis, H. M. The judgement
Petrakis, H. M. The legacy of Leontis
Petrakis, H. M. Matsoukas
Petrakis, H. M. The miracle
Petrakis, H. M. Pa and the sad turkeys
Petrakis, H. M. Pericles on 31st Street
Petrakis, H. M. The return of Katerina
Petrakis, H. M. The shearing of Samson
Petrakis, H. M. The siege of Minerva
Petrakis, H. M. The song of Rhodanthe
Petrakis, H. M. The waves of night
Petrakis, H. M. The wooing of Ariadne
Thomas, J. Half frame
Greektown. Estleman, L. D.

Greeley, Andrew M., 1928-
Anne Marie
  U.S. Catholic 49:18-24 Mr '84
Count the ways
  U.S. Catholic 51:26-32 Je '86
A handful of tinsel
  Ladies' Home Journal 101:84+ D '84
How Father Grinch stole Christmas
  U.S. Catholic 49:32-7 D '84
Martina
  The Literary Review (Madison, N.J.)
  31:333-42 Spr '88
The priest and Jenny Martin
  Redbook 162:60-4+ Ap '84
Sionna Marie
  U.S. Catholic 53:30-4 Ja '88
Green, Evan
Marginals
  The New press anthology #2
Peters in Shinjuku: a set of miniatures
  The New press anthology #1
Green, Hannah, 1932- *See* Greenberg, Joanne, 1932-
Green, J. C., and Proctor, George W.
The night of the Piasa
  Nightmares in Dixie; ed. by F. McSherry; C. G. Waugh and M. H. Greenberg
Green, Janet
The tallest man in the world
  Ellery Queen's Crimes and punishments
Green, Jesse
An every-afternoon affair
  Mademoiselle 93:128+ Ag '87
Green, Joseph, 1706-1780
The ruby wand of Asrazel
  Magic in Ithkar 2; ed. by A. Norton and R. Adams
Green, Michael
Measuring the light
  L. Ron Hubbard presents Writers of the future
Green, Sharon
A quiet day at the fair
  Magic in Ithkar 4; ed. by A. Norton and R. Adams
Green are the meadows. Böll, H.
The **green** behind the glass. Geras, A.
The **green** bottle. Wiebe, D. E.
Green Brother. Waldrop, H.
The **green** chrysanthemum. An, S.-G.
Green days in Brunei. Sterling, B.
Green grass, blue sky, white house. Morris, W.
Green grow the rushes. Hungerford, T. A. G.
Green head. Davie, E.
Green in High Hallack. Stuart, K.
The **green** lamp. Grin, A.
The **green** leaves. Ogot, G.
The **green** life. Haas, B.
Green life. Mihelic, J.

The **green** magician. De Camp, L. S., and Pratt, F.
The **green** man. Jones, K.
Green marmalade. Houbein, L.
Green Mars. Robinson, K. S.
Green messiah. Yolen, J.
The **green** road to Quephanda. Rendell, R.
Green sealing wax. Colette
Green shoes. Boerema, R.
The **green** silk shirt. Böll, H.
Green tea. Le Fanu, J. S.
Green things. Thompson, K.
The **green** village. Peattie, M. R.
Green winter. Francis, M.
The **green** woman. Collins, M.
Greenbaum, O'Reilly & Stephens. Gangemi, K.
Greenberg, Alvin
Closed Mondays
  Stiller's pond; ed. by J. Agee; R. Blakely and S. Welch
The conservation of matter
  Greenberg, A. The man in the cardboard mask
The man in the cardboard mask
  Greenberg, A. The man in the cardboard mask
No loose ends
  The North American Review 272:51-5 D '87
Sue: a meditation on history
  Greenberg, A. The man in the cardboard mask
The true story of how my grandfather was smuggled out of the old country in a pickle barrel in order to escape military conscription
  Greenberg, A. The man in the cardboard mask
What would I know?
  Greenberg, A. The man in the cardboard mask
Where do folk sayings come from?
  Greenberg, A. The man in the cardboard mask
Greenberg, Barbara, 1940-, and Chambers, George
Monday
  Chicago Review 34 no4:42-53 '85
Greenberg, Barbara L.
Important things
  Sudden fiction; ed. by R. Shapard and J. Thomas
Greenberg, Joanne, 1932-
Days of awe
  New women and new fiction; ed. by S. Cahill
The Pope skis faster than that!
  50 Plus 28:52-63+ F '88
The supremacy of the Hunza
  The Interior country; ed. by A. Blackburn
Greenbriar. Eighner, L.

Greenburg, Joanne
Certain distant suns
Black water; ed. by A. Manguel
Greene, Graham, 1904-
Across the bridge
Greene, G. Collected short stories
Alas, poor Maling
Greene, G. Collected short stories
Awful when you think of it
Greene, G. Collected short stories
The basement room
Greene, G. Collected short stories
Beauty
Greene, G. Collected short stories
The blue film
Greene, G. Collected short stories
Brother
Greene, G. Collected short stories
The case for the defence
Greene, G. Collected short stories
The Penguin classic crime omnibus
Chagrin in three parts
Greene, G. Collected short stories
A chance for Mr. Lever
Greene, G. Collected short stories
Cheap in August
Greene, G. Collected short stories
The World of the short story; ed. by
C. Fadiman
A day saved
Greene, G. Collected short stories
The destructor
Greene, G. Collected short stories
A discovery in the woods
Greene, G. Collected short stories
Doctor Crombie
Greene, G. Collected short stories
Dream of a strange land
Greene, G. Collected short stories
A drive in the country
Greene, G. Collected short stories
The end of the party
Child's ploy; ed. by M. Muller and B.
Pronzini
Greene, G. Collected short stories
The hint of an explanation
Greene, G. Collected short stories
I spy
Greene, G. Collected short stories
The innocent
Greene, G. Collected short stories
The invisible Japanese gentlemen
Greene, G. Collected short stories
The Penguin book of modern British
short stories
Jubilee
Greene, G. Collected short stories
A little place off the Edgeware Road
Black water; ed. by A. Manguel
Greene, G. Collected short stories
May we borrow your husband?
Greene, G. Collected short stories

Men at work
Greene, G. Collected short stories
Mortmain
Greene, G. Collected short stories
The Treasury of English short stories;
ed. by N. Sullivan
The over-night bag
Greene, G. Collected short stories
Proof positive
Greene, G. Collected short stories
The root of all evil
Greene, G. Collected short stories
The second death
Christian short stories; ed. by M. Booth
Greene, G. Collected short stories
A shocking accident
Greene, G. Collected short stories
Special duties
Greene, G. Collected short stories
Two gentle people
The Art of the tale; ed. by D. Halpern
Greene, G. Collected short stories
Under the garden
Greene, G. Collected short stories
A visit to Morin
Greene, G. Collected short stories
The Substance of things hoped for; ed.
by J. B. Breslin
When Greek meets Greek
Greene, G. Collected short stories
Greene, Philip L.
The Stella school
The North American Review 273:34-7 Je
'88
They got it all
The Literary Review (Madison, N.J.)
27:191-200 Wint '84
A **greenhouse** for Maureen. Barclay, B.
Greening, John
Pleasure trips
P.E.N. new fiction I
The **greening** of Bed-Stuy. Pohl, F.
GREENLAND
Millman, L. The wrong-handed man
Greenleaf, Stephen
Iris
The Eyes have it; ed. by R. J. Randisi
The Mammoth book of private eye
stories; ed. by B. Pronzini and M. H.
Greenberg
The Year's best mystery and suspense
stories, 1985
Greenleaf. O'Connor, F.
Greenshaw's Folly. Christie, A.
**GREENWICH VILLAGE (NEW YORK,
N.Y.)** *See* New York (N.Y.)—Green-
wich Village
Greenwood, Robert
Arcadia
Greenwood, R. Arcadia, and other
stories

Greenwood, Robert—*Continued*
Archetypes
Greenwood, R. Arcadia, and other stories
The cannon
Greenwood, R. Arcadia, and other stories
Charley Wales
Greenwood, R. Arcadia, and other stories
A gift to the future
Greenwood, R. Arcadia, and other stories
The last survivor of Sierra Flat
Greenwood, R. Arcadia, and other stories
Like Lucifer
Greenwood, R. Arcadia, and other stories
Mind and body
Greenwood, R. Arcadia, and other stories
Mokli
Greenwood, R. Arcadia, and other stories
The other world
Greenwood, R. Arcadia, and other stories
Seed grain
Greenwood, R. Arcadia, and other stories
Snake eyes
Greenwood, R. Arcadia, and other stories

GREGORY IX POPE, ca. 1170-1241
About
Schwob, M. The narrative of Pope Gregory IX
Gregory, Ormond *See* Robbins, W. Wayne
Gregory. Ioannides, P.
Greg's peg. Auchincloss, L.
Grekova, I.
One summer in the city
The Barsukov Triangle, The two-toned blond & other stories; ed. by C. R. Proffer & E. Proffer
Grenon, Joan
A new dress for Maggie
Short story international 61
Grenville, Kate, 1950-
Blast off
Grenville, K. Bearded ladies
Country pleasures
Grenville, K. Bearded ladies
Dropping dance
Room to move; ed. by S. Falkiner
Having a wonderful time
Grenville, K. Bearded ladies
Junction
Grenville, K. Bearded ladies
Making tracks
Grenville, K. Bearded ladies

Meeting the folks
Grenville, K. Bearded ladies
No such thing as a free lunch
Grenville, K. Bearded ladies
Refractions
Grenville, K. Bearded ladies
Rosalie's folly
Grenville, K. Bearded ladies
Home and away; ed. by R. Creswell
Slow dissolve
Grenville, K. Bearded ladies
The space between
Grenville, K. Bearded ladies
A summer aunt
Grenville, K. Bearded ladies
The test is, if they drown
Grenville, K. Bearded ladies
Greta. Burns, M.
Grey, Zane, 1872-1939
Don
Roger Caras' Treasury of great dog stories
The land of the wild musk-ox
Grey, Z. The wolf tracker, and other animal tales
Roping lions in the Grand Canyon
Grey, Z. The wolf tracker, and other animal tales
Strange partners of Two-Fold Bay
Grey, Z. The wolf tracker, and other animal tales
Tappan's burro
The Western hall of fame; ed. by B. Pronzini and M. H. Greenberg
The wolf tracker
Grey, Z. The wolf tracker, and other animal tales
The grey day. Rhys, J.
The grey dog. Ferron, J.
The grey horse. Prichard, K. S.
The grey ones. Priestley, J. B.
A grey sleeve. Crane, S.
Gribiche. Colette
Grids and doglegs. Blaise, C.
GRIEF *See* Bereavement
Grief counselor. Smith, J.
Griesemer, John
Comfort stations
Our roots grow deeper than we know; ed. by L. Gutkind
The deck
The Massachusetts Review 25:44-56 Spr '84
North to south
The Literary Review (Madison, N.J.) 28:17-22 Fall '84
Grieve now. Redfield, C.
Griff!. Clarke, A. C.
Griffin, Pauline
Covenant
Magic in Ithkar 3; ed. by A. Norton and R. Adams

Griffin, Pauline—*Continued*
Oath-bound
  Tales of the Witch World [1]
Griffin, Susan
Cradles of light
  Erotic interludes; ed. by L. Barbach
GRIFFITH, D. W. (DAVID WARK), 1875-1948
About
Kaminsky, S. M. Busted blossoms
GRIFFITH, DAVID WARK *See* Griffith, D. W. (David Wark), 1875-1948
Griffiths, Ella
Autumn crocus
  John Creasey's Crime collection, 1984
The dead don't steal
  John Creasey's Crime collection, 1986
Griggs, Terry
India
  The New press anthology #1
The **Griggsby** papers. Ritchie, J.
Grillet, Alain Robbe- *See* Robbe-Grillet, Alain, 1922-
Grim want and misery. *See* Taylor, R. Jim July Starr
Grimes, Prudy
Indian summer
  The North American Review 269:41 Mr '84
Grimm, Mary
Book of dreams
  The New Yorker 63:29-33 Je 22 '87
Stealing time
  The New Yorker 62:36-8 O 27 '86
We
  The New Yorker 64:36-42 O 17 '88
Grin, A. (Aleksandr), 1880-1932
The arm
  Grin, A. Selected short stories
Augustus Esborn's marriage
  Grin, A. Selected short stories
The death of Romelink
  Grin, A. Selected short stories
Fire and water
  Grin, A. Selected short stories
Gatt, Witt and Redott
  Grin, A. Selected short stories
The green lamp
  Grin, A. Selected short stories
He came and went
  Grin, A. Selected short stories
The heart of the wilderness
  Grin, A. Selected short stories
The legend of Ferguson
  Grin, A. Selected short stories
The long journey
  Grin, A. Selected short stories
Mystery on a moonlit night
  Grin, A. Selected short stories
The oranges
  Grin, A. Selected short stories
The pillory
  Grin, A. Selected short stories

The Port Commandant
  Grin, A. Selected short stories
Reno Island
  Grin, A. Selected short stories
Ships in Liss
  Grin, A. Selected short stories
The snake
  Grin, A. Selected short stories
Voice and eye
  Grin, A. Selected short stories
The voice of the siren
  Grin, A. Selected short stories
The window in the forest
  Grin, A. Selected short stories
Grin, Aleksandr *See* Grin, A. (Aleksandr), 1880-1932
Grindal, Richard *See* Grayson, Richard
Griner, Paul
Worboys' transaction
  The Graywolf annual 4
Gringo city. Klass, P.
The **grinning** god. Futrelle, M.
Grinning underneath. Brady, M.
Grippes and Poche. Gallant, M.
The **grisly** folk. Wells, H. G.
Grizzard, Lewis
Good men of God
  A Collection of classic Southern humor; ed. by G. W. Koon
GROCERS
Bedard, B. Hubbard Squash
Camoin, F. A. Miami
Canin, E. Star Food
Cooper, J. C. $100 and nothing!
Mazel, D. The storekeeper
O'Hara, J. Fatimas and kisses
Petrakis, H. M. A hand for tomorrow
Petrakis, H. M. Matsoukas
Groff, David
Nobody's child
  Men on men 2; ed. by G. Stambolian
Grom's story: naked lady. Taylor, C.
Groping. Hull, H. R.
Gross, Henry H.
Cubeworld
  Mathenauts: tales of mathematical wonder; ed. by R. Rucker
La **Grosse** Fifi. Rhys, J.
Grossman, Lynn
The sleeves
  Hot type; ed. by J. Miller
Grossmith, Robert
The book of ands
  Critical Quarterly 30:27-33 Aut '88
Paragrams and anadigms
  The Literary Review (Madison, N.J.) 27:201-13 Wint '84
Grotto of the dancing deer. Simak, C. D.
Groucho. Goulart, R.
The **Ground** Hostess. Wyndham, F.
Ground zero. Willson, H.
Grounded. Cameron, P.
Grounds for love. Nevai, L.

Group beating. Yun, H.-G.
GROUPS, SOCIAL *See* Social groups
Grow old along with me. Asimov, I.
Grow old along with me, the best is yet to be. Lively, P.
Growing. Viramontes, H. M.
Growing boys. Aickman, R.
Growing old. Maupassant, G. de
Growing pains. Torres, A.
The **growing** stone. Camus, A.
Growing things at Bad Luck Pond. Rose, D. A.
Growing up. Gaitens, E.
Growing up Bronx. Rosen, G.
Grrrrr!. Sisskind, M.
Grubb, Davis, 1919-1982
Cry havoc
    Nightmares in Dixie; ed. by F. McSherry; C. G. Waugh and M. H. Greenberg
The horsehair trunk
    Rod Serling's Night gallery reader
The **grudge**. Terhune, A. P.
Grumley, Michael, 1941-1988
Life drawing
    Men on men; ed. by G. Stambolian
Gryphon. Baxter, C.
Grzimek, Martin, 1950-
Finlandia
    Grzimek, M. Heartstop
Heartstop
    Grzimek, M. Heartstop
Timestop
    Grzimek, M. Heartstop
Gu Hua, 1942-
The log cabin overgrown with creepers
    Short story international 44
GUADALAJARA (MEXICO) *See* Mexico—Guadalajara
GUADELOUPE
Crampsey, R. A. Felicity
GUAM
Bishop, M. Patriots
Pritchard, M. Dead finish
GUANAJA ISLAND (HONDURAS)
Shepard, L. Black coral
Shepard, L. A traveler's tale
GUARD DUTY
Böll, H. In the darkness
The **guardian**. Spivack, K.
GUARDIAN AND WARD
    See also Adoption
Saki. Sredni Vashtar
Guardian angel. Clarke, A. C.
Guardian angel. Latimer, M.
Guardian of the law. Fisher, R.
Guardians of the secret. Curry, G. S., and Conroy, M.
GUATEMALA
Burke, J. L. Lower me down with a golden chain
Klass, P. Gringo city

Shepard, L. The end of life as we know it
Shepard, L. R&r
Politics
    See Politics—Guatemala
GUATEMALAN REFUGEES *See* Refugees, Guatemalan
La **güera**. Campbell, E.
Guerin and the presidential revue. Standiford, L.
GUERRILLAS
    See also World War, 1939-1945—Underground movements
Angel, A. The guerrillero
Bishop, M. Vernalfest morning
Chipulina, E. G. The procession
Gordimer, N. Oral history
Havemann, E. A farm at Raraba
Mcauley, P. J. The king of the hill
Mukherjee, B. The middleman
Salisbury, R. Aniwaya, Anikawa, and the killer teen-agers
The **guerrillero**. Angel, A.
The **guest**. Herman, E.
The **guest**. Rubião, M.
Guest for the weekend. Ferreira, R.
Guest-room in Hell. Byrne, L.
Guesting. Sladek, J. T.
GUESTS
Bates, H. E. The chords of youth
Bissoondath, N. A short visit to a failed artist
Bowen, E. The visitor
Buzzati, D. The gnawing worm
Carlson, R. Max
Conley, R. J. Calf Roper's house guest
Engberg, S. Household
Flynn, R. Pictures
Freeman, M. E. W. The twelfth guest
Gordon, M. The murderer guest
Hawthorne, N. The ambitious guest
Haylock, J. The worries of Laurence Ridley
Le Fanu, J. S. Carmilla
MacLaverty, B. In the hills above Lugano
Morgan, S. Household expenses
O'Brien, E. Ways
Ocampo, S. The guests
O'Connor, F. A Temple of the Holy Ghost
Phelps, E. S. No news
Roberts, N. The upstairs people
Rooke, L. Why Agnes left
Rule, J. Seaweed and song
Sandel, C. A mystery
Son, C.-S. Walking in the snow
Sorrentino, F. The life of the party
Spark, M. The twins
Sprengnether, M. The camper
Stead, C. The hotel-keeper's story
Stewart, M. The wedding guest
Suckow, R. Midwestern primitive
Tuohy, F. Live bait
Warner, S. T. Mr. Mackenzie's last hour

GUESTS—*Continued*
  Watmough, D. Who shall be the judge?
  Welch, D. Alex Fairburn
  Weldon, F. Weekend
  Wodehouse, P. G. Uncle Fred flits by
The **guests**. Ocampo, S.
The **guests**. Potter, N. A. J.
GUEVARA, CHE *See* Guevara, Ernesto, 1928-1967
GUEVARA, ERNESTO, 1928-1967
                    About
  Broun, H. Finding Florida
Guha the judge. Al Sharuni, Y.
Guidance. De Queiroz, D. S.
GUIDED MISSILE BASES
  Barthelme, D. Game
Guido, Beatriz
  The usurper
    Other fires; ed. by A. Manguel
Guild and the Indian woman. Gorman, E.
GUILT
          See also Sin
  Buzzati, D. Barnabo of the mountains
  Card, O. S. Eumenides in the fourth floor lavatory
  Clark, D. Answer to prayer
  Courtois, P. J. The silent couple
  Crabtree, L. V. Wildcat John
  Dubus, A. The curse
  Dubus, A. A father's story
  Endō, S. Mothers
  Francis, H. E. A chronicle of love
  Friedman, P. A period of grace
  Gardner, J. Redemption
  Grant, C. L. If Damon comes
  Hansen, J. The Anderson boy
  Hartley, L. P. The thought
  Hawthorne, N. The minister's black veil
  Hawthorne, N. Roger Malvin's burial
  Highsmith, P. Under a dark angel's eye
  Honig, D. Voices in dead man's well
  Hulme, K. Hooks and feelers
  Jakes, J. I still see Sally
  Kawabata, Y. There is a God
  Matheson, R. C. Echoes
  O'Faoláin, S. Lovers of the lake
  Pancake, B. D. The honored dead
  Phelan, F. The battle of boiling water
  Poe, E. A. The tell-tale heart
  Pritchard, M. Photograph of Luisa
  Pronzini, B. Waiting, waiting . . .
  Pronzini, B., and Malzberg, B. N. Rebound
  Rulfo, J. Talpa
  Schwartz, S. To Leningrad in winter
  Silverberg, R. The feast of St. Dionysus
  Silvis, R. Trash man
  So, K.-W. The heir
  Taylor, P. H. The hand of Emmagene
  Valenzuela, L. Nihil obstat
  Valenzuela, L. Strange things happen here
  Wilmot, T. Skeleton in the cupboard
  Windsor, G. Far on the ringing plains
Guilt. Lish, G.

Guilt-edged blonde. Macdonald, R.
Guilty witness. Hershman, M.
Guin, Wyman
  The delegate from Guapanga
    Election Day 2084; ed. by I. Asimov and M. H. Greenberg
  The root and the ring
    Masterpieces of fantasy and enchantment; ed. by D. G. Hartwell
GUINEA FOWL
  McHaney, T. L. The habits of guineas
GUINEA PIGS
  Schwartz, L. S. What I did for love
GUITARISTS
  Berry, R. M. Metempsychosis
  Cain, J. M. Cigarette girl
  Chappell, F. Blue dive
  Daniels, C. Honky-Tonk Avenue
  Gingher, M. No news
  Hillis, R. Eagle flies on Friday; greyhound runs at dawn
  Murray, A. Gasoline Point, Alabama
  Shiner, L. Jeff Beck
The **gulag** computer: dead souls in the terminal. Claiborne, S.
Gulf. Heinlein, R. A.
Gulf. Woodman, A.
The **Gulf** wars. Sterling, B.
Gulik, Robert Hans van, 1910-1967
  The coffins of the Emperor
    The Ethnic detectives; ed. by B. Pronzini and M. H. Greenberg
  The murder on the lotus pond
    Great detectives; ed. by D. W. McCullough
Gullard, Pamela
  About fame
    Mademoiselle 94:162+ Ag '88
Gulliver, the story of a tall man. Wolfe, T.
The **gully**. Banks, R.
Gummerman, Jay
  The assassin
    Chicago Review 34:118-24 Spr '84
The **gun** and the hat. Garrett, G. P.
Gun-shy. Fenton, E.
Gundown. Cain, P.
The **gunfight**. Taylor, A.
Gunn, James E., 1923-
  Donor
    Fantastic stories; ed. by M. H. Greenberg and P. L. Price
  Feeding time
    100 great fantasy short short stories; ed. by I. Asimov; T. Carr and M. H. Greenberg
  Kindergarten
    Young extraterrestrials; ed. by I. Asimov; M. H. Greenberg and C. G. Waugh
  Out of my head
    Afterlives; ed. by P. Sargent and I. Watson
Gunnar's sword. Bly, C.

Gunnell, Bryn
The home-coming
Critical Quarterly 29:3-13 Spr '87
Gunpowder god. Piper, H. B.
GUNS *See* Firearms
GUP, or Falling in love in Helsinki. Weldon, F.
GUPPIES
Cohen, M. Death of a guppy
Gurganus, Allan
Adult art
Men on men 2; ed. by G. Stambolian
America competes
Harper's 277:51-8 Jl '88
A body tends to shine
The Paris Review 27:168-90 Spr '85
It had wings
Harper's 272:36-7 F '86
The Paris Review 27:12-16 Wint '85
Gurlas. Thorman, C.
Gurley, George H.
The seventh day
Missouri short fiction; ed. by C. Beasley
Gurnah, Abdulrazak
Bossy
African short stories; ed. by C. Achebe and C. L. Innes
The **guru** and his mother. Claiborne, S.
GURUS
Essop, A. The yogi
Jhabvala, R. P. How I became a holy mother
Gus Zernial and me. Spinelli, J.
Gusewelle, C. W. (Charles W.)
Horst Wessel
Missouri short fiction; ed. by C. Beasley
Gusewelle, Charles W. *See* Gusewelle, C. W. (Charles W.)
Gustafson, Jon
Beast
L. Ron Hubbard presents Writers of the future v2
Gustafsson, Lars, 1936-
The art of surviving November
Gustafsson, L. Stories of happy people
The bird in the breast
Gustafsson, L. Stories of happy people
The four railroads of Iserlohn
Gustafsson, L. Stories of happy people
The fugitives discover that they knew nothing
Gustafsson, L. Stories of happy people
The girl in the blue cap
Gustafsson, L. Stories of happy people
Greatness strikes where it pleases [Variant title: The truly great strikes wherever it wants]
Gustafsson, L. Stories of happy people
Out of the pain
Gustafsson, L. Stories of happy people
The truly great strikes wherever it wants [Variant title: Greatness strikes where it pleases]
New directions in prose and poetry 48
Uncle Sven and the Cultural Revolution
Gustafsson, L. Stories of happy people
A water story
Gustafsson, L. Stories of happy people
The Paris Review 26:23-36 Fall '84
What does not kill us, tends to make us stronger
Gustafsson, L. Stories of happy people
Guthrie, Thomas Anstey *See* Anstey, F., 1856-1934
Guy 'Micko' Delaney. Hogan, D.
Guyal of Sfere. Vance, J.
Guyot, Gabriele *See* Wohmann, Gabriele, 1932-
Guy's early retirement. Villefranche, A.-M.
Guys under their fedoras. La Puma, S.
Gwala, Mafika
Reflections in a cell
African short stories; ed. by C. Achebe and C. L. Innes
Gwen. Kincaid, J.
Gwenanda and the Supremes. Pohl, F.
GYNECOLOGISTS
Windsor, G. Reasons for going into gynaecology
GYPSIES
Blei, N. Skarda
Bloch, R. The double whammy
Haldeman, J. W. Armaja das
Hoch, E. D. The luck of a gypsy
Mansfield, K. How Pearl Button was kidnapped
Mears, S. S. Thirty horses for your daughter
Nowakowski, M. Gorgio
O'Brien, F.-J. The wondersmith
Ornstien, E. The admission ticket
Rios, A. Eyes like they say the devil has
Vogan, S. The confession of the Finch
Gypsies. Lee, A.
Gypsies. Potter, N. A. J.
Gypsy moths. Beattie, A.

H

H as in homicide. Treat, L.
H. D. (Hilda Doolittle), 1886-1961
Two Americans
New Directions in prose and poetry 51
The **H** Street sledding record. Carlson, R.
Ha, Kun-Chan
Ill-fated father and son
Two travelers, and other Korean short stories
The spring song
Two travelers, and other Korean short stories

Ha, Kun-Chan—*Continued*
The white paper beard
Two travelers, and other Korean short stories
Haake, Katharine
Another kind of nostalgia
Haake, K. No reason on earth
Bear and other pale giants
Haake, K. No reason on earth
Burning the lost country
Haake, K. No reason on earth
The meaning of their names
Haake, K. No reason on earth
Natural histories
Haake, K. No reason on earth
One pair red, one pair blue
Haake, K. No reason on earth
Recently I've discovered my mistake
Haake, K. No reason on earth
A scrap of green silk
Haake, K. No reason on earth
Wait until heaven
Haake, K. No reason on earth
Haas, Barbara
Dying in the goldenwest
Haas, B. When California was an island
The Virginia Quarterly Review 62:463-77 Summ '86
Garden of glass
The Georgia Review 41:556-69 Fall '87
The green life
Haas, B. When California was an island
Like a cactus in a field of corn
Haas, B. When California was an island
On Mu
Haas, B. When California was an island
Princess Gilda talks to the unborn
Haas, B. When California was an island
When California was an island
Haas, B. When California was an island
The Hudson Review 37:21-40 Spr '84
A wolf in the heart
Haas, B. When California was an island
You'll remember me long after
Haas, B. When California was an island
The **Habbitson** stories. Ahern, T.
The **habit**. Coleman, W.
Habit. Colette
The **habit** of friendship. Frucht, A.
The **habit** of loving. Lessing, D. M.
Habits. Kalpakian, L.
Habits of contact. Jeffrey, T.
The **habits** of guineas. McHaney, T. L.
Hacendado. Reasoner, J. M.
Hack. Burke, J. L.
The **hack**. Swados, H.
Hackberry. Benedict, P.
Had I a hundred mouths. Goyen, W.
Hadj. Ellison, H.
Hady, Wageh Abd el *See* El Hady, Wageh Abd

Haensel, Regine
Goldenrod
The Old dance; ed. by B. Burnard
Haggard, H. Rider (Henry Rider), 1856-1925
Black heart and white heart
Baker's dozen: 13 short fantasy novels
Witches; ed. by I. Asimov; M. H. Greenberg and C. G. Waugh
Only a dream
Spirits, spooks, and other sinister creatures; ed. by H. Hoke
Haggard, Henry Rider *See* Haggard, H. Rider (Henry Rider), 1856-1925
Hagy, Alyson Carol
Infrared signature
Hagy, A. C. Madonna on her back
Madonna on her back
Hagy, A. C. Madonna on her back
The North American Review 271:41-6 S '86
Mister Makes
Hagy, A. C. Madonna on her back
No kind of name
Hagy, A. C. Madonna on her back
The Sewanee Review 94:240-52 Spr '86
Nongqause
Hagy, A. C. Madonna on her back
Shoreline
Hagy, A. C. Madonna on her back
Stadia
Hagy, A. C. Madonna on her back
Michigan Quarterly Review 25:351-62 Spr '86
Where men go to cry
Hagy, A. C. Madonna on her back
The Virginia Quarterly Review 62:634-53 Aut '86
Haien, Jeannette
The summer of my last chance
The Massachusetts Review 28:461-73 Aut '87
Haig, Michael
Eighteen hours in Frankfurt
Home and away; ed. by R. Creswell
Hail and farewell. Bradbury, R.
Hail Mary. Fante, J.
Hail to the chief. Garrett, R.
Hail to the chief. Sackett, S.
Hail to the chief. Silverberg, R.
The **Haile** Selassie Funeral Train. Davenport, G.
Haines, Harry A.
Dancing with gloom and broken noses
The Georgia Review 42:153-9 Spr '88
HAIR
Colette. The judge
Colette. Newly shorn
Crane, S. The angel-child
Maupassant, G. de. One phase of love
Robbins, T. The hair of the beast
Stoker, B. The secret of the growing gold
Hair. Kawabata, Y.
The **hair** and the teeth. Bird, C.

Hair jewellery. Atwood, M.
The hair of the beast. Robbins, T.
The hair of the widow. Somerlott, R.
Haircut. Lardner, R.
A hairdresser. Colette
HAIRDRESSERS See Beauty shops
Hairline fractures. Kalpakian, L.
Hair's breath. Shwartz, S. M.
Hairston, Loyle
    The revolt of Brud Bascomb
        Mississippi writers v1: Fiction; ed. by D.
        Abbott
HAITI
    Cave, H. B. Footprints in Perdu
    Working, R. Resurrectionists
            Politics
        See Politics—Haiti
            Port-au-Prince
    Gold, H. A Haitian gentleman
    Gold, H. Max and the pacemaker
    Gold, H. Paternity
    Gold, H. Ti-Moune
A Haitian gentleman. Gold, H.
HAITIANS
            Cuba
    Benítez-Rojo, A. Heaven and earth
The Hajji. Essop, A.
Hajji Musa and the Hindu fire-walker. Es-
    sop, A.
Hakanono. Charlton, W.
Hakim Driver. Monar, R.
The halberdier of the Little Rheinschloss.
    Henry, O.
Haldeman, Jack C., 1941-
    Mortimer Snodgrass Turtle
        100 great fantasy short short stories; ed.
        by I. Asimov; T. Carr and M. H.
        Greenberg
    Playing for keeps
        Tales from Isaac Asimov's science fiction
        magazine: short stories for young
        adults
    Still frame
        Shadows 7
    Wet behind the ears
        Tales from Isaac Asimov's science fiction
        magazine: short stories for young
        adults
    (jt. auth) See Dozois, Gardner R., and
        Haldeman, Jack C., 1941-
Haldeman, Joe W.
    Armaja das
        Masters of darkness; ed. by D. Etchison
    Blood brothers
        Haldeman, J. W. Dealing in futures
    Blood sisters
        Haldeman, J. W. Dealing in futures
    DX
        In the field of fire; ed. by J. Van B.
        Dann and J. Dann
    Hero
        Space wars; created by P. Anderson

    Lindsay and the red city blues
        Haldeman, J. W. Dealing in futures
    Manifest destiny
        Haldeman, J. W. Dealing in futures
        The Year's best science fiction, first an-
        nual collection
    The monster
        Cutting edge; ed. by D. Etchison
    More than the sum of his parts
        Haldeman, J. W. Dealing in futures
        Nebula awards 21
        The Year's best science fiction, third an-
        nual collection
    No future in it
        Haldeman, J. W. Dealing in futures
    The pilot
        Haldeman, J. W. Dealing in futures
    Seasons
        Haldeman, J. W. Dealing in futures
    Seven and the stars
        Haldeman, J. W. Dealing in futures
    A !tangled web
        Haldeman, J. W. Dealing in futures
    Tricentennial
        The Hugo winners v4
    You can never go back
        Haldeman, J. W. Dealing in futures
Haldeman, Linda
    Bird of paradise
        Magic in Ithkar 2; ed. by A. Norton and
        R. Adams
Hale, Edward Everett, 1822-1909
    Hands off
        Alternative histories; ed. by C. G.
        Waugh and M. H. Greenberg
Hale, Nancy, 1908-1988
    A part
        The Virginia Quarterly Review 61:76-8
        Wint '85
Haley, Russell, 1934-
    The cosmetic factory
        Haley, R. Real illusions
    Dogmaster
        Haley, R. Real illusions
    Except that they move and talk
        Haley, R. Real illusions
    Fischer's mirror
        Haley, R. Real illusions
    Fog
        Haley, R. Real illusions
    Grand-uncle's legs
        Haley, R. Real illusions
    Looping the loop
        Haley, R. Real illusions
    Occam's electric razor
        Haley, R. Real illusions
    The palace of Kandahar
        Haley, R. Real illusions
    The Polish village
        Haley, R. Real illusions
    Real illusions
        Haley, R. Real illusions

Haley, Russell, 1934-—*Continued*
Search party
    Haley, R. Real illusions
Story
    Haley, R. Real illusions
Stroke
    Haley, R. Real illusions
Half a loaf. Willson, H.
Half a mussel shell. Tallent, E.
Half a partner. Brand, M.
Half a rupee worth. Narayan, R. K.
The **half** acre. Roy, J.
The **half** brother. Wyndham, F.
HALF-BROTHERS
    Gaskell, E. C. The half-brothers
    Hogan, D. Guy 'Micko' Delaney
    London, J. The house of pride
    Lurie, M. Lessons
    Wyndham, F. The half brother
The **half-brothers.** Gaskell, E. C.
HALF-CASTES *See* Mixed bloods
'**Half** Chick'. Briefs, E. C.
The **half-crazy.** Colette
Half frame. Thomas, J.
Half-holiday. So, K.-W.
The **half-invisible** man. Pronzini, B., and
    Wallmann, J. M.
Half life. Carlson, R.
A **half-life** ahead. Gilliatt, P.
Half measures. Lewis, T.
Half past eight. Alford, E.
Half past four. Le Guin, U. K.
Half-pint homicide. Bradbury, R.
HALF-SISTERS
    Milton, E. Entrechat
    Rambach, P. When the animals leave
Half the way back. Nesbitt, J. D.
The **half-wit** of Xeenemuende. Nesvadba, J.
The **Halfway** Diner. Sayles, J.
Haliburton. Percy, H. R.
HALIFAX (N.S.) *See* Canada—Halifax
Hall, David
The smell in Bertha's house
    Prize stories, Texas Institute of Letters;
    ed. by M. Terry
Hall, Deborah
Reunion
    Stories and poems from close to home;
    ed. by F. Salas
Hall, Donald, 1928-
Mrs. Thing
    The Sewanee Review 94:231-9 Spr '86
Princess Ostrich
    Southern Humanities Review 22:35-8
    Wint '88
The world is a bed
    The Georgia Review 40:155-67 Spr '86
    Necessary fictions; ed. by S. W. Lind-
    berg and S. Corey
Hall, James B., 1918-
How J. B. Hartley saw his father
    Sudden fiction; ed. by R. Shapard and
    J. Thomas

My work in California
    The Interior country; ed. by A. Black-
    burn
Old man finds what was lost
    New Directions in prose and poetry 51
Hall, James W. *See* Hall, Jim, 1947-
Hall, Jim, 1947-
Arabella
    The Southern Review (Baton Rouge, La.)
    24:907-13 Aut '88
Gas
    The Georgia Review 41:349-59 Summ '87
    New stories from the South: the year's
    best, 1988
Paper products
    The Georgia Review 39:604-16 Fall '85
Survival week
    The Kenyon Review ns10:67-79 Fall '88
Hall, Joan Joffe
Thief in the brambles
    Michigan Quarterly Review 26:497-502
    Summ '87
Hall, Lawrence Sargent
The ledge
    American short story masterpieces; ed.
    by R. Carver and T. Jenks
    The Best Maine stories; ed. by S. Phip-
    pen; C. Waugh and M. Greenberg
Hall, Martha Lacy, 1923-
The authoress
    The Virginia Quarterly Review 64:633-50
    Aut '88
The birthday party
    The Southern Review (Baton Rouge, La.)
    22:876-91 O '86
Crab Celestine
    The Southern Review (Baton Rouge, La.)
    23:435-48 Spr '87
Doll
    Hall, M. L. Music lesson
Joanna
    Hall, M. L. Music lesson
    Selected stories from The Southern
    review, 1965-1985
Just a little sore throat
    Hall, M. L. Music lesson
Lucky Lafe
    Hall, M. L. Music lesson
The man who gave brother double
    pneumonia
    Hall, M. L. Music lesson
Music lesson
    Hall, M. L. Music lesson
The painter
    Hall, M. L. Music lesson
The peaceful eye
    Hall, M. L. Music lesson
    Mississippi writers v1: Fiction; ed. by D.
    Abbott
Privacy
    Hall, M. L. Music lesson
    The Sewanee Review 92:36-47 Wint '84

Hall, Martha Lacy, 1923-—_Continued_
The visit
Hall, M. L. Music lesson
Hall, Mary Ann Taylor- _See_ Taylor-Hall,
Mary Ann
Hall, Melissa Mia
The glass doorknob
After midnight; ed. by C. L. Grant
Rapture
Shadows 7
Hall, Oakley M.
Blind man
The Antioch Review 43:92-116 Wint '85
Hall, Richard Walter
Backwards
Hall, R. Letter from a great-uncle &
other stories
Men on men; ed. by G. Stambolian
The lesson of the master
Hall, R. Letter from a great-uncle &
other stories
Letter from a great-uncle
Hall, R. Letter from a great-uncle &
other stories
The lost chord
Hall, R. Letter from a great-uncle &
other stories
The night visitors
Hall, R. Letter from a great-uncle &
other stories
The piano
Hall, R. Letter from a great-uncle &
other stories
The Purple Prince
Hall, R. Letter from a great-uncle &
other stories
A rose in Murcia
Hall, R. Letter from a great-uncle &
other stories
Hall, Tom T.
Another dark and stormy night
Hall, T. T. The acts of life
Backbone of the nation
Hall, T. T. The acts of life
The boardinghouse ballad
Hall, T. T. The acts of life
Camouflage
Hall, T. T. The acts of life
Civic pride
Hall, T. T. The acts of life
The day Jimmy killed the rabbit
Hall, T. T. The acts of life
An early spring morning remembered and
understood
Hall, T. T. The acts of life
The eleven dollar story
Hall, T. T. The acts of life
From Hank in Nashville
Hall, T. T. The acts of life
The gate
Hall, T. T. The acts of life
Holding up the other end
Hall, T. T. The acts of life

The last fly of summer
Hall, T. T. The acts of life
A letter from home
Hall, T. T. The acts of life
Murphy Walls and the Oriental hummer
Hall, T. T. The acts of life
Wet stump
Hall, T. T. The acts of life
Homewords: a book of Tennessee
writers; ed. by D. Paschall
Why my walls shake
Hall, T. T. The acts of life
The wooden box
Hall, T. T. The acts of life
Hall of Fame. Chowder, K.
The **Hall** of the Meteorites. Morris, M.
Hallam. Washburn, L. J.
Hallas, Richard _See_ Knight, Eric Mowbray,
1897-1943
Halley, Anne
Reading the signs
The Southern Review (Baton Rouge, La.)
20:673-92 Jl '84
A Rosenkavalier
Stand one; ed. by M. Blackburn; J.
Silkin and L. Tracy
Halley's passing. McDowell, M.
Halliday, Mark, 1949-
Coping with Paul
The North American Review 273:33 Je
'88
Cuba night
The Ohio Review no42:16-17 '88
Flaming doorway
The North American Review 270:37-41
Je '85
Halligan, Marion, 1940-
A cage of gold
Halligan, M. The living hothouse
Down to earth
Halligan, M. The living hothouse
The ego in Arcadia
Halligan, M. The living hothouse
Family album
Halligan, M. The living hothouse
Fat chance
Halligan, M. The living hothouse
The Gauter letters
Halligan, M. The living hothouse
A gigolo, Miss Emery?
Halligan, M. The living hothouse
Hard sausage
Halligan, M. The living hothouse
A leisurely drowning
Halligan, M. The living hothouse
The living hothouse
Halligan, M. The living hothouse
The marble angel
Halligan, M. The living hothouse
Mozart is best
Halligan, M. The living hothouse
The noise of the lorries
Halligan, M. The living hothouse

Halligan, Marion, 1940-—*Continued*
The oak bed
  Halligan, M. The living hothouse
Paris vicarious
  Halligan, M. The living hothouse
Pity the dumb beast
  Halligan, M. The living hothouse
The porch of Paradise
  Halligan, M. The living hothouse
Remember the rug
  Halligan, M. The living hothouse
Thrift
  Halligan, M. The living hothouse
Trespassers or guests?
  Halligan, M. The living hothouse
A whiff of brimstone
  Halligan, M. The living hothouse
HALLOWEEN
Bloch, R. Pranks
Campbell, R. Apples
Gardner, C. S. Three faces of the night
Grant, C. L. Eyes
Heise, K. Trick or treat
Jones, D. C. Halloween and other sacred events
Liben, M. Trick or treat
Long, F. B. Lover in the wildwood
Martone, M. X-ray
McCammon, R. R. He'll come knocking at your door
McDowell, M. Miss Mack
Pronzini, B. Pumpkin
Rule, J. You cannot judge a pumpkin's happiness by the smile upon his face
Ryan, A. The Halloween house
Smith, G. N. Hollow eyes
Strieber, W. The Nixon mask
Tem, S. R. Trickster
Tremayne, P. The Samhain Feis
Wilson, G. Yesterday's witch
Winter, D. E. Masks
Halloween. Asimov, I.
Halloween. Ruffolo, L.
Halloween. Winters, J.
Halloween and other sacred events. Jones, D. C.
The **Halloween** house. Ryan, A.
The **Halloween** party. Chabon, M.
Halloween, Via Dolorosa. Working, R.
HALLUCINATIONS AND ILLUSIONS
  See also Personality disorders
Ballard, J. G. The terminal beach
Benedict, D. Unknown feathers
Berdnyk, O. The apostle of immortality, a tale of the unprecedented
Berdnyk, O. A chorus of elements
Berriault, G. Works of the imagination
Bierce, A. An occurrence at Owl Creek Bridge
Blythe, R. A bit simple
Bradbury, R. One night in your life
Bradley, M. Z. The day of the butterflies
Brown, F. Don't look behind you

Burrage, A. M. The waxwork
Campbell, E. Piranesi's dream
Card, O. S. Eumenides in the fourth floor lavatory
Carey, P. Report on the shadow industry
Cheever, J. The swimmer
Chekhov, A. P. The Black Monk
Cowper, R. Paradise beach
Cullen, E. J. First sight
Dick, P. K. Frozen journey
Drake, M. Tea break
Edkins, A. What's eating you?
Ellison, H. The silver corridor
Faik, S. The head and the bottle
Faik, S. The man who forgot the city
Faik, S. Psst, psst!
Fisher, M. F. K. A question answered
Gibson, W. The Gernsback continuum
Godwin, G. Dream children
Hichens, R. How love came to Professor Guildea
Hogg, J. Strange letter of a lunatic
James, M. R. The rose garden
Josipovici, G. Steps
Kittredge, W. Blue stone
Kittredge, W. Momentum is always the weapon
Le Fanu, J. S. Green tea
Longyear, B. B. The house of if
Lovecraft, H. P. The shunned house
Lynn, E. A. The island
Maugham, W. S. The taipan
Maupassant, G. de. The inn
McLaughlin, L. In the plane
Miller, W. M. The little creeps
Oates, J. C. Lamb of Abyssalia
Oliphant, M. The library window
Ozick, C. Levitation
Poe, E. A. The sphinx
Pollack, R. The protector
Priestley, J. B. The grey ones
Pronzini, B. A lot on his mind
Risse, H. Traffic accident
Rodoreda, M. The gentleman and the moon
Rooke, L. The birth control king of the Upper Volta
Ryan, A. Pietà
Sanders, S. R. Time and again
Shepard, L. Black coral
Shepard, L. The end of life as we know it
Shepard, L. Salvador
Silverberg, R. In entropy's jaws
Stern, S. Bruno's metamorphosis
Tem, S. R. Preparations for the game
Tevis, W. S. Out of luck
Wells, H. G. The door in the wall
Wells, H. G. The moth
Wells, H. G. The remarkable case of Davidson's eyes
Wyndham, F. The Ground Hostess
Halmôm. Yi, K.-S.

Halperin, Irving
Live and let live
Prairie Schooner 59:55-64 Wint '85
The **halt**. Colette
Hamamssy, Abdelal el *See* El Hamamssy,
Abdelal
Hamburgers. Coleman, W.
Hamerton, Philip Gilbert, 1834-1894
Cats
Roger Caras' Treasury of great cat
stories
Hamilton, Alex, 1930-
Moonlighting
Streets of stone; ed. by M. Burgess and
H. Whyte
Hamilton, Dale Colleen
Blood, sweat, and fears
Hear the silence; ed. by I. Zahava
Hamilton, Dennis
The alteration
Masques; ed. by J. N. Williamson
Fish story
Masques II; ed. by J. N. Williamson
Hamilton, Edmond, 1904-1977
Devolution
Amazing science fiction anthology: The
war years, 1936-1945; ed. by M. H.
Greenberg
He that hath wings
Young mutants; ed. by I. Asimov; M.
H. Greenberg and C. G. Waugh
Requiem
Amazing stories: 60 years of the best
science fiction
The stars, my brothers
Amazing stories: visions of other worlds
World without sex
Sensuous science fiction from the weird
and spicy pulps; ed. by S. Jaffery
Hamilton, Margaret, 1902-1985
Jenny Stairy's hat
Streets of stone; ed. by M. Burgess and
H. Whyte
Hamilton, Nan
Made for each other
Murder California style; ed. by J. L.
Breen and J. Ball
Hamilton, R. C.
Da Vinci is dead
The Antioch Review 42:140-55 Spr '84
Prize stories, 1985
Tiger's eye
The Antioch Review 43:486-95 Fall '85
Hamilton, Virginia, 1936-
Sheema's journey
Seventeen 43:202-3+ Ap '84
Hamlet. Wendt, A.
Hamlin's story. Taylor, C.
Hammer, Charles
The new roof
Missouri short fiction; ed. by C. Beasley

Hammer, Signe
Strangers in the universe
Erotic interludes; ed. by L. Barbach
The **Hammerpond** Park burglary. Wells, H.
G.
Hammett, Dashiell, 1894-1961
Bodies piled up
The Black mask boys; ed. by W. F.
Nolan
If they hang you
Great American love stories; ed. by L.
Rosenthal
A man called Spade
Great detectives; ed. by D. W. McCul-
lough
They can only hang you once
Great detectives; ed. by D. W. McCul-
lough
Too many have lived
Great detectives; ed. by D. W. McCul-
lough
Hammett, Samuel Dashiell *See* Hammett,
Dashiell, 1894-1961
Hammick, Georgina
A few problems in the Day Case Unit
Critical Quarterly 28:19-31 Aut '86
Hammond, Diane Coplin
Undercurrents
Mademoiselle 92:108+ Ag '86
HAMPSHIRE (ENGLAND) *See* England—
Hampshire
Hampton, Susan
Conrad's bear
Transgressions; ed. by D. Anderson
Ham's wife. Forsh, O.
HAMSTERS
Highsmith, P. Hamsters vs Websters
Hamsters vs Websters. Highsmith, P.
Han, Mal-Suk
Mr. Kim, the Bohemian minstrel
Hospital room 205, and other Korean
short stories
Han, Mu-Suk
The rock
Hospital room 205, and other Korean
short stories
Shadow
Hospital room 205, and other Korean
short stories
Han, Sung-Won
The cave
Early spring, mid-summer, and other
Korean short stories
Hanalei. Heckathorn, J.
HAND
Barker, C. The body politic
Chase, V. The search
Colette. The hand
Harvey, W. F. The beast with five fingers
The **hand**. Colette
A **hand** for tomorrow. Petrakis, H. M.
Hand in glove. Aickman, R.
Hand in glove. Bowen, E.

Hand of a wanker. McGrath, P.

The **hand** of Emmagene. Taylor, P. H.

Hand of fate. Lutz, J.

The **hand** that fed me. Rosenfeld, I.

HAND-TO-HAND FIGHTING

    See also Boxing; Karate; Kung fu; Wrestling

    Algren, N. The face on the barroom floor

    Bates, H. E. Silas and Goliath

    Carver, R. Bicycles, muscles, cigarettes

    Crane, S. The blue hotel

    Crane, S. The city urchin and the chaste villagers

    Crane, S. The fight

    Hemingway, E. A man of the world

    Lansdale, J. R. The pit

    Liben, M. Homage to Benny Leonard

    Moore, G. Two men

    Morris, W. A fight between a white boy and a black boy in the dusk of a fall afternoon in Omaha, Nebraska

    Ríos, A. Then they'd watch comedies

    Schwartz, S. Slow-motion

    Shukshin, V. M. Shiva dancing

Hand upon the waters. Faulkner, W.

HANDBAGS

    Williams, T. A lady's beaded bag

A **handful** of ball-points, a heartful of love. Swados, H.

A **handful** of dates. Ṣālih, al-Ṭ.

A **handful** of tinsel. Greeley, A. M.

A **handful** of white daffodils. Rinser, L.

The **handgun**. DeMarinis, R.

Handke, Peter, 1942-

    Child story

    Handke, P. Slow homecoming

    The lesson of Mont Sainte-Victoire

    Handke, P. Slow homecoming

    The long way around

    Handke, P. Slow homecoming

    Repetition

    The New Yorker 64:28-36 F 29 '88

    Slow homecoming

    The New Yorker 60:50-6 D 10 '84

The **handler**. Knight, D. F.

Handprints on the Moon. Hartmann, W. K.

The **hands**. Campbell, R.

Hands. Smith, G. B.

The **hands**: a story. Bonner, M.

Hands across America. Hauptman, W.

The **hands** around the neck. Moravia, A.

The **hands** of God. Ferreira, R.

The **hands** of Jesse James. See Taylor, R. Jim Reed

The **hands** of Mr. Ottermole. Burke, T.

Hands off. Hale, E. E.

The **handshake** deal. Mordden, E.

The **handsomest** drowned man in the world. García Márquez, G.

Handyman. Coskran, K.

HANDYMEN *See* Hired men

HANDYWOMEN *See* Hired women

Hang head, vandal! Clifton, M.

Hang out your washing on the Siegfried Line. Sawai, G.

The **hanged** man. Tremblay, M.

The **hanged** man's bride. Dickens, C.

The **hanging** man. Pronzini, B.

The **hanging** man. Virgo, S.

The **hanging** of Mose Miller. Conley, R. J.

The **hanging** tree. Johnson, D. M.

The **hanging** tree. Ritchie, J.

HANGINGS

    Andreyev, L. The seven who were hanged

    Barthelme, D. Some of us had been threatening our friend Colby

    Bierce, A. An occurrence at Owl Creek Bridge

    Crane, S. Moonlight on the snow

    Melville, H. Billy Budd, Sailor

    O'Brien, F.-J. A dead secret

    Pronzini, B. The hanging man

    Read, O. An Arkansas hanging

    Schwob, M. The 'Papier Rouge'

    Thompson, K. A local hanging

    Tremblay, M. The hanged man

    Wegner, H. A death in a quiet town

Hangover. MacDonald, J. D.

Hangover. Runyon, C.

Hank. Bonosky, P.

A **hank** of hair, a piece of bone. Nordan, L.

Hankla, Cathryn, 1958-

    The baby, the parrot

    Hankla, C. Learning the mother tongue

    A box for dreams

    Hankla, C. Learning the mother tongue

    The cartoonist

    Hankla, C. Learning the mother tongue

    Fishing

    Hankla, C. Learning the mother tongue

    If it were dark

    Hankla, C. Learning the mother tongue

    In search of literary heroes

    Hankla, C. Learning the mother tongue

    Learning the mother tongue

    Hankla, C. Learning the mother tongue

    The moped massacre

    Hankla, C. Learning the mother tongue

    Skeleton

    Hankla, C. Learning the mother tongue

    The strawberry patch

    Hankla, C. Learning the mother tongue

Hankla, Susan

    Nervous couple

    Michigan Quarterly Review 23:264-7 Spr '84

Hanley, Lynne

    War stories

    The Massachusetts Review 28:107-14 Spr '87

Hannah, Barry

    All the old harkening faces at the rail

    A Modern Southern reader; ed. by B. Forkner and P. Samway

Hannah, Barry—*Continued*
Even Greenland
  Hannah, B. Captain Maximus
  Sudden fiction; ed. by R. Shapard and
    J. Thomas
Fans
  Hannah, B. Captain Maximus
Getting ready
  Hannah, B. Captain Maximus
Horning in--A
  A Collection of classic Southern humor;
    ed. by G. W. Koon
I am shaking to death
  Hannah, B. Captain Maximus
Idaho
  Hannah, B. Captain Maximus
It spoke of exactly the things
  Hannah, B. Captain Maximus
Power and light
  Hannah, B. Captain Maximus
Ride, fly, penetrate, loiter
  The Georgia Review 40:168-73 Spr '86
  Hannah, B. Captain Maximus
  Necessary fictions; ed. by S. W. Lind-
    berg and S. Corey
Sources agree rock swoon has no past
  Harper's 272:37 Je '86
Testimony of pilot
  Mississippi writers v1: Fiction; ed. by D.
    Abbott
  Stories of the modern South; ed. by B.
    Forkner and P. Samway
Water liars
  American short story masterpieces; ed.
    by R. Carver and T. Jenks
Hannah. Whitaker, M.
Hannah's example. Tallent, E.
Hannibal's elephants. Silverberg, R.
Hannie's journal. Delius, A.
Hanniya, Akram
A death in Palestine
  Harper's 274:29-31 Ap '87
Hannum, Alberta Pierson
Turkey hunt
  Civil War women; ed. by F. McSherry;
    C. G. Waugh and M. Greenberg
Hans Cassebeer and the virgin's rose. Cohen,
  A.
Han's crime. Shiga, N.
Hans Pfeifer. Gordon, G.
Hans Phaall. Poe, E. A.
Hansel. Keillor, G.
Hansen, Joseph
The Anderson boy
  Hansen, J. Brandstetter & others
  The Year's best mystery and suspense
    stories, 1984
Death of an otter
  Hansen, J. Bohannon's book
Election day
  Hansen, J. Brandstetter & others
Merely players
  Hansen, J. Bohannon's book

Snipe hunt
  Hansen, J. Bohannon's book
  Murder California style; ed. by J. L.
    Breen and J. Ball
Surf
  Hansen, J. Brandstetter & others
  The Mammoth book of private eye
    stories; ed. by B. Pronzini and M. H.
    Greenberg
The Tango Bear
  Hansen, J. Bohannon's book
  Hansen, J. Brandstetter & others
Willow's money
  Hansen, J. Brandstetter & others
Witch's broom
  Hansen, J. Bohannon's book
Hansen, Karl
Dreams unwind
  Omni (New York, N.Y.) 7:62-4+ My '85
Hansen, Ron
Nebraska
  The Bread Loaf anthology of contem-
    porary American short stories; ed. by
    R. Pack and J. Parini
  Harper's 273:32-4+ D '86
  Prairie Schooner 60:5-9 Summ '86
Red letter days
  Michigan Quarterly Review 27:566-76
    Fall '88
Sleepless
  The Paris Review 30:136-53 Wint '88
True romance
  The Best of the West; ed. by J. Thomas
  Esquire 101:182-4+ My '84
  The Esquire fiction reader v1
Hanson, Deborah
The whisper business
  The Womansleuth anthology; ed. by I.
    Zahava
Hap, Lim Beng *See* Lim Beng Hap
Hapa hapa/half and half. Saiki, J.
A **happening** in Barbados. Meriwether, L.
The **happiest** man in all Kodny. Sholem
  Aleichem
Happily ever after. Yellin, L. N.
HAPPINESS
    See also Joy and sorrow
Bates, H. E. A happy man
Brodkey, H. Verona: a young woman
  speaks
Hartley, L. P. The crossways
Heckathorn, J. Hanalei
Keillor, G. New Year's
Maupassant, G. de. Happiness
Paley, G. Midrash on happiness
Rhys, J. Tout Montparnasse and a lady
Robinson, S. God is an iron
Happiness. Abish, W.
Happiness. Maupassant, G. de
Happiness. Parise, G.
Happiness. Prichard, K. S.
Happiness. Woolf, V.

Happiness does not come in colors. Cooper, J. C.

The **happiness** farm. Bukoski, A.

Happiness of the garden variety. Richard, M.

Happy, Elizabeth
 A collection of letters
  Missouri short fiction; ed. by C. Beasley

Happy. Oates, J. C.

Happy August the Tenth. Williams, T.

A **happy** birthday. MacLaverty, B.

Happy birthday Harry & Lucille. O'Neal, D. R.

Happy birthday (Lucia). Mohr, N.

The **happy** brotherhood. Gilbert, M.

Happy Christmas. Barnard, R.

The **happy** corpse story. Carrington, L.

O **happy** day! Ryman, G.

Happy Diwali. Hospital, J. T.

Happy endings. Atwood, M.

The **happy** failure. Melville, H.

Happy fortieth, Ed and Shirley. Sanford, A.

A **happy** home. Takahashi, T.

Happy hour. Silva, B.

A **happy** man. Bates, H. E.

Happy new year. Fonseca, R.

Happy New Year, Mr. Ganaway. Fleming, B.

Happy release. Shannon, D.

Happy times. Lurie, M.

Happy trails! Hiemstra, M. R.

Hara, Tamiki, 1905-1951
 The land of heart's desire
  The Crazy iris, and other stories of the atomic aftermath; ed. by K. Ōe
 Summer flower
  The Crazy iris, and other stories of the atomic aftermath; ed. by K. Ōe

Harabin, Virginia
 Saturday, Sunday
  The Paris Review 27:115-24 Fall '85

Harada, Yasuko
 Evening bells
  The Mother of dreams, and other short stories; ed. by M. Ueda

Harbor town. Kawabata, Y.

HARBORS
   Massachusetts
 Lovecraft, H. P. The shadow over Innsmouth

Harcourt, Palma
 A box of books
  John Creasey's Crime collection, 1984

Hard candy. Williams, T.

Hard feelings. King, F. H.

Hard luck. Sholem Aleichem

Hard sausage. Halligan, M.

Hard sell. Anthony, P.

Hard to be good. Barich, B.

Hard to get. Johnson, M.

The **hard** way. Leonard, E.

A **hard** way to die. Irvine, R. R.

Hard winter. Conroy, J.

The **hard** worker. Colette

Hardesty, Carolyn
 Punk love in the library john
  The North American Review 271:44-5 Je '86

Hardfought. Bear, G.

Hardhats. Mordden, E.

Harding, Lee, 1937-
 Limbo
  Australian science fiction; ed. by V. Ikin

Harding, Mark
 Visit
  P.E.N. new fiction I

Hardly ever. Boyd, W.

Hardly working. Thorman, R.

Hardware. Silverberg, R.

The **hardware** man. O'Hara, J.

Hardwood. Gimbel, A.

Hardy, Jonathan Gathorne- *See* Gathorne-Hardy, Jonathan

Hardy, Thomas, 1840-1928
 The mayor of Casterbridge [excerpt]
  Inspired by drink; ed. by Joan Digby and John Digby
 Old Mrs. Chundle
  Christian short stories; ed. by M. Booth
 The three strangers
  Isaac Asimov presents the best crime stories of the 19th century
 A tradition of eighteen hundred and four
  The Treasury of English short stories; ed. by N. Sullivan
 The withered arm
  Charles Keeping's Classic tales of the macabre

The **Hardys**. Humphrey, W.

HARE, WILLIAM
   About
 Schwob, M. Burke and Hare, murderers

HARELIP *See* Face—Abnormalities and deformities

HAREM LIFE
 Maupassant, G. de. Châli
 Sandel, C. The women in the bath-house

Hare's house. Rendell, R.

Harington, Donald
 Beginning
  Arkansas in short fiction; ed. by W. M. Baker and E. C. Simpson

Haris, Petros, 1902-
 Before the dawn
  Haris, P. The longest night
 A dead city
  Haris, P. The longest night
 Four and a half
  Haris, P. The longest night
 Lights on the sea
  Haris, P. The longest night
 Not a bird in the sky
  Haris, P. The longest night
 Of love and darkness
  Haris, P. The longest night
 Reinforced concrete
  Haris, P. The longest night

Haris, Petros, 1902-—*Continued*
The third son
Haris, P. The longest night
A young man's dance
Haris, P. The longest night
Harland, Marion, 1830-1922
One old maid
Old maids; ed. by S. Koppelman
HARLEM (NEW YORK, N.Y.) *See* New
York (N.Y.)—Harlem
Harlem. Dumas, H.
A **Harlem** game. Dumas, H.
The **harlequin** tea set. Christie, A.
Harlow, Enid
David's song
The Southern Review (Baton Rouge, La.)
24:615-26 Summ '88
Morning light
Southwest Review 69:119-28 Spr '84
A **harmless** affair. Stead, C.
HARMONICA
Bonnie, F. Take a seat, not a solo
Patchett, A. All little colored children
should play the harmonica
Harmonica. Asscher-Pinkhof, C.
Harmony. Kauffman, J.
Harmony of the world. Baxter, C.
Harness, Charles L.
Signals
Synergy v1
Harold's Trudy. Pascoe, B.
The **harp** of the winds. Canzoneri, R.
Harper, F. E. W. *See* Harper, Frances Ellen
Watkins, 1825-1911
Harper, Frances Ellen Watkins, 1825-1911
The two offers
Old maids; ed. by S. Koppelman
Harper, Richard B.
Bale jumpers
A Matter of crime v1
Harper Conan & Singer David. Pangborn,
E.
HARPISTS
Pangborn, E. Harper Conan & Singer
David
Harrington, Evans
The prisoners [excerpt]
Mississippi writers v1: Fiction; ed. by D.
Abbott
Harrington, Joyce
The adventure of the Gowanus abduction
The New adventures of Sherlock
Holmes; ed. by M. H. Greenberg and
C. L. R. Waugh
The au pair girl
A Matter of crime v1
The Year's best mystery and suspense
stories, 1988
Birdbrain
Murder in Manhattan; ed. by B. Adler
Dispatching Bootsie
Hound dunnit; ed. by I. Asimov; M. H.
Greenberg and C. L. R. Waugh

A letter to Amy
The Year's best mystery & suspense
stories, 1986
Night crawlers
Distant danger; ed. by J. Van de
Wetering
A place of her own
Manhattan mysteries; ed. by B. Pronzini;
C. L. R. Waugh and M. H. Greenberg
Harris, Bev
Light
Alberta bound; ed. by F. Stenson
Harris, Elizabeth
The world record holder
New stories from the South: the year's
best, 1986
Southwest Review 70:396-412 Summ '85
Harris, Frank, 1851-1931
The holy man
Christian short stories; ed. by M. Booth
Harris, Helen, 1955-
The foot
Winter's tales, new ser. v4
Harris, Herbert
Death at the barbecue
John Creasey's Crime collection, 1987
Detective's wife
John Creasey's Crime collection, 1985
The doctor afraid of blood
John Creasey's Crime collection, 1986
Give him an inch . . .
John Creasey's Crime collection, 1984
Harris, James Thomas *See* Harris, Frank,
1851-1931
Harris, Joel Chandler, 1848-1908
The wonderful Tar-Baby story
The Norton book of American short
stories
**Harris, John Wyndham Parkes Lucas
Beynon** *See* Wyndham, John, 1903-
1969
Harris, MacDonald, 1921-
The dog mafia
Harris, M. The Cathay stories and other
fictions
Dr. Pettigot's face
Harris, M. The Cathay stories and other
fictions
The fun dome
Harris, M. The Cathay stories and other
fictions
The linguist
Harris, M. The Cathay stories and other
fictions
Little Eddy
Harris, M. The Cathay stories and other
fictions
The martyred poet
Harris, M. The Cathay stories and other
fictions
The orphan bassoonist
Harris, M. The Cathay stories and other
fictions

Harris, MacDonald, 1921-—*Continued*
The photograph
  Harris, M. The Cathay stories and other fictions
Polo's trip
  Harris, M. The Cathay stories and other fictions
Harris, Mark, 1922-
Titwillow
  Michigan Quarterly Review 25:511-24 Summ '86
Harris. Matheson, S.
Harrison, Barbara Grizzuti
In the name of the father
  Partisan Review 53 no3:414-26 '86
Wheel-of-fortune
  The North American Review 272:57-8 Je '87

Harrison, Claire
The leopard
  Ladies' Home Journal 101:66+ My '84
Harrison, Harry, 1925-
After the storm
  The Planets; ed. by B. Preiss
Or battle's sound
  Space wars; created by P. Anderson
Run from the fire
  Time wars; ed. by C. Waugh and M. H. Greenberg
The view from the top of the tower
  Tales from the planet Earth
War with the robots
  Machines that think; ed. by I. Asimov; P. S. Warrick and M. H. Greenberg
Harrison, Jim, 1937-
Dalva: how it happened to me
  Esquire 109:185-92 Ap '88
Harrison, M. John (Michael John), 1945-
Egnaro
  Harrison, M. J. The ice monkey, and other stories
The Great God Pan
  Prime evil; ed. by D. E. Winter
The ice monkey
  Harrison, M. J. The ice monkey, and other stories
The incalling
  Harrison, M. J. The ice monkey, and other stories
The new rays
  Harrison, M. J. The ice monkey, and other stories
The quarry
  Harrison, M. J. The ice monkey, and other stories
Running down
  Harrison, M. J. The ice monkey, and other stories
Settling the world
  Harrison, M. J. The ice monkey, and other stories

Small heirlooms
  The Year's best fantasy, first annual collection
Harrison, Michael, 1907-
Sherlock Holmes and "The woman": an explanatory memoir by Dr. John H. Watson, MD.
  The New adventures of Sherlock Holmes; ed. by M. H. Greenberg and C. L. R. Waugh
Harrison, Michael John *See* Harrison, M. John (Michael John), 1945-
Harrison, Sam
My mother's piano
  Américas 37:12-14 Mr/Ap '85
Harrison, Susie Frances
The idyl of the island
  The Oxford book of Canadian short stories in English
Harrow Street at Linden. Oates, J. C.
Harry. Timperley, R.
Harry: a ferret. Highsmith, P.
Harry and Sylvia and Sylvia and so on. Everman, W. D.
Harry and the dancer. Bukoski, A.
Harry the woman killer. Matthews, J.
Hart, Jane
Eva
  McCall's 111:98-9+ Mr '84
Harte, Bret, 1836-1902
The idyl of Red Gulch
  Westeryear; ed. by E. Gorman
The outcasts of Poker Flat
  Christian short stories; ed. by M. Booth
  The Norton book of American short stories
  The Second reel West; ed. by B. Pronzini and M. H. Greenberg
  The Western hall of fame; ed. by B. Pronzini and M. H. Greenberg
Hartley, L. P. (Leslie Poles), 1895-1972
Apples
  Hartley, L. P. The complete short stories of L. P. Hartley
A change of ownership
  Hartley, L. P. The complete short stories of L. P. Hartley
A condition of release
  Hartley, L. P. The complete short stories of L. P. Hartley
Conrad and the dragon
  Hartley, L. P. The complete short stories of L. P. Hartley
The corner cupboard
  Hartley, L. P. The complete short stories of L. P. Hartley
The cotillon
  Hartley, L. P. The complete short stories of L. P. Hartley
The crossways
  Hartley, L. P. The complete short stories of L. P. Hartley

Hartley, L. P. (Leslie Poles), 1895-1972—
Continued
The face
  Hartley, L. P. The complete short stories
    of L. P. Hartley
Fall in at the double
  Hartley, L. P. The complete short stories
    of L. P. Hartley
Feet foremost
  Hartley, L. P. The complete short stories
    of L. P. Hartley
A high dive
  Hartley, L. P. The complete short stories
    of L. P. Hartley
Hilda's letter
  Hartley, L. P. The complete short stories
    of L. P. Hartley
Home, sweet home
  Hartley, L. P. The complete short stories
    of L. P. Hartley
Interference
  Hartley, L. P. The complete short stories
    of L. P. Hartley
The island
  Hartley, L. P. The complete short stories
    of L. P. Hartley
The killing bottle
  Hartley, L. P. The complete short stories
    of L. P. Hartley
Monkshood Manor
  Hartley, L. P. The complete short stories
    of L. P. Hartley
Mr. Blandfoot's picture
  Hartley, L. P. The complete short stories
    of L. P. Hartley
Mrs. Carteret receives
  Hartley, L. P. The complete short stories
    of L. P. Hartley
Night fears
  Hartley, L. P. The complete short stories
    of L. P. Hartley
Noughts and crosses
  Hartley, L. P. The complete short stories
    of L. P. Hartley
Pains and pleasures
  Hartley, L. P. The complete short stories
    of L. P. Hartley
The pampas clump
  Hartley, L. P. The complete short stories
    of L. P. Hartley
Paradise Paddock
  Hartley, L. P. The complete short stories
    of L. P. Hartley
Per far l'amore
  Hartley, L. P. The complete short stories
    of L. P. Hartley
Please do not touch
  Hartley, L. P. The complete short stories
    of L. P. Hartley

Podolo
  Hartley, L. P. The complete short stories
    of L. P. Hartley
  Roger Caras' Treasury of great cat
    stories
The prayer
  Hartley, L. P. The complete short stories
    of L. P. Hartley
The price of the absolute
  Hartley, L. P. The complete short stories
    of L. P. Hartley
The pylon
  Hartley, L. P. The complete short stories
    of L. P. Hartley
A rewarding experience
  Hartley, L. P. The complete short stories
    of L. P. Hartley
Roman charity
  Hartley, L. P. The complete short stories
    of L. P. Hartley
The shadow on the wall
  Hartley, L. P. The complete short stories
    of L. P. Hartley
The silver clock
  Hartley, L. P. The complete short stories
    of L. P. Hartley
Simonetta Perkins
  Hartley, L. P. The complete short stories
    of L. P. Hartley
Someone in the lift
  Hartley, L. P. The complete short stories
    of L. P. Hartley
A summons
  Hartley, L. P. The complete short stories
    of L. P. Hartley
The thought
  Hartley, L. P. The complete short stories
    of L. P. Hartley
  The Penguin book of horror stories
Three, or four, for dinner
  Hartley, L. P. The complete short stories
    of L. P. Hartley
A tonic
  Hartley, L. P. The complete short stories
    of L. P. Hartley
The travelling grave
  Hartley, L. P. The complete short stories
    of L. P. Hartley
  Lost souls; ed. by J. Sullivan
Two for the river
  Hartley, L. P. The complete short stories
    of L. P. Hartley
The two Vaynes
  Hartley, L. P. The complete short stories
    of L. P. Hartley
Up the garden path
  Hartley, L. P. The complete short stories
    of L. P. Hartley
A very present help
  Hartley, L. P. The complete short stories
    of L. P. Hartley

Hartley, L. P. (Leslie Poles), 1895-1972—
Continued
A visitor from down under
Black water; ed. by A. Manguel
Hartley, L. P. The complete short stories
of L. P. Hartley
The Oxford book of English ghost
stories
W.S.
Hartley, L. P. The complete short stories
of L. P. Hartley
The waits
Hartley, L. P. The complete short stories
of L. P. Hartley
The white wand
Hartley, L. P. The complete short stories
of L. P. Hartley
Witheling End
Hartley, L. P. The complete short stories
of L. P. Hartley
Won by a fall
Hartley, L. P. The complete short stories
of L. P. Hartley
Hartley, Leslie Poles *See* Hartley, L. P. (Les-
lie Poles), 1895-1972
Hartman, W. Sherwood
Poltergeist
Alfred Hitchcock's Mortal errors
Hartmann, William K.
Handprints on the Moon
The Planets; ed. by B. Preiss
Hartmut
Gentility
Southern Exposure (Durham, N.C.)
15:56-7 Summ '87
Haruf, Kent
Private debts/public holdings
The Best American short stories, 1987
Harum scarum. Abbott, K.
HARVARD UNIVERSITY
Updike, J. The Christian roommates
The **harvest**. Garcia, J. S.
Harvey, Joan
Plagiarism
Between C & D; ed. by J. Rose and
C. Texier
Harvey, W. F. (William Fryer), 1885-1937
The beast with five fingers
The Penguin book of horror stories
The clock
The Oxford book of English ghost
stories
Harvey, William Fryer *See* Harvey, W. F.
(William Fryer), 1885-1937
Harvor, Elisabeth
The age of unreason
Harvor, E. If only we could drive like
this forever
Heart trouble
Harvor, E. If only we could drive like
this forever

If only we could drive like this forever
Harvor, E. If only we could drive like
this forever
The students' soirée
Harvor, E. If only we could drive like
this forever
A sweetheart
Harvor, E. If only we could drive like
this forever
The teller's cage
Harvor, E. If only we could drive like
this forever
To supper in the morning and to bed at
noon
Harvor, E. If only we could drive like
this forever
Has anybody here seen me? Symons, J.
Hasan as a king. Tamer, Z.
Hasegawa, Hisako *See* Hirota, Yukiko, 1937-
Hašek, Jaroslav, 1883-1923
The good Soldier Švejk [excerpt]
Inspired by drink; ed. by Joan Digby
and John Digby
HASIDISM
Schwartz, H. Rooms of the soul
Haslam, Gerald W., 1937-
Hawk's flight: an American fable
Earth power coming; ed. by S. J. Ortiz
Trophies
Stories and poems from close to home;
ed. by F. Salas
Hass story. Soldatow, S.
Hassell, Harriett
History of the South
The Art of fiction in the heart of Dixie;
ed. by P. D. Beidler
Hassler, Jon
Rufus at the door
Stiller's pond; ed. by J. Agee; R. Blakely
and S. Welch
The **hat**. Boyle, T. C.
The **hat**. Spivack, K.
The **hat** incident. Kawabata, Y.
The **hat** of my mother. Steele, M.
The **hatchet** man in the lighthouse. Peden,
W.
HATE
See also Misogyny
Benson, E. F. The bath-chair
Hensley, J. L. Shut the final door
Keeling, N. Agathe
London, J. Diable: a dog
Oates, J. C. The Jesuit
Parise, G. Hate
Pronzini, B. Black wind
Proulx, A. On the Antler
Sorrentino, F. The fetid tale of Antulín
Tamer, Z. Snow at the end of the night
Thomas, M. Abdullah and Mariam
Hate. Parise, G.
Hate is nothing. Bonner, M.
The **hateful** word. Welch, D.
The **haters**. Wollheim, D. A.

Hathaway, William
Friends with you
  The Southern Review (Baton Rouge, La.)
  20:153-66 Ja '84
The secretsharer
  The Hudson Review 38:427-44 Aut '85
Hathor's pets. St. Clair, M.
Hatrack River. Card, O. S.
HATRED *See* Hate
Hatred. Nowakowski, M.
HATS
Bates, H. E. The spring hat
Daniels, C. Lacy Mallard
Henry, O. The red roses of Tonia
O'Connor, F. Everything that rises must
  converge
Steele, M. The hat of my mother
Warner, S. T. Some effects of a hat
Haukeness, Helen
Up in the bush
  The North American Review 269:44-5 D
  '84
The **Haulage** company. Malet, L.
Haunted. Oates, J. C.
The **haunted** actress. Brett, S.
The **haunted** and the haunters. Lytton, E. B.
  L., Baron
The **haunted** boy. McCullers, C.
Haunted by name our ignorant lips. Mat-
  thews, J.
The **haunted** chamber. Radcliffe, A. W.
Haunted ground. La Farge, O.
A **haunted** house. Woolf, V.
HAUNTED HOUSES *See* Ghost stories
A **haunted** island. Blackwood, A.
The **haunted** mind. Hawthorne, N.
The **haunted** trailer. Arthur, R.
The **haunter** of the dark. Lovecraft, H. P.
The **haunting**. Casper, S.
The **haunting** of the Lingards. Willett, J.
The **haunting** of Y-12. Sarrantonio, A.
Hauptman, William, 1942-
Boom town
  Hauptman, W. Good rockin' tonight
The desert
  Hauptman, W. Good rockin' tonight
Good rockin' tonight
  Hauptman, W. Good rockin' tonight
Hands across America
  Hauptman, W. Good rockin' tonight
Kozmic Blues
  Hauptman, W. Good rockin' tonight
Moon walking
  Hauptman, W. Good rockin' tonight
Pure sex
  Hauptman, W. Good rockin' tonight
Sierra wave
  Hauptman, W. Good rockin' tonight
Stormchaser
  Hauptman, W. Good rockin' tonight

Hauser, Marianne, 1910-
The seersucker suit
  American made; ed. by M. Leyner; C.
  White and T. Glynn
Hausmann, Jocelyn
Offices of instruction
  The Ploughshares reader: new fiction for
  the eighties
Haute cuisine. Dávila, A.
HAVANA (CUBA) *See* Cuba—Havana
Havazelet, Ehud
Glass
  Havazelet, E. What is it then between
  us?
Jillie
  Havazelet, E. What is it then between
  us?
  The New generation; ed. by A. Kaufman
Natalie Wood's amazing eyes
  20 under 30; ed. by D. Spark
  Havazelet, E. What is it then between
  us?
No word for mercy
  Havazelet, E. What is it then between
  us?
The only thing you've got
  Havazelet, E. What is it then between
  us?
Resident
  Havazelet, E. What is it then between
  us?
Solace
  Havazelet, E. What is it then between
  us?
  The North American Review 272:19-21
  Je '87
What everyone wants
  Havazelet, E. What is it then between
  us?
What is it then between us?
  Havazelet, E. What is it then between
  us?
Have a nice death. Fraser, A.
Havemann, Ernst
The animal lover
  Havemann, E. Bloodsong, and other
  stories of South Africa
The bloodsong
  The Atlantic 257:56-61 F '86
  Havemann, E. Bloodsong, and other
  stories of South Africa
Death of the nation
  The Atlantic 256:82-6 O '85
  The Editors' choice v3; ed. by G. E.
  Murphy, Jr.
  Havemann, E. Bloodsong, and other
  stories of South Africa
The exiles
  The Atlantic 260:103-6 N '87

Havemann, Ernst—*Continued*

A farm at Raraba
  The Atlantic 259:56-60 Ja '87
  Havemann, E. Bloodsong, and other stories of South Africa
  Somehow tenderness survives; ed. by H. Rochman

The going home of Ntambo
  Havemann, E. Bloodsong, and other stories of South Africa

Incident at Mhlaba Jail
  The Atlantic 258:42-4 S '86
  Havemann, E. Bloodsong, and other stories of South Africa

An interview
  Havemann, E. Bloodsong, and other stories of South Africa

My father's son
  The Atlantic 259:48-52 Je '87

The prophet Elijah
  The Paris Review 30:136-46 Spr '88

Pure Hamitic strain
  Havemann, E. Bloodsong, and other stories of South Africa

The self-destruction of the Ama Gabe
  Havemann, E. Bloodsong, and other stories of South Africa

Spirits do not forgive
  Havemann, E. Bloodsong, and other stories of South Africa

Tom and Beauty
  Havemann, E. Bloodsong, and other stories of South Africa

Having a woman at lunch. Hazel, P.
Having a wonderful time. Grenville, K.
Having fun. Cooper, J. C.
Having fun. Schulman, H.
Having it both ways. Houbein, L.
Having the human thing of joy. Abbott, L. K.
Having words. Thompson, J.

Havird, Ashley Mace

At Aunt Charlotte's
  The Virginia Quarterly Review 63:409-25 Summ '87

HAWAII

Baber, A. The surfer
Garfield, B. Scrimshaw
Heller, S. The player and the giant
Holt, J. D. "God sent you into that Gomorrah this morning to bring up the truth"
Kirk-Kuwaye, C. Complete with fireworks above Magic Island
Lee, L. Born and bred
London, J. Chun Ah Chun
London, J. Good-by, Jack
London, J. The house of pride
London, J. Koolau the leper
London, J. The sheriff of Kona
MacMillan, I. C. The rock
Misitano, R. A. Deep water
Ōe, K. The clever rain tree

Onopa, R. The man who swam through jellyfish, through men-of-war
Saiki, J. Bus stop
Saiki, J. Hapa hapa/half and half
Saiki, J. Petty larceny
Saiki, J. Plumeria days
Saiki, J. Retrospective
Sinclair, M. J. P. Secrets
Stevenson, R. L. The bottle imp
Stevenson, R. L. The isle of voices
Wakayama, M. Watching fire
Watanabe, S. A. Colors
Watanabe, S. A. The seabirds

Plantation life
  See Plantation life—Hawaii

Honolulu

Heckathorn, J. Hanalei
Heller, S. Auteur
Heller, S. A matter of style
Heller, S. The rainbow man
Lum, D. H. Y. Primo doesn't take back bottles anymore

Lanai

Heller, S. The red dust of Lanai

Maui

Heller, S. Postcard from Lahaina
McPherson, M. That was last year

Molokai

Nelson, V. Coming back

Oahu

Holt, J. D. The pool
Lum, D. H. Y. The Moiliili Bag Man
Yamanaka, C. What the ironwood whispered

Waikiki

Heller, S. The man who drank a thousand beers
Heller, S. The rainbow syndrome
Lagory, M. Seaside idle
McPherson, M. Beachboy
Molinaro, U. Bird in ambush

Hawaii. Keillor, G.

HAWAIIAN ISLANDS *See* Hawaii

The **hawk.** Wright, D. L.

The **hawk** and the dome of hell. Rafferty, S. S.

Hawk of the Sudan. Goodis, D.

Hawkes, G. W.

At the walls of Jericho
  The Atlantic 260:79-82 O '87

Hawkes, John, 1925-

A little bit of the old slap and tickle
  New directions in prose and poetry 50
The traveler
  Buying time; ed. by S. Walker

Hawk's flight: an American fable. Haslam, G. W.

Hawsmoot. Sandberg, P. L.

Hawthorne, Nathaniel, 1804-1864

The ambitious guest
  Hawthorne, N. Nathaniel Hawthorne's tales

Hawthorne, Nathaniel, 1804-1864 — *Continued*

The artist of the beautiful
  Hawthorne, N. Nathaniel Hawthorne's tales

The birthmark
  Hawthorne, N. Nathaniel Hawthorne's tales
  Mystery in the mainstream; ed. by B. Pronzini; M. H. Greenberg and B. N. Malzberg

The Celestial rail-road
  Hawthorne, N. Nathaniel Hawthorne's tales

The Christmas banquet
  Christmas ghosts; ed. by K. Cramer and D. G. Hartwell
  Masterpieces of terror and the supernatural; ed. by M. Kaye and S. Kaye

Drowne's wooden image
  Hawthorne, N. Nathaniel Hawthorne's tales

Earth's holocaust
  Hawthorne, N. Nathaniel Hawthorne's tales

Endicott and the Red Cross
  Hawthorne, N. Nathaniel Hawthorne's tales

Ethan Brand
  Hawthorne, N. Nathaniel Hawthorne's tales

Feathertop
  Hawthorne, N. Nathaniel Hawthorne's tales
  Masterpieces of fantasy and enchantment; ed. by D. G. Hartwell

Foot-prints on the sea-shore
  Short stories of the sea; ed. by G. C. Solley and E. Steinbaugh

The gentle boy
  Hawthorne, N. Nathaniel Hawthorne's tales

The gray champion
  Hawthorne, N. Nathaniel Hawthorne's tales

The haunted mind
  Hawthorne, N. Nathaniel Hawthorne's tales

Main-street
  Hawthorne, N. Nathaniel Hawthorne's tales

The man of Adamant
  Hawthorne, N. Nathaniel Hawthorne's tales

The May-Pole of Merry Mount
  Hawthorne, N. Nathaniel Hawthorne's tales

The minister's black veil
  Hawthorne, N. Nathaniel Hawthorne's tales

Mr. Higginbotham's catastrophe
  Isaac Asimov presents the best crime stories of the 19th century

My kinsman, Major Molineux
  Hawthorne, N. Nathaniel Hawthorne's tales

Rappaccini's daughter
  Great American love stories; ed. by L. Rosenthal
  Hawthorne, N. Nathaniel Hawthorne's tales

Roger Malvin's burial
  Hawthorne, N. Nathaniel Hawthorne's tales

Wakefield
  Hawthorne, N. Nathaniel Hawthorne's tales

Young Goodman Brown [Variant title: The Salem Mass]
  The Dark descent; ed. by D. G. Hartwell
  Hawthorne, N. Nathaniel Hawthorne's tales
  The Norton book of American short stories

Haxton, Josephine *See* Douglas, Ellen

Hayashi, Fumiko, 1904-1951
A late chrysanthemum
  A Late chrysanthemum; tr. by L. Dunlop

Hayashi, Kyoko, 1930-
The empty can
  The Crazy iris, and other stories of the atomic aftermath; ed. by K. Ōe

Haycox, Ernest, 1899-1950
A day in town
  The Western hall of fame; ed. by B. Pronzini and M. H. Greenberg
Stage to Lordsburg
  The Western hall of fame; ed. by B. Pronzini and M. H. Greenberg

Haydar, Haydar
The ants and the qat
  Modern Syrian short stories; ed. by M. G. Azrak

Hayes, Joseph Arnold, 1918-
Act of rage
  Good Housekeeping 206:201-4+ Ap '88

Hayes, Lesley
Kiss good night to the princess, frog
  Short story international 44

Hayes, Mcnevin
The cottage in winter
  The Clarion awards; ed. by D. Knight

Hayes, R. Chetwynd- *See* Chetwynd-Hayes, R., 1919-

Haylock, John
Choice
  Short story international 48
Fan mail
  Short story international 45
Love problems
  Short story international 71
A sort of retirement
  Short story international 66

Haylock, John—*Continued*
Tomiko
  Short story international 60
Traveling towards Boris
  Short story international 57
The worries of Laurence Ridley
  Short story international 69
Hayman, Ronald, 1932-
Urchins
  P.E.N. new fiction I
Haynes, David
Taking Miss Kezee to the polls
  Stiller's pond; ed. by J. Agee; R. Blakely
  and S. Welch
Haynes, Dorothy K. (Dorothy Kate)
Thou shalt not suffer a witch . . .
  The Penguin book of horror stories
Hays, Donald
The Dixie Association [excerpt]
  The New writers of the South; ed. by
  C. East
Hazards of war. Chipulina, E. G.
Hazel, Paul
Having a woman at lunch
  Prime evil; ed. by D. E. Winter
Hazell and the patriot. Yuill, P. B.
Hazzard, Shirley, 1931-
Forgiving
  Ladies' Home Journal 101:173-5 Ja '84
The place to be
  The New Yorker 63:26-36+ Je 29 '87
  Prize stories, 1988
Weekend
  The Treasury of English short stories;
  ed. by N. Sullivan
He. Josipovici, G.
He?. Maupassant, G. de
He. Porter, K. A.
He came and went. Grin, A.
He came as a beer-truck driver. Böll, H.
"He cometh and he passeth by!". Wakefield,
  H. R.
He couldn't boogie-woogie worth a damn.
  Algren, N.
He korero. Taylor, A.
He of the assembly. Bowles, P.
He swung and he missed. Algren, N.
He tauware kawa, he kawa tauware. Hulme,
  K.
He that hath wings. Hamilton, E.
He the fisher. Petroski, C.
He walked around the horses. Piper, H. B.
He was a good lion. Markham, B.
He was a man! (But he did himself wrong).
  Cooper, J. C.
He was reaching for a shovel. Abbott, K.
He was there when they came across the
  bridge on their bicycles. Austin, D.
He wasn't there. Asimov, I.
He who sows hope in the flesh. Tindall, G.
He won't go down to the park with me
  today. Austin, D.
He wrote to the rats. Ralph, J.

Head, Bessie, 1937-1986
The lovers
  The Penguin book of Southern African
  stories
Snapshots of a wedding
  African short stories; ed. by C. Achebe
  and C. L. Innes
The **head** and the bottle. Faik, S.
A **head** in the marshes. Pu Zong
The **head** man. Bloch, R.
Head of the line. Carroll, G. H.
Head over heels. Gifkins, M.
The **headdress**. Murphy, Y.
Heading home. Shaw, J. B.
Headlights. Campbell, W. B.
Headlines. Bliss, C. D.
Headlines for Whitey. McLay, F.
HEADMASTERS *See* School superintendents
  and principals; Teachers
HEADMISTRESSES *See* School superinten-
  dents and principals; Teachers
Heal. Cadigan, P.
Heald, Tim
The case of the frozen diplomat
  Ellery Queen's Prime crimes 2
A jumbo death
  Winter's crimes 18
Healey, Judith
Flowers in January
  Stiller's pond; ed. by J. Agee; R. Blakely
  and S. Welch
Healey, Rose Million
A neat crime
  The Womansleuth anthology; ed. by I.
  Zahava
Healing. Bail, M.
The **healing**. Boucher, S.
Healing. Fraser, K.
The **healing**. Nimmo, D.
The **healing**. Norris, H.
The **healing** touch. Chidester, A.
Health. Krist, G.
Health. Williams, J.
**HEALTH RESORTS, WATERING
  PLACES, ETC.**
  See also Summer resorts
  Beerbohm, M. A. V. Laider
  Halligan, M. A whiff of brimstone
  Sagan, F. The distant cousin
  Williams, J. Health
The **healthiest** girl in town. Stafford, J.
Hear anything from Bakersfield? Eisenstein,
  S.
Hear that long train moan. Everett, P. L.
Hear the nightingale sing. Gordon, C.
Hear the whistle blowing. Ryan, A.
Hearing from Wayne. Franzen, B.
Hearings. Wilson, B.

Hearn, Lafcadio, 1850-1904
The boy who drew cats
  Great ghost stories; ed. by B. A. Schwartz
  Young witches & warlocks; ed. by I. Asimov; M. H. Greenberg and C. G. Waugh
Of a promise kept
  Black water; ed. by A. Manguel
Oshidori
  Masterpieces of terror and the supernatural; ed. by M. Kaye and S. Kaye
Rokuro-Kubi
  Devils & demons; ed. by M. Kaye and S. Kaye
Hearon, Shelby, 1931-
The British Museum
  Southwest Review 71:383-8 Summ '86
War and peace
  Southwest Review 69:379-83 Aut '84
HEART
Wolfe, T. No more rivers
Diseases
Anderson, S. Unlighted lamps
Booth, B. Still life
Chopin, K. The story of an hour
Clarke, A. C. Death and the senator
Corrington, J. W. The actes and monuments
Drewitz, I. The news
Ford, J. H. Fishes, birds and sons of men
Gold, H. Max and the pacemaker
Hall, M. L. Music lesson
Li Chao. Spring chill
Norris, H. The light on the water
St. Clair, M. The listening child
Welty, E. Death of a traveling salesman
Wilner, H. The quarterback speaks to his god
Heart. Swick, M.
Heart and soul. Giles, M.
Heart as nails. Caponegro, M.
Heart attack. Apple, M.
The **heart** in the egg. Carr, J.
Heart leaves. Ball, B.
The **heart** of God. Rey Rosa, R.
The **heart** of my heart. Schulman, H.
Heart of the Dutch country. Stark, S. S.
The **heart** of the wilderness. Grin, A.
Heart songs. Proulx, A.
Heart trouble. Harvor, E.
Heartburn. Calisher, H.
The **hearth**. Crowley, A.
Heartland. Dokey, R.
Heartland. Oates, J. C.
The **heart's** advantage. Shacochis, B.
Heart's desire. Soman, F. J.
Hearts do not in eyes shine. Kessel, J.
Hearts of a shark. Vogan, S.
Heartstop. Grzimek, M.
Heat. Rhys, J.
Heat wave. Donson, C.

Heath, Aloîse Buckley
A Heath Christmas-carol program
  National Review 38:48-50 D 31 '86
A Trapp family Christmas
  National Review 40:34-5+ D 30 '88
A **Heath** Christmas-carol program. Heath, A. B.
Heathen ways. Rahmann, P.
HEAVEN
  See also Angels
Edmonds, W. D. Moses
Jolley, E. The representative
Lee, H. Death Valley Scotty
Sheckley, R. Five minutes early
Twain, M. Captain Stormfield's visit to heaven
Heaven. Gaitskill, M.
Heaven and earth. Benítez-Rojo, A.
Heaven full of astronauts. James-French, D.
Heaven in your mind. Winton, T.
Heaven on a summer night. Beattie, A.
Heaven vs. hell. Kilgore, D.
The **heavenly** animal. Phillips, J. A.
Heavenly bliss. Tabucchi, A.
The **heavenly** blue answer. Cross, R. A.
Heavey, Jean
Never get another dog
  The Saturday Evening Post 258:64-7+ N '86
The **heavy** splash. Cooper, L.
The **heavy** stone. West, J.
Hebe laughs. Ekström, M.
Hebel, Johann Peter, 1760-1826
Kannitverstan
  German romantic stories; ed. by F. G. Ryder
An unexpected reunion
  German romantic stories; ed. by F. G. Ryder
  German stories; ed. by H. Steinhauer
Hébert, Anne
The torrent
  The Oxford book of French-Canadian short stories
Hébert, François
Prowling around Little Red Riding Hood
  Invisible fictions; ed. by G. Hancock
Hébert, Louis-Philippe, 1850-1917
The hotel
  Invisible fictions; ed. by G. Hancock
A text concerning strawberries
  Invisible fictions; ed. by G. Hancock
Hecht, Ben, 1894-1964
Miracle in the rain
  The Saturday Evening Post 256:48-51+ Ja/F '84
  The Saturday Evening Post 256:68+ Mr '84
  The Saturday Evening Post 256:34-36 Ap '84
Miracle of the fifteen murderers
  Kill or cure; ed. by M. Muller and B. Pronzini

Hecht, Ben, 1894-1964—_Continued_
Specter of the Rose
The Deadly arts; ed. by B. Pronzini and
M. Muller
Hecht, Deborah C.
Summer dreams
Good Housekeeping 202:164-5+ Je '86
Heckathorn, John
Hanalei
Passages to the dream shore; ed. by F.
Stewart
The **Hector** Quesadilla story. Boyle, T. C.
Hedge, Pennie
Snap dragon
Winter's tales, new ser. v3
The **hedge** between. Armstrong, C.
A **hedge** of rosemary. Jolley, E.
Hedin, Mary
The Princess of Calistoga
Ploughshares 14 no1:45-57 '88
Heffernan, Maryclare J.
The bonds of love
Ladies' Home Journal 105:105-7 Mr '88
Simple celebrations
Ladies' Home Journal 104:88+ F '87
Sprung traps
Ladies' Home Journal 102:96-7+ Ja '85
Too tired for love
Redbook 171:40+ S '88
Hegi, Ursula
Breaking the rules
The North American Review 273:38-41
Mr '88
Unearned pleasures
Prairie Schooner 59:96-8 Spr '85
Heidbrink, James R.
Of ancient swords and evil mist
Tales of the Witch World [1]
Heideman, Eric M.
Roger, Mr. Whilkie!
The Year's best mystery and suspense
stories, 1988
Time and chance
L. Ron Hubbard presents Writers of the
future v3
Heilbrun, Carolyn G., 1926-
_For works written by this author under
other names see_ Cross, Amanda,
1926-
HEINE, HEINRICH, 1797-1856
About
Pasternak, B. L. The Apelles mark
Heinemann, Larry
Good morning to you, Lieutenant
Soldiers & civilians; ed. by T. Jenks
Heinesen, William, 1900-
The ballad of the Toft Boy
Heinesen, W. Laterna magica
The fall
Heinesen, W. Laterna magica
The fire-pump test
Heinesen, W. Laterna magica
Laterna magica
Heinesen, W. Laterna magica
The lucky stone
Heinesen, W. Laterna magica
Master Jakob and Miss Urd
Heinesen, W. Laterna magica
The miracle
Heinesen, W. Laterna magica
The silent guests
Heinesen, W. Laterna magica
Stubborn Stina
Heinesen, W. Laterna magica
**Heinlein, Robert A. (Robert Anson), 1907-
1988**
Beyond doubt [Variant title: Lyle Monroe
and Elma Wentz]
Election Day 2084; ed. by I. Asimov
and M. H. Greenberg
Gulf
[Analog]: Writers' choice v2
Our fair city
Masterpieces of fantasy and enchant-
ment; ed. by D. G. Hartwell
Heinrich Heine and the grain dance. Jolas,
E.
The **heir**. Al Shaikh, A.
Heir. Rand, P.
The **heir**. So, K.-W.
Heir apparent. Bloch, R.
Heir to the realm. Johnson, W.
The **heiress** of Glenmahowley. Doyle, Sir A.
C.
HEIRESSES _See_ Inheritance and succession;
Wealth
HEIRLOOMS
Cheever, J. The lowboy
Doyle, Sir A. C. The Musgrave ritual
Sams, F. Saba (an affirmation)
HEIRS _See_ Inheritance and succession;
Wealth
The **heirs**. José, F. S.
Heirs apparent. Abernathy, R.
Heirs of the Perisphere. Waldrop, H.
Heise, Kenan
The addition to Aunt Ella's house
Heise, K. Aunt Ella stories
Aunt Ella and my first communion
Heise, K. Aunt Ella stories
Aunt Ella gits it
Heise, K. Aunt Ella stories
Aunt Ella's funeral
Heise, K. Aunt Ella stories
Aunt Ella's taxes
Heise, K. Aunt Ella stories
Children's crusade
Heise, K. Aunt Ella stories
The chocolate Easter bunny
Heise, K. Aunt Ella stories
The condemned movie
Heise, K. Aunt Ella stories
"Don't pick any apples for your Aunt El-
la"
Heise, K. Aunt Ella stories

Heise, Kenan—_Continued_
Eating out
  Heise, K. Aunt Ella stories
Ferndale fights the flies
  Heise, K. Aunt Ella stories
Ferndale fireworks
  Heise, K. Aunt Ella stories
The heroine of Ferndale
  Heise, K. Aunt Ella stories
The little boy who was left behind
  Heise, K. Aunt Ella stories
Long pants day at last
  Heise, K. Aunt Ella stories
My Aunt Ella
  Heise, K. Aunt Ella stories
My father's confession
  Heise, K. Aunt Ella stories
The mystery of the Higgins coupe
  Heise, K. Aunt Ella stories
Shazam
  Heise, K. Aunt Ella stories
Trick or treat
  Heise, K. Aunt Ella stories
The Woodward Avenue streetcar
  Heise, K. Aunt Ella stories
Heitkamp, Kristen
The yellow deer
  Missouri short fiction; ed. by C. Beasley
Hejmadi, Padma
Uncle Monkey
  The Massachusetts Review 29:599-608
  Wint '88/'89
Heker, Liliana
The stolen party
  Other fires; ed. by A. Manguel
Helen. Bell, M.
HELEN OF TROY (LEGENDARY CHARACTER)
Givner, J. Laocoön, my father
Helen, thy beauty is to me—. Fante, J.
Helfman, Elizabeth S.
Voices in the wind
  The Year's best fantasy, first annual collection
HELL
Asimov, I. The brazen locked room
Barker, C. Hell's event
Benford, G. Newton sleep
Bishop, M. Scrimptalon's test
Creveling, W. Thinking the unthinkable
Elkin, S. The conventional wisdom
Hogg, J. The expedition to Hell
Hogg, J. George Dobson's expedition to Hell
Kaye, M. Damned funny
McCormack, F. Hell-bent
Sallis, J. Miranda-Escobedo
Singer, I. B. Sabbath in Gehenna
Stevenson, R. L. The bottle imp
Williams, C. Et in sempiternum pereant
Young, P. ja. The helldivers
Hell. Matheson, R. C.
Hell. Piñera, V.

Hell-bent. McCormack, F.
Hell-bent. Patten, L. B.
Hell-bent men and their cities. Dodd, S. M.
He'll come knocking at your door. McCammon, R. R.
A **hell** of a story. Keating, H. R. F.
Hell on both sides of the gate. Timperley, R.
Hell screen. Akutagawa, R.
A **hell** so fearsome. Espino González, M. A.
The **helldivers**. Young, P. ja
Heller, Peter
A little tatter of sky
  Harper's 275:28+ Ag '87
Heller, Steve, 1949-
Auteur
  Heller, S. The man who drank a thousand beers
The Crow Woman
  Prize stories, 1985
The man who drank a thousand beers
  Heller, S. The man who drank a thousand beers
A matter of style
  Heller, S. The man who drank a thousand beers
The player and the giant
  Heller, S. The man who drank a thousand beers
Postcard from Lahaina
  Heller, S. The man who drank a thousand beers
The rainbow man
  Heller, S. The man who drank a thousand beers
The rainbow syndrome
  Heller, S. The man who drank a thousand beers
The red dust of Lanai
  Heller, S. The man who drank a thousand beers
  Passages to the dream shore; ed. by F. Stewart
The summer game
  Heller, S. The man who drank a thousand beers
Hellerstein, David
Killer butterfly
  The North American Review 272:39-43 Je '87
The spirit of the Grove
  The North American Review 269:16-21 S '84
"Hello?". Dadswell, M.
Hello from Ture. Bukoski, A.
Hello, Lenin! Hello, Stalin! How's the revolution today? Granit, A.
Hell's event. Barker, C.
Hell's half hour. Bradbury, R.
Hell's kettle. Gardner, E. S.
Hell's playground. Silva, B.
Help. Apple, M.
Help wanted, male. Stout, R.

Helping. Stone, R.
The **helping** hand. Sheckley, R.
Helpless. Seema, N.
Helplessness. Vercors
Helprin, Mark
Letters from the Samantha
American short story masterpieces; ed.
by R. Carver and T. Jenks
The Norton book of American short
stories
Mar Nueva
The New Yorker 64:28-40+ My 30 '88
North light
Soldiers & civilians; ed. by T. Jenks
The Pacific
The Atlantic 257:74-80 Mr '86
The Bread Loaf anthology of contem-
porary American short stories; ed. by
R. Pack and J. Parini
Great American love stories; ed. by L.
Rosenthal
Palais de Justice
Short story international 42
The Schreuderspitze
The World of the short story; ed. by
C. Fadiman
HELSINKI (FINLAND) *See* Finland—
Helsinki
Hemensley, Kris, 1946-
The book (Chez Claude Mauriac)
Transgressions; ed. by D. Anderson
Hemenway, Phillip
Our lady of the barbershop
The Antioch Review 42:433-48 Fall '84
Hemingway, Ernest, 1899-1961
An African story
Hemingway, E. The complete short
stories of Ernest Hemingway
After the storm
Hemingway, E. The complete short
stories of Ernest Hemingway
Short stories of the sea; ed. by G. C.
Solley and E. Steinbaugh
An Alpine idyll
Hemingway, E. The complete short
stories of Ernest Hemingway
The ash heel's tendon
The New York Times Magazine p21+ Ag
18 '85
Banal story
Hemingway, E. The complete short
stories of Ernest Hemingway
The battler
Hemingway, E. The complete short
stories of Ernest Hemingway
Look who's talking; ed. by B. Weber
Big two-hearted river: part I
Hemingway, E. The complete short
stories of Ernest Hemingway
Big two-hearted river: part II
Hemingway, E. The complete short
stories of Ernest Hemingway

Black ass at the cross roads
Hemingway, E. The complete short
stories of Ernest Hemingway
The butterfly and the tank
Hemingway, E. The complete short
stories of Ernest Hemingway
A canary for one
Hemingway, E. The complete short
stories of Ernest Hemingway
The capital of the world
Hemingway, E. The complete short
stories of Ernest Hemingway
Cat in the rain
Hemingway, E. The complete short
stories of Ernest Hemingway
Che ti dice la patria?
Hemingway, E. The complete short
stories of Ernest Hemingway
A clean, well-lighted place
Hemingway, E. The complete short
stories of Ernest Hemingway
Inspired by drink; ed. by Joan Digby
and John Digby
Cross-country snow
Hemingway, E. The complete short
stories of Ernest Hemingway
Crossroads—an anthology
The New York Times Magazine p19-20
Ag 18 '85
A day's wait
Hemingway, E. The complete short
stories of Ernest Hemingway
The denunciation
Hemingway, E. The complete short
stories of Ernest Hemingway
The doctor and the doctor's wife
Hemingway, E. The complete short
stories of Ernest Hemingway
The end of something
Hemingway, E. The complete short
stories of Ernest Hemingway
The faithful bull
Hemingway, E. The complete short
stories of Ernest Hemingway
Fathers and sons
Hemingway, E. The complete short
stories of Ernest Hemingway
Fifty grand
Hemingway, E. The complete short
stories of Ernest Hemingway
The gambler, the nun, and the radio
Hemingway, E. The complete short
stories of Ernest Hemingway
Get a seeing-eyed dog
Hemingway, E. The complete short
stories of Ernest Hemingway
God rest you merry, gentlemen
Hemingway, E. The complete short
stories of Ernest Hemingway
The good lion
Hemingway, E. The complete short
stories of Ernest Hemingway

Hemingway, Ernest, 1899-1961—*Continued*

Great news from the mainland
  Hemingway, E. The complete short stories of Ernest Hemingway

Hills like white elephants
  Hemingway, E. The complete short stories of Ernest Hemingway
  The Norton book of American short stories

Homage to Switzerland
  Hemingway, E. The complete short stories of Ernest Hemingway

I guess everything reminds you of something
  Hemingway, E. The complete short stories of Ernest Hemingway

In another country
  Hemingway, E. The complete short stories of Ernest Hemingway

Indian camp
  Hemingway, E. The complete short stories of Ernest Hemingway
  The Nobel reader; ed. by J. Eisen and S. Troy

The killers
  Hemingway, E. The complete short stories of Ernest Hemingway

Landscape with figures
  Hemingway, E. The complete short stories of Ernest Hemingway

The last good country
  Hemingway, E. The complete short stories of Ernest Hemingway

The light of the world
  Hemingway, E. The complete short stories of Ernest Hemingway

A man of the world
  Hemingway, E. The complete short stories of Ernest Hemingway

The mercenaries
  The New York Times Magazine p16-18 Ag 18 '85

The mother of a queen
  Hemingway, E. The complete short stories of Ernest Hemingway

Mr. and Mrs. Elliot
  Hemingway, E. The complete short stories of Ernest Hemingway

My old man
  Hemingway, E. The complete short stories of Ernest Hemingway
  The World of the short story; ed. by C. Fadiman

A natural history of the dead
  Hemingway, E. The complete short stories of Ernest Hemingway

Night before battle
  Hemingway, E. The complete short stories of Ernest Hemingway

Nobody ever dies
  Hemingway, E. The complete short stories of Ernest Hemingway

Now I lay me
  Hemingway, E. The complete short stories of Ernest Hemingway

Old man at the bridge
  Hemingway, E. The complete short stories of Ernest Hemingway

On the quai in Smyrna
  Hemingway, E. The complete short stories of Ernest Hemingway

One reader writes
  Hemingway, E. The complete short stories of Ernest Hemingway

One trip across
  Hemingway, E. The complete short stories of Ernest Hemingway

Out of season
  Hemingway, E. The complete short stories of Ernest Hemingway

The porter
  Hemingway, E. The complete short stories of Ernest Hemingway

A pursuit race
  Hemingway, E. The complete short stories of Ernest Hemingway

The revolutionist
  Hemingway, E. The complete short stories of Ernest Hemingway

The sea change
  Hemingway, E. The complete short stories of Ernest Hemingway

The short happy life of Francis Macomber
  Hemingway, E. The complete short stories of Ernest Hemingway

A simple enquiry
  Hemingway, E. The complete short stories of Ernest Hemingway

The snows of Kilimanjaro
  Hemingway, E. The complete short stories of Ernest Hemingway

Soldier's home
  Hemingway, E. The complete short stories of Ernest Hemingway

Summer people
  Hemingway, E. The complete short stories of Ernest Hemingway

Ten Indians
  Hemingway, E. The complete short stories of Ernest Hemingway

The three-day blow
  Hemingway, E. The complete short stories of Ernest Hemingway

Today is Friday
  Hemingway, E. The complete short stories of Ernest Hemingway

The tradesman's return
  Hemingway, E. The complete short stories of Ernest Hemingway

A train trip
  Esquire 108:162-4+ D '87
  Hemingway, E. The complete short stories of Ernest Hemingway

Hemingway, Ernest, 1899-1961—*Continued*
The undefeated
Hemingway, E. The complete short stories of Ernest Hemingway
Under the ridge
Hemingway, E. The complete short stories of Ernest Hemingway
Up in Michigan
Great American love stories; ed. by L. Rosenthal
Hemingway, E. The complete short stories of Ernest Hemingway
A very short story
Hemingway, E. The complete short stories of Ernest Hemingway
Sudden fiction; ed. by R. Shapard and J. Thomas
A way you'll never be
Hemingway, E. The complete short stories of Ernest Hemingway
Wine of Wyoming
Hemingway, E. The complete short stories of Ernest Hemingway
About
Murphy, M. Lesson number one
Waldrop, H. Fair game
Hemingway. Joens, H.
Hemingway slept here. Milofsky, D.
Hemley, Robin, 1958-
All you can eat
Hemley, R. All you can eat
Clues
Hemley, R. All you can eat
Digging a hole
Hemley, R. All you can eat
Dropping the baby
Hemley, R. All you can eat
Installations
Hemley, R. All you can eat
Looking for kin
Hemley, R. All you can eat
The mouse town
Hemley, R. All you can eat
Polish luggage
Hemley, R. All you can eat
Rainwalkers
Hemley, R. All you can eat
Riding The Whip
20 under 30; ed. by D. Spark
Hemley, R. All you can eat
A sentimental wolf
Hemley, R. All you can eat
The trumpet player and his wife
Hemley, R. All you can eat
What's that in your ear?
Hemley, R. All you can eat
Hemmerchts, Kristien, 1955-
The sixth of the sixth of the year nineteen sixty-six
First fictions: Introduction 9
Words
First fictions: Introduction 9

Hempel, Amy
Beg, sl tog, inc, cont, rep
Hempel, A. Reasons to live
New women and new fiction; ed. by S. Cahill
Breathing Jesus
Hempel, A. Reasons to live
Celia is back
Hempel, A. Reasons to live
Going
Hempel, A. Reasons to live
In a tub
Hempel, A. Reasons to live
In the cemetery where Al Jolson is buried
The Editors' choice: new American stories v1
Hempel, A. Reasons to live
Making things whole
Mademoiselle 91:128+ My '85
The man in Bogotá
Hempel, A. Reasons to live
The most girl part of you
New American short stories; ed. by G. Norris
Nashville gone to ashes
Hempel, A. Reasons to live
Pool Night
Hempel, A. Reasons to live
San Francisco
Harper's 270:29-30 Ap '85
Hempel, A. Reasons to live
Three popes walk into a bar
Hempel, A. Reasons to live
Today will be a quiet day
The Best American short stories, 1986
Hempel, A. Reasons to live
The Pushcart prize XI
Tonight is a favor to Holly
Hempel, A. Reasons to live
When it's human instead of when it's dog
Hempel, A. Reasons to live
Why I'm here
Hempel, A. Reasons to live
The hen. Rodoreda, M.
Henderson, Dion, 1921-
Broken treaty
Roger Caras' Treasury of great dog stories
The test
Roger Caras' Treasury of great dog stories
Henderson, M. R.
Dream house
Murder in Los Angeles; ed. by J. L. Breen and others
Henderson, Zenna, 1917-
Come on, wagon!
Young mutants; ed. by I. Asimov; M. H. Greenberg and C. G. Waugh
Stevie and The Dark
Young witches & warlocks; ed. by I. Asimov; M. H. Greenberg and C. G. Waugh

Henderson, Zenna, 1917——*Continued*
Subcommittee
　　Young extraterrestrials; ed. by I. Asimov;
　　　M. H. Greenberg and C. G. Waugh
Henderson. Rose, M.
Hendrie, Laura
Armadillo
　　The Best of the West; ed. by J. Thomas
Hendrix, Howard V.
In the smoke
　　L. Ron Hubbard presents Writers of the
　　future v2
Hendry, J. F.
The disinherited
　　Streets of stone; ed. by M. Burgess and
　　　H. Whyte
Henley, Patricia
As luck would have it
　　Henley, P. Friday night at Silver Star
The birthing
　　Henley, P. Friday night at Silver Star
　　The Pushcart prize XII
Black ice
　　Henley, P. Friday night at Silver Star
Friday night at Silver Star
　　Henley, P. Friday night at Silver Star
Let me call you sweetheart
　　Henley, P. Friday night at Silver Star
Moving in
　　Henley, P. Friday night at Silver Star
Picking time
　　Henley, P. Friday night at Silver Star
Victory
　　Henley, P. Friday night at Silver Star
Henne Fire. Singer, I. B.
Henry, Gordon
Sleeping in rain
　　Earth power coming; ed. by S. J. Ortiz
Henry, O., 1862-1910
An adjustment of nature
　　Henry, O. The gift of the Magi, and
　　other stories
After twenty years
　　Henry, O. The gift of the Magi, and
　　other stories
An afternoon miracle
　　Henry, O. O. Henry's Texas stories
　　The Western hall of fame; ed. by B.
　　　Pronzini and M. H. Greenberg
Art and the bronco
　　Henry, O. O. Henry's Texas stories
The buyer from Cactus City
　　Henry, O. O. Henry's Texas stories
The caballero's way
　　Henry, O. O. Henry's Texas stories
The Caliph, cupid, and the clock
　　Henry, O. The gift of the Magi, and
　　other stories
A call loan
　　Henry, O. O. Henry's Texas stories
The clarion call
　　Henry, O. The gift of the Magi, and
　　other stories

The complete life of John Hopkins
　　Henry, O. The gift of the Magi, and
　　other stories
The cop and the anthem
　　Henry, O. The gift of the Magi, and
　　other stories
　　Manhattan mysteries; ed. by B. Pronzini;
　　　C. L. R. Waugh and M. H. Greenberg
The defeat of the city
　　Henry, O. The gift of the Magi, and
　　other stories
A departmental case
　　Henry, O. O. Henry's Texas stories
A double-dyed deceiver
　　Henry, O. O. Henry's Texas stories
Dougherty's eye-opener
　　Henry, O. The gift of the Magi, and
　　other stories
The dream
　　Black water; ed. by A. Manguel
The enchanted kiss
　　Henry, O. The gift of the Magi, and
　　other stories
　　Henry, O. O. Henry's Texas stories
A fog in Santone
　　Henry, O. O. Henry's Texas stories
Friends in San Rosario
　　Henry, O. O. Henry's Texas stories
The furnished room
　　Henry, O. The gift of the Magi, and
　　other stories
Georgia's ruling
　　Henry, O. O. Henry's Texas stories
The gift of the Magi
　　Henry, O. The gift of the Magi, and
　　other stories
　　Ladies' Home Journal 102:126-8+ D '85
The halberdier of the Little Rheinschloss
　　Henry, O. The gift of the Magi, and
　　other stories
The hiding of Black Bill
　　Henry, O. O. Henry's Texas stories
The higher abdication
　　Henry, O. O. Henry's Texas stories
The higher pragmatism
　　Henry, O. The gift of the Magi, and
　　other stories
Hygeia at the Solito
　　Henry, O. O. Henry's Texas stories
The Indian Summer of Dry Valley Johnson
　　Henry, O. O. Henry's Texas stories
Jimmy Hayes and Muriel
　　Henry, O. O. Henry's Texas stories
The last of the troubadours
　　Henry, O. O. Henry's Texas stories
The lonesome road
　　Henry, O. The gift of the Magi, and
　　other stories
　　Henry, O. O. Henry's Texas stories
　　Westeryear; ed. by E. Gorman

Henry, O., 1862-1910—*Continued*
The lost blend
  Through a glass, darkly; ed. by B. Woelfel
Lost on dress parade
  Henry, O. The gift of the Magi, and other stories
Madame Bo-Peep, of the ranches
  Henry, O. O. Henry's Texas stories
Mammon and the archer
  Henry, O. The gift of the Magi, and other stories
  The Norton book of American short stories
The memento
  Henry, O. The gift of the Magi, and other stories
Memoirs of a yellow dog
  Henry, O. The gift of the Magi, and other stories
  Roger Caras' Treasury of great dog stories
Nemesis and the candy man
  Henry, O. The gift of the Magi, and other stories
The octopus marooned
  Henry, O. O. Henry's Texas stories
One thousand dollars
  Henry, O. The gift of the Magi, and other stories
The passing of Black Eagle
  Henry, O. O. Henry's Texas stories
  The Second reel West; ed. by B. Pronzini and M. H. Greenberg
The pint flask
  Inspired by drink; ed. by Joan Digby and John Digby
The princess and the puma
  Henry, O. O. Henry's Texas stories
The rathskeller and the rose
  Henry, O. The gift of the Magi, and other stories
The red roses of Tonia
  Henry, O. O. Henry's Texas stories
The renaissance at Charleroi
  Henry, O. The gift of the Magi, and other stories
A retrieved reformation
  Henry, O. The gift of the Magi, and other stories
Roads of destiny
  Henry, O. The gift of the Magi, and other stories
The romance of a busy broker
  Henry, O. The gift of the Magi, and other stories
Rus in urbe
  Henry, O. The gift of the Magi, and other stories
Schools and schools
  Henry, O. The gift of the Magi, and other stories

Seats of the haughty
  Henry, O. O. Henry's Texas stories
A service of love
  Henry, O. The gift of the Magi, and other stories
The third ingredient
  Henry, O. The gift of the Magi, and other stories
Two renegades
  A Treasury of Civil War stories; ed. by M. H. Greenberg and B. Pronz
Henry, Rick
Subject: Petri Ganton
  Between C & D; ed. by J. Rose and C. Texier
Henry, Will
  For works by this author under other names see Fisher, Clay, 1912-
Henry, Will, 1912-
The streets of Laredo
  Westeryear; ed. by E. Gorman
Henry. Smith, C. W.
Henry and the golden mine. Benét, S. V.
Henry's eighth. McCoy, E.
The Henshaws. Mathers, P.
Hensley, Joe L., 1926-
All that mattered
  Hensley, J. L. Robak's firm
The decision
  Hensley, J. L. Robak's firm
Dog man
  Hensley, J. L. Robak's firm
Finder
  Hensley, J. L. Robak's firm
The home
  Hensley, J. L. Robak's firm
Judicial discretion
  Hensley, J. L. Robak's firm
On the rocks
  Hensley, J. L. Robak's firm
Paint doctor
  Kill or cure; ed. by M. Muller and B. Pronzini
The profession
  Hensley, J. L. Robak's firm
The retiree
  Hensley, J. L. Robak's firm
Savant
  Hensley, J. L. Robak's firm
Searcher
  Hensley, J. L. Robak's firm
Shut the final door [Variant title: Shut the last door]
  The Black Lizard anthology of crime fiction; ed. by E. Gorman
Tourist
  Hensley, J. L. Robak's firm
Trial
  Hensley, J. L. Robak's firm
Truly yours, John R. Jacks
  Hensley, J. L. Robak's firm
Whistler
  Hensley, J. L. Robak's firm

Henson, Robert
Billie loses her job
    Prime number; ed. by A. L. Weir
Hentz, Caroline Lee
Wild Jack; or, The stolen child
    The Art of fiction in the heart of Dixie;
    ed. by P. D. Beidler
Heptaporos in Phrygia. Parotti, P.
Her. Francis, H. E.
Her. Martínez-Serros, H.
Her book. Akins, E.
Her day. Upward, E.
Her ex-lover. Birtha, B.
Her first ball. Mansfield, K.
Her furry face. Kennedy, L.
Her kind of man. Soman, F. J.
Her letters. Chopin, K.
Her life: a fragment. Lurie, M.
Her mother's daughter. Russell, T.
Her mother's daughter. Trevor, W.
Her mother's eye. Kawabata, Y.
Her secret. Bittle, C. R.
Her story. Spofford, H. E. P.
Her trademark. O'Faolain, J.
Her valiant heart. Pilcher, R.
Hera. Taylor, A.
The **herald.** Codrescu, A.
The **heraldry** of the body. McGregor, C.
The **herb** of death. Christie, A.
Herbert, Frank
By the book
    Herbert, F. Eye
Cease fire
    Herbert, F. Eye
Committee of the whole
    Election Day 2084; ed. by I. Asimov
    and M. H. Greenberg
Death of a city
    Herbert, F. Eye
Dragon in the sea
    Herbert, F. Eye
Frogs and scientists
    Herbert, F. Eye
Heretics of Dune
    Omni (New York, N.Y.) 6:54-6+ Mr '84
A matter of traces
    Herbert, F. Eye
Murder will in
    Herbert, F. Eye
Operation Syndrome
    [Analog]: Writers' choice v2
Passage for piano
    Herbert, F. Eye
Rat race
    Herbert, F. Eye
The road to Dune
    Herbert, F. Eye
Seed stock
    Herbert, F. Eye
Songs of a sentient flute
    Medea: Harlan's world; ed. by H. Ellison
The tactful saboteur
    Herbert, F. Eye

Transcript: Mercury program
    The Planets; ed. by B. Preiss
Try to remember
    Herbert, F. Eye
Herbert, James, 1943-
Maurice and Mog
    Masques II; ed. by J. N. Williamson
Herbert, Susan
The little Ice Age
    The Kenyon Review ns6:46-65 Wint '84
Herbert, Zbigniew
The Gordian knot
    The Kenyon Review ns6:34-40 Summ '84
Mirror
    Encounter (London, England) 62:3-7 Ja
    '84
HERBS
Austin, M. H. Old Spanish gardens
Choe, I.-N. The color of mugwort
Herbst, Josephine, 1892-1969
The enemy
    Writing red; ed. by C. Nekola and P.
    Rabinowitz
Here at the Starlight Motel. Barrett, A.
Here be dragons. Blythe, R.
Here come the Maples. Updike, J.
Here comes the sun. Hospital, J. T.
Here, in this sacred grotto. Kraman, C.
Here in time and not. Abbott, L. K.
Here is Einbaum. Morris, W.
Here lies another blackmailer. Pronzini, B.
Here, take my words. Brodine, K.
Here there be tygers. King, S.
Here to get my baby out of jail. Shivers,
    L.
Here to learn. Bowles, P.
Here we go again, Alice. Silman, R.
Here you are. Barthelme, S.
HERESIES AND HERETICS
Martin, G. R. R. The way of cross and
    dragon
Schwob, M. Frate Dolcino, heretic
The **heretic.** Humphries, J.
Heretics of Dune. Herbert, F.
Heritage. Moffatt, D.
The **heritage.** Panneton, P.
Herman, Ellen
Dangers of the world
    Seventeen 47:206-7+ S '88
The guest
    The Massachusetts Review 29:493-504
    Fall '88
Herman, Michelle
Auslander
    20 under 30; ed. by D. Spark
    The North American Review 271:16-25
    Je '86
Hermann, John
South fork
    The Yale Review 74:107-18 Aut '84
HERMAPHRODITISM
Arias, R. Lupe
Conroy, J. The morphadite

HERMAPHRODITISM—*Continued*
Gathorne-Hardy, J. Peiter and Paulina
Kotzwinkle, W. Mr. Jones's convention
Sage, V. Nada
Valenzuela, L. Legend of the self-sufficient child
White, C. The order of virility
HERMES, TRISMEGISTUS
About
Zelazny, R. But not the herald
Hermes. Kessler, J. F.
The **hermit.** Gorky, M.
The **hermit** of Treasure Peaks. Davis, S.
HERMITS
See also Recluses
Crane, S. Four men in a cave
Gorky, M. The hermit
Hawthorne, N. The man of Adamant
Jhabvala, R. P. In the mountains
Melville, H. Hood's Isle and the hermit Oberlus
Preus, M. A novel theory of extinction
Valenzuela, L. The redtown chronicles
Hernández, Juan José
The lady-killers
The Literary Review (Madison, N.J.) 31:171-6 Wint '88
Queens
Short story international 66
Herndon, Ursule *See* Molinaro, Ursule
Herne, Alex
Saying grace
The North American Review 272:6-10 Je '87
Hero. Haldeman, J. W.
Hero. Ioannidou Adamidou, I.
A **hero.** Narayan, R. K.
The **hero.** Overholser, W. D.
Hero. Pronzini, B.
Hero. Wheatcroft, J.
Hero of the mines. Prichard, K. S.
HEROD I, THE GREAT, KING OF JUDEA, 73 B.C.-4 B.C.
About
Hurston, Z. N. Herod on trial
Herod on trial. Hurston, Z. N.
HEROES
Asimov, I. C-chute
Banks, R. The gully
Baykurt, F. The wolf
Crane, S. A mystery of heroism: a detail of an American battle
Doyle, Sir A. C. The death voyage
Drake, D. Dreams in amber
Dunsany, E. J. M. D. P., Baron. The sword of Welleran
Howard, R. E. The people of the Black Circle
Howard, R. E. Red nails
Lupoff, R. A. God of the Naked Unicorn
MacDougall, C. A small hotel
Mikhailov, V. Brook on Iapetus
Thurber, J. The greatest man in the world

Wellman, M. W. The seeker in the fortress
Wheatcroft, J. Hero
Yourcenar, M. The end of Marko Kral-jević
Yourcenar, M. Marko's smile
The **heroes.** Algren, N.
Heroes. Chernoff, M.
Heroes. Paxson, D. L.
Heroes and villains. Bumpus, J.
Heroic measures/vital signs. Corrington, J. W.
HEROIN
Boswell, R. Dancing in the movies
The **heroine** of Ferndale. Heise, K.
HEROISM
See also Courage; Heroes
HERONS
Jewett, S. O. A white heron
Hero's moon. Bradley, M. Z.
The **hero's** son. Eunson, D.
Herostratos, incendiary. Schwob, M.
Herrick, Amy
Chicken Little
The Kenyon Review ns7:66-79 Wint '85
In the air, over our heads
The Editors' choice v4; ed. by G. E. Murphy, Jr.
Herrick, Ann Crowder
The fall fling
'Teen 30:42+ O '86
What are friends for?
'Teen 28:30-2+ Ja '84
Herring, Robert, 1938-
HUB [excerpt]
Homewords: a book of Tennessee writers; ed. by D. Paschall
Mississippi writers v1: Fiction; ed. by D. Abbott
Herriot, James
The stolen car
Ladies' Home Journal 103:66+ Ag '86
Herschel, Jan
Geometry
The Clarion awards; ed. by D. Knight
Herschell. Summers, H. S.
Herself in love. Wiggins, M.
Hersey, John, 1914-
God's typhoon
The Atlantic 261:72-8 Ja '88
Mr. Quintillian
The Yale Review 77:1-24 Aut '87
Requiescat
The Paris Review 30:98-115 Summ '88
The terrorist
Esquire 108:114-15+ Ag '87
Hershenow, Nicholas
Opening day
The North American Review 270:53-5 S '85
Hershman, Morris
Guilty witness
Kill or cure; ed. by M. Muller and B. Pronzini

Hershman, Morris—*Continued*
When a felon needs a friend
The Deadly arts; ed. by B. Pronzini and M. Muller
The **Hertford** Manuscript. Cowper, R.
HERTFORDSHIRE (ENGLAND) *See* England—Hertfordshire
Hervey, Evelyn *See* Keating, H. R. F. (Henry Reymond Fitzwalter), 1926-
He's all mine. De Haven, T.
Hess, Mark Steven
Where you have been, where you are going
Prairie Schooner 62:79-85 Spr '88
Hess, Sonya
Something in the air
Redbook 166:74+ Mr '86
Hesse, Hermann, 1877-1962
Inside and outside
The Nobel reader; ed. by J. Eisen and S. Troy
A man by the name of Ziegler
Black water; ed. by A. Manguel
Robert Aghion
On being foreign; ed. by T. J. Lewis and R. E. Jungman
Hey, look at me! Finney, J.
Heyen, William, 1940-
Open letter to Oates
TriQuarterly no73:87-92 Fall '88
Heym, Stefan, 1913-
My Richard
Voices East and West: German short stories since 1945
Heynen, Jim, 1940-
The boys
Harper's 270:32-3 Ap '85
The old waitress
The North American Review 269:41 Mr '84
Heyrman, Peter
Funeral for a friend
A Matter of crime v2
Heyst, A. (Axel) *See* Grabowski, Z. Anthony (Zbigniew Anthony), 1903-
Hiatus. Naqvi, T.
Hic haec hoc. Gilliatt, P.
Hic sunt leones. Nowotny, J.
Hiccup's tale. Schlossberg, E.
Hichens, Robert, 1864-1950
How love came to Professor Guildea
Black water; ed. by A. Manguel
Dark banquet; ed. by L. Child
The Dark descent; ed. by D. G. Hartwell
Hidalgos. Shacochis, B.
Hidden symptoms. Madden, D.
A **hidden** thing. Hunnicutt, E.
The **hidden** woman. Colette
Hide and seek. Asimov, I.
Hide and seek. Clarke, A. C.
Hide and seek. Klein, G.
Hide-out for a hero. Carunungan, C. A.

Hideout, Younger's Bend c1874. See Taylor, R. Eddy the boy
Hidey hole. Tem, S. R.
Hiding. Burt, S.
Hiding. Minot, S.
The **hiding** of Black Bill. Henry, O.
Hiemstra, Marvin R.
Happy trails!
The North American Review 270:40-1 S '85
Hieroglyphic tales. Walpole, H.
Higazy, Fouad
The source of the Nile is Cairo's Muqattam Hills
Egyptian tales and short stories of the 1970s and 1980s
Higgins, George V., 1939-
A case of Chivas Regal
Murder and mystery in Boston; ed. by C. L. R. Waugh; F. D. McSherry and M. H. Greenberg
Higgins, Joanna
The importance of high places in a flat town
Prairie Schooner 61:27-42 Spr '87
Stella Silvernoll and the El Grecos
Prairie Schooner 59:64-82 Summ '85
High barbary. Durrell, L.
High bridge. Conroy, J.
High-carded. Patten, L. B.
High dive. Fremlin, C.
A **high** dive. Hartley, L. P.
The **high** divers. Conroy, J.
High-grade. Overholser, W. D.
High heels. Straayer, A. C.
The **high** life in space. O'Neill, G. K.
High-low-jack. Olmstead, R.
The **high** price of everything. Coskran, K.
High rise. Keillor, G.
High school. Beattie, A.
High school. Sholem Aleichem
HIGH SCHOOLS *See* School life
High stakes. Lutz, J.
High-stepper. Bonner, M.
High-tech insolence. Baker, R.
The **high** test. Pohl, F.
High tide. Marquand, J. P.
High yaller. Fisher, R.
The **higher** abdication. Henry, O.
Higher animals. Bird, C.
The **higher** pragmatism. Henry, O.
The **highest** treason. Garrett, R.
Highland hearts. Stewart, I.
Highsmith, Patricia, 1921-
The black house
Highsmith, P. The black house
Blow it
Highsmith, P. The black house
The bravest rat in Venice
Highsmith, P. The animal-lover's book of beastly murder

Highsmith, Patricia, 1921——*Continued*

The button
Highsmith, P. Mermaids on the golf course

Chorus girl's absolutely final performance
Highsmith, P. The animal-lover's book of beastly murder

Chris's last party
Highsmith, P. Mermaids on the golf course

A clock ticks at Christmas
Highsmith, P. Mermaids on the golf course

The cruellest month
Highsmith, P. Mermaids on the golf course

The day of reckoning
Highsmith, P. The animal-lover's book of beastly murder

Djemal's revenge [Variant title: The tale of Djemal]
Highsmith, P. The animal-lover's book of beastly murder

The dream of the Emma C
Highsmith, P. The black house

Eddie and the monkey robberies
Highsmith, P. The animal-lover's book of beastly murder

Engine horse
Highsmith, P. The animal-lover's book of beastly murder

Goat ride
Highsmith, P. The animal-lover's book of beastly murder

Hamsters vs Websters
Highsmith, P. The animal-lover's book of beastly murder

Harry: a ferret
Highsmith, P. The animal-lover's book of beastly murder

I am not as efficient as other people
Highsmith, P. Mermaids on the golf course

I despise your life
Highsmith, P. The black house

In the dead of truffle season
Highsmith, P. The animal-lover's book of beastly murder

The kite
Highsmith, P. The black house

The legless A
Omni (New York, N.Y.) 10:50+ Ap '88

Mermaids on the golf course
Highsmith, P. Mermaids on the golf course

Ming's biggest prey
Highsmith, P. The animal-lover's book of beastly murder

The mobile bed-object
The Penguin classic crime omnibus

Not in this life, maybe the next [Variant title: The nature of the thing]
Highsmith, P. Mermaids on the golf course

Not one of us
Highsmith, P. The black house

Notes from a respectable cockroach
Highsmith, P. The animal-lover's book of beastly murder

Old folks at home
Highsmith, P. The black house

The quest for Blank Claveringi
Masterpieces of terror and the supernatural; ed. by M. Kaye and S. Kaye

The romantic
Highsmith, P. Mermaids on the golf course

A shot from nowhere
Highsmith, P. Mermaids on the golf course

Something the cat dragged in
Highsmith, P. The black house

The stuff of madness
Highsmith, P. Mermaids on the golf course

The terrapin
The Penguin book of horror stories

The terrors of basket-weaving
Highsmith, P. The black house

There I was, stuck with Bubsy
Highsmith, P. The animal-lover's book of beastly murder

Those awful dawns
The Mammoth book of modern crime stories; ed. by G. Hardinge

Under a dark angel's eye
Highsmith, P. The black house

When in Rome
Highsmith, P. The black house

Where the action is
Highsmith, P. Mermaids on the golf course

Highspeed linear Main St. Broun, H.

Highway 71. Eighner, L.

Highway robbery. Rivanera, L.

Highway trade. Domini, J.

Hijacked heart. Bell, A.

The **hijacker.** Winters, J.

HIJACKING OF AIRPLANES
Lutz, J. Discount fare

Hike and Calcutta. O'Kelly, S.

Hilbert, Betsy
Alligator love
The North American Review 271:34-5 S '86

Hilda's letter. Hartley, L. P.

Hilda's wedding. Jolley, E.

Hildebidle, John
.240, lifetime
Partisan Review 53 no1:56-66 '86

Hildegarde Withers is back. Palmer, S.

Hildesheimer, Wolfgang, 1916-
Why I transformed myself into a nightingale
  The Art of the tale; ed. by D. Halpern
Hiles, Robert
'Blessed are the geeks'
  The Kenyon Review ns8:95-106 Wint '86
Howard an Monroe
  The Kenyon Review ns10:31-44 Summ '88
Hill, Barry, 1943-
Lizards
  The Australian short story; ed. by L. Hergenhan
Hill, Elizabeth
Marriage at noon
  Short story international 53
The piano
  Short story international 60
Hill, James
The malachite beads
  Short story international 53
Hill, Kathleen
Flood
  The Hudson Review 40:71-7 Spr '87
Solstice
  Prairie Schooner 61:3-10 Spr '87
Hill, Rebecca
Blue Rise [excerpt]
  Mississippi writers v1: Fiction; ed. by D. Abbott
Hill, Reginald, 1936-
Auteur theory
  Hill R. There are no ghosts in the Soviet Union
Bring back the cat!
  Hill R. There are no ghosts in the Soviet Union
The bull ring
  Hill R. There are no ghosts in the Soviet Union
Crowded hour
  Hill R. There are no ghosts in the Soviet Union
Exit line
  John Creasey's Crime collection, 1987
  The Year's best mystery and suspense stories, 1988
Poor Emma
  Hill R. There are no ghosts in the Soviet Union
There are no ghosts in the Soviet Union
  Hill R. There are no ghosts in the Soviet Union
The worst crime known to man
  Masterpieces of mystery and suspense; ed. by M. H. Greenberg
  The Year's best mystery and suspense stories, 1985
Hill climbing by boat. Warren, J.
Hillabold, Jean
Yellow roses
  The Old dance; ed. by B. Burnard

Hillerman, Tony
The witch, Yazzie, and the nine of clubs
  The Ethnic detectives; ed. by B. Pronzini and M. H. Greenberg
Hillis, Rick
Eagle flies on Friday; greyhound runs at dawn
  The Old dance; ed. by B. Burnard
Hillmer, Jacquelin
New day coming
  Stiller's pond; ed. by J. Agee; R. Blakely and S. Welch
The **hills.** Grace, P.
The **hills** and the creeks (Albany, 1850). Kennedy, W.
Hills like white elephants. Hemingway, E.
The **hills** of Andorra. Chernoff, M.
The **hilt.** Lish, G.
Him with his foot in his mouth. Bellow, S.
HIMALAYA MOUNTAINS
  Robinson, K. S. Escape from Kathmandu
  Robinson, K. S. Mother goddess of the world
Hinchman, Jane
Where the magic waits
  Good Housekeeping 201:146-7 N '85
Hindsight. Hood, M.
HINDUS
  Basu, R. Sambal and Putki
  Mukherjee, B. Hindus
  Narayan, R. K. House opposite
  Narayan, R. K. Nitya
            England
    See also East Indians—England
Hindus. Mukherjee, B.
Hine e Hine. Taylor, A.
The **hinge.** Gilliatt, P.
The **hint** of an explanation. Greene, G.
A **hint** of danger. Bankier, W.
HIPPIES
    See also Bohemianism; Collective settlements
  Abbott, L. K. Be free, die young
  Clark, M. A diet of bananas and Nietzsche
  Clayton, J. J. Cambridge is sinking!
  Daniels, C. Swami Swafford
  Gilchrist, E. Defender of the Little Falaya
  Glasser, P. Mexico
  Haake, K. A scrap of green silk
  Hagy, A. C. Infrared signature
  Hauptman, W. Kozmic Blues
  MacLean, K. The missing man
  Morris, W. Since when do they charge admission
  Parise, G. Liking
  Phillips, J. A. Fast lanes
  Phillips, J. A. Rayme
  Taylor, P. E. Answering the inquisitor
  Taylor, P. E. Bird prayer and no amen
  Taylor, P. E. Entering the house of the 'Lord
  Taylor, P. E. An independent meditation
  Taylor, P. E. Kingdom come

HIPPIES—*Continued*
Taylor, P. E. Leaping Leo
Taylor, P. E. Sermon on the rat
Taylor, P. E. Who's that knocking? Is it you?
Thompson, S. L.A.
Wilding, M. I am monarch of all I survey
Hippolyte's claim. Maupassant, G. de
Hirabayashi, Taiko, 1905-1972
A woman to call mother
The Mother of dreams, and other short stories; ed. by M. Ueda
Hiraiwa, Yumie
Lady of the evening faces
The Mother of dreams, and other short stories; ed. by M. Ueda
Hiram's ghost. Wilds, M. C.
HIRED KILLERS
Lutz, J. The very best
McGerr, P. In the clear
Mukherjee, B. Loose ends
Murphy, W. An element of surprise
Ritchie, J. The crime machine
Spillane, M. Everybody's watching me
HIRED MEN
Chute, C. "Ollie, oh . . . "
Crawford, I. V. Extradited
Daniels, C. Christmas at the line shack
Everett, P. L. Cry about a nickel
Freeman, C. Crime of the century
Freeman, C. Not everyone can be a soldier
Freeman, C. That is no country for old men
MacDonald, D. R. Of one kind
Morrison, J. The Prophet of Pandaloop
O'Connor, F. Greenleaf
Richard, M. Happiness of the garden variety
Stuart, J. Old Gore
Waters, F. The woman at Otowi Crossing [excerpt]
Yu, C.-Y. The relationship
HIRED WOMEN
Cartagena Portalatín, A. "Colita"
Cooper, J. C. About love and money; or, Love's lore and money's myth
Garro, E. The tree
Mphahlele, E. Mrs. Plum
Panneton, P. The heritage
Purdy, J. Scrap of paper
Salter, J. Foreign shores
Sanford, W. M. Black child
Wicomb, Z. Ash on my sleeve
HIROSHIMA (JAPAN) *See* Japan— Hiroshima
Hirota, Yukiko, 1937-
An invitation to a movie
Short story international 59
Hirsch, Gary
The housing correspondence of prisoner number 100293/8
Short story international 63
His. Oestreicher, D.

His and hearse. Bloch, R.
His brother Joe 1914-1964. Mason, R.
His cheatin' heart. Wilson, R., Jr.
His color. Stark, S. S.
His defense. Edwards, H. S.
His easiest case. Škvorecký, J.
His everlasting mansion. King, F. H.
His father's earth. Wolfe, T.
His first love. Stacey, K.
His grandma's wedding. Conley, R. J.
His heart could break. Rice, C.
His idea of a mother. Boyle, K.
His mistress's voice. Roth, P.
His moment of glory. Rawet, S.
His mother. Gallant, M.
His mother's image. Ramos, M.
His name was Legion. Pronzini, B.
His new mittens. Crane, S.
His nor hers. Rule, J.
His own boss. Ziem, J.
His own key. Ríos, A.
His own where. Jordan, J.
His unconquerable enemy. Morrow, W. C.
His wife. Chekhov, A. P.
A **hiss** of dragon. Benford, G., and Laidlaw, M.
Histoire vache. Boyd, W.
HISTORIANS
Auchincloss, L. Greg's peg
Chavez, A. My ancestor—Don Pedro
Fuentes, C. Aura
Willis, C. Fire watch
Zhang Jie. An unfinished record
Historic moments: the discovery of love. Claiborne, S.
The **historical** mistake. Raines, H.
History. Berry, R. M.
History lesson. Leedom-Ackerman, J.
The **history** of England, part four. Rooke, L.
The **history** of Frank James. Taylor, R.
A **history** of Indiana. Kercheval, J. L.
The **history** of peanut butter. Kinsella, W. P.
A **history** of small ideas. Busch, F.
The **history** of the church in America. Kercheval, J. L.
History of the South. Hassell, H.
The **history** of X. Josephson, M.
History; or, The four pictures of Vludka. Lish, G.
The **hit.** Petroski, C.
Hit-and-run. Dunlap, S.
Hit and run. Schor, S.
HIT-AND-RUN DRIVERS
Dubus, A. A father's story
Dunlap, S. Hit-and-run
Pronzini, B. A lot on his mind
Wilmot, T. Skeleton in the cupboard
The **hit** man. Boyle, T. C.
Hit or miss. Wellen, E.
Hit the baby! Brown, R.
The **hitch.** Wheatcroft, J.

Hitchcock, George, 1850-1913
An invitation to the hunt
   Black water; ed. by A. Manguel
HITCHHIKERS
Algren, N. Kingdom City to Cairo
Barthelme, S. The friend
Barthelme, S. Liars
Barthelme, S. That's no reason
Bausch, R. The man who knew Belle Starr
Cowan, P. Mobiles
Deaver, P. F. Long Pine
Garrett, G. P. Time of bitter children
Hauptman, W. Stormchaser
Jolley, E. Woman in a lampshade
Kerr, D. Get your jive on highway five
Mardeusz, S. The back-seat talker
Oates, J. C. Romance
Rogers, T. N. R. Galb's elbow
Subramanian, U. Hitchhikers
Hitchhikers. Subramanian, U.
The **hitchhiking** game. Kundera, M.

HITLER, ADOLF, 1889-1945
About
Benford, G. Valhalla
Davenport, G. Bronze leaves and red
Yolen, J. Angelica
Hitler's daughter. Federspiel, J.
The **hitmaker.** Morgan, C.
Hizzoner's water supply. Tomlinson, G.
"HMS Marlborough will enter harbour".
   Monsarrat, N.

HO CHI MINH CITY (VIETNAM) *See*
   Vietnam—Ho Chi Minh City

HOAXES
Allen, G. The episode of the Mexican seer
Asimov, I. He wasn't there
Block, L. A little off the top
Caldwell, E. The courting of Susie Brown
Davis, S. A miner's Christmas carol
Doyle, Sir A. C. Selecting a ghost. The
   ghosts of Goresthorpe Grange
Eisenberg, L. The Chameleon
Gardner, M. Mysterious Smith
Gardner, M. Nora says "check."
Lutz, J. Something like murder
Nagibin, ÎÙ. M. Olezhka got married
Nesin, A. The first woman who under-
   stood me
O'Kelly, S. The can with the diamond
   notch
Poe, E. A. Hans Phaall
Poe, E. A. The spectacles
Poe, E. A. The unparalleled adventure of
   one Hans Pfaall
Ritchie, J. The crime machine
Sackett, S. Hail to the chief
Shiga, N. Akanishi Kakita
Smith, C. A. Morthylla
Wells, H. G. A deal in ostriches
Williams, T. The killer chicken and the
   closet queen

Hobana, Ion
Night broadcast
   The Penguin world omnibus of science
   fiction
The **hobby.** McCormack, E. P.
Hobbyist. Brown, F.
Hobo. Bloch, R.
HOBOES *See* Homeless
HOBOKEN (N.J.) *See* New Jersey—
   Hoboken
Hobson, Geary
The talking that trees does
   Earth power coming; ed. by S. J. Ortiz
Hoch, Edward D., 1930-
The Athanasia League
   Hoch, E. D. Leopold's way
Captain Leopold and the ghost-killer
   Hoch, E. D. Leopold's way
Captain Leopold goes home
   Hoch, E. D. Leopold's way
Captain Leopold goes to the dogs
   Great modern police stories; ed. by B.
   Pronzini and M. H. Greenberg
   Hound dunnit; ed. by I. Asimov; M. H.
   Greenberg and C. L. R. Waugh
Captain Leopold looks for the cause
   Ellery Queen's Crimes and punishments
Captain Leopold plays a hunch
   Hoch, E. D. Leopold's way
Captain Leopold's secret
   The Year's best mystery & suspense
   stories, 1986
Christmas is for cops
   Hoch, E. D. Leopold's way
Circus
   Hoch, E. D. Leopold's way
The crime of the century
   Manhattan mysteries; ed. by B. Pronzini;
   C. L. R. Waugh and M. H. Greenberg
Day for a picnic
   Child's ploy; ed. by M. Muller and B.
   Pronzini
Death in the harbor
   Hoch, E. D. Leopold's way
Deceptions
   The Year's best mystery and suspense
   stories, 1984
Dreaming is a lonely thing
   Alfred Hitchcock's Mortal errors
End of the day
   Hoch, E. D. Leopold's way
The faceless thing
   Masterpieces of terror and the super-
   natural; ed. by M. Kaye and S. Kaye
Five-day forecast
   Ellery Queen's Prime crimes
A flash of red
   A Matter of crime v1
The great American novel
   Chapter & hearse; ed. by M. Muller and
   B. Pronzini
The house by the ferris
   Hoch, E. D. Leopold's way

Hoch, Edward D., 1930-—_Continued_
I'd know you anywhere
  A Treasury of World War II stories; ed.
    by B. Pronzini and M. H. Greenberg
The Jersey Devil
  Hoch, E. D. Leopold's way
The Judges of Hades
  Hoch, E. D. The quests of Simon Ark
Just one more
  100 great fantasy short short stories; ed.
    by I. Asimov; T. Carr and M. H.
    Greenberg
The last unicorns
  100 great fantasy short short stories; ed.
    by I. Asimov; T. Carr and M. H.
    Greenberg
Last year's murder
  Ellery Queen's Prime crimes 2
Leopold and the broken bride
  The Year's best mystery and suspense
    stories, 1988
The Leopold locked room
  Crime of my life; ed. by B. Garfield
  Hoch, E. D. Leopold's way
The luck of a gypsy
  The Ethnic detectives; ed. by B. Pronzini
    and M. H. Greenberg
The magic bullet
  Death locked in; ed. by D. G. Greene
    and R. C. S. Adey
The maiden's sacrifice
  100 great fantasy short short stories; ed.
    by I. Asimov; T. Carr and M. H.
    Greenberg
The man from nowhere
  Hoch, E. D. The quests of Simon Ark
The man who came back
  Manhattan mysteries; ed. by B. Pronzini;
    C. L. R. Waugh and M. H. Greenberg
The maze and the monster
  Devils & demons; ed. by M. Kaye and
    S. Kaye
A melee of diamonds
  Hoch, E. D. Leopold's way
The melting man
  The Deadly arts; ed. by B. Pronzini and
    M. Muller
The most dangerous man
  Last laughs; ed. by G. Mcdonald
  The Penguin classic crime omnibus
The most dangerous man alive
  Hoch, E. D. Leopold's way
The mummy from the sea
  Hoch, E. D. The quests of Simon Ark
Murder at the Bouchercon
  Chapter & hearse; ed. by M. Muller and
    B. Pronzini
Mystery at Wimbledon
  Women's Sports & Fitness 8:33-6+ My
    '86
  Women's Sports & Fitness 8:34 Je '86

No crime for Captain Leopold
  Hoch, E. D. Leopold's way
The oblong room
  Hoch, E. D. Leopold's way
The other eye
  The Mammoth book of private eye
    stories; ed. by B. Pronzini and M. H.
    Greenberg
The people of the peacock
  Baker's dozen: 13 short espionage novels
A place for bleeding
  Hoch, E. D. Leopold's way
The problem of the Boston Common
  Murder and mystery in Boston; ed. by
    C. L. R. Waugh; F. D. McSherry and
    M. H. Greenberg
The problem of the county fair
  Uncollected crimes; ed. by B. Pronzini
    and M. H. Greenberg
The problem of the covered bridge
  Kill or cure; ed. by M. Muller and B.
    Pronzini
The problem of the fatal fireworks
  Tales from Ellery Queen's Mystery
    Magazine: short stories for young
    adults
The rainy-day bandit
  Hoch, E. D. Leopold's way
The rented scar
  The Eyes have it; ed. by R. J. Randisi
The return of the speckled band
  The New adventures of Sherlock
    Holmes; ed. by M. H. Greenberg and
    C. L. R. Waugh
Reunion
  Hoch, E. D. Leopold's way
The ring with the velvet ropes
  Rod Serling's Night gallery reader
The spy who went to the opera
  The Deadly arts; ed. by B. Pronzini and
    M. Muller
The spy's story
  The Year's best mystery and suspense
    stories, 1987
Sword for a sinner
  Hoch, E. D. The quests of Simon Ark
The theft of nothing at all
  Ellery Queen's Memorable characters
The theft of the circus poster
  The Wickedest show on earth; ed. by
    M. Muller and B. Pronzini
The theft of the four of spades
  Masterpieces of mystery and suspense;
    ed. by M. H. Greenberg
The theft of the overdue library book
  Murder and mystery in Chicago; ed. by
    C. R. Waugh; F. D. McSherry and M.
    H. Greenberg
Too long at the fair
  The Wickedest show on earth; ed. by
    M. Muller and B. Pronzini

Hoch, Edward D., 1930-—Continued
The treasure of Jack the Ripper
    Hoch, E. D. The quests of Simon Ark
Uncle Max
    Child's ploy; ed. by M. Muller and B. Pronzini
The unicorn's daughter
    Hoch, E. D. The quests of Simon Ark
The vanished steamboat
    The Year's best mystery and suspense stories, 1985
The vanishing of Velma
    Hoch, E. D. Leopold's way
The Vicar of Hell
    Hoch, E. D. The quests of Simon Ark
Village of the dead
    Hoch, E. D. The quests of Simon Ark
The vultures of Malabar
    Distant danger; ed. by J. Van de Wetering
Who rides with Santa Anna?
    100 great fantasy short short stories; ed. by I. Asimov; T. Carr and M. H. Greenberg
Winter run
    Hitchcock in prime time; ed. by F. M. Nevins and M. H. Greenberg
The witch of Park Avenue
    Hoch, E. D. The quests of Simon Ark
Zoo
    Young extraterrestrials; ed. by I. Asimov; M. H. Greenberg and C. G. Waugh
Hochstein, Rolaine
The Caravaggio kid
    The Antioch Review 45:206-11 Spr '87
Sadie and the brat
    The North American Review 271:52-5 S '86
She should have died hereafter
    The Literary Review (Madison, N.J.) 27:229-38 Wint '84
    Prize stories, 1985
HOCKEY
Kinsella, W. P. Truth
Hoctel, Patrick
Bad pictures
    Men on men; ed. by G. Stambolian
Hodge, Jane Aiken
Suicide, or murder?
    The Mammoth book of modern crime stories; ed. by G. Hardinge
Hodgell, P. C. (Patricia C.), 1951-
Stranger blood
    Imaginary lands; ed. by R. McKinley
Hodgell, Patricia C. *See* Hodgell, P. C. (Patricia C.), 1951-
Hodgins, Jack, 1939-
By the river
    The Oxford book of Canadian short stories in English
Hodgson, William Hope, 1877-1918
The derelict
    The Penguin book of horror stories

The finding of the Graiken
    Mysterious sea stories; ed. by W. Pattrick
The thing in the weeds
    Sea captains' tales; ed. by A. Enfield
The voice in the night
    Dark company; ed. by L. Child
    Lost souls; ed. by J. Sullivan
Hodl. Sholem Aleichem
Hoeing. Skrzynecki, P.
Hoffman, Nina Kiriki
Ants
    Shadows 9
Lost lives
    The Clarion awards; ed. by D. Knight
The shadow of a hawk
    Shadows 8
A step into darkness
    L. Ron Hubbard presents Writers of the future
Hoffman, William, 1925-
Altarpiece
    Hoffman, W. By land, by sea
    The Sewanee Review 95:413-29 Summ '87
Cuttings
    Hoffman, W. By land, by sea
Faces at the window
    Hoffman, W. By land, by sea
    The Sewanee Review 94:216-30 Spr '86
Fathers and daughters
    Hoffman, W. By land, by sea
Indian gift
    Hoffman, W. By land, by sea
    The Sewanee Review 93:337-53 Summ '85
Landfall
    Hoffman, W. By land, by sea
Lover
    Hoffman, W. By land, by sea
    The Virginia Quarterly Review 60:629-44 Aut '84
Moon lady
    Hoffman, W. By land, by sea
Moorings
    Hoffman, W. By land, by sea
    The Sewanee Review 92:20-35 Wint '84
Night sport
    The Atlantic 258:56-62 O '86
Patriot
    Hoffman, W. By land, by sea
The question of rain
    Hoffman, W. By land, by sea
Smoke
    Hoffman, W. By land, by sea
    The Sewanee Review 93:39-55 Wint '85
Sweet Armageddon
    The Virginia Quarterly Review 64:491-512 Summ '88
Hoffmann, E. T. A. (Ernst Theodor Amadeus), 1776-1822
Don Juan
    German stories; ed. by H. Steinhauer

Hoffmann, E. T. A. (Ernst Theodor Amadeus), 1776-1822—_Continued_
The entail
The Penguin book of ghost stories
Hoffmann, Ernst Theodor Amadeus _See_ Hoffmann, E. T. A. (Ernst Theodor Amadeus), 1776-1822
Hoffmeier's Antelope. Swift, G.
Hofmann, Gert
Arno
Hofmann, G. Balzac's horse, and other stories
Casanova and the extra
Hofmann, G. Balzac's horse, and other stories
A conversation about Balzac's horse
Hofmann, G. Balzac's horse, and other stories
The cramp
Hofmann, G. Balzac's horse, and other stories
Moth
Hofmann, G. Balzac's horse, and other stories
The night
Hofmann, G. Balzac's horse, and other stories
Tolstoy's head
Hofmann, G. Balzac's horse, and other stories
Hofstadter, Douglas R., 1945-
The tale of Happiton
Mathenauts: tales of mathematical wonder; ed. by R. Rucker
Hogan, Desmond
Guy 'Micko' Delaney
Winter's tales, new ser. v4
Players
Winter's tales, new ser. v2
Ties
P.E.N. new fiction I
The vicar's wife
Winter's tales, new ser. v3
Hogan, Linda
Amen
Earth power coming; ed. by S. J. Ortiz
Friends and fortunes
The Pushcart prize XI
Stand one; ed. by M. Blackburn; J. Silkin and L. Tracy
New shoes
Earth power coming; ed. by S. J. Ortiz
Hogan, Linda Henderson
That horse: 1921
Southern Exposure (Durham, N.C.) 13:41-4 N/D '85
Hogg, James, 1770-1835
The barber of Duncow—a real ghost story
Hogg, J. Selected stories and sketches
The Brownie of the Black Haggs
Hogg, J. Selected stories and sketches

The Cameronian preacher's tale
Christian short stories; ed. by M. Booth
Hogg, J. Selected stories and sketches
The expedition to Hell [Variant title: George Dobson's expedition to Hell]
The Penguin book of horror stories
George Dobson's expedition to Hell [Variant title: The expedition to Hell]
Hogg, J. Selected stories and sketches
Mary Burnet
Hogg, J. Selected stories and sketches
Mr. Adamson of Laverhope
Hogg, J. Selected stories and sketches
The mysterious bride
Hogg, J. Selected stories and sketches
The Treasury of English short stories; ed. by N. Sullivan
On the separate existence of the soul
Hogg, J. Selected stories and sketches
Sound morality
Hogg, J. Selected stories and sketches
Strange letter of a lunatic
Hogg, J. Selected stories and sketches
Tibby Hyslop's dream
Hogg, J. Selected stories and sketches
The unearthly witness
Hogg, J. Selected stories and sketches
Hold me fast, don't let me pass. Munro, A.
Hold on. Goddin, N.
Hold tight, my love. Gerber, M. J.
Holden, David
The onion grass season
Encounter (London, England) 67:21-4 N '86
Holden, Mark
The field
Southwest Review 69:434-43 Aut '84
Holder, Nancy
Blood gothic
Shadows 8
Moving night
The Best of Shadows; ed. by C. L. Grant
Shadows 9
Holding, James, 1907-
A good kid
Alfred Hitchcock's Crimewatch
The grave robber
Ellery Queen's Prime crimes 2
Monkey king
Alfred Hitchcock's Grave suspicions
A padlock for Charlie Draper
Alfred Hitchcock's Mortal errors
The Treasure of Pachacamac
Distant danger; ed. by J. Van de Wetering
Holding. Winton, T.
Holding on. Norris, G.
Holding on. Pfeil, F.
Holding up the other end. Hall, T. T.

Holditch, W. Kenneth
  One of these mornings
    Mississippi writers v1: Fiction; ed. by D. Abbott
The **holdout**. Dash, J.
The **holdouts**. Reed, K.
HOLDUPS See Robbery
The **hole**. Maupassant, G. de
The **hole** in the wall. Chesterton, G. K.
The **hole** in the window. Gee, M.
The **holiday**. Fremlin, C.
Holiday. Matheson, R. C.
Holiday. Oates, J. C.
Holiday. Porter, K. A.
The **holiday** bread. Tripodi, C.
Holiday Haven. Thompson, K.
The **holiday** house. Kelly, G.
Holiday houseguest. Maron, M.
Holiday memory. Thomas, D.
HOLIDAYS
    See also All Saints' Day; Christmas
    stories; Fourth of July; New Year;
    Saint Patrick's Day; Thanksgiving Day;
    Vacations; Valentine's Day; Yom Kip-
    pur
Nagibin, ĨŬ. M. Elijah's Day
Ornstien, E. The admission ticket
Skrzynecki, P. The biggest bonfire of all
The **holidays**. Connelly, J.
Holidays. Ruffolo, L.
The **holiness** of Azédarac. Smith, C. A.
Holing out. Jackson, G.
Holland, Barbara
  The bonus
    McCall's 113:129-31 Ag '86
Holland, Noy
  River day
    Ploughshares 14 no2/3:180-8 '88
HOLLAND See Netherlands
Hollander, John
  The twin's story
    Partisan Review 51 no4/52 no1:530-4 '84/'85
Holleran, Andrew
  Friends at evening
    Men on men; ed. by G. Stambolian
  A house divided
    First love/last love; ed. by M. Denneny; C. Ortleb and T. Steele
  Ties
    First love/last love; ed. by M. Denneny; C. Ortleb and T. Steele
Holley, Maria Bruno- See Bruno-Holley, Maria
Hollingshead, Greg
  Rat with tangerine
    Alberta bound; ed. by F. Stenson
Hollow eyes. Smith, G. N.
The **hollow** man. Burke, T.
The **hollow** men. Wolfe, T.
The **hollow** nut. Colette

Holloway, John
  Deserving Princess
    The Hudson Review 41:449-56 Aut '88
HOLLY, BUDDY, 1936-1959
    About
  Dozois, G. R., and others. Touring
  Waldrop, H. Save a place in the lifeboat for me
The **holly** wreath. Moyes, P.
The **hollyhock** sowers. Wolfe, T.
HOLLYWOOD (CALIF.) See California—Hollywood
Hollywood guns. Washburn, L. J.
The **holm** oak. Norris, L.
Holman, John
  On earth
    The New Yorker 64:42-9 D 5 '88
  Squabble
    The New Yorker 63:25-30 Ja 4 '88
Holme, Timothy
  Dureddu
    Winter's crimes 18
Holmes, Charlotte
  Metropolitan
    New stories from the South: the year's best, 1988
Holmes, Nancy, 1921-
  Bugs
    Alberta bound; ed. by F. Stenson
Holmstrom, David
  Ice cream at noon
    McCall's 114:97-8 Ag '87
HOLOCAUST, JEWISH (1933-1945)
  Auswaks, A. Mrs. Halprin and the lottery
  Avery, M. The Holocaust remembrance service
  Borowski, T. This way for the gas, ladies and gentlemen
  Ellison, H. The boulevard of broken dreams
  Fink, I. Aryan papers
  Fink, I. Behind the hedge
  Fink, I. The black beast
  Fink, I. A conversation
  Fink, I. The garden that floated away
  Fink, I. Inspector von Galoshinsky
  Fink, I. Jean-Christophe
  Fink, I. Jump!
  Fink, I. The key game
  Fink, I. The other shore
  Fink, I. The pig
  Fink, I. A scrap of time
  Fink, I. The shelter
  Fink, I. Splinter
  Fink, I. A spring morning
  Fink, I. The tenth man
  Fink, I. Titina
  Fink, I. Traces
  Klíma, I. Miriam
  Kornblatt, J. R. Flo
  Lustig, A. Blue day
  Ozick, C. The shawl
Holocaust envy. Eisenstein, S.

The **Holocaust** remembrance service. Avery, M.

Holt, John Dominis
"God sent you into that Gomorrah this morning to bring up the truth"
  Passages to the dream shore; ed. by F. Stewart
The pool
  Passages to the dream shore; ed. by F. Stewart

Holt, T. E.
Apocalypse
  The Georgia Review 40:174-87 Spr '86
  Necessary fictions; ed. by S. W. Lindberg and S. Corey

Holy Annie. MacDonald, D. R.
HOLY GRAIL *See* Grail
Holy mackerel. Broinowski, A.
The **holy** man. Harris, F.
Holy quarrel. Dick, P. K.
The **holy** six. Thomas, D.
Holy Spirit. Crabtree, L. V.
The **holy** terror. Maxwell, W.
The **holy** wristwatch. Sharat Chandra, G. S.

Holz, Cynthia
Jack M.
  The New press anthology #2

Homage. Mazel, D.
Homage to Benny Leonard. Liben, M.
Homage to Switzerland. Hemingway, E.

HOME
Blythe, R. At Swan Gates
Jolley, E. Pear tree dance
Home. Belloc, H.
Home. See Chekhov, A. P. At home
Home. Gordimer, N.
Home. Grau, S. A.
The **home**. Hensley, J. L.
Home. King, F. H.
Home. Minot, S.
Home. Phillips, J. A.
Home. Rambach, P.
Home. Robison, J.
Home again, home again. Gallant, J.
Home again, home again. O'Connor, T. F.
Home alone. Finney, J.
A **home** away from home. Bloch, R.
A **home** away from home. Humphrey, W.
The **home** boy. Constantine, D.
The **home-coming**. Gunnell, B.
Home-coming. So, C.-I.
Home-coming. Suckow, R.
Home cooking. Samples, H.

HOME ECONOMICS
Fisher, M. F. K. The unswept emptiness
Gass, W. H. Order of insects
Home fires. Long, D.
Home for Christmas. Stewart, I.
Home for supper. Bonosky, P.
Home for the day. Pilcher, R.
Home from the war. Hunnewell, E.
Home is. Lurie, M.

Home is the Blue Moon Cafe. Camoin, F. A.
Home is the hangman. Zelazny, R.
Home is the hunter. Kuttner, H.
Home ownership. Bail, M.
Home safe. Wilbur, E.
Home sickness. Moore, G.
Home, sweet home. Fante, J.
Home, sweet home. Hartley, L. P.
Home sweet home. Wicomb, Z.
Home to Marie. Beattie, A.
Home to Uncle Ollie's. Conroy, J.
Home to wagonhouses. Whitaker, M.
Homecoming. Arden, W.
Homecoming. Bradbury, R.
Homecoming. Keillor, G.
The **homecoming**. Longyear, B. B.
Homecoming. Petrakis, H. M.
Homecoming. Shwartz, S. M.
Homecoming. West, J.
The **homecoming** stranger. Zhao Zhenkai

HOMECOMINGS
Alden, P. B. Ladies' luncheon
Algren, N. The brothers' house
Biggle, L. Orphan of the void
Blythe, R. Period return
Brender à Brandis, M. The living Christmas tree
Dawkins, C. The mourner
Doyle, Sir A. C. The lonely Hampshire cottage
Ellison, H. Basilisk
Faik, S. A dot on the map
Fernando, C. The bird of paradise
Garland, H. The return of a private
Gide, A. The return of the prodigal son
Goyen, W. Rhody's path
Greene, G. Under the garden
Hospital, J. T. After long absence
Houbein, L. Round trip
Ishiguro, K. A family supper
Kamal Muhamed, M. The leg
Keillor, G. Exiles
Keillor, G. Homecoming
Kessler, J. F. The old muse
Mohr, N. Brief miracle (Virginia)
Moore, G. Home sickness
Moore, S. Dove shooting
Norris, L. The holm oak
Oates, J. C. Heartland
O'Hara, J. The girl from California
Olmstead, R. A place to stay
Petrakis, H. M. Homecoming
Proulx, A. In the pit
Suckow, R. Home-coming
Welch, D. Full circle
Wexler, J. Two year's absence
Williams, T. The knightly guest
Winton, T. Laps
Wolfe, T. Return
Homefaring. Silverberg, R.
HOMELESS
Abbott, K. Yellow rock

HOMELESS—*Continued*
Adams, A. The oasis
Alderson, T. Vigil
Algren, N. Design for departure
Bloch, R. Hobo
Blythe, R. The packhorse path
Bradbury, R. The dead man
Briskin, M. Preservation
Campbell, R. Mackintosh Willy
Coleman, W. Reba
Crane, S. An excursion ticket
Crane, S. An experiment in misery
Day, R. C. Uccello
Ellison, H. Soft monkey
Gallagher, T. King Death
Goldberg, L. One more river
Hemingway, E. The battler
Henry, O. The Caliph, cupid, and the clock
Henry, O. The cop and the anthem
Henry, O. The higher abdication
Henry, O. The passing of Black Eagle
Houbein, L. The basement of happiness
Hunter, E. The beatings
Ingalls, R. The man who was left behind
Krisman, S. No marks for Rolf
Lum, D. H. Y. The Moiliili Bag Man
Lum, D. H. Y. Primo doesn't take back bottles anymore
Maupassant, G. de. A vagabond
Mayhar, A. In the tank
Mazel, D. The flying ark
Middleton, R. On the Brighton Road
Millman, L. The 545 pound boy
O, Y. The bird of passage
O'Connor, F. The life you save may be your own
Pfeil, F. The fame of price
Pronzini, B. Sweet fever
Sagan, F. Tears in the red wine
Schwartz, L. S. The last frontier
Sherman, C. W. Glory
Smith, A. Cornfield with lights
Valle, C. Diary entry #6
Walters, A. L. The warriors
Warren, R. P. Blackberry winter
Williams, T. A lady's beaded bag
Williams, T. The poet
Wolfe, T. The bums at sunset

HOMER

Parodies, travesties, etc.
Ferron, J. The Sirens
Ferron, J. Ulysses
Homer. La Chapelle, M.
Homer-snake. Crabtree, L. V.
HOMES *See* Houses
Homes and gardens. Kuffel, F.
HOMES FOR THE ELDERLY *See* Old age homes
Homesick at home. Chesterton, G. K.
The **homesick** Buick. MacDonald, J. D.
Homesickness. Cook, H.

The **homestead**. See Muschg, A. The scythe hand; or, The homestead
Homestead crescent. Krahn, R.
HOMESTEADING
See also Frontier and pioneer life
Curry, P. S. Geranium House
Overholser, W. D. Book-l'arnin' and the equalizer
Overholser, W. D. The patriarch of Gunsight Flat
Hometown. Kawabata, Y.
Homework. Cameron, P.
HOMOSEXUALITY
See also Bisexuality; Lesbianism
Adams, A. Time in Santa Fe
Allbeury, T. The party of the second part
Barker, C. In the hills, the cities
Barnett, A. Snapshot
Barrus, T. Life sucks; or, Ernest Hemingway never slept here
Baxter, C. The model
Benderson, B. A visit from Mom
Benner, R. The business card
Boone, B. David's charm
Borgman, C. F. A queer red spirit
Bowles, P. Pages from Cold Point
Brett, S. Big Boy, Little Boy
Burt, S. Hiding
Burt, S. Welcome
Burt, S. Wh'appen?
Callaghan, B. The black queen
Cameron, P. Excerpts from Swan Lake
Cameron, P. Jump or dive
Campbell, E. Out of empty cisterns
Coe, C. Anything you want
Conner, M. Vamp
Cooper, D. George: Wednesday, Thursday, Friday
Cooper, D. The outsiders
Coriolan, J. As you'd like it
Coriolan, J. Counting coup
Coriolan, J. Dream stud
Coriolan, J. The G'issimo
Coriolan, J. In the Blair's Lair
Coriolan, J. Interview in the number two dressing-room
Coriolan, J. Kindred
Coriolan, J. A marriage, a mantra, a massage
D'Allesandro, S. Nothing ever just disappears
Davis, C. The boys in the bars
Dawson, F. Kid stuff
Dixon, M. Red leaves
Dlugos, T. Generation
Ebon, W. Death of a lover
Ebon, W. The doctorate
Ebon, W. Little girl from Little Rock
Ebon, W. The supermarket manager's daughter
Eighner, L. Bayou boy
Eighner, L. Bertner: emergency room
Eighner, L. Biker boy

HOMOSEXUALITY—*Continued*

Eighner, L. The burnout kid
Eighner, L. Cherryhurst
Eighner, L. A cowboy Christmas
Eighner, L. Duel
Eighner, L. Fairview
Eighner, L. Greenbriar
Eighner, L. Highway 71
Eighner, L. Montrose Boulevard
Eighner, L. Park
Eighner, L. Texarkana
Eighner, L. Waugh
Eighner, L. Westheimer
Eighner, L. Windsor
Eighner, L. Woodhead
Eighner, L. Yoakum: the cruising circuit
Eisenstein, S. Post coitus tristus
Faik, S. The blanket
Faik, S. There is a snake in Alemdağ
Feinberg, D. B. The age of anxiety
Ferreira, R. The gold chain
Ferrell, A. Why people get cancer
Ferro, R. Frank's party
Ferro, R. Second son [excerpt]
Fisk, N. Find the lady
Forrest, K. V. The test
Fox, J. Choice
Fox, J. Over the Pyrenees
Franklin, P. Catalytic converter
Franklin, P. A DimEn is forever
Franklin, P. For merit
Franklin, P. Grease hunger
Franklin, P. A little peace
Franklin, P. The luck of the Irish
Franklin, P. New clothes
Franklin, P. Stale beer and roses
Franklin, P. Tzigane
Franklin, P. The uncertainty of strangers
Galgut, D. The night the blood
Garber, E. K. The lover
Gathorne-Hardy, J. The man who laughed
Glickman, G. Magic
Glück, R. Sex story
Gold, H. Blind, blind date
Gold, H. From Proust to Dada
Gooch, B. Maine
Gooch, B. Spring
Greene, G. May we borrow your husband?
Groff, D. Nobody's child
Grumley, M. Life drawing
Gurganus, A. Adult art
Hall, R. W. Backwards
Hall, R. W. The lesson of the master
Hall, R. W. Letter from a great-uncle
Hall, R. W. The lost chord
Hall, R. W. The night visitors
Hall, R. W. The piano
Hall, R. W. The Purple Prince
Hall, R. W. A rose in Murcia
Hemingway, E. The mother of a queen
Hoctel, P. Bad pictures
Hogan, D. Ties
Holleran, A. Friends at evening

Holleran, A. A house divided
Holleran, A. Ties
Hopes, D. B. Once in Syracuse
Hori, T. Les joues en feu
Innaurato, A. Solidarity
Janowitz, T. Patterns
Jolley, E. The fellow passenger
Killian, K. September
King, F. H. Hard feelings
Kinsella, W. P. Punchlines
Klass, P. Officemate with pink feathers
Lawrence, D. H. The Prussian officer
Leavitt, D. Ayor
Leavitt, D. Dedicated
Leavitt, D. Territory
Lerman, E. Remedies
MacLaverty, B. The drapery man
Mathers, P. A change for the better
McCourt, J. I go back to the mais oui
McKinley, J. Alastair and Jeremy
McQueen, J. The myna birds
Meinke, P. The twisted river
Mordden, E. Beach blanket mah-jongg
Mordden, E. The Boffer
Mordden, E. The dinner party
Mordden, E. Do-it-yourself S & M
Mordden, E. The ghost of Champ McQuest
Mordden, E. The handshake deal
Mordden, E. Hardhats
Mordden, E. The right boy for Cosgrove
Mordden, E. The tale of the changeling
Mordden, E. Uptown, downtown: a tour through the gay metropolis
Mordden, E. The woggle
Mortimer, J. C. Rumpole and the bright seraphim
Navarre, Y. Allan Bloom
Oates, J. C. Blackmail
Oates, J. C. The quarrel
Pangborn, E. The night wind
Picano, F. The most golden Bulgari
Plante, D. The crack
Povod, R. Things to do today
Purdy, J. The candles of your eyes
Purdy, J. Dawn
Purdy, J. In this corner . . .
Purdy, J. Rapture
Purdy, J. Some of these days
Ramírez, S. The siege
Raphael, L. Dancing on Tishe B'av
Rees, D. An apple for the preacher
Rees, D. At 21st Street
Rees, D. Canes
Rees, D. Cliff
Rees, D. Departures
Rees, D. Gay cat burglar seeks same for long-lasting relationship
Rees, D. The gilded youth of Los Gatos
Rees, D. In the fast lane
Rees, D. In the same boat
Rees, D. Open scholarship
Rees, D. Pip

HOMOSEXUALITY—*Continued*
  Rees, D. Plums
  Rees, D. The queen of queens
  Rees, D. Quiet days in Los Gatos
  Rees, D. Robin
  Rees, D. The year of the bulls
  Russ, J. Bodies
  Russ, J. The mystery of the young gentleman
  Ryan, N. Stavrogin
  Ryman, G. O happy day!
  Sams, F. Porphyria's lover
  Simpson, J. A party for idiot
  Smiley, J. Jeffrey, believe me
  Soldatow, S. Hass story
  Soldatow, S. Michael
  Soldatow, S. Practising dying
  Soldatow, S. Quick exchanges
  Soldatow, S. Strangers
  Soldatow, S. Writing it down 1972-1975
  Stambolian, G. Encounters
  Thomas, T. L. Broken tool
  Thompson, J. Of his bones are coral made
  Thompson, R. Under the swaying curtain
  Thurm, M. Sanctuary
  Tremain, R. Dinner for one
  Trevor, W. Torridge
  Umans, R. Connie
  Umans, R. Speech
  Underwood, M. OK for murder
  Valenzuela, L. Nihil obstat
  Watmough, D. All at sea
  Watmough, D. Bowen Island confessions
  Watmough, D. Closeted
  Watmough, D. Connecticut countess
  Watmough, D. In the mood
  Watmough, D. Return of the native
  Watmough, D. Seduction
  Watmough, D. Who shall be the judge?
  Weinstein, J. A Jean-Marie cookbook
  Welch, D. The barn
  Welch, D. A party
  Welch, D. Touchett's party
  Welch, D. When I was thirteen
  White, E. A man of the world
  White, E. An oracle
  Williams, T. Hard candy
  Williams, T. The killer chicken and the closet queen
  Williams, T. Mama's old stucco house
  Williams, T. The mysteries of the Joy Rio
  Williams, T. One arm
  Williams, T. Two on a party
  Windsor, G. The life of a man's man
  Zinnes, H. Wings
HOMOSEXUALS *See* Homosexuality; Lesbianism
The **hon**. Kelman, J.
HONDURAS
    See also Bahia Islands (Honduras); Guanaja Island (Honduras)
  Shepard, L. Aymara
Honest. Leonard, T.
The **honest** blackmailer. Moyes, P.

The **Honest** Company. Baumbach, J.
An **honest** deal. Maupassant, G. de
HONESTY
    See also Truthfulness and falsehood
  Rizkalla, J. A janitor for sale
  Stern, R. M. Present for Minna
  Wells, H. G. A slip under the microscope
Honesty. Cullen, E. J.
Honey. Beattie, A.
Honey. Evans, E.
The **honey** boys. McKnight, R.
Honeycomb. Friesner, E. M.
Honeymoon. Albarelli, D.
Honeymoon. Gerber, M. J.
Honeymoon. Gordon, P.
Honeymoon. Shaw, J. B.
The **honeymoon**. Spivack, K.
Honeymoon. Whitaker, M.
HONEYMOONS
  Albarelli, D. Honeymoon
  Bowles, P. Call at Corazón
  Colette. The hand
  Garrett, G. P. The sleeping beauty
  Greene, G. May we borrow your husband?
  Ingalls, R. St. George and the nightclub
  Rizkalla, J. The black figurine
  Sisskind, M. The apparition
  Whitaker, M. Honeymoon
  Wilson, B. Il circo delle donne
Hong, Song-Won
  A boy in search of rest
    Home-coming, and other Korean short stories
HONG KONG
  Grandbois, A. May Blossom
  Kaikō, T. The crushed pellet
HONGKONG *See* Hong Kong
Hongry fire. Bonner, M.
Hong's bluff. Wu, W. F.
Honig, Donald
  First date
    Good Housekeeping 198:144-5 My '84
  My escaped convict
    Alfred Hitchcock's Crimewatch
  Nice work if you can get it
    Alfred Hitchcock's Grave suspicions
  Voices in dead man's well
    Alfred Hitchcock's Mortal errors
Honig, Lucy, 1948-
  No friends, all strangers
    The Best American short stories, 1988
Honky-Tonk Avenue. Daniels, C.
HONOLULU (HAWAII) *See* Hawaii—Honolulu
HONOR
  Brentano, C. The story of good Caspar and fair Annie
  Doyle, Sir A. C. A regimental scandal
Honor among thieves. Archer, J.
Honor bright. Schiffman, C.
Honorable enemies. Anderson, P.
The **honored** dead. Pancake, B. D.

Honwana, Luís Bernardo, 1942-
Papa, snake & I
African short stories; ed. by C. Achebe and C. L. Innes

Hood, Ann, 1956-
At war with Amy
McCall's 114:152+ S '87

Hood, Hugh
Breaking off
Making it new; ed. by J. Metcalf
Flying a red kite
The Oxford book of Canadian short stories in English
Going out as a ghost
The Literary Review (Madison, N.J.) 28:389-99 Spr '85
The small birds
Making it new; ed. by J. Metcalf

Hood, Mary
After Moore
The Georgia Review 40:491-517 Summ '86
Hood, M. And Venus is blue
New stories from the South: the year's best, 1987
And Venus is blue
Hood, M. And Venus is blue
A country girl
Hood, M. How far she went
Desire call of the wild hen
Hood, M. And Venus is blue
Doing this, saying that, to applause
Hood, M. How far she went
Finding the chain
Hood, M. And Venus is blue
The goodwife Hawkins
Hood, M. And Venus is blue
Hindsight
Hood, M. How far she went
How far she went
Hood, M. How far she went
The New writers of the South; ed. by C. East
Inexorable progress
The Best American short stories, 1984
The Editors' choice: new American stories v1
Hood, M. How far she went
Lonesome road blues
Hood, M. How far she went
A man among men
Hood, M. How far she went
Manly conclusions
The Georgia Review 40:188-95 Spr '86
Hood, M. How far she went
Necessary fictions; ed. by S. W. Lindberg and S. Corey
Moths
Hood, M. And Venus is blue
The Kenyon Review ns6:25-35 Fall '84
Nobody's fool
Hood, M. And Venus is blue
The Kenyon Review ns8:64-73 Summ '86

Solomon's seal
Hood, M. How far she went
New American short stories; ed. by G. Norris
Something good for Ginnie
The Georgia Review 39:479-504 Fall '85
Hood, M. And Venus is blue
New stories from the South: the year's best, 1986
The Pushcart prize XI

Hoodoo. Porter, C.

Hood's Isle and the hermit Oberlus. Melville, H.

Hooked. Nevai, L.

Hooks and feelers. Hulme, K.

Hooper, Johnson Jones, 1815?-1863
Fighting the "tiger" and other speculations
The Art of fiction in the heart of Dixie; ed. by P. D. Beidler

Hooray for Haralambos. Loukakis, A.

Hoover, Judith
Proteus
The Georgia Review 40:196-204 Spr '86
Necessary fictions; ed. by S. W. Lindberg and S. Corey

Hoover, Paul, 1946-
Demonstration
The New Yorker 63:40-6 O 5 '87

Hoover's men. Waldrop, H.

Hop-frog. Poe, E. A.

Hop, skip, and jump. Liben, M.

Hop skip jump. Malzberg, B. N.

Hopalong sits in. Mulford, C. E.

Hope. Sisskind, M.

Hope chest. Sexson, L.

Hopes, David B. (David Brendan)
Once in Syracuse
Men on men 2; ed. by G. Stambolian

Hopi. West, P.

Hopkins, Diane
Being occupied
The Massachusetts Review 25:61-78 Spr '84

Hopkins, James *See* Nolan, William F., 1928-

Hopley, George, 1903-1968
For works written by this author under other names see Irish, William, 1903-1968; Woolrich, Cornell, 1903-1968

Hopley-Woolrich, Cornell George *See* Woolrich, Cornell, 1903-1968

Hora. Asscher-Pinkhof, C.

Horace and Margaret's fifty-second. Baxter, C.

Horace Chooney, M.D. West, J.

Horan, Hillary
The first good-bye
Redbook 169:29-30 Ag '87

Horatio's trick. Beattie, A.

Horgan, Paul, 1903-
To the castle
A Treasury of World War II stories; ed.
by B. Pronzini and M. H. Greenberg
Hori, Tatsuo, 1904-1953
Les joues en feu
The Shōwa anthology 1
Horizontal light. Spain, C.
Le **Horla**. Maupassant, G. de
Horn, Andrew
The making of Musa Maikudi
A Good deal; ed. by M. Heath and F.
M. Robinson
Horn man. Howard, C.
The **horn** of Elfland. Jeppson, J. O.
The **horn** of plenty. Nowakowski, M.
Horne, Lewis, 1932-
The last dancer
The Old dance; ed. by B. Burnard
Taking care
Prize stories, 1987
The Virginia Quarterly Review 61:603-19
Aut '85
HORNED TOADS
Henry, O. Jimmy Hayes and Muriel
The **hornets'** nest. Feng Jicai
Horning in--A. Hannah, B.
Hornung, Ernest William, 1866-1921
A bad night
Hornung, E. W. The complete short
stories of Raffles—the amateur cracks-
man
The chest of silver
Hornung, E. W. The complete short
stories of Raffles—the amateur cracks-
man
A costume piece
Hornung, E. W. The complete short
stories of Raffles—the amateur cracks-
man
The criminologists' club
Hornung, E. W. The complete short
stories of Raffles—the amateur cracks-
man
The fate of Faustina
Hornung, E. W. The complete short
stories of Raffles—the amateur cracksman
The field of Philippi
Hornung, E. W. The complete short
stories of Raffles—the amateur cracksman
Gentlemen and players
Hornung, E. W. The complete short
stories of Raffles—the amateur cracksman
The gift of the emperor
Hornung, E. W. The complete short
stories of Raffles—the amateur cracksman

The Ides of March
Hornung, E. W. The complete short
stories of Raffles—the amateur cracks-
man
A Jubilee present
Hornung, E. W. The complete short
stories of Raffles—the amateur cracks-
man
The knees of the gods
Hornung, E. W. The complete short
stories of Raffles—the amateur cracks-
man
The last laugh
Hornung, E. W. The complete short
stories of Raffles—the amateur cracks-
man
The last word
Hornung, E. W. The complete short
stories of Raffles—the amateur cracks-
man
Nine points of the law
Hornung, E. W. The complete short
stories of Raffles—the amateur cracks-
man
No sinecure
Hornung, E. W. The complete short
stories of Raffles—the amateur cracks-
man
An old flame
Hornung, E. W. The complete short
stories of Raffles—the amateur cracks-
man
Out of paradise
Hornung, E. W. The complete short
stories of Raffles—the amateur cracks-
man
Le premier pas
Hornung, E. W. The complete short
stories of Raffles—the amateur cracksman
The raffles relics
Hornung, E. W. The complete short
stories of Raffles—the amateur cracksman
The rest cure
Hornung, E. W. The complete short
stories of Raffles—the amateur cracksman
The return match
Hornung, E. W. The complete short
stories of Raffles—the amateur cracksman
The spoils of sacrilege
Hornung, E. W. The complete short
stories of Raffles—the amateur cracksman
To catch a thief
Hornung, E. W. The complete short
stories of Raffles—the amateur cracksman

Hornung, Ernest William, 1866-1921—*Continued*
  A trap to catch a cracksman
    Hornung, E. W. The complete short stories of Raffles—the amateur cracksman
  Wilful murder
    Hornung, E. W. The complete short stories of Raffles—the amateur cracksman
  The wrong house
    Hornung, E. W. The complete short stories of Raffles—the amateur cracksman
Horrer Howce. St. Clair, M.
The **horrible**. Maupassant, G. de
The **horrible** horns. Gardner, M.
The **horror** at his heels. Blassingame, W.
The **horror** from the bridge. Campbell, R.
The **horror** of the heights. Doyle, Sir A. C.
The **horror** on the #33. Shea, M.
Horror show. Thompson, S.
HORROR STORIES
    See also Ghost stories; Murder stories; Supernatural phenomena; Vampires; Werewolves
Aickman, R. The fetch
Aickman, R. Hand in glove
Aickman, R. The hospice
Aickman, R. The same dog
Aickman, R. The stains
Aickman, R. The swords
Akutagawa, R. Hell screen
Allan, J. N. The aquarist
Antieau, K. Cycles
Antieau, K. Sanctuary
Arnold, H. F. The night wire
Arnold, M. Pilgrims to the cathedral
The Astrologer's prediction
Atherton, G. F. H. The striding place
Baker, R. High-tech insolence
Baker, S. Nesting instinct
Barker, C. The age of desire
Barker, C. The body politic
Barker, C. The Book of Blood
Barker, C. The Book of Blood (a postscript): on Jerusalem Street
Barker, C. Cabal
Barker, C. Coming to grief
Barker, C. Down, Satan!
Barker, C. Dread
Barker, C. Human remains
Barker, C. In the hills, the cities
Barker, C. The inhuman condition
Barker, C. Jacqueline Ess: her will and testament
Barker, C. The life of death
Barker, C. The midnight meat train
Barker, C. Pig blood blues
Barker, C. Rawhead Rex
Barker, C. Sex, death and starshine
Barker, C. Son of celluloid
Barker, C. Twilight at the towers

Bear, G. If I die before I wake
Beaumont, C. Fritzchen
Bensink, J. R. Lake George in high August
Bierce, A. The boarded window
Bierce, A. A watcher by the dead
Bishop, M. In the memory room
Bishop, M. A tapestry of little murders
Blassingame, W. The horror at his heels
Blassingame, W. The tongueless horror
Bloch, R. Almost human
Bloch, R. The animal fair
Bloch, R. The beasts of Barsac
Bloch, R. Beelzebub
Bloch, R. The big kick
Bloch, R. The bogey man will get you
Bloch, R. Constant reader
Bloch, R. The cure
Bloch, R. Dead-end doctor
Bloch, R. The deadliest art
Bloch, R. Double whammy
Bloch, R. Enoch
Bloch, R. Everybody needs a little love
Bloch, R. Final performance
Bloch, R. Founding fathers
Bloch, R. Freak show
Bloch, R. Frozen fear
Bloch, R. The goddess of wisdom
Bloch, R. The head man
Bloch, R. A home away from home
Bloch, R. The hungry house
Bloch, R. I like blondes
Bloch, R. The man who collected Poe
Bloch, R. Mannikins of horror
Bloch, R. The masterpiece
Bloch, R. Nina
Bloch, R. The plot is the thing
Bloch, R. Show biz
Bloch, R. The skull of the Marquis de Sade
Bloch, R. Sweets to the sweet
Bloch, R. Tell your fortune
Bloch, R. Terror in Cut-throat Cove
Bloch, R. Terror in the night
Bloch, R. The thinking cap
Bloch, R. The tunnel of love
Bloch, R. Water's edge
Bloch, R. You got to have brains
Boucher, A. Mr. Lupescu
Bowles, P. A distant episode
Boyett, S. R. The answer tree
Bracken, M. Of memories dying
Bradbury, R. The emissary
Bradbury, R. Homecoming
Bradbury, R. Skeleton
Bradbury, R. The small assassin
Bradbury, R. The thing at the top of the stairs
Bradbury, R. Trapdoor
Braddon, M. E. Good Lady Ducayne
Braun, L. J. The sin of Madame Phloi
Brennan, J. P. Canavan's back yard
Brennan, J. P. Road to Granville
Bretnor, R. Markham

HORROR STORIES—*Continued*
Bretnor, R. No other gods
Brown, F. The spherical ghoul
Browne, C. The lesson
Bryant, E. Author's notes
Bryant, E. The transfer
Burks, A. J. Dance of the damned
Burrage, A. M. One who saw
Byrne, L. Guest-room in Hell
Cady, J. By reason of darkness
Campbell, R. Among the pictures are these
Campbell, R. Before the storm
Campbell, R. Blacked out
Campbell, R. Call first
Campbell, R. Calling card
Campbell, R. The church in High Street
Campbell, R. Cold print
Campbell, R. Dolls
Campbell, R. The faces at Pine Dunes
Campbell, R. The hands
Campbell, R. The horror from the bridge
Campbell, R. The inhabitant of the lake
Campbell, R. The insects from Shaggai
Campbell, R. The invocation
Campbell, R. Loveman's comeback
Campbell, R. Mackintosh Willy
Campbell, R. Merry May
Campbell, R. The moon-lens
Campbell, R. Old clothes
Campbell, R. The other side
Campbell, R. The render of the veils
Campbell, R. The room in the castle
Campbell, R. The scar
Campbell, R. Second sight
Campbell, R. The seductress
Campbell, R. The show goes on
Campbell, R. The tugging
Campbell, R. The voice of the beach
Campbell, R. Where the heart is
Campbell, R. The words that count
Carter, R. The pleasure
Casper, S. Spring-fingered Jack
Castle, M. Party time
Cave, H. B. Death tolls the bell
Chambers, R. W. The repairer of reputations
Chambers, R. W. The yellow sign
Charlton, W. Hakanono
Chetwynd-Hayes, R. The fly-by-night
Chittum, I. The monster of Poot Holler
Clifford, L. L. The new mother
Cobb, I. S. Fishhead
Conner, M. Stillborn
Counselman, M. E. Night court
Crawford, F. M. The upper berth
Crump, R. Anthony's wives
Cunningham, J. Decoys
Dahl, R. The landlady
Dann, J. Visitors
Davidson, A. Naples
Davis, F. C. The mole men want your eyes
De la Mare, W. A:B:O.

Derleth, A. W. Carousel
Dickens, C. Captain Murderer and the Devil's bargain
Disch, T. M. The roaches
Donaldson, S. R. The conqueror worm
Doyle, Sir A. C. The adventure of the speckled band
Doyle, Sir A. C. The horror of the heights
Doyle, Sir A. C. Lot no 249
Doyle, Sir A. C. The winning shot
Du Maurier, Dame D. The birds
Edgell, J. Did you see the window-cleaner?
Elflandsson, G. Icarus
Ellison, H. Footsteps
Ellison, H. I have no mouth, and I must scream
Ellison, H. The whimper of whipped dogs
Ely, D. The academy
Etchemendy, N. The tuckahoe
Etchison, D. The blood kiss
Etchison, D. Somebody like you
Etchison, D. Talking in the dark
Etchison, D., and Johnson, M. The spot
Farber, S. N. Return of the dust vampires
Farley, R. M. The living mist
Ferrara, P. Rising waters
Ferreira, R. Shark
Fisher, L. Overnight
Fleming-Roberts, G. T. Moulder of monsters
Ford, J. M. Preflash
Ford, J. M. Tales from the original gothic
Fox, J. Intimately, with rain
Fox, J. The skins you love to touch
Frost, G. From Hell, again
Gallagher, S. By the river, Fontainebleau
Gallagher, S. Old red shoes
Gardner, C. S. The man who loved water
Gardner, C. S. Overnight guest
Gardner, C. S. Three faces of the night
Gardner, C. S. Walk home alone
Garris, M. A life in the cinema
Garton, R. Sinema
Gilchrist, M. Dame Inowslad
Gilchrist, M. My friend
Gilchrist, M. Roxana runs lunatick
Godfrey, P. The lady and the dragon
Goldsmith, H. Do ye hear the children weeping?
Grant, C. L. Ellen, in her time
Grant, C. L. If Damon comes
Grant, C. L. Pride
Graves, R. Earth to earth
Gray, A. The Everlasting Club
Gray, A. The true history of Anthony Ffryar
Grubb, D. Cry havoc
Grubb, D. The horsehair trunk
Haldeman, J. C. Still frame
Hall, M. M. The glass doorknob
Hamilton, D. Fish story
Harrison, M. J. The Great God Pan
Hartley, L. P. A change of ownership

HORROR STORIES—*Continued*

Hartley, L. P. Podolo
Hartley, L. P. Someone in the lift
Hartley, L. P. The thought
Hartley, L. P. The waits
Harvey, W. F. The beast with five fingers
Hazel, P. Having a woman at lunch
Henderson, Z. Stevie and The Dark
Highsmith, P. The quest for Blank Claveringi
Hoch, E. D. The faceless thing
Hoch, E. D. The maze and the monster
Hodgson, W. H. The derelict
Hodgson, W. H. The thing in the weeds
Hoffman, N. K. Ants
Holder, N. Moving night
Horvitz, L. A. The fishing village of Roebush
Horvitz, L. A. Marriage vows
Household, G. Taboo
Ingalls, R. Captain Hendrik's story
Ingalls, R. Inheritance
Ingalls, R. People to people
Ingalls, R. Third time lucky
Irving, W. The adventure of the German student
Jackson, S. The lottery
Jackson, S. The lovely house
Jacobson, E., and Jacobson, E. Corpses on parade
Jakes, J. And the monsters walk
James, F. Arms of the flame goddess
James, F. Dance of the bloodless ones
Jennings, J. Tiger hunt
Jones, K. The green man
Kearns, R. Grave angels
Kenny, W. A country home
Kersh, G. Men without bones
King, S. Beachworld
King, S. The cat from hell
King, S. Crouch end
King, S. Gramma
King, S. Here there be tygers
King, S. The Jaunt
King, S. The man who would not shake hands
King, S. The mist
King, S. Mrs. Todd's shortcut
King, S. The Night Flier
King, S. The night of the tiger
King, S. Nona
King, S. Quitters, Inc.
King, S. The raft
King, S. The reach
King, S. The reaper's image
King, S. Survivor type
King, S. Uncle Otto's truck
King, S. Word processor of the gods
Kisner, J. The litter
Klein, T. E. D. Children of the kingdom
Klein, T. E. D. Nadelman's god
Klein, T. E. D. Petey
Knoles, D. The first day of spring
Knox, J. H. The buyer of souls

Koontz, D. Down in the darkness
Kushner, E. Night laughter
Kuttner, H. The graveyard rats
Laidlaw, M. Muzak for torso murders
Laidlaw, M. Sneakers
Langford, D. Cold spell
Lansdale, J. R. Dog, Cat, and Baby
Lansdale, J. R. Down by the sea near the great big rock
Lansdale, J. R. Night they missed the horror show
Laski, M. The tower
Le Fanu, J. S. Carmilla
Le Fanu, J. S. Schalken the painter
Leiber, F. The dead man
Leiber, F. The girl with the hungry eyes
Lem, S. The mask
Level, M. A madman
Level, M. Night and silence
Ligotti, T. Alice's last adventure
Little, B. The backroom
Lovecraft, H. P. The call of Cthulhu
Lovecraft, H. P. The colour out of space
Lovecraft, H. P. Cool air
Lovecraft, H. P. The Dunwich horror
Lovecraft, H. P. In the vault
Lovecraft, H. P. The music of Erich Zann
Lovecraft, H. P. The outsider
Lovecraft, H. P. Pickman's model
Lovecraft, H. P. The picture in the house
Lovecraft, H. P. The rats in the walls
Lovecraft, H. P. The shadow over Innsmouth
Lovecraft, H. P. The statement of Randolph Carter
Lovecraft, H. P. The thing on the doorstep
Lovecraft, H. P. The whisperer in darkness
Lyons, J. Trust me
Machen, A. The great god Pan
Machen, A. Novel of the white powder
MacLennan, P. Good-by, Miss Patterson
Malden, R. H. Between sunset and moonrise
Martin, G. R. R. The Pear-shaped Man
Martin, V. Sea lovers
Massie, E. Sick'un
Matheson, R. Big surprise
Matheson, R. Graveyard shift
Matheson, R. C. Beholder
Matheson, R. C. Cancelled
Matheson, R. C. Dead end
Matheson, R. C. Dust
Matheson, R. C. The good always comes back
Matheson, R. C. Goosebumps
Matheson, R. C. Hell
Matheson, R. C. Intruder
Matheson, R. C. Mugger
Matheson, R. C. Red
Matheson, R. C. Third wind
Matheson, R. C., and Matheson, R. Where there's a will
Maupassant, G. de. The flayed hand

HORROR STORIES—*Continued*

Maupassant, G. de. Le Horla
Mayhar, A. In the tank
Mayhar, A. A night in Possum Holler
Mayhar, A. Nor disregard the humblest voice
McCammon, R. R. Nightcrawlers
McCormack, E. P. Festival
McDowell, M. Halley's passing
McGrath, P. The Black Hand of the Raj
McGrath, P. Hand of a wanker
McGrath, P. Marmilion
Merritt, A. The moon pool
Merritt, A. The pool of the stone god
Metcalfe, J. The feasting dead
Metcalfe, J. Mr. Meldrum's mania
The Monk of horror; or, The Conclave of corpses
Monteleone, T. F. The night is freezing fast
Morrell, D. For these and all my sins
Morris, W. Lindenborg pool
Morrow, W. C. His unconquerable enemy
Morton, S. L. Now you see me
Nash, O. The three d's
Nesbit, E. Man-size in marble
Nolan, W. F. Ceremony
Nolan, W. F. Trust not a man
Nolan, W. F. The Yard
Noyes, A. Midnight express
Oates, J. C. Haunted
O'Brien, F.-J. The lost room
O'Brien, F.-J. What was it?
O'Brien, F.-J. The wondersmith
Onions, O. The beckoning fair one
Pacheco, J. E. The amusement park
Pangborn, E. Longtooth
Perry, M. C. Stumps
Phillips, J. A. Bluegill
Pizarnik, A. The bloody countess
Poe, E. A. Berenice
Poe, E. A. The black cat
Poe, E. A. The cask of Amontillado
Poe, E. A. A descent into the maelström
Poe, E. A. The fall of the House of Usher
Poe, E. A. Ligeia
Poe, E. A. Morella
Poe, E. A. Ms. found in a bottle
Poe, E. A. The oblong box
Poe, E. A. The pit and the pendulum
Poe, E. A. The tell-tale heart
Poe, E. A. William Wilson
Pronzini, B. Peekaboo
Proulx, M. ABC
Ptacek, K. Dead possums
Quinliven, J. O. Beauty for sale
Quiroga, H. The feather pillow
Reamy, T. Beyond the cleft
Reaves, J. M. Werewind
Rendell, R. Loopy
Robbins, W. W. A beast is born
Robbins, W. W. Test-tube Frankenstein
Rogers, W. Sleep with me—and death
Rolt, L. T. C. Bosworth summit pound

Rolt, L. T. C. The mine
Rosemund, V. L. The thing from the old seaman's mouth
Royle, N. Irrelativity
Rud, A. M. Ooze
Russ, J. "I had vacantly crumpled it into my pocket . . . but by God, Eliot, it was a photograph from life!"
Russ, J. My dear Emily
Russell, R. Czadek
Russell, R. Sardonicus
Ryan, A. The bones wizard
Ryan, A. The East Beaverton monster
Ryan, A. I shall not leave England now
Ryan, A. The lovely and talented Maxine Kane
Ryan, A. Memory and desire
Ryan, A. The rose of Knock
Ryan, A. Sand
Ryan, A. Sheets
Saki. The wolves of Cernogratz
Salmonson, J. A. The blind man
Salmonson, J. A. The house that knew no hate
Sarrantonio, A. Wish
Schow, D. J. Pamela's get
Shea, M. The autopsy
Shea, M. Fat Face
Sheckley, R. Warm
Shepard, L. How the wind spoke at Madaket
Shepard, L. The night of White Bhairab
Shields, R. Mistress of the blood-drinkers
Silva, D. B. Ice sculptures
Silva, D. B. The turn of time
Silverberg, R. Not our brother
Simms, W. G. The arm-chair of Tustenuggee
Skipp, J. Film at eleven
Skipp, J., and Spector, C. Gentlemen
Smith, C. A planet named Shayol
Smith, C. A. The dweller in the gulf
Smith, C. A. The return of the sorcerer
Smith, C. A. The tale of Satampra Zeiros
Smith, C. A. The vaults of Yoh-Vombis
Smith, G. N. Hollow eyes
Snow, J. The anchor
Sohl, J. Cabin number six
Spector, C. Lifecast
St. Clair, M. Brenda
St. Clair, M. Horrer Howce
Stevenson, R. L. The body snatchers
Stevenson, R. L. Thrawn Janet
Stoker, B. Dracula's guest
Stoker, B. The judge's house
Stoker, B. The secret of the growing gold
Stoker, B. The squaw
Straub, P. Blue rose
Strieber, W. The pool
Sturgeon, T. Bright segment
Sturgeon, T. It
Sturgeon, T. The professor's teddy bear
Sullivan, T. Knucklebones

HORROR STORIES—*Continued*

Sullivan, T. The extension
Sullivan, T. The man who drowned puppies
Sullivan, T. A night at the head of a grave
Swain, E. G. The man with the roller
Taylor, B. Our last nanny
Tem, S. R. Father's Day
Tem, S. R. Hidey hole
Tem, S. R. Little cruelties
Tidmarsh, W. M. Bronze
Tieck, J. L. Wake not the dead
Tremblay, M. The octagonal room
Tuttle, L. Bug house
Tuttle, L. Jamie's grave
Vandegrift, G. White mother of shadows
Vandercook, J. W. The challenge
Wagner, K. E. Endless night
Wagner, K. E. Sticks
Wagner, K. E. Where the summer ends
Wakefield, H. R. Blind man's buff
Wakefield, H. R. Old man's beard
Watson, I. Salvage rites
Webb, S. A demon in rosewood
Wells, H. G. The flowering of the strange orchid
Wells, H. G. Pollock and the Porroh man
Wells, H. G. The valley of spiders
White, T. H. The troll
Wiater, S. Moist dreams
Williams, T. Desire and the black masseur
Williamson, C. Return of the neon fireball
Wilson, F. P. Cuts
Wilson, H. Please, no strawberries
Wilson, P. F. Soft
Wilson, R. The thing that stared
Winter, D. E. Masks
Winter, D. E. Splatter
Wolfe, G. In the house of gingerbread
Wollheim, D. A. The rag thing
Woolrich, C. Jane Brown's body
Wright, T. M. A world without toys
Yarbro, C. Q. Lapses

Horror, we got. Waldrop, H.

Horsdal, Maralyn

An educated taste
    Through a glass, darkly; ed. by B. Woelfel
The **horse.** Tinker, L.
A **horse** and two goats. Narayan, R. K.

HORSE BREEDING

Beekman, E. M. Frisian horses
Reed, R. The slicker
Rooke, L. The woman who talked to horses

Horse camp. Le Guin, U. K.
Horse collars. Kinsella, W. P.
Horse dreams. Inness-Brown, E.
The **horse** in the bedroom. Sullivan, C.
The **horse-leech** hath two daughters. Lofts, N.
The **horse** on the escalator. Gardner, M.

HORSE RACING

See also Jockeys

Beckett, R. Forty Susan Sangsters stride out at the Wellington Boot
Byram, G. The wonder horse
Cain, J. M. Pay-off girl
Doyle, Sir A. C. Silver Blaze
Faust, I. The year of the hot jock
Francis, D. The gift
Francis, D. Twenty-one good men and true
Gee, M. The losers
Killingsworth, S. Born to ride
Lawrence, D. H. The rocking-horse winner
Markham, B. The quitter
Mayer, R. The system
Mortimer, J. C. Rumpole's last case
Oates, J. C. Raven's Wing
Randisi, R. J. The nickel derby
Reed, R. The slicker
Robison, M. Culpability
Rooke, L. Friendship and property
Sisskind, M. The apparition
Womersley, J. The year granpa won the Melbourne Cup

The **horse-shade.** See Poe, E. A. Metzengerstein
Horse story. Loesch, C.
The **horse** that drank beer. Rosa, J. G.
Horse thief. See Opatoshu, J. Romance of a horse thief

HORSE THIEVES

Doyle, Sir A. C. Silver Blaze
Jahnn, H. H. Stolen horses
Mears, S. S. Thirty horses for your daughter
Opatoshu, J. Romance of a horse thief
Saroyan, W. The beautiful white horse
The **horse** thieves of Ballysaggert. Cleeve, B.

HORSE TRADING

Stuart, J. Horse-trading trembles
Horse-trading trembles. Stuart, J.
Horse year. Boylan, J.
The **horsebreaker.** Schott, M.
The **horsehair.** Stark, S. S.
The **horsehair** trunk. Grubb, D.

HORSEMANSHIP

Bates, H. E. Death of a huntsman
Crace, J. Cross-country
Grey, Z. Roping lions in the Grand Canyon
O'Hara, J. It must have been spring

HORSES

Banks, R. The neighbor
Brand, M. Dark Rosaleen
Burt, S. Anyone else would learn
Byram, G. The wonder horse
Carrington, L. The seventh horse
Clark, G. At Lowry's
Conroy, J. Charley was our darlin'
Cook-Lynn, E. The power of horses
Crane, S. Horses—one dash
Crane, S. One dash—horses
De Larrabeiti, M. The curse of Igamor

HORSES—*Continued*
Federspiel, J. Death of a foal
Freeman, C. That is no country for old men
Frost, G. Sardofa's horseshoes
Gardner, M. The horse on the escalator
Gilchrist, E. Nineteen forty-one
Highsmith, P. Engine horse
Hudson, W. H. The story of a piebald horse
Hughes, T. The rain horse
Levinson, B. ". . . .and he chose a mule"
Loesch, C. Horse story
MacLeod, A. In the fall
Markham, B. The captain and his horse
Markham, B. Something I remember
Markham, B. The splendid outcast
Michalson, G. The tail of his luck
Miller, A. The misfits
Ocampo, S. Livio Roca
O'Hara, J. We'll have fun
Poe, E. A. Metzengerstein
Prichard, K. S. The grey horse
Richard, M. Happiness of the garden variety
Robinson, L. Telepathic rein
Robison, M. In the woods
Schott, M. The horsebreaker
Springer, N. The prince out of the past
Tallent, E. Sweet disposition
Tinker, L. The horse
Valenzuela, L. My everyday colt
Walker, A. Am I Blue?
Woodman, A. Waiting for the broken horse
Horses. Mrożek, S.
The **horse's** ha. Thomas, D.
The **horses** of Diomedes. Christie, A.
Horses--one dash. See Crane, S. One dash—horses
Horses—one dash. Crane, S.
Horsey horsey. Virgo, S.
Horst Wessel. Gusewelle, C. W.
Hortensia. Ruta, S.
Horvitz, Leslie Alan
The fishing village of Roebush
    Shadows 9
Marriage vows
    After midnight; ed. by C. L. Grant
Pictures of a woman gone
    Midnight; ed. by C. L. Grant
The **hospice.** Aickman, R.
Hospital, Janette Turner, 1942-
After long absence
    Hospital, J. T. Dislocations
After the fall
    Hospital, J. T. Dislocations
Amazing Grace
    Ladies' Home Journal 103:114+ Je '86
Ashes to ashes
    Hospital, J. T. Dislocations
The baroque ensemble
    Hospital, J. T. Dislocations

The bloody past, the wandering future
    Hospital, J. T. Dislocations
The dark wood
    Hospital, J. T. Dislocations
The Dominican season
    The Editors' choice v4; ed. by G. E. Murphy, Jr.
Expatriate
    Prairie Schooner 62:55-63 Wint '88/'89
Golden girl
    Hospital, J. T. Dislocations
Happy Diwali
    Hospital, J. T. Dislocations
    The North American Review 271:26-30 S '86
Here comes the sun
    The Editors' choice: new American stories v2
The inside story
    Hospital, J. T. Dislocations
The mango tree
    The Yale Review 75:601-9 Summ '86
Morgan Morgan
    Hospital, J. T. Dislocations
Mosie
    Hospital, J. T. Dislocations
Moving out
    Hospital, J. T. Dislocations
The owl-bander
    Hospital, J. T. Dislocations
Port after port, the same baggage
    Hospital, J. T. Dislocations
Some have called thee mighty and dreadful
    Hospital, J. T. Dislocations
Waiting
    Hospital, J. T. Dislocations
You gave me hyacinths
    Hospital, J. T. Dislocations
Hospital. Grace, P.
Hospital barrack. Asscher-Pinkhof, C.
Hospital room 205. Choe, C.-H.
The **hospital:** seeing him there almost dead. McGarry, J.
Hospital ship rams U-boat. MacLean, A.
HOSPITALS AND SANATORIUMS
Alcott, L. M. The brothers
Anderman, J. Night shift in emergency
Baker, S. The sins of the fathers
Bellamy, J. D. Roth's deadman
Böll, H. Lohengrin's death
Bonosky, P. Charity ward
Briskin, M. Two hours in the life of Steven Malinowski
Butler, O. E. The evening and the morning and the night
Buzzati, D. Seven floors
Calisher, H. Gargantua
Carver, R. Where I'm calling from
Chekhov, A. P. An unpleasant business
Choe, C.-H. Hospital room 205
Clark, J. Passage by water
Cordor, S. M. In the hospital
Crayford, K. Duncan

HOSPITALS AND SANATORIUMS —
Continued
Crehan, S. The operation
Dann, J. Camps
Davie, E. Bones and bouquets
Davin, D. Jaundiced
Drewe, R. Stingray
Dub, O. The rebel wolf and Petrina
Endō, S. The day before
Endō, S. A forty-year-old man
Endō, S. Incredible voyage
Endō, S. Retreating figures
Farber, S. N. Return of the dust vampires
Ferguson, P. Indefinite nights
Ferguson, P. Inside knowledge
Ferguson, P. The quality of mercy
Ferguson, P. Sister Hilary
Forrest, K. V. Survivor
Gault, C. Mary Beth
Gojawiczyńska, P. Two women
Goulart, R. Calling Dr. Clockwork
Halligan, M. Mozart is best
Hankla, C. If it were dark
Harvor, E. The age of unreason
Havazelet, E. No word for mercy
Hempel, A. Going
Hirabayashi, T. A woman to call mother
Horn, A. The making of Musa Maikudi
Johnson, J. The children's wing
Kinsella, W. P. Lark song
Klíma, I. Friday morning: an orderly's tale
Kratz, E. Poppa
Matthews, J. The gray lady
Matthiessen, P. Midnight turning gray
McClure, J. The last place on earth
McElroy, C. J. A dance with a dolly with
    a hole in her stocking
McElroy, C. J. Jesus and Fat Tuesday
McGarry, J. The hospital: seeing him there
    almost dead
McPherson, M. That was last year
Mohr, N. Happy birthday (Lucia)
Morris, W. The safe place
Murphy, D. Roller
Murphy, P. Checking in
Murphy, P. Terminals
Narayan, R. K. A breath of Lucifer
Nonhebel, C. Popcorn
Oates, J. C. Face
Ocampo, S. Visions
O'Kelly, S. Nan Hogan's house
Pirandello, L. A challenge
Rhys, J. Outside the machine
Rhys, J. Rapunzel, Rapunzel
Roth, H. H. This time
Schwartz, L. S. The wrath-bearing tree
Stafford, J. The interior castle
Thomas, J. My journal as the fishwoman
Tuohy, F. A reprieve
Tuohy, F. A special relationship
Updike, J. The city
Vanderhaeghe, G. A taste for perfection
Verma, N. The dead and the dying

Verma, N. The difference
Viola, A. Excerpts from Sunnyview journal
Weaver, G. Flowers: memento mori
Welch, D. Leaves from a young person's
    notebook
West, J. I'll ask him to come sooner
Wilbur, E. Wind and birds and human
    voices
Williams, W. C. Jean Beicke
Wilner, H. Consultations
Wilner, H. In my roommate's room
Wilner, H. Lead
Wilner, H. St. Denis
Wilner, H. Ward action
Wilner, H. Whitestone & Greenberg
Wolitzer, H. Mother
Zhang Jie. Under the hawthorn
Zhang Jie. An unfinished record
Hostage. Banks, R.
HOSTAGES
Harris, H. Detective's wife
Ioannides, P. Gregory
Pritchett, M. Fashion in the Third World
Spillane, M. Tomorrow I die
Waugh, E. The man who liked Dickens
Hostages. Mooney, M.
Hostages. Zwicky, F.
Hostess. Asimov, I.
Hostess. Mangum, D.
Hot. Mort, J.
Hot air pilot. Ritchie, J.
Hot and cold. Piñera, V.
Hot as a pistol. Wilson, K.
Hot-collared mule. Stuart, J.
A **hot** day in Nuevo Laredo. Swados, H.
Hot day on the Gold Coast. Shacochis, B.
Hot dogs and the Sox. Klinkowitz, J.
Hot eyes, cold eyes. Block, L.
Hot ice. Dybek, S.
Hot night homicide. Arden, W.
Le **Hot** Sport. Lafferty, R. A.
HOT SPRINGS
Johnston, S. Jesse and Louise
Hot water. Woolrich, C.
The **hotel**. Hébert, L.-P.
Hotel. Parise, G.
The **hotel**. Singer, I. B.
Hotel. Swift, G.
Hotel des Boobs. Lodge, D.
Hotel Joy. Faik, S.
The **hotel-keeper's** story. Stead, C.
Hotel mind slaves. Cross, R. A.
A **hotel** on Broadwalk. Gibson, S.
Hotel Savoy. Roth, J.
HOTELS, TAVERNS, ETC.
Adams, A. La Señora
Adams, G. G. A small hotel
Aickman, R. The hospice
Algren, N. The face on the barroom floor
Ariyoshi, S. The Tomoshibi
Balzac, H. de. The red inn
Bankier, W. One clear sweet clue
Bell, M. S. Zero db

HOTELS, TAVERNS, ETC.—*Continued*

Bloch, R. Impractical joker
Böll, H. Drinking in Petöcki
Brondoli, M. Coldbeer at the Only
Brondoli, M. Showdown
Brown, G. M. The chamber of poetry
Burns, M. After hours
Cain, J. M. Two o'clock blonde
Campbell, W. B. Moose
Carter, M. Teacher
Carver, R. Gazebo
Chappell, F. Blue dive
Chesterton, G. K. The two taverns
Christman, R. The Mai-Loan and the man who could fly
Codrescu, A. A bar in Brooklyn
Colette. The Sémiramis bar
Colter, C. An untold story
Coppard, A. E. Dusky Ruth
Crane, S. The blue hotel
Crane, S. The third violet
Crane, S. Twelve o'clock
Cullen, E. J. Better bars and garden
Daniels, C. The story of uneasy rider
Davie, E. The stamp
Davie, E. A traveller's room
Davis, C. The boys in the bars
Dickens, C. The bagman's story
Dickens, C. Mr. Testator's visitation
Dunn, D. A night out at the Club Harmonica
Faik, S. Hotel Joy
Federspiel, J. The Monderau chronicle
Flaherty, G. The main chance
Flores, C. N. Yellow flowers
Fox, W. P. You don't smell it: you drink it
Fritch, C. E. The curse of Hooligan's Bar
Garrett, G. P. Love is a cold kingdom
Gilbert, W. S. Creatures of impulse
Gotthelf, J. How Christen wins a bride
Hannah, B. Fans
Haris, P. A young man's dance
Hébert, L.-P. The hotel
Hemingway, E. An Alpine idyll
Hemingway, E. A man of the world
Henley, P. Friday night at Silver Star
Henry, O. The lost blend
Henry, O. The octopus marooned
Highsmith, P. Notes from a respectable cockroach
Hill, J. The malachite beads
Jeffrey, W. A case for quiet
Kawabata, Y. Harbor town
Kercheval, J. L. Underground women
Kinsella, W. P. King of the street
Klíma, I. My country
Lawson, H. Shooting the moon
Lurie, M. American shoes
Lurie, M. A social life
Lynch, L. At a bar I: The Jersey dyke
Lynch, L. At a bar II: In the morning
Lynch, L. At a bar IV: White wine

Lynch, L. At a bar V: Summer storm
Lynch, L. At a bar VI: Winter sun
Lynch, L. At a bar VIII: The long slow-burning fuse
Lynch, L. At a bar IX: Halloween
MacDougall, C. A small hotel
McKinley, J. Chambers
Meinke, P. Even crazy old barmaids need love
Moorhouse, F. The New York bell captain
O'Brien, E. In the hours of darkness
O'Hara, J. Olive
Pallant, C. A neighborhood bar
Pavese, C. Misogyny
Peterson, M. Like boats
Petrakis, H. M. The ballad of Daphne and Apollo
Petrakis, H. M. Pericles on 31st Street
Pierce, C. Chez les petits suisses
Pohl, F. The kindly isle
Power, V. Night
Pronzini, B. A case for quiet
Pronzini, B. A dip in the Poole
Rabelais, F. Gargantua and pantagruel [excerpt]
Raphael, F. Forgetting it
Rees, D. In the fast lane
Regent, P. Mr. Parsley's lunchtime pursuit
Rhys, J. Tigers are better-looking
Robinson, S. Fivesight
Rossi, A. Working
Roth, J. Hotel Savoy
Sampson, J. Qazia and a ferret-fetch
Sanford, W. M. The forest fire
Sharat Chandra, G. S. Iyer's Hotel
Sheehan, R. Optics
Sheehan, R. Telescope
Silverberg, R. Multiples
Silverberg, R. The regulars
Somers, A. The burial
Spark, M. The ormolu clock
St. Pierre, P. H. Cabin fever
Stead, C. The hotel-keeper's story
Stead, C. The woman in the bed
Swift, G. Hotel
Taylor, A. Old mates
Taylor, A. Pa mai
Tem, S. R. Bloodwolf
Tem, S. R. The men & women of Rivendale
Thomas, D. Old Garbo
Thompson, S. The Don
Trevor, W. Beyond the pale
Tuohy, F. Thunderbolt
Updike, D. Social studies
Van Greenaway, P. A western
Vogan, S. No other women
Walter, E. Christmas night
West, J. Gallup Poll
Williams, B. The lovers
Wolfe, G. Checking out
Woodman, A. Vinyl repair

HOTELS, TAVERNS, ETC.—*Continued*
  Woolrich, C. The room with something
    wrong
  Yarbro, C. Q. Cabin 33
  Ziem, J. Clarifications
Hothouse. Aldiss, B. W.
HOTLINES (TELEPHONE COUNSELING)
  Tabucchi, A. Voices
The **hotter** flash. Jeppson, J. O.
Houbein, Lolo
  The basement of happiness
    Houbein, L. Everything is real
  Child of two sisters
    Houbein, L. Everything is real
  Every poet's pipe-dream
    Houbein, L. Everything is real
  Everything is real
    Houbein, L. Everything is real
  Fighting for peace
    Houbein, L. Everything is real
  Footprints of Maria
    Houbein, L. Everything is real
  Green marmalade
    Houbein, L. Everything is real
  Having it both ways
    Houbein, L. Everything is real
  I shall live until I die
    Houbein, L. Everything is real
  Magic of this moment
    Houbein, L. Everything is real
  The marriage of the beautiful lady who
    had a mind of her own
    Houbein, L. Everything is real
  No stranger
    Houbein, L. Everything is real
  Not without rain
    Houbein, L. Everything is real
  Reluctant revolutionaries
    Houbein, L. Everything is real
  Round trip
    Houbein, L. Everything is real
  The serene revolution
    Houbein, L. Everything is real
  A serious courtship
    Houbein, L. Everything is real
  The sixth sense
    Houbein, L. Everything is real
  Survival switch
    Houbein, L. Everything is real
  Talking to the dark
    Houbein, L. Everything is real
  Three good reasons
    Houbein, L. Everything is real
HOUDINI, HARRY, 1874-1926
                About
  Willis, C. Substitution trick
Houdini's wife. Adams, G. G.
The **hound**. Lovecraft, H. P.
The **hounds** of youth. Rawls, W.
The **hour** after Westerly. Coates, R. M.
Hour of the beast. Bedard, B.
The **hour** of the ungovernable. Covino, M.
The **house**. Cowan, P.

The **house**. Fleutiaux, P.
The **house**. Maurois, A.
House. Walwicz, A.
House arrest. Larson, E.
The **house** by the ferris. Hoch, E. D.
The **house** by the moat. Shiga, N.
House call. Browne, H.
House call. Collins, M. A.
House call. Pronzini, B.
A **house** divided. Holleran, A.
A **house** divided. Walton, D.
The **house** friend. Singer, I. B.
A **house** full of Maude. McElroy, C. J.

House furniture. See Poe, E. A. The philoso-
    phy of furniture
House hunting. Oates, J. C.
The **house** in Goblin Wood. Carr, J. D.
House mothers. Williamson, J. N.
The **house** of being. Colasanti, M.
House of bones. Silverberg, R.
The **house** of crime. McConnor, V.
The **House** of Darkness. Queen, E.
The **house** of fear. Carrington, L.
The **house** of funerals. Scott, L.
The **House** of Hands. Inoue, M.
House of heroes. La Chapelle, M.
The **house** of if. Longyear, B. B.
House of joy. Šmahelová, H.
The **House** of Kaa. Sale, R.
The **house** of my dreams. O'Brien, E.
The **House** of offence. Austin, M. H.
The **house** of pride. London, J.
The **house** of sounds. Shiel, M. P.
The **house** of sugar. Ocampo, S.
The **house** of the beehives. Calvino, I.
House of the blue woman. Osborn, C.
The **house** of the famous poet. Spark, M.
The **house** of the far and lost. Wolfe, T.
The **house** of the nightmare. White, E. L.
The **House** of the Twin Jewels. Feyrer, G.
A **house** of women. Plante, D.
The **house** on Lafayette Street. Nayman, M.
The **house** on Plymouth Street. Curtiss, U.
    R.
The **house** on the hill. Pilcher, R.
House opposite. Narayan, R. K.
The **house** plans. Davis, L.
House poison. Fraser, A.
The **house** sitter. Robison, J.
House taken over. Cortázar, J.
The **house** that Jack built. Wellen, E.
The **house** that knew no hate. Salmonson,
    J. A.
The **house** that was. Futrelle, J.
House—with ghost. Derleth, A. W.

Household, Geoffrey, 1900-1988

  Taboo
    The Penguin book of horror stories
Household. Engberg, S.
Household. Kawabata, Y.
A **household**. Stead, C.

HOUSEHOLD EMPLOYEES
        See also Butlers; Cooks; Hired men;
    Hired women; Housekeepers; Maids
    (Servants); Nursemaids; Valets
Household expenses. Morgan, S.
Householder. Skelton, R.
The **housekeeper.** Burk, R.
Housekeeper. Grau, S. A.
The **housekeeper.** Pritchard, M.

HOUSEKEEPERS
    Beattie, A. Heaven on a summer night
    Blythe, R. Dear dead Pippa
    Burk, R. The housekeeper
    Carver, R. Fever
    Davis, D. S. Mrs. Norris observes
    Dunn, D. Something for little Robert
    Gilliatt, P. F.R.A.N.K.
    Grau, S. A. Housekeeper
    Hartley, L. P. The corner cupboard
    Huggan, I. Queen Esther
    Kang, S.-J. Another Eve
    King, F. H. I lived for you
    McLaverty, M. The priest's housekeeper
    Powers, J. F. The valiant woman
    Pritchard, M. The housekeeper
    Raphael, F. On the black list
    Spark, M. Another pair of hands
    Spingarn, L. P. Ingermann
    Tuohy, F. The license
    Warner, S. T. One thing leading to
        another
    Wolfe, T. 'E: a recollection
Housekeeping. Asscher-Pinkhof, C.
The **housemaid.** Davis, L.
HOUSEMAIDS *See* Maids (Servants)
Houseraising. Allen, J. C.

HOUSES
        See also Apartment houses; Summer
    homes
    Bail, M. Home ownership
    Bates, H. E. The evolution of Saxby
    Beattie, A. Lofty
    Bellow, S. Leaving the yellow house
    Bilenkin, D. The genius house
    Blei, N. Dwelling
    Blythe, R. Immediate possession
    Botwinik, B. Rivals
    Bradbury, R. Trapdoor
    Buchan, J. Fullcircle
    Burrage, A. M. Smee
    Cable, G. W. Belles Demoiselles plantation
    Calvino, I. The Argentine ant
    Calvino, I. The house of the beehives
    Canin, E. Where we are now
    Clark, E. Hurry, hurry
    Cortázar, J. House taken over
    Cowan, P. The house
    Curtiss, U. R. The house on Plymouth
        Street
    Davis, L. The house plans
    Dundas, R. Booker's End
    Fahy, C. The glow of copper
    Ferrara, P. Rising waters

    Finney, J. Where the Cluetts are
    Greenwood, R. Seed grain
    Haley, R. Real illusions
    Halligan, M. The oak bed
    Hartley, L. P. Two for the river
    Heise, K. The addition to Aunt Ella's
        house
    Highsmith, P. The black house
    Hornung, E. W. The rest cure
    Hornung, E. W. The spoils of sacrilege
    Humphrey, W. The Hardys
    Jackson, S. The lovely house
    Jolley, E. Mr. Parker's valentine
    Keillor, G. High rise
    Kessler, J. F. Perceval
    Klein, T. E. D. Petey
    Leman, B. Window
    Lovecraft, H. P. The shunned house
    MacDonald, D. R. Eyestone
    Melville, H. The piazza
    Muschg, A. The country house; or, Defaul-
        ted presence
    O'Brien, F.-J. The lost room
    O'Kelly, S. Nan Hogan's house
    Onions, O. The rope in the rafters
    Poe, E. A. The fall of the House of Usher
    Reamy, T. Insects in amber
    Rifaat, A. My world of the unknown
    Robison, J. Set off
    Roche, S. Structurally sound
    Rooke, L. Break and enter
    Russ, J. Nor custom stale
    Sandel, C. The sisters
    Sexson, L. Chalk line
    Shaw, H. The gipsies
    Shiel, M. P. The house of sounds
    Spark, M. The house of the famous poet
    Stafford, J. The liberation
    Thomas, D. Brember
    Tuttle, L. Bug house
    Welch, D. A picture in the snow
    Wells, H. G. The red room
    Wright, T. M. A world without toys
HOUSES, DESERTED *See* Deserted houses
The **houses** of the city. Berriault, G.
Housesitting. Krist, G.
The **housewife.** Jhabvala, R. P.
The **housing** correspondence of prisoner
    number 100293/8. Hirsch, G.

HOUSING PROJECTS *See* Public housing
Houston, Robert, 1940-
    Lawfully
        The Bread Loaf anthology of contem-
        porary American short stories; ed. by
        R. Pack and J. Parini

HOUSTON (TEX.) *See* Texas—Houston
Houston, Houston, do you read? Tiptree, J.
How?. Ignatow, R. G.
How. Moore, L.
How beautiful with shoes. Steele, W. D.
How big the world is. Klass, P.
How birds sleep. Rose, D. A.

How can Herod bear the light. Asscher-Pinkhof, C.

How can I tell you? O'Hara, J.

How can she get along without me? Gerber, M. J.

How Celia changed her mind. Cooke, R. T.

How Christen wins a bride. Gotthelf, J.

How come my dog don't bark? Goulart, R.

How do you do? May I marry you? Clayton, S.

How does your garden grow? Christie, A.

How Dorothy kept away the spring. Russ, J.

How Esco Mize got religion. McCulla, J.

How far she went. Hood, M.

How Father Grinch stole Christmas. Greeley, A. M.

How he does it. Clarke, A. C.

How he got the Legion of Honor. Maupassant, G. de

How I became a holy mother. Jhabvala, R. P.

How I became a Jew. Blaise, C.

How I became a jeweler. Weinstein, L.

How I became a shadow. Purdy, J.

How I contemplated the world from the Detroit House of Correction and began my life over again. Oates, J. C.

How I found my brother. Baxter, C.

How I found the superman. Chesterton, G. K.

How I kept our house while my husband was away. Pak, W.-S.

How I learned to raise the dead of Bergen County. Krist, G.

How I lived and how I died. Piñera, V.

How I met Idi at the Bassi Dakaru restaurant. McKnight, R.

How I missed the million dollar round table. Kinsella, W. P.

How it happened. Asimov, I.

How it happened. Burns, M.

How it happens. McGarry, J.

How J. B. Hartley saw his father. Hall, J. B.

How Joggeli finds a wife: a country tale. Gotthelf, J.

How Krabat lost Smjala. Brězan, J.

How like a god. Bloch, R.

How love came to Professor Guildea. Hichens, R.

How many boys? Kauffman, J.

How many miles to Babylon? Norton, A.

How Mickey made it. Phillips, J. A.

How Mr. Hogan robbed a bank. Steinbeck, J.

How much can a man bear? Jia Pingwa

How much money did you make today, little man? Winters, J.

How one woman kept her husband. Jackson, H. H.

How Pearl Button was kidnapped. Mansfield, K.

How "Pink" was reformed. Ade, G.

How poetry came into the world and why God doesn't write it. Willard, N.

How some people feel about Jesus. Cullen, E. J.

How spoilers bleed. Barker, C.

How Stonewall came back. Bellah, J. W.

How the barber finally got himself into a fable. Saroyan, W.

How the corn came. Austin, M. H.

How the crab apple grew. Keillor, G.

How the Devil came down Division Street. Algren, N.

How the jungle soldiers became sons of heaven. Claudius, E.

How the monkey lost the fruit of his labor. Cabrera, L.

How the old man died. Ferron, J.

How the story ends. Vanderhaeghe, G.

How the two Ivans quarreled. See Gogol', N. V. The tale of how Ivan Ivanovich quarreled with Ivan Nikiforovich

How the wind spoke at Madaket. Shepard, L.

How they pass the time in Pelpel. Silverberg, R.

How things are put together. Burns, C.

How time has flown. Nowakowski, M.

How to be an other woman. Moore, L.

How to become a writer. Moore, L.

How to bury a dog. Olmstead, R.

How to choose a wife. Saroyan, W.

How to fix a roof. Wilson, B.

How to impress an editor. Pohl, F.

How to live alone. Frucht, A.

How to make major scientific discoveries at home in your spare time. Sladek, J. T.

How to quit smoking. Giles, M.

How to run the country. St. Pierre, P. H.

How to sound like an expert. Benford, G.

How to start a pharmaceuticals business. Carrington, L.

How to talk to your mother (notes). Moore, L.

How to tell a true war story. O'Brien, T.

How to write a Blackwood article. Poe, E. A.

How to write a novel. Lish, G.

How to write a poem. Lish, G.

How Wang-Fo was saved. Yourcenar, M.

How we saved the human race. Gerrold, D.

How you play the game. Baumbach, J.

Howard, Clark

Animals
    The Year's best mystery & suspense stories, 1986

Custer's ghost
    The Year's best mystery and suspense stories, 1984

Howard, Clark—*Continued*
The Dublin eye
Ellery Queen's Prime crimes 2
The Year's best mystery and suspense stories, 1985
Enough rope for two
Hitchcock in prime time; ed. by F. M. Nevins and M. H. Greenberg
Horn man
The Black Lizard anthology of crime fiction; ed. by E. Gorman
The Deadly arts; ed. by B. Pronzini and M. Muller
Last chance in Singapore
Distant danger; ed. by J. Van de Wetering
The last revival
Alfred Hitchcock's Mortal errors
New Orleans getaway
Tales from Ellery Queen's Mystery Magazine: short stories for young adults
Return to the OK Corral
Tales from Ellery Queen's Mystery Magazine: short stories for young adults
Scalplock
The Year's best mystery and suspense stories, 1987
Spook house
The Wickedest show on earth; ed. by M. Muller and B. Pronzini

Howard, Hayden
The dipping of the candlemaker
Murder and mystery in Boston; ed. by C. L. R. Waugh; F. D. McSherry and M. H. Greenberg

Howard, Marghanita Laski *See* Laski, Marghanita, 1915-1988

Howard, Robert Ervin, 1906-1936
The people of the Black Circle
Wizards; ed. by I. Asimov; M. H. Greenberg and C. G. Waugh
Red nails
Baker's dozen: 13 short fantasy novels

Howard, Volney E.
The midnight voyage of the Seagull
Yankee witches; ed. by C. G. Waugh; M. H. Greenberg and F. D. McSherry

Howard an Monroe. Hiles, R.
Howdy Doody is dead. White, C.
Howdy Doody time. Sams, F.

Howe, Fanny
The Ruth tractate
American made; ed. by M. Leyner; C. White and T. Glynn

Howell, Carol
The part-timer
The North American Review 272:24-32 Mr '87

Howell, Carol Cosek
The mother-daughter cookbook
Redbook 167:44+ S '86

Howes, Craig
The resurrection man
Passages to the dream shore; ed. by F. Stewart

How's your mother? Brett, S.

Hoyle, Fred
Blackmail
Great science fiction; ed. by I. Asimov; M. H. Greenberg and C. G. Waugh
The magnetosphere
Science Digest 93:70-1+ Ja '85

Hoyt, Myron S.
Buffalo, sun and strawberries
Hoyt, M. S. Rainbow, river & tree
Clay songs
Hoyt, M. S. Rainbow, river & tree
The flowers at Anat Qesh
Hoyt, M. S. Rainbow, river & tree
An island of curving stone
Hoyt, M. S. Rainbow, river & tree
Lyrical voices
Hoyt, M. S. Rainbow, river & tree
The manuscript
Hoyt, M. S. Rainbow, river & tree
The monastery floor
Hoyt, M. S. Rainbow, river & tree
Park taxi
Hoyt, M. S. Rainbow, river & tree
The peg
Hoyt, M. S. Rainbow, river & tree
The pool
Hoyt, M. S. Rainbow, river & tree
The river giantess
Hoyt, M. S. Rainbow, river & tree
Small suns
Hoyt, M. S. Rainbow, river & tree
Tree
Hoyt, M. S. Rainbow, river & tree
The wind wizard
Hoyt, M. S. Rainbow, river & tree

Hoyt, Richard, 1941-
Private investigations
The Eyes have it; ed. by R. J. Randisi

Hsiu, Hsiu
The trap
Short story international 54

Huang, Chun-ming
I love Mary
The Unbroken chain; ed. by J. S. M. Lau

Huang Qingyun
Annals of a fossil
Roses and thorns; ed. by P. Link

Hub. Herring, R.

Hubbard, P. M. (Philip Maitland), 1910-1980
Mary
The Mammoth book of modern crime stories; ed. by G. Hardinge

Hubbard, Philip Maitland *See* Hubbard, P. M. (Philip Maitland), 1910-1980

Hubbard Squash. Bedard, B.
Huby falling. Barstow, S.

Huddle, David, 1942-
Apache
  The Bread Loaf anthology of contemporary American short stories; ed. by R. Pack and J. Parini
The crossing
  Prairie Schooner 62:42-7 Spr '88
Summer of the magic show
  New stories from the South: the year's best, 1986
Hudec, Goran
The ring
  The Penguin world omnibus of science fiction
Hudson, Helen
A daughter's duty
  Redbook 169:31-2+ Ag '87
Hudson, W. H. (William Henry), 1841-1922
The story of a piebald horse
  The Treasury of English short stories; ed. by N. Sullivan
Hudson, William Henry *See* Hudson, W. H. (William Henry), 1841-1922
Huebler. Bail, M.
Huff, T. S.
What little girls are made of
  Magic in Ithkar 3; ed. by A. Norton and R. Adams
Huggan, Isabel, 1943-
Celia behind me
  Huggan, I. The Elizabeth stories
Getting out of Garten
  Huggan, I. The Elizabeth stories
Into the green stillness
  Huggan, I. The Elizabeth stories
Jack of hearts
  Huggan, I. The Elizabeth stories
Queen Esther
  Huggan, I. The Elizabeth stories
Sawdust
  Huggan, I. The Elizabeth stories
Secrets
  Huggan, I. The Elizabeth stories
Sorrows of the flesh
  Huggan, I. The Elizabeth stories
Hugh. Freeman, A. H.
Hugh Merrow. James, H.
Hughes, Dorothy Belle Flanagan, 1904-
Everybody needs a mink
  Uncollected crimes; ed. by B. Pronzini and M. H. Greenberg
Sherlock Holmes and the muffin
  The New adventures of Sherlock Holmes; ed. by M. H. Greenberg and C. L. R. Waugh
The spotted pup
  Murder and mystery in Chicago; ed. by C. R. Waugh; F. D. McSherry and M. H. Greenberg
Hughes, Edward James *See* Hughes, Ted, 1930-

Hughes, Fielden
'Dear ghost . . .'
  The Penguin book of ghost stories
Hughes, James
An open house
  Mississippi writers v1: Fiction; ed. by D. Abbott
Hughes, Langston, 1902-1967
Slave on the block
  The Norton book of American short stories
Thank you, m'am
  Sudden fiction; ed. by R. Shapard and J. Thomas
Hughes, Lucinda
Western women are tough
  The Virginia Quarterly Review 60:242-54 Spr '84
Hughes, Mary Gray
The stuttering priest
  Editor's choice II; ed. by M. Sklar and M. Biggs
Hughes, Monica
The singing float
  Dragons and dreams; ed. by J. Yolen; M. H. Greenberg and C. G. Waugh
Hughes, Ted, 1930-
The rain horse
  The Penguin book of modern British short stories
Hughes, Tom
This house and my home
  The Antioch Review 44:416-23 Fall '86
Hugo, Victor, 1802-1885
A wild cannon dooms the Claymore
  Men at sea; ed. by B. Aymar
Hugo. MacLaverty, B.
The Hulk. Wilson, B.
Hull, Helen R.
Alley ways
  Hull, H. R. Last September
Discovery
  Hull, H. R. Last September
The fire
  Between mothers & daughters; ed. by S. Koppelman
  Hull, H. R. Last September
The fusing
  Hull, H. R. Last September
Groping
  Hull, H. R. Last September
Last September
  Hull, H. R. Last September
Separation
  Hull, H. R. Last September
Hulme, Keri
The cicadas of summer
  Hulme, K. Te Kaihau: the windeater
A drift in dream
  Hulme, K. Te Kaihau: the windeater
He tauware kawa, he kawa tauware
  Hulme, K. Te Kaihau: the windeater

Hulme, Keri—*Continued*
Hooks and feelers
  Hulme, K. Te Kaihau: the windeater
Kaibutsu-san
  Hulme, K. Te Kaihau: the windeater
King bait
  Hulme, K. Te Kaihau: the windeater
Kiteflying party at Doctors' Point
  Hulme, K. Te Kaihau: the windeater
  Women's work; ed. by M. McLeod and
    L. Wevers
The knife and the stone
  Hulme, K. Te Kaihau: the windeater
A nightsong for the shining cuckoo
  Hulme, K. Te Kaihau: the windeater
One whale, singing
  Hulme, K. Te Kaihau: the windeater
  Through other eyes; ed. by I. Zahava
  Women's work; ed. by M. McLeod and
    L. Wevers
Planetesimal
  Hulme, K. Te Kaihau: the windeater
Stations on the way to Avalon
  Hulme, K. Te Kaihau: the windeater
Swansong
  Hulme, K. Te Kaihau: the windeater
A tally of the souls of sheep
  Hulme, K. Te Kaihau: the windeater
Te Kaihau: the windeater
  Hulme, K. Te Kaihau: the windeater
Unnamed islands in the unknown sea
  Hulme, K. Te Kaihau: the windeater
While my guitar gently sings
  Hulme, K. Te Kaihau: the windeater
A window drunken in the brain
  Hulme, K. Te Kaihau: the windeater
The **human** angle. Tenn, W.
Human ashes. Oda, K.
The **human** fly. Humphrey, W.
Human moments in World War III. DeLillo,
  D.
Human remains. Barker, C.
Human repetends. Clarke, M.
HUMAN SACRIFICE *See* Sacrifice, Human
Humiliation. Maupassant, G. de
Humming. Boucher, S.
The **hummingbird** kimono. Gingher, M.
HUMOR
          See also Parodies; Practical jokes;
  Satire
Abbott, L. K. A modern story of Woe and
  Lovecraft
Alexan, J. The locusts
Allen, W. Count Dracula
Anthony, P. Up Schist Crick
Arthur, R. The haunted trailer
Asimov, I. How it happened
Asimov, I. I'm in Marsport without Hilda
Asimov, I. Jokester
Asimov, I. Paté de foie gras
Astley, T. Seeing Mrs. Landers
Avery, M. The Komedy Kabaret
Babbitt, N. Simple sentences

Baldwin, J. G. Samuel Hele, Esq.
Barr, J. G. John Bealle's accident—or,
  How the widow Dudu treated insanity
Barrett, N., Jr. Perpetuity blues
Barthelme, D. The king of jazz
Bates, H. E. A funny thing
Bates, H. E. The revelation
Belloc, H. Home
Botwinik, B. The boarder
Botwinik, B. Esperanto
Bower, B. M. When the cook fell ill
Boyle, T. C. I dated Jane Austen
Brautigan, R. 1/3, 1/3, 1/3
Brautigan, R. Revenge of the lawn
Brown, F. Hobbyist
Burkert, R. The stone inscription of Caleb
  Pellor
Busby, F. M. Once upon a unicorn
Butler, E. P. Getting rid of Fluff
Caldwell, E. The courting of Susie Brown
Calvino, I. Autumn: the garden of stub-
  born cats
Cooper, J. C. Spooks
Crane, S. The carriage-lamps
Crane, S. The knife
Crane, S. Lynx-hunting
De Camp, L. S. Divide and rule
Dixon, S. Milk is very good for you
Doyle, Sir A. C. The heiress of Glen-
  mahowley
Doyle, Sir A. C. The Parish Magazine
Doyle, Sir A. C. Selecting a ghost. The
  ghosts of Goresthorpe Grange
Dozois, G. R., and others. Afternoon at
  Schrafft's
Dunn, D. Getting used to it
Ellison, H. Prince Myshkin, and hold the
  relish
Fairman, P. W. The dark road home
Ferguson, N. The Monroe Doctrine
Fox, W. P. Doug Broome, hamburger king
Franzen, B. 37 years
Franzen, B. The Gene Norman Collection
Franzen, B. The long donut hole
Franzen, B. Mom and Pop biz
Franzen, B. Peacekeeper
Gardner, C. S. Demon luck
Gardner, M. The horse on the escalator
Gardner, M. Ranklin Felano Doosevelt
Goulart, R. How come my dog don't
  bark?
Greene, G. The root of all evil
Grizzard, L. Good men of God
Harrington, J. Dispatching Bootsie
Harrison, H. The view from the top of
  the tower
Hays, D. The Dixie Association [excerpt]
Henry, O. The cop and the anthem
Henry, O. Lost on dress parade
Henry, O. Mammon and the archer
Henry, O. A service of love
Hooper, J. J. Fighting the "tiger" and
  other speculations

HUMOR—*Continued*

Humphrey, W. The rainmaker
Izgü, M. The attack by yoghurt
Janowitz, T. You and The Boss
Kawabata, Y. Lavatory Buddahood
Kinsella, W. P. The bear went over the mountain
Kinsella, W. P. Dancing
Kinsella, W. P. The Indian Nation Cultural Exchange Program
Kinsella, W. P. The managers
Kinsella, W. P. The performance
Kinsella, W. P. Real Indians
Kinsella, W. P. The truck
Kinsella, W. P. Truth
Law, W. Lincoln's doctor's son's dog
Lawson, H. The loaded dog
Leacock, S. B. The marine excursion of the Knights of Pythias
Lish, G. The friend
Lish, G. I'm wide
London, J. The one thousand dozen
Lurie, M. A king of the road
Lutz, J. The butcher, the baker
Marquis, D. Blood will tell
Matheson, R. C. Sentences
Melville, H. I and my chimney
Montgomery, M. I got a gal
Moorcock, M. Elric at the end of time
Nicol, A. The truly married woman
Nowakowski, M. The confidential call
O'Connor, F. The drunkard
Pearson, T. R. A short history of a small place [excerpt]
Pilcher, R. An evening to remember
Poe, E. A. King Pest
Poe, E. A. Loss of breath
Poe, E. A. Why the little Frenchman wears his hand in a sling
Poe, E. A. 'X-ing a paragrab'
Pulaski, J. Father of the bride
Ríos, A. La boda
Roiter, H. Only Sam knows
Rosenfeld, I. The misfortunes of the Flapjacks
Rule, J. A chair for George
Rule, J. A migrant Christmas
Rule, J. Musical beds
Rule, J. Seaweed and song
Rule, J. You cannot judge a pumpkin's happiness by the smile upon his face
Runyon, D. The idyll of Miss Sarah Brown
Saki. Laura
Saki. The philanthropist and the happy cat
Saki. Tobermory
Sams, F. Run with the horsemen [excerpt]
Sayles, J. At the anarchists' convention
Schulberg, B. Señor Discretion himself
Shacochis, B. Hot day on the Gold Coast
Sheckley, R. The demons
Sholem Aleichem. The automatic exemption

Sholem Aleichem. Baranovich Station
Sholem Aleichem. Burned out
Sholem Aleichem. Chava
Sholem Aleichem. Competitors
Sholem Aleichem. Eighteen from Pereshchepena
Sholem Aleichem. Elul
Sholem Aleichem. Fated for misfortune
Sholem Aleichem. A game of sixty-six
Sholem Aleichem. Go climb a tree if you don't like it
Sholem Aleichem. The happiest man in all Kodny
Sholem Aleichem. Hard luck
Sholem Aleichem. High school
Sholem Aleichem. Lekh-lekho
Sholem Aleichem. The man from Buenos Aires
Sholem Aleichem. The miracle of Hoshana Rabbah
Sholem Aleichem. Rabchik, a Jewish dog
Sholem Aleichem. Shprintze
Sholem Aleichem. The slowpoke express
Sholem Aleichem. The tallis koton
Sholem Aleichem. Tevye blows a small fortune
Sholem Aleichem. Tevye leaves for the land of Israel
Sholem Aleichem. Tevye strikes it rich
Sholem Aleichem. Third class
Sholem Aleichem. Today's children
Sholem Aleichem. The wedding that came without its band
Silverberg, R. The Science Fiction Hall of Fame
Sorrells, R. T. The blacktop champion of Ickey Honey
Sorrentino, F. Ars poetica
Sorrentino, F. The fetid tale of Antulín
Sorrentino, F. The life of the party
Spark, M. The first year of my life
Stark, S. S. The Barlip run
Steadman, M. John Fletcher's night of love
Stewart, J. I. M. Napier into Ffinch
Thackeray, W. M. The devil's wager
Thompson, T. A wollopin' good chew
Thurber, J. The greatest man in the world
Thurber, J. The unicorn in the garden
Toole, J. K. A confederacy of dunces [excerpt]
Tracy, J. Spirit weather
Trevanian. The sacking of Miss Plimsoll
Twain, M. 3,000 years among the microbes
Twain, M. The canvasser's tale
Twain, M. The notorious jumping frog of Calaveras County
Van Greenaway, P. The immortal coil
Van Greenaway, P. Indefinite article
Volsky, P. The tenancy of Mr. Eex
Waldrop, H. The ugly chickens
Wells, H. G. The Hammerpond Park burglary

HUMOR—*Continued*

Welty, E. Why I live at the P.O.
Welty, E. The wide net
Wild, M. Tied in knots
Wilde, O. The Canterville ghost
Wodehouse, P. G. The artistic career of Corky
Wodehouse, P. G. Aunt Agatha takes the count
Wodehouse, P. G. The aunt and the sluggard
Wodehouse, P. G. Bertie changes his mind
Wodehouse, P. G. Bingo and the little woman
Wodehouse, P. G. Clustering round young Bingo
Wodehouse, P. G. Comrade Bingo
Wodehouse, P. G. The delayed exit of Claude and Eustace
Wodehouse, P. G. Episode of the dog McIntosh
Wodehouse, P. G. Fixing it for Freddie
Wodehouse, P. G. The go-getter
Wodehouse, P. G. The great sermon handicap
Wodehouse, P. G. Indian summer of an uncle
Wodehouse, P. G. The inferiority complex of old Sippy
Wodehouse, P. G. Jeeves and the Chump Cyril
Wodehouse, P. G. Jeeves and the greasy bird
Wodehouse, P. G. Jeeves and the hard-boiled egg
Wodehouse, P. G. Jeeves and the impending doom
Wodehouse, P. G. Jeeves and the kid Clementina
Wodehouse, P. G. Jeeves and the old school chum
Wodehouse, P. G. Jeeves and the song of songs
Wodehouse, P. G. Jeeves and the unbidden guest
Wodehouse, P. G. Jeeves and the Yule-tide spirit
Wodehouse, P. G. Jeeves in the springtime
Wodehouse, P. G. Jeeves makes an omelette
Wodehouse, P. G. Jeeves takes charge
Wodehouse, P. G. The love that purifies
Wodehouse, P. G. The Metropolitan touch
Wodehouse, P. G. Open house
Wodehouse, P. G. The ordeal of young Tuppy
Wodehouse, P. G. Pig-hoo-o-o-o-ey!
Wodehouse, P. G. The purity of the turf
Wodehouse, P. G. The rummy affair of old Biffy
Wodehouse, P. G. Scoring off Jeeves
Wodehouse, P. G. Sir Roderick comes to lunch
Wodehouse, P. G. The spot of art
Wodehouse, P. G. The story of Webster
Wodehouse, P. G. Ukridge's dog college
Wodehouse, P. G. Uncle Fred flits by
Wodehouse, P. G. Unpleasantness at Bludleigh Court
Wodehouse, P. G. Without the option
Woodman, A. The pleasure garden of the root vegetables
Woodman, A. The shoebox of desire

HUMOROUS STORIES *See* Humor

Humphrey, William

The ballad of Jesse Neighbours
　Humphrey, W. The collected stories of William Humphrey
Dolce far' niente
　Humphrey, W. The collected stories of William Humphrey
The fauve
　Humphrey, W. The collected stories of William Humphrey
A fresh snow
　Humphrey, W. The collected stories of William Humphrey
A good Indian
　Humphrey, W. The collected stories of William Humphrey
The Hardys
　Humphrey, W. The collected stories of William Humphrey
A home away from home
　Humphrey, W. The collected stories of William Humphrey
The human fly
　Humphrey, W. The collected stories of William Humphrey
In sickness and health
　Humphrey, W. The collected stories of William Humphrey
A job of the plains
　Humphrey, W. The collected stories of William Humphrey
The last husband
　Humphrey, W. The collected stories of William Humphrey
The last of the Caddoes
　Humphrey, W. The collected stories of William Humphrey
Man with a family
　Humphrey, W. The collected stories of William Humphrey
Mouth of brass
　Humphrey, W. The collected stories of William Humphrey
The patience of a saint
　Humphrey, W. The collected stories of William Humphrey
The pump
　Humphrey, W. The collected stories of William Humphrey
Quail for Mr. Forester
　Humphrey, W. The collected stories of William Humphrey

Humphrey, William—*Continued*
The rainmaker
  Humphrey, W. The collected stories of
    William Humphrey
Report cards
  Humphrey, W. The collected stories of
    William Humphrey
The shell
  Humphrey, W. The collected stories of
    William Humphrey
Sister
  Humphrey, W. The collected stories of
    William Humphrey
A voice from the woods
  Humphrey, W. The collected stories of
    William Humphrey
Humphreys, Josephine
Dreams of sleep [excerpt]
  The New writers of the South; ed. by
    C. East
Humphries, Jefferson, 1955-
The heretic
  Michigan Quarterly Review 24:584-7 Fall
    '85
Quincy
  Selected stories from The Southern
    review, 1965-1985
  The Southern Review (Baton Rouge, La.)
    21:512-21 Ap '85
Humphries, Jenny Stone
The make-believe ballroom
  The North American Review 270:16-19
    Je '85
The **hunchback** cat. Crispin, E.
Hunchback Madonna. Chavez, A.
The **hunchback** of Seoul. Kwon, T.-U.
HUNCHBACKS
  Day, R. C. Leaning man
  Kwon, T.-U. The hunchback of Seoul
  McCullers, C. The ballad of the sad café
  O'Brien, F.-J. The wondersmith
  West, J. Breach of promise
A **hundred** paths. Summers, H. S.
Hundred year war. Wetherell, W. D.
Huneven, Michelle
The foot
  Harper's 270:59-66 My '85
Hung jury. Ritchie, J.
Hungarian night. Morand, P.
HUNGARIANS
England
  Dorr, L. A D-minor fugue
  Swift, G. Gabor
United States
  Dorr, L. An early Christmas
  Dorr, L. The immigrant
  Dorr, L. Lazarus
  Dorr, L. Vladimir's kitchen
HUNGARY
20th century
  Dorr, L. Neither death nor life
  Dorr, L. The wedding anniversary
  Marosi, G. The milk-boy

World War, 1939-1945
  See World War, 1939-1945—
  Hungary
Budapest
  Gallant, M. His mother
  Oates, J. C. Old Budapest
  Rhys, J. Vienne
HUNGER
  See also Starvation
  Böll, H. The taste of bread
  Edkins, A. What's eating you?
  Gorky, M. One autumn evening
  Kang, K.-A. The underground village
  Liu, Q. The good luck bun
  Maupassant, G. de. A vagabond
Hunger. Asscher-Pinkhof, C.
Hunger. Parise, G.
Hunger. Rhys, J.
Hunger. Shacochis, B.
Hunger at Bévera. Calvino, I.
Hungerford, Hesba Brinsmead *See* Brins-
  mead, H. F. (Hesba Fay), 1922-
Hungerford, T. A. G. (Thomas Arthur Guy),
  1915-
Green grow the rushes
  The Australian short story; ed. by L.
    Hergenhan
Hungerford, Thomas Arthur Guy *See*
  Hungerford, T. A. G. (Thomas Arthur
  Guy), 1915-
HUNGERFORD (AUSTRALIA) *See* Austra-
  lia—Hungerford
Hungerford. Lawson, H.
Hungers. Crapser, W.
The **hungry** eye. Bloch, R.
The **hungry** girls. Eakins, P.
The **hungry** house. Bloch, R.
Hungry lion. Field, I.
A **hunk** of burning love. Camoin, F. A.
Hunktown. Mason, B. A.
Hunnewell, Elizabeth
Home from the war
  The Virginia Quarterly Review 61:681-90
    Aut '85
Hunnicutt, Ellen
All kinds of flowers
  Hunnicutt, E. In the music library
Amos
  Hunnicutt, E. In the music library
At St. Theresa's College for Women
  Hunnicutt, E. In the music library
Bargaining
  Hunnicutt, E. In the music library
The Bengal tiger
  Hunnicutt, E. In the music library
Bringing the news
  Hunnicutt, E. In the music library
Energy
  Hunnicutt, E. In the music library
A hidden thing
  Hunnicutt, E. In the music library
In the music library
  Hunnicutt, E. In the music library

Hunnicutt, Ellen—*Continued*
There is a balm in Gilead
  Hunnicutt, E. In the music library
When I was married
  Hunnicutt, E. In the music library
Hunt, Leigh, 1784-1859
The cat by the fire
  Roger Caras' Treasury of great cat stories
The **hunt**. Jolley, E.
Hunt the hunter. Neville, K.
Hunter, Evan, 1926-
  For works written by this author under other names see McBain, Ed, 1926-
The beatings
  Manhattan mysteries; ed. by B. Pronzini; C. L. R. Waugh and M. H. Greenberg
The fallen angel
  The Wickedest show on earth; ed. by M. Muller and B. Pronzini
The interview
  Mystery in the mainstream; ed. by B. Pronzini; M. H. Greenberg and B. N. Malzberg
The **hunter**. Doctorow, E. L.
Hunter. Grau, S. A.
The **hunter**. Littlebird, L.
HUNTERS *See* Hunting
The **hunters**. Miller, S.
Hunters. Ross, V.
Hunters in the fields of August. Kalpakian, L.
Hunters in the snow. Wolff, T.
Hunter's moon. Anderson, P.
HUNTING
  See also Duck hunting; Fox hunting; Trappers and trapping; Whaling
Aldiss, B. W. Poor little warrior!
Bates, H. E. The shooting party
Benson, R. H. The watcher
Block, L. Click!
Calvino, I. Man in the wasteland
Campbell, W. B. Moose
Carrington, L. The three hunters
Crane, S. Killing his bear
Cunningham, J. Decoys
Dabrowska, C. Huntress
Dabrowska, C. Red stag
Dorr, L. The wedding anniversary
Dunsany, E. J. M. D. P., Baron. In a dim room
Ford, R. Going to the dogs
Gordimer, N. A hunting accident
Grey, Z. The land of the wild musk-ox
Grey, Z. Roping lions in the Grand Canyon
Grey, Z. The wolf tracker
Grin, A. The window in the forest
Hemingway, E. An African story
Hemingway, E. Fathers and sons
Herring, R. Hub [excerpt]
Hitchcock, G. An invitation to the hunt
Hornung, E. W. The spoils of sacrilege

Humphrey, W. The shell
Kittredge, W. We are not in this together
Lee, T. Bright burning tiger
Lutz, J. The wounded tiger
Markham, B. The captain and his horse
Matthiessen, P. The wolves of Aguila
Maupassant, G. de. A cock crowed
Maupassant, G. de. The deaf-mute
Mazel, D. Choosing
McGuane, T. Flight
McGuane, T. Sportsmen
McGuane, T. Two hours to kill
Mrożek, S. The fall of an Eagle's Nest
Neville, K. Hunt the hunter
O'Connor, F. Wildcat
Olmstead, R. What to do first
Percy, W. The second coming [excerpt]
Ross, V. Hunters
Shepard, L. The jaguar hunter
Solensten, J. Two: a story of numbers
Waldrop, H. Fair game
Walsh, T. The killer instinct
Wodehouse, P. G. Unpleasantness at Bludleigh Court
Wolff, T. Hunters in the snow
Woolf, V. The shooting party
A **hunting** accident. Gordimer, N.
HUNTING ACCIDENTS
Blyton, C. The final solution
Dilworth, S. The seeney stretch
Hemingway, E. The short happy life of Francis Macomber
Hemingway, E. The snows of Kilimanjaro
Kittredge, W. The waterfowl tree
Olmstead, R. The boon
Quammen, D. Walking out
Hunting for hoot owls. West, J.
The **hunting** of Lord Etsalian's daughter. Bell, C.
Huntress. Dabrowska, C.
Huraniyyah, Sa'id
Another hard winter
  Modern Syrian short stories; ed. by M. G. Azrak
Hurd, Jerrie W.
Raising wild birds
  The Antioch Review 43:49-64 Wint '85
Hurdle. Anthony, P.
Hurricane Hazel. Atwood, M.
HURRICANES
Goyen, W. Precious door
Schwartz, J. Faith
Hurry, hurry. Clark, E.
Hurry, hurry, hurry! Gallico, P.
Hurry up and love me. Coates, R. A.
Hurst, Fannie, 1889-1968
The nth commandment
  "May your days be merry and bright" and other Christmas stories by women; ed. by S. Koppelman
Oats for the woman
  Between mothers & daughters; ed. by S. Koppelman

Hurston, Zora Neale, 1907-1960
Book of Harlem
　Hurston, Z. N. Spunk
Cock Robin Beale Street
　Hurston, Z. N. Spunk
The Eatonville anthology
　The Norton book of American short
　　stories
The gilded six-bits
　Hurston, Z. N. Spunk
　A Modern Southern reader; ed. by B.
　　Forkner and P. Samway
Herod on trial
　Hurston, Z. N. Spunk
Isis [Variant title: Drenched in light]
　Hurston, Z. N. Spunk
Muttsy
　Hurston, Z. N. Spunk
Spunk
　Hurston, Z. N. Spunk
Story in Harlem slang
　Hurston, Z. N. Spunk
Sweat
　Hurston, Z. N. Spunk
Hurting much? Woolrich, C.
Hurwood, Bernhardt J.
The vampire cat of Nabeshima
　Devils & demons; ed. by M. Kaye and
　　S. Kaye
Husain, Akhtar
Dejection
　Short story international 60
A **husband** and a father. Thompson, K.
A **husband** and a home of her own and nice
　things. Drake, R.
HUSBAND AND WIFE
　　See also Desertion and nonsupport;
　　Marriage
Abbott, L. K. Having the human thing of
　joy
Adams, G. G. Houdini's wife
Adams, G. G. The purchase of order
Ade, G. The fable of the honest money-
　maker and the partner of his joys,
　such as they were
Alcott, L. M. A pair of eyes; or, Modern
　magic
Algren, N. Stickman's laughter
Amis, M. Let me count the times
Anderman, J. Shabby lodgings
Andersen, B. The phone call
Andrić, I. Thirst
Ardizzone, T. The evening news
Asimov, I. Hostess
Asscher-Pinkhof, C. Island
Asscher-Pinkhof, C. Star wife
Astley, T. Seeing Mrs. Landers
Atwood, M. Scarlet ibis
Atwood, M. When it happens
Aymé, M. The state of grace
Ballantyne, S. Letters to the darkness
Ballantyne, S. Life on earth
Ballantyne, S. You are here

Barthelme, D. Affection
Barthelme, F. Gila Flambé
Barthelme, F. Parents
Bates, H. E. Elaine
Bates, H. E. The evolution of Saxby
Baumbach, J. Mother and father
Bausch, R. Spirits
Baxter, C. Saul and Patsy are getting com-
　fortable in Michigan
Baxter, C. Surprised by joy
Beasley, C. Blue oraciones
Benedict, D. Unknown feathers
Bernard, K. Bird-watching
Bernard, K. Walking
Blei, N. Dwelling
Bloch, R. His and hearse
Block, L. The dangerous business
Böll, H. And there was the evening and
　the morning . . .
Bonner, M. The prison-bound
Borgen, J. Song of stars
Botwinik, B. The radicals
Bowles, P. Call at Corazón
Bradbury, R. Come, and bring Constance!
Bradbury, R. A touch of petulance
Brennan, J. P. Rhea
Brigham, B. The lottery drawing
Briskin, M. Marshall in Rome
Brown, L. Facing the music
Bukoski, A. The happiness farm
Bukoski, A. I, Lillian
Bukoski, A. Route of the zephyrs
Burns, M. How it happened
Busch, F. Comrades
Camoin, F. A. Cheerful wisdom
Camus, A. The adulterous woman
Canin, E. We are nighttime travelers
Canin, E. Where we are now
Caponegro, M. Tales from the next village
Carlson, R. Half life
Carlson, R. Life before science
Carlson, R. Milk
Carlson, R. The time I died
Carlson, R. The uses of videotape
Carter, R. Sixties into eighties won't go
Carver, R. After the denim
Carver, R. Are these actual miles?
Carver, R. Feathers
Carver, R. Neighbors
Carver, R. The student's wife
Carver, R. Whoever was using this bed
Carver, W. With voice of joy and praise
Cary, J. New women
Casey, G. Short-shift Saturday
Castillo, R. C. The miracle
Chambers, G. March 11
Chavez, A. The bell that sang again
Chavez, A. The lean years
Cheever, J. The enormous radio
Cheever, J. The pot of gold
Chekhov, A. P. The party
Chipulina, E. G. Sirocco
Chipulina, E. G. Square peg, round hole

HUSBAND AND WIFE—*Continued*
Ch'oe, S. Point
Choyce, L. Dancing the night away
Claiborne, S. Okinawa's wife
Clark, M. A moment of illumination
Clark, M. "'Twere best not know myself"
Clarke, A. C. A man
Colette. "Châ"
Colette. In the flower of age
Colette. The other wife
Colette. The rainy moon
Collins, L. Driving back from the funeral
Colvin, C. All living things
Cook, H. Exodus
Coskran, K. An African river
Coskran, K. Facing Mount Kenya
Coskran, K. Natural causes
Courtois, P. J. The silent couple
Cowley, J. The silk
Crabtree, L. V. Holy Spirit
Crane, S. The bride comes to Yellow Sky
Curley, D. The inlet
Curtiss, U. R. Snowball
Davis, L. Visit to her husband
Dawson, F. The fourth surprise
Day, R. C. Relative motion
De Jong, D. Vagabundus Vinea
DeMarinis, R. The coming triumph of the free world
DeMarinis, R. Culture shocks
DeMarinis, R. The handgun
DeMarinis, R. Your burden is lifted, love returns
DeMarinis, R. Your story
Derleth, A. W. House—with ghost
Dodd, S. M. Public appearances
Drewitz, I. The news
Dubus, A. They now live in Texas
Ekström, M. Perfect
El-Bisatie, M. A conversation from the third floor
Eldridge, M. Chanson d'automne
Ellin, S. The orderly world of Mr. Appleby
Ellison, H. Do-it-yourself
Endō, S. A man sixty
Engberg, S. Boiling river
Engberg, S. Northern light
Evans, E. Crime in Italy
Feng Jicai. The tall woman and her short husband
Ferguson, W. Dies irae
Ferron, J. Back to Val-d'Or
Ferron, J. How the old man died
Ferron, J. The sea-lion
Ferron, J. The wool nightshirt and the horsehair tunic
Fink, I. A conversation
Finney, E. J. Bed of roses
Flowerday, E. Rubbish day
Ford, J. H. Fishes, birds and sons of men
Frame, R. Rowena Fletcher
Freeman, J. The Joan Crawford letter
Freeman, J. The rake people

Fremlin, C. High dive
Fremlin, C. The woman who had everything
Frucht, A. Fate and the poet
Frucht, A. Fruit of the month
Frucht, A. Midnight
Gallant, M. The ice wagon going down the street
Gallant, M. Rue de Lille
Garrett, G. P. The strong man
Gault, C. At dusk / just when / the light is filled with birds
Gault, C. Dinner for two
Gault, C. This bright night
Gifkins, M. Local time
Gilchrist, E. Memphis
Gilchrist, E. Traceleen at dawn
Giles, M. Heart and soul
Giles, M. The planter box
Gilliatt, P. Come back if it doesn't get better
Gilliatt, P. Stephanie, Stephen, Steph, Steve
Gilliatt, P. The tactics of hunger
Gilman, C. P. The yellow wallpaper
Glasgow, E. The difference
Glover, D. H. Fire drill
Gogol', N. V. Old-world landowners
Gordimer, N. Terminal
Grace, P. The geranium
Greenberg, A. Where do folk sayings come from?
Greene, G. The blue film
Greene, G. Mortmain
Grzimek, M. Finlandia
Haake, K. Another kind of nostalgia
Haake, K. Natural histories
Haake, K. Recently I've discovered my mistake
Hauptman, W. Sierra wave
Hawkes, J. A little bit of the old slap and tickle
Hawkes, J. The traveler
Hawthorne, N. The birthmark
Hemingway, E. The doctor and the doctor's wife
Hemley, R. All you can eat
Hemley, R. Dropping the baby
Hemley, R. Rainwalkers
Hemley, R. A sentimental wolf
Henry, O. The defeat of the city
Henry, O. Dougherty's eye-opener
Henry, O. The gift of the Magi
Highsmith, P. The terrors of basket-weaving
Hillabold, J. Yellow roses
Hoffman, W. Altarpiece
Hoffman, W. Landfall
Hofmann, G. The cramp
Hogan, D. The vicar's wife
Holt, T. E. Apocalypse
Hood, M. The goodwife Hawkins
Horne, L. The last dancer

HUSBAND AND WIFE—*Continued*

Hulme, K. One whale, singing
Humphrey, W. Dolce far' niente
Humphrey, W. The Hardys
Humphrey, W. In sickness and health
Hunnicutt, E. Bringing the news
Hurston, Z. N. The gilded six-bits
Ingalls, R. Something to write home about
Ioannidou Adamidou, I. The beggar
Ioannidou Adamidou, I. Conversation
Jackson, S. The beautiful stranger
Jackson, S. The summer people
James, H. The author of Beltraffio
Johnson, H. Victoria
Johnston, G. Strong-man from Piraeus
Jolley, E. Adam's bride
Jolley, E. Mr. Parker's valentine
Jolley, E. The travelling entertainer
Jonker, I. The goat
Just, W. S. I'm worried about you
Kauffman, J. The Easter we lived in Detroit
Kavaler, R. Local habitations
Kawabata, Y. The bound husband
Kawabata, Y. Eggs
Kawabata, Y. Household
Kawabata, Y. The incident of the dead face
Kawabata, Y. Mother
Kawabata, Y. The rainy station
Kawabata, Y. The Sliding Rock
Kawabata, Y. Thunder in autumn
Kidman, F. A strange delight
Kilworth, G. The rose bush
Klass, P. A gift of sweet mustard
Klass, P. In Africa
Klinkowitz, J. Sweet Jayne
Krause, P. Second sight
Krist, G. Ty and Janet
Landolfi, T. Rain
Lane, P. Apple peels and knives
Larimer, J. If you want company, turn on the radio
Latimer, M. Monday morning
Latimer, M. Mr. and Mrs. Arnold
Lavers, N. Big dog
Lawson, H. A double buggy at Lahey's Creek
Lee, H. Tamsen Donner's decision
Lim, C. The marriage
Lish, G. Everything I know
Lish, G. Mr. and Mrs. North
Lispector, C. The obedient
Loizeaux, W. Beside the Passaic
Long, D. Home fires
López Heredia, J. The retiree
Lott, J. The Janeites
Loukakis, A. Billy and the birds
Loukakis, A. Perfect holiday sounds
Lurie, M. An immaculate conception
Lutz, J. Autumn madness
Lutz, J. Dear Dorie
MacMahon, B. Exile's return
Martin, H. R. Mrs. Gladfelter's revolt

Mason, B. A. Big Bertha stories
Mason, B. A. Shiloh
Matheson, R. C. Dead end
Matthews, J. A marriage of solipsists
Matthews, J. Quest for an unnamed place
Matthews, J. "This moment is ours alone"
Matthews, J. The tree beyond
Mattison, A. The colorful alphabet
Maupassant, G. de. A crisis
Maupassant, G. de. In the wood
Maupassant, G. de. A meeting
Maupassant, G. de. The real one and the other
Maupassant, G. de. Toine
Maupassant, G. de. Useless beauty
McLaughlin, L. The absent toy
McLaughlin, L. Moving house
McQueen, J. The myna birds
Melville, H. I and my chimney
Moffatt, D. When Roger got married
Monem, H. A. The thief
Monreal, D. N. Lola's return
Montero, M. Last night at dawn
Montero, M. Thirteen and a turtle
Montgomery, M. I got a gal
Moravia, A. The belt
Moravia, A. The hands around the neck
Moravia, A. The woman with the black cloak
Morazzoni, M. Order in the house
Morris, M. Burning issues
Morris, M. The typewriter
Morris, W. Fiona
Morris, W. The ram in the thicket
Morris, W. Wishing you and your loved ones every happiness
Morrison, J. The blind man's story
Moskowitz, F. The change
Moskowitz, F. They all ran after the farmer's wife
Moskowitz, F. Whoever finds this: I love you
Mukherjee, B. A wife's story
Mukherjee, B. The world according to Hsü
Murphy, P. The small businessman's wife
Nagibin, ÍÛ. M. Needed urgently: gray human hair
Nagibin, ÍÛ. M. The newlywed
Nagibin, ÍÛ. M. The outsider
Nagibin, ÍÛ. M. The peak of success
Nagibin, ÍÛ. M. Somebody else's heart
Nestor, T. G. Byway of the rose
Nevai, L. Likely houses
Nevai, L. The Nile
Neville, S. Rapture
Ng'maryo, E. S. Ivory bangles
Nicol, A. The truly married woman
Nova, C. The prince
Oates, J. C. Blue-bearded lover
O'Brien, D. Eminent domain
O'Brien, E. Number 10
Ocampo, S. The expiation
O'Connor, F. Parker's back

HUSBAND AND WIFE—*Continued*

O'Faoláin, S. The fur coat
O'Hara, J. Are we leaving tomorrow?
O'Hara, J. Flight
O'Hara, J. Free
O'Hara, J. In the silence
Olmstead, R. A pair of bulls
Ozaki, S. River deer
Packer, N. H. Early morning, lonely ride
Paley, G. Love
Papaellinas, G. Christos Mavromatis is a welder
Parise, G. Italy
Pascoe, B. Cobber: The cat men of Genoa
Pascoe, B. Harold's Trudy
Payne, P. The pure in heart
Peterson, M. Crows
Peterson, M. Traveling
Petrakis, H. M. A day's journey
Petrakis, H. M. End of winter
Petrakis, H. M. The journal of a wife beater
Petrakis, H. M. The legacy of Leontis
Petrakis, H. M. The shearing of Samson
Pilcher, R. Home for the day
Pil'niãk, B. A year of their life
Piñera, V. Hot and cold
Pirandello, L. The black shawl
Plomer, W. When the sardines came
Potter, N. A. J. A private space
Power, U. The private life of Mrs. Herman
Prichard, K. S. The bride of Far-away
Prichard, K. S. The cow
Pritchett, M. Peach seed
Pritchett, V. S. The Spanish bed
Pronzini, B. Black wind
Pronzini, B. The imperfect crime
Pronzini, B. Mrs. Rakubian
Pronzini, B., and Malzberg, B. N. Multiples
Rabasa, G. The lion. The eagle. The wolf
Rand, P. Mr. and Mrs. Noonan
Rasputin, V. G. Vasili and Vasilisa
Reed, K. The bride of Bigfoot
Reed, K. Frontiers
Reed, K. The marriage bug
Rifaat, A. Another evening at the club
Ríos, A. The birthday of Mrs. Piñeda
Robison, M. Yours
Rodoreda, M. Love
Rogers, T. N. R. Crater Lake
Rooke, L. Break and enter
Rooke, L. Conversations with Ruth: the farmer's tale
Rooke, L. The woman's guide to home companionship
Rose, D. A. The good-bye present
Rosenbaum, K. Low tide
Rule, J. The investment years
Rule, J. One can of soup at a time
Rushin, P. Speed of light
Saiki, J. The fisherman
Sanders, S. R. The cry

Sargent, P. Shrinker
Schulman, H. Before and after: snapshots
Schulman, H. East Jesus
Schwartz, J. This time, yesterday morning
Schwartz, L. S. Rough strife
Schwartz, L. S. Sound is second sight
Selvon, S. If winter comes
Shacochis, B. Where Pelham fell
Shaw, I. The man who married a French wife
Sheckley, R. Fear in the night
Sheckley, R. The helping hand
Sheckley, R. The life of anybody
Shiga, N. Infatuation
Silva, B. No joy in the morning
Silva, B. The thesis
Silverberg, R. The changeling
Silverberg, R. Many mansions
Simmie, L. You tell me your dreams
Simmons, C. Eva and the apple tree
Singer, I. B. Short Friday
Skelton, R. The man who sang in his sleep
Snelling, W. J. Weenokhenchah Wandeeteekah
Sorrentino, F. The life of the party
Spark, M. The Black Madonna
Sperling, L. The book of life
Sprengnether, M. The camper
Stead, C. Street idyll
Steele, M. Color the daydream yellow
Steele, M. The death of a chimp
Stern, D. The interpretation of dreams by Sigmund Freud: a story
Stern, R. G. Dr. Cahn's visit
Stevens, J. A. The sacrifice
Strand, M. Dog life
Suckow, R. The man of the family
Suckow, R. Three, counting the cat
Suter, J. F. Doctor's orders
Swados, H. The man in the toolhouse
Swift, G. Seraglio
Symons, J. Love affair
Tallent, E. Favor
Tallent, E. The forgiveness trick
Tallent, E. Grant of easement
Tallent, E. Hannah's example
Tallent, E. Sweet disposition
Taylor, A. Casey and Sarah
Tem, S. R. Sleep
Tenorio, F. H. Tata Fino
Trollope, A. Returning home
Updike, J. Pygmalion
Updike, J. Unstuck
Van Vechten, C. Parties [excerpt]
Vanderhaeghe, G. Reunion
Vaughn, S. Sweet talk
Verma, N. An inch and a half above ground
Vines, H. The ginsing gatherers
Vogan, S. The crane wife
Wagoner, D. Wild goose chase
Watson, S. Brother Oedipus

HUSBAND AND WIFE—*Continued*
Weldon, F. Weekend
Welty, E. The wide net
West, J. Flow gently, sweet aspirin
West, J. A. Gladys's Gregory
Wharton, E. Afterward
Wharton, E. Bewitched
Whelan, G. Children in the park
Whitaker, M. Home to wagonhouses
Whitaker, M. The wife
White, P. Five-twenty
Wilbur, E. Sundays
Willett, J. Anticipatory grief
Willett, J. The haunting of the Lingards
Willett, J. Melinda falling
Williams, T. Sand
Williams, T. Tent worms
Williams, W. C. A face of stone
Wilner, H. Desert couple
Wilner, H. The quarterback speaks to his god
Wilson, R., Jr. Payment in kind
Windsor, G. In the house of the dead
Windsor, G. Wedding presents for breakfast
Winton, T. A measure of eloquence
Winton, T. Neighbours
Winton, T. Scission
Wolff, T. Desert breakdown, 1968
Wolff, T. Say yes
Woolf, V. The legacy
Wright, R. Man of all work
Yi, S. Wings
Yngve, R. The quail
Zwicky, F. The courts of the lord
A **husband** is missing. Flora, F.
A **husband's** return. Trevor, W.
Hush my mouth. Elgin, S. H.
Huss, Sandy
Coupon for blood
TriQuarterly no73:7-18 Fall '88
Hussey, Leigh Ann
The white wolf
Werewolves; ed. by J. Yolen and M. H. Greenberg
Huston, Ned
Pliny's commentaries
Universe 17
Hutman, Norma
The land of the leaves
L. Ron Hubbard presents Writers of the future
Hutnik, Ivan
The fire on the other side of the glass
Encounter (London, England) 62:7-8 F '84
Hutton, Suky
Chickweed
The North American Review 271:16-20 D '86
Huxley, Aldous, 1894-1963
Fard
The Treasury of English short stories; ed. by N. Sullivan

The Gioconda smile
Mystery in the mainstream; ed. by B. Pronzini; M. H. Greenberg and B. N. Malzberg
Huybensz, Joanne
Burial
Américas 37:44-6 N/D '85
Huynh, Quang Nhuong
The family's secret move
Missouri short fiction; ed. by C. Beasley
The **huzul** flute. Wegner, H.
Hval. Sandel, C.
Hwang, Sok-Yong
The road to Samp'o
The Road to Sampo, and other Korean short stories
Hwang, Sunwŏn
Cranes
Flowers of fire; ed. by P. H. Lee
Hyams, Edward
Exorcizing Baldassare
The Penguin book of ghost stories
Hyde, Elisabeth
Code blue!
Redbook 167:42-4+ My '86
Redbook 167:38-40+ Je '86
Family matters
McCall's 111:61-4 Ag '84
HYDROGEN BOMB *See* Atomic bomb
Hygeia at the Solito. Henry, O.
Hyne, C. J. Cutcliffe
The liner and the iceberg
Sea captains' tales; ed. by A. Enfield
Hyon, Chin-Gon
The death of my grandmother
The Unenlightened, and other Korean short stories
Fire
Flowers of fire; ed. by P. H. Lee
A **hyperborean** brew. London, J.
HYPNOSIS *See* Hypnotism
The **hypnotic** mailbox. Austin, D.
HYPNOTISM
Doyle, Sir A. C. The parasite
Goulart, R. Please stand by
Poe, E. A. The case of M. Valdemar
Poe, E. A. The facts in the case of M. Valdemar
Poe, E. A. The facts of M. Valdemar's case
Poe, E. A. Mesmeric revelation
Poe, E. A. A tale of the ragged mountains
Russell, E. F. Mesmerica
Stephen, J. Blood relations
Straub, P. Blue rose
HYPOCHONDRIA
Bradbury, R. Skeleton
Daniels, C. Mrs. Eloise
Hartley, L. P. A tonic
Harvor, E. Heart trouble
Stafford, J. The liberation
Williams, W. C. Mind and body
The **hypochondriac.** Swift, G.

HYPOCRISY
Blais, M.-C. An act of pity
Pierce, C. A summer afternoon
Potter, N. A. J. Pen pals
Shiga, N. A memory of Yamashina
A **hypothetical** lizard. Moore, A.

HYSTERECTOMY
Schwartz, L. S. So you're going to have
a new body!

I

I always get the cuties. MacDonald, J. D.
I am airport. Kinsella, W. P.
I am an employee. Austin, D.
I am Bigfoot. Carlson, R.
I am Candy Jones. Indiana, G.
I am counting with you all the way. Drake,
R.
I am Greenwald, my father's son. Komie,
L. B.
I am having an adventure. Klass, P.
I am Miss America. Schulman, H.
I am monarch of all I survey. Wilding, M.
I am not as efficient as other people. High-
smith, P.
I am returning. Russell, R.
I am shaking to death. Hannah, B.
I am the burning bush. Keizer, G.
I am twenty-one. Robison, M.
I and my chimney. Melville, H.
I ate her heart. Shacochis, B.
I break into houses. Cullen, E. J.
I can find my way out. Marsh, Dame N.
I can't forget her. Böll, H.
I can't get drunk. Boyle, K.
I can't help saying goodbye. Mackenzie, A.
I can't sleep anymore. Schwartz, S.
I can't sta-and it . . . . Rasputin, V. G.
I dated Jane Austen. Boyle, T. C.
I despise your life. Highsmith, P.
I do dwell. Davidson, L.
I do not like thee, Dr. Feldman. Slesar, H.
"I don't believe this". Gerber, M. J.
I don't know what he's doing now. Drake,
R.
I don't understand it. Pronzini, B.
I get by. Robison, M.
I go back to the mais oui. McCourt, J.
I got a gal. Montgomery, M.
I guess everything reminds you of something.
Hemingway, E.
I had a date with Lady Janet. O'Donnell,
P.
I had a hunch, and . . . Powell, T.
"I had vacantly crumpled it into my pocket
. . . but by God, Eliot, it was a
photograph from life!". Russ, J.
I have looked for Carrie. Ignatow, R. G.
I have no mouth, and I must scream. El-
lison, H.

I hope I shall arrive soon. Dick, P. K.
I just kept on smiling. Burt, S.
I kept grumbling. Faik, S.
I like blondes. Bloch, R.
I, Lillian. Bukoski, A.
I live in you. Stead, C.
I lived for you. King, F. H.
I look out for Ed Wolfe. Elkin, S.
I lost my love to the space shuttle 'Colum-
bia'. Broderick, D.
I love Galesburg in the springtime. Finney,
J.
I love Mary. Huang, C.-M.
I [love] NY. Bell, M. S.
"I love ya, baby". Gallico, P.
I love you, Ray Chrysler. La Follette, M.
W.
I made you. Miller, W. M.
I met a lady. Warner, S. T.
I miss dancing with you. Winters, J.
I never eat crabmeat now. St. Aubin de
Terán, L.
I never have been a well woman. Drake,
R.
I.O.U.—one bullet. Cushman, D.
I pay my rent. See Kinsella, W. P. Gabon
I read my nephew stories. Mordden, E.
"I remember my grandpa". Capote, T.
I, robot. Binder, E.
I, rocket. Bradbury, R.
"I," said the fly. Alter, R. E.
I see a long journey. Ingalls, R.
I see you never. Bradbury, R.
I shall live until I die. Houbein, L.
I shall not leave England now. Ryan, A.
I should worry. Kees, W.
I spy. Greene, G.
I spy a stranger. Rhys, J.
I stand alone. Winters, J.
I stand here ironing. Olsen, T.
I still see Sally. Jakes, J.
I suppose you are wondering why we are
here? Bradbury, R.
I swear I always wished you were a pos-
sibility. Brondoli, M.
I told mama not to come. Loukakis, A.
I try to look out for my family. Cullen, E.
J.
I used to live here once. Rhys, J.
I want to be a horse. Mrożek, S.
I want to be a soldier. Winters, J.
I want to be alone. Craig, D.
I want to go live with daddy. Swick, M.
I was an infinitely hot and dense dot.
Leyner, M.
I was behind the couch all the time. Win-
ters, J.
I went to the market place to see the world!
Oy, Mama, oy! Granit, A.
I will be our saviour from the bad smell.
Wendt, A.

Ibargüengoitia, Jorge, 1928-1983
What became of pampa hash?
Anthology of contemporary Latin American literature, 1960-1984
Ibrahim, Ibrahim, 1932-
The gap in Kaltouma's fence
Arabic short stories; tr. by D. Johnson-Davies
Ibuse, Masuji, 1898-
The crazy iris
The Crazy iris, and other stories of the atomic aftermath; ed. by K. Ōe
Kuchisuke's valley
The Shōwa anthology 1
Icarus. Elflandsson, G.
Ice. Thurm, M.
ICE AGE See Prehistoric times
Ice castle. Birtha, B.
Ice cream at noon. Holmstrom, D.
Ice cream birth. Sexson, L.
Ice days. Bukoski, A.
The **ice** dragon. Martin, G. R. R.
The **ice** fish. Johnson, W.
Ice fishing. Clark, G.
Ice flowers. Thompson, J.
ICE HOCKEY See Hockey
The **ice** monkey. Harrison, M. J.
Ice music. Manfredi, R.
Ice sculptures. Silva, D. B.
The **ice** wagon going down the street. Gallant, M.
Ice water. Broun, H.
An **iced** cake with cherries. Stead, C.
ICELAND
Sigurdsardóttir, J. Nothing to tell
Icera. Ocampo, S.
Ich bin ein Berliner. Oates, J. C.
ICONS
Leskov, N. S. The sealed angel
Malzberg, B. N. Icons
Sharat Chandra, G. S. Iyer's Hotel
Icons. Malzberg, B. N.
I'd know you anywhere. Hoch, E. D.
Ida. Dorris, M.
IDAHO
Carver, W. With voice of joy and praise
Idaho. Hannah, B.
An **idea**. Pirandello, L.
The **idea** trap. Zebrowski, G.
An **ideal** family. Mansfield, K.
The **ideal** village. Updike, J.
IDEALISM
Asimov, I. "In a good cause--"
Idenborough. Warner, S. T.
IDENTITY See Personality
Identity. Blaise, C.
The **Ides** of March. Hornung, E. W.
The **idiocy** of rural life. Pfeil, F.
Idiots. Day, R. C.
Idiot's crusade. Simak, C. D.
Idiots first. Malamud, B.
The **idler**. Bitov, A.

Idlibi, Ulfat al- See Al-Idlibi, Ulfat
Idling. Ardizzone, T.
The **idol**. Pavese, C.
The **Idol** House of Astarte. Christie, A.
The **Idol** of the Flies. Rice, J.
Idris, Yusuf
The chair carrier
Arabic short stories; tr. by D. Johnson-Davies
Kill her
Encounter (London, England) 64:3-7 Mr '85
Idris' pig. St. Clair, M.
The **idyl** of Red Gulch. Harte, B.
The **idyl** of the island. Harrison, S. F.
The **idyll** of Miss Sarah Brown. Runyon, D.
If. Dawson, F.
If a body. Wasylyk, S.
If a woodchuck could chuck wood. Wetherell, W. D.
If big brother says so. Rudoski, A.
If Damon comes. Grant, C. L.
If ever I should leave you. Sargent, P.
If garlic be the food of love . . . . Durrell, L.
If I die before I wake. Bear, G.
If I don't go now I never will. Buisson, J.
"**If** I forget thee, oh Earth . . . ". Clarke, A. C.
"**If** I had a daughter . . .". Colette
If I had three wishes. Foltz, L.
If it were dark. Hankla, C.
If not us, then who? Matthews, J.
If only: only if . . . . Clarke, A. C.
If only we could drive like this forever. Harvor, E.
If she knowed what I knowed, she never would woke. Drake, R.
If the dead could talk. Woolrich, C.
If the driver vanishes. . . . Garratt, P. T.
If the river was whiskey. Boyle, T. C.
If there be magic. Dunn, M.
If there were no Benny Cemoli. Dick, P. K.
If they hang you. Hammett, D.
If they knew Yvonne. Dubus, A.
If this be madness. Block, L.
If winter comes. Selvon, S.
If you ever go. Benedict, E.
If you take my hand, my son. Castle, M.
If you want company, turn on the radio. Larimer, J.
Ignatow, Rose Graubart
A careless man of the 20th century
Ignatow, R. G. Surplus love, and other stories
A clown
Ignatow, R. G. Surplus love, and other stories
Colors
Ignatow, R. G. Surplus love, and other stories

Ignatow, Rose Graubart—*Continued*
A dream can never complete itself
Ignatow, R. G. Surplus love, and other stories
Dreams & disappointments
Ignatow, R. G. Surplus love, and other stories
Dreams for sale
Ignatow, R. G. Surplus love, and other stories
How?
Ignatow, R. G. Surplus love, and other stories
I have looked for Carrie
Ignatow, R. G. Surplus love, and other stories
It deals with people first
Ignatow, R. G. Surplus love, and other stories
New artists, new jungle
Ignatow, R. G. Surplus love, and other stories
The penny story
Ignatow, R. G. Surplus love, and other stories
The pool of life
Ignatow, R. G. Surplus love, and other stories
Resurrection
Ignatow, R. G. Surplus love, and other stories
Sheep in the meadow
Ignatow, R. G. Surplus love, and other stories
Stealing the bread
Ignatow, R. G. Surplus love, and other stories
Surplus love
Ignatow, R. G. Surplus love, and other stories
An **ignoble** martyr. Davis, R. H.
The **iguana** killer. Ríos, A.
Igur and the mountain. Aldiss, B. W.
Ikaros. Kessler, J. F.
Ike and Nina. Boyle, T. C.
Ike at the mike. Waldrop, H.
Ikhlasi, Walïd
Wondering who . . .
Modern Syrian short stories; ed. by M. G. Azrak
Ile Forest. Le Guin, U. K.
Île Sèche. Minot, S.
I'll ask him to come sooner. West, J.
I'll be waiting for you when the swimming pool is empty. Tiptree, J.
I'll cut your throat again, Kathleen. Brown, F.
Ill-fated father and son. Ha, K.-C.
I'll fight you. Brooks, J.
Ill met in Lankhmar. Leiber, F.
The **ill-omened** groom. Maupassant, G. de
ILLEGAL ALIENS *See* Undocumented aliens

ILLEGITIMACY
See also Unmarried mothers
Bonner, M. One boy's story
Botwinik, B. The glazier
Bowles, P. Allal
Castillo, A. Ghost talk
Faulkner, W. Wash
Goyen, W. Had I a hundred mouths
Lacy, R. The natural father
Leitão, L. The son
MacMahon, B. Exile's return
Maupassant, G. de. Simon's papa
Naipaul, S. The father, the son and the Holy Ghost
Norris, H. The love child
Oates, J. C. Baby
O'Connor, F. A set of variations on a borrowed theme
Olson, D. A voice from the leaves
Petrakis, H. M. The bastards of Thanos
Pronzini, B. All the long years
Rand, P. Charades
Rooke, L. Winter is lovely, isn't summer hell
Saunders, C. R. Outsteppin' Fetchit
Shaik, F. Before echo
Singer, I. B. The secret
Stegner, W. E. The women on the wall
Thomas, D. Just like little dogs
Walker, M. Jubilee [excerpt]
Illianna comes home. Kinsella, W. P.

ILLINOIS
Johnson, C. R. The education of Mingo
Kinsella, W. P. K Mart
Lott, J. The Janeites
White, C. More crimes against the people of Illinois

Chicago
Anderson, S. Milk bottles
Bellow, S. Cousins
Bellow, S. A silver dish
Bellow, S. What kind of day did you have?
Bellow, S. Zetland: by a character witness
Blei, N. Skarda
Blei, N. Stars
Bloch, R. Yours truly, Jack the Ripper
Dybek, S. Blight
Dybek, S. Hot ice
Dybek, S. Pet Milk
Gans, B. M. And here in Chicago it's 78°
Kessler, J. F. Aeaea
Klinkowitz, J. Sweet home Chicago
Martínez-Serros, H. Distillation
Painter, P. Sylvia
Sanders, S. R. Wake
Stockanes, A. E. Ladies who knit for a living
Wright, R. The man who went to Chicago

Galesburg
Finney, J. I love Galesburg in the springtime

ILLITERACY *See* Literacy
ILLNESS
> *See also* Invalids; Mental illness; Terminal illness

Adler, W. The angel of mercy
Anderson, J. The milk
Ardizzone, T. My mother's stories
Asscher-Pinkhof, C. Madonna
Asscher-Pinkhof, C. Operation
Asscher-Pinkhof, C. Promenade
Ballantyne, S. You are here
Banks, R. Indisposed
Barstow, S. The middle of the journey
Benedict, D. Unknown feathers
Big Eagle, D. The journey
Bioy Casares, A. Venetian masks
Bryan, J. Y. Frontier vigil
Campbell, W. B. The baby
Canin, E. The year of getting to know us
Chernoff, M. Degan dying
Davie, E. Thorns and gifts
Dixon, S. Will as a boy
Drake, R. A cool day in August
Harrison, M. J. The quarry
Hemingway, E. A day's wait
Humphrey, W. In sickness and health
Johnston, G. The verdict
Jolley, E. The agent in travelling
Jolley, E. Grasshoppers
Kawabata, Y. The white flower
Laberge, A. The patient
Llewellyn, K. Croup
Lurie, M. Architecture
Massie, E. Sick'un
McGahern, J. All sorts of impossible things
Mills, W. To pass him out
Moore, S. Dove shooting
Morris, W. Glimpse into another country
Norris, H. The healing
O'Connor, F. The enduring chill
Petrakis, H. M. Zena Dawn
Russ, J. How Dorothy kept away the spring
Shiga, N. The razor
Shimaki, K. The black cat
Shimaki, K. The centipede
Shimaki, K. The red frog
Shimaki, K. The wasps
Sholem Aleichem. The happiest man in all Kodny
Sladek, J. T. The kindly ones
Thurm, M. Secrets
Verma, N. The dead and the dying
Verma, N. Under cover of darkness
West, J. The linden trees
Whelan, G. Playing with shadows
Williams, T. Mother Yaws
Wilner, H. Air
Wilner, H. Desert couple
Wilner, H. In my roommate's room
Wilner, H. Whitestone & Greenberg
Working, R. Charis

Yi, K.-S. The Unenlightened
Yŏm, S. The last moment
Zhang Jie. Under the hawthorn
Illusion. Rhys, J.
The **illusion.** Skelton, R.
The **illusionist.** Trujillo, R.
ILLUSIONS *See* Hallucinations and illusions
ILLUSTRATORS
Colwin, L. The lone pilgrim
Wagner, K. E. Sticks
Ilya. Mazel, D.
Im, Ok-In
The new life
> Hospital room 205, and other Korean short stories

I'm glad you asked. Abbott, L. K.
I'm going down to watch the horses come alive. Wagner, R. E.
I'm in Marsport without Hilda. Asimov, I.
I'm in the book. Estleman, L. D.
I'm not a Communist. Böll, H.
"I'm not so dumb!". Bradbury, R.
I'm scared. Finney, J.
I'm stupid and my wife is stupid. Sisskind, M.
I'm subtle. Mrożek, S.
I'm wide. Lish, G.
I'm worried about you. Just, W. S.
I'm your horse in the night. Valenzuela, L.
The **image.** Singer, I. B.
Image of departure. Wheatcroft, J.
IMAGINARY ANIMALS *See* Mythical animals
The **imaginary** assassin. Mukherjee, B.
IMAGINARY CITIES
Bishop, M. Storming the bijou, mon amour
Carter, A. The kiss
Decarnin, C. The book of time
Gorodischer, A. Man's dwelling place
Grahn, J. Ernesta
Harris, M. The linguist
Harris, M. The martyred poet
Herbert, F. Death of a city
Hoyt, M. S. The flowers at Anat Qesh
Silverberg, R. Getting across
Smith, C. A. The city of the singing flame
Smith, C. A. The seven geases
Sterling, B. Dinner in Audoghast
Valenzuela, L. City of the unknown
Valenzuela, L. The gift of words
Wells, H. G. The country of the blind
Wells, H. G. In the abyss
Westall, R. The Big Rock Candy Mountain
Wilder, C. Something coming through
An **imaginary** journey to the moon. Sabah, V.
IMAGINARY KINGDOMS
Campbell, L. A sum of moments
De Larrabeiti, M. The curse of Igamor
Dickinson, P. Flight
Duane, D. Lior and the sea

IMAGINARY KINGDOMS—*Continued*
Dunsany, E. J. M. D. P., Baron. The sword of Welleran
Gilbert, W. S. The wicked world
Gray, A. The end of the Axletree
Gray, A. Five letters from an eastern empire
Gray, A. The start of the Axletree
Hodgell, P. C. Stranger blood
Howard, R. E. The people of the Black Circle
Kilworth, G. Blind windows
Lynn, E. A. The gods of Reorth
McAuley, P. J. The temporary king
"Oo-a-deen"; or, The mysteries of the interior unveiled
Piper, H. B. Ministry of disturbance
Robbins, T. The hair of the beast
Roberts, K. Kitemaster
Tiptree, J. All this and heaven too
Van Greenaway, P. Cadenza
Walker, W. Arnaud's nixie
Walker, W. The unseen soldier
Warner, S. T. The Duke of Orkney's Leonardo
Warner, S. T. An improbable story
Warner, S. T. Narrative of events preceding the death of Queen Ermine
Warner, S. T. Queen Mousie
Yolen, J. Evian Steel
An **imaginary** line. Ruta, S.
Imaginary lives. Eis, J.

IMAGINARY PLAYMATES
Gingher, M. Toy Paris
Timperley, R. Harry
Wier, A. Bob and the other man

IMAGINARY WARS AND BATTLES
Anderson, P. No truce with kings
Anderson, P. Operation afreet
DeLillo, D. Human moments in World War III
Dick, P. K. If there were no Benny Cemoli
Donaldson, S. R. Gilden-Fire
Flynn, M. The forest of time
Gentle, M. Anukazi's daughter
Howard, R. E. The people of the Black Circle
Murphy, G. R. War
Rata. The invasion of Sydney
Redd, D. On the deck of the Flying Bomb
Sullivan, J. A. Welcome to freedom
Tiptree, J. Beam us home
Tiptree, J. Yanqui Doodle
Wells, H. G. A dream of Armageddon
Wells, H. G. The land ironclads
Whitlock, D. The million-dollar wound
Imagination. Lish, G.
The **imagination** of disaster. Gordon, M.
Imagine a day at the end of your life. Beattie, A.
Imagine kissing Pete. O'Hara, J.
The **Imam**. Saint, R.

The **imbecile**. Pirandello, L.
Imbert, Enrique Anderson *See* Anderson Imbert, Enrique, 1910-
The **imitation** demon. Kuttner, R.
The **imitation** of the rose. Lispector, C.
An **immaculate** conception. Lurie, M.
The **immanence** of God in the tropics. Rosen, G. H.
Immediate family. Lipman, E.
Immediate possession. Blythe, R.
Immensee. Storm, T.
Immersion. Mathers, P.
The **immigrant**. Dorr, L.

IMMIGRANTS
Batistich, A. All mixed up
Bell, J. L. The curlew's cry
Bonosky, P. The cathedral
Botwinik, B. The Bubbe
Brender à Brandis, M. All that counts
Brender à Brandis, M. The little old Dutch church bell
Brodkey, H. Ceil
Bukoski, A. The children of strangers
Codrescu, A. Monsieur Teste in America
Davidson, A. The Slovo stove
Edwards, C. Prima vera
Ferron, J. Chronicle of Anse Saint-Roch
Hogan, L. Friends and fortunes
Holmes, N. Bugs
Kinsella, W. P. K Mart
Kornblatt, J. R. Pa
Martone, M. Watch out
Mukherjee, B. Danny's girl
Saroyan, W. Madness in the family
Schnitzler, A. America
Schwartz, L. S. The melting pot
Skrzynecki, P. The biggest bonfire of all
Skrzynecki, P. The chainsaw incident
Skrzynecki, P. Indian mynas
Skrzynecki, P. Lilies
Skrzynecki, P. Pick-and-shovel hero
Skrzynecki, P. The red-back spider
Skrzynecki, P. The wild dogs
Stead, C. An iced cake with cherries
Thorman, C. Fifty years of eternal vigilance
The **immortal**. Nakagami, K.
The **Immortal** Bard. Asimov, I.
The **immortal** coil. Van Greenaway, P.
The **immortal** dog. Matthews, J.
Immortal night. Benford, G.
The **immortal** soul of Tommy O'. Costello, K.

IMMORTALITY
Amis, M. The immortals
Berdnyk, O. The apostle of immortality, a tale of the unprecedented
Bloch, R. Forever and amen
Bloch, R. The living end
Brunner, J. Elixir for the emperor
Budrys, A. The end of summer
De Celles, M. Recurrence

IMMORTALITY—*Continued*
Ellison, H. Chained to the fast lane in the Red Queen's race
Ellison, H. Deal from the bottom
Gunn, J. E. Donor
Kessel, J. The pure product
Oates, J. C. Further confessions
Rao, B. S. Victims of time
Shelley, M. W. The mortal immortal
Silverberg, R. Sailing to Byzantium
Simak, C. D. Grotto of the dancing deer
Stableford, B. M. And he not busy being born . . .
Immortality. Kawabata, Y.
Immortality. Sauro, J.
The **immortals**. Amis, M.
The **immortals**. Conley, R. J.
Immune dreams. Watson, I.
Imogene. McElroy, C. J.
Imp among aunts. Lish, G.
The **imp** of the perverse. Poe, E. A.
The **imperfect** crime. Pronzini, B.
IMPERIALISM
Leitão, L. The colonial bishop's visit
IMPERSONATIONS
This subject is used for stories dealing with individuals who assume or act the character of another. For tales describing a condition in which one individual shows in alternation two very different characters see subject: Dual personality
See also Impostors; Mistaken identity; Transvestism
Ballard, J. G. The man who walked on the moon
Bloch, R. Ego trip
Bloch, R. The living dead
Bloch, R. Talent
Correa, H. Alter ego
De Camp, L. S. The wheels of if
Delany, S. R. Time considered as a helix of semi-precious stones
Dexter, C. At the Lulu-Bar Motel
Garfield, B. Trust Charlie
Hauptman, W. Good rockin' tonight
Henry, O. Lost on dress parade
Henry, O. The rathskeller and the rose
Hoch, E. D. The people of the peacock
Knight, D. F. The handler
Lawson, H. The geological spieler
McGrath, P. The skewer
Moore, A. A hypothetical lizard
Nevins, F. M., Jr. The garrulous Garrity grand scam
Poe, E. A. The oblong box
Prince, H. Requiem for a busted flush
Prior, A. Be lucky
Rafferty, S. S. The Massachusetts peep-o'night
Russ, J. The mystery of the young gentleman
Russ, J. What did you do during the revolution, Grandma?
Swanwick, M. The feast of Saint Janis
Updike, J. Pygmalion

Vachss, A. H. It's a hard world
Walton, D. A house divided
West, J. Tom Wolfe's my name
Wodehouse, P. G. Comrade Bingo
Wodehouse, P. G. Without the option
Wright, R. Man of all work
Zangwill, I. Cheating the gallows
IMPERSONATORS, FEMALE
Bloch, R. The man who knew women
IMPERSONATORS, MALE
Lynch, L. Fruitstand II: Honeydew moon
An **implied** acquaintance. Ahern, T.
The **implosion**. Calvino, I.
The **impolite** sex. Maupassant, G. de
Importance. Mujica Láinez, M.
The **importance** of being Percy. Skelton, R.
The **importance** of high places in a flat town. Higgins, J.
The **important** thing. Williams, T.
Important things. Greenberg, B. L.
The **important** things. Schell, J.
The **imposition**. Power, V.
Imposter. Dick, P. K.
The **impostor**. Leedom-Ackerman, J.
IMPOSTORS
See also Impersonations
Bowles, P. Mejdoub
Bumpus, J. The outdoorsman
Bush, J. The problem of Li T'ang
Chisholm, L. Someone else's house
Fremlin, C. The post-graduate thesis
Marlowe, D. J. Give-and-take
Maupassant, G. de. Under the yoke
Reach, J. A time to remember
Sembene, O. The false prophet
St. Pierre, P. H. December Nilsen
Welch, D. Brave and cruel
IMPOTENCE
Wang, C.-H. The story of three springs
Impractical joker. Bloch, R.
The **impresario**. Singer, I. B.
IMPRESSARIOS
Gilliatt, P. The position of the planets
An **impression** of the Regency. Doyle, Sir A. C.
Impressions. Wilson, R.
Imprints. Waters, M.
IMPROBABLE STORIES
See also Fantasies
Arias, R. Lupe
Bates, H. E. Finger wet, finger dry
Baumbach, J. The great Cape Cod shock scare
Bloch, R. A case of the stubborns
Bradbury, R. Come, and bring Constance!
Cabrera, L. How the monkey lost the fruit of his labor
Calisher, H. Heartburn
Chavez, A. My ancestor—Don Pedro
Chesterton, G. K. The angry street
Chesterton, G. K. A crazy tale
Chesterton, G. K. A nightmare
Chipulina, E. G. A man called Lovac

IMPROBABLE STORIES—*Continued*

Conroy, J. The Boomer's fireman's fast sooner hound
Conroy, J. The demon bricksetter from Williamson County
Conroy, J. The high divers
Conroy, J. The sissy from the Hardscrabble County rock quarries
Conroy, J. Slappy Hooper, world's biggest, fastest, and bestest sign painter
Davis, L. The brother-in-law
Dembling, A. The dragon of Dunloon
Digby, J. The one and only bottle
Doyle, Sir A. C. The American's tale
Fox, R. A fable
Gogol', N. V. The nose
Grant, C. L. Spinning tales with the dead
Hankla, C. The baby, the parrot
Harris, M. The dog mafia
Hartley, L. P. The travelling grave
Henry, O. Seats of the haughty
Hoyt, M. S. The peg
Kinsella, W. P. The gerbil that ate Los Angeles
Körner, W. Bleep, crash, zap, wow: accidents in the Ruhr
Laidlaw, M. Love comes to the middleman
Laidlaw, M. The random man
Landolfi, T. Chicken fate
Landolfi, T. Words in commotion
London, J. A hyperborean brew [excerpt]
Lover, S. Ye marvelous legend of Tom Connor's cat
Mathers, P. The Henshaws
Moore, G. The strange story of the three golden fishes
Neff, O. The Porton Potion
Ocampo, S. Thus were their faces
Pallant, C. A neighborhood bar
Parker, R. The wheelbarrow boy
Piñera, V. The dummy
Piñera, V. The face
Piñera, V. A few beers
Piñera, V. Meat
Piñera, V. The philanthropist
Pronzini, B. The man who collected "The Shadow"
Pronzini, B. Outrageous
Purdy, J. Mud Toe the cannibal
Rabasa, G. The lion. The eagle. The wolf
Rooke, L. A bolt of white cloth
Rooke, L. Saks Fifth Avenue
Rooke, L. Why the heathens are no more
Saki. Tobermory
Sālim, G. The power of darkness
Sargent, P. Shrinker
Somers, A. The fall
Thorpe, T. B. The big bear of Arkansas
Traba, M. Conformity
Wells, H. G. The truth about Pyecraft
An **improbable** story. Warner, S. T.
The **improper** princess. Wrede, P. C.

In a bamboo garden. Fagan, A.
In a café. Rhys, J.
In a dim room. Dunsany, E. J. M. D. P., Baron
In a dream. Blinkin, M.
In a dry season. Lawson, H.
"In a good cause--". Asimov, I.
In a grove. Akutagawa, R.
In a lighted house. Scarfe, E.
In a Mexican garden. Stone, R.
In a Park Row restaurant. Crane, S.
In a Petri dish upstairs. Turner, G.
In a piney wood. Alden, P. B.
In a tub. Hempel, A.
In a world like this. Kress, N.
In absentia. Bowles, P.
In Africa. Klass, P.
In Alaska. Schwartz, S.
In all realities. Kirkhart, R.
In and out of the arms of the law. Taylor, C.
In and out of the cat bag. Janowitz, T.
In another country. Bovey, J.
In another country. Hemingway, E.
In another country. Morris, W.
In another language. Bonnie, F.
In case you don't come back. Kenney, S.
In Christ there is no east or west. Nussey, K.
In country. Mason, B. A.
In darkness. Durban, P.
In Delphine's bed. La Puma, S.
In entropy's jaws. Silverberg, R.
In family. Mattison, A.
In Fiona's country. Ruta, S.
In foreign country. Pritchard, M.
In foreign tongues. Busch, F.
In France they kiss on Main Street. McWey, M.
In Friedenstadt. Böll, H.
In front of the Temple of Luxor, 31 July 1980. Villemaire, Y.
In frozen time. Rucker, R. von B.
In God's country. Schulman, H.
In going is a drama. Moskowitz, F.
In heat. Crace, J.
In hiding. Ehlenbeck, S.
In high country. Shaw, J. B.
In his sweetheart's livery. Maupassant, G. de
In hock. McLaughlin, L.
In jeopardy. Diamond, R. G.
In Kew Gardens. Malamud, B.
In lonely lands. Ellison, H.
In memory of . . . Lutz, J.
In memory of an aristocrat. Williams, T.
In midst of life. Tiptree, J.
In my dream I always hear a step on the stairs. Moravia, A.
In my mother's footsteps. Stacey, K.
In my roommate's room. Wilner, H.
In one place. Troy, J.
In our state. Drury, T.
In Paracas with Jimmy. Bryce Echenique, A.

In pastures green. Jones, D. C.
In port. See Maupassant, G. de. The port
In praise of creeping things. Cockrell, C.
In recent history. Steinbach, M.
In retirement. Malamud, B.
In return. Stern, R. G.
In search of a story. Faik, S.
In search of dignity. Lispector, C.
In search of literary heroes. Hankla, C.
In search of the rattlesnake plantain. At-
 wood, M.
In search of the reader. Böll, H.
In season. Campbell, W. B.
In self-defense. Sorrentino, F.
In Siberia it is very cold. Goldberg, L.
In sickness and health. Humphrey, W.
In silence. Pirandello, L.
In spring. Evans, E.
In the abyss. Wells, H. G.
In the air. Byatt, A. S.
In the air, over our heads. Herrick, A.
In the American society. Jen, G.
In the archives. Wilson, B.
In the attic of the house. Rule, J.
In the Avu observatory. Wells, H. G.
In the barn. Anthony, P.
In the beginning. Klass, M.
In the beginning there was humming. Metz-
 ger, D.
In the Blair's Lair. Coriolan, J.
In the blink of an eye. Federici, C. M.
In the boudoir. Colette
In the cards. Bloch, R.
In the castle. Moyer, K.
In the cemetery where Al Jolson is buried.
 Hempel, A.
In the circle of nowhere. Cox, I. E., Jr.
In the city of sleep. Coleman, W.
In the clear. McGerr, P.
In the conservatory. Bird, C.
In the cotton country. Woolson, C. F.
In the country of last things. Auster, P.
In the court room. Maupassant, G. de
In the cutting of a drink. Aidoo, C. A. A.
In the dark years. Tuohy, F.
In the darkness. Böll, H.
In the dead hours. Irvine, R. R.
In the dead of truffle season. Highsmith, P.
In the deep heart's core. Birtha, B.
In the depths of a coal mine. Crane, S.
In the direction of the beginning. Thomas,
 D.
In the drawer. Mrożek, S.
In the dreamhouse. Galyan, D.
In the fall. MacLeod, A.
In the fast lane. Rees, D.
In the fertile land. Josipovici, G.
In the flesh. Barker, C.
In the flower of age. Colette
In the garden. Brown, S. H.
In the garden. Mayhew, A. J.
In the garden. Paley, G.
In the garden. Rooke, L.
In the garden. Thomas, D.
In the group. Silverberg, R.
In the heart of the heart of the country.
 Gass, W. H.
In the hills above Lugano. MacLaverty, B.
In the hills, the cities. Barker, C.
In the hospital. Cordor, S. M.
In the hotel. Tuohy, F.
In the hours of darkness. O'Brien, E.
In the House of Double Minds. Silverberg,
 R.
In the house of gingerbread. Wolfe, G.
In the house of glass. Chowder, K.
In the house of the dead. Windsor, G.
In the ice house. Edwards, K. A.
In the icebound hothouse. Goyen, W.
In the islands. Murphy, P.
In the Jardin des plantes. Chase, C.
In the jaws of danger. Anthony, P.
In the kingdom of the golden dust. Bissoon-
 dath, N.
In the land of the married. Miller, K. T.
In the life. Birtha, B.
In the lost lands. Martin, G. R. R.
In the Luxemburg Gardens. Rhys, J.
In the memory room. Bishop, M.
In the midnight hour. Benbow, M.
In the Miro District. Taylor, P. H.
In the modern vein: an unsympathetic love
 story. Wells, H. G.
In the mood. Watmough, D.
In the moonlight. Maupassant, G. de
In the mountains. Jhabvala, R. P.
In the music library. Hunnicutt, E.
In the name of the father. Harrison, B. G.
In the orchard. Woolf, V.
In the park. Wolfe, T.
In the penal colony. Kafka, F.
In the penny arcade. Millhauser, S.
In the pit. Proulx, A.
In the plane. McLaughlin, L.
In the presence of mine enemies. Frazier,
 L., Jr.
In the problem pit. Pohl, F.
In the Rambla de Cataluña. Campbell, E.
In the realm of the herons. Kaplan, D. M.
In the red room. Bowles, P.
In the roof garden. Ade, G.
In the rubbish tin. Taylor, A.
In the Rue de l'Arrivée. Rhys, J.
In the same boat. Rees, D.
In the season of the rains. Russo, R. P.
In the secret places of the stairs. Blei, N.
In the service of evil. Tilton, L.
In the sickbay. Branham, R. V.
In the silence. O'Hara, J.
In the smoke. Hendrix, H. V.
In the spirit of socialism. Aćin-Kosta, M.
In the spring. Fante, J.
In the spring. Maupassant, G. de
In the street. Fleutiaux, P.
In the surprise of life. Stark, S. S.
In the tank. Mayhar, A.

In the tower. McDevitt, J.
In the town of Ballymuck. Power, V.
In the train. Davie, E.
In the train station. Monreal, D. N.
In the tunnel. Gallant, M.
In the Valley of the Thundering Hoofs. Böll, H.
In the vast house. Welch, D.
In the vault. Lovecraft, H. P.
In the village. Crystal, S.
In the water-butt. Pound, E.
In the west country. Norris, L.
In the Western tradition. Eisenstein, P.
In the white night. Beattie, A.
In the winter of her days . . . Litchfield, R. M.
In the wood. Maupassant, G. de
In the woods. Robison, M.
In the Year of the Mouse. Murray, C.
In the Yucatán. Powers, P. E.
In the zoo. Stafford, J.
In this corner . . . Purdy, J.
In this country, but in another language, my aunt refuses to marry the men everyone wants her to. Paley, G.
In this life. Olmstead, R.
In this place of illusion. Schiff, T.
In time for the human race. Wiggins, P. J.
In Tír na nÓg. McCourt, J.
In traction. Oates, J. C.
In transit. Davin, D.
In various rôles. Maupassant, G. de
In which language is one called Schnecken-röder? Böll, H.
In which Peter Mavromatis lives up to his name. Papaellinas, G.
In winter the snow never stops. Covino, M.
In youth is pleasure. Gallant, M.
The **inaugural** meeting. Kinsella, W. P.
The **incalling**. Harrison, M. J.
The **incense-burner**. Morrison, J.

INCEST
Carpenter, D. The father's love
Clarke, A. C. The smell
Cook, H. A Canadian education
Drewe, R. The silver medallist
El Rahman, M. A. Gentlemen eating gentlemen
Harris, H. The foot
Huggan, I. Into the green stillness
Jolley, E. Two men running
Lannes, R. Goodbye, dark love
Moyer, K. Tumbling
Murphy, Y. The headdress
Muschg, A. The scythe hand; or, The homestead
Pritchett, M. Flying lessons
Robinson, S. God is an iron
Simpson, M. Lawns
Sims, L. Behind my lace curtain
Swift, G. Hotel
Thomas, D. The burning baby
Yourcenar, M. Anna, soror . . .

Incest rock. Coffman, B.
An **inch** and a half above ground. Verma, N.
An **incident**. Shiga, N.
Incident at Huacaloc. Cowper, R.
Incident at Mhlaba Jail. Havemann, E.
Incident at Owl Creek. See Bierce, A. An occurrence at Owl Creek Bridge
Incident at the Gaumont. Digby, J.
Incident at the old tin bridge. Wegner, R.
Incident in a far country. Aldiss, B. W.
Incident in a neighborhood tavern. Pronzini, B.
An **incident** in the Ghobashi household. Rifaat, A.
The **incident** of the dead face. Kawabata, Y.
Incident on the afternoon of November third. Shiga, N.
Incidental music. Sagan, F.
Incomprehensible. Blinkin, M.
Incorporation. Matheson, R. C.
The **incorrect** hour. Spark, D.
The **incredible** and sad tale of innocent Eréndira and her heartless grandmother. García Márquez, G.
The **incredible** survival. Poe, E. A.
The **incredible** theft. Christie, A.
Incredible voyage. Endō, S.
An **incurable** malady. Claiborne, S.
Indecent dreams. Lustig, A.
Indefinite article. Van Greenaway, P.
Indefinite nights. Ferguson, P.
Independence. Claeson, E.
INDEPENDENCE DAY (UNITED STATES) *See* Fourth of July
Independence day. Crichton, S.
Independence Day. Dilworth, S.
Independence Day. Ruffolo, L.
The **independent** fiend. Linzner, G.
An **independent** meditation. Taylor, P. E.
Indestructible union. Piñera, V.

INDIA
Narayan, R. K. Attila
Narayan, R. K. The blind dog
Narayan, R. K. Naga
British occupation, 1765-1947
Hesse, H. Robert Aghion
Kipling, R. Lispeth
Kipling, R. The return of Imray
Lee, T. Foreign skins
Maupassant, G. de. Châli
McGrath, P. The Black Hand of the Raj
Morrow, W. C. His unconquerable enemy
Pilcher, R. Amita
Tagore, Sir R. The Cabuliwallah
Webster, C. The feud
Wells, H. G. The Rajah's treasure
20th century
Dullas, I. Shanti, simple, sweet and—sinister!
Dullas, I. X marks the spot
Grenville, K. The space between
Mistry, R. Auspicious occasion

INDIA—20th century—*Continued*
Sastri, P. Rival candidates
1947-
Aithal, S. K., and Rothfork, J. Moksha
Basu, R. Sambal and Putki
Bloch, R. Untouchable
Desai, A. Games at twilight
Fagan, A. In a bamboo garden
Hospital, J. T. Ashes to ashes
Houbein, L. Round trip
Jhabvala, R. P. An experience of India
Jhabvala, R. P. The housewife
Jhabvala, R. P. The man with the dog
Jhabvala, R. P. On bail
Jhabvala, R. P. Passion
Jhabvala, R. P. Rose petals
Jhabvala, R. P. A spiritual call
Jhabvala, R. P. Two more under the Indian sun
Ramchandani, K. Gitley
Rubin, D. Longing for America
Sharat Chandra, G. S. Bhat's return
Sharat Chandra, G. S. Iyer's Hotel
Subramanian, U. Portrait of a woman
Van de Wetering, J. The yoga yo-yo
Verma, N. Maya Darpan
Marriage customs
See Marriage customs—India
Politics
See Politics—India
Rural life
Jhabvala, R. P. Desecration
Jhabvala, R. P. How I became a holy mother
Jhabvala, R. P. In the mountains
Narayan, R. K. Annamalai
Narayan, R. K. Another community
Narayan, R. K. A breath of Lucifer
Narayan, R. K. A career
Narayan, R. K. Chippy
Narayan, R. K. Dodu
Narayan, R. K. The evening gift
Narayan, R. K. Four rupees
Narayan, R. K. Fruition at forty
Narayan, R. K. Half a rupee worth
Narayan, R. K. A hero
Narayan, R. K. A horse and two goats
Narayan, R. K. House opposite
Narayan, R. K. Like the sun
Narayan, R. K. The mute companions
Narayan, R. K. Nitya
Narayan, R. K. Old man of the temple
Narayan, R. K. The Roman image
Narayan, R. K. A snake in the grass
Narayan, R. K. Under the banyan tree
Narayan, R. K. The watchman
Sharat Chandra, G. S. Maya
Bombay
Chand, M. The gift of Sunday
Jhabvala, R. P. Bombay
Sadhu, A. Ziprya
Delhi
Jhabvala, R. P. My first marriage

Mysore
Sharat Chandra, G. S. The holy wristwatch
India. Griggs, T.
Indian burial. Carr, P. M.
Indian camp. Hemingway, E.
The **Indian** Gardens. Robison, J.
Indian gift. Hoffman, W.
Indian Joe. Kinsella, W. P.
Indian mynas. Skrzynecki, P.
The **Indian** Nation Cultural Exchange Program. Kinsella, W. P.
Indian poker. Fischer, C. E.
Indian rope trick. Davidson, L.
Indian summer. Grimes, P.
Indian summer. Updike, D.
Indian summer of an uncle. Wodehouse, P. G.
The **Indian** Summer of Dry Valley Johnson. Henry, O.
The **Indian** well. Clark, W. V. T.
Indiana, Gary
I am Candy Jones
Between C & D; ed. by J. Rose and C. Texier
INDIANA
Conroy, J. High bridge
Gass, W. H. In the heart of the heart of the country
Thompson, J. Birds in air
Frontier and pioneer life
See Frontier and pioneer life—Indiana
INDIANS OF CENTRAL AMERICA
See also Mayas
Holding, J. The Treasure of Pachacamac
La Farge, O. The door in the wall
Wolfe, T. Polyphemus
INDIANS OF MEXICO
See also Aztecs
Anaya, R. A. B. Traven is alive and well in Cuernavaca
Bowles, P. Pastor Dowe at Tacaté
Silverberg, R. Not our brother
Valadés, E. Permission for death is granted
INDIANS OF NORTH AMERICA
See also names of specific tribes or nations
Algren, N. The heroes
Allen, P. G. Tough love
Austin, M. H. The basket maker
Austin, M. H. The Basket Woman: first story
Austin, M. H. The Basket Woman: second story
Austin, M. H. A case of conscience
Austin, M. H. The divorcing of Sina
Austin, M. H. The lost mine of Fisherman's Peak
Austin, M. H. Mahala Joe
Austin, M. H. The medicine of Bow-Returning
Austin, M. H. The Walking Woman
Bell, M. S. Today is a good day to die

INDIANS OF NORTH AMERICA — *Continued*

Benedict, S. Tahotahontanekentseratkerontakwenhakie

Big Eagle, D. The journey

Bruchac, J. Turtle meat

Carpenter, L. The ebbing

Carr, P. M. Indian burial

Conley, R. J. The endless dark of the night

Cook-Lynn, E. A good chance

Cook-Lynn, E. The power of horses

Cox, I. E., Jr. In the circle of nowhere

Doubiago, S. Ramon/Ramona

Erdrich, L. American Horse

Erdrich, L. Saint Marie

Erdrich, L. Snares

Ferguson, W. The claims adjuster

Forbes, J. Only approved Indians can play: made in USA

Green, J. C., and Proctor, G. W. The night of the Piasa

Greenwood, R. A gift to the future

Hemingway, E. Indian camp

Hogan, L. Amen

Hogan, L. New shoes

Kees, W. The ceremony

Kenny, M. Yaikni

Kinsella, W. P. Dancing

Kinsella, W. P. Pretend dinners

Kinsella, W. P. To look at the Queen

Littlebird, L. The hunter

Messenger, B. Give it back to the Indians

Morrell, D. The storm

Niatum, D. She keeps the dance turning like the earth

Petrakis, H. M. The victim

Pritchard, M. Ramon: souvenirs

Pronzini, B., and Wallmann, J. M. Coyote and Quarter Moon

Revard, C. Report to the nation: claiming Europe

Rosen, S. The deerhide

Salisbury, R. Aniwaya, Anikawa, and the killer teen-agers

Salisbury, R. The gleams

Salisbury, R. The sonofabitch and the dog

Sanders, T. E. Ave Lutie

Simms, W. G. The arm-chair of Tustenuggee

Snelling, W. J. Weenokhenchah Wandeeteekah

Tenn, W. Eastward ho!

Vizenor, G. R. Reservation café: the origins of American Indian instant coffee

Waldrop, H. Green Brother

Waldrop, H. Mary Margaret Road-Grader

Walters, A. L. Apparitions

Walters, A. L. The Devil and Sister Lena

Walters, A. L. Going home

Walters, A. L. The laws

Walters, A. L. The resurrection of John Stink

Walters, A. L. The sun is not merciful

Waters, F. The woman at Otowi Crossing [excerpt]

Wellman, M. W. A star for a warrior

Captivities

Johnson, D. M. Lost sister

Johnson, D. M. A man called Horse

Schaefer, J. W. Sergeant Houck

Legends

Austin, M. H. The Coyote-Spirit and the Weaving Woman

Austin, M. H. How the corn came

Blue Cloud, P. Coyote meets Raven

Blue Cloud, P. Stinkbug

Blue Cloud, P. Waterbugs

Greenwood, R. Mokli

Grey, Z. The land of the wild musk-ox

Lee, H. The legend of Chief Little Sitting Bear

Sears, V. L. Sticktalk

Sladek, J. T. Ursa Minor

Walters, A. L. Mythomania

Reservations

Kinsella, W. P. Lark song

Rites and ceremonies

Dann, J. Bad medicine

Hamilton, D. C. Blood, sweat, and fears

Social life and customs

Jack, R. The pebble people

Kinsella, W. P. The performance

Lopez, B. H. Winter count 1973: geese, they flew over in a storm

Tall Mountain, M. The sinh of Niguudzagha

Wars

Bean, A. The warhorse of Spotted Tail

Brown, C. A winter's tale

Garcia y Robertson, R. The moon of popping trees

Haslam, G. W. Hawk's flight: an American fable

Poe, E. A. The man that was used up

Arkansas

Hobson, G. The talking that trees does

California

Lee, H. The slaves of Stony Creek

West, J. Up a tree

Canada

Blackwood, A. A haunted island

Burns, M. The men on my window

Burns, M. Suburbs of the Arctic Circle

Grenon, J. A new dress for Maggie

Kinsella, W. P. The bear went over the mountain

Kinsella, W. P. Beef

Kinsella, W. P. Between

Kinsella, W. P. Butterflies

Kinsella, W. P. Caraway

Kinsella, W. P. Dance me outside

Kinsella, W. P. Feathers

Kinsella, W. P. The fog

INDIANS OF NORTH AMERICA—Canada—*Continued*
  Kinsella, W. P. Gooch
  Kinsella, W. P. Horse collars
  Kinsella, W. P. Illianna comes home
  Kinsella, W. P. The inaugural meeting
  Kinsella, W. P. Indian Joe
  Kinsella, W. P. The Indian Nation Cultural Exchange Program
  Kinsella, W. P. The kid in the stove
  Kinsella, W. P. Linda Star
  Kinsella, W. P. Longhouse
  Kinsella, W. P. The managers
  Kinsella, W. P. The McGuffin
  Kinsella, W. P. Panache
  Kinsella, W. P. Penance
  Kinsella, W. P. The practical education of Constable B. B. Bobowski
  Kinsella, W. P. Real Indians
  Kinsella, W. P. The truck
  Kinsella, W. P. Truth
  Kinsella, W. P. Ups and downs
  Mitchell, W. O. Patterns
  Reininger, C. Cache reward
Louisiana
  Wier, A. Campbell Oakley's gospel sun shines on Roy Singing Grass
Michigan
  Dilworth, S. Mad Dog Queen
Montana
  Welch, J. Winter in the blood [excerpt]
Nevada
  Sanchez, T. Red Reno honkers
Oklahoma
  Humphrey, W. A good Indian
Pacific Northwest
  Dauenhauer, N. Egg boat
Texas
  Taylor, P. E. A clouded visit with Rolling Thunder
Virginia
  Carter, A. Our Lady of the Massacre
Yukon Territory
  Handke, P. The long way around
  London, J. The law of life
  London, J. Nam-Bok, the unveracious
  London, J. Negore, the Coward
  London, J. The sickness of Lone Chief
INDIANS OF SOUTH AMERICA
  Card, O. S. America
  Castellanos, R. Death of the tiger
Indirect method. King, F. H.
Indisposed. Banks, R.
INDIVIDUALITY
  Greenwood, R. The last survivor of Sierra Flat
  Kōda, R. The five-storied pagoda
  Pollack, E. The vanity of small differences
INDOCHINESE WAR, 1946-1954
  Claudius, E. How the jungle soldiers became sons of heaven
  Ziem, J. Something's missing

INDOCTRINATION, FORCED *See* Brainwashing
Industrial accident. Correy, L.
INDUSTRIAL ACCIDENTS
  Bonosky, P. The delegate
  Bonosky, P. Johnny Cucu's record
  Correy, L. Industrial accident
  Nichols, R. Free fall (R's account)
  Samarakis, A. The mother
  Williams, W. C. The paid nurse
INDUSTRIAL RELATIONS
  Schulze, A. Eighteen minutes
Industrial valley. McKenney, R.
INDUSTRIALISTS *See* Capitalists and financiers
Ineligible. Crowley, A.
Inexorable progress. Hood, M.
Inexperience. Tuohy, F.
The **inexperienced** ghost. Wells, H. G.
The **Infant** Hercules. Gathorne-Hardy, J.
The **infant** prodigy. Mann, T.
INFANTICIDE
  Caldwell, E. Daughter
  James, H. The author of Beltraffio
  Joubert, E. Milk
  Kranes, D. Cordials
  Maupassant, G. de. Rosalie Prudent
  McBain, E. Small homicide
  Mérimée, P. Mateo Falcone
Infantiev. Bitov, A.
INFANTS
  Asscher-Pinkhof, C. Baby in the basket
  Asscher-Pinkhof, C. A laundry basket full
  Asscher-Pinkhof, C. New mother
  Barthelme, D. The baby
  Benford, G. Freezeframe
  Bingham, S. Fear
  Bloch, R. Nina
  Bradbury, R. The small assassin
  Carlson, R. Blood and its relationship to water
  Carver, R. Popular mechanics
  Case, D. Fengriffen
  Cheuse, A. The quest for Ambrose Bierce
  Colwin, L. Old flames
  Dixon, S. Reversal
  Dixon, S. Wheels
  Frazee, S. The man who made a beeline
  Greene, G. Awful when you think of it
  Kessler, J. F. A Theban ostrakon
  Lipman, E. After Emily
  Little, B. The backroom
  McGarry, J. The babysitter
  Pollack, R. Angel baby
  Ryan, A. Babies from heaven
  Sandel, C. There's a war on
  Spark, M. The first year of my life
  Spivack, K. Loving
  Strand, M. The tiny baby
  Sturgeon, T. Brat
  Thompson, J. Dreams of a new mother
  Tiptree, J. Morality meat
  Whelan, G. Children in the park

Infatuated. Albarelli, D.
Infatuation. Shiga, N.
The **inferiority** complex of old Sippy. Wodehouse, P. G.
The **infernal** machine. Lutz, J.
Infestation. Aldiss, B. W.
The **infidel**. Schwartz, L. S.
Infield. Deaver, P. F.
The **infinite** passion of expectation. Berriault, G.
Infinks. Chernoff, M.
Infirtaris inoaknoneis. Federspiel, J.
Influencing the hell out of time and Teresa Golowitz. Godwin, P.
The **informal** execution of Soupbone Pew. Runyon, D.
INFORMERS
    See also Treason
    Asimov, I. The sign
    Gordimer, N. A city of the dead, a city of the living
    Gordimer, N. Crimes of conscience
    Gordimer, N. Oral history
    Klíma, I. Monday morning: a black market tale
Infrared signature. Hagy, A. C.
Ing, Dean
    Sam and the Banzai runner
        Omni (New York, N.Y.) 8:60-2+ Ja '86
    Sam and the sudden blizzard machine
        Omni book of science fiction 1
Ingalls, Rachel
    Blessed art thou
        Ingalls, R. I see a long journey
    Captain Hendrik's story
        Ingalls, R. The pearlkillers
    Early morning sightseer
        Ingalls, R. Something to write home about
    I see a long journey
        Ingalls, R. I see a long journey
    Inheritance
        Ingalls, R. The pearlkillers
    The man who was left behind
        Ingalls, R. Something to write home about
    On ice
        Ingalls, R. I see a long journey
    People to people
        Ingalls, R. The pearlkillers
    Something to write home about
        Ingalls, R. Something to write home about
    St. George and the nightclub
        Ingalls, R. Something to write home about
    Theft
        Ingalls, R. Something to write home about
    Third time lucky
        Ingalls, R. The pearlkillers
The **ingenuity** of Captain Spink. Roberts, M.
Ingermann. Spingarn, L. P.

Ingots of gold. Christie, A.
Ingram, Willis J. *See* Harris, Mark, 1922-
The **inhabitant** of the lake. Campbell, R.
The **inhabitants** of Venus. Shaw, I.
Inhabiting the interspaces. Maddern, P. C.
Inheritance. Farmer, B.
Inheritance. Ingalls, R.
The **inheritance**. O'Brien, D.
The **inheritance**. Rey Rosa, R.
The **inheritance**. Zacharia, D.
INHERITANCE AND SUCCESSION
    See also Wills
    Addison, J. A story of an heir
    Ade, G. The judge's son
    Asimov, I. The one and only east
    Asimov, I. The pointing finger
    Asimov, I. The stamp
    Baxt, G. Stroke of genius
    Böll, H. Black sheep
    Brand, C. Double cross
    Brown, G. M. Magi
    Brown, G. M. The skald in the cave
    Cable, G. W. Belles Demoiselles plantation
    Christie, A. The Lemesurier inheritance
    Crowley, A. The stone of Cybele
    Del Rey, L. The still waters
    Donaldson, S. R. Daughter of Regals
    Gifkins, M. Head over heels
    Gilbert, M. The curious conspiracy
    Gilbert, W. S. Diamonds
    Gilchrist, M. The stone dragon
    Goyen, W. The Texas principessa
    Hall, T. T. The wooden box
    Hansen, J. Willow's money
    Henry, O. One thousand dollars
    Hoch, E. D. The theft of the circus poster
    Hogg, J. The unearthly witness
    Ingalls, R. Inheritance
    Jacobs, W. W. The white cat
    James, P. D. Great Aunt Allie's flypapers
    Jennings, G. Tom cat
    Kessler, J. F. Sphinx
    Knox, B. Deerglen Queen
    Le Fanu, J. S. Squire Toby's will
    Matthews, J. Haunted by name our ignorant lips
    Panneton, P. The heritage
    Pirandello, L. Aunt Michelina
    Potter, N. A. J. Legacies
    Queen, E. Last man to die
    Rand, P. Heir
    Read, P. P. Son and heir
    Rice, J. The crossroads
    Sams, F. The widow's mite
    Sexson, L. Intestate and without issue
    Shibaki, Y. Ripples
    Warren, J. Ready money
    Waugh, H. The beneficiaries
    Wells, H. G. The lost inheritance
    Wexler, J. The bequest
    Whitaker, M. No stone for Jochebed
    Woods, S. Every tale condemns me
    Yu, C.-Y. The relationship

The **inhuman** condition. Barker, C.

The **initiation**. Longyear, B. B.

An **Injustice** revealed
  Black water; ed. by A. Manguel

The **ink**. Carrier, R.

Inks, Caralyn
  Mandrake
    Magic in Ithkar 4; ed. by A. Norton and R. Adams
  Nine words in winter
    Tales of the Witch World [1]

Inks, Caralyn, and Miller, Georgia
  Eyes of the seer
    Magic in Ithkar 3; ed. by A. Norton and R. Adams

Inland. Erbe, P.

Inland passage. Rule, J.

The **inlet**. Curley, D.

The **inn**. Maupassant, G. de

Inn Essence. Lombreglia, R.

Innaurato, Albert
  Solidarity
    Men on men 2; ed. by G. Stambolian

The **inner** circle. Queen, E.

The **inner** garden. Eisenstein, S.

The **inner** room. Aickman, R.

Innes, Michael, 1906-
  For works written by this author under other names see Stewart, J. I. M. (John Innes Mackintosh), 1906-
  Tragedy of a handkerchief
    Ellery Queen's Crimes and punishments

Inness-Brown, Elizabeth, 1954-
  Horse dreams
    The New Yorker 61:28-9 S 2 '85

INNKEEPERS *See* Hotels, taverns, etc.

Innocence. Brodkey, H.

INNOCENT III, POPE, 1160 or 61-1216
About
  Schwob, M. The narrative of Pope Innocent III

The **innocent**. Greene, G.

INNS *See* Hotels, taverns, etc.

An **inopportune** visit. Bowles, P.

Inoue, Mitsuharu
  The House of Hands
    The Crazy iris, and other stories of the atomic aftermath; ed. by K. Oe

Inoue, Yasushi, 1907-
  A marriage interview
    The Mother of dreams, and other short stories; ed. by M. Ueda
  Under the shadow of Mt. Bandai
    The Shōwa anthology 2

Inquiries. Lewis, B. L.

INQUISITION
  Poe, E. A. The pit and the pendulum

INSANE, CRIMINAL AND DANGEROUS
  See also Insanity; Mentally ill
  Andreyev, L. The thought
  Avallone, M. Walter ego
  Bloch, R. The screaming people

Chambers, R. W. The repairer of reputations
Collins, M. The motive
Dixon, S. The news
Dixon, S. Ray
Evans, J. Purple prose
Hensley, J. L. Whistler
Ocampo, S. The fury
Pronzini, B. Mrs. Rakubian
Shannon, D. They will call it insane
Shaw, J. B. On the river road
Shea, M. The Angel of Death

The **insane**. Williams, W. C.

INSANE ASYLUMS *See* Mentally ill—Care and treatment

INSANITY
  See also Insane, Criminal and dangerous; Mental illness; Personality disorders
  Adams, G. G. Bow wow and good-bye
  Aiken, C. Silent snow, secret snow
  Aldiss, B. W. The girl who sang
  Arden, W. Homecoming
  The Astrologer's prediction
  Atherton, G. F. H. The foghorn
  Berdnyk, O. The constellation of green fish, a tale of the unprecedented
  Blinkin, M. The mysterious secret
  Bloch, R. Beelzebub
  Bloch, R. Mannikins of horror
  Bonner, M. High-stepper
  Bowles, P. In the red room
  Boyd, W. My girl in skintight jeans
  Bumpus, J. Popinjay's African notes
  Campbell, R. Next time you'll know me
  Case, D. Fengriffen
  Colette. The half-crazy
  Collins, W. Mad Monkton
  Connolly, P. Dead flower
  Curtiss, U. R. Something green and growing
  Dahl, R. Man from the south
  Dick, P. K. Strange memories of death
  Dickens, C. A madman's manuscript
  Dickens, M. Activity time
  Doyle, Sir A. C. A pastoral horror
  Ekström, M. Balzac's valet
  Everett, P. L. Chacón, Chacón
  Federspiel, J. The man who brought happiness
  Ferron, J. Back to Val-d'Or
  Ferron, J. Mélie and the bull
  Ferron, J. The parrot
  Fink, I. Crazy
  Fraser, A. Who's been sitting in my car?
  Gogol', N. V. Diary of a madman
  Greene, G. A little place off the Edgeware Road
  Grin, A. Fire and water
  Haldeman, J. W. More than the sum of his parts
  Hecht, B. Specter of the Rose
  Herbert, F. Operation Syndrome

INSANITY—*Continued*
Hesse, H. A man by the name of Ziegler
Houbein, L. Footprints of Maria
Ignatow, R. G. Stealing the bread
Kessler, J. F. Cheiron
Kiely, B. Through the fields in gloves
Klein, T. E. D. Petey
Kotzwinkle, W. A man who knew his birds
Landolfi, T. The labrenas
Le Guin, U. K. SQ
Lowden, D. The old mob
Lutz, J. Understanding electricity
March, W. Not worthy of a Wentworth
Maupassant, G. de. The diary of a madman
Maupassant, G. de. Francis
Maupassant, G. de. Le Horla
McKinley, J. Kafka in suburbia
McKinley, J. Ozark episode
Moon, S.-T. The sound of the gong
Morrell, D. Orange is for anguish, blue for insanity
Motsisi, C. Boy-boy
Muscillo, D. Sister Coxall's revenge
Neville, K. Ballenger's people
Nolan, W. F. My name is Dolly
Ocampo, S. The punishment
"Oo-a-deen"; or, The mysteries of the interior unveiled
Owens, B. A little piece of room
Priestley, J. B. The grey ones
Pronzini, B., and Malzberg, B. N. Another burnt-out case
Rendell, R. Loopy
Rey Rosa, R. The inheritance
Russell, R. Sardonicus
Singer, I. B. The slaughterer
Singmaster, D. Stella Artois
Spark, M. Come along, Marjorie
Spark, M. The leaf-sweeper
St. Clair, M. Wryneck, draw me
Steele, W. D. How beautiful with shoes
Stevenson, R. L. The merry men
Thomas, D. The dress
Thompson, J. Ice flowers
Thompson, J. Having words
Vizyēnos, G. M. The consequences of the old story
Watson, I. To the Pump Room with Jane
Wicomb, Z. Jan Klinkies
Windsor, G. Press conferences of Ambassador Sweeney
Wodehouse, P. G. Sir Roderick comes to lunch
Woolf, V. Solid objects
Yi, H.-C. Torn flesh
The **inscribed** copy of the Kreutzer sonata. Saroyan, W.
The **insect** world. Rhys, J.
INSECTS
Aldiss, B. W. Hothouse
Barrett, N., Jr. Diner

Butler, O. E. Bloodchild
Card, O. S. Eumenides in the fourth floor lavatory
Gass, W. H. Order of insects
Holmes, N. Bugs
Hulme, K. The cicadas of summer
Kawabata, Y. The grasshopper and the bell cricket
Melville, H. The apple-tree table; or, Original spiritual manifestations
Shimaki, K. The wasps
The **insects** are winning: At least they'll have candlelight. Garrett, G. P.
The **insects** are winning: The moth. Garrett, G. P.
The **insects** from Shaggai. Campbell, R.
Insects in amber. Reamy, T.
Insecurity. Bissoondath, N.
Inside and outside. Hesse, H.
Inside dope. Adams, G. G.
Inside knowledge. Ferguson, P.
Inside out. Rucker, R. von B.
The **inside** story. Hospital, J. T.
Inside the frame. Coover, R.
Inside the violet. Rose, D. A.
Insider trading. Ephron, N.
Insight. Watson, I.
Insight at Flame Lake. Amis, M.
INSOMNIA
Aickman, R. Into the wood
Carver, R. The student's wife
Colette. Sleepless nights
Davis, L. Liminal: the little man
Hemingway, E. Now I lay me
Liben, M. The caller
Lutz, J. The Insomniacs Club
O'Brien, E. In the hours of darkness
Rhys, J. A night
Schwartz, L. S. Acquainted with the night
Schwartz, S. I can't sleep anymore
Insomnia. Piñera, V.
The **Insomniacs** Club. Lutz, J.
Inspecting the vaults. McCormack, E. P.
Inspector Ghote and the noted British author. Keating, H. R. F.
Inspector Ghote and the test match. Keating, H. R. F.
Inspector Maigret pursues. Simenon, G.
Inspector Saito's small satori. Van de Wetering, J.
Inspector von Galoshinsky. Fink, I.
INSPIRATION *See* Creation (Literary, artistic, etc.)
Installations. Hemley, R.
Instant of the hour after. McCullers, C.
INSTRUCTORS *See* Teachers
Instrument of justice. Ferrars, E.
Instruments of liberation. McCarthy, C.
Instruments of seduction. Rush, N.
Insulation. Frame, J.
INSURANCE
Beman, B. Set 'em up, Joe

INSURANCE—*Continued*
  Gilchrist, E. The lower garden district free gravity mule blight; or, Rhoda, a fable
  Henry, O. A departmental case
  Ignatow, R. G. It deals with people first
  Sholem Aleichem. Burned out
INSURANCE, LIFE *See* Life insurance
INSURANCE BROKERS
  Gilchrist, E. The perfect stone
  Kinsella, W. P. How I missed the million dollar round table
  Sheckley, R. The demons
The **intellectual** awakening in Burton's Row. Ade, G.
INTELLECTUALS
      See also Scholars
  Ch'en, Y.-C. The comedy of Narcissa T'ang
  Colum, P. Three men
  Freeman, C. The exile, the housekeeper, and Flora, the beauty of Rome
  Gilliatt, P. The wind-child factor
  Johnston, G. Vale, Pollini!
INTELLIGENCE AGENTS *See* Secret service
INTER-RACIAL MARRIAGE *See* Interracial marriage
Intercourse. Rose, D. A.
An **interest** in life. Paley, G.
INTERFAITH MARRIAGE
  Archer, J. Christina Rosenthal
  Gordon, M. Delia
  Liberman, S. Drifting
  O'Brien, E. The Connor girls
  Olmstead, R. Bruno and Rachel
  Ozick, C. Levitation
  Pulaski, J. Father of the bride
  Silverberg, R. The mutant season
Interference. Hartley, L. P.
Interference. Menaker, D.
Interior. Eldridge, M.
The **interior** castle. Stafford, J.
Interlocking pieces. Gloss, M.
The **intermediary**. Liben, M.
Intermission. Coover, R.
An **international** episode. James, H.
INTERNATIONAL INTRIGUE
      See also Adventure; Secret service; Spies
  Fleming, I. Octopussy
  Garfield, B. Trust Charlie
  Piper, H. B. Operation RSVP
INTERNATIONAL MARRIAGES
  James, H. Lady Barberina
  Jhabvala, R. P. Two more under the Indian sun
  Osborn, C. The new castle
  Peterson, M. Two cats
  Rule, J. Joy
  Sharat Chandra, G. S. Bhat's return
  Thompson, B. Tattoo
  Tuohy, F. The Admiral and the nuns
  Wiebe, D. E. The art of Vietnam

Interollo, Lisa
  The quickening
      The Editors' choice: new American stories v2
      Seventeen 43:154-5+ N '84
INTERPLANETARY COMMUNICATION
      See Interstellar communication
INTERPLANETARY TRAVEL *See* Interplanetary voyages
INTERPLANETARY VISITORS
      See also Martians
  Abbott, L. K. The unfinished business of childhood
  Aldani, L. S is for snake
  Anderson, P. Delenda est
  Anderson, P. No truce with kings
  Anderson, P., and Dickson, G. R. The adventure of the misplaced hound
  Anthony, P. Beak by beak
  Asimov, I. Does a bee care?
  Asimov, I. Found!
  Asimov, I. Hostess
  Bakhnov, V. According to scientific data
  Bates, H. Farewell to the master
  Bear, G. Tangents
  Beattie, A. It's just another day in Big Bear City, California
  Benford, G. Of space-time and the river
  Benford, G. White creatures
  Benford, G., and Carter, P. A. Proserpina's daughter
  Biggle, L. Who's on first?
  Bishop, M. Alien graffiti
  Bloch, R. I like blondes
  Bloch, R. Space-born
  Bloch, R. Welcome, stranger
  Bloch, R. Where the buffalo roam
  Bone, J. F. On the fourth planet
  Bone, J. F. Tween
  Boren, T. Sliding rock
  Budrys, A. Shadow on the stars
  Cadigan, P. Angel
  Cadigan, P. Roadside rescue
  Campbell, J. W., Jr. Who goes there?
  Carneiro, A. Life as an ant
  Carr, T., and Carr, C. Some are born cats
  Chandler, A. B. Don't knock the rock
  Charnas, S. M. Listening to Brahms
  Clarke, A. C. Guardian angel
  Clarke, A. C. Rescue party
  Clemence, B. All the livelong night
  Del Rey, L. For I am a jealous people!
  Di Filippo, P. Phylogenesis
  Dick, P. K. Explorers we
  Dickson, G. R. The cloak and the staff
  Dickson, G. R. Rex and Mr. Rejilla
  Dickson, G. R. Show me the way to go home
  Dickson, G. R. Who dares a Bulbur eat?
  Dilov, L. Forward, mankind!
  Ellison, H. The sky is burning
  Ellison, H. Strange wine

INTERPLANETARY VISITORS — *Continued*

Ellison, H. The wind beyond the mountains
Fairman, P. W. The cosmic frame
Federici, C. M. 'Oh, Lenore!' came the echo
Forrest, K. V. The gift
Forrest, K. V. Mother was an alien
Forrest, K. V. Xessex
Forward, R. L. The singing diamond
Garrett, R. A little intelligence
Haldeman, J. C. Playing for keeps
Haldeman, J. W. Seven and the stars
Hamilton, E. Devolution
Harness, C. L. Signals
Harrison, H. The view from the top of the tower
Herbert, F. Rat race
Herbert, F. Try to remember
Johnson, C. R. Popper's disease
Kilworth, G. Almost heaven
Kilworth, G. The invisible foe
Kinsella, W. P. Reports concerning the death of the Seattle Albatross are somewhat exaggerated
Kotzwinkle, W. Star cruisers, welcome
Kress, N. Out of all them bright stars
Kuttner, H., and Moore, C. L. Or else
Lafferty, R. A. Polity and custom of the Camiroi
Larionova, O. A tale of kings
Laumer, K. Doorstep
Long, F. B. The Mississippi saucer
Longyear, B. B. The homecoming
Lovecraft, H. P. The whisperer in darkness
Martin, G. R. R. Run to starlight
Morressy, J. The last Jerry Fagin Show
Nesvadba, J. The divided Carla
Neville, K. Bettyann
Oliver, C. Transfusion
Pohl, F. The children of night
Pohl, F. Sitting around the pool, soaking up the rays
Pohl, F. We servants of the stars
Reed, K. Shan
Reynolds, M. The adventure of the extraterrestrial
Robinson, S. User friendly
Robinson, S., and Robinson, J. Stardance
Rodgers, A. The boy who came back from the dead
Rucker, R. von B. Inside out
Russ, J. Foul fowl
Russ, J. Reasonable people
Russ, J. Souls
Russell, E. F. Diabologic
Russell, E. F. The witness
Russell, R. I am returning
Schmidt, S. The unreachable star
Shea, M. The Angel of Death
Sheckley, R. The monsters
Sheckley, R. The native problem

Sheckley, R. Shape
Shepard, L. A traveler's tale
Shepard, L. Voyage South from Thousand Willows
Shockley, G. W. The coming of the Goonga
Silverberg, R. Against Babylon
Silverberg, R. Amanda and the alien
Silverberg, R. Blindsight
Silverberg, R. The iron star
Simak, C. D. Idiot's crusade
Simak, C. D. Skirmish
Sladek, J. T. Guesting
Sladek, J. T. White hat
Soukup, M. Frenchmen and plumbers
St. Clair, M. Child of void
St. Clair, M. The wines of earth
Stone, M. The Plasting Project
Strugatskiĭ, B. N., and Strugatskiĭ, A. N. The visitors
Sturgeon, T. Poker Face
Sucharitkul, S. Fiddling for water buffaloes
Tiptree, J. Beam us home
Tiptree, J. Second going
Tiptree, J. The women men don't see
Tong Enzheng. The middle kingdom
Vesity, A. The first day
Vinge, V. Gemstone
Wagner, K. E. An awareness of angels
Waldrop, H. Flying saucer rock & roll
Watson, I. When the timegate failed
Wilson, G. The substitute
Wilson, R. Farewell party
Wyndham, J. Phoney meteor
Ye Yonglie. The Thursday events
Zheng Wenguang. The mirror image of the earth

INTERPLANETARY VOYAGES
        See also Science fiction; Space flight
Bishop, M. The gospel according to Gamaliel Crucis; or, The astrogator's testimony
Bradley, M. Z. Death between the stars
Clarke, A. C. Breaking strain
Del Rey, L. Though dreamers die
Ellison, H. Mealtime
Finney, J. Of missing persons
Forrest, K. V. O captain, my captain
Haldeman, J. W. Hero
Haldeman, J. W. A !tangled web
Kelly, J. P., and Kessel, J. Friend
Knight, D. F. Strangers on paradise
Martin, G. R. R. Nightflyers
McDevitt, J. Promises to keep
Niven, L. The borderland of Sol
Robinett, S. Number 13
Rocklynne, R. They fly so high
Schmitz, J. H. The witches of Karres
Sheckley, R. All the things you are
Sheckley, R. Restricted area
Smith, C. A. Master of the asteroid
Smith, C. A. The vaults of Yoh-Vombis
Smith, C. A. A voyage to Sfanomoë

INTERPLANETARY VOYAGES — *Continued*
Tiptree, J. The only neat thing to do
Tiptree, J. With delicate mad hands
Van Ewyck, A. The lens
Walsh, J. M. The wreck in the void
Wolfe, G. Alien stones
INTERPLANETARY WARS
Anderson, P. Tomorrow's children
Anthony, P. The alien rulers
Anthony, P. The whole truth
Asimov, I. C-chute
Bear, G. Hardfought
Bradbury, R. I, rocket
Budrys, A. Shadow on the stars
Dick, P. K. Imposter
Ellison, H. Battlefield
Garrett, R. The highest treason
Godwin, T. Too soon to die
Haldeman, J. W. You can never go back
Harrison, H. Or battle's sound
Leinster, M. Keyhole
Longyear, B. B. Enemy mine
Miller, W. M. I made you
Reynolds, M. Prone
Saberhagen, F. Smasher
Sheckley, R. Fool's mate
Smith, C. The game of rat and dragon
Vinge, J. D. Mother & child
Wodhams, J. One clay foot
The **interpretation** of dreams by Sigmund Freud: a story. Stern, D.
INTERPRETERS *See* Translators
INTERRACIAL MARRIAGE
Austin, M. H. A case of conscience
Austin, M. H. Papago wedding
Bonham, F. Chivaree
Chua, R. The morning after
Coleman, W. Lonnie's cousin
Durham, E. M. Deepening dusk
Hungerford, T. A. G. Green grow the rushes
Kinsella, W. P. Illianna comes home
Thomas, M. Second rains
Thompson, B. Crossing
Walker, A. Kindred spirits
Yamamoto, M. Betty-san
An **interrupted** story. Buzzati, D.
Interruptions. Covino, M.
The **intersection.** Ardizzone, T.
INTERSTELLAR COLONIES *See* Space colonies
INTERSTELLAR COMMUNICATION
Cartier, F. A. The signals
Hamilton, E. Requiem
McDevitt, J. Cryptic
Russell, E. F. Top secret
Smith, G. O. Beam pirate
Sturgeon, T. The Martian and the moron
Vinge, J. D. Eyes of amber
Wolfe, G. Alien stones
Interurban queen. Lafferty, R. A.
The **interval.** Williams, T.

An **interval** of time. Dadswell, M.
An **interview.** Colette
An **interview.** Havemann, E.
The **interview.** Hunter, E.
The **interview.** Jhabvala, R. P.
The **interview.** Komie, L. B.
The **interview.** Singer, I. B.
The **interview.** Upward, E.
Interview in the number two dressing-room. Coriolan, J.
Interview with a gentleman farmer. Boston, B.
Interview with the author of Caryatids. Dennison, G.
Interview with the drag queen. Mordden, E.
INTERVIEWING
Barthelme, D. January
Barthelme, D. Lightning
Colette. An interview
Covino, M. In winter the snow never stops
Gilliatt, P. Nobody's business
Hunter, E. The interview
Komie, L. B. The interview
Lessing, D. M. One off the short list
McCormack, E. P. Anyhow in a corner
Rooke, L. Agnes and the cobwebs
Sisskind, M. Twenty questions
Updike, J. One more interview
Intestate and without issue. Sexson, L.
Intimacy. Carver, R.
Intimacy. Collins, L.
An **intimacy** beyond words. Covino, M.
Intimately, with rain. Fox, J.
Into a further dimension. Papaellinas, G.
Into gold. Lee, T.
Into that good night. Stevens, J.
Into the green stillness. Huggan, I.
Into the night life. Miller, H.
Into the parlor. Reed, K.
Into the sketch. Pirandello, L.
Into the wood. Aickman, R.
Introducing your friends. Bird, C.
The **introduction.** Woolf, V.
An **introduction** to opera. Canzoneri, R.
Intruder. Matheson, R. C.
The **intruder.** Pavese, C.
The **intruders.** Kelen, S.
Intruders of sleepless nights. Painter, P.
The **intrusion.** Asimov, I.
INTUITION
Ghose, Z. A translator's fiction
Wetherell, W. D. Nickel a throw
Willis, C. And come from miles around
INUIT
Apple, M. Eskimo love
Lenz, S. The amusement-doctor
London, J. A hyperborean brew [excerpt]
Munro, A. Eskimo
Thériault, Y. Nuliak
INVALIDS
See also Paraplegics
Apollinaire, G. The deified invalid

INVALIDS—*Continued*
Best, E. Sunday
Boyle, K. Convalescence
Bradbury, R. The emissary
Buzzati, D. Seven floors
Dixon, S. Wheels
Fitzgerald, M. J. Il bell'uomo
Freeman, C. The exile, the housekeeper, and Flora, the beauty of Rome
Fremlin, C. A lovely day to die
Graves, Mrs. A. J. Mary and Ellen Grosvenor; or, The two sisters
Halligan, M. A cage of gold
James, H. The middle years
Klass, P. The secret lives of dieters
Lofts, N. Now you have me
Norris, L. Shaving
Pavese, C. Loyalty
Pirandello, L. A breath of air
Sandel, C. Madame
Stead, C. The woman in the bed
Thanet, O. Sist' Chaney's black silk
Tremain, R. My wife is a White Russian
Tyler, A. The geologist's maid
Viola, A. Excerpts from Sunnyview journal
Wells, H. G. Through a window
Wharton, E. Ethan Frome
White, P. Five-twenty
The **invasion** of Sydney. Rata
The **invasion** of the Church of the Holy Ghost. Kirk, R.
Inventing the Abbotts. Miller, S.
Inventing the kiss. Shaw, J. B.
Invention of a language. Kohlhaase, W.
The **invention** of flight. Neville, S.
INVENTIONS
Buzzati, D. The time machine
Dick, P. K. Service call
Dick, P. K. The short happy life of the brown oxford
Keller, G. D. Papi invented the automatic jumping bean
King, S. The Jaunt
Lafferty, R. A. Flaming-arrow
Melville, H. The happy failure
Sturgeon, T. Microcosmic god
Twain, M. From The "London Times" of 1904
Inventions. Schulman, H.
INVENTORS
Aldrich, T. B. Out of his head
Asimov, I. Obituary
Bloch, R. The golden opportunity of Lefty Feep
Clarke, A. C. Moving spirit
Herbert, F. A matter of traces
Paley, G. This is a story about my friend George, the toy inventor
Targan, B. Surviving adverse seasons
Inventory. Barrett, L.
The **inventory** at Fontana Bella. Williams, T.
The **inversion.** Roberts, N.
The **invested** libido. St. Clair, M.

The **investigator.** Finney, E. J.
The **investment.** Wilson, B.
The **investment** years. Rule, J.
INVESTMENTS
Friedman, B. J. Business is business
Lafferty, R. A. Interurban queen
St. Pierre, P. H. The owner of the gang
INVISIBILITY
O'Brien, F.-J. What was it?
Pronzini, B. The man who collected "The Shadow"
Reed, K. The visible partner
Ward, L. The marbled horn
The **invisible** cat. Wright, B. R.
The **invisible** foe. Kilworth, G.
Invisible hands. Carr, J. D.
The **invisible** Japanese gentlemen. Greene, G.
Invisible life. Nelson, K.
Invisible malls. Kalfus, K.
The **invisible** man. Chesterton, G. K.
Invisible woman. Boylan, J.
Invisible worm. Abrahams, L.
An **invitation.** Mazel, D.
An **invitation** to a movie. Hirota, Y.
Invitation to the dance. Rhys, J.
An **invitation** to the hunt. Hitchcock, G.
The **invocation.** Campbell, R.
Ioannides, Panos
Gregory
    Short story international 62
The unseen aspect
    Short story international 60
Ioannidou Adamidou, Irena
The beggar
    Short story international 69
Conversation
    Short story international 64
Hero
    Short story international 52
Iocasta. Kessler, J. F.
Iona Moon. Thon, M. R.
Ionian white and gold. Spillard, A.
IOWA
Kinsella, W. P. Distances
Kinsella, W. P. Frank Pierce, Iowa
Suckow, R. Home-coming
The **Ipswich** Phial. Garrett, R.
IRA *See* Irish Republican Army
IRAN
Jahnn, H. H. Sassanidian king
Lester, C. S. Dogs and foreigners
                    Tehran
Farnsworth, K. A. Counterpoint
IRANIANS
                    United States
Thompson, J. Foreigners
Wolfe, G. Seven American nights
Ireland, Aileen
Paukenmesse
    Encounter (London, England) 71:19-20 N '88

IRELAND

See also Northern Ireland

Bradbury, R. Banshee

Bradbury, R. One for his lordship, and one for the road!

Leonard, H. The anticlerical pup

Lover, S. Ye marvelous legend of Tom Connor's cat

Tremayne, P. Tavesher

Virgo, S. Shan Val Mór

18th century

Sheehan, R. Boy with an injured eye

19th century

Crane, S. A fishing village

Le Fanu, J. S. Sir Dominick's bargain

20th century

Behan, B. The last of Mrs. Murphy

MacIntyre, T. Boarding

MacLaverty, B. Anodyne

MacLaverty, B. The bull with the hard hat

MacLaverty, B. The deep end

MacLaverty, B. Hugo

MacLaverty, B. A present for Christmas

MacLaverty, B. A rat and some renovations

MacLaverty, B. St. Paul could hit the nail on the head

MacLaverty, B. Where the tides meet

O'Brien, F. The martyr's crown

O'Connor, F. Judas

O'Flaherty, L. The stolen ass

Plunkett, J. The scoop

Power, V. In the town of Ballymuck

Power, V. Night

Sheehan, R. Several sweet ecstasies

Trevor, W. Beyond the pale

Wall, M. "They also serve . . ."

Walsh, T. My other grandmother

College life

See College life—Ireland

Farm life

See Farm life—Ireland

Rural life

Behan, B. The confirmation suit

Colum, P. Catherine Mulamphy and the man from the north

Colum, P. The death of the rich man

Colum, P. Eilis: a woman's story

Colum, P. The flute player's story

Colum, P. Land hunger

Colum, P. The little pension

Colum, P. Marcus of Clooney

Colum, P. Marriage

Colum, P. The Peacocks of Baron's Hall

Colum, P. Pilgrimage home

Colum, P. The slopes of Tara

Doyle, Sir A. C. The heiress of Glenmahowley

Kiely, B. Bloodless Byrne of a Monday

Kiely, B. A journey to the seven streams

Kiely, B. Mock battle

Kiely, B. Secondary top

Kiely, B. A walk in the wheat

Le Fanu, J. S. The white cat of Drumgunniol

McGahern, J. The recruiting officer

McLaverty, M. The priest's housekeeper

Millman, L. The standing stone

Moore, G. At the turn of the road

Moore, G. A flood

Moore, G. Home sickness

Moore, G. A letter to Rome

Moore, G. The strange story of the three golden fishes

Moore, G. The voice of the mountain

Nestor, T. Once upon a dream

Nestor, T. G. The last fling

O'Brien, E. The bachelor

O'Brien, E. The Connor girls

O'Brien, E. The creature

O'Brien, E. Irish revel

O'Brien, E. A rose in the heart of New York

O'Brien, E. The rug

O'Brien, E. Savages

O'Brien, E. A scandalous woman

O'Brien, E. The small-town lovers

O'Brien, E. Tough men

O'Faoláin, S. Lovers of the lake

O'Kelly, S. Hike and Calcutta

O'Kelly, S. The man with the gift

O'Kelly, S. Michael and Mary

O'Kelly, S. Nan Hogan's house

O'Kelly, S. The weaver's grave

Power, V. The operation

Power, V. The threshold

Tracy, H. A rest and a change

Trevor, W. Beyond the pale

Trevor, W. Bodily secrets

Trevor, W. The news from Ireland

Trevor, W. The property of Colette Nervi

Trevor, W. The wedding in the garden

Van Greenaway, P. Indefinite article

Clare

Collier, J. The lady on the grey

Donegal (County)

Bernen, R. Sacrament of the sick

Bernen, R. Two lives

Bernen, R. The windcharger

Ryan, A. Bundoran, Co. Donegal

Dublin

Albarelli, D. Honeymoon

Colum, P. A Dublin day

Colum, P. Three men

Glavin, A. One for sorrow

Joyce, J. The boarding house

Kiely, B. Through the fields in gloves

McCarthy, T. Mammy's boy

Power, V. An eye for an eye

Power, V. The ragged rascal ran

Sheehan, R. Universitas

Kildare

Power, V. No cigarettes, no matches, no lights allowed

Mayo (County)

Ryan, A. The rose of Knock

Irene. Bell, M. S.
Irene. Moskowitz, F.
Irina. Gallant, M.
Iris. Greenleaf, S.
Iris Holmes. Johnston, S.
Irish, William, 1903-1968
   *For works written by this author under
      other names see* Woolrich, Cornell,
      1903-1968
The corpse in the Statue of Liberty
   Manhattan mysteries; ed. by B. Pronzini;
      C. L. R. Waugh and M. H. Greenberg
The dancing detective [Variant title: Dime
   a dance]
The Deadly arts; ed. by B. Pronzini and
   M. Muller
IRISH
                    Australia
Jones, R. Ring of Kerry
Morrison, J. The busting of Rory
   O'Mahony
                    England
Hogan, D. Ties
MacLaverty, B. Between two shores
O'Brien, E. Cords
Sheehan, R. Optics
Sproat, R. Almost graceful like a dancer
Tremayne, P. The pooka
                    France
Moore, G. 'Emma Bovary'
O'Faolain, J. Her trademark
                    Italy
Trevor, W. On the Zattere
                    Majorca
Glavin, A. One for sorrow
                    United States
Davis, D. S. Sweet William
Gordon, M. Agnes
Gordon, M. Delia
Gordon, M. Eileen
Gordon, M. The neighborhood
Moore, G. Home sickness
O'Brien, E. Ways
Ryan, A. The bones wizard
Schulberg, B. Murder on the waterfront
Wolfe, T. On leprechauns
IRISH DIALECT See Dialect stories—Irish
The **Irish** gentleman and the little French-
   man. See Poe, E. A. Why the little
   Frenchman wears his hand in a sling
The **Irish** information office. Murphy, P.
IRISH REPUBLICAN ARMY
   Gilbert, M. The killing of Michael Fin-
      negan
Irish revel. O'Brien, E.
Iron, Ralph See Schreiner, Olive, 1855-1920
The **iron-bark** chip. Lawson, H.
Iron Beard leaves home. Lepiano, J.
Iron fish. Kono, T.
The **iron** hand. Durrell, L.
Iron masks. Cho, H.-I.
The **iron** star. Silverberg, R.
An **ironic** Yetta Montana. Friedman, B. J.

IRONY
   See also Satire
Akutagawa, R. 'Autumn Mountain'
Alexander, D. The man who went to Tal-
   tavul's
Archer, J. Not the real thing
Archer, J. The steal
Asscher-Pinkhof, C. White lie
Balfour, B. J. Some days are like that
Bloch, R. Daybroke
Block, L. As good as a rest
Böll, H. Adventures of a haversack
Borgen, J. The swan
Boyle, K. The first lover
Boyle, K. To the pure
Chekhov, A. P. The bet
Colegate, I. Distant cousins
Curley, D. Billy Will's song
Cushman, D. I.O.U.—one bullet
Disch, T. M. Canned goods
Ellison, H. Strange wine
Faik, S. Good deeds are never forgotten
Farmer, P. J. The sliced-crosswise only-on-
   Tuesday world
Forester, C. S. The turning of the tide
Fuentes, C. The two Elenas
Gilbert, W. S. The burglar's story
Halligan, M. Trespassers or guests?
Henry, O. The furnished room
Henry, O. The gift of the Magi
Henry, O. The last of the troubadours
Hoch, E. D. The last unicorns
Hoch, E. D. The maiden's sacrifice
Kimball, R. W. Destination
Klíma, I. Sunday morning: a foolish tale
Klíma, I. Wednesday morning: a Christmas
   conspiracy tale
Leaton, A. Gita's story
Lenz, S. The amusement-doctor
Lish, G. The problem of the preface
Lofts, N. Debt of gratitude
Lutz, J. Pure rotten
MacLean, A. McCrimmon and the blue
   moonstones
Maupassant, G. de. The diamond necklace
Moyes, P. The honest blackmailer
Pritchett, V. S. Tea with Mrs. Bittell
Pronzini, B. Bank job
Pronzini, B. Connoisseur
Proulx, A. Electric arrows
Read, O. Big Bill and Little Bill
Roth, J. Fallmerayer the stationmaster
Scholz, C. The menagerie of Babel
Schwob, M. The firebrands
Sciascia, L. End game
Slesar, H. The day of the execution
Slesar, H. A victim must be found
Spark, M. The fortune-teller
Sturges, A. E. Only a matter of time
Tenn, W. Eastward ho!
Tyre, N. A nice place to stay
Valdez, O. J. A dollar's worth
Valenzuela, L. The celery munchers

IRONY—*Continued*
Valenzuela, L. The censors
Valenzuela, L. Love of animals
Valenzuela, L. A story about greenery
Valenzuela, L. The verb to kill
Warren, J. The Corn Dolly
Warren, J. A special occasion
Wells, H. G. A family elopement
Wells, H. G. The new Faust
Wells, H. G. The Rajah's treasure
Willson, H. Half a loaf
Wolfe, T. Justice is blind
An **irony**. Van Wert, W. F.
The **irony** of hate. Rendell, R.
Irrelativity. Royle, N.
Irrelevant ideas. Matthews, J.
Irvine, R. R. (Robert R.)
A hard way to die
The Deadly arts; ed. by B. Pronzini and
M. Muller
In the dead hours
Murder California style; ed. by J. L.
Breen and J. Ball
Irvine, Robert R. *See* Irvine, R. R. (Robert
R.)
Irving, John, 1942-
Trying to save Piggy Sneed
The Bread Loaf anthology of contem-
porary American short stories; ed. by
R. Pack and J. Parini
Irving, Washington, 1783-1859
The adventure of the German student
[Variant title: The tale of the German
student]
Charles Keeping's Book of classic ghost
stories
Great ghost stories; ed. by B. A.
Schwartz
The Devil and Tom Walker
The Norton book of American short
stories
Is that what people do? Sheckley, R.
Is the Devil a gentleman? Quinn, S.
Is there too much sex in soaps? Mesler, C.
Is this civilization? Broun, H.
Is your name Joe? Algren, N.
"Is your wife here, honey?"**. Skrzynecki, P.
Isaac and the undertaker's daughter. *See*
Stern, S. The theft of Lily
Isaac Trimble's tale. Matthews, J.
Ishiguro, Kazuo, 1954-
A family supper
The Penguin book of modern British
short stories
Ishikawa, Jun, 1899-
Moon gems
The Shōwa anthology 1
Ishikawa, Tatsuzo
The affair of the arabesque inlay
Murder in Japan; ed. by J. L. Apostolou
and M. H. Greenberg
Ishmael in love. Silverberg, R.
Isis. Hurston, Z. N.

Iskander, Fazil'
Grandfather
The Barsukov Triangle, The two-toned
blond & other stories; ed. by C. R.
Proffer & E. Proffer
Isla. Kolankiewicz, S. J.
ISLAM
See also Muslims
McElroy, C. J. Farm day
Island. Asscher-Pinkhof, C.
The **island**. Francis, H. E.
The **island**. Hartley, L. P.
Island. Jones, E. P.
The **island**. Lynn, E. A.
Island. MacLeod, A.
An **island** of curving stone. Hoyt, M. S.
The **island** of Dr. Circe. Sladek, J. T.
The **island** of the fay. Poe, E. A.
The **island** of Ven. Berriault, G.
ISLANDS
See also Tasmania (Australia); also
names of individual islands
Aickman, R. The wine-dark sea
Barker, C. Scape-goats
Blackwood, A. A haunted island
Coover, R. Quenby and Ola, Swede and
Carl
Doyle, Sir A. C. Our midnight visitor
Faik, S. A dot on the map
Friedman, P. The family
Gifkins, M. Matching the blue
Grin, A. Reno Island
Haris, P. Lights on the sea
Hartley, L. P. Podolo
Houbein, L. Green marmalade
King, F. H. His everlasting mansion
Kolankiewicz, S. J. Isla
MacLeod, A. Island
Poe, E. A. The island of the fay
Pronzini, B. Smuggler's Island
Rule, J. Power failure
Smith, C. A. The uncharted isle
Virgo, S. Brother Dael's new year
Wells, H. G. Æpyornis Island
Wolfe, G. The death of Doctor Island
Woolson, C. F. The Lady of Little Fishing
Woolson, C. F. St. Clair Flats
Islands. Loukakis, A.
ISLANDS OF THE INDIAN OCEAN
See also Kerguelen Islands
ISLANDS OF THE PACIFIC
See also Solomon Islands
Ballard, J. G. The terminal beach
Bates, H. E. The white wind
Maugham, W. S. Red
Melville, H. Hood's Isle and the hermit
Oberlus
Merritt, A. The moon pool
The **isle** of dreams. Fühmann, F.
Isle of illusion. Severance, C.
The **isle** of the torturers. Smith, C. A.
The **isle** of voices. Stevenson, R. L.
Isley's stranger. Fisher, C.

Ismini. Farmer, B.
Isn't it something? Kauffman, J.
Isn't she lovely? Waldie, S.
Isolated incidents. Mukherjee, B.
Isometropia. Dodd, S. M.
Isosceles. Wilhelm, K.
ISRAEL
    See also Jerusalem; Negev (Israel);
    Zionism
  Amichai, Y. The Bar Mitzvah party
  Amichai, Y. Nina of Ashkelon
  Amichai, Y. The world is a room
  Eisenstein, S. The sacrifice
  Kessler, J. F. Esau
  Mazel, D. Karen
  Mazel, D. A story of hope
  Metzger, D. The tree on the mountain
            Tel Aviv
  Kaniuk, Y. The parched earth
  Shaw, I. Medal from Jerusalem
Israel and his children. Botwinik, B.
ISRAEL-ARAB WAR, 1973
  Helprin, M. North light
  Mazel, D. Sacrifices
ISRAELI SOLDIERS *See* Soldiers—Israel
ISRAELIS
    See also Jews
            Italy
  Shamosh, A. Lily, Africa and I
ISRAELITES *See* Jews
Israeloff, Roberta, 1952-
  City ball
    Editor's choice II; ed. by M. Sklar and
    M. Biggs
ISTANBUL (TURKEY) *See* Turkey—Istan-
    bul
It. Dawson, F.
It. Sturgeon, T.
It burns me up! Bradbury, R.
It could happen. Camoin, F. A.
It deals with people first. Ignatow, R. G.
It doesn't pay to be good. Sholem Aleichem
It had to be you. Lentricchia, M.
It had wings. Gurganus, A.
It must have been spring. O'Hara, J.
It opens your eyes. Morrison, J.
It so happens. Sisskind, M.
It spoke of exactly the things. Hannah, B.
It sure is cold here at night. Freeman, J.
It takes a thief. Miller, A.
It was an awful shame. MacLeod, C.
It wasn't all dancing. Brown, M. W.
ITALIAN AMERICANS
  La Puma, S. The boys of Bensonhurst
  La Puma, S. The gangster's ghost
  La Puma, S. Gravesend Bay
  La Puma, S. Guys under their fedoras
  La Puma, S. The jilted groom
  La Puma, S. The mouthpiece
  La Puma, S. Wear it in good health
  Mukherjee, B. Orbiting
The **Italian** cousin. Villefranche, A.-M.

ITALIAN RIVIERA *See* Riviera (France and
    Italy)
ITALIAN SOLDIERS *See* Soldiers—Italy
ITALIANS
            Australia
  Kalamaras, V. The shot
  Skrzynecki, P. Empty cages
            Canada
  Edwards, C. Prima vera
            England
  Hornung, E. W. The last laugh
            France
  Apollinaire, G. The departure of the
    shadow
  Apollinaire, G. Giovanni Moroni
  Sandel, C. The silken thread
            New York (N.Y.)
  Dawkins, C. The mourner
  Paolucci, A. Ciao, mio tesoro
  Paolucci, A. Rarà
  Pulaski, J. Music story
            Soviet Union
  Parise, G. Marriage
            United States
  Ardizzone, T. Nonna
  Briskin, M. Vincenzo and Giulia
  Fante, J. First Communion
  Fante, J. A kidnaping in the family
  Fante, J. My father's God
  Fante, J. A nun no more
  Fante, J. The odyssey of a Wop
  Fante, J. One of us
  Fante, J. A wife for Dino Rossi
  Humphrey, W. Dolce far' niente
  Kalpakian, L. Hunters in the fields of
    August
  Labozzetta, M. Making the wine
  Osborn, C. The new castle
  Paolucci, A. The oracle is dumb or cheat
  Schinto, J. The disappearance
ITALY
    See also Capri; Sicily
  Davidson, A. Duke Pasquale's ring
  Kleist, H. von. The beggarwoman of
    Locarno
  Pirandello, L. Sun and shade
            16th century
  Kotzwinkle, W. Sun, moon, and storm
            19th century
  Lee, V. A wicked voice
  Sagan, F. "La Futura"
            20th century
  Calvino, I. The adventure of a traveler
  Calvino, I. Autumn: the garden of stub-
    born cats
  Calvino, I. Man in the wasteland
  Calvino, I. Sleeping like dogs
  Cheever, J. The world of apples
  Fitzgerald, M. J. The fire eater
  Furlong, M. The garden
  Garrett, G. P. A wreath for Garibaldi
  Hemingway, E. Che ti dice la patria?
  Hemingway, E. Out of season

ITALY—20th century—*Continued*
King, F. H. The soutane
King, F. H. Sundays
King, F. H. Unmaking
Laski, M. The tower
Moravia, A. Jewellery
Paolucci, A. Don Giacomo
Paolucci, A. Lights
Parise, G. Mother
Parise, G. Youth
Pasternak, B. L. The Apelles mark
Pavese, C. Festival night
Pavese, C. First love
Pavese, C. Friends
Pavese, C. Gaol birds
Pavese, C. The intruder
Pavese, C. Misogyny
Pavese, C. The three girls
Pavese, C. Wedding trip
Pirandello, L. The lonely man
Sciascia, L. A matter of conscience
Aristocracy
See Aristocracy—Italy
Communism
See Communism—Italy
Farm life
See Farm life—Italy
Peasant life
See Peasant life—Italy
Rural life
Calvino, I. A goatherd at luncheon
Calvino, I. Hunger at Bévera
Déon, M. Umbrian afternoon
Forster, E. M. The story of a panic
Gordimer, N. Sins of the third age
Kleist, H. von. The Marquise of O—
Parise, G. Work
Pavese, C. The cornfield
Pavese, C. Land of exile
World War, 1939-1945
See World War, 1939-1945—Italy
Amalfi
Williams, T. Man bring this up road
Florence
Day, R. C. The pleasures of the senses
Gold, H. From Proust to Dada
Schwob, M. The plague
Genoa
Swados, H. Something a little special
Milan
Hemingway, E. In another country
Parise, G. Poise
Naples
Conrad, J. Il Conde
Davidson, A. Naples
Hornung, E. W. The fate of Faustina
Yourcenar, M. Anna, soror . . .
Padua
Hawthorne, N. Rappaccini's daughter
Pisa
Garrett, G. P. The strong man
Portofino
Sisk, F. The fly swatter

Rome
Ahern, T. An implied acquaintance
Eldridge, M. Tourist
Ellin, S. The twelfth statue
Gilliatt, P. Autumn of a dormouse
Highsmith, P. When in Rome
James, H. Daisy Miller
Kleist, H. von. The foundling
Morand, P. The Roman night
Parise, G. Freedom
Parise, G. Rome
Pritchard, M. Disturbing no one
Ryan, A. Pietà
Tuscany
Grenville, K. Country pleasures
Venice
Aiken, J. The cat who lived in a drainpipe
Baker, S. Sea change
Gilbert, W. S. Angela
Harris, M. The orphan bassoonist
Hartley, L. P. Podolo
Hartley, L. P. Simonetta Perkins
Highsmith, P. The bravest rat in Venice
Poe, E. A. The assignation
Poe, E. A. The visionary
Robinson, K. S. Venice drowned
Italy. Parise, G.
Item. Slesar, H.
Ithaca. Cooley, N.
ITINERANT CLERGY
Lowrey, P. H. The great speckled bird
It's a hard world. Vachss, A. H.
It's a man's drink, tonic water. Digby, J.
It's a pity. Mrozek, S.
It's all a matter of luck. Gardner, T. S.
It's important to believe. Russ, J.
It's just another day in Big Bear City, California. Beattie, A.
It's just one Elvis. Ball, B.
It's just the way it is. Bates, H. E.
It's quiet now. Mhlope, G.
It's six a.m. do you know where you are? McInerney, J.
It's such a beautiful day. Asimov, I.
It's the fault of the Tlaxcaltecas. Garro, E.
It's the same old story. Austin, D.
Itself surprised. Zelazny, R.
Ivan Fiodorovich Shponka and his aunt. Gogol', N. V.
I've stuttered all my life. Moravia, A.
Ivory bangles. Ng'maryo, E. S.
The **ivory** comb. Arnason, E.
The **ivory** dancer. Ekwensi, C.
The **ivy-covered** castle. Winters, J.
The **ivy** in the chimney. Wilcox, J.
Iyer's Hotel. Sharat Chandra, G. S.
Izgü, Muzaffer
Apollo's thing
Short story international 71
The attack by yoghurt
Short story international 59
Devoted Moslem Ismail Effendi
Short story international 55

Izzo, Francis E.
Tank
Tales from Isaac Asimov's science fiction magazine: short stories for young adults

J

"J". McBain, E.
J. Habakuk Jephson's statement. Doyle, Sir A. C.
J. P. and the water tower. Ruffin, P.
Jablokov, Alexander
At the cross-time jaunters' ball
The Year's best science fiction, fifth annual collection
Jack, Roger
The pebble people
Earth power coming; ed. by S. J. Ortiz
Jack Ellyat at Gettysburg. Benét, S. V.
Jack Frost. Jacobsen, J.
Jack M. Holz, C.
Jack of diamonds. Spencer, E.
Jack of hearts. Huggan, I.
JACK THE RIPPER
About
Baker, S. The sins of the fathers
Bloch, R. A toy for Juliette
Bloch, R. Yours truly, Jack the Ripper
Clemens, S. A good night's work
Ellison, H. The prowler in the city at the edge of the world
Ford, J. M. Street of dreams
Frost, G. From Hell, again
Grant, C. L. My shadow is the fog
Hoch, E. D. The treasure of Jack the Ripper
McLaughlin, C. The lodge of Jahbulon
Nicoll, G. Dead air
Nolan, W. F. The final stone
Shepard, L. Jack's decline
Somtow, S. P. Anna and the Ripper of Siam
Sullivan, T. Knucklebones
Turtledove, H. Gentlemen of the shade
Wagner, K. E. An awareness of angels
Wolfe, G. Game in the pope's head
Jackal's meal. Dickson, G. R.
Jacklighting. Beattie, A.
Jack's decline. Shepard, L.
Jack's garden. Naipaul, V. S.
Jack's girl. Kadohata, C.
Jackson, Gordon
Billy's girl
Sudden fiction; ed. by R. Shapard and J. Thomas
Jackson, Graham, 1947-
The decline of Western Hill
Jackson, G. The decline of Western Hill
Fly in the ointment
Jackson, G. The decline of Western Hill

The fly-screen
Jackson, G. The decline of Western Hill
Holing out
Jackson, G. The decline of Western Hill
Pyjamas
Jackson, G. The decline of Western Hill
Structural unemployment
Jackson, G. The decline of Western Hill
Sweet things
Jackson, G. The decline of Western Hill
Jackson, Helen Hunt, 1830-1885
How one woman kept her husband
The Other woman; ed. by S. Koppelman
Jackson, Margaret Weymouth
The magical geranium
The Saturday Evening Post 259:64-9+ Jl/Ag '87
Jackson, Shirley, 1919-1965
The beautiful stranger
The Dark descent; ed. by D. G. Hartwell
The lottery
The Norton book of American short stories
The lovely house
Witches' brew; ed. by M. Muller and B. Pronzini
The renegade
Haunting women; ed. by A. Ryan
Seven types of ambiguity
Chapter & hearse; ed. by M. Muller and B. Pronzini
The summer people
The Dark descent; ed. by D. G. Hartwell
JACKSON (MISS.) *See* Mississippi—Jackson
Jacob, Suzanne
Surviving
Intimate strangers; ed. by M. Cohen and W. Grady
Jacob. Kessler, J. F.
Jacobi, Carl, 1908-
Revelations in black
Vampires; ed. by A. Ryan
Jacobs, Harvey
My rose and my glove
Omni (New York, N.Y.) 6:56-7+ My '84
Stardust
Omni (New York, N.Y.) 9:44-6+ Ag '87
Jacobs, M. G.
Minor surgery and a poker game
Omni (New York, N.Y.) 7:70-2+ Mr '85
Jacobs, W. W. (William Wymark), 1863-1943
A black affair
Roger Caras' Treasury of great cat stories
The monkeys paw
Black water; ed. by A. Manguel
Dark company; ed. by L. Child
The Oxford book of English ghost stories

Jacobs, W. W. (William Wymark), 1863-1943—*Continued*
Outsailed
Sea captains' tales; ed. by A. Enfield
The white cat
Roger Caras' Treasury of great cat stories

Jacobs, William Wymark *See* Jacobs, W. W. (William Wymark), 1863-1943

Jacob's angel. Barton, M.

Jacob's ladder. Bell, S.

Jacobsen, Josephine
Adios, Mr. Moxley
Prairie Schooner 59:43-9 Spr '85
The friends
Prairie Schooner 59:36-49 Summ '85
Jack Frost
The Substance of things hoped for; ed. by J. B. Breslin
Life signs
McCall's 113:100-1 Ap '86
The mango community
Prize stories, 1985
The night the playoffs were rained out
Prairie Schooner 61:66-73 Summ '87
Trial run
Prairie Schooner 60:3-18 Wint '86

Jacobson, Dan
Beggar my neighbour
Echad 2: South African Jewish voices
Brian
The New Yorker 60:28-33 Ag 13 '84
A day in the country
Somehow tenderness survives; ed. by H. Rochman
The Treasury of English short stories; ed. by N. Sullivan

Jacobson, Edith, and Jacobson, Ejler
Corpses on parade
Selected tales of grim and grue from the horror pulps; ed. by S. Jaffery

Jacoby, Joan
Diary of a polesitter
Echad 2: South African Jewish voices

Jacqueline Ess: her will and testament. Barker, C.

JADE
Holding, J. Monkey king

Jade Blue. Bryant, E.

Jade Buddhas, red bridges, fruits of love. Gilchrist, E.

Jæger, Frank
Spring evening with Faust
Prairie Schooner 62:3-18 Fall '88

Jafek, Bev
You've come a long way, Mickey Mouse
The Best American short stories, 1985

Jaffe, Harold
Brother Wolf
Jaffe, H. Beasts
New directions in prose and poetry 49
Giraffe
Jaffe, H. Beasts

John Crow
Jaffe, H. Beasts
Monkey
Jaffe, H. Beasts
Mussel
Jaffe, H. Beasts
Pelican
American made; ed. by M. Leyner; C. White and T. Glynn
Jaffe, H. Beasts
Persian lamb
Jaffe, H. Beasts
The Pushcart prize XII
Salamander
Jaffe, H. Beasts
Sheep
Jaffe, H. Beasts
Sidewinder
Jaffe, H. Beasts

Jaffee, Annette Williams, 1945-
Rosie
Ploughshares 14 no1:119-24 '88

Jaffer's chicken. Leitão, L.

The **jaguar** hunter. Shepard, L.

JAGUARS
Shepard, L. The jaguar hunter

Jahnn, Hans Henny, 1894-1959
A boy weeps
Jahnn, H. H. Thirteen uncanny stories
The diver
Jahnn, H. H. Thirteen uncanny stories
The gardener
Jahnn, H. H. Thirteen uncanny stories
Kebad Kenya
Jahnn, H. H. Thirteen uncanny stories
The marmalade eaters
Jahnn, H. H. Thirteen uncanny stories
A master selects his servant
Jahnn, H. H. Thirteen uncanny stories
Mov
Jahnn, H. H. Thirteen uncanny stories
Ragna and Nils
Jahnn, H. H. Thirteen uncanny stories
Sassanidian king
Jahnn, H. H. Thirteen uncanny stories
The slave's story
Jahnn, H. H. Thirteen uncanny stories
Stolen horses
Jahnn, H. H. Thirteen uncanny stories
The story of the twins
Jahnn, H. H. Thirteen uncanny stories
The watchmaker
Jahnn, H. H. Thirteen uncanny stories

The **jailer's** son. Ferron, J.

Jairus' daughter. Ponsoldt, S.

Jak the tout. Böll, H.

Jake. Botwinik, B.

The **Jake** Pond. Crabtree, L. V.

Jakes, John, 1932-
And the monsters walk
Wizards; ed. by I. Asimov; M. H. Greenberg and C. G. Waugh

Jakes, John, 1932——*Continued*
  Dr. Sweetkill
    Baker's dozen: 13 short espionage novels
  I still see Sally
    Uncollected crimes; ed. by B. Pronzini
      and M. H. Greenberg
  The man who wanted to be in the movies
    The Deadly arts; ed. by B. Pronzini and
      M. Muller
  Political machine
    Election Day 2084; ed. by I. Asimov
      and M. H. Greenberg
  The sellers of the dream
    Baker's dozen: 13 short science fiction
      novels
  Storm in a bottle
    Baker's dozen: 13 short fantasy novels
  There's no vinism like chauvinism
    Amazing stories: 60 years of the best
      science fiction
JAMAICA
  Bowles, P. Pages from Cold Point
  Katz, S. The stolen stories
                    Kingston
  Shacochis, B. The pelican
JAMAICANS
                    England
  Mortimer, J. C. Rumpole and the confes-
    sion of guilt
Jamboree. Williamson, J.
Jameison, Leland
  East from Botwood
    A Treasury of World War II stories; ed.
      by B. Pronzini and M. H. Greenberg
James, Darius
  Negrophobia
    Between C & D; ed. by J. Rose and
      C. Texier
James, Francis
  Arms of the flame goddess
    Selected tales of grim and grue from the
      horror pulps; ed. by S. Jaffery
  Dance of the bloodless ones
    The Weirds; ed. by S. Jaffery
JAMES, FRANK, 1844-1915
                    About
  Taylor, R. The history of Frank James
James, Henry, 1843-1916
  The author of Beltraffio
    James, H. The figure in the carpet, and
      other stories
  Brooksmith
    James H. Henry James' shorter master-
      piece v1
  A bundle of letters
    The Best Maine stories; ed. by S. Phip-
      pen; C. Waugh and M. Greenberg
  The chaperon
    James H. Henry James' shorter master-
      pieces v1
  The Coxon Fund
    James H. Henry James' shorter master-
      pieces v1

Daisy Miller
    Great American love stories; ed. by L.
      Rosenthal
  The death of the lion
    James H. Henry James' shorter master-
      pieces v1
    James, H. The figure in the carpet, and
      other stories
  The figure in the carpet
    James H. Henry James' shorter master-
      pieces v2
    James, H. The figure in the carpet, and
      other stories
  The friends of the friends
    Black water; ed. by A. Manguel
    The Oxford book of English ghost
      stories
  The great good place
    James H. Henry James' shorter master-
      pieces v2
  Hugh Merrow
    The New York Times Magazine p55+ O
      26 '86
  An international episode
    James H. An international episode, and
      other stories
  John Delavoy
    James H. Henry James' shorter master-
      pieces v2
    James, H. The figure in the carpet, and
      other stories
  The jolly corner
    Dark company; ed. by L. Child
    The Dark descent; ed. by D. G. Hart-
      well
  Lady Barberina
    James H. An international episode, and
      other stories
  The lesson of the master
    James, H. The figure in the carpet, and
      other stories
  The middle years
    James H. Henry James' shorter master-
      pieces v1
    James, H. The figure in the carpet, and
      other stories
    The Norton book of American short
      stories
  The next time
    James H. Henry James' shorter master-
      pieces v2
    James, H. The figure in the carpet, and
      other stories
  Nona Vincent
    James H. Henry James' shorter master-
      pieces v1
  Paste
    James H. Henry James' shorter master-
      pieces v2
  The Pension Beaurepas
    James H. An international episode, and
      other stories

James, Henry, 1843-1916—_Continued_
The private life
James, H. The figure in the carpet, and other stories
The romance of certain old clothes
The Penguin book of horror stories
Sir Edmund Orme
The Penguin book of ghost stories
The way it came
James H. Henry James' shorter masterpieces v2

JAMES, JESSE WOODSON, 1847-1882
About
Taylor, R. Billy Gashade and glory
Taylor, R. Charley Ford betrayed
Taylor, R. The James boys ride again
Taylor, R. Mrs. Jesse James, mourning
Taylor, R. The tragedy of Bob Ford

James, M. R. (Montague Rhodes), 1862-1936
The ash-tree
The Dark descent; ed. by D. G. Hartwell
Lost souls; ed. by J. Sullivan
Count Magnus
Lost souls; ed. by J. Sullivan
An episode of cathedral history
Vampires; ed. by A. Ryan
Lost hearts
Handle with care; ed. by J. Kahn
The Penguin book of horror stories
Young ghosts; ed. by I. Asimov; M. H. Greenberg and C. G. Waugh
The mezzotint
Dark company; ed. by L. Child
'Oh, whistle, and I'll come to you, my lad'
Charles Keeping's Classic tales of the macabre
The Oxford book of English ghost stories
The rose garden
The Penguin book of ghost stories
Wailing well
Charles Keeping's Book of classic ghost stories

James, Montague Rhodes _See_ James, M. R. (Montague Rhodes), 1862-1936

James, P. D.
The girl who loved graveyards
The Mammoth book of modern crime stories; ed. by G. Hardinge
Great Aunt Allie's flypapers
John Creasey's Crime collection, 1985
Memories don't die
Redbook 163:36+ Jl '84
The murder of Santa Claus
Great detectives; ed. by D. W. McCullough
The victim
Masterpieces of mystery and suspense; ed. by M. H. Greenberg
The Penguin classic crime omnibus

James, Stuart
Mission #6
The Virginia Quarterly Review 63:479-97 Summ '87
Mission No. 1
The Sewanee Review 95:219-37 Spr '87
Mission no. 16
The Sewanee Review 96:584-600 Fall '88
"Then face to face"
The Sewanee Review 94:521-40 Fall '86
The **James** boys ride again. Taylor, R.
James Dean's widow. Schulman, H.

JAMES FAMILY
About
Taylor, R. Zerelda James Samuel

James-French, Dayv
Cows
The Antioch Review 46:327-40 Summ '88
Domestic order
The Antioch Review 43:36-48 Wint '85
Heaven full of astronauts
The Antioch Review 45:129-49 Spr '87

Jamie's grave. Tuttle, L.
Jammed. Lindsey, J.
Jan Klinkies. Wicomb, Z.
Janda, N. L. _See_ Aldani, Lino
Jane Brown's body. Woolrich, C.
The **Jane** from Hell's Kitchen. Paul, P.

Janecky, J. Y.
The red dress
'Teen 31:28+ D '87

The **Janeites.** Lott, J.
A **janitor** for sale. Rizkalla, J.
Il **janitoro.** Ade, G.

JANITORS
Dixon, S. The clean-up man
Lish, G. What is left to link us
Lynch, L. Mary's garden
Pascoe, B. Cobber: Peach Face
Rizkalla, J. A janitor for sale
West, J. The battle of the suits

Janka Doodle. Stark, S. S.

Janowitz, Tama
Case history #4: Fred
Harper's 272:34+ Je '86
Janowitz, T. Slaves of New York
Case history #15: Melinda
Janowitz, T. Slaves of New York
Case history #179: Tina
Between C & D; ed. by J. Rose and C. Texier
Conviction
The New generation; ed. by A. Kaufman
Engagements
Janowitz, T. Slaves of New York
The New Yorker 61:30-8 S 2 '85
Fondue
Janowitz, T. Slaves of New York
In and out of the cat bag
Janowitz, T. Slaves of New York
Kurt and Natasha, a relationship
Janowitz, T. Slaves of New York

Janowitz, Tama—*Continued*
Life in the pre-Cambrian era
   Janowitz, T. Slaves of New York
Lunch involuntary
   Janowitz, T. Slaves of New York
Matches
   Janowitz, T. Slaves of New York
Modern saint #271
   Janowitz, T. Slaves of New York
The new acquaintances
   Janowitz, T. Slaves of New York
Ode to heroine of the future
   Janowitz, T. Slaves of New York
On and off the African veldt
   Janowitz, T. Slaves of New York
Patterns
   Janowitz, T. Slaves of New York
   The New Yorker 61:38-46 F 3 '86
Physics
   Janowitz, T. Slaves of New York
   The New Yorker 61:33-40 S 30 '85
The slaves in New York
   Janowitz, T. Slaves of New York
   The New Yorker 60:22-7 D 31 '84
Snowball
   Janowitz, T. Slaves of New York
Spells
   Janowitz, T. Slaves of New York
   The New Yorker 61:42-50 N 25 '85
Sun poisoning
   Janowitz, T. Slaves of New York
Turkey talk
   Janowitz, T. Slaves of New York
Who's on first?
   Janowitz, T. Slaves of New York
You and The Boss
   Janowitz, T. Slaves of New York
January. Barthelme, D.
Janus. Beattie, A.
Janus. Van Greenaway, P.
JAPAN
Akutagawa, R. Hell screen
Davenport, G. Fifty-seven views of
   Fujiyama
Endō, S. The day before
Endō, S. Incredible voyage
Hearn, L. Of a promise kept
Kaikō, T. Duel
Kawabata, Y. The white horse
Levy, D. Proletarian Zen
Shiga, N. Akanishi Kakita
Shiga, N. An incident
Shiga, N. The razor
Shiga, N. Seibei and his gourds
Shiga, N. The shopboy's god
Sterling, B. Flowers of Edo
Tanizaki, J. Tattoo
####### 16th century
Kōda, R. The bearded samurai
####### 20th century
Buck, P. S. The enemy
Enchi, F. Blind man's buff
Harada, Y. Evening bells

Haylock, J. Love problems
Ibuse, M. Kuchisuke's valley
Ishiguro, K. A family supper
Kaikō, T. A certain voice
Kaikō, T. The fishing hole (Ana)
Kaikō, T. Five thousand runaways
Kaikō, T. The laughingstock
Kawabata, Y. Autumn rain
Kawabata, Y. Bamboo-leaf boats
Kawabata, Y. Beyond death
Kawabata, Y. The blind man and the girl
Kawabata, Y. The bound husband
Kawabata, Y. Earth
Kawabata, Y. Eggs
Kawabata, Y. Glass
Kawabata, Y. Gleanings from snow country
Kawabata, Y. God's bones
Kawabata, Y. Goldfish on the roof
Kawabata, Y. The grasshopper and the bell cricket
Kawabata, Y. The hat incident
Kawabata, Y. Her mother's eye
Kawabata, Y. Immortality
Kawabata, Y. The incident of the dead face
Kawabata, Y. The jay
Kawabata, Y. Lavatory Buddahood
Kawabata, Y. Love suicides
Kawabata, Y. The maidens' prayers
Kawabata, Y. Makeup
Kawabata, Y. The man who did not smile
Kawabata, Y. The neighbors
Kawabata, Y. The O-Shin Jizo
Kawabata, Y. One person's happiness
Kawabata, Y. A pet dog's safe birthing
Kawabata, Y. The rainy station
Kawabata, Y. A saw and childbirth
Kawabata, Y. The silver fifty-sen pieces
Kawabata, Y. The silverberry thief
Kawabata, Y. The Sliding Rock
Kawabata, Y. A smile outside the night stall
Kawabata, Y. The snakes
Kawabata, Y. Snow
Kawabata, Y. Socks
Kawabata, Y. Summer shoes
Kawabata, Y. A sunny place
Kawabata, Y. Tabi
Kawabata, Y. Thank you
Kawabata, Y. There is a God
Kawabata, Y. Thunder in autumn
Kawabata, Y. Umbrella
Kawabata, Y. Up in the tree
Kawabata, Y. The weaker vessel
Kawabata, Y. The white flower
Kawabata, Y. The Wife of the Autumn Wind
Kawabata, Y. The wife's search
Kawabata, Y. The young lady of Suruga
Kawabata, Y. The younger sister's clothes
King, F. H. A corner of a foreign field
King, F. H. The Festival of the Dead

JAPAN—20th century—*Continued*
King, F. H. Indirect method
Mori, Y. Be it ever so humble
Nagai, K. Nude
Ooka, S. The mother of dreams
Rampo, E. The Red Chamber
Setouchi, H. Pheasant
Shiga, N. As far as Abashiri
Shiga, N. A gray moon
Shiga, N. Incident on the afternoon of November third
Shiga, N. Kuniko
Shiga, N. A memory of Yamashina
Shiga, N. The paper door
Shiga, N. Rain frogs
Shiga, N. The razor
Tsushima, Y. Clearing the thickets
Tsushima, Y. An embrace
Tsushima, Y. The shooting gallery
Yasuoka, S. Bad company
Yasuoka, S. The moth
Yasuoka, S. Rain
Yasuoka, S. Thick the new leaves
1945-
Abe, A. Friends
Abe, K. Song of a dead girl
Ariyoshi, S. The Tomoshibi
Dazai, O. The lady who entertained
Eisenstein, S. All the monkeys
Endō, S. Despicable bastard
Endō, S. My belongings
Endō, S. Old friends
Hara, T. The land of heart's desire
Hayashi, K. The empty can
Hiraiwa, Y. Lady of the evening faces
Hirota, Y. An invitation to a movie
Ibuse, M. The crazy iris
Inoue, M. The House of Hands
Inoue, Y. A marriage interview
Ishikawa, J. Moon gems
Matsumoto, S. Wait a year and a half
Mishima, Y. Three million yen
Ota, Y. Fireflies
Sata, I. The colorless paintings
Shibaki, Y. Ripples
Takenishi, H. The rite
Tsuboi, S. Umbrella on a moonlit night
Tsushima, Y. The chrysanthemum beetle
Tsushima, Y. Missing
Tsushima, Y. A sensitive season
Tsushima, Y. The silent traders
Tsushima, Y. South wind
Van de Wetering, J. The new disciple
Yasuoka, S. Gloomy pleasures
Yasuoka, S. A view by the sea
College life
See College life—Japan
Marriage customs
See Marriage customs—Japan
Prisoners and prisons
See Prisoners and prisons—Japan
Rural life
Fuerst, R. E. The plight of the dragonfly

Inoue, Y. Under the shadow of Mt. Bandai
Kōda, R. Encounter with a skull
Kōda, R. The five-storied pagoda
Minakami, T. Mulberry child
Shiga, N. At Kinosaki
Shiga, N. The house by the moat
Yano, T. The legend of the paper spaceship
Hiroshima
Hara, T. Summer flower
Mrożek, S. The pastor
Oda, K. Human ashes
Kyoto
Kawabata, Y. Autumn rain
King, F. H. The goat
Nagasaki
Hayashi, K. The empty can
Inoue, M. The House of Hands
Tokyo
Endō, S. The war generation
Green, E. Marginals
Green, E. Peters in Shinjuku: a set of miniatures
Haylock, J. Fan mail
Tsutsui, Y. Standing woman
Tuohy, F. The broken bridge
Tuohy, F. Nocturne with neon lights
Woolrich, C. Tokyo, 1941
Unzen
Endō, S. Unzen
Yokohama
Bissoondath, N. The cage
JAPANESE
Australia
Rata. The invasion of Sydney
Yamamoto, M. Betty-san
Yamamoto, M. Chair in the rain
Yamamoto, M. Father Goose
Yamamoto, M. Powers
Austria
Rhys, J. Vienne
Canada
Bissoondath, N. The cage
China
Kawabata, Y. Water
England
Haylock, J. Choice
Kawabata, Y. Riding clothes
King, F. H. Loss
Tuohy, F. A summer pilgrim
Guam
Bishop, M. Patriots
Hawaii
Nunes, S. A small obligation
Saiki, J. The arrangement
Saiki, J. Arrival of the picture brides
Saiki, J. Family business
Saiki, J. The fisherman
Saiki, J. My wartime job
Saiki, J. Nocturne
Saiki, J. The old ways
Saiki, J. Once, a lotus garden

JAPANESE—Hawaii—*Continued*
Saiki, J. Revelation
Saiki, J. Samurai
Saiki, J. Sisters
Saiki, J. Suspect alien
Saiki, J. The visit
Saiki, J. Windows
Saiki, P. S. Communion
Korea
Yi, H. The woman who fulled clothes
Taiwan
Chu, T.-J. Autumn note
United States
Apple, M. Small island republics
Bellah, J. W. Day of terror
Saiki, J. The wood rose
Wolfe, T. Katamoto
Yamamoto, H. Seventeen syllables
JAPANESE AMERICANS
Apple, M. Small island republics
A **Japanese** play. Starr, V.
JAPANESE SOLDIERS *See* Soldiers—Japan
Jar-boy. Baukin, L.
A **jar** of emeralds. Giles, M.
Jarley's. Thomas, D.
Jarman, Mark
Goose, dog, fish, stars
    Alberta bound; ed. by F. Stenson
The **jarrah** thieves. Jolley, E.
Jarvis, Mark C.
Collaboration
    From mind to mind: tales of communication from Analog
Jasmin, Claude, 1930-
Lulu the tailor
    The Oxford book of French-Canadian short stories
Jasmine. Mukherjee, B.
Jaundiced. Davin, D.
The **Jaunt**. King, S.
Jauss, David
Freeze
    New England Review and Bread Loaf Quarterly 11:8-21 Aut '88
Jaws. Barthelme, D.
The **jaws** of life. Willett, J.
The **jay**. Kawabata, Y.
Jay Score. Russell, E. F.
JAZZ MUSIC
Barthelme, D. The king of jazz
Bonnie, F. Take a seat, not a solo
Gardner, M. The fall of Flatbush Smith
Gardner, M. Sibyl sits in
Howard, C. Horn man
Shacochis, B. Lord Short Shoe wants the monkey
The **jealous** apprentice. Aiken, J.
Jealous-hearted me. Packer, N. H.
JEALOUSY
Andreyev, L. The thought
Apollinaire, G. The favorite
Archer, J. A chapter of accidents
Bloch, R. Impractical joker

Bloch, R. That old black magic
Bonner, M. A sealed pod
Brewer, G. Fool's gold
Bukoski, A. Route of the zephyrs
Camoin, F. A. A hunk of burning love
Campbell, W. B. The favour
Campbell, W. B. Headlights
Colette. Clever dogs
Colette. A dead end
Colter, C. A gift
Colter, C. The lookout
Colum, P. Catherine Mulamphy and the man from the north
Curtiss, U. R. Something green and growing
Dibble, J. B. To sleep, perchance to dream
Drewe, R. Eighty per cent humidity
Enright, E. A distant bell
Fisher, R. The promised land
Fremlin, C. Dangerous sport
Greenwood, R. Charley Wales
Guido, B. The usurper
Hannah, B. Water liars
Henry, O. Schools and schools
Hernández, J. J. Queens
Hoch, E. D. The problem of the county fair
Humphrey, W. A voice from the woods
James, H. The romance of certain old clothes
James, H. The way it came
Johnston, G. Strong-man from Piraeus
Kawabata, Y. A smile outside the night stall
Kundera, M. The hitchhiking game
Maupassant, G. de. Am I insane
Maupassant, G. de. A wife's confession
McCormack, E. P. The fugue
Moore, G. A Russian husband
Moore, G. Two men
Mori, Y. Spring storm
Nagibin, IŪ. M. Shurik
Nielsen, H. The deadly Mrs. Haversham
Pritchett, V. S. A family man
Pronzini, B. The hanging man
Rees, D. Quiet days in Los Gatos
Regent, P. Feet of clay
Sims, G. Family butcher
Singer, I. B. The impresario
Swan, A. Monsoon
Taylor, C. Loving thy neighbor
Taylor, P. A. The swan-boat murder
Thomas, M. Shellers
Tsushima, Y. The chrysanthemum beetle
Vaughn, S. Sweet talk
Weber, T. The night of the sea serpent
Wellen, E. Born victims
Ziem, J. Before the thunderstorm
Jealousy. Faik, S.
Jealousy. Michaels, L.
Jean and Little Aunt. Livesey, M.
Jean Beicke. Williams, W. C.
Jean-Christophe. Fink, I.

A **Jean-Marie** cookbook. Weinstein, J.
Jean Paul, 1763-1825
  Army-chaplain Schmelzle's journey to Flätz
    German romantic novellas, by H. von
    Kleist and Jean Paul
  The life of Maria Wuz, the merry-hearted
    Dominie of Auenthal [Variant title:
    Life of the cheerful schoolmaster
    Maria Wutz]
    German romantic novellas, by H. von
    Kleist and Jean Paul
Jean-Pierre. Spencer, E.
Jean Sandwich, the sponsor and I. Watson,
    I.
JEANNE D'ARC, SAINT *See* Joan, of Arc,
    Saint, 1412-1431
Jeannette's hands. Latham, P.
Jeeves and the Chump Cyril. Wodehouse, P.
    G.
Jeeves and the greasy bird. Wodehouse, P.
    G.
Jeeves and the hard-boiled egg. Wodehouse,
    P. G.
Jeeves and the impending doom.
    Wodehouse, P. G.
Jeeves and the kid Clementina. Wodehouse,
    P. G.
Jeeves and the old school chum. Wodehouse,
    P. G.
Jeeves and the song of songs. Wodehouse,
    P. G.
Jeeves and the unbidden guest. Wodehouse,
    P. G.
Jeeves and the Yule-tide spirit. Wodehouse,
    P. G.
Jeeves in the springtime. Wodehouse, P. G.
Jeeves makes an omelette. Wodehouse, P. G.
Jeeves takes charge. Wodehouse, P. G.
Jeff Beck. Shiner, L.
Jefferson I: home in your hands. Lynch, L.
Jefferson II: in and out of the darkness.
    Lynch, L.
Jefferson III: family and friends. Lynch, L.
Jefferson IV: around every base till she was
    home. Lynch, L.
Jeffrey, Tim
  Habits of contact
    Editor's choice II; ed. by M. Sklar and
    M. Biggs
Jeffrey, William
  A case for quiet
    Alfred Hitchcock's Mortal errors
Jeffrey, believe me. Smiley, J.
Jeffty is five. Ellison, H.
Jemima Shore's first case. Fraser, A.
Jen, Gish
  Eating crazy
    The Yale Review 74:425-33 Spr '85
  In the American society
    The New generation; ed. by A. Kaufman
    The Southern Review (Baton Rouge, La.)
    22:606-19 Summ '86

The water-faucet vision
  The Best American short stories, 1988
The white umbrella
  The Yale Review 73:401-9 Spr '84
Jen, the fox fairy. See Shen, C.-C. Miss Jen
Jenkins, Will F.
  Uneasy home-coming
    The Penguin book of horror stories
Jennie's lessons to Peter on how to behave
  like a cat. Gallico, P.
Jennifer's lover. Silverberg, R.
Jennifer's wedding day. Soman, F. J.
Jennings, Gary
  Tom cat
    Magicats! Ed. by J. Dann and G. Dozois
Jennings, Jor
  Tiger hunt
    L. Ron Hubbard presents Writers of the
    future
Jennings, Philip Sidney
  The copy cats
    Encounter (London, England) 66:3-7 Mr
    '86
Jenny. Willett, J.
Jenny Stairy's hat. Hamilton, M.
Jeopardies. Mazel, D.
Jeppson, J. O., 1926-
  August angst
    Jeppson, J. O. The mysterious cure, and
    other stories of Pshrinks Anonymous
  The beanstalk analysis
    Jeppson, J. O. The mysterious cure, and
    other stories of Pshrinks Anonymous
  Consternation and empire
    Jeppson, J. O. The mysterious cure, and
    other stories of Pshrinks Anonymous
  The curious consultation
    Jeppson, J. O. The mysterious cure, and
    other stories of Pshrinks Anonymous
  The horn of Elfland
    Jeppson, J. O. The mysterious cure, and
    other stories of Pshrinks Anonymous
  The hotter flash
    Jeppson, J. O. The mysterious cure, and
    other stories of Pshrinks Anonymous
  A million shades of green
    Jeppson, J. O. The mysterious cure, and
    other stories of Pshrinks Anonymous
  The mysterious cure
    Jeppson, J. O. The mysterious cure, and
    other stories of Pshrinks Anonymous
  The Noodge Factor
    Jeppson, J. O. The mysterious cure, and
    other stories of Pshrinks Anonymous
  A pestilence of psychoanalysts
    Jeppson, J. O. The mysterious cure, and
    other stories of Pshrinks Anonymous
  Seasonal special
    Jeppson, J. O. The mysterious cure, and
    other stories of Pshrinks Anonymous
  The time-warp trauma
    Jeppson, J. O. The mysterious cure, and
    other stories of Pshrinks Anonymous

Jeppson, J. O., 1926-—*Continued*
The ultimate biofeedback device
Jeppson, J. O. The mysterious cure, and other stories of Pshrinks Anonymous
Jeremy Franklin Simmons. McElroy, C. J.
Jeremy's first hunt. Gordon, A.
Jericho and the cardboard box. Pentecost, H.
Jericho, Jericho, Jericho. Lytle, A.
Jerk the giant killer. Bloch, R.
Jeroboam. Maupassant, G. de
Jerome, Jerome K. (Jerome Klapka), 1859-1927
The dancing partner
Handle with care; ed. by J. Kahn
The **Jersey** Devil. Hoch, E. D.
JERUSALEM
Amichai, Y. Battle for the hill
Amichai, Y. Love in reverse
Amichai, Y. The snow
Amichai, Y. Terrible spring
Gold, H. Contingency planning
Lewitt, M. All the storms and sun-sets
Liphshitz, A. Gates of joy
Liphshitz, A. The last stage
Liphshitz, A. Three women
Liphshitz, A. Under the horses' hooves
Mazel, D. The wall
Poe, E. A. A tale of Jerusalem
Thomas, J. Talma Levy is falling
Trevor, W. Death in Jerusalem
Siege, 70 A.D.
Doyle, Sir A. C. The centurion
Jerusalem & home. Avery, M.
The **Jervis** Bay. MacLean, A.
Jespersen, Ruth
Yport
Stand one; ed. by M. Blackburn; J. Silkin and L. Tracy
Jesse and Louise. Johnston, S.
Jesse and Meribeth. Munro, A.
Jesse James betrayed. See Taylor, R. Charley Ford betrayed
Jessie. Forrest, K. V.
Jester. Murphy, P.
JESTERS *See* Fools and jesters
Jesu, Joy of Man's Desiring. Tournier, M.
The **Jesuit.** Oates, J. C.
JESUITS
L'Heureux, J. Clothing
McGrath, P. Ambrose Syme
Oates, J. C. The Jesuit
Ryan, A. Following the way
Jesus and Fat Tuesday. McElroy, C. J.
JESUS CHRIST
About
Boisvert, C. The prophet
Cullen, E. J. First sight
Olson, T. The scourging at the pillar
Sawai, G. The day I sat with Jesus on the sun deck and a wind came up and blew my kimono open and he saw my breasts

Wilde, O. The selfish giant
Crucifixion
Hemingway, E. Today is Friday
Kilworth, G. Let's go to Golgotha!
Jesus Christ and the plaster squirrels. Abbott, K.
The **Jesus** Flag. MacLeod, J. L.
Jesus knew. O'Donnell, E. P.
The **jet** ruler. Liang Xiaosheng
Jeter, K. W.
The new floor
Omni (New York, N.Y.) 11:182+ O '88
The **Jew** from Babylon. Singer, I. B.
The **Jewbird.** Malamud, B.
A **jewel** for a friend. Cooper, J. C.
The **jewel** of Arwen. Bradley, M. Z.
Jewel of the moon. Kotzwinkle, W.
JEWEL ROBBERIES *See* Robbery
The **jewel** robbery at the Grand Metropolitan. Christie, A.
JEWELERS
Leskov, N. S. The mountain
Lessing, D. M. Out of the fountain
Marlowe, D. J. By means unlovely
Mathews, P. S. Well met in Ithkar
Naipaul, S. The tenant
Sandel, C. Hval
Weinstein, L. How I became a jeweler
Woolf, V. The Duchess and the jeweller
The **jeweller's** boy. Kiely, B.
Jewellery. Moravia, A.
JEWELRY
See also Diamonds; Emeralds; Jade; Necklaces; Pearls; Rings
Archer, J. Not the real thing
Chipulina, E. G. Diamonds are forever
Crowley, A. The stone of Cybele
Garfield, B. King's X
Ingalls, R. Inheritance
Maupassant, G. de. The false gems
Sandel, C. The bracelet
Jewels. Gekiere, M.
Jewels in an angel's wing. Watson, I.
Jewett, Sarah Orne, 1849-1909
All my sad captains
Short stories of the sea; ed. by G. C. Solley and E. Steinbaugh
The foreigner
Haunted women; ed. by A. Bendixen
Lady Ferry
Haunted New England; ed. by C. G. Waugh; M. H. Greenberg and F. D. McSherry
Mrs. Parkins's Christmas Eve
"May your days be merry and bright" and other Christmas stories by women; ed. by S. Koppelman
A white heron
The Best Maine stories; ed. by S. Phippen; C. Waugh and M. Greenberg
The Norton book of American short stories
Through other eyes; ed. by I. Zahava

JEWISH-ARAB RELATIONS
  Liphshitz, A. Jum'a and Jamila
  Liphshitz, A. Under the horses' hooves
JEWISH-BLACK RELATIONS *See* Black-
  Jewish relations
JEWISH CHILDREN
  Asscher-Pinkhof, C. Adventurer
  Asscher-Pinkhof, C. Bath
  Asscher-Pinkhof, C. Bogeyman
  Asscher-Pinkhof, C. Breakdown
  Asscher-Pinkhof, C. Expensive purchase
  Asscher-Pinkhof, C. First worry
  Asscher-Pinkhof, C. Flap of wings
  Asscher-Pinkhof, C. Good luck songs
  Asscher-Pinkhof, C. Good night—good
    morning
  Asscher-Pinkhof, C. Grandson
  Asscher-Pinkhof, C. Harmonica
  Asscher-Pinkhof, C. Hora
  Asscher-Pinkhof, C. Hospital barrack
  Asscher-Pinkhof, C. How can Herod bear
    the light
  Asscher-Pinkhof, C. Hunger
  Asscher-Pinkhof, C. Market woman
  Asscher-Pinkhof, C. Merry child
  Asscher-Pinkhof, C. Missed chance
  Asscher-Pinkhof, C. Neighbor below
  Asscher-Pinkhof, C. Packages
  Asscher-Pinkhof, C. Passage to Heaven
  Asscher-Pinkhof, C. Return
  Asscher-Pinkhof, C. Star dance
  Asscher-Pinkhof, C. Transfer
  Asscher-Pinkhof, C. Transport night
  Asscher-Pinkhof, C. Tucking in
  Asscher-Pinkhof, C. Unloading
  Asscher-Pinkhof, C. White lie
  Asscher-Pinkhof, C. Women's talk
  Barnea, L. My grandfather
  Pulaski, J. Religious instruction
JEWISH HOLOCAUST (1933-1945) *See*
  Holocaust, Jewish (1933-1945)
JEWISH REFUGEES *See* Refugees, Jewish
JEWISH WOMEN
  Blinkin, M. Women
  Briskin, M. Giant sequoia
  Morand, P. Hungarian night
  Paley, G. In this country, but in another
    language, my aunt refuses to marry
    the men everyone wants her to
JEWS
      See also Antisemitism; Hasidism; Is-
    raelis; Jewish-Arab relations; Jewish
    women; Judaism; World War, 1939-
    1945—Jews
  Amichai, Y. The times my father died
  Ansky, S. Behind a mask
  Asscher-Pinkhof, C. French
  Bellow, S. Him with his foot in his mouth
  Blinkin, M. The little calf
  Botwinik, B. The Bubbe
  Damon, P. Davidson among the chosen
  Gold, H. Christmas in Dakar
  Lewitt, M. All the storms and sun-sets

  Lurie, M. Tell me what you want
  Maupassant, G. de. Lost!
  Maupassant, G. de. The Venus of Braniza
  Mazel, D. Karen
  Mazel, D. A story of hope
  Mazel, D. Strawberries
  Mazel, D. A visit with Esta
  Mazel, D. The wall
  Moskowitz, F. Fanny's comfort station
  Moskowitz, F. The runaround
  Moskowitz, F. Thelma
  Moskowitz, F. Whoever finds this: I love
    you
  Neugeboren, J. Uncle Nathan
  Ozick, C. Levitation
  Rose, D. A. Summer heat
  Shaham, N. S/S Cairo City
  Shaw, I. The inhabitants of Venus
  Sholem Aleichem. Rabchik, a Jewish dog
  Silverberg, R. The dybbuk of Mazel Tov
    IV
  Singer, I. B. The dead fiddler
  Singer, I. B. Henne Fire
  Singer, I. B. Miracles
  Singer, I. B. One day of happiness
  Singer, I. B. Strangers
  Sperling, L. The book of life
  Stern, S. Aaron makes a match
  Stern, S. The book of Mordecai
  Stern, S. Bruno's metamorphosis
  Stern, S. Goldfinch & Son
  Stern, S. The theft of Lily
  Waldrop, H. Horror, we got
  Wolfenstein, M. Chayah
              Marriage customs
          See Marriage customs—Jews
              Persecutions
          See also Holocaust, Jewish (1933-
  1945)
              Religion
          See Judaism
              Australia
  Bergner, H. The actor
  Collins, A. The trouble with Felix
  Liberman, S. Two years in exile
  Lurie, M. Bobbeh
  Lurie, M. Popov
  Waten, J. Mother
  Waten, J. Well, what do you say to my
    boy?
  Zwicky, F. Hostages
          Bronx (New York, N.Y.)
  Rosen, G. Growing up Bronx
          Brooklyn (New York, N.Y.)
  Briskin, M. Before and after Celeste
  Granit, A. Fire is burning on our street!
  Granit, A. Free the canaries from their
    cages!
  Granit, A. Hello, Lenin! Hello, Stalin!
    How's the revolution today?
  Granit, A. No golden tombstones for me!
  Granit, A. The penny is for God!

JEWS—Brooklyn (New York, N.Y.)—*Continued*

Granit, A. Tessie, don't give away the raisin; without it, you're lost!

Granit, A. They're killing Jews on Sackman Street!

Granit, A. "When we produce prostitutes and thieves, we shall be a normal people!"—Jabotinsky

Mazel, D. Sadie

Singer, I. B. The last gaze

California

Sisskind, M. Hope

Canada

Avery, M. The Canadian Diaspora

Avery, M. Jerusalem & home

Avery, M. The Komedy Kabaret

Avery, M. Nazis, communists, Presbyterians & Jews in Norman Bethune's hometown

Avery, M. Promised land Newfoundland

Avery, M. Soviet jewellery

Choyce, L. Major repairs

Richler, M. The summer my grandmother was supposed to die

Roiter, H. Only Sam knows

China

Auswaks, A. The dowry

Eastern Europe

Bergelson, D. At the depot

Opatoshu, J. Romance of a horse thief

Sholem Aleichem. Rabchik, a Jewish dog

Wegner, H. The counter of Lvov

England

Sinclair, C. Bedbugs

Trevor, W. A complicated nature

France

Cohen, M. Sentimental meetings

Eisenstein, S. A place of refuge

Fink, I. Night of surrender

Germany

Eisenstein, S. The Kassel ballet

Wickstrom, L. Vines

Haiti

Gold, H. Max and the pacemaker

Italy

Briskin, M. Florence, May '86

Briskin, M. My father and Signor Corelli

Malamud, B. The last Mohican

Shamosh, A. Trip

Kansas

Mazel, D. The discovery

Lithuania

Botwinik, B. Shabbas

Mendele Mokher Seforim. Of bygone days

Mexico

Glantz, M. From genealogies

Shamosh, A. A nature reserve

Miami Beach (Fla.)

Ozick, C. Rosa

Singer, I. B. The hotel

Michigan

Baxter, C. Saul and Patsy are getting comfortable in Michigan

Netherlands

Asscher-Pinkhof, C. After eight

Asscher-Pinkhof, C. Caravan

Asscher-Pinkhof, C. Grandson

Asscher-Pinkhof, C. Market woman

Asscher-Pinkhof, C. Passage to Hell

Asscher-Pinkhof, C. Promenade

Asscher-Pinkhof, C. Shopping

Asscher-Pinkhof, C. Star dance

Mazel, D. A longing to live

Van de Wetering, J. Jacob Sanders' final solution

New Jersey

Granit, A. Come into the hallway, for five cents!

New York (N.Y.)

Apple, M. Blood relatives

Apple, M. Stranger at the table

Asimov, I. Unto the fourth generation

Blinkin, M. Card game

Blinkin, M. In a dream

Blinkin, M. Smoke

Botwinik, B. The boarder

Botwinik, B. Israel and his children

Botwinik, B. The last young man

Botwinik, B. A man

Botwinik, B. Mendel the Tinsmith

Botwinik, B. Shabbas

Botwinik, B. Yankel

Canin, E. The carnival dog, the buyer of diamonds

Epstein, L. The magic flute

Epstein, L. Music of the spheres

Epstein, L. The Steinway quintet

Field, B. Three sisters

Granit, A. Usher

Janowitz, T. Modern saint #271

Kumin, M. Opening the door on Sixty-Second Street

Liben, M. Homage to Benny Leonard

Liben, M. Hop, skip, and jump

Malamud, B. Idiots first

Malamud, B. The Jewbird

Malamud, B. My son the murderer

Michaels, L. Murderers

Paley, G. The contest

Paley, G. Telling

Prose, F. Electricity

Pulaski, J. Music story

Pulaski, J. The romance

Schwartz, L. S. The opiate of the people

Shaham, N. The salt of the earth

Singer, I. B. Advice

Stern, S. Rudolph Finkl's apprenticeship

New York (State)

Botwinik, B. Jake

Mazel, D. Choosing

New Zealand

Brasch, C. Dunedin

JEWS—*Continued*

Pennsylvania

Greenberg, J. Days of awe

Poland

Ansky, S. Behind a mask
Barnea, L. My grandfather
Botwinik, B. The general strike
Chasek, J. A ticket to America
Fink, I. Crazy
Nałkowska, Z. At the railroad track
Oates, J. C. My Warszawa: 1980
Singer, I. B. The black wedding
Singer, I. B. The divorce
Singer, I. B. Gimpel the fool
Singer, I. B. The image
Singer, I. B. The Jew from Babylon
Singer, I. B. The mistake
Singer, I. B. A nest egg for paradise
Singer, I. B. On the way to the poorhouse
Singer, I. B. The pocket remembered
Singer, I. B. The recluse
Singer, I. B. Remnants
Singer, I. B. Short Friday
Singer, I. B. The Spinoza of Market Street
Singer, I. B. Why Heisherik was born
Stead, C. The Azhdanov tailors
Weissenberg, I. M. A shtetl

South Africa

Jacobson, D. A day in the country
Levinson, B. The night Motke Behr
  danced
Simon, B. Our war

Soviet Union

Blinkin, M. Doctor Machover
Blinkin, M. Family life: a chapter
Blinkin, M. The freethinker: a shtetl
  atheist
Blinkin, M. Incomprehensible
Blinkin, M. The mysterious secret
Blinkin, M. A simple life
Blinkin, M. Troubles
Blinkin, M. Women
Botwinik, B. Discovered
Botwinik, B. Israel and his children
Botwinik, B. Mendel the Tinsmith
Botwinik, B. Rivals
Gorky, M. Cain and Artyom
Kuncewiczowa, M. Strange Rachel
Malaparte, C. The Soroca girls
Sholem Aleichem. The automatic exemption
Sholem Aleichem. Baranovich Station
Sholem Aleichem. Burned out
Sholem Aleichem. Chava
Sholem Aleichem. Competitors
Sholem Aleichem. Eighteen from Peresh-
  chepena
Sholem Aleichem. Elul
Sholem Aleichem. Fated for misfortune
Sholem Aleichem. A game of sixty-six
Sholem Aleichem. Go climb a tree if you
  don't like it

Sholem Aleichem. The happiest man in all
  Kodny
Sholem Aleichem. Hard luck
Sholem Aleichem. High school
Sholem Aleichem. Hodl
Sholem Aleichem. Lekh-lekho
Sholem Aleichem. The man from Buenos
  Aires
Sholem Aleichem. The miracle of Hoshana
  Rabbah
Sholem Aleichem. Shprintze
Sholem Aleichem. The slowpoke express
Sholem Aleichem. The tallis koton
Sholem Aleichem. The tenth man
Sholem Aleichem. Tevye blows a small
  fortune
Sholem Aleichem. Tevye leaves for the
  land of Israel
Sholem Aleichem. Tevye strikes it rich
Sholem Aleichem. Third class
Sholem Aleichem. Today's children
Sholem Aleichem. The wedding that came
  without its band

Tennessee

Stern, S. Shimmele fly-by-night

United States

Algren, N. So help me
Amichai, Y. The orgy
Apple, M. The American bakery
Apple, M. The eighth day
Bellow, S. Cousins
Botwinik, B. Death went astray
Botwinik, B. Esperanto
Botwinik, B. The glazier
Botwinik, B. The mother's Yom Kippur
Botwinik, B. The one I didn't marry
Botwinik, B. The radicals
Botwinik, B. Shabbas morning
Botwinik, B. A shoemaker for a husband
Boucher, S. The healing
Brodkey, H. Falling and ascending bodies:
  four passages
Brown, R. A good deal
Corrington, J. W. The actes and monu-
  ments
Ellison, H. The boulevard of broken
  dreams
Friedman, B. J. The mourner
Friedman, B. J. The war criminal
Goldberg, L. One more river
Gordon, M. Temporary shelter
Granit, A. I went to the market place to
  see the world! Oy, Mama, oy!
Greenburg, J. Certain distant suns
Lish, G. Mr. Goldbaum
Lish, G. Resurrection
Mazel, D. The angel's overcoat
Mazel, D. Aunt Leah
Mazel, D. Dragons and puppies
Mazel, D. The flying ark
Mazel, D. Homage
Mazel, D. Ilya
Mazel, D. Jeopardies

JEWS—United States—*Continued*
Mazel, D. Late prayers
Mazel, D. A matter of pride
Mazel, D. Mr. Bernshtein
Mazel, D. Mr. Tessler
Mazel, D. Our Zaideh
Mazel, D. Sacrifices
Mazel, D. A spoonful of kindness
Mazel, D. Sprucy wages
Mazel, D. The storekeeper
Mazel, D. Surprises
Mazel, D. An unsung Solomon
Mazel, D. The well
McCullers, C. The aliens
Moskowitz, F. Every airborne particle
Moskowitz, F. In going is a drama
Narell, I. Papa's tea
Oates, J. C. Last days
Paley, G. Dreamer in a dead language
Paley, G. The loudest voice
Penner, J. Emotion recollected in tranquillity
Raphael, L. Dancing on Tishe B'av
Ravin, B. L. Cabin class to Pubjanice
Roth, P. Eli, the fanatic
Schwartz, S. To Leningrad in winter
Singer, I. B. Confused
Singer, I. B. A peephole in the gate
Singer, I. B. The secret
Singer, I. B. A telephone call on Yom Kippur
Stern, S. The gramophone
Stern, S. Lazar Malkin enters heaven
Stern, S. Leonard Shapiro banished from dreams
Stern, S. The Lord and Morton Gruber
Stern, S. Moishe the Just
Wilk, M. Singing with Skulnick
Vermont
Stern, S. The ghost and Saul Bozoff
Jeyfo. Baykurt, F.
Jezeri and her beast go to the fair and find more excitement than they want. Clayton, J.
Jhabvala, Ruth Prawer
The aliens
The Literary Review (Madison, N.J.) 29:437-51 Summ '86
Bombay
Jhabvala, R. P. Out of India
Desecration
Jhabvala, R. P. Out of India
An experience of India
Jhabvala, R. P. Out of India
Farid and Farida
The New Yorker 60:40-50 O 15 '84
The housewife
Jhabvala, R. P. Out of India
How I became a holy mother
Jhabvala, R. P. Out of India
In the mountains
Jhabvala, R. P. Out of India

The interview
Jhabvala, R. P. Out of India
The man with the dog
Jhabvala, R. P. Out of India
My first marriage
Jhabvala, R. P. Out of India
On bail
Jhabvala, R. P. Out of India
Passion
Jhabvala, R. P. Out of India
Rose petals
Jhabvala, R. P. Out of India
A spiritual call
Jhabvala, R. P. Out of India
Two more under the Indian sun
Jhabvala, R. P. Out of India
The widow
Jhabvala, R. P. Out of India
Jia Pingwa
Family chronicle of a wooden bowl maker
The Chinese Western; ed. by Zhu Hong
How much can a man bear?
The Chinese Western; ed. by Zhu Hong
Shasha and the pigeons
Short story international 65
The **jigsaw** girl. Gallagher, S.
The **jigsaw** puzzle. Loukakis, A.
Jillie. Havazelet, E.
The **jilted** groom. La Puma, S.
JILTING
Berdnyk, O. The constellation of green fish, a tale of the unprecedented
Brown, M. W. Disturber of the peace
Humphrey, W. The ballad of Jesse Neighbours
Moore, G. Home sickness
The **jilting** of Granny Weatherall. Porter, K. A.
The **jilting** of Jane. Wells, H. G.
Jim Chance. Thomas, M.
Jim July Starr. Taylor, R.
Jim Reed. Taylor, R.
Jimbie. Prichard, K. S.
Jiménez, Francisco, 1943-
The circuit
Cuentos Chicanos; ed. by R. A. Anaya and A. Márquez
Jimmy Durante lost in Antarctica. Boylan, J.
Jimmy Goggles the god. Wells, H. G.
Jimmy Hayes and Muriel. Henry, O.
Jimmy Rose. Melville, H.
Jimmy the dancer: necromancer. Pascoe, B.
Jin He
Reencounter
Roses and thorns; ed. by P. Link
Jin's first Christmas. Kupfer, F.
The **jinx.** Dickinson, C.
Jitomates. Martínez-Serros, H.
JOAN, OF ARC, SAINT, 1412-1431
About
Jones, J. Superbity
Kress, N. With the original cast

The **Joan** Crawford letter. Freeman, J.
Joanna. Hall, M. L.
Joanna loves Jesus. Lampart, J.
The **job**. Kinsella, W. P.
Job inaction. Zahn, T.
A **job** of the plains. Humphrey, W.
The **jockey**. McCullers, C.
JOCKEYS
  Faust, I. The year of the hot jock
  Hemingway, E. My old man
  Killingsworth, S. Born to ride
  McCullers, C. The jockey
Jody after the war. Bryant, E.
Joe. Wallace, P.
Joe will take me home. Nunes, S.
Joe Wilson's courtship. Lawson, H.
Joens, Harley
  Hemingway
    The North American Review 271:48 Je
    '86
Joe's dead. Roth, H. H.
Johann Sebastian Brahms. Malzberg, B. N.
JOHANNESBURG (SOUTH AFRICA) *See*
    South Africa—Johannesburg
John Archer's nose. Fisher, R.
John Bealle's accident—or, How the widow
    Dudu treated insanity. Barr, J. G.
John Charrington's wedding. Nesbit, E.
John Crow. Jaffe, H.
John Delavoy. James, H.
John Duffy's brother. O'Brien, F.
John Fletcher's night of love. Steadman, M.
JOHN PAUL II, POPE, 1920-
    About
  Kinsella, W. P. The fog
John Thomas Bird. Nordan, L.
Johnnieruth. Birtha, B.
Johnny Appleseed. Neville, S.
Johnny Cucu's record. Bonosky, P.
Johnny Lingo's eight-cow wife. McGerr, P.
Johnny Mnemonic. Gibson, W.
Johnny Pye and the Fool-killer. Benét, S. V.
Johnny Ray. Ríos, A.
Johnson, B. S. (Bryan Stanley), 1933-1973
  Everyone knows somebody who's dead
    New directions in prose and poetry 49
  A few selected sentences
    The Penguin book of modern British
    short stories
Johnson, Bryan Stanley *See* Johnson, B. S.
    (Bryan Stanley), 1933-1973
Johnson, Charles Richard, 1948-
  Alēthia
    Johnson, C. R. The sorcerer's apprentice
  China
    Johnson, C. R. The sorcerer's apprentice
  The education of Mingo
    Johnson, C. R. The sorcerer's apprentice
  Exchange value
    Johnson, C. R. The sorcerer's apprentice
  Menagerie, a child's fable
    Johnson, C. R. The sorcerer's apprentice

Moving pictures
    Johnson, C. R. The sorcerer's apprentice
    The North American Review 270:45-7 S
    '85
  Sudden fiction; ed. by R. Shapard and
    J. Thomas
Popper's disease
    Johnson, C. R. The sorcerer's apprentice
The sorcerer's apprentice
    Johnson, C. R. The sorcerer's apprentice
Johnson, David
  Another savage day in the belly of the
    whale
    Stiller's pond; ed. by J. Agee; R. Blakely
    and S. Welch
Johnson, Denis, 1949-
  Two men
    The New Yorker 64:41-4+ S 19 '88
  Work
    The New Yorker 64:36-8 N 14 '88
Johnson, Dennis
  The big sway
    The New generation; ed. by A. Kaufman
Johnson, Dorothy M., 1905-1984
  The hanging tree
    She won the West; ed. by M. Muller
    and B. Pronzini
  Lost sister
    The Western hall of fame; ed. by B.
      Pronzini and M. H. Greenberg
    Westward the women; ed. by V. Piekar-
      ski
  A man called Horse
    The Second reel West; ed. by B. Pron-
      zini and M. H. Greenberg
    The Western hall of fame; ed. by B.
      Pronzini and M. H. Greenberg
Johnson, George Clayton, 1929-
  Devlin's dream
    100 great fantasy short short stories; ed.
    by I. Asimov; T. Carr and M. H.
    Greenberg
  The man with the hoe
    Cutting edge; ed. by D. Etchison
  Sea change
    Masters of darkness; ed. by D. Etchison
Johnson, Greg
  Crazy ladies
    Prize stories, 1986
  The reliquary
    Prairie Schooner 58:15-30 Fall '84
  Wintering
    The Virginia Quarterly Review 60:84-101
    Wint '84
Johnson, Hilding
  Victoria
    The Best American short stories, 1988
Johnson, Jeffrey A., 1956-
  At D'Ambrosia's
    Stiller's pond; ed. by J. Agee; R. Blakely
    and S. Welch

Johnson, Joyce, 1935-
The children's wing
  Prize stories, 1987
The fall of Texas
  The Bread Loaf anthology of contemporary American short stories; ed. by R. Pack and J. Parini
  The New Yorker 61:40-2 N 11 '85
Launching day, 1962
  The New Yorker 63:30-5 Ap 13 '87
Johnson, L. T.
(jt. auth) See Russell, Eric Frank, 1905-, and Johnson, L. T.
JOHNSON, LYNDON B. (LYNDON BAINES), 1908-1973
        About
Boylan, J. Thirty-six miracles of Lyndon Johnson
Johnson, Margot
Hard to get
  Seventeen 43:92-3+ Ja '84
Johnson, Mark
(jt. auth) See Etchison, Dennis, 1943-, and Johnson, Mark
JOHNSON, ROBERT, d. 1938
        About
Boyle, T. C. Stones in my passway, hellhound on my trail
Johnson, Susan B.
A gift from the past
  'Teen 28:14+ Jl '84
Johnson, Timothy Joel
Mr. Pat's magical ride
  Redbook 170:168+ D '87
Reclamation
  The Yale Review 73:551-60 Summ '84
Johnson, W. Ryerson
Enough gold
  Wild westerns; ed. by B. Pronzini
White water
  The Ethnic detectives; ed. by B. Pronzini and M. H. Greenberg
Johnson, Wayne D.
What happened to Red Deer
  Ploughshares 14 no2/3:41-59 '88
Johnson, Willis, 1938-
The girl who would be Russian
  Johnson, W. The girl who would be Russian, and other stories
  The Southern Review (Baton Rouge, La.) 21:144-61 Ja '85
The great Valentinova
  Johnson, W. The girl who would be Russian, and other stories
Heir to the realm
  Johnson, W. The girl who would be Russian, and other stories
The ice fish
  Johnson, W. The girl who would be Russian, and other stories
The last song of exile
  Johnson, W. The girl who would be Russian, and other stories

Prayer for the dying
  The Best Maine stories; ed. by S. Phippen; C. Waugh and M. Greenberg
  Johnson, W. The girl who would be Russian, and other stories
  Prize stories, 1984
Sarajevo
  Johnson, W. The girl who would be Russian, and other stories
Johnston, Betty
Never the right time
  Room to move; ed. by S. Falkiner
Johnston, George, 1912-1970
Astypalaian knife
  Johnston, G. and Clift, C. Strong-man from Piraeus, and other stories
The dying day of Francis Bainsbridge
  Johnston, G. and Clift, C. Strong-man from Piraeus, and other stories
Requiem mass
  Johnston, G. and Clift, C. Strong-man from Piraeus, and other stories
Sponge boat
  Johnston, G. and Clift, C. Strong-man from Piraeus, and other stories
Strong-man from Piraeus
  Johnston, G. and Clift, C. Strong-man from Piraeus, and other stories
Vale, Pollini!
  Johnston, G. and Clift, C. Strong-man from Piraeus, and other stories
The verdict
  Johnston, G. and Clift, C. Strong-man from Piraeus, and other stories
Johnston, Harold
The shadow falls
  Australian science fiction; ed. by V. Ikin
Johnston, Sibyl
Iris Holmes
  Hot type; ed. by J. Miller
Jesse and Louise
  Greening wheat: fifteen Mormon short stories
JOHNSTOWN (PA.) *See* Pennsylvania—Johnstown
The **Johnstown** Polka. Stark, S. S.
Joiner. Whitehead, J.
A **joint** communique. Burns, M.
The **joke.** Brown, F.
Joker. Gottlieb, E.
Joker and wife. Gee, M.
JOKES, PRACTICAL *See* Practical jokes
Jokester. Asimov, I.
Jolas, Eugene, 1894-1952
Heinrich Heine and the grain dance
  New directions in prose and poetry 50
Jolley, Elizabeth, 1923-
Adam's bride [Variant title: The bench]
  Jolley, E. Woman in a lampshade
The agent in travelling
  Jolley, E. Stories
Another holiday for the Prince
  Jolley, E. Stories

Jolley, Elizabeth, 1923- —*Continued*
Bathroom dance
  Prairie Schooner 62:5-16 Wint '88/'89
  Transgressions; ed. by D. Anderson
Bill Sprockett's land
  Jolley, E. Stories
Butter butter butter for a boat
  Jolley, E. Woman in a lampshade
Clever and pretty
  Jolley, E. Woman in a lampshade
Dingle the fool
  Jolley, E. Woman in a lampshade
Fairfields
  The New Yorker 61:28-36 Jl 22 '85
The fellmonger
  The New Yorker 62:26-33 Jl 14 '86
The fellow passenger
  Home and away; ed. by R. Creswell
  Jolley, E. Stories
Five acre virgin
  Jolley, E. Stories
A gentleman's agreement
  Jolley, E. Stories
Grasshoppers
  Jolley, E. Stories
A hedge of rosemary
  Jolley, E. Stories
Hilda's wedding
  Jolley, E. Woman in a lampshade
The hunt
  Grand Street 7:30-44 Spr '88
The jarrah thieves
  Jolley, E. Stories
The last crop
  Jolley, E. Woman in a lampshade
The libation
  Jolley, E. Woman in a lampshade
The long distant lecture
  Jolley, E. Stories
Mr. Parker's valentine
  Jolley, E. Stories
My father's moon
  The Pushcart prize XII
A new world
  Jolley, E. Stories
Night runner
  Room to move; ed. by S. Falkiner
One bite for Christmas
  Jolley, E. Stories
One Christmas knitting
  Jolley, E. Woman in a lampshade
Outink to Uncle's place
  Jolley, E. Stories
The outworks of the kingdom
  Jolley, E. Stories
Paper children
  Jolley, E. Woman in a lampshade
Pear tree dance
  Jolley, E. Woman in a lampshade
The performance
  Jolley, E. Stories
The play reading
  Jolley, E. Woman in a lampshade

The representative
  Jolley, E. Woman in a lampshade
The shed
  Jolley, E. Woman in a lampshade
The shepherd on the roof
  Jolley, E. Stories
'Surprise! Surprise!' from Matron
  Jolley, E. Stories
The travelling entertainer
  Jolley, E. Stories
Two men running
  Jolley, E. Woman in a lampshade
Uncle Bernard's proposal
  Jolley, E. Woman in a lampshade
The wedding of the painted doll
  Jolley, E. Stories
Wednesdays and Fridays
  Jolley, E. Woman in a lampshade
Winter nelis
  The Australian short story; ed. by L.
    Hergenhan
  Jolley, E. Stories
Woman in a lampshade
  Jolley, E. Woman in a lampshade
The **jolly** corner. James, H.
A **jolly** fellow. Maupassant, G. de
JONAH (BIBLICAL FIGURE)
          About
Davenport, G. Jonah
Jonah. Davenport, G.
Jonah. Doubiago, S.
Jones, Adam Mars- *See* Mars-Jones, Adam,
  1954-
Jones, Barry
The shadows on the lawn: an adventure
  of Sherlock Holmes
  The New adventures of Sherlock
    Holmes; ed. by M. H. Greenberg and
    C. L. R. Waugh
Jones, Cori
Daddy Rat
  The North American Review 272:44-51
  Je '87
Jones, Diana Wynne
Carol Oneir's hundredth dream
  Dragons and dreams; ed. by J. Yolen;
    M. H. Greenberg and C. G. Waugh
Jones, Douglas C.
Halloween and other sacred events
  Jones, D. C. Hickory cured
In pastures green
  Jones, D. C. Hickory cured
Knights of the Flaming Circle
  Jones, D. C. Hickory cured
The last fastball
  Jones, D. C. Hickory cured
The Law
  Jones, D. C. Hickory cured
Once a year
  Jones, D. C. Hickory cured
Raised in the wilderness
  Jones, D. C. Hickory cured

Jones, Douglas C.—*Continued*
The saga of Slaven Budd
  Jones, D. C. Hickory cured
The trombone and the lady
  Jones, D. C. Hickory cured
Trusty
  Jones, D. C. Hickory cured
Jones, Edward P.
Island
  The Ploughshares reader: new fiction for
  the eighties
Jones, Eldred Durosimi
A man can try
  African short stories in English; ed. by
  J. de Grandsaigne
Jones, Gwyneth, 1936-
The snow apples
  The Year's best fantasy, first annual
  collection
Jones, Helen
Roses of Eden
  Harper's 273:70-2 Jl '86
Jones, James, 1921-1977
The way it is
  A Treasury of World War II stories; ed.
  by B. Pronzini and M. H. Greenberg
Jones, Jo
Superbity
  Stepping out; ed. by A. Oosthuizen
Jones, Joan
Between brothers
  McCall's 113:173-5 My '86
Jones, Joanna, 1922-
*For works written by this author under
  other names see* Burke, John, 1922-
Jones, Kelvyn
The green man
  Midnight; ed. by C. L. Grant
Jones, Louis Beynon
The whole idea of Cindy Potts
  Hot type; ed. by J. Miller
Jones, Madison, 1925-
A beginning
  Homewords: a book of Tennessee
  writers; ed. by D. Paschall
The fugitives
  A Modern Southern reader; ed. by B.
  Forkner and P. Samway
  Stories of the modern South; ed. by B.
  Forkner and P. Samway
Jones, Paul
Beautiful rebel
  A Treasury of Civil War stories; ed. by
  M. H. Greenberg and B. Pronzini
Jones, Raymond F., 1930-1982
The children's room
  Young mutants; ed. by I. Asimov; M.
  H. Greenberg and C. G. Waugh
Jones, Rosemary
Ring of Kerry
  Room to move; ed. by S. Falkiner
Jones' Victoria Cross. Gilbert, W. S.
Jonesed. Coleman, W.

Jonker, Ingrid
The goat
  The Penguin book of Southern African
  stories
JOPLIN, JANIS, 1943-1970
                    About
Dozois, G. R., and others. Touring
Swanwick, M. The feast of Saint Janis
Jordan, A. C.
The king of the waters
  The Penguin book of Southern African
  stories
Jordan, June, 1936-
His own where
  Great American love stories; ed. by L.
  Rosenthal
Jordan, Neil, 1951-
Night in Tunisia
  The Treasury of English short stories;
  ed. by N. Sullivan
JORDAN
        See also Jerusalem
Jordan County. Foote, S.
Jorgensen, Bruce W.
A song for one still voice
  Greening wheat: fifteen Mormon short
  stories
Jorgenson, Ivar
*For works written by this author under
  other names see* Silverberg, Robert
Jorinda and Jorindel. Gallant, M.
José, Elias
Returning from the lost land
  The Literary Review (Madison, N.J.)
  27:469-80 Summ '84
José, F. Sionil (Francisco Sionil), 1924-
Friendship
  Short story international 54
The heirs
  Short story international 67
Modesty aside
  Short story international 52
Progress
  Short story international 49
Two interviews
  Short story international 59
JOSEPH (BIBLICAL FIGURE)
                    About
Böll, H. The tidings of Bethlehem
Joseph, Toni Y.
Broken bonds
  Ms. 14:89-90+ O '85
Joseph. Maupassant, G. de
Josephina Anna Maria. Prichard, K. S.
Josephson, Mary
The history of X
  Artforum 26:122-3 Ap '88
Joshua. Francis, H. E.
Josie. Palmer, V.
Josipovici, Gabriel, 1940-
Absence and echo
  Josipovici, G. In the fertile land

Josipovici, Gabriel, 1940——*Continued*
  The bird cage
    Josipovici, G. In the fertile land
  The bitter end
    Josipovici, G. In the fertile land
  Brothers
    Josipovici, G. In the fertile land
  A changeable report
    Josipovici, G. In the fertile land
  Children's games
    P.E.N. new fiction I
  Children's voices
    Josipovici, G. In the fertile land
  Death of the word
    Josipovici, G. In the fertile land
  Exile
    Josipovici, G. In the fertile land
  Fuga
    Josipovici, G. In the fertile land
  Getting better
    Josipovici, G. In the fertile land
  He
    Josipovici, G. In the fertile land
  In the fertile land
    Josipovici, G. In the fertile land
  Memories of a mirrored room in Hamburg
    Josipovici, G. In the fertile land
  Second person looking out
    Josipovici, G. In the fertile land
  Steps
    Josipovici, G. In the fertile land
  That which is hidden is that which is
      shown; that which is shown is that
      which is hidden
    Josipovici, G. In the fertile land
  Volume IV, pp. 167-9
    Josipovici, G. In the fertile land
  Waiting
    Josipovici, G. In the fertile land
Jots and tittles. Durrell, L.
Joubert, Elsa
  Milk
    The Penguin book of Southern African
      stories
Les **joues** en feu. Hori, T.
The **journal** of a wife beater. Petrakis, H.
  M.
The **journal** of Julius Rodman. Poe, E. A.
The **journal** of Mistress Joan Martyn. Woolf,
  V.
JOURNALISM
  Brown, F. The night the world ended
  Carlson, R. I am Bigfoot
  Singer, I. B. The missing line
JOURNALISTS
      See also Women journalists
  Al-Kouni, I. The drumming sands
  Barr, R. The chemistry of anarchy
  Barthelme, D. January
  Barthelme, D. Lightning
  Bates, H. Farewell to the master
  Bloch, R. The warm farewell
  Bloch, R. Word of honor
  Bourjaily, V. The Duchess
  Broun, H. Cycling posture
  Burke, J. L. Lower me down with a gol-
      den chain
  Cade, T. Mississippi Ham Rider
  Calisher, H. A Christmas carillon
  Callaghan, M. Last spring they came over
  Cheuse, A. The quest for Ambrose Bierce
  Colette. An interview
  Colwin, L. Frank and Billy
  Costa, C. The best bid
  Covino, M. In winter the snow never
      stops
  Coxe, G. H. Seed of suspicion
  Crane, S. Death and the child
  Crane, S. "God rest ye, merry gentlemen"
  Day, R. C. Relative motion
  Ebon, W. Little girl from Little Rock
  Finney, J. I love Galesburg in the spring-
      time
  Francis, D. The gift
  Gallagher, T. Desperate measures
  Girion, B. Another blue-eyed quarterback
  Girion, B. With a little gold pencil
  Hanson, D. The whisper business
  Highsmith, P. Where the action is
  Hood, M. A country girl
  Irvine, R. R. In the dead hours
  Jackson, G. Holing out
  James, H. The death of the lion
  Johnson, D. Another savage day in the
      belly of the whale
  José, F. S. Modesty aside
  José, F. S. Two interviews
  Kaikō, T. Festivities by the river
  Kinsella, W. P. Searching for Freddy
  Kipling, R. A matter of fact
  Klinkowitz, J. Metaphors
  Lafferty, R. A. Magazine section
  Lovesey, P. Arabella's answer
  MacDonald, J. D. The legend of Joe Lee
  Mathers, P. Micki New
  Niven, L. Flash crowd
  Nowakowski, M. The vetting session
  O'Hara, J. Fatimas and kisses
  O'Hara, J. Ninety minutes away
  Pascoe, B. Gravity and levity
  Plunkett, J. The scoop
  Poe, E. A. How to write a Blackwood ar-
      ticle
  Poe, E. A. The Signora Psyche Zenobia
  Pronzini, B., and Malzberg, B. N. Rebound
  Raphael, F. Still life
  Reed, R. The slicker
  Rhys, J. Tigers are better-looking
  Romun, I. Christmas is over
  Rubin, L. D. The St. Anthony Chorale
  Sanguinetti, E. A Yankee inquisitor
  Schwartz, J. Crazy
  Schwartz, J. Faith
  Singer, I. B. The interview
  Tenn, W. The human angle
  Thomas, D. Old Garbo

JOURNALISTS—Continued
  Wasylyk, S. Funeral in a small town
  Wells, H. G. The land ironclads
  Wharton, E. The last asset
  Willett, J. The best of Betty
  Wilson, R. Farewell party
  Wolfe, T. The newspaper
  Wolfe, T. Old Man Rivers
  Wollaston, N. Walkabout
  Working, R. Shooting
JOURNALS See Diaries, Stories about;
    Diaries (Stories in diary form)
Journey. Anderman, J.
The **journey.** Big Eagle, D.
Journey. Gahagan, J.
Journey in. Mathers, P.
A **journey** in the snow. Roberts, N.
Journey of love. Rachlin, N.
Journey to Petrópolis. Lispector, C.
A **journey** to the antiworld. Berdnyk, O.
The **journey** to the dead. Updike, J.
A **journey** to the seven streams. Kiely, B.
JOURNEYS See Overland journeys; Voyages
    and travels
Journey's end. Colette
Joy. Rule, J.
JOY AND SORROW
    See also Crying; Happiness
  Abbott, L. K. The end of grief
  Böll, H. My sad face
  Hagy, A. C. Stadia
  Kittredge, W. Momentum is always the
    weapon
  Sanford, W. M. Mary
  Smith, R. The princess, the Boeing, and
    the hot pastrami sandwich
  Willett, J. Anticipatory grief
Joyce, James, 1882-1941
  The boarding house
    The Best of Irish wit and wisdom; ed.
      by J. McCarthy
    The Treasury of English short stories;
      ed. by N. Sullivan
      About
  Davenport, G. The Haile Selassie Funeral
    Train
Joyce. Doubiago, S.
Joyce made easy. Lish, G.
The **joys** of speculating. Dadswell, M.
Juan de Dios. Ferreira, R.
Juan Rambellais et al., A history of Bitic
    literature. Lem, S.
Juarez, Hélène
  The answer
    Murder California style; ed. by J. L.
      Breen and J. Ball
JUAREZ (MEXICO) See Mexico—Juarez
Jubal, the Ringer. O'Brien, F.-J.
Jubilee. Greene, G.
Jubilee. Walker, M.
A **Jubilee** present. Hornung, E. W.

JUDAISM
    See also Hasidism; Jews; Yom Kip-
    pur; Zionism
  Asscher-Pinkhof, C. Celebrations
  Asscher-Pinkhof, C. Old tales
  Kessler, J. F. Saul of Tarsus
  Paley, G. At that time; or, The history
    of a joke
  Roth, P. The conversion of the Jews
Judas. Brunner, J.
Judas. O'Connor, F.
Judas in the square. Nowakowski, M.
JUDAS ISCARIOT
      About
  Young, R. F. A drink of darkness
The **Judas** target. Dundee, W. D.
The **Judas** tree. Welch, D.
Jude. Benson, P.
The **judge.** Colette
The **judge** and literature. Kuhlman, T. A.
The **judgement.** Petrakis, H. M.
Judgement Day. O'Connor, F.
JUDGES
  Auchincloss, L. The Fabbri tape
  Hensley, J. L. Judicial discretion
  Jolley, E. Adam's bride
  Komie, L. B. The judge's chambers
  Pohl, F. Gwenanda and the Supremes
  Trippett, F. Child Ellen [excerpt]
The **judge's** chambers. Komie, L. B.
The **judge's** house. Stoker, B.
The **Judges** of Hades. Hoch, E. D.
The **judge's** son. Ade, G.
Judgment. Sams, F.
Judgment. Sandor, M.
Judgment. Wheeler, K.
JUDGMENT DAY
  Wells, H. G. A vision of judgment
A **judgment** in the mountains. Benét, S. V.
The **judgment** of Neave. Lewitt, S. N.
A **judgment** worthy of Solomon. Mundstock,
    K.
Judicial discretion. Hensley, J. L.
A **judicious** half inch. Curtiss, U. R.
Judson, John
  And cordiality
    The Ohio Review no42:24-48 '88
Judy's kiss. Wandor, M.
JUGGLERS AND JUGGLING
  Colette. Florie
  Leskov, N. S. Pamphalon the entertainer
  Shiga, N. Han's crime
The **jughead** file. Van de Wetering, J.
The **Jules** Verne steam balloon. Davenport,
    G.
Julia. Wain, J.
Julia & the damned. Worton, M.
The **Julian** Mondays. Gash, J.
Julie. Codrescu, A.
Julie in the funhouse. Willett, J.
Julie Romain. Maupassant, G. de
Julius Caesar and the werewolf. Gardner, J.

JULY, JIM
About
Taylor, R. Jim July Starr
July. Rice, L.
July 7th. McCorkle, J.
JULY FOURTH *See* Fourth of July
The July ghost. Byatt, A. S.
Jum'a and Jamila. Liphshitz, A.
A jumbo death. Heald, T.
Jump!. Fink, I.
The jump. Lasdun, J.
Jump or dive. Cameron, P.
Jumping from high places. Rose, D. A.
Junction. Grenville, K.
June. Drake, R.
The June cross. Nowakowski, M.
The June woman. Koger, L.
June's night. Wesseler, M.
Jungle dove. Pintauro, J.
The jungle rot kid on the nod. Farmer, P. J.
JUNGLES
Aikin, J. My life in the jungle
Aldiss, B. W. Hothouse
Card, O. S. America
Kersh, G. Men without bones
Smith, C. A. The maze of Maal Dweb
Junior. Bradbury, R.
Junior partner. Goulart, R.
The juniper tree. Straub, P.
Junk trade. Makuck, P.
JUPITER (PLANET)
Benford, G. The future of the Jovian system
Clarke, A. C. A meeting with Medusa
Strugatskiĭ, A. N., and Strugatskiĭ, B. N. The way to Amalteia
Jupiter V. Clarke, A. C.
Jurisprudence. Kelley, L. P.
JURY DUTY *See* Trials
Just, Ward S.
About Boston
Prize stories, 1985
The Costa Brava, 1959
Prize stories, 1986
The Virginia Quarterly Review 61:211-29 Spr '85
I'm worried about you
Soldiers & civilians; ed. by T. Jenks
Just a little sore throat. Hall, M. L.
Just a little thing. Vander Putten, J.
Just a poor working girl. Kaiser, H. D.
Just a touch. Al Makhzangy, M.
Just another day. Rifaat, A.
Just another working mom. Cirone, P. B.
Just before the wedding. Dash, J.
Just eighteen months. Matsumoto, S.
Just for kicks. Franco, A.
Just good friends. Archer, J.
Just like a tree. Gaines, E. J.
Just like little dogs. Thomas, D.
Just like Robert De Niro. Cox, A.
Just my type. Dickerson, K.

Just not my type. Franco, M.
Just one more. Hoch, E. D.
Just trying to help. Miller, H. R.
Just turn like a gear. Gautreaux, T.
Just what it says. Fuentes Millán, H.
Justice, Donald Rodney, 1925-
The artificial moonlight
The Best American short stories, 1984
Prize stories, 1984
Little elegy for cello and piano
The North American Review 269:53-5 Je '84
JUSTICE
Benford, G. Valhalla
Böll, H. The Balek scales
Lai, H. The steelyard
Justice. Wendt, A.
Justice is blind. Wolfe, T.
Justine laughs at death. Willett, J.
JUVENILE DELINQUENCY
Abbott, K. Spanish Castle
Algren, N. A lot you got to holler
Barker, C. Pig blood blues
Biggle, L. Who's on first?
Carver, R. Bicycles, muscles, cigarettes
Cather, W. Paul's case
Colter, C. Mary's convert
Curtiss, U. R. The pool sharks
Garrett, G. P. The last of the Spanish blood
Gilbert, M. The happy brotherhood
Greene, G. The destructor
Hemingway, E. The last good country
Howard, C. Spook house
Hughes, L. Thank you, m'am
Lowry, B. So far from the road, so long until morning
Meinke, P. The ponoes
Oates, J. C. How I contemplated the world from the Detroit House of Correction and began my life over again
O'Connor, F. The lame shall enter first
Phillips, J. A. Lechery
Queen, E. Object lesson
Sproat, R. Stunning the punters
Tyler, A. Teenage wasteland

K

K. Bumpus, J.
K Mart. Kinsella, W. P.
Kadohata, Cynthia
Charlie-O
The New Yorker 62:42-8 O 20 '86
Jack's girl
The New Yorker 63:44-50 D 7 '87
Marigolds
The New Yorker 62:36-9 F 9 '87
Seven moons
Grand Street 7:73-80 Summ '88

Kadrey, Richard
Fire catcher
Omni (New York, N.Y.) 8:60-2+ Ag '86
KAFIRS (AFRICAN PEOPLE) *See* Xhosa
(African people); Zulus (African people)
Kafka, Franz, 1883-1924
Before the law
German stories; ed. by H. Steinhauer
An everyday heroism
German stories; ed. by H. Steinhauer
In the penal colony
Black water; ed. by A. Manguel
The Penguin book of horror stories
The World of the short story; ed. by
C. Fadiman
The knock at the manor gate
German stories; ed. by H. Steinhauer
About
Buzzati, D. Kafka's houses
Davenport, G. The chair
Gordimer, N. Letter from his father
McKinley, J. Kafka in suburbia
KAFKA, HERMANN
About
Gordimer, N. Letter from his father
Kafka in suburbia. McKinley, J.
Kafkas. Wiggins, M.
Kafka's houses. Buzzati, D.
Kagan, Norman
Four brands of impossible
Mathenauts: tales of mathematical won-
der; ed. by R. Rucker
The mathenauts
Mathenauts: tales of mathematical won-
der; ed. by R. Rucker
Kahawai. Grace, P.
Kaibutsu-san. Hulme, K.
Kaikō, Takeshi, 1930-
Building a shell mound
Kaikō, T. Five thousand runaways
A certain voice
The Mother of dreams, and other short
stories; ed. by M. Ueda
The crushed pellet
Kaikō, T. Five thousand runaways
Short story international 63
The Shōwa anthology 2
Duel
Kaikō, T. Five thousand runaways
Festivities by the river
Kaikō, T. Five thousand runaways
The fishing hole (Ana)
Kaikō, T. Five thousand runaways
Five thousand runaways
Kaikō, T. Five thousand runaways
The laughingstock
Kaikō, T. Five thousand runaways
Monster and toothpick
Kaikō, T. Five thousand runaways
Kaiser, Harold D.
Just a poor working girl
A Matter of crime v2

Kajii, Motojirō, 1901-1932
Mating
The Shōwa anthology 1
Kalamaras, Vasso
The shot
Room to move; ed. by S. Falkiner
Kalfus, Ken
Bouquet
The North American Review 273:24-7 D
'88
Invisible malls
The North American Review 271:34-5 Je
'86
Notice
The North American Review 270:44 S
'85
KALI (INDIAN DEITY)
Yourcenar, M. Kali beheaded
Kali beheaded. Yourcenar, M.
Kalinikhta [good night]. Faik, S.
Kalpakian, Laura
And departing leave behind us
Kalpakian, L. Fair Augusto, and other
stories
Bare root season
Kalpakian, L. Fair Augusto, and other
stories
The battle of Manila
Winter's tales, new ser. v3
A Christmas cordial
Winter's tales, new ser. v4
Fair Augusto
Kalpakian, L. Fair Augusto, and other
stories
Habits
Kalpakian, L. Fair Augusto, and other
stories
Hairline fractures
Kalpakian, L. Fair Augusto, and other
stories
Hunters in the fields of August
Kalpakian, L. Fair Augusto, and other
stories
The land of lucky strike
Kalpakian, L. Fair Augusto, and other
stories
The last dream before waking
Kalpakian, L. Fair Augusto, and other
stories
The last page
Kalpakian, L. Fair Augusto, and other
stories
Sonata in G minor
Kalpakian, L. Fair Augusto, and other
stories
A time change
Kalpakian, L. Fair Augusto, and other
stories
Veteran's Day
Kalpakian, L. Fair Augusto, and other
stories
Stand one; ed. by M. Blackburn; J.
Silkin and L. Tracy

Kalpakian, Laura—*Continued*
Youth in Asia
Kalpakian, L. Fair Augusto, and other stories
Kamal Muhamed, Muhamed
The leg
Egyptian tales and short stories of the 1970s and 1980s
Kamenetz, Rodger, 1950-
Fault lines
The North American Review 270:48-50 D '85
Kamikaze. Wheatcroft, J.
Kamine, Mark
Some talk
The Massachusetts Review 27:121-6 Spr '86
Kaminsky, Stuart M.
Busted blossoms
The Mammoth book of private eye stories; ed. by B. Pronzini and M. H. Greenberg
Mean streets; ed. by R. J. Randisi
The final toast
The New adventures of Sherlock Holmes; ed. by M. H. Greenberg and C. L. R. Waugh
The man who shot Lewis Vance
The Eyes have it; ed. by R. J. Randisi
Kamkondo, Dede
The sacrifice; an African story
The North American Review 271:46-7 Je '86
Kamminga, Afiena
Moleman
Short story international 51
KAMPUCHEA *See* Cambodia
Kamstra, Jerry
Big Sur pig
Stories and poems from close to home; ed. by F. Salas
Kanafānī, Ghassān
The Slave Fort
Arabic short stories; tr. by D. Johnson-Davies
Kanai, Mieko, 1947-
Platonic love
The Shōwa anthology 2
Kane, Henry
Suicide is scandalous
The Mammoth book of private eye stories; ed. by B. Pronzini and M. H. Greenberg
Kang, Kyong-Ae
The underground village
Hospital room 205, and other Korean short stories
Kang, Sin-Jae
Another Eve
Hospital room 205, and other Korean short stories

Nursery tale for a dreary day
Hospital room 205, and other Korean short stories
The young zelkova
Flowers of fire; ed. by P. H. Lee
Kaniuk, Yoram
The parched earth
Short story international 43
Kannitverstan. Hebel, J. P.
KANSAS
Mazel, D. The discovery
Wheeler, K. Judgment
Wilhelm, K. The girl who fell into the sky
Yates, R. The right thing
Frontier and pioneer life
See Frontier and pioneer life—Kansas
Kansas City
McKinley, J. Chambers
Kansas. Gamble, J. S.
KANSAS CITY (KAN.) *See* Kansas—Kansas City
Kansas heat. Robinson, H.
Kant, Hermann
A bit of the South Sea
Short story international 48
Kant, Uwe
A letter to comrade Ernst L.
Voices East and West: German short stories since 1945
Kantner, Rob
Fly away home
Mean streets; ed. by R. J. Randisi
Left for dead
An Eye for justice; ed. by R. J. Randisi
The rat line
The Eyes have it; ed. by R. J. Randisi
Kantor, MacKinlay, 1904-1977
Easter flowers
The Saturday Evening Post 256:62-3+ Ap '84
The voice of Bugle Ann
Roger Caras' Treasury of great dog stories
Kapitan Lee. Chon, K.-Y.
Kaplan, David Michael
Anne Rey
Kaplan, D. M. Comfort
Comfort
The Atlantic 258:42-9 Ag '86
Kaplan, D. M. Comfort
Doe season
The Atlantic 256:106-10+ N '85
The Best American short stories, 1986
Kaplan, D. M. Comfort
Elias Schneebaum
Kaplan, D. M. Comfort
Elisabetta, Carlotta, Catherine (raising the demon)
Kaplan, D. M. Comfort
In the realm of the herons
Kaplan, D. M. Comfort

Kaplan, David Michael—*Continued*
Love, your only mother
  Kaplan, D. M. Comfort
Magic
  Kaplan, D. M. Comfort
The man with Picasso's eyes
  Kaplan, D. M. Comfort
A Mexican tale
  Kaplan, D. M. Comfort
Summer people
  Kaplan, D. M. Comfort
Tidewatcher
  Kaplan, D. M. Comfort
Kaplan, James
The new age
  The New Yorker 60:34-5 Je 11 '84
Kaplan, Johanna, 1942-
Close calls
  Commentary 81:51-6 My '86
Kaplický, Václav
Theatrum magnum
  Short story international 42
Karaghala's daughter. Gardiner, J. R.
Karamora. Gorky, M.
KARATE
  Huynh, Q. N. The family's secret move
Karbo, Karen
Disarming Big Mad
  The Massachusetts Review 28:93-106 Spr
    '87
KAREL V, EMPEROR OF GERMANY *See*
  Charles V, Holy Roman Emperor,
  1500-1558
Karen. Mazel, D.
A **karmic** lover. Gold, H.
Karr, Phyllis Ann
The toe
  100 great fantasy short short stories; ed.
    by I. Asimov; T. Carr and M. H.
    Greenberg
Kasarjian, Janna Vaughan
Looking for love
  'Teen 30:28-9+ Mr '86
Kaschnitz, Marie Luise, 1901-1974
The fat child
  Short story international 47
  Voices East and West: German short
    stories since 1945
On Day X
  TriQuarterly no71:24-32 Wint '88
Kassandra. Kessler, J. F.
The **Kassel** ballet. Eisenstein, S.
Kassem, Abdel-Hakim
The trial of the small black woman
  Arabic short stories; tr. by D. Johnson-
    Davies
Katamoto. Wolfe, T.
Kate and Allie and Kate. Painter, P.
Kate Bixby's queerness. Austin, M. H.

Katerli, Nina
The Barsukov Triangle
  The Barsukov Triangle, The two-toned
    blond & other stories; ed. by C. R.
    Proffer & E. Proffer
Katey Foster's two boys. Rose, D. A.
Kathenor, Sansoucy
The Cinderella caper
  L. Ron Hubbard presents Writers of the
    future v2
Katherine la Dentellière, whore. Schwob, M.
Kathleen's field. Trevor, W.
Katkov, Norman
Where wisdom waits
  Good Housekeeping 203:104-5+ Ag '86
Kattan, Naîm, 1928-
The neighbour
  The Oxford book of French-Canadian
    short stories
Katz, Laura Battey
Recovery
  The Yale Review 74:240-52 Wint '85
Katz, Steve, 1935-
Death of the band
  Katz, S. Stolen stories
Friendship
  Katz, S. Stolen stories
Made of wax
  Katz, S. Stolen stories
Mongolian Whiskey
  Katz, S. Stolen stories
On self-knowledge
  Katz, S. Stolen stories
One on one
  Katz, S. Stolen stories
The Perfect Life
  Katz, S. Stolen stories
Smooth
  Katz, S. Stolen stories
The stolen stories
  Katz, S. Stolen stories
Three essays
  Katz, S. Stolen stories
Two essays
  Katz, S. Stolen stories
Two seaside yarns
  Katz, S. Stolen stories
The zippo stories
  American made; ed. by M. Leyner; C.
    White and T. Glynn
Katz. Algren, N.
Kauffman, Janet, 1945-
The Alvordton Spa and Sweat Shop
  Kauffman, J. Places in the world a
    woman could walk
At first it looks like nothing
  Kauffman, J. Places in the world a
    woman could walk
At odds
  Kauffman, J. Places in the world a
    woman could walk

Kauffman, Janet, 1945-—_Continued_
Breaking the news to Doll
  Kauffman, J. Places in the world a
    woman could walk
The Easter we lived in Detroit
  The Paris Review 26:173-81 Summ '84
  The Pushcart prize X
Harmony
  The Editors' choice: new American
    stories v2
  Kauffman, J. Places in the world a
    woman could walk
How many boys?
  Kauffman, J. Places in the world a
    woman could walk
Isn't it something?
  Kauffman, J. Places in the world a
    woman could walk
Machinery
  The New Yorker 62:32-4 Ap 14 '86
Marguerite Landmine
  The Paris Review 29:188-93 Summ '87
The mechanics of good times
  Kauffman, J. Places in the world a
    woman could walk
My mother has me surrounded
  Kauffman, J. Places in the world a
    woman could walk
Obscene gestures for women
  The Paris Review 30:88-98 Fall '88
Patriotic
  Kauffman, J. Places in the world a
    woman could walk
Places in the world a woman could walk
  Kauffman, J. Places in the world a
    woman could walk
Where I'd quit
  The New Yorker 62:30-1 F 16 '87
Who has lived from a child with chickens
  Kauffman, J. Places in the world a
    woman could walk
  Through other eyes; ed. by I. Zahava
Kaufman, Bel
Sunday in the park
  Sudden fiction; ed. by R. Shapard and
    J. Thomas
Kaufman, Lynne
Change of heart
  Good Housekeeping 205:40+ Ag '87
Objects of affection
  McCall's 111:57-9 Ag '84
Silver linings
  McCall's 113:127-8 Ag '86
Welcome home
  Good Housekeeping 203:122-3 Ag '86
Kavaler, Rebecca
Depression glass
  Kavaler, R. Tigers in the wood
Little Boy Blue
  Kavaler, R. Tigers in the wood
Local habitations
  Kavaler, R. Tigers in the wood

The perfume of love
  Kavaler, R. Tigers in the wood
Those grand old songs
  Kavaler, R. Tigers in the wood
Tigers in the wood
  Kavaler, R. Tigers in the wood
The Zeigarnik effect
  Kavaler, R. Tigers in the wood
Kawabata, Yasunari, 1899-1972
At the pawnshop
  Kawabata, Y. Palm-of-the-hand stories
Autumn rain
  Kawabata, Y. Palm-of-the-hand stories
  The Mother of dreams, and other short
    stories; ed. by M. Ueda
Bamboo-leaf boats
  Kawabata, Y. Palm-of-the-hand stories
Beyond death
  The Mother of dreams, and other short
    stories; ed. by M. Ueda
The blind man and the girl
  Kawabata, Y. Palm-of-the-hand stories
The bound husband
  Kawabata, Y. Palm-of-the-hand stories
Canaries
  Kawabata, Y. Palm-of-the-hand stories
A child's viewpoint
  Kawabata, Y. Palm-of-the-hand stories
Death mask
  Kawabata, Y. Palm-of-the-hand stories
Earth
  Kawabata, Y. Palm-of-the-hand stories
Eggs
  Kawabata, Y. Palm-of-the-hand stories
Faces
  Kawabata, Y. Palm-of-the-hand stories
The girl who approached the fire
  Kawabata, Y. Palm-of-the-hand stories
Glass
  Kawabata, Y. Palm-of-the-hand stories
Gleanings from snow country
  Kawabata, Y. Palm-of-the-hand stories
God's bones
  Kawabata, Y. Palm-of-the-hand stories
Goldfish on the roof
  Kawabata, Y. Palm-of-the-hand stories
The grasshopper and the bell cricket
  Kawabata, Y. Palm-of-the-hand stories
  A Late chrysanthemum; tr. by L. Dun-
    lop
Hair
  Kawabata, Y. Palm-of-the-hand stories
Harbor town
  Kawabata, Y. Palm-of-the-hand stories
The hat incident
  Kawabata, Y. Palm-of-the-hand stories
Her mother's eye
  Kawabata, Y. Palm-of-the-hand stories
Hometown
  Kawabata, Y. Palm-of-the-hand stories
Household
  Kawabata, Y. Palm-of-the-hand stories

Kawabata, Yasunari, 1899-1972—*Continued*
Immortality
  Kawabata, Y. Palm-of-the-hand stories
The incident of the dead face
  Kawabata, Y. Palm-of-the-hand stories
The jay
  Kawabata, Y. Palm-of-the-hand stories
Lavatory Buddahood
  Kawabata, Y. Palm-of-the-hand stories
Love suicides
  Kawabata, Y. Palm-of-the-hand stories
The maidens' prayers
  Kawabata, Y. Palm-of-the-hand stories
Makeup
  Kawabata, Y. Palm-of-the-hand stories
The man who did not smile
  Kawabata, Y. Palm-of-the-hand stories
Morning nails
  Kawabata, Y. Palm-of-the-hand stories
Mother
  Kawabata, Y. Palm-of-the-hand stories
The neighbors
  Kawabata, Y. Palm-of-the-hand stories
The O-Shin Jizo
  Kawabata, Y. Palm-of-the-hand stories
One arm
  The Art of the tale; ed. by D. Halpern
  The Shōwa anthology 2
One person's happiness
  Kawabata, Y. Palm-of-the-hand stories
A pet dog's safe birthing
  Kawabata, Y. Palm-of-the-hand stories
Photograph
  Kawabata, Y. Palm-of-the-hand stories
The rainy station
  Kawabata, Y. Palm-of-the-hand stories
Riding clothes
  Kawabata, Y. Palm-of-the-hand stories
The ring
  Kawabata, Y. Palm-of-the-hand stories
The rooster and the dancing girl
  Kawabata, Y. Palm-of-the-hand stories
Samurai descendant
  Kawabata, Y. Palm-of-the-hand stories
A saw and childbirth
  Kawabata, Y. Palm-of-the-hand stories
The silver fifty-sen pieces
  Kawabata, Y. Palm-of-the-hand stories
The silverberry thief
  Kawabata, Y. Palm-of-the-hand stories
  A Late chrysanthemum; tr. by L. Dun-
    lop
Sleeping habit
  Kawabata, Y. Palm-of-the-hand stories
The Sliding Rock
  Kawabata, Y. Palm-of-the-hand stories
A smile outside the night stall
  Kawabata, Y. Palm-of-the-hand stories
The snakes
  Kawabata, Y. Palm-of-the-hand stories
Snow
  Kawabata, Y. Palm-of-the-hand stories

Socks
  The Mother of dreams, and other short
    stories; ed. by M. Ueda
The sparrow's matchmaking
  Kawabata, Y. Palm-of-the-hand stories
Summer shoes
  Kawabata, Y. Palm-of-the-hand stories
A sunny place
  Kawabata, Y. Palm-of-the-hand stories
Tabi
  Kawabata, Y. Palm-of-the-hand stories
Thank you
  Kawabata, Y. Palm-of-the-hand stories
There is a God
  Kawabata, Y. Palm-of-the-hand stories
Thunder in autumn
  Kawabata, Y. Palm-of-the-hand stories
Toward winter
  Kawabata, Y. Palm-of-the-hand stories
Umbrella
  Kawabata, Y. Palm-of-the-hand stories
Up in the tree
  Kawabata, Y. Palm-of-the-hand stories
Water
  Kawabata, Y. Palm-of-the-hand stories
The weaker vessel
  Kawabata, Y. Palm-of-the-hand stories
The white flower
  Kawabata, Y. Palm-of-the-hand stories
The white horse
  Kawabata, Y. Palm-of-the-hand stories
The Wife of the Autumn Wind
  Kawabata, Y. Palm-of-the-hand stories
The wife's search
  Kawabata, Y. Palm-of-the-hand stories
The young lady of Suruga
  Kawabata, Y. Palm-of-the-hand stories
  A Late chrysanthemum; tr. by L. Dun-
    lop
The younger sister's clothes
  Kawabata, Y. Palm-of-the-hand stories
Yuriko
  Kawabata, Y. Palm-of-the-hand stories
Kay, Hunter
The fifth generation
  Stories of the modern South; ed. by B.
    Forkner and P. Samway
Kay, Jackie
Since Agnes left
  Stepping out; ed. by A. Oosthuizen
Kay Petman's coloured pencils. Bird, C.
Kaye, Frances W.
Nebraska, sweet Nebraska land
  Prairie Schooner 60:93-8 Wint '86
Kaye, Marvin
Damned funny
  Devils & demons; ed. by M. Kaye and
    S. Kaye
Kaye Wayfaring in "Avenged". McCourt, J.
Kazakov, Yuri
Nikishka's secrets
  The World of the short story; ed. by
    C. Fadiman

Kearns, Richard
From Bach to broccoli
Dragons of light; ed. by O. S. Card
Grave angels
Terry Carr's Best science fiction and fantasy of the year #16
The Year's best science fiction, fourth annual collection
Keas on Ida. Parotti, P.
Keating, H. R. F. (Henry Reymond Fitzwalter), 1926-
The all-bad hat
John Creasey's Crime collection, 1986
Caught and bowled, Mrs. Craggs
Keating, H. R. F. Mrs. Craggs: crimes cleaned up
A crime child
Tales from Ellery Queen's Mystery Magazine: short stories for young adults
A dangerous thing, Mrs. Craggs
Keating, H. R. F. Mrs. Craggs: crimes cleaned up
Dead-letter drop
Tales from Ellery Queen's Mystery Magazine: short stories for young adults
The five senses of Mrs. Craggs
Keating, H. R. F. Mrs. Craggs: crimes cleaned up
A hell of a story
Ellery Queen's Memorable characters
John Creasey's Crime collection, 1984
Ready or not; ed. by J. Kahn
Inspector Ghote and the noted British author
John Creasey's Crime collection, 1985
Inspector Ghote and the test match
The Ethnic detectives; ed. by B. Pronzini and M. H. Greenberg
Mrs. Craggs and a certain lady's town house
Keating, H. R. F. Mrs. Craggs: crimes cleaned up
Mrs. Craggs and a sad case of simony
Keating, H. R. F. Mrs. Craggs: crimes cleaned up
Mrs. Craggs and the late Prince Albert
Keating, H. R. F. Mrs. Craggs: crimes cleaned up
Mrs. Craggs and the living dead
Keating, H. R. F. Mrs. Craggs: crimes cleaned up
Mrs. Craggs and the Lords spiritual and temporal
Keating, H. R. F. Mrs. Craggs: crimes cleaned up
Mrs. Craggs and the pale Ella
Keating, H. R. F. Mrs. Craggs: crimes cleaned up
Mrs. Craggs and the round blue immortals
Keating, H. R. F. Mrs. Craggs: crimes cleaned up

Mrs. Craggs gives a dose of physic
Keating, H. R. F. Mrs. Craggs: crimes cleaned up
Mrs. Craggs hears the nightingale
Keating, H. R. F. Mrs. Craggs: crimes cleaned up
Mrs. Craggs sings a different tune
Keating, H. R. F. Mrs. Craggs: crimes cleaned up
Mrs. Craggs's sixth sense
Keating, H. R. F. Mrs. Craggs: crimes cleaned up
The Old Haddock
John Creasey's Crime collection, 1987
An upright woman
The Mammoth book of modern crime stories; ed. by G. Hardinge
Keating, Henry Reymond Fitzwalter *See* Keating, H. R. F. (Henry Reymond Fitzwalter), 1926-
Kebad Kenya. Jahnn, H. H.
Keeley, Edmund
Cambodian diary
The Pushcart prize IX
Keeling, Julian
Leslie's house
Critical Quarterly 30:27-33 Summ '88
Keeling, Nora
Agathe
Keeling, N. Chasing her own tail
Berthilde's holiday
Keeling, N. Chasing her own tail
Big Herb
Keeling, N. Chasing her own tail
Chasing her own tail
Keeling, N. Chasing her own tail
George's eyes & the red ball
Keeling, N. Chasing her own tail
The little axe
Keeling, N. Chasing her own tail
Mine
Keeling, N. Chasing her own tail
A **keen** observer of footwear. Bernen, R.
Keening. Norris, L.
Keep out. Brown, F.
Keep us safe. La Chapelle, M.
Keep your money side up. Searls, H.
Keeping count. Picoult, J.
Keeping house with Freud. Whelan, G.
Keeping in touch with Holly. Lipman, E.
Keeping kosher. See Apple, M. Stranger at the table
Keeping order. Whelan, G.
Keeping pace with the rest of the world. Mankiller, W.
Keeping the customer satisfied. Killough, L., and Killough, H. P.
Keepsake. Schinto, J.
Kees, Weldon
The brothers
Kees, W. The ceremony & other stories
The ceremony
Kees, W. The ceremony & other stories

Kees, Weldon—*Continued*
Do you like the mountains?
  Kees, W. The ceremony & other stories
The evening of the Fourth of July
  Kees, W. The ceremony & other stories
Farewell to Frognall
  Kees, W. The ceremony & other stories
Gents 50¢/Ladies 25¢
  Kees, W. The ceremony & other stories
I should worry
  Kees, W. The ceremony & other stories
Letter from Maine
  Kees, W. The ceremony & other stories
The library: four sketches
  Kees, W. The ceremony & other stories
Mrs. Lutz
  Kees, W. The ceremony & other stories
Public library
  Kees, W. The ceremony & other stories
The Purcells
  Kees, W. The ceremony & other stories
The sign
  Kees, W. The ceremony & other stories
So cold outside
  Kees, W. The ceremony & other stories
Keesing, Nancy
End of the affair
  Room to move; ed. by S. Falkiner
Garden Island people
  Echad 4: Jewish writing from down under: Australia and New Zealand
Keillor, Garrison
Aprille
  Keillor, G. Leaving home
Brethren
  Keillor, G. Leaving home
Chicken
  Keillor, G. Leaving home
Christmas dinner
  Keillor, G. Leaving home
Christmas in Lake Wobegon
  Ladies' Home Journal 103:74+ D '86
  The Saturday Evening Post 259:60-3 D '87
Collection
  Keillor, G. Leaving home
Corinne
  Keillor, G. Leaving home
Dale
  Keillor, G. Leaving home
Darlene makes a move
  Keillor, G. Leaving home
David and Agnes, a romance
  Keillor, G. Leaving home
Du, du liegst mir im herzen
  Keillor, G. Leaving home
Easter
  Keillor, G. Leaving home
Eloise
  Keillor, G. Leaving home
End of an era
  The New Yorker 61:31-2 O 28 '85

Everything's up-to-date in South Roxy
  The New York Times Magazine p18-20 Ag 14 '88
Exiles
  Keillor, G. Leaving home
A glass of Wendy
  Keillor, G. Leaving home
Goodbye to the lake
  Keillor, G. Leaving home
Hansel
  Keillor, G. Leaving home
Hawaii
  Keillor, G. Leaving home
High rise
  Keillor, G. Leaving home
Homecoming
  Keillor, G. Leaving home
How the crab apple grew
  Keillor, G. Leaving home
The killer
  Keillor, G. Leaving home
A Lake Wobegon Christmas—such were the joys
  The New York Times Book Review 90:7 D 8 '85
Lake Wobegon games
  Sports Illustrated 65:124-8+ D 22-29 '86
Leaving home
  The Atlantic 260:47-53 S '87
Life is good
  Keillor, G. Leaving home
Lyle's roof
  Keillor, G. Leaving home
My name is Yon Yonson
  The New York Times Magazine p77-8+ D 18 '88
New Year's
  Keillor, G. Leaving home
Out in the cold
  Keillor, G. Leaving home
Pontoon boat
  Keillor, G. Leaving home
Post office
  Keillor, G. Leaving home
The royal family
  Keillor, G. Leaving home
Seeds
  Keillor, G. Leaving home
The speeding ticket
  Keillor, G. Leaving home
State Fair
  Keillor, G. Leaving home
A ten-dollar bill
  Keillor, G. Leaving home
Thanksgiving
  Keillor, G. Leaving home
A trip to Grand Rapids
  Keillor, G. Leaving home
Truckstop
  Keillor, G. Leaving home
Where did it go wrong?
  Keillor, G. Leaving home

Keillor, Garrison—*Continued*
Whose child is this?
U.S. Catholic 51:27-31 F '86

Keisler, Paula
Swimmer
The Massachusetts Review 25:182-96
Summ '84

Keisling, William
A fire in the box that could truly light
the world
The North American Review 272:40-1 D
'87

Keith, Don Lee
When the morning comes
Mississippi writers v1: Fiction; ed. by D.
Abbott

Keizer, Gregg
Chimera dreams
Omni (New York, N.Y.) 8:52-4+ Je '86
I am the burning bush
Omni book of science fiction 3

Kelele. Coleman, W.

Kelen, Stephen
The intruders
Short story international 67

Keller, David Henry, 1886-1966
The lost language
Young mutants; ed. by I. Asimov; M.
H. Greenberg and C. G. Waugh
The revolt of the pedestrians
Amazing stories: 60 years of the best
science fiction

Keller, Gary D.
Mocha in Disneyland
Keller, G. D. Tales of El Huitlacoche
The mojado who offered up his tapeworms
to the public weal
Keller, G. D. Tales of El Huitlacoche
Papi invented the automatic jumping bean
Keller, G. D. Tales of El Huitlacoche
The raza who scored big in Anáhuac
Keller, G. D. Tales of El Huitlacoche

Keller, Gottfried, 1819-1890
The little legend of the dance
German stories; ed. by H. Steinhauer

Kelley, Leo P., 1928-
Jurisprudence
Alfred Hitchcock's Grave suspicions

Kelly, Carla
A season for heroes
She won the West; ed. by M. Muller
and B. Pronzini

Kelly, Carmel
Park
Transgressions; ed. by D. Anderson
The waters of Vanuatu
Home and away; ed. by R. Creswell

Kelly, Clara
Where's grandma's home?
'Teen 32:32 Jl '88

Kelly, David
(jt. auth) See Colless, Ted, and Kelly,
David

Kelly, Gwen, 1922-
The holiday house
Room to move; ed. by S. Falkiner

Kelly, James P. (James Patrick)
Glass cloud
The Year's best science fiction, fifth an-
nual collection
The prisoner of Chillon
Terry Carr's Best science fiction and fan-
tasy of the year #16
The Year's best science fiction, fourth
annual collection
Solstice
Mirrorshades; ed. by B. Sterling
The Year's best science fiction, third an-
nual collection

**Kelly, James P. (James Patrick), and Kessel,
John**
Friend
The Year's best science fiction, second
annual collection

Kelly, Maeve
Pilgrim's tale
The Massachusetts Review 28:441-52 Aut
'87

Kelly, Patrick, 1917-
*For works written by this author under
other names see* Allbeury, Ted,
1917-

Kelly, Robert, 1935-
Rosary
Sudden fiction; ed. by R. Shapard and
J. Thomas

Kelly, Terence, 1920-
Their first American
Short story international 70

Kelly, Valerie
Berlioz & the ghetto blaster
Erotic interludes; ed. by L. Barbach

Kelly country. Chandler, A. B.

Kelm, Karlton
Musical evenings
The Literary Review (Madison, N.J.)
28:23-33 Fall '84

Kelman, James
The hon
Streets of stone; ed. by M. Burgess and
H. Whyte
Remember young Cecil
Streets of stone; ed. by M. Burgess and
H. Whyte

Kelso's lady. Lurie, M.

Kelvingrove Park. Ure, J.

Kély, Entmount *See* Keeley, Edmund

Kempson, Joan
The flyaway heart
Good Housekeeping 201:96-7 Jl '85

Kennedy, Daniel
After all these years
Redbook 168:48+ Ap '87

Kennedy, Leigh
Her furry face
  The Year's best science fiction, first annual collection
The silent cradle
  The Best of Shadows; ed. by C. L. Grant
Tropism
  Afterlives; ed. by P. Sargent and I. Watson
KENNEDY, ROBERT F., 1925-1968
                About
Barthelme, D. Robert Kennedy saved from drowning
Kennedy, Thomas E., 1944-
Years in Kaldar
  The Literary Review (Madison, N.J.) 31:315-27 Spr '88
Kennedy, William, 1928-
The hills and the creeks (Albany, 1850)
  Harper's 276:55-62 Mr '88
Kenneth, Jan
The drowning
  Redbook 165:72-4+ O '85
  Redbook 166:52-4+ N '85
Kenney, Susan, 1941-
The checkup
  Redbook 170:48-9+ F '88
In case you don't come back
  The Hudson Review 38:214-34 Summ '85
Nativity
  Ladies' Home Journal 103:86+ D '86
The well
  McCall's 113:160-1+ S '86
Kenny, Maurice, 1929-
Yaikni
  Earth power coming; ed. by S. J. Ortiz
Kenny, Wade
A country home
  Whispers V
Kent, Alexander
      See also Reeman, Douglas
KENTUCKY
Stuart, J. Hot-collared mule
                20th century
Attaway, W. Blood on the forge [excerpt]
Gilchrist, E. Music
Madden, D. The singer
Neville, S. Kentucky people
Stuart, J. Battle with the bees
Stuart, J. The champion
Stuart, J. Competition at Slush Creek
Stuart, J. Evidence is high proof
Stuart, J. Fight number twenty-five
Stuart, J. Horse-trading trembles
Stuart, J. Land of our enemies
Stuart, J. No hero
Stuart, J. No petty thief
Stuart, J. The slipover sweater
Stuart, J. Testimony of trees
Stuart, J. To market, to market
Stuart, J. When mountain men make peace
Zugsmith, L. Room in the world

                Coal mines and mining
  See Coal mines and mining—Kentucky
                Farm life
  See Farm life—Kentucky
                Politics
  See Politics—Kentucky
Kentucky. Boswell, R.
Kentucky people. Neville, S.
KENYA
Hill, J. The malachite beads
Ngugi wa Thiong'o. Minutes of glory
Ngugi wa Thiong'o. The return
Satterthwait, W. The smoke people
                Farm life
  See Farm life—Kenya
                Race relations
Thomas, M. She hears, falling, the seed
Kenyatta, Jomo, ca. 1891-1978
The gentlemen of the jungle
  African short stories; ed. by C. Achebe and C. L. Innes
Kepa. Grace, P.
The **kepi.** Colette
Keppel, Tim
Oyster shells
  The Literary Review (Madison, N.J.) 29:55-64 Fall '85
Ker, the god killer. Ferguson, J.
Kercheval, Jesse Lee
A clean house
  Kercheval, J. L. The dogeater
The dogeater
  Kercheval, J. L. The dogeater
A history of Indiana
  Kercheval, J. L. The dogeater
The history of the church in America
  Kercheval, J. L. The dogeater
La mort au moyen âge
  Kercheval, J. L. The dogeater
Tertiary care
  Kercheval, J. L. The dogeater
Underground women
  20 under 30; ed. by D. Spark
  Kercheval, J. L. The dogeater
Willy
  Kercheval, J. L. The dogeater
The **kerchief.** Agnon, S. Y.
KERGUELEN ISLANDS
Charlton, W. Hakanono
The **Kerman** kill. Gault, W. C.
The **kerosene** stove. Al-Wardani, M.
Kerouac. Galyan, D.
Kerr, Don
Get your jive on highway five
  The Old dance; ed. by B. Burnard
Kerr, Laurie
Passion fruit
  Stories and poems from close to home; ed. by F. Salas
Kerr, M. E.
Do you want my opinion?
  Seventeen 43:192-3+ S '84

Kerr, Raymond
Animal prison
Whole Earth Review no56:114-17 Fall
'87
Kerrigan, Philip, 1959-
West wind
Winter's crimes 18
Kersh, Gerald, 1911-1968
Comrade death
The Penguin book of horror stories
Men without bones
Lost souls; ed. by J. Sullivan
Kerslake, Susan
Foreigner
TriQuarterly no71:83-6 Wint '88
Kesey, Ken
Dream of Jeannie
The Esquire fiction reader v1
Kessel, John
Credibility
In the field of fire; ed. by J. Van B.
Dann and J. Dann
Hearts do not in eyes shine
The Year's best science fiction, first an-
nual collection
The pure product
The Year's best science fiction, fourth
annual collection
(jt. auth) See Kelly, James P. (James
Patrick), and Kessel, John
Kessler, Jascha Frederick, 1929-
Aeaea
Kessler, J. F. Classical illusions
Afrodite
Kessler, J. F. Classical illusions
The bird cage
Kessler, J. F. Classical illusions
Cheiron
Kessler, J. F. Classical illusions
Corinth
Kessler, J. F. Classical illusions
Courtly love
Kessler, J. F. Classical illusions
Dafne
Kessler, J. F. Classical illusions
Esau
Kessler, J. F. Classical illusions
The foundation
Kessler, J. F. Classical illusions
Gnosis
Kessler, J. F. Classical illusions
Hermes
Kessler, J. F. Classical illusions
Ikaros
Kessler, J. F. Classical illusions
Iocasta
Kessler, J. F. Classical illusions
Jacob
Kessler, J. F. Classical illusions
Kassandra
Kessler, J. F. Classical illusions
Maya
Kessler, J. F. Classical illusions

Medea
Kessler, J. F. Classical illusions
Moses
Kessler, J. F. Classical illusions
The old muse
Kessler, J. F. Classical illusions
Perceval
Kessler, J. F. Classical illusions
Rhadamanthys
Kessler, J. F. Classical illusions
Saul of Tarsus
Kessler, J. F. Classical illusions
Sphinx
Kessler, J. F. Classical illusions
Teiresias
Kessler, J. F. Classical illusions
A Theban ostrakon
Kessler, J. F. Classical illusions
Valley
Kessler, J. F. Classical illusions
Xanthippe
Kessler, J. F. Classical illusions
Kessler, Rod
Mr. Integrity for 1987
The North American Review 272:38-9 Mr
'87
Kew Gardens. Woolf, V.
The **key**. Asimov, I.
The **key**. Staples, G.
A **key** for Dolcina. Seepaul, L.
The **key** game. Fink, I.
Key Largo. Ballantyne, S.
KEY WEST (FLA.) *See* Florida—Key West
The **key** word. Asimov, I.
Keyhole. Leinster, M.
The **keynote.** Thompson, K.
Khan, Ismith, 1925-
Shadows move in the Britannia Bar
Short story international 50
Kharal, Naseem
The dead end
Short story international 62
KHMER REFUGEES *See* Refugees, Khmer
**KHRUSHCHEV, NINA PETROVNA,
1900?-1984**
About
Boyle, T. C. Ike and Nina
Khudayyir, Mohammed
Clocks like horses
Arabic short stories; tr. by D. Johnson-
Davies
Khuri, Colette
Sarab
Modern Syrian short stories; ed. by M.
G. Azrak
KIBBUTZIM *See* Collective settlements—Is-
rael
Kibera, Leonard
A silent song
African short stories in English; ed. by
J. de Grandsaigne

Kibera, Leonard—*Continued*
  The spider's web
    African short stories; ed. by C. Achebe
      and C. L. Innes
Kickback for a killer. Searls, H.
Kicking on. Lurie, M.
The **Kicking** Twelfth. Crane, S.
The **kid**. Briskin, M.
The **Kid**. Lee, M.
Kid in a bin. Carter, R.
The **kid** in command. Marmur, J.
The **kid** in the stove. Kinsella, W. P.
Kid MacArthur. Vaughn, S.
Kid stuff. Dawson, F.
Kid victory. Salas, F.
Kid zero. Sulivan, J.
Kidman, Fiona, 1940-
  Flower man
    Women's work; ed. by M. McLeod and
      L. Wevers
  A strange delight
    Women's work; ed. by M. McLeod and
      L. Wevers
A **kidnaping** in the family. Fante, J.
The **kidnapped** Prime Minister. Christie, A.
The **kidnappers**. Painter, P.
KIDNAPPING
  See also Hostages
  Block, L. The most unusual snatch
  Blythe, W. The taming power of the small
  Bradbury, R. Dead men rise up never
  Christie, A. The adventure of Johnnie
    Waverly
  Doyle, Sir A. C. An exciting Christmas
    Eve; or, My lecture on dynamite
  Doyle, Sir A. C. The Greek interpreter
  Flanagan, M. Wild garlic
  Garve, A. Flight from danger
  Gilbert, M. The unstoppable man
  Hentz, C. L. Wild Jack; or, The stolen
    child
  Highsmith, P. When in Rome
  Hoch, E. D. A place for bleeding
  Honig, D. Nice work if you can get it
  Ingalls, R. I see a long journey
  Keating, H. R. F. A hell of a story
  King, S. Popsy
  Lutz, J. Buried treasure
  Lutz, J. Mail order
  Lutz, J. Pure rotten
  Mansfield, K. How Pearl Button was kid-
    napped
  Muir, A. The reptile
  Oates, J. C. The abduction
  O'Donnell, P. A better day to die
  Painter, P. The kidnappers
  Pritchett, M. Fashion in the Third World
  Rendell, R. The price of joy
  Rooke, L. The shut-in number
  Sisk, F. Dogbane
  Walsh, T. The killer instinct
  Washburn, L. J. On the prod
  Wellen, E. Scents in the dark

Woolrich, C. The book that squealed
The **kid's** guide to divorce. Moore, L.
Kiely, Benedict
  Bloodless Byrne of a Monday
    Kiely, B. A letter to Peachtree & nine
      other stories
  Eton Crop
    Kiely, B. A letter to Peachtree & nine
      other stories
  The jeweller's boy
    Kiely, B. A letter to Peachtree & nine
      other stories
  A journey to the seven streams
    The Best of Irish wit and wisdom; ed.
      by J. McCarthy
  A letter to Peachtree
    Kiely, B. A letter to Peachtree & nine
      other stories
  Mock battle
    Kiely, B. A letter to Peachtree & nine
      other stories
  The python
    Kiely, B. A letter to Peachtree & nine
      other stories
  Secondary top
    Kiely, B. A letter to Peachtree & nine
      other stories
  Through the fields in gloves
    Kiely, B. A letter to Peachtree & nine
      other stories
  A walk in the wheat
    Kiely, B. A letter to Peachtree & nine
      other stories
  Your left foot is crazy
    Kiely, B. A letter to Peachtree & nine
      other stories
Kikimora. Rhys, J.
Kilberg, Garnett
  A position of trying
    The Literary Review (Madison, N.J.)
      30:609-14 Summ '87
KILBINNIN (SCOTLAND) *See* Scotland—
  Kilbinnin
Kilbinnin men. Dunn, D.
KILDARE (IRELAND) *See* Ireland—Kildare
Kilgore, Davida
  Bingo
    Kilgore, D. Last summer
    Stiller's pond; ed. by J. Agee; R. Blakely
      and S. Welch
  The day we discovered we were black
    Kilgore, D. Last summer
  The deterioration of 47th Street
    Kilgore, D. Last summer
  The dietary exploits of Bessie
    Kilgore, D. Last summer
  Heaven vs. hell
    Kilgore, D. Last summer
  Last summer "How I spent my summer
    vacation" by Diana Lancaster
    Kilgore, D. Last summer
  Three alarm fire
    Kilgore, D. Last summer

Kilgore, Davida—*Continued*
  Unpaid debts
    Kilgore, D. Last summer
Kill day on the government wharf. Thomas,
    A. C.
Kill her. Idris, Y.
Killdeer. Martínez-Serros, H.
The **killer.** Flynn, R.
The **killer.** Keillor, G.
The **killer.** Mailer, N.
The **killer.** Murphy, Y.
Killer butterfly. Hellerstein, D.
The **killer** chicken and the closet queen. Wil-
    liams, T.
A **killer** in the dark. Alter, R. E.
The **killer** instinct. Walsh, T.
The **killer** poet. Strand, M.
The **killers.** Hemingway, E.
Killers' club car. Tepperman, E. C.
Killian, Kevin
  September
    Men on men; ed. by G. Stambolian
The **killing.** Pronzini, B.
Killing. Updike, J.
The **killing** bottle. Hartley, L. P.
Killing his bear. Crane, S.
Killing lizards. Boyd, W.
The **killing** of a hedgehog. Falkiner, S.
The **killing** of Michael Finnegan. Gilbert, M.
Killing the bees. Schwartz, L. S.
Killings. Dubus, A.
Killingsworth, Sharon
  Born to ride
    Stories and poems from close to home;
      ed. by F. Salas
Killough, H. Patrick
  (jt. auth) See Killough, Lee, and Killough,
    H. Patrick
Killough, Lee, and Killough, H. Patrick
  Keeping the customer satisfied
    Isaac Asimov's Tomorrow's voices
Kilworth, Garry
  Almost heaven
    Kilworth, G. The songbirds of pain
  Blind windows
    Kilworth, G. The songbirds of pain
  The dissemblers
    Kilworth, G. The songbirds of pain
  God's cold lips
    Kilworth, G. The songbirds of pain
  The invisible foe
    Kilworth, G. The songbirds of pain
  Let's go to Golgotha!
    Kilworth, G. The songbirds of pain
  The looking-glass man
    Omni (New York, N.Y.) 10:76-8+ Mr '88
  Lord of the dance
    Kilworth, G. The songbirds of pain
  The man who collected bridges
    Kilworth, G. The songbirds of pain
  Oubliette
    Kilworth, G. The songbirds of pain

  Paper moon
    Omni (New York, N.Y.) 9:60-2+ Ja '87
  The rose bush
    Kilworth, G. The songbirds of pain
  Scarlet fever
    Kilworth, G. The songbirds of pain
  The songbirds of pain
    Kilworth, G. The songbirds of pain
    Omni (New York, N.Y.) 7:46-8+ Ag '85
  Spiral sands
    Interzone: the 2nd anthology; ed. by J.
      Clute; D. Pringle and S. Ounsley
  Sumi dreams of a paper frog
    Kilworth, G. The songbirds of pain
Kim, Chu-Yong
  The moon-welcoming flower
    The Road to Sampo, and other Korean
      short stories
Kim, I-Sok
  Tombstone without an inscription
    The Unenlightened, and other Korean
      short stories
Kim, Song-Han
  Badby
    A Respite, and other Korean short
      stories
Kim, Sung-Ok
  Good bargain
    Home-coming, and other Korean short
      stories
  Operation
    Home-coming, and other Korean short
      stories
  Record of a journey to Mujin
    Home-coming, and other Korean short
      stories
  Seoul: winter 1964 [Variant title: Seoul—
    1964 winter]
    Flowers of fire; ed. by P. H. Lee
    Home-coming, and other Korean short
      stories
Kim, Tongin
  Potato
    Flowers of fire; ed. by P. H. Lee
Kim, Tongni
  Portrait of a shaman
    Flowers of fire; ed. by P. H. Lee
Kim, Won-Il
  The spirit of the darkness
    Early spring, mid-summer, and other
      Korean short stories
Kim, Yisök
  The cuckoo
    Flowers of fire; ed. by P. H. Lee
Kim, Yong Ik
  The first election
    Short story international 64
  From below the bridge
    Short story international 54
  The gold watch
    Short story international 48
  Gourd Dance Song
    Short story international 59

Kim, Yong Ik—*Continued*
The snake man
Short story international 56
The taste of salt
Short story international 43
Village wine
Short story international 62
Kim, Yu-Jong
The visitor
The Unenlightened, and other Korean
short stories
Kimball, Richard W.
Destination
Southwest tales; ed. by Alurista and X.
Rojas-Urista
The **Kimberly** toughs. Conroy, J.
Kimbriel, Katharine Eliska
Night calls
Werewolves; ed. by J. Yolen and M. H.
Greenberg
Kincaid, Jamaica
Gwen
The New Yorker 60:46-52 Ap 16 '84
The long rain
The New Yorker 60:28-36 Jl 30 '84
Somewhere, Belgium
The New Yorker 60:44-51 My 14 '84
A walk to the jetty
The New Yorker 60:45-51 N 5 '84
Kincaid, Nanci
Like the old wolf in all those wolf stories
New stories from the South: the year's
best, 1988
A **kind** of dying. Barrett, M.
KINDERGARTEN
Steele, M. The cat and the coffee drinkers
Kindergarten. Gunn, J. E.
Kindling point. Muller, M.
Kindly dig your grave. Ellin, S.
The **kindly** isle. Pohl, F.
The **kindly** ones. Sladek, J. T.
KINDNESS
Crane, S. The men in the storm
Sanders, S. R. The fire woman
Kindness. Dale, C.
Kindred. Coriolan, J.
Kindred spirits. Walker, A.
King, Cynthia
The gift of love
Good Housekeeping 207:242+ D '88
King, Francis Henry, 1923-
Appetites
King, F. H. One is a wanderer
The Brighton Belle
King, F. H. One is a wanderer
A corner of a foreign field
King, F. H. One is a wanderer
The Festival of the Dead
King, F. H. One is a wanderer
The goat
King, F. H. One is a wanderer
Hard feelings
King, F. H. One is a wanderer

His everlasting mansion
King, F. H. One is a wanderer
Home
King, F. H. One is a wanderer
I lived for you
King, F. H. One is a wanderer
Indirect method
King, F. H. One is a wanderer
Loss
King, F. H. One is a wanderer
Mess
King, F. H. One is a wanderer
The mouse
King, F. H. One is a wanderer
A scent of mimosa
Black water; ed. by A. Manguel
King, F. H. One is a wanderer
The silence is rest?
King, F. H. One is a wanderer
So hurt and humiliated
King, F. H. One is a wanderer
The soutane
King, F. H. One is a wanderer
Sundays
King, F. H. One is a wanderer
The tradesman
Winter's tales, new ser. v4
The tree
King, F. H. One is a wanderer
Unmaking
King, F. H. One is a wanderer
Voices
King, F. H. One is a wanderer
King, Grace Elizabeth, 1852-1932
Bayou l'Ombre: an incident of the war
Civil War women; ed. by F. McSherry;
C. G. Waugh and M. Greenberg
The little convent girl
Mississippi River tales; ed. by F.
McSherry; C. G. Waugh and M. H.
Greenberg
The story of a day
Haunted women; ed. by A. Bendixen
King, Rufus, 1893-1966
Malice in wonderland
Witches; ed. by I. Asimov; M. H.
Greenberg and C. G. Waugh
King, Stephen, 1947-
The ballad of the flexible bullet
King, S. Skeleton crew
Beachworld
King, S. Skeleton crew
Big wheels: a tale of the laundry game
(milkman #2)
King, S. Skeleton crew
Cain rose up
King, S. Skeleton crew
The cat from hell
Magicats! Ed. by J. Dann and G. Dozois
Crouch end
The Dark descent; ed. by D. G. Hart-
well

King, Stephen, 1947—— *Continued*

The doctor's case
  The New adventures of Sherlock Holmes; ed. by M. H. Greenberg and C. L. R. Waugh

The end of the whole mess
  Omni (New York, N.Y.) 9:72-4+ O '86

Gramma
  King, S. Skeleton crew

Here there be tygers
  King, S. Skeleton crew

The Jaunt
  King, S. Skeleton crew

The man who would not shake hands
  The Best of Shadows; ed. by C. L. Grant
  King, S. Skeleton crew

The mist
  King, S. Skeleton crew

The monkey
  The Dark descent; ed. by D. G. Hartwell
  King, S. Skeleton crew
  The Mammoth book of short horror novels; ed. by M. Ashley

Morning deliveries (milkman #1)
  King, S. Skeleton crew

Mrs. Todd's shortcut
  King, S. Skeleton crew
  Redbook 163:56+ My '84

The Night Flier
  Prime evil; ed. by D. E. Winter

The night of the tiger
  The Best horror stories from the Magazine of fantasy and science fiction

Nona
  King, S. Skeleton crew

One for the road
  Young monsters; ed. by I. Asimov; M. H. Greenberg and C. G. Waugh

Popsy
  Masques II; ed. by J. N. Williamson

Quitters, Inc.
  Masterpieces of mystery and suspense; ed. by M. H. Greenberg

The raft
  King, S. Skeleton crew

The reach [Variant title: Do the dead sing]
  The Dark descent; ed. by D. G. Hartwell
  King, S. Skeleton crew

The reaper's image
  King, S. Skeleton crew

The revelations of 'Becka Paulson
  Rolling Stone p80-1+ Jl 19-Ag 2 '84

Survivor type
  King, S. Skeleton crew

Uncle Otto's truck
  King, S. Skeleton crew

The wedding gig
  King, S. Skeleton crew

Word processor of the gods [Variant title: The word processor]
  King, S. Skeleton crew

King, Susan Petigru *See* Bowen, Susan Petigru, 1824-1875

King, Tappan

Boogie Man
  Devils & demons; ed. by M. Kaye and S. Kaye

The king. Clarke, T.

The king and his three daughters. Walpole, H.

King and shepherd. Brown, G. M.

King bait. Hulme, K.

King Death. Gallagher, T.

The king in pawn. Gilbert, M.

The king in the golden mask. Schwob, M.

The king is threatened. Ekström, M.

KING KONG (MOTION PICTURE)

Farmer, P. J. After King Kong fell

King Kong: a meditation. Bernard, K.

King Mike. Faik, S.

The king of beasts. Farmer, P. J.

The king of clubs. Christie, A.

The king of jazz. Barthelme, D.

King of safety. Martone, M.

The king of Siam. Govier, K.

King of the Bloodies. Friedman, B. J.

The King of the Cats. Benét, S. V.

The king of the elves. Dick, P. K.

King of the hill. Girion, B.

King of the Hill. Liben, M.

The king of the hill. Mcauley, P. J.

King of the mountain. Garrett, G. P.

A king of the road. Lurie, M.

King of the street. Kinsella, W. P.

The king of the waters. Jordan, A. C.

The king of the wood. Crowley, A.

King Pest. Poe, E. A.

King Solomon. Rosenfeld, I.

King Solomon's ring. Zelazny, R.

The king who had to be queen too. Winters, J.

Kingdom City to Cairo. Algren, N.

Kingdom come. Gallant, M.

Kingdom come. McAllister, B.

Kingdom come. Taylor, P. E.

The kingdom of earth. Williams, T.

Kingdom of the heart. Ledbetter, E.

The kingfisher. Norris, L.

KINGS AND RULERS

  See also Courts and courtiers

Apollinaire, G. The moon king

Barthelme, D. The palace at four A.M.

Baum, L. F. The queen of Quok

Böll, H. Recollections of a young king

Brown, G. M. King and shepherd

Brown, G. M. Magi

Brunner, J. Elixir for the emperor

Coleridge, S. Phantasmion [excerpt]

Crowley, A. The god of Ibreez

Crowley, A. The hearth

KINGS AND RULERS—*Continued*
Crowley, A. The oracle of the Corycian cave
Cullen, E. J. Larmer said he would be King
Ford, J. M. As above, so below
Jahnn, H. H. Sassanidian king
Lee, T. A lynx with lions
Morazzoni, M. The last assignment
Morris, K. The sapphire necklace
Mukherjee, B. Courtly vision
Rooke, L. The history of England, part four
Schwob, M. The king in the golden mask
Shefner, E. Troubles of a tattooed king
Smith, C. A. The death of Malygris
Smith, C. A. The garden of Adompha
Smith, C. A. The seven geases
Vance, J. The new prime
Vinge, J. D. The storm king
Vizyēnos, G. M. The only journey of his life
Walker, W. Ashiepattle
Walpole, H. The peach in brandy: a Milesian tale
Wells, H. G. The Rajah's treasure
A **king's** son. Maupassant, G. de
King's X. Garfield, B.
Kingsbury, Donald, 1929-
The moon goddess and the son
Baker's dozen: 13 short science fiction novels
Kingsolver, Barbara
Rose-Johnny
New stories from the South: the year's best, 1988
The Virginia Quarterly Review 63:88-109 Wint '87
KINGSTON (JAMAICA) *See* Jamaica—Kingston
Kinsella, W. P.
The Alligator Report—with questions for discussion
Kinsella, W. P. The Alligator Report
Barefoot and pregnant in Des Moines
The Virginia Quarterly Review 60:319-29 Spr '84
The bear went over the mountain
Kinsella, W. P. The Fencepost chronicles
Beef
Kinsella, W. P. The Fencepost chronicles
Between
Kinsella, W. P. Dance me outside
The book buyers
Kinsella, W. P. The Alligator Report
Books by the pound
Kinsella, W. P. The Alligator Report
Butterflies
Kinsella, W. P. Dance me outside
Caraway
Kinsella, W. P. Dance me outside
Dance me outside
Kinsella, W. P. Dance me outside

Dancing
Kinsella, W. P. The Fencepost chronicles
Diehard
Kinsella, W. P. The further adventures of Slugger McBatt
Distances
Kinsella, W. P. The further adventures of Slugger McBatt
Sport (New York, N.Y.) 78:66-8+ Jl '87
Doves and proverbs
Kinsella, W. P. The Alligator Report
The East End Umbrella Company endowment for the arts
Kinsella, W. P. The Alligator Report
The Eddie Scissons syndrome
Kinsella, W. P. The further adventures of Slugger McBatt
Electrico utensilio
Kinsella, W. P. The Alligator Report
Feathers
Kinsella, W. P. Dance me outside
The fog
Kinsella, W. P. The Fencepost chronicles
Frank Pierce, Iowa
Kinsella, W. P. The further adventures of Slugger McBatt
The further adventures of Slugger McBatt
Kinsella, W. P. The further adventures of Slugger McBatt
Gabon [Variant title: I pay my rent]
Kinsella, W. P. The Alligator Report
The North American Review 270:33-4 S '85
The gerbil that ate Los Angeles
Kinsella, W. P. The Alligator Report
Gooch
Kinsella, W. P. Dance me outside
The history of peanut butter
Kinsella, W. P. The Alligator Report
Horse collars
Kinsella, W. P. Dance me outside
How I missed the million dollar round table
Kinsella, W. P. The Alligator Report
I am airport
Kinsella, W. P. The Alligator Report
Illianna comes home
Kinsella, W. P. Dance me outside
The inaugural meeting
Kinsella, W. P. Dance me outside
Indian Joe
Kinsella, W. P. The Fencepost chronicles
The Indian Nation Cultural Exchange Program
Kinsella, W. P. The Fencepost chronicles
The job
Kinsella, W. P. The Alligator Report
K Mart
Kinsella, W. P. The further adventures of Slugger McBatt
The kid in the stove
Kinsella, W. P. Dance me outside

Kinsella, W. P.—*Continued*
King of the street
  Kinsella, W. P. The Alligator Report
Lark song
  Kinsella, W. P. Dance me outside
The letter writer
  Kinsella, W. P. The Alligator Report
Linda Star
  Kinsella, W. P. Dance me outside
Longhouse
  Kinsella, W. P. Dance me outside
The managers
  Kinsella, W. P. The Fencepost chronicles
Marco in paradise
  Kinsella, W. P. The Alligator Report
The McGuffin
  Kinsella, W. P. Dance me outside
Nursie
  Here's the story: fiction with heart; ed.
    by M. Sklar
A page from the marriage manual for
    Songhees brides
  Kinsella, W. P. The Alligator Report
Panache
  Kinsella, W. P. Dance me outside
Penance
  Kinsella, W. P. Dance me outside
The performance
  Kinsella, W. P. The Fencepost chronicles
The post office octopus
  Kinsella, W. P. The Alligator Report
The practical education of Constable B. B.
    Bobowski
  Kinsella, W. P. The Fencepost chronicles
Preserving fireweed for the White Pass and
    Yukon Railroad
  Kinsella, W. P. The Alligator Report
Pretend dinners
  Love stories for the time being; ed. by
    G. D. Chipps and B. Henderson
Punchlines
  Kinsella, W. P. The further adventures
    of Slugger McBatt
Real Indians
  Kinsella, W. P. The Fencepost chronicles
The Redemption Center
  Kinsella, W. P. The Alligator Report
Reports concerning the death of the Seattle
    Albatross are somewhat exaggerated
  Kinsella, W. P. The further adventures
    of Slugger McBatt
The resurrection of Troutfishing in Ameri-
    ca Shorty
  Kinsella, W. P. The Alligator Report
Searching for Freddy
  Kinsella, W. P. The further adventures
    of Slugger McBatt
The secret
  Kinsella, W. P. The Alligator Report
The silver porcupine
  Kinsella, W. P. The Alligator Report
Strawberry stew
  Kinsella, W. P. The Alligator Report

Syzygy
  Kinsella, W. P. The Alligator Report
The thrill of the grass
  The Oxford book of Canadian short
    stories in English
To look at the Queen
  Kinsella, W. P. The Fencepost chronicles
The truck
  Kinsella, W. P. The Fencepost chronicles
Truth
  Kinsella, W. P. The Fencepost chronicles
Ups and downs
  Kinsella, W. P. Dance me outside
The Valley of the Schmoon
  Kinsella, W. P. The further adventures
    of Slugger McBatt
The Vancouver chapter of the Howard G.
    Scharff Memorial Society
  Kinsella, W. P. The Alligator Report
Voyeur
  Kinsella, W. P. The Alligator Report
KINSHIP
    See also Tribes
Kiosk encounter. Davie, E.
Kip, Leonard
The ghosts at Grantley
  Christmas ghosts; ed. by K. Cramer and
    D. G. Hartwell
Kipling, Rudyard, 1865-1936
The cat that walked by himself
  Roger Caras' Treasury of great cat
    stories
Dayspring mishandled
  Dark arrows; ed. by A. Manguel
The devil and the deep sea
  Short stories of the sea; ed. by G. C.
    Solley and E. Steinbaugh
East and West
  On being foreign; ed. by T. J. Lewis and
    R. E. Jungman
Lispeth
  The Nobel reader; ed. by J. Eisen and
    S. Troy
Mary Postgate
  The Treasury of English short stories;
    ed. by N. Sullivan
A matter of fact
  Mysterious sea stories; ed. by W. Pat-
    trick
The return of Imray [Variant title:
    Recrudescence of Imray]
  Mystery in the mainstream; ed. by B.
    Pronzini; M. H. Greenberg and B. N.
    Malzberg
  The Penguin book of ghost stories
"They"
  Dark banquet; ed. by L. Child
The wish house
  Black water; ed. by A. Manguel
The wreck of the Visigoth
  Short stories of the sea; ed. by G. C.
    Solley and E. Steinbaugh

Kipling, Rudyard, 1865-1936—Continued
Parodies, travesties, etc.
Boyle, T. C. Rupert Beersley and the Beggar Master of Sivani-Hoota
Kipp, George Grover
Farewell gesture
Alfred Hitchcock's Crimewatch
Lessons from a pro
Alfred Hitchcock's Mortal errors
Kirchheimer, Gloria L.
A case of dementia
The North American Review 269:10-13 Mr '84
Kirk, Michael, 1928-
For works written by this author under other names see Knox, Bill, 1928-
Kirk, Russell
Balgrummo's hell
The Best horror stories from the Magazine of fantasy and science fiction
An encounter by Mortstone pond
Kirk, R. Watchers at the strait gate
Fate's purse
Kirk, R. Watchers at the strait gate
The invasion of the Church of the Holy Ghost
Kirk, R. Watchers at the strait gate
Lex Talionis
Kirk, R. Watchers at the strait gate
The peculiar demesne of Archvicar Gerontion
Kirk, R. Watchers at the strait gate
The reflex-man in Whinnymuir Close
Kirk, R. Watchers at the strait gate
Sorworth Place
Rod Serling's Night gallery reader
The surly sullen bell
Kirk, R. Watchers at the strait gate
There's a long, long trail a-winding
The Dark descent; ed. by D. G. Hartwell
The Mammoth book of short horror novels; ed. by M. Ashley
Uncle Isaiah
Kirk, R. Watchers at the strait gate
Watchers at the strait gate
Kirk, R. Watchers at the strait gate
What shadows we pursue
Kirk, R. Watchers at the strait gate
Kirk, Stephen
Morrison's reaction
The Best American short stories, 1984
Kirk-Kuwaye, Chris
Complete with fireworks above Magic Island
Passages to the dream shore; ed. by F. Stewart
Kirkhart, Roberta
In all realities
Prairie Schooner 62:102-9 Summ '88
KIRKPATRICK, JEANE J., 1926-
About
Ruta, S. Hortensia

Kiser, Rosemarie
Sequins
50 Plus 28:37-44 Ag '88
Kismet. Rhys, J.
Kisner, James
The litter
Masques II; ed. by J. N. Williamson
The **kiss.** Carter, A.
The **kiss.** Chekhov, A. P.
The **kiss.** Gingher, M.
The **kiss.** Landolfi, T.
Kiss good night to the princess, frog. Hayes, L.
Kiss of the cobra. Woolrich, C.
Kiss the father. Rossiter, S.
Kisses. Campbell, W. B.
The **kissing** booth. Bukoski, A.
Kissmeowt and the healing friar. Major, A. R.
Kiswana Browne. Naylor, G.
A **kitchen** allegory. Fisher, M. F. K.
The **kitchen** child. Carter, A.
Kitchen conversation. McKinley, J.
The **kite.** Highsmith, P.
The **kite.** Rifaat, A.
The **kite** man. Dunn, R.
Kiteflying party at Doctors' Point. Hulme, K.
Kiteley, Brian
Still life with insects
The Best American short stories, 1988
Kitemaster. Roberts, K.
KITES
Boylan, J. The string
Garve, A. Flight from danger
Highsmith, P. The kite
Hulme, K. Kiteflying party at Doctors' Point
Roberts, K. Kitemaster
Kitten. Zapolska, G.
Kittredge, William
Agriculture
The Pushcart prize X
Balancing water
The Paris Review 29:14-27 Fall '87
Be careful what you want
The Paris Review 27:191-214 Fall '85
Blue stone
Kittredge, W. We are not in this together
Flight
Kittredge, W. We are not in this together
Momentum is always the weapon
Kittredge, W. We are not in this together
Phantom Silver
The Graywolf annual 4
The soap bear
Kittredge, W. We are not in this together

Kittredge, William—*Continued*
Thirty-four seasons of winter
  Kittredge, W. We are not in this
    together
The underground river
  The Best of the West; ed. by J. Thomas
  Kittredge, W. We are not in this
    together
The Van Gogh field
  The Interior country; ed. by A. Black-
    burn
The waterfowl tree
  Kittredge, W. We are not in this
    together
We are not in this together
  Kittredge, W. We are not in this
    together
  Writers of the purple sage; ed. by R.
    Martin and M. Barasch
Kitty partners. Apple, M.
KKK *See* Ku Klux Klan
Klara. Sandel, C.
Klass, Fruma
Before the rainbow
  Synergy v3
Klass, Morton
In the beginning
  Great science fiction; ed. by I. Asimov;
    M. H. Greenberg and C. G. Waugh
Klass, Perri, 1958-
The almond torte equilibrium
  First love/last love; ed. by M. Denneny;
    C. Ortleb and T. Steele
  Klass, P. I am having an adventure
The anatomy of the brain
  Klass, P. I am having an adventure
Bloomingdale's
  Klass, P. I am having an adventure
Clytemnestra in the suburbs
  Klass, P. I am having an adventure
Cowboy time
  Klass, P. I am having an adventure
A gift of sweet mustard
  Klass, P. I am having an adventure
Gingerbread men
  Klass, P. I am having an adventure
Gringo city
  Klass, P. I am having an adventure
How big the world is
  Klass, P. I am having an adventure
I am having an adventure
  Klass, P. I am having an adventure
In Africa
  Klass, P. I am having an adventure
Murderers don't cook for themselves
  Klass, P. I am having an adventure
Nineteen lists
  Klass, P. I am having an adventure
Not a good girl
  Klass, P. I am having an adventure
  Prize stories, 1984
Officemate with pink feathers
  Klass, P. I am having an adventure

A romance—in brief
  Mademoiselle 90:126+ O '84
The secret lives of dieters
  Klass, P. I am having an adventure
Television will betray us all
  Klass, P. I am having an adventure
Theme and variations
  Klass, P. I am having an adventure
Trivia
  Klass, P. I am having an adventure
Two New Jersey stories: Hudson Towers
  Klass, P. I am having an adventure
Two New Jersey stories: Stealing
  Klass, P. I am having an adventure
Klass, Philip *See* Tenn, William, 1920-
KLEE, PAUL, 1879-1940
                About
Barthelme, D. Engineer-private Paul Klee
  misplaces an aircraft between Milbert-
  shofen and Cambrai, March 1916
Klein, Carol
Emancipation
  Prairie Schooner 60:3-25 Fall '86
Klein, Elizabeth
Fishbein's fast
  Prairie Schooner 60:71-91 Fall '86
Klein, Gérard
Hide and seek
  Omni (New York, N.Y.) 9:56+ Je '87
Klein, R. E.
Mrs. Rahlo's closet
  Bringing down the moon; ed. by J. An-
    derson
Klein, T. E. D., 1947-
Black man with a horn
  Klein, T. E. D. Dark gods
Children of the kingdom
  Klein, T. E. D. Dark gods
Nadelman's god
  Klein, T. E. D. Dark gods
  The Mammoth book of short horror
    novels; ed. by M. Ashley
Petey
  Klein, T. E. D. Dark gods
Kleist, Heinrich von, 1777-1811
Anecdote from the last Prussian war
  German romantic stories; ed. by F. G.
    Ryder
The beggarwoman of Locarno
  German romantic stories; ed. by F. G.
    Ryder
  The Penguin book of ghost stories
Betrothal in Santo Domingo [Variant title:
    The engagement in Santo Domingo]
  German romantic novellas, by H. von
    Kleist and Jean Paul
The earthquake in Chile
  German romantic novellas, by H. von
    Kleist and Jean Paul
  German stories; ed. by H. Steinhauer
The foundling
  Dark arrows; ed. by A. Manguel

Kleist, Heinrich von, 1777-1811—*Continued*
The Marquise of O—
German romantic novellas, by H. von
Kleist and Jean Paul
Michael Kohlhaas
German romantic novellas, by H. von
Kleist and Jean Paul
Story of a remarkable single combat
German romantic stories; ed. by F. G.
Ryder
KLEPTOMANIA
Klass, P. Clytemnestra in the suburbs
Whelan, G. Spies and lovers
Klíma, Ivan
Friday morning: an orderly's tale; (with a
story inserted in a hatbox)
Klíma, I. My merry mornings
Miriam
Klíma, I. My first loves
Monday morning: a black market tale
Klíma, I. My merry mornings
My country
Klíma, I. My first loves
Saturday morning: a thief's tale
Klíma, I. My merry mornings
Sunday morning: a foolish tale
Klíma, I. My merry mornings
Short story international 67
Thursday morning: an erotic tale
Klíma, I. My merry mornings
The tightrope walkers
Klíma, I. My first loves
The truth game
Klíma, I. My first loves
Tuesday morning: a sentimental story
Klíma, I. My merry mornings
Short story international 59
Wednesday   morning: a   Christmas
conspiracy tale
Klíma, I. My merry mornings
Klimasewiski, Marshall N.
Tanner and JunHee
Ploughshares 14 no2/3:120-7 '88
Klinkowitz, Jerome
Adolph Menjou's tryout camp
Klinkowitz, J. Short season, and other
stories
Ambience
Klinkowitz, J. Short season, and other
stories
Ball two
Klinkowitz, J. Short season, and other
stories
Baseball bingo
Klinkowitz, J. Short season, and other
stories
Beer night in Bettendorf
Klinkowitz, J. Short season, and other
stories
BP
Klinkowitz, J. Short season, and other
stories

Bus trip
Klinkowitz, J. Short season, and other
stories
Cheap seats
Klinkowitz, J. Short season, and other
stories
Costy Pedraza's greatest pitch
Klinkowitz, J. Short season, and other
stories
Eddie and the niña
Klinkowitz, J. Short season, and other
stories
Five bad hands and the wild mouse folds
Klinkowitz, J. Short season, and other
stories
Freddie's up
Klinkowitz, J. Short season, and other
stories
Game time
Klinkowitz, J. Short season, and other
stories
Hot dogs and the Sox
Klinkowitz, J. Short season, and other
stories
The language game
Klinkowitz, J. Short season, and other
stories
Mack's stats
Klinkowitz, J. Short season, and other
stories
Metaphors
Klinkowitz, J. Short season, and other
stories
The moment of release
Sport (New York, N.Y.) 79:70-3 Jl '88
Nicknames
Klinkowitz, J. Short season, and other
stories
Pregame
Klinkowitz, J. Short season, and other
stories
Rain date
Klinkowitz, J. Short season, and other
stories
Release
Klinkowitz, J. Short season, and other
stories
Road work
Klinkowitz, J. Short season, and other
stories
Short season
Klinkowitz, J. Short season, and other
stories
The squeeze is on
Klinkowitz, J. Short season, and other
stories
Sweet home Chicago
Klinkowitz, J. Short season, and other
stories
Sweet Jayne
Klinkowitz, J. Short season, and other
stories

Klinkowitz, Jerome—*Continued*
The swoon wagon
  Klinkowitz, J. Short season, and other
    stories
Workouts
  Klinkowitz, J. Short season, and other
    stories
Klitzee one—God zero. Michaelson, L. W.
Klobouk, Jiri
The music teacher
  Partisan Review 54:255-61 Spr '87
KLONDIKE RIVER VALLEY (YUKON)
London, J. The Sun-Dog Trail
Kneel to the rising sun. Caldwell, E.
The **knees** of the gods. Hornung, E. W.
The **knife**. Crane, S.
The **knife** and the stone. Hulme, K.
KNIFE THROWING
Böll, H. The man with the knives
Maupassant, G. de. The artist
Shiga, N. Han's crime
Knight, Damon Francis, 1922-
Forever
  Omni book of science fiction 2
Four in one
  Robert Silverberg's Worlds of wonder
God's nose
  100 great fantasy short short stories; ed.
    by I. Asimov; T. Carr and M. H.
    Greenberg
The handler
  100 great fantasy short short stories; ed.
    by I. Asimov; T. Carr and M. H.
    Greenberg
O
  Universe 14
Strangers on paradise
  The Year's best science fiction, fourth
    annual collection
Knight, Eric Mowbray, 1897-1943
Lassie come-home
  Roger Caras' Treasury of great dog
    stories
Knight, Wallace E.
The resurrection man
  Full measure; ed. by D. Sennett
Knight, death and the devil. Kociancich, V.
Knight of shallows. Lee, R. B.
A **knight** of teeth. Mathers, P.
KNIGHTHOOD *See* Knights and knighthood
The **knightly** guest. Williams, T.
KNIGHTS AND KNIGHTHOOD
  See also Chivalry
Denevi, M. A dog in Durer's etching 'The
  knight, death and the devil'
Henry, O. The halberdier of the Little
  Rheinschloss
Kleist, H. von. Story of a remarkable
  single combat
Kociancich, V. Knight, death and the devil
La Motte-Fouqué, F. H. K., Freiherr von.
  Undine
Zelazny, R. The George business

Knights of Puntukas. Thorman, C.
Knights of the Flaming Circle. Jones, D. C.
KNITTING
Hempel, A. Beg, sl tog, inc, cont, rep
The **knitting**. Mattison, A.
The **knock** at the manor gate. Kafka, F.
Knoles, David
The first day of spring
  Masques; ed. by J. N. Williamson
Knowing what I know now. Perowne, B.
Knowledge. Abrahams, L.
Knowledge. Lish, G.
Known for her frankness. Gilliatt, P.
Knox, Bill, 1928-
Deerglen Queen
  Through a glass, darkly; ed. by B. Woel-
    fel
KNOX, JOHN, 1505-1572
                    About
McCormack, E. P. Knox abroad
Knox, John H.
The buyer of souls
  Selected tales of grim and grue from the
    horror pulps; ed. by S. Jaffery
Knox, William, 1928-
  *For works written by this author under
    other names see* Knox, Bill, 1928-
Knox abroad. McCormack, E. P.
KNOXVILLE (TENN.) *See* Tennessee—
  Knoxville
The **knuckle** buster. Osborne, G.
Knucklebones. Sullivan, T.
Knuttel, William
Fugue
  The Clarion awards; ed. by D. Knight
Ko, Haruto
Black market blues
  Murder in Japan; ed. by J. L. Apostolou
    and M. H. Greenberg
Kobin, Joann
"Loving your characters"
  The Literary Review (Madison, N.J.)
    31:89-99 Fall '87
The meat man's death
  The North American Review 269:21-4 Je
    '84
Koch, Claude
Bread and butter questions
  Prize stories, 1985
You taught us good
  Our roots grow deeper than we know;
    ed. by L. Gutkind
Kociancich, Vlady
Knight, death and the devil
  Other fires; ed. by A. Manguel
Kōda, Rohan, 1867-1947
The bearded samurai
  Kōda, R. Pagoda, skull & samurai
Encounter with a skull
  Kōda, R. Pagoda, skull & samurai
The five-storied pagoda
  Kōda, R. Pagoda, skull & samurai

Koea, Shonagh
Meat
  Women's work; ed. by M. McLeod and
    L. Wevers
Koenig, Joseph
A perfect gentleman
  A Matter of crime v2
Koger, Lisa
The June woman
  Seventeen 44:175-7+ Je '85
Kohler, Sheila
The mountain
  Prize stories, 1988
Kohlhaase, Wolfgang
Invention of a language
  Voices East and West: German short
    stories since 1945
Koizumi, Yakumo *See* Hearn, Lafcadio, 1850-
  1904
Kojima, Nobuo, 1915-
Stars
  The Shōwa anthology 1
The **Kokod** warriors. Vance, J.
Kolankiewicz, Sandra J.
El amor no tiene orgullo
  The North American Review 270:54-6 D
    '85
Isla
  Sudden fiction; ed. by R. Shapard and
    J. Thomas
Kolm, Ron
Duke & Jill
  Between C & D; ed. by J. Rose and
    C. Texier
The **Komedy** Kabaret. Avery, M.
Komie, Lowell B.
The balloon of William Fuerst
  Komie, L. B. The judge's chambers, and
    other stories
The butterfly
  Komie, L. B. The judge's chambers, and
    other stories
The Christmas party
  Komie, L. B. The judge's chambers, and
    other stories
The cornucopia of Julia K.
  Komie, L. B. The judge's chambers, and
    other stories
I am Greenwald, my father's son
  Komie, L. B. The judge's chambers, and
    other stories
The interview
  Komie, L. B. The judge's chambers, and
    other stories
The judge's chambers
  Komie, L. B. The judge's chambers, and
    other stories
The law clerk's lament
  Komie, L. B. The judge's chambers, and
    other stories
The loves of David Freund
  Komie, L. B. The judge's chambers, and
    other stories

Mentoring
  Komie, L. B. The judge's chambers, and
    other stories
Picasso is dead
  Komie, L. B. The judge's chambers, and
    other stories
Podhoretz revisited
  Komie, L. B. The judge's chambers, and
    other stories
Professor Strauss's gift
  Komie, L. B. The judge's chambers, and
    other stories
Konas, Gary
What genius
  Universe 16
Kong Jiesheng
On the other side of the stream
  Roses and thorns; ed. by P. Link
Kono, Taeko, 1926-
Crimson markings
  The Literary Review (Madison, N.J.)
    30:184-93 Wint '87
Iron fish
  The Shōwa anthology 2
Konopnicka, Maria
Banasiowa
  Russian and Polish women's fiction; ed.
    by H. Goscilo
Urbanowa
  Russian and Polish women's fiction; ed.
    by H. Goscilo
Konwicki, Tadeusz
A minor apocalypse [excerpt]
  The Pushcart prize IX
Koolau the leper. London, J.
Koontz, Dean, 1945-
Down in the darkness
  The Architecture of fear; ed. by K.
    Cramer and P. D. Pautz
Kooser, Ted
Dogs
  Prairie Schooner 58:53-65 Fall '84
Korabelnikov, Oleg
Tower of birds
  Earth and elsewhere, by K. Bulychev
    and others
Kore 87. Le Guin, U. K.
KOREA
                    20th century
Cho, H.-I. Iron masks
Cho, S.-H. The bony-fish that came into
  my net
Choe, I.-H. Christmas carol
Ch'oe, S. Point
Chon, K.-Y. Kapitan Lee
Han, M.-S. Mr. Kim, the Bohemian
  minstrel
Han, M.-S. The rock
Kim, S.-O. Record of a journey to Mujin
Kim, Y. The cuckoo
Kim, Y. I. The gold watch
Kim, Y. I. Gourd Dance Song
Kim, Y. I. Village wine

KOREA—20th century—*Continued*
Pak, K.-N. A time of disbelief
Pak, W.-S. How I kept our house while
    my husband was away
Sexson, L. Ice cream birth
Sin, S.-U. Pyŏn's death
So, C.-I. Home-coming
So, C.-I. The river
Son, C.-S. The rainy season
Sonu, H. Flowers of fire
Sonu, H. The mirror
Sonu, H. The story of a peculiar pain
Sonu, H. The terrorist
Sonu, H. Thoughts of home
Yi, H. The woman who fulled clothes
Yi, H.-C. Midnight
Yi, P. A stray bullet
Yŏm, S. The last moment
Yu, C.-Y. Relationship
Yun, H.-G. Group beating
            College life
    See College life—Korea
            Communism
    See Communism—Korea
            Farm life
    See Farm life—Korea
            Marriage customs
    See Marriage customs—Korea
            Politics
    See Politics—Korea
        Prisoners and prisons
    See Prisoners and prisons—Korea
            Rural life
An, S.-G. The green chrysanthemum
Ha, K.-C. The spring song
Han, S.-W. The cave
Hwang, S.-Y. The road to Samp'o
Hyon, C.-G. Fire
Kim, C.-Y. The moon-welcoming flower
Kim, S.-O. Operation
Kim, T. Portrait of a shaman
Kim, W.-I. The spirit of the darkness
Kim, Y. I. The snake man
Kim, Y. I. The taste of salt
Kim, Y.-J. The visitor
Kye, Y.-M. Adada the idiot
Moon, S.-T. Last sound of the gong
Na, T.-H. The water-mill
O, Y.-G. Two travelers
So, C.-I. The way to Kŭmsansa temple
So, K.-W. The heir
Song, Y. Overnight at Matthew's
Sonu, H. The colonel and his friend
Yi, C.-J. Target
Yi, H. The buckwheat season
            Pyongyang
Kim, T. Potato
            Seoul
Byatt, A. S. Loss of face
Cho, S.-H. On the overhead bridge
Chon, K.-Y. Driver's assistant
Chon, S.-G. Wings that will carry us both
Kang, S.-J. The young zelkova

Kim, S.-O. Seoul: winter 1964
Kwon, T.-U. The hunchback of Seoul
O, Y. The bird of passage
So, K.-W. Half-holiday
Yi, K.-S. Halmôm
Yi, S. Wings
            Yenang
Yi, P.-J. The wind and landscape of
    Yenang
KOREAN SOLDIERS *See* Soldiers—Korea
KOREAN WAR, 1950-1953
Boswell, R. Little Bear
Burke, J. L. We Build Churches, Inc.
Hwang, S. Cranes
Kwon, T.-U. The hunchback of Seoul
O, S.-W. A respite
Sonu, H. One way
Sonu, H. Spark of life
Yu, H.-J. D.M.Z.
            Aerial operations
Song, P.-S. Debris
            Casualties
Ha, K.-C. Ill-fated father and son
Ha, K.-C. The white paper beard
Kornblatt, Joyce Reiser
Daniel
    Kornblatt, J. R. Breaking bread
Fire blight
    The Atlantic 254:60-4 Ag '84
Flo
    Kornblatt, J. R. Breaking bread
Lila
    Kornblatt, J. R. Breaking bread
Offerings
    The Georgia Review 39:67-77 Spr '85
    Prize stories, 1986
Pa
    Kornblatt, J. R. Breaking bread
Susan
    Kornblatt, J. R. Breaking bread
Kornbluth, C. M. (Cyril M.), 1924-1958
The little black bag
    Robert Silverberg's Worlds of wonder
    Rod Serling's Night gallery reader
The mindworm
    Vampires; ed. by A. Ryan
Two dooms
    Hitler victorious; ed. by G. Benford and
    M. H. Greenberg
Kornbluth, Cyril M. *See* Kornbluth, C. M.
    (Cyril M.), 1924-1958
Körner, Wolfgang
Bleep, crash, zap, wow: accidents in the
    Ruhr
    Voices East and West: German short
    stories since 1945
KOSINSKI, JERZY N., 1933-
            About
Bumpus, J. K

Kosta, Miloš Aćin- See Aćin-Kosta, Miloš
Kosztolányi, Dezso
The wondrous visitation of Krisztina Hrussz
Short story international 63
Kotzwinkle, William
The curio shop
Kotzwinkle, W. Jewel of the moon
The day Stokowski saved the world
Kotzwinkle, W. Jewel of the moon
Disturbance reported on a pipeline
Kotzwinkle, W. Jewel of the moon
Fading tattoo
Kotzwinkle, W. Jewel of the moon
Fana
Kotzwinkle, W. Jewel of the moon
Fragments of papyrus from the temple of the older gods
Omni (New York, N.Y.) 10:84-6+ Ap '88
Jewel of the moon
Kotzwinkle, W. Jewel of the moon
Letter to a swan
Kotzwinkle, W. Jewel of the moon
A man who knew his birds
Kotzwinkle, W. Jewel of the moon
Omni (New York, N.Y.) 7:52-4+ F '85
The man who wasn't there
Omni (New York, N.Y.) 8:48-50+ F '86
Mr. Jones's convention
Kotzwinkle, W. Jewel of the moon
Postcard found in a trunk
Kotzwinkle, W. Jewel of the moon
Star cruisers, welcome
Kotzwinkle, W. Jewel of the moon
Sun, moon, and storm
Kotzwinkle, W. Jewel of the moon
Tell her you love her with a ring from Dave's House of Diamonds
Kotzwinkle, W. Jewel of the moon
That winter when Prince Borisov was everybody's favorite
Kotzwinkle, W. Jewel of the moon
Victory at North Antor
Kotzwinkle, W. Jewel of the moon
Kotzwinkle, William, and Shiarella, Robert
The philosophy of Sebastian Trump; or, The art of outrage
Devils & demons; ed. by M. Kaye and S. Kaye
Kouni, Ibrahim al- See Al-Kouni, Ibrahim
Kozmic Blues. Hauptman, W.
Krahn, Ruth
Homestead crescent
Alberta bound; ed. by F. Stenson
Kraman, Cynthia
Here, in this sacred grotto
The Southern Review (Baton Rouge, La.) 23:666-70 Summ '87
Kramer, Kathryn
Seeds of conflict
Soldiers & civilians; ed. by T. Jenks

Kranes, David
Cordials
Love stories for the time being; ed. by G. D. Chipps and B. Henderson
The phantom Mercury of Nevada
The Best of the West; ed. by J. Thomas
Sudden modeling
The North American Review 269:15-20 Je '84
The whorehouse picnic
The Interior country; ed. by A. Blackburn
Kraski, Glenn
Wings of eucalyptus leaves
Stories and poems from close to home; ed. by F. Salas
Kratz, Ed
Poppa
Bringing down the moon; ed. by J. Anderson
Krause, Pat
Second sight
The Old dance; ed. by B. Burnard
Kreisel, Henry, 1922-
The broken globe
Alberta bound; ed. by F. Stenson
Kreitman, Esther
The new world
The Yale Review 73:525-32 Summ '84
Kress, Nancy
Against a crooked stile
Kress, N. Trinity, and other stories
Borovsky's hollow woman
Kress, N. Trinity, and other stories
Casey's empire
Kress, N. Trinity, and other stories
Explanations, Inc.
Kress, N. Trinity, and other stories
In a world like this
Omni (New York, N.Y.) 11:140-2+ O '88
Night win
Kress, N. Trinity, and other stories
Out of all them bright stars
Kress, N. Trinity, and other stories
Nebula awards 21
The Year's best science fiction, third annual collection
Shadows on the cave wall
Kress, N. Trinity, and other stories
Talp hunt
Kress, N. Trinity, and other stories
Ten thousand pictures, one word
Kress, N. Trinity, and other stories
Trinity
Kress, N. Trinity, and other stories
The Year's best science fiction, second annual collection
With the original cast
Kress, N. Trinity, and other stories
(jt. auth) See Duntemann, Jeff, and Kress, Nancy

Kriegel, Leonard, 1933-
Love and politics in New York
Partisan Review 54:383-93 Summ '87
Kriegel, Marilyn Harris
Love letters
Erotic interludes; ed. by L. Barbach
KRIS KRINGLE *See* Santa Claus
Krisman, Sue
No marks for Rolf
Winter's tales, new ser. v4
Krist, Gary
The canonization
Krist, G. The Garden State
Evidence
Krist, G. The Garden State
Health
The Hudson Review 40:367-89 Aut '87
Krist, G. The Garden State
Housesitting
Krist, G. The Garden State
How I learned to raise the dead of Bergen
County
Krist, G. The Garden State
Layover
Krist, G. The Garden State
Tribes of northern New Jersey
Krist, G. The Garden State
Ty and Janet
The Hudson Review 39:566-84 Wint '87
Krist, G. The Garden State
Krivich, M, and Olgin, O.
Plays and wins
Aliens, travelers, and other strangers; by
B. and A. Strugatsky and others
Kroll, Jeri
The Electrolux man
Room to move; ed. by S. Falkiner
Krueger, Rudolf M.
She wanted strawberries and love
Partisan Review 51 no1:75-8 '84
Kruse, Lily
Delivery
Américas 40:50-2 Ja/F '88
Krysl, Marilyn, 1942-
And Judith, daughter of Ester, raised the
sword above her head
Krysl, M. Mozart, Westmoreland, and
me
The artichoke
Sudden fiction; ed. by R. Shapard and
J. Thomas
Bondage
Krysl, M. Mozart, Westmoreland, and
me
Désirs
Krysl, M. Mozart, Westmoreland, and
me
Fallout
Krysl, M. Mozart, Westmoreland, and
me
The fur of the bear
Krysl, M. Mozart, Westmoreland, and
me

Macroscopic phenomena
Krysl, M. Mozart, Westmoreland, and
me
Mother
Krysl, M. Mozart, Westmoreland, and
me
Mother and child
Krysl, M. Mozart, Westmoreland, and
me
Mozart, Westmoreland, and me
Krysl, M. Mozart, Westmoreland, and
me
Snegurochka
Krysl, M. Mozart, Westmoreland, and
me
Something unforgivable
Krysl, M. Mozart, Westmoreland, and
me
Sons
Krysl, M. Mozart, Westmoreland, and
me
We are ready
Love, struggle & change; ed. by I.
Zahava
Krystal goes mystical. Lopatin, J.
KU KLUX KLAN
Bloch, R. The warm farewell
Doyle, Sir A. C. The five orange pips
Kuchisuke's valley. Ibuse, M.
Kuffel, Frances
Homes and gardens
The Massachusetts Review 26:93-103 Spr
'85
Kuhlman, Thomas Ashford
The judge and literature
Prairie Schooner 59:77-87 Spr '85
The **kumara** plant. Taylor, A.
Kumin, Maxine, 1925-
Creature comforts
Mademoiselle 93:152+ Mr '87
Opening the door on Sixty-Second Street
Selected stories from The Southern
review, 1965-1985
West
The Ploughshares reader: new fiction for
the eighties
Kump, Eileen Gibbons
Everncere
Greening wheat: fifteen Mormon short
stories
Kuncewiczowa, Maria
Strange Rachel
Russian and Polish women's fiction; ed.
by H. Goscilo
Kundera, Milan
The hitchhiking game
The World of the short story; ed. by
C. Fadiman
Let the old dead make room for the
young dead
The Art of the tale; ed. by D. Halpern
The unbearable lightness of being
The New Yorker 60:42-54+ Mr 19 '84

KUNG FU
Johnson, C. R. China
Kuniko. Shiga, N.
Kunstler, James Howard
The rise, fall, and redemption of Mooski
   Toffski Offski
   The Editors' choice: new American
      stories v2
Kupfer, Fern
For better, for worse . . . but not for
   lunch
   Redbook 162:57+ Ap '84
For the love of my sons
   Redbook 170:40+ F '88
Jin's first Christmas
   Ladies' Home Journal 105:108+ D '88
Kurahashi, Yumiko, 1935-
The monastery
   The Shōwa anthology 2
Kureishi, Hanif
The Buddha of suburbia
   Harper's 274:45-51 Je '87
Kurland, Michael, 1938-
(jt. auth) See Pronzini, Bill, and Kurland,
   Michael, 1938-
Kurt and Natasha, a relationship. Janowitz,
   T.
Kurtz, Katherine
Catalyst
   Moonsinger's friends; ed. by S. Shwartz
Kusenberg, Kurt
Odd tippling
   On being foreign; ed. by T. J. Lewis and
      R. E. Jungman
Who am I?
   Voices East and West: German short
      stories since 1945
Kushner, Ellen
Night laughter
   After midnight; ed. by C. L. Grant
Kuttner, Henry, 1915-1958
The dark world
   Kuttner, H. The startling worlds of
      Henry Kuttner
The graveyard rats
   Devils & demons; ed. by M. Kaye and
      S. Kaye
Home is the hunter
   Robert Silverberg's Worlds of wonder
The portal in the picture
   Kuttner, H. The startling worlds of
      Henry Kuttner
Valley of the Flame
   Kuttner, H. The startling worlds of
      Henry Kuttner
**Kuttner, Henry, 1915-1958, and Moore, C.
   L. (Catherine Lucille), 1911-**
Or else
   Amazing stories: visions of other worlds
Kuttner, Robert
The imitation demon
   Devils & demons; ed. by M. Kaye and
      S. Kaye

Kuwaye, Chris Kirk- *See* Kirk-Kuwaye, Chris
Kuznets, Miriam
Signs of life
   The Antioch Review 45:185-9 Spr '87
Kuznetsova, Agnia
Storms of a cruel fate
   Short story international 65
Kwon, Tae-Ung
The hunchback of Seoul
   Two travelers, and other Korean short
      stories
Kye, Yong-Muk
Adada the idiot
   The Unenlightened, and other Korean
      short stories
KYOTO (JAPAN) *See* Japan—Kyoto

L

L.A.. Thompson, S.
L.A. child. Brandt, P.
La Chapelle, Mary
Accidents
   La Chapelle, M. House of heroes, and
      other stories
Anna in a small town
   La Chapelle, M. House of heroes, and
      other stories
Drinking
   La Chapelle, M. House of heroes, and
      other stories
Faith
   La Chapelle, M. House of heroes, and
      other stories
The gate house
   La Chapelle, M. House of heroes, and
      other stories
Homer
   La Chapelle, M. House of heroes, and
      other stories
House of heroes
   La Chapelle, M. House of heroes, and
      other stories
Keep us safe
   Redbook 170:68+ Ap '88
The meadow bell
   La Chapelle, M. House of heroes, and
      other stories
Superstitions
   La Chapelle, M. House of heroes, and
      other stories
The understanding
   La Chapelle, M. House of heroes, and
      other stories
La Farge, Oliver, 1901-1963
The door in the wall
   On being foreign; ed. by T. J. Lewis and
      R. E. Jungman

La Farge, Oliver, 1901-1963—*Continued*
Haunted ground
Haunted New England; ed. by C. G.
Waugh; M. H. Greenberg and F. D.
McSherry
La Follette, Melvin Walker
I love you, Ray Chrysler
The North American Review 273:22-4 Mr
'88
La Forme, Audrey
Telephone poles
Earth power coming; ed. by S. J. Ortiz
La Guma, Alex
Blankets
African short stories in English; ed. by
J. de Grandsaigne
**La Motte-Fouqué, Friedrich Heinrich Karl,
Freiherr von, 1777-1843**
Undine
German romantic stories; ed. by F. G.
Ryder
La Puma, Salvatore
The boys of Bensonhurst
La Puma, S. The boys of Bensonhurst
The gangster's ghost
The Kenyon Review ns9:50-9 Wint '87
Prize stories, 1988
La Puma, S. The boys of Bensonhurst
Gravesend Bay
La Puma, S. The boys of Bensonhurst
Guys under their fedoras
The Antioch Review 44:77-87 Wint '86
La Puma, S. The boys of Bensonhurst
In Delphine's bed
The Southern Review (Baton Rouge, La.)
23:680-91 Summ '87
The jilted groom
La Puma, S. The boys of Bensonhurst
The mouthpiece
La Puma, S. The boys of Bensonhurst
Wear it in good health
La Puma, S. The boys of Bensonhurst
Laberge, Albert
The patient
The Oxford book of French-Canadian
short stories
LABOR AND LABORING CLASSES
See also Apprentices; Farm workers;
Labor unions; Migrant labor; Strikes
and lockouts
Ahmed, F. The wicked city
Anderman, J. Sinking wells
Bonosky, P. The cathedral
Bonosky, P. Poor Joey
Bonosky, P. A sweet tooth
Chekhov, A. P. My life
Dennison, G. Oilers and sweepers
Dickinson, C. Arcadia
Dorr, L. A D-minor fugue
Forshaw, T. The mateship syndrome
Grace, P. The wall
Granit, A. Hello, Lenin! Hello, Stalin!
How's the revolution today?

Hemley, R. Looking for kin
Hood, M. Moths
Kay, H. The fifth generation
Kharal, N. The dead end
Liphshitz, A. The last stage
Liphshitz, A. Master of his fate
Lu Wenfu. Tang Qiaodi
Morrison, J. Lena
Oates, J. C. Surf City
Rodoreda, M. Love
Shukshin, V. M. Roubles in words, kopeks
in figures
Stead, C. The Azhdanov tailors
Weissenberg, I. M. A shtetl
Ziem, J. His own boss
Labor Day dinner. Munro, A.
LABOR UNIONS
See also Labor and laboring classes;
Strikes and lockouts
José, F. S. Two interviews
Koch, C. You taught us good
Long, D. The last photograph of Lyle Pet-
tibone
Morrison, J. Lena
Nowakowski, M. The secret face
Labozzetta, Marisa
Making the wine
When I am an old woman I shall wear
purple; ed. by S. K. Martz
The **labrenas.** Landolfi, T.
Labyrinth. Essop, A.
LABYRINTHS
Lunn, R. Mirrors
Lack of sleep. Naipaul, S.
Lackendara. Power, V.
Lackey, Mercedes
Fiddler fair
Magic in Ithkar 3; ed. by A. Norton and
R. Adams
Were-hunter
Tales of the Witch World [1]
Lacunae. Wagner, K. E.
Lacy, Ed, 1911-1968
You can't win 'em (at) all
Alfred Hitchcock's Crimewatch
Lacy, Robert
The natural father
The Best American short stories, 1988
Stiller's pond; ed. by J. Agee; R. Blakely
and S. Welch
Lacy Mallard. Daniels, C.
LADDERS
Sansom, W. The vertical ladder
Ladders to success. Valenzuela, L.
Ladenheim, Kala, 1950-
Mokele Mbembe
Editor's choice II; ed. by M. Sklar and
M. Biggs
Ladies. Coleman, W.
Ladies in the snow. Bird, C.
Ladies' luncheon. Alden, P. B.
Ladies who knit for a living. Stockanes, A.
E.

A **ladle** for pure water. Varlamova, I.
The **lady** and the dragon. Godfrey, P.
The **lady** and the merman. Yolen, J.
Lady Barberina. James, H.
Lady, be good. Moreland, J.
Lady Ferry. Jewett, S. O.
The **lady** from Ferme-Neuve. Ferron, J.
The **lady** from hell. Thomas, E.
The **lady** from Lucknow. Mukherjee, B.
Lady Godiva's horse. Rooke, L.
Lady, I did it. Liben, M.
Lady in the dark. Canning, V.
The **lady** in the looking-glass: a reflection. Woolf, V.
The **lady** in the plaid shawl. Gilbert, W. S.
The **Lady** in White. Donaldson, S. R.
Lady into fox. Garnett, D.
The **lady-killers.** Hernández, J. J.
Lady Macbeth of Mtsensk. Leskov, N. S.
The **Lady** Margaret. Roberts, K.
The **Lady** of Little Fishing. Woolson, C. F.
Lady of Spain. Taylor, R.
Lady of the evening faces. Hiraiwa, Y.
The **lady** of the museums. Véry, P.
The **lady** on the grey. Collier, J.
The **lady** on the plane. Dilworth, S.
Lady Weare and the Bodhisattva. Tennant, K.
The **lady** who entertained. Dazai, O.
Lady with a knife. Parker, P. S.
Ladybug, Ladybug. Swofford, A.
A **lady's** beaded bag. Williams, T.
Lafayette, farewell. Bradbury, R.
Lafferty, R. A.
 Company in the wings
  The Year's best science fiction, second annual collection
 Flaming-arrow
  Magic in Ithkar 2; ed. by A. Norton and R. Adams
 Golden gate
  The Year's best science fiction, first annual collection
 Le Hot Sport
  Terry's universe; ed. by B. Meacham
 Interurban queen
  Alternative histories; ed. by C. G. Waugh and M. H. Greenberg
 Magazine section
  The Year's best science fiction, third annual collection
 Nor limestone islands
  The Best from Universe
 Polity and custom of the Camiroi
  Election Day 2084; ed. by I. Asimov and M. H. Greenberg
 Primary education of the Camiroi
  Young extraterrestrials; ed. by I. Asimov; M. H. Greenberg and C. G. Waugh
Lagerkvist, Pär, 1891-1974
 The myth of mankind
  The Nobel reader; ed. by J. Eisen and S. Troy

Lagerlöf, Selma, 1858-1940
 The peace of God
  The Nobel reader; ed. by J. Eisen and S. Troy
Lagier, Jennifer
 Tending the flock
  When I am an old woman I shall wear purple; ed. by S. K. Martz
Lagory, Michael
 Seaside idle
  Passages to the dream shore; ed. by F. Stewart
LAHORE (PAKISTAN) *See* Pakistan—Lahore
Lai, Ho
 The steelyard
  The Unbroken chain; ed. by J. S. M. Lau
Laidlaw, Marc
 400 boys
  Mirrorshades; ed. by B. Sterling
 Bruno's shadow
  Omni (New York, N.Y.) 10:40-2+ Ag '88
 Love comes to the middleman
  Mathenauts: tales of mathematical wonder; ed. by R. Rucker
 Muzak for torso murders
  Cutting edge; ed. by D. Etchison
 The random man
  Tales from Isaac Asimov's science fiction magazine: short stories for young adults
 Sea of tranquillity
  Omni (New York, N.Y.) 7:66-8+ F '85
 Sneakers
  The Best of Shadows; ed. by C. L. Grant
 (jt. auth) See Benford, Gregory, 1941-, and Laidlaw, Marc
 (jt. auth) See Rucker, Rudy von Bitter, 1946-, and Laidlaw, Marc
Láinez, Manuel Mujica *See* Mujica Láinez, Manuel, 1910-1984
Lake, David J.
 Re-deem the time
  Australian science fiction; ed. by V. Ikin
The **lake.** Bradbury, R.
The **lake.** Simmons, P.
Lake George in high August. Bensink, J. R.
The **lake** was full of artificial things. Fowler, K. J.
A **Lake** Wobegon Christmas—such were the joys. Keillor, G.
Lake Wobegon games. Keillor, G.
LAKES
 King, S. The raft
Lamb, Wendy
 Scenes of passion
  Mademoiselle 90:116+ My '84
Lamb of Abyssalia. Oates, J. C.
The **lamb** of the Flying U. Bower, B. M.

Lambert, Nina
  All for the love of David
    Good Housekeeping 203:200-1+ N '86
  Look toward tomorrow
    Good Housekeeping 206:114-15 F '88
Lamburn, Nell
  Tom's thatch
    The Year's best mystery and suspense
    stories, 1987
The **lame** shall enter first. O'Connor, F.
Lament for a son. Wexler, J.
The **lament** of the salesman. Covino, M.
L'Amour, Louis, 1908-1988
  Booty for a badman
    The Saturday Evening Post 260:62-5+ S
    '88
    The Saturday Evening Post 260:78+ O
    '88
  The gift of Cochise
    Reader's Digest 125:102-6 S '84
L'amour. Boylan, C.
The **lamp.** Christie, A.
The **lamp.** Grace, P.
The **lamp** at noon. Ross, S.
Lampart, Jacob
  Joanna loves Jesus
    Commentary 84:44-50 Ag '87
The **lampshade** vendor. Woodman, A.
Lan Lung. Chin, M. L.
LANAI (HAWAII) See Hawaii—Lanai
Lancastria. MacLean, A.
Lance's story: art sucks. Taylor, C.
Land, Susan
  Old glass-new glass
    The Literary Review (Madison, N.J.)
    29:227-34 Wint '86
The **land.** Austin, M. H.
The **land** beyond. Murphy, R.
Land deal. Murnane, G.
Land fishers. Wilson, R., Jr.
Land hunger. Colum, P.
The **land** ironclads. Wells, H. G.
Land of exile. Pavese, C.
The **land** of heart's desire. Hara, T.
The **land** of lucky strike. Kalpakian, L.
Land of our enemies. Stuart, J.
The **land** of the dead. Wagoner, D.
Land of the free, home of the brave. Crap-
    ser, W.
The **land** of the leaves. Hutman, N.
Land of the midnight sun. Lipman, E.
The **land** of the wild musk-ox. Grey, Z.
LAND REFORM See Land tenure
LAND TENURE
  Walters, A. L. The sun is not merciful
Land where my fathers died. Dubus, A.
Landfall. Hoffman, W.
LANDLADIES See Landlord and tenant
The **landlady.** Dahl, R.
Landlady. Sodowsky, R. E.
The **landlord.** Rizkalla, J.

LANDLORD AND TENANT
  See also Tenant farming
  Barthelme, D. The new owner
  Bell, M. S. The lie detector
  Clayton, J. J. Bodies like mouths
  Dahl, R. The landlady
  Dullas, I. Shanti, simple, sweet and—
    sinister!
  Essop, A. The visitation
  Fisher, M. F. K. The second time around
  Hartley, L. P. Interference
  Highsmith, P. Old folks at home
  King, F. H. The Brighton Belle
  Lee, H. The Bodega War
  Lofts, N. Now you have me
  Lombreglia, R. Men under water
  Lurie, M. Good people in the house
  McElroy, C. J. Exercises
  Moore, G. Dried fruit
  Naipaul, S. Lack of sleep
  Naipaul, S. The tenant
  Osborn, C. Amnesia's child
  Petrakis, H. M. Pericles on 31st Street
  Pierce, C. The tenants at Auxillac
  Purdy, J. Some of these days
  Rizkalla, J. The landlord
  Robison, J. Time alone
  Rule, J. In the attic of the house
  Sanford, W. M. Mr. Carmichael's room
  Stead, C. The captain's house
  Stead, C. A routine
  Steele, M. The man in the doll house
  Taylor, P. E. Kingdom come
  Thomas, J. Sparkle in five
  Thorman, C. Blue haired chickens
  Valenzuela, L. The celery munchers
  Volsky, P. The tenancy of Mr. Eex
  Wexler, J. The bequest
  Williams, T. The mattress by the tomato
    patch
  Wilson, B. The investment
Landlord of the Crystal Fountain. Whitaker,
    M.
LANDLORDS See Landlord and tenant
Landolfi, Tommaso, 1908-1979
  An abstract concept
    Landolfi, T. Words in commotion, and
    other stories
  The ampulla
    Landolfi, T. Words in commotion, and
    other stories
  Chicken fate
    Landolfi, T. Words in commotion, and
    other stories
  Dialogue of the greater systems
    Landolfi, T. Words in commotion, and
    other stories
  The eclipse
    Landolfi, T. Words in commotion, and
    other stories
  The eternal province
    Landolfi, T. Words in commotion, and
    other stories

Landolfi, Tommaso, 1908-1979—*Continued*
The gnat
  Landolfi, T. Words in commotion, and other stories
Gogol's wife
  The Art of the tale; ed. by D. Halpern
  Landolfi, T. Words in commotion, and other stories
The grace of God
  Landolfi, T. Words in commotion, and other stories
The kiss
  Landolfi, T. Words in commotion, and other stories
The labrenas
  Landolfi, T. Words in commotion, and other stories
Literary prize
  Landolfi, T. Words in commotion, and other stories
Maria Giuseppa
  Landolfi, T. Words in commotion, and other stories
Personaphilological-dramatic conference with implications
  Landolfi, T. Words in commotion, and other stories
Prefigurations: Prato
  Landolfi, T. Words in commotion, and other stories
Prize in spite of
  Landolfi, T. Words in commotion, and other stories
The provincial night
  Landolfi, T. Words in commotion, and other stories
Rain
  Landolfi, T. Words in commotion, and other stories
The test
  Landolfi, T. Words in commotion, and other stories
Two wakes
  Landolfi, T. Words in commotion, and other stories
Uxoricide
  Landolfi, T. Words in commotion, and other stories
The werewolf
  Landolfi, T. Words in commotion, and other stories
A woman's breast
  Landolfi, T. Words in commotion, and other stories
Words in commotion
  Landolfi, T. Words in commotion, and other stories

Landon, Perceval, 1869-1927
Thurnley Abbey
  The Book of the dead; ed. by A. K. Russell
  The Penguin book of horror stories
  Spirits, spooks, and other sinister creatures; ed. by H. Hoke
Landor's cottage. Poe, E. A.
The **lands** beyond the world. Moorcock, M.
The **landscape**. Colette
LANDSCAPE ARCHITECTS
  Poe, E. A. The landscape garden
The **landscape** garden. Poe, E. A.
LANDSCAPE GARDENING
  See also Trees
  Poe, E. A. The domain of Arnheim
  Poe, E. A. The landscape garden
The **landscape** of dreams. Lutz, J.
The **landscape** painter. Ferron, J.
Landscape with figures. Hemingway, E.
A **landscape** with walls. Fitzgerald, M. J.
The **landscaper**. Blei, N.
Landscaping. Ephron, N.
LANDSLIDES
  Hawthorne, N. The ambitious guest
The **landsman's** tale. Stockton, F.
Lane, Patrick, 1939-
Apple peels and knives
  The Old dance; ed. by B. Burnard
Lang, Allen
Sweet smell of murder
  Alfred Hitchcock's Crimewatch
The **Lang** women. Masters, O.
Langford, David
Cold spell
  After midnight; ed. by C. L. Grant
Langford, Michael N.
Wood
  Afterlives; ed. by P. Sargent and I. Watson
Langston James McHenry. Steadman, M.
LANGUAGE AND LANGUAGES
  See also English language; French language; Latin language
  Anvil, C. Babel II
  Anvil, C. A rose by other name . . .
  Boucher, A. Barrier
  Buzzati, D. The prohibited word
  Elgin, S. H. Hush my mouth
  Elgin, S. H. Modulation in all things
  Hankla, C. Learning the mother tongue
  Herbert, F. Songs of a sentient flute
  Herbert, F. Try to remember
  Keller, D. H. The lost language
  Klinkowitz, J. The language game
  Kohlhaase, W. Invention of a language
  Landolfi, T. Dialogue of the greater systems
  Le Guin, U. K. "The author of the acacia seeds" and other extracts from the Journal of the Association of Therolinguistics
  Le Guin, U. K. She unnames them

LANGUAGE AND LANGUAGES — *Continued*
Lem, S. Juan Rambellais et al., A history of Bitic literature
Pei, M. The bones of Charlemagne
Piper, H. B. Omnilingual
Warner, S. T. The mother tongue
The **language** game. Klinkowitz, J.
The **language** of love. Sheckley, R.
The **language** of the sea. Gilman, C.
Lanham, Cathryn
The pink-eyed monster
The Antioch Review 46:308-16 Summ '88
Lanier, Sterling E.
A father's tale
Sherlock Holmes through time and space
Lannes, Roberta
Goodbye, dark love
Cutting edge; ed. by D. Etchison
Lannoy, Violet Dias
The story of Jesus—according to Mokuba, the beloved tribesman
The Literary Review (Madison, N.J.) 29:456-70 Summ '86
Lansdale, Joe R., 1951-
Dog, Cat, and Baby
Masques II; ed. by J. N. Williamson
Down by the sea near the great big rock
Masques; ed. by J. N. Williamson
Duck hunt
After midnight; ed. by C. L. Grant
Night they missed the horror show
Silver scream; ed. by D. J. Schow
The pit
The Black Lizard anthology of crime fiction; ed. by E. Gorman
Trains not taken
Westeryear; ed. by E. Gorman
Lansky, Ellen
What she really did
Stiller's pond; ed. by J. Agee; R. Blakely and S. Welch
Lantern stalk. Winton, T.
Lao Hong
The gap
Roses and thorns; ed. by P. Link
Laocoön, my father. Givner, J.
LAOS
London, J. Travelling
Lap dissolves. Coover, R.
Lapidary nights. Randall, M.
Lappin and Lapinova. Woolf, V.
Laps. Winton, T.
The **lapse.** Wheatcroft, J.
Lapses. Yarbro, C. Q.
Larabi's ox. Ardizzone, T.
Larbaud. See Dennison, G. A tale of Pierrot
LARCENY *See* Theft
The **larder.** Lurie, M.
Lardner, Ring, 1885-1933
Champion
The Norton book of American short stories

Haircut
Look who's talking; ed. by B. Weber
The **large** ant. Fast, H.
Larger than oneself. Aickman, R.
Larimer, Judith
If you want company, turn on the radio
Stories and poems from close to home; ed. by F. Salas
Larionova, Olga
A tale of kings
Earth and elsewhere, by K. Bulychev and others
Lark song. Kinsella, W. P.
Larmer said he would be King. Cullen, E. J.
Larrabeiti, Michael de *See* De Larrabeiti, Michael
Larry. Gallant, M.
Larsen's. Sandel, C.
Larson, Erik
House arrest
Omni (New York, N.Y.) 8:44-6+ S '86
Larson, Lynne
Original sin
Greening wheat: fifteen Mormon short stories
LaRue, Dorie
Only visiting this planet
The Southern Review (Baton Rouge, La.) 24:914-23 Aut '88
LAS VEGAS (NEV.) *See* Nevada—Las Vegas
LaSalle, Peter
The Burkes and the blue
The Literary Review (Madison, N.J.) 29:301-11 Spr '86
Dolphin dreaming
Prize stories, 1988
Sleeping
Southwest Review 70:518-33 Aut '85
Lasdun, James
The jump
Encounter (London, England) 71:20-6 S/O '88
Property
Encounter (London, England) 62:3-6 F '84
Snow
The Paris Review 29:210-15 Fall '87
Laser, Michael
The American queen
The Massachusetts Review 26:128-38 Spr '85
Mr. Ng at the Great Wall
The Massachusetts Review 29:136-48 Spr '88
LASERS
Herbert, F. Committee of the whole
Lash, Kenneth, 1918-1985
The unnecessary overcoat
The Massachusetts Review 26:595-602 Wint '85

Lashuay, Nanette
The anniversary party
The Kenyon Review ns8:69-81 Fall '86
Laski, Marghanita, 1915-1988
The tower
The Penguin book of ghost stories
Lasseter, Rollin A.
Voices
The Sewanee Review 96:369-77 Summ
'88
Lassie come-home. Knight, E. M.
Lasswitz, Kurd, 1848-1910
The universal library
Great science fiction; ed. by I. Asimov;
M. H. Greenberg and C. G. Waugh
The **last** adventure. Doderer, H. von
The **last** and only messenger. Schwartz, J.
The **last** angler. Li Hangyu
The **last** answer. Asimov, I.
The **last** antelope. Austin, M. H.
The **last** asset. Wharton, E.
The **last** assignment. Morazzoni, M.
Last birds. Faik, S.
The **last** bottle in the world. Ellin, S.
Last Chance. Warren, J.
Last chance in Singapore. Howard, C.
The **last** circus. Bradbury, R.
The **last** class. Daudet, A.
Last courtesies. Leffland, E.
The **last** crop. Jolley, E.
Last dance. Edler, P. R.
The **last** dancer. Horne, L.
The **last** day of summer. Ch'en, Y.-C.
The **last** day of violence. St. Pierre, P. H.
The **last** day the circus came to town. Win-
ters, J.
Last days. Oates, J. C.
The **last** days of (parallel?) Earth. Sheckley,
R.
The **last** demon. Singer, I. B.
Last descent to earth. Lish, G.
The **last** diet. Gilchrist, E.
The **last** dream. Freeman, L.
The **last** dream before waking. Kalpakian, L.
Last drink is on the house. Soldatow, S.
The **last** escapade. Petrakis, H. M.
The **last** explorer. Drewe, R.
Last factory blues. Thomas, J.
Last fair deal. Everett, P. L.
The **last** fastball. Jones, D. C.
The **last** fire. Colette
The **last** fling. Nestor, T. G.
The **last** fly of summer. Hall, T. T.
The **last** frontier. Schwartz, L. S.
The **last** game. Glasser, P.
The **last** gaze. Singer, I. B.
The **last** gentleman. Percy, W.
The **last** good country. Hemingway, E.
The **last** hieroglyph. Smith, C. A.
The **last** hunt. Nagibin, ĪŪ. M.
The **last** hunt. Teixeira, K.
The **last** husband. Humphrey, W.
The **last** hussar. Mrożek, S.

The **last** illusion. Barker, C.
The **last** incantation. Smith, C. A.
The **last** Jerry Fagin Show. Morressy, J.
The **last** laugh. Hornung, E. W.
The **last** laugh. Martínez-Serros, H.
The **last** laugh. Raine, N. R.
Last lessons. Menaker, D.
The **last** loneliness. Sturges, A. E.
The **last** love of Prince Genji. Yourcenar,
M.
The **last** man. Shelley, M. W.
Last man to die. Queen, E.
The **last** meeting of the Butlers Club. Bush,
J.
The **last** Mohican. Malamud, B.
The **last** moment. Yŏm, S.
The **last** Mrs. Aspair. Trow, G. W. S.
Last night. McFarland, D.
Last night and every night. Tiptree, J.
Last night at dawn. Montero, M.
Last night I dreamt of you. Tahir, B.
The **last** of it. Osborn, C.
The **last** of Mrs. Murphy. Behan, B.
The **last** of the Caddoes. Humphrey, W.
The **last** of the gold star mothers. Bly, C.
The **last** of the Huggermuggers: a giant story.
Cranch, C. P.
The **last** of the masters. Dick, P. K.
The **last** of the midnight gardeners. Wilmot,
T.
Last of the old buffalo hunters. Garrett, G.
P.
The **last** of the Spanish blood. Garrett, G.
P.
The **last** of the troubadours. Henry, O.
The **last** of the whaleburgers. Sladek, J. T.
Last of the wild ones. Zelazny, R.
The **last** one mo once golden oldies revival.
Wilson, F. P.
The **last** page. Kalpakian, L.
The **last** parting. Pak, Y.-J.
The **last** party. Davis, D. S.
The **last** person. East, C.
The **last** photograph of Lyle Pettibone. Long,
D.
The **last** place on earth. McClure, J.
The **last** possible moment. Cameron, P.
The **last** question. Asimov, I.
The **last** resort. Dixon, S.
The **last** resource. Doyle, Sir A. C.
Last respects. Baldwin, D.
The **last** revival. Howard, C.
The **last** rite. Lee, Y.-H.
The **last** romantic. Springstubb, T.
Last September. Hull, H. R.
The **last** song of exile. Johnson, W.
Last sound of the gong. Moon, S.-T.
Last spring they came over. Callaghan, M.
The **last** stage. Liphshitz, A.
The **last** step. Maupassant, G. de
Last summer "How I spent my summer
vacation" by Diana Lancaster. Kilgore,
D.

The **last** survivor of Sierra Flat. Greenwood, R.
The **last** time I saw Harris. Elflandsson, G.
The **last** unicorns. Hoch, E. D.
The **last** visit. Cameron, E.
The **last** voyage of the ghost ship. García Márquez, G.
The **last** wizard. Davidson, A.
The **last** word. Hornung, E. W.
The **last** word was love. Saroyan, W.
Last year at Pittsburgh. Claiborne, S.
Last year's murder. Hoch, E. D.
The **last** young man. Botwinik, B.
Lasting impression. Weinstein, L.
A **late** chrysanthemum. Hayashi, F.
The **late** date. Alford, E.
A **late** encounter with the enemy. O'Connor, F.
A **late** flowering. Lofts, N.
Late in the season. Matthiessen, P.
The **late** Mr. Elvesham. See Wells, H. G. The story of the late Mr. Elvesham
Late prayers. Mazel, D.
A **late** Sunday afternoon by the Huron. Baxter, C.
The **late** sunlight. Anderson, J.
The **late** unlamented. Craig, J.
Laterna magica. Heinesen, W.
Latham, John
Can the blind lead the blind?
Critical Quarterly 28:45-50 Aut '86
Latham, Philip
Jeannette's hands
Great science fiction; ed. by I. Asimov; M. H. Greenberg and C. G. Waugh
Latimer, Margery, 1899-1932
Death of Mrs. Vanderwood
Latimer, M. Guardian angel, and other stories
The family
Latimer, M. Guardian angel, and other stories
Gisela
Latimer, M. Guardian angel, and other stories
Guardian angel
Latimer, M. Guardian angel, and other stories
Marriage eve
Latimer, M. Guardian angel, and other stories
Monday morning
Latimer, M. Guardian angel, and other stories
Mr. and Mrs. Arnold
Latimer, M. Guardian angel, and other stories
Nellie Bloom
Latimer, M. Guardian angel, and other stories
Two in love
Latimer, M. Guardian angel, and other stories

LATIN AMERICA
Klinkowitz, J. Costy Pedraza's greatest pitch
LATIN LANGUAGE
Maupassant, G. de. The question of Latin
Latin lover. Lynch, M.
The **latter-day** triumph of Graves. Gifkins, M.
The **laugh**. Brodkey, H.
Laugh track. Ellison, H.
The **laughing** butcher. Brown, F.
Laughing Pig. Regent, P.
The **laughingstock**. Kaikō, T.
Laughter in the leaves. De Lint, C.
The **laughter** of Slim Malone. Brand, M.
Laumer, Keith, 1925-
Doorstep
Young extraterrestrials; ed. by I. Asimov; M. H. Greenberg and C. G. Waugh
The timesweepers
Time wars; ed. by C. Waugh and M. H. Greenberg
Launching day, 1962. Johnson, J.
LAUNDRESSES
Maupassant, G. de. The Devil
Mazel, D. Sadie
A **laundry** basket full. Asscher-Pinkhof, C.
Laura. Saki
The **Laurel** and Hardy love affair. Bradbury, R.
Laurence, Margaret, 1926-1987
The loons
The Oxford book of Canadian short stories in English
LAUSANNE (SWITZERLAND) *See* Switzerland—Lausanne
Lavatory Buddahood. Kawabata, Y.
Lavender blue. Marshall, D. R.
Lavers, Norman
Big dog
The Editors' choice v3; ed. by G. E. Murphy, Jr.
The North American Review 270:27-32 S '85
Prize stories, 1987
Rumors
American made; ed. by M. Leyner; C. White and T. Glynn
Lavin, John
By any other name
Streets of stone; ed. by M. Burgess and H. Whyte
Lavin, Mary, 1912-
A cup of tea
Inspired by drink; ed. by Joan Digby and John Digby
Eterna
The Treasury of English short stories; ed. by N. Sullivan
The face of hate
Selected stories from The Southern review, 1965-1985

Lavin, Mary, 1912-—*Continued*
The living
    The World of the short story; ed. by
    C. Fadiman
A voice from the dead (a monologue)
    The Best of Irish wit and wisdom; ed.
    by J. McCarthy
Lavinia: an old story. Paley, G.
Law, Warner
Lincoln's doctor's son's dog
    Hound dunnit; ed. by I. Asimov; M. H.
    Greenberg and C. L. R. Waugh
The **Law.** Jones, D. C.

LAW AND LAWYERS
    See also Judges; Trials; Women law-
    yers
Ade, G. The fable of the lawyer who
    brought in a minority report
Allbeury, T. The party of the second part
Asimov, I. A loint of paw
Asimov, I. What time is it?
Auchincloss, L. Equitable awards
Auchincloss, L. The Fabbri tape
Auchincloss, L. The senior partner's ethics
Auchincloss, L. Suttee
Block, L. The Ehrengraf appointment
Block, L. The Ehrengraf experience
Block, L. The Ehrengraf method
Carlson, R. Milk
Chekhov, A. P. At home
Clarke, A. C. How he does it
Corrington, J. W. The actes and monu-
    ments
Cullen, E. J. Pleadings
Cushman, D. I.O.U.—one bullet
Gangemi, K. Greenbaum, O'Reilly &
    Stephens
Gilbert, M. The curious conspiracy
Gilbert, W. S. My maiden brief
Gilliatt, P. Nobody's business
Gillie, W. T. Motor-driven
Gogol', N. V. The tale of how Ivan
    Ivanovich quarreled with Ivan
    Nikiforovich
Harrison, H. Run from the fire
Helprin, M. Palais de Justice
Hensley, J. L. The home
Hensley, J. L. The profession
Hensley, J. L. Trial
Hensley, J. L. Whistler
Higgins, G. V. A case of Chivas Regal
Just, W. S. About Boston
Koenig, J. A perfect gentleman
Komie, L. B. The balloon of William
    Fuerst
Komie, L. B. The butterfly
Komie, L. B. The Christmas party
Komie, L. B. The cornucopia of Julia K.
Komie, L. B. I am Greenwald, my father's
    son
Komie, L. B. The interview
Komie, L. B. The law clerk's lament
Komie, L. B. Mentoring

Komie, L. B. Podhoretz revisited
Le Fanu, J. S. Mr. Justice Harbottle
Lipsky, E. Tiger in the night
Lofts, N. A late flowering
Lopatin, J. Our perfect partners
Masur, H. Q. The $2,000,000 defense
McGuane, T. Partners
Melville, H. Bartleby the scrivener
Mortimer, J. C. Rumpole and the age for
    retirement
Mortimer, J. C. Rumpole and the alterna-
    tive society
Mortimer, J. C. Rumpole and the blind
    tasting
Mortimer, J. C. Rumpole and the boat
    people
Mortimer, J. C. Rumpole and the bright
    seraphim
Mortimer, J. C. Rumpole and the case of
    identity
Mortimer, J. C. Rumpole and the confes-
    sion of guilt
Mortimer, J. C. Rumpole and the course
    of true love
Mortimer, J. C. Rumpole and the dear
    departed
Mortimer, J. C. Rumpole and the expert
    witness
Mortimer, J. C. Rumpole and the fascist
    beast
Mortimer, J. C. Rumpole and the gentle
    art of blackmail
Mortimer, J. C. Rumpole and the genuine
    article
Mortimer, J. C. Rumpole and the golden
    thread
Mortimer, J. C. Rumpole and the heavy
    brigade
Mortimer, J. C. Rumpole and the
    Honourable Member
Mortimer, J. C. Rumpole and the judge's
    elbow
Mortimer, J. C. Rumpole and the last
    resort
Mortimer, J. C. Rumpole and the learned
    friends
Mortimer, J. C. Rumpole and the Man of
    God
Mortimer, J. C. Rumpole and the married
    lady
Mortimer, J. C. Rumpole and the official
    secret
Mortimer, J. C. Rumpole and the old boy
    net
Mortimer, J. C. Rumpole and the old, old
    story
Mortimer, J. C. Rumpole and the rotten
    apple
Mortimer, J. C. Rumpole and the show-
    folk
Mortimer, J. C. Rumpole and the spirit
    of Christmas

LAW AND LAWYERS—_Continued_
Mortimer, J. C. Rumpole and the sporting life
Mortimer, J. C. Rumpole and the winter break
Mortimer, J. C. Rumpole and the younger generation
Mortimer, J. C. Rumpole's last case
O'Brien, E. The love object
Overholser, W. D. Lawyer two-fist
Post, M. D. The forgotten witness
Post, M. D. The sheriff of Gullmore
Post, M. D., and Suter, J. F. The tree in the forest
Raphael, F. Benchmark
Risse, H. Traffic accident
Robison, J. Time alone
Roth, P. Eli, the fanatic
Sams, F. Big Star woman
Shukshin, V. M. The court case
Shukshin, V. M. The sufferings of young Vaganov
Singer, I. B. The litigants
Slesar, H. The day of the execution
Train, A. C. The Viking's daughter
Trippett, F. Child Ellen [excerpt]
Williams, T. The killer chicken and the closet queen
Wolfe, T. Justice is blind
The **law** clerk's lament. Komie, L. B.
Law of averages. Barthelme, F.
The **law** of life. London, J.
Law of the hunted ones. Leonard, E.
Law-Yone, Wendy
Ankle
Grand Street 7:7-24 Spr '88
The **lawd** don't like ugly. Williams, S. A.
Lawfully. Houston, R.
Lawler, Pat
After the wedding
Good Housekeeping 207:112-13 Ag '88
Celebration
McCall's 114:136+ Ap '87
A matter of responsibility
McCall's 114:66+ F '87
Lawn City. Cullen, E. J.
Lawns. Simpson, M.
Lawrence, D. H. (David Herbert), 1885-1930
Odour of chrysanthemums
The World of the short story; ed. by C. Fadiman
The Prussian officer
The Treasury of English short stories; ed. by N. Sullivan
Rex
Roger Caras' Treasury of great dog stories
The rocking-horse winner
Black water; ed. by A. Manguel
Child's ploy; ed. by M. Muller and B. Pronzini
The Dark descent; ed. by D. G. Hartwell

Lawrence, David Herbert _See_ Lawrence, D. H. (David Herbert), 1885-1930
Lawrence, Kathleen Rockwell
With this ring . . .
Redbook 165:58+ Ag '85
The **laws.** Walters, A. L.
Laws of nature. Murphy, Y.
Lawson, Henry, 1867-1922
Bill, the ventriloquial rooster
Lawson, H. The Penguin Henry Lawson
The boozers' home
Inspired by drink; ed. by Joan Digby and John Digby
Brighten's sister-in-law
Lawson, H. The Penguin Henry Lawson
The bush undertaker
Lawson, H. The Penguin Henry Lawson
A child in the dark, and a foreign father
Lawson, H. The Penguin Henry Lawson
A double buggy at Lahey's Creek
Lawson, H. The Penguin Henry Lawson
The drover's wife
Lawson, H. The Penguin Henry Lawson
The geological spieler
Lawson, H. The Penguin Henry Lawson
Hungerford
Lawson, H. The Penguin Henry Lawson
In a dry season
Lawson, H. The Penguin Henry Lawson
The iron-bark chip
Lawson, H. The Penguin Henry Lawson
Joe Wilson's courtship
Lawson, H. The Penguin Henry Lawson
The loaded dog
Lawson, H. The Penguin Henry Lawson
Mitchell: a character sketch
Lawson, H. The Penguin Henry Lawson
An old mate of your father's
Lawson, H. The Penguin Henry Lawson
On the edge of a plain
Lawson, H. The Penguin Henry Lawson
Our pipes
Lawson, H. The Penguin Henry Lawson
'Rats'
Lawson, H. The Penguin Henry Lawson
Shooting the moon
Lawson, H. The Penguin Henry Lawson
'Some day'
Lawson, H. The Penguin Henry Lawson
Telling Mrs. Baker
Lawson, H. The Penguin Henry Lawson
The union buries its dead
The Australian short story; ed. by L. Hergenhan
Lawson, H. The Penguin Henry Lawson
"Water them geraniums"
The Australian short story; ed. by L. Hergenhan
Lawson, H. The Penguin Henry Lawson
Lawson, Sylvia, 1932-
PASTA MOMA
Home and away; ed. by R. Creswell

LAWSUITS *See* Law and lawyers
Lawyer two-fist. Overholser, W. D.
LAWYERS *See* Law and lawyers
The **lay** of the land. Milofsky, D.
Layfield, Sharyn
The Coggios
The Ploughshares reader: new fiction for the eighties
Sudden fiction; ed. by R. Shapard and J. Thomas
The **laying** on of hands. Millman, L.
Layland, Penelope
The death of the fat man
Room to move; ed. by S. Falkiner
Layover. Krist, G.
Layover in El Paso. Lowry, R.
Lazar Malkin enters heaven. Stern, S.
Lazarre, Jane
The circus
Ms. 14:44-7+ Ag '85
Penetrations
Love, struggle & change; ed. by I. Zahava
LAZARUS (BIBLICAL FIGURE)
About
Andreyev, L. Lazarus
Lazarus. Andreyev, L.
Lazarus. Dorr, L.
Laziness. Parise, G.
A **Lazofsky.** Myers, L.
Lazy sons. Calvino, I.
Le Braz, Anatole
The owl
Masterpieces of terror and the supernatural; ed. by M. Kaye and S. Kaye
Le Fanu, Joseph Sheridan, 1814-1873
Carmilla
Masterpieces of terror and the supernatural; ed. by M. Kaye and S. Kaye
Vampires; ed. by A. Ryan
Green tea
The Book of the dead; ed. by A. K. Russell
Dark company; ed. by L. Child
Lost souls; ed. by J. Sullivan
Mr. Justice Harbottle
The Book of the dead; ed. by A. K. Russell
The Dark descent; ed. by D. G. Hartwell
The Penguin book of ghost stories
Passage in the secret history of an Irish countess
Death locked in; ed. by D. G. Greene and R. C. S. Adey
Schalken the painter
The Dark descent; ed. by D. G. Hartwell
Lost souls; ed. by J. Sullivan
Sir Dominick's bargain
Devils & demons; ed. by M. Kaye and S. Kaye

Squire Toby's will
The Oxford book of English ghost stories
The white cat of Drumgunniol
The Treasury of English short stories; ed. by N. Sullivan
Le Guin, Ursula K., 1929-
"The author of the acacia seeds" and other extracts from the Journal of the Association of Therolinguistics [Variant title: The author of the acacia seeds]
Through other eyes; ed. by I. Zahava
Buffalo gals, won't you come out tonight
The Year's best fantasy, first annual collection
The Year's best science fiction, fifth annual collection
Daddy's big girl
Omni (New York, N.Y.) 9:48-50+ Ja '87
The evil eye
Seventeen 43:192-3+ S '84
Half past four
The New Yorker 63:34-44+ S 28 '87
Horse camp
The New Yorker 62:22-3 Ag 25 '86
Ile Forest
American short story masterpieces; ed. by R. Carver and T. Jenks
Kore 87
Terry's universe; ed. by B. Meacham
The ones who walk away from Omelas
Black water; ed. by A. Manguel
The Norton book of American short stories
The rule of names
Fantastic stories; ed. by M. H. Greenberg and P. L. Price
Masterpieces of fantasy and enchantment; ed. by D. G. Hartwell
Schrödinger's cat
The Best from Universe
Magicats! Ed. by J. Dann and G. Dozois
Semley's necklace
Amazing stories: 60 years of the best science fiction
Wizards; ed. by I. Asimov; M. H. Greenberg and C. G. Waugh
She unnames them
Hear the silence; ed. by I. Zahava
The New Yorker 60:27 Ja 21 '85
The ship ahoy
The New Yorker 63:40-5 N 2 '87
Small change
Afterlives; ed. by P. Sargent and I. Watson
SQ
Short story international 47
Time in the valley
The Hudson Review 37:537-48 Wint '84/ '85
The trouble with the cotton people
The Year's best science fiction, second annual collection

Le Guin, Ursula K., 1929-—*Continued*
The visionary
  Omni (New York, N.Y.) 7:100-2+ O '84
Le Sueur, Meridel
Sequel to love
  Writing red; ed. by C. Nekola and P.
  Rabinowitz
Leach, A. R.
A captain out of Etruria
  The Other woman; ed. by S. Koppelman
Leacock, Stephen Butler, 1869-1944
The marine excursion of the Knights of
  Pythias
  The Oxford book of Canadian short
  stories in English
Lead. Wilner, H.
LEAD MINES AND MINING
Rolt, L. T. C. The mine
Leaf season. Updike, J.
The **leaf-sweeper.** Spark, M.
The **lean.** Wilkinson, R.
The **lean** years. Chavez, A.
Leanderthal lady. Taylor, C.
Leaning man. Day, R. C.
Leaping Leo. Taylor, P. E.
Lear, Anne
The adventure of the global traveler
  Sherlock Holmes through time and space
Lear, Peter *See* Lovesey, Peter
Learn a trade. Updike, J.
"Learn! Learn!". Martínez-Serros, H.
Learn the hard way. Frazee, S.
Learn to say good-bye. West, J.
LEARNING AND SCHOLARSHIP *See*
  Scholars
Learning by heart. Livesey, M.
The **learning** maze. Bloch, R.
Learning the mother tongue. Hankla, C.
Learning theory. McConnell, J. V.
Learning to be a mother. Rhys, J.
Learning to bowl an out-swinger. Clark, M.
Learning to dream. Nelson, K.
Learning to swim. Swift, G.
Leask, Ian Graham
The anobiid
  Stiller's pond; ed. by J. Agee; R. Blakely
  and S. Welch
The **leather** jacket. Pavese, C.
The **leather** man. Doctorow, E. L.
Leatherwood, Kristi
Orange grove
  TriQuarterly no73:57-79 Fall '88
Leaton, Anne
Destiny
  Leaton, A. Mayakovsky, my love
Gita's story [Variant title: This domain,
  that domain]
  Leaton, A. Mayakovsky, my love
Little pictures
  Leaton, A. Mayakovsky, my love
Mayakovsky, my love
  Leaton, A. Mayakovsky, my love

Tracks to the cold country
  Leaton, A. Mayakovsky, my love
"Leave my daughter alone!".** Glickman, J.
Leave of absence. Ruffolo, L.
LEAVE-TAKINGS *See* Farewells
Leaves from a young person's notebook.
  Welch, D.
Leaving home. Keillor, G.
Leaving home. Miller, S.
Leaving Johanna. Thurm, M.
Leaving Sasha; or, The bed makes the man.
  Block, S.
Leaving the party. Gallant, M.
Leaving the yellow house. Bellow, S.
Leavitt, David, 1961-
Aliens
  20 under 30; ed. by D. Spark
  Leavitt, D. Family dancing
Ayor
  Men on men 2; ed. by G. Stambolian
Counting months
  The Editors' choice: new American
  stories v1
  Leavitt, D. Family dancing
  Prize stories, 1984
Danny in transit
  Leavitt, D. Family dancing
Dedicated
  First love/last love; ed. by M. Denneny;
  C. Ortleb and T. Steele
  Leavitt, D. Family dancing
Family dancing
  Leavitt, D. Family dancing
The lost cottage
  Leavitt, D. Family dancing
Out here
  Leavitt, D. Family dancing
Radiation
  Leavitt, D. Family dancing
Spouse night
  Winter's tales, new ser. v4
Territory
  Leavitt, D. Family dancing
  Look who's talking; ed. by B. Weber
LEBANESE   United States
Gilchrist, E. The emancipator
Salloum, V. Sitty Victoria
Sams, F. Saba (an affirmation)
Lebar, Alvin B., 1922-1988
The giver
  America 155:400-1 D 20 '86
Leblanc, Maurice, 1864-1941
Drops that trickle away
  Great French detective stories; ed. by T.
  J. Hale
The mysterious railway-passenger
  Great French detective stories; ed. by T.
  J. Hale
Lechery. Phillips, J. A.
LeClaire, Anne D.
Brothers in honor
  Redbook 169:64-9+ S '87
  Redbook 169:64-6+ O '87

LECTURES AND LECTURING
See also Speeches, addresses, etc.
Byatt, A. S. Loss of face
Greene, G. Proof positive
James, H. The Coxon Fund
Mattison, A. Art is lost
Yi, M.-Y. Early spring, mid-summer

Ledbetter, Eve
Come September
Good Housekeeping 199:170-1 S '84
Kingdom of the heart
Good Housekeeping 204:100-1 Ja '87
Stars in her eyes
Good Housekeeping 203:154-5 Jl '86
This summer's promise
Good Housekeeping 206:96+ My '88
Whirlwind romance
Good Housekeeping 201:174-5 S '85

The **ledge**. Hall, L. S.

Lee, Andrea, 1953-
The days of the Thunderbirds
The New Yorker 60:34-42 Jl 9 '84
Fine points
The New Yorker 60:38-41 My 21 '84
Gypsies
The New Yorker 60:37-9 Je 18 '84
Negatives
The New Yorker 60:34-8 O 1 '84

Lee, Audrey
The ride
Short story international 50
Waiting for her train
Our roots grow deeper than we know;
ed. by L. Gutkind

Lee, Camilla
Prescription for love
Redbook 164:49-50+ Mr '85

Lee, Cucu
One Florida night
Erotic interludes; ed. by L. Barbach

Lee, Harper, 1926-
Christmas
The Art of fiction in the heart of Dixie;
ed. by P. D. Beidler

Lee, Hector, 1908-
The Bodega War
Lee, H. The Bodega War, and other
tales from western lore
The celebrated Millard County Dramatic
Stock Company
Lee, H. The Bodega War, and other
tales from western lore
Death Valley Scotty
Lee, H. The Bodega War, and other
tales from western lore
Down the hole
Lee, H. The Bodega War, and other
tales from western lore
Going home
Lee, H. The Bodega War, and other
tales from western lore

The legend of Chief Little Sitting Bear
Lee, H. The Bodega War, and other
tales from western lore
Lucia and old lace
Lee, H. The Bodega War, and other
tales from western lore
The Mink Creek ghost
Lee, H. The Bodega War, and other
tales from western lore
On becoming somebody
Lee, H. The Bodega War, and other
tales from western lore
Remme's ride
Lee, H. The Bodega War, and other
tales from western lore
The slaves of Stony Creek
Lee, H. The Bodega War, and other
tales from western lore
Tamsen Donner's decision
Lee, H. The Bodega War, and other
tales from western lore
There could be a lesson in it somewhere
Lee, H. The Bodega War, and other
tales from western lore
Unto her a child was born
Lee, H. The Bodega War, and other
tales from western lore

Lee, Lanning
Born and bred
Passages to the dream shore; ed. by F.
Stewart

Lee, Linda
Stealing time for love
Redbook 166:44+ N '85

Lee, Manfred, 1905-1971
*For works written by this author in
collaboration with Frederic Dannay
see* Queen, Ellery

Lee, Michael
The Kid
The Yale Review 76:261-7 Wint '87

Lee, Nancy
The great defender
'Teen 32:24+ F '88

Lee, Rand B.
Full fathom five my father lies
Worlds apart; ed. by C. Decarnin; E.
Garber and L. Paleo
Knight of shallows
The Year's best science fiction, first an-
nual collection

Lee, Tanith
Because our skins are finer
Lee, T. Dreams of dark and light
Bite-me-not; or, Fleur de feu
Lee, T. Dreams of dark and light
Vampires; ed. by A. Ryan
Black as ink
Lee, T. Dreams of dark and light
Bright burning tiger
Lee, T. Dreams of dark and light
Cyrion in wax
Lee, T. Dreams of dark and light

Lee, Tanith—*Continued*
A day in the skin; or, The century we
    were out of them
  Lee, T. Dreams of dark and light
The dry season
  Lee, T. Dreams of dark and light
Elle est trois, (la mort)
  Lee, T. Dreams of dark and light
Foreign skins
  Lee, T. Dreams of dark and light
  The Year's best science fiction, second
    annual collection
The gorgon
  The Best of Shadows; ed. by C. L.
    Grant
  Lee, T. Dreams of dark and light
Into gold
  The Year's best science fiction, fourth
    annual collection
A lynx with lions
  Lee, T. Dreams of dark and light
Magritte's secret agent
  Lee, T. Dreams of dark and light
Medra
  Lee, T. Dreams of dark and light
Nunc dimittis
  Lee, T. Dreams of dark and light
  The Year's best science fiction, first an-
    nual collection
Odds against the gods
  Lee, T. Dreams of dark and light
The pale girl, the dark mage, and the
    green sea
  Moonsinger's friends; ed by S. Shwartz
Prince Amilec
  Don't bet on the prince; ed. by J. Zipes
The princess and her future
  Devils & demons; ed. by M. Kaye and
    S. Kaye
Red as blood
  Young monsters; ed. by I. Asimov; M.
    H. Greenberg and C. G. Waugh
La reine blanche
  Lee, T. Dreams of dark and light
A room with a vie
  Lee, T. Dreams of dark and light
Simon's wife
  Haunting women; ed. by A. Ryan
Sirriamnis
  Lee, T. Dreams of dark and light
Southern lights
  Lee, T. Dreams of dark and light
Tamastara
  Lee, T. Dreams of dark and light
Three days
  The Dark descent; ed. by D. G. Hart-
    well
  Shadows 7
When the clock strikes
  Lee, T. Dreams of dark and light
  Masterpieces of terror and the super-
    natural; ed. by M. Kaye and S. Kaye

Wolfland
  Don't bet on the prince; ed. by J. Zipes
  Lee, T. Dreams of dark and light
Written in water
  Lee, T. Dreams of dark and light
Lee, Vernon, 1856-1935
A wicked voice
  The Oxford book of English ghost
    stories
Lee, William M.
A message from Charity
  Witches; ed. by I. Asimov; M. H.
    Greenberg and C. G. Waugh
  Yankee witches; ed. by C. G. Waugh;
    M. H. Greenberg and F. D. McSherry
  Young witches & warlocks; ed. by I.
    Asimov; M. H. Greenberg and C. G.
    Waugh
Lee, Yu-hwa
The last rite
  The Other woman; ed. by S. Koppelman
Leebron, Fred
Cuisinart
  The New generation; ed. by A. Kaufman
Leedom-Ackerman, Joanne, 1948-
The beginning of violence
  Leedom-Ackerman, J. No marble angels
Death stalks a building once it enters
  Leedom-Ackerman, J. No marble angels
Eurlanda's box
  Leedom-Ackerman, J. No marble angels
History lesson
  Leedom-Ackerman, J. No marble angels
The impostor
  Leedom-Ackerman, J. No marble angels
No marble angels
  Leedom-Ackerman, J. No marble angels
Of imagination
  Leedom-Ackerman, J. No marble angels
Sissy Mamma's wig
  Leedom-Ackerman, J. No marble angels
The tutor
  Leedom-Ackerman, J. No marble angels
LeFanu, Joseph Sheridan *See* Le Fanu,
    Joseph Sheridan, 1814-1873
Leffland, Ella
Last courtesies
  New women and new fiction; ed. by S.
    Cahill
Left alone. Ekström, M.
Left for dead. Kantner, R.
The left-handers. Grass, G.
Left or right? Gardner, M.
The leg. Bitov, A.
The leg. Kamal Muhamed, M.
LEGACIES *See* Inheritance and succession
Legacies. Alden, P. B.
Legacies. Potter, N. A. J.
The legacy. Rahman, T.
Legacy. Schell, J.
Legacy. Schwartz, S.
The legacy. Woolf, V.
The legacy of Beau Kremel. Wolf, S.

The **legacy** of Frank Finklestein. Blum, J.
  J.
The **legacy** of Leontis. Petrakis, H. M.
LEGAL PROFESSION *See* Law and lawyers
Legend for a painting. O'Faolain, J.
A **legend** of Barlagh cave. O'Brien, F.-J.
The **legend** of Chief Little Sitting Bear. Lee,
  H.
The **legend** of Ferguson. Grin, A.
The **legend** of Joe Lee. MacDonald, J. D.
A **legend** of Saint Francis. Chesterton, G. K.
The **legend** of the bell rock. Marryat, F.
The **legend** of the paper spaceship. Yano,
  T.
Legend of the self-sufficient child. Valen-
  zuela, L.
The **legend** of the seven who found the true
  egg of lightning. Watson, I.
The **legend** of the sword. Chesterton, G. K.
The **legend** of Wooley Swamp. Daniels, C.
A **legendary** lover. Adams, A.
Legends. See Taylor, R. Sam Starr
LEGENDS AND FOLK TALES
  See also Grail
  Abramov, F. Olesha's cabin
  Brown, G. M. A winter legend
  Carter, A. The kiss
  De Lint, C. Laughter in the leaves
  Ferron, J. Summer Lethe
  Forsh, O. The little mermaid Rotozeyechka
  Harris, J. C. The wonderful Tar-Baby story
  Hoyt, M. S. Clay songs
  Hoyt, M. S. The river giantess
  Matthews, J. The tour of the sleeping
    steamboat
  Metzger, D. In the beginning there was
    humming
  Michaelson, L. W. An early frost
  Russ, J. Russalka; or, The seacoast of
    Bohemia
  Shukshin, V. M. Before the cock crows
    thrice
  Stein, J. Why the moon is small and dark
    when the sun is big and shiny
  Tsui, K. Why the sea is salty
  Van Den Heever, T. Outa Sem and Father
    Christmas
  Wells, H. G. The flying man
  Willis, C. The father of the bride
  Yolen, J. Great-grandfather dragon's tale
  Yolen, J. The moon ribbon
  Zipes, J. D. A fairy tale for our time
    Africa
  Brownlee, F. Dove and jackal
  Havemann, E. The going home of Ntambo
  Havemann, E. The self-destruction of the
    Ama Gabe
  Jordan, A. C. The king of the waters
  Kenyatta, J. The gentlemen of the jungle
  Marais, E. N. Little-reed-alone-in-the-
    whirlpool
  Ntuli, D. B. Z. Once in a century

Australia
  Roe, P., and Muecke, S. Mirdinan
  Scott, G. F. The bunyip dies
    Balkan Peninsula
  Yourcenar, M. The end of Marko Kral-
    jević
  Yourcenar, M. Marko's smile
  Yourcenar, M. The milk of death
    China
  Ch'en, H.-Y. 'Twixt soul and body
  Li, F.-Y. The carp
  Li, F.-Y. Old Chang
  Li, F.-Y. Rain-making
  Li, F.-Y. The tiger
  Li, K.-T. The Beldame Feng
  Liu, F. Wang Hsieh; or Dark robe land
  Pu, S.-L. The Tou lass
  Pu, S.-L. Yellow pride
  Pu, S.-L. Yüeh Chung
  Shen, C.-C. Miss Jen
  Yourcenar, M. How Wang-Fo was saved
    France
  Schwob, M. The death of Odjigh
    Germany
  Borchert, W. The three dark kings
  Brězan, J. How Krabat lost Smjala
  Keller, G. The little legend of the dance
    Greece
  Tennant, E. Philomela
  Yourcenar, M. The man who loved the
    Nereids
    Hungary
  Brust, S. Csucskári
    India
  Yourcenar, M. Kali beheaded
    Ireland
  Virgo, S. Tinker tale
    Japan
  Hearn, L. Rokuro-Kubi
  Hurwood, B. J. The vampire cat of
    Nabeshima
  Nakagami, K. The immortal
    Scotland
  Brown, G. M. The feast at Paplay
  Hogg, J. Mary Burnet
  Vinge, J. D. Tam Lin
    Southern States
  Daniels, C. The legend of Wooley Swamp
    Soviet Union
  Gogol', N. V. A bewitched place
  Gogol', N. V. St. John's Eve
  Gogol', N. V. Taras Bulba
  Gogol', N. V. A terrible vengeance
    United States
  Irving, W. The Devil and Tom Walker
    Wales
  Sir Galahad and the Holy Grail
LEGISLATION
  Lafferty, R. A. Polity and custom of the
    Camiroi
The **legless** A. Highsmith, P.
LeGuin, Ursula *See* Le Guin, Ursula K.,
  1929-

Leiber, Fritz, 1910-
Belsen Express
  The Dark descent; ed. by D. G. Hartwell
Catch that zeppelin!
  The Hugo winners v4
The curse of the smalls and the stars
  Leiber, F. The knight and knave of swords
The dead man
  Rod Serling's Night gallery reader
The girl with the hungry eyes
  Rod Serling's Night gallery reader
  Vampires; ed. by A. Ryan
Ill met in Lankhmar
  Baker's dozen: 13 short fantasy novels
The mer she
  Leiber, F. The knight and knave of swords
A rite of spring
  The Best from Universe
Sea magic
  Leiber, F. The knight and knave of swords
Slack Lankhmar afternoon featuring Hisvet
  Terry's universe; ed. by B. Meacham
Smoke ghost
  The Dark descent; ed. by D. G. Hartwell
Space-time for springers
  Magicats! Ed. by J. Dann and G. Dozois
  Masterpieces of fantasy and enchantment; ed. by D. G. Hartwell
  Roger Caras' Treasury of great cat stories
Yesterday house
  Isaac Asimov presents the best science fiction firsts
Leidiger, Lynda
Snake head
  The New generation; ed. by A. Kaufman
Leila Lee. Oates, J. C.
Leiningen versus the ants. Stephenson, C.
Leinster, Murray
Devil's henchman
  Witches; ed. by I. Asimov; M. H. Greenberg and C. G. Waugh
Keyhole
  Young extraterrestrials; ed. by I. Asimov; M. H. Greenberg and C. G. Waugh
A logic named Joe
  Isaac Asimov presents the best science fiction firsts
  Machines that think; ed. by I. Asimov; P. S. Warrick and M. H. Greenberg
Sidewise in time
  The Mammoth book of classic science fiction; ed. by I. Asimov; C. G. Waugh and M. H. Greenberg
A **leisurely** drowning. Halligan, M.
Leitão, Lino
The colonial bishop's visit
  Short story international 63

Dona Amalia Quadros
  Short story international 47
Jaffer's chicken
  Short story international 56
The son
  Short story international 49
Leith, Rena
Loaded dice
  The Clarion awards; ed. by D. Knight
Lejeune, Anthony, 1928-
Something on everyone
  The Mammoth book of modern crime stories; ed. by G. Hardinge
Lekh-lekho. Sholem Aleichem
Lem, Stanisław
Cezary Strzybisz, Necrobes
  Lem, S. Imaginary magnitude
Golem XIV
  Lem, S. Imaginary magnitude
Juan Rambellais et al., A history of Bitic literature
  Lem, S. Imaginary magnitude
The mask
  The Slaying of the dragon; ed. by F. Rottensteiner
Reginald Gulliver, Eruntics
  Lem, S. Imaginary magnitude
Vestrand's Extelopedia in 44 magnetomes
  Lem, S. Imaginary magnitude
Leman, Bob
Window
  The Best horror stories from the Magazine of fantasy and science fiction
Lemay, Pamphile
Blood and gold
  The Oxford book of French-Canadian short stories
Lemelin, Roger, 1919-
The Stations of the Cross
  The Oxford book of French-Canadian short stories
The **Lemesurier** inheritance. Christie, A.
LEMMINGS
  Comfort, A. The lemmings
The **lemmings.** Comfort, A.
The **lemon.** Thomas, D.
The **lemon** drop story. Outlaw, L. L.
Lena. Gallant, M.
Lena. Morrison, J.
L'Engle, Madeleine, 1918-
Poor little Saturday
  Witches; ed. by I. Asimov; M. H. Greenberg and C. G. Waugh
  Young ghosts; ed. by I. Asimov; M. H. Greenberg and C. G. Waugh
Lengyel, Peter
Rising sun; or, The celebration of heartfelt joy
  The Penguin world omnibus of science fiction
LENINGRAD (SOVIET UNION) See Soviet Union—Leningrad

SHORT STORY INDEX, 1984-1988

Lennon, John, 1940-1980
No flies on Frank
The Penguin book of horror stories
About
Boylan, J. Thirty-six miracles of Lyndon Johnson
Lenny dying, Pacific standard time. Thompson, J.
The **lens**. Van Ewyck, A.
Lentricchia, Melissa
Ensemble
The Kenyon Review ns10:23-39 Wint '88
It had to be you
Antaeus 60:138-45 Spr '88
Some enchanted evening
The Kenyon Review ns8:77-86 Summ '86
Lenz, Siegfried, 1926-
The amusement-doctor
Voices East and West: German short stories since 1945
Leo. Stark, S. S.
Leo Youngdahl, R.I.P. Block, L.
Leon, Henry Cecil *See* Cecil, Henry, 1902-1976
Leonard, Elmore, 1925-
The captives
The Second reel West; ed. by B. Pronzini and M. H. Greenberg
The hard way
Westeryear; ed. by E. Gorman
Law of the hunted ones
Wild westerns; ed. by B. Pronzini
Leonard, Hugh
The anticlerical pup
The Best of Irish wit and wisdom; ed. by J. McCarthy
Leonard, Tom, 1944-
Honest
Streets of stone; ed. by M. Burgess and H. Whyte
Mr. Endrews speaks
Streets of stone; ed. by M. Burgess and H. Whyte
Leonard Shapiro banished from dreams. Stern, S.
LEONARDO, DA VINCI, 1452-1519
About
Anderson, P. The light
The **leopard**. Harrison, C.
Leopard in a temple. Lish, G.
The **Leopard** Man's story. London, J.
LEOPARDS
Roberts, C. G. D. Do seek their meat from God
Leopold and the broken bride. Hoch, E. D.
The **Leopold** locked room. Hoch, E. D.
Leopoldina's dream. Ocampo, S.
The **leper**. Gallagher, T.
Lepiano, Jenifer
Iron Beard leaves home
The North American Review 269:22-6 Mr '84

LEPRECHAUNS
Fritch, C. E. The curse of Hooligan's Bar
LEPROSY
Endō, S. Despicable bastard
Greene, G. Dream of a strange land
London, J. Good-by, Jack
London, J. Koolau the leper
London, J. The sheriff of Kona
Monreal, D. N. Leprosy
Schwob, M. The king in the golden mask
Leprosy. Monreal, D. N.
Lerch, Sharon
Waiting
The Literary Review (Madison, N.J.) 30:73-80 Fall '86
Lerman, Eleanor
Remedies
First love/last love; ed. by M. Denneny; C. Ortleb and T. Steele
The **Lernean** Hydra. Christie, A.
Leroux, Gaston, 1868-1927
The mystery of the four husbands
Great French detective stories; ed. by T. J. Hale
LeSabre. Rinehart, S.
LESBIANISM
See also Homosexuality
Aquino, J. We've been invited to a party
Banks, B. A. Miss Esther's land
Bingham, S. Reunion
Birtha, B. Both ways
Birtha, B. Her ex-lover
Birtha, B. Ice castle
Birtha, B. In the life
Birtha, B. Johnnieruth
Birtha, B. Past halfway
Birtha, B. Pencil sketches for a story: the gray whelk shell
Boucher, S. Humming
Brady, M. Care in the holding
Brady, M. Early autumn exchange
Brady, M. The field is full of daisies and I'm afraid to pass
Brady, M. On the way to the ERA
Brady, M. The question she put to herself
Brady, M. Seneca morning
Brondoli, M. I swear I always wished you were a possibility
Broun, H. By the numbers
Bumpus, J. Plenty of time
Bumpus, J. Shame
Chernin, K. An American in Paris
Colette. "Gitanette"
Corinne, T. A. The woman in love
DeLynn, J. Sex
Donnelly, N. The scavenger hunt
Farmer, B. Gerontissa
Forrest, K. V. Benny's place
Forrest, K. V. Force majeur
Forrest, K. V. Mandy Larkin
Forrest, K. V. O captain, my captain
Forrest, K. V. The test
Fraser, A. Have a nice death

LESBIANISM—*Continued*
Frucht, A. Fruit of the month
Gaitskill, M. Other factors
Gearhart, S. M. Roxie raccoon
Gomez, J. No day too long
Grau, S. A. Home
Greene, G. Chagrin in three parts
Haake, K. A scrap of green silk
Hansen, J. Willow's money
Hemingway, E. The sea change
Janowitz, T. Ode to heroine of the future
Jolley, E. The bathroom dance
Jolley, E. Grasshoppers
Jolley, E. The libation
Kay, J. Since Agnes left
Klass, P. The almond torte equilibrium
Livia, A. 5 1/2 Charlotte Mews
London, J. The girls love each other
Lynch, L. The abrupt edge
Lynch, L. At a bar I: The Jersey dyke
Lynch, L. At a bar II: In the morning
Lynch, L. At a bar III: Sally the bartender goes on jury duty
Lynch, L. At a bar IV: White wine
Lynch, L. At a bar V: Summer storm
Lynch, L. At a bar VI: Winter sun
Lynch, L. At a bar VII: The florist shop
Lynch, L. At a bar VIII: The long slow-burning fuse
Lynch, L. At a bar IX: Halloween
Lynch, L. At a bar X: How they got together
Lynch, L. Augusta Brennan I: The coat
Lynch, L. Augusta Brennan II: The tracks
Lynch, L. The awakening
Lynch, L. Babe and Evie I: Sunshine
Lynch, L. Babe and Evie II: Thanksgiving
Lynch, L. Cookie and Toni
Lynch, L. Dutch and Sybil I: Eleanor Roosevelt's garden
Lynch, L. Dutch and Sybil II: Beachfront hotel
Lynch, L. From a novel in progress: Dusty eats out
Lynch, L. Fruitstand I: Oranges out of season
Lynch, L. Fruitstand II: Honeydew moon
Lynch, L. Jefferson I: home in your hands
Lynch, L. Jefferson II: in and out of the darkness
Lynch, L. Jefferson III: family and friends
Lynch, L. Jefferson IV: around every base till she was home
Lynch, L. The LoPresto Traveling Magic Show
Lynch, L. Marie-Christine I: Valentine's Day
Lynch, L. Marie-Christine II
Lynch, L. Marie-Christine III: a butch named Dinah
Lynch, L. Mary's garden
Lynch, L. The mirror
Lynch, L. Natural food
Lynch, L. Night 'n day
Lynch, L. Pleasure Park
Lynch, L. The swashbuckler, afterward: the Easter feast
Lynch, L. That old Studebaker
Lynn, E. A. The woman who loved the moon
Malinowitz, H. Water skiing
Moffett, J. Surviving
Moravia, A. The thing
Noonan, B. Fruit drink
Nugent, B. City of boys
Pastan, R. Underground
Pollack, R. Angel baby
Pollack, R. Black Rose and White Rose
Rees, D. Quiet days in Los Gatos
Rule, J. Dulce
Rule, J. First love/last love
Rule, J. His nor hers
Rule, J. In the attic of the house
Rule, J. Inland passage
Rule, J. A perfectly nice man
Rule, J. The real world
Russ, J. Everyday depressions
Russ, J. What did you do during the revolution, Grandma?
Russ, J. When it changed
Salmonson, J. A. The prodigal daughter
Scarfe, E. In a lighted house
Shockley, A. A. A birthday remembered
Smiley, J. The pleasure of her company
Spivack, K. The honeymoon
Stone, M. The Plasting Project
Taylor, C. The new and the old, the old and the new
Taylor, C. These women
Tsui, K. Why the sea is salty
Tuohy, F. At home with the Colonel
Tuohy, F. A reprieve
Welch, D. In the vast house
Weldon, F. Threnody
Wells, J. Two willow chairs
Wilson, B. Emily's arrows
Wilson, B. The Hulk
Wilson, B. Phantom limb pain
Wilson, B. Walking on the moon
Wilson, K. Hot as a pistol
Ziem, J. So much happiness

LESBOS ISLAND (GREECE)
Farmer, B. Gerontissa

Leskov, N. S. (Nikolaï Semenovich), 1831-1895

An apparition in the Engineers' Castle
Leskov, N. S. The sealed angel, and other stories

The cattle pen
Leskov, N. S. The sealed angel, and other stories

Lady Macbeth of Mtsensk
Leskov, N. S. Lady Macbeth of Mtsensk, and other stories

Leskov, N. S. (Nikolaĭ Semenovich), 1831-1895—*Continued*
The mountain
  Leskov, N. S. The sealed angel, and other stories
Musk-Ox
  Leskov, N. S. Lady Macbeth of Mtsensk, and other stories
Pamphalon the entertainer
  Leskov, N. S. Lady Macbeth of Mtsensk, and other stories
A robbery
  Leskov, N. S. The sealed angel, and other stories
The sealed angel
  Leskov, N. S. Lady Macbeth of Mtsensk, and other stories
  Leskov, N. S. The sealed angel, and other stories
The sentry
  Classic European short stories; ed. by R. Beum
A winter's day
  Leskov, N. S. Lady Macbeth of Mtsensk, and other stories
Leskov, Nikolaĭ Semenovich *See* Leskov, N. S. (Nikolaĭ Semenovich), 1831-1895
Lesley, Craig
The catch
  The Interior country; ed. by A. Blackburn
Leslie, Paul
Exits
  The Editors' choice v3; ed. by G. E. Murphy, Jr.
  Seventeen 44:206-7+ Ap '85
Leslie in California. Dubus, A.
Leslie's house. Keeling, J.
Lessing, Doris May, 1919-
The habit of loving
  The Art of the tale; ed. by D. Halpern
The old Chief Mshlanga
  Somehow tenderness survives; ed. by H. Rochman
An old woman and her cat
  Through other eyes; ed. by I. Zahava
One off the short list
  The World of the short story; ed. by C. Fadiman
Out of the fountain
  The Penguin book of Southern African stories
The real thing
  Partisan Review 55:555-80 Fall '88
To room nineteen
  The Penguin book of modern British short stories
Two potters
  The Treasury of English short stories; ed. by N. Sullivan
Womb ward
  The New Yorker 63:41-3 D 7 '87
The **lesson**. Brown, S.

The **lesson**. Browne, C.
A **lesson** for Bernard. Villefranche, A.-M.
A **lesson** for the teacher. O'Connor, K.
A **lesson** in dance. Cook, H.
A **lesson** in the classics. Whelan, G.
A **lesson** in traveling light. Eisenberg, D.
Lesson number one. Murphy, M.
The **lesson** of Mont Sainte-Victoire. Handke, P.
The **lesson** of the master. Hall, R. W.
The **lesson** of the master. James, H.
The **lesson** which is sufficient unto the day thereof. Lish, G.
Lessons. Lurie, M.
Lessons from a pro. Kipp, G. G.
Lest we remember. Asimov, I.
Lester, Catherine Stripe
Dogs and foreigners
  Short story international 61
Lester, DeeGee
Ann Marie's advice
  'Teen 30:42+ N '86
Ghost makers
  'Teen 28:68+ Je '84
Wind screams
  'Teen 32:42+ Mr '88
  'Teen 32:52+ Ap '88
Let him live. Brown, M. W.
Let it be. Crapser, W.
Let it pass. Gallant, M.
Let me call you sweetheart. Henley, P.
Let me count the times. Amis, M.
Let the old dead make room for the young dead. Kundera, M.
Let them call it jazz. Rhys, J.
Let us know. Vreuls, D.
Let us now praise unknown women and our mothers who begat us. Maitland, S.
Lethal legacy for the lady. Searls, H.
Letourneau, Mona
Pulsars
  Seventeen 43:246-7+ Mr '84
Let's all die together. Searls, H.
Let's go to Golgotha! Kilworth, G.
Let's go to Indio! Wesling, D.
Let's hear it for a beautiful guy. Friedman, B. J.
A **letter**. Colette
The **letter**. Davis, L.
The **letter**. Dixon, S.
A **letter**. Feng Jicai
Letter. Lurie, M.
A **letter**. Rodoreda, M.
Letter found on a corpse. Maupassant, G. de
Letter from a great-uncle. Hall, R. W.
Letter from a stranger. Wheatcroft, J.
Letter from an old people's home. Mrożek, S.
Letter from Casablanca. Tabucchi, A.
A **letter** from God. Watson, I.
A **letter** from her past. Smolens, J.
Letter from his father. Gordimer, N.
A **letter** from home. Hall, T. T.

Letter from Maine. Kees, W.
A letter from the Cleary's. Willis, C.
A letter from the Queen. Lewis, S.
A letter home [1]. Crapser, W.
A letter home [2]. Crapser, W.
A letter home [3]. Crapser, W.
A letter home [4]. Crapser, W.
The letter in the cedarchest. Goyen, W.
The letter scene. Sontag, S.
Letter to a swan. Kotzwinkle, W.
A letter to Amy. Harrington, J.
A letter to comrade Ernst L. Kant, U.
Letter to his son. Brett, S.
Letter to John Lennon. Ballantyne, S.
Letter to my daughter. Saroff, S. S.
A letter to Nick Carraway: fifty years after.
    Brenner, G.
A letter to Peachtree. Kiely, B.
A letter to Rome. Moore, G.
Letter to the institution. Cullen, E. J.
The letter writer. Kinsella, W. P.

LETTERS, STORIES ABOUT

Abbott, L. K. Time and fear and somehow
    love
Ahern, T. Unsophar and Onsopur
Auchincloss, L. The "fulfillment" of Grace
    Eliot
Brender à Brandis, M. All that counts
Brondoli, M. The love letter hack
Chopin, K. Her letters
Dixon, S. The letter
Etchison, D. Talking in the dark
Franzen, B. Mom and Pop biz
Freeman, J. The Joan Crawford letter
Gallagher, T. The woman who saved Jesse
    James
Geras, A. Love letters
Gogol', N. V. The lost letter
Gordimer, N. Rags and bones
Greene, G. Mortmain
Halligan, M. The Gauter letters
Happy, E. A collection of letters
Harris, M. The photograph
Hartley, L. P. Hilda's letter
Ignatow, R. G. A dream can never com-
    plete itself
Jolley, E. The performance
Kees, W. Letter from Maine
Kinsella, W. P. The letter writer
Lovesey, P. Did you tell Daddy?
MacLaverty, B. Secrets
Malamud, B. In retirement
Moore, G. A letter to Rome
Morrison, J. Appointment at Princess Gate
Munro, A. A queer streak
Poe, E. A. The purloined letter
Razzak, A. I. A. Voices from near and
    far
Schinto, J. The friendships of girls un-
    popular together
Schulberg, B. Señor Discretion himself
Sciascia, L. A matter of conscience
Shaw, I. Act of faith

Swados, H. The letters
Vreuls, D. The Mary mystery
Wharton, E. Pomegranate seed
Wharton, E. The touchstone
Wilhelm, K. Forever yours, Anna
Williamson, C. The personal touch

LETTERS (STORIES IN LETTER FORM)

Aldani, L. S is for snake
Aquin, H. Back on April eleventh
Archer, J. Christina Rosenthal
Ardizzone, T. My father's laugh
Auchincloss, L. The seagull
Ballantyne, S. Perpetual care
Barstow, S. The middle of the journey
Barthelme, D. Letters to the editore
Benét, S. V. The curfew tolls
Bowles, P. In absentia
Bowles, P. Unwelcome words
Boyle, K. Letters of a lady
Campbell, E. They're talking about Cher-
    nobyl today
Campos-De Metro, J. The feather
Carr, J. D. The gentleman from Paris
Chang, H.-kuo. Red boy
Charmatz, A. Sailing, through program
    management
Colette. A letter
Collins, W. The biter bit
Conroy, F. The mysterious case of R
Cortázar, J. Bestiary
Crapser, W. A letter home [1]
Crapser, W. A letter home [2]
Crapser, W. A letter home [3]
Crapser, W. A letter home [4]
Doyle, Sir A. C. The centurion
Drake, M. The feast to end all feasts
Drake, M. Remembrance of things past
Duke, M. The notif
Eisenstein, S. The Kassel ballet
Flanagan, M. A parma violet room
Gilchrist, M. The writings of Althea
    Swarthmoor
Glasser, P. Easily and well
Gordimer, N. Letter from his father
Gray, A. Five letters from an eastern em-
    pire
Hall, T. T. Backbone of the nation
Hall, T. T. From Hank in Nashville
Hall, T. T. A letter from home
Helprin, M. Letters from the Samantha
Hemingway, E. One reader writes
Hirsch, G. The housing correspondence of
    prisoner number 100293/8
Hogg, J. Strange letter of a lunatic
Hornung, E. W. The last word
Ishikawa, T. The affair of the arabesque
    inlay
Jackson, G. Structural unemployment
James, H. A bundle of letters
Jolley, E. Wednesdays and Fridays
Kant, U. A letter to comrade Ernst L.
Kawabata, Y. Canaries
Kawabata, Y. One person's happiness

LETTERS (STORIES IN LETTER FORM)—*Continued*
King, F. H. The silence is rest?
Kriegel, M. H. Love letters
Lavers, N. Rumors
Lish, G. For Jeromé—with love and kisses
Loewald, U. Cycle
Lurie, M. Letter
Lutz, J. Pure rotten
Matheson, R. Graveyard shift
Matheson, R. C. Graduation
Matthew, J. R. The letters of Mrs. J. L. Hartle
Maupassant, G. de. The impolite sex
Maupassant, G. de. Letter found on a corpse
Maupassant, G. de. The relic
Maupassant, G. de. Words of love
McCullers, C. Correspondence
Moravia, A. The thing
Nahin, P. J. Publish and perish
Narayan, R. K. Uncle's letters
Ocampo, S. The clock house
O'Hara, J. Pal Joey
Pasternak, B. L. Letters from Tula
Piper, H. B. Operation RSVP
Poe, E. A. Hans Phaall
Poe, E. A. The unparalleled adventure of one Hans Pfaall
Pronzini, B. Dear poisoner
Reed, K. Alumni fund
Rodoreda, M. The dolls' room
Rodoreda, M. A letter
Rosenfeld, I. The hand that fed me
Rostopchina, E. P., grafiníã. Rank and money
Sams, F. Saba (an affirmation)
Sarrantonio, A. Letters from camp
Shaham, N. S/S Cairo City
Sheckley, R. The shaggy average American man story
Shukshin, V. M. The postscript
Sims, G. Remember Mrs. Fitz
Sorrells, R. T. A fan of the game
Sterling, B. The beautiful and the sublime
Still, J. Pattern of a man
Tabucchi, A. Letter from Casablanca
Walton, D. One blood
Willett, J. The best of Betty
Wolfe, T. One of the girls in our party
Zhang Xian. The widow
The **letters**. Swados, H.
Letters from camp. Sarrantonio, A.
Letters from home. Fowler, K. J.
Letters from the Samantha. Helprin, M.
Letters from Tula. Pasternak, B. L.
Letters of a lady. Boyle, K.
The **letters** of Mrs. J. L. Hartle. Matthew, J. R.
Letters to the darkness. Ballantyne, S.
Letters to the editore. Barthelme, D.
Letting go. Grau, S. A.

LEUKEMIA
Gold, H. A death on the East Side
Lewis, T. Vincristine
Level, Maurice, 1875-1926
A madman
   Devils & demons; ed. by M. Kaye and S. Kaye
Night and silence
   Masterpieces of terror and the supernatural; ed. by M. Kaye and S. Kaye
Leventhal, Alice Walker *See* Walker, Alice, 1944-
Levi, Jan Heller
For the love of Katie
   Redbook 165:48+ My '85
The perfect couple
   Redbook 164:58+ F '85
A small dose of magic
   Redbook 167:56+ S '86
Levi, Primo, 1919-1987
Children of the wind
   Harper's 272:32-3 Mr '86
Lorenzo's return
   The New York Review of Books 32:3-4 N 7 '85
The story of C
   Harper's 269:28-9 N '84
Leviathan. Wolff, T.
Levine, David M.
A festival of parrots
   The Antioch Review 46:49-53 Wint '88
Levine, Norman, 1923-
Django, Karfunkelstein, & roses
   Encounter (London, England) 65:3-6 D '85
A Maritime story
   Encounter (London, England) 69:15-19 Jl/Ag '87
A small piece of blue
   The Literary Review (Madison, N.J.) 28:400-10 Spr '85
   Making it new; ed. by J. Metcalf
Something happened here
   Encounter (London, England) 67:20-5 Je '86
   The New press anthology #1
We all begin in a little magazine
   Making it new; ed. by J. Metcalf
   The Oxford book of Canadian short stories in English
Levinson, Bernard
". . . .and he chose a mule"
   Echad 2: South African Jewish voices
The night Motke Behr danced
   Echad 2: South African Jewish voices
Tokai
   Echad 2: South African Jewish voices
Levinson, Richard
(jt. auth) *See* Link, William, and Levinson, Richard

Levinson, Richard, and Link, William
Child's play
  Murder California style; ed. by J. L.
  Breen and J. Ball
LEVITATION
  Asimov, I. Belief
Levitation. Ozick, C.
LEVITTOWN (N.Y.) *See* New York
  (State)—Levittown
Levy, Deborah
Proletarian Zen
  P.E.N. new fiction I
Lewd and lascivious conjugations. Dadswell,
  M.
Lewin, Michael Z.
The reluctant detective
  The Eyes have it; ed. by R. J. Randisi
  The Mammoth book of modern crime
  stories; ed. by G. Hardinge
  Winter's crimes 16
  The Year's best mystery and suspense
  stories, 1985
Lewis, Bart L.
Inquiries
  Américas 36:20-2 Jl/Ag '84
Lewis, Flossie
The River Temz
  Commentary 86:41-6 S '88
Lewis, Geraldine
Why can't I kiss daddy good-night?
  Redbook 166:66+ D '85
Lewis, Norman
A weekend in Havana
  Foreign exchange; ed. by J. Evans
Lewis, Sara E.
Family secrets
  Seventeen 46:112-13+ Ja '87
The first weekend
  The New Yorker 62:44-52 D 8 '86
One whole day
  The New Yorker 61:44-9 Mr 18 '85
Perfect combinations
  The New Yorker 60:34-41 Ag 20 '84
Trouble people
  The Editors' choice v4; ed. by G. E.
  Murphy, Jr.
  Seventeen 45:164-5+ My '86
Lewis, Sinclair, 1885-1951
A letter from the Queen
  The Nobel reader; ed. by J. Eisen and
  S. Troy
Lewis, Trudy
Half measures
  New stories from the South: the year's
  best, 1988
Vincristine
  New stories from the South: the year's
  best, 1987

Lewitt, Maria, 1924-
All the storms and sun-sets
  Echad 4: Jewish writing from down un-
  der: Australia and New Zealand
Lewitt, S. N.
The judgment of Neave
  Tales of the Witch World 2
Lewitt, Shariann
The shaman flute
  Magic in Ithkar 2; ed. by A. Norton and
  R. Adams
Lex Talionis. Kirk, R.
Lexicographicide. Liyong, T. lo
LEYLA (BIBLICAL FIGURE)
          About
Givner, J. The testament of Leyla
Leyner, Mark
I was an infinitely hot and dense dot
  Harper's 277:36-8 N '88
Ode to autumn
  American made; ed. by M. Leyner; C.
  White and T. Glynn
L'Heureux, John
The anatomy of desire
  Sudden fiction; ed. by R. Shapard and
  J. Thomas
Clothing
  The Best American short stories, 1985
The comedian
  The Atlantic 254:106-11 N '84
  Prize stories, 1986
  The Substance of things hoped for; ed.
  by J. B. Breslin
Li, Ch'iao
The spheric man
  The Unbroken chain; ed. by J. S. M.
  Lau
Li, Fu-yen
The carp [Variant title: Man who became
  a fish]
  Tales of the supernatural; ed. by H. C.
  Chang
Old Chang
  Tales of the supernatural; ed. by H. C.
  Chang
Rain-making [Variant title: Li Ching and
  the rain god]
  Tales of the supernatural; ed. by H. C.
  Chang
The tiger
  Tales of the supernatural; ed. by H. C.
  Chang
Li, Kung-tso
The Beldame Feng
  Tales of the supernatural; ed. H. C.
  Chang
Li, Yung-p'ing
The rain from the sun
  The Unbroken chain; ed. by J. S. M.
  Lau

Li Chao
  Spring chill
    Contemporary Chinese literature; ed. by
      M. S. Duke
Li Ching and the rain god. See Li, F.-Y.
    Rain-making
Li Hangyu
  The last angler
    Short story international 68
Li Ping
  Autumn
    Contemporary Chinese literature; ed. by
      M. S. Duke
Liang, Lee Kok
  The pei-pa
    Short story international 65
Liang Xiaosheng
  The Chinese language
    The Antioch Review 46:254-6 Spr '88
  The jet ruler
    Short story international 46
The **liar**. Wolff, T.
LIARS
  Algren, N. Poor man's pennies
  Brand, C. The whispering
  Carver, R. Why, honey?
  Fremlin, C. Dangerous sport
  Hannah, B. All the old harkening faces at
    the rail
  Hannah, B. Water liars
  Kinsella, W. P. The Eddie Scissons syn-
    drome
  Painter, P. Something to do
  Pritchett, V. S. A family man
  Stead, C. An iced cake with cherries
  Stead, C. Life is difficult
  Wolff, T. The liar
Liars. Barthelme, S.
The **libation**. Jolley, E.
LIBEL
  Archer, J. The loophole
Libel. Covino, M.
Liben, Meyer
  Armistice Day
    Liben, M. New York street games and
      other stories and sketches
  The ball
    Liben, M. New York street games and
      other stories and sketches
  Ball of fire
    Liben, M. New York street games and
      other stories and sketches
  Brenner's dream
    Liben, M. New York street games and
      other stories and sketches
  The caller
    Liben, M. New York street games and
      other stories and sketches
  Change of heart
    Liben, M. New York street games and
      other stories and sketches

A dream of collaboration
    Liben, M. New York street games and
      other stories and sketches
  Frimmell's successor
    Liben, M. New York street games and
      other stories and sketches
  The garden
    Liben, M. New York street games and
      other stories and sketches
  Homage to Benny Leonard
    Liben, M. New York street games and
      other stories and sketches
  Hop, skip, and jump
    Liben, M. New York street games and
      other stories and sketches
  The intermediary
    Liben, M. New York street games and
      other stories and sketches
  King of the Hill
    Liben, M. New York street games and
      other stories and sketches
  Lady, I did it
    Liben, M. New York street games and
      other stories and sketches
  Minkin copying
    Liben, M. New York street games and
      other stories and sketches
  Mr. Mintz retires
    Liben, M. New York street games and
      other stories and sketches
  No sale 1
    Liben, M. New York street games and
      other stories and sketches
  No sale 2
    Liben, M. New York street games and
      other stories and sketches
  Not quite alone on the telephone
    Liben, M. New York street games and
      other stories and sketches
  A note on chivalry
    Liben, M. New York street games and
      other stories and sketches
  One
    Liben, M. New York street games and
      other stories and sketches
  Past due
    Liben, M. New York street games and
      other stories and sketches
  The perils of trade
    Liben, M. New York street games and
      other stories and sketches
  The pharmacist
    Liben, M. New York street games and
      other stories and sketches
  Pinkham: the enchanted isles
    Liben, M. New York street games and
      other stories and sketches
  The record
    Liben, M. New York street games and
      other stories and sketches
  The relay race
    Liben, M. New York street games and
      other stories and sketches

Liben, Meyer—_Continued_
Suspension points . . .
    Liben, M. New York street games and
    other stories and sketches
The Tolstoy movie
    Liben, M. New York street games and
    other stories and sketches
The Tolstoy quotation
    Liben, M. New York street games and
    other stories and sketches
Trick or treat
    Liben, M. New York street games and
    other stories and sketches
Uncle Benny
    Liben, M. New York street games and
    other stories and sketches
The winners
    Liben, M. New York street games and
    other stories and sketches
You're it
    Liben, M. New York street games and
    other stories and sketches
Liberated. Cooper, J. C.
Liberation. Davin, D.
The **liberation.** Stafford, J.
The **liberation** of the Youngers. Taylor, R.
LIBERIA
Cordor, S. M. A farewell to the old order
Cordor, S. M. In the hospital
Darling, J. The matchstick hut
Liberman, Serge, 1942-
Drifting
    Echad 4: Jewish writing from down un-
    der: Australia and New Zealand
Seeds
    Transgressions; ed. by D. Anderson
Two years in exile
    Echad 4: Jewish writing from down un-
    der: Australia and New Zealand
LIBERTY
Aldiss, B. W. Incident in a far country
Asimov, I. The Bicentennial Man
Berdnyk, O. The apostle of immortality,
    a tale of the unprecedented
Ferron, J. The pigeon and the parakeet
Narayan, R. K. The blind dog
Sandel, C. The child who loved roads
Yorke, M. Gifts from the bridegroom
Liberty. Sarrantonio, A.
LIBRARIANS
Adams, G. G. A teller's tale
Boucher, A. QL 696.C9
Dabrowska, M. Miss Vincent
Ferguson, N. The second third of C
Kees, W. The sign
McGerr, P. The day of the bookmobile
Painter, P. Something to do
Sage, V. Obscurity
Shibaki, Y. Ripples
Wagar, W. W. A woman's life
West, J. The condemned librarian
Williams, T. Something about him
Woolrich, C. The book that squealed

LIBRARIES
Blochman, L. G. Murder walks in marble
    halls
Emshwiller, C. The circular library of
    stones
Granit, A. Songs my mother taught me
    that are not in Hamlet; or, "Come
    into my house, Horatio! there are
    more things under the mattress than
    are dreamt of in your philosophy!"
Kees, W. The library: four sketches
Kees, W. Public library
Lindsay, F. The people of the book
Stockton, F. The landsman's tale
Wetherell, W. D. Why I love America
Wilson, B. In the archives
The **library.** Calisher, H.
The **library** book. Asimov, I.
The **library:** four sketches. Kees, W.
The **library** window. Oliphant, M.
LIBYA
Al-Kouni, I. The drumming sands
The **licences** to eat meat. Belben, R.
The **license.** Tuohy, F.
Lichen. Munro, A.
Lichtenberg, Jacqueline
Through the moon gate
    Tales of the Witch World 2
Lickety-split. Coleman, W.
Licorice lozenges. french safety pins. and
    jelly snakes. Sweeney, B.
The **lie** detector. Bell, M. S.
Lieber, Todd
Country things
    The Editors' choice v4; ed. by G. E.
    Murphy, Jr.
Steers
    The Yale Review 76:32-41 Aut '86
Liebscher, Walt
Do androids dream of electric love?
    Worlds apart; ed. by C. Decarnin; E.
    Garber and L. Paleo
Liederman, Erica
Animal stew
    The North American Review 269:28-35
    Mr '84
LIÈGE (BELGIUM) _See_ Belgium—Liège
Lies. Canin, E.
LIFE (BIOLOGY)
Ballard, J. G. Time of passage
LIFE (PHILOSOPHY OF LIFE)
Barrada, M. Life by instalments
Barth, J. Night-sea journey
Bitov, A. Notes from the corner
Colless, T., and Kelly, D. The lost world:
    signs of life
Drake, R. A ticket as long as your arm
Hodgson, W. H. The derelict
Jean Paul. The life of Maria Wuz, the
    merry-hearted Dominie of Auenthal
Landolfi, T. An abstract concept
Li Ping. Autumn
Owens, M. We find Harris again

LIFE (PHILOSOPHY OF LIFE) — *Continued*

Sheckley, R. Cordle to onion to carrot
Life after death. Cullinan, E.
The **life** and death of Martha. Matthew, J. R.
The **life** and times of Major Fiction. Baumbach, J.
Life as an ant. Carneiro, A.
Life before science. Carlson, R.
Life being the best. Boyle, K.
Life between meals. DeMarinis, R.
Life by instalments. Barrada, M.
Life drawing. Grumley, M.
Life drawing. McGraw, E.
A **life** for the theater. Cullen, E. J.
Life in a furniture store. Russ, J.
Life in death. Poe, E. A.
Life in our time. Bloch, R.
A **life** in the cinema. Garris, M.
Life in the pre-Cambrian era. Janowitz, T.
Life in windy weather. Bitov, A.

LIFE INSURANCE

Gallagher, T. Beneficiaries
Life is an adventure, with risks. Schwartz, L. S.
Life is difficult. Stead, C.
Life is good. Keillor, G.
Life jackets. Moyer, K.
A **life** membership. Tuohy, F.
The **life** of a man's man. Windsor, G.
The **life** of anybody. Sheckley, R.
The **life** of art. Garner, H.
Life of Beethoven. Smith, P. J.
Life of Buddha. Shepard, L.
The **life** of death. Barker, C.
The **life** of Maria Wuz, the merry-hearted Dominie of Auenthal. Jean Paul
Life of the cheerful schoolmaster Maria Wutz. See Jean Paul. The life of Maria Wuz, the merry-hearted Dominie of Auenthal
The **life** of the imagination. Gordimer, N.
Life of the party. Bail, M.
The **life** of the party. Sorrentino, F.
The **life** of the stripe. Anthony, P.
Life on earth. Ballantyne, S.

LIFE ON OTHER PLANETS

See also Interplanetary visitors; Interstellar communication
Aldani, L. Quo vadis, Francisco?
Anderson, P. Honorable enemies
Anderson, P. Hunter's moon
Anthony, P. In the jaws of danger
Anthony, P. Quinquepedalian
Ash, P. Minds meet
Asimov, I. Blind alley
Asimov, I. Strikebreaker
Asimov, I. What is this thing called love?
Asimov, I. Youth
Bear, G. Hardfought
Benford, G. Titan falling

Benford, G., and Laidlaw, M. A hiss of dragon
Bilenkin, D. Crossing of the paths
Bloch, R. The baldheaded mirage
Bloch, R. Broomstick ride
Bloch, R. The old college try
Bone, J. F. On the fourth planet
Bova, B. A small kindness
Bova, B. To touch a star
Bradbury, R. The love affair
Bradley, M. Z. Death between the stars
Bradley, M. Z. The wind people
Bretnor, R. Dr. Birdmouse
Burdick, B. S. From time to time
Butler, O. E. Bloodchild
Carr, J. Blind spot
Carr, T. The Dance of the Changer and the Three
Clarke, A. C. Before Eden
Clarke, A. C. A meeting with Medusa
Clement, H. Seasoning
Del Rey, L. The still waters
Dick, P. K. Colony
Dick, P. K. Rautavaara's case
Dickson, G. R. The faithful wilf
Dickson, G. R. Jackal's meal
Dickson, G. R. A matter of technique
Dickson, G. R. A wobble in Wockii futures
Effinger, G. A. The aliens who knew, I mean, everything
Elgin, S. H. For the sake of Grace
Elgin, S. H. Modulation in all things
Ellison, H. Hadj
Ellison, H. Nothing from my noon meal
Ellison, H. With Virgil Oddum at the East Pole
Farmer, P. J. Mother
Farmer, P. J. My sister's brother
Farmer, P. J. Uranus; or, UFO versus IRS
Fraser, J. Utopian dreams
Godwin, T. Too soon to die
Gold, H. L. No charge for alterations
Guin, W. The delegate from Guapanga
Haldeman, J. W. Hero
Haldeman, J. W. Seasons
Hamilton, E. The stars, my brothers
Herbert, F. Seed stock
Herbert, F. Songs of a sentient flute
Hoch, E. D. Zoo
Kilworth, G. The man who collected bridges
Knight, D. F. Four in one
Lafferty, R. A. Polity and custom of the Camiroi
Lafferty, R. A. Primary education of the Camiroi
Le Guin, U. K. Semley's necklace
Leinster, M. Keyhole
Longyear, B. B. Adagio
Longyear, B. B. Catch the sun
Longyear, B. B. Enemy mine
Longyear, B. B. The homecoming

LIFE ON OTHER PLANETS—*Continued*

Martin, G. R. R. And seven times never kill man

Martin, G. R. R. Nor the many-colored fires of a star ring

Martin, G. R. R. Sandkings

Martin, G. R. R. A song for Lya

Martin, G. R. R. The way of cross and dragon

McDevitt, J. In the tower

Merril, J. The shrine of temptation

Moore, C. L. The bright illusion

Neville, K. The forest of Zil

Niven, L. Flare time

Norton, A. Teddi

Pohl, F. The high test

Pohl, F. Swanilda's song

Potter, R. The red sickness

Randall, M. Lapidary nights

Russell, E. F. Diabologic

Russell, E. F. Mechanistria

Russell, E. F. Mesmerica

Russell, E. F. Symbiotica

Saberhagen, F. Smasher

Schmitz, J. H. Novice

Schmitz, J. H. The witches of Karres

Shaw, B. Small world

Sheckley, R. All the things you are

Sheckley, R. The language of love

Sheckley, R. The monsters

Silverberg, R. The dybbuk of Mazel Tov IV

Silverberg, R. Sunrise on Pluto

Silverberg, R. The trouble with Sempoanga

Silverberg, R. Waiting for the earthquake

Smith, C. The crime and glory of Commander Suzdal

Smith, C. A. Master of the asteroid

Smith, S. A. The amber frog

St. Clair, M. An egg a month from all over

St. Clair, M. Hathor's pets

Sterling, B. Sunken gardens

Stone, M. The Plasting Project

Sturgeon, T. Why dolphins don't bite

Tiptree, J. Come live with me

Tiptree, J. The only neat thing to do

Tiptree, J. The peacefulness of Vivyan

Tiptree, J. With delicate mad hands

Van Ewyck, A. The lens

Vance, J. The gift of gab

Vance, J. The Kokod warriors

Vinge, J. D. Eyes of amber

Vinge, J. D. Mother & child

Wagar, W. W. Madonna of the red sun

Watson, I. The artistic touch

Wilhelm, K. The promise

Williamson, J. At the human limit

Williamson, J. Farside station

Willis, C. The Sidon in the mirror

Wyndham, J. The lost machine

Yolen, J. Cockfight

Zelazny, R. Dreadsong

Zelazny, R. King Solomon's ring

Life on the moon. Smith, L.

Life on this planet. Cohen, M.

Life, passion, and death of Glutton da Silva, the man who ate films. Da Costa, F. M.

Life-sentence. Oldfield, J.

Life signs. Jacobsen, J.

Life story. Woodman, A.

Life sucks; or, Ernest Hemingway never slept here. Barrus, T.

The **life** you live (may not be your own). Cooper, J. C.

The **life** you save may be your own. O'Connor, F.

Lifecast. Spector, C.

Lifeguard. Updike, J.

LIFESAVING

Douglas, E. On the lake

Kotzwinkle, W. Tell her you love her with a ring from Dave's House of Diamonds

Sanford, W. M. Wreck

Updike, J. Lifeguard

A **lifestyle.** Sorrentino, F.

Ligeia. Poe, E. A.

Liggett, Byron

The Cat Man

Magicats! Ed. by J. Dann and G. Dozois

LIGHT

Davie, E. Bulbs

The **light.** Anderson, P.

Light. Harris, B.

The **light** at the end of the tunnel. DeGrazia, E.

Light dark. Moss, R.

Light fingers. Slesar, H.

The **light-house.** Poe, E. A.

LIGHT HOUSES *See* Lighthouses

Light in dark places. Bonner, M.

Light of other days. Shaw, B.

The **light** of the world. Hemingway, E.

A **light** on the road to Woodstock. Peters, E.

The **light** on the sea. Wickham, J.

The **light** on the water. Norris, H.

Light timber. Potter, N. A. J.

Light verse. Asimov, I.

Light-years. Thurm, M.

The **lighted** window. Roy, J.

LIGHTHOUSES

Alcott, L. M. Ariel. A legend of the lighthouse

MacLeod, A. Island

Osborn, M. Maine

Poe, E. A. The light-house

Steele, W. D. The woman at Seven Brothers

Lightly. Tallent, E.

Lightning. Barthelme, D.

LIGHTNING CONDUCTORS

Melville, H. The lightning-rod man

The **lightning-rod** man. Melville, H.

Lights. Mathers, P.
Lights. Paolucci, A.
Lights, action—killer! Ballard, W. T.
The **lights** of the carrousel. Amado, J.
Lights on the sea. Haris, P.
Ligotti, Thomas
  Alice's last adventure
    Prime evil; ed. by D. E. Winter
'Lijah. Smith, E. V.
Like a bad dream. Böll, H.
Like a bug on a windshield. Block, L.
Like a cactus in a field of corn. Haas, B.
Like a lamb to slaughter. Block, L.
Like a leaf. McGuane, T.
Like a Maori prince. Mathers, P.
Like a thief in the night. Block, L.
Like all other men. McGahern, J.
Like boats. Peterson, M.
Like brothers. Schulman, H.
Like Lucifer. Greenwood, R.
Like sisters. Schulman, H.
Like that. McCullers, C.
Like the Hully-Gully but not so slow.
    Finger, A.
Like the old wolf in all those wolf stories.
    Kincaid, N.
Like the sun. Narayan, R. K.
Like visitant of air. West, J.
Like you used to do. Abbott, K.
Likely houses. Nevai, L.
Liking. Parise, G.
Lila. Kornblatt, J. R.
Lila the werewolf. Beagle, P. S.
Lilie Lala. Maupassant, G. de
LILIES
  Bates, H. E. The lily
Lilies. London, J.
Lilies. Skrzynecki, P.
Lilith's. Campbell, R.
The **lily**. Bates, H. E.
Lily. Broughton, T. A.
Lily. Smiley, J.
Lily, Africa and I. Shamosh, A.
The **Lily** of the Valley rest area. Tournier,
    M.
The **lily-white** boys. Maxwell, W.
Lily's Deli. Mazel, D.
Lily's party. Purdy, J.
Lim, Catherine
  Love
    Short story international 57
  The marriage
    Short story international 46
  The ugly one
    Short story international 65
Lim. Nimmo, H. A.
Lim Beng Hap
  Tricked again
    Short story international 64
LIMA (PERU) *See* Peru—Lima
Lima beans. Small, D.
Limbo. Harding, L.

LIME-KILNS
  Hawthorne, N. Ethan Brand
LIMERICKS
  Gardner, M. The virgin from Kalamazoo
  Saroyan, W. There was a young lady of
    Perth
Liminal: the little man. Davis, L.
The **limitations** of Jason Packard. McElroy,
    C. J.
Limited access. Sanford, A.
Lin, Hai-yin
  Lunar New Year's feast
    The Unbroken chain; ed. by J. S. M.
    Lau
Lin Jinlan
  The transcript
    Roses and thorns; ed. by P. Link
Linaweaver, Brad
  Moon of ice
    Hitler victorious; ed. by G. Benford and
    M. H. Greenberg
  Shadow quest
    Magic in Ithkar 2; ed. by A. Norton and
    R. Adams
Linaweaver, Brad, and Linaweaver, Cynthia
  Dream pirates' jewel
    Tales of the Witch World 2
Linaweaver, Cynthia
  (jt. auth) See Linaweaver, Brad, and
    Linaweaver, Cynthia
LINCOLN, ABRAHAM, 1809-1865
                  About
  Singmaster, E. The battleground
Lincoln's doctor's son's dog. Law, W.
Linda Star. Kinsella, W. P.
The **linden** trees. West, J.
Lindenborg pool. Morris, W.
Lindop, Audrey Erskine- *See* Erskine-Lindop,
    Audrey, 1921-
Lindsay, Frederic
  The people of the book
    Streets of stone; ed. by M. Burgess and
    H. Whyte
Lindsay and the red city blues. Haldeman,
    J. W.
Lindsey, Jim
  Jammed
    The Antioch Review 43:79-91 Wint '85
The **line**. Robison, J.
A **line** of communication. Davies, V.
Linebarger, Paul M. A., 1913-1966
    *For works written by this author under
    other names see* Smith, Cordwainer,
    1913-1966
Linehan, Patricia
  One last hunting pack
    The Clarion awards; ed. by D. Knight
The **liner** and the iceberg. Hyne, C. J. C.
Lines. Davie, E.
Lingo. Gilliatt, P.
The **linguist**. Harris, M.

Linington, Elizabeth, 1921-
  *For works written by this author under
  other names see* Shannon, Dell,
  1921-
Link, William
  (jt. auth) See Levinson, Richard, and Link,
  William
Link, William, and Levinson, Richard
  One bad winter's day
  Alfred Hitchcock's Mortal errors
Links. Morris, M.
Linzner, Gordon, 1949-
  The independent fiend
  Bringing down the moon; ed. by J. An-
  derson
Lion. Garrett, G. P.
The **lion**. Mrożek, S.
The **lion** at morning. Wolfe, T.
The **lion** that learned algebra. Pak, L. H.
The **lion**. The eagle. The wolf. Rabasa, G.
Lionizing. Poe, E. A.
LIONS
  Carter, A. The courtship of Mr. Lyon
  Garrett, G. P. Lion
  Grey, Z. Roping lions in the Grand
    Canyon
  Hemingway, E. The short happy life of
    Francis Macomber
  London, J. The Leopard Man's story
  Markham, B. Brothers are the same
  Markham, B. He was a good lion
The **lions** are asleep this night. Waldrop, H.
Lior and the sea. Duane, D.
Lip service résumé. Dilworth, S.
Lipenga, Ken
  The road to Migowi
    The Penguin book of Southern African
    stories
Liphshitz, Arye, 1901-
  Gates of joy
    Liphshitz, A. We built Jerusalem
  Jum'a and Jamila
    Liphshitz, A. We built Jerusalem
  The last stage
    Liphshitz, A. We built Jerusalem
  A man and his house
    Liphshitz, A. We built Jerusalem
  Master of his fate
    Liphshitz, A. We built Jerusalem
  The monk
    Liphshitz, A. We built Jerusalem
  Three women
    Liphshitz, A. We built Jerusalem
  Under the horses' hooves
    Liphshitz, A. We built Jerusalem
Lipman, Elinor
  After Emily
    Ladies' Home Journal 102:86+ Ap '85
    Lipman, E. Into love and out again
  Baby's first Christmas
    Lipman, E. Into love and out again
  Back to normal
    Lipman, E. Into love and out again

Catering
    Lipman, E. Into love and out again
  A daughter your age
    Lipman, E. Into love and out again
  The day woman
    Lipman, E. Into love and out again
  Frankie's soup
    Lipman, E. Into love and out again
  Good news
    Lipman, E. Into love and out again
  Immediate family
    Lipman, E. Into love and out again
  Keeping in touch with Holly
    Lipman, E. Into love and out again
  Land of the midnight sun
    Lipman, E. Into love and out again
  Memorial Day
    Lipman, E. Into love and out again
  My cousin Veronica
    Ladies' Home Journal 103:82+ My '86
  Obit
    Lipman, E. Into love and out again
  They'll smile at you if you're with me
    Lipman, E. Into love and out again
  Thick and thin
    Lipman, E. Into love and out again
  You're right, I know you're right
    Lipman, E. Into love and out again
Lippman, Amy
  Private lies
    Mademoiselle 92:218+ S '86
Lipsky, David
  Three thousand dollars
    The Best American short stories, 1986
    The New Yorker 61:43-50 N 11 '85
Lipsky, Eleazar
  The quality of mercy
    Manhattan mysteries; ed. by B. Pronzini;
      C. L. R. Waugh and M. H. Greenberg
  Tiger in the night
    Ellery Queen's Crimes and punishments
Lipsyte, Robert
  Red carpet treatment
    100 great fantasy short short stories; ed.
      by I. Asimov; T. Carr and M. H.
      Greenberg
LIQUOR INDUSTRY *See* Liquor traffic
Liquor makes you smart. Loos, A.
LIQUOR TRAFFIC
    See also Moonshiners
  Grau, S. A. White girl, fine girl
  Osborn, C. Reversals
  Wetherell, W. D. Calm seas and a
    prosperous voyage
LISBON (PORTUGAL) *See* Portugal—Lis-
bon
Lish, Gordon
  Agony
    Lish, G. Mourner at the door
  Balzano & Son
    The Antioch Review 46:5-6 Wint '88
    Lish, G. Mourner at the door

Lish, Gordon—*Continued*
Behold the incredible revenge of the shifted P. O. V.
  Lish, G. Mourner at the door
Can you top this?
  The Antioch Review 44:15-16 Wint '86
  Lish, G. Mourner at the door
The death of me
  Lish, G. Mourner at the door
The dog
  Lish, G. Mourner at the door
Don't die
  Lish, G. Mourner at the door
[Entitled story]
  Lish, G. What I know so far
Everything I know
  Lish, G. What I know so far
Fear: four examples
  Harper's 269:33 Ag '84
  Lish, G. What I know so far
Fish story
  Lish, G. Mourner at the door
Fleur
  Lish, G. What I know so far
For Jeromé—with love and kisses
  Lish, G. What I know so far
  Prize stories, 1984
For Rupert—with no promises
  Lish, G. What I know so far
Frank Sinatra or Carleton Carpenter
  Lish, G. What I know so far
The friend
  Lish, G. Mourner at the door
  Southwest Review 69:278-84 Summ '84
Guilt
  Lish, G. What I know so far
The hilt
  Lish, G. Mourner at the door
History; or, The four pictures of Vludka
  Lish, G. Mourner at the door
How to write a novel
  Lish, G. What I know so far
How to write a poem
  Lish, G. What I know so far
I'm wide
  Lish, G. What I know so far
Imagination
  Lish, G. What I know so far
Imp among aunts
  Lish, G. What I know so far
Joyce made easy
  Harper's 272:22-3 Ap '86
Knowledge
  Lish, G. Mourner at the door
Last descent to earth
  Lish, G. Mourner at the door
  Southwest Review 71:68-70 Wint '86
Leopard in a temple
  Lish, G. Mourner at the door
The lesson which is sufficient unto the day thereof
  Lish, G. Mourner at the door

The merry chase
  The Antioch Review 43:5-8 Wint '85
  Lish, G. Mourner at the door
  The Pushcart prize XI
  Sudden fiction; ed. by R. Shapard and J. Thomas
Mr. and Mrs. North
  Lish, G. Mourner at the door
Mr. Goldbaum
  Lish, G. Mourner at the door
  The Pushcart prize XII
My true story
  Lish, G. Mourner at the door
On the business of generating transforms
  Lish, G. Mourner at the door
The problem of the preface
  Lish, G. Mourner at the door
The psoriasis diet
  Lish, G. What I know so far
Resurrection
  Lish, G. Mourner at the door
  Prize stories, 1986
Shit
  Lish, G. Mourner at the door
Spell bereavement
  Lish, G. Mourner at the door
Three
  Lish, G. What I know so far
The traitor
  Lish, G. Mourner at the door
Two families
  Lish, G. What I know so far
Weight
  Lish, G. What I know so far
What is left to link us
  Lish, G. What I know so far
What my mother's father was really the father of
  Lish, G. Mourner at the door
The wire
  Lish, G. Mourner at the door
Lispector, Clarice, 1924-1977
The egg and the chicken
  Lispector, C. The foreign legion
The evolution of myopia
  Lispector, C. The foreign legion
Family ties
  Women's fiction from Latin America; ed. by E. P. Garfield
The fifth story
  Lispector, C. The foreign legion
The foreign legion
  Lispector, C. The foreign legion
The imitation of the rose
  Other fires; ed. by A. Manguel
In search of dignity
  Short story international 68
Journey to Petrópolis
  Lispector, C. The foreign legion
Love
  Women's fiction from Latin America; ed. by E. P. Garfield

Lispector, Clarice, 1924-1977—*Continued*
  The message
    Lispector, C. The foreign legion
  The misfortunes of Sofia
    Lispector, C. The foreign legion
  Monkeys
    Lispector, C. The foreign legion
  The obedient
    Lispector, C. The foreign legion
  Pig Latin
    Ms. 13:68-9 Jl '84
  The sharing of bread
    Lispector, C. The foreign legion
  A sincere friendship
    Lispector, C. The foreign legion
  The solution
    Lispector, C. The foreign legion
  Temptation
    Lispector, C. The foreign legion
Lispeth. Kipling, R.
"Listen buddy, we don't throw gutter balls here". Ashley, F.
Listen to reason. Tallent, E.
Listening. Paley, G.
The **listening** child. St. Clair, M.
Listening to Brahms. Charnas, S. M.
Listfield, Emily
  Porcupines and other travesties
    20 under 30; ed. by D. Spark
Litchfield, R. M.
  In the winter of her days . . .
    Critical Quarterly 29:45-6 Spr '87
LITERACY
  Botwinik, B. Esperanto
  Finger, C. J. Eric
LITERARY AGENTS
  Gilliatt, P. Known for her frankness
  Stegner, W. E. Field guide to the western birds
LITERARY CRITICS
  Bloch, R. The play's the thing
  Gilchrist, E. Looking over Jordan
  James, H. The death of the lion
  James, H. The figure in the carpet
  James, H. John Delavoy
  James, H. The next time
  Poe, E. A. The literary life of Thingum Bob, Esq.
  Wolfe, T. Portrait of a literary critic
LITERARY FORGERIES AND MYSTIFICATION
  Kipling, R. Dayspring mishandled
  Queen, E. Abraham Lincoln's clue
LITERARY LIFE
    See also Authors
The **literary** life of Thingum Bob, Esq. Poe, E. A.
Literary prize. Landolfi, T.
LITERARY PRIZES *See* Rewards (Prizes, etc.)
Literature. Colette

LITHUANIA
  Rural life
  Dickson, M. M. The farmer
LITHUANIANS
  United States
  Kornblatt, J. R. Pa
  Thorman, C. Blue haired chickens
  Thorman, C. God giving Lithuania to the world
  Thorman, C. Knights of Puntukas
  Thorman, C. No job too small
  Thorman, C. Society for the benefit of the Daughters of Vilnius
  Thorman, C. Sweet chickadee of grace
The **litigants**. Singer, I. B.
The **litter**. Kisner, J.
Littke, Lael
  Away in a manger
    McCall's 114:21-2+ D '86
  The bantam phantom
    Spirits, spooks, and other sinister creatures; ed. by H. Hoke
  A feline felony
    Roger Caras' Treasury of great cat stories
Little, Bentley
  The backroom
    Bringing down the moon; ed. by J. Anderson
Little, John, 1939-
  Wild rabbits
    Mississippi writers v1: Fiction; ed. by D. Abbott
Little, John R.
  Tommy's Christmas
    100 great fantasy short short stories; ed. by I. Asimov; T. Carr and M. H. Greenberg
The **little** affair in Paris. Durrell, L.
The **little** American executive. Murphy, P.
Little Apple Hard to Peel. Brown, F.
The **little** axe. Keeling, N.
Little Bear. Boswell, R.
The **little** bear who didn't know who he was. Winters, J.
LITTLE BIG HORN, BATTLE OF THE, 1876
  Bell, M. S. Today is a good day to die
  Howard, C. Custer's ghost
A **little** bit of the old slap and tickle. Hawkes, J.
The **little** black bag. Kornbluth, C. M.
The **little** black train. Wellman, M. W.
Little blood-button. Oates, J. C.
The **little** Bouilloux girl. Colette
Little Boy Blue. Kavaler, R.
Little boy lost. Wheeler, H. C.
The **little** boy who was left behind. Heise, K.
A **little** boy's Christmas list. Winters, J.
Little by little they come back for you. Covino, M.
The **little** calf. Blinkin, M.

The **little** cask. Maupassant, G. de
A **little** collar for the monkey. West, J.
The **little** convent girl. King, G. E.
The **little** cousins. Taylor, P. H.
The **little** creeps. Miller, W. M.
Little cruelties. Tem, S. R.
A **little** demon. Stead, C.
A **little** different. Ballard, W. T.
The **little** dirty girl. Russ, J.
Little Eddy. Harris, M.
Little elegy for cello and piano. Justice, D. R.
Little expressionless animals. Wallace, D. F.
Little extras. McGuane, T.
Little Face. Thompson, J.
A **little** fairy tale. Poniatowska, E.
Little Francis. Carrington, L.
Little frog. Zapolska, G.
The **little** Gatsby. Tabucchi, A.
The **little** ghost. Walpole, Sir H.
Little girl. Ângelo, I.
The **little** girl and the rapeseed flower. Shiga, N.
Little girl from Little Rock. Ebon, W.
The **little** girl from town. Suckow, R.
The **little** girl in green. Aslan, I.
Little girl lost. Stefaniak, M. H.
Little Goethe. Sage, V.
The **little** governess. Mansfield, K.
A **little** holiday. O'Brien, E.
The **little** house. Bowles, P.
The **little** Ice Age. Herbert, S.
A **little** intelligence. Garrett, R.
Little Jesus. Crabtree, L. V.
The **little** knife. Chabon, M.
Little knives. Duke, M.
Little lamb. Pronzini, B.
A **little** larceny. Pronzini, B.
The **little** legend of the dance. Keller, G.
Little lost robot. Asimov, I.
Little Louise Roque. Maupassant, G. de
The **little** man who wasn't all there. Bloch, R.
The **little** mermaid Rotozeyechka. Forsh, O.
Little Mim. Gilbert, W. S.
The **little** monster. Anderson, P.
Little mooses. Campos-De Metro, J.
Little mother up the Mörderberg. Wells, H. G.
The **little** movement. Dick, P. K.
A **little** of what you fancy. McDaniel, M. C.
A **little** off the top. Block, L.
The **little** old Dutch church bell. Brender à Brandis, M.
The **little** old man of Batignolles. Gaboriau, E.
A **little** peace. Franklin, P.
The **little** pension. Colum, P.
Little pictures. Leaton, A.
A **little** piece of room. Owens, B.
A **little** place off the Edgeware Road. Greene, G.

The **little** puppy that could. Amis, M.
Little recipes from modern magic. Apollinaire, G.

LITTLE RED RIDING HOOD
        Parodies, travesties, etc.
   Hébert, F. Prowling around Little Red Riding Hood
Little Red Riding Hood. Ferron, J.
Little-reed-alone-in-the-whirlpool. Marais, E. N.
The **little** regiment. Crane, S.
LITTLE ROCK (ARK.) *See* Arkansas—Little Rock
The **little** room. Wynne, M. Y.
Little sharks. Elman, R.
A **little** something. Colwin, L.
A **little** something for us tempunauts. Dick, P. K.
Little sunshine. Nowakowski, M.
A **little** surprise. Abbott, K.
A **little** tatter of sky. Heller, P.
Little terror. Barnard, R.
The **little** things. Asimov, I.
Little things. Carver, R.
Little touches. Shyer, M. F.
A **little** walk. Maupassant, G. de
Little whale, the painter of reality. See Aksenov, V. P. Little whale, varnisher of reality
Little whale, varnisher of reality. Aksenov, V. P.
Little white bundle. Asscher-Pinkhof, C.
Little white girl. Mencken, S. H.
A **little** white lye. Brown, F.
Little wife. Oates, J. C.
Littlebird, Larry
  The hunter
    Earth power coming; ed. by S. J. Ortiz
Liu, Fu
  Wang Hsieh; or Dark robe land
    Tales of the supernatural; ed. by H. C. Chang
Liu, M. E.
  Enlisting
    Commentary 84:41-4 Jl '87
Liu, Qingbang
  The good luck bun
    Roses and thorns; ed. by P. Link
Liu, Ta-jen
  Chrysalis
    The Unbroken chain; ed. by J. S. M. Lau
Live and let live. Halperin, I.
Live bait. Tuohy, F.
Live life deeply. West, J.
Live performance. Carden, S.
Live souls. Blaine, M.
Lively, Penelope, 1933-
  Corruption
    Encounter (London, England) 62:3-8 Mr '84

Lively, Penelope, 1933--—*Continued*
The Crimean hotel
  Encounter (London, England) 67:10-14 Jl/Ag '86
Grow old along with me, the best is yet to be
  New women and new fiction; ed. by S. Cahill
A long night at Abu Simbel
  Encounter (London, England) 63:3-7 N '84
A **lively** friend. Maupassant, G. de
Lives of a cat. Franco, M.
Lives of the poets. Doctorow, E. L.
Livesey, Margot
The acrobat's grave
  Livesey, M. Learning by heart
Jean and Little Aunt
  Livesey, M. Learning by heart
Learning by heart
  Livesey, M. Learning by heart
Obituary
  Livesey, M. Learning by heart
  The New press anthology #1
Peter and the asteroids
  Livesey, M. Learning by heart
The ring
  Livesey, M. Learning by heart
The salt course
  Livesey, M. Learning by heart
A small price
  Livesey, M. Learning by heart
A story to be illustrated by Max Ernst
  Livesey, M. Learning by heart
Umbrellas
  Livesey, M. Learning by heart
Livia, Anna
5 1/2 Charlotte Mews
  Stepping out; ed. by A. Oosthuizen
Living. Cooper, J. C.
Living. Cowan, P.
The **living**. Lavin, M.
Living alone in Iota. Abbott, L. K.
The **living** Christmas tree. Brender à Brandis, M.
The **living** dead. Bloch, R.
The **living** end. Bloch, R.
The **living** hothouse. Halligan, M.
Living in the jungle. Soukup, M.
The **living** mist. Farley, R. M.
Living out the past. Gifkins, M.
Living together. Friedman, B. J.
The **living** torpedo. Yates, T.
Living with snakes. Curley, D.
Livio Roca. Ocampo, S.
Liyong, Taban lo
Lexicographicide
  African short stories in English; ed. by J. de Grandsaigne
The **lizard**. Gottlieb, E.
LIZARDS
Gingher, M. Camouflage
Hill, B. Lizards

Williams, T. The night of the Iguana
Lizards. Hill, B.
Llewellyn, Kate
Croup
  Room to move; ed. by S. Falkiner
Llosa, Mario Vargas *See* Vargas Llosa, Mario, 1936-
Lloyd, Tracey
McIver in Bombay
  Encounter (London, England) 64:3-6 Ja '85
Llywelyn, Morgan
Fletcher found
  Magic in Ithkar [1]; ed. by A. Norton and R. Adams
Me, tree
  Devils & demons; ed. by M. Kaye and S. Kaye
The silverlord
  Magic in Ithkar 3; ed. by A. Norton and R. Adams
Lo Bosco, Rocco
The birthday present
  Here's the story: fiction with heart; ed. by M. Sklar
Lo Liyong, Taban *See* Liyong, Taban lo
Loaded dice. Leith, R.
The **loaded** dog. Lawson, H.
LOANS
      See also Moneylenders
Brondoli, M. Borrowing
Carver, R. Elephant
Coleman, W. Buying primo time
Henry, O. A call loan
Oates, J. C. Yarrow
The **lob**. Wetherell, W. D.
Lobotomy shoals. Brantingham, J.
LOBSTERS
Brown, S. The lesson
MacLeod, A. Vision
Train, A. C. The Viking's daughter
Local anaesthetic. Flanagan, R.
Local customs. Thomas, A. C.
Local habitations. Kavaler, R.
A **local** hanging. Thompson, K.
Local heroes. Choyce, L.
Local time. Gifkins, M.
LOCH NESS MONSTER
Dickson, G. R. The mortal and the monster
Lock. Connelly, J.
The **locket**. Chopin, K.
Lockridge, Frances Louise Davis, 1896-1963, and Lockridge, Richard, 1898-1982
Captain Heimrich stumbles
  Great modern police stories; ed. by B. Pronzini and M. H. Greenberg
Lockridge, Richard, 1898-1982
(jt. auth) See Lockridge, Frances Louise Davis, 1896-1963, and Lockridge, Richard, 1898-1982
LOCKS AND KEYS
Rendell, R. The whistler

LOCKS AND KEYS—*Continued*
Sorrentino, F. A lifestyle
Locomotion. Evans, E.
The **locomotive**. Piñera, V.
Locust. Robertson, M. E.
LOCUSTS
Alexan, J. The locusts
Kawabata, Y. The grasshopper and the bell cricket
The **locusts**. Alexan, J.
Lodge, David, 1935-
Hotel des Boobs
The Penguin book of modern British short stories
The **lodge** of Jahbulon. McLaughlin, C.
The **lodger**. Moffatt, D.
Lodging for the night. Aiken, J.
A **lodging** for the night. Stevenson, R. L.
Loesch, Cheryl
Horse story
Stiller's pond; ed. by J. Agee; R. Blakely and S. Welch
Loeser, Katinka
Shelf life
The Yale Review 73:391-400 Spr '84
Loewald, Uyen
Bond
Short story international 70
Cycle
Short story international 53
Prosperity
Short story international 49
The **loft**. Skiles, D.
Lofts, Norah, 1904-1983
Debt of gratitude
Lofts, N. Saving face, and other stories
Gateway to happiness?
Lofts, N. Saving face, and other stories
God's own elect
Lofts, N. Saving face, and other stories
The horse-leech hath two daughters
Lofts, N. Saving face, and other stories
A late flowering
Lofts, N. Saving face, and other stories
Lord, who is my neighbour?
Lofts, N. Saving face, and other stories
The natives are friendly
Lofts, N. Saving face, and other stories
Now you have me
Lofts, N. Saving face, and other stories
Saving face
Lofts, N. Saving face, and other stories
Lofty. Beattie, A.
The **log**. Maupassant, G. de
The **log** cabin overgrown with creepers. Gu Hua
Logarithms. Singer, I. B.
Logger Linkhorn's 1928 Buick. Abbott, K.
LOGGERS
Abramov, F. Olesha's cabin
Fréchette, L. Tom Cariboo
MacLean, N. Logging and pimping and "your pal, Jim"

Olmstead, R. Cody's story
Pascoe, B. Splitter
Logging and pimping and "your pal, Jim". MacLean, N.
LOGIC
Lutz, J. Dead man
Russell, E. F. Diabologic
A **logic** named Joe. Leinster, M.
Logopandocy. Gray, A.
Logue, Mary
Boundary waters
Stiller's pond; ed. by J. Agee; R. Blakely and S. Welch
Lohengrin's death. Böll, H.
A **loint** of paw. Asimov, I.
Loizeaux, William
Beside the Passaic
A Good deal; ed. by M. Heath and F. M. Robinson
The Massachusetts Review 28:50-70 Spr '87
"Lola". Colette
Lola. Sandel, C.
Lola's return. Monreal, D. N.
Lollipop and the tar baby. Varley, J.
Lombreglia, Ralph
Inn Essence
The Atlantic 260:46-51+ Jl '87
The Best American short stories, 1988
Men under water
The Atlantic 257:53-6+ Ja '86
The Best American short stories, 1987
London, Jack, 1876-1916
All Gold Canyon [Variant title: All Gold Cañon]
London, J. Young wolf: the early adventure stories of Jack London
At the rainbow's end
London, J. Young wolf: the early adventure stories of Jack London
Brown Wolf
London, J. Young wolf: the early adventure stories of Jack London
Chun Ah Chun
London, J. Jack London's Tales of Hawaii
A daughter of the aurora
London, J. Young wolf: the early adventure stories of Jack London
Diable: a dog [Variant title: The devil dog]
London, J. Young wolf: the early adventure stories of Jack London
For the love of a man
London, J. Young wolf: the early adventure stories of Jack London
Roger Caras' Treasury of great dog stories
The Ghost loses her seal-hunting boats
Men at sea; ed. by B. Aymar
Good-by, Jack
London, J. Jack London's Tales of Hawaii

London, Jack, 1876-1916—*Continued*

The house of pride
    London, J. Jack London's Tales of Hawaii

A hyperborean brew [excerpt]
    Inspired by drink; ed. by Joan Digby and John Digby

Koolau the leper
    London, J. Jack London's Tales of Hawaii

The law of life
    London, J. Young wolf: the early adventure stories of Jack London

The Leopard Man's story
    The Deadly arts; ed. by B. Pronzini and M. Muller

Love of life
    London, J. Young wolf: the early adventure stories of Jack London

Make westing
    Mysterious sea stories; ed. by W. Pattrick
    Sea captains' tales; ed. by A. Enfield
    Short stories of the sea; ed. by G. C. Solley and E. Steinbaugh

Moon-face
    Masterpieces of terror and the supernatural; ed. by M. Kaye and S. Kaye

Nam-Bok, the unveracious
    London, J. Young wolf: the early adventure stories of Jack London

Negore, the Coward
    London, J. Young wolf: the early adventure stories of Jack London

The one thousand dozen
    London, J. Young wolf: the early adventure stories of Jack London

The sheriff of Kona
    London, J. Jack London's Tales of Hawaii

The sickness of Lone Chief
    London, J. Young wolf: the early adventure stories of Jack London

The Sun-Dog Trail
    London, J. Young wolf: the early adventure stories of Jack London

That Spot
    Roger Caras' Treasury of great dog stories

To build a fire
    The Norton book of American short stories

To the man on the trail
    London, J. Young wolf: the early adventure stories of Jack London

Which make men remember
    London, J. Young wolf: the early adventure stories of Jack London

The white silence
    London, J. Young wolf: the early adventure stories of Jack London

London, Joan, 1948-

Burning off
    London, J. Sister ships, and other stories

Enough rope
    London, J. Sister ships, and other stories

First night
    London, J. Sister ships, and other stories

The girls love each other
    London, J. Sister ships, and other stories

Lilies
    London, J. Sister ships, and other stories

New Year
    London, J. Sister ships, and other stories

Sister ships
    London, J. Sister ships, and other stories

Travelling
    London, J. Sister ships, and other stories

LONDON (ENGLAND) *See* England—London

LONDON BRIDGE (LAKE HAVASU CITY, ARIZ.)

Nolan, W. F. The final stone

The **lone** pilgrim. Colwin, L.

A **lone** woman. Tamer, Z.

LONELINESS

Abbott, K. Like you used to do
Barnard, M. The persimmon tree
Bird, C. Woodpecker Point
Bukoski, A. Harry and the dancer
Burns, M. Greta
Burt, S. Fellow passengers
Burt, S. The single tractor track
Campion, E. Good morning wardrobe
Carver, R. Why don't you dance?
Cinca, S. The voice
Colette. Clouk alone
Colter, C. The beach umbrella
Colter, C. Rapport
Conrad, J. An outpost of progress
Cook, H. Cracked wheat
Cooper, J. C. Down that lonesome road
Curtiss, U. R. Good neighbor
Davis, L. Five signs of disturbance
Drake, R. Sisters
Ellison, H. Count the clock that tells the time
Fleming, B. Beach party
Flynn, R. Pictures
Garfield, B. Scrimshaw
Gilchrist, E. The young man
Gilliatt, P. The nuisance
Grau, S. A. The beginning
Grenville, K. Dropping dance
Gustafsson, L. Out of the pain
Hagy, A. C. No kind of name
Hall, D. The smell in Bertha's house
Hauptman, W. Kozmic Blues
Highsmith, P. Not in this life, maybe the next
Hood, M. Lonesome road blues
Kawabata, Y. The rainy station
Keeling, N. Mine
Kim, S.-O. Seoul: winter 1964

LONELINESS—Continued

Leedom-Ackerman, J. The impostor
Lish, G. I'm wide
Listfield, E. Porcupines and other travesties
MacIntyre, F. G. The prisoner of gravity
MacLaverty, B. Remote
Malamud, B. The model
Moravia, A. The devil comes and goes
Nolan, W. F. Trust not a man
Norris, H. The Christmas wife
Norris, H. The love child
Oates, J. C. Desire
O'Brien, E. Christmas roses
O'Hara, J. The friends of Miss Julia
O'Hara, J. The pretty daughters
Pak, Y.-J. The last parting
Parise, G. Simplicity
Pirandello, L. The lonely man
Rasputin, V. G. Mum's gone out somewhere
Rifaat, A. Telephone call
Ross, V. An understated look
Rubin, L. D. The St. Anthony Chorale
Ruffolo, L. You'll lose them before Thanksgiving
Schulman, H. To die from
Schwartz, L. S. Mrs. Saunders writes to the world
Schwartz, L. S. Plaisir d'amour
Shaw, J. B. Saturday night in Pinedale, Wyoming
Silvis, R. Murphy
Spivack, K. The hat
Stafford, J. Children are bored on Sunday
Swados, H. A question of loneliness
Thompson, J. Yarn
Verma, N. A splinter of the sun
Vogan, S. The crane wife
Welch, D. Constance, Lady Willet
Wexler, J. Women who live in small rooms
Wolfe, T. The anatomy of loneliness
Wolfe, T. No door
Wolff, T. Sister
Yamamoto, M. Chair in the rain
The **lonely** Hampshire cottage. Doyle, Sir A. C.
The **lonely** man. Pirandello, L.
Lonesome. Abrahams, P.
The **lonesome** road. Henry, O.
Lonesome road blues. Hood, M.
The **lonesomes** ain't no spring picnic. Miller, B.

Long, David, 1948-

Alex's fire
Long, D. The flood of '64
Clearance
The Graywolf annual 4
Long, D. The flood of '64
Compensation
Long, D. The flood of '64
Cooper Loftus
Long, D. The flood of '64

The Sewanee Review 93:354-71 Summ '85
The flood of '64
Long, D. The flood of '64
Great blue
Long, D. The flood of '64
Home fires
The Best of the West; ed. by J. Thomas
Prime number; ed. by A. L. Weir
Writers of the purple sage; ed. by R. Martin and M. Barasch
The last photograph of Lyle Pettibone
Long, D. The flood of '64
New American short stories; ed. by G. Norris
The Oriental Limited
Long, D. The flood of '64
Solstice
Long, D. The flood of '64
V-E Day
Long, D. The flood of '64

Long, Frank Belknap, 1903-

Lover in the wildwood
Halloween horrors; ed. by A. Ryan
The Mississippi saucer
Young extraterrestrials; ed. by I. Asimov; M. H. Greenberg and C. G. Waugh
The **long** bow. Chesterton, G. K.
The **long** chance. Shannon, D.
A **long** day in the town. McCormack, E. P.
Long distance. Smiley, J.
The **long** distant lecture. Jolley, E.
Long division. Bradbury, R.
The **long** donut hole. Franzen, B.
The **long** dress. Pirandello, L.
A **long** fourth. Taylor, P. H.
A **long** freeze. Minot, S.

LONG ISLAND (N.Y.)

Pierce, C. A summer afternoon
Rose, D. A. The good-bye present
The **long** journey. Grin, A.
Long knives. Dunn, J. R.
A **long**, long time. Banks, C.
A **long** mile. Pavel, O.
The **long** night. Bradbury, R.
A **long** night at Abu Simbel. Lively, P.
The **long** night of waiting. Norton, A.
The **long** night of winter. Rifaat, A.
Long pants day at last. Heise, K.
Long Pine. Deaver, P. F.
The **long** rain. Kincaid, J.
The **long** reconciliation. Viramontes, H. M.
Long shot. Vinge, V.
Long story short. Boyd, W.
A **long** time ago. Clark, M.
A **long** time coming, a long time gone. Durban, P.
A **long** time dying. Nolan, W. F.
A **long** wail. Crews, H.
The **long** way around. Handke, P.
A **long** way from home. O'Brien, E.
The **long** way home. Bradbury, R.
The **long** white. Dilworth, S.

The **longest** season. Modrack, B. A.
LONGEVITY
> *See also* Aging; Rejuvenation

Cox, A. J. Evergreen
Silverberg, R. Capricorn games
Silverberg, R. To be continued
Swift, G. The watch
Longhouse. Kinsella, W. P.
Longing. Thompson, K.
Longing for America. Rubin, D.
A **longing** to live. Mazel, D.
Longrigg, Roger, 1929-
> The chair
>> The Mammoth book of modern crime stories; ed. by G. Hardinge

LONGSHORE WORKERS
Gorky, M. Chelkash
Mathers, P. Journey in
Miller, J. F. A lover of nature
Schulberg, B. Murder on the waterfront
LONGSHOREMEN *See* Longshore workers
Longtooth. Pangborn, E.
Longyear, Barry B.
> Adagio
>> Longyear, B. B. It came from Schenectady
>> *Omni (New York, N.Y.)* 6:64-6+ S '84
> Catch the sun
>> Longyear, B. B. It came from Schenectady
> Collector's item
>> Longyear, B. B. It came from Schenectady
> Dreams
>> Longyear, B. B. It came from Schenectady
> Enemy mine
>> Baker's dozen: 13 short science fiction novels
>> The Hugo winners v5
> The homecoming
>> Longyear, B. B. It came from Schenectady
> The house of if
>> Longyear, B. B. It came from Schenectady
> The initiation
>> Longyear, B. B. It came from Schenectady
> The portrait of Baron Negay
>> Longyear, B. B. It came from Schenectady
> SHAWNA, Ltd.
>> Longyear, B. B. It came from Schenectady
> A time for terror
>> Longyear, B. B. It came from Schenectady
> Twist ending
>> Longyear, B. B. It came from Schenectady

Where do you get your ideas?
> Longyear, B. B. It came from Schenectady

Lonnie's cousin. Coleman, W.
Looie follows me. MacDonald, J. D.
Look at Violet now! Dyer, S.
Look of love. Piñera, V.
Look toward tomorrow. Lambert, N.
The **lookalike.** Wilhelm, K.
Looking at water. Spivack, K.
Looking for kin. Hemley, R.
Looking for love. Kasarjian, J. V.
Looking for love. Troy, J.
Looking for love again. Tinsley, M. B.
Looking for Malibu. Drewe, R.
Looking for the Golden Gate. Wilson, B.
Looking for work. Murphy, P.
The **looking-glass** man. Kilworth, G.
Looking in windows. Sussman, E.
Looking like Virginia Woolf. McLaughlin, L.
Looking over Jordan. Gilchrist, E.
The **lookout.** Colter, C.
The **loons.** Laurence, M.
The **loophole.** Archer, J.
Looping the loop. Haley, R.
Loopy. Rendell, R.
Loos, Anita, 1894-1981
> Liquor makes you smart
>> The Norton book of American short stories

Loose connections. Claiborne, S.
Loose ends. Mukherjee, B.
Lopatin, Judy
> Budapest dangereux
>> Lopatin, J. Modern romances
> The death of Joe Dassin
>> Lopatin, J. Modern romances
> Dominica
>> Lopatin, J. Modern romances
> Etiology of the new war
>> Lopatin, J. Modern romances
> Fast and loose, a historical romance
>> Lopatin, J. Modern romances
> Krystal goes mystical
>> Lopatin, J. Modern romances
> Los Angeles
>> Lopatin, J. Modern romances
> Modern romances
>> Lopatin, J. Modern romances
> A murder history
>> Lopatin, J. Modern romances
> The mystery of Madame Kitten
>> Lopatin, J. Modern romances
> Nuit blanche
>> Lopatin, J. Modern romances
> Our perfect partners
>> Lopatin, J. Modern romances
> A phantasm, a bird—
>> Lopatin, J. Modern romances
> The real life of Viviane Romance
>> Lopatin, J. Modern romances
> Retrospective on Weegee
>> Lopatin, J. Modern romances

Lopatin, Judy—*Continued*
Trixie Taylor, hospital nurse
Lopatin, J. Modern romances
Visitation of the ghost
Lopatin, J. Modern romances
Lopez, Barry Holstun, 1945-
Winter count 1973: geese, they flew over
in a storm
The Interior country; ed. by A. Black-
burn
Lopez and the Maya bull. Brigham, B.
López Heredia, José
The retiree
Anthology of contemporary Latin Ameri-
can literature, 1960-1984
The **LoPresto** Traveling Magic Show. Lynch,
L.
Lord, Nancy
Marks
The Antioch Review 44:345-54 Summ '86
Waiting for the thaw
Ploughshares 14 no1:67-77 '88
The **Lord** and Morton Gruber. Stern, S.
Lord Brummel; or, How not to get noticed.
Campanile, A.
Lord Chugger of cheer. Saroyan, W.
Lord Mountdrago. Maugham, W. S.
The **lord** of Central Park. Davidson, A.
Lord of hosts. Willis, C.
Lord of silence. Brown, G. M.
Lord of the dance. Kilworth, G.
The **Lord** of the Dynamos. Wells, H. G.
Lord Short Shoe wants the monkey.
Shacochis, B.
Lord Sweatrag. Gallacher, T.
Lord, who is my neighbour? Lofts, N.
Lordan, Beth
Running out
The Atlantic 257:74-8 My '86
The widow
The Atlantic 260:63-7 Ag '87
LORD'S SUPPER
Greene, G. The hint of an explanation
Lore. Bauer, D.
Lorenzo's collection. Brownstein, M.
Lorenzo's return. Levi, P.
Lorimer, Graeme, and Lorimer, Sarah
Navy blues
Ladies' Home Journal 101:169-72 Ja '84
LOS ANGELES (CALIF.) *See* California—
Los Angeles
Los Angeles. Lopatin, J.
LOS GATOS (CALIF.) *See* California—Los
Gatos
The **loser.** MacDuff, L.
The **losers.** Gee, M.
Losers pay. Meinke, P.
Loshikl. Singer, I. B.
Losing color. Stern, R. G.
Losing game. Swan, G.
Losing things. Lurie, M.
Losing your cool. Morris, M.
Loss. King, F. H.

Loss of breath. Poe, E. A.
Loss of face. Byatt, A. S.
Losses. Burke, J. L.
Lost. Gault, C.
Lost. Martone, M.
Lost!. Maupassant, G. de
Lost American. Stead, C.
Lost and found. McInerney, J.
Lost and found. Nowaira, A.
Lost and found. Richie, K. M.
Lost and found. Willis, C.
The **lost** blend. Henry, O.
The **lost** boy. Brown, G. M.
The **lost** boy. Wolfe, T.
LOST CHILDREN
Heise, K. The little boy who was left
behind
Hoyt, M. S. Buffalo, sun and strawberries
Martone, M. Lost
Stifter, A. Rock crystal
The **lost** chord. Hall, R. W.
The **lost** cottage. Leavitt, D.
The **lost** D.O. Clarke, T.
Lost Dorsai. Dickson, G. R.
The **lost** explorer. McGrath, P.
Lost generation. Davis, D. S.
The **lost** ghost. Freeman, M. E. W.
A **lost** grave. Malamud, B.
Lost hearts. James, M. R.
Lost in space. Boylan, J.
The **lost** inheritance. Wells, H. G.
The **lost** key. Rey Rosa, R.
The **lost** language. Keller, D. H.
Lost leader. Gilbert, M.
The **lost** letter. Gogol', N. V.
Lost lives. Hoffman, N. K.
The **lost** machine. Wyndham, J.
The **lost** mine. Christie, A.
The **lost** mine of Fisherman's Peak. Austin,
M. H.
The **lost** mistress. Gilchrist, M.
Lost on dress parade. Henry, O.
The **lost** room. O'Brien, F.-J.
The **lost** salt gift of blood. MacLeod, A.
The **lost** sheep. Givner, J.
Lost sister. Johnson, D. M.
The **lost** skipper. Runciman, J.
Lost sons. Salter, J.
Lost soul. Sheckley, J.
Lost souls. Barker, C.
The **lost**, strayed, stolen. Fisher, M. F. K.
Lost time. Armitage, R.
Lost time accident. Whittier, G. B.
Lost valley of the gods. Winters, J.
The **lost** world: signs of life. Colless, T., and
Kelly, D.
LOT (BIBLICAL FIGURE)
About
Givner, J. The testament of Leyla
Lot. Moore, W.
A **lot** in common. Geng, V.
Lot no. 17. Finney, E. J.
Lot no 249. Doyle, Sir A. C.

A **lot** on his mind. Pronzini, B.
A **lot** you got to holler. Algren, N.
Lots. Rosofsky, I.
Lots of luck, kid! Okudzhava, B. S.
Lott, Bret
  Open house
    The Yale Review 73:561-7 Summ '84
  Sleeping through
    Michigan Quarterly Review 26:317-23 Spr
    '87
  This plumber
    20 under 30; ed. by D. Spark
Lott, James
  The center
    The Southern Review (Baton Rouge, La.)
    20:720-30 Jl '84
  The Janeites
    Prize stories, 1987
    The Virginia Quarterly Review 62:437-49
    Summ '86
LOTTERIES
  Apollinaire, G. The departure of the
    shadow
  Auswaks, A. Mrs. Halprin and the lottery
  Böll, H. Black sheep
  Borges, J. L. The lottery in Babylon
  Brigham, B. The lottery drawing
  Clark, M. H. Lucky day
  Franzen, B. After I won the lottery
  Hoch, E. D. The theft of nothing at all
  Jackson, S. The lottery
  Kinsella, W. P. The truck
  Mathers, P. The Henshaws
  Morrison, J. It opens your eyes
  Oates, J. C. Surf City
The **lottery**. Jackson, S.
The **lottery** drawing. Brigham, B.
The **lottery** in Babylon. Borges, J. L.
The **Lotus**. Rhys, J.
LOUD-SPEAKERS *See* Loudspeakers
The **loudest** voice. Paley, G.
LOUDSPEAKERS
  West, J. Public-address system
Louie, David Wong
  Displacement
    Ploughshares 14 no2/3:77-91 '88
Louisa. Freeman, M. E. W.
LOUISIANA
  Goyen, W. Arthur Bond
  King, G. E. The story of a day
  McGrath, P. Marmilion
            19th century
  Cable, G. W. Belles Demoiselles plantation
  King, G. E. Bayou l'Ombre: an incident
    of the war
            20th century
  Benedict, P. Fat Tuesday
  Burke, J. L. The convict
  Burke, J. L. The pilot
  Holmes, C. Metropolitan
  Kincaid, N. Like the old wolf in all those
    wolf stories
  Shaik, F. Before echo

  Wilcox, J. North Gladiola [excerpt]
            New Orleans
  Adcock, T. L. Thrown-away child
  Boeckman, C. You can get away with
    murder
  Dew, R. F. Two girls wearing perfume in
    the summer
  Ellison, H. On the downhill side
  Franklin, P. The uncertainty of strangers
  Gifkins, M. Metamorphosis
  Gilchrist, E. Looking over Jordan
  Gilchrist, E. There's a Garden of Eden
  Gilchrist, E. Traceleen's diary
  Henry, O. The renaissance at Charleroi
  Howard, C. Horn man
  Pynchon, T. The small rain
  Shaik, F. The mayor of New Orleans; just
    talking jazz
  Toole, J. K. A confederacy of dunces [ex-
    cerpt]
  Welty, E. No place for you, my love
  Williams, T. The angel in the alcove
  Williams, T. The coming of something to
    Widow Holly
  Williams, T. In memory of an aristocrat
  Woolrich, C. Dark melody of madness
Louisiana shade. Anderson, K. E.
Loukakis, Angelo, 1951-
  Being here now
    Loukakis, A. Vernacular dreams
  Billy and the birds
    Loukakis, A. Vernacular dreams
  The cheerfulness of the bush
    Loukakis, A. Vernacular dreams
  Hooray for Haralambos
    Loukakis, A. Vernacular dreams
  I told mama not to come
    Loukakis, A. Vernacular dreams
  Islands
    Home and away; ed. by R. Creswell
    Loukakis, A. Vernacular dreams
  The jigsaw puzzle
    Loukakis, A. Vernacular dreams
  My neighbour's death
    Loukakis, A. Vernacular dreams
  Only in the truth
    Loukakis, A. Vernacular dreams
  Our own business
    Loukakis, A. Vernacular dreams
  Partying on parquet
    Loukakis, A. Vernacular dreams
    Transgressions; ed. by D. Anderson
  Perfect holiday sounds
    Loukakis, A. Vernacular dreams
  Single lens reflex
    Loukakis, A. Vernacular dreams
  This wizened creature
    Loukakis, A. Vernacular dreams
  To Mrs. Starkey
    Loukakis, A. Vernacular dreams
  Velodrome
    Loukakis, A. Vernacular dreams

Loulou; or, The domestic life of the language. Atwood, M.

Lou's corner. Burke, M.

Love, John M.
A cry for help
Redbook 168:70+ Ap '87

LOVE
See also Friendship
Austin, M. H. Bitterness of women
Austin, M. H. The Woman at the Eighteen-Mile
Baldwin, D. The shadow watchers
Bonner, M. One true love
Carver, R. What we talk about when we talk about love
Claiborne, S. Historic moments: the discovery of love
Cooper, J. C. At long last
Cooper, J. C. Red-winged blackbirds
Dixon, S. Reversal
Fitzgerald, M. J. Il bell'uomo
Friesner, E. M. Honeycomb
Gaskell, E. C. The three eras of Libbie Marsh
Girion, B. To Francie, with love
Henry, O. One thousand dollars
Jones, D. C. The last fastball
Jones, G. The snow apples
Kawabata, Y. The Wife of the Autumn Wind
Keillor, G. Hansel
Kosztolányi, D. The wondrous visitation of Krisztina Hrussz
Lee, L. Born and bred
Llywelyn, M. Me, tree
Malinowitz, H. Water skiing
Martin, G. R. R. In the lost lands
Mordden, E. The handshake deal
Oates, J. C. Secret
Pacheco, J. E. August afternoon
Phelps, E. S. Comrades
Roberts, N. The inversion
Rooke, L. A bolt of white cloth
Rossiter, S. Pandora
Saiki, P. S. Communion
Shiga, N. Akanishi Kakita
Shiga, N. The paper door
Sutherland, M. Codling-moth
Wilde, O. The fisherman and his soul
Williams, J. Taking care
Zhang Jie. Emerald
Zhang Jie. Love must not be forgotten

LOVE, PLATONIC
Leavitt, D. Dedicated
Maupassant, G. de. Châli
Thompson, S. Montauk

Love. Colette
Love. Lim, C.
Love. Lispector, C.
Love. Maupassant, G. de
Love. Paley, G.
Love. Rodoreda, M.
The **love** affair. Bradbury, R.

Love affair. Symons, J.

LOVE AFFAIRS
See also Courtship; Love stories; Lovers; Marriage problems
Abrahams, L. Invisible worm
Abrahams, L. The moment
Adams, A. Sintra
Aickman, R. The next glade
Aiken, J. Lodging for the night
al-Ujayli, A. al--S. Madness
Alden, P. B. The reunion
Alden, P. B. Two women
Algren, N. Please don't talk about me when I'm gone
Anderson, J. Outdoor friends
Apple, M. The eighth day
Apple, M. Eskimo love
Apple, M. Small island republics
Aquin, H. Back on April eleventh
Archer, J. The perfect murder
Ardizzone, T. The transplant
Astley, T. The scenery never changes
Atwood, M. The salt garden
Atwood, M. Spring song of the frogs
Auchincloss, L. The "fulfillment" of Grace Eliot
Austin, D. And now he was beginning to feel uneasy about the weather
Austin, M. H. The fakir
Balzac, H. de. La Grande Bretêche
Banks, R. Sarah Cole: a type of love story
Barnard, R. The woman in the wardrobe
Barrett, L. Out with the crowd
Barstow, S. Foreign parts
Barstow, S. Rue
Barthelme, D. Terminus
Barthelme, F. Cleo
Barthelme, S. Beach
Barthelme, S. Michael
Barthelme, S. Zach
Baxter, C. Gershwin's second prelude
Baxter, C. Harmony of the world
Baxter, C. The model
Baxter, C. Weights
Beattie, A. Janus
Beattie, A. Sunshine and shadow
Beattie, A. Weekend
Beckett, S. First love
Bedard, B. The fifth letter
Bedford, J. Campaign
Bellow, S. What kind of day did you have?
Berger, J. Play me something
Bird, C. The right stuff
Bitov, A. The forest
Bitov, A. The garden
Bitov, A. The third story
Blei, N. In the secret places of the stairs
Bloch, R. Nina
Block, L. The books always balance
Boeckman, C. You can get away with murder
Bonner, M. High-stepper

LOVE AFFAIRS—*Continued*

Bonner, M. Patch quilt
Bonner, M. A sealed pod
Bowles, P. Here to learn
Boyd, W. The care and attention of swimming pools
Boyd, W. The coup
Boylan, J. Bride of Frankenstein
Boyle, T. C. All shook up
Brady, M. Wilderness journal
Bridge, A. The Buick saloon
Brodkey, H. Innocence
Brondoli, M. Showdown
Broun, H. No smoking
Brown, A. The back way to Fantasyland
Brown, M. W. Disturber of the peace
Caldwell, E. Return to Lavinia
Calisher, H. The library
Camoin, F. A. A hunk of burning love
Campos-De Metro, J. Shooting for Jupiter
Carter, A. Black Venus
Carter, A. Flesh and the mirror
Carver, R. Menudo
Chand, M. The gift of Sunday
Chekhov, A. P. The duel
Ch'en, Y.-C. Night freight
Choyce, L. Family protection
Ciment, J. Money
Claiborne, S. Acid rain
Claiborne, S. The future of conglomerates
Clifford, F. Turn and turn about
Cohen, A. Hans Cassebeer and the virgin's rose
Cohen, M. Life on this planet
Colegate, I. The girl who had lived among artists
Coleman, W. Without visible means
Colette. The cure
Colette. A dead end
Colette. "Gitanette"
Colette. Morning glories
Colette. The other table
Colette. The return
Colette. The victim
Colter, C. Girl friend
Colwin, L. A country wedding
Colwin, L. Frank and Billy
Colwin, L. French movie
Colwin, L. A little something
Colwin, L. The lone pilgrim
Colwin, L. My mistress
Colwin, L. Old flames
Colwin, L. Swan song
Conroy, F. Roses
Cowan, P. The brown grass
Cowan, P. Seminar
Creswell, R. Epithalamium
Crowley, A. The king of the wood
Davie, E. In the train
Davie, E. The stamp
Davies, D. A quiet man
Davis, L. Break it down
Davis, L. A few things wrong with me

Davis, L. Mr. Burdoff's visit to Germany
Davis, L. Once a very stupid man
Davis, S. The hermit of Treasure Peaks
Deaver, P. F. Fiona's rooms
Deaver, P. F. Geneseo
Deaver, P. F. Marguerite Howe
Deaver, P. F. Why I shacked up with Martha
DeMarinis, R. Culture shocks
Dennison, G. The carbon paper poet
Dennison, G. The sufficiency of everyday life: Avenue A and Eleventh Street, 1963
Dinesen, I. The cloak
Disch, T. M. Concepts
Dixon, S. End of Magna
Dixon, S. For a man your age
Dixon, S. Meeting Aline
Dorr, L. At a certain angle
Dorr, L. Two hundred yards past Wordsworth's house
Doubiago, S. Vets
Dowell, C. The surgeon
Drewe, R. Baby oil
Drewe, R. Eighty per cent humidity
Driskell, L. V. Martha Jean
Dub, O. The rebel wolf and Petrina
Dubus, A. Miranda over the valley
Dullas, I. X marks the spot
Dundas, R. The uniform
Dunn, D. Ever let the fancy roam
Edwards, M. F. Roses
Eisenberg, D. Flotsam
Eisenberg, D. A lesson in traveling light
Eisenberg, D. Rafe's coat
Eisenberg, D. Transactions in a foreign currency
Eisenberg, D. What it was like, seeing Chris
Eisenreich, H. A farewell to love
Eisenreich, H. A friend of the family
Eisenstein, S. All the monkeys
Ekwensi, C. The ivory dancer
Eldridge, M. Wayside
Ellin, S. Mrs. Mouse
Ellison, H. Prince Myshkin, and hold the relish
Evans, E. Honey
Evans, E. Small acts
Faik, S. My father's second home
Fante, J. The wrath of God
Farmer, B. Maria's girl
Farmer, B. Saint Kay's day
Farmer, B. Snake
Farmer, B. Summer on ice
Ferreira, R. Facade
Finger, A. A tragedy
Fitzgerald, M. J. Creases
Fitzgerald, M. J. Falling sickness
Fitzgerald, M. J. Perspective on the first you
Flaherty, G. The man who wore sunlight
Flanagan, M. A view of Manhattan

LOVE AFFAIRS—*Continued*

Flanagan, R. Comedy of Eros
Fleming, B. The bookman's tale
Flores, C. N. Yellow flowers
Fraser, K. The emerald city
Fremlin, C. Dangerous sport
Friedman, B. J. Marching through Delaware
Frucht, A. Fate and the poet
Frucht, A. Winter
Gallagher, T. At mercy
Gallant, M. In the tunnel
García Márquez, G. Eyes of a blue dog
Gardner, C. S. Overnight guest
Garner, H. A thousand miles from the ocean
Garro, E. It's the fault of the Tlaxcaltecas
Gathorne-Hardy, J. The man who laughed
Gault, C. Albatross
Geras, A. The whole truth
Gifkins, M. The latter-day triumph of Graves
Gifkins, M. Natural histories
Gifkins, M. Playing for keeps
Gilchrist, E. Anna, Part 1
Gilchrist, E. Drunk with love
Gilchrist, E. First Manhattans
Gilchrist, E. Jade Buddhas, red bridges, fruits of love
Gilchrist, E. There's a Garden of Eden
Gilchrist, M. Roxana runs lunatick
Gilchrist, M. The writings of Althea Swarthmoor
Gilliatt, P. When are you going back?
Glasser, P. Mexico
Glover, D. H. The seeker, the snake and the baba
Gold, H. Annique
Gold, H. A dark Norwegian person
Gold, H. Paris and Cleveland are voyages
Gold, H. San Francisco petal
Gold, H. Stages
Gold, H. What's become of your creature?
Gold, H. Winter of '73
Goodman, I. White boy
Gordimer, N. City lovers
Gordimer, N. The life of the imagination
Gordimer, N. Town lovers
Gordon, M. The other woman
Gordon, M. Watching the tango
Grau, S. A. The way back
Greenberg, A. The conservation of matter
Greenberg, A. What would I know?
Grekova, I. One summer in the city
Grenville, K. Making tracks
Grubb, D. The horsehair trunk
Grumley, M. Life drawing
Gustafsson, L. The art of surviving November
Gustafsson, L. The fugitives discover that they knew nothing
Haake, K. Burning the lost country
Haake, K. The meaning of their names
Haake, K. A scrap of green silk

Haas, B. You'll remember me long after
Hagy, A. C. Nongqause
Haley, R. Search party
Hall, D. The world is a bed
Halligan, M. Down to earth
Harris, H. The foot
Hartley, L. P. Up the garden path
Hartley, L. P. A very present help
Hauptman, W. Pure sex
Havazelet, E. Glass
Havazelet, E. No word for mercy
Havemann, E. Tom and Beauty
Hemingway, E. The end of something
Hemingway, E. Summer people
Hemingway, E. A very short story
Henson, R. Billie loses her job
Highsmith, P. Blow it
Highsmith, P. The mobile bed-object
Highsmith, P. Something the cat dragged in
Highsmith, P. The stuff of madness
Hill, R. Crowded hour
Hillis, R. Eagle flies on Friday; greyhound runs at dawn
Hirota, Y. An invitation to a movie
Hoffman, W. Lover
Hospital, J. T. Here comes the sun
Houbein, L. Footprints of Maria
Hulme, K. A drift in dream
Hulme, K. A window drunken in the brain
Humphreys, J. Dreams of sleep [excerpt]
Hurst, F. Oats for the woman
Hurston, Z. N. Spunk
Ibargüengoitia, J. What became of pampa hash?
Jahnn, H. H. The slave's story
Janowitz, T. Spells
Johnson, D. The big sway
Jones, E. D. A man can try
Joyce, J. The boarding house
Kaikō, T. A certain voice
Kawabata, Y. One arm
Keeling, N. Berthilde's holiday
Keeling, N. Big Herb
Kelly, C. The waters of Vanuatu
Kessler, J. F. Courtly love
Kessler, J. F. Kassandra
Kessler, J. F. Medea
Kim, S.-O. Record of a journey to Mujin
King, F. H. Loss
Klass, P. The anatomy of the brain
Klass, P. In Africa
Klass, P. Not a good girl
Klíma, I. The tightrope walkers
Klíma, I. The truth game
Koenig, J. A perfect gentleman
Kranes, D. Cordials
Krysl, M. Macroscopic phenomena
Landolfi, T. The eternal province
Leebron, F. Cuisinart
Leitão, L. Jaffer's chicken
Liben, M. The intermediary
Lish, G. What is left to link us

LOVE AFFAIRS—*Continued*

Livesey, M. A small price
Lofts, N. A late flowering
Lofts, N. The natives are friendly
Lovesey, P. The secret lover
Lurie, M. Kelso's lady
Lurie, M. Rewards
Lynch, M. Latin lover
Mason, B. A. Residents and transients
Matsumoto, S. The secret alibi
Mattison, A. Bears
Mattison, A. Cake night
Mattison, A. New Haven
Maupassant, G. de. An adventure
Maupassant, G. de. Caught
Maupassant, G. de. A deer park in the provinces
Maupassant, G. de. False alarm
Maupassant, G. de. The farmer's wife
Maupassant, G. de. Lost!
Maupassant, G. de. The mountebanks
Maupassant, G. de. The new sensation
Maupassant, G. de. Room no. eleven
Maupassant, G. de. A rupture
Maupassant, G. de. The Venus of Braniza
McCormack, E. P. The fugue
McDonald, S. Falling
McGerr, P. In the clear
McGuane, T. Like a leaf
McGuane, T. Partners
McGuane, T. To skin a cat
McKnight, R. Peaches
McPherson, J. A. The story of a scar
Michaels, L. Crossbones
Michaelson, L. W. The burglar face
Michalson, G. The tail of his luck
Milton, B. The cigarette boat
Mitchell, K. The centre of gravity
Mooney, M. Hostages
Moore, G. An episode in married life
Moore, L. How to be an other woman
Moorhouse, F. Buenaventura Durruti's funeral
Morand, P. Borealis
Mordden, E. Beach blanket mah-jongg
Morgan, C. The hitmaker
Mori, Y. Be it ever so humble
Morris, M. Copies
Morris, M. The Hall of the Meteorites
Morris, M. Links
Morris, M. Losing your cool
Morris, M. Summer share
Mortimer, J. C. Rumpole and the sporting life
Mukherjee, B. Fighting for the rebound
Mukherjee, B. The lady from Lucknow
Mukherjee, B. Orbiting
Mukherjee, B. Saints
Munro, A. Bardon bus
Munro, A. Lichen
Munro, A. Prue
Nabokov, V. V. Spring in Fialta
Nagibin, ĪŪ. M. Needed urgently: gray human hair

Nagibin, ĪŪ. M. Olezhka got married
Nevai, L. Mr. Feathers
Nimmo, D. Wake and call me mother
Nooteboom, C. Mokusei: a love story
Nugent, B. Tough as a man
Oakes, P. You're in my story
Oates, J. C. Adultress
Oates, J. C. Ancient airs, voices
Oates, J. C. Anecdote
Oates, J. C. Double solitaire
Oates, J. C. The man whom women adored
Oates, J. C. Manslaughter
Oates, J. C. Old Budapest
Oates, J. C. Ruth
Oates, J. C. The seasons
Oates, J. C. Sentimental journey
Oates, J. C. Superstitious
O'Brien, D. Cowboy on the Concord bridge
O'Brien, E. Baby blue
O'Brien, E. The call
O'Brien, E. The love object
O'Brien, E. Mrs. Reinhardt
O'Brien, E. Over
O'Brien, E. Paradise
O'Brien, E. The plan
O'Brien, E. The return
O'Brien, E. A scandalous woman
O'Brien, E. Violets
Osborn, C. The accidental trip to Jamaica
Osborn, C. Other people's mail
Paley, G. The expensive moment
Paley, G. Listening
Pancake, B. D. Trilobits
Parise, G. Fascination
Parise, G. Youth
Pascoe, B. Cobber: The cat men of Genoa
Pascoe, B. Nautilus
Pascoe, B. Neither did I
Pavese, C. The cornfield
Pavese, C. The family
Pavese, C. Suicides
Penner, J. Emotion recollected in tranquillity
Peterson, L. S. The gift
Peterson, M. To dance
Petrakis, H. M. The ballad of Daphne and Apollo
Petrakis, H. M. End of winter
Petrakis, H. M. The last escapade
Pfeil, F. The fame of price
Phillips, J. A. How Mickey made it
Phillips, J. A. El Paso
Pierce, C. When things get back to normal
Pirandello, L. Into the sketch
Plomer, W. When the sardines came
Pointon, S. Framed
Poretz, D. Birthing
Potter, N. A. J. A thin place
Pritchett, M. People
Pronzini, B. Little lamb
Raines, H. The historical mistake

LOVE AFFAIRS—*Continued*
Raphael, F. Similar triangles
Raphael, F. Still life
Rhys, J. Vienne
Rifaat, A. Mansoura
Rizkalla, J. The servant of the last hour
Roberts, N. Fire Island
Robison, M. Adore her
Robison, M. For real
Rogers, T. N. R. Waterlilies
Rooke, L. The history of England, part four
Rooke, L. Lady Godiva's horse
Rooke, L. Narcissus consulted
Rose, D. A. How birds sleep
Ross, V. Hunters
Ross, V. Thanksgiving
Ross, V. That summer
Ruffolo, L. Leave of absence
Ruffolo, L. Words of love
Rule, J. A matter of numbers
Russell, R. The bell
Sagan, F. Partway round the course
Sagan, F. A question of timing
Sagan, F. Tears in the red wine
Sage, V. Destroying angel
Salas, G. Police report
Salter, J. The fields at dusk
Sanchez, T. Red Reno honkers
Sandberg, P. L. The rhyme of Lancelot
Sandel, C. The bracelet
Sandel, C. Klara
Sandel, C. The ways of love
Sanders, S. R. The recovery of vision
Schinto, J. Sounds of the rude world
Schlobin, R. C. For lovers only
Schwartz, L. S. Grand staircases
Schwartz, L. S. The infidel
Schwartz, L. S. The melting pot
Scott, R. Diary of a woman
Seepaul, L. A sleeping pill for the doctor
Shacochis, B. I ate her heart
Shamosh, A. Lily, Africa and I
Shaw, J. B. The cat who fought the rain
Shaw, J. B. The courtship of the thin girl
Sheil, G. Dogs, in Denpasar
Shiga, N. Kuniko
Shiga, N. A memory of Yamashina
Shivers, L. Here to get my baby out of jail [excerpt]
Silva, B. Bits & pieces
Silver, R. Fearful symmetry
Silverberg, R. The affair
Silverberg, R. The Science Fiction Hall of Fame
Silvis, R. The fatalist
Singer, I. B. Confused
Singer, I. B. The house friend
Singer, I. B. Miracles
Singer, I. B. Remnants
Singer, I. B. A telephone call on Yom Kippur
Singer, I. B. The trap
Skelton, R. The bride

Smiley, J. Jeffrey, believe me
Smiley, J. Long distance
Sorrells, R. T. When Etta Reece danced
Spark, M. The fortune-teller
Spark, M. A member of the family
Spencer, E. The skater
Spivack, K. Annoyances
Spivack, K. The sacrifice
Spofford, H. E. P. The amber gods
Steele, M. Another love story
Stockanes, A. E. Ladies who knit for a living
Strand, M. Zadar
Stýblová, V. Scalpel, please
Suckow, R. Susan and the doctor
Tabucchi, A. The backwards game
Tallent, E. Faux pas
Tallent, E. Listen to reason
Tallent, E. No one's a mystery
Tallent, E. Two ghosts of us
Taylor, C. The tribe
Taylor, D. J. Dreams of leaving
Taylor, R. Where are our M.I.A.'s?
Thomas, J. My journal as the fishwoman
Thomas, M. Mama Angelina's
Thompson, J. Robert's song
Thompson, J. Accidents
Thompson, J. A courtship
Thompson, J. Danny's chick
Thompson, J. Little Face
Thompson, J. Remembering Sonny
Thompson, J. Sex life of the sponge
Thompson, K. Night train through the snow to Montreal
Thompson, K. Promises
Thompson, S. Close-ups
Thompson, S. The Don
Thompson, S. Horror show
Thompson, S. L.A.
Thurm, M. California
Titcher, M. Someone-else
Tremain, R. Current account
Treviño, J. S. A very old man
Trevor, W. Cocktails at Doney's
Tripp, M. The casebook Casanova
Tsushima, Y. The chrysanthemum beetle
Updike, D. Bachelor of arts
Updike, D. Social studies
Updike, D. Spring
Updike, D. Winter
Updike, J. A constellation of events
Updike, J. More stately mansions
Valenzuela, L. Fourth version
Van de Wetering, J. A tasty tidbit
Vanderhaeghe, G. The watcher
Varlamova, I. A ladle for pure water
Verma, N. The man and the girl
Verma, N. Weekend
Vészi, E. Chapters from the life of Vera Angi
Vinge, J. D. Tam Lin
Vogan, S. China across the bay
Vogan, S. Hearts of a shark

LOVE AFFAIRS—*Continued*

Vreuls, D. Beebee
Warner, S. T. I met a lady
Watt, N. The mule driver and the carrot
Weinzweig, H. Causation
Wexler, J. World of women
Wharton, E. Souls belated
Whitaker, M. Strange music
Whitaker, M. Sultan Jekker
White, C. Metaphysics in the Midwest
Whittington, H. B. Swamp search
Wiater, S. Moist dreams
Wicomb, Z. Ash on my sleeve
Willett, J. The jaws of life
Williams, B. The lovers
Williams, T. Rubio y Morena
Windsor, G. The life of a man's man
Wolfe, T. April, late April
Wolfenstein, M. Chayah
Working, R. Pictures of her snake
Yourcenar, M. An obscure man
Zapolska, G. Virtue (a sketch for a novel)
Ziem, J. Clarifications
ZoBell, B. Avenida revolucion
Love and like. Gold, H.
Love and other lessons. Shaw, J. B.
Love and other lost causes. Ruffolo, L.
Love and politics in New York. Kriegel, L.
Love and potatoes. Ephron, N.
Love and the branch manager. Shimizu, I.
Love and tiddlywinks. Gardner, M.
The Love Chapter. Waters, M.
The love child. Norris, H.
Love comes to the middleman. Laidlaw, M.
Love day. Styron, W.
Love, death, and the ladies' drill team. West, J.
Love for lunch. Geras, A.
A love for the infinite. Cohen, M.
Love hurts. Boyd, W.
Love in reverse. Amichai, Y.
Love in vain. Shiner, L.
Love is a cold kingdom. Garrett, G. P.
Love is the crooked thing. Abbott, L. K.
Love is the plan the plan is death. Tiptree, J.
Love letter. Faik, S.
The love letter. Finney, J.
The love letter hack. Brondoli, M.
Love letters. Geras, A.
Love letters. Kriegel, M. H.
Love life. Mason, B. A.
Love must not be forgotten. Zhang Jie
The love object. O'Brien, E.
Love of animals. Valenzuela, L.
The love of Christ. Clark, M.
Love of life. London, J.
The love of long ago. Maupassant, G. de
Love problems. Haylock, J.
Love song. Cusack, I. L.
A love song for Christmas. Doig, D. T.
Love spells. Rice, L.
The love starter. Boylan, J.
Love-starved. Grant, C. L.

LOVE STORIES

See also Courtship; Love affairs; Lovers

Abbey, E. Black sun [excerpt]
Abbott, K. You can't miss it
Abbott, L. K. Be free, die young
Abbott, L. K. The eldest of things
Abbott, L. K. Living alone in Iota
Abbott, L. K. Love is the crooked thing
Abbott, L. K. When our dream world finds us, and these hard times are gone
Ade, G. Our private romance
Ahern, T. An implied acquaintance
Ahern, T. Monsters
Ahern, T. Unsophar and Onsopur
al-Shayib, F. East is east
Alberts, L. Veterans
Aldiss, B. W. The girl who sang
Aldiss, B. W. A romance of the equator
Amichai, Y. Love in reverse
Amichai, Y. The world is a room
Anderson, P. Rachaela
Anderson, P. The Saturn game
Antieau, K. Sanctuary
Apollinaire, G. The posthumous fiance
Apollinaire, G. Saint Adorata
Archer, J. Christina Rosenthal
Asimov, I. True love
Atherton, G. F. H. The conquest of Doña Jacoba
Atherton, G. F. H. The wash-tub mail
Atwood, M. Hair jewellery
Atwood, M. Hurricane Hazel
Atwood, M. Two stories about Emma: Walking on water
Austin, D. It's the same old story
Austin, M. H. The divorcing of Sina
Bail, M. A, B, C, D, E, F, G, H, I, J, K, L, M, N, O, P, Q, R, S, T, U, V, W, X, Y, Z
Ball, B. Heart leaves
Banks, R. Success story
Barich, B. Too much electricity
Barthelme, D. Great days
Barthelme, F. Reset
Barton, M. Jacob's angel
Bates, H. E. A month by the lake
Bates, H. E. Nina
Bates, H. E. A Silas idyll
Baumbach, J. The errant melancholy of twilight
Bausch, R. Wise men at their end
Baxter, C. Stained glass
Baxter, C. Winter journey
Beattie, A. Skeletons
Beattie, A. When can I see you again?
Bell, M. S. Monkey Park
Berger, J. The time of the cosmonauts
Berriault, G. The infinite passion of expectation
Bester, A. Galatea Galante
Bioy Casares, A. Venetian masks

LOVE STORIES—*Continued*

Bird, C. Buttercup and Wendy
Birtha, B. Pencil sketches for a story: the gray whelk shell
Bishop, M. The monkey's bride
Böll, H. He came as a beer-truck driver
Böll, H. My pal with the long hair
Böll, H. Parting
Böll, H. Rendezvous with Margret; or, Happy ending
Boswell, R. Dancing in the movies
Boswell, R. The darkness of love
Boswell, R. Flipflops
Bradbury, R. The Laurel and Hardy love affair
Bradbury, R. The love affair
Bradley, M. Z. Blood will tell
Brantingham, J. Giraffe Tuesday
Brězan, J. How Krabat lost Smjala
Brondoli, M. The love letter hack
Bunin, I. A. Sunstroke
Busch, F. Defense
Busch, F. The news
Cain, J. M. Cigarette girl
Cain, J. M. Pay-off girl
Calisher, H. Saratoga, hot
Calvino, I. The adventure of a photographer
Calvino, I. The adventure of a poet
Calvino, I. The adventure of a reader
Calvino, I. The adventure of a traveler
Cameron, E. The dark mirror
Cameron, P. Archeology
Cameron, P. The last possible moment
Cameron, P. Odd jobs
Camoin, F. A. It could happen
Campbell, W. B. The thaw
Campos-De Metro, J. And there was Bert
Canin, E. Lies
Canin, E. We are nighttime travelers
Cather, W. Coming, Aphrodite!
Chavez, A. A Romeo and Juliet story in early New Mexico
Chernoff, M. That summer
Chipulina, E. G. The catalyst
Choi, Y. H. Bloomington, Fall 1971
Chopin, K. The locket
Chua, R. The morning after
Clarke, T. A rite of passion
Clift, C. Three old men of Lerici
Colegate, I. A glimpse of Sion's glory
Colette. Clouk's fling
Colette. The pearls
Collier, J. Evening primrose
Cooper, J. C. Color me real
Cooper, J. C. Feeling for life
Cooper, J. C. The free and the caged
Cooper, J. C. Happiness does not come in colors
Cooper, J. C. When life begins!
Cowan, P. Escape
Cowan, P. Requiem
Cowan, P. Shadow

Curley, D. The first baseman
Curley, D. Living with snakes
Dadswell, M. Backtracking
Daniels, C. The legend of Wooley Swamp
Daniels, C. Trudy
Davie, E. A botanist's romance
Davis, L. Story
Davis, R. H. An ignoble martyr
Dazai, O. The garden lantern
De Haven, T. Clap hands! Here comes Charley
De Haven, T. He's all mine
De Haven, T. Where we'll never grow old
DeMarinis, R. Romance: a prose villanelle
Desaulniers, J. Age
DiFranco, A. M. The garden of redemption
Dinesen, I. The cloak
Dorr, L. A D-minor fugue
Dorr, L. A slight momentary affliction
Doubiago, S. Jonah
Doubiago, S. Ramon/Ramona
Doyle, Sir A. C. Bones. The April fool of Harvey's Sluice
Doyle, Sir A. C. The colonel's choice
Doyle, Sir A. C. The confession
Doyle, Sir A. C. The fate of the Evangeline
Doyle, Sir A. C. Gentlemanly Joe
Doyle, Sir A. C. Our Derby sweepstakes
Drewe, R. After Noumea
Dubus, A. Finding a girl in America
Dubus, A. Graduation
Dunn, M. If there be magic
Effinger, G. A. Babes on bawd way
Eichendorff, J., Freiherr von. Memoirs of a good-for-nothing
Eisenstein, P. In the Western tradition
Ekström, M. The king is threatened
Engberg, S. Pastorale
Engberg, S. Riffraff
Engel, M. Anita's dance
Evans, E. Relics
Everett, P. L. Still hunting
Everett, P. L. The weather and women treat me fair
Faik, S. Fear of loving
Faik, S. Love letter
Faik, S. A love story
Faik, S. Tomb with an arbor
Faik, S. Waiting for love
Fante, J. The dreamer
Fante, J. Helen, thy beauty is to me—
Farmer, B. Maria's girl
Federici, C. M. 'Oh, Lenore!' came the echo
Feeney, J. A married woman
Ferguson, W. The teacher
Ferrandino, J. Ten cents a dance
Ferreira, R. A color for that fear
Fink, I. Night of surrender
Fitzgerald, M. J. Glass
Fitzgerald, Z. Miss Ella

LOVE STORIES—*Continued*

Foltz-Gray, D. Departed coming back
Fox, R. A fable
Francis, H. E. A chronicle of love
Freeman, C. The ride
Freeman, M. E. W. Silence
Freeman, M. E. W. The twelfth guest
Friedman, B. J. Living together
Frucht, A. Nuns in love
Frucht, A. Peace and passivity
Frucht, A. Trees at night
Fuentes, C. Aura
Gaitskill, M. Daisy's Valentine
Gardner, M. Sibyl sits in
Gass, W. H. In the heart of the heart of the country
Gault, W. C. The cackle bladder
Geras, A. Alice
Geras, A. Don't sing love songs . . .
Geras, A. The green behind the glass
Geras, A. Love letters
Geras, A. Monday
Geras, A. Snapshots of paradise
Geras, A. Tea in the Wendy House
Gifkins, M. Summer is the Côte d'Azur
Gilbert, W. S. Angela
Gilbert, W. S. Diamonds
Gilbert, W. S. An elixir of love
Gilchrist, E. The starlight express
Gilchrist, M. The lost mistress
Gilchrist, M. The manuscript of Francis Shackerley
Gilchrist, M. The Noble Courtesan
Gilchrist, M. The stone dragon
Gildner, G. Sleepy time gal
Giles, M. How to quit smoking
Gilliatt, P. As is
Gilliatt, P. Teeth
Gingher, M. The hummingbird kimono
Girion, B. Another blue-eyed quarterback
Girion, B. The makeover of Meredith Kaplan
Girion, B. Trophy
Givner, J. First love
Glasser, P. Easily and well
Glavin, A. One for sorrow
Glover, D. H. Red
Godwin, G. St. George
Goethe, J. W. von. The attorney
Gordimer, N. Crimes of conscience
Gordon, M. The only son of the doctor
Granit, A. Tessie, don't give away the raisin; without it, you're lost!
Gray, P. W. Too soon solos
Grin, A. The oranges
Grin, A. The pillory
Grin, A. The snake
Grin, A. Voice and eye
Gunn, J. E. Donor
Gustafsson, L. A water story
Haas, B. The green life
Haas, B. On Mu
Haas, B. A wolf in the heart
Hagy, A. C. Madonna on her back

Hagy, A. C. No kind of name
Hagy, A. C. Where men go to cry
Haldeman, L. Bird of paradise
Hall, M. M. Rapture
Han, M.-S. Shadow
Hannah, B. Horning in--A
Hannah, B. I am shaking to death
Hannah, B. It spoke of exactly the things
Hansen, J. Willow's money
Haris, P. Of love and darkness
Harrison, S. F. The idyl of the island
Hartley, L. P. The pampas clump
Hartley, L. P. Simonetta Perkins
Hartley, L. P. The white wand
Havazelet, E. Jillie
Haylock, J. Love problems
Head, B. The lovers
Hebel, J. P. An unexpected reunion
Heinesen, W. Master Jakob and Miss Urd
Hempel, A. The most girl part of you
Henley, P. As luck would have it
Henry, O. An adjustment of nature
Henry, O. The buyer from Cactus City
Henry, O. The halberdier of the Little Rheinschloss
Henry, O. The higher pragmatism
Henry, O. Madame Bo-Peep, of the ranches
Henry, O. Nemesis and the candy man
Henry, O. The princess and the puma
Henry, O. The romance of a busy broker
Henry, O. Rus in urbe
Henry, O. The third ingredient
Highsmith, P. I am not as efficient as other people
Hoffman, W. Fathers and daughters
Hogg, J. The mysterious bride
Holz, C. Jack M.
Hood, M. Lonesome road blues
Hopes, D. B. Once in Syracuse
Hornung, E. W. The fate of Faustina
Hornung, E. W. Out of paradise
Horvitz, L. A. The fishing village of Roebush
Ioannides, P. The unseen aspect
Jackson, G. Pyjamas
Janowitz, T. The new acquaintances
Jordan, J. His own where
Just, W. S. The Costa Brava, 1959
Kang, S.-J. The young zelkova
Kauffman, J. At first it looks like nothing
Kauffman, J. The mechanics of good times
Kawabata, Y. Beyond death
Kawabata, Y. The blind man and the girl
Khuri, C. Sarab
King, G. E. The story of a day
Kipling, R. Lispeth
Klima, I. Tuesday morning: a sentimental story
Komie, L. B. Professor Strauss's gift
Kong Jiesheng. On the other side of the stream
Kotzwinkle, W. Fana

LOVE STORIES—*Continued*

Kotzwinkle, W. Tell her you love her with a ring from Dave's House of Diamonds

Kranes, D. The whorehouse picnic

Krist, G. Health

Krist, G. How I learned to raise the dead of Bergen County

Kundera, M. The hitchhiking game

Kunstler, J. H. The rise, fall, and redemption of Mooski Toffski Offski

La Motte-Fouqué, F. H. K., Freiherr von. Undine

La Puma, S. The boys of Bensonhurst

La Puma, S. Gravesend Bay

Landolfi, T. The gnat

Lawson, H. Joe Wilson's courtship

Le Guin, U. K. Ile Forest

Leach, A. R. A captain out of Etruria

Lee, T. Medra

Lee, W. M. A message from Charity

Lem, S. The mask

Liben, M. The garden

Lim, C. Love

Liphshitz, A. The last stage

Lipman, E. Good news

Lipman, E. They'll smile at you if you're with me

Livesey, M. A story to be illustrated by Max Ernst

Long, D. Compensation

Long, D. V-E Day

Lopatin, J. Fast and loose, a historical romance

Lopatin, J. Modern romances

Loukakis, A. Our own business

Lurie, M. The muted love song of Edvard Nils

Lynn, E. A. At the Embassy Club

Markham, B. Appointment in Khartoum

Markham, B. Your heart will tell you

Martone, M. A short, short story complete on these two pages

Maupassant, G. de. Happiness

Maupassant, G. de. Letter found on a corpse

Maupassant, G. de. Margot's tapers

Maupassant, G. de. Moonlight

Maupassant, G. de. The sequel to a divorce

Maupassant, G. de. Under the yoke

Maupassant, G. de. Virtue in the ballet

Mayer, R. The system

Mayhar, A. Neither rest nor refuge

McCullers, C. Instant of the hour after

McElroy, C. J. Exercises

McEwan, I. First love, last rites

McKinley, R. The stone fey

McMurtry, L. Texasville [excerpt]

Metzger, D. The tree on the mountain

Miller, J. J. Ouroboros

Mohr, N. Happy birthday (Lucia)

Moore, C. L. The bright illusion

Moore, G. At the turn of the road

Moore, G. Dried fruit

Moore, G. An episode in bachelor life

Moore, L. Amahl and the Night Visitors: a guide to the tenor of love

Moore, L. How

Moore, M. J. Summer sand

Morand, P. The Roman night

Moravia, A. My daughter is called Giulia too

Moravia, A. That damned gun

Morris, W. The lover and the beloved

Mphahlele, E. The coffee-cart girl

Mrożek, S. A forester in love

Mrożek, S. I'm subtle

Mukherjee, B. Angela

Nagibin, IŪ. M. By a quiet lake

Nestor, T. Once upon a dream

Nestor, T. G. Byway of the rose

Neugeboren, J. Uncle Nathan

Nolan, W. F. Of time and Kathy Benedict

Norris, H. The light on the water

Norris, H. Money man

Norris, H. Mrs. Moonlight

Oates, J. C. Détente

Oba, M. The Pale Fox

O'Brien, E. Courtship

O'Faolain, J. Her trademark

O'Kelly, S. Michael and Mary

Opatoshu, J. Romance of a horse thief

Osborn, C. Man Dancing

Overholser, W. D. Winchester wedding

Overholser, W. D. The wooing of Rosy Malone

Painter, P. A man of his time

Paolucci, A. The oracle is dumb or cheat

Parise, G. Patience, spring

Parise, G. Poise

Pascoe, B. Cicadas

Pavese, C. The idol

Pavese, C. Loyalty

Pearlman, E. Conveniences

Pei, L. The cold room

Petchsingh, T. The third encounter

Peterson, M. Coming about

Petrakis, H. M. Chrisoula

Petrakis, H. M. The eyes of love

Petrakis, H. M. The song of Rhodanthe

Phillips, E. O. Stephanotis

Pindar, S. Aunt Mable's love story

Piñón, N. Bird of paradise

Pirandello, L. An idea

Pirandello, L. The trip

Poverman, C. E. Beautiful

Prichard, K. S. Painted finches

Pritchett, V. S. The Camberwell beauty

Proulx, M. Feint of heart

Purdy, J. In this corner . . .

Rand, P. Circe

Raphael, F. Private views

Rasulov, M.-R. The eve of love

Reed, R. Treading in the afterglow

Roberts, K. The Lady Margaret

Robison, J. Time alone

LOVE STORIES—*Continued*

Rodoreda, M. Memory of Caux
Rodoreda, M. Rain
Rodoreda, M. That wall, that mimosa
Roscoe, P. Never tears for California
Rosenfeld, I. The hand that fed me
Roshchin, M. The ever-blossoming garden
Rossi, A. Breakfast, lunch, and dinner
Rostopchina, E. P., grafinīā. Rank and
     money
Roth, H. H. This time
Roth, J. Fallmerayer the stationmaster
Rubin, L. D. The St. Anthony Chorale
Sargent, P. If ever I should leave you
Schwartz, J. Chloe Hummel of the Chicago
     White Sox
Schwartz, S. In Alaska
Schwebel, B. A gift for Lucrecia
Seabrook, W. B. The witch's vengeance
Seghers, A. The reed
Shacochis, B. The heart's advantage
Shaw, J. B. Love and other lessons
Sheckley, R. Can you feel anything when
     I do this?
Shukshin, V. M. The sufferings of young
     Vaganov
Sillitoe, L. Four walls and an empty door
Silva, B. Hell's playground
Silverberg, R. Needle in a timestack
Singer, I. B. Burial at sea
Singer, I. B. Dazzled
Singer, I. B. The last gaze
Singer, I. B. Strong as death is love
Spencer, E. The cousins
Spencer, E. Jean-Pierre
Spivack, K. Sleep
Sproat, R. The fascination of the vanity
Stark, S. S. Heart of the Dutch country
Stead, C. A harmless affair
Stewart, J. I. M. André
Stockton, F. The great staircase at Land-
     over Hall
Stone, K. Summer of a stick man
Strand, M. True loves
Stuart, J. The slipover sweater
Sturgeon, T. The silken-swift . . .
Sturgeon, T. The touch of your hand
Swan, A. Monsoon
Swift, G. The tunnel
Tallent, E. Why I love country music
Tamer, Z. City in ashes
Taylor, R. The fiddler
Thériault, Y. The whale
Theroux, P. An unofficial rose
Thomas, A. C. Breaking the ice
Thomas, A. C. Relics
Thomas, J. Santorini gray
Thomas, J. Sparkle in five
Thomas, M. Abdullah and Mariam
Tiptree, J. Love is the plan the plan is death
Tremain, R. La plume de mon amı
Trevor, W. The property of Colette Nervi
Trevor, W. The wedding in the garden

Updike, D. Summer
Valenzuela, L. I'm your horse in the night
Valenzuela, L. Rituals of rejection
Valenzuela, L. The word "killer"
Valgardson, W. D. Bloodflowers
Vardeman, R. E. The Road of Dreams
     and death
Vaughan, M. C. Fruits of sorrow; or, An
     old maid's story
Vines, H. The ginsing gatherers
Vizyēnos, G. M. The consequences of the
     old story
Vreuls, D. Stoke Sobel in Polk
Walpole, H. A true love story
Walsh, T. Girl in danger
Walters, A. L. The resurrection of John
     Stink
Warren, J. Ready money
Welch, D. Anna Dillon
Welch, D. The fire in the wood
Weldon, F. Au pair
Wells, H. G. In the modern vein: an
     unsympathetic love story
Wexler, J. Simon goes to London
Wharton, E. The touchstone
Whitaker, M. Accident
Whitaker, M. The apprentice
Whitaker, M. Frost in April
Whitaker, M. Hannah
Whitaker, M. Spring day at Slater's End
Wicomb, Z. Behind the Bougainvillea
Wicomb, Z. You can't get lost in Cape
     Town
Wiggins, M. Herself in love
Wilbur, E. Perfection
Wilhelm, K. The girl who fell into the sky
Willard, N. Theo's girl
Williams, J. The debt
Williams, J. The wedding
Williams, T. The interval
Williams, T. Something about him
Williams, T. Two on a party
Willis, C. Blued moon
Wodehouse, P. G. Comrade Bingo
Wodehouse, P. G. The go-getter
Wodehouse, P. G. Open house
Wolff, T. Our story begins
Woolrich, C. If the dead could talk
Woolrich, C. Jane Brown's body
Woolson, C. F. At the château of Corinne
Woolson, C. F. Felipa
Woolson, C. F. The street of the Hyacinth
Wyatt, M. Sincerely yours
Yoshiyuki, J. Are the trees green?
Yourcenar, M. Aphrodissia, the widow
Yourcenar, M. The last love of Prince
     Genji
Yourcenar, M. The man who loved the
     Nereids
Zahn, T. The giftie gie us
Zhang Jie. An unfinished record
Zhang Jie. Who knows how to live?

LOVE STORIES—*Continued*

Zhang Kangkang, and Mei Jin. The tolling of a distant bell

Ziem, J. The classy woman

Love stories. O'Donnell, B.

A **love** story. Barrett, W. E.

A **love** story. Faik, S.

Love story. Reed, K.

Love suicides. Kawabata, Y.

The **love** that purifies. Wodehouse, P. G.

Love the ones you're with. Smith, L.

Love to Patsy. Tuohy, F.

Love under glass. Franklin, P.

Love, your only mother. Kaplan, D. M.

Lovecraft, H. P. (Howard Phillips), 1890-1937

The call of Cthulhu

The Dark descent; ed. by D. G. Hartwell

Lovecraft, H. P. The Dunwich horror, and others

The colour out of space [Variant title: Monster of terror]

Lovecraft, H. P. The Dunwich horror, and others

Cool air

Lovecraft, H. P. The Dunwich horror, and others

Rod Serling's Night gallery reader

The Dunwich horror

Lovecraft, H. P. The Dunwich horror, and others

The haunter of the dark

Lovecraft, H. P. The Dunwich horror, and others

The hound

Devils & demons; ed. by M. Kaye and S. Kaye

In the vault

Lovecraft, H. P. The Dunwich horror, and others

The music of Erich Zann

Lovecraft, H. P. The Dunwich horror, and others

Masterpieces of terror and the supernatural; ed. by M. Kaye and S. Kaye

The outsider

Lovecraft, H. P. The Dunwich horror, and others

Pickman's model

Lovecraft, H. P. The Dunwich horror, and others

Rod Serling's Night gallery reader

The picture in the house

Lovecraft, H. P. The Dunwich horror, and others

The rats in the walls

The Dark descent; ed. by D. G. Hartwell

Lovecraft, H. P. The Dunwich horror, and others

The shadow out of time

Dark company; ed. by L. Child

Lovecraft, H. P. The Dunwich horror, and others

The Mammoth book of classic science fiction; ed. by I. Asimov; C. G. Waugh and M. H. Greenberg

The shadow over Innsmouth

Lovecraft, H. P. The Dunwich horror, and others

The shunned house

Haunted New England; ed. by C. G. Waugh; M. H. Greenberg and F. D. McSherry

The statement of Randolph Carter

Charles Keeping's Classic tales of the macabre

The Terrible Old Man

Lovecraft, H. P. The Dunwich horror, and others

The thing on the doorstep

Lovecraft, H. P. The Dunwich horror, and others

Yankee witches; ed. by C. G. Waugh; M. H. Greenberg and F. D. McSherry

The whisperer in darkness

Lovecraft, H. P. The Dunwich horror, and others

About

Klein, T. E. D. Black man with a horn

Lovecraft, Howard Phillips *See* Lovecraft, H. P. (Howard Phillips), 1890-1937

The **loved** one. Wolfert, A.

Loved to death. Cooper, J. C.

Lovelorn in the U.S.A. Morris, M.

The **lovely** and talented Maxine Kane. Ryan, A.

A **lovely** day. Winston, C.

A **lovely** day to die. Fremlin, C.

The **lovely** house. Jackson, S.

A **lovely** morning. Yourcenar, M.

A **lovely** morning to die. See Fremlin, C. A lovely day to die

The **lovely** troubled daughters of our old crowd. Updike, J.

Loveman's comeback. Campbell, R.

Lover, Samuel, 1797-1868

Ye marvelous legend of Tom Connor's cat

Roger Caras' Treasury of great cat stories

The **lover.** Garber, E. K.

Lover. Hoffman, W.

The **lover** and the beloved. Morris, W.

The **lover** and the tell-tale. Crane, S.

Lover in the wildwood. Long, F. B.

The **lover** of horses. Gallagher, T.

A **lover** of nature. Miller, J. F.

The **lover** of women. Miller, S.

LOVERS

Abbott, K. A 1957 Ford

Aquino, J. We've been invited to a party

Benedict, P. Getting over Arnette

Birtha, B. Her ex-lover

LOVERS—*Continued*
Böll, H. The embrace
Böll, H. The rain gutter
Bradbury, R. Promises, promises
Brady, M. Care in the holding
Broun, H. Cycling posture
Broun, H. South Sea sensations
Carter, E. All the men are called McCabe
DeMarinis, R. Queen
Doubiago, S. Chappaquiddick
Finger, A. Cross-country
Flook, M. Richard's girl
Gaitskill, M. A romantic weekend
Gordon, M. Out of the fray
Harvor, E. A sweetheart
Hemingway, E. Get a seeing-eyed dog
Hemingway, E. The sea change
Hemingway, E. Up in Michigan
Hemley, R. Installations
Hospital, J. T. Happy Diwali
Jhabvala, R. P. The man with the dog
Jhabvala, R. P. Passion
Katz, S. Friendship
Kawabata, Y. Death mask
Kawabata, Y. God's bones
Kawabata, Y. Sleeping habit
Kawabata, Y. A sunny place
La Chapelle, M. Drinking
McCormack, E. P. Festival
Miller, G. W. Wiping the slate clean
Ocampo, S. Lovers
Prichard, K. S. The rabbit trapper's wife
Pritchett, M. The Venus tree
Prose, F. Everything is about animals
Ryan, A. The lovely and talented Maxine
     Kane
Thorman, C. God giving Lithuania to the
     world
Updike, D. Due cappuccini
Verma, N. The difference
Williams, S. A. Tell Martha not to moan
The **lovers**. Head, B.
Lovers. Ocampo, S.
Lovers. Sorrells, R. T.
Lovers. Thurm, M.
The **lovers**. Williams, B.
Lovers of the lake. O'Faoláin, S.
Love's an itinerant. Given, A.
Love's awakening. Maupassant, G. de
Love's celebration. Outlaw, L. L.
Love's heresy. Bishop, M.
The **loves** of Alonzo Fitz Clarence and
     Rosannah Ethelton. Twain, M.
The **loves** of David Freund. Komie, L. B.
The **loves** of Lady Coldpence. Gardner, M.
Lovesey, Peter
Arabella's answer
     John Creasey's Crime collection, 1985
The curious computer
     The New adventures of Sherlock
     Holmes; ed. by M. H. Greenberg and
     C. L. R. Waugh
Curl up and dye
     John Creasey's Crime collection, 1987
Did you tell Daddy?
     John Creasey's Crime collection, 1986
The secret lover
     The Mammoth book of modern crime
     stories; ed. by G. Hardinge
     Winter's crimes 17
     The Year's best mystery & suspense
     stories, 1986
Loving. Spivack, K.
Loving. Sutherland, M.
Loving Belle Starr. See Taylor, R. The fidd-
     ler
Loving pictures. See Giles, M. Baby pictures
Loving strangers. Portnoy, M.
Loving thy neighbor. Taylor, C.
"Loving your characters". Kobin, J.
Low, David
Winterblossom Garden
     The Ploughshares reader: new fiction for
     the eighties
Low-lands. Pynchon, T.
Low rider. Daugherty, T.
Low tide. Rosenbaum, K.
The **lowboy**. Cheever, J.
Lowden, Desmond
The old mob
     The Mammoth book of modern crime
     stories; ed. by G. Hardinge
Lowe, Ramona
The woman in the window
     Writing red; ed. by C. Nekola and P.
     Rabinowitz
Lowenstein, Andrea Freud
The mother right
     Stepping out; ed. by A. Oosthuizen
LOWER EAST SIDE (NEW YORK, N.Y.)
     See New York (N.Y.)—Lower East
     Side
The **lower** garden district free gravity mule
     blight; or, Rhoda, a fable. Gilchrist,
     E.
Lower me down with a golden chain. Burke,
     J. L.
The **Lower** Pontalba. Morgan, B.
Lowrey, P. H.
The great speckled bird
     Mississippi writers v1: Fiction; ed. by D.
     Abbott
Lowry, Beverly
Come back, Lolly Ray [excerpt]
     Mississippi writers v1: Fiction; ed. by D.
     Abbott
     The New writers of the South; ed. by
     C. East
Out of the blue
     Southwest Review 73:255-72 Spr '88
So far from the road, so long until mor-
     ning
     Prize stories, Texas Institute of Letters;
     ed. by M. Terry

Lowry, Malcolm, 1909-1957
Strange comfort afforded by the profession
The Penguin book of modern British short stories
Lowry, Robert
Layover in El Paso
A Treasury of World War II stories; ed. by B. Pronzini and M. H. Greenberg
Loyalty. Pavese, C.
Loyalty erosion. Willson, H.
The **loyalty** of Esau Common. Wells, H. G.
Lu Wenfu, 1928-
The boundary wall
Lu Wenfu. The gourmet, and other stories of modern China
The doorbell
Lu Wenfu. The gourmet, and other stories of modern China
The gourmet
Lu Wenfu. The gourmet, and other stories of modern China
Graduation
Lu Wenfu. The gourmet, and other stories of modern China
The man from a peddlers' family
Lu Wenfu. The gourmet, and other stories of modern China
Tang Qiaodi
Lu Wenfu. The gourmet, and other stories of modern China
World of dreams, a valediction
Lu Wenfu. The gourmet, and other stories of modern China
Luban, Marianne
Tomorrow you'll forget
Stiller's pond; ed. by J. Agee; R. Blakely and S. Welch
LUBLIN (POLAND) *See* Poland—Lublin
Luc and his father. Gallant, M.
Luce-Kapler, Rebecca
The Rawleigh man
Alberta bound; ed. by F. Stenson
Lucia and old lace. Lee, H.
Luciano, Elizabeth
Dressing down
Mademoiselle 94:104+ F '88
Lucifer. Zelazny, R.
Lucille would have known. Burke, J.
Luck. Prichard, K. S.
Luck. Sanford, W. M.
Luck. Tuohy, F.
Luck is no lady. Bloch, R.
The **luck** of a gypsy. Hoch, E. D.
Luck of Riley. Frazee, S.
The **luck** of the Devil. Fremlin, C.
The **luck** of the Irish. Franklin, P.
The **luck** of the Tavy. 'Taffrail'
The **luckiest** man in the world. Silvis, R.
A **lucky** burglar. Maupassant, G. de
Lucky day. Clark, M. H.
A **lucky** dog. Brand, M.
Lucky Lafe. Hall, M. L.
The **lucky** one. Bache, E.

Lucky penny. Barnes, L.
The **lucky** stone. Heinesen, W.
The **lucky** strike. Robinson, K. S.
Lucrecia's poisons. Coutinho, S.
Lucy. Swan-Goodchild, A.
Lucy comes to stay. Bloch, R.
Ludmila. Backus, J. L.
Luella Miller. Freeman, M. E. W.
Luftig, Richard
A promise is a promise
'Teen 29:52+ My '85
Luisa. Fletcher, C.
Lukora. Wolfe, G.
Luks, Allan
The doctor & the social worker
Encounter (London, England) 68:16-22 Ja '87
Lull, Roderick
No dogs allowed
The Saturday Evening Post 259:42-5+ N '87
Lull after the storm. Rehman, S.
Lullaby. Gorky, M.
Lullaby. Silko, L.
Lulu the tailor. Jasmin, C.
Lum, Darrell H. Y.
The Moiliili Bag Man
Passages to the dream shore; ed. by F. Stewart
Primo doesn't take back bottles anymore
Passages to the dream shore; ed. by F. Stewart
Yahk fahn, Auntie
Passages to the dream shore; ed. by F. Stewart
LUMBER INDUSTRY
See also Loggers
Cassutt, M. Stillwater, 1896
Jolley, E. The jarrah thieves
Rooke, L. Sing me no love songs, I'll say you no prayers
LUMBERJACKS *See* Loggers
LUMBERMEN *See* Loggers
Lunar frisson. Clark, G.
Lunar New Year's feast. Lin, H.-Y.
The **lunatics.** Robinson, K. S.
Lunch at Archibald's. Dilworth, S.
Lunch break. Shi Tiesheng
Lunch-hour magic. Finney, J.
Lunch in winter. Trevor, W.
Lunch involuntary. Janowitz, T.
LUNCHEONS
Adams, A. Waiting for Stella
Alden, P. B. Ladies' luncheon
Lispector, C. The sharing of bread
Lurie, M. Kicking on
Lurie, M. Sunday lunch
O'Brien, E. Violets
Lunchtime, August 1938. Rava, S.
Lundwall, Sam J.
Time everlasting
Tales from the planet Earth

Lunn, Richard
Mirrors
Transgressions; ed. by D. Anderson
Lupe. Arias, R.
Lupoff, Richard A., 1935-
God of the Naked Unicorn
Sherlock Holmes through time and space
Lurchers. Norris, L.
The **lure.** Morris, M.
Lurie, Morris
Africa wall
Echad 4: Jewish writing from down un-
der: Australia and New Zealand
Lurie, M. Outrageous behaviour
American shoes
Lurie, M. Outrageous behaviour
Architecture
Lurie, M. The night we ate the sparrow
Bannister
Lurie, M. Outrageous behaviour
Bobbeh
Echad 4: Jewish writing from down un-
der: Australia and New Zealand
Camille Pissaro 1830-1903
Lurie, M. The night we ate the sparrow
The card-players
Lurie, M. Outrageous behaviour
The day the bottom fell out of Yugoslavia
Lurie, M. Outrageous behaviour
The death of Rappaport
Lurie, M. Outrageous behaviour
Fenner
Lurie, M. Outrageous behaviour
A fool in winter
Lurie, M. Outrageous behaviour
French toothpaste
Lurie, M. Outrageous behaviour
Good people in the house
Lurie, M. Outrageous behaviour
Happy times
Lurie, M. Outrageous behaviour
Her life: a fragment
Lurie, M. Outrageous behaviour
Home is
Lurie, M. Outrageous behaviour
An immaculate conception
Lurie, M. Outrageous behaviour
Kelso's lady
Lurie, M. The night we ate the sparrow
Kicking on
Lurie, M. The night we ate the sparrow
A king of the road
Lurie, M. Outrageous behaviour
The larder
Lurie, M. Outrageous behaviour
Lessons
Lurie, M. The night we ate the sparrow
Letter
Lurie, M. The night we ate the sparrow
Losing things
Lurie, M. The night we ate the sparrow
The muted love song of Edvard Nils
Lurie, M. Outrageous behaviour

My greatest ambition
Lurie, M. Outrageous behaviour
Outrageous behaviour
Lurie, M. Outrageous behaviour
A partial portrait of my father, his birth-
days, my gifts, bottled in bond
Lurie, M. The night we ate the sparrow
Popov
Lurie, M. Outrageous behaviour
Pride and joy
Lurie, M. Outrageous behaviour
Rappaport lays an egg
Lurie, M. Outrageous behaviour
A red fox, a Polish lady, a Russian
samovar
Lurie, M. Outrageous behaviour
Repository
Lurie, M. Outrageous behaviour
Rewards
Lurie, M. The night we ate the sparrow
Running nicely
The Australian short story; ed. by L.
Hergenhan
Lurie, M. Outrageous behaviour
Russian boxes
Lurie, M. The night we ate the sparrow
Skylight in Lausanne
Lurie, M. Outrageous behaviour
A social life
Lurie, M. Outrageous behaviour
Sunday lunch
Lurie, M. Outrageous behaviour
Swallows
Lurie, M. The night we ate the sparrow
Tell me what you want
Lurie, M. The night we ate the sparrow
Two artists
Lurie, M. The night we ate the sparrow
Warts
Lurie, M. Outrageous behaviour
Were they pretty?
Lurie, M. The night we ate the sparrow
What is my secret identity?
Lurie, M. Outrageous behaviour
Lusawort's meditation. McCormack, E. P.
Lush triumphant. McGrath, P.
Lust. Minot, S.
Lustig, Arnošt
Blue day
Lustig, A. Indecent dreams
The girl with the scar
Lustig, A. Indecent dreams
Indecent dreams
Lustig, A. Indecent dreams
Lute Goin's sawmill. Conroy, J.
Lutz, John, 1939-
All business
Ellery Queen's Prime crimes 2
Autumn madness
Lutz, J. Better mousetraps
Big game
Lutz, J. Better mousetraps

Lutz, John, 1939—— *Continued*
Buried treasure
  Lutz, J. Better mousetraps
The butcher, the baker
  Lutz, J. Better mousetraps
Close calls
  Lutz, J. Better mousetraps
The day of the picnic
  Lutz, J. Better mousetraps
Dead man
  Lutz, J. Better mousetraps
Dear Dorie
  Lutz, J. Better mousetraps
Deeper and deeper
  Lutz, J. Better mousetraps
Discount fare
  Lutz, J. Better mousetraps
  Uncollected crimes; ed. by B. Pronzini
    and M. H. Greenberg
The explosives expert
  Lutz, J. Better mousetraps
Fractions
  Lutz, J. Better mousetraps
Games for adults
  Lutz, J. Better mousetraps
Hand of fate
  Lutz, J. Better mousetraps
High stakes
  Lutz, J. Better mousetraps
  The Year's best mystery and suspense
    stories, 1985
In memory of . . .
  Lutz, J. Better mousetraps
The infernal machine
  The New adventures of Sherlock
    Holmes; ed. by M. H. Greenberg and
    C. L. R. Waugh
The Insomniacs Club
  Lutz, J. Better mousetraps
The landscape of dreams
  Child's ploy; ed. by M. Muller and B.
    Pronzini
  Lutz, J. Better mousetraps
Mail order
  Lutz, J. Better mousetraps
Mortal combat
  Lutz, J. Better mousetraps
The music from downstairs
  Lutz, J. Better mousetraps
No small problem
  Alfred Hitchcock's Crimewatch
  Lutz, J. Better mousetraps
On guard
  Lutz, J. Better mousetraps
One man's manual
  Lutz, J. Better mousetraps
The other runner
  Lutz, J. Better mousetraps
Pure rotten
  Lutz, J. Better mousetraps
The real shape of the coast
  Lutz, J. Better mousetraps

Ride the lightning
  The Mammoth book of private eye
    stories; ed. by B. Pronzini and M. H.
    Greenberg
  The Year's best mystery & suspense
    stories, 1986
The second shot
  Lutz, J. Better mousetraps
The shooting of Curly Dan
  Lutz, J. Better mousetraps
Something for the dark
  Lutz, J. Better mousetraps
Something like murder
  Lutz, J. Better mousetraps
The thunder of guilt
  Mean streets; ed. by R. J. Randisi
Tough
  The Black Lizard anthology of crime fic-
    tion; ed. by E. Gorman
Trickle down
  Lutz, J. Better mousetraps
Typographical error
  The Eyes have it; ed. by R. J. Randisi
Understanding electricity
  Lutz, J. Better mousetraps
Until you are dead
  Lutz, J. Better mousetraps
The very best
  Alfred Hitchcock's Mortal errors
The weapon
  Alfred Hitchcock's Grave suspicions
The wounded tiger
  Lutz, J. Better mousetraps
Lutz, John, 1939-, and Pachter, Josh
DDS 10752 Libra
  An Eye for justice; ed. by R. J. Randisi
Luzon. Turner, R. F.
Lydia McQueen. Dykeman, W.
Lyle Monroe and Elma Wentz. See Heinlein,
    R. A. Beyond doubt
Lyle's roof. Keillor, G.
Lynch, Lee, 1945-
The abrupt edge
  Lynch, L. Old dyke tales
At a bar I: The Jersey dyke
  Lynch, L. Old dyke tales
At a bar II: In the morning
  Lynch, L. Old dyke tales
At a bar III: Sally the bartender goes on
    jury duty
  Lynch, L. Old dyke tales
At a bar IV: White wine
  Lynch, L. Old dyke tales
At a bar V: Summer storm
  Lynch, L. Old dyke tales
At a bar VI: Winter sun
  Lynch, L. Home in your hands
At a bar VII: The florist shop
  Lynch, L. Home in your hands
At a bar VIII: The long slow-burning fuse
  Lynch, L. Home in your hands
At a bar IX: Halloween
  Lynch, L. Home in your hands

Lynch, Lee, 1945—Continued
At a bar X: How they got together
Lynch, L. Home in your hands
Augusta Brennan I: The coat
Lynch, L. Old dyke tales
Augusta Brennan II: The tracks
Lynch, L. Old dyke tales
The awakening
Lynch, L. Old dyke tales
Babe and Evie I: Sunshine
Lynch, L. Home in your hands
Babe and Evie II: Thanksgiving
Lynch, L. Home in your hands
Cookie and Toni
Lynch, L. Old dyke tales
Dutch and Sybil I: Eleanor Roosevelt's
garden
Lynch, L. Home in your hands
Dutch and Sybil II: Beachfront hotel
Lynch, L. Home in your hands
From a novel in progress: Dusty eats out
Lynch, L. Home in your hands
Fruitstand I: Oranges out of season
Lynch, L. Old dyke tales
Fruitstand II: Honeydew moon
Lynch, L. Old dyke tales
Jefferson I: home in your hands
Lynch, L. Home in your hands
Jefferson II: in and out of the darkness
Lynch, L. Home in your hands
Jefferson III: family and friends
Lynch, L. Home in your hands
Jefferson IV: around every base till she
was home
Lynch, L. Home in your hands
The LoPresto Traveling Magic Show
Lynch, L. Old dyke tales
Marie-Christine I: Valentine's Day
Lynch, L. Home in your hands
Marie-Christine II
Lynch, L. Home in your hands
Marie-Christine III: a butch named Dinah
Lynch, L. Home in your hands
Mary's garden
Lynch, L. Old dyke tales
The mirror
Lynch, L. Old dyke tales
Natural food
Lynch, L. Old dyke tales
Night 'n day
Lynch, L. Home in your hands
Pleasure Park
Lynch, L. Old dyke tales
The swashbuckler, afterward: the Easter
feast
Lynch, L. Home in your hands
That old Studebaker
Lynch, L. Old dyke tales
Lynch, Marta
Latin lover
Other fires; ed. by A. Manguel
LYNCHING
Baldwin, J. Going to meet the man

Bradley, D. 197903042100 (Sunday)
Caldwell, E. Saturday afternoon
Dumas, H. Rope of wind
Faulkner, W. Dry September
McKnight, R. Rebirth
Wright, R. Big boy leaves home
Lynds, Dennis, 1924-
*For works written by this author under
other names see Arden, William,
1924-; Collins, Michael, 1924-; Sad-
ler, Mark, 1924-*
Yellow gal
The Black Lizard anthology of crime fic-
tion; ed. by E. Gorman
Lynn, David H.
Wild flowers
The Virginia Quarterly Review 64:671-85
Aut '88
Lynn, Elizabeth A.
At the Embassy Club
Omni (New York, N.Y.) 6:92-4+ Je '84
The Year's best science fiction, second
annual collection
The gods of Reorth
Worlds apart; ed. by C. Decarnin; E.
Garber and L. Paleo
The island
Haunted New England; ed. by C. G.
Waugh; M. H. Greenberg and F. D.
McSherry
The red hawk
Masterpieces of fantasy and enchant-
ment; ed. by D. G. Hartwell
The woman who loved the moon
Kindred spirits; ed. by J. M. Elliot
LYNX
Stuart, J. Fight number twenty-five
Lynx-hunting. Crane, S.
A **lynx** with lions. Lee, T.
Lyons, Arthur
Dead copy
An Eye for justice; ed. by R. J. Randisi
Missing in Miami
Mean streets; ed. by R. J. Randisi
Trouble in paradise
The Mammoth book of private eye
stories; ed. by B. Pronzini and M. H.
Greenberg
Lyons, Joseph, 1918-
Trust me
The Architecture of fear; ed. by K.
Cramer and P. D. Pautz
Lyrical voices. Hoyt, M. S.
Lyrics for Puerto Rican salsa and three
soneos by request. Vega, A. L.
LYSERGIC ACID DIETHYLAMIDE
Campbell, R. The faces at Pine Dunes
Doubiago, S. The art of seeing with one's
own eyes
Hoch, E. D. The oblong room

Lytle, Andrew
Jericho, Jericho, Jericho
  Homewords: a book of Tennessee
    writers; ed. by D. Paschall
  A Modern Southern reader; ed. by B.
    Forkner and P. Samway
Lytton, Edward Bulwer Lytton, Baron, 1803-1873
The haunted and the haunters
  The Book of the dead; ed. by A. K.
    Russell

M

M. M. B.
The mystery of the Hotel de l'Orme
  Death locked in; ed. by D. G. Greene
    and R. C. S. Adey
Macabre. Colter, C.
MACABRE STORIES *See* Horror stories
Macaulay, Richard
What a boy wants
  The Saturday Evening Post 257:50-3+
    Jl/Ag '85
Macauley, Cameron
Compassion
  The North American Review 273:14-19
    Je '88
The **Macauley** circuit. Silverberg, R.
MacCall, Libby
Mrs. Henderson talks to God
  Ellery Queen's Crimes and punishments
MacDonald, D. R.
The Chinese rifle
  MacDonald, D. R. Eyestone
Eyestone
  MacDonald, D. R. Eyestone
  Southwest Review 71:27-40 Wint '86
The flowers of Bermuda
  MacDonald, D. R. Eyestone
  The Pushcart prize XI
  The Sewanee Review 93:387-400 Summ
    '85
Holy Annie
  MacDonald, D. R. Eyestone
Of one kind
  MacDonald, D. R. Eyestone
Poplars
  MacDonald, D. R. Eyestone
Sailing
  MacDonald, D. R. Eyestone
The wharf king
  MacDonald, D. R. Eyestone
Work
  MacDonald, D. R. Eyestone
Macdonald, J. D. (James David), 1908-
(jt. auth) *See* Doyle, Debra, and Mac-
  donald, J. D. (James David), 1908-
Macdonald, James David *See* Macdonald, J.
  D. (James David), 1908-

MacDonald, John D. (John Dann), 1916-1986
Amphiskios
  Time wars; ed. by C. Waugh and M.
    H. Greenberg
Betrayed
  Baker's dozen: 13 short espionage novels
Bimini kill
  The Year's best mystery and suspense
    stories, 1988
The fatal flaw
  Redbook 165:99-102+ O '85
Hangover
  Crime of my life; ed. by B. Garfield
  Hitchcock in prime time; ed. by F. M.
    Nevins and M. H. Greenberg
The homesick Buick
  Masterpieces of mystery and suspense;
    ed. by M. H. Greenberg
I always get the cuties
  Great modern police stories; ed. by B.
    Pronzini and M. H. Greenberg
The legend of Joe Lee
  Nightmares in Dixie; ed. by F. McSher-
    ry; C. G. Waugh and M. H. Green-
    berg
Looie follows me
  Child's ploy; ed. by M. Muller and B.
    Pronzini
Squealer
  Uncollected crimes; ed. by B. Pronzini
    and M. H. Greenberg
Macdonald, Ross, 1915-1983
Guilt-edged blonde
  The Mammoth book of private eye
    stories; ed. by B. Pronzini and M. H.
    Greenberg
Midnight blue
  Masterpieces of mystery and suspense;
    ed. by M. H. Greenberg
The sleeping dog
  Hound dunnit; ed. by I. Asimov; M. H.
    Greenberg and C. L. R. Waugh
MacDougall, Carl
A small hotel
  Streets of stone; ed. by M. Burgess and
    H. Whyte
MacDuff, Lynn
Forever
  'Teen 31:32+ Ja '87
The loser
  'Teen 31:88+ S '87
Mach, Michael
A Christmas promise
  Redbook 172:64+ D '88
Machado, Anibal Monteiro
The piano
  The World of the short story; ed. by
    C. Fadiman
Machaon at Tricca. Parotti, P.
Machen, Arthur, 1863-1947
The great god Pan
  Dark company; ed. by L. Child

Machen, Arthur, 1863-1947—*Continued*
A new Christmas carol
    Christmas ghosts; ed. by K. Cramer and
    D. G. Hartwell
Novel of the white powder [Variant title:
    White powder]
    Devils & demons; ed. by M. Kaye and
    S. Kaye
The white people
    Lost souls; ed. by J. Sullivan
Machine dreams. Phillips, J. A.
The **machine** stops. Forster, E. M.
The **machine** that won the war. Asimov, I.
Machinery. Kauffman, J.
MACHINERY AND CIVILIZATION *See*
    Technology and civilization
MACHINERY AND MACHINISTS
    Barthelme, D. The explanation
    Gallacher, T. A friend of Dosser Farr
    Gallacher, T. Lord Sweatrag
    Gallacher, T. Portrait of Isa Mulvenny
    Marshall, J. The old woman
    Wells, H. G. The Lord of the Dynamos
MacHinery and the cauliflowers. MacLean,
    A.
Macinnes, Patricia
    View from Kwaj
        The New generation; ed. by A. Kaufman
        Seventeen 47:202-3+ Ap '88
MacIntyre, F. Gwynplaine
    The prisoner of gravity
        Isaac Asimov's Tomorrow's voices
MacIntyre, Tom
    Boarding
        Short story international 46
Mackay, Shen
    Babushka in the blue bus
        The Times Literary Supplement
        no4441:535 My 13-19 '88
Mackenzie, Ann
    I can't help saying goodbye
        Young mutants; ed. by I. Asimov; M.
        H. Greenberg and C. G. Waugh
Mackintosh Willy. Campbell, R.
Mack's stats. Klinkowitz, J.
MacLachlan, Patricia
    All the names of Baby Hag
        Dragons and dreams; ed. by J. Yolen;
        M. H. Greenberg and C. G. Waugh
MacLaverty, Bernard
    Across the street
        MacLaverty, B. The Great Profundo, and
        other stories
    Anodyne
        MacLaverty, B. Secrets, and other stories
    The beginnings of a sin
        The Substance of things hoped for; ed.
        by J. B. Breslin
    Between two shores
        MacLaverty, B. Secrets, and other stories
    The break
        MacLaverty, B. The Great Profundo, and
        other stories

The bull with the hard hat
    MacLaverty, B. Secrets, and other stories
Death of a parish priest
    MacLaverty, B. The Great Profundo, and
    other stories
The deep end
    MacLaverty, B. Secrets, and other stories
The drapery man
    MacLaverty, B. The Great Profundo, and
    other stories
End of season
    MacLaverty, B. The Great Profundo, and
    other stories
The exercise
    MacLaverty, B. Secrets, and other stories
For my wife's eyes only
    Redbook 164:70+ F '85
The Great Profundo
    MacLaverty, B. The Great Profundo, and
    other stories
A happy birthday
    MacLaverty, B. Secrets, and other stories
Hugo
    MacLaverty, B. Secrets, and other stories
In the hills above Lugano
    MacLaverty, B. The Great Profundo, and
    other stories
The miraculous candidate
    MacLaverty, B. Secrets, and other stories
More than just the disease
    MacLaverty, B. The Great Profundo, and
    other stories
A pornographer woos
    MacLaverty, B. Secrets, and other stories
A present for Christmas
    MacLaverty, B. Secrets, and other stories
A rat and some renovations
    MacLaverty, B. Secrets, and other stories
Remote
    MacLaverty, B. The Great Profundo, and
    other stories
Secrets
    MacLaverty, B. Secrets, and other stories
    The Treasury of English short stories;
    ed. by N. Sullivan
Some surrender
    MacLaverty, B. The Great Profundo, and
    other stories
St. Paul could hit the nail on the head
    MacLaverty, B. Secrets, and other stories
Umberto Verdi, chimney sweep
    MacLaverty, B. Secrets, and other stories
Where the tides meet
    MacLaverty, B. Secrets, and other stories
Words the happy say
    MacLaverty, B. The Great Profundo, and
    other stories
MacLean, Alistair, 1922-1987
    The Arandora Star
        MacLean, A. The lonely sea
    City of Benares
        MacLean, A. The lonely sea

MacLean, Alistair, 1922-1987—_Continued_
The Dileas
 MacLean, A. The lonely sea
The gold watch
 MacLean, A. The lonely sea
Hospital ship rams U-boat
 Men at sea; ed. by B. Aymar
The Jervis Bay
 MacLean, A. The lonely sea
Lancastria
 MacLean, A. The lonely sea
MacHinery and the cauliflowers
 MacLean, A. The lonely sea
McCrimmon and the blue moonstones
 MacLean, A. The lonely sea
The Meknes
 MacLean, A. The lonely sea
Rawalpindi
 MacLean, A. The lonely sea
Rendezvous
 MacLean, A. The lonely sea
The sinking of the Bismarck
 MacLean, A. The lonely sea
St. George and the dragon
 MacLean, A. The lonely sea
They sweep the seas
 MacLean, A. The lonely sea
MacLean, Katherine
The missing man
 Manhattan mysteries; ed. by B. Pronzini;
  C. L. R. Waugh and M. H. Greenberg
The other
 100 great fantasy short short stories; ed.
  by I. Asimov; T. Carr and M. H.
  Greenberg
Perchance to dream
 100 great fantasy short short stories; ed.
  by I. Asimov; T. Carr and M. H.
  Greenberg
Rescue squad
 [Analog]: Writers' choice v2
MacLean, Norman, 1902-
Logging and pimping and "your pal, Jim"
 Writers of the purple sage; ed. by R.
  Martin and M. Barasch
MacLennan, Phyllis
Good-by, Miss Patterson
 Young monsters; ed. by I. Asimov; M.
  H. Greenberg and C. G. Waugh
MacLeod, Alistair
As birds bring forth the sun
 MacLeod, A. The lost salt gift of blood
The boat
 MacLeod, A. The lost salt gift of blood
The closing down of summer
 MacLeod, A. The lost salt gift of blood
In the fall
 MacLeod, A. The lost salt gift of blood
Island
 MacLeod, A. The lost salt gift of blood

The lost salt gift of blood
 MacLeod, A. The lost salt gift of blood
 Selected stories from The Southern
  review, 1965-1985
The road to Rankin's Point
 MacLeod, A. The lost salt gift of blood
Second spring
 MacLeod, A. The lost salt gift of blood
To everything there is a season
 MacLeod, A. The lost salt gift of blood
Vision
 MacLeod, A. The lost salt gift of blood
Winter dog
 MacLeod, A. The lost salt gift of blood
MacLeod, Charlotte
It was an awful shame
 Murder and mystery in Boston; ed. by
  C. L. R. Waugh; F. D. McSherry and
  M. H. Greenberg
MacLeod, James Lewis
The Jesus flag
 The Georgia Review 40:205-16 Spr '86
 Necessary fictions; ed. by S. W. Lind-
  berg and S. Corey
MacLeod, Robert, 1928-
 _For works written by this author under
  other names see_ Knox, Bill, 1928-
MacMahon, Bryan
Exile's return
 The Best of Irish wit and wisdom; ed.
  by J. McCarthy
MacMillan, Ian C., 1940-
The rock
 Passages to the dream shore; ed. by F.
  Stewart
Macroscopic phenomena. Krysl, M.
Mad Dog Queen. Dilworth, S.
Mad like Lasseter. Sheil, G.
Mad Monkton. Collins, W.
The **mad** tea-party. Queen, E.
The **mad** woman. Maupassant, G. de
Madam Amalia Bessarabo. Nowakowski, M.
Madame. Sandel, C.
Madame Baptiste. Maupassant, G. de
Madame Bo-Peep, of the ranches. Henry, O.
Madame Charpentier and her children. Nas-
 lund, S. J.
Madame Parisse. Maupassant, G. de
Madame Zelena finally comes clean. Carlson,
 R.
Madame Zilensky and the King of Finland.
 McCullers, C.
Madden, David, 1933-
A fever of dying
 Homewords: a book of Tennessee
  writers; ed. by D. Paschall
No trace
 Selected stories from The Southern
  review, 1965-1985
The singer
 Stories of the modern South; ed. by B.
  Forkner and P. Samway

Madden, David, 1933-—*Continued*
Willis Carr at Bleak House
The Bread Loaf anthology of contemporary American short stories; ed. by R. Pack and J. Parini
The Southern Review (Baton Rouge, La.) 21:522-33 Ap '85
Madden, Deirdre
Hidden symptoms
First fictions: Introduction 9
Maddern, Philippa C.
Inhabiting the interspaces
Australian science fiction; ed. by V. Ikin
Maddox, Tom
The mind like a strange balloon
Omni (New York, N.Y.) 7:60-2+ Je '85
The robot and the one you love
Omni (New York, N.Y.) 10:42-4+ Mr '88
Snake-eyes
Mirrorshades; ed. by B. Sterling
Omni (New York, N.Y.) 8:44-6+ Ap '86
The Year's best science fiction, fourth annual collection
Maddren, Gerry
Fit for felony
The Womansleuth anthology; ed. by I. Zahava
Made for each other. Hamilton, N.
Made for each other. Outlaw, L. L.
Made for each other. Stewart, I.
Made in heaven. Updike, J.
Made of wax. Katz, S.
Made to last. Durban, P.
Mademoiselle. Maupassant, G. de
Mademoiselle Fifi. Maupassant, G. de
Madison, Claudia
Ball game
The North American Review 272:36-7 Mr '87
A **madman**. Level, M.
The **madman**. Wady, T.
The **madman** of Fort Ratonneau. Arnim, L. A., Freiherr von
A **madman's** manuscript. Dickens, C.
MADNESS *See* Insanity; Mental illness
Madness. al-Ujayli, A. al--S.
Madness in the family. Saroyan, W.
Madonna. Asscher-Pinkhof, C.
The **madonna**. Barker, C.
Madonna of the red sun. Wagar, W. W.
Madonna on her back. Hagy, A. C.
Madonna with cat. Petroski, C.
MADRID (SPAIN) *See* Spain—Madrid
The **madwoman** of Cherry Vale. Rooke, L.
The **maestro**. Mazel, D.
MAFIA
See also Gangsters
Brennan, D. The trouble shooters
Davidson, A. The lord of Central Park
Kaiser, H. D. Just a poor working girl
Longyear, B. B. The initiation
Pohl, F. The blister
Mafioso. Malerba, L.

Magazine section. Lafferty, R. A.
Maggie: a girl of the streets. Crane, S.
MAGI
Borchert, W. The three dark kings
Magi. Brown, G. M.
MAGIC
See also Supernatural phenomena; Talismans; Witchcraft
Alcott, L. M. The fate of the Forrests
Anderson, P. Operation afreet
Apollinaire, G. Little recipes from modern magic
Baum, L. F. The dummy that lived
Baum, L. F. The glass dog
Baum, L. F. The magic bonbons
Bloodwine, G. Three knives in Ithkar
Brown, A. R. The clockwork woman
Brown, A. R. Were-sisters
Broxon, M. D. First do no harm
Broxon, M. D. Flux of fortune
Carroll, L. E. The very last party at #13 Mallory Way
Carter, A. The donkey prince
Carter, L. The goblinry of Ais
Cherryh, C. J. Of law and magic
Chin, M. L. Catmagic
Clark, J. The magic carpet
Cogswell, T. R. The wall around the world
Crispin, A. C. The amiable assassin
Curry, G. S., and Conroy, M. Guardians of the secret
De Camp, L. S. The eye of Tandyla
De Camp, L. S., and Pratt, F. The green magician
De Lint, C. Uncle Dobbin's Parrot Fair
DeWeese, G. The beggar and his cat
Donaldson, S. R. Daughter of Regals
Donaldson, S. R. The Lady in White
Easton, M. C. Flarrin red-chin
Effinger, G. A. Babes on bawd way
Finney, J. Lunch-hour magic
Friesner, E. M. Honeycomb
Frost, G. Sardofa's horseshoes
Gardner, C. S. Demon luck
Gilbert, W. S. The triumph of vice
Goulart, R. Please stand by
Green, S. A quiet day at the fair
Griffin, P. Covenant
Guin, W. The root and the ring
Haldeman, L. Bird of paradise
Hankla, C. The strawberry patch
Harrison, M. J. The incalling
Huff, T. S. What little girls are made of
Inks, C. Mandrake
Inks, C., and Miller, G. Eyes of the seer
Kaplan, D. M. Magic
Kearns, R. From Bach to broccoli
Lackey, M. Fiddler fair
Lafferty, R. A. Flaming-arrow
Lee, T. La reine blanche
Llywelyn, M. Fletcher found
Llywelyn, M. The silverlord
Manuel, J. The wizard postponed

MAGIC—*Continued*

Mayhar, A. Esmene's eyes
Mayhar, A. To trap a demon
McKillip, P. A. Baba Yaga and the sorcerer's son
Meier, S. Trave
Miesel, S. The book-healer
Moorcock, M. The lands beyond the world
Neville, S. Johnny Appleseed
Niven, L. Convergent series
Niven, L. What good is a glass dagger?
Norton, A. Swamp dweller
O'Malley, K. The demon's gift
Painter, P. The visitor
Pierce, M. A. The woman who loved reindeer
Rausch, B. Snows of yesteryear
Rouland, S. L. SunDark in Ithkar
Sampson, J. Qazia and a ferret-fetch
Schlobin, R. C. For lovers only
Schutz, J. W. Dragon's horn
Severance, C. Day of strange fortune
Shwartz, S. M. Hair's breath
Shwartz, S. M. Homecoming
Smith, C. A. The colossus of Ylourgne
Smith, C. A. The coming of the white worm
Smith, C. A. The holiness of Azédarac
Springer, N. The prince out of the past
Stevenson, R. L. The bottle imp
Stuart, K. The singing eggs
Waters, E. Cold spell
Weinbaum, S. G. Dawn of flame
Wells, H. G. The magic shop
Wolf, R. Cat and muse
Zahn, T. The talisman
Magic. Bronstein, E.
Magic. Glickman, G.
Magic. Kaplan, D. M.
Magic. Morris, W.
The **magic** barrel. Malamud, B.
The **magic** bonbons. Baum, L. F.
The **magic** bullet. Hoch, E. D.
The **magic** carpet. Clark, J.
Magic castle. Barthelme, F.
The **magic** chalk. Abe, K.
The **magic** circle. Gingher, M.
The **magic** fishbone. Dickens, C.
The **magic** flute. Epstein, L.
The **magic** hour. Eubanks, G.
Magic in a world of magic. Cameron, A.
Magic lantern. Dazai, O.
Magic lantern. Richards, S. S.
Magic of this moment. Houbein, L.
The **magic** shop. Wells, H. G.
The **magic** strength of need. Cooper, J. C.
The **magic** umbrella. Asimov, I.
The **magical** geranium. Jackson, M. W.

MAGICIANS

Asimov, I. The Cross of Lorraine
Barker, C. The last illusion
Betancourt, J. G. Vernon's dragon

Bloch, R. The little man who wasn't all there
Bloch, R. Son of a witch
Bloch, R. That old black magic
Boisvert, C. A slice of nothingness
Bradley, M. Z. The secret of the Blue Star
Brown, F. Armageddon
Buzzati, D. The five brothers
Carter, L. Geydelle's protective
Davidson, A. The last wizard
De Larrabeiti, M. Malagan and the Lady of Rascas
Dozois, G. R., and others. Afternoon at Schrafft's
Duane, D. Lior and the sea
Dunn, M. If there be magic
Gardner, C. S. A drama of dragons
Gardner, C. S. A malady of magicks
Gardner, M. Merlina and the colored ice
Gardner, M. Mysterious Smith
Goldman, L. Temporarily at liberty
Gordon, M. The magician's wife
Green, J. The ruby wand of Asrazel
Haldeman, J. W. Blood brothers
Hoover, J. Proteus
Howard, R. E. The people of the Black Circle
Huddle, D. Summer of the magic show
Jakes, J. And the monsters walk
Johnson, C. R. The sorcerer's apprentice
Le Guin, U. K. The rule of names
Lee, T. Cyrion in wax
Lewitt, S. The shaman flute
Linaweaver, B. Shadow quest
Martin, G. R. R. In the lost lands
Pronzini, B., and Kurland, M. Vanishing act
Regent, P. Ziggy's last dance
Skelton, R. The illusion
Smith, C. A. The last incantation
Smith, C. A. The maze of Maal Dweb
Stevenson, R. L. The isle of voices
Vance, J. Mazirian the Magician
Wellman, M. W. The seeker in the fortress
Williams, J. Petronella
Zelazny, R. Tower of ice
The **magician's** wife. Gordon, M.

Magid, Ibrahim Abd al *See* Al Magid, Ibrahim Abd
Magna takes the calls. Dixon, S.
Magnetism. Maupassant, G. de
The **magnetosphere**. Hoyle, F.
Magnolia. Covington, V.
Mago's bride. Estleman, L. D.
Magritte's secret agent. Lee, T.
Magush. Ocampo, S.
Mahala Joe. Austin, M. H.

Maheux-Forcier, Louise, 1929-

ABC
　Intimate strangers; ed. by M. Cohen and W. Grady

Maheux-Forcier, Louise, 1929——*Continued*
The carnation
   The Oxford book of French-Canadian short stories
Mahfouz, Naguib *See* Maḥfūz, Najīb, 1912-
Maḥfūz, Najīb, 1912-
The conjurer made off with the dish
   The Art of the tale; ed. by D. Halpern
The time and the place
   Short story international 49
Mahogany. Pil'nīāk, B.
The **mahogany** table. Warner, S. T.
The **Mai-Loan** and the man who could fly. Christman, R.
The **maid** on the shore. Sherman, D.
Maiden names. Miriam, L.
The **maidens'** prayers. Kawabata, Y.
The **maiden's** sacrifice. Hoch, E. D.
MAIDS (SERVANTS)
Adams, A. La Señora
Ade, G. Effie Whittlesy
Antoni, R. W. Two-head Fred and Tree-foot Frieda
Apple, M. Help
Christie, A. The case of the perfect maid
Coskran, K. Graven images
Davis, L. The housemaid
Dazai, O. The lady who entertained
Fink, I. Behind the hedge
Floyd, P. L. Secrets
Gilchrist, E. Miss Crystal's maid name Traceleen, she's talking, she's telling everything she knows
Gilchrist, E. Traceleen, she's still talking
Gilchrist, E. Traceleen's diary
Gilchrist, E. Traceleen's telling a story called "A bad year"
Gordimer, N. Blinder
Hogan, L. New shoes
Leedom-Ackerman, J. No marble angels
Maupassant, G. de. The story of a farm-girl
Moore, G. An episode in bachelor life
Painter, P. Sylvia
Rifaat, A. The flat in Nakshabandi Street
Rifaat, A. The long night of winter
Rodoreda, M. Therafina
Ruta, S. Carmela
Shiga, N. The paper door
Singer, I. B. Dazzled
Thomas, D. The true story
Tournier, M. The Woodcock
Trevor, W. The wedding in the garden
Tyler, A. The geologist's maid
Walker, M. Jubilee [excerpt]
Wegner, H. Cyankali
Wegner, H. The stoning of Stanislava
Wharton, E. All Souls'
Maigret at the crossroads. Simenon, G.
Maigret mystified. Simenon, G.
Maigret stonewalled. Simenon, G.
Mail order. Lutz, J.
Mail-order clone. Willis, C.

Mailer, Norman
The killer
   Mystery in the mainstream; ed. by B. Pronzini; M. H. Greenberg and B. N. Malzberg
The paper house
   A Treasury of World War II stories; ed. by B. Pronzini and M. H. Greenberg
A piece of harlot's ghost
   Esquire 110:80-2+ Jl '88
Maillet, Antonine, 1929-
Two saints
   The Oxford book of French-Canadian short stories
The **main** chance. Flaherty, G.
Main-street. Hawthorne, N.
Main street: 1953. Russ, J.
MAINE
   See also White Mountains (N.H. and Me.)
Auchincloss, L. Greg's peg
Brown, S. The lesson
Cummings, R. Berrying
Fahy, C. A clock in San Diego
Gooch, B. Maine
Hoyt, M. S. The peg
King, S. The mist
King, S. One for the road
Minot, S. The navigator
Minot, S. Small Point Bridge
Ruffolo, L. Leave of absence
Train, A. C. The Viking's daughter
Van de Wetering, J. A great sight
Van de Wetering, J. A tasty tidbit
Wilson, B. Looking for the Golden Gate
       Farm life
   See Farm life—Maine
Maine. Gooch, B.
Maine. Osborn, M.
Maiolo, Joseph
A wry sleep of boys
   The Sewanee Review 96:566-83 Fall '88
Mairowitz, David Zane
The tidings brought to Sylvie
   The Massachusetts Review 29:505-18 Fall '88
Maitland, Sara, 1950-
Let us now praise unknown women and our mothers who begat us
   Stepping out; ed. by A. Oosthuizen
Major, A. R.
Kissmeowt and the healing friar
   Magic in Ithkar 2; ed. by A. Norton and R. Adams
La Verdad: the magic sword
   Tales of the Witch World 2
Major, André, 1942-
The good old days
   Intimate strangers; ed. by M. Cohen and W. Grady

Major, Clarence
Tattoo
American made; ed. by M. Leyner; C. White and T. Glynn
Major repairs. Choyce, L.
Major Stede Bonnet, pirate by vagary. Schwob, M.
The **Major** steps out. Regent, P.
MAJORCA (SPAIN)
Glavin, A. One for sorrow
Mak, Ali al- See Al-Mak, Ali
Makar Zherebtsov. Shukshin, V. M.
The **make-believe** ballroom. Humphries, J. S.
Make it never happened. Bickel, B.
Make love not war. Bellamy, J. D.
Make westing. London, J.
The **makeover** of Meredith Kaplan. Girion, B.
The **maker** of coffins. Bates, H. E.
Makeup. Clark, M.
Makeup. Kawabata, Y.
Makhzangy, Mohammed al See Al Makhzangy, Mohammed
Making a convert. Maupassant, G. de
Making amends. Packer, N. H.
Making change. Busch, F.
Making good. See Muschg, A. Reparations; or, Making good
Making it work. Rushin, P.
The **making** of Musa Maikudi. Horn, A.
Making the wine. Labozzetta, M.
Making things whole. Hempel, A.
Making tracks. Grenville, K.
The **makin's.** Bonner, M.
Makuck, Peter, 1940-
Bound away
The Yale Review 76:74-90 Aut '86
Filling the igloo
Selected stories from The Southern review, 1965-1985
The Southern Review (Baton Rouge, La.) 20:632-44 Jl '84
Junk trade
The Hudson Review 41:274-88 Summ '88
Persistence
The Yale Review 73:418-28 Spr '84
Mal. Roth, H. H.
Mal and fem. Carter, R.
Malachi's Cove. Trollope, A.
The **malachite** beads. Hill, J.
MALADJUSTED CHILDREN See Emotionally disturbed children
A **malady** of magicks. Gardner, C. S.
Malagan and the Lady of Rascas. De Larrabeiti, M.
Malamud, Bernard, 1914-1986
Alma redeemed
Commentary 78:30-4 Jl '84
Idiots first
The Norton book of American short stories

In Kew Gardens
Partisan Review 51 no4/52 no1:536-40 '84/'85
In retirement
Full measure; ed. by D. Sennett
The Jewbird
The World of the short story; ed. by C. Fadiman
The last Mohican
The Art of the tale; ed. by D. Halpern
A lost grave
Esquire 103:204-6 My '85
The Esquire fiction reader v2
Sudden fiction; ed. by R. Shapard and J. Thomas
The magic barrel
American short story masterpieces; ed. by R. Carver and T. Jenks
Great American love stories; ed. by L. Rosenthal
Look who's talking; ed. by B. Weber
The model
Prize stories, 1984
My son the murderer
Mystery in the mainstream; ed. by B. Pronzini; M. H. Greenberg and B. N. Malzberg
Malaparte, Curzio, 1898-1957
The Soroca girls
The Pushcart prize IX
MALARIA
L'Engle, M. Poor little Saturday
MALAYA
See also Malaysia
MALAYSIA
Hsiu, H. The trap
Race relations
Clarke, T. Apai
Clarke, T. The champion
Clarke, T. The day nothing happened
Clarke, T. The king
Clarke, T. The lost D.O.
Clarke, T. A posthumous gift
Clarke, T. The red
Clarke, T. A rite of passion
Clarke, T. The truth
Clarke, T. The wee manok
Clarke, T. The well
Clarke, T. The Wo family
Malden, R. H. (Richard Henry), 1879-1951
Between sunset and moonrise
Lost souls; ed. by J. Sullivan
Malden, Richard Henry See Malden, R. H. (Richard Henry), 1879-1951
The **Maldive** chronicles. Bernard, K.
Male. Acker, K.
The **malediction.** Williams, T.
Malenov's revenge. Cohen, A.
Malerba, Luigi
Mafioso
The Literary Review (Madison, N.J.) 28:253-6 Wint '85

Malet, Léo
The Haulage company
  Great French detective stories; ed. by T.
    J. Hale
Mali is very dangerous. McKnight, R.
Malice. White, C.
Malice aforethought. Wollheim, D. A.
Malice at the mike. Breen, J. L.
Malice in wonderland. King, R.
MALICIOUS MISCHIEF
  Bonosky, P. Home for supper
  Gilchrist, E. Dede's talking, it's her turn
  Lofts, N. Lord, who is my neighbour?
Malinowitz, Harriet
Water skiing
  Love, struggle & change; ed. by I.
    Zahava
Maloney, J. J., 1940-
The Mid-City Meat Company
  Missouri short fiction; ed. by C. Beasley
Malouf, David, 1934-
The empty lunch-tin
  Transgressions; ed. by D. Anderson
The sun in winter
  Home and away; ed. by R. Creswell
MALPRACTICE
  Enayetullah, A. Enemy
MALTA
  Barstow, S. Foreign parts
Malterre, Elona
Touching the buffalo
  Alberta bound; ed. by F. Stenson
Malzberg, Barry N.
Chained
  100 great fantasy short short stories; ed.
    by I. Asimov; T. Carr and M. H.
    Greenberg
Going down
  Kindred spirits; ed. by J. M. Elliot
Hop skip jump
  Omni (New York, N.Y.) 11:104+ O '88
Icons
  Omni book of science fiction 2
Johann Sebastian Brahms
  Universe 15
On the campaign trail
  Election Day 2084; ed. by I. Asimov
    and M. H. Greenberg
The Queen of Lower Saigon
  In the field of fire; ed. by J. Van B.
    Dann and J. Dann
Reason seven
  Omni (New York, N.Y.) 7:46-8+ My '85
Spree
  Witches; ed. by I. Asimov; M. H.
    Greenberg and C. G. Waugh
To mark the times we had
  Omni (New York, N.Y.) 7:62 N '84
(jt. auth) See Pronzini, Bill, and Malzberg,
  Barry N.
Mama Angelina's. Thomas, M.
Mama sings the blues. McCafferty, J. E.
Mama Tuddi done over. Rooke, L.

Mama won't budge. Mee, S.
Mama's old stucco house. Williams, T.
Mamaya. Diaconú, A.
Mamie. Mancuso, C.
MAMMALS, FOSSIL *See* Fossils
MAMMOGRAPHY
  Hampton, S. Conrad's bear
  Oates, J. C. Pinch
Mammon and the archer. Henry, O.
Mammy's boy. McCarthy, T.
MAN
  Aldiss, B. W. A romance of the equator
  Anthony, P. Small mouth, bad taste
  Bates, H. Alas, all thinking
  Colegate, I. Distant cousins
  Del Rey, L. The faithful
  Morressy, J. Final version
  Wolfe, T. So this is man
  Zelazny, R. For a breath I tarry
MAN, PREHISTORIC
    See also Prehistoric times
  Simak, C. D. Grotto of the dancing deer
A **man.** Botwinik, B.
A **man.** Clarke, A. C.
The **man.** Dawson, F.
A **man** among men. Hood, M.
Man and daughter in the cold. Updike, J.
A **man** and his god. Morris, J.
A **man** and his habit. Faik, S.
A **man** and his house. Liphshitz, A.
Man and his world. Blaise, C.
A **man** and some others. Crane, S.
The **man** and the girl. Verma, N.
Man around a maypole. Espina-Moore, L.
A **man** around the house. Pritchard, M.
Man as plaything, life as mockery. Bissoon-
    dath, N.
The **man** at Gantt's place. Frazee, S.
Man at low volume. Doucette, R. J.
The **man** at Quitobaquito. Nelson, K.
The **man** at the gate. Schwartz, L. S.
Man bites dog. Queen, E.
Man bring this up road. Williams, T.
A **man** by the name of Ziegler. Hesse, H.
A **man** called Horse. Johnson, D. M.
A **man** called Lovac. Chipulina, E. G.
A **man** called Spade. Hammett, D.
A **man** can try. Jones, E. D.
A **man** can't even swindle any more. Nesin,
    A.
Man Dancing. Osborn, C.
Man descending. Vanderhaeghe, G.
The **man** from a peddlers' family. Lu Wenfu
The **man** from Buenos Aires. Sholem
    Aleichem
The **man** from Mars. Atwood, M.
The **man** from nowhere. Hoch, E. D.
Man from the south. Dahl, R.
The **man** from the White Mountains. Willis,
    T.
Man, God ain't like that. . . . Wright, R.
The **man** he used to be. Bauer-Stuchly, J.
The **man** I married. Pinsoneault, D.

A man in a million. Bates, M.
The man in black. Whitaker, M.
The man in Bogotá. Hempel, A.
A man in Louisiana. McGuane, T.
A man in love. Carrington, L.
The man in the armchair. Benítez-Rojo, A.
The man in the attic and the woman on the main floor. Óskar, J.
The man in the cardboard mask. Greenberg, A.
The man in the doll house. Steele, M.
The man in the green bathrobe. Rooke, L.
A man in the house. Colter, C.
The man in the moon. Maxwell, W.
Man in the night. Morrison, J.
The man in the toolhouse. Swados, H.
Man in the wasteland. Calvino, I.
Man-Mountain Gentian. Waldrop, H.
The man of Adamant. Hawthorne, N.
Man of all work. Wright, R.
A man of his time. Painter, P.
A man of mystery. Naipaul, S.
The man of the crowd. Poe, E. A.
The man of the family. Suckow, R.
Man of the house. Pilcher, R.
A man of the world. Hemingway, E.
A man of the world. White, E.
The man on the 'bidgee. Morrison, J.
The man on the motorcycle. Cohen, S.
Man overboard! Crawford, F. M.
A man sixty. Endō, S.
Man-size in marble. Nesbit, E.
The man that corrupted Hadleyburg. Twain, M.
The man that was used up. Poe, E. A.
A man told me the story of his life. Paley, G.
The man who. Spinrad, N.
The man who always wanted to travel. Bryant, E.
Man who became a fish. See Li, F.-Y. The carp
The man who became a soprano. Updike, J.
The man who brought happiness. Federspiel, J.
The man who came back. Hoch, E. D.
The man who collected bridges. Kilworth, G.
The man who collected photographs. Rutishauser, P.
The man who collected Poe. Bloch, R.
The man who collected "The Shadow". Pronzini, B.
The man who could not see devils. Russ, J.
The man who could work miracles. Wells, H. G.
The man who cursed and the good Lutheran boy. DeGrazia, E.
The man who did not smile. Kawabata, Y.
The man who disappeared. Meade, L. T., and Eustace, R.

The man who doesn't know what a tooth or a toothache is. Faik, S.
The man who drank a thousand beers. Heller, S.
The man who drowned puppies. Sullivan, T.
The man who floated in time. Silverberg, R.
The man who forgot the city. Faik, S.
The man who gave brother double pneumonia. Hall, M. L.
The man who hated. Sambrot, W.
The man who killed a shadow. Wright, R.
The man who knew Belle Starr. Bausch, R.
The man who knew Cary Grant. Schwartz, J.
A man who knew his birds. Kotzwinkle, W.
The man who knew how. Sayers, D. L.
The man who knew women. Bloch, R.
The man who laughed. Gathorne-Hardy, J.
The man who lied about a woman. Austin, M. H.
The man who liked Dickens. Waugh, E.
The man who liked noise. Savage, E.
The man who lived underground. Wright, R.
The man who looked young. Summers, H. S.
The man who loved Detroit. Broder, G. K.
The man who loved his kind. Woolf, V.
The man who loved Levittown. Wetherell, W. D.
The man who loved the Nereids. Yourcenar, M.
The man who loved water. Gardner, C. S.
The man who made a beeline. Frazee, S.
The man who married a French wife. Shaw, I.
The man who married Mom. Doig, D. T.
The man who met Picasso. Swanwick, M.
The man who murdered in public. Vickers, R.
The man who nursed grievances. Underwood, M.
The man who painted the dragon Griaule. Shepard, L.
The man who planted trees. Giono, J.
The man who sang in his sleep. Skelton, R.
The man who saved himself. Flaherty, G.
The man who saw the flood. Wright, R.
The man who saw the lizard eat his child. Brandão, I. de L.
The man who saw through Heaven. Steele, W. D.
The man who shot Lewis Vance. Kaminsky, S. M.
The man who sold rope to the Gnoles. St. Clair, M.
The man who stopped trains. Barcelo, F.
The man who swam through jellyfish, through men-of-war. Onopa, R.
The man who walked home. Tiptree, J.
The man who walked on the moon. Ballard, J. G.
The man who walked pigeons. Sorrells, R. T.

The **man** who wanted to be in the movies. Jakes, J.

The **man** who was a cosmic string. Rucker, R. von B.

The **man** who was almost a man. Wright, R.

The **man** who was left behind. Ingalls, R.

The **man** who was loved by women. Austin, M. H.

The **man** who wasn't there. Kotzwinkle, W.

The **man** who watched the glaciers run. Wilkerson, C.

The **man** who went to Chicago. Wright, R.

The **man** who went to Taltavul's. Alexander, D.

The **man** who went too far. Benson, E. F.

The **man** who wore sunlight. Flaherty, G.

The **man** who would be God. Ruffin, P.

The **man** who would not go away. Minot, S.

The **man** who would not shake hands. King, S.

The **man** whom women adored. Oates, J. C.

Man with a family. Humphrey, W.

Man with a hobby. Bloch, R.

The **man** with a nose. Wells, H. G.

The **man** with clam eyes. Thomas, A. C.

The **man** with Picasso's eyes. Kaplan, D. M.

The **man** with the bag full of boomerangs in the Bois de Boulogne. McElroy, J.

The **man** with the blue eyes. Maupassant, G. de

The **man** with the cigarette. Palma, C.

The **man** with the dog. Jhabvala, R. P.

The **man** with the dogs. Maupassant, G. de

The **man** with the gift. O'Kelly, S.

The **man** with the hoe. Johnson, G. C.

The **man** with the knives. Böll, H.

The **man** with the roller. Swain, E. G.

The **man** with the twisted lip. Doyle, Sir A. C.

Manacled. Crane, S.

The **management** of grief. Mukherjee, B.

The **manageress** and the mirage. Drewe, R.

The **managers**. Kinsella, W. P.

MANCHESTER (ENGLAND) *See* England—Manchester

Mancuso, Carolina

Mamie
Love, struggle & change; ed. by I. Zahava

Mandiargues, André Pieyre de *See* Pieyre de Mandiargues, André, 1909-

Mandikini. Benford, G.

The **mandoline**. Whitaker, M.

Mandrake. Inks, C.

Mandy Larkin. Forrest, K. V.

Manea, Norman

The sweater
TriQuarterly no72:7-16 Spr/Summ '88

Maneuvers. Summers, B.

Manfredi, Renée

Ice music
Michigan Quarterly Review 27:313-27 Spr '88

Mange. Matthews, J.

The **manger** is empty. Wangerin, W.

The **mango** community. Jacobsen, J.

The **mango** tree. Hospital, J. T.

Mangum, Donald

Hostess
The New Yorker 63:33 S 28 '87

MANHATTAN (NEW YORK, N.Y.) *See* New York (N.Y.)—Manhattan

Manhattan night's entertainment. See Davidson, A. The lord of Central Park

MANHUNTS

See also Adventure

Anderson, P. Eutopia

Frazee, S. My brother down there

Honig, D. My escaped convict

Rhodes, E. M. Pasó por aquí

Sheckley, R. The prize of peril

Sheckley, R. Seventh victim

Wells, H. G. Through a window

Woolrich, C. New York blues

Maniaty, Tony

'Who was that masked man?'
Home and away; ed. by R. Creswell

Manifest destiny. Haldeman, J. W.

Manikins. Varley, J.

MANILA (PHILIPPINES) *See* Philippines—Manila

MANITOBA *See* Canada—Manitoba

Mankiewicz, Don M.

Two rolls, no coffee
Ellery Queen's Crimes and punishments

Mankiller, Wilma

Keeping pace with the rest of the world
Southern Exposure (Durham, N.C.) 13:72-6 N/D '85

Manley, Frank

The baptism of water
New England Review and Bread Loaf Quarterly 11:43-57 Aut '88

The rain of terror
The Southern Review (Baton Rouge, La.) 24:872-92 Aut '88

Manly conclusions. Hood, M.

Mann, Thomas, 1875-1955

A difficult hour
German stories; ed. by H. Steinhauer

The infant prodigy
The Nobel reader; ed. by J. Eisen and S. Troy

The wardrobe
The Penguin book of ghost stories

Mannequin. Rhys, J.

Manners, Margaret

Squeakie's first case
Witches; ed. by I. Asimov; M. H. Greenberg and C. G. Waugh

MANNERS AND CUSTOMS

Halligan, M. Trespassers or guests?

MANNERS AND CUSTOMS—*Continued*
O'Hara, J. Are we leaving tomorrow?
Warren, J. Fetters
Mannikins of horror. Bloch, R.
Mannita's garden cove. Dabydeen, C.
Manor, Jason *See* Hall, Oakley M.
MANORS *See* Houses
Manosque. Pierce, C.
Man's dwelling place. Gorodischer, A.
Mansfield, Katherine, 1888-1923
At the bay
   Mansfield, K. The garden-party
Bliss
   The Treasury of English short stories;
   ed. by N. Sullivan
The canary
   Mansfield, K. The garden-party
The doll's house
   Mansfield, K. The garden-party
The fly
   Mansfield, K. The garden-party
   The World of the short story; ed. by
   C. Fadiman
The garden party
   Early sorrow: ten stories of youth; ed.
   by C. Zolotow
   Mansfield, K. The garden-party
Her first ball
   Mansfield, K. The garden-party
How Pearl Button was kidnapped
   Child's ploy; ed. by M. Muller and B.
   Pronzini
   Mansfield, K. The garden-party
An ideal family
   Mansfield, K. The garden-party
The little governess
   On being foreign; ed. by T. J. Lewis and
   R. E. Jungman
New dresses
   Mansfield, K. The garden-party
Ole Underwood
   Mansfield, K. The garden-party
Prelude
   Mansfield, K. The garden-party
Six years after
   Mansfield, K. The garden-party
The stranger
   Mansfield, K. The garden-party
Taking the veil
   Mansfield, K. The garden-party
The voyage
   Mansfield, K. The garden-party
The woman at the store
   Mansfield, K. The garden-party
           About
King, F. H. A scent of mimosa
Mansfield, Kathleen Beauchamp *See* Mans-
   field, Katherine, 1888-1923
MANSIONS *See* Houses
Manslaughter. Oates, J. C.
Mansoura. Rifaat, A.

Mantel, Hilary
Dog days
   Encounter (London, England) 68:15-21
   My '87
Manuel, Juan
The wizard postponed
   Black water; ed. by A. Manguel
The **manuscript.** Bruce-Novoa
The **manuscript.** Hoyt, M. S.
The **manuscript** of Francis Shackerley. Gil-
   christ, M.
MANUSCRIPTS
Apollinaire, G. Little recipes from modern
   magic
Austin, D. The hypnotic mailbox
De la Torre, L. The missing Shakespeare
   manuscript
Dickens, C. A madman's manuscript
Hoyt, M. S. The manuscript
James, H. The death of the lion
King, F. H. Loss
Kirk, R. The reflex-man in Whinnymuir
   Close
"Oo-a-deen"; or, The mysteries of the in-
   terior unveiled
Pasternak, B. L. The Apelles mark
Smith, C. A. The chain of Aforgomon
Smith, C. A. The end of the story
Many mansions. Silverberg, R.
Manzione, Joseph
Candle in a cosmic wind
   The Year's best science fiction, fifth an-
   nual collection
The **Mao** button. Feng Jicai
MAORIS
Hulme, K. He tauware kawa, he kawa
   tauware
Hulme, K. A nightsong for the shining
   cuckoo
Hulme, K. While my guitar gently sings
Taylor, A. Bread and hunger
Taylor, A. The carving
Taylor, A. Casey and Sarah
Taylor, A. Fish heads
Taylor, A. Hera
Taylor, A. Hine e Hine
Taylor, A. The kumara plant
Taylor, A. Old mates
Taylor, A. Pa mai
Taylor, A. Pou
The **map.** Wolfe, G.
MAP DRAWING
Ferron, J. The provinces
The **map** of love. Thomas, D.
Maps to anywhere. Cooper, B.
Mar Nueva. Helprin, M.
Maraini, Dacia
My hands
   The Literary Review (Madison, N.J.)
   27:315-35 Spr '84

Marais, Eugène N.
Little-reed-alone-in-the-whirlpool
The Penguin book of Southern African stories
Maramzin, Vladimir
The two-toned blond: a reciprocal tale
The Barsukov Triangle, The two-toned blond & other stories; ed. by C. R. Proffer & E. Proffer
The **marathon** runner. Winters, J.
The **marble** angel. Halligan, M.
Marble Mildred. Collins, M. A.
The **marbled** horn. Ward, L.
MARBLES
Creekmore, H. The chain in the heart [excerpt]
March, William, 1893-1954
Not worthy of a Wentworth
The Art of fiction in the heart of Dixie; ed. by P. D. Beidler
The **march**. Colter, C.
March 11. Chambers, G.
A **March** Christmas. Alcott, L. M.
March of dimes. Martone, M.
The **marchers**. Dumas, H.
Marching through Delaware. Friedman, B. J.
Marching to Byzantium. Corodimas, P.
Marco in paradise. Kinsella, W. P.
Marcus, J. S.
The art of cartography
Harper's 273:65-8 D '86
Under water
The New Yorker 61:30-2 S 30 '85
Wartime
Antaeus 60:168-71 Spr '88
Marcus: a Gothic tale. Auchincloss, L.
Marcus of Clooney. Colum, P.
Mardeusz, Steven
The back-seat talker
Stories and poems from close to home; ed. by F. Salas
Mardon, Deirdre
Stranded
Redbook 169:70+ O '87
Marechera, Dambudzo
Protista
African short stories; ed. by C. Achebe and C. L. Innes
The slow sound of his feet
The Penguin book of Southern African stories
Mares, E. A., 1938-
Florinto
Cuentos Chicanos; ed. by R. A. Anaya and A. Márquez
Margaret, are you grieving? Bliss, C. D.
Margaret of the imperfections. Sexson, L.
Margaritas. Yunker, T.
Margery's prom. McGarry, J.
Marginals. Green, E.
Margot's tapers. Maupassant, G. de
Marguerite Howe. Deaver, P. F.
Marguerite Landmine. Kauffman, J.

Le **mari** terrible. Wells, H. G.
Maria. Doucette, R. J.
Maria Giuseppa. Landolfi, T.
Maria's girl. Farmer, B.
MARIE CELESTE (BRIGANTINE)
Doyle, Sir A. C. J. Habakuk Jephson's statement
Marie-Christine I: Valentine's Day. Lynch, L.
Marie-Christine II. Lynch, L.
Marie-Christine III: a butch named Dinah. Lynch, L.
Marielle. Bled, R. N.
MARIENBAD (CZECHOSLOVAKIA) *See* Czechoslovakia—Marienbad
Marigolds. Kadohata, C.
MARIHUANA *See* Marijuana
MARIJUANA
Birtha, B. The saints and sinners run
Bowles, P. He of the assembly
Campbell, E. Maundy Thursday
Campos-De Metro, J. Stock
Carver, R. What's in Alaska
Choyce, L. Billy Botzweiler's last dance
Jones, M. A beginning
MARINE ANIMALS
Shea, M. Polyphemus
MARINE BIOLOGY
See also Marine animals
MARINE CORPS (U.S.) *See* United States. Marine Corps
The **marine** excursion of the Knights of Pythias. Leacock, S. B.
MARINES (U.S.) *See* United States. Marine Corps
Marines signaling under fire at Guantanamo. Crane, S.
Marita. Mason, B. A.
A **Maritime** story. Levine, N.
Mark Haverly. Davis, S.
Mark of the Moon Man. Davis, F. C.
The **mark** on the wall. Woolf, V.
The **marked** man. Curtiss, U. R.
The **Market** Basing mystery. Christie, A.
Market woman. Asscher-Pinkhof, C.
MARKETS
Halligan, M. Hard sausage
Stuart, J. To market, to market
Thomas, N. At the market
Markham, Beryl, 1902-1986
Appointment in Khartoum
Markham, B. The splendid outcast
Brothers are the same
Markham, B. The splendid outcast
The captain and his horse
Markham, B. The splendid outcast
He was a good lion
Through other eyes; ed. by I. Zahava
The quitter
Markham, B. The splendid outcast
Something I remember
Markham, B. The splendid outcast

Markham, Beryl, 1902-1986—*Continued*
The splendid outcast
  Markham, B. The splendid outcast
The transformation
  Markham, B. The splendid outcast
Your heart will tell you
  Markham, B. The splendid outcast
Markham, Robert, 1922-
  For works written by this author under other names see Amis, Kingsley, 1922-
Markham. Bretnor, R.
Markheim. Stevenson, R. L.
Markings. Thurm, M.
Marko's smile. Yourcenar, M.
Marks. Lord, N.
Marlene's sister. Strauss, B.
Marlowe, Dan James, 1914-
By means unlovely
  Murder California style; ed. by J. L. Breen and J. Ball
The donor
  Alfred Hitchcock's Crimewatch
Give-and-take
  Alfred Hitchcock's Mortal errors
Marlowe, Stephen, 1928-
The shill
  The Wickedest show on earth; ed. by M. Muller and B. Pronzini
Wanted—dead and alive
  The Mammoth book of private eye stories; ed. by B. Pronzini and M. H. Greenberg
The **marmalade** eaters. Jahnn, H. H.
Marmariadis, Yannis *See* Haris, Petros, 1902-
Marmilion. McGrath, P.
Marmosets. Glasser, P.
Marmur, Jacland
The kid in command
  A Treasury of World War II stories; ed. by B. Pronzini and M. H. Greenberg
Maron, Margaret
Deadhead coming down
  Distant danger; ed. by J. Van de Wetering
Holiday houseguest
  McCall's 112:112-13+ D '84
Marosi, Gyula
The milk-boy
  Short story international 55
Marotta, Kenny
A seamstress
  The Virginia Quarterly Review 61:95-105 Wint '85
Marquand, John P. (John Phillips), 1893-1960
High tide
  A Treasury of Civil War stories; ed. by M. H. Greenberg and B. Pronzini
Márquez, Gabriel García *See* García Márquez, Gabriel, 1928-

Marquis, Don, 1878-1937
Blood will tell
  Roger Caras' Treasury of great dog stories
The **marquis.** Maupassant, G. de
The **Marquis** de Fumerol. Maupassant, G. de
The **Marquise** of O—. Kleist, H. von
MARRAKESH (MOROCCO) *See* Morocco—Marrakesh
MARRIAGE
  See also Childless marriage; Divorce; Family life; Husband and wife; Interfaith marriage; Interracial marriage; Marriage problems; Weddings
Abbott, K. A 50-50 marriage
Abbott, K. Mary Lou and the perfect husband
Abbott, L. K. Time and fear and somehow love
Adams, G. G. Inside dope
Alden, P. B. Blue mountains
Alden, P. B. Feeding the eagles
Apple, M. Business talk
Arredondo, I. The shunammite
Banks, R. Captions
Barthelme, F. Black tie
Baumbach, J. Children of divorced parents
Beattie, A. In the white night
Beattie, A. Times
Bedford, J. Through road
Bonner, M. On the altar
Botwinik, B. The last young man
Bowen, S. P. A marriage of persuasion
Bowen, S. P. Old maidism versus marriage
Boyle, K. Astronomer's wife
Brooks, G. The young couple at home
Brown, A. Natalie Blayne
Burns, M. Greta
Calisher, H. The sound track
Camoin, F. A. Sometimes the wrong thing is the right thing
Camoin, F. A. A special case
Camoin, F. A. Things I did to make it possible
Campbell, W. B. Kisses
Carneiro, A. A perfect marriage
Carver, R. Distance
Cho, H.-I. Iron masks
Christmas, R. A. Another angel
Chua, R. Second thoughts
Clark, M. H. Lucky day
Clift, C. Wild Emperor
Collins, L. A summer's day
Collins, L. When the pipes froze
Colum, P. Eilis: a woman's story
Colum, P. Marcus of Clooney
Colum, P. Marriage
Connelly, J. The holidays
Connelly, J. Partner
Cooper, J. C. About love and money; or, Love's lore and money's myth
Cooper, J. C. Funeral plans

MARRIAGE—*Continued*

Cope, J. Ekaterina

Coriolan, J. A marriage, a mantra, a massage

Dadswell, M. On the way to the Goat

Dickens, C. The Boots at the Holly-Tree Inn

Dixon, S. Don

Drake, R. A cool day in August

Eldridge, M. Adult education

Eldridge, M. Cream sponge on Sunday

Ellin, S. The last bottle in the world

Engberg, S. Soliloquy

Evans, E. Crime in Italy

Ferron, J. Back to Kentucky

Ferron, J. The wedding bouquet

Flaherty, G. Something to talk like a family about

Flanagan, R. Teller's ticket

Ford, R. Fireworks

Friedman, B. J. The pledges

Gallant, M. Lena

Gardner, M. Love and tiddlywinks

Garrett, G. P. The insects are winning: At least they'll have candlelight

Garrett, G. P. The insects are winning: The moth

Gee, M. The losers

Gee, M. A retired life

Gifkins, M. A final fling

Gilchrist, E. Adoration

Gilchrist, M. Midsummer madness

Gilliatt, P. Broderie anglaise

Gilliatt, P. Fred and Arthur

Gilliatt, P. Nobody's business

Glasser, P. Steering clear

Glasser, P. Visit

Goff, I. A ticket to Odessa

Gordon, M. Mrs. Cassidy's last year

Gordon, M. Now I am married

Gordon, M. Safe

Grin, A. Augustus Esborn's marriage

Gustafsson, L. The four railroads of Iserlohn

Halligan, M. A leisurely drowning

Hartley, L. P. The face

Hauser, M. The seersucker suit

Heckathorn, J. Hanalei

Henry, O. The lonesome road

Horvitz, L. A. Marriage vows

Houbein, L. The marriage of the beautiful lady who had a mind of her own

Houbein, L. A serious courtship

Hull, H. R. The fusing

James, H. The lesson of the master

Jhabvala, R. P. My first marriage

Kaufman, B. Sunday in the park

Kavaler, R. The perfume of love

Keillor, G. Du, du liegst mir im herzen

Keillor, G. Truckstop

Kim, C.-Y. The moon-welcoming flower

Kim, Y.-J. The visitor

Kinsella, W. P. A page from the marriage manual for Songhees brides

Klíma, I. Friday morning: an orderly's tale

Kotzwinkle, W. That winter when Prince Borisov was everybody's favorite

Krysl, M. Désirs

Krysl, M. Something unforgivable

Leaton, A. Tracks to the cold country

Leitão, L. Dona Amalia Quadros

Lessing, D. M. Out of the fountain

Lipman, E. Frankie's soup

Lipman, E. Immediate family

Martin, H. R. A poet though married

Mason, B. A. Hunktown

Matthews, J. Harry the woman killer

Maupassant, G. de. The last step

McCoy, E. Henry's eighth

McCullers, C. Art and Mr. Mahoney

McCullers, C. Who has seen the wind?

McGregor, C. The heraldry of the body

Mooney, M. Fidelity savings

Mrożek, S. A fact

Mukherjee, B. Visitors

Munro, A. Lichen

Nielsen, H. Never trust a woman

Oates, J. C. Harrow Street at Linden

O'Brien, D. Weightless

O'Flaherty, L. Milking time

Paley, G. The story hearer

Paley, G. Wants

Parise, G. Marriage

Pavese, C. The villa on the hill

Pilcher, R. An evening to remember

Potter, N. A. J. The bigamist

Pritchard, M. With wings cross water

Pritchett, V. S. The Camberwell beauty

Pu, S.-L. Yüeh Chung

Raddall, T. H. The wedding gift

Rand, P. A soldier of fortunes

Raphael, F. Benchmark

Regent, P. Summer pudding

Ríos, A. The birthday of Mrs. Piñeda

Roberts, N. Flames

Rooke, L. The madwoman of Cherry Vale

Rooke, L. Saks Fifth Avenue

Rooke, L. Sing me no love songs, I'll say you no prayers

Ruffolo, L. Birthday

Russell, C. Retiring man

Russell, R. American Gothic

Ruta, S. The autograph

Saiki, P. S. Communion

Saki. Tea

Sandel, C. Larsen's

Saroyan, W. How to choose a wife

Schwob, M. Blanche the bloody

Sedgwick, C. M. Old maids

Shefner, E. The common body

Slesinger, T. Mother to dinner

Smith, E. E. The good husband

Spark, M. The twins

Spencer, E. Jack of diamonds

Spivack, K. The honeymoon

MARRIAGE—*Continued*
Stead, C. My friend, Lafe Tilly
Steele, Sir R. The wedding of Jenny Distaff
Stockanes, A. E. Ladies who knit for a living
Strand, M. Mr. and Mrs. Baby
Struthers, A. Gathering evidence
Tallent, E. Half a mussel shell
Taylor, A. Hine e Hine
Taylor, P. E. At the altar
Taylor, P. H. A long fourth
Taylor-Hall, M. A. Banana boats
Thanet, O. Why Abbylonia surrendered
Thomas, A. C. Kill day on the government wharf
Thompson, J. New bed
Thompson, J. Of his bones are coral made
Thompson, K. A blunt affair
Thompson, K. Green things
Trevor, W. Bodily secrets
Tuohy, F. Dreams of unfair women
Updike, J. Made in heaven
Updike, J. Slippage
Vinge, J. D. Phoenix in the ashes
Wells, H. G. The devotee of art
Wexler, J. Your eighteenth birthday was a long time ago
Whitaker, M. Blackberry day
Wilbur, E. Ned
Wilbur, E. The success and the little failure
Willett, J. The jaws of life
Willett, J. Under the bed
Wolff, T. Leviathan
Woodman, A. TV guide
Woodman, A. Waiting for the broken horse
Woolf, V. Lappin and Lapinova
Wynne, M. Y. The little room
Zhang Jie. Love must not be forgotten

MARRIAGE, CHILDLESS *See* Childless marriage

MARRIAGE, INTERFAITH *See* Interfaith marriage

MARRIAGE, INTERRACIAL *See* Interracial marriage

Marriage. Colum, P.
The **marriage**. Lim, C.
Marriage. Parise, G.
A **marriage**, a mantra, a massage. Coriolan, J.
Marriage and the family. Williams, D.
Marriage at noon. Hill, E.

MARRIAGE BROKERS
Buck, P. S. The good deed
Malamud, B. The magic barrel
Mukherjee, B. Danny's girl
Petrakis, H. M. The siege of Minerva
Saiki, J. Arrival of the picture brides
The **marriage** bug. Reed, K.

MARRIAGE COUNSELING *See* Marriage problems

MARRIAGE CUSTOMS
Cordor, S. M. A farewell to the old order
Saiki, J. The arrangement
Saiki, J. Once, a lotus garden
Jews
Auswaks, A. The dowry
Shamosh, A. My sister the bride
Africa
Head, B. The lovers
Nicol, A. The truly married woman
China
Pu, S.-L. The Tou lass
Greece
Johnston, G. Astypalaian knife
India
Basu, R. Sambal and Putki
Begamudré, V. A promise we shall wake in the pink city after harvest
Sharat Chandra, G. S. Maya
Japan
Inoue, Y. A marriage interview
Kawabata, Y. A child's viewpoint
Kawabata, Y. The sparrow's matchmaking
Korea
Ha, K.-C. The spring song
Mexico
Sepúlveda, E. Elba Nazario
Turkey
Faik, S. The wedding night
Marriage eve. Latimer, M.
A **marriage** interview. Inoue, Y.
A **marriage** of convenience. Scobie, S.
A **marriage** of persuasion. Bowen, S. P.
A **marriage** of solipsists. Matthews, J.
The **marriage** of the beautiful lady who had a mind of her own. Houbein, L.

MARRIAGE PROBLEMS
See also Divorce; Family life; Interfaith marriage; Love affairs
Abbott, K. Back to nature
Abbott, K. Like you used to do
Aćin-Kosta, M. A psychological warrior
Adams, A. Ocracoke Island
Adams, A. Separate planes
Adams, A. You are what you own: a notebook
Adams, G. G. Inside dope
Adisa, O. P. Bake-Face
Ahern, T. The anatomist of Petrus Borel
Alcott, L. M. A double tragedy. An actor's story
Alcott, L. M. The fate of the Forrests
Aldiss, B. W. The girl who sang
Alter, R. E. To catch a big one
An, S.-G. The green chrysanthemum
Anderson, J. Outdoor friends
Apple, M. Kitty partners
Archer, J. A chapter of accidents
Ardizzone, T. The transplant
Atwood, M. Bluebeard's egg
Atwood, M. The salt garden
Auchincloss, L. The seagull
Auchincloss, L. The takeover

MARRIAGE PROBLEMS—*Continued*

Austin, M. H. The return of Mr. Wills
Bail, M. The drover's wife
Banks, R. Adultery
Banks, R. Indisposed
Banks, R. Mistake
Banks, R. Queen for a Day
Barbey d'Aurevilly, J. A woman's vengeance
Barstow, S. The apples of paradise
Barstow, S. The glad eye
Barstow, S. Work in progress
Barthelme, D. 110 West Sixty-First Street
Barthelme, D. Bluebeard
Barthelme, D. Jaws
Barthelme, F. Chroma
Barthelme, F. Perfect things
Barthelme, S. Beach
Barthelme, S. Get-together
Barthelme, S. Their house
Bates, H. E. Death of a huntsman
Bauer, D. Lore
Baumbach, J. Mr. and Mrs. McFeely at home and away
Baumbach, J. Passion?
Bausch, R. All the way in Flagstaff, Arizona
Bausch, R. Contrition
Bausch, R. Police dreams
Baxt, G. The woman I envied
Baxter, C. Xavier speaking
Baykurt, F. The airplane ticket
Beattie, A. It's just another day in Big Bear City, California
Beattie, A. Spiritus
Beattie, A. Summer people
Bedard, B. Hour of the beast
Beekman, E. M. Frisian horses
Bellamy, J. D. Saving the boat people
Bennett, J. G. Dependents
Benton, K. C. Cast for murder
Bergland, M. An embarrassment of ordinary riches
Birdsell, S. Night travellers
Bishop, M. The monkey's bride
Bissoondath, N. There are a lot of ways to die
Blaise, C. Translation
Blei, N. The chair trick
Blinkin, M. Card game
Blinkin, M. Family life: a chapter
Blinkin, M. In a dream
Blinkin, M. Smoke
Bloch, R. Fat chance
Bloch, R. A good imagination
Bloch, R. Life in our time
Bloch, R. A matter of life
Bloch, R. Method for murder
Block, L. You could call it blackmail
Blythe, R. The church mouse
Blyton, C. The final solution
Bombal, M. L. The tree
Bonner, M. Hate is nothing

Bonner, M. Stones for bread
Bonnie, F. Mistrial
Bonnie, F. Wide load, where are you?
Bonosky, P. Poor Joey
Boswell, R. The darkness of love
Boswell, R. Edward and Jill
Botwinik, B. The glazier
Bourjaily, V. The Amish farmer
Boyd, W. Killing lizards
Boyd, W. Love hurts
Boyle, T. C. All shook up
Bradley, M. Z. The engine
Brett, S. Parking space
Brett, S. Private areas
Brett, S. Unwilling sleep
Brondoli, M. Showdown
Brooks, J. Wrong play
Brown, F. Witness in the dark
Brown, L. Facing the music
Brown, M. W. Good-bye, Cliff
Bukoski, A. Stan and Ollie
Burke, J. L. The pilot
Burns, M. How it happened
Burns, M. A joint communique
Busch, F. Comrades
Busch, F. Dog song
Cain, J. M. The baby in the icebox
Caldwell, E. August afternoon
Caldwell, E. Yellow girl
Calisher, H. A Christmas carillon
Camoin, F. A. Miami
Campbell, W. B. The favour
Campos-De Metro, J. Stock
Carlson, R. Bigfoot stole my wife
Carrington, L. Monsieur Cyril de Guindre
Carter, M. The things that would never be mine
Carver, R. Blackbird pie
Carver, R. Careful
Carver, R. Fever
Carver, R. Gazebo
Carver, R. Menudo
Carver, R. Nobody said anything
Carver, R. One more thing
Carver, R. Popular mechanics
Carver, R. A serious talk
Carver, R. So much water so close to home
Carver, R. The third thing that killed my father off
Carver, R. Vitamins
Carver, R. What do you do in San Francisco?
Carver, R. Where I'm calling from
Cheever, J. The country husband
Cheever, J. The five-forty-eight
Cheever, J. The music teacher
Chekhov, A. P. His wife
Chekhov, A. P. My wife
Chekhov, A. P. Peasant women
Chekhov, A. P. Terror
Chekhov, A. P. The two Volodyas
Cheuse, A. The Tennessee waltz

MARRIAGE PROBLEMS—*Continued*

Chopin, K. Her letters
Claiborne, S. The future of conglomerates
Clark, M. A moment of illumination
Clark, M. "'Twere best not know myself"
Clarke, A. C. A man
Clarke, A. C. The smell
Cohen, A. The monumental sculptor
Cohen, M. Golden whore of the heartland
Coleman, W. Lickety-split
Colette. Dawn
Colette. The hidden woman
Colette. The respite
Colette. The return
Collier, J. Bird of prey
Colter, C. Overnight trip
Colum, P. Catherine Mulamphy and the man from the north
Colwin, L. My mistress
Colwin, L. Swan song
Cooke, R. T. How Celia changed her mind
Cooper, J. C. $100 and nothing!
Cooper, J. C. Liberated
Cooper, J. C. Say what you Willomay!
Corrington, J. W. Pleadings
Cortázar, J. Stories I tell myself
Coskran, K. Graven images
Coskran, K. Natural causes
Cowan, P. Living
Coxe, G. H. Seed of suspicion
Cullen, E. J. One-eyed Jacks
Curley, D. The contrivance
Curley, D. The other two
Dadswell, M. The bed
Dai Qing. Anticipation
Daniels, L. They're coming for you
Davidson, L. Indian rope trick
Davie, E. The return
Davis, D. S. Till death do us part
Davis, G. P. African story
Davis, K. Roach bait
Davis, L. Visit to her husband
De Queiroz, R. Metonymy; or, The husband's revenge
DeMarinis, R. Under the wheat
DeMarinis, R. Your burden is lifted, love returns
Deming, R. The better bargain
Dickens, C. The Baron of Grogzwig
Dickens, C. A madman's manuscript
Dickinson, C. Risk
Dilworth, S. The seeney stretch
Dixon, S. Goodbye to goodbye
Dixon, S. The last resort
Dixon, S. Moving on
Doctorow, E. L. The foreign legation
Doctorow, E. L. Lives of the poets
Donaldson, S. R. The conqueror worm
Dowell, C. The surgeon
Doyle, Sir A. C. The colonel's choice
Doyle, Sir A. C. The retirement of Signor Lambert
Doyle, Sir A. C. A sordid affair
Drake, M. The prison

Drake, R. Shoot, child, what you talking about?
Drewe, R. Looking for Malibu
Dubus, A. Adultery
Dubus, A. Delivering
Dubus, A. The fat girl
Dubus, A. Leslie in California
Dubus, A. Molly
Dubus, A. Over the hill
Dubus, A. The pretty girl
Dubus, A. We don't live here anymore
Duecker, K. Saving the dead
Duke, M. Little knives
Duke, M. The notif
Dunn, D. South America
Durban, P. In darkness
Durban, P. Made to last
Edgerton, C. Raney [excerpt]
Eisenstein, S. The weight goes on the downhill ski
Endō, S. My belongings
Engberg, S. Common happiness
Engberg, S. Fourth brother
Engberg, S. Trio
Erdrich, L. Flesh and blood
Estleman, L. D. The tree on Execution Hill
Evans, E. Another moon
Faik, S. Jealousy
Faust, I. Melanie and the purple people eaters
Feng Jicai. Numbskull
Ferguson, W. Freedom
Ferré, R. Sleeping beauty
Ferreira, R. A road somewhere
Ferron, J. The woman next door
Findley, T. Dinner along the Amazon
Finney, E. J. The investigator
Flanagan, R. Naked to naked goes
Flora, F. Where's Milo
Flores, C. N. Yellow flowers
Flynn, R. The saviour of the bees
Foltz-Gray, D. Departed coming back
Ford, R. Empire
Ford, R. Going to the dogs
Ford, R. Great Falls
Forrest, K. V. Force majeur
Franklin, P. A little peace
Franzen, B. Something the matter with Dad
Fraser, A. The night mother
Fraser, A. On the battlements
Freeman, J. Going out to sea
Fremlin, C. The luck of the Devil
Fremlin, C. The sensory deprivation tank
Fremlin, C. A strong shoulder to weep on
Fremlin, C. Test case
Friedman, P. Blackburn
Fuentes, C. The two Elenas
Gallagher, T. At mercy
Gallagher, T. Beneficiaries
Galsworthy, J. The neighbors
Gans, B. M. And here in Chicago it's 78°

MARRIAGE PROBLEMS—*Continued*

Gant, P. The revolver
Gardner, C. S. The man who loved water
Gardner, M. The horse on the escalator
Garrett, G. P. More geese than swans
Garrett, G. P. A record as long as your arm
Garrett, G. P. What's the matter with Mary Jane?
Garro, E. It's the fault of the Tlaxcaltecas
Gault, C. This bright night
Gault, C. This now fenceless world
Gee, M. The champion
Gee, M. Down in the world
Gee, M. A sleeping face
Gerber, M. J. At the fence
Gerber, M. J. Honeymoon
Gifkins, M. The dispossessed
Gilchrist, E. Miss Crystal's maid name Traceleen, she's talking, she's telling everything she knows
Gilchrist, E. Traceleen's diary
Giles, M. Chocolate footballs
Giles, M. A jar of emeralds
Giles, M. Peril
Gilliatt, P. Come back if it doesn't get better
Gilliatt, P. Foreigners
Gilliatt, P. Nobody's business
Gilman, C. P. Turned
Gingher, M. Wearing glasses
Glasser, P. Away out and over
Glover, D. H. Dog attempts to drown man in Saskatoon
Gold, H. Paris and Cleveland are voyages
Gold, H. What's become of your creature?
Gordimer, N. The life of the imagination
Gordimer, N. Sins of the third age
Grau, S. A. The way back
Graves, Mrs. A. J. Mary and Ellen Grosvenor; or, The two sisters
Greene, G. The basement room
Greene, G. Two gentle people
Greenwood, R. Charley Wales
Greenwood, R. Mind and body
Grenville, K. Rosalie's folly
Grzimek, M. Timestop
Gustafsson, L. The art of surviving November
Haake, K. Another kind of nostalgia
Haake, K. Natural histories
Haake, K. One pair red, one pair blue
Haake, K. Recently I've discovered my mistake
Haake, K. Wait until heaven
Haas, B. Dying in the goldenwest
Haas, B. When California was an island
Hall, M. L. Music lesson
Halligan, M. Pity the dumb beast
Halligan, M. A whiff of brimstone
Hansen, J. The Anderson boy
Hansen, R. True romance
Harper, F. E. W. The two offers
Harris, B. Light

Harris, E. The world record holder
Hartley, L. P. The island
Hartley, L. P. Won by a fall
Harvor, E. The teller's cage
Hauptman, W. Sierra wave
Havazelet, E. Natalie Wood's amazing eyes
Heinesen, W. The fall
Hemingway, E. A canary for one
Hemingway, E. Mr. and Mrs. Elliot
Hemingway, E. The short happy life of Francis Macomber
Hemmerchts, K. The sixth of the sixth of the year nineteen sixty-six
Hempel, A. Three popes walk into a bar
Highsmith, P. Mermaids on the golf course
Highsmith, P. Those awful dawns
Highsmith, P. When in Rome
Hill, R. The worst crime known to man
Hirota, Y. An invitation to a movie
Hoch, E. D. Dreaming is a lonely thing
Hollingshead, G. Rat with tangerine
Hood, M. After Moore
Hood, M. Inexorable progress
Hood, M. Solomon's seal
Horne, L. The last dancer
Hospital, J. T. After the fall
Houbein, L. Not without rain
Houbein, L. The sixth sense
Houbein, L. Three good reasons
Huang, C.-M. I love Mary
Huggan, I. Secrets
Humphrey, W. The last husband
Hurston, Z. N. Sweat
Huxley, A. The Gioconda smile
Hyon, C.-G. Fire
Ignatow, R. G. How?
Ingalls, R. St. George and the nightclub
Jackson, G. Sweet things
Jackson, H. H. How one woman kept her husband
Jhabvala, R. P. Desecration
Jhabvala, R. P. An experience of India
Jhabvala, R. P. On bail
Johnson, W. Sarajevo
Johnston, G. Requiem mass
Jolley, E. The performance
Jolley, E. Woman in a lampshade
Justice, D. R. The artificial moonlight
Kalpakian, L. Hairline fractures
Kalpakian, L. Youth in Asia
Kauffman, J. The Alvordton Spa and Sweat Shop
Kavaler, R. The Zeigarnik effect
Kawabata, Y. Earth
Kawabata, Y. Riding clothes
Kawabata, Y. The wife's search
Keeling, N. Agathe
Keeling, N. The little axe
Kees, W. The Purcells
Kessel, J. Hearts do not in eyes shine
Kessler, J. F. Corinth
Kessler, J. F. Iocasta
Kessler, J. F. Xanthippe

MARRIAGE PROBLEMS—*Continued*

Kilgore, D. Heaven vs. hell
Kilgore, D. Three alarm fire
Kim, Y. I. The snake man
Kim, Y. I. The taste of salt
Kinsella, W. P. Between
Kinsella, W. P. Nursie
Kittredge, W. Agriculture
Klass, P. In Africa
Krist, G. Ty and Janet
Kye, Y.-M. Adada the idiot
Lansdale, J. R. Trains not taken
Lao Hong. The gap
Le Guin, U. K. Ile Forest
Le Guin, U. K. She unnames them
Leaton, A. Mayakovsky, my love
Lee, T. Simon's wife
Leidiger, L. Snake head
Lessing, D. M. The habit of loving
Lessing, D. M. To room nineteen
Liben, M. Past due
Lim, C. The marriage
Lipman, E. Catering
Lish, G. The wire
Livesey, M. The ring
Livesey, M. Umbrellas
Loizeaux, W. Beside the Passaic
Long, D. Clearance
Long, D. Solstice
López Heredia, J. The retiree
Loukakis, A. The cheerfulness of the bush
Lunn, R. Mirrors
Lurie, M. Kelso's lady
Lurie, M. Letter
Lutz, J. Hand of fate
Lutz, J. The landscape of dreams
Lynch, L. The awakening
MacDonald, D. R. Eyestone
MacDonald, J. D. Bimini kill
MacLaverty, B. Between two shores
MacLaverty, B. The bull with the hard hat
MacMahon, B. Exile's return
Maheux-Forcier, L. ABC
Malamud, B. A lost grave
Mancuso, C. Mamie
Mansfield, K. Bliss
Mansfield, K. The stranger
Markham, B. The transformation
Mars-Jones, A. Structural anthropology
Marshall, O. Don't blame yourself at all
Martin, V. The cat in the attic
Martin, V. Spats
Matthews, J. Irrelevant ideas
Matthews, J. The secret hour
Matthiessen, P. Late in the season
Mattison, A. The colorful alphabet
Maugham, W. S. The colonel's lady
Maupassant, G. de. An adventure
Maupassant, G. de. An artifice
Maupassant, G. de. The avenger
Maupassant, G. de. How he got the Legion of Honor
Maupassant, G. de. Jeroboam
Maupassant, G. de. Marroca

Maupassant, G. de. A mésalliance
Maupassant, G. de. Monsieur Parent
Maupassant, G. de. A New Year's gift
Maupassant, G. de. The rabbit
Maupassant, G. de. Ugly
Maupassant, G. de. The upstart
Mayberry, F. V. No tomorrows
Mayers, C. Police calls
McGuane, T. Little extras
McGuane, T. The rescue
McKinley, J. Kafka in suburbia
McKinley, J. Kitchen conversation
McKinley, J. Moriarty's return
McKinley, J. Praying for a Fickleman
McQueen, J. Acorns
Meinke, P. A decent life
Mesler, C. Is there too much sex in soaps?
Miller, J. F. A lover of nature
Miller, S. Leaving home
Miller, S. Tyler and Brina
Millman, L. Midnight at the dump
Millman, L. The wrong-handed man
Moffatt, D. When Roger got married
Mohr, N. The artist (Inez)
Mohr, N. Aunt Rosana's rocker (Zoraida)
Monreal, D. N. The young wife
Mooney, M. Eros and crazy
Moore, G. A faithful heart
Moore, G. A Russian husband
Moore, L. To fill
Moravia, A. The belt
Morgan, S. Household expenses
Morris, M. The Hall of the Meteorites
Morris, M. Orphans of the Storm
Morris, W. The cat in the picture
Mortimer, J. C. Rumpole and the old, old story
Moskowitz, F. In going is a drama
Moyer, K. In the castle
Muller, M. Kindling point
Munro, A. Circle of prayer
Munro, A. Fits
Murphy, Y. Laws of nature
Muschg, A. The blue man
Na, T.-H. The water-mill
Nagibin, ÍU. M. The peak of success
Nagibin, ÍU. M. The runaway
Naipaul, S. The dolly house
Naipaul, S. The tenant
Narayan, R. K. The shelter
Nelson, K. Invisible life
Nelson, K. This light is for those at sea
Nesin, A. For a crate of lemons
Nordan, L. Wild dog
Norris, H. The cloven tree
Norris, H. The light on the water
Norris, H. The quarry
Oates, J. C. Accident
Oates, J. C. Ancient airs, voices
Oates, J. C. Bad habits
Oates, J. C. Détente
Oates, J. C. Double solitaire
Oates, J. C. The Jesuit

MARRIAGE PROBLEMS—*Continued*

Oates, J. C. Leila Lee
Oates, J. C. Raven's Wing
Oates, J. C. Tick
Oates, J. C. Train
Oates, J. C. The tryst
O'Brien, E. Baby blue
O'Brien, E. Mrs. Reinhardt
O'Brien, E. The small-town lovers
O'Brien, T. Quantum jumps
Ocampo, S. The prayer
O'Donnell, P. The Soo girl charity
O'Faoláin, S. Lovers of the lake
O'Grady, D. Geography lesson
O'Hara, J. Fatimas and kisses
O'Hara, J. The girl from California
O'Hara, J. Imagine kissing Pete
O'Hara, J. Natica Jackson
O'Hara, J. Zero
Olmstead, R. Bruno and Rachel
Olmstead, R. The mason
Olmstead, R. What to do first
Osborn, C. The last of it
Osborn, C. Other people's mail
Osborn, M. Maine
Ozick, C. The suitcase
Padayachee, D. A first encounter of the
marital kind
Painter, P. Intruders of sleepless nights
Paley, G. An interest in life
Panning, A. Pigs
Panova, V. F. Evdokia
Pascoe, B. Nautilus
Pascoe, B. Neither did I
Pascoe, B. That's what friends are for
Pavese, C. Wedding trip
Peterson, M. Coastal
Peterson, M. Like boats
Peterson, M. Two cats
Petrakis, H. M. The judgement
Petrakis, H. M. Song of songs
Pfeil, F. The idiocy of rural life
Pfeil, F. The quality of light in Maine
Phelps, E. S. No news
Phelps, E. S. The true story of Guenever
Pirandello, L. Candelora
Pirandello, L. The fish trap
Pohl, F. The blister
Pohl, F. My life as a born-again pig
Potter, N. A. J. The guests
Price, R. Truth and lies
Pritchard, M. Taking hold of Renee
Pritchett, M. The barrel racer
Pritchett, M. Peach seed
Pritchett, V. S. A family man
Pronzini, B. Deathwatch
Pronzini, B. His name was Legion
Prose, F. Useful ceremonies
Proulx, A. Bedrock
Proulx, A. A run of bad luck
Proulx, A. The wer-trout
Purdy, J. Short Papa
Rabasa, G. The lion. The eagle. The wolf

Ramírez, S. A bed of bauxite in Weipa
Raphael, F. Aperitif
Raphael, F. Forgetting it
Raphael, F. Oxbridge blues
Raphael, F. Similar triangles
Raphael, F. Someone else
Raphael, F. Still life
Raphael, F. That was Tory
Raymond, I. Taking a chance on Jack
Rees, D. Pip
Rendell, R. The clinging woman
Rendell, R. The fever tree
Rendell, R. The price of joy
Rendell, R. The vinegar mother
Rifaat, A. Badriyya and her husband
Rifaat, A. Distant view of a minaret
Rifaat, A. The long night of winter
Roberts, N. Training for Alaska
Robison, J. Envy
Robison, J. The line
Robison, M. Culpability
Rodoreda, M. The salamander
Rogers, T. N. R. You can do anything
Rooke, L. Dirty heels of the fine young
children
Rooke, L. The woman who talked to
horses
Rose, D. A. So long, million miles
Ross, S. The lamp at noon
Ross, V. Dark secrets
Rucker, R. von B. Inside out
Ruffolo, L. Commercials
Rule, J. The end of summer
Rule, J. The pruning of the apple trees
Runyon, C. Hangover
Rushin, P. Speed of light
Ruta, S. Carmela
Sagan, F. Aftermath of a duel
Sagan, F. The cat and the casino
Sagan, F. Incidental music
Sagan, F. Third person singular
Samples, H. Home cooking
Sams, F. Porphyria's lover
Sandberg, P. L. Calloway's climb
Sandel, C. Avalanche
Sandel, C. The child
Sandel, C. The picture from Hull
Sandel, C. Thank you, doctor
Sanders, S. R. The fire woman
Saroyan, W. What a world, said the bicy-
cle rider
Schmidt, H. J. Shoe
Schwartz, L. S. The age of analysis
Schwartz, L. S. The sound of Velcro
Schwartz, S. Monkey business
Schwartz, S. Society of Friends
Sciascia, L. End game
Sciascia, L. A matter of conscience
Scofield, S. Trespass
Seabrooke, D. Secrets
Sexson, L. Chalk line
Sharat Chandra, G. S. Bhat's return
Shaw, J. B. The trail to the ledge

MARRIAGE PROBLEMS—*Continued*

Sheckley, R. The last days of (parallel?) Earth
Shiga, N. Infatuation
Shiga, N. Rain frogs
Shivers, L. Here to get my baby out of jail [excerpt]
Sillitoe, A. The fishing-boat picture
Silva, B. No joy in the morning
Silverberg, R. Jennifer's lover
Silverberg, R. Needle in a timestack
Sims, G. Family butcher
Singer, I. B. Advice
Singer, I. B. Burial at sea
Singer, I. B. Disguised
Singer, I. B. Gimpel the fool
Singer, I. B. The image
Singer, I. B. The impresario
Singer, I. B. The mistake
Sisskind, M. The dawn of a new day
Sisskind, M. The devotions of Jean Blysema
Sladek, J. T. The last of the whaleburgers
Slesar, H. Item
Slesar, H. A victim must be found
Smiley, J. The age of grief
Smiley, J. Lily
Smiley, J. The pleasure of her company
Smith, E. E. Weather prediction
Smith, R. The princess, the Boeing, and the hot pastrami sandwich
Sohl, J. Cabin number six
Sorrells, R. T. The phone call
Spencer, B. The small things that save us
Spencer, E. The business venture
Spencer, E. The finder
Spencer, E. Jean-Pierre
Spivack, K. The guardian
Spivack, K. Loving
Spivack, K. My friend who lives in a commune
Spivack, K. The sacrifice
Spivack, K. Surviving
Spivack, K. Terms
Spofford, H. E. P. Her story
St. Clair, M. New ritual
St. Pierre, P. H. Frenchie's wife
Stark, S. S. The Appaloosa house
Stark, S. S. Best Quality Glass Company, New York
Stark, S. S. The dealers' yard
Stark, S. S. The horsehair
Starkman, E. M. Anniversary
Stead, C. About the house
Stead, C. The fathers
Stead, C. UNO 1945
Steele, M. Another love story
Stern, S. Leonard Shapiro banished from dreams
Stewart, R. Beans!
Stone, R. Not for love
Stowe, R. The pizza
Strand, M. Cephalus
Subramanian, U. Portrait of a woman

Summers, H. S. Amaryllis & the telephone
Summers, H. S. The man who looked young
Svendsen, L. Flight
Swados, H. The balcony
Swados, H. Something a little special
Swados, H. Year of grace
Swartz, J. After the yarn is spun
Swick, M. Heart
Swift, G. Cliffedge
Swift, G. The hypochondriac
Swift, G. Learning to swim
Symons, J. The best chess player in the world
Symons, J. The boiler
Tallent, E. Hannah's example
Tallent, E. Two ghosts of us
Taylor, C. Hamlin's story
Taylor, P. E. Kingdom come
Tenorio, F. H. Tata Fino
Thackeray, W. M. Dennis Haggarty's wife
Thomas, A. C. Goodbye Harold, good luck
Thomas, J. Barbecue
Thomas, J. Last factory blues
Thomas, M. Come to Africa and save your marriage
Thomas, M. A thief in my house
Thompson, B. Tattoo
Thompson, J. Ice flowers
Thompson, J. Having words
Thompson, K. Getting saved
Thompson, K. The keynote
Thompson, K. What happened
Thorman, C. Anchovy trees
Thorman, C. No job too small
Thurm, M. Floating
Thurm, M. Grace
Thurm, M. Light-years
Thurm, M. Lovers
Thurm, M. Markings
Thurm, M. Secrets
Thurm, M. Skaters
Thurm, M. Winter
Tindall, G. He who sows hope in the flesh
Tournier, M. The fetishist
Tournier, M. The Woodcock
Travis, L. Tom's burn
Tremain, R. Dinner for one
Tremain, R. My wife is a White Russian
Tremayne, P. The pooka
Trevor, W. Beyond the pale
Trevor, W. Running away
Tuohy, F. The Admiral and the nuns
Tuohy, F. In the dark years
Tuohy, F. Nocturne with neon lights
Turnley, J. E. The best foot forward
Tyler, A. The artificial family
Updike, D. The end of the reign
Updike, J. Beautiful husbands
Updike, J. Killing
Updike, J. The other
Updike, J. The other woman
Updike, J. Separating

MARRIAGE PROBLEMS—*Continued*

Valenzuela, L. A family for Clotilde
Van Langenberg, C. An unfinished head
Vander Putten, J. Just a little thing
Vanderhaeghe, G. Going to Russia
Vanderhaeghe, G. Man descending
Vanderhaeghe, G. Reunion
Vanderhaeghe, G. Sam, Soren, and Ed
Varley, J. Options
Vega, A. L. ADJ, Inc.
Viramontes, H. M. The long reconciliation
Virgo, S. Horsey horsey
Vivante, A. Can-can
Walker, A. The abortion
Walker, A. Coming apart
Walser, M. The move
Walters, A. L. Going home
Wang Zhecheng, and Wen Xiaoyu. Nest egg
Warner, S. T. Idenborough
Weber, T. The night of the sea serpent
Welch, S. The time, the place, the loved one
Weldon, F. Alopecia
Weldon, F. Threnody
Wells, H. G. A family elopement
Wells, H. G. Le mari terrible
Wells, H. G. The purple pileus
Wendt, A. A talent
West, J. Mother's Day
Wharton, E. Ethan Frome
Wheeler, K. Judgment
Whelan, G. Spies and lovers
Whitaker, M. Time for chapel
White, P. Willy-Wagtails by moonlight
Wiebe, D. E. Passage to India
Wilhelm, K. Isosceles
Wilkinson, R. The bitch
Willett, J. The haunting of the Lingards
Williams, J. Rot
Williams, T. Something by Tolstoi
Williams, T. Three players of a summer game
Williams, T. The vine
Wilner, H. Air
Wilson, B. Il circo delle donne
Wilson, B. Stalingrad
Wilson, L. A. The raising
Windsor, G. A real little marriage-wrecker
Winton, T. Minimum of two
Winton, T. More
Winton, T. Wake
Yamamoto, H. Seventeen syllables
Yi, S. A discontinued knot
Yi, S. Wings
Yorke, M. The wrath of Zeus
Zapolska, G. Kitten
Zapolska, G. Little frog
Ziem, J. Before the thunderstorm
Ziem, J. Something's missing
Zwicky, F. The courts of the lord

MARRIAGE PROPOSALS

Baum, L. F. The glass dog
Baum, L. F. The queen of Quok

Cameron, P. Nuptials & heathens
Doyle, Sir A. C. The voice of science
Fisher, M. F. K. Another love story
Lipman, E. Back to normal
Moore, G. Under the fan
Pirandello, L. The long dress
Regent, P. The proposal
Silverberg, R. To be continued
Sparling, E. E. Daughter of Lescale
Trevor, W. Lunch in winter
Van Zleer, D. Violet's choice
Whitaker, M. Landlord of the Crystal Fountain

Marriage vows. Horvitz, L. A.

Married. Mooney, M.

The **married** land. Bell, C. G.

A **married** woman. Feeney, J.

Marrington, Pauline

The beautiful journey
    Home and away; ed. by R. Creswell

Marroca. Maupassant, G. de

Marryat, Frederick, 1792-1848

The legend of the bell rock
    Mysterious sea stories; ed. by W. Patrick

The midshipman
    Men at sea; ed. by B. Aymar

MARS (PLANET)

Anthony, P. Hard sell
Anthony, P. Hurdle
Asimov, I. The Martian way
Bishop, M. Out of the mouths of Olympus
Bishop, M. Vox Olympica
Bradbury, R. The love affair
Clifton, M. Hang head, vandal!
Cowper, R. The scent of silverdill
Dick, P. K. A game of unchance
Farmer, P. J. My sister's brother
Matheson, R. C. Dust
Miller, W. M. Crucifixus etiam
Piper, H. B. Omnilingual
Robinson, K. S. Green Mars
Smith, C. A. The dweller in the gulf
St. Clair, M. Idris' pig
Sterling, B. Sunken gardens
Vinge, J. D. Voices from the dust

Mars-Jones, Adam, 1954-

Structural anthropology
    The Penguin book of modern British short stories

Marsh, Dame Ngaio, 1899-1982

Chapter and verse
    Chapter & hearse; ed. by M. Muller and B. Pronzini

Death on the air
    Masterpieces of mystery and suspense; ed. by M. H. Greenberg

I can find my way out
    Death locked in; ed. by D. G. Greene and R. C. S. Adey

Marshall, Alan, 1902-
Trees can speak
  The Australian short story; ed. by L. Hergenhan
Marshall, Donald R., 1934-
Lavender blue
  Greening wheat: fifteen Mormon short stories
Marshall, Joyce
The old woman
  The Oxford book of Canadian short stories in English
Marshall, Owen
Don't blame yourself at all
  Short story international 68
The master of big jingles
  Short story international 51
The paper parcel
  Short story international 55
Marshall in Rome. Briskin, M.
MARSHALL ISLANDS
Macinnes, P. View from Kwaj
Marsten, Richard, 1926-
  For works written by this author under other names see Hunter, Evan, 1926-; McBain, Ed, 1926-
Mårtensson, Bertil
Myxomatosis forte
  The Penguin world omnibus of science fiction
Martha, Henry *See* Harris, Mark, 1922-
Martha Jean. Driskell, L. V.
MARTIAL LAW
Nowakowski, M. The distributor
Nowakowski, M. The peacock
The **Martian** and the moron. Sturgeon, T.
Martian tales. Tsyganov, V.
The **Martian** way. Asimov, I.
MARTIANS
  See also Interplanetary visitors; Mars (Planet)
Bradbury, R. The love affair
Brown, F. Keep out
Clarke, A. C. Jupiter V
Fraser, J. Utopian dreams
Jeppson, J. O. A million shades of green
Kersh, G. Men without bones
Moore-Bentley, M. A. A woman of Earth
Tsyganov, V. Martian tales
Martians. Abbott, L. K.
Martin, Claire
The gift
  The Oxford book of French-Canadian short stories
Martin, David
Amazing powers
  Stand one; ed. by M. Blackburn; J. Silkin and L. Tracy
Martin, Donald
Footprints in a ghost town
  Alfred Hitchcock's Crimewatch

Martin, George R. R.
And seven times never kill man
  Martin, G. R. R. Nightflyers
The exit to San Breta
  Fantastic stories; ed. by M. H. Greenberg and P. L. Price
The ice dragon
  Dragons of light; ed. by O. S. Card
In the lost lands
  A Very large array; ed. by M. M. Snodgrass
The monkey treatment
  The Year's best science fiction, first annual collection
Nightflyers
  Martin, G. R. R. Nightflyers
Nor the many-colored fires of a star ring
  Martin, G. R. R. Nightflyers
Override
  Martin, G. R. R. Nightflyers
The pear-shaped man
  Omni (New York, N.Y.) 10:62-4+ O '87
  The Year's best fantasy, first annual collection
Portraits of his children
  Nebula awards 21
Run to starlight
  The Science fictional Olympics; ed. by I. Asimov; M. H. Greenberg and C. G. Waugh
Sandkings
  The Hugo winners v5
  Omni book of science fiction 1
A song for Lya
  Martin, G. R. R. Nightflyers
Under siege
  Omni (New York, N.Y.) 8:76-8+ O '85
  The Year's best science fiction, third annual collection
The way of cross and dragon
  The Hugo winners v5
Weekend in a war zone
  Martin, G. R. R. Nightflyers
Martin, Helen Reimensnyder
Mrs. Gladfelter's revolt
  Between mothers & daughters; ed. by S. Koppelman
A poet though married
  The Other woman; ed. by S. Koppelman
Martin, Jane
Twirler
  Sudden fiction; ed. by R. Shapard and J. Thomas
Martin, Russell
Cliff Dwellers
  Writers of the purple sage; ed. by R. Martin and M. Barasch
Martin, Valerie
The cat in the attic
  Martin, V. The consolation of nature, and other stories

Martin, Valerie—*Continued*
The consolation of nature
  Martin, V. The consolation of nature, and other stories
Death goes to a party
  Martin, V. The consolation of nature, and other stories
Elegy for dead animals
  Martin, V. The consolation of nature, and other stories
The freeze
  Martin, V. The consolation of nature, and other stories
The parallel world
  Martin, V. The consolation of nature, and other stories
Sea lovers
  Martin, V. The consolation of nature, and other stories
Spats
  Martin, V. The consolation of nature, and other stories
The way of the world
  Martin, V. The consolation of nature, and other stories
The woman who was never satisfied
  Martin, V. The consolation of nature, and other stories
Martina. Greeley, A. M.
Martine. Ferron, J.
Martine continued. Ferron, J.
Martínez-Serros, Hugo, 1930-
The birthday present
  Martínez-Serros, H. The last laugh, and other stories
Distillation
  Martínez-Serros, H. The last laugh, and other stories
Father Palomo
  Martínez-Serros, H. The last laugh, and other stories
Her
  Martínez-Serros, H. The last laugh, and other stories
Jitomates
  Martínez-Serros, H. The last laugh, and other stories
Killdeer
  Martínez-Serros, H. The last laugh, and other stories
The last laugh
  Martínez-Serros, H. The last laugh, and other stories
"Learn! Learn!"
  Martínez-Serros, H. The last laugh, and other stories
Octavo
  Martínez-Serros, H. The last laugh, and other stories
Ricardo's war
  Martínez-Serros, H. The last laugh, and other stories

Victor and David
  Martínez-Serros, H. The last laugh, and other stories
Martini, Clem
Breath of God
  Alberta bound; ed. by F. Stenson
Martins, Anna Maria
Collage
  The Literary Review (Madison, N.J.) 27:496-503 Summ '84
Martone, Michael
An accident
  Martone, M. Safety patrol
Biograph
  The Norton book of American short stories
Carbonation
  Martone, M. Safety patrol
King of safety
  Martone, M. Safety patrol
Lost
  Martone, M. Safety patrol
March of dimes
  Martone, M. Safety patrol
Nein
  Martone, M. Safety patrol
Parting
  Martone, M. Safety patrol
The safety patrol
  Martone, M. Safety patrol
A short, short story complete on these two pages
  Martone, M. Safety patrol
The third day of trials
  Martone, M. Safety patrol
Watch out
  Martone, M. Safety patrol
X-ray
  Martone, M. Safety patrol
The **martyred** poet. Harris, M.
MARTYRS
  Endō, S. Unzen
The **martyr's** crown. O'Brien, F.
MARUT, RET See Traven, B.
Marva Jean Howard confesses. Adams, G. G.
MARY, BLESSED VIRGIN, SAINT
  About
  Valenzuela, L. Trial of the Virgin
Mary. Hubbard, P. M.
Mary. Sanford, W. M.
Mary and Ellen Grosvenor; or, The two sisters. Graves, Mrs. A. J.
Mary Beth. Gault, C.
Mary Burnet. Hogg, J.
Mary in the mountains. Tilghman, C.
Mary Lou and the perfect husband. Abbott, K.
Mary Margaret Road-Grader. Waldrop, H.
Mary, Mary so contrary. Stefaniak, M. H.
The **Mary** mystery. Vreuls, D.
Mary Postgate. Kipling, R.
Mary will be good for Warren. Dawson, F.

MARYLAND
 See also Chesapeake Bay (Md. and Va.)
Baltimore
Leedom-Ackerman, J. Of imagination
Leedom-Ackerman, J. The tutor
Mary's convert. Colter, C.
Mary's garden. Lynch, L.
MASAI (AFRICAN PEOPLE)
Markham, B. Brothers are the same
Masefield, John, 1878-1967
Ambitious Jimmy Hicks
 Short stories of the sea; ed. by G. C. Solley and E. Steinbaugh
Being ashore
 Short stories of the sea; ed. by G. C. Solley and E. Steinbaugh
Davy Jones's gift
 Mysterious sea stories; ed. by W. Patrick
 Short stories of the sea; ed. by G. C. Solley and E. Steinbaugh
Don Alfonso's treasure hunt
 Sea captains' tales; ed. by A. Enfield
On growing old
 Short stories of the sea; ed. by G. C. Solley and E. Steinbaugh
The **mask**. Coalhouse, V.
The **mask**. DeGrazia, E.
The **mask**. Lem, S.
The **masked** crusader. Pentecost, H.
MASKS (FOR THE FACE)
Kawabata, Y. The man who did not smile
Leidiger, L. Snake head
Lynn, E. A. At the Embassy Club
Moravia, A. What use have I got for carnival?
Schwob, M. The king in the golden mask
Walpole, Sir H. The silver mask
Yi, C.-J. The dream of a mask
MASKS (SCULPTURE)
Silverberg, R. Not our brother
Masks. Sheehan, R.
Masks. Winter, D. E.
MASOCHISM
Gaitskill, M. A romantic weekend
Gaitskill, M. Secretary
Hemley, R. Riding The Whip
Kilworth, G. The dissemblers
Matheson, R. C. Mr. Right
Moravia, A. The belt
Raphael, F. That was Tory
Mason, Bobbie Ann
Big Bertha stories
 Prize stories, 1986
 Soldiers & civilians; ed. by T. Jenks
Blue country
 The Graywolf annual 2
Bumblebees
 The New Yorker 63:32-40 Mr 9 '87
 Prize stories, 1988
Coyotes
 The New Yorker 64:29-38 Je 13 '88

Do you know what it means to Miss New Orleans?
 The Paris Review 26:79-92 Fall '84
Drawing names
 The New writers of the South; ed. by C. East
Graveyard day
 Love stories for the time being; ed. by G. D. Chipps and B. Henderson
Hunktown
 The Atlantic 253:56-64 Ja '84
 The Graywolf annual [1]
In country
 The New Yorker 61:38-48+ Je 3 '85
Love life
 The New Yorker 60:42-50 O 29 '84
Marita
 Mother Jones 13:41-6 My '88
Memphis
 The New Yorker 64:34-42 F 22 '88
Midnight magic
 The New Yorker 63:26-33 Ag 24 '87
Residents and transients
 Great American love stories; ed. by L. Rosenthal
Shiloh
 American short story masterpieces; ed. by R. Carver and T. Jenks
 New women and new fiction; ed. by S. Cahill
Sorghum
 The Paris Review 30:206-21 Summ '88
State champions
 Harper's 274:68-72+ F '87
Wish
 The New Yorker 64:28-32 Ag 15 '88
Mason, Lisa
Arachne
 Omni (New York, N.Y.) 10:108-10+ D '87
Mason, Robert
His brother Joe 1914-1964
 The Virginia Quarterly Review 63:340-4 Spr '87
The **mason**. Olmstead, R.
MASONS (SECRET ORDER) *See* Freemasons
The **masque** of the Red Death. Poe, E. A.
MASQUERADES
Colette. The hidden woman
Martin, V. Death goes to a party
Poe, E. A. Hop-frog
Poe, E. A. The masque of the Red Death
Sayers, D. L. The queen's square
The **mass** of Saint Sécaire. Crowley, A.
MASSACHUSETTS
 See also Charles River (Mass.); Nantucket Island (Mass.)
17th century
Barker, S. The fog on Pemble Green
Hawthorne, N. The gentle boy
Hawthorne, N. Main-street

MASSACHUSETTS — 17th century — *Continued*
  Hawthorne, N. My kinsman, Major Molineux
      18th century
  Irving, W. The Devil and Tom Walker
      20th century
  Clayton, J. J. Fantasy for a Friday afternoon
  Dubus, A. Townies
  Mason, B. A. Blue country
  Updike, D. Agawam
  Updike, J. More stately mansions
      Boston
  Flaherty, G. Blood
  Flaherty, G. Filthy the man
  Flaherty, G. The main chance
  Flaherty, G. The man who saved himself
  Flaherty, G. The man who wore sunlight
  Flaherty, G. Something to talk like a family about
  Flaherty, G. The terrible speed of mercy
  Flaherty, G. Whom God hath promised
  Gates, D. China Blue
  Hawthorne, N. The gray champion
  Helprin, M. Palais de Justice
  Hoch, E. D. The problem of the Boston Common
  Just, W. S. About Boston
  Klass, P. The almond torte equilibrium
  Lovecraft, H. P. Pickman's model
  MacLeod, C. It was an awful shame
  O'Connor, W. D. The ghost
  Rafferty, S. S. The Massachusetts peep-o'night
  Robison, J. The line
  Taylor, P. A. The swan-boat murder
      Cambridge
  Clayton, J. J. Cambridge is sinking!
      Cape Cod
  Goldman, E. S. Way to the dump
  Nelson, K. This light is for those at sea
  Schulman, H. Inventions
  Theroux, P. Yard sale
      Salem
  Hawthorne, N. Main-street
  Howard, V. E. The midnight voyage of the Seagull
  Pyle, H. The Salem wolf
      Worcester
  Ferguson, W. The claims adjuster
The **Massachusetts** peep-o'night. Rafferty, S. S.
Massacre at Cottonwood Springs. Patten, L. B.
MASSACRES
  Arnold, M. Pilgrims to the cathedral
  Gordimer, N. Oral history
  Kleist, H. von. Betrothal in Santo Domingo
  Wilhelm, K. The village
MASSAGE
  Colette. A masseuse

Massé. Wilson, L. A.
A **masseuse**. Colette
Massie, Elizabeth
  Sick'un
      Bringing down the moon; ed. by J. Anderson
Massimo. Day, R. C.
The **"master"**. Colette
The **master** & servant act. Mathers, P.
Master Jakob and Miss Urd. Heinesen, W.
A **master** of Babylon. Pangborn, E.
The **master** of big jingles. Marshall, O.
Master of ceremonies. Murphy, P.
The **master** of Doornvlei. Mphahlele, E.
Master of his fate. Liphshitz, A.
The **master** of Rampling gate. Rice, A.
Master of the asteroid. Smith, C. A.
Master race. Oates, J. C.
A **master** selects his servant. Jahnn, H. H.
Master Therion *See* Crowley, Aleister, 1875-1947
A **master** time. Still, J.
The **masterpiece**. Bloch, R.
Masters, Olga, 1919-
  The Lang women
      Room to move; ed. by S. Falkiner
  The rages of Mrs. Torrens
      The Australian short story; ed. by L. Hergenhan
MASTURBATION
  Amis, M. Let me count the times
  Clark, D. Answer to prayer
  Franklin, P. A little peace
  Griffin, S. Cradles of light
  Huggan, I. Sawdust
  McGrath, P. Hand of a wanker
  Moravia, A. The woman with the black cloak
  Murphy, Y. The headdress
  Soldatow, S. White noise
  Watmough, D. Sacred & secular
Masuji, Ibuse
  The carp
      The Literary Review (Madison, N.J.)
      28:34-7 Fall '84
Masur, Harold Q.
  The $2,000,000 defense
      Hitchcock in prime time; ed. by F. M. Nevins and M. H. Greenberg
  Dead game
      Alfred Hitchcock's Mortal errors
  Framed for murder
      Crime of my life; ed. by B. Garfield
Match-boxes. Bowering, G.
Matches. Janowitz, T.
Matching the blue. Gifkins, M.
MATCHMAKERS *See* Marriage brokers
The **matchmakers**. Tuohy, F.
MATCHMAKING
  Cooper, J. C. Down that lonesome road
  Durrell, L. 'Noblesse oblige'
The **matchstick** hut. Darling, J.
Mateo Falcone. Mérimée, P.

Maternity. Eldridge, M.
The **mateship** syndrome. Forshaw, T.
Mathabane, Mark
  The road to Alexandra
    Somehow tenderness survives; ed. by H.
    Rochman
MATHEMATICIANS
  Dnieprov, A. The Maxwell equations
  Leiber, F. A rite of spring
  Leinster, M. Sidewise in time
  Orr, W. F. Euclid alone
  Pohl, F. Schematic man
MATHEMATICS
        See also Arithmetic
  Gross, H. H. Cubeworld
  Kagan, N. The mathenauts
  Krisman, S. No marks for Rolf
  Rucker, R. von B. A new golden age
  Sakers, D. The finagle fiasco
The **mathenauts**. Kagan, N.
Mathers, Peter, 1931-
  Arthur & Alwyn
    Mathers, P. A change for the better
  Chains
    Mathers, P. A change for the better
  A change for the better
    Mathers, P. A change for the better
  The chemical works
    Mathers, P. A change for the better
  Getting there
    Mathers, P. A change for the better
  The Henshaws
    Mathers, P. A change for the better
  Immersion
    Mathers, P. A change for the better
  Journey in
    Mathers, P. A change for the better
  A knight of teeth
    Mathers, P. A change for the better
  Lights
    Mathers, P. A change for the better
  Like a Maori prince
    Mathers, P. A change for the better
  The master & servant act
    Mathers, P. A change for the better
  Micki New
    Mathers, P. A change for the better
  Minutes
    Mathers, P. A change for the better
  Picking a loser
    Mathers, P. A change for the better
  Plaster, culture, rape and deprivation
    Mathers, P. A change for the better
  A small drop
    Mathers, P. A change for the better
  Something touchy and delicate again
    Mathers, P. A change for the better
  Sound worm
    Mathers, P. A change for the better
Matheson, Richard, 1926-
  Big surprise
    Rod Serling's Night gallery reader

  Born of man and woman
    The Dark descent; ed. by D. G. Hart-
    well
  Buried talents
    Masques II; ed. by J. N. Williamson
  Dance of the dead
    Masters of darkness; ed. by D. Etchison
  Dress of white silk
    The Best horror stories from the
    Magazine of fantasy and science fiction
  Drink my blood [Variant title: Blood son]
    Vampires; ed. by A. Ryan
  Graveyard shift
    Masterpieces of terror and the super-
    natural; ed. by M. Kaye and S. Kaye
  The near departed
    Masques II; ed. by J. N. Williamson
  Old haunts
    Young ghosts; ed. by I. Asimov; M. H.
    Greenberg and C. G. Waugh
  Shoo fly
    Omni (New York, N.Y.) 11:50-2+ N '88
  The test
    Isaac Asimov presents the best science
    fiction firsts
  (jt. auth) See Matheson, Richard Christian,
    and Matheson, Richard, 1926-
Matheson, Richard Christian
  Beholder
    Matheson, R. C. Scars and other
    distinguishing marks
  Break-up
    Matheson, R. C. Scars and other
    distinguishing marks
  Cancelled
    Matheson, R. C. Scars and other
    distinguishing marks
  Commuters
    Matheson, R. C. Scars and other
    distinguishing marks
  Conversation piece
    Matheson, R. C. Scars and other
    distinguishing marks
  The Dark Ones
    Matheson, R. C. Scars and other
    distinguishing marks
  Dead end
    Matheson, R. C. Scars and other
    distinguishing marks
  Deathbed
    Masques II; ed. by J. N. Williamson
  Dust
    Matheson, R. C. Scars and other
    distinguishing marks
  Echoes
    Matheson, R. C. Scars and other
    distinguishing marks
  The good always comes back
    Matheson, R. C. Scars and other
    distinguishing marks
  Goosebumps
    Matheson, R. C. Scars and other
    distinguishing marks

Matheson, Richard Christian—*Continued*
Graduation
Matheson, R. C. Scars and other distinguishing marks
Hell
Matheson, R. C. Scars and other distinguishing marks
Silver scream; ed. by D. J. Schow
Holiday
Matheson, R. C. Scars and other distinguishing marks
Incorporation
Matheson, R. C. Scars and other distinguishing marks
Intruder
Matheson, R. C. Scars and other distinguishing marks
Mobius
Matheson, R. C. Scars and other distinguishing marks
Mr. Right
Matheson, R. C. Scars and other distinguishing marks
Mugger
Matheson, R. C. Scars and other distinguishing marks
Obsolete
Matheson, R. C. Scars and other distinguishing marks
Red
Matheson, R. C. Scars and other distinguishing marks
Sentences
Matheson, R. C. Scars and other distinguishing marks
Sirens
Silver scream; ed. by D. J. Schow
Third wind
Masques; ed. by J. N. Williamson
Masters of darkness; ed. by D. Etchison
Matheson, R. C. Scars and other distinguishing marks
Timed exposure
Matheson, R. C. Scars and other distinguishing marks
Unknown drives
Matheson, R. C. Scars and other distinguishing marks
Vampire
Cutting edge; ed. by D. Etchison
Matheson, R. C. Scars and other distinguishing marks
Matheson, Richard Christian, and Matheson, Richard, 1926-
Where there's a will
Matheson, R. C. Scars and other distinguishing marks
Matheson, Shirlee
Harris
Alberta bound; ed. by F. Stenson

Mathews, Aidan
Nephritis
Stand one; ed. by M. Blackburn; J. Silkin and L. Tracy
Mathews, Harry
Singular pleasures
Grand Street 7:36-49 Wint '88
Mathews, Patricia Shaw
Darkness over Mirhold
Tales of the Witch World 2
Well met in Ithkar
Magic in Ithkar [1]; ed. by A. Norton and R. Adams
Matinee. Colette
Matinee at the Bijou. Covino, M.
Mating. Kajii, M.
MATRIARCHS *See* Mothers
MATRIARCHY
Bond, N. Pilgrimage
Russ, J. When it changed
Tiptree, J. Houston, Houston, do you read?
Yolen, J. Evian Steel
MATRICIDE *See* Parricide
Matsoukas. Petrakis, H. M.
Matsumoto, Seicho
Just eighteen months
Ellery Queen's Prime crimes
The secret alibi
Murder in Japan; ed. by J. L. Apostolou and M. H. Greenberg
Wait a year and a half
The Mother of dreams, and other short stories; ed. by M. Ueda
The woman who took the local paper
Murder in Japan; ed. by J. L. Apostolou and M. H. Greenberg
MATSUO, BASHO, 1644-1694
About
Davenport, G. Fifty-seven views of Fujiyama
MATTER
Asimov, I. Eyes do more than see
A **matter** of conscience. Sciascia, L.
A **matter** of dignity. Monreal, D. N.
A **matter** of disguise. Bruno-Holley, M.
A **matter** of ethics. Randisi, R. J.
A **matter** of experience. Toole, W.
A **matter** of fact. Kipling, R.
A **matter** of form. Gold, H. L.
A **matter** of life. Bloch, R.
A **matter** of numbers. Rule, J.
A **matter** of pride. Mazel, D.
A **matter** of public notice. Davis, D. S.
A **matter** of responsibility. Lawler, P.
A **matter** of style. Heller, S.
A **matter** of taste. Godwin, P.
A **matter** of technique. Dickson, G. R.
A **matter** of traces. Herbert, F.
Matthew, Jean R.
Amy Rose, 1947
Matthew, J. R. Testimony

Matthew, Jean R.—*Continued*
  Bar song
    Matthew, J. R. Testimony
  Family visit
    Matthew, J. R. Testimony
  The letters of Mrs. J. L. Hartle
    Matthew, J. R. Testimony
  The life and death of Martha
    Matthew, J. R. Testimony
  Sweet Letty
    Matthew, J. R. Testimony
  Testimony
    Matthew, J. R. Testimony
Matthews, Jack
  The amnesia ballet
    Matthews, J. Ghostly populations
  Amos Bond, the gunsmith
    Matthews, J. Ghostly populations
  The betrayal of the fives
    Matthews, J. Ghostly populations
  Bothering
    The Kenyon Review ns10:87-96 Wint '88
  Brumbacher breathing
    The Southern Review (Baton Rouge, La.)
      20:710-19 Jl '84
  The burial
    The Georgia Review 40:217-30 Spr '86
    Necessary fictions; ed. by S. W. Lind-
      berg and S. Corey
  A cat may look
    Matthews, J. Crazy women
  Critical decisions of early years
    The Kenyon Review ns7:54-66 Fall '85
  Dark, dark
    The Antioch Review 42:224-33 Spr '84
    Matthews, J. Ghostly populations
  Five women
    Matthews, J. Crazy women
  The ghost of First Crow
    Matthews, J. Ghostly populations
  Ghostly populations
    Matthews, J. Ghostly populations
  The grave at Mount Nebo
    Matthews, J. Crazy women
  The gray lady
    Matthews, J. Crazy women
  Harry the woman killer
    Matthews, J. Crazy women
  Haunted by name our ignorant lips
    Matthews, J. Crazy women
  If not us, then who?
    Matthews, J. Ghostly populations
  The immortal dog
    Matthews, J. Ghostly populations
  Irrelevant ideas
    Matthews, J. Crazy women
  Isaac Trimble's tale
    The Kenyon Review ns6:42-52 Fall '84
  Mange
    Matthews, J. Crazy women
  A marriage of solipsists
    Matthews, J. Crazy women

  Quest for an unnamed place
    Matthews, J. Ghostly populations
  A questionnaire for Rudolph Gordon
    Sudden fiction; ed. by R. Shapard and
      J. Thomas
  Return to an unknown city
    Matthews, J. Ghostly populations
  The secret hour
    Matthews, J. Ghostly populations
  The sound of a girl singing
    Matthews, J. Crazy women
  The story Mac told
    Matthews, J. Ghostly populations
  Tableau with three ghostly women
    Matthews, J. Ghostly populations
  Taking stock
    Matthews, J. Ghostly populations
  "This moment is ours alone"
    Matthews, J. Crazy women
  The tour of the sleeping steamboat
    Matthews, J. Ghostly populations
  Toward a distant train
    Matthews, J. Ghostly populations
  The tree beyond
    Matthews, J. Crazy women
  The two of them together
    Matthews, J. Crazy women
  The visionary land
    Matthews, J. Ghostly populations
  A woman of properties
    Matthews, J. Crazy women
Matthews, Sebastian
  Story-telling
    *New England Review and Bread Loaf
      Quarterly* 11:42 Aut '88
Matthiessen, Peter
  The fifth day
    Matthiessen, P. Midnight turning gray
  Late in the season
    Matthiessen, P. Midnight turning gray
  Midnight turning gray
    Matthiessen, P. Midnight turning gray
  On the River Styx
    Esquire 104:79-81+ Ag '85
    The Esquire fiction reader v2
  A replacement
    Matthiessen, P. Midnight turning gray
  Sadie
    Matthiessen, P. Midnight turning gray
  Travelin man
    Matthiessen, P. Midnight turning gray
  The wolves of Aguila
    Matthiessen, P. Midnight turning gray
Mattison, Alice
  Art is lost
    Mattison, A. Great wits
  Bears
    Mattison, A. Great wits
    The New Yorker 63:34-43 Mr 16 '87
  Cake night
    Mattison, A. Great wits
  The colorful alphabet
    Mattison, A. Great wits

Mattison, Alice—*Continued*
A date with Dmitri
  Mattison, A. Great wits
Exactments
  Mattison, A. Great wits
The flight of Andy Burns
  The New Yorker 64:28-32 Je 20 '88
Great wits
  Mattison, A. Great wits
  The New Yorker 62:34-42 My 19 '86
In family
  Mattison, A. Great wits
  The New Yorker 62:42-5 Ap 21 '86
The knitting
  Mattison, A. Great wits
  The New Yorker 61:38-40 Ap 8 '85
The May dance
  Mattison, A. Great wits
The Middle Ages
  Mattison, A. Great wits
  The New Yorker 61:38-40 Je 10 '85
New Haven
  Mattison, A. Great wits
  The New Yorker 61:33-8 O 28 '85
Painting day
  Mattison, A. Great wits
Sleeping giant
  Mattison, A. Great wits
They all went up to Amsterdam
  Mattison, A. Great wits
  The New Yorker 61:24-5 Jl 29 '85
The **mattress** by the tomato patch. Williams, T.
A **mature** and civilized relationship. Sorrells, R. T.
Matuszewicz, J. Michael
Power times one
  Tales from Isaac Asimov's science fiction magazine: short stories for young adults
Maud Island. Caldwell, E.
Maugham, Somerset *See* Maugham, W. Somerset (William Somerset), 1874-1965
Maugham, W. Somerset (William Somerset), 1874-1965
Before the party
  Mystery in the mainstream; ed. by B. Pronzini; M. H. Greenberg and B. N. Malzberg
The colonel's lady
  The Treasury of English short stories; ed. by N. Sullivan
The facts of life
  The World of the short story; ed. by C. Fadiman
A friend in need
  Devils & demons; ed. by M. Kaye and S. Kaye
Lord Mountdrago
  Black water; ed. by A. Manguel

Red
  Short stories of the sea; ed. by G. C. Solley and E. Steinbaugh
The taipan
  The Oxford book of English ghost stories
The traitor
  Baker's dozen: 13 short espionage novels
Maugham, William Somerset *See* Maugham, W. Somerset (William Somerset), 1874-1965
MAUI (HAWAII) *See* Hawaii—Maui
Maundy Thursday. Campbell, E.
Maupassant, Guy de, 1850-1893
The accent
  Maupassant, G. de. The collected stories of Guy de Maupassant
The accursed bread
  Maupassant, G. de. The collected stories of Guy de Maupassant
An adventure
  Maupassant, G. de. The collected stories of Guy de Maupassant
An affair of state
  Maupassant, G. de. The collected stories of Guy de Maupassant
After
  Maupassant, G. de. The collected stories of Guy de Maupassant
After death
  Maupassant, G. de. The collected stories of Guy de Maupassant
All over
  Maupassant, G. de. The collected stories of Guy de Maupassant
Am I insane
  Maupassant, G. de. The collected stories of Guy de Maupassant
An artifice
  Maupassant, G. de. The collected stories of Guy de Maupassant
The artist
  Maupassant, G. de. The collected stories of Guy de Maupassant
The artist's wife
  Maupassant, G. de. The collected stories of Guy de Maupassant
The assassin
  Maupassant, G. de. The collected stories of Guy de Maupassant
At sea
  Short stories of the sea; ed. by G. C. Solley and E. Steinbaugh
The avenger
  Maupassant, G. de. The collected stories of Guy de Maupassant
The awakening
  Maupassant, G. de. The collected stories of Guy de Maupassant
Babette
  Maupassant, G. de. The collected stories of Guy de Maupassant

Maupassant, Guy de, 1850-1893—*Continued*
A bad error
Maupassant, G. de. The collected stories
of Guy de Maupassant
Ball-of-fat [Variant title: Ball of tallow]
Maupassant, G. de. The collected stories
of Guy de Maupassant
The bed
Maupassant, G. de. The collected stories
of Guy de Maupassant
Bed no. 29
Maupassant, G. de. The collected stories
of Guy de Maupassant
"Bell"
Maupassant, G. de. The collected stories
of Guy de Maupassant
Bellflower
Maupassant, G. de. The collected stories
of Guy de Maupassant
Benoist
Maupassant, G. de. The collected stories
of Guy de Maupassant
Bertha
Maupassant, G. de. The collected stories
of Guy de Maupassant
Beside a dead man
Maupassant, G. de. The collected stories
of Guy de Maupassant
The blind man
Maupassant, G. de. The collected stories
of Guy de Maupassant
Boitelle
Maupassant, G. de. The collected stories
of Guy de Maupassant
Bric-à-brac
Maupassant, G. de. The collected stories
of Guy de Maupassant
The carter's wench
Maupassant, G. de. The collected stories
of Guy de Maupassant
Caught
Maupassant, G. de. The collected stories
of Guy de Maupassant
Châli
Maupassant, G. de. The collected stories
of Guy de Maupassant
The charm dispelled
Maupassant, G. de. The collected stories
of Guy de Maupassant
Christening
Maupassant, G. de. The collected stories
of Guy de Maupassant
Christmas Eve
Maupassant, G. de. The collected stories
of Guy de Maupassant
The clown
Maupassant, G. de. The collected stories
of Guy de Maupassant
A cock crowed
Maupassant, G. de. The collected stories
of Guy de Maupassant

The colonel's ideas
Maupassant, G. de. The collected stories
of Guy de Maupassant
Complication
Maupassant, G. de. The collected stories
of Guy de Maupassant
The conservatory
Maupassant, G. de. The collected stories
of Guy de Maupassant
Consideration
Maupassant, G. de. The collected stories
of Guy de Maupassant
The Corsican bandit
Maupassant, G. de. The collected stories
of Guy de Maupassant
A costly outing
Maupassant, G. de. The collected stories
of Guy de Maupassant
Countess Satan
Maupassant, G. de. The collected stories
of Guy de Maupassant
A country excursion
Maupassant, G. de. The collected stories
of Guy de Maupassant
A crisis
Maupassant, G. de. The collected stories
of Guy de Maupassant
The dancers
Maupassant, G. de. The collected stories
of Guy de Maupassant
A dead woman's secret
Maupassant, G. de. The collected stories
of Guy de Maupassant
The deaf-mute
Maupassant, G. de. The collected stories
of Guy de Maupassant
The debt
Maupassant, G. de. The collected stories
of Guy de Maupassant
A deer park in the provinces
Maupassant, G. de. The collected stories
of Guy de Maupassant
Delila
Maupassant, G. de. The collected stories
of Guy de Maupassant
The Devil
Maupassant, G. de. The collected stories
of Guy de Maupassant
The diamond necklace
Maupassant, G. de. The collected stories
of Guy de Maupassant
The diary of a madman
Maupassant, G. de. The collected stories
of Guy de Maupassant
The double pins
Maupassant, G. de. The collected stories
of Guy de Maupassant
Doubtful happiness
Maupassant, G. de. The collected stories
of Guy de Maupassant
The duel
Maupassant, G. de. The collected stories
of Guy de Maupassant

Maupassant, Guy de, 1850-1893—*Continued*
The Englishman
  Maupassant, G. de. The collected stories
    of Guy de Maupassant
An enthusiast
  Maupassant, G. de. The collected stories
    of Guy de Maupassant
Epiphany
  Maupassant, G. de. The collected stories
    of Guy de Maupassant
A fair exchange
  Maupassant, G. de. The collected stories
    of Guy de Maupassant
False alarm
  Maupassant, G. de. The collected stories
    of Guy de Maupassant
The false gems
  Maupassant, G. de. The collected stories
    of Guy de Maupassant
A family
  Maupassant, G. de. The collected stories
    of Guy de Maupassant
The farmer's wife
  Maupassant, G. de. The collected stories
    of Guy de Maupassant
A fashionable woman
  Maupassant, G. de. The collected stories
    of Guy de Maupassant
The father
  Maupassant, G. de. The collected stories
    of Guy de Maupassant
Fecundity
  Maupassant, G. de. The collected stories
    of Guy de Maupassant
The first snowfall
  Maupassant, G. de. The collected stories
    of Guy de Maupassant
A fishing excursion
  Maupassant, G. de. The collected stories
    of Guy de Maupassant
The flayed hand
  Masterpieces of terror and the super-
    natural; ed. by M. Kaye and S. Kaye
Florentine
  Maupassant, G. de. The collected stories
    of Guy de Maupassant
Forbidden fruit
  Maupassant, G. de. The collected stories
    of Guy de Maupassant
Forgiveness
  Maupassant, G. de. The collected stories
    of Guy de Maupassant
Francis
  Maupassant, G. de. The collected stories
    of Guy de Maupassant
A French Enoch Arden
  Maupassant, G. de. The collected stories
    of Guy de Maupassant
Ghosts
  Maupassant, G. de. The collected stories
    of Guy de Maupassant

Good reasons
  Maupassant, G. de. The collected stories
    of Guy de Maupassant
Graveyard sirens
  Maupassant, G. de. The collected stories
    of Guy de Maupassant
Growing old
  Maupassant, G. de. The collected stories
    of Guy de Maupassant
Happiness
  Maupassant, G. de. The collected stories
    of Guy de Maupassant
He?
  Maupassant, G. de. The collected stories
    of Guy de Maupassant
Hippolyte's claim
  Maupassant, G. de. The collected stories
    of Guy de Maupassant
The hole
  Maupassant, G. de. The collected stories
    of Guy de Maupassant
An honest deal
  Maupassant, G. de. The collected stories
    of Guy de Maupassant
Le Horla
  The Penguin book of ghost stories
The horrible
  Maupassant, G. de. The collected stories
    of Guy de Maupassant
How he got the Legion of Honor
  Maupassant, G. de. The collected stories
    of Guy de Maupassant
Humiliation
  Maupassant, G. de. The collected stories
    of Guy de Maupassant
The ill-omened groom
  Maupassant, G. de. The collected stories
    of Guy de Maupassant
The impolite sex
  Maupassant, G. de. The collected stories
    of Guy de Maupassant
In his sweetheart's livery
  Maupassant, G. de. The collected stories
    of Guy de Maupassant
In the court room
  Maupassant, G. de. The collected stories
    of Guy de Maupassant
In the moonlight
  Maupassant, G. de. The collected stories
    of Guy de Maupassant
In the spring
  Maupassant, G. de. The collected stories
    of Guy de Maupassant
In the wood
  Maupassant, G. de. The collected stories
    of Guy de Maupassant
In various rôles
  Maupassant, G. de. The collected stories
    of Guy de Maupassant
The inn
  Maupassant, G. de. The collected stories
    of Guy de Maupassant

Maupassant, Guy de, 1850-1893—*Continued*

Jeroboam
  Maupassant, G. de. The collected stories
    of Guy de Maupassant
A jolly fellow
  Maupassant, G. de. The collected stories
    of Guy de Maupassant
Joseph
  Maupassant, G. de. The collected stories
    of Guy de Maupassant
Julie Romain
  Maupassant, G. de. The collected stories
    of Guy de Maupassant
A king's son
  Maupassant, G. de. The collected stories
    of Guy de Maupassant
The last step
  Maupassant, G. de. The collected stories
    of Guy de Maupassant
Letter found on a corpse
  Maupassant, G. de. The collected stories
    of Guy de Maupassant
Lilie Lala
  Maupassant, G. de. The collected stories
    of Guy de Maupassant
The little cask
  Inspired by drink; ed. by Joan Digby
    and John Digby
  Maupassant, G. de. The collected stories
    of Guy de Maupassant
Little Louise Roque
  Maupassant, G. de. The collected stories
    of Guy de Maupassant
A little walk
  Maupassant, G. de. The collected stories
    of Guy de Maupassant
A lively friend
  Maupassant, G. de. The collected stories
    of Guy de Maupassant
The log
  Maupassant, G. de. The collected stories
    of Guy de Maupassant
Lost!
  Maupassant, G. de. The collected stories
    of Guy de Maupassant
Love
  Classic European short stories; ed. by R.
    Beum
  Maupassant, G. de. The collected stories
    of Guy de Maupassant
The love of long ago
  Maupassant, G. de. The collected stories
    of Guy de Maupassant
Love's awakening
  Maupassant, G. de. The collected stories
    of Guy de Maupassant
A lucky burglar
  Maupassant, G. de. The collected stories
    of Guy de Maupassant
The mad woman
  Maupassant, G. de. The collected stories
    of Guy de Maupassant

Madame Baptiste
  Maupassant, G. de. The collected stories
    of Guy de Maupassant
Madame Parisse
  Maupassant, G. de. The collected stories
    of Guy de Maupassant
Mademoiselle
  Maupassant, G. de. The collected stories
    of Guy de Maupassant
Mademoiselle Fifi
  Classic European short stories; ed. by R.
    Beum
  Maupassant, G. de. The collected stories
    of Guy de Maupassant
Magnetism
  Maupassant, G. de. The collected stories
    of Guy de Maupassant
Making a convert
  Maupassant, G. de. The collected stories
    of Guy de Maupassant
The man with the blue eyes
  Maupassant, G. de. The collected stories
    of Guy de Maupassant
The man with the dogs
  Maupassant, G. de. The collected stories
    of Guy de Maupassant
Margot's tapers
  Maupassant, G. de. The collected stories
    of Guy de Maupassant
The marquis
  Maupassant, G. de. The collected stories
    of Guy de Maupassant
The Marquis de Fumerol
  Maupassant, G. de. The collected stories
    of Guy de Maupassant
Marroca
  Maupassant, G. de. The collected stories
    of Guy de Maupassant
A meeting
  Maupassant, G. de. The collected stories
    of Guy de Maupassant
A mésalliance
  Maupassant, G. de. The collected stories
    of Guy de Maupassant
A miracle
  Maupassant, G. de. The collected stories
    of Guy de Maupassant
Miss Harriet
  Maupassant, G. de. The collected stories
    of Guy de Maupassant
A mistake
  Maupassant, G. de. The collected stories
    of Guy de Maupassant
Mme. Tellier's excursion
  Maupassant, G. de. The collected stories
    of Guy de Maupassant
Mohammed Fripouli
  Maupassant, G. de. The collected stories
    of Guy de Maupassant
Monsieur Parent
  Maupassant, G. de. The collected stories
    of Guy de Maupassant

Maupassant, Guy de, 1850-1893—*Continued*
Moonlight
  Classic European short stories; ed. by R. Beum
  Maupassant, G. de. The collected stories of Guy de Maupassant
La Morillonne
  Maupassant, G. de. The collected stories of Guy de Maupassant
Mother and son!!!
  Maupassant, G. de. The collected stories of Guy de Maupassant
The mountebanks
  Maupassant, G. de. The collected stories of Guy de Maupassant
My landlady
  Maupassant, G. de. The collected stories of Guy de Maupassant
My twenty-five days
  Maupassant, G. de. The collected stories of Guy de Maupassant
My uncle Sosthenes
  Maupassant, G. de. The collected stories of Guy de Maupassant
The new sensation
  Maupassant, G. de. The collected stories of Guy de Maupassant
A New Year's gift
  Maupassant, G. de. The collected stories of Guy de Maupassant
A night in Whitechapel
  Maupassant, G. de. The collected stories of Guy de Maupassant
The noncommissioned officer
  Maupassant, G. de. The collected stories of Guy de Maupassant
A Normandy joke
  Maupassant, G. de. The collected stories of Guy de Maupassant
The Odalisque of Senichou
  Maupassant, G. de. The collected stories of Guy de Maupassant
An odd feast
  Maupassant, G. de. The collected stories of Guy de Maupassant
An old maid [Variant title: Queen Hortense]
  Maupassant, G. de. The collected stories of Guy de Maupassant
On cats
  Maupassant, G. de. The collected stories of Guy de Maupassant
On perfumes
  Maupassant, G. de. The collected stories of Guy de Maupassant
On the river
  Maupassant, G. de. The collected stories of Guy de Maupassant
One phase of love
  Maupassant, G. de. The collected stories of Guy de Maupassant

The orderly
  Maupassant, G. de. The collected stories of Guy de Maupassant
A passion
  Maupassant, G. de. The collected stories of Guy de Maupassant
A peculiar case
  Maupassant, G. de. The collected stories of Guy de Maupassant
A philosopher
  Maupassant, G. de. The collected stories of Guy de Maupassant
A piece of string
  Maupassant, G. de. The collected stories of Guy de Maupassant
Poor Andrew
  Maupassant, G. de. The collected stories of Guy de Maupassant
A poor girl
  Maupassant, G. de. The collected stories of Guy de Maupassant
The port [Variant title: In port]
  Maupassant, G. de. The collected stories of Guy de Maupassant
A practical joke
  Maupassant, G. de. The collected stories of Guy de Maupassant
Profitable business
  Maupassant, G. de. The collected stories of Guy de Maupassant
A queer night in Paris
  Maupassant, G. de. The collected stories of Guy de Maupassant
The question of Latin
  Maupassant, G. de. The collected stories of Guy de Maupassant
The rabbit
  Maupassant, G. de. The collected stories of Guy de Maupassant
The real one and the other
  Maupassant, G. de. The collected stories of Guy de Maupassant
Regret
  Maupassant, G. de. The collected stories of Guy de Maupassant
The relic
  Maupassant, G. de. The collected stories of Guy de Maupassant
The relics
  Maupassant, G. de. The collected stories of Guy de Maupassant
The rendezvous
  Maupassant, G. de. The collected stories of Guy de Maupassant
Revenge
  Maupassant, G. de. The collected stories of Guy de Maupassant
Room no. eleven
  Maupassant, G. de. The collected stories of Guy de Maupassant
Rosalie Prudent
  Maupassant, G. de. The collected stories of Guy de Maupassant

Maupassant, Guy de, 1850-1893—*Continued*

A rupture
  Maupassant, G. de. The collected stories
    of Guy de Maupassant
Saved
  Maupassant, G. de. The collected stories
    of Guy de Maupassant
Selfishness
  Maupassant, G. de. The collected stories
    of Guy de Maupassant
Semillante
  Maupassant, G. de. The collected stories
    of Guy de Maupassant
Sentiment
  Maupassant, G. de. The collected stories
    of Guy de Maupassant
The sequel to a divorce
  Maupassant, G. de. The collected stories
    of Guy de Maupassant
The signal
  Maupassant, G. de. The collected stories
    of Guy de Maupassant
Simon's papa
  Maupassant, G. de. The collected stories
    of Guy de Maupassant
Solitude
  Maupassant, G. de. The collected stories
    of Guy de Maupassant
The spasm
  Maupassant, G. de. The collected stories
    of Guy de Maupassant
The specter
  Maupassant, G. de. The collected stories
    of Guy de Maupassant
The story of a farm-girl
  Maupassant, G. de. The collected stories
    of Guy de Maupassant
A strange fancy
  Maupassant, G. de. The collected stories
    of Guy de Maupassant
The substitute
  Maupassant, G. de. The collected stories
    of Guy de Maupassant
Suicides
  Maupassant, G. de. The collected stories
    of Guy de Maupassant
Sympathy
  Maupassant, G. de. The collected stories
    of Guy de Maupassant
That pig of a Morin
  Maupassant, G. de. The collected stories
    of Guy de Maupassant
The thief
  Maupassant, G. de. The collected stories
    of Guy de Maupassant
The tobacco shop
  Maupassant, G. de. The collected stories
    of Guy de Maupassant
Toine
  Maupassant, G. de. The collected stories
    of Guy de Maupassant

The traveler's story
  Maupassant, G. de. The collected stories
    of Guy de Maupassant
A traveler's tale
  Maupassant, G. de. The collected stories
    of Guy de Maupassant
Two little soldiers
  Maupassant, G. de. The collected stories
    of Guy de Maupassant
Ugly
  Maupassant, G. de. The collected stories
    of Guy de Maupassant
The umbrella
  Maupassant, G. de. The collected stories
    of Guy de Maupassant
Under the yoke
  Maupassant, G. de. The collected stories
    of Guy de Maupassant
An unfortunate likeness
  Maupassant, G. de. The collected stories
    of Guy de Maupassant
An unreasonable woman
  Maupassant, G. de. The collected stories
    of Guy de Maupassant
The upstart
  Maupassant, G. de. The collected stories
    of Guy de Maupassant
A useful house
  Maupassant, G. de. The collected stories
    of Guy de Maupassant
Useless beauty
  Maupassant, G. de. The collected stories
    of Guy de Maupassant
A vagabond
  Maupassant, G. de. The collected stories
    of Guy de Maupassant
The Venus of Braniza
  Maupassant, G. de. The collected stories
    of Guy de Maupassant
The victim
  Maupassant, G. de. The collected stories
    of Guy de Maupassant
Virtue!
  Maupassant, G. de. The collected stories
    of Guy de Maupassant
Virtue in the ballet
  Maupassant, G. de. The collected stories
    of Guy de Maupassant
Waiter, a bock!
  Inspired by drink; ed. by Joan Digby
    and John Digby
  Maupassant, G. de. The collected stories
    of Guy de Maupassant
Was it a dream?
  Maupassant, G. de. The collected stories
    of Guy de Maupassant
The watchdog
  Maupassant, G. de. The collected stories
    of Guy de Maupassant
A way to wealth
  Maupassant, G. de. The collected stories
    of Guy de Maupassant

Maupassant, Guy de, 1850-1893—*Continued*
The wedding night
Maupassant, G. de. The collected stories of Guy de Maupassant
The White Lady
Maupassant, G. de. The collected stories of Guy de Maupassant
The white wolf
Maupassant, G. de. The collected stories of Guy de Maupassant
Who knows?
The Penguin book of horror stories
A wife's confession
Maupassant, G. de. The collected stories of Guy de Maupassant
The will
Maupassant, G. de. The collected stories of Guy de Maupassant
Woman's wiles
Maupassant, G. de. The collected stories of Guy de Maupassant
The wooden shoes
Maupassant, G. de. The collected stories of Guy de Maupassant
Words of love
Maupassant, G. de. The collected stories of Guy de Maupassant
Mauriac, François, 1885-1970
A Christmas tale
The Substance of things hoped for; ed. by J. B. Breslin
Maurice and Mog. Herbert, J.
Maurois, André, 1885-1967
The house
100 great fantasy short short stories; ed. by I. Asimov; T. Carr and M. H. Greenberg
Rod Serling's Night gallery reader
Mawyer, Gary D.
Soapstone
Southern Exposure (Durham, N.C.) 13:24-7 Jl/Ag '85
Max. Carlson, R.
Max. Schwartz, J.
Max and the pacemaker. Gold, H.
Maximum security. Oates, J. C.
Max's Christmas. Wells, R.
Maxwell, William, 1908-
The holy terror
The New Yorker 62:34-8 Mr 17 '86
The lily-white boys
The Paris Review 28:132-8 Summ/Fall '86
The man in the moon
The New Yorker 60:46-55 N 12 '84
My father's friends
The New Yorker 59:30-4 Ja 30 '84
The Pilgrimage
The Art of the tale; ed. by D. Halpern
Maxwell and I. Gilbert, W. S.
The **Maxwell** equations. Dnieprov, A.

May, Naomi
Minnie's treasure
Encounter (London, England) 66:3-11 F '86
May, Paula
Resonance ritual
L. Ron Hubbard presents Writers of the future v3
May angels lead you home. Stark, S. S.
May Blossom. Grandbois, A.
The **May** dance. Mattison, A.
A **May** night; or, The drowned maiden. Gogol', N. V.
The **May-Pole** of Merry Mount. Hawthorne, N.
May the best man win. Schmidt, S.
May we borrow your husband? Greene, G.
May your days be merry and bright. Shore, W.
Maya. Kessler, J. F.
Maya. Sharat Chandra, G. S.
Maya Darpan. Verma, N.
Mayakovsky, my love. Leaton, A.
MAYAS
Monterroso, A. The eclipse
Mayberry, Florence V.
No tomorrows
Ellery Queen's Memorable characters
Mayberry. Cullen, E. J.
Mayberry '86. Cullen, E. J.
Mayer, Debby
The secretary
The New Yorker 64:36-41 N 28 '88
Mayer, Musa
One last ride
Seventeen 44:178-9+ O '85
Mayer, Robert
The system
Writers of the purple sage; ed. by R. Martin and M. Barasch
Mayers, Carroll
Police calls
Alfred Hitchcock's Grave suspicions
Mayes, Sharon S.
Auto erotic
Erotic interludes; ed. by L. Barbach
Mayhar, Ardath, 1930-
Esmene's eyes
Magic in Ithkar [1]; ed. by A. Norton and R. Adams
In the tank
Masques II; ed. by J. N. Williamson
Neither rest nor refuge
Tales of the Witch World [1]
A night in Possum Holler
After midnight; ed. by C. L. Grant
Nor disregard the humblest voice
Shadows 9
To trap a demon
Magic in Ithkar 4; ed. by A. Norton and R. Adams

Mayhew, Anna Jean
In the garden
  L. Ron Hubbard presents Writers of the
    future
Mayo, Jim, 1908-1988
  *For works written by this author under
    other names see* L'Amour, Louis,
    1908-1988
MAYO   (IRELAND: COUNTY)   *See*
    Ireland—Mayo (County)
The **mayor** of Casterbridge. Hardy, T.
The **mayor** of New Orleans; just talking jazz.
    Shaik, F.
MAYORS
  García Márquez, G. One of these days
  Kim, Y. I. Village wine
  Shaik, F. The mayor of New Orleans; just
    talking jazz
The **maze** and the monster. Hoch, E. D.
The **maze** of Maal Dweb. Smith, C. A.
Mazel, David
  The angel's overcoat
    Mazel, D. My heart's world
  Aunt Leah
    Mazel, D. My heart's world
  Children of the universe
    Mazel, D. My heart's world
  Choosing
    Mazel, D. My heart's world
  A crossing
    Mazel, D. My heart's world
  A dance
    Mazel, D. My heart's world
  The discovery
    Mazel, D. My heart's world
  Dragons and puppies
    Mazel, D. My heart's world
  The flying ark
    Mazel, D. My heart's world
  Friends
    Mazel, D. My heart's world
  Homage
    Mazel, D. My heart's world
  Ilya
    Mazel, D. My heart's world
  An invitation
    Mazel, D. My heart's world
  Jeopardies
    Mazel, D. My heart's world
  Karen
    Mazel, D. My heart's world
  Late prayers
    Mazel, D. My heart's world
  Lily's Deli
    Mazel, D. My heart's world
  A longing to live
    Mazel, D. My heart's world
  The maestro
    Mazel, D. My heart's world
  A matter of pride
    Mazel, D. My heart's world
  The merry-go-round
    Mazel, D. My heart's world

Mr. Bernshtein
  Mazel, D. My heart's world
Mr. Tessler
  Mazel, D. My heart's world
Old folks
  Mazel, D. My heart's world
Our Zaideh
  Mazel, D. My heart's world
Proverb of the parched
  Mazel, D. My heart's world
Sacrifices
  Mazel, D. My heart's world
Sadie
  Mazel, D. My heart's world
A self-portrait
  Mazel, D. My heart's world
Shining
  Mazel, D. My heart's world
A spoonful of kindness
  Mazel, D. My heart's world
Sprucy wages
  Mazel, D. My heart's world
The storekeeper
  Mazel, D. My heart's world
A story of hope
  Mazel, D. My heart's world
Strawberries
  Mazel, D. My heart's world
Surprises
  Mazel, D. My heart's world
An unsung Solomon
  Mazel, D. My heart's world
A visit with Esta
  Mazel, D. My heart's world
The wall
  Mazel, D. My heart's world
The well
  Mazel, D. My heart's world
When you swing upon a star
  Mazel, D. My heart's world
Mazirian the Magician. Vance, J.
Mazzari, Louis
Stickpins
  The Antioch Review 42:345-51 Summ '84
McAllister, Bruce, 1946-
The ark
  Omni (New York, N.Y.) 7:44-6+ S '85
Dream baby
  In the field of fire; ed. by J. Van B.
    Dann and J. Dann
  The Year's best science fiction, fifth an-
    nual collection
The girl who loved animals
  Omni (New York, N.Y.) 10:100-2+ My
    '88
Kingdom come
  Omni (New York, N.Y.) 9:60-2+ F '87
Mcauley, Paul J.
The king of the hill
  Interzone: the 2nd anthology; ed. by J.
    Clute; D. Pringle and S. Ounsley

Mcauley, Paul J.—*Continued*
The temporary king
The Year's best science fiction, fifth annual collection

McBain, Ed, 1926-
For works written by this author under other names see Hunter, Evan, 1926-
Consolation
Uncollected crimes; ed. by B. Pronzini and M. H. Greenberg
Death flight
The Mammoth book of private eye stories; ed. by B. Pronzini and M. H. Greenberg
"J"
The Ethnic detectives; ed. by B. Pronzini and M. H. Greenberg
Nightshade
Great modern police stories; ed. by B. Pronzini and M. H. Greenberg
Sadie when she died
Great detectives; ed. by D. W. McCullough
Small homicide
Manhattan mysteries; ed. by B. Pronzini; C. L. R. Waugh and M. H. Greenberg

McBain, Hugh
Supper on the wall
Streets of stone; ed. by M. Burgess and H. Whyte

McBride's list. Blair, R.

McCafferty, Jane E.
Mama sings the blues
Mademoiselle 92:178+ O '86

McCaffrey, Anne
Dragonrider
Time wars; ed. by C. Waugh and M. H. Greenberg
A flock of geese
Moonsinger's friends; ed. by S. Shwartz

McCall, Anthony *See* Kane, Henry

McCammon, Robert R.
He'll come knocking at your door
Halloween horrors; ed. by A. Ryan
Night calls the Green Falcon
Silver scream; ed. by D. J. Schow
Nightcrawlers
Masques; ed. by J. N. Williamson

McCandless, D. B.
Cash or credit
Hard-boiled dames; ed. by B. A. Drew

McCandless, Holloway
Wet afternoons in Paris
Mademoiselle 92:98+ F '86

McCann, Richard
My mother's clothes: the school of beauty and shame
The Atlantic 257:109-16 Ap '86
The Editors' choice v4; ed. by G. E. Murphy, Jr.
Men on men 2; ed. by G. Stambolian

McCarthy, Cormac, 1933-
Instruments of liberation
Homewords: a book of Tennessee writers; ed. by D. Paschall

McCarthy, Thomas, 1954-
Mammy's boy
P.E.N. new fiction I

McClanahan, Ed
The Congress of Wonders
Esquire 110:236-40+ D '88

McClintock, Mike
Red suspenders
Country Journal 15:34-9 N '88

McCloy, Helen, 1904-
Chinoiserie
The Crime of my life; ed. by B. Garfield
The other side of the curtain
Kill or cure; ed. by M. Muller and B. Pronzini

McClure, James, 1939-
The last place on earth
The Mammoth book of modern crime stories; ed. by G. Hardinge
Winter's crimes 17
Remember that joke, Harry?
Winter's crimes 16

McCluskey, John (John A.), 1944-
The best teacher in Georgia
The Southern Review (Baton Rouge, La.) 21:658-71 Jl '85
Stories of the modern South; ed. by B. Forkner and P. Samway

McCollum, Lynn
Cheer for me
'Teen 28:54+ Ag '84

McConkey, James
A family record
The New Yorker 61:42-51 Mr 25 '85

McConnell, Charles R.
Sidney, Seth and S.A.M.
Last laughs; ed. by G. Mcdonald

McConnell, James V.
Learning theory
Great science fiction; ed. by I. Asimov; M. H. Greenberg and C. G. Waugh

McConnell, Jean
Come soar with me
Good Housekeeping 204:110+ Ap '87
Fancy meeting you
Good Housekeeping 199:182-3 N '84
Germination period
John Creasey's Crime collection, 1984

McConnor, John Vincent *See* McConnor, Vincent

McConnor, Vincent
The house of crime
Murder in Los Angeles; ed. by J. L. Breen and others

McCorkle, Jill, 1958-
First union blues
New stories from the South: the year's best, 1988

McCorkle, Jill, 1958----*Continued*
July 7th [excerpt]
    The New writers of the South; ed. by
    C. East
The spell of her beautiful garden
    Seventeen 43:136-7+ O '84
McCorkle, Kate
War story
    The North American Review 272:46-7 D
    '87
McCormack, Eric P.
Anyhow in a corner
    McCormack, E. P. Inspecting the vaults
Captain Joe
    McCormack, E. P. Inspecting the vaults
Eckhardt at a window
    McCormack, E. P. Inspecting the vaults
Edward and Georgina
    McCormack, E. P. Inspecting the vaults
Festival
    McCormack, E. P. Inspecting the vaults
The fragment
    McCormack, E. P. Inspecting the vaults
The fugue
    McCormack, E. P. Inspecting the vaults
The hobby
    McCormack, E. P. Inspecting the vaults
Inspecting the vaults
    McCormack, E. P. Inspecting the vaults
Knox abroad
    McCormack, E. P. Inspecting the vaults
A long day in the town
    McCormack, E. P. Inspecting the vaults
Lusawort's meditation
    McCormack, E. P. Inspecting the vaults
No country for old men
    McCormack, E. P. Inspecting the vaults
The one-legged men
    McCormack, E. P. Inspecting the vaults
One picture of Trotsky
    McCormack, E. P. Inspecting the vaults
Sad stories in Patagonia
    McCormack, E. P. Inspecting the vaults
The swath
    McCormack, E. P. Inspecting the vaults
A train of gardens—Part I: Ireneus Fludd
    McCormack, E. P. Inspecting the vaults
A train of gardens—Part II: the machine
    McCormack, E. P. Inspecting the vaults
Twins
    McCormack, E. P. Inspecting the vaults
McCormack, Ford
Hell-bent
    Devils & demons; ed. by M. Kaye and
    S. Kaye
McCourt, James, 1941-
I go back to the mais oui
    Men on men 2; ed. by G. Stambolian
In Tír na nÓg
    The New Yorker 63:30-40 F 15 '88
Kaye Wayfaring in "Avenged"
    McCourt, J. Kaye Wayfaring in
    "Avenged"

The Scan of Illyria
    McCourt, J. Kaye Wayfaring in
    "Avenged"
Something sensational to read in the train
    McCourt, J. Kaye Wayfaring in
    "Avenged"
Wayfaring at Waverly in Silver Lake
    The New Yorker 61:42-51 N 4 '85
Winter meeting
    McCourt, J. Kaye Wayfaring in
    "Avenged"
McCoy, Elizabeth, 1903-
Henry's eighth
    Murder California style; ed. by J. L.
    Breen and J. Ball
McCoy, Horace, 1897-1955
Frost flies alone
    The Black mask boys; ed. by W. F.
    Nolan
McCreary, Lew
Static discharge
    The Ploughshares reader: new fiction for
    the eighties
McCrimmon and the blue moonstones.
    MacLean, A.
McCrory, Moy
Strangers
    Stepping out; ed. by A. Oosthuizen
McCulla, James
How Esco Mize got religion
    The Editors' choice v3; ed. by G. E.
    Murphy, Jr.
McCullers, Carson, 1917-1967
The aliens
    McCullers, C. Collected stories
Art and Mr. Mahoney
    McCullers, C. Collected stories
The ballad of the Sad Café
    Great American love stories; ed. by L.
    Rosenthal
    McCullers, C. Collected stories
Breath from the sky
    McCullers, C. Collected stories
Correspondence
    McCullers, C. Collected stories
Court in the West eighties
    McCullers, C. Collected stories
A domestic dilemma
    Look who's talking; ed. by B. Weber
    McCullers, C. Collected stories
The haunted boy
    McCullers, C. Collected stories
Instant of the hour after
    McCullers, C. Collected stories
The jockey
    McCullers, C. Collected stories
Like that
    Early sorrow: ten stories of youth; ed.
    by C. Zolotow
    McCullers, C. Collected stories

McCullers, Carson, 1917-1967—_Continued_
Madame Zilensky and the King of Finland
McCullers, C. Collected stories
The World of the short story; ed. by
C. Fadiman
The orphanage
McCullers, C. Collected stories
Poldi
McCullers, C. Collected stories
The sojourner
McCullers, C. Collected stories
Stories of the modern South; ed. by B.
Forkner and P. Samway
Sucker
McCullers, C. Collected stories
A tree. A rock. A cloud
McCullers, C. Collected stories
Untitled piece
McCullers, C. Collected stories
Who has seen the wind?
McCullers, C. Collected stories
Wunderkind
McCullers, C. Collected stories

McCulloch, Jeanne
Going back
The North American Review 273:30-5 Mr
'88

McDaniel, Mary Catherine
A little of what you fancy
L. Ron Hubbard presents Writers of the
future v3

McDaniel, Wilma Elizabeth
A dream of Grand Junction
Earth power coming; ed. by S. J. Ortiz
Shamrock Road
Earth power coming; ed. by S. J. Ortiz

McDermott, Alice
She knew what she wanted
Redbook 166:44+ F '86

McDevitt, Jack
Cryptic
The Year's best science fiction, first an-
nual collection
In the tower
Universe 17
Promises to keep
The Year's best science fiction, second
annual collection
Tidal effects
Universe 15

McDonald, Camden
My life at Magnum
Critical Quarterly 30:63-8 Aut '88

Mcdonald, Gregory, 1937-
The nine best movies
Last laughs; ed. by G. Mcdonald
The robbery
The Year's best mystery and suspense
stories, 1985

McDonald, Jeanne
Settlement
Homewords: a book of Tennessee
writers; ed. by D. Paschall

McDonald, Sara
Falling
The Old dance; ed. by B. Burnard
McDonald, Steven Edward
Silken dragon
Dragons of light; ed. by O. S. Card
McDonald, Walter
The track
Prize stories, Texas Institute of Letters;
ed. by M. Terry
McDowell, Michael, 1950-
Halley's passing
The Year's best fantasy, first annual
collection
The Year's best science fiction, fifth an-
nual collection
Miss Mack
Halloween horrors; ed. by A. Ryan
McElroy, Colleen J.
A brief spell by the river
McElroy, C. J. Jesus and Fat Tuesday,
and other short stories
A dance with a dolly with a hole in her
stocking
McElroy, C. J. Jesus and Fat Tuesday,
and other short stories
Exercises
McElroy, C. J. Jesus and Fat Tuesday,
and other short stories
Farm day
McElroy, C. J. Jesus and Fat Tuesday,
and other short stories
A house full of Maude
McElroy, C. J. Jesus and Fat Tuesday,
and other short stories
Imogene
McElroy, C. J. Jesus and Fat Tuesday,
and other short stories
Jeremy Franklin Simmons
McElroy, C. J. Jesus and Fat Tuesday,
and other short stories
Jesus and Fat Tuesday
McElroy, C. J. Jesus and Fat Tuesday,
and other short stories
The limitations of Jason Packard
McElroy, C. J. Jesus and Fat Tuesday,
and other short stories
More than a notion
McElroy, C. J. Jesus and Fat Tuesday,
and other short stories
Sister Detroit
McElroy, C. J. Jesus and Fat Tuesday,
and other short stories
Sun, wind and water
McElroy, C. J. Jesus and Fat Tuesday,
and other short stories
Take mama's picture out of the light
McElroy, C. J. Jesus and Fat Tuesday,
and other short stories
Under the equinox
McElroy, C. J. Jesus and Fat Tuesday,
and other short stories

McElroy, Joseph
Daughter of the revolution
Prize stories, 1985
The man with the bag full of boomerangs
in the Bois de Boulogne
Partisan Review 51 no1:70-4 '84
McEwan, Ian
The child in time
Esquire 108:69-72 Ag '87
First love, last rites
The Art of the tale; ed. by D. Halpern
Psychopolis
The Penguin book of modern British
short stories
McFall, Lynne, 1948-
The one true story of the world
Prairie Schooner 58:41-8 Fall '84
McFarland, Dennis
Last night
The New generation; ed. by A. Kaufman
Seducing Alice
Mademoiselle 92:190+ O '86
McGahern, John, 1934-
All sorts of impossible things
The Ploughshares reader: new fiction for
the eighties
Eddie Mac
The New Yorker 60:46-53 D 3 '84
Like all other men
The Yale Review 74:415-24 Spr '85
Oldfashioned
The Yale Review 73:367-90 Spr '84
The recruiting officer
The Substance of things hoped for; ed.
by J. B. Breslin
McGarry, Jean
Another Sunday story
Chicago Review 36 no1:10-13 '88
The babysitter
McGarry, J. Airs of Providence
Every hour that goes by grows younger
Southwest Review 72:404-13 Summ '87
The hospital: seeing him there almost dead
McGarry, J. Airs of Providence
How it happens
Chicago Review 36 no1:14-18 '88
Margery's prom
McGarry, J. Airs of Providence
One of them gets married
McGarry, J. Airs of Providence
Ozark winter
The North American Review 273:13-17
D '88
Penmanship
McGarry, J. Airs of Providence
Providence, 1934: the house at the beach
McGarry, J. Airs of Providence
Providence, 1948: the most complimentary
thing
McGarry, J. Airs of Providence
Providence, 1954: watch
McGarry, J. Airs of Providence

Providence, 1956: toy box
McGarry, J. Airs of Providence
Providence, 1957: an accident
McGarry, J. Airs of Providence
Providence, 1960: cavities
McGarry, J. Airs of Providence
Providence, 1966: ducks and lucks
McGarry, J. Airs of Providence
Providence, 1970: behind this soft eclipse
McGarry, J. Airs of Providence
Stayed back
McGarry, J. Airs of Providence
They meet a boy
McGarry, J. Airs of Providence
Uncle Maggot
The Southern Review (Baton Rouge, La.)
23:906-15 Aut '87
McGarvey, Craig
Sense of wonder, sense of awe
Sudden fiction; ed. by R. Shapard and
J. Thomas
McGerr, Patricia
The day of the bookmobile
Handle with care; ed. by J. Kahn
In the clear
Ellery Queen's Crimes and punishments
Johnny Lingo's eight-cow wife
Reader's Digest 132:138-41 F '88
McGinn, Colin
Totalled
Critical Quarterly 29:95-7 Wint '87
McGlamry, Beverly
Only a matter of time
The Womansleuth anthology; ed. by I.
Zahava
McGrath, Patrick
Ambrose Syme
McGrath, P. Blood and water, and other
tales
The angel
McGrath, P. Blood and water, and other
tales
The Arnold Crombeck story
McGrath, P. Blood and water, and other
tales
The Black Hand of the Raj
McGrath, P. Blood and water, and other
tales
Blood and water
McGrath, P. Blood and water, and other
tales
Blood disease
McGrath, P. Blood and water, and other
tales
The boot's tale
McGrath, P. Blood and water, and other
tales
The e(rot)ic potato
McGrath, P. Blood and water, and other
tales
Hand of a wanker
McGrath, P. Blood and water, and other
tales

McGrath, Patrick—*Continued*
The lost explorer
  McGrath, P. Blood and water, and other tales
Lush triumphant
  Between C & D; ed. by J. Rose and C. Texier
  McGrath, P. Blood and water, and other tales
Marmilion
  McGrath, P. Blood and water, and other tales
The skewer
  McGrath, P. Blood and water, and other tales
McGrath, William M.
The evening of Mr. Boch's baloney factory
  Short story international 64
McGraw, Erin
Accepted wisdom
  The North American Review 272:56-60 D '87
Bodies at sea
  The Georgia Review 41:67-80 Spr '87
Life drawing
  The Georgia Review 40:475-86 Summ '86
Preparation
  The North American Review 270:20-3 Je '85
Until it comes closer
  The Georgia Review 42:487-503 Fall '88
McGregor, Craig
The heraldry of the body
  Transgressions; ed. by D. Anderson
McGuane, Thomas, 1938-
Dogs
  Harper's 272:31-2+ Je '86
  McGuane, T. To skin a cat
The El Western
  Writers of the purple sage; ed. by R. Martin and M. Barasch
Flight
  Esquire 106:42-3+ Ag '86
  McGuane, T. To skin a cat
Like a leaf
  The Editors' choice: new American stories v1
  McGuane, T. To skin a cat
Little extras
  McGuane, T. To skin a cat
A man in Louisiana
  The Editors' choice v4
  McGuane, T. To skin a cat
The millionaire
  McGuane, T. To skin a cat
Partners
  McGuane, T. To skin a cat
The rescue
  McGuane, T. To skin a cat
The road atlas
  McGuane, T. To skin a cat
A skirmish
  McGuane, T. To skin a cat

Sportsmen
  The Best American short stories, 1986
  McGuane, T. To skin a cat
To skin a cat
  McGuane, T. To skin a cat
Two hours to kill
  McGuane, T. To skin a cat
The **McGuffin.** Kinsella, W. P.
McHaney, Thomas L.
The habits of guineas
  Mississippi writers v1: Fiction; ed. by D. Abbott
McIlrath, J. Harley
Flies
  The North American Review 269:42-3 Je '84
McIlroy, Christopher
All my relations
  The Best American short stories, 1986
McInerney, Jay
It's six a.m. do you know where you are?
  Look who's talking; ed. by B. Weber
Lost and found
  Esquire 110:112-18 Jl '88
The real Tad Allagash
  Ms. 14:38-42+ Ag '85
Reunion
  Esquire 107:178-80+ Mr '87
She dreams of Johnny
  Gentlemen's Quarterly 58:228-9+ Mr '88
Smoke
  The Atlantic 259:68-72+ Mr '87
Story of my life
  Esquire 108:106-8+ Ag '87
McIver in Bombay. Lloyd, T.
McKay, Jean, 1943-
Mr. Appledorn
  The New press anthology #1
McKenna, Bridget
The old organ trail
  L. Ron Hubbard presents Writers of the future v2
McKenney, Ruth, 1911-1972
Industrial valley [excerpt]
  Writing red; ed. by C. Nekola and P. Rabinowitz
McKillip, Patricia A., 1948-
Baba Yaga and the sorcerer's son
  Dragons and dreams; ed. by J. Yolen; M. H. Greenberg and C. G. Waugh
The old woman and the storm
  Imaginary lands; ed. by R. McKinley
McKimmey, James
Choices of the heart
  Good Housekeeping 198:162-3+ Ap '84
McKinley, James
Alastair and Jeremy
  McKinley, J. Acts of love
Chambers
  McKinley, J. Acts of love
Each new springtime, each new summer
  McKinley, J. Acts of love

McKinley, James—*Continued*
A Fickleman jogs
  McKinley, J. Acts of love
Gloves and fishes
  McKinley, J. Acts of love
Kafka in suburbia
  McKinley, J. Acts of love
Kitchen conversation
  McKinley, J. Acts of love
Moriarty's return
  McKinley, J. Acts of love
Ozark episode
  McKinley, J. Acts of love
Praying for a Fickleman
  McKinley, J. Acts of love
Traveler's advisory
  McKinley, J. Acts of love
  Missouri short fiction; ed. by C. Beasley
McKinley, Robin
The stone fey
  Imaginary lands; ed. by R. McKinley
McKnight, Reginald, 1956-
First I look at the purse
  McKnight, R. Moustapha's eclipse
Getting to be like the studs
  McKnight, R. Moustapha's eclipse
The honey boys
  McKnight, R. Moustapha's eclipse
How I met Idi at the Bassi Dakaru
    restaurant
  McKnight, R. Moustapha's eclipse
Mali is very dangerous
  The Massachusetts Review 27:317-29
    Summ '86
  McKnight, R. Moustapha's eclipse
Peaches
  McKnight, R. Moustapha's eclipse
Rebirth
  McKnight, R. Moustapha's eclipse
Uncle Moustapha's eclipse
  McKnight, R. Moustapha's eclipse
  Prairie Schooner 59:3-10 Summ '85
The voice
  McKnight, R. Moustapha's eclipse
Who Big Bob?
  McKnight, R. Moustapha's eclipse
McLaughlin, Cooper
The lodge of Jahbulon
  Ripper! Ed. by G. Dozois and S. Casper
McLaughlin, Lissa, 1952-
The absent toy
  McLaughlin, L. Troubled by his complexion
Before the rain
  McLaughlin, L. Troubled by his complexion
A decent interval
  McLaughlin, L. Troubled by his complexion
In hock
  McLaughlin, L. Troubled by his complexion

In the plane
  McLaughlin, L. Troubled by his complexion
Looking like Virginia Woolf
  McLaughlin, L. Troubled by his complexion
Moving house
  McLaughlin, L. Troubled by his complexion
Mrs. Shreeve and Mrs. Bolero
  McLaughlin, L. Troubled by his complexion
Nancy
  McLaughlin, L. Troubled by his complexion
Paris
  McLaughlin, L. Troubled by his complexion
Shattering
  McLaughlin, L. Troubled by his complexion
The snow
  McLaughlin, L. Troubled by his complexion
The stomach
  McLaughlin, L. Troubled by his complexion
A teacher of the blind
  McLaughlin, L. Troubled by his complexion
Troubled by his complexion
  McLaughlin, L. Troubled by his complexion
McLaverty, Michael
The priest's housekeeper
  The Best of Irish wit and wisdom; ed.
    by J. McCarthy
McLay, Farquhar
Headlines for Whitey
  Streets of stone; ed. by M. Burgess and
    H. Whyte
McLean, Anne, 1951-
Snakebite
  Fatal recurrences; ed. by H. Hugh and
    P. O'Brien
McLoughlin, Jane B.
Straight no chaser
  Critical Quarterly 30:64-8 Wint '88
McMahon, Pat *See* Hoch, Edward D., 1930-
McMillan, Florri
She never knew what hit her
  Redbook 163:171-4 S '84
McMillan, Terry
Men who are good with their hands
  Esquire 110:100-2+ Jl '88
McMurtry, Larry
Texasville [excerpt]
  Great American love stories; ed. by L.
    Rosenthal
McNeal, Tom
True
  The Best of the West; ed. by J. Thomas

McNeill, Christine
Double-glazing
Critical Quarterly 30:72-9 Spr '88
McPherson, Diane
Day after day, like a terrible fish
Through other eyes; ed. by I. Zahava
McPherson, James Alan, 1943-
The story of a scar
American short story masterpieces; ed.
by R. Carver and T. Jenks
McPherson, Jessamyn West *See* West, Jessamyn, d. 1984
McPherson, Michael
Beachboy
Passages to the dream shore; ed. by F.
Stewart
That was last year
Passages to the dream shore; ed. by F.
Stewart
McQueen, James, 1934-
Acorns
Short story international 49
The myna birds
Short story international 57
Uphill runner
Short story international 71
McWey, Michael
Accidents will happen
Seventeen 45:122-3+ F '86
Cruise control
Seventeen 46:212-13+ Ap '87
Dad, I need you now
Redbook 163:50+ Ag '84
In France they kiss on Main Street
Seventeen 44:344-5+ Ag '85
Me/days. Benford, G.
Me and Deke. Daniels, C.
Me and my sister. Rifaat, A.
Me and Will. Michaelson, L. W.
Me man Angel. Adisa, O. P.
Me, tree. Llywelyn, M.
Meade, L. T., 1854-1914, and Eustace, Robert
The man who disappeared
Death locked in; ed. by D. G. Greene
and R. C. S. Adey
The **meadow.** Davenport, G.
The **meadow** bell. La Chapelle, M.
Mealtime. Ellison, H.
Mean men are big. Overholser, W. D.
A **mean** teacher. Sisskind, M.
The **meaning** of their names. Haake, K.
Meanwhile, back at the bromide. Sheckley, R.
Mears, Sheila Sandray
Thirty horses for your daughter
Short story international 49
A **measure** of eloquence. Winton, T.
Measuring the light. Green, M.
Meat. Koea, S.
Meat. Piñera, V.
Meat. Smith, K.
The **meat** man's death. Kobin, J.

The **mechanic.** Clement, H.
MECHANICS (PERSONS)
Abbott, K. Back to nature
Griner, P. Worboys' transaction
Thurber, J. The greatest man in the world
The **mechanics** of good times. Kauffman, J.
Mechanistria. Russell, E. F.
Les **Méchins.** Ferron, J.
Meckel, Christoph
The crow
Short story international 43
The fire
Short story international 61
The sand ball
Short story international 56
Medal from Jerusalem. Shaw, I.
MEDALS
Archer, J. Not the real thing
Chavez, A. The Colonel and the santo
Moore, R. The soldier shows his medal
Windsor, G. The Victoria Cross of
Timothy O'Hea
Meddlesome Jack. Caldwell, E.
Medea. Kessler, J. F.
Medea's kiss. Freriks, K.
Media event. Baxter, C.
The **medical** finger. Queen, E.
MEDICAL LIFE *See* Physicians
MEDICAL RESEARCH *See* Medicine, Experimental
MEDICAL STUDENTS *See* Students
MEDICINE
See also Surgery
MEDICINE, EXPERIMENTAL
Harrison, M. J. The new rays
Kilworth, G. The songbirds of pain
Mårtensson, B. Myxomatosis forte
Matheson, R. C. Conversation piece
Strugatskiĭ, A. N., and Strugatskiĭ, B. N.
Six matches
Sykes, S. C. Rockabye Baby
Wagner, K. E. Lacunae
Williams, W. J. Side effects
MEDICINE, PRACTICE OF *See* Physicians
The **medicine** man. Caldwell, E.
Medicine man. DeMarinis, R.
The **medicine** of Bow-Returning. Austin, M. H.
MEDICINES, PATENT, PROPRIETARY, ETC.
Caldwell, E. The medicine man
García Márquez, G. Blacamán the good, vendor of miracles
Wells, H. G. The truth about Pyecraft
MEDITATION
Adams, G. G. Doing yoga
Boucher, S. The healing
Meditation on play, thoughts on death. Collins, L.
Mediterranean lifestyle: the parvis pry. Ebejer, F.

MEDITERRANEAN REGION
See also Corsica
Chipulina, E. G. Sirocco
Lavers, N. Big dog
MEDIUMS *See* Spiritualism
Medon in Thrace. Parotti, P.
Medra. Lee, T.
MEDUSA (GREEK MYTHOLOGY)
Lee, T. The gorgon
Moore, C. L. Shambleau
Medusa. Sturgeon, T.
Mee, Susie
Mama won't budge
Redbook 168:58+ N '86
A **meeting**. Maupassant, G. de
Meeting. Rasputin, V. G.
Meeting Aline. Dixon, S.
Meeting at the crossroad. Davis, D. S.
The **meeting** at the mixed club. Apollinaire, G.
A **meeting** in Georgestown. Bing, J.
A **meeting** in middle age. Trevor, W.
Meeting Mossie. Moore, S. J.
The **meeting** of the stones. Boyle, K.
Meeting the folks. Grenville, K.
Meeting the head examiner. Murphy, P.
A **meeting** with Medusa. Clarke, A. C.
Meeting you. Vreuls, D.
MEETINGS
Austin, D. A pear
Lu Wenfu. The boundary wall
Murphy, P. Meeting the head examiner
Meetings. Rossi, A.
Meges at Dulichium. Parotti, P.
Mei Jin
(jt. auth) See Zhang Kangkang, and Mei Jin
Meier, Shirley
Peacock eyes
Tales of the Witch World 2
Trave
Magic in Ithkar 4; ed. by A. Norton and R. Adams
Meihem in ce klasrum. Edwards, D.
MEINHOF, ULRIKE, 1934-1976
About
Smith, J. Ulrike Meinhof
Meinke, Peter
Alice's brother
Meinke, P. The piano tuner
The bracelet
Meinke, P. The piano tuner
Conversation with a pole
Meinke, P. The piano tuner
A decent life
Meinke, P. The piano tuner
Doubles
The Virginia Quarterly Review 64:291-9 Spr '88
Even crazy old barmaids need love
Meinke, P. The piano tuner
Losers pay
Meinke, P. The piano tuner

The piano tuner
The Atlantic 253:70-4 F '84
The Best American short stories, 1985
Meinke, P. The piano tuner
The ponoes
Meinke, P. The piano tuner
Ruby lemons
Meinke, P. The piano tuner
Sealink
Meinke, P. The piano tuner
The starlings of Leicester Square
Meinke, P. The piano tuner
The twisted river
Meinke, P. The piano tuner
Uncle George and Uncle Stefan
Prize stories, 1986
The water-tree
Meinke, P. The piano tuner
Winter term
Meinke, P. The piano tuner
Meira Chand *See* Chand, Meira
Meiring, Jane
Bird of my voice
Short story international 58
Meissner, William
The outfielder
Stiller's pond; ed. by J. Agee; R. Blakely and S. Welch
Mejdoub. Bowles, P.
The **Meknes**. MacLean, A.
Melancholy. Parise, G.
Melanie and the purple people eaters. Faust, I.
MELBOURNE (AUSTRALIA) *See* Australia—Melbourne
A **melee** of diamonds. Hoch, E. D.
Melencolia I. Stewart, J. I. M.
Mélie and the bull. Ferron, J.
Melinda falling. Willett, J.
Melissa & Henry—September 10, 1983. Cameron, P.
Mellonta Tauta. Poe, E. A.
Melpo. Farmer, B.
Mel's back. Fries, W. H.
The **melting** man. Hoch, E. D.
The **melting** pot. Schwartz, L. S.
Melusina. Flanagan, M.
Melville, Herman, 1819-1891
The apple-tree table; or, Original spiritual manifestations
Melville, H. Pierre, Israel Potter, The piazza tales, The confidence-man, Uncollected prose, Billy Budd, Sailor
Bartleby the scrivener [Variant title: Bartleby]
Melville, H. Pierre, Israel Potter, The piazza tales, The confidence-man, Uncollected prose, Billy Budd, Sailor
The bell-tower
Melville, H. Pierre, Israel Potter, The piazza tales, The confidence-man, Uncollected prose, Billy Budd, Sailor

Melville, Herman, 1819-1891—*Continued*
Benito Cereno
　Melville, H. Pierre, Israel Potter, The
　piazza tales, The confidence-man, Un-
　collected prose, Billy Budd, Sailor
　Sea captains' tales; ed. by A. Enfield
　Short stories of the sea; ed. by G. C.
　Solley and E. Steinbaugh
Billy Budd, Sailor [Variant title: Billy
　Budd, foretopman]
　Melville, H. Pierre, Israel Potter, The
　piazza tales, The confidence-man, Un-
　collected prose, Billy Budd, Sailor
The chase
　Men at sea; ed. by B. Aymar
Cock-a-doodle-doo; or, The crowing of the
　noble cock beneventano
　Melville, H. Pierre, Israel Potter, The
　piazza tales, The confidence-man, Un-
　collected prose, Billy Budd, Sailor
The encantadas; or, Enchanted isles
　Melville, H. Pierre, Israel Potter, The
　piazza tales, The confidence-man, Un-
　collected prose, Billy Budd, Sailor
The fiddler
　Melville, H. Pierre, Israel Potter, The
　piazza tales, The confidence-man, Un-
　collected prose, Billy Budd, Sailor
The 'Gees
　Melville, H. Pierre, Israel Potter, The
　piazza tales, The confidence-man, Un-
　collected prose, Billy Budd, Sailor
The happy failure
　Melville, H. Pierre, Israel Potter, The
　piazza tales, The confidence-man, Un-
　collected prose, Billy Budd, Sailor
Hood's Isle and the hermit Oberlus
　Mysterious sea stories; ed. by W. Pat-
　trick
I and my chimney
　Melville, H. Pierre, Israel Potter, The
　piazza tales, The confidence-man, Un-
　collected prose, Billy Budd, Sailor
Jimmy Rose
　Melville, H. Pierre, Israel Potter, The
　piazza tales, The confidence-man, Un-
　collected prose, Billy Budd, Sailor
The lightning-rod man
　Melville, H. Pierre, Israel Potter, The
　piazza tales, The confidence-man, Un-
　collected prose, Billy Budd, Sailor
The paradise of bachelors
　Melville, H. Pierre, Israel Potter, The
　piazza tales, The confidence-man, Un-
　collected prose, Billy Budd, Sailor
The piazza
　Great American love stories; ed. by L.
　Rosenthal
　Melville, H. Pierre, Israel Potter, The
　piazza tales, The confidence-man, Un-
　collected prose, Billy Budd, Sailor

Poor man's pudding
　Melville, H. Pierre, Israel Potter, The
　piazza tales, The confidence-man, Un-
　collected prose, Billy Budd, Sailor
Rich man's crumbs
　Melville, H. Pierre, Israel Potter, The
　piazza tales, The confidence-man, Un-
　collected prose, Billy Budd, Sailor
The tartarus of maids
　Melville, H. Pierre, Israel Potter, The
　piazza tales, The confidence-man, Un-
　collected prose, Billy Budd, Sailor
The two temples: Temple first
　Melville, H. Pierre, Israel Potter, The
　piazza tales, The confidence-man, Un-
　collected prose, Billy Budd, Sailor
The two temples: Temple second
　Melville, H. Pierre, Israel Potter, The
　piazza tales, The confidence-man, Un-
　collected prose, Billy Budd, Sailor
About
Beaulieu, V. L. Monsieur Melville [excerpt]
Melville, Jennie *See* Butler, Gwendoline
A **member** of the family. Alden, P. B.
A **member** of the family. Spark, M.
The **memento**. Henry, O.
Memento homo. Miller, W. M.
Memento mori. Pronzini, B.
Memo on Kathy O'Rourke. Sher, J.
Memoir, cut short. Thompson, S.
Memoirs of a good-for-nothing. Eichendorff,
　J., Freiherr von
Memoirs of a novelist. Woolf, V.
Memoirs of a yellow dog. Henry, O.
MEMORIAL DAY
　Mitchell, M. E. For the honor of the com-
　pany
　Phelps, E. S. Comrades
Memorial Day. Cameron, P.
Memorial Day. Lipman, E.
The **memorial** hour. Miller, W.
MEMORIAL SERVICE
　East, C. A tribute to the general
Memorial service. Gerber, M. J.
Memories. Dazai, O.
Memories don't die. James, P. D.
Memories of a mirrored room in Hamburg.
　Josipovici, G.
Memories of a vanished period. Welch, D.
Memories of colonialism. Regent, P.
Memories of the assassination attempt. Win-
　dsor, G.
Memories of the Space Age. Ballard, J. G.
Memories of Uncle Neddy. Bishop, E.
Memories of unhousement. Blaise, C.
MEMORY
　　See also Amnesia
　Abbott, K. We have another ape
　Alford, E. The late date
　Asimov, I. Lest we remember
　Bates, H. E. The return
　Beattie, A. Jacklighting
　Beattie, A. Snow

MEMORY—*Continued*
Bitov, A. The soldier
Briskin, M. Vincenzo and Giulia
Budrys, A. The end of summer
Burke, J. L. Hack
Carver, W. With voice of joy and praise
Chipulina, E. G. Good clean fun
Christmas, R. A. Another angel
Covington, V. Magnolia
Desnoues, L. Philéas
Dixon, S. Don
Dixon, S. Wheels
Dozois, G. R. A dream at noonday
Ekström, M. Hebe laughs
Eliade, M. Nineteen roses
Ellison, H. When Auld's acquaintance is forgot
Endō, S. Retreating figures
Faik, S. The test
Farmer, P. J. Sketches among the ruins of my mind
Flaherty, G. The man who saved himself
Fleming, B. The bookman's tale
Fuentes, C. The doll queen
Garcia, L. G. The wedding
Geras, A. Tea in the Wendy House
Gilliatt, P. Stephanie, Stephen, Steph, Steve
Givner, J. The celebrant
Grau, S. A. Flight
Gustafsson, L. The bird in the breast
Gustafsson, L. Greatness strikes where it pleases
Gustafsson, L. The truly great strikes wherever it wants
Haley, R. Grand-uncle's legs
Heller, S. Postcard from Lahaina
Heller, S. The rainbow man
Hoover, J. Proteus
Ignatow, R. G. Resurrection
James, P. D. The girl who loved graveyards
Johnston, G. The verdict
Kawabata, Y. A sunny place
Kessel, J. Hearts do not in eyes shine
King, S. The monkey
Kittredge, W. Flight
Kittredge, W. The Van Gogh field
Kohler, S. The mountain
La Guma, A. Blankets
Li Ping. Autumn
Littlebird, L. The hunter
Loukakis, A. Being here now
Loukakis, A. Only in the truth
Lutz, J. The landscape of dreams
MacLaverty, B. Umberto Verdi, chimney sweep
Malouf, D. The empty lunch-tin
Matthews, J. Quest for an unnamed place
McCluskey, J. The best teacher in Georgia
McDaniel, W. E. Shamrock Road
Michaelson, L. W. Butcherdom
Moravia, A. A bad memory block

Norris, L. The holm oak
Norris, L. Sing it again, Wordsworth
Oates, J. C. Eleuthéria
Oates, J. C. Two doors
Olsen, T. I stand here ironing
Osborn, C. Amnesia's child
Osborn, C. House of the blue woman
Papaellinas, G. A merchant's widow
Parise, G. Memory
Phillips, J. A. Bess
Prosser, H. L. Summer wine
Ransom, W. M. The aftermath
Rasputin, V. G. Meeting
Reed, K. Into the parlor
Rhys, J. Temps perdi
Sandel, C. To Lukas
Schnitzler, A. America
Schreiner, O. The woman's rose
Schwartz, L. S. The two portraits of Rembrandt
Selmi, H. Distant seas
Sheckley, R. The mnemone
Silva, B. Hell's playground
Silva, B. Precious
Sinclair, M. J. P. Secrets
Sproat, R. Almost graceful like a dancer
Storm, T. Immensee
Summers, H. S. Herschell
Takenishi, H. The rite
Thomas, A. C. Relics
Thomas, D. Holiday memory
Thompson, J. Robert's song
Thompson, J. The white impala
Ty-Casper, L. Application for a small life
Updike, J. One more interview
Updike, J. Still of some use
Vreuls, D. Stoke Sobel in Polk
Wagner, K. E. Lacunae
Wagner, R. E. I'm going down to watch the horses come alive
Wallace, S. R. Dark steps
Warren, J. Ugly Douglas & company
Watson, S. The rumble seat
Weidman, J. My father sits in the dark
Wheatcroft, J. Letter from a stranger
Whitaker, M. Hannah
Wilson, B. Hearings
Windsor, G. My father's version of the nurses' story
Yarbro, C. Q. Lapses
Zhang Xian. The widow
Memory. Day, R. C.
Memory. Parise, G.
A **memory.** Welty, E.
Memory and desire. Ryan, A.
Memory of Caux. Rodoreda, M.
A **memory** of Yamashina. Shiga, N.

MEMPHIS (TENN.) *See* Tennessee—Memphis
Memphis. Gilchrist, E.
Memphis. Mason, B. A.

MEN

See also Single men

Adams, G. G. Inside dope

Austin, D. Men without women

Claiborne, S. Flotsam and Jetsam

DeMarinis, R. Good wars

Gallagher, T. The wimp

Ignatow, R. G. A careless man of the 20th century

Kiely, B. Bloodless Byrne of a Monday

Kiely, B. Mock battle

Lott, B. This plumber

Nowotny, J. Hic sunt leones

Oates, J. C. The man whom women adored

Oates, J. C. Surf City

Shukshin, V. M. Moving to the country

Summers, H. S. The man who looked young

Men. Boyle, K.

The **men** & women of Rivendale. Tem, S. R.

Men and gold and bread. Brown, G. M.

Men are like children, like the beasts. Day, R. C.

Men at work. Greene, G.

The **men** in her life. Schweitzer, G.

The **men** in her life. Soman, F. J.

The **men** in the storm. Crane, S.

Men like us. Drake, D.

Men of Old Catawba. See Wolfe, T. Old Catawba

The **men** on my window. Burns, M.

Men under water. Lombreglia, R.

Men who are good with their hands. McMillan, T.

The **men** who discovered forbidden chairs. Brandão, I. de L.

Men without bones. Kersh, G.

Men without women. Austin, D.

Mena Keyfer. Waterhouse, C.

Menagerie, a child's fable. Johnson, C. R.

The **menagerie** of Babel. Scholz, C.

Menaker, Daniel

Brothers
 The Graywolf annual [1]

Continuing care
 The New Yorker 61:42-50 D 9 '85

Interference
 The New Yorker 60:37-45 F 18 '85

Last lessons
 The New Yorker 62:24-33 Je 23 '86

The old left
 A Grand Street reader; ed. by B. Sonnenberg
 Prize stories, 1984

The ravages of time
 The New Yorker 61:36-42 My 27 '85

The three-mile hill is five miles long
 Full measure; ed. by D. Sennett

Mencken, Sara Haardt, 1898-1935

Little white girl
 The Art of fiction in the heart of Dixie; ed. by P. D. Beidler

Mencken stuff. Richards, J.

Mendel the Tinsmith. Botwinik, B.

Mendele Mokher Seforim, 1835?-1917

Of bygone days
 A Shtetl, and other Yiddish novellas; ed. by R. R. Wisse

Mendocino. Packer, A.

Meneseteung. Munro, A.

Menestheus at Athens. Parotti, P.

MENGELE, JOSEF

About

Shepard, L. Mengele

Mengele. Shepard, L.

Mengele in Jerusalem. Reich, T.

MENINGITIS

Williams, W. C. Danse pseudomacabre

MENNONITES

Bourjaily, V. The Amish farmer

Huggan, I. Queen Esther

MENOMINEE INDIANS

Henson, R. Billie loses her job

MENSERVANTS

Colette. The judge

Hartley, L. P. Pains and pleasures

Jahnn, H. H. A master selects his servant

Livesey, M. A story to be illustrated by Max Ernst

Maupassant, G. de. The farmer's wife

MENSTRUATION

Shange, N. Sassafrass, Cypress & Indigo [excerpt]

Williams, T. Completed

MENTAL DEPRESSION

Akutagawa, R. Cogwheels

Akutagawa, R. A fool's life

Alderson, T. Michelson in the desert

Bell, M. S. Zero db

Cohen, R. Shamsky and other casualties

Davis, L. Therapy

Deaver, P. F. Silent retreats

Deaver, P. F. Wilbur Gray falls in love with an idea

Flook, M. All the girls had gone

Gilliatt, P. Foreigners

Halligan, M. A leisurely drowning

Minot, S. Sparks

Oates, J. C. In traction

O'Hara, J. How can I tell you?

Robison, M. An amateur's guide to the night

Schwartz, L. S. The man at the gate

Tabucchi, A. Voices

Wendt, A. The birth and death of the miracle man

Wilson, B. Disaster

Yasuoka, S. Rain

MENTAL DISORDERS *See* Mental illness

MENTAL HOSPITALS *See* Mentally ill—Care and treatment

MENTAL ILLNESS

See also Dual personality; Hallucinations and illusions; Nervous breakdown; Paranoia; Personality disorders; Schizophrenia

Aickman, R. Into the wood
Alderson, T. Tim's back home
Alderson, T. Vigil
Ballard, J. G. Myths of the near future
Ballard, J. G. News from the sun
Barker, C. Babel's children
Bates, H. E. A happy man
Berriault, G. The bystander
Bird, C. Woodpecker Point
Bloch, R. Man with a hobby
Bloch, R. The plot is the thing
Böll, H. Christmas not just once a year
Boylan, J. The love starter
Boyle, T. C. Two ships
Brand, C. Bless this house
Brooks, J. A value
Campbell, E. They're talking about Chernobyl today
Carpenter, D. The father's love
Cheever, J. The five-forty-eight
Chernoff, M. Respect for the dead
Claiborne, S. Rubble
Coleman, W. Reba
Conroy, F. Midair
Crapser, W. Wild child
Crayford, K. Duncan
Crispin, E. We know you're busy writing, but we thought you wouldn't mind if we just dropped in for a minute
Dadswell, M. A vignette of Susannah
DeMarinis, R. The coming triumph of the free world
DeMarinis, R. Mole
DeMarinis, R. Pagans
Dixon, S. Speak
Dodd, S. M. Coelostat
Dodd, S. M. Potions
Dozois, G. R., and Haldeman, J. C. Executive clemency
Dubus, A. After the game
Ebon, W. Agua prieta
Eisenstein, S. Holocaust envy
Ellin, S. Robert
Emshwiller, C. The circular library of stones
Eskapa, S. Between the sheets
Faik, S. The futile man
Ferguson, W. A summer at Estabrook
Flaherty, G. The terrible speed of mercy
Flook, M. A walk in the city
García Márquez, G. Nabo: the black man who made the angels wait
Garrett, G. P. A game of catch
Gathorne-Hardy, J. Mothers
Gilchrist, E. Crazy, crazy, now showing everywhere
Gilman, C. P. The yellow wallpaper
Golding, W. Miss Pulkinhorn

Gordon, M. Billy
Harris, M. The photograph
Havazelet, E. Glass
Havazelet, E. Resident
Hemley, R. Digging a hole
Hensley, J. L. The retiree
Hofmann, G. Moth
Hoyt, M. S. An island of curving stone
Hulme, K. Kiteflying party at Doctors' Point
Hulme, K. Planetesimal
Hunnicutt, E. Amos
Ingalls, R. Something to write home about
Johnson, G. Crazy ladies
Jolley, E. One Christmas knitting
Jolley, E. Two men running
Kang, S.-J. Another Eve
King, S. The ballad of the flexible bullet
Kittredge, W. Blue stone
La Chapelle, M. Faith
La Chapelle, M. House of heroes
La Chapelle, M. The meadow bell
Labozzetta, M. Making the wine
Lavers, N. Rumors
Li, C. The spheric man
Lispector, C. The imitation of the rose
Lutz, J. The music from downstairs
Lutz, J. No small problem
MacLean, K. The other
Mansfield, K. Ole Underwood
Matthiessen, P. Midnight turning gray
Mattison, A. The knitting
McCullers, C. The haunted boy
McCullers, C. Who has seen the wind?
McGrath, P. The skewer
McGuane, T. Like a leaf
Michaelson, L. W. The burning bush
Montgomerie, W. Daft Jenny
Moravia, A. I've stuttered all my life
Morrison, J. Christ, the Devil and the lunatic
Murphy, P. Cross purposes
Nelson, K. This light is for those at sea
Nolan, W. F. Saturday's shadow
O'Brien, E. The house of my dreams
Oe, K. The clever rain tree
Olson, D. Enter the stranger
Perkins, F. The changes
Phillips, J. A. 1934
Russ, J. Life in a furniture store
Saiki, J. The fisherman
Schwartz, J. Crazy
Schwartz, L. S. Plaisir d'amour
Scott, D. C. The Desjardins
Shaw, J. B. Some of the things I did not do
Sheckley, R. The petrified world
Shiel, M. P. The house of sounds
Shirley, J. What Cindy saw
Sligo, J. Burnham camp
St. Clair, M. The invested libido
Steele, M. The glass-brick apartment
Stern, S. Rudolph Finkl's apprenticeship

MENTAL ILLNESS—*Continued*
Stone, R. Not for love
Swofford, A. Ladybug, Ladybug
Takahashi, T. A happy home
Tem, S. R. Little cruelties
Thomas, D. The mouse and the woman
Tuohy, F. In the hotel
Vanderhaeghe, G. Going to Russia
Varley, J. Manikins
Vogan, S. Miss Buick of 1942
Welch, S. The time, the place, the loved one
West, J. The day of the hawk
Wiesinger, S. Cane Road
Wilson, B. Pity
Wilson, B. Starfish
Wolfe, G. All the hues of Hell

MENTAL TELEPATHY *See* Telepathy
MENTAL TESTS
Forrest, K. V. The test
Malzberg, B. N. Johann Sebastian Brahms
Rampo, E. The psychological test

MENTALLY HANDICAPPED
See also Mentally handicapped children
Campbell, W. B. Moose
Cook, H. Easter lily
Crace, J. The world with one eye shut
Day, R. C. Massimo
El-Bisatie, M. My brother
Flanagan, J. Chinook
Gault, C. This now fenceless world
Gbadamosi, R. A. Death by the waterfall
Gustafsson, L. Greatness strikes where it pleases
Gustafsson, L. The truly great strikes wherever it wants
Haake, K. The meaning of their names
Harland, M. One old maid
Hassler, J. Rufus at the door
Hensley, J. L. Savant
Hoyt, M. S. Park taxi
Huggan, I. Into the green stillness
Jolley, E. Adam's bride
Jolley, E. Dingle the fool
Kye, Y.-M. Adada the idiot
Lardner, R. Haircut
Maupassant, G. de. Bertha
Maupassant, G. de. Mademoiselle
Maupassant, G. de. The rabbit
McGarry, J. Providence, 1948: the most complimentary thing
Meinke, P. Ruby lemons
Milenski, P. Tickits
Nonhebel, C. Popcorn
Robinson, K. S. Ridge running
Rossiter, S. Secrets
Rudin, J. Sellin' some wood
Sexson, L. Hope chest
Sheehan, R. The ark
Smith, P. C. The patchwork quilt
Spivack, K. Surviving
Stephan, M. The tub

Van Name, M. L. My sister, my self
Wells, H. G. Our little neighbour
Windsor, G. The sad music of men
Winton, T. Thomas Awkner floats

MENTALLY HANDICAPPED CHILDREN
Carter, R. Composition
Dadswell, M. Self-exposure
Finger, A. Basic skills
Grant, C. L. Eyes
Highsmith, P. The button
Matheson, S. Harris
Nesvadba, J. The half-wit of Xeenemuende
Nowakowski, M. The silver bird
Porter, K. A. He
Saiki, J. Samurai
Strachan, T. A father's love
Warren, J. The Corn Dolly

MENTALLY ILL
See also Insane, Criminal and dangerous
Care and treatment
Alford, E. The late date
Berriault, G. The bystander
Bloch, R. A home away from home
Bloch, R. Terror in the night
Botwinik, B. The glazier
Ch'en, Y.-C. Poor poor dumb mouths
Dilov, L. Forward, mankind!
Drake, R. Were you there?
Ferguson, P. Patrick
García Márquez, G. Bitterness for three sleepwalkers
Godfrey, P. Time out of mind
Ignatow, R. G. The pool of life
Jolley, E. The performance
Lutz, J. The real shape of the coast
Munro, A. Circle of prayer
Poe, E. A. The system of Doctor Tarr and Professor Fether
Sheehan, R. The ark
Stead, C. Private matters
Wilson, B. White mountains in the moon
Wolfe, G. The death of Doctor Island
Yasuoka, S. A view by the sea

Mentoring. Komie, L. B.
Menudo. Carver, R.
The **mer** she. Leiber, F.
MERCENARIES *See* Soldiers of fortune
The **mercenaries.** Hemingway, E.
MERCENARY SOLDIERS *See* Soldiers of fortune
MERCHANT MARINE *See* Seamen
MERCHANTS
See also Department stores
Bloch, R. The gods are not mocked
Brown, M. W. The barbecue
Conroy, J. The siren
Dixon, S. The package store
Elkin, S. The conventional wisdom
Friel, G. Onlookers
Gorky, M. Creatures that once were men
Holding, J. A padlock for Charlie Draper
Kees, W. I should worry

MERCHANTS—*Continued*
Liben, M. No sale 1
Liben, M. No sale 2
Liben, M. Pinkham: the enchanted isles
Liben, M. Uncle Benny
Lofts, N. The natives are friendly
Morazzoni, M. Girl in a turban
Sandel, C. Larsen's
Sproat, R. A small difference only
Suckow, R. The man of the family
Wells, H. G. A catastrophe
Winslow, T. S. The best man in town
Wolfe, T. The lost boy
A **merchant's** widow. Papaellinas, G.
Mercurial. Robinson, K. S.
MERCURY (PLANET)
Herbert, F. Transcript: Mercury program
Robinson, K. S. Mercurial
Mercury. Murphy, Y.
MERCY DEATH *See* Euthanasia
Mercy flights. Peterson, M.
Meredith, Christopher
Shifts
New England Review and Bread Loaf Quarterly 10:410-13 Summ '88
Meredith, Jerry, and Smirl, D. E.
Dream in a bottle
L. Ron Hubbard presents Writers of the future v2
Merely players. Hansen, J.
Merica, Elizabeth
Out of place
The Georgia Review 42:555-66 Fall '88
A **merican**. Treitel, J.
Mérigot Marchès. Schwob, M.
Mérimée, Prosper, 1803-1870
Mateo Falcone
Classic European short stories; ed. by R. Beum
The Penguin book of horror stories
Meriones at Gortyn. Parotti, P.
Meriwether, Louise, 1923-
A happening in Barbados
The Other woman; ed. by S. Koppelman
Merkin, Daphne
Enchantment
The New Yorker 60:42-6 Ap 2 '84
MERLIN
Swanwick, M. The dragon line
Merlina and the colored ice. Gardner, M.
Merlini *See* Rawson, Clayton, 1906-1971
A **mermaid** on a blue horse: a tale with two endings. Morrissey, M.
MERMAIDS
Alcott, L. M. Ariel. A legend of the lighthouse
Bradbury, R. Undersea guardians
De Camp, L. S. Nothing in the rules
Forsh, O. The little mermaid Rotozeyechka
Martin, V. Sea lovers
Morrissey, M. A mermaid on a blue horse: a tale with two endings

Russ, J. Russalka; or, The seacoast of Bohemia
Shiner, L. Till human voices wake us
Wilde, O. The fisherman and his soul
Mermaids. Beattie, A.
Mermaids on the golf course. Highsmith, P.
MERMEN
Shiner, L. Till human voices wake us
Yolen, J. The lady and the merman
Merops in Mysia. Parotti, P.
MERRICK, JOSEPH CAREY, 1862 or 3-1890
About
Sinclair, I. Brides of the pleiades
Merril, Judith, 1923-
The shrine of temptation
Fantastic stories; ed. by M. H. Greenberg and P. L. Price
Merrill, Lew
The robot awakes
Sensuous science fiction from the weird and spicy pulps; ed. by S. Jaffery
Merriman, Catherine
Silly mothers
New England Review and Bread Loaf Quarterly 10:424-34 Summ '88
That special day
New England Review and Bread Loaf Quarterly 11:168-75 Wint '88
Merritt, Abraham, 1882-1943
The moon pool
Masterpieces of fantasy and enchantment; ed. by D. G. Hartwell
The pool of the stone god
Masterpieces of terror and the supernatural; ed. by M. Kaye and S. Kaye
The **merry** chase. Lish, G.
Merry child. Asscher-Pinkhof, C.
Merry Christmas, Marge! Childress, A.
The **merry-go-round**. Mazel, D.
The **merry-go-round**. Pulaski, J.
MERRY-GO-ROUNDS
Crane, S. The pace of youth
Derleth, A. W. Carousel
Ryan, A. Bundoran, Co. Donegal
Merry May. Campbell, R.
The **merry** men. Stevenson, R. L.
Merseyside fairy story collective
Snow White
Don't bet on the prince; ed. by J. Zipes
Merwin, W. S. (William Stanley), 1927-
Foie gras
The New Yorker 60:46-60+ N 19 '84
Merwin, William Stanley *See* Merwin, W. S. (William Stanley), 1927-
A **mésalliance**. Maupassant, G. de
Mesler, Corey
Is there too much sex in soaps?
Here's the story: fiction with heart; ed. by M. Sklar
The **mesmeric** mountain. Crane, S.
Mesmeric revelation. Poe, E. A.
Mesmerica. Russell, E. F.

Mess. King, F. H.

The **message**. Lispector, C.

Message found in a copy of Flatland. Rucker, R. von B.

A **message** from Charity. Lee, W. M.

The **message** in the message. Ritchie, J.

Message to a messy man. Stallings, F.

A **message** to the King of Brobdingnag. Cowper, R.

Messenger, Bill

Give it back to the Indians
Isaac Asimov's Tomorrow's voices

The **messenger**. Dickerson, K.

MESSENGERS

Böll, H. Breaking the news

Livia, A. 5 1/2 Charlotte Mews

Winton, T. Thomas Awkner floats

Messing about in boats. Van de Wetering, J.

Met by moonlight. Crompton, A. E.

The **metamorfalsis**. Brossard, J.

METAMORPHOSIS

Bowles, P. Allal

Bradbury, R. Chrysalis

Bryant, E. The transfer

Collier, J. The lady on the grey

Cortázar, J. Axolotl

Garnett, D. Lady into fox

Gray, A. The comedy of the white dog

Hildesheimer, W. Why I transformed myself into a nightingale

Kawabata, Y. Yuriko

Korabelnikov, O. Tower of birds

Meckel, C. The crow

Piñón, N. The new kingdom

Rodoreda, M. The river and the boat

Silverberg, R. At the conglomeroid cocktail party

Sonnemann, W. K. The council of drones

Valenzuela, L. My everyday colt

Valenzuela, L. The snow white watchman

Yolen, J. Words of power

Metamorphosis. Dé, C., and Dandurand, A.

Metamorphosis. Gifkins, M.

Metanoia: medicine. Rusenas, I.

Metaphor for murder. See Brett, S. The nuggy bar

Metaphors. Klinkowitz, J.

Metaphysics in the Midwest. White, C.

Metaxas, Eric

The wild ride of Miss Impala George
Blair & Ketchum's Country Journal 13:22-5 Ja '86

Metcalf, John, 1938-

Gentle as flowers make the stones
Making it new; ed. by J. Metcalf

Single gents only
The Literary Review (Madison, N.J.) 28:411-24 Spr '85
Making it new; ed. by J. Metcalf

Metcalfe, John, 1891-1965

The feasting dead
The Mammoth book of short horror novels; ed. by M. Ashley

Mr. Meldrum's mania
The Penguin book of horror stories

Metcalfe, Rowan

The cat
Women's work; ed. by M. McLeod and L. Wevers

Metempsychosis. Berry, R. M.

Method for murder. Bloch, R.

METHUSELAH (BIBLICAL FIGURE)
About

Singer, I. B. The death of Methuselah

Metonymy; or, The husband's revenge. De Queiroz, R.

Metropolitan. Holmes, C.

The **Metropolitan** touch. Wodehouse, P. G.

Metz, Jerred

Angel rolling the heavens together
Missouri short fiction; ed. by C. Beasley

Metzengerstein. Poe, E. A.

Metzger, Deena

Blood oranges
Erotic interludes; ed. by L. Barbach

In the beginning there was humming
Hear the silence; ed. by I. Zahava

The tree on the mountain
Hear the silence; ed. by I. Zahava

MEXICAN AMERICANS
See also Mexicans—United States

Arias, R. Lupe

Armas, J. El tonto del Barrio

Bruce-Novoa. The manuscript

Candelaria, N. El patrón

Castillo, A. Ghost talk

Chávez, D. Willow game

Flores, C. N. Yellow flowers

Garcia, L. G. The wedding

Jiménez, F. The circuit

Keller, G. D. Mocha in Disneyland

Keller, G. D. The raza who scored big in Anáhuac

Mares, E. A. Florinto

Martínez-Serros, H. The birthday present

Martínez-Serros, H. Father Palomo

Martínez-Serros, H. Her

Martínez-Serros, H. Jitomates

Martínez-Serros, H. Killdeer

Martínez-Serros, H. The last laugh

Martínez-Serros, H. Victor and David

Monreal, D. N. In the train station

Monreal, D. N. A matter of dignity

Monreal, D. N. The new neighbor

Monreal, D. N. The visit

Monreal, D. N. The weight lifters

Nichols, J. T. The Milagro beanfield war [excerpt]

Padilla, M. Papel

Salinas, M. The scholarship jacket

Suarez, M. The migrant

Treviño, J. S. A very old man

MEXICAN AMERICANS—*Continued*
Vargas, K. The corpse
Mexican dust. Adams, A.
A **Mexican** fairy tale. Carrington, L.
MEXICAN REVOLUTION *See* Mexico—20th century
A **Mexican** tale. Kaplan, D. M.
The **Mexican** tattoo. Conley, R. J.
MEXICAN WAR, 1845-1848 *See* United States—War with Mexico, 1845-1848
MEXICANS
United States
Bradbury, R. I see you never
Burk, R. The housekeeper
Burke, J. L. Uncle Sidney and the Mexicans
Castillo, R. C. The miracle
Connell, E. S. The fisherman from Chihuahua
Crane, S. A man and some others
De la Torre, A. Diamond eyes and pig tails
Dybek, S. Hot ice
Evans, M. Xavier's folly
Everett, P. L. Chacón, Chacón
Gallegos, M. Florence and the new shoes
Henry, O. An afternoon miracle
Keller, G. D. The mojado who offered up his tapeworms to the public weal
Martínez-Serros, H. "Learn! Learn!"
Monreal, D. N. Lola's return
Monreal, D. N. The weight lifters
Monreal, D. N. The young wife
Osborn, C. House of the blue woman
Peña, D. One story too many
Phillips, J. A. El Paso
Ramos, M. His mother's image
Ríos, A. La boda
Valdez, O. J. A dollar's worth
Viramontes, H. M. Growing
Viramontes, H. M. Neighbors
West, J. Foot-shaped shoes
MEXICO
Bowles, P. Señor Ong and Señor Ha
Carrington, L. A Mexican fairy tale
Cheuse, A. The quest for Ambrose Bierce
19th century
Crane, S. Horses—one dash
Crane, S. One dash—horses
20th century
Boswell, R. Flipflops
Campbell, E. Maundy Thursday
Carr, P. M. Night of the luminarias
Fuentes, C. The two Elenas
Garro, E. The tree
Greene, G. Across the bridge
Keller, G. D. The raza who scored big in Anáhuac
Kuttner, H., and Moore, C. L. Or else
Pacheco, J. E. Battles in the desert
Pacheco, J. E. The pleasure principle
Ríos, A. The child
Roscoe, P. Never tears for California

Schulberg, B. Señor Discretion himself
Schwebel, B. A gift for Lucrecia
Schwebel, B. El Señor Lector
Stone, R. Not for love
Swados, H. The tree of life
Valdés, G. Recuerdo
College life
See College life—Mexico
Marriage customs
See Marriage customs—Mexico
Prisoners and prisons
See Prisoners and prisons—Mexico
Ranch life
See Ranch life—Mexico
Rural life
Bowles, P. Pastor Dowe at Tacaté
Ríos, A. The iguana killer
Rulfo, J. Talpa
Silverberg, R. Not our brother
Cuernavaca
Anaya, R. A. B. Traven is alive and well in Cuernavaca
Guadalajara
Rand, P. The nephew
Juarez
Keller, G. D. Papi invented the automatic jumping bean
Mexico City
Campbell, E. La güera
Crane, S. The five white mice
Crane, S. The wise men: a detail of American life in Mexico
Curley, D. Revenge
Puerto Vallarta
Gébler, C. Puerto Vallarta
Tijuana
Silvis, R. Prayer and old jokes
ZoBell, B. Avenida revolucion
Yucatan
Tiptree, J. Beyond the dead reef
Tiptree, J. The women men don't see
Mexico. Bass, R.
Mexico. Glasser, P.
MEXICO CITY (MEXICO) *See* Mexico—Mexico City
The **mezzotint.** James, M. R.
Mhlope, Gcina
It's quiet now
Somehow tenderness survives; ed. by H. Rochman
The toilet
Somehow tenderness survives; ed. by H. Rochman
La **Mi-Carême.** Ferron, J.
Mi Li: a Chinese fairy tale. Walpole, H.
MIAMI (FLA.) *See* Florida—Miami
Miami. Camoin, F. A.
MICE
Aiken, J. The cat who lived in a drainpipe
Bloch, R. The Pied Piper fights the Gestapo
Coppard, A. E. Arabesque—the mouse
Davis, L. The mouse

MICE—*Continued*

Granit, A. I went to the market place to see the world! Oy, Mama, oy!

Klinkowitz, J. Five bad hands and the wild mouse folds

Kress, N. Against a crooked stile

Mayhar, A. Nor disregard the humblest voice

Parise, G. Liking

Mice. Tester, W.

Michael. Barthelme, S.

Michael. Soldatow, S.

Michael. Warren, J.

Michael and Mary. O'Kelly, S.

Michael Egerton. Price, R.

Michael Kohlhaas. Kleist, H. von

Michael Surfax, whaler. Brown, G. M.

Michaels, Leonard, 1933-

Crossbones

Sudden fiction; ed. by R. Shapard and J. Thomas

The deal

The Art of the tale; ed. by D. Halpern

Jealousy

Harper's 274:36-7 Mr '87

The Paris Review 28:250-2 Summ/Fall '86

Murderers

American short story masterpieces; ed. by R. Carver and T. Jenks

Toiler

Partisan Review 51 no4/52 no1:540-51 '84/'85

Stories and poems from close to home; ed. by F. Salas

Michaelson, L. W., 1920-

All my darlings

Michaelson, L. W. On my being dead, and other stories

The burglar face

Michaelson, L. W. On my being dead, and other stories

The burning bush

Michaelson, L. W. On my being dead, and other stories

Butcherdom

Michaelson, L. W. On my being dead, and other stories

An early frost

Michaelson, L. W. On my being dead, and other stories

The Ferrari

Michaelson, L. W. On my being dead, and other stories

The flying Dutchman

Michaelson, L. W. On my being dead, and other stories

The goldfish

Michaelson, L. W. On my being dead, and other stories

Klitzee one—God zero

Michaelson, L. W. On my being dead, and other stories

Me and Will

Michaelson, L. W. On my being dead, and other stories

On my being dead

Michaelson, L. W. On my being dead, and other stories

Phocian

Michaelson, L. W. On my being dead, and other stories

The rabbit that lost its nose

Michaelson, L. W. On my being dead, and other stories

The rhyme in Freddy's face

Michaelson, L. W. On my being dead, and other stories

The tennis bum

Michaelson, L. W. On my being dead, and other stories

Michali among the roses. Eisenstein, S.

Michalson, Greg

The tail of his luck

Missouri short fiction; ed. by C. Beasley

MICHELANGELO BUONARROTI, 1475-1564

Pietà

Ryan, A. Pietà

Michel's courtship adventures. Gotthelf, J.

Michelson in the desert. Alderson, T.

Michener, James A. (James Albert), 1907-

Coral Sea

A Treasury of World War II stories; ed. by B. Pronzini and M. H. Greenberg

MICHIGAN

Baxter, C. A late Sunday afternoon by the Huron

Baxter, C. Saul and Patsy are getting comfortable in Michigan

Dilworth, S. The long white

Hemingway, E. Up in Michigan

Kauffman, J. At first it looks like nothing

Wagner, R. E. I'm going down to watch the horses come alive

Ann Arbor

Baxter, C. Weights

Baxter, C. The would-be father

Detroit

Conroy, J. Bull market

DeGrazia, E. The cat-hater

DeGrazia, E. Enemy country

Kauffman, J. The Easter we lived in Detroit

Oates, J. C. How I contemplated the world from the Detroit House of Correction and began my life over again

MICKEY MOUSE (CARTOON CHARACTER)

Jafek, B. You've come a long way, Mickey Mouse

The **Mickey** Mouse Olympics. Sullivan, T.

Micki New. Mathers, P.

Microcosmic god. Sturgeon, T.

MICROORGANISMS
Potter, R. The red sickness
Twain, M. 3,000 years among the microbes
The **microscope**. Shukshin, V. M.
MICROSCOPE AND MICROSCOPY
O'Brien, F.-J. The diamond lens
The **Mid-City** Meat Company. Maloney, J. J.
Mid-May's eldest child. Alford, E.
Midair. Conroy, F.
MIDDLE AGE
See also Aging
Adams, A. The oasis
Ashley, M. A. Gracefully afraid
Claiborne, S. Scenes from a novel: replenishing Ava
Colette. Alix's refusal
Colette. Chéri
Deaver, P. F. Geneseo
Deaver, P. F. Infield
Deaver, P. F. Long Pine
Deaver, P. F. Marguerite Howe
Deaver, P. F. Silent retreats
Deaver, P. F. Why I shacked up with Martha
Deaver, P. F. Wilbur Gray falls in love with an idea
Delbanco, N. The consolation of philosophy
DeMarinis, R. The flowers of boredom
Dixon, S. For a man your age
Drake, R. The birthday picture
Eisenberg, D. Broken glass
Fisher, M. F. K. Answer in the affirmative
Fowler, K. J. The faithful companion at forty
Freeman, J. The Botanic Gardens
Friedman, P. An unexpected death
Gifkins, M. Living out the past
Haley, R. Fog
Harvor, E. The students' soirée
Havazelet, E. Glass
Kawabata, Y. The white horse
Komie, L. B. Picasso is dead
Lessing, D. M. The habit of loving
McQueen, J. Uphill runner
Mooney, M. Eros and crazy
Mooney, M. The numbers
Muschg, A. The blue man
Robison, M. Your errant mom
Ross, V. An understated look
Ruffolo, L. Birthday
Rule, J. First love/last love
Stern, D. The interpretation of dreams by Sigmund Freud: a story
Updike, J. The afterlife
Updike, J. Deaths of distant friends
Wolff, T. Leviathan
Middle-aged Martha Anne. Seamon, H. R.
MIDDLE AGES
See also Chivalry; Knights and knighthood

The **Middle** Ages. Mattison, A.
MIDDLE CLASSES
Barstow, S. Good
Chekhov, A. P. With friends
Hull, H. R. Alley ways
Hull, H. R. Discovery
Pfeil, F. The night game
Prose, F. Everyone had a lobster
Pym, B. So, some tempestuous morn
The **middle** classes. Schwartz, L. S.
The **middle** drawer. Calisher, H.
MIDDLE EAST
Al-Mak, A. Forty-one minarets
Grandbois, A. The thirteenth
The **middle** kingdom. Tong Enzheng
Middle name. Asimov, I.
The **middle** of the journey. Barstow, S.
MIDDLE WESTERN STATES
Deaver, P. F. Arcola girls
Suckow, R. Midwestern primitive
The **middle** years. James, H.
The **middleman**. Mukherjee, B.
Middleton, Harry
December's pecans
Blair & Ketchum's Country Journal 12:22-3 D '85
Middleton, Richard, 1941-
On the Brighton Road
The Oxford book of English ghost stories
Young ghosts; ed. by I. Asimov; M. H. Greenberg and C. G. Waugh
Middleton, Simon
Small world
Critical Quarterly 30:29-33 Wint '88
Middleton, Stanley, 1919-
The noise
Critical Quarterly 29:53-62 Wint '87
MIDGETS *See* Dwarfs
Midnight. Frucht, A.
Midnight. Yi, H.-C.
Midnight angel. Dow, L.
Midnight at the dump. Millman, L.
Midnight blue. Macdonald, R.
Midnight caller. Franco, M.
The **midnight** clear. Flynn, R.
Midnight dreams. Doig, D. T.
Midnight express. Noyes, A.
Midnight magic. Mason, B. A.
The **midnight** meat train. Barker, C.
Midnight promise. Cross, C.
The **midnight** strangler. Ritchie, J.
Midnight turning gray. Matthiessen, P.
A **midnight** visitor. Bangs, J. K.
The **midnight** voyage of the Seagull. Howard, V. E.
Midrash on happiness. Paley, G.
The **midshipman**. Marryat, F.
Midshipman, the cat. Adams, J. C.
Midsummer madness. Gilchrist, M.
MIDWEST *See* Middle Western States
Midwestern primitive. Suckow, R.

MIDWIVES
Ferguson, P. Inside knowledge
Miesel, Sandra, 1941-
The book-healer
Magic in Ithkar 4; ed. by A. Norton and R. Adams
The salt garden
Tales of the Witch World 2
The shadow hart
Moonsinger's friends; ed by S. Shwartz
Mighty long time. Plumpp, S.
The **mighty** Titanic is sinking. Edric, R.
The **migrant**. Suarez, M.
A **migrant** Christmas. Rule, J.
MIGRANT LABOR
Caldwell, E. Picking cotton
Henley, P. Picking time
Jiménez, F. The circuit
Pronzini, B. I don't understand it
Suarez, M. The migrant
Williams, S. A. The lawd don't like ugly
Migrants. Tallent, E.
The **migration** of the bag ladies. Porterfield, N.
Mihelic, John
Green life
Stiller's pond; ed. by J. Agee; R. Blakely and S. Welch
Mikhailov, Vladimir
Brook on Iapetus
Aliens, travelers, and other strangers; by B. and A. Strugatsky and others
Milady, Fawzi Abdel Kader el See El Milady, Fawzi Abdel Kader
Milady bigamy. De la Torre, L.
The **Milagro** beanfield war. Nichols, J. T.
Milagros, on Mercurio Street. Filippi, C. L.
Milán, Victor
Feast of John the Baptist
A Very large array; ed. by M. M. Snodgrass
MILAN (ITALY) See Italy—Milan
The **mile** run. Engberg, S.
Milenski, Paul
Tickits
Sudden fiction; ed. by R. Shapard and J. Thomas
Miles. Dawson, F.
Miles City, Montana. Munro, A.
Miles from Coconut Grove. Dilworth, S.
The **Milesian** virgins. Schwob, M.
Milford Junction, 1939: a brief encounter. Coover, R.
MILITARY DESERTION See Desertion, Military
MILITARY EDUCATION
Salter, J. Lost sons
MILITARY INTELLIGENCE
Bishop, M. Cold war orphans
MILITARY MANEUVERS
See also War games
Amichai, Y. Dicky's death
Morrison, J. The fugitive

MILITARY OCCUPATION
Chon, K.-Y. Kapitan Lee
MILITARY SCHOOLS See Military education
MILITARY SERVICE, COMPULSORY See Draft
MILITARY TRAINING CAMPS
Saucier, M. Pukes!
Winton, T. Lantern stalk
The **milk**. Anderson, J.
Milk. Carlson, R.
Milk. Farmer, B.
Milk. Joubert, E.
Milk bottles. Anderson, S.
The **milk-boy**. Marosi, G.
Milk from a maiden's breast. Scarborough, E.
Milk is very good for you. Dixon, S.
The **milk** of death. Yourcenar, M.
The **milk** of knowledge. Watson, I.
The **milk** run. Stead, C.
Milking time. O'Flaherty, L.
The **mill**. Bates, H. E.
The **mill-race**. Thurlby, J.
MILL TOWNS
Bonosky, P. Hank
Bonosky, P. A quiet summer's day
Masters, O. The rages of Mrs. Torrens
Updike, J. More stately mansions
Millar, Kenneth See Macdonald, Ross, 1915-1983
Millard, Peter, 1932-
The diamond
The Old dance; ed. by B. Burnard
The **Millennium** Garden of the New Jerusalem. Cahoon, B.
Miller, Ann
The stones of Sharnon
Tales of the Witch World 2
Miller, Arthur, 1915-
It takes a thief
Mystery in the mainstream; ed. by B. Pronzini; M. H. Greenberg and B. N. Malzberg
The misfits
American short story masterpieces; ed. by R. Carver and T. Jenks
Miller, Birthalene
The lonesomes ain't no spring picnic
Mississippi writers v1: Fiction; ed. by D. Abbott
Miller, Deborah
Schweitzer's camera
The Antioch Review 45:156-63 Spr '87
Miller, Ellen Votaw
Blackberries
The North American Review 272:48 Mr '87
Energy
Michigan Quarterly Review 24:433-9 Summ '85

Miller, G. Wayne
Wiping the slate clean
Masques II; ed. by J. N. Williamson
Miller, Georgia
(jt. auth) See Inks, Caralyn, and Miller, Georgia
Miller, Heather Ross
Just trying to help
Redbook 166:66+ Mr '86
Miller, Henry, 1891-1980
Into the night life
New directions in prose and poetry 50
Miller, J. Fullerton
A lover of nature
Streets of stone; ed. by M. Burgess and H. Whyte
Miller, John J., 1932-1985
Ouroboros
A Very large array; ed. by M. M. Snodgrass
Miller, Katherine T.
In the land of the married
Mademoiselle 94:152+ Ap '88
Miller, Michael D.
Tyson's turn
L. Ron Hubbard presents Writers of the future
Miller, P. Schuyler (Peter Schuyler), 1912-1974
Over the river
Vampires; ed. by A. Ryan
Miller, Peter Schuyler *See* Miller, P. Schuyler (Peter Schuyler), 1912-1974
Miller, Sasha
To rebuild the eyrie
Tales of the Witch World [1]
Miller, Sue
Appropriate affect
Miller, S. Inventing the Abbotts, and other stories
The birds and the bees
Miller, S. Inventing the Abbotts, and other stories
Calling
Miller, S. Inventing the Abbotts, and other stories
Expensive gifts
Miller, S. Inventing the Abbotts, and other stories
The Ploughshares reader: new fiction for the eighties
Inventing the Abbotts
The Editors' choice v4; ed. by G. E. Murphy, Jr.
Miller, S. Inventing the Abbotts, and other stories
Leaving home
Miller, S. Inventing the Abbotts, and other stories
The lover of women
The Best American short stories, 1987
Mademoiselle 92:148+ Mr '86

The quality of life
The Atlantic 258:118-24 N '86
Miller, S. Inventing the Abbotts, and other stories
Slides
Miller, S. Inventing the Abbotts, and other stories
Travel
Miller, S. Inventing the Abbotts, and other stories
Tyler and Brina
The Atlantic 255:59-63+ My '85
Miller, S. Inventing the Abbotts, and other stories
What Ernest says
Miller, S. Inventing the Abbotts, and other stories
Miller, Suzanne
The hunters
Erotic interludes; ed. by L. Barbach
Miller, Wade
The memorial hour
Kill or cure; ed. by M. Muller and B. Pronzini
Miller, Walter M., 1923-
Crucifixus etiam
The Substance of things hoped for; ed. by J. B. Breslin
I made you
Machines that think; ed. by I. Asimov; P. S. Warrick and M. H. Greenberg
The little creeps
Amazing science fiction anthology: The wild years, 1946-1955; ed. by M. H. Greenberg
Memento homo
Amazing stories: 60 years of the best science fiction
Millhauser, Steven
August Eschenburg
Millhauser, S. In the penny arcade
Cathay
A Grand Street reader; ed. by B. Sonnenberg
Millhauser, S. In the penny arcade
A day in the country
Millhauser, S. In the penny arcade
In the penny arcade
The Hudson Review 37:199-208 Summ '84
Millhauser, S. In the penny arcade
A protest against the sun
Millhauser, S. In the penny arcade
Rain
The Paris Review 30:215-21 Fall '88
The sledding party
Millhauser, S. In the penny arcade
Snowmen
Millhauser, S. In the penny arcade
The **million** dollar bond robbery. Christie, A.
Million-dollar brainstorm. Algren, N.
A **million-dollar** tramp. Ballard, W. T.
The **million-dollar** wound. Whitlock, D.

A **million** shades of green. Jeppson, J. O.
The **millionaire**. McGuane, T.
MILLIONAIRES
>   *See also* Capitalists and financiers; Wealth

Crane, S. An experiment in luxury
London, J. Good-by, Jack
Lurie, M. Pride and joy
Poe, E. A. The domain of Arnheim
Poe, E. A. The landscape garden
Ramírez, S. To Jackie with all our heart
Millman, Lawrence
The 545 pound boy
>   Millman, L. The wrong-handed man

Annie Bardwell gets back her cutlery
>   Millman, L. The wrong-handed man

The great snake massacre
>   Millman, L. The wrong-handed man

The laying on of hands
>   Millman, L. The wrong-handed man

Midnight at the dump
>   Millman, L. The wrong-handed man

Nightrangers
>   Millman, L. The wrong-handed man

The pickling of Rewt Chaney
>   Millman, L. The wrong-handed man

The preserved woman
>   Millman, L. The wrong-handed man

Prudence
>   Millman, L. The wrong-handed man

Scenes from the island
>   Millman, L. The wrong-handed man

The standing stone
>   Millman, L. The wrong-handed man

The triumph of literacy
>   Millman, L. The wrong-handed man

The wrong-handed man
>   Millman, L. The wrong-handed man

Mills, Lia
Best friends and other strangers
>   *'Teen* 31:64+ S '87

Mills, William, 1935-
Sweet Tickfaw run softly, till I end my song
>   Selected stories from The Southern review, 1965-1985

To pass him out
>   Mississippi writers v1: Fiction; ed. by D. Abbott

Milofsky, David
Hemingway slept here
>   *Prairie Schooner* 58:71-85 Fall '84

The lay of the land
>   *Prairie Schooner* 60:43-54 Spr '86

Spider
>   *Prairie Schooner* 62:81-7 Summ '88

Milosevic, Mario
Up above the world so high
>   The Clarion awards; ed. by D. Knight

Milton, Barbara, 1947-
The cigarette boat
>   Love stories for the time being; ed. by G. D. Chipps and B. Henderson
>   The Pushcart prize IX

Promiscuity
>   *The North American Review* 271:32-3 S '86

Milton, Edith
Dwyer's girl
>   *The Kenyon Review* ns6:92-105 Spr '84

Entrechat
>   The Best American short stories, 1988
>   *The Kenyon Review* ns9:16-30 Summ '87

Milton Freabe. Austin, D.
Mimi. Dadswell, M.
Mimoso. Ocampo, S.
Minakami, Tsutomu, 1919-
Mulberry child
>   The Shōwa anthology 2

MIND AND BODY
Aldani, L. S is for snake
Aldiss, B. W. Infestation
Armer, K. M. On the inside track
Bing, J. The Owl of Bear Island
Carneiro, A. Life as an ant
Dann, J. Blind shemmy
Dilov, L. Contacts of a fourth kind
Foray, V. Duplex
Nesvadba, J. The divided Carla
Robinson, S. User friendly
Sheckley, R. Warm
Silverberg, R. Passengers
Simak, C. D. Idiot's crusade
Sucharitkul, S. Fiddling for water buffaloes
Tong Enzheng. The middle kingdom
Vinge, J. D. Psiren
Zahn, T. Dragon pax
Zajdel, J. A. Particularly difficult territory
Mind and body. Greenwood, R.
Mind and body. Williams, W. C.
MIND CONTROL *See* Brainwashing
The **mind** like a strange balloon. Maddox, T.
Mind over matter. Queen, E.
Mind over matters: headset. Cadigan, P.
MIND READING *See* Telepathy
Minds meet. Ash, P.
The **mindworm**. Kornbluth, C. M.
Mine. Keeling, N.
The **mine**. Rolt, L. T. C.
MINE ACCIDENTS
Sun Shaoshan. Eight hundred meters below
Wegner, H. Miner's tattoo
Mine field. Calvino, I.
MINERS *See* Coal mines and mining; Diamond mines and mining; Gold mines and mining; Mines and mining
A **miner's** Christmas carol. Davis, S.
Miner's tattoo. Wegner, H.
MINES, MILITARY
Federspiel, J. The sapper: a romance

MINES AND MINING
See also Coal mines and mining; Diamond mines and mining; Gold mines and mining

Austin, M. H. The lost mine of Fisherman's Peak

Casey, G. Short-shift Saturday

Conroy, J. The fields of golden glow

Conroy, J. That Skinner Bottoms winter

Davis, S. Mark Haverly

Davis, S. The pocket-miner

Dhlomo, R. R. R. The death of Masaba

Dilworth, S. Winter mines

Doyle, Sir A. C. The stone of Boxman's Drift

Forward, R. L. The singing diamond

Frazee, S. Luck of Riley

Hebel, J. P. An unexpected reunion

Hoffman, W. Patriot

Lee, H. Down the hole

Levine, N. A small piece of blue

MacLeod, A. The closing down of summer

Martin, G. R. R. Override

Mason, B. A. Big Bertha stories

Prichard, K. S. Hero of the mines

Robinson, K. S. Coming back to Dixieland

Robinson, K. S. The lunatics

Sandham, A. A. The conscientious cat

Short, L. Swindle at Piute Sink

St. Pierre, P. H. The owner of the gang

Tallent, E. Why I love country music

Twain, M. Dick Baker's cat

Ming's biggest prey. Highsmith, P.

Minh-Quan
My milk goes dry
Inspired by drink; ed. by Joan Digby and John Digby

MINIATURE OBJECTS
Sorrentino, F. Piccirilli

Minimum of two. Winton, T.

MINING TOWNS
Conroy, J. The siren
Sullivan, T. Whores in the pulpit

The **minister.** Piñera, V.

MINISTERS *See* Clergy

The **minister's** black veil. Hawthorne, N.

Ministry of disturbance. Piper, H. B.

The **Mink** Creek ghost. Lee, H.

Minkhoff, Robert
Better tomorrow
New England Review and Bread Loaf Quarterly 11:117-24 Wint '88

Minkin copying. Liben, M.

MINNEAPOLIS (MINN.) *See* Minnesota—Minneapolis

MINNESOTA
20th century
Baxter, C. Cataract
Baxter, C. The crank
Bly, C. The dignity of life
Bly, C. Gunnar's sword
Bly, C. The last of the gold star mothers
Bly, C. The mouse roulette wheel

Bly, C. Talk of heroes
Farm life
See Farm life—Minnesota
Minneapolis
Kinsella, W. P. Diehard
Stillwater
Cassutt, M. Stillwater, 1896

Minnie the Moocher's hair. Pulaski, J.

Minnie's treasure. May, N.

A **minor** apocalypse. Konwicki, T.

Minor surgery and a poker game. Jacobs, M. G.

Minot, Stephen
Home
The Sewanee Review 94:555-70 Fall '86
A long freeze
The Virginia Quarterly Review 63:661-71 Aut '87
The seawall
New American short stories; ed. by G. Norris
Small Point Bridge
The Best Maine stories; ed. by S. Phippen; C. Waugh and M. Greenberg

Minot, Susan
Allowance
The New Yorker 61:37-41 Ap 29 '85
Hiding
A Grand Street reader; ed. by B. Sonnenberg
Look who's talking; ed. by B. Weber
The Pushcart prize IX
Île Sèche
Grand Street 7:16-22 Wint '88
Lust
Great American love stories; ed. by L. Rosenthal
The Paris Review 26:98-107 Spr '84
Prize stories, 1985
The man who would not go away
The Paris Review 30:76-80 Wint '88
The navigator
The Graywolf annual 2
The solo
Gentlemen's Quarterly 58:173-4+ My '88
Sparks
The New generation; ed. by A. Kaufman
Thanksgiving Day
20 under 30; ed. by D. Spark
Thorofare
The Best American short stories, 1984

The **minstrels.** Valenzuela, L.

Minton, Karen
Reading sign
The Georgia Review 42:755-69 Wint '88

Minus, Ed
The furniture store
The Yale Review 76:569-86 Summ '87

Minutes. Mathers, P.

Minutes of glory. Ngugi wa Thiong'o

The **miracle.** Castillo, R. C.

The **miracle.** Fremlin, C.

The **miracle.** Heinesen, W.

A **miracle**. Maupassant, G. de
The **miracle**. Paynter, J.
The **miracle**. Petrakis, H. M.
Miracle at Chimayo. Perea, R. L.
The **miracle** in Sweet Hollow. Crabtree, L. V.
Miracle in the rain. Hecht, B.
The **miracle** of Glendyne. Power, V.
The **miracle** of Hoshana Rabbah. Sholem Aleichem
Miracle of the fifteen murderers. Hecht, B.
MIRACLES
  Boisvert, C. The prophet
  Brown, G. M. The box of fish
  Brown, G. M. An epiphany tale
  Desnoues, L. The poplars
  Erdrich, L. Saint Marie
  France, A. The ocean Christ
  Fremlin, C. The miracle
  Heinesen, W. The miracle
  Leskov, N. S. The sealed angel
  Maupassant, G. de. A miracle
  Milán, V. Feast of John the Baptist
  Molnar, A. K. The crosstie
  Power, V. The miracle of Glendyne
  Rushdie, S. The Prophet's hair
  Stern, S. Moishe the Just
  Wells, H. G. The man who could work miracles
Miracles. Singer, I. B.
Miracles do happen. Queen, E.
The **miraculous** candidate. MacLaverty, B.
The **mirage**. Winters, J.
Miranda-Escobedo. Sallis, J.
Miranda over the valley. Dubus, A.
Mirdinan. Roe, P., and Muecke, S.
The **mire** of Almendares. Cabrera, L.
Miriam, Libbi
  Maiden names
    Family: stories from the interior; ed. by G. G. Chavis
Miriam. Capote, T.
Miriam. Klíma, I.
Miror. Giguère, R.
Mirror. Herbert, Z.
The **mirror**. Lynch, L.
Mirror. Robison, M.
The **mirror**. Sonu, H.
The **mirror** at the beach. Faik, S.
Mirror games. Colette
The **mirror** image of the earth. Zheng Wenguang
Mirror-play. See Colette. Mirror games
MIRRORS
  Bloch, R. The hungry house
  Gardner, C. S. Overnight guest
  King, S. The reaper's image
  Shaw, B. Light of other days
  Sonu, H. The mirror
  Whitehead, H. S. C. The trap
  Woolf, V. The lady in the looking-glass: a reflection
  Yarbro, C. Q. The spider glass

Mirrors. Grace, P.
Mirrors. Lunn, R.
The **misbehaviour** of things. Brooks, D.
MISCARRIAGE OF JUSTICE
  Kleist, H. von. Michael Kohlhaas
MISCEGENATION
    See also Interracial marriage
  Caldwell, E. Return to Lavinia
  Caldwell, E. Yellow girl
  Child, L. M. F. The quadroons
  Gordimer, N. Country lovers
  Rhys, J. Pioneers, oh, pioneers
  Saiki, J. Hapa hapa/half and half
  Saiki, J. The visit
  Williams, T. Miss Coynte of Greene
MISERS
  Botwinik, B. The one I didn't marry
  Jewett, S. O. Mrs. Parkins's Christmas Eve
  Johnson, C. R. Exchange value
  Valdez, O. J. A dollar's worth
The **misfit**. Colette
The **misfits**. Miller, A.
The **misfortunes** of Sofia. Lispector, C.
The **misfortunes** of the Flapjacks. Rosenfeld, I.
Mishima, Yukio, 1925-1970
  Patriotism
    The Art of the tale; ed. by D. Halpern
  Three million yen
    The World of the short story; ed. by C. Fadiman
            About
  Bishop, M. The Yukio Mishima Cultural Association of Kudzu Valley, Georgia
Misitano, Ralph Anthony
  Deep water
    Passages to the dream shore; ed. by F. Stewart
MISOGYNY
  Kavaler, R. Tigers in the wood
  Pirandello, L. The trap
Misogyny. Pavese, C.
Miss Antonina. Orzeszkowa, E.
Miss Armstrong's homicide. Davis, S.
Miss Bell. Patron, J. F.
Miss Buick of 1942. Vogan, S.
Miss Cameron at Christmas. Pilcher, R.
Miss Clay County 1960. Coskran, K.
Miss Coynte of Greene. Williams, T.
Miss Crystal's maid name Traceleen, she's talking, she's telling everything she knows. Gilchrist, E.
Miss Cynthie. Fisher, R.
Miss Darkness. Brown, F.
Miss Effie, the Peabody, and Father Time. Drake, R.
Miss Elisabetha. Woolson, C. F.
Miss Ella. Fitzgerald, Z.
Miss Esperson. Derleth, A. W.
Miss Esther's land. Banks, B. A.
Miss Foote. Thomas, A. C.
"**Miss** Grief". Woolson, C. F.
Miss Harriet. Maupassant, G. de

Miss Jen. Shen, C.-C.
Miss Mack. McDowell, M.
Miss Mahalia and the still. Owen, G.
Miss Marple tells a story. Christie, A.
Miss Mouse and the fourth dimension. Sheckley, R.
Miss Olive's retreat. Pfeil, F.
Miss Pinkerton's apocalypse. Spark, M.
Miss Prinks. Dickson, G. R.
Miss Pryme. Woolf, V.
Miss Pulkinhorn. Golding, W.
Miss Venezuela. Wilson, B.
Miss Vincent. Dabrowska, M.
Miss Winchelsea's heart. Wells, H. G.
Missed chance. Asscher-Pinkhof, C.
MISSILES See Munitions
Missing. Tsushima, Y.

MISSING CHILDREN
See also Lost children
Carter, R. Kid in a bin
Duecker, K. Saving the dead
Russ, J. Come closer
Missing in Miami. Lyons, A.
The missing ingredient. Northern, M. L.
The missing line. Singer, I. B.
The missing man. MacLean, K.
The missing person. Wolff, T.

MISSING PERSONS
See also Missing children
Abbott, L. K. Martians
Arnold, M. The girl in the mirror
Carter, N. The mystery of room no. 11
Christie, A. The disappearance of Mr. Davenheim
Cross, A. Tania's no where
Dundas, R. Six faces of Feridah Challoner
Everett, P. L. Gaining the door
Forrest, K. V. Jessie
Fowles, J. The enigma
Gardner, M. The dome of many colors
Gault, W. C. The Kerman kill
Gerber, M. J. Tragic lives
Gordon, G. Hans Pfeifer
Greenwood, R. Snake eyes
Hankla, C. A box for dreams
Hawthorne, N. Wakefield
Henry, O. The renaissance at Charleroi
Hofmann, G. The cramp
Horvitz, L. A. Pictures of a woman gone
Kaikō, T. Five thousand runaways
King, R. Malice in wonderland
Kinsella, W. P. Searching for Freddy
Kipling, R. The return of Imray
Klein, T. E. D. Black man with a horn
Kranes, D. The phantom Mercury of Nevada
Long, D. The Oriental Limited
Meade, L. T., and Eustace, R. The man who disappeared
Morand, P. Hungarian night
Morris, M. The bus of dreams
Morris, W. To Calabria
Nielsen, H. A woman is missing

Norris, H. Starwood
Pronzini, B. Thin air
Rawson, C. Off the face of the earth
Regent, P. Laughing Pig
Rolt, L. T. C. Bosworth summit pound
Rooke, L. The madwoman of Cherry Vale
Sheckley, R. Fishing season
Skrzynecki, P. The Superman t-shirt
Taylor, P. H. The old forest
Trevor, W. Cocktails at Doney's
Wells, H. G. The Plattner story
Missing persons. Wilson, L. A.
The missing Shakespeare manuscript. De la Torre, L.
The mission. Cave, H. B.
Mission #6. James, S.
Mission No. 1. James, S.
Mission no. 16. James, S.

MISSIONARIES
Barich, B. The end of the world
Bowles, P. Pastor Dowe at Tacaté
Durban, P. All set about with fever trees
Hesse, H. Robert Aghion
Johnson, H. Victoria
Klein, T. E. D. Black man with a horn
Peterson, J. Yellow dust
Peterson, L. S. The gift
Steele, W. D. The man who saw through Heaven

MISSIONS
Chavez, A. Hunchback Madonna

MISSISSIPPI
19th century
Foote, S. Jordan County [excerpt]
Sullivan, C. The horse in the bedroom
Welty, E. First love
20th century
Bennett, L. The convert
Caldwell, P. A sense of place
Canzoneri, R. The harp of the winds
Corrington, J. W. The actes and monuments
Gilchrist, E. Summer, an elegy
Hall, M. L. Doll
Hall, M. L. Joanna
Hall, M. L. Lucky Lafe
Hall, M. L. The man who gave brother double pneumonia
Hall, M. L. The painter
Hall, M. L. The peaceful eye
Hall, M. L. Privacy
Hall, M. L. The visit
Hill, R. Blue Rise [excerpt]
Hughes, J. An open house
McGuane, T. A man in Louisiana
Morris, W. Good old boy [excerpt]
Nordan, L. The Sears and Roebuck catalog game
Nordan, L. Sugar among the chickens
Nordan, L. Sugar, the eunuchs, and Big G.B.
Nordan, L. The talker at the freak-show
Norris, G. Holding on

MISSISSIPPI—20th century—*Continued*
Percy, W. The moviegoer [excerpt]
Sanders, S. R. Walking to sleep
Spencer, E. The business venture
Spencer, E. The finder
Spencer, E. First dark
Spencer, E. A southern landscape
Taylor, M. D. Roll of thunder, hear my cry [excerpt]
Welty, E. Why I live at the P.O.
Whitehead, J. Joiner [excerpt]
Young, A. Snakes [excerpt]
Farm life
See Farm life—Mississippi
Prisoners and prisons
See Prisoners and prisons—Mississippi
Jackson
Whitehead, H. S. C. The fireplace
Mississippi Ham Rider. Cade, T.
MISSISSIPPI RIVER
Dumas, H. Ark
Dumas, H. Fever
Dumas, H. Wandering in the wilderness
Dumas, H. The white horse
Gibson, W. Murnane and the Illinois
O'Donnell, E. P. Jesus knew
MISSISSIPPI RIVER VALLEY
Douglas, E. On the lake
The **Mississippi** saucer. Long, F. B.
MISSOURI
Conroy, J. Charley was our darlin'
Conroy, J. The fields of golden glow
Conroy, J. The Kimberly toughs
Conroy, J. The morphadite
Conroy, J. Paving gang—on a job in Missouri
Conroy, J. The siren
Kantor, M. The voice of Bugle Ann
McElroy, C. J. A brief spell by the river
McKinley, J. Ozark episode
Stafford, J. Woden's day
Coal mines and mining
See Coal mines and mining—Missouri
Farm life
See Farm life—Missouri
Saint Louis
Dawson, F. The blue in the sky
Taylor, P. H. The little cousins
Williams, T. Oriflamme
MISSOURI RIVER
Poe, E. A. The journal of Julius Rodman
The **mist**. King, S.
Mistake. Banks, R.
A **mistake**. Maupassant, G. de
The **mistake**. Singer, I. B.
Mistaken identify. Sproat, R.
MISTAKEN IDENTITY
See also Impersonations
Brett, S. Big Boy, Little Boy
Davis, S. A fair exchange
Dawson, C. Supergrass

Day, R. C. Grace
Ely, D. The running man
Friedenkraft, G. Anne
Gardner, M. Good dancing, sailor!
Garrett, G. P. Farmer in the dell
Henderson, M. R. Dream house
Hoch, E. D. The man who came back
Hornung, E. W. A bad night
Kusenberg, K. Who am I?
Leskov, N. S. A robbery
Mortimer, J. C. Rumpole and the case of identity
Olson, D. Another me
Romun, I. Christmas is over
Wellen, E. Hit or miss
The **mistaken** smile. Erskine-Lindop, A.
Mister Al. Sheil, G.
Mister Argus. Erdrich, L.
Mister Death and the redheaded woman. Eustis, H.
Mister Dog. Ellis, M.
Mister Makes. Hagy, A. C.
Mister Period. Clark, G.
Mistletoe. Bradley, J.
Mistress Bearberry & lovers. Curtis, J.
The **mistress** of Goldman's Antiques. Gerber, M. J.
Mistress of the blood-drinkers. Shields, R.
Mistress Sary. Tenn, W.
Mistrial. Bonnie, F.
Mistry, Rohinton, 1952-
Auspicious occasion
  The New press anthology #2
A **misunderstood** artist. Wells, H. G.
Mitchell, Edward Page
The devilish rat
  Devils & demons; ed. by M. Kaye and S. Kaye
An uncommon sort of spectre
  Young ghosts; ed. by I. Asimov; M. H. Greenberg and C. G. Waugh
Mitchell, Ken
The centre of gravity
  The Old dance; ed. by B. Burnard
The great electrical revolution
  Dark arrows; ed. by A. Manguel
Mitchell, Maria, 1818-1889
View from the mud
  The North American Review 271:38-9 Mr '86
Mitchell, Mary E.
For the honor of the company
  A Treasury of Civil War stories; ed. by M. H. Greenberg and B. Pronzini
Mitchell, W. O. (William Ormond), 1914-
Patterns
  Alberta bound; ed. by F. Stenson
Mitchell, William Ormond *See* Mitchell, W. O. (William Ormond), 1914-
Mitchell: a character sketch. Lawson, H.
Mitrani. Mujica, B.

MIXED BLOODS
> *See also* Mulattoes

Atherton, G. F. H. The conquest of Doña
> Jacoba

Brand, M. Outcast

Prichard, K. S. Flight

Prichard, K. S. N'goola

Mixed marriage. Reaver, C.

The **mixer**. Wodehouse, P. G.

Mixing cocktails. Rhys, J.

Mme. Tellier's excursion. Maupassant, G. de

The **mnemone**. Sheckley, R.

The **mobile** bed-object. Highsmith, P.

Mobiles. Cowan, P.

Mobius. Matheson, R. C.

The **moccasins**. O'Hara, J.

Mocha in Disneyland. Keller, G. D.

Mock battle. Kiely, B.

The **model**. Baxter, C.

The **model**. Bloch, R.

The **model**. Malamud, B.

MODELS, ARTISTS' *See* Artists' models

MODELS, FASHION *See* Fashion models

MODELS AND MODELMAKING
> Swanwick, M., and Gibson, W. Dogfight

Modern life. Mrożek, S.

Modern romances. Lopatin, J.

Modern saint #271. Janowitz, T.

A **modern** Snowwhite. Viidikas, V.

A **modern** story of Woe and Lovecraft. Ab-
> bott, L. K.

Modesty aside. José, F. S.

Modrack, Barbara Arno
> Baby's first Christmas
>> *Seventeen* 45:124-5 D '86
> The longest season
>> *Seventeen* 45:298-9+ Ag '86

Modulation in all things. Elgin, S. H.

Moffatt, Deborah
> Heritage
>> *Critical Quarterly* 28:23-30 Wint '86
> The lodger
>> First fictions: Introduction 9
> When Roger got married
>> First fictions: Introduction 9
> Willie's war
>> First fictions: Introduction 9

Moffett, Judith, 1942-
> Surviving
>> Nebula awards 22
>> Terry Carr's Best science fiction and fan-
>> tasy of the year #16
>> The Year's best science fiction, fourth
>> annual collection

Mogan, Jewel
> Étude
>> *The North American Review* 272:37 D
>> '87

Mohammed Fripouli. Maupassant, G. de

MOHAMMEDANISM *See* Islam

MOHAMMEDANS *See* Muslims

MOHAVE DESERT (CALIF.) *See* Mojave
> Desert (Calif.)

Mohr, Nicholasa
> The artist (Inez)
>> Mohr, N. Rituals of survival
> Aunt Rosana's rocker (Zoraida)
>> Mohr, N. Rituals of survival
> Brief miracle (Virginia)
>> Mohr, N. Rituals of survival
> Happy birthday (Lucia)
>> Mohr, N. Rituals of survival
> A Thanksgiving celebration (Amy)
>> Mohr, N. Rituals of survival
> A time with a future (Carmela)
>> Mohr, N. Rituals of survival

Moikangoa, C. E.
> Sebolelo comes home
>> The Penguin book of Southern African
>> stories

The **Moiliili** Bag Man. Lum, D. H. Y.

Moishe the Just. Stern, S.

Moist dreams. Wiater, S.

The **mojado** who offered up his tapeworms
> to the public weal. Keller, G. D.

MOJAVE DESERT (CALIF.)
> Boucher, S. The healing
> Working, R. The monkey

Mokele Mbembe. Ladenheim, K.

Mokli. Greenwood, R.

Moksha. Aithal, S. K., and Rothfork, J.

Mokusei: a love story. Nooteboom, C.

Mole. DeMarinis, R.

The **mole** men want your eyes. Davis, F.
> C.

Moleman. Kamminga, A.

Molinaro, Ursule
> Apocalyptic flirtation
>> American made; ed. by M. Leyner; C.
>> White and T. Glynn
> Bird in ambush
>> New directions in prose and poetry 52

Moline, Stephen
> Two gifts
>> *Prairie Schooner* 62:111-12 Wint '88/'89

Molla's heart attack. Rölvaag, O. E.

Molly. Dubus, A.

Molly's dog. Adams, A.

Molnar, A. K.
> The crosstie
>> Bringing down the moon; ed. by J. An-
>> derson

MOLOKAI (HAWAII) *See* Hawaii—Molokai

Mom and Pop biz. Franzen, B.

Mom makes a wish. Yaffe, J.

Mom sings an aria. Yaffe, J.

The **moment**. Abrahams, L.

The **moment** before the gun went off.
> Gordimer, N.

A **moment** of illumination. Clark, M.

The **moment** of release. Klinkowitz, J.

Moment of wisdom. Fisher, M. F. K.

Moments of being: 'Slater's pins have no
> points'. Woolf, V.

Moments of stress. Colette

Momentum. Woolrich, C.

Momentum is always the weapon. Kittredge, W.
Momma's boy. Apple, M.
Mom's clean sweep. Wood, M.
MONACO
    Monte Carlo
Maugham, W. S. The facts of life
Monar, Rooplall
Hakim Driver
 The Literary Review (Madison, N.J.) 29:473-80 Summ '86
Monarch. Cooper, C. R.
The **monarch** butterfly. Rothberg, A.
Monarchs. Clarke, L.
MONASTERIES *See* Monasticism and religious orders
The **monastery.** Kurahashi, Y.
The **monastery.** Rey Rosa, R.
The **monastery** floor. Hoyt, M. S.
MONASTICISM AND RELIGIOUS ORDERS
   See also Convent life; Jesuits; Monks
Bowles, P. The circular valley
Cowper, R. The custodians
Daudet, A. The elixir
Hoyt, M. S. The monastery floor
McCormack, E. P. The fragment
Spark, M. Come along, Marjorie
Monday. Caponegro, M.
Monday. Geras, A.
Monday. Greenberg, B., and Chambers, G.
A **Monday** in April. Asimov, I.
Monday morning. Latimer, M.
Monday morning: a black market tale. Klíma, I.
Monday or Tuesday. Woolf, V.
The **Monderau** chronicle. Federspiel, J.
Mondeschein, Brian
To vault over the moon
 Women's Sports & Fitness 9:48-50+ Ap '87
Monem, Hassan Abdel
The thief
 Egyptian tales and short stories of the 1970s and 1980s
MONEY
   See also Finance
Auchincloss, L. The takeover
Bonner, M. The makin's
Bonner, M. Stones for bread
Bradfield, S. Unmistakably the finest
Carter, A. A. The fortune hunter
Clarke, A. C. Griff!
Dubus, A. Anna
Fernando, C. Of bread and power
Friedman, B. J. Business is business
Garrett, G. P. Bread from stones
Greenwood, R. The other world
Hemingway, E. The mother of a queen
Henry, O. One thousand dollars
Ignatow, R. G. The penny story
Kees, W. Letter from Maine

Keillor, G. A ten-dollar bill
Lipsky, D. Three thousand dollars
Miller, A. It takes a thief
Mooney, M. The mysteries of banking
Sproat, R. Firework night isn't in it
Willson, H. Half a loaf
Money. Ciment, J.
Money can't buy a home. Shulman, A. K.
Money man. Norris, H.
The **money** preacher. Winters, J.
MONEYLENDERS
   See also Loans; Pawnbrokers
Hornung, E. W. Wilful murder
Smith, C. A. The weird of Avoosl Wuthoqquan
Mongolian Whiskey. Katz, S.
MONGOOSES
Kaikō, T. Duel
The **mongrel.** Nowakowski, M.
Monique and Gérard discuss art. Villefranche, A.-M.
Monitor. Dillon, M.
The **monk.** Liphshitz, A.
The **Monk** of horror; or, The Conclave of corpses
 The Penguin book of horror stories
Monkey. Jaffe, H.
The **monkey.** King, S.
The **monkey.** Working, R.
Monkey business. Schwartz, S.
Monkey business. Wodehouse, P. G.
Monkey king. Holding, J.
Monkey Park. Bell, M. S.
The **monkey** treatment. Martin, G. R. R.
The **monkey** wrench. Dickson, G. R.
MONKEYS
Benson, E. F. Monkeys
Bishop, M. The monkey's bride
Campos-De Metro, J. The grape's vine, the horse's mouth
Highsmith, P. Eddie and the monkey robberies
Lispector, C. Monkeys
Martin, G. R. R. The monkey treatment
Narayan, R. K. The mute companions
Shacochis, B. Lord Short Shoe wants the monkey
Monkeys. Benson, E. F.
Monkeys. Lispector, C.
The **monkey's** bride. Bishop, M.
The **monkey's** paw. Jacobs, W. W.
MONKS
   See also Monasticism and religious orders
Böll, H. The Staech affair
Canton, W. The song of the Minster
Chekhov, A. P. The Black Monk
Chipulina, E. G. The procession
Daudet, A. The elixir
Farmer, P. J. Sail on! Sail on!
Ingalls, R. Blessed art thou
Jhabvala, R. P. How I became a holy mother

MONKS—*Continued*
King, F. H. The soutane
Liphshitz, A. The monk
Major, A. R. Kissmeowt and the healing friar
The Monk of horror; or, The Conclave of corpses
Schwob, M. Frate Dolcino, heretic
Ts'ai-hua, T. The feast of "Flower-Pattern" wine
Monkshood Manor. Hartley, L. P.
Monologue. Mrożek, S.
Monologue by a man in black. Clark, M.
Monologue for Danny. Simon, B.
Monologue of a waiter. Böll, H.
Monologue of Isabel watching it rain in Macondo. García Márquez, G.
Monologue of the movie mogul. Covino, M.
Monologue—Tangier 1975. Bowles, P.
Monreal, David Nava
  Anything is possible
    Monreal, D. N. The new neighbor & other stories
  Down in Las Vegas
    Monreal, D. N. The new neighbor & other stories
  The eleventh round
    Monreal, D. N. The new neighbor & other stories
  Faces
    Monreal, D. N. The new neighbor & other stories
  In the train station
    Monreal, D. N. The new neighbor & other stories
  Leprosy
    Monreal, D. N. The new neighbor & other stories
  Lola's return
    Southwest tales; ed. by Alurista and X. Rojas-Urista
  A matter of dignity
    Monreal, D. N. The new neighbor & other stories
  The new neighbor
    Monreal, D. N. The new neighbor & other stories
  The visit
    Monreal, D. N. The new neighbor & other stories
  The weight lifters
    Monreal, D. N. The new neighbor & other stories
    Southwest tales; ed. by Alurista and X. Rojas-Urista
  The young wife
    Monreal, D. N. The new neighbor & other stories
MONROE, MARILYN, 1926-1962
                  About
Ferguson, N. The Monroe Doctrine
Tillman, L. Dead talk
The **Monroe** Doctrine. Ferguson, N.

Monsarrat, Nicholas, 1910-
  "HMS Marlborough will enter harbour"
    Short stories of the sea; ed. by G. C. Solley and E. Steinbaugh
  Night shoot
    Sea captains' tales; ed. by A. Enfield
Monsieur Cyril de Guindre. Carrington, L.
Monsieur Jim. Padgett, R.
Monsieur les Deux Chapeaux. Munro, A.
Monsieur Maurice. Colette
Monsieur Melville. Beaulieu, V. L.
Monsieur Parent. Maupassant, G. de
Monsieur Teste in America. Codrescu, A.
Monsoon. Swan, A.
The **monster.** Crane, S.
The **monster.** Haldeman, J. W.
Monster and toothpick. Kaikō, T.
Monster mash. Smith, S.
The **monster** mine. P.G.M.
The **monster** of Poot Holler. Chittum, I.
Monster of terror. See Lovecraft, H. P. The colour out of space
MONSTERS
Barker, C. The skins of the fathers
Bishop, M. Seasons of belief
Bradbury, R. The thing at the top of the stairs
Card, O. S. Eumenides in the fourth floor lavatory
Chetwynd-Hayes, R. The fly-by-night
Chittum, I. The monster of Poot Holler
Gunn, J. E. Feeding time
Hoch, E. D. The faceless thing
Hodgson, W. H. The derelict
King, S. The mist
Klein, T. E. D. Children of the kingdom
Lovecraft, H. P. The call of Cthulhu
Matheson, R. Born of man and woman
Metcalfe, J. Mr. Meldrum's mania
Morton, S. L. Now you see me
Reitz, J. Monsters
Smith, C. A. The dweller in the gulf
St. Clair, M. Brenda
Sturgeon, T. It
Sturgeon, T. The professor's teddy bear
Tolkien, J. R. R. Riddles in the dark
Webb, S. The thing that goes burp in the night
Monsters. Ahern, T.
Monsters. Reitz, J.
The **monsters.** Sheckley, R.
MONT SAINTE-VICTOIRE (FRANCE)
Handke, P. The lesson of Mont Sainte-Victoire
MONTANA
Willis, C. And come from miles around
                  20th century
Boyle, T. C. On for the long haul
Ford, R. Communist
Ford, R. Winterkill
Haake, K. Burning the lost country
Long, D. The last photograph of Lyle Pettibone

MONTANA—20th century—*Continued*
MacLean, N. Logging and pimping and "your pal, Jim"
McGuane, T. The El Western
Welch, J. Winter in the blood [excerpt]
Wilson, B. Thin ice

Frontier and pioneer life
See Frontier and pioneer life—Montana

Ranch life
See Ranch life—Montana
Montauk. Thompson, S.
MONTE CARLO (MONACO) *See* Monaco—Monte Carlo
Monteleone, Thomas F.
The night is freezing fast
Masques II; ed. by J. N. Williamson
MONTEREY (CALIF.) *See* California—Monterey
Montero, Mayra
Last night at dawn
Reclaiming Medusa; ed. by D. L. Vélez
Thirteen and a turtle
Reclaiming Medusa; ed. by D. L. Vélez
Monterroso, Augusto
The eclipse
Winter's tales, new ser. v4
MONTEZUMA II, EMPEROR OF MEXICO, ca. 1480-1520
About
Barthelme, D. Cortés and Montezuma
Montgomerie, Lee
War and/or peace
Interzone: the 2nd anthology; ed. by J. Clute; D. Pringle and S. Ounsley
Montgomerie, William
Daft Jenny
Streets of stone; ed. by M. Burgess and H. Whyte
Montgomery, Marion
I got a gal
A Collection of classic Southern humor; ed. by G. W. Koon
A **month** by the lake. Bates, H. E.
Montiel's widow. García Márquez, G.
MONTREAL (QUÉBEC) *See* Canada—Montreal
Montrose Boulevard. Eighner, L.
The **monument.** Mrożek, S.
The **monument.** Sanford, W. M.
The **monumental** sculptor. Cohen, A.
MONUMENTS
See also Sculpture
Chandler, A. B. Don't knock the rock
Mrożek, S. The monument
Wells, H. G. The pearl of love
Monuments. Burns, M.
Monzó, Quim
Anis del mono
Harper's 273:33-4 O '86
Moody, Hiram
Gambit declined
The Antioch Review 45:194-205 Spr '87

Twister
The Paris Review 30:60-3 Wint '88
Moon, Soon-Tae
Last sound of the gong
Short story international 60
The sound of the gong
Early spring, mid-summer, and other Korean short stories
MOON
See also Space flight to the moon
Asimov, I. The key
Caldwell, P. A sense of place
Kingsbury, D. The moon goddess and the son
Leinster, M. Keyhole
Longyear, B. B. A time for terror
Lynn, E. A. The woman who loved the moon
Miller, W. M. I made you
Poe, E. A. Hans Phaall
Poe, E. A. The unparalleled adventure of one Hans Pfaall
Robinson, K. S. The lunatics
Rodoreda, M. The gentleman and the moon
Sladek, J. T. An explanation for the disappearance of the moon
Spark, M. The Playhouse called Remarkable
Stein, J. Why the moon is small and dark when the sun is big and shiny
Varley, J. Tango Charlie and Foxtrot Romeo
Wellen, E. Shapes to come
Willson, H. Moonset near Magdalena
The **moon** cookies. Girion, B.
Moon Face. Conley, R. J.
Moon-face. London, J.
The **moon-fixer.** Drake, R.
Moon gems. Ishikawa, J.
The **moon** goddess and the son. Kingsbury, D.
The **moon** in the Orange Street Skating Rink. Munro, A.
The **moon** king. Apollinaire, G.
Moon lady. Hoffman, W.
The **moon-lens.** Campbell, R.
Moon mirror. Norton, A.
Moon of ice. Linaweaver, B.
The **moon** of popping trees. Garcia y Robertson, R.
The **moon** pool. Merritt, A.
The **moon** ribbon. Yolen, J.
Moon walk. Barrett, L.
Moon walking. Hauptman, W.
The **moon-welcoming** flower. Kim, C.-Y.
Mooney, Michael
Ancient voices
Mooney, M. Ancient voices, and other stories
A civilized man
Mooney, M. Ancient voices, and other stories

Mooney, Michael—*Continued*
　Eros and crazy
　　Mooney, M. Ancient voices, and other stories
　Fidelity savings
　　Mooney, M. Ancient voices, and other stories
　Hostages
　　Mooney, M. Ancient voices, and other stories
　Married
　　Mooney, M. Ancient voices, and other stories
　The mysteries of banking
　　Mooney, M. Ancient voices, and other stories
　The numbers
　　Mooney, M. Ancient voices, and other stories
　The peach orchard
　　Mooney, M. Ancient voices, and other stories
Moonlight. Maupassant, G. de
Moonlight. Wertime, R.
Moonlight on the snow. Crane, S.
Moonlighting. Hamilton, A.
The **moonlit** road. Bierce, A.
The **moon's** revenge. Aiken, J.
Moonset near Magdalena. Willson, H.
MOONSHINERS
　Clarke, A. C. Moving spirit
　Fox, W. P. You don't smell it: you drink it
　Kinsella, W. P. The practical education of Constable B. B. Bobowski
　Owen, G. Miss Mahalia and the still
　Rawlings, M. K. Gal young un
　Stuart, J. Evidence is high proof
Moorcock, Michael, 1939-
　Elric at the end of time
　　Masterpieces of fantasy and enchantment; ed. by D. G. Hartwell
　The lands beyond the world
　　Baker's dozen: 13 short fantasy novels
Moore, Alan
　A hypothetical lizard
　　The Year's best fantasy, first annual collection
Moore, Alison
　At Abu Ali
　　The North American Review 272:50 D '87
　Disappearing act
　　The North American Review 273:51-3 S '88
Moore, Brian, 1921-
　The sight
　　Black water; ed. by A. Manguel
Moore, C. L. (Catherine Lucille), 1911-
　The bright illusion
　　[Analog]: Writers' choice v2
　No woman born
　　Robert Silverberg's Worlds of wonder

　Shambleau
　　Vampires; ed. by A. Ryan
　(jt. auth) See Kuttner, Henry, 1915-1958, and Moore, C. L. (Catherine Lucille), 1911-
Moore, Catherine Lucille *See* Moore, C. L. (Catherine Lucille), 1911-
Moore, George, 1852-1933
　At the turn of the road
　　Moore, G. In minor keys
　Dried fruit
　　Moore, G. In minor keys
　'Emma Bovary'
　　Moore, G. In minor keys
　An episode in bachelor life
　　Moore, G. In minor keys
　An episode in married life
　　Moore, G. In minor keys
　A faithful heart
　　Moore, G. In minor keys
　A flood
　　Moore, G. In minor keys
　Home sickness
　　On being foreign; ed. by T. J. Lewis and R. E. Jungman
　A letter to Rome
　　The Best of Irish wit and wisdom; ed. by J. McCarthy
　Parted
　　Moore, G. In minor keys
　A Russian husband
　　Moore, G. In minor keys
　A strange death
　　Moore, G. In minor keys
　The strange story of the three golden fishes
　　Moore, G. In minor keys
　Two men
　　Moore, G. In minor keys
　Under the fan
　　Moore, G. In minor keys
　The voice of the mountain
　　Moore, G. In minor keys
Moore, Lorrie
　Amahl and the Night Visitors: a guide to the tenor of love
　　20 under 30; ed. by D. Spark
　　Moore, L. Self-help
　Go like this
　　Moore, L. Self-help
　How
　　Moore, L. Self-help
　How to be an other woman
　　Moore, L. Self-help
　How to become a writer
　　New women and new fiction; ed. by S. Cahill
　How to talk to your mother (notes)
　　Moore, L. Self-help
　The kid's guide to divorce
　　Look who's talking; ed. by B. Weber
　　Moore, L. Self-help

Moore, Lorrie—_Continued_
To fill
Moore, L. Self-help
What is seized
Moore, L. Self-help
Moore, Lucia
The deep valley
Westward the women; ed. by V. Piekarski
Moore, Mary Jane
Summer sand
Short story international 43
Moore, Raylyn
Getting back to before it began
100 great fantasy short short stories; ed. by I. Asimov; T. Carr and M. H. Greenberg
Moore, Ruth
The soldier shows his medal
The Best Maine stories; ed. by S. Phippen; C. Waugh and M. Greenberg
Moore, Sandra
Dove shooting
Homewords: a book of Tennessee writers; ed. by D. Paschall
Moore, Susan J.
The beautiful intruder
'Teen 32:34+ N '88
Meeting Mossie
'Teen 31:62+ Mr '87
Moore, Ward, 1903-
Frank Merriwell in the White House
Election Day 2084; ed. by I. Asimov and M. H. Greenberg
Lot
Beyond Armageddon; ed. by W. M. Miller and M. H. Greenberg
Peacebringer
Amazing science fiction anthology: The wild years, 1946-1955; ed. by M. H. Greenberg
Moore-Bentley, Mary Ann
A woman of Earth
Australian science fiction; ed. by V. Ikin
Moorhead, Finola
Waiting for Colombo: a close-up
Room to move; ed. by S. Falkiner
Moorhouse, Frank
The airport, the pizzeria, the motel, the rented car, and the mysteries of life
The Australian short story; ed. by L. Hergenhan
Buenaventura Durruti's funeral
Transgressions; ed. by D. Anderson
The Coca-Cola Kid
Inspired by drink; ed. by Joan Digby and John Digby
The New York bell captain
Home and away; ed. by R. Creswell
Moorings. Hoffman, W.
Moose. Campbell, W. B.
Moose. Sternberg, A.
Moot. Colter, C.

The **moped** massacre. Hankla, C.
A **moral** exigency. Freeman, M. E. W.
Moral questions of our time. Ephron, N.
MORALITY
    See also Ethics; Good and evil
Lagerlöf, S. The peace of God
Morality meat. Tiptree, J.
Morality play. Weaver, G.
Moran, Daniel Keys
(jt. auth) See Prebehalla, Gladys, and Moran, Daniel Keys
Moran, Virginia A. K.
Down by the river
The Virginia Quarterly Review 60:45-56 Wint '84
Morand, Paul, 1888-1976
Aurora
Morand, P. Fancy goods [and] Open all night
Borealis
Morand, P. Fancy goods [and] Open all night
The Paris Review 26:188-203 Spr '84
Catalan night
Morand, P. Fancy goods [and] Open all night
Clarissa
Morand, P. Fancy goods [and] Open all night
Delphine
Morand, P. Fancy goods [and] Open all night
Hungarian night
Morand, P. Fancy goods [and] Open all night
The Roman night
Morand, P. Fancy goods [and] Open all night
The six-day night
Morand, P. Fancy goods [and] Open all night
Turkish night
Morand, P. Fancy goods [and] Open all night
Moravia, Alberto, 1907-
A bad memory block
Moravia, A. Erotic tales
The belt
Moravia, A. Erotic tales
The devil can't save the world
Moravia, A. Erotic tales
The devil comes and goes
Moravia, A. Erotic tales
The hands around the neck
Moravia, A. Erotic tales
In my dream I always hear a step on the stairs
Moravia, A. Erotic tales
I've stuttered all my life
Moravia, A. Erotic tales
Jewellery
The Art of the tale; ed. by D. Halpern

Moravia, Alberto, 1907-—*Continued*
My daughter is called Giulia too
  Moravia, A. Erotic tales
The owner of the flat
  Moravia, A. Erotic tales
Revealing thunder
  Moravia, A. Erotic tales
The sign of the operation
  Moravia, A. Erotic tales
That damned gun
  Moravia, A. Erotic tales
There was a basket down by the Tiber
  Moravia, A. Erotic tales
There's a neutron bomb for ants too
  Moravia, A. Erotic tales
The thing
  Moravia, A. Erotic tales
To the unknown god
  Moravia, A. Erotic tales
The voyeur's stroll
  Moravia, A. Erotic tales
What use have I got for carnival?
  Moravia, A. Erotic tales
The woman in the customs officer's house
  Moravia, A. Erotic tales
The woman with the black cloak
  Moravia, A. Erotic tales
Moray eel. Eisenstein, S.
Morazzoni, Marta, 1950-
The dignity of Signor Da Ponte
  Morazzoni, M. Girl in a turban
Girl in a turban
  Morazzoni, M. Girl in a turban
The last assignment
  Morazzoni, M. Girl in a turban
Order in the house
  Morazzoni, M. Girl in a turban
The white door
  Morazzoni, M. Girl in a turban
Mordden, Ethan, 1947-
Beach blanket mah-jongg
  Mordden, E. Everybody loves you
The Boffer
  Mordden, E. Everybody loves you
The complete death of the clown dog
  Mordden, E. Everybody loves you
The dinner party
  Mordden, E. Everybody loves you
Do-it-yourself S & M
  Mordden, E. Everybody loves you
The ghost of Champ McQuest
  Mordden, E. Everybody loves you
The handshake deal
  Mordden, E. Everybody loves you
Hardhats
  Men on men; ed. by G. Stambolian
I read my nephew stories
  Mordden, E. Everybody loves you
  The New Yorker 64:24-32 Ag 29 '88
Interview with the drag queen
  First love/last love; ed. by M. Denneny;
    C. Ortleb and T. Steele

The right boy for Cosgrove
  Mordden, E. Everybody loves you
The tale of the changeling
  Mordden, E. Everybody loves you
The talking dog of the world
  The New Yorker 64:25-30 Jl 11 '88
Uptown, downtown: a tour through the
  gay metropolis
  First love/last love; ed. by M. Denneny;
    C. Ortleb and T. Steele
The woggle
  Mordden, E. Everybody loves you
More. Winton, T.
More crimes against the people of Illinois.
  White, C.
More friend than lodger. Wilson, Sir A.
More geese than swans. Garrett, G. P.
More life. Strand, M.
More precious than gold. Cherry, K.
More sinned against. Wagner, K. E.
More stately mansions. Updike, J.
More than a notion. McElroy, C. J.
More than just the disease. MacLaverty, B.
More than meets the eye. Ritchie, J.
More than money. Rule, J.
More than the sum of his parts. Haldeman,
  J. W.
The **more** things change . . . Pierce, J. P.
Moreland, Jane
  Lady, be good
  Mademoiselle 92:112+ Je '86
Morella. Poe, E. A.
Morgan, Berry, 1919-
The auction
  The New Yorker 61:32-8 Ja 27 '86
The Lower Pontalba
  The New Yorker 60:46-7 Mr 12 '84
Mr. Doll
  The New Yorker 62:48-53 N 17 '86
The organ piece
  Mississippi writers v1: Fiction; ed. by D.
    Abbott
Morgan, Cynthia
The hitmaker
  Omni book of science fiction 1
Morgan, Kay
Goodnight piece
  The North American Review 272:28-31
    D '87
North Dakota
  The North American Review 271:47-51
    Mr '86
Morgan, Speer, 1949-
Household expenses
  Missouri short fiction; ed. by C. Beasley
Morgan and Joanna. Engberg, S.
Morgan Morgan. Hospital, J. T.
MORGUES
Brown, F. The spherical ghoul
Hong, S.-W. A boy in search of rest

Mori, Yōko
Be it ever so humble
   The Mother of dreams, and other short stories; ed. by M. Ueda
Spring storm
   The Mother of dreams, and other short stories; ed. by M. Ueda
Moriarty's return. McKinley, J.
Morice, Anne
Young man on a train
   Winter's crimes 18
La **Morillonne**. Maupassant, G. de
Morio, Kita
Along the mountain ridge
   The Literary Review (Madison, N.J.) 31:301-10 Spr '88
Morison, Scot
Brother
   The Old dance; ed. by B. Burnard
MORMONISM *See* Mormons and Mormonism
MORMONS AND MORMONISM
Brooks, J. The outsider
Card, O. S. Salvage
Carver, W. With voice of joy and praise
Cassity, K. The age-old problem of who
Christmas, R. A. Another angel
Farnsworth, K. A. Counterpoint
Freeman, J. The death of a Mormon elder
Kalpakian, L. And departing leave behind us
Kalpakian, L. Sonata in G minor
Kump, E. G. Everncere
Larson, L. Original sin
Peterson, J. Yellow dust
Peterson, L. S. The gift
Sillitoe, L. Four walls and an empty door
Wright, D. L. The hawk
The **morning** after. Chua, R.
Morning child. Dozois, G. R.
Morning deliveries (milkman #1). King, S.
Morning glories. Colette
Morning light. Harlow, E.
Morning nails. Kawabata, Y.
Morning on the Wissahiccon. Poe, E. A.
Morning song. Wright, B. R.
MOROCCO
Bowles, P. Allal
Bowles, P. He of the assembly
Bowles, P. Here to learn
Bowles, P. The little house
Bowles, P. Mejdoub
Mrabet, M. Doctor Safi

        Marrakesh
Haldeman, J. W. Lindsay and the red city blues

        Tangier
Bowles, P. The eye
Lurie, M. Africa wall
Lurie, M. Swallows
The **morphadite**. Conroy, J.

Morrell, David, 1943-
For these and all my sins
   Whispers V
Orange is for anguish, blue for insanity
   Prime evil; ed. by D. E. Winter
The storm
   The Best of Shadows; ed. by C. L. Grant
   Shadows 7
Morressy, John
Final version
   100 great fantasy short short stories; ed. by I. Asimov; T. Carr and M. H. Greenberg
The last Jerry Fagin Show
   Omni book of science fiction 1
Morrill, George P.
Act of honor
   A Treasury of World War II stories; ed. by B. Pronzini and M. H. Greenberg
Morris, Janet, 1946-
A man and his god
   Baker's dozen: 13 short fantasy novels
Morris, Kenneth
The eyeless dragons: a Chinese story
   Masterpieces of fantasy and enchantment; ed. by D. G. Hartwell
The regent of the North
   Masterpieces of fantasy and enchantment; ed. by D. G. Hartwell
The sapphire necklace
   Masterpieces of fantasy and enchantment; ed. by D. G. Hartwell
Morris, Mary, 1947-
Alewives
   Morris, M. The bus of dreams
The banana fever
   Morris, M. The bus of dreams
Burning issues
   Morris, M. The bus of dreams
The bus of dreams
   Morris, M. The bus of dreams
Conquering space
   Morris, M. The bus of dreams
Copies
   Love stories for the time being; ed. by G. D. Chipps and B. Henderson
   Morris, M. The bus of dreams
   The Pushcart prize IX
Death apples
   Morris, M. The bus of dreams
The Hall of the Meteorites
   Morris, M. The bus of dreams
Links
   Morris, M. The bus of dreams
Losing your cool
   Morris, M. The bus of dreams
Lovelorn in the U.S.A.
   Mademoiselle 92:146+ D '86
The lure
   The Bread Loaf anthology of contemporary American short stories; ed. by R. Pack and J. Parini

Morris, Mary, 1947-——Continued
Orphans of the Storm
　Morris, M. The bus of dreams
　The Paris Review 26:112-22 Wint '84
Shining path
　Morris, M. The bus of dreams
Summer share
　Morris, M. The bus of dreams
The typewriter
　Morris, M. The bus of dreams
The watermelon people
　Morris, M. The bus of dreams
Morris, Sara, 1922-
　*For works written by this author under
　other names see* Burke, John, 1922-
Morris, William, 1834-1896
Lindenborg pool
　Masterpieces of fantasy and enchant-
　ment; ed. by D. G. Hartwell
Morris, Willie
Good old boy [excerpt]
　Mississippi writers v1: Fiction; ed. by D.
　Abbott
Morris, Wright, 1910-
The cat in the picture
　Morris, W. Collected stories, 1948-1986
The cat's meow
　Morris, W. Collected stories, 1948-1986
The character of the lover
　Morris, W. Collected stories, 1948-1986
Country music
　Morris, W. Collected stories, 1948-1986
　The New Yorker 61:38-41 Mr 11 '85
The customs of the country
　Morris, W. Collected stories, 1948-1986
Drrdla
　Morris, W. Collected stories, 1948-1986
Fellow-creatures
　The Best American short stories, 1985
　Morris, W. Collected stories, 1948-1986
　The New Yorker 60:28-31 D 31 '84
A fight between a white boy and a black
　boy in the dusk of a fall afternoon
　in Omaha, Nebraska
　Morris, W. Collected stories, 1948-1986
Fiona
　Morris, W. Collected stories, 1948-1986
Glimpse into another country
　The Best American short stories, 1984
　Morris, W. Collected stories, 1948-1986
　Prize stories, 1985
Going into exile
　Morris, W. Collected stories, 1948-1986
　The New Yorker 59:42-5 F 6 '84
Green grass, blue sky, white house
　Morris, W. Collected stories, 1948-1986
Here is Einbaum
　Morris, W. Collected stories, 1948-1986
In another country
　Morris, W. Collected stories, 1948-1986
The lover and the beloved
　Morris, W. Collected stories, 1948-1986

Magic
　Morris, W. Collected stories, 1948-1986
The origin of sadness
　Morris, W. Collected stories, 1948-1986
The ram in the thicket
　Morris, W. Collected stories, 1948-1986
Real losses, imaginary gains
　Morris, W. Collected stories, 1948-1986
The safe place
　Morris, W. Collected stories, 1948-1986
Since when do they charge admission
　Morris, W. Collected stories, 1948-1986
The sound tape
　Morris, W. Collected stories, 1948-1986
Things that matter
　Morris, W. Collected stories, 1948-1986
　The New Yorker 62:39-42 Mr 17 '86
To Calabria
　Morris, W. Collected stories, 1948-1986
　The New Yorker 60:36-9 Jl 23 '84
Victrola
　Morris, W. Collected stories, 1948-1986
Wishing you and your loved ones every
　happiness
　Morris, W. Collected stories, 1948-1986
MORRIS-DANCE
Kilworth, G. Lord of the dance
Morrison, Arthur, 1863-1945
The affair of the 'Avalanche Bicycle and
　Tyre Co., Limited'
　Isaac Asimov presents the best crime
　stories of the 19th century
Morrison, Jack, 1912-
A dash of murder
　Alfred Hitchcock's Grave suspicions
Morrison, John, 1904-
Appointment at Princess Gate
　Morrison, J. This freedom
Black night in Collingwood
　Morrison, J. This freedom
The blind man's story
　Morrison, J. This freedom
Bushfire
　Morrison, J. This freedom
The busting of Rory O'Mahony
　Morrison, J. This freedom
The children
　Morrison, J. This freedom
Christ, the Devil and the lunatic
　Morrison, J. This freedom
The fugitive
　Morrison, J. This freedom
The incense-burner
　The Australian short story; ed. by L.
　Hergenhan
It opens your eyes
　Morrison, J. This freedom
Lena
　Morrison, J. This freedom
Man in the night
　Morrison, J. This freedom
The man on the 'bidgee
　Morrison, J. This freedom

Morrison, John, 1904-—*Continued*
The Prophet of Pandaloop
  Morrison, J. This freedom
Sailors belong ships
  Morrison, J. This freedom
This freedom
  Morrison, J. This freedom
The ticket
  Morrison, J. This freedom
Morrison, Maggie
Which way is home?
  'Teen 30:52+ Ag '86
Morrison's reaction. Kirk, S.
Morrissey, Michael
A mermaid on a blue horse: a tale with
  two endings
  Short story international 63
Morrissey. Ferguson, W.
MORRO BAY (CALIF.)
Fisher, M. F. K. Another love story
Morrow, Bradford, 1951-
Cutt's grace
  New directions in prose and poetry 52
Morrow, James
Diary of a mad deity
  Synergy v2
Veritas
  Synergy v1
**Morrow, W. C. (William Chambers), 1854-
  1923**
His unconquerable enemy
  Masterpieces of terror and the super-
    natural; ed. by M. Kaye and S. Kaye
Morrow, William Chambers *See* Morrow, W.
  C. (William Chambers), 1854-1923
Mors ex vita. Palma, C.
Morsels. Bernard, K.
Mort, Graham
The saw mill
  Critical Quarterly 29:33-6 Spr '87
Mort, John, 1947-
Hot
  Missouri short fiction; ed. by C. Beasley
Tanks
  Soldiers & civilians; ed. by T. Jenks
La **mort** au moyen âge. Kercheval, J. L.
Mortal. Davin, D.
The **mortal** and the monster. Dickson, G.
  R.
Mortal combat. Lutz, J.
The **mortal** immortal. Shelley, M. W.
The **mortal** sin. Ocampo, S.
MORTALITY
Burns, M. Monuments
Hospital, J. T. Some have called thee
  mighty and dreadful
Swift, G. The watch
Treviño, J. S. A very old man
Morthylla. Smith, C. A.
MORTICIANS *See* Undertakers and under-
  taking

Mortimer, John Clifford, 1923-
Rumpole and the age for retirement
  Mortimer, J. C. The first Rumpole om-
    nibus
Rumpole and the alternative society
  Mortimer, J. C. The first Rumpole om-
    nibus
Rumpole and the blind tasting
  Mortimer, J. C. The second Rumpole
    omnibus
Rumpole and the boat people
  Mortimer, J. C. Rumpole for the defence
  Mortimer, J. C. The second Rumpole
    omnibus
Rumpole and the bright seraphim
  Mortimer, J. C. The second Rumpole
    omnibus
Rumpole and the case of identity
  Mortimer, J. C. The first Rumpole om-
    nibus
Rumpole and the confession of guilt
  Mortimer, J. C. Rumpole for the defence
  Mortimer, J. C. The second Rumpole
    omnibus
Rumpole and the course of true love
  Mortimer, J. C. The first Rumpole om-
    nibus
Rumpole and the dear departed
  Mortimer, J. C. Rumpole for the defence
  Mortimer, J. C. The second Rumpole
    omnibus
Rumpole and the expert witness
  Mortimer, J. C. Rumpole for the defence
  Mortimer, J. C. The second Rumpole
    omnibus
Rumpole and the fascist beast
  Mortimer, J. C. The first Rumpole om-
    nibus
Rumpole and the female of the species
  Mortimer, J. C. The second Rumpole
    omnibus
Rumpole and the gentle art of blackmail
  Mortimer, J. C. Rumpole for the defence
  Mortimer, J. C. The second Rumpole
    omnibus
Rumpole and the genuine article
  Mortimer, J. C. The second Rumpole
    omnibus
Rumpole and the golden thread
  Mortimer, J. C. The second Rumpole
    omnibus
Rumpole and the heavy brigade
  Mortimer, J. C. The first Rumpole om-
    nibus
Rumpole and the Honourable Member
  Mortimer, J. C. The first Rumpole om-
    nibus
Rumpole and the judge's elbow
  Mortimer, J. C. The second Rumpole
    omnibus
Rumpole and the last resort
  Mortimer, J. C. The second Rumpole
    omnibus

Mortimer, John Clifford, 1923— *Continued*
Rumpole and the learned friends
    Mortimer, J. C. The first Rumpole omnibus
Rumpole and the Man of God
    Mortimer, J. C. The first Rumpole omnibus
Rumpole and the married lady
    Mortimer, J. C. The first Rumpole omnibus
Rumpole and the official secret
    Mortimer, J. C. The second Rumpole omnibus
Rumpole and the old boy net
    Mortimer, J. C. The second Rumpole omnibus
Rumpole and the old, old story
    Mortimer, J. C. The second Rumpole omnibus
Rumpole and the rotten apple
    Mortimer, J. C. Rumpole for the defence
    Mortimer, J. C. The second Rumpole omnibus
Rumpole and the showfolk
    Mortimer, J. C. The first Rumpole omnibus
Rumpole and the spirit of Christmas
    Mortimer, J. C. Rumpole for the defence
    Mortimer, J. C. The second Rumpole omnibus
Rumpole and the sporting life
    Mortimer, J. C. The second Rumpole omnibus
Rumpole and the winter break
    Mortimer, J. C. The second Rumpole omnibus
Rumpole and the younger generation
    Mortimer, J. C. The first Rumpole omnibus
Rumpole's last case
    Mortimer, J. C. The second Rumpole omnibus
Mortimer, Penelope, 1918-
The skylight
    Venomous tales of villainy and vengeance; ed. by H. Hoke
Mortimer Snodgrass Turtle. Haldeman, J. C.
Mortmain. Greene, G.
Morton, Sheri Lee
Now you see me
    Shadows 9
Moscóv-Selím. Vizyēnos, G. M.
MOSCOW (SOVIET UNION) *See* Soviet Union—Moscow
MOSES (BIBLICAL FIGURE)
                    About
Asimov, I. How it happened
Moses, Jennifer
New York girls are different
    Mademoiselle 90:110+ Mr '84
Right girl, wrong guy
    Mademoiselle 90:96+ Jl '84
Moses. Edmonds, W. D.
Moses. Kessler, J. F.

Mosie. Hospital, J. T.
Moskowitz, Cheryl
The present
    P.E.N. new fiction I
Moskowitz, Faye
The change
    Moskowitz, F. Whoever finds this: I love you
Every airborne particle
    Moskowitz, F. Whoever finds this: I love you
Fanny's comfort station
    Moskowitz, F. Whoever finds this: I love you
In going is a drama
    Moskowitz, F. Whoever finds this: I love you
Irene
    Moskowitz, F. Whoever finds this: I love you
Presents
    Moskowitz, F. Whoever finds this: I love you
The runaround
    Moskowitz, F. Whoever finds this: I love you
Thelma
    Moskowitz, F. Whoever finds this: I love you
They all ran after the farmer's wife
    Moskowitz, F. Whoever finds this: I love you
Whoever finds this: I love you
    Moskowitz, F. Whoever finds this: I love you
Moss, Rose
Exile
    The Penguin book of Southern African stories
Light dark
    Echad 2: South African Jewish voices
The shopping trip
    Echad 2: South African Jewish voices
The **most** dangerous man. Hoch, E. D.
The **most** dangerous man alive. Hoch, E. D.
The **most** girl part of you. Hempel, A.
The **most** golden Bulgari. Picano, F.
The **most** obstinate man in Paris. Simenon, G.
The **most** profound caress. Cortázar, J.
A **most** unusual murder. Bloch, R.
The **most** unusual snatch. Block, L.
The **moth.** See Garrett, G. P. The insects are winning: The moth
Moth. Hofmann, G.
The **moth.** Wells, H. G.
The **moth.** Yasuoka, S.
Moth summer. Reed, J. R.
Mother. Farmer, P. J.
The **mother.** Ginzburg, N.
A **mother.** Gojawiczyńska, P.
Mother. Kawabata, Y.
Mother. Krysl, M.

The **mother**. Oates, J. C.
Mother. Paley, G.
Mother. Parise, G.
The **mother**. Samarakis, A.
Mother. Sandel, C.
Mother. Waten, J.
Mother. Wolitzer, H.
Mother & child. Vinge, J. D.
Mother and child. Krysl, M.
Mother and daughter. Bentley, P.
Mother and doctor. Fuentes, C.
Mother and father. Baumbach, J.
Mother and son!!! Maupassant, G. de
Mother Christmas. Tournier, M.
The **mother-daughter** cookbook. Howell, C. C.
Mother earth. Pil'niāk, B.
Mother goddess of the world. Robinson, K. S.
Mother Goose gets married. Yang, K.
The **mother** in the house of grass. Tsushima, Y.
The **mother** next door. Ariail, J.
The **mother** of a queen. Hemingway, E.
The **mother** of dreams. Ooka, S.
Mother of the bride. Bird, C.
The **mother** right. Lowenstein, A. F.
Mother to dinner. Slesinger, T.
The **mother** tongue. Warner, S. T.
Mother was an alien. Forrest, K. V.
Mother Yaws. Williams, T.
MOTHERHOOD See Mothers
Mothering Sunday. Thomas, A. C.
MOTHERS
    See also Mothers and daughters; Mothers and sons; Mothers-in-law; Stepmothers
Agnon, S. Y. The kerchief
Asscher-Pinkhof, C. Comforting milk
Asscher-Pinkhof, C. New mother
Bambara, T. C. My man Bovanne
Batistich, A. All mixed up
Bingham, S. Fear
Bonner, M. Hongry fire
Botwinik, B. The mother's Yom Kippur
Brodkey, H. Ceil
Browne, H. House call
Chernoff, M. Enough
Clifford, L. L. The new mother
Dadswell, M. Mrs. McGrath
De Queiroz, D. S. Guidance
Deaver, P. F. Geneseo
DeMarinis, R. Gent
Ekström, M. The child's garden
Eldridge, M. Interior
Eldridge, M. Maternity
Evans, E. Desert birds
Fisher, D. C. As ye sow—
García Márquez, G. Tuesday siesta
Gilchrist, E. Adoration
Giles, M. Baby pictures
Giles, M. Rough translations
Gojawiczyńska, P. A mother

Han, S.-W. The cave
Jolley, E. The last crop
Jolley, E. The play reading
Joubert, E. Milk
MacLaverty, B. Umberto Verdi, chimney sweep
Masters, O. The rages of Mrs. Torrens
Mattison, A. Painting day
Mohr, N. Aunt Rosana's rocker (Zoraida)
Moore, G. An episode in married life
Moore-Bentley, M. A. A woman of Earth
Munro, A. The progress of love
Paley, G. Faith in a tree
Paley, G. Mother
Potter, N. A. J. Legacies
Rhys, J. Learning to be a mother
Rifaat, A. Just another day
Robison, M. Your errant mom
Samarakis, A. The mother
Shore, W. May your days be merry and bright
Singmaster, D. Stella Artois
Spivack, K. Loving
Steele, M. The hat of my mother
Takahashi, T. The necklace of flowers
Thomas, A. C. Mothering Sunday
Vinge, J. D. Mother & child
White, C. The phantom limb
Wilbur, E. A certain view
Williams, W. C. A face of stone
Wilson, B. Pity
Wu, C.-L. The doctor's mother
Yates, R. Oh, Joseph, I'm so tired
Yourcenar, M. The milk of death
Mothers. Endō, S.
Mothers. Gathorne-Hardy, J.
MOTHERS AND DAUGHTERS
    See also Parent and child
Abbott, K. The commercial break
Aidoo, C. A. A. Certain winds from the south
Al-Shaykh, H. The Persian carpet
Alcott, L. M. A March Christmas
Alden, P. B. Ladies' luncheon
Alford, E. The late date
Alther, L. Termites
Asscher-Pinkhof, C. See again
Atwood, M. Significant moments in the life of my mother
Auchincloss, L. America first
Austin, M. H. Kate Bixby's queerness
Barich, B. Where the mountains are
Barthelme, S. Mrs. Sims
Bentley, P. Mother and daughter
Berry, R. M. Paradise lost
Bonner, M. On the altar
Bowen, E. Coming home
Bowen, S. P. A marriage of persuasion
Bowles, P. The echo
Boylan, E. My daughter, the murderer
Brady, M. Corsage
Brady, M. Early autumn exchange
Brady, M. Grinning underneath

MOTHERS AND DAUGHTERS — *Continued*

Briskin, M. Present tense
Brown, A. The way of peace
Brown, M. W. The cure
Brown, S. H. Communion
Busch, F. Comrades
Byatt, A. S. The next room
Byatt, A. S. Rose-coloured teacups
Calisher, H. Gargantua
Calisher, H. The middle drawer
Campbell, W. B. The baby
Campbell, W. B. Birthday party
Campos-De Metro, J. Shooting for Jupiter
Canin, E. Pitch memory
Choe, I.-N. The color of mugwort
Ciment, J. Astronomy
Cohen, A. On her feet again
Coleman, W. The seamstress
Colette. Secrets
Cooper, J. C. Swimming to the top of the rain
Coskran, K. The high price of everything
Crayford, K. Duncan
Crone, M. Crocheting
Davis, L. The housemaid
Day, R. C. The violation
Du Maurier, Dame D. Split second
Dubus, A. Molly
Durham, E. M. Deepening dusk
Eldridge, M. Fragment
Eldridge, M. Wayside
Evans, E. Locomotion
Evans, E. The sleeping gypsy
Fante, J. A kidnaping in the family
Farmer, B. Inheritance
Faulkner, W. Skirmish at Sartoris
Fisher, M. F. K. Another love story
Fisher, M. F. K. A delayed meeting
Floyd, P. L. When Mother played Moonshine
Freeman, J. What is this movie?
Fremlin, C. Don't be frightened
Fremlin, C. A lovely day to die
Gallant, M. Going ashore
Gare, N. The child
Gathorne-Hardy, J. Mothers
Gee, M. Buried treasure, old bones
Giles, M. Old souls
Giles, M. Self-defense
Giles, M. What do you say?
Gilliatt, P. Come back if it doesn't get better
Gingher, M. My mother's confession
Girion, B. A very brief season
Glasgow, E. The shadowy third
Glover, D. H. Fire drill
Gordimer, N. A correspondence course
Grau, S. A. The beginning
Harvor, E. A sweetheart
Harvor, E. The teller's cage
Hemley, R. Polish luggage
Hirabayashi, T. A woman to call mother

Hiraiwa, Y. Lady of the evening faces
Hogan, L. New shoes
Hospital, J. T. After long absence
Hospital, J. T. Here comes the sun
Houbein, L. No stranger
Huggan, I. Secrets
Hull, H. R. The fire
Hull, H. R. Separation
James, H. The chaperon
James, H. Sir Edmund Orme
Janowitz, T. Fondue
Jhabvala, R. P. In the mountains
Jolley, E. Paper children
Jones, L. B. The whole idea of Cindy Potts
Kaplan, D. M. Anne Rey
Kaplan, D. M. Comfort
Kaplan, D. M. Love, your only mother
Kauffman, J. My mother has me surrounded
Kavaler, R. Those grand old songs
Kawabata, Y. Faces
Kawabata, Y. The silver fifty-sen pieces
Kawabata, Y. Thank you
Klass, P. Television will betray us all
Krahn, R. Homestead crescent
Krysl, M. Mother
Krysl, M. Mother and child
Kumin, M. West
Laberge, A. The patient
Lavin, M. A cup of tea
Leedom-Ackerman, J. History lesson
Lipman, E. Keeping in touch with Holly
Lish, G. The friend
London, J. The girls love each other
London, J. Lilies
Lowenstein, A. F. The mother right
Lynch, L. The awakening
Maitland, S. Let us now praise unknown women and our mothers who begat us
Malterre, E. Touching the buffalo
March, W. Not worthy of a Wentworth
Martini, C. Breath of God
Mason, B. A. Graveyard day
Masters, O. The Lang women
Matthew, J. R. The letters of Mrs. J. L. Hartle
Matthews, J. The sound of a girl singing
Maupassant, G. de. The accent
Moon, S.-T. Last sound of the gong
Moore, G. A faithful heart
Moore, L. How to talk to your mother (notes)
Moore, L. What is seized
Morris, M. Death apples
Moussa, S. Benevolence
Munro, A. The peace of Utrecht
Murphy, Y. Believer in death
Murphy, Y. The escape
Murphy, Y. Mercury
Naylor, G. Kiswana Browne
Neely, J. Skin angels
Neville, S. The invention of flight

MOTHERS AND DAUGHTERS—*Continued*

Neville, S. Rain forest
Nunes, S. A small obligation
Oates, J. C. April
Oates, J. C. Happy
Oates, J. C. Mule
O'Brien, E. Cords
O'Brien, E. A rose in the heart of New York
Olsen, T. I stand here ironing
Owens, M. We find Harris again
Ozick, C. The shawl
Painter, P. The kidnappers
Papaellinas, G. You told me
Perkins, F. The changes
Phelps, E. S. Old Mother Goose
Phillips, J. A. Home
Phillips, J. A. Something that happened
Pierce, C. When things get back to normal
Pilcher, R. The white birds
Portnoy, M. Loving strangers
Potter, N. A. J. Safe home
Pritchard, M. Companions
Pritchett, M. The Venus tree
Reed, K. The wait
Rendell, R. The vinegar mother
Riches, B. Fall
Rifaat, A. An incident in the Ghobashi household
Rifaat, A. Thursday lunch
Roberts, N. A proper introduction
Robison, J. Eleven
Ross, V. The girls
Ross, V. Thanksgiving
Rule, J. The real world
Russ, J. Autobiography of my mother
Russ, J. Elf hill
Russ, J. Old thoughts, old presences: The autobiography of my mother
Ruta, S. Stalin in the Bronx
Sage, V. Destroying angel
Sandel, C. Alberta
Sanford, W. M. Fools
Schulman, H. Not a free show
Schwartz, L. S. Over the hill
Schwartz, L. S. The Thousand Islands
Schwartz, L. S. What I did for love
Scofield, S. Trespass
Setouchi, H. Pheasant
Shaik, F. Before echo
Shange, N. Christmas for Sassafrass, Cypress & Indigo
Shields, C. Family secrets
Shockley, A. A. A birthday remembered
Silva, B. Smile
Slesinger, T. Mother to dinner
Smiley, J. Dynamite
Spark, M. The pawnbroker's wife
Spencer, E. First dark
Spivack, K. Generations
Straayer, A. C. High heels
Suckow, R. Midwestern primitive
Swados, H. A hot day in Nuevo Laredo
Swados, H. The peacocks of Avignon

Taylor, A. In the rubbish tin
Taylor, P. H. A walled garden
Taylor, R. Pearl Starr alive in Arizona
Thomas, A. C. The dance
Thompson, J. The afternoon of the poetess
Thompson, J. Dreams of a new mother
Thompson, K. A mother's cry
Thompson, S. Ashes
Thompson, S. The birthday party
Thurm, M. Romance
Trevor, W. Her mother's daughter
Tsushima, Y. Clearing the thickets
Tsushima, Y. Missing
Valdés, G. Recuerdo
Vogan, S. Mozart in the afternoon
Walker, A. Everyday use
Walters, A. L. Apparitions
Warren, J. Fetters
Weldon, F. Au pair
West, J. A little collar for the monkey
West, J. Mother's Day
West, J. The second (or perhaps third) time round
West, J. Up a tree
West, J. The wake
Whittier, G. Turning out
Wilbur, E. Wealth
Williams, J. Escapes
Williams, S. A. The lawd don't like ugly
Williams, T. The dark room
Wilson, B. Sense and sensitivity
Winston, C. A lovely day
Winton, T. The water was dark and it went forever down
Wright, B. R. Morning song
Yolen, J. The moon ribbon
Mothers and shadows. Traba, M.

MOTHERS AND SONS
    See also Parent and child
Abbott, K. Jesus Christ and the plaster squirrels
Abbott, L. K. Having the human thing of joy
Abbott, L. K. Time and fear and somehow love
Adams, G. G. Houdini's wife
Aickman, R. Growing boys
Al-Mak, A. Forty-one minarets
Apple, M. Momma's boy
Arden, W. Homecoming
Ardizzone, T. My mother's stories
Asimov, I. My son, the physicist
Auchincloss, L. Greg's peg
Auchincloss, L. The reckoning
Banks, R. The child screams and looks back at you
Banks, R. My mother's memoirs, my father's lie, and other true stories
Banks, R. Queen for a Day
Barthelme, S. Zorro
Bates, H. E. The butterfly
Bates, H. E. The maker of coffins
Baumbach, J. Familiar games

MOTHERS AND SONS—_Continued_

Bausch, R. Ancient history
Berger, J. The accordion player
Berriault, G. The houses of the city
Bonnie, F. Too hot
Bowen, E. Tears, idle tears
Boyle, K. Convalescence
Boyle, K. Winter in Italy
Bretnor, R. Markham
Briskin, M. Preservation
Broughton, T. A. Lily
Brown, G. M. Gold dust
Brown, G. M. Lord of silence
Bukoski, A. Ice days
Burgin, R. The victims
Carver, R. Boxes
Carver, R. Why, honey?
Cather, W. The burglar's Christmas
Claeson, E. Independence
Claiborne, S. The guru and his mother
Cohen, M. Café Le Dog
Colter, C. The frog hunters
Colter, C. The march
Connolly, L. C. Echoes
Conroy, F. Celestial events
Cooper, S. Terminal Island
Crane, S. George's mother
Crane, S. His new mittens
Curley, D. The contrivance
Davis, L. Liminal: the little man
Dunn, D. Something for little Robert
Endō, S. Mothers
Engberg, S. Riffraff
Faik, S. The mirror at the beach
Faik, S. Samovar
Farmer, B. Melpo
Farmer, P. J. Mother
Ferron, J. Black cargo ships of war
Fink, I. Splinter
Flythe, S. Walking, walking
Foote, S. Jordan County [excerpt]
Ford, R. Communist
Forrest, K. V. Benny's place
Frazier, I. Dating your mom
Friedman, B. J. A different ball game
Friedman, B. J. The scientist
Gaines, E. J. The sky is gray
Gallant, M. His mother
Gallant, M. Up north
Gardam, J. Showing the flag
Garrett, G. P. Thus the early gods
Ginzburg, N. The mother
Gold, H. Max and the pacemaker
Gordon, M. Billy
Granit, A. No golden tombstones for me!
Haake, K. One pair red, one pair blue
Haley, R. Fog
Harvor, E. If only we could drive like this
    forever
Harvor, E. To supper in the morning and
    to bed at noon
Hébert, A. The torrent
Hemmerchts, K. Words

Heym, S. My Richard
Highsmith, P. The terrapin
Hofmann, G. Casanova and the extra
Hospital, J. T. Mosie
Houbein, L. I shall live until I die
Humphrey, W. The last of the Caddoes
Humphrey, W. The patience of a saint
Jahnn, H. H. The marmalade eaters
Johnson, J. A. At D'Ambrosia's
Jolley, E. Butter butter butter for a boat
Jolley, E. The shed
Jolley, E. Wednesdays and Fridays
Josipovici, G. Waiting
Kalpakian, L. The battle of Manila
Kamal Muhamed, M. The leg
Kavaler, R. Little Boy Blue
Konopnicka, M. Urbanowa
Krysl, M. Sons
Kump, E. G. Everncere
Kundera, M. Let the old dead make room
    for the young dead
Laidlaw, M. Muzak for torso murders
Lazarre, J. Penetrations
Leavitt, D. Territory
Lee, H. On becoming somebody
Lewis, S. E. Trouble people
Livesey, M. Jean and Little Aunt
Lofts, N. The horse-leech hath two
    daughters
Lofts, N. Saving face
Long, D. V-E Day
Lowry, B. So far from the road, so long
    until morning
MacLaverty, B. Anodyne
Malouf, D. The empty lunch-tin
Mansfield, K. Six years after
Martone, M. March of dimes
Matthews, J. Harry the woman killer
Maupassant, G. de. Mother and son!!!
McCann, R. My mother's clothes: the
    school of beauty and shame
McCullers, C. The haunted boy
McKinley, J. Each new springtime, each
    new summer
Miller, S. Expensive gifts
Mortimer, P. The skylight
Moskowitz, F. Irene
Motsisi, C. Boy-boy
Mukherjee, B. Saints
Mungoshi, C. Coming of the dry season
Nagibin, ÍÙ. M. Somebody else's heart
Narayan, R. K. At the portal
Nevai, L. The sad-womb son
Oates, J. C. The mother
O'Brien, E. The creature
O'Brien, E. In the hours of darkness
O'Connor, F. The comforts of home
O'Connor, F. The enduring chill
O'Connor, F. Everything that rises must
    converge
O'Connor, F. Greenleaf
O'Connor, F. Why do the heathen rage?
O'Connor, F. Judas

MOTHERS AND SONS—*Continued*

Ordan, D. Any minute Mom should come blasting through the door

Pak, S.-J. Ten minutes to seven

Paley, G. Listening

Paley, G. A subject of childhood

Paley, G. The used-boy raisers

Parise, G. Fascination

Parise, G. Mother

Parr, W. Street star

Pascoe, B. Sirens

Petchsingh, T. The sacrifice

Petrakis, H. M. The prison

Pilcher, R. Tea with the professor

Pil'niāk, B. The Nizhni Novgorod Otkos

Porter, K. A. He

Powell, P. Edisto [excerpt]

Pritchett, M. Flying lessons

Pritchett, M. The principles of flotation

Prose, F. Women and children first

Purdy, J. Encore

Purdy, J. Eventide

Rambach, P. Home

Ramos, M. His mother's image

Rasputin, V. G. Mum's gone out somewhere

Razzak, A. I. A. Voices from near and far

Reed, K. Chicken soup

Robison, J. The ecstasy of the animals

Rooke, L. Agnes and the cobwebs

Rooke, L. The birth control king of the Upper Volta

Rossiter, S. Combinations

Rule, J. A good kid in a troubled world

Rule, J. Musical beds

Saki. The Easter egg

Sandel, C. Mother

Sanford, W. M. Allie

Sanford, W. M. Saved

Saroyan, W. Cowards

Shaw, J. B. Some of the things I did not do

Sorrells, R. T. The all-time master grand-master of solitaire

Summers, H. S. Fortunato & the night visitor

Symons, J. The dream is better

Tabucchi, A. Dolores Ibarruri sheds bitter tears

Taylor, P. E. Turning thirty-eight

Taylor, R. Eddy the boy

Thurm, M. Starlight

Toole, J. K. A confederacy of dunces [excerpt]

Traba, M. Mothers and shadows [excerpt]

Trevor, W. Death in Jerusalem

Tsushima, Y. The shooting gallery

Tuohy, F. Discontinued lines

Updike, D. Apples

Valenzuela, L. The minstrels

Valenzuela, L. The son of Kermaria

Walker, A. Strong horse tea

Walters, A. L. The laws

Watson, S. Brother Oedipus

Welch, D. At sea

Wells, H. G. Little mother up the Mörderberg

Wheeler, H. C. Little boy lost

Whelan, G. Sympathy notes

White, T. Only yesterday

Wilbur, E. Safe

Wilk, M. Singing with Skulnick

Williams, T. The killer chicken and the closet queen

Williams, T. Mama's old stucco house

Williamson, B. The toy killer

Wilner, H. St. Denis

Wolff, T. The liar

Wolff, T. The other Miller

Yaffe, J. Mom sings an aria

Yano, T. The legend of the paper spaceship

Yi, H. The woman who fulled clothes

A **mother's** cry. Thompson, K.

Mother's Day. Nevai, L.

Mother's Day. Thompson, S.

Mother's Day. West, J.

A **mother's** good-bye. Goldreich, G.

MOTHERS-IN-LAW

Botwinik, B. Death went astray

Bowles, P. The little house

Briskin, M. Giant sequoia

Brown, M. W. New dresses

Edgerton, C. Raney [excerpt]

Edwards, H. S. His defense

Fisher, M. F. K. A delayed meeting

Givner, J. Conversation pieces

Grau, S. A. Letting go

Miller, S. Leaving home

Pak, W.-S. How I kept our house while my husband was away

Ross, J. Unfinished business

A **mother's** secret. Weber, N.

The **mother's** Yom Kippur. Botwinik, B.

MOTHS

Poe, E. A. The sphinx

Moths. Hood, M.

The **moths.** Viramontes, H. M.

MOTION PICTURE ACTORS AND ACTRESSES

Bloch, R. All on a golden afternoon

Bloch, R. The movie people

Busby, F. M. Once upon a unicorn

Friedman, B. J. An ironic Yetta Montana

Hill, R. Auteur theory

McCourt, J. Kaye Wayfaring in "Avenged"

McCourt, J. The Scan of Illyria

McCourt, J. Something sensational to read in the train

McCourt, J. Winter meeting

Narayan, R. K. The antidote

Nielsen, H. Death scene

Nolan, W. F. Saturday's shadow

O'Hara, J. Drawing room B

O'Hara, J. The girl from California

O'Hara, J. Natica Jackson

MOTION PICTURE ACTORS AND AC-TRESSES—*Continued*
Raphael, F. For Joannie
Wagner, K. E. More sinned against
Woolrich, C. Hot water
Woolrich, C. Preview of death
MOTION PICTURE CRITICS
Mcdonald, G. The nine best movies
MOTION PICTURE DIRECTORS *See* Motion picture producers and directors
MOTION PICTURE PRODUCERS AND DIRECTORS
Boyett, S. R. The answer tree
Broun, H. South Sea sensations
Claiborne, S. Visions and revisions
Covino, M. Monologue of the movie mogul
Ellin, S. The twelfth statue
Etchison, D. Deadspace
Garris, M. A life in the cinema
Hunter, E. The interview
Lombreglia, R. Men under water
Petroski, C. The hit
Picano, F. The most golden Bulgari
Wallace, W. Up home
MOTION PICTURE THEATERS
Arnold, M. Pilgrims to the cathedral
Campbell, R. The show goes on
Greene, G. A little place off the Edgeware Road
Straub, P. The juniper tree
Williams, T. The mysteries of the Joy Rio
MOTION PICTURES
Apple, M. Child's play
Barker, C. Son of celluloid
Barthelme, D. The film
Bernard, K. The films of R. Nixon
Bishop, M. Storming the bijou, mon amour
Bloch, R. The movie people
Bloch, R. The plot is the thing
Bloch, R. Sock finish
Bloch, R. Talent
Bryant, E. The cutter
Coover, R. Charlie in the house of rue
Coover, R. Intermission
Coover, R. The phantom of the movie palace
Covino, M. Matinee at the Bijou
Drake, R. Mrs. Picture Show Green
Dybek, S. Bijou
Essop, A. Film
Etchison, D. The blood kiss
Garton, R. Sinema
Granit, A. No golden tombstones for me!
Greene, G. The blue film
Havazelet, E. Natalie Wood's amazing eyes
Heise, K. The condemned movie
Jakes, J. The man who wanted to be in the movies
Johnson, C. R. Moving pictures
Keillor, G. The killer
King, F. H. The goat

Liben, M. The Tolstoy movie
Madden, D. The singer
Milton, B. The cigarette boat
Muir, A. The reptile
Percy, W. The moviegoer [excerpt]
Rucker, R. von B. Tales of Houdini
Russell, R. Ding-dong, the lizard's dead
Shea, M. The extra
Sladek, J. T. White hat
Spector, C. Lifecast
Villiers, A. J. The windjammer film
Waldrop, H. French scenes
Wiebe, D. E. Omega I
Williams, W. J. Video star
Williamson, C. Return of the neon fireball
Winter, D. E. Splatter
Wodehouse, P. G. Monkey business
The **motive**. Collins, M.
The **motive**. Shannon, D.
Motive for murder. Powell, T.
Motive v. opportunity. Christie, A.
MOTOR BUSES *See* Buses
Motor-driven. Gillie, W. T.
MOTORCYCLE DRIVERS
Hankla, C. The moped massacre
Kinsella, W. P. King of the street
Mathers, P. Chains
Mathers, P. Plaster, culture, rape and deprivation
Taylor, P. E. A call from brotherland
The **motorcycle** riders. Schinto, J.
MOTORCYCLES
Kinsella, W. P. The job
Schinto, J. The motorcycle riders
Motsisi, Casey
Boy-boy
  The Penguin book of Southern African stories
Moudy, Walter F.
The survivor
  The Science fictional Olympics; ed. by I. Asimov; M. H. Greenberg and C. G. Waugh
Moulder of monsters. Fleming-Roberts, G. T.
Mountain. Davies, P. H.
The **mountain**. Kohler, S.
The **mountain**. Leskov, N. S.
The **mountain**. Piñera, V.
MOUNTAIN CLIMBING *See* Mountaineering
MOUNTAIN LIFE
Southern States
See also Appalachian highlanders
Barnhill, S. Near places, far places
O'Connor, F. The life you save may be your own
Smith, P. C. The patchwork quilt
Spillane, M. Stand up and die!
Still, J. A master time
Stuart, J. Battle with the bees
Stuart, J. The champion
Stuart, J. Coming down the mountain
Stuart, J. Competition at Slush Creek

MOUNTAIN LIFE—Southern States—*Continued*

Stuart, J. Fight number twenty-five
Stuart, J. Horse-trading trembles
Stuart, J. Hot-collared mule
Stuart, J. Land of our enemies
Stuart, J. No hero
Stuart, J. No petty thief
Stuart, J. Old Gore
Stuart, J. Road number one
Stuart, J. The slipover sweater
Stuart, J. Testimony of trees
Stuart, J. Thirty-two votes before breakfast
Stuart, J. To market, to market
Stuart, J. When mountain men make peace
Williams, T. The kingdom of earth

MOUNTAIN LIONS *See* Pumas

MOUNTAIN MEADOWS MASSACRE, 1857

Bean, A. The warhorse of Spotted Tail
The **mountain** top. Nestor, T. G.

MOUNTAIN WHITES (SOUTHERN STATES) *See* Appalachian highlanders

MOUNTAINEERING

Crane, S. The mesmeric mountain
Harrison, M. J. The ice monkey
Helprin, M. The Schreuderspitze
Maupassant, G. de. The inn
O'Brien, D. Weightless
Piñera, V. The fall
Robinson, K. S. Green Mars
Robinson, K. S. Ridge running
Sandberg, P. L. Calloway's climb
Sandberg, P. L. Gabe's fall
Sandberg, P. L. The old bull moose of the woods
Wells, H. G. Little mother up the Mörderberg
Woolf, V. The symbol

MOUNTAINS

See also Adirondack Mountains (N.Y.); Andes; Himalaya Mountains; Mont Sainte-Victoire (France); Rocky Mountains; Sierra Nevada Mountains (Calif. and Nev.); Volcanoes; White Mountains (N.H. and Me.)

Black, S. The cloud child
Clift, C. Wild Emperor
Vreuls, D. Estarolly's mountain
The **mountebanks**. Maupassant, G. de

Mountzoures, H. L.

At the tutor's
The New Yorker 62:36-41 Je 16 '86
By the sea
Redbook 170:62+ Ap '88
The **mourner**. Dawkins, C.
The **mourner**. Friedman, B. J.

MOURNING *See* Bereavement

Mourning. See Taylor, R. Mrs. Jesse James, mourning

MOURNING CUSTOMS *See* Funeral rites and ceremonies

Mourning Henry. Ballantyne, S.

Mouse. Brown, F.
The **mouse**. Davis, L.
The **mouse**. King, F. H.
The **mouse** and the woman. Thomas, D.
The **mouse** roulette wheel. Bly, C.
The **mouse** town. Hemley, R.
The **mouse-trap**. Slesinger, T.
Mousetrap. Crichton, M.

Moussa, Sabry

Benevolence
Egyptian tales and short stories of the 1970s and 1980s

MOUSTACHE *See* Mustache

Mouth of brass. Humphrey, W.
The **mouth** of the cave. O'Brien, E.
The **mouthpiece**. La Puma, S.
Mov. Jahnn, H. H.
The **move**. Walser, M.
Movements of the hand. Moyer, K.
Movie music. Swick, M.
The **movie** people. Bloch, R.
The **moviegoer**. Percy, W.

MOVING (HOUSEHOLD GOODS)

Bausch, R. Spirits
Beattie, A. The big outside world
Bradbury, R. Long division
Brady, M. Strike it rich
Carver, R. Boxes
Gallagher, T. King Death
Henley, P. Moving in
McLaughlin, L. Moving house
O'Brien, D. Final touches
Ruffolo, L. Independence Day
Schinto, J. Keepsake
Schwartz, L. S. The painters
Still, J. The moving
Tallent, E. Black holes
Vogan, S. The strength of steel
The **moving**. Still, J.
Moving house. McLaughlin, L.
Moving in. Henley, P.
Moving night. Holder, N.
Moving on. Dixon, S.
Moving out. Hospital, J. T.

MOVING PICTURE INDUSTRY *See* Motion pictures

MOVING PICTURES *See* Motion pictures

Moving pictures. Johnson, C. R.
Moving spirit. Clarke, A. C.
Moving to the country. Shukshin, V. M.

Mowat, John

Violators towed away
Encounter (London, England) 70:15-20 Ap '88
Moxon's master. Bierce, A.

Moyano, Daniel

The story of the green Falcon and the marvelous flute
The Massachusetts Review 27:401-17 Fall/Wint '86
Short story international 69
Unspoken words
Partisan Review 55:409-28 Summ '88

Moyer, Kermit, 1943-
Coming unbalanced
Moyer, K. Tumbling
The Southern Review (Baton Rouge, La.)
23:629-44 Summ '87
The compass of the heart
Moyer, K. Tumbling
In the castle
Moyer, K. Tumbling
The Sewanee Review 95:349-58 Summ
'87
Life jackets
Moyer, K. Tumbling
Movements of the hand
Moyer, K. Tumbling
Ruth's daughter
The Hudson Review 41:19-44 Spr '88
Moyer, K. Tumbling
Tumbling
The Hudson Review 38:579-608 Wint '86
Moyer, K. Tumbling
Moyes, Patricia
The holly wreath
Ellery Queen's Prime crimes
The honest blackmailer
Masterpieces of mystery and suspense;
ed. by M. H. Greenberg
**MOZART, JOHANN CHRYSOSTOM
WOLFGANG AMADEUS** *See*
Mozart, Wolfgang Amadeus, 1756-1791
**MOZART, WOLFGANG AMADEUS, 1756-
1791**
About
Krysl, M. Mozart, Westmoreland, and me
Morazzoni, M. The white door
Sterling, B., and Shiner, L. Mozart in mir-
rorshades
Don Juan
Hoffmann, E. T. A. Don Juan
Mozart in mirrorshades. Sterling, B., and
Shiner, L.
Mozart in the afternoon. Vogan, S.
Mozart is best. Halligan, M.
Mozart, Westmoreland, and me. Krysl, M.
Mozart you can't give them. Gerber, M. J.
Mozart's Clarinet Concerto. Dunn, D.
Mphahlele, Ezekiel
The coffee-cart girl
African short stories; ed. by C. Achebe
and C. L. Innes
The master of Doornvlei
African short stories in English; ed. by
J. de Grandsaigne
Mrs. Plum
The Penguin book of Southern African
stories
Mr. Adamson of Laverhope. Hogg, J.
Mr. and Mrs. Arnold. Latimer, M.
Mr. and Mrs. Baby. Strand, M.
Mr. and Mrs. Elliot. Hemingway, E.
Mr. and Mrs. Martins. Van Steen, E.
Mr. and Mrs. McFeely at home and away.
Baumbach, J.

Mr. and Mrs. Noonan. Rand, P.
Mr. and Mrs. North. Lish, G.
Mr. Appledorn. McKay, J.
Mr. Arcularis. Aiken, C.
Mr. Barry. Stiles, M. B.
Mr. Bernshtein. Mazel, D.
Mr. Binks' day off. Crane, S.
Mr. Blandfoot's picture. Hartley, L. P.
Mr. Brisher's treasure. Wells, H. G.
Mr. Bulmer's golden carp. Bingham, J.
Mr. Burdoff's visit to Germany. Davis, L.
Mr. Carmichael's room. Sanford, W. M.
Mr. de la Torre. Dundas, R.
Mr. Dnarley's pigs. Warren, J.
Mr. Doll. Morgan, B.
Mr. Endrews speaks. Leonard, T.
Mr. Evening. Purdy, J.
Mr. Feathers. Nevai, L.
Mr. Felix. Gosling, P.
Mr. Goldbaum. Lish, G.
Mr. Higginbotham's catastrophe. Hawthorne,
N.
Mr. Integrity for 1987. Kessler, R.
Mr. Jones. Wharton, E.
Mr. Jones's convention. Kotzwinkle, W.
Mr. Justice Harbottle. Le Fanu, J. S.
Mr. Kim, the Bohemian minstrel. Han,
M.-S.
Mr. Lazenbee. Willett, J.
Mr. Ledbetter's vacation. Wells, H. G.
Mr. Lupescu. Boucher, A.
Mr. Mackenzie's last hour. Warner, S. T.
Mr. Macnamee. Dadswell, M.
Mr. Malone. Wolfe, T.
Mr. Marshall's doppelganger. Wells, H. G.
Mr. McAlligator. Warren, J.
Mr. Meldrum's mania. Metcalfe, J.
Mr. Mintz retires. Liben, M.
Mr Moonreddy. Essop, A.
Mr. Murdoch's ghost. Frede, R.
Mr. Ng at the Great Wall. Laser, M.
Mr. Parker's valentine. Jolley, E.
Mr. Parsley's lunchtime pursuit. Regent, P.
Mr. Pat's magical ride. Johnson, T. J.
Mr. Payson's satirical Christmas. Ade, G.
Mr. Quintillian. Hersey, J.
Mr. Reed goes to dinner. Dumonte, E.
Mr. Right. Matheson, R. C.
Mr. Simpson. Szucsany, D.
Mr. Skelmersdale in Fairyland. Wells, H. G.
Mr. Smith kicks the bucket. Brown, F.
Mr. Sookhoo and the carol singers. Naipaul,
S.
Mr. Steinway. Bloch, R.
Mr. Strang and the purloined memo. Brit-
tain, W.
Mr. Strang picks up the pieces. Brittain, W.
Mr. Tessler. Mazel, D.
Mr. Testator's visitation. Dickens, C.
Mr. Tivy. Sisskind, M.
Mr. Walsh's mare. Gibbons, R.
Mr. Wilde's second chance. Russ, J.

Mrabet, Mohammed, 1940-
Doctor Safi
   The Art of the tale; ed. by D. Halpern
Mrożek, Sławomir
Art
   Mrożek, S. The elephant
The background to an era
   Mrożek, S. The elephant
Birthday
   Mrożek, S. The elephant
Children
   Mrożek, S. The elephant
The chronicle of a besieged city
   Mrożek, S. The elephant
A citizen's fate
   Mrożek, S. The elephant
The co-operative
   Mrożek, S. The elephant
A confession about Bobby
   Mrożek, S. The elephant
A drummer's adventure
   Mrożek, S. The elephant
The elephant
   Mrożek, S. The elephant
An event
   Mrożek, S. The elephant
A fact
   Mrożek, S. The elephant
The fall of an Eagle's Nest
   Short story international 51
A forester in love
   Mrożek, S. The elephant
From the darkness
   Mrożek, S. The elephant
The giraffe
   Mrożek, S. The elephant
Golden thoughts
   Mrożek, S. The elephant
Horses
   Mrożek, S. The elephant
I want to be a horse
   Mrożek, S. The elephant
I'm subtle
   Mrożek, S. The elephant
In the drawer
   Mrożek, S. The elephant
It's a pity
   Mrożek, S. The elephant
The last hussar
   Mrożek, S. The elephant
Letter from an old people's home
   Mrożek, S. The elephant
The lion
   Mrożek, S. The elephant
Modern life
   Mrożek, S. The elephant
Monologue
   Mrożek, S. The elephant
The monument
   Mrożek, S. The elephant
My uncle's stories
   Mrożek, S. The elephant

On a journey [Variant title: Enroute]
   Mrożek, S. The elephant
The parable of the miraculous escape
   Mrożek, S. The elephant
The parson and the band
   Mrożek, S. The elephant
The pastor
   Mrożek, S. The elephant
Peer Gynt
   Mrożek, S. The elephant
   Short story international 49
Poetry
   Mrożek, S. The elephant
The sceptic
   Mrożek, S. The elephant
Siesta
   Mrożek, S. The elephant
A silent hero
   Mrożek, S. The elephant
Spring in Poland
   Mrożek, S. The elephant
The swan
   Mrożek, S. The elephant
Tiny
   Mrożek, S. The elephant
The trial
   Mrożek, S. The elephant
The ugupu bird
   Short story international 64
The veteran
   Mrożek, S. The elephant
Mrs. Amworth. Benson, E. F.
Mrs. Carteret receives. Hartley, L. P.
Mrs. Cassidy's last year. Gordon, M.
Mrs. Clendon's place. Brennan, J. P.
Mrs. Craggs and a certain lady's town house.
   Keating, H. R. F.
Mrs. Craggs and a sad case of simony.
   Keating, H. R. F.
Mrs. Craggs and the late Prince Albert.
   Keating, H. R. F.
Mrs. Craggs and the living dead. Keating,
   H. R. F.
Mrs. Craggs and the Lords spiritual and
   temporal. Keating, H. R. F.
Mrs. Craggs and the pale Ella. Keating, H.
   R. F.
Mrs. Craggs and the round blue immortals.
   Keating, H. R. F.
Mrs. Craggs gives a dose of physic. Keating,
   H. R. F.
Mrs. Craggs hears the nightingale. Keating,
   H. R. F.
Mrs. Craggs sings a different tune. Keating,
   H. R. F.
Mrs. Craggs's sixth sense. Keating, H. R. F.
Mrs. Dalloway in Bond Street. Woolf, V.
Mrs. Effie. Daniels, C.
Mrs. Eglantine. Bates, H. E.
Mrs. Eloise. Daniels, C.
Mrs. English. Drake, R.
Mrs. Gladfelter's revolt. Martin, H. R.
Mrs. Halprin and the lottery. Auswaks, A.

Mrs. Henderson. Wyndham, F.
Mrs. Henderson talks to God. MacCall, L.
Mrs. Jesse James, mourning. Taylor, R.
Mrs. Lutz. Kees, W.
Mrs. McGrath. Dadswell, M.
Mrs. Moonlight. Norris, H.
Mrs. Mouse. Ellin, S.
Mrs. Norris observes. Davis, D. S.
Mrs. Pacal's bike-athon. Giammatteo, H.
Mrs. Parkins's Christmas Eve. Jewett, S. O.
Mrs. Picture Show Green. Drake, R.
Mrs. Pilate's duty. Conrad, B.
Mrs. Plum. Mphahlele, E.
Mrs. Rahlo's closet. Klein, R. E.
Mrs. Rakubian. Pronzini, B.
Mrs. Reinhardt. O'Brien, E.
Mrs. Rogers. Warren, J.
Mrs. Saunders writes to the world. Schwartz, L. S.
Mrs. Shreeve and Mrs. Bolero. McLaughlin, L.
Mrs. Sims. Barthelme, S.
Mrs. Teeters' tomato jar. Fisher, M. F. K.
Mrs. Thing. Hall, D.
Mrs. Todd's shortcut. King, S.
Ms. found in a bottle. Poe, E. A.
Ms. found in an abandoned time machine. Silverberg, R.
Ms. Grossberg's legs. Ephron, N.
Mud Toe the cannibal. Purdy, J.
Mudd, E. J.
Stop that music!
Redbook 169:46+ My '87
Mudpuppies. Touzalin, R.
Muecke, Stephen, 1951-
(jt. auth) See Roe, Paddy, 1912-, and Muecke, Stephen, 1951-
Mufti, Masud
Good luck
Short story international 50
Mugger. Matheson, R. C.
Muggers' moon. Pronzini, B.
MUGGING
Dawson, F. Night
Matthews, J. The amnesia ballet
Pronzini, B. Muggers' moon
Muheim, Harry
The dusty drawer
Hitchcock in prime time; ed. by F. M. Nevins and M. H. Greenberg
Muir, Augustus
The reptile
The Penguin book of horror stories
Muir, John, 1838-1914
An adventure with a dog [Variant title: An adventure with a dog and a glacier]
Roger Caras' Treasury of great dog stories
Mujica, Barbara
Mitrani
The Literary Review (Madison, N.J.) 27:357-71 Spr '84

Mujica Láinez, Manuel, 1910-1984
Importance
Black water; ed. by A. Manguel
Mukherjee, Bharati
Angela
The Best American short stories, 1985
Mukherjee, B. Darkness
Buried lives
Mukherjee, B. The middleman, and other stories
Courtly vision
Mukherjee, B. Darkness
Danny's girl
Mukherjee, B. The middleman, and other stories
A father
Mukherjee, B. Darkness
Fathering
Mukherjee, B. The middleman, and other stories
Fighting for the rebound
Mukherjee, B. The middleman, and other stories
Hindus
Mukherjee, B. Darkness
The imaginary assassin
Mukherjee, B. Darkness
Isolated incidents
Mukherjee, B. Darkness
Jasmine
Mukherjee, B. The middleman, and other stories
The lady from Lucknow
Mukherjee, B. Darkness
The Oxford book of Canadian short stories in English
Loose ends
Mukherjee, B. The middleman, and other stories
The management of grief
Mukherjee, B. The middleman, and other stories
The middleman
The Editors' choice v4
Mukherjee, B. The middleman, and other stories
Nostalgia
Mukherjee, B. Darkness
Orbiting
Mukherjee, B. The middleman, and other stories
Saints
Mukherjee, B. Darkness
Tamurlane
Mukherjee, B. Darkness
The tenant
The Best American short stories, 1987
The Literary Review (Madison, N.J.) 29:481-92 Summ '86
Mukherjee, B. The middleman, and other stories
Visitors
Mukherjee, B. Darkness

Mukherjee, Bharati—*Continued*
A wife's story
  Mukherjee, B. The middleman, and other stories
The world according to Hsü
  Mukherjee, B. Darkness
MULATTOES
Alcott, L. M. The brothers
Andrews, R. Appalachee Red [excerpt]
Bonner, M. A sealed pod
Caldwell, E. Yellow girl
Cooper, J. C. Color me real
Mulberry child. Minakami, T.
Mulder, Michael
San Diego dilemma
  A Matter of crime v2
Muldoon and the numbers game. Fish, R. L.
Mule. Oates, J. C.
The **mule** driver and the carrot. Watt, N.
Mulford, Clarence E.
Hopalong sits in
  Wild westerns; ed. by B. Pronzini
Mulikita, Fwanyanga M.
The tender crop
  African short stories in English; ed. by J. de Grandsaigne
Mullen, Jane Ann
Brotherly love
  Mademoiselle 91:140+ Ap '85
Mullen, Robert
At the beach
  P.E.N. new fiction I
Muller, Donna Nitz
The old woman's blessing
  Stiller's pond; ed. by J. Agee; R. Blakely and S. Welch
Muller, Marcia
The broken men
  The Mammoth book of private eye stories; ed. by B. Pronzini and M. H. Greenberg
  Women sleuths; ed. by M. H. Greenberg and B. Pronzini
Deceptions
  A Matter of crime v1
Kindling point
  Witches' brew; ed. by M. Muller and B. Pronzini
The Sanchez sacraments
  The Ethnic detectives; ed. by B. Pronzini and M. H. Greenberg
  The Year's best mystery & suspense stories, 1986
Sweet cactus wine
  She won the West; ed. by M. Muller and B. Pronzini
The time of the wolves
  Westeryear; ed. by E. Gorman
Wild mustard
  The Eyes have it; ed. by R. J. Randisi

Muller, Robert, 1923-
General Patton did not sleep here
  Short story international 60
Of science and love
  Short story international 44
Mulrine, Stephen
A cold coming
  Streets of stone; ed. by M. Burgess and H. Whyte
MULTIPLE PERSONALITY
  See also Dual personality; Personality disorders
Bendel, S. K. The woman in the shadows
MULTIPLE SCLEROSIS
Sutherland, M. Loving
Multiples. Pronzini, B., and Malzberg, B. N.
Multiples. Silverberg, R.
MUMMIES
Benson, E. F. Monkeys
Bradbury, R. Colonel Stonesteel's genuine home-made truly Egyptian mummy
Crowley, J. Antiquities
Doyle, Sir A. C. Lot no 249
Poe, E. A. Some words with a mummy
The **mummies** of Guanajuato. Whelan, G.
The **mummy** from the sea. Hoch, E. D.
Mum's gone out somewhere. Rasputin, V. G.
Mumú. Turgenev, I. S.
Mun, Sun-Tae *See* Moon, Soon-Tae
Munby, A. N. L. (Alan Noel Latimer), 1913-1974
A Christmas game
  Christmas ghosts; ed. by K. Cramer and D. G. Hartwell
An encounter in the mist
  The Oxford book of English ghost stories
Munby, Alan Noel Latimer *See* Munby, A. N. L. (Alan Noel Latimer), 1913-1974
Mundo's sign. Shacochis, B.
Mundstock, Karl
A judgment worthy of Solomon
  Voices East and West: German short stories since 1945
Mungoshi, Charles
Coming of the dry season
  African short stories in English; ed. by J. de Grandsaigne
MUNICH (GERMANY) *See* Germany—Munich
Municipal noir. Broun, H.
MUNITIONS
Franzen, B. Peacekeeper
Munro, Alice
Bardon bus
  The World of the short story; ed. by C. Fadiman
Circle of prayer
  The Best American short stories, 1987
  Munro, A. The progress of love
  The Paris Review 28:31-51 Summ/Fall '86

Munro, Alice—*Continued*
Eskimo
Munro, A. The progress of love
Fits
Munro, A. The progress of love
Five points
The New Yorker 64:34-43 Mr 14 '88
Hold me fast, don't let me pass
The Atlantic 262:58-66+ D '88
Jesse and Meribeth
Munro, A. The progress of love
Labor Day dinner
Short story international 65
Lichen
Munro, A. The progress of love
The New Yorker 61:26-36 Jl 15 '85
Meneseteung
The New Yorker 63:28-38 Ja 11 '88
Miles City, Montana
Munro, A. The progress of love
New American short stories; ed. by G. Norris
The New Yorker 60:30-40 Ja 14 '85
Monsieur les Deux Chapeaux
The Best American short stories, 1986
Munro, A. The progress of love
The New press anthology #2
The moon in the Orange Street Skating Rink
Munro, A. The progress of love
The New Yorker 62:26-36+ Mr 31 '86
Oh, what avails
The New Yorker 63:42-52+ N 16 '87
Oranges and apples
The New Yorker 64:36-48+ O 24 '88
The peace of Utrecht
The Oxford book of Canadian short stories in English
The progress of love
Munro, A. The progress of love
The New Yorker 61:35-46+ O 7 '85
Prue
The Treasury of English short stories; ed. by N. Sullivan
A queer streak
Munro, A. The progress of love
Royal beatings
Making it new; ed. by J. Metcalf
Secrets between friends
Mademoiselle 91:116+ N '85
Walker Brothers cowboy
The Graywolf annual 2
The Literary Review (Madison, N.J.) 28:425-37 Spr '85
White dump
Munro, A. The progress of love
The New Yorker 62:25-39+ Jl 28 '86
Who do you think you are?
Making it new; ed. by J. Metcalf
Working for a living
A Grand Street reader; ed. by B. Sonnenberg

Munro, H. H. (Hector Hugh) *See* Saki, 1870-1916
Munves, James, 1922-
Bogotá
The New Yorker 62:35-6 D 22 '86
Daughters
The New Yorker 62:28-9 My 26 '86
MURASAKI SHIKIBU, b. 978?
Parodies, travesties, etc.
Yourcenar, M. The last love of Prince Genji
Murder. Anderson Imbert, E.
The **murder.** Böll, H.
Murder. Chekhov, A. P.
Murder à la mode. Grayson, R.
Murder at the Bouchercon. Hoch, E. D.
Murder between the sheets. Grafton, S.
Murder by mail. Nebel, F.
Murder by proxy. Bodkin, M. M.
Murder deluxe. Pentecost, H.
A **murder** history. Lopatin, J.
Murder in miniature. Caplan, N.
Murder in one scene. Wheeler, H. C.
Murder in the mews. Christie, A.
Murder in wax. Woolrich, C.
Murder most kind. Gill, B. M.
Murder of a novel Parisian style amid the frenzy of France's literary merry-go-round. Russo, A.
Murder of an African prince. Russo, A.
The **murder** of Santa Claus. James, P. D.
The **murder** of the governor. De la Torre Bueno, T.
Murder off limits. Ritchie, J.
Murder on the flux line. Reimer, I.
The **murder** on the lotus pond. Gulik, R. H. van
Murder on the waterfront. Schulberg, B.
MURDER STORIES
See also Assassination; Crime and criminals; Fratricide; Infanticide; International intrigue; Murderers; Mystery and detective stories; Parricide; Poisons; Strangling; Violence
Abe, K. The dream soldier
Aickman, R. The trains
Akutagawa, R. In a grove
Allyn, D. The puddle diver
Alter, R. E. To catch a big one
Amis, M. Bujak and the strong force; or, God's dice
Anderson Imbert, E. Murder
Andreyev, L. The thought
Archer, J. The perfect murder
Asimov, I. Light verse
Asimov, I. The little things
Asimov, I. Nothing might happen
Asimov, I. The sign
Asimov, I. What time is it?
Avallone, M. Walter ego
Balzac, H. de. La Grande Bretêche
Bankier, W. A hint of danger
Bankier, W. One clear sweet clue

MURDER STORIES—*Continued*

Barker, C. New murders in the Rue Morgue
Barker, C. Revelations
Barker, S. The fog on Pemble Green
Barnard, R. Happy Christmas
Barnard, R. Little terror
Barnard, R. The woman in the wardrobe
Barthelme, S. Samaritan
Baum, L. F. The suicide of Kiaros
Bausch, R. The man who knew Belle Starr
Baxt, G. Stroke of genius
Bedard, B. The fifth letter
Bedard, B. Hour of the beast
Bedard, B. Sweet Billy
Benjamin, D. Things will look brighter in the morning
Bester, A. Fondly Fahrenheit
Bierce, A. The moonlit road
Billington, R. The photograph
Bird, C. The best thing to do
Bishop, M. A tapestry of little murders
Blaisten, I. Uncle Facundo
Bloch, R. Betsy Blake will live forever
Bloch, R. Crime in rhyme
Bloch, R. The deadliest art
Bloch, R. Enoch
Bloch, R. Final performance
Bloch, R. The gloating place
Bloch, R. A good imagination
Bloch, R. His and hearse
Bloch, R. Hobo
Bloch, R. The hungry eye
Bloch, R. Impractical joker
Bloch, R. Life in our time
Bloch, R. The living end
Bloch, R. Luck is no lady
Bloch, R. Lucy comes to stay
Bloch, R. The man who knew women
Bloch, R. Man with a hobby
Bloch, R. Method for murder
Bloch, R. A most unusual murder
Bloch, R. Night school
Bloch, R. Pin-up girl
Bloch, R. The play's the thing
Bloch, R. A quiet funeral
Bloch, R. Reaper
Bloch, R. The screaming people
Bloch, R. See how they run
Bloch, R. String of pearls
Bloch, R. That old black magic
Bloch, R. 'Til death do us part
Bloch, R. Yours truly, Jack the Ripper
Blochman, L. G. Murder walks in marble halls
Block, L. Click!
Block, L. Hot eyes, cold eyes
Block, L. If this be madness
Block, L. Like a bug on a windshield
Block, L. Passport in order
Block, L. With a smile for the ending
Boeckman, C. You can get away with murder

Bonner, M. High-stepper
Bonner, M. Nothing new
Borges, J. L. Emma Zunz
Bowles, P. In the red room
Boyd, W. Bizarre situations
Boyd, W. Love hurts
Boylan, E. My daughter, the murderer
Bradbury, R. And so died Riabouchinska
Bradbury, R. The candy skull
Bradbury, R. A careful man dies
Bradbury, R. Dead men rise up never
Bradbury, R. Four-way funeral
Bradbury, R. Hell's half hour
Bradbury, R. "I'm not so dumb!"
Bradbury, R. It burns me up!
Bradbury, R. The long night
Bradbury, R. The long way home
Bradbury, R. The trunk lady
Bradbury, R. Yesterday I lived!
Braddon, M. E. The shadow in the corner
Brand, C. Bless this house
Breen, J. L. Starstruck
Breen, J. L. A thumb on the scales
Brennan, J. P. An ordinary brick house
Brett, S. Big Boy, Little Boy
Brett, S. Double glazing
Brett, S. How's your mother?
Brett, S. The nuggy bar
Brett, S. Parking space
Brett, S. Private areas
Brett, S. The thirteenth killer
Brewer, G. Fool's gold
Brown, F. The Djinn murder
Brown, F. Granny's birthday
Brown, F. Hobbyist
Brown, F. Little Apple Hard to Peel
Brown, F. Murder while you wait
Brown, F. Nightmare in yellow
Brown, F. A voice behind him
Browne, H. House call
Bryant, E. The cutter
Burgess, F. Exit, stage right
Burke, J. Lucille would have known
Burke, T. The hands of Mr. Ottermole
Burns, M. The men on my window
Burrage, A. M. The waxwork
Bush, J. The last meeting of the Butlers Club
Butler, G. Chicken feed
Butler, G. The sisterhood
Buzzati, D. The gnawing worm
Cain, J. M. The baby in the icebox
Campbell, R. Lilith's
Campbell, R. The other woman
Campbell, R. The will of Stanley Brooke
Canning, V. Lady in the dark
Caplan, N. Murder in miniature
Carr, J. The heart in the egg
Carver, R. The third thing that killed my father off
Chastain, T. Directed verdict
Chekhov, A. P. Murder
Chipulina, E. G. Square peg, round hole

MURDER STORIES—*Continued*

Clarke, A. C. A short acquaintance
Clayton, J. Jezeri and her beast go to the fair and find more excitement than they want
Cobb, I. S. Fishhead
Codrescu, A. Samba de los agentes
Cohen, A. Malenov's revenge
Cole, G. D. H., and Cole, M. The toys of death
Coleman, W. Dream 5281
Coleman, W. Kelele
Coleman, W. Word monkey
Colette. The murderer
Collins, M. The motive
Cortázar, J. Return trip tango
Cowper, R. Paradise beach
Coxe, G. H. Seed of suspicion
Craig, J. This day's evil
Crispin, E. We know you're busy writing, but we thought you wouldn't mind if we just dropped in for a minute
Curtiss, U. R. Good neighbor
Curtiss, U. R. The house on Plymouth Street
Curtiss, U. R. A judicious half inch
Curtiss, U. R. The old barn on the pond
Curtiss, U. R. Point of no return
Curtiss, U. R. The right perspective
Curtiss, U. R. Snowball
Dale, C. Business lunch
Dale, C. Good investments
Dale, C. Kindness
Daniels, L. They're coming for you
Davidson, L. I do dwell
Davidson, L. Indian rope trick
Davis, D. S. Born killer
Davis, D. S. By the scruff of the soul
Davis, D. S. The last party
Davis, D. S. Lost generation
Davis, D. S. Meeting at the crossroad
Davis, D. S. Natural causes
Davis, D. S. Spring fever
Davis, D. S. Till death do us part
Davis, S. A fair exchange
Davis, S. Miss Armstrong's homicide
Dawson, C. Supergrass
Dawson, C. To have and to hold
Day, R. C. Uccello
Dé, C., and Dandurand, A. Case still open
Deming, R. The better bargain
Derleth, A. W. House—with ghost
Dibble, J. B. To sleep, perchance to dream
Donson, C. Heat wave
Doyle, Sir A. C. The lonely Hampshire cottage
Doyle, Sir A. C. A pastoral horror
Doyle, Sir A. C. Uncle Jeremy's household
Drewe, R. The bodysurfers
DuBois, B. Final marks, final secrets
Dubus, A. Killings
Dubus, A. Townies
Dullas, I. Shanti, simple, sweet and— sinister!

Dullas, I. X marks the spot
Dunlap, S. Hit-and-run
Eberhart, M. G. Dangerous widows
El Rahman, M. A. Gentlemen eating gentlemen
Elflandsson, G. The devil don't dance with strangers
Ellenberger, D. The sewing machine
Ellin, S. The Blessington method
Ellin, S. The last bottle in the world
Ellin, S. The orderly world of Mr. Appleby
Ellison, H. Do-it-yourself
Epstein, L. The magic flute
Erskine-Lindop, A. The mistaken smile
Estleman, L. D. Bodyguards shoot second
Estleman, L. D. The tree on Execution Hill
Etchison, D. You can go now
Evans, J. Purple prose
Evans, M. Candles in the bottom of the pool
Everett, P. L. Esteban
Faulkner, W. Hand upon the waters
Faulkner, W. Pantaloon in black
Faulkner, W. A rose for Emily
Faulkner, W. Smoke
Faulkner, W. Wash
Ferrars, E. Instrument of justice
Ferreira, R. A date at nine
Ferreira, R. Facade
Ferreira, R. The gold chain
Ferreira, R. Twilight hunt
Fischer, C. E. Indian poker
Fish, R. L. Muldoon and the numbers game
Fisher, P. W. The pickup
Fisher, R. John Archer's nose
Fontana, D. C. Cut to: murder
Forester, C. S. The turning of the tide
Forsyth, F. There are no snakes in Ireland
Fox, G. Return to Venice
Fraser, A. Boots
Fraser, A. Death of an old dog
Fraser, A. Have a nice death
Fraser, A. Who would kill a cat?
Freeman, L. The last dream
Fremlin, C. Accommodation vacant
Fremlin, C. Bluebeard's key
Fremlin, C. A case of maximum need
Fremlin, C. Etiquette for dying
Fremlin, C. The holiday
Fremlin, C. The luck of the Devil
Fremlin, C. A strong shoulder to weep on
Fremlin, C. Test case
Gaines, E. J. Robert Louis Stevenson Banks, a.k.a. Chimley
Galsworthy, J. The neighbors
Gamble, J. S. Kansas
Gardner, C. S. The man who loved water
Gardner, M. At the feet of Karl Klodhopper
Garfield, B. Scrimshaw
Garfield, B. The view

MURDER STORIES—*Continued*

Garro, E. The tree
Gash, J. The Julian Mondays
Gates, D. China Blue
Gault, W. C. The cackle bladder
Gbadamosi, R. A. Death by the waterfall
Gifkins, M. The latter-day triumph of Graves
Gilbert, A. A day of encounters
Gilbert, D. The canoe
Gilbert, M. Audited and found correct
Gilchrist, E. The emancipator
Gilchrist, E. Memphis
Gilchrist, M. The manuscript of Francis Shackerley
Gilchrist, M. My friend
Gilchrist, M. Roxana runs lunatick
Gilford, C. B. The forgiving ghost
Gill, B. M. A certain kind of skill
Gill, B. M. Murder most kind
Godfrey, P. And turn the hour
Godfrey, P. The shadow behind the face
Godfrey, P. Time out of mind
Gordimer, N. Country lovers
Gores, J. Pahua
Gosling, P. The perfect alibi
Goulart, R. Out of the inkwell
Goyen, W. The white rooster
Graham, W. The circus
Greenwood, R. Charley Wales
Griffiths, E. Autumn crocus
Griffiths, E. The dead don't steal
Hamilton, N. Made for each other
Hanson, D. The whisper business
Harcourt, P. A box of books
Harrington, J. The au pair girl
Harrington, J. Birdbrain
Harrington, J. Night crawlers
Harris, H. The doctor afraid of blood
Hartley, L. P. The island
Hartley, L. P. The killing bottle
Hartley, L. P. The two Vaynes
Hartley, L. P. W.S.
Heald, T. The case of the frozen diplomat
Hecht, B. Miracle of the fifteen murderers
Heideman, E. M. Roger, Mr. Whilkie!
Hemingway, E. The butterfly and the tank
Henderson, M. R. Dream house
Henry, O. The clarion call
Hensley, J. L. The decision
Hensley, J. L. Dog man
Hensley, J. L. Finder
Hensley, J. L. On the rocks
Hensley, J. L. The retiree
Hensley, J. L. Searcher
Hensley, J. L. Tourist
Hensley, J. L. Truly yours, John R. Jacks
Highsmith, P. The black house
Highsmith, P. The button
Highsmith, P. The day of reckoning
Highsmith, P. Djemal's revenge
Highsmith, P. Eddie and the monkey robberies
Highsmith, P. Engine horse
Highsmith, P. Goat ride
Highsmith, P. Hamsters vs Websters
Highsmith, P. Harry: a ferret
Highsmith, P. Ming's biggest prey
Highsmith, P. The mobile bed-object
Highsmith, P. Not one of us
Highsmith, P. Old folks at home
Highsmith, P. A shot from nowhere
Highsmith, P. Something the cat dragged in
Highsmith, P. The terrapin
Highsmith, P. There I was, stuck with Bubsy
Hill, R. Auteur theory
Hill, R. The bull ring
Hill, R. Crowded hour
Hill, R. Poor Emma
Hill, R. The worst crime known to man
Hoch, E. D. Deceptions
Hoch, E. D. Dreaming is a lonely thing
Hoch, E. D. Last year's murder
Hoch, E. D. The man who came back
Hoch, E. D. The melting man
Hoch, E. D. Murder at the Bouchercon
Hoch, E. D. The problem of the Boston Common
Hoch, E. D. The problem of the county fair
Hoch, E. D. Too long at the fair
Hoch, E. D. Winter run
Hodge, J. A. Suicide, or murder?
Hogg, J. The barber of Duncow—a real ghost story
Hogg, J. The Cameronian preacher's tale
Hogg, J. The mysterious bride
Holding, J. A good kid
Holme, T. Dureddu
Honig, D. Voices in dead man's well
Hornung, E. W. The last laugh
Hornung, E. W. Wilful murder
Howard, C. Last chance in Singapore
Humphrey, W. Mouth of brass
Huxley, A. The Gioconda smile
Ikhlasi, W. Wondering who . . .
Ingalls, R. Captain Hendrik's story
Ingalls, R. People to people
Irish, W. The dancing detective
Irvine, R. R. A hard way to die
Irvine, R. R. In the dead hours
Jaffe, H. Persian lamb
Jahnn, H. H. The gardener
James, M. R. Lost hearts
James, P. D. The girl who loved graveyards
James, P. D. The victim
Jones, D. C. Raised in the wilderness
Juarez, H. The answer
Katz, S. Death of the band
Kauffman, J. Isn't it something?
Kelley, L. P. Jurisprudence
Kharal, N. The dead end
King, F. H. The tradesman
King, R. Malice in wonderland

MURDER STORIES—*Continued*

King, S. The ballad of the flexible bullet
King, S. Big wheels: a tale of the laundry game (milkman #2)
King, S. Cain rose up
King, S. Morning deliveries (milkman #1)
King, S. Nona
Kinsella, W. P. Dance me outside
Kipling, R. The return of Imray
Kipp, G. G. Lessons from a pro
Kirk, R. Lex Talionis
Kirk, R. The surly sullen bell
Kirk, R. What shadows we pursue
Kittredge, W. The soap bear
Kittredge, W. The underground river
Landolfi, T. The provincial night
Lang, A. Sweet smell of murder
Lannes, R. Goodbye, dark love
Lansdale, J. R. Duck hunt
Lansdale, J. R. Night they missed the horror show
Le Guin, U. K. Ile Forest
Leaton, A. Little pictures
Lemay, P. Blood and gold
Lennon, J. No flies on Frank
Leskov, N. S. Lady Macbeth of Mtsensk
Levinson, R., and Link, W. Child's play
Li, F.-Y. The tiger
Lispector, C. The solution
London, J. Make westing
London, J. Moon-face
Longrigg, R. The chair
Lopatin, J. Dominica
Lopatin, J. A murder history
Lopatin, J. The real life of Viviane Romance
Lovecraft, H. P. The Terrible Old Man
Lovesey, P. Arabella's answer
Lovesey, P. The secret lover
Lutz, J. Autumn madness
Lutz, J. Big game
Lutz, J. The butcher, the baker
Lutz, J. Close calls
Lutz, J. The day of the picnic
Lutz, J. Dead man
Lutz, J. Dear Dorie
Lutz, J. Deeper and deeper
Lutz, J. The explosives expert
Lutz, J. Games for adults
Lutz, J. Hand of fate
Lutz, J. In memory of . . .
Lutz, J. The landscape of dreams
Lutz, J. Mortal combat
Lutz, J. The music from downstairs
Lutz, J. No small problem
Lutz, J. The other runner
Lutz, J. The real shape of the coast
Lutz, J. The second shot
Lutz, J. The shooting of Curly Dan
Lutz, J. Something for the dark
Lutz, J. Something like murder
Lutz, J. Until you are dead
Lutz, J. The very best
Lutz, J. The weapon

Lutz, J. The wounded tiger
MacCall, L. Mrs. Henderson talks to God
MacDonald, J. D. Bimini kill
MacDonald, J. D. Hangover
Madden, D. Hidden symptoms
Mansfield, K. The woman at the store
Marlowe, S. The shill
Marryat, F. The legend of the bell rock
Matheson, R. The near departed
Matheson, R. C. Graduation
Matheson, R. C. Mobius
Matheson, R. C. Timed exposure
Matsumoto, S. Wait a year and a half
Matthews, J. Amos Bond, the gunsmith
Maugham, W. S. Before the party
Maupassant, G. de. The assassin
Maupassant, G. de. The deaf-mute
Maupassant, G. de. Little Louise Roque
Maupassant, G. de. Revenge
Maupassant, G. de. A wife's confession
Mayberry, F. V. No tomorrows
McBain, E. Sadie when she died
McCammon, R. R. Night calls the Green Falcon
McCloy, H. Chinoiserie
McCloy, H. The other side of the curtain
McClure, J. The last place on earth
McConnell, J. Germination period
McConnor, V. The house of crime
McCormack, E. P. No country for old men
McCoy, E. Henry's eighth
McElroy, C. J. Farm day
McGerr, P. In the clear
McGrath, P. Ambrose Syme
McGrath, P. The Arnold Crombeck story
McGrath, P. Blood and water
McGrath, P. Blood disease
McGrath, P. Marmilion
McGuane, T. Like a leaf
Montero, M. Thirteen and a turtle
Morris, W. The customs of the country
Mortimer, J. C. Rumpole and the expert witness
Mortimer, J. C. Rumpole and the heavy brigade
Mortimer, J. C. Rumpole and the sporting life
Mortimer, J. C. Rumpole and the winter break
Moussa, S. Benevolence
Mulder, M. San Diego dilemma
Muller, M. Sweet cactus wine
Munro, A. Fits
Muscillo, D. Sister Coxall's revenge
Natsuki, S. The pawnshop murder
Newman, K. Patricia's profession
Nielsen, H. The deadly Mrs. Haversham
Nielsen, H. Death scene
Nielsen, H. A woman is missing
Nielsen, H. You can't trust a man
Nolan, W. F. The final stone
Nolan, W. F. My name is Dolly

MURDER STORIES—*Continued*

Nolan, W. F. Pirate's moon
Oates, J. C. Fin de siècle
Oates, J. C. Haunted
Oates, J. C. Last days
Oates, J. C. Manslaughter
Oates, J. C. The white cat
Oates, J. C. The witness
O'Brien, F.-J. The diamond lens
O'Callaghan, M. The sweet old lady who sits in the park
Ocampo, S. The perfect crime
O'Connor, F. The comforts of home
O'Connor, F. A good man is hard to find
O'Connor, F. The Partridge festival
O'Cork, S. Well worth it
O'Donnell, P. The Soo girl charity
O'Hara, J. Fatimas and kisses
Olson, D. Blood relatives
Olson, D. Enter the stranger
Owens, B. A little piece of room
Palmer, S. Riddle of the marble blade
Palmieri, A. Force of habit
Paynter, J. The miracle
Piñera, V. A few beers
Poe, E. A. The cask of Amontillado
Poe, E. A. The imp of the perverse
Poe, E. A. The tell-tale heart
Porges, A. Dead drunk
Powell, T. I had a hunch, and . . .
Powell, T. Motive for murder
Powell, T. Till death do not us part
Price, A. The Chinaman's garden
Prichard, K. S. Painted finches
Pronzini, B. Buttermilk
Pronzini, B. Connoisseur
Pronzini, B. Dear poisoner
Pronzini, B. Don't spend it all in one place
Pronzini, B. For love
Pronzini, B. Here lies another blackmailer
Pronzini, B. Hero
Pronzini, B. His name was Legion
Pronzini, B. I don't understand it
Pronzini, B. The imperfect crime
Pronzini, B. Little lamb
Pronzini, B. Mrs. Rakubian
Pronzini, B. Outrageous
Pronzini, B. The pattern
Pronzini, B. Perfect timing
Pronzini, B. Putting the pieces back
Pronzini, B. Retirement
Pronzini, B. The same old grind
Pronzini, B. The storm tunnel
Pronzini, B. The terrarium principle
Pronzini, B. Thirst
Pronzini, B. Under the skin
Pronzini, B., and Kurland, M. Vanishing act
Pronzini, B., and Malzberg, B. N. Another burnt-out case
Pronzini, B., and Wallmann, J. M. The half-invisible man
Purdy, J. Ruthanna Elder

Rafferty, S. S. The Massachusetts peep-o'night
Rambach, P. Winter ends
Randall, M. Lapidary nights
Rathjen, C. H. A debt to Doc
Regent, P. Stepan
Rendell, R. Bribery and corruption
Rendell, R. The convolvulus clock
Rendell, R. A dark blue perfume
Rendell, R. Father's day
Rendell, R. Fen Hall
Rendell, R. Hare's house
Rendell, R. The irony of hate
Rendell, R. Loopy
Rendell, R. The new girl friend
Rendell, R. The orchard walls
Resnicow, H. Greater love than this . .

Rey Rosa, R. The beggar's knife
Rey Rosa, R. A widespread belief
Rice, J. The crossroads
Richards, J. Deadtime
Richardson, M. Tower of silence
Riddell, J. H., Mrs. A strange Christmas game
Ritchie, J. The $5,000 getaway
Ritchie, J. Anyone for murder?
Ritchie, J. The crime machine
Ritchie, J. Piggy bank killer
Ritchie, J. Sound alibi
Ritchie, J. The wastebasket
Robinson, K. S. The disguise
Rodoreda, M. The dolls' room
Romun, I. Christmas is over
Runyon, C. Hangover
Russell, R. Ding-dong, the lizard's dead
Ryan, A. Hear the whistle blowing
Sampson, R. Rain in Pinton County
Satterthwait, W. The smoke people
Saunders, C. R. Outsteppin' Fetchit
Savage, E. The man who liked noise
Sayers, D. L. The man who knew how
Schulberg, B. Murder on the waterfront
Schwob, M. Burke and Hare, murderers
Schwob, M. The veiled man
Sciascia, L. End game
Seidman, M. Perchance to dream
Sexson, L. Deer crossing
Shannon, D. Flash attachment
Shannon, D. Happy release
Shannon, D. Rannysore
Shannon, D. They will call it insane
Shea, M. Fat Face
Shea, M. Uncle Tuggs
Sheckley, J. Bargain cinema
Sheckley, R. The helping hand
Sheckley, R. The swamp
Shirley, J. Triggering
Silverberg, R. How they pass the time in Pelpel
Simenon, G. Blessed are the meek
Simmons, D. Carrion comfort
Simpson, D. Two's company

MURDER STORIES—*Continued*

Sims, G. Family butcher
Sims, G. Remember Mrs. Fitz
Sinclair, I. Brides of the pleiades
Sisk, F. Ashes for an urn
Sisk, F. The fly swatter
Sisk, F. The return of Crazy Bill
Slesar, H. A choice of witnesses
Slesar, H. I do not like thee, Dr. Feldman
Slesar, H. Item
Smith, J. Grief counselor
Smith, P. C. The crazy
Smith, P. C. The night Helen was killed
Spark, M. The Portobello Road
Speed, J. Fair's fair
St. James, B. The Valencia orange murder
Stead, C. The triskelion
Stevenson, R. L. The body snatchers
Stevenson, R. L. Markheim
Strand, M. The killer poet
Strieber, W. Vaudeville
Stuart, I. The steep dark stairs
Stubbs, J. The belvedere
Symons, J. The best chess player in the world
Symons, J. The birthmark
Symons, J. The boiler
Symons, J. The flaw
Symons, J. Has anybody here seen me?
Symons, J. Love affair
Tamer, Z. Small sun
Taylor, P. A. The swan-boat murder
Thomas, D. The true story
Thomas, D. The vest
Thomas, M. The Texan
Thompson, J. This world, then the fireworks
Thompson, K. A local hanging
Thomson, J. Dead ground
Tobey, F. S. You drive, dear
Tournier, M. The red dwarf
Treat, L. Give the devil his due
Treat, L. Who's innocent?
Tripp, M. Fixation
Twain, M. The facts concerning the recent carnival of crime in Connecticut
Tyre, N. Carnival day
Tyre, N. A nice place to stay
Tyre, N. Reflections on murder
Underwood, M. OK for murder
Vachss, A. H. It's a hard world
Van de Wetering, J. A tasty tidbit
Varley, J. Manikins
Vizyēnos, G. M. Who was my brother's killer?
Wainwright, J. W. A wise child
Walter, E. Christmas night
Wasylyk, S. Funeral in a small town
Wellen, E. Born victims
Wellen, E. Hit or miss
Wells, H. G. The cone
Wendt, A. Justice
Westlake, D. E. Never shake a family tree
Wheatcroft, J. Kamikaze

Wheeler, H. C. All the way to the moon
Whitehead, H. S. C. The fireplace
Whittington, H. B. Swamp search
Williams, A. Being a murderer myself
Williams, D. The bully
Williams, D. Three's a crowd
Willis, C. The Sidon in the mirror
Willis, T. The gallows
Willis, T. The man from the White Mountains
Wilmot, T. The last of the midnight gardeners
Wilmot, T. Open and shut case
Wilson, H. Please, no strawberries
Wolfe, G. Redbeard
Wolfe, T. The child by tiger
Woods, S. Every tale condemns me
Woolrich, C. The corpse and the kid
Woolrich, C. The dancing detective
Woolrich, C. Death at the Burlesque
Woolrich, C. Fire escape
Woolrich, C. Momentum
Wright, B. R. The invisible cat
Wright, B. R. Morning song
Wright, B. R. Sweet remembrance
Wright, R. The man who killed a shadow
Yarbro, C. Q. Do not forsake me, O my darlin'
Zangwill, I. The big Bow mystery

MURDER TRIALS *See* Trials
Murder under the microscope. Russell, W.
Murder walks in marble halls. Blochman, L. G.
Murder while you wait. Brown, F.
Murder will in. Herbert, F.
The **murderer**. Colette
The **murderer** guest. Gordon, M.
MURDERERS
　　See also Murder stories
Algren, N. A bottle of milk for mother
Barnard, R. Little Terror
Bausch, R. The man who knew Belle Starr
Beekman, E. M. Frisian horses
Bird, C. Higher animals
Boucher, A. Elsewhen
Bradbury, R. At midnight, in the month of June
Bukoski, A. Twelve below zero
Cadigan, P. The edge
Carter, A. The Fall River axe murders
Colette. The omelette
Crichton Smith, I. Timoshenko
Dale, C. Faery tale
De Queiroz, R. Metonymy; or, The husband's revenge
Dickens, C. A confession found in a prison in the time of Charles the Second
Dickens, C. The hanged man's bride
Dowell, C. The surgeon
Doyle, Sir A. C. The mystery of the lost special
Dubus, A. Rose

MURDERERS—*Continued*
Ellison, H. Deal from the bottom
Eskapa, S. Between the sheets
Forrest, K. V. Benny's place
Glasgow, E. The shadowy third
Gordon, M. The murderer guest
Greenwood, R. Archetypes
Haldeman, J. W. The monster
Hogg, J. The Brownie of the Black Haggs
Hulme, K. Kiteflying party at Doctors' Point
Jaffe, H. Sheep
Koea, S. Meat
Kuttner, H. Home is the hunter
Laidlaw, M. Muzak for torso murders
Landolfi, T. Uxoricide
London, J. Which make men remember
Marryat, F. The legend of the bell rock
Maupassant, G. de. The man with the blue eyes
McDowell, M. Halley's passing
Oates, J. C. Testimony
Painter, P. Patterns
Paynter, J. Fifty-eight cents
Pizarnik, A. The bloody countess
Poe, E. A. The black cat
Pouvoir, J. L. The death triple
Rampo, E. The psychological test
Reimer, I. Murder on the flux line
Shiner, L. Love in vain
Smith, P. C. The patchwork quilt
Sodowsky, R. E. Landlady
Straub, P. Blue rose
Sullivan, T. Knucklebones
Taylor, B. Forget-me-not
Valenzuela, L. The word "killer"
Wagner, K. E. An awareness of angels
White, C. You've changed
Wideman, J. E. Tommy
Williams, T. One arm
Winton, T. Scission
Murderers. Michaels, L.
Murderers don't cook for themselves. Klass, P.
The **murders** in the Rue Morgue. Poe, E. A.

Murguía, Julián
The old gaucho
Américas 38:50-2 Mr/Ap '86
Murke's collected silences. Böll, H.

Murnane, Gerald, 1939-
Land deal
Transgressions; ed. by D. Anderson
Murnane and the Illinois. Gibson, W.

Murphy, Douglas
Roller
Bringing down the moon; ed. by J. Anderson

Murphy, G. Read
War
Australian science fiction; ed. by V. Ikin

Murphy, Michael, 1930-
Lesson number one
Missouri short fiction; ed. by C. Beasley
Murphy, Pat
Art in the war zone
Universe 14
In the islands
Amazing stories: 60 years of the best science fiction
The Year's best science fiction, first annual collection
Rachel in love
The Year's best science fiction, fifth annual collection
With four lean hounds
Young witches & warlocks; ed. by I. Asimov; M. H. Greenberg and C. G. Waugh
Murphy, Peter, 1945-
The alarm system
Murphy, P. The moving shadow problem
The appointment
Murphy, P. The moving shadow problem
Approaching substance
Murphy, P. The moving shadow problem
Beyond the moving shadow problem
Murphy, P. The moving shadow problem
Cane toads
Murphy, P. The moving shadow problem
The chapter on love
Murphy, P. The moving shadow problem
Checking in
Murphy, P. The moving shadow problem
The cleaner
Murphy, P. The moving shadow problem
Cross purposes
Murphy, P. The moving shadow problem
Getting out
Murphy, P. The moving shadow problem
The Irish information office
Murphy, P. The moving shadow problem
Jester
Murphy, P. The moving shadow problem
The little American executive
Murphy, P. The moving shadow problem
Looking for work
Murphy, P. The moving shadow problem

Murphy, Peter, 1945-—Continued
Master of ceremonies
Murphy, P. The moving shadow problem
Meeting the head examiner
Murphy, P. The moving shadow problem
The Santa class test
Murphy, P. The moving shadow problem
The small businessman's wife
Murphy, P. The moving shadow problem
Terminals
Murphy, P. The moving shadow problem
Murphy, Robert
The land beyond
The Saturday Evening Post 260:44-7+ Mr '88
The Saturday Evening Post 260:26+ Ap '88
The warmhearted polar bear
The Saturday Evening Post 260:62-5+ D '88
Murphy, Thomas M.
The answers they have
Stories and poems from close to home; ed. by F. Salas
Murphy, Warren
An element of surprise
Murder in Manhattan; ed. by B. Adler
Murphy, Yannick
Ball and socket
Murphy, Y. Stories in another language
Believer in death
Murphy, Y. Stories in another language
The children inside the trunk
Murphy, Y. Stories in another language
The escape
Murphy, Y. Stories in another language
A good father
Murphy, Y. Stories in another language
The headdress
The Antioch Review 44:481-5 Fall '86
Murphy, Y. Stories in another language
The killer
Murphy, Y. Stories in another language
Laws of nature
Murphy, Y. Stories in another language
Mercury
The Antioch Review 44:105-10 Wint '86
Murphy, Y. Stories in another language
Red, red
Murphy, Y. Stories in another language
Rough seas
Murphy, Y. Stories in another language
The slit
Murphy, Y. Stories in another language
Stories in another language
Murphy, Y. Stories in another language
The summer the men landed on the moon
Murphy, Y. Stories in another language
Tidal air
Murphy, Y. Stories in another language

Southwest Review 71:512-16 Aut '86
The toys
Murphy, Y. Stories in another language
Where dead is best
Murphy, Y. Stories in another language
Murphy. Silvis, R.
Murphy Walls and the Oriental hummer. Hall, T. T.
Murray, Albert
Gasoline Point, Alabama
The Art of fiction in the heart of Dixie; ed. by P. D. Beidler
Murray, Carole
In the Year of the Mouse
The North American Review 272:102-3 S '87
Murray, Wendell Carl
Desire, and other topics
Homewords: a book of Tennessee writers; ed. by D. Paschall
Murrey, Mary
Dream evolution
The North American Review 271:47-51 S '86
Muschg, Adolf, 1934-
The blue man
Muschg, A. The blue man, and other stories
Brami's view
Muschg, A. The blue man, and other stories
The country house; or, Defaulted presence
Muschg, A. The blue man, and other stories
Dinnertime
Muschg, A. The blue man, and other stories
Grandfather's little pleasure
Muschg, A. The blue man, and other stories
Reparations; or, Making good
Muschg, A. The blue man, and other stories
The scythe hand; or, The homestead
Muschg, A. The blue man, and other stories
Muscillo, Dawn
Sister Coxall's revenge
The Penguin book of horror stories
The **museum.** Richardson, M.
MUSEUMS
See also Waxworks
Bail, M. Portrait of electricity
Barthelme, D. At the Tolstoy Museum
Faust, I. Simon Girty go ape
Hornung, E. W. A Jubilee present
Hornung, E. W. The raffles relics
Nabokov, V. V. The visit to the museum
The **Musgrave** ritual. Doyle, Sir A. C.
MUSIC
See also Popular music
Dick, P. K. The Preserving Machine
Dybek, S. Chopin in winter

MUSIC—*Continued*
Lutz, J. The music from downstairs
Silverberg, R. The Macauley circuit

MUSIC, POPULAR *See* Popular music
Music. Gilchrist, E.
Music. Trevor, W.
The **music-box**. Whitaker, M.

MUSIC CRITICS
Baxter, C. Harmony of the world
The **music** from downstairs. Lutz, J.

MUSIC HALL ENTERTAINERS *See* Entertainers

MUSIC HALLS (VARIETY THEATERS, CABARETS, ETC.)
Colette. "La Fenice"
Colette. Gribiche
Colette. The misfit
Colette. The quick-change artist
Colette. "The strike, oh, Lord, the strike!"
Oates, J. C. Señorita
Woolrich, C. Death at the Burlesque
Music lesson. Hall, M. L.
The **music** of Erich Zann. Lovecraft, H. P.
Music of the spheres. Epstein, L.
The **music** of the spheres. Tournier, M.
The **music** of the violin. Ndebele, N.
Music story. Pulaski, J.
The **music** teacher. Cheever, J.
The **music** teacher. Klobouk, J.

MUSIC TEACHERS
Baxter, C. Gershwin's second prelude
Carter, M. Teacher
Cheever, J. The music teacher
Cohen, M. At the Empress Hotel
Dadswell, M. Mr. Macnamee
Drake, R. I am counting with you all the way
Hall, M. L. Doll
Hunnicutt, E. At St. Theresa's College for Women
Hunnicutt, E. Bargaining
Hunnicutt, E. There is a balm in Gilead
Jhabvala, R. P. The housewife
Lewis, T. Vincristine
Mazel, D. An invitation
McCullers, C. Madame Zilensky and the King of Finland
McCullers, C. Wunderkind
Petrakis, H. M. The eyes of love
Schwartz, L. S. The middle classes
Thompson, J. Naomi counting time
Zwicky, F. Hostages
Musical beds. Rule, J.
Musical evenings. Kelm, K.

MUSICAL INSTRUMENTS
Whitaker, M. The music-box
A **musical** interlude. Charnas, S. M.
Musical overdoses. Tallis, R.

MUSICIANS
See also Accordionists; Cellists; Clarinetists; Conductors (Music); Drummers; Flutists; Guitarists; Harpists; Oboe players; Organists; Pianists; Saxophonists; Trombonists; Trumpet players; Violinists
Abish, W. Happiness
Asscher-Pinkhof, C. Dance
Barich, B. Too much electricity
Bishop, M. Out of the mouths of Olympus
Bishop, M. Vox Olympica
Cade, T. Mississippi Ham Rider
Chekhov, A. P. Rothschild's fiddle
Ch'en, Y.-C. A couple of generals
Coleman, W. Take it up at the bridge
Dawson, F. The blue in the sky
Dawson, F. Miles
Dumas, H. Will the circle be unbroken?
Eichendorff, J., Freiherr von. Memoirs of a good-for-nothing
Epstein, L. The magic flute
Epstein, L. Music of the spheres
Epstein, L. The Steinway quintet
Fisher, R. Common meter
Gallant, M. Bonaventure
Gingher, M. The hummingbird kimono
Gray, P. W. Too soon solos
Hall, D. The world is a bed
Hall, T. T. From Hank in Nashville
Herbert, F. Passage for piano
Hood, M. Lonesome road blues
King, S. The wedding gig
King, T. Boogie Man
MacDonald, D. R. Work
Mathers, P. The chemical works
Matthew, J. R. Bar song
Moss, R. Exile
Ndebele, N. Uncle
Neville, S. Rondo
Nussey, K. In Christ there is no east or west
Patchett, A. All little colored children should play the harmonica
Plumpp, S. Mighty long time
Proulx, A. Heart songs
Ryan, A. The bones wizard
Shacochis, B. I ate her heart
Sorrells, R. T. Three rivers
Thompson, S. Notes
Vreuls, D. Boys and music
Waldrop, H. Ike at the mike
Wellman, M. W. The little black train
Winton, T. Gravity
Yarbro, C. Q. Cabin 33
Musk-Ox. Leskov, N. S.

MUSLIM WOMEN
Rifaat, A. Badriyya and her husband
Rifaat, A. Bahiyya's eyes
Rifaat, A. Distant view of a minaret
Rifaat, A. An incident in the Ghobashi household
Rifaat, A. Just another day

MUSLIM WOMEN—*Continued*
Rifaat, A. The kite
Rifaat, A. Telephone call
MUSLIMS
    See also Islam; Muslim women
Bates, A. J. A ceremony of innocence
Bowles, J. A. Everything is nice
Bowles, P. He of the assembly
Bowles, P. The time of friendship
Essop, A. Aziz Khan
Essop, A. The betrayal
Essop, A. Film
Essop, A. Gladiators
Essop, A. The Hajji
Essop, A. Hajji Musa and the Hindu fire-
    walker
Essop, A. The target
Izgü, M. Devoted Moslem Ismail Effendi
Owoyele, D. The will of Allah
Şālih, al-Ṭ. A handful of dates
Sembene, O. The false prophet
Mussel. Jaffe, H.
Must. Asscher-Pinkhof, C.
MUSTACHE
Maupassant, G. de. Good reasons
Mrożek, S. A forester in love
The **mustard** plaster. Bessette, G.
The **mutant** season. Silverberg, R.
MUTATION (BIOLOGY)
    See also Albinos
Aldiss, B. W. Hothouse
Anderson, P. Tomorrow's children
Bear, G. Blood music
Byram, G. The wonder horse
Donaldson, S. R. Mythological beast
Hamilton, E. He that hath wings
Jones, R. F. The children's room
Knight, D. F. Four in one
Murphy, P. In the islands
Neville, K. Underground movement
Rebetez-Cortes, R. The new prehistory
Reynolds, M. Optical illusion
Silverberg, R. The mutant season
Silverberg, R. This is the road
Wolfe, G. Seven American nights
The **mute** companions. Narayan, R. K.
MUTE PERSONS
Brown, G. M. Lord of silence
Hoyt, M. S. The monastery floor
Keller, D. H. The lost language
Kye, Y.-M. Adada the idiot
Marechera, D. The slow sound of his feet
Maupassant, G. de. The deaf-mute
Sandel, C. Bernhardt
The **muted** horn. Davis, D. S.
The **muted** love song of Edvard Nils. Lurie,
    M.
MUTILATION
Jahnn, H. H. The diver
Jahnn, H. H. The slave's story
Williamson, B. The toy killer
MUTINY
Doyle, Sir A. C. The Gloria Scott

Doyle, Sir A. C. A true story of the
    tragedy of Flowery Land
Melville, H. Benito Cereno
Melville, H. Billy Budd, Sailor
Thomason, J. Mutiny
Wouk, H. The mutiny
Mutiny. Thomason, J.
The **mutiny**. Wouk, H.
Muttsy. Hurston, Z. N.
Mutual of Omaha. Gordon, G.
Muzak for torso murders. Laidlaw, M.
My adventure in Norfolk. Alan, A. J.
My ancestor—Don Pedro. Chavez, A.
My Aunt Ella. Heise, K.
My belongings. Endō, S.
My bird doesn't sing anymore. Winters, J.
My brother. El-Bisatie, M.
My brother and the perfect people. Weaver,
    G.
My brother down there. Frazee, S.
My Christina. Rodoreda, M.
My Coney Island uncle. Swados, H.
My corset maker. Colette
My country. Klíma, I.
My country 'tis not only of thee. Aldiss, B.
    W.
My cousin comes to Jo'burg. Mzamane, M.
My cousin Veronica. Lipman, E.
My daughter is called Giulia too. Moravia,
    A.
My daughter, the murderer. Boylan, E.
My dear Emily. Russ, J.
My dear Uncle Sherlock. Pentecost, H.
My dream of flying to Wake Island. Ballard,
    J. G.
My enemy's enemy. Amis, K.
My escaped convict. Honig, D.
My everyday colt. Valenzuela, L.
My expensive leg. Böll, H.
My father and Signor Corelli. Briskin, M.
My father, at the wheel. Willett, J.
My father sits in the dark. Weidman, J.
My father, the cat. Slesar, H.
My father's axe. Winton, T.
My father's confession. Heise, K.
My father's cough. Böll, H.
My father's friends. Maxwell, W.
My father's God. Fante, J.
My father's laugh. Ardizzone, T.
My father's moon. Jolley, E.
My father's second home. Faik, S.
My father's son. Havemann, E.
My father's version of the nurses' story.
    Windsor, G.
My final adventure. Tamer, Z.
My first aeroplane. Wells, H. G.
My first and only house. Adams, A.
My first goose. Babel', I.
My first marriage. Jhabvala, R. P.
My first script. Burns, E.
My flannel knickers. Carrington, L.
My friend. Gilchrist, M.
My friend, Lafe Tilly. Stead, C.

My friend who lives in a commune. Spivack, K.

My girl in skintight jeans. Boyd, W.

My goddaughter. Colette

My grandfather. Barnea, L.

My grandmother's japonicas. Beaumont, C.

My greatest ambition. Lurie, M.

My hands. Maraini, D.

My hometown is gone—I mean gone. Winters, J.

My idiot uncle. Chae, M.-S.

My journal as the fishwoman. Thomas, J.

My kid brother, K'ang-hsiung. Ch'en, Y.-C.

My kinsman, Major Molineux. Hawthorne, N.

My landlady. Maupassant, G. de

My last flight south. Winters, J.

My latest sun. Wiebe, D. E.

My life. Chekhov, A. P.

My life as a born-again pig. Pohl, F.

My life at Magnum. McDonald, C.

My life in the jungle. Aikin, J.

My life on the snowplow. Freeman, C.

My life up till now. Dixon, S.

My livelihood. Dickinson, C.

My love affair with English. See Apple, M. The American bakery

My love affair with James I. Tremain, R.

My maiden brief. Gilbert, W. S.

My man Bovanne. Bambara, T. C.

My milk goes dry. Minh-Quan

My mistress. Colwin, L.

My mother has me surrounded. Kauffman, J.

My mother is a cow. Carrington, L.

My mother was a witch. Tenn, W.

My mother's clothes: the school of beauty and shame. McCann, R.

My mother's confession. Gingher, M.

My mother's goofy song. Fante, J.

My mother's memoirs, my father's lie, and other true stories. Banks, R.

My mother's mother. O'Brien, E.

My mother's night out. See Steele, M. The hat of my mother

My mother's piano. Harrison, S.

My mother's secret life. Brett, S. A.

My mother's sin. Vizyēnos, G. M.

My mother's stories. Ardizzone, T.

My name is Dolly. Nolan, W. F.

My name is Yon Yonson. Keillor, G.

My neighbour's death. Loukakis, A.

My old man. Hemingway, E.

My other grandmother. Walsh, T.

My pal with the long hair. Böll, H.

My perseus. Gault, C.

My picture left in Scotland. Garrett, G. P.

My platonic sweetheart. Twain, M.

My queer Dean! Queen, E.

My real estate. Apple, M.

My Richard. Heym, S.

My romance. Shyer, M. F.

My room. Padgett, R.

My rose and my glove. Jacobs, H.

My sad face. Böll, H.

My shadow is the fog. Grant, C. L.

My sister, my self. Van Name, M. L.

My sister the bride. Shamosh, A.

My sister's brother. Farmer, P. J.

My sister's marriage. Rich, C.

My son the murderer. Malamud, B.

My son, the physicist. Asimov, I.

My summer scenes. Ahern, T.

My sweetheart's house. Drake, R.

My true story. Lish, G.

My twenty-five days. Maupassant, G. de

My Uncle Fred. Böll, H.

My uncle Sosthenes. Maupassant, G. de

My uncle's stories. Mrożek, S.

My uncle's story. Norris, L.

My Warszawa: 1980. Oates, J. C.

My wartime job. Saiki, J.

My wife. Chekhov, A. P.

My wife is a White Russian. Tremain, R.

My work in California. Hall, J. B.

My world of the unknown. Rifaat, A.

Myers, Lou
  A Lazofsky
  The New Yorker 63:22-4 Ja 4 '88

Myles *See* O'Brien, Flann, 1911-1966

The myna birds. McQueen, J.

Myśliwski, Wieslaw
  Stone upon stone
  Short story international 68

MYSORE (INDIA) *See* India—Mysore

The mysteries of banking. Mooney, M.

The mysteries of life in an orderly manner. West, J.

The mysteries of the Joy Rio. Williams, T.

The mysterious bride. Hogg, J.

The mysterious case of Miss V. Woolf, V.

The mysterious case of R. Conroy, F.

The mysterious cure. Jeppson, J. O.

Mysterious Kôr. Bowen, E.

The mysterious portrait. See Gogol', N. V. The portrait

The mysterious railway-passenger. Leblanc, M.

The mysterious secret. Blinkin, M.

Mysterious Smith. Gardner, M.

The Mysterious stranger
  Vampires; ed. by A. Ryan

Mystery. Parise, G.

A mystery. Sandel, C.

MYSTERY AND DETECTIVE STORIES
    See also Crime and criminals; International intrigue; Murder stories

Asimov, I. The magic umbrella

Asimov, I. Never out of sight

Asimov, I. The speck

Charteris, L. The sizzling saboteur

Chisholm, L. Someone else's house

Christie, A. The apples of the Hesperides

Christie, A. The Arcadian Deer

Christie, A. Problem at sea

Christie, A. The Stymphalean birds

MYSTERY AND DETECTIVE STORIES
—*Continued*

Davis, D. S. A matter of public notice
Dumonte, E. Mr. Reed goes to dinner
Futrelle, J. The phantom motor
Gardner, M. Private Eye Oglesby
Garrett, R. A little intelligence
Hoch, E. D. The magic bullet
Hodgson, W. H. The finding of the Graiken
Hornung, E. W. The gift of the emperor
Maupassant, G. de. The ill-omened groom
McCormack, E. P. Eckhardt at a window
Pronzini, B. Strangers in the fog
Pronzini, B., and Malzberg, B. N. Prose Bowl
Queen, E. Cold money
Rawson, C. Off the face of the earth
Rinehart, M. R. The splinter
Robinson, K. S. Mercurial
Wolfe, G. Slaves of silver

Australia
Moorhead, F. Waiting for Colombo: a close-up

Austria
Pronzini, B. The web

Bahamas
Stephens, W. M. Water Witch

Bahrain
Pachter, J. The beer drinkers
Pachter, J. The Dilmun Exchange
Pachter, J. The night of power

Belgium
Christie, A. The chocolate box

Brazil
Hoch, E. D. The mummy from the sea

Canada
Bankier, W. Beliveau pays
Bankier, W. The dog who hated jazz
Johnson, W. R. White water

Canary Islands
Christie, A. The companion

China
Gulik, R. H. van. The coffins of the Emperor
Gulik, R. H. van. The murder on the lotus pond

Czechoslovakia
Škvorecký, J. Aristotelian logic
Škvorecký, J. The case of the horizontal trajectory
Škvorecký, J. Crime in a girls' high school
Škvorecký, J. Death on needlepoint
Škvorecký, J. The end of an old tom-cat
Škvorecký, J. His easiest case
Škvorecký, J. The scientific method
Škvorecký, J. The supernatural powers of Lieutenant Boruvka
Škvorecký, J. That sax solo
Škvorecký, J. Whose deduction?

Egypt
Christie, A. The adventure of the Egyptian tomb

England
Ambler, E. The case of the emerald sky
Ambler, E. Case of the gentlemen poet
Anderson, P., and Dickson, G. R. The adventure of the misplaced hound
Bentley, E. C. The unknown peer
Bodkin, M. M. Murder by proxy
Bramah, E. The coin of Dionysius
Brand, C. Double cross
Breen, J. L. The adventure of the unique Holmes
Brett, S. The haunted actress
Brett, S. Tickled to death
Carr, J. D. The house in Goblin Wood
Carr, J. D. Invisible hands
Carr, J. D. The proverbial murder
Chesterton, G. K. The blue cross
Chesterton, G. K. The bottomless well
Chesterton, G. K. The Donnington affair [Father Brown solves]
Chesterton, G. K. The Donnington affair [Max Pemberton presents the puzzle of]
Chesterton, G. K. The garden of smoke
Chesterton, G. K. The hole in the wall
Chesterton, G. K. The invisible man
Chesterton, G. K. The shadow of the shark
Chesterton, G. K. The singular speculation of the house agent
Chesterton, G. K. The three horsemen of the apocalypse
Chesterton, G. K. The tremendous adventure of Major Brown
Chesterton, G. K. When doctors agree
Chesterton, G. K. The White Pillars murder
Chesterton, G. K. The wrong shape
Christie, A. The adventure of Johnnie Waverly
Christie, A. The adventure of the cheap flat
Christie, A. The adventure of the Clapham cook
Christie, A. The adventure of the Italian nobleman
Christie, A. The adventure of "The Western Star"
Christie, A. The affair at the bungalow
Christie, A. The affair at the victory ball
Christie, A. The Augean stables
Christie, A. The bloodstained pavement
Christie, A. The blue geranium
Christie, A. The capture of Cerberus
Christie, A. The case of the caretaker
Christie, A. The case of the perfect maid
Christie, A. A Christmas tragedy
Christie, A. The Cornish mystery
Christie, A. The Cretan bull
Christie, A. Dead man's mirror
Christie, A. Death by drowning
Christie, A. The disappearance of Mr. Davenheim

MYSTERY AND DETECTIVE STORIES
—England—*Continued*

Christie, A. The double clue
Christie, A. Double sin
Christie, A. The dream
Christie, A. The flock of Geryon
Christie, A. Four-and-twenty blackbirds
Christie, A. The four suspects
Christie, A. The Girdle of Hyppolita
Christie, A. The girl in the train
Christie, A. Greenshaw's Folly
Christie, A. The harlequin tea set
Christie, A. The herb of death
Christie, A. The horses of Diomedes
Christie, A. How does your garden grow?
Christie, A. The Idol House of Astarte
Christie, A. The incredible theft
Christie, A. Ingots of gold
Christie, A. The jewel robbery at the Grand Metropolitan
Christie, A. The kidnapped Prime Minister
Christie, A. The king of clubs
Christie, A. The Lemesurier inheritance
Christie, A. The Lernean Hydra
Christie, A. The lost mine
Christie, A. The Market Basing mystery
Christie, A. The million dollar bond robbery
Christie, A. Miss Marple tells a story
Christie, A. Motive v. opportunity
Christie, A. Murder in the mews
Christie, A. The mystery of Hunter's Lodge
Christie, A. The mystery of the Bagdad Chest
Christie, A. The Nemean lion
Christie, A. The Plymouth Express
Christie, A. Sanctuary
Christie, A. Strange jest
Christie, A. The submarine plans
Christie, A. Tape-measure murder
Christie, A. The theft of the royal ruby
Christie, A. The third-floor flat
Christie, A. The thumbmark of St. Peter
Christie, A. The tragedy at Marsdon Manor
Christie, A. The Tuesday Night Club
Christie, A. The under dog
Christie, A. The veiled lady
Christie, A. Wasps' nest
Christie, A. Yellow Iris
Collins, W. The biter bit
Crispin, E. The hunchback cat
Crispin, E., and Bush, G. Who killed Baker?
Crowley, A. Big game
Crowley, A. The conduct of John Briggs
Crowley, A. Ineligible
Crowley, A. Not good enough
Crowley, A. Outside the bank's routine
De la Torre, L. The adventure of the persistent marksman
De la Torre, L. The first locked room
De la Torre, L. Milady bigamy
De la Torre, L. The second sight of Dr. Sam: Johnson
Derleth, A. W. The adventure of the spurious Tamerlane
Dickens, C. A pair of gloves
Dickens, C. To be read at dusk
Dirckx, J. H. The adventure of the oval window
Doyle, Sir A. C. The adventure of the Beryl Coronet
Doyle, Sir A. C. The adventure of the blue carbuncle
Doyle, Sir A. C. The adventure of the Bruce-Partington plans
Doyle, Sir A. C. The adventure of the copper beeches
Doyle, Sir A. C. The adventure of the devil's foot
Doyle, Sir A. C. The adventure of the engineer's thumb
Doyle, Sir A. C. The adventure of the noble bachelor
Doyle, Sir A. C. The adventure of the speckled band
Doyle, Sir A. C. The Boscombe Valley mystery
Doyle, Sir A. C. The cardboard box
Doyle, Sir A. C. A case of identity
Doyle, Sir A. C. The copper beeches
Doyle, Sir A. C. The crooked man
Doyle, Sir A. C. The final problem
Doyle, Sir A. C. The five orange pips
Doyle, Sir A. C. The Gloria Scott
Doyle, Sir A. C. The Greek interpreter
Doyle, Sir A. C. The man with the twisted lip
Doyle, Sir A. C. The Musgrave ritual
Doyle, Sir A. C. The mystery of the lost special
Doyle, Sir A. C. The naval treaty
Doyle, Sir A. C. The red-headed league
Doyle, Sir A. C. The reigate squires
Doyle, Sir A. C. The resident patient
Doyle, Sir A. C. A scandal in Bohemia
Doyle, Sir A. C. Silver Blaze
Doyle, Sir A. C. The stockbroker's clerk
Doyle, Sir A. C. The yellow face
Dunsany, E. J. M. D. P., Baron. The two bottles of relish
Farmer, P. J. The problem of the sore bridge—among others
Ferrars, E. X. A very small clue
Fraser, A. The case of the Parr children
Fraser, A. Doctor Zeit
Fraser, A. House poison
Fraser, A. Swimming will be the death of you
Fraser, A. Your appointment is cancelled
Gilbert, M. Breach of the peace
Gilbert, M. Cash in hand
Gilbert, M. The Coulman handicap
Gilbert, M. Dangerous structure

MYSTERY AND DETECTIVE STORIES
—England—*Continued*

Gilbert, M. Death watch
Gilbert, M. The happy brotherhood
Gilbert, M. The king in pawn
Gilbert, M. Lost leader
Gilbert, M. The night the cat stayed out
Gilbert, M. Nothing ever happens on Highside
Gilbert, M. The oyster catcher
Gilbert, M. Paris in summer
Gilbert, M. The prophet and the bird
Gilbert, M. The Sark Lane Mission
Gilbert, M. A sense of history
Gilbert, M. Source seven
Gilbert, M. The two footmen
Gilbert, M. Voyage into illusion
Gilbert, M. Who has seen the wind?
Harrington, J. The adventure of the Gowanus abduction
Harris, H. Death at the barbecue
Harrison, M. Sherlock Holmes and "The woman": an explanatory memoir by Dr. John H. Watson, MD.
Hill, R. Bring back the cat!
Hoch, E. D. The return of the speckled band
Hoch, E. D. The treasure of Jack the Ripper
Hoch, E. D. The Vicar of Hell
Hornung, E. W. Nine points of the law
Hornung, E. W. The return match
Hughes, D. B. F. Sherlock Holmes and the muffin
Innes, M. Tragedy of a handkerchief
James, P. D. Great Aunt Allie's flypapers
James, P. D. The murder of Santa Claus
Jones, B. The shadows on the lawn: an adventure of Sherlock Holmes
Kaminsky, S. M. The final toast
Keating, H. R. F. Caught and bowled, Mrs. Craggs
Keating, H. R. F. A dangerous thing, Mrs. Craggs
Keating, H. R. F. The five senses of Mrs. Craggs
Keating, H. R. F. Mrs. Craggs and a certain lady's town house
Keating, H. R. F. Mrs. Craggs and a sad case of simony
Keating, H. R. F. Mrs. Craggs and the late Prince Albert
Keating, H. R. F. Mrs. Craggs and the living dead
Keating, H. R. F. Mrs. Craggs and the Lords spiritual and temporal
Keating, H. R. F. Mrs. Craggs and the pale Ella
Keating, H. R. F. Mrs. Craggs and the round blue immortals
Keating, H. R. F. Mrs. Craggs gives a dose of physic
Keating, H. R. F. Mrs. Craggs hears the nightingale
Keating, H. R. F. Mrs. Craggs sings a different tune
Keating, H. R. F. Mrs. Craggs's sixth sense
Keating, H. R. F. The Old Haddock
King, S. The doctor's case
Lamburn, N. Tom's thatch
Lewin, M. Z. The reluctant detective
Lovesey, P. The curious computer
Lutz, J. The infernal machine
Marsh, Dame N. Chapter and verse
Marsh, Dame N. Death on the air
Marsh, Dame N. I can find my way out
Meade, L. T., and Eustace, R. The man who disappeared
Morrison, A. The affair of the 'Avalanche Bicycle and Tyre Co., Limited'
Moyes, P. The holly wreath
O'Donnell, P. I had a date with Lady Janet
Perowne, B. Knowing what I know now
Perowne, B. Raffles on the trail of the hound
Peters, E. Come to dust
Peters, E. A light on the road to Woodstock
Powell, J. Death in the Christmas hour
Reynolds, M. The adventure of the extraterrestrial
Ruse, G. A. The phantom chamber
Russell, W. Murder under the microscope
Saberhagen, F. Adventure of the metal murderer
Sale, R. The House of Kaa
Saunders, C. M. The wax witness
Sayers, D. L. The Dragon's head
Sayers, D. L. The necklace of pearls
Sayers, D. L. The queen's square
Symons, J. Credit to Shakespeare
Vickers, R. The man who murdered in public
Wellen, E. The house that Jack built
Wellen, E. Voiceover
Wynne, A. The Cyprian bees

France

Allen, G. The episode of the Mexican seer
Carraud, J. For piano and vocal accompaniment
Chesterton, G. K. The finger of stone
Crowley, A. The artistic temperament
Dearmore, E. The adventure of the perpetual husbands
Decrest, J. The amethyst fly
Doyle, Sir A. C. The red-headed league
Gaboriau, E. The little old man of Batignolles
Garrett, R. The Ipswich Phial
Gilbert, M. The conspirators
Grayson, R. Murder à la mode
Leblanc, M. Drops that trickle away
Leblanc, M. The mysterious railway-passenger

MYSTERY AND DETECTIVE STORIES
—France—*Continued*

Leroux, G. The mystery of the four husbands

M. M. B. The mystery of the Hotel de l'Orme

Malet, L. The Haulage company

Perowne, B. Raffles and operation champagne

Peyrou, M. The sleeping sword

Poe, E. A. The murders in the Rue Morgue

Poe, E. A. The mystery of Marie Rogêt

Poe, E. A. The purloined letter

Simenon, G. The drowned men's inn

Simenon, G. Inspector Maigret pursues

Simenon, G. Maigret at the crossroads

Simenon, G. Maigret mystified

Simenon, G. Maigret stonewalled

Simenon, G. The most obstinate man in Paris

Simenon, G. Storm over the Channel

Véry, P. The lady of the museums

Véry, P. Watch the red balloons

Germany
Farmer, P. J. A Scarletin study

Tyre, N. Beyond the wall

Greece
Brett, S. The girls in Villa Costas

Christie, A. Triangle at Rhodes

India
Hoch, E. D. The vultures of Malabar

Keating, H. R. F. The all-bad hat

Keating, H. R. F. Inspector Ghote and the noted British author

Keating, H. R. F. Inspector Ghote and the test match

Indonesia
Lanier, S. E. A father's tale

Ireland
Aiken, J. The black cliffs

Braly, D. The gallowglass

Darling, J. A bite of the pie

Le Fanu, J. S. Passage in the secret history of an Irish countess

Italy
Carr, J. D. "As drink the dead . . . "

Ellin, S. The twelfth statue

Fraser, A. The girl who wanted to see Venice

Fraser, A. Jemima Shore's first case

Škvorecký, J. Falling light

Škvorecký, J. A tried and proven method

Japan
Matsumoto, S. Just eighteen months

Matsumoto, S. The woman who took the local paper

Van de Wetering, J. Inspector Saito's small satori

Van de Wetering, J. Messing about in boats

Van de Wetering, J. Saito and the fox girl

Van de Wetering, J. Saito and the sacred stick

Van de Wetering, J. Saito and the Shogun

Van de Wetering, J. Saito and the twenty-sen stamp

Van de Wetering, J. Saito versus Saito

Van de Wetering, J. Saito versus Satan

Van de Wetering, J. Saito's small oversight

Van de Wetering, J. Saito's summary

Van de Wetering, J. Samurai Saito

Malaysia
Harris, H. Give him an inch . . .

Mexico
Muller, M. The Sanchez sacraments

Somerlott, R. The hair of the widow

Netherlands
Van de Wetering, J. The deadly egg

Van de Wetering, J. Houseful of mussels

Van de Wetering, J. Letter present

Van de Wetering, J. The machine gun and the mannequin

Van de Wetering, J. The sergeant's cat

Van de Wetering, J. Six this, six that

Van de Wetering, J. Sure, blue, and dead, too

Van de Wetering, J. There goes Ravelaar

North Africa
Hoch, E. D. Village of the dead

Northern Ireland
Howard, C. The Dublin eye

Philippines
Whitfield, R. The black sampan

Poland
Gilbert, M. The emergency exit affair

Romania
Hoch, E. D. The luck of a gypsy

South Africa
Godfrey, P. Out of this world

Soviet Union
Hill, R. There are no ghosts in the Soviet Union

Switzerland
Christie, A. The Erymanthian boar

Tahiti
Peirce, H. Goldfish

United States
Adams, C. F. Flowers for Violet

Aldrich, T. B. Out of his head

Alter, R. E. "I," said the fly

Anderson, L. The Domino Lady doubles back

Arden, W. Hot night homicide

Armstrong, C. The enemy

Armstrong, C. The hedge between

Armstrong, C. The other shoe

Asimov, I. Can you prove it?

Asimov, I. The driver

Asimov, I. The Good Samaritan

Asimov, I. Halloween

Asimov, I. The intrusion

Asimov, I. The key word

Asimov, I. A Monday in April

Asimov, I. Neither brute nor human

MYSTERY AND DETECTIVE STORIES
—United States—*Continued*
Asimov, I. The Phoenician bauble
Asimov, I. Quicker than the eye
Asimov, I. The redhead
Asimov, I. Sixty million trillion combinations
Asimov, I. The ultimate crime
Asimov, I. The woman in the bar
Asimov, I. The wrong house
Asimov, I. The year of the action
Ball, J. Good evening, Mr. Tibbs
Ball, J. One for Virgil Tibbs
Ballard, W. T. Gamblers don't win
Ballard, W. T. Lights, action—killer!
Ballard, W. T. A little different
Ballard, W. T. A million-dollar tramp
Ballard, W. T. Scars of murder
Barnes, L. Lucky penny
Barnes, L. A trouble of fools [excerpt]
Bellem, R. L. Diamonds of death
Blochman, L. G. But the patient died
Block, L. By the dawn's early light
Block, L. Death of the Mallory Queen
Block, L. The Ehrengraf appointment
Block, L. The Ehrengraf experience
Block, L. The Ehrengraf method
Block, L. Like a lamb to slaughter
Block, L. Out of the window
Block, L. That kind of a day
Boucher, A. Elsewhen
Boucher, A. QL 696.C9
Brandner, G. The pigeon hunters
Breen, J. L. All-star team
Breen, J. L. Malice at the mike
Brittain, W. The artificial liar
Brittain, W. Mr. Strang and the purloined memo
Brittain, W. Mr. Strang picks up the pieces
Brown, F. Before she kills
Brown, F. Blue murder
Brown, F. The case of the dancing sandwiches
Brown, F. Cry silence
Brown, F. The dangerous people
Brown, F. The four blind men
Brown, F. I'll cut your throat again, Kathleen
Brown, F. The joke
Brown, F. The laughing butcher
Brown, F. A little white lye
Brown, F. Miss Darkness
Brown, F. Mr. Smith kicks the bucket
Brown, F. The night the world ended
Brown, F. The spherical ghoul
Brown, F. Witness in the dark
Brown, R. Hit the baby!
Browne, H. So dark for April
Burt, E. No witnesses
Butler, E. P. Philo Gubb's greatest case
Cain, P. Gundown
Carpenter, H., and Carpenter, L. The disappearing diamond

Carr, J. D. The gentleman from Paris
Carter, N. The mystery of room no. 11
Chadwick, P. Fangs of the cobra
Chambers, W. The Duchess pulls a fast one
Chandler, R. Blackmailers don't shoot
Chandler, R. Trouble is my business
Chandler, R. Wrong pigeon
Charteris, L. The well-meaning mayor
Chastain, T. Directed verdict
Chesbro, G. C. Candala
Christie, A. The case of the missing will
Collins, M. Black in the snow
Collins, M. Eighty million dead
Collins, M. The oldest killer
Collins, M. A reason to die
Collins, M. A. House call
Collins, M. A. Marble Mildred
Collins, M. A. Scrap
Collins, M. A. The strawberry teardrop
Commings, J. The X Street murders
Costa, C. The best bid
Coxe, G. H. The doctor takes a case
Craig, J. The late unlamented
Cross, A. Tania's no where
Daly, C. J. Not my corpse
Daly, C. J. Three gun Terry
Davis, D. S. Backward, turn backward
Davis, D. S. Mrs. Norris observes
Davis, F. C. Fingers of fear
Davis, F. C. Mark of the Moon Man
Davis, R. H. Gallegher
Dent, L. The tank of terror
Du Lac, L. "What's cooking? murder?"
Dubus, A. Land where my fathers died
Dundee, W. D. Body count
Dundee, W. D. The Judas target
Dundee, W. D. Shooting match
Eberhart, M. G. The calico dog
Eberhart, M. G. Easter devil
Ellin, S. Unacceptable procedures
Ellis, J. One step to murder
Estleman, L. D. Blond and blue
Estleman, L. D. Bloody July
Estleman, L. D. Bodyguards shoot second
Estleman, L. D. Dead soldier
Estleman, L. D. Eight Mile and Dequindre
Estleman, L. D. Fast burn
Estleman, L. D. Greektown
Estleman, L. D. I'm in the book
Estleman, L. D. The prettiest dead girl in Detroit
Estleman, L. D. Robbers' roost
Estleman, L. D. State of grace
Farr, D. Sam's conscience
Fleming-Roberts, G. T. The death master
Flora, F. A husband is missing
Flora, F. Where's Milo
Flynn, T. T. The deadly orchid
Footner, H. Wolves of Monte Carlo
Forrest, K. V. Jessie
Francis, J. Sniped at
Friedman, B. J. Our Lady of the Lockers

MYSTERY AND DETECTIVE STORIES
—United States—*Continued*

Futrelle, J. The house that was
Futrelle, J. The scarlet thread
Futrelle, J. The stolen Rubens
Futrelle, J. The superfluous finger
Futrelle, M. The grinning god
Gallico, P. Hurry, hurry, hurry!
Gardner, E. S. Hell's kettle
Gardner, T. S. You could have done better
Gault, W. C. April in peril
Gault, W. C. Night work
Gault, W. C. Stolen star
Gault, W. C. Take care of yourself
Gores, J. Smart guys don't snore
Gorman, E. The reason why
Goulart, R. Back on my feet again
Goulart, R. Please stand by
Grafton, S. Non Sung Smoke
Grafton, S. The Parker shotgun
Grafton, S. She didn't come home
Greenleaf, S. Iris
Hammett, D. Bodies piled up
Hammett, D. If they hang you
Hammett, D. A man called Spade
Hammett, D. They can only hang you once
Hammett, D. Too many have lived
Hansen, J. Death of an otter
Hansen, J. Election day
Hansen, J. Merely players
Hansen, J. Snipe hunt
Hansen, J. Surf
Hansen, J. The Tango Bear
Hansen, J. Witch's broom
Healey, R. M. A neat crime
Hershman, M. Guilty witness
Hillerman, T. The witch, Yazzie, and the nine of clubs
Hoch, E. D. The Athanasia League
Hoch, E. D. Captain Leopold and the ghost-killer
Hoch, E. D. Captain Leopold goes home
Hoch, E. D. Captain Leopold goes to the dogs
Hoch, E. D. Captain Leopold looks for the cause
Hoch, E. D. Captain Leopold plays a hunch
Hoch, E. D. Captain Leopold's secret
Hoch, E. D. Christmas is for cops
Hoch, E. D. Circus
Hoch, E. D. Death in the harbor
Hoch, E. D. End of the day
Hoch, E. D. Five-day forecast
Hoch, E. D. The house by the ferris
Hoch, E. D. The Jersey Devil
Hoch, E. D. The Judges of Hades
Hoch, E. D. Leopold and the broken bride
Hoch, E. D. The Leopold locked room
Hoch, E. D. The man from nowhere
Hoch, E. D. A melee of diamonds

Hoch, E. D. The most dangerous man alive
Hoch, E. D. No crime for Captain Leopold
Hoch, E. D. The oblong room
Hoch, E. D. The other eye
Hoch, E. D. A place for bleeding
Hoch, E. D. The problem of the covered bridge
Hoch, E. D. The rainy-day bandit
Hoch, E. D. The rented scar
Hoch, E. D. Reunion
Hoch, E. D. Sword for a sinner
Hoch, E. D. The theft of nothing at all
Hoch, E. D. The theft of the overdue library book
Hoch, E. D. The unicorn's daughter
Hoch, E. D. The vanished steamboat
Hoch, E. D. The vanishing of Velma
Hoch, E. D. The witch of Park Avenue
Howard, H. The dipping of the candlemaker
Hoyt, R. Private investigations
Hughes, D. B. F. The spotted pup
Irish, W. The corpse in the Statue of Liberty
Kaminsky, S. M. Busted blossoms
Kaminsky, S. M. The man who shot Lewis Vance
Kane, H. Suicide is scandalous
Kantner, R. Fly away home
Kantner, R. Left for dead
Kantner, R. The rat line
Kipp, G. G. Farewell gesture
Lipsky, E. Tiger in the night
Lockridge, F. L. D., and Lockridge, R. Captain Heimrich stumbles
Lutz, J. Ride the lightning
Lutz, J. The thunder of guilt
Lutz, J. Typographical error
Lutz, J., and Pachter, J. DDS 10752 Libra
Lyons, A. Dead copy
Lyons, A. Missing in Miami
Lyons, A. Trouble in paradise
MacDonald, J. D. I always get the cuties
Macdonald, R. Guilt-edged blonde
Macdonald, R. Midnight blue
Macdonald, R. The sleeping dog
Maddren, G. Fit for felony
Manners, M. Squeakie's first case
Marlowe, S. Wanted—dead and alive
Martin, D. Footprints in a ghost town
Masur, H. Q. Dead game
Masur, H. Q. Framed for murder
McBain, E. Death flight
McBain, E. "J"
McBain, E. Small homicide
McCandless, D. B. Cash or credit
McClure, J. Remember that joke, Harry?
McCoy, H. Frost flies alone
Mcdonald, G. The nine best movies
McGlamry, B. Only a matter of time
Muller, M. The broken men

MYSTERY AND DETECTIVE STORIES
—United States—*Continued*

Muller, M. Deceptions
Muller, M. The Sanchez sacraments
Muller, M. Wild mustard
Nebel, F. Murder by mail
Nebel, F. Rough justice
Nevins, F. M., Jr. The Dogsbody case
Nolan, W. F. A long time dying
Olson, D. On consignment
Ottolengui, R. The nameless man
Page, N. Satan's hoof
Palmer, S. Hildegarde Withers is back
Paretsky, S. At the old swimming hole
Paretsky, S. Three-Dot Po
Parker, P. S. Lady with a knife
Parry, H. T. The Plum Point Ladies
Parry, H. T. The punchboards
Paul, P. The Jane from Hell's Kitchen
Penfold, N. Death on Goose Hill
Pentecost, H. Chambrun and the double event
Pentecost, H. Chambrun and the electronic ear
Pentecost, H. Chambrun and the melting swan
Pentecost, H. Chambrun and the obvious clue
Pentecost, H. Chambrun gets the message
Pentecost, H. Death to the hunter
Pentecost, H. Jericho and the cardboard box
Pentecost, H. The masked crusader
Pentecost, H. Murder deluxe
Pentecost, H. My dear Uncle Sherlock
Pentecost, H. Pierre Chambrun and the black days
Pentecost, H. Pierre Chambrun and the last fling
Pentecost, H. Pierre Chambrun and the sad song
Pentecost, H. Pierre Chambrun and the war for peace
Pentecost, H. Pierre Chambrun defends himself
Pentecost, H. Pierre Chambrun's dilemma
Poe, E. A. The gold-bug
Poe, E. A. Thou art the man
Prather, R. S. Dead giveaway
Pronzini, B. Ace in the hole
Pronzini, B. Cache and carry
Pronzini, B. Cat's-paw
Pronzini, B. Incident in a neighborhood tavern
Pronzini, B. Memento mori
Pronzini, B. Proof of guilt
Pronzini, B. Sanctuary
Pronzini, B. Skeleton rattle your mouldy leg
Pronzini, B. Smuggler's Island
Pronzini, B. Something wrong
Pronzini, B. Stacked deck
Pronzini, B. Thin air

Pronzini, B., and Wallmann, J. M. Coyote and Quarter Moon
Queen, E. Abraham Lincoln's clue
Queen, E. The adventure of the bearded lady
Queen, E. The adventure of the hanging acrobat
Queen, E. The bearded lady
Queen, E. The Dauphin's doll
Queen, E. The death of Don Juan
Queen, E. GI story
Queen, E. The glass-domed clock
Queen, E. The House of Darkness
Queen, E. The inner circle
Queen, E. Last man to die
Queen, E. The mad tea-party
Queen, E. Man bites dog
Queen, E. The medical finger
Queen, E. Mind over matter
Queen, E. Miracles do happen
Queen, E. My queer Dean!
Queen, E. Mystery at the Library of Congress
Queen, E. Snowball in July
Queen, E. Terror town
Queen, E. The three widows
Queen, E. Wedding anniversary
Rafferty, S. S. The greatest cook in Christendom
Rafferty, S. S. The hawk and the dome of hell
Randisi, R. J. Deathlist
Randisi, R. J. A matter of ethics
Randisi, R. J. The nickel derby
Randisi, R. J. The vanishing virgin
Reach, A. S. Father Crumlish remembers his Poe
Reasoner, J. M. Death and the dancing shadows
Reasoner, J. M. The safest place in the world
Rice, C. His heart could break
Ritchie, J. The 23 brown paper bags
Ritchie, J. The alphabet murders
Ritchie, J. Bedlam at the Budgie
Ritchie, J. Box in a box
Ritchie, J. By child undone
Ritchie, J. The connecting link
Ritchie, J. Dial an alibi
Ritchie, J. The fifth grave
Ritchie, J. The final truth
Ritchie, J. Finger exercise
Ritchie, J. The gourmet kidnaper
Ritchie, J. The Griggsby papers
Ritchie, J. The hanging tree
Ritchie, J. Hung jury
Ritchie, J. The message in the message
Ritchie, J. The midnight strangler
Ritchie, J. More than meets the eye
Ritchie, J. Murder off limits
Ritchie, J. No wider than a nickel
Ritchie, J. Nobody tells me anything
Ritchie, J. An odd pair of socks

MYSTERY AND DETECTIVE STORIES
—United States—*Continued*

Ritchie, J. The O'Leary conspiracy
Ritchie, J. The school bus caper
Ritchie, J. The sliver of evidence
Ritchie, J. Some days are like that
Ritchie, J. Take another look
Ritchie, J. The two percent solution
Ritchie, J. Variations on a scheme
Ritchie, J. The Willinger predicament
Ritchie, J. Win some, lose some
Rossoff, A. The Whisperer prowls
Rudin, J. Sellin' some wood
Rudloff, S. A. A cup of coffee
Russell, R. Before he kills
Sale, R. Double trouble
Savage, E. The girl and the ghost
Searls, H. A dish of homicide
Searls, H. For auld lang crime
Searls, H. Keep your money side up
Searls, H. Kickback for a killer
Searls, H. Lethal legacy for the lady
Searls, H. Let's all die together
Searls, H. Shiv for your supper
Shannon, D. Accident
Shannon, D. The bronze cat
Shannon, D. The cat
Shannon, D. The clue
Shannon, D. The long chance
Shannon, D. The motive
Shannon, D. Novelties
Shannon, D. The ring
Spillane, M. Trouble . . . come and get it!
Stevenson, J. The blind alley
Stodghill, D. Wrongful death
Stout, R. A dog in the daytime
Stout, R. Help wanted, male
Stout, R. See no evil
Tepperman, E. C. Killers' club car
Thomas, E. The lady from hell
Tinsley, T. Riddle in silk
Toole, W. A matter of experience
Treat, L. H as in homicide
Twohy, R. Case blue
Ullman, J. M. Dead ringer
Van Derveer, M. The quiet investigation
Washburn, L. J. Hallam
Washburn, L. J. Hollywood guns
Wasylyk, S. The exoneration of Phineas Droogan
Wasylyk, S. The spring that Ellie died
Waugh, H. The beneficiaries
Waugh, H. Galton and the yelling boys
Weber, T. The Wells Plan
Weinstein, L. Lasting impression
Wellman, M. W. A star for a warrior
Wheeler, H. C. Murder in one scene
Wheeler, H. C. Puzzle for Poppy
Whitfield, R. Sal the Dude
Widmer, H. The corpse laughs
Wilson, K. Hot as a pistol
Woolrich, C. The body upstairs

Woolrich, C. Dead on her feet
Woolrich, C. The death of me
Woolrich, C. The detective's dilemma
Woolrich, C. Hurting much?
Woolrich, C. Kiss of the cobra
Woolrich, C. Murder in wax
Woolrich, C. Preview of death
Woolrich, C. Red liberty
Woolrich, C. The room with something wrong
Woolrich, C. The showboat murders
Woolrich, C. Walls that hear you
Yaffe, J. Mom makes a wish
Yaffe, J. One of the family
Yorke, C. B. Snowbound
Mystery at the Library of Congress. Queen, E.
Mystery at Wimbledon. Hoch, E. D.
A **mystery** of heroism: a detail of an American battle. Crane, S.
The **mystery** of Hunter's Lodge. Christie, A.
The **mystery** of Madame Kitten. Lopatin, J.
The **mystery** of Marie Rogêt. Poe, E. A.
The **mystery** of room no. 11. Carter, N.
The **mystery** of Sasassa Valley. Doyle, Sir A. C.
The **mystery** of the back-roomer. Ade, G.
The **mystery** of the Bagdad Chest. Christie, A.
The **mystery** of the desert giants. Vaughan, R. E.
The **mystery** of the four husbands. Leroux, G.
The **mystery** of the Higgins coupe. Heise, K.
The **mystery** of the Hotel de l'Orme. M. M. B.
The **mystery** of the lost special. Doyle, Sir A. C.
The **mystery** of the young gentleman. Russ, J.
Mystery on a moonlit night. Grin, A.
Mystery story. Fitzgerald, M. J.
Mystic games. Saroyan, W.

MYSTICISM
Hesse, H. Inside and outside
Mystification. Poe, E. A.
The **myth.** Creech, W. G.
The **myth** of mankind. Lagerkvist, P.

MYTHICAL ANIMALS
See also Dragons; Unicorns; Vampires; Werewolves

Anthony, P. Possible to rue
De Larrabeiti, M. The curse of Igamor
Huang Qingyun. Annals of a fossil
Martin, G. R. R. Nor the many-colored fires of a star ring
Robinson, K. S. Escape from Kathmandu
Stivens, D. The gentle basilisk
Wells, H. G. In the Avu observatory
Wells, H. G. The sea-raiders
Zelazny, R. Unicorn variations
The **mythical** kid. Dickinson, D.
Mythological beast. Donaldson, S. R.

MYTHOLOGY

See also Helen of Troy (Legendary character); Medusa (Greek mythology); Mythical animals; Orpheus (Greek mythology); Sirens (Mythology)

Brin, D. Thor meets Captain America

Petrakis, H. M. The ballad of Daphne and Apollo

Schwob, M. Arachné

Silverberg, R. Breckenridge and the continuum

Tennant, E. Philomela

Mythomania. Walters, A. L.

Myths of the near future. Ballard, J. G.

Myxomatosis forte. Mårtensson, B.

Mzamane, Mbulelo

My cousin comes to Jo'burg

The Penguin book of Southern African stories

N

Na, To-Hyang

The water-mill

The Unenlightened, and other Korean short stories

Nabo: the black man who made the angels wait. García Márquez, G.

Nabokov, Vladimir Vladimirovich, 1899-1977

The fight

The New Yorker 60:34-6 F 18 '85

First love

The World of the short story; ed. by C. Fadiman

Spring in Fialta

The Art of the tale; ed. by D. Halpern

The visit to the museum

Black water; ed. by A. Manguel

Nada. Sage, V.

Nadelman's god. Klein, T. E. D.

Naga, Abu el Ma'ati Abu el See El Naga, Abu el Ma'ati Abu

Naga. Narayan, R. K.

Nagai, Kafū

Nude

The Mother of dreams, and other short stories; ed. by M. Ueda

Nagai, Tatsuo

The nutcracker

The Kenyon Review ns6:13-20 Wint '84

NAGASAKI (JAPAN) See Japan—Nagasaki

NAGASHINO, BATTLE OF, 1575

Kōda, R. The bearded samurai

Nagibin, Íŭrii Markovich, 1920-

The abandoned path

Nagibin, I. M. The peak of success, and other stories

By a quiet lake

Nagibin, I. M. The peak of success, and other stories

Echo

Nagibin, I. M. The peak of success, and other stories

Elijah's Day

Nagibin, I. M. The peak of success, and other stories

The last hunt

Nagibin, I. M. The peak of success, and other stories

Needed urgently: gray human hair

Nagibin, I. M. The peak of success, and other stories

The newlywed

Nagibin, I. M. The peak of success, and other stories

The night guest

Nagibin, I. M. The peak of success, and other stories

Olezhka got married

Nagibin, I. M. The peak of success, and other stories

The outsider

Nagibin, I. M. The peak of success, and other stories

The peak of success

Nagibin, I. M. The peak of success, and other stories

The runaway

Nagibin, I. M. The peak of success, and other stories

Shurik

Nagibin, I. M. The peak of success, and other stories

Somebody else's heart

Nagibin, I. M. The peak of success, and other stories

Winter oak

Nagibin, I. M. The peak of success, and other stories

Nahin, Paul J.

Publish and perish

Great science fiction; ed. by I. Asimov; M. H. Greenberg and C. G. Waugh

Naipaul, Shiva, 1945-1985

The beauty contest

Naipaul, S. Beyond the dragon's mouth

The dolly house

Naipaul, S. Beyond the dragon's mouth

The father, the son and the Holy Ghost

Naipaul, S. Beyond the dragon's mouth

Lack of sleep

Naipaul, S. Beyond the dragon's mouth

A man of mystery

Naipaul, S. Beyond the dragon's mouth

Mr. Sookhoo and the carol singers

Naipaul, S. Beyond the dragon's mouth

The political education of Clarissa Forbes

Naipaul, S. Beyond the dragon's mouth

The tenant

Naipaul, S. Beyond the dragon's mouth

Naipaul, V. S. (Vidiadhar Surajprasad), 1932-

The enigma of arrival
The New Yorker 62:26-43+ Ag 11 '86
Jack's garden
The New Yorker 62:36-46+ O 6 '86

Naipaul, Vidiadhar Surajprasad *See* Naipaul, V. S. (Vidiadhar Surajprasad), 1932-

Nairobi. Oates, J. C.

Najari Levon's old country advice to the young Americans on how to live with a snake. Saroyan, W.

Nakagami, Kenji, 1946-

The immortal
The Shōwa anthology 2
The **naked** lady. Bell, M. S.
Naked to naked goes. Flanagan, R.

Nałkowska, Zofia

At the railroad track
Russian and Polish women's fiction; ed. by H. Goscilo

Rock bottom
Russian and Polish women's fiction; ed. by H. Goscilo

Nam, Chong-Hyon

Chaos
A Respite, and other Korean short stories

Nam. Wilson, R., Jr.
Nam-Bok, the unveracious. London, J.
The **name.** Conley, R. J.
The **name.** Pavese, C.
A **name** for herself. Tufel, A.
Name the general. Bonnie, F.
The **nameless** man. Ottolengui, R.

NAMES, PERSONAL

Asimov, I. Middle name
Asimov, I. Unto the fourth generation
Baumbach, J. The Honest Company
Benedict, S. Tahotahontanekent-seratkerontakwenhakie
Bonnie, F. In another language
Griggs, T. India
Kessler, J. F. Teiresias
Le Guin, U. K. The rule of names
Lish, G. The lesson which is sufficient unto the day thereof
MacLachlan, P. All the names of Baby Hag
Mazel, D. Friends
Olson, D. Another me
Stewart, J. I. M. Napier into Ffinch
Wells, H. G. Miss Winchelsea's heart
Wetherell, W. D. The lob
Wolfe, T. Arnold Pentland
The **names** and faces of heroes. Price, R.
The **names** of the nation. Wolfe, T.
Naming the enemy. Cobbold, D.
Nan Hogan's house. O'Kelly, S.
Nancy. McLaughlin, L.
Naninja and Janey. Prichard, K. S.

NANNIES *See* Governesses; Nursemaids

NANTUCKET ISLAND (MASS.)

Shepard, L. How the wind spoke at Madaket

Naomi counting time. Thompson, J.
Napier into Ffinch. Stewart, J. I. M.

NAPLES (ITALY) *See* Italy—Naples

Naples. Davidson, A.

NAPOLEON I, EMPEROR OF THE FRENCH, 1769-1821

About

Apollinaire, G. The eagle hunt
Benét, S. V. The curfew tolls
Hoch, E. D. Who rides with Santa Anna?
Windsor, G. Memories of the assassination attempt

Naqvi, Tahira

Hiatus
The Massachusetts Review 29:744-61 Wint '88/'89

Naranjo, Carmen

Ondina
Women's fiction from Latin America; ed. by E. P. Garfield
Why kill the Countess?
Women's fiction from Latin America; ed. by E. P. Garfield

Narayan, R. K., 1906-

All avoidable talk
Narayan, R. K. Under the banyan tree, and other stories
Annamalai
Narayan, R. K. Under the banyan tree, and other stories
Another community
Narayan, R. K. Under the banyan tree, and other stories
The antidote
Narayan, R. K. Under the banyan tree, and other stories
At the portal
Narayan, R. K. Under the banyan tree, and other stories
Attila
Roger Caras' Treasury of great dog stories
The blind dog
Roger Caras' Treasury of great dog stories
A breath of Lucifer
Narayan, R. K. Under the banyan tree, and other stories
A career
Narayan, R. K. Under the banyan tree, and other stories
Chippy
Narayan, R. K. Under the banyan tree, and other stories
Crime and punishment
Narayan, R. K. Under the banyan tree, and other stories

Narayan, R. K., 1906-—*Continued*
Dodu
  Narayan, R. K. Under the banyan tree,
  and other stories
The evening gift
  Narayan, R. K. Under the banyan tree,
  and other stories
Flavour of coconut
  Narayan, R. K. Under the banyan tree,
  and other stories
Four rupees
  Narayan, R. K. Under the banyan tree,
  and other stories
Fruition at forty
  Narayan, R. K. Under the banyan tree,
  and other stories
Half a rupee worth
  Narayan, R. K. Under the banyan tree,
  and other stories
A hero
  Narayan, R. K. Under the banyan tree,
  and other stories
A horse and two goats
  Narayan, R. K. Under the banyan tree,
  and other stories
House opposite
  A Grand Street reader; ed. by B. Son-
  nenberg
  The Literary Review (Madison, N.J.)
  29:493-5 Summ '86
  Narayan, R. K. Under the banyan tree,
  and other stories
Like the sun
  Narayan, R. K. Under the banyan tree,
  and other stories
The mute companions
  Narayan, R. K. Under the banyan tree,
  and other stories
Naga
  The Art of the tale; ed. by D. Halpern
Nitya
  Narayan, R. K. Under the banyan tree,
  and other stories
Old man of the temple
  Narayan, R. K. Under the banyan tree,
  and other stories
The Roman image
  Narayan, R. K. Under the banyan tree,
  and other stories
The shelter
  Narayan, R. K. Under the banyan tree,
  and other stories
A snake in the grass
  Narayan, R. K. Under the banyan tree,
  and other stories
Uncle's letters
  Narayan, R. K. Under the banyan tree,
  and other stories
Under the banyan tree
  Narayan, R. K. Under the banyan tree,
  and other stories
  The Treasury of English short stories;
  ed. by N. Sullivan

The watchman
  Narayan, R. K. Under the banyan tree,
  and other stories
NARCISSISM
  Clark, M. At the exhibition
  Conroy, F. Roses
  Hospital, J. T. The baroque ensemble
Narcissus bay. Welch, D.
Narcissus consulted. Rooke, L.
NARCOTIC HABIT
  Bloch, R. The unpardonable crime
  Campos-De Metro, J. Evvy's brother
  Crapser, W. Nicky Martinez
  Ferron, J. Les Méchins
  Gerber, M. J. Memorial service
  Havazelet, E. What is it then between us?
  Hemingway, E. A pursuit race
  Kang, S.-J. Nursery tale for a dreary day
  Neville, K. The price of Simeryl
  Stone, R. In a Mexican garden
  Williams, T. Completed
  Williams, W. C. Old Doc Rivers
NARCOTICS
  See also Marijuana
  Field, I. Hungry lion
  Fisher, R. The city of refuge
  Friedman, B. J. The adventurer
  Gilbert, M. The Sark Lane Mission
  Heald, T. The case of the frozen diplomat
  Kipp, G. G. Farewell gesture
  Lutz, J. All business
  MacLean, A. MacHinery and the
  cauliflowers
  Mortimer, J. C. Rumpole and the alterna-
  tive society
  Oates, J. C. Fin de siècle
  Pronzini, B. Cain's mark
  Tuohy, F. A survivor in Salvador
  Willson, H. Half a loaf
Narell, Irena
  Papa's tea
  Family: stories from the interior; ed. by
  G. G. Chavis
Narodny Rasprava. Wiebe, D. E.
The **narrative** of Arthur Gordon Pym of
  Nantucket. Poe, E. A.
Narrative of events preceding the death of
  Queen Ermine. Warner, S. T.
The **narrative** of Pope Gregory IX. Schwob,
  M.
The **narrative** of Pope Innocent III. Schwob,
  M.
Narrative of the whale truck essex.
  Wetherell, W. D.
NASA *See* United States. National
  Aeronautics and Space Administration
Nash, Ogden, 1902-1971
  The three d's
  Yankee witches; ed. by C. G. Waugh;
  M. H. Greenberg and F. D. McSherry
NASHVILLE (TENN.) *See* Tennessee—
  Nashville
Nashville gone to ashes. Hempel, A.

Naslund, Sena Jeter

Madame Charpentier and her children
Michigan Quarterly Review 27:605-16
Fall '88

The perfecting of the Chopin Valse no. 14
The Georgia Review 39:826-34 Wint '85

Nastes at Miletus. Parotti, P.

Natalie Blayne. Brown, A.

Natalie Wood's amazing eyes. Havazelet, E.

Natasha. Rasputin, V. G.

Nathan's rime. Quammen, D.

Natica Jackson. O'Hara, J.

NATIONAL AERONAUTICS AND SPACE ADMINISTRATION (U.S.) *See* United States. National Aeronautics and Space Administration

The **National** Circus of Argentina. Roscoe, P.

The **national** debt. Apple, M.

The **national** pastime. Cheever, J.

The **national** pastime. Spinrad, N.

NATIONAL SOCIALISM

See also Germany—1918-1945

Bailey, H. The fall of Frenchy Steiner

Bear, G. Through road no whither

Brin, D. Thor meets Captain America

Burt, S. QB/3854/294 & 6

DiFranco, A. M. The garden of redemption

Ellison, H. The boulevard of broken dreams

Fleming, B. War memorial

Friedman, B. J. The war criminal

Goldsmith, H. Do ye hear the children weeping?

Leaton, A. Gita's story

Leiber, F. Belsen Express

Linaweaver, B. Moon of ice

Shippey, T. Enemy transmissions

Waldrop, H. Der untergang des Abendlandesmenschen

The **National** Theatre's burning down. Anderman, J.

NATIONALISM

Eisenstein, S. From in Albania

Native country. Gordimer, N.

The **native** problem. Sheckley, R.

The **natives** are friendly. Lofts, N.

Nativity. Kenney, S.

Natsuki, Shizuko, 1938-

The pawnshop murder
Murder in Japan; ed. by J. L. Apostolou and M. H. Greenberg

The sole of the foot
Murder in Japan; ed. by J. L. Apostolou and M. H. Greenberg

Natural causes. Coskran, K.

Natural causes. Davis, D. S.

The **natural** father. Lacy, R.

Natural food. Lynch, L.

Natural histories. Gifkins, M.

Natural histories. Haake, K.

A **natural** history of the dead. Hemingway, E.

NATURALISTS

Rose, D. A. Tasting leaves

NATURE

Calvino, I. The adventure of a poet

Calvino, I. The house of the beehives

Colum, P. The slopes of Tara

Covino, M. The coming of snow

Grzimek, M. Finlandia

Handke, P. The lesson of Mont Sainte-Victoire

Ioannides, P. The unseen aspect

Kessler, J. F. Afrodite

Martin, V. The parallel world

Moore, G. The voice of the mountain

Thomas, D. The crumbs of one man's year

Thomas, D. In the direction of the beginning

Nature. Eldridge, M.

NATURE CONSERVATION

Cowan, P. The tractor

The **nature** of poetry. Blythe, R.

The **nature** of the thing. See Highsmith, P. Not in this life, maybe the next

A **nature** reserve. Shamosh, A.

Natzler, Caroline

Water wings
Critical Quarterly 30:37-49 Spr '88

Nautilus. Pascoe, B.

NAVAHO INDIANS *See* Navajo Indians

Navajo Café. Schwartz, S.

NAVAJO INDIANS

Austin, M. H. The man who was loved by women

Austin, M. H. White wisdom

Boren, T. Sliding rock

Chavez, A. A desert idyll

Eastlake, W. The death of Sun

Schwartz, S. Navajo Café

Silko, L. Lullaby

NAVAL BATTLES

See also Sea stories; World War, 1914-1918—Naval operations; World War, 1939-1945—Naval operations

Cooper, J. F. The Ariel defeats the Alacrity

Forester, C. S. The sinking of the Bismarck

Hugo, V. A wild cannon dooms the Claymore

MacLean, A. Hospital ship rams U-boat

Reade, C. Agra outwits two pirate ships

Robinson, W. The blow-up of the Mohawk

Thomson, V. The battle of Bonhomme Richard and Serapis

NAVAL OFFICERS *See* Great Britain. Royal Navy—Officers; United States. Navy—Officers

The **naval** treaty. Doyle, Sir A. C.

Navarre, Yves, 1940-
Allan Bloom
First love/last love; ed. by M. Denneny;
C. Ortleb and T. Steele
Navas, Deborah
Blood
The North American Review 273:57-9 S
'88
Navigating the night. Risley, S.
The **navigator.** Minot, S.
Navy blues. Lorimer, G., and Lorimer, S.
Naylor, Gloria
Kiswana Browne
Look who's talking; ed. by B. Weber
Nayman, Michele
The house on Lafayette Street
Echad 4: Jewish writing from down un-
der: Australia and New Zealand
Nazareth, Peter
Rosie's theme
The Literary Review (Madison, N.J.)
29:496-506 Summ '86
NAZIS *See* National socialism
Nazis, communists, Presbyterians & Jews in
Norman Bethune's hometown. Avery,
M.
NAZISM *See* National socialism
Ndebele, Njabulo
Fools
Ndebele, N. Fools, and other stories
The music of the violin
Ndebele, N. Fools, and other stories
The prophetess
Ndebele, N. Fools, and other stories
The test
Ndebele, J. Fools, and other stories
Uncle
Ndebele, N. Fools, and other stories
NEANDERTHAL RACE
See also Man, Prehistoric
Asimov, I. The ugly little boy
Farmer, P. J. The alley man
Klass, M. In the beginning
Silverberg, R. House of bones
The **near** departed. Matheson, R.
NEAR EAST *See* Middle East
Near Forelanders Kop. Colvin, C.
Near November. Akins, E.
Near Pala. Rush, N.
Near places, far places. Barnhill, S.
Nearly departed. Cadigan, P.
A **neat** crime. Healey, R. M.
Nebel, Frederick, 1903-1967
Murder by mail
Hard-boiled dames; ed. by B. A. Drew
Rough justice
The Black mask boys; ed. by W. F.
Nolan
NEBRASKA
Crane, S. The blue hotel
Hansen, R. Nebraska
Potter, N. A. J. Legacies

Farm life
See Farm life—Nebraska
Nebraska. Hansen, R.
Nebraska Crane. Wolfe, T.
Nebraska, sweet Nebraska land. Kaye, F. W.
The **necklace.** See Maupassant, G. de. The
diamond necklace
The **necklace** of flowers. Takahashi, T.
The **necklace** of pearls. Sayers, D. L.
NECKLACES
Kessler, J. F. Kassandra
Le Guin, U. K. Semley's necklace
Maupassant, G. de. The diamond necklace
Spofford, H. E. P. The amber gods
Necromancy in Naat. Smith, C. A.
NECROPHILIA
Lannes, R. Goodbye, dark love
Smith, C. A. Necromancy in Naat
Nectar. Feng Jicai
Ned. Wilbur, E.
Ned Jumper. Russell, T.
Need-fire. Shannon, D.
Needed urgently: gray human hair. Nagibin,
ÍŪ. M.
Needle in a timestack. Silverberg, R.
NEEDLEWORK
Ferron, J. Ulysses
Norton, A. Through the needle's eye
Needlework. Dunn, D.
Neely, Jessica
Skin angels
The Best American short stories, 1986
Neery Christmas. Weaver, G.
Neff, Ondrej
The Porton Potion
Short story international 71
Negatives. Lee, A.
NEGEV (ISRAEL)
Amichai, Y. Dicky's death
Negore, the Coward. London, J.
The **Negro** in the well. Caldwell, E.
NEGROES *See* Blacks
Negrophobia. James, D.
The **neighbor.** Banks, R.
Neighbor below. Asscher-Pinkhof, C.
The **neighborhood.** Gordon, M.
Neighborhood. Spivack, K.
A **neighborhood** bar. Pallant, C.
The **neighborhood** coffeehouse. Faik, S.
NEIGHBORS
Abbott, K. When this van is rockin' don't
bother knockin'
Ade, G. The intellectual awakening in Bur-
ton's Row
Austin, M. H. The Castro baby
Bail, M. Life of the party
Beattie, A. Honey
Bell, J. L. The curlew's cry
Bell, M. S. The forgotten bridge
Blei, N. Stars
Blythe, R. And the green grass grew all
around
Böll, H. A peach tree in his garden stands

NEIGHBORS—*Continued*
Bonnie, F. Two widows
Briskin, M. Theresa McCann and Joe
Canin, E. Emperor of the air
Carver, R. Neighbors
Chesterton, G. K. A real discovery
Coleman, W. Kelele
Cooper, J. C. The watcher
Csiffary, S. Russian songs
Curtiss, U. R. Good neighbor
Dick, P. K. Chains of air, web of aether
Dick, P. K. Strange memories of death
Dickinson, C. With or without
Dodd, S. M. Walls
Ellin, S. Mrs. Mouse
Floyd, P. L. The summer no one was poor
Frucht, A. Trees at night
Galsworthy, J. The neighbors
Gerber, M. J. At the fence
Gifkins, M. Local time
Goodman, I. White boy
Greenwood, R. Arcadia
Greenwood, R. Snake eyes
Hall, T. T. Why my walls shake
Halligan, M. The marble angel
Halligan, M. The noise of the lorries
Hoffman, W. Moorings
Hofmann, G. Arno
Hospital, J. T. Moving out
Jewett, S. O. Mrs. Parkins's Christmas Eve
Jolley, E. Winter nelis
Kattan, N. The neighbour
Kawabata, Y. The neighbors
Kincaid, N. Like the old wolf in all those wolf stories
Kinsella, W. P. Syzygy
Klíma, I. Monday morning: a black market tale
Krist, G. Evidence
Lawson, H. 'Water them geraniums'
Leedom-Ackerman, J. Sissy Mamma's wig
Lofts, N. Lord, who is my neighbour?
Lurie, M. Popov
MacLaverty, B. Across the street
Matthews, J. The secret hour
Mazel, D. The maestro
McGarry, J. The babysitter
Mihelic, J. Green life
Monreal, D. N. The new neighbor
Morris, W. Fellow-creatures
Neville, S. Kentucky people
Nussey, K. In Christ there is no east or west
Oates, J. C. Harrow Street at Linden
Osborn, C. Running around America
Paley, G. In the garden
Petrakis, H. M. Zena Dawn
Pilcher, R. The house on the hill
Pilcher, R. Miss Cameron at Christmas
Prichard, K. S. The grey horse
Pulaski, J. The merry-go-round
Robison, J. The house sitter

Rossi, A. Notes
Schinto, J. Shadow bands
Shukshin, V. M. The court case
Smiley, J. The pleasure of her company
Sorrentino, F. The fetid tale of Antulín
Sorrentino, F. In self-defense
Stark, S. S. Janka Doodle
Still, J. The moving
Tallent, E. Favor
Tallent, E. Grant of easement
Taylor, C. Loving thy neighbor
Taylor, P. E. News from El Corazon: in the composing room
Thompson, J. Ice flowers
Thompson, K. Getting ready to go camping down in Maine
Traba, M. Conformity
Trevor, W. A complicated nature
Updike, J. Getting into the set
Valenzuela, L. Papito's story
Wells, H. G. Our little neighbour
Wetherell, W. D. The man who loved Levittown
Wheatcroft, J. The shadow of a bear
Winton, T. Neighbours
Winton, T. Scission
Yamamoto, M. Powers
Neighbors. Carver, R.
Neighbors. Fines, B.
The **neighbors.** Galsworthy, J.
The **neighbors.** Kawabata, Y.
Neighbors. Petersen, W.
Neighbors. Thomas, M.
Neighbors. Viramontes, H. M.
The **neighbour.** Kattan, N.
Neighbours. Winton, T.
Nein. Martone, M.
Neither brute nor human. Asimov, I.
Neither brute nor human. Wagner, K. E.
Neither death nor life. Dorr, L.
Neither did I. Pascoe, B.
Neither rest nor refuge. Mayhar, A.
Nellie Bloom. Latimer, M.
Nelsen, Robert S.
Something big
    TriQuarterly no71:46-51 Wint '88
Nelson, Antonya
Dog problems
    The North American Review 273:38-43 Je '88
One-way ticket
    Mademoiselle 90:176+ S '84
Nelson, Jill
Best foot forward
    Essence 15:80-1+ Ap '85
The ol' ball game
    Essence 16:76-7+ D '85
Nelson, Kent
Acts of love
    Mademoiselle 90:130+ Ag '84
Discoveries
    The Southern Review (Baton Rouge, La.) 22:634-50 Summ '86

Nelson, Kent—*Continued*
Invisible life
The Best American short stories, 1986
The Virginia Quarterly Review 61:20-43
Wint '85
Learning to dream
The Southern Review (Baton Rouge, La.)
24:380-95 Spr '88
The man at Quitobaquito
The Southern Review (Baton Rouge, La.)
20:693-700 Jl '84
Roses and limes
The Virginia Quarterly Review 62:669-80
Aut '86
This light is for those at sea
Selected stories from The Southern
review, 1965-1985
Nelson, Mariah Burton
Echoes in an empty gym
Women's Sports & Fitness 7:24-5+ Ja/F
'85
Nelson, Penelope
The dowry
Room to move; ed. by S. Falkiner
Nelson, Peter, 1953-
The newest blessing
Redbook 166:86+ D '85
Sylvia and the visitor
Seventeen 44:144-5+ N '85
Sylvia Smith-Smith and . . . the cigar-
smoking ghost
Seventeen 46:120-1+ Je '87
Seventeen 46:122-3+ Jl '87
Sylvia Smith-Smith strikes back
Seventeen 43:168-9+ My '84
Sylvia Smith-Smith's Christmas surprise
Seventeen 47:102-3+ D '88
Sylvia Smith-Smith's mixed-up masquerade
Seventeen 46:150-1+ O '87
Sylvia Smith-Smith's practically perfect,
highly irregular prom date
Seventeen 45:216-17+ Mr '86
Nelson, Victoria, 1945-
Coming back
Passages to the dream shore; ed. by F.
Stewart
Nelson, Violet
A pocket full of snow
'Teen 32:54-5+ D '88
The **Nemean** lion. Christie, A.
Nemesis and the candy man. Henry, O.
Neons. Walwicz, A.
Neoptolemus in Phthia. Parotti, P.
NEPAL
Shepard, L. The night of white Bhairab
The **nephew.** Rand, P.
NEPHEWS
Abrams, L. Secrets men keep
Davie, E. The free fur coat
Gogol', N. V. Ivan Fiodorovich Shponka
and his aunt
Hartley, L. P. Apples
Jolley, E. The jarrah thieves

Lesley, C. The catch
Mordden, E. I read my nephew stories
Pronzini, B. Here lies another blackmailer
Turgenev, I. S. Clara Militch
Nephritis. Mathews, A.
NEPTUNE (PLANET)
Williamson, J. At the human limit
Nérault, François
The dusty sunbeam
Short story international 52
NERVOUS BREAKDOWN
Abe, A. Friends
Chekhov, A. P. A nervous breakdown
Crapser, W. Remains
Loukakis, A. I told mama not to come
Oates, J. C. The others
Roth, P. Eli, the fanatic
A **nervous** breakdown. Chekhov, A. P.
Nervous couple. Hankla, S.
Nesanovich, Stella
The pearl
The Southern Review (Baton Rouge, La.)
20:934-50 O '84
Nesbit, E. (Edith), 1858-1924
John Charrington's wedding
The Dark descent; ed. by D. G. Hart-
well
Venomous tales of villainy and
vengeance; ed. by H. Hoke
Man-size in marble
The Oxford book of English ghost
stories
Nesbit, Edith *See* Nesbit, E. (Edith), 1858-
1924
Nesbitt, John D.
Half the way back
Here's the story: fiction with heart; ed.
by M. Sklar
Nesin, Aziz
The first woman who understood me
Short story international 45
For a crate of lemons
Short story international 64
A man can't even swindle any more
Short story international 62
Regulations for meatball peddlers
Short story international 42
Socialism is coming—stand aside!
Short story international 52
Tactics
Short story international 54
The university committee's sociological
study of a village
Short story international 49
The **Nest.** Anderson, P.
Nest egg. Wang Zhecheng, and Wen Xiaoyu
A **nest** egg for paradise. Singer, I. B.
Nesting instinct. Baker, S.
Nestor, T. G.
Byway of the rose
Short story international 66
The last fling
Short story international 49

Nestor, T. G.—*Continued*
The mountain top
Short story international 63
Ulick's Island
Short story international 47
Nestor, Tom
Once upon a dream
Short story international 58
Nesvadba, Josef
The divided Carla
Tales from the planet Earth
The half-wit of Xeenemuende
The Penguin world omnibus of science
fiction
The **net**. Tzu, O.-Y.
NETHERLANDS
Brender à Brandis, M. The living Christ-
mas tree
Dundas, R. The uniform
          Amsterdam
Mazel, D. A longing to live
Neugeboren, Jay, 1938-
Cold storage
The Massachusetts Review 26:63-80 Spr
'85
Don't worry about the kids
The Georgia Review 41:121-39 Spr '87
Prize stories, 1988
Uncle Nathan
The Ploughshares reader: new fiction for
the eighties
NEURASTHENIA *See* Nervous breakdown
NEUROLOGISTS
Calisher, H. Heartburn
NEUROSES
Barnard, R. Happy Christmas
Brett, S. Double glazing
Brulotte, G. The elevator messengers
Bullen, F. T. The debt of the whale
Campbell, E. Squares of opposition, signs
of disorder
Campbell, R. The sunshine club
Cather, W. Paul's case
Claiborne, S. Acid rain
Davis, L. The fears of Mrs. Orlando
Davis, L. Five signs of disturbance
Davis, L. The housemaid
Davis, L. Sketches for a life of Wassilly
Ferguson, W. Morrissey
Gallagher, T. The lover of horses
Gilchrist, E. Defender of the Little Falaya
Glover, D. H. Fire drill
Gowan, L. The decline and fall of Howard
Dawn
Greenberg, A. The man in the cardboard
mask
Happy, E. A collection of letters
Harrington, J. Birdbrain
Ishikawa, J. Moon gems
Leaton, A. Mayakovsky, my love
Lee, T. Black as ink
Martin, V. The woman who was never
satisfied

Matthews, J. The grave at Mount Nebo
Matthews, J. The tree beyond
Michaelson, L. W. The Ferrari
Michaelson, L. W. The tennis bum
Miller, S. Calling
Montero, M. Thirteen and a turtle
Mordden, E. The ghost of Champ
McQuest
Oates, J. C. Sentimental journey
Oates, J. C. Superstitious
O'Brien, T. Quantum jumps
Olson, D. Another me
Painter, P. The next time I meet Buddy
Rich
Pascoe, B. Gravity and levity
Piñera, V. The decoration
Purdy, J. Some of these days
Roberts, N. The exterminator
Sage, V. Crusoe
Sheehan, R. Every angel is terrible
Skelton, R. Sarah
Soucy, J.-Y. The red boots
Spark, M. Come along, Marjorie
Spark, M. You should have seen the mess
Spillane, M. The girl behind the hedge
St. Clair, M. Wryneck, draw me
Stark, S. S. The Barlip run
Swift, G. Hoffmeier's Antelope
Tem, S. R. At the bureau
Vanderhaeghe, G. Going to Russia
Welty, E. A memory
Wheatcroft, J. The hitch
Wilson, B. Drive-away
Winters, Y. The brink of darkness
Wolfe, T. Arnold Pentland
NEUROTICS *See* Neuroses
The **neutral** man. Carrington, L.
Neutral zone. Cummins, A.
NEUTRON BOMB
Moravia, A. There's a neutron bomb for
ants too
Neutron star. Niven, L.
NEVADA
See also Sierra Nevada Mountains
(Calif. and Nev.)
Clark, W. V. T. The Indian well
Davis, S. The pocket-miner
Kranes, D. The phantom Mercury of
Nevada
Kranes, D. The whorehouse picnic
Sanchez, T. Red Reno honkers
Updike, J. Nevada
      Frontier and pioneer life
See Frontier and pioneer life—
Nevada
        Las Vegas
Gerber, M. J. Honeymoon
Gilliatt, P. The position of the planets
Monreal, D. N. Down in Las Vegas
Schwartz, J. Faith
Nevada. Updike, J.
The **Nevada** School of Acting. Troy, J.

Nevai, Lucia, 1945-
Baby wood
  Nevai, L. Star game
Close
  The New Yorker 64:36-9 N 7 '88
Connor's lake
  Nevai, L. Star game
Diamond twill
  Nevai, L. Star game
Grounds for love
  Mademoiselle 90:62+ Ja '84
Hooked
  Nevai, L. Star game
Likely houses
  Nevai, L. Star game
Mother's Day
  Nevai, L. Star game
  Prairie Schooner 60:30-6 Wint '86
Mr. Feathers
  Nevai, L. Star game
The Nile
  Nevai, L. Star game
Red spikes
  Nevai, L. Star game
Resident artist
  Nevai, L. Star game
The sad-womb son
  Nevai, L. Star game
The star game
  The Literary Review (Madison, N.J.)
    31:65-70 Fall '87
  Nevai, L. Star game
"Stranger in paradise"
  Nevai, L. Star game
Temp
  Nevai, L. Star game
Never bet the devil your head. Poe, E. A.
Never bet your head. See Poe, E. A. Never
  bet the devil your head
Never blue. Soldatow, S.
Never get another dog. Heavey, J.
Never meet again. Budrys, A.
Never out of sight. Asimov, I.
Never quite a Hollywood star. Revard, C.
Never say good-bye. Soman, F. J.
Never shake a family tree. Westlake, D. E.
Never talk to strangers. Christman, K.
Never tears for California. Roscoe, P.
Never tell anyone. Wilhelm, K.
Never the right time. Johnston, B.
Never trust a woman. Nielsen, H.
Never visit Venice. Aickman, R.
Neville, Kris (Kris Ottman), 1925-1980
Ballenger's people
  Neville, K. The science fiction of Kris
    Neville
Bettyann
  Neville, K. The science fiction of Kris
    Neville
Cold war
  Neville, K. The science fiction of Kris
    Neville

The forest of Zil
  Amazing stories: visions of other worlds
  Neville, K. The science fiction of Kris
    Neville
From the government printing office
  Neville, K. The science fiction of Kris
    Neville
Hunt the hunter
  Neville, K. The science fiction of Kris
    Neville
New apples in the garden
  Neville, K. The science fiction of Kris
    Neville
Old Man Henderson
  Neville, K. The science fiction of Kris
    Neville
Overture
  Neville, K. The science fiction of Kris
    Neville
The price of Simeryl
  Neville, K. The science fiction of Kris
    Neville
Underground movement
  Neville, K. The science fiction of Kris
    Neville
Neville, Susan
Banquet
  Neville, S. The invention of flight
The beekeeper
  Neville, S. The invention of flight
Cousins
  Neville, S. The invention of flight
The invention of flight
  Neville, S. The invention of flight
Johnny Appleseed
  Neville, S. The invention of flight
Kentucky people
  Neville, S. The invention of flight
Rain forest
  Neville, S. The invention of flight
Rapture
  Neville, S. The invention of flight
Rondo
  Neville, S. The invention of flight
Second coming
  Neville, S. The invention of flight
Nevins, Francis M., Jr.
The Dogsbody case
  Hound dunnit; ed. by I. Asimov; M. H.
    Greenberg and C. L. R. Waugh
The garrulous Garrity grand scam
  Manhattan mysteries; ed. by B. Pronzini;
    C. L. R. Waugh and M. H. Greenberg
Nevsky Prospekt. Gogol', N. V.
New, J.
Crossing demon
  P.E.N. new fiction I
The **new** accelerator. Wells, H. G.
The **new** acquaintances. Janowitz, T.
A **new** act. Berle, M.
The **new** age. Kaplan, J.
The **new** and the old, the old and the new.
  Taylor, C.

New apples in the garden. Neville, K.
New artists, new jungle. Ignatow, R. G.
New bed. Thompson, J.
New best friends. Adams, A.
NEW BRUNSWICK *See* Canada—New Brunswick
NEW CALEDONIA
  Russell, J. The fourth man
The new castle. Osborn, C.
The new catacomb. Doyle, Sir A. C.
A new Christmas carol. Machen, A.
New clothes. Franklin, P.
New day coming. Hillmer, J.
The new disciple. Van de Wetering, J.
The new dress. Woolf, V.
A new dress for Maggie. Grenon, J.
New dresses. Brown, M. W.
New dresses. Mansfield, K.
A new Eden? Sligo, J.
NEW ENGLAND
          17th century
  Franklin, B. The speech of Polly Baker
  Hawthorne, N. Endicott and the Red Cross
          19th century
  Brown, A. The way of peace
  Cooke, R. T. How Celia changed her mind
  Davis, R. H. An ignoble martyr
  Freeman, M. E. W. Louisa
  Lovecraft, H. P. The picture in the house
  Wharton, E. Ethan Frome
          20th century
  Dubus, A. Adultery
  Dubus, A. Finding a girl in America
  Dubus, A. The pretty girl
  Dubus, A. We don't live here anymore
  Sarton, M. The silent minister
  Sligo, J. A new Eden?
  Williams, J. The skater
  Wilson, B. Disaster
          Farm life
  See Farm life—New England
      Frontier and pioneer life
  See Frontier and pioneer life—New England
NEW ENGLAND DIALECT *See* Dialect stories—New England
The new Faust. Wells, H. G.
The new floor. Jeter, K. W.
The new girl friend. Rendell, R.
A new golden age. Rucker, R. von B.
NEW GUINEA
          Native peoples
  Carter, R. Prints in the valley
NEW HAMPSHIRE
      See also White Mountains (N.H. and Me.)
  Banks, R. Firewood
  Banks, R. Sarah Cole: a type of love story
New Haven. Mattison, A.
NEW HEBRIDES *See* Vanuatu
The new honesty. Busch, F.
NEW JERSEY
  Campos-De Metro, J. Shooting for Jupiter

Damon, P. Davidson among the chosen
          Atlantic City
  Faust, I. Bar bar bar
          Hoboken
  Bell, M. S. The lie detector
          Newark
  Bell, M. S. Irene
  Campos-De Metro, J. Bands
  Campos-De Metro, J. Evvy's brother
  Campos-De Metro, J. The grape's vine, the horse's mouth
  Campos-De Metro, J. Stock
          Trenton
  O'Hara, J. The girl from California
The new kingdom. Piñón, N.
The new life. Ahern, T.
The new life. Im, O.-I.
A new life. Nowakowski, M.
A new life. Shaw, J. B.
New man. Crapser, W.
New men, old ways. Thomas, R.
NEW MEXICO
      See also Carlsbad Caverns National Park (N.M.)
  Austin, M. H. Blue roses
  Barrett, N., Jr. Sallie C.
  Boren, T. Sliding rock
  Charnas, S. M. A musical interlude
  Chavez, A. The ardent commandant
  Chavez, A. The bell that sang again
  Chavez, A. A desert idyll
  Chavez, A. Hunchback Madonna
  Chavez, A. The lean years
  Chavez, A. The penitente thief
  Chavez, A. A Romeo and Juliet story in early New Mexico
  Chavez, A. The Tesuque Pony Express
  Chavez, A. Wake for Don Corsinio
  Evans, M. Xavier's folly
  Rhodes, E. M. Pasó por aquí
      Frontier and pioneer life
  See Frontier and pioneer life—New Mexico
          Albuquerque
  Mares, E. A. Florinto
          Santa Fe
  Adams, A. Time in Santa Fe
  Gardner, M. Old man gloom
The New Moon Party. Boyle, T. C.
New mother. Asscher-Pinkhof, C.
The new mother. Clifford, L. L.
New murders in the Rue Morgue. Barker, C.
The new neighbor. Monreal, D. N.
NEW ORLEANS (LA.) *See* Louisiana—New Orleans
New Orleans getaway. Howard, C.
The new owner. Barthelme, D.
The new prehistory. Rebetez-Cortes, R.
The new prime. Vance, J.
The new rays. Harrison, M. J.
New ritual. St. Clair, M.
The new roof. Hammer, C.

New Rose Hotel. Gibson, W.
The new season. Bloch, R.
The new sensation. Maupassant, G. de
New shoes. Hogan, L.
NEW SOUTH WALES (AUSTRALIA) See
   Australia—New South Wales
NEW SOUTHWEST See Southwestern
States
A new tradition. Schell, J.
New villa. Chekhov, A. P.
New women. Cary, J.
A new world. Jolley, E.
The new world. Kreitman, E.
NEW YEAR
   Bitov, A. The garden
   Brown, G. M. Darkness and light
   DeMarinis, R. Pagans
   Eskapa, S. White and injured
   Kawabata, Y. Snow
   London, J. New Year
   Vanderhaeghe, G. Man descending
   Wakayama, M. Watching fire
New Year. London, J.
New Year's. Keillor, G.
A New Year's gift. Maupassant, G. de
NEW YORK (N.Y.)
   Auchincloss, L. The Stations of the Cross
   Davidson, A. The lord of Central Park
   Duane, D. Uptown local
   Finney, J. The coin collector
   MacLean, K. The missing man
   Sheckley, R. The people trap
      19th century
   Auchincloss, L. A diary of old New York
   Auchincloss, L. The wedding guest
   Hoch, E. D. The crime of the century
   James, H. The jolly corner
      20th century
   Austin, D. The detective
   Barker, C. The midnight meat train
   Biggs, M. The other Catherine Irene
   Busch, F. Defense
   Cheever, J. Reunion
   Davis, D. S. Mrs. Norris observes
   Doctorow, E. L. Lives of the poets
   Epstein, L. Music of the spheres
   Friedman, B. H. Whispers
   Friedman, B. J. Detroit Abe
   Friedman, B. J. Our Lady of the Lockers
   Gangemi, K. Greenbaum, O'Reilly &
      Stephens
   Gold, H. A selfish story
   Hauptman, W. Moon walking
   Henry, O. The buyer from Cactus City
   Henry, O. Rus in urbe
   Hoch, E. D. Murder at the Bouchercon
   Honig, L. No friends, all strangers
   Ignatow, R. G. Colors
   Ignatow, R. G. New artists, new jungle
   Janowitz, T. Conviction
   Johnson, J. The children's wing
   Kessler, J. F. Courtly love
   Kessler, J. F. Ikaros

   Kessler, J. F. Teiresias
   Kiely, B. The python
   Lurie, M. Her life: a fragment
   Lynch, L. Fruitstand I: Oranges out of
      season
   Mazel, D. The maestro
   Mordden, E. The handshake deal
   Mordden, E. Uptown, downtown: a tour
      through the gay metropolis
   Morris, M. Losing your cool
   Mukherjee, B. Hindus
   Paley, G. Faith in a tree
   Paolucci, A. Buried treasure
   Paolucci, A. Ciao, mio tesoro
   Pulaski, J. Minnie the Moocher's hair
   Pulaski, J. Religious instruction
   Rose, J. The sunshine of Paradise Alley
   Shaham, N. The salt of the earth
   Stephens, M. Everlast
   Swados, H. The dancer
   Swados, H. Nights in the gardens of
      Brooklyn
   Swados, H. A story for Teddy
   Texier, C. The fedora
   Thurm, M. California
   Wexler, J. Alleywalk
      Politics
      See Politics—New York (N.Y.)
      Bronx
   Faust, I. Bunny Berigan in the elephants'
      graveyard
   Kessler, J. F. The old muse
   Kotzwinkle, W. Star cruisers, welcome
   Paley, G. Ruthy and Edie
   Ryan, A. Waiting for the papers
      Brooklyn
   Bell, M. S. The forgotten bridge
   Bell, M. S. The lie detector
   Ellin, S. The day of the bullet
   Granit, A. The penny is for God!
   Granit, A. Songs my mother taught me
      that are not in Hamlet; or, "Come
      into my house, Horatio! there are
      more things under the mattress than
      are dreamt of in your philosophy!"
   Granit, A. Tessie, don't give away the
      raisin; without it, you're lost!
   La Puma, S. The boys of Bensonhurst
   La Puma, S. The gangster's ghost
   La Puma, S. Gravesend Bay
   La Puma, S. The jilted groom
   La Puma, S. The mouthpiece
   La Puma, S. Wear it in good health
   Mazel, D. Sadie
   Neugeboren, J. Uncle Nathan
   Pohl, F. The greening of Bed-Stuy
   Pulaski, J. Music story
   Schwartz, L. S. The middle classes
   Schwartz, L. S. The two portraits of Rem-
      brandt
   Swados, H. My Coney Island uncle
   Updike, D. Winter
   Wolfe, T. The hollow men

NEW YORK (N.Y.)—Brooklyn—*Continued*
Wolfe, T. No door
Wolfe, T. Only the dead know Brooklyn
Coney Island
Crane, S. Coney Island's failing days
Rosenfeld, I. Coney Island revisited
Greenwich Village
Bell, M. S. I [love] NY
Calisher, H. Real impudence
Cather, W. Coming, Aphrodite!
Farris, J. You can keep your razors & guns but check your loud mouths at the door
Janowitz, T. Kurt and Natasha, a relationship
Kolm, R. Duke & Jill
Lerman, E. Remedies
Yates, R. Oh, Joseph, I'm so tired
Harlem
Dumas, H. Harlem
Dumas, H. A Harlem game
Faust, I. The Dalai Lama of Harlem
Fisher, R. Blades of steel
Fisher, R. The city of refuge
Fisher, R. Common meter
Fisher, R. Ezekiel
Fisher, R. Ezekiel learns
Fisher, R. Miss Cynthie
Fisher, R. The promised land
Fisher, R. Ringtail
Fisher, R. The South lingers on
Hurston, Z. N. Book of Harlem
Hurston, Z. N. Muttsy
Hurston, Z. N. Story in Harlem slang
Lower East Side
Botwinik, B. Israel and his children
Botwinik, B. Yankel
Crane, S. When man falls, a crowd gathers
Dennison, G. The sufficiency of everyday life: Avenue A and Eleventh Street, 1963
Epstein, L. The magic flute
Epstein, L. The Steinway quintet
Forer, A. U. Thanksgiving with Trudy
McGrath, P. The angel
Weidman, J. Good man, bad man
Manhattan
Barker, C. Lost souls
Barnett, A. Snapshot
Baxt, G. The woman I envied
Beattie, A. The big outside world
Beattie, A. Cards
Benderson, B. A visit from Mom
Broun, H. The deep blue eastern sky
Brown, F. Mouse
Calisher, H. The sound track
Calisher, H. Survival techniques
Cheever, J. The enormous radio
Cheever, J. The pot of gold
Ciment, J. Money
Clayton, J. J. Bodies like mouths
Crane, S. Adventures of a novelist
Crane, S. The broken-down van

Crane, S. An experiment in misery
Crane, S. The fire
Crane, S. In a Park Row restaurant
Cullinan, E. Life after death
Disch, T. M. The roaches
Ellin, S. The nine-to-five man
Ellison, H. Soft monkey
Ellison, H. The whimper of whipped dogs
Faust, I. Simon Girty go ape
Feinberg, D. B. The age of anxiety
Fox, W. P. You don't smell it: you drink it
Gaitskill, M. Daisy's Valentine
Gaitskill, M. Other factors
Gaitskill, M. Trying to be
Gilliatt, P. As we have learnt from Freud, there are no jokes
Gold, H. A death on the East Side
Grant, C. L. Out there
Henry, O. The cop and the anthem
Henry, O. Mammon and the archer
Holleran, A. Ties
Hospital, J. T. Here comes the sun
Hospital, J. T. Mosie
Hughes, L. Slave on the block
Hunter, E. The beatings
Innaurato, A. Solidarity
Interollo, L. The quickening
Janowitz, T. On and off the African veldt
Janowitz, T. Spells
Johnson, J. The fall of Texas
Kessler, J. F. The bird cage
Kilgore, D. The deterioration of 47th Street
Klein, T. E. D. Children of the kingdom
Kotzwinkle, W. The day Stokowski saved the world
Kotzwinkle, W. Mr. Jones's convention
Kunstler, J. H. The rise, fall, and redemption of Mooski Toffski Offski
Kuttner, H. Home is the hunter
Leiber, F. Catch that zeppelin!
Liben, M. A note on chivalry
Linzner, G. The independent fiend
Lish, G. The traitor
MacLean, K. Rescue squad
Manners, M. Squeakie's first case
McCullers, C. Court in the West eighties
McGrath, P. Lush triumphant
Melville, H. Bartleby the scrivener
Menaker, D. The old left
Moorhouse, F. The New York bell captain
Morris, W. Glimpse into another country
Nugent, B. City of boys
Oates, J. C. Nairobi
Palmer, S. Riddle of the marble blade
Pentecost, H. Jericho and the cardboard box
Pohl, F. The blister
Pohl, F. Gwenanda and the Supremes
Pohl, F. Second-hand sky
Pohl, F. When New York hit the fan

NEW YORK (N.Y.) — Manhattan — Continued
Pronzini, B. The man who collected "The Shadow"
Purdy, J. In this corner . . .
Rafferty, S. S. The hawk and the dome of hell
Robinson, S. By any other name
Schulman, H. To die from
Schwartz, J. Chloe Hummel of the Chicago White Sox
Schwartz, J. Crazy
Schwartz, J. Max
Schwartz, J. Waiting weeping
Schwartz, L. S. Epistemology, sex, and the shedding of light
Schwartz, L. S. The painters
Tevis, W. S. Out of luck
Thurm, M. Away from the heart
Thurm, M. Leaving Johanna
Tuohy, F. Windows
Wilson, P. F. Soft
Wolfe, T. The birthday
Wolfe, T. Death the proud brother
Woolrich, C. New York blues
Zelazny, R. Deadboy Donner and the Filstone Cup
NEW YORK (N.Y.). STATUE OF LIBERTY See Statue of Liberty (New York, N.Y.)
NEW YORK (STATE)
See also Adirondack Mountains (N.Y.); Long Island (N.Y.)
Thompson, J. Applause, applause
19th century
Crane, S. The third violet
20th century
Halley, A. A Rosenkavalier
Kessler, J. F. Afrodite
Mukherjee, B. Saints
Thompson, S. Montauk
Walsh, T. The killer instinct
Farm life
See Farm life—New York (State)
Buffalo
Swados, H. The man in the toolhouse
Levittown
Wetherell, W. D. The man who loved Levittown
New York City
See New York (N.Y.)
Oneida County
Busch, F. The new honesty
Saratoga Springs
Calisher, H. Saratoga, hot
The New York bell captain. Moorhouse, F.
New York blues. Woolrich, C.
New York girls are different. Moses, J.
NEW YORK TIMES
Stark, S. S. The Barlip run
The "New Yorker" story. Bayles, M.
NEW ZEALAND
Brasch, C. Dunedin

Dabrowska, C. Huntress
Frame, J. Insulation
Gee, M. The champion
Gee, M. Eleventh holiday
Gee, M. The hole in the window
Gee, M. Joker and wife
Gee, M. Right-hand man
Grace, P. Butterflies
Grace, P. Electric city
Grace, P. Fishing
Grace, P. Flies
Grace, P. The geranium
Grace, P. Going for the bread
Grace, P. The hills
Grace, P. Hospital
Grace, P. Kahawai
Grace, P. The lamp
Grace, P. The urupa
Grace, P. Waimarie
Grace, P. The wall
Haley, R. Fog
Haley, R. The palace of Kandahar
Hill, E. The piano
Hulme, K. The cicadas of summer
Hulme, K. A drift in dream
Hulme, K. He tauware kawa, he kawa tauware
Hulme, K. Kaibutsu-san
Hulme, K. King bait
Hulme, K. The knife and the stone
Hulme, K. A nightsong for the shining cuckoo
Hulme, K. Stations on the way to Avalon
Hulme, K. Swansong
Hulme, K. A tally of the souls of sheep
Hulme, K. Te Kaihau: the windeater
Hulme, K. Unnamed islands in the unknown sea
Hulme, K. While my guitar gently sings
Hulme, K. A window drunken in the brain
Lawson, H. The geological spieler
Mansfield, K. The woman at the store
Marshall, O. The paper parcel
Sligo, J. Burnham camp
Sligo, J. Going home
Farm life
See Farm life—New Zealand
Rural life
Feeney, J. A married woman
Gee, M. The widow
Taylor, A. Bread and hunger
Taylor, A. Hera
Auckland
Morrissey, M. A mermaid on a blue horse: a tale with two endings
Wellington
Haley, R. Looping the loop
NEW ZEALAND. ARMY
Officers
Davin, D. Coming and going

NEWARK (N.J.) *See* New Jersey—Newark

Newbound, Christopher
Tennis or what
Seventeen 46:164-5+ My '87

The **newest** blessing. Nelson, P.

NEWFOUNDLAND *See* Canada—Newfoundland

Newly shorn. Colette

The **newlywed.** Nagibin, ÍŪ. M.

Newman, Kim
Dreamers
Interzone: the first anthology; ed. by J.
Clute; C. Greenland and D. Pringle
Patricia's profession
Interzone: the 2nd anthology; ed. by J.
Clute; D. Pringle and S. Ounsley

The **news.** Busch, F.

The **news.** Dixon, S.

The **news.** Drewitz, I.

News from El Corazon: in the composing room. Taylor, P. E.

The **news** from Ireland. Trevor, W.

News from the sun. Ballard, J. G.

The **news** of my suicide. Patchett, A.

The **newspaper.** Wolfe, T.

NEWSPAPER PUBLISHERS *See* Publishers and publishing

NEWSPAPER VENDORS
Burke, M. Lou's corner
Warren, J. Mr. Dnarley's pigs

NEWSPAPERMEN *See* Journalists

NEWSPAPERS
Barthelme, D. Pepperoni
Codrescu, A. The herald
Durrell, L. Frying the flag
Gallant, M. With a capital T
Henry, O. The clarion call
Matsumoto, S. The woman who took the local paper
Nowakowski, M. Wastepaper
Rhys, J. Again the Antilles
Richards, J. Mencken stuff
Silverberg, R. What we learned from this morning's newspaper
Wells, H. G. The queer story of Brownlow's newspaper

Newton sleep. Benford, G.

The **next** best thing to happy. Cameron, P.

Next boat from Douala. Boyd, W.

The **next** day. Asimov, I.

The **next** dwarf. Sladek, J. T.

The **next** glade. Aickman, R.

Next of kin. Girion, B.

The **next** room. Byatt, A. S.

The **next** time. James, H.

The **next** time I meet Buddy Rich. Painter, P.

Next time you'll know me. Campbell, R.

Ng, Fae Myenne
A red sweater
The Pushcart prize XII

Nga tui. Taylor, A.

Ng'maryo, Eric Sikujua
Ivory bangles
African short stories in English; ed. by J. de Grandsaigne

N'goola. Prichard, K. S.

Ngugi, James *See* Ngugi wa Thiong'o, 1938-

Ngugi wa Thiong'o, 1938-
Minutes of glory
African short stories; ed. by C. Achebe and C. L. Innes
The return
African short stories in English; ed. by J. de Grandsaigne

Nhuong, Huynh Quang
Fighting crickets
TriQuarterly no72:17-25 Spr/Summ '88

NIAGARA FALLS (N.Y.) *See* New York (State)—Niagara Falls

Niagara Falls. Winters, J.

Niatum, Duane, 1938-
She keeps the dance turning like the earth
Earth power coming; ed. by S. J. Ortiz

NICARAGUA
Ramírez, S. To Jackie with all our heart

Nicaragua is white. Ramírez, S.

NICARAGUANS
                    Germany
Ramírez, S. Saint Nikolaus

NICE (FRANCE) *See* France—Nice

A **nice** place to stay. Tyre, N.

Nice white people. Everett, P. L.

Nice work if you can get it. Honig, D.

Nichols, Janet
Recapitulation
The New Yorker 60:27-9 Ag 6 '84

Nichols, John Treadwell, 1940-
The Milagro beanfield war [excerpt]
The Interior country; ed. by A. Blackburn
Writers of the purple sage; ed. by R. Martin and M. Barasch

Nichols, Robert
Free fall (R's account)
New directions in prose and poetry 48

Nicholson, Margaret Beda *See* Yorke, Margaret

Nickel a throw. Wetherell, W. D.

The **nickel** derby. Randisi, R. J.

NICKNAMES
Yi, M.-Y. Early spring, mid-summer

Nicknames. Klinkowitz, J.

Nicky Martinez. Crapser, W.

Nicol, Abioseh
The truly married woman
African short stories in English; ed. by J. de Grandsaigne

Nicolai, Dan
Day out
Stiller's pond; ed. by J. Agee; R. Blakely and S. Welch

Nicolas Oyseleur, judge. Schwob, M.

Nicole liberated. Villefranche, A.-M.

Nicoll, Gregory
Dead air
  Ripper! Ed. by G. Dozois and S. Casper
NICOSIA (CYPRUS) *See* Cyprus—Nicosia
NIECES
Thompson, J. The birch tree
Wilson, B. How to fix a roof
Nielsen, Helen, 1918-
The deadly Mrs. Haversham
  Uncollected crimes; ed. by B. Pronzini
  and M. H. Greenberg
Death scene
  Hitchcock in prime time; ed. by F. M.
  Nevins and M. H. Greenberg
Never trust a woman
  Alfred Hitchcock's Grave suspicions
A woman is missing
  Alfred Hitchcock's Crimewatch
You can't trust a man
  The Deadly arts; ed. by B. Pronzini and
  M. Muller
Nielsen, Marianne O.
The trout
  L. Ron Hubbard presents Writers of the
  future v2
NIGERIA
Achebe, C. The sacrificial egg
Ekwensi, C. The ivory dancer
Parise, G. Hunger
Regent, P. Memories of colonialism
Thomas, M. Summer opportunity
      Civil War, 1967-1970
Achebe, C. Civil peace
NIGHT
Wexler, J. For Ann
Night. Dawson, F.
The **night**. Hofmann, G.
Night. Power, V.
A **night**. Rhys, J.
Night and silence. Level, M.
A **night** at the head of a grave. Sullivan,
  T.
Night before battle. Hemingway, E.
The **night** before Chancellorsville. Fitzgerald,
  F. S.
The **night** between the second and the third.
  Ekström, M.
Night broadcast. Hobana, I.
Night calls. Kimbriel, K. E.
Night calls the Green Falcon. McCammon,
  R. R.
NIGHT CLUBS
Cain, J. M. Cigarette girl
Coleman, W. The stare down
McGrath, P. Hand of a wanker
Woolrich, C. The showboat murders
Night court. Counselman, M. E.
Night crawlers. Harrington, J.
Night cries. See Giles, M. Old souls
Night fears. Hartley, L. P.
The **Night** Flier. King, S.
Night flight to Miami. Wiebe, D. E.
Night flight to Stockholm. Wiebe, D. E.

Night fragrance. Furui, Y.
Night freight. Ch'en, Y.-C.
The **night** game. Pfeil, F.
The **night** George Wolfe died. Conley, R. J.
The **night** guest. Nagibin, ÍŪ. M.
The **night** Helen was killed. Smith, P. C.
Night hound's moon. Schaub, M. H.
A **night** in June. Williams, W. C.
A **night** in Possum Holler. Mayhar, A.
A **night** in the garden. Dickinson, C.
A **night** in the Indian Ocean. Stead, C.
Night in Tunisia. Jordan, N.
A **night** in Whitechapel. Maupassant, G. de
The **night** is freezing fast. Monteleone, T.
  F.
Night laughter. Kushner, E.
Night life. Finney, E. J.
The **night** mother. Fraser, A.
The **night** Motke Behr danced. Levinson, B.
Night moves. Powers, T.
Night 'n day. Lynch, L.
The **night** of power. Pachter, J.
Night of surrender. Fink, I.
The **night** of the angels. Zalygin, S.
Night of the cooters. Waldrop, H.
The **night** of the curlews. García Márquez,
  G.
The **night** of the festival. El Milady, F. A.
  K.
The **night** of the Iguana. Williams, T.
Night of the luminarias. Carr, P. M.
The **night** of the Piasa. Green, J. C., and
  Proctor, G. W.
The **night** of the sea serpent. Weber, T.
The **night** of the tiger. King, S.
The **night** of white Bhairab. Shepard, L.
Night on Mispec Moor. Niven, L.
Night out 1925. Rhys, J.
A **night** out at the Club Harmonica. Dunn,
  D.
The **night** patrol. Nowakowski, M.
Night piece for Julia. West, J.
Night run. O'Cork, S.
Night runner. Jolley, E.
Night school. Bloch, R.
Night-sea journey. Barth, J.
Night shift in emergency. Anderman, J.
Night shoot. Monsarrat, N.
Night-side. Oates, J. C.
Night. Sleep. Death. The stars. Oates, J. C.
Night sport. Hoffman, W.
Night stalk. Forester, C. S.
The **night** the blood. Galgut, D.
The **night** the cat stayed out. Gilbert, M.
The **night** the playoffs were rained out.
  Jacobsen, J.
The **night** the world ended. Brown, F.
Night they missed the horror show. Lansdale, J. R.
Night train through the snow to Montreal.
  Thompson, K.
The **night** train to Lost Valley. Derleth, A.
  W.

Night travellers. Birdsell, S.
Night visions. Dann, J.
The **night** visitor. Poniatowska, E.
The **night** visitors. Hall, R. W.
Night walk. Painter, P.
The **night** walk. Upward, E.
Night win. Kress, N.
The **night** wind. Pangborn, E.
The **night** wire. Arnold, H. F.
A **night** with Kant. Crichton Smith, I.
Night work. Gault, W. C.
Nightcrawlers. McCammon, R. R.
Nightfall. Asimov, I.
Nightflyers. Martin, G. R. R.
NIGHTINGALES
  Hildesheimer, W. Why I transformed myself into a nightingale
A **nightmare.** Chesterton, G. K.
The **nightmare.** Saidi, W.
Nightmare in yellow. Brown, F.
Nightmares. Watson, I.
Nightrangers. Millman, L.
Nights. Asscher-Pinkhof, C.
Nights and days. Finney, E. J.
Nights in the gardens of Brooklyn. Swados, H.
Nightshade. McBain, E.
A **nightsong** for the shining cuckoo. Hulme, K.
A **nighttime** story. See Collins, L. Fears
Nihil obstat. Valenzuela, L.
NIHILISM
      See also Anarchism and anarchists
Nikishka's secrets. Kazakov, Y.
The **Nile.** Nevai, L.
Nilsam's friend. Winton, T.
Nimmo, Dorothy
  The healing
    First fictions: Introduction 9
  Rabbits
    First fictions: Introduction 9
  Wake and call me mother
    First fictions: Introduction 9
Nimmo, H. Arlo
  Lim
    Short story international 46
Nimram. Gardner, J.
Nina. Bates, H. E.
Nina. Bloch, R.
Nina of Ashkelon. Amichai, Y.
The **nine** best movies. Mcdonald, G.
The **nine** billion names of God. Clarke, A. C.
Nine dollars' worth of mumble. Caldwell, E.
Nine occasions. Rey Rosa, R.
Nine points of the law. Hornung, E. W.
The **nine-to-five** man. Ellin, S.
Nine words in winter. Inks, C.
Nineteen fifty-four: days of the roomers. See Stead, C. 1954: days of the roomers
A **nineteen** fifty-seven Ford. See Abbott, K. A 1957 Ford
Nineteen forty-one. Gilchrist, E.

Nineteen lists. Klass, P.
Nineteen roses. Eliade, M.
Nineteen seventy five has come and gone. See Drake, R. 1975 has come and gone
Nineteen thirty-four. See Phillips, J. A. 1934
Nineteen twenty-eight story. See Agee, J. 1928 story
Ninety minutes away. O'Hara, J.
Ninety-nine point six. See West, J. 99.6
A **ninety-six-year-old** big sister. Gold, H.
Nisbet, Robert
  Dorme-toi, mon petit
    New England Review and Bread Loaf Quarterly 10:454-60 Summ '88
Nitya. Narayan, R. K.
Niven, Larry
  The borderland of Sol
    The Hugo winners v4
  Convergent series
    Mathenauts: tales of mathematical wonder; ed. by R. Rucker
  Flare time
    Medea: Harlan's world; ed. by H. Ellison
  Flash crowd
    Baker's dozen: 13 short science fiction novels
  Neutron star
    Isaac Asimov presents the best science fiction firsts
  Night on Mispec Moor
    Robert Adams' Book of soldiers
  What good is a glass dagger?
    Wizards; ed. by I. Asimov; M. H. Greenberg and C. G. Waugh
Nixon, Cornelia
  Snapshot
    Michigan Quarterly Review 24:588-95 Fall '85
NIXON, RICHARD M. (RICHARD MILHOUS), 1913-
      About
  Bumpus, J. The attack on San Clemente
  Strieber, W. The Nixon mask
The **Nixon** mask. Strieber, W.
Nizer, Louis
  The zipper
    Short story international 65
The **Nizhni** Novgorod Otkos. Pil'niāk, B.
No!. Dai Qing
No. 252 Rue M le Prince. Cram, R. A.
No alarming symptoms. Varshavsky, I.
No charge for alterations. Gold, H. L.
No cigarettes, no matches, no lights allowed. Power, V.
No country for old men. McCormack, E. P.
No crime for Captain Leopold. Hoch, E. D.
No cure for it. Wolfe, T.
No day too long. Gomez, J.
No dogs allowed. Lull, R.
No door. Wolfe, T.
No fairies at the bottom of the garden. Titcher, M.

No fish for the cat. Clark, N. M.
No flies on Frank. Lennon, J.
No friend like a new friend. Auchincloss, L.
No friends, all strangers. Honig, L.
No future in it. Haldeman, J. W.
No golden tombstones for me! Granit, A.
No handicap. Post, J.
No hero. Stuart, J.
No job too small. Thorman, C.
No joy in the morning. Silva, B.
No kidding!?! Franco, M.
No kind of name. Hagy, A. C.
No loose ends. Greenberg, A.
No luggage? Whitaker, M.
No man's laughter. Algren, N.
No marble angels. Leedom-Ackerman, J.
No marks for Rolf. Krisman, S.
No memory comes. Winton, T.
No more. Phillips, J. L.
No more rivers. Wolfe, T.
No-name baby. Wesley, V. W.
No news. Gingher, M.
No news. Phelps, E. S.
No, no, and no. Cortázar, J.
No one looks out anymore. Ferreira, R.
No one will ever love you as much. Smith,
    L.
No one's a mystery. Tallent, E.
No other gods. Bretnor, R.
No other women. Vogan, S.
No pets. Stokes, T.
No petty thief. Stuart, J.
No place for you, my love. Welty, E.
No Pulitzer for Pinsker. Epstein, J.
No raincloud for the trees, no wings above
    the mountain. Tamer, Z.
No room at the inn. Ferber, E.
No sale 1. Liben, M.
No sale 2. Liben, M.
No-sided professor. Gardner, M.
No sinecure. Hornung, E. W.
No small problem. Lutz, J.
No smoking. Broun, H.
No sore losers. Rand, N.
No sound of footsteps in the treetops. An-
    derman, J.
No spring chicken. Pierce, A. W.
No stone for Jochebed. Whitaker, M.
No stranger. Houbein, L.
No such thing as a free lunch. Grenville, K.
No tears for Schmeck. Böll, H.
No tomorrows. Mayberry, F. V.
No trace. Madden, D.
No truce with kings. Anderson, P.
No wider than a nickel. Ritchie, J.
No witnesses. Burt, E.
No woman born. Moore, C. L.
No word for mercy. Havazelet, E.

NOAH (BIBLICAL FIGURE)
About
Klass, F. Before the rainbow
The Noah heritage. Dorman, S.

NOBILITY See Aristocracy
The Noble Courtesan. Gilchrist, M.
'Noblesse oblige'. Durrell, L.
Nobody ever dies. Hemingway, E.
Nobody said anything. Carver, R.
Nobody tells me anything. Ritchie, J.
Nobody's business. Gilliatt, P.
Nobody's child. Groff, D.
Nobody's fool. Hood, M.
Nocturne. Saiki, J.
Nocturne with neon lights. Tuohy, F.
Noel. Plemmons, M.
The noise. Middleton, S.
Noise of strangers. Garrett, G. P.
The noise of the lorries. Halligan, M.
The noise was heard afar off. Dorr, L.
Nolan, B. See O'Brien, Flann, 1911-1966
Nolan, William F., 1928-
Ceremony
    Midnight; ed. by C. L. Grant
Dead call
    100 great fantasy short short stories; ed.
        by I. Asimov; T. Carr and M. H.
        Greenberg
The final stone
    Cutting edge; ed. by D. Etchison
A long time dying
    The Eyes have it; ed. by R. J. Randisi
My name is Dolly
    The Year's best fantasy, first annual
        collection
Of time and Kathy Benedict
    Whispers V
Pirate's moon
    Murder in Los Angeles; ed. by J. L.
        Breen and others
A real nice guy
    Murder California style; ed. by J. L.
        Breen and J. Ball
Saturday's shadow
    Masters of darkness; ed. by D. Etchison
Sungrab
    Distant danger; ed. by J. Van de
        Wetering
Trust not a man
    Masques; ed. by J. N. Williamson
The Yard
    Masques II; ed. by J. N. Williamson
Nomad and viper. Oz, A.
Non Sung Smoke. Grafton, S.
Nona. King, S.
Nona Vincent. James, H.
The noncommissioned officer. Maupassant, G.
de
Nongqause. Hagy, A. C.
Nonhebel, Clare
Popcorn
    Winter's tales, new ser. v3
Nonie. Brodkey, H.
Nonna. Ardizzone, T.
NONVIOLENCE
Sonu, H. Flowers of fire
The Noodge Factor. Jeppson, J. O.

Noonan, Bode
Fruit drink
    Hear the silence; ed. by I. Zahava
Nooteboom, Cees, 1933-
Mokusei: a love story
    Winter's tales, new ser. v1
Nor custom stale. Russ, J.
Nor disregard the humblest voice. Mayhar, A.
Nor limestone islands. Lafferty, R. A.
Nor the many-colored fires of a star ring. Martin, G. R. R.
Nora says "check.". Gardner, M.
Nordan, Lewis
The all-girl football team
    Nordan, L. The all-girl football team
The attendant
    Nordan, L. The all-girl football team
The farmers' daughter
    Nordan, L. The all-girl football team
A hank of hair, a piece of bone
    The Southern Review (Baton Rouge, La.) 24:366-79 Spr '88
John Thomas Bird
    Nordan, L. The all-girl football team
The Sears and Roebuck catalog game
    Nordan, L. The all-girl football team
The sin eater
    Mississippi writers v1: Fiction; ed. by D. Abbott
Storyteller
    Arkansas in short fiction; ed. by W. M. Baker and E. C. Simpson
    The New writers of the South; ed. by C. East
Sugar among the chickens
    Nordan, L. The all-girl football team
Sugar, the eunuchs, and Big G.B.
    New stories from the South: the year's best, 1987
    Nordan, L. The all-girl football team
    The Southern Review (Baton Rouge, La.) 22:860-75 O '86
The talker at the freak-show
    Nordan, L. The all-girl football team
Wild dog
    Nordan, L. The all-girl football team
Nordin, Signe
The carp
    The Georgia Review 41:763-6 Wint '87
Nor'easter. Robison, J.
NORFOLK (ENGLAND) *See* England—Norfolk
Norfolk, 1969. Tilghman, C.
Normal experience. Francis, H. E.
The **Norman** Fisher Memorial Ski Race. Burns, M.
NORMANDY (FRANCE) *See* France—Normandy
A **Normandy** joke. Maupassant, G. de
Norris, Benjamin Franklin *See* Norris, Frank, 1870-1902

Norris, Frank, 1870-1902
The ship that saw a ghost
    Short stories of the sea; ed. by G. C. Solley and E. Steinbaugh
Norris, Gloria
Holding on
    New stories from the South: the year's best, 1986
    Prize stories, 1985
    The Sewanee Review 92:175-93 Spr '84
Revive us again
    Mississippi writers v1: Fiction; ed. by D. Abbott
    Prize stories, 1984
Norris, Helen, 1916-
A bee in amber
    The Southern Review (Baton Rouge, La.) 23:692-708 Summ '87
The Christmas wife
    Norris, H. The Christmas wife
    Prime number; ed. by A. L. Weir
The cloven tree
    Norris, H. Water into wine
The cormorant
    Norris, H. Water into wine
    The Sewanee Review 96:179-204 Spr '88
The healing
    Norris, H. The Christmas wife
The light on the water
    Norris, H. Water into wine
    The Southern Review (Baton Rouge, La.) 24:349-65 Spr '88
The love child
    Norris, H. The Christmas wife
    Prize stories, 1984
Money man
    Norris, H. The Christmas wife
Mrs. Moonlight
    Norris, H. Water into wine
    The Sewanee Review 94:253-71 Spr '86
The pearl sitter
    Norris, H. Water into wine
    The Southern Review (Baton Rouge, La.) 22:157-73 Ja '86
The quarry
    Norris, H. The Christmas wife
    Prize stories, 1985
The singing well
    Norris, H. The Christmas wife
    Prize stories, 1987
Starwood
    Norris, H. The Christmas wife
Water into wine
    Norris, H. Water into wine
    The Sewanee Review 95:430-47 Summ '87
White hyacinths
    Norris, H. Water into wine
Norris, Kathleen, 1947-
Conversation
    Stiller's pond; ed. by J. Agee; R. Blakely and S. Welch

Norris, Leslie, 1921-
Blackberries
  Norris, L. The girl from Cardigan
A flight of geese
  Norris, L. The girl from Cardigan
Gamblers
  Norris, L. The girl from Cardigan
The girl from Cardigan
  The New Yorker 62:38-44 S 29 '86
  Norris, L. The girl from Cardigan
The holm oak
  Norris, L. The girl from Cardigan
In the west country
  Norris, L. The girl from Cardigan
Keening
  The Sewanee Review 95:543-52 Fall '87
The kingfisher
  The New Yorker 60:31-3 Jl 23 '84
  Norris, L. The girl from Cardigan
Lurchers
  Norris, L. The girl from Cardigan
My uncle's story
  Norris, L. The girl from Cardigan
A piece of archangel
  Norris, L. The girl from Cardigan
A professional man
  Norris, L. The girl from Cardigan
Reverse for Dennis
  Norris, L. The girl from Cardigan
Shaving
  Norris, L. The girl from Cardigan
Sing it again, Wordsworth
  Norris, L. The girl from Cardigan
Some opposites of good
  New England Review and Bread Loaf Quarterly 10:465-73 Summ '88
  Norris, L. The girl from Cardigan
The wind, the cold wind
  Norris, L. The girl from Cardigan
North. Blaise, C.
NORTH AFRICA
  See also Sahara
Bowles, P. The delicate prey
Bowles, P. A distant episode
Camus, A. The renegade
Sterling, B. Dinner in Audoghast
A **North** American education. Blaise, C.
NORTH CAROLINA
Owen, G. Miss Mahalia and the still
Price, R. Uncle Grant
Raleigh
Gingher, M. My mother's confession
Leedom-Ackerman, J. No marble angels
NORTH DAKOTA
Erdrich, L. The beet queen
Erdrich, L. Fleur
North Dakota. Morgan, K.
North Gladiola. Wilcox, J.
North light. Helprin, M.
North of peace. Wetherell, W. D.
North of the Sangro. Davin, D.
North to south. Griesemer, J.
North wind. Butler, G.

Northern, Mary Lou
The missing ingredient
  Redbook 167:48-50 Ag '86
NORTHERN IRELAND
Forsyth, F. There are no snakes in Ireland
MacLaverty, B. A happy birthday
MacLaverty, B. Some surrender
McCrory, M. Strangers
Belfast
Lavin, M. The face of hate
Madden, D. Hidden symptoms
Northern light. Engberg, S.
NORTHERN RHODESIA *See* Zambia
NORTHMEN *See* Vikings
Northrup, Jim
The odyssey
  Stiller's pond; ed. by J. Agee; R. Blakely and S. Welch
NORTHUMBERLAND (ENGLAND) *See* England—Northumberland
Norton, Alice Mary *See* Norton, Andre, 1912-
Norton, Andre, 1912-
Desirable lakeside residence
  Norton, A. Moon mirror
How many miles to Babylon?
  Norton, A. Moon mirror
The long night of waiting
  Norton, A. Moon mirror
Moon mirror
  Norton, A. Moon mirror
Of the shaping of Ulm's heir
  Tales of the Witch World [1]
One spell wizard
  Norton, A. Moon mirror
Outside
  Norton, A. Moon mirror
Spider silk
  Baker's dozen: 13 short fantasy novels
Swamp dweller
  Magic in Ithkar [1]; ed. by A. Norton and R. Adams
Teddi
  Norton, A. Moon mirror
Through the needle's eye
  Norton, A. Moon mirror
The toymaker's snuffbox
  Norton, A. Moon mirror
Wizard's world
  Witches; ed. by I. Asimov; M. H. Greenberg and C. G. Waugh
Norton, Mary, 1903-
Paul's tale
  Ready or not; ed. by J. Kahn
NORWAY
Carter, R. Tergiversator
Garrett, R. Frost and thunder
Sandel, C. Papen
Oslo
Jahnn, H. H. A boy weeps

NORWEGIANS
See also Vikings
France
Sandel, C. Artist's Christmas
United States
Bly, C. Talk of heroes
Cather, W. On the divide
Gold, H. A dark Norwegian person
Rölvaag, O. E. The boy who had no jack-knife
Rölvaag, O. E. The butter war in Greenfield
Rölvaag, O. E. The Christmas offering
Rölvaag, O. E. Molla's heart attack
Rölvaag, O. E. When the wind is in the south
Rölvaag, O. E. Whitebear and Graybear: an Indian legend

NOSE
Knight, D. F. God's nose
Poe, E. A. Lionizing
Wells, H. G. The man with a nose
The **nose**. Gogol', N. V.

NOSTALGIA
Adams, A. My first and only house
Adams, G. G. Alice remembers
Asimov, I. C-chute
Blei, N. Stars
Bowles, P. Unwelcome words
Campos, J. All the roses
Casper, S. Spring fever
Chesterton, G. K. Homesick at home
Deaver, P. F. Marguerite Howe
Ellison, H. Jeffty is five
Fahy, C. The glow of copper
Faust, I. Bunny Berigan in the elephants' graveyard
Fetler, J. The dust of Yuri Serafimovich
Gaitskill, M. An affair, edited
Greene, G. The innocent
Kawabata, Y. Water
Kawabata, Y. The white horse
Mazel, D. A dance
Mazel, D. Ilya
Morrison, J. The incense-burner
Pfeil, F. The collected works of Brown
Sigurdsardóttir, J. Nothing to tell
Sonu, H. Thoughts of home
Still, J. The moving
Theroux, P. Yard sale
Nostalgia. Colette
Nostalgia. Mukherjee, B.
Nostalgia. Parise, G.
Nostalgia; or, Grease spots. Böll, H.
Not a bird in the sky. Haris, P.
Not a free show. Schulman, H.
Not a good girl. Klass, P.
Not a leg to stand on. Boyle, T. C.
Not all wolves. Turtledove, H.
Not always to the strong. Zahn, T.
"**Not** as the world giveth": a friendship story. Gale, Z.

Not even the bones will be left to tell the story. Covino, M.
Not everyone can be a soldier. Freeman, C.
Not for love. Stone, R.
Not for publication. Gordimer, N.
Not good enough. Crowley, A.
Not in this life, maybe the next. Highsmith, P.
Not-knowing. Barthelme, D.
Not marrying Martha. Danes, J. J.
Not my corpse. Daly, C. J.
Not one of us. Highsmith, P.
Not our brother. Silverberg, R.
Not quite alone on the telephone. Liben, M.
Not snow nor rain. DeFord, M. A.
Not substantial things. Davin, D.
Not the news. Cook, P.
Not the real thing. Archer, J.
Not without rain. Houbein, L.
Not worthy of a Wentworth. March, W.
Not yet Jayette. Boyd, W.

NOTARIES
Maupassant, G. de. A fair exchange
Maupassant, G. de. A queer night in Paris
The **notary** gets caught. Gotthelf, J.
Notch. Gorky, M.
Note box. Penn, B. A.
A **note** on chivalry. Liben, M.
A **note** on experts: Dexter Vespasian Joyner. Wolfe, T.
Notes. Rossi, A.
Notes. Thompson, S.
Notes from a respectable cockroach. Highsmith, P.
Notes from the corner. Bitov, A.
Notes I made on the man I was. Abbott, L. K.
Notes of a condottiere. Canessa, G.
Notes of Manfredo Rangel, reporter (about Kramer). Sant'Anna, S.
Notes on a necessary pact. Fisher, M. F. K.
Notes on veritarian bookfighting. Brint, S.
Notes toward an understanding of my father's novel. Durban, P.
Nothing. Pirandello, L.
Nothing. Tamer, Z.
Nothing ever happens on Highside. Gilbert, M.
Nothing ever just disappears. D'Allesandro, S.
Nothing from my noon meal. Ellison, H.
Nothing from nothing comes. Ramsland, K.
Nothing happened. Coombs, M.
Nothing in the rules. De Camp, L. S.
Nothing might happen. Asimov, I.
Nothing new. Bonner, M.
Nothing to tell. Sigurdsardóttir, J.
The **nothingness** forest. Ekström, M.
The **notice**. Essop, A.
Notice. Kalfus, K.
The **notif**. Duke, M.
The **notorious** jumping frog of Calaveras County. Twain, M.

Noughts and crosses. Hartley, L. P.
Nourse, Alan Edward, 1928-
  Second sight
    Young mutants; ed. by I. Asimov; M.
    H. Greenberg and C. G. Waugh
Nova, Craig
  The prince
    The Best American short stories, 1987
    Esquire 105:168-71+ My '86
NOVA SCOTIA *See* Canada—Nova Scotia
Novakovich, Josip
  The apple
    Ploughshares 14 no2/3:15-31 '88
  Yahbo the hawk
    *New England Review and Bread Loaf
    Quarterly* 11:81-94 Aut '88
Novel of the white powder. Machen, A.
A **novel** theory of extinction. Preus, M.
NOVELISTS *See* Authors
Novelties. Shannon, D.
Novelty act. Dick, P. K.
November 14, 1864. Berry, R. M.
November and December: Billy, 1969. Phil-
  lips, J. A.
Novena. Brady, M.
Novice. Schmitz, J. H.
Novitski, Paul
  Nuclear fission
    Kindred spirits; ed. by J. M. Elliot
Now, Baby, do you know one thing? Drake,
  R.
Now I am married. Gordon, M.
Now I lay me. Hemingway, E.
(Now + n, now - n). Silverberg, R.
Now we are three. Chapman, B.
Now we know. O'Hara, J.
Now you have me. Lofts, N.
Now you see me. Morton, S. L.
Nowaira, Amira
  Lost and found
    Egyptian tales and short stories of the
    1970s and 1980s
Nowakowski, Marek
  2072 days
    Nowakowski, M. The canary, and other
    tales of martial law
    Short story international 69
  The canary
    Nowakowski, M. The canary, and other
    tales of martial law
  The confidential call
    Nowakowski, M. The canary, and other
    tales of martial law
  CPD
    Nowakowski, M. The canary, and other
    tales of martial law
  The distributor
    Nowakowski, M. The canary, and other
    tales of martial law
  The enemy
    Nowakowski, M. The canary, and other
    tales of martial law

The forest
    Nowakowski, M. The canary, and other
    tales of martial law
Gorgio
    Nowakowski, M. The canary, and other
    tales of martial law
Hatred
    Nowakowski, M. The canary, and other
    tales of martial law
The horn of plenty
    Nowakowski, M. The canary, and other
    tales of martial law
How time has flown
    Nowakowski, M. The canary, and other
    tales of martial law
Judas in the square
    Nowakowski, M. The canary, and other
    tales of martial law
The June cross
    Nowakowski, M. The canary, and other
    tales of martial law
Little sunshine
    Nowakowski, M. The canary, and other
    tales of martial law
Madam Amalia Bessarabo
    Nowakowski, M. The canary, and other
    tales of martial law
The mongrel
    Nowakowski, M. The canary, and other
    tales of martial law
A new life
    Nowakowski, M. The canary, and other
    tales of martial law
The night patrol
    Nowakowski, M. The canary, and other
    tales of martial law
On the bus
    Nowakowski, M. The canary, and other
    tales of martial law
The peacock
    Nowakowski, M. The canary, and other
    tales of martial law
The search
    Nowakowski, M. The canary, and other
    tales of martial law
The secret face
    Nowakowski, M. The canary, and other
    tales of martial law
The shadow
    Nowakowski, M. The canary, and other
    tales of martial law
A short street
    Nowakowski, M. The canary, and other
    tales of martial law
Silent night, holy night
    Nowakowski, M. The canary, and other
    tales of martial law
The silver bird
    Nowakowski, M. The canary, and other
    tales of martial law
The soldiers and the girl
    Nowakowski, M. The canary, and other
    tales of martial law

Nowakowski, Marek—*Continued*
The spring walk
  Nowakowski, M. The canary, and other
    tales of martial law
Squad ready for action
  Nowakowski, M. The canary, and other
    tales of martial law
The state of war
  Nowakowski, M. The canary, and other
    tales of martial law
The steel-clawed glove
  Nowakowski, M. The canary, and other
    tales of martial law
The taxi driver's story
  Nowakowski, M. The canary, and other
    tales of martial law
The vetting session
  Nowakowski, M. The canary, and other
    tales of martial law
The washing machine
  Nowakowski, M. The canary, and other
    tales of martial law
Wastepaper
  Nowakowski, M. The canary, and other
    tales of martial law
The well-matched couple
  Nowakowski, M. The canary, and other
    tales of martial law
  Short story international 60
Nowotny, Joachim
Hic sunt leones
  Voices East and West: German short
    stories since 1945
Pimpush
  Short story international 60
Noyes, Alfred, 1880-1958
Midnight express
  Lost souls; ed. by J. Sullivan
The **nth** commandment. Hurst, F.
Ntuli, D. B. Z.
Once in a century
  The Penguin book of Southern African
    stories
Nuclear. Eldridge, M.
NUCLEAR BOMB *See* Atomic bomb
NUCLEAR ENERGY
Asimov, I. "Breeds there a man . . .?"
Clifton, M. Hang head, vandal!
Nahin, P. J. Publish and perish
Piper, H. B. Operation RSVP
Nuclear fission. Novitski, P.
Nuclear holocaust. Oates, J. C.
NUCLEAR POWER *See* Nuclear energy
NUCLEAR POWER PLANTS
Drake, D. Men like us
Frazier, R. The daily Chernobyl
NUCLEAR WARFARE
  See also Atomic bomb
Aldiss, B. W. The gods in flight
Barthelme, D. Game
Bishop, M. Diary of a dead man
Bloch, R. The past master
Edwards, M. After-images

Fialkowski, K. A perfect Christmas evening
Forrest, K. V. Survivor
Hendrix, H. V. In the smoke
Oates, J. C. Nuclear holocaust
Pohl, F. Fermi and frost
Regent, P. Ziggy's last dance
Scholz, C. A draft of canto ci
Swanwick, M. Covenant of souls
Upward, E. Over the cliff
Watson, I. Returning home
NUCLEAR WEAPONS
O'Brien, T. Quantum jumps
Upward, E. The interview
Nude. Nagai, K.
Nudelman, Jane Cutler
A precious gift
  Redbook 165:69-70+ My '85
NUDITY
Bernard, K. Preparations
Calvino, I. The adventure of a bather
Camoin, F. A. Sometimes the wrong thing
  is the right thing
Haley, R. The palace of Kandahar
Lodge, D. Hotel des Boobs
Miller, S. Slides
Morand, P. Borealis
Parise, G. Mystery
Taylor, C. Grom's story: naked lady
Vanderhaeghe, G. Going to Russia
Nuetzel, Charles
A day for dying
  The Science fictional Olympics; ed. by
    I. Asimov; M. H. Greenberg and C.
    G. Waugh
Nugent, Beth
City of boys
  The Best American short stories, 1985
  The Editors' choice: new American
    stories v2
  The North American Review 269:26-31
    S '84
Tough as a man
  The Editors' choice: new American
    stories v1
What Susan saw
  Mademoiselle 90:102+ N '84
The **nuggy** bar. Brett, S.
The **nuisance.** Gilliatt, P.
Nuit blanche. Lopatin, J.
Nuliak. Thériault, Y.
Number 10. O'Brien, E.
Number 13. Phelps, E. S.
Number 13. Robinett, S.
The **numbers.** Mooney, M.
Numbskull. Feng Jicai
A **nun** no more. Fante, J.
Nunc dimittis. Lee, T.
Nunes, Natalia
Clastomina
  Short story international 71
Nunes, Shirley
The boy who wouldn't say his name
  Ladies' Home Journal 104:56+ Jl '87

Nunes, Shirley—*Continued*
Joe will take me home
Ladies' Home Journal 103:115+ Je '86
Nunes, Susan
A small obligation
Passages to the dream shore; ed. by F. Stewart
NUNS
Bernard, K. Sister Francetta and the pig baby
Böll, H. The taste of bread
Doyle, Sir A. C. The confession
Erdrich, L. Saint Marie
Fante, J. A nun no more
Fante, J. Scoundrel
Ferron, J. Martine
Ferron, J. The pigeon and the parakeet
Franklin, P. Splendor and black wool
Garrett, R. A little intelligence
Gaspé, P. A. de. Rose Latulipe
Hemingway, E. The gambler, the nun, and the radio
Hulme, K. A drift in dream
Lavin, M. Eterna
Lipsky, E. The quality of mercy
Nestor, T. Once upon a dream
O'Brien, E. Sister Imelda
Potter, N. A. J. Light timber
Rhys, J. The bishop's feast
Rummel, M. K. White-out
Russ, J. Souls
Shamosh, A. Trip
Thorman, C. Sweet chickadee of grace
Wegner, H. The stoning of Stanislava
Nuns in love. Frucht, A.
Nuptials & heathens. Cameron, P.
Nurse Lugton's curtain. Woolf, V.
The **nursemaid**. Rodoreda, M.
NURSEMAIDS
Alcott, L. M. Taming a Tartar
Furlong, M. The drum
Gad, H. The blue weapon
Lipman, E. The day woman
Rodoreda, M. The nursemaid
Taylor, B. Our last nanny
Tuohy, F. Ructions; or, A historical footnote to the Cold War
Yaffe, J. One of the family
Nursery. Asscher-Pinkhof, C.
NURSERY SCHOOLS
Rooke, L. Some people will tell you the situation at Henny Penny Nursery is getting intolerable
Nursery tale for a dreary day. Kang, S.-J.
NURSES AND NURSING
Broun, H. Ruby Dawn, private duty nurse
Campbell, W. B. The thaw
Christie, A. The blue geranium
Cohen, M. The sins of Tomas Benares
Dann, J. Camps
Ferguson, P. Indefinite nights
Ferguson, P. Inside knowledge
Ferguson, P. Patrick

Ferguson, P. The products of conception
Ferguson, P. The quality of mercy
Ferguson, P. Sister Hilary
Fitzgerald, F. S. An alcoholic case
Garrett, G. P. The witness
Glasgow, E. The shadowy third
Harvor, E. The age of unreason
Jolley, E. The bathroom dance
Jolley, E. Hilda's wedding
Jolley, E. Night runner
L'Heureux, J. The anatomy of desire
Lofts, N. Saving face
Lopatin, J. Trixie Taylor, hospital nurse
McAllister, B. Dream baby
McElroy, C. J. A dance with a dolly with a hole in her stocking
Metcalfe, R. The cat
Moravia, A. To the unknown god
Munro, A. Eskimo
Muscillo, D. Sister Coxall's revenge
Narayan, R. K. A breath of Lucifer
Spark, M. The curtain blown by the breeze
Tang Dong. The progress of the military patrol car
Tuohy, F. A special relationship
Williams, W. C. The paid nurse
Nursie. Kinsella, W. P.
NURSING HOMES
Alford, E. Mid-May's eldest child
Ballantyne, S. Key Largo
Busch, F. Comrades
Conner, M. J. Bunco
Flaherty, G. The man who saved himself
Gosling, P. Mr. Felix
Gustafsson, L. The bird in the breast
Gustafsson, L. Greatness strikes where it pleases
Gustafsson, L. The truly great strikes wherever it wants
Jolley, E. 'Surprise! Surprise!' from Matron
Michaelson, L. W. All my darlings
Shannon, D. Happy release
Whelan, G. The dogs in Renoir's garden
Wiebe, D. E. Elegy
The **nuse** man. St. Clair, M.
Nussbaum, Al
An easy score
Alfred Hitchcock's Mortal errors
Nussey, Kent
In Christ there is no east or west
The New generation; ed. by A. Kaufman
The **nutcracker**. Nagai, T.
Nye, Naomi Shihab
The cookies
The Georgia Review 40:231-3 Spr '86
Necessary fictions; ed. by S. W. Lindberg and S. Corey
One eye on the Indian
Prairie Schooner 58:3-10 Fall '84
A wild of sand
Southwest Review 71:170-8 Spr '86

NYMPHOMANIA
McGuane, T. Like a leaf
O'Connor, F. The comforts of home
Painter, P. The sorting out

O

O, Sang-Won
A respite
A Respite, and other Korean short
stories
O, Yŏngsu
The bird of passage
Flowers of fire; ed. by P. H. Lee
O, Yu-Gwon
Two travelers
Two travelers, and other Korean short
stories
O. Knight, D. F.
O **captain,** my captain. Forrest, K. V.
O **homo,** o femina, o tempora. Wilhelm, K.
'O, if I could but shiver!'. Stead, C.
The **O** in José. Aldiss, B. W.
The **O-Shin** Jizo. Kawabata, Y.
OAHU (HAWAII) See Hawaii—Oahu
Oak. Yourgrau, B.
The **oak** bed. Halligan, M.
Oakes, Philip, 1928-
You're in my story
Winter's tales, new ser. v2
OAKLAND (CALIF.) See California—Oak-
land
The **oasis.** Adams, A.
Oates, Joyce Carol, 1938-
The abduction
Oates, J. C. The assignation
Seventeen 46:176-7+ N '87
Accident
Oates, J. C. The assignation
Ace
Oates, J. C. The assignation
Adultress
Oates, J. C. The assignation
Ancient airs, voices
The Antioch Review 44:17-39 Wint '86
Oates, J. C. Raven's Wing
Prize stories, 1987
Anecdote
Oates, J. C. The assignation
April
Oates, J. C. Raven's Wing
The assignation
Antaeus 60:172-5 Spr '88
Oates, J. C. The assignation
August evening
Oates, J. C. The assignation
Baby
Oates, J. C. Raven's Wing
Back country
Shenandoah: an anthology; ed. by J.
Boatwright

Bad habits
Oates, J. C. The assignation
Ballad
Southwest Review 70:216-29 Spr '85
Ballerina
The Georgia Review 40:234-49 Spr '86
Necessary fictions; ed. by S. W. Lind-
berg and S. Corey
The bingo master
Witches' brew; ed. by M. Muller and
B. Pronzini
Blackmail
New directions in prose and poetry 48
Blue-bearded lover
Oates, J. C. The assignation
The boy
Oates, J. C. The assignation
The boy friend
The Massachusetts Review 29:9-19 Spr
'88
The bystander
Oates, J. C. The assignation
Canal Road
The Southern Review (Baton Rouge, La.)
20:610-31 Jl '84
Capital punishment
The Southern Review (Baton Rouge, La.)
23:916-34 Aut '87
Death Valley
Esquire 110:120-5 Jl '88
Desire
Oates, J. C. The assignation
Détente
Love stories for the time being; ed. by
G. D. Chipps and B. Henderson
Oates, J. C. Last days
Selected stories from The Southern
review, 1965-1985
The double-edged knife
Redbook 169:50+ My '87
Double solitaire
Michigan Quarterly Review 25:336-46 Spr
'86
Oates, J. C. Raven's Wing
Eleuthéria
Oates, J. C. The assignation
Face
Oates, J. C. The assignation
Fin de siècle
Oates, J. C. The assignation
"For I will consider my cat Jeoffry"
Michigan Quarterly Review 23:385-99
Summ '84
Foster home
The Virginia Quarterly Review 64:91-107
Wint '88
Funland
Oates, J. C. Last days
Further confessions
The Slaying of the dragon; ed. by F.
Rottensteiner
Geese
Ploughshares 14 no1:92-103 '88

Oates, Joyce Carol, 1938-—*Continued*
Getting to know all about you
  The Southern Review (Baton Rouge, La.)
    24:640-58 Summ '88
Golden gloves
  Oates, J. C. Raven's Wing
Happy
  Oates, J. C. Raven's Wing
  Sudden fiction; ed. by R. Shapard and
    J. Thomas
Harrow Street at Linden
  Oates, J. C. Raven's Wing
Haunted
  The Architecture of fear; ed. by K.
    Cramer and P. D. Pautz
  The Year's best fantasy, first annual
    collection
Heartland
  Oates, J. C. The assignation
Holiday
  Oates, J. C. The assignation
House hunting
  The Kenyon Review ns9:26-41 Fall '87
How I contemplated the world from the
    Detroit House of Correction and began
    my life over again
  The Norton book of American short
    stories
  The World of the short story; ed. by
    C. Fadiman
Ich bin ein Berliner
  Oates, J. C. Last days
In traction
  Oates, J. C. The assignation
The Jesuit
  Oates, J. C. Raven's Wing
Lamb of Abyssalia
  Oates, J. C. Last days
Last days
  Oates, J. C. Last days
Leila Lee
  Winter's tales, new ser. v3
Little blood-button
  Oates, J. C. Raven's Wing
Little wife
  The Kenyon Review ns8:42-61 Spr '86
  Oates, J. C. Raven's Wing
The man whom women adored
  Oates, J. C. Last days
Manslaughter
  Oates, J. C. Raven's Wing
Master race
  Partisan Review 51 no4/52 no1:566-90
    '84/'85
  Prize stories, 1986
  Winter's tales, new ser. v2
Maximum security
  Oates, J. C. The assignation
The mother
  Oates, J. C. Raven's Wing
Mule
  Oates, J. C. The assignation

My Warszawa: 1980
  Oates, J. C. Last days
Nairobi
  The Best American short stories, 1984
  Oates, J. C. Raven's Wing
Night-side
  The Dark descent; ed. by D. G. Hart-
    well
Night. Sleep. Death. The stars
  Oates, J. C. Last days
Nuclear holocaust
  Oates, J. C. Raven's Wing
Old Budapest
  Oates, J. C. Last days
One flesh
  Oates, J. C. The assignation
Only son
  Oates, J. C. The assignation
The others
  Oates, J. C. The assignation
Our wall
  Oates, J. C. Last days
Party
  Oates, J. C. The assignation
Photographer's model
  Oates, J. C. The assignation
Picnic
  Oates, J. C. The assignation
Pinch
  Oates, J. C. The assignation
The quarrel
  Oates, J. C. The assignation
Quartet
  New directions in prose and poetry 50
Raven's Wing
  The Best American short stories, 1985
  Esquire 102:94-6+ Ag '84
  The Esquire fiction reader v1
  Oates, J. C. Raven's Wing
Romance
  Oates, J. C. The assignation
Ruth
  Short story international 51
The seasons
  Oates, J. C. Raven's Wing
  Prize stories, 1985
Secret
  Oates, J. C. The assignation
Secret observations on the goat-girl
  Oates, J. C. The assignation
Secrets
  Mademoiselle 92:156+ N '86
Señorita
  Oates, J. C. The assignation
A sentimental encounter
  Oates, J. C. The assignation
Sentimental journey
  Mystery in the mainstream; ed. by B.
    Pronzini; M. H. Greenberg and B. N.
    Malzberg
Sharpshooting
  Oates, J. C. The assignation

Oates, Joyce Carol, 1938— *Continued*
Shelter
  Oates, J. C. The assignation
Shopping
  Ms. 15:50-3+ Mr '87
Slow
  Oates, J. C. The assignation
The stadium
  Oates, J. C. The assignation
  Omni (New York, N.Y.) 11:103 O '88
Stroke
  Oates, J. C. The assignation
Sundays in summer
  Michigan Quarterly Review 26:218-27
    Wint '87
Superstitious
  Oates, J. C. The assignation
Surf City
  The Bread Loaf anthology of contemporary American short stories; ed. by R. Pack and J. Parini
  Oates, J. C. Raven's Wing
  Partisan Review 53 no3:372-89 '86
Testimony
  Oates, J. C. Raven's Wing
  The Southern Review (Baton Rouge, La.) 22:600-5 Summ '86
A theory of knowledge
  Full measure; ed. by D. Sennett
Tick
  Oates, J. C. The assignation
A touch of the flu
  Oates, J. C. The assignation
The track
  Gentlemen's Quarterly 58:329+ S '88
Train
  Oates, J. C. The assignation
The tryst
  The Art of the tale; ed. by D. Halpern
Two doors
  Oates, J. C. The assignation
Visitation rights
  Oates, J. C. The assignation
  TriQuarterly no73:83-6 Fall '88
Where are you going, where have you been?
  American short story masterpieces; ed. by R. Carver and T. Jenks
The white cat
  A Matter of crime v2
The witness
  Oates, J. C. Last days
Yarrow
  Prize stories, 1988
Oath-bound. Griffin, P.
Oats for the woman. Hurst, F.
Oba, Minako, 1930-
The Pale Fox
  The Shōwa anthology 2
The **obedient**. Lispector, C.
OBESITY
Bausch, R. What feels like the world
Bloch, R. Fat chance

Bukoski, A. The happiness farm
Bukoski, A. This heat
Carver, R. Fat
Carver, R. They're not your husband
Daniels, C. Mrs. Eloise
DeMarinis, R. Life between meals
Drake, R. First date
Du Lac, L. "What's cooking? murder?"
Dubus, A. The fat girl
Gilchrist, E. The gauzy edge of paradise
Gilchrist, E. The last diet
Halligan, M. Fat chance
Kaschnitz, M. L. The fat child
King, S. Quitters, Inc.
King, S. The wedding gig
Lipman, E. Thick and thin
Lish, G. Weight
MacIntyre, F. G. The prisoner of gravity
Martin, G. R. R. The monkey treatment
Maupassant, G. de. Toine
Pritchard, M. La Bête: a figure study
Ríos, A. Pato
Schwob, M. The fat man
Tessier, T. Food
Wells, H. G. The truth about Pyecraft
West, J. A. Gladys's Gregory
Wicomb, Z. When the train comes
Windsor, G. Edging around the fat man
Wolff, T. Hunters in the snow
Obit. Lipman, E.
OBITUARIES
Asimov, I. Obituary
Block, L. Leo Youngdahl, R.I.P.
Hofmann, G. Arno
Johnson, B. S. Everyone knows somebody who's dead
Leedom-Ackerman, J. The impostor
Lipman, E. Obit
Livesey, M. Obituary
Woolf, V. Sympathy
Obituary. Asimov, I.
Obituary. Livesey, M.
Object lesson. Queen, E.
The **object** of the attack. Ballard, J. G.
Objects. Fitzgerald, M. J.
The **objects.** Ocampo, S.
Objects of affection. Kaufman, L.
The **oblong** box. Poe, E. A.
The **oblong** room. Hoch, E. D.
OBOE PLAYERS
Gardner, M. Sibyl sits in
O'Brien, Dan, 1947-
Cowboy on the Concord bridge
  O'Brien, D. Eminent domain
Crossing Spider Creek
  The Best of the West; ed. by J. Thomas
Eminent domain
  O'Brien, D. Eminent domain
Final touches
  O'Brien, D. Eminent domain
The Georgia breeze
  O'Brien, D. Eminent domain

O'Brien, Dan, 1947-—_Continued_
The inheritance
  O'Brien, D. Eminent domain
Seals
  O'Brien, D. Eminent domain
Strand of wire
  O'Brien, D. Eminent domain
Weightless
  O'Brien, D. Eminent domain
The wild geese
  O'Brien, D. Eminent domain
Winter cat
  O'Brien, D. Eminent domain
O'Brien, Edna
Another time
  The New Yorker 64:39-46 N 14 '88
Baby blue
  O'Brien, E. A fanatic heart
The bachelor
  O'Brien, E. A fanatic heart
The call
  O'Brien, E. A fanatic heart
Christmas roses
  O'Brien, E. A fanatic heart
The Connor girls
  O'Brien, E. A fanatic heart
Cords [Variant title: Which of those two
  ladies is he married to?]
  The Treasury of English short stories;
    ed. by N. Sullivan
Courtship
  O'Brien, E. A fanatic heart
The creature
  O'Brien, E. A fanatic heart
The doll
  O'Brien, E. A fanatic heart
Epitaph
  The New Yorker 63:34-41 Ap 27 '87
Ghosts
  O'Brien, E. A fanatic heart
The house of my dreams
  O'Brien, E. A fanatic heart
In the hours of darkness
  The Penguin book of modern British
    short stories
Irish revel [Variant title: Come into the
  drawing-room, Doris]
  O'Brien, E. A fanatic heart
A little holiday
  The New Yorker 63:26-8 Jl 27 '87
A long way from home
  Redbook 165:76+ My '85
The love object
  O'Brien, E. A fanatic heart
The mouth of the cave
  O'Brien, E. A fanatic heart
Mrs. Reinhardt
  O'Brien, E. A fanatic heart
My mother's mother
  O'Brien, E. A fanatic heart
Number 10
  O'Brien, E. A fanatic heart

Over
  O'Brien, E. A fanatic heart
Paradise
  O'Brien, E. A fanatic heart
The plan
  O'Brien, E. A fanatic heart
The return
  O'Brien, E. A fanatic heart
A rose in the heart of New York
  O'Brien, E. A fanatic heart
The rug
  O'Brien, E. A fanatic heart
Savages
  O'Brien, E. A fanatic heart
A scandalous woman
  O'Brien, E. A fanatic heart
Sister Imelda
  The Art of the tale; ed. by D. Halpern
  O'Brien, E. A fanatic heart
The small-town lovers
  O'Brien, E. A fanatic heart
Tough men
  O'Brien, E. A fanatic heart
Violets
  O'Brien, E. A fanatic heart
Ways
  O'Brien, E. A fanatic heart
O'Brien, Fitz-James, 1828-1862
The Bohemian
  O'Brien, F.-J. The supernatural tales of
    Fitz-James O'Brien v1
The child that loved a grave
  O'Brien, F.-J. The supernatural tales of
    Fitz-James O'Brien v1
A dead secret
  O'Brien, F.-J. The supernatural tales of
    Fitz-James O'Brien v1
The diamond lens
  Isaac Asimov presents the best science
    fiction firsts
  O'Brien, F.-J. The supernatural tales of
    Fitz-James O'Brien v1
Jubal, the Ringer
  O'Brien, F.-J. The supernatural tales of
    Fitz-James O'Brien v1
A legend of Barlagh cave
  O'Brien, F.-J. The supernatural tales of
    Fitz-James O'Brien v1
The lost room
  O'Brien, F.-J. The supernatural tales of
    Fitz-James O'Brien v1
The pot of tulips
  O'Brien, F.-J. The supernatural tales of
    Fitz-James O'Brien v1
Seeing the world
  O'Brien, F.-J. The supernatural tales of
    Fitz-James O'Brien v1

O'Brien, Fitz-James, 1828-1862—*Continued*
What was it?
The Dark descent; ed. by D. G. Hartwell
Isaac Asimov presents the best science fiction firsts
O'Brien, F.-J. The supernatural tales of Fitz-James O'Brien v1
The wondersmith
O'Brien, F.-J. The supernatural tales of Fitz-James O'Brien v1
O'Brien, Flann, 1911-1966
John Duffy's brother
Black water; ed. by A. Manguel
The martyr's crown
The Best of Irish wit and wisdom; ed. by J. McCarthy
O'Brien, Tim
The ghost soldiers
Soldiers & civilians; ed. by T. Jenks
Going after Cacciato
The Ploughshares reader: new fiction for the eighties
How to tell a true war story
Esquire 108:208-10+ O '87
Quantum jumps
The Pushcart prize X
The things they carried
The Best American short stories, 1987
The Bread Loaf anthology of contemporary American short stories; ed. by R. Pack and J. Parini
The Editors' choice v4; ed. by G. E. Murphy, Jr.
Esquire 106:76-81 Ag '86
The Graywolf annual 4
Underground tests
The Esquire fiction reader v2
Obscene gestures for women. Kauffman, J.
An **obscure** man. Yourcenar, M.
Obscurity. Sage, V.
Obsession. Essop, A.
Obsessions. Wyndham, F.
Obsolete. Matheson, R. C.
OBSTETRICIANS *See* Physicians
Obstfeld, Raymond
Someone's in the kitchen with Dinah
Murder California style; ed. by J. L. Breen and J. Ball
OBSTINACY
Heinesen, W. Stubborn Stina
The **obvious** factor. Asimov, I.
O'Callaghan, Maxine
The sweet old lady who sits in the park
Murder California style; ed. by J. L. Breen and J. Ball
Ocampo, Silvina, 1889-1952
The autobiography of Irene
Ocampo, S. Leopoldina's dream
Azabache
Ocampo, S. Leopoldina's dream
The basement
Ocampo, S. Leopoldina's dream

The bed
Ocampo, S. Leopoldina's dream
Carl Herst
Ocampo, S. Leopoldina's dream
The clock house
Ocampo, S. Leopoldina's dream
The doll
Ocampo, S. Leopoldina's dream
The expiation
Ocampo, S. Leopoldina's dream
The friends
Black water; ed. by A. Manguel
Ocampo, S. Leopoldina's dream
The fury
Ocampo, S. Leopoldina's dream
The guests
Ocampo, S. Leopoldina's dream
The house of sugar
Ocampo, S. Leopoldina's dream
Icera
Ocampo, S. Leopoldina's dream
Leopoldina's dream
Ocampo, S. Leopoldina's dream
Livio Roca
Ocampo, S. Leopoldina's dream
Lovers
Ocampo, S. Leopoldina's dream
Magush
Ocampo, S. Leopoldina's dream
Mimoso
Ocampo, S. Leopoldina's dream
The mortal sin
Ocampo, S. Leopoldina's dream
The objects
Ocampo, S. Leopoldina's dream
The perfect crime
Ocampo, S. Leopoldina's dream
The photographs
Ocampo, S. Leopoldina's dream
The prayer
Ocampo, S. Leopoldina's dream
The punishment
Ocampo, S. Leopoldina's dream
Report on Heaven and Hell
Ocampo, S. Leopoldina's dream
Revelation
Ocampo, S. Leopoldina's dream
The sibyl
Ocampo, S. Leopoldina's dream
Thus were their faces
Ocampo, S. Leopoldina's dream
Two reports
Other fires; ed. by A. Manguel
The velvet dress
Ocampo, S. Leopoldina's dream
Visions
Ocampo, S. Leopoldina's dream
Voice on the telephone
Ocampo, S. Leopoldina's dream
The wedding
Ocampo, S. Leopoldina's dream
Occam's electric razor. Haley, R.

Occomy, Marita Odette Bonner *See* Bonner, Marita, 1899-1971

OCCULTISM

> *See also* Alchemy; Fortune telling; Supernatural phenomena; Superstition; Witchcraft

Broster, D. K. Couching at the door

Harrison, M. J. The incalling

Lytton, E. B. L., Baron. The haunted and the haunters

Naipaul, S. The tenant

Smith, C. A. The return of the sorcerer

Wakefield, H. R. "He cometh and he passeth by!"

OCCUPATIONS

Austin, M. H. Kate Bixby's queerness

Böll, H. Action will be taken

Conroy, J. Bun Grady

Davie, E. A field in space

Updike, J. Learn a trade

An **occurrence** at Owl Creek Bridge. Bierce, A.

OCEAN

Alcott, L. M. Ariel. A legend of the lighthouse

Brantingham, J. Lobotomy shoals

Dann, J. Between the windows of the sea

García Márquez, G. The sea of lost time

MacMillan, I. C. The rock

Rodoreda, M. The sea

Rucker, R. von B., and Laidlaw, M. Probability pipeline

Tiptree, J. Beyond the dead reef

The **ocean** Christ. France, A.

OCEAN TRAVEL

> *See also* Whaling; Yachts and yachting

Adams, G. Coral dance

Asimov, I. Out of sight

Boylan, J. There's the sea

Christie, A. Problem at sea

Crawford, F. M. The upper berth

Dickens, C. The wreck of the Golden Mary

Ferron, J. Chronicle of Anse Saint-Roch

Fisher, M. F. K. The weather within

Fitzgerald, F. S. The rough crossing

Fremlin, C. The bonus years

Hornung, E. W. The gift of the emperor

Hospital, J. T. Port after port, the same baggage

Howard, V. E. The midnight voyage of the Seagull

Jolley, E. The fellow passenger

Kipling, R. The wreck of the Visigoth

London, J. Sister ships

Marrington, P. The beautiful journey

Moyer, K. Life jackets

O'Hara, J. Our friend the sea

Poe, E. A. The oblong box

Rule, J. Inland passage

Singer, I. B. The enemy

Stead, C. A night in the Indian Ocean

Swados, H. The letters

Tomlinson, H. M. The derelict

Twain, M. About all kinds of ships

Twain, M. "The great dark"

OCEANIA *See* Islands of the Pacific

O'Connor, Flannery

An afternoon in the woods

> O'Connor, F. Collected stories

The artificial nigger

> The Art of the tale; ed. by D. Halpern
>
> Christian short stories; ed. by M. Booth
>
> O'Connor, F. Collected stories
>
> The World of the short story; ed. by C. Fadiman

The barber

> O'Connor, F. Collected stories

A circle in the fire

> O'Connor, F. Collected stories

The comforts of home

> O'Connor, F. Collected stories

The crop

> O'Connor, F. Collected stories

The displaced person

> O'Connor, F. Collected stories

The enduring chill

> O'Connor, F. Collected stories
>
> The Substance of things hoped for; ed. by J. B. Breslin

Everything that rises must converge

> Family: stories from the interior; ed. by G. G. Chavis
>
> Look who's talking; ed. by B. Weber
>
> O'Connor, F. Collected stories

The geranium

> O'Connor, F. Collected stories

Good country people

> The Dark descent; ed. by D. G. Hartwell
>
> O'Connor, F. Collected stories
>
> Stories of the modern South; ed. by B. Forkner and P. Samway

A good man is hard to find

> American short story masterpieces; ed. by R. Carver and T. Jenks
>
> O'Connor, F. Collected stories

Greenleaf

> O'Connor, F. Collected stories

Judgement Day

> O'Connor, F. Collected stories
>
> Witches' brew; ed. by M. Muller and B. Pronzini

The lame shall enter first

> O'Connor, F. Collected stories

A late encounter with the enemy

> O'Connor, F. Collected stories

The life you save may be your own

> A Modern Southern reader; ed. by B. Forkner and P. Samway
>
> O'Connor, F. Collected stories

Parker's back

> O'Connor, F. Collected stories

The Partridge festival

> O'Connor, F. Collected stories

O'Connor, Flannery—*Continued*
Revelation
  A Collection of classic Southern humor; ed. by G. W. Koon
  The Norton book of American short stories
  O'Connor, F. Collected stories
The river
  O'Connor, F. Collected stories
A stroke of good fortune
  O'Connor, F. Collected stories
  Shenandoah: an anthology; ed. by J. Boatwright
A Temple of the Holy Ghost
  O'Connor, F. Collected stories
The train
  O'Connor, F. Collected stories
The turkey
  O'Connor, F. Collected stories
A view of the woods
  O'Connor, F. Collected stories
Why do the heathen rage?
  O'Connor, F. Collected stories
Wildcat
  O'Connor, F. Collected stories
O'Connor, Frank, 1903-1966
The drunkard
  The World of the short story; ed. by C. Fadiman
Judas
  The Treasury of English short stories; ed. by N. Sullivan
Old-age pensioners
  Full measure; ed. by D. Sennett
The party
  The Best of Irish wit and wisdom; ed. by J. McCarthy
A set of variations on a borrowed theme [Variant title: Variations on a theme]
  The Art of the tale; ed. by D. Halpern
O'Connor, Kathleen
And through the woods
  Redbook 172:68+ N '88
A lesson for the teacher
  Redbook 167:54+ Ag '86
To count the ways
  Good Housekeeping 206:68+ F '88
O'Connor, Mary Flannery *See* O'Connor, Flannery
O'Connor, Philip F.
Gerald's song
  Sudden fiction; ed. by R. Shapard and J. Thomas
O'Connor, Teresa F., 1943-
Home again, home again
  The Antioch Review 44:458-66 Fall '86
O'Connor, William Douglas, 1832-1889
The ghost
  Christmas ghosts; ed. by K. Cramer and D. G. Hartwell

O'Cork, Shannon
Night run
  Tales from Ellery Queen's Mystery Magazine: short stories for young adults
Well worth it
  The Year's best mystery and suspense stories, 1985
Ocracoke Island. Adams, A.
The **octagonal** room. Tremblay, M.
Octavo. Martínez-Serros, H.
October. Barich, B.
October. Colette
The **October** Bagman. Blythe, R.
OCTOPUS
  Crane, S. The octopush
  Hodgson, W. H. The thing in the weeds
The **octopus** marooned. Henry, O.
The **octopush.** Crane, S.
Octopussy. Fleming, I.
Oda, Katsuzō
Human ashes
  The Crazy iris, and other stories of the atomic aftermath; ed. by K. Oe
The **Odalisque** of Senichou. Maupassant, G. de
An **odd** feast. Maupassant, G. de
Odd jobs. Cameron, P.
An **odd** pair of socks. Ritchie, J.
Odd tippling. Kusenberg, K.
Odds against the gods. Lee, T.
Ode to a baby robin. Winters, J.
Ode to a sea gull. Winters, J.
Ode to autumn. Leyner, M.
Ode to heroine of the future. Janowitz, T.
Ode to the big school. Stark, S. S.
ODESSA (UKRAINE) *See* Ukraine—Odessa
Odios at Alybe. Parotti, P.
Odom, Judy
Sole owners of the mountain
  Homewords: a book of Tennessee writers; ed. by D. Paschall
O'Donnell, Brophy
Love stories
  McCall's 112:100-1+ Ap '85
O'Donnell, E. P.
Jesus knew
  Mississippi River tales; ed. by F. McSherry; C. G. Waugh and M. H. Greenberg
O'Donnell, Kevin, 1957-
Rock garden
  Omni (New York, N.Y.) 8:46-8+ Jl '86
O'Donnell, Lawrence
Clash by night
  Robert Adams' Book of soldiers
O'Donnell, Patricia
Desire
  The North American Review 273:34-5 S '88
Farber and Mr. White
  The New Yorker 59:46-9 F 6 '84

O'Donnell, Patricia—*Continued*
A visit
 The North American Review 269:41-3 D
 '84
O'Donnell, Peter
A better day to die
 O'Donnell, P. Pieces of Modesty
The giggle-wrecker
 Baker's dozen: 13 short espionage novels
 O'Donnell, P. Pieces of Modesty
I had a date with Lady Janet
 O'Donnell, P. Pieces of Modesty
A perfect night to break your neck
 O'Donnell, P. Pieces of Modesty
Salamander Four
 O'Donnell, P. Pieces of Modesty
The Soo girl charity
 O'Donnell, P. Pieces of Modesty
ODORS
García Márquez, G. The sea of lost time
Wendt, A. I will be our saviour from the
 bad smell
Odour of chrysanthemums. Lawrence, D. H.
The **odyssey**. Northrup, J.
The **odyssey** of a Wop. Fante, J.
Ōe, Kenzaburō
The clever rain tree
 The Shōwa anthology 2
The day another Izumi Shikibu was born
 The Literary Review (Madison, N.J.)
 30:232-44 Wint '87
Oestreicher, Deb
His
 The North American Review 273:49-51
 Je '88
Of a promise kept. Hearn, L.
Of ancient swords and evil mist. Heidbrink,
 J. R.
Of bread and power. Fernando, C.
Of bygone days. Mendele Mokher Seforim
Of generations. Campbell, W. B.
Of gumleaves and clove-scented cigarettes.
 Sheil, G.
Of his bones are coral made. Thompson, J.
Of imagination. Leedom-Ackerman, J.
Of Jimmy Harris. Bonner, M.
Of law and magic. Cherryh, C. J.
Of love and darkness. Haris, P.
Of memories dying. Bracken, M.
Of missing persons. Finney, J.
Of one kind. MacDonald, D. R.
Of science and love. Muller, R.
Of space-time and the river. Benford, G.
Of the shaping of Ulm's heir. Norton, A.
Of time and Kathy Benedict. Nolan, W. F.
O'Faolain, Julia, 1932-
Her trademark
 The Best of Irish wit and wisdom; ed.
 by J. McCarthy
Legend for a painting
 The Treasury of English short stories;
 ed. by N. Sullivan

O'Faoláin, Seán, 1900-
The fur coat
 The Best of Irish wit and wisdom; ed.
 by J. McCarthy
Lovers of the lake
 The World of the short story; ed. by
 C. Fadiman
Sinners
 The Treasury of English short stories;
 ed. by N. Sullivan
Ofelia's transfiguration. Daviú, M.
Off the face of the earth. Rawson, C.
Off track. Windsor, P.
An **offering**. Apple, M.
The **offering**. Wallace, D.
Offerings. Kornblatt, J. R.
Office affairs. Werner, C.
Office romance. Fleming, T. J.
Officemate with pink feathers. Klass, P.
The **officer** takes a wife. Weldon, F.
Offices of instruction. Hausmann, J.
Official Americans. Rush, N.
O'Flaherty, Liam, 1896-1984
Milking time
 Inspired by drink; ed. by Joan Digby
 and John Digby
Spring sowing
 The Treasury of English short stories;
 ed. by N. Sullivan
The stolen ass
 The Best of Irish wit and wisdom; ed.
 by J. McCarthy
OGLALA INDIANS
Howard, C. Custer's ghost
Ogot, Grace, 1930-
The green leaves
 African short stories; ed. by C. Achebe
 and C. L. Innes
O'Grady, Desmond, 1935-
Geography lesson
 Short story international 70
Say one for Leo
 Short story international 53
 U.S. Catholic 49:31-4 Ag '84
Sterner's double vision
 Short story international 47
Oh, Joseph, I'm so tired. Yates, R.
'Oh, Lenore!' came the echo. Federici, C. M.
Oh, that shoestore used to be mine. Tetu,
 R.
Oh, what avails. Munro, A.
'Oh, whistle, and I'll come to you, my lad'.
 James, M. R.
Oh, ye of little faith. Goldswain, R.
O'Hara, John, 1905-1970
Are we leaving tomorrow?
 O'Hara, J. Collected stories of John
 O'Hara
Bread alone
 O'Hara, J. Collected stories of John
 O'Hara

O'Hara, John, 1905-1970—*Continued*

Can I stay here?
  O'Hara, J. Collected stories of John O'Hara

Common sense should tell you
  O'Hara, J. Collected stories of John O'Hara

Do you like it here?
  O'Hara, J. Collected stories of John O'Hara

The doctor's son
  O'Hara, J. Collected stories of John O'Hara

Drawing room B
  O'Hara, J. Collected stories of John O'Hara

Exactly eight thousand dollars exactly
  O'Hara, J. Collected stories of John O'Hara

Fatimas and kisses
  O'Hara, J. Collected stories of John O'Hara

The flatted saxophone
  O'Hara, J. Collected stories of John O'Hara

Flight
  The World of the short story; ed. by C. Fadiman

Free
  O'Hara, J. Collected stories of John O'Hara

The friends of Miss Julia
  O'Hara, J. Collected stories of John O'Hara

The gentleman in the tan suit
  O'Hara, J. Collected stories of John O'Hara

The girl from California
  O'Hara, J. Collected stories of John O'Hara

Good-by, Herman
  O'Hara, J. Collected stories of John O'Hara

Graven image
  O'Hara, J. Collected stories of John O'Hara

The hardware man
  O'Hara, J. Collected stories of John O'Hara

How can I tell you?
  O'Hara, J. Collected stories of John O'Hara

Imagine kissing Pete
  Great American love stories; ed. by L. Rosenthal
  O'Hara, J. Collected stories of John O'Hara

In the silence
  O'Hara, J. Collected stories of John O'Hara

It must have been spring
  O'Hara, J. Collected stories of John O'Hara

The moccasins
  O'Hara, J. Collected stories of John O'Hara

Natica Jackson
  O'Hara, J. Collected stories of John O'Hara

Ninety minutes away
  O'Hara, J. Collected stories of John O'Hara

Now we know
  O'Hara, J. Collected stories of John O'Hara

Olive
  O'Hara, J. Collected stories of John O'Hara

Our friend the sea
  O'Hara, J. Collected stories of John O'Hara

Over the river and through the wood
  The Norton book of American short stories
  O'Hara, J. Collected stories of John O'Hara

Pal Joey
  Look who's talking; ed. by B. Weber
  O'Hara, J. Collected stories of John O'Hara

The pig
  O'Hara, J. Collected stories of John O'Hara

The pretty daughters
  O'Hara, J. Collected stories of John O'Hara

Price's always open
  O'Hara, J. Collected stories of John O'Hara

Too young
  O'Hara, J. Collected stories of John O'Hara

We'll have fun
  O'Hara, J. Collected stories of John O'Hara

Winter dance
  O'Hara, J. Collected stories of John O'Hara

Zero
  O'Hara, J. Collected stories of John O'Hara

O'Harra, Doug

On the lake
  The Antioch Review 45:212-23 Spr '87

OHIO

19th century

Cary, A. An old maid's story

20th century

McKenney, R. Industrial valley
Sanders, S. R. The fire woman
Sanders, S. R. Prophet
Smiley, J. Lily
Thomas, J. Barbecue

OHIO—*Continued*
Farm life
See Farm life—Ohio
Frontier and pioneer life
See Frontier and pioneer life—Ohio
Cincinnati
Blaise, C. How I became a Jew
Cleveland
Bloch, R. Man with a hobby
OIL INDUSTRY *See* Petroleum industry
OIL WELLS *See* Petroleum industry
Oilers and sweepers. Dennison, G.
Oilers and sweepers cantata. See Dennison,
G. Oilers and sweepers
OJIBWA INDIANS *See* Chippewa Indians
OK for murder. Underwood, M.
The **O'Keefe** luck. Overholser, W. D.
O'Kelly, Seumas, 1881-1918
The can with the diamond notch
The Best of Irish wit and wisdom; ed.
by J. McCarthy
Hike and Calcutta
O'Kelly, S. The weaver's grave
The man with the gift
O'Kelly, S. The weaver's grave
Michael and Mary
O'Kelly, S. The weaver's grave
Nan Hogan's house
O'Kelly, S. The weaver's grave
The weaver's grave
O'Kelly, S. The weaver's grave
Okinawa's wife. Claiborne, S.
OKLAHOMA
Heller, S. The Crow Woman
Humphrey, W. The ballad of Jesse Neigh-
bours
Humphrey, W. A job of the plains
Humphrey, W. The rainmaker
Farm life
See Farm life—Oklahoma
Tulsa
Gardner, M. Good dancing, sailor!
Okri, Ben
Disparities
P.E.N. new fiction I
The dream-vendor's August
The Paris Review 29:18-45 Wint '87
Oktoberfest. Wolfe, T.
Okudzhava, Bulat Shalvovich, 1924-
Lots of luck, kid! [Variant title: Good
luck, schoolboy]
The Barsukov Triangle, The two-toned
blond & other stories; ed. by C. R.
Proffer & E. Proffer
Singular misfortunes amidst a parade of
successes
Short story international 45
Ol Antoine's wooden overcoat. St. Pierre, P.
H.
The **ol'** ball game. Nelson, J.
Olaf's calling. Paulson, A. B.
Olalla. Stevenson, R. L.
An **old** 3 A.M. story. Clayton, J. J.

OLD AGE
See also Aging; Elderly
Adler, W. The angel of mercy
Aiken, J. Smell
Alden, P. B. Legacies
Aldiss, B. W. Consolations of age
Alford, E. Mid-May's eldest child
Anderson, S. Death in the woods
Ardizzone, T. Nonna
Armer, K. M. On the inside track
Arnold, M. The old woman
Austin, D. He won't go down to the park
with me today
Bache, E. Pigeons
Barich, B. The end of the world
Barstow, S. The running and the lame
Barthelme, S. Mrs. Sims
Barthelme, S. Stoner's lament
Bates, A. J. A ceremony of innocence
Bates, H. E. The chords of youth
Bates, H. E. Time
Bates, H. E. Where the cloud breaks
Bausch, R. Wise men at their end
Baxter, C. The cliff
Baxter, C. Horace and Margaret's fifty-
second
Baxter, C. The would-be father
Beckett, S. The calmative
Behan, B. The last of Mrs. Murphy
Bellow, S. Leaving the yellow house
Berriault, G. The infinite passion of
expectation
Bessette, G. The mustard plaster
Blei, N. In the secret places of the stairs
Blei, N. This horse of a body of mine
Bloch, R. Reaper
Bly, C. Gunnar's sword
Blythe, R. Here be dragons
Bonnie, F. The bulk tour
Bonnie, F. Squatter's rights
Botwinik, B. Death went astray
Botwinik, B. Jake
Bowles, P. The little house
Boyle, T. C. Not a leg to stand on
Bradbury, R. Junior
Braddon, M. E. Good Lady Ducayne
Brand, C. Bless this house
Braund, M. What's on the telly tonight?
Brentano, C. The story of good Caspar
and fair Annie
Brigham, B. The lottery drawing
Brown, M. W. The amaryllis
Brown, M. W. The cure
Brown, M. W. New dresses
Bruchac, J. Turtle meat
Burke, J. L. Hack
Burt, S. The single tractor track
Calvino, I. Hunger at Bévera
Cameron, P. Excerpts from Swan Lake
Cameron, P. Grounded
Campion, E. Good morning wardrobe
Campos, J. All the roses
Campos-De Metro, J. The feather

OLD AGE—*Continued*

Canin, E. We are nighttime travelers
Carlisle, A. Don't it make you wonder
Carroll, G. H. Head of the line
Cheever, J. The world of apples
Chetwynd-Hayes, R. The colored transmission
Choe, C.-H. When the cricket chirrs
Clark, M. Makeup
Colette. The burglar
Colter, C. Moot
Conroy, J. Bun Grady
Covington, V. Magnolia
Curley, D. Visiting the dead
Curtiss, U. R. Good neighbor
Dadswell, M. Backtracking
Dai Qing. No!
Davie, E. Lines
Davis, L. The cottages
Davis, L. What an old woman will wear
Day, H. When Dustin "called on"
DeGrazia, E. Brothers of the tiger
Dickens, M. Activity time
Dodd, S. M. One hundred years of solicitude: The meditations of Ursula
Dodd, S. M. Snowbird
Drake, R. I never have been a well woman
Drake, R. Sisters
Drake, R. The veteran
Drewe, R. The last explorer
Dunn, D. Old women without gardens
Ekström, M. The eagle cage
El Ghitany, G. Buzzing
Eldridge, M. Antique
Eldridge, M. Paterson's Flats
Ellin, S. The Blessington method
Ellison, H. Paladin of the lost hour
Endō, S. A man sixty
Epstein, L. The Steinway quintet
Fagan, A. In a bamboo garden
Fahy, C. The glow of copper
Farmer, B. Gerontissa
Faust, I. Bar bar bar
Federspiel, J. Oranges on her windowsill
Federspiel, J. The survivor
Feng Jicai. Chrysanthemums
Ferguson, W. Space Invaders
Ferron, J. The parakeet
Ferron, J. The parrot
Fetler, J. The dust of Yuri Serafimovich
Fink, I. Behind the hedge
Fisher, M. F. K. A kitchen allegory
Fisher, M. F. K. The oldest man
Fisher, M. F. K. A question answered
Fisher, M. F. K. The reunion
Fisher, M. F. K. The unswept emptiness
Fisher, R. Miss Cynthie
Flaherty, G. The man who saved himself
Fontane, T. A woman in my years
Freeman, C. That is no country for old men
Fremlin, C. A case of maximum need

Fremlin, C. High dive
Fremlin, C. A lovely day to die
Fuentes, C. Aura
Gale, Z. "Not as the world giveth": a friendship story
Gallagher, T. Girls
Gallagher, T. The woman who saved Jesse James
Gallant, M. Lena
Garcia, L. G. The wedding
Garrett, G. P. Good-bye, good-bye, be always kind and true
Gee, M. A glorious morning, comrade
Giles, M. Rough translations
Gilliatt, P. As is
Gilliatt, P. Splendid lives
Girion, B. The moon cookies
Gold, H. Cohorts
Gold, H. A ninety-six-year-old big sister
Gordimer, N. Enemies
Gordon, M. Mrs. Cassidy's last year
Gordon, M. Out of the fray
Gosling, P. Mr. Felix
Grant, C. L. My shadow is the fog
Grau, S. A. Flight
Greenberg, A. The true story of how my grandfather was smuggled out of the old country in a pickle barrel in order to escape military conscription
Greenwood, R. The last survivor of Sierra Flat
Gustafsson, L. The bird in the breast
Haldeman, J. C. Still frame
Hall, D. The smell in Bertha's house
Hall, J. B. Old man finds what was lost
Hall, M. L. Doll
Hall, R. W. Backwards
Hall, T. T. Why my walls shake
Halley, A. A Rosenkavalier
Halligan, M. A cage of gold
Hardy, T. Old Mrs. Chundle
Hayashi, F. A late chrysanthemum
Haylock, J. The worries of Laurence Ridley
Haynes, D. Taking Miss Kezee to the polls
Heinesen, W. Master Jakob and Miss Urd
Heller, S. The rainbow syndrome
Hemingway, E. Old man at the bridge
Hemingway, E. The undefeated
Hemley, R. A sentimental wolf
Hoffman, W. Lover
Hospital, J. T. The dark wood
Hospital, J. T. Moving out
Hull, H. R. Last September
Humphrey, W. The Hardys
Humphries, J. Quincy
Hyon, C.-G. The death of my grandmother
Ibuse, M. Kuchisuke's valley
Ingalls, R. On ice
Jackson, G. Sweet things
Jackson, S. The summer people
Jacobsen, J. Jack Frost
Jhabvala, R. P. The man with the dog

OLD AGE—*Continued*

Jolley, E. A hedge of rosemary
Kalpakian, L. The battle of Manila
Kalpakian, L. A Christmas cordial
Kavaler, R. Those grand old songs
Keesing, N. End of the affair
Keith, D. L. When the morning comes
Kenny, M. Yaikni
Kercheval, J. L. A clean house
Kercheval, J. L. The dogeater
Kercheval, J. L. The history of the church in America
Kercheval, J. L. La mort au moyen âge
Kercheval, J. L. Tertiary care
King, F. H. The Brighton Belle
King, F. H. The tradesman
Kipling, R. The wish house
Klíma, I. Thursday morning: an erotic tale
Knight, W. E. The resurrection man
Komie, L. B. The judge's chambers
Konopnicka, M. Banasiowa
Lagier, J. Tending the flock
Lee, H. There could be a lesson in it somewhere
Leedom-Ackerman, J. Death stalks a building once it enters
Lessing, D. M. An old woman and her cat
Lispector, C. In search of dignity
Lispector, C. Journey to Petrópolis
Lofts, N. Now you have me
Lott, J. The Janeites
Lutz, J. Tough
Lynch, L. Augusta Brennan I: The coat
Lynch, L. Augusta Brennan II: The tracks
Lynch, L. Babe and Evie I: Sunshine
Lynch, L. Dutch and Sybil I: Eleanor Roosevelt's garden
Lynch, L. Dutch and Sybil II: Beachfront hotel
Lynch, L. Mary's garden
Lynch, L. Pleasure Park
MacDonald, D. R. Poplars
MacDonald, D. R. Sailing
MacDonald, D. R. Work
Maheux-Forcier, L. The carnation
Malamud, B. In retirement
Mansfield, K. An ideal family
Mansfield, K. The little governess
Matheson, R. The test
Matthews, J. The ghost of First Crow
Matthews, J. The immortal dog
Matthews, J. Return to an unknown city
Maupassant, G. de. Julie Romain
Maupassant, G. de. The marquis
Maupassant, G. de. Sympathy
Mazel, D. Aunt Leah
McCormack, E. P. Captain Joe
McGarry, J. Providence, 1970: behind this soft eclipse
McLaughlin, L. Mrs. Shreeve and Mrs. Bolero
Menaker, D. The old left

Menaker, D. The three-mile hill is five miles long
Michaelson, L. W. All my darlings
Minot, S. Small Point Bridge
Moore, G. 'Emma Bovary'
Morris, M. The banana fever
Morris, W. Real losses, imaginary gains
Morris, W. Victrola
Moskowitz, F. Fanny's comfort station
Murphy, P. Checking in
Murphy, Y. The toys
Muschg, A. The country house; or, Defaulted presence
Muschg, A. Dinnertime
Myśliwski, W. Stone upon stone
Narayan, R. K. Under the banyan tree
Neville, K. Old Man Henderson
Norris, G. Holding on
Norris, H. The love child
Norris, H. Mrs. Moonlight
Nowakowski, M. The canary
Nye, N. S. The cookies
Oates, J. C. A theory of knowledge
O'Brien, E. Christmas roses
O'Connor, F. The geranium
O'Connor, F. Judgement Day
O'Connor, F. Old-age pensioners
O'Hara, J. The friends of Miss Julia
O'Hara, J. Over the river and through the wood
O'Kelly, S. The weaver's grave
Osborn, C. Amnesia's child
Osborn, C. Ancient history
Osborn, C. The circuit rider
Osborn, C. The last of it
Osborn, C. Man Dancing
Osborn, C. Running around America
Ozick, C. Rosa
Painter, P. Suppertime
Paley, G. Dreamer in a dead language
Paley, G. In the garden
Parise, G. Fear
Parise, G. Nostalgia
Parise, G. Work
Pearlman, D. Taking from the top
Petrakis, H. M. A hand for tomorrow
Petrakis, H. M. The last escapade
Pfeil, F. The collected works of Brown
Pfeil, F. Skeeter's last reflections
Phelps, E. S. Old Mother Goose
Pilcher, R. The tree
Poe, E. A. The man of the crowd
Pollard, J. A. Old woman
Porter, K. A. The jilting of Granny Weatherall
Potter, N. A. J. The bigamist
Potter, N. A. J. A short vacation
Price, R. The Warrior Princess Ozimba
Pritchard, M. A dying man
Pritchett, V. S. The spree
Pritchett, V. S. Tea with Mrs. Bittell
Pym, B. Across a crowded room
Reed, K. Great Escape Tours Inc.

OLD AGE—*Continued*

Reed, K. The revenge of the senior citizens: a novella
Rhys, J. Good-bye Marcus, good-bye Rose
Rhys, J. Sleep it off lady
Rifaat, A. Bahiyya's eyes
Rifaat, A. Just another day
Ross, V. Dreams & sleep
Rossiter, S. Civil War
Rossiter, S. Star light, star bright
Rule, J. In the attic of the house
Rule, J. Power failure
Ruta, S. The bus
Sanford, A. Limited access
Sarton, M. The silent minister
Schinto, J. The original dog
Sexson, L. Turning
Shacochis, B. Where Pelham fell
Shaham, N. The salt of the earth
Sheil, G. Mad like Lasseter
Sigurdsardóttir, J. Nothing to tell
Silvis, R. One night with a girl by the Seine
Singer, I. B. The hotel
Singer, I. B. The Spinoza of Market Street
Slesar, H. The day of the execution
Smith, D. W. One last dance
Smith, W. A. Delivery
Sperling, L. The book of life
Spilman, R. The old man tells his story and gets it wrong
Sproat, R. When the sailor was far away
St. Pierre, P. H. December Nilsen
Stark, S. S. The Johnstown Polka
Steele, M. What to do till the postman comes
Stephens, M. Everlast
Stern, R. G. Dr. Cahn's visit
Stern, S. The book of Mordecai
Stockanes, A. E. Ladies who knit for a living
Storm, T. Immensee
Summers, H. S. Concerning, I suppose my father
Summerville, J. Paper fires
Tallent, E. The evolution of birds of paradise
Tamer, Z. A summary of what happened to Mohammed al-Mahmoudi
Tetu, R. Oh, that shoestore used to be mine
Thomas, A. C. Miss Foote
Thomas, D. The end of the river
Thorman, C. Fifty years of eternal vigilance
Thurm, M. Ice
Treviño, J. S. A very old man
Tuohy, F. A summer pilgrim
Upward, E. The white-pinafored black cat
Vanderhaeghe, G. Dancing bear
Vanderhaeghe, G. How the story ends
Vivante, A. The soft core
Waldrop, H. Fair game
Walters, A. L. The sun is not merciful

Watanabe, S. A. Colors
Weaver, G. Some killers
Welch, D. Evergreen Seaton-Leverett
Welty, E. A worn path
West, P. The place in flowers where pollen rests
Wetherell, W. D. The man who loved Levittown
Whatley, W. Something to lose
Whelan, G. The dogs in Renoir's garden
Whelan, G. The mummies of Guanajuato
Whelan, G. Playing with shadows
Whitaker, M. Hannah
White, P. Five-twenty
Wiebe, D. E. Elegy
Williams, T. Hard candy
Williams, T. The inventory at Fontana Bella
Williams, T. Man bring this up road
Willson, H. Duke City alchemist
Wilson, L. A. From the bottom up
Wolfe, T. The lion at morning
Wolfe, T. Old Man Rivers
Yi, K.-S. Halmôm
Zambreno, M. F. A way out
Zapolska, G. Virtue (a sketch for a novel)
Zhang Jie. An unfinished record

OLD AGE HOMES

See also Nursing homes

Blackman, M. The Golden Shadows old west museum
Bly, C. Gunnar's sword
Brodine, K. Here, take my words
Choyce, L. Dancing the night away
DeMarinis, R. Red chair
Ekström, M. The king is threatened
Hensley, J. L. The home
Jolley, E. A new world
Paley, G. Dreamer in a dead language
Russ, J. Elf hill
Watmough, D. Closeted
Old-age pensioners. O'Connor, F.
The **old** Army game. Garrett, G. P.
The **old** barn on the pond. Curtiss, U. R.

OLD BELIEVERS

Leskov, N. S. The sealed angel
Old bottles. Bowering, G.
Old Budapest. Oates, J. C.
The **old** bull moose of the woods. Sandberg, P. L.
Old Catawba. Wolfe, T.
Old Chang. Li, F.-Y.
The **old** Chief Mshlanga. Lessing, D. M.
Old clothes. Campbell, R.
The **old** college try. Bloch, R.
The **old** couple. Codrescu, A.
The **old** darkness. Sargent, P.
Old Doc Rivers. Williams, W. C.
Old enough to be your father . . . Sammān, G.
An **old-established** school. Upward, E.
Old farmhouse roof. Olson, J. N.

An **old-fashioned** bird Christmas. St. Clair, M.
Old fires. Currey, R.
The **old** flame. Boler, R.
An **old** flame. Hornung, E. W.
Old flames. Colwin, L.
Old folks. Mazel, D.
Old folks at home. Highsmith, P.
The **old** forest. Taylor, P. H.
Old friends. Davis, D. S.
Old friends. Endō, S.
Old Garbo. Thomas, D.
The **old** gaucho. Murguía, J.
The **old** general and the lost granddaughter. Wilson, A. J. E.
Old glass-new glass. Land, S.
Old Gore. Stuart, J.
The **old** guard. Boylan, R. B.
The **Old** Haddock. Keating, H. R. F.
Old haunts. Matheson, R.
The **old** heathen. Ferron, J.
An **old** Indian buries an old friend. Winters, J.
Old Joe. Conley, R. J.
OLD LADIES *See* Old age
The **old** left. Menaker, D.
An **old** maid. Maupassant, G. de
Old maidism versus marriage. Bowen, S. P.
OLD MAIDS *See* Single women
Old maids. Finger, A.
Old maids. Sedgwick, C. M.
An **old** maid's story. Cary, A.
An **old** maid's story. See Vaughan, M. C. Fruits of sorrow; or, An old maid's story
The **old** man. Du Maurier, Dame D.
Old man at the bridge. Hemingway, E.
Old man finds what was lost. Hall, J. B.
Old man gloom. Gardner, M.
Old Man Henderson. Neville, K.
The **old** man of the peepul-tree. Crowley, A.
Old man of the temple. Narayan, R. K.
Old Man Rivers. Wolfe, T.
The **old** man tells his story and gets it wrong. Spilman, R.
Old man's beard. Wakefield, H. R.
The **old** man's dying. Shukshin, V. M.
An **old** mate of your father's. Lawson, H.
Old mates. Taylor, A.
OLD MEN *See* Old age
The **old** men know. Grant, C. L.
Old men shall dream dreams. Dorr, L.
Old Mickey Flip had a marvelous ship. White, L. A.
The **old** mob. Lowden, D.
Old Mother Goose. Phelps, E. S.
Old Mrs. Chundle. Hardy, T.
The **old** muse. Kessler, J. F.
The **old** nurse's story. Gaskell, E. C.
The **old** organ trail. McKenna, B.
Old pictures. Russ, J.
Old Ramón and the devil. Ferrari, H.
Old Red. Gordon, C.

Old red shoes. Gallagher, S.
The **old** school. Stead, C.
Old souls. Giles, M.
Old Spanish gardens. Austin, M. H.
Old tales. Asscher-Pinkhof, C.
Old thoughts, old presences: Daddy's girl. Russ, J.
Old thoughts, old presences: The autobiography of my mother. Russ, J.
Old Toad. Gravel, G.
The **old** track. Prichard, K. S.
The **old** waitress. Heynen, J.
The **old** ways. Saiki, J.
Old wildwood. Goyen, W.
The **old** woman. Arnold, M.
The **old** woman. Marshall, J.
Old woman. Pollard, J. A.
The **old** woman. Rasputin, V. G.
An **old** woman and her cat. Lessing, D. M.
The **old** woman and the storm. McKillip, P. A.
Old Woman Magoun. Freeman, M. E. W.
The **old** woman's blessing. Muller, D. N.
OLD WOMEN *See* Old age
Old women without gardens. Dunn, D.
Old words for new. Bukiet, M. J.
Old-world landowners. Gogol', N. V.
The **oldest** killer. Collins, M.
The **oldest** man. Fisher, M. F. K.
Oldfashioned. McGahern, J.
Oldfield, Jenny
  Life-sentence
    Stand one; ed. by M. Blackburn; J. Silkin and L. Tracy
Ole and Trufa. Singer, I. B.
Ole Underwood. Mansfield, K.
The **O'Leary** conspiracy. Ritchie, J.
Olesen, Kristi
  Beast and beauty
    The Clarion awards; ed. by D. Knight
Olesha's cabin. Abramov, F.
Olezhka got married. Nagibin, ÍŪ. M.
Olgin, O.
  (jt. auth) See Krivich, M, and Olgin, O.
Oliphant, Margaret, 1828-1897
  The library window
    The Book of the dead; ed. by A. K. Russell
  The open door
    The Penguin book of ghost stories
Olive. O'Hara, J.
Oliveira, Lolio Lourenco de
  Adelaide
    Américas 37:49-51 Jl/Ag '85
Oliver, Chad, 1928-
  Any more at home like you?
    Science Digest 92:66-9+ S '84
  One night at Medicine Tail
    Westeryear; ed. by E. Gorman
  Transfusion
    Great science fiction; ed. by I. Asimov; M. H. Greenberg and C. G. Waugh

Oliver, Symmes Chadwick See Oliver, Chad, 1928-
"Ollie, oh . . . ". Chute, C.
Ollivant, Alfred, 1874-1927
  The tailless tyke at bay
    Roger Caras' Treasury of great dog stories
Olmstead, Robert
  The boon
    Olmstead, R. River dogs
  Bruno and Rachel
    Olmstead, R. River dogs
  Cody's story
    Olmstead, R. River dogs
  A good cow
    Olmstead, R. River dogs
  High-low-jack
    The Graywolf annual 4
  How to bury a dog
    Olmstead, R. River dogs
  In this life
    Olmstead, R. River dogs
  The mason
    Olmstead, R. River dogs
  Onions
    Olmstead, R. River dogs
  A pair of bulls
    Olmstead, R. River dogs
  A place to stay
    Olmstead, R. River dogs
  River dogs
    Olmstead, R. River dogs
  What to do first
    Olmstead, R. River dogs
Olof Lindstrom goes fishing. Ade, G.
Olsen, Paul
  Crossing
    The Southern Review (Baton Rouge, La.) 20:464-73 Ap '84
Olsen, Theodore V.
  Vengeance station
    Westeryear; ed. by E. Gorman
Olsen, Tillie
  I stand here ironing
    Between mothers & daughters; ed. by S. Koppelman
    The Norton book of American short stories
Olson, Donald
  Another me
    Ellery Queen's Prime crimes 2
  Blood relatives
    Alfred Hitchcock's Mortal errors
  Enter the stranger
    Alfred Hitchcock's Crimewatch
  On consignment
    Ellery Queen's Prime crimes
  A voice from the leaves
    Alfred Hitchcock's Grave suspicions
Olson, Jon N.
  Old farmhouse roof
    The Antioch Review 44:161-6 Spr '86

Olson, Toby
  The scourging at the pillar
    New directions in prose and poetry 50
The **Olympians.** Resnick, M.
OLYMPIC GAMES
  Pouvoir, J. L. The death triple
  Sullivan, T. The Mickey Mouse Olympics
Olympus Hills. Carlson, R.
O'Malley, Kathleen
  The demon's gift
    Magic in Ithkar 4; ed. by A. Norton and R. Adams
O'Malley, Mary Dolling See Bridge, Ann, 1889-1974
Omega I. Wiebe, D. E.
The **omelette.** Colette
OMENS
  Everett, P. L. The bear as symbol
  Stead, C. The triskelion
An **ominous** baby. Crane, S.
Omnilingual. Piper, H. B.
On a journey. Mrożek, S.
On and off the African veldt. Janowitz, T.
On bail. Jhabvala, R. P.
On becoming somebody. Lee, H.
On being a son. Dennison, G.
On being courteous when compelled to break the law. Böll, H.
On cats. Maupassant, G. de
On consignment. Olson, D.
On Day X. Kaschnitz, M. L.
On each other's time. Gilliatt, P.
On earth. Holman, J.
On for the long haul. Boyle, T. C.
On freedom. Working, R.
On golden seas. Clarke, A. C.
On growing old. Masefield, J.
On guard. Lutz, J.
On guard! Pronzini, B.
On her feet again. Cohen, A.
On ice. Ingalls, R.
On leprechauns. Wolfe, T.
On Mu. Haas, B.
On my being dead. Michaelson, L. W.
On my way to paradise. Wolverton, D.
On not shooting sitting birds. Rhys, J.
On official business. Chekhov, A. P.
On perfumes. Maupassant, G. de
On private property. Chesterton, G. K.
On secular education. Chesterton, G. K.
On self-knowledge. Katz, S.
On the Aberdonian. Regent, P.
On the altar. Bonner, M.
On the Antler. Proulx, A.
On the battlements. Fraser, A.
On the black list. Raphael, F.
On the Brighton Road. Middleton, R.
On the bus. Nowakowski, M.
On the business of generating transforms. Lish, G.
On the campaign trail. Malzberg, B. N.
On the day that E. M. Forster died. Byatt, A. S.

On the deck. Barthelme, D.
On the deck of the Flying Bomb. Redd, D.
On the divide. Cather, W.
On the downhill side. Ellison, H.
On the edge. Farber, S. N.
On the edge of a plain. Lawson, H.
On the flats. Rosen, G. H.
On the fourth planet. Bone, J. F.
On the hook. Böll, H.
On the inside track. Armer, K. M.
On the lake. Douglas, E.
On the lake. O'Harra, D.
On the meaning of life. Ratushinskaya, I.
On the Orient, North. Bradbury, R.
On the other side of the stream. Kong Jiesheng
On the overhead bridge. Cho, S.-H.
On the prod. Washburn, L. J.
On the quai in Smyrna. Hemingway, E.
On the rebound. Purdy, J.
On the river. Maupassant, G. de
On the river road. Shaw, J. B.
On the River Styx. Matthiessen, P.
On the rocks. Hensley, J. L.
On the roof. Zenowich, C.
On the run. Boyle, K.
On the separate existence of the soul. Hogg, J.
On the side porch. Drake, R.
On the slab. Ellison, H.
On the turn. Frahm, L.
On the uses of torture. Anthony, P.
On the way to the ERA. Brady, M.
On the way to the Goat. Dadswell, M.
On the way to the poorhouse. Singer, I. B.
On the Yankee station. Boyd, W.
On the Zattere. Trevor, W.
On this good ground. Virgo, S.
On vacation. Claiborne, S.
On voyage. White, S.
Once, a lotus garden. Saiki, J.
Once a thief. Pronzini, B.
Once a very stupid man. Davis, L.
Once a year. Jones, D. C.
Once in a century. Ntuli, D. B. Z.
Once in Europa. Berger, J.
Once in Syracuse. Hopes, D. B.
Once upon a dream. Nestor, T.
Once upon a time. Abbott, L. K.
Once upon a unicorn. Busby, F. M.
Ondina. Naranjo, C.
One. Liben, M.
One afternoon. Billington, R.
One afternoon, Adam . . . See Calvino, I. Adam, one afternoon
One against Thebes. See Gordon, C. The dragon's teeth
The one and only bottle. Digby, J.
The one and only east. Asimov, I.
One arm. Kawabata, Y.
One arm. Williams, T.
One autumn evening. Gorky, M.

One bad winter's day. Link, W., and Levinson, R.
One bite for Christmas. Jolley, E.
One blood. Walton, D.
One boy's story. Bonner, M.
One can of soup at a time. Rule, J.
One chance. De Lint, C.
One Christmas knitting. Jolley, E.
One clay foot. Wodhams, J.
One clear sweet clue. Bankier, W.
One dash--horses. See Crane, S. Horses—one dash
One dash—horses. Crane, S.
One day after Saturday. García Márquez, G.
One day in November. Sandel, C.
One day in the life of a white-collar worker. Ch'en, Y.-C.
One day in the short happy life of Anna Banana. Fahy, C.
One day of happiness. Singer, I. B.
One dollar ninety eight. See Porges, A. $1.98
One evening. Colette
One eye on the Indian. Nye, N. S.
One-eyed Jacks. Cullen, E. J.
One-eyed sky. Evans, M.
One flesh. Oates, J. C.
One Florida night. Lee, C.
One for his lordship, and one for the road! Bradbury, R.
One for sorrow. Glavin, A.
One for the road. King, S.
One for Virgil Tibbs. Ball, J.
One hundred dollars and nothing! See Cooper, J. C. $100 and nothing!
One hundred ten West Sixty-First Street. See Barthelme, D. 110 West Sixty-First Street
One hundred years of solicitude: The meditations of Ursula. Dodd, S. M.
One husband too many. Carrig, J.
The one I didn't marry. Botwinik, B.
One last dance. Smith, D. W.
One last hunting pack. Linehan, P.
One last ride. Mayer, M.
The one-legged men. McCormack, E. P.
One man's manual. Lutz, J.
One more interview. Updike, J.
One more martini. Gardner, M.
One more river. Goldberg, L.
One more thing. Carver, R.
One night at Medicine Tail. Oliver, C.
One night in your life. Bradbury, R.
One night with a girl by the Seine. Silvis, R.
One of a kind. Barnes, J.
One of my families. Compton, J.
One of the family. Yaffe, J.
One of the girls in our party. Wolfe, T.
One of the missing. Bierce, A.
One of the three is still alive. Calvino, I.
One of them gets married. McGarry, J.
One of these days. García Márquez, G.
One of these mornings. Holditch, W. K.

One of those days. Pronzini, B.
One of those things. Chipulina, E. G.
One of two. Brown, R.
One of us. Fante, J.
One off the short list. Lessing, D. M.
One old maid. Harland, M.
One on one. Katz, S.
One pair red, one pair blue. Haake, K.
One person's happiness. Kawabata, Y.
One phase of love. Maupassant, G. de
One picture of Trotsky. McCormack, E. P.
One-play Oscar. Fante, J.
One reader writes. Hemingway, E.
One regret. Brown, M. W.
One siren or another. Valenzuela, L.
One size fits all. Thomas, A. C.
One special moment. Soman, F. J.
One spell wizard. Norton, A.
One step to murder. Ellis, J.
One story too many. Peña, D.
One summer in the city. Grekova, I.
One summer night. Bierce, A.
One thing leading to another. Warner, S. T.
One third, one third, one third. See Brautigan, R. 1/3, 1/3, 1/3
One thousand dollars. Henry, O.
One thousand dollars a word. Block, L.
The one thousand dozen. London, J.
One to nine hundred ninety nine. See Asimov, I. 1 to 999
One trip across. Hemingway, E.
One true love. Bonner, M.
The one true story of the world. McFall, L.
One-two-three little Indians. Garner, H.
One warm Saturday. Thomas, D.
One way. Sonu, H.
One-way ticket. Nelson, A.
One way to tomorrow. Whiteford, W. N.
One whale, singing. Hulme, K.
The one who came to save me. Piñera, V.
One who saw. Burrage, A. M.
One whole day. Lewis, S. E.
One winter in Eden. Bishop, M.
One winter's evening. Shi Tiesheng
One with the lot. Bird, C.
One year later. Sagan, F.

O'Neal, Deborah Rose
Happy birthday Harry & Lucille
The Southern Review (Baton Rouge, La.) 24:659-70 Summ '88

ONEIDA COUNTY (N.Y.) *See* New York (State)—Oneida County

ONEIDA INDIANS
Harrison, H. Run from the fire

O'Neil, Dennis
Report on a broken bridge
Ellery Queen's Memorable characters

O'Neill, Egan, 1921-
For works written by this author under other names see Shannon, Dell, 1921-

O'Neill, Gerard K.
The high life in space
Omni (New York, N.Y.) 7:72-4+ O '84
The ones who walk away from Omelas. Le Guin, U. K.
The onion grass season. Holden, D.

Onions, Oliver, 1873-1961
The beckoning fair one
Dark company; ed. by L. Child
The Dark descent; ed. by D. G. Hartwell
The cigarette case
The Oxford book of English ghost stories
The rope in the rafters
The Mammoth book of short horror novels; ed. by M. Ashley
Onions. Olmstead, R.
Onlookers. Friel, G.
Only a dream. Haggard, H. R.
Only a little of so much. Zwicky, F.
Only a matter of time. McGlamry, B.
Only a matter of time. Sturges, A. E.
Only approved Indians can play: made in USA. Forbes, J.
The only daughter. Rooke, L.
Only in the truth. Loukakis, A.
The only journey of his life. Vizyēnos, G. M.
Only natural. Ruffner, B.
The only neat thing to do. Tiptree, J.
The only real day. Chin, F.
Only Sam knows. Roiter, H.
Only son. Oates, J. C.
The only son of the doctor. Gordon, M.
Only the dead know Brooklyn. Wolfe, T.
The only thing you've got. Havazelet, E.
Only visiting this planet. LaRue, D.
Only yesterday. White, T.

Onopa, Robert
The man who swam through jellyfish, through men-of-war
Passages to the dream shore; ed. by F. Stewart

ONTARIO *See* Canada—Ontario
Onward Jerusalem. Penner, J.
"Oo-a-deen"; or, The mysteries of the interior unveiled
Australian science fiction; ed. by V. Ikin
The oogenesis of Bird City. Farmer, P. J.

Ooka, Shōhei
The mother of dreams
The Mother of dreams, and other short stories; ed. by M. Ueda
Oom. Gardner, M.

Oosthuizen, Ann
A fine romance
Stepping out; ed. by A. Oosthuizen
Ooze. Rud, A. M.

Opatoshu, Joseph
　Romance of a horse thief [Variant title: Horse thief]
　　A Shtetl, and other Yiddish novellas; ed. by R. R. Wisse
An **open** (and closed) marriage. Binchy, M.
Open and shut case. Wilmot, T.
The **open** boat. Crane, S.
The **open** door. Oliphant, M.
Open ground. Wan Zhi
An **open** house. Hughes, J.
Open house. Lott, B.
Open house. Wodehouse, P. G.
Open letter to Oates. Heyen, W.
Open scholarship. Rees, D.
Open twenty-four hours. Pritchett, M.
The **open** window. Saki
Opening. Barthelme, D.
Opening a vein. Pronzini, B., and Malzberg, B. N.
Opening day. Hershenow, N.
Opening the door on Sixty-Second Street. Kumin, M.
Openings. Shapiro, G.

OPERA
　Ade, G. Il janitoro
　Charnas, S. M. A musical interlude
　Gilliatt, P. Addio
　Hoch, E. D. The spy who went to the opera
　Weinzweig, H. Causation
Operate and maintain. Stone, R.
Operation. Asscher-Pinkhof, C.
The **operation.** Crehan, S.
Operation. Kim, S.-O.
The **operation.** Power, V.
Operation afreet. Anderson, P.
Operation Buena Vista. Faust, I.
Operation P-Button. Dickson, G. R.
Operation RSVP. Piper, H. B.
Operation salamander. Anderson, P.
Operation Syndrome. Herbert, F.
Operation wild ass. Ellis, L. R.
OPERATIONS, SURGICAL *See* Surgery
The **operetta.** Drake, R.
The **opiate** of the people. Schwartz, L. S.
OPIUM
　Colette. The screen
　Gates, E. A yellow man and a white
　Taher, B. Advice from a sensible young man
OPIUM TRADE
　Bowles, P. Señor Ong and Señor Ha
　Jia Pingwa. Family chronicle of a wooden bowl maker
　Ríos, A. The child
The **oppressed.** Winton, T.
Optical illusion. Reynolds, M.
Optics. Sheehan, R.
An **optimistic** story. Böll, H.
Optimists. Ford, R.
Options. Varley, J.

OPTOMETRISTS
　Bird, C. The enlargement of Bethany
　Botwinik, B. Esperanto
　Spark, M. The dark glasses
Or battle's sound. Harrison, H.
Or else. Kuttner, H., and Moore, C. L.
The **oracle.** Bloch, R.
An **oracle.** White, E.
The **oracle** is dumb or cheat. Paolucci, A.
The **oracle** of the Corycian cave. Crowley, A.
ORACLES
　Borges, J. L. Paracelsus and the rose
　Crowley, A. The oracle of the Corycian cave
　Silverberg, R. In the House of Double Minds
Oral history. Gordimer, N.
Orange grove. Leatherwood, K.
Orange is for anguish, blue for insanity. Morrell, D.
The **oranges.** Grin, A.
Oranges and apples. Munro, A.
Oranges on her windowsill. Federspiel, J.
ORANGUTANS
　Kennedy, L. Her furry face
　Poe, E. A. The murders in the Rue Morgue
　Willis, C. Samaritan
Orbiting. Mukherjee, B.
Orbits. Busch, F.
The **orchard** walls. Rendell, R.
The **orchards.** Thomas, D.
ORCHIDS
　Wells, H. G. The flowering of the strange orchid
Ordan, David
　Any minute Mom should come blasting through the door
　　Sudden fiction; ed. by R. Shapard and J. Thomas
The **ordeal** of young Tuppy. Wodehouse, P. G.
Order and disorder. Byrd, L. M.
Order in the house. Morazzoni, M.
Order of insects. Gass, W. H.
The **order** of virility. White, C.
The **orderly.** Maupassant, G. de
The **orderly** world of Mr. Appleby. Ellin, S.
An **ordinary** brick house. Brennan, J. P.
An **ordinary** night. Watson, S.
Ore. Bail, M.
OREGON
　Overholser, W. D. Book-l'arnin' and the equalizer
　Overholser, W. D. The patriarch of Gunsight Flat
　Overholser, W. D. The petticoat brigade
　　Farm life
　　See Farm life—Oregon
O'Reilly, Montagu
　The romantic museum
　　New directions in prose and poetry 50

ORGAN
  Jahnn, H. H. A boy weeps
The **organ** piece. Morgan, B.
ORGANISTS
  Franzen, B. The volunteer organist
  Knuttel, W. Fugue
  Pasternak, B. L. Suboctave story
ORGASM
  Brodkey, H. Innocence
The **orgy**. Amichai, Y.
ORIENT AND OCCIDENT *See* East and
  West
The **Oriental** Limited. Long, D.
Oriflamme. Williams, T.
The **origin** of sadness. Morris, W.
The **original** dog. Schinto, J.
Original sin. Larson, L.
Originals. Sargent, P.
Orion. Winterson, J.
ORKNEY (SCOTLAND)
  Brown, G. M. The battle in the hills
  Brown, G. M. A candle for milk and grass
  Brown, G. M. The feast at Paplay
The **ormolu** clock. Spark, M.
An **ornery** kind of kid. Saroyan, W.
ORNITHOLOGISTS
  Kotzwinkle, W. A man who knew his
    birds
  Tallent, E. The evolution of birds of
    paradise
  Thomas, A. C. Elevation
Ornstien, Edwin
  The admission ticket
    Short story international 65
  English for immigrants
    Short story international 54
The **orphan** bassoonist. Harris, M.
Orphan of the void. Biggle, L.
The **orphanage**. McCullers, C.
ORPHANS
  Baxter, C. The would-be father
  Boyle, K. His idea of a mother
  Dodd, S. M. Coelostat
  Fines, B. Neighbors
  Gallant, M. Orphans' progress
  Hall, T. T. The last fly of summer
  Hoyt, M. S. The monastery floor
  James, M. R. Lost hearts
  Lurie, M. Sunday lunch
  MacDonald, J. D. Looie follows me
  Maupassant, G. de. Margot's tapers
  Ocampo, S. The doll
  Pavese, C. Festival night
  Phillips, J. A. Machine dreams [excerpt]
  Sexson, L. Ice cream birth
  Spinelli, J. Gus Zernial and me
  Vaughan, M. C. Fruits of sorrow; or, An
    old maid's story
  Vreuls, D. Beebee
  Warren, J. Erika
  Wilson, L. A. The raising
Orphans of the Storm. Morris, M.
Orphans' progress. Gallant, M.

Orphée, Elvira, 1930-
  Angel's last conquest [excerpt]
    Women's fiction from Latin America; ed.
      by E. P. Garfield
  The silken whale
    Women's fiction from Latin America; ed.
      by E. P. Garfield
ORPHEUS (GREEK MYTHOLOGY)
  Fitzgerald, M. J. Eurydice
Orr, William F.
  Euclid alone
    Mathenauts: tales of mathematical won-
      der; ed. by R. Rucker
Orr Mount. Dunn, D.
Ortalda, Claire
  Close to home
    Stories and poems from close to home;
      ed. by F. Salas
**ORTHODOX   EASTERN   CHURCH,
    GREEK**
  Haris, P. Not a bird in the sky
Orzeszkowa, Eliza
  Miss Antonina
    Russian and Polish women's fiction; ed.
      by H. Goscilo
Osborn, Carolyn, 1934-
  The accidental trip to Jamaica
    Prize stories, Texas Institute of Letters;
      ed. by M. Terry
  Amnesia's child
    Osborn, C. The fields of memory
  Ancient history
    Osborn, C. The fields of memory
  The circuit rider
    Osborn, C. The fields of memory
  Dreamer when last seen
    Osborn, C. The fields of memory
  The greats
    The Antioch Review 46:46-8 Wint '88
  House of the blue woman
    Osborn, C. The fields of memory
  The last of it
    Osborn, C. The fields of memory
  Man Dancing
    Osborn, C. The fields of memory
  The new castle
    Osborn, C. The fields of memory
  Other people's mail
    Osborn, C. The fields of memory
  Reversals
    Osborn, C. The fields of memory
  Running around America
    Osborn, C. The fields of memory
  Stalking strangers
    Osborn, C. The fields of memory
Osborn, Margaret
  Maine
    The Best Maine stories; ed. by S. Phip-
      pen; C. Waugh and M. Greenberg
Osborn, Millicent
  The flounder
    The North American Review 273:52-3 Je
      '88

Osborne, David
For works written by this author under other names see Silverberg, Robert
Osborne, George
The knuckle buster
Southern Exposure (Durham, N.C.) 12:14-16 Jl/Ag '84
Oshidori. Hearn, L.
Osier, John, 1938-
The ritual
Homewords: a book of Tennessee writers; ed. by D. Paschall
Osinsky, Vladimir
Spaceship
Aliens, travelers, and other strangers; by B. and A. Strugatsky and others
Óskar, Jón
The man in the attic and the woman on the main floor
Short story international 44
OSLO (NORWAY) *See* Norway—Oslo
Oslo. Crone, M.
The **ostrich**. Bedard, B.
OSTRICHES
Wells, H. G. A deal in ostriches
Oswald in the Lone Star State. DeLillo, D.
Ota, Yōko
Fireflies
The Crazy iris, and other stories of the atomic aftermath; ed. by K. Oe
Other. Bass, R.
The **other**. MacLean, K.
The **other**. Updike, J.
The **other** Catherine Irene. Biggs, M.
The **other** Ellen. Gault, C.
The **other** eye. Hoch, E. D.
The **other** face. Shallash, S.
Other factors. Gaitskill, M.
Other lives. Prose, F.
The **other** Miller. Wolff, T.
Other people's mail. Osborn, C.
Other people's marriages. Wolfe, L.
The **other** room. Austin, D.
The **other** runner. Lutz, J.
The **other** shoe. Armstrong, C.
The **other** shore. Fink, I.
The **other** side. Campbell, R.
The **other** side of death. García Márquez, G.
The **other** side of summer. Stephen, J.
The **other** side of the curtain. McCloy, H.
The **other** side of the lake. Aldiss, B. W.
The **other** side of the wall. Shaham, N.
The **other** table. Colette
The **other** train phenomenon. Bowker, R.
The **other** two. Curley, D.
The **other** two. Wharton, E.
Other weapons. Valenzuela, L.
The **other** wife. Colette
The **other** woman. Campbell, R.
The **other** woman. Gordon, M.
The **other** woman. Updike, J.
The **other** world. Greenwood, R.

The **other** world I see. Abbott, L. K.
The **others**. Oates, J. C.
Others. Sallis, J.
OTTERS
Saki. Laura
Otto, Lon, 1948-
The Bert and Ernie show
Stiller's pond; ed. by J. Agee; R. Blakely and S. Welch
Ottolengui, Rodriguez
The nameless man
Isaac Asimov presents the best crime stories of the 19th century
Oubliette. Kilworth, G.
OUIJA BOARDS
Muller, M. Kindling point
Our Derby sweepstakes. Doyle, Sir A. C.
Our fair city. Heinlein, R. A.
Our family doctors. Daly, P.
Our fighting cock. Abid, A.
Our first year together. Tinsley, M. B.
Our friend Méritarte. Apollinaire, G.
Our friend the sea. O'Hara, J.
Our house. Thomas, E.
Our Janice. Gardiner, J. R.
Our lady of the barbershop. Hemenway, P.
Our lady of the beehives. Farmer, B.
Our Lady of the Lockers. Friedman, B. J.
Our Lady of the Massacre. Carter, A.
Our Lady of the Sauropods. Silverberg, R.
Our-Lady-of-the-Swallows. Yourcenar, M.
Our last nanny. Taylor, B.
Our little neighbour. Wells, H. G.
Our midnight visitor. Doyle, Sir A. C.
Our own business. Loukakis, A.
Our perfect partners. Lopatin, J.
Our pipes. Lawson, H.
Our private romance. Ade, G.
Our resident djinn. Tiptree, J.
Our shining star. Phillips, D. M.
Our story begins. Wolff, T.
Our town. Robinson, K. S.
Our wall. Oates, J. C.
Our war. Simon, B.
Our war and how we won it. Cullen, E. J.
Our Zaideh. Mazel, D.
Ouroboros. Miller, J. J.
Ours. Connelly, J.
Ousmane, Sembene *See* Sembene, Ousmane, 1923-
Out here. Leavitt, D.
Out in the cold. Keillor, G.
Out of all them bright stars. Kress, N.
Out of empty cisterns. Campbell, E.
Out of his head. Aldrich, T. B.
Out of luck. Tevis, W. S.
Out of my head. Gunn, J. E.
Out of order. Davie, E.
Out of paradise. Hornung, E. W.
Out of place. Merica, E.
Out of place. Sargent, P.
Out of season. Hemingway, E.
Out of sight. Asimov, I.

Out of the blue. Lowry, B.
Out of the fountain. Lessing, D. M.
Out of the fray. Gordon, M.
Out of the inkwell. Goulart, R.
Out of the lion's belly. Glickfeld, C. L.
Out of the mouths of Olympus. Bishop, M.
Out of the pain. Gustafsson, L.
Out of the window. Block, L.
Out of this world. Godfrey, P.
Out of time. Bova, B.
Out on the marsh. Updike, D.
Out on the res. Abbott, K.
Out there. Grant, C. L.
Out with the crowd. Barrett, L.
Outa Sem and Father Christmas. Van Den
  Heever, T.
Outcast. Brand, M.
Outcast breed. See Brand, M. Outcast
The **outcasts** of Poker Flat. Harte, B.
Outdoor friends. Anderson, J.
OUTDOOR LIFE
  See also Country life; Wilderness
  survival
  Campbell, W. B. In season
  Freeman, M. E. W. The Cat
  Muir, J. An adventure with a dog
  Olmstead, R. The boon
  Wegner, R. Incident at the old tin bridge
The **outdoorsman**. Bumpus, J.
Outen, Karen E.
  The Peter story
    Essence 15:78-80+ Ag '84
OUTER SPACE
  See also Space flight
  Communication
  See Interstellar communication
  Exploration
  Anderson, P. The Saturn game
  Asimov, I. Sucker bait
  Asimov, I. Youth
  Bishop, M. Close encounter with the deity
  Brin, D. The warm space
  Clarke, A. C. Jupiter V
  Clarke, A. C. Rescue party
  Dick, P. K. Colony
  Haldeman, J. W. Tricentennial
  Niven, L. Neutron star
  Smith, C. The crime and glory of Com-
    mander Suzdal
  St. Clair, M. Prott
  Vinge, V. Long shot
  Watson, I. Bud
  Wolfe, G. Alien stones
  Zheng Wenguang. The mirror image of the
    earth
The **outfielder**. Meissner, W.
Outink to Uncle's place. Jolley, E.
Outlaw, Louise Lee
  The lemon drop story
    Good Housekeeping 201:62+ D '85
  Love's celebration
    Good Housekeeping 200:136-7 Je '85

Made for each other
    Good Housekeeping 199:144-5 Ag '84
A stranger's charm
    Good Housekeeping 202:172-3 Je '86
Outlaw trail. Barker, S. O.
OUTLAWS
  See also Brigands and robbers
  Abbott, L. K. The purpose of this creature
    man
  Broun, H. Blood Aspens
  Conley, R. J. The hanging of Mose Miller
  Conley, R. J. The name
  Estleman, L. D. Mago's bride
  Frazee, S. Learn the hard way
  Henry, O. The passing of Black Eagle
  Henry, W. The streets of Laredo
  Leonard, E. Law of the hunted ones
  Rhodes, E. M. Pasó por aquí
  Taylor, R. The liberation of the Youngers
Outlaw's wife. Overholser, W. D.
An **outpost** of progress. Conrad, J.
Outrageous. Pronzini, B.
Outrageous behaviour. Lurie, M.
Outrider. Wilson, M.
Outsailed. Jacobs, W. W.
Outside. Norton, A.
Outside the bank's routine. Crowley, A.
Outside the machine. Rhys, J.
The **outsider**. Brooks, J.
The **outsider**. Lovecraft, H. P.
The **outsider**. Nagibin, IU. M.
The **outsider**. Shukshin, V. M.
The **outsiders**. Cooper, D.
The **outspan**. Fitzpatrick, J. P.
Outsteppin' Fetchit. Saunders, C. R.
The **outworks** of the kingdom. Jolley, E.
The **oval** lady. Carrington, L.
The **oval** portrait. Poe, E. A.
Ovenmen. Zimpel, L.
Over. O'Brien, E.
Over and under. Abbott, K.
The **over-night** bag. Greene, G.
Over the cliff. Upward, E.
Over the hill. Dubus, A.
Over the hill. Schwartz, L. S.
Over the mountain. Godwin, G.
Over the purple hills. Schwartz, J.
Over the Pyrenees. Fox, J.
Over the river. Miller, P. S.
Over the river and through the wood.
  O'Hara, J.
Over the river and through the woods. Dyer,
  S.
Over there. Al Magid, I. A.
Over there. Dawson, F.
The **overcoat**. Gogol', N. V.
The **overcoat**. Swanwick, M.
The **overcoat** II. Boyle, T. C.
Overhead in a balloon. Gallant, M.
Overholser, Wayne D., 1906-
  Beecher Island
    Overholser, W. D. The best Western
      stories of Wayne D. Overholser

Overholser, Wayne D., 1906-—*Continued*
Book-l'arnin' and the equalizer
　Overholser, W. D. The best Western
　　stories of Wayne D. Overholser
Debt cancelled
　Overholser, W. D. The best Western
　　stories of Wayne D. Overholser
The hero
　Overholser, W. D. The best Western
　　stories of Wayne D. Overholser
High-grade
　Overholser, W. D. The best Western
　　stories of Wayne D. Overholser
Lawyer two-fist
　Wild westerns; ed. by B. Pronzini
Mean men are big
　Overholser, W. D. The best Western
　　stories of Wayne D. Overholser
The O'Keefe luck
　Overholser, W. D. The best Western
　　stories of Wayne D. Overholser
Outlaw's wife
　Overholser, W. D. The best Western
　　stories of Wayne D. Overholser
The patriarch of Gunsight Flat
　Overholser, W. D. The best Western
　　stories of Wayne D. Overholser
The petticoat brigade
　Overholser, W. D. The best Western
　　stories of Wayne D. Overholser
Smart
　Overholser, W. D. The best Western
　　stories of Wayne D. Overholser
The steadfast
　Overholser, W. D. The best Western
　　stories of Wayne D. Overholser
Steel to the west
　Overholser, W. D. The best Western
　　stories of Wayne D. Overholser
They hanged Wild Bill Murphy
　Overholser, W. D. The best Western
　　stories of Wayne D. Overholser
Winchester wedding
　Overholser, W. D. The best Western
　　stories of Wayne D. Overholser
The wooing of Rosy Malone
　Overholser, W. D. The best Western
　　stories of Wayne D. Overholser
OVERLAND JOURNEYS
Flynn, R. The great plain
Vaughn, S. Sweet talk
The **overlap**. Bovey, J.
Overnight. Fisher, L.
Overnight at Matthew's. Song, Y.
Overnight guest. Gardner, C. S.
Overnight to many distant cities. Barthelme, D.
Overnight trip. Colter, C.
Override. Martin, G. R. R.
Overture. Neville, K.
Overture and beginners please. Rhys, J.
Overture and incidental music for A mid-summer night's dream. Carter, A.

OVID, 43 B.C.-17 or 18
　Parodies, travesties, etc.
Strand, M. Cephalus
Owen, Guy
Miss Mahalia and the still
　Short story international 45
Owens, Barbara
A little piece of room
　Distant danger; ed. by J. Van de Wetering
Owens, Michele
We find Harris again
　Hot type; ed. by J. Miller
The **owl**. Le Braz, A.
The **owl-bander**. Hospital, J. T.
The **Owl** of Bear Island. Bing, J.
OWLS
Conley, R. J. Wesley's story
West, J. Hunting for hoot owls
The **owner** of the flat. Moravia, A.
The **owner** of the gang. St. Pierre, P. H.
Owoyele, David
The will of Allah
　African short stories; ed. by C. Achebe and C. L. Innes
Oxbridge blues. Raphael, F.
OXFORD (ENGLAND) *See* England—Oxford
OXFORD UNIVERSITY *See* University of Oxford
Oxfords. Cummins, W.
OYSLELEUR, NICOLAS
　About
Schwob, M. Nicolas Oyseleur, judge
The **oyster** catcher. Gilbert, M.
Oyster shells. Keppel, T.
Oz, Amos
Nomad and viper
　The Art of the tale; ed. by D. Halpern
Ozaki, Shiro
River deer
　A Late chrysanthemum; tr. by L. Dunlop
The wagtail's nest
　A Late chrysanthemum; tr. by L. Dunlop
Ozark episode. McKinley, J.
Ozark winter. McGarry, J.
Ozick, Cynthia
At Fumicaro
　The New Yorker 60:32-8+ Ag 6 '84
Levitation
　The Norton book of American short stories
The pagan rabbi
　Black water; ed. by A. Manguel
Rosa
　The Best American short stories, 1984
　Prize stories, 1984

Ozick, Cynthia—*Continued*
The shawl
The Bread Loaf anthology of contemporary American short stories; ed. by R. Pack and J. Parini
New women and new fiction; ed. by S. Cahill
The World of the short story; ed. by C. Fadiman
The suitcase
The Art of the tale; ed. by D. Halpern
Trust [excerpt]
Buying time; ed. by S. Walker

P

P.G.M.
The monster mine
Australian science fiction; ed. by V. Ikin
Pa. Kornblatt, J. R.
Pa and the sad turkeys. Petrakis, H. M.
Pa mai. Taylor, A.
The **pace** of youth. Crane, S.
Pacheco, José Emilio, 1939-
Acheron
Pacheco, J. E. Battles in the desert & other stories
The amusement park
New directions in prose and poetry 48
August afternoon
Pacheco, J. E. Battles in the desert & other stories
Battles in the desert
Pacheco, J. E. Battles in the desert & other stories
The captive
Pacheco, J. E. Battles in the desert & other stories
The pleasure principle
Pacheco, J. E. Battles in the desert & other stories
The sunken park
Pacheco, J. E. Battles in the desert & other stories
You wouldn't understand
Pacheco, J. E. Battles in the desert & other stories
Pachter, Josh
The beer drinkers
The Ethnic detectives; ed. by B. Pronzini and M. H. Greenberg
The Dilmun Exchange
The Year's best mystery and suspense stories, 1985
The night of power
The Year's best mystery and suspense stories, 1987
(jt. auth) See Lutz, John, 1939-, and Pachter, Josh
The **Pacific.** Helprin, M.
Pacific theater. Bennett, J. G.

The **pack.** Stephenson, M.
The **package** store. Dixon, S.
Packages. Asscher-Pinkhof, C.
Packard, Chris
Tornado weather
Michigan Quarterly Review 25:582-9 Summ '86
Packer, Ann
Mendocino
The New Yorker 64:38-44 Je 6 '88
Packer, Miriam
The condition
Fatal recurrences; ed. by H. Hugh and P. O'Brien
Packer, Nancy Huddleston
Early morning, lonely ride
Prime number; ed. by A. L. Weir
Jealous-hearted me
The Southern Review (Baton Rouge, La.) 24:893-906 Aut '88
Making amends
Southwest Review 70:95-105 Wint '85
The **packhorse** path. Blythe, R.
Paco and I at sea. Thomas, J.
Padayachee, Deena
A first encounter of the marital kind
Short story international 68
Padgett, Lewis
The piper's son
From mind to mind: tales of communication from Analog
Padgett, Ron
Monsieur Jim
The Paris Review 26:102-3 Summ '84
My room
The Paris Review 26:104-5 Summ '84
Padilla, Mike
Papel
Hot type; ed. by J. Miller
A **padlock** for Charlie Draper. Holding, J.
PADUA (ITALY) *See* Italy—Padua
PAETUS, PUBLIUS CLODIUS THRASEA
See Thrasea Paetus, Publius Clodius, d. 66
The **pagan** rabbi. Ozick, C.
PAGANISM
See also Religion, Primitive
Machen, A. The white people
Morrison, J. Christ, the Devil and the lunatic
Ozick, C. The pagan rabbi
Wells, H. G. Jimmy Goggles the god
Pagans. DeMarinis, R.
Page, Frank
The spear thrower
Short story international 71
Page, Norvell
Satan's hoof
A Cent a story! Ed. by G. G. Roberts
Page, Patricia
Thrift
The New Yorker 60:44-9 Ap 30 '84

Page, Thomas Nelson
The burial of the guns
A Treasury of Civil War stories; ed. by M. H. Greenberg and B. Pronzini
A **page** from the marriage manual for Songhees brides. Kinsella, W. P.
The **pageant** of ghosts. Gilchrist, M.
Pages from a young girl's journal. Aickman, R.
Pages from Cold Point. Bowles, P.
Paget, Violet See Lee, Vernon, 1856-1935
PAGODAS
Kōda, R. The five-storied pagoda
Lafferty, R. A. Nor limestone islands
Pahua. Gores, J.
The **paid** nurse. Williams, W. C.
Paik, Binney
Ramón
Seventeen 47:258-9+ Mr '88
Pain, Barry, 1865-1928
Rose Rose
The Oxford book of English ghost stories
PAIN
See also Suffering
Haldeman, J. W. Lindsay and the red city blues
Kirk, S. Morrison's reaction
Sonu, H. The story of a peculiar pain
Steele, M. The silent scream
Strieber, W. Pain
Tilton, L. In the service of evil
Pain. Strieber, W.
A **painful** affair. Gallant, M.
Pains and pleasures. Hartley, L. P.
Paint doctor. Hensley, J. L.
Painted finches. Prichard, K. S.
Painter, Pamela
Astral travel
The Virginia Quarterly Review 61:318-21 Spr '85
The bridge
Sudden fiction; ed. by R. Shapard and J. Thomas
Getting to know the weather
Painter, P. Getting to know the weather
The Sewanee Review 93:173-82 Spr '85
Intruders of sleepless nights
Painter, P. Getting to know the weather
The Ploughshares reader: new fiction for the eighties
Kate and Allie and Kate
Redbook 168:54+ Mr '87
The kidnappers
The North American Review 269:49-52 Je '84
Painter, P. Getting to know the weather
A man of his time
Painter, P. Getting to know the weather
The next time I meet Buddy Rich
Painter, P. Getting to know the weather
Prime number; ed. by A. L. Weir

Night walk
Painter, P. Getting to know the weather
Patterns
Painter, P. Getting to know the weather
Pearls before wine
Mademoiselle 92:92+ Jl '86
The real story
Harper's 273:58-9+ O '86
The runaway wife
Redbook 167:40+ Ag '86
Something to do
Ms. 15:58-60+ Ag '86
Painter, P. Getting to know the weather
The sorting out
Painter, P. Getting to know the weather
Suppertime
Painter, P. Getting to know the weather
Sylvia
Painter, P. Getting to know the weather
The visitor
Painter, P. Getting to know the weather
Winter evenings: spring night
Painter, P. Getting to know the weather
The **painter.** Hall, M. L.
PAINTERS
See also Women painters
Abrahams, L. Invisible worm
Akutagawa, R. Hell screen
Blei, N. The landscaper
Bloch, R. The masterpiece
Burns, M. Collected bear stories
Cather, W. Coming, Aphrodite!
Chambers, R. W. The yellow sign
Chipulina, E. G. Diamonds are forever
Colette. The landscape
Conroy, J. Slappy Hooper, world's biggest, fastest, and bestest sign painter
Cowan, P. The beach
Dunn, D. Kilbinnin men
Eldridge, M. Flight
Farmer, P. J. Riders of the purple wage
Ferron, J. The landscape painter
Gallant, M. Speck's idea
Gardner, M. The horrible horns
Gilchrist, M. Excerpts from Witherton's journal: also a letter of Crystalla's
Gogol', N. V. The portrait
Hall, M. L. The painter
Henry, O. Art and the bronco
Humphrey, W. The fauve
Ignatow, R. G. Colors
Ignatow, R. G. New artists, new jungle
Ignatow, R. G. Sheep in the meadow
Ioannides, P. The unseen aspect
Jeppson, J. O. A million shades of green
Kuncewiczowa, M. Strange Rachel
Le Fanu, J. S. Schalken the painter
Longyear, B. B. The portrait of Baron Negay
Lovecraft, H. P. Pickman's model
Malamud, B. The model
Maramzin, V. The two-toned blond: a reciprocal tale

PAINTERS—*Continued*
Maupassant, G. de. The artist's wife
Maupassant, G. de. Miss Harriet
Pain, B. Rose Rose
Paolucci, A. Buried treasure
Parise, G. Freedom
Pirandello, L. Candelora
Pirandello, L. The fish trap
Pritchard, M. The housekeeper
Raphael, F. On the black list
Rhys, J. Tea with an artist
Roberts, N. For luck
Saiki, J. Retrospective
Sandel, C. Artist's Christmas
Sata, I. The colorless paintings
Shaw, H. The gipsies
Silvis, R. Prayer and old jokes
Skelton, R. Portrait of Duck
Tem, S. R. The painters are coming today
Wells, H. G. The devotee of art
Wells, H. G. The temptation of Harringay
West, J. A time of learning
Wright, R. Man, God ain't like that. . .

Yourcenar, M. How Wang-Fo was saved
Yourcenar, M. The sadness of Cornelius
     Berg
PAINTERS, INDUSTRIAL
Chekhov, A. P. My life
Gallagher, T. Turpentine
Schwartz, L. S. The painters
The **painters**. Schwartz, L. S.
The **painters** are coming today. Tem, S. R.
The **painter's** daughter. Bedford, W.
Painting day. Mattison, A.
PAINTINGS
Akutagawa, R. 'Autumn Mountain'
Bail, M. The drover's wife
Bloch, R. The past master
Chesterton, G. K. A picture of Tuesday
Cowper, R. Paradise beach
Davis, D. S. The purple is everything
DeMarinis, R. The swimmer in hard light
Hornung, E. W. Nine points of the law
Josipovici, G. Absence and echo
Kotzwinkle, W. Sun, moon, and storm
Le Fanu, J. S. Schalken the painter
Lemelin, R. The Stations of the Cross
Lurie, M. The day the bottom fell out of
     Yugoslavia
Lurie, M. An immaculate conception
Matheson, R. C. Beholder
Morazzoni, M. Girl in a turban
Petroski, C. Madonna with cat
Ribeyro, J. R. The double
Ritchie, J. Who's got the lady?
Silva, B. The artist
Wiebe, D. E. The art of Vietnam
Woolf, V. A simple melody
A **pair** of bulls. Olmstead, R.
A **pair** of duelling pistols. Warner, S. T.
A **pair** of eyes; or, Modern magic. Alcott,
     L. M.

A **pair** of glasses. Gallagher, T.
A **pair** of gloves. Dickens, C.
A **pair** of hands. Quiller-Couch, Sir A. T.
Pak, Kyong-Ni
A time of disbelief
     Hospital room 205, and other Korean
     short stories
Pak, Leopoldo H.
The lion that learned algebra
     Américas 36:16-19 Mr/Ap '84
Pak, Si-Jong
Ten minutes to seven
     Early spring, mid-summer, and other
     Korean short stories
Pak, Wan-So
How I kept our house while my husband
     was away
     Hospital room 205, and other Korean
     short stories
Pak, Yong-Jun
The last parting
     The Unenlightened, and other Korean
     short stories
Pak, Yong-Suk
Eroica Symphony
     Two travelers, and other Korean short
     stories
PAKISTAN
Kharal, N. The dead end
Rahman, T. Bingo
Rahman, T. The legacy
Thompson, B. Crossing
     Civil War, 1971
     See Bangladesh—Revolution, 1971
     Lahore
Thompson, B. Tattoo
Pal Joey. O'Hara, J.
The **palace** at four A.M. Barthelme, D.
The **palace** at midnight. Silverberg, R.
The **Palace** of Culture. Tuohy, F.
The **palace** of Kandahar. Haley, R.
PALACES
Eichendorff, J., Freiherr von. Memoirs of
     a good-for-nothing
Smith, C. A. The end of the story
Paladin of the lost hour. Ellison, H.
Palais de Justice. Helprin, M.
Pale Anna. Böll, H.
The **Pale** Fox. Oba, M.
The **pale** girl, the dark mage, and the green
     sea. Lee, T.
"**Pale** trembling youth". Pugmire, W. H., and
     Salmonson, J. A.
PALESTINE
     See also Israel; Jerusalem
Davin, D. Unwrung withers
Liphshitz, A. Jum'a and Jamila
Liphshitz, A. A man and his house
Liphshitz, A. Master of his fate
Liphshitz, A. The monk
PALESTINIAN ARABS
     See also Jewish-Arab relations
Liphshitz, A. Jum'a and Jamila

PALESTINIAN ARABS—*Continued*
Liphshitz, A. Under the horses' hooves
Paley, Grace
Anxiety
Paley, G. Later the same day
At that time; or, The history of a joke
Paley, G. Later the same day
The contest
The Art of the tale; ed. by D. Halpern
Dreamer in a dead language
Full measure; ed. by D. Sennett
Paley, G. Later the same day
The expensive moment
Paley, G. Later the same day
Short story international 68
Faith in a tree
Buying time; ed. by S. Walker
Friends
Paley, G. Later the same day
In the garden
Paley, G. Later the same day
In this country, but in another language,
my aunt refuses to marry the men
everyone wants her to
Paley, G. Later the same day
An interest in life
Great American love stories; ed. by L.
Rosenthal
Lavinia: an old story
Paley, G. Later the same day
Listening
Paley, G. Later the same day
The loudest voice
"May your days be merry and bright"
and other Christmas stories by wom-
en; ed. by S. Koppelman
Love
Paley, G. Later the same day
A man told me the story of his life
Paley, G. Later the same day
Midrash on happiness
Prize stories, 1987
Mother
Paley, G. Later the same day
Sudden fiction; ed. by R. Shapard and
J. Thomas
Ruthy and Edie
Paley, G. Later the same day
Somewhere else
Paley, G. Later the same day
The story hearer
Paley, G. Later the same day
Prize stories, 1984
A subject of childhood
The Norton book of American short
stories
Telling
The Best American short stories, 1986
This is a story about my friend George,
the toy inventor
Paley, G. Later the same day

The used-boy raisers
American short story masterpieces; ed.
by R. Carver and T. Jenks
Wants
Look who's talking; ed. by B. Weber
Zagrowsky tells
Short story international 60
Palindrome. Disch, T. M.
The **Palladian** Bridge. Tuohy, F.
Pallant, Cheryl
A neighborhood bar
Inspired by drink; ed. by Joan Digby
and John Digby
PALM SPRINGS (CALIF.) *See* California—
Palm Springs
Palma, Clemente, 1872-1944
Aboard the cart
Palma, C. Malignant tales
The man with the cigarette
Palma, C. Malignant tales
Mors ex vita
Palma, C. Malignant tales
The story of the man who was not born
Palma, C. Malignant tales
PALMA (SPAIN) *See* Spain—Palma
Palmer, Edward Vance *See* Palmer, Vance,
1885-1959
Palmer, Michael, 1953-
Esmerelda's hands
Bringing down the moon; ed. by J. An-
derson
Palmer, Stuart, 1905-1968
Hildegarde Withers is back
Manhattan mysteries; ed. by B. Pronzini;
C. L. R. Waugh and M. H. Greenberg
Riddle of the marble blade
Uncollected crimes; ed. by B. Pronzini
and M. H. Greenberg
Palmer, Vance, 1885-1959
Josie
The Australian short story; ed. by L.
Hergenhan
Palmer, William
Bel
Critical Quarterly 30:88-101 Summ '88
Palmieri, Anthony
Force of habit
Short story international 62
PALMISTRY
Beerbohm, M. A. V. Laider
La **Paloma**; or, The food of love. Bender,
H.
Palwick, Susan
Ever after
The Year's best fantasy, first annual
collection
The Year's best science fiction, fifth an-
nual collection
Pamela's get. Schow, D. J.
The **pampas** clump. Hartley, L. P.
Pamphalon the entertainer. Leskov, N. S.
PAN (DEITY)
Benson, E. F. The man who went too far

Panache. Kinsella, W. P.
PANAMA
Swados, H. Tease
       Panama City
Morris, M. The bus of dreams
PANAMA CANAL
Watt, N. The mule driver and the carrot
PANAMA CITY (PANAMA) *See* Panama—
Panama City
Pancake, Breece D'J, d. 1979
The honored dead
  Soldiers & civilians; ed. by T. Jenks
The salvation of me
  The Substance of things hoped for; ed.
  by J. B. Breslin
Trilobites
  Stories of the modern South; ed. by B.
  Forkner and P. Samway
Pandora. Rossiter, S.
Pangborn, Edgar
Harper Conan & Singer David
  Worlds apart; ed. by C. Decarnin; E.
  Garber and L. Paleo
Longtooth
  The Best horror stories from the
  Magazine of fantasy and science fiction
A master of Babylon
  Beyond Armageddon; ed. by W. M. Mil-
  ler and M. H. Greenberg
The night wind
  The Best from Universe
  Kindred spirits; ed. by J. M. Elliot
Pick-up for Olympus
  100 great fantasy short short stories; ed.
  by I. Asimov; T. Carr and M. H.
  Greenberg
Panneton, Philippe, 1895-1960
The heritage
  The Oxford book of French-Canadian
  short stories
Panning, Anne
Pigs
  Stiller's pond; ed. by J. Agee; R. Blakely
  and S. Welch
Panova, Vera Fedorovna, 1905-1973
Evdokia
  Russian and Polish women's fiction; ed.
  by H. Goscilo
Panshin, Alexei, 1940-
Down to the worlds of men
  Intergalactic empires; ed. by I. Asimov;
  M. H. Greenberg and C. G. Waugh
Pantaloon in black. Faulkner, W.
PANTHERS
Balzac, H. de. A passion in the desert
Dollarhide, L. The gift
Pants on fire. Baker, N.
Paolo Uccello, painter. Schwob, M.
Paolucci, Anne
Buried treasure
  Paolucci, A. Sepia tones
Ciao, mio tesoro
  Paolucci, A. Sepia tones

Don Giacomo
  Paolucci, A. Sepia tones
Lights
  Paolucci, A. Sepia tones
The oracle is dumb or cheat
  Paolucci, A. Sepia tones
Rarà
  Paolucci, A. Sepia tones
A small clearing
  Paolucci, A. Sepia tones
Papa Benjamin. See Woolrich, C. Dark
  melody of madness
Papa, snake & I. Honwana, L. B.
PAPACY *See* Catholic faith; Popes
Papaellinas, George, 1954-
Around the crate
  Papaellinas, G. Ikons
Christos Mavromatis is a welder
  Papaellinas, G. Ikons
In which Peter Mavromatis lives up to his
  name
  Papaellinas, G. Ikons
Into a further dimension
  Papaellinas, G. Ikons
A merchant's widow
  Papaellinas, G. Ikons
Peter Mavromatis rides the tail of the
  donkey
  Papaellinas, G. Ikons
Peter's song
  Papaellinas, G. Ikons
You told me
  Papaellinas, G. Ikons
PAPAGO INDIANS
Austin, M. H. Papago wedding
Papago wedding. Austin, M. H.
Papa's tea. Narell, I.
Papel. Padilla, M.
Papen. Sandel, C.
Paper children. Jolley, E.
The **paper** door. Shiga, N.
Paper dragons. Blaylock, J. P.
Paper fires. Summerville, J.
The **paper** house. Mailer, N.
PAPER INDUSTRY
Melville, H. The tartarus of maids
PAPER MAKING AND TRADE *See* Paper
  industry
Paper moon. Kilworth, G.
The **paper** parcel. Marshall, O.
Paper products. Hall, J.
The **paper** route. Choyce, L.
PAPERMAKING INDUSTRY *See* Paper in-
  dustry
PAPERS *See* Manuscripts
Papi invented the automatic jumping bean.
  Keller, G. D.
The **'Papier** Rouge'. Schwob, M.
Papini, Giovanni
The sick gentleman's last visit
  Black water; ed. by A. Manguel
Papito's story. Valenzuela, L.
Pap's mules. Peck, S. M.

PAPUA NEW GUINEA
O'Grady, D. Sterner's double vision
The **parable** of the miraculous escape.
Mrożek, S.

PARABLES
See also Allegories
Banks, R. The fish
Borges, J. L. The lottery in Babylon
Ekström, M. The night between the second
and the third
Grin, A. The green lamp
Hogg, J. On the separate existence of the
soul
Kafka, F. Before the law
Mrożek, S. The parable of the miraculous
escape
Ratushinskaya, I. On the meaning of life
Roth, J. The bust of the emperor
Roth, J. Hotel Savoy
Schwartz, L. S. The last frontier
Schwob, M. The fat man
Sholem Aleichem. Rabchik, a Jewish dog
Singer, I. B. Logarithms
Vinge, J. D. The storm king
Paracelsus and the rose. Borges, J. L.

PARADES
Alford, E. Half past eight
Lowry, B. Come back, Lolly Ray [excerpt]
Paradise. Bail, M.
Paradise. Frucht, A.
Paradise. O'Brien, E.
Paradise beach. Cowper, R.
Paradise lost. Berry, R. M.
The **paradise** of bachelors. Melville, H.
The **paradise** of human fishes. Chesterton,
G. K.
Paradise Paddock. Hartley, L. P.
Paradise sheldrake. Dabrowska, C.
Paragrams and anadigms. Grossmith, R.
The **parakeet**. Ferron, J.

PARAKEETS
Anthony, P. Beak by beak
Parallel play. Ephron, N.
The **parallel** world. Martin, V.

PARALYSIS
See also Paraplegics
Fremlin, C. A lovely day to die
Gilbert, W. S. Angela
Matthews, J. The gray lady
Miller, S. Appropriate affect
Morazzoni, M. Order in the house
Russell, R. Sardonicus
Sillitoe, L. Four walls and an empty door

PARANOIA
DeMarinis, R. Mole
Heideman, E. M. Roger, Mr. Whilkie!
Lutz, J. On guard
Sage, V. Crusoe
Sprengnether, M. The camper
Wilmot, T. Skeleton in the cupboard
Paranoid fantasy #1. Watt-Evans, L.

PARAPLEGICS
Hulme, K. A nightsong for the shining
cuckoo
Pronzini, B. Unchained
The **parasite**. Doyle, Sir A. C.

PARASITES
Quiroga, H. The feather pillow
Snodgrass, M. Requiem
Paratuga will return. Federspiel, J.
The **parched** earth. Kaniuk, Y.
The **pardoner's** tale. Silverberg, R.
Paré, Paul
Five fables
Invisible fictions; ed. by G. Hancock

PARENT AND CHILD
See also Conflict of generations;
Fathers and daughters; Fathers and
sons; Mothers and daughters; Mothers
and sons
Asscher-Pinkhof, C. Madonna
Asscher-Pinkhof, C. Safety
Atwood, M. In search of the rattlesnake
plantain
Atwood, M. Unearthing suite
Bachmann, I. Everything
Banks, R. Children's story
Bausch, R. What feels like the world
Blinkin, M. Smoke
Bonnie, F. Mistrial
Botwinik, B. Shabbas morning
Botwinik, B. A shoemaker for a husband
Bowles, C. The song of the fisherman
Bowles, P. In the red room
Bradbury, R. I suppose you are wondering
why we are here?
Bradbury, R. The small assassin
Bradfield, S. Unmistakably the finest
Brender à Brandis, M. Foreigner in the
family
Briskin, M. Two women, one child
Brodkey, H. Verona: a young woman
speaks
Buzzati, D. A difficult evening
Cameron, P. Fear of math
Campbell, R. The faces at Pine Dunes
Canin, E. Star Food
Caponegro, M. Deformity
Carlson, R. Milk
Carver, R. A small, good thing
Clayton, J. J. An old 3 A.M. story
Corrington, J. W. Pleadings
Cullen, E. J. I try to look out for my
family
Curley, D. Trinity
Curtiss, U. R. Change of climate
Dahl, R. Royal jelly
Dixon, S. Reversal
Dixon, S. Wheels
Dixon, S. Will as a boy
Doctorow, E. L. Willi
Du Fresne, Y. Christmas (Shirley Temple
is a wife and mother)
Dubus, A. The winter father

PARENT AND CHILD—*Continued*
Dunn, D. Bobby's room
Durban, P. In darkness
Durban, P. This heat
El Milady, F. A. K. The night of the festival
Engberg, S. A daughter's heart
Faust, I. Melanie and the purple people eaters
Fetler, A. The third count
Fuentes, C. The doll queen
Gaitskill, M. Heaven
Gallant, M. Jorinda and Jorindel
Gallant, M. Luc and his father
Gardner, M. The three cowboys
Girion, B. To Francie, with love
Given, A. Love's an itinerant
Givner, J. The decline and fall of a reasonable woman
Gold, H. Paternity
Gordon, M. Temporary shelter
Grau, S. A. Letting go
Greenberg, B. L. Important things
Greenberg, J. Days of awe
Halley, A. A Rosenkavalier
Hayes, L. Kiss good night to the princess, frog
Hood, H. Flying a red kite
Houbein, L. The serene revolution
Huggan, I. Sawdust
Johnston, S. Iris Holmes
Jones, D. W. Carol Oneir's hundredth dream
Jones, R. F. The children's room
Kaufman, B. Sunday in the park
Kavaler, R. The perfume of love
Keillor, G. Thanksgiving
King, F. H. The mouse
Krause, P. Second sight
Kress, N. Talp hunt
Krysl, M. Bondage
Krysl, M. Désirs
Lipman, E. Baby's first Christmas
Lipsky, D. Three thousand dollars
Lipsky, E. The quality of mercy
Lish, G. What my mother's father was really the father of
Lofts, N. God's own elect
Lutz, J. The landscape of dreams
Marosi, G. The milk-boy
Matthews, J. A questionnaire for Rudolph Gordon
Matthews, J. The two of them together
Mattison, A. The Middle Ages
Mattison, A. They all went up to Amsterdam
McGuane, T. The millionaire
Minh-Quan. My milk goes dry
Minot, S. Thorofare
Moore, L. The kid's guide to divorce
Moyer, K. In the castle
Murphy, Y. Tidal air
Narayan, R. K. Nitya

Oates, J. C. Visitation rights
Paley, G. Anxiety
Potter, N. A. J. Talking to trees
Prichard, K. S. Yoirimba
Pritchard, M. In foreign country
Pritchard, M. A private landscape
Prose, F. Everyday disorders
Rive, R. Resurrection
Roberts, N. Dancing in Trolley Square
Robison, J. Transfer
Rodoreda, M. The hen
Rooke, L. The only daughter
Rooke, L. Why the heathens are no more
Rossiter, S. Kiss the father
Schulman, H. James Dean's widow
Schwartz, L. S. The age of analysis
Seema, N. Helpless
Silva, B. Yellow bird
Spark, M. The twins
Spencer, E. Jack of diamonds
Stern, R. G. Dr. Cahn's visit
Sturges, A. E. Pianoforte
Swift, G. Hotel
Swift, G. Learning to swim
Tarkington, B. Blue milk
Thompson, S. The baby in mid-air
Thurm, M. Light-years
Thurm, M. Markings
Thurm, M. Snow-child
Travis, L. Tom's burn
Tremain, R. The Colonel's daughter
Tyler, A. Teenage wasteland
Updike, J. Learn a trade
Updike, J. Separating
Vaughan, D. The death of a champion
Walton, D. One blood
West, J. Alive and real
West, J. Crimson Ramblers of the world, farewell
Wexler, J. Two year's absence
Wicomb, Z. Bowl like hole
Parent conference. Erbaugh, H.
Parents. Barthelme, F.
Paretsky, Sara
At the old swimming hole
  Mean streets; ed. by R. J. Randisi
  Murder and mystery in Chicago; ed. by C. R. Waugh; F. D. McSherry and M. H. Greenberg
Three-Dot Po
  The Eyes have it; ed. by R. J. Randisi
Pargeter, Edith *See* Peters, Ellis, 1913-
Parini, Jay
Astray in the suburbs
  The Virginia Quarterly Review 62:490-8 Summ '86
PARIS (FRANCE) *See* France—Paris
Paris. McLaughlin, L.
Paris, 1959. Plante, D.
Paris and Cleveland are voyages. Gold, H.
Paris in summer. Gilbert, M.
Paris leaves me cold. Crone, M.
Paris vicarious. Halligan, M.

Parise, Goffredo
Boredom
Harper's 270:31-2 Je '85
Parise, G. Solitudes
Dream
Parise, G. Solitudes
Fascination
Parise, G. Solitudes
Fatherhood
Parise, G. Solitudes
Fear
Parise, G. Solitudes
Freedom
Parise, G. Solitudes
Happiness
Parise, G. Solitudes
Hate
Parise, G. Solitudes
Hotel
Parise, G. Solitudes
Hunger
Parise, G. Solitudes
Italy
Parise, G. Solitudes
Laziness
Parise, G. Solitudes
Liking
Parise, G. Solitudes
Marriage
Parise, G. Solitudes
Melancholy
Parise, G. Solitudes
Memory
Parise, G. Solitudes
Mother
Parise, G. Solitudes
Mystery
Parise, G. Solitudes
Nostalgia
Parise, G. Solitudes
Patience, spring
Parise, G. Solitudes
Patriotism
Parise, G. Solitudes
Poetry
Parise, G. Solitudes
Poise
Parise, G. Solitudes
Poverty
Parise, G. Solitudes
Rome
Parise, G. Solitudes
Sea
Parise, G. Solitudes
Sex
Parise, G. Solitudes
Simplicity
Parise, G. Solitudes
Solitude
Parise, G. Solitudes
War
Parise, G. Solitudes

Work
Parise, G. Solitudes
Youth
Parise, G. Solitudes
The **Parish** Magazine. Doyle, Sir A. C.
Park. Eighner, L.
Park. Kelly, C.
The **park**. Piñera, V.
The **Park** Avenue Social Review visits the
Drought Dinner in Eagle Grove, Iowa.
Franzen, B.
Park taxi. Hoyt, M. S.
Parker, Dorothy, 1893-1967
The standard of living
The Norton book of American short
stories
A telephone call
Great American love stories; ed. by L.
Rosenthal
**PARKER, JOHN F. (JOHN FREDERICK),
1933-**
About
Alexander, D. The man who went to Tal-
tavul's
Parker, Percy Spurlark
Lady with a knife
Ellery Queen's Prime crimes
Parker, Richard
The wheelbarrow boy
Young monsters; ed. by I. Asimov; M.
H. Greenberg and C. G. Waugh
The **Parker** shotgun. Grafton, S.
Parker's back. O'Connor, F.
Parking space. Brett, S.
Parkinson, Terry L.
The blue man
Shadows 8
The father figure
Shadows 9
Sleep
After midnight; ed. by C. L. Grant
PARKS
See also Amusement parks; Wilder-
ness areas; Zoos
Baxter, C. A late Sunday afternoon by the
Huron
Faik, S. The park's mornings, evenings,
nights
Gault, C. At dusk / just when / the light
is filled with birds
Kelly, C. Park
The **park's** mornings, evenings, nights. Faik,
S.
Parlour 4. Stewart, J. I. M.
A **parma** violet room. Flanagan, M.
PAROCHIAL SCHOOLS *See* Church
schools
PARODIES
Dumonte, E. Mr. Reed goes to dinner
Russ, J. Everyday depressions
Sladek, J. T. White hat

Parotti, Phillip, 1941-
Antiphus on Tmolus
  Parotti, P. The Trojan generals talk
Diator beyond Olympus
  Parotti, P. The Trojan generals talk
Diomedes at Aulis
  Parotti, P. The Greek generals talk
Eurypylus at Dodona
  Parotti, P. The Greek generals talk
Facing west
  The Sewanee Review 96:549-65 Fall '88
Heptaporos in Phrygia
  Parotti, P. The Trojan generals talk
Keas on Ida
  Parotti, P. The Trojan generals talk
Machaon at Tricca
  Parotti, P. The Greek generals talk
Medon in Thrace
  Parotti, P. The Trojan generals talk
Meges at Dulichium
  Parotti, P. The Greek generals talk
Menestheus at Athens
  Parotti, P. The Greek generals talk
Meriones at Gortyn
  Parotti, P. The Greek generals talk
Merops in Mysia
  Parotti, P. The Trojan generals talk
Nastes at Miletus
  Parotti, P. The Trojan generals talk
Neoptolemus in Phthia
  Parotti, P. The Greek generals talk
Odios at Alybe
  Parotti, P. The Trojan generals talk
Pheidippus at Cos
  Parotti, P. The Greek generals talk
Polydamas on the Plain
  Parotti, P. The Trojan generals talk
Pyracchmes beneath Laurion
  Parotti, P. The Trojan generals talk
Sinon at Elis
  Parotti, P. The Greek generals talk
Thersites at Mytilene
  Parotti, P. The Greek generals talk
Thoas at Pylene
  Parotti, P. The Greek generals talk
Thrasymedes at Pylos
  Parotti, P. The Greek generals talk
A Trojan general talks
  The Sewanee Review 95:185-98 Spr '87
Parr, Wallace
Street star
  Men on men; ed. by G. Stambolian
PARRICIDE
Benson, E. F. The confession of Charles
  Linkworth
Humphrey, W. The patience of a saint
O'Connor, F. A view of the woods
Sims, L. Behind my lace curtain
Willett, J. Julie in the funhouse
Parris, P. B.
Carmen Miranda's navel
  The Kenyon Review ns9:71-7 Summ '87
The **parrot**. Ferron, J.

PARROTS
Ciment, J. Small claims
Collier, J. Bird of prey
Hankla, C. The baby, the parrot
Hichens, R. How love came to Professor
  Guildea
Pascoe, B. Cobber: Peach Face
Prichard, K. S. The galah
Sandel, C. Papen
Woolf, V. The widow and the parrot: a
  true story
Parry, Henry T.
The Plum Point Ladies
  Alfred Hitchcock's Crimewatch
The punchboards
  Tales from Ellery Queen's Mystery
  Magazine: short stories for young
  adults
The **parson** and the band. Mrożek, S.
A **part**. Hale, N.
A **part** of him revealed. Polizzi, C.
A **part** of the institution. Suckow, R.
A **part** of the world. Gansovsky, S.
Part-time father. Clayton, J. J.
The **part-timer**. Howell, C.
Parted. Moore, G.
A **partial** portrait of my father, his birthdays,
  my gifts, bottled in bond. Lurie, M.
Particularly difficult territory. Zajdel, J. A.
PARTIES
  See also Birthdays; Children's par-
  ties; Dinners
Allen, R. The woman in the shadows
Amichai, Y. The Bar Mitzvah party
Bail, M. Life of the party
Barthelme, S. Here you are
Bates, H. E. Country society
Bates, H. E. A party for the girls
Beattie, A. Lofty
Blaise, C. Grids and doglegs
Blythe, R. Take your partners
Brady, M. On the way to the ERA
Brett, S. Tickled to death
Briskin, M. By evil and kindness
Bye, C. Box social
Cárdenas, M. But what if I liked the
  Panchos, not the Beatles
Carlson, R. Olympus Hills
Davis, D. S. The last party
Digby, J. The champagne party
Evans, M. Candles in the bottom of the
  pool
Fisher, M. F. K. The reunion
Fleming, B. Beach party
Gallant, M. Thank you for the lovely tea
Geras, A. Snapshots of paradise
Hardy, T. The three strangers
Hartley, L. P. The cotillon
Hulme, K. Planetesimal
Janowitz, T. Matches
Johnson, J. The fall of Texas
Justice, D. R. The artificial moonlight
Kilgore, D. Heaven vs. hell

PARTIES—*Continued*
Klein, T. E. D. Petey
Komie, L. B. The Christmas party
Krysl, M. Something unforgivable
Leavitt, D. Family dancing
Liben, M. A note on chivalry
Loukakis, A. Partying on parquet
Mansfield, K. The garden party
Mansfield, K. Her first ball
Marshall, O. The paper parcel
McGarry, J. Margery's prom
Millhauser, S. The sledding party
Moorhouse, F. The Coca-Cola Kid
Murphy, P. The alarm system
Newman, K. Patricia's profession
Oates, J. C. Party
O'Brien, E. Irish revel
Oe, K. The clever rain tree
O'Hara, J. The moccasins
O'Hara, J. Winter dance
Ozick, C. Levitation
Piñera, V. The ball
Pynchon, T. Entropy
Richardson, H. H. "And women must
    weep"
Rosenfeld, I. George
Schulman, H. Like brothers
Silverberg, R. Capricorn games
Simpson, J. A party for idiot
Skelton, R. The importance of being Percy
Sorrentino, G. The gala cocktail party
Spark, M. Daisy Overend
Steele, M. Where she brushed her hair
Stegner, W. E. Field guide to the western
    birds
Tallent, E. The fence party
Taylor, P. H. The little cousins
Thompson, J. The Christmas party
Thurm, M. Still life
Truss, J. The party
Tuohy, F. Evening in Connecticut
Ullmann, A. Those in peril in the air
Vogan, S. Sunday's no name band
Warren, J. Mrs. Rogers
Warren, J. The underground banquet
Watmough, D. In the mood
Welch, D. A party
Wilson, R. Farewell party
Woolf, V. The evening party
Woolf, V. The shooting party
Yates, R. The best of everything
Parties. Van Vechten, C.
Parties and storms. Rose, D. A.
Parting. Böll, H.
A **parting**. Dixon, S.
Parting. Martone, M.
Parting shots. Cook, M.
PARTINGS (FAREWELLS) *See* Farewells
PARTISANS *See* Guerrillas
The **partitions**. Bail, M.
Partner. Connelly, J.
Partners. McGuane, T.
The **Partridge** festival. O'Connor, F.

The **parts**. Piñera, V.
The **parts** of speech. Weaver, G.
Partway round the course. Sagan, F.
The **party**. Carr, P. E.
The **party**. Chekhov, A. P.
Party. Oates, J. C.
The **party**. O'Connor, F.
The **party**. Rosenfeld, I.
The **party**. Truss, J.
A **party**. Welch, D.
A **party** for idiot. Simpson, J.
A **party** for the girls. Bates, H. E.
A **party** in the country. Wohmann, G.
The **party** of the second part. Allbeury, T.
Party time. Castle, M.
Partying on parquet. Loukakis, A.
Pascoe, Bruce, 1947-
Black velvet night
    Pascoe, B. Night animals
The carbide lamp
    Pascoe, B. Night animals
Cicadas
    Pascoe, B. Night animals
Cobber: Peach Face
    Pascoe, B. Night animals
Cobber: The cat men of Genoa
    Pascoe, B. Night animals
Dreaming
    Pascoe, B. Night animals
Flour for your grave
    Pascoe, B. Night animals
Friday night
    Pascoe, B. Night animals
Funny man
    Pascoe, B. Night animals
Gravity and levity
    Pascoe, B. Night animals
Harold's Trudy
    Pascoe, B. Night animals
Jimmy the dancer: necromancer
    Pascoe, B. Night animals
Nautilus
    Pascoe, B. Night animals
Neither did I
    Pascoe, B. Night animals
Primary colours
    Pascoe, B. Night animals
Sirens
    Pascoe, B. Night animals
The slaughters of the bulumwaal butcher
    Pascoe, B. Night animals
Soldier goes to ground
    Pascoe, B. Night animals
Splitter
    Pascoe, B. Night animals
That's what friends are for
    Pascoe, B. Night animals
Thylacine
    Pascoe, B. Night animals
Work-horses
    Pascoe, B. Night animals
El **Paso**. Phillips, J. A.
Pasó por aquí. Rhodes, E. M.

Passage by water. Clark, J.
Passage for piano. Herbert, F.
A **passage** in Earth. Broderick, D.
Passage in the secret history of an Irish countess. Le Fanu, J. S.
Passage to Dilfar. Zelazny, R.
Passage to Heaven. Asscher-Pinkhof, C.
Passage to Hell. Asscher-Pinkhof, C.
Passage to India. Wiebe, D. E.
The **passenger**. Calisher, H.
Passengers. Silverberg, R.
Passing as a flower in the city of the dead. Farber, S. N.
Passing away. See Taylor, R. Zerelda James Samuel
The **passing** of Black Eagle. Henry, O.
The **passing** of the ice. Petrakis, H. M.
The **passing** of the pack. Coville, B.
Passion?. Baumbach, J.
Passion. Jhabvala, R. P.
A **passion**. Maupassant, G. de
Passion fruit. Kerr, L.
A **passion** in the desert. Balzac, H. de
The **passion** of Marisol. Costa, S.
The **passion** of the artist is nothing compared to the passion of the businessman. Covino, M.
Passport in order. Block, L.
Past due. Liben, M.
Past halfway. Birtha, B.
The **past** is a doomed parachutist. Austin, D.
The **past** master. Bloch, R.
PASTA MOMA. Lawson, S.
Pastan, Rachel
 Sounds of a summer night
  Mademoiselle 94:130+ My '88
 Underground
  The Editors' choice v4; ed. by G. E. Murphy, Jr.
  The Georgia Review 40:883-90 Wint '86
Paste. James, H.
Pasternak, Boris Leonidovich, 1890-1960
 The Apelles mark [Variant title: Il tratto di Apelle]
  Pasternak, B. L. The voice of prose v1
 Letters from Tula
  Pasternak, B. L. The voice of prose v1
 Suboctave story
  Pasternak, B. L. The voice of prose v1
 Without love
  Pasternak, B. L. The voice of prose v1
 Zhenya Luvers' childhood [Variant title: Zhenia's childhood]
  Pasternak, B. L. The voice of prose v1
The **pastor**. Mrożek, S.
Pastor Dowe at Tacaté. Bowles, P.
A **pastoral** horror. Doyle, Sir A. C.
Pastorale. Engberg, S.
PASTORS See Clergy
PATAGONIA (ARGENTINA AND CHILE)
 McCormack, E. P. Sad stories in Patagonia
Patch quilt. Bonner, M.

Patchett, Ann
 All little colored children should play the harmonica
  20 under 30; ed. by D. Spark
  The Paris Review 26:180-92 Wint '84
 The news of my suicide
  Seventeen 47:104-5+ F '88
The **patchwork** quilt. Smith, P. C.
Paté de foie gras. Asimov, I.
PATENT MEDICINES See Medicines, patent, proprietary, etc.
The **patented** gate and the mean hamburger. Warren, R. P.
Paternity. Gold, H.
Paterson's Flats. Eldridge, M.
The **path** doubles back. Rey Rosa, R.
PATHOLOGISTS See Physicians
The **patience** of a saint. Humphrey, W.
Patience, spring. Parise, G.
The **patient**. Laberge, A.
Pato. Ríos, A.
Paton, Alan
 A drink in the passage
  The Treasury of English short stories; ed. by N. Sullivan
 Sunlight in Trebizond Street
  The Penguin book of Southern African stories
The **patriarch**. Colette
The **patriarch** of Gunsight Flat. Overholser, W. D.
Patricia, Edith, and Arnold. Thomas, D.
Patricia's profession. Newman, K.
Patrick, Q. See Wheeler, Hugh Callingham, 1912-1987
Patrick. Ferguson, P.
Patriot. Hoffman, W.
Patriotic. Kauffman, J.
Patriotism. Mishima, Y.
Patriotism. Parise, G.
Patriots. Bishop, M.
Patron, J. F. (Joseph F.)
 Miss Bell
  Short story international 65
 The wallet
  Short story international 62
Patron, Joseph F. See Patron, J. F. (Joseph F.)
El **patrón**. Candelaria, N.
Patten, Lewis B.
 Dobbs Ferry
  Patten, L. B. The best western stories of Lewis B. Patten
 Hell-bent
  Patten, L. B. The best western stories of Lewis B. Patten
 High-carded
  Patten, L. B. The best western stories of Lewis B. Patten
 Massacre at Cottonwood Springs
  Patten, L. B. The best western stories of Lewis B. Patten

Patten, Lewis B.—*Continued*
  Nester kid
    Patten, L. B. The best western stories
      of Lewis B. Patten
  Payday
    Patten, L. B. The best western stories
      of Lewis B. Patten
  The rough string
    Patten, L. B. The best western stories
      of Lewis B. Patten
  They called him a killer
    Patten, L. B. The best western stories
      of Lewis B. Patten
  Too good with a gun
    Patten, L. B. The best western stories
      of Lewis B. Patten
  The winter of his life
    Patten, L. B. The best western stories
      of Lewis B. Patten
    The Western hall of fame; ed. by B.
      Pronzini and M. H. Greenberg
The **pattern**. Pronzini, B.
Pattern of a man. Still, J.
Patterning. Surface, D.
Patterns. Cadigan, P.
Patterns. Janowitz, T.
Patterns. Mitchell, W. O.
Patterns. Painter, P.
Patton, Frances Gray
  First principles
    "May your days be merry and bright"
      and other Christmas stories by wom-
      en; ed. by S. Koppelman
Paukenmesse. Ireland, A.
Paul, Jean *See* Jean Paul, 1763-1825
Paul, Perry
  The Jane from Hell's Kitchen
    Hard-boiled dames; ed. by B. A. Drew
Paul's case. Cather, W.
Paul's eyes. Wilson, A.
Paul's tale. Norton, M.
Paulson, A. B.
  College life
    The Georgia Review 40:250-8 Spr '86
    Necessary fictions; ed. by S. W. Lind-
      berg and S. Corey
  Olaf's calling
    The Georgia Review 38:721-6 Wint '84
Pavel, Ota
  A long mile
    Antaeus 60:79-86 Spr '88
  They might even kill you
    Antaeus 60:72-8 Spr '88
Pavel, Thomas G., 1941-
  The Persian mirror
    Invisible fictions; ed. by G. Hancock
Pavese, Cesare
  The beggars
    Pavese, C. Stories
  The cornfield
    Pavese, C. Stories
  The evil eye
    Pavese, C. Stories

  Evocation
    Pavese, C. Stories
  The family
    Pavese, C. Stories
  Festival night
    Pavese, C. Stories
  First love
    Pavese, C. Stories
  Free will
    Pavese, C. Stories
  Friends
    Pavese, C. Stories
  Gaol birds
    Pavese, C. Stories
  The idol
    Pavese, C. Stories
  The intruder
    Pavese, C. Stories
  Land of exile
    Pavese, C. Stories
  The leather jacket
    Pavese, C. Stories
  Loyalty
    Pavese, C. Stories
  Misogyny
    Pavese, C. Stories
  The name
    Pavese, C. Stories
  Suicides
    The Art of the tale; ed. by D. Halpern
    Pavese, C. Stories
  Summer storm
    Pavese, C. Stories
  The three girls
    Pavese, C. Stories
  The villa on the hill
    Pavese, C. Stories
  Wedding trip
    Pavese, C. Stories
Paving gang—on a job in Missouri. Conroy,
  J.
Pawn promotion. Vester, L.
PAWNBROKERS
  Irving, W. The Devil and Tom Walker
  Kawabata, Y. At the pawnshop
  Natsuki, S. The pawnshop murder
  Spark, M. The pawnbroker's wife
The **pawnbroker's** wife. Spark, M.
PAWNEE INDIANS
  Walters, A. L. The warriors
The **pawnshop** murder. Natsuki, S.
Paxson, Diana L.
  Heroes
    Tales of the Witch World 2
  Sky sister
    Moonsinger's friends; ed. by S. Shwartz
Pay-off girl. Cain, J. M.
Payday. Patten, L. B.
Payday. Ziem, J.
Payment. Bliss, C. D.
Payment in kind. Wilson, R., Jr.

Payne, Nellie
Bush tea and sympathy
Américas 38:25-7 Ja/F '86
Payne, Peggy
The pure in heart
New stories from the South: the year's best, 1987
Paynter, Jane
The miracle
Ellery Queen's Prime crimes 2
Paynter, Jennifer
Fifty-eight cents
Room to move; ed. by S. Falkiner
Payson, Heather Lee
Dressing up
The North American Review 273:41-5 D '88
PEACE
Brady, M. Seneca morning
Childress, A. Merry Christmas, Marge!
Henderson, Z. Subcommittee
Keillor, G. Brethren
Moore, W. Peacebringer
Spiro, G. Utopia
Wetherell, W. D. North of peace
Peace. Watson, I.
Peace and passivity. Frucht, A.
The **peace** of God. Lagerlöf, S.
The **peace** of Utrecht. Munro, A.
Peace on earth, good will to men. Coutinho, E.
Peacebringer. Moore, W.
The **peaceful** eye. Hall, M. L.
The **peacefulness** of Vivyan. Tiptree, J.
Peacekeeper. Franzen, B.
The **peacemaker.** Dozois, G. R.
The **peach** dance. Edmundson, M.
The **peach** in brandy: a Milesian tale. Walpole, H.
The **peach** orchard. Mooney, M.
Peach seed. Pritchett, M.
A **peach** tree in his garden stands. Böll, H.
Peaches. McKnight, R.
The **peaches.** Thomas, D.
The **peacock.** Nowakowski, M.
Peacock blue. Camoin, F. A.
Peacock eyes. Meier, S.
PEACOCKS
Carver, R. Feathers
Colum, P. The Peacocks of Baron's Hall
Peacocks. Finney, E. J.
The **peacocks** of Avignon. Swados, H.
The **Peacocks** of Baron's Hall. Colum, P.
The **peak** of success. Nagibin, IU. M.
A **peal** from the past. Wainwright, J. W.
PEANUT BUTTER
Kinsella, W. P. The history of peanut butter
The **peanut** girl. Allen, R.
A **pear.** Austin, D.
The **pear-shaped** man. Martin, G. R. R.
Pear tree dance. Jolley, E.
The **pearl.** Nesanovich, S.

PEARL FISHING
Shea, M. The pearls of the vampire queen
The **pearl** of love. Wells, H. G.
The **pearl** sitter. Norris, H.
Pearl Starr alive in Arizona. Taylor, R.
Pearlman, Daniel
Rising action
New England Review and Bread Loaf Quarterly 10:298-327 Spr '88
Taking from the top
Synergy v2
Pearlman, Edith
Conveniences
Prize stories, 1984
Settlers
Commentary 81:63-7 Ja '86
Their pride and joy
Redbook 171:82+ My '88
PEARLS
Bloch, R. String of pearls
Colette. The photographer's wife
Ingalls, R. Inheritance
James, H. Paste
Norris, H. The pearl sitter
Sayers, D. L. The necklace of pearls
Sexson, L. Margaret of the imperfections
The **pearls.** Colette
Pearls before wine. Painter, P.
The **pearls** of the vampire queen. Shea, M.
Pears. Desaulniers, J.
Pearson, T. R., 1956-
A short history of a small place [excerpt]
The New writers of the South; ed. by C. East
PEASANT LIFE
Aldiss, B. W. The blue background
Aldiss, B. W. Igur and the mountain
Woodman, A. The church of summer sausage
Woodman, A. The pleasure garden of the root vegetables
Argentina
Valenzuela, L. The door
France
Berger, J. The accordion player
Berger, J. Boris is buying horses
Berger, J. Once in Europa
Berger, J. The time of the cosmonauts
Maupassant, G. de. The Devil
Maupassant, G. de. The rabbit
Italy
Berger, J. Play me something
Soviet Union
Gogol', N. V. The fair at Sorochintsy
Peasant women. Chekhov, A. P.
Peattie, Elia Wilkinson
Their dear little ghost
Christmas ghosts; ed. by K. Cramer and D. G. Hartwell
Peattie, Margaret Rhodes
The green village
The Saturday Evening Post 257:64-8+ N '85

The **pebble** people. Jack, R.

Peck, Claudia
  The gentle art of making enemies
    Magic in Ithkar 4; ed. by A. Norton and
    R. Adams

Peck, Richard
  The size of the universe
    Southwest Review 71:493-509 Aut '86

Peck, Samuel Minturn
  Pap's mules
    The Art of fiction in the heart of Dixie;
    ed. by P. D. Beidler

A **peculiar** case. Maupassant, G. de
The **peculiar** demesne of Archvicar Gerontion. Kirk, R.

PEDDLERS AND PEDDLING
  Blythe, R. The October Bagman
  Botwinik, B. Shabbas
  Hawthorne, N. Mr. Higginbotham's
    catastrophe
  Lu Wenfu. The man from a peddlers'
    family
  McKnight, R. Mali is very dangerous
  Nesin, A. Regulations for meatball pedd-
    lers
  Parise, G. Work
  Sholem Aleichem. Competitors
  Tagore, Sir R. The Cabuliwallah
  Vinge, J. D., and Vinge, V. The peddler's
    apprentice
  Yi, H. The buckwheat season
The **peddler's** apprentice. Vinge, J. D., and
  Vinge, V.
Peddling in the dark. Asscher-Pinkhof, C.

Peden, William
  The hatchet man in the lighthouse
    Sudden fiction; ed. by R. Shapard and
    J. Thomas

PEDOPHILIA
  Monreal, D. N. The new neighbor
  Moravia, A. The devil can't save the
    world
  Thorman, C. Gurlas
Peekaboo. Pronzini, B.
A **peephole** in the gate. Singer, I. B.
Peer Gynt. Mrożek, S.
The **peewit's** nest. Skrzynecki, P.
The **peg.** Hoyt, M. S.

Pei, Lowry
  The cold room
    The Best American short stories, 1984

Pei, Mario, 1901-
  The bones of Charlemagne
    Great science fiction; ed. by I. Asimov;
    M. H. Greenberg and C. G. Waugh
The **pei-pa.** Liang, L. K.

Peirce, Hayford
  Goldfish
    The Ethnic detectives; ed. by B. Pronzini
    and M. H. Greenberg
Peiter and Paulina. Gathorne-Hardy, J.

Pejovich, Ted
  Places on the water
    The Kenyon Review ns10:58-9 Spr '88

PEKING (CHINA) See China—Beijing
Pelican. Jaffe, H.
The **pelican.** Shacochis, B.
Pelicans in flight. Ballantyne, S.

Pellegrini, Domingos, Jr.
  The biggest bridge in the world
    The Literary Review (Madison, N.J.)
    27:504-13 Summ '84
Pen pals. Potter, N. A. J.

Peña, Devon
  One story too many
    Southwest tales; ed. by Alurista and X.
    Rojas-Urista
Penance. Kinsella, W. P.
Pencil sketches for a story: the gray whelk
  shell. Birtha, B.
Penelope. Bitov, A.
Penetrations. Lazarre, J.

Penfold, Nita
  Death on Goose Hill
    The Womansleuth anthology; ed. by I.
    Zahava

PENIS
  Lurie, M. Warts
  Moravia, A. To the unknown god
The **penitente** thief. Chavez, A.
Penmanship. McGarry, J.

Penn, Barbara Allison
  Note box
    U.S. Catholic 49:34-9 N '84

Pennell, H. Barrett, Jr.
  The quality of mercy
    The Saturday Evening Post 259:64-5 O
    '87

Penner, Jonathan, 1940-
  Emotion recollected in tranquillity
    The Pushcart prize IX
  Onward Jerusalem
    Commentary 79:47-51 My '85
  Smoke
    The Paris Review 29:220-30 Spr '87
  Things to be thrown away
    The Best American short stories, 1984

Penney, Alexandra
  Champagne for one
    Ladies' Home Journal 101:90+ Je '84

PENNSYLVANIA
    See also Wissahickon Creek (Pa.)
  Griesemer, J. Comfort stations
  O'Hara, J. Imagine kissing Pete
  O'Hara, J. In the silence
  Stark, S. S. The Barlip run
  Stark, S. S. Heart of the Dutch country
  Stark, S. S. His color
  Stark, S. S. In the surprise of life
  Taylor, R. Where are our M.I.A.'s?
  Wideman, J. E. Tommy

PENNSYLVANIA—*Continued*
Farm life
See Farm life—Pennsylvania
Johnstown
Stark, S. S. The Johnstown Polka
Philadelphia
Birtha, B. The saints and sinners run
Davis, R. H. Gallegher
O'Hara, J. Ninety minutes away
Rile, K. Solid walls
Spinelli, J. Gus Zernial and me
Pittsburgh
Blaise, C. Grids and doglegs
Phelan, F. The battle of boiling water
Pennsylvania. Robinson, F. M.
PENNSYLVANIA DUTCH
Martin, H. R. Mrs. Gladfelter's revolt
Martin, H. R. A poet though married
O'Hara, J. Fatimas and kisses
Van Zleer, D. Violet's choice
PENNSYLVANIA DUTCH DIALECT *See*
Dialect stories—Pennsylvania Dutch
The **penny-a-worder.** Woolrich, C.
The **penny** is for God! Granit, A.
Penny Royal. Yaw, Y.
The **penny** story. Ignatow, R. G.
The **Pension** Beaurepas. James, H.
PENSIONS
Colum, P. The little pension
Yasuoka, S. Gloomy pleasures
Pentecost, Hugh, 1903-
Chambrun and the double event
  Pentecost, H. Murder round the clock:
  Pierre Chambrun's crime file
Chambrun and the electronic ear
  Pentecost, H. Murder round the clock:
  Pierre Chambrun's crime file
Chambrun and the melting swan
  Pentecost, H. Murder round the clock:
  Pierre Chambrun's crime file
Chambrun and the obvious clue
  Pentecost, H. Murder round the clock:
  Pierre Chambrun's crime file
Chambrun gets the message
  Hound dunnit; ed. by I. Asimov; M. H.
  Greenberg and C. L. R. Waugh
  Pentecost, H. Murder round the clock:
  Pierre Chambrun's crime file
Death to the hunter
  Hard-boiled dames; ed. by B. A. Drew
Jericho and the cardboard box
  Manhattan mysteries; ed. by B. Pronzini;
  C. L. R. Waugh and M. H. Greenberg
The masked crusader
  Pentecost, H. Murder round the clock:
  Pierre Chambrun's crime file
Murder deluxe
  Pentecost, H. Murder round the clock:
  Pierre Chambrun's crime file
My dear Uncle Sherlock
  Handle with care; ed. by J. Kahn

Pierre Chambrun and the black days
  Pentecost, H. Murder round the clock:
  Pierre Chambrun's crime file
Pierre Chambrun and the last fling
  Pentecost, H. Murder round the clock:
  Pierre Chambrun's crime file
Pierre Chambrun and the sad song
  Pentecost, H. Murder round the clock:
  Pierre Chambrun's crime file
Pierre Chambrun and the war for peace
  Pentecost, H. Murder round the clock:
  Pierre Chambrun's crime file
Pierre Chambrun defends himself
  Pentecost, H. Murder round the clock:
  Pierre Chambrun's crime file
Pierre Chambrun's dilemma
  Pentecost, H. Murder round the clock:
  Pierre Chambrun's crime file
Pentecost Sunday. García Márquez, G.
People. Pritchett, M.
The **people** of the Black Circle. Howard, R.
  E.
The **people** of the book. Lindsay, F.
The **people** of the peacock. Hoch, E. D.
People to people. Ingalls, R.
The **people** trap. Sheckley, R.
The **people** v. Abe Lathan, colored. Caldwell,
  E.
Pepperoni. Barthelme, D.
PEPYS, SAMUEL, 1633-1703
About
Turtledove, H. And so to bed
Per far l'amore. Hartley, L. P.
Perceval. Kessler, J. F.
Perchance to dream. MacLean, K.
Perchance to dream. Seidman, M.
Percy, H. R.
Haliburton
  Short story international 42
Percy, Walker, 1916-
The last gentleman [excerpt]
  Mississippi writers v1: Fiction; ed. by D.
  Abbott
The moviegoer [excerpt]
  Mississippi writers v1: Fiction; ed. by D.
  Abbott
The promiscuous self
  The Substance of things hoped for; ed.
  by J. B. Breslin
The second coming [excerpt]
  Mississippi writers v1: Fiction; ed. by D.
  Abbott
Perea, Robert L.
Miracle at Chimayo
  Earth power coming; ed. by S. J. Ortiz
Small arms fire
  Cuentos Chicanos; ed. by R. A. Anaya
  and A. Márquez
Perec, Georges, 1936-1982
The winter journey
  Encounter (London, England) 65:3-5
  Jl/Ag '85

Perez, Norah
 Elizabeth
  Ladies' Home Journal 103:48+ O '86
Perfect. Ekström, M.
The **perfect** alibi. Gosling, P.
A **perfect** Christmas evening. Fialkowski, K.
Perfect combinations. Lewis, S. E.
The **perfect** couple. Levi, J. H.
A **perfect** crime. Austin, D.
The **perfect** crime. Ocampo, S.
Perfect friends. Schell, J.
The **perfect** game. Ramírez, S.
A **perfect** gentleman. Koenig, J.
A **perfect** gentleman on wheels. Wells, H. G.
Perfect holiday sounds. Loukakis, A.
The **Perfect** Life. Katz, S.
A **perfect** marriage. Carneiro, A.
The **perfect** match. Stewart, I.
The **perfect** model. Sharp, M.
The **perfect** murder. Archer, J.
A **perfect** night to break your neck. O'Don-
  nell, P.
Perfect pitch. Gallacher, T.
The **perfect** stone. Gilchrist, E.
Perfect things. Barthelme, F.
Perfect timing. Pronzini, B.
Perfect vision. Thurm, M.
The **perfect** woman. Sheckley, R.
The **perfecting** of the Chopin Valse no. 14.
  Naslund, S. J.
PERFECTION
 Hawthorne, N. The birthmark
 Maupassant, G. de. The artist
Perfection. Wilbur, E.
A **perfectly** nice man. Rule, J.
The **performance**. Jolley, E.
The **performance**. Kinsella, W. P.
PERFORMERS *See* Entertainers
The **perfume** of love. Kavaler, R.
PERFUMES
 Regent, P. A delicate nose
**PERGOLESI, GIOVANNI BATTISTA,
 1710-1736**
  About
 Silverberg, R. Gianni
Pericles on 31st Street. Petrakis, H. M.
Peril. Giles, M.
The **perilous** flight of Henry O'Grady. Sher-
  win, J.
The **perils** of trade. Liben, M.
A **period** of grace. Friedman, P.
Period return. Blythe, R.
PERIODICALS, PUBLISHING OF
 Doyle, Sir A. C. The Parish Magazine
Perkins, Fionna
 The changes
  When I am an old woman I shall wear
  purple; ed. by S. K. Martz
Perlman, Helen Harris
 Twelfth summer
  Family: stories from the interior; ed. by
  G. G. Chavis
Permafrost. Zelazny, R.

Permission for death is granted. Valadés, E.
Pero venceremos. Algren, N.
Perowne, Barry, 1908-
 Knowing what I know now
  Ellery Queen's Memorable characters
 Raffles and operation champagne
  Through a glass, darkly; ed. by B. Woel-
  fel
 Raffles on the trail of the hound
  Hound dunnit; ed. by I. Asimov; M. H.
  Greenberg and C. L. R. Waugh
Perpetual care. Ballantyne, S.
Perpetuity blues. Barrett, N., Jr.
PERRAULT, CHARLES, 1628-1703
  Parodies, travesties, etc.
 Ferron, J. Little Red Riding Hood
Perry, Michael Clark
 Stumps
  Bringing down the moon; ed. by J. An-
  derson
Perry, Richard, 1944-
 Blues for my father, my mother, and me
 Selected stories from The Southern
  review, 1965-1985
  The Southern Review (Baton Rouge, La.)
  21:641-50 Jl '85
PERSECUTION
  See also Atrocities; Martyrs
 Feng Jicai. The tall woman and her short
  husband
 Hawthorne, N. The gentle boy
Persecution is for you. Thorman, C.
PERSIA *See* Iran
The **Persian** carpet. Al-Shaykh, H.
Persian lamb. Jaffe, H.
The **Persian** mirror. Pavel, T. G.
The **Persian's** grave. Davin, D.
The **persimmon** tree. Barnard, M.
Persistence. Makuck, P.
The **persistence** of vision. Varley, J.
Personal escort. Buzzati, D.
The **personal** touch. Williamson, C.
PERSONALITY
 Aksenov, V. P. Rendezvous
 Asimov, I. He wasn't there
 Austin, M. H. The portrait
 Austin, M. H. White wisdom
 Biggle, L. Orphan of the void
 Bonnie, F. In another language
 Brooks, J. Doing the voices
 Dann, J. Camps
 Ferron, J. Cadieu
 Kilworth, G. Oubliette
 Kress, N. Talp hunt
 Lurie, M. Bannister
 Mukherjee, B. Hindus
 Pavel, T. G. The Persian mirror
 Potter, N. A. J. A private space
 Pritchard, M. Rocking on water, floating
  in glass
 Silverberg, R. The changeling
 Tournier, M. Tristan Vox
 Van Greenaway, P. Janus

PERSONALITY—*Continued*
Wells, H. G. The sad story of a dramatic critic

PERSONALITY DISORDERS
See also Dual personality; Hallucinations and illusions; Insane, Criminal and dangerous; Multiple personality
Amis, M. Insight at Flame Lake
Barthelme, D. Game
Böll, H. Across the bridge
Böll, H. On the hook
Botwinik, B. A man
Bowker, R. The other train phenomenon
Bryant, E. Teeth marks
Carter, R. Within
Chute, C. "Ollie, oh . . . "
Crace, J. The prospect from the silver hill
Curtiss, U. R. Change of climate
Disch, T. M. The Asian shore
Dixon, S. Change
Dixon, S. A parting
Elkin, S. A poetics for bullies
Ellison, H. All the sounds of fear
Ferguson, P. The dry familiar plains
Havazelet, E. Natalie Wood's amazing eyes
Havazelet, E. What is it then between us?
Hébert, A. The torrent
Highsmith, P. The terrors of basketweaving
Hoch, E. D. The ring with the velvet ropes
Josipovici, G. Getting better
Malzberg, B. N. The Queen of Lower Saigon
McGuane, T. Dogs
Miller, W. The memorial hour
Morrow, J. Diary of a mad deity
Moskowitz, C. The present
O'Brien, F.-J. The diamond lens
Ocampo, S. The basement
Ocampo, S. The expiation
Ocampo, S. The objects
O'Connor, F. A good man is hard to find
Prose, F. Everyone had a lobster
Rooke, L. Why the heathens are no more
Schwartz, L. S. The age of analysis
Sharouni, Y. Glimpses from the life of Maugoud Abdul Maugoud and two postscripts
Symons, J. The dream is better
Taylor, P. E. News from El Corazon: in the composing room
Thomas, A. C. Compulsory figures
Thomas, D. The true story
White, C. The phantom limb
Wiebe, D. E. Omega I
Wolff, T. The other Miller
Yarbro, C. Q. Cabin 33
Yasuoka, S. Gloomy pleasures
Personaphilological-dramatic conference with implications. Landolfi, T.
Perspective on the first you. Fitzgerald, M. J.

PERTH (SCOTLAND) *See* Scotland—Perth
PERU
Cowper, R. Incident at Huacaloc
Horvitz, L. A. Pictures of a woman gone
Vargas Llosa, M. The challenge
Lima
Lynch, M. Latin lover
PERUVIANS
United States
Ribeyro, J. R. Alienation
Pesetsky, Bette, 1932-
Piers the impostor
The Paris Review 28:14-27 Spr '86
The Prince of Wales
The New Yorker 64:36-40 S 19 '88
A walker's manual
New women and new fiction; ed. by S. Cahill
A **pestilence** of psychoanalysts. Jeppson, J. O.
Pestonjee's tower of silence. Cooper, D.
A **pet** dog's safe birthing. Kawabata, Y.
Pet Milk. Dybek, S.
Petchsingh, Trirat
The sacrifice
Short story international 54
The third encounter
Short story international 45
The two moons of Vira's world
Short story international 65
Peter and the asteroids. Livesey, M.
Peter and the wolf. Carter, A.
Peter Foxe. Boyle, K.
Peter Mavromatis rides the tail of the donkey. Papaellinas, G.
Peter Pendulum, the business man. Poe, E. A.
The **Peter** story. Outen, K. E.
Peter the Rock. Coggeshall, R.
Peter Two. Shaw, I.
Peters, Ellis, 1913-
Come to dust
Winter's crimes 16
A light on the road to Woodstock
The Mammoth book of modern crime stories; ed. by G. Hardinge
Winter's crimes 17
Peters, Stephen
Spring concert
Stiller's pond; ed. by J. Agee; R. Blakely and S. Welch
Peters in Shinjuku: a set of miniatures. Green, E.
Peter's song. Papaellinas, G.
Petersen, William
Neighbors
The North American Review 270:44 S '85
Peterson, Joseph
Yellow dust
Greening wheat: fifteen Mormon short stories

Peterson, Levi S., 1933-
  The gift
    Greening wheat: fifteen Mormon short
    stories
Peterson, Mary
  The carved table
    Peterson, M. Mercy flights
    The Ploughshares reader: new fiction for
    the eighties
  Coastal
    Peterson, M. Mercy flights
  Coming about
    Peterson, M. Mercy flights
  Crows
    Peterson, M. Mercy flights
  Like boats
    Peterson, M. Mercy flights
  Mercy flights
    Peterson, M. Mercy flights
  To dance
    Peterson, M. Mercy flights
  Traveling
    Peterson, M. Mercy flights
  Two cats
    Peterson, M. Mercy flights
  With Evelyn
    Peterson, M. Mercy flights
Petey. Klein, T. E. D.
Petra. Bear, G.
Petra. Codrescu, A.
Petra. Wilson, R., Jr.
Petrakis, Harry Mark
  The ballad of Daphne and Apollo
    Petrakis, H. M. Collected stories
  The bastards of Thanos
    Petrakis, H. M. Collected stories
  Between sleep and death
    Petrakis, H. M. Collected stories
  The castle
    Petrakis, H. M. Collected stories
  Chrisoula
    Petrakis, H. M. Collected stories
  Courtship of the blue widow
    Petrakis, H. M. Collected stories
  Dark eye
    Petrakis, H. M. Collected stories
  A day's journey
    Petrakis, H. M. Collected stories
  End of winter
    Petrakis, H. M. Collected stories
  The eyes of love
    Petrakis, H. M. Collected stories
  A hand for tomorrow
    Petrakis, H. M. Collected stories
  Homecoming
    Petrakis, H. M. Collected stories
  The journal of a wife beater
    Petrakis, H. M. Collected stories
  The judgement
    Petrakis, H. M. Collected stories
  The last escapade
    Petrakis, H. M. Collected stories

  The legacy of Leontis
    Petrakis, H. M. Collected stories
  Matsoukas
    Petrakis, H. M. Collected stories
  The miracle
    Petrakis, H. M. Collected stories
  Pa and the sad turkeys
    Petrakis, H. M. Collected stories
  The passing of the ice
    Petrakis, H. M. Collected stories
  Pericles on 31st Street
    Petrakis, H. M. Collected stories
  The prison
    Petrakis, H. M. Collected stories
  The return of Katerina
    Petrakis, H. M. Collected stories
  Rosemary
    Petrakis, H. M. Collected stories
  The shearing of Samson
    Petrakis, H. M. Collected stories
  The siege of Minerva
    Petrakis, H. M. Collected stories
  The song of Rhodanthe
    Petrakis, H. M. Collected stories
  Song of songs
    Petrakis, H. M. Collected stories
  The sweet life
    Petrakis, H. M. Collected stories
  The victim
    Petrakis, H. M. Collected stories
  The waves of night
    Petrakis, H. M. Collected stories
  The witness
    Petrakis, H. M. Collected stories
  The wooing of Ariadne
    Petrakis, H. M. Collected stories
  Zena Dawn
    Petrakis, H. M. Collected stories
The petrified world. Sheckley, R.
PETROLEUM INDUSTRY
  Böll, H. The railway station of Zimpren
  Cameron, E. Ace in the hole
  Hauptman, W. Boom town
  Hauptman, W. Hands across America
  Hoch, E. D. A flash of red
  Humphrey, W. A home away from home
  Humphrey, W. The pump
  Sanford, W. M. Fever in the South
  Sanford, W. M. Luck
  Sanford, W. M. Windfall
Petronella. Williams, J.
PETRONIUS ARBITER
              About
  Schwob, M. Petronius, novelist
  Sheehan, R. The death of Petronius
Petronius, novelist. Schwob, M.
Petroski, Catherine
  Beautiful my mane in the wind
    Prize stories, Texas Institute of Letters;
    ed. by M. Terry
  He the fisher
    The North American Review 270:34-5 Je
    '85

Petroski, Catherine—*Continued*
The hit
New Directions in prose and poetry 51
Madonna with cat
New directions in prose and poetry 48
The Shakespeare man
Prairie Schooner 58:5-12 Summ '84
PETS
Asimov, I. Sure thing
Clift, C. The small animus
Everman, W. D. Harry and Sylvia and
Sylvia and so on
Franklin, P. Love under glass
Hempel, A. Today will be a quiet day
Johnson, C. R. Menagerie, a child's fable
King, F. H. The mouse
Lispector, C. The foreign legion
Lispector, C. Monkeys
Lutz, J. In memory of . . .
Martin, G. R. R. Sandkings
Morris, W. Fellow-creatures
Neville, K. Old Man Henderson
Rule, J. Seaweed and song
St. Clair, M. Hathor's pets
Tarkington, B. Blue milk
Tsushima, Y. The silent traders
Warren, J. Ugly Douglas & company
Waters, M. Imprints
The **petticoat** brigade. Overholser, W. D.
Petty larceny. Saiki, J.
Peyrou, Manuel
The sleeping sword
Short story international 63
Pfeil, Fred
The collected works of Brown
Pfeil, F. Shine on
The fame of price
Pfeil, F. Shine on
Holding on
Pfeil, F. Shine on
The idiocy of rural life
The Georgia Review 40:259-74 Spr '86
Necessary fictions; ed. by S. W. Lind-
berg and S. Corey
Miss Olive's retreat
Pfeil, F. Shine on
The night game
Pfeil, F. Shine on
Plus you
TriQuarterly no72:48-71 Spr/Summ '88
Poker fugue
Pfeil, F. Shine on
The quality of light in Maine
Pfeil, F. Shine on
Shine on
Pfeil, F. Shine on
Skeeter's last reflections
Pfeil, F. Shine on
A **phantasm**, a bird—. Lopatin, J.
Phantasmion. Coleridge, S.
The **phantom** chamber. Ruse, G. A.
The **phantom** coach. Edwards, A. A. B.
The **phantom** death. Russell, W. C.

The **phantom** limb. White, C.
Phantom limb pain. Wilson, B.
The **phantom** Mercury of Nevada. Kranes,
D.
The **phantom** motor. Futrelle, J.
The **phantom** of the movie palace. Coover,
R.
Phantom pleasure. Chernoff, M.
Phantom Silver. Kittredge, W.
The **pharmacist**. Liben, M.
PHARMACISTS
See also Medicines, patent,
proprietary, etc.
Enayetullah, A. Enemy
Gilbert, W. S. The poisoned postage stamp
Greene, G. When Greek meets Greek
Kang, S.-J. Nursery tale for a dreary day
Liben, M. The pharmacist
MacLaverty, B. Hugo
Mathers, P. A small drop
Yaffe, J. Mom sings an aria
PHAROAHS *See* Egypt—Kings and rulers
Pheasant. Setouchi, H.
Phebican. Fitzgerald, M. J.
Pheidippus at Cos. Parotti, P.
Phelan, Francis
The battle of boiling water
The Graywolf annual [1]
Phelps, Elizabeth Stuart, 1844-1911
Comrades
Civil War women; ed. by F. McSherry;
C. G. Waugh and M. Greenberg
No news
The Other woman; ed. by S. Koppelman
Number 13
Old maids; ed. by S. Koppelman
Old Mother Goose
Between mothers & daughters; ed. by S.
Koppelman
"May your days be merry and bright"
and other Christmas stories by wom-
en; ed. by S. Koppelman
The true story of Guenever
Haunted women; ed. by A. Bendixen
Phenomena. Carlson, R.
PHILADELPHIA (PA.) *See* Pennsylvania—
Philadelphia
The **philanthropist**. Piñera, V.
The **philanthropist** and the happy cat. Saki
PHILANTHROPISTS
García Márquez, G. The sea of lost time
PHILANTHROPY *See* Endowments; Philan-
thropists
Philéas. Desnoues, L.
PHILIPPINES
Bowles, C. The song of the fisherman
Espina-Moore, L. Man around a maypole
José, F. S. Friendship
José, F. S. The heirs
José, F. S. Modesty aside
José, F. S. Two interviews
Nimmo, H. A. Lim
Roberts, N. A second wife

PHILIPPINES—*Continued*
Tiempo, E. Un bel di
Politics
See Politics—Philippines
Manila
Haylock, J. A sort of retirement
José, F. S. Progress
Phillips, Dale Ray
What men love for
The Atlantic 261:46-51 Ap '88
Phillips, Darlene M.
Our shining star
Redbook 167:67-9+ My '86
Phillips, Edward O.
Stephanotis
Fatal recurrences; ed. by H. Hugh and
P. O'Brien
Phillips, Jayne Anne, 1952-
1934
Stories of the modern South; ed. by B.
Forkner and P. Samway
Bess
Esquire 102:58-60+ Ag '84
The Esquire fiction reader v1
New American short stories; ed. by G.
Norris
Phillips, J. A. Fast lanes
Blind girls
Sudden fiction; ed. by R. Shapard and
J. Thomas
Blue moon
Phillips, J. A. Fast lanes
Bluegill
Phillips, J. A. Fast lanes
Fast lanes
Phillips, J. A. Fast lanes
The heavenly animal
American short story masterpieces; ed.
by R. Carver and T. Jenks
Home
Love stories for the time being; ed. by
G. D. Chipps and B. Henderson
New women and new fiction; ed. by S.
Cahill
How Mickey made it
Phillips, J. A. Fast lanes
Lechery
The Norton book of American short
stories
Machine dreams [excerpt]
The New writers of the South; ed. by
C. East
November and December: Billy, 1969
Soldiers & civilians; ed. by T. Jenks
El Paso
The Ploughshares reader: new fiction for
the eighties
Rayme
Phillips, J. A. Fast lanes
Something that happened
Phillips, J. A. Fast lanes

Phillips, John L.
No more
The North American Review 270:56-7 S
'85
Phillips, Max
Blonde hairs
The Antioch Review 46:438-49 Fall '88
Phillips, Rog
Game preserve
Beyond Armageddon; ed. by W. M. Mil-
ler and M. H. Greenberg
The yellow pill
Handle with care; ed. by J. Kahn
Phillips, Thomas Hal
The shadow of an arm
Mississippi writers v1: Fiction; ed. by D.
Abbott
Philo Gubb's greatest case. Butler, E. P.
Philomela. Tennant, E.
A **philosopher.** Maupassant, G. de
PHILOSOPHERS
Hesse, H. Inside and outside
Johnston, G. Vale, Pollini!
Longyear, B. B. SHAWNA, Ltd.
Palma, C. The story of the man who was
not born
Poe, E. A. Bon-bon
Singer, I. B. The Spinoza of Market Street
Stewart, J. I. M. Melencolia I
Vivante, A. The soft core
Warner, S. T. An improbable story
White, C. Critical theory
The **philosophy** of furniture. Poe, E. A.
PHILOSOPHY OF LIFE *See* Life (Philoso-
phy of life)
The **philosophy** of Sebastian Trump; or, The
art of outrage. Kotzwinkle, W., and
Shiarella, R.
Phippen, Sanford, 1942-
Step-over toe-hold
The Best Maine stories; ed. by S. Phip-
pen; C. Waugh and M. Greenberg
Phipps, Helene Juarez
The saintmaker's wife
Distant danger; ed. by J. Van de
Wetering
Phocian. Michaelson, L. W.
The **Phoenician** bauble. Asimov, I.
PHOENIX (ARIZ.) *See* Arizona—Phoenix
The **phoenix.** Wohlfeld, V.
Phoenix in the ashes. Vinge, J. D.
Phog. Anthony, P.
The **phone** call. Andersen, B.
The **phone** call. Sorrells, R. T.
Phone-in. Gilliatt, P.
Phoney meteor. Wyndham, J.
Phosphates. Broun, H.
The **photograph.** Billington, R.
The **photograph.** Harris, M.
Photograph. Kawabata, Y.
Photograph of Luisa. Pritchard, M.

PHOTOGRAPHERS

See also Women photographers

Ahern, T. An implied acquaintance
Aldiss, B. W. The blue background
Apple, M. Eskimo love
Bail, M. Huebler
Baillie, A. Snap
Bowles, P. Tapiama
Broun, H. Highspeed linear Main St.
Calvino, I. The adventure of a photographer
Carter, M. The things that would never be mine
DeMarinis, R. Billy Ducks among the Pharoahs
Drake, R. The birthday picture
Godfrey, P. The lady and the dragon
Haldeman, J. C. Still frame
Hoch, E. D. Just one more
Klass, P. Clytemnestra in the suburbs
Leedom-Ackerman, J. Of imagination
Leiber, F. The girl with the hungry eyes
Long, D. The last photograph of Lyle Pettibone
Lopatin, J. Retrospective on Weegee
Loukakis, A. Single lens reflex
Mazel, D. Karen
Morris, M. Shining path
Nooteboom, C. Mokusei: a love story
Oates, J. C. Testimony
Papaellinas, G. In which Peter Mavromatis lives up to his name
Pritchard, M. Photograph of Luisa
Taylor, D. J. Dreams of leaving
Thomas, J. Half frame
Thornton, V. Another Sunday morning
Tournier, M. Veronica's shrouds
Working, R. Pictures of her snake
The **photographer's** Missus. See Colette. The photographer's wife
Photographer's model. Oates, J. C.
The **photographer's** wife. Colette

PHOTOGRAPHS

Block, L. Click!
Greenwood, R. A gift to the future
Highsmith, P. Where the action is
Kawabata, Y. Photograph
Lish, G. Agony
Lynch, L. The abrupt edge
Miller, S. Slides
Ocampo, S. The photographs
Piñera, V. The album
Regent, P. At Manoli's sheepfold
Rossi, A. Athletes and artists
Skelton, R. Sarah
Viramontes, H. M. Snapshots
Vreuls, D. The Alice P. Gamboe strip
The **photographs**. Ocampo, S.
Photographs of Stanley's grandfather. Dunn, D.

PHRENOLOGY

Brown, C. A winter's tale
Phyllis and Rosamond. Woolf, V.

Phylogenesis. Di Filippo, P.

PHYSICAL FITNESS

Ramírez, S. Charles Atlas also dies

PHYSICALLY HANDICAPPED

See also Blind; Deaf; Hunchbacks; Paraplegics; Physically handicapped children

Abrahams, L. Knowledge
Bradley, M. Z. Blood will tell
Card, O. S. The fringe
Card, O. S. A sepulcher of songs
Clark, M. The love of Christ
Colvin, C. Near Forelanders Kop
Conroy, J. The siren
Ferreira, R. The hands of God
Ferreira, R. Juan de Dios
Fleming, B. Beach party
Fuentes, C. The doll queen
Gordon, M. Eileen
Grin, A. The voice of the siren
Harrison, M. J. The quarry
Hensley, J. L. Shut the final door
Ioannidou Adamidou, I. The beggar
Ioannidou Adamidou, I. Conversation
Kotzwinkle, W. The day Stokowski saved the world
Landolfi, T. The eternal province
Maupassant, G. de. "Bell"
Maupassant, G. de. Bellflower
Mayhar, A. Esmene's eyes
McGerr, P. The day of the bookmobile
McKinley, J. Gloves and fishes
Morison, S. Brother
Nordan, L. The attendant
Norris, H. Money man
Oates, J. C. Golden gloves
Pritchard, M. Dead finish
Roberts, N. The upstairs people
Rose, D. A. Envy the dead
Schulman, H. I am Miss America
Shi Tiesheng. One winter's evening
Silver, R. Fearful symmetry
Šmahelová, H. House of joy
Son, C.-S. The rainy season
Spencer, B. The small things that save us
Sykes, S. C. Rockabye Baby
Welch, D. The diamond badge
Wheatcroft, J. The shadow of a bear
Wiebe, D. E. Night flight to Stockholm
Wolfe, T. The bell remembered
Yu, C.-Y. Relationship

PHYSICALLY HANDICAPPED CHILDREN

Brown, G. M. An epiphany tale
Clift, C. Even the thrush has wings
Danby, M. Robbie
Figueredo, D. H. Tell the night
Fremlin, C. The miracle
Gaskell, E. C. The three eras of Libbie Marsh
Gorky, M. Lullaby
Hagy, A. C. Mister Makes
Huggan, I. Sorrows of the flesh

PHYSICIANS

See also Gynecologists; Psychiatrists; Surgeons; Veterinarians; Women physicians

Ade, G. The Alfalfa European Hotel
Anderson, S. Unlighted lamps
Andreyev, L. The thought
Bierce, A. A watcher by the dead
Blish, J. A dusk of idols
Blochman, L. G. But the patient died
Bower, B. M. When the cook fell ill
Bowles, P. Rumor and a ladder
Boyle, K. Winter in Italy
Broxon, M. D. First do no harm
Broxon, M. D. Flux of fortune
Bryan, J. Y. Frontier vigil
Buck, P. S. The enemy
Busch, F. A history of small ideas
Busch, F. Rise and fall
Campbell, R. The moon-lens
Carr, J. Blind spot
Chekhov, A. P. The duel
Chekhov, A. P. His wife
Chekhov, A. P. An unpleasant business
Chesterton, G. K. When doctors agree
Chon, K.-Y. Kapitan Lee
Cohen, M. The sins of Tomas Benares
Colette. Armande
Collins, L. The doctor's house
Collins, W. The dead hand
Coxe, G. H. The doctor takes a case
Crane, S. The monster
Davis, L. The bone
Eighner, L. Bertner: emergency room
Endō, S. Incredible voyage
Essop, A. The betrayal
Ferron, J. Armageddon
Ferron, J. The lady from Ferme-Neuve
Ferron, J. Les Méchins
Ferron, J. Tiresome company
Fleming, B. War memorial
Gallant, M. The doctor
Gifkins, M. Natural histories
Gordimer, N. The life of the imagination
Gordon, M. The only son of the doctor
Goulart, R. Calling Dr. Clockwork
Greene, G. Doctor Crombie
Greene, G. Dream of a strange land
Hall, M. L. Just a little sore throat
Halley, A. A Rosenkavalier
Hartley, L. P. A tonic
Hawthorne, N. Rappaccini's daughter
Hecht, B. Miracle of the fifteen murderers
Hemingway, E. God rest you merry, gentlemen
Hemingway, E. Indian camp
Hensley, J. L. Savant
Hoch, E. D. The problem of the Boston Common
Hospital, J. T. The dark wood
Jackson, G. The decline of Western Hill
Jahnn, H. H. The diver

James, H. Lady Barberina
James, H. The middle years
Johnson, C. R. Popper's disease
Johnson, D. M. The hanging tree
Jolley, E. The fellow passenger
Kaplický, V. Theatrum magnum
Kornbluth, C. M. The little black bag
Lavin, M. Eterna
Le Fanu, J. S. Green tea
Leiber, F. The dead man
Malamud, B. In retirement
Mattison, A. Exactments
Maupassant, G. de. An affair of state
Maupassant, G. de. An artifice
Maupassant, G. de. The last step
Mrabet, M. Doctor Safi
Mukherjee, B. Angela
Murphy, G. R. War
Murphy, P. Terminals
O'Hara, J. The doctor's son
Parotti, P. Machaon at Tricca
Phelps, E. S. No news
Porges, A. Dead drunk
Pronzini, B. House call
Purdy, J. Ruthanna Elder
Rhys, J. Pioneers, oh, pioneers
Ritchie, J. Sound alibi
Rush, N. Instruments of seduction
Russell, R. Sardonicus
Sams, F. Big Star woman
Sams, F. Saba (an affirmation)
Schulman, H. East Jesus
Seepaul, L. A sleeping pill for the doctor
Shaw, J. B. The courtship of the thin girl
Sheehan, R. Boy with an injured eye
Sladek, J. T. The kindly ones
Smith, W. A. Delivery
Starkman, E. M. Anniversary
Stýblová, V. Scalpel, please
Swados, H. A chance encounter
Swados, H. My Coney Island uncle
Swift, G. The hypochondriac
Verne, J. The storm
Watson, I. Sunstroke
West, J. Horace Chooney, M.D.
Williams, W. C. Ancient gentility
Williams, W. C. Comedy entombed: 1930
Williams, W. C. Danse pseudomacabre
Williams, W. C. A face of stone
Williams, W. C. The girl with a pimply face
Williams, W. C. Jean Beicke
Williams, W. C. A night in June
Williams, W. C. Old Doc Rivers
Williams, W. C. The use of force
Williams, W. J. Side effects
Wolff, T. The liar
Wynne, A. The Cyprian bees
Yasuoka, S. The moth
A physician's log. Dubbs, C.

PHYSICISTS

Asimov, I. Belief

PHYSICISTS—*Continued*
Asimov, I. The last answer
Asimov, I. My son, the physicist
Asimov, I. Spell my name with an S
Berry, R. M. A decisive refutation of Herbert Dingle's objection to Einstein's twin paradox; or, Gravitas
Breuer, M. J. The gostak and the doshes
Gustafsson, L. The girl in the blue cap
Kornbluth, C. M. Two dooms
McDevitt, J. Tidal effects
Physics. Janowitz, T.

PIANISTS
Bates, H. E. Nina
Baxter, C. Gershwin's second prelude
Baxter, C. Harmony of the world
Bender, H. La Paloma; or, The food of love
Bloch, R. Mr. Steinway
Browne, C. The lesson
Cohen, M. Life on this planet
Colette. The accompanist
Davie, E. Accompanists
Drake, R. I am counting with you all the way
Ferguson, W. Morrissey
Ferguson, W. A summer at Estabrook
Hall, R. W. The lost chord
Hall, R. W. The piano
Henry, O. A service of love
Houbein, L. Child of two sisters
Mann, T. The infant prodigy
McCullers, C. Wunderkind
McElroy, C. J. The limitations of Jason Packard
Meinke, P. The piano tuner
Palmer, M. Esmerelda's hands
Sarah, R. Première arabesque
Shelnutt, E. Angel
Silverberg, R. The Macauley circuit
Stegner, W. E. Field guide to the western birds
Swados, H. Where does your music come from?
Tournier, M. Jesu, Joy of Man's Desiring
Whitaker, M. The mandoline
Williams, S. A. Tell Martha not to moan
Williams, T. Resemblance between a violin case and a coffin

PIANO
Bloch, R. Mr. Steinway
Giles, M. Heart and soul
Hill, E. The piano
Machado, A. M. The piano
Mathers, P. Journey in
Maupassant, G. de. False alarm
Sturges, A. E. Pianoforte
The **piano.** Hall, R. W.
The **piano.** Hill, E.
The **piano.** Machado, A. M.
Piano lessons. Van Wert, W. F.
The **piano** tuner. Meinke, P.

PIANO TUNERS
Boylan, J. Lost in space
Meinke, P. The piano tuner
Weinzweig, H. Causation
Pianoforte. Sturges, A. E.
Pianola. Wheeler, K.
The **piazza.** Melville, H.
Picano, Felice, 1944-
The most golden Bulgari
Men on men; ed. by G. Stambolian
PICASSO, PABLO, 1881-1973
About
Swanwick, M. The man who met Picasso
Picasso is dead. Komie, L. B.
Piccirilli. Sorrentino, F.
Pick-and-shovel hero. Skrzynecki, P.
Pick-up for Olympus. Pangborn, E.
The **pickets.** Chambers, R. W.
Pickett's charge. Boylan, J.
Picking a loser. Mathers, P.
Picking cotton. Caldwell, E.
The **picking** season. Sheil, G.
Picking time. Henley, P.
The **pickling** of Rewt Chaney. Millman, L.
Pickman's model. Lovecraft, H. P.
The **pickpocket.** Spillane, M.
PICKPOCKETS *See* Thieves
The **pickup.** Fisher, P. W.
The **picnic.** Gathorne-Hardy, J.
Picnic. Oates, J. C.
Picnic at Amapolas. Doerr, H.
Picnic time. Saroyan, W.
PICNICS
Bingham, S. Reunion
Carrington, L. How to start a pharmaceuticals business
Colette. April
Crane, S. Shame
Emshwiller, C. Day at the beach
Gauger, R. The vacuum-packed picnic
Maupassant, G. de. A country excursion
Saroyan, W. Picnic time
Summers, H. S. A hundred paths
Thomas, D. A story
Pico Rico, mandorico. Ferré, R.
Picoult, Jodi
Keeping count
Seventeen 46:126-7+ F '87
Road stop
Seventeen 46:330-1+ Ag '87
The **picture.** Caldwell, E.
The **picture** from Hull. Sandel, C.
The **picture** in the house. Lovecraft, H. P.
A **picture** in the snow. Welch, D.
A **picture** of Tuesday. Chesterton, G. K.
Pictures. Flynn, R.
Pictures made of stones. Shepard, L.
Pictures of a woman gone. Horvitz, L. A.
Pictures of her snake. Working, R.
PIDGIN ENGLISH DIALECT *See* Dialect stories—Pidgin English
Pie dance. Giles, M.
A **piece** of archangel. Norris, L.

A **piece** of harlot's ghost. Mailer, N.
A **piece** of my heart. Ford, R.
A **piece** of string. Maupassant, G. de
The **Pied** Piper fights the Gestapo. Bloch, R.
Pied piper of Hamelin. Asscher-Pinkhof, C.
Pierce, Anne Whitney
No spring chicken
The Virginia Quarterly Review 62:85-104 Wint '86
Remarkable
The Virginia Quarterly Review 64:316-35 Spr '88
Pierce, Constance
Chez les petits suisses
Pierce, C. When things get back to normal
The gourmand
Pierce, C. When things get back to normal
Manosque
Pierce, C. When things get back to normal
A summer afternoon
Pierce, C. When things get back to normal
The tenants at Auxillac
Pierce, C. When things get back to normal
What I did for Aunt Berthe
Pierce, C. When things get back to normal
When things get back to normal
Pierce, C. When things get back to normal
Woman waiting for train at dusk
Pierce, C. When things get back to normal
Pierce, Jackie Peters
Great Pumpkins I have known & loved
'Teen 29:34-5+ O '85
The more things change . . .
'Teen 30:60-3 Je '86
Pierce, John Robinson, 1910-
Choice
Great science fiction; ed. by I. Asimov; M. H. Greenberg and C. G. Waugh
Pierce, Meredith Ann
The woman who loved reindeer
Moonsinger's friends; ed. by S. Shwartz
Pierre. Steward, D. E.
Pierre Chambrun and the black days. Pentecost, H.
Pierre Chambrun and the last fling. Pentecost, H.
Pierre Chambrun and the sad song. Pentecost, H.
Pierre Chambrun and the war for peace. Pentecost, H.
Pierre Chambrun defends himself. Pentecost, H.
Pierre Chambrun's dilemma. Pentecost, H.
Piers the impostor. Pesetsky, B.

Pierson, Amanda
Drawn from life
Ploughshares 14 no2/3:167-77 '88
Pietà. Ryan, A.
Pieyre de Mandiargues, André, 1909-
Clorinda
Black water; ed. by A. Manguel
The **pig.** Fink, I.
The **pig.** O'Hara, J.
Pig blood blues. Barker, C.
Pig-hoo-o-o-o-ey!. Wodehouse, P. G.
Pig Latin. Lispector, C.
Pig thieves on Ptolemy: a tale of the Tricentennial. Daugherty, L.
The **pigeon** and the parakeet. Ferron, J.
Pigeon feathers. Updike, J.
Pigeon, fly! Carrington, L.
The **pigeon** hunters. Brandner, G.
PIGEONS
Bache, E. Pigeons
Jia Pingwa. Shasha and the pigeons
Lee, L. Born and bred
McKnight, R. Mali is very dangerous
Miller, J. F. A lover of nature
Sorrells, R. T. The man who walked pigeons
Whelan, G. The showing
Pigeons. Bache, E.
Pigeons. Vick, F.
Piggy bank killer. Ritchie, J.
PIGS
Barker, C. Pig blood blues
Bates, H. E. The sow and Silas
Highsmith, P. In the dead of truffle season
McLaughlin, L. In hock
Still, J. A master time
Wodehouse, P. G. Pig-hoo-o-o-o-ey!
Pigs. Panning, A.
Pilar, your curls. Filippi, C. L.
Pilcher, Rosamunde, 1924-
Amita
Pilcher, R. The blue bedroom, and other stories
The before-Christmas present
Pilcher, R. The blue bedroom, and other stories
The blue bedroom
Pilcher, R. The blue bedroom, and other stories
Change of heart
Good Housekeeping 198:134-5+ Je '84
Christmas wedding
Good Housekeeping 203:162-3+ D '86
An evening to remember
Pilcher, R. The blue bedroom, and other stories
Garden of love
Good Housekeeping 200:108-9+ Ap '85
The gift of love
Good Housekeeping 202:96+ My '86
Gilbert
Pilcher, R. The blue bedroom, and other stories

Pilcher, Rosamunde, 1924-—*Continued*
Her valiant heart
 Good Housekeeping 206:48+ Mr '88
Home for the day
 Pilcher, R. The blue bedroom, and other stories
The house on the hill
 Pilcher, R. The blue bedroom, and other stories
Man of the house
 Good Housekeeping 198:116-17+ Mr '84
Miss Cameron at Christmas
 Pilcher, R. The blue bedroom, and other stories
Promise of tomorrow
 Good Housekeeping 201:168-9+ S '85
The secrets of life
 Good Housekeeping 201:136-7+ O '85
Spanish ladies
 Ladies' Home Journal 105:94+ Ag '88
 Pilcher, R. The blue bedroom, and other stories
Tea with the professor
 Pilcher, R. The blue bedroom, and other stories
Toby
 Pilcher, R. The blue bedroom, and other stories
The tree
 Pilcher, R. The blue bedroom, and other stories
Uninvited disaster
 Redbook 167:74+ My '86
The white birds
 Pilcher, R. The blue bedroom, and other stories
Pilgrimage. Bond, N.
The **Pilgrimage.** Maxwell, W.
Pilgrimage home. Colum, P.
Pilgrimage to Earth. Sheckley, R.
PILGRIMAGES *See* Pilgrims and pilgrimages
Pilgrims. Gordon, R.
PILGRIMS AND PILGRIMAGES
 O'Faoláin, S. Lovers of the lake
 Rulfo, J. Talpa
Pilgrim's tale. Kelly, M.
Pilgrims to the cathedral. Arnold, M.
Pillar of fire. Foote, S.
The **pillory.** Grin, A.
The **pillows.** St. Clair, M.
Pil'niāk, Boris, 1894-1937
Chinese story
 Pil'niāk, B. Chinese story, and other tales
A dog's life
 Pil'niāk, B. Chinese story, and other tales
Mahogany
 Pil'niāk, B. Chinese story, and other tales

Mother earth
 Pil'niāk, B. Chinese story, and other tales
The Nizhni Novgorod Otkos
 Pil'niāk, B. Chinese story, and other tales
The tale of the unextinguished moon
 Pil'niāk, B. Chinese story, and other tales
A year of their life
 Pil'niāk, B. Chinese story, and other tales
The **pilot.** Burke, J. L.
The **pilot.** Haldeman, J. W.
The **pilot-messenger.** Shelnutt, E.
PILOTS, AIRPLANE *See* Air pilots
Pimple, Dennis J.
Arcadus Arcane
 L. Ron Hubbard presents Writers of the future
PIMPS
 See also Prostitutes
 Coleman, W. Big dreams
 Friedman, B. J. Detroit Abe
 MacLean, N. Logging and pimping and "your pal, Jim"
 Sholem Aleichem. The man from Buenos Aires
 Vogan, S. No other women
Pimpush. Nowotny, J.
The **pin.** Bloch, R.
Pin-up girl. Bloch, R.
Pinch. Oates, J. C.
Pincherle, Alberto *See* Moravia, Alberto, 1907-
Pindar, Susan
Aunt Mable's love story
 Old maids; ed. by S. Koppelman
Piñera, Virgilio
An a posteriori ghost
 Piñera, V. Cold tales
The Actæon case
 Piñera, V. Cold tales
Affairs of amputees
 Piñera, V. Cold tales
The album
 Piñera, V. Cold tales
Argument against the free-standing bathtub
 Piñera, V. Cold tales
The balcony
 Piñera, V. Cold tales
The ball
 Piñera, V. Cold tales
The battle
 Piñera, V. Cold tales
The candy
 Piñera, V. Cold tales
The conflict
 Piñera, V. Cold tales
The death of the birds
 Piñera, V. Cold tales
The decoration
 Piñera, V. Cold tales

Piñera, Virgilio—*Continued*
Design for a dream
  Piñera, V. Cold tales
The dummy
  Piñera, V. Cold tales
The employ of darkness
  Piñera, V. Cold tales
The face
  Piñera, V. Cold tales
The fall
  Piñera, V. Cold tales
A few beers
  Piñera, V. Cold tales
A few children
  Piñera, V. Cold tales
Graphomania
  Piñera, V. Cold tales
The great staircase of the legislative palace
  Piñera, V. Cold tales
Hell
  Piñera, V. Cold tales
Hot and cold
  Piñera, V. Cold tales
How I lived and how I died
  Piñera, V. Cold tales
Indestructible union
  Piñera, V. Cold tales
Insomnia
  Piñera, V. Cold tales
The locomotive
  Piñera, V. Cold tales
Look of love
  Piñera, V. Cold tales
Meat
  Piñera, V. Cold tales
The minister
  Piñera, V. Cold tales
The mountain
  Piñera, V. Cold tales
The one who came to save me
  Piñera, V. Cold tales
The park
  Piñera, V. Cold tales
The parts
  Piñera, V. Cold tales
The philanthropist
  Piñera, V. Cold tales
A saving nakedness
  Piñera, V. Cold tales
The store
  Piñera, V. Cold tales
Swimming
  Piñera, V. Cold tales
The switch
  Piñera, V. Cold tales
The transformation
  Piñera, V. Cold tales
The trip
  Piñera, V. Cold tales
An unexpected delivery
  Piñera, V. Cold tales
The wedding
  Piñera, V. Cold tales

Ping. Beckett, S.
The **pink-eyed** monster. Lanham, C.
PINKERTON'S NATIONAL DETECTIVE AGENCY
  Davenport, G. Les exploits de Nat Pinkerton de jour en jour: un texte de René Magritte translated and improved
Pinkham: the enchanted isles. Liben, M.
Pinkhof, Clara Asscher- *See* Asscher-Pinkhof, Clara
Pinkwater, Daniel Manus, 1941-
Devil in the drain
  Devils & demons; ed. by M. Kaye and S. Kaye
Wempires
  Omni (New York, N.Y.) 11:103-4 O '88
Pinkwater, Manus *See* Pinkwater, Daniel Manus, 1941-
Piñón, Nélida
Bird of paradise
  Women's fiction from Latin America; ed. by E. P. Garfield
The new kingdom
  Women's fiction from Latin America; ed. by E. P. Garfield
Pin's fee wife. Whitaker, M.
Pinsky, Robert
Clara and Benedict
  The Yale Review 73:263-7 Wint '84
Pinsoneault, Donna
The man I married
  Good Housekeeping 207:124-5 Jl '88
The **pint** flask. Henry, O.
Pintauro, Joseph
Jungle dove
  Men on men 2; ed. by G. Stambolian
PIONEER LIFE *See* Frontier and pioneer life
Pioneers, oh, pioneers. Rhys, J.
Pip. Rees, D.
Pipe line. Conroy, J.
Piper, H. Beam, 1904-1964
Down Styphon!
  Robert Adams' Book of soldiers
Gunpowder god
  Time wars; ed. by C. Waugh and M. H. Greenberg
He walked around the horses
  Alternative histories; ed. by C. G. Waugh and M. H. Greenberg
Ministry of disturbance
  Intergalactic empires; ed. by I. Asimov; M. H. Greenberg and C. G. Waugh
Omnilingual
  From mind to mind: tales of communication from Analog
Operation RSVP
  Amazing science fiction anthology: The wild years, 1946-1955; ed. by M. H. Greenberg
Piper at the gates of dawn. Cowper, R.
The **piper's** son. Padgett, L.
Pipkin Grove. Stewart, J. I. M.

PIRACY *See* Pirates
Pirandello, Luigi, 1867-1936
Aunt Michelina
    Pirandello, L. Tales of suicide
The black shawl
    Pirandello, L. Tales of suicide
A breath of air
    The Nobel reader; ed. by J. Eisen and
    S. Troy
By himself
    Pirandello, L. Tales of suicide
Candelora
    Pirandello, L. Tales of suicide
A challenge
    Pirandello, L. Tales of suicide
The fish trap
    Pirandello, L. Tales of suicide
An idea
    Pirandello, L. Tales of suicide
The imbecile
    Pirandello, L. Tales of suicide
In silence
    Pirandello, L. Tales of suicide
Into the sketch
    Pirandello, L. Tales of suicide
The lonely man
    Pirandello, L. Tales of suicide
The long dress
    Pirandello, L. Tales of suicide
Nothing
    Pirandello, L. Tales of suicide
The stuffed bird
    Pirandello, L. Tales of suicide
Sun and shade
    Pirandello, L. Tales of suicide
Sunrise
    Pirandello, L. Tales of suicide
This makes two!
    Pirandello, L. Tales of suicide
The trap
    Pirandello, L. Tales of suicide
The trip
    Pirandello, L. Tales of suicide
While the heart suffered
    Pirandello, L. Tales of suicide
Piranesi's dream. Campbell, E.
The **pirate** of the Round Pond. Dunsany, E.
    J. M. D. P., Baron
PIRATES
Barthelme, D. Captain Blood
Davidson, A. The lord of Central Park
Dunsany, E. J. M. D. P., Baron. A story
    of land and sea
Hoch, E. D. The crime of the century
Masefield, J. Don Alfonso's treasure hunt
Reade, C. Agra outwits two pirate ships
Sabatini, R. The blank shot
Schwob, M. Major Stede Bonnet, pirate by
    vagary
Schwob, M. The sleeping city
Pirates. Rand, P.
Pirate's moon. Nolan, W. F.

PISA (ITALY) *See* Italy—Pisa
Pisces. Cook, H.
PISSARRO, CAMILLE, 1830-1903
                    About
    Lurie, M. Camille Pissaro 1830-1903
Pit. Benedict, P.
The **pit.** Croft, M.
The **pit.** Lansdale, J. R.
The **pit** and the pendulum. Poe, E. A.
Pitch memory. Canin, E.
Pitched out. Friedman, B. J.
The **pitcher.** Dubus, A.
PITTSBURGH (PA.) *See* Pennsylvania—Pitts-
    sburgh
Pity. Wilson, B.
The **pity** of it all. Barstow, S.
Pity the dumb beast. Halligan, M.
Pitzen, Jim
The village
    Prize stories, 1987
Pizarnik, Alejandra, 1936-1972
The bloody countess
    Other fires; ed. by A. Manguel
PIZARRO, FRANCISCO
                    About
    De la Torre Bueno, T. The murder of the
    governor
The **pizza.** Stowe, R.
Pizza time. Apple, M.
Place. Flynn, R.
A **place** for bleeding. Hoch, E. D.
The **place** in flowers where pollen rests.
    West, P.
A **place** of her own. Harrington, J.
The **place** of its quietude. Valenzuela, L.
Place of meeting. Beaumont, C.
A **place** of our own. Cecala, K. P.
A **place** of refuge. Eisenstein, S.
Place of the throwing-stick. Bryning, F.
The **place** to be. Hazzard, S.
A **place** to stay. Olmstead, R.
Places in the world a woman could walk.
    Kauffman, J.
Places on the water. Pejovich, T.
PLAGIARISM
Böll, H. No tears for Schmeck
Bush, J. The problem of Li T'ang
Plagiarism. Harvey, J.
PLAGUE
                See also Disasters
Broxon, M. D. Flux of fortune
Cowper, R. The Hertford Manuscript
Poe, E. A. The masque of the Red Death
Potter, R. The red sickness
Ross, R. T. The craft of death
Schwob, M. The plague
Shelley, M. W. The last man
Thomas, D. The horse's ha
The **plague.** Buzzati, D.
The **plague.** Schwob, M.
The **plain,** the endless plain. Aldiss, B. W.
Plaisir d'amour. Schwartz, L. S.
The **plan.** O'Brien, E.

Plan "B" for Buck. Schwab, P. V.
The **plane** in the woods. Backman, B.
A **planet** named Shayol. Smith, C.
Planet of peril. St. Maur, H.
The **planet** of the dead. Smith, C. A.
Planetesimal. Hulme, K.
PLANETS, MINOR
  Berdnyk, O. The alien secret
  Bradley, M. Z. Hero's moon
  Forward, R. L. The singing diamond
  Preuss, P. Small bodies
  Sheckley, R. Beside still waters
The **planets.** Dawson, F.
Plans for an escape to Carmelo. Bioy
  Casares, A.
Plant, Richard
  Cecil grounded
    The Antioch Review 44:282-97 Summ '86
    Prize stories, 1988
PLANTATION LIFE
  Caldwell, E. The end of Christy Tucker
  King, G. E. Bayou l'Ombre: an incident
    of the war
  Lytle, A. Jericho, Jericho, Jericho
  Smith, E. V. 'Lijah
  Spark, M. The go-away bird
                    Brazil
  Stephenson, C. Leiningen versus the ants
                    Hawaii
  Heller, S. The summer game
Plante, David
  The crack
    First love/last love; ed. by M. Denneny;
    C. Ortleb and T. Steele
  A house of women
    The New Yorker 62:30-2 Ap 28 '86
  Paris, 1959
    The New Yorker 60:44-54+ Je 4 '84
The **planter** box. Giles, M.
PLANTS
        See also Poison ivy; Poisonous
        plants; Weeds
  Brown, M. W. The amaryllis
  Cowper, R. A message to the King of
    Brobdingnag
  Hartley, L. P. The pampas clump
  Nolan, W. F. Trust not a man
  Valenzuela, L. A story about greenery
PLANTS, POISONOUS *See* Poisonous
  plants
Plaster, culture, rape and deprivation.
  Mathers, P.
The **Plasting** Project. Stone, M.
The **plateau.** Willis, C.
Plato at Scratch Daniels. Falco, E.
Platonic love. Kanai, M.
The **Plattner** story. Wells, H. G.
The **play.** Dixon, S.
Play me something. Berger, J.
The **play** reading. Jolley, E.
Playboy and the slime god. See Asimov, I.
  What is this thing called love?

PLAYBOY ENTERPRISES, INC.
  Sisskind, M. The Playboy Rabbit
The **Playboy** Rabbit. Sisskind, M.
The **player** and the giant. Heller, S.
Player in the symphony. Pritchard, S.
Players. Hogan, D.
The **playground.** Bradbury, R.
PLAYGROUNDS
  Bradbury, R. The playground
The **Playhouse** called Remarkable. Spark, M.
PLAYING CARDS *See* Cards
Playing for keeps. Gifkins, M.
Playing for keeps. Haldeman, J. C.
Playing with fire. Shaw, J. B.
Playing with shadows. Whelan, G.
Plays and wins. Krivich, M., and Olgin, O.
The **play's** the thing. Bloch, R.
PLAYWRIGHTS *See* Dramatists
Pleadings. Corrington, J. W.
Pleadings. Cullen, E. J.
Please do not touch. Hartley, L. P.
Please don't talk about me when I'm gone.
  Algren, N.
Please, no strawberries. Wilson, H.
"Please, please me". Sadoff, I.
Please stand by. Goulart, R.
PLEASURE *See* Happiness
The **pleasure.** Carter, R.
Pleasure. Soldatow, S.
The **pleasure** garden of the root vegetables.
  Woodman, A.
The **pleasure** of her company. Smiley, J.
Pleasure Park. Lynch, L.
The **pleasure** principle. Pacheco, J. E.
Pleasure trips. Greening, J.
Pleasures of the flesh. Regent, P.
The **pleasures** of the senses. Day, R. C.
The **pledges.** Friedman, B. J.
Plemmons, Michael
  Noel
    The North American Review 270:33 Je
    '85
  Sudden fiction; ed. by R. Shapard and
    J. Thomas
Plenty of furniture. See Thomas, D. Adven-
  tures in the skin trade: Plenty of
  furniture
Plenty of time. Bumpus, J.
The **plight** of the dragonfly. Fuerst, R. E.
Pliny's commentaries. Huston, N.
Pliscou, Lisa
  Shower check
    Ms. 17:76-80 Ag '88
Plomer, William, 1903-1973
  When the sardines came
    The Penguin book of Southern African
    stories
The **plot** is the thing. Bloch, R.
Plotting Elsa. Barbasch, A.
Plum blossoms in the snow. Feng Jicai
The **Plum** Point Ladies. Parry, H. T.
PLUMBERS
  Boyle, K. Astronomer's wife

PLUMBERS—*Continued*
  Evans, M. Xavier's folly
  Lott, B. This plumber
  Treat, L. Suburban tigress
  Whitaker, M. The apprentice
  Yamamoto, M. Father Goose
La **plume** de ma tante. Adams, G. G.
La **plume** de mon ami. Tremain, R.
The **plumed** knight. Wolfe, T.
Plumeria days. Saiki, J.
Plumpp, Sterling, 1940-
  Mighty long time
    Mississippi writers v1: Fiction; ed. by D.
    Abbott
Plums. Rees, D.
Plunder. Somers, A.
Plunkett, Edward John Moreton Drax, Baron
    Dunsany *See* Dunsany, Edward John
    Moreton Drax Plunkett, Baron, 1878-
    1957
Plunkett, James
  The scoop
    The Best of Irish wit and wisdom; ed.
    by J. McCarthy
Plus you. Pfeil, F.
PLUTO (PLANET)
  Benford, G., and Carter, P. A. Proserpina's
    daughter
  Lovecraft, H. P. The whisperer in darkness
  Silverberg, R. Sunrise on Pluto
The **Plymouth** Express. Christie, A.
POACHING
    See also Hunting
  Brown, S. The lesson
  Wallin, L. The redneck poacher's son [ex-
    cerpt]
A **pocket** full of snow. Nelson, V.
The **pocket-miner**. Davis, S.
The **pocket** remembered. Singer, I. B.
Podhoretz revisited. Komie, L. B.
Podolo. Hartley, L. P.
Podulka, Fran
  Translations
    The North American Review 272:42-3 Mr
    '87
Poe, Edgar Allan, 1809-1849
  The Angel of the Odd
    Poe, E. A. Poetry and tales
    Poe, E. A. The unabridged Edgar Allan
    Poe
  The assignation [Variant title: The
    visionary]
    Poe, E. A. Poetry and tales
  The balloon-hoax
    Poe, E. A. Poetry and tales
    Poe, E. A. The unabridged Edgar Allan
    Poe
  Berenice
    Poe, E. A. Poetry and tales
    Poe, E. A. Tales of suspense
    Poe, E. A. The unabridged Edgar Allan
    Poe

The black cat
  Charles Keeping's Book of classic ghost
    stories
  Poe, E. A. Poetry and tales
  Poe, E. A. Tales of suspense
  Poe, E. A. Tales of terror
  Poe, E. A. The unabridged Edgar Allan
    Poe
  Roger Caras' Treasury of great cat
    stories
Bon-bon
  Poe, E. A. Poetry and tales
  Poe, E. A. The unabridged Edgar Allan
    Poe
The business man [Variant title: Peter Pen-
    dulum, the business man]
  Poe, E. A. Poetry and tales
The case of M. Valdemar [Variant title:
    The facts in the case of M. Valdemar]
  The Penguin book of horror stories
The cask of Amontillado
  The Book of the dead; ed. by A. K.
    Russell
  Inspired by drink; ed. by Joan Digby
    and John Digby
  Poe, E. A. Poetry and tales
  Poe, E. A. Tales of suspense
  Poe, E. A. Tales of terror
  Poe, E. A. The unabridged Edgar Allan
    Poe
  Through a glass, darkly; ed. by B. Woel-
    fel
The colloquy of Monos and Una
  Poe, E. A. Poetry and tales
  Poe, E. A. The unabridged Edgar Allan
    Poe
The conversation of Eiros and Charmion
    [Variant title: The destruction of the
    world]
  Isaac Asimov presents the best science
    fiction firsts
  Poe, E. A. Poetry and tales
  Poe, E. A. The unabridged Edgar Allan
    Poe
A descent into the maelström
  Poe, E. A. Poetry and tales
  Poe, E. A. Tales of terror
  Poe, E. A. The unabridged Edgar Allan
    Poe
The devil in the belfry
  Poe, E. A. Poetry and tales
  Poe, E. A. The unabridged Edgar Allan
    Poe
Diddling considered as one of the exact
    sciences [Variant title: Raising the
    wind]
  Poe, E. A. Poetry and tales
The domain of Arnheim
  Poe, E. A. Poetry and tales
The Duc de l'Omelette
  Poe, E. A. Poetry and tales
  Poe, E. A. The unabridged Edgar Allan
    Poe

Poe, Edgar Allan, 1809-1849—*Continued*

Eleonora
 Poe, E. A. Poetry and tales
 Poe, E. A. The unabridged Edgar Allan
 Poe
The facts in the case of M. Valdemar
 [Variant title: The case of M. Valdemar]
 Black water; ed. by A. Manguel
 Poe, E. A. Poetry and tales
 Poe, E. A. Tales of suspense
The facts of M. Valdemar's case [Variant
 title: The case of M. Valdemar]
 Poe, E. A. The unabridged Edgar Allan
 Poe
The fall of the House of Usher
 Charles Keeping's Classic tales of the
 macabre
 Dark company; ed. by L. Child
 The Dark descent; ed. by D. G. Hartwell
 Poe, E. A. Poetry and tales
 Poe, E. A. Tales of suspense
 Poe, E. A. Tales of terror
 Poe, E. A. The unabridged Edgar Allan
 Poe
The Folio Club
 Poe, E. A. Poetry and tales
Four beasts in one—the homo-cameleopard
 [Variant title: Epimanes]
 Poe, E. A. Poetry and tales
 Poe, E. A. The unabridged Edgar Allan
 Poe
The gold-bug
 Poe, E. A. Poetry and tales
 Poe, E. A. Tales of suspense
 Poe, E. A. The unabridged Edgar Allan
 Poe
Hans Phaall [Variant title: The unparalled
 adventure of one Hans Pfaall]
 Poe, E. A. The unabridged Edgar Allan
 Poe
Hop-frog
 Dark arrows; ed. by A. Manguel
 Masterpieces of terror and the supernatural; ed. by M. Kaye and S. Kaye
 Poe, E. A. Poetry and tales
 Poe, E. A. Tales of suspense
 Poe, E. A. Tales of terror
 Poe, E. A. The unabridged Edgar Allan
 Poe
 The Wickedest show on earth; ed. by
 M. Muller and B. Pronzini
How to write a Blackwood article [Variant
 title: The Psyche Zenobia]
 Poe, E. A. Poetry and tales
The imp of the perverse
 Poe, E. A. Poetry and tales
 Poe, E. A. Tales of suspense
 Poe, E. A. The unabridged Edgar Allan
 Poe
The incredible survival
 Men at sea; ed. by B. Aymar

The island of the fay
 Poe, E. A. Poetry and tales
 Poe, E. A. The unabridged Edgar Allan
 Poe
The journal of Julius Rodman
 Poe, E. A. Poetry and tales
 Poe, E. A. The unabridged Edgar Allan
 Poe
King Pest
 Poe, E. A. Poetry and tales
 Poe, E. A. The unabridged Edgar Allan
 Poe
Landor's cottage
 Poe, E. A. Poetry and tales
 Poe, E. A. The unabridged Edgar Allan
 Poe
The landscape garden
 Poe, E. A. The unabridged Edgar Allan
 Poe
Life in death [Variant title: The oval portrait]
 Poe, E. A. The unabridged Edgar Allan
 Poe
Ligeia
 Poe, E. A. Poetry and tales
 Poe, E. A. Tales of terror
 Poe, E. A. The unabridged Edgar Allan
 Poe
The light-house
 Poe, E. A. Poetry and tales
Lionizing [Variant title: Some passages in
 the life of a lion (Lionizing)]
 Poe, E. A. Poetry and tales
 Poe, E. A. The unabridged Edgar Allan
 Poe
The literary life of Thingum Bob, Esq.
 Poe, E. A. Poetry and tales
 Poe, E. A. The unabridged Edgar Allan
 Poe
Loss of breath
 Poe, E. A. Poetry and tales
 Poe, E. A. The unabridged Edgar Allan
 Poe
The man of the crowd
 Poe, E. A. Poetry and tales
 Poe, E. A. The unabridged Edgar Allan
 Poe
The man that was used up
 Poe, E. A. Poetry and tales
 Poe, E. A. The unabridged Edgar Allan
 Poe
The masque of the Red Death
 Poe, E. A. Poetry and tales
 Poe, E. A. Tales of suspense
 Poe, E. A. Tales of terror
 Poe, E. A. The unabridged Edgar Allan
 Poe
Mellonta Tauta
 Poe, E. A. Poetry and tales
 Poe, E. A. The unabridged Edgar Allan
 Poe

Poe, Edgar Allan, 1809-1849—*Continued*

Mesmeric revelation
Poe, E. A. Poetry and tales
Poe, E. A. The unabridged Edgar Allan Poe

Metzengerstein [Variant title: The horse-shade]
Poe, E. A. Poetry and tales
Poe, E. A. Tales of suspense
Poe, E. A. The unabridged Edgar Allan Poe

Morella
Poe, E. A. Poetry and tales
Poe, E. A. Tales of suspense
Poe, E. A. The unabridged Edgar Allan Poe

Morning on the Wissahiccon [Variant title: The Elk]
Poe, E. A. Poetry and tales
Poe, E. A. The unabridged Edgar Allan Poe

Ms. found in a bottle
Mysterious sea stories; ed. by W. Patrick
Poe, E. A. Poetry and tales
Poe, E. A. Tales of terror
Poe, E. A. The unabridged Edgar Allan Poe
Short stories of the sea; ed. by G. C. Solley and E. Steinbaugh

The murders in the Rue Morgue
Poe, E. A. Poetry and tales
Poe, E. A. Tales of suspense
Poe, E. A. The unabridged Edgar Allan Poe

The mystery of Marie Rogêt
Poe, E. A. Poetry and tales
Poe, E. A. The unabridged Edgar Allan Poe

Mystification [Variant title: Von Jung, the mystic]
Poe, E. A. Poetry and tales

The narrative of Arthur Gordon Pym of Nantucket
Poe, E. A. Poetry and tales
Poe, E. A. The unabridged Edgar Allan Poe

Never bet the devil your head [Variant title: Never bet your head]
Poe, E. A. Poetry and tales
Poe, E. A. The unabridged Edgar Allan Poe

The oblong box
Poe, E. A. Poetry and tales
Poe, E. A. Tales of suspense
Poe, E. A. The unabridged Edgar Allan Poe

The oval portrait [Variant title: Life in death]
Poe, E. A. Poetry and tales

Peter Pendulum, the business man [Variant title: The business man]
Poe, E. A. The unabridged Edgar Allan Poe

The philosophy of furniture [Variant title: House furniture]
Poe, E. A. Poetry and tales
Poe, E. A. The unabridged Edgar Allan Poe

The pit and the pendulum
The Book of the dead; ed. by A. K. Russell
Poe, E. A. Poetry and tales
Poe, E. A. Tales of suspense
Poe, E. A. Tales of terror
Poe, E. A. The unabridged Edgar Allan Poe

The power of words
Poe, E. A. Poetry and tales
Poe, E. A. The unabridged Edgar Allan Poe

The premature burial
Poe, E. A. Poetry and tales
Poe, E. A. Tales of suspense
Poe, E. A. The unabridged Edgar Allan Poe

The purloined letter
Isaac Asimov presents the best crime stories of the 19th century
Poe, E. A. Poetry and tales
Poe, E. A. Tales of suspense
Poe, E. A. The unabridged Edgar Allan Poe

Raising the wind [Variant title: Diddling considered as one of the exact sciences]
Poe, E. A. The unabridged Edgar Allan Poe

The scythe of time [Variant title: A predicament]
Poe, E. A. The unabridged Edgar Allan Poe

Shadow—a parable
Poe, E. A. Poetry and tales
Poe, E. A. The unabridged Edgar Allan Poe

The Signora Psyche Zenobia [Variant title: How to write a Blackwood article]
Poe, E. A. The unabridged Edgar Allan Poe

Silence—a fable [Variant title: Siope (Silence)]
Poe, E. A. Poetry and tales

Siope (Silence) [Variant title: Silence--a fable]
Poe, E. A. The unabridged Edgar Allan Poe

Some words with a mummy
Poe, E. A. Poetry and tales
Poe, E. A. The unabridged Edgar Allan Poe

Poe, Edgar Allan, 1809-1849—*Continued*
The spectacles
  Poe, E. A. Poetry and tales
  Poe, E. A. The unabridged Edgar Allan
    Poe
The sphinx
  Poe, E. A. Poetry and tales
  Poe, E. A. The unabridged Edgar Allan
    Poe
A succession of Sundays [Variant title:
    Three Sundays in a week]
  Poe, E. A. The unabridged Edgar Allan
    Poe
The system of Doctor Tarr and Professor
    Fether
  Poe, E. A. Poetry and tales
  Poe, E. A. The unabridged Edgar Allan
    Poe
A tale of Jerusalem
  Poe, E. A. Poetry and tales
  Poe, E. A. The unabridged Edgar Allan
    Poe
A tale of the ragged mountains
  Poe, E. A. Poetry and tales
  Poe, E. A. Tales of suspense
  Poe, E. A. The unabridged Edgar Allan
    Poe
The tell-tale heart
  Great ghost stories; ed. by B. A.
    Schwartz
  The Norton book of American short
    stories
  Poe, E. A. Poetry and tales
  Poe, E. A. Tales of suspense
  Poe, E. A. Tales of terror
  Poe, E. A. The unabridged Edgar Allan
    Poe
Thou art the man
  The Penguin classic crime omnibus
  Poe, E. A. Poetry and tales
  Poe, E. A. The unabridged Edgar Allan
    Poe
The thousand-and-second tale of
    Scheherazade
  Poe, E. A. Poetry and tales
  Poe, E. A. The unabridged Edgar Allan
    Poe
Three Sundays in a week [Variant title:
    Succession of Sundays]
  Poe, E. A. Poetry and tales
The unparalleled adventure of one Hans
    Pfaall [Variant title: Hans Phaall]
  Poe, E. A. Poetry and tales
The visionary [Variant title: The as-
    signation]
  Poe, E. A. The unabridged Edgar Allan
    Poe
Von Jung, the mystific [Variant title:
    Mystification]
  Poe, E. A. The unabridged Edgar Allan
    Poe

Von Kempelen and his discovery
  Poe, E. A. Poetry and tales
  Poe, E. A. The unabridged Edgar Allan
    Poe
Why the little Frenchman wears his hand
    in a sling [Variant title: The Irish gen-
    tleman and the little Frenchman]
  Poe, E. A. Poetry and tales
  Poe, E. A. The unabridged Edgar Allan
    Poe
William Wilson
  Poe, E. A. Poetry and tales
  Poe, E. A. Tales of suspense
  Poe, E. A. The unabridged Edgar Allan
    Poe
'X-ing a paragrab'
  Poe, E. A. Poetry and tales
  Poe, E. A. The unabridged Edgar Allan
    Poe

About

Bloch, R. The man who collected Poe
Carter, A. The cabinet of Edgar Allan Poe
A **poem** of ecstasy. Aksenov, V. P.
Poems of John the Baptist. Chang, Y.-H.
The **poet**. Austin, D.
Poet. Silva, B.
The **poet**. Williams, T.
The **poet** assassinated. Apollinaire, G.
A **poet** in the classroom. Rizkalla, J.
A **poet** though married. Martin, H. R.
A **poetics** for bullies. Elkin, S.

POETRY

Cullen, E. J. Trying to grow up American
Dadswell, M. Retirement
Dennison, G. The carbon paper poet
Hershman, M. When a felon needs a
    friend
Ignatow, R. G. It deals with people first
Kawabata, Y. The Wife of the Autumn
    Wind
Liben, M. The garden
Lish, G. How to write a poem
McGrath, P. Ambrose Syme
Willard, N. How poetry came into the
    world and why God doesn't write it
Poetry. Mrozek, S.
Poetry. Parise, G.

POETS

See also Troubadours; Women poets
Abbott, L. K. Youth on Mars
Abrahams, L. Invisible worm
Agee, J. 1928 story
Aksenov, V. P. A poem of ecstasy
Apollinaire, G. The poet assassinated
Atwood, M. Loulou; or, The domestic life
    of the language
Austin, D. The poet
Baumbach, J. A famous Russian poet
Beerbohm, M. Enoch Soames
Borges, J. L. The Aleph
Brondoli, M. I swear I always wished you
    were a possibility
Broster, D. K. Couching at the door

POETS—*Continued*

Brown, G. M. The chamber of poetry
Brown, G. M. Gold dust
Brown, G. M. Lord of silence
Brown, G. M. The satirist
Brown, G. M. The skald in the cave
Cheever, J. The world of apples
Collier, J. Evening primrose
Colum, P. A Dublin day
Cook-Lynn, E. A good chance
Dawson, F. Miles
Elgin, S. H. For the sake of Grace
Elgin, S. H. Modulation in all things
Frucht, A. Fate and the poet
Gilbert, W. S. The poisoned postage stamp
Goyen, W. In the icebound hothouse
Hall, T. T. Murphy Walls and the Oriental hummer
Henry, O. Roads of destiny
Herbert, F. Songs of a sentient flute
Herman, M. Auslander
Hofmann, G. Arno
Houbein, L. Every poet's pipe-dream
Ignatow, R. G. Dreams & disappointments
Kilworth, G. Spiral sands
Landolfi, T. Dialogue of the greater systems
Mann, T. A difficult hour
Matthews, J. The gray lady
Metcalf, J. Gentle as flowers make the stones
Morazzoni, M. The dignity of Signor Da Ponte
Mrożek, S. Poetry
Paley, G. Dreamer in a dead language
Parise, G. Memory
Parise, G. Poetry
Penner, J. Emotion recollected in tranquillity
Petrakis, H. M. The bastards of Thanos
Pirandello, L. Nothing
Poe, E. A. The literary life of Thingum Bob, Esq.
Reynolds, M. The Devil finds work
Ripley, B. Desert owls
Rizkalla, J. A poet in the classroom
Schwob, M. Cecco Angiolieri, malevolent poet
Sheehan, R. Boy with an injured eye
Slayter, E. The silver fish
Smiley, J. Lily
Smith, C. A. Morthylla
Sorrentino, F. Ars poetica
Strand, M. The killer poet
Taylor, C. Catherine and Michael
Taylor, C. Lance's story: art sucks
Taylor, P. E. Entering the house of the 'Lord
Taylor, P. E. Leaping Leo
Thomas, D. Adventures in the skin trade: A fine beginning
Thomas, D. Adventures in the skin trade: Four lost souls
Thomas, D. Adventures in the skin trade: Plenty of furniture
Tuohy, F. A summer pilgrim
Upward, E. At the Ferry Inn
Vizyēnos, G. M. Between Peiraeus and Naples
White, C. A disciplined life
Williams, T. Field of blue children
Williams, T. The poet
Williams, T. Sabbatha and solitude
Wodehouse, P. G. Unpleasantness at Bludleigh Court
Zeiss, T. R. At the post office

Pohl, Frederik, 1919-
Adeste fideles
  Omni (New York, N.Y.) 10:68-70+ D '87
The blister
  Pohl, F. The years of the city
The children of night
  Election Day 2084; ed. by I. Asimov and M. H. Greenberg
The dark shadow
  The Universe; ed. by B. Preiss
Day million
  Robert Silverberg's Worlds of wonder
Farmer on the dole
  Omni book of science fiction 3
Fermi and frost
  The Year's best science fiction, third annual collection
The greening of Bed-Stuy
  Nebula awards 20
  Pohl, F. The years of the city
Gwenanda and the Supremes
  Pohl, F. The years of the city
The high test
  Tales from Isaac Asimov's science fiction magazine: short stories for young adults
How to impress an editor
  L. Ron Hubbard presents Writers of the future v3
In the problem pit
  Baker's dozen: 13 short science fiction novels
The kindly isle
  The Year's best science fiction, second annual collection
My life as a born-again pig
  Synergy v1
Schematic man
  Mathenauts: tales of mathematical wonder; ed. by R. Rucker
Second-hand sky
  Pohl, F. The years of the city
Sitting around the pool, soaking up the rays
  Tales from the planet Earth
Swanilda's song
  Medea: Harlan's world; ed. by H. Ellison
We servants of the stars
  Tales from the planet Earth

Pohl, Frederik, 1919-—*Continued*
When New York hit the fan
  Pohl, F. The years of the city
Point. Ch'oe, S.
Point of no return. Curtiss, U. R.
The **pointing** finger. Asimov, I.
Pointon, Susan
Framed
  Home and away; ed. by R. Creswell
Poise. Parise, G.
POISON *See* Poisons
POISON IVY
Heise, K. Aunt Ella gits it
POISON PEN LETTERS *See* Letters,
  Stories about
The **poisoned** postage stamp. Gilbert, W. S.
POISONING
  See also Poisons
Alcott, L. M. The fate of the Forrests
Ambler, E. The case of the emerald sky
Armstrong, C. The splintered Monday
Asimov, I. The winnowing
Bloch, R. Fat chance
Bowles, P. The little house
Carr, J. D. "As drink the dead . . . "
Christie, A. The Cornish mystery
Dale, C. Faery tale
Duke, M. Little knives
Faik, S. Filbert
Flanagan, M. Cream sauce
Flora, F. A husband is missing
Hartley, L. P. Please do not touch
Hensley, J. L. The home
Hoch, E. D. Day for a picnic
Hoch, E. D. The problem of the Boston
  Common
James, P. D. Great Aunt Allie's flypapers
Jeffrey, W. A case for quiet
Matsumoto, S. The woman who took the
  local paper
McConnell, J. Germination period
Morrison, J. A dash of murder
Nevins, F. M., Jr. The Dogsbody case
Pascoe, B. Flour for your grave
Piñera, V. The candy
Pronzini, B. A case for quiet
Pronzini, B. Dear poisoner
Pronzini, B. The same old grind
Russell, W. C. The phantom death
Sage, V. Destroying angel
Wasylyk, S. If a body
Weaver, G. Some killers
Wheeler, H. C. Puzzle for Poppy
Woolrich, C. Death sits in the dentist's
  chair
Yaffe, J. Mom sings an aria
POISONOUS GASES
  See also Chemical warfare
Boylan, J. Weasels
Michaelson, L. W. The rabbit that lost its
  nose
POISONOUS PLANTS
Hawthorne, N. Rappaccini's daughter

POISONOUS SNAKES
Forsyth, F. There are no snakes in Ireland
Russell, W. C. The phantom death
POISONS
  See also Poison ivy; Poisoning;
    Poisonous gases
Bloch, R. A matter of life
Brunner, J. Elixir for the emperor
Christie, A. How does your garden grow?
Doyle, Sir A. C. The adventure of the
  devil's foot
Drewe, R. Stingray
Poisson d'Avril. Ross, M., and Somerville,
  E. A. Œ.
POKER (GAME)
Apple, M. Kitty partners
Crane, S. A poker game
Davis, S. A Carson poker incident
Huggan, I. Jack of hearts
King, S. The man who would not shake
  hands
Klinkowitz, J. Five bad hands and the
  wild mouse folds
Mulford, C. E. Hopalong sits in
Painter, P. Winter evenings: spring night
Pfeil, F. Poker fugue
Sturgeon, T. Poker Face
Updike, J. Poker night
Poker Face. Sturgeon, T.
Poker fugue. Pfeil, F.
A **poker** game. Crane, S.
Poker night. Updike, J.
POLAND
Singer, I. B. The pocket remembered
                    16th century
Gogol', N. V. Taras Bulba
                    19th century
Konopnicka, M. Banasiowa
Konopnicka, M. Urbanowa
                    20th century
Anderman, J. Bitter red star
Anderman, J. Breathless
Anderman, J. Chain of pure hearts
Anderman, J. Czarnoleka: Black Meadow
Anderman, J. Empty . . . sort of
Anderman, J. Journey
Anderman, J. The National Theatre's burn-
  ing down
Anderman, J. Night shift in emergency
Anderman, J. No sound of footsteps in the
  treetops
Anderman, J. Poland still?
Anderman, J. Prison sickness
Anderman, J. A sense of
Anderman, J. Sinking wells
Anderman, J. The three kings
Anderman, J. Topical subject
Anderman, J. Turkish baths
Anderman, J. VICTO . . .
Anderman, J. White night
Anderman, J. World of worlds
Dabrowska, M. Miss Vincent
Mrożek, S. The elephant

POLAND—20th century—*Continued*

Mrożek, S. The parable of the miraculous escape

Mrożek, S. Spring in Poland

Nowakowski, M. 2072 days

Nowakowski, M. The canary

Nowakowski, M. The confidential call

Nowakowski, M. CPD

Nowakowski, M. The distributor

Nowakowski, M. The enemy

Nowakowski, M. The forest

Nowakowski, M. Gorgio

Nowakowski, M. Hatred

Nowakowski, M. The horn of plenty

Nowakowski, M. How time has flown

Nowakowski, M. Judas in the square

Nowakowski, M. The June cross

Nowakowski, M. Little sunshine

Nowakowski, M. Madam Amalia Bessarabo

Nowakowski, M. The mongrel

Nowakowski, M. A new life

Nowakowski, M. The night patrol

Nowakowski, M. On the bus

Nowakowski, M. The peacock

Nowakowski, M. The search

Nowakowski, M. The secret face

Nowakowski, M. The shadow

Nowakowski, M. A short street

Nowakowski, M. Silent night, holy night

Nowakowski, M. The silver bird

Nowakowski, M. The soldiers and the girl

Nowakowski, M. The spring walk

Nowakowski, M. Squad ready for action

Nowakowski, M. The state of war

Nowakowski, M. The steel-clawed glove

Nowakowski, M. The taxi driver's story

Nowakowski, M. The vetting session

Nowakowski, M. The washing machine

Nowakowski, M. Wastepaper

Nowakowski, M. The well-matched couple

Singer, I. B. The bond

Singer, I. B. The conference

Singer, I. B. Dazzled

Singer, I. B. The interview

Army—Officers

Nowakowski, M. The enemy

College life

See College life—Poland

Communism

See Communism—Poland

Rural life

Chasek, J. A ticket to America

Myśliwski, W. Stone upon stone

Roth, J. The bust of the emperor

Singer, I. B. The divorce

Singer, I. B. The litigants

Singer, I. B. Strong as death is love

World War, 1939-1945

See World War, 1939-1945—Poland

Lublin

Singer, I. B. A nest egg for paradise

Warsaw

Anderman, J. Day of mist and cloud

Anderman, J. Shabby lodgings

Clark, M. Still hope for God

Gilliatt, P. The hinge

Konwicki, T. A minor apocalypse [excerpt]

Oates, J. C. My Warszawa: 1980

Singer, I. B. The bitter truth

Singer, I. B. Loshikl

Poland still? Anderman, J.

The **polar** bears. Sandel, C.

POLAR REGIONS *See* Antarctic regions; Arctic regions

Poldi. McCullers, C.

POLES

Australia

Skrzynecki, P. The black madonna

Skrzynecki, P. The Superman t-shirt

Skrzynecki, P. The white eagle

Brazil

Tuohy, F. A survivor in Salvador

Egypt

Rizkalla, J. A poet in the classroom

England

Amis, M. Bujak and the strong force; or, God's dice

Tuohy, F. The trap

Warner, S. T. The mother tongue

United States

Bukoski, A. The children of strangers

Dybek, S. Chopin in winter

Gordon, M. Temporary shelter

Granit, A. They're killing Jews on Sackman Street!

Komie, L. B. Professor Strauss's gift

Kornblatt, J. R. Flo

Meinke, P. Uncle George and Uncle Stefan

O'Connor, F. The displaced person

Singer, I. B. The smuggler

Stark, S. S. Janka Doodle

Thorman, C. Anchovy trees

POLICE

Andreyev, L. At the station

Ashwood-Collins, A. Film at eleven

Bonosky, P. Charity ward

Eliade, M. The cape

Everett, P. L. Esteban

Harris, H. Detective's wife

Hensley, J. L. All that mattered

Herbert, F. Rat race

Izgü, M. Apollo's thing

Kiely, B. Secondary top

Lutz, J. All business

MacDonald, J. D. Squealer

Mayers, C. Police calls

Post, J. No handicap

Powell, T. I had a hunch, and . . .

Thompson, K. Longing

Wright, R. The man who lived underground

Arkansas

Jones, D. C. The Law

California

See also Police—Los Angeles (Calif.)

Working, R. On freedom

POLICE—*Continued*

Canada

Clarke, A. C. Doing right

Kinsella, W. P. Marco in paradise

Kinsella, W. P. The practical education of Constable B. B. Bobowski

England

See also Police—London (England)

Ambler, E. Case of the gentlemen poet

Georgia

Caldwell, E. Candy-Man Beechum

Hollywood (Calif.)

See Police—Los Angeles (Calif.)

Ireland

Shannon, D. Conundrum

London (England)

Fowles, J. The enigma

Gilbert, M. Counterplot

Gilbert, M. Rough justice

Gilbert, M. The unstoppable man

Hornung, E. W. The raffles relics

King, S. Crouch end

Mortimer, J. C. Rumpole and the rotten apple

Sproat, R. Mistaken identify

Los Angeles (Calif.)

Ellroy, J. The black dahlia [excerpt]

Nebraska

Fischer, C. E. Indian poker

New York (N.Y.)

Asimov, I. The thirteenth day of Christmas

Boswell, R. The darkness of love

Henry, O. After twenty years

Henry, O. The clarion call

Henry, O. The cop and the anthem

Katz, S. Death of the band

Longyear, B. B. The initiation

MacLean, K. The missing man

McBain, E. Nightshade

McBain, E. Sadie when she died

Walsh, T. Girl in danger

Westlake, D. E. After I'm gone

Westlake, D. E. The best-friend murder

Westlake, D. E. Come back, come back

Westlake, D. E. The death of a bum

Westlake, D. E. The feel of the trigger

Westlake, D. E. The sound of murder

Woolrich, C. Red liberty

Oklahoma

Conley, R. J. Badger

Poland

Anderman, J. Empty . . . sort of

Saint Louis (Mo.)

Woolrich, C. The showboat murders

San Diego (Calif.)

McClure, J. Remember that joke, Harry?

Nolan, W. F. Saturday's shadow

Singapore

MacLean, A. MacHinery and the cauliflowers

South Africa

Havemann, E. An interview

United States

Ellin, S. Unacceptable procedures

Farr, D. Sam's conscience

Finney, J. The face in the photo

Fisher, R. Guardian of the law

Kipp, G. G. Farewell gesture

Lang, A. Sweet smell of murder

Rathjen, C. H. A debt to Doc

Twain, M. The stolen white elephant

Working, R. Shooting

Police calls. Mayers, C.

Police dreams. Bausch, R.

Police report. Salas, G.

Polidori, John William, 1795-1821

The vampyre

Vampires; ed. by A. Ryan

Polikushka. Silone, I.

Polish luggage. Hemley, R.

POLISH REFUGEES *See* Refugees, Polish

POLISH SOLDIERS *See* Soldiers—Poland

The **Polish** village. Haley, R.

POLITICAL CAMPAIGNS *See* Politics

POLITICAL CORRUPTION *See* Corruption (in politics)

POLITICAL CRIMES AND OFFENSES

See also Assassination; Political prisoners; Terrorism

Pil'nīāk, B. The tale of the unextinguished moon

POLITICAL DEFECTORS *See* Defectors

The **political** education of Clarissa Forbes. Naipaul, S.

POLITICAL ETHICS

See also Power (Social sciences)

POLITICAL INTRIGUE *See* International intrigue; Politics

Political machine. Jakes, J.

POLITICAL PRISONERS

Aćin-Kosta, M. The rape

Anderman, J. Bitter red star

Anderman, J. Breathless

Anderman, J. Czarnoleka: Black Meadow

Anderman, J. No sound of footsteps in the treetops

Anderman, J. Prison sickness

Chappell, F. The snow that is nothing in the triangle

Gordimer, N. A correspondence course

Lin Jinlan. The transcript

Ruta, S. An imaginary line

Valenzuela, L. Fourth version

POLITICIANS *See* Politics

POLITICS

See also Suffrage; Utopias; Women in politics

Ambler, E. The blood bargain

Bova, B. A small kindness

Bryant, E. Teeth marks

García Márquez, G. Death constant beyond love

Gee, M. Right-hand man

Gilliatt, P. The hinge

Guin, W. The delegate from Guapanga

POLITICS—*Continued*
Heinlein, R. A. Beyond doubt
Jakes, J. Political machine
Lewis, S. A letter from the Queen
Monreal, D. N. A matter of dignity
Neville, K. The price of Simeryl
Rosenfeld, I. The party
Singer, I. B. Sabbath in Gehenna
Still, J. Pattern of a man
Tamer, Z. Nothing
Tamer, Z. A summary of what happened to Mohammed al-Mahmoudi
Weinbaum, S. G. Shifting seas
Williams, O. The angel's gift
Africa
Gordimer, N. At the rendezvous of victory
Australia
Clark, M. A democrat on the Ganges
Clark, M. Monologue by a man in black
Canada
St. Pierre, P. H. How to run the country
Central America
Ferguson, W. The teacher
China
Paley, G. The expensive moment
Shen Rong. Troubled Sunday
England
Bailey, H. The fall of Frenchy Steiner
Fowles, J. The enigma
Lejeune, A. Something on everyone
Maugham, W. S. Lord Mountdrago
Tuohy, F. Dreams of unfair women
Wells, H. G. Wayde's essence
Florida
Garrett, G. P. King of the mountain
France
Maupassant, G. de. Countess Satan
Maupassant, G. de. A lively friend
Germany
Grass, G. The left-handers
Guatemala
Ruta, S. The bus
Haiti
Gold, H. A Haitian gentleman
India
Chipulina, E. G. Your obedient servant
Kentucky
Stuart, J. Governor Warburton's right-hand man
Stuart, J. Road number one
Stuart, J. Thirty-two votes before breakfast
Korea
Kim, Y. I. The first election
New York (N.Y.)
Weidman, J. Good man, bad man
Philippines
José, F. S. Friendship
South Africa
Essop, A. The betrayal
Essop, A. Ten years
Goldswain, R. Dube's first day
Ndebele, N. Fools

South America
Ruta, S. In Fiona's country
Tennessee
Taylor, R. The Tennessee war of the roses
Trinidad and Tobago
Naipaul, S. The political education of Clarissa Forbes
Turkey
Nesin, A. Socialism is coming—stand aside!
United States
Apple, M. Small island republics
Boyle, T. C. The New Moon Party
Farmer, P. J. The oogenesis of Bird City
Garrett, R. Hail to the chief
Hall, T. T. Backbone of the nation
Hoch, E. D. Day for a picnic
Malzberg, B. N. On the campaign trail
Moore, W. Frank Merriwell in the White House
Wilner, H. Recovery room
West Indies
Bissoondath, N. Digging up the mountains
Yugoslavia
Aćin-Kosta, M. Boulevard of the revolution

Politics between us. Tunstall, T.
Polity and custom of the Camiroi. Lafferty, R. A.
Polizzi, Catherine
A part of him revealed
McCall's 145:150-2 Mr '87
Pollack, Eileen
The vanity of small differences
The New generation; ed. by A. Kaufman
Prairie Schooner 61:43-55 Summ '87
Xylem and phloem
The Literary Review (Madison, N.J.) 29:321-32 Spr '86
Pollack, Rachel
Angel baby
Interzone: the first anthology; ed. by J. Clute; C. Greenland and D. Pringle
Black Rose and White Rose
Kindred spirits; ed. by J. M. Elliot
The protector
Interzone: the 2nd anthology; ed. by J. Clute; D. Pringle and S. Ounsley
Pollard, Jean Ann, 1934-
Old woman
Haunted New England; ed. by C. G. Waugh; M. H. Greenberg and F. D. McSherry
Pollitt, Katha
Sonata for two pianos
Ms. 15:64-6+ My '87
Pollock and the Porroh man. Wells, H. G.
Pollyanna. Rossi, A.
Polo's trip. Harris, M.
Poltergeist. Hartman, W. S.
Polydamas on the Plain. Parotti, P.

POLYGAMY
See also Mormons and Mormonism
POLYNESIA
See also Rarotonga Island (Cook Islands); Samoan Islands
Gores, J. Pahua
POLYNESIANS
See also Maoris
Polyphemus. Shea, M.
Polyphemus. Wolfe, T.
Pomegranate seed. Wharton, E.
Pomerance, Murray
Belles excentriques
The Kenyon Review ns10:110-20 Fall '88
Sicilian vespers
The Kenyon Review ns10:100-9 Fall '88
Pomfret. Bovey, J.
Ponce, Mary Helen
Los tisicos
Southwest tales; ed. by Alurista and X. Rojas-Urista
PONDS
Crabtree, L. V. The Jake Pond
Poniatowska, Elena
A little fairy tale
The Massachusetts Review 27:467-71 Fall/Wint '86
The night visitor
Other fires; ed. by A. Manguel
The ponoes. Meinke, P.
Ponsoldt, Susan
The dyer's art
The Southern Review (Baton Rouge, La.) 24:169-81 Wint '88
Jairus' daughter
The Georgia Review 38:607-17 Fall '84
Pontoon boat. Keillor, G.
Pontoppidan, Henrik, 1857-1943
Eagle's flight
The Nobel reader; ed. by J. Eisen and S. Troy
The pooka. Tremayne, P.
The pool. Holt, J. D.
The pool. Hoyt, M. S.
The pool. Strieber, W.
Pool Night. Hempel, A.
The pool of life. Ignatow, R. G.
The pool of the stone god. Merritt, A.
The pool sharks. Curtiss, U. R.
Poole, Fiona Farrell
Airmen
Women's work; ed. by M. McLeod and L. Wevers
POOR See Poverty
The poor. Tem, S. R.
Poor Andrew. Maupassant, G. de
The poor are always with us. Wolff, T.
Poor Emma. Hill, R.
A poor girl. Maupassant, G. de
Poor Joey. Bonosky, P.
Poor little Saturday. L'Engle, M.
Poor little warrior! Aldiss, B. W.
Poor man's pennies. Algren, N.

Poor man's pudding. Melville, H.
Poor poor dumb mouths. Ch'en, Y.-C.
Popcorn. Nonhebel, C.
The Pope of the chimps. Silverberg, R.
The Pope skis faster than that! Greenberg, J.
POPES
Silverberg, R. Good news from the Vatican
Popinjay's African notes. Bumpus, J.
The poplars. Desnoues, L.
Poplars. MacDonald, D. R.
Popov, Evgeny
Three tales
The Barsukov Triangle, The two-toned blond & other stories; ed. by C. R. Proffer & E. Proffer
Popov. Lurie, M.
Poppa. Kratz, E.
Popper's disease. Johnson, C. R.
Popsy. King, S.
Popular mechanics. Carver, R.
POPULAR MUSIC
Bender, H. La Paloma; or, The food of love
Pak, Y.-S. Eroica Symphony
Wegner, H. Butcher's beguine
POPULAR SONGS See Popular music
POPULATION
Anderson, P. Welcome
Asimov, I. The winnowing
Gerrold, D. How we saved the human race
Sheckley, R. The people trap
PORCELAIN
Spark, M. Miss Pinkerton's apocalypse
The porch of Paradise. Halligan, M.
Porcupines and other travesties. Listfield, E.
Porcupines at the university. Barthelme, D.
Pore Perrie. Goyen, W.
Poretz, Doraine
Birthing
Erotic interludes; ed. by L. Barbach
Porges, Arthur
$1.98
100 great fantasy short short stories; ed. by I. Asimov; T. Carr and M. H. Greenberg
Dead drunk
Alfred Hitchcock's Grave suspicions
A pornographer woos. MacLaverty, B.
PORNOGRAPHY
Bloch, R. Crook of the month
Burt, S. Floral Street
Endō, S. Mothers
Greene, G. The blue film
Lem, S. Cezary Strzybisz, Necrobes
Loukakis, A. Single lens reflex
MacLaverty, B. A pornographer woos
Newman, K. Dreamers
Taylor, D. J. Dreams of leaving
Walker, A. Coming apart
Porphyria's lover. Sams, F.

The **port**. Maupassant, G. de

Port after port, the same baggage. Hospital, J. T.

PORT-AU-PRINCE (HAITI) *See* Haiti—Port-au-Prince

The **Port** Commandant. Grin, A.

PORT OF SPAIN (TRINIDAD AND TOBAGO) *See* Trinidad and Tobago—Port of Spain

Portable cities. Austin, D.

The **portal** in the picture. Kuttner, H.

Porte Cochere. Taylor, P. H.

Porter, Connie
Hoodoo
The Southern Review (Baton Rouge, La.) 24:396-400 Spr '88

Porter, Hal
At Aunt Sophia's
The Australian short story; ed. by L. Hergenhan
A double because it's snowing
The Australian short story; ed. by L. Hergenhan

Porter, Joe Ashby
Duckwalking
Harper's 269:28-30 D '84
The Pushcart prize IX
Retrieval
Raritan 7:70-85 Spr '88

Porter, Katherine Anne, 1890-1980
He
The World of the short story; ed. by C. Fadiman
Holiday
Stories of the modern South; ed. by B. Forkner and P. Samway
The jilting of Granny Weatherall
Look who's talking; ed. by B. Weber
A Modern Southern reader; ed. by B. Forkner and P. Samway
Theft
The Norton book of American short stories

Porter, William Sydney *See* Henry, O., 1862-1910

The **porter**. Hemingway, E.

Porterfield, Nolan
1,000 unknown facts about country music
The North American Review 271:12-17 Mr '86
The migration of the bag ladies
Missouri short fiction; ed. by C. Beasley

Portfolio. Copeland, A.

Portnoy, Marsha
Loving strangers
Family: stories from the interior; ed. by G. G. Chavis
Sunday with someone new
McCall's 112:94-5+ F '85

The **Portobello** Road. Spark, M.

PORTOFINO (ITALY) *See* Italy—Portofino

The **Porton** Potion. Neff, O.

The **portrait**. Austin, M. H.

The **portrait**. Colette

The **portrait**. Gogol', N. V.

Portrait of a freethinker. Clark, M.

Portrait of a girl in glass. Williams, T.

Portrait of a literary critic. Wolfe, T.

Portrait of a shaman. Kim, T.

Portrait of a woman. Subramanian, U.

The **portrait** of Baron Negay. Longyear, B. B.

Portrait of Duck. Skelton, R.

Portrait of electricity. Bail, M.

A **portrait** of Elmer. Faulkner, W.

Portrait of Isa Mulvenny. Gallacher, T.

Portrait of the artist by another. Auchincloss, L.

PORTRAITS
Colette. The portrait
Gogol', N. V. The portrait
Leach, A. R. A captain out of Etruria
Martin, G. R. R. Portraits of his children
Poe, E. A. Life in death
Poe, E. A. The oval portrait
Portraits. Woolf, V.

Portraits of his children. Martin, G. R. R.

PORTUGAL
20th century
Adams, A. Sintra
Nunes, N. Clastomina
Lisbon
Chipulina, E. G. The catalyst
Doyle, Sir A. C. The confession
Oates, J. C. Further confessions

PORTUGUESE
Canada
Kinsella, W. P. Electrico utensilio
Mozambique
Tabucchi, A. Theatre

The **position** of the planets. Gilliatt, P.

A **position** of trying. Kilberg, G.

POSSESSION, DEMONIAC *See* Demoniac possession

Possible to rue. Anthony, P.

Possum triptych. Wing, B.

Post, Judith
No handicap
The Womansleuth anthology; ed. by I. Zahava

Post, Melville Davisson, 1869-1930
The forgotten witness
Ellery Queen's Memorable characters
The sheriff of Gullmore
Isaac Asimov presents the best crime stories of the 19th century

Post, Melville Davisson, 1869-1930, and Suter, John F.
The tree in the forest
Ellery Queen's Prime crimes 2

Post cards. Cullen, E. J.

Post coitus tristus. Eisenstein, S.

The **post-graduate** thesis. Fremlin, C.

Post-modernism. Apple, M.

Post office. Keillor, G.

The **post** office octopus. Kinsella, W. P.

POSTAGE STAMPS
Asimov, I. The stamp
Brittain, W. The boy who read Agatha
  Christie
Davie, E. The stamp
Wolfe, T. The lost boy
POSTAL CARDS
Garner, H. Postcards from surfers
Woodman, A. Foreign postcard
POSTAL SERVICE
Carver, R. What do you do in San
  Francisco?
DeFord, M. A. Not snow nor rain
Johnson, C. R. China
Kinsella, W. P. The post office octopus
Matthews, J. Tableau with three ghostly
  women
Maupassant, G. de. A mistake
Painter, P. Patterns
Shukshin, V. M. Makar Zherebtsov
Sillitoe, A. The fishing-boat picture
Steele, M. What to do till the postman
  comes
Welty, E. Why I live at the P.O.
Zeiss, T. R. At the post office
The **postcard**. Böll, H.
The **postcard**. Winters, J.
Postcard found in a trunk. Kotzwinkle, W.
Postcard from Lahaina. Heller, S.
Postcards from surfers. Garner, H.
The **poster**. Silva, B.
POSTERS
Hoch, E. D. The theft of the circus poster
The **posthumous** fiance. Apollinaire, G.
A **posthumous** gift. Clarke, T.
Postscript. Dadswell, M.
The **postscript**. Shukshin, V. M.
The **pot** of gold. Cheever, J.
The **pot** of tulips. O'Brien, F.-J.
Potato. Kim, T.
POTATO FAMINES See Famines
Potential. Asimov, I.
Potions. Dodd, S. M.
The **potlatch** of Esmeralda. Tuohy, F.
Potter, Nancy A. J.
The bigamist
  Potter, N. A. J. Legacies
Calendar Day
  Potter, N. A. J. Legacies
The guests
  Potter, N. A. J. Legacies
Gypsies
  Potter, N. A. J. Legacies
Legacies
  Potter, N. A. J. Legacies
Light timber
  Potter, N. A. J. Legacies
Pen pals
  Potter, N. A. J. Legacies
A private space
  Potter, N. A. J. Legacies
Safe home
  Potter, N. A. J. Legacies

A short vacation
  Potter, N. A. J. Legacies
Talking to trees
  Potter, N. A. J. Legacies
A thin place
  Potter, N. A. J. Legacies
Viewing the remains
  Potter, N. A. J. Legacies
The woman who would not stay home
  Potter, N. A. J. Legacies
Potter, Robert
The red sickness
  Australian science fiction; ed. by V. Ikin
POTTERS AND POTTERY
Atwood, M. Loulou; or, The domestic life
  of the language
Hoyt, M. S. Clay songs
Lessing, D. M. Two potters
O'Connor, P. F. Gerald's song
Potter's field. Boylan, J.
POTTERY
Van de Wetering, J. The new disciple
Pou. Taylor, A.
POULTRY
  See also Guinea fowl
Colette. The fox
Davidson, A. Full chicken richness
Williams, A. Being a murderer myself
Pound, Ezra, 1885-1972
In the water-butt
  The Paris Review 28:303-8 Summ/Fall
  '86
Pouvillon, Emile
Duck shooting
  Classic European short stories; ed. by R.
  Beum
Pouvoir, J. L.
The death triple
  Tales from Ellery Queen's Mystery
  Magazine: short stories for young
  adults
Poverman, C. E., 1944-
Beautiful
  The Pushcart prize XII
POVERTY
Ade, G. The judge's son
Al-Qa'id, Y. Three meaningless tales
Aldiss, B. W. Igur and the mountain
Bell, M. S. The naked lady
Blaise, C. South
Blinkin, M. In a dream
Boehm, L. Two-bit piece
Böll, H. Business is business
Böll, H. A case for Kop
Böll, H. I'm not a Communist
Böll, H. In Friedenstadt
Böll, H. On the hook
Bonner, M. Black fronts
Bonner, M. Tin can
Bonner, M. The whipping
Brennan, J. P. Mrs. Clendon's place
Caldwell, E. Daughter
Caldwell, E. Kneel to the rising sun

POVERTY—*Continued*

Calisher, H. Survival techniques
Calvino, I. Desire in November
Calvino, I. Sleeping like dogs
Chappell, F. Children of strikers
Chukri, M. Flower Crazy
Cooper, J. C. Feeling for life
Cooper, J. C. Red-winged blackbirds
Cooper, J. C. Sisters of the rain
Coskran, K. The high price of everything
Crane, S. An experiment in misery
Crane, S. The men in the storm
Crowley, A. The old man of the peepul-tree
Davidson, A. Naples
Davis, R. H. An ignoble martyr
Dazai, O. A golden picture
Dumas, H. A boll of roses
Faik, S. A certain kind of people
Faik, S. I kept grumbling
Ferreira, R. Dream with no name
Ferreira, R. The gravedigger
Ferron, J. The bridge
Freeman, M. E. W. Louisa
Gaines, E. J. The sky is gray
Galsworthy, J. The broken boot
Goldsmith, O. A curious inconsistency of the Man in Black
González, C. A. Toño
Gorky, M. Creatures that once were men
Gorky, M. Evil-doers
Gorky, M. Lullaby
Gorky, M. One autumn evening
Gotthelf, J. The broommaker of Rychiswyl
Gotthelf, J. Elsi the unusual farm maid
Granit, A. Fire is burning on our street!
Granit, A. Free the canaries from their cages!
Grenon, J. A new dress for Maggie
Hagy, A. C. Mister Makes
Hauptman, W. Moon walking
Henry, O. The third ingredient
Highsmith, P. A clock ticks at Christmas
Humphrey, W. A job of the plains
Kelen, S. The intruders
Kim, T. Potato
Kim, W.-I. The spirit of the darkness
La Puma, S. The mouthpiece
Lai, H. The steelyard
Latimer, M. Gisela
Lavin, J. By any other name
Lavin, M. The face of hate
Lee, A. Waiting for her train
Lessing, D. M. An old woman and her cat
Liang, L. K. The pei-pa
Matthew, J. R. Amy Rose, 1947
Matthew, J. R. The life and death of Martha
Melville, H. Poor man's pudding
Melville, H. Rich man's crumbs
Minakami, T. Mulberry child

Mohr, N. A Thanksgiving celebration (Amy)
Moore, G. Parted
Narayan, R. K. Four rupees
Narayan, R. K. A horse and two goats
Porterfield, N. The migration of the bag ladies
Pu, S.-L. Yellow pride
Qiao Shi. Providing a meal
Ragab, M. A taste of success
Rasputin, V. G. French lessons
Rhys, J. Discourse of a lady standing a dinner to a down-and-out friend
Rhys, J. In the Rue de l'Arrivée
Ribeyro, J. R. Vultures without feathers
Robinson, K. S. Down and out in the year 2000
Rooke, L. The problem shop
Rooke, L. Winter is lovely, isn't summer hell
Sadhu, A. Ziprya
Seema, N. Helpless
Shacochis, B. Redemption songs
Silvis, R. One night with a girl by the Seine
Son, C.-S. Walking in the snow
St. Pierre, P. H. The owner of the gang
St. Pierre, P. H. Sarah's copper
Stewart, J. I. M. Sweets from a stranger
Swados, H. The balcony
Tamer, Z. Sun for the young
Tem, S. R. The poor
Trevor, W. The news from Ireland
Truss, J. The party
Tung, N. Fire
Turner, B. The shoes
Valenzuela, L. Blue water-man
Wang Zhecheng, and Wen Xiaoyu. Nest egg
Warner, S. T. A breaking wave
Watson, I. Salvage rites
Wegner, H. But America is far
Wetherell, W. D. If a woodchuck could chuck wood
Whitaker, M. Eve
Wojnarowicz, D. Self portrait in twenty-three rounds
Yun, H.-G. Group beating
Zhu Lin. Downpour on a leaky roof

Poverty. Parise, G.

Povod, Reinaldo

Things to do today
　Between C & D; ed. by J. Rose and C. Texier

Povolo, Gilda

Getting even
　'Teen 29:44+ Ag '85

Powell, James, 1932-

Death in the Christmas hour
　Sherlock Holmes through time and space

Powell, Padgett
Edisto [excerpt]
The New writers of the South; ed. by
C. East
Flood
Grand Street 7:29-31 Wint '88
Voice from the grave
Esquire 107:100-3 Ja '87
Powell, Talmage, 1920-
I had a hunch, and . . .
Alfred Hitchcock's Crimewatch
Motive for murder
The Wickedest show on earth; ed. by
M. Muller and B. Pronzini
Till death do not us part
Alfred Hitchcock's Grave suspicions
Power, Udana
The private life of Mrs. Herman
Erotic interludes; ed. by L. Barbach
Power, Victor
The bullfight
Power, V. The town of Ballymuck
An eye for an eye
Power, V. The town of Ballymuck
The imposition
Power, V. The town of Ballymuck
In the town of Ballymuck
Power, V. The town of Ballymuck
Lackendara
Power, V. The town of Ballymuck
The miracle of Glendyne
Short story international 70
Night
Short story international 62
No cigarettes, no matches, no lights al-
lowed
Power, V. The town of Ballymuck
The operation
Power, V. The town of Ballymuck
The ragged rascal ran
Power, V. The town of Ballymuck
The threshold
Power, V. The town of Ballymuck
POWER (SOCIAL SCIENCES)
Sturgeon, T. Microcosmic god
Zelazny, R. King Solomon's ring
Power and light. Hannah, B.
Power failure. Rule, J.
The **power** of darkness. Sālim, G.
The **power** of horses. Cook-Lynn, E.
The **power** of words. Poe, E. A.
POWER RESOURCES
Bernen, R. The windcharger
Power stories. Russell, R.
Power times one. Matuszewicz, J. M.
Powers, J. F. (James Farl), 1917-
The valiant woman
The Norton book of American short
stories
The warm sand
The Substance of things hoped for; ed.
by J. B. Breslin

Powers, James Farl *See* Powers, J. F. (James
Farl), 1917-
Powers, Patricia E.
In the Yucatán
The Kenyon Review ns9:40-51 Summ '87
The settlement
The Kenyon Review ns7:1-9 Spr '85
The visualizers
The Massachusetts Review 28:229-41
Summ '87
Powers, Richard, 1957-
The best place for it
The New Yorker 63:28-35 F 1 '88
Powers, Tim
Night moves
The Year's best science fiction, fourth
annual collection
Powers. Yamamoto, M.
Poyer, D. C.
Three soldiers
Robert Adams' Book of soldiers
The **practical** education of Constable B. B.
Bobowski. Kinsella, W. P.
A **practical** joke. Maupassant, G. de.
The **practical** joke. Shannon, D.
PRACTICAL JOKES
Bloch, R. Pranks
Boylan, J. The rescue
Brett, S. Tickled to death
Bukoski, A. This heat
Conroy, J. Freight car repair yard pranks
Gilbert, W. S. Tom Poulton's joke
Gilbert, W. S. Wide awake
Hartley, L. P. Three, or four, for dinner
Hartley, L. P. The travelling grave
Henry, O. The pint flask
Kawabata, Y. The hat incident
Kinsella, W. P. The practical education of
Constable B. B. Bobowski
Lardner, R. Haircut
Lopatin, J. Etiology of the new war
Maupassant, G. de. A practical joke
Maupassant, G. de. The question of Latin
Plunkett, J. The scoop
Prichard, K. S. The frogs of Quirra-Quirra
Pronzini, B. The dispatching of George
Ferris
Saki. The open window
Shannon, D. The practical joke
Watt, N. The mule driver and the carrot
Wodehouse, P. G. Something squishy
Wood, Mrs. H. The ghost
Practically engaged. Cameron, P.
Practising dying. Soldatow, S.
PRAGUE (CZECHOSLOVAKIA) *See* Czech-
oslovakia—Prague
PRAIRIE LIFE
Ross, S. The lamp at noon
Prairie sun. Bryant, E.
PRANKS *See* Practical jokes
Pranks. Bloch, R.

Prather, Richard S., 1921-
Dead giveaway
The Mammoth book of private eye stories; ed. by B. Pronzini and M. H. Greenberg
Pratt, Fletcher, 1897-1956
(jt. auth) See De Camp, L. Sprague (Lyon Sprague), 1907-, and Pratt, Fletcher, 1897-1956
Pray for China. Austin, D.
The **prayer**. Hartley, L. P.
The **prayer**. Ocampo, S.
Prayer and old jokes. Silvis, R.
Prayer for the dying. Johnson, W.
PRAYERS
al-Rahib, H. The ablution
Brender à Brandis, M. To grow into a man
Brown, M. W. Let him live
Chekhov, A. P. The requiem
Fante, J. Hail Mary
Hoffman, W. The question of rain
MacLaverty, B. The miraculous candidate
Mazel, D. Late prayers
Munro, A. Circle of prayer
Wells, H. G. Answer to prayer
Whittier, G. B. Lost time accident
Praying for a Fickleman. McKinley, J.
Prebehalla, Gladys, and Moran, Daniel Keys
Realtime
Tales from Isaac Asimov's science fiction magazine: short stories for young adults
Precious. Silva, B.
Precious door. Goyen, W.
A **precious** gift. Nudelman, J. C.
Precious memories. Schell, J.
A **precious** memory. Doig, D. T.
Precipice-encurled. Byatt, A. S.
PRECOGNITIONS *See* Premonitions
A **predicament**. See Poe, E. A. The scythe of time
PREDICTIONS *See* Prophecies
Prefigurations: Prato. Landolfi, T.
Preflash. Ford, J. M.
Pregame. Klinkowitz, J.
PREGNANCY
See also Abortion
Ardizzone, T. The evening news
Blinkin, M. Smoke
Boyle, T. C. Caviar
Bradley, M. Z. Centaurus changeling
Coleman, W. Ladies
Coleman, W. The screamer
Collins, L. The doctor's house
Cordor, S. M. In the hospital
Edwards, C. Prima vera
Fitzgerald, M. J. Communions
Gare, N. The child
Gilchrist, E. The Double Happiness Bun
Gilchrist, E. Drunk with love
Gilchrist, E. The starlight express
Hempel, A. Beg, sl tog, inc, cont, rep

Hulme, K. One whale, singing
Jahnn, H. H. Ragna and Nils
Jonker, I. The goat
Kaikō, T. The laughingstock
Klass, P. The almond torte equilibrium
Kleist, H. von. The Marquise of O—
Lacy, R. The natural father
Leedom-Ackerman, J. Death stalks a building once it enters
L'Heureux, J. The comedian
Lipman, E. After Emily
Lipman, E. They'll smile at you if you're with me
Miller, B. The lonesomes ain't no spring picnic
Moskowitz, F. Presents
Mukherjee, B. A father
Nielsen, M. O. The trout
Oates, J. C. Golden gloves
O'Connor, F. A stroke of good fortune
Painter, P. The sorting out
Pavese, C. The villa on the hill
Phillips, J. A. Bluegill
Pilcher, R. The white birds
Rifaat, A. An incident in the Ghobashi household
Rogers, T. N. R. Crater Lake
Russo, A. The target
Schwartz, J. This time, yesterday morning
Schwartz, L. S. Rough strife
Sexson, L. When the pie was opened
Spivack, K. Terms
Steele, M. Where she brushed her hair
Stevens, J. A. Families
Swift, G. The hypochondriac
Thurm, M. Floating
Trippett, F. Child Ellen [excerpt]
Van Zleer, D. Violet's choice
Whittier, G. Turning out
Wolff, T. Desert breakdown, 1968
Yamamoto, M. Father Goose
Zahn, T. The final report on the lifeline experiment
PREHISTORIC ANIMALS *See* Fossils
PREHISTORIC MAN *See* Man, Prehistoric; Prehistoric times
PREHISTORIC TIMES
Anderson, P. The little monster
Anderson, P. Wildcat
Drake, D. Time safari
Schwob, M. The death of Odjigh
Wells, H. G. The grisly folk
Wells, H. G. A story of the stone age
PREJUDICES
See also Antisemitism; Race relations
Abrahams, P. Lonesome
Baldwin, J. Going to meet the man
Bonosky, P. Charity ward
Brown, F. Keep out
Buck, P. S. The enemy
Burns, M. Suburbs of the Arctic Circle
Clark, M. A moment of illumination

PREJUDICES—*Continued*
Coleman, W. Eyes and teeth
Cook-Lynn, E. A good chance
Coskran, K. Handyman
Cox, E. Andax and Odi
DeGrazia, E. The cat-hater
Dubus, A. Deaths at sea
Dubus, A. Sorrowful mysteries
Dumas, H. Double nigger
Ferreira, R. Facade
Ferreira, R. A road somewhere
Fisher, R. Dust
Fisher, R. High yaller
Fisher, R. Ringtail
Grace, P. Going for the bread
Honwana, L. B. Papa, snake & I
Jacobson, D. A day in the country
Kelly, C. A season for heroes
Lee, H. Christmas
Martínez-Serros, H. Her
Martínez-Serros, H. Victor and David
Melville, H. The 'Gees
Mencken, S. H. Little white girl
O'Connor, F. The geranium
O'Connor, F. Revelation
O'Connor, F. The train
Pacheco, J. E. You wouldn't understand
Pilcher, R. Amita
Pynchon, T. The secret integration
Rahman, T. The legacy
Saiki, J. Windows
Sambrot, W. Black night, white night; or, The battle of Dingle on the Dangle
Sheckley, R. The native problem
Sproat, R. Stunning the punters
Toomer, J. Becky
Prelude. Mansfield, K.

PREMATURE BURIAL
Bierce, A. One summer night
Pacheco, J. E. The captive
Palma, C. Aboard the cart
Poe, E. A. Berenice
Poe, E. A. The fall of the House of Usher
Poe, E. A. The premature burial
Sullivan, T. The extension
Walters, A. L. The resurrection of John Stink
Zola, É. The death of Olivier Bécaille
The **premature** burial. Poe, E. A.
Le **premier** pas. Hornung, E. W.
Première arabesque. Sarah, R.

PREMONITIONS
Campbell, E. The forty and eight
Robinson, S. Fivesight
Schwob, M. Train 081
St. Clair, M. The listening child
Woods, S. Every tale condemns me
Preparation. McGraw, E.
Preparations. Bernard, K.
Preparations for the game. Tem, S. R.
Prescription for love. Lee, C.
The **presence** by the fire. Wells, H. G.

Presences. See Taylor, R. Glory
The **present**. Moskowitz, C.
A **present** for Christmas. MacLaverty, B.
Present for Minna. Stern, R. M.
Present tense. Briskin, M.
Presents. Eisenberg, D.
Presents. Moskowitz, F.
Preservation. Briskin, M.
The **preserved** woman. Millman, L.
Preserving fireweed for the White Pass and Yukon Railroad. Kinsella, W. P.
The **Preserving** Machine. Dick, P. K.
President Sahib's blue period. Qazi, J.
El **presidente** de Méjico. Algren, N.
PRESIDENTS
United States
Baumbach, J. From the life of the president
Dick, P. K. Novelty act
Dozois, G. R., and Haldeman, J. C. Executive clemency
Lewis, N. A weekend in Havana
Strand, M. The President's resignation
Wolfe, T. The four lost men
United States—Election
Asimov, I. Franchise
Eisenberg, L. The Chameleon
Garrett, R. Hail to the chief
Schmidt, S. May the best man win
Shaara, M. 2066: Election Day
The **President's** resignation. Strand, M.
PRESLEY, ELVIS, 1935-1977
About
Boylan, J. Elvis in space
Boyle, T. C. All shook up
Dozois, G. R., and others. Touring
Hauptman, W. Good rockin' tonight
Waldrop, H. Ike at the mike
Press conferences of Ambassador Sweeney. Windsor, G.
Press enter. Varley, J.
Preston, Marcia
A Christmas romance
'Teen 29:38-9+ D '85
Pretend dinners. Kinsella, W. P.
Pretend we're French. Freeman, J.
The **prettiest** dead girl in Detroit. Estleman, L. D.
Pretty birdie. Garrett, G. P.
Pretty boy crossover. Cadigan, P.
The **pretty** daughters. O'Hara, J.
A **pretty** fine life. Claiborne, S.
The **pretty** girl. Dubus, A.
Pretty pictures. Rooke, L.
Preus, Margi
A novel theory of extinction
Stiller's pond; ed. by J. Agee; R. Blakely and S. Welch
Preuss, Paul, 1942-
Small bodies
The Planets; ed. by B. Preiss
Preventing snow. Drury, T.
Preview of death. Woolrich, C.

Prewar quality. Clayton, J. J.
Pribus, Marilyn
  The calendar chest
    Tales from Ellery Queen's Mystery
      Magazine: short stories for young
      adults
Price, Anthony
  The Boudicca killing
    The Mammoth book of modern crime
      stories; ed. by G. Hardinge
  The Chinaman's garden
    John Creasey's Crime collection, 1984
Price, Reynolds, 1933-
  Michael Egerton
    Early sorrow: ten stories of youth; ed.
      by C. Zolotow
  The names and faces of heroes
    Shenandoah: an anthology; ed. by J.
      Boatwright
  Truth and lies
    Selected stories from The Southern
      review, 1965-1985
  Uncle Grant
    A Modern Southern reader; ed. by B.
      Forkner and P. Samway
  The Warrior Princess Ozimba
    Stories of the modern South; ed. by B.
      Forkner and P. Samway
The **price** of joy. Rendell, R.
The **price** of lightning. Carr, J.
The **price** of parting. Ware, L.
The **price** of Simeryl. Neville, K.
The **price** of the absolute. Hartley, L. P.
The **price** of the harness. Crane, S.
Price's always open. O'Hara, J.
Prices' bewitched cow. Crabtree, L. V.
Prichard, Katharine Susannah, 1884-1969
  Bad debts
    Prichard, K. S. Tribute
  The bride of Far-away
    Prichard, K. S. Tribute
  Communists are always young
    Prichard, K. S. Tribute
  The cooboo
    Prichard, K. S. Tribute
  The cow
    Prichard, K. S. Tribute
  The curse
    Prichard, K. S. Tribute
  Flight
    Prichard, K. S. Tribute
  The frogs of Quirra-Quirra
    Prichard, K. S. Tribute
  The galah
    Prichard, K. S. Tribute
  Genieve
    Prichard, K. S. Tribute
  The grey horse
    Prichard, K. S. Tribute
  Happiness
    The Australian short story; ed. by L.
      Hergenhan
    Prichard, K. S. Tribute

Hero of the mines
  Prichard, K. S. Tribute
Jimble
  Prichard, K. S. Tribute
Josephina Anna Maria
  Prichard, K. S. Tribute
Luck
  Prichard, K. S. Tribute
Naninja and Janey
  Prichard, K. S. Tribute
N'goola
  Prichard, K. S. Tribute
The old track
  Prichard, K. S. Tribute
Painted finches
  Prichard, K. S. Tribute
The rabbit trapper's wife
  Prichard, K. S. Tribute
The siren of Sandy Gap
  Prichard, K. S. Tribute
Yoirimba
  Prichard, K. S. Tribute
A young comrade
  Prichard, K. S. Tribute
Pride. Grant, C. L.
Pride and joy. Lurie, M.
PRIDE AND VANITY
  Botwinik, B. A shoemaker for a husband
  Colette. The little Bouilloux girl
  Curley, D. Billy Will's song
  Erdrich, L. Flesh and blood
  Fühmann, F. The isle of dreams
  Grey, Z. The wolf tracker
  Keillor, G. Lyle's roof
  Kilworth, G. The songbirds of pain
  Mazel, D. Choosing
  Oates, J. C. Blackmail
  O'Connor, F. A view of the woods
  Overholser, W. D. The hero
  Shelley, M. W. The transformation
  Spivack, K. Generations
  Sproat, R. The fascination of the vanity
Pride of lions. Thomson, G.
The **priest**. Auswaks, A.
The **priest** and Jenny Martin. Greeley, A. M.
Priest Effendi. Faik, S.
PRIESTESSES
  Vinge, J. D. Mother & child
Priestley, J. B. (John Boynton), 1894-1984
  The grey ones
    Black water; ed. by A. Manguel
Priestley, John Boynton See Priestley, J. B.
  (John Boynton), 1894-1984
PRIESTS See Catholic priests; Clergy; Cler-
  gy, Anglican and Episcopal
PRIESTS, BUDDHIST See Buddhist priests
PRIESTS, CATHOLIC See Catholic priests
The **priest's** housekeeper. McLaverty, M.
Prikli. Tournier, M.
Prima vera. Edwards, C.
Primary colours. Pascoe, B.
Primary education of the Camiroi. Lafferty,
  R. A.

Primavera. Dugan, M.
Primo doesn't take back bottles anymore. Lum, D. H. Y.
Prince, Harry
  Requiem for a busted flush [Variant title: Game plan]
    Murder California style; ed. by J. L. Breen and J. Ball
The **prince.** Nova, C.
Prince Amilec. Lee, T.
Prince Myshkin, and hold the relish. Ellison, H.
The **Prince** of Wales. Pesetsky, B.
The **prince** out of the past. Springer, N.
PRINCES
    See also Princesses
  Carr, J. The price of lightning
  Carter, A. The donkey prince
  Kotzwinkle, W. That winter when Prince Borisov was everybody's favorite
  Nova, C. The prince
  Springer, N. Bright-eyed black pony
Princess!. Watson, J.
The **princess** and her future. Lee, T.
The **princess** and the puma. Henry, O.
The **princess** and the zucchini. Thomas, A. C.
Princess Gilda talks to the unborn. Haas, B.
The **Princess** of Calistoga. Hedin, M.
Princess Ostrich. Hall, D.
The **princess,** the Boeing, and the hot pastrami sandwich. Smith, R.
The **princess** who stood on her own two feet. Desy, J.
PRINCESSES
  Alcott, L. M. Taming a Tartar
  Brown, G. M. A winter legend
  Desy, J. The princess who stood on her own two feet
  Hartley, L. P. Conrad and the dragon
  Paxson, D. L. Sky sister
  Shefner, E. Royal bones
  Thomas, A. C. The princess and the zucchini
  Wellman, M. W. The seeker in the fortress
  Wilde, O. The birthday of the Infanta
  Williams, J. Petronella
  Wrede, P. C. The improper princess
PRINCETON UNIVERSITY
  Bell, M. S. The structure and meaning of dormitory and food services
The **principles** of flotation. Pritchett, M.
Print dresses. Riskin, M.
PRINTERS AND PRINTING
  Conroy, J. The type louse
  Doyle, Sir A. C. The Parish Magazine
  Poe, E. A. 'X-ing a paragrab'
PRINTING *See* Printers and printing
Prints in the valley. Carter, R.
Prior, Allan, 1922-
  Be lucky
    John Creasey's Crime collection, 1987

The **prison.** Drake, M.
The **prison.** Petrakis, H. M.
The **prison-bound.** Bonner, M.
PRISON CAMPS *See* World War, 1939-1945—Prisoners and prisons
PRISON ESCAPES *See* Escapes
Prison sickness. Anderman, J.
A **prisoner.** Rey Rosa, R.
The **prisoner** of Chillon. Kelly, J. P.
The **prisoner** of gravity. MacIntyre, F. G.
PRISONERS, CONDEMNED
  Twain, M. From The "London Times" of 1904
PRISONERS, POLITICAL *See* Political prisoners
The **prisoners.** Harrington, E.
PRISONERS AND PRISONS
    See also Ex-convicts; Political prisoners; Prisoners of war
  Algren, N. Depend on Aunt Elly
  Bernard, K. Firm ground
  Böll, H. The cage
  Brown, F. Cain
  Canessa, G. Notes of a condottiere
  Chandler, A. B. The cage
  Crace, J. The world with one eye shut
  Daviú, M. Ofelia's transfiguration
  Dinesen, I. The cloak
  Farley, R. M. The living mist
  Ferreira, R. The hands of God
  Finney, E. J. Bed of roses
  Ford, R. Sweethearts
  Frazier, L., Jr. In the presence of mine enemies
  Gautreaux, T. Just turn like a gear
  Gorky, M. Karamora
  Gorky, M. Notch
  Hall, T. T. The eleven dollar story
  Harrington, J. A letter to Amy
  Hartley, L. P. Roman charity
  Henry, O. The dream
  Hershman, M. When a felon needs a friend
  Hill, R. Exit line
  Hospital, J. T. The inside story
  Ingalls, R. Theft
  Jaffe, H. Salamander
  Josipovici, G. A changeable report
  Kafka, F. The knock at the manor gate
  Kawabata, Y. Earth
  Longyear, B. B. The house of if
  Mailer, N. The killer
  McCormack, E. P. Inspecting the vaults
  Oates, J. C. Maximum security
  Pavese, C. Gaol birds
  Pavese, C. The intruder
  Poe, E. A. The pit and the pendulum
  Ramírez, S. The centerfielder
  Rhys, J. Let them call it jazz
  Sanders, S. R. Walking to sleep
  Sayles, J. The Halfway Diner
  Silva, B. Happy hour
  Silverberg, R. The pardoner's tale

PRISONERS AND PRISONS—*Continued*
Singer, I. B. Loshikl
White, C. A disciplined life
Wilder, C. Something coming through
    Africa
Gwala, M. Reflections in a cell
    Australia
Prichard, K. S. A young comrade
    Egypt
El-Bisatie, M. A conversation from the third floor
    England
Auswaks, A. The familiar
    France
Rhys, J. From a French prison
Rhys, J. The Sidi
    Japan
Endō, S. Fuda-no-Tsuji
    Korea
Yi, K.-S. The Unenlightened
    Mexico
Algren, N. El presidente de Méjico
    Mississippi
Harrington, E. The prisoners [excerpt]
    South Africa
Balfour, C. To the torturor
Havemann, E. Incident at Mhlaba Jail
Paton, A. Sunlight in Trebizond Street
    Soviet Union
Grin, A. The oranges
Shalamov, V. T. Condensed milk
Tolstoy, L., graf. God sees the truth but waits
    United States
Connell, R. Brother Orchid
De la Torre, A. Diamond eyes and pig tails
Garrett, G. P. Noise of strangers
Marlowe, D. J. The donor
Oates, J. C. How I contemplated the world from the Detroit House of Correction and began my life over again
Pintauro, J. Jungle dove
Pohl, F. The greening of Bed-Stuy
Rees, D. Gay cat burglar seeks same for long-lasting relationship
Ritchie, J. The $5,000 getaway
PRISONERS OF WAR
  See also Concentration camps; World War, 1939-1945—Prisoners and prisons
Boyle, K. Men
Chipulina, E. G. Hazards of war
Davin, D. Finders and losers
Davin, D. North of the Sangro
Davin, D. The Persian's grave
DiFranco, A. M. The garden of redemption
Dorr, L. The noise was heard afar off
Ellison, H. Basilisk
Fink, I. Inspector von Galoshinsky
Hwang, S. Cranes

MacLean, A. The Arandora Star
Price, A. The Chinaman's garden
Roth, J. Hotel Savoy
Whitaker, M. The mandoline
PRISONS *See* Prisoners and prisons
Pritchard, Melissa
La Bête: a figure study
 Pritchard, M. Spirit seizures
Companions
 Pritchard, M. Spirit seizures
A dance with Alison
 Pritchard, M. Spirit seizures
 The Southern Review (Baton Rouge, La.)
  23:874-8 Aut '87
Dead finish
 Pritchard, M. Spirit seizures
Disturbing no one
 Pritchard, M. Spirit seizures
A dying man
 Pritchard, M. Spirit seizures
The housekeeper
 Pritchard, M. Spirit seizures
In foreign country
 Pritchard, M. Spirit seizures
A man around the house
 Pritchard, M. Spirit seizures
Photograph of Luisa
 Pritchard, M. Spirit seizures
A private landscape
 Pritchard, M. Spirit seizures
Prize stories, 1984
Ramon: souvenirs
 Pritchard, M. Spirit seizures
Rocking on water, floating in glass
 Pritchard, M. Spirit seizures
Shed of grace
 Pritchard, M. Spirit seizures
Spirit seizures
 Pritchard, M. Spirit seizures
Taking hold of Renee
 Pritchard, M. Spirit seizures
With wings cross water
 Pritchard, M. Spirit seizures
Pritchard, Selwyn
Top of the class
 Critical Quarterly 30:73-86 Summ '88
Pritchard, Stanford
Player in the symphony
 New England Review and Bread Loaf Quarterly 10:337-50 Spr '88
Pritchett, Michael, 1961-
The barrel racer
 Pritchett, M. The Venus tree
Close water
 Pritchett, M. The Venus tree
Fashion in the Third World
 Pritchett, M. The Venus tree
Flying lessons
 Pritchett, M. The Venus tree
Open twenty-four hours
 Pritchett, M. The Venus tree
Peach seed
 Pritchett, M. The Venus tree

Pritchett, Michael, 1961-—*Continued*
People
  Pritchett, M. The Venus tree
The principles of flotation
  Pritchett, M. The Venus tree
Trinity
  Pritchett, M. The Venus tree
The Venus tree
  Pritchett, M. The Venus tree
Pritchett, V. S. (Victor Sawdon), 1900-
The Camberwell beauty
  The World of the short story; ed. by C. Fadiman
Cocky olly
  The New Yorker 64:20-32+ Ag 1 '88
A family man
  The Penguin book of modern British short stories
The saint
  The Art of the tale; ed. by D. Halpern
The Spanish bed
  Short story international 47
The spree
  The Treasury of English short stories; ed. by N. Sullivan
A story of Don Juan
  The Oxford book of English ghost stories
Tea with Mrs. Bittell
  Full measure; ed. by D. Sennett
Pritchett, Victor Sawdon *See* Pritchett, V. S. (Victor Sawdon), 1900-
Privacy. Hall, M. L.
The **privacy** of storm. Schaap, J. C.
Private areas. Brett, S.
Private debts/public holdings. Haruf, K.
PRIVATE DETECTIVES *See* Detectives, Private
Private Eye Oglesby. Gardner, M.
A **private** ghost. Cary, J.
The **private** history of a campaign that failed. Twain, M.
Private investigations. Hoyt, R.
A **private** landscape. Pritchard, M.
Private lesson. Cameron, L.
Private lies. Lippman, A.
The **private** life. James, H.
The **private** life of Mrs. Herman. Power, U.
Private matters. Stead, C.
Private property. Silko, L.
PRIVATE SCHOOLS *See* School life
A **private** space. Potter, N. A. J.
Private tuition by Mr Bose. Desai, A.
Private views. Raphael, F.
The **privileged** class. Aćin-Kosta, M.
Prize in spite of. Landolfi, T.
The **prize** of peril. Sheckley, R.
PRIZES *See* Rewards (Prizes, etc.)
Prizes. Frame, J.
PROBABILITIES
  Asimov, I. Spell my name with an S
  Gardner, M. Left or right?

Probability pipeline. Rucker, R. von B., and Laidlaw, M.
Probably Shakespeare. West, J.
The **problem.** Gray, A.
Problem at sea. Christie, A.
PROBLEM CHILDREN *See* Emotionally disturbed children
The **problem** of Li T'ang. Bush, J.
A **problem** of numbers. Asimov, I.
The **problem** of the Boston Common. Hoch, E. D.
The **problem** of the county fair. Hoch, E. D.
The **problem** of the covered bridge. Hoch, E. D.
The **problem** of the fatal fireworks. Hoch, E. D.
The **problem** of the preface. Lish, G.
The **problem** of the sore bridge—among others. Farmer, P. J.
The **problem** shop. Rooke, L.
Problematical species. Barthelme, S.
The **procession.** Chipulina, E. G.
The **procession.** Upward, E.
PROCESSIONS
  Mrożek, S. It's a pity
PROCURERS *See* Pimps
The **prodigal** daughter. Salmonson, J. A.
The **prodigal** parent. Gallant, M.
Prodigies. Falco, E.
The **products** of conception. Ferguson, P.
PROFANITY *See* Swearing
Profession. Asimov, I.
The **profession.** Hensley, J. L.
A **professional** man. Norris, L.
Professor and colonel. Berman, R.
Professor Strauss's gift. Komie, L. B.
PROFESSORS *See* Teachers
The **professor's** teddy bear. Sturgeon, T.
Profitable business. Maupassant, G. de
Profumo, David
  The blind man eats many flies
    Foreign exchange; ed. by J. Evans
Progenitor. Curval, P.
Prognosis. Spielberg, P.
A **program** for writers. Schwartz, S.
PROGRAMMING (COMPUTERS)
  Asimov, I. True love
Progress. José, F. S.
The **progress** of love. Munro, A.
The **progress** of the military patrol car. Tang Dong
The **prohibited** word. Buzzati, D.
Proletarian Zen. Levy, D.
A **prologue** to America. Wolfe, T.
Prologue to an adventure. Thomas, D.
Promenade. Asscher-Pinkhof, C.
Prometheus. Gray, A.
Prometheus's ghost. Williamson, C.
PROMISCUITY
  Brand, C. The whispering
  Caldwell, E. Picking cotton

PROMISCUITY—*Continued*
Colegate, I. The girl who had lived among artists
Cooper, J. C. Sins leave scars
Dubus, A. Graduation
Flanagan, M. Simple pleasures
Gilchrist, E. The Double Happiness Bun
Meriwether, L. A happening in Barbados
Miller, S. Inventing the Abbotts
Miller, S. The lover of women
Percy, W. The promiscuous self
Phillips, J. A. Lechery
Tremain, R. Words with Marigold
Williams, T. Miss Coynte of Greene
Promiscuity. Milton, B.
The **promiscuous** self. Percy, W.
The **promise**. Wilhelm, K.
A **promise** is a promise. Luftig, R.
The **promise** of America. Wolfe, T.
Promise of rain. Taylor, P. H.
The **promise** of the fruit. Ahlswede, A.
Promise of tomorrow. Pilcher, R.
A **promise** we shall wake in the pink city after harvest. Begamudré, V.
The **promised** land. Fisher, R.
Promised land Newfoundland. Avery, M.
The **promised** village. Federspiel, J.
PROMISES
Austin, M. H. Mahala Joe
Goethe, J. W. von. The attorney
Promises. Thompson, K.
Promises, promises. Bradbury, R.
Promises to keep. McDevitt, J.
Promising signs. Garber, L. J.
Prone. Reynolds, M.
Pronzini, Bill
Ace in the hole
Mean streets; ed. by R. J. Randisi
The Year's best mystery and suspense stories, 1987
All the long years
Westeryear; ed. by E. Gorman
Bank job
Ellery Queen's Crimes and punishments
Uncollected crimes; ed. by B. Pronzini and M. H. Greenberg
Black wind
Pronzini, B. Graveyard plots
Pronzini, B. Small felonies
Buttermilk
Pronzini, B. Small felonies
Cache and carry
Pronzini, B. Small felonies
Cain's mark
Pronzini, B. Graveyard plots
A case for quiet
Pronzini, B. Small felonies
Cat's-paw
Masterpieces of mystery and suspense; ed. by M. H. Greenberg
Pronzini, B. Graveyard plots
The Year's best mystery and suspense stories, 1984

Caught in the act
Pronzini, B. Graveyard plots
Changes
Pronzini, B. Graveyard plots
Pronzini, B. Small felonies
The clincher
Pronzini, B. Small felonies
A cold foggy day
The Black Lizard anthology of crime fiction; ed. by E. Gorman
Pronzini, B. Small felonies
Connoisseur
Through a glass, darkly; ed. by B. Woelfel
A craving for originality
Chapter & hearse; ed. by M. Muller and B. Pronzini
Manhattan mysteries; ed. by B. Pronzini; C. L. R. Waugh and M. H. Greenberg
Pronzini, B. Graveyard plots
Dear poisoner
Pronzini, B. Small felonies
Deathwatch
Pronzini, B. Small felonies
Defect
Pronzini, B. Small felonies
A dip in the Poole
Pronzini, B. Small felonies
The dispatching of George Ferris
Pronzini, B. Small felonies
Don't spend it all in one place
Pronzini, B. Small felonies
The facsimile shop
Pronzini, B. Small felonies
For love
Pronzini, B. Small felonies
The hanging man
Pronzini, B. Graveyard plots
Here lies another blackmailer
Child's ploy; ed. by M. Muller and B. Pronzini
Pronzini, B. Small felonies
Hero
Pronzini, B. Small felonies
His name was Legion
Pronzini, B. Graveyard plots
Pronzini, B. Small felonies
House call
Pronzini, B. Small felonies
I don't understand it
Pronzini, B. Graveyard plots
The imperfect crime
Pronzini, B. Small felonies
Incident in a neighborhood tavern
An Eye for justice; ed. by R. J. Randisi
Pronzini, B. Small felonies
The killing
Pronzini, B. Small felonies
Little lamb
Pronzini, B. Small felonies
A little larceny
Pronzini, B. Small felonies

Pronzini, Bill—*Continued*
A lot on his mind
   Pronzini, B. Graveyard plots
The man who collected "The Shadow"
   Pronzini, B. Small felonies
Memento mori
   Pronzini, B. Small felonies
Mrs. Rakubian
   Pronzini, B. Small felonies
Muggers' moon
   Pronzini, B. Small felonies
On guard!
   Pronzini, B. Small felonies
Once a thief
   Pronzini, B. Small felonies
One of those days
   Pronzini, B. Small felonies
Outrageous
   Pronzini, B. Small felonies
The pattern
   Pronzini, B. Graveyard plots
Peekaboo
   Pronzini, B. Graveyard plots
   Pronzini, B. Small felonies
Perfect timing
   Pronzini, B. Small felonies
Proof of guilt
   Pronzini, B. Graveyard plots
The prophecy
   100 great fantasy short short stories; ed.
     by I. Asimov; T. Carr and M. H.
     Greenberg
Pumpkin
   Halloween horrors; ed. by A. Ryan
Putting the pieces back
   Pronzini, B. Graveyard plots
Retirement
   Pronzini, B. Small felonies
The same old grind
   Pronzini, B. Small felonies
Sanctuary
   Pronzini, B. Graveyard plots
Shell game
   Pronzini, B. Small felonies
Skeleton rattle your mouldy leg
   The Eyes have it; ed. by R. J. Randisi
   The Mammoth book of private eye
     stories; ed. by B. Pronzini and M. H.
     Greenberg
   Pronzini, B. Graveyard plots
   The Year's best mystery and suspense
     stories, 1985
Skeletons
   Pronzini, B. Small felonies
Smuggler's Island
   Alfred Hitchcock's Grave suspicions
   Pronzini, B. Graveyard plots
Something wrong
   Pronzini, B. Small felonies
Stacked deck
   The Year's best mystery and suspense
     stories, 1988

The storm tunnel
   Pronzini, B. Small felonies
Strangers in the fog
   Pronzini, B. Graveyard plots
Sweet fever
   Pronzini, B. Graveyard plots
   Pronzini, B. Small felonies
The terrarium principle
   Pronzini, B. Small felonies
Thin air
   Death locked in; ed. by D. G. Greene
     and R. C. S. Adey
Thirst
   Pronzini, B. Small felonies
Tiger, tiger
   Pronzini, B. Small felonies
Toy
   Pronzini, B. Small felonies
   Shadows 8
Two weeks every summer
   Pronzini, B. Graveyard plots
Unchained
   Pronzini, B. Small felonies
Under the skin
   Pronzini, B. Graveyard plots
   Pronzini, B. Small felonies
Waiting, waiting . . .
   Pronzini, B. Small felonies
The web
   Alfred Hitchcock's Mortal errors
Whodunit
   Pronzini, B. Small felonies
Words do not a book make
   Pronzini, B. Small felonies
Pronzini, Bill, and Kurland, Michael, 1938-
Vanishing act
   The Deadly arts; ed. by B. Pronzini and
     M. Muller
Pronzini, Bill, and Malzberg, Barry N.
Another burnt-out case
   The Wickedest show on earth; ed. by
     M. Muller and B. Pronzini
Multiples
   Pronzini, B. Graveyard plots
Opening a vein
   100 great fantasy short short stories; ed.
     by I. Asimov; T. Carr and M. H.
     Greenberg
Prose Bowl
   The Science fictional Olympics; ed. by
     I. Asimov; M. H. Greenberg and C.
     G. Waugh
Rebound
   Pronzini, B. Graveyard plots
Pronzini, Bill, and Wallmann, Jeffrey M.,
1941-
Coyote and Quarter Moon
   Hound dunnit; ed. by I. Asimov; M. H.
     Greenberg and C. L. R. Waugh
The half-invisible man
   Great modern police stories; ed. by B.
     Pronzini and M. H. Greenberg
Proof of guilt. Pronzini, B.

Proof positive. Greene, G.
The **proper** circumstances. Warner, S. T.
A **proper** introduction. Roberts, N.
The **proper** maintenance of lists. Sellers, J. F.
PROPERTY
    See also Real estate
Lofts, N. The horse-leech hath two daughters
Sandel, C. The broad versus the narrow outlook
Property. Lasdun, J.
The **property** of Colette Nervi. Trevor, W.
PROPHECIES
The Astrologer's prediction
Buzzati, D. Duelling stories
Cowper, R. The custodians
Dick, P. K. What'll we do with Ragland Park?
Faik, S. Hotel Joy
Faik, S. Last birds
Grant, C. L. The old men know
Haggard, H. R. Black heart and white heart
Haldeman, J. W. Manifest destiny
Kinsella, W. P. Frank Pierce, Iowa
Lafferty, R. A. Le Hot Sport
Pribus, M. The calendar chest
Pronzini, B. The prophecy
Schwob, M. The Milesian virgins
St. Clair, M. The boy who predicted earthquakes
Stewart, J. I. M. Pipkin Grove
Walpole, H. Mi Li: a Chinese fairy tale
Yarbro, C. Q. Do not forsake me, O my darlin'
The **prophecy**. Pronzini, B.
A **prophecy** of monsters. Smith, C. A.
The **prophet**. Boisvert, C.
Prophet. Sanders, S. R.
The **prophet** and the bird. Gilbert, M.
The **prophet** Elijah. Havemann, E.
The **prophet** in the sea. Gauvreau, C.
The **Prophet** of Pandaloop. Morrison, J.
The **prophetess**. Ndebele, N.
PROPHETS
Sterling, B. Dinner in Audoghast
Stern, S. The Lord and Morton Gruber
The **Prophet's** hair. Rushdie, S.
The **proposal**. Regent, P.
Proposal and disposal. Sisskind, M.
Prose, Francine, 1947-
The bandit was my neighbor
    Prose, F. Women and children first
Creature comforts
    Prose, F. Women and children first
Criminals
    Prose, F. Women and children first
Electricity
    Prose, F. Women and children first
Everyday disorders
    Prose, F. Women and children first

Everyone had a lobster
    Prose, F. Women and children first
Everything is about animals
    Prose, F. Women and children first
Other lives
    The Bread Loaf anthology of contemporary American short stories; ed. by R. Pack and J. Parini
    Prose, F. Women and children first
    The Pushcart prize XI
Tangerine dreams
    Redbook 170:52+ D '87
Tibetan time
    Prose, F. Women and children first
Tomatoes
    The New Yorker 62:35-41 Ap 7 '86
    Prose, F. Women and children first
Useful ceremonies
    Prose, F. Women and children first
Women and children first
    The New Yorker 62:32-7 Ja 19 '87
    Prose, F. Women and children first
Prose Bowl. Pronzini, B., and Malzberg, B. N.
Proserpina's daughter. Benford, G., and Carter, P. A.
The **prospect** from the silver hill. Crace, J.
A **prospect** of the sea. Thomas, D.
Prospecting. Wendt, A.
PROSPECTORS
Clark, W. V. T. The Indian well
Crace, J. The prospect from the silver hill
Grey, Z. Tappan's burro
Johnson, W. R. Enough gold
Lawson, H. The loaded dog
London, J. All Gold Canyon
Marshall, A. Trees can speak
Prichard, K. S. The bride of Far-away
Prichard, K. S. Genieve
Prichard, K. S. Luck
Sheckley, R. Beside still waters
Vinge, J. D. Phoenix in the ashes
Prospects for an expedition. Federspiel, J.
Prosperity. Loewald, U.
Prosser, Harold Lee
Summer wine
    Missouri short fiction; ed. by C. Beasley
PROSTITUTES
    See also Pimps
Aidoo, C. A. A. In the cutting of a drink
Andreyev, L. Darkness
Asher, H. W. Three happy Japanese
Austin, M. H. The House of offence
Barbey d'Aurevilly, J. A woman's vengeance
Barker, C. Human remains
Beman, B. A cowboy for a madam
Blinkin, M. Incomprehensible
Borchert, W. Do stay, Giraffe
Calvino, I. Dollars and the demimondaine
Calvino, I. Transit bed
Carter, A. Our Lady of the Massacre
Chekhov, A. P. A nervous breakdown

PROSTITUTES—*Continued*
Ch'en, Y.-C. Roses in June
Chipulina, E. G. The catalyst
Chukri, M. Flower Crazy
Crane, S. Adventures of a novelist
Crane, S. Maggie: a girl of the streets
Crapser, W. R&R
Dangor, A. A strange romance
Daniels, C. Honky-Tonk Avenue
Effinger, G. A. Babes on bawd way
Eighner, L. Highway 71
Eighner, L. Westheimer
Ellison, H. The very last day of a good woman
Faik, S. A love story
Faik, S. The mirror at the beach
Ferreira, R. A color for that fear
Feyrer, G. The House of the Twin Jewels
Gaitskill, M. Something nice
Gaitskill, M. Trying to be
García Márquez, G. The incredible and sad tale of innocent Eréndira and her heartless grandmother
García Márquez, G. The woman who came at six o'clock
Gogol', N. V. Nevsky Prospekt
Gorky, M. One autumn evening
Gorky, M. Red
Greene, G. Jubilee
Hamilton, D. The alteration
Haycox, E. Stage to Lordsburg
Haylock, J. Tomiko
Hemingway, E. The light of the world
Hsiu, H. The trap
Jaffe, H. Brother Wolf
Janowitz, T. Modern saint #271
Kawabata, Y. The O-Shin Jizo
Kim, T. Potato
Kinsella, W. P. Horse collars
Kinsella, W. P. Linda Star
Kinsella, W. P. The Vancouver chapter of the Howard G. Scharff Memorial Society
Klass, P. Two New Jersey stories: Hudson Towers
Kotzwinkle, W. Mr. Jones's convention
Kotzwinkle, W. Sun, moon, and storm
Kranes, D. The whorehouse picnic
Lee, T. Black as ink
Lopatin, J. Dominica
Lopatin, J. The mystery of Madame Kitten
Lustig, A. Blue day
Mailer, N. The paper house
Major, C. Tattoo
Malaparte, C. The Soroca girls
Maupassant, G. de. Ball-of-fat
Maupassant, G. de. Florentine
Maupassant, G. de. Graveyard sirens
Maupassant, G. de. Mademoiselle Fifi
Maupassant, G. de. Mme. Tellier's excursion
Maupassant, G. de. La Morillonne
Maupassant, G. de. A poor girl
Maupassant, G. de. The port
Maupassant, G. de. Sympathy
McElroy, C. J. Imogene
Mufti, M. Good luck
Muschg, A. Grandfather's little pleasure
Nagai, K. Nude
Naipaul, S. The father, the son and the Holy Ghost
Naipaul, S. Lack of sleep
Narayan, R. K. House opposite
O'Hara, J. Ninety minutes away
Pavese, C. The idol
Petrakis, H. M. Rosemary
Ramírez, S. A bed of bauxite in Weipa
Rhys, J. La Grosse Fifi
Rhys, J. Night out 1925
Rose, D. A. Summer heat
Sandel, C. Shit-Katrine
Schwob, M. Katherine la Dentellière, whore
Shea, M. Fat Face
Sims, L. Behind my lace curtain
Singer, I. B. On the way to the poorhouse
Spillane, M. "Sex is my vengeance"
Steadman, M. John Fletcher's night of love
Sullivan, T. Whores in the pulpit
Tuohy, F. A survivor in Salvador
Tuohy, F. Two private lives
Vega, A. L. Lyrics for Puerto Rican salsa and three soneos by request
Watt, N. As good as gold
Williams, T. The yellow bird
Winton, T. The woman at the well
Wojnarowicz, D. Self portrait in twenty-three rounds
Wolfe, T. The face of the war
Yarbro, C. Q. The end of the carnival
Yi, S. A discontinued knot
Yi, S. Wings
Ziem, J. So much happiness

PROSTITUTION
See also Prostitutes
Hall, T. T. Civic pride
A **protective** fuzz. Esposito, M.
The **protector**. Pollack, R.
A **protest** against the sun. Millhauser, S.
Proteus. Hoover, J.
Protista. Marechera, D.
Prott. St. Clair, M.
Proud. Crapser, W.
Proulx, Annie
Bedrock
Proulx, A. Heart songs, and other stories
Electric arrows
Proulx, A. Heart songs, and other stories
Heart songs
Esquire 106:196-8+ O '86
Proulx, A. Heart songs, and other stories
In the pit
Proulx, A. Heart songs, and other stories
On the Antler
Proulx, A. Heart songs, and other stories

Proulx, Annie—*Continued*
A run of bad luck
    Proulx, A. Heart songs, and other stories
Stone City
    Proulx, A. Heart songs, and other stories
The unclouded day
    Proulx, A. Heart songs, and other stories
The wer-trout
    Proulx, A. Heart songs, and other stories
Proulx, Monique
ABC
    Invisible fictions; ed. by G. Hancock
Feint of heart
    Intimate strangers; ed. by M. Cohen and
    W. Grady
PROVENCE (FRANCE) *See* France—
Provence
Proverb of the parched. Mazel, D.
The **proverbial** murder. Carr, J. D.
PROVIDENCE (R.I.) *See* Rhode Island—
Providence
Providence. Gault, C.
Providence, 1934: the house at the beach.
McGarry, J.
Providence, 1948: the most complimentary
thing. McGarry, J.
Providence, 1954: watch. McGarry, J.
Providence, 1956: toy box. McGarry, J.
Providence, 1957: an accident. McGarry, J.
Providence, 1960: cavities. McGarry, J.
Providence, 1966: ducks and lucks. McGarry,
J.
Providence, 1970: behind this soft eclipse.
McGarry, J.
Providence will provide. Sokoloff, T. C.
Providing a meal. Qiao Shi
The **provinces.** Ferron, J.
The **provincial** night. Landolfi, T.
The **prowler** in the city at the edge of the
world. Ellison, H.
Prowling around Little Red Riding Hood.
Hébert, F.
Prudence. Millman, L.
Prue. Munro, A.
The **pruning** of the apple trees. Rule, J.
The **Prussian** officer. Lawrence, D. H.
Prying loose. Choyce, L.
Psiren. Vinge, J. D.
The **psoriasis** diet. Lish, G.
Psst, psst! Faik, S.
The **Psyche** Zenobia. See Poe, E. A. How
to write a Blackwood article
The **Psyche** Zenobia. See Poe, E. A. The
Signora Psyche Zenobia
PSYCHIATRISTS
    See also Mentally ill—Care and
treatment; Psychoanalysts; Women psy-
chiatrists
Ballard, J. G. The object of the attack
Barthelme, S. Samaritan
Bickel, B. Make it never happened
Bloch, R. All on a golden afternoon
Bloch, R. The screaming people

Bloch, R. The world-timer
Calisher, H. Heartburn
Campbell, R. The sunshine club
Charnas, S. M. Unicorn tapestry
Davis, L. Therapy
Ellison, H. All the sounds of fear
Friedman, B. J. The war criminal
Harris, M. The fun dome
Jeppson, J. O. August angst
Jeppson, J. O. The beanstalk analysis
Jeppson, J. O. Consternation and empire
Jeppson, J. O. The curious consultation
Jeppson, J. O. The horn of Elfland
Jeppson, J. O. The hotter flash
Jeppson, J. O. A million shades of green
Jeppson, J. O. The mysterious cure
Jeppson, J. O. The Noodge Factor
Jeppson, J. O. Seasonal special
Jeppson, J. O. The time-warp trauma
Jeppson, J. O. The ultimate biofeedback
    device
Langford, M. N. Wood
Lutz, J. Big game
Lutz, J. The second shot
MacLean, K. The other
Miller, W. The memorial hour
Mukherjee, B. Nostalgia
Phillips, R. The yellow pill
Ramchandani, K. Gitley
Ramsland, K. Nothing from nothing comes
Sheckley, R. The petrified world
Silverberg, R. A sea of faces
Spark, M. The dark glasses
St. Clair, M. Short in the chest
Thomas, J. My journal as the fishwoman
Treat, L. Give the devil his due
Williams, W. C. The insane
Yarbro, C. Q. Cabin 33
PSYCHIC PHENOMENA *See* Extrasensory
perception; Occultism; Spiritualism;
Supernatural phenomena
PSYCHICAL RESEARCH
Oates, J. C. Night-side
PSYCHOANALYSIS
Atwood, M. The sin eater
PSYCHOANALYSTS
Bloch, R. See how they run
Cadigan, P. Nearly departed
Conroy, F. The mysterious case of R
Freeman, L. The last dream
Friedman, B. J. The Candide of copiers
Gilliatt, P. Staying in bed
Harris, M. Dr. Pettigot's face
Herbert, F. Operation Syndrome
Jeppson, J. O. A pestilence of psy-
choanalysts
Lutz, J. No small problem
Maugham, W. S. Lord Mountdrago
Schwartz, L. S. The age of analysis
Weldon, F. Threnody
Whelan, G. Keeping house with Freud
PSYCHOKINESIS
Bixby, J. The draw

PSYCHOKINESIS—*Continued*
Block, L. The boy who disappeared clouds
Jakes, J. And the monsters walk
The **psychological** test. Rampo, E.
Psychological warfare at Cassino. Davin, D.
A **psychological** warrior. Aćin-Kosta, M.
PSYCHOLOGISTS
Berriault, G. The infinite passion of expectation
Dawson, F. If
Faust, I. Melanie and the purple people eaters
Finger, A. Basic skills
La Chapelle, M. Faith
La Chapelle, M. House of heroes
Moffett, J. Surviving
Silverberg, R. A thousand paces along the Via Dolorosa
PSYCHOLOGY
Barker, C. Dread
PSYCHOPATHS *See* Insane, Criminal and dangerous; Personality disorders
Psychopolis. McEwan, I.
PSYCHOTHERAPISTS *See* Psychotherapy
PSYCHOTHERAPY
Bace, K. M. Sterile relationships
Busch, F. In foreign tongues
Coleman, W. Ladies
Eisenstein, S. The weight goes on the downhill ski
Flook, M. A walk in the city
Fowler, K. J. The lake was full of artificial things
Gunn, J. E. Feeding time
La Chapelle, M. Faith
La Chapelle, M. House of heroes
Michaelson, L. W. On my being dead
Pohl, F. In the problem pit
Silverberg, R. A sea of faces
Wilson, B. Sense and sensitivity
Ptacek, Kathryn
Dead possums
The Year's best fantasy, first annual collection
Pu, Sung-ling, 1640-1715
The cricket
Tales of the supernatural; ed. by H. C. Chang
The Tou lass
Tales of the supernatural; ed. by H. C. Chang
Yellow pride
Tales of the supernatural; ed. by H. C. Chang
Yüeh Chung
Tales of the supernatural; ed. by H. C. Chang
Pu Zong
A head in the marshes
The Antioch Review 46:157-64 Spr '88
Public-address system. West, J.
Public appearances. Dodd, S. M.

PUBLIC HOUSING
Hirsch, G. The housing correspondence of prisoner number 100293/8
Public library. Kees, W.
A **public** pool. Adams, A.
PUBLIC PROSECUTORS
Struthers, A. Gathering evidence
PUBLIC SCHOOLS *See* School life
PUBLIC UTILITIES
See also Electricity
PUBLICITY
Bloch, R. Betsy Blake will live forever
Bloch, R. Show biz
Pohl, F. The children of night
Publish and perish. Nahin, P. J.
PUBLISHERS AND PUBLISHING
See also Newspapers
Asimov, I. The next day
Gardner, M. The loves of Lady Coldpence
Hartley, L. P. Noughts and crosses
Hoch, E. D. The great American novel
Hoch, E. D. The Judges of Hades
Hoch, E. D. Murder at the Bouchercon
Hoch, E. D. The unicorn's daughter
Hoch, E. D. The Vicar of Hell
Kress, N. Shadows on the cave wall
Lasswitz, K. The universal library
Levine, N. We all begin in a little magazine
Oosthuizen, A. A fine romance
Pohl, F. How to impress an editor
Russo, A. Murder of a novel Parisian style amid the frenzy of France's literary merry-go-round
Wilson, Sir A. More friend than lodger
PUBS *See* Hotels, taverns, etc.
The **puddle** diver. Allyn, D.
PUEBLO INDIANS
Martin, R. Cliff Dwellers
Silko, L. Private property
Silko, L. Yellow Woman
PUERTO RICANS
Ferré, R. Sleeping beauty
Valle, C. Diary entry #1
Vega, A. L. Three love aerobics
New York (N.Y.)
Michaels, L. The deal
Mohr, N. Happy birthday (Lucia)
Pulaski, J. Alone or with others
Pulaski, J. Don Juan, the senior citizen
Pulaski, J. Father of the bride
United States
Mohr, N. The artist (Inez)
Mohr, N. Aunt Rosana's rocker (Zoraida)
Mohr, N. Brief miracle (Virginia)
Mohr, N. A Thanksgiving celebration (Amy)
Mohr, N. A time with a future (Carmela)
PUERTO RICO
Ferré, R. Pico Rico, mandorico
Filippi, C. L. Milagros, on Mercurio Street
Montero, M. Last night at dawn

PUERTO VALLARTA (MEXICO) *See* Mexico—Puerto Vallarta
Puerto Vallarta. Gébler, C.
A puff of roses. Taylor, J.
PUGILISM *See* Boxing
Pugmire, W. H., and Salmonson, Jessica Amanda
  "Pale trembling youth"
    Cutting edge; ed. by D. Etchison
Pukes!. Saucier, M.
Pulaski, Jack
  Alone or with others
    Pulaski, J. The St. Veronica gig stories
  Don Juan, the senior citizen
    Pulaski, J. The St. Veronica gig stories
  Father of the bride
    Pulaski, J. The St. Veronica gig stories
  The merry-go-round
    Pulaski, J. The St. Veronica gig stories
  Minnie the Moocher's hair
    The Ploughshares reader: new fiction for the eighties
    Pulaski, J. The St. Veronica gig stories
  Music story
    Pulaski, J. The St. Veronica gig stories
  Religious instruction
    Pulaski, J. The St. Veronica gig stories
  The romance
    Pulaski, J. The St. Veronica gig stories
The Pulaski Guards. Bukoski, A.
Pulitzer. Contou-Carrère, E. J.
Pulsars. Letourneau, M.
PUMAS
  Grey, Z. Don
The pump. Humphrey, W.
Pumpkin. Farmer, B.
Pumpkin. Pronzini, B.
The punchboards. Parry, H. T.
Punchlines. Kinsella, W. P.
PUNIC WAR, 2D, 218-201 B.C.
  Anderson, P. Delenda est
PUNISHMENT
  Burt, S. I just kept on smiling
  Chernoff, M. Two times two
  Herschel, J. Geometry
  Moore, G. A Russian husband
  Smith, C. A planet named Shayol
  Sturgeon, T. Shadow, shadow on the wall
  Walters, A. L. The laws
The punishment. Ocampo, S.
The punishment of Oscar. Wexelblatt, R.
Punk love in the library john. Hardesty, C.
PUNS
  Asimov, I. Death of a Foy
  Asimov, I. Jokester
  Asimov, I. Sure thing
  Farber, S. N. The great dormitory mystery
  Farmer, P. J. Riders of the purple wage
Pupil. Barthelme, F.
PUPPETS AND PUPPET PLAYS
  Brown, A. R. The clockwork woman
  Petrakis, H. M. Dark eye
  Schutz, J. W. Dragon's horn

Puppo, Alberto
  The tree
    Américas 39:50-2 N/D '87
The Purcells. Kees, W.
The purchase of order. Adams, G. G.
Purdin, Scott
  Fly to fly
    The North American Review 270:46-9 Je '85
Purdy, James, 1923-
  The candles of your eyes
    First love/last love; ed. by M. Denneny; C. Ortleb and T. Steele
    Purdy, J. The candles of your eyes, and thirteen other stories
  Dawn
    Purdy, J. The candles of your eyes, and thirteen other stories
  Encore
    Family: stories from the interior; ed. by G. G. Chavis
  Eventide
    The Art of the tale; ed. by D. Halpern
  How I became a shadow
    Purdy, J. The candles of your eyes, and thirteen other stories
  In this corner . . .
    Men on men 2; ed. by G. Stambolian
  Lily's party
    Purdy, J. The candles of your eyes, and thirteen other stories
  Mr. Evening
    Purdy, J. The candles of your eyes, and thirteen other stories
  Mud Toe the cannibal
    The Antioch Review 42:135-9 Spr '84
    Purdy, J. The candles of your eyes, and thirteen other stories
  On the rebound
    Purdy, J. The candles of your eyes, and thirteen other stories
  Rapture
    New directions in prose and poetry 50
    Purdy, J. The candles of your eyes, and thirteen other stories
  Ruthanna Elder
    Purdy, J. The candles of your eyes, and thirteen other stories
  Scrap of paper
    Purdy, J. The candles of your eyes, and thirteen other stories
  Short Papa
    Early sorrow: ten stories of youth; ed. by C. Zolotow
    Purdy, J. The candles of your eyes, and thirteen other stories
  Sleep tight
    Purdy, J. The candles of your eyes, and thirteen other stories

Purdy, James, 1923- — *Continued*
   Some of these days
      First love/last love; ed. by M. Denneny;
         C. Ortleb and T. Steele
      Purdy, J. The candles of your eyes, and
         thirteen other stories
   Summer tidings
      Purdy, J. The candles of your eyes, and
         thirteen other stories
Pure Hamitic strain. Havemann, E.
The **pure** in heart. Payne, P.
The **pure** product. Kessel, J.
Pure rotten. Lutz, J.
Pure sex. Hauptman, W.
PURITANS
   Hawthorne, N. The gentle boy
   Hawthorne, N. The May-Pole of Merry
      Mount
The **purity** of the turf. Wodehouse, P. G.
The **purloined** letter. Poe, E. A.
The **purple** is everything. Davis, D. S.
The **purple** pileus. Wells, H. G.
The **Purple** Prince. Hall, R. W.
Purple prose. Evans, J.
The **purpose** of this creature man. Abbott,
   L. K.
Purse. Gilliatt, P.
Pursuit of excellence. Yount, R.
A **pursuit** race. Hemingway, E.
Push no more. Silverberg, R.
The **pusher**. Varley, J.
Pushing the point. Schulman, H.
Pushkin, Aleksandr Sergeevich, 1799-1837
   The queen of spades
      Black water; ed. by A. Manguel
      The Penguin book of ghost stories
Put yourself in my shoes. Carver, R.
Putting a black-leg on shore. Drake, B.
Putting out an old flame. Yellin, L. N.
Putting the pieces back. Pronzini, B.
Puzzle. Rule, J.
Puzzle for Poppy. Wheeler, H. C.
PUZZLES
   Asimov, I. The Cross of Lorraine
   Asimov, I. The one and only east
   Asimov, I. A problem of numbers
   Mrożek, S. The background to an era
Pygmalion. Updike, J.
Pyjamas. Jackson, G.
Pyle, Howard, 1853-1911
   The Salem wolf
      Yankee witches; ed. by C. G. Waugh;
         M. H. Greenberg and F. D. McSherry
The **pylon**. Hartley, L. P.
Pym, Barbara
   Across a crowded room
      Pym, B. Civil to strangers, and other
         writings
   The Christmas visit
      Pym, B. Civil to strangers, and other
         writings

   Goodbye Balkan capital
      Pym, B. Civil to strangers, and other
         writings
   So, some tempestuous morn
      Pym, B. Civil to strangers, and other
         writings
Pynchon, Thomas
   Entropy
      Pynchon, T. Slow learner
   Low-lands
      Pynchon, T. Slow learner
   The secret integration
      Pynchon, T. Slow learner
   The small rain
      Pynchon, T. Slow learner
   Under the rose
      Pynchon, T. Slow learner
PYONGYANG (KOREA) *See* Korea—
   Pyongyang
Pyŏn's death. Sin, S.-U.
Pyracchmes beneath Laurion. Parotti, P.
Pyrotechnics. Smith, I.
PYRRHON, OF ELIS, ca. 365-275 B.C.
      About
   Davenport, G. Pyrrhon of Elis
Pyrrhon of Elis. Davenport, G.
The **python**. Kiely, B.

Q

Qa'id, Yusuf al- *See* Al-Qa'id, Yusuf
Qazi, Javaid
   President Sahib's blue period
      The Massachusetts Review 29:683-700
      Wint '88/'89
Qazia and a ferret-fetch. Sampson, J.
QB/3854/294 & 6. Burt, S.
Qiao Shi
   Providing a meal
      Contemporary Chinese literature; ed. by
         M. S. Duke
QL 696.C9. Boucher, A.
QUACKS AND QUACKERY
   Caldwell, E. The medicine man
   Horn, A. The making of Musa Maikudi
   Mrabet, M. Doctor Safi
QUADROONS *See* Mulattoes
The **quadroons**. Child, L. M. F.
Quah Kung Yu
   Equality
      The Penguin world omnibus of science
         fiction
The **quail**. Yngve, R.
Quail for Mr. Forester. Humphrey, W.
QUAILS
   Yngve, R. The quail
QUAKERS *See* Society of Friends
The **quality** of life. Miller, S.
The **quality** of light in Maine. Pfeil, F.
The **quality** of mercy. Ferguson, P.
The **quality** of mercy. Lipsky, E.

The **quality** of mercy. Pennell, H. B., Jr.
Quammen, David, 1948-
  Nathan's rime
    Quammen, D. Blood line
  Uriah's letter
    Quammen, D. Blood line
  Walking out
    American short story masterpieces; ed.
      by R. Carver and T. Jenks
    Quammen, D. Blood line
    Writers of the purple sage; ed. by R.
      Martin and M. Barasch
QUANTRILL, WILLIAM CLARKE, 1837-
1865
        About
  Taylor, R. Quantrill
Quantrill. Taylor, R.
Quantum jumps. O'Brien, T.
The **quarrel**. Oates, J. C.
QUARRELING
  Bates, H. E. Elaine
  Carver, R. The calm
  Carver, R. One more thing
  Carver, R. Popular mechanics
  Colette. The rendezvous
  Davis, L. Story
  Francis, H. E. Her
  Morrison, J. It opens your eyes
  Parise, G. Patience, spring
  Sladek, J. T. Breakfast with the Mur-
    gatroyds
  Williams, T. Happy August the Tenth
  Wolff, T. Hunters in the snow
QUARRIES AND QUARRYING
  Conroy, J. The sissy from the Hardscrab-
    ble County rock quarries
  Harrison, M. J. The quarry
  St. Clair, M. Brenda
The **quarry**. Harrison, M. J.
The **quarry**. Norris, H.
The **quarry**. Woods, C.
The **quarterback** speaks to his god. Wilner,
  H.
Quartet. Oates, J. C.
QUÉBEC (PROVINCE) *See* Canada—
  Québec (Province)
Queen, Ellery
  Abraham Lincoln's clue [Variant title: The
    adventure of Abraham Lincoln's clue]
    Great detectives; ed. by D. W. McCul-
      lough
    Masterpieces of mystery and suspense;
      ed. by M. H. Greenberg
    Queen, E. The best of Ellery Queen
  The adventure of the bearded lady
    [Variant title: The bearded lady]
    The Penguin classic crime omnibus
  The adventure of the hanging acrobat
    The Deadly arts; ed. by B. Pronzini and
      M. Muller
  The bearded lady [Variant title: The
    adventure of the bearded lady]
    Queen, E. The best of Ellery Queen

  Cold money
    Ellery Queen's Memorable characters
  The Dauphin's doll [Variant title: The
    adventure of the Dauphin's doll]
    Queen, E. The best of Ellery Queen
  The death of Don Juan
    Ellery Queen's Crimes and punishments
  GI story
    Queen, E. The best of Ellery Queen
  The glass-domed clock [Variant title: The
    adventure of the glass-domed clock]
    Queen, E. The best of Ellery Queen
  The House of Darkness
    The Wickedest show on earth; ed. by
      M. Muller and B. Pronzini
  The inner circle
    Queen, E. The best of Ellery Queen
  Last man to die
    Queen, E. The best of Ellery Queen
  The mad tea-party [Variant title: The
    adventure of the mad tea-party]
    Queen, E. The best of Ellery Queen
  Man bites dog
    Queen, E. The best of Ellery Queen
  The medical finger
    Manhattan mysteries; ed. by B. Pronzini;
      C. L. R. Waugh and M. H. Greenberg
  Mind over matter
    Queen, E. The best of Ellery Queen
  Miracles do happen
    Queen, E. The best of Ellery Queen
  My queer Dean!
    Queen, E. The best of Ellery Queen
  Mystery at the Library of Congress
    Chapter & hearse; ed. by M. Muller and
      B. Pronzini
  Object lesson
    Handle with care; ed. by J. Kahn
  Snowball in July
    Queen, E. The best of Ellery Queen
  Terror town
    Hitchcock in prime time; ed. by F. M.
      Nevins and M. H. Greenberg
  The three widows
    Queen, E. The best of Ellery Queen
  Wedding anniversary
    Queen, E. The best of Ellery Queen
Queen. DeMarinis, R.
Queen Esther. Huggan, I.
Queen for a Day. Banks, R.
Queen Hortense. See Maupassant, G. de. An
  old maid
Queen Mousie. Warner, S. T.
The **Queen** of Lower Saigon. Malzberg, B.
  N.
The **queen** of queens. Rees, D.
The **queen** of Quok. Baum, L. F.
The **Queen** of Sheba's nightmare. Russell, B.
The **queen** of spades. Pushkin, A. S.
QUEENS
     See also Courts and courtiers; also
    names of queens
  Lee, T. La reine blanche

QUEENS—*Continued*

Smith, C. A. The death of Ilalotha

Tiptree, J. All this and heaven too

Walpole, H. The peach in brandy: a Milesian tale

Queens. Hernández, J. J.

The **queen's** square. Sayers, D. L.

A **queer** night in Paris. Maupassant, G. de

A **queer** red spirit. Borgman, C. F.

The **queer** story of Brownlow's newspaper. Wells, H. G.

A **queer** streak. Munro, A.

Quenby and Ola, Swede and Carl. Coover, R.

Quentin, Patrick *See* Wheeler, Hugh Callingham, 1912-1987

The **quest** for Ambrose Bierce. Cheuse, A.

Quest for an unnamed place. Matthews, J.

The **quest** for Blank Claveringi. Highsmith, P.

The **question**. Ellin, S.

Question and answer. Bernard, K.

A **question** answered. Fisher, M. F. K.

The **question** my son asked. See Ellin, S. The question

The **question** of Latin. Maupassant, G. de

Question of light. Rossiter, S.

A **question** of loneliness. Swados, H.

The **question** of rain. Hoffman, W.

A **question** of re-entry. Ballard, J. G.

A **question** of timing. Sagan, F.

The **question** she put to herself. Brady, M.

A **questionnaire** for Rudolph Gordon. Matthews, J.

Quest's end. Zelazny, R.

The **quick-change** artist. Colette

Quick exchanges. Soldatow, S.

The **quickening**. Bishop, M.

The **quickening**. Interollo, L.

Quicker than the eye. Asimov, I.

Quicktime. Ellison, H.

A **quiet** day at the fair. Green, S.

Quiet days in Los Gatos. Rees, D.

A **quiet** funeral. Bloch, R.

The **quiet** investigation. Van Derveer, M.

A **quiet** man. Davies, D.

A **quiet** summer's day. Bonosky, P.

Quiller-Couch, Sir Arthur Thomas, 1863-1944

A pair of hands

Young ghosts; ed. by I. Asimov; M. H. Greenberg and C. G. Waugh

The roll-call of the reef

The Oxford book of English ghost stories

Short stories of the sea; ed. by G. C. Solley and E. Steinbaugh

Quincy. Humphries, J.

Quinliven, J. O.

Beauty for sale

The Weirds; ed. by S. Jaffery

Quinn, Seabury, 1889-1969

Is the Devil a gentleman?

Yankee witches; ed. by C. G. Waugh; M. H. Greenberg and F. D. McSherry

Quinquepedalian. Anthony, P.

Quiroga, Horacio, 1878-1937

The dead man

The World of the short story; ed. by C. Fadiman

The feather pillow

Black water; ed. by A. Manguel

Quite early one morning. Thomas, D.

The **quitter**. Markham, B.

Quitters, Inc. King, S.

Quo vadis, Francisco? Aldani, L.

Quoirez, Françoise *See* Sagan, Françoise, 1935-

QUOTATIONS

Sheckley, R. The mnemone

R

R&R. Crapser, W.

R&r. Shepard, L.

Raab, Scott

Goodbye and good luck

The North American Review 271:26-32 Je '86

Rabasa, George

The lion. The eagle. The wolf

Stiller's pond; ed. by J. Agee; R. Blakely and S. Welch

RABBIS

Avery, M. The Singing Rabbi

Davenport, G. The chair

Kessler, J. F. Saul of Tarsus

Liben, M. Hop, skip, and jump

Malamud, B. The magic barrel

Michaels, L. Murderers

Ozick, C. The pagan rabbi

Singer, I. B. The last demon

Singer, I. B. The recluse

Rabbit. Campbell, W. B.

The **rabbit**. Maupassant, G. de

RABBIT HUNTING

Campbell, W. B. Rabbit

Little, J. Wild rabbits

MacLaverty, B. Where the tides meet

A **rabbit** in the garden. Bowen, J.

The **rabbit** that lost its nose. Michaelson, L. W.

The **rabbit** that loved cats. Saunders, J.

The **rabbit** trapper's wife. Prichard, K. S.

RABBITS

Carrington, L. White rabbits

Conroy, J. Uncle Ollie's rabbit hunt

Everett, P. L. Nice white people

Regent, P. Summer pudding

Rifaat, A. Degrees of death

Woolf, V. Lappin and Lapinova

Rabbits. Nimmo, D.

Rabchik, a Jewish dog. Sholem Aleichem
Rabelais, François, 1490-1553?
Gargantua and pantagruel [excerpt]
Inspired by drink; ed. by Joan Digby and John Digby
Rabie, Jan
Drought
The Penguin book of Southern African stories
Rabindranath Tagore *See* Tagore, Sir Rabindranath, 1861-1941
Rabinowitz, Sholem Yakov *See* Sholem Aleichem, 1859-1916
RACCOONS
Campbell, W. B. Death is always part of dinner
Smith, G. B. Hands
The **race.** Bates, H. E.
Race at morning. Faulkner, W.
RACE PROBLEMS *See* Race relations
RACE RELATIONS
See also Antisemitism; Black-Jewish relations; Blacks; Culture conflict; Interracial marriage; Miscegenation; Prejudices
Coleman, W. Jonesed
Dubus, A. Deaths at sea
Duff, G. Fire ants
Field, B. Three sisters
Flynn, R. Champion of the world
Gifkins, M. Metamorphosis
Healey, J. Flowers in January
Mathers, P. Like a Maori prince
Meriwether, L. A happening in Barbados
O'Connor, F. The barber
Saiki, J. Nocturne
Sanford, W. M. Black child
Swados, H. Bobby Shafter's gone to sea
Wilner, H. Emergency room bicentennial
Africa
See Africa—Race relations
Kenya
See Kenya—Race relations
Malaysia
See Malaysia—Race relations
South Africa
See South Africa—Race relations
United States
See United States—Race relations
RACEHORSES *See* Horses
Rachaela. Anderson, P.
Rachel in love. Murphy, P.
Rachlin, Nahid
Journey of love
Redbook 171:42-4+ Je '88
RACIAL INTERMARRIAGE *See* Interracial marriage
Racine and the tablecloth. Byatt, A. S.
RACING
See also Automobile races; Bicycle racing; Boat racing; Dog racing; Horse racing; Yacht racing
Crace, J. Cross-country

Ing, D. Sam and the sudden blizzard machine
O'Connor, F. Old-age pensioners
RACISM *See* Antisemitism; Prejudices; Race relations
RACKETEERS *See* Crime and criminals; Gangsters; Mafia
RACKETS *See* Gambling
Rackham, Jeff
Rebecca Winwar's flanks had withered
The Georgia Review 38:93-100 Spr '84
A **racy** romance. Snelson, R.
Radcliffe, Ann Ward, 1764-1823
The haunted chamber
Witches' brew; ed. by M. Muller and B. Pronzini
Raddall, Thomas H.
The wedding gift
The Oxford book of Canadian short stories in English
RADIATION
Physiological effect
Bryant, E. Jody after the war
Inoue, M. The House of Hands
Sata, I. The colorless paintings
Yarbro, C. Q. The end of the carnival
Radiation. Leavitt, D.
RADICALISM *See* Radicals and radicalism
The **radicals.** Botwinik, B.
RADICALS AND RADICALISM
See also Anarchism and anarchists
Ardizzone, T. The intersection
Cohen, R. Shamsky and other casualties
O'Brien, T. Underground tests
Rosenfeld, I. The party
Smiley, J. Dynamite
Tremain, R. The Colonel's daughter
RADIGUET, RAYMOND, 1903-1923
About
Lopatin, J. Fast and loose, a historical romance
RADIO
Anvil, C. Two-way communication
Cheever, J. The enormous radio
Dagg, M. The second coming of Little Richard [excerpt]
Morgan, S. Household expenses
Sturgeon, T. The Martian and the moron
Swados, H. The letters
RADIO BROADCASTING
Martin, C. The gift
Nicoll, G. Dead air
RADIO PROGRAMS
Böll, H. Murke's collected silences
DeMarinis, R. Red chair
Gilliatt, P. Phone-in
Lessing, D. M. One off the short list
Wier, A. Campbell Oakley's gospel sun shines on Roy Singing Grass
Radio Smith. Daniels, C.
RADIOACTIVITY *See* Radiation—Physiological effect

RADIUM

Twain, M. Sold to Satan

Rafe's coat. Eisenberg, D.

Raffel, Dawn

Design

The North American Review 272:22-6 Je '87

Rafferty, S. S.

The greatest cook in Christendom

Alfred Hitchcock's Crimewatch

The hawk and the dome of hell

Manhattan mysteries; ed. by B. Pronzini; C. L. R. Waugh and M. H. Greenberg

The Massachusetts peep-o'night

Murder and mystery in Boston; ed. by C. L. R. Waugh; F. D. McSherry and M. H. Greenberg

Raffles and operation champagne. Perowne, B.

Raffles on the trail of the hound. Perowne, B.

The **raffles** relics. Hornung, E. W.

The **raft**. King, S.

Raftery's ghost. Skelton, R.

The **rag** thing. Wollheim, D. A.

Ragab, Mona

A taste of success

Egyptian tales and short stories of the 1970s and 1980s

The **rages** of Mrs. Torrens. Masters, O.

The **ragged** rascal ran. Power, V.

Ragna and Nils. Jahnn, H. H.

The **ragpicker's** boy. Croft, B.

Rags and bones. Gordimer, N.

Rahib, Hani al- *See* Al-Rahib, Hani

Rahman, Mahfouz Abd el *See* El Rahman, Mahfouz Abd

Rahman, Tariq

Bingo

Short story international 64

The legacy

Short story international 45

Rahmann, Patricia

Heathen ways

Editor's choice II; ed. by M. Sklar and M. Biggs

The **railroad**. Rosenfeld, I.

RAILROAD ACCIDENTS

Dickens, C. The signalman

Ford, R. Optimists

Heise, K. The heroine of Ferndale

Martone, M. An accident

Moore, G. Two men

Sholem Aleichem. The miracle of Hoshana Rabbah

Railroad standard time. Chin, F.

RAILROADS

    See also Street railroads; Subways

Finney, J. The third level

Pronzini, B. Sweet fever

Tuohy, F. The white stick

Construction

Overholser, W. D. Steel to the west

Employees

Arreola, J. J. The switchman

Böll, H. On the hook

Böll, H. This is Tibten!

Conroy, J. Anyplace but here

Conroy, J. Freight car repair yard pranks

Conroy, J. Greedy-Gut Gus, the car toad

Dickens, C. The signalman

Lawson, H. The iron-bark chip

Lutz, J. The shooting of Curly Dan

Roberts, K. The Lady Margaret

Rosenfeld, I. The railroad

Schwob, M. Train 081

Stuart, J. The Anglo-Saxons of Auxierville

Stuart, J. Fast-Train Ike

Wolfe, T. The far and the near

Models

Everett, P. L. Hear that long train moan

Gustafsson, L. The four railroads of Iserlohn

McCormack, E. P. The hobby

Stations

Andreyev, L. At the station

Bergelson, D. At the depot

Böll, H. My pal with the long hair

Butler, G. The sisterhood

Nowakowski, M. The peacock

Trains

Arreola, J. J. The switchman

Conroy, J. The Boomer's fireman's fast sooner hound

Doyle, Sir A. C. The mystery of the lost special

McElroy, C. J. A brief spell by the river

O'Brien, F. John Duffy's brother

Ryan, A. Hear the whistle blowing

Stuart, J. Fast-Train Ike

Travel

Bates, H. E. Elaine

Böll, H. Across the bridge

Böll, H. The train was on time

Bradbury, R. On the Orient, North

Calisher, H. The passenger

Carver, R. The compartment

Crane, S. An excursion ticket

Cullen, E. J. The second law of thermodynamics

Davenport, G. The Haile Selassie Funeral Train

Davie, E. Couchettes

Doyle, Sir A. C. The recollections of Captain Wilkie

Durrell, L. The ghost train

Edkins, A. What's eating you?

Fitzgerald, F. S. The night before Chancellorsville

Gallant, M. Up north

Gordimer, N. Enemies

Greene, G. Awful when you think of it

Haig, M. Eighteen hours in Frankfurt

Hemingway, E. The porter

Hemingway, E. A train trip

Hemley, R. Installations

RAILROADS—Travel—*Continued*
  Kawabata, Y. The young lady of Suruga
  Kipling, R. East and West
  Lansdale, J. R. Trains not taken
  Martin, V. The way of the world
  Mathers, P. Arthur & Alwyn
  Maupassant, G. de. A meeting
  Maupassant, G. de. A traveler's tale
  Nowakowski, M. The steel-clawed glove
  O'Connor, F. The train
  Pak, Y.-J. The last parting
  Regent, P. On the Aberdonian
  Ross, M., and Somerville, E. A. Œ. Pois-
    son d'Avril
  Schulze, A. Eighteen minutes
  Shiga, N. As far as Abashiri
  Shiga, N. A gray moon
  Sholem Aleichem. Third class
  Smith, A. Cornfield with lights
  Updike, D. Agawam
  Whitaker, M. Landlord of the Crystal
    Fountain
  Wolfe, T. Dark in the forest, strange as
    time
  Woolf, V. An unwritten novel
The **railway** station of Zimpren. Böll, H.
Rain. Aya, K.
Rain. Landolfi, T.
Rain. Millhauser, S.
The **rain**. Rif'iyyah, Y.
Rain. Rodoreda, M.
Rain. Shaw, D.
Rain. Yasuoka, S.
The **rain** and other children. Rey Rosa, R.
RAIN AND RAINFALL
  Dumas, H. Rain god
  Ellison, H. Rain, rain, go away
  García Márquez, G. Monologue of Isabel
    watching it rain in Macondo
  Hoffman, W. The question of rain
  Li, F.-Y. Rain-making
  McLaughlin, L. Before the rain
  Ndebele, N. The test
  Yasuoka, S. Rain
The **rain** dance. Spence, A.
Rain date. Klinkowitz, J.
Rain forest. Neville, S.
RAIN FORESTS
  Wollaston, N. Walkabout
Rain frogs. Shiga, N.
The **rain** from the sun. Li, Y.-P.
Rain god. Dumas, H.
The **rain** gutter. Böll, H.
The **rain** horse. Hughes, T.
Rain in Pinton County. Sampson, R.
Rain in the heart. Taylor, P. H.
Rain-making. Li, F.-Y.
The **rain** of terror. Manley, F.
Rain, rain, go away. Ellison, H.
The **rainbow** man. Heller, S.
The **rainbow** painter. Vannice, J.
The **rainbow** syndrome. Heller, S.
Raindrops from heaven. Dowling, L.

Raine, Norman Reilly
  The last laugh
    Sea captains' tales; ed. by A. Enfield
Raine, William MacLeod
  Doan whispers
    Wild westerns; ed. by B. Pronzini
Raines, Howell
  The historical mistake
    The Art of fiction in the heart of Dixie;
      ed. by P. D. Beidler
Rainfall. Rogers, T. N. R.
The **rainmaker**. Humphrey, W.
RAINMAKERS
  Humphrey, W. The rainmaker
Rainwalkers. Hemley, R.
Rainy day. De Carteret, G. M.
The **rainy-day** bandit. Hoch, E. D.
The **rainy** moon. Colette
The **rainy** season. Son, C.-S.
The **rainy** station. Kawabata, Y.
Raised in the wilderness. Jones, D. C.
The **raising**. Wilson, L. A.
Raising the wind. Poe, E. A.
Raising wild birds. Hurd, J. W.
The **Rajah's** treasure. Wells, H. G.
The **rake** people. Freeman, J.
RALEIGH (N.C.) *See* North Carolina—
    Raleigh
Ralph, Julian, 1853-1903
  He wrote to the rats
    Roger Caras' Treasury of great cat
      stories
Ram him, damn him! Bedford-Jones, H.
The **ram** in the thicket. Morris, W.
Ram Ram. Ray, D.
Rambach, Peggy
  The crescent
    Rambach, P. When the animals leave
  Home
    Rambach, P. When the animals leave
  When the animals leave
    Rambach, P. When the animals leave
  Winter ends
    Rambach, P. When the animals leave
Ramblers and spinners. Wooton, C.
Ramchandani, Kamala
  Gitley
    Short story international 63
Ramírez, Sergio, 1942-
  A bed of bauxite in Weipa
    Ramírez, S. Stories
  The centerfielder
    Ramírez, S. Stories
  Charles Atlas also dies
    Ramírez, S. Stories
  Nicaragua is white
    Ramírez, S. Stories
  The perfect game
    Ramírez, S. Stories
  Saint Nikolaus
    Ramírez, S. Stories
  The siege
    Ramírez, S. Stories

Ramírez, Sergio, 1942-—Continued
To Jackie with all our heart
Ramírez, S. Stories
Ramírez Muñoz, M. Pilar
Up-country
Américas 38:50-2 Jl/Ag '86
Ramón. Paik, B.
Ramon/Ramona. Doubiago, S.
Ramon: souvenirs. Pritchard, M.
Ramos, Manuel
His mother's image
Southwest tales; ed. by Alurista and X.
Rojas-Urista
Rampling, Anne See Rice, Anne, 1941-
Rampo, Edogawa
The psychological test
Murder in Japan; ed. by J. L. Apostolou
and M. H. Greenberg
The Red Chamber
Murder in Japan; ed. by J. L. Apostolou
and M. H. Greenberg
Ramsland, Katherine
Nothing from nothing comes
Masques II; ed. by J. N. Williamson
Ramspeck, Doug
Conrat!
Seventeen 45:176-7+ Ap '86
RANCH LIFE
See also Cowboys
Brand, M. Dust storm
Brand, M. The sun stood still
Brand, M. The third bullet
DeMarinis, R. Romance: a prose villanelle
Australia
Cowan, P. The fence
Cowan, P. Living
Morrison, J. The Prophet of Pandaloop
Prichard, K. S. The cooboo
Prichard, K. S. Happiness
California
Atherton, G. F. H. The conquest of Doña
Jacoba
Brand, M. The golden day
Canada
St. Pierre, P. H. A day with a deer, a
bear and Norah Smith
St. Pierre, P. H. Frenchie's wife
St. Pierre, P. H. How to run the country
St. Pierre, P. H. Sale of one small ranch
Mexico
Bowles, P. At Paso Rojo
Reasoner, J. M. Hacendado
Montana
Bower, B. M. The lamb of the Flying U
Pronzini, B. All the long years
New Mexico
Anaya, R. A. The silence of the llano
McIlroy, C. All my relations
Texas
Henry, O. The higher abdication
Henry, O. Hygeia at the Solito
Osborn, C. House of the blue woman
Osborn, C. Stalking strangers

Western States
Curry, P. S. The brushoff
Henry, O. The last of the troubadours
Pritchett, M. Open twenty-four hours
Sandoz, M. The girl in the Humbert
Wyoming
Fisher, C. Isley's stranger
Rand, Naomi
No sore losers
Here's the story: fiction with heart; ed.
by M. Sklar
Rand, Peter, 1940-
Baby Boy
Rand, P. The private rich
The butler
Rand, P. The private rich
Charades
Rand, P. The private rich
Circe
Rand, P. The private rich
Cousins
Rand, P. The private rich
A grandson of the Golden West
Rand, P. The private rich
Heir
Rand, P. The private rich
Mr. and Mrs. Noonan
Rand, P. The private rich
The nephew
Rand, P. The private rich
Pirates
Rand, P. The private rich
Settembrino's mother
Rand, P. The private rich
A soldier of fortunes
Rand, P. The private rich
Randall, Marta
Big dome
The Planets; ed. by B. Preiss
Lapidary nights
Universe 17
Thank you, Mr. Halifax
Omni (New York, N.Y.) 7:62+ N '84
Randall, Robert
For works written by this author under
other names see Silverberg, Robert
Randall's band. Buckley, D.
Randisi, Robert J.
Deathlist
The Eyes have it; ed. by R. J. Randisi
A matter of ethics
The Black Lizard anthology of crime fic-
tion; ed. by E. Gorman
The nickel derby
The Mammoth book of private eye
stories; ed. by B. Pronzini and M. H.
Greenberg
The vanishing virgin
An Eye for justice; ed. by R. J. Randisi
Randolph, Georgiana Ann See Rice, Craig,
1908-1957
The random man. Laidlaw, M.
Randy's gift. Romberger, J.

Raney. Edgerton, C.
Rank and money. Rostopchina, E. P., grafiniä
Ranklin Felano Doosevelt. Gardner, M.
Rannysore. Shannon, D.
Ransom, W. M.
  The aftermath
    Earth power coming; ed. by S. J. Ortiz
Rao, B. Sridhar
  Victims of time
    The Penguin world omnibus of science fiction
RAPE
  Andreyev, L. The abyss
  Ardizzone, T. The daughter and the tradesman
  Atwood, M. Rape fantasies
  Barthelme, S. The friend
  Baynton, B. The chosen vessel
  Bloch, R. Untouchable
  Bryant, E. The transfer
  Coleman, W. The Dufus Rufus
  Davis, D. S. Old friends
  Day, R. C. The violation
  Dixon, M. Red leaves
  Dubus, A. The curse
  Dubus, A. The pretty girl
  Ellison, H. Broken glass
  Everett, P. L. Cry about a nickel
  Goyen, W. Had I a hundred mouths
  Grenville, K. Refractions
  Hauptman, W. Sierra wave
  Heinemann, L. Good morning to you, Lieutenant
  Highsmith, P. Where the action is
  Hunnicutt, E. Bringing the news
  Joubert, E. Milk
  Kavaler, R. Tigers in the wood
  Kinsella, W. P. Caraway
  Kleist, H. von. Story of a remarkable single combat
  Li, Y.-P. The rain from the sun
  Lish, G. Everything I know
  MacDonald, J. D. Squealer
  Matthews, J. A woman of properties
  McElroy, C. J. A brief spell by the river
  McGuane, T. Like a leaf
  Moon, S.-T. Last sound of the gong
  Mortimer, J. C. Rumpole and the Honourable Member
  Oates, J. C. Master race
  O'Donnell, P. A better day to die
  Pavese, C. Summer storm
  Rees, D. Gay cat burglar seeks same for long-lasting relationship
  Schinto, J. From a juror's notebook
  Singer, I. B. One day of happiness
  Somers, A. Plunder
  Tamer, Z. The stale loaf
  Thorman, C. Sweet chickadee of grace
  Wiesinger, S. Cane Road
  Willett, J. Under the bed
  Williams, T. Big Black: a Mississippi idyll

  Williamson, J. N. House mothers
  Winton, T. Minimum of two
The **rape**. Aćin-Kosta, M.
Rape fantasies. Atwood, M.
Raphael, Frederic, 1931-
  Aperitif
    Raphael, F. Oxbridge blues, and other stories
  Benchmark
    Raphael, F. Oxbridge blues, and other stories
  Cheap day
    Raphael, F. Oxbridge blues, and other stories
  For Joannie
    Raphael, F. Oxbridge blues, and other stories
  Forgetting it
    Raphael, F. Oxbridge blues, and other stories
  On the black list
    Raphael, F. Oxbridge blues, and other stories
  Oxbridge blues
    Raphael, F. Oxbridge blues, and other stories
  Private views
    Raphael, F. Oxbridge blues, and other stories
  Similar triangles
    Raphael, F. Oxbridge blues, and other stories
  Sleeps six
    Raphael, F. Oxbridge blues, and other stories
  Someone else
    Raphael, F. Oxbridge blues, and other stories
  Still life
    Raphael, F. Oxbridge blues, and other stories
  That was Tory
    Raphael, F. Oxbridge blues, and other stories
  Welcome aboard
    Raphael, F. Oxbridge blues, and other stories
  You don't remember me
    Raphael, F. Oxbridge blues, and other stories
Raphael, Lev
  Dancing on Tishe B'av
    Men on men 2; ed. by G. Stambolian
  Roy's Jewish problem
    Commentary 80:62-6 S '85
Rapoport, Louis
  The staged 60's
    Commentary 82:47-52 Jl '86
Rappaccini's daughter. Hawthorne, N.
Rappaport lays an egg. Lurie, M.
Rappoport, Solomon *See* Ansky, S., 1863-1920
Rapport. Colter, C.

Rapture. Hall, M. M.
Rapture. Neville, S.
Rapture. Purdy, J.
Rapunzel, Rapunzel. Rhys, J.
Raquel. Doubiago, S.
Rarà. Paolucci, A.
Rara avis. Boyle, T. C.
RARE BOOKS
  Lovecraft, H. P. The picture in the house
The **rarer** thing. Garrett, G. P.
RAROTONGA ISLAND (COOK ISLANDS)
  McQueen, J. The myna birds
RAS TAFARI MOVEMENT
  Katz, S. The stolen stories
Rasputin, Valentin Grigor'evich
  French lessons
    Rasputin, V. G. You live and love, and
    other stories
  I can't sta-and it . . .
    Rasputin, V. G. You live and love, and
    other stories
  Meeting
    Rasputin, V. G. You live and love, and
    other stories
  Mum's gone out somewhere
    Rasputin, V. G. You live and love, and
    other stories
  Natasha
    Rasputin, V. G. You live and love, and
    other stories
  The old woman
    Rasputin, V. G. You live and love, and
    other stories
  Rudolfio
    The Barsukov Triangle, The two-toned
    blond & other stories; ed. by C. R.
    Proffer & E. Proffer
    Rasputin, V. G. You live and love, and
    other stories
  Vasili and Vasilisa
    Rasputin, V. G. You live and love, and
    other stories
  What shall I tell the crow?
    Rasputin, V. G. You live and love, and
    other stories
  You live and love
    Rasputin, V. G. You live and love, and
    other stories
Rassim. Aćin-Kosta, M.
Rasulov, Mahomed-Rasul
  The eve of love
  Short story international 53
A **rat** and some renovations. MacLaverty, B.
The **rat** line. Kantner, R.
Rat race. Herbert, F.
Rat with tangerine. Hollingshead, G.
Rata
  The invasion of Sydney
  Australian science fiction; ed. by V. Ikin
Rathjen, Carl Henry
  A debt to Doc
  Alfred Hitchcock's Crimewatch
The **rathskeller** and the rose. Henry, O.

The **ration** runners. Böll, H.
Ratner, Debra
  The dreams of all men
    The Yale Review 74:434-46 Spr '85
Ratón ladrón. Shuttle, P.
RATS
  Fisher, M. F. K. A question answered
  Hébert, L.-P. The hotel
  Highsmith, P. The bravest rat in Venice
  Kuttner, H. The graveyard rats
  Lanier, S. E. A father's tale
  Lovecraft, H. P. The rats in the walls
  MacLaverty, B. A rat and some renova-
    tions
  Martin, V. The consolation of nature
  McEwan, I. First love, last rites
  Mitchell, E. P. The devilish rat
  Murphy, P. The cleaner
  Narayan, R. K. Flavour of coconut
  Ralph, J. He wrote to the rats
  Stoker, B. The judge's house
  Taylor, P. E. Sermon on the rat
'Rats'. Lawson, H.
The **rats** in the walls. Lovecraft, H. P.
RATTLESNAKES
  Alter, R. E. A killer in the dark
  Hurston, Z. N. Sweat
Ratushinskaya, Irina
  On the meaning of life
    The Pushcart prize XII
Rausch, Barbara
  Snows of yesteryear
    The Clarion awards; ed. by D. Knight
Rautavaara's case. Dick, P. K.
Rava, Susan
  Lunchtime, August 1938
    Prairie Schooner 59:3-12 Spr '85
The **ravages** of time. Menaker, D.
Raven, Simon, 1927-
  The bottle of 1912
    The Oxford book of English ghost
    stories
RAVENS
  St. Clair, M. An old-fashioned bird Christ-
    mas
Raven's Wing. Oates, J. C.
Ravin, Bernice Lewis
  Cabin class to Pubjanice
    A Good deal; ed. by M. Heath and F.
    M. Robinson
Rawalpindi. MacLean, A.
Rawet, Samuel
  His moment of glory
    The Literary Review (Madison, N.J.)
    27:411-13 Summ '84
Rawhead Rex. Barker, C.
The **Rawleigh** man. Luce-Kapler, R.
Rawlings, Marjorie Kinnan, 1896-1953
  Gal young un
    The Other woman; ed. by S. Koppelman

Rawls, Wilson, 1913-
The hounds of youth
The Saturday Evening Post 258:68-73+
Ja/F '86
The Saturday Evening Post 258:50-55+ Mr
'86
The Saturday Evening Post 258:68-73+ Ap
'86
Rawson, Clayton, 1906-1971
Off the face of the earth
Death locked in; ed. by D. G. Greene
and R. C. S. Adey
Ray, David, 1932-
Ram Ram
Missouri short fiction; ed. by C. Beasley
Ray. Dixon, S.
Rayfiel, Thomas
Watch the closing doors
Grand Street 7:49-71 Spr '88
Rayme. Phillips, J. A.
Raymond, Ilene
Taking a chance on Jack
The Editors' choice: new American
stories v2
Mademoiselle 90:127+ Ap '84
Prize stories, 1985
Raymond's run. Bambara, T. C.
The **raza** who scored big in Anáhuac. Keller,
G. D.
The **razor.** Shiga, N.
Razzak, Abdul Ilah Abdul
Voices from near and far
Arabic short stories; tr. by D. Johnson-
Davies
Re-deem the time. Lake, D. J.
Reach, Alice Scanlan
Father Crumlish remembers his Poe
Ellery Queen's Memorable characters
Reach, James
A time to remember
Ellery Queen's Memorable characters
The **reach.** King, S.
Reach for the sky. Shepard, J.
Reach for tomorrow. Thomas, R.
Read, Opie
An Arkansas hanging
Arkansas in short fiction; ed. by W. M.
Baker and E. C. Simpson
Big Bill and Little Bill
Arkansas in short fiction; ed. by W. M.
Baker and E. C. Simpson
Read, Piers Paul, 1941-
Son and heir
Winter's tales, new ser. v2
Reade, Charles, 1814-1884
Agra outwits two pirate ships
Men at sea; ed. by B. Aymar
Reading sign. Minton, K.
Reading the paper. Carlson, R.
Reading the signs. Halley, A.
Ready money. Warren, J.

REAGAN, RONALD, 1911-
About
Blumlein, M. Tissue ablation and variant
regeneration: a case report
The **real** bad friend. Bloch, R.
A **real** discovery. Chesterton, G. K.
REAL ESTATE
Apple, M. My real estate
Calisher, H. The tenth child
Canin, E. Where we are now
Dadswell, M. The joys of speculating
Henry, O. Georgia's ruling
Howes, C. The resurrection man
Jolley, E. Bill Sprockett's land
Jolley, E. A gentleman's agreement
Jolley, E. The outworks of the kingdom
Matthews, J. A woman of properties
Pronzini, B. Caught in the act
Singer, I. B. The litigants
Stuart, J. From the mountains of Pike
Wolfe, T. Boom town
REAL ESTATE BUSINESS
Apple, M. My real estate
Beattie, A. Janus
Fahy, C. The rock
Gifkins, M. The dispossessed
A **real** hard rain. Everett, P. L.
Real illusions. Haley, R.
Real impudence. Calisher, H.
Real Indians. Kinsella, W. P.
The **real** life of Viviane Romance. Lopatin,
J.
A **real** little marriage-wrecker. Windsor, G.
Real losses, imaginary gains. Morris, W.
A **real** nice guy. Nolan, W. F.
The **real** one and the other. Maupassant, G.
de
REAL PROPERTY *See* Real estate
The **real** shape of the coast. Lutz, J.
The **real** story. Painter, P.
The **real** Tad Allagash. McInerney, J.
The **real** thing. Lessing, D. M.
The **real** world. Rule, J.
Reality. Valladares, A.
Realtime. Prebehalla, G., and Moran, D. K.
Realty. Barrett, L.
Reamy, Tom, 1935-1977
Beyond the cleft
Nightmares in Dixie; ed. by F. McSher-
ry; C. G. Waugh and M. H. Green-
berg
Insects in amber
The Best horror stories from the
Magazine of fantasy and science fiction
Reaney, James, 1926-
The bully
The Oxford book of Canadian short
stories in English
Reap it as you sow it. Bonner, M.
Reaper. Bloch, R.
The **reaper's** image. King, S.
Reason. Asimov, I.
The **reason.** Dawson, F.

Reason seven. Malzberg, B. N.
A reason to die. Collins, M.
The reason why. Gorman, E.
Reasonable people. Russ, J.
Reasoner, James M.
  Death and the dancing shadows
    The Black Lizard anthology of crime fic-
    tion; ed. by E. Gorman
  Hacendado
    Westeryear; ed. by E. Gorman
  The safest place in the world
    An Eye for justice; ed. by R. J. Randisi
REASONING
  Gardner, M. The dome of many colors
  Landolfi, T. An abstract concept
Reasons for going into gynaecology. Windsor,
  G.
Reata's peril trek. Brand, M.
Reaver, Chap
  Mixed marriage
    Southern Exposure (Durham, N.C.)
    13:40-1 S/O '85
Reaves, J. Michael
  Werewind
    The Best horror stories from the
    Magazine of fantasy and science fiction
Reba. Bell, M.
Reba. Coleman, W.
Reba. Walmsley, A.
Rebecca Winwar's flanks had withered. Rack-
  ham, J.
The rebel wolf and Petrina. Dub, O.
REBELLIONS See Revolutions
Rebels. Shiner, L.
The rebels. Winters, J.
Rebetez-Cortes, René
  The new prehistory
    The Penguin world omnibus of science
    fiction
Rebirth. McKnight, R.
Rebound. Pronzini, B., and Malzberg, B. N.
Recalling Cinderella. Fowler, K. J.
Recapitulation. Nichols, J.
Recently I've discovered my mistake. Haake,
  K.
The reckoning. Auchincloss, L.
Reclamation. Johnson, T. J.
The recluse. Singer, I. B.
A recluse and his guest. Williams, T.
RECLUSES
    See also Hermits
  Anaya, R. A. The silence of the llano
  Aucamp, H. Soup for the sick
  Austin, D. Milton Freabe
  Bates, H. E. Where the cloud breaks
  Boylan, J. Invisible woman
  Calvino, I. The house of the beehives
  Dick, P. K. Chains of air, web of aether
  Faulkner, W. A rose for Emily
  Grant, C. L. Out there
  Haley, R. The palace of Kandahar
  Helprin, M. The Schreuderspitze
  Jeffrey, W. A case for quiet

Kanafānī, G. The Slave Fort
Rhys, J. Pioneers, oh, pioneers
Williams, T. A recluse and his guest
A recollection. Gallant, M.
Recollections of a young king. Böll, H.
The recollections of Captain Wilkie. Doyle,
  Sir A. C.
RECONCILIATION
  Aldiss, B. W. Consolations of age
  Stuart, J. When mountain men make peace
The reconciliation. Wells, H. G.
A reconciliation. Wooton, C.
The record. Liben, M.
A record as long as your arm. Garrett, G.
  P.
Record of a journey to Mujin. Kim, S.-O.
The recording. Wolfe, G.
Recourse. Gallagher, T.
Recovery. Crone, M.
Recovery. Katz, L. B.
The recovery of vision. Sanders, S. R.
Recovery room. Wilner, H.
Recrudescence of Imray. See Kipling, R. The
  return of Imray
The recruiting officer. McGahern, J.
RECTORS See Catholic priests; Clergy,
  Anglican and Episcopal
Recuerdo. Valdés, G.
Recurrence. De Celles, M.
Recurrent dreams. Rey Rosa, R.
The red. Clarke, T.
Red. Glover, D. H.
Red. Gorky, M.
Red. Matheson, R. C.
Red. Maugham, W. S.
RED ARMY (SOVIET UNION) See Soviet
  Union. Red Army
Red as blood. Lee, T.
The red-back spider. Skrzynecki, P.
The red-backed spiders. Cowan, P.
The red badge of courage. Crane, S.
Red Beard's daughter. Essop, A.
The red boots. Soucy, J.-Y.
Red boy. Chang, H.-kuo
The red bread. Aćin-Kosta, M.
Red carpet treatment. Lipsyte, R.
Red chair. DeMarinis, R.
The Red Chamber. Rampo, E.
The red cocoon. Abe, K.
The red dress. Janecky, J. Y.
The red dress. Rothberg, A.
The red dust of Lanai. Heller, S.
The red dwarf. Tournier, M.
A red fox, a Polish lady, a Russian samovar.
  Lurie, M.
The red frog. Shimaki, K.
Red glass. Walter, R.
The red hawk. Lynn, E. A.
The red-headed league. Doyle, Sir A. C.
The red inn. Balzac, H. de
Red leaves. Dixon, M.
Red letter days. Hansen, R.
Red liberty. Woolrich, C.

Red nails. Howard, R. E.

Red noise. Sladek, J. T.

Red, red. Murphy, Y.

Red Reno honkers. Sanchez, T.

The **red** room. Wells, H. G.

The **red** roses of Tonia. Henry, O.

The **red** sickness. Potter, R.

Red spikes. Nevai, L.

Red stag. Dabrowska, C.

Red star, winter orbit. Sterling, B., and Gibson, W.

Red suspenders. McClintock, M.

A **red** sweater. Ng, F. M.

Red-winged blackbirds. Cooper, J. C.

Red Wolf. Rosenfeld, I.

Redbeard. Wolfe, G.

Redd, David

On the deck of the Flying Bomb
Interzone: the first anthology; ed. by J. Clute; C. Greenland and D. Pringle

Redding, Sandra

Tin of Tube Rose
When I am an old woman I shall wear purple; ed. by S. K. Martz

REDEMPTION *See* Atonement

Redemption. Gardner, J.

The **Redemption** Center. Kinsella, W. P.

Redemption songs. Shacochis, B.

Redfield, Cinda

Grieve now
The North American Review 269:15-19 Mr '84

Redfish. Bass, R.

The **redhead**. Asimov, I.

The **redhead**. Gilliatt, P.

A **redhead** named Sabina. Campos, J.

Redmond. Schulze, K.

The **redneck** poacher's son. Wallin, L.

The **redtown** chronicles. Valenzuela, L.

REDUCING

Kilgore, D. The dietary exploits of Bessie

Reed, Diana

Bizarre births
The Georgia Review 42:71-91 Spr '88

REED, JIM

About

Taylor, R. Jim Reed

Reed, John R.

Moth summer
Michigan Quarterly Review 23:412-21 Summ '84

Reed, Kit, 1932-

Alumni fund
Reed, K. The revenge of the senior citizens ** plus

The bride of Bigfoot
Reed, K. The revenge of the senior citizens ** plus

Chicken soup
Reed, K. The revenge of the senior citizens ** plus

Dog days
Reed, K. The revenge of the senior citizens ** plus

Final tribute
Reed, K. The revenge of the senior citizens ** plus

Frontiers
Reed, K. The revenge of the senior citizens ** plus

Great Escape Tours Inc.
Reed, K. The revenge of the senior citizens ** plus

The holdouts
Reed, K. The revenge of the senior citizens ** plus

Into the parlor
Reed, K. The revenge of the senior citizens ** plus

Love story
Reed, K. The revenge of the senior citizens ** plus

The marriage bug
Reed, K. The revenge of the senior citizens ** plus

The revenge of the senior citizens: a novella
Reed, K. The revenge of the senior citizens ** plus

Shan
Reed, K. The revenge of the senior citizens ** plus

Sisohpromatem
Reed, K. The revenge of the senior citizens ** plus

A unique service
Reed, K. The revenge of the senior citizens ** plus

The visible partner
Reed, K. The revenge of the senior citizens ** plus

The wait
Nightmares in Dixie; ed. by F. McSherry; C. G. Waugh and M. H. Greenberg

Reed, Lillian Craig *See* Reed, Kit, 1932-

Reed, Robert

Treading in the afterglow
Universe 16

Reed, Ron

The slicker
Short story international 42

The **reed**. Seghers, A.

Reeman, Douglas

Trouble cargo
Sea captains' tales; ed. by A. Enfield

Reencounter. Jin He

Rees, David, 1936-

An apple for the preacher
Rees, D. Islands

At 21st Street
Rees, D. Islands

Canes
Rees, D. Islands

Rees, David, 1936-—Continued
Cliff
  Rees, D. Islands
Departures
  Rees, D. Islands
Gay cat burglar seeks same for long-lasting
    relationship
  Rees, D. Islands
The gilded youth of Los Gatos
  Rees, D. Islands
In the fast lane
  Rees, D. Islands
In the same boat
  Rees, D. Islands
Open scholarship
  Rees, D. Islands
Pip
  Rees, D. Islands
Plums
  Rees, D. Islands
The queen of queens
  Rees, D. Islands
Quiet days in Los Gatos
  Rees, D. Islands
Robin
  Rees, D. Islands
The year of the bulls
  Rees, D. Islands
Reeve, F. D. (Franklin D.), 1928-
The riverman
  The Sewanee Review 95:359-68 Summ
    '87
Soda pop
  The North American Review 269:50-2 Mr
    '84
Reeve, Franklin D. *See* Reeve, F. D. (Frank-
    lin D.), 1928-
The **Reeve's** tale. Chaucer, G.
Reflections in a cell. Gwala, M.
Reflections in the ice. Curley, D.
Reflections on murder. Tyre, N.
The **reflex-man** in Whinnymuir Close. Kirk,
    R.
REFORMATORIES
Algren, N. The children
REFORMERS
Gordon, M. The only son of the doctor
Hawthorne, N. Earth's holocaust
Refractions. Grenville, K.
Refugee. Clarke, A. C.
REFUGEES
    See also Exiles
Baillie, A. Snap
Bissoondath, N. Man as plaything, life as
    mockery
Greening, J. Pleasure trips
Lin, H.-Y. Lunar New Year's feast
O'Connor, F. The displaced person
Rhys, J. I spy a stranger
Sandel, C. To Lukas
REFUGEES, GERMAN
Matthews, J. "This moment is ours alone"
Seghers, A. The reed

Serling, R. The escape route
REFUGEES, GUATEMALAN
Ruta, S. At the border
REFUGEES, JEWISH
Briskin, M. By evil and kindness
Briskin, M. Florence, May '86
Briskin, M. My father and Signor Corelli
Briskin, M. Vincenzo and Giulia
Liberman, S. Drifting
Morris, W. Here is Einbaum
Ozick, C. Rosa
Zwicky, F. Hostages
REFUGEES, KHMER
Bellamy, J. D. Saving the boat people
REFUGEES, POLISH
Singer, I. B. Runners to nowhere
REFUGEES, RUSSIAN
Schwartz, L. S. The opiate of the people
REFUGEES, VIETNAMESE
Houbein, L. Survival switch
Refugees. Bullard, S.
REFUSE AND REFUSE DISPOSAL
Carlson, R. The Governor's Ball
Farmer, P. J. The alley man
Irving, J. Trying to save Piggy Sneed
Martínez-Serros, H. Distillation
Silvis, R. Trash man
Regarding the problem of new-born pigs in
    winter. Shen Rong
REGENCY ENGLAND *See* England—19th
    century
REGENERATION
Clement, H. The mechanic
Johnson, G. C. Sea change
Moore, C. L. No woman born
Varshavsky, I. No alarming symptoms
Regent, Peter
At Manoli's sheepfold
  Regent, P. Laughing Pig, and other
    stories
A delicate nose
  Regent, P. Laughing Pig, and other
    stories
Feet of clay
  Regent, P. Laughing Pig, and other
    stories
Great Pan is dead!
  Regent, P. Laughing Pig, and other
    stories
Laughing Pig
  Regent, P. Laughing Pig, and other
    stories
The Major steps out
  Regent, P. Laughing Pig, and other
    stories
Memories of colonialism
  Regent, P. Laughing Pig, and other
    stories
Mr. Parsley's lunchtime pursuit
  Regent, P. Laughing Pig, and other
    stories

Regent, Peter—*Continued*
On the Aberdonian
Regent, P. Laughing Pig, and other
stories
Pleasures of the flesh
Regent, P. Laughing Pig, and other
stories
The proposal
Regent, P. Laughing Pig, and other
stories
Schoolboy war
Regent, P. Laughing Pig, and other
stories
Stepan
Regent, P. Laughing Pig, and other
stories
Summer pudding
Regent, P. Laughing Pig, and other
stories
The ugliest man in the world
Regent, P. Laughing Pig, and other
stories
Ziggy's last dance
Regent, P. Laughing Pig, and other
stories
The **regent** of the North. Morris, K.
Regier, Gail
Talking to the sun
The Atlantic 260:76-80 S '87
A **regimental** scandal. Doyle, Sir A. C.
Reginald Gulliver, Eruntics. Lem, S.
The **region** between. Ellison, H.
The **region** of the heart. Dumont, F.
Regret. Maupassant, G. de
The **regulars**. Silverberg, R.
Regulations for meatball peddlers. Nesin, A.
Rehman, Shafiqur
Lull after the storm
Short story international 71
Reich, Tova
Gifted and talented
Commentary 80:56-61 Jl '85
Mengele in Jerusalem
Harper's 272:64-8 Je '86
Solidarity
The Atlantic 253:70-80 Ja '84
Reichs-peace. Finch, S.
The **reigate** squires. Doyle, Sir A. C.
Reimer, Isabel
Murder on the flux line
Short story international 52
REINCARNATION
Bradbury, R. The Laurel and Hardy love
affair
Clarke, M. Human repetends
Clee, M. A. Encounter on the ladder
Gilgun, J. Cow
Goulart, R. Groucho
Kress, N. With the original cast
Lee, T. Tamastara
Lee, T. Three days
Merril, J. The shrine of temptation
Nesin, A. Tactics

Poe, E. A. A tale of the ragged mountains
Pohl, F. My life as a born-again pig
Saki. Laura
Scholz, C. Galileo complains
Smith, E. E. Teragram
Strand, M. More life
La **reine** blanche. Lee, T.
Reinforced concrete. Haris, P.
Reininger, Cathy
Cache reward
Alberta bound; ed. by F. Stenson
Reitci, John George *See* Ritchie, Jack, 1922-
1983
Reitz, Jean
Monsters
L. Ron Hubbard presents Writers of the
future v3
REJUVENATION
Bradbury, R. Hail and farewell
Relationship. Yu, C.-Y.
Relative motion. Day, R. C.
RELATIVES *See* Family life
RELATIVITY (PHYSICS)
See also Gravitation; Space and time
Asimov, I. The billiard ball
Breuer, M. J. The gostak and the doshes
The **relaxed** anarchist. Austin, D.
The **relay** race. Liben, M.
Release. Klinkowitz, J.
The **release**. Rey Rosa, R.
The **relic**. Maupassant, G. de
Relics. Evans, E.
The **relics**. Maupassant, G. de
Relics. Thomas, A. C.
RELIGION
See also Biblical stories; Buddhism;
Catholic faith; Christianity; Clergy;
Conversion; Faith; God; Judaism;
Mormons and Mormonism; Religion,
Primitive
Auchincloss, L. The Stations of the Cross
Barthelme, D. January
Barton, M. Jacob's angel
Bishop, M. The gospel according to
Gamaliel Crucis; or, The astrogator's
testimony
Broun, H. Cows on the drag strip
Campbell, R. The hands
Caponegro, M. The convention
Chekhov, A. P. Murder
Choe, I.-H. Christmas carol
Cowley, J. God loves you, Miss Rosewater
Dick, P. K. Rautavaara's case
Ferron, J. The Buddhist
Ferron, J. Cadieu
Fisher, R. The backslider
Fisher, R. The South lingers on
Gilchrist, E. First Manhattans
Harris, F. The holy man
Houston, R. Lawfully
Huggan, I. Secrets
Kercheval, J. L. The history of the church
in America

RELIGION—*Continued*
Kim, S.-H. Badby
Kinsella, W. P. The Redemption Center
Martin, G. R. R. And seven times never kill man
Martin, G. R. R. A song for Lya
Martin, G. R. R. The way of cross and dragon
McCulla, J. How Esco Mize got religion
Norris, G. Revive us again
Pritchard, M. Disturbing no one
Pritchett, V. S. The saint
Rees, D. An apple for the preacher
Roberts, K. Kitemaster
Rogers, S. The crumb
Rossiter, S. Sinners
Sanders, S. R. Prophet
Sawai, G. The day I sat with Jesus on the sun deck and a wind came up and blew my kimono open and he saw my breasts
Sheckley, J. Lost soul
Silverberg, R. The Pope of the chimps
Singer, I. B. The accuser and the accused
Spark, M. The gentile Jewesses
Sturgeon, T. Why dolphins don't bite
Sturges, A. E. The last loneliness
Tiptree, J. Our resident djinn
Tiptree, J. Second going
Updike, J. Pigeon feathers
Vanderhaeghe, G. How the story ends
Walters, A. L. The Devil and Sister Lena
Watson, I. Cold light
Weaver, G. The Bearded Lady
Williamson, J. Farside station
Woolson, C. F. The Lady of Little Fishing
Woolson, C. F. St. Clair Flats

RELIGION, PRIMITIVE
See also Paganism
McCormack, E. P. A train of gardens— Part I: Ireneus Fludd
Religious instruction. Pulaski, J.

RELIGIOUS LIBERTY
Hawthorne, N. Endicott and the Red Cross

RELIGIOUS LIFE *See* Convent life; Monasticism and religious orders

RELIGIOUS PERSECUTION *See* Persecution

The **reliquary**. Johnson, G.
The **reluctant** detective. Lewin, M. Z.
A **reluctant** grandmother. Clayton, S.
Reluctant revolutionaries. Houbein, L.
Remains. Crapser, W.
A **remark** concerning a little something about the devil. Bakhnov, V.
Remarkable. Pierce, A. W.
The **remarkable** case of Davidson's eyes. Wells, H. G.

REMARRIAGE
Botwinik, B. A shoemaker for a husband
Busch, F. A history of small ideas
Clayton, J. J. Part-time father
Davis, L. The sock

DeMarinis, R. Gent
Engberg, S. The mile run
Ford, R. Sweethearts
Gallagher, T. Beneficiaries
Gilchrist, E. Dede's talking, it's her turn
Greenberg, A. What would I know?
Miller, S. The quality of life
Nagibin, ÍŪ. M. The outsider
Oates, J. C. Happy
Peterson, M. The carved table
Price, R. Michael Egerton
Roberts, N. A second wife
Ross, V. That summer
Rossi, A. Athletes and artists
Singer, I. B. Strangers
Steele, M. The girl from Carthage
Tallent, E. Black holes
Thurm, M. Aftermath
Thurm, M. Flying
Thurm, M. Sounds
Updike, J. Beautiful husbands
Wang, C.-H. The story of three springs
Williams, J. The wedding
Remedies. Lerman, E.
Remember Mrs. Fitz. Sims, G.
Remember that joke, Harry? McClure, J.
Remember the Errol-mo! Drake, R.
Remember the rug. Halligan, M.
Remember young Cecil. Kelman, J.
Remembering Sonny. Thompson, J.
Remembrance of things past. Drake, M.
Remme's ride. Lee, H.
Remnants. Singer, I. B.
Remote. MacLaverty, B.
RENAISSANCE
See also Italy—16th century
The **renaissance** at Charleroi. Henry, O.
Rendell, Ruth, 1930-
Bribery and corruption
Rendell, R. The new girl friend, and other stories of suspense
The clinging woman
The Penguin classic crime omnibus
The convolvulus clock
John Creasey's Crime collection, 1987
Rendell, R. The new girl friend, and other stories of suspense
The Year's best mystery & suspense stories, 1986
A dark blue perfume
Rendell, R. The new girl friend, and other stories of suspense
Father's day
Rendell, R. The new girl friend, and other stories of suspense
The Year's best mystery and suspense stories, 1985
Fen Hall
Rendell, R. The new girl friend, and other stories of suspense
The fever tree
Masterpieces of mystery and suspense; ed. by M. H. Greenberg

Rendell, Ruth, 1930---- *Continued*
The green road to Quephanda
  Rendell, R. The new girl friend, and other stories of suspense
Hare's house
  Rendell, R. The new girl friend, and other stories of suspense
The irony of hate
  The Mammoth book of modern crime stories; ed. by G. Hardinge
Loopy
  Haunting women; ed. by A. Ryan
  Rendell, R. The new girl friend, and other stories of suspense
The new girl friend
  Rendell, R. The new girl friend, and other stories of suspense
  The Year's best mystery and suspense stories, 1984
The orchard walls
  Rendell, R. The new girl friend, and other stories of suspense
The price of joy
  Ellery Queen's Crimes and punishments
The vinegar mother
  Ready or not; ed. by J. Kahn
The whistler
  Rendell, R. The new girl friend, and other stories of suspense
The **render** of the veils. Campbell, R.
Rendering Byzantium. Working, R.
Rendezvous. Aksenov, V. P.
The **rendezvous.** Colette
Rendezvous. MacLean, A.
The **rendezvous.** Maupassant, G. de
A **rendezvous** in Averoigne. Smith, C. A.
Rendezvous with Margret; or, Happy ending. Böll, H.
The **renegade.** Camus, A.
The **renegade.** Jackson, S.
Reno Island. Grin, A.
The **rented** scar. Hoch, E. D.
Renwick, Joyce
  Still lives
    The Sewanee Review 94:73-91 Wint '86
The **repairer** of reputations. Chambers, R. W.
Reparations; or, Making good. Muschg, A.
REPENTANCE
    See also Sin
  Botwinik, B. The one I didn't marry
  Chekhov, A. P. Rothschild's fiddle
  Gardner, M. The sixth ship
  Sanford, W. M. Saved
Repetition. Handke, P.
A **replacement.** Matthiessen, P.
The **replacement.** Robbe-Grillet, A.
Report cards. Humphrey, W.
Report from the World Federation of Displaced Writers. Federman, R.
Report on a broken bridge. O'Neil, D.
Report on Heaven and Hell. Ocampo, S.
Report on the shadow industry. Carey, P.

Report to the nation: claiming Europe. Revard, C.
REPORTERS *See* Journalists
Reports from Cahabon. Rey Rosa, R.
Repository. Lurie, M.
The **representative.** Jolley, E.
Reprieve. Toyne, M.
A **reprieve.** Tuohy, F.
REPRODUCTION, ARTIFICIAL
  Bioy Casares, A. Venetian masks
  Varley, J. Lollipop and the tar baby
  Willis, C. Mail-order clone
  Zebrowski, G. The Eichmann variations
REPRODUCTION, ASEXUAL
  Asimov, I. What is this thing called love?
  Bloch, R. Forever and amen
  Lafferty, R. A. Magazine section
  Scortia, T. N. Flowering Narcissus
  Shepard, L. A Spanish lesson
  Tiptree, J. Houston, Houston, do you read?
The **reptile.** Muir, A.
The **requiem.** Chekhov, A. P.
Requiem. Cowan, P.
Requiem. Hamilton, E.
Requiem. Snodgrass, M.
Requiem for a busted flush. Prince, H.
Requiem for a universe. Anderson, P.
Requiem mass. Johnston, G.
Requiescat. Hersey, J.
Rerun. Tyler, A.
Rescheduling. Bernard, K.
The **rescue.** Boylan, J.
The **rescue.** Colter, C.
The **rescue.** McGuane, T.
RESCUE OPERATIONS *See* Search and rescue operations
Rescue party. Clarke, A. C.
Rescue squad. MacLean, K.
The **rescuer.** Dixon, S.
The **rescuer.** Walker, W.
RESCUES
  Bradley, M. Z. Hero's moon
  Crane, S. The open boat
  Doyle, Sir A. C. Gentlemanly Joe
  Doyle, Sir A. C. Touch and go: a midshipman's story
  Duecker, K. Saving the dead
  Ellis, M. Mister Dog
  Gaskell, E. C. The half-brothers
  Gustafsson, L. A water story
  Highsmith, P. The dream of the Emma C
  MacLean, A. The Dileas
  MacLean, K. Rescue squad
  Markham, B. Your heart will tell you
  Terry, W. S. The bottomless well
  Tiptree, J. Excursion fare
  Upward, E. Over the cliff
RESEARCH
  Kinsella, W. P. The Eddie Scissons syndrome
  Kress, N. Explanations, Inc.

RESEARCH—*Continued*
Le Guin, U. K. SQ
Nahin, P. J. Publish and perish
Wilhelm, K. Forever yours, Anna
Research. Apple, M.

RESEARCH WORKERS
Conley, R. J. Calf Roper's house guest
Pei, L. The cold room
Resemblance between a violin case and a coffin. Williams, T.
Reservation café: the origins of American Indian instant coffee. Vizenor, G. R.
Reset. Barthelme, F.
Resident. Havazelet, E.
Resident artist. Nevai, L.
The **resident** patient. Doyle, Sir A. C.
Residents and transients. Mason, B. A.

RESISTANCE MOVEMENTS (WORLD WAR, 1939-1945) *See* World War, 1939-1945—Underground movements

Resnick, Mike, 1942-
The Olympians
The Science fictional Olympics; ed. by I. Asimov; M. H. Greenberg and C. G. Waugh

Resnicow, Herbert
Greater love than this . . .
Distant danger; ed. by J. Van de Wetering
The **resolution** of muscle. Eidus, J.
Resonance ritual. May, P.

RESORTS *See* Hotels, taverns, etc. Summer resorts
Respect for the dead. Chernoff, M.
The **respecter** of persons. Dundas, R.
The **respite.** Colette
A **respite.** O, S.-W.
The **rest.** Crapser, W.
A **rest** and a change. Tracy, H.
The **rest** cure. Hornung, E. W.

RESTAURANTS, LUNCHROOMS, ETC.
Barthelme, F. Gila Flambé
Bell, M. S. The structure and meaning of dormitory and food services
Broun, H. Fryed cutlets
Camoin, F. A. Home is the Blue Moon Cafe
Carter, R. Kid in a bin
Colette. The other wife
Connell, E. S. The fisherman from Chihuahua
Crane, S. In a Park Row restaurant
Dadswell, M. Supper after the show
Dale, C. Business lunch
Davidson, A. Full chicken richness
Dozois, G. R., and others. Afternoon at Schrafft's
Dunn, D. Twin-sets and pickle forks
Epstein, L. The magic flute
Epstein, L. Music of the spheres
Epstein, L. The Steinway quintet
Faik, S. The neighborhood coffeehouse
Fox, W. P. Doug Broome, hamburger king

García Márquez, G. The woman who came at six o'clock
Gardner, E. S. Danger out of the past
Goldman, F. Fili
Greene, G. Brother
Greene, G. The invisible Japanese gentlemen
Heise, K. Eating out
Hemingway, E. A clean, well-lighted place
Hemingway, E. The killers
Horsdal, M. An educated taste
Ioannidou Adamidou, I. The beggar
Ioannidou Adamidou, I. Conversation
Jen, G. In the American society
Kees, W. Mrs. Lutz
Lombreglia, R. Inn Essence
Lowe, R. The woman in the window
Luban, M. Tomorrow you'll forget
Maheux-Forcier, L. The carnation
Maxwell, W. The Pilgrimage
Mazel, D. Lily's Deli
McCullers, C. The ballad of the sad café
McCullers, C. A tree. A rock. A cloud
Muschg, A. Dinnertime
Norris, G. Holding on
O'Hara, J. Price's always open
Pacheco, J. E. Acheron
Painter, P. Getting to know the weather
Parise, G. Poise
Petrakis, H. M. Pa and the sad turkeys
Petrakis, H. M. Rosemary
Poe, E. A. Bon-bon
Pronzini, B. Black wind
Raphael, F. Aperitif
Rhys, J. In a café
Roscoe, P. Never tears for California
Sharp, M. The perfect model
Suckow, R. Midwestern primitive
Warren, R. P. The patented gate and the mean hamburger
Wheatcroft, J. Sunday breakfast
Wijenaike, P. The visitor
Winton, T. Death belongs to the dead, his father told him, and sadness to the sad
Yun, H.-G. Group beating

RESTORATION ENGLAND *See* England—17th century
Restraint. Barthelme, F.
Restricted area. Sheckley, R.
Résumé. Willett, J.

RESURRECTION
Blish, J. A work of art
Bloch, R. The man who collected Poe
Smith, C. A. The empire of the necromancers
Resurrection. Ignatow, R. G.
Resurrection. Lish, G.
Resurrection. Rive, R.
The **resurrection** man. Howes, C.
The **resurrection** man. Knight, W. E.
The **resurrection** of John Stink. Walters, A. L.

The **resurrection** of Troutfishing in America
    Shorty. Kinsella, W. P.
Resurrectionists. Working, R.
A **retired** life. Gee, M.
The **retiree**. Hensley, J. L.
The **retiree**. López Heredia, J.
RETIREMENT
    See also Old age
Ade, G. The fable of the man who was
    going to retire
Baranskaya, N. The retirement party
Claiborne, S. Okinawa's wife
Digby, J. The champagne party
Fisher, M. F. K. Diplomatic, retired
Gee, M. A retired life
Goldman, E. S. Way to the dump
Gordimer, N. Sins of the third age
Haylock, J. A sort of retirement
Kiteley, B. Still life with insects
Liben, M. Mr. Mintz retires
Mortimer, J. C. Rumpole and the age for
    retirement
Murphy, P. Beyond the moving shadow
    problem
O'Brien, E. Christmas roses
Prichard, K. S. Yoirimba
Russell, C. Retiring man
Taylor, P. H. Two ladies in retirement
Vaughan, D. The death of a champion
West, J. Hunting for hoot owls
Wheatcroft, J. Image of departure
Whelan, G. A dwelling place for dragons
Whelan, G. First light
Whelan, G. The showing
Whitaker, M. Blackberry day
Retirement. Dadswell, M.
Retirement. Pronzini, B.
The **retirement** of Signor Lambert. Doyle, Sir
    A. C.
The **retirement** party. Baranskaya, N.
Retiring man. Russell, C.
Retreating figures. Endō, S.
Retrieval. Porter, J. A.
A **retrieved** reformation. Henry, O.
Retrospective. Saiki, J.
Retrospective on Weegee. Lopatin, J.
RETROSPECTIVE STORIES
Agee, J. 1928 story
Bartlett, H. Some notes on evolution
Bellow, S. Him with his foot in his mouth
Camoin, F. A. Peacock blue
Camoin, F. A. A special case
Dazai, O. Memories
Dixon, S. Will as a boy
Ellin, S. The day of the bullet
Faik, S. White gold
Flynn, R. The boy from Chillicothe
Flynn, R. Waiting for the postman
Gordon, C. Old Red
Halligan, M. The noise of the lorries
Houbein, L. Talking to the dark
Humphrey, W. A fresh snow
Ingalls, R. The man who was left behind

Kavaler, R. Depression glass
Madden, D. Willis Carr at Bleak House
Martin, V. The way of the world
Matthews, J. The burial
McCullers, C. Untitled piece
Munro, A. Royal beatings
Munro, A. Who do you think you are?
Nye, N. S. The cookies
Phillips, E. O. Stephanotis
Power, V. Lackendara
Rasputin, V. G. Natasha
Rodoreda, M. Memory of Caux
Sawai, G. Hang out your washing on the
    Siegfried Line
Skrzynecki, P. The biggest bonfire of all
Skrzynecki, P. The white eagle
Stafford, J. In the zoo
Thompson, J. Birds in air
Thompson, J. Remembering Sonny
Tremain, R. Wedding night
Wilbur, E. Faith
Wolff, T. The liar
Return. Asscher-Pinkhof, C.
The **return**. Bates, H. E.
The **return**. Colette
The **return**. Davie, E.
The **return**. Gilchrist, M.
The **return**. Ngugi wa Thiong'o
The **return**. O'Brien, E.
Return. Wolfe, T.
Return journey. Thomas, D.
The **return** match. Hornung, E. W.
The **return** of a private. Garland, H.
The **return** of Crazy Bill. Sisk, F.
The **return** of Imray. Kipling, R.
The **return** of Katerina. Petrakis, H. M.
The **return** of Mr. Wills. Austin, M. H.
The **return** of possibility. Covino, M.
Return of the dust vampires. Farber, S. N.
Return of the native. Watmough, D.
Return of the neon fireball. Williamson, C.
The **return** of the prodigal. Wolfe, T.
The **return** of the prodigal son. Gide, A.
The **return** of the Robins family. Chastain,
    T.
The **return** of the sorcerer. Smith, C. A.
The **return** of the speckled band. Hoch, E.
    D.
Return to an unknown city. Matthews, J.
Return to Lavinia. Caldwell, E.
Return to the fold. Zahn, T.
Return to the OK Corral. Howard, C.
Return to Venice. Fox, G.
Return trip tango. Cortázar, J.
Return trips. Adams, A.
Return visit. Anderman, J.
Returning from the lost land. José, E.
Returning home. Trollope, A.
Returning home. Watson, I.
Returns. Vreuls, D.
The **reunion**. Alden, P. B.
Reunion. Bingham, S.
Reunion. Cheever, J.

The **reunion**. Fisher, M. F. K.
Reunion. Hall, D.
Reunion. Hoch, E. D.
Reunion. McInerney, J.
Reunion. Vanderhaeghe, G.
Reunion on the avenue. Böll, H.
Reunion with Drüng. Böll, H.
REUNIONS
  Abbott, K. The sea lion
  Baxter, C. How I found my brother
  Bingham, S. Reunion
  Blackwood, A. Secret worship
  Bowen, S. P. Old maidism versus marriage
  Bracken, M. Of memories dying
  Busch, F. Stand, and be recognized
  Carver, R. Chef's house
  De Bruyn, G. Someday he really will come home
  Endō, S. Fuda-no-Tsuji
  Endō, S. Old friends
  Foltz-Gray, D. Departed coming back
  Garfield, B. Scrimshaw
  Garrett, G. P. Love is a cold kingdom
  Gilliatt, P. On each other's time
  Gold, H. Young man, old days
  Grenville, K. Slow dissolve
  Henry, O. The higher abdication
  Hood, M. A country girl
  Hornung, E. W. The field of Philippi
  Houbein, L. No stranger
  Howard, C. Custer's ghost
  Kalpakian, L. Habits
  Kessler, J. F. Aeaea
  Kessler, J. F. Esau
  Kundera, M. Let the old dead make room for the young dead
  Leavitt, D. Out here
  Matthew, J. R. Family visit
  Moorhouse, F. The airport, the pizzeria, the motel, the rented car, and the mysteries of life
  Mordden, E. The Boffer
  Muller, R. General Patton did not sleep here
  Phelps, E. S. Old Mother Goose
  Rule, J. Slogans
  Salter, J. Lost sons
  Schulman, H. Like brothers
  Stark, S. S. His color
  Straayer, A. C. High heels
  Summers, H. S. A hundred paths
  Taylor, P. H. Rain in the heart
  Thompson, J. Applause, applause
  Trevor, W. Torridge
Revard, Carter
  Never quite a Hollywood star
    The Massachusetts Review 25:115-24 Spr '84
  Report to the nation: claiming Europe
  Earth power coming; ed. by S. J. Ortiz
The **revealed** life of Cole Younger. Taylor, R.
Revealing thunder. Moravia, A.

The **revelation**. Bates, H. E.
Revelation. Ocampo, S.
Revelation. O'Connor, F.
Revelation. Saiki, J.
Revelations. Barker, C.
Revelations in black. Jacobi, C.
The **revelations** of 'Becka Paulson. King, S.
REVENGE
  Adcock, T. L. Thrown-away child
  Aiken, J. Smell
  Auchincloss, L. The reckoning
  Ballard, J. G. The dead astronaut
  Barbey d'Aurevilly, J. A woman's vengeance
  Barker, C. Cabal
  Bell, C. The hunting of Lord Etsalian's daughter
  Binder, E. Adam Link's vengeance
  Bishop, M. Within the walls of Tyre
  Bloch, R. The animal fair
  Bloch, R. The gods are not mocked
  Bloch, R. Night school
  Borges, J. L. Emma Zunz
  Bowles, P. The delicate prey
  Boyd, W. On the Yankee station
  Bradley, M. Z. Treason of the blood
  Brand, M. Outcast
  Braun, L. J. The sin of Madame Phloi
  Braund, M. What's on the telly tonight?
  Brennan, D. The trouble shooters
  Brunner, J. Elixir for the emperor
  Calvino, I. One of the three is still alive
  Canin, E. Emperor of the air
  Cohen, A. Malenov's revenge
  Conley, R. J. The hanging of Mose Miller
  Cooper, J. C. $100 and nothing!
  Crane, S. This majestic lie
  Curley, D. Revenge
  Daugherty, S. R. Claws of the white hawk
  De Queiroz, R. Metonymy; or, The husband's revenge
  Derleth, A. W. Miss Esperson
  Doyle, Sir A. C. The new catacomb
  Doyle, Sir A. C. The retirement of Signor Lambert
  Doyle, Sir A. C. The winning shot
  Dubus, A. Killings
  Dunlap, S. Hit-and-run
  Dunsany, E. J. M. D. P., Baron. The pirate of the Round Pond
  Ellin, S. The last bottle in the world
  Farris, J. Fire enough for you
  Faulkner, W. A bear hunt
  Field, I. Hungry lion
  Fisher, R. Ringtail
  Forsyth, F. There are no snakes in Ireland
  Foster, A. D. Why Johnny can't speed
  Garfield, B. King's X
  Gaskell, E. C. The old nurse's story
  Gault, W. C. The cackle bladder
  Gilchrist, E. Traceleen, she's still talking
  Gill, B. M. A certain kind of skill
  Godwin, T. Too soon to die

REVENGE—*Continued*

Gogol', N. V. A terrible vengeance

Goldsmith, H. Do ye hear the children weeping?

Gorky, M. Red

Gorman, E. Guild and the Indian woman

Hamilton, D. The alteration

Hansen, J. The Anderson boy

Havemann, E. The animal lover

Henry, O. The caballero's way

Hensley, J. L. All that mattered

Hensley, J. L. Finder

Hensley, J. L. Judicial discretion

Hensley, J. L. Searcher

Hensley, J. L. Tourist

Hill, R. Auteur theory

Hoch, E. D. The man who came back

Hogg, J. The Cameronian preacher's tale

Hood, M. Manly conclusions

Hornung, E. W. The last laugh

Howard, C. Enough rope for two

Howard, C. Return to the OK Corral

Howard, C. Scalplock

Ingalls, R. People to people

Kinsella, W. P. Caraway

Kipling, R. Mary Postgate

Kirk, R. The reflex-man in Whinnymuir Close

Kittredge, W. We are not in this together

Kleist, H. von. The foundling

Kleist, H. von. Michael Kohlhaas

Kress, N. Borovsky's hollow woman

Le Fanu, J. S. Squire Toby's will

Lee, T. A lynx with lions

Lee, T. When the clock strikes

Leedom-Ackerman, J. Sissy Mamma's wig

Leiber, F. The dead man

Li, Y.-P. The rain from the sun

London, J. The Leopard Man's story

London, J. Which make men remember

Lovesey, P. Curl up and dye

Lowden, D. The old mob

Lutz, J. Close calls

Lutz, J. The second shot

Mars-Jones, A. Structural anthropology

Matthews, J. A woman of properties

Maupassant, G. de. Monsieur Parent

Maupassant, G. de. The Odalisque of Senichou

Maupassant, G. de. Semillante

McConnell, C. R. Sidney, Seth and S.A.M.

Meinke, P. Losers pay

Mitchell, K. The great electrical revolution

Moore, A. A hypothetical lizard

Morrison, J. Appointment at Princess Gate

Morrow, W. C. His unconquerable enemy

Muheim, H. The dusty drawer

Nussbaum, A. An easy score

O'Brien, T. The ghost soldiers

O'Donnell, P. I had a date with Lady Janet

O'Kelly, S. Hike and Calcutta

Ollivant, A. The tailless tyke at bay

Olsen, T. V. Vengeance station

Paynter, J. Fifty-eight cents

Poe, E. A. The cask of Amontillado

Poe, E. A. Hop-frog

Pribus, M. The calendar chest

Pronzini, B. A lot on his mind

Pronzini, B. Putting the pieces back

Pronzini, B. Sweet fever

Pronzini, B., and Kurland, M. Vanishing act

Purdy, J. How I became a shadow

Rendell, R. The whistler

Runyon, D. The informal execution of Soupbone Pew

Rush, N. Bruns

Russell, R. I am returning

Saki. Sredni Vashtar

Schweitzer, D. Caliban's revenge

Serling, R. The escape route

Shalamov, V. T. Condensed milk

Shaw, I. The inhabitants of Venus

Sherman, D. The maid on the shore

Silvis, R. The fatalist

Sinclair, C. Bedbugs

Sinclair, M. The victim

Sisk, F. Ashes for an urn

Spillane, M. The girl behind the hedge

Stephenson, M. The pack

Stoker, B. The secret of the growing gold

Stoker, B. The squaw

Stuart, J. Coming down the mountain

Swados, H. Tease

Twain, M. The man that corrupted Hadleyburg

Underwood, M. The man who nursed grievances

Valadés, E. Permission for death is granted

Van de Wetering, J. A great sight

Vander Putten, J. Just a little thing

Vinge, J. D. Eyes of amber

Wagner, K. E. More sinned against

Walter, E. Come and get me

Webster, C. The feud

Wells, H. G. The cone

Whitaker, M. The man in black

Williams, D. The bully

Williams, T. The vengeance of Nitocris

Willis, T. The man from the White Mountains

Winton, T. Minimum of two

Woolrich, C. Hurting much?

Yerxa, L. Carrion crypt

Revenge. Curley, D.

Revenge. Gilchrist, E.

Revenge. Maupassant, G. de

The **revenge** of the Adolphus. Crane, S.

Revenge of the lawn. Brautigan, R.

The **revenge** of the senior citizens: a novella. Reed, K.

Reverdy. West, J.

Reversal. Dixon, S.

Reversals. Osborn, C.

Reverse for Dennis. Norris, L.

Revill, Pat
Book review
P.E.N. new fiction I
REVIVALS
Black, S. The biggest tent in the world
Brown, M. W. Tongues of flame
Goyen, W. Rhody's path
Norris, G. Revive us again
West, J. There ought to be a judge
Revive us again. Norris, G.
The **revolt** of Brud Bascomb. Hairston, L.
The **revolt** of the pedestrians. Keller, D. H.
Revolution on a bicycle. Giardinelli, M.
REVOLUTIONARIES *See* Revolutionists
Revolutionaries. Abbott, L. K.
The **revolutionary**. Bissoondath, N.
The **revolutionist**. Hemingway, E.
REVOLUTIONISTS
Ahern, T. Chenken and Nartzarzen in
several days on the town
Álvarez Gardeazábal, G. Donaldo Arrieta
Andreyev, L. Darkness
Andreyev, L. The seven who were hanged
Bissoondath, N. Counting the wind
Bissoondath, N. The revolutionary
Bloch, R. The oracle
Dorr, L. An early Christmas
Gordimer, N. A city of the dead, a city
of the living
Gordimer, N. Something out there
Gorky, M. Karamora
Hemingway, E. Nobody ever dies
Hemingway, E. The revolutionist
Houbein, L. Reluctant revolutionaries
Jin He. Reencounter
Kim, W.-I. The spirit of the darkness
Morand, P. Catalan night
O'Brien, F. The martyr's crown
Price, A. The Boudicca killing
Rocklynne, R. They fly so high
Shepard, L. Aymara
Silva, B. The poster
Silvis, R. The luckiest man in the world
Sonu, H. Spark of life
Thompson, J. Foreigners
Vészi, E. Chapters from the life of Vera
Angi
REVOLUTIONS
See also Coups d'état; Revolutionists
Anderson, P. The Nest
Dixon, S. Encountering revolution
Enayetullah, A. This also happened
Morris, M. The banana fever
Mukherjee, B. The world according to Hsü
Naranjo, C. Why kill the Countess?
Piper, H. B. Ministry of disturbance
Ryman, G. O happy day!
Thomas, M. Choobeedoo Yum-yum and
the ANC
Thomas, M. Second rains
Trebelo, J. La Cueva Del Círculo Sin Fin
The **revolver**. Gant, P.
A **rewarding** experience. Hartley, L. P.

REWARDS (PRIZES, ETC.)
Crawford, I. V. Extradited
Frame, J. Prizes
Landolfi, T. Literary prize
Rewards. Lurie, M.
Rex. Lawrence, D. H.
Rex. Vincent, H.
Rex and Mr. Rejilla. Dickson, G. R.
Rey Rosa, Rodrigo, 1958-
The animal
Rey Rosa, R. The beggar's knife
The beggar's knife
Rey Rosa, R. The beggar's knife
The black room
Rey Rosa, R. The beggar's knife
The book
Rey Rosa, R. The beggar's knife
The heart of God
Rey Rosa, R. The beggar's knife
The inheritance
Rey Rosa, R. The beggar's knife
The lost key
Rey Rosa, R. The beggar's knife
The monastery
Rey Rosa, R. The beggar's knife
Nine occasions
Rey Rosa, R. The beggar's knife
The path doubles back
Rey Rosa, R. The beggar's knife
A prisoner
Rey Rosa, R. The beggar's knife
The rain and other children
Rey Rosa, R. The beggar's knife
Recurrent dreams
Rey Rosa, R. The beggar's knife
The release
Rey Rosa, R. The beggar's knife
Reports from Cahabon
Rey Rosa, R. The beggar's knife
The river bed
Rey Rosa, R. The beggar's knife
The seeing eye
Rey Rosa, R. The beggar's knife
The sign
Rey Rosa, R. The beggar's knife
Son and father
Rey Rosa, R. The beggar's knife
The sorcerer's son
Rey Rosa, R. The beggar's knife
Sunrise
Rey Rosa, R. The beggar's knife
Uncertain readings
Rey Rosa, R. The beggar's knife
A version of my death
Rey Rosa, R. The beggar's knife
A widespread belief
Rey Rosa, R. The beggar's knife
The widow of Don Juan Manuel
Rey Rosa, R. The beggar's knife
A yellow cat
Rey Rosa, R. The beggar's knife

Reynolds, Mack
The adventure of the extraterrestrial
Sherlock Holmes through time and space
The Devil finds work
100 great fantasy short short stories; ed.
by I. Asimov; T. Carr and M. H.
Greenberg
Optical illusion
Young monsters; ed. by I. Asimov; M.
H. Greenberg and C. G. Waugh
Prone
Young mutants; ed. by I. Asimov; M.
H. Greenberg and C. G. Waugh
Your soul comes C.O.D.
100 great fantasy short short stories; ed.
by I. Asimov; T. Carr and M. H.
Greenberg
Reynolds, Sallie
Cusie
Prairie Schooner 60:67-82 Spr '86
Rhadamanthys. Kessler, J. F.
Rhea. Brennan, J. P.
Rheinheimer, Kurt
Baltimore
Michigan Quarterly Review 27:473-86
Summ '88
Umpire
New stories from the South: the year's
best, 1986
RHINE RIVER
Böll, H. Undine's mighty father
Rhodabeh. Rustomji, R.
RHODE ISLAND
Brondoli, M. Sixty-three questions
Dodd, S. M. Rue
Nolan, W. F. Ceremony
Robison, J. Time alone
Providence
Bloch, R. The shadow from the steeple
Lovecraft, H. P. The haunter of the dark
Rhodes, Eugene Manlove
Pasó por aquí
The Western hall of fame; ed. by B.
Pronzini and M. H. Greenberg
RHODES (GREECE)
Ingalls, R. Early morning sightseer
Ingalls, R. Something to write home about
Ingalls, R. St. George and the nightclub
RHODESIA, NORTHERN *See* Zambia
RHODESIA, SOUTHERN *See* Zimbabwe
Rhody's path. Goyen, W.
The **rhyme** in Freddy's face. Michaelson, L.
W.
The **rhyme** of Lancelot. Sandberg, P. L.
Rhys, Jean
Again the Antilles
Rhys, J. The collected short stories
At the Villa d'Or
Rhys, J. The collected short stories
Before the deluge
Rhys, J. The collected short stories
The bishop's feast
Rhys, J. The collected short stories

The blue bird
Rhys, J. The collected short stories
The Chevalier of the Place Blanche
Rhys, J. The collected short stories
The day they burned the books
Rhys, J. The collected short stories
Discourse of a lady standing a dinner to
a down-and-out friend
Rhys, J. The collected short stories
Fishy waters
Rhys, J. The collected short stories
From a French prison
Rhys, J. The collected short stories
Good-bye Marcus, good-bye Rose
Rhys, J. The collected short stories
The grey day
Rhys, J. The collected short stories
La Grosse Fifi
Rhys, J. The collected short stories
Heat
Rhys, J. The collected short stories
Hunger
Rhys, J. The collected short stories
I spy a stranger
Rhys, J. The collected short stories
I used to live here once
Rhys, J. The collected short stories
Illusion
Rhys, J. The collected short stories
In a café
Rhys, J. The collected short stories
In the Luxemburg Gardens
Rhys, J. The collected short stories
In the Rue de l'Arrivée
Rhys, J. The collected short stories
The insect world
Rhys, J. The collected short stories
Invitation to the dance
Rhys, J. The collected short stories
Kikimora
Rhys, J. The collected short stories
Kismet
Rhys, J. The collected short stories
Learning to be a mother
Rhys, J. The collected short stories
Let them call it jazz
Rhys, J. The collected short stories
The lotus
The Penguin book of modern British
short stories
Rhys, J. The collected short stories
Mannequin
Rhys, J. The collected short stories
Mixing cocktails
Rhys, J. The collected short stories
A night
Rhys, J. The collected short stories
Night out 1925
Rhys, J. The collected short stories
On not shooting sitting birds
Rhys, J. The collected short stories
Outside the machine
Rhys, J. The collected short stories

Rhys, Jean—*Continued*
Overture and beginners please
 Rhys, J. The collected short stories
Pioneers, oh, pioneers [Variant title: Dear darling Mr. Ramage]
 Rhys, J. The collected short stories
Rapunzel, Rapunzel
 Rhys, J. The collected short stories
The Sidi
 Rhys, J. The collected short stories
Sleep it off, lady
 Full measure; ed. by D. Sennett
 Rhys, J. The collected short stories
A solid house
 Rhys, J. The collected short stories
The sound of the river
 Haunting women; ed. by A. Ryan
 Rhys, J. The collected short stories
A spiritualist
 Rhys, J. The collected short stories
Tea with an artist
 Rhys, J. The collected short stories
Temps perdi
 Rhys, J. The collected short stories
Tigers are better-looking
 Rhys, J. The collected short stories
Till September Petronella
 Rhys, J. The collected short stories
Tout Montparnasse and a lady
 Rhys, J. The collected short stories
Trio
 Rhys, J. The collected short stories
Vienne
 Rhys, J. The collected short stories
The whistling bird
 Rhys, J. The collected short stories
Who knows what's up in the attic?
 Rhys, J. The collected short stories
Ribeiro, João Ubaldo, 1941-
Alaindelon de la Patrie
 A Good deal; ed. by M. Heath and F. M. Robinson
 The Massachusetts Review 27:449-57 Fall/Wint '86
Ribeyro, Julio Ramón
Alienation
 On being foreign; ed. by T. J. Lewis and R. E. Jungman
The double
 Anthology of contemporary Latin American literature, 1960-1984
Vultures without feathers
 Anthology of contemporary Latin American literature, 1960-1984
Ricardo's war. Martínez-Serros, H.
Rice, Anne, 1941-
The master of Rampling gate
 Redbook 162:50-6+ F '84
Rice, Craig, 1908-1957
His heart could break
 Murder and mystery in Chicago; ed. by C. R. Waugh; F. D. McSherry and M. H. Greenberg

Rice, Jackson *See* Lish, Gordon
Rice, Jane
The crossroads
 The Year's best mystery & suspense stories, 1986
The Idol of the Flies
 Witches' brew; ed. by M. Muller and B. Pronzini
Rice, Luanne
July
 The Massachusetts Review 25:9-18 Spr '84
Love spells
 McCall's 114:164+ N '86
Rich, Cynthia
My sister's marriage
 Family: stories from the interior; ed. by G. G. Chavis
The **rich** brother. Wolff, T.
Rich man's crumbs. Melville, H.
RICH PEOPLE *See* Wealth
Richard, Mark, 1955-
Happiness of the garden variety
 New stories from the South: the year's best, 1988
Strays
 Esquire 110:106-8+ Jl '88
Richards, Joel
The bridge sings
 Isaac Asimov's Tomorrow's voices
Deadtime
 Universe 14
Mencken stuff
 Universe 17
Richards, Susan Starr
Magic lantern
 The Kenyon Review ns8:78-89 Spr '86
Richard's girl. Flook, M.
Richardson, Henry Handel, 1870-1946
"And women must weep"
 The Australian short story; ed. by L. Hergenhan
Richardson, Maurice
Tower of silence
 The Mammoth book of modern crime stories; ed. by G. Hardinge
Richardson, Miles
The museum
 The Southern Review (Baton Rouge, La.) 20:919-27 O '84
Riches, Brenda
Fall
 The Old dance; ed. by B. Burnard
Richie, Kathleen M.
Lost and found
 Américas 39:49-51 My/Je '87
Richler, Mordecai, 1931-
The summer my grandmother was supposed to die
 The Oxford book of Canadian short stories in English
Richter, Johann Paul Friedrich *See* Jean Paul, 1763-1825

Rick's first visit to the A & W. Abbott, K.
RICKSHAW MEN
   Kim, I.-S. Tombstone without an inscription
Riddell, Charlotte Eliza Lawson Cowan *See*
   Riddell, J. H., Mrs., 1832-1906
Riddell, J. H., Mrs., 1832-1906
   A strange Christmas game
      Christmas ghosts; ed. by K. Cramer and
      D. G. Hartwell
Riddle in silk. Tinsley, T.
Riddle of the marble blade. Palmer, S.
Riddles in the dark. Tolkien, J. R. R.
The **ride**. Freeman, C.
The **ride**. Lee, A.
Ride a golden horse. Toland, S.
Ride, fly, penetrate, loiter. Hannah, B.
Ride the lightning. Lutz, J.
The **rider** on the pale horse. See Eustis, H.
   Mister Death and the redheaded
   woman
Riders of the purple wage. Farmer, P. J.
Ridge running. Robinson, K. S.
Riding clothes. Kawabata, Y.
The **riding** lesson. Wagoner, D.
Riding The Whip. Hemley, R.
Rif. Barthelme, D.
Rifaat, Alifa
   Another evening at the club
      Arabic short stories; tr. by D. Johnson-
      Davies
   At the time of the jasmine
      Rifaat, A. Distant view of a minaret,
      and other stories
   Badriyya and her husband
      Rifaat, A. Distant view of a minaret,
      and other stories
   Bahiyya's eyes
      Rifaat, A. Distant view of a minaret,
      and other stories
   Degrees of death
      Rifaat, A. Distant view of a minaret,
      and other stories
   Distant view of a minaret
      Rifaat, A. Distant view of a minaret,
      and other stories
   The flat in Nakshabandi Street
      Rifaat, A. Distant view of a minaret,
      and other stories
   An incident in the Ghobashi household
      African short stories; ed. by C. Achebe
      and C. L. Innes
      Rifaat, A. Distant view of a minaret,
      and other stories
   Just another day
      Rifaat, A. Distant view of a minaret,
      and other stories
   The kite
      Rifaat, A. Distant view of a minaret,
      and other stories
   The long night of winter
      Rifaat, A. Distant view of a minaret,
      and other stories

   Mansoura
      Rifaat, A. Distant view of a minaret,
      and other stories
   Me and my sister
      Rifaat, A. Distant view of a minaret,
      and other stories
   My world of the unknown
      Rifaat, A. Distant view of a minaret,
      and other stories
   Telephone call
      Rifaat, A. Distant view of a minaret,
      and other stories
   Thursday lunch
      Rifaat, A. Distant view of a minaret,
      and other stories
Riffraff. Engberg, S.
Rif'iyyah, Yasin
   The rain
      Modern Syrian short stories; ed. by M.
      G. Azrak
Rigby, Rita
   The day my nose stopped growing
      '*Teen* 30:26+ Ap '86
The **right** boy for Cosgrove. Mordden, E.
The **right** chemistry. Schweer, K.
The **right** day to kill a pike. Blythe, R.
Right girl, wrong guy. Moses, J.
Right-hand man. Gee, M.
The **right** perspective. Curtiss, U. R.
Right questions. Stiles, J.
The **right** stuff. Bird, C.
The **right** thing. Boswell, R.
The **right** thing. Yates, R.
Rile, Karen
   Solid walls
      Our roots grow deeper than we know;
      ed. by L. Gutkind
Rinehart, Mary Roberts, 1876-1958
   The splinter
      Kill or cure; ed. by M. Muller and B.
      Pronzini
Rinehart, Steven
   LeSabre
      The Georgia Review 42:106-19 Spr '88
The **ring**. Hudec, G.
The **ring**. Kawabata, Y.
The **ring**. Livesey, M.
The **ring**. Shannon, D.
Ring of Kerry. Jones, R.
The **ring**; or, A girl confesses. Schinto, J.
The **ring** with the velvet ropes. Hoch, E. D.
The **ringbarker's** daughter. Eldridge, M.
The **ringdove** sign. Davenport, G.
The **ringer**. Dixon, S.
RINGS
   Disch, T. M. Ringtime
   Guin, W. The root and the ring
   Lynch, L. Pleasure Park
   Sabah, M. 'l--D. The destroyer of families
Ringtail. Fisher, R.
Ringtime. Disch, T. M.

Rinser, Luise
A handful of white daffodils
Voices East and West: German short stories since 1945

Ríos, Alberto
The birthday of Mrs. Piñeda
Ríos, A. The iguana killer
La boda
Cuentos Chicanos; ed. by R. A. Anaya and A. Márquez
Ríos, A. The iguana killer
The child
Ríos, A. The iguana killer
Eyes like they say the devil has
Ríos, A. The iguana killer
A friend, brother maybe
Ríos, A. The iguana killer
His own key
Ríos, A. The iguana killer
The iguana killer
Ríos, A. The iguana killer
Johnny Ray
Ríos, A. The iguana killer
Pato
Ríos, A. The iguana killer
The secret lion
The Pushcart prize X
Ríos, A. The iguana killer
Then they'd watch comedies
Ríos, A. The iguana killer
The way spaghetti feels
Ríos, A. The iguana killer

RIOTS
Havemann, E. Spirits do not forgive
Ingalls, R. Theft
Niven, L. Flash crowd
Vester, L. Pawn promotion
Rip-off!. Girion, B.
Ripe plums. Frayne, A.
Ripley, Bill
Desert owls
The Best of the West; ed. by J. Thomas
Ripley, Jack See Wainwright, John William, 1921-
Ripples. Shibaki, Y.
Rise and fall. Busch, F.
The **rise,** fall, and redemption of Mooski Toffski Offski. Kunstler, J. H.
Rising action. Pearlman, D.
Rising sun; or, The celebration of heartfelt joy. Lengyel, P.
Rising waters. Ferrara, P.
Risk. Dickinson, C.
The **risk** of love. Stacey, K.
Riskin, Mary
Print dresses
Alberta bound; ed. by F. Stenson
Risley, Susannah
Navigating the night
Mademoiselle 92:134+ Ap '86

Risse, Heinz
Traffic accident
Voices East and West: German short stories since 1945

Ritchie, Jack, 1922-1983
The 23 brown paper bags
Ritchie, J. The adventures of Henry Turnbuckle
The $5,000 getaway
Uncollected crimes; ed. by B. Pronzini and M. H. Greenberg
The alphabet murders
Ritchie, J. The adventures of Henry Turnbuckle
Anyone for murder?
Hitchcock in prime time; ed. by F. M. Nevins and M. H. Greenberg
Bedlam at the Budgie
Ritchie, J. The adventures of Henry Turnbuckle
Box in a box
Ritchie, J. The adventures of Henry Turnbuckle
By child undone
Great modern police stories; ed. by B. Pronzini and M. H. Greenberg
Chicken Charley
A Treasury of World War II stories; ed. by B. Pronzini and M. H. Greenberg
The connecting link
Ritchie, J. The adventures of Henry Turnbuckle
The crime machine
Alfred Hitchcock's Crimewatch
Dial an alibi
Ritchie, J. The adventures of Henry Turnbuckle
The fifth grave
Ritchie, J. The adventures of Henry Turnbuckle
The final truth
Ritchie, J. The adventures of Henry Turnbuckle
Finger exercise
Ritchie, J. The adventures of Henry Turnbuckle
The gourmet kidnaper
Ritchie, J. The adventures of Henry Turnbuckle
The Griggsby papers
Ritchie, J. The adventures of Henry Turnbuckle
The hanging tree
Ritchie, J. The adventures of Henry Turnbuckle
Hot air pilot
A Treasury of World War II stories; ed. by B. Pronzini and M. H. Greenberg
Hung jury
Ritchie, J. The adventures of Henry Turnbuckle

Ritchie, Jack, 1922-1983—*Continued*

The message in the message
  Ritchie, J. The adventures of Henry Turnbuckle
The midnight strangler
  Ritchie, J. The adventures of Henry Turnbuckle
More than meets the eye
  Ritchie, J. The adventures of Henry Turnbuckle
Murder off limits
  Ritchie, J. The adventures of Henry Turnbuckle
No wider than a nickel
  Ritchie, J. The adventures of Henry Turnbuckle
Nobody tells me anything
  Ritchie, J. The adventures of Henry Turnbuckle
An odd pair of socks
  Ritchie, J. The adventures of Henry Turnbuckle
The O'Leary conspiracy
  Ritchie, J. The adventures of Henry Turnbuckle
Piggy bank killer
  Alfred Hitchcock's Grave suspicions
The school bus caper
  Ellery Queen's Crimes and punishments
  Ritchie, J. The adventures of Henry Turnbuckle
The sliver of evidence
  Ritchie, J. The adventures of Henry Turnbuckle
Some days are like that
  Ritchie, J. The adventures of Henry Turnbuckle
Sound alibi
  Kill or cure; ed. by M. Muller and B. Pronzini
Take another look
  Ritchie, J. The adventures of Henry Turnbuckle
The two percent solution
  Ritchie, J. The adventures of Henry Turnbuckle
Variations on a scheme
  Ritchie, J. The adventures of Henry Turnbuckle
The wastebasket
  Alfred Hitchcock's Mortal errors
Who's got the lady?
  The Deadly arts; ed. by B. Pronzini and M. Muller
The Willinger predicament
  Ritchie, J. The adventures of Henry Turnbuckle
Win some, lose some
  Ritchie, J. The adventures of Henry Turnbuckle
The **rite**. Takenishi, H.
Rite of failure. Shwartz, S. M.
A **rite** of passion. Clarke, T.

A **rite** of spring. Leiber, F.
Rites. Colette
RITES AND CEREMONIES
  Crowley, A. The burning of Melcarth
  Markham, B. Brothers are the same
  Shannon, D. Need-fire
  Silverberg, R. The feast of St. Dionysus
  Taylor, P. E. Spring water celebration
  Tiptree, J. I'll be waiting for you when the swimming pool is empty
The **ritual**. Osier, J.
Rituals. Fein, N.
Rituals of rejection. Valenzuela, L.
Rival candidates. Sastri, P.
The **rivalry**. Easton, R.
Rivals. Botwinik, B.
The **rivals**. Colette
The **rivals**. Garrett, G. P.
Rivanera, Luisa
  Highway robbery
    Américas 37:12-14 Ja/F '85
Rivarola Matto, Juan Bautista
  Soul brother
    Américas 39:48-50 Mr/Ap '87
Rive, Richard, 1931-
  The bench
    The Penguin book of Southern African stories
  Resurrection
    African short stories in English; ed. by J. de Grandsaigne
The **river**. O'Connor, F.
The **river**. So, C.-I.
The **river** and the boat. Rodoreda, M.
The **river** bed. Rey Rosa, R.
River day. Holland, N.
River deer. Ozaki, S.
River dogs. Olmstead, R.
The **river** giantess. Hoyt, M. S.
River house. Young, S.
The **River** Temz. Lewis, F.
RIVERBOATS *See* Steamboats
The **riverman**. Reeve, F. D.
RIVERS
    See also Charles River (Mass.); Danube River; Mississippi River; Missouri River; Rhine River; Seine River (France)
  Valenzuela, L. Generous impediments float downriver
RIVIERA (FRANCE AND ITALY)
  Greene, G. Chagrin in three parts
  Greene, G. May we borrow your husband?
Rizkalla, John
  The black figurine
    Short story international 71
  The dummy in the jeep
    Short story international 66
  A janitor for sale
    Short story international 56
  The landlord
    Short story international 68

Rizkalla, John—*Continued*
A poet in the classroom
  Short story international 58
The servant of the last hour
  Short story international 61
Roach bait. Davis, K.
The **roaches**. Disch, T. M.
The **road** atlas. McGuane, T.
Road number one. Stuart, J.
The **Road** of Dreams and death. Vardeman, R. E.
A **road** somewhere. Ferreira, R.
Road stop. Picoult, J.
The **road** to Alexandra. Mathabane, M.
The **road** to Dune. Herbert, F.
Road to Granville. Brennan, J. P.
The **Road** to Hell. Fante, J.
The **road** to Migowi. Lipenga, K.
The **road** to Rankin's Point. MacLeod, A.
The **road** to Samp'o. Hwang, S.-Y.
Road work. Klinkowitz, J.
ROADS
  Conroy, J. Paving gang—on a job in Missouri
  Cortázar, J. The southern thruway
  Prichard, K. S. The old track
  Sandel, C. The child who loved roads
  Stuart, J. Road number one
  Tournier, M. The Lily of the Valley rest area
Roads of destiny. Henry, O.
Roadside rescue. Cadigan, P.
Robb, Jacquie
  Twilight fantasy
    Erotic interludes; ed. by L. Barbach
Robbe-Grillet, Alain, 1922-
  The replacement
    The Art of the tale; ed. by D. Halpern
ROBBER BARONS *See* Capitalists and financiers
ROBBERS *See* Brigands and robbers; Robbery
Robbers' roost. Estleman, L. D.
ROBBERY
    See also Bank robbers; Theft
  Barnes, L. Lucky penny
  Bird, C. The hair and the teeth
  Brand, M. The laughter of Slim Malone
  Coskran, K. Miss Clay County 1960
  Curley, D. Revenge
  Day, R. C. Two paces east
  Dixon, S. The package store
  Dubus, A. Anna
  Ferreira, R. Bagasse
  Finney, E. J. Nights and days
  Gerber, M. J. The mistress of Goldman's Antiques
  Gilbert, M. The king in pawn
  Hartley, L. P. Please do not touch
  Hornung, E. W. Out of paradise
  Howard, C. New Orleans getaway
  Ko, H. Black market blues
  Lacy, E. You can't win 'em (at) all
  Mayers, C. Police calls
  McBain, E. Consolation
  McElroy, C. J. A brief spell by the river
  Miller, A. It takes a thief
  Natsuki, S. The sole of the foot
  Nussbaum, A. An easy score
  Oates, J. C. The bystander
  O'Donnell, P. A perfect night to break your neck
  Pronzini, B. Don't spend it all in one place
  Sadler, M. The choice
  Thompson, K. Robbing motels
  Wells, H. G. The Hammerpond Park burglary
A **robbery**. Leskov, N. S.
The **robbery**. Mcdonald, G.
Robbie. Asimov, I.
Robbie. Danby, M.
Robbing motels. Thompson, K.
Robbins, Tom
  The hair of the beast
    The Esquire fiction reader v1
Robbins, W. Wayne
  A beast is born
    The Weirds; ed. by S. Jaffery
  Test-tube Frankenstein
    Sensuous science fiction from the weird and spicy pulps; ed. by S. Jaffery
Robert. Ellin, S.
Robert Aghion. Hesse, H.
Robert Kennedy saved from drowning. Barthelme, D.
Robert Louis Stevenson Banks, a.k.a. Chimley. Gaines, E. J.
Roberts, Charles G. D., 1860-1943
  Do seek their meat from God
    The Oxford book of Canadian short stories in English
Roberts, Keith, 1935-
  Kitemaster
    Interzone: the first anthology; ed. by J. Clute; C. Greenland and D. Pringle
  The Lady Margaret
    Alternative histories; ed. by C. G. Waugh and M. H. Greenberg
  Weihnachtsabend
    Hitler victorious; ed. by G. Benford and M. H. Greenberg
Roberts, Morley
  The ingenuity of Captain Spink
    Sea captains' tales; ed. by A. Enfield
Roberts, Nancy, 1941-
  The bruise
    Roberts, N. Women and other bodies of water
  Dancing in Trolley Square
    Roberts, N. Women and other bodies of water
  The exterminator
    Roberts, N. Women and other bodies of water

Roberts, Nancy, 1941——_Continued_
Fire Island
  Roberts, N. Women and other bodies of
    water
Flames
  Roberts, N. Women and other bodies of
    water
For luck
  Roberts, N. Women and other bodies of
    water
The inversion
  Roberts, N. Women and other bodies of
    water
A proper introduction
  Roberts, N. Women and other bodies of
    water
A second wife
  Roberts, N. Women and other bodies of
    water
Training for Alaska
  Roberts, N. Women and other bodies of
    water
The upstairs people
  The North American Review 272:19-23
    Mr '87
  Roberts, N. Women and other bodies of
    water
Water babies
  Roberts, N. Women and other bodies of
    water
Roberts, Neil
A journey in the snow
  Critical Quarterly 29:3-8 Summ '87
Roberts, Roxanne
The egghead
  'Teen 32:40+ Je '88
Roberts, Sheila, 1942-
The butcher shop
  The Penguin book of Southern African
    stories
Robert's song. Thompson, J.
**Robertson, Ethel Florence Lindesay Richard-
son** _See_ Richardson, Henry Handel,
    1870-1946
Robertson, Mary Elsie, 1937-
The baptism
  Arkansas in short fiction; ed. by W. M.
    Baker and E. C. Simpson
Locust
  Arkansas in short fiction; ed. by W. M.
    Baker and E. C. Simpson
Robertson, R. Garcia y _See_ Garcia y Robert-
son, R.
Robin. Rees, D.
Robinett, Stephen
Number 13
  Omni book of science fiction 3
Robinson, Arthur
The boy on the train
  The New Yorker 64:36-43 Ap 11 '88

Robinson, Barbara
The funny tale of . . . Vergil, the laid-back
    dog
  Redbook 170:30+ Ja '88
A funny thing about mother
  Redbook 171:56+ My '88
The wedding of Willard and what's her
    name
  McCall's 114:89-93 Je '87
Robinson, Fred Miller, 1942-
Pennsylvania
  TriQuarterly no73:31-44 Fall '88
Robinson, Holly
Kansas heat
  The North American Review 269:36-40
    Mr '84
Robinson, Jeanne
(jt. auth) See Robinson, Spider, and
    Robinson, Jeanne
Robinson, Kim Stanley
Black air
  Robinson, K. S. The planet on the table
  The Year's best science fiction, first an-
    nual collection
Coming back to Dixieland
  Robinson, K. S. The planet on the table
The disguise
  Robinson, K. S. The planet on the table
Down and out in the year 2000
  The Year's best science fiction, fourth
    annual collection
Escape from Kathmandu
  Terry Carr's Best science fiction and fan-
    tasy of the year #16
Green Mars
  The Year's best science fiction, third an-
    nual collection
The lucky strike
  Alternative histories; ed. by C. G.
    Waugh and M. H. Greenberg
  Nebula awards 20
  Robinson, K. S. The planet on the table
  Universe 14
  The Year's best science fiction, second
    annual collection
The lunatics
  Terry's universe; ed. by B. Meacham
Mercurial
  Robinson, K. S. The planet on the table
  Universe 15
Mother goddess of the world
  The Year's best science fiction, fifth an-
    nual collection
Our town
  Omni (New York, N.Y.) 9:88-90+ N '86
Ridge running
  Robinson, K. S. The planet on the table
Stone eggs
  Robinson, K. S. The planet on the table
Venice drowned
  Robinson, K. S. The planet on the table

Robinson, Lou
Telepathic rein
Through other eyes; ed. by I. Zahava
Robinson, Margaret A.
The fundamentals
Ladies' Home Journal 105:84+ Ja '88
A woman of her tribe
Seventeen 44:160-1+ S '85
Robinson, Marilynne
Connie Bronson
The Paris Review 28:294-302 Summ/Fall
'86
Robinson, Michael Arden
The first kill
Critical Quarterly 29:41-5 Summ '87
Fishing
Critical Quarterly 30:102-6 Spr '88
Robinson, Roxana
Charity dance
The Southern Review (Baton Rouge, La.)
23:185-93 Ja '87
Robinson, Spider
By any other name
The Hugo winners v4
Fivesight
Omni book of science fiction 2
God is an iron
Omni book of science fiction 1
User friendly
Tales from the planet Earth
Robinson, Spider, and Robinson, Jeanne
Stardance
The Hugo winners v4
Robinson, William
The blow-up of the Mohawk
Men at sea; ed. by B. Aymar
Robinson. Faik, S.
Robison, James
The ecstasy of the animals
Robison, J. Rumor, and other stories
Eleven
Robison, J. Rumor, and other stories
Envy
Robison, J. Rumor, and other stories
The foundry
Robison, J. Rumor, and other stories
Home
Robison, J. Rumor, and other stories
The house sitter
Robison, J. Rumor, and other stories
The Indian Gardens
The New Yorker 60:30-2 S 3 '84
Robison, J. Rumor, and other stories
The line
Robison, J. Rumor, and other stories
Nor'easter
Robison, J. Rumor, and other stories
Rumor
Robison, J. Rumor, and other stories
Set off
Robison, J. Rumor, and other stories
Time alone
Robison, J. Rumor, and other stories

Transfer
Robison, J. Rumor, and other stories
Robison, Mary
Adore her
Robison, M. Believe them
Again, again, again
Robison, M. Believe them
An amateur's guide to the night
Look who's talking; ed. by B. Weber
Culpability
Robison, M. Believe them
For real
The New Yorker 62:42-4 N 10 '86
Robison, M. Believe them
I am twenty-one
New women and new fiction; ed. by S.
Cahill
I get by
The New Yorker 62:27-9 Jl 21 '86
Prize stories, 1987
Robison, M. Believe them
In the woods
The New Yorker 60:42-3 Mr 26 '84
Robison, M. Believe them
Mirror
The New Yorker 61:30-4 Ag 12 '85
Robison, M. Believe them
Seizing control
The New Yorker 63:35-6 My 25 '87
Robison, M. Believe them
Trying
The New Yorker 62:36-41 S 8 '86
Robison, M. Believe them
While home
The New Yorker 60:42-7 My 21 '84
Robison, M. Believe them
Your errant mom
Robison, M. Believe them
Yours
Sudden fiction; ed. by R. Shapard and
J. Thomas
Robot AL-76 goes astray. Asimov, I.
The **robot** and the one you love. Maddox,
T.
The **robot** awakes. Merrill, L.
Robot dreams. Asimov, I.
The **robot** who looked like me. Sheckley, R.
Robotgnomics. Sheckley, R.
ROBOTS
Armer, K. M. BCO equipment
Asimov, I. The Bicentennial Man
Asimov, I. Evidence
Asimov, I. The evitable conflict
Asimov, I. Jokester
Asimov, I. Light verse
Asimov, I. Little lost robot
Asimov, I. Reason
Asimov, I. Robbie
Asimov, I. Robot AL-76 goes astray
Asimov, I. Robot dreams
Asimov, I. Runaround
Asimov, I. Sally
Asimov, I. Satisfaction guaranteed

ROBOTS—*Continued*

Bates, H. Farewell to the master
Benford, G. Mandikini
Bester, A. Fondly Fahrenheit
Bierce, A. Moxon's master
Binder, E. Adam Link's vengeance
Binder, E. I, robot
Blaylock, J. P. Paper dragons
Bloch, R. The new season
Bloch, R. Terror over Hollywood
Brin, D. Bubbles
Brin, D. The warm space
Brunner, J. Judas
Brunner, J. What friends are for
Cadigan, P. Pretty boy crossover
Del Rey, L. Though dreamers die
Dick, P. K. Autofac
Dick, P. K. The defenders
Dick, P. K. The electric ant
Dick, P. K. Explorers we
Dick, P. K. Imposter
Dick, P. K. The last of the masters
Dick, P. K. The little movement
Dick, P. K. Sales pitch
Dick, P. K. Second Variety
Dick, P. K. To serve the master
Dnieprov, A. The Maxwell equations
Donaldson, S. R. Animal lover
Duntemann, J., and Kress, N. Borovsky's hollow woman
Ellison, H. Back to the drawing boards
Ewart, C. A day in the life
Fisk, N. Find the lady
Franklin, P. A DimEn is forever
Gibson, W. The winter market
Gilliatt, P. F.R.A.N.K.
Goulart, R. Calling Dr. Clockwork
Haldeman, J. W. More than the sum of his parts
Harrison, H. War with the robots
Huston, N. Pliny's commentaries
Ing, D. Sam and the sudden blizzard machine
Jerome, J. K. The dancing partner
Konas, G. What genius
Kress, N. Borovsky's hollow woman
Laumer, K. The timesweepers
Lem, S. The mask
Liebscher, W. Do androids dream of electric love?
Matheson, R. C. Obsolete
Merrill, L. The robot awakes
Miller, W. M. I made you
Moore, C. L. No woman born
Moore, W. Frank Merriwell in the White House
Pohl, F. Farmer on the dole
Quah Kung Yu. Equality
Reed, K. The marriage bug
Reed, K. A unique service
Russell, E. F. Mechanistria
Saberhagen, F. Adventure of the metal murderer

Scortia, T. N. Flowering Narcissus
Sheckley, R. The battle
Sheckley, R. Beside still waters
Sheckley, R. Can you feel anything when I do this?
Sheckley, R. The perfect woman
Sheckley, R. The robot who looked like me
Silverberg, R. Good news from the Vatican
Simak, C. D. Skirmish
Sladek, J. T. Absent friends
Smith, C. Scanners live in vain
Soukup, M. Dress rehearsal
St. Clair, M. Horrer Howce
St. Clair, M. Short in the chest
Sterling, B. Green days in Brunei
Tiptree, J. The girl who was plugged in
Van Vogt, A. E. Fulfillment
Vincent, H. Rex
Vinge, V. Long shot
Williams, R. M. Robot's return
Williamson, J. Jamboree
Wolfe, G. Slaves of silver
Wolfe, G. Sonya, Crane Wessleman, and Kittee
Wolfe, G. War beneath the tree
Wyndham, J. The lost machine
Zelazny, R. Home is the hangman
Zelazny, R. Last of the wild ones
Robot's return. Williams, R. M.
Robotvendor Rex. Sheckley, R.
Roche, Stanley
Structurally sound
    Women's work; ed. by M. McLeod and L. Wevers
The **rock**. Fahy, C.
The **rock**. Han, M.-S.
The **rock**. MacMillan, I. C.
Rock bottom. Nałkowska, Z.
ROCK CLIMBING
Rees, D. Cliff
Sandberg, P. L. The devil's thumb
Sandberg, P. L. Hawsmoot
Rock crystal. Stifter, A.
Rock garden. O'Donnell, K.
ROCK MUSIC
Abbott, L. K. The unfinished business of childhood
Cadigan, P. Rock on
Calisher, H. Real impudence
Choyce, L. Billy Botzweiler's last dance
Covino, M. In winter the snow never stops
Hauptman, W. Good rockin' tonight
Mukherjee, B. Isolated incidents
Phillips, J. A. How Mickey made it
Reed, K. Final tribute
Shirley, J. Freezone
Spinrad, N. The big flash
Waldrop, H. Flying saucer rock & roll
Wilson, F. P. The last one mo once golden oldies revival

ROCK MUSICIANS *See* Rock music
Rock on. Cadigan, P.
Rock Springs. Ford, R.
The **rock** star and the lifeguard. Collins, J.
Rockabye Baby. Sykes, S. C.
The **rocking-horse** winner. Lawrence, D. H.
Rocking on water, floating in glass. Pritchard, M.
Rocklynne, Ross
They fly so high
Amazing science fiction anthology: The wild years, 1946-1955; ed. by M. H. Greenberg
ROCKY MOUNTAINS
Poe, E. A. The journal of Julius Rodman
RODEOS
Ellis, L. R. The great rodeo fix
Norris, K. Conversation
Rodgers, Alan
The boy who came back from the dead
Masques II; ed. by J. N. Williamson
Rodoreda, Mercè, 1909-
The dolls' room
Rodoreda, M. My Christina & other stories
The elephant
Rodoreda, M. My Christina & other stories
A flock of lambs in all colors
Rodoreda, M. My Christina & other stories
The gentleman and the moon
Rodoreda, M. My Christina & other stories
The hen
Rodoreda, M. My Christina & other stories
A letter
Rodoreda, M. My Christina & other stories
Love
Rodoreda, M. My Christina & other stories
Memory of Caux
Rodoreda, M. My Christina & other stories
My Christina
Rodoreda, M. My Christina & other stories
The nursemaid
Rodoreda, M. My Christina & other stories
Rain
The Art of the tale; ed. by D. Halpern
Rodoreda, M. My Christina & other stories
The river and the boat
Rodoreda, M. My Christina & other stories
The salamander
Rodoreda, M. My Christina & other stories

The sea
Rodoreda, M. My Christina & other stories
That wall, that mimosa
Rodoreda, M. My Christina & other stories
Therafina
Rodoreda, M. My Christina & other stories
A white geranium petal
Rodoreda, M. My Christina & other stories
Rodowsky, Colby
Those special afternoons
McCall's 112:96-7+ Mr '85
Rodríguez, Alicia María Zorrilla de *See* Zorrilla de Rodríguez, Alicia María
Roe, Paddy, 1912-, and Muecke, Stephen, 1951-
Mirdinan
Transgressions; ed. by D. Anderson
Rofihe, Rick
Boys who do the bop
The New Yorker 64:34-7 Je 6 '88
Father must
The New Yorker 64:35-6 O 10 '88
Roger Malvin's burial. Hawthorne, N.
Roger, Mr. Whilkie! Heideman, E. M.
Rogers, Jennifer
Along came a stranger
Good Housekeeping 203:144-5 O '86
Rogers, Sunny
The crumb
New stories from the South: the year's best, 1988
Rogers, T. N. R.
Crater Lake
Rogers, T. N. R. Too far from home
Galb's elbow
Rogers, T. N. R. Too far from home
Rainfall
The North American Review 273:42-5 Mr '88
Rogers, T. N. R. Too far from home
Waterlilies
Rogers, T. N. R. Too far from home
You can do anything
Rogers, T. N. R. Too far from home
Rogers, Wayne, 1933-
Sleep with me—and death
Selected tales of grim and grue from the horror pulps; ed. by S. Jaffery
ROGUES AND VAGABONDS
Andreyev, L. The abyss
Eichendorff, J., Freiherr von. Memoirs of a good-for-nothing
Lawson, H. The geological spieler
Lawson, H. On the edge of a plain
Lawson, H. Our pipes
Lawson, H. 'Some day'
Somers, A. Plunder

Rohde, Barbara
Solo flight
  McCall's 111:82-3+ Je '84
Roiter, Howard
Only Sam knows
  Fatal recurrences; ed. by H. Hugh and
    P. O'Brien
Rokuro-Kubi. Hearn, L.
Roll call. Asscher-Pinkhof, C.
The **roll-call** of the reef. Quiller-Couch, Sir
  A. T.
A **roll** in the hay. Winters, J.
Roll them bones. Easton, T. A.
Roller. Murphy, D.
Rolling thunder. Abbott, L. K.
**Rolt, L. T. C. (Lionel Thomas Caswell),
  1910-1974**
Bosworth summit pound
  The Oxford book of English ghost
    stories
The mine
  Lost souls; ed. by J. Sullivan
Rolt, Lionel Thomas Caswell *See* Rolt, L.
  T. C. (Lionel Thomas Caswell), 1910-
  1974
Rölvaag, Ole Edvart, 1876-1931
The boy who had no jackknife
  Rölvaag, O. E. When the wind is in the
    south, and other stories
The butter war in Greenfield
  Rölvaag, O. E. When the wind is in the
    south, and other stories
The Christmas offering
  Rölvaag, O. E. When the wind is in the
    south, and other stories
Molla's heart attack
  Rölvaag, O. E. When the wind is in the
    south, and other stories
When the wind is in the south
  Rölvaag, O. E. When the wind is in the
    south, and other stories
Whitebear and Graybear: an Indian legend
  Rölvaag, O. E. When the wind is in the
    south, and other stories
Roman business. Szell, T.
ROMAN CATHOLIC CHURCH *See* Catho-
  lic faith
ROMAN CATHOLIC RELIGION *See* Cath-
  olic faith
Roman charity. Hartley, L. P.
ROMAN EMPIRE *See* Rome
The **Roman** image. Narayan, R. K.
The **Roman** night. Morand, P.
ROMAN SOLDIERS *See* Soldiers—Rome
Romance. Oates, J. C.
The **romance**. Pulaski, J.
Romance. Thurm, M.
The **romance**. Young-Bruehl, E.
Romance: a prose villanelle. DeMarinis, R.
A **romance**—in brief. Klass, P.
The **romance** of a busy broker. Henry, O.
Romance of a horse thief. Opatoshu, J.

The **romance** of certain old clothes. James,
  H.
A **romance** of the equator. Aldiss, B. W.
ROMANCES (LOVE STORIES) *See* Love
  affairs; Love stories
ROMANIA
Eliade, M. The cape
ROMANIANS
Barnes, J. One of a kind
                United States
Herman, M. Auslander
ROMANS
                Palestine
Doyle, Sir A. C. The centurion
The **romantic**. Highsmith, P.
The **romantic** museum. O'Reilly, M.
A **romantic** weekend. Gaitskill, M.
Romarias dos mutilados. Fox, H.
Romberger, Judy
Randy's gift
  'Teen 29:68+ D '85
ROME
Crowley, A. The king of the wood
Lee, T. Into gold
Schwob, M. Clodia, shameless matron
Swann, T. B. Where is the bird of fire?
                510-30 B.C.
Gardner, J. Julius Caesar and the werewolf
                30 B.C.-476 A.D.
Andreyev, L. Lazarus
Brunner, J. Elixir for the emperor
Sheehan, R. The death of Petronius
Sheehan, R. Masks
ROME (ITALY) *See* Italy—Rome
Rome. Parise, G.
Romen Basu *See* Basu, Romen
A **Romeo** and Juliet story in early New Mex-
  ico. Chavez, A.
Romero, Norberto Luis
The city
  Short story international 57
Symmetries
  Short story international 52
Romun, Isak
Christmas is over
  Ellery Queen's Prime crimes 2
Ronald, James
The woman who hated children
  The Saturday Evening Post 256:60-3+ S
    '84
Rondo. Neville, S.
Ronk-Lifson, Martha
Eddie
  The Southern Review (Baton Rouge, La.)
    24:627-31 Summ '88
Ronnie so long at the fair. Summers, M.
ROOFS
Hammer, C. The new roof
Wilson, B. How to fix a roof
The **Rooinek**. Bosman, H. C.

Rooke, Leon
Agnes and the cobwebs
Rooke, L. Sing me no love songs, I'll say you no prayers
The birth control king of the Upper Volta
Rooke, L. Sing me no love songs, I'll say you no prayers
A bolt of white cloth
Rooke, L. A bolt of white cloth
Break and enter
Rooke, L. Sing me no love songs, I'll say you no prayers
Conversations with Ruth: the farmer's tale
Rooke, L. Sing me no love songs, I'll say you no prayers
Dirty heels of the fine young children
Rooke, L. A bolt of white cloth
Dream Lady
Rooke, L. A bolt of white cloth
The end of the revolution and other stories
The Literary Review (Madison, N.J.) 28:438-55 Spr '85
Friendship and property
Rooke, L. Sing me no love songs, I'll say you no prayers
The history of England, part four
Rooke, L. Sing me no love songs, I'll say you no prayers
In the garden
The Art of the tale; ed. by D. Halpern
Rooke, L. Sing me no love songs, I'll say you no prayers
Lady Godiva's horse
Rooke, L. Sing me no love songs, I'll say you no prayers
The madwoman of Cherry Vale
Rooke, L. A bolt of white cloth
Mama Tuddi done over
Rooke, L. Sing me no love songs, I'll say you no prayers
The man in the green bathrobe
Rooke, L. Sing me no love songs, I'll say you no prayers
Narcissus consulted
Rooke, L. Sing me no love songs, I'll say you no prayers
The only daughter
Rooke, L. A bolt of white cloth
Pretty pictures
Harper's 275:31-2 Jl '87
The problem shop
Making it new; ed. by J. Metcalf
Saks Fifth Avenue
A Grand Street reader; ed. by B. Sonnenberg
Rooke, L. A bolt of white cloth
Saloam frigid with time's legacy while Mrs. Willoughby Bight-Davies sits naked through the night on a tree stump awaiting the lizard that will make her loins go boom-boom
Rooke, L. A bolt of white cloth

The shut-in number
Rooke, L. Sing me no love songs, I'll say you no prayers
Sing me no love songs, I'll say you no prayers
Rooke, L. Sing me no love songs, I'll say you no prayers
Some people will tell you the situation at Henny Penny Nursery is getting intolerable
Rooke, L. Sing me no love songs, I'll say you no prayers
Why Agnes left
Rooke, L. Sing me no love songs, I'll say you no prayers
Why the heathens are no more
Rooke, L. A bolt of white cloth
Winter is lovely, isn't summer hell
Making it new; ed. by J. Metcalf
The woman who talked to horses
The Oxford book of Canadian short stories in English
Rooke, L. Sing me no love songs, I'll say you no prayers
The Yale Review 73:410-17 Spr '84
The woman's guide to home companionship
Rooke, L. A bolt of white cloth
Rookie. Sorrells, R. T.
The **room.** Carrier, R.
The **room** in the castle. Campbell, R.
The **room** in the Driskill. Campbell, E.
The **room** in the tower. Benson, E. F.
Room in the world. Zugsmith, L.
Room no. eleven. Maupassant, G. de
A **room** of her own. Chute, P.
A **room** of their own. Verma, N.
A **room** with a vie. Lee, T.
The **room** with something wrong. Woolrich, C.
Room with two beds. Tamer, Z.
ROOMING HOUSES *See* Boarding houses
ROOMMATES
Bass, R. Cats and students, bubbles and abysses
Bumpus, J. Shame
Ciment, J. Money
Kalpakian, L. Habits
Rossi, A. Bums on needles and pins
Scarfe, E. In a lighted house
Williams, T. Happy August the Tenth
The **rooms** of paradise. Watson, I.
Rooms of the soul. Schwartz, H.
Roosevelt, Eleanor, 1884-1962
Christmas 1940
McCall's 114:95-7 Ja '87
The **rooster** and the dancing girl. Kawabata, Y.
ROOSTERS
Goyen, W. The white rooster
Melville, H. Cock-a-doodle-doo; or, The crowing of the noble cock beneventano
Nordan, L. Sugar among the chickens

ROOSTERS—*Continued*
  Purdy, J. How I became a shadow
  Stuart, J. The champion
The **root** and the ring. Guin, W.
The **root** of all evil. Greene, G.
The **roots** of the world. Chesterton, G. K.
The **rope** in the rafters. Onions, O.
Rope of wind. Dumas, H.
Roping lions in the Grand Canyon. Grey, Z.
Rosa, João Guimarães
  The horse that drank beer
    Inspired by drink; ed. by Joan Digby and John Digby
  The third bank of the river
    Black water; ed. by A. Manguel
Rosa, Rodrigo Rey *See* Rey Rosa, Rodrigo, 1958-
Rosa. Ozick, C.
Rosa the beautiful. Allende, I.
Rosalie Prudent. Maupassant, G. de
Rosalie's folly. Grenville, K.
Rosary. Kelly, R.
Roscoe, Patrick, 1962-
  The National Circus of Argentina
    The New press anthology #2
  Never tears for California
    The New press anthology #1
Rose, Daniel Asa
  About the sea
    Rose, D. A. Small family with rooster
  Arturo and Eve
    Rose, D. A. Small family with rooster
  Avoiding the shoals of passion
    Rose, D. A. Small family with rooster
  Betraying Jilly
    Rose, D. A. Small family with rooster
  The elephant story (The stroke, I)
    Rose, D. A. Small family with rooster
  Envy the dead
    Rose, D. A. Small family with rooster
  The escargot story (The stroke, II)
    Rose, D. A. Small family with rooster
  The good-bye present
    Rose, D. A. Small family with rooster
  Growing things at Bad Luck Pond
    Rose, D. A. Small family with rooster
  How birds sleep
    Rose, D. A. Small family with rooster
  Inside the violet
    Rose, D. A. Small family with rooster
  Intercourse
    Rose, D. A. Small family with rooster
  Jumping from high places
    Rose, D. A. Small family with rooster
  Katey Foster's two boys
    Rose, D. A. Small family with rooster
  Parties and storms
    Rose, D. A. Small family with rooster
  Small family with rooster
    Rose, D. A. Small family with rooster
  So long, million miles
    Rose, D. A. Small family with rooster

  Stranger in the house
    Rose, D. A. Small family with rooster
  Summer heat
    Rose, D. A. Small family with rooster
  Tasting leaves
    Rose, D. A. Small family with rooster
Rose, George B.
  William Wilson
    Arkansas in short fiction; ed. by W. M. Baker and E. C. Simpson
Rose, Joel
  The sunshine of Paradise Alley
    Between C & D; ed. by J. Rose and C. Texier
Rose, Meredith
  Henderson
    Through other eyes; ed. by l. Zahava
Rose. Dubus, A.
The **rose** bush. Kilworth, G.
A **rose** by other name . . . Anvil, C.
Rose by the water. Schwartz, A.
Rose-coloured teacups. Byatt, A. S.
A **rose** for Emily. Faulkner, W.
A **rose** for Miss Caroline. Gordon, A.
The **rose** garden. James, M. R.
A **rose** in Murcia. Hall, R. W.
A **rose** in the heart of New York. O'Brien, E.
Rose-Johnny. Kingsolver, B.
Rose Latulipe. Gaspé, P. A. de
The **rose** of Knock. Ryan, A.
Rose petals. Jhabvala, R. P.
Rose Rose. Pain, B.
Rosella, in stages. Broun, H.
Rosemary. Petrakis, H. M.
Rosemund, Victor L.
  The thing from the old seaman's mouth
    L. Ron Hubbard presents Writers of the future
Rosen, George H., 1946-
  The immanence of God in the tropics
    The Yale Review 73:503-17 Summ '84
  On the flats
    Harper's 277:53-8 O '88
Rosen, Gerald
  Growing up Bronx
    Stories and poems from close to home; ed. by F. Salas
Rosen, Stephen
  The deerhide
    Stiller's pond; ed. by J. Agee; R. Blakely and S. Welch
Rosenbaum, Karen
  Low tide
    Greening wheat: fifteen Mormon short stories
Rosenberg, Janice
  Becky Henderson's other life
    Seventeen 43:354-5+ Ag '84
Rosenberg, L. M.
  The walker
    Prairie Schooner 58:5-19 Wint '84

Rosenfeld, Isaac, 1918-1956
Coney Island revisited
   Rosenfeld, I. Preserving the hunger
George
   Rosenfeld, I. Preserving the hunger
The hand that fed me
   Rosenfeld, I. Preserving the hunger
King Solomon
   Rosenfeld, I. Preserving the hunger
The misfortunes of the Flapjacks
   Rosenfeld, I. Preserving the hunger
The party
   Rosenfeld, I. Preserving the hunger
The railroad
   Rosenfeld, I. Preserving the hunger
Red Wolf
   Rosenfeld, I. Preserving the hunger
Wolfie
   Rosenfeld, I. Preserving the hunger
The world of the ceiling
   Rosenfeld, I. Preserving the hunger
A **Rosenkavalier**. Halley, A.
ROSES
Eisenstein, S. Michali among the roses
Lispector, C. The imitation of the rose
Ryan, A. The rose of Knock
Roses. Conroy, F.
Roses. Edwards, M. F.
Roses and limes. Nelson, K.
Roses in June. Ch'en, Y.-C.
Roses of Eden. Jones, H.
Roshchin, Mikhail
The ever-blossoming garden
   Short story international 70
Rosie. Deaver, P. F.
Rosie. Jaffee, A. W.
Rosie's theme. Nazareth, P.
Rosofsky, Iris
Lots
   The Southern Review (Baton Rouge, La.)
   20:429-40 Ap '84
Ross, Bob
Chicago
   Prairie Schooner 60:54-61 Summ '86
Ross, Jean
Fortunes and old perfumes
   The North American Review 270:50-2 S
   '85
Unfinished business
   Shenandoah: an anthology; ed. by J.
   Boatwright
**Ross, Martin, 1862-1915, and Somerville,
Edith Anna Œnone, 1858-1949**
Poisson d'Avril
   The Best of Irish wit and wisdom; ed.
   by J. McCarthy
Ross, R. T. (Robert Thomas), 1924-
The craft of death
   Men at sea; ed. by B. Aymar
Ross, Robert Thomas *See* Ross, R. T.
(Robert Thomas), 1924-

Ross, Sinclair
The lamp at noon
   The Oxford book of Canadian short
   stories in English
Ross, Veronica
Dark secrets
   Ross, V. Dark secrets
Dreams & sleep
   Ross, V. Dark secrets
The girls
   Ross, V. Dark secrets
Hunters
   Ross, V. Dark secrets
Thanksgiving
   Ross, V. Dark secrets
That summer
   Ross, V. Dark secrets
An understated look
   Ross, V. Dark secrets
Whistling
   Ross, V. Dark secrets
Rossi, Agnes, 1957-
Athletes and artists
   Rossi, A. Athletes and artists
Back in the days
   Rossi, A. Athletes and artists
Breakfast, lunch, and dinner
   Rossi, A. Athletes and artists
Bums on needles and pins
   Rossi, A. Athletes and artists
Meetings
   Rossi, A. Athletes and artists
Notes
   Rossi, A. Athletes and artists
Pollyanna
   Rossi, A. Athletes and artists
Teeth and nails
   Rossi, A. Athletes and artists
Winter rentals
   Rossi, A. Athletes and artists
Working
   Rossi, A. Athletes and artists
Rossiter, Sarah
Civil war
   The North American Review 272:65-71
   Mr '87
   Rossiter, S. Beyond this bitter air
Combinations
   Rossiter, S. Beyond this bitter air
Kiss the father
   The Massachusetts Review 26:119-27 Spr
   '85
   Rossiter, S. Beyond this bitter air
Pandora
   Rossiter, S. Beyond this bitter air
Question of light
   Rossiter, S. Beyond this bitter air
Secrets
   Rossiter, S. Beyond this bitter air
Sinners
   Rossiter, S. Beyond this bitter air
Skinner
   Rossiter, S. Beyond this bitter air

Rossiter, Sarah—*Continued*
Star light, star bright
Rossiter, S. Beyond this bitter air
Tea party
Rossiter, S. Beyond this bitter air
Rossner, Judith
The unfaithful father
Mademoiselle 92:134+ Ag '86
Rossoff, Alexis
The Whisperer prowls
A Cent a story! Ed. by G. G. Roberts
Rosta, Helen
Belinda's seal
Alberta bound; ed. by F. Stenson
Rostopchina, Evdokiiã Petrovna, grafinĩã, 1811-1858
Rank and money
Russian and Polish women's fiction; ed. by H. Goscilo
Rot. Williams, J.
Roth, Henry H.
Beginnings
New England Review and Bread Loaf Quarterly 10:262-71 Spr '88
Joe's dead
The Literary Review (Madison, N.J.) 31:43-6 Fall '87
Mal
The North American Review 269:48-9 Mr '84
This time
New directions in prose and poetry 52
Roth, Joseph, 1894-1939
The bust of the emperor
Roth, J. Hotel Savoy; Fallmerayer the stationmaster [and] The bust of the emperor
Fallmerayer the stationmaster
Roth, J. Hotel Savoy; Fallmerayer the stationmaster [and] The bust of the emperor
Hotel Savoy
Roth, J. Hotel Savoy; Fallmerayer the stationmaster [and] The bust of the emperor
Roth, Philip
The conversion of the Jews
American short story masterpieces; ed. by R. Carver and T. Jenks
Eli, the fanatic
The World of the short story; ed. by C. Fadiman
His mistress's voice
Partisan Review 53 no2:155-76 '86
Rothberg, Abraham
The monarch butterfly
Southwest Review 71:97-119 Wint '86
The red dress
Prime number; ed. by A. L. Weir
Rothfork, John
(jt. auth) See Aithal, S. K., and Rothfork, John

Rothman, Chuck
The transformation
Isaac Asimov's Tomorrow's voices
Roth's deadman. Bellamy, J. D.
Rothschild's fiddle. Chekhov, A. P.
Roubles in words, kopeks in figures. Shukshin, V. M.
The **rough** crossing. Fitzgerald, F. S.
Rough justice. Gilbert, M.
Rough justice. Nebel, F.
Rough seas. Murphy, Y.
Rough strife. Schwartz, L. S.
The **rough** string. Patten, L. B.
Rough translations. Giles, M.
Rouland, S. Lee
SunDark in Ithkar
Magic in Ithkar 3; ed. by A. Norton and R. Adams
Round trip. Houbein, L.
Roushdi, Zeinab
Celebrating the Prophet's birthday
Egyptian tales and short stories of the 1970s and 1980s
Route 23: 10th and Bigler to Bethlehem Pike. Birtha, B.
Route of the zephyrs. Bukoski, A.
A **routine**. Stead, C.
Rowe, Marsha
'Who's she—the cat's mother?'
Stepping out; ed. by A. Oosthuizen
Rowena Fletcher. Frame, R.
Roxana runs lunatick. Gilchrist, M.
Roxie raccoon. Gearhart, S. M.
Roy, Gabrielle, 1909-1983
Ely! Ely! Ely!
The Oxford book of French-Canadian short stories
Roy, Jude
La boucherie
The Southern Review (Baton Rouge, La.) 23:477-82 Spr '87
A dream
The Southern Review (Baton Rouge, La.) 20:207-11 Ja '84
The half acre
The Southern Review (Baton Rouge, La.) 23:471-6 Spr '87
The lighted window
The Southern Review (Baton Rouge, La.) 20:199-203 Ja '84
She sang only on Sundays
The Southern Review (Baton Rouge, La.) 20:204-6 Ja '84
Royal beatings. Munro, A.
Royal bones. Shefner, E.
The **royal** command. See Carrington, L. The royal summons
The **royal** family. Keillor, G.
Royal jelly. Dahl, R.
The **royal** summons. Carrington, L.
Royle, Nicholas
Irrelativity
Cutting edge; ed. by D. Etchison

Roy's Jewish problem. Raphael, L.
The **rubber** ball. Beaulieu, V. L.
Rubber heels. Conroy, J.
Rubbish day. Flowerday, E.
Rubble. Claiborne, S.
Rubião, Murilo
  The guest
    Latin American Literary Review 16:82-8
    Ja/Je '88
Rubin, David, 1924-
  Longing for America
    On being foreign; ed. by T. J. Lewis and
    R. E. Jungman
Rubin, Louis Decimus, 1923-
  The shores of Tripoli
    The Southern Review (Baton Rouge, La.)
    20:900-11 O '84
  The St. Anthony Chorale
    Selected stories from The Southern
    review, 1965-1985
Rubio y Morena. Williams, T.
Ruby Dawn, private duty nurse. Broun, H.
Ruby lemons. Meinke, P.
The **ruby** wand of Asrazel. Green, J.
Rubyfruit jungle. Brown, R. M.
Ruch, Teri
  Claire's lover's church
    A Grand Street reader; ed. by B. Son-
    nenberg
    The New generation; ed. by A. Kaufman
    The Pushcart prize IX
Rucker, Rudy von Bitter, 1946-
  In frozen time
    Afterlives; ed. by P. Sargent and I. Wat-
    son
  Inside out
    Synergy v1
  The man who was a cosmic string
    The Universe; ed. by B. Preiss
  Message found in a copy of Flatland
    Mathenauts: tales of mathematical won-
    der; ed. by R. Rucker
  A new golden age
    Mathenauts: tales of mathematical won-
    der; ed. by R. Rucker
  Tales of Houdini
    Mirrorshades; ed. by B. Sterling
Rucker, Rudy von Bitter, 1946-, and Laidlaw,
  Marc
  Probability pipeline
    Synergy v2
Ructions; or, A historical footnote to the
  Cold War. Tuohy, F.
Rud, Anthony M.
  Ooze
    Nightmares in Dixie; ed. by F. McSher-
    ry; C. G. Waugh and M. H. Green-
    berg
Rude awakening. Disch, T. M.
Rudin, John
  Sellin' some wood
    Hound dunnit; ed. by I. Asimov; M. H.
    Greenberg and C. L. R. Waugh

Rudloff, Stephen A.
  A cup of coffee
    A Matter of crime v2
Rudolfio. Rasputin, V. G.
Rudolph Finkl's apprenticeship. Stern, S.
Rudoski, Alice
  If big brother says so
    Ready or not; ed. by J. Kahn
Rue. Barstow, S.
Rue. Dodd, S. M.
Rue de Lille. Gallant, M.
Ruffin, Paul
  The fox
    Ploughshares 14 no2/3:94-8 '88
  J. P. and the water tower
    The Southern Review (Baton Rouge, La.)
    21:503-11 Ap '85
  The man who would be God
    The Best of the West; ed. by J. Thomas
Ruffner, Ben
  Only natural
    The Southern Review (Baton Rouge, La.)
    24:427-34 Spr '88
Ruffolo, Lisa
  Birthday
    Ruffolo, L. Holidays
  Candy
    Ruffolo, L. Holidays
  Commercials
    Ruffolo, L. Holidays
  Halloween
    Ruffolo, L. Holidays
  Holidays
    Ruffolo, L. Holidays
  Independence Day
    Ruffolo, L. Holidays
  Leave of absence
    Ruffolo, L. Holidays
  Love and other lost causes
    Mademoiselle 94:170+ O '88
  Words of love
    Ruffolo, L. Holidays
  You'll lose them before Thanksgiving
    Ruffolo, L. Holidays
Rufus at the door. Hassler, J.
The **rug.** O'Brien, E.
RUGBY FOOTBALL
  Sutherland, M. Loving
RUGS
  Archer, J. The steal
  O'Brien, E. The rug
Ruhen, Olaf
  Christmas on the island
    The Saturday Evening Post 256:46-9+ D
    '84
Rule, Jane, 1931-
  Blessed are the dead
    Rule, J. Inland passage
  A chair for George
    Rule, J. Inland passage
  Dulce
    Rule, J. Inland passage

Rule, Jane, 1931——_Continued_
The end of summer
  Rule, J. Inland passage
First love/last love
  First love/last love; ed. by M. Denneny;
    C. Ortleb and T. Steele
A good kid in a troubled world
  Rule, J. Inland passage
His nor hers
  Rule, J. Inland passage
In the attic of the house
  Editor's choice II; ed. by M. Sklar and
    M. Biggs
Inland passage
  Rule, J. Inland passage
The investment years
  Rule, J. Inland passage
Joy
  Rule, J. Inland passage
A matter of numbers
  Rule, J. Inland passage
A migrant Christmas
  Rule, J. Inland passage
More than money
  Rule, J. Inland passage
Musical beds
  Rule, J. Inland passage
One can of soup at a time
  Rule, J. Inland passage
A perfectly nice man
  The Other woman; ed. by S. Koppelman
Power failure
  Rule, J. Inland passage
The pruning of the apple trees
  Rule, J. Inland passage
Puzzle
  Rule, J. Inland passage
The real world
  Rule, J. Inland passage
Seaweed and song
  Rule, J. Inland passage
Slogans
  The Oxford book of Canadian short
    stories in English
  Rule, J. Inland passage
You cannot judge a pumpkin's happiness
    by the smile upon his face
  Rule, J. Inland passage
The **rule** of names. Le Guin, U. K.
Rules for a normal relationship. Cherry, K.
Rules of the game. Tan, A.
Rulfo, Juan, 1918-1986
Talpa
  The Art of the tale; ed. by D. Halpern
RUMANIA _See_ Romania
The **rumble** seat. Watson, S.
Rumkowsky was right. Fein, Y.
Rummel, Mary Kay
White-out
  Stiller's pond; ed. by J. Agee; R. Blakely
    and S. Welch
The **rummy** affair of old Biffy. Wodehouse,
  P. G.

Rumor. Robison, J.
Rumor and a ladder. Bowles, P.
Rumors. Lavers, N.
Rumpole and the age for retirement. Mortimer, J. C.
Rumpole and the alternative society. Mortimer, J. C.
Rumpole and the blind tasting. Mortimer, J. C.
Rumpole and the boat people. Mortimer, J. C.
Rumpole and the bright seraphim. Mortimer, J. C.
Rumpole and the case of identity. Mortimer, J. C.
Rumpole and the confession of guilt. Mortimer, J. C.
Rumpole and the course of true love. Mortimer, J. C.
Rumpole and the dear departed. Mortimer, J. C.
Rumpole and the expert witness. Mortimer, J. C.
Rumpole and the fascist beast. Mortimer, J. C.
Rumpole and the female of the species. Mortimer, J. C.
Rumpole and the gentle art of blackmail. Mortimer, J. C.
Rumpole and the genuine article. Mortimer, J. C.
Rumpole and the golden thread. Mortimer, J. C.
Rumpole and the heavy brigade. Mortimer, J. C.
Rumpole and the Honourable Member. Mortimer, J. C.
Rumpole and the judge's elbow. Mortimer, J. C.
Rumpole and the last resort. Mortimer, J. C.
Rumpole and the learned friends. Mortimer, J. C.
Rumpole and the Man of God. Mortimer, J. C.
Rumpole and the married lady. Mortimer, J. C.
Rumpole and the official secret. Mortimer, J. C.
Rumpole and the old boy net. Mortimer, J. C.
Rumpole and the old, old story. Mortimer, J. C.
Rumpole and the rotten apple. Mortimer, J. C.
Rumpole and the showfolk. Mortimer, J. C.
Rumpole and the spirit of Christmas. Mortimer, J. C.
Rumpole and the sporting life. Mortimer, J. C.
Rumpole and the winter break. Mortimer, J. C.

Rumpole and the younger generation. Mortimer, J. C.

Rumpole's last case. Mortimer, J. C.

Run from the fire. Harrison, H.

A **run** of bad luck. Proulx, A.

Run to starlight. Martin, G. R. R.

Run with the horsemen. Sams, F.

Runaround. Asimov, I.

The **runaround.** Moskowitz, F.

Runaway. Caldwell, E.

The **runaway.** Nagibin, ÍŪ. M.

The **runaway** wife. Painter, P.

RUNAWAYS (CHILDREN)

  Bowles, P. Here to learn

  Crane, S. His new mittens

  Fante, J. In the spring

  Hemingway, E. The last good country

  Kawabata, Y. Summer shoes

  Oates, J. C. The witness

  Phelps, E. S. Old Mother Goose

  So, K.-W. The heir

  West, J. Live life deeply

  Wright, R. Almos' a man

  Wright, R. The man who was almost a man

  Yu, H.-J. D.M.Z.

RUNAWAYS (YOUTH)

  Barrett, N., Jr. Perpetuity blues

  Cook, H. Clown

  Flook, M. Dancing with my sister Jane

  Gamble, J. S. Kansas

  Gilchrist, E. Traceleen's telling a story called "A bad year"

  Klass, P. Two New Jersey stories: Hudson Towers

  Moyer, K. Tumbling

  Oates, J. C. Little wife

  Peña, D. One story too many

  Sanders, S. R. Fetching the dead

Runciman, James

  The lost skipper

    Sea captains' tales; ed. by A. Enfield

The **runner.** DeLillo, D.

Runners to nowhere. Singer, I. B.

RUNNING

  Apple, M. Carbo-loading

  Bambara, T. C. Raymond's run

  Barcelo, F. The man who stopped trains

  Bates, H. E. The race

  Bonnie, F. The state meet

  Crace, J. Cross-country

  Crane, S. The wise men: a detail of American life in Mexico

  Ellison, H. Gnomebody

  Haas, B. Princess Gilda talks to the unborn

  Liben, M. The relay race

  Lurie, M. Running nicely

  Lutz, J. The other runner

  Matheson, R. C. Third wind

  McDonald, W. The track

  McKinley, J. A Fickleman jogs

  O'Cork, S. Night run

  Pouvoir, J. L. The death triple

  Resnick, M. The Olympians

  Shacochis, B. Hot day on the Gold Coast

  Sheil, G. Mister Al

  Thompson, J. The white impala

  Watanabe, S. A. The seabirds

The **running** and the lame. Barstow, S.

Running around America. Osborn, C.

Running away. Trevor, W.

Running down. Harrison, M. J.

Running from love. Bache, E.

Running from love. Willey, M.

The **running** man. Ely, D.

Running nicely. Lurie, M.

Running out. Lordan, B.

Runyon, Alfred Damon See Runyon, Damon, 1880-1946

Runyon, Charles

  Hangover

    Hitchcock in prime time; ed. by F. M. Nevins and M. H. Greenberg

Runyon, Damon, 1880-1946

  The idyll of Miss Sarah Brown

    Great American love stories; ed. by L. Rosenthal

  The informal execution of Soupbone Pew

    Masterpieces of terror and the supernatural; ed. by M. Kaye and S. Kaye

Rupert Beersley and the Beggar Master of Sivani-Hoota. Boyle, T. C.

A **rupture.** Maupassant, G. de

RURAL LIFE See Country life

Rus in urbe. Henry, O.

Ruse, Gary Alan, 1946-

  The phantom chamber

    The New adventures of Sherlock Holmes; ed. by M. H. Greenberg and C. L. R. Waugh

Rusenas, Irena

  Metanoia: medicine

    Coevolution Quarterly no42:14-21 Summ '84

Rush, Norman

  Alone in Africa

    Rush, N. Whites

  Bruns

    The Best American short stories, 1984

    Rush, N. Whites

  Instruments of seduction

    The Best American short stories, 1985

    The Paris Review 26:146-60 Fall '84

    Rush, N. Whites

  Near Pala

    The New Yorker 60:50-6 My 7 '84

    Rush, N. Whites

  Official Americans

    The New Yorker 61:36-46+ F 10 '86

    Rush, N. Whites

  Thieving

    A Grand Street reader; ed. by B. Sonnenberg

    Rush, N. Whites

The **rush.** Bernen, R.

Rushdie, Salman
Good advice is rarer than rubies
The New Yorker 63:26-8 Je 22 '87
The Prophet's hair
The Penguin book of modern British
short stories
Untime of the Imam
Harper's 277:53-6+ D '88
Rushin, Pat
Making it work
The North American Review 269:43-7 S
'84
Speed of light
Sudden fiction; ed. by R. Shapard and
J. Thomas
Russ, Joanna, 1937-
Autobiography of my mother
Between mothers & daughters; ed. by S.
Koppelman
Bodies
Russ, J. Extra(ordinary) people
The clichés from outer space
Russ, J. The hidden side of the moon
Come closer
Russ, J. The hidden side of the moon
Elf hill
Russ, J. The hidden side of the moon
Everyday depressions
Russ, J. Extra(ordinary) people
Existence
Russ, J. The hidden side of the moon
The experimenter
Russ, J. The hidden side of the moon
Foul fowl
Russ, J. The hidden side of the moon
How Dorothy kept away the spring
Russ, J. The hidden side of the moon
"I had vacantly crumpled it into my
pocket . . . but by God, Eliot, it was
a photograph from life!"
Russ, J. The hidden side of the moon
It's important to believe
Russ, J. The hidden side of the moon
Life in a furniture store
Russ, J. The hidden side of the moon
The little dirty girl
Russ, J. The hidden side of the moon
Main street: 1953
Russ, J. The hidden side of the moon
The man who could not see devils
Masterpieces of fantasy and enchant-
ment; ed. by D. G. Hartwell
Mr. Wilde's second chance
100 great fantasy short short stories; ed.
by I. Asimov; T. Carr and M. H.
Greenberg
Russ, J. The hidden side of the moon
My dear Emily
The Dark descent; ed. by D. G. Hart-
well
The mystery of the young gentleman
Russ, J. Extra(ordinary) people
Worlds apart; ed. by C. Decarnin; E.
Garber and L. Paleo
Nor custom stale
Russ, J. The hidden side of the moon
Old pictures
Russ, J. The hidden side of the moon
Old thoughts, old presences: Daddy's girl
Russ, J. The hidden side of the moon
Old thoughts, old presences: The
autobiography of my mother
Russ, J. The hidden side of the moon
Reasonable people
Russ, J. The hidden side of the moon
Russalka; or, The seacoast of Bohemia
Don't bet on the prince; ed. by J. Zipes
Souls
Russ, J. Extra(ordinary) people
Sword blades and poppy seed
Russ, J. The hidden side of the moon
This afternoon
Russ, J. The hidden side of the moon
This night, at my fire
Russ, J. The hidden side of the moon
The throaways
Russ, J. The hidden side of the moon
The view from this window
Russ, J. The hidden side of the moon
Visiting
Russ, J. The hidden side of the moon
Visiting day
Russ, J. The hidden side of the moon
What did you do during the revolution,
Grandma?
Russ, J. Extra(ordinary) people
When it changed
Kindred spirits; ed. by J. M. Elliot
Window dressing
Russ, J. The hidden side of the moon
Russalka; or, The seacoast of Bohemia.
Russ, J.
Russell, Bertrand, 1872-1970
The Queen of Sheba's nightmare
Devils & demons; ed. by M. Kaye and
S. Kaye
Russell, Chrys
Retiring man
Short story international 45
Russell, Eric Frank, 1905-
Diabologic
Intergalactic empires; ed. by I. Asimov;
M. H. Greenberg and C. G. Waugh
Displaced person
100 great fantasy short short stories; ed.
by I. Asimov; T. Carr and M. H.
Greenberg
Jay Score
Russell, E. F. Men, Martians and
machines
Mechanistria
Russell, E. F. Men, Martians and
machines

Russell, Eric Frank, 1905-—*Continued*
Mesmerica
  Russell, E. F. Men, Martians and machines
Symbiotica
  Russell, E. F. Men, Martians and machines
Top secret
  From mind to mind: tales of communication from Analog
The witness
  Young extraterrestrials; ed. by I. Asimov; M. H. Greenberg and C. G. Waugh
Russell, Eric Frank, 1905-, and Johnson, L. T.
Seeker of tomorrow
  The Mammoth book of classic science fiction; ed. by I. Asimov; C. G. Waugh and M. H. Greenberg
Russell, John
The fourth man
  The Penguin book of horror stories
Russell, Randee, 1946-
Power stories
  Editor's choice II; ed. by M. Sklar and M. Biggs
Russell, Ray
American Gothic
  Masques II; ed. by J. N. Williamson
Before he kills
  Murder and mystery in Chicago; ed. by C. R. Waugh; F. D. McSherry and M. H. Greenberg
The bell
  Cutting edge; ed. by D. Etchison
Czadek
  Masques; ed. by J. N. Williamson
Ding-dong, the lizard's dead
  Murder in Los Angeles; ed. by J. L. Breen and others
I am returning
  Devils & demons; ed. by M. Kaye and S. Kaye
Sardonicus
  Masterpieces of terror and the supernatural; ed. by M. Kaye and S. Kaye
Russell, Tom
Her mother's daughter
  The Georgia Review 39:136-63 Spr '85
Ned Jumper
  The Georgia Review 42:342-83 Summ '88
Witness
  Southwest Review 69:312-27 Summ '84
Russell, William
Murder under the microscope
  Isaac Asimov presents the best crime stories of the 19th century
Russell, William Clark, 1844-1911
A bewitched ship
  Mysterious sea stories; ed. by W. Patrick
Can these dry bones live?
  Sea captains' tales; ed. by A. Enfield

The phantom death
  Men at sea; ed. by B. Aymar
RUSSIA *See* Soviet Union
RUSSIA. RED ARMY *See* Soviet Union. Red Army
Russian boxes. Lurie, M.
A **Russian** husband. Moore, G.
RUSSIAN REFUGEES *See* Refugees, Russian
RUSSIAN REVOLUTION, 1905 *See* Soviet Union—1900-1917
RUSSIAN REVOLUTION, 1917-1921 *See* Soviet Union—1917-1945
RUSSIAN SOLDIERS *See* Soldiers—Soviet Union
Russian songs. Csiffary, S.
RUSSIANS
Alaska
London, J. Negore, the Coward
Australia
Sheiner, R. Brass on the cannons
Tremain, R. My wife is a White Russian
China
McCloy, H. Chinoiserie
Pil'niāk, B. Chinese story
France
Apollinaire, G. The posthumous fiance
Maupassant, G. de. The marquis
Germany
Cohen, A. Malenov's revenge
Majorca
Pronzini, B. Defect
Poland
Nowakowski, M. Madam Amalia Bessarabo
Turkey
Morand, P. Turkish night
United States
Bellow, S. Zetland: by a character witness
Chernoff, M. Bop
Cohen, A. Malenov's revenge
Csiffary, S. Russian songs
Eisenstein, S. Boris
Fetler, J. The dust of Yuri Serafimovich
Hofmann, G. Tolstoy's head
Johnson, W. The girl who would be Russian
Johnson, W. The great Valentinova
Johnson, W. Heir to the realm
Johnson, W. The ice fish
Johnson, W. The last song of exile
Johnson, W. Prayer for the dying
Johnson, W. Sarajevo
Mazel, D. Ilya
Oates, J. C. Détente
Silvis, R. One night with a girl by the Seine
Stead, C. Life is difficult
Russo, Albert
Murder of a novel Parisian style amid the frenzy of France's literary merry-go-round
  Short story international 68

Russo, Albert—*Continued*
Murder of an African prince
Short story international 53
The Sephardic sisters
Short story international 47
The target
Short story international 58
The universe of Mama Malkia
Short story international 70
Russo, Richard, 1949-
The dowry
Prairie Schooner 59:3-25 Fall '85
Russo, Richard Paul
In the season of the rains
In the field of fire; ed. by J. Van B.
Dann and J. Dann
RUSTLERS, CATTLE *See* Cattle thieves
Rustomji, Roshni
Rhodabeh
The Literary Review (Madison, N.J.)
29:527-37 Summ '86
Ruta, Suzanne
The actor
Ruta, S. Stalin in the Bronx, and other
stories
At the border
Ruta, S. Stalin in the Bronx, and other
stories
The autograph
Ruta, S. Stalin in the Bronx, and other
stories
The bus
Ruta, S. Stalin in the Bronx, and other
stories
Carmela
Ruta, S. Stalin in the Bronx, and other
stories
Hortensia
Ruta, S. Stalin in the Bronx, and other
stories
An imaginary line
Ruta, S. Stalin in the Bronx, and other
stories
In Fiona's country
Ruta, S. Stalin in the Bronx, and other
stories
The shoe clerk
Ruta, S. Stalin in the Bronx, and other
stories
Soldier's rest
Ruta, S. Stalin in the Bronx, and other
stories
Stalin in the Bronx
Ruta, S. Stalin in the Bronx, and other
stories
Ruth. Oates, J. C.
The **Ruth** tractate. Howe, F.
Ruthanna Elder. Purdy, J.
Ruth's daughter. Moyer, K.
Ruthy and Edie. Paley, G.
Rutishauser, P.
The man who collected photographs
Critical Quarterly 29:47-53 Spr '87

Ryan, Alan, 1943-
Babies from heaven
Ryan, A. The bones wizard
The bones wizard
Ryan, A. The bones wizard
Bundoran, Co. Donegal
Ryan, A. The bones wizard
The East Beaverton monster
Whispers V
Following the way
The Best of Shadows; ed. by C. L.
Grant
Ryan, A. The bones wizard
Vampires; ed. by A. Ryan
The Halloween house
Halloween horrors; ed. by A. Ryan
Hear the whistle blowing
After midnight; ed. by C. L. Grant
Ryan, A. The bones wizard
I shall not leave England now
Shadows 7
The lovely and talented Maxine Kane
Ryan, A. The bones wizard
Memory and desire
Ryan, A. The bones wizard
Pietà
Ryan, A. The bones wizard
The rose of Knock
Ryan, A. The bones wizard
Sand
Ryan, A. The bones wizard
Shadows 8
Sheets
Ryan, A. The bones wizard
Waiting for the papers
Ryan, A. The bones wizard
Ryan, Noel
Stavrogin
First love/last love; ed. by M. Denneny;
C. Ortleb and T. Steele
The **Ryans**. Ford, K.
Ryman, Geoff
O happy day!
Interzone: the first anthology; ed. by J.
Clute; C. Greenland and D. Pringle
Rymer, James Malcolm, 1814-1881
Varney the vampyre; or, The feast of
blood [excerpt]
Vampires; ed. by A. Ryan
Rynas, Stephen
The apprentice sorcerer
Yankee witches; ed. by C. G. Waugh;
M. H. Greenberg and F. D. McSherry

S

S/S Cairo City. Shaham, N.
S F. Soutter, A.
S is for snake. Aldani, L.
S.L.. Brodkey, H.

Saadawi, Nawal el- *See* El-Saadawi, Nawal
Saba (an affirmation). Sams, F.
Sabah, Muyhi 'l-Din, 1925-1962
 The destroyer of families
  Modern Syrian short stories; ed. by M.
   G. Azrak
Sabah, Victor
 An imaginary journey to the moon
  The Penguin world omnibus of science
   fiction
Sabatini, Rafael, 1875-1950
 The blank shot
  Sea captains' tales; ed. by A. Enfield
The **sabbat** at Mofflaines. Schwob, M.
SABBATH
 Botwinik, B. Shabbas
 Botwinik, B. Shabbas morning
Sabbath in Gehenna. Singer, I. B.
Sabbatha and solitude. Williams, T.
Sabbatical. Bloch, R.
Sabbatical. Evans, D.
Saberhagen, Fred, 1930-
 Adventure of the metal murderer
  Omni book of science fiction 3
  Sherlock Holmes through time and space
 Smasher
  A Very large array; ed. by M. M. Snod-
   grass
SABOTAGE
 Chipulina, E. G. The exiles
 Herbert, F. The tactful saboteur
 Knox, B. Deerglen Queen
SABOTEURS *See* Sabotage
Sacastrú, Martín, 1914-
 *For works written by this author under
  other names see* Bioy Casares, Adol-
  fo, 1914-
The **sack.** Sheehan, R.
Sackett, Sam
 Hail to the chief
  Election Day 2084; ed. by I. Asimov
   and M. H. Greenberg
The **sacking** of Miss Plimsoll. Trevanian
Sacrament of the sick. Bernen, R.
Sacred & secular. Watmough, D.
SACRIFICE
 Desy, J. The princess who stood on her
  own two feet
 Poe, E. A. A tale of Jerusalem
SACRIFICE, HUMAN
 Amis, M. The little puppy that could
 Campbell, R. Merry May
 Clee, M. A. Dust
 Derleth, A. W. The night train to Lost
  Valley
 Dozois, G. R. The peacemaker
 Hoch, E. D. The maiden's sacrifice
 Kessler, J. F. Valley
 Lee, T. The dry season
 Linaweaver, B. Shadow quest
 Lovecraft, H. P. The shadow over Inns-
  mouth
 Strieber, W. Pain

 Wells, H. G. The Lord of the Dynamos
The **sacrifice.** Dozois, G. R.
The **sacrifice.** Eisenstein, S.
Sacrifice. Gottlieb, E.
The **sacrifice.** Petchsingh, T.
The **sacrifice.** Spivack, K.
The **sacrifice.** Stevens, J. A.
The **sacrifice;** an African story. Kamkondo,
 D.
Sacrifices. Mazel, D.
The **sacrificial** egg. Achebe, C.
The **sad** music of men. Windsor, G.
Sad stories in Patagonia. McCormack, E. P.
The **sad** story of a dramatic critic. Wells,
 H. G.
'A **sad** tale's best for winter'. Spark, M.
The **sad-womb** son. Nevai, L.
Sa'dāwī, Nawāl *See* El-Saadawi, Nawal
The **saddest** pleasure. Baranay, I.
SADE, MARQUIS DE, 1740-1814
         About
 Bloch, R. The skull of the Marquis de
  Sade
Sadhu, Arun
 Ziprya
  Short story international 64
Sadie. Matthiessen, P.
Sadie. Mazel, D.
Sadie and the brat. Hochstein, R.
Sadie when she died. McBain, E.
SADISM
      See also Cruelty
 Bloch, R. A toy for Juliette
 Conner, M. Vamp
 Cooper, D. George: Wednesday, Thursday,
  Friday
 Elkin, S. A poetics for bullies
 Ellison, H. The prowler in the city at the
  edge of the world
 Flanagan, M. White places
 Gaitskill, M. A romantic weekend
 Gaitskill, M. Secretary
 Hofmann, G. The night
 Landolfi, T. Maria Giuseppa
 Lawrence, D. H. The Prussian officer
 Martínez-Serros, H. Her
 O'Donnell, P. The Soo girl charity
Sadler, Mark, 1924-
 *For works written by this author under
  other names see* Arden, William,
  1924-; Collins, Michael, 1924-;
  Lynds, Dennis, 1924-
The **choice**
 Alfred Hitchcock's Mortal errors
The **sadness** of Cornelius Berg. Yourcenar,
 M.
Sadoff, Ira
 "Please, please me"
  The Antioch Review 44:355-66 Summ '86
Safe. Gordon, M.
Safe. Wilbur, E.
Safe home. Potter, N. A. J.
The **safe** place. Morris, W.

SAFES
Asimov, I. Getting the combination
The **safest** place in the world. Reasoner, J. M.
Safety. Asscher-Pinkhof, C.
The **safety** patrol. Martone, M.
Safransky, Rosa
Can a Morris Minor break the speed of sound?
Prairie Schooner 62:101-4 Wint '88/'89
The **saga** of Slaven Budd. Jones, D. C.
Sagan, Carl, 1934-
Contact
Discover 6:49-60+ O '85
Sagan, Françoise, 1935-
Aftermath of a duel
Sagan, F. Incidental music
The cat and the casino
Sagan, F. Incidental music
A country outing
Sagan, F. Incidental music
The distant cousin
Sagan, F. Incidental music
A dog's night
Roger Caras' Treasury of great dog stories
The exchange
Sagan, F. Incidental music
"La Futura"
Sagan, F. Incidental music
Incidental music
Sagan, F. Incidental music
One year later
Sagan, F. Incidental music
Partway round the course
Sagan, F. Incidental music
A question of timing
Sagan, F. Incidental music
Tears in the red wine
Sagan, F. Incidental music
Third person singular
Sagan, F. Incidental music
Sage, Victor
Bagley's progress
Sage, V. Dividing lines
Crusoe
Sage, V. Dividing lines
Destroying angel
Sage, V. Dividing lines
Little Goethe
Sage, V. Dividing lines
Nada
Sage, V. Dividing lines
Obscurity
Sage, V. Dividing lines
SAHARA
Balzac, H. de. A passion in the desert
Saidi, William
The nightmare
African short stories in English; ed. by J. de Grandsaigne
SAIGON (VIETNAM) *See* Vietnam—Ho Chi Minh City

Saiki, Jessica
The arrangement
Saiki, J. Once, a lotus garden, and other stories
Arrival of the picture brides
Saiki, J. Once, a lotus garden, and other stories
Bus stop
Saiki, J. Once, a lotus garden, and other stories
Family business
Saiki, J. Once, a lotus garden, and other stories
The fisherman
Saiki, J. Once, a lotus garden, and other stories
Hapa hapa/half and half
Saiki, J. Once, a lotus garden, and other stories
My wartime job
Saiki, J. Once, a lotus garden, and other stories
Nocturne
Saiki, J. Once, a lotus garden, and other stories
The old ways
Saiki, J. Once, a lotus garden, and other stories
Once, a lotus garden
Saiki, J. Once, a lotus garden, and other stories
Petty larceny
Saiki, J. Once, a lotus garden, and other stories
Plumeria days
Saiki, J. Once, a lotus garden, and other stories
Retrospective
Saiki, J. Once, a lotus garden, and other stories
Revelation
Saiki, J. Once, a lotus garden, and other stories
Samurai
Saiki, J. Once, a lotus garden, and other stories
Sisters
Saiki, J. Once, a lotus garden, and other stories
Suspect alien
Saiki, J. Once, a lotus garden, and other stories
The visit
Saiki, J. Once, a lotus garden, and other stories
Windows
Saiki, J. Once, a lotus garden, and other stories
The wood rose
Saiki, J. Once, a lotus garden, and other stories

Saiki, Patsy S.
Communion
Passages to the dream shore; ed. by F. Stewart
Sail 25. Vance, J.
Sail on! Sail on! Farmer, P. J.
Sailing. MacDonald, D. R.
The **sailing** ship. Gaitens, E.
Sailing, through program management. Charmatz, A.
Sailing to Byzantium. Silverberg, R.
The **sailor-boy's** tale. Dinesen, I.
SAILORS *See* Seamen
Sailors belong ships. Morrison, J.
Saint, Robert
The Imam
Stories and poems from close to home; ed. by F. Salas
The **saint.** Pritchett, V. S.
Saint Adorata. Apollinaire, G.
Saint-Aubin, Horace de *See* Balzac, Honoré de, 1799-1850
Saint Cecilia's son. Eaton, C. E.
SAINT CROIX (VIRGIN ISLANDS OF THE U.S.)
Dubus, A. At St. Croix
Saint Kay's day. Farmer, B.
SAINT LOUIS (MO.) *See* Missouri—Saint Louis
Saint Marie. Erdrich, L.
Saint Nikolaus. Ramírez, S.
SAINT PATRICK'S DAY
Morrison, J. The busting of Rory O'Mahony
SAINT PETERSBURG (FLA.) *See* Florida—Saint Petersburg
SAINT PETERSBURG (SOVIET UNION) *See* Soviet Union—Leningrad
A **saint** (unknown) with two donors. Warner, S. T.
SAINT VALENTINE'S DAY *See* Valentine's Day
The **saintmaker's** wife. Phipps, H. J.
SAINTS
Apollinaire, G. Saint Adorata
Bowles, P. An inopportune visit
Chavez, A. The bell that sang again
Chavez, A. Hunchback Madonna
Karr, P. A. The toe
Piñera, V. The balcony
Sexson, L. Margaret of the imperfections
Williams, T. Chronicle of a demise
Saints. Mukherjee, B.
The **saints** and sinners run. Birtha, B.
Saipan the shoeshine man. Anderson, C. R.
Saito and the fox girl. Van de Wetering, J.
Saito and the sacred stick. Van de Wetering, J.
Saito and the Shogun. Van de Wetering, J.
Saito and the twenty-sen stamp. Van de Wetering, J.
Saito versus Saito. Van de Wetering, J.
Saito versus Satan. Van de Wetering, J.

Saito's small oversight. Van de Wetering, J.
Saito's summary. Van de Wetering, J.
Sakers, Don
The finagle fiasco
Mathenauts: tales of mathematical wonder; ed. by R. Rucker
Saki, 1870-1916
The Easter egg
Masterpieces of terror and the supernatural; ed. by M. Kaye and S. Kaye
Gabriel-Ernest
Young monsters; ed. by I. Asimov; M. H. Greenberg and C. G. Waugh
Laura
Black water; ed. by A. Manguel
The open window
Great ghost stories; ed. by B. A. Schwartz
The philanthropist and the happy cat
Roger Caras' Treasury of great cat stories
Sredni Vashtar
Dark arrows; ed. by A. Manguel
Tea
Inspired by drink; ed. by Joan Digby and John Digby
Tobermory
Masterpieces of fantasy and enchantment; ed. by D. G. Hartwell
Roger Caras' Treasury of great cat stories
The Treasury of English short stories; ed. by N. Sullivan
The wolves of Cernogratz
Spirits, spooks, and other sinister creatures; ed. by H. Hoke
Sakrete. Barthelme, D.
Saks Fifth Avenue. Rooke, L.
Sal the Dude. Whitfield, R.
Salama, Fathy
Friends' eyes
Egyptian tales and short stories of the 1970s and 1980s
Salamander. Jaffe, H.
The **salamander.** Rodoreda, M.
Salamander Four. O'Donnell, P.
Salas, Floyd, 1931-
Kid victory
Stories and poems from close to home; ed. by F. Salas
Salas, Gregory
Police report
Stories and poems from close to home; ed. by F. Salas
Sale, Richard, 1911-
The benevolent ghost and Captain Lowrie
Mysterious sea stories; ed. by W. Patrick
Double trouble
Hard-boiled dames; ed. by B. A. Drew
The House of Kaa
A Cent a story! Ed. by G. G. Roberts
Sale of one small ranch. St. Pierre, P. H.

SALEM (MASS.) *See* Massachusetts—Salem

The **Salem** Mass. See Hawthorne, N. Young Goodman Brown

The **Salem** wolf. Pyle, H.

SALES PERSONNEL AND SELLING
Anthony, P. Hard sell
Anthony, P. Hurdle
Broun, H. Cows on the drag strip
Carver, R. Collectors
Carver, R. Vitamins
Coates, R. M. The hour after Westerly
Cobb, W. The stone soldier
Colette. The saleswoman
De Haven, T. Clap hands! Here comes Charley
Derleth, A. W. The night train to Lost Valley
Ellis, L. R. The great rodeo fix
Frame, J. Insulation
Franzen, B. The long donut hole
Gallagher, T. Turpentine
Greene, G. A chance for Mr. Lever
Humphrey, W. A good Indian
Jolley, E. Outink to Uncle's place
Jolley, E. The travelling entertainer
Kees, W. So cold outside
Klíma, I. Wednesday morning: a Christmas conspiracy tale
Kroll, J. The Electrolux man
Luce-Kapler, R. The Rawleigh man
Lurie, M. Were they pretty?
Lutz, J. Mail order
McKinley, J. Traveler's advisory
Nevai, L. Likely houses
Norris, H. Water into wine
O'Connor, F. Good country people
O'Hara, J. How can I tell you?
Ryan, A. Sheets
St. Clair, M. The man who sold rope to the Gnoles
Weaver, G. The Bearded Lady
Wilson, B. Take Louise Nevelson
Wodehouse, P. G. The go-getter
Wolfe, T. The Company
Woodman, A. The lampshade vendor
Sales pitch. Dick, P. K.

SALESMEN AND SALESMENSHIP *See* Sales personnel and selling

The **saleswoman**. Colette

Salient facts. Covino, M.

SALIERI, ANTONIO, 1750-1825
About
Morazzoni, M. The dignity of Signor Da Ponte

Ṣāliḥ, al-Ṭayyib, 1929-
The Cypriot man
Arabic short stories; tr. by D. Johnson-Davies
A handful of dates
African short stories; ed. by C. Achebe and C. L. Innes

Sālim, George
The power of darkness
Modern Syrian short stories; ed. by M. G. Azrak

Salinas, Marta
The scholarship jacket
Cuentos Chicanos; ed. by R. A. Anaya and A. Márquez

Salisbury, Ralph
Aniwaya, Anikawa, and the killer teen-agers
Earth power coming; ed. by S. J. Ortiz
The gleams
Earth power coming; ed. by S. J. Ortiz
The sonofabitch and the dog
Earth power coming; ed. by S. J. Ortiz

Sallie C. Barrett, N., Jr.

Sallis, James, 1944-
Miranda-Escobedo
100 great fantasy short short stories; ed. by I. Asimov; T. Carr and M. H. Greenberg
Others
The Georgia Review 39:372-6 Summ '85

Salloum, Vicki
Sitty Victoria
When I am an old woman I shall wear purple; ed. by S. K. Martz

Sally. Asimov, I.

Sally's birthday. Farmer, B.

Salmawy, Mohammed
A concerto for the nay
Egyptian tales and short stories of the 1970s and 1980s

Salmón, Filéncio
Zapatos
Harper's 277:30-2+ O '88

SALMON FISHING
Dauenhauer, N. Egg boat
Kazakov, Y. Nikishka's secrets

A **salmon** for the White House. Train, A. C.

Salmonson, Jessica Amanda
Angel's exchange
Masques; ed. by J. N. Williamson
The blind man
Shadows 8
Eagle-worm
Dragons of light; ed. by O. S. Card
The house that knew no hate
The Architecture of fear; ed. by K. Cramer and P. D. Pautz
The prodigal daughter
Kindred spirits; ed. by J. M. Elliot
The trilling princess
Devils & demons; ed. by M. Kaye and S. Kaye

Saloam frigid with time's legacy while Mrs. Willoughby Bight-Davies sits naked through the night on a tree stump awaiting the lizard that will make her loins go boom-boom. Rooke, L.

The **salt** course. Livesey, M.

The **salt** garden. Atwood, M.
The **salt** garden. Miesel, S.
SALT LAKE CITY (UTAH) *See* Utah—Salt
    Lake City
The **salt** of the earth. Shaham, N.
Salter, James
  Akhnilo
    American short story masterpieces; ed.
      by R. Carver and T. Jenks
  American express
    Esquire 109:125-32 F '88
  The fields at dusk
    Esquire 102:101-2+ Ag '84
    The Esquire fiction reader v1
  Foreign shores
    The Best American short stories, 1984
  Lost sons
    A Grand Street reader; ed. by B. Son-
      nenberg
    Prize stories, 1984
    Soldiers & civilians; ed. by T. Jenks
  Twenty minutes
    Grand Street 7:7-13 Wint '88
Salvador. Shepard, L.
SALVAGE
  Bloch, R. Terror in Cut-throat Cove
  Gallacher, T. A friend of Dosser Farr
  Hemingway, E. After the storm
  Raine, N. R. The last laugh
Salvage. Card, O. S.
Salvage rites. Watson, I.
SALVATION
      See also Atonement
  Thackeray, W. M. The devil's wager
The **salvation** of me. Pancake, B. D.
Salvatore, Diane
  The comforts of home
    Ladies' Home Journal 105:96+ My '88
Sam and the Banzai runner. Ing, D.
Sam and the sudden blizzard machine. Ing,
    D.
Sam Hall. Anderson, P.
Sam, Soren, and Ed. Vanderhaeghe, G.
Sam Starr. Taylor, R.
Samarakis, Antonis
  The flesh
    Short story international 69
  The mother
    Short story international 58
Samaritan. Barthelme, S.
Samaritan. Willis, C.
Samba de los agentes. Codrescu, A.
Sambal and Putki. Basu, R.
Sambrot, William
  Black night, white night; or, The battle of
    Dingle on the Dangle
    A Treasury of World War II stories; ed.
      by B. Pronzini and M. H. Greenberg
  The man who hated
    A Treasury of World War II stories; ed.
      by B. Pronzini and M. H. Greenberg
The **same** dog. Aickman, R.
The **same** old grind. Pronzini, B.

The **Samhain** Feis. Tremayne, P.
Sammān, Ghādah
  Old enough to be your father . . .
    Modern Syrian short stories; ed. by M.
      G. Azrak
SAMOAN ISLANDS
  Maugham, W. S. Red
  Theroux, P. Yard sale
  Wendt, A. The balloonfish and the ar-
    madillo
  Wendt, A. The birth and death of the
    miracle man
  Wendt, A. Birthdays
  Wendt, A. Crocodile
  Wendt, A. Daughter of the mango season
  Wendt, A. Elena's son
  Wendt, A. Exam failure praying
  Wendt, A. Hamlet
  Wendt, A. I will be our saviour from the
    bad smell
  Wendt, A. Justice
  Wendt, A. Prospecting
  Wendt, A. A talent
Samovar. Faik, S.
Samples, Henry
  Home cooking
    Homewords: a book of Tennessee
      writers; ed. by D. Paschall
Sampson, Judith
  Qazia and a ferret-fetch
    Magic in Ithkar [1]; ed. by A. Norton
      and R. Adams
Sampson, Robert, 1927-
  Far eyes
    A Matter of crime v1
  Rain in Pinton County
    The Year's best mystery and suspense
      stories, 1987
Sams, Ferrol, 1922-
  Big Star woman
    Sams, F. The widow's mite & other
      stories
  Fubar
    Sams, F. The widow's mite & other
      stories
  Fulfillment
    Sams, F. The widow's mite & other
      stories
  Howdy Doody time
    Sams, F. The widow's mite & other
      stories
  Judgment
    Sams, F. The widow's mite & other
      stories
  Porphyria's lover
    Sams, F. The widow's mite & other
      stories
  Run with the horsemen [excerpt]
    A Collection of classic Southern humor;
      ed. by G. W. Koon
  Saba (an affirmation)
    Sams, F. The widow's mite & other
      stories

Sams, Ferrol, 1922-—*Continued*
The widow's mite
Sams, F. The widow's mite & other stories
Sam's conscience. Farr, D.
Samuel Hele, Esq. Baldwin, J. G.
SAMURAI
Kawabata, Y. Toward winter
Kōda, R. The bearded samurai
Shiga, N. Akanishi Kakita
Sterling, B. Flowers of Edo
Samurai. Saiki, J.
Samurai descendant. Kawabata, Y.
Samurai Saito. Van de Wetering, J.
San Diego dilemma. Mulder, M.
SAN FRANCISCO (CALIF.) *See* California—San Francisco
San Francisco. Hempel, A.
San Francisco petal. Gold, H.
SANATORIUMS *See* Hospitals and sanatoriums
Sanchez, Thomas, 1944-
Red Reno honkers
Stories and poems from close to home; ed. by F. Salas
The Sanchez sacraments. Muller, M.
Sanctuary. Antieau, K.
Sanctuary. Christie, A.
Sanctuary. Pronzini, B.
Sanctuary. Thurm, M.
SAND, GEORGE, 1804-1876
About
Russ, J. Sword blades and poppy seed
Sand. Ryan, A.
Sand. Williams, T.
Sand. Yourgrau, B.
The sand ball. Meckel, C.
Sandberg, Peter Lars, 1934-
B-Tower west wall
Sandberg, P. L. Gabe's fall, and other climbing stories
Calloway's climb
Sandberg, P. L. Gabe's fall, and other climbing stories
The devil's thumb
Sandberg, P. L. Gabe's fall, and other climbing stories
Gabe's fall
McCall's 115:99-100+ Ag '88
Sandberg, P. L. Gabe's fall, and other climbing stories
Hawsmoot
Sandberg, P. L. Gabe's fall, and other climbing stories
The old bull moose of the woods
Sandberg, P. L. Gabe's fall, and other climbing stories
The rhyme of Lancelot
Sandberg, P. L. Gabe's fall, and other climbing stories
To have and to hold
Good Housekeeping 204:102-3+ Je '87

SANDBURG, CARL, 1878-1967
About
Blei, N. The ghost of Sandburg's phizzog
Sandel, Cora, 1880-1974
Alberta
Sandel, C. The silken thread
Allie
Sandel, C. The silken thread
The art of murder
Sandel, C. Cora Sandel: selected short stories
Artist's Christmas
Sandel, C. The silken thread
Avalanche
Sandel, C. The silken thread
Bernhardt
Sandel, C. Cora Sandel: selected short stories
The bracelet
Sandel, C. The silken thread
The broad versus the narrow outlook
Sandel, C. The silken thread
Carmen and Maia
Sandel, C. The silken thread
The child
Sandel, C. Cora Sandel: selected short stories
The child who loved roads
Sandel, C. Cora Sandel: selected short stories
The flight to America
Sandel, C. Cora Sandel: selected short stories
Hval
Sandel, C. Cora Sandel: selected short stories
Klara
Sandel, C. Cora Sandel: selected short stories
Larsen's
Sandel, C. Cora Sandel: selected short stories
Lola
Sandel, C. Cora Sandel: selected short stories
Madame
Sandel, C. The silken thread
Mother
Sandel, C. Cora Sandel: selected short stories
A mystery
Sandel, C. Cora Sandel: selected short stories
One day in November
Sandel, C. The silken thread
Papen
Sandel, C. Cora Sandel: selected short stories
The picture from Hull
Sandel, C. The silken thread
The polar bears
Sandel, C. The silken thread

Sandel, Cora, 1880-1974—*Continued*
Shit-Katrine
  Sandel, C. Cora Sandel: selected short
    stories
The silken thread
  Sandel, C. The silken thread
Simple memories
  Sandel, C. The silken thread
The sisters
  Sandel, C. Cora Sandel: selected short
    stories
Thank you, doctor
  Sandel, C. Cora Sandel: selected short
    stories
There's a war on
  Sandel, C. The silken thread
To Lukas
  Sandel, C. Cora Sandel: selected short
    stories
Two cats in Paris and one in Florence
  Sandel, C. The silken thread
The ways of love
  Sandel, C. Cora Sandel: selected short
    stories
The women in the bath-house
  Sandel, C. The silken thread
Sanders, Barry
Feldman and Goldman, barbers
  The North American Review 273:44-8 Je
    '88
Sanders, H. G.
Boom job
  The Paris Review 28:77-83 Spr '86
Smiling time
  The Paris Review 28:84-6 Spr '86
Sanders, Scott R. (Scott Russell), 1945-
America is one long bloody fight
  The Georgia Review 40:275-6 Spr '86
  Necessary fictions; ed. by S. W. Lind-
    berg and S. Corey
The anatomy lesson
  100 great fantasy short short stories; ed.
    by I. Asimov; T. Carr and M. H.
    Greenberg
  Tales from Isaac Asimov's science fiction
    magazine: short stories for young
    adults
The cry
  Sanders, S. R. Fetching the dead
Fetching the dead
  Sanders, S. R. Fetching the dead
The fire woman
  Sanders, S. R. Fetching the dead
Prophet
  Sanders, S. R. Fetching the dead
The recovery of vision
  Sanders, S. R. Fetching the dead
Time and again
  Sanders, S. R. Fetching the dead
Travels in the interior
  Omni (New York, N.Y.) 8:98-100+ D '85
Wake
  Sanders, S. R. Fetching the dead

Walking to sleep
  Sanders, S. R. Fetching the dead
Sanders, Thomas E.
Ave Lutie
  Short story international 65
Sanders, Walter
Dreaming of Grandpa
  The North American Review 272:20-2 D
    '87
Going to school
  The North American Review 270:35-8 S
    '85
A visit to Aunt Ivy's
  The North American Review 269:22-5 S
    '84
Sandham, Agnes A.
The conscientious cat
  Roger Caras' Treasury of great cat
    stories
Sandkings. Martin, G. R. R.
Sandor, Marjorie
The Gittel
  20 under 30; ed. by D. Spark
  The Best American short stories, 1985
  The Georgia Review 38:509-22 Fall '84
Judgment
  The Yale Review 77:578-88 Summ '88
Still life
  The Best American short stories, 1988
  The Georgia Review 41:465-72 Fall '87
Sandoz, Mari, 1896-1966
The girl in the Humbert
  She won the West; ed. by M. Muller
    and B. Pronzini
The vine
  Westward the women; ed. by V. Piekar-
    ski
SANDSTORMS *See* Storms
Sanford, Annette
Grandmother's little girl
  Redbook 166:46+ Ap '86
Happy fortieth, Ed and Shirley
  The North American Review 270:28-30
    Mr '85
Limited access
  New stories from the South: the year's
    best, 1988
Sanford, Winifred M., 1890-
Allie
  Sanford, W. M. Windfall, and other
    stories
Black child
  Sanford, W. M. Windfall, and other
    stories
The blue spruce
  Sanford, W. M. Windfall, and other
    stories
Fever in the South
  Sanford, W. M. Windfall, and other
    stories
Fools
  Sanford, W. M. Windfall, and other
    stories

Sanford, Winifred M., 1890——*Continued*
The forest fire
Sanford, W. M. Windfall, and other stories
Luck
Sanford, W. M. Windfall, and other stories
Mary
Sanford, W. M. Windfall, and other stories
The monument
Sanford, W. M. Windfall, and other stories
Mr. Carmichael's room
Sanford, W. M. Windfall, and other stories
Saved
Sanford, W. M. Windfall, and other stories
Windfall
Sanford, W. M. Windfall, and other stories
Wreck
Sanford, W. M. Windfall, and other stories
Sanguinetti, Elise
A Yankee inquisitor
The Art of fiction in the heart of Dixie; ed. by P. D. Beidler
SANITATION
Blish, J. A dusk of idols
Sansom, William, 1912-
The vertical ladder
The World of the short story; ed. by C. Fadiman
SANTA BARBARA (CALIF.) *See* California—Santa Barbara
The **Santa** class test. Murphy, P.
SANTA CLAUS
Daniels, C. A Carolina Christmas carol
Ferreira, R. Are you stone-cold, Santa Claus?
Hartley, L. P. Someone in the lift
Little, J. R. Tommy's Christmas
Matheson, R. C. Holiday
Ramírez, S. Saint Nikolaus
Van Gelder, G. Santa's tenth reindeer
Santa Claus. Yunker, R.
SANTA CRUZ (CALIF.) *See* California—Santa Cruz
SANTA FE (N.M.) *See* New Mexico—Santa Fe
Santa knows. Woodruff, E.
SANTA MONICA (CALIF.) *See* California—Santa Monica
Santa Monica. Carlson, R.
Sant'Anna, Sérgio
Notes of Manfredo Rangel, reporter (about Kramer)
The Literary Review (Madison, N.J.) 27:450-68 Summ '84
Santa's tenth reindeer. Van Gelder, G.

SANTO DOMINGO (DOMINICAN REPUBLIC) *See* Dominican Republic—Santo Domingo
Santorini gray. Thomas, J.
The **sapper**: a romance. Federspiel, J.
The **sapphire** necklace. Morris, K.
Sara. Yarbrough, S.
Sarab. Khuri, C.
Sarah, Robyn
Première arabesque
Fatal recurrences; ed. by H. Hugh and P. O'Brien
Sarah. Skelton, R.
Sarah Cole: a type of love story. Banks, R.
Sarah runs the weasel. Williams, W. J.
Sarah's copper. St. Pierre, P. H.
Sarajevo. Johnson, W.
Saratoga, hot. Calisher, H.
SARATOGA SPRINGS (N.Y.) *See* New York (State)—Saratoga Springs
Sardofa's horseshoes. Frost, G.
Sardonicus. Russell, R.
Saree of the gods. Sharat Chandra, G. S.
Sargent, Pamela
If ever I should leave you
Afterlives; ed. by P. Sargent and I. Watson
The old darkness
The Best horror stories from the Magazine of fantasy and science fiction
Originals
Universe 15
Out of place
Magicats! Ed. by J. Dann and G. Dozois
Roger Caras' Treasury of great cat stories
Shrinker
Tales from Isaac Asimov's science fiction magazine: short stories for young adults
The **Sark** Lane Mission. Gilbert, M.
Sarkadi, Imre
The deserter
Short story international 58
Saroff, Steve S.
A family man
Redbook 167:66+ S '86
Letter to my daughter
Redbook 162:46+ Ja '84
Saroyan, William, 1908-1981
The beautiful white horse
Child's ploy; ed. by M. Muller and B. Pronzini
Cowards
Saroyan, W. Madness in the family
The duel
Saroyan, W. Madness in the family
Fire
Saroyan, W. Madness in the family
A Fresno fable
Saroyan, W. Madness in the family
Gaston
Saroyan, W. Madness in the family

Saroyan, William, 1908-1981—*Continued*
How the barber finally got himself into a fable
  Saroyan, W. Madness in the family
How to choose a wife
  Saroyan, W. Madness in the family
The inscribed copy of the Kreutzer sonata
  Saroyan, W. Madness in the family
The last word was love
  Saroyan, W. Madness in the family
Lord Chugger of cheer
  Saroyan, W. Madness in the family
Madness in the family
  Saroyan, W. Madness in the family
Mystic games
  Saroyan, W. Madness in the family
Najari Levon's old country advice to the young Americans on how to live with a snake
  Saroyan, W. Madness in the family
An ornery kind of kid
  The Saturday Evening Post 258:46-9+ S '86
Picnic time
  Saroyan, W. Madness in the family
There was a young lady of Perth
  Saroyan, W. Madness in the family
There's one in every school
  Ladies' Home Journal 101:175-7 Ja '84
Twenty is the greatest time in any man's life
  Saroyan, W. Madness in the family
What a world, said the bicycle rider
  Saroyan, W. Madness in the family
Sarrantonio, Al
The haunting of Y-12
  Great ghost stories; ed. by B. A. Schwartz
Letters from camp
  100 great fantasy short short stories; ed. by I. Asimov; T. Carr and M. H. Greenberg
Liberty
  Westeryear; ed. by E. Gorman
Wish
  The Best of Shadows; ed. by C. L. Grant
  Shadows 8
Sarraute, Nathalie
XXII
  The Art of the tale; ed. by D. Halpern
Sarton, May, 1912-
The donkey
  Through other eyes; ed. by I. Zahava
The silent minister
  Buying time; ed. by S. Walker
SASKATCHEWAN *See* Canada—Saskatchewan
SASQUATCH
Pangborn, E. Longtooth
Reed, K. The bride of Bigfoot
Sassafrass, Cypress & Indigo. Shange, N.
Sassanidian king. Jahnn, H. H.

Sastri, Prema
Rival candidates
  Short story international 48
Sata, Ineko, 1904-
The colorless paintings
  The Crazy iris, and other stories of the atomic aftermath; ed. by K. Oe
SATANISM
  See also Demoniac possession
Blackwood, A. Secret worship
Wellman, M. W. School for the unspeakable
West, J. Alive and real
Satan's hoof. Page, N.
SATIRE
  See also Humor; Irony; Parodies
Abbott, L. K. We get smashed and our endings are swift
Aksenov, V. P. A poem of ecstasy
Aksenov, V. P. Surplussed barrelware
Apple, M. Child's play
Apple, M. Free agents
Apple, M. The national debt
Apple, M. An offering
Apple, M. Pizza time
Asimov, I. The feeling of power
Aymé, M. The state of grace
Bail, M. Ore
Bail, M. The partitions
Bail, M. Portrait of electricity
Baker, R. High-tech insolence
Banks, R. Children's story
Barthelme, D. The educational experience
Barthelme, D. Engineer-private Paul Klee misplaces an aircraft between Milbertshofen and Cambrai, March 1916
Barthelme, D. The film
Barthelme, D. The flight of pigeons from the palace
Barthelme, D. Game
Barthelme, D. The genius
Barthelme, D. Letters to the editore
Barthelme, D. Pepperoni
Barthelme, D. Porcupines at the university
Barthelme, D. Some of us had been threatening our friend Colby
Barthelme, D. The temptation of St. Anthony
Barthelme, D. The wound
Beckett, R. Forty Susan Sangsters stride out at the Wellington Boot
Bedard, B. South Dakota samaritans
Bernard, K. The films of R. Nixon
Bernard, K. King Kong: a meditation
Berry, R. M. Metempsychosis
Berry, R. M. Paradise lost
Bird, C. Cherries jubilee; or, Whichever way you look at it
Bishop, M. The Bob Dylan Tambourine Software & Satori Support Services Consortium, Ltd.

SATIRE—*Continued*

Bishop, M. The gospel according to Gamaliel Crucis; or, The astrogator's testimony

Bishop, M. The Yukio Mishima Cultural Association of Kudzu Valley, Georgia

Blinkin, M. The freethinker: a shtetl atheist

Bloch, R. The golden opportunity of Lefty Feep

Bloch, R. Jerk the giant killer

Bloch, R. The little man who wasn't all there

Bloch, R. The Pied Piper fights the Gestapo

Bloch, R. A snitch in time

Bloch, R. Son of a witch

Bloch, R. Time wounds all heels

Bloch, R. The weird doom of Floyd Scrilch

Bloch, R. Welcome, stranger

Bloch, R. Word of honor

Bloch, R. The world-timer

Blumlein, M. Tissue ablation and variant regeneration: a case report

Böll, H. Murke's collected silences

Böll, H. My expensive leg

Böll, H. My sad face

Böll, H. On being courteous when compelled to break the law

Böll, H. The railway station of Zimpren

Boston, B. Interview with a gentleman farmer

Boyle, T. C. Ike and Nina

Boyle, T. C. The New Moon Party

Boyle, T. C. On for the long haul

Boyle, T. C. Rara avis

Boyle, T. C. We are Norsemen

Boyle, T. C. Whales weep

Broderick, D. I lost my love to the space shuttle 'Columbia'

Bumpus, J. The attack on San Clemente

Bumpus, J. K

Calisher, H. Real impudence

Calisher, H. Saratoga, hot

Calisher, H. The tenth child

Charmatz, A. Sailing, through program management

Chekhov, A. P. Peasant women

Chesterton, G. K. Chivalry begins at home

Chesterton, G. K. Concerning grocers as gods

Chesterton, G. K. The conversion of an anarchist

Chesterton, G. K. The dragon at hide-and-seek

Chesterton, G. K. Dukes

Chesterton, G. K. A fish story

Chesterton, G. K. How I found the superman

Chesterton, G. K. A legend of Saint Francis

Chesterton, G. K. The legend of the sword

Chesterton, G. K. The long bow

Chesterton, G. K. On private property

Chesterton, G. K. On secular education

Chesterton, G. K. The paradise of human fishes

Chesterton, G. K. A real discovery

Chesterton, G. K. The second miracle

Chesterton, G. K. The sword of wood

Claiborne, S. Scenes from a novel: replenishing Ava

Codrescu, A. The herald

Collier, J. Evening primrose

Colum, P. Three men

Cook, P. Not the news

Cooper, L. Class notes

Coover, R. Cartoon

Coover, R. Charlie in the house of rue

Coover, R. Intermission

Coover, R. Lap dissolves

Coover, R. The phantom of the movie palace

Coover, R. Shootout at Gentry's Junction

Coover, R. You must remember this

Cullen, E. J. Mayberry

Cullen, E. J. Our war and how we won it

Cullen, E. J. Worrying

Dadswell, M. Lewd and lascivious conjugations

Davis, L. City employment

Dick, P. K. Autofac

Dick, P. K. Novelty act

Dickson, G. R. Operation P-Button

Dunn, D. Ever let the fancy roam

Dunn, D. A night out at the Club Harmonica

Dunn, D. Wives in the garden

Durrell, L. All to scale

Durrell, L. Aunt Norah

Durrell, L. Call of the sea

Durrell, L. Case history

Durrell, L. A corking evening

Durrell, L. Cry wolf

Durrell, L. Drage's divine discontent

Durrell, L. For immediate release

Durrell, L. Frying the flag

Durrell, L. The game's the thing

Durrell, L. High barbary

Durrell, L. If garlic be the food of love . . .

Durrell, L. The iron hand

Durrell, L. Jots and tittles

Durrell, L. 'Noblesse oblige'

Durrell, L. Sauve qui peut

Durrell, L. Seraglios and imbroglios

Durrell, L. Smoke, the embassy cat

Durrell, L. Something à la carte?

Durrell, L. Stiff upper lip

Durrell, L. The swami's secret

Durrell, L. Taking the consequences

Durrell, L. The unspeakable attaché

Durrell, L. La valise

Durrell, L. What-ho on the Rialto!

SATIRE—*Continued*

Durrell, L. Where the bee sucks . . .
Durrell, L. White man's milk
Elkin, S. The conventional wisdom
Epstein, L. The magic flute
Epstein, L. Music of the spheres
Epstein, L. The Steinway quintet
Farmer, P. J. Don't wash the carats
Farmer, P. J. The jungle rot kid on the nod
Farmer, P. J. The king of beasts
Farmer, P. J. Riders of the purple wage
Faust, I. The double snapper
Faust, I. Melanie and the purple people eaters
Federman, R. Report from the World Federation of Displaced Writers
Feng Jicai. The Mao button
Feng Jicai. The street-sweeping show
Forbes, J. Only approved Indians can play: made in USA
Franklin, P. Love under glass
Frazier, I. Dating your mom
Gangemi, K. Greenbaum, O'Reilly & Stephens
Gilbert, W. S. The fairy's dilemma
Gilbert, W. S. The poisoned postage stamp
Gilbert, W. S. The triumph of vice
Gilliatt, P. On each other's time
Gilliatt, P. Phone-in
Givner, J. First love
Glynn, T. The world's most amazing prophet, a.k.a. Wallace Mumford Amazon Polleau
Gogol', N. V. The tale of how Ivan Ivanovich quarreled with Ivan Nikiforovich
Grass, G. The left-handers
Greene, G. Alas, poor Maling
Greene, G. Awful when you think of it
Hawthorne, N. Earth's holocaust
Heinlein, R. A. Beyond doubt
Jackson, G. Structural unemployment
Jean Paul. Army-chaplain Schmelzle's journey to Flätz
Jeppson, J. O. The Noodge Factor
Jeppson, J. O. A pestilence of psychoanalysts
Johnston, G. Vale, Pollini!
Jolley, E. The representative
Katz, S. Friendship
Katz, S. Mongolian Whiskey
Kinsella, W. P. The job
Kinsella, W. P. The Redemption Center
Kleist, H. von. The earthquake in Chile
Kotzwinkle, W. Star cruisers, welcome
Kotzwinkle, W., and Shiarella, R. The philosophy of Sebastian Trump; or, The art of outrage
Kress, N. Explanations, Inc.
Kusenberg, K. Odd tippling
Lafferty, R. A. Primary education of the Camiroi
Lem, S. Cezary Strzybisz, Necrobes

Lem, S. Golem XIV
Lem, S. Juan Rambellais et al., A history of Bitic literature
Lem, S. Reginald Gulliver, Eruntics
Lem, S. Vestrand's Extelopedia in 44 magnetomes
Leskov, N. S. The cattle pen
Leskov, N. S. A winter's day
Lewis, N. A weekend in Havana
Lish, G. How to write a poem
Littke, L. A feline felony
Longyear, B. B. Where do you get your ideas?
Loos, A. Liquor makes you smart
Lutz, J. Discount fare
Malamud, B. The Jewbird
Malzberg, B. N. On the campaign trail
Maron, M. Deadhead coming down
Mathers, P. Immersion
Mathers, P. Micki New
Mathers, P. Minutes
Mathers, P. Picking a loser
Melville, H. The lightning-rod man
Moore, G. A letter to Rome
Moore, W. Frank Merriwell in the White House
Moorhouse, F. The New York bell captain
Mrożek, S. Art
Mrożek, S. The background to an era
Mrożek, S. Birthday
Mrożek, S. Children
Mrożek, S. The chronicle of a besieged city
Mrożek, S. A citizen's fate
Mrożek, S. The co-operative
Mrożek, S. A confession about Bobby
Mrożek, S. A drummer's adventure
Mrożek, S. The elephant
Mrożek, S. An event
Mrożek, S. A fact
Mrożek, S. The fall of an Eagle's Nest
Mrożek, S. The giraffe
Mrożek, S. Horses
Mrożek, S. I want to be a horse
Mrożek, S. It's a pity
Mrożek, S. The last hussar
Mrożek, S. Letter from an old people's home
Mrożek, S. The lion
Mrożek, S. Modern life
Mrożek, S. The monument
Mrożek, S. My uncle's stories
Mrożek, S. On a journey
Mrożek, S. The pastor
Mrożek, S. Peer Gynt
Mrożek, S. Poetry
Mrożek, S. The sceptic
Mrożek, S. Siesta
Mrożek, S. Spring in Poland
Mrożek, S. The swan
Mrożek, S. Tiny
Mrożek, S. The trial
Mrożek, S. The veteran

SATIRE—*Continued*

Nesin, A. A man can't even swindle any more
Paley, G. At that time; or, The history of a joke
Paley, G. Wants
Percy, W. The promiscuous self
Pierce, C. Manosque
Pierce, C. The tenants at Auxillac
Pinkwater, D. M. Devil in the drain
Poe, E. A. The business man
Poe, E. A. The devil in the belfry
Poe, E. A. Diddling considered as one of the exact sciences
Poe, E. A. The Folio Club
Poe, E. A. Four beasts in one—the homo-cameleopard
Poe, E. A. How to write a Blackwood article
Poe, E. A. Lionizing
Poe, E. A. The literary life of Thingum Bob, Esq.
Poe, E. A. The man that was used up
Poe, E. A. Mellonta Tauta
Poe, E. A. Never bet the devil your head
Poe, E. A. Peter Pendulum, the business man
Poe, E. A. Raising the wind
Poe, E. A. The scythe of time
Poe, E. A. The Signora Psyche Zenobia
Pronzini, B. A craving for originality
Ramírez, S. Nicaragua is white
Ramírez, S. To Jackie with all our heart
Reed, K. Alumni fund
Regent, P. Laughing Pig
Regent, P. The Major steps out
Revard, C. Report to the nation: claiming Europe
Rooke, L. The history of England, part four
Rooke, L. Some people will tell you the situation at Henny Penny Nursery is getting intolerable
Russ, J. The clichés from outer space
Russ, J. Existence
Russ, J. The throaways
Ruta, S. The shoe clerk
Saki. The open window
Saki. The philanthropist and the happy cat
Saki. Tobermory
Salmonson, J. A. The trilling princess
Schwartz, S. A program for writers
Sheckley, J. Lost soul
Sheckley, R. All the things you are
Sheckley, R. Pilgrimage to Earth
Silverberg, R. Good news from the Vatican
Sisskind, M. Hope
Sladek, J. T. Absent friends
Sladek, J. T. After Flaubert
Sladek, J. T. Calling all gumdrops!
Sladek, J. T. An explanation for the disappearance of the moon
Sladek, J. T. Fables
Sladek, J. T. Great mysteries explained!
Sladek, J. T. Guesting
Sladek, J. T. How to make major scientific discoveries at home in your spare time
Sladek, J. T. The island of Dr. Circe
Sladek, J. T. The kindly ones
Sladek, J. T. The last of the whaleburgers
Smith, J. Grief counselor
Smith, R. Cape Breton is the thought control centre of Canada
Sorrentino, G. The gala cocktail party
Spark, M. The Playhouse called Remarkable
Spinrad, N. The national pastime
Stewart, J. I. M. Pipkin Grove
Strand, M. Dog life
Strand, M. The President's resignation
Sturgeon, T. Microcosmic god
Sullivan, T. The Mickey Mouse Olympics
Twain, M. The man that corrupted Hadleyburg
Twain, M. The private history of a campaign that failed
Twain, M. The secret history of Eddypus, the world-empire
Twain, M. The stolen white elephant
Valenzuela, L. The gift of words
Van Greenaway, P. Cadenza
Vizenor, G. R. Reservation café: the origins of American Indian instant coffee
Waldrop, H. Heirs of the Perisphere
Waldrop, H. Horror, we got
Wells, H. G. The loyalty of Esau Common
Wetherell, W. D. Narrative of the whale truck essex
Wharton, E. Xingu
White, C. Metaphysics in the Midwest
White, C. More crimes against the people of Illinois
Wiebe, D. E. At the Rotonde
Wiebe, D. E. Going to the mountain
Wiebe, D. E. Night flight to Stockholm
Williams, T. The knightly guest
Windsor, G. Press conferences of Ambassador Sweeney
Wolfe, T. Fame and the poet
Wolfe, T. A note on experts: Dexter Vespasian Joyner
Wolfe, T. On leprechauns
Wrede, P. C. The improper princess
The **satirist**. Brown, G. M.
Satisfaction guaranteed. Asimov, I.
Satran, Karen
Boy on the loose!
Seventeen 44:176-7+ My '85
Satterthwait, Walter
The smoke people
Distant danger; ed. by J. Van de Wetering
Saturday. Gallant, M.
Saturday afternoon. Caldwell, E.

Saturday afternoons. Tabucchi, A.
Saturday morning: a thief's tale. Klíma, I.
Saturday night in Pinedale, Wyoming. Shaw, J. B.
Saturday, Sunday. Harabin, V.
Saturday's shadow. Nolan, W. F.
SATURN (PLANET)
Zelazny, R. Dreadsong
The Saturn game. Anderson, P.
Saucier, Michael
Pukes!
Stories and poems from close to home; ed. by F. Salas
Saul and Patsy are getting comfortable in Michigan. Baxter, C.
Saul of Tarsus. Kessler, J. F.
Saunders, Carl McK.
The wax witness
A Cent a story! Ed. by G. G. Roberts
Saunders, Charles R.
Outsteppin' Fetchit
Masques II; ed. by J. N. Williamson
Saunders, Judith
The rabbit that loved cats
The North American Review 271:38-40 S '86
Sauro, Joan
Immortality
U.S. Catholic 52:32-7 N '87
Sauve qui peut. Durrell, L.
Sauvinet, Jeri
Temporary islands
The Antioch Review 46:54-64 Wint '88
Savage, Ernest, 1918-
The girl and the ghost
Ellery Queen's Prime crimes 2
The man who liked noise
Ellery Queen's Memorable characters
Savage, John, 1931-
The getaway
The Saturday Evening Post 260:46-7+ N '88
Savage, Les
Dangerous orders
Wild westerns; ed. by B. Pronzini
Savage, Richard
The boy from the woods
The Saturday Evening Post 257:70-2+ Ap '85
Savages. O'Brien, E.
Savannah River payday. Caldwell, E.
Savant. Hensley, J. L.
Save a place in the lifeboat for me. Waldrop, H.
Saved. Maupassant, G. de
Saved. Sanford, W. M.
SAVING AND THRIFT
Cooper, J. C. Liberated
Faulkner, W. Thrift
Saving face. Bishop, M.
Saving face. Lofts, N.
A saving nakedness. Piñera, V.
Saving the boat people. Bellamy, J. D.

Saving the dead. Duecker, K.
The saviour of the bees. Flynn, R.
Savoias out of Sapporo. Whitehouse, A.
A saw and childbirth. Kawabata, Y.
The saw mill. Mort, G.
Sawai, Gloria
The day I sat with Jesus on the sun deck and a wind came up and blew my kimono open and he saw my breasts
The Oxford book of Canadian short stories in English
Hang out your washing on the Siegfried Line
Alberta bound; ed. by F. Stenson
Sawdust. Huggan, I.
SAWMILLS
Conroy, J. Lute Goin's sawmill
Sawyer, Robert J.
The contest
100 great fantasy short short stories; ed. by I. Asimov; T. Carr and M. H. Greenberg
SAXOPHONISTS
Bonnie, F. Name the general
Hannah, B. Testimony of pilot
Say one for Leo. O'Grady, D.
Say what you Willomay! Cooper, J. C.
Say yes. Wolff, T.
Sayers, Dorothy L. (Dorothy Leigh), 1893-1957
The Cyprian cat
Roger Caras' Treasury of great cat stories
Witches' brew; ed. by M. Muller and B. Pronzini
The Dragon's head
Chapter & hearse; ed. by M. Muller and B. Pronzini
The man who knew how
The Penguin classic crime omnibus
The necklace of pearls
Masterpieces of mystery and suspense; ed. by M. H. Greenberg
The queen's square
Great detectives; ed. by D. W. McCullough
Saying grace. Herne, A.
Sayles, John, 1950-
At the anarchists' convention
Full measure; ed. by D. Sennett
The Halfway Diner
The Atlantic 259:59-68 Je '87
Prize stories, 1988
Tan
Soldiers & civilians; ed. by T. Jenks
Treasure
Esquire 109:168-70+ Mr '88
Says Velma. Crowell, D.
Sayyed, Salah Abd el *See* El Sayyed, Salah Abd
Scalpel, please. Stýblová, V.
Scalplock. Howard, C.
The Scan of Illyria. McCourt, J.

A **scandal** in Bohemia. Doyle, Sir A. C.
A **scandalous** woman. O'Brien, E.
Scanners live in vain. Smith, C.
Scape-goats. Barker, C.
The **scar.** Campbell, R.
Scarborough, Elizabeth
   Milk from a maiden's breast
     Tales of the Witch World [1]
   Wolf from the door
     Werewolves; ed. by J. Yolen and M. H.
     Greenberg
SCARECROWS
   Hawthorne, N. Feathertop
Scarfe, Eunice
   The five o'clock train
     The New press anthology #1
   In a lighted house
     The Old dance; ed. by B. Burnard
Scarlet fever. Kilworth, G.
Scarlet ibis. Atwood, M.
The **scarlet** thread. Futrelle, J.
A **Scarletin** study. Farmer, P. J.
Scars of murder. Ballard, W. T.
Scarth, Lynda
   The funeral
     Women's work; ed. by M. McLeod and
     L. Wevers
Scatterbrain. Su Ye
The **scavenger** hunt. Donnelly, N.
The **scenery** never changes. Astley, T.
Scenes from a novel: replenishing Ava. Claiborne, S.
Scenes from the homefront. Vogan, S.
Scenes from the island. Millman, L.
Scenes from the life of a British naval officer. Woolf, V.
Scenes of passion. Lamb, W.
A **scent** of mimosa. King, F. H.
The **scent** of silverdill. Cowper, R.
Scents in the dark. Wellen, E.
The **sceptic.** Mrożek, S.
Schaap, James C., 1948-
   The privacy of storm
     Stiller's pond; ed. by J. Agee; R. Blakely
     and S. Welch
Schad, Cynthia M.
   Close to autumn
     Ploughshares 14 no2/3:33-8 '88
Schaefer, Jack Warner, 1907-
   Cat nipped
     Roger Caras' Treasury of great cat
     stories
   Sergeant Houck
     The Second reel West; ed. by B. Pronzini and M. H. Greenberg
   Stubby Pringle's Christmas
     The Western hall of fame; ed. by B.
     Pronzini and M. H. Greenberg
Schaeffer, Susan Fromberg
   Bluebeard's second wife
     Great American love stories; ed. by L.
     Rosenthal

Schafler, Nathan
   The social hour
     Short story international 49
SCHALCKEN, GODFRIED, 1643-1706
           About
   Le Fanu, J. S. Schalken the painter
Schalken the painter. Le Fanu, J. S.
Schaub, Mary H.
   The cards of Eldrianza
     Magic in Ithkar 2; ed. by A. Norton and
     R. Adams
   Night hound's moon
     Tales of the Witch World [1]
Schell, Jessie
   Alvira, Lettie, and Pip
     Mississippi writers v1: Fiction; ed. by D.
     Abbott
   Caring for Rosie
     McCall's 113:80+ My '86
   The important things
     McCall's 112:52+ Jl '85
   Legacy
     McCall's 112:68+ Je '85
   A new tradition
     McCall's 114:78+ Jl '87
   Perfect friends
     McCall's 115:56+ Jl '88
   Precious memories
     McCall's 113:151-4 Je '86
   Time for a change
     McCall's 112:94-5+ Ap '85
Schematic man. Pohl, F.
Scherzo with TV antenna. Ferguson, W.
Schiff, Tracy
   In this place of illusion
     Mademoiselle 91:60 Jl '85
Schiffman, Carl
   Honor bright
     The Literary Review (Madison, N.J.)
     30:91-102 Fall '86
Schinto, Jeanne, 1951-
   Before sewing one must cut
     *New England Review and Bread Loaf
     Quarterly* 11:145-56 Wint '88
     Schinto, J. Shadow bands
   Caddies' Day
     The Best American short stories, 1984
     Schinto, J. Shadow bands
   The disappearance
     Schinto, J. Shadow bands
     The Yale Review 77:441-62 Spr '88
   The eel man
     Schinto, J. Shadow bands
   The friendships of girls unpopular together
     Schinto, J. Shadow bands
   From a juror's notebook
     Schinto, J. Shadow bands
   Keepsake
     Schinto, J. Shadow bands
   The motorcycle riders
     Schinto, J. Shadow bands
   The original dog
     Schinto, J. Shadow bands

Schinto, Jeanne, 1951—— *Continued*
The ring; or, A girl confesses
Schinto, J. Shadow bands
Shadow bands
Schinto, J. Shadow bands
Sounds of the rude world
Schinto, J. Shadow bands
The **schism.** Blythe, R.

SCHIZOPHRENIA
See also Dual personality; Personality disorders
Bloch, R. Lucy comes to stay
Bloch, R. The real bad friend
Hoffman, N. K. Ants
Lutz, J. One man's manual
Oates, J. C. Last days
Paley, G. Zagrowsky tells
Silverberg, R. Multiples
Vester, L. Pawn promotion
Schlifkin on my books. Epstein, J.

Schlobin, Roger C.
For lovers only
Magic in Ithkar [1]; ed. by A. Norton and R. Adams

Schlossberg, Edwin
Hiccup's tale
Life 11:186-7+ D '88

Schmahmann, David R.
Baptie in her homeland
The Yale Review 77:600-6 Summ '88

Schmidt, Arno, 1914-1979
Great Cain
The Review of Contemporary Fiction 8:38-50 Spr '88
Tall Grete
The Review of Contemporary Fiction 8:51-2 Spr '88

Schmidt, Heidi Jon
Shoe
20 under 30; ed. by D. Spark
A Grand Street reader; ed. by B. Sonnenberg

Schmidt, Stanley
May the best man win
Election Day 2084; ed. by I. Asimov and M. H. Greenberg
The unreachable star
[Analog]: Writers' choice v2

Schmitz, James H., 1911-
Novice
Roger Caras' Treasury of great cat stories
The witches of Karres
Witches; ed. by I. Asimov; M. H. Greenberg and C. G. Waugh
Schmoozing. Conard, B.

Schneider, Rolf
Border crossers
Voices East and West: German short stories since 1945

Schnitzler, Arthur, 1862-1931
America
On being foreign; ed. by T. J. Lewis and R. E. Jungman
The blind Geronimo and his brother
German stories; ed. by H. Steinhauer

Schnurre, Wolfdietrich
Diary of a dayfly
Voices East and West: German short stories since 1945

Schoemperlen, Diane, 1954-
Clues
Alberta bound; ed. by F. Stenson
Crimes of passion
The Old dance; ed. by B. Burnard

SCHOLARS
See also Intellectuals
Anderson, J. The late sunlight
Asimov, I. The winds of change
Blinkin, M. Doctor Machover
Bowles, P. A distant episode
Byatt, A. S. Precipice-encurled
Cao Guanlong. Three professors
Chu, T.-J. Autumn note
Cowan, P. Seminar
Dai Qing. Anticipation
Day, R. C. Two paces east
Dennison, G. The carbon paper poet
Fisher, M. F. K. The reunion
Gallant, M. Kingdom come
Gilliatt, P. Foreigners
Halligan, M. The Gauter letters
Johnson, C. R. Alēthia
King, F. H. Loss
Meinke, P. The twisted river
Morris, W. The origin of sadness
Morris, W. To Calabria
Muller, R. Of science and love
Oates, J. C. A sentimental encounter
Oates, J. C. A theory of knowledge
Sheckley, R. The mnemone
Stewart, J. I. M. Two strings to his bow
Tuohy, F. A summer pilgrim
Wang Zhecheng, and Wen Xiaoyu. Nest egg
Wheatcroft, J. Image of departure
Wheatcroft, J. The lapse
The **scholarship** jacket. Salinas, M.

Scholz, Carter
A draft of canto ci
Afterlives; ed. by P. Sargent and I. Watson
Galileo complains
Terry Carr's Best science fiction and fantasy of the year #16
The menagerie of Babel
Universe 14
Transients
Terry's universe; ed. by B. Meacham
The **school.** Barthelme, D.
The **school** bus caper. Ritchie, J.
School days. Abrams, R.
School for the unspeakable. Wellman, M. W.

The **school** for witches. Thomas, D.
SCHOOL LIFE
Abbott, K. The ghost of the senior banquet
Abbott, K. A little surprise
Alexin, A. The class photograph
Asimov, I. The fun they had
Bausch, R. What feels like the world
Baxter, C. Gryphon
Block, L. The boy who disappeared clouds
Bonosky, P. The first robin in the world
Boylan, J. Pickett's charge
Card, O. S. The fringe
Dillon, M. Monitor
Farnsworth, K. A. Counterpoint
Gingher, M. The magic circle
Gonzalez, N. V. M. The blue skull and the dark palms
Hassler, J. Rufus at the door
Herschel, J. Geometry
Kilgore, D. The day we discovered we were black
Lispector, C. The misfortunes of Sofia
MacDonald, J. D. Squealer
MacIntyre, T. Boarding
Martínez-Serros, H. Her
Martínez-Serros, H. Octavo
Martone, M. The safety patrol
Mattison, A. The Middle Ages
McKnight, R. The honey boys
Miller, S. What Ernest says
Mrożek, S. A confession about Bobby
Norris, L. Some opposites of good
Ríos, A. Johnny Ray
Ríos, A. The way spaghetti feels
Robbe-Grillet, A. The replacement
Salinas, M. The scholarship jacket
Schwartz, J. Over the purple hills
Skrzynecki, P. Empty cages
Soldatow, S. White noise
St. Pierre, P. H. The education of Phyllisteen
Stark, S. S. Ode to the big school
Willis, C. All my darling daughters
Wood, Mrs. H. The ghost
Australia
Anderson, J. Against the wall
Clark, M. Discovery
Houbein, L. Survival switch
Stead, C. The old school
Canada
Bye, C. Box social
Matheson, S. Harris
Reaney, J. The bully
Egypt
Attia, N. Games
England
Boyd, W. Hardly ever
Byatt, A. S. Racine and the tablecloth
Gathorne-Hardy, J. The Infant Hercules
Geras, A. Monday
Hornung, E. W. The field of Philippi

Mortimer, J. C. Rumpole and the course of true love
Rees, D. Canes
Rees, D. Open scholarship
Rhys, J. Overture and beginners please
Trevor, W. Torridge
Tuohy, F. The Palladian Bridge
Watmough, D. The cross-country run
Wheeler, H. C. Little boy lost
Wyndham, F. Mrs. Henderson
Ireland
MacLaverty, B. The exercise
O'Brien, E. Sister Imelda
Power, V. The imposition
Italy
Landolfi, T. Prefigurations: Prato
Japan
Hayashi, K. The empty can
Tanizaki, J. The thief
New Zealand
Gee, M. Schooldays
Haley, R. Looping the loop
Kidman, F. Flower man
Poland
Nowakowski, M. The enemy
Samoan Islands
Wendt, A. Crocodile
Scotland
Leonard, T. Mr. Endrews speaks
United States
Auchincloss, L. Marcus: a Gothic tale
Auchincloss, L. Portrait of the artist by another
Barthelme, D. The school
Blaise, C. Grids and doglegs
Blaise, C. How I became a Jew
Blew, M. C. Forby and the Mayan maidens
Bonnie, F. The state meet
Ciment, J. Self-portrait with vanishing point
Crane, S. The lover and the tell-tale
Digby, J. It's a man's drink, tonic water
Drake, R. Football Queen
Ely, D. The academy
Fante, J. Big leaguer
Flook, M. The fairway
Gilchrist, E. Victory over Japan
Girion, B. King of the hill
Girion, B. With a little gold pencil
Goyen, W. The grasshopper's burden
Humphrey, W. Report cards
Ignatow, R. G. I have looked for Carrie
Kotzwinkle, W. Victory at North Antor
Lewis, S. E. Trouble people
Liben, M. The garden
McElroy, C. J. Jeremy Franklin Simmons
McGarry, J. Penmanship
McGarry, J. Providence, 1957: an accident
Morris, W. Good old boy [excerpt]
Nash, O. The three d's
Nordan, L. The all-girl football team
O'Hara, J. Do you like it here?

SCHOOL LIFE—United States—*Continued*
Ríos, A. His own key
Slesinger, T. White on black
Stuart, J. The slipover sweater
Taylor, M. D. Roll of thunder, hear my cry [excerpt]
Tyler, A. Teenage wasteland
Whitman, W. Death in the school-room
Wales
Norris, L. Reverse for Dennis
SCHOOL SUPERINTENDENTS AND PRINCIPALS
Böll, H. Daniel the Just
Carter, R. Within
Davie, E. The gift
Görlich, G. The decision
West, J. Flow gently, sweet aspirin
SCHOOL TEACHERS *See* Teachers
Schoolboy war. Regent, P.
Schooldays. Gee, M.
The **schoolmaster.** Smith, P.
SCHOOLS *See* School life
Schools and schools. Henry, O.
Schools and stocks. Davis, S.
SCHOPENHAUER, ARTHUR, 1788-1860
About
Maupassant, G. de. Beside a dead man
Schor, Sandra
Hit and run
The Sewanee Review 96:378-88 Summ '88
Schott, Max, 1935-
The horsebreaker
The Interior country; ed. by A. Blackburn
Schow, David J.
Pamela's get
The Year's best fantasy, first annual collection
Schraft, Constance
Signals
The New Yorker 62:38-41 My 5 '86
Schramm, Wilbur Lang, 1907-1987
Dan Peters and Casey Jones
The Saturday Evening Post 256:50-3+ O '84

Grandpa Hopewell and his flying tractor
The Saturday Evening Post 259:36+ My/Je '87
The Saturday Evening Post 259:42-5+ Ap '87
There are no ordinary men in Iowa
The Saturday Evening Post 257:46-51+ Ap '85
Schreiner, Olive, 1855-1920
The woman's rose
The Penguin book of Southern African stories
The **Schreuderspitze.** Helprin, M.
Schrödinger's cat. Le Guin, U. K.
Schrödinger's kitten. Effinger, G. A.

Schulberg, Budd
The barracudas
Short story international 53
Murder on the waterfront
Mystery in the mainstream; ed. by B. Pronzini; M. H. Greenberg and B. N. Malzberg
Señor Discretion himself
Short story international 50
Schulman, Helen
Before and after: snapshots
The Antioch Review 45:150-5 Spr '87
Schulman, H. Not a free show
Body snatchers
The Antioch Review 46:7-19 Wint '88
East Jesus
Schulman, H. Not a free show
Good practice
Schulman, H. Not a free show
Having fun
Schulman, H. Not a free show
The heart of my heart
Schulman, H. Not a free show
I am Miss America
Schulman, H. Not a free show
In God's country
Schulman, H. Not a free show
Inventions
Schulman, H. Not a free show
James Dean's widow
Schulman, H. Not a free show
Like brothers
Schulman, H. Not a free show
Like sisters
Schulman, H. Not a free show
Not a free show
Schulman, H. Not a free show
Pushing the point
The Antioch Review 44:111-13 Wint '86
Schulman, H. Not a free show
Siblings
Schulman, H. Not a free show
To die from
Schulman, H. Not a free show
We were of two minds
The North American Review 272:40-1 Mr '87
Schulman, H. Not a free show
Schultz, Stephen B.
World champion
The North American Review 269:44-6 Mr '84
Schulz, Bruno, 1892-1942
Father's last escape
Black water; ed. by A. Manguel
Schulze, Axel
Eighteen minutes
Harper's 271:36-7 D '85
Voices East and West: German short stories since 1945

Schulze, Kenneth
Redmond
   L. Ron Hubbard presents Writers of the
      future v2
Schutz, J. W.
Dragon's horn
   Magic in Ithkar [1]; ed. by A. Norton
      and R. Adams
Schutzman, Steven
The bank robbery
   Sudden fiction; ed. by R. Shapard and
      J. Thomas
Schwab, Penney V.
Plan "B" for Buck
   'Teen 28:40+ S '84
Schwaid, Alfred
Splittin a dime
   Chicago Review 34:125-37 Spr '84
Schwartz, Adam
The grammar of love
   The New Yorker 64:24-32 Jl 18 '88
Schwartz, Andrew
Rose by the water
   New England Review and Bread Loaf
      Quarterly 11:196-206 Wint '88
Schwartz, Hillel, 1948-
Compset
   Michigan Quarterly Review 24:197-8 Spr
      '85
Schwartz, Howard, 1945-
Rooms of the soul
   Missouri short fiction; ed. by C. Beasley
Schwartz, Jonathan
Chloe Hummel of the Chicago White Sox
   Schwartz, J. The man who knew Cary
      Grant
Crazy
   Schwartz, J. The man who knew Cary
      Grant
Day trip
   Schwartz, J. The man who knew Cary
      Grant
Faith
   Schwartz, J. The man who knew Cary
      Grant
The last and only messenger
   Schwartz, J. The man who knew Cary
      Grant
The man who knew Cary Grant
   Schwartz, J. The man who knew Cary
      Grant
Max
   Schwartz, J. The man who knew Cary
      Grant
Over the purple hills
   Schwartz, J. The man who knew Cary
      Grant
This time, yesterday morning
   Schwartz, J. The man who knew Cary
      Grant
Waiting weeping
   Schwartz, J. The man who knew Cary
      Grant

Schwartz, Lynne Sharon
The accounting
   Schwartz, L. S. Acquainted with the
      night, and other stories
Acquainted with the night
   Schwartz, L. S. Acquainted with the
      night, and other stories
The age of analysis
   Schwartz, L. S. Acquainted with the
      night, and other stories
The death of Harriet Gross
   Schwartz, L. S. Acquainted with the
      night, and other stories
Epistemology, sex, and the shedding of
   light
   Schwartz, L. S. Acquainted with the
      night, and other stories
Grand staircases
   Schwartz, L. S. Acquainted with the
      night, and other stories
The infidel
   Michigan Quarterly Review 26:612-47
      Fall '87
   Schwartz, L. S. The melting pot, and
      other subversive stories
Killing the bees
   Schwartz, L. S. The melting pot, and
      other subversive stories
The last frontier
   Schwartz, L. S. The melting pot, and
      other subversive stories
Life is an adventure, with risks
   Schwartz, L. S. Acquainted with the
      night, and other stories
The man at the gate
   Schwartz, L. S. Acquainted with the
      night, and other stories
The melting pot
   Schwartz, L. S. The melting pot, and
      other subversive stories
The middle classes
   Schwartz, L. S. Acquainted with the
      night, and other stories
Mrs. Saunders writes to the world
   Schwartz, L. S. Acquainted with the
      night, and other stories
The opiate of the people
   Schwartz, L. S. Acquainted with the
      night, and other stories
Over the hill
   Schwartz, L. S. Acquainted with the
      night, and other stories
The painters
   The Bread Loaf anthology of contem-
      porary American short stories; ed. by
      R. Pack and J. Parini
   Schwartz, L. S. The melting pot, and
      other subversive stories
Plaisir d'amour
   Schwartz, L. S. Acquainted with the
      night, and other stories

Schwartz, Lynne Sharon—*Continued*
Rough strife
  Love stories for the time being; ed. by
    G. D. Chipps and B. Henderson
So you're going to have a new body!
  Schwartz, L. S. The melting pot, and
    other subversive stories
Sound is second sight
  Schwartz, L. S. Acquainted with the
    night, and other stories
The sound of Velcro
  Schwartz, L. S. The melting pot, and
    other subversive stories
The subversive divorce
  Schwartz, L. S. The melting pot, and
    other subversive stories
The sunfish and the mermaid
  Schwartz, L. S. Acquainted with the
    night, and other stories
The Thousand Islands
  The North American Review 272:22-4 S
    '87
  Schwartz, L. S. The melting pot, and
    other subversive stories
The two portraits of Rembrandt
  Schwartz, L. S. The melting pot, and
    other subversive stories
What I did for love
  Prairie Schooner 61:3-18 Summ '87
  Schwartz, L. S. The melting pot, and
    other subversive stories
The wrath-bearing tree
  Schwartz, L. S. Acquainted with the
    night, and other stories
Schwartz, Sheila, 1929-
Double lives
  The Atlantic 255:70-6 Mr '85
A tough life
  TriQuarterly no72:72-90 Spr/Summ '88
Schwartz, Steven, 1950-
Down under
  The Virginia Quarterly Review 61:498-
    511 Summ '85
I can't sleep anymore
  Schwartz, S. To Leningrad in winter
In Alaska
  Schwartz, S. To Leningrad in winter
Legacy
  The Antioch Review 46:497-509 Fall '88
Monkey business
  Schwartz, S. To Leningrad in winter
Navajo Café
  Schwartz, S. To Leningrad in winter
A program for writers
  Schwartz, S. To Leningrad in winter
Slow-motion
  Schwartz, S. To Leningrad in winter
Society of Friends
  Schwartz, S. To Leningrad in winter
To Leningrad in winter
  Schwartz, S. To Leningrad in winter
Schwartz between the galaxies. Silverberg, R.

Schwarz, Adele Aron
Snapshots
  Ladies' Home Journal 103:114+ N '86
SCHWARZSCHILD, KARL, 1873-1916
About
  Willis, C. Schwarzschild radius
Schwarzschild radius. Willis, C.
Schwebel, Bruno
A gift for Lucrecia
  Short story international 51
El Señor Lector
  Short story international 59
Schweer, Kendra
The right chemistry
  'Teen 29:28-9+ Ja '85
Schweitzer, Darrell, 1952-
Caliban's revenge
  Devils & demons; ed. by M. Kaye and
    S. Kaye
Schweitzer, Gertrude, 1909-
The best of friends
  Good Housekeeping 206:122-3 Mr '88
The men in her life
  Good Housekeeping 200:148-9+ Mr '85
Something special
  Good Housekeeping 198:168-9 Ap '84
Who is my love?
  Good Housekeeping 204:124-5+ Mr '87
Schweitzer's camera. Miller, D.
Schwob, Marcel, 1867-1905
The amber-trader
  Schwob, M. The king in the golden
    mask, and other writings
Arachné
  Schwob, M. The king in the golden
    mask, and other writings
Blanche the bloody
  Schwob, M. The king in the golden
    mask, and other writings
Burke and Hare, murderers
  Schwob, M. The king in the golden
    mask, and other writings
Cecco Angiolieri, malevolent poet
  Schwob, M. The king in the golden
    mask, and other writings
Clodia, shameless matron
  Schwob, M. The king in the golden
    mask, and other writings
Crates, cynic
  Schwob, M. The king in the golden
    mask, and other writings
The death of Odjigh
  Schwob, M. The king in the golden
    mask, and other writings
The Dom
  Schwob, M. The king in the golden
    mask, and other writings
The embalming-women
  Schwob, M. The king in the golden
    mask, and other writings
Empedocles, reputed god
  Schwob, M. The king in the golden
    mask, and other writings

Schwob, Marcel, 1867-1905—*Continued*
The fat man
  Schwob, M. The king in the golden mask, and other writings
The firebrands
  Schwob, M. The king in the golden mask, and other writings
The flute
  Schwob, M. The king in the golden mask, and other writings
Frate Dolcino, heretic
  Schwob, M. The king in the golden mask, and other writings
Herostratos, incendiary
  Schwob, M. The king in the golden mask, and other writings
Katherine la Dentellière, whore
  Schwob, M. The king in the golden mask, and other writings
The king in the golden mask
  Schwob, M. The king in the golden mask, and other writings
Major Stede Bonnet, pirate by vagary
  Schwob, M. The king in the golden mask, and other writings
Mérigot Marchès
  Schwob, M. The king in the golden mask, and other writings
The Milesian virgins
  Schwob, M. The king in the golden mask, and other writings
The narrative of Pope Gregory IX
  Schwob, M. The king in the golden mask, and other writings
The narrative of Pope Innocent III
  Schwob, M. The king in the golden mask, and other writings
Nicolas Oyseleur, judge
  Schwob, M. The king in the golden mask, and other writings
Paolo Uccello, painter
  Schwob, M. The king in the golden mask, and other writings
The 'Papier Rouge'
  Schwob, M. The king in the golden mask, and other writings
Petronius, novelist
  Schwob, M. The king in the golden mask, and other writings
The plague
  Schwob, M. The king in the golden mask, and other writings
The sabbat at Mofflaines
  Schwob, M. The king in the golden mask, and other writings
Septima, enchantress
  Schwob, M. The king in the golden mask, and other writings
A skeleton
  Schwob, M. The king in the golden mask, and other writings

The sleeping city
  Schwob, M. The king in the golden mask, and other writings
The strigae
  Schwob, M. The king in the golden mask, and other writings
Sufrah, geomancer
  Schwob, M. The king in the golden mask, and other writings
Train 081
  Schwob, M. The king in the golden mask, and other writings
The veiled man
  Schwob, M. The king in the golden mask, and other writings

Sciascia, Leonardo
The American aunt
  Sciascia, L. Sicilian uncles
Antimony
  Sciascia, L. Sicilian uncles
The death of Stalin
  Sciascia, L. Sicilian uncles
End game
  Short story international 64
'Forty-eight'
  Sciascia, L. Sicilian uncles
A matter of conscience
  Short story international 62

SCIENCE FICTION
  See also End of the world; Extrasensory perception; Fantasies; Future, Stories of the; Interplanetary visitors; Interplanetary voyages; Interplanetary wars; Life on other planets; Robots; Space colonies; Space flight; Space ships; Time travel

Aldani, L. S is for snake
Aldiss, B. W. Infestation
Aldridge, R. Click
Anderson, P. The discovery of the past
Anderson, P. Eutopia
Anderson, P. Flight to forever
Anderson, P. Requiem for a universe
Anderson, P. Sam Hall
Anderson, P. Tomorrow's children
Anderson, P. Vulcan's forge
Anthony, P. The bridge
Anthony, P. Getting through University
Anthony, P. Gone to the dogs
Anthony, P. Hard sell
Anthony, P. Hurdle
Anthony, P. On the uses of torture
Anthony, P. The toaster
Anthony, P. Within the cloud
Anvil, C. Babel II
Anvil, C. A rose by other name . . .
Asimov, I. Belief
Asimov, I. "Breeds there a man . . .?"
Asimov, I. The dead past
Asimov, I. The end of eternity
Asimov, I. Evidence

SCIENCE FICTION—*Continued*

Asimov, I. The evitable conflict
Asimov, I. Eyes do more than see
Asimov, I. The fun they had
Asimov, I. Grow old along with me
Asimov, I. The Immortal Bard
Asimov, I. Jokester
Asimov, I. Little lost robot
Asimov, I. Nightfall
Asimov, I. Runaround
Asimov, I. Satisfaction guaranteed
Bakhnov, V. According to scientific data
Bakhnov, V. A remark concerning a little something about the devil
Bear, G. Blood music
Bear, G. Hardfought
Bear, G. Tangents
Bell, S. Jacob's ladder
Benford, G. At the double solstice
Benford, G. Mandikini
Berdnyk, O. The alien secret
Berdnyk, O. A journey to the antiworld
Berdnyk, O. Two abysses
Bernard, K. Sister Francetta and the pig baby
Binder, E. I, robot
Bing, J. The Owl of Bear Island
Bishop, M. Dogs' lives
Bishop, M. A short history of the bicycle: 401 B.C. to 2677 A.D.
Bishop, M. Vox Olympica
Bloch, R. How like a god
Bloch, R. The model
Bloch, R. Word of honor
Bova, B. Brothers
Bradbury, R. Chrysalis
Bradbury, R. Uncle Elinar
Bradfield, S. The Flash! Kid
Bradley, M. Z. Bird of prey
Bradley, M. Z. Blood will tell
Bradley, M. Z. Centaurus changeling
Bradley, M. Z. The day of the butterflies
Bradley, M. Z. The engine
Bradley, M. Z. The secret of the Blue Star
Bradley, M. Z. To keep the oath
Bradley, M. Z. The wild one
Branham, R. V. In the sickbay
Brin, D. The fourth vocation of George Gustaf
Broderick, D. A passage in Earth
Brown, F. Answer
Brown, F. Keep out
Brunner, J. Judas
Bryant, E. Jade Blue
Bulychev, K. Another's memory
Campbell, J. W., Jr. Who goes there?
Card, O. S. The fringe
Card, O. S. A sepulcher of songs
Carneiro, A. Life as an ant
Carpenter, L. The ebbing
Carr, J. The heart in the egg
Carr, J. Webrider
Chandler, A. B. Don't knock the rock

Clark, J. D. Minus planet
Clarke, A. C. Before Eden
Clarke, A. C. Dial F for Frankenstein
Clarke, A. C. Dog Star
Clarke, A. C. Refugee
Clarke, A. C. The songs of distant Earth
Clifton, M. Hang head, vandal!
Cogswell, T. R. The wall around the world
Cole, E. B. Fighting Philosopher
Colegate, I. Distant cousins
Conner, M. Vamp
Correy, L. Industrial accident
Cowper, R. The custodians
Cowper, R. A message to the King of Brobdingnag
Cowper, R. Paradise beach
Cowper, R. The scent of silverdill
Cox, E. Andax and Odi
Cox, I. E., Jr. In the circle of nowhere
Cramer, K. Forbidden knowledge
Cross, R. A. The forever summer
Curval, P. Progenitor
Dabbs, D. E. Arriki
Davidson, A. The Slovo stove
De Camp, L. S. Nothing in the rules
De Celles, M. Recurrence
DeFord, M. A. Not snow nor rain
Dick, P. K. The alien mind
Dick, P. K. Chains of air, web of aether
Dick, P. K. The exit door leads in
Dick, P. K. Frozen journey
Dick, P. K. A game of unchance
Dick, P. K. Holy quarrel
Dick, P. K. I hope I shall arrive soon
Dick, P. K. The Preserving Machine
Dick, P. K. The short happy life of the brown oxford
Dick, P. K. War game
Dickson, G. R. Catch a tartar
Dickson, G. R. Lost Dorsai
Dickson, G. R. Miss Prinks
Dickson, G. R. The mortal and the monster
Dickson, G. R. Soupstone
Dilov, L. Contacts of a fourth kind
Disch, T. M. Ringtime
Dumas, H. The distributors
Effinger, G. A. The aliens who knew, I mean, everything
Effinger, G. A. From downtown at the buzzer
Ellison, H. In lonely lands
Ellison, H. On the slab
Ellison, H. When Auld's acquaintance is forgot
Farmer, P. J. The alley man
Farmer, P. J. The god business
Fast, H. The large ant
Federici, C. M. In the blink of an eye
Feyrer, G. The House of the Twin Jewels
Finch, S. Reichs-peace
Finney, J. The coin collector
Finney, J. Such interesting neighbors

SCIENCE FICTION—*Continued*

Fitch, M. They that go down to the sea in ships
Fitzgerald, M. J. Glass
Ford, J. M. Street of dreams
Fowler, K. J. Recalling Cinderella
Friedenkraft, G. Anne
Gardner, M. Left or right?
Gardner, M. No-sided professor
Gardner, M. Oom
Gardner, M. Thang
Garratt, P. T. If the driver vanishes. . .
Garrett, R. The Ipswich Phial
Gauger, R. The vacuum-packed picnic
Gentle, M. Anukazi's daughter
Gibson, W. The winter market
Gilman, C. The language of the sea
Gold, H. L. A matter of form
Gorodischer, A. Man's dwelling place
Green, M. Measuring the light
Gross, H. H. Cubeworld
Gunn, J. E. Kindergarten
Haldeman, J. W. Seven and the stars
Hall, J. B. My work in California
Hamilton, E. World without sex
Harding, L. Limbo
Harrison, H. The view from the top of the tower
Heinlein, R. A. Gulf
Henderson, Z. Come on, wagon!
Henderson, Z. Subcommittee
Herbert, F. By the book
Herbert, F. Cease fire
Herbert, F. Committee of the whole
Herbert, F. Frogs and scientists
Herbert, F. Murder will in
Herbert, F. The road to Dune
Herbert, F. The tactful saboteur
Hoffman, N. K. Lost lives
Hoffman, N. K. A step into darkness
Jeppson, J. O. August angst
Jeppson, J. O. The beanstalk analysis
Jeppson, J. O. Consternation and empire
Jeppson, J. O. The curious consultation
Jeppson, J. O. The mysterious cure
Jeppson, J. O. Seasonal special
Jeppson, J. O. The ultimate biofeedback device
Kagan, N. The mathenauts
Keizer, G. I am the burning bush
Killough, L., and Killough, H. P. Keeping the customer satisfied
Kilworth, G. Oubliette
King, S. Beachworld
Klass, M. In the beginning
Knight, D. F. O
Kornbluth, C. M. The little black bag
Kornbluth, C. M. The mindworm
Kress, N. Casey's empire
Kress, N. Explanations, Inc.
Kress, N. Talp hunt
Kress, N. Trinity
Kuttner, H. The dark world

Kuttner, H. The portal in the picture
Kuttner, H. Valley of the Flame
Lafferty, R. A. Company in the wings
Lafferty, R. A. Golden gate
Lafferty, R. A. Interurban queen
Lafferty, R. A. Magazine section
Langford, M. N. Wood
Larionova, O. A tale of kings
Lasswitz, K. The universal library
Le Guin, U. K. Schrödinger's cat
Le Guin, U. K. The trouble with the cotton people
Lee, R. B. Full fathom five my father lies
Lee, T. A day in the skin; or, The century we were out of them
Lee, T. Medra
Lee, T. Written in water
Leinster, M. A logic named Joe
Leman, B. Window
Lengyel, P. Rising sun; or, The celebration of heartfelt joy
Longyear, B. B. A time for terror
Longyear, B. B. Twist ending
Longyear, B. B. Where do you get your ideas?
Lynn, E. A. At the Embassy Club
MacIntyre, F. G. The prisoner of gravity
Maddern, P. C. Inhabiting the interspaces
Maddox, T. Snake-eyes
Martin, G. R. R. Override
Martin, G. R. R. Weekend in a war zone
Matheson, R. Born of man and woman
Matheson, R. Dance of the dead
Matheson, R. Dress of white silk
McDaniel, M. C. A little of what you fancy
Meredith, J., and Smirl, D. E. Dream in a bottle
Merrill, L. The robot awakes
Messenger, B. Give it back to the Indians
Miller, W. M. Memento homo
Milosevic, M. Up above the world so high
Moore, C. L. No woman born
Moore, C. L. Shambleau
Moore, W. Lot
Moore, W. Peacebringer
Murphy, P. Art in the war zone
Nesvadba, J. The divided Carla
Nesvadba, J. The half-wit of Xeenemuende
Neville, K. Ballenger's people
Neville, K. Hunt the hunter
Neville, K. Overture
Newman, K. Dreamers
Niven, L. The borderland of Sol
Olesen, K. Beast and beauty
Orr, W. F. Euclid alone
Pangborn, E. The night wind
Phillips, R. The yellow pill
Pimple, D. J. Arcadus Arcane
Piper, H. B. He walked around the horses
Piper, H. B. Ministry of disturbance
Piper, H. B. Operation RSVP
Pohl, F. The dark shadow

SCIENCE FICTION—*Continued*

Pohl, F. My life as a born-again pig
Pollack, R. The protector
Preuss, P. Small bodies
Randall, M. Big dome
Reed, K. Dog days
Reed, K. Frontiers
Reed, K. Love story
Reed, K. Sisohpromatem
Reed, K. The visible partner
Reed, K. The wait
Resnicow, H. Greater love than this . . .
Richards, J. The bridge sings
Robinson, K. S. The lucky strike
Robinson, S. User friendly
Rucker, R. von B. The man who was a cosmic string
Rucker, R. von B. Message found in a copy of Flatland
Rucker, R. von B. A new golden age
Rucker, R. von B., and Laidlaw, M. Probability pipeline
Sakers, D. The finagle fiasco
Sarrantonio, A. The haunting of Y-12
Scholz, C. Galileo complains
Scholz, C. Transients
Shaw, B. Light of other days
Sheckley, R. Pilgrimage to Earth
Sheckley, R. The prize of peril
Sheckley, R. The Skag Castle
Shiner, L. Till human voices wake us
Shippey, T. Enemy transmissions
Shirley, J. Triggering
Shirley, J. What Cindy saw
Silverberg, R. At the conglomeroid cocktail party
Silverberg, R. The desert of stolen dreams
Silverberg, R. Our Lady of the Sauropods
Silverberg, R. The Science Fiction Hall of Fame
Silverberg, R. A sea of faces
Silverberg, R. To be continued
Silverberg, R. We know who we are
Simmons, D. Carrion comfort
Sladek, J. T. Answers
Smith, C. The game of rat and dragon
Smith, C. A planet named Shayol
Smith, C. A. The planet of the dead
Smith, C. A. A prophecy of monsters
Sonderlund, N. O. The angel from hell
St. Clair, M. Brightness falls from the air
St. Clair, M. The causes
St. Clair, M. Idris' pig
St. Clair, M. The invested libido
St. Clair, M. New ritual
St. Clair, M. The pillows
St. Clair, M. Prott
St. Maur, H. Planet of peril
Sterling, B. Cicada Queen
Stevens, J. A. Families
Stokes, T. No pets
Strugatskiĭ, A. N., and Strugatskiĭ, B. N. The way to Amalteia

Sturgeon, T. Medusa
Sturgeon, T. Microcosmic god
Sturgeon, T. The traveling Crag
Sturgeon, T. Two percent inspiration
Sucharitkul, S. Fiddling for water buffaloes
Thomas, T. L. Broken tool
Tiptree, J. Excursion fare
Tiptree, J. I'll be waiting for you when the swimming pool is empty
Tiptree, J. Love is the plan the plan is death
Tiptree, J. The peacefulness of Vivyan
Tooker, R. Zenith Rand, planet vigilante
Tsutsui, Y. Standing woman
Twain, M. From The "London Times" of 1904
Van Name, M. L. My sister, my self
Vance, J. The new prime
Varley, J. Options
Varley, J. The pusher
Varshavsky, I. No alarming symptoms
Varshavsky, I. The secrets of the genre
Vester, L. Pawn promotion
Vinge, J. D. Psiren
Vinge, J. D. Voices from the dust
Vonarburg, E. Cold bridge
Wagner, K. E. Neither brute nor human
Waldrop, H. Heirs of the Perisphere
Waldrop, H. Ike at the mike
Waldrop, H. Man-Mountain Gentian
Watson, I. The call of the wild: the dog-flea version
Watson, I. Cold light
Watson, I. Immune dreams
Watson, I. A letter from God
Watson, I. The thousand cuts
Watson, I. The world science fiction convention of 2080
Weinbaum, S. G. Shifting seas
Wellman, M. W. Vandy, Vandy
Wells, H. G. The crystal egg
Wells, H. G. The Time Machine
Wilhelm, K. The girl who fell into the sky
Wilkerson, C. The man who watched the glaciers run
Williams, O. The angel's gift
Williams, R. M. Robot's return
Williams, W. J. Side effects
Williamson, J. Wolves of darkness
Willis, C. Blued moon
Willis, C. Lost and found
Willis, C. Schwarzschild radius
Wolfe, G. All the hues of Hell
Wolfe, G. The death of Doctor Island
Wolverton, D. On my way to paradise
Ye Yonglie. The Thursday events
Young, P. ja. The helldivers
Zahn, T. Dragon pax
Zahn, T. Teamwork
Zajdel, J. A. Particularly difficult territory
Zebrowski, G. The Eichmann variations
Zebrowski, G. Gödel's doom

The **Science** Fiction Hall of Fame. Silverberg, R.

SCIENTIFIC EXPEDITIONS
  Anderson, P. The Saturn game
  Colegate, I. Distant cousins
  McCormack, E. P. Sad stories in Patagonia
  Silverberg, R. Breckenridge and the continuum
  Silverberg, R. The iron star

SCIENTIFIC EXPERIMENTS *See* Experiments, Scientific
The **scientific** method. Cohen, R.
The **scientific** method. Škvorecký, J.

SCIENTIFIC RESEARCH *See* Research
The **scientist.** Friedman, B. J.

SCIENTISTS
  See also Anthropologists; Archeologists; Astronomers; Bacteriologists; Biochemists; Biologists; Chemists; Inventors; Physicists; Women scientists
  Asimov, I. "Breeds there a man . . .?"
  Asimov, I. Flies
  Asimov, I. A problem of numbers
  Berdnyk, O. A journey to the antiworld
  Bloch, R. Life in our time
  Bloch, R. The living end
  Budrys, A. Never meet again
  Bumpus, J. Popinjay's African notes
  Crace, J. In heat
  Doyle, Sir A. C. An exciting Christmas Eve; or, My lecture on dynamite
  Doyle, Sir A. C. The parasite
  Finch, S. Reichs-peace
  Hartmann, W. K. Handprints on the Moon
  Hawthorne, N. The birthmark
  Lovecraft, H. P. Cool air
  Meade, L. T., and Eustace, R. The man who disappeared
  Moravia, A. The devil can't save the world
  Mrożek, S. The ugupu bird
  Pohl, F. The dark shadow
  Robinson, S. By any other name
  Rud, A. M. Ooze
  Sterling, B. The beautiful and the sublime
  Strugatskiĭ, A. N., and Strugatskiĭ, B. N. The way to Amalteia
  Temple, W. F. The four-sided triangle
  Van de Wetering, J. A tale with an end
  Vinge, J. D. Voices from the dust
  Wilhelm, K. The promise
Scission. Winton, T.
Scobie, Stephen
  A marriage of convenience
    The New press anthology #1
Scofield, Sandra
  Trespass
    The Ploughshares reader: new fiction for the eighties
The **scoop.** Plunkett, J.
Scoring off Jeeves. Wodehouse, P. G.

Scortia, Thomas N., 1926-
  Flowering Narcissus
    Kindred spirits; ed. by J. M. Elliot
SCOTLAND
  See also Orkney (Scotland)
    16th century
  Hogg, J. Mary Burnet
    17th century
  Hogg, J. The barber of Duncow—a real ghost story
  Hogg, J. The Brownie of the Black Haggs
  Hogg, J. The Cameronian preacher's tale
  McCormack, E. P. The fragment
    18th century
  Hogg, J. The mysterious bride
  Hogg, J. The unearthly witness
  Kirk, R. The reflex-man in Whinnymuir Close
  Scott, Sir W. Wandering Willie's tale
    19th century
  Dickens, C. The story of the bagman's uncle
  Doyle, Sir A. C. Touch and go: a midshipman's story
  Hogg, J. On the separate existence of the soul
  Hogg, J. Strange letter of a lunatic
  Stevenson, R. L. The merry men
    20th century
  Crampsey, R. A. Felicity
  Crichton Smith, I. Timoshenko
  Dunn, D. Getting used to it
  Dunn, D. Mozart's Clarinet Concerto
  Dunn, D. Something for little Robert
  Gallacher, T. A friend of Dosser Farr
  Gallacher, T. Lord Sweatrag
  Gallacher, T. Perfect pitch
  Gallacher, T. Portrait of Isa Mulvenny
  Gallacher, T. Store quarter
  Knox, B. Deerglen Queen
  MacDonald, D. R. The flowers of Bermuda
  McCormack, E. P. Captain Joe
  McCormack, E. P. The one-legged men
    Coal mines and mining
  See Coal mines and mining—Scotland
    Rural life
  Doyle, Sir A. C. Our midnight visitor
  Dundas, R. The climber on the hill
  Dunn, D. The bagpiping people
  Dunn, D. The canoes
  Dunn, D. Fishermen
  Dunn, D. Wives in the garden
  Hogg, J. Mr. Adamson of Laverhope
  Hogg, J. Sound morality
  Hogg, J. Tibby Hyslop's dream
  Kirk, R. Sorworth Place
  Livesey, M. The acrobat's grave
  Oliphant, M. The library window
  Oliphant, M. The open door
    Edinburgh
  Green, J. The tallest man in the world

SCOTLAND—Edinburgh—*Continued*
  Stewart, J. I. M. Sweets from a stranger
         Glasgow
  Costello, K. The immortal soul of Tommy O'
  Dunn, D. South America
  Friel, G. Onlookers
  Gaitens, E. Growing up
  Gaitens, E. The sailing ship
  Gilkison, A. Atthis
  Gray, A. The crank that made the revolution
  Hamilton, A. Moonlighting
  Hendry, J. F. The disinherited
  Kelman, J. Remember young Cecil
  Lavin, J. By any other name
  Leonard, T. Mr. Endrews speaks
  Lindsay, F. The people of the book
  MacDougall, C. A small hotel
  McBain, H. Supper on the wall
  McLay, F. Headlines for Whitey
  Montgomerie, W. Daft Jenny
  Mulrine, S. A cold coming
  Spence, A. The rain dance
  Spence, A. Tinsel
  Thornton, V. Another Sunday morning
  Turner, B. The shoes
  Ure, J. Kelvingrove Park
         Kilbinnin
  Dunn, D. Kilbinnin men
         Perth
  Davie, E. A traveller's room
SCOTS
         Canada
  McCormack, E. P. One picture of Trotsky
         Egypt
  MacLean, A. McCrimmon and the blue moonstones
         Germany
  Muir, A. The reptile
Scott, Duncan Campbell, 1862-1947
  The Desjardins
    The Oxford book of Canadian short stories in English
Scott, G. Firth
  The bunyip dies
    Australian science fiction; ed. by V. Ikin
Scott, Gail
  Car wrecks and bleeding hearts
    Fatal recurrences; ed. by H. Hugh and P. O'Brien
Scott, Jody
  The American Book of the Dead
    Afterlives; ed. by P. Sargent and I. Watson
Scott, Lawrence
  The house of funerals
    Winter's tales, new ser. v4
Scott, Rosie
  Diary of a woman
    Women's work; ed. by M. McLeod and L. Wevers

Scott, Sir Walter, 1771-1832
  The tapestried chamber
    The Book of the dead; ed. by A. K. Russell
    The Oxford book of English ghost stories
    The Treasury of English short stories; ed. by N. Sullivan
  Wandering Willie's tale
    The Penguin book of ghost stories
SCOTTISH DIALECT *See* Dialect stories—Scottish
Scoundrel. Fante, J.
The scourging at the pillar. Olson, T.
The scoutmaster. Taylor, P. H.
Scrap. Collins, M. A.
A scrap of green silk. Haake, K.
Scrap of paper. Purdy, J.
A scrap of time. Fink, I.
Scratch scratch. Dixon, S.
The screamer. Coleman, W.
The screaming people. Bloch, R.
The screaming woman. Bradbury, R.
The screen. Colette
Scrimptalon's test. Bishop, M.
Scrimshaw. Garfield, B.
SCRIPTWRITERS *See* Authors
SCULPTORS
    See also Women sculptors
  Barthelme, S. Michael
  Bell, M. S. The naked lady
  Cohen, A. The monumental sculptor
  Colum, P. Pilgrimage home
  Donaldson, S. R. Unworthy of the angel
  Garrett, G. P. The rarer thing
  Gilliatt, P. Teeth
  Hoch, E. D. The melting man
  O'Donnell, P. Salamander Four
  Palmer, S. Riddle of the marble blade
  Rand, P. Heir
  Rose, D. A. Jumping from high places
  Tremain, R. Current account
  Wolfe, T. Katamoto
  Woods, C. The quarry
SCULPTURE
    See also Masks (Sculpture); Monuments; Soap sculpture; Statues; Wood carving
  Bloch, R. Mannikins of horror
The scythe. Bernen, R.
The scythe hand; or, The homestead. Muschg, A.
The scythe of Saturn. Wickert, M.
The scythe of time. Poe, E. A.
SEA *See* Ocean
The sea. Eldridge, M.
Sea. Parise, G.
The sea. Rodoreda, M.
SEA ANIMALS *See* Marine animals
SEA CAPTAINS *See* Seamen; Shipmasters
Sea change. Baker, S.
The sea change. Hemingway, E.
Sea change. Johnson, G. C.

The **sea** devil. Gordon, A.
The **sea** fairies. Stanton, M.
The **sea** is always the same. Warner, S. T.
The **sea** lion. Abbott, K.
The **sea-lion**. Ferron, J.
Sea lovers. Martin, V.
Sea magic. Leiber, F.

SEA MONSTERS
        See also Loch Ness monster
 Bloch, R. Terror in Cut-throat Cove
 Curry, G. S. Sea-serpents of Domnudale
 Kipling, R. A matter of fact
A **sea** of faces. Silverberg, R.
The **sea** of lost time. García Márquez, G.
Sea of tranquillity. Laidlaw, M.
The **sea-rabbit;** or, The artist of life. Walker,
     W.
The **sea-raiders**. Wells, H. G.
Sea-serpents of Domnudale. Curry, G. S.
The **sea** snake. Eis, J.

SEA STORIES
        See also Seamen; Whaling; also
     names of wars with the subdivision
     Naval operations
 Baumbach, J. The great Cape Cod shock
     scare
 Bradbury, R. Undersea guardians
 Collins, W. "Blow up with the brig"
 Conrad, J. The black mate
 Conrad, J. The gale
 Conrad, J. The secret sharer
 Conrad, J. Typhoon
 Conrad, J. Youth
 Cooper, J. F. The Ariel defeats the
     Alacrity
 Crane, S. Flanagan and his short
     filibustering adventure
 Crane, S. The open boat
 Crane, S. The revenge of the Adolphus
 Doyle, Sir A. C. The fate of the
     Evangeline
 Doyle, Sir A. C. J. Habakuk Jephson's
     statement
 Doyle, Sir A. C. Touch and go: a midship-
     man's story
 Doyle, Sir A. C. A true story of the
     tragedy of Flowery Land
 Du Maurier, Dame D. Escort
 Dunsany, E. J. M. D. P., Baron. A story
     of land and sea
 Forester, C. S. The sinking of the Bis-
     marck
 France, A. The ocean Christ
 Grey, Z. Strange partners of Two-Fold Bay
 Hodgson, W. H. The finding of the
     Graiken
 Hoffman, W. Landfall
 Hugo, V. A wild cannon dooms the
     Claymore
 Ingalls, R. Captain Hendrik's story
 Kipling, R. A matter of fact
 London, J. The Ghost loses her seal-
     hunting boats

 London, J. Make westing
 MacLachlan, P. All the names of Baby
     Hag
 MacLean, A. The Dileas
 MacLean, A. Hospital ship rams U-boat
 Marryat, F. The midshipman
 Masefield, J. Being ashore
 Melville, H. Benito Cereno
 Norris, F. The ship that saw a ghost
 Poe, E. A. The incredible survival
 Poe, E. A. Ms. found in a bottle
 Poe, E. A. The narrative of Arthur
     Gordon Pym of Nantucket
 Raine, N. R. The last laugh
 Robinson, W. The blow-up of the Mohawk
 Russell, W. C. A bewitched ship
 Russell, W. C. Can these dry bones live?
 Russell, W. C. The phantom death
 Sale, R. The benevolent ghost and Captain
     Lowrie
 Schwob, M. The flute
 Sturgeon, T. Cargo
 Thomson, V. The battle of Bonhomme
     Richard and Serapis
 Verne, J. Captain Nemo's revenge
 Villiers, A. J. The windjammer film
 Wallace, L. Ben-Hur escapes from the
     Astroea
 Wetjen, A. R. Duty
 Wolfe, G. A cabin on the coast
 Wouk, H. The mutiny
 Yourcenar, M. An obscure man
Sea wrack. Bradley, M. Z.
The **seabirds**. Watanabe, S. A.
Seabright, Idris See St. Clair, Margaret
Seabrook, W. B.
 The witch's vengeance
     Handle with care; ed. by J. Kahn
Seabrooke, Deborah
 Secrets
     The Best American short stories, 1985
     The Virginia Quarterly Review 60:119-33
       Wint '84
The **seagull**. Auchincloss, L.

SEAGULLS
 Faik, S. An episode of two
The **sealed** angel. Leskov, N. S.
A **sealed** pod. Bonner, M.
Sealink. Meinke, P.

SEALS (ANIMALS)
 Lee, T. Because our skins are finer
 Sherman, D. The maid on the shore
Seals. O'Brien, D.

SEAMEN
        See also Sea stories; Shipmasters;
     Vikings
 Boylan, C. Villa Marta
 Burnet, D. Fog
 Collins, W. "Blow up with the brig"
 Conrad, J. The gale
 Coppard, A. E. Ahoy, sailor boy!
 Costello, K. The immortal soul of Tommy
     O'

SEAMEN—*Continued*

Crane, S. The open boat
Crawford, F. M. Man overboard!
Dinesen, I. The sailor-boy's tale
Faik, S. Robinson
Gallacher, T. A friend of Dosser Farr
Gallacher, T. Portrait of Isa Mulvenny
Gardner, M. Good dancing, sailor!
Gardner, M. The sixth ship
Grin, A. The Port Commandant
Grin, A. Reno Island
Grin, A. Ships in Liss
Hemingway, E. On the quai in Smyrna
Hodgson, W. H. The thing in the weeds
Ingalls, R. Captain Hendrik's story
Khudayyir, M. Clocks like horses
Liu, F. Wang Hsieh; or Dark robe land
MacDonald, J. D. Bimini kill
MacLean, A. McCrimmon and the blue
   moonstones
Marryat, F. The legend of the bell rock
Marryat, F. The midshipman
Masefield, J. Ambitious Jimmy Hicks
Masefield, J. On growing old
Maupassant, G. de. The port
Melville, H. Billy Budd, Sailor
Morrison, J. Sailors belong ships
Naipaul, S. The father, the son and the
   Holy Ghost
Petrakis, H. M. The bastards of Thanos
Poe, E. A. King Pest
Poe, E. A. The narrative of Arthur
   Gordon Pym of Nantucket
Robinson, K. S. Black air
Runciman, J. The lost skipper
Sproat, R. When the sailor was far away
Swados, H. Bobby Shafter's gone to sea
Watt, N. As good as gold
Wheatcroft, J. Kamikaze
Wyatt, M. Sincerely yours
Zelazny, R. And I alone am escaped to
   tell thee

Seamon, Hollis Rowan
Middle-aged Martha Anne
   The Hudson Review 37:557-66 Wint '84/
   '85

The **seamstress**. Coleman, W.
The **seamstress**. Colette
A **seamstress**. Marotta, K.
SEAMSTRESSES *See* Dressmakers
Seance. Sharman, J.
SEANCES *See* Spiritualism
The **search**. Chase, V.
The **search**. Nowakowski, M.

SEARCH AND RESCUE OPERATIONS

Lesley, C. The catch
Roberts, C. G. D. Do seek their meat
   from God
Search party. Haley, R.
Searcher. Hensley, J. L.
Searching for Freddy. Kinsella, W. P.
The **searchlight**. Woolf, V.
Searchlight operator. Faik, S.

Searls, Hank
A dish of homicide
   Searls, H. The adventures of Mike Blair
For auld lang crime
   Searls, H. The adventures of Mike Blair
Keep your money side up
   Searls, H. The adventures of Mike Blair
Kickback for a killer
   Searls, H. The adventures of Mike Blair
Lethal legacy for the lady
   Searls, H. The adventures of Mike Blair
Let's all die together
   Searls, H. The adventures of Mike Blair
Shiv for your supper
   Searls, H. The adventures of Mike Blair
Sears, Vickie L.
Sticktalk
   Hear the silence; ed. by I. Zahava
The **Sears** and Roebuck catalog game.
   Nordan, L.

SEASHORE

Ahern, T. Monsters
Ballard, J. G. The drowned giant
Campbell, R. The voice of the beach
Cowan, P. Canary
Davie, E. Shoe in the sand
Drewe, R. The bodysurfers
Drewe, R. Shark logic
Gold, H. Susanna at the beach
Haley, R. Except that they move and talk
Hawthorne, N. Foot-prints on the sea-shore
Hayman, R. Urchins
Kanafānī, G. The Slave Fort
Kauffman, J. My mother has me surround-
   ed
Mansfield, K. At the bay
Mathers, P. A knight of teeth
Millhauser, S. A protest against the sun
Moore, M. J. Summer sand
Morris, W. Since when do they charge
   admission
Rosenbaum, K. Low tide
St. Aubin de Terán, L. I never eat crab-
   meat now
Warner, S. T. The sea is always the same
Seaside idle. Lagory, M.

SEASIDE RESORTS

Cole, G. D. H., and Cole, M. The toys
   of death
Lurie, M. Pride and joy
MacLaverty, B. Anodyne
O'Brien, E. Paradise
Parise, G. Sea
Woolf, V. The watering place
A **season** for heroes. Kelly, C.
A **season** for Idols. Dudley, W.
A **season** of acceptance. Fosdick, C. J.
Seasonal rain. Flynn, R.
Seasonal special. Jeppson, J. O.
Seasoning. Clement, H.
Seasons. Haldeman, J. W.
The **seasons**. Oates, J. C.
Season's greetings. Gillette, V.

Seasons of belief. Bishop, M.
The seasons of love. Shyer, M. F.
Seaton's aunt. De la Mare, W.
Seats of the haughty. Henry, O.
SEATTLE (WASH.) See Washington
    (State)—Seattle
The seawall. Minot, S.
Seaweed and song. Rule, J.
Sebastian, Lee
    For works written by this author under
        other names see Silverberg, Robert
Sebolelo comes home. Moikangoa, C. E.
Secession chapter. Sharman, J.
Sechler, Teena
    A drummer's gift
        Redbook 170:60-1 D '87
Second best. Floyd, P. L.
A second chance. Bosniak, M. E.
Second chance. Finney, J.
Second chance. Soman, F. J.
Second coming. Currer, B.
The second coming. Gores, J.
Second coming. Neville, S.
The second coming. Percy, W.
The second coming of Little Richard. Dagg,
    M.
The second death. Greene, G.
The second generation. Crane, S.
Second going. Tiptree, J.
Second-hand man. Dove, R.
Second-hand sky. Pohl, F.
A second impression. Dickerson, K.
The second law of thermodynamics. Cullen,
    E. J.
The second miracle. Chesterton, G. K.
The second (or perhaps third) time round.
    West, J.
The second part. Dixon, S.
Second person looking out. Josipovici, G.
The second Pete. Abbott, K.
Second rains. Thomas, M.
The second shot. Lutz, J.
SECOND SIGHT See Clairvoyance; Ex-
    trasensory perception
Second sight. Campbell, R.
Second sight. Krause, P.
Second sight. Nourse, A. E.
The second sight of Dr. Sam: Johnson. De
    la Torre, L.
Second son. Ferro, R.
Second spring. MacLeod, A.
The second third of C. Ferguson, N.
Second thoughts. Chua, R.
The second time around. Fisher, M. F. K.
Second Variety. Dick, P. K.
A second wife. Roberts, N.
Secondary top. Kiely, B.
Secret. Asscher-Pinkhof, C.
The secret. Kinsella, W. P.
Secret. Oates, J. C.
The secret. Singer, I. B.
SECRET AGENTS See Secret service; Spies
The secret alibi. Matsumoto, S.

The secret dog. Cameron, P.
The secret face. Nowakowski, M.
The secret history of Eddypus, the world-
    empire. Twain, M.
The secret hour. Matthews, J.
The secret integration. Pynchon, T.
The secret lion. Rios, A.
The secret lives of dieters. Klass, P.
The secret lover. Lovesey, P.
The secret meeting with Mr. Eliot. Whelan,
    G.
Secret observations on the goat-girl. Oates,
    J. C.
The secret of the Blue Star. Bradley, M. Z.
The secret of the growing gold. Stoker, B.
The secret of the holy places. Austin, M.
    H.
SECRET SERVICE
    See also International intrigue;
        World War, 1914-1918—Secret service
Aćin-Kosta, M. The privileged class
Asimov, I. Hide and seek
Barrett, W. E. Dealers in doom
Gilbert, M. Emergency exit
Gilbert, M. The spoilers
Jakes, J. Dr. Sweetkill
Maugham, W. S. The traitor
Yarbro, C. Q. Do I dare to eat a peach?
    England
    See Secret service—Great Britain
    Great Britain
Allbeury, T. Time spent in reconnaissance
Gilbert, M. The African tree-beavers
Gilbert, M. The killing of Michael Fin-
    negan
O'Donnell, P. The giggle-wrecker
The secret sharer. Conrad, J.
SECRET SOCIETIES
Böll, H. A peach tree in his garden stands
Doyle, Sir A. C. An exciting Christmas
    Eve; or, My lecture on dynamite
Greene, G. The root of all evil
Matthews, J. The betrayal of the fives
West, J. The mysteries of life in an order-
    ly manner
The secret to not getting stuck. Woodruff,
    J.
Secret worship. Blackwood, A.
SECRETARIES
Brett, S. Unwilling sleep
Cheever, J. The five-forty-eight
Colter, C. Macabre
Gaitskill, M. Secretary
Greene, G. Special duties
Mathers, P. Minutes
Murphy, P. Jester
Nevai, L. Temp
O'Hara, J. The gentleman in the tan suit
Parker, D. The standard of living
Russ, J. Existence
Saiki, J. The wood rose
Slesinger, T. The mouse-trap
Tabucchi, A. Heavenly bliss

SECRETARIES—*Continued*
    Taylor, P. E. Afoot in a field of men
    Trevanian. The sacking of Miss Plimsoll
    Walpole, Sir H. The silver mask
    Wilson, L. A. The snipe hunters
Secretary. Gaitskill, M.
The **secretary**. Mayer, D.
Secrets. Bryant, S. K.
Secrets. Colette
Secrets. Floyd, P. L.
Secrets. Huggan, I.
Secrets. MacLaverty, B.
Secrets. Oates, J. C.
Secrets. Rossiter, S.
Secrets. Seabrooke, D.
Secrets. Sinclair, M. J. P.
Secrets. Thurm, M.
Secrets. Winton, T.
Secrets between friends. Munro, A.
Secrets men keep. Abrams, L.
The **secrets** of life. Pilcher, R.
The **secrets** of Miss Plimsoll, private
    secretary. See Trevanian. The sacking
    of Miss Plimsoll
The **secrets** of phylogeny, or What Jason
    knew. Carter, B.
The **secrets** of the genre. Varshavsky, I.
The **secretsharer**. Hathaway, W.
SECTS
    Aickman, R. Larger than oneself
    Bishop, M. Out of the mouths of Olympus
    Lofts, N. God's own elect
Security. Davie, E.
Sedgwick, Catharine Maria, 1789-1867
    Old maids
        Old maids; ed. by S. Koppelman
Seducing Alice. McFarland, D.
SEDUCTION
    Bowles, J. A. Señorita Córdoba
    Choyce, L. The paper route
    Coleman, W. Lonnie's cousin
    Colter, C. Mary's convert
    Cook, H. Cracked wheat
    Ferguson, W. Scherzo with TV antenna
    Ford, R. Empire
    Hagy, A. C. Shoreline
    Kaplan, D. M. Comfort
    Major, A. The good old days
    Maupassant, G. de. A country excursion
    Maupassant, G. de. Joseph
    Neville, S. Johnny Appleseed
    Oates, J. C. The boy
    Oates, J. C. Where are you going, where
        have you been?
    Petrakis, H. M. Courtship of the blue
        widow
    Russ, J. The view from this window
    Stephan, M. The tub
    Williams, T. Twenty-seven wagons full of
        cotton
    Wolfe, T. Fame and the poet
    Ziem, J. Statement
Seduction. Watmough, D.

The **seductress**. Campbell, R.
See again. Asscher-Pinkhof, C.
See how they run. Bloch, R.
See no evil. Stout, R.
Seed grain. Greenwood, R.
Seed of suspicion. Coxe, G. H.
Seed stock. Herbert, F.
Seeds. Keillor, G.
Seeds. Liberman, S.
Seeds of conflict. Kramer, K.
The **seeing** eye. Rey Rosa, R.
Seeing Mrs. Landers. Astley, T.
Seeing the world. Campbell, R.
Seeing the world. O'Brien, F.-J.
The **seeker** in the fortress. Wellman, M. W.
Seeker of tomorrow. Russell, E. F., and
    Johnson, L. T.
The **seeker,** the snake and the baba. Glover,
    D. H.
Seeking its level. Bird, C.
Seema, Nighat
    Helpless
        Short story international 48
The **seeney** stretch. Dilworth, S.
Seepaul, Lionel
    A key for Dolcina
        Short story international 71
    A sleeping pill for the doctor
        Short story international 61
    Sou-Sou money
        Short story international 45
The **seersucker** suit. Hauser, M.
Segal, Erich, 1937-
    The whole world is watching
        TV Guide 36:26-30 Ag 6-12 '88
        TV Guide 36:32-4+ Ag 13-19 '88
Segal, Lore Groszmann
    An absence of cousins
        The New Yorker 63:22-9 Ag 17 '87
Seghers, Anna, 1900-1983
    The reed
        Voices East and West: German short
        stories since 1945
SEGREGATION *See* Race relations
Seibei and his gourds. Shiga, N.
Seidman, Michael
    Perchance to dream
        The Black Lizard anthology of crime fic-
        tion; ed. by E. Gorman
SEINE RIVER (FRANCE)
    Maupassant, G. de. On the river
Seitlin, Percy
    Short story shortening
        The Antioch Review 42:427-32 Fall '84
Seizing control. Robison, M.
Selecting a ghost. The ghosts of Goresthorpe
    Grange. Doyle, Sir A. C.
Self-defense. Giles, M.
The **self-destruction** of the Ama Gabe.
    Havemann, E.
The **self-esteem** of Marcel Chalon. Vil-
    lefranche, A.-M.

SELF-MADE MEN
See also Success
Wells, H. G. Wayde's essence
Self-portrait. Dixon, S.
A **self-portrait.** Mazel, D.
Self portrait in twenty-three rounds. Wojnarowicz, D.
Self-portrait with vanishing point. Ciment, J.
SELF-SACRIFICE
Doyle, Sir A. C. The colonel's choice
Freeman, M. E. W. A moral exigency
Grin, A. The snake
Harte, B. The outcasts of Poker Flat
Kipling, R. The wish house
Smith, C. A. The city of the singing flame
The **selfish** giant. Wilde, O.
A **selfish** story. Gold, H.
SELFISHNESS
Endō, S. Despicable bastard
Rush, N. Near Pala
Whelan, G. Children in the park
Selfishness. Maupassant, G. de
The **seller** of watches. Vreuls, D.
Sellers, James F.
The proper maintenance of lists
Chicago Review 34:51-8 Summ '84
The **sellers** of the dream. Jakes, J.
Sellin' some wood. Rudin, J.
Selling out. Eldridge, M.
SELMA (ALA.) *See* Alabama—Selma
Selmi, Habib
Distant seas
Arabic short stories; tr. by D. Johnson-Davies
Selvon, Samuel
If winter comes
Alberta bound; ed. by F. Stenson
Sembene, Ousmane, 1923-
The false prophet
African short stories; ed. by C. Achebe and C. L. Innes
Semillante. Maupassant, G. de
Seminar. Cowan, P.
SEMINARIANS
Chekhov, A. P. The student
Gogol', N. V. Viy
Matthews, J. If not us, then who?
Updike, J. Lifeguard
Watmough, D. False start
The **Sémiramis** bar. Colette
Semley's necklace. Le Guin, U. K.
The **sempstress.** Colette
SENATE (U.S.) *See* United States. Congress. Senate
Seneca morning. Brady, M.
SENEGAL
McKnight, R. Uncle Moustapha's eclipse
Sembene, O. The false prophet
Dakar
Gold, H. Christmas in Dakar
The **senior** partner's ethics. Auchincloss, L.
Señor Discretion himself. Schulberg, B.
El **Señor** Lector. Schwebel, B.

Señor Ong and Señor Ha. Bowles, P.
La **Señora.** Adams, A.
Señorita. Oates, J. C.
Señorita Córdoba. Bowles, J. A.
Sense and sensitivity. Wilson, B.
A **sense** of. Anderman, J.
A **sense** of history. Gilbert, M.
A **sense** of humor. Brown, A.
A **sense** of place. Caldwell, P.
The **sense** of the meeting. Conroy, F.
Sense of wonder, sense of awe. McGarvey, C.
"The **sensible** thing". Fitzgerald, F. S.
A **sensitive** season. Tsushima, Y.
The **sensory** deprivation tank. Fremlin, C.
Sentence. Barthelme, D.
Sentence commuted. Berberova, N.
Sentences. Matheson, R. C.
Sentiment. Maupassant, G. de
A **sentimental** encounter. Oates, J. C.
Sentimental journey. Oates, J. C.
A **sentimental** journey. Stern, S.
Sentimental meetings. Cohen, M.
A **sentimental** wolf. Hemley, R.
The **sentimentality** of William Tavener. Cather, W.
The **sentinel.** Clarke, A. C.
The **sentinel** at the edge of the world. Wind, D.
The **sentry.** Leskov, N. S.

SEOUL (KOREA) *See* Korea—Seoul
Seoul: winter 1964. Kim, S.-O.
Separate planes. Adams, A.
Separating. Updike, J.
Separation. Hull, H. R.
The **Sephardic** sisters. Russo, A.

SEPOY REBELLION *See* India—British occupation, 1765-1947
September. Killian, K.
September crickets. Campbell, E.
September in the rain. Dawson, F.
September morn. Garrett, G. P.
Septima, enchantress. Schwob, M.
A **sepulcher** of songs. Card, O. S.

Sepúlveda, Enid

Elba Nazario
Southwest tales; ed. by Alurista and X. Rojas-Urista
The **sequel** to a divorce. Maupassant, G. de
Sequel to love. Le Sueur, M.
Sequins. Kiser, R.
Ser Visal's tale. Donaldson, S. R.
Seraglio. Swift, G.
Seraglios and imbroglios. Durrell, L.
The **Seraph** and the Zambesi. Spark, M.
The **serene** revolution. Houbein, L.
Sergeant Carmichael. Bates, H. E.
Sergeant Houck. Schaefer, J. W.

SERGEANTS *See* Soldiers
A **serious** courtship. Houbein, L.
A **serious** talk. Carver, R.

Serling, Rod, 1924-1975
The changing of the guard
Young ghosts; ed. by I. Asimov; M. H. Greenberg and C. G. Waugh
The escape route
Rod Serling's Night gallery reader
Sermon on the rat. Taylor, P. E.
Serotta, Edward
The cabbie wore red
Road & Track 39:58-60 D '87
The **serrated** edge. Bryant, E.
Serros, Hugo Martínez- *See* Martínez-Serros, Hugo, 1930-
The **servant** of the last hour. Rizkalla, J.
SERVANTS
See also Black servants; also types of household employees
Barstow, S. Rue
Bates, H. E. The mill
Brooks, J. Doing the voices
Carver, R. Fat
Cary, J. A private ghost
Colter, C. A chance meeting
Faik, S. The bundle
Gilman, C. P. Turned
Huxley, A. Fard
Mathers, P. The master & servant act
Maupassant, G. de. The wooden shoes
Na, T.-H. The water-mill
Narayan, R. K. A snake in the grass
Nunes, N. Clastomina
Spark, M. Another pair of hands
Swan-Goodchild, A. Lucy
Taylor, P. H. Two ladies in retirement
Thompson, B. Tattoo
Weldon, F. Au pair
Wells, H. G. The jilting of Jane
Whelan, G. Playing with shadows
Whitaker, M. Pin's fee wife
Yi, K.-S. Halmôm
Service call. Dick, P. K.
Service for the burial of the dead. Willis, C.
A **service** of love. Henry, O.
SERVICE STATIONS *See* Automobiles— Service stations
Servitude. Ferron, J.
Set 'em up, Joe. Beman, B.
A **set** of variations on a borrowed theme. O'Connor, F.
Set off. Robison, J.
Sethi, Robbie Clipper
The bride wore red
Mademoiselle 93:154+ Ap '87
Cow tipping in the land of the truck farms
The Literary Review (Madison, N.J.) 31:221-9 Wint '88
Setouchi, Harumi
Pheasant
The Mother of dreams, and other short stories; ed. by M. Ueda
Settembrino's mother. Rand, P.

Settle, Mary Lee
The days of October
Gentlemen's Quarterly 58:253+ O '88
Settlement. McDonald, J.
The **settlement.** Powers, P. E.
The **settlement** of Mars. Busch, F.
A **settlement** of wages. Bonnie, F.
Settlers. Pearlman, E.
Settling the world. Harrison, M. J.
Seven American nights. Wolfe, G.
Seven and the stars. Haldeman, J. W.
Seven come heaven? Wnorowska, D.
The **seven** dreams and the reality of Perrine Blanc. Carpentier, A.
Seven floors. Buzzati, D.
The **seven** geases. Smith, C. A.
Seven moons. Kadohata, C.
Seven prophecies of Egypt. Freeman, C.
Seven stories. See Buzzati, D. Seven floors
Seven types of ambiguity. Jackson, S.
The **seven** who were hanged. Andreyev, L.
Seventeen syllables. Yamamoto, H.
The **seventh** day. Gurley, G. H.
The **seventh** horse. Carrington, L.
Seventh victim. Sheckley, R.
Several sweet ecstasies. Sheehan, R.
Several uses for the heart. Shaw, J. B.
Severance, Carol
Day of strange fortune
Magic in Ithkar 4; ed. by A. Norton and R. Adams
Isle of illusion
Tales of the Witch World [1]
SEVILLE (SPAIN) *See* Spain—Seville
The **sewing** machine. Ellenberger, D.
SEX
Abbott, K. Harum scarum
Abbott, K. Tell the truth
Amichai, Y. The orgy
Anthony, P. The bridge
Banks, C. A long, long time
Barker, C. Sex, death and starshine
Barthelme, F. Cut glass
Beasley, C. Blue oraciones
Bernard, K. The Maldive chronicles
Billington, R. One afternoon
Blaise, C. A North American education
Block, S. Leaving Sasha; or, The bed makes the man
Boyd, W. Histoire vache
Bradbury, R. Junior
Bradley, M. Z. The engine
Brondoli, M. Sixty-three questions
Brondoli, M. What do you think about three times a day?
Bumpus, J. Plenty of time
Camoin, F. A. La vida
Campbell, R. Dolls
Campbell, R. Loveman's comeback
Campbell, R. The other woman
Campbell, R. The seductress
Campbell, R. Stages
Campos-De Metro, J. And there was Bert

SEX—*Continued*

Caponegro, M. The Star Cafe
Cheever, J. The world of apples
Claiborne, S. Flotsam and Jetsam
Clark, G. Lunar frisson
Colette. One evening
Connelly, J. Teamwork
Conroy, F. Gossip
Coover, R. You must remember this
Cox, A. Twentieth frame
Crowell, D. Work
Curval, P. Progenitor
Dadswell, M. Lewd and lascivious conjugations
Davenport, G. Apples and pears: Het Erewhonisch schetsboek: Messidor-Vendémiaire 1981
Davenport, G. The bicycle rider
Davenport, G. The ringdove sign
DeGrazia, E. The enemy
Dixon, S. Milk is very good for you
Doubiago, S. The whore
Drake, R. Remember the Errol-mo!
Drewe, R. The view from the sandhills
Dubus, A. If they knew Yvonne
Eisenstein, S. The contortionist
Eisenstein, S. Post coitus tristus
Eldridge, M. Chanson d'automne
Elliott, L. T. Flint/steel sparks on tropic moon-night
Ellison, H. A boy and his dog
Ellison, H. Footsteps
Feyrer, G. The House of the Twin Jewels
Fitzgerald, M. J. A landscape with walls
Flanagan, M. A view of Manhattan
Ford, R. Children
Forrest, K. V. Xessex
Friedman, B. J. The tax man
Gardiner, J. R. Game farm
Gathorne-Hardy, J. The Infant Hercules
Gathorne-Hardy, J. Peiter and Paulina
Gébler, C. Puerto Vallarta
Gee, M. Buried treasure, old bones
Gold, H. The smallest part
Gordon, M. Safe
Gordon, M. Violation
Greene, G. Cheap in August
Greene, G. Doctor Crombie
Grenville, K. Blast off
Griffin, S. Cradles of light
Hammer, S. Strangers in the universe
Harris, M. The linguist
Healey, J. Flowers in January
Huggan, I. Getting out of Garten
Huggan, I. Sawdust
Jaffe, H. Pelican
Jahnn, H. H. The marmalade eaters
Janowitz, T. Kurt and Natasha, a relationship
Kalpakian, L. Fair Augusto
Katz, S. Mongolian Whiskey
Katz, S. Smooth
Kawabata, Y. Samurai descendant

Kelly, V. Berlioz & the ghetto blaster
Kilgore, D. The dietary exploits of Bessie
Klass, P. Cowboy time
Klass, P. Not a good girl
Klíma, I. Thursday morning: an erotic tale
Kotzwinkle, W. Jewel of the moon
Kranes, D. Cordials
Kriegel, M. H. Love letters
Kurahashi, Y. The monastery
Lee, C. One Florida night
London, J. Sister ships
Matthews, J. Five women
Mayes, S. S. Auto erotic
McCormack, E. P. A train of gardens—Part I: Ireneus Fludd
McElroy, C. J. A house full of Maude
Metzger, D. Blood oranges
Miller, S. The hunters
Minot, S. Lust
Mooney, M. Eros and crazy
Moskowitz, F. The runaround
Moyer, K. The compass of the heart
Moyer, K. Life jackets
Mukherjee, B. The middleman
Mukherjee, B. Nostalgia
Murphy, Y. Laws of nature
Murphy, Y. Rough seas
Nakagami, K. The immortal
Norris, K. Conversation
Oates, J. C. The mother
Oates, J. C. Where are you going, where have you been?
Parise, G. Sex
Petrakis, H. M. Song of songs
Petrakis, H. M. The sweet life
Pierce, C. A summer afternoon
Pintauro, J. Jungle dove
Poretz, D. Birthing
Power, U. The private life of Mrs. Herman
Purdy, J. Lily's party
Robb, J. Twilight fantasy
Rogers, T. N. R. Galb's elbow
Rosenfeld, I. Coney Island revisited
Rosenfeld, I. George
Rosenfeld, I. Wolfie
Royle, N. Irrelativity
Rucker, R. von B. Inside out
Salter, J. Foreign shores
Sams, F. Big Star woman
Sams, F. Porphyria's lover
Schwartz, J. Chloe Hummel of the Chicago White Sox
Shaham, N. The other side of the wall
Sheckley, R. The future lost
Sheckley, R. The future of sex: speculative journalism
Sheckley, R. The shaggy average American man story
Silver, R. Fearful symmetry
Silverberg, R. In the group
Silverberg, R. Push no more
Silvis, R. The luckiest man in the world

SEX—*Continued*
  Singer, I. B. The interview
  Sisskind, M. I'm stupid and my wife is
    stupid
  Sisskind, M. The Playboy Rabbit
  Smith, R. The Continental
  Sorrells, R. T. Lovers
  Starr, V. A Japanese play
  Stern, S. Aaron makes a match
  Stern, S. A sentimental journey
  Stern, S. The theft of Lily
  Summers, M. Ronnie so long at the fair
  Swados, H. Tease
  Texier, C. The fedora
  Thompson, J. Defoliation
  Tournier, M. The red dwarf
  Valenzuela, L. Other weapons
  Van Greenaway, P. The immortal coil
  Vega, A. L. Three love aerobics
  Villefranche, A.-M. The arrangements of
    Françoise Dumoutier
  Villefranche, A.-M. Christophe and the vir-
    gin
  Villefranche, A.-M. Dr. Faguet amuses
    himself
  Villefranche, A.-M. Ginette on the Metro
  Villefranche, A.-M. Guy's early retirement
  Villefranche, A.-M. The Italian cousin
  Villefranche, A.-M. A lesson for Bernard
  Villefranche, A.-M. Monique and Gérard
    discuss art
  Villefranche, A.-M. Nicole liberated
  Villefranche, A.-M. The self-esteem of
    Marcel Chalon
  Villefranche, A.-M. The solicitude of
    Pauline Devreux
  Viramontes, H. M. The long reconciliation
  Wagner, K. E. More sinned against
  Walker, A. Coming apart
  Watmough, D. False start
  Welch, D. Alex Fairburn
  Williams, T. The kingdom of earth
  Williams, T. The mattress by the tomato
    patch
  Wilner, H. Ward action
  Zabriskie, G. Games
  Zebrowski, G. Starcrossed
Sex. DeLynn, J.
Sex. Parise, G.
Sex, death and starshine. Barker, C.
Sex in Australia from the man's point of
    view. Wilding, M.
"Sex is my vengeance". Spillane, M.
Sex life of the sponge. Thompson, J.
SEX PROBLEMS
        See also Hermaphroditism; Im-
    potence; Incest; Marriage problems;
    Promiscuity; Sexual perversion; Trans-
    sexuals; Transvestism; Voyeurs
  Austin, D. A perfect crime
  Bace, K. M. Sterile relationships
  Brodkey, H. Innocence
  Keeling, N. Agathe

  Lessing, D. M. One off the short list
  Malzberg, B. N. Going down
  Raphael, F. Cheap day
  Tamer, Z. The face of the moon
  Thompson, J. Sex life of the sponge
  Tuohy, F. Two private lives
  Watmough, D. Connecticut countess
SEX ROLE
  Atwood, M. Simmering
  Blumlein, M. The brains of rats
  Carter, R. Mal and fem
  Chung, L.-H. Together through thick and
    thin
  Hull, H. R. Discovery
  Hull, H. R. The fusing
  Hull, H. R. Groping
  Hull, H. R. Last September
  Hull, H. R. Separation
  Jeppson, J. O. The Noodge Factor
  Kornblatt, J. R. Lila
  Lispector, C. The message
  Nordan, L. The all-girl football team
  Russ, J. Bodies
  Russ, J. The mystery of the young gen-
    tleman
  Sage, V. Nada
  Seepaul, L. A key for Dolcina
Sex story. Glück, R.
Sexson, Lynda
  The apocalypse of Mary the unbeliever
    Sexson, L. Margaret of the imperfections
  Chalk line
    Sexson, L. Margaret of the imperfections
  Deer crossing
    Sexson, L. Margaret of the imperfections
  Foxglove
    Sexson, L. Margaret of the imperfections
  Hope chest
    Sexson, L. Margaret of the imperfections
  Ice cream birth
    Sexson, L. Margaret of the imperfections
  Intestate and without issue
    Sexson, L. Margaret of the imperfections
  Margaret of the imperfections
    Sexson, L. Margaret of the imperfections
  Starlings, mute swans, a goose, an impos-
    sible angel, evening grosbeaks, an
    ostrich, some ducks, and a sparrow
    Sexson, L. Margaret of the imperfections
  Turning
    Sudden fiction; ed. by R. Shapard and
      J. Thomas
  When the pie was opened
    Sexson, L. Margaret of the imperfections
SEXTONS
  Dickens, C. The story of the goblins who
    stole a sexton
  Granit, A. With a herring in one hand
    and a bottle of schnapps in the other;
    oh! how he did dance!
SEXUAL INSTINCT
  Bird, C. One with the lot

SEXUAL INSTINCT—*Continued*
Böll, H. In the Valley of the Thundering Hoofs
Boyd, W. Hardly ever
Calvino, I. Adam, one afternoon
Calvino, I. The adventure of a soldier
Cowan, P. A window in Mrs X's place
Durban, P. World of women
Eldridge, M. Candlebark
Fox, J. The superhero
Franklin, P. Splendor and black wool
Franklin, P. Stale beer and roses
Gooch, B. Spring
Harington, D. Beginning
Henley, P. Picking time
Hori, T. Les joues en feu
Huggan, I. Queen Esther
Jordan, N. Night in Tunisia
Marshall, D. R. Lavender blue
McGarvey, C. Sense of wonder, sense of awe
Miller, S. The birds and the bees
Miller, S. Tyler and Brina
Miller, S. What Ernest says
Morris, M. Alewives
Redding, S. Tin of Tube Rose
Regent, P. Pleasures of the flesh
Russ, J. Old thoughts, old presences: Daddy's girl
Schulman, H. Like sisters
Schwartz, L. S. The sunfish and the mermaid
Schwartz, S. Slow-motion
Silvis, R. A walk in the moonlight
Spark, D. Summer of the Dead Frogs
Stewart, J. I. M. André
Tamer, Z. Death of the jasmine
Tamer, Z. A lone woman
Tamer, Z. Room with two beds
Welch, D. The barn
Yates, R. A compassionate leave
Ziem, J. Statement
SEXUAL PERVERSION
Austin, D. She fell asleep sunbathing on the grass outside her apartment building
Bernard, K. Dirty old man
Bloch, R. A toy for Juliette
Camoin, F. A. Cheerful wisdom
Campbell, R. Lilith's
Ekström, M. When we are home alone we dance all around the house
Federspiel, J. The Turk
Jackson, G. Pyjamas
Kennedy, L. Her furry face
Landolfi, T. A woman's breast
Mishima, Y. Three million yen
Moravia, A. The sign of the operation
Tournier, M. The fetishist
SEXUALLY TRANSMITTED DISEASES
Boyd, W. Next boat from Douala
MacLaverty, B. Between two shores
Silverberg, R. The trouble with Sempoanga

Swados, H. The letters
Shaara, Michael, 1929-1988
2066: Election Day
Election Day 2084; ed. by I. Asimov and M. H. Greenberg
Machines that think; ed. by I. Asimov; P. S. Warrick and M. H. Greenberg
Shabbas. Botwinik, B.
Shabbas morning. Botwinik, B.
Shabby lodgings. Anderman, J.
Shacochis, Bob
Dead reckoning
Look who's talking; ed. by B. Weber
Shacochis, B. Easy in the islands
Easy in the islands
The Editors' choice v3; ed. by G. E. Murphy, Jr.
Shacochis, B. Easy in the islands
The heart's advantage
Shacochis, B. Easy in the islands
Hidalgos
Harper's 276:54-60+ My '88
Hot day on the Gold Coast
The Pushcart prize X
Shacochis, B. Easy in the islands
Hunger
Missouri short fiction; ed. by C. Beasley
Shacochis, B. Easy in the islands
I ate her heart
The New generation; ed. by A. Kaufman
Lord Short Shoe wants the monkey
Shacochis, B. Easy in the islands
Mundo's sign
Shacochis, B. Easy in the islands
The pelican
Shacochis, B. Easy in the islands
Redemption songs
The Editors' choice: new American stories v2
Esquire 101:236-43+ Mr '84
The Esquire fiction reader v1
Shacochis, B. Easy in the islands
Where Pelham fell
Esquire 105:104-6+ Ja '86
New stories from the South: the year's best, 1987
Soldiers & civilians; ed. by T. Jenks
Shades. Shepard, L.
SHADES AND SHADOWS
Apollinaire, G. The departure of the shadow
Shadow. Cowan, P.
Shadow. Han, M.-S.
The **shadow.** Nowakowski, M.
Shadow—a parable. Poe, E. A.
Shadow bands. Schinto, J.
The **shadow** behind the face. Godfrey, P.
The **shadow** falls. Johnston, H.
The **shadow** from the steeple. Bloch, R.
The **shadow** hart. Miesel, S.
The **shadow** in the corner. Braddon, M. E.
The **shadow** of a bear. Wheatcroft, J.
The **shadow** of a hawk. Hoffman, N. K.

The **shadow** of an arm. Phillips, T. H.
The **shadow** of space. Farmer, P. J.
The **shadow** of the shark. Chesterton, G. K.
Shadow on the stars. Budrys, A.
The **shadow** on the wall. Hartley, L. P.
The **shadow** out of time. Lovecraft, H. P.
The **shadow** over Innsmouth. Lovecraft, H.
     P.
Shadow quest. Linaweaver, B.
Shadow, shadow on the wall. Sturgeon, T.
The **shadow** watchers. Baldwin, D.
Shadows. Boyd, S.
Shadows move in the Britannia Bar. Khan,
     I.
The **shadows** of evening. Zahn, T.
The **shadows** of the living. Blythe, R.
Shadows on the cave wall. Kress, N.
The **shadows** on the lawn: an adventure of
     Sherlock Holmes. Jones, B.
The **shadowy** third. Glasgow, E.
The **shaggy** average American man story.
     Sheckley, R.
A **shaggy** love story. Beattie, A.
Shaham, Nathan
  The other side of the wall
     Shaham, N. The other side of the wall
  S/S Cairo City
     Shaham, N. The other side of the wall
  The salt of the earth
     Shaham, N. The other side of the wall
Shaik, Fatima, 1952-
  Before echo
     Shaik, F. The mayor of New Orleans
  Charity begins at home
     The Southern Review (Baton Rouge, La.)
     23:935-49 Aut '87
  Climbing Monkey Hill
     Shaik, F. The mayor of New Orleans
  The mayor of New Orleans; just talking
     jazz
     Shaik, F. The mayor of New Orleans
Shaikh, Ahmed al *See* Al Shaikh, Ahmed
SHAKESPEARE, WILLIAM, 1564-1616
                    About
Asimov, I. The Immortal Bard
Borges, J. L. Shakespeare's memory
De la Torre, L. The missing Shakespeare
     manuscript
Lear, A. The adventure of the global
     traveler
Michaelson, L. W. Me and Will
                   Hamlet
Symons, J. Credit to Shakespeare
           A midsummer night's dream
Carter, A. Overture and incidental music
     for A midsummer night's dream
                   Othello
Epstein, L. Music of the spheres
Innes, M. Tragedy of a handkerchief
          Parodies, travesties, etc.
Malzberg, B. N. Chained
Schweitzer, D. Caliban's revenge
The **Shakespeare** man. Petroski, C.

Shakespeare's memory. Borges, J. L.
Shalamov, Varlam Tikhonovich
  Condensed milk
     Inspired by drink; ed. by Joan Digby
        and John Digby
Shallash, Salma
  The other face
     Egyptian tales and short stories of the
        1970s and 1980s
The **shaman** flute. Lewitt, S.
Shambleau. Moore, C. L.
Shame. Bumpus, J.
Shame. Crane, S.
A **shame**. Gault, C.
Shamosh, Amnon
  Bells
     Short story international 52
  Lily, Africa and I
     Short story international 68
  My sister the bride
     Short story international 54
  A nature reserve
     Short story international 66
  Trip
     Short story international 58
Shamrock Road. McDaniel, W. E.
Shamsky and other casualties. Cohen, R.
Shan. Reed, K.
Shan-fei, communist. Smedley, A.
Shan Val Mór. Virgo, S.
Shange, Ntožake
  Christmas for Sassafrass, Cypress & Indigo
     "May your days be merry and bright"
        and other Christmas stories by wom-
        en; ed. by S. Koppelman
  Sassafrass, Cypress & Indigo [excerpt]
     Buying time; ed. by S. Walker
SHANGHAI (CHINA) *See* China—Shanghai
Shanidar. Zindell, D.
Shannon, Beth Tashery
  Asilomarian lecture (The dirmal life of the
     inhabitats)
     The Pushcart prize IX
Shannon, Dell, 1921-
  Accident
     Shannon, D. Murder by the tale
  The bronze cat
     Shannon, D. Murder by the tale
  The cat
     Shannon, D. Murder by the tale
  The clue
     Shannon, D. Murder by the tale
  Conundrum
     Shannon, D. Murder by the tale
  Flash attachment
     Shannon, D. Murder by the tale
  Happy release
     Shannon, D. Murder by the tale
  The long chance
     Shannon, D. Murder by the tale
  The motive
     Shannon, D. Murder by the tale

Shannon, Dell, 1921-—_Continued_
Need-fire
Shannon, D. Murder by the tale
Novelties
Shannon, D. Murder by the tale
The practical joke
Shannon, D. Murder by the tale
Rannysore
Shannon, D. Murder by the tale
The ring
Shannon, D. Murder by the tale
They will call it insane
Shannon, D. Murder by the tale
Shannon, Jacqueline
The adventures of Strike-out Stratton
'Teen 29:18+ Ap '85
Christmas in the aisles
'Teen 28:26+ D '84
December roses
'Teen 30:40+ D '86
Surprise in disguise
'Teen 28:32 O '84
Valentine rhymes!
'Teen 30:24+ F '86
Shanti, simple, sweet and—sinister! Dullas,
I.
Shapard, Robert, 1942-
Tamazanchale
The Literary Review (Madison, N.J.)
31:186-7 Wint '88
Shapcott, Thomas W.
Telephones
Home and away; ed. by R. Creswell
Shape. Sheckley, R.
Shapes to come. Wellen, E.
Shapiro, Gerald
Openings
The Kenyon Review ns10:1-16 Spr '88
Shapiro, Jane
Down in Florida
The New Yorker 63:35-40 F 8 '88
Volpone
The New Yorker 63:37-43 N 30 '87
Sharat Chandra, G. S.
Bhat's return
Missouri short fiction; ed. by C. Beasley
Short story international 61
The holy wristwatch
Short story international 47
Iyer's Hotel
Short story international 65
Maya
Short story international 55
Saree of the gods
On being foreign; ed. by T. J. Lewis and
R. E. Jungman
SHARECROPPERS _See_ Tenant farming
Sharif, M. T.
The butcher sultan and the musical
brothers
The Antioch Review 46:89-101 Wint '88
The **sharing** of bread. Lispector, C.
Shark. Ferreira, R.

Shark logic. Drewe, R.
SHARKS
Dubus, A. Blessings
Ferreira, R. Shark
Misitano, R. A. Deep water
Vogan, S. Hearts of a shark
Sharman, Jack
Seance
The Southern Review (Baton Rouge, La.)
20:701-9 Jl '84
Secession chapter
The Southern Review (Baton Rouge, La.)
23:449-70 Spr '87
Sharouni, Yusuf
Glimpses from the life of Maugoud Abdul
Maugoud and two postscripts
Arabic short stories; tr. by D. Johnson-
Davies
Sharp, Margery, 1905-
The perfect model
Ellery Queen's Memorable characters
SHARPSHOOTERS
DeGrazia, E. The sniper
Nolan, W. F. A real nice guy
Sharpshooting. Oates, J. C.
Sharuni, Ya'qub al _See_ Al Sharuni, Ya'qub
Shasha and the pigeons. Jia Pingwa
Shattering. McLaughlin, L.
SHAVING
García Márquez, G. Dialogue with the
mirror
Shaving. Norris, L.
Shaw, Bob
Dream fighter
The Science fictional Olympics; ed. by
I. Asimov; M. H. Greenberg and C.
G. Waugh
Light of other days
Robert Silverberg's Worlds of wonder
Skirmish on a summer morning
Time wars; ed. by C. Waugh and M.
H. Greenberg
Small world
The Penguin world omnibus of science
fiction
Shaw, Dave
Rain
The Massachusetts Review 28:313-24
Summ '87
Shaw, Felicity _See_ Morice, Anne
Shaw, Helen
The gipsies
Women's work; ed. by M. McLeod and
L. Wevers
Shaw, Irwin, 1913-1984
Act of faith
A Treasury of World War II stories; ed.
by B. Pronzini and M. H. Greenberg
The eighty-yard run
The Norton book of American short
stories
The inhabitants of Venus
Short story international 56

Shaw, Irwin, 1913-1984—*Continued*
  The man who married a French wife
    Short story international 63
  Medal from Jerusalem
    The World of the short story; ed. by
      C. Fadiman
  Peter Two
    Ready or not; ed. by J. Kahn
  Then we were three
    Short story international 48
Shaw, Janet Beeler, 1937-
  The cat who fought the rain
    Shaw, J. B. Some of the things I did
      not do
  The courtship of the thin girl
    Shaw, J. B. Some of the things I did
      not do
  The geese at Presque Isle
    Shaw, J. B. Some of the things I did
      not do
  Heading home
    McCall's 111:104-5+ S '84
  Honeymoon
    McCall's 112:102-3+ My '85
  In high country
    Family: stories from the interior; ed. by
      G. G. Chavis
    Shaw, J. B. Some of the things I did
      not do
  Inventing the kiss
    Shaw, J. B. Some of the things I did
      not do
  Love and other lessons
    Shaw, J. B. Some of the things I did
      not do
  A new life
    The Editors' choice: new American
      stories v1
    Prime number; ed. by A. L. Weir
    Shaw, J. B. Some of the things I did
      not do
  On the river road
    Stiller's pond; ed. by J. Agee; R. Blakely
      and S. Welch
  Playing with fire
    Redbook 165:58+ Jl '85
  Saturday night in Pinedale, Wyoming
    Shaw, J. B. Some of the things I did
      not do
  Several uses for the heart
    The Sewanee Review 94:27-44 Wint '86
  Some of the things I did not do
    Shaw, J. B. Some of the things I did
      not do
  The trail to the ledge
    Family: stories from the interior; ed. by
      G. G. Chavis
    Shaw, J. B. Some of the things I did
      not do
  What his wife knew
    Redbook 168:50+ D '86
The **shawl**. Ozick, C.
Shawm of the stars. Speer, H.

SHAWNA, Ltd. Longyear, B. B.
Shawno. Dennison, G.
Shayib, Fu'ad al- *See* Al-Shayib, Fu'ad
Shaykh, Hanan al- *See* Al-Shaykh, Hanan
Shazam. Heise, K.
She didn't come home. Grafton, S.
She dreams of Johnny. McInerney, J.
She fell asleep sunbathing on the grass out-
  side her apartment building. Austin,
  D.
She hears, falling, the seed. Thomas, M.
She keeps the dance turning like the earth.
  Niatum, D.
She knew what she wanted. McDermott, A.
She never knew what hit her. McMillan, F.
She sang only on Sundays. Roy, J.
She should have died hereafter. Hochstein,
  R.
She sits on the bridge. Tapahonso, L.
She unnames them. Le Guin, U. K.
She wanted strawberries and love. Krueger,
  R. M.
Shea, John
  A down-and-out disciple meets his match
    U.S. Catholic 52:27-9 Ap '87
Shea, Michael, 1946-
  The Angel of Death
    Shea, M. Polyphemus
  The autopsy
    The Best horror stories from the
      Magazine of fantasy and science fiction
    The Dark descent; ed. by D. G. Hart-
      well
    Shea, M. Polyphemus
  The extra
    Shea, M. Polyphemus
  Fat Face
    The Year's best fantasy, first annual
      collection
  The horror on the #33
    Shea, M. Polyphemus
  The pearls of the vampire queen
    Shea, M. Polyphemus
  Polyphemus
    Shea, M. Polyphemus
  Uncle Tuggs
    Shea, M. Polyphemus
The **shearing** of Samson. Petrakis, H. M.
SHEBA, QUEEN OF
                    About
  Russell, B. The Queen of Sheba's night-
    mare
Sheckley, Jay
  Bargain cinema
    Silver scream; ed. by D. J. Schow
  Lost soul
    Devils & demons; ed. by M. Kaye and
      S. Kaye
Sheckley, Robert, 1928-
  The accountant
    Sheckley, R. Is that what people do?
  All the things you are
    Sheckley, R. Is that what people do?

Sheckley, Robert, 1928---*Continued*

The battle
Sheckley, R. Is that what people do?
Beside still waters
Sheckley, R. Is that what people do?
Can you feel anything when I do this?
Sheckley, R. Is that what people do?
Cordle to onion to carrot
Sheckley, R. Is that what people do?
Cost of living
The Penguin world omnibus of science
fiction
The demons
Devils & demons; ed. by M. Kaye and
S. Kaye
Fear in the night
Sheckley, R. Is that what people do?
Fishing season
Sheckley, R. Is that what people do?
Five minutes early
Sheckley, R. Is that what people do?
Fool's mate
Sheckley, R. Is that what people do?
The future lost
Sheckley, R. Is that what people do?
The future of sex: speculative journalism
Sheckley, R. Is that what people do?
Good-bye forever to Mr. Pain
Sheckley, R. Is that what people do?
The helping hand
Sheckley, R. Is that what people do?
Is that what people do?
Sheckley, R. Is that what people do?
The language of love
Sheckley, R. Is that what people do?
The last days of (parallel?) Earth
Sheckley, R. Is that what people do?
The life of anybody
Sheckley, R. Is that what people do?
Meanwhile, back at the bromide
Sheckley, R. Is that what people do?
Miss Mouse and the fourth dimension
Mathenauts: tales of mathematical won-
der; ed. by R. Rucker
Sheckley, R. Is that what people do?
The mnemone
Sheckley, R. Is that what people do?
The monsters
Robert Silverberg's Worlds of wonder
Sheckley, R. Is that what people do?
The native problem
Sheckley, R. Is that what people do?
The people trap
The Science fictional Olympics; ed. by
I. Asimov; M. H. Greenberg and C.
G. Waugh
The perfect woman
Amazing stories: 60 years of the best
science fiction
The petrified world
Sheckley, R. Is that what people do?
Pilgrimage to Earth
Sheckley, R. Is that what people do?

The prize of peril
Sheckley, R. Is that what people do?
Restricted area
Amazing science fiction anthology: The
wild years, 1946-1955; ed. by M. H.
Greenberg
The robot who looked like me
Sheckley, R. Is that what people do?
Robotgnomics
Omni (New York, N.Y.) 7:112-14+ D '84
Robotvendor Rex
Omni (New York, N.Y.) 8:62-4+ F '86
Seventh victim
Sheckley, R. Is that what people do?
The shaggy average American man story
Sheckley, R. Is that what people do?
Shape
Sheckley, R. Is that what people do?
Shootout in the toy shop
Sheckley, R. Is that what people do?
Silversmith wishes
Sheckley, R. Is that what people do?
The Skag Castle
Sheckley, R. Is that what people do?
The store of the worlds
Beyond Armageddon; ed. by W. M. Mil-
ler and M. H. Greenberg
Sheckley, R. Is that what people do?
The swamp
Sheckley, R. Is that what people do?
Warm
Sheckley, R. Is that what people do?
Wild Talents, Inc.
Sheckley, R. Is that what people do?
A wind is rising
Sheckley, R. Is that what people do?
The **shed**. Jolley, E.
Shed of grace. Pritchard, M.
Sheehan, Ronan, 1953-
The ark
Sheehan, R. Boy with an injured eye
Boy with an injured eye
Sheehan, R. Boy with an injured eye
The death of Petronius
Sheehan, R. Boy with an injured eye
Every angel is terrible
Sheehan, R. Boy with an injured eye
Masks
Sheehan, R. Boy with an injured eye
Optics
Sheehan, R. Boy with an injured eye
The sack
Sheehan, R. Boy with an injured eye
Several sweet ecstasies
Sheehan, R. Boy with an injured eye
Telescope
Sheehan, R. Boy with an injured eye
Universitas
Sheehan, R. Boy with an injured eye
Sheema's journey. Hamilton, V.
SHEEP
Bernen, R. The extra wether
Earle, A. M. The witch sheep

Sheep. Jaffe, H.
Sheep. Tamer, Z.
SHEEP FARMING *See* Sheep
Sheep in the meadow. Ignatow, R. G.
Sheer Energy. Bedard, B.
The sheeted dead. Grant, C. L.
Sheets. Brashler, A.
Sheets. Ryan, A.
Sheffield, Anne
Strawberry moon
The Massachusetts Review 26:571-6 Wint
'85
Sheffield, Charles
Dies irae
The Planets; ed. by B. Preiss
Skystalk
Great science fiction; ed. by I. Asimov;
M. H. Greenberg and C. G. Waugh
Shefner, Evelyn, 1919-
The common body
Shefner, E. Common body, royal bones
Royal bones
Shefner, E. Common body, royal bones
Troubles of a tattooed king
Shefner, E. Common body, royal bones
Sheil, Graham
Dogs, in Denpasar
Short story international 43
Mad like Lasseter
Short story international 51
Mister Al
Short story international 66
Of gumleaves and clove-scented cigarettes
Short story international 42
The picking season
Short story international 58
Sheiner, Robin
Brass on the cannons
Room to move; ed. by S. Falkiner
Sheldon, Alice Hastings Bradley *See* Tiptree,
James, 1916-1987
Sheldon, Raccoona, 1916-1987
See also Tiptree, James, 1916-1987
Shelf life. Loeser, K.
The shell. Humphrey, W.
Shell game. Pronzini, B.
Shellers. Thomas, M.
Shelley, Mary Wollstonecraft, 1797-1851
The last man
Witches' brew; ed. by M. Muller and
B. Pronzini
The mortal immortal
The Book of the dead; ed. by A. K.
Russell
The transformation
Masterpieces of terror and the super-
natural; ed. by M. Kaye and S. Kaye
Shelley, Rick
At the flood
Universe 16
SHELLS
Lurie, M. The larder
The shells of Horace. Auchincloss, L.

Shelnutt, Eve, 1943-
Angel
Stories of the modern South; ed. by B.
Forkner and P. Samway
The pilot-messenger
The Ploughshares reader: new fiction for
the eighties
Voice
New stories from the South: the year's
best, 1988
The shelter. Fink, I.
The shelter. Narayan, R. K.
Shelter. Oates, J. C.
Shen, Chi-chi
Miss Jen [Variant title: The fox fairy]
Tales of the supernatural; ed. by H. C.
Chang
Shen Rong
A freakish girl
The Antioch Review 46:166-9 Spr '88
Regarding the problem of new-born pigs
in winter
The Literary Review (Madison, N.J.)
27:346-56 Spr '84
Troubled Sunday
Contemporary Chinese literature; ed. by
M. S. Duke
Shepard, Jim
Atomic tourism
The Atlantic 256:80-3 S '85
Reach for the sky
The New Yorker 63:28-9 S 7 '87
Who we are, what we're doing
Southwest Review 73:398-9 Summ '88
Shepard, Lucius
Aymara
Terry Carr's Best science fiction and fan-
tasy of the year #16
Black coral
Shepard, L. The jaguar hunter
Universe 14
The Year's best science fiction, second
annual collection
Delta sly honey
In the field of fire; ed. by J. Van B.
Dann and J. Dann
The Year's best fantasy, first annual
collection
The end of life as we know it
Shepard, L. The jaguar hunter
The etheric transmitter
The Clarion awards; ed. by D. Knight
How the wind spoke at Madaket
The Mammoth book of short horror
novels; ed. by M. Ashley
Shepard, L. The jaguar hunter
Jack's decline
Ripper! Ed. by G. Dozois and S. Casper
The jaguar hunter
Shepard, L. The jaguar hunter
The Year's best science fiction, third an-
nual collection

Shepard, Lucius—*Continued*
Life of Buddha
  Omni (New York, N.Y.) 10:52-4+ My '88
The man who painted the dragon Griaule
  Nebula awards 20
  Shepard, L. The jaguar hunter
Mengele
  Shepard, L. The jaguar hunter
  Universe 15
The night of White Bhairab
  The Best horror stories from the
    Magazine of fantasy and science fiction
  Shepard, L. The jaguar hunter
Pictures made of stones
  Omni (New York, N.Y.) 9:68-70+ S '87
  The Year's best fantasy, first annual
    collection
R&r
  Nebula awards 22
  Shepard, L. The jaguar hunter
  The Year's best science fiction, fourth
    annual collection
Salvador
  Beyond Armageddon; ed. by W. M. Mil-
    ler and M. H. Greenberg
  Shepard, L. The jaguar hunter
  The Year's best science fiction, second
    annual collection
Shades
  In the field of fire; ed. by J. Van B.
    Dann and J. Dann
  The Year's best science fiction, fifth an-
    nual collection
A Spanish lesson
  Shepard, L. The jaguar hunter
  The Year's best science fiction, third an-
    nual collection
A traveler's tale
  Shepard, L. The jaguar hunter
Voyage South from Thousand Willows
  Universe 16
Youthful folly
  Omni (New York, N.Y.) 11:105-11 N '88
The **shepherd** on the roof. Jolley, E.
SHEPHERDS
  Austin, M. H. The last antelope
  Berger, J. Boris is buying horses
  Bernen, R. Brock
  Bernen, R. Fox
  Bernen, R. A keen observer of footwear
  Brown, G. M. King and shepherd
  Calvino, I. A goatherd at luncheon
  Chavez, A. The black ewe
  Faik, S. Jealousy
  Henry, O. The hiding of Black Bill
  Henry, O. Roads of destiny
  Maupassant, G. de. La Morillonne
  Oz, A. Nomad and viper
  Regent, P. At Manoli's sheepfold
  Shamosh, A. Bells
Shepperson, Janet
The sound of the river
  Critical Quarterly 30:20-6 Aut '88

Sher, Jack, 1913-1988
Memo on Kathy O'Rourke
  The Saturday Evening Post 258:46-9+ Ap
    '86
  The Saturday Evening Post 259:68-70+
    My/Je '86
Sheridan, Jennifer K.
'Teen talkout!: hidden secrets
  'Teen 30:37 Ja '86
The **sheriff** of Gullmore. Post, M. D.
The **sheriff** of Kona. London, J.
SHERIFFS
  Andrews, R. Appalachee Red [excerpt]
  Benjamin, D. Things will look brighter in
    the morning
  Brand, M. The laughter of Slim Malone
  Carlson, R. Phenomena
  Clark, N. M. No fish for the cat
  Crane, S. The bride comes to Yellow Sky
  Crane, S. In a Park Row restaurant
  Daniels, C. Chatham County
  Ellison, H. The end of the time of Leinard
  Garrett, G. P. Noise of strangers
  Hoch, E. D. Winter run
  Kelley, L. P. Jurisprudence
  Kittredge, W. The soap bear
  London, J. The sheriff of Kona
  Long, D. The flood of '64
  Overholser, W. D. Debt cancelled
  Overholser, W. D. High-grade
  Penfold, N. Death on Goose Hill
  Post, M. D. The sheriff of Gullmore
  Pronzini, B. Changes
  Waldrop, H. Night of the cooters
Sherlock Holmes and the muffin. Hughes,
  D. B. F.
Sherlock Holmes and "The woman": an ex-
  planatory memoir by Dr. John H.
  Watson, MD. Harrison, M.
Sherman, C. H.
Tapestry
  Devils & demons; ed. by M. Kaye and
    S. Kaye
Sherman, Charlotte Watson
Glory
  When I am an old woman I shall wear
    purple; ed. by S. K. Martz
Sherman, Delia
The maid on the shore
  The Year's best fantasy, first annual
    collection
Sherman was right. Fuller, R. G.
Sherwin, Jane
The perilous flight of Henry O'Grady
  McCall's 114:102-4 Ag '87
Shi, Mo *See* Zhao Zhenkai
Shi Tiesheng
Blacky
  Contemporary Chinese literature; ed. by
    M. S. Duke
Lunch break
  Contemporary Chinese literature; ed. by
    M. S. Duke

Shi Tiesheng—*Continued*
One winter's evening
   Contemporary Chinese literature; ed. by
   M. S. Duke
Shiarella, Robert
(jt. auth) See Kotzwinkle, William, and
   Shiarella, Robert
Shibaki, Yoshiko, 1914-
Ripples
   Short story international 71
   The Shōwa anthology 2
Shibusawa, Tatsuhiko
Fish scales
   The Literary Review (Madison, N.J.)
   30:245-56 Wint '87
Shiel, Matthew Phipps, 1865-1947
The house of sounds
   Dark banquet; ed. by L. Child
Shields, Carol
Family secrets
   The Old dance; ed. by B. Burnard
Shields, Ralston
Mistress of the blood-drinkers
   The Weirds; ed. by S. Jaffery
Shifting seas. Weinbaum, S. G.
Shifts. Meredith, C.
Shiga, Naoya, 1883-1971
Akanishi Kakita
   Shiga, Naoya. The paper door, and other
   stories
As far as Abashiri
   Shiga, Naoya. The paper door, and other
   stories
At Kinosaki
   A Late chrysanthemum; tr. by L. Dun-
   lop
   Shiga, Naoya. The paper door, and other
   stories
A gray moon
   A Late chrysanthemum; tr. by L. Dun-
   lop
   Shiga, Naoya. The paper door, and other
   stories
Han's crime [Variant title: The death of
   the knife-thrower's wife]
   Murder in Japan; ed. by J. L. Apostolou
   and M. H. Greenberg
   Shiga, Naoya. The paper door, and other
   stories
The house by the moat
   The Literary Review (Madison, N.J.)
   29:347-52 Spr '86
   Shiga, Naoya. The paper door, and other
   stories
An incident [Variant title: An accident]
   Shiga, Naoya. The paper door, and other
   stories
Incident on the afternoon of November
   third
   Shiga, Naoya. The paper door, and other
   stories

Infatuation
   A Late chrysanthemum; tr. by L. Dun-
   lop
   Shiga, Naoya. The paper door, and other
   stories
Kuniko
   Shiga, Naoya. The paper door, and other
   stories
The little girl and the rapeseed flower
   Shiga, Naoya. The paper door, and other
   stories
A memory of Yamashina
   Shiga, Naoya. The paper door, and other
   stories
The paper door
   Shiga, Naoya. The paper door, and other
   stories
Rain frogs
   Shiga, Naoya. The paper door, and other
   stories
The razor
   A Late chrysanthemum; tr. by L. Dun-
   lop
   Murder in Japan; ed. by J. L. Apostolou
   and M. H. Greenberg
   Shiga, Naoya. The paper door, and other
   stories
Seibei and his gourds
   Shiga, Naoya. The paper door, and other
   stories
The shopboy's god
   Shiga, Naoya. The paper door, and other
   stories
The **shill.** Marlowe, S.
Shiloh. Foote, S.
Shiloh. Mason, B. A.
Shimaki, Kensaku
The black cat
   A Late chrysanthemum; tr. by L. Dun-
   lop
The centipede
   A Late chrysanthemum; tr. by L. Dun-
   lop
The red frog
   A Late chrysanthemum; tr. by L. Dun-
   lop
The wasps
   A Late chrysanthemum; tr. by L. Dun-
   lop
Shimao, Toshio, 1917-
With Maya
   The Shōwa anthology 1
Shimizu, Ikkō
Love and the branch manager
   Harper's 272:27-8 Je '86
Shimmele fly-by-night. Stern, S.
Shine on. Pfeil, F.
Shiner, Edith
(jt. auth) See Shiner, Lewis, and Shiner,
   Edith
Shiner, Lewis
Deserted cities of the heart
   Omni (New York, N.Y.) 6:68-70+ F '84

Shiner, Lewis—*Continued*
Jeff Beck
The Year's best science fiction, fourth annual collection
Love in vain
Ripper! Ed. by G. Dozois and S. Casper
Rebels
Omni (New York, N.Y.) 10:64-6+ N '87
Till human voices wake us
Mirrorshades; ed. by B. Sterling
Twilight time
The Year's best science fiction, second annual collection
The war at home
In the field of fire; ed. by J. Van B. Dann and J. Dann
The Year's best science fiction, third annual collection
(jt. auth) See Sterling, Bruce, and Shiner, Lewis
Shiner, Lewis, and Shiner, Edith
Things that go quack in the night
Tales from Isaac Asimov's science fiction magazine: short stories for young adults
Shining. Mazel, D.
Shining path. Morris, M.
A **ship**. Faik, S.
The **ship** ahoy. Le Guin, U. K.
SHIP CAPTAINS *See* Shipmasters
A **ship** loaded with crabs. Calvino, I.
Ship-sister, star-sister. Silverberg, R.
The **ship** that saw a ghost. Norris, F.
SHIPMASTERS
Brown, G. M. Andrina
Brown, G. M. Michael Surfax, whaler
Bullen, F. T. The debt of the whale
Conrad, J. The secret sharer
Conrad, J. Typhoon
Drake, B. Putting a black-leg on shore
Helprin, M. Letters from the Samantha
Hyne, C. J. C. The liner and the iceberg
Jahnn, H. H. Mov
Jewett, S. O. All my sad captains
London, J. The Ghost loses her seal-hunting boats
Lovecraft, H. P. The Terrible Old Man
Maupassant, G. de. Selfishness
Melville, H. The chase
Reade, C. Agra outwits two pirate ships
Roberts, M. The ingenuity of Captain Spink
Severance, C. Day of strange fortune
Sherman, D. The maid on the shore
Twain, M. Captain Stormfield's visit to heaven
Valenzuela, L. One siren or another
Watson, I. To the Pump Room with Jane
Wilson, E. From Flores
Shippey, Tom
Enemy transmissions
Hitler victorious; ed. by G. Benford and M. H. Greenberg

SHIPPING
See also Panama Canal
Bates, H. E. Summer in Salandar
SHIPS
See also Shipping; Steamboats; Submarines
Bioy Casares, A. The first class passenger
Crane, S. Stephen Crane's own story
Dinesen, I. From 'Peter and Rosa'
Faik, S. A ship
Faik, S. The Stelyanos Hrisopulos
Fitzgerald, F. S. The rough crossing
Gaitens, E. Growing up
Gallico, P. Jennie's lessons to Peter on how to behave like a cat
Highsmith, P. The dream of the Emma C
Jacobs, W. W. A black affair
Mansfield, K. The voyage
Sturgeon, T. Cargo
Thomas, J. Paco and I at sea
Twain, M. About all kinds of ships
Wheatcroft, J. Kamikaze
Officers
See Shipmasters
Ships in Liss. Grin, A.
SHIPWRECKS AND CASTAWAYS
See also Survival (after airplane accidents, shipwrecks, etc.)
Anderson, P. Eve times four
Barker, C. Scape-goats
Cranch, C. P. The last of the Huggermuggers: a giant story
Crane, S. Flanagan and his short filibustering adventure
Crane, S. The open boat
Crane, S. Stephen Crane's own story
Defoe, D. Crusoe visits the wreck
Dickens, C. The wreck of the Golden Mary
Doyle, Sir A. C. Touch and go: a midshipman's story
García Márquez, G. The last voyage of the ghost ship
Grin, A. The death of Romelink
Harrison, H. After the storm
Hemingway, E. After the storm
Hoch, E. D. The maze and the monster
Hodgson, W. H. The voice in the night
Hulme, K. Unnamed islands in the unknown sea
Hyne, C. J. C. The liner and the iceberg
Kipling, R. The devil and the deep sea
Kipling, R. The wreck of the Visigoth
Longyear, B. B. Adagio
MacLean, A. The Dileas
Masefield, J. Davy Jones's gift
Matthews, J. The tour of the sleeping steamboat
Poe, E. A. The incredible survival
Poe, E. A. Ms. found in a bottle
Quiller-Couch, Sir A. T. The roll-call of the reef

SHIPWRECKS AND CASTAWAYS—*Continued*
  Rodoreda, M. My Christina
  Ross, R. T. The craft of death
  Smith, C. A. The uncharted isle
  Stevenson, R. L. The merry men
  Stockton, F. The landsman's tale
  Sturges, A. E. Only a matter of time
  Wetjen, A. R. Duty
  Wilson, E. From Flores
Shirley, John, 1953-
  Freezone
    Mirrorshades; ed. by B. Sterling
  Triggering
    Omni book of science fiction 2
  What Cindy saw
    Interzone: the first anthology; ed. by J.
      Clute; C. Greenland and D. Pringle
Shirley, John, 1953-, and Sterling, Bruce
  The unfolding
    Interzone: the 2nd anthology; ed. by J.
      Clute; D. Pringle and S. Ounsley
Shirley. Teles, H.
Shit. Lish, G.
Shit-Katrine. Sandel, C.
Shiv for your supper. Searls, H.
Shiva dancing. Shukshin, V. M.
Shivers, Louise
  Here to get my baby out of jail [excerpt]
    The New writers of the South; ed. by
      C. East
A **shocking** accident. Greene, G.
Shockley, Ann Allen, 1927-
  A birthday remembered
    Between mothers & daughters; ed. by S.
      Koppelman
  The world of Rosie Polk
    Black American Literature Forum
      21:113-32 Spr/Summ '87
Shockley, Gary W.
  The coming of the Goonga
    The Clarion awards; ed. by D. Knight
Shoe. Schmidt, H. J.
The **shoe** clerk. Ruta, S.
Shoe in the sand. Davie, E.
Shoe trees. Van Wert, W. F.
The **shoebox** of desire. Woodman, A.
A **shoemaker** for a husband. Botwinik, B.
SHOEMAKERS
  Naipaul, S. A man of mystery
The **shoes.** Turner, B.
The **shoes** of death. Borden, J.
Sholem Aleichem, 1859-1916
  The automatic exemption
    Sholom Aleichem. Tevye the dairyman
      and The railroad stories
  Baranovich Station [Variant title: The station at Baranovitch]
    Sholom Aleichem. Tevye the dairyman
      and The railroad stories
  Burned out
    Sholom Aleichem. Tevye the dairyman
      and The railroad stories

Chava
  Sholom Aleichem. Tevye the dairyman
    and The railroad stories
Competitors
  Sholom Aleichem. Tevye the dairyman
    and The railroad stories
Eighteen from Pereshchepena
  Sholom Aleichem. Tevye the dairyman
    and The railroad stories
Elul
  Sholom Aleichem. Tevye the dairyman
    and The railroad stories
Fated for misfortune
  Sholom Aleichem. Tevye the dairyman
    and The railroad stories
A game of sixty-six
  Sholom Aleichem. Tevye the dairyman
    and The railroad stories
Go climb a tree if you don't like it
  Sholom Aleichem. Tevye the dairyman
    and The railroad stories
The happiest man in all Kodny
  Sholom Aleichem. Tevye the dairyman
    and The Railroad stories
Hard luck
  Sholom Aleichem. Tevye the dairyman
    and The railroad stories
High school
  Sholom Aleichem. Tevye the dairyman
    and The railroad stories
Hodl
  Sholom Aleichem. Tevye the dairyman
    and The railroad stories
It doesn't pay to be good
  Sholom Aleichem. Tevye the dairyman
    and The railroad stories
Lekh-lekho
  Sholom Aleichem. Tevye the dairyman
    and The railroad stories
The man from Buenos Aires
  Sholom Aleichem. Tevye the dairyman
    and The railroad stories
The miracle of Hoshana Rabbah
  Sholom Aleichem. Tevye the dairyman
    and The railroad stories
Rabchik, a Jewish dog
  Roger Caras' Treasury of great dog stories
Shprintze
  Sholom Aleichem. Tevye the dairyman
    and The railroad stories
The slowpoke express
  Sholom Aleichem. Tevye the dairyman
    and The railroad stories
The tallis koton
  Sholom Aleichem. Tevye the dairyman
    and The railroad stories
The tenth man
  Sholom Aleichem. Tevye the dairyman
    and The railroad stories
Tevye blows a small fortune
  Sholom Aleichem. Tevye the dairyman
    and The railroad stories

Sholem Aleichem, 1859-1916—*Continued*
Tevye leaves for the land of Israel
    Sholom Aleichem. Tevye the dairyman
        and The railroad stories
Tevye strikes it rich
    Sholom Aleichem. Tevye the dairyman
        and The railroad stories
Third class
    Sholom Aleichem. Tevye the dairyman
        and The railroad stories
Today's children
    Sholom Aleichem. Tevye the dairyman
        and The railroad stories
The wedding that came without its band
    Sholom Aleichem. Tevye the dairyman
        and The railroad stories
Shomlo, Ana
Surgical Department A
    The Literary Review (Madison, N.J.)
        29:215-21 Wint '86
Shōno, Junzō, 1921-
Still life
    The Shōwa anthology 1
Shoo fly. Matheson, R.
Shoot, child, what you talking about? Drake,
    R.
SHOOTING
Calvino, I. The crow comes last
Clark, G. Ice fishing
Coleman, W. The twinight of Reverend
    Jones
Cox, E. A sounding brass
Crane, S. Lynx-hunting
Doyle, Sir A. C. The winning shot
Ellin, S. Mrs. Mouse
Ferré, R. Sleeping beauty
Leaton, A. Tracks to the cold country
Nordan, L. Sugar, the eunuchs, and Big
    G.B.
Nordan, L. Wild dog
Oates, J. C. Sharpshooting
Osier, J. The ritual
Salas, G. Police report
Spark, M. The go-away bird
Shooting. Working, R.
Shooting for Jupiter. Campos-De Metro, J.
The **shooting** gallery. Tsushima, Y.
Shooting match. Dundee, W. D.
The **shooting** of Curly Dan. Lutz, J.
The **shooting** party. Bates, H. E.
The **shooting** party. Woolf, V.
A **shooting** season. Tremain, R.
Shooting the moon. Lawson, H.
Shootout at Gentry's Junction. Coover, R.
Shootout in the toy shop. Sheckley, R.
The **shopboy's** god. Shiga, N.
SHOPKEEPERS *See* Merchants
SHOPLIFTING
Abbott, K. A can of smoked oysters
Barstow, S. Good
Callaghan, M. A wedding-dress
Canin, E. Pitch memory
Canin, E. Star Food

Davis, D. S. The Devil and his due
Gilbert, M. Counterplot
Girion, B. Rip-off!
Goldman, L. Temporarily at liberty
Interollo, L. The quickening
Klass, P. Two New Jersey stories: Stealing
Pronzini, B. Tiger, tiger
Rendell, R. The convolvulus clock
Taylor, C. In and out of the arms of the
    law
SHOPPING
Coskran, K. The high price of everything
Dodd, S. M. Browsing
Girion, B. A very brief season
Kawabata, Y. The silver fifty-sen pieces
Murphy, P. The Irish information office
Parise, G. Poverty
Shopping. Asscher-Pinkhof, C.
Shopping. Oates, J. C.
SHOPPING BAG LADIES *See* Homeless
The **shopping** trip. Moss, R.
Shorblac: a driver's story. Zhang Xianliang
Shore, Wilma
May your days be merry and bright
    "May your days be merry and bright"
        and other Christmas stories by wom-
        en; ed. by S. Koppelman
Shoreline. Hagy, A. C.
The **shores** of Tripoli. Rubin, L. D.
Short, Luke, 1908-1975
Swindle at Piute Sink
    Wild westerns; ed. by B. Pronzini
A **short** acquaintance. Clarke, A. C.
A **short** course in Nietzschean ethics. Baxter,
    C.
Short Friday. Singer, I. B.
The **short** happy life of Francis Macomber.
    Hemingway, E.
The **short** happy life of the brown oxford.
    Dick, P. K.
A **short** history of a small place. Pearson,
    T. R.
A **short** history of the bicycle: 401 B.C. to
    2677 A.D. Bishop, M.
Short in the chest. St. Clair, M.
Short Papa. Purdy, J.
Short season. Klinkowitz, J.
Short-shift Saturday. Casey, G.
A **short,** short story complete on these two
    pages. Martone, M.
A **short** story. Bowering, G.
Short story contest. Aguinis, M.
Short story shortening. Seitlin, P.
A **short** street. Nowakowski, M.
A **short** vacation. Potter, N. A. J.
A **short** visit to a failed artist. Bissoondath,
    N.
The **shot.** Kalamaras, V.
A **shot** from nowhere. Highsmith, P.
Show biz. Bloch, R.
The **show** goes on. Campbell, R.
Show me the way to go home. Dickson, G.
    R.

The **show** must go on. Bloch, R.
The **showboat** murders. Woolrich, C.
Showdown. Brondoli, M.
Shower check. Pliscou, L.
"Showin' off". Crane, S.
The **showing**. Whelan, G.
Showing the flag. Gardam, J.
Showing the flag. Tuohy, F.
Shprintze. Sholem Aleichem
The **shrapnel** of their friends. Crane, S.
The **shrine** of temptation. Merril, J.
Shrinker. Sargent, P.
'Shrooms. Coleman, W.
A **shtetl**. Weissenberg, I. M.
Shukshin, Vasilii Makarovich, 1929-1974
  Before the cock crows thrice
    Shukshin, V. M. Roubles in words,
      kopeks in figures, and other stories
  The court case
    Shukshin, V. M. Roubles in words,
      kopeks in figures, and other stories
  Makar Zherebtsov
    The Barsukov Triangle, The two-toned
      blond & other stories; ed. by C. R.
      Proffer & E. Proffer
  The microscope
    Shukshin, V. M. Roubles in words,
      kopeks in figures, and other stories
  Moving to the country
    Shukshin, V. M. Roubles in words,
      kopeks in figures, and other stories
  The old man's dying
    Shukshin, V. M. Roubles in words,
      kopeks in figures, and other stories
  The outsider
    Shukshin, V. M. Roubles in words,
      kopeks in figures, and other stories
  The postscript
    Shukshin, V. M. Roubles in words,
      kopeks in figures, and other stories
  Roubles in words, kopeks in figures
    Shukshin, V. M. Roubles in words,
      kopeks in figures, and other stories
  Shiva dancing
    Shukshin, V. M. Roubles in words,
      kopeks in figures, and other stories
  Stefan
    Shukshin, V. M. Roubles in words,
      kopeks in figures, and other stories
  The sufferings of young Vaganov
    Shukshin, V. M. Roubles in words,
      kopeks in figures, and other stories
Shulman, Alix Kates
  Money can't buy a home
    Redbook 165:66+ Je '85
The **shunammite**. Arredondo, I.
The **shunned** house. Lovecraft, H. P.
Shurik. Nagibin, ÏU. M.
The **shut-in** number. Rooke, L.
Shut the final door. Hensley, J. L.
Shuttle, Penelope, 1947-
  Ratón ladrón
    P.E.N. new fiction I

Shwartz, Susan M.
  Hair's breath
    Magic in Ithkar 3; ed. by A. Norton and
      R. Adams
  Homecoming
    Magic in Ithkar [1]; ed. by A. Norton
      and R. Adams
  Rite of failure
    Tales of the Witch World 2
  The wolf's flock
    Werewolves; ed. by J. Yolen and M. H.
      Greenberg
Shyer, Marlene Fanta
  A dream for tomorrow
    Good Housekeeping 200:154-5 Mr '85
  The first move
    McCall's 113:84-5 Ja '86
  Little touches
    Ladies' Home Journal 105:96+ Ap '88
  My romance
    Good Housekeeping 199:118-19+ Jl '84
  The seasons of love
    Good Housekeeping 205:124-5+ Jl '87
  Tomorrow's magic
    Good Housekeeping 204:138-9 Ap '87
  Waiting for a poet
    McCall's 113:138-41 Jl '86
SIAMESE CATS *See* Cats
SIAMESE TWINS
  Bishop, M. Collaborating
  Bradbury, R. Corpse carnival
  Powell, T. Motive for murder
  Romero, N. L. Symmetries
Siba'i, Fadil al- *See* Al-Siba'i, Fadil
SIBERIA (SOVIET UNION)
  Colegate, I. Distant cousins
  Goldberg, L. In Siberia it is very cold
  Korabelnikov, O. Tower of birds
Siblings. Schulman, H.
The **sibyl**. Ocampo, S.
Sibyl sits in. Gardner, M.
SIBYLS *See* Oracles
Sicilian vespers. Pomerance, M.
SICILIANS
  Prose, F. The bandit was my neighbor
                Spain
  Sciascia, L. Antimony
SICILY
  Pirandello, L. The long dress
  Pirandello, L. The trip
  Sciascia, L. The American aunt
  Sciascia, L. The death of Stalin
  Sciascia, L. 'Forty-eight'
The **sick** child. Colette
SICK CHILDREN
  Banks, R. The child screams and looks
    back at you
  Bonosky, P. Walk to the moon
  Briskin, M. Two hours in the life of
    Steven Malinowski
  Colette. The sick child
  Freeman, J. Going out to sea
  Johnson, J. The children's wing

SICK CHILDREN—*Continued*
Lawson, H. Brighten's sister-in-law
Lewis, T. Vincristine
McCullers, C. Breath from the sky
Vizyénos, G. M. My mother's sin
Walker, A. Strong horse tea
Williams, W. C. Jean Beicke
Williams, W. C. The use of force
The **sick** gentleman's last visit. Papini, G.
The **sickness** of Lone Chief. London, J.
Sick'un. Massie, E.
Side effects. Williams, W. J.
Sidewinder. Jaffe, H.
Sidewise in time. Leinster, M.
The **Sidi.** Rhys, J.
Sidney, Seth and S.A.M. McConnell, C. R.
The **Sidon** in the mirror. Willis, C.
The **siege.** Ramírez, S.
The **siege** of Minerva. Petrakis, H. M.
SIERRA LEONE
Wells, H. G. Pollock and the Porroh man
SIERRA NEVADA MOUNTAINS (CALIF. AND NEV.)
Sandham, A. A. The conscientious cat
Sierra wave. Hauptman, W.
Siesta. Mrożek, S.
The **sight.** Moore, B.
The **sign.** Asimov, I.
The **sign.** Kees, W.
The **sign.** Rey Rosa, R.
The **sign** of the operation. Moravia, A.
SIGN PAINTING
Conroy, J. Slappy Hooper, world's biggest, fastest, and bestest sign painter
Mathers, P. A small drop
Thompson, T. A wollopin' good chew
West, J. A time of learning
The **signal.** Maupassant, G. de
The **signalman.** Dickens, C.
The **signals.** Cartier, F. A.
Signals. Harness, C. L.
Signals. Schraft, C.
Significant moments in the life of my mother. Atwood, M.
The **signing.** Dixon, S.
The **Signora** Psyche Zenobia. Poe, E. A.
The **Signora** Zenobia. See Poe, E. A. How to write a Blackwood article
SIGNS (OMENS) *See* Omens
Signs. Czarny, H.
SIGNS AND SIGNBOARDS
Asimov, I. The Cross of Lorraine
Ha, K.-C. The white paper beard
Signs and wonders. Becker, L.
Signs of life. Kuznets, M.
Sigurdsardóttir, Jakobína
Nothing to tell
Short story international 56
SIKHS
Mukherjee, B. The management of grief
     Scotland
Thomson, G. Pride of lions

SIKSIKA INDIANS
Frazee, S. Great medicine
Silas and Goliath. Bates, H. E.
A **Silas** idyll. Bates, H. E.
Silas the good. Bates, H. E.
Silber, Joan
The city, seen from the water, 1924
The Paris Review 29:101-14 Spr '87
The **silence.** Bail, M.
Silence. Freeman, M. E. W.
Silence—a fable. Poe, E. A.
The **silence** is rest? King, F. H.
The **silence** of the llano. Anaya, R. A.
The **silent** couple. Courtois, P. J.
The **silent** cradle. Kennedy, L.
The **silent** guests. Heinesen, W.
A **silent** hero. Mrożek, S.
The **silent** minister. Sarton, M.
Silent night, holy night. Nowakowski, M.
Silent retreats. Deaver, P. F.
The **silent** scream. Steele, M.
Silent snow, secret snow. Aiken, C.
A **silent** song. Kibera, L.
The **silent** speech of love. Ding Ling
The **silent** traders. Tsushima, Y.
The **silent** treatment. Desnoues, L.
The **silk.** Cowley, J.
The **silk** handkerchief. Faik, S.
Silken dragon. McDonald, S. E.
The **silken-swift** . . . . Sturgeon, T.
The **silken** thread. Sandel, C.
The **silken** whale. Orphée, E.
Silko, Leslie
Lullaby
 The Interior country; ed. by A. Blackburn
Private property
 Earth power coming; ed. by S. J. Ortiz
Yellow Woman
 The Best of the West; ed. by J. Thomas
 Westward the women; ed. by V. Piekarski
 Writers of the purple sage; ed. by R. Martin and M. Barasch
Sillitoe, Alan
The fishing-boat picture
 The Penguin book of modern British short stories
Sillitoe, Linda, 1948-
Four walls and an empty door
 Greening wheat: fifteen Mormon short stories
Silly mothers. Merriman, C.
Silman, Roberta, 1934-
Here we go again, Alice
McCall's 116:65+ N '88
Silone, Ignazio, 1900-1978
Polikushka
 The Substance of things hoped for; ed. by J. B. Breslin
Silva, Beverly
The artist
 Silva, B. The cat, and other stories

Silva, Beverly—*Continued*
The bathetic fallacy
   Silva, B. The cat, and other stories
Bits & pieces
   Silva, B. The cat, and other stories
The cat
   Silva, B. The cat, and other stories
Happy hour
   Silva, B. The cat, and other stories
Hell's playground
   Silva, B. The cat, and other stories
No joy in the morning
   Silva, B. The cat, and other stories
Poet
   Silva, B. The cat, and other stories
The poster
   Silva, B. The cat, and other stories
Precious
   Silva, B. The cat, and other stories
A small western town
   Silva, B. The cat, and other stories
Smile
   Silva, B. The cat, and other stories
The thesis
   Silva, B. The cat, and other stories
The woes of a single woman and her car
   Silva, B. The cat, and other stories
Yellow bird
   Silva, B. The cat, and other stories
Silva, David B., 1950-
Ice sculptures
   Masques II; ed. by J. N. Williamson
The turn of time
   Masques; ed. by J. N. Williamson
Silver, Rebecca
Fearful symmetry
   Erotic interludes; ed. by L. Barbach
The **silver** bird. Nowakowski, M.
Silver Blaze. Doyle, Sir A. C.
The **silver** butterfly. Buck, P. S.
The **silver** clock. Hartley, L. P.
The **silver** corridor. Ellison, H.
The **silver** DeSoto. Floyd, P. L.
A **silver** dish. Bellow, S.
Silver dollars. Barber, P.
The **silver** fifty-sen pieces. Kawabata, Y.
The **silver** fish. Slayter, E.
Silver Fox. Evans, E.
Silver linings. Kaufman, L.
The **silver** mask. Walpole, Sir H.
The **silver** medallist. Drewe, R.
The **silver** porcupine. Kinsella, W. P.
Silver sugar from Bombay. Thomas, M.
Silverberg, Robert
The affair
   The Year's best science fiction, second
      annual collection
Against Babylon
   Omni (New York, N.Y.) 8:86-8+ My '86
   The Year's best science fiction, fourth
      annual collection
Amanda and the alien
   Omni book of science fiction 3

As is
   Venomous tales of villainy and
      vengeance; ed. by H. Hoke
At the conglomeroid cocktail party
   Silverberg, R. The conglomeroid cocktail
      party
Blindsight
   Terry Carr's Best science fiction and fan-
      tasy of the year #16
Breckenridge and the continuum
   Silverberg, R. Beyond the safe zone
Caliban
   Silverberg, R. Beyond the safe zone
Capricorn games
   Silverberg, R. Beyond the safe zone
Caught in the organ draft
   Silverberg, R. Beyond the safe zone
Chalice of death
   Intergalactic empires; ed. by I. Asimov;
      M. H. Greenberg and C. G. Waugh
The changeling
   Silverberg, R. The conglomeroid cocktail
      party
The desert of stolen dreams
   Baker's dozen: 13 short science fiction
      novels
The dybbuk of Mazel Tov IV
   Silverberg, R. Beyond the safe zone
The far side of the bell-shaped curve
   Silverberg, R. The conglomeroid cocktail
      party
The feast of St. Dionysus
   Silverberg, R. Beyond the safe zone
Gate of horn, gate of ivory
   Universe 14
Getting across
   Silverberg, R. Beyond the safe zone
Gianni
   Silverberg, R. The conglomeroid cocktail
      party
Good news from the Vatican
   The Best from Universe
   Silverberg, R. Beyond the safe zone
Hail to the chief
   Omni (New York, N.Y.) 7:60-2 N '84
Hannibal's elephants
   Omni (New York, N.Y.) 11:82-4+ O '88
Hardware
   Omni (New York, N.Y.) 10:134-6+ O '87
Homefaring
   Nebula awards #19
House of bones
   Terry's universe; ed. by B. Meacham
How they pass the time in Pelpel
   Silverberg, R. The conglomeroid cocktail
      party
In entropy's jaws
   Silverberg, R. Beyond the safe zone
In the group
   Silverberg, R. Beyond the safe zone
In the House of Double Minds
   Silverberg, R. Beyond the safe zone

Silverberg, Robert—*Continued*
The iron star
    The Universe; ed. by B. Preiss
Ishmael in love
    Silverberg, R. Beyond the safe zone
Jennifer's lover
    Silverberg, R. The conglomeroid cocktail
    party
The Macauley circuit
    Machines that think; ed. by I. Asimov;
    P. S. Warrick and M. H. Greenberg
The man who floated in time
    Silverberg, R. The conglomeroid cocktail
    party
Many mansions
    Silverberg, R. Beyond the safe zone
Ms. found in an abandoned time machine
    Silverberg, R. Beyond the safe zone
Multiples
    The Year's best science fiction, first an-
    nual collection
The mutant season
    Silverberg, R. Beyond the safe zone
Needle in a timestack
    Silverberg, R. The conglomeroid cocktail
    party
Not our brother
    Silverberg, R. The conglomeroid cocktail
    party
(Now + n, now - n)
    Silverberg, R. Beyond the safe zone
Our Lady of the Sauropods
    Silverberg, R. The conglomeroid cocktail
    party
The palace at midnight
    Omni book of science fiction 1
    Silverberg, R. The conglomeroid cocktail
    party
The pardoner's tale
    The Year's best science fiction, fifth an-
    nual collection
Passengers
    Kindred spirits; ed. by J. M. Elliot
The Pope of the chimps
    Silverberg, R. The conglomeroid cocktail
    party
Push no more
    Silverberg, R. Beyond the safe zone
The regulars
    Silverberg, R. The conglomeroid cocktail
    party
Sailing to Byzantium
    Nebula awards 21
    The Year's best science fiction, third an-
    nual collection
Schwartz between the galaxies
    Silverberg, R. Beyond the safe zone
The Science Fiction Hall of Fame
    Silverberg, R. Beyond the safe zone
A sea of faces
    Silverberg, R. Beyond the safe zone
Ship-sister, star-sister
    Silverberg, R. Beyond the safe zone

Some notes on the pre-dynastic epoch
    Silverberg, R. Beyond the safe zone
Sunrise on Pluto
    The Planets; ed. by B. Preiss
This is the road
    Silverberg, R. Beyond the safe zone
A thousand paces along the Via Dolorosa
    Silverberg, R. The conglomeroid cocktail
    party
To be continued
    Analog: Writers' choice v2
Trips
    Silverberg, R. Beyond the safe zone
The trouble with Sempoanga
    Silverberg, R. The conglomeroid cocktail
    party
Waiting for the earthquake
    Medea: Harlan's world; ed. by H. Ellison
    Omni book of science fiction 2
    Silverberg, R. The conglomeroid cocktail
    party
We know who we are
    Amazing stories: visions of other worlds
What we learned from this morning's
    newspaper
    Silverberg, R. Beyond the safe zone
When we went to see the end of the
    world
    Silverberg, R. Beyond the safe zone
The wind and the rain
    Silverberg, R. Beyond the safe zone
The **silverberry** thief. Kawabata, Y.
Silverfish. Dew, R. F.
The **silverlord**. Llywelyn, M.
Silversmith wishes. Sheckley, R.
Silvis, Randall, 1950-
The fatalist
    Silvis, R. The luckiest man in the world
The luckiest man in the world
    Silvis, R. The luckiest man in the world
Murphy
    Short story international 42
One night with a girl by the Seine
    Silvis, R. The luckiest man in the world
Prayer and old jokes
    Silvis, R. The luckiest man in the world
Trash man
    Silvis, R. The luckiest man in the world
A walk in the moonlight
    Silvis, R. The luckiest man in the world
Simak, Clifford D., 1904-1988
Grotto of the dancing deer
    The Hugo winners v5
Idiot's crusade
    Young monsters; ed. by I. Asimov; M.
    H. Greenberg and C. G. Waugh
Skirmish
    Amazing science fiction anthology: The
    wild years, 1946-1955; ed. by M. H.
    Greenberg

Simenon, Georges, 1903-1989
Blessed are the meek
The Crime of my life; ed. by B. Garfield
The drowned men's inn
Great modern police stories; ed. by B. Pronzini and M. H. Greenberg
Inspector Maigret pursues
The Penguin classic crime omnibus
Maigret at the crossroads
Simenon, G. Maigret at the crossroads
Maigret mystified
Simenon, G. Maigret at the crossroads
Maigret stonewalled
Simenon, G. Maigret at the crossroads
The most obstinate man in Paris
The Ethnic detectives; ed. by B. Pronzini and M. H. Greenberg
Storm over the Channel [Variant title: Storm in the Channel]
Great French detective stories; ed. by T. J. Hale
Similar triangles. Raphael, F.
Simmering. Atwood, M.
Simmie, Lois, 1932-
You tell me your dreams
The Old dance; ed. by B. Burnard
Simmons, Catherine
Eva and the apple tree
Alberta bound; ed. by F. Stenson
Simmons, Dan
Carrion comfort
Omni book of science fiction 3
The Year's best science fiction, first annual collection
E-ticket to Namland
Omni (New York, N.Y.) 10:108-10+ N '87
Eyes I dare not meet in dreams
Omni book of science fiction 2
Two minutes forty-five seconds
Omni (New York, N.Y.) 10:110+ Ap '88
Simmons, David
Sjambok
The Antioch Review 46:510-13 Fall '88
Simmons, Philip
The lake
The Massachusetts Review 28:128-44 Spr '87
Simms, William Gilmore, 1806-1870
The arm-chair of Tustenuggee
Nightmares in Dixie; ed. by F. McSherry; C. G. Waugh and M. H. Greenberg
Simon, Barney
The birds
Echad 2: South African Jewish voices
The fourth day of Christmas
Echad 2: South African Jewish voices
Monologue for Danny
Echad 2: South African Jewish voices
Our war
Echad 2: South African Jewish voices

Simon. Barthelme, D.
Simon Girty go ape. Faust, I.
Simon goes to London. Wexler, J.
Simonetta Perkins. Hartley, L. P.
Simon's papa. Maupassant, G. de
Simon's wife. Lee, T.
Simple celebrations. Heffernan, M. J.
A **simple** enquiry. Hemingway, E.
A **simple** life. Blinkin, M.
A **simple** melody. Woolf, V.
Simple memories. Sandel, C.
Simple pleasures. Flanagan, M.
Simple sentences. Babbitt, N.
Simplicity. Parise, G.
Simpson, Dorothy, 1933-
Two's company
John Creasey's Crime collection, 1984
Simpson, John
A party for idiot
First love/last love; ed. by M. Denneny; C. Ortleb and T. Steele
Simpson, Mona
Approximations
20 under 30; ed. by D. Spark
Lawns
The Best American short stories, 1986
The Pushcart prize XI
Three maids' children
The New generation; ed. by A. Kaufman
You leave them
The Paris Review 27:81-92 Fall '85
Sims, George *See* Cain, Paul, 1902-1966
Sims, George, 1923-
Family butcher
The Mammoth book of modern crime stories; ed. by G. Hardinge
Remember Mrs. Fitz
John Creasey's Crime collection, 1987
Sims, LaVonne
Behind my lace curtain
Ellery Queen's Prime crimes 2
Sin, Sang-Ung
Pyŏn's death
The Road to Sampo, and other Korean short stories
SIN
See also Guilt; Repentance
Hawthorne, N. Ethan Brand
Ocampo, S. The mortal sin
Sinclair, M. Where their fire is not quenched
Singer, I. B. A nest egg for paradise
Sladek, J. T. The next dwarf
Sin. Bonosky, P.
The **sin** eater. Atwood, M.
The **sin** eater. Nordan, L.
The **sin** of Madame Phloi. Braun, L. J.
SINATRA, FRANK, 1915-
About
Lish, G. Frank Sinatra or Carleton Carpenter
Sinatra. Dodd, S. M.
Since Agnes left. Kay, J.

Since when do they charge admission. Morris, W.
A sincere friendship. Lispector, C.
Sincerely, yours. Bukiet, M. J.
Sincerely yours. Wyatt, M.
Sinclair, Clive, 1948-
Bedbugs
   The Penguin book of modern British short stories
Sinclair, Iain
Brides of the pleiades
   P.E.N. new fiction I
Sinclair, Marjorie Jane Putnam
Secrets
   Passages to the dream shore; ed. by F. Stewart
Sinclair, May, 1863-1946
The victim
   The Oxford book of English ghost stories
The Villa Désirée
   Haunting women; ed. by A. Ryan
Where their fire is not quenched
   Witches' brew; ed. by M. Muller and B. Pronzini
Sindbad. Barthelme, D.
Sinema. Garton, R.
Sing it again, Wordsworth. Norris, L.
Sing me no love songs, I'll say you no prayers. Rooke, L.
SINGAPORE
Howard, C. Last chance in Singapore
Kilworth, G. The invisible foe
Wong, S. H. The feminist
Singer, Isaac Bashevis, 1904-
The accuser and the accused
   Singer, I. B. The death of Methuselah, and other stories
Advice
   Singer, I. B. The image, and other stories
The bitter truth
   Singer, I. B. The death of Methuselah, and other stories
The black wedding
   Masterpieces of terror and the supernatural; ed. by M. Kaye and S. Kaye
The bond
   Singer, I. B. The image, and other stories
Burial at sea
   The New Yorker 61:39-43 O 14 '85
   Singer, I. B. The death of Methuselah, and other stories
The conference
   Singer, I. B. The image, and other stories
Confused
   Singer, I. B. The image, and other stories

Dazzled
   The New Yorker 61:40-3 Mr 18 '85
   Singer, I. B. The death of Methuselah, and other stories
The dead fiddler
   The World of the short story; ed. by C. Fadiman
The death of Methuselah
   Singer, I. B. The death of Methuselah, and other stories
Disguised
   The New Yorker 62:34-8 S 22 '86
   Singer, I. B. The death of Methuselah, and other stories
The divorce
   Singer, I. B. The image, and other stories
The enemy
   Singer, I. B. The image, and other stories
Gifts
   Singer, I. B. The death of Methuselah, and other stories
Gimpel the fool
   The Norton book of American short stories
Henne Fire
   The Art of the tale; ed. by D. Halpern
The hotel
   Singer, I. B. The death of Methuselah, and other stories
The house friend
   The New Yorker 61:26-9 Jl 1 '85
   Singer, I. B. The death of Methuselah, and other stories
The image
   The New Yorker 60:43-50 O 8 '84
   Singer, I. B. The image, and other stories
The impresario
   Harper's 272:57-61 Ap '86
   Singer, I. B. The death of Methuselah, and other stories
The interview
   Singer, I. B. The image, and other stories
The Jew from Babylon
   Singer, I. B. The death of Methuselah, and other stories
The last demon
   Devils & demons; ed. by M. Kaye and S. Kaye
The last gaze
   Partisan Review 55:210-18 Spr '88
   Singer, I. B. The death of Methuselah, and other stories
The litigants
   Singer, I. B. The image, and other stories
Logarithms
   Singer, I. B. The death of Methuselah, and other stories

Singer, Isaac Bashevis, 1904-—_Continued_
Loshikl
  Partisan Review 52 no2:22-30 '85
    Singer, I. B. The image, and other
    stories
Miracles
    Singer, I. B. The image, and other
    stories
The missing line
  Partisan Review 55:205-10 Spr '88
    Singer, I. B. The death of Methuselah,
    and other stories
The mistake
  The New Yorker 60:36-40 F 4 '85
    Singer, I. B. The image, and other
    stories
A nest egg for paradise
    Singer, I. B. The image, and other
    stories
Ole and Trufa
  Reader's Digest 127:143-5 N '85
On the way to the poorhouse
    Singer, I. B. The image, and other
    stories
One day of happiness
    Singer, I. B. The image, and other
    stories
A peephole in the gate
    Singer, I. B. The death of Methuselah,
    and other stories
The pocket remembered
    Singer, I. B. The image, and other
    stories
The recluse
  The New Yorker 62:30-3 Jl 21 '86
    Singer, I. B. The death of Methuselah,
    and other stories
Remnants
    Singer, I. B. The image, and other
    stories
Runners to nowhere
    Singer, I. B. The death of Methuselah,
    and other stories
Sabbath in Gehenna
    Singer, I. B. The death of Methuselah,
    and other stories
The secret
    Singer, I. B. The image, and other
    stories
Short Friday
    The Nobel reader; ed. by J. Eisen and
    S. Troy
The slaughterer
    Buying time; ed. by S. Walker
The smuggler
    Singer, I. B. The death of Methuselah,
    and other stories
The Spinoza of Market Street
    Great American love stories; ed. by L.
    Rosenthal
Strangers
    Singer, I. B. The image, and other
    stories

Strong as death is love
  Partisan Review 51 no4/52 no1:601-7
  '84/'85
    Singer, I. B. The image, and other
    stories
A telephone call on Yom Kippur
    Singer, I. B. The image, and other
    stories
The trap
    Singer, I. B. The death of Methuselah,
    and other stories
Twice Chanukah
  Ladies' Home Journal 102:72+ D '85
Why Heisherik was born
    Singer, I. B. The image, and other
    stories
The **singer**. Madden, D.

SINGERS
Baxter, C. Harmony of the world
Colette. The tenor
Colum, P. The little pension
De Haven, T. Clap hands! Here comes
    Charley
Desnoues, L. The silent treatment
Dick, P. K. What'll we do with Ragland
    Park?
Doyle, Sir A. C. The retirement of Signor
    Lambert
Dumas, H. The voice
Durban, P. A long time coming, a long
    time gone
Durrell, L. La valise
Forrest, K. V. Mandy Larkin
Geras, A. Don't sing love songs . . .
Gilliatt, P. Addio
Gomez, J. No day too long
Hill, J. The malachite beads
Hoyt, M. S. Lyrical voices
Kim, Y. I. Gourd Dance Song
Lee, V. A wicked voice
Leskov, N. S. A robbery
Lynds, D. Yellow gal
Madden, D. The singer
Mathers, P. Lights
Matthews, J. "This moment is ours alone"
Maupassant, G. de. Virtue!
McKnight, R. The voice
Nielsen, H. You can't trust a man
Pangborn, E. Harper Conan & Singer
    David
Petrakis, H. M. The ballad of Daphne and
    Apollo
Phelps, E. S. Old Mother Goose
Pohl, F. Swanilda's song
Shacochis, B. Lord Short Shoe wants the
    monkey
Shwartz, S. M. Homecoming
Sladek, J. T. Red noise
Sproat, R. A former security with Helen
    Damnation
Valenzuela, L. City of the unknown
Wetherell, W. D. Volpi's farewell

SINGING AND VOICE CULTURE
Ade, G. The fable of Lutie, the false alarm, and how she finished about the time that she started
Fisher, D. C. As ye sow—
Gallacher, T. Perfect pitch
Jhabvala, R. P. The housewife
Johnston, S. Jesse and Louise
Skelton, R. The man who sang in his sleep
West, J. The singing lesson
The **singing** diamond. Forward, R. L.
The **singing** eggs. Stuart, K.
The **singing** float. Hughes, M.
The **singing** lesson. West, J.
Singing on the Titanic. Glasser, P.
The **Singing** Rabbi. Avery, M.
The **singing** sands. Frazee, S.
Singing stars and stripes forever. Dawson, F.
The **singing** well. Norris, H.
Singing with Skulnick. Wilk, M.
Single gents only. Metcalf, J.
Single lens reflex. Loukakis, A.

SINGLE MEN
        See also Unmarried couples; Widowers
Austin, D. Men without women
Barthelme, S. Failing all else
Berger, J. The accordion player
Botwinik, B. The last young man
Broun, H. Cycling posture
Choyce, L. Prying loose
Colette. The tender shoot
Cooper, J. C. Too hep to be happy!
Dorr, L. Old men shall dream dreams
Fante, J. A wife for Dino Rossi
Fetler, A. The third count
Fitzgerald, M. J. Bachelor life
Gaitskill, M. An affair, edited
Gholson, C. Temple to the economics of love
Glasser, P. Marmosets
Halligan, M. The marble angel
Harris, M. The photograph
Hauptman, W. Kozmic Blues
Hauptman, W. Stormchaser
Hospital, J. T. The baroque ensemble
Hunnicutt, E. Amos
Kawabata, Y. Gleanings from snow country
Kawabata, Y. The ring
Kawabata, Y. The sparrow's matchmaking
Kawabata, Y. There is a God
Krist, G. Evidence
Lofts, N. Gateway to happiness?
Maupassant, G. de. An enthusiast
Maupassant, G. de. Who knows?
Melville, H. The paradise of bachelors
Murphy, P. Cane toads
Murphy, P. Cross purposes
Naranjo, C. Ondina

Nesin, A. The first woman who understood me
Nevai, L. Connor's lake
Nowakowski, M. How time has flown
O'Brien, E. The bachelor
O'Faolain, J. Her trademark
Okudzhava, B. S. Singular misfortunes amidst a parade of successes
Painter, P. A man of his time
Pavese, C. The family
Petchsingh, T. The third encounter
Petrakis, H. M. The prison
Pfeil, F. Holding on
Power, V. The ragged rascal ran
Pritchett, M. Trinity
Rogers, S. The crumb
Rogers, T. N. R. Galb's elbow
Saiki, J. Revelation
Saki. Tea
Tahir, B. Last night I dreamt of you
Trevor, W. A meeting in middle age
Ullmann, A. Those in peril in the air
Updike, D. Social studies
Vega, A. L. Three love aerobics
Wilbur, E. Perfection

SINGLE-PARENT FAMILY
Cox, E. A sounding brass
Gallant, M. Going ashore
Glasser, P. Singing on the Titanic
Hogan, L. New shoes
Jolley, E. The last crop
Keillor, G. Eloise
Miller, S. Expensive gifts
Oates, J. C. Mule
Oates, J. C. A touch of the flu
Pascoe, B. Work-horses
Pirandello, L. In silence
Rambach, P. The crescent
Salter, J. Foreign shores
Spivack, K. Dorothy
Sproat, R. Black madonna two-wheel gypsy queen
Summers, H. S. Herschell
Tallent, E. Migrants
Taylor, P. E. News from El Corazon: in the composing room
Thompson, J. The stud
Thurm, M. Squirrels
Winton, T. Getting ahead
The **single** tractor track. Burt, S.

SINGLE WOMEN
        See also Unmarried couples; Unmarried mothers; Widows
Adams, A. Tide pools
Adams, G. G. A teller's tale
Barrett, L. Realty
Barthelme, S. Failing all else
Bates, H. E. The spring hat
Bird, C. Seeking its level
Blaushild, L. Witness
Blythe, R. Everything a man needs
Blythe, R. The schism
Botwinik, B. Rivals

SINGLE WOMEN—*Continued*

Bowen, S. P. Old maidism versus marriage
Boylan, J. The love starter
Boylan, J. There's the sea
Broughton, T. A. Lily
Broun, H. The deep blue eastern sky
Broun, H. Is this civilization?
Broun, H. No smoking
Brown, A. A sense of humor
Burt, S. Fellow passengers
Carr, P. M. Indian burial
Carter, A. A. The fortune hunter
Carter, E. All the men are called McCabe
Cary, A. An old maid's story
Chasek, J. A ticket to America
Chavez, A. The ardent commandant
Chekhov, A. P. A woman's kingdom
Chernoff, M. Don't send poems, send money
Clarke, A. C. A short acquaintance
Coleman, W. Dream 5281
Coleman, W. The stare down
Cooke, R. T. How Celia changed her mind
Crabtree, L. V. Homer-snake
Cullinan, E. Life after death
Dazai, O. Magic lantern
Dickson, G. R. Miss Prinks
Digby, J. Incident at the Gaumont
Drake, R. Still swinging
Drake, R. The veteran
Du Fresne, Y. Christmas (Shirley Temple is a wife and mother)
Dundas, R. Mr. de la Torre
Eisenberg, D. Broken glass
Eldridge, M. Fragment
Eldridge, M. Together
Eldridge, M. Tourist
Engel, M. Anita's dance
Faulkner, W. Dry September
Fernando, C. Of bread and power
Fetler, A. The third count
Finger, A. Old maids
Fitzgerald, M. J. Communions
Fitzgerald, M. J. Falling sickness
Fitzgerald, M. J. A landscape with walls
Fitzgerald, Z. Miss Ella
Forsh, O. Ham's wife
Fox, J. Garage sale
Freeman, J. The Botanic Gardens
Freeman, M. E. W. Louisa
Frucht, A. Nuns in love
Frucht, A. Winter
Gallant, M. A painful affair
Garner, H. A thousand miles from the ocean
Gaskell, E. C. The three eras of Libbie Marsh
Gee, M. Buried treasure, old bones
Geras, A. Alice
Gilchrist, E. The gauzy edge of paradise
Gilchrist, E. Jade Buddhas, red bridges, fruits of love
Gilchrist, E. Looking over Jordan

Golding, W. Miss Pulkinhorn
Gordimer, N. Rags and bones
Granit, A. Come into the hallway, for five cents!
Grenville, K. The test is, if they drown
Halligan, M. Fat chance
Halligan, M. A gigolo, Miss Emery?
Halligan, M. Remember the rug
Hamilton, M. Jenny Stairy's hat
Harland, M. One old maid
Harper, F. E. W. The two offers
Hartley, L. P. The silver clock
Hayashi, F. A late chrysanthemum
Highsmith, P. The romantic
Hogg, J. Tibby Hyslop's dream
Hospital, J. T. The dark wood
Hospital, J. T. Happy Diwali
Hull, H. R. Last September
Hulme, K. A window drunken in the brain
Hunnicutt, E. When I was married
Janowitz, T. Case history #15: Melinda
Janowitz, T. Fondue
Janowitz, T. Matches
Janowitz, T. Patterns
Kawabata, Y. Autumn rain
Kawabata, Y. Bamboo-leaf boats
Kawabata, Y. The jay
Kawabata, Y. Morning nails
Kawabata, Y. The white flower
Keeling, N. Berthilde's holiday
Keeling, N. George's eyes & the red ball
Keeling, N. Mine
Klass, P. Not a good girl
Krist, G. Housesitting
Latimer, M. Nellie Bloom
Lofts, N. Debt of gratitude
Lofts, N. A late flowering
Lofts, N. The natives are friendly
MacDonald, D. R. Of one kind
MacLaverty, B. End of season
MacLaverty, B. Remote
Marrington, P. The beautiful journey
Matthews, J. Haunted by name our ignorant lips
Maupassant, G. de. Miss Harriet
Maupassant, G. de. An old maid
McCorkle, J. First union blues
Mihelic, J. Green life
Nevai, L. Diamond twill
Nevai, L. Mr. Feathers
Nevai, L. "Stranger in paradise"
Ngugi wa Thiong'o. Minutes of glory
Norris, G. Revive us again
Norris, H. Water into wine
Oates, J. C. The assignation
Oates, J. C. Shelter
O'Brien, E. The Connor girls
O'Connor, F. The crop
O'Faolain, J. Her trademark
Orzeszkowa, E. Miss Antonina
Oz, A. Nomad and viper
Parise, G. Solitude
Pavese, C. The family

SINGLE WOMEN—*Continued*
Petrakis, H. M. The prison
Petrakis, H. M. The song of Rhodanthe
Phelps, E. S. Number 13
Phillips, J. A. The heavenly animal
Pierce, C. What I did for Aunt Berthe
Pilcher, R. Miss Cameron at Christmas
Pindar, S. Aunt Mable's love story
Prichard, K. S. The siren of Sandy Gap
Rhys, J. The Chevalier of the Place Blanche
Rhys, J. In the Rue de l'Arrivée
Rhys, J. The insect world
Rhys, J. Who knows what's up in the attic?
Robinson, L. Telepathic rein
Rölvaag, O. E. Molla's heart attack
Rooke, L. In the garden
Sams, F. Fulfillment
Sandel, C. The ways of love
Sarton, M. The donkey
Schulman, H. Inventions
Schulman, H. James Dean's widow
Schulman, H. To die from
Sedgwick, C. M. Old maids
Seepaul, L. Sou-Sou money
Silva, B. The cat
Silva, B. Happy hour
Silva, B. Poet
Silva, B. A small western town
Singer, I. B. One day of happiness
Singer, I. B. The Spinoza of Market Street
Smiley, J. Lily
Sproat, R. The fascination of the vanity
Stern, S. Aaron makes a match
Stuart, R. M. The Woman's Exchange of Simpkinsville
Suckow, R. Susan and the doctor
Targan, B. Surviving adverse seasons
Taylor, A. The absolutely ordinary family
Texier, C. The fedora
Thorman, C. Binkas sausage
Tiptree, J. The women men don't see
Traba, M. Conformity
Trevor, W. The ballroom of romance
Trevor, W. Lunch in winter
Tsushima, Y. Clearing the thickets
Tsushima, Y. An embrace
Tsushima, Y. A sensitive season
Tuohy, F. A ghost garden
Ullmann, A. Those in peril in the air
Updike, J. The lovely troubled daughters of our old crowd
Vaughan, M. C. Fruits of sorrow; or, An old maid's story
Vega, A. L. Three love aerobics
Vogan, S. Angels in the snow
Vreuls, D. The seller of watches
Walpole, Sir H. The silver mask
Waters, F. The woman at Otowi Crossing [excerpt]
Whelan, G. Beneath the fig trees
Williams, T. Happy August the Tenth
Williams, T. The night of the Iguana
Williams, T. Oriflamme
Wilson, B. Drive-away
Wilson, B. Emily's arrows
Wilson, L. A. Massé
Winton, T. Distant lands
Wolfe, G. Sonya, Crane Wessleman, and Kittee
Wolff, T. Sister
Woolf, V. Miss Pryme
Woolf, V. Moments of being: 'Slater's pins have no points'
Woolson, C. F. Crowder's Cove: a story of the war
Woolson, C. F. Miss Elisabetha
Yunker, T. Margaritas
ZoBell, B. Avenida revolucion

Singmaster, Deborah
Stella Artois
  P.E.N. new fiction I
Singmaster, Elsie, 1879-1958
The battleground
  Civil War women; ed. by F. McSherry; C. G. Waugh and M. Greenberg
Singular misfortunes amidst a parade of successes. Okudzhava, B. S.
Singular pleasures. Mathews, H.
The **singular** speculation of the house agent. Chesterton, G. K.
The **sinh** of Niguudzagha. Tall Mountain, M.
Sinking house. Boyle, T. C.
The **sinking** of the Bismarck. Forester, C. S.
The **sinking** of the Bismarck. MacLean, A.
Sinking wells. Anderman, J.
Sinners. O'Faoláin, S.
Sinners. Rossiter, S.
Sinon at Elis. Parotti, P.
Sins against animals. Gillette, J. B.
Sins and virtues. Crace, J.
Sins leave scars. Cooper, J. C.
The **sins** of the fathers. Baker, S.
Sins of the third age. Gordimer, N.
The **sins** of Tomas Benares. Cohen, M.
Sintra. Adams, A.
Sionna Marie. Greeley, A. M.
Siope (Silence). Poe, E. A.
SIOUX INDIANS *See* Dakota Indians
Sir Dominick's bargain. Le Fanu, J. S.
Sir Edmund Orme. James, H.
Sir Galahad and the Holy Grail
  Christian short stories; ed. by M. Booth
Sir Roderick comes to lunch. Wodehouse, P. G.
Sir Thomas More in the Hall of Languages. Falco, E.
The **siren**. Conroy, J.
Siren business. Christie, A.
The **siren** of Sandy Gap. Prichard, K. S.
SIRENS (MYTHOLOGY)
  Ferron, J. The Sirens
  Forster, E. M. The story of the siren
  Valenzuela, L. One siren or another
The **Sirens**. Ferron, J.

Sirens. Matheson, R. C.
Sirens. Pascoe, B.
Sirens and voices. Swan, G.
Sirocco. Chipulina, E. G.
Sirriamnis. Lee, T.
Sis. Barthelme, F.
Sisk, Frank
  Ashes for an urn
    Ellery Queen's Prime crimes 2
  Dogbane
    Last laughs; ed. by G. Mcdonald
  The fly swatter
    Alfred Hitchcock's Crimewatch
  The return of Crazy Bill
    Alfred Hitchcock's Grave suspicions
Sisohpromatem. Reed, K.
Sisskind, Mitch
  The apparition
    Sisskind, M. Visitations
  The dawn of a new day
    Sisskind, M. Visitations
  A day I'll never forget
    Sisskind, M. Visitations
  The devotions of Jean Blysema
    Sisskind, M. Visitations
  Grrrrr!
    Sisskind, M. Visitations
  Hope
    Sisskind, M. Visitations
  I'm stupid and my wife is stupid
    Sisskind, M. Visitations
  It so happens
    Sisskind, M. Visitations
  A mean teacher
    Sisskind, M. Visitations
  Mr. Tivy
    Sisskind, M. Visitations
  The Playboy Rabbit
    Sisskind, M. Visitations
  Proposal and disposal
    Sisskind, M. Visitations
  Twenty questions
    Sisskind, M. Visitations
The **sissy** from the Hardscrabble County
  rock quarries. Conroy, J.
Sissy Mamma's wig. Leedom-Ackerman, J.
Sist' Chaney's black silk. Thanet, O.
Sister. Humphrey, W.
Sister. Wolff, T.
Sister Coxall's revenge. Muscillo, D.
Sister Detroit. McElroy, C. J.
Sister Francetta and the pig baby. Bernard,
  K.
Sister Hilary. Ferguson, P.
Sister Imelda. O'Brien, E.
Sister love. Campbell, E.
Sister ships. London, J.
The **sisterhood**. Butler, G.
SISTERS
    See also Brothers and sisters; Half-
    sisters; Stepsisters; Twins
  Ade, G. The fable of sister Mae, who did
    as well as could be expected

Alden, P. B. At the beach
Anderson, J. Under the house
Asscher-Pinkhof, C. Trust
Bausch, R. The wife's tale
Bird, C. In the conservatory
Boyle, K. The first lover
Campbell, E. September crickets
Caponegro, M. Heart as nails
Carrington, L. The sisters
Chernoff, M. The spirit of giving
Colette. The rainy moon
Colter, C. The rescue
Cooper, J. C. Loved to death
Davis, D. S. By the scruff of the soul
Davis, K. Roach bait
Davis, L. Two sisters
Dew, R. F. Two girls wearing perfume in
  the summer
Ekström, M. Left alone
Essop, A. Two sisters
Evans, E. Blue news
Farmer, B. Pumpkin
Ferré, R. Pico Rico, mandorico
Field, B. Three sisters
Finney, E. J. Lot no. 17
Flook, M. Dancing with my sister Jane
Geras, A. The green behind the glass
Gerber, M. J. "I don't believe this"
Giles, M. Old souls
Glasser, P. What doesn't kill me
Gordon, M. Delia
Goyen, W. Zamour; or, A tale of in-
  heritance
Graves, Mrs. A. J. Mary and Ellen Gros-
  venor; or, The two sisters
Guido, B. The usurper
Haake, K. Wait until heaven
Hagy, A. C. Madonna on her back
Hall, M. L. Joanna
Harland, M. One old maid
Hempel, A. San Francisco
Henry, O. The higher pragmatism
Houbein, L. Child of two sisters
Jackson, H. H. How one woman kept her
  husband
James, H. The romance of certain old
  clothes
Janowitz, T. Ode to heroine of the future
Jolley, E. Clever and pretty
Jolley, E. Dingle the fool
Kawabata, Y. Tabi
Kawabata, Y. The younger sister's clothes
Kornblatt, J. R. Flo
La Chapelle, M. The gate house
Leavitt, D. Out here
Levy, D. Proletarian Zen
Livesey, M. Jean and Little Aunt
Logue, M. Boundary waters
Loukakis, A. The jigsaw puzzle
MacLaverty, B. End of season
Matthew, J. R. The letters of Mrs. J. L.
  Hartle
Mattison, A. The May dance

SISTERS—*Continued*

  Maupassant, G. de. Moonlight
  McCullers, C. Like that
  McGarry, J. Penmanship
  Miriam, L. 'Maiden names
  Moore, G. 'Emma Bovary'
  Morris, M. The bus of dreams
  Morris, M. Orphans of the Storm
  Munro, A. The peace of Utrecht
  Munro, A. The progress of love
  Ng, F. M. A red sweater
  Oates, J. C. Double solitaire
  Peterson, L. S. The gift
  Pritchard, M. A man around the house
  Pritchard, M. Shed of grace
  Raphael, F. Welcome aboard
  Rich, C. My sister's marriage
  Rifaat, A. Me and my sister
  Robertson, M. E. The baptism
  Roscoe, P. The National Circus of Argentina
  Sandel, C. The art of murder
  Sandel, C. The sisters
  Schell, J. Alvira, Lettie, and Pip
  Sedgwick, C. M. Old maids
  Sexson, L. Deer crossing
  Shelnutt, E. Voice
  Sherman, C. H. Tapestry
  Smith, L. Cakewalk
  Stafford, J. In the zoo
  Stuart, R. M. The Woman's Exchange of Simpkinsville
  Taylor, P. H. The little cousins
  Thanet, O. Sist' Chaney's black silk
  Thurm, M. Secrets
  Traba, M. All in a lifetime
  Updike, J. The other
  Walker, A. Kindred spirits
  Walters, A. L. The warriors
  Warner, S. T. The mahogany table
  Welty, E. Why I live at the P.O.
  West, J. Reverdy
  Whitaker, M. X
  Whitehead, J. Joiner [excerpt]
  Woolf, V. Phyllis and Rosamond
  Wyndham, F. Ursula
  Yi, H.-C. Torn flesh
The **sisters**. Carrington, L.
Sisters. Drake, R.
Sisters. Saiki, J.
The **sisters**. Sandel, C.

SISTERS AND BROTHERS *See* Brothers and sisters

SISTERS-IN-LAW
  Hazzard, S. Weekend
  Kauffman, J. Places in the world a woman could walk
  McFarland, D. Last night
  Russo, A. The Sephardic sisters
Sisters of the rain. Cooper, J. C.
Sitting. Francis, H. E.
Sitting and spinning. Taylor, C.

Sitting around the pool, soaking up the rays. Pohl, F.
Sitty Victoria. Salloum, V.
Sivriada nights. Faik, S.
The **six-day** night. Morand, P.
Six days you shall labor. Dumas, H.
Six faces of Feridah Challoner. Dundas, R.
Six feet of the country. Gordimer, N.
Six matches. Strugatskiĭ, A. N., and Strugatskiĭ, B. N.
Six this, six that. Van de Wetering, J.
Six years after. Mansfield, K.
The **sixth** of the sixth of the year nineteen sixty-six. Hemmerchts, K.
The **sixth** sense. Houbein, L.
The **sixth** ship. Gardner, M.
Sixties into eighties won't go. Carter, R.
Sixty million trillion combinations. Asimov, I.
Sixty-three questions. Brondoli, M.
The **size** of the universe. Peck, R.
The **sizzling** saboteur. Charteris, L.
Sjambok. Simmons, D.
The **Skag** Castle. Sheckley, R.
The **skald** in the cave. Brown, G. M.
Skarda. Blei, N.
The **skater**. Spencer, E.
The **skater**. Williams, J.
Skaters. Thurm, M.
Skeeter's last reflections. Pfeil, F.
Skeleton. Bradbury, R.
Skeleton. Hankla, C.
A **skeleton**. Schwob, M.
Skeleton in the closet. Anderson, K. J., and Fortier, R.
Skeleton in the cupboard. Wilmot, T.
Skeleton rattle your mouldy leg. Pronzini, B.
SKELETONS
  Carrington, L. The skeleton's holiday
  Sanders, S. R. The anatomy lesson
  Taylor, C. Leanderthal lady
Skeletons. Beattie, A.
Skeletons. Pronzini, B.
The **skeleton's** holiday. Carrington, L.
Skelton, Robin
  The angel
    Skelton, R. The man who sang in his sleep
  The bride
    Skelton, R. The man who sang in his sleep
  Finder
    Skelton, R. The man who sang in his sleep
  Householder
    Skelton, R. The man who sang in his sleep
  The illusion
    Skelton, R. The man who sang in his sleep
  The importance of being Percy
    Skelton, R. The man who sang in his sleep

Skelton, Robin—*Continued*
  The man who sang in his sleep
    Skelton, R. The man who sang in his
      sleep
  Portrait of Duck
    Skelton, R. The man who sang in his
      sleep
  Raftery's ghost
    Skelton, R. The man who sang in his
      sleep
  Sarah
    Skelton, R. The man who sang in his
      sleep
Sketches among the ruins of my mind. Far-
  mer, P. J.
Sketches by Boz. Dickens, C.
Sketches for a life of Wassilly. Davis, L.
The **skewer**. McGrath, P.
Skiles, Don, 1939-
  The loft
    Between C & D; ed. by J. Rose and
      C. Texier
SKIN
                    Diseases
  MacLaverty, B. More than just the disease
  Williams, W. C. Danse pseudomacabre
Skin and blood. Bryant, E.
Skin angels. Neely, J.
SKIN DIVING
  Allyn, D. The puddle diver
  Heller, S. A matter of style
  Kim, Y. I. The taste of salt
  MacMillan, I. C. The rock
Skinner. Rossiter, S.
The **skins** of the fathers. Barker, C.
The **skins** you love to touch. Fox, J.
Skipp, John
  Film at eleven
    Silver scream; ed. by D. J. Schow
Skipp, John, and Spector, Craig
  Gentlemen
    The Architecture of fear; ed. by K.
      Cramer and P. D. Pautz
    The Year's best fantasy, first annual
      collection
A **skirmish**. McGuane, T.
Skirmish. Simak, C. D.
Skirmish at Sartoris. Faulkner, W.
Skirmish on a summer morning. Shaw, B.
SKIS AND SKIING
  Archer, J. A chapter of accidents
  Burns, M. The Norman Fisher Memorial
    Ski Race
  Hemingway, E. Cross-country snow
  Sanford, W. M. The blue spruce
  Shaw, I. The inhabitants of Venus
  Updike, J. Man and daughter in the cold
  Vreuls, D. Estarolly's mountain
Skrzynecki, Peter, 1945-
  The biggest bonfire of all
    Skrzynecki, P. The wild dogs
  The black madonna
    Skrzynecki, P. The wild dogs

The chainsaw incident
  Skrzynecki, P. The wild dogs
Empty cages
  Skrzynecki, P. The wild dogs
Hoeing
  Skrzynecki, P. The wild dogs
Indian mynas
  Skrzynecki, P. The wild dogs
"Is your wife here, honey?"
  Skrzynecki, P. The wild dogs
Lilies
  Skrzynecki, P. The wild dogs
The peewit's nest
  Skrzynecki, P. The wild dogs
Pick-and-shovel hero
  Skrzynecki, P. The wild dogs
The red-back spider
  Skrzynecki, P. The wild dogs
The Superman t-shirt
  Skrzynecki, P. The wild dogs
The white eagle
  Skrzynecki, P. The wild dogs
The wild dogs
  Skrzynecki, P. The wild dogs
The **skull** of the Marquis de Sade. Bloch,
  R.
Škvorecký, Josef
  Aristotelian logic
    Škvorecký, J. The mournful demeanour
      of Lieutenant Boruvka
  The case of the horizontal trajectory
    Škvorecký, J. The mournful demeanour
      of Lieutenant Boruvka
  Crime in a girls' high school
    Škvorecký, J. The Mournful demeanour
      of Lieutenant Boruvka
  Death on needlepoint
    Škvorecký, J. The mournful demeanour
      of Lieutenant Boruvka
  The end of an old tom-cat
    Škvorecký, J. The mournful demeanour
      of Lieutenant Boruvka
  Falling light
    Škvorecký, J. The mournful demeanour
      of Lieutenant Boruvka
  His easiest case
    Škvorecký, J. The mournful demeanour
      of Lieutenant Boruvka
  The scientific method
    Škvorecký, J. The mournful demeanour
      of Lieutenant Boruvka
  The supernatural powers of Lieutenant
    Boruvka
    Škvorecký, J. The mournful demeanour
      of Lieutenant Boruvka
  That sax solo
    Škvorecký, J. The mournful demeanour
      of Lieutenant Boruvka
  A tried and proven method
    Škvorecký, J. The mournful demeanour
      of Lieutenant Boruvka

Škvorecký, Josef—*Continued*
Whose deduction?
Škvorecký, J. The mournful demeanour of Lieutenant Boruvka
The **sky** is burning. Ellison, H.
The **sky** is gray. Gaines, E. J.
Sky sister. Paxson, D. L.
The **skylight**. Mortimer, P.
Skylight in Lausanne. Lurie, M.
Skystalk. Sheffield, C.
Slack Lankhmar afternoon featuring Hisvet. Leiber, F.
Sladek, John Thomas
Absent friends
Sladek, J. T. The lunatics of Terra
After Flaubert
Sladek, J. T. The lunatics of Terra
Answers
Sladek, J. T. The lunatics of Terra
The brass monkey
Sladek, J. T. The lunatics of Terra
Breakfast with the Murgatroyds
Sladek, J. T. The lunatics of Terra
Calling all gumdrops!
Sladek, J. T. The lunatics of Terra
An explanation for the disappearance of the moon
Sladek, J. T. The lunatics of Terra
Fables
Sladek, J. T. The lunatics of Terra
Great mysteries explained!
Sladek, J. T. The lunatics of Terra
Guesting
Sladek, J. T. The lunatics of Terra
How to make major scientific discoveries at home in your spare time
Sladek, J. T. The lunatics of Terra
The island of Dr. Circe
Sladek, J. T. The lunatics of Terra
The kindly ones
Sladek, J. T. The lunatics of Terra
The last of the whaleburgers
Sladek, J. T. The lunatics of Terra
The next dwarf
Sladek, J. T. The lunatics of Terra
Red noise
Sladek, J. T. The lunatics of Terra
Ursa Minor
Sladek, J. T. The lunatics of Terra
White hat
Sladek, J. T. The lunatics of Terra
Slappy Hooper, world's biggest, fastest, and bestest sign painter. Conroy, J.
Slater, Judith
A father's wish
Redbook 169:48-50 Jl '87
The **slaughterer**. Singer, I. B.
SLAUGHTERING AND SLAUGHTER-HOUSES
Clark, G. At Lowry's
McPherson, D. Day after day, like a terrible fish

Pascoe, B. The **slaughters** of the bulumwaal butcher
Still, J. A master time
Jews
Singer, I. B. The slaughterer
The **slaughters** of the bulumwaal butcher. Pascoe, B.
The **Slave** Fort. Kanafānī, G.
Slave on the block. Hughes, L.
SLAVE SHIPS
Melville, H. Benito Cereno
SLAVE TRADE
Maupassant, G. de. The Odalisque of Senichou
Melville, H. Benito Cereno
SLAVERY
　　See also Blacks; Fugitive slaves; Slave trade
Aldiss, B. W. Incident in a far country
Anderson, P. The Nest
Child, L. M. F. The quadroons
Cox, I. E., Jr. In the circle of nowhere
Donaldson, S. R. Ser Visal's tale
Faulkner, W. Was
Johnson, C. R. The education of Mingo
Robinson, K. S. The lunatics
Schwob, M. Septima, enchantress
Yourcenar, M. An obscure man
SLAVES *See* Slavery
The **slaves** in New York. Janowitz, T.
Slaves of silver. Wolfe, G.
The **slaves** of Stony Creek. Lee, H.
The **slave's** story. Jahnn, H. H.
The **slaying** of the dragon. Buzzati, D.
Slayter, Eric
The silver fish
P.E.N. new fiction I
The **sledding** party. Millhauser, S.
SLEEP
Coleman, W. In the city of sleep
Lurie, M. Fenner
Parkinson, T. L. Sleep
Rey Rosa, R. The sign
Skelton, R. The man who sang in his sleep
Woolf, V. In the orchard
Sleep. Parkinson, T. L.
Sleep. Spivack, K.
Sleep. Tem, S. R.
Sleep it off lady. Rhys, J.
Sleep tight. Purdy, J.
Sleep well of nights. Davidson, A.
Sleep with me—and death. Rogers, W.
Sleeping. LaSalle, P.
Sleeping beauty. Ferré, R.
The **sleeping** beauty. Garrett, G. P.
The **sleeping** city. Schwob, M.
The **sleeping** dog. Macdonald, R.
A **sleeping** face. Gee, M.
Sleeping giant. Mattison, A.
The **sleeping** gypsy. Evans, E.
Sleeping habit. Kawabata, Y.
Sleeping in rain. Henry, G.

Sleeping like dogs. Calvino, I.
A **sleeping** pill for the doctor. Seepaul, L.
The **sleeping** sword. Peyrou, M.
Sleeping through. Lott, B.
Sleeping together. Connelly, J.
Sleepless. Hansen, R.
Sleepless nights. Colette
Sleeps six. Raphael, F.
Sleepy Hollow. Cullen, E. J.
Sleepy time gal. Gildner, G.
The **sleeves**. Grossman, L.
SLEIGHS AND SLEDGES
    Pasternak, B. L. Without love
Sleight of wit. Dickson, G. R.
Slesar, Henry, 1927-
    A choice of witnesses
      Alfred Hitchcock's Mortal errors
    The day of the execution
      Hitchcock in prime time; ed. by F. M.
        Nevins and M. H. Greenberg
    The first crime of Ruby Martinson
      Alfred Hitchcock's Grave suspicions
    I do not like thee, Dr. Feldman
      Last laughs; ed. by G. Mcdonald
    Item
      Alfred Hitchcock's Crimewatch
    Light fingers
      Last laughs; ed. by G. Mcdonald
    My father, the cat
      Magicats! Ed. by J. Dann and G. Dozois
      Roger Caras' Treasury of great cat
        stories
    A victim must be found
      Ellery Queen's Crimes and punishments
Slesinger, Tess, 1905-1945
    Mother to dinner
      Between mothers & daughters; ed. by S.
        Koppelman
    The mouse-trap
      Writing red; ed. by C. Nekola and P.
        Rabinowitz
    White on black
      The Norton book of American short
        stories
A **slice** of nothingness. Boisvert, C.
The **sliced-crosswise** only-on-Tuesday world.
    Farmer, P. J.
The **slicker**. Reed, R.
Slides. Miller, S.
Sliding rock. Boren, T.
The **Sliding** Rock. Kawabata, Y.
A **slight** momentary affliction. Dorr, L.
Sligo, John, 1944-
    Burnham camp
      Sligo, J. Final things
    Going home
      Sligo, J. Final things
    A new Eden?
      Sligo, J. Final things
A **slip** under the microscope. Wells, H. G.
The **slipover** sweater. Stuart, J.
Slippage. Updike, J.
Slipstream. Ford, C.

The **slit**. Murphy, Y.
The **sliver** of evidence. Ritchie, J.
Slogans. Rule, J.
The **slopes** of Tara. Colum, P.
The **Slovo** stove. Davidson, A.
Slow. Oates, J. C.
Slow birds. Watson, I.
Slow dissolve. Grenville, K.
Slow grounder. Broun, H.
Slow homecoming. Handke, P.
Slow-motion. Schwartz, S.
The **slow** sound of his feet. Marechera, D.
Slowly. Cameron, P.
The **slowpoke** express. Sholem Aleichem
The **slugger** heart. Campos-De Metro, J.
SLUM LIFE
    Crane, S. Maggie: a girl of the streets
    McKinley, J. Chambers
             Korea
    Kim, T. Potato
             Peru
    Morris, M. Shining path
SLUMS *See* Slum life
Šmahelová, Helena
    House of joy
      Short story international 56
Small, Deborah
    Lima beans
      Chicago Review 34 no4:56-62 '85
Small acts. Evans, E.
The **small** animus. Clift, C.
Small arms fire. Perea, R. L.
The **small** assassin. Bradbury, R.
The **small** birds. Hood, H.
Small bodies. Preuss, P.
The **small** businessman's wife. Murphy, P.
Small change. Boulanger, D.
Small change. Le Guin, U. K.
Small claims. Ciment, J.
A **small** clearing. Paolucci, A.
A **small** crime. Wexler, J.
A **small** difference only. Sproat, R.
A **small** dose of magic. Levi, J. H.
A **small** drop. Mathers, P.
Small family with rooster. Rose, D. A.
A **small**, good thing. Carver, R.
Small-hands Chen. Wang Zengqi
Small heirlooms. Harrison, M. J.
Small homicide. McBain, E.
A **small** hotel. Adams, G. G.
A **small** hotel. MacDougall, C.
Small island republics. Apple, M.
A **small** kindness. Bova, B.
A **small** miracle of fishhooks and straight
    pins. Bunch, D. R.
Small mouth, bad taste. Anthony, P.
A **small** obligation. Nunes, S.
A **small** paradise. Cortázar, J.
A **small** piece of blue. Levine, N.
Small Point Bridge. Minot, S.
A **small** price. Livesey, M.
The **small** rain. Pynchon, T.
Small sun. Tamer, Z.

Small suns. Hoyt, M. S.
The **small** things that save us. Spencer, B.

SMALL TOWN LIFE

Abbott, K. Rick's first visit to the A & W

Adams, G. G. Bow wow and good-bye

Adams, G. G. Inside dope

Adams, G. G. Marva Jean Howard confesses

Akins, E. George Bailey fishing

Arthur, R. The wonderful day

Barrett, N., Jr. Diner

Barrett, N., Jr. Perpetuity blues

Bauer, D. Lore

Bedard, B. The fifth letter

Bedard, B. Hour of the beast

Bedard, B. Stalking

Bell, M. S. Monkey Park

Benedict, P. Getting over Arnette

Bly, C. The dignity of life

Bly, C. The last of the gold star mothers

Bonosky, P. A bird in her hair

Boswell, R. Kentucky

Bradbury, R. Colonel Stonesteel's genuine home-made truly Egyptian mummy

Brondoli, M. Coldbeer at the Only

Broun, H. Municipal noir

Broun, H. Phosphates

Brown, G. M. Gold dust

Brown, M. W. The barbecue

Busch, F. The new honesty

Caldwell, P. A sense of place

Capote, T. Children on their birthdays

Carlson, R. Phenomena

Carver, R. What do you do in San Francisco?

Chishimba, M. Weekend of carousal

Clark, G. Mister Period

Clayton, J. J. Fantasy for a Friday afternoon

Conroy, J. The Kimberly toughs

Conroy, J. The morphadite

Coskran, K. Miss Clay County 1960

Crane, S. The monster

Cullen, E. J. Mayberry

Daniels, C. Chatham County

Derleth, A. W. The night train to Lost Valley

Dilworth, S. The long white

Drake, R. 1975 has come and gone

Drake, R. A husband and a home of her own and nice things

Drake, R. If she knowed what I knowed, she never would woke

Drake, R. Mrs. English

Drake, R. Still swinging

Drake, R. Up on the corner, on the dogleg

Drake, R. Were you there?

Faulkner, W. A rose for Emily

Finger, A. Old maids

Freeman, C. Before he went out west

Freeman, C. The bride of Ambrose

Freeman, C. Dreaming of Africa

Freeman, C. The exile, the housekeeper, and Flora, the beauty of Rome

Freeman, C. My life on the snowplow

Freeman, C. Not everyone can be a soldier

Freeman, C. The ride

Freeman, C. Seven prophecies of Egypt

Freeman, C. The song of Roland

Gallagher, T. Recourse

Garrett, G. P. Pretty birdie

Gass, W. H. In the heart of the heart of the country

Gingher, M. No news

Goyen, W. Figure over the town

Goyen, W. Tongues of men and of angels

Greenwood, R. The cannon

Greenwood, R. The other world

Hall, M. L. Lucky Lafe

Hall, M. L. The man who gave brother double pneumonia

Hall, M. L. The painter

Hall, M. L. Privacy

Hall, M. L. The visit

Hall, T. T. Camouflage

Hall, T. T. Civic pride

Hall, T. T. Holding up the other end

Haruf, K. Private debts/public holdings

Haslam, G. W. Trophies

Heinesen, W. The ballad of the Toft Boy

Hoffman, W. Moon lady

Humphrey, W. The human fly

Humphrey, W. The patience of a saint

Jewett, S. O. The foreigner

Jones, D. C. Halloween and other sacred events

Jones, D. C. In pastures green

Jones, D. C. Knights of the Flaming Circle

Jones, D. C. The last fastball

Jones, D. C. The Law

Jones, D. C. Once a year

Jones, D. C. Raised in the wilderness

Jones, D. C. The saga of Slaven Budd

Jones, D. C. The trombone and the lady

Jones, D. C. Trusty

Keillor, G. Goodbye to the lake

Keillor, G. Hawaii

Keillor, G. Post office

Krahn, R. Homestead crescent

Kramer, K. Seeds of conflict

La Chapelle, M. Anna in a small town

Lang, A. Sweet smell of murder

Latimer, M. Nellie Bloom

Lee, H. Unto her a child was born

Lee, H. Christmas

Lowry, B. Come back, Lolly Ray [excerpt]

Luban, M. Tomorrow you'll forget

MacDonald, J. D. Looie follows me

Martone, M. Lost

Miller, S. Inventing the Abbotts

Miller, S. The lover of women

Millman, L. The 545 pound boy

Millman, L. Annie Bardwell gets back her cutlery

Millman, L. The laying on of hands

SMALL TOWN LIFE—*Continued*

Millman, L. The pickling of Rewt Chaney

Millman, L. The preserved woman

Millman, L. The triumph of literacy

Morris, W. Green grass, blue sky, white house

Moskowitz, F. The change

Moskowitz, F. Thelma

Munro, A. Fits

Munro, A. Jesse and Meribeth

Munro, A. The moon in the Orange Street Skating Rink

Munro, A. A queer streak

Nevai, L. Hooked

Nevai, L. Red spikes

Neville, S. The invention of flight

Nicolai, D. Day out

Norris, L. The girl from Cardigan

Oates, J. C. April

Oates, J. C. The bingo master

Oates, J. C. Little wife

O'Connor, F. Revelation

O'Connor, F. The turkey

Osborn, C. Ancient history

Painter, P. Getting to know the weather

Painter, P. The next time I meet Buddy Rich

Pancake, B. D. The honored dead

Pancake, B. D. The salvation of me

Pancake, B. D. Trilobites

Pearson, T. R. A short history of a small place [excerpt]

Pfeil, F. Poker fugue

Pritchard, M. Companions

Robison, M. Again, again, again

Sams, F. Run with the horsemen [excerpt]

Sanders, S. R. The fire woman

Sanders, S. R. Prophet

Sanford, W. M. Allie

Sexson, L. The apocalypse of Mary the unbeliever

Sexson, L. Intestate and without issue

Silva, B. A small western town

Sligo, J. A new Eden?

Sorrells, R. T. The blacktop champion of Ickey Honey

Spencer, E. The business venture

Spencer, E. First dark

Stafford, J. The healthiest girl in town

Stark, S. S. Heart of the Dutch country

Stribling, T. S. The colonel's predicament

Stuart, R. M. The Woman's Exchange of Simpkinsville

Suckow, R. The crick

Suckow, R. The little girl from town

Suckow, R. The man of the family

Suckow, R. What have I?

Taylor, P. E. The god-chaser

Taylor, P. H. Promise of rain

Taylor, P. H. What you hear from 'em?

Thanet, O. Why Abbylonia surrendered

Thompson, J. Birds in air

Twain, M. The man that corrupted Hadleyburg

Updike, D. Agawam

Updike, J. One more interview

Updike, J. When everyone was pregnant

Waldrop, H. Night of the cooters

Welty, E. Why I live at the P.O.

West, J. The Calla Lily Cleaners & Dyers

Wilbur, E. Faith

Wilbur, E. Ned

Wilcox, J. North Gladiola [excerpt]

Wilson, L. A. The raising

Winslow, T. S. The best man in town

Winton, T. Distant lands

Wolfe, T. The return of the prodigal

Zigal, T. Curios

The **small-town** lovers. O'Brien, E.

A **small** triumph. Glaze, E.

A **small** western town. Silva, B.

Small world. Middleton, S.

Small world. Shaw, B.

The **smallest** part. Gold, H.

Smart. Overholser, W. D.

Smart guys don't snore. Gores, J.

Smasher. Saberhagen, F.

Smedley, Agnes, 1890-1950

Shan-fei, communist

Writing red; ed. by C. Nekola and P. Rabinowitz

Smeds, Dave

Dragon touched

Dragons of light; ed. by O. S. Card

Goats

In the field of fire; ed. by J. Van B. Dann and J. Dann

Smee. Burrage, A. M.

Smell. Aiken, J.

The **smell.** Clarke, A. C.

The **smell** in Bertha's house. Hall, D.

Smile. Silva, B.

The **smile.** Tamer, Z.

The **smile** of a turtle. DeMarinis, R.

A **smile** outside the night stall. Kawabata, Y.

The **smiles** of Konarak. *See* Dennison, G. The sufficiency of everyday life: Avenue A and Eleventh Street, 1963

Smiley, Jane, 1949-

The age of grief

Smiley, J. The age of grief

Dynamite

Smiley, J. The age of grief

Jeffrey, believe me

Smiley, J. The age of grief

Lily

The Atlantic 254:76-80+ Jl '84

The Best American short stories, 1985

Prize stories, 1985

Smiley, J. The age of grief

Long distance

The Atlantic 259:68-75 Ja '87

Prize stories, 1988

Smiley, J. The age of grief

Smiley, Jane, 1949-—*Continued*
The pleasure of her company
Smiley, J. The age of grief
Smiling time. Sanders, H. G.
Smirl, D. E.
(jt. auth) See Meredith, Jerry, and Smirl, D. E.
Smith, Alicia
Cornfield with lights
Stories and poems from close to home; ed. by F. Salas
Smith, C. W. (Charles William), 1940-
Henry
Southwest Review 69:413-32 Aut '84
Smith, Charles William *See* Smith, C. W. (Charles William), 1940-
Smith, Charlie, 1947-
Canaan [excerpt]
The New writers of the South; ed. by C. East
Crystal River
The Editors' choice: new American stories v1
Smith, Clark Ashton, 1893-1961
The chain of Aforgomon
Smith, C. A. A rendezvous in Averoigne
The charnel god
Smith, C. A. A rendezvous in Averoigne
The city of the singing flame
Smith, C. A. A rendezvous in Averoigne
The colossus of Ylourgne
Smith, C. A. A rendezvous in Averoigne
The coming of the white worm
Smith, C. A. A rendezvous in Averoigne
The dark eidolon
Smith, C. A. A rendezvous in Averoigne
The death of Ilalotha
Smith, C. A. A rendezvous in Averoigne
The death of Malygris
Smith, C. A. A rendezvous in Averoigne
The dweller in the gulf
Smith, C. A. A rendezvous in Averoigne
The empire of the necromancers
Smith, C. A. A rendezvous in Averoigne
The end of the story
Smith, C. A. A rendezvous in Averoigne
The garden of Adompha
Smith, C. A. A rendezvous in Averoigne
Genius loci
Smith, C. A. A rendezvous in Averoigne
The holiness of Azédarac
Smith, C. A. A rendezvous in Averoigne
The isle of the torturers
Smith, C. A. A rendezvous in Averoigne
The last hieroglyph
Smith, C. A. A rendezvous in Averoigne
The last incantation
Smith, C. A. A rendezvous in Averoigne
Master of the asteroid
Smith, C. A. A rendezvous in Averoigne
The maze of Maal Dweb
Smith, C. A. A rendezvous in Averoigne

Morthylla
Smith, C. A. A rendezvous in Averoigne
Necromancy in Naat
Smith, C. A. A rendezvous in Averoigne
The planet of the dead
Smith, C. A. A rendezvous in Averoigne
A prophecy of monsters
100 great fantasy short short stories; ed. by I. Asimov; T. Carr and M. H. Greenberg
A rendezvous in Averoigne
Smith, C. A. A rendezvous in Averoigne
Vampires; ed. by A. Ryan
The return of the sorcerer
Rod Serling's Night gallery reader
The seven geases
Smith, C. A. A rendezvous in Averoigne
The tale of Satampra Zeiros
Smith, C. A. A rendezvous in Averoigne
The uncharted isle
Smith, C. A. A rendezvous in Averoigne
The vaults of Yoh-Vombis
Smith, C. A. A rendezvous in Averoigne
A voyage to Sfanomoë
Smith, C. A. A rendezvous in Averoigne
The weird of Avoosl Wuthoqquan
Smith, C. A. A rendezvous in Averoigne
Xeethra
Smith, C. A. A rendezvous in Averoigne
Smith, Cordwainer, 1913-1966
The crime and glory of Commander Suzdal
Amazing stories: visions of other worlds
Space wars; created by P. Anderson
Drunkboat
Amazing stories: 60 years of the best science fiction
The game of rat and dragon
Magicats! Ed. by J. Dann and G. Dozois
Roger Caras' Treasury of great cat stories
A planet named Shayol
Intergalactic empires; ed. by I. Asimov; M. H. Greenberg and C. G. Waugh
Scanners live in vain
Robert Silverberg's Worlds of wonder
Smith, Dean Wesley
Flawless execution
The Clarion awards; ed. by D. Knight
One last dance
L. Ron Hubbard presents Writers of the future
Smith, Edgar Valentine
'Lijah
The Art of fiction in the heart of Dixie; ed. by P. D. Beidler
Smith, Elaine Campbell
Anniversary
The Southern Review (Baton Rouge, La.) 24:632-9 Summ '88
The engagement
The Southern Review (Baton Rouge, La.) 23:897-905 Aut '87

Smith, Ernest Bramah *See* Bramah, Ernest, 1868-1942
Smith, Evelyn E.
The good husband
  100 great fantasy short short stories; ed. by I. Asimov; T. Carr and M. H. Greenberg
Teragram
  Young witches & warlocks; ed. by I. Asimov; M. H. Greenberg and C. G. Waugh
Weather prediction
  100 great fantasy short short stories; ed. by I. Asimov; T. Carr and M. H. Greenberg
Smith, Frank E. *See* Craig, Jonathan, 1919-
Smith, George O.
Beam pirate
  From mind to mind: tales of communication from Analog
Smith, Gregory Blake
Geography
  The Antioch Review 42:156-71 Spr '84
Hands
  The New generation; ed. by A. Kaufman
Snowblind
  The Kenyon Review ns6:11-19 Summ '84
Smith, Guy Newman
Hollow eyes
  Halloween horrors; ed. by A. Ryan
Smith, Iain Crichton *See* Crichton Smith, Iain
Smith, Ingrid
Baptism of desire
  The Southern Review (Baton Rouge, La.) 24:408-26 Spr '88
Dead man's spoons
  The North American Review 273:30-3 S '88
Pyrotechnics
  The Southern Review (Baton Rouge, La.) 23:950-64 Aut '87
Smith, James Melvin *See* Summerville, James, 1947-
Smith, Jim *See* Summerville, James, 1947-
Smith, Joe
Ulrike Meinhof
  Editor's choice II; ed. by M. Sklar and M. Biggs
Smith, John Marke
Three times around
  The Saturday Evening Post 256:56-9+ N '84
Smith, Julie
Grief counselor
  Last laughs; ed. by G. Mcdonald
Smith, Ken
Meat
  The Atlantic 261:80-5 Je '88
Smith, Lee, 1944-
Cakewalk
  A Collection of classic Southern humor; ed. by G. W. Koon

Good-bye, sweetheart
  Redbook 166:52+ F '86
Life on the moon
  New stories from the South: the year's best, 1987
Love the ones you're with
  Redbook 169:48+ Ag '87
No one will ever love you as much
  Redbook 171:44+ S '88
Smith, Lia
Someone in the neighborhood
  Ms. 15:62-3+ Ag '86
Smith, Patrick D., 1927-
Forever Island [excerpt]
  Mississippi writers v1: Fiction; ed. by D. Abbott
Smith, Pauline, 1882-1959
The schoolmaster
  The Penguin book of Southern African stories
Smith, Pauline C.
The crazy
  Alfred Hitchcock's Grave suspicions
The night Helen was killed
  Alfred Hitchcock's Mortal errors
The patchwork quilt
  Alfred Hitchcock's Crimewatch
Smith, Peter J.
Life of Beethoven
  The Hudson Review 40:251-78 Summ '87
Smith, Ray, 1949-
Cape Breton is the thought control centre of Canada
  The Oxford book of Canadian short stories in English
The Continental
  The New press anthology #2
The princess, the Boeing, and the hot pastrami sandwich
  The New press anthology #1
Smith, Sherwood
Monster mash
  Werewolves; ed. by J. Yolen and M. H. Greenberg
Smith, Stephanie A.
The amber frog
  Tales from Isaac Asimov's science fiction magazine: short stories for young adults
Smith, W. A.
The birdbath
  New England Review and Bread Loaf Quarterly 10:274-7 Spr '88
Delivery
  New stories from the South: the year's best, 1986
SMITHSONIAN INSTITUTION
Bates, H. Farewell to the master
Smoke. Blinkin, M.
Smoke. Faulkner, W.
Smoke. Hoffman, W.
Smoke. McInerney, J.
Smoke. Penner, J.

Smoke ghost. Leiber, F.
The smoke people. Satterthwait, W.
Smoke, the embassy cat. Durrell, L.
Smoker. Flanagan, R.
SMOKING
  Eisenberg, D. Days
  King, S. Quitters, Inc.
  Meinke, P. Alice's brother
Smolens, John
  Disciple pigeons
    The Massachusetts Review 28:334-42
      Summ '87
  A letter from her past
    Redbook 170:62+ N '87
Smooth. Katz, S.
Smorgasbord. Wolff, T.
The smuggler. Singer, I. B.
SMUGGLERS *See* Smuggling
Smuggler's Island. Pronzini, B.
SMUGGLING
  Carr, P. M. Night of the luminarias
  Darling, J. The matchstick hut
  Ebon, W. Agua prieta
  El Makk, A. The case
  Fish, R. L. The wager
  Hemingway, E. One trip across
  Hemingway, E. The tradesman's return
  Kipp, G. G. Farewell gesture
  Maupassant, G. de. The man with the
    dogs
  Roberts, M. The ingenuity of Captain
    Spink
  Sayles, J. Tan
  Shacochis, B. Hot day on the Gold Coast
  Stern, R. M. Present for Minna
Smyth, Paul
  A death in Souvála
    The Kenyon Review ns7:1-8 Summ '85
SNAILS
  Highsmith, P. The quest for Blank
    Claveringi
Snake. Farmer, B.
The snake. Grin, A.
Snake eyes. Greenwood, R.
Snake-eyes. Maddox, T.
Snake head. Leidiger, L.
A snake in the grass. Narayan, R. K.
The snake man. Kim, Y. I.
Snakebite. McLean, A.
SNAKES
  Bloch, R. Nina
  Bowles, P. Allal
  Crabtree, L. V. Homer-snake
  Curley, D. Living with snakes
  Honwana, L. B. Papa, snake & I
  Howard, C. Last chance in Singapore
  Kaikō, T. Duel
  Kiely, B. The python
  Lawson, H. The drover's wife
  Millman, L. The great snake massacre
  Muir, A. The reptile
  Ratushinskaya, I. On the meaning of life

Saroyan, W. Najari Levon's old country
    advice to the young Americans on
    how to live with a snake
  Wodehouse, P. G. Something squishy
  Working, R. Pictures of her snake
The snakes. Kawabata, Y.
Snakes. Young, A.
Snap. Baillie, A.
Snap dragon. Hedge, P.
Snapshot. Barnett, A.
Snapshot. Nixon, C.
Snapshots. Schwarz, A. A.
Snapshots. Viramontes, H. M.
Snapshots of a wedding. Head, B.
Snapshots of paradise. Geras, A.
Snares. Erdrich, L.
Sneakers. Laidlaw, M.
Snegurochka. Krysl, M.
Snelling, William Joseph
  Weenokhenchah Wandeeteekah
    Mississippi River tales; ed. by F.
      McSherry; C. G. Waugh and M. H.
      Greenberg
Snelson, Robin
  A racy romance
    Redbook 166:63-5 Ja '86
Snipe hunt. Hansen, J.
The snipe hunters. Wilson, L. A.
Sniped at. Francis, J.
The sniper. DeGrazia, E.
A snitch in time. Bloch, R.
Snobs and marriage. Thackeray, W. M.
SNOBS AND SNOBBISHNESS
  Heker, L. The stolen party
  Pierce, C. The tenants at Auxillac
  Raphael, F. Oxbridge blues
  Sagan, F. Third person singular
  Saiki, J. Retrospective
  Tuohy, F. Fingers in the door
  Wells, H. G. A perfect gentleman on
    wheels
  Whelan, G. Playing with shadows
Snodgrass, Melinda
  Futures yet unseen
    Tales of the Witch World 2
  Requiem
    A Very large array; ed. by M. M. Snod-
      grass
Snodgrass, Richard
  Down in the greenwood O
    *New England Review and Bread Loaf
      Quarterly* 10:283-92 Spr '88
Snow, Jack
  The anchor
    Masterpieces of terror and the super-
      natural; ed. by M. Kaye and S. Kaye
Snow, Karen
  Ghindi
    The North American Review 270:20-6 Mr
      '85
SNOW
  Aiken, C. Silent snow, secret snow
  Amichai, Y. The snow

SNOW—*Continued*
Covino, M. The coming of snow
Flanagan, M. White places
Hall, T. T. Another dark and stormy night
Jewett, S. O. Mrs. Parkins's Christmas Eve
Liben, M. King of the Hill
Maupassant, G. de. The inn
The **snow**. Amichai, Y.
Snow. Baxter, C.
Snow. Beattie, A.
Snow. Crowley, J.
Snow. Kawabata, Y.
Snow. Lasdun, J.
The **snow**. McLaughlin, L.
Snow. Thompson, S.
The **snow** apples. Jones, G.
Snow at the end of the night. Tamer, Z.
Snow-child. Thurm, M.
SNOW STORMS *See* Storms
The **snow** that is nothing in the triangle. Chappell, F.
Snow White. Merseyside fairy story collective
SNOW WHITE AND THE SEVEN DWARFS
    Parodies, travesties, etc.
Merseyside fairy story collective. Snow White
The **snow** white watchman. Valenzuela, L.
Snowball. Curtiss, U. R.
Snowball. Janowitz, T.
Snowball in July. Queen, E.
Snowbird. Dodd, S. M.
Snowblind. Smith, G. B.
Snowbound. Yorke, C. B.
Snowfall. Ford, K.
The **snowman**. Winters, J.
Snowmen. Millhauser, S.
The **snows** of Kilimanjaro. Hemingway, E.
Snows of yesteryear. Rausch, B.
SNOWSTORMS *See* Storms
Snyder, Zilpha Keatley
  The three men
    Dragons and dreams; ed. by J. Yolen; M. H. Greenberg and C. G. Waugh
So, Chong-In
  Home-coming
    Home-coming, and other Korean short stories
  The river
    Flowers of fire; ed. by P. H. Lee
  The way to Kŭmsansa temple
    Home-coming, and other Korean short stories
So, Ki-Won
  Half-holiday
    Two travelers, and other Korean short stories
  The heir
    Flowers of fire; ed. by P. H. Lee
So. Dawson, F.
So cold outside. Kees, W.
So dark for April. Browne, H.

So far from the road, so long until morning. Lowry, B.
So help me. Algren, N.
So hurt and humiliated. King, F. H.
So long, million miles. Rose, D. A.
So much happiness. Ziem, J.
So much water so close to home. Carver, R.
So, some tempestuous morn. Pym, B.
So this is man. Wolfe, T.
So what are you going to do now if you're a friend of Jim's? Franzen, B.
So you're going to have a new body! Schwartz, L. S.
The **soap** bear. Kittredge, W.
The **soap** must go on. Stanton, W.
SOAP SCULPTURE
Kittredge, W. The soap bear
Soapstone. Mawyer, G. D.
SOCCER
Durrell, L. The game's the thing
SOCIAL CLASSES
    See also Class distinction
Cheng, C.-W. Betel Palm Village
Cullen, E. J. Gorbachev's wife
Gordon, M. The neighborhood
James, H. Daisy Miller
Lavin, M. A cup of tea
Oates, J. C. How I contemplated the world from the Detroit House of Correction and began my life over again
O'Hara, J. Price's always open
Updike, J. Getting into the set
Wyndham, F. Obsessions
SOCIAL GROUPS
Silverberg, R. In the group
The **social** hour. Schafler, N.
SOCIAL ISOLATION
Baynton, B. The chosen vessel
Dixon, S. The bridge
A **social** life. Lurie, M.
SOCIAL PROBLEMS
    See also Crime and criminals; Divorce; Drug abuse; Homeless; Juvenile delinquency; Narcotic habit; Poverty; Prejudices; Prostitution; Race relations; Slum life; Suicide; Technology and civilization; Unemployed; Violence
SOCIAL SATIRE *See* Satire
SOCIAL STATUS
Bonner, M. Hate is nothing
Bonner, M. On the altar
Colter, C. The lookout
Hartley, L. P. Mr. Blandfoot's picture
Hartley, L. P. Mrs. Carteret receives
Liben, M. The winners
March, W. Not worthy of a Wentworth
Miller, S. Inventing the Abbotts
Miller, S. The lover of women
O'Hara, J. Graven image
Thackeray, W. M. Snobs and marriage
Tuohy, F. A war of liberation

SOCIAL STATUS—*Continued*
  Wolfe, T. Old Man Rivers
Social studies. Updike, D.
SOCIAL WORKERS
  Brett, S. Double glazing
  Grenon, J. A new dress for Maggie
  Loukakis, A. My neighbour's death
  Williams, T. The dark room
SOCIALISM
  Botwinik, B. Discovered
  Botwinik, B. The general strike
  Botwinik, B. Mendel the Tinsmith
  Chesterton, G. K. Concerning grocers as
    gods
  Johnston, H. The shadow falls
Socialism is coming—stand aside! Nesin, A.
SOCIETY, PRIMITIVE
  Byatt, A. S. The dried witch
  Crace, J. In heat
  Gallant, M. Kingdom come
  Greenberg, J. The supremacy of the Hunza
  Kessler, J. F. Valley
  Schwob, M. The amber-trader
A **society**. Woolf, V.
Society for the benefit of the Daughters of
    Vilnius. Thorman, C.
SOCIETY OF FRIENDS
  Hawthorne, N. The gentle boy
Society of Friends. Schwartz, S.
SOCIOLOGISTS
  McCormack, E. P. A train of gardens—
    Part I: Ireneus Fludd
  McCormack, E. P. A train of gardens—
    Part II: the machine
Sociology. Govier, K.
The **sock**. Davis, L.
Sock finish. Bloch, R.
Socks. Campbell, W. B.
Socks. Kawabata, Y.
Soda pop. Reeve, F. D.
Sodowsky, Roland E.
  Landlady
    Prize stories, Texas Institute of Letters;
      ed. by M. Terry
Sofa art. Dickinson, C.
Soft. Wilson, P. F.
The **soft** core. Vivante, A.
Soft monkey. Ellison, H.
Soft voices at Passenham. White, T. H.
SOFTBALL
  Curley, D. The first baseman
  Janowitz, T. Who's on first?
Sohl, Jerry
  Cabin number six
  Whispers V
The **sojourner**. McCullers, C.
Sokoloff, Thelma C.
  Providence will provide
    Last laughs; ed. by G. Mcdonald
Solace. Havazelet, E.
SOLAR ENERGY
  Asimov, I. The last question
  Clarke, A. C. The wind from the sun

S'Olcarias's sons. Swallow, L.
Sold to Satan. Twain, M.
Soldati, Mario, 1906-
  Footsteps in the snow
    The Penguin book of ghost stories
Soldatow, Sasha, 1947-
  Details, before the event
    Soldatow, S. Private—do not open
  Hass story
    Soldatow, S. Private—do not open
  Last drink is on the house
    Soldatow, S. Private—do not open
  Michael
    Soldatow, S. Private—do not open
  Never blue
    Soldatow, S. Private—do not open
  Pleasure
    Soldatow, S. Private—do not open
  Practising dying
    Soldatow, S. Private—do not open
  Quick exchanges
    Soldatow, S. Private—do not open
  Strangers
    Soldatow, S. Private—do not open
  White noise
    Soldatow, S. Private—do not open
  Writing it down 1972-1975
    Soldatow, S. Private—do not open
The **soldier**. Bitov, A.
Soldier goes to ground. Pascoe, B.
A **soldier** of fortunes. Rand, P.
The **soldier** shows his medal. Moore, R.
SOLDIERS
  Algren, N. That's the way it's always been
  Anderson, P. Among thieves
  Apollinaire, G. The case of the masked
    corporal, that is, the poet resuscitated
  Bradbury, R. By the numbers!
  Burke, J. L. We Build Churches, Inc.
  Calvino, I. The crow comes last
  Chang, T.-C. Birds of a feather
  Crowley, A. The mass of Saint Sécaire
  Davin, D. Below the heavens
  Davin, D. Bourbons
  Davin, D. Cassino casualty
  Davin, D. Danger's flower
  Davin, D. The dog and the dead
  Davin, D. Finders and losers
  Davin, D. In transit
  Davin, D. Liberation
  Davin, D. Mortal
  Davin, D. North of the Sangro
  Davin, D. The Persian's grave
  Davin, D. Psychological warfare at Cassino
  Davin, D. Under the bridge
  Davin, D. When mum died
  Dickson, G. R. Lost Dorsai
  Dickson, G. R. Warrior
  Drake, D. Dragon's teeth
  Garrett, G. P. Don't take no for an
    answer
  Garrett, G. P. The old Army game
  Garrett, G. P. Texarkana was a crazy town

SOLDIERS—*Continued*

Garrett, G. P. Unmapped country
Garrett, G. P. What's the purpose of the bayonet?
Garrett, R. Despoilers of the golden empire
Grin, A. Mystery on a moonlit night
Jakes, J. There's no vinism like chauvinism
London, J. Koolau the leper
Lowry, R. Layover in El Paso
Maupassant, G. de. Epiphany
McCormack, E. P. No country for old men
Niven, L. Night on Mispec Moor
O'Donnell, L. Clash by night
Piper, H. B. Down Styphon!
Poyer, D. C. Three soldiers
Rodoreda, M. That wall, that mimosa
Salisbury, R. The gleams
Salisbury, R. The sonofabitch and the dog
Sarkadi, I. The deserter
Schwob, M. Mérigot Marchès
Sheckley, R. Fool's mate
Singer, I. B. Why Heisherik was born
St. Clair, M. Short in the chest
Sullivan, J. A. Welcome to freedom
Tamer, Z. The ancient gate
Turtledove, H. A difficult undertaking
Wagner, K. E. Cold light
Wells, H. G. The loyalty of Esau Common
Zelazny, R. Passage to Dilfar

Australia

Cowan, P. Drift
Pascoe, B. Soldier goes to ground
Winton, T. Lantern stalk

Canada

Jameison, L. East from Botwood
St. Pierre, P. H. The last day of violence

Czechoslovakia

Hašek, J. The good Soldier Švejk [excerpt]

France

Arnim, L. A., Freiherr von. The madman of Fort Ratonneau
Balzac, H. de. The red inn
Colette. The kepi
Hemingway, E. Black ass at the cross roads
Hill, R. The bull ring
Maupassant, G. de. Bed no. 29
Maupassant, G. de. The colonel's ideas
Maupassant, G. de. Two little soldiers

Germany

Böll, H. Adventures of a haversack
Böll, H. And where were you, Adam?
Böll, H. Between trains in X
Böll, H. Broommakers
Böll, H. The casualty
Böll, H. Cause of death: hooked nose
Böll, H. Children are civilians too
Böll, H. Drinking in Petöcki
Böll, H. Green are the meadows
Böll, H. I can't forget her

Böll, H. In the darkness
Böll, H. Jak the tout
Böll, H. The murder
Böll, H. My Uncle Fred
Böll, H. Pale Anna
Böll, H. The ration runners
Böll, H. Reunion on the avenue
Böll, H. Reunion with Drüng
Böll, H. A soldier's legacy
Böll, H. That time we were in Odessa
Böll, H. The train was on time
Böll, H. The unknown soldier
Böll, H. Vingt-et-un
Böll, H. Vive la France!
Böll, H. When the war broke out
Böll, H. When the war was over
Brentano, C. The story of good Caspar and fair Annie
Calvino, I. Animal woods
Kleist, H. von. Anecdote from the last Prussian war
Lawrence, D. H. The Prussian officer
Maupassant, G. de. Mademoiselle Fifi
Morrill, G. P. Act of honor
Wellman, M. W. The Devil is not mocked

Great Britain

Alter, R. E. The exile
Amis, K. My enemy's enemy
Cowper, R. Brothers
Crane, S. "And if he wills, we must die"
Crane, S. The Kicking Twelfth
Crane, S. The shrapnel of their friends
Crowley, A. The stone of Cybele
Davin, D. Not substantial things
Doyle, Sir A. C. That veteran
Goodis, D. Hawk of the Sudan
Hartley, L. P. Fall in at the double
Morrill, G. P. Act of honor
Sambrot, W. The man who hated

Israel

Amichai, Y. Dicky's death
Amichai, Y. The world is a room
Helprin, M. North light

Italy

Hemingway, E. A simple enquiry

Japan

Abe, K. The dream soldier
Bishop, M. Patriots
Hensley, J. L. Paint doctor
Kojima, N. Stars
Lim Beng Hap. Tricked again
Mishima, Y. Patriotism
Reed, K. The holdouts
Shiga, N. Incident on the afternoon of November third

Korea

O, S.-W. A respite
Pak, S.-J. Ten minutes to seven
Song, P.-S. Debris
Sonu, H. The colonel and his friend
Sonu, H. Flowers of fire
Yi, H.-C. The sultriness of a cold evening

SOLDIERS—*Continued*
Poland
Nowakowski, M. The soldiers and the girl
Rome
Doyle, Sir A. C. The centurion
Hemingway, E. Today is Friday
South Africa
Havemann, E. A farm at Raraba
Soviet Union
See also Cossacks
Babel', I. My first goose
Okudzhava, B. S. Lots of luck, kid!
Pushkin, A. S. The queen of spades
Spain
Ferguson, W. Cortez
United States
Abbott, K. Rick's first visit to the A & W
Abbott, L. K. Rolling thunder
Abbott, L. K. We get smashed and our endings are swift
Algren, N. The heroes
Alter, R. E. Bummer's roost
Bishop, M. Patriots
Boswell, R. Little Bear
Bouma, J. L. Final mission
Brinsmead, H. F. The twilight road
Carunungan, C. A. Hide-out for a hero
Chambers, R. W. The pickets
Chavez, A. The Colonel and the santo
Ch'en, Y.-C. Roses in June
Choe, I.-H. The end of the highway
Crane, S. The clan of no-name
Crane, S. The red badge of courage
Crane, S. Virtue in war
Crapser, W. Baptism of fire
Crapser, W. Billy Sunday
Crapser, W. The descent
Crapser, W. Education of a pointman
Crapser, W. For Timothy Baer
Crapser, W. Hungers
Crapser, W. A letter home [1]
Crapser, W. A letter home [2]
Crapser, W. A letter home [3]
Crapser, W. A letter home [4]
Crapser, W. New man
Crapser, W. Nicky Martinez
Crapser, W. Proud
Crapser, W. R&R
Crapser, W. Remains
Crapser, W. The rest
Crapser, W. The wall: Michael Bowle
DeGrazia, E. The cat-hater
DeGrazia, E. The death of Sin
DeGrazia, E. The enemy
DeGrazia, E. The girl and two old men
DeGrazia, E. The light at the end of the tunnel
DeGrazia, E. The man who cursed and the good Lutheran boy
DeGrazia, E. The mask
DeGrazia, E. The sniper
DeGrazia, E. Zabel's choice

Ehrhart, W. D. Vietnam-Perkasie
Flynn, R. Christmas in a very small place
Flynn, R. The feelings of the dead
Flynn, R. The killer
Foote, S. Pillar of fire
Frazier, R. Across those endless skies
Fuller, R. G. Sherman was right
Hemingway, E. Black ass at the cross roads
Hemingway, E. Night before battle
Hemingway, E. Now I lay me
Hemingway, E. Under the ridge
Hemingway, E. A way you'll never be
Mailer, N. The paper house
McDonald, W. The track
Michener, J. A. Coral Sea
Moore, R. The soldier shows his medal
Mort, J. Hot
Mort, J. Tanks
Muller, R. General Patton did not sleep here
Murphy, D. Roller
O'Brien, T. The ghost soldiers
O'Brien, T. Going after Cacciato
O'Brien, T. The things they carried
Pitzen, J. The village
Ritchie, J. Chicken Charley
Ruta, S. The actor
Schaefer, J. W. Cat nipped
Shaw, I. Act of faith
Shaw, I. Medal from Jerusalem
Shepard, L. Salvador
Smeds, D. Goats
Styron, W. Love day
Taylor, P. H. Rain in the heart
Tiptree, J. Yanqui Doodle
Wetherell, W. D. Spitfire autumn
Whitehouse, A. Bataan landing
Wilhelm, K. The village
Wolff, T. The other Miller
Wolff, T. Soldier's joy
Yates, R. A compassionate leave
Vietnam
Shepard, L. Delta Sly Honey
The **soldiers** and the girl. Nowakowski, M.
Soldier's home. Hemingway, E.
Soldier's joy. Wolff, T.
A **soldier's** legacy. Böll, H.
SOLDIERS OF FORTUNE
Gardner, E. S. The danger zone
Soldier's rest. Ruta, S.
The **sole** of the foot. Natsuki, S.
Sole owners of the mountain. Odom, J.
Solensten, John
Two: a story of numbers
   Stiller's pond; ed. by J. Agee; R. Blakely and S. Welch
SOLICITORS *See* Law and lawyers
The **solicitude** of Pauline Devreux. Villefranche, A.-M.
A **solid** house. Rhys, J.
Solid objects. Woolf, V.
Solid walls. Rile, K.

Solidarity. Innaurato, A.
Solidarity. Reich, T.
Soliloquy. Engberg, S.
Solitaire. Eldridge, M.
SOLITUDE
 Bradley, M. Z. Elbow room
 Chekhov, A. P. The bet
 Fisher, M. F. K. A kitchen allegory
 Martin, V. The parallel world
Solitude. Maupassant, G. de
Solitude. Parise, G.
The **solo.** Minot, S.
Solo flight. Rohde, B.
Solo pass. De Feo, R.
SOLOMON, KING OF ISRAEL
 About
 Russell, B. The Queen of Sheba's night-
 mare
Solomon, Barbara Probst
 America you have gone and left me
 Partisan Review 53 no4:563-76 '86
SOLOMON ISLANDS
 Wollaston, N. Walkabout
Solomon's seal. Hood, M.
Solstice. Hill, K.
Solstice. Kelly, J. P.
Solstice. Long, D.
The **solution.** Lispector, C.
Solwitz, Sharon
 All the men she loved and lost
 Mademoiselle 93:162+ N '87
Soman, Florence Jane
 Enchanted evening
 Good Housekeeping 206:124-5 Ap '88
 Heart's desire
 Good Housekeeping 198:130-1 Mr '84
 Her kind of man
 Good Housekeeping 202:130-1 Ap '86
 Jennifer's wedding day
 Good Housekeeping 201:112-13+ Ag '85
 The men in her life
 Good Housekeeping 205:128+ O '87
 Never say good-bye
 Good Housekeeping 198:144-5 F '84
 One special moment
 Good Housekeeping 200:120-1+ F '85
 Second chance
 Good Housekeeping 206:86-7 Ja '88
 Vital statistics
 Good Housekeeping 204:62+ Je '87
 When dreams come true
 Good Housekeeping 203:138-9+ Jl '86
 When fortune smiles
 Good Housekeeping 202:172-3 Mr '86
 When strangers meet
 Good Housekeeping 200:120-1 Ap '85
Some are born cats. Carr, T., and Carr, C.
'Some' day'. Lawson, H.
Some days are like that. Balfour, B. J.
Some days are like that. Ritchie, J.
Some effects of a hat. Warner, S. T.
Some enchanted evening. Lentricchia, M.

Some have called thee mighty and dreadful.
 Hospital, J. T.
Some killers. Weaver, G.
Some notes on evolution. Bartlett, H.
Some notes on the pre-dynastic epoch. Sil-
 verberg, R.
Some of the things I did not do. Shaw, J.
 B.
Some of these days. Purdy, J.
Some of us had been threatening our friend
 Colby. Barthelme, D.
Some one is watching. Wilhelm, K.
Some opposites of good. Norris, L.
Some passages in the life of a lion
 (Lionizing). See Poe, E. A. Lionizing
Some people will tell you the situation at
 Henny Penny Nursery is getting in-
 tolerable. Rooke, L.
Some surrender. MacLaverty, B.
Some talk. Kamine, M.
Some things I won't do. Thompson, K.
Some words with a mummy. Poe, E. A.
Somebody else's heart. Nagibin, IŪ. M.
Somebody like you. Etchison, D.
Someday he really will come home. De
 Bruyn, G.
Someone else. Raphael, F.
Someone-else. Titcher, M.
Someone else's house. Chisholm, L.
Someone has been disarranging these roses.
 Garcia Márquez, G.
Someone in the lift. Hartley, L. P.
Someone in the neighborhood. Smith, L.
Someone should know this story. Gerber, M.
 J.
Someone's in the kitchen with Dinah. Obst-
 feld, R.
Somerlott, Robert
 The hair of the widow
 The Ethnic detectives; ed. by B. Pronzini
 and M. H. Greenberg
Somers, Armonia, 1920-
 The burial
 Women's fiction from Latin America; ed.
 by E. P. Garfield
 The fall
 Other fires; ed. by A. Manguel
 Plunder
 Women's fiction from Latin America; ed.
 by E. P. Garfield
 The tunnel
 Women's fiction from Latin America; ed.
 by E. P. Garfield
Somers, Jane *See* Lessing, Doris May, 1919-
SOMERSET (ENGLAND) *See* England—
 Somerset
Somerville, Edith Anna Œnone, 1858-1949
 (jt. auth) See Ross, Martin, 1862-1915, and
 Somerville, Edith Anna Œnone, 1858-
 1949
Something à la carte? Durrell, L.
Something a little special. Swados, H.
Something about him. Williams, T.

Something big. Nelsen, R. S.
Something by Tolstoi. Williams, T.
Something called San Francisco. Furman, L.
Something coming through. Wilder, C.
Something for little Robert. Dunn, D.
Something for the dark. Lutz, J.
Something good for Ginnie. Hood, M.
Something green and growing. Curtiss, U. R.
Something happened here. Levine, N.
Something I remember. Markham, B.
Something in the air. Hess, S.
Something like a risk. Calcagno, A.
Something like murder. Lutz, J.
Something nice. Gaitskill, M.
Something on everyone. Lejeune, A.
Something out there. Gordimer, N.
Something sensational to read in the train.
   McCourt, J.
Something similar would be a boarding
   house. Austin, D.
Something special. Schweitzer, G.
Something squishy. Wodehouse, P. G.
Something that happened. Phillips, J. A.
Something the cat dragged in. Highsmith, P.
Something the matter with Dad. Franzen, B.
Something to do. Painter, P.
Something to lose. Whatley, W.
Something to remember you by. Goldreich,
   G.
Something to talk like a family about.
   Flaherty, G.
Something to write home about. Ingalls, R.
Something touchy and delicate again.
   Mathers, P.
Something unforgivable. Krysl, M.
Something wrong. Pronzini, B.
Something you won't understand. Akins, E.
Something's missing. Ziem, J.
Sometimes pain waits. Barnes, Y.
Sometimes the wrong thing is the right thing.
   Camoin, F. A.
Sometimes, when it's slow on the 2 1/2's.
   Burns, G.
Somewhere, Belgium. Kincaid, J.
Somewhere else. Paley, G.
Somewhere geese are flying. Gildner, G.
SOMNAMBULISM
   Gilbert, W. S. Wide awake
Somtow, S. P.
   Anna and the Ripper of Siam
      Ripper! Ed. by G. Dozois and S. Casper
Son, Chang-Sop
   The rainy season
      Flowers of fire; ed. by P. H. Lee
   Walking in the snow
      A Respite, and other Korean short
      stories
Son, So-Hui
   At the end of the world
      Hospital room 205, and other Korean
      short stories
The son. Leitão, L.
The son. Swift, G.

Son and father. Rey Rosa, R.
Son and heir. Read, P. P.
Son, father, judge. Bartov, H.
Son of a witch. Bloch, R.
Son of celluloid. Barker, C.
The son of Kermaria. Valenzuela, L.
Sonata for harp and bicycle. Aiken, J.
Sonata for two pianos. Pollitt, K.
Sonata in G minor. Kalpakian, L.
Sonderlund, Nils O.
   The angel from hell
      Sensuous science fiction from the weird
      and spicy pulps; ed. by S. Jaffery
Song, Pyong-Su
   Debris
      Two travelers, and other Korean short
      stories
Song, Yong
   Cock-fighting
      Home-coming, and other Korean short
      stories
   Overnight at Matthew's
      Home-coming, and other Korean short
      stories
The song. Dawson, F.
A song for Lya. Martin, G. R. R.
A song for one still voice. Jorgensen, B. W.
Song from the highest tower. Tager, M.
Song of a dead girl. Abe, K.
Song of a drowning sailor: a fabliau. Garrett,
   G. P.
The song of Rhodanthe. Petrakis, H. M.
The song of Roland. Freeman, C.
Song of songs. Petrakis, H. M.
Song of stars. Borgen, J.
The song of the fisherman. Bowles, C.
Song of the geometry instructor. Berry, R.
   M.
The song of the Minster. Canton, W.
The song of the wren. Bates, H. E.
Song of willow. Summers, M.
Song on Royal Street. Blessing, R.
The songbirds of pain. Kilworth, G.
SONGS
   Asimov, I. Yankee Doodle went to town
   Maupassant, G. de. The accursed bread
   Rhys, J. Let them call it jazz
SONGS, POPULAR See Popular music
Songs my mother taught me that are not
   in Hamlet; or, "Come into my house,
   Horatio! there are more things under
   the mattress than are dreamt of in
   your philosophy!". Granit, A.
Songs of a sentient flute. Herbert, F.
The songs of distant Earth. Clarke, A. C.
SONGWRITERS See Composers
Sonnemann, W. K.
   The council of drones
      Amazing science fiction anthology: The
      war years, 1936-1945; ed. by M. H.
      Greenberg
Sonny's blues. Baldwin, J.
The sonofabitch and the dog. Salisbury, R.

SONS *See* Fathers and sons; Mothers and sons
Sons. Krysl, M.
SONS-IN-LAW
Bonnie, F. Squatter's rights
Bumpus, J. Heroes and villains
The **sons** of Chan. Chin, F.
Sontag, Susan, 1933-
Description (of a description)
Harper's 270:32-4 Ja '85
The letter scene
The New Yorker 62:24-32 Ag 18 '86
Unguided tour
The Art of the tale; ed. by D. Halpern
The way we live now
The Best American short stories, 1987
The New Yorker 62:42-51 N 24 '86
Sonu, Hwi
The colonel and his friend
One way, and other Korean short stories
Flowers of fire
Flowers of fire; ed. by P. H. Lee
The mirror
One way, and other Korean short stories
One way
One way, and other Korean short stories
Spark of life
One way, and other Korean short stories
The story of a peculiar pain
One way, and other Korean short stories
The terrorist
One way, and other Korean short stories
Thoughts of home
One way, and other Korean short stories
Sonya, Crane Wessleman, and Kittee. Wolfe, G.
The **Soo** girl charity. O'Donnell, P.
Sophie's Sunday afternoon. Ade, G.
Sopwith Hall. Warner, S. T.
The **sorcerer's** apprentice. Johnson, C. R.
The **sorcerer's** son. Rey Rosa, R.
SORCERY *See* Witchcraft
A **sordid** affair. Doyle, Sir A. C.
Sorghum. Mason, B. A.
The **Soroca** girls. Malaparte, C.
Sorrells, Robert T., 1932-
The all-time master grand-master of solitaire
Sorrells, R. T. The blacktop champion of Ickey Honey, and other stories
The blacktop champion of Ickey Honey
Sorrells, R. T. The blacktop champion of Ickey Honey, and other stories
Charley Billy
Sorrells, R. T. The blacktop champion of Ickey Honey, and other stories
Drowning
Sorrells, R. T. The blacktop champion of Ickey Honey, and other stories
A fan of the game
Sorrells, R. T. The blacktop champion of Ickey Honey, and other stories

Lovers
Sorrells, R. T. The blacktop champion of Ickey Honey, and other stories
The man who walked pigeons
Sorrells, R. T. The blacktop champion of Ickey Honey, and other stories
A mature and civilized relationship
Sorrells, R. T. The blacktop champion of Ickey Honey, and other stories
The phone call
Sorrells, R. T. The blacktop champion of Ickey Honey, and other stories
Rookie
Sorrells, R. T. The blacktop champion of Ickey Honey, and other stories
Talking to the boy
Sorrells, R. T. The blacktop champion of Ickey Honey, and other stories
Three rivers
Sorrells, R. T. The blacktop champion of Ickey Honey, and other stories
When Etta Reece danced
Sorrells, R. T. The blacktop champion of Ickey Honey, and other stories
Sorrentino, Fernando
Ars poetica
Sorrentino, F. Sanitary centennial, and selected short stories
The fetid tale of Antulín
Sorrentino, F. Sanitary centennial, and selected short stories
In self-defense
Sorrentino, F. Sanitary centennial, and selected short stories
The life of the party
Sorrentino, F. Sanitary centennial, and selected short stories
A lifestyle
Sorrentino, F. Sanitary centennial, and selected short stories
Piccirilli
Sorrentino, F. Sanitary centennial, and selected short stories
Sorrentino, Gilbert, 1929-
The gala cocktail party
The Pushcart prize IX
Sorrowful mysteries. Dubus, A.
Sorrows of the flesh. Huggan, I.
Sorry fugu. Boyle, T. C.
A **sort** of eligible man. Swick, M.
A **sort** of retirement. Haylock, J.
The **sorting** out. Painter, P.
Sorworth Place. Kirk, R.
Sou-Sou money. Seepaul, L.
Soucy, Jean-Yves
The red boots
Intimate strangers; ed. by M. Cohen and W. Grady
Soukup, Martha
Dress rehearsal
Universe 16

Soukup, Martha—*Continued*
Frenchmen and plumbers
 A Very large array; ed. by M. M. Snodgrass
Living in the jungle
 L. Ron Hubbard presents Writers of the future v3

SOUL
 See also Transmigration
Duntemann, J., and Kress, N. Borovsky's hollow woman
Ellison, H. Laugh track
Hogg, J. On the separate existence of the soul
Kilworth, G. The dissemblers
Kirk, R. The peculiar demesne of Archvicar Gerontion
Kōda, R. Encounter with a skull
Kress, N. Borovsky's hollow woman
Llywelyn, M. Me, tree
Reynolds, M. Your soul comes C.O.D.
Wilde, O. The fisherman and his soul
Soul brother. Rivarola Matto, J. B.
Souls. Russ, J.
Souls belated. Wharton, E.
Sound alibi. Ritchie, J.
Sound effects. Ely, D.
Sound is second sight. Schwartz, L. S.
Sound morality. Hogg, J.
The **sound** of a girl singing. Matthews, J.
The **sound** of murder. Westlake, D. E.
The **sound** of the gong. Moon, S.-T.
The **sound** of the river. Rhys, J.
The **sound** of the river. Shepperson, J.
The **sound** of Velcro. Schwartz, L. S.
SOUND RECORDINGS
 Doyle, Sir A. C. The voice of science
Ellison, H. Laugh track
Sladek, J. T. Red noise
Wolfe, G. The recording
The **sound** tape. Morris, W.
The **sound** track. Calisher, H.
Sound worm. Mathers, P.
A **sounding** brass. Cox, E.
Soundings in feet and fathoms. Steinbach, M.
Sounds. Thurm, M.
Sounds of a summer night. Pastan, R.
Sounds of the rude world. Schinto, J.
Soup for the sick. Aucamp, H.
Soupstone. Dickson, G. R.
The **source** of the Nile is Cairo's Muqattam Hills. Higazy, F.
Source seven. Gilbert, M.
Sources agree rock swoon has no past. Hannah, B.
The **soutane**. King, F. H.
SOUTH (U.S.) *See* Southern States
South. Blaise, C.
SOUTH AFRICA
 Hornung, E. W. The knees of the gods
19th century
Doyle, Sir A. C. The mystery of Sasassa Valley

Doyle, Sir A. C. The stone of Boxman's Drift
Fitzpatrick, J. P. The outspan
Smith, P. The schoolmaster
20th century
Abrahams, L. Invisible worm
Abrahams, L. Knowledge
Colvin, C. Near Forelanders Kop
Davis, G. P. African story
Eskapa, S. White and injured
Essop, A. The betrayal
Essop, A. The commandment
Essop, A. Labyrinth
Essop, A. Ten years
Godfrey, P. The lady and the dragon
Gordimer, N. The bridegroom
Gordimer, N. A correspondence course
Gordimer, N. Crimes of conscience
Havemann, E. The animal lover
Havemann, E. A farm at Raraba
Jonker, I. The goat
Levinson, B. ". . . .and he chose a mule"
Lipenga, K. The road to Migowi
Mhlope, G. It's quiet now
Ndebele, N. The music of the violin
Ndebele, N. The prophetess
Ndebele, N. The test
Ndebele, N. Uncle
Roberts, S. The butcher shop
Spark, M. The curtain blown by the breeze
Spark, M. The pawnbroker's wife
Spark, M. The Seraph and the Zambesi
Farm life
 See Farm life—South Africa
Native peoples
Delius, A. Hannie's journal
Essop, A. Two sisters
Gordimer, N. Blinder
Gordimer, N. A city of the dead, a city of the living
Gordimer, N. Not for publication
Gordimer, N. Six feet of the country
Havemann, E. A farm at Raraba
Moikangoa, C. E. Sebolelo comes home
Moss, R. Exile
Motsisi, C. Boy-boy
Mphahlele, E. Mrs. Plum
Mzamane, M. My cousin comes to Jo'burg
Ntuli, D. B. Z. Once in a century
Wicomb, Z. Ash on my sleeve
Wicomb, Z. Bowl like hole
Wicomb, Z. A fair exchange
Wicomb, Z. Home sweet home
Wicomb, Z. Jan Klinkies
Wicomb, Z. A trip to the Gifberge
Wicomb, Z. You can't get lost in Cape Town
Politics
 See Politics—South Africa
Prisoners and prisons
 See Prisoners and prisons—South Africa

SOUTH AFRICA—*Continued*

Race relations

Abrahams, P. Crackling day
Abrahams, P. Lonesome
Aucamp, H. Soup for the sick
Balfour, C. To the torturor
Becker, J. The stench
Cripps, A. S. Fuel of fire
Dangor, A. A strange romance
Dhlomo, R. R. R. The death of Masaba
Eskapa, S. Between the sheets
Essop, A. Black and white
Essop, A. Gerty's brother
Goldswain, R. Dube's first day
Gordimer, N. Blinder
Gordimer, N. A chip of glass ruby
Gordimer, N. City lovers
Gordimer, N. A city of the dead, a city of the living
Gordimer, N. Country lovers
Gordimer, N. Something out there
Gordimer, N. Town lovers
Havemann, E. Bloodsong
Havemann, E. Death of the Nation
Havemann, E. Incident at Mhlaba Jail
Havemann, E. An interview
Havemann, E. Pure Hamitic strain
Havemann, E. Spirits do not forgive
Jacobson, D. Beggar my neighbour
Jacobson, D. A day in the country
Lessing, D. M. The old Chief Mshlanga
Mathabane, M. The road to Alexandra
Mhlope, G. The toilet
Moss, R. Light dark
Mphahlele, E. The master of Doornvlei
Mphahlele, E. Mrs. Plum
Ndebele, N. Fools
Paton, A. A drink in the passage
Rabie, J. Drought
Rive, R. The bench
Rive, R. Resurrection
Sutherland, M. Loving
Wicomb, Z. When the train comes

Cape Town

Black, S. The cloud child
Simon, B. Monologue for Danny
Wicomb, Z. Behind the Bougainvillea
Wicomb, Z. A clearing in the bush
Wicomb, Z. When the train comes

Johannesburg

Gordimer, N. Native country
Mzamane, M. My cousin comes to Jo'burg
Williams, A. Being a murderer myself

SOUTH AFRICAN SOLDIERS *See* Soldiers—South Africa

SOUTH AFRICANS

See also Afrikaners

United States

Moss, R. Exile

Zambia

Gordimer, N. Abroad

SOUTH AMERICA

See also Amazon River Valley

Davidson, A. Sleep well of nights
García Márquez, G. Monologue of Isabel watching it rain in Macondo
García Márquez, G. There are no thieves in this town
Hudson, W. H. The story of a piebald horse

Politics

See Politics—South America

South America. Dunn, D.

SOUTH CAROLINA

See also Sullivan's Island (S.C.)

Poe, E. A. The gold-bug
Sorrells, R. T. The blacktop champion of Ickey Honey
Wolfe, T. Old Catawba

Charleston

Rand, P. Circe
Shange, N. Sassafrass, Cypress & Indigo [excerpt]
Smith, C. Canaan [excerpt]

South Dakota samaritans. Bedard, B.

South fork. Hermann, J.

The **South** lingers on. Fisher, R.

SOUTH SEA ISLANDS *See* Islands of the Pacific

South Sea sensations. Broun, H.

South wind. Tsushima, Y.

SOUTH YEMEN *See* Yemen (People's Democratic Republic)

A **southern** landscape. Spencer, E.

Southern lights. Lee, T.

SOUTHERN RHODESIA *See* Zimbabwe

SOUTHERN STATES

Abbott, L. K. A modern story of Woe and Lovecraft
Adams, A. New best friends
Akins, E. George Bailey fishing
Alderson, T. The auction
Bass, R. The watch
Benedict, P. Booze
Benedict, P. Dog
Benedict, P. Hackberry
Blaise, C. South
Bloch, R. The warm farewell
Boyle, T. C. Not a leg to stand on
Brown, M. W. Let him live
Child, L. M. F. The quadroons
Cullen, E. J. The baddest, baddest days
Daniels, C. Lacy Mallard
East, C. A tribute to the general
Faulkner, W. Dry September
Faulkner, W. Skirmish at Sartoris
Fitzgerald, Z. Miss Ella
Fox, W. P. Doug Broome, hamburger king
Gardiner, J. R. Game farm
Garrett, G. P. Noise of strangers
Garrett, G. P. Song of a drowning sailor: a fabliau
Gordon, C. Hear the nightingale sing
Gordon, C. Old Red

SOUTHERN STATES—*Continued*
Grizzard, L. Good men of God
Hall, J. Gas
Hannah, B. Getting ready
Hannah, B. Horning in--A
Hannah, B. Ride, fly, penetrate, loiter
Hassell, H. History of the South
Hood, M. Desire call of the wild hen
Hood, M. Moths
Hood, M. Nobody's fool
Humphrey, W. A fresh snow
Hurston, Z. N. The Eatonville anthology
Kingsolver, B. Rose-Johnny
McDowell, M. Miss Mack
Montgomery, M. I got a gal
Moyer, K. Ruth's daughter
O'Connor, F. An afternoon in the woods
O'Connor, F. The barber
O'Connor, F. A circle in the fire
O'Connor, F. The displaced person
O'Connor, F. The geranium
O'Connor, F. A late encounter with the enemy
O'Connor, F. The life you save may be your own
O'Connor, F. Parker's back
O'Connor, F. The Partridge festival
O'Connor, F. Revelation
O'Connor, F. The river
O'Connor, F. A stroke of good fortune
O'Connor, F. A Temple of the Holy Ghost
O'Connor, F. The train
Powell, P. Edisto [excerpt]
Quammen, D. Uriah's letter
Richard, M. Happiness of the garden variety
Sams, F. Big Star woman
Sams, F. Fubar
Sams, F. Judgment
Sams, F. Run with the horsemen [excerpt]
Schell, J. Alvira, Lettie, and Pip
Shelnutt, E. Voice
Smith, L. Cakewalk
Steadman, M. John Fletcher's night of love
Steele, M. The cat and the coffee drinkers
Stribling, T. S. The colonel's predicament
Taylor, P. E. The god-chaser
Waldrop, H. The ugly chickens
Wallin, L. The redneck poacher's son [excerpt]
Wellman, M. W. Coven
Whisnant, L. Wallwork
Williams, T. The knightly guest
Wolfe, T. Boom town
Woolson, C. F. Miss Elisabetha
Farm life
See Farm life—Southern States
Mountain life
See Mountain life—Southern States
SOUTHERN STATES DIALECT *See*
Dialect stories—Southern States
The **southern** thruway. Cortázar, J.

SOUTHWEST, NEW *See* Southwestern States
SOUTHWESTERN STATES
Evans, M. Candles in the bottom of the pool
Keller, G. D. The mojado who offered up his tapeworms to the public weal
Soutter, Andy
S F
P.E.N. new fiction I
Soviet jewellery. Avery, M.
SOVIET SOLDIERS *See* Soldiers—Soviet Union
SOVIET UNION
See also Lithuania; Siberia (Soviet Union); Ukraine
Abernathy, R. Heirs apparent
Alexin, A. The class photograph
Auswaks, A. The priest
Gogol', N. V. The overcoat
Kotzwinkle, W. That winter when Prince Borisov was everybody's favorite
Kuznetsova, A. Storms of a cruel fate
Pasternak, B. L. Letters from Tula
16th century
Gogol', N. V. Taras Bulba
19th century
Chekhov, A. P. At a country house
Chekhov, A. P. Murder
Chekhov, A. P. New villa
Chekhov, A. P. With friends
Forsh, O. Ham's wife
Gorky, M. Cain and Artyom
Gorky, M. Creatures that once were men
Leskov, N. S. Lady Macbeth of Mtsensk
Leskov, N. S. Musk-Ox
Leskov, N. S. The sealed angel
Leskov, N. S. A winter's day
Rostopchina, E. P., grafiniá. Rank and money
Turgenev, I. S. Clara Militch
Wiebe, D. E. Narodny Rasprava
1900-1917
Andreyev, L. Darkness
Botwinik, B. Discovered
Chekhov, A. P. At home
Chekhov, A. P. The Black Monk
Chekhov, A. P. The two Volodyas
Chekhov, A. P. A woman's kingdom
Leskov, N. S. The cattle pen
Leskov, N. S. The sealed angel
Pil'niāk, B. The Nizhni Novgorod Otkos
Pushkin, A. S. The queen of spades
Wiebe, D. E. At the Rotonde
20th century
Goff, I. A ticket to Odessa
Panova, V. F. Evdokia
1917-1945
Böll, H. Children are civilians too
Pil'niāk, B. A dog's life
1945-
Aksenov, V. P. Rendezvous
Aksenov, V. P. Super-deluxe

SOVIET UNION—1945-—*Continued*
Baranskaya, N. The retirement party
Bitov, A. The big balloon
Bitov, A. The forest
Bitov, A. The garden
Bitov, A. The idler
Bitov, A. Infantiev
Bitov, A. The leg
Bitov, A. Notes from the corner
Bitov, A. Penelope
Bitov, A. The soldier
Bitov, A. The taste
Bitov, A. The third story
Grekova, I. One summer in the city
Katerli, N. The Barsukov Triangle
Maramzin, V. The two-toned blond: a reciprocal tale
Okudzhava, B. S. Singular misfortunes amidst a parade of successes
Patron, J. F. The wallet
Popov, E. Three tales
Rasputin, V. G. Rudolfio
Shukshin, V. M. The microscope
Shukshin, V. M. Moving to the country
Shukshin, V. M. The sufferings of young Vaganov
Aristocracy
See Aristocracy—Soviet Union
Army
Leskov, N. S. The sentry
Okudzhava, B. S. Lots of luck, kid!
Communism
See Communism—Soviet Union
Peasant life
See Peasant life—Soviet Union
Prisoners and prisons
See Prisoners and prisons—Soviet Union
Revolution of 1917
See Soviet Union—1917-1945
Rural life
Abramov, F. Olesha's cabin
Aksenov, V. P. Surplussed barrelware
Backus, J. L. Ludmila
Berdnyk, O. The apostle of immortality, a tale of the unprecedented
Bitov, A. Life in windy weather
Bunin, I. A. Sunstroke
Chekhov, A. P. The fiancée
Chekhov, A. P. My life
Chekhov, A. P. My wife
Chekhov, A. P. On official business
Chekhov, A. P. Peasant women
Chekhov, A. P. The requiem
Chekhov, A. P. Rothschild's fiddle
Chekhov, A. P. The student
Chekhov, A. P. Terror
Chekhov, A. P. Three years
Gogol', N. V. The coach
Gogol', N. V. Ivan Fiodorovich Shponka and his aunt
Gogol', N. V. Old-world landowners
Harris, F. The holy man

Iskander, F. Grandfather
Kazakov, Y. Nikishka's secrets
Leskov, N. S. Musk-Ox
Leskov, N. S. A robbery
Moore, G. A Russian husband
Nagibin, ÍŪ. M. Elijah's Day
Nagibin, ÍŪ. M. Olezhka got married
Nagibin, ÍŪ. M. Winter oak
Pasternak, B. L. Zhenya Luvers' childhood
Pil'nīāk, B. Mahogany
Pil'nīāk, B. Mother earth
Pil'nīāk, B. A year of their life
Rasputin, V. G. French lessons
Rasputin, V. G. The old woman
Rasputin, V. G. Vasili and Vasilisa
Rasputin, V. G. What shall I tell the crow?
Rasputin, V. G. You live and love
Rasulov, M.-R. The eve of love
Shalamov, V. T. Condensed milk
Shukshin, V. M. Before the cock crows thrice
Shukshin, V. M. The court case
Shukshin, V. M. Makar Zherebtsov
Shukshin, V. M. The old man's dying
Shukshin, V. M. The outsider
Shukshin, V. M. Roubles in words, kopeks in figures
Shukshin, V. M. Shiva dancing
Shukshin, V. M. Stefan
Tolstoy, L., graf. God sees the truth but waits
Varlamova, I. A ladle for pure water
Zalygin, S. The night of the angels
Bessarabia
Blythe, R. Here be dragons
Leningrad
Gogol', N. V. Nevsky Prospekt
Gogol', N. V. The portrait
Leskov, N. S. An apparition in the Engineers' Castle
Shukshin, V. M. The postscript
Thubron, C. The ear
Moscow
Bulychev, K. Another's memory
Trifonov, ÍŪ. Games at dusk
SOVIET UNION. ARMY *See* Soviet Union. Red Army
SOVIET UNION. RED ARMY
Officers
Bunin, I. A. Sunstroke
Chekhov, A. P. The kiss
Gogol', N. V. The coach
Gogol', N. V. Nevsky Prospekt
Pil'nīāk, B. The tale of the unextinguished moon
The **sow** and Silas. Bates, H. E.
SPACE AND TIME
See also Relativity (Physics); Time travel
Asimov, I. The ugly little boy
Ballard, J. G. Memories of the Space Age
Ballard, J. G. Myths of the near future

SPACE AND TIME—*Continued*
Blish, J. Common time
Bloch, R. The world-timer
Burdick, B. S. From time to time
Carr, T. Thus I refute
Du Maurier, Dame D. Split second
Edwards, M. After-images
Ellison, H. Jeffty is five
Farmer, P. J. The shadow of space
Flynn, M. The forest of time
Godwin, P. Stroke of mercy
Harrison, H. Run from the fire
Lee, R. B. Knight of shallows
Leinster, M. Sidewise in time
Longyear, B. B. Collector's item
Neville, K. The forest of Zil
Norton, A. The long night of waiting
Rucker, R. von B. In frozen time
Silverberg, R. Breckenridge and the continuum
Silverberg, R. The changeling
Varley, J. The pusher
Wells, H. G. The queer story of Brownlow's newspaper
Willis, C. Chance
The **space** between. Grenville, K.
SPACE BIOLOGY
Vance, J. The gift of gab
Space-born. Bloch, R.
SPACE COLONIES
Anthony, P. The alien rulers
Bakhnov, V. The fifth on the left
Chandler, A. B. The cage
Farber, S. N. Passing as a flower in the city of the dead
Federici, C. M. 'Oh, Lenore!' came the echo
Haldeman, J. W. Tricentennial
Herbert, F. Passage for piano
Herbert, F. Seed stock
Miller, W. M. Crucifixus etiam
Neville, K. The price of Simeryl
Panshin, A. Down to the worlds of men
Russ, J. When it changed
Sheckley, R. The native problem
Silverberg, R. The trouble with Sempoanga
Tsyganov, V. Martian tales
Watson, I. The milk of knowledge
Watson, I. Peace
SPACE FLIGHT
See also Astronauts; Interplanetary voyages; Science fiction
Anderson, P. The light
Anderson, P. Vulcan's forge
Anthony, P. The ghost galaxies
Asimov, I. Does a bee care?
Baumgart, D. All you can eat
Berdnyk, O. The alien secret
Berdnyk, O. A chorus of elements
Blish, J. Common time
Bloch, R. The strange flight of Richard Clayton
Boylan, J. Elvis in space

Campbell, L. A sum of moments
Dick, P. K. Frozen journey
Ellison, H. Back to the drawing boards
Ellison, H. Commuter's problem
Ellison, H. Nothing from my noon meal
Fitch, M. They that go down to the sea in ships
Kelly, J. P. Glass cloud
King, S. The Jaunt
Longyear, B. B. SHAWNA, Ltd.
Meckel, C. The sand ball
Messenger, B. Give it back to the Indians
Mikhailov, V. Brook on Iapetus
Osinsky, V. Spaceship
Richards, J. The bridge sings
Schmidt, S. The unreachable star
Sheckley, R. A wind is rising
Silverberg, R. Schwartz between the galaxies
Silverberg, R. Ship-sister, star-sister
Smith, C. Drunkboat
Varley, J. Lollipop and the tar baby
Watson, I. Nightmares
Wolfe, G. All the hues of hell
Zahn, T. Cascade point
SPACE FLIGHT TO JUPITER
Clarke, A. C. A meeting with Medusa
SPACE FLIGHT TO MARS
Ballard, J. G. The cage of sand
Silverberg, R. The feast of St. Dionysus
SPACE FLIGHT TO THE MOON
Anderson, P. The light
Bishop, M. Cold war orphans
Clarke, A. C. The sentinel
Gauger, R. The vacuum-packed picnic
Hartmann, W. K. Handprints on the Moon
Morris, M. Conquering space
Sabah, V. An imaginary journey to the moon
Space Invaders. Ferguson, W.
Space invaders. Wilhelm, P.
SPACE PROBES
Meckel, C. The sand ball
Zebrowski, G. Starcrossed
SPACE SHIPS
Anderson, P. Eve times four
Anderson, P. Third stage
Asimov, I. The Martian way
Bradbury, R. I, rocket
Brin, D. Bubbles
Bryning, F. Place of the throwing-stick
Clarke, A. C. Hide and seek
Clarke, A. C. Jupiter V
Clarke, A. C. Refugee
DeLillo, D. Human moments in World War III
Dick, P. K. The alien mind
Dickson, G. R. Sleight of wit
Farmer, P. J. The shadow of space
Hamilton, E. Requiem
Johnson, C. R. Popper's disease
Russell, E. F. Jay Score

SPACE SHIPS—*Continued*
Vance, J. Sail 25
Walsh, J. M. The wreck in the void
White, L. A. Old Mickey Flip had a marvelous ship
Wilcox, D. The voyage that lasted 600 years
Wolfe, G. Alien stones
SPACE STATIONS
Asimov, I. Reason
Bradley, M. Z. Elbow room
Bradley, M. Z. Hero's moon
Harness, C. L. Signals
Kingsbury, D. The moon goddess and the son
Kress, N. Borovsky's hollow woman
Neville, K. Cold war
Sheckley, R. A wind is rising
Sterling, B., and Gibson, W. Red star, winter orbit
Turner, G. In a Petri dish upstairs
Varley, J. Tango Charlie and Foxtrot Romeo
Young, P. ja. The helldivers
Space-time for springers. Leiber, F.
SPACE TRAVEL *See* Space flight
Spaceship. Osinsky, V.
Spackman, W. M. (William Mode), 1905-
Declarations of intent
Southwest Review 72:455-74 Aut '87
Spackman, William Mode *See* Spackman, W. M. (William Mode), 1905-
Spain, Chris
Horizontal light
The Antioch Review 46:20-6 Wint '88
Spain, John *See* Adams, Cleve Franklin, 1895-1949
SPAIN
Anderson, P. The little monster
Rodoreda, M. Therafina
17th century
Wilde, O. The birthday of the Infanta
19th century
Stevenson, R. L. Olalla
Civil War, 1936-1939
Hemingway, E. The butterfly and the tank
Hemingway, E. The denunciation
Hemingway, E. Landscape with figures
Hemingway, E. Night before battle
Hemingway, E. Old man at the bridge
Hemingway, E. Under the ridge
Moorhouse, F. Buenaventura Durruti's funeral
Sciascia, L. Antimony
Rural life
Morris, W. In another country
Sage, V. Nada
Barcelona
Adams, A. Barcelona
Costa Brava
Just, W. S. The Costa Brava, 1959
Madrid
Hemingway, E. The capital of the world

Sanders, S. R. The cry
Majorca
See Majorca (Spain)
Palma
Boylan, C. Villa Marta
Seville
Bishop, M. The quickening
SPANIARDS
Moore, L. The deep valley
Tuohy, F. The potlatch of Esmeralda
Philippines
José, F. S. The heirs
SPANISH AMERICAN WAR, 1898 *See* United States—War of 1898
SPANISH AMERICANS
Austin, M. H. Old Spanish gardens
SPANISH ARMADA, 1588 *See* Armada, 1588
The **Spanish** bed. Pritchett, V. S.
Spanish Castle. Abbott, K.
SPANISH CIVIL WAR, 1936-1939 *See* Spain—Civil War, 1936-1939
SPANISH INQUISITION *See* Inquisition
Spanish ladies. Pilcher, R.
A **Spanish** lesson. Shepard, L.
The **Spanish** letter. Wolfe, T.
SPANISH SOLDIERS *See* Soldiers—Spain
Spare change. Taylor, C.
Spark, Debra, 1962-
The incorrect hour
The New generation; ed. by A. Kaufman
The North American Review 271:10-15 Je '86
Summer of the dead frogs
Esquire 104:88-91+ Ag '85
The Esquire fiction reader v2
Spark, Muriel
Alice Long's dachshunds
Spark, M. The stories of Muriel Spark
The Substance of things hoped for; ed. by J. B. Breslin
Another pair of hands
The New Yorker 61:46-50 My 13 '85
Spark, M. The stories of Muriel Spark
Winter's tales, new ser. v3
Bang-bang you're dead
Spark, M. The stories of Muriel Spark
The Black Madonna
Spark, M. The stories of Muriel Spark
Come along, Marjorie
Spark, M. The stories of Muriel Spark
The curtain blown by the breeze
Spark, M. The stories of Muriel Spark
Daisy Overend
Spark, M. The stories of Muriel Spark
The dark glasses
Spark, M. The stories of Muriel Spark
The dragon
The New Yorker 61:24-9 Ag 12 '85
Spark, M. The stories of Muriel Spark
Winter's tales, new ser. v2

Spark, Muriel—*Continued*

The executor
  Spark, M. The stories of Muriel Spark
  Winter's tales, new ser. v1
The fathers' daughters
  Spark, M. The stories of Muriel Spark
  The Treasury of English short stories;
    ed. by N. Sullivan
The first year of my life
  Spark, M. The stories of Muriel Spark
The fortune-teller
  Spark, M. The stories of Muriel Spark
The gentile Jewesses
  Spark, M. The stories of Muriel Spark
The go-away bird
  Spark, M. The stories of Muriel Spark
The house of the famous poet
  Haunting women; ed. by A. Ryan
  The Penguin book of modern British
    short stories
  Spark, M. The stories of Muriel Spark
The leaf-sweeper
  The Penguin book of ghost stories
  Spark, M. The stories of Muriel Spark
A member of the family
  Spark, M. The stories of Muriel Spark
Miss Pinkerton's apocalypse
  Spark, M. The stories of Muriel Spark
The ormolu clock
  Spark, M. The stories of Muriel Spark
The pawnbroker's wife
  Spark, M. The stories of Muriel Spark
The Playhouse called Remarkable
  Spark, M. The stories of Muriel Spark
The Portobello Road
  The Penguin book of horror stories
  Spark, M. The stories of Muriel Spark
'A sad tale's best for winter'
  Spark, M. The stories of Muriel Spark
The Seraph and the Zambesi
  Spark, M. The stories of Muriel Spark
The twins
  Spark, M. The stories of Muriel Spark
You should have seen the mess
  Spark, M. The stories of Muriel Spark
Spark of life. Sonu, H.
Sparking. Steinbach, M.
Sparkle in five. Thomas, J.
Sparkling celluloid. Cooper, R. R.
Sparks. Minot, S.
Sparling, E. Earl
Daughter of Lescale
  Mississippi River tales; ed. by F.
    McSherry; C. G. Waugh and M. H.
    Greenberg
Sparrow's fall. Springer, N.
The **sparrow's** matchmaking. Kawabata, Y.
SPAS *See* Health resorts, watering places,
    etc.
The **spasm.** Maupassant, G. de
Spats. Martin, V.
Speak. Dixon, S.
The **spear** thrower. Page, F.

A **special** case. Camoin, F. A.
Special duties. Greene, G.
A **special** occasion. Warren, J.
A **special** relationship. Tuohy, F.
The **speck.** Asimov, I.
The **speckled** band. See Doyle, Sir A. C. The
    adventure of the speckled band
Speck's idea. Gallant, M.
The **spectacles.** Poe, E. A.
A **spectator** sport. Givner, J.
The **specter.** Maupassant, G. de
Specter of the Rose. Hecht, B.
Spector, Craig
Lifecast
  Silver scream; ed. by D. J. Schow
  (jt. auth) See Skipp, John, and Spector,
    Craig
A **spectre** of ancient dust. Dadswell, M.
Speech. Umans, R.
The **speech** of Polly Baker. Franklin, B.
Speech sounds. Butler, O. E.
SPEECHES, ADDRESSES, ETC.
  See also Lectures and lecturing
  Ade, G. Dubley, '89
  O'Kelly, S. The man with the gift
  Warner, S. T. Chloroform for all
Speed, Jane
Fair's fair
  Ready or not; ed. by J. Kahn
Speed of light. Rushin, P.
Speeding. Breault, M. E.
The **speeding** ticket. Keillor, G.
Speer, Hugh
Shawm of the stars
  Sensuous science fiction from the weird
    and spicy pulps; ed. by S. Jaffery
Spell bereavement. Lish, G.
Spell my name with an S. Asimov, I.
The **spell** of her beautiful garden. McCorkle,
    J.
Spells. Janowitz, T.
Spence, Alan
The rain dance
  Streets of stone; ed. by M. Burgess and
    H. Whyte
Tinsel
  Streets of stone; ed. by M. Burgess and
    H. Whyte
Spencer, Brent
The small things that save us
  The Atlantic 254:60-4+ O '84
  The Editors' choice: new American
    stories v2
Spencer, Elizabeth
The business venture
  Prize stories, 1988
  The Southern Review (Baton Rouge, La.)
    23:403-34 Spr '87
  Spencer, E. Jack of diamonds, and other
    stories

Spencer, Elizabeth—Continued

The cousins
Prize stories, 1986
Selected stories from The Southern review, 1965-1985
The Southern Review (Baton Rouge, La.) 21:449-81 Ap '85
Spencer, E. Jack of diamonds, and other stories

The day before
Mississippi writers v1: Fiction; ed. by D. Abbott

The finder
Stories of the modern South; ed. by B. Forkner and P. Samway

First dark
A Modern Southern reader; ed. by B. Forkner and P. Samway

Jack of diamonds
The Kenyon Review ns8:1-25 Summ '86
The Pushcart prize XII
Spencer, E. Jack of diamonds, and other stories

Jean-Pierre
Spencer, E. Jack of diamonds, and other stories

The skater
The North American Review 273:20-6 Je '88
Spencer, E. Jack of diamonds, and other stories

A southern landscape
Mississippi writers v1: Fiction; ed. by D. Abbott

SPENDTHRIFTS
Rule, J. More than money

Sperling, Leone, 1937-
The book of life
Room to move; ed. by S. Falkiner

The **spheric** man. Li, C.

The **spherical** ghoul. Brown, F.

Sphinx. Kessler, J. F.

The **sphinx.** Poe, E. A.

Spider. Milofsky, D.

The **spider** glass. Yarbro, C. Q.

Spider silk. Norton, A.

SPIDERS
Bloch, R. The masterpiece
Cowan, P. The red-backed spiders
James, M. R. The ash-tree
Norton, A. Spider silk
Wells, H. G. The valley of spiders

The **spider's** web. Kibera, L.

Spielberg, Peter
Prognosis
American made; ed. by M. Leyner; C. White and T. Glynn

SPIES
See also International intrigue; Secret service
Anderson, P. Honorable enemies
Aquino, J. We've been invited to a party
Asimov, I. Never out of sight

Asimov, I. Out of sight
Asimov, I. The speck
Barker, C. Twilight at the towers
Barrett, W. E. Dealers in doom
Boucher, A. QL 696.C9
Carr, J. D. Strictly diplomatic
Cassiday, B. Deep-sleep
Clark, M. Monologue by a man in black
Clarke, A. C. Hide and seek
Crane, S. This majestic lie
Doyle, Sir A. C. The adventure of the Bruce-Partington plans
Ekström, M. When we are home alone we dance all around the house
Gibson, W. New Rose Hotel
Gilbert, M. Emergency exit
Gilbert, M. The emergency exit affair
Harrison, H. After the storm
Hartley, L. P. Roman charity
Hemingway, E. The denunciation
Hoch, E. D. The people of the peacock
Hoch, E. D. The spy who went to the opera
Hoch, E. D. The spy's story
Keating, H. R. F. Dead-letter drop
Lee, H. Lucia and old lace
MacLean, A. Rendezvous
Marquand, J. P. High tide
Maugham, W. S. The traitor
Mortimer, J. C. Rumpole and the official secret
O'Donnell, P. The giggle-wrecker
Parise, G. Hotel
Pynchon, T. Under the rose
Roberts, K. Weihnachtsabend
Schulze, K. Redmond
Tuohy, F. Ructions; or, A historical footnote to the Cold War
Wilmot, T. The finger of suspicion
Woolrich, C. Tokyo, 1941

Spies and lovers. Whelan, G.

Spillane, Mickey, 1918-

Everybody's watching me
Spillane, M. Tomorrow I die

The girl behind the hedge
Spillane, M. Tomorrow I die

The gold fever tapes
Spillane, M. Tomorrow I die

The pickpocket
Spillane, M. Tomorrow I die

"Sex is my vengeance"
Spillane, M. Tomorrow I die

Stand up and die!
Spillane, M. Tomorrow I die

Tomorrow I die
Spillane, M. Tomorrow I die

Trouble . . . come and get it!
Spillane, M. Tomorrow I die

Spillard, Anne
Ionian white and gold
Foreign exchange; ed. by J. Evans

Spilman, Richard
 The old man tells his story and gets it
  wrong
   The Editors' choice v3; ed. by G. E.
   Murphy, Jr.
Spinelli, Jerry, 1941-
 Gus Zernial and me
  Our roots grow deeper than we know;
  ed. by L. Gutkind
Spingarn, Lawrence Perry, 1917-
 Ingermann
  Short story international 58
Spinning tales with the dead. Grant, C. L.
The **Spinoza** of Market Street. Singer, I. B.
Spinrad, Norman
 The big flash
  Beyond Armageddon; ed. by W. M. Mil-
  ler and M. H. Greenberg
 The man who
  Omni (New York, N.Y.) 7:112 N '84
 The national pastime
  The Science fictional Olympics; ed. by
  I. Asimov; M. H. Greenberg and C.
  G. Waugh
SPINSTERS *See* Single women
A **spinster's** confession regarding her sorrows.
  Bukoski, A.
Spiral sands. Kilworth, G.
The **spirit** of Belle Starr. *See* Taylor, R.
  Eddy the man
The **spirit** of giving. Chernoff, M.
The **spirit** of the darkness. Kim, W.-I.
The **spirit** of the Grove. Hellerstein, D.
Spirit seizures. Pritchard, M.
The **spirit** sweep. Davis, J. T.
Spirit weather. Tracy, J.
Spirits. Bausch, R.
Spirits do not forgive. Havemann, E.
A **spiritual** call. Jhabvala, R. P.
SPIRITUALISM
 Byatt, A. S. The next room
 Deaver, P. F. Arcola girls
 Edric, R. A well-spent life
 Grahn, J. Ernesta
 Haas, B. On Mu
 Haas, B. Princess Gilda talks to the un-
  born
 Oates, J. C. Night-side
 O'Brien, F.-J. The diamond lens
 Pritchard, M. Spirit seizures
 Sears, V. L. Sticktalk
 Sims, G. Remember Mrs. Fitz
 Wakefield, H. R. "He cometh and he pas-
  seth by!"
A **spiritualist**. Rhys, J.
Spiritus. Beattie, A.
Spiro, György
 Utopia
  Short story international 70
Spiro, Joanna
 The year of loving dangerously
  Mademoiselle 92:130+ My '86
Spitfire autumn. Wetherell, W. D.

Spivack, Kathleen
 Annoyances
  Spivack, K. The honeymoon
 The donkey
  Spivack, K. The honeymoon
 Dorothy
  The North American Review 270:31 Je
  '85
  Spivack, K. The honeymoon
 For art's sake
  The North American Review 271:36-7 Je
  '86
 Generations
  Spivack, K. The honeymoon
 The guardian
  Spivack, K. The honeymoon
 The hat
  Spivack, K. The honeymoon
 The honeymoon
  The North American Review 269:20-1 Mr
  '84
  Spivack, K. The honeymoon
 Looking at water
  The Kenyon Review ns10:15-17 Fall '88
 Loving
  The North American Review 270:30-1 Je
  '85
  Spivack, K. The honeymoon
 My friend who lives in a commune
  Spivack, K. The honeymoon
 Neighborhood
  The North American Review 272:34-5 Mr
  '87
 The sacrifice
  Spivack, K. The honeymoon
 Sleep
  Spivack, K. The honeymoon
 Surviving
  Spivack, K. The honeymoon
 Terms
  Spivack, K. The honeymoon
Splatter. Winter, D. E.
Splendid lives. Gilliatt, P.
The **splendid** outcast. Markham, B.
Splendor and black wool. Franklin, P.
Splices. Draycott, M.
Splinter. Fink, I.
The **splinter**. Rinehart, M. R.
A **splinter** of the sun. Verma, N.
The **splintered** Monday. Armstrong, C.
SPLIT PERSONALITY *See* Dual personality
Split second. Du Maurier, Dame D.
Splitter. Pascoe, B.
Splittin a dime. Schwaid, A.
**Spofford, Harriet Elizabeth Prescott, 1835-
  1921**
 The amber gods
  Haunted women; ed. by A. Bendixen
 Her story
  The Other woman; ed. by S. Koppelman
The **spoilers**. Gilbert, M.
The **spoils** of sacrilege. Hornung, E. W.
Spokane. Coster, G.

Sponge boat. Johnston, G.
SPONGE FISHING
Johnston, G. Sponge boat
Spook house. Howard, C.
Spooks. Cooper, J. C.
Spooner. Farjeon, E.
A **spoonful** of kindness. Mazel, D.
SPORTS
    See also Athletes; Ball games; Coaching (Athletics); Games; Swimming; Track (Athletics)
Faust, I. Melanie and the purple people eaters
Liben, M. Hop, skip, and jump
Willson, H. Tufts and Wink
Sportsmen. McGuane, T.
The **spot**. Etchison, D., and Johnson, M.
The **spot** of art. Wodehouse, P. G.
The **spotted** pup. Hughes, D. B. F.
Spouse night. Leavitt, D.
The **spread** of Ian Nicol. Gray, A.
Sprecher, Lorrie
  A cure for boredom, dumpy spirits
    The North American Review 271:36 S '86
Spree. Malzberg, B. N.
The **spree**. Pritchett, V. S.
Sprengnether, Madelon
  The camper
    Stiller's pond; ed. by J. Agee; R. Blakely and S. Welch
SPRING
Amichai, Y. Terrible spring
Colette. April
Colette. Bygone spring
Colette. The last fire
Crane, S. Mr. Binks' day off
Pirandello, L. A breath of air
Updike, D. Spring
Spring. Gooch, B.
Spring. Updike, D.
Spring baby, early sorrow. Wilbur, E.
Spring chill. Li Chao
Spring cleaning. Broughton, T. A.
Spring concert. Peters, S.
Spring day at Slater's End. Whitaker, M.
Spring evening with Faust. Jæger, F.
Spring fever. Casper, S.
Spring fever. Davis, D. S.
Spring-fingered Jack. Casper, S.
Spring flower. Aćin-Kosta, M.
The **spring** hat. Bates, H. E.
Spring in Fialta. Nabokov, V. V.
Spring in Poland. Mrożek, S.
A **spring** morning. Fink, I.
The **spring** song. Ha, K.-C.
Spring song of the frogs. Atwood, M.
Spring sowing. O'Flaherty, L.
Spring storm. Mori, Y.
The **spring** that Ellie died. Wasylyk, S.
The **spring** walk. Nowakowski, M.
Spring water celebration. Taylor, P. E.

Springer, Nancy
  Bright-eyed black pony
    Moonsinger's friends; ed. by S. Shwartz
  The prince out of the past
    Magic in Ithkar [1]; ed. by A. Norton and R. Adams
  Sparrow's fall
    U.S. Catholic 53:32-7 Ap '88
SPRINGSTEEN, BRUCE
      About
  Janowitz, T. You and The Boss
Springstubb, Tricia, 1950-
  The last romantic
    McCall's 112:82-3+ Ag '85
Sproat, Robert
  Almost graceful like a dancer
    Sproat, R. Stunning the punters
  Black madonna two-wheel gypsy queen
    Sproat, R. Stunning the punters
  The fascination of the vanity
    Sproat, R. Stunning the punters
  Firework night isn't in it
    Sproat, R. Stunning the punters
  A former security with Helen Damnation
    Sproat, R. Stunning the punters
  Mistaken identify
    Sproat, R. Stunning the punters
  A small difference only
    Sproat, R. Stunning the punters
  Stunning the punters
    Sproat, R. Stunning the punters
  When the sailor was far away
    Sproat, R. Stunning the punters
Sprucy wages. Mazel, D.
Sprung traps. Heffernan, M. J.
Spunk. Hurston, Z. N.
A **spy** in the domain of Arnheim. Bishop, M.
The **spy** who went to the opera. Hoch, E. D.
The **spy's** story. Hoch, E. D.
SQ. Le Guin, U. K.
Squabble. Holman, J.
Squad ready for action. Nowakowski, M.
Square peg, round hole. Chipulina, E. G.
Squares of opposition, signs of disorder. Campbell, E.
Squatter's rights. Bonnie, F.
The **squaw**. Stoker, B.
Squeakie's first case. Manners, M.
Squealer. MacDonald, J. D.
The **squeeze** is on. Klinkowitz, J.
Squire Dinwiddy. Caldwell, E.
Squire Toby's will. Le Fanu, J. S.
The **squirrel** who was scared. Tracy, D.
SQUIRRELS
Kercheval, J. L. A history of Indiana
Narayan, R. K. At the portal
Squirrels. Thurm, M.
The **squirt** and the monkey. See Stout, R. See no evil
Sredni Vashtar. Saki

SRI LANKA
  Bowles, P. In the red room
  Fernando, C. The bird of paradise
  Fernando, C. Of bread and power
  Mukherjee, B. Buried lives
  Swan, A. Monsoon
  Swan-Goodchild, A. Lucy
St. Amy's tale. Card, O. S.
The St. Anthony Chorale. Rubin, L. D.
St. Aubin de Terán, Lisa, 1953-
  I never eat crabmeat now
    Foreign exchange; ed. by J. Evans
St. Clair, Joy
  Gold rings & orange blossoms
    'Teen 31:42+ Jl '87
St. Clair, Margaret
  The boy who predicted earthquakes
    Rod Serling's Night gallery reader
  Brenda
    Rod Serling's Night gallery reader
    St. Clair, M. The best of Margaret St.
      Clair
  Brightness falls from the air
    St. Clair, M. The best of Margaret St.
      Clair
  The causes
    St. Clair, M. The best of Margaret St.
      Clair
  Child of void
    St. Clair, M. The best of Margaret St.
      Clair
  An egg a month from all over
    St. Clair, M. The best of Margaret St.
      Clair
  The gardener
    St. Clair, M. The best of Margaret St.
      Clair
  The goddess on the street corner
    Masterpieces of fantasy and enchant-
      ment; ed. by D. G. Hartwell
  Hathor's pets
    St. Clair, M. The best of Margaret St.
      Clair
  Horrer Howce
    St. Clair, M. The best of Margaret St.
      Clair
  Idris' pig
    St. Clair, M. The best of Margaret St.
      Clair
  The invested libido
    St. Clair, M. The best of Margaret St.
      Clair
  The listening child
    St. Clair, M. The best of Margaret St.
      Clair
    Young mutants; ed. by I. Asimov; M.
      H. Greenberg and C. G. Waugh
  The man who sold rope to the Gnoles
    100 great fantasy short short stories; ed.
      by I. Asimov; T. Carr and M. H.
      Greenberg
    St. Clair, M. The best of Margaret St.
      Clair

New ritual
    St. Clair, M. The best of Margaret St.
      Clair
  The nuse man
    St. Clair, M. The best of Margaret St.
      Clair
  An old-fashioned bird Christmas
    St. Clair, M. The best of Margaret St.
      Clair
  The pillows
    St. Clair, M. The best of Margaret St.
      Clair
  Prott
    St. Clair, M. The best of Margaret St.
      Clair
  Short in the chest
    St. Clair, M. The best of Margaret St.
      Clair
  The wines of earth
    Inspired by drink; ed. by Joan Digby
      and John Digby
    St. Clair, M. The best of Margaret St.
      Clair
  Wryneck, draw me
    St. Clair, M. The best of Margaret St.
      Clair
St. Clair Flats. Woolson, C. F.
St. Denis. Wilner, H.
St. George. Godwin, G.
St. George and the dragon. MacLean, A.
St. George and the nightclub. Ingalls, R.
St. James, Bernard
  The Valencia orange murder
    Murder in Manhattan; ed. by B. Adler
St. John's Eve. Gogol′, N. V.
St. Maur, Henri
  Planet of peril
    Sensuous science fiction from the weird
      and spicy pulps; ed. by S. Jaffery
ST. PATRICK'S DAY See Saint Patrick's
    Day
St. Paul could hit the nail on the head.
    MacLaverty, B.
ST. PAUL'S CATHEDRAL (LONDON,
    ENGLAND)
  Willis, C. Fire watch
ST. PETERSBURG (SOVIET UNION) See
    Soviet Union—Leningrad
St. Pierre, Paul H., 1923-
  Cabin fever
    St. Pierre, P. Smith and other events
  A day with a deer, a bear and Norah
    Smith
    St. Pierre, P. Smith and other events
  December Nilsen
    St. Pierre, P. Smith and other events
  Dry storm
    St. Pierre, P. Smith and other events
  The education of Phyllisteen
    St. Pierre, P. Smith and other events
  Frenchie's wife
    St. Pierre, P. Smith and other events

St. Pierre, Paul H., 1923-—*Continued*
How to run the country
St. Pierre, P. Smith and other events
The last day of violence
St. Pierre, P. Smith and other events
Ol Antoine's wooden overcoat
St. Pierre, P. Smith and other events
The owner of the gang
St. Pierre, P. Smith and other events
Sale of one small ranch
St. Pierre, P. Smith and other events
Sarah's copper
St. Pierre, P. Smith and other events
The **St. Stephen Martyr Bears.** Doyle, B.
ST. VALENTINE'S DAY *See* Valentine's Day
Stableford, Brian M.
And he not busy being born . . .
Interzone: the 2nd anthology; ed. by J. Clute; D. Pringle and S. Ounsley
STABLEMEN
García Márquez, G. Nabo: the black man who made the angels wait
O'Hara, J. We'll have fun
Stacey, Karen
The biopsy report
Redbook 167:22+ Ag '86
His first love
Redbook 165:68+ Ag '85
In my mother's footsteps
Redbook 163:32+ Ag '84
The risk of love
Redbook 164:38+ Ja '85
Stacked deck. Pronzini, B.
Stadia. Hagy, A. C.
The **stadium.** Oates, J. C.
The **Staech** affair. Böll, H.
Stafford, Jean, 1915-1979
Children are bored on Sunday
The Art of the tale; ed. by D. Halpern
The healthiest girl in town
The Interior country; ed. by A. Blackburn
In the zoo
The Norton book of American short stories
The interior castle
The World of the short story; ed. by C. Fadiman
The liberation
Look who's talking; ed. by B. Weber
Woden's day
Shenandoah: an anthology; ed. by J. Boatwright
STAFFORDSHIRE (ENGLAND) *See* England—Staffordshire
STAGE LIFE *See* Theater life
Stage to Lordsburg. Haycox, E.
STAGECOACH LINES
Haycox, E. Stage to Lordsburg
The **staged** 60's. Rapoport, L.
Stages. Campbell, R.
Stages. Gold, H.

Stained glass. Baxter, C.
The **stains.** Aickman, R.
The **staircase.** Boulanger, D.
STAIRS
Wallace, S. R. Dark steps
Stairs again. Cortázar, J.
Stale beer and roses. Franklin, P.
The **stale** loaf. Tamer, Z.
STALIN, JOSEPH, 1879-1953
About
Ruta, S. Stalin in the Bronx
Sciascia, L. The death of Stalin
Stalin in the Bronx. Ruta, S.
Stalingrad. Wilson, B.
Stalking. Bedard, B.
Stalking strangers. Osborn, C.
Stallings, Fran
Message to a messy man
Redbook 163:82+ O '84
Stambolian, George
Encounters
First love/last love; ed. by M. Denneny; C. Ortleb and T. Steele
STAMMERING
Marechera, D. The slow sound of his feet
The **stamp.** Asimov, I.
The **stamp.** Davie, E.
Stan and Ollie. Bukoski, A.
Stand, and be recognized. Busch, F.
Stand in a row and learn. Abbott, L. K.
Stand up and die! Spillane, M.
The **standard** of living. Parker, D.
Standiford, Les
Guerin and the presidential revue
Editor's choice II; ed. by M. Sklar and M. Biggs
The **standing** stone. Millman, L.
Standing woman. Tsutsui, Y.
Stanton, Maura
The sea fairies
Michigan Quarterly Review 25:642-54 Fall '86
Stanton, Will
Chester's Christmas surprise
McCall's 115:154+ D '87
The soap must go on
Redbook 165:36-8+ Ag '85
Stanton: the man and his times. Van Wert, W. F.
Staples, George
The key
Antaeus 60:93-121 Spr '88
The **star.** Gray, A.
The **star.** Wells, H. G.
The **Star** Cafe. Caponegro, M.
Star cruisers, welcome. Kotzwinkle, W.
Star dance. Asscher-Pinkhof, C.
Star Food. Canin, E.
A **star** for a warrior. Wellman, M. W.
Star game. Nevai, L.
Star light, star bright. Rossiter, S.
STAR TREK (TELEVISION PROGRAM)
Tiptree, J. Beam us home

Star wife. Asscher-Pinkhof, C.
Starburst. Cummins, A.
Starcrossed. Zebrowski, G.
Stardance. Robinson, S., and Robinson, J.
Stardust. Jacobs, H.
The **stare** down. Coleman, W.
Starer, Robert
Continuo
The New Yorker 61:23-7 Ja 6 '86
Starfish. Wilson, B.
Stark, Richard
For works written by this author under other names see Westlake, Donald E.
Stark, Sharon Sheehe
The Appaloosa house
Stark, S. S. The dealers' yard, and other stories
Autumnscape
The Massachusetts Review 25:286-99 Summ '84
The Barlip run
Stark, S. S. The dealers' yard, and other stories
Best Quality Glass Company, New York
Stark, S. S. The dealers' yard, and other stories
The dealers' yard
Stark, S. S. The dealers' yard, and other stories
Heart of the Dutch country
Stark, S. S. The dealers' yard, and other stories
His color
Stark, S. S. The dealers' yard, and other stories
The horsehair
Stark, S. S. The dealers' yard, and other stories
In the surprise of life
Stark, S. S. The dealers' yard, and other stories
Janka Doodle
Stark, S. S. The dealers' yard, and other stories
The Johnstown Polka
The Best American short stories, 1985
Stark, S. S. The dealers' yard, and other stories
Leo
The Atlantic 261:54-8+ My '88
May angels lead you home
The Atlantic 258:60-5 D '86
Ode to the big school
Stark, S. S. The dealers' yard, and other stories
A wrestler's tale
Stark, S. S. The dealers' yard, and other stories
Starke, Henderson *See* Neville, Kris (Kris Ottman), 1925-1980

Starkman, Elaine Marcus
Anniversary
Family: stories from the interior; ed. by G. G. Chavis
Starlight. Thurm, M.
The **starlight** express. Gilchrist, E.
Starlings, mute swans, a goose, an impossible angel, evening grosbeaks, an ostrich, some ducks, and a sparrow. Sexson, L.
The **starlings** of Leicester Square. Meinke, P.
STARR, BELLE, 1848-1889
About
Taylor, R. The death of Belle Starr
Taylor, R. Eddy the boy
Taylor, R. Eddy the man
Taylor, R. The fiddler
Taylor, R. Jim July Starr
Taylor, R. Jim Reed
Taylor, R. Pearl Starr alive in Arizona
Taylor, R. Sam Starr
STARR, JIM JULY *See* July, Jim
STARR, SAM
About
Taylor, R. Sam Starr
Starr, Victoria
A Japanese play
Erotic interludes; ed. by L. Barbach
STARS
Asimov, I. The last question
Asimov, I. Nightfall
Bova, B. To touch a star
Wells, H. G. The star
Stars. Blei, N.
Stars. Kojima, N.
Stars in her eyes. Ledbetter, E.
The **stars**, my brothers. Hamilton, E.
Starstruck. Breen, J. L.
The **start** of the Axletree. Gray, A.
STARVATION
Arias, R. Lupe
Chatto, J. The atheist
Choe, I.-N. The color of mugwort
Milán, V. Feast of John the Baptist
Parise, G. Hunger
Rhys, J. Hunger
The **starveling**. Colette
Starwood. Norris, H.
Stashed. Coleman, W.
The **state** against Sam Tucker. Stephens, W. M.
State champions. Mason, B. A.
State Fair. Keillor, G.
The **state** meet. Bonnie, F.
The **state** of grace. Aymé, M.
The **state** of grace. Brodkey, H.
State of grace. Estleman, L. D.
The **state** of the art. Grabowski, Z. A.
State of the streets. Taylor, C.
The **state** of war. Nowakowski, M.
The **stately** roller coaster. Tremain, R.
Statement. Ziem, J.

The **statement** of Randolph Carter. Lovecraft, H. P.
The **States**. Wilson, R., Jr.
Static discharge. McCreary, L.
The **station** at Baranovitch. *See* Sholem Aleichem. Baranovich Station
The **Stations** of the Cross. Auchincloss, L.
The **Stations** of the Cross. Lemelin, R.
Stations on the way to Avalon. Hulme, K.
STATISTICS
  Böll, H. At the bridge
The **statue** I stole from the Louvre. Faik, S.
STATUE OF LIBERTY (NEW YORK, N.Y.)
  Irish, W. The corpse in the Statue of Liberty
  Woolrich, C. Red liberty
STATUES
  Ellin, S. The twelfth statue
  Faik, S. The statue I stole from the Louvre
  Hartley, L. P. The two Vaynes
  Narayan, R. K. A horse and two goats
  Paton, A. A drink in the passage
  Tidmarsh, W. M. Bronze
  Warner, S. T. A saint (unknown) with two donors
  Wolf, R. Cat and muse
STATUETTES *See* Art objects; Statues
The **status** quo. Carlson, R.
Stavrogin. Ryan, N.
A **stay** by the river. Engberg, S.
Stayed back. McGarry, J.
Staying in bed. Gilliatt, P.
Stead, Christina, 1902-1983
  1954: days of the roomers
    Stead, C. Ocean of story
  About the house
    Stead, C. Ocean of story
  Accents
    Stead, C. Ocean of story
  The Azhdanov tailors
    Stead, C. Ocean of story
  The boy
    Stead, C. Ocean of story
  The captain's house
    Stead, C. Ocean of story
  The fathers
    Stead, C. Ocean of story
  A harmless affair
    Stead, C. Ocean of story
  The hotel-keeper's story
    Stead, C. Ocean of story
  A household
    Stead, C. Ocean of story
  I live in you
    Stead, C. Ocean of story
  An iced cake with cherries
    Stead, C. Ocean of story
  Life is difficult
    Stead, C. Ocean of story

  A little demon
    Stead, C. Ocean of story
  Lost American
    Stead, C. Ocean of story
  The milk run
    Stead, C. Ocean of story
  My friend, Lafe Tilly
    Stead, C. Ocean of story
  A night in the Indian Ocean
    Stead, C. Ocean of story
  'O, if I could but shiver!'
    Stead, C. Ocean of story
  The old school
    Stead, C. Ocean of story
  Private matters
    Stead, C. Ocean of story
  A routine
    Stead, C. Ocean of story
  Street idyll
    Stead, C. Ocean of story
  La Toussaint (All Saints' Day, November 1)
    Stead, C. Ocean of story
  Trains
    Stead, C. Ocean of story
  The triskelion
    The Australian short story; ed. by L. Hergenhan
  Uncle Morgan at the Nats
    Stead, C. Ocean of story
  UNO 1945
    Stead, C. Ocean of story
  The woman in the bed
    Stead, C. Ocean of story
  Yac, yac
    Stead, C. Ocean of story
The **steadfast**. Overholser, W. D.
Steadman, Mark
  John Fletcher's night of love
    A Collection of classic Southern humor; ed. by G. W. Koon
  Langston James McHenry
    The Southern Review (Baton Rouge, La.) 22:577-88 Summ '86
The **steal**. Archer, J.
Stealing the bread. Ignatow, R. G.
Stealing time. Grimm, M.
Stealing time for love. Lee, L.
Steam gives way to sail. Gilliatt, P.
STEAM SHOVELS
  Stuart, J. No petty thief
STEAMBOATS
  Bedford-Jones, H. Ram him, damn him!
  Drake, B. Putting a black-leg on shore
  Dumas, H. Ark of bones
  Gibson, W. Murnane and the Illinois
  King, G. E. The little convent girl
  Leacock, S. B. The marine excursion of the Knights of Pythias
The **steel-clawed** glove. Nowakowski, M.
STEEL INDUSTRY
  Wells, H. G. The cone
Steel to the west. Overholser, W. D.

Steele, Max, 1922-
Ah love! Ah me!
   Steele, M. The hat of my mother
Another love story
   Steele, M. The hat of my mother
The cat and the coffee drinkers
   Steele, M. The hat of my mother
Color the daydream yellow
   Steele, M. The hat of my mother
The death of a chimp
   Steele, M. The hat of my mother
Forget the geraniums
   Steele, M. The hat of my mother
The girl from Carthage
   Steele, M. The hat of my mother
The glass-brick apartment
   Steele, M. The hat of my mother
The hat of my mother [Variant title: My mother's night out]
   Steele, M. The hat of my mother
The man in the doll house
   Steele, M. The hat of my mother
The silent scream
   Steele, M. The hat of my mother
The Tin Can
   Steele, M. The hat of my mother
What to do till the postman comes
   Steele, M. The hat of my mother
Where she brushed her hair [Variant title: Fiction, fact and dream]
   Steele, M. The hat of my mother
Steele, Sir Richard, 1672-1729
The wedding of Jenny Distaff
   The Treasury of English short stories; ed. by N. Sullivan
Steele, Wilbur Daniel
How beautiful with shoes
   Great American love stories; ed. by L. Rosenthal
The man who saw through Heaven
   The Norton book of American short stories
The woman at Seven Brothers
   Haunted New England; ed. by C. G. Waugh; M. H. Greenberg and F. D. McSherry
The **steelyard**. Lai, H.
The **steep** dark stairs. Stuart, I.
STEEPLECHASING See Horse racing
Steering clear. Glasser, P.
Steers. Lieber, T.
Stefan. Shukshin, V. M.
Stefaniak, Mary Helen
America, the beautiful
   The Yale Review 77:402-17 Spr '88
Little girl lost
   Redbook 164:48+ Ja '85
Mary, Mary so contrary
   Redbook 163:36+ Ag '84
Stegner, Wallace Earle, 1909-
The blue-winged teal
   Family: stories from the interior; ed. by G. G. Chavis

Field guide to the western birds
   The Interior country; ed. by A. Blackburn
The women on the wall
   A Treasury of World War II stories; ed. by B. Pronzini and M. H. Greenberg
Stein, Gertrude, 1874-1946
A water-fall and a piano
   New directions in prose and poetry 50
Stein, Judith, 1935-
Why the moon is small and dark when the sun is big and shiny
   Hear the silence; ed. by I. Zahava
Steinbach, Meredith
In recent history
   Southwest Review 73:319-42 Summ '88
Soundings in feet and fathoms
   The Massachusetts Review 26:33-46 Spr '85
Sparking
   The Antioch Review 43:480-5 Fall '85
Steinbeck, John, 1902-1968
The chrysanthemums
   The Nobel reader; ed. by J. Eisen and S. Troy
How Mr. Hogan robbed a bank
   Mystery in the mainstream; ed. by B. Pronzini; M. H. Greenberg and B. N. Malzberg
The **Steinway** quintet. Epstein, L.
Stella Artois. Singmaster, D.
The **Stella** school. Greene, P. L.
Stella Silvernoll and the El Grecos. Higgins, J.
The **Stelyanos** Hrisopulos. Faik, S.
Stemple, Jane H. Yolen See Yolen, Jane
The **stench**. Becker, J.
A **step** into darkness. Hoffman, N. K.
Step-over toe-hold. Phippen, S.
Stepan. Regent, P.
STEPBROTHERS
   See also Half-brothers
Kittredge, W. Thirty-four seasons of winter
Lo Bosco, R. The birthday present
Minot, S. The seawall
STEPCHILDREN
   See also Stepdaughters
STEPDAUGHTERS
Flanagan, M. Melusina
Moravia, A. The sign of the operation
Peterson, M. With Evelyn
Stepdaughters. Apple, M.
STEPFATHERS
Benedict, P. All the dead
Cameron, P. Memorial Day
Freeman, J. Family attractions
Hood, M. Finding the chain
Millman, L. Nightrangers
Pilcher, R. Gilbert
Rambach, P. Home
Simpson, M. Approximations
Stead, C. The fathers
Tyler, A. The artificial family

Stephan, Martin
The tub
Voices East and West: German short stories since 1945
Stephanie, Stephen, Steph, Steve. Gilliatt, P.
Stephanotis. Phillips, E. O.
Stephen, Jaci
Blood relations
First fictions: Introduction 9
The other side of summer
First fictions: Introduction 9
Stephen Crane's own story. Crane, S.
Stephens, Michael
Everlast
Hot type; ed. by J. Miller
Stephens, William M.
The state against Sam Tucker
Alfred Hitchcock's Grave suspicions
Water Witch
Alfred Hitchcock's Crimewatch
Stephenson, Carl
Leiningen versus the ants
The Penguin book of horror stories
Stephenson, Michael
The pack
Short story international 43
STEPMOTHERS
Billington, R. The photograph
Derleth, A. W. Carousel
Fraser, A. Death of an old dog
Hurst, F. Oats for the woman
Im, O.-I. The new life
Livesey, M. Learning by heart
Mukherjee, B. Fathering
Munro, A. Royal beatings
Oates, J. C. Leila Lee
Oates, J. C. Night. Sleep. Death. The stars
Pacheco, J. E. The sunken park
Pilcher, R. The blue bedroom
Son, S.-H. At the end of the world
Thurm, M. Floating
Winter, D. E. Masks
Steps. Carrier, R.
Steps. Josipovici, G.
STEPSISTERS
See also Half-sisters
Kang, S.-J. The young zelkova
Schulman, H. We were of two minds
Sterile relationships. Bace, K. M.
STERILITY
Boyle, T. C. Caviar
Eisenberg, L. Dr. Snow Maiden
Rooke, L. Saloam frigid with time's legacy while Mrs. Willoughby Bight-Davies sits naked through the night on a tree stump awaiting the lizard that will make her loins go boom-boom
Wilson, B. Pity
Sterling, Bruce
The beautiful and the sublime
The Year's best science fiction, fourth annual collection

Cicada Queen
The Year's best science fiction, first annual collection
Dinner in Audoghast
The Year's best science fiction, third annual collection
Flowers of Edo
The Year's best science fiction, fifth annual collection
Green days in Brunei
The Year's best science fiction, third annual collection
The Gulf wars
Omni (New York, N.Y.) 10:52-4+ F '88
Sunken gardens
Omni (New York, N.Y.) 6:58-9+ Je '84
The Year's best science fiction, second annual collection
(jt. auth) See Shirley, John, 1953-, and Sterling, Bruce
Sterling, Bruce, and Gibson, William, 1948-
Red star, winter orbit
Mirrorshades; ed. by B. Sterling
Omni book of science fiction 3
Sterling, Bruce, and Shiner, Lewis
Mozart in mirrorshades
Mirrorshades; ed. by B. Sterling
Omni (New York, N.Y.) 7:68-70+ S '85
Stern, Daniel, 1928-
Brooksmith by Henry James: a story
Raritan 8:92-101 Summ '88
The interpretation of dreams by Sigmund Freud: a story
The Best American short stories, 1987
Prize stories, 1987
Stern, Philip Van Doren, 1900-1984
The greatest gift
McCall's 113:147-50 D '85
Stern, Richard G., 1928-
Dr. Cahn's visit
Full measure; ed. by D. Sennett
In return
Encounter (London, England) 71:10-14 Jl/Ag '88
Losing color
The Antioch Review 44:40-1 Wint '86
Stern, Richard Martin, 1915-
Present for Minna
Crime of my life; ed. by B. Garfield
Stern, Steve, 1947-
Aaron makes a match
Stern, S. Isaac and the undertaker's daughter
Stern, S. Lazar Malkin enters heaven
The book of Mordecai
Stern, S. Isaac and the undertaker's daughter
Stern, S. Lazar Malkin enters heaven
Bruno's metamorphosis
Stern, S. Isaac and the undertaker's daughter
The ghost and Saul Bozoff
Stern, S. Lazar Malkin enters heaven

Stern, Steve, 1947-—_Continued_
Goldfinch & Son
  Stern, S. Isaac and the undertaker's
    daughter
The gramophone
  Stern, S. Lazar Malkin enters heaven
Lazar Malkin enters heaven
  Stern, S. Lazar Malkin enters heaven
Leonard Shapiro banished from dreams
  Stern, S. Lazar Malkin enters heaven
The Lord and Morton Gruber
  Stern, S. Lazar Malkin enters heaven
Moishe the Just
  Stern, S. Lazar Malkin enters heaven
Rudolph Finkl's apprenticeship
  Stern, S. Isaac and the undertaker's
    daughter
A sentimental journey
  Stern, S. Isaac and the undertaker's
    daughter
Shimmele fly-by-night
  Homewords: a book of Tennessee
    writers; ed. by D. Paschall
  Stern, S. Lazar Malkin enters heaven
The theft of Lily [Variant title: Isaac and
  the undertaker's daughter]
  Stern, S. Isaac and the undertaker's
    daughter
Sternberg, Alan
Blazer
  The New Yorker 64:33-8 Mr 21 '88
Moose
  The New Yorker 64:32-8 S 12 '88
Sterner's double vision. O'Grady, D.
STEVEDORES _See_ Longshore workers
Stevens, James
Into that good night
  Afterlives; ed. by P. Sargent and I. Watson
Stevens, Julie A.
Families
  Isaac Asimov's Tomorrow's voices
The sacrifice
  Midnight; ed. by C. L. Grant
Stevens, R. L. _See_ Hoch, Edward D., 1930-
Stevenson, John, 1926-
The blind alley
  Murder California style; ed. by J. L.
    Breen and J. Ball
Stevenson, M. M.
First day
  The North American Review 272:36 D
    '87
Stevenson, Robert Louis, 1850-1894
The body snatchers
  Charles Keeping's Book of classic ghost
    stories
  The Penguin book of horror stories
The bottle imp
  Black water; ed. by A. Manguel
  Masterpieces of terror and the supernatural; ed. by M. Kaye and S. Kaye
The isle of voices
  Dark arrows; ed. by A. Manguel
A lodging for the night
  The Treasury of English short stories;
    ed. by N. Sullivan
Markheim
  Christian short stories; ed. by M. Booth
  Devils & demons; ed. by M. Kaye and
    S. Kaye
The merry men
  Short stories of the sea; ed. by G. C.
    Solley and E. Steinbaugh
Olalla
  Classic European short stories; ed. by R.
    Beum
Thrawn Janet
  Dark banquet; ed. by L. Child
Stevie and The Dark. Henderson, Z.
Steward, D. E.
Pierre
  Editor's choice II; ed. by M. Sklar and
    M. Biggs
Stewart, Deborah
Beyond their reach
  The North American Review 270:36 Je
    '85
Stewart, Isobel
Bless the child
  Good Housekeeping 205:80+ D '87
Highland hearts
  Good Housekeeping 203:182-3+ S '86
Home for Christmas
  Ladies' Home Journal 104:100+ D '87
Made for each other
  Good Housekeeping 202:106+ F '86
The perfect match
  Good Housekeeping 204:118-19+ F '87
Tomorrow's promise
  Good Housekeeping 207:78+ O '88
The true believer
  Good Housekeeping 202:116-17 Ja '86
**Stewart, J. I. M. (John Innes Mackintosh),
  1906-**
  _For works written by this author under
    other names see_ Innes, Michael,
    1906-
André
  Stewart, J. I. M. Parlour 4, and other
    stories
The dyslexia factor
  Stewart, J. I. M. Parlour 4, and other
    stories
Melencolia I
  Stewart, J. I. M. Parlour 4, and other
    stories
Napier into Ffinch
  Stewart, J. I. M. Parlour 4, and other
    stories
Parlour 4
  Stewart, J. I. M. Parlour 4, and other
    stories

Stewart, J. I. M. (John Innes Mackintosh), 1906-—*Continued*
Pipkin Grove
  Stewart, J. I. M. Parlour 4, and other stories
Sweets from a stranger
  Stewart, J. I. M. Parlour 4, and other stories
Tom Dick and Harry
  Stewart, J. I. M. Parlour 4, and other stories
Two strings to his bow
  Stewart, J. I. M. Parlour 4, and other stories
Stewart, John Innes Mackintosh *See* Stewart, J. I. M. (John Innes Mackintosh), 1906-
Stewart, Molly
The wedding guest
  Short story international 70
Stewart, Natacha, d. 1986
The dacha
  The New Yorker 61:38-44 My 20 '85
Stewart, Robert, 1946-
Beans!
  Missouri short fiction; ed. by C. Beasley
Stewed beans. Austin, M. H.
The **stick.** Abe, K.
Stickman's laughter. Algren, N.
Stickpins. Mazzari, L.
Sticks. Wagner, K. E.
Sticktalk. Sears, V. L.
Stiff upper lip. Durrell, L.
Stifter, Adalbert, 1805-1868
Rock crystal
  German stories; ed. by H. Steinhauer
Stiles, Jan
Right questions
  'Teen 29:34-5+ Ap '85
Stiles, Martha Bennett
Mr. Barry
  Southwest Review 70:489-95 Aut '85
Still, James, 1906-
A master time
  Short story international 51
The moving
  Sudden fiction; ed. by R. Shapard and J. Thomas
Pattern of a man
  Short story international 43
Still frame. Haldeman, J. C.
Still hope for God. Clark, M.
Still hunting. Everett, P. L.
Still life. Booth, B.
Still life. Raphael, F.
Still life. Sandor, M.
Still life. Shōno, J.
Still life. Thurm, M.
Still life with insects. Kiteley, B.
Still lives. Renwick, J.
Still of some use. Updike, J.
Still points. Woodman, A.
Still swinging. Drake, R.

The **still** waters. Del Rey, L.
Stillborn. Conner, M.
Stiller's pond. Agee, J.
STILLWATER (MINN.) *See* Minnesota—Stillwater
Stillwater, 1896. Cassutt, M.
Stingray. Drewe, R.
Stinkbug. Blue Cloud, P.
Stivens, Dal, 1911-
The gentle basilisk
  Australian science fiction; ed. by V. Ikin
The unicorn
  The Australian short story; ed. by L. Hergenhan
Stock. Campos-De Metro, J.
STOCK EXCHANGE
Henry, O. The romance of a busy broker
Stockanes, Anthony E., 1935-
Ladies who knit for a living
  Prime number; ed. by A. L. Weir
The **stockbroker's** clerk. Doyle, Sir A. C.
Stocks, Doug
Therapeutic bondage
  Stories and poems from close to home; ed. by F. Salas
Stockton, Frank, 1834-1902
The Bee-man of Orn
  Masterpieces of fantasy and enchantment; ed. by D. G. Hartwell
The great staircase at Landover Hall
  Christmas ghosts; ed. by K. Cramer and D. G. Hartwell
The landsman's tale
  Men at sea; ed. by B. Aymar
Stodghill, Dick
Wrongful death
  Mean streets; ed. by R. J. Randisi
Stoke Sobel in Polk. Vreuls, D.
Stoker, Bram, 1847-1912
The burial of the rats
  Devils & demons; ed. by M. Kaye and S. Kaye
Dracula's guest [Variant title: Dracula's daughter]
  Masterpieces of terror and the supernatural; ed. by M. Kaye and S. Kaye
  Vampires; ed. by A. Ryan
The judge's house
  Charles Keeping's Classic tales of the macabre
  The Oxford book of English ghost stories
The secret of the growing gold
  Great ghost stories; ed. by B. A. Schwartz
The squaw
  Dark arrows; ed. by A. Manguel
Stokes, Tawn
No pets
  L. Ron Hubbard presents Writers of the future v3
The **stolen** ass. O'Flaherty, L.
The **stolen** bacillus. Wells, H. G.

The **stolen** body. Wells, H. G.
The **stolen** car. Herriot, J.
Stolen flowers. Winters, J.
Stolen horses. Jahnn, H. H.
The **stolen** party. Heker, L.
The **stolen** Rubens. Futrelle, J.
Stolen star. Gault, W. C.
The **stolen** stories. Katz, S.
The **stolen** white elephant. Twain, M.
Stoll, Patricia
  The age of fish
    The North American Review 270:24-8 Je
    '85
STOMACH
  Greene, G. Alas, poor Maling
  McLaughlin, L. The stomach
The **stomach**. McLaughlin, L.
Stone, Alma
  A fine zoo day
    The North American Review 271:11-15
    S '86
Stone, Kathryn
  Summer of a stick man
    Room to move; ed. by S. Falkiner
Stone, Merlin
  The Plasting Project
    Hear the silence; ed. by I. Zahava
Stone, Robert, 1937-
  Absence of mercy
    Harper's 275:61-8 N '87
  Helping
    The Best American short stories, 1988
    The New Yorker 63:28-38+ Je 8 '87
  In a Mexican garden
    The Esquire fiction reader v2
  Not for love
    The Esquire fiction reader v1
  Operate and maintain
    Soldiers & civilians; ed. by T. Jenks
STONE CARVING
  Bear, G. Petra
Stone City. Proulx, A.
The **stone** door. Carrington, L.
The **stone** dragon. Gilchrist, M.
Stone eggs. Robinson, K. S.
The **stone** fey. McKinley, R.
The **stone** inscription of Caleb Pellor. Burkert, R.
Stone lives. Di Filippo, P.
The **stone** of Boxman's Drift. Doyle, Sir A. C.
The **stone** of Cybele. Crowley, A.
The **stone** soldier. Cobb, W.
Stone upon stone. Myśliwski, W.
STONECUTTERS
  Hawthorne, N. Ethan Brand
  Lafferty, R. A. Nor limestone islands
STONEHENGE (ENGLAND)
  Kelly, J. P. Solstice
Stoner's lament. Barthelme, S.
Stones for bread. Bonner, M.
Stones in my passway, hellhound on my trail. Boyle, T. C.

The **stones** of Sharnon. Miller, A.
Stonewall Jackson's wife. Wiggins, M.
The **stoning** of Stanislava. Wegner, H.
Stop that music! Mudd, E. J.
The **store**. Piñera, V.
The **store** of the worlds. Sheckley, R.
Store quarter. Gallacher, T.
The **storekeeper**. Mazel, D.
STORES
  Bambara, T. C. Christmas Eve at Johnson's Drugs N Goods
  Evans, E. Desert birds
  O'Hara, J. The hardware man
STORIES ABOUT LETTERS See Letters, Stories about
Stories from a first reader. Borchert, W.
Stories I tell myself. Cortázar, J.
Stories I'd rather not tell. Ashour, L.
Stories in another language. Murphy, Y.
STORIES IN DIARY FORM See Diaries (Stories in diary form)
STORIES OF THE FUTURE See Future, Stories of the
Stories told by an artist. Crane, S.
Storm, Theodor, 1817-1888
  Immensee
    Classic European short stories; ed. by R. Beum
The **storm**. Morrell, D.
The **storm**. Verne, J.
Storm in a bottle. Jakes, J.
Storm in the Channel. See Simenon, G. Storm over the Channel
The **storm** king. Vinge, J. D.
Storm over the Channel. Simenon, G.
The **storm** tunnel. Pronzini, B.
Stormchaser. Hauptman, W.
Storming the bijou, mon amour. Bishop, M.
STORMS
    See also Hurricanes; Tornadoes; Typhoons
  Berry, R. M. Song of the geometry instructor
  Chekhov, A. P. On official business
  Conrad, J. The gale
  Crane, S. The men in the storm
  DeMarinis, R. Under the wheat
  Derleth, A. W. The drifting snow
  Dickens, C. The wreck of the Golden Mary
  Doyle, Sir A. C. Touch and go: a midshipman's story
  Dundas, R. As small as your shadow
  Edwards, A. A. B. The phantom coach
  Hall, T. T. Another dark and stormy night
  Harte, B. The outcasts of Poker Flat
  Hogg, J. Mr. Adamson of Laverhope
  Jewett, S. O. The foreigner
  King, S. The mist
  King, S. One for the road
  Kipling, R. The wreck of the Visigoth
  Lee, H. Tamsen Donner's decision

STORMS—*Continued*

Link, W., and Levinson, R. One bad winter's day

Lish, G. [Entitled story]

Martínez-Serros, H. Distillation

McKillip, P. A. The old woman and the storm

Melville, H. Benito Cereno

Morrell, D. The storm

Reamy, T. Insects in amber

Reaves, J. M. Werewind

Robinson, K. S. Venice drowned

Robison, J. Nor'easter

Rose, D. A. Inside the violet

Schaap, J. C. The privacy of storm

Schwob, M. The flute

So, C.-I. The way to Kŭmsansa temple

Stifter, A. Rock crystal

Updike, J. Unstuck

Wells, H. G. The thing in No. 7

Wouk, H. The mutiny

Storms of a cruel fate. Kuznetsova, A.

Story. Davis, L.

Story. Haley, R.

A **story.** Thomas, D.

A **story** about greenery. Valenzuela, L.

Story for Susan. Thompson, J.

A **story** for Teddy. Swados, H.

The **story** hearer. Paley, G.

Story in a mirror. Aichinger, I.

Story in Harlem slang. Hurston, Z. N.

The **story** Mac told. Matthews, J.

The **story** of a day. King, G. E.

The **story** of a farm-girl. Maupassant, G. de

The **story** of a panic. Forster, E. M.

The **story** of a peculiar pain. Sonu, H.

The **story** of a piebald horse. Hudson, W. H.

Story of a remarkable single combat. Kleist, H. von

The **story** of a scar. McPherson, J. A.

A **story** of an heir. Addison, J.

The **story** of an hour. Chopin, K.

The **story** of an old man and a dog. Zhang Xianliang

The **story** of C. Levi, P.

The **story** of Davidson's eyes. See Wells, H. G. The remarkable case of Davidson's eyes

A **story** of Don Juan. Pritchett, V. S.

The **story** of good Caspar and fair Annie. Brentano, C.

The **story** of Honest Casper and Fair Annie. See Brentano, C. The story of good Caspar and fair Annie

A **story** of hope. Mazel, D.

A **story** of inland life. Eckstein, B.

The **story** of Jesus—according to Mokuba, the beloved tribesman. Lannoy, V. D.

A **story** of land and sea. Dunsany, E. J. M. D. P., Baron

Story of my life. McInerney, J.

Story of my weight. Calcagno, A.

The **story** of the bagman's uncle. Dickens, C.

A **story** of the days to come. Wells, H. G.

The **story** of the goblins who stole a sexton. Dickens, C.

The **story** of the green Falcon and the marvelous flute. Moyano, D.

The **story** of the Last Trump. Wells, H. G.

The **story** of the late Mr. Elvesham. Wells, H. G.

The **story** of the man who was not born. Palma, C.

The **story** of the siren. Forster, E. M.

A **story** of the stone age. Wells, H. G.

The **story** of the twins. Jahnn, H. H.

Story of the warrior and the captive. Borges, J. L.

The **story** of three springs. Wang, C.-H.

The **story** of uneasy rider. Daniels, C.

The **story** of Webster. Wodehouse, P. G.

Story-telling. Matthews, S.

A **story** to be illustrated by Max Ernst. Livesey, M.

STORY WITHIN A STORY

Adams, G. G. La plume de ma tante

al-Ujayli, A. al--S. Madness

Alarcón, P. A. de. The tall woman

Allende, I. Rosa the beautiful

Antoni, R. W. Frogchild on the day of Corpus Christi

Austin, M. H. How the corn came

Balzac, H. de. The red inn

Baumbach, J. How you play the game

Bayles, M. The "New Yorker" story

Benét, S. V. A judgment in the mountains

Bishop, M. Seasons of belief

Bourjaily, V. The Amish farmer

Boyd, W. Long story short

Brentano, C. The story of good Caspar and fair Annie

Campbell, R. Next time you'll know me

Campos, J. A redhead named Sabina [excerpt]

Chang, Y.-H. Poems of John the Baptist

Clarke, A. C. Hide and seek

Claudius, E. How the jungle soldiers became sons of heaven

Crawford, F. M. For the blood is the life

De Lint, C. Uncle Dobbin's Parrot Fair

Dickens, C. Sketches by Boz [excerpt]

Dilov, L. Contacts of a fourth kind

Doyle, Sir A. C. The American's tale

Ellin, S. Beidenbauer's flea

Faik, S. First letter from a reader

Ferron, J. Martine continued

Fish, R. L. The wager

Fréchette, L. Tom Cariboo

Gardner, M. The three cowboys

Gogol', N. V. A May night; or, The drowned maiden

Goldsmith, O. A curious inconsistency of the Man in Black

Greene, G. The hint of an explanation

STORY WITHIN A STORY—*Continued*

Jahnn, H. H. A master selects his servant

James, M. R. An episode of cathedral history

Jewett, S. O. The foreigner

Kiely, B. Eton Crop

Landon, P. Thurnley Abbey

Latimer, M. Nellie Bloom

Lemay, P. Blood and gold

Lish, G. The hilt

Lish, G. The problem of the preface

Lispector, C. The fifth story

Lodge, D. Hotel des Boobs

Longyear, B. B. Twist ending

Lover, S. Ye marvelous legend of Tom Connor's cat

Lutz, J. The shooting of Curly Dan

Machen, A. The white people

MacLaverty, B. Hugo

Maillet, A. Two saints

Maramzin, V. The two-toned blond: a reciprocal tale

Maugham, W. S. Red

Maupassant, G. de. The white wolf

Melville, H. The chase

Merritt, A. The moon pool

Morris, W. Lindenborg pool

Muller, M. The time of the wolves

Norris, L. A flight of geese

Nowotny, J. Hic sunt leones

Orphée, E. Angel's last conquest [excerpt]

Pavel, T. G. The Persian mirror

Radcliffe, A. W. The haunted chamber

Rifaat, A. Mansoura

Rooke, L. Saloam frigid with time's legacy while Mrs. Willoughby Bight-Davies sits naked through the night on a tree stump awaiting the lizard that will make her loins go boom-boom

Rose, D. A. Katey Foster's two boys

Russell, E. F., and Johnson, L. T. Seeker of tomorrow

Russell, R. Power stories

Saroyan, W. Najari Levon's old country advice to the young Americans on how to live with a snake

Schwartz, L. S. The melting pot

Singer, I. B. The enemy

Singer, I. B. Loshikl

Singer, I. B. Runners to nowhere

Singer, I. B. The secret

Sisskind, M. Hope

Skelton, R. The bride

Spofford, H. E. P. Her story

Steele, M. Where she brushed her hair

Thomas, D. Where Tawe flows

Traba, M. Mothers and shadows [excerpt]

Twain, M. The notorious jumping frog of Calaveras County

Varshavsky, I. The secrets of the genre

Vizyēnos, G. M. The only journey of his life

Vreuls, D. Beebee

Weaver, G. Morality play

Wells, H. G. The apple

Wetherell, W. D. Calm seas and a prosperous voyage

Wolff, T. Our story begins

Woolson, C. F. The Lady of Little Fishing

Yarbro, C. Q. The spider glass

Yi, M.-Y. Early spring, mid-summer

Storyteller. Nordan, L.

STORYTELLING

Abbott, L. K. The final proof of fate and circumstance

Abbott, L. K. When our dream world finds us, and these hard times are gone

Abbott, L. K. Where is Garland Steeples now?

Aldiss, B. W. The O in José

Bauer, D. Lore

Bear, G. The white horse child

Burns, M. Collected bear stories

Buzzati, D. Duelling stories

Cameron, A. Magic in a world of magic

Campbell, E. The ghost of an apprehension

Carter, R. Cityman

Cowper, R. Piper at the gates of dawn

Curley, D. Reflections in the ice

Doyle, Sir A. C. The cabman's story

Doyle, Sir A. C. That veteran

Faik, S. Searchlight operator

Ghose, Z. A translator's fiction

Kinsella, W. P. The kid in the stove

Kirk, R. The peculiar demesne of Archvicar Gerontion

Lish, G. Shit

Mason, B. A. Big Bertha stories

McKillip, P. A. The old woman and the storm

Moore, G. The strange story of the three golden fishes

Narayan, R. K. Under the banyan tree

Nordan, L. Storyteller

Poe, E. A. The thousand-and-second tale of Scheherazade

Schwebel, B. El Señor Lector

Sexson, L. Turning

Shaik, F. The mayor of New Orleans; just talking jazz

Walpole, H. Hieroglyphic tales

Stout, Rex, 1886-1975

A dog in the daytime [Variant title: Die like a dog]

Hound dunnit; ed. by I. Asimov; M. H. Greenberg and C. L. R. Waugh

Help wanted, male

Masterpieces of mystery and suspense; ed. by M. H. Greenberg

See no evil [Variant title: The squirt and the monkey]

Great detectives; ed. by D. W. McCullough

STOVES

Davidson, A. The Slovo stove

STOWAWAYS
Redd, D. On the deck of the Flying Bomb
Stowe, Harriet Beecher, 1811-1896
The ghost in the Cap'n Brown House
Haunted women; ed. by A. Bendixen
Stowe, Rebecca
The pizza
Hot type; ed. by J. Miller
Straayer, Arny Christine
High heels
Between mothers & daughters; ed. by S.
Koppelman
Strachan, Tom
A father's love
Stand one; ed. by M. Blackburn; J.
Silkin and L. Tracy
The **Stradivarius**. Thorman, R.
Straight, Susan
Back
Ploughshares 14 no2/3:140-4 '88
The box
TriQuarterly no73:45-56 Fall '88
Buddah
TriQuarterly no71:33-45 Wint '88
Straight from the deathbed. Gerber, M. J.
Straight no chaser. McLoughlin, J. B.
Straight razor. Eisenstein, S.
Strand, Mark, 1934-
Cephalus
Strand, M. Mr. and Mrs. Baby, and
other stories
Dog life
Strand, M. Mr. and Mrs. Baby, and
other stories
Sudden fiction; ed. by R. Shapard and
J. Thomas
Drogo
Strand, M. Mr. and Mrs. Baby, and
other stories
The general
Strand, M. Mr. and Mrs. Baby, and
other stories
The killer poet
Strand, M. Mr. and Mrs. Baby, and
other stories
More life
Strand, M. Mr. and Mrs. Baby, and
other stories
Mr. and Mrs. Baby
Strand, M. Mr. and Mrs. Baby, and
other stories
The President's resignation
Strand, M. Mr. and Mrs. Baby, and
other stories
The tiny baby
Strand, M. Mr. and Mrs. Baby, and
other stories
True loves
Strand, M. Mr. and Mrs. Baby, and
other stories
Two stories
Strand, M. Mr. and Mrs. Baby, and
other stories

Under water
The Antioch Review 42:172-6 Spr '84
Strand, M. Mr. and Mrs. Baby, and
other stories
Wooley
Strand, M. Mr. and Mrs. Baby, and
other stories
Zadar
Michigan Quarterly Review 23:334-8
Summ '84
Strand, M. Mr. and Mrs. Baby, and
other stories
Strand of wire. O'Brien, D.
Stranded. Mardon, D.
A **strange** Christmas game. Riddell, J. H.,
Mrs.
Strange comfort afforded by the profession.
Lowry, M.
A **strange** death. Moore, G.
A **strange** delight. Kidman, F.
A **strange** elation. Wilbur, E.
A **strange** fancy. Maupassant, G. de
The **strange** flight of Richard Clayton. Bloch,
R.
Strange jest. Christie, A.
Strange letter of a lunatic. Hogg, J.
Strange memories of death. Dick, P. K.
Strange music. Whitaker, M.
The **strange** orchid. See Wells, H. G. The
flowering of the strange orchid
Strange partners of Two-Fold Bay. Grey, Z.
Strange prey. Chesbro, G. C.
Strange Rachel. Kuncewiczowa, M.
A **strange** romance. Dangor, A.
The **strange** story of Peter Schlemihl.
Chamisso, A. von
The **strange** story of the three golden fishes.
Moore, G.
Strange things happen here. Valenzuela, L.
Strange wine. Ellison, H.
The **stranger**. Bar Yosef, Y.
The **stranger**. Gardner, M.
Stranger at the table. Apple, M.
"**Stranger,** bear word to the Spartans we .
. .". Böll, H.
Stranger blood. Hodgell, P. C.
"**Stranger** in paradise". Nevai, L.
Stranger in the house. Rose, D. A.
Strangers. McCrory, M.
Strangers. Singer, I. B.
Strangers. Soldatow, S.
A **stranger's** charm. Outlaw, L. L.
Strangers in the fog. Pronzini, B.
Strangers in the universe. Hammer, S.
Strangers on paradise. Knight, D. F.
STRANGLING
Forester, C. S. The turning of the tide
Hartley, L. P. Per far l'amore
Ingalls, R. St. George and the nightclub
Stratton, Marilynn
Before summer comes
Alberta bound; ed. by F. Stenson

Straub, Joseph
The Gioconda aria
The Massachusetts Review 28:115-27 Spr '87
Straub, Peter
Blue rose
Cutting edge; ed. by D. Etchison
The juniper tree
Prime evil; ed. by D. E. Winter
Strauss, Botho, 1944-
Marlene's sister
The Literary Review (Madison, N.J.) 30:493-506 Summ '87
STRAUSS, RICHARD, 1864-1949
About
Blish, J. A work of art
Strawberries. Mazel, D.
Strawberry moon. Sheffield, A.
The **strawberry** patch. Hankla, C.
Strawberry stew. Kinsella, W. P.
The **strawberry** teardrop. Collins, M. A.
A **stray** bullet. Yi, P.
Strays. Richard, M.
STREAM OF CONSCIOUSNESS
Barthelme, D. The school
Barthelme, D. Sentence
Beckett, S. The calmative
Bowles, P. Monologue—Tangier 1975
Bowles, P. Tangier 1975
Brooks, D. The misbehaviour of things
Camus, A. The renegade
Coleman, W. Fat Lena
DeGrazia, E. The enemy
DeGrazia, E. The girl and two old men
Dixon, S. The beginning of something
Dixon, S. Meeting Aline
Dixon, S. Self-portrait
Faik, S. Four plus signs
Faik, S. Kalinikhta [good night]
Faust, I. Gary Dis-Donc
Flanagan, R. Berzerk
Francis, H. E. A chronicle of love
García Márquez, G. Dialogue with the mirror
García Márquez, G. The other side of death
García Márquez, G. Someone has been disarranging these roses
García Márquez, G. The third resignation
Gilkison, A. Atthis
Gottlieb, E. The lizard
Hara, T. The land of heart's desire
Jolley, E. The long distant lecture
Kilworth, G. Oubliette
Le Guin, U. K. Kore 87
Liben, M. Suspension points . . .
Lish, G. Last descent to earth
Lish, G. The traitor
Moore, L. To fill
Moorhead, F. Waiting for Colombo: a close-up
Neville, S. Second coming
Okri, B. Disparities

Paolucci, A. A small clearing
Phillips, J. A. How Mickey made it
Porter, K. A. The jilting of Granny Weatherall
Szucsany, D. Mr. Simpson
Thomas, D. Prologue to an adventure
Valenzuela, L. The verb to kill
Wali, M. A. A. At a woman's house
Wilson, B. Hearings
Woolf, V. The mark on the wall
Woolf, V. The new dress
Street, Emmet *See* Behan, Brendan
Street, James, 1924-
Weep no more, my lady
Mississippi writers v1: Fiction; ed. by D. Abbott
Street idyll. Stead, C.
Street of dreams. Ford, J. M.
The **street** of the Hyacinth. Woolson, C. F.
STREET RAILROADS
See also Trolley buses
Crane, S. The broken-down van
Street star. Parr, W.
The **street-sweeping** show. Feng Jicai
The **streets** of Laredo. Henry, W.
The **strength** of steel. Vogan, S.
Strete, Craig, 1950-
The game of cat and eagle
In the field of fire; ed. by J. Van B. Dann and J. Dann
Stribling, T. S. (Thomas Sigismund), 1881-1965
The colonel's predicament
The Art of fiction in the heart of Dixie; ed. by P. D. Beidler
Stribling, Thomas Sigismund *See* Stribling, T. S. (Thomas Sigismund), 1881-1965
Strictly diplomatic. Carr, J. D.
The **striding** place. Atherton, G. F. H.
Strieber, Whitley
The Nixon mask
Halloween horrors; ed. by A. Ryan
Pain
Cutting edge; ed. by D. Etchison
The pool
Prime evil; ed. by D. E. Winter
Vaudeville
Murder in Manhattan; ed. by B. Adler
The **strigae.** Schwob, M.
Strike and fade. Dumas, H.
Strike it rich. Brady, M.
"The **strike,** oh, Lord, the strike!". Colette
Strikebreaker. Asimov, I.
STRIKES AND LOCKOUTS
Asimov, I. Strikebreaker
Botwinik, B. The general strike
Conroy, J. Uncle Ollie finds a new market
Conroy, J. Uncle Ollie's rabbit hunt
Dickinson, C. A night in the garden
Kinsella, W. P. The thrill of the grass
Lawson, S. PASTA MOMA
Long, D. The last photograph of Lyle Pettibone

STRIKES AND LOCKOUTS—*Continued*
Slesinger, T. The mouse-trap
Weissenberg, I. M. A shtetl
The **string**. Boylan, J.
The **string**. See Maupassant, G. de. A piece of string
String of pearls. Bloch, R.
The **string** quartet. Woolf, V.
Stroke. Haley, R.
Stroke. Oates, J. C.
Stroke of genius. Baxt, G.
A **stroke** of good fortune. O'Connor, F.
Stroke of mercy. Godwin, P.
Strong as death is love. Singer, I. B.
Strong horse tea. Walker, A.
The **strong** man. Garrett, G. P.
Strong-man from Piraeus. Johnston, G.
The **strong** one. Winton, T.
A **strong** shoulder to weep on. Fremlin, C.
Structural anthropology. Mars-Jones, A.
Structural unemployment. Jackson, G.
Structurally sound. Roche, S.
The **structure** and meaning of dormitory and food services. Bell, M. S.
Strugatškiĭ, Arkadiĭ Natanovich
(jt. auth) See Strugatškiĭ, Boris Natanovich, and Strugatškiĭ, Arkadiĭ Natanovich
Strugatškiĭ, Arkadiĭ Natanovich, and Strugatškiĭ, Boris Natanovich
Six matches
The Penguin world omnibus of science fiction
The way to Amalteia
Earth and elsewhere, by K. Bulychev and others
Strugatškiĭ, Boris Natanovich
(jt. auth) See Strugatškiĭ, Arkadiĭ Natanovich, and Strugatškiĭ, Boris Natanovich
Strugatškiĭ, Boris Natanovich, and Strugatškiĭ, Arkadiĭ Natanovich
The visitors
Aliens, travelers, and other strangers; by B. and A. Strugatsky and others
Struth. Deveson, R.
Struthers, Ann
Gathering evidence
Here's the story: fiction with heart; ed. by M. Sklar
Stuart, Floyd C.
This is a delta
The Georgia Review 41:509-20 Fall '87
Stuart, Ian, 1922-1987 *See* MacLean, Alistair, 1922-1987
Stuart, Ian, 1927-
The steep dark stairs
John Creasey's Crime collection, 1986
Stuart, Jesse, 1907-1984
The Anglo-Saxons of Auxierville
Stuart, J. Clearing in the sky & other stories

Battle with the bees
Stuart, J. Clearing in the sky & other stories
The champion
Stuart, J. Clearing in the sky & other stories
Clearing in the sky
Stuart, J. Clearing in the sky & other stories
Coming down the mountain
Stuart, J. Clearing in the sky & other stories
Competition at Slush Creek
Stuart, J. Clearing in the sky & other stories
Evidence is high proof
Stuart, J. Clearing in the sky & other stories
Fast-Train Ike
Nightmares in Dixie; ed. by F. McSherry; C. G. Waugh and M. H. Greenberg
Fight number twenty-five
Stuart, J. Clearing in the sky & other stories
From the mountains of Pike
The Georgia Review 40:277-88 Spr '86
Necessary fictions; ed. by S. W. Lindberg and S. Corey
Governor Warburton's right-hand man
Stuart, J. Clearing in the sky & other stories
Horse-trading trembles
Stuart, J. Clearing in the sky & other stories
Hot-collared mule
Stuart, J. Clearing in the sky & other stories
Land of our enemies
Stuart, J. Clearing in the sky & other stories
No hero
Stuart, J. Clearing in the sky & other stories
No petty thief
Stuart, J. Clearing in the sky & other stories
Old Gore
Stuart, J. Clearing in the sky & other stories
Road number one
Stuart, J. Clearing in the sky & other stories
The slipover sweater
Stuart, J. Clearing in the sky & other stories
Testimony of trees
Stuart, J. Clearing in the sky & other stories
Thirty-two votes before breakfast
Stuart, J. Clearing in the sky & other stories

Stuart, Jesse, 1907-1984—*Continued*
To market, to market
  Stuart, J. Clearing in the sky & other stories
When mountain men make peace
  Stuart, J. Clearing in the sky & other stories
Stuart, Kiel
Green in High Hallack
  Tales of the Witch World [1]
The singing eggs
  Magic in Ithkar 3; ed. by A. Norton and R. Adams
Stuart, Ruth McEnery
The Woman's Exchange of Simpkinsville
  Arkansas in short fiction; ed. by W. M. Baker and E. C. Simpson
Stubblefield, Charles
A Christmas story
  Prairie Schooner 59:3-34 Wint '85
Stubborn Stina. Heinesen, W.
STUBBORNNESS *See* Obstinacy
Stubbs, Jean, 1926-
The belvedere
  The Mammoth book of modern crime stories; ed. by G. Hardinge
Stubby Pringle's Christmas. Schaefer, J. W.
Stuchly, Judy Bauer- *See* Bauer-Stuchly, Judy
The **stud**. Thompson, J.
The **student**. Chekhov, A. P.
The **student**. Taube, M.
The **student**. Tuohy, F.
Student, petty thief, TV star. Bowering, G.
STUDENTS
    See also College life; College students; School life; Seminarians; Youth
Ansky, S. Behind a mask
Bernard, K. The girl who might or might not have read Sartre
Böll, H. Daniel the Just
Boylan, J. Final exam
Bryce Echenique, A. In Paracas with Jimmy
Canin, E. The carnival dog, the buyer of diamonds
Carlson, R. Half life
Cho, S.-H. On the overhead bridge
Clark, M. Learning to bowl an out-swinger
Clarke, A. C. If only: only if . . .
Clayton, J. J. Cambridge is sinking!
Dadswell, M. Mimi
Day, R. C. Annunciation
Durrell, L. The little affair in Paris
Flanagan, R. Close dancing
Francis, H. E. The sudden trees
Fremlin, C. The sensory deprivation tank
Girion, B. King of the hill
Girion, B. The makeover of Meredith Kaplan
Girion, B. Rip-off!
Girion, B. Trophy
Harvor, E. The age of unreason
Harvor, E. The students' soirée

Harvor, E. To supper in the morning and to bed at noon
Haylock, J. Tomiko
Hospital, J. T. You gave me hyacinths
Hunnicutt, E. In the music library
Ioannidou Adamidou, I. Hero
Kawabata, Y. The young lady of Suruga
Kercheval, J. L. A clean house
Kessler, J. F. Rhadamanthys
Klass, P. The anatomy of the brain
MacLaverty, B. The Great Profundo
MacLaverty, B. The miraculous candidate
McKnight, R. First I look at the purse
McKnight, R. Getting to be like the studs
McKnight, R. The honey boys
Monreal, D. N. A matter of dignity
Morrell, D. Orange is for anguish, blue for insanity
Murphy, P. The chapter on love
Murphy, T. M. The answers they have
Ndebele, N. Fools
Nesbitt, J. D. Half the way back
Nimmo, D. The healing
Nowakowski, M. The confidential call
O'Brien, E. Sister Imelda
Petchsingh, T. The two moons of Vira's world
Rasputin, V. G. French lessons
Robison, M. An amateur's guide to the night
Robison, M. Trying
Sabah, V. An imaginary journey to the moon
Salama, F. Friends' eyes
Salinas, M. The scholarship jacket
Sanders, S. R. The anatomy lesson
Simpson, M. Three maids' children
Sorrells, R. T. Lovers
St. Pierre, P. H. The education of Phyllisteen
Stevenson, R. L. The body snatchers
Swanwick, M. The man who met Picasso
Thompson, J. Naomi counting time
Tuohy, F. The trap
Vesity, A. The first day
Wendt, A. Hamlet
Wicomb, Z. A clearing in the bush
Williams, S. And say good-bye to yourself
Wilson, B. Phantom limb pain
Wolff, T. Smorgasbord
Yasuoka, S. Thick the new leaves
The **students'** soirée. Harvor, E.
The **student's** wife. Carver, R.
The **stuff** of madness. Highsmith, P.
The **stuffed** bird. Pirandello, L.
Stuffing. Ellison, H.
Stumps. Perry, M. C.
Stung. Creamer, E. S.
Stung. Winters, J.
Stunning the punters. Sproat, R.
STUNT MEN
Beaulieu, V. L. The rubber ball
Hartley, L. P. A high dive

STUNT MEN—*Continued*
Humphrey, W. The human fly
MacLaverty, B. The Great Profundo
Sturgeon, Theodore, 1918-1985
Brat
Sturgeon, T. Alien cargo
Bright segment
The Dark descent; ed. by D. G. Hartwell
Sturgeon, T. Alien cargo
Cargo
Sturgeon, T. Alien cargo
It
Sturgeon, T. Alien cargo
The Martian and the moron
Sturgeon, T. Alien cargo
Medusa [Variant title: To marry Medusa]
Sturgeon, T. Alien cargo
Microcosmic god
Sturgeon, T. Alien cargo
Poker Face
Sturgeon, T. Alien cargo
The professor's teddy bear
Masterpieces of terror and the supernatural; ed. by M. Kaye and S. Kaye
Shadow, shadow on the wall
Sturgeon, T. Alien cargo
The silken-swift . . .
Masterpieces of fantasy and enchantment; ed. by D. G. Hartwell
The touch of your hand
Sturgeon, T. Alien cargo
The traveling Crag
Sturgeon, T. Alien cargo
Twink
Sturgeon, T. Alien cargo
Two percent inspiration
Sturgeon, T. Alien cargo
A way of thinking
Amazing science fiction anthology: The wild years, 1946-1955; ed. by M. H. Greenberg
Why dolphins don't bite
Medea: Harlan's world; ed. by H. Ellison
Won't you walk—
[Analog]: Writers' choice v2
Sturgeon, T. Alien cargo
Sturges, A. E.
The last loneliness
Short story international 51
Only a matter of time
Short story international 65
Pianoforte
Short story international 54
The **stuttering** priest. Hughes, M. G.
Stýblová, Valja
Scalpel, please
Short story international 50
The **Stymphalean** birds. Christie, A.
Styron, William, 1925-
Love day
The Esquire fiction reader v2

Su Ye
Scatterbrain
Short story international 52
Suarez, Mario
The migrant
Cuentos Chicanos; ed. by R. A. Anaya and A. Márquez
Subcommittee. Henderson, Z.
A **subject** of childhood. Paley, G.
Subject: Petri Ganton. Henry, R.
The **submarine** plans. Christie, A.
SUBMARINE WARFARE *See* World War, 1939-1945—Naval operations—Submarine
SUBMARINES
Chard, J. The call of the running tide
Gores, J. Pahua
Verne, J. Captain Nemo's revenge
Suboctave story. Pasternak, B. L.
Subramani
Tell me where the train goes
The Literary Review (Madison, N.J.) 29:538-44 Summ '86
Subramanian, Usha
Hitchhikers
Short story international 44
Portrait of a woman
Short story international 46
The **substitute.** Maupassant, G. de
The **substitute.** Wilson, G.
Substitution trick. Willis, C.
SUBURBAN LIFE
See also Commuters
Auchincloss, L. The seagull
Boyle, T. C. Rara avis
Cheever, J. The country husband
Cheever, J. The swimmer
Cullen, E. J. Lawn City
Delbanco, N. The consolation of philosophy
Ellison, H. Commuter's problem
Humphrey, W. The last husband
McCullers, C. A domestic dilemma
Painter, P. Sylvia
Roth, P. Eli, the fanatic
Silverberg, R. What we learned from this morning's newspaper
Tuohy, F. Evening in Connecticut
Wetherell, W. D. The man who loved Levittown
Suburban tigress. Treat, L.
SUBURBS *See* Suburban life
Suburbs of the Arctic Circle. Burns, M.
SUBVERSIVE ACTIVITIES
See also Terrorism
Gilbert, M. The African tree-beavers
The **subversive** divorce. Schwartz, L. S.
SUBWAYS
Ade, G. When father meets father
Ashwood-Collins, A. Film at eleven
Barker, C. The midnight meat train
Bernard, K. Dirty old man
Bowker, R. The other train phenomenon

SUBWAYS—*Continued*
Duane, D. Uptown local
Fox, R. A fable
Honig, L. No friends, all strangers
Linzner, G. The independent fiend
Lish, G. The traitor
Molnar, A. K. The crosstie
SUCCESS
    See also Ambition; Self-made men
Barthelme, D. 110 West Sixty-First Street
Drake, R. The moon-fixer
Mori, Y. Spring storm
Rand, P. Charades
Stewart, J. I. M. Two strings to his bow
Swados, H. A glance in the mirror
Van Greenaway, P. The immortal coil
Wells, H. G. Wayde's essence
Wolff, T. The rich brother
Ziem, J. Clever
The **success** and the little failure. Wilbur, E.
Success story. Banks, R.
SUCCESSION *See* Inheritance and succession
The **succession**. Goodman, A.
A **succession** of Sundays. Poe, E. A.
Such interesting neighbors. Finney, J.
Sucharitkul, Somtow
Fiddling for water buffaloes
    Tales from the planet Earth
    The Year's best science fiction, fourth
    annual collection
Sucher, Cheryl Pearl
Erich Auerbach leaves Istanbul
    Michigan Quarterly Review 23:84-94
    Wint '84
Sucker. McCullers, C.
Sucker bait. Asimov, I.
Suckert, Curzio *See* Malaparte, Curzio, 1898-1957
Suckow, Ruth, 1892-1960
The crick
    Suckow, R. A Ruth Suckow omnibus
A great Mollie
    Suckow, R. A Ruth Suckow omnibus
Home-coming
    Suckow, R. A Ruth Suckow omnibus
The little girl from town
    Suckow, R. A Ruth Suckow omnibus
The man of the family
    Suckow, R. A Ruth Suckow omnibus
Midwestern primitive
    Suckow, R. A Ruth Suckow omnibus
A part of the institution
    Suckow, R. A Ruth Suckow omnibus
Susan and the doctor
    Suckow, R. A Ruth Suckow omnibus
Three, counting the cat
    Suckow, R. A Ruth Suckow omnibus
Visiting
    Suckow, R. A Ruth Suckow omnibus
What have I?
    Suckow, R. A Ruth Suckow omnibus

SUDAN
Ahmed, F. The wicked city
El Makk, A. The case
Horn, A. The making of Musa Maikudi
A **sudden** enthusiasm. Crowley, B.
Sudden modeling. Kranes, D.
A **sudden** story. Coover, R.
The **sudden** trees. Francis, H. E.
Sue: a meditation on history. Greenberg, A.
SUFFERING
    See also Good and evil; Pain
Ellison, H. Strange wine
Goyen, W. Arthur Bond
Mann, T. A difficult hour
West, J. Night piece for Julia
The **sufferings** of young Vaganov. Shukshin, V. M.
The **sufficiency** of everyday life: Avenue A and Eleventh Street, 1963. Dennison, G.
SUFFOLK (ENGLAND) *See* England—Suffolk
SUFFRAGE
Twain, M. The curious republic of Gondour
Sufrah, geomancer. Schwob, M.
Sugar. Byatt, A. S.
Sugar among the chickens. Nordan, L.
Sugar, the eunuchs, and Big G.B. Nordan, L.
SUICIDE
Abe, A. Friends
Akutagawa, R. A fool's life
Amis, M. Insight at Flame Lake
An, S.-G. The green chrysanthemum
Aquin, H. Back on April eleventh
Archer, J. Christina Rosenthal
Asscher-Pinkhof, C. Dawn
Asscher-Pinkhof, C. Secret
Asscher-Pinkhof, C. Transport night
Austin, D. He was there when they came across the bridge on their bicycles
Balfour, B. J. Some days are like that
Barker, C. Jacqueline Ess: her will and testament
Basu, R. Sambal and Putki
Bates, H. E. A great day for Bonzo
Baxt, G. The woman I envied
Bedard, B. Hour of the beast
Bishop, M. The Yukio Mishima Cultural Association of Kudzu Valley, Georgia
Böll, H. Beside the river
Boylan, J. Bride of Frankenstein
Bruce-Novoa. The manuscript
Burns, M. A joint communique
Burt, S. The General's toothache
Busch, F. Dog song
Campos-De Metro, J. The feather
Carver, R. The third thing that killed my father off
Cather, W. Paul's case
Chang, Y.-H. Poems of John the Baptist
Cohen, A. On her feet again

SUICIDE—*Continued*
Coleman, W. Hamburgers
Colette. The landscape
Colette. The photographer's wife
Crampsey, R. A. Felicity
Dann, J. Between the windows of the sea
Dann, J. Night visions
Davies, D. A quiet man
De Queiroz, D. S. Guidance
DeMarinis, R. Disneyland
DeMarinis, R. Gent
Dennison, G. On being a son
DeWeese, G. Everything's going to be all right
Dick, P. K. The electric ant
Dickens, C. The Baron of Grogzwig
Dilworth, S. Winter mines
Dodd, S. M. Berkie
Dowell, C. The surgeon
Dubus, A. Over the hill
East, C. The last person
Eldridge, M. Together
Ellison, H. The sky is burning
Espina-Moore, L. Man around a maypole
Faik, S. Psst, psst!
Flanagan, M. Death in Sussex
Frazier, L., Jr. In the presence of mine enemies
Fremlin, C. The woman who had everything
Gardner, M. The horrible horns
Geras, A. The whole truth
Gerber, M. J. Memorial service
Gilchrist, E. Traceleen's telling a story called "A bad year"
Gilchrist, M. The lost mistress
Givner, J. A climate of extremes
Gordimer, N. Oral history
Gordimer, N. Terminal
Gordon, M. Agnes
Gowan, L. The decline and fall of Howard Dawn
Goyen, W. In the icebound hothouse
Greenberg, A. The conservation of matter
Haake, K. Wait until heaven
Haldeman, J. W. The monster
Haldeman, J. W. The pilot
Hall, M. L. The painter
Hall, M. L. The peaceful eye
Hall, T. T. Holding up the other end
Harrington, J. The au pair girl
Hartley, L. P. The cotillon
Hartley, L. P. The pampas clump
Hartley, L. P. Up the garden path
Havazelet, E. What everyone wants
Hempel, A. The man in Bogotá
Henry, O. The furnished room
Henry, R. Subject: Petri Ganton
Hensley, J. L. The decision
Heyrman, P. Funeral for a friend
Highsmith, P. The stuff of madness
Hoch, E. D. The ring with the velvet ropes
Hoch, E. D. Uncle Max
Hood, M. And Venus is blue
Hood, M. Doing this, saying that, to applause
Hood, M. Inexorable progress
Ingalls, R. Early morning sightseer
Janowitz, T. Ode to heroine of the future
Jhabvala, R. P. Desecration
Johnston, G. Requiem mass
Josipovici, G. He
Kalpakian, L. Fair Augusto
Kavaler, R. Little Boy Blue
Kawabata, Y. Love suicides
Keizer, G. I am the burning bush
Kerrigan, P. West wind
Kilworth, G. The rose bush
Kim, S.-O. Seoul: winter 1964
King, F. H. The tradesman
Kinsella, W. P. Caraway
Kinsella, W. P. K Mart
Kurahashi, Y. The monastery
Lessing, D. M. To room nineteen
Lofts, N. God's own elect
Lutz, J. Something for the dark
Lynch, L. At a bar I: The Jersey dyke
MacLaverty, B. Across the street
MacLaverty, B. Hugo
Madden, D. No trace
Matheson, R. C. Echoes
Matthews, J. If not us, then who?
Maupassant, G. de. The duel
Maupassant, G. de. Little Louise Roque
Maupassant, G. de. A little walk
Maupassant, G. de. Madame Baptiste
Maupassant, G. de. Miss Harriet
Maupassant, G. de. Sentiment
Maupassant, G. de. Suicides
McGuane, T. Flight
McQueen, J. Uphill runner
Meinke, P. The twisted river
Mishima, Y. Patriotism
Moore, G. At the turn of the road
Moore, L. Go like this
Moorhouse, F. The Coca-Cola Kid
Morice, A. Young man on a train
Muschg, A. Brami's view
Nagibin, IŪ. M. The peak of success
Naipaul, S. The dolly house
Narayan, R. K. The watchman
Nelson, V. Coming back
Nordan, L. The Sears and Roebuck catalog game
Norris, L. Reverse for Dennis
Nunes, N. Clastomina
Oates, J. C. Ancient airs, voices
Oates, J. C. Ich bin ein Berliner
Oates, J. C. Last days
Oates, J. C. The tryst
O'Hara, J. The hardware man
O'Hara, J. Our friend the sea
O'Neil, D. Report on a broken bridge
Ozick, C. The pagan rabbi
Palma, C. The man with the cigarette

SUICIDE—*Continued*

Pascoe, B. Cicadas
Pavese, C. Suicides
Pfeil, F. Shine on
Phillips, J. A. Blue moon
Pil'niāk, B. The Nizhni Novgorod Otkos
Piñera, V. An a posteriori ghost
Pirandello, L. Aunt Michelina
Pirandello, L. The black shawl
Pirandello, L. By himself
Pirandello, L. Candelora
Pirandello, L. The fish trap
Pirandello, L. An idea
Pirandello, L. The imbecile
Pirandello, L. In silence
Pirandello, L. Into the sketch
Pirandello, L. The lonely man
Pirandello, L. The long dress
Pirandello, L. Nothing
Pirandello, L. The stuffed bird
Pirandello, L. Sun and shade
Pirandello, L. Sunrise
Pirandello, L. This makes two!
Pirandello, L. The trap
Pirandello, L. The trip
Pirandello, L. While the heart suffered
Pronzini, B. Deathwatch
Prose, F. Creature comforts
Pugmire, W. H., and Salmonson, J. A. "Pale trembling youth"
Regent, P. The Major steps out
Rendell, R. The clinging woman
Robinson, S. God is an iron
Rucker, R. von B. In frozen time
Sandel, C. The art of murder
Schulman, H. The heart of my heart
Schwob, M. The Milesian virgins
Shaw, J. B. Some of the things I did not do
Shiga, N. Kuniko
Sin, S.-U. Pyŏn's death
Singer, I. B. One day of happiness
Smith, D. W. Flawless execution
Son, S.-H. At the end of the world
Sorrells, R. T. Talking to the boy
Spillane, M. The girl behind the hedge
Stevens, J. Into that good night
Strand, M. Two stories
Strieber, W. The pool
Swift, G. Cliffedge
Symons, J. The boiler
Tahir, B. Last night I dreamt of you
Taylor, P. H. The hand of Emmagene
Taylor, R. Charley Ford betrayed
Thomas, J. Half frame
Thompson, J. Having words
Thorman, C. No job too small
Tung, N. Fire
Valenzuela, L. All about suicide
Van de Wetering, J. The jughead file
Waldrop, H. Fair game
Welch, D. A fragment of a life story
West, J. Up a tree

Westlake, D. E. Come back, come back
Williams, B. The lovers
Wilmot, J. Dirt angel
Wilner, H. Lead
Wolfe, T. The hollow men
Woolf, V. The legacy
Woolrich, C. If the dead could talk
Yaryura-Tobías, A. The voyeur
Yun, H.-G. Group beating
Zhang Jie. Under the hawthorn
Suicide is scandalous. Kane, H.
The **suicide** of Kiaros. Baum, L. F.
Suicide, or murder? Hodge, J. A.
Suicides. Maupassant, G. de
Suicides. Pavese, C.
The **suitcase**. Ozick, C.
Suited to be a fish. See Li, F.-Y. The carp
Sukenick, Ronald
At this very instant
American made; ed. by M. Leyner; C. White and T. Glynn
Sulayman, Nabil
The wrath of Shaykh Muhammad Al-Ajami
Modern Syrian short stories; ed. by M. G. Azrak
Sulivan, Jean, 1913-1980
The beginning of science
Cross Currents 35:434-8 Wint '85/'86
Kid zero
Cross Currents 35:443-51 Wint '85/'86
Why do straight lines curve for no reason?
Cross Currents 35:439-42 Wint '85/'86
Sulkin, Sidney
Broder's loves
TriQuarterly no71:7-23 Wint '88
Sullivan, Chester
The horse in the bedroom
Mississippi writers v1: Fiction; ed. by D. Abbott
Sullivan, Jay A.
Welcome to freedom
L. Ron Hubbard presents Writers of the future v2
Sullivan, Thomas
The extension
Midnight; ed. by C. L. Grant
The man who drowned puppies
Masques II; ed. by J. N. Williamson
The Mickey Mouse Olympics
The Science fictional Olympics; ed. by I. Asimov; M. H. Greenberg and C. G. Waugh
A night at the head of a grave
Shadows 8
Whores in the pulpit
Westeryear; ed. by E. Gorman
Sullivan, Tim
Knucklebones
Ripper! Ed. by G. Dozois and S. Casper
Sullivan, Tom *See* Sullivan, Thomas
SULLIVAN'S ISLAND (S.C.)
Poe, E. A. The gold-bug

Sultan, Muzaffar
  The butterfly collector
    Modern Syrian short stories; ed. by M.
      G. Azrak
Sultan Jekker. Whitaker, M.
The **sultriness** of a cold evening. Yi, H.-C.
The **sum** of love. Dubus, E. N.
A **sum** of moments. Campbell, L.
Sumi dreams of a paper frog. Kilworth, G.
A **summary** of what happened to Moham-
  med al-Mahmoudi. Tamer, Z.
SUMMER
  Anderson, S. Milk bottles
  Bates, H. E. Summer in Salandar
  Brooks, B. Summer in Sydney
  Collins, L. A summer's day
  Henry, O. Rus in urbe
  Hood, H. The small birds
  Kiely, B. The python
  Kilgore, D. Last summer "How I spent
    my summer vacation" by Diana
    Lancaster
  McGarry, J. Stayed back
  Morris, M. Losing your cool
  Updike, D. Summer
  Wexler, J. For Ann
Summer. Updike, D.
A **summer** afternoon. Pierce, C.
Summer, an elegy. Gilchrist, E.
A **summer** at Estabrook. Ferguson, W.
A **summer** aunt. Grenville, K.
SUMMER CAMPS
  Carpenter, D. The father's love
  Colter, C. The frog hunters
  Ferguson, W. Terror
  Gault, C. The other Ellen
  Gordon, M. The thorn
  Harrington, J. A place of her own
  Harvor, E. If only we could drive like this
    forever
  Klass, P. Trivia
  Levinson, R., and Link, W. Child's play
  Lish, G. The death of me
  Long, D. Great blue
  Nevai, L. Baby wood
  Parise, G. Melancholy
  Price, R. Michael Egerton
  Roiter, H. Only Sam knows
  Sarrantonio, A. Letters from camp
Summer dreams. Hecht, D. C.
A **summer** experience. Ge Wujue
Summer flower. Hara, T.
Summer flying. Eiferman, L.
The **summer** game. Heller, S.
Summer heat. Rose, D. A.
SUMMER HOMES
  Alden, P. B. Feeding the eagles
  Beattie, A. Spiritus
  Beattie, A. Summer people
  Gilchrist, E. Defender of the Little Falaya
  Greenberg, A. Sue: a meditation on history
  Laurence, M. The loons
  Leavitt, D. The lost cottage

  Loukakis, A. Perfect holiday sounds
  McGarry, J. Providence, 1934: the house
    at the beach
  Proulx, A. In the pit
  Stephen, J. The other side of summer
  Stratton, M. Before summer comes
Summer in Salandar. Bates, H. E.
Summer in Sydney. Brooks, B.
Summer is the Côte d'Azur. Gifkins, M.
Summer Lethe. Ferron, J.
The **summer** my grandmother was supposed
  to die. Richler, M.
The **summer** no one was poor. Floyd, P. L.
Summer of a stick man. Stone, K.
The **summer** of my last chance. Haien, J.
Summer of sanctity. Bonnie, K. F.
Summer of the Dead Frogs. Spark, D.
Summer of the magic show. Huddle, D.
Summer on ice. Farmer, B.
Summer opportunity. Thomas, M.
Summer people. Beattie, A.
Summer people. Hemingway, E.
The **summer** people. Jackson, S.
Summer people. Kaplan, D. M.
A **summer** pilgrim. Tuohy, F.
Summer pudding. Regent, P.
The **summer** rebellion. Calisher, H.
SUMMER RESORTS
  Cameron, E. The girl on the beach
  Clayton, J. J. Bodies of the rich
  Franzen, B. Come stay with us
  Gee, M. Eleventh holiday
  Hoch, E. D. Winter run
  Jackson, S. The summer people
  Kerr, L. Passion fruit
  O'Hara, J. Price's always open
  Raphael, F. Sleeps six
  Thomas, A. C. Local customs
  Wagner, R. E. I'm going down to watch
    the horses come alive
Summer sand. Moore, M. J.
Summer share. Morris, M.
Summer shoes. Kawabata, Y.
Summer shore. Grau, S. A.
Summer storm. Pavese, C.
The **summer** the men landed on the moon.
  Murphy, Y.
Summer tidings. Purdy, J.
SUMMER VACATIONS *See* Vacations
Summer visit. Bittle, C. R.
Summer wine. Prosser, H. L.
Summers, Barbara
  Fryday
    Essence 18:68-70+ N '87
  Maneuvers
    Essence 17:55-6+ Mr '87
Summers, Hollis Spurgeon, 1916-
  Amaryllis & the telephone
    Summers, H. Standing room
  Concerning, I suppose my father
    Summers, H. Standing room
  Diving
    Summers, H. Standing room

Summers, Hollis Spurgeon, 1916- — Continued
Dolly
  Summers, H. Standing room
Fortunato & the night visitor
  Summers, H. Standing room
Herschell
  Summers, H. Standing room
A hundred paths
  Summers, H. Standing room
The man who looked young
  Summers, H. Standing room
The vireo's nest
  Summers, H. Standing room
Summers, Merna
Ronnie so long at the fair
  Alberta bound; ed. by F. Stenson
Song of willow
  The Old dance; ed. by B. Burnard
A **summer's** day. Collins, L.
Summerville, James, 1947-
Paper fires
  Homewords: a book of Tennessee
  writers; ed. by D. Paschall
A **summing** up. Woolf, V.
A **summons**. Hartley, L. P.
SUN
Janowitz, T. Sun poisoning
Stein, J. Why the moon is small and dark
  when the sun is big and shiny
Willis, C. Daisy, in the sun
Sun and shade. Pirandello, L.
The **sun** and the rain. Wolfe, T.
The **Sun-Dog** Trail. London, J.
Sun for the young. Tamer, Z.
The **sun** in winter. Malouf, D.
The **sun** is not merciful. Walters, A. L.
Sun, moon, and storm. Kotzwinkle, W.
Sun poisoning. Janowitz, T.
Sun Shaoshan
Eight hundred meters below
  Short story international 50
The **sun** stood still. Brand, M.
Sun, wind and water. McElroy, C. J.
SunDark in Ithkar. Rouland, S. L.
SUNDAY
Poe, E. A. A succession of Sundays
Poe, E. A. Three Sundays in a week
Sunday. Best, E.
Sunday at the zoo. Dybek, S.
Sunday breakfast. Wheatcroft, J.
The **Sunday** drive. Gass, W. H.
Sunday in the park. Kaufman, B.
Sunday lunch. Lurie, M.
Sunday morning: a foolish tale. Klíma, I.
Sunday rodeos. Warren, D.
Sunday with someone new. Portnoy, M.
Sundays. King, F. H.
Sundays. Wilbur, E.
Sundays in summer. Oates, J. C.
Sunday's no name band. Vogan, S.
The **sunfish** and the mermaid. Schwartz, L.
  S.

Sungrab. Nolan, W. F.
Sunken gardens. Sterling, B.
The **sunken** park. Pacheco, J. E.
Sunlight in Trebizond Street. Paton, A.
Sunny. Furman, L.
A **sunny** place. Kawabata, Y.
The **sunrise**. Atwood, M.
Sunrise. Pirandello, L.
Sunrise. Rey Rosa, R.
Sunrise on Pluto. Silverberg, R.
Sunshine and shadow. Beattie, A.
The **sunshine** club. Campbell, R.
The **sunshine** of Paradise Alley. Rose, J.
Sunstroke. Bunin, I. A.
Sunstroke. Watson, I.
Super-deluxe. Aksenov, V. P.
Superbity. Jones, J.
The **superfluous** finger. Futrelle, J.
Supergrass. Dawson, C.
The **superhero**. Fox, J.
The **Superman** t-shirt. Skrzynecki, P.
The **supermarket** manager's daughter. Ebon,
  W.
SUPERNATURAL PHENOMENA
  See also Demoniac possession;
  Ghost stories; Horror stories
Aickman, R. Larger than oneself
Aickman, R. Your tiny hand is frozen
Alarcón, P. A. de. The tall woman
Arthur, R. The wonderful day
Barker, C. The forbidden
Barker, C. The last illusion
Baxter, C. Through the safety net
Benson, E. F. The man who went too far
Bierce, A. The damned thing
Bishop, M. A spy in the domain of Arn-
  heim
Blackwood, A. The transfer
Blackwood, A. The willows
Bloch, R. The unspeakable betrothal
Bradbury, R. Banshee
Bradbury, R. Promises, promises
Bradbury, R. The wind
Brennan, J. P. Mrs. Clendon's place
Brown, G. M. The lost boy
Campbell, R. Old clothes
Campbell, R. Seeing the world
Capote, T. Miriam
Card, O. S. Hatrack River
Chopin, K. Her letters
Christie, A. The dressmaker's doll
Clarke, M. Human repetends
Coville, B. The box
Cowper, R. What did the Deazies do?
Crowley, J. Antiquities
Davis, D. S. The muted horn
De la Mare, W. The creatures
Dickens, C. Mr. Testator's visitation
Doyle, Sir A. C. The parasite
Doyle, Sir A. C. The winning shot
Finney, J. I love Galesburg in the spring-
  time
Finney, J. I'm scared

SUPERNATURAL PHENOMENA — *Continued*

Finney, J. Where the Cluetts are
Freeman, M. E. W. Silence
Gallagher, T. Turpentine
García Márquez, G. The last voyage of the ghost ship
Grant, C. L. Out there
Green, J. C., and Proctor, G. W. The night of the Piasa
Hardy, T. The withered arm
Harrison, M. J. Running down
Hartley, L. P. The corner cupboard
Hartley, L. P. Paradise Paddock
Harvey, W. F. The clock
Hearn, L. The boy who drew cats
Hensley, J. L. Savant
Hodgson, W. H. The voice in the night
Hoffman, N. K. The shadow of a hawk
Horvitz, L. A. Pictures of a woman gone
Howard, V. E. The midnight voyage of the Seagull
Hughes, M. The singing float
James, M. R. An episode of cathedral history
James, M. R. The mezzotint
Kearns, R. Grave angels
King, F. H. Voices
Kipling, R. The wish house
Kirk, R. The reflex-man in Whinnymuir Close
Kirk, R. There's a long, long trail a-winding
Klein, R. E. Mrs. Rahlo's closet
Le Fanu, J. S. The white cat of Drumgunniol
Lee, T. Because our skins are finer
Leiber, F. Belsen Express
Leiber, F. Smoke ghost
Lopatin, J. Budapest dangereux
Lovecraft, H. P. The colour out of space
Lovecraft, H. P. The Dunwich horror
Lovecraft, H. P. The haunter of the dark
Lovecraft, H. P. The shunned house
MacDonald, J. D. The legend of Joe Lee
Machen, A. Novel of the white powder
Martin, V. Death goes to a party
Matthews, J. The amnesia ballet
Maupassant, G. de. The Englishman
Maupassant, G. de. Who knows?
Maurois, A. The house
Michaelson, L. W. An early frost
Michaelson, L. W. The flying Dutchman
Michaelson, L. W. The goldfish
Murphy, D. Roller
Norton, A. How many miles to Babylon?
O'Brien, F.-J. The Bohemian
O'Brien, F.-J. The wondersmith
Palma, C. Mors ex vita
Palmer, M. Esmerelda's hands
Percy, H. R. Haliburton
Phelps, E. S. The true story of Guenever
Poe, E. A. Metzengerstein
Poe, E. A. The narrative of Arthur Gordon Pym of Nantucket
Pronzini, B. Toy
Ramos, M. His mother's image
Reamy, T. Insects in amber
Rhys, J. A spiritualist
Rifaat, A. My world of the unknown
Rodoreda, M. The dolls' room
Rodoreda, M. A letter
Russell, W. C. A bewitched ship
Sarrantonio, A. The haunting of Y-12
Sheckley, R. Shootout in the toy shop
Sheckley, R. Wild Talents, Inc.
Shiel, M. P. The house of sounds
Simmons, D. Carrion comfort
Singer, I. B. The enemy
Singer, I. B. The missing line
Singer, I. B. A telephone call on Yom Kippur
Smith, C. A. The chain of Aforgomon
Smith, C. A. Genius loci
Snyder, Z. K. The three men
Stevenson, R. L. The isle of voices
Sturgeon, T. Cargo
Swain, E. G. The man with the roller
Tem, S. R. The battering
Thomas, D. Brember
Thomas, D. Jarley's
Trebelo, J. La Cueva Del Círculo Sin Fin
Verne, J. The storm
Walter, E. Christmas night
Warner, S. T. The proper circumstances
Waters, F. The woman at Otowi Crossing [excerpt]
Wells, H. G. The inexperienced ghost
Wells, H. G. The stolen body
Whitehead, H. S. C. The trap
Wiebe, R. H. The angel of the tar sands
Williamson, J. N. House mothers
Willis, C. Blued moon
Willson, H. Duke City alchemist
Woodforde, C. Cushi
Wynne, M. Y. The little room
Yerxa, L. Carrion crypt
The **supernatural** powers of Lieutenant Boruvka. Škvorecký, J.

SUPERSTITION

See also Occultism; Omens; Talismans; Vampires; Voodooism; Werewolves

Anderson, P. Eutopia
Ardizzone, T. The eyes of children
Ardizzone, T. World without end
Bishop, M. And the marlin spoke
Bishop, M. Love's heresy
Bowles, P. An inopportune visit
Brown, G. M. A candle for milk and grass
Chesterton, G. K. The second miracle
Chon, S.-G. Wings that will carry us both
Collins, M. The green woman
Conley, R. J. The endless dark of the night
Conley, R. J. The witch of Goingsnake

SUPERSTITION—*Continued*
Crace, J. Talking Skull
Crane, S. The black dog
Crowley, A. The mass of Saint Sécaire
Davis, S. Mark Haverly
Dumas, H. Ark of bones
Dumas, H. Devil bird
Dumas, H. Echo tree
Dumas, H. Fever
Dumas, H. Rain god
Earle, A. M. The witch sheep
El Hady, W. A. Who's superstitious?
Fisher, R. John Archer's nose
Fitzgerald, M. J. Objects
Grin, A. Ships in Liss
Hillmer, J. New day coming
Hoffman, W. The question of rain
Holt, J. D. "God sent you into that Gomorrah this morning to bring up the truth"
Kawabata, Y. The maidens' prayers
Kawabata, Y. The Sliding Rock
Kawabata, Y. Thunder in autumn
Kipling, R. The return of Imray
Lane, P. Apple peels and knives
Mrożek, S. From the darkness
Ocampo, S. The house of sugar
Ocampo, S. Leopoldina's dream
O'Grady, D. Sterner's double vision
Palma, C. The man with the cigarette
Ralph, J. He wrote to the rats
Rummel, M. K. White-out
Russell, W. C. Can these dry bones live?
Shannon, D. Conundrum
Smith, C. A. The colossus of Ylourgne
Tennant, K. Lady Weare and the Bodhisattva
Thomas, M. Neighbors
Thomas, M. She hears, falling, the seed
Valgardson, W. D. Bloodflowers
Warner, S. T. A widow's quilt
Superstitions. La Chapelle, M.
Superstitious. Oates, J. C.
The **supper.** Borowski, T.
Supper after the show. Dadswell, M.
Supper on the wall. McBain, H.
Suppertime. Painter, P.
The **supremacy** of the Hunza. Greenberg, J.
Supreme Court defends 50 racial equivalence in nationwide police departments. Dawson, F.
Sure thing. Asimov, I.
Surf. Hansen, J.
Surf City. Oates, J. C.
Surface, David
  Patterning
    The North American Review 270:40 S '85
Surfacing. Ferriss, L.
The **surfer.** Baber, A.
The **surfer.** Böll, H.
Surfiction. Wideman, J. E.
The **surgeon.** Dowell, C.

SURGEONS
    See also Physicians; Women physicians
Benson, E. F. Monkeys
Chen Rong. At middle age
Glasgow, E. The shadowy third
SURGERY
    See also Amputation; Brain—Surgery; Transplantation of organs, tissues, etc.
Bishop, M. Saving face
Blumlein, M. Tissue ablation and variant regeneration: a case report
Endō, S. A forty-year-old man
Farmer, P. J. Don't wash the carats
Gold, H. L. A matter of form
Grace, P. Hospital
Jahnn, H. H. Mov
King, S. Survivor type
Oates, J. C. Double solitaire
Stafford, J. The interior castle
Wells, H. G. Under the knife
Wilner, H. Facial nerve
Wilner, H. Recovery room
Surgical Department A. Shomlo, A.
The **surly** sullen bell. Kirk, R.
Surplus love. Ignatow, R. G.
Surplussed barrelware. Aksenov, V. P.
SURPRISE ENDINGS
Aldani, L. S is for snake
Betancourt, J. G. Vernon's dragon
Bloch, R. In the cards
Bloch, R. Man with a hobby
Bloch, R. 'Til death do us part
Bloch, R. Yours truly, Jack the Ripper
Brand, C. Bless this house
Brown, F. Nightmare in yellow
Cecil, H. The wanted man
Chopin, K. The locket
Davidson, A. The last wizard
Dozois, G. R. The sacrifice
Dunsany, E. J. M. D. P., Baron. In a dim room
Fish, R. L. The wager
Fisher, M. F. K. The reunion
Forsyth, F. There are no snakes in Ireland
Henry, O. The rathskeller and the rose
Little, J. R. Tommy's Christmas
Marlowe, D. J. The donor
Poe, E. A. The system of Doctor Tarr and Professor Fether
Pronzini, B. Changes
Pronzini, B. Sweet fever
Sagan, F. The exchange
Sarrantonio, A. Letters from camp
Spillane, M. Tomorrow I die
Stark, S. S. Best Quality Glass Company, New York
Wolff, T. The other Miller
Woolrich, C. The penny-a-worder
Surprise in disguise. Shannon, J.
'Surprise! Surprise!' from Matron. Jolley, E.
Surprised by joy. Baxter, C.

Surprises. Mazel, D.

SURREALISM

Ahern, T. Dr. Zifhart leaves for Atlantic City

Barthelme, D. The wound

Barthelme, S. Chat

Bell, M. Decatur

Bumpus, J. Heroes and villains

Carrington, L. As they rode along the edge

Carrington, L. Cast down by sadness

Carrington, L. The debutante

Carrington, L. Et in bellicus lunarum medicalis

Carrington, L. The happy corpse story

Carrington, L. The house of fear

Carrington, L. How to start a pharmaceuticals business

Carrington, L. Little Francis

Carrington, L. A man in love

Carrington, L. A Mexican fairy tale

Carrington, L. Monsieur Cyril de Guindre

Carrington, L. My flannel knickers

Carrington, L. My mother is a cow

Carrington, L. The neutral man

Carrington, L. The oval lady

Carrington, L. Pigeon, fly!

Carrington, L. The royal summons

Carrington, L. The seventh horse

Carrington, L. The sisters

Carrington, L. The skeleton's holiday

Carrington, L. The stone door

Carrington, L. The three hunters

Carrington, L. Uncle Sam Carrington

Carrington, L. Waiting

Carrington, L. White rabbits

Codrescu, A. Monsieur Teste in America

DeMarinis, R. Blind euchre

Edson, R. Dinner time

Eliade, M. The cape

Farris, J. You can keep your razors & guns but check your loud mouths at the door

Federspiel, J. An earthquake in my family

Federspiel, J. Infirtaris inoaknoneis

Ferguson, W. Cortez

Ferré, R. Pico Rico, mandorico

Ferré, R. The youngest doll

Gholson, C. Temple to the economics of love

Haley, R. Dogmaster

Haley, R. Occam's electric razor

Haley, R. Real illusions

Haley, R. Stroke

Hauser, M. The seersucker suit

Ingalls, R. Blessed art thou

Kurahashi, Y. The monastery

McCormack, E. P. Inspecting the vaults

Naranjo, C. Ondina

Norris, H. Starwood

O'Reilly, M. The romantic museum

Ozick, C. The shawl

Pierce, C. What I did for Aunt Berthe

Piñón, N. The new kingdom

Ruch, T. Claire's lover's church

Schulz, B. Father's last escape

Schwartz, L. S. The last frontier

Thomas, D. The lemon

Valenzuela, L. All about suicide

Valenzuela, L. Blue water-man

Valenzuela, L. Cat's eye

Valenzuela, L. The celery munchers

Valenzuela, L. Country carnival

Valenzuela, L. Flea market

Valenzuela, L. Generous impediments float downriver

Valenzuela, L. The gift of words

Valenzuela, L. Legend of the self-sufficient child

Valenzuela, L. My everyday colt

Valenzuela, L. Papito's story

Valenzuela, L. The place of its quietude

Valenzuela, L. The redtown chronicles

Valenzuela, L. A story about greenery

Valenzuela, L. Strange things happen here

SURREY (ENGLAND) *See* England—Surrey

SURVIVAL (AFTER AIRPLANE ACCIDENTS, SHIPWRECKS, ETC.)

See also Shipwrecks and castaways; Wilderness survival

Aldiss, B. W. The gods in flight

Atwood, M. A travel piece

Boyle, T. C. On for the long haul

Butler, O. E. Speech sounds

Defoe, D. Crusoe visits the wreck

Dubus, A. Blessings

Evarts, H. G. The trap

Farmer, P. J. Mother

Godwin, T. Too soon to die

Grau, S. A. Hunter

King, S. Survivor type

London, J. Love of life

Song, P.-S. Debris

Sturges, A. E. The last loneliness

Tiptree, J. The women men don't see

Willis, C. A letter from the Cleary's

Survival switch. Houbein, L.

Survival techniques. Calisher, H.

Survival week. Hall, J.

Surviving. Jacob, S.

Surviving. Moffett, J.

Surviving. Spivack, K.

Surviving adverse seasons. Targan, B.

The **survivor**. Federspiel, J.

Survivor. Forrest, K. V.

The **survivor**. Moudy, W. F.

A **survivor** in Salvador. Tuohy, F.

Survivor type. King, S.

Susan. Kornblatt, J. R.

Susan and the doctor. Suckow, R.

Susanna at the beach. Gold, H.

SUSHI

Shiga, N. The shopboy's god

Suspect alien. Saiki, J.

Suspense item. Gilliatt, P.

Suspension points . . . . Liben, M.

SUSSEX (ENGLAND) *See* England—Sussex

SUSSEX DIALECT *See* Dialect stories—
English—Sussex

Sussman, Ellen
Looking in windows
Redbook 170:68+ Mr '88

Suter, John F.
Doctor's orders
Kill or cure; ed. by M. Muller and B.
Pronzini
(jt. auth) See Post, Melville Davisson,
1869-1930, and Suter, John F.

Sutherland, Margaret
Codling-moth
Women's work; ed. by M. McLeod and
L. Wevers
Loving
Women's work; ed. by M. McLeod and
L. Wevers

Suttee. Auchincloss, L.

Sutter, Barton
You ain't dead yet
Stiller's pond; ed. by J. Agee; R. Blakely
and S. Welch

The **Sutton** Pie Safe. Benedict, P.

Svendsen, Linda
Flight
The New generation; ed. by A. Kaufman

Swados, Harvey
The balcony
Swados, H. Nights in the gardens of
Brooklyn
Bobby Shafter's gone to sea
Swados, H. Nights in the gardens of
Brooklyn
A chance encounter
Swados, H. Nights in the gardens of
Brooklyn
Claudine's book
Swados, H. Nights in the gardens of
Brooklyn
The dancer
Swados, H. Nights in the gardens of
Brooklyn
A glance in the mirror
Swados, H. Nights in the gardens of
Brooklyn
The hack
Swados, H. Nights in the gardens of
Brooklyn
A handful of ball-points, a heartful of love
Swados, H. Nights in the gardens of
Brooklyn
A hot day in Nuevo Laredo
Swados, H. Nights in the gardens of
Brooklyn
The letters
Swados, H. Nights in the gardens of
Brooklyn
The man in the toolhouse
Swados, H. Nights in the gardens of
Brooklyn

My Coney Island uncle
Swados, H. Nights in the gardens of
Brooklyn
Nights in the gardens of Brooklyn
Swados, H. Nights in the gardens of
Brooklyn
The peacocks of Avignon
Swados, H. Nights in the gardens of
Brooklyn
A question of loneliness
Swados, H. Nights in the gardens of
Brooklyn
Something a little special
Swados, H. Nights in the gardens of
Brooklyn
A story for Teddy
Swados, H. Nights in the gardens of
Brooklyn
Tease
Swados, H. Nights in the gardens of
Brooklyn
The tree of life
Swados, H. Nights in the gardens of
Brooklyn
Where does your music come from?
Swados, H. Nights in the gardens of
Brooklyn
Year of grace
Swados, H. Nights in the gardens of
Brooklyn

Swain, E. G. (Edmund Gill), 1861-1938
Bone to his bone
The Oxford book of English ghost
stories
The man with the roller
Lost souls; ed. by J. Sullivan

Swain, Edmund Gill *See* Swain, E. G. (Edmund Gill), 1861-1938

Swallow, Lisa
S'Olcarias's sons
Tales of the Witch World 2

Swallows. Lurie, M.

Swami Swafford. Daniels, C.

The **swami's** secret. Durrell, L.

The **swamp**. Sheckley, R.

Swamp dweller. Norton, A.

Swamp search. Whittington, H. B.

SWAMPS
Daniels, C. The legend of Wooley Swamp
Sheckley, R. The swamp

Swan, Annette
Monsoon
Short story international 43

Swan, Gladys, 1934-
Carnival for the gods
The Sewanee Review 92:355-69 Summ
'84
Losing game
The Interior country; ed. by A. Black-
burn
Sirens and voices
The Sewanee Review 94:4-26 Wint '86

The **swan**. Borgen, J.

The **swan**. Mrożek, S.
The **swan**. Wohmann, G.
The **swan-boat** murder. Taylor, P. A.
Swan-Goodchild, Annette
Lucy
Short story international 70
Swan song. Colwin, L.
Swanilda's song. Pohl, F.
Swann, Roberta Metz
Weather report
The North American Review 270:51-3 D
'85
Swann, Thomas Burnett
Where is the bird of fire?
Baker's dozen: 13 short fantasy novels
SWANS
Borgen, J. The swan
Cunningham, J. Decoys
Drewe, R. The silver medallist
Du Maurier, Dame D. The old man
Hartley, L. P. Two for the river
Wodehouse, P. G. Jeeves and the impend-
ing doom
Wohmann, G. The swan
SWANSEA (WALES) *See* Wales—Swansea
Swansong. Hulme, K.
Swanwick, Michael
Covenant of souls
Omni (New York, N.Y.) 9:90-2+ D '86
The Year's best science fiction, fourth
annual collection
The dragon line
Terry's universe; ed. by B. Meacham
The feast of Saint Janis
Beyond Armageddon; ed. by W. M. Mil-
ler and M. H. Greenberg
The man who met Picasso
Omni book of science fiction 2
The overcoat
Omni (New York, N.Y.) 10:54+ Ap '88
Trojan horse
Omni (New York, N.Y.) 7:88-90+ D '84
The Year's best science fiction, second
annual collection
(jt. auth) See Dozois, Gardner R., and
others
**Swanwick, Michael, and Gibson, William,
1948-**
Dogfight
Omni (New York, N.Y.) 7:44-6+ Jl '85
The Year's best science fiction, third an-
nual collection
Swartz, Jill
After the yarn is spun
The New press anthology #1
The **swashbuckler**, afterward: the Easter feast.
Lynch, L.
The **swath**. McCormack, E. P.
SWEARING
DeGrazia, E. The man who cursed and
the good Lutheran boy
Sweat. Hurston, Z. N.
The **sweater**. Manea, N.

SWEDEN
Ekström, M. Hebe laughs
Ekström, M. When we are home alone we
dance all around the house
Lagerlöf, S. The peace of God
Morand, P. Borealis

Göteborg
Gustafsson, L. The girl in the blue cap

SWEDES
See also Vikings

China
Gustafsson, L. Uncle Sven and the Cultural Revolution

United States
Coover, R. Quenby and Ola, Swede and
Carl
Gustafsson, L. The art of surviving
November
Gustafsson, L. What does not kill us,
tends to make us stronger
Sanford, W. M. The blue spruce
West, J. A little collar for the monkey

Sweeney, Bronwyn
Licorice lozenges. french safety pins. and
jelly snakes.
Room to move; ed. by S. Falkiner
The **sweeper**. Burrage, A. M.
Sweet Armageddon. Hoffman, W.
Sweet Billy. Bedard, B.
Sweet cactus wine. Muller, M.
Sweet chickadee of grace. Thorman, C.
Sweet disposition. Tallent, E.
Sweet fever. Pronzini, B.
Sweet home Chicago. Klinkowitz, J.
Sweet Jayne. Klinkowitz, J.
Sweet Letty. Matthew, J. R.
The **sweet** life. Petrakis, H. M.
The **sweet** old lady who sits in the park.
O'Callaghan, M.
Sweet remembrance. Wright, B. R.
Sweet smell of murder. Lang, A.
Sweet talk. Vaughn, S.
Sweet things. Jackson, G.
Sweet Tickfaw run softly, till I end my song.
Mills, W.
A **sweet** tooth. Bonosky, P.
Sweet William. Davis, D. S.
Sweeter than the flesh of birds. Garrett, G.
P.
A **sweetheart**. Harvor, E.
Sweethearts. Ford, R.
Sweetlip. Drewe, R.
Sweets from a stranger. Stewart, J. I. M.
Sweets to the sweet. Bloch, R.
Swenson, John
Christmas in port
The Antioch Review 42:352-61 Summ '84
Swenson, Karen
The difference
Prairie Schooner 58:43-54 Summ '84

Swick, Marly
Heart
New stories from the South: the year's best, 1987
I want to go live with daddy
Redbook 163:60+ S '84
Movie music
The North American Review 270:38-43 D '85
A sort of eligible man
Redbook 171:88+ O '88
Swift, Graham, 1949-
Chemistry
Swift, G. Learning to swim, and other stories
Cliffedge
Swift, G. Learning to swim, and other stories
Gabor
Swift, G. Learning to swim, and other stories
Hoffmeier's Antelope
Swift, G. Learning to swim, and other stories
Hotel
Swift, G. Learning to swim, and other stories
The hypochondriac
Swift, G. Learning to swim, and other stories
Learning to swim
Swift, G. Learning to swim, and other stories
Seraglio
The Penguin book of modern British short stories
Swift, G. Learning to swim, and other stories
The son
Swift, G. Learning to swim, and other stories
The tunnel
Swift, G. Learning to swim, and other stories
The watch
Swift, G. Learning to swim, and other stories
Swift, Margaret *See* Drabble, Margaret, 1939-
The **swimmer**. Cheever, J.
Swimmer. Keisler, P.
The **swimmer** in hard light. DeMarinis, R.
SWIMMING
Adams, A. A public pool
Calvino, I. The adventure of a bather
Cheever, J. The swimmer
Curley, D. The contrivance
De Camp, L. S. Nothing in the rules
Drewe, R. The silver medallist
Gold, H. Susanna at the beach
Haldeman, J. C. Wet behind the ears
Hartley, L. P. A condition of release
Hemingway, E. Summer people
Maugham, W. S. A friend in need

Munro, A. Miles City, Montana
Nordan, L. John Thomas Bird
O'Brien, E. Paradise
Strand, M. Under water
Swift, G. Learning to swim
Winton, T. Laps
Winton, T. The water was dark and it went forever down
Yermakov, N. A glint of gold
Swimming. Conrad, B.
Swimming. Piñera, V.
Swimming in the sand. Abaza, S.
Swimming to the top of the rain. Cooper, J. C.
Swimming will be the death of you. Fraser, A.
Swindle at Piute Sink. Short, L.
SWINDLERS AND SWINDLING
See also Business—Unscrupulous methods
Bingham, J. Mr. Bulmer's golden carp
Cameron, E. Ace in the hole
Conroy, J. Lute Goin's sawmill
Cozzens, J. G. Clerical error
Dahl, R. Taste
Dexter, C. At the Lulu-Bar Motel
Evans, E. Silver Fox
García Márquez, G. Blacamán the good, vendor of miracles
Garfield, B. King's X
Garrett, G. P. The confidence man
Garrett, G. P. Time of bitter children
Gilbert, W. S. The lady in the plaid shawl
Greene, G. When Greek meets Greek
Hamilton, N. Made for each other
Harris, H. Give him an inch . . .
Hill, R. Crowded hour
Jolley, E. A gentleman's agreement
Keillor, G. The speeding ticket
Kinsella, W. P. Distances
Kinsella, W. P. The managers
Mortimer, J. C. Rumpole and the boat people
Naipaul, S. Mr. Sookhoo and the carol singers
Nesin, A. A man can't even swindle any more
Nevins, F. M., Jr. The garrulous Garrity grand scam
O'Brien, E. Tough men
Pronzini, B. A little larceny
Rhys, J. The Chevalier of the Place Blanche
Russ, J. The experimenter
Sams, F. Howdy Doody time
Sanders, S. R. Wake
Selvon, S. If winter comes
Shacochis, B. Lord Short Shoe wants the monkey
Symons, J. The best chess player in the world
Wendt, A. A talent
Swingers and squares. Cooper, J. C.

Swinging round a circle. Dadswell, M.
SWISS ALPS *See* Alps
The **switch**. Piñera, V.
SWITCHBOARD HOTLINES *See* Hotlines
  (Telephone counseling)
The **switchman**. Arreola, J. J.
SWITZERLAND
  Berriault, G. Works of the imagination
  Gallant, M. Irina
  Hemingway, E. Cross-country snow
  Hemingway, E. Homage to Switzerland
  Kotzwinkle, W. Letter to a swan
  Pierce, C. Chez les petits suisses
  Welch, D. When I was thirteen
              Farm life
    See Farm life—Switzerland
              Rural life
  Gotthelf, J. The broommaker of Rychiswyl
  Gotthelf, J. Elsi the unusual farm maid
  Gotthelf, J. How Christen wins a bride
  Gotthelf, J. How Joggeli finds a wife: a
    country tale
  Gotthelf, J. Michel's courtship adventures
  Gotthelf, J. The notary gets caught
  Hemingway, E. An Alpine idyll
  Muschg, A. The country house; or, Defaul-
    ted presence
  Muschg, A. The scythe hand; or, The
    homestead
              Basle
  Stead, C. Trains
              Lausanne
  Lurie, M. Skylight in Lausanne
              Vevey
  James, H. Daisy Miller
Swofford, Avon
  Ladybug, Ladybug
    Isaac Asimov's Tomorrow's voices
The **swoon** wagon. Klinkowitz, J.
Sword blades and poppy seed. Russ, J.
Sword for a sinner. Hoch, E. D.
The **sword** of Welleran. Dunsany, E. J. M.
  D. P., Baron
The **sword** of wood. Chesterton, G. K.
SWORDS
  Dunsany, E. J. M. D. P., Baron. The
    sword of Welleran
  Yolen, J. Evian Steel
The **swords**. Aickman, R.
SYDNEY (AUSTRALIA) *See* Australia—Sy-
  dney
Sydney to Brisbane. Burt, D.
Sykes, S. C.
  Rockabye Baby
    The Year's best science fiction, third an-
    nual collection
Sylvia. Painter, P.
Sylvia and the visitor. Nelson, P.
Sylvia Smith-Smith and . . . the cigar-
  smoking ghost. Nelson, P.
Sylvia Smith-Smith strikes back. Nelson, P.
Sylvia Smith-Smith's Christmas surprise.
  Nelson, P.

Sylvia Smith-Smith's mixed-up masquerade.
  Nelson, P.
Sylvia Smith-Smith's practically perfect, high-
  ly irregular prom date. Nelson, P.
SYMBIOSIS
  Russell, E. F. Symbiotica
Symbiotica. Russell, E. F.
The **symbol**. Woolf, V.
A **symbol** of our love. Goldreich, G.
SYMBOLISM
        See also Allegories; Parables
  Abe, K. The flood
  Aksenov, V. P. Rendezvous
  Barth, J. Night-sea journey
  Benedict, P. Booze
  Benedict, P. Fat Tuesday
  Boyle, T. C. The Hector Quesadilla story
  Buzzati, D. The plague
  Cheever, J. The lowboy
  Curley, D. The inlet
  Curley, D. Wild geese
  Endō, S. The day before
  Endō, S. A forty-year-old man
  Faik, S. The mirror at the beach
  Gilliatt, P. The hinge
  Hagy, A. C. Stadia
  Hempel, A. Pool Night
  Kawabata, Y. One arm
  Kawabata, Y. Socks
  Kilworth, G. The rose bush
  Miller, H. Into the night life
  Moravia, A. There's a neutron bomb for
    ants too
  Morris, M. Losing your cool
  Muschg, A. The blue man
  Oba, M. The Pale Fox
  Pierce, C. Chez les petits suisses
  Poe, E. A. The narrative of Arthur
    Gordon Pym of Nantucket
  Rey Rosa, R. The path doubles back
  Rosa, J. G. The third bank of the river
  Roy, G. Ely! Ely! Ely!
  Schwartz, L. S. Killing the bees
  Shimaki, K. The red frog
  Stark, S. S. The horsehair
  Tamer, Z. The face of the moon
  Tamer, Z. My final adventure
  Thomas, D. Gaspar, Melchior, Balthasar
  Thomas, D. The holy six
  Thomas, D. Prologue to an adventure
  Watson, S. Brother Oedipus
  Wilson, B. Stalingrad
Symmetries. Romero, N. L.
Symmetries. Valenzuela, L.
Symons, Julian, 1912-
  The best chess player in the world
    John Creasey's Crime collection, 1987
  The birthmark
    Winter's crimes 17
  The boiler
    John Creasey's Crime collection, 1984

Symons, Julian, 1912-—*Continued*
  Credit to Shakespeare
    The Deadly arts; ed. by B. Pronzini and
      M. Muller
  The dream is better
    Masterpieces of mystery and suspense;
      ed. by M. H. Greenberg
  The flaw
    John Creasey's Crime collection, 1986
    The Mammoth book of modern crime
      stories; ed. by G. Hardinge
  Has anybody here seen me?
    The Year's best mystery and suspense
      stories, 1988
  Love affair
    John Creasey's Crime collection, 1985
Sympathy. Maupassant, G. de
Sympathy. Woolf, V.
Sympathy notes. Whelan, G.
SYRIA
  Poe, E. A. Four beasts in one—the homo-
    cameleopard
SYRIANS
               United States
  Conroy, J. The siren
The **system.** Mayer, R.
The **system** of Doctor Tarr and Professor
    Fether. Poe, E. A.
Syzygy. Kinsella, W. P.
Szell, Timea
  The first portrait
    The Southern Review (Baton Rouge, La.)
      20:406-18 Ap '84
  Roman business
    The Southern Review (Baton Rouge, La.)
      23:888-96 Aut '87
Szucsany, Désirée
  Mr. Simpson
    Intimate strangers; ed. by M. Cohen and
      W. Grady

T

Tabi. Kawabata, Y.
Table for two. Winters, J.
Tableau with three ghostly women. Mat-
    thews, J.
TABLES
  Melville, H. The apple-tree table; or,
    Original spiritual manifestations
  Warner, S. T. The mahogany table
The **tables.** Gault, C.
TABOO *See* Superstition
Taboo. Household, G.
Tabucchi, Antonio, 1943-
  The backwards game
    Tabucchi, A. Letter from Casablanca
  Dolores Ibarruri sheds bitter tears
    Tabucchi, A. Letter from Casablanca
  Heavenly bliss
    Tabucchi, A. Letter from Casablanca

  Letter from Casablanca
    Tabucchi, A. Letter from Casablanca
  The little Gatsby
    Tabucchi, A. Letter from Casablanca
  Saturday afternoons
    Tabucchi, A. Letter from Casablanca
  Theatre
    Tabucchi, A. Letter from Casablanca
  Voices
    Tabucchi, A. Letter from Casablanca
The **tactful** saboteur. Herbert, F.
Tactics. Nesin, A.
The **tactics** of hunger. Gilliatt, P.
'Taffrail'
  The luck of the Tavy
    Sea captains' tales; ed. by A. Enfield
Tafolla, Carmen
  You don't know Marta
    Southern Exposure (Durham, N.C.)
      14:42-3 Ja/F '86
Tager, Marcia
  Song from the highest tower
    The Literary Review (Madison, N.J.)
      29:17-23 Fall '85
Tagore, Sir Rabindranath, 1861-1941
  The Cabuliwallah
    The Nobel reader; ed. by J. Eisen and
      S. Troy
Taher, Bahaa
  Advice from a sensible young man
    Arabic short stories; tr. by D. Johnson-
      Davies
Tahir, Baha'
  Last night I dreamt of you
    Egyptian tales and short stories of the
      1970s and 1980s
TAHITI
  Bates, H. E. Mrs. Eglantine
  Farmer, B. Darling Odile
Tahotahontanekent-seratkerontakwenhakie.
    Benedict, S.
The **tail** of his luck. Michalson, G.
The **tailless** tyke at bay. Ollivant, A.
TAILORS
  Blinkin, M. A simple life
  Jasmin, C. Lulu the tailor
  Simenon, G. Blessed are the meek
  Stead, C. The Azhdanov tailors
Táim ainnis. Cornell, J. C.
The **taipan.** Maugham, W. S.
TAIPEI (TAIWAN) *See* Taiwan—Taipei
TAIWAN
  Apple, M. Small island republics
  Ch'en, Y.-C. The comedy of Narcissa
    T'ang
  Ch'en, Y.-C. The country village teacher
  Ch'en, Y.-C. A couple of generals
  Ch'en, Y.-C. The dying
  Ch'en, Y.-C. The last day of summer
  Ch'en, Y.-C. My kid brother, K'ang-hsiung
  Ch'en, Y.-C. Night freight
  Ch'en, Y.-C. One day in the life of a
    white-collar worker

TAIWAN—*Continued*
Ch'en, Y.-C. Poor poor dumb mouths
Cheng, C.-W. Betel Palm Village
Chu, T.-J. Autumn note
Chung, L.-H. Together through thick and thin
Lai, H. The steelyard
Lin, H.-Y. Lunar New Year's feast
Tung, N. Fire
Wang, C.-H. The story of three springs
Wu, C.-L. The doctor's mother
Yang, K. Mother Goose gets married
Farm life
See Farm life—Taiwan
Taipei
Tzu, O.-Y. The net
TAIZZ (YEMEN) *See* Yemen (People's Democratic Republic)—Taizz
Takahashi, Tetsuro
A happy home
Short story international 46
The necklace of flowers
Short story international 68
Take a seat, not a solo. Bonnie, F.
Take another look. Ritchie, J.
Take care of yourself. Gault, W. C.
Take it up at the bridge. Coleman, W.
Take Louise Nevelson. Wilson, B.
Take mama's picture out of the light. McElroy, C. J.
Take your partners. Blythe, R.
Takenishi, Hiroko
The rite
The Crazy iris, and other stories of the atomic aftermath; ed. by K. Oe
The **takeover**. Auchincloss, L.
Takes. Dixon, S.
Taking a chance on Jack. Raymond, I.
Taking a second look. Burke, J. L.
Taking care. Horne, L.
Taking care. Williams, J.
Taking from the top. Pearlman, D.
Taking hold of Renee. Pritchard, M.
Taking Miss Kezee to the polls. Haynes, D.
Taking stock. Matthews, J.
Taking the consequences. Durrell, L.
Taking the discipline. Copeland, A.
Taking the road not taken. Ephron, N.
Taking the veil. Mansfield, K.
The **tale** of Djemal. See Highsmith, P. Djemal's revenge
The **tale** of dragons and dreamers. Delany, S. R.
The **tale** of Happiton. Hofstadter, D. R.
The **tale** of how Ivan Ivanovich quarreled with Ivan Nikiforovich. Gogol', N. V.
A **tale** of Jerusalem. Poe, E. A.
A **tale** of kings. Larionova, O.
A **tale** of no more demands. Broun, H.
A **tale** of Pierrot. Dennison, G.
The **tale** of Satampra Zeiros. Smith, C. A.
The **tale** of the bagman's uncle. See Dickens, C. The story of the bagman's uncle

The **tale** of the changeling. Mordden, E.
The **tale** of the German student. See Irving, W. The adventure of the German student
A **tale** of the ragged mountains. Poe, E. A.
The **tale** of the unextinguished moon. Pil'nīāk, B.
Talent. Bloch, R.
A **talent**. Wendt, A.
Tales from the next village. Caponegro, M.
Tales from the original gothic. Ford, J. M.
Tales of Houdini. Rucker, R. von B.
The **talisman**. Zahn, T.
TALISMANS
Carter, L. Geydelle's protective
Green, J. The ruby wand of Asrazel
Major, A. R. Kissmeowt and the healing friar
Ward, L. The marbled horn
Talk of heroes. Bly, C.
Talk show. Baxter, C.
The **talker** at the freak-show. Nordan, L.
The **talking** dog of the world. Mordden, E.
Talking in the dark. Etchison, D.
The **talking** memories. Apollinaire, G.
Talking Skull. Crace, J.
The **talking** that trees does. Hobson, G.
Talking to the boy. Sorrells, R. T.
Talking to the dark. Houbein, L.
Talking to the sun. Regier, G.
Talking to trees. Potter, N. A. J.
Tall dames go walking. Wolf, R.
Tall Grete. Schmidt, A.
Tall Mountain, Mary
The sinh of Niguudzagha
Earth power coming; ed. by S. J. Ortiz
TALL STORIES *See* Improbable stories
The **tall** woman. Alarcón, P. A. de
The **tall** woman and her short husband. Feng Jicai
Tallent, Elizabeth, 1954-
Black holes
The Graywolf annual 2
The New Yorker 61:30-5 Jl 1 '85
Tallent, E. Time with children
The evolution of birds of paradise
Prize stories, 1984
Faux pas
The New Yorker 63:36-9 Ap 6 '87
Tallent, E. Time with children
Favor
The Best American short stories, 1987
The New Yorker 62:46-52 Ap 21 '86
Tallent, E. Time with children
The fence party
The New Yorker 61:36-40 S 16 '85
Tallent, E. Time with children
The forgiveness trick
The New Yorker 62:32-5 S 1 '86
Tallent, E. Time with children
Grant of easement
The New Yorker 60:32-6 D 24 '84
Tallent, E. Time with children

Tallent, Elizabeth, 1954-—*Continued*
Half a mussel shell
  The Graywolf annual [1]
Hannah's example
  The New Yorker 63:28-34 Je 15 '87
  Tallent, E. Time with children
Lightly
  The Esquire fiction reader v2
Listen to reason
  Tallent, E. Time with children
Migrants
  The Editors' choice v4; ed. by G. E. Murphy, Jr.
  The Paris Review 28:219-29 Spr '86
  Tallent, E. Time with children
No one's a mystery
  The Best of the West; ed. by J. Thomas
  Harper's 271:28-9 Ag '85
  Sudden fiction; ed. by R. Shapard and J. Thomas
  Tallent, E. Time with children
Sweet disposition
  The New Yorker 61:36-42 Ap 1 '85
  Tallent, E. Time with children
Time with children
  The New Yorker 61:26-32 Ja 13 '86
  Tallent, E. Time with children
Two ghosts of us
  Tallent, E. Time with children
Why I love country music
  Writers of the purple sage; ed. by R. Martin and M. Barasch
The **tallest** man in the world. Green, J.
Tallis, Raymond
Musical overdoses
  Encounter (London, England) 69:23-6 Je '87
The **tallis** koton. Sholem Aleichem
Tallow ball. See Maupassant, G. de. Ball-of-fat
A **tally** of the souls of sheep. Hulme, K.
Talma Levy is falling. Thomas, J.
Talp hunt. Kress, N.
Talpa. Rulfo, J.
Talus. Finney, E. J.
Tam Lin. Vinge, J. D.
Tamastara. Lee, T.
Tamazanchale. Shapard, R.
Tamer, Zakaria
The ancient gate
  Tamer, Z. Tigers on the tenth day, and other stories
An angry man
  Tamer, Z. Tigers on the tenth day, and other stories
City in ashes
  Tamer, Z. Tigers on the tenth day, and other stories
The day Genghis Khan became angry
  Tamer, Z. Tigers on the tenth day, and other stories

Death of the black hair
  Tamer, Z. Tigers on the tenth day, and other stories
Death of the jasmine
  Tamer, Z. Tigers on the tenth day, and other stories
The enemy
  Tamer, Z. Tigers on the tenth day, and other stories
The face of the moon
  Tamer, Z. Tigers on the tenth day, and other stories
The family
  Tamer, Z. Tigers on the tenth day, and other stories
Genghis Khan
  Tamer, Z. Tigers on the tenth day, and other stories
Hasan as a king
  Tamer, Z. Tigers on the tenth day, and other stories
A lone woman
  Tamer, Z. Tigers on the tenth day, and other stories
My final adventure
  Tamer, Z. Tigers on the tenth day, and other stories
No raincloud for the trees, no wings above the mountain
  Tamer, Z. Tigers on the tenth day, and other stories
Nothing
  Tamer, Z. Tigers on the tenth day, and other stories
Room with two beds
  Tamer, Z. Tigers on the tenth day, and other stories
Sheep
  Tamer, Z. Tigers on the tenth day, and other stories
Small sun
  Arabic short stories; tr. by D. Johnson-Davies
The smile
  Tamer, Z. Tigers on the tenth day, and other stories
Snow at the end of the night
  Tamer, Z. Tigers on the tenth day, and other stories
The stale loaf
  Tamer, Z. Tigers on the tenth day, and other stories
A summary of what happened to Mohammed al-Mahmoudi
  Tamer, Z. Tigers on the tenth day, and other stories
Sun for the young
  Tamer, Z. Tigers on the tenth day, and other stories
Tigers on the tenth day
  Tamer, Z. Tigers on the tenth day, and other stories

Tamer, Zakaria—*Continued*
The water's crime
Tamer, Z. Tigers on the tenth day, and other stories
Taming a Tartar. Alcott, L. M.
The **taming** of the nightmare. Chesterton, G. K.
The **taming** power of the small. Blythe, W.
Tāmir, Zakarīyā
The thunderbolt
Modern Syrian short stories; ed. by M. G. Azrak
TAMPA (FLA.) *See* Florida—Tampa
Tamsen Donner's decision. Lee, H.
Tamurlane. Mukherjee, B.
Tan, Amy
Rules of the game
Seventeen 45:160-2+ N '86
Tan. Sayles, J.
Tang Dong
The progress of the military patrol car
The Chinese Western; ed. by Zhu Hong
Tang Qiaodi. Lu Wenfu
Tangents. Bear, G.
Tangerine dreams. Prose, F.
TANGIER (MOROCCO) *See* Morocco—Tangier
Tangier 1975. Bowles, P.
A **!tangled** web. Haldeman, J. W.
The **Tango** Bear. Hansen, J.
Tango Charlie and Foxtrot Romeo. Varley, J.
Tania's no where. Cross, A.
Tanizaki, Jun'ichirō, 1886-1965
Tattoo [Variant title: The tattooer]
Black water; ed. by A. Manguel
The thief
Murder in Japan; ed. by J. L. Apostolou and M. H. Greenberg
Tank. Izzo, F. E.
The **tank** of terror. Dent, L.
TANKS (MILITARY SCIENCE)
Mayhar, A. In the tank
Wells, H. G. The land ironclads
Tanks. Mort, J.
Tanner and JunHee. Klimasewiski, M. N.
TANZANIA
Thomas, M. Choobeedoo Yum-yum and the ANC
Thomas, M. Silver sugar from Bombay
Thomas, M. The Texan
Tapahonso, Luci, 1953-
She sits on the bridge
Earth power coming; ed. by S. J. Ortiz
Tape-measure murder. Christie, A.
TAPE RECORDINGS
Bell, M. S. Zero db
The **tapestried** chamber. Scott, Sir W.
Tapestry. Sherman, C. H.
A **tapestry** of little murders. Bishop, M.
Tapiama. Bowles, P.
Tappan's burro. Grey, Z.

TARANTULAS
Reed, K. Love story
Taras Bulba. Gogol', N. V.
Targan, Barry
Drexel's Garage
Southwest Review 69:183-93 Spr '84
The editor of A
The Georgia Review 40:289-96 Spr '86
Necessary fictions; ed. by S. W. Lindberg and S. Corey
Surviving adverse seasons
Prime number; ed. by A. L. Weir
The **target.** Essop, A.
The **target.** Russo, A.
Target. Yi, C.-J.
Tarkington, Booth, 1869-1946
Blue milk
Roger Caras' Treasury of great dog stories
TAROT
Klein, T. E. D. Petey
Tarr, Judith
Defender of the faith
Moonsinger's friends; ed. by S. Shwartz
The **tartarus** of maids. Melville, H.
TASMANIA (AUSTRALIA)
Bird, C. Woodpecker Point
The **taste.** Bitov, A.
Taste. Dahl, R.
A **taste** for perfection. Vanderhaeghe, G.
The **taste** of bread. Böll, H.
A **taste** of earth. Bird, C.
The **taste** of melon. Deal, B.
The **taste** of salt. Kim, Y. I.
A **taste** of success. Ragab, M.
Tasting leaves. Rose, D. A.
Tata Fino. Tenorio, F. H.
Tatabisako. Cabrera, L.
Tate, James, 1943-
Welcome signs
The North American Review 272:42-3 D '87
Tattoo. Major, C.
Tattoo. Tanizaki, J.
Tattoo. Thompson, B.
The **tattooer.** See Tanizaki, J. Tattoo
TATTOOING
Dann, J. Tattoos
Hartley, L. P. Mr. Blandfoot's picture
O'Connor, F. Parker's back
Tanizaki, J. Tattoo
Tattoos. Dann, J.
Taube, Myron
The student
Our roots grow deeper than we know; ed. by L. Gutkind
Tauscher, Donna
August heat
Ms. 15:53-4+ D '86
TAVERNS *See* Hotels, taverns, etc.
Tavesher. Tremayne, P.

Tawfiq, Sahar
A visit to the old city
Egyptian tales and short stories of the 1970s and 1980s
TAX EVASION
Archer, J. The loophole
Friedman, B. J. The tax man
The **tax** man. Friedman, B. J.
TAXATION
Heise, K. Aunt Ella's taxes
The **taxi** driver's story. Nowakowski, M.
TAXIDERMY
Franklin, P. Love under glass
Highsmith, P. The stuff of madness
Rossi, A. Teeth and nails
Wells, H. G. The triumphs of a taxidermist
Taylor, Andrew
The absolutely ordinary family
Home and away; ed. by R. Creswell
Taylor, Apirana
Bread and hunger
Taylor, A. He rau aroha
Bye bye Billy
Taylor, A. He rau aroha
The carving
Taylor, A. He rau aroha
Casey and Sarah
Taylor, A. He rau aroha
Chudka popoy ugh cha cha
Taylor, A. He rau aroha
Fish heads
Taylor, A. He rau aroha
The gunfight
Taylor, A. He rau aroha
He korero
Taylor, A. He rau aroha
Hera
Taylor, A. He rau aroha
Hine e Hine
Taylor, A. He rau aroha
In the rubbish tin
Taylor, A. He rau aroha
The kumara plant
Taylor, A. He rau aroha
Nga tui
Taylor, A. He rau aroha
Old mates
Taylor, A. He rau aroha
Pa mai
Taylor, A. He rau aroha
Pou
Taylor, A. He rau aroha
Taylor, Bernard, 1934-
Forget-me-not
After midnight; ed. by C. L. Grant
Our last nanny
After midnight; ed. by C. L. Grant
Taylor, Chuck
Borg's last word
Taylor, C. The lights of the city: stories from Austin

Catherine and Michael
Taylor, C. The lights of the city: stories from Austin
Denver's story
Taylor, C. The lights of the city: stories from Austin
Dutko's story
Taylor, C. The lights of the city: stories from Austin
Grom's story: naked lady
Taylor, C. The lights of the city: stories from Austin
Hamlin's story
Taylor, C. The lights of the city: stories from Austin
In and out of the arms of the law
Taylor, C. The lights of the city: stories from Austin
Lance's story: art sucks
Taylor, C. The lights of the city: stories from Austin
Leanderthal lady
Taylor, C. The lights of the city: stories from Austin
Loving thy neighbor
Taylor, C. The lights of the city: stories from Austin
The new and the old, the old and the new
Taylor, C. The lights of the city: stories from Austin
Sitting and spinning
Taylor, C. The lights of the city: stories from Austin
Spare change
Taylor, C. The lights of the city: stories from Austin
State of the streets
Taylor, C. The lights of the city: stories from Austin
These women
Taylor, C. The lights of the city: stories from Austin
The tribe
Taylor, C. The lights of the city: stories from Austin
Wince's story
Taylor, C. The lights of the city: stories from Austin
Taylor, D. J. (David John)
Dreams of leaving
P.E.N. new fiction I
Taylor, David John *See* Taylor, D. J. (David John)
Taylor, Eleanor Ross, 1920-
Early deaths
The Virginia Quarterly Review 61:655-66 Aut '85
Taylor, Joe
A puff of roses
The Virginia Quarterly Review 63:684-96 Aut '87

Taylor, Mildred D.
Roll of thunder, hear my cry [excerpt]
   Mississippi writers v1: Fiction; ed. by D.
   Abbott

Taylor, Pat Ellis, 1941-
Acquiring point of view
   Taylor, P. E. Afoot in a field of men
Afoot in a field of men
   Taylor, P. E. Afoot in a field of men
Answering the inquisitor
   Taylor, P. E. Afoot in a field of men
At the altar
   Taylor, P. E. Afoot in a field of men
Bird prayer and no amen
   Taylor, P. E. Afoot in a field of men
A call from brotherland
   Taylor, P. E. Afoot in a field of men
A clouded visit with Rolling Thunder
   Taylor, P. E. Afoot in a field of men
Descent into brotherland
   Taylor, P. E. Afoot in a field of men
Entering the house of the 'Lord
   Taylor, P. E. Afoot in a field of men
The god-chaser
   Taylor, P. E. Afoot in a field of men
An independent meditation
   Taylor, P. E. Afoot in a field of men
Kingdom come
   Taylor, P. E. Afoot in a field of men
Leaping Leo
   Taylor, P. E. Afoot in a field of men
News from El Corazon: in the composing
   room
   Taylor, P. E. Afoot in a field of men
Sermon on the rat
   Taylor, P. E. Afoot in a field of men
Spring water celebration
   Taylor, P. E. Afoot in a field of men
Turning thirty-eight
   Taylor, P. E. Afoot in a field of men
Who's that knocking? Is it you?
   Taylor, P. E. Afoot in a field of men

Taylor, Peter Hillsman, 1917-
Allegiance
   Taylor, P. H. The old forest, and other
   stories
Bad dreams
   Taylor, P. H. The old forest, and other
   stories
A friend and protector [Variant title: Who
   was Jesse's friend and protector?]
   The Art of the tale; ed. by D. Halpern
   Taylor, P. H. The old forest, and other
   stories
The gift of the prodigal
   Taylor, P. H. The old forest, and other
   stories
   The World of the short story; ed. by
   C. Fadiman

The hand of Emmagene
   Homewords: a book of Tennessee
   writers; ed. by D. Paschall
   Shenandoah: an anthology; ed. by J.
   Boatwright
In the Miro District
   A Modern Southern reader; ed. by B.
   Forkner and P. Samway
The little cousins
   Taylor, P. H. The old forest, and other
   stories
A long fourth
   Taylor, P. H. The old forest, and other
   stories
The old forest
   Taylor, P. H. The old forest, and other
   stories
Porte Cochere
   Taylor, P. H. The old forest, and other
   stories
Promise of rain
   Taylor, P. H. The old forest, and other
   stories
Rain in the heart
   Taylor, P. H. The old forest, and other
   stories
The scoutmaster
   Taylor, P. H. The old forest, and other
   stories
Two ladies in retirement
   Taylor, P. H. The old forest, and other
   stories
A walled garden
   Sudden fiction; ed. by R. Shapard and
   J. Thomas
   Taylor, P. H. The old forest, and other
   stories
What you hear from 'em?
   Stories of the modern South; ed. by B.
   Forkner and P. Samway

Taylor, Phoebe Atwood, 1909-1976
The swan-boat murder
   Murder and mystery in Boston; ed. by
   C. L. R. Waugh; F. D. McSherry and
   M. H. Greenberg

Taylor, Robert, 1941-
Billy Gashade and glory [Variant title: The
   James boys ride again]
   Taylor, R. Loving Belle Starr
Charley Ford betrayed [Variant title: Jesse
   James betrayed]
   Taylor, R. Loving Belle Starr
The death of Belle Starr
   Taylor, R. Loving Belle Starr
Eddy the boy [Variant title: Hideout,
   Younger's Bend c1874]
   Taylor, R. Loving Belle Starr
Eddy the man [Variant title: The spirit of
   Belle Starr]
   Taylor, R. Loving Belle Starr
Fiddle and bow
   Southwest Review 70:55-67 Wint '85

Taylor, Robert, 1941——*Continued*
The fiddler [Variant title: Loving Belle Starr]
    Taylor, R. Loving Belle Starr
Glory [Variant title: Presences]
    Taylor, R. Loving Belle Starr
The history of Frank James
    Taylor, R. Loving Belle Starr
The James boys ride again
    The Georgia Review 40:297-306 Spr '86
    Necessary fictions; ed. by S. W. Lindberg and S. Corey
Jim July Starr [Variant title: Grim want and misery]
    Taylor, R. Loving Belle Starr
Jim Reed [Variant title: The hands of Jesse James]
    Taylor, R. Loving Belle Starr
Lady of Spain
    The Best American short stories, 1987
    The Hudson Review 39:33-52 Spr '86
    New stories from the South: the year's best, 1987
    Prize stories, 1987
The liberation of the Youngers
    Taylor, R. Loving Belle Starr
Mrs. Jesse James, mourning [Variant title: Mourning]
    Taylor, R. Loving Belle Starr
Pearl Starr alive in Arizona
    Taylor, R. Loving Belle Starr
Quantrill
    Taylor, R. Loving Belle Starr
The revealed life of Cole Younger
    Editor's choice II; ed. by M. Sklar and M. Biggs
Sam Starr [Variant title: Legends]
    Taylor, R. Loving Belle Starr
The Tennessee war of the roses
    New American short stories; ed. by G. Norris
The tragedy of Bob Ford [Variant title: The tragedy of Jesse James]
    Taylor, R. Loving Belle Starr
Where are our M.I.A.'s?
    Our roots grow deeper than we know; ed. by L. Gutkind
Zerelda James Samuel [Variant title: Passing away]
    Taylor, R. Loving Belle Starr
Taylor, Samuel W.
Wily woman
    The Saturday Evening Post 258:64-8+ O '86
Taylor-Hall, Mary Ann
Advanced beginners
    The Kenyon Review ns10:68-82 Spr '88
Banana boats
    The Best American short stories, 1988
    The Paris Review 29:170-99 Fall '87
Te Kaihau: the windeater. Hulme, K.
Tea. Saki
Tea break. Drake, M.

Tea in the Wendy House. Geras, A.
Tea party. Rossiter, S.
Tea with an artist. Rhys, J.
Tea with Mrs. Bittell. Pritchett, V. S.
Tea with the professor. Pilcher, R.
Teacher. Carter, M.
The **teacher.** Ferguson, W.
A **teacher** of the blind. McLaughlin, L.
TEACHERS
    See also Students; Tutors
Abbott, L. K. The eldest of things
Aćin-Kosta, M. In the spirit of socialism
Adams, A. Ocracoke Island
Aldiss, B. W. The girl who sang
Alexin, A. The class photograph
Ardizzone, T. The evening news
Asimov, I. The dead past
Asimov, I. Unique is where you find it
Auchincloss, L. Marcus: a Gothic tale
Auchincloss, L. Portrait of the artist by another
Barich, B. Giorgio's mother
Barthelme, D. The school
Barthelme, F. Pupil
Bass, R. Cats and students, bubbles and abysses
Bausch, R. Spirits
Baxter, C. Gryphon
Bedard, B. Benedict's dove
Bernard, K. The girl who might or might not have read Sartre
Berry, R. M. Song of the geometry instructor
Birtha, B. In the deep heart's core
Bishop, M. One winter in Eden
Bishop, M. The Yukio Mishima Cultural Association of Kudzu Valley, Georgia
Bissoondath, N. An arrangement of shadows
Blaise, C. A class of new Canadians
Böll, H. Broommakers
Böll, H. No tears for Schmeck
Boswell, R. Edward and Jill
Bourjaily, V. The Amish farmer
Bourjaily, V. The Duchess
Bowles, P. The time of friendship
Boyle, K. Life being the best
Bradbury, M. Composition
Brittain, W. Mr. Strang picks up the pieces
Brooks, J. A value
Broun, H. Is this civilization?
Burke, J. L. Taking a second look
Bush, J. The problem of Li T'ang
Byatt, A. S. Loss of face
Cameron, P. Fear of math
Camoin, F. A. A special case
Campbell, E. Duties and liabilities
Campbell, R. The other side
Carlson, R. Half life
Chappell, F. The snow that is nothing in the triangle
Ch'en, Y.-C. The country village teacher
Ch'en, Y.-C. The last day of summer

TEACHERS—*Continued*

Chernoff, M. Two times two
Christmas, R. A. Another angel
Clayton, J. J. Fantasy for a Friday afternoon
Cohen, M. Golden whore of the heartland
Coleman, W. Watching the sunset
Cowan, P. The tins
Cullen, E. J. Worrying
Dadswell, M. Retirement
Daudet, A. The last class
Derleth, A. W. The dark boy
Dixon, S. Eating the placenta
Doctorow, E. L. The hunter
Dorr, L. Old men shall dream dreams
Drewe, R. Shark logic
Dubus, A. Finding a girl in America
Dunn, D. Ever let the fancy roam
Eastlake, W. The death of Sun
Eldridge, M. Candlebark
Eldridge, M. Flight
Eldridge, M. Solitaire
Eldridge, M. Walking the dog
Ellin, S. Robert
Faik, S. Jealousy
Faik, S. The village teacher and the herdsboy
Feng Jicai. A letter
Ferguson, W. Scherzo with TV antenna
Ferguson, W. Space Invaders
Ferguson, W. The teacher
Fink, I. Titina
Finney, J. The face in the photo
Francis, H. E. The sudden trees
Friedman, B. J. Detroit Abe
Gallagher, T. A pair of glasses
Gardner, M. One more martini
Garrett, G. P. The gun and the hat
Garrett, G. P. Last of the old buffalo hunters
Garrett, G. P. My picture left in Scotland
Garrett, G. P. What's the matter with Mary Jane?
Gilliatt, P. As is
Gilliatt, P. F.R.A.N.K.
Gingher, M. Wearing glasses
Givner, J. First love
Glickfeld, C. L. Out of the lion's belly
Gold, H. A dark Norwegian person
Gonzalez, N. V. M. The blue skull and the dark palms
Görlich, G. The decision
Gould, R. The child and the poet
Gustafsson, L. What does not kill us, tends to make us stronger
Hall, R. W. The lesson of the master
Halligan, M. A gigolo, Miss Emery?
Halligan, M. A leisurely drowning
Halligan, M. Remember the rug
Harte, B. The idyl of Red Gulch
Harvor, E. The students' soirée
Haylock, J. Tomiko
Hoffman, N. K. The shadow of a hawk

Hospital, J. T. The baroque ensemble
Hospital, J. T. The inside story
Hospital, J. T. You gave me hyacinths
Houbein, L. Having it both ways
Huggan, I. Sorrows of the flesh
Hull, H. R. Discovery
Jean Paul. The life of Maria Wuz, the merry-hearted Dominie of Auenthal
Kercheval, J. L. La mort au moyen âge
Kessler, J. F. Rhadamanthys
Kiely, B. Secondary top
Kim, Y. I. The gold watch
King, F. H. A corner of a foreign field
Kirk, R. The surly sullen bell
Klíma, I. Sunday morning: a foolish tale
Koch, C. You taught us good
Komie, L. B. Professor Strauss's gift
Leaton, A. Destiny
Lee, H. On becoming somebody
Leedom-Ackerman, J. History lesson
Lewis, S. A letter from the Queen
Liang Xiaosheng. The jet ruler
Liben, M. The garden
Lish, G. Imagination
Lispector, C. The misfortunes of Sofia
Lofts, N. God's own elect
Longyear, B. B. Collector's item
Lopez, B. H. Winter count 1973: geese, they flew over in a storm
Lovecraft, H. P. The call of Cthulhu
MacLennan, P. Good-by, Miss Patterson
Martin, H. R. A poet though married
Martínez-Serros, H. The birthday present
Martínez-Serros, H. Her
Martínez-Serros, H. Octavo
Martone, M. The safety patrol
Martone, M. Watch out
Massie, E. Sick'un
Maupassant, G. de. Revenge
Mazel, D. Mr. Bernshtein
Mazel, D. A spoonful of kindness
McGahern, J. All sorts of impossible things
McGahern, J. The recruiting officer
McLaughlin, L. A teacher of the blind
Mrożek, S. Poetry
Mukherjee, B. The tenant
Murphy, P. The chapter on love
Murphy, P. Meeting the head examiner
Nagibin, IŪ. M. Winter oak
Narayan, R. K. Crime and punishment
Ndebele, N. Fools
Nowaira, A. Lost and found
Oates, J. C. The boy
Oates, J. C. The Jesuit
O'Brien, E. The doll
O'Connor, F. The barber
Ornstien, E. English for immigrants
Orzeszkowa, E. Miss Antonina
Overholser, W. D. Book-l'arnin' and the equalizer
Owen, G. Miss Mahalia and the still
Parker, R. The wheelbarrow boy

TEACHERS—*Continued*

Paulson, A. B. College life

Pilcher, R. Tea with the professor

Proulx, M. ABC

Queen, E. Object lesson

Rasputin, V. G. French lessons

Ray, D. Ram Ram

Rizkalla, J. A poet in the classroom

Robison, J. Rumor

Ruffolo, L. Halloween

Ruffolo, L. You'll lose them before Thanksgiving

Rule, J. A matter of numbers

Saiki, J. Suspect alien

Serling, R. The changing of the guard

Sharouni, Y. Glimpses from the life of Maugoud Abdul Maugoud and two postscripts

Sinclair, C. Bedbugs

Sisskind, M. A mean teacher

Sokoloff, T. C. Providence will provide

Son, C.-S. Walking in the snow

Sorrells, R. T. Drowning

Stafford, J. The liberation

Steele, M. The cat and the coffee drinkers

Steele, M. The Tin Can

Tamer, Z. Death of the jasmine

Targan, B. Surviving adverse seasons

Terry, M. The antichrist

Thompson, S. Close-ups

Tuohy, F. The broken bridge

Tuohy, F. The candidate

Tuohy, F. Evening in Connecticut

Tuohy, F. In the dark years

Tuohy, F. The trap

Updike, D. Social studies

Updike, J. More stately mansions

Updike, J. Slippage

Upward, E. An old-established school

Vanderhaeghe, G. The expatriates' party

Vesity, A. The first day

Warren, J. Mr. McAlligator

Wellen, E. Chalk talk

Wells, H. G. The apple

Wells, H. G. Mr. Ledbetter's vacation

Wendt, A. Crocodile

Wendt, A. Hamlet

Wesseler, M. June's night

West, J. The condemned librarian

West, J. The singing lesson

Wheatcroft, J. Image of departure

Wheatcroft, J. The lapse

Whelan, G. Beneath the fig trees

Whelan, G. Children in the park

Whelan, G. A lesson in the classics

Whelan, G. The showing

White, C. Metaphysics in the Midwest

Whitman, W. Death in the school-room

Wilson, B. Phantom limb pain

Wolfe, T. For professional appearance

Wolfe, T. One of the girls in our party

Wolfe, T. The plumed knight

Wright, B. R. Morning song

Yates, R. The right thing

Yoshiyuki, J. Are the trees green?

Team venture. Clayton, J.

Teamwork. Connelly, J.

Teamwork. Zahn, T.

Tears, idle tears. Bowen, E.

Tears in the red wine. Sagan, F.

Tease. Swados, H.

TECHNOLOGY AND CIVILIZATION

Benford, G. At the double solstice

Card, O. S. St. Amy's tale

Dorr, L. Neither death nor life

Flynn, M. The forest of time

Hall, J. B. My work in California

Kress, N. Shadows on the cave wall

Watson, I. The emir's clock

Teddi. Norton, A.

Teddy and I go Kong. Bernard, K.

TEDDY BEARS

Sladek, J. T. Ursa Minor

Teen angel. Gingher, M.

'Teen talkout!: hidden secrets. Sheridan, J. K.

Teenage wasteland. Tyler, A.

TEENAGERS *See* Adolescence; Youth

TEETH

Ahern, T. Dr. Zifhart leaves for Atlantic City

Faik, S. The man who doesn't know what a tooth or a toothache is

Mathers, P. A knight of teeth

Poe, E. A. Berenice

Diseases

Burt, S. The General's toothache

Gusewelle, C. W. Horst Wessel

Teeth. Gilliatt, P.

Teeth and nails. Rossi, A.

Teeth marks. Bryant, E.

TEHRAN (IRAN) *See* Iran—Tehran

Teiresias. Kessler, J. F.

Teixeira, Kevin

The last hunt

Stories and poems from close to home; ed. by F. Salas

TEL AVIV (ISRAEL) *See* Israel—Tel Aviv

TELECOMMUNICATION

See also Telegraph; Telephone; Television

Austin, D. Pray for China

Clarke, A. C. Dial F for Frankenstein

Disch, T. M. Concepts

TELEGRAPH

Mrożek, S. On a journey

TELEKINESIS *See* Psychokinesis

Teleky, Richard

The album

The Antioch Review 43:133-9 Spr '85

Telepathic rein. Robinson, L.

TELEPATHY

Anderson, P. Honorable enemies

Anderson, P. Requiem for a universe

Barcelo, F. The man who stopped trains

Bloch, R. Space-born

Bone, J. F. Tween

TELEPATHY—*Continued*
Bradley, M. Z. Centaurus changeling
Bradley, M. Z. Death between the stars
Cadigan, P. Nearly departed
Carroll, J. Friend's best man
Chesbro, G. C. Strange prey
Dickson, G. R. Fleegl of Fleegl
Dickson, G. R. Rex and Mr. Rejilla
Dickson, G. R. Show me the way to go home
Ellison, H. Broken glass
Federici, C. M. 'Oh, Lenore!' came the echo
Foray, V. Duplex
Killough, L., and Killough, H. P. Keeping the customer satisfied
Kornbluth, C. M. The mindworm
Kratz, E. Poppa
Kress, N. Night win
Lee, W. M. A message from Charity
Leinster, M. Keyhole
Lewitt, S. The shaman flute
Longyear, B. B. The house of if
MacLean, K. Rescue squad
Major, A. R. Kissmeowt and the healing friar
Martin, G. R. R. Nightflyers
Martin, G. R. R. A song for Lya
Mayhar, A. Esmene's eyes
Neville, K. Underground movement
Norton, A. Outside
Norton, A. Swamp dweller
Norton, A. Teddi
Padgett, L. The piper's son
Poe, E. A. A tale of the ragged mountains
Powell, T. I had a hunch, and . . .
Reamy, T. Insects in amber
Sargent, P. Out of place
Schmitz, J. H. Novice
Shaw, B. Dream fighter
Silverberg, R. The affair
Silverberg, R. Ship-sister, star-sister
Simmons, D. Eyes I dare not meet in dreams
Smith, C. The game of rat and dragon
St. Clair, M. Prott
Stevens, J. Into that good night
Tiptree, J. Come live with me
Vinge, J. D. Psiren
Wollheim, D. A. Malice aforethought
Yano, T. The legend of the paper spaceship
Zahn, T. The dreamsender
Zelazny, R. King Solomon's ring
TELEPHONE
Aickman, R. Your tiny hand is frozen
Baxter, C. The crank
Bukoski, A. The woman who ate cat food
Cinca, S. The voice
Dadswell, M. "Hello?"
Fremlin, C. A case of maximum need
Gustafsson, L. The girl in the blue cap
Kauffman, J. How many boys?

Liben, M. The caller
Liben, M. Not quite alone on the telephone
Lurie, M. What is my secret identity?
Miller, S. Calling
Nolan, W. F. Dead call
Sullivan, T. The extension
Twain, M. The loves of Alonzo Fitz Clarence and Rosannah Ethelton
The telephone. Delfino, A. M.
A telephone call. Parker, D.
Telephone call. Rifaat, A.
A telephone call from David. Baxter, A.
A telephone call on Yom Kippur. Singer, I. B.
TELEPHONE COUNSELING *See* Hotlines (Telephone counseling)
Telephone poles. La Forme, A.
Telephones. Shapcott, T. W.
Teles, Hélio
Shirley
Américas 37:48-50 S/O '85
TELESCOPE
Woolf, V. The searchlight
Telescope. Sheehan, R.
TELEVISION
Abbott, K. The commercial break
Ashwood-Collins, A. Film at eleven
Chetwynd-Hayes, R. The colored transmission
Daniels, C. Mrs. Effie
Etchison, D. Deathtracks
Houbein, L. Everything is real
Irvine, R. R. A hard way to die
Kessler, J. F. A Theban ostrakon
Lopatin, J. Los Angeles
Murphy, P. Approaching substance
Robinson, S., and Robinson, J. Stardance
TELEVISION ANNOUNCERS *See* Television announcing
TELEVISION ANNOUNCING
Chowder, K. Hall of Fame
O'Brien, E. The love object
TELEVISION BROADCASTING *See* Television announcing
TELEVISION PRODUCERS AND DIRECTORS
Fontana, D. C. Cut to: murder
TELEVISION PROGRAMS
Baumbach, J. Mr. and Mrs. McFeely at home and away
Bloch, R. The new season
Cullen, E. J. Mayberry
Evans, E. Will
Faust, I. The double snapper
Goulart, R. Groucho
Herbert, F. Transcript: Mercury program
Jafek, B. You've come a long way, Mickey Mouse
Morgan, C. The hitmaker
Morressy, J. The last Jerry Fagin Show
Sheckley, R. The life of anybody
Sheckley, R. The prize of peril

TELEVISION PROGRAMS—*Continued*
Spinrad, N. The big flash
Weaver, G. Morality play
Rating
Hoyle, F. Blackmail
Television, trashbags and love. Butler, K.
Television will betray us all. Klass, P.
Tell her you love her with a ring from Dave's House of Diamonds. Kotzwinkle, W.
Tell Martha not to moan. Williams, S. A.
Tell me what you want. Lurie, M.
Tell me where the train goes. Subramani
The **tell-tale** heart. Poe, E. A.
Tell the night. Figueredo, D. H.
Tell the truth. Abbott, K.
Tell your fortune. Bloch, R.
The **teller's** cage. Harvor, E.
A **teller's** tale. Adams, G. G.
Teller's ticket. Flanagan, R.
Telles, Lygia Fagundes
Tigrela
Other fires; ed. by A. Manguel
Telling. Paley, G.
Telling Mrs. Baker. Lawson, H.
Telpaz, Gideon
Four camels out of the desert
Partisan Review 53 no1:43-55 '86
Tem, Steve Rasnic, 1950-
At the bureau
100 great fantasy short short stories; ed. by I. Asimov; T. Carr and M. H. Greenberg
The Best of Shadows; ed. by C. L. Grant
The battering
Shadows 8
Bloodwolf
Shadows 9
Father's Day
Whispers V
The giveaway
100 great fantasy short short stories; ed. by I. Asimov; T. Carr and M. H. Greenberg
Hidey hole
Masques II; ed. by J. N. Williamson
Little cruelties
Cutting edge; ed. by D. Etchison
The men & women of Rivendale
Vampires; ed. by A. Ryan
The painters are coming today
100 great fantasy short short stories; ed. by I. Asimov; T. Carr and M. H. Greenberg
The poor
100 great fantasy short short stories; ed. by I. Asimov; T. Carr and M. H. Greenberg
Preparations for the game
Masters of darkness; ed. by D. Etchison

Sleep
100 great fantasy short short stories; ed. by I. Asimov; T. Carr and M. H. Greenberg
Trickster
Halloween horrors; ed. by A. Ryan
Temp. Nevai, L.
Temple, Willard
The eternal duffer
The Saturday Evening Post 256:68-70+ Ja/F '84
Temple, William F.
The four-sided triangle
Amazing science fiction anthology: The war years, 1936-1945; ed. by M. H. Greenberg
A **Temple** of the Holy Ghost. O'Connor, F.
Temple to the economics of love. Gholson, C.
TEMPLES, BUDDHIST
Pak, K.-N. A time of disbelief
Temporarily at liberty. Goldman, L.
Temporary islands. Sauvinet, J.
The **temporary** king. McAuley, P. J.
Temporary shelter. Gordon, M.
Temps perdi. Rhys, J.
Temptation. Lispector, C.
The **temptation** of Harringay. Wells, H. G.
The **temptation** of St. Anthony. Barthelme, D.
Temptations. Christensen, K.
Ten cents a dance. Ferrandino, J.
A **ten-dollar** bill. Keillor, G.
Ten Indians. Hemingway, E.
Ten minute stop. Williams, T.
Ten minutes to seven. Pak, S.-J.
The **ten-second** election. Asimov, I.
Ten thousand pictures, one word. Kress, N.
Ten years. Essop, A.
The **tenancy** of Mr. Eex. Volsky, P.
The **tenant**. Mukherjee, B.
The **tenant**. Naipaul, S.
TENANT FARMING
Caldwell, E. The people v. Abe Lathan, colored
Caldwell, E. Wild flowers
Faulkner, W. Barn burning
Lee, H. The Bodega War
O'Connor, F. The displaced person
Wright, R. The man who saw the flood
The **tenants** at Auxillac. Pierce, C.
The **tender** crop. Mulikita, F. M.
The **tender** shoot. Colette
Tending the flock. Lagier, J.
Tenn, William, 1920-
Eastward ho!
Beyond Armageddon; ed. by W. M. Miller and M. H. Greenberg
The human angle
100 great fantasy short short stories; ed. by I. Asimov; T. Carr and M. H. Greenberg

Tenn, William, 1920——_Continued_
Mistress Sary
　　Young witches & warlocks; ed. by I.
　　Asimov; M. H. Greenberg and C. G.
　　Waugh
My mother was a witch
　　Witches; ed. by I. Asimov; M. H.
　　Greenberg and C. G. Waugh
Tennant, Emma
Philomela
　　The Penguin book of modern British
　　short stories
Tennant, Kylie, 1912-1988
Lady Weare and the Bodhisattva
　　Room to move; ed. by S. Falkiner
TENNESSEE
Forrest, K. V. Mandy Larkin
19th century
Madden, D. A fever of dying
Taylor, R. The Tennessee war of the roses
Woolson, C. F. Crowder's Cove: a story
　　of the war
20th century
Drake, R. Mrs. Picture Show Green
Durban, P. A long time coming, a long
　　time gone
Taylor, P. H. Bad dreams
Taylor, P. H. A long fourth
Taylor, P. H. Porte Cochere
Taylor, P. H. Two ladies in retirement
Taylor, P. H. What you hear from 'em?
Williams, T. Mother Yaws
Wilson, L. A. Country blues for Melissa
Wilson, L. A. From the bottom up
Wilson, L. A. The raising
Wilson, L. A. The snipe hunters
Farm life
　　See Farm life—Tennessee
Politics
　　See Politics—Tennessee
Knoxville
Alther, L. Termites
Wagner, K. E. Where the summer ends
Memphis
Taylor, P. H. The old forest
Taylor, P. H. A walled garden
Nashville
Hall, T. T. From Hank in Nashville
Leedom-Ackerman, J. The beginning of
　　violence
Taylor, P. H. The hand of Emmagene
Taylor, P. H. In the Miro District
Taylor, P. H. The scoutmaster
The **Tennessee** waltz. Cheuse, A.
The **Tennessee** war of the roses. Taylor, R.
Tenney, Elizabeth Mackintosh
Audition
　　McCall's 112:102-3+ S '85
TENNIS
Dunn, D. The tennis court
Hill, R. The worst crime known to man
Maugham, W. S. The facts of life

Sorrells, R. T. The blacktop champion of
　　Ickey Honey
Wetherell, W. D. The lob
The **tennis** bum. Michaelson, L. W.
The **tennis** court. Dunn, D.
Tennis or what. Newbound, C.
Tennis whites. Drake, R.
The **tenor**. Colette
Tenorio, Francisca H.
Tata Fino
　　Southwest tales; ed. by Alurista and X.
　　Rojas-Urista
A **tent** in agony. Crane, S.
Tent worms. Williams, T.
The **tenth** child. Calisher, H.
The **tenth** man. Fink, I.
The **tenth** man. Sholem Aleichem
Tepperman, Emile C.
Killers' club car
　　A Cent a story! Ed. by G. G. Roberts
Teragram. Smith, E. E.
Tergiversator. Carter, R.
Terhune, Albert Payson, 1872-1942
The coming of Lad
　　Roger Caras' Treasury of great dog
　　stories
The grudge
　　Roger Caras' Treasury of great dog
　　stories
Terhune, Mary Virginia Hawes _See_ Harland,
　　Marion, 1830-1922
Terminal. Gordimer, N.
The **terminal** beach. Ballard, J. G.
TERMINAL ILLNESS
Adams, A. Elizabeth
Aiken, C. Mr. Arcularis
Baber, A. The surfer
Ballantyne, S. Letters to the darkness
Broughton, T. A. Duck season
Crews, H. A long wail
Deaver, P. F. Rosie
Ekström, M. Death's midwives
Evans, E. In spring
Francis, H. E. The sudden trees
Friel, G. Onlookers
Gardner, J. Nimram
Gordimer, N. Terminal
Hagy, A. C. Where men go to cry
Hoffman, W. Smoke
Klíma, I. Friday morning: an orderly's tale
Leavitt, D. Counting months
MacLeod, A. The road to Rankin's Point
Moore, L. Go like this
Ocampo, S. Revelation
Prose, F. Tomatoes
Robison, M. Yours
Sligo, J. Going home
Updike, J. Poker night
Vanderhaeghe, G. A taste for perfection
Weaver, G. Flowers: memento mori
Terminal Island. Cooper, S.
Terminals. Murphy, P.
Terminus. Barthelme, D.

Termites. Alther, L.
Terms. Spivack, K.
The **terrapin**. Highsmith, P.
The **terrarium** principle. Pronzini, B.
The **Terrible** Old Man. Lovecraft, H. P.
A **terrible** revenge. See Gogol', N. V. A terrible vengeance
The **terrible** speed of mercy. Flaherty, G.
Terrible spring. Amichai, Y.
A **terrible** vengeance. Gogol', N. V.
A **terribly** strange bed. Collins, W.
Territory. Leavitt, D.
Terror. Chekhov, A. P.
Terror. Ferguson, W.
Terror in Cut-throat Cove. Bloch, R.
Terror in the night. Bloch, R.
Terror over Hollywood. Bloch, R.
Terror town. Queen, E.
TERRORISM
>See also Subversive activities; Violence

Asimov, I. Dollars and cents
Banks, R. Hostage
Bell, S. Jacob's ladder
Jaffe, H. Mussel
Moravia, A. In my dream I always hear a step on the stairs
Mukherjee, B. The management of grief
Regent, P. A delicate nose
Sheffield, C. Skystalk
Sonu, H. The terrorist
Valenzuela, L. Love of animals
The **terrorist**. Hersey, J.
The **terrorist**. Sonu, H.
TERRORISTS See Terrorism
The **terrors** of basket-weaving. Highsmith, P.
Terry, Marshall, 1931-
The antichrist
Prize stories, Texas Institute of Letters; ed. by M. Terry
Terry, Walter S.
The bottomless well
The Georgia Review 40:307-19 Spr '86
Necessary fictions; ed. by S. W. Lindberg and S. Corey
Tertiary care. Kercheval, J. L.
Tesich, Nadja
Easy money
Mademoiselle 90:98+ Je '84
Tessie, don't give away the raisin; without it, you're lost! Granit, A.
Tessier, Thomas
Food
Prime evil; ed. by D. E. Winter
The **test**. Faik, S.
The **test**. Forrest, K. V.
The **test**. Garrett, G. P.
The **test**. Henderson, D.
The **test**. Landolfi, T.
The **test**. Matheson, R.
The **test**. Ndebele, N.
Test. Thomas, T. L.
Test case. Fremlin, C.

The **test** is, if they drown. Grenville, K.
TEST PILOTS See Air pilots
Test-tube Frankenstein. Robbins, W. W.
The **testament** of Leyla. Givner, J.
Tester, William
Mice
Prairie Schooner 61:88-94 Summ '87
Testimony. Matthew, J. R.
Testimony. Oates, J. C.
Testimony of pilot. Hannah, B.
Testimony of trees. Stuart, J.
The **Tesuque** Pony Express. Chavez, A.
Tetu, Randeane
Depth of field
The Massachusetts Review 29:267-76 Summ '88
Fourth of July
The Massachusetts Review 27:127-30 Spr '86
Oh, that shoestore used to be mine
When I am an old woman I shall wear purple; ed. by S. K. Martz
Tevis, Walter S., 1928-1984
Out of luck
Omni book of science fiction 2
Tevye blows a small fortune. Sholem Aleichem
Tevye leaves for the land of Israel. Sholem Aleichem
Tevye strikes it rich. Sholem Aleichem
The **Texan**. Thomas, M.
Texarkana. Eighner, L.
Texarkana was a crazy town. Garrett, G. P.
TEXAS
>See also Alamo (San Antonio, Tex.)

Henry, O. Art and the bronco
Henry, O. The buyer from Cactus City
Henry, O. The caballero's way
Henry, O. A double-dyed deceiver
Henry, O. Georgia's ruling
Henry, O. The Indian Summer of Dry Valley Johnson
Henry, O. The octopus marooned
Henry, O. The red roses of Tonia
Wier, A. Bob and the other man
19th century
Bryan, J. Y. Frontier vigil
20th century
Camoin, F. A. Home is the Blue Moon Cafe
Camoin, F. A. A hunk of burning love
Duff, G. Fire ants
Garrett, G. P. Texarkana was a crazy town
Goyen, W. Tongues of men and of angels
Hauptman, W. Hands across America
Hauptman, W. Stormchaser
Henry, O. The passing of Black Eagle
Humphrey, W. The human fly
Humphrey, W. The last of the Caddoes
Humphrey, W. Mouth of brass
Humphrey, W. Quail for Mr. Forester
Kay, H. The fifth generation
Mayhar, A. A night in Possum Holler

TEXAS—20th century—*Continued*
McMurtry, L. Texasville [excerpt]
Osborn, C. The circuit rider
Osborn, C. The new castle
Osborn, C. Reversals
Osborn, C. Running around America
Ruffin, P. The man who would be God
Sanford, W. M. Fever in the South
Sanford, W. M. Luck
Scofield, S. Trespass
Williams, J. Health
Farm life
See Farm life—Texas
Alamo
See Alamo (San Antonio, Tex.)
Austin
Taylor, C. Denver's story
Taylor, C. Dutko's story
Taylor, C. Grom's story: naked lady
Taylor, C. Hamlin's story
Taylor, C. In and out of the arms of the law
Taylor, C. Lance's story: art sucks
Taylor, C. Leanderthal lady
Taylor, C. Loving thy neighbor
Taylor, C. The new and the old, the old and the new
Taylor, C. Sitting and spinning
Taylor, C. State of the streets
Taylor, C. These women
Taylor, C. The tribe
Taylor, C. Wince's story
Taylor, P. E. An independent meditation
Taylor, P. E. Spring water celebration
Taylor, P. E. Turning thirty-eight
Dallas
Taylor, P. E. Afoot in a field of men
Taylor, P. E. Answering the inquisitor
Taylor, P. E. Bird prayer and no amen
Taylor, P. E. Descent into brotherland
Taylor, P. E. Entering the house of the 'Lord
Taylor, P. E. Leaping Leo
Taylor, P. E. Who's that knocking? Is it you?
El Paso
Camoin, F. A. La vida
Phillips, J. A. El Paso
Taylor, P. E. At the altar
Houston
Furman, L. Eldorado
The **Texas** principessa. Goyen, W.
TEXAS RANGERS
Henry, O. Jimmy Hayes and Muriel
Kittredge, W. Phantom Silver
Reasoner, J. M. Hacendado
Texasville. McMurtry, L.
Texier, Catherine
The fedora
Between C & D; ed. by J. Rose and C. Texier
A **text** concerning strawberries. Hébert, L.-P.

TEXTILE INDUSTRY
See also Weavers
Thackeray, William Makepeace, 1811-1863
Dennis Haggarty's wife
Christian short stories; ed. by M. Booth
The devil's wager
Devils & demons; ed. by M. Kaye and S. Kaye
Snobs and marriage
The Treasury of English short stories; ed. by N. Sullivan
THAILAND
Bowles, P. You have left your lotus pods on the bus
Petchsingh, T. The third encounter
Petchsingh, T. The two moons of Vira's world
Somtow, S. P. Anna and the Ripper of Siam
Sucharitkul, S. Fiddling for water buffaloes
THAIS
United States
Lombreglia, R. Inn Essence
Thaler, Susan
Coming home
McCall's 116:67-9+ D '88
Forever with you
Good Housekeeping 198:126-7+ F '84
Thalia. Dumas, H.
Thanet, Octave
Sist' Chaney's black silk
Arkansas in short fiction; ed. by W. M. Baker and E. C. Simpson
Why Abbylonia surrendered
Arkansas in short fiction; ed. by W. M. Baker and E. C. Simpson
Thang. Gardner, M.
Thank you. Kawabata, Y.
Thank you, doctor. Sandel, C.
Thank you for the lovely tea. Gallant, M.
Thank you, m'am. Hughes, L.
Thank you, Mr. Halifax. Randall, M.
Thanksgiving. Keillor, G.
Thanksgiving. Ross, V.
Thanksgiving. Winters, J.
A **Thanksgiving** celebration (Amy). Mohr, N.
THANKSGIVING DAY
Abbott, K. The fort
Everett, P. L. Still hunting
Ferguson, W. The family
Gerber, M. J. Witnesses
Minot, S. Thanksgiving Day
Mohr, N. A Thanksgiving celebration (Amy)
Mukherjee, B. Orbiting
Wetherell, W. D. If a woodchuck could chuck wood
Thanksgiving Day. Minot, S.
Thanksgiving with Trudy. Forer, A. U.
That damned gun. Moravia, A.
That day. Vercors
That evening sun. Faulkner, W.

That evening sun go down. *See* Faulkner, W. That evening sun

That horse: 1921. Hogan, L. H.

That is no country for old men. Freeman, C.

That kind of a day. Block, L.

That old black magic. Bloch, R.

That old Studebaker. Lynch, L.

That pig of a Morin. Maupassant, G. de

That sax solo. Škvorecký, J.

That Skinner Bottoms winter. Conroy, J.

That special day. Merriman, C.

That Spot. London, J.

That summer. Chernoff, M.

That summer. Ross, V.

That time we were in Odessa. Böll, H.

That veteran. Doyle, Sir A. C.

That wall, that mimosa. Rodoreda, M.

That was last year. McPherson, M.

That was Tory. Raphael, F.

That which is hidden is that which is shown; that which is shown is that which is hidden. Josipovici, G.

That winter when Prince Borisov was everybody's favorite. Kotzwinkle, W.

That woman. Walsh, R.

That wonderful lizard of ours. Doran, J.

That's no reason. Barthelme, S.

That's the way it's always been. Algren, N.

That's what friends are for. Pascoe, B.

The **thaw**. Campbell, W. B.

Thayer, Nancy, 1943-

Vanished!

Redbook 163:60-2+ My '84

Redbook 163:34-35+ Je '84

Redbook 163:50-52+ Jl '84

THEATER LIFE

See also Actors; Actresses; also names of actors and actresses

Barthelme, D. Opening

Burgess, F. Exit, stage right

Carter, A. The cabinet of Edgar Allan Poe

Colette. Arrival and rehearsal

Colette. A bad morning

Colette. The cashier

Colette. The circus horse

Colette. The halt

Colette. Journey's end

Colette. Matinee

Colette. The misfit

Colette. Nostalgia

Colette. The starveling

Colette. The workroom

Covino, M. Matinee at the Bijou

Crane, S. Manacled

Dennison, G. Interview with the author of Caryatids

Friedman, B. J. The best we have

Hogan, D. Players

Lee, H. The celebrated Millard County Dramatic Stock Company

Marsh, Dame N. I can find my way out

Melville, H. The two temples: Temple second

Robinson, K. S. The disguise

Theatre. Tabucchi, A.

THEATRICAL TROUPES *See* Theater life

Theatrum magnum. Kaplický, V.

A **Theban** ostrakon. Kessler, J. F.

THEFT

See also Embezzlement; Robbery; Thieves

Abbott, K. Blood, binoculars, and a blizzard

Adams, A. Barcelona

Aiken, J. The jealous apprentice

Aiken, J. Smell

Algren, N. A lot you got to holler

Arnason, E. The ivory comb

Austin, D. A perfect crime

Bloch, R. The past master

Böll, H. On being courteous when compelled to break the law

Burt, S. I just kept on smiling

Chernoff, M. Respect for the dead

Connelly, J. Lock

Connelly, J. Sleeping together

Crane, S. A great mistake

Davis, S. A miner's Christmas carol

Dazai, O. The garden lantern

De Camp, L. S. The eye of Tandyla

Digby, J. The champagne party

Fante, J. My mother's goofy song

Freeman, C. Crime of the century

Futrelle, J. The stolen Rubens

Gibson, W. Burning chrome

Gillie, W. T. Motor-driven

Gorky, M. The affair of the clasps

Hartley, L. P. The silver clock

Hoch, E. D. Dreaming is a lonely thing

Hoch, E. D. The theft of nothing at all

Hoch, E. D. The theft of the four of spades

Holding, J. A good kid

Holmes, C. Metropolitan

Hornung, E. W. A bad night

Hornung, E. W. The chest of silver

Hornung, E. W. A costume piece

Hornung, E. W. The criminologists' club

Hornung, E. W. Gentlemen and players

Hornung, E. W. The Ides of March

Hornung, E. W. A Jubilee present

Hornung, E. W. Nine points of the law

Hornung, E. W. The spoils of sacrilege

Hornung, E. W. A trap to catch a cracksman

Hornung, E. W. The wrong house

Horsdal, M. An educated taste

Izgü, M. Apollo's thing

Johnson, C. R. Exchange value

Johnston, G. The dying day of Francis Bainsbridge

Jolley, E. The travelling entertainer

Lish, G. What is left to link us

Lofts, N. Saving face

THEFT—*Continued*
MacLeod, C. It was an awful shame
Matthiessen, P. On the River Styx
Mcdonald, G. The robbery
McGahern, J. The recruiting officer
McKnight, R. The voice
Montero, M. Last night at dawn
Muschg, A. Reparations; or, Making good
Ozick, C. The suitcase
Padilla, M. Papel
Queen, E. The Dauphin's doll
Queen, E. Object lesson
Rifaat, A. Another evening at the club
Rush, N. Thieving
Rushdie, S. The Prophet's hair
Sayers, D. L. The necklace of pearls
Schinto, J. The ring; or, A girl confesses
Sembene, O. The false prophet
Thorman, C. Binkas sausage
Thurm, M. Away from the heart
Tremain, R. The Colonel's daughter
Valenzuela, L. Strange things happen here
Ward, L. The marbled horn
Whelan, G. Beneath the fig trees
Zangwill, I. Cheating the gallows
Theft. Ingalls, R.
Theft. Porter, K. A.
Theft in a pastry shop. Calvino, I.
The **theft** of Lily. Stern, S.
The **theft** of nothing at all. Hoch, E. D.
The **theft** of the circus poster. Hoch, E. D.
The **theft** of the four of spades. Hoch, E. D.
The **theft** of the overdue library book. Hoch, E. D.
The **theft** of the royal ruby. Christie, A.
Their dear little ghost. Peattie, E. W.
Their first American. Kelly, T.
Their house. Barthelme, S.
Their pride and joy. Pearlman, E.
Thelma. Moskowitz, F.
Theme and variations. Klass, P.
"Then face to face". James, S.
Then they'd watch comedies. Ríos, A.
Then we were three. Shaw, I.
Theology. Atwood, M.
A theory of knowledge. Oates, J. C.
Theo's girl. Willard, N.
Therafina. Rodoreda, M.
Therapeutic bondage. Stocks, D.
Therapy. Davis, L.
There are a lot of ways to die. Bissoondath, N.
There are no ghosts in the Soviet Union. Hill, R.
There are no ordinary men in Iowa. Schramm, W. L.
There are no snakes in Ireland. Forsyth, F.
There are no thieves in this town. García Márquez, G.
There could be a lesson in it somewhere. Lee, H.
There goes Ravelaar. Van de Wetering, J.

There I was, stuck with Bubsy. Highsmith, P.
There is a balm in Gilead. Hunnicutt, E.
There is a God. Kawabata, Y.
There is a snake in Alemdağ. Faik, S.
There ought to be a judge. West, J.
There was a basket down by the Tiber. Moravia, A.
There was a young lady of Perth. Saroyan, W.
There were three. Bonner, M.
There will come soft rains. Bradbury, R.
There's a Garden of Eden. Gilchrist, E.
There's a long, long trail a-winding. Kirk, R.
There's a neutron bomb for ants too. Moravia, A.
There's a war on. Sandel, C.
There's no vinism like chauvinism. Jakes, J.
There's one in every school. Saroyan, W.
There's the sea. Boylan, J.
Theresa McCann and Joe. Briskin, M.
Thériault, Marie-José
The thirty-first bird
Invisible fictions; ed. by G. Hancock
Thériault, Yves, 1915-1983
Nuliak
Invisible fictions; ed. by G. Hancock
The whale
The Oxford book of French-Canadian short stories
Theroux, Paul
An unofficial rose
Short story international 66
Yard sale
On being foreign; ed. by T. J. Lewis and R. E. Jungman
Short story international 43
Thersites at Mytilene. Parotti, P.
These women. Taylor, C.
The thesis. Silva, B.
"They". Kipling, R.
They all ran after the farmer's wife. Moskowitz, F.
They all went up to Amsterdam. Mattison, A.
"They also serve . . .". Wall, M.
They called him a killer. Patten, L. B.
They can only hang you once. Hammett, D.
They fly so high. Rocklynne, R.
They got it all. Greene, P. L.
They grind exceeding small. Williams, B. A., Jr.
They hanged Wild Bill Murphy. Overholser, W. D.
They meet a boy. McGarry, J.
They might even kill you. Pavel, O.
They never even see me. Williamson, J. N.
They now live in Texas. Dubus, A.
They put their heads together. Asscher-Pinkhof, C.
They sleep without dreaming. Gilliatt, P.
They sweep the seas. MacLean, A.

They that go down to the sea in ships. Fitch, M.

They will call it insane. Shannon, D.

They'll smile at you if you're with me. Lipman, E.

They're coming for you. Daniels, L.

They're killing Jews on Sackman Street! Granit, A.

They're not your husband. Carver, R.

They're talking about Chernobyl today. Campbell, E.

Thibault, David
A woman like Dilsie
Arkansas in short fiction; ed. by W. M. Baker and E. C. Simpson

Thibault, Jacques Anatole *See* France, Anatole, 1844-1924

Thick and thin. Lipman, E.

Thick the new leaves. Yasuoka, S.

The **thief**. Andreyev, L.

The **thief**. Maupassant, G. de

The **thief**. Monem, H. A.

The **thief**. Tanizaki, J.

Thief. Wilson, R., Jr.

A **thief** in my house. Thomas, M.

Thief in the brambles. Hall, J. J.

THIEVES
See also Cattle thieves; Horse thieves; Kleptomania; Theft

Abbott, K. Yellow rock

Achebe, C. Civil peace

Algren, N. No man's laughter

Andreyev, L. The thief

Bellow, S. A silver dish

Bloch, R. String of pearls

Block, L. As good as a rest

Block, L. Like a thief in the night

Block, L. Weekend guests

Boyle, T. C. Not a leg to stand on

Brett, S. Don't know much about art

Brittain, W. Mr. Strang and the purloined memo

Brittain, W. Mr. Strang picks up the pieces

Calvino, I. Theft in a pastry shop

Campbell, E. In the Rambla de Cataluña

Canning, V. Lady in the dark

Chavez, A. The penitente thief

Cherryh, C. J. To take a thief

Colette. The burglar

Collins, W. The biter bit

Conley, R. J. The name

Croft, M. The pit

Cullen, E. J. I break into houses

Curtiss, U. R. A beneficial walk

Curtiss, U. R. The marked man

Dazai, O. Magic lantern

DeMarinis, R. Billy Ducks among the Pharoahs

Doyle, Sir A. C. Our midnight visitor

Doyle, Sir A. C. The recollections of Captain Wilkie

Faik, S. The silk handkerchief

Farr, D. Sam's conscience

Faust, I. Simon Girty go ape

Ford, R. Rock springs

Fremlin, C. The bonus years

García Márquez, G. There are no thieves in this town

Gardam, J. Benevolence

Gardner, M. The conspicuous turtle

Gardner, M. Old man gloom

Gilbert, W. S. The burglar's story

Gorky, M. Chelkash

Gorky, M. Chums

Gosling, P. Mr. Felix

Granit, A. They're killing Jews on Sackman Street!

Haldeman, J. W. Lindsay and the red city blues

Henry, O. A retrieved reformation

Highsmith, P. Eddie and the monkey robberies

Hoch, E. D. The theft of the circus poster

Holding, J. The grave robber

Holding, J. Monkey king

Holding, J. A padlock for Charlie Draper

Hornung, E. W. Gentlemen and players

Hornung, E. W. The Ides of March

Hornung, E. W. No sinecure

Hornung, E. W. To catch a thief

Howard, C. Last chance in Singapore

Ingalls, R. Theft

Jenkins, W. F. Uneasy home-coming

Johnson, G. C. Sea change

Jolley, E. Another holiday for the Prince

Kawabata, Y. Her mother's eye

Kessler, J. F. Hermes

Kim, Y.-J. The visitor

Klíma, I. Saturday morning: a thief's tale

Leiber, F. Ill met in Lankhmar

Lutz, J. The Insomniacs Club

Lutz, J. Tough

Maupassant, G. de. The ill-omened groom

Maupassant, G. de. A lucky burglar

Maupassant, G. de. The rabbit

Miller, A. It takes a thief

Narayan, R. K. A career

Nielsen, H. Never trust a woman

Ocampo, S. The sibyl

O'Donnell, P. A perfect night to break your neck

Ogot, G. The green leaves

Owoyele, D. The will of Allah

Painter, P. Intruders of sleepless nights

Parise, G. Fear

Peters, E. Come to dust

Powell, T. Till death do not us part

Pritchard, M. A man around the house

Pritchett, V. S. Tea with Mrs. Bittell

Pronzini, B. A dip in the Poole

Pronzini, B. House call

Pronzini, B. The killing

Pronzini, B. On guard!

Pronzini, B. Once a thief

Pronzini, B. One of those days

Pronzini, B. Two weeks every summer

THIEVES—*Continued*

Purdy, J. Sleep tight

Ritchie, J. Who's got the lady?

Robinson, S. God is an iron

Sagan, F. The exchange

Sharp, M. The perfect model

Sholem Aleichem. Hard luck

Shuttle, P. Ratón ladrón

Slesar, H. The first crime of Ruby Martinson

Slesar, H. Light fingers

Sokoloff, T. C. Providence will provide

Stead, C. An iced cake with cherries

Stevenson, R. L. A lodging for the night

Stuart, J. No petty thief

Sun Shaoshan. Eight hundred meters below

Tanizaki, J. The thief

Tyre, N. A nice place to stay

Valenzuela, L. Vision out of the corner of one eye

Wallace, P. Joe

Walters, A. L. The laws

Weinstein, L. How I became a jeweler

Wilson, R., Jr. Land fishers

Wilson, R., Jr. Thief

Wodehouse, P. G. The mixer

Thieving. Rush, N.

Thin air. Pronzini, B.

Thin ice. Wilson, B.

A **thin** place. Potter, N. A. J.

The **thing**. Moravia, A.

The **thing** at the top of the stairs. Bradbury, R.

The **thing** from the old seaman's mouth. Rosemund, V. L.

The **thing** in No. 7. Wells, H. G.

The **thing** in the weeds. Hodgson, W. H.

The **thing** on the doorstep. Lovecraft, H. P.

The **thing** that goes burp in the night. Webb, S.

The **thing** that stared. Wilson, R.

The **thing** waiting outside. Williamson, B.

Things best forgotten. Bissoondath, N.

Things I did to make it possible. Camoin, F. A.

Things that go quack in the night. Shiner, L., and Shiner, E.

Things that matter. Morris, W.

The **things** that would never be mine. Carter, M.

The **things** they carried. O'Brien, T.

Things to be thrown away. Penner, J.

Things to do today. Povod, R.

Things to draw. Andres, K.

Things will look brighter in the morning. Benjamin, D.

Think of wives in old China. Wolfe, L.

Thinking about babies. Yellin, L. N.

The **thinking** cap. Bloch, R.

Thinking of you. Von Stamwitz, A.

Thinking the unthinkable. Creveling, W.

Thiong'o, Ngugi wa *See* Ngugi wa Thiong'o, 1938-

The **third** bank of the river. Rosa, J. G.

The **third** bullet. Brand, M.

Third class. Sholem Aleichem

The **third** count. Fetler, A.

The **third** day of trials. Martone, M.

The **third** encounter. Petchsingh, T.

The **third-floor** flat. Christie, A.

The **third** ingredient. Henry, O.

The **third** level. Finney, J.

The **third** party. Trevor, W.

Third person singular. Sagan, F.

The **third** resignation. García Márquez, G.

The **third** son. Haris, P.

Third stage. Anderson, P.

The **third** story. Bitov, A.

The **third** thing that killed my father off. Carver, R.

Third time lucky. Ingalls, R.

The **third** violet. Crane, S.

The **third** voice. Ferguson, W.

Third wind. Matheson, R. C.

Thirst. Andrić, I.

Thirst. Pronzini, B.

Thirteen and a turtle. Montero, M.

The **thirteenth**. Grandbois, A.

The **thirteenth** day of Christmas. Asimov, I.

The **thirteenth** killer. Brett, S.

The **thirty-first** bird. Thériault, M.-J.

Thirty-four seasons of winter. Kittredge, W.

Thirty horses for your daughter. Mears, S. S.

Thirty-seven just to take a fall. Everett, P. L.

Thirty-seven years. See Franzen, B. 37 years

Thirty-six miracles of Lyndon Johnson. Boylan, J.

Thirty-two votes before breakfast. Stuart, J.

This afternoon. Russ, J.

This also happened. Enayetullah, A.

This bright night. Gault, C.

This day's evil. Craig, J.

This domain, that domain. See Leaton, A. Gita's story

This freedom. Morrison, J.

This heat. Bukoski, A.

This heat. Durban, P.

This horse of a body of mine. Blei, N.

This house and my home. Hughes, T.

This is a delta. Stuart, F. C.

This is a story about my friend George, the toy inventor. Paley, G.

This is the road. Silverberg, R.

This is Tibten! Böll, H.

This light is for those at sea. Nelson, K.

This majestic lie. Crane, S.

This makes two! Pirandello, L.

"**This** moment is ours alone". Matthews, J.

This night, at my fire. Russ, J.

This now fenceless world. Gault, C.

This plumber. Lott, B.

This summer's promise. Ledbetter, E.

This time. Roth, H. H.

This time, yesterday morning. Schwartz, J.

This uncle. Franzen, B.
This way for the gas, ladies and gentlemen.
  Borowski, T.
This wizened creature. Loukakis, A.
This world, then the fireworks. Thompson,
  J.
Thoas at Pylene. Parotti, P.
Thomas, Audrey Callahan
  Breaking the ice
    Thomas, A. C. Goodbye Harold, good
    luck
  Compulsory figures
    Thomas, A. C. Goodbye Harold, good
    luck
  The dance
    Thomas, A. C. Goodbye Harold, good
    luck
  Degrees
    Thomas, A. C. Goodbye Harold, good
    luck
  Elevation
    Thomas, A. C. Goodbye Harold, good
    luck
  Goodbye Harold, good luck
    Thomas, A. C. Goodbye Harold, good
    luck
  Kill day on the government wharf
    The Oxford book of Canadian short
    stories in English
  Local customs
    Thomas, A. C. Goodbye Harold, good
    luck
  The man with clam eyes
    Thomas, A. C. Goodbye Harold, good
    luck
  Miss Foote
    Thomas, A. C. Goodbye Harold, good
    luck
  Mothering Sunday
    Thomas, A. C. Goodbye Harold, good
    luck
  One size fits all
    Thomas, A. C. Goodbye Harold, good
    luck
  The princess and the zucchini
    Thomas, A. C. Goodbye Harold, good
    luck
  Relics
    Thomas, A. C. Goodbye Harold, good
    luck
Thomas, Dorothy
  The car
    The Saturday Evening Post 256:52-5+
    My/Je '84
Thomas, Dylan, 1914-1953
  An adventure from a work in progress
    Thomas, D. The collected stories
  Adventures in the skin trade: A fine begin-
    ning
    Thomas, D. The collected stories
  Adventures in the skin trade: Four lost
    souls
    Thomas, D. The collected stories

Adventures in the skin trade: Plenty of
  furniture
  Thomas, D. The collected stories
After the fair
  Thomas, D. The collected stories
Brember
  Thomas, D. The collected stories
The burning baby
  The Penguin book of modern British
  short stories
  Thomas, D. The collected stories
A child's Christmas in Wales
  Thomas, D. The collected stories
The crumbs of one man's year
  Thomas, D. The collected stories
The dress
  Thomas, D. The collected stories
The end of the river
  Thomas, D. The collected stories
The enemies
  Thomas, D. The collected stories
Extraordinary little cough
  Thomas, D. The collected stories
The fight
  Thomas, D. The collected stories
The followers
  Thomas, D. The collected stories
Gaspar, Melchior, Balthasar
  Thomas, D. The collected stories
Holiday memory
  Thomas, D. The collected stories
The holy six
  Thomas, D. The collected stories
The horse's ha
  Thomas, D. The collected stories
In the direction of the beginning
  Thomas, D. The collected stories
In the garden
  Thomas, D. The collected stories
Jarley's
  Thomas, D. The collected stories
Just like little dogs
  Thomas, D. The collected stories
The lemon
  Thomas, D. The collected stories
The map of love
  Thomas, D. The collected stories
The mouse and the woman
  Thomas, D. The collected stories
Old Garbo
  Thomas, D. The collected stories
One warm Saturday
  Thomas, D. The collected stories
The orchards
  Thomas, D. The collected stories
Patricia, Edith, and Arnold
  Thomas, D. The collected stories
The peaches
  Thomas, D. The collected stories
Prologue to an adventure
  Thomas, D. The collected stories
A prospect of the sea
  Thomas, D. The collected stories

Thomas, Dylan, 1914-1953—*Continued*
Quite early one morning
  Thomas, D. The collected stories
Return journey
  Thomas, D. The collected stories
The school for witches
  Thomas, D. The collected stories
A story
  Thomas, D. The collected stories
The tree
  Masterpieces of terror and the super-
    natural; ed. by M. Kaye and S. Kaye
  Thomas, D. The collected stories
The true story
  Thomas, D. The collected stories
  The Treasury of English short stories;
    ed. by N. Sullivan
The vest
  Thomas, D. The collected stories
A visit to grandpa's
  Thomas, D. The collected stories
The visitor
  Thomas, D. The collected stories
Where Tawe flows
  Thomas, D. The collected stories
Who do you wish was with us?
  Thomas, D. The collected stories
Thomas, Elizabeth
Driving into the light
  The North American Review 272:44-5 Mr
    '87
Our house
  Writing red; ed. by C. Nekola and P.
    Rabinowitz
Thomas, Eugene
The lady from hell
  Hard-boiled dames; ed. by B. A. Drew
Thomas, James, 1946-
Barbecue
  Thomas, J. Pictures, moving
Blood money
  Thomas, J. Pictures, moving
Christmas in Calpe
  Thomas, J. Pictures, moving
Half frame
  Thomas, J. Pictures, moving
Last factory blues
  Thomas, J. Pictures, moving
My journal as the fishwoman
  Thomas, J. Pictures, moving
Paco and I at sea
  Thomas, J. Pictures, moving
Santorini gray
  Thomas, J. Pictures, moving
Sparkle in five
  Thomas, J. Pictures, moving
Talma Levy is falling
  Thomas, J. Pictures, moving
Thomas, Maria, 1941-1989
Abdullah and Mariam
  Thomas, M. Come to Africa and save
    your marriage, and other stories

Charlie Speed
  The Antioch Review 44:5-14 Wint '86
Choobeedoo Yum-yum and the ANC
  Thomas, M. Come to Africa and save
    your marriage, and other stories
Come to Africa and save your marriage
  Thomas, M. Come to Africa and save
    your marriage, and other stories
Jim Chance
  Thomas, M. Come to Africa and save
    your marriage, and other stories
Mama Angelina's
  Thomas, M. Come to Africa and save
    your marriage, and other stories
Neighbors
  Thomas, M. Come to Africa and save
    your marriage, and other stories
Second rains
  Thomas, M. Come to Africa and save
    your marriage, and other stories
She hears, falling, the seed
  Thomas, M. Come to Africa and save
    your marriage, and other stories
Shellers
  Thomas, M. Come to Africa and save
    your marriage, and other stories
Silver sugar from Bombay
  Thomas, M. Come to Africa and save
    your marriage, and other stories
Summer opportunity
  Thomas, M. Come to Africa and save
    your marriage, and other stories
The Texan
  Thomas, M. Come to Africa and save
    your marriage, and other stories
A thief in my house
  Thomas, M. Come to Africa and save
    your marriage, and other stories
Why the sky is so far away
  Thomas, M. Come to Africa and save
    your marriage, and other stories
Thomas, Nigel
At the market
  Fatal recurrences; ed. by H. Hugh and
    P. O'Brien
Thomas, Richard, 1920-
New men, old ways
  Short story international 49
Thomas, Rosie
Reach for tomorrow
  Good Housekeeping 205:200-1+ S '87
Thomas, Theodore L.
Broken tool
  Kindred spirits; ed. by J. M. Elliot
Test
  The Best horror stories from the
    Magazine of fantasy and science fiction
Thomas Awkner floats. Winton, T.
Thomason, John
Mutiny
  Short stories of the sea; ed. by G. C.
    Solley and E. Steinbaugh

Thompson, Arthur Leonard Bell, 1917-1975
*For works written by this author under
other names see* Clifford, Francis,
1917-1975

Thompson, Barbara
Crossing
The Pushcart prize IX
Tattoo
Love stories for the time being; ed. by
G. D. Chipps and B. Henderson
Shenandoah: an anthology; ed. by J.
Boatwright

Thompson, Edward Anthony *See* Lejeune,
Anthony, 1928-

Thompson, Jean, 1950-
Accidents
Thompson, J. Little Face, and other
stories
Applause, applause
New women and new fiction; ed. by S.
Cahill
The best it could be
Thompson, J. Little Face, and other
stories
Birds in air
Prime number; ed. by A. L. Weir
A courtship
Thompson, J. Little Face, and other
stories
Danny's chick
Thompson, J. Little Face, and other
stories
Fire dreams
The New Yorker 64:32-8 O 31 '88
Foreigners
Thompson, J. Little Face, and other
stories
Having words
Thompson, J. Little Face, and other
stories
Lenny dying, Pacific standard time
Thompson, J. Little Face, and other
stories
Little Face
Thompson, J. Little Face, and other
stories
Naomi counting time
Thompson, J. Little Face, and other
stories
Of his bones are coral made
Thompson, J. Little Face, and other
stories
Remembering Sonny
Thompson, J. Little Face, and other
stories
Sex life of the sponge
Thompson, J. Little Face, and other
stories

Thompson, Jim
This world, then the fireworks
The Black Lizard anthology of crime fic-
tion; ed. by E. Gorman

Thompson, Joyce
The afternoon of the poetess
Thompson, J. East is west of here
The birch tree
Thompson, J. East is west of here
The Christmas party
Thompson, J. East is west of here
The copper mine
Thompson, J. East is west of here
Defoliation
Thompson, J. East is west of here
Dreams of a new mother
Thompson, J. East is west of here
Ice flowers
Thompson, J. East is west of here
New bed
Thompson, J. East is west of here
Robert's song
Thompson, J. East is west of here
Story for Susan
Thompson, J. East is west of here
The stud
Thompson, J. East is west of here
The white impala
Thompson, J. East is west of here
Yarn
Thompson, J. East is west of here

Thompson, Kent
A blunt affair
Thompson, K. A local hanging, and
other stories
Getting ready to go camping down in
Maine
Thompson, K. A local hanging, and
other stories
Getting saved
Thompson, K. A local hanging, and
other stories
Goodbye
Thompson, K. A local hanging, and
other stories
Green things
Thompson, K. A local hanging, and
other stories
Holiday Haven
Thompson, K. A local hanging, and
other stories
A husband and a father
Thompson, K. A local hanging, and
other stories
The keynote
Thompson, K. A local hanging, and
other stories
A local hanging
Thompson, K. A local hanging, and
other stories
Longing
Thompson, K. A local hanging, and
other stories
A mother's cry
Thompson, K. A local hanging, and
other stories

Thompson, Kent—*Continued*
Night train through the snow to Montreal
Thompson, K. A local hanging, and other stories
Promises
Thompson, K. A local hanging, and other stories
Robbing motels
Thompson, K. A local hanging, and other stories
Some things I won't do
Thompson, K. A local hanging, and other stories
What happened
Thompson, K. A local hanging, and other stories
Thompson, Robert
Under the swaying curtain
Missouri short fiction; ed. by C. Beasley
Thompson, Sandra
Ashes
Thompson, S. Close-ups
The baby in mid-air
Thompson, S. Close-ups
The birthday party
Thompson, S. Close-ups
Close-ups
Thompson, S. Close-ups
The Don
Thompson, S. Close-ups
Horror show
Thompson, S. Close-ups
L.A.
Thompson, S. Close-ups
Memoir, cut short
Thompson, S. Close-ups
Montauk
Thompson, S. Close-ups
Mother's Day
Thompson, S. Close-ups
Notes
Thompson, S. Close-ups
Snow
Thompson, S. Close-ups
Thompson, Thomas, 1913-
Blood on the sun
The Western hall of fame; ed. by B. Pronzini and M. H. Greenberg
A wollopin' good chew
Wild westerns; ed. by B. Pronzini
Thomson, Geddes
Pride of lions
Streets of stone; ed. by M. Burgess and H. Whyte
Thomson, June, 1930-
Dead ground
John Creasey's Crime collection, 1986
Thomson, Valentine
The battle of Bonhomme Richard and Serapis
Men at sea; ed. by B. Aymar

Thon, Melanie Rae
Iona Moon
The Hudson Review 41:433-47 Aut '88
Thor meets Captain America. Brin, D.
THOREAU, HENRY DAVID, 1817-1862
About
West, J. Like visitant of air
Thorman, Carolyn
Anchovy trees
Thorman, C. Fifty years of eternal vigilance, and other stories
Binkas sausage
Thorman, C. Fifty years of eternal vigilance, and other stories
Blue haired chickens
Thorman, C. Fifty years of eternal vigilance, and other stories
Fifty years of eternal vigilance
Thorman, C. Fifty years of eternal vigilance, and other stories
God giving Lithuania to the world
Thorman, C. Fifty years of eternal vigilance, and other stories
Gurlas
Thorman, C. Fifty years of eternal vigilance, and other stories
Knights of Puntukas
Thorman, C. Fifty years of eternal vigilance, and other stories
No job too small
Thorman, C. Fifty years of eternal vigilance, and other stories
Persecution is for you
Thorman, C. Fifty years of eternal vigilance, and other stories
Society for the benefit of the Daughters of Vilnius
Thorman, C. Fifty years of eternal vigilance, and other stories
Sweet chickadee of grace
Thorman, C. Fifty years of eternal vigilance, and other stories
Thorman, Richard
The box of contents
The Virginia Quarterly Review 61:433-52 Summ '85
The family man
The Sewanee Review 95:369-87 Summ '87
Hardly working
The Sewanee Review 93:507-25 Fall '85
The Stradivarius
The Southern Review (Baton Rouge, La.) 20:387-405 Ap '84
The **thorn**. Gordon, M.
Thorns and gifts. Davie, E.
Thornton, Valerie
Another Sunday morning
Streets of stone; ed. by M. Burgess and H. Whyte
Thorofare. Minot, S.
Thoroughly modern magic. Cross, C.

Thorpe, Thomas Bangs, 1815-1878
 The big bear of Arkansas
  Arkansas in short fiction; ed. by W. M.
   Baker and E. C. Simpson
Those awful dawns. Highsmith, P.
Those grand old songs. Kavaler, R.
Those in peril in the air. Ullmann, A.
Those special afternoons. Rodowsky, C.
Thou art the man. Poe, E. A.
Thou shalt not suffer a witch . . . . Haynes,
 D. K.
Though dreamers die. Del Rey, L.
The **thought**. Andreyev, L.
The **thought**. Hartley, L. P.
THOUGHT CONTROL *See* Brainwashing
THOUGHT TRANSFERENCE *See*
 Telepathy
Thoughts of home. Sonu, H.
THOUSAND AND ONE NIGHTS *See*
 Arabian nights
The **thousand-and-second** tale of
 Scheherazade. Poe, E. A.
The **thousand** cuts. Watson, I.
The **Thousand** Islands. Schwartz, L. S.
A **thousand** miles from the ocean. Garner,
 H.
THOUSAND NIGHTS AND A NIGHT *See*
 Arabian nights
A **thousand** paces along the Via Dolorosa.
 Silverberg, R.
Thrapp, Dan
 Gravedigger
  Editor's choice II; ed. by M. Sklar and
   M. Biggs
THRASEA PAETUS, PUBLIUS CLODIUS,
 d. 66
              About
 Sheehan, R. Masks
Thrasymedes at Pylos. Parotti, P.
Thrawn Janet. Stevenson, R. L.
The **threatening** three. Gault, W. C.
Three. Lish, G.
Three alarm fire. Kilgore, D.
Three ambiguous visitors. Fainlight, R.
The **three** cats. Warner, S. T.
Three, counting the cat. Suckow, R.
The **three** cowboys. Gardner, M.
The **three** dark kings. Borchert, W.
The **three** dark Magi. See Borchert, W. The
 three dark kings
The **three-day** blow. Hemingway, E.
Three days. Lee, T.
The **three** dogs. Chesterton, G. K.
Three-Dot Po. Paretsky, S.
The **three** d's. Nash, O.
The **three** eras of Libbie Marsh. Gaskell, E.
 C.
Three essays. Katz, S.
Three faces of the night. Gardner, C. S.
The **three** girls. Pavese, C.
Three good reasons. Houbein, L.
Three gun Terry. Daly, C. J.
Three happy Japanese. Asher, H. W.

The **three** horsemen of the apocalypse.
 Chesterton, G. K.
The **three** hunters. Carrington, L.
The **three** kings. Anderman, J.
Three knives in Ithkar. Bloodwine, G.
Three love aerobics. Vega, A. L.
Three maids' children. Simpson, M.
Three meaningless tales. Al-Qaʻid, Y.
Three men. Colum, P.
The **three** men. Snyder, Z. K.
The **three-mile** hill is five miles long.
 Menaker, D.
Three million yen. Mishima, Y.
The **three** numbers. Asimov, I.
Three o'clock. Wolfe, T.
Three o'clock and woodstream. Gaines, C.
The **three** of us. Frede, R.
Three old men of Lerici. Clift, C.
Three, or four, for dinner. Hartley, L. P.
Three pictures. Woolf, V.
Three players of a summer game. Williams,
 T.
Three popes walk into a bar. Hempel, A.
Three professors. Cao Guanlong
Three rivers. Sorrells, R. T.
Three sisters. Field, B.
Three soldiers. Poyer, D. C.
THREE STOOGES (COMEDY TEAM)
 Boylan, J. Fugue for violin and Three
  Stooges
The **three** strangers. Hardy, T.
Three Sundays in a week. Poe, E. A.
Three tales. Popov, E.
Three thousand dollars. Lipsky, D.
Three times around. Smith, J. M.
Three vignettes. Wilbur, E.
The **three** widows. Queen, E.
Three women. Liphshitz, A.
Three years. Chekhov, A. P.
Three's a crowd. Williams, D.
Threnody. Weldon, F.
The **threshold**. Power, V.
Thrift. Faulkner, W.
Thrift. Halligan, M.
Thrift. Page, P.
The **thrill** of the grass. Kinsella, W. P.
The **throaways**. Russ, J.
Through a window. Wells, H. G.
Through road. Bedford, J.
Through road no whither. Bear, G.
Through the eyes of a cat. Virgo, S.
Through the fields in gloves. Kiely, B.
Through the moon gate. Lichtenberg, J.
Through the needle's eye. Norton, A.
Through the safety net. Baxter, C.
The **thrower-away**. Böll, H.
Thrown-away child. Adcock, T. L.
Thrust counter thrust. Dumas, H.
Thubron, Colin, 1939-
 The ear
  Foreign exchange; ed. by J. Evans
A **thumb** on the scales. Breen, J. L.
The **thumbmark**. Wells, H. G.

The **thumbmark** of St. Peter. Christie, A.
Thumbs up, thumbs down. Buckley, W. F.
Thunder in autumn. Kawabata, Y.
The **thunder** of guilt. Lutz, J.
The **thunderbolt**. Tāmir, Z.
Thunderbolt. Tuohy, F.
Thurber, James, 1894-1961
  The catbird seat
    Reader's Digest 131:138-44 Ag '87
  The greatest man in the world
    The World of the short story; ed. by
      C. Fadiman
  The unicorn in the garden
    The Norton book of American short
      stories
Thurlby, James
  The mill-race
    Encounter (London, England) 70:8-11 My
      '88
Thurm, Marian
  Aftermath
    Thurm, M. Floating
  Away from the heart
    Thurm, M. These things happen
  California
    Thurm, M. Floating
  Floating
    Thurm, M. Floating
  Flying
    Thurm, M. These things happen
  Grace
    Thurm, M. Floating
  Ice
    The Editors' choice v3; ed. by G. E.
      Murphy, Jr.
    Ms. 13:52-4+ F '85
    Thurm, M. These things happen
  Leaving Johanna
    Thurm, M. These things happen
  Light-years
    Thurm, M. Floating
  Lovers
    Thurm, M. These things happen
  Markings
    Thurm, M. Floating
  Perfect vision
    Ms. 14:52-4+ Mr '86
  Romance
    Thurm, M. These things happen
  Sanctuary
    Thurm, M. These things happen
  Secrets
    Thurm, M. Floating
  Skaters
    Thurm, M. Floating
  Snow-child
    Thurm, M. These things happen
  Sounds
    Thurm, M. These things happen
  Squirrels
    Thurm, M. These things happen
  Starlight
    Thurm, M. Floating

Still life
  Thurm, M. Floating
Unmarried states
  Mademoiselle 90:112+ D '84
Winter
  Thurm, M. Floating
Thurnley Abbey. Landon, P.
The **Thursday** events. Ye Yonglie
Thursday lunch. Rifaat, A.
Thursday morning: an erotic tale. Klíma, I.
Thurston, Robert
  Was that house there yesterday?
    Universe 16
Thus I refute. Carr, T.
Thus the early gods. Garrett, G. P.
Thus were their faces. Ocampo, S.
Thy sting. Broderick, D.
Thylacine. Pascoe, B.
Ti-Moune. Gold, H.
Tibby Hyslop's dream. Hogg, J.
TIBET (CHINA) *See* China—Tibet
Tibetan time. Prose, F.
Tick. Oates, J. C.
The **tick** is full. Wooton, C.
The **ticket**. Foster, M.
The **ticket**. Morrison, J.
A **ticket** as long as your arm. Drake, R.
A **ticket** to America. Chasek, J.
A **ticket** to Odessa. Goff, I.
Tickits. Milenski, P.
Tickled to death. Brett, S.
Tidal air. Murphy, Y.
Tidal effects. McDevitt, J.
Tide pools. Adams, A.
TIDES
  Frahm, L. On the turn
Tidewatcher. Kaplan, D. M.
The **tidings** brought to Sylvie. Mairowitz, D.
  Z.
The **tidings** of Bethlehem. Böll, H.
Tidmarsh, W. M.
  Bronze
    Venomous tales of villainy and
      vengeance; ed. by H. Hoke
Tieck, Johann Ludwig
  Wake not the dead [Variant title: The
    bride of the grave]
    Masterpieces of terror and the super-
      natural; ed. by M. Kaye and S. Kaye
Tied in knots. Wild, M.
Tiempo, Edith
  Un bel di
    Short story international 69
Ties. Hogan, D.
Ties. Holleran, A.
The **tiger**. Li, F.-Y.
Tiger by the tail. Curtiss, U. R.
Tiger hunt. Jennings, J.
Tiger in the night. Lipsky, E.
Tiger, tiger. Pronzini, B.
TIGERS
  Anthony, P. Encounter
  Cain, J. M. The baby in the icebox

TIGERS—*Continued*
Cortázar, J. Bestiary
Dunsany, E. J. M. D. P., Baron. In a dim room
Kilworth, G. God's cold lips
King, S. Here there be tygers
King, S. The night of the tiger
Lee, T. Bright burning tiger
Li, F.-Y. The tiger
Narayan, R. K. A hero
Tamer, Z. Tigers on the tenth day
Telles, L. F. Tigrela
Tigers are better-looking. Rhys, J.
Tiger's eye. Hamilton, R. C.
Tigers in the wood. Kavaler, R.
Tigers on the tenth day. Tamer, Z.
The **tighten** up. Barry, L.
The **tightrope** walkers. Klíma, I.
Tigrela. Telles, L. F.
TIJUANA (MEXICO) *See* Mexico—Tijuana
'Til death do us part. Bloch, R.
Tilghman, Christopher
  Mary in the mountains
    Ploughshares 14 no2/3:153-65 '88
  Norfolk, 1969
    The Virginia Quarterly Review 62:237-52 Spr '86
Till death do not us part. Powell, T.
Till death do us part. Davis, D. S.
Till death us do part. Böll, H.
Till human voices wake us. Shiner, L.
Till September Petronella. Rhys, J.
Tillinghast, David
  The great fire
    The Virginia Quarterly Review 60:465-72 Summ '84
Tillman, Lynne
  Dead talk
    Between C & D; ed. by J. Rose and C. Texier
Tilton, Alice *See* Taylor, Phoebe Atwood, 1909-1976
Tilton, Lois
  In the service of evil
    Bringing down the moon; ed. by J. Anderson
TIME
    See also Clocks and watches
  Amis, M. The time disease
  Anderson, P. The discovery of the past
  Anderson, P. Flight to forever
  Asimov, I. The Immortal Bard
  Asimov, I. What if . . .
  Ballard, J. G. News from the sun
  Brown, G. M. A winter legend
  Buzzati, D. The time machine
  Eliade, M. Youth without youth
  Ellison, H. Count the clock that tells the time
  Farmer, P. J. Sail on! Sail on!
  Finney, J. Second chance
  Fitzgerald, M. J. Experiment with time
  Hofstadter, D. R. The tale of Happiton

  Hoover, J. Proteus
  Kilworth, G. Lord of the dance
  Lovecraft, H. P. The shadow out of time
  Neville, K. The forest of Zil
  Silverberg, R. In entropy's jaws
  Stone, M. The Plasting Project
  Watson, I. The emir's clock
  Wells, H. G. The new accelerator
  Wilkerson, C. The man who watched the glaciers run
TIME, TRAVELS IN *See* Time travel
Time. Bates, H. E.
Time alone. Adams, A.
Time alone. Robison, J.
Time and again. Sanders, S. R.
Time and chance. Heideman, E. M.
Time and fear and somehow love. Abbott, L. K.
TIME AND SPACE *See* Space and time
The **time** and the place. Maḥfūẓ, N.
A **time** change. Kalpakian, L.
Time considered as a helix of semi-precious stones. Delany, S. R.
The **time** disease. Amis, M.
Time everlasting. Lundwall, S. J.
Time for a change. Schell, J.
Time for chapel. Whitaker, M.
A **time** for terror. Longyear, B. B.
The **time** I died. Carlson, R.
Time in Santa Fe. Adams, A.
Time in the valley. Le Guin, U. K.
Time is money. Busch, F.
The **time** is not yet ripe. Zhang Jie
Time Lucy went. Warren, J.
The **time** machine. Buzzati, D.
The **Time Machine**. Wells, H. G.
TIME MACHINES
  Anderson, P. Wildcat
  Asimov, I. The dead past
  Asimov, I. A loint of paw
  Bloch, R. Crime machine
  Bradbury, R. The Toynbee convector
  Bryant, E. Jade Blue
  Davidson, A. Full chicken richness
  Davies, D. A quiet man
  Finney, J. Such interesting neighbors
  Miller, J. J. Ouroboros
  Wells, H. G. The Time Machine
Time of bitter children. Garrett, G. P.
A **time** of disbelief. Pak, K.-N.
The **time** of friendship. Bowles, P.
A **time** of learning. West, J.
Time of passage. Ballard, J. G.
The **time** of the cosmonauts. Berger, J.
The **time** of the wolves. Muller, M.
Time out of mind. Godfrey, P.
Time safari. Drake, D.
Time spent in reconnaissance. Allbeury, T.
The **time**, the place, the loved one. Welch, S.
Time to go. Dixon, S.
Time to laugh. Aiken, J.
Time to laugh again. Franco, M.

A **time** to remember. Crossman, P. R.
A **time** to remember. Reach, J.

TIME TRAVEL
Aldiss, B. W. Poor little warrior!
Anderson, P. Delenda est
Anderson, P. The little monster
Anderson, P. The Nest
Anderson, P. Welcome
Anderson, P. Wildcat
Asimov, I. The end of eternity
Asimov, I. Obituary
Asimov, I. The winds of change
Bates, H. Alas, all thinking
Bear, G. Through road no whither
Benford, G. Valhalla
Bloch, R. The past master
Bloch, R. Sabbatical
Bloch, R. A snitch in time
Bloch, R. Time wounds all heels
Bloch, R. A toy for Juliette
Boucher, A. Barrier
Boucher, A. Elsewhen
Bradbury, R. A touch of petulance
Bradley, M. Z. Exiles of tomorrow
Breuer, M. J. The gostak and the doshes
Bryant, E. Prairie sun
Budrys, A. Never meet again
Bulychev, K. The empty house
Burrage, A. M. Between the minute and the hour
Chandler, A. B. Kelly country
Cowper, R. The Hertford Manuscript
De Camp, L. S. The wheels of if
De Camp, L. S., and Pratt, F. The green magician
Dick, P. K. Breakfast at twilight
Dick, P. K. A little something for us tempunauts
Dick, P. K. Service call
Drake, D. Time safari
Duane, D. Uptown local
Dunn, J. R. Long knives
Eisenstein, P. In the Western tradition
Ellison, H. Escapegoat
Ellison, H. The prowler in the city at the edge of the world
Ellison, H. Quicktime
Finney, J. The face in the photo
Finney, J. The third level
Flynn, M. The forest of time
Gansovsky, S. Vincent Van Gogh
Garrett, R. Frost and thunder
Gilbert, W. S. Foggerty's fairy
Haldeman, J. W. No future in it
Hale, E. E. Hands off
Harris, M. Polo's trip
Howard, V. E. The midnight voyage of the Seagull
Hudec, G. The ring
Jablokov, A. At the cross-time jaunters' ball
Jeppson, J. O. The hotter flash
Jeppson, J. O. The time-warp trauma

Kilworth, G. Let's go to Golgotha!
Kornbluth, C. M. The little black bag
Lake, D. J. Re-deem the time
Laumer, K. The timesweepers
Lear, A. The adventure of the global traveler
Lee, R. B. Knight of shallows
Lee, W. M. A message from Charity
Leiber, F. Catch that zeppelin!
Leinster, M. Sidewise in time
MacDonald, J. D. Amphiskios
Malzberg, B. N. Johann Sebastian Brahms
Martin, G. R. R. Under siege
May, P. Resonance ritual
McCaffrey, A. Dragonrider
McCaffrey, A. A flock of geese
Moorcock, M. Elric at the end of time
Nolan, W. F. Of time and Kathy Benedict
Norton, A. The long night of waiting
Oliver, C. Transfusion
Pei, M. The bones of Charlemagne
Piper, H. B. Gunpowder god
Reed, K. Into the parlor
Richards, J. Deadtime
Richards, J. Mencken stuff
Robinson, K. S. Stone eggs
Russ, J. Bodies
Russ, J. The experimenter
Russell, E. F., and Johnson, L. T. Seeker of tomorrow
Ryan, A. I shall not leave England now
Sargent, P. If ever I should leave you
Schmidt, S. May the best man win
Shaw, B. Skirmish on a summer morning
Sheckley, R. The future lost
Sheckley, R. The store of the worlds
Shepard, L. Aymara
Shepard, L. The etheric transmitter
Shiner, L. Twilight time
Silverberg, R. The far side of the bell-shaped curve
Silverberg, R. Gianni
Silverberg, R. Homefaring
Silverberg, R. House of bones
Silverberg, R. Jennifer's lover
Silverberg, R. The man who floated in time
Silverberg, R. Many mansions
Silverberg, R. Ms. found in an abandoned time machine
Silverberg, R. Needle in a timestack
Silverberg, R. (Now + n, now - n)
Silverberg, R. Sailing to Byzantium
Silverberg, R. What we learned from this morning's newspaper
Silverberg, R. When we went to see the end of the world
St. Clair, M. The nuse man
Swanwick, M. The dragon line
Tiptree, J. Backward, turn backward
Tiptree, J. Houston, Houston, do you read?
Tiptree, J. The man who walked home

TIME TRAVEL—*Continued*
Twain, M. Time-travel contexts from A Connecticut Yankee in King Arthur's Court
Watson, I. Insight
Watson, I. When the timegate failed
White, T. Only yesterday
Whiteford, W. N. One way to tomorrow
Willis, C. Fire watch
Time-travel contexts from A Connecticut Yankee in King Arthur's Court. Twain, M.
The **time-warp** trauma. Jeppson, J. O.
A **time** with a future (Carmela). Mohr, N.
Time with children. Tallent, E.
Time wounds all heels. Bloch, R.
Timed exposure. Matheson, R. C.
Times. Beattie, A.
The **times** my father died. Amichai, Y.
Time's rub. Benford, G.
Timestop. Grzimek, M.
The **timesweepers**. Laumer, K.
Timoshenko. Crichton Smith, I.
Timperley, Rosemary, 1920-
Christmas meeting
Christmas ghosts; ed. by K. Cramer and D. G. Hartwell
Harry
Lost souls; ed. by J. Sullivan
Hell on both sides of the gate
Haunting women; ed. by A. Ryan
Tim's back home. Alderson, T.
Tin can. Bonner, M.
The **Tin** Can. Steele, M.
Tin container. Faik, S.
Tin of Tube Rose. Redding, S.
Tindall, Gillian
Faith
Encounter (London, England) 68:19-22 Mr '87
He who sows hope in the flesh
Winter's tales, new ser. v1
Tinker, Libby
The horse
Whispers V
Tinker tale. Virgo, S.
TINKERS
Nestor, T. G. The last fling
Steinbeck, J. The chrysanthemums
Tinkham, Bill
Doppelganger
Stiller's pond; ed. by J. Agee; R. Blakely and S. Welch
The **tins**. Cowan, P.
Tinsel. Spence, A.
Tinsley, Molly Best
Looking for love again
Redbook 163:73-4+ S '84
Our first year together
Redbook 167:32+ Je '86
Welcome advance
Prairie Schooner 62:67-76 Fall '88

Tinsley, Theodore
Riddle in silk
Hard-boiled dames; ed. by B. A. Drew
Tiny. Mrożek, S.
The **tiny** baby. Strand, M.
Tippens, Elizabeth
Good-bye, Columbus Avenue
Mademoiselle 94:100+ Je '88
Tiptree, James, 1916-1987
All this and heaven too
Tiptree, J. Crown of stars
Backward, turn backward
Synergy v2
Tiptree, J. Crown of stars
Beam us home
Tiptree, J. Byte beautiful
Beyond the dead reef
The Year's best science fiction, first annual collection
Come live with me
Tiptree, J. Crown of stars
The Earth doth like a snake renew
Tiptree, J. Crown of stars
Excursion fare
Tiptree, J. Byte beautiful
The girl who was plugged in
The Other woman; ed. by S. Koppelman
Houston, Houston, do you read?
The Hugo winners v4
Worlds apart; ed. by C. Decarnin; E. Garber and L. Paleo
I'll be waiting for you when the swimming pool is empty
Tiptree, J. Byte beautiful
In midst of life
Tiptree, J. Crown of stars
Last night and every night
Tiptree, J. Crown of stars
Love is the plan the plan is death
Great science fiction; ed. by I. Asimov; M. H. Greenberg and C. G. Waugh
Tiptree, J. Byte beautiful
The man who walked home
Amazing stories: 60 years of the best science fiction
Tiptree, J. Byte beautiful
Morality meat
Tiptree, J. Crown of stars
The only neat thing to do
The Year's best science fiction, third annual collection
Our resident djinn
Tiptree, J. Crown of stars
The peacefulness of Vivyan
Tiptree, J. Byte beautiful
Second going
Tiptree, J. Crown of stars
Universe 17
With delicate mad hands
Tiptree, J. Byte beautiful
The women men don't see
Between mothers & daughters; ed. by S. Koppelman

Tiptree, James, 1916-1987—*Continued*
Yanqui Doodle
  Tiptree, J. Crown of stars
Your faces, o my sisters! Your faces filled
  of light!
  Tiptree, J. Byte beautiful
Tiresome company. Ferron, J.
Tiritilli, Patricia
The winner's touch
  'Teen 31:26+ My '87
Los **tisicos**. Ponce, M. H.
Tissue ablation and variant regeneration: a
  case report. Blumlein, M.
Titan falling. Benford, G.
TITANIC (STEAMSHIP)
Ellison, H. Escapegoat
Titcher, Margot
No fairies at the bottom of the garden
  Short story international 44
Someone-else
  Short story international 62
The **Tithonian** Factor. Cowper, R.
Titina. Fink, I.
Titwillow. Harris, M.
Tlön, Uqbar, Orbis Tertius. Borges, J. L.
To be continued. Silverberg, R.
To be read at dusk. Dickens, C.
To build a fire. London, J.
To Calabria. Morris, W.
To catch a big one. Alter, R. E.
To catch a thief. Hornung, E. W.
To count the ways. O'Connor, K.
To dance. Peterson, M.
To die from. Schulman, H.
To eat or not to eat. Dadswell, M.
To everything there is a season. MacLeod,
  A.
To fill. Moore, L.
To Francie, with love. Girion, B.
To grow into a man. Brender à Brandis, M.
To have and to hold. Dawson, C.
To have and to hold. Sandberg, P. L.
To Jackie with all our heart. Ramírez, S.
To keep the oath. Bradley, M. Z.
To Leningrad in winter. Schwartz, S.
To look at the Queen. Kinsella, W. P.
To Lukas. Sandel, C.
To mark the times we had. Malzberg, B. N.
To market, to market. Stuart, J.
To marry Medusa. See Sturgeon, T. Medusa
To Mrs. Starkey. Loukakis, A.
To pass him out. Mills, W.
To rebuild the eyrie. Miller, S.
To remain a ripple people. Barber, K.
To room nineteen. Lessing, D. M.
To serve the master. Dick, P. K.
To skin a cat. McGuane, T.
To sleep, perchance to dream. Dibble, J. B.
To supper in the morning and to bed at
  noon. Harvor, E.
To take a thief. Cherryh, C. J.
To the castle. Horgan, P.
To the Chicago Abyss. Bradbury, R.

To the man on the trail. London, J.
To the Pump Room with Jane. Watson, I.
To the pure. Boyle, K.
To the rescue. Glimm, A.
To the torturor. Balfour, C.
To the unknown god. Moravia, A.
To touch a star. Bova, B.
To trap a demon. Mayhar, A.
To vault over the moon. Mondeschein, B.
The **toaster**. Anthony, P.
TOBACCO HABIT *See* Smoking
The **tobacco** shop. Maupassant, G. de
Tobermory. Saki
Tobey, Fred S.
You drive, dear
  Last laughs; ed. by G. Mcdonald
Tobin, Greg
The damned
  Westeryear; ed. by E. Gorman
Toby. Pilcher, R.
Today is a good day to die. Bell, M. S.
Today is Friday. Hemingway, E.
Today will be a quiet day. Hempel, A.
Today's children. Sholem Aleichem
The **toe**. Karr, P. A.
Together. Eldridge, M.
Together and apart. Woolf, V.
Together through thick and thin. Chung,
  L.-H.
Toiler. Michaels, L.
The **toilet**. Mhlope, G.
Toine. Maupassant, G. de
Tokai. Levinson, B.
TOKYO (JAPAN) *See* Japan—Tokyo
Tokyo, 1941. Woolrich, C.
Toland, Stewart
Ride a golden horse
  The Saturday Evening Post 256:66-8+ N
  '84

  The Saturday Evening Post 256:26+ D
  '84
**Tolkien, J. R. R. (John Ronald Reuel), 1892-
1973**
Riddles in the dark
  Masterpieces of terror and the super-
  natural; ed. by M. Kaye and S. Kaye
Tolkien, John Ronald Reuel *See* Tolkien, J.
  R. R. (John Ronald Reuel), 1892-1973
The **tolling** of a distant bell. Zhang Kang-
  kang, and Mei Jin
Tolstoy, Leo, graf, 1828-1910
God sees the truth but waits [Variant title:
  God sees the truth but is in no hurry
  to reveal it]
  Classic European short stories; ed. by R.
  Beum
  Mystery in the mainstream; ed. by B.
  Pronzini; M. H. Greenberg and B. N.
  Malzberg

About

Barthelme, D. At the Tolstoy Museum
Liben, M. The Tolstoy movie
The **Tolstoy** movie. Liben, M.

The **Tolstoy** quotation. Liben, M.
Tolstoy's head. Hofmann, G.
Tolstoy's son. Cullen, E. J.
Tom and Beauty. Havemann, E.
Tom Cariboo. Fréchette, L.
Tom cat. Jennings, G.
Tom Dick and Harry. Stewart, J. I. M.
Tom Poulton's joke. Gilbert, W. S.
Tom Thumb runs away. Tournier, M.
Tom Wolfe's my name. West, J.
Tomatoes. Prose, F.
Tomb with an arbor. Faik, S.
The **tombstone.** Bradbury, R.
Tombstone without an inscription. Kim, I.-S.
TOMBSTONES
  Brown, M. W. Good-bye, Cliff
  Finney, J. Hey, look at me!
Tomiko. Haylock, J.
Tomlinson, Gerald, 1933-
  Hizzoner's water supply
  Last laughs; ed. by G. Mcdonald
Tomlinson, H. M. (Henry Major), 1873-1958
  The derelict
  Short stories of the sea; ed. by G. C.
    Solley and E. Steinbaugh
Tomlinson, Henry Major See Tomlinson, H.
    M. (Henry Major), 1873-1958
Tommy. Wideman, J. E.
Tommy's Christmas. Little, J. R.
Tomorrow I die. Spillane, M.
Tomorrow you'll forget. Luban, M.
Tomorrow's children. Anderson, P.
Tomorrow's magic. Shyer, M. F.
Tomorrow's promise. Stewart, I.
The **Tomoshibi.** Ariyoshi, S.
Tom's burn. Travis, L.
Tom's thatch. Lamburn, N.
Toner, Gerald R.
  Benefit of the bargain
    The Saturday Evening Post 260:54-7+ D
    '88
  Caroling on command
    The Saturday Evening Post 259:42-5+ D
    '87
  The Christmas visitation
    The Saturday Evening Post 258:60-3+ D
    '86
Tong Enzheng
  The middle kingdom
  Tales from the planet Earth
The **tongueless** horror. Blassingame, W.
Tongues of flame. Brown, M. W.
Tongues of men and of angels. Goyen, W.
A **tonic.** Hartley, L. P.
Tonight is a favor to Holly. Hempel, A.
Toño. González, C. A.
El **tonto** del Barrio. Armas, J.
Too early spring. Benét, S. V.
Too good with a gun. Patten, L. B.
Too hep to be happy! Cooper, J. C.
Too hot. Bonnie, F.
Too long at the fair. Hoch, E. D.
Too many have lived. Hammett, D.

Too many trips to Heidelberg. Böll, H.
Too much electricity. Barich, B.
Too soon solos. Gray, P. W.
Too soon to die. Godwin, T.
Too tired for love. Heffernan, M. J.
Too young. O'Hara, J.
Tooker, Richard
  Zenith Rand, planet vigilante
  Sensuous science fiction from the weird
    and spicy pulps; ed. by S. Jaffery
Toole, John Kennedy, 1937-1969
  A confederacy of dunces [excerpt]
  A Collection of classic Southern humor;
    ed. by G. W. Koon
Toole, Wyc
  A matter of experience
  Alfred Hitchcock's Mortal errors
Toomer, Jean, 1894-1967
  Becky
  The Norton book of American short
    stories
Tooth fairy. Carr, C.
Top hat. Coover, R.
Top of the class. Pritchard, S.
Top secret. Russell, E. F.
Topical subject. Anderman, J.
Topolino. Eicher, T.
Torn flesh. Yi, H.-C.
Tornado weather. Packard, C.
TORNADOES
  Floyd, P. L. The voice in the whirlwind
  Franzen, B. What the twister did
  Hauptman, W. Stormchaser
  Kauffman, J. Places in the world a woman
    could walk
TORONTO (ONT.) See Canada—Toronto
The **torrent.** Hébert, A.
Torres, Antônio
  Growing pains
    The Literary Review (Madison, N.J.)
    27:492-5 Summ '84
Torridge. Trevor, W.
TORSVAN, TRAVEN See Traven, B.
TORTURE
  Anthony, P. On the uses of torture
  Balfour, C. To the torturor
  Ellison, H. Basilisk
  Gorky, M. Red
  Maloney, J. J. The Mid-City Meat Com-
    pany
  Oates, J. C. Testimony
  Poe, E. A. The pit and the pendulum
  Smith, C. A. The isle of the torturers
  Yourcenar, M. Marko's smile
Total immersion. Goodman, A.
TOTALITARIANISM
    See also Communism; Dictators;
    Fascism; National socialism
  Aksenov, V. P. Destruction of Pompeii (a
    story for Bella)
  Aksenov, V. P. Rendezvous
  Anderman, J. Day of mist and cloud
  Anderman, J. Return visit

TOTALITARIANISM—_Continued_
Benét, S. V. A judgment in the mountains
Böll, H. My sad face
Haley, R. The cosmetic factory
Kaikō, T. The crushed pellet
Lengyel, P. Rising sun; or, The celebration of heartfelt joy
Moyano, D. The story of the green falcon and the marvelous flute
Mrożek, S. A drummer's adventure
Salama, F. Friends' eyes
Sturgeon, T. The touch of your hand
Upward, E. The night walk
Totalled. McGinn, C.
Totally nude live girls. Donohue, G.
Toti, Gianni
The translator
The Literary Review (Madison, N.J.) 28:308 Wint '85
The **Tou** lass. Pu, S.-L.
Touch and go: a midshipman's story. Doyle, Sir A. C.
A **touch** of petulance. Bradbury, R.
A **touch** of tenderness. Wallace, M. C.
A **touch** of the flu. Oates, J. C.
The **touch** of the monkey god. Glazer, D.
The **touch** of your hand. Sturgeon, T.
Touchett's party. Welch, D.
Touching the buffalo. Malterre, E.
The **touchstone**. Wharton, E.
Tough. Lutz, J.
Tough as a man. Nugent, B.
A **tough** life. Schwartz, S.
Tough love. Allen, P. G.
Tough men. O'Brien, E.
The **tour** of the sleeping steamboat. Matthews, J.
Touring. Dozois, G. R., and others
Tourist. Eldridge, M.
Tourist. Hensley, J. L.
TOURIST TRADE
    See also Travel agents
Aickman, R. The Cicerones
Barich, B. October
Barker, C. Rawhead Rex
Berriault, G. The island of Ven
Bonnie, F. The bulk tour
Colette. The rendezvous
Cowper, R. Incident at Huacaloc
Drake, D. Time safari
Dunn, D. The bagpiping people
Faik, S. By the fountain
Grenville, K. Having a wonderful time
Grenville, K. The space between
Hall, J. B. My work in California
Haylock, J. Traveling towards Boris
Ingalls, R. Early morning sightseer
Ingalls, R. Something to write home about
Ingalis, R. St. George and the nightclub
Izgü, M. The attack by yoghurt
Kinsella, W. P. Real Indians
Matthews, J. The tour of the sleeping steamboat

Matthiessen, P. On the River Styx
Morris, W. In another country
Niven, L. Flare time
Onopa, R. The man who swam through jellyfish, through men-of-war
Paley, G. Somewhere else
Regent, P. Stepan
Sheil, G. Of gumleaves and clove-scented cigarettes
Shukshin, V. M. The postscript
Tyre, N. Beyond the wall
TOURISTS _See_ Tourist trade
Tournier, Michel
The Adam family
    Tournier, M. The fetishist
Amandine; or, The two gardens
    Tournier, M. The fetishist
Blandine, or The father's visit
    Partisan Review 54:247-54 Spr '87
Death and the maiden
    The Art of the tale; ed. by D. Halpern
    Tournier, M. The fetishist
The end of Robinson Crusoe
    Tournier, M. The fetishist
The fetishist
    Tournier, M. The fetishist
Jesu, Joy of Man's Desiring
    Tournier, M. The fetishist
The Lily of the Valley rest area
    Tournier, M. The fetishist
Mother Christmas
    Tournier, M. The fetishist
The music of the spheres
    Winter's tales, new ser. v2
Prikli
    Tournier, M. The fetishist
The red dwarf
    Tournier, M. The fetishist
Tom Thumb runs away
    Tournier, M. The fetishist
Tristan Vox
    Tournier, M. The fetishist
Veronica's shrouds
    Tournier, M. The fetishist
The Woodcock
    Tournier, M. The fetishist
Toussaint. Turner, R. F.
La Toussaint (All Saints' Day, November 1). Stead, C.
Tout Montparnasse and a lady. Rhys, J.
Touzalin, Robert
Mudpuppies
    L. Ron Hubbard presents Writers of the future v2
Toward a distant train. Matthews, J.
Toward winter. Kawabata, Y.
The **tower**. Laski, M.
Tower of birds. Korabelnikov, O.
Tower of ice. Zelazny, R.
Tower of silence. Richardson, M.
TOWERS
Laski, M. The tower
Poe, E. A. The devil in the belfry

A **town** like Kansas. Vreuls, D.
Town lovers. Gordimer, N.
Town smokes. Benedict, P.
Town wanted. Brown, F.
Towne, Stuart See Rawson, Clayton, 1906-1971
Townies. Dubus, A.
Toy. Pronzini, B.
A **toy** for Juliette. Bloch, R.
The **toy** killer. Williamson, B.
Toy Paris. Gingher, M.
The **toymaker's** snuffbox. Norton, A.
The **Toynbee** convector. Bradbury, R.
Toyne, Marcus
Reprieve
Encounter (London, England) 66:9-11 Ap '86
TOYS
See also Teddy bears
Aickman, R. The inner room
Bradley, M. Z. Bird of prey
Bunch, D. R. A small miracle of fishhooks and straight pins
Crane, S. An ominous baby
Dick, P. K. The little movement
Dick, P. K. War game
King, S. The monkey
Mazel, D. Friends
Mazel, D. The merry-go-round
Millhauser, S. August Eschenburg
Powell, J. Death in the Christmas hour
Pronzini, B. Toy
Shannon, D. Rannysore
Williamson, B. The toy killer
Wolfe, G. War beneath the tree
The **toys.** Murphy, Y.
The **toys** of death. Cole, G. D. H., and Cole, M.
Traba, Marta
All in a lifetime
Women's fiction from Latin America; ed. by E. P. Garfield
Conformity
Women's fiction from Latin America; ed. by E. P. Garfield
Mothers and shadows [excerpt]
Women's fiction from Latin America; ed. by E. P. Garfield
Traceleen at dawn. Gilchrist, E.
Traceleen, she's still talking. Gilchrist, E.
Traceleen's diary. Gilchrist, E.
Traceleen's telling a story called "A bad year". Gilchrist, E.
Traces. Fink, I.
TRACK (ATHLETICS)
Dennison, G. A tale of Pierrot
Gilchrist, E. Revenge
The **track.** McDonald, W.
The **track.** Oates, J. C.
TRACKLESS TROLLEYS See Trolley buses
Tracks to the cold country. Leaton, A.
Tractatus cantatus. Berry, R. M.
The **tractor.** Cowan, P.

TRACTORS
Waldrop, H. Mary Margaret Road-Grader
Tracy, Don
The squirrel who was scared
The Saturday Evening Post 258:60-3+ My/Je '86
Tracy, Honor
A rest and a change
The Best of Irish wit and wisdom; ed. by J. McCarthy
Tracy, Jack, 1945-
Spirit weather
Tales from Ellery Queen's Mystery Magazine: short stories for young adults
The **trade.** Gault, C.
The **trade-off.** Trott, S.
TRADERS
Aldiss, B. W. Igur and the mountain
Böll, H. A case for Kop
Haggard, H. R. Black heart and white heart
Le Guin, U. K. The trouble with the cotton people
Martin, G. R. R. Nor the many-colored fires of a star ring
Schwob, M. The amber-trader
The **tradesman.** King, F. H.
The **tradesman's** return. Hemingway, E.
TRADING POSTS
Conrad, J. An outpost of progress
A **tradition** of eighteen hundred and four. Hardy, T.
Traffic accident. Risse, H.
TRAFFIC ACCIDENTS
See also Hit-and-run drivers
Abbott, K. The ghost of the senior banquet
Abbott, L. K. The final proof of fate and circumstance
Bates, H. E. Death of a huntsman
Baxter, C. Saul and Patsy are getting comfortable in Michigan
Bedard, B. Sheer Energy
Bloch, R. Ego trip
Bradbury, R. The crowd
Brady, M. The field is full of daisies and I'm afraid to pass
Busch, F. Dog song
Carver, R. A small, good thing
Chon, K.-Y. Driver's assistant
Connolly, L. C. Echoes
Conroy, F. Car games
Conroy, J. Uncle Ollie on trial
Counselman, M. E. Night court
Cowan, P. The corner
Deaver, P. F. The valence of common ions
Ferron, J. Armageddon
Finger, A. Cars
Grzimek, M. Timestop
Hospital, J. T. Some have called thee mighty and dreadful

TRAFFIC ACCIDENTS—*Continued*
Humphrey, W. A good Indian
Jakes, J. I still see Sally
Jolley, E. Adam's bride
Jolley, E. The performance
King, S. The man who would not shake hands
Leavitt, D. Aliens
Long, D. Home fires
Matheson, R. C. Unknown drives
Matheson, R. C. Vampire
Michaelson, L. W. The flying Dutchman
Morris, W. Country music
Murphy, Y. Tidal air
Nolan, W. F. The Yard
Oates, J. C. Ruth
O'Connor, F. A good man is hard to find
Ptacek, K. Dead possums
Ryan, A. Memory and desire
Schwartz, S. Navajo Café
St. Pierre, P. H. Sarah's copper
Strachan, T. A father's love
Taher, B. Advice from a sensible young man
Thomas, T. L. Test
Tindall, G. He who sows hope in the flesh
Walters, A. L. Going home
Warren, J. Crash
Wilner, H. Lead
Yarbro, C. Q. Lapses

TRAFFIC ENGINEERING
Cortázar, J. The southern thruway
The **tragedians**. Doyle, Sir A. C.
A **tragedy**. Finger, A.
The **tragedy** at Marsdon Manor. Christie, A.
Tragedy of a handkerchief. Innes, M.
The **tragedy** of Bob Ford. Taylor, R.
The **tragedy** of Jesse James. See Taylor, R. The tragedy of Bob Ford
Tragic lives. Gerber, M. J.
The **trail** to the ledge. Shaw, J. B.

TRAILER PARKS
Brady, M. Grinning underneath
Claiborne, S. Final words
Potter, N. A. J. A thin place

TRAILERPARKS *See* Trailer parks

Train, Arthur Cheney, 1875-1945
A salmon for the White House
   The Saturday Evening Post 259:64-8+ My/Je '87
   The Saturday Evening Post 259:36+ Jl/Ag '87
The Viking's daughter
   The Best Maine stories; ed. by S. Phippen; C. Waugh and M. Greenberg
The **train**. See Böll, H. The train was on time
The **train**. Cherry, K.
Train. Oates, J. C.
The **train**. O'Connor, F.
Train 081. Schwob, M.
The **train** and the city. Wolfe, T.
The **train** at eleven. Eid, H.

A **train** of gardens—Part I: Ireneus Fludd. McCormack, E. P.
A **train** of gardens—Part II: the machine. McCormack, E. P.
TRAIN TRAVEL *See* Railroads—Travel
A **train** trip. Hemingway, E.
The **train** was on time. Böll, H.
Training for Alaska. Roberts, N.
TRAINS *See* Railroads—Trains
The **trains**. Aickman, R.
Trains. Stead, C.
Trains not taken. Lansdale, J. R.
The **traitor**. Lish, G.
The **traitor**. Maugham, W. S.
TRAITORS *See* Treason
TRAMPS *See* Homeless
Transactions in a foreign currency. Eisenberg, D.
Transatlantic passage. Blue, A.
TRANSCENDENTALISM
   See also Idealism
The **transcript**. Lin Jinlan
Transcript: Mercury program. Herbert, F.
Transfer. Asscher-Pinkhof, C.
The **transfer**. Blackwood, A.
The **transfer**. Bryant, E.
Transfer. Robison, J.
The **transformation**. Markham, B.
The **transformation**. Piñera, V.
The **transformation**. Rothman, C.
The **transformation**. Shelley, M. W.
Transfusion. Oliver, C.
Transients. Scholz, C.
Transit. Conroy, F.
Transit bed. Calvino, I.
Transit of earth. Clarke, A. C.
Translation. Blaise, C.
Translations. Podulka, F.
The **translator**. Toti, G.
TRANSLATORS
   Ghose, Z. A translator's fiction
   Herman, M. Auslander
A **translator's** fiction. Ghose, Z.
TRANSMIGRATION
   See also Reincarnation
   Bloch, R. The movie people
   Chin, M. L. Catmagic
   Lee, T. A day in the skin; or, The century we were out of them
   Li, F.-Y. The carp
   Michaelson, L. W. Phocian
   Mitchell, E. P. The devilish rat
   Poe, E. A. Morella
   Pu, S.-L. The cricket
   Shirley, J. Triggering
   Tessier, T. Food
   Wells, H. G. The new Faust
   Wells, H. G. The story of the late Mr. Elvesham
The **transplant**. Ardizzone, T.
TRANSPLANTATION OF ORGANS, TISSUES, ETC.
   Apple, M. Free agents

TRANSPLANTATION OF ORGANS, TIS-SUES, ETC.—Continued

Ballantyne, S. Life on earth
Bird, C. Cherries jubilee; or, Whichever way you look at it
Gloss, M. Interlocking pieces
Marlowe, D. J. The donor
Matheson, R. C. Conversation piece
Nagibin, ĪŪ. M. Somebody else's heart
Silverberg, R. Caught in the organ draft
Transport night. Asscher-Pinkhof, C.

TRANSPORTATION

See also Traffic engineering
Niven, L. Flash crowd

TRANSSEXUALS

Gold, H. Blind, blind date
Hamilton, D. The alteration
Ingalls, R. Blessed art thou
Regent, P. Great Pan is dead!
Symons, J. Has anybody here seen me?
Varley, J. Options
Wagner, K. E. Lacunae

TRANSVESTISM

Apollinaire, G. The meeting at the mixed club
Fitzgerald, M. J. Bachelor life
Jasmin, C. Lulu the tailor
McCann, R. My mother's clothes: the school of beauty and shame
McCormack, E. P. Edward and Georgina
Mordden, E. Interview with the drag queen
Parr, W. Street star
Rendell, R. The new girl friend
The trap. Evarts, H. G.
The trap. Hsiu, H.
The trap. Pirandello, L.
The trap. Singer, I. B.
The trap. Tuohy, F.
The trap. Whitehead, H. S. C.
A trap to catch a cracksman. Hornung, E. W.
Trapdoor. Bradbury, R.
A Trapp family Christmas. Heath, A. B.

TRAPPERS AND TRAPPING

Bail, M. The silence
Campbell, W. B. Death is always part of dinner
Kamminga, A. Moleman
Prichard, K. S. The rabbit trapper's wife
TRAPPING See Trappers and trapping
Trash man. Silvis, R.
Il tratto di Apelle. See Pasternak, B. L. The Apelles mark
Trave. Meier, S.

TRAVEL

Bloy, L. The captives of Longjumeau
Bond, N. Pilgrimage
Campbell, R. Seeing the world
Choe, I.-H. The end of the highway
Colette. The halt
Colette. Journey's end
Cullen, E. J. Post cards

Curley, D. Wild geese
Doubiago, S. Chappaquiddick
Finger, A. Cross-country
Fisher, M. F. K. The oldest man
Hall, T. T. Another dark and stormy night
Hemingway, E. Che ti dice la patria?
Klass, P. How big the world is
Mullen, R. At the beach
Potter, N. A. J. The guests
Potter, N. A. J. The woman who would not stay home
Smith, R. The princess, the Boeing, and the hot pastrami sandwich
Sontag, S. Unguided tour
Trollope, A. Returning home
Van de Wetering, J. The yoga yo-yo
Warner, S. T. I met a lady
Warner, S. T. The sea is always the same
Warner, S. T. A view of Exmoor
Travel. Miller, S.

TRAVEL AGENTS

Finney, J. Of missing persons
Hospital, J. T. The Dominican season
A travel piece. Atwood, M.
The traveler. Hawkes, J.

TRAVELERS

See also Visitors, Foreign
Aksenov, V. P. Surplussed barrelware
Barr, J. G. John Bealle's accident—or, How the widow Dudu treated insanity
Bates, H. E. Summer in Salandar
Bedard, B. South Dakota samaritans
Berdnyk, O. The apostle of immortality, a tale of the unprecedented
Berdnyk, O. A journey to the antiworld
Birtha, B. In the deep heart's core
Bissoondath, N. Continental drift
Bradbury, R. One night in your life
Broun, H. Development
Carver, W. With voice of joy and praise
Clark, M. A democrat on the Ganges
Clift, C. Three old men of Lerici
Conley, R. J. The Mexican tattoo
Cowan, P. Collector
Dantin, L. You're coughing?
Davenport, G. Fifty-seven views of Fujiyama
Davidson, A. Great is Diana
Davie, E. Couchettes
Davie, E. A traveller's room
Eid, H. The train at eleven
Faik, S. Hotel Joy
Faik, S. In search of a story
Fleming, B. The bookman's tale
Ford, R. Empire
Gifkins, M. Matching the blue
Grin, A. The arm
Grin, A. The long journey
Gusewelle, C. W. Horst Wessel
Harris, M. The linguist
Harris, M. The martyred poet
Harris, M. The orphan bassoonist
Harris, M. Polo's trip

TRAVELERS—*Continued*
Hawkes, J. The traveler
Haylock, J. Traveling towards Boris
Hwang, S.-Y. The road to Samp'o
Jolley, E. The libation
Jolley, E. The long distant lecture
Just, W. S. I'm worried about you
Kim, C.-Y. The moon-welcoming flower
Kusenberg, K. Odd tippling
Leavitt, D. Ayor
Lewitt, M. All the storms and sun-sets
London, J. Travelling
Lurie, M. Africa wall
Lurie, M. Bannister
Lurie, M. The day the bottom fell out of Yugoslavia
Lurie, M. A fool in winter
Lurie, M. French toothpaste
Lurie, M. Home is
Lurie, M. A red fox, a Polish lady, a Russian samovar
Mansfield, K. The little governess
McCourt, J. I go back to the mais oui
Nayman, M. The house on Lafayette Street
O, Y.-G. Two travelers
Phillips, J. A. Fast lanes
Raphael, F. Cheap day
Revard, C. Report to the nation: claiming Europe
Ríos, A. The child
Rooke, L. The only daughter
Roy, G. Ely! Ely! Ely!
Scholz, C. Transients
Smith, C. Crystal River
Thomas, J. Paco and I at sea
Vreuls, D. Meeting you
Vreuls, D. Returns
Wells, H. G. A misunderstood artist
Williams, J. The skater
Wilson, B. Looking for the Golden Gate
Traveler's advisory. McKinley, J.
The **traveler's** story. Maupassant, G. de
A **traveler's** tale. Maupassant, G. de
A **traveler's** tale. Shepard, L.
Travelin man. Matthiessen, P.
Traveling. Peterson, M.
The **traveling** companion. Andersen, H. C.
The **traveling** Crag. Sturgeon, T.
Traveling light. Burnett, W. R.
Traveling towards Boris. Haylock, J.
A **traveller's** room. Davie, E.
Travelling. London, J.
The **travelling** entertainer. Jolley, E.
The **travelling** grave. Hartley, L. P.
Travels in the interior. Sanders, S. R.
TRAVELS IN TIME *See* Time travel
Travels with my father. Fox, P.
TRAVEN, B.
About
Anaya, R. A. B. Traven is alive and well in Cuernavaca
Traverso, Dino Buzzati *See* Buzzati, Dino, 1906-1972

Travis, Lori
Tom's burn
Stories and poems from close to home; ed. by F. Salas
Treading in the afterglow. Reed, R.
Treadway, Jessica
And give you peace
The Hudson Review 37:431-42 Aut '84
Frozen
The Hudson Review 39:435-48 Aut '86
TREASON
See also Defectors; Spies
Abe, K. The dream soldier
Barrett, W. E. The destroyer
Benét, S. V. A judgment in the mountains
Chon, K.-Y. Kapitan Lee
Garrett, R. The highest treason
Lee, T. A lynx with lions
MacDonald, J. D. Betrayed
Maugham, W. S. The traitor
Treason of the blood. Bradley, M. Z.
Treasure. Sayles, J.
The **treasure** in the forest. Wells, H. G.
The **treasure** of Jack the Ripper. Hoch, E. D.
The **Treasure** of Pachacamac. Holding, J.
TREASURE-TROVE *See* Buried treasure
Treat, Lawrence
Give the devil his due
Crime of my life; ed. by B. Garfield
H as in homicide
Great modern police stories; ed. by B. Pronzini and M. H. Greenberg
Suburban tigress
Hitchcock in prime time; ed. by F. M. Nevins and M. H. Greenberg
Who's innocent?
Alfred Hitchcock's Crimewatch
TREATIES
Kinsella, W. P. Beef
Trebelo, John
La Cueva Del Círculo Sin Fin
Bringing down the moon; ed. by J. Anderson
The **tree**. Bombal, M. L.
The **tree**. Garro, E.
Tree. Hoyt, M. S.
The **tree**. King, F. H.
The **tree**. Pilcher, R.
The **tree**. Puppo, A.
The **tree**. Thomas, D.
A **tree**. A rock. A cloud. McCullers, C.
The **tree** beyond. Matthews, J.
Tree day. Delany, S.
The **tree** in the forest. Post, M. D., and Suter, J. F.
The **tree** of life. Swados, H.
The **tree** of pride. Chesterton, G. K.
The **tree** on Execution Hill. Estleman, L. D.
The **tree** on the mountain. Metzger, D.
TREES
See also Apple trees; Christmas trees; Willow trees

TREES—*Continued*
Blackwood, A. The willows
Canin, E. Emperor of the air
Chávez, D. Willow game
Chesterton, G. K. The tree of pride
Desnoues, L. Philéas
Hoffman, W. Cuttings
Huraniyyah, S. Another hard winter
King, F. H. The tree
Llywelyn, M. Me, tree
Mason, B. A. Bumblebees
Rendell, R. Fen Hall
St. Clair, M. The gardener
Stuart, J. Testimony of trees
Thompson, J. The birch tree
Tsutsui, Y. Standing woman
Trees at night. Frucht, A.
Trees can speak. Marshall, A.
Treitel, Jonathan
The flambé'd thing
Critical Quarterly 30:95-8 Spr '88
A merican
Critical Quarterly 30:106-10 Aut '88
Tremain, Rose
Autumn in Florida
Tremain, R. The Colonel's daughter, and other stories
The Colonel's daughter
Tremain, R. The Colonel's daughter, and other stories
Current account
Tremain, R. The Colonel's daughter, and other stories
Dinner for one
Tremain, R. The Colonel's daughter, and other stories
The garden of the Villa Mollini
Critical Quarterly 28:3-22 Wint '86
My love affair with James I
Tremain, R. The Colonel's daughter, and other stories
My wife is a white Russian
The Penguin book of modern British short stories
Tremain, R. The Colonel's daughter, and other stories
La plume de mon ami
Foreign exchange; ed. by J. Evans
A shooting season
Tremain, R. The Colonel's daughter, and other stories
The stately roller-coaster
Encounter (London, England) 62:8-10 Ja '84
Tremain, R. The Colonel's daughter, and other stories
Wedding night
Tremain, R. The Colonel's daughter, and other stories
Wildtrack
Winter's tales, new ser. v2
Will and Lou's boy
The Paris Review 27:13-19 Summ '85

Words with Marigold
Tremain, R. The Colonel's daughter, and other stories
Tremayne, Peter
The pooka
Shadows 8
The Samhain Feis
Halloween horrors; ed. by A. Ryan
Tavesher
Shadows 9
Tremblay, Michel, 1942-
The devil and the mushroom
The Oxford book of French-Canadian short stories
The eye of the idol
Invisible fictions; ed. by G. Hancock
The ghost of Don Carlos
Invisible fictions; ed. by G. Hancock
The hanged man
Invisible fictions; ed. by G. Hancock
The octagonal room
Invisible fictions; ed. by G. Hancock
The **tremendous** adventure of Major Brown.
Chesterton, G. K.
TRENTON (N.J.) *See* New Jersey—Trenton
TRESPASS
Garrett, G. P. Thus the early gods
Rooke, L. Break and enter
Trespass. Scofield, S.
Trespassers or guests? Halligan, M.
Trevanian
The sacking of Miss Plimsoll [Variant title: The secrets of Miss Plimsoll, private secretary]
The Editors' choice: new American stories v2
Treviño, Jesús Salvador
A very old man
Cuentos Chicanos; ed. by R. A. Anaya and A. Márquez
Trevor, William, 1928-
August Saturday
The New Yorker 64:34-44 My 9 '88
The ballroom of romance
The Treasury of English short stories; ed. by N. Sullivan
Beyond the pale
The Art of the tale; ed. by D. Halpern
Bodily secrets
Encounter (London, England) 62:3-11 My '84
Trevor, W. The news from Ireland & other stories
Cocktails at Doney's
The New Yorker 61:41-8 Ap 8 '85
Trevor, W. The news from Ireland & other stories
A complicated nature
The World of the short story; ed. by C. Fadiman
Death in Jerusalem
The Best of Irish wit and wisdom; ed. by J. McCarthy

Trevor, William, 1928——*Continued*
  Family sins
    The New Yorker 63:28-38 Jl 6 '87
  Frau Messinger
    The New Yorker 63:30-9 Mr 2 '87
  Her mother's daughter
    Trevor, W. The news from Ireland &
      other stories
  A husband's return
    Grand Street 7:56-70 Summ '88
  Kathleen's field
    The New Yorker 62:36-45 My 12 '86
  Lunch in winter
    Trevor, W. The news from Ireland &
      other stories
  A meeting in middle age
    The Penguin book of modern British
      short stories
  Music
    Encounter (London, England) 65:3-10 Je
      '85
    Trevor, W. The news from Ireland &
      other stories
  The news from Ireland
    The New Yorker 62:44-52+ Mr 10 '86
    Trevor, W. The news from Ireland &
      other stories
  On the Zattere
    The New Yorker 60:44-52 S 10 '84
    Trevor, W. The news from Ireland &
      other stories
  The property of Colette Nervi
    Trevor, W. The news from Ireland &
      other stories
  Running away
    The Atlantic 253:116-20+ Ap '84
    Trevor, W. The news from Ireland &
      other stories
  The third party
    The New Yorker 62:35-44 Ap 14 '86
  Torridge
    Dark arrows; ed. by A. Manguel
  A trinity
    The New Yorker 63:38-48 My 11 '87
  Two more gallants
    Trevor, W. The news from Ireland &
      other stories
  Virgins
    The New Yorker 61:38-50 Mr 4 '85
    Trevor, W. The news from Ireland &
      other stories
  The wedding in the garden
    The New Yorker 61:41-7 Je 10 '85
    Trevor, W. The news from Ireland &
      other stories
Trial. Hensley, J. L.
The **trial**. Mrożek, S.
Trial by fire. Whitman, S.
The **trial**, execution, and burial of Homer
  Phelps. Crane, S.
The **trial** for murder. Dickens, C.
The **trial** of the small black woman. Kassem,
  A.-H.

Trial of the Virgin. Valenzuela, L.
Trial run. Jacobsen, J.
TRIALS
        See also War crime trials; Witnesses
Aćin-Kosta, M. Spring flower
Apple, M. Free agents
Archer, J. The perfect murder
Bennett, L. The convert
Cho, S.-H. The bony-fish that came into
  my net
Clarke, A. C. Moving spirit
Conroy, J. Uncle Ollie on trial
Crane, S. An eloquence of grief
De la Torre, L. Milady bigamy
Dickens, C. The trial for murder
Edwards, H. S. His defense
El Makk, A. The case
Franklin, B. The speech of Polly Baker
Frazee, S. Due process
Gilbert, W. S. My maiden brief
Greene, G. The case for the defence
Hensley, J. L. The profession
Hensley, J. L. Trial
Hensley, J. L. Whistler
Hurston, Z. N. Herod on trial
Jones, J. Superbity
Koenig, J. A perfect gentleman
Le Fanu, J. S. Mr. Justice Harbottle
Lynch, L. At a bar III: Sally the bartender
  goes on jury duty
Masur, H. Q. The $2,000,000 defense
Maupassant, G. de. The assassin
Maupassant, G. de. Hippolyte's claim
Maupassant, G. de. The hole
Maupassant, G. de. In the court room
Maupassant, G. de. Rosalie Prudent
McCloy, H. The other side of the curtain
Mortimer, J. C. Rumpole and the age for
  retirement
Mortimer, J. C. Rumpole and the alterna-
  tive society
Mortimer, J. C. Rumpole and the blind
  tasting
Mortimer, J. C. Rumpole and the boat
  people
Mortimer, J. C. Rumpole and the case of
  identity
Mortimer, J. C. Rumpole and the confes-
  sion of guilt
Mortimer, J. C. Rumpole and the course
  of true love
Mortimer, J. C. Rumpole and the dear
  departed
Mortimer, J. C. Rumpole and the expert
  witness
Mortimer, J. C. Rumpole and the fascist
  beast
Mortimer, J. C. Rumpole and the female
  of the species
Mortimer, J. C. Rumpole and the gentle
  art of blackmail
Mortimer, J. C. Rumpole and the genuine
  article

TRIALS—*Continued*

Mortimer, J. C. Rumpole and the golden thread

Mortimer, J. C. Rumpole and the heavy brigade

Mortimer, J. C. Rumpole and the Honourable Member

Mortimer, J. C. Rumpole and the last resort

Mortimer, J. C. Rumpole and the learned friends

Mortimer, J. C. Rumpole and the Man of God

Mortimer, J. C. Rumpole and the married lady

Mortimer, J. C. Rumpole and the official secret

Mortimer, J. C. Rumpole and the old boy net

Mortimer, J. C. Rumpole and the old, old story

Mortimer, J. C. Rumpole and the rotten apple

Mortimer, J. C. Rumpole and the show-folk

Mortimer, J. C. Rumpole and the younger generation

Mortimer, J. C. Rumpole's last case

Muschg, A. Reparations; or, Making good

Muschg, A. The scythe hand; or, The homestead

Oates, J. C. Manslaughter

O'Flaherty, L. The stolen ass

Overholser, W. D. Lawyer two-fist

Pohl, F. Gwenanda and the Supremes

Post, M. D. The forgotten witness

Post, M. D., and Suter, J. F. The tree in the forest

Rhys, J. Fishy waters

Rooke, L. Agnes and the cobwebs

Russell, E. F. The witness

Schinto, J. From a juror's notebook

Shiga, N. Han's crime

Stephens, W. M. The state against Sam Tucker

TRIALS (FRAUD)

Gilbert, M. Rough justice

Triangle at Rhodes. Christie, A.

The **tribe**. Taylor, C.

TRIBES

See also Clans

Aldiss, B. W. Consolations of age

Aldiss, B. W. The plain, the endless plain

Castellanos, R. Death of the tiger

Lewitt, S. The shaman flute

Tribes of northern New Jersey. Krist, G.

A **tribute** to the general. East, C.

Tricentennial. Haldeman, J. W.

Trick or treat. Heise, K.

Trick or treat. Liben, M.

Trick scenery. Barthelme, F.

Tricked again. Lim Beng Hap

Trickle down. Lutz, J.

Trickster. Tem, S. R.

Tricky customers. Chatto, J.

A **tried** and proven method. Škvorecký, J.

Trifonov, ÍÛrii Valentinovich, 1925-1981

Games at dusk

The Barsukov Triangle, The two-toned blond & other stories; ed. by C. R. Proffer & E. Proffer

Triggering. Shirley, J.

Triggerman. Bone, J. F.

The **trilling** princess. Salmonson, J. A.

Trilobites. Pancake, B. D.

Trimble, Barbara Margaret *See* Gill, B. M.

TRINIDAD AND TOBAGO

Bissoondath, N. Dancing

Naipaul, S. The father, the son and the Holy Ghost

Naipaul, S. A man of mystery

Naipaul, S. Mr. Sookhoo and the carol singers

Naipaul, S. The political education of Clarissa Forbes

Seepaul, L. A sleeping pill for the doctor

Politics

See Politics—Trinidad and Tobago

Port of Spain

Khan, I. Shadows move in the Britannia Bar

Naipaul, S. The beauty contest

TRINIDADIANS

Canada

Clarke, A. C. How he does it

United States

Mukherjee, B. Jasmine

Trinity. Curley, D.

Trinity. Kress, N.

Trinity. Pritchett, M.

A **trinity**. Trevor, W.

Trio. Engberg, S.

Trio. Rhys, J.

The **trip**. Piñera, V.

The **trip**. Pirandello, L.

Trip. Shamosh, A.

A **trip** to Czardis. Granberry, E.

A **trip** to Grand Rapids. Keillor, G.

A **trip** to the Gifberge. Wicomb, Z.

Tripodi, Carlos

The holiday bread

Américas 36:18-21 Ja/F '84

Tripp, Miles, 1923-

The casebook Casanova

Winter's crimes 17

Fixation

The Mammoth book of modern crime stories; ed. by G. Hardinge

Form

Winter's crimes 16

Trippett, Frank

Child Ellen [excerpt]

Mississippi writers v1: Fiction; ed. by D. Abbott

Trips. Silverberg, R.

Triptych I. Bell, M. S.

Triptych II. Bell, M. S.
Triptych 2. Bell, M. S.
The triskelion. Stead, C.
Tristan Vox. Tournier, M.
Triumph!. Dawson, F.
The triumph and the celery stick. Desnoues, L.
The triumph of literacy. Millman, L.
The triumph of night. Wharton, E.
The triumph of vice. Gilbert, W. S.
The triumphs of a taxidermist. Wells, H. G.
Trivia. Klass, P.
Trixie Taylor, hospital nurse. Lopatin, J.
A Trojan general talks. Parotti, P.
Trojan horse. Swanwick, M.
TROJAN WAR
    Parotti, P. Antiphus on Tmolus
    Parotti, P. Diator beyond Olympus
    Parotti, P. Diomedes at Aulis
    Parotti, P. Eurypylus at Dodona
    Parotti, P. Heptaporos in Phrygia
    Parotti, P. Keas on Ida
    Parotti, P. Machaon at Tricca
    Parotti, P. Medon in Thrace
    Parotti, P. Meges at Dulichium
    Parotti, P. Menestheus at Athens
    Parotti, P. Meriones at Gortyn
    Parotti, P. Merops in Mysia
    Parotti, P. Nastes at Miletus
    Parotti, P. Neoptolemus in Phthia
    Parotti, P. Odios at Alybe
    Parotti, P. Pheidippus at Cos
    Parotti, P. Polydamas on the Plain
    Parotti, P. Pyracchmes beneath Laurion
    Parotti, P. Sinon at Elis
    Parotti, P. Thersites at Mytilene
    Parotti, P. Thoas at Pylene
    Parotti, P. Thrasymedes at Pylos
The troll. White, T. H.
TROLLEY BUSES
    Birtha, B. Route 23: 10th and Bigler to Bethlehem Pike
    Lafferty, R. A. Interurban queen
Trollope, Anthony, 1815-1882
    Malachi's Cove
        Short stories of the sea; ed. by G. C. Solley and E. Steinbaugh
    Returning home
        The Treasury of English short stories; ed. by N. Sullivan
TROLLS See Fairies
The trombone and the lady. Jones, D. C.
TROMBONISTS
    Barthelme, D. The king of jazz
    Gardner, M. Sibyl sits in
Trophies. Haslam, G. W.
Trophy. Girion, B.
Tropism. Kennedy, L.
Trott, Suzanne
    The trade-off
        Seventeen 45:88-9 Ja '86
TROUBADOURS
    Henry, O. The last of the troubadours

Trouble cargo. Reeman, D.
Trouble . . . come and get it! Spillane, M.
Trouble in paradise. Lyons, A.
Trouble is my business. Chandler, R.
A trouble of fools. Barnes, L.
Trouble people. Lewis, S. E.
The trouble shooters. Brennan, D.
The trouble with Felix. Collins, A.
The trouble with Sempoanga. Silverberg, R.
The trouble with the cotton people. Le Guin, U. K.
Troubled by his complexion. McLaughlin, L.
Troubled Sunday. Shen Rong
Troubles. Blinkin, M.
Troubles of a tattooed king. Shefner, E.
TROUSERS
    Heise, K. Long pants day at last
The trout. Nielsen, M. O.
The trout stream. Welch, D.
Trow, George W. S.
    The last Mrs. Aspair
        The New Yorker 59:42-54+ F 13 '84
    What I want
        The New Yorker 60:45 Mr 12 '84
Troy, Judy
    Birthday
        The New Yorker 59:33 Ja 9 '84
    Flowers
        The New Yorker 64:34-5 N 28 '88
    Geometry
        The New Yorker 62:33-4 F 9 '87
    In one place
        The New Yorker 60:42-3 S 10 '84
    Looking for love
        The New Yorker 63:32-3 Mr 16 '87
    The Nevada School of Acting
        The New Yorker 61:28-9 Je 24 '85
TROY (ANCIENT CITY)
        See also Trojan War
The truck. Kinsella, W. P.
TRUCK DRIVERS
    Bedard, B. Sheer Energy
    Block, L. Like a bug on a windshield
    Bonnie, F. Wide load, where are you?
    Kauffman, J. The mechanics of good times
    Long, D. Home fires
    Maron, M. Deadhead coming down
    Tournier, M. The Lily of the Valley rest area
    Zhang Xianliang. Shorblac: a driver's story
TRUCKS
                Accidents
            See Traffic accidents
Truckstop. Keillor, G.
Trudy. Daniels, C.
True. McNeal, T.
True adventures. Bukoski, A.
The true believer. Stewart, I.
The true history of Anthony Ffryar. Gray, A.
True love. Asimov, I.
A true love story. Walpole, H.
True loves. Strand, M.

The **true** marriage. Walker, W.
True romance. Hansen, R.
The **true** story. Thomas, D.
The **true** story of Guenever. Phelps, E. S.
The **true** story of how my grandfather was smuggled out of the old country in a pickle barrel in order to escape military conscription. Greenberg, A.
A **true** story of the tragedy of Flowery Land. Doyle, Sir A. C.

Trueblood, Harriett
The courage of Millie Baldwin
Redbook 168:42+ Mr '87

Truesdale, C. W.
Doña baby
Stiller's pond; ed. by J. Agee; R. Blakely and S. Welch

Trujillo, Renato
The illusionist
Fatal recurrences; ed. by H. Hugh and P. O'Brien

The **truly** great strikes wherever it wants. Gustafsson, L.
The **truly** married woman. Nicol, A.
Truly yours, John R. Jacks. Hensley, J. L.
The **trumpet** player and his wife. Hemley, R.

TRUMPET PLAYERS
Bankier, W. One clear sweet clue
Gardner, M. The fall of Flatbush Smith
Howard, C. Horn man
Shaik, F. The mayor of New Orleans; just talking jazz

TRUMPETERS *See* Trumpet players
The **trunk** lady. Bradbury, R.

Truss, Jan, 1925-
The party
Alberta bound; ed. by F. Stenson

Trust. Asscher-Pinkhof, C.
Trust. Ozick, C.
Trust Charlie. Garfield, B.
Trust me. Lyons, J.
Trust me. Updike, J.
Trust not a man. Nolan, W. F.
Trusty. Jones, D. C.
The **truth.** Clarke, T.
Truth. Kinsella, W. P.
The **truth** about Pyecraft. Wells, H. G.
Truth and lies. Price, R.
The **truth** game. Klíma, I.
Truth to tell. Wallace, P.

TRUTHFULNESS AND FALSEHOOD
See also Honesty
Asimov, I. The obvious factor
Austin, M. H. The man who lied about a woman
Banks, R. My mother's memoirs, my father's lie, and other true stories
Barstow, S. Huby falling
Beerbohm, M. A. V. Laider
Blinkin, M. The mysterious secret
Bloch, R. Word of honor
Broun, H. Cows on the drag strip

Castle, M. If you take my hand, my son
Crane, S. The knife
DuBois, B. Final marks, final secrets
Furman, L. Eldorado
Grin, A. The legend of Ferguson
Higgins, G. V. A case of Chivas Regal
Leaton, A. Gita's story
Lish, G. Everything I know
Lish, G. History; or, The four pictures of Vludka
MacDonald, J. D. Squealer
Milton, E. Entrechat
Morrow, J. Veritas
Narayan, R. K. Like the sun
Norris, H. The pearl sitter
Price, R. Truth and lies
Schwob, M. The Dom
Singer, I. B. The bitter truth
Stafford, J. The healthiest girl in town
Swados, H. Claudine's book
Tetu, R. Oh, that shoestore used to be mine
Thériault, Y. The whale
Wallace, P. Truth to tell
Wolff, T. The liar

Try to remember. Herbert, F.
Trying. Robison, M.
Trying to be. Gaitskill, M.
Trying to grow up American. Cullen, E. J.
Trying to save Piggy Sneed. Irving, J.
The **tryst.** Oates, J. C.

Ts'ai-hua, Tuan
The feast of "Flower-Pattern" wine
Inspired by drink; ed. by Joan Digby and John Digby

TSILKOTIN INDIANS
St. Pierre, P. H. The education of Phyllisteen
St. Pierre, P. H. Ol Antoine's wooden overcoat
St. Pierre, P. H. Sarah's copper

Tsuboi, Sakae, 1900-
Umbrella on a moonlit night
The Mother of dreams, and other short stories; ed. by M. Ueda

Tsui, Kitty
Why the sea is salty
Hear the silence; ed. by I. Zahava

Tsushima, Yūko
The chrysanthemum beetle
Tsushima, Y. The shooting gallery
Clearing the thickets
Tsushima, Y. The shooting gallery
An embrace
Tsushima, Y. The shooting gallery
Missing
Tsushima, Y. The shooting gallery
The mother in the house of grass
The Literary Review (Madison, N.J.) 30:265-96 Wint '87
A sensitive season
Tsushima, Y. The shooting gallery

Tsushima, Yūko—*Continued*
  The shooting gallery
    Tsushima, Y. The shooting gallery
  The silent traders
    The Shōwa anthology 2
    Tsushima, Y. The shooting gallery
  South wind
    Tsushima, Y. The shooting gallery
Tsutsui, Yasutaka
  Standing woman
    Omni book of science fiction 1
Tsyganov, Valery
  Martian tales
    Aliens, travelers, and other strangers; by
      B. and A. Strugatsky and others
TUAMOTU ISLANDS *See* Islands of the
  Pacific
The **tub**. Stephan, M.
TUBERCULOSIS
  Henry, O. A fog in Santone
  Henry, O. Hygeia at the Solito
  Óskar, J. The man in the attic and the
    woman on the main floor
  Ponce, M. H. Los tisicos
  Welch, D. Anna Dillon
  West, J. 99.6
  West, J. The condemned librarian
  West, J. Homecoming
  West, J. I'll ask him to come sooner
  Williams, T. The angel in the alcove
  Yi, P.-J. The wind and landscape of
    Yenang
The **tuckahoe**. Etchemendy, N.
Tucker, Eva
  Fertility doll
    Encounter (London, England) 65:3-6 N
      '85
Tucking in. Asscher-Pinkhof, C.
Tuesday morning: a sentimental story.
  Klíma, I.
The **Tuesday** Night Club. Christie, A.
Tuesday siesta. García Márquez, G.
Tufel, Alice
  A name for herself
    Tales from Ellery Queen's Mystery
      Magazine: short stories for young
      adults
Tufts and Wink. Willson, H.
The **tugging**. Campbell, R.
TULSA (OKLA.) *See* Oklahoma—Tulsa
Tumbleweed Christmas. Flynn, R.
Tumbling. Moyer, K.
Tung, Nien
  Fire
    The Unbroken chain; ed. by J. S. M.
      Lau
The **tunnel**. Somers, A.
The **tunnel**. Swift, G.
The **tunnel** of love. Bloch, R.
Tunstall, Tricia
  Politics between us
    The Antioch Review 44:42-60 Wint '86

Tuohy, Frank, 1925-
  The Admiral and the nuns
    Tuohy, F. The collected stories
  At home with the Colonel
    Tuohy, F. The collected stories
  The broken bridge
    Tuohy, F. The collected stories
  The candidate
    Tuohy, F. The collected stories
  Discontinued lines
    Tuohy, F. The collected stories
  Dreams of unfair women
    Winter's tales, new ser. v1
  Evening in Connecticut
    Tuohy, F. The collected stories
  Fingers in the door
    Tuohy, F. The collected stories
  A floral tribute
    Tuohy, F. The collected stories
  A ghost garden
    Tuohy, F. The collected stories
  In the dark years
    Tuohy, F. The collected stories
  In the hotel
    Tuohy, F. The collected stories
  Inexperience
    Tuohy, F. The collected stories
  The license
    Tuohy, F. The collected stories
  A life membership
    Tuohy, F. The collected stories
  Live bait
    Tuohy, F. The collected stories
  Love to Patsy
    Tuohy, F. The collected stories
  Luck
    Tuohy, F. The collected stories
  The matchmakers
    Tuohy, F. The collected stories
  Nocturne with neon lights
    Tuohy, F. The collected stories
  The Palace of Culture
    Tuohy, F. The collected stories
  The Palladian Bridge
    Tuohy, F. The collected stories
  The potlatch of Esmeralda
    Tuohy, F. The collected stories
  A reprieve
    Tuohy, F. The collected stories
  Ructions; or, A historical footnote to the
    Cold War
    Tuohy, F. The collected stories
  Showing the flag
    Tuohy, F. The collected stories
  A special relationship
    Tuohy, F. The collected stories
  The student
    Tuohy, F. The collected stories
  A summer pilgrim
    Tuohy, F. The collected stories
  A survivor in Salvador
    Tuohy, F. The collected stories

Tuohy, Frank, 1925——Continued
Thunderbolt
  Tuohy, F. The collected stories
The trap
  Tuohy, F. The collected stories
Two private lives
  Tuohy, F. The collected stories
A war of liberation
  Tuohy, F. The collected stories
The white stick
  Tuohy, F. The collected stories
Windows
  Tuohy, F. The collected stories
A young girl
  Tuohy, F. The collected stories
Tupelo nights. Bradley, J. E.
Turgenev, Ivan Sergeevich, 1818-1883
Bubnoff and the Devil
  Masterpieces of terror and the supernatural; ed. by M. Kaye and S. Kaye
Clara Militch
  The Dark descent; ed. by D. G. Hartwell
Mumú
  Roger Caras' Treasury of great dog stories
The **Turk.** Federspiel, J.
TURKEY
Baykurt, F. The wolf
Faik, S. A city morning and a man
Faik, S. Coming of age on Kasikadasi
Faik, S. In search of a story
Faik, S. The mirror at the beach
Faik, S. Samovar
Hemingway, E. On the quai in Smyrna
Izgü, M. The attack by yoghurt
Izgü, M. Devoted Moslem Ismail Effendi
Nesin, A. The first woman who understood me
Nesin, A. Regulations for meatball peddlers
Farm life
  See Farm life—Turkey
Marriage customs
  See Marriage customs—Turkey
Politics
  See Politics—Turkey
Rural life
Baykurt, F. The airplane ticket
Baykurt, F. Jeyfo
Faik, S. Good deeds are never forgotten
Faik, S. My father's second home
Faik, S. Priest Effendi
Faik, S. Searchlight operator
Faik, S. Sivriada nights
Faik, S. The Stelyanos Hrisopulos
Faik, S. Tomb with an arbor
Faik, S. The village teacher and the herdsboy
Faik, S. The wedding night
Faik, S. White gold
Leaton, A. Destiny

Nesin, A. The university committee's sociological study of a village
Bursa
Faik, S. The silk handkerchief
Ephesus
Schwob, M. Herostratos, incendiary
Istanbul
Brondoli, M. The death of the vice consul
Disch, T. M. The Asian shore
Faik, S. The barometer
Faik, S. By the fountain
Faik, S. A certain kind of people
Faik, S. The futile man
Faik, S. Last birds
Faik, S. The park's mornings, evenings, nights
Faik, S. There is a snake in Alemdağ
Morand, P. Turkish night
Nesin, A. Socialism is coming—stand aside!
Swift, G. Seraglio
Vizyēnos, G. M. Who was my brother's killer?
The **turkey.** O'Connor, F.
Turkey hunt. Hannum, A. P.
Turkey talk. Janowitz, T.
TURKISH BATHS
al-Idlibi, U. The women's baths
Anderman, J. Turkish baths
Williams, T. Desire and the black masseur
Turkish baths. Anderman, J.
Turkish night. Morand, P.
TURKS
Vizyēnos, G. M. Moscóv-Selím
Africa
Maupassant, G. de. Mohammed Fripouli
Turn about. Faulkner, W.
Turn and turn about. Clifford, F.
Turn away. Gorman, E.
The **turn** of time. Silva, D. B.
Turnabout. Elman, R.
TURNCOATS See Defectors
Turned. Gilman, C. P.
Turner, Bill
The shoes
  Streets of stone; ed. by M. Burgess and H. Whyte
Turner, George, 1916-
In a Petri dish upstairs
  Australian science fiction; ed. by V. Ikin
Turner, Ronald F.
Luzon
  The Yale Review 74:507-17 Summ '85
Toussaint
  Harper's 275:41-2 N '87
Turning. Sexson, L.
The **turning** of the tide. Forester, C. S.
Turning out. Whittier, G.
Turning thirty-eight. Taylor, P. E.
Turnley, Jean E.
The best foot forward
  Short story international 67
Turpentine. Gallagher, T.

Turtle. Everett, P. L.
Turtle meat. Bruchac, J.
Turtledove, Harry
And so to bed
  Terry Carr's Best science fiction and fantasy of the year #16
  The Year's best science fiction, fourth annual collection
A difficult undertaking
  Robert Adams' Book of soldiers
Gentlemen of the shade
  Ripper! Ed. by G. Dozois and S. Casper
Not all wolves
  Werewolves; ed. by J. Yolen and M. H. Greenberg
TURTLES
Gardner, M. The conspicuous turtle
Haldeman, J. C. Mortimer Snodgrass Turtle
Highsmith, P. The terrapin
Matthiessen, P. Late in the season
TUSCANY (ITALY) *See* Italy—Tuscany
The **tutor**. Leedom-Ackerman, J.
TUTORS
Briskin, M. A boy like Astrid's mother
Leedom-Ackerman, J. The tutor
Schwartz, J. Max
Tuttle, Lisa, 1952-
Bug house
  The Best horror stories from the Magazine of fantasy and science fiction
Jamie's grave
  The Best of Shadows; ed. by C. L. Grant
  The Year's best fantasy, first annual collection
TV guide. Woodman, A.
Twain, Mark, 1835-1910
3,000 years among the microbes
  Twain, M. The science fiction of Mark Twain
About all kinds of ships
  Short stories of the sea; ed. by G. C. Solley and E. Steinbaugh
The canvasser's tale
  Masterpieces of fantasy and enchantment; ed. by D. G. Hartwell
Captain Stormfield's visit to heaven
  Twain, M. The science fiction of Mark Twain
A curious pleasure excursion
  Twain, M. The science fiction of Mark Twain
The curious republic of Gondour
  Twain, M. The science fiction of Mark Twain
Dick Baker's cat
  Roger Caras' Treasury of great cat stories
A dog's tale
  Roger Caras' Treasury of great dog stories

The facts concerning the recent carnival of crime in Connecticut
  The Norton book of American short stories
From The "London Times" of 1904
  Twain, M. The science fiction of Mark Twain
A ghost story
  Great ghost stories; ed. by B. A. Schwartz
"The great dark"
  Twain, M. The science fiction of Mark Twain
The loves of Alonzo Fitz Clarence and Rosannah Ethelton
  Twain, M. The science fiction of Mark Twain
The man that corrupted Hadleyburg
  Isaac Asimov presents the best crime stories of the 19th century
My platonic sweetheart
  Twain, M. The science fiction of Mark Twain
The notorious jumping frog of Calaveras County [Variant title: The celebrated jumping frog of Calaveras County]
  The Western hall of fame; ed. by B. Pronzini and M. H. Greenberg
The private history of a campaign that failed
  A Treasury of Civil War stories; ed. by M. H. Greenberg and B. Pronzini
The secret history of Eddypus, the world-empire
  Twain, M. The science fiction of Mark Twain
Sold to Satan
  Twain, M. The science fiction of Mark Twain
The stolen white elephant
  Masterpieces of mystery and suspense; ed. by M. H. Greenberg
Time-travel contexts from A Connecticut Yankee in King Arthur's Court
  Twain, M. The science fiction of Mark Twain
Tweedsmuir, John Buchan, Baron *See* Buchan, John, 1875-1940
Tween. Bone, J. F.
The **twelfth** guest. Freeman, M. E. W.
The **twelfth** statue. Ellin, S.
Twelfth summer. Perlman, H. H.
Twelve below zero. Bukoski, A.
Twelve o'clock. Crane, S.
Twentieth frame. Cox, A.
Twenty-five August 1983. See Borges, J. L. 25 August 1983
Twenty is the greatest time in any man's life. Saroyan, W.
Twenty minutes. Salter, J.
Twenty-one good men and true. Francis, D.
Twenty questions. Sisskind, M.

Twenty-seven wagons full of cotton. Williams, T.

Twenty-six men and a girl. Gorky, M.

The twenty three brown paper bags. See Ritchie, J. The 23 brown paper bags

XXII. Sarraute, N.

"'Twere best not know myself". Clark, M.

Twice Chanukah. Singer, I. B.

Twice shy. Edwards, M. F.

Twilight at the towers. Barker, C.

Twilight fantasy. Robb, J.

Twilight hunt. Ferreira, R.

The twilight road. Brinsmead, H. F.

Twilight time. Shiner, L.

Twilight's last gleamings. Burroughs, W. S.

Twin-sets and pickle forks. Dunn, D.

The twinight of Reverend Jones. Coleman, W.

Twink. Sturgeon, T.

TWINS

   See also Siamese twins

   Carr, J. The heart in the egg

   Covino, M. Salient facts

   Crawford, F. M. Man overboard!

   Duke, M. The notif

   García Márquez, G. The other side of death

   Greene, G. The case for the defence

   Greene, G. The end of the party

   Harland, M. One old maid

   Hartley, L. P. The face

   Jahnn, H. H. Ragna and Nils

   Jahnn, H. H. The story of the twins

   Moyer, K. Tumbling

   Osborn, C. Reversals

   Sonu, H. The story of a peculiar pain

   Updike, J. The other

   Wegner, H. The huzul flute

Twins. McCormack, E. P.

The twins. Spark, M.

The twin's story. Hollander, J.

Twirler. Martin, J.

Twirling. Bradley, J.

Twist ending. Longyear, B. B.

The twisted river. Meinke, P.

The twister. Boles, P. D.

Twister. Moody, H.

'Twixt soul and body. Ch'en, H.-Y.

Two: a story of numbers. Solensten, J.

Two abysses. Berdnyk, O.

Two Americans. H. D.

Two are better than one. Whelan, G.

Two artists. Lurie, M.

Two-bit piece. Boehm, L.

The two bottles of relish. Dunsany, E. J. M. D. P., Baron

Two cats. Peterson, M.

Two cats in Paris and one in Florence. Sandel, C.

Two dooms. Kornbluth, C. M.

Two doors. Oates, J. C.

The two Elenas. Fuentes, C.

Two essays. Katz, S.

Two families. Lish, G.

Two fathers. Conn, C. W.

The two footmen. Gilbert, M.

Two for the river. Hartley, L. P.

Two gentle people. Greene, G.

Two ghosts of us. Tallent, E.

Two gifts. Moline, S.

Two girls wearing perfume in the summer. Dew, R. F.

The two-gun man. White, S. E.

Two-head Fred and Tree-foot Frieda. Antoni, R. W.

Two hours in the life of Steven Malinowski. Briskin, M.

Two hours to kill. McGuane, T.

Two hundred yards past Wordsworth's house. Dorr, L.

Two in love. Latimer, M.

Two interviews. José, F. S.

Two ladies in retirement. Taylor, P. H.

Two little soldiers. Maupassant, G. de

Two lives. Bernen, R.

Two men. Johnson, D.

Two men. Moore, G.

Two men running. Jolley, E.

The two million dollar defense. See Masur, H. Q. The $2,000,000 defense

Two minutes forty-five seconds. Simmons, D.

The two moons of Vira's world. Petchsingh, T.

Two more gallants. Trevor, W.

Two more under the Indian sun. Jhabvala, R. P.

Two New Jersey stories: Hudson Towers. Klass, P.

Two New Jersey stories: Stealing. Klass, P.

Two o'clock blonde. Cain, J. M.

The two of them together. Matthews, J.

The two offers. Harper, F. E. W.

Two on a party. Williams, T.

Two paces east. Day, R. C.

Two percent inspiration. Sturgeon, T.

The two percent solution. Ritchie, J.

The two portraits of Rembrandt. Schwartz, L. S.

Two potters. Lessing, D. M.

Two private lives. Tuohy, F.

Two renegades. Henry, O.

Two reports. Ocampo, S.

Two rolls, no coffee. Mankiewicz, D. M.

Two saints. Maillet, A.

Two seaside yarns. Katz, S.

Two ships. Boyle, T. C.

The two sides of things. Weaver, G.

Two sisters. Davis, L.

Two sisters. Essop, A.

The two sisters. See Graves, Mrs. A. J. Mary and Ellen Grosvenor; or, The two sisters

Two stories. Strand, M.

Two stories about Emma: The whirlpool rapids. Atwood, M.

Two stories about Emma: Walking on water. Atwood, M.
Two strings to his bow. Stewart, J. I. M.
Two tales of a trip. Graham, J.
The two taverns. Chesterton, G. K.
The two temples: Temple first. Melville, H.
The two temples: Temple second. Melville, H.
Two thousand seventy two days. See Nowakowski, M. 2072 days
Two thousand sixty six: Election Day. See Shaara, M. 2066: Election Day
Two times two. Chernoff, M.
The two-toned blond: a reciprocal tale. Maramzin, V.
Two travelers. O, Y.-G.
The two Vaynes. Hartley, L. P.
The two Volodyas. Chekhov, A. P.
Two wakes. Landolfi, T.
Two-way communication. Anvil, C.
Two weeks every summer. Pronzini, B.
Two widows. Bonnie, F.
Two willow chairs. Wells, J.
Two women. Alden, P. B.
Two women. Gojawiczyńska, P.
Two women at nightfall. Woods, C.
Two women, one child. Briskin, M.
Two year's absence. Wexler, J.
Two years in exile. Liberman, S.
Twohy, Robert
  Case blue
    Ellery Queen's Prime crimes
Two's a crowd. Dyer, S.
Two's company. Simpson, D.
Ty and Janet. Krist, G.
Ty-Casper, Linda
  Application for a small life
  Short story international 56
TYCOONS See Millionaires
Tyler, Anne, 1941-
  The artificial family
    Love stories for the time being; ed. by G. D. Chipps and B. Henderson
    Selected stories from The Southern review, 1965-1985
  The geologist's maid
    Stories of the modern South; ed. by B. Forkner and P. Samway
  Rerun
    The New Yorker 64:20-32 Jl 4 '88
  Teenage wasteland
    The Editors' choice: new American stories v1
    New women and new fiction; ed. by S. Cahill
Tyler, S. G.
  Alice's snazzy pajamas
    The North American Review 270:39 S '85
Tyler and Brina. Miller, S.
The type louse. Conroy, J.
The typewriter. Morris, M.

TYPEWRITERS
  Asimov, I. Dollars and cents
Typhoon. Conrad, J.
TYPHOONS
  Conrad, J. Typhoon
TYPHUS FEVER
  Ferron, J. Chronicle of Anse Saint-Roch
TYPISTS
  Brautigan, R. 1/3, 1/3, 1/3
  Colette. The rainy moon
  Rhys, J. The insect world
  Wilding, M. The words she types
Typographical error. Lutz, J.
Tyre, Nedra, 1921-
  Beyond the wall
    Alfred Hitchcock's Mortal errors
  Carnival day
    Child's ploy; ed. by M. Muller and B. Pronzini
    The Wickedest show on earth; ed. by M. Muller and B. Pronzini
  A nice place to stay
    Masterpieces of mystery and suspense; ed. by M. H. Greenberg
  Reflections on murder
    Chapter & hearse; ed. by M. Muller and B. Pronzini
Tyson's turn. Miller, M. D.
Tzigane. Franklin, P.
Tzu, Ou-yang
  The net
    The Unbroken chain; ed. by J. S. M. Lau

U

U-BOATS See Submarines
U.F.O.'S See Flying saucers
UCCELLO, PAOLO, 1396 or 7-1475
  About
  Schwob, M. Paolo Uccello, painter
Uccello. Day, R. C.
The ugliest man in the world. Regent, P.
The ugliest pilgrim. Betts, D.
UGLINESS
  Austin, M. H. Bitterness of women
  Betts, D. The ugliest pilgrim
  Maupassant, G. de. Ugly
  Regent, P. The ugliest man in the world
  Silverberg, R. Caliban
  Wells, H. G. The man with a nose
Ugly. Maupassant, G. de
The ugly chickens. Waldrop, H.
Ugly Douglas & company. Warren, J.
The ugly little boy. Asimov, I.
The ugly one. Lim, C.
Uglypuss. Atwood, M.
UGOLINO, OF SEGNI See Gregory IX, Pope, ca. 1170-1241
The ugupu bird. Mrożek, S.

Ujayli, Abd al-Salam al- *See* Al-Ujayli, Abd al-Salam
UKRAINE
Berdnyk, O. A chorus of elements
Gogol', N. V. The fair at Sorochintsy
Gogol', N. V. A May night; or, The drowned maiden
Gogol', N. V. Old-world landowners
Gogol', N. V. The tale of how Ivan Ivanovich quarreled with Ivan Nikiforovich
Gogol', N. V. Viy
Odessa
Böll, H. That time we were in Odessa
UKRAINIANS
Canada
Kreisel, H. The broken globe
Matheson, S. Harris
Ukridge's dog college. Wodehouse, P. G.
ULCERS
Phillips, J. A. Something that happened
Ulick's Island. Nestor, T. G.
Ullman, James M.
Dead ringer
Murder and mystery in Chicago; ed. by C. R. Waugh; F. D. McSherry and M. H. Greenberg
Ullman, Natacha *See* Stewart, Natacha, d. 1986
Ullmann, Alexis
Those in peril in the air
Hot type; ed. by J. Miller
Ulrike Meinhof. Smith, J.
The **ultimate** biofeedback device. Jeppson, J. O.
The **ultimate** crime. Asimov, I.
Ulysses. Ferron, J.
Umans, Richard
Connie
First love/last love; ed. by M. Denneny; C. Ortleb and T. Steele
Speech
Men on men; ed. by G. Stambolian
Umbach, Eberle
Belly on a stick
Whole Earth Review no56:8-11 Fall '87
Umberto Verdi, chimney sweep. MacLaverty, B.
Umbrella. Kawabata, Y.
The **umbrella.** Maupassant, G. de
Umbrella dance. Day, R. C.
Umbrella on a moonlit night. Tsuboi, S.
UMBRELLAS
Asimov, I. The magic umbrella
Colter, C. The beach umbrella
Kinsella, W. P. The East End Umbrella Company endowment for the arts
Maupassant, G. de. The umbrella
Umbrellas. Livesey, M.
Umbrian afternoon. Déon, M.
Umpire. Rheinheimer, K.
UN *See* United Nations
Unacceptable procedures. Ellin, S.

The **unbearable** lightness of being. Kundera, M.
UNBORN CHILD *See* Fetus
Uncertain readings. Rey Rosa, R.
The **uncertainty** of strangers. Franklin, P.
Unchained. Pronzini, B.
The **uncharted** isle. Smith, C. A.
The **uncle.** Garber, E. K.
Uncle. Ndebele, N.
Uncle Aron. Dovlatov, S.
Uncle Benny. Liben, M.
Uncle Bernard's proposal. Jolley, E.
Uncle Dobbin's Parrot Fair. De Lint, C.
Uncle Elinar. Bradbury, R.
Uncle Facundo. Blaisten, I.
Uncle Fred flits by. Wodehouse, P. G.
Uncle George and Uncle Stefan. Meinke, P.
Uncle Grant. Price, R.
Uncle Isaiah. Kirk, R.
Uncle Jeremy's household. Doyle, Sir A. C.
Uncle Leopold. Dovlatov, S.
Uncle Maggot. McGarry, J.
Uncle Max. Hoch, E. D.
Uncle Monkey. Hejmadi, P.
Uncle Morgan at the Nats. Stead, C.
Uncle Moustapha's eclipse. McKnight, R.
Uncle Nathan. Neugeboren, J.
Uncle Ollie finds a new market. Conroy, J.
Uncle Ollie on trial. Conroy, J.
Uncle Ollie's rabbit hunt. Conroy, J.
Uncle Ollie's spite fence. Conroy, J.
Uncle Otto's truck. King, S.
Uncle Sam Carrington. Carrington, L.
Uncle Sidney and the Mexicans. Burke, J. L.
Uncle Sven and the Cultural Revolution. Gustafsson, L.
Uncle Tom's daybook. Floyd, P. L.
Uncle Tuggs. Shea, M.
Uncle Vanya. Woolf, V.
UNCLES
See also Nephews
Al-Wardani, M. The kerosene stove
Apple, M. Blood relatives
Arredondo, I. The shunammite
Asimov, I. Unique is where you find it
Bates, H. E. The death of Uncle Silas
Bates, H. E. Finger wet, finger dry
Bates, H. E. A funny thing
Bates, H. E. The lily
Bates, H. E. The race
Bates, H. E. The return
Bates, H. E. The revelation
Bates, H. E. The shooting party
Bates, H. E. Silas and Goliath
Bates, H. E. A Silas idyll
Bates, H. E. Silas the good
Bates, H. E. The sow and Silas
Bates, H. E. The wedding
Baxter, C. The would-be father
Bishop, E. Memories of Uncle Neddy
Blei, N. The chair trick
Blythe, R. The nature of poetry

UNCLES—*Continued*

Blythe, R. The October Bagman
Blythe, R. The right day to kill a pike
Böll, H. Black sheep
Böll, H. My Uncle Fred
Boylan, J. The love starter
Caldwell, E. Maud Island
Cameron, P. Jump or dive
Camoin, F. A. Cheerful wisdom
Carter, R. Cityman
Chae, M.-S. My idiot uncle
Conroy, J. "A barrel of fun"
Conroy, J. Home to Uncle Ollie's
Conroy, J. Uncle Ollie finds a new market
Conroy, J. Uncle Ollie on trial
Conroy, J. Uncle Ollie's rabbit hunt
Conroy, J. Uncle Ollie's spite fence
Coriolan, J. Kindred
Cullen, E. J. What Uncle Tom did
Dai Houying. Father's milk is also blood transformed
Davie, E. Thorns and gifts
Dazai, O. Chiyojo
Dennison, G. A tale of Pierrot
Dickens, C. The story of the bagman's uncle
Eighner, L. Greenbriar
Franzen, B. This uncle
Gallant, M. Dédé
Hall, R. W. Letter from a great-uncle
Hartley, L. P. Apples
Hauptman, W. Boom town
Heise, K. Aunt Ella's funeral
Hoch, E. D. Uncle Max
Jhabvala, R. P. Bombay
Jolley, E. Outink to Uncle's place
Jolley, E. The outworks of the kingdom
Jolley, E. Uncle Bernard's proposal
Kiely, B. Eton Crop
Kirk, R. Uncle Isaiah
Leskov, N. S. A robbery
Liben, M. Uncle Benny
MacDonald, D. R. Poplars
McGarry, J. Providence, 1948: the most complimentary thing
Meinke, P. Uncle George and Uncle Stefan
Melville, H. The happy failure
Menaker, D. The three-mile hill is five miles long
Mrożek, S. The giraffe
Muschg, A. Brami's view
Muschg, A. Dinnertime
Narayan, R. K. Uncle's letters
Ndebele, N. Uncle
Neugeboren, J. Uncle Nathan
Norris, L. A flight of geese
Norris, L. My uncle's story
Oates, J. C. Photographer's model
Osborn, C. Stalking strangers
Potter, N. A. J. Light timber
Power, V. The operation
Pronzini, B. Here lies another blackmailer
Purdy, J. Rapture

Rand, N. No sore losers
Regent, P. Pleasures of the flesh
Ross, V. Whistling
Ruta, S. Soldier's rest
Stead, C. Uncle Morgan at the Nats
Summers, M. Song of willow
Swados, H. My Coney Island uncle
Swados, H. The tree of life
Swift, G. Hoffmeier's Antelope
Taylor, P. H. A friend and protector
Taylor, P. H. The scoutmaster
Thomas, D. A story
Thorman, C. Gurlas
Tremblay, M. The ghost of Don Carlos
Vanderhaeghe, G. How the story ends
Walters, A. L. The warriors
Wasylyk, S. If a body
Watson, S. The Black Farm
Watson, S. The rumble seat
Weaver, G. The two sides of things
Wells, H. G. The lost inheritance
Wetherell, W. D. Calm seas and a prosperous voyage
Wicomb, Z. Jan Klinkies
Wilson, B. Starfish
Wodehouse, P. G. Uncle Fred flits by
Wolfe, G. The recording
Uncle's letters. Narayan, R. K.
The **unclouded** day. Proulx, A.
An **uncommon** sort of spectre. Mitchell, E. P.
The **undefeated**. Hemingway, E.
Under a dark angel's eye. Highsmith, P.
Under cover of darkness. Verma, N.
The **under** dog. Christie, A.
Under siege. Martin, G. R. R.
Under the banyan tree. Narayan, R. K.
Under the bed. Willett, J.
Under the bell jar. Daviau, D.-M.
Under the bridge. Davin, D.
Under the equinox. McElroy, C. J.
Under the fan. Moore, G.
Under the garden. Greene, G.
Under the hawthorn. Zhang Jie
Under the horses' hooves. Liphshitz, A.
Under the house. Anderson, J.
Under the influence. Dubus, E. N.
Under the knife. Wells, H. G.
Under the ridge. Hemingway, E.
Under the rose. Pynchon, T.
Under the shadow of Mt. Bandai. Inoue, Y.
Under the skin. Pronzini, B.
Under the swaying curtain. Thompson, R.
Under the wheat. DeMarinis, R.
Under the yoke. Maupassant, G. de
Under water. Marcus, J. S.
Under water. Strand, M.
Undercurrents. Hammond, D. C.
Underground. Bloch, R.
Underground. Pastan, R.
The **underground** banquet. Warren, J.
Underground movement. Neville, K.

UNDERGROUND MOVEMENTS (WORLD WAR, 1939-1945) See World War, 1939-1945—Underground movements

The **underground** river. Kittredge, W.

Underground tests. O'Brien, T.

The **underground** village. Kang, K.-A.

Underground women. Kercheval, J. L.

Undersea guardians. Bradbury, R.

The **understanding**. La Chapelle, M.

Understanding electricity. Lutz, J.

An **understated** look. Ross, V.

UNDERTAKERS AND UNDERTAKING

Bloch, R. 'Til death do us part

Bly, C. The dignity of life

Ferron, M. The weaker sex

Lovecraft, H. P. In the vault

Stuart, J. Competition at Slush Creek

UNDERWATER COLONIES

Berdnyk, O. Two abysses

UNDERWATER EXPLORATION

Chesterton, G. K. The paradise of human fishes

Daley, R. The cannons of the Atocha

Gores, J. Pahua

Wells, H. G. In the abyss

Wells, H. G. Jimmy Goggles the god

Underwood, Michael, 1916-

The man who nursed grievances
Winter's crimes 17

OK for murder
The Mammoth book of modern crime stories; ed. by G. Hardinge

UNDERWORLD

See also Crime and criminals; Gangsters; Mafia

Undine. La Motte-Fouqué, F. H. K., Freiherr von

Undine's mighty father. Böll, H.

UNDOCUMENTED ALIENS

Keller, G. D. The mojado who offered up his tapeworms to the public weal

Mukherjee, B. Jasmine

Mukherjee, B. Tamurlane

Mulder, M. San Diego dilemma

Pritchett, M. Fashion in the Third World

Viramontes, H. M. The broken web

Unearned pleasures. Hegi, U.

Unearthing suite. Atwood, M.

The **unearthly** witness. Hogg, J.

Uneasy home-coming. Jenkins, W. F.

UNEMPLOYED

Baxter, C. Weights

Bell, M. S. The lie detector

Böll, H. An optimistic story

Böll, H. What a racket

Carver, R. Collectors

Connelly, J. The holidays

Connelly, J. Partner

Conroy, J. Hard winter

Dickinson, C. My livelihood

Dorr, L. The immigrant

Elkin, S. I look out for Ed Wolfe

Fitzgerald, P. The axe

Ford, R. Fireworks

Friedman, B. J. The pledges

Gaitens, E. The sailing ship

Gans, B. M. And here in Chicago it's 78°

Gorky, M. Evil-doers

Greenberg, A. Where do folk sayings come from?

Halligan, M. The porch of Paradise

Houbein, L. The serene revolution

Jhabvala, R. P. The interview

Johnson, G. C. The man with the hoe

La Forme, A. Telephone poles

La Puma, S. The mouthpiece

MacLaverty, B. A happy birthday

Matthew, J. R. Amy Rose, 1947

Norris, L. My uncle's story

Northrup, J. The odyssey

Pavese, C. Friends

Raymond, I. Taking a chance on Jack

Schwartz, L. S. The man at the gate

Shaw, J. B. The geese at Presque Isle

Taylor, A. Casey and Sarah

Tuohy, F. Luck

Wetherell, W. D. If a woodchuck could chuck wood

Wilson, B. The investment

Zahn, T. Job inaction

Zugsmith, L. Room in the world

The **Unenlightened**. Yi, K.-S.

An **unexpected** death. Friedman, P.

An **unexpected** delivery. Piñera, V.

Unexpected guests. Böll, H.

An **unexpected** reunion. Hebel, J. P.

The **unfaithful** father. Rossner, J.

Unfinished business. Ross, J.

The **unfinished** business of childhood. Abbott, L. K.

An **unfinished** head. Van Langenberg, C.

An **unfinished** record. Zhang Jie

UNFINISHED STORIES

Buzzati, D. An interrupted story

Poe, E. A. The light-house

Sholem Aleichem. Baranovich Station

The **unfolding**. Shirley, J., and Sterling, B.

An **unfortunate** likeness. Maupassant, G. de

Unguided tour. Sontag, S.

The **unicorn**. Stivens, D.

The **unicorn** in the garden. Thurber, J.

Unicorn tapestry. Charnas, S. M.

Unicorn variations. Zelazny, R.

UNICORNS

Busby, F. M. Once upon a unicorn

Donaldson, S. R. Mythological beast

Dozois, G. R. The sacrifice

Hoch, E. D. The last unicorns

Stivens, D. The unicorn

Sturgeon, T. The silken-swift . . .

Zelazny, R. Unicorn variations

The **unicorn's** daughter. Hoch, E. D.

UNIDENTIFIED FLYING SAUCERS See Flying saucers

The **uniform**. Dundas, R.

Uninvited disaster. Pilcher, R.
The union buries its dead. Lawson, H.
UNION OF SOVIET SOCIALIST REPUBLICS *See* Soviet Union
Unique is where you find it. Asimov, I.
A unique service. Reed, K.
UNITED NATIONS
 Anvil, C. A rose by other name . . .
 Muller, R. Of science and love
UNITED STATES
  See also Middle Western States; Southern States; Southwestern States; Western States; also names of individual states
To 1776
Freeman, M. E. W. Silence
19th century
Bowen, S. P. A marriage of persuasion
Bowen, S. P. Old maidism versus marriage
Card, O. S. Hatrack River
Dall, C. W. H. Annie Gray: a tale
Johnson, C. R. The education of Mingo
War with Mexico, 1845-1848
McCarthy, C. Instruments of liberation
Civil War, 1861-1865
Alcott, L. M. The brothers
Aldrich, T. B. The white feather
Alter, R. E. Bummer's roost
Alter, R. E. The centennial comment
Altsheler, J. At the twelfth hour
Bedford-Jones, H. Ram him, damn him!
Bellah, J. W. How Stonewall came back
Benét, S. V. The die-hard
Benét, S. V. Jack Ellyat at Gettysburg
Bierce, A. An occurrence at Owl Creek Bridge
Burke, J. L. When it's Decoration Day
Chopin, K. The locket
Conley, R. J. The immortals
Cooke, R. T. A woman
Crane, S. A grey sleeve
Crane, S. The little regiment
Crane, S. A mystery of heroism: a detail of an American battle
Crane, S. The red badge of courage
De Forest, J. W. The brigade commander
Dowdey, C. Weep not for them
Dykeman, W. Lydia McQueen
Elgin, S. H. Hush my mouth
Faulkner, W. Skirmish at Sartoris
Fitzgerald, F. S. The night before Chancellorsville
Foote, S. Pillar of fire
Foote, S. Shiloh [excerpt]
Gordon, C. Hear the nightingale sing
Hannum, A. P. Turkey hunt
Henry, O. Two renegades
Jones, P. Beautiful rebel
King, G. E. Bayou l'Ombre: an incident of the war
Lee, H. Lucia and old lace
Madden, D. A fever of dying
Madden, D. Willis Carr at Bleak House

Marquand, J. P. High tide
Mitchell, M. E. For the honor of the company
Overholser, W. D. The petticoat brigade
Page, T. N. The burial of the guns
Peck, S. M. Pap's mules
Sanders, S. R. America is one long bloody fight
Savage, L. Dangerous orders
Singmaster, E. The battleground
Sullivan, C. The horse in the bedroom
Twain, M. The private history of a campaign that failed
Welty, E. The burning
Williams, J. A. Captain Blackman [excerpt]
Wolfe, T. Chickamauga
Wolfe, T. The plumed knight
Woodrell, D. Woe to live on
Woolson, C. F. Crowder's Cove: a story of the war
Woolson, C. F. In the cotton country
War of 1898
Crane, S. The clan of no-name
Crane, S. An episode of war
Crane, S. "God rest ye, merry gentlemen"
Crane, S. Marines signaling under fire at Guantanamo
Crane, S. The price of the harness
Crane, S. The revenge of the Adolphus
Crane, S. The second generation
Crane, S. This majestic lie
Crane, S. Virtue in war
20th century
Kornblatt, J. R. Susan
Shiner, L. Twilight time
Wolfe, T. A prologue to America
Wolfe, T. The promise of America
College life
 See College life—United States
Politics
 See Politics—United States
Presidents
 See Presidents—United States
Prisoners and prisons
 See Prisoners and prisons—United States
Race relations
Andrews, R. Appalachee Red [excerpt]
Bishop, M. One winter in Eden
Bloch, R. The warm farewell
Bonner, M. Nothing new
Bonner, M. One boy's story
Bradley, D. 197903042100 (Sunday)
Brown, M. W. Beyond New Forks
Brown, M. W. Fruit of the season
Brown, M. W. Let him live
Burke, J. L. The convict
Burke, J. L. Uncle Sidney and the Mexicans
Caldwell, E. Kneel to the rising sun
Child, L. M. F. The quadroons
Childress, A. Merry Christmas, Marge!
Conroy, J. The cement king

UNITED STATES — Race relations — *Continued*
  Coskran, K. Handyman
  Dubus, A. Sorrowful mysteries
  Dumas, H. Fon
  Dumas, H. Goodbye, sweetwater
  Dumas, H. Rope of wind
  Dumas, H. Thrust counter thrust
  Gates, E. A yellow man and a white
  Hall, M. L. The visit
  Hughes, L. Slave on the block
  Johnson, C. R. The education of Mingo
  Jones, D. C. Knights of the Flaming Circle
  Kilgore, D. The day we discovered we
    were black
  Leedom-Ackerman, J. Sissy Mamma's wig
  Lynch, L. At a bar V: Summer storm
  Matthiessen, P. On the River Styx
  McKnight, R. Getting to be like the studs
  McKnight, R. The honey boys
  McKnight, R. Peaches
  McKnight, R. Rebirth
  Mencken, S. H. Little white girl
  Miller, S. What Ernest says
  O'Connor, F. Revelation
  Pintauro, J. Jungle dove
  Schinto, J. The original dog
  Schinto, J. Shadow bands
  Schwartz, L. S. The middle classes
  Shaik, F. Climbing Monkey Hill
  Spencer, E. The business venture
UNITED STATES. ARMY
  Alderson, T. At salt river
  Alderson, T. FTX; Fort Irwin
  Algren, N. The heroes
  Bonnie, F. Name the general
  Garrett, G. P. The old Army game
  Garrett, G. P. Unmapped country
  Garrett, G. P. What's the purpose of the
    bayonet?
  Pynchon, T. The small rain
        Officers
  Anthony, P. The life of the stripe
  Asimov, I. Yankee Doodle went to town
  Bennett, J. G. Dependents
  Brown, H. A walk in the sun
  Crane, S. Virtue in war
  DeGrazia, E. The death of Sin
  Hoch, E. D. I'd know you anywhere
  Morris, W. The safe place
  O'Brien, T. The things they carried
  Vaughn, S. Able, Baker, Charlie, Dog
UNITED STATES. ARMY. CAVALRY
  Bell, M. S. Today is a good day to die
  Bellah, J. W. Big hunt
  Bellah, J. W. Command
  Kelly, C. A season for heroes
UNITED STATES. CONGRESS
  Crane, S. The second generation
UNITED STATES. CONGRESS. SENATE
  Clarke, A. C. Death and the senator
  Herbert, F. Committee of the whole

**UNITED STATES. DEPT. OF JUSTICE.
  FEDERAL BUREAU OF INVESTI-
  GATION** *See* United States. Federal
  Bureau of Investigation
**UNITED STATES. FEDERAL BUREAU
  OF INVESTIGATION**
  Fleming, B. War memorial
UNITED STATES. MARINE CORPS
  Crane, S. Marines signaling under fire at
    Guantanamo
  Dubus, A. Cadence
  Dubus, A. Over the hill
  Flanagan, R. Smoker
  Saucier, M. Pukes!
  Wheeler, H. C. The fat cat
        Officers
  Dubus, A. The captain
**UNITED   STATES.   NATIONAL
  AERONAUTICS AND SPACE AD-
  MINISTRATION**
  Asimov, I. Out of sight
UNITED STATES. NAVY
        Officers
  Dubus, A. The dark men
The **universal** library. Lasswitz, K.
The **universe** of Mama Malkia. Russo, A.
Universitas. Sheehan, R.
The **university** committee's sociological study
    of a village. Nesin, A.
UNIVERSITY LIFE *See* College life
The **university** of man. Dumas, H.
UNIVERSITY OF OXFORD
  Stewart, J. I. M. The dyslexia factor
UNIVERSITY STUDENTS *See* College life
Unknown drives. Matheson, R. C.
Unknown feathers. Benedict, D.
The **unknown** peer. Bentley, E. C.
The **unknown** soldier. Böll, H.
Unlighted lamps. Anderson, S.
Unloading. Asscher-Pinkhof, C.
Unmaking. King, F. H.
Unmapped country. Garrett, G. P.
UNMARRIED COUPLES
  Alden, P. B. In a piney wood
  Atwood, M. Uglypuss
  Beattie, A. Sunshine and shadow
  Beattie, A. Weekend
  Carver, R. Boxes
  Cherches, P. Dirty windows
  Connelly, J. Ours
  Connelly, J. Sleeping together
  Covino, M. The foreigners
  Dodd, S. M. Walls
  Evans, E. Blue news
  Ford, R. Rock Springs
  Francis, H. E. Her
  Frucht, A. Engagements
  Girion, B. Next of kin
  Gray, A. The comedy of the white dog
  Halligan, M. The oak bed
  Janowitz, T. Physics
  Klass, P. Clytemnestra in the suburbs
  Klass, P. Nineteen lists

UNMARRIED COUPLES—*Continued*
  Klass, P. The secret lives of dieters
  Klass, P. Theme and variations
  Kolm, R. Duke & Jill
  La Chapelle, M. Drinking
  Lawson, S. PASTA MOMA
  Lively, P. Grow old along with me, the best is yet to be
  MacLaverty, B. In the hills above Lugano
  Miller, S. Travel
  Munro, A. Labor Day dinner
  Niatum, D. She keeps the dance turning like the earth
  Pearlman, E. Conveniences
  Proulx, A. Heart songs
  Rooke, L. Winter is lovely, isn't summer hell
  Sanford, W. M. Wreck
  Schwartz, L. S. The man at the gate
  Sisskind, M. Proposal and disposal
  Spark, D. The incorrect hour
  Thurm, M. Leaving Johanna

UNMARRIED MOTHERS
  Abbott, K. Mary Lou and the perfect husband
  Birdsell, S. The wild plum tree
  Briskin, M. Two women, one child
  Campbell, W. B. The thaw
  Child, L. M. F. The quadroons
  Essop, A. Two sisters
  Franklin, B. The speech of Polly Baker
  Freeman, C. The bride of Ambrose
  Freeman, J. Clearfield
  Geras, A. Tea in the Wendy House
  Gilman, C. P. Turned
  Gorky, M. Lullaby
  Hagy, A. C. Mister Makes
  Ignatow, R. G. It deals with people first
  Jolley, E. Hilda's wedding
  Le Sueur, M. Sequel to love
  Lee, H. Unto her a child was born
  Lipman, E. Baby's first Christmas
  Lipman, E. Back to normal
  Lipman, E. The day woman
  Lipman, E. Good news
  Lipman, E. They'll smile at you if you're with me
  McGuane, T. The millionaire
  Montgomerie, W. Daft Jenny
  Mundstock, K. A judgment worthy of Solomon
  Oldfield, J. Life-sentence
  Prose, F. Electricity
  Sandel, C. The art of murder
  Sanders, T. E. Ave Lutie
  Shaw, J. B. Love and other lessons
  Shwartz, S. M. Homecoming
  Tsushima, Y. South wind
  Whitaker, M. Five for silver
  Wilbur, E. Faith
  Williams, S. A. Tell Martha not to moan
Unmarried states. Thurm, M.
Unmistakably the finest. Bradfield, S.

Unnamed islands in the unknown sea. Hulme, K.
The **unnecessary** overcoat. Lash, K.
UNO 1945. Stead, C.
An **unofficial** rose. Theroux, P.
Unpaid debts. Kilgore, D.
The **unparalleled** adventure of one Hans Pfaall. Poe, E. A.
The **unpardonable** crime. Bloch, R.
An **unpleasant** business. Chekhov, A. P.
Unpleasantness at Bludleigh Court. Wodehouse, P. G.
The **unreachable** star. Schmidt, S.
An **unreasonable** woman. Maupassant, G. de
The **unseen** aspect. Ioannides, P.
The **unseen** soldier. Walker, W.
Unsophar and Onsopur. Ahern, T.
The **unspeakable** attaché. Durrell, L.
The **unspeakable** betrothal. Bloch, R.
Unspoken words. Moyano, D.
The **unstoppable** man. Gilbert, M.
Unstuck. Updike, J.
An **unsung** Solomon. Mazel, D.
An **unswallowable** love. Gibson, D.
The **unswept** emptiness. Fisher, M. F. K.
Der **untergang** des Abendlandesmenschen. Waldrop, H.
Until it comes closer. McGraw, E.
Until you are dead. Lutz, J.
Untime of the Imam. Rushdie, S.
Untitled—Ink on paper. Ballantyne, S.
Untitled piece. McCullers, C.
Untitled/wailing landscape. De Walef, A. N.
Unto her a child was born. Lee, H.
Unto the fourth generation. Asimov, I.
An **untold** story. Colter, C.
Untouchable. Bloch, R.
UNWED MOTHERS *See* Unmarried mothers
Unwelcome words. Bowles, P.
Unwilling sleep. Brett, S.
Unworthy of the angel. Donaldson, S. R.
An **unwritten** novel. Woolf, V.
Unwrung withers. Davin, D.
UNZEN (JAPAN) *See* Japan—Unzen
Unzen. Endō, S.
Up a tree. West, J.
Up above the world so high. Milosevic, M.
Up among the eagles. Valenzuela, L.
Up-country. Ramírez Muñoz, M. P.
Up home. Wallace, W.
Up in Michigan. Hemingway, E.
Up in the bush. Haukeness, H.
Up in the tree. Kawabata, Y.
Up north. Gallant, M.
Up on the corner, on the dogleg. Drake, R.
Up Schist Crick. Anthony, P.
Up the garden path. Hartley, L. P.
Updike, David
  Agawam
    Updike, D. Out on the marsh
  Apples
    Updike, D. Out on the marsh

Updike, David—*Continued*
Bachelor of Arts
The New Yorker 59:35-7 Ja 30 '84
Updike, D. Out on the marsh
The cushion of time
Updike, D. Out on the marsh
Due cappuccini
The New Yorker 62:39-46 O 27 '86
Updike, D. Out on the marsh
The end of the reign
The New Yorker 60:42-8 O 22 '84
Updike, D. Out on the marsh
First impressions
Updike, D. Out on the marsh
Indian summer
Updike, D. Out on the marsh
Out on the marsh
Updike, D. Out on the marsh
Social studies
Updike, D. Out on the marsh
Spring
Updike, D. Out on the marsh
Summer
20 under 30; ed. by D. Spark
Updike, D. Out on the marsh
Winter
Updike, D. Out on the marsh
Updike, John
The afterlife
The Best American short stories, 1987
The New Yorker 62:34-41 S 15 '86
Beautiful husbands
Updike, J. Trust me
Bech in Czech
The New Yorker 63:32-42+ Ap 20 '87
Brother grasshopper
The New Yorker 63:40-6 D 14 '87
The burglar alarm
The New Yorker 63:30-1 Mr 9 '87
The Christian roommates
American short story masterpieces; ed.
by R. Carver and T. Jenks
The city
Updike, J. Trust me
Conjunction
The New Yorker 63:29-32 Jl 27 '87
A constellation of events
The New Yorker 61:30-4 F 25 '85
Updike, J. Trust me
Deaths of distant friends
Updike, J. Trust me
Getting into the set
Updike, J. Trust me
Here come the Maples
Great American love stories; ed. by L.
Rosenthal
The ideal village
Updike, J. Trust me
The journey to the dead
The New Yorker 64:26-34 My 23 '88
Killing
Updike, J. Trust me

Leaf season
The New Yorker 62:47-52+ O 13 '86
Prize stories, 1988
Updike, J. Trust me
Learn a trade
Updike, J. Trust me
Lifeguard
Short stories of the sea; ed. by G. C.
Solley and E. Steinbaugh
The lovely troubled daughters of our old
crowd
Updike, J. Trust me
Made in heaven
The Atlantic 255:48-51+ Ap '85
New American short stories; ed. by G.
Norris
Updike, J. Trust me
Man and daughter in the cold
Family: stories from the interior; ed. by
G. G. Chavis
The man who became a soprano
The New Yorker 64:28-35 D 26 '88
More stately mansions
Updike, J. Trust me
Nevada
The Best of the West; ed. by J. Thomas
One more interview
Updike, J. Trust me
The other
Prize stories, 1985
Updike, J. Trust me
The other woman
The New Yorker 61:32-40+ D 23 '85
Updike, J. Trust me
Pigeon feathers
The World of the short story; ed. by
C. Fadiman
Poker night
The Bread Loaf anthology of contem-
porary American short stories; ed. by
R. Pack and J. Parini
Esquire 102:40-3 Ag '84
The Esquire fiction reader v1
Updike, J. Trust me
Pygmalion
Sudden fiction; ed. by R. Shapard and
J. Thomas
Updike, J. Trust me
Separating
The Art of the tale; ed. by D. Halpern
Slippage
The New Yorker 60:48-51 F 20 '84
Updike, J. Trust me
Still of some use
Updike, J. Trust me
Trust me
Updike, J. Trust me
Unstuck
Updike, J. Trust me
The wallet
Updike, J. Trust me

Updike, John—*Continued*
  When everyone was pregnant
    The Norton book of American short
      stories
  Wildlife
    Esquire 108:62-4+ Ag '87
Uphill runner. McQueen, J.
The **upper** berth. Crawford, F. M.
An **upright** woman. Keating, H. R. F.
Uprising in East Germany. Ziem, J.
Ups and downs. Kinsella, W. P.
Upson, William Hazlett
  Botts runs for his life
    The Saturday Evening Post 257:62-5+
      My/Je '85
The **upstairs** people. Roberts, N.
The **upstart**. Maupassant, G. de
Upstream. Canzoneri, R.
Uptown, downtown: a tour through the gay
  metropolis. Mordden, E.
Uptown local. Duane, D.
The **upturned** face. Crane, S.
Upward, Edward
  At the Ferry Inn
    Upward, E. The night walk, and other
      stories
  Her day
    Upward, E. The night walk, and other
      stories
  The interview
    Upward, E. The night walk, and other
      stories
  The night walk
    Upward, E. The night walk, and other
      stories
  An old-established school
    Upward, E. The night walk, and other
      stories
  Over the cliff
    Upward, E. The night walk, and other
      stories
  The procession
    Upward, E. The night walk, and other
      stories
  The white-pinafored black cat
    Upward, E. The night walk, and other
      stories
URANUS (PLANET)
  Farmer, P. J. Uranus; or, UFO versus IRS
  Sheffield, C. Dies irae
Uranus; or, UFO versus IRS. Farmer, P. J.
Urban renewal. Boyle, T. C.
Urbanowa. Konopnicka, M.
Urchins. Hayman, R.
Ure, Joan
  Kelvingrove Park
    Streets of stone; ed. by M. Burgess and
      H. Whyte
Uriah's letter. Quammen, D.
Ursa Minor. Sladek, J. T.
Ursula. Wyndham, F.
The **urupa**. Grace, P.
The **use** of force. Williams, W. C.

The **used**. Estleman, L. D.
The **used-boy** raisers. Paley, G.
Used goods. Goldleaf, S.
Useful ceremonies. Prose, F.
A **useful** house. Maupassant, G. de
Useless beauty. Maupassant, G. de
User friendly. Robinson, S.
The **uses** of videotape. Carlson, R.
Usher. Granit, A.
The **usurper**. Guido, B.
UTAH
  Alderson, T. Michelson in the desert
                    Salt Lake City
  Bedard, B. The ostrich
  Wright, D. L. The hawk
Utley, Steven, and Waldrop, Howard
  Custer's last jump
    Alternative histories; ed. by C. G.
      Waugh and M. H. Greenberg
Utopia. Cooper, B.
Utopia. Spiro, G.
Utopian dreams. Fraser, J.
UTOPIAS
  Anderson, P. Eutopia
  Bailey, H. The fall of Frenchy Steiner
  Bloch, R. The world-timer
  Bradley, M. Z. The climbing wave
  Grin, A. The heart of the wilderness
  Harrison, M. J. Settling the world
  Knight, D. F. Strangers on paradise
  Le Guin, U. K. The ones who walk away
    from Omelas
The **uttermost** farthing. Benson, A. C.
Uxoricide. Landolfi, T.

V

V-E Day. Long, D.
VACATIONS
  Adams, G. G. The purchase of order
  Ade, G. What they had laid out for their
    vacation
  Alden, P. B. At the beach
  Amichai, Y. Nina of Ashkelon
  Atwood, M. Scarlet ibis
  Bartlett, B. Fearful children [excerpt]
  Berthiaume, A. A change of air
  Block, L. As good as a rest
  Bowles, P. In the red room
  Boylan, C. Villa Marta
  Boyle, K. The first lover
  Busch, F. Critics
  Busch, F. The settlement of Mars
  Campos, J. A redhead named Sabina [ex-
    cerpt]
  Claiborne, S. On vacation
  Clark, M. A long time ago
  Cook, H. Pisces
  Covino, M. The foreigners
  Crane, S. Mr. Binks' day off
  Dunn, D. The canoes

VACATIONS—*Continued*
Eisenstein, S. Moray eel
Eisenstein, S. The weight goes on the downhill ski
Friedman, B. J. Let's hear it for a beautiful guy
Galloway, F. Vida's child
Garner, H. Postcards from surfers
Garrett, G. P. Thus the early gods
Gee, M. The widow
Gingher, M. Aurora Island
Haake, K. Natural histories
Janowitz, T. Sun poisoning
Jespersen, R. Yport
Jolley, E. Grasshoppers
Just, W. S. The Costa Brava, 1959
Keillor, G. Hawaii
Kelly, G. The holiday house
Kessler, J. F. Medea
Kilgore, D. Last summer "How I spent my summer vacation" by Diana Lancaster
Kinsella, W. P. Ups and downs
Klíma, I. My country
Komie, L. B. Picasso is dead
Lavers, N. Big dog
Levine, N. We all begin in a little magazine
Lynch, L. The mirror
Moore, M. J. Summer sand
Morrell, D. The storm
Mullen, R. At the beach
Munro, A. Eskimo
Murphy, Y. The summer the men landed on the moon
Nagibin, IÛ. M. Echo
O'Brien, E. The return
Papaellinas, G. Peter Mavromatis rides the tail of the donkey
Parise, G. Nostalgia
Parise, G. Simplicity
Porter, K. A. Holiday
Pritchard, M. With wings cross water
Pronzini, B. Two weeks every summer
Rogers, T. N. R. Crater Lake
Ross, V. That summer
Rule, J. A migrant Christmas
Sheckley, R. Cordle to onion to carrot
Shepard, L. R&r
Slesar, H. I do not like thee, Dr. Feldman
Stewart, J. I. M. Parlour 4
Thompson, K. Getting ready to go camping down in Maine
Tracy, H. A rest and a change
Tremain, R. Autumn in Florida
Updike, J. Leaf season
Wegner, H. The huzul flute
Wheatcroft, J. Hero
Whelan, G. A lesson in the classics
Whelan, G. The mummies of Guanajuato
Wiesinger, S. Cane Road
Wilson, B. Crater Lake
Wohmann, G. The swan

Vachss, Andrew H.
It's a hard world
A Matter of crime v1
VACUUM CLEANERS
Carver, R. Collectors
Kroll, J. The Electrolux man
The **vacuum-packed** picnic. Gauger, R.
A **vagabond.** Maupassant, G. de
VAGABONDS *See* Rogues and vagabonds
Vagabundus Vinea. De Jong, D.
VAGRANTS *See* Homeless
Valadés, Edmundo
Permission for death is granted
Dark arrows; ed. by A. Manguel
Valdés, Guadalupe
Recuerdo
Between mothers & daughters; ed. by S. Koppelman
Valdez, O. J.
A dollar's worth
Southwest tales; ed. by Alurista and X. Rojas-Urista
Vale, Pollini! Johnston, G.
The **valence** of common ions. Deaver, P. F.
The **Valencia** orange murder. St. James, B.
Valentine rhymes! Shannon, J.
VALENTINE'S DAY
Lynch, L. Marie-Christine I: Valentine's Day
Valenzuela, Luisa, 1938-
All about suicide
Valenzuela, L. Open door
The attainment of knowledge
Valenzuela, L. Open door
The best shod
Valenzuela, L. Open door
The blue water man
Valenzuela, L. Open door
Women's fiction from Latin America; ed. by E. P. Garfield
Cat's eye
Valenzuela, L. Open door
The celery munchers
Valenzuela, L. Open door
The censors
Valenzuela, L. Open door
City of the unknown
Valenzuela, L. Open door
Country carnival
Valenzuela, L. Open door
The door
Valenzuela, L. Open door
A family for Clotilde
Valenzuela, L. Open door
Flea market
Valenzuela, L. Open door
Fourth version
Valenzuela, L. Other weapons
Generous impediments float downriver
Valenzuela, L. Open door
The gift of words
Valenzuela, L. Open door

Valenzuela, Luisa, 1938——_Continued_
  The girl who turned into cider
    Harper's 268:30 Mr '84
  I'm your horse in the night
    The Art of the tale; ed. by D. Halpern
    Valenzuela, L. Other weapons
    Women's fiction from Latin America; ed.
      by E. P. Garfield
  Ladders to success
    Valenzuela, L. Open door
  Legend of the self-sufficient child
    Valenzuela, L. Open door
  Love of animals
    Valenzuela, L. Open door
  The minstrels
    Valenzuela, L. Open door
  My everyday colt
    Valenzuela, L. Open door
  Nihil obstat
    Valenzuela, L. Open door
  One siren or another
    Valenzuela, L. Open door
  Other weapons
    Valenzuela, L. Other weapons
    Women's fiction from Latin America; ed.
      by E. P. Garfield
  Papito's story
    Valenzuela, L. Open door
  The place of its quietude
    Valenzuela, L. Open door
  The redtown chronicles
    Valenzuela, L. Open door
  Rituals of rejection
    Valenzuela, L. Other weapons
  The snow white watchman
    Valenzuela, L. Open door
  The son of Kermaria
    Valenzuela, L. Open door
  A story about greenery
    Valenzuela, L. Open door
  Strange things happen here
    Valenzuela, L. Open door
  Symmetries
    Grand Street 8:35-44 Aut '88
  Trial of the Virgin
    Valenzuela, L. Open door
  Up among the eagles
    Valenzuela, L. Open door
  The verb to kill
    Valenzuela, L. Open door
  Vision out of the corner of one eye
    Valenzuela, L. Open door
  The word "killer"
    Valenzuela, L. Other weapons
VALETS
  Ekström, M. Balzac's valet
  Wodehouse, P. G. The artistic career of
    Corky
  Wodehouse, P. G. Aunt Agatha takes the
    count
  Wodehouse, P. G. The aunt and the slug-
    gard
  Wodehouse, P. G. Bertie changes his mind

  Wodehouse, P. G. Bingo and the little
    woman
  Wodehouse, P. G. Clustering round young
    Bingo
  Wodehouse, P. G. Comrade Bingo
  Wodehouse, P. G. The delayed exit of
    Claude and Eustace
  Wodehouse, P. G. Episode of the dog
    McIntosh
  Wodehouse, P. G. Fixing it for Freddie
  Wodehouse, P. G. The great sermon hand-
    icap
  Wodehouse, P. G. Indian summer of an
    uncle
  Wodehouse, P. G. The inferiority complex
    of old Sippy
  Wodehouse, P. G. Jeeves and the Chump
    Cyril
  Wodehouse, P. G. Jeeves and the greasy
    bird
  Wodehouse, P. G. Jeeves and the hard-
    boiled egg
  Wodehouse, P. G. Jeeves and the impend-
    ing doom
  Wodehouse, P. G. Jeeves and the kid
    Clementina
  Wodehouse, P. G. Jeeves and the old
    school chum
  Wodehouse, P. G. Jeeves and the song of
    songs
  Wodehouse, P. G. Jeeves and the unbid-
    den guest
  Wodehouse, P. G. Jeeves and the Yule-tide
    spirit
  Wodehouse, P. G. Jeeves in the springtime
  Wodehouse, P. G. Jeeves makes an
    omelette
  Wodehouse, P. G. Jeeves takes charge
  Wodehouse, P. G. The love that purifies
  Wodehouse, P. G. The Metropolitan touch
  Wodehouse, P. G. The ordeal of young
    Tuppy
  Wodehouse, P. G. The purity of the turf
  Wodehouse, P. G. The rummy affair of
    old Biffy
  Wodehouse, P. G. Scoring off Jeeves
  Wodehouse, P. G. Sir Roderick comes to
    lunch
  Wodehouse, P. G. The spot of art
  Wodehouse, P. G. Without the option
Valgardson, W. D., 1939-
  Bloodflowers
    The Oxford book of Canadian short
      stories in English
Valhalla. Benford, G.
The valiant woman. Powers, J. F.
La valise. Durrell, L.
Valladares, Armando
  Reality
    Anthology of contemporary Latin Ameri-
      can literature, 1960-1984

Valle, Carmen
Diary entry #1
Reclaiming Medusa; ed. by D. L. Vélez
Diary entry #6
Reclaiming Medusa; ed. by D. L. Vélez
The **Valley**. Burroughs, W. S.
Valley. Kessler, J. F.
The **valley** of sin. Abbott, L. K.
The **valley** of spiders. Wells, H. G.
Valley of the Flame. Kuttner, H.
The **Valley** of the Schmoon. Kinsella, W. P.
VALLEYS
Bowles, P. The circular valley
A **value**. Brooks, J.
Vamp. Conner, M.
Vampire. Matheson, R. C.
VAMPIRE BATS See Bats
The **vampire** cat of Nabeshima. Hurwood, B. J.
VAMPIRES
Aickman, R. Pages from a young girl's journal
Allen, W. Count Dracula
Beaumont, C. Place of meeting
Benson, E. F. Mrs. Amworth
Benson, E. F. The room in the tower
Bloch, R. The living dead
Bloch, R. Underground
Bradbury, R. Homecoming
Byron, G. G. B., 6th Baron. Fragment of a novel
Charnas, S. M. A musical interlude
Charnas, S. M. Unicorn tapestry
Chetwynd-Hayes, R. The werewolf and the vampire
Crawford, F. M. For the blood is the life
Derleth, A. W. The drifting snow
Elflandsson, G. The last time I saw Harris
Forrest, K. V. O captain, my captain
Freeman, M. E. W. Luella Miller
Fritch, C. E. The curse of Hooligan's Bar
Gomez, J. No day too long
Goulart, R. Glory
Grant, C. L. Love-starved
Hall, M. M. Rapture
Holder, N. Blood gothic
Hurwood, B. J. The vampire cat of Nabeshima
Jacobi, C. Revelations in black
King, S. The Night Flier
King, S. One for the road
King, S. Popsy
Kornbluth, C. M. The mindworm
Kushner, E. Night laughter
Le Fanu, J. S. Carmilla
Lee, T. Bite-me-not; or, Fleur de feu
Lee, T. Nunc dimittis
Lichtenberg, J. Through the moon gate
Matheson, R. Drink my blood
Matheson, R. C. Vampire
McDowell, M. Halley's passing
Miller, P. S. Over the river
The Mysterious stranger

Nolan, W. F. Ceremony
Palwick, S. Ever after
Polidori, J. W. The vampyre
Pronzini, B., and Malzberg, B. N. Opening a vein
Russ, J. My dear Emily
Russell, R. American Gothic
Ryan, A. Following the way
Rymer, J. M. Varney the vampyre; or, The feast of blood [excerpt]
Schulze, K. Redmond
Shea, M. The pearls of the vampire queen
Smith, C. A. The end of the story
Smith, C. A. A rendezvous in Averoigne
Smith, E. E. The good husband
Stoker, B. Dracula's guest
Tem, S. R. The men & women of Rivendale
Tenn, W. The human angle
Tieck, J. L. Wake not the dead
Tilton, L. In the service of evil
Turtledove, H. Gentlemen of the shade
Van de Wetering, J. Jacob Sanders' final solution
Wagar, W. W. A woman's life
Wagner, K. E. Beyond any measure
Waldrop, H. Der untergang des Abendlandesmenschen
Wellman, M. W. Coven
Wellman, M. W. The Devil is not mocked
Wellman, M. W. School for the unspeakable
Yarbro, C. Q. Cabin 33
Yarbro, C. Q. The spider glass
The **vampyre**. Polidori, J. W.
Van Arkel, Jo
Everyday living
The Literary Review (Madison, N.J.) 29:47-50 Fall '85
Van de Wetering, Janwillem, 1931-
The deadly egg
Van de Wetering, J. The sergeant's cat, and other stories
A great sight
Van de Wetering, J. The sergeant's cat, and other stories
The Year's best mystery and suspense stories, 1984
Houseful of mussels
Van de Wetering, J. The sergeant's cat, and other stories
Inspector Saito's small satori
The Ethnic detectives; ed. by B. Pronzini and M. H. Greenberg
Van de Wetering, J. Inspector Saito's small satori
Jacob Sanders' final solution
Van de Wetering, J. The sergeant's cat, and other stories
The jughead file
Distant danger; ed. by J. Van de Wetering

Van de Wetering, Janwillem, 1931- — *Continued*
Letter present
Van de Wetering, J. The sergeant's cat,
and other stories
The machine gun and the mannequin
Van de Wetering, J. The sergeant's cat,
and other stories
Messing about in boats
Van de Wetering, J. Inspector Saito's
small satori
The new disciple
Van de Wetering, J. The sergeant's cat,
and other stories
Saito and the fox girl
Van de Wetering, J. Inspector Saito's
small satori
Saito and the sacred stick
Van de Wetering, J. Inspector Saito's
small satori
Saito and the Shogun
Van de Wetering, J. Inspector Saito's
small satori
Saito and the twenty-sen stamp
Van de Wetering, J. Inspector Saito's
small satori
Saito versus Saito
Van de Wetering, J. Inspector Saito's
small satori
Saito versus Satan
Van de Wetering, J. Inspector Saito's
small satori
Saito's small oversight
Van de Wetering, J. Inspector Saito's
small satori
Saito's summary
Van de Wetering, J. Inspector Saito's
small satori
Samurai Saito
Van de Wetering, J. Inspector Saito's
small satori
The sergeant's cat
Van de Wetering, J. The sergeant's cat,
and other stories
Six this, six that
Van de Wetering, J. The sergeant's cat,
and other stories
Sure, blue, and dead, too
Van de Wetering, J. The sergeant's cat,
and other stories
A tale with an end
Van de Wetering, J. The sergeant's cat,
and other stories
A tasty tidbit
Van de Wetering, J. The sergeant's cat,
and other stories
There goes Ravelaar
Van de Wetering, J. The sergeant's cat,
and other stories
The yoga yo-yo
Van de Wetering, J. The sergeant's cat,
and other stories

Van Den Heever, Toon
Outa Sem and Father Christmas
The Penguin book of Southern African
stories
Van Derveer, Max
The quiet investigation
Alfred Hitchcock's Mortal errors
Van Ewyck, Annemarie
The lens
The Penguin world omnibus of science
fiction
Van Gelder, Gordon
Santa's tenth reindeer
100 great fantasy short short stories; ed.
by I. Asimov; T. Carr and M. H.
Greenberg
VAN GOGH, VINCENT *See* Gogh, Vincent
van, 1853-1890
The **Van Gogh** field. Kittredge, W.
Van Greenaway, Peter, 1929-
Cadenza
Van Greenaway, P. The immortal coil
The exhibition
Van Greenaway, P. The immortal coil
The immortal coil
Van Greenaway, P. The immortal coil
Indefinite article
Van Greenaway, P. The immortal coil
Janus
Van Greenaway, P. The immortal coil
A western
Van Greenaway, P. The immortal coil
Van Gulik, Robert *See* Gulik, Robert Hans
van, 1910-1967
Van Herk, Aritha, 1954-
Waiting for the rodeo
Alberta bound; ed. by F. Stenson
Van Langenberg, Carolyn
An unfinished head
Transgressions; ed. by D. Anderson
Van Name, Mark L.
My sister, my self
Isaac Asimov's Tomorrow's voices
Van Steen, Edla
Mr. and Mrs. Martins
The Literary Review (Madison, N.J.)
27:442-5 Summ '84
Van Vechten, Carl, 1880-1964
Parties [excerpt]
Inspired by drink; ed. by Joan Digby
and John Digby
Van Vogt, A. E. (Alfred Elton), 1912-
Fulfillment
Machines that think; ed. by I. Asimov;
P. S. Warrick and M. H. Greenberg
The witch
Witches; ed. by I. Asimov; M. H.
Greenberg and C. G. Waugh
Van Vogt, Alfred Elton *See* Van Vogt, A.
E. (Alfred Elton), 1912-
Van Wert, William F.
The blue hotel
Southwest Review 71:206-21 Spr '86

Van Wert, William F.—*Continued*
  Fear of trembling
    The Georgia Review 42:132-46 Spr '88
  An irony
    The Literary Review (Madison, N.J.)
      30:543-52 Summ '87
  Piano lessons
    The Georgia Review 41:19-33 Spr '87
  Shoe trees
    The Yale Review 77:418-34 Spr '88
  Stanton: the man and his times
    The Antioch Review 46:27-36 Wint '88
Van Zleer, Doris
  Violet's choice
    Short story international 71
Vance, Jack, 1916-
  The gift of gab
    From mind to mind: tales of communi-
      cation from Analog
  Guyal of Sfere
    Baker's dozen: 13 short fantasy novels
  The Kokod warriors
    The Science fictional Olympics; ed. by
      I. Asimov; M. H. Greenberg and C.
      G. Waugh
  Mazirian the Magician
    Wizards; ed. by I. Asimov; M. H.
      Greenberg and C. G. Waugh
  The new prime
    Robert Silverberg's Worlds of wonder
  Sail 25
    Amazing stories: visions of other worlds
Vance, John Holbrook *See* Vance, Jack,
  1916-
VANCOUVER (B.C.) *See* Canada—
  Vancouver
The **Vancouver** chapter of the Howard G.
  Scharff Memorial Society. Kinsella, W.
  P.
VANCOUVER ISLAND (B.C.)
  Gallant, M. The prodigal parent
  Kinsella, W. P. The East End Umbrella
    Company endowment for the arts
  Kinsella, W. P. The secret
  Kinsella, W. P. The silver porcupine
VANDALISM
  Burke, M. Lou's corner
  Clifton, M. Hang head, vandal!
  Pronzini, B. A craving for originality
Vandegrift, George
  White mother of shadows
    The Weirds; ed. by S. Jaffery
Vander Putten, Joan
  Just a little thing
    Devils & demons; ed. by M. Kaye and
      S. Kaye
Vandercook, John W.
  The challenge
    Haunted New England; ed. by C. G.
      Waugh; M. H. Greenberg and F. D.
      McSherry

Vanderhaeghe, Guy, 1951-
  Cages
    Vanderhaeghe, G. Man descending
  Dancing bear
    The Oxford book of Canadian short
      stories in English
    Vanderhaeghe, G. Man descending
  Drummer
    Vanderhaeghe, G. Man descending
  The expatriates' party
    Vanderhaeghe, G. Man descending
  Going to Russia
    Vanderhaeghe, G. Man descending
  How the story ends
    Vanderhaeghe, G. Man descending
  Man descending
    Vanderhaeghe, G. Man descending
  Reunion
    The Old dance; ed. by B. Burnard
    Vanderhaeghe, G. Man descending
  Sam, Soren, and Ed
    Vanderhaeghe, G. Man descending
  A taste for perfection
    Vanderhaeghe, G. Man descending
  The watcher
    Vanderhaeghe, G. Man descending
  What I learned from Caesar
    Vanderhaeghe, G. Man descending
Vandy, Vandy. Wellman, M. W.
Vanished!. Thayer, N.
The **vanished** steamboat. Hoch, E. D.
Vanishing act. Pronzini, B., and Kurland, M.
The **vanishing** of Velma. Hoch, E. D.
The **vanishing** virgin. Randisi, R. J.
VANITY *See* Egoism
The **vanity** of small differences. Pollack, E.
Vannice, Judith
  The rainbow painter
    Seventeen 44:72-3+ Ja '85
VANUATU
  Kelly, C. The waters of Vanuatu
Vardeman, Robert E.
  The Road of Dreams and death
    Tales of the Witch World [1]
Vargas, Kika
  The corpse
    Cuentos Chicanos; ed. by R. A. Anaya
      and A. Márquez
Vargas Llosa, Mario, 1936-
  The challenge
    The Art of the tale; ed. by D. Halpern
Variant text. Goodman, A.
VARIATION (BIOLOGY) *See* Mutation (Bi-
  ology)
Variation on a man. Cadigan, P.
Variations on a scheme. Ritchie, J.
Variations on a theme. See O'Connor, F. A
  set of variations on a borrowed theme
Varieties of exile. Gallant, M.

Varlamova, Inna
A ladle for pure water
The Barsukov Triangle, The two-toned
blond & other stories; ed. by C. R.
Proffer & E. Proffer
Russian and Polish women's fiction; ed.
by H. Goscilo
Varley, John, 1947-
Lollipop and the tar baby
Worlds apart; ed. by C. Decarnin; E.
Garber and L. Paleo
Manikins
Amazing stories: 60 years of the best
science fiction
Options
The Best from Universe
The persistence of vision
The Hugo winners v4
Press enter
Nebula awards 20
The Year's best science fiction, second
annual collection
The pusher
The Hugo winners v5
Tango Charlie and Foxtrot Romeo
Terry Carr's Best science fiction and fan-
tasy of the year #16
Varney the vampyre; or, The feast of blood.
Rymer, J. M.
Varshavsky, Ilya
No alarming symptoms
Aliens, travelers, and other strangers; by
B. and A. Strugatsky and others
The secrets of the genre
Aliens, travelers, and other strangers; by
B. and A. Strugatsky and others
Vasili and Vasilisa. Rasputin, V. G.
VAUDEVILLE
See also Music halls (Variety
theaters, cabarets, etc.)
Vaudeville. Strieber, W.
Vaughan, Dai
The death of a champion
Stand one; ed. by M. Blackburn; J.
Silkin and L. Tracy
Vaughan, Mary C.
Fruits of sorrow; or, An old maid's story
Old maids; ed. by S. Koppelman
Vaughan, Ralph E.
The mystery of the desert giants
'Teen 32:38-40+ Jl '88
Vaughn, Stephanie
Able, Baker, Charlie, Dog
Soldiers & civilians; ed. by T. Jenks
Kid MacArthur
The New Yorker 60:46-56 D 17 '84
Prize stories, 1986
Sweet talk
Love stories for the time being; ed. by
G. D. Chipps and B. Henderson
The **vaults** of Yoh-Vombis. Smith, C. A.

Vega, Ana Lydia
ADJ, Inc.
Reclaiming Medusa; ed. by D. L. Vélez
Lyrics for Puerto Rican salsa and three
soneos by request
The Pushcart prize XI
Three love aerobics
Reclaiming Medusa; ed. by D. L. Vélez
VEGETARIANS
Houbein, L. A serious courtship
The **veil.** El Saadawi, N.
The **veiled** lady. Christie, A.
The **veiled** man. Schwob, M.
Veins visible. Bissoondath, N.
Velodrome. Loukakis, A.
The **velvet** dress. Ocampo, S.
Venables, Terry, 1943-
*For works written by this author in
collaboration with Gordon M. Wil-
liams see Yuill, P. B.*
VENDETTA *See* Revenge
VENDING STANDS
Crane, S. A great mistake
Lynch, L. Fruitstand I: Oranges out of
season
VENEREAL DISEASES *See* Sexually trans-
mitted diseases
Venetian masks. Bioy Casares, A.
VENEZUELA
Peterson, J. Yellow dust
Scott, L. The house of funerals
VENEZUELANS
United States
Wilson, B. Miss Venezuela
VENGEANCE *See* Revenge
The **vengeance** of Nitocris. Williams, T.
Vengeance station. Olsen, T. V.
VENICE (CALIF.) *See* California—Venice
VENICE (ITALY) *See* Italy—Venice
Venice drowned. Robinson, K. S.
VENTRILOQUISTS
Apollinaire, G. The talking memories
Bishop, M. Voices
Bloch, R. Final performance
Bradbury, R. And so died Riabouchinska
Russell, W. C. Can these dry bones live?
VENUS (PLANET)
Clarke, A. C. Before Eden
Dickson, G. R. The monkey wrench
Randall, M. Big dome
Russell, E. F., and Johnson, L. T. Seeker
of tomorrow
The **Venus** of Braniza. Maupassant, G. de
The **Venus** tree. Pritchett, M.
The **verb** to kill. Valenzuela, L.
Verbal transcription: 6 A.M. Williams, W.
C.
Vercors, 1902-
Helplessness
The Antioch Review 45:315-21 Summ '87
That day
The Antioch Review 45:310-14 Summ '87
La **Verdad:** the magic sword. Major, A. R.

Verdery, Daniel

Gardener

The Sewanee Review 92:48-57 Wint '84

The **verdict**. Johnston, G.

Veritas. Morrow, J.

Verma, Nirmal, 1929-

The burning bush

Verma, N. Maya Darpan, and other stories

Verma, N. The world elsewhere, and other stories

The dead and the dying

Verma, N. Maya Darpan, and other stories

Verma, N. The world elsewhere, and other stories

The difference

Verma, N. Maya Darpan, and other stories

Verma, N. The world elsewhere, and other stories

Exile

Verma, N. Maya Darpan, and other stories

Verma, N. The world elsewhere, and other stories

An inch and a half above ground

Verma, N. Maya Darpan, and other stories

Verma, N. The world elsewhere, and other stories

The man and the girl

Verma, N. Maya Darpan, and other stories

Verma, N. The world elsewhere, and other stories

Maya Darpan

Verma, N. Maya Darpan, and other stories

Verma, N. The world elsewhere, and other stories

A room of their own

Verma, N. Maya Darpan, and other stories

Verma, N. The world elsewhere, and other stories

A splinter of the sun

Verma, N. Maya Darpan, and other stories

Verma, N. The world elsewhere, and other stories

Under cover of darkness

Verma, N. Maya Darpan, and other stories

Verma, N. The world elsewhere, and other stories

Weekend

Verma, N. Maya Darpan, and other stories

Verma, N. The world elsewhere, and other stories

The world elsewhere

Verma, N. Maya Darpan, and other stories

Verma, N. The world elsewhere, and other stories

VERMONT

Freeman, C. Before he went out west

Freeman, C. The bride of Ambrose

Freeman, C. Crime of the century

Freeman, C. Dreaming of Africa

Freeman, C. The exile, the housekeeper, and Flora, the beauty of Rome

Freeman, C. My life on the snowplow

Freeman, C. Not everyone can be a soldier

Freeman, C. The ride

Freeman, C. Seven prophecies of Egypt

Harper, R. B. Bale jumpers

Lewis, S. A letter from the Queen

O'Brien, E. Ways

Robison, J. The Indian Gardens

Updike, J. Leaf season

Wetherell, W. D. North of peace

VERMOUTH *See* Wine and wine making

Vernalfest morning. Bishop, M.

Verne, Jules, 1828-1905

Captain Nemo's revenge

Men at sea; ed. by B. Aymar

The storm

Black water; ed. by A. Manguel

Vernon's dragon. Betancourt, J. G.

Verona: a young woman speaks. Brodkey, H.

Veronica's shrouds. Tournier, M.

A **version** of my death. Rey Rosa, R.

The **vertical** fields. Dawson, F.

The **vertical** ladder. Sansom, W.

Vervaecke, Kris

Black dirt

Prairie Schooner 59:23-32 Spr '85

Véry, Pierre

The lady of the museums

Great French detective stories; ed. by T. J. Hale

Watch the red balloons

Great French detective stories; ed. by T. J. Hale

A **very** Baltic story. Becher, U.

The **very** best. Lutz, J.

A **very** brief season. Girion, B.

The **very** last day of a good woman. Ellison, H.

The **very** last party at #13 Mallory Way. Carroll, L. E.

A **very** old man. Treviño, J. S.

A **very** old man with enormous wings. García Márquez, G.

A **very** present help. Hartley, L. P.

A **very** short story. Hemingway, E.

A **very** small clue. Ferrars, E. X.

A **very** special relationship. Gilbert, M.

Vesity, Art
  The first day
    Tales from Isaac Asimov's science fiction magazine: short stories for young adults
The **vest**. Thomas, D.
Vester, Lee
  Pawn promotion
    Isaac Asimov's Tomorrow's voices
Vestrand's Extelopedia in 44 magnetomes. Lem, S.
Vészi, Endre
  Chapters from the life of Vera Angi
    Short story international 47
The **veteran**. Crane, S.
The **veteran**. Drake, R.
The **veteran**. Mrozek, S.
VETERANS
  Bausch, R. The man who knew Belle Starr
  Bernard, K. Teddy and I go Kong
  Bloch, R. You could be wrong
  Bonnie, F. A settlement of wages
  Garrett, G. P. Wounded soldier
  L'Heureux, J. The anatomy of desire
  Mrozek, S. The veteran
  Norris, H. The cormorant
  Shacochis, B. Where Pelham fell
VETERANS (AMERICAN CIVIL WAR, 1861-1865)
  Ahlswede, A. The promise of the fruit
  Alter, R. E. The centennial comment
  Benét, S. V. The die-hard
  Crane, S. The veteran
  Garland, H. The return of a private
  Henry, O. Two renegades
  Mitchell, M. E. For the honor of the company
  O'Connor, F. A late encounter with the enemy
  Phelps, E. S. Comrades
  Shacochis, B. Where Pelham fell
VETERANS (CRIMEAN WAR, 1853-1856)
  Doyle, Sir A. C. That veteran
VETERANS (KOREAN WAR, 1950-1953)
  Counselman, M. E. Night court
  Hall, T. T. Murphy Walls and the Oriental hummer
  So, K.-W. Half-holiday
  Whisnant, L. Across from the Motoheads
VETERANS (SPANISH CIVIL WAR, 1936-1939)
  Algren, N. Pero venceremos
VETERANS (VIETNAMESE WAR, 1961-1975)
  Abbott, K. He was reaching for a shovel
  Abbott, L. K. Category Z
  Abbott, L. K. I'm glad you asked
  Abbott, L. K. Stand in a row and learn
  Abbott, L. K. When our dream world finds us, and these hard times are gone
  Abbott, L. K. Where is Garland Steeples now?

Alberts, L. Veterans
Arden, W. Homecoming
Barth, S. The broken dam
Barthelme, S. That's no reason
Baxter, C. Xavier speaking
Blei, N. An American presence
Boswell, R. The right thing
Boyd, W. On the Yankee station
Cady, J. By reason of darkness
Camoin, F. A. Home is the Blue Moon Cafe
Casper, S. Covenant with a dragon
Crapser, W. Land of the free, home of the brave
Crapser, W. Let it be
Crapser, W. Wild child
Currey, R. Waiting for trains
Deaver, P. F. Wilbur Gray falls in love with an idea
DeGrazia, E. Enemy country
Dubus, A. Dressed like summer leaves
Ellison, H. Basilisk
Flaherty, G. The main chance
Grant, C. L. The sheeted dead
Harrington, J. A letter to Amy
Heinemann, L. Good morning to you, Lieutenant
Kalpakian, L. Veteran's Day
Kessel, J. Credibility
Mason, B. A. Big Bertha stories
Masur, H. Q. Dead game
McCammon, R. R. Nightcrawlers
McKinley, J. Gloves and fishes
Mukherjee, B. Fathering
Mukherjee, B. Loose ends
Russo, R. P. In the season of the rains
Shepard, L. Shades
Stone, R. Helping
Stone, R. Operate and maintain
Taylor, P. E. A call from brotherland
Taylor, P. E. Descent into brotherland
Taylor, R. Where are our M.I.A.'s?
Vaughn, S. Kid MacArthur
Weaver, G. Canavan's knee
Wiebe, D. E. The art of Vietnam
Wilbur, E. Wind and birds and human voices
Wolff, T. Soldier's joy
VETERANS (WORLD WAR, 1914-1918)
  Bradbury, R. Lafayette, farewell
  Garrett, G. P. Good-bye, good-bye, be always kind and true
  Hemingway, E. Soldier's home
  Parise, G. Patriotism
  Pavese, C. Friends
VETERANS (WORLD WAR, 1939-1945)
  Böll, H. Business is business
  Böll, H. Green are the meadows
  Böll, H. My expensive leg
  Böll, H. The waiting-room
  Clark, G. Blood blossom
  Collins, M. The motive
  Hall, M. L. Lucky Lafe

VETERANS (WORLD WAR, 1939-1945)—
Continued
  McKinley, J. Chambers
  Moffatt, D. Willie's war
  Sanders, S. R. Wake
  Sanders, S. R. Walking to sleep
  Spilman, R. The old man tells his story
    and gets it wrong
  Swados, H. Nights in the gardens of
    Brooklyn
Veterans. Alberts, L.
Veterans. Beal, M. F.
Veteran's Day. Kalpakian, L.
VETERINARIANS
  Thompson, J. Ice flowers
Vets. Doubiago, S.
The **vetting** session. Nowakowski, M.
VEVEY (SWITZERLAND) *See* Switzer-
  land—Vevey
The **Vicar** of Hell. Hoch, E. D.
The **vicar's** wife. Hogan, D.
Vick, Frank
  Pigeons
    The Yale Review 76:91-100 Aut '86
Vickers, Hugo
  Vuidons les tonneaux
    Winter's tales, new ser. v3
Vickers, Roy, d. 1965
  The man who murdered in public
    The Penguin classic crime omnibus
The **victim.** Colette
The **victim.** Garrett, G. P.
The **victim.** James, P. D.
The **victim.** Maupassant, G. de
The **victim.** Petrakis, H. M.
The **victim.** Sinclair, M.
A **victim** must be found. Slesar, H.
The **victims.** Burgin, R.
Victims of time. Rao, B. S.
VICTO . . . . Anderman, J.
Victor and David. Martínez-Serros, H.
VICTORIA (B.C.) *See* Canada—Victoria
Victoria. Johnson, H.
The **Victoria** Cross of Timothy O'Hea. Win-
  dsor, G.
VICTORIAN ENGLAND *See* England—19th
  century
Victory. Henley, P.
Victory at North Antor. Kotzwinkle, W.
Victory over Japan. Gilchrist, E.
Victrola. Morris, W.
La **vida.** Camoin, F. A.
Vida's child. Galloway, F.
VIDEO GAMES
  Casper, S. Spring-fingered Jack
  Pimple, D. J. Arcadus Arcane
  Sladek, J. T. Answers
Video star. Williams, W. J.
VIENNA (AUSTRIA) *See* Austria—Vienna
Vienne. Rhys, J.
VIETNAM
  Kaikō, T. Building a shell mound
  Loewald, U. Bond

  Loewald, U. Cycle
  Minh-Quan. My milk goes dry
      Ho Chi Minh City
  Murphy, Y. Red, red
        Saigon
    See Vietnam—Ho Chi Minh City
Vietnam-Perkasie. Ehrhart, W. D.
VIETNAMESE
        Australia
  Houbein, L. Survival switch
  Loewald, U. Cycle
      United States
  Casper, S. Covenant with a dragon
  Sayles, J. Tan
VIETNAMESE REFUGEES *See* Refugees,
  Vietnamese
VIETNAMESE SOLDIERS *See* Soldiers—
  Vietnam
VIETNAMESE WAR, 1961-1975
  Abbott, L. K. Rolling thunder
  Abbott, L. K. We get smashed and our
    endings are swift
  Abbott, L. K. When our dream world
    finds us, and these hard times are
    gone
  Aldiss, B. W. My country 'tis not only of
    thee
  Ardizzone, T. The intersection
  Boswell, R. The right thing
  Bova, B. Brothers
  Cady, J. By reason of darkness
  Ch'en, Y.-C. Roses in June
  Christman, R. The Mai-Loan and the man
    who could fly
  Colter, C. The march
  Crapser, W. Baptism of fire
  Crapser, W. Billy Sunday
  Crapser, W. The descent
  Crapser, W. Education of a pointman
  Crapser, W. For Timothy Baer
  Crapser, W. Hungers
  Crapser, W. A letter home [1]
  Crapser, W. A letter home [2]
  Crapser, W. A letter home [3]
  Crapser, W. A letter home [4]
  Crapser, W. New man
  Crapser, W. Nicky Martinez
  Crapser, W. Proud
  Crapser, W. R&R
  Crapser, W. Remains
  Crapser, W. The rest
  Crapser, W. The wall: Michael Bowle
  Crapser, W. The war enters
  Cross, R. A. The heavenly blue answer
  Curley, D. Billy Will's song
  DeGrazia, E. Brothers of the tiger
  DeGrazia, E. The cat-hater
  DeGrazia, E. The death of Sin
  DeGrazia, E. The enemy
  DeGrazia, E. Enemy country
  DeGrazia, E. The girl and two old men
  DeGrazia, E. The light at the end of the
    tunnel

VIETNAMESE WAR, 1961-1975 — *Continued*

DeGrazia, E. The man who cursed and the good Lutheran boy
DeGrazia, E. The mask
DeGrazia, E. The sniper
DeGrazia, E. Zabel's choice
Ehrhart, W. D. Vietnam-Perkasie
Flynn, R. The feelings of the dead
Flynn, R. The killer
Fowler, K. J. Letters from home
Frazier, R. Across those endless skies
Haldeman, J. W. DX
Haldeman, J. W. The monster
Kaikō, T. Festivities by the river
Kaikō, T. Monster and toothpick
Loewald, U. Prosperity
Malzberg, B. N. The Queen of Lower Saigon
Mason, B. A. Big Bertha stories
McAllister, B. Dream baby
Mort, J. Tanks
O'Brien, T. The ghost soldiers
O'Brien, T. Going after Cacciato
O'Brien, T. The things they carried
Pak, S.-J. Ten minutes to seven
Pancake, B. D. The honored dead
Pascoe, B. Friday night
Pascoe, B. Soldier goes to ground
Perea, R. L. Small arms fire
Pitzen, J. The village
Sayles, J. Tan
Shepard, L. Delta Sly Honey
Shepard, L. Shades
Shiner, L. The war at home
Strete, C. The game of cat and eagle
The **view**. Garfield, B.
A **view** by the sea. Yasuoka, S.
View from Kwaj. Macinnes, P.
View from the mud. Mitchell, M.
The **view** from the sandhills. Drewe, R.
The **view** from the top of the tower. Harrison, H.
The **view** from this window. Russ, J.
A **view** of Exmoor. Warner, S. T.
A **view** of Manhattan. Flanagan, M.
The **view** of me from Mars. Abbott, L. K.
A **view** of the woods. O'Connor, F.
Viewing the remains. Potter, N. A. J.
Vigil. Alderson, T.
VIGILANCE COMMITTEES
Banks, R. The gully
DeRosso, H. A. Vigilante
Doyle, Sir A. C. The last resource
Overholser, W. D. Steel to the west
Vigilante. DeRosso, H. A.
A **vignette** of Susannah. Dadswell, M.
Viidikas, Vicki
A modern Snowwhite
Room to move; ed. by S. Falkiner
VIKINGS
Boyle, T. C. We are Norsemen
Brown, G. M. The day of the ox

Morris, K. The regent of the North
Russ, J. Souls
The **Viking's** daughter. Train, A. C.
Vilela, Luiz
The ants
The Literary Review (Madison, N.J.) 27:481-2 Summ '84
The **Villa** Désirée. Sinclair, M.
Villa Marta. Boylan, C.
The **villa** on the hill. Pavese, C.
The **village**. Pitzen, J.
The **village**. Wilhelm, K.
Village of the dead. Hoch, E. D.
The **village** teacher and the herdsboy. Faik, S.
Village wine. Kim, Y. I.
Villefranche, Anne-Marie, 1899-1980
The arrangements of Françoise Dumoutier
Villefranche, A.-M. Joie d'amour
Christophe and the virgin
Villefranche, A.-M. Joie d'amour
Dr. Faguet amuses himself
Villefranche, A.-M. Joie d'amour
Ginette on the Metro
Villefranche, A.-M. Joie d'amour
Guy's early retirement
Villefranche, A.-M. Joie d'amour
The Italian cousin
Villefranche, A.-M. Joie d'amour
A lesson for Bernard
Villefranche, A.-M. Joie d'amour
Monique and Gérard discuss art
Villefranche, A.-M. Joie d'amour
Nicole liberated
Villefranche, A.-M. Joie d'amour
The self-esteem of Marcel Chalon
Villefranche, A.-M. Joie d'amour
The solicitude of Pauline Devreux
Villefranche, A.-M. Joie d'amour
Villemaire, Yolande, 1949-
In front of the Temple of Luxor, 31 July 1980
Invisible fictions; ed. by G. Hancock
Villiers, Alan John, 1903-
The windjammer film
Sea captains' tales; ed. by A. Enfield
VILLON, FRANÇOIS, b. 1431
About
Stevenson, R. L. A lodging for the night
Vincent, Harl
Rex
Machines that think; ed. by I. Asimov; P. S. Warrick and M. H. Greenberg
Vincent Van Gogh. Gansovsky, S.
Vincenzo and Giulia. Briskin, M.
Vincristine. Lewis, T.
Vine, Barbara
See also Rendell, Ruth, 1930-
The **vine**. Sandoz, M.
The **vine**. Williams, T.
The **vinegar** mother. Rendell, R.

Vines, Howell
The ginsing gatherers
The Art of fiction in the heart of Dixie;
ed. by P. D. Beidler
Vines. Wickstrom, L.
VINEYARDS *See* Wine and wine making
Vinge, Joan D., 1948-
Eyes of amber
The Hugo winners v4
Mother & child
Vinge, J. D. Phoenix in the ashes
Phoenix in the ashes
Vinge, J. D. Phoenix in the ashes
Psiren
Vinge, J. D. Phoenix in the ashes
The storm king
Vinge, J. D. Phoenix in the ashes
Tam Lin
Imaginary lands; ed. by R. McKinley
Voices from the dust
Vinge, J. D. Phoenix in the ashes
Vinge, Joan D., 1948-, and Vinge, Vernor
The peddler's apprentice
Vinge, J. D. Phoenix in the ashes
Vinge, Vernor
Gemstone
The Year's best science fiction, first an-
nual collection
Long shot
Great science fiction; ed. by I. Asimov;
M. H. Greenberg and C. G. Waugh
Machines that think; ed. by I. Asimov;
P. S. Warrick and M. H. Greenberg
(jt. auth) See Vinge, Joan D., 1948-, and
Vinge, Vernor
Vingt-et-un. Böll, H.
Vinyl repair. Woodman, A.
Vinz, Mark
Fireworks
Stiller's pond; ed. by J. Agee; R. Blakely
and S. Welch
Viola, Ann
Excerpts from Sunnyview journal
Love, struggle & change; ed. by I.
Zahava
The **violation.** Day, R. C.
Violation. Gordon, M.
Violators towed away. Mowat, J.
VIOLENCE
See also Child abuse; Riots; Ter-
rorism; Wife abuse
Abbott, L. K. Youth on Mars
Barthelme, S. Beach
Benedict, P. All the dead
Benedict, P. Pit
Boyle, T. C. Greasy Lake
Boyle, T. C. On for the long haul
Bumpus, J. Chums
Burt, S. Wh'appen?
Cook, H. Easter lily
Cullen, E. J. Down time Tyler, Texas
Danby, M. Robbie
Daniels, C. Honky-Tonk Avenue

Eisenstein, S. Straight razor
Ellison, H. A boy and his dog
Ellison, H. The whimper of whipped dogs
Evans, E. Small acts
Flaherty, G. Whom God hath promised
Garrett, G. P. Texarkana was a crazy town
Goyen, W. Had I a hundred mouths
Goyen, W. Precious door
Goyen, W. Tongues of men and of angels
Grin, A. The window in the forest
Hannah, B. Fans
Hood, M. How far she went
Kaikō, T. Duel
Kersh, G. Comrade death
King, S. Nona
Lansdale, J. R. The pit
Lavin, M. The face of hate
Leffland, E. Last courtesies
Lynds, D. Yellow gal
Matthews, J. A cat may look
McGuane, T. To skin a cat
Mukherjee, B. Tamurlane
Murphy, Y. Red, red
Narayan, R. K. Another community
Nicolai, D. Day out
Nuetzel, C. A day for dying
Olson, D. A voice from the leaves
Overholser, W. D. They hanged Wild Bill
Murphy
Parise, G. Hate
Ríos, A. A friend, brother maybe
Sheehan, R. The sack
Skipp, J. Film at eleven
Sonu, H. The terrorist
Spillane, M. Stand up and die!
Swanwick, M. The feast of Saint Janis
Tamer, Z. An angry man
Tamer, Z. City in ashes
Tamer, Z. The day Genghis Khan became
angry
Tamer, Z. Death of the jasmine
Tamer, Z. The family
Tamer, Z. My final adventure
Tamer, Z. Nothing
Thompson, S. Mother's Day
Tiptree, J. Your faces, o my sisters! Your
faces filled of light!
Vance, J. The Kokod warriors
Vanderhaeghe, G. Cages
Vanderhaeghe, G. The watcher
Viramontes, H. M. The Cariboo Cafe
Wilner, H. Emergency room bicentennial
Winter, D. E. Splatter
Working, R. Rendering Byzantium
Violets. O'Brien, E.
Violet's choice. Van Zleer, D.
The **violin** of his mind. Cherry, K.
VIOLINISTS
Aiken, J. The moon's revenge
Asscher-Pinkhof, C. Pied piper of Hamelin
Bates, H. E. The maker of coffins
Daniels, C. The devil went down to Geor-
gia

VIOLINISTS—*Continued*
Lovecraft, H. P. The music of Erich Zann
Melville, H. The fiddler
Norris, H. White hyacinths
Pascoe, B. Jimmy the dancer: necromancer
Singer, I. B. The dead fiddler
Swados, H. The man in the toolhouse
Williams, T. Resemblance between a violin case and a coffin

Viramontes, Helena Maria, 1954-
Birthday
  Viramontes, H. M. The moths, and other stories
The broken web
  Viramontes, H. M. The moths, and other stories
The Cariboo Cafe
  Viramontes, H. M. The moths, and other stories
Growing
  Viramontes, H. M. The moths, and other stories
The long reconciliation
  Viramontes, H. M. The moths, and other stories
The moths
  Viramontes, H. M. The moths, and other stories
Neighbors
  Viramontes, H. M. The moths, and other stories
Snapshots
  Viramontes, H. M. The moths, and other stories

The **vireo's** nest. Summers, H. S.
The **virgin** from Kalamazoo. Gardner, M.
VIRGIN ISLANDS OF THE UNITED STATES
  See also Saint Croix (Virgin Islands of the U.S.)
VIRGIN MARY *See* Mary, Blessed Virgin, Saint
VIRGINIA
  See also Chesapeake Bay (Md. and Va.)
Betts, D. Benson Watts is dead and in Virginia
Brondoli, M. Borrowing
Brondoli, M. What do you think about three times a day?
Phillips, J. A. 1934
Rogers, S. The crumb
Rubin, L. D. The St. Anthony Chorale
VIRGINITY
  See also Celibacy
Dubus, A. Molly
Halligan, M. Thrift
Oates, J. C. The bingo master
Virgins. Trevor, W.
Virgo, Seán, 1940-
Brother Dael's new year
  Virgo, S. Through the eyes of a cat

The hanging man
  Virgo, S. Through the eyes of a cat
Horsey horsey
  Virgo, S. Through the eyes of a cat
On this good ground
  Virgo, S. Through the eyes of a cat
Shan Val Mór
  Virgo, S. Through the eyes of a cat
Through the eyes of a cat
  Virgo, S. Through the eyes of a cat
Tinker tale
  Virgo, S. Through the eyes of a cat
Virtue!. Maupassant, G. de
Virtue (a sketch for a novel). Zapolska, G.
Virtue in the ballet. Maupassant, G. de
Virtue in war. Crane, S.
Virus X. Gallant, M.
VIRUSES
Gerrold, D. How we saved the human race
The **visible** partner. Reed, K.
VISION
  See also Eye
Packer, M. The condition
Williams, C. Et in sempiternum pereant
Vision. MacLeod, A.
A **vision** of judgment. Wells, H. G.
Vision out of the corner of one eye. Valenzuela, L.
The **visionary**. Le Guin, U. K.
The **visionary**. Poe, E. A.
The **visionary** land. Matthews, J.
VISIONS
  See also Dreams; Hallucinations and illusions
Apollinaire, G. The eagle hunt
Castillo, R. C. The miracle
Cherryh, C. J. Cassandra
Coggeshall, R. Peter the Rock
Lovecraft, H. P. The shadow out of time
Maḥfūz, N. The time and the place
Ocampo, S. Visions
Sisskind, M. It so happens
Zahn, T. The Cassandra
Visions. Ocampo, S.
Visions and revisions. Claiborne, S.
Visit. Glasser, P.
The **visit**. Hall, M. L.
Visit. Harding, M.
The **visit**. Monreal, D. N.
A **visit**. O'Donnell, P.
The **visit**. Saiki, J.
A **visit** from Mom. Benderson, B.
A **visit** to Aunt Ivy's. Sanders, W.
A **visit** to grandpa's. Thomas, D.
Visit to her husband. Davis, L.
A **visit** to Morin. Greene, G.
The **visit** to the museum. Nabokov, V. V.
A **visit** to the old city. Tawfiq, S.
A **visit** with Esta. Mazel, D.
The **visitation**. Bear, G.
The **visitation**. Essop, A.
The **visitation**. Whalen, T.

Visitation of the ghost. Lopatin, J.
Visitation rights. Oates, J. C.
VISITING
 Adler, W. The angel of mercy
 Brender à Brandis, M. All that counts
 Carver, R. Feathers
 Carver, R. What's in Alaska
 Engberg, S. A stay by the river
 Gerber, M. J. Someone should know this
  story
 Harington, D. Beginning
 Kawabata, Y. Autumn rain
 Leavitt, D. Territory
 Moore, G. A strange death
 Oates, J. C. Nairobi
 O'Brien, E. Courtship
 O'Brien, E. My mother's mother
 O'Hara, J. Good-by, Herman
 O'Hara, J. The pretty daughters
 Parise, G. Solitude
 Rifaat, A. Thursday lunch
 Rose, D. A. Small family with rooster
 Smiley, J. Lily
 Suckow, R. Visiting
 Thompson, J. The stud
 Thurm, M. Lovers
 Updike, J. The afterlife
 Wasylyk, S. If a body
 Weaver, G. Neery Christmas
 Welch, D. The trout stream
 Wolf, S. The legacy of Beau Kremel
Visiting. Russ, J.
Visiting. Suckow, R.
Visiting day. Russ, J.
Visiting the dead. Curley, D.
The **visitor.** Bowen, E.
The **visitor.** Frahm, L.
The **visitor.** Kim, Y.-J.
The **visitor.** Painter, P.
The **visitor.** Thomas, D.
The **visitor.** Wijenaike, P.
The **visitor.** Winters, J.
A **visitor** from down under. Hartley, L. P.

VISITORS, FOREIGN
 Atwood, M. The man from Mars
 Brown, G. M. An epiphany tale
 Nichols, R. Free fall (R's account)
 Rooke, L. A bolt of white cloth
 Valenzuela, L. Up among the eagles
Visitors. Barthelme, D.
Visitors. Dann, J.
Visitors. Mukherjee, B.
The **visitors.** Strugatskiĭ, B. N., and
  Strugatskiĭ, A. N.

VISITORS FROM OUTER SPACE *See* In-
 terplanetary visitors
The **visualizers.** Powers, P. E.
Vital statistics. Soman, F. J.
Vitamins. Carver, R.

VITICULTURE *See* Wine and wine making
Vivante, Arturo
 Can-can
  Sudden fiction; ed. by R. Shapard and
   J. Thomas
 Fioretta
  The Massachusetts Review 29:319-29
   Summ '88
 The soft core
  Full measure; ed. by D. Sennett
Vive la France! Böll, H.
VIVISECTION *See* Medicine, Experimental
Viy. Gogol', N. V.
Vizenor, Gerald Robert, 1934-
 Reservation café: the origins of American
  Indian instant coffee
 Earth power coming; ed. by S. J. Ortiz
Vizyēnos, G. M. (Geōrgios M.), 1849-1896
 Between Peiraeus and Naples
  Vizyēnos, G. M. My mother's sin, and
   other stories
 The consequences of the old story
  Vizyēnos, G. M. My mother's sin, and
   other stories
 Moscóv-Selím
  Vizyēnos, G. M. My mother's sin, and
   other stories
 My mother's sin
  Vizyēnos, G. M. My mother's sin, and
   other stories
 The only journey of his life
  Vizyēnos, G. M. My mother's sin, and
   other stories
 Who was my brother's killer?
  Vizyēnos, G. M. My mother's sin, and
   other stories
Vizyēnos, Geōrgios M. *See* Vizyēnos, G. M.
 (Geōrgios M.), 1849-1896
Vladimir's kitchen. Dorr, L.
Vogan, Sara
 Angels in the snow
  Vogan, S. Scenes from the homefront
 China across the bay
  Vogan, S. Scenes from the homefront
 The confession of the Finch
  Vogan, S. Scenes from the homefront
 The crane wife
  Vogan, S. Scenes from the homefront
 Hearts of a shark
  Vogan, S. Scenes from the homefront
 Miss Buick of 1942
  Vogan, S. Scenes from the homefront
 Mozart in the afternoon
  Vogan, S. Scenes from the homefront
 No other women
  Vogan, S. Scenes from the homefront
 Scenes from the homefront
  Vogan, S. Scenes from the homefront
 The strength of steel
  Vogan, S. Scenes from the homefront
 Sunday's no name band
  The Graywolf annual 2
  Vogan, S. Scenes from the homefront

The voice. Cinca, S.
The voice. Dumas, H.
The voice. McKnight, R.
Voice. Shelnutt, E.
Voice and eye. Grin, A.
A voice behind him. Brown, F.
A voice from the dead (a monologue). Lavin, M.
Voice from the grave. Powell, P.
A voice from the leaves. Olson, D.
A voice from the woods. Humphrey, W.
The voice in the night. Hodgson, W. H.
The voice in the whirlwind. Floyd, P. L.
The voice of Bugle Ann. Kantor, M.
The voice of science. Doyle, Sir A. C.
The voice of the beach. Campbell, R.
The voice of the mountain. Moore, G.
The voice of the siren. Grin, A.
The voice of unhousement. Blaise, C.
Voice on the telephone. Ocampo, S.
Voiceover. Wellen, E.
Voices. Bishop, M.
Voices. King, F. H.
Voices. Lasseter, R. A.
Voices. Tabucchi, A.
Voices from near and far. Razzak, A. I. A.
Voices from the dust. Vinge, J. D.
Voices from the moon. Dubus, A.
Voices in dead man's well. Honig, D.
Voices in the wind. Helfman, E. S.
Voices lost in snow. Gallant, M.
The voices of El Dorado. Goldsmith, H.

VOLCANOES
Inoue, Y. Under the shadow of Mt. Bandai
Rhys, J. Heat

Volkmer, Jon
The elevator man
Prairie Schooner 60:123-9 Summ '86

Volpi's farewell. Wetherell, W. D.
Volpone. Shapiro, J.

Volsky, Paula
The tenancy of Mr. Eex
Devils & demons; ed. by M. Kaye and S. Kaye

Volume IV, pp. 167-9. Josipovici, G.
The volunteer organist. Franzen, B.

VOLUNTEER WORKERS
Matthews, J. The gray lady

Von Chamisso, Adelbert *See* Chamisso, Adelbert von, 1781-1838

Von Doderer, Heimito *See* Doderer, Heimito von, 1896-1966

Von Goethe, Johann Wolfgang *See* Goethe, Johann Wolfgang von, 1749-1832

Von Jung, the mystific. Poe, E. A.
Von Kempelen and his discovery. Poe, E. A.

Von Kleist, Heinrich *See* Kleist, Heinrich von, 1777-1811

Von Stamwitz, Alicia
Thinking of you
Redbook 166:42-3 F '86

Vonarburg, Elisabeth
Cold bridge
Invisible fictions; ed. by G. Hancock

Vonnegut, Kurt, 1922-
The boy who hated girls
The Saturday Evening Post 260:42-5+ S '88
A dream of the future (not excluding lobsters)
Esquire 104:74-6 Ag '85
The Esquire fiction reader v2

VOODOOISM
See also Zombies
Adcock, T. L. Thrown-away child
Goulart, R. Junior partner
Haldeman, J. W. Lindsay and the red city blues
Khan, I. Shadows move in the Britannia Bar
Lee, T. Cyrion in wax
Spector, C. Lifecast
Sturgeon, T. A way of thinking
Tenn, W. Mistress Sary
Wilson, F. P. Cuts
Woolrich, C. Dark melody of madness

Vorsatz, Fred
From noon to midnight
Stories and poems from close to home; ed. by F. Salas

Vox Olympica. Bishop, M.
The voyage. Mansfield, K.
Voyage into illusion. Gilbert, M.
Voyage of the heart. Cherry, K.
The voyage of their life. Adams, G.
Voyage South from Thousand Willows. Shepard, L.
The voyage that lasted 600 years. Wilcox, D.
A voyage to Sfanomoë. Smith, C. A.

VOYAGES AND TRAVELS
See also Adventure; Air travel; Railroads—Travel; Sea stories; Tourist trade; Travelers
Adams, G. G. The purchase of order
Aickman, R. The trains
al-Ujayli, A. al--S. Madness
Ballantyne, S. Flaubert in Miami Beach
Birtha, B. Past halfway
Donaldson, S. R. Gilden-Fire
Dumas, H. The university of man
Flynn, R. The great plain
Ingalls, R. Captain Hendrik's story
Jean Paul. Army-chaplain Schmelzle's journey to Flätz
MacLeod, A. Vision
Munro, A. Miles City, Montana
Robinson, K. S. Mother goddess of the world
Stern, S. A sentimental journey
Vizyēnos, G. M. Between Peiraeus and Naples
Warren, J. Hill climbing by boat
Voyeur. Kinsella, W. P.

The **voyeur**. Yaryura-Tobías, A.
VOYEURS
Campbell, R. Stages
Drewe, R. The view from the sandhills
Halligan, M. Paris vicarious
Highsmith, P. When in Rome
Michaels, L. Murderers
Moravia, A. The voyeur's stroll
Shaw, J. B. The trail to the ledge
Sheckley, R. Is that what people do?
Starr, V. A Japanese play
The **voyeur's** stroll. Moravia, A.
Vreuls, Diane
The Alice P. Gamboe strip
  Vreuls, D. Let us know
Beebee
  Shenandoah: an anthology; ed. by J.
    Boatwright
  Vreuls, D. Let us know
Boys and music
  Vreuls, D. Let us know
Estarolly's mountain
  Vreuls, D. Let us know
Facing the cold
  Vreuls, D. Let us know
Let us know
  Vreuls, D. Let us know
The Mary mystery
  Vreuls, D. Let us know
Meeting you
  Vreuls, D. Let us know
Returns
  Vreuls, D. Let us know
The seller of watches
  Vreuls, D. Let us know
Stoke Sobel in Polk
  Vreuls, D. Let us know
A town like Kansas
  Vreuls, D. Let us know
Vuidons les tonneaux. Vickers, H.
Vulcan. Behrens, P.
Vulcan's forge. Anderson, P.
The **vultures** of Malabar. Hoch, E. D.
Vultures without feathers. Ribeyro, J. R.

W

W.S.. Hartley, L. P.
Wa Thiong'o, James *See* Ngugi wa Thiong'o,
  1938-
Wady, Taha
The madman
  Egyptian tales and short stories of the
    1970s and 1980s
Wagar, W. Warren
Madonna of the red sun
  Synergy v1
A woman's life
  Afterlives; ed. by P. Sargent and I. Wat-
    son
The **wager**. Fish, R. L.

WAGERS
Archer, J. Honor among thieves
Chekhov, A. P. The bet
Crane, S. The wise men: a detail of Amer-
  ican life in Mexico
Dahl, R. Man from the south
Dahl, R. Taste
Daniels, C. Radio Smith
Faulkner, W. Was
Fish, R. L. The wager
Fox, W. P. You don't smell it: you drink
  it
Poe, E. A. Never bet the devil your head
Street, J. Weep no more, my lady
Thackeray, W. M. The devil's wager
Twain, M. The notorious jumping frog of
  Calaveras County
Wolff, T. The poor are always with us
Wagner, Karl Edward
An awareness of angels
  Ripper! Ed. by G. Dozois and S. Casper
Beyond any measure
  Whispers V
Cold light
  Robert Adams' Book of soldiers
Endless night
  The Architecture of fear; ed. by K.
    Cramer and P. D. Pautz
Lacunae
  Cutting edge; ed. by D. Etchison
More sinned against
  Silver scream; ed. by D. J. Schow
Neither brute nor human
  Masters of darkness; ed. by D. Etchison
Sticks
  The Dark descent; ed. by D. G. Hart-
    well
Where the summer ends
  Nightmares in Dixie; ed. by F. McSher-
    ry; C. G. Waugh and M. H. Green-
    berg
Wagner, Robert E.
I'm going down to watch the horses come
  alive
  Short story international 45
WAGON TRAINS
Bosman, H. C. The Rooinek
Lee, H. Tamsen Donner's decision
Wagoner, David
The land of the dead
  The Georgia Review 41:365-79 Summ '87
The riding lesson
  Southwest Review 72:515-27 Aut '87
Wild goose chase
  The Georgia Review 40:320-8 Spr '86
  Necessary fictions; ed. by S. W. Lind-
    berg and S. Corey
The **wagtail's** nest. Ozaki, S.
WAIKIKI (HAWAII) *See* Hawaii—Waikiki
Wailing well. James, M. R.
Waimarie. Grace, P.

Wain, John
  Julia
    The American Scholar 54:78-88 Wint
      '84/'85
Wainwright, John William, 1921-
  A peal from the past
    Winter's crimes 18
  A wise child
    The Mammoth book of modern crime
      stories; ed. by G. Hardinge
    Winter's crimes 17
Wait. Connelly, J.
The **wait.** Reed, K.
Wait a year and a half. Matsumoto, S.
Wait until heaven. Haake, K.
Waiter, a bock! Maupassant, G. de
WAITERS
  Böll, H. Monologue of a waiter
  Goldman, F. Fili
  Henry, O. The halberdier of the Little
    Rheinschloss
  McCarthy, T. Mammy's boy
  Singer, I. B. The enemy
  Whelan, G. A lesson in the classics
Waiting. Carrington, L.
Waiting. Dubus, A.
Waiting. Hospital, J. T.
Waiting. Josipovici, G.
Waiting. Lerch, S.
Waiting for a poet. Shyer, M. F.
Waiting for Carrie. Dagon, J.
Waiting for Colombo: a close-up. Moorhead,
  F.
Waiting for her train. Lee, A.
Waiting for His Excellency. Carlin, M. M.
Waiting for love. Faik, S.
Waiting for Stella. Adams, A.
Waiting for the broken horse. Woodman, A.
Waiting for the earthquake. Silverberg, R.
Waiting for the forty-one union. Gold, H.
Waiting for the papers. Ryan, A.
Waiting for the postman. Flynn, R.
Waiting for the rodeo. Van Herk, A.
Waiting for the thaw. Lord, N.
Waiting for trains. Currey, R.
The **waiting-room.** Böll, H.
Waiting, waiting . . . . Pronzini, B.
Waiting weeping. Schwartz, J.
WAITRESSES
  Arnow, H. L. S. Fra Lippi and me
  Bates, H. E. The flame
  Camoin, F. A. A hunk of burning love
  Carver, R. Fat
  Carver, R. They're not your husband
  Coleman, W. The Friday night shift at the
    Taco House blues (wah-wah)
  Connelly, J. Agency
  Covino, M. Little by little they come back
    for you
  Dubus, A. Waiting
  Dunn, D. Twin-sets and pickle forks
  Finney, E. J. Night life
  Fox, G. Return to Venice

  Gomez, J. Don't explain
  Hartley, L. P. The face
  Heller, S. Auteur
  Kees, W. Mrs. Lutz
  Mphahlele, E. The coffee-cart girl
  Ngugi wa Thiong'o. Minutes of glory
  Painter, P. Getting to know the weather
  Rambach, P. Winter ends
  Seepaul, L. A key for Dolcina
The **waits.** Hartley, L. P.
Wakayama, Mary
  Watching fire
    Passages to the dream shore; ed. by F.
      Stewart
Wake. Sanders, S. R.
The **wake.** West, J.
Wake. Winton, T.
Wake and call me mother. Nimmo, D.
Wake for Don Corsinio. Chavez, A.
Wake for the living. Bradbury, R.
Wake not the dead. Tieck, J. L.
Wakefield, H. Russell (Herbert Russell),
  1889-1964
  Blind man's buff
    Dark banquet; ed. by L. Child
  "He cometh and he passeth by!"
    Lost souls; ed. by J. Sullivan
  Old man's beard
    The Oxford book of English ghost
      stories
Wakefield, Herbert Russell *See* Wakefield, H.
  Russell (Herbert Russell), 1889-1964
Wakefield. Hawthorne, N.
Walcote. Wells, H. G.
Walcott, Derek
  Cafe Martinique
    House & Garden 157:140-1+ Mr '85
Walden, Wesley
  The belly of darkness
    TriQuarterly no72:102-25 Spr/Summ '88
Waldie, Scott
  Isn't she lovely?
    Redbook 167:72-6+ S '86
Waldrop, Howard
  Dr. Hudson's secret gorilla
    Waldrop, H. Howard who?
  Fair game
    Afterlives; ed. by P. Sargent and I. Wat-
      son
    The Year's best science fiction, fourth
      annual collection
  Flying saucer rock & roll
    Omni (New York, N.Y.) 7:80-2+ Ja '85
    The Year's best science fiction, third an-
      nual collection
  French scenes
    Synergy v2
  God's hooks!
    Waldrop, H. Howard who?
  Green Brother
    Waldrop, H. Howard who?

Waldrop, Howard—*Continued*
  Heirs of the Perisphere
    Nebula awards 21
    Waldrop, H. Howard who?
  Hoover's men
    Omni (New York, N.Y.) 11:190+ O '88
  Horror, we got
    Waldrop, H. Howard who?
  Ike at the mike
    Omni book of science fiction 1
    Waldrop, H. Howard who?
  The lions are asleep this night
    Omni (New York, N.Y.) 8:48-50+ Ag '86
  Man-Mountain Gentian
    Waldrop, H. Howard who?
    The Year's best science fiction, first annual collection
  Mary Margaret Road-Grader
    Waldrop, H. Howard who?
  Night of the cooters
    Omni (New York, N.Y.) 9:92-4+ Ap '87
    The Year's best science fiction, fifth annual collection
  Save a place in the lifeboat for me
    Waldrop, H. Howard who?
  The ugly chickens
    The Best from Universe
    Waldrop, H. Howard who?
  Der untergang des Abendlandesmenschen
    Waldrop, H. Howard who?
  Wild, wild horses
    Omni (New York, N.Y.) 10:80-2+ Je '88
  ". . . the world, as we know't."
    Waldrop, H. Howard who?
  (jt. auth) See Utley, Steven, and Waldrop, Howard
WALES
  Brooks, J. I'll fight you
          Rural life
  Rossiter, S. Tea party
  Thomas, D. A child's Christmas in Wales
  Thomas, D. The enemies
  Thomas, D. Extraordinary little cough
  Thomas, D. The fight
  Thomas, D. The holy six
  Thomas, D. Old Garbo
  Thomas, D. The orchards
  Thomas, D. Patricia, Edith, and Arnold
  Thomas, D. The peaches
  Thomas, D. Quite early one morning
  Thomas, D. The school for witches
  Thomas, D. The tree
  Thomas, D. Where Tawe flows
  Thomas, D. Who do you wish was with us?
  Walter, E. Come and get me
          Swansea
  Thomas, D. Return journey
Wali, Mohammed Ahmed Abdul
  At a woman's house
    Arabic short stories; tr. by D. Johnson-Davies
Walk home alone. Gardner, C. S.

A **walk** in the city. Flook, M.
A **walk** in the moonlight. Silvis, R.
A **walk** in the sun. Brown, H.
A **walk** in the wheat. Kiely, B.
The **walk-on**. Ardizzone, T.
A **walk** to the jetty. Kincaid, J.
Walk to the moon. Bonosky, P.
Walkabout. Wollaston, N.
Walker, Alice, 1944-
  The abortion
    Buying time; ed. by S. Walker
  Am I Blue?
    Through other eyes; ed. by I. Zahava
  Coming apart
    The Other woman; ed. by S. Koppelman
  Cuddling
    Essence 16:74-6+ Jl '85
  Everyday use
    Between mothers & daughters; ed. by S. Koppelman
    The Norton book of American short stories
  Kindred spirits
    Esquire 104:106-7+ Ag '85
    Prize stories, 1986
  Strong horse tea
    Stories of the modern South; ed. by B. Forkner and P. Samway
Walker, Margaret, 1915-
  Jubilee [excerpt]
    Mississippi writers v1: Fiction; ed. by D. Abbott
Walker, Wendy
  Arnaud's nixie
    Walker, W. The sea-rabbit; or, The artist of life
  Ashiepattle
    Walker, W. The sea-rabbit; or, The artist of life
  The cathedral
    Walker, W. The sea-rabbit; or, The artist of life
  The cleverness of Elsie
    Walker, W. The sea-rabbit; or, The artist of life
  The contract with the beast
    Walker, W. The sea-rabbit; or, The artist of life
  The rescuer
    Walker, W. The sea-rabbit; or, The artist of life
  The sea-rabbit; or, The artist of life
    Walker, W. The sea-rabbit; or, The artist of life
  The true marriage
    Walker, W. The sea-rabbit; or, The artist of life
  The unseen soldier
    Walker, W. The sea-rabbit; or, The artist of life
The **walker**. Rosenberg, L. M.
Walker Brothers cowboy. Munro, A.
A **walker's** manual. Pesetsky, B.

WALKING
Dixon, S. Down the road
Haley, R. Fischer's mirror
Keller, D. H. The revolt of the pedestrians
Pesetsky, B. A walker's manual
Porter, J. A. Duckwalking
Wexler, J. Alleywalk
Walking. Bernard, K.
Walking in the snow. Son, C.-S.
Walking on the moon. Wilson, B.
Walking out. Quammen, D.
Walking the dog. Eldridge, M.
Walking to sleep. Sanders, S. R.
Walking, walking. Flythe, S.
The **Walking** Woman. Austin, M. H.
Wall, Mervin
"They also serve . . ."
The Best of Irish wit and wisdom; ed. by J. McCarthy
The **wall.** Grace, P.
The **wall.** Mazel, D.
The **wall** around the world. Cogswell, T. R.
The **wall:** Michael Bowle. Crapser, W.
WALL STREET (NEW YORK, N.Y.)
See also Stock exchange
Wallace, Daniel
Father all over again
Prairie Schooner 62:92-9 Spr '88
The offering
The Yale Review 77:589-99 Summ '88
Ways to skin a cat
The North American Review 272:44-5 D '87
Wallace, David Foster
Little expressionless animals
The Paris Review 30:21-59 Spr '88
Wallace, Lew, 1827-1905
Ben-Hur escapes from the Astroea
Men at sea; ed. by B. Aymar
Wallace, Mary Catherine
A touch of tenderness
U.S. Catholic 50:34-9 Ja '85
Wallace, Penelope
Joe
John Creasey's Crime collection, 1985
Truth to tell
John Creasey's Crime collection, 1986
Wallace, S. R.
Dark steps
P.E.N. new fiction I
Wallace, Warren
Up home
Prize stories, 1987
A **walled** garden. Taylor, P. H.
The **wallet.** Patron, J. F.
The **wallet.** Updike, J.
Wallin, Luke
The redneck poacher's son [excerpt]
Mississippi writers v1: Fiction; ed. by D. Abbott
Wallmann, Jeffrey M., 1941-
(jt. auth) See Pronzini, Bill, and Wallmann, Jeffrey M., 1941-

WALLPAPER
McBain, H. Supper on the wall
Walls. Dodd, S. M.
Walls that hear you. Woolrich, C.
Wallwork. Whisnant, L.
Walmsley, Amelie
Reba
The North American Review 270:44-7 D '85
Walpole, Horace, 1717-1797
The bird's nest
Masterpieces of fantasy and enchantment; ed. by D. G. Hartwell
The dice-box: a fairy tale
Masterpieces of fantasy and enchantment; ed. by D. G. Hartwell
Hieroglyphic tales
Masterpieces of fantasy and enchantment; ed. by D. G. Hartwell
The king and his three daughters
Masterpieces of fantasy and enchantment; ed. by D. G. Hartwell
Mi Li: a Chinese fairy tale
Masterpieces of fantasy and enchantment; ed. by D. G. Hartwell
The peach in brandy: a Milesian tale
Masterpieces of fantasy and enchantment; ed. by D. G. Hartwell
A true love story
Masterpieces of fantasy and enchantment; ed. by D. G. Hartwell
Walpole, Sir Hugh, 1884-1941
Bachelors
The Treasury of English short stories; ed. by N. Sullivan
The little ghost
The Oxford book of English ghost stories
The silver mask
Lost souls; ed. by J. Sullivan
Walser, Martin, 1927-
The move
Short story international 50
Walsh, James Morgan
The wreck in the void
Australian science fiction; ed. by V. Ikin
Walsh, Rodolfo
That woman
Winter's tales, new ser. v3
Walsh, T.
My other grandmother
P.E.N. new fiction I
Walsh, Thomas, 1908-
Girl in danger
Ellery Queen's Memorable characters
The killer instinct
Ellery Queen's Crimes and punishments
Walt and Will. Apple, M.
Walter, Elizabeth
Christmas night
Christmas ghosts; ed. by K. Cramer and D. G. Hartwell

Walter, Elizabeth—*Continued*
  Come and get me
    The Penguin book of ghost stories
Walter, Robert
  Red glass
    Seventeen 45:100-1 Jl '86
Walter ego. Avallone, M.
Walters, Anna Lee, 1946-
  Apparitions
    Walters, A. L. The sun is not merciful
  The Devil and Sister Lena
    Walters, A. L. The sun is not merciful
  Going home
    Walters, A. L. The sun is not merciful
  The laws
    Walters, A. L. The sun is not merciful
  Mythomania
    Walters, A. L. The sun is not merciful
  The resurrection of John Stink
    Walters, A. L. The sun is not merciful
  The sun is not merciful
    Walters, A. L. The sun is not merciful
  The warriors
    Earth power coming; ed. by S. J. Ortiz
    Walters, A. L. The sun is not merciful
Walton, David
  A house divided
    A Grand Street reader; ed. by B. Son-
      nenberg
  One blood
    Hot type; ed. by J. Miller
WALTON, ISAAC *See* Walton, Izaak, 1593-
  1683
WALTON, IZAAK, 1593-1683
                    About
  Waldrop, H. God's hooks!
Walwicz, Ania
  House
    Transgressions; ed. by D. Anderson
  Neons
    Transgressions; ed. by D. Anderson
Wampum. Barrett, L.
Wan Zhi
  Open ground
    Contemporary Chinese literature; ed. by
      M. S. Duke
Wandering in the wilderness. Dumas, H.
Wandering Willie's tale. Scott, Sir W.
Wandor, Michelene, 1940-
  Judy's kiss
    Stepping out; ed. by A. Oosthuizen
Wang, Chen-ho
  The story of three springs
    The Unbroken chain; ed. by J. S. M.
      Lau
Wang Anyi
  The destination
    Short story international 61
Wang Hongzhen, and Zhou Peisheng
  Weishan Lake
    Short story international 60
Wang Hsieh; or Dark robe land. Liu, F.

Wang Jiada
  Daughter of the Yellow River
    The Chinese Western; ed. by Zhu Hong
Wang Meng
  Anecdotes of Chairman Maimaiti
    The Chinese Western; ed. by Zhu Hong
  Eye of the night
    Roses and thorns; ed. by P. Link
  A gray pigeon
    The Antioch Review 46:197-202 Spr '88
  The wind on the plateau
    Short story international 66
Wang Zengqi
  Small-hands Chen
    Harper's 277:39+ Ag '88
Wang Zhecheng, and Wen Xiaoyu
  Nest egg
    Roses and thorns; ed. by P. Link
Wangerin, Walter
  The manger is empty
    Christianity Today 29:20-5 D 13 '85
Wanted—dead and alive. Marlowe, S.
The **wanted** man. Cecil, H.
Wanting an orange. Woiwode, L.
Wanting only to be heard. Driscoll, J.
Wants. Paley, G.
WAR
        See   *also*   Chemical   warfare;
        Imaginary   wars   and   battles;   Inter-
        planetary wars; Nuclear warfare; also
        names of individual wars
  Altsheler, J. At the twelfth hour
  Amichai, Y. Battle for the hill
  Amichai, Y. Dicky's death
  Amichai, Y. The world is a room
  Asimov, I. "In a good cause--"
  Asimov, I. The machine that won the war
  Bates, H. E. A happy man
  Bierce, A. One of the missing
  Böll, H. Adventures of a haversack
  Borchert, W. Stories from a first reader
  Carrier, R. The ink
  Cherryh, C. J. Cassandra
  Crane, S. "And if he wills, we must die"
  Crane, S. Death and the child
  Crane, S. An episode of war
  Crane, S. The Kicking Twelfth
  Crane, S. The price of the harness
  Crane, S. The shrapnel of their friends
  Crane, S. The upturned face
  Cullen, E. J. Our war and how we won
    it
  DeGrazia, E. Brothers of the tiger
  DeGrazia, E. Enemy country
  DeGrazia, E. The light at the end of the
    tunnel
  DeGrazia, E. Zabel's choice
  DeMarinis, R. Good wars
  Dick, P. K. Breakfast at twilight
  Dick, P. K. The defenders
  Dick, P. K. The last of the masters
  Dick, P. K. To serve the master
  Dozois, G. R. Morning child

WAR—*Continued*

Godwin, P. Stroke of mercy
Grubb, D. Cry havoc
Harrison, H. War with the robots
Havemann, E. A farm at Raraba
Herbert, F. Cease fire
Hoch, E. D. I'd know you anywhere
Hornung, E. W. The knees of the gods
Houbein, L. Fighting for peace
Ioannides, P. Gregory
Jakes, J. There's no vinism like chauvinism
Kilworth, G. Sumi dreams of a paper frog
Martin, G. R. R. Weekend in a war zone
Moudy, W. F. The survivor
Murphy, P. Art in the war zone
O'Connor, P. F. Gerald's song
Rehman, S. Lull after the storm
Saiki, J. Family business
Shepard, L. R&r
Shepard, L. Salvador
Shiner, L. The war at home
Simon, B. Our war
Spiro, G. Utopia
Thomas, D. Gaspar, Melchior, Balthasar
Tremblay, M. The devil and the mushroom
Vogan, S. Scenes from the homefront
Wells, H. G. The land ironclads
Wolfe, T. The four lost men
Zahn, T. Not always to the strong
Zalygin, S. The night of the angels

Casualties

Arnim, L. A., Freiherr von. The madman of Fort Ratonneau
Bierce, A. Chickamauga
Dozois, G. R. A dream at noonday
Hannum, A. P. Turkey hunt
McAllister, B. Dream baby
Whitlock, D. The million-dollar wound
Winton, T. The woman at the well
War. Murphy, G. R.
War. Parise, G.

WAR AND CHILDREN

Aćin-Kosta, M. Spring flower
Asscher-Pinkhof, C. Breakdown
Asscher-Pinkhof, C. Return
Asscher-Pinkhof, C. Women's talk
Bird, C. Goczka
Gold, H. Contingency planning
War and/or peace. Montgomerie, L.
War and peace. Hearon, S.
The war at home. Shiner, L.
War beneath the tree. Wolfe, G.

WAR CORRESPONDENTS *See* Journalists

WAR CRIME TRIALS

Hazzard, S. The place to be
Serling, R. The escape route
The war criminal. Friedman, B. J.

WAR CRIMINALS

Burke, J. L. The pilot
Dick, P. K. If there were no Benny Cemoli

Dorr, L. An early Christmas
Federspiel, J. Oranges on her windowsill
Serling, R. The escape route
Stark, S. S. Janka Doodle
The war enters. Crapser, W.
War game. Dick, P. K.

WAR GAMES

Moudy, W. F. The survivor
Wilson, B. Stalingrad
The war generation. Endō, S.
War memorial. Fleming, B.
A war of eyes. Coleman, W.
The war of heaven. Currey, R.
A war of liberation. Tuohy, F.

WAR OF THE ROSES *See* England—15th century

War stories. Hanley, L.
War story. McCorkle, K.
War with Japan. Barthelme, F.
War with the robots. Harrison, H.

Ward, Elizabeth Stuart Phelps *See* Phelps, Elizabeth Stuart, 1844-1911

Ward, Lynn
The marbled horn
Magic in Ithkar 2; ed. by A. Norton and R. Adams
Ward action. Wilner, H.

Wardani, Mahmoud al- *See* Al-Wardani, Mahmoud
The wardrobe. Mann, T.

Ware, Leon
The price of parting
The Saturday Evening Post 256:48-9+ Mr '84

The warhorse of Spotted Tail. Bean, A.

WARLOCKS *See* Witchcraft

Warm. Sheckley, R.
The warm farewell. Bloch, R.
The warm sand. Powers, J. F.
The warm space. Brin, D.
The warmhearted polar bear. Murphy, R.

Warner, Charles Dudley, 1829-1900
Calvin, the cat [Variant title: Calvin—his life and death]
Roger Caras' Treasury of great cat stories

Warner, Marina, 1946-
After Titian's Susannah and the elders
Ms. 12:74-5+ Ja '84

Warner, Sylvia Townsend, 1893-1978
A breaking wave
Warner, S. T. One thing leading to another, and other stories
Chloroform for all
Warner, S. T. One thing leading to another, and other stories
The Duke of Orkney's Leonardo
Warner, S. T. One thing leading to another, and other stories
I met a lady
Warner, S. T. One thing leading to another, and other stories

Warner, Sylvia Townsend, 1893-1978—_Continued_

Idenborough
  The Treasury of English short stories; ed. by N. Sullivan
An improbable story
  Warner, S. T. One thing leading to another, and other stories
The mahogany table
  Warner, S. T. One thing leading to another, and other stories
The mother tongue
  Warner, S. T. One thing leading to another, and other stories
Mr. Mackenzie's last hour
  Warner, S. T. One thing leading to another, and other stories
Narrative of events preceding the death of Queen Ermine
  Warner, S. T. One thing leading to another, and other stories
One thing leading to another
  Warner, S. T. One thing leading to another, and other stories
A pair of duelling pistols
  Warner, S. T. One thing leading to another, and other stories
The proper circumstances
  Warner, S. T. One thing leading to another, and other stories
Queen Mousie
  Warner, S. T. One thing leading to another, and other stories
A saint (unknown) with two donors
  Warner, S. T. One thing leading to another, and other stories
The sea is always the same
  Warner, S. T. One thing leading to another, and other stories
Some effects of a hat
  Warner, S. T. One thing leading to another, and other stories
Sopwith Hall
  Warner, S. T. One thing leading to another, and other stories
The three cats
  Warner, S. T. One thing leading to another, and other stories
A view of Exmoor
  Warner, S. T. One thing leading to another, and other stories
A widow's quilt
  Warner, S. T. One thing leading to another, and other stories

Warren, Dianne
Sunday rodeos
  The Old dance; ed. by B. Burnard

Warren, Joyce
Anny's men
  Warren, J. The underground banquet, and other stories

The Corn Dolly
  Warren, J. The underground banquet, and other stories
Crash
  Warren, J. The underground banquet, and other stories
Erika
  Warren, J. The underground banquet, and other stories
Fetters
  Warren, J. The underground banquet, and other stories
Hill climbing by boat
  Warren, J. The underground banquet, and other stories
Last Chance
  Warren, J. The underground banquet, and other stories
Michael
  Warren, J. The underground banquet, and other stories
Mr. Dnarley's pigs
  Warren, J. The underground banquet, and other stories
Mr. McAlligator
  Warren, J. The underground banquet, and other stories
Mrs. Rogers
  Warren, J. The underground banquet, and other stories
Ready money
  Warren, J. The underground banquet, and other stories
A special occasion
  Warren, J. The underground banquet, and other stories
Time Lucy went
  Warren, J. The underground banquet, and other stories
Ugly Douglas & company
  Warren, J. The underground banquet, and other stories
The underground banquet
  Warren, J. The underground banquet, and other stories
Wedding garment
  Warren, J. The underground banquet, and other stories

Warren, Robert Penn, 1905-
Blackberry winter
  Stories of the modern South; ed. by B. Forkner and P. Samway
The patented gate and the mean hamburger
  The World of the short story; ed. by C. Fadiman

Warren, Rosalind
Auto repair
  Seventeen 47:144-5+ N '88
Warrior. Dickson, G. R.
The **Warrior** Princess Ozimba. Price, R.
Warriors. Doubiago, S.
The **warriors.** Walters, A. L.

WARSAW (POLAND) *See* Poland—Warsaw
Wartime. Marcus, J. S.
WARTS
  Lurie, M. Warts
Warts. Lurie, M.
Was. Faulkner, W.
Was it a dream? Maupassant, G. de
Was that house there yesterday? Thurston, R.
Wash. Faulkner, W.
The wash-tub mail. Atherton, G. F. H.
Washburn, L. J.
  The battle of Reno's Bend
    Westeryear; ed. by E. Gorman
  Hallam
    The Eyes have it; ed. by R. J. Randisi
  Hollywood guns
    An Eye for justice; ed. by R. J. Randisi
  On the prod
    A Matter of crime v2
WASHERWOMEN *See* Laundresses
The washing machine. Nowakowski, M.
Washington, Alex *See* Harris, Mark, 1922-
WASHINGTON (D.C.)
  Aquino, J. We've been invited to a party
  Bates, H. Farewell to the master
  Pynchon, T. Entropy
  Wolfe, G. Seven American nights
WASHINGTON (STATE)
                    Seattle
  Kinsella, W. P. The resurrection of Trout-
    fishing in America Shorty
WASPS
  Federspiel, J. The wasps
  Shimaki, K. The wasps
The wasps. Federspiel, J.
The wasps. Shimaki, K.
Wasps' nest. Christie, A.
The wastebasket. Ritchie, J.
Wastepaper. Nowakowski, M.
Wasylyk, Stephen
  The exoneration of Phineas Droogan
    Ellery Queen's Prime crimes
  Funeral in a small town
    Alfred Hitchcock's Grave suspicions
  If a body
    Alfred Hitchcock's Mortal errors
  The spring that Ellie died
    The Year's best mystery and suspense
    stories, 1984
Watanabe, Sylvia A.
  Colors
    Love, struggle & change; ed. by I.
    Zahava
  The seabirds
    Passages to the dream shore; ed. by F.
    Stewart
The watch. Bass, R.
The watch. Swift, G.
Watch out. Martone, M.
Watch the closing doors. Rayfiel, T.
Watch the red balloons. Véry, P.
Watch without time. Campbell, E.

The watchdog. Maupassant, G. de
The watcher. Benson, R. H.
The watcher. Cooper, J. C.
The watcher. Vanderhaeghe, G.
A watcher by the dead. Bierce, A.
Watchers at the strait gate. Kirk, R.
Watching fire. Wakayama, M.
Watching the sunset. Coleman, W.
Watching the tango. Gordon, M.
The watchmaker. Jahnn, H. H.
The watchman. Colette
The watchman. Narayan, R. K.
WATCHMEN
  Colette. The watchman
  Davie, E. Security
  Hartley, L. P. Night fears
  Kees, W. The evening of the Fourth of
    July
  Narayan, R. K. The watchman
  O'Connor, F. The party
  Valenzuela, L. The snow white watchman
  Wright, R. Big black good man
Waten, Judah, 1911-
  Mother
    The Australian short story; ed. by L.
    Hergenhan
  Well, what do you say to my boy?
    Echad 4: Jewish writing from down un-
    der: Australia and New Zealand
WATER
          See also Wells
  Boyle, K. Career
  Dubus, A. At St. Croix
  Thomas, M. Neighbors
  Valenzuela, L. Blue water-man
Water. Kawabata, Y.
Water babies. Roberts, N.
A water-fall and a piano. Stein, G.
The water-faucet vision. Jen, G.
The water ghost of Harrowby Hall. Bangs,
  J. K.
Water into wine. Norris, H.
Water liars. Hannah, B.
Water-message. Barth, J.
The water-mill. Na, T.-H.
Water skiing. Malinowitz, H.
A water story. Gustafsson, L.
'Water them geraniums'. Lawson, H.
The water-tree. Meinke, P.
The water was dark and it went forever
    down. Winton, T.
Water wings. Natzler, C.
Water witch. Benedict, P.
Water Witch. Stephens, W. M.
The Water Works. Doctorow, E. L.
Waterbugs. Blue Cloud, P.
The waterfowl tree. Kittredge, W.
Waterhouse, Carole
  Mena Keyfer
    The Massachusetts Review 26:158-68 Spr
    '85
The watering place. Woolf, V.
Waterlilies. Rogers, T. N. R.

The **watermelon** people. Morris, M.
WATERMELONS
  Conroy, J. Home to Uncle Ollie's
  Crane, S. The knife
  Mazel, D. Proverb of the parched
Waters *See* Russell, William
Waters, Elisabeth
  Cold spell
    Magic in Ithkar [1]; ed. by A. Norton
    and R. Adams
Waters, Frank, 1902-
  The woman at Otowi Crossing [excerpt]
    The Interior country; ed. by A. Black-
    burn
Waters, Martha
  Imprints
    Through other eyes; ed. by I. Zahava
  The Love Chapter
    Hear the silence; ed. by I. Zahava
Waters, Thomas *See* Russell, William
The **water's** crime. Tamer, Z.
Water's edge. Bloch, R.
The **waters** of Vanuatu. Kelly, C.
Watkins, Frances Ellen *See* Harper, Frances
    Ellen Watkins, 1825-1911
Watmough, David, 1932-
  All at sea
    Watmough, D. The Connecticut countess
  Bowen Island confessions
    Watmough, D. The Connecticut countess
  Closeted
    Watmough, D. The Connecticut countess
  Connecticut countess
    Watmough, D. The Connecticut countess
  Cousin Petherick and the will
    Watmough, D. The Connecticut countess
  The cross-country run
    Watmough, D. The Connecticut countess
  False start
    Watmough, D. The Connecticut countess
  In the mood
    Watmough, D. The Connecticut countess
  Return of the native
    Watmough, D. The Connecticut countess
  Sacred & secular
    Watmough, D. The Connecticut countess
  Seduction
    Watmough, D. The Connecticut countess
  Who shall be the judge?
    Watmough, D. The Connecticut countess
Watson, Ian, 1943-
  The artistic touch
    Watson, I. Sunstroke, and other stories
  Bud
    Watson, I. Sunstroke, and other stories
  The call of the wild: the dog-flea version
    Watson, I. Sunstroke, and other stories
  Cold light
    Terry Carr's Best science fiction and fan-
    tasy of the year #16
  The emir's clock
    The Year's best science fiction, fifth an-
    nual collection

Flame and the healer
    Watson, I. Sunstroke, and other stories
Immune dreams
    Mathenauts: tales of mathematical won-
    der; ed. by R. Rucker
Insight
    Watson, I. Sunstroke, and other stories
Jean Sandwich, the sponsor and I
    Watson, I. Sunstroke, and other stories
Jewels in an angel's wing
    Synergy v1
The legend of the seven who found the
    true egg of lightning
    Universe 16
A letter from God
    Watson, I. Sunstroke, and other stories
The milk of knowledge
    Watson, I. Sunstroke, and other stories
Nightmares
    Watson, I. Sunstroke, and other stories
Peace
    Watson, I. Sunstroke, and other stories
Returning home
    Watson, I. Sunstroke, and other stories
The rooms of paradise
    Afterlives; ed. by P. Sargent and I. Wat-
    son
    Watson, I. Sunstroke, and other stories
Salvage rites
    The Best horror stories from the
    Magazine of fantasy and science fiction
Slow birds
    Nebula awards #19
    The Year's best science fiction, first an-
    nual collection
Sunstroke
    Watson, I. Sunstroke, and other stories
The thousand cuts
    Watson, I. Sunstroke, and other stories
To the Pump Room with Jane
    Watson, I. Sunstroke, and other stories
When the timegate failed
    Interzone: the 2nd anthology; ed. by J.
    Clute; D. Pringle and S. Ounsley
The world science fiction convention of
    2080
    Watson, I. Sunstroke, and other stories
Watson, Jean
Princess!
    Women's work; ed. by M. McLeod and
    L. Wevers
Watson, Sheila
And the four animals
    Watson, S. Five stories
Antigone
    Watson, S. Five stories
The Black Farm
    Watson, S. Five stories
Brother Oedipus
    Watson, S. Five stories
The rumble seat
    Watson, S. Five stories

Watson, Susan
An ordinary night
Ploughshares 14 no2/3:70-4 '88
Watt, Nigel
As good as gold
Short story international 61
The mule driver and the carrot
Short story international 52
Watt-Evans, Lawrence, 1954-
Paranoid fantasy #1
100 great fantasy short short stories; ed.
by I. Asimov; T. Carr and M. H.
Greenberg
Waugh, Evelyn, 1903-1966
The man who liked Dickens
The Penguin book of horror stories
Waugh, Hillary, 1920-
The beneficiaries
Ellery Queen's Prime crimes 2
Galton and the yelling boys
The Crime of my life; ed. by B. Gar-
field
Waugh. Eighner, L.
The **waves** of night. Petrakis, H. M.
The **wax** witness. Saunders, C. M.
The **waxwork.** Burrage, A. M.
WAXWORKS
Burrage, A. M. The waxwork
Federspiel, J. An earthquake in my family
Thomas, D. Jarley's
The **way** back. Grau, S. A.
The **way** it came. James, H.
The **way** it is. Jones, J.
The **way** of cross and dragon. Martin, G.
R. R.
The **way** of peace. Brown, A.
The **way** of the world. Martin, V.
A **way** of thinking. Sturgeon, T.
A **way** out. Zambreno, M. F.
The **way** spaghetti feels. Ríos, A.
The **way** to Amalteia. Strugatskiĭ, A. N., and
Strugatskiĭ, B. N.
The **way** to Budjerra Heights. Anderson, J.
The **way** to Kŭmsansa temple. So, C.-I.
Way to the dump. Goldman, E. S.
A **way** to wealth. Maupassant, G. de
The **way** we live now. Sontag, S.
A **way** with men. Franco, M.
A **way** you'll never be. Hemingway, E.
Wayde's essence. Wells, H. G.
Wayfaring at Waverly in Silver Lake.
McCourt, J.
Wayne. Franzen, B.
Ways. O'Brien, E.
The **ways** of love. Sandel, C.
Ways to skin a cat. Wallace, D.
The **ways** we surfed. Franzen, B.
Wayside. Eldridge, M.
We. Grimm, M.
We all begin in a little magazine. Levine,
N.
We are nighttime travelers. Canin, E.
We are Norsemen. Boyle, T. C.

We are not in this together. Kittredge, W.
We are ready. Krysl, M.
We Build Churches, Inc. Burke, J. L.
We don't live here anymore. Dubus, A.
We find Harris again. Owens, M.
We get smashed and our endings are swift.
Abbott, L. K.
We have another ape. Abbott, K.
We know who we are. Silverberg, R.
We know you're busy writing, but we
thought you wouldn't mind if we just
dropped in for a minute. Crispin, E.
We often think of Lenin at the clothespin
factory. Davenport, G.
We servants of the stars. Pohl, F.
We were of two minds. Schulman, H.
The **weaker** sex. Ferron, M.
The **weaker** vessel. Kawabata, Y.
WEALTH
See also Capitalists and financiers;
Millionaires
Blinkin, M. Troubles
Bowles, P. In absentia
Calisher, H. Saratoga, hot
Campbell, W. B. Birthday party
Cho, S.-H. The bony-fish that came into
my net
Colum, P. The death of the rich man
Daniels, C. Curtis Loach
Franzen, B. After I won the lottery
Gerber, M. J. Someone should know this
story
Goyen, W. Where's Esther?
Greenwood, R. Charley Wales
Henry, O. Mammon and the archer
Humphrey, W. A job of the plains
Humphrey, W. The pump
Ingalls, R. I see a long journey
Ingalls, R. On ice
Johnson, C. R. Exchange value
Kees, W. The Purcells
King, F. H. His everlasting mansion
Mathers, P. The Henshaws
McGuane, T. To skin a cat
Michaelson, L. W. The tennis bum
Mooney, M. Hostages
Mooney, M. The peach orchard
O'Hara, J. Common sense should tell you
Parker, D. The standard of living
Pierce, C. A summer afternoon
Rand, P. Baby Boy
Rand, P. The butler
Rand, P. Charades
Rand, P. Circe
Rand, P. Cousins
Rand, P. A grandson of the Golden West
Rand, P. Heir
Rand, P. Mr. and Mrs. Noonan
Rand, P. The nephew
Rand, P. Pirates
Rand, P. Settembrino's mother
Rand, P. A soldier of fortunes
Rhys, J. At the Villa d'Or

WEALTH—*Continued*
  Rogers, S. The crumb
  Ruffin, P. The man who would be God
  Stead, C. A night in the Indian Ocean
  Tremain, R. The Colonel's daughter
  Tremain, R. Current account
  Welch, D. The trout stream
  Wilbur, E. Wealth
  Williams, T. A lady's beaded bag
Wealth. Wilbur, E.
The weapon. Lutz, J.
WEAPONS See Arms and armor; Munitions; Nuclear weapons
Wear it in good health. La Puma, S.
Wearing glasses. Gingher, M.
Weasels. Boylan, J.
WEATHER
        See also Storms
  Faik, S. The barometer
  Mrożek, S. A citizen's fate
  Ramírez, S. Nicaragua is white
  Smith, E. E. Weather prediction
  Strand, M. The President's resignation
  Weinbaum, S. G. Shifting seas
The **weather** and women treat me fair.
    Everett, P. L.
Weather prediction. Smith, E. E.
Weather report. Swann, R. M.
The **weather** within. Fisher, M. F. K.
Weaver, Gordon
  The Bearded Lady
    Weaver, G. Morality play
  Canavan's knee
    Weaver, G. Morality play
  Flowers: memento mori
    Weaver, G. Morality play
  Morality play
    Weaver, G. Morality play
  My brother and the perfect people
    Weaver, G. Morality play
  Neery Christmas
    Weaver, G. Morality play
  The parts of speech
    The Kenyon Review ns6:76-101 Summ '84
  Some killers
    Weaver, G. Morality play
  The two sides of things
    Prime number; ed. by A. L. Weir
  Whiskey, whiskey, gin, gin, gin
    The Pushcart prize X
WEAVERS
  Cherryh, C. J. To take a thief
  Mazel, D. A visit with Esta
  Meier, S. Trave
  Norton, A. Spider silk
The **weaver's** grave. O'Kelly, S.
The **web**. Pronzini, B.
Webb, Sharon, 1936-
  A demon in rosewood
    Shadows 8

The thing that goes burp in the night
    Dragons and dreams; ed. by J. Yolen;
    M. H. Greenberg and C. G. Waugh
Webbing. Frazier, I.
Weber, Nancy, 1942-
  A mother's secret
    Redbook 165:46-8+ Je '85
Weber, Thomasina
  The night of the sea serpent
    Alfred Hitchcock's Grave suspicions
  The Wells Plan
    Alfred Hitchcock's Crimewatch
Webrider. Carr, J.
Webster, Charles
  The feud
    Short story international 43
Webster, Noah, 1928-
    *For works written by this author under
      other names see Knox, Bill, 1928-*
The **wedding**. Bates, H. E.
The **wedding**. Carrier, R.
The **wedding**. Cinca, S.
Wedding. Cravens, G.
The **wedding**. Garcia, L. G.
The **wedding**. Ocampo, S.
The **wedding**. Piñera, V.
The **wedding**. Williams, J.
The **wedding**. Winters, J.
WEDDING ANNIVERSARIES
  Baxter, C. Horace and Margaret's fifty-second
  Brewster, E. Golden anniversary
  Colette. The bracelet
  Keillor, G. Du, du liegst mir im herzen
The **wedding** anniversary. Dorr, L.
Wedding anniversary. Queen, E.
The **wedding** bouquet. Ferron, J.
A **wedding-dress**. Callaghan, M.
Wedding garment. Warren, J.
The **wedding** gift. Raddall, T. H.
The **wedding** gig. King, S.
The **wedding** guest. Auchincloss, L.
The **wedding** guest. Stewart, M.
A **wedding** in the family. Blythe, R.
The **wedding** in the garden. Trevor, W.
The **wedding** night. Faik, S.
The **wedding** night. Maupassant, G. de
Wedding night. Tremain, R.
The **wedding** of Jenny Distaff. Steele, Sir R.
The **wedding** of the painted doll. Jolley, E.
The **wedding** of Willard and what's her name. Robinson, B.
A **wedding** parable. Beutner, E. F.
Wedding presents for breakfast. Windsor, G.
A **wedding** surprise. Gottfried, T.
The **wedding** that came without its band.
    Sholem Aleichem
Wedding trip. Pavese, C.
WEDDINGS
  Auchincloss, L. The wedding guest
  Bates, H. E. The wedding
  Blythe, R. A wedding in the family

WEDDINGS—_Continued_
Cameron, P. Melissa & Henry—September 10, 1983
Campbell, W. B. Headlights
Colwin, L. A country wedding
Dixon, S. Time to go
Drake, R. Fairy tale
Fitzgerald, F. S. The bridal party
Garcia, L. G. The wedding
Gilchrist, E. Dede's talking, it's her turn
Gilchrist, E. Revenge
Gilliatt, P. Catering
Grau, S. A. Ending
Head, B. Snapshots of a wedding
Hoch, E. D. Leopold and the broken bride
Hornung, E. W. A bad night
Houston, R. Lawfully
Jolley, E. The wedding of the painted doll
Lee, Y.-H. The last rite
Lipman, E. Memorial Day
Mason, B. A. Blue country
Maupassant, G. de. The accursed bread
Maupassant, G. de. A Normandy joke
McGarry, J. One of them gets married
Moskowitz, F. Presents
Nesbit, E. John Charrington's wedding
O'Hara, J. The flatted saxophone
Pilcher, R. Spanish ladies
Ríos, A. La boda
Spence, A. The rain dance
Stewart, M. The wedding guest
Thurm, M. Flying
Tremain, R. Wedding night
Ts'ai-hua, T. The feast of "Flower-Pattern" wine
Warren, J. Wedding garment
Wharton, E. The last asset
Wilson, B. Thin ice
Woodman, A. The bear tamers
Yorke, M. Gifts from the bridegroom
Wednesday afternoon. Brooks, B.
Wednesday morning: a Christmas conspiracy tale. Klíma, I.
Wednesdays and Fridays. Jolley, E.
The wee manok. Clarke, T.
The weed king. Conroy, J.
WEEDS
Conroy, J. The weed king
Prichard, K. S. The curse
Weeds. DeMarinis, R.
WEEGEE, 1899-1968
About
Lopatin, J. Retrospective on Weegee
A week in South Dakota. Gildner, G.
Weekend. Beattie, A.
Weekend. Hazzard, S.
Weekend. Verma, N.
Weekend. Welch, D.
Weekend. Weldon, F.
Weekend guests. Block, L.
Weekend in a war zone. Martin, G. R. R.
A weekend in Havana. Lewis, N.
Weekend of carousal. Chishimba, M.

Weenokhenchah Wandeeteekah. Snelling, W. J.
Weep no more, my lady. Clark, M. H.
Weep no more, my lady. Street, J.
Weep not for them. Dowdey, C.
WEEPING _See_ Crying
Weesner, Theodore
Getting serious
The New Yorker 60:30-5 Jl 16 '84
Wegner, Hart
But America is far
Wegner, H. Houses of ivory
Butcher's beguine
Wegner, H. Houses of ivory
The counter of Lvov
Wegner, H. Houses of ivory
Cyankali
Wegner, H. Houses of ivory
A death in a quiet town
Wegner, H. Houses of ivory
The huzul flute
Wegner, H. Houses of ivory
Miner's tattoo
Wegner, H. Houses of ivory
The stoning of Stanislava
Wegner, H. Houses of ivory
Wegner, Robert
Incident at the old tin bridge
Short story international 55
Weidman, Jerome, 1913-
Good man, bad man
Child's ploy; ed. by M. Muller and B. Pronzini
My father sits in the dark
The Norton book of American short stories
Weight. Lish, G.
The weight goes on the downhill ski. Eisenstein, S.
The weight lifters. Monreal, D. N.
Weightless. O'Brien, D.
WEIGHTLESSNESS
Robinson, S., and Robinson, J. Stardance
Weights. Baxter, C.
Weihnachtsabend. Roberts, K.
Weinbaum, Stanley G.
Dawn of flame
The Mammoth book of classic science fiction; ed. by I. Asimov; C. G. Waugh and M. H. Greenberg
Shifting seas
Amazing science fiction anthology: The war years, 1936-1945; ed. by M. H. Greenberg
Weiner, Ellis
Errata
The Paris Review 26:124-9 Spr '84
Weinheber, Josef
The affair
Southern Humanities Review 22:347-52 Fall '88

Weinstein, Jeff
A Jean-Marie cookbook
Love stories for the time being; ed. by
G. D. Chipps and B. Henderson
Weinstein, Louis, 1909-
How I became a jeweler
Tales from Ellery Queen's Mystery
Magazine: short stories for young
adults
Lasting impression
Ellery Queen's Prime crimes
Weinzweig, Helen, 1915-
Causation
The Oxford book of Canadian short
stories in English
The **weird** doom of Floyd Scrilch. Bloch, R.
The **weird** of Avoosl Wuthoqquan. Smith, C.
A.
Weishan Lake. Wang Hongzhen, and Zhou
Peisheng
Weissenberg, I. M.
A shtetl
A Shtetl, and other Yiddish novellas; ed.
by R. R. Wisse
Welch, Denton
Alex Fairburn
Welch, D. The stories of Denton Welch
Anna Dillon
Welch, D. The stories of Denton Welch
At sea
Welch, D. The stories of Denton Welch
The barn
Welch, D. The stories of Denton Welch
Brave and cruel
Welch, D. The stories of Denton Welch
The coffin on the hill
Welch, D. The stories of Denton Welch
Constance, Lady Willet
Welch, D. The stories of Denton Welch
The diamond badge
Welch, D. The stories of Denton Welch
The earth's crust
Welch, D. The stories of Denton Welch
Evergreen Seaton-Leverett
Welch, D. The stories of Denton Welch
The fire in the wood
Welch, D. The stories of Denton Welch
A fragment of a life story
Welch, D. The stories of Denton Welch
Full circle
Welch, D. The stories of Denton Welch
Ghosts
Welch, D. The stories of Denton Welch
The hateful word
Welch, D. The stories of Denton Welch
In the vast house
Welch, D. The stories of Denton Welch
The Judas tree
Welch, D. The stories of Denton Welch
Leaves from a young person's notebook
Welch, D. The stories of Denton Welch
Memories of a vanished period
Welch, D. The stories of Denton Welch

Narcissus bay
Welch, D. The stories of Denton Welch
A party
Welch, D. The stories of Denton Welch
A picture in the snow
Welch, D. The stories of Denton Welch
Touchett's party
Welch, D. The stories of Denton Welch
The trout stream
Welch, D. The stories of Denton Welch
Weekend
Welch, D. The stories of Denton Welch
When I was thirteen
Welch, D. The stories of Denton Welch
Welch, James, 1940-
Winter in the blood [excerpt]
Writers of the purple sage; ed. by R.
Martin and M. Barasch
Welch, Susan
The time, the place, the loved one
Love stories for the time being; ed. by
G. D. Chipps and B. Henderson
Welcome. Anderson, P.
Welcome. Burt, S.
Welcome aboard. Raphael, F.
Welcome advance. Tinsley, M. B.
Welcome home. Kaufman, L.
Welcome signs. Tate, J.
Welcome, stranger. Bloch, R.
Welcome to freedom. Sullivan, J. A.
Weldon, Fay
Alopecia
New women and new fiction; ed. by S.
Cahill
Au pair
Foreign exchange; ed. by J. Evans
GUP, or Falling in love in Helsinki
Ms. 17:71-5 Ag '88
The officer takes a wife
Redbook 163:72+ O '84
Threnody
The Treasury of English short stories;
ed. by N. Sullivan
Weekend
The Penguin book of modern British
short stories
The **well.** Clarke, T.
The **well.** Ferreira, R.
The **well.** Kenney, S.
The **well.** Mazel, D.
We'll have fun. O'Hara, J.
A **well-kept** secret. Winters, J.
The **well-matched** couple. Nowakowski, M.
The **well-meaning** mayor. Charteris, L.
Well met in Ithkar. Mathews, P. S.
A **well-spent** life. Edric, R.
Well, what do you say to my boy? Waten,
J.
Well worth it. O'Cork, S.
Wellen, Edward
Born victims
Ellery Queen's Prime crimes 2

Wellen, Edward—*Continued*
Chalk talk
    100 great fantasy short short stories; ed. by I. Asimov; T. Carr and M. H. Greenberg
Hit or miss
    Alfred Hitchcock's Grave suspicions
The house that Jack built
    The New adventures of Sherlock Holmes; ed. by M. H. Greenberg and C. L. R. Waugh
Scents in the dark
    Alfred Hitchcock's Mortal errors
Shapes to come
    From mind to mind: tales of communication from Analog
Voiceover
    Sherlock Holmes through time and space
WELLINGTON (N.Z.) *See* New Zealand—Wellington
Wellman, Manly Wade, 1903-1986
Coven
    Nightmares in Dixie; ed. by F. McSherry; C. G. Waugh and M. H. Greenberg
The Devil is not mocked
    Rod Serling's Night gallery reader
The little black train
    The Best horror stories from the Magazine of fantasy and science fiction
School for the unspeakable
    Vampires; ed. by A. Ryan
The seeker in the fortress
    Wizards; ed. by I. Asimov; M. H. Greenberg and C. G. Waugh
A star for a warrior
    The Ethnic detectives; ed. by B. Pronzini and M. H. Greenberg
Vandy, Vandy
    The Dark descent; ed. by D. G. Hartwell
The witch's cat
    Magicats! Ed. by J. Dann and G. Dozois
    Roger Caras' Treasury of great cat stories
Wells, Dee
What they did for love
    Ladies' Home Journal 101:88+ Je '84
Wells, H. G. (Herbert George), 1866-1946
Æpyornis Island
    Wells, H. G. The complete short stories of H. G. Wells
Answer to prayer
    Wells, H. G. The man with a nose, and the other uncollected short stories of H. G. Wells
The apple
    Wells, H. G. The complete short stories of H. G. Wells
The Argonauts of the air
    Wells, H. G. The complete short stories of H. G. Wells

The beautiful suit
    Wells, H. G. The complete short stories of H. G. Wells
A catastrophe
    Wells, H. G. The complete short stories of H. G. Wells
The cone
    Wells, H. G. The complete short stories of H. G. Wells
The country of the blind
    Wells, H. G. The complete short stories of H. G. Wells
The crystal egg
    Wells, H. G. The complete short stories of H. G. Wells
A deal in ostriches
    Wells, H. G. The complete short stories of H. G. Wells
The devotee of art
    Wells, H. G. The man with a nose, and the other uncollected short stories of H. G. Wells
The diamond maker
    Wells, H. G. The complete short stories of H. G. Wells
The door in the wall
    Black water; ed. by A. Manguel
    Wells, H. G. The complete short stories of H. G. Wells
A dream of Armageddon
    Wells, H. G. The complete short stories of H. G. Wells
The empire of the ants
    Wells, H. G. The complete short stories of H. G. Wells
A family elopement
    Wells, H. G. The man with a nose, and the other uncollected short stories of H. G. Wells
Filmer
    Wells, H. G. The complete short stories of H. G. Wells
The flowering of the strange orchid [Variant title: The strange orchid]
    Wells, H. G. The complete short stories of H. G. Wells
The flying man
    Wells, H. G. The complete short stories of H. G. Wells
The grisly folk
    Wells, H. G. The complete short stories of H. G. Wells
The Hammerpond Park burglary
    Wells, H. G. The complete short stories of H. G. Wells
In the abyss
    Mysterious sea stories; ed. by W. Patrick
    Wells, H. G. The complete short stories of H. G. Wells
In the Avu observatory
    Wells, H. G. The complete short stories of H. G. Wells

Wells, H. G. (Herbert George), 1866-1946
—*Continued*

In the modern vein: an unsympathetic love story
Wells, H. G. The complete short stories of H. G. Wells

The inexperienced ghost
Dark banquet; ed. by L. Child
The Penguin book of ghost stories
Wells, H. G. The complete short stories of H. G. Wells

The jilting of Jane
Wells, H. G. The complete short stories of H. G. Wells

Jimmy Goggles the god
Wells, H. G. The complete short stories of H. G. Wells

The land ironclads
Isaac Asimov presents the best science fiction firsts
Wells, H. G. The complete short stories of H. G. Wells

Little mother up the Mörderberg
Wells, H. G. The complete short stories of H. G. Wells

The Lord of the Dynamos
Wells, H. G. The complete short stories of H. G. Wells

The lost inheritance
Wells, H. G. The complete short stories of H. G. Wells

The loyalty of Esau Common
Wells, H. G. The man with a nose, and the other uncollected short stories of H. G. Wells

The magic shop
Wells, H. G. The complete short stories of H. G. Wells

The man who could work miracles
Wells, H. G. The complete short stories of H. G. Wells

The man with a nose
Wells, H. G. The man with a nose, and the other uncollected short stories of H. G. Wells

Le mari terrible
Wells, H. G. The man with a nose, and the other uncollected short stories of H. G. Wells

Miss Winchelsea's heart
Wells, H. G. The complete short stories of H. G. Wells

A misunderstood artist
Wells, H. G. The man with a nose, and the other uncollected short stories of H. G. Wells

The moth
Wells, H. G. The complete short stories of H. G. Wells

Mr. Brisher's treasure
Mystery in the mainstream; ed. by B. Pronzini; M. H. Greenberg and B. N. Malzberg
The Treasury of English short stories; ed. by N. Sullivan
Wells, H. G. The complete short stories of H. G. Wells

Mr. Ledbetter's vacation
Wells, H. G. The complete short stories of H. G. Wells

Mr. Marshall's doppelganger
Wells, H. G. The man with a nose, and the other uncollected short stories of H. G. Wells

Mr. Skelmersdale in Fairyland
Wells, H. G. The complete short stories of H. G. Wells

My first aeroplane
Wells, H. G. The complete short stories of H. G. Wells

The new accelerator
Wells, H. G. The complete short stories of H. G. Wells

The new Faust
Wells, H. G. The man with a nose, and the other uncollected short stories of H. G. Wells

Our little neighbour
Wells, H. G. The man with a nose, and the other uncollected short stories of H. G. Wells

The pearl of love
Wells, H. G. The complete short stories of H. G. Wells

A perfect gentleman on wheels
Wells, H. G. The man with a nose, and the other uncollected short stories of H. G. Wells

The Plattner story
Lost souls; ed. by J. Sullivan
Wells, H. G. The complete short stories of H. G. Wells

Pollock and the Porroh man
Wells, H. G. The complete short stories of H. G. Wells

The presence by the fire
Wells, H. G. The man with a nose, and the other uncollected short stories of H. G. Wells

The purple pileus
Wells, H. G. The complete short stories of H. G. Wells

The queer story of Brownlow's newspaper
Wells, H. G. The man with a nose, and the other uncollected short stories of H. G. Wells

The Rajah's treasure
Wells, H. G. The man with a nose, and the other uncollected short stories of H. G. Wells

Wells, H. G. (Herbert George), 1866-1946
—*Continued*
The reconciliation
　Wells, H. G. The complete short stories
　　of H. G. Wells
The red room
　Great ghost stories; ed. by B. A.
　　Schwartz
　The Oxford book of English ghost
　　stories
　Wells, H. G. The complete short stories
　　of H. G. Wells
The remarkable case of Davidson's eyes
　[Variant title: The story of Davidson's
　eyes]
　Wells, H. G. The complete short stories
　　of H. G. Wells
The sad story of a dramatic critic
　Wells, H. G. The complete short stories
　　of H. G. Wells
The sea-raiders
　The Penguin book of horror stories
　Wells, H. G. The complete short stories
　　of H. G. Wells
A slip under the microscope
　Wells, H. G. The complete short stories
　　of H. G. Wells
The star
　Wells, H. G. The complete short stories
　　of H. G. Wells
The stolen bacillus
　Wells, H. G. The complete short stories
　　of H. G. Wells
The stolen body
　Wells, H. G. The complete short stories
　　of H. G. Wells
A story of the days to come
　Wells, H. G. The complete short stories
　　of H. G. Wells
The story of the Last Trump
　Wells, H. G. The complete short stories
　　of H. G. Wells
The story of the late Mr. Elvesham
　[Variant title: The late Mr. Elvesham]
　Charles Keeping's Classic tales of the
　　macabre
　Wells, H. G. The complete short stories
　　of H. G. Wells
A story of the stone age
　Wells, H. G. The complete short stories
　　of H. G. Wells
The temptation of Harringay
　Devils & demons; ed. by M. Kaye and
　　S. Kaye
　Wells, H. G. The complete short stories
　　of H. G. Wells
The thing in No. 7
　Wells, H. G. The man with a nose, and
　　the other uncollected short stories of
　　H. G. Wells
Through a window
　Wells, H. G. The complete short stories
　　of H. G. Wells

The thumbmark
　Wells, H. G. The man with a nose, and
　　the other uncollected short stories of
　　H. G. Wells
The Time Machine
　Wells, H. G. The complete short stories
　　of H. G. Wells
The treasure in the forest
　Wells, H. G. The complete short stories
　　of H. G. Wells
The triumphs of a taxidermist
　Wells, H. G. The complete short stories
　　of H. G. Wells
The truth about Pyecraft
　Wells, H. G. The complete short stories
　　of H. G. Wells
Under the knife
　Wells, H. G. The complete short stories
　　of H. G. Wells
The valley of spiders
　Wells, H. G. The complete short stories
　　of H. G. Wells
A vision of judgment
　Wells, H. G. The complete short stories
　　of H. G. Wells
Walcote
　Wells, H. G. The man with a nose, and
　　the other uncollected short stories of
　　H. G. Wells
Wayde's essence
　Wells, H. G. The man with a nose, and
　　the other uncollected short stories of
　　H. G. Wells
The wild asses of the devil
　Wells, H. G. The man with a nose, and
　　the other uncollected short stories of
　　H. G. Wells
　　　　Parodies, travesties, etc.
　Cowper, R. The Hertford Manuscript
Wells, Herbert George *See* Wells, H. G.
　(Herbert George), 1866-1946
Wells, Jess
Two willow chairs
　When I am an old woman I shall wear
　　purple; ed. by S. K. Martz
Wells, Rosemary, 1943-
Max's Christmas
　Parents 63:151-2+ D '88
WELLS
Anderman, J. Sinking wells
Annan, K. Ding dong bell
Caldwell, E. The Negro in the well
Mazel, D. The well
Narayan, R. K. Four rupees
O'Cork, S. Well worth it
Terry, W. S. The bottomless well
The **Wells** Plan. Weber, T.
WELSH
　　　　United States
Austin, D. The hypnotic mailbox

Welty, Eudora, 1909-

The burning

Civil War women; ed. by F. McSherry; C. G. Waugh and M. Greenberg

Death of a traveling salesman

The World of the short story; ed. by C. Fadiman

First love

Mississippi writers v1: Fiction; ed. by D. Abbott

A memory

Mississippi writers v1: Fiction; ed. by D. Abbott

No place for you, my love

The Art of the tale; ed. by D. Halpern

Great American love stories; ed. by L. Rosenthal

Why I live at the P.O.

A Collection of classic Southern humor; ed. by G. W. Koon

Look who's talking; ed. by B. Weber

Mississippi writers v1: Fiction; ed. by D. Abbott

The Norton book of American short stories

The wide net

Stories of the modern South; ed. by B. Forkner and P. Samway

A worn path

A Modern Southern reader; ed. by B. Forkner and P. Samway

Wempires. Pinkwater, D. M.

Wen Xiaoyu

(jt. auth) See Wang Zhecheng, and Wen Xiaoyu

Wendt, Albert, 1939-

The balloonfish and the armadillo

Wendt, A. The birth and death of the miracle man

The birth and death of the miracle man

Wendt, A. The birth and death of the miracle man

Birthdays

Wendt, A. The birth and death of the miracle man

Crocodile

Wendt, A. The birth and death of the miracle man

Daughter of the mango season

Wendt, A. The birth and death of the miracle man

Elena's son

Wendt, A. The birth and death of the miracle man

Exam failure praying

Wendt, A. The birth and death of the miracle man

Hamlet

Wendt, A. The birth and death of the miracle man

I will be our saviour from the bad smell

Wendt, A. The birth and death of the miracle man

Justice

Wendt, A. The birth and death of the miracle man

Prospecting

Wendt, A. The birth and death of the miracle man

A talent

Wendt, A. The birth and death of the miracle man

The **wer-trout**. Proulx, A.

Were-hunter. Lackey, M.

Were-sisters. Brown, A. R.

Were they pretty? Lurie, M.

Were you there? Drake, R.

Werewind. Reaves, J. M.

The **werewolf**. Landolfi, T.

The **werewolf** and the vampire. Chetwynd-Hayes, R.

The **werewolf's** gift. Emerson, R.

WEREWOLVES

Beagle, P. S. Lila the werewolf

Bixby, J. The young one

Case, D. Fengriffen

Cave, H. B. Footprints in Perdu

Chetwynd-Hayes, R. The werewolf and the vampire

Coville, B. The passing of the pack

Crider, B. Wolf night

Crispin, A. C. Bloodspell

Crompton, A. E. Met by moonlight

Davol, M. W. Flesh and blood

De Lint, C. One chance

Doyle, D., and Macdonald, J. D. Bad blood

Emerson, R. The werewolf's gift

Ferron, J. The grey dog

Friesner, E. M. A winter's night

Gardner, J. Julius Caesar and the werewolf

Grant, C. L. Pride

Hoch, E. D. Just one more

Hussey, L. A. The white wolf

Kimbriel, K. E. Night calls

Lee, T. Wolfland

Martin, G. R. R. In the lost lands

Niven, L. What good is a glass dagger?

Pyle, H. The Salem wolf

Saki. Gabriel-Ernest

Saki. The wolves of Cernogratz

Scarborough, E. Wolf from the door

Shwartz, S. M. The wolf's flock

Smith, C. A. A prophecy of monsters

Smith, S. Monster mash

Stoker, B. Dracula's guest

Tem, S. R. Bloodwolf

Turtledove, H. Not all wolves

Whittington, M. K. Wolfskin

Yolen, J. Green messiah

Werner, Caryn

Office affairs

Seventeen 47:92-3+ Ja '88

Wertime, Richard
Moonlight
    The Ploughshares reader: new fiction for
    the eighties
WERWOLVES *See* Werewolves
Wesley, Valerie Wilson
No-name baby
    Essence 17:138 My '86
Wesley's story. Conley, R. J.
Wesling, Donald
Let's go to Indio!
    Southwest Review 70:198-211 Spr '85
Wesseler, Marlis
June's night
    The Old dance; ed. by B. Burnard
West, Jessamyn, d. 1984
99.6
    West, J. Collected stories of Jessamyn
    West
Alive and real
    West, J. Collected stories of Jessamyn
    West
Aloha, farewell to thee
    West, J. Collected stories of Jessamyn
    West
The battle of the suits
    West, J. Collected stories of Jessamyn
    West
Breach of promise
    West, J. Collected stories of Jessamyn
    West
The Calla Lily Cleaners & Dyers
    West, J. Collected stories of Jessamyn
    West
Child of the century
    West, J. Collected stories of Jessamyn
    West
The condemned librarian
    West, J. Collected stories of Jessamyn
    West
Crimson Ramblers of the world, farewell
    West, J. Collected stories of Jessamyn
    West
The day of the hawk
    West, J. Collected stories of Jessamyn
    West
Flow gently, sweet aspirin
    West, J. Collected stories of Jessamyn
    West
Foot-shaped shoes
    West, J. Collected stories of Jessamyn
    West
Gallup Poll
    West, J. Collected stories of Jessamyn
    West
Grand opening
    West, J. Collected stories of Jessamyn
    West
The heavy stone
    West, J. Collected stories of Jessamyn
    West

Homecoming
    West, J. Collected stories of Jessamyn
    West
Horace Chooney, M.D.
    West, J. Collected stories of Jessamyn
    West
Hunting for hoot owls
    West, J. Collected stories of Jessamyn
    West
I'll ask him to come sooner
    West, J. Collected stories of Jessamyn
    West
Learn to say good-bye
    West, J. Collected stories of Jessamyn
    West
Like visitant of air
    West, J. Collected stories of Jessamyn
    West
The linden trees
    West, J. Collected stories of Jessamyn
    West
A little collar for the monkey
    West, J. Collected stories of Jessamyn
    West
Live life deeply
    West, J. Collected stories of Jessamyn
    West
Love, death, and the ladies' drill team
    West, J. Collected stories of Jessamyn
    West
Mother's Day
    West, J. Collected stories of Jessamyn
    West
The mysteries of life in an orderly manner
    West, J. Collected stories of Jessamyn
    West
Night piece for Julia
    West, J. Collected stories of Jessamyn
    West
Probably Shakespeare
    West, J. Collected stories of Jessamyn
    West
Public-address system
    West, J. Collected stories of Jessamyn
    West
Reverdy
    West, J. Collected stories of Jessamyn
    West
The second (or perhaps third) time round
    West, J. Collected stories of Jessamyn
    West
The singing lesson
    West, J. Collected stories of Jessamyn
    West
There ought to be a judge
    West, J. Collected stories of Jessamyn
    West
A time of learning
    West, J. Collected stories of Jessamyn
    West
Tom Wolfe's my name
    West, J. Collected stories of Jessamyn
    West

West, Jessamyn, d. 1984—*Continued*
  Up a tree
    West, J. Collected stories of Jessamyn West
  The wake
    West, J. Collected stories of Jessamyn West
West, John Anthony
  Gladys's Gregory
    The Best horror stories from the Magazine of fantasy and science fiction
West, Paul, 1930-
  Hopi
    The Kenyon Review ns8:99-106 Fall '86
  The place in flowers where pollen rests
    The Pushcart prize XII
West, Dame Rebecca, 1892-1983
  The gray men
    Witches' brew; ed. by M. Muller and B. Pronzini
WEST (U.S.) *See* Western States
West. Kumin, M.
WEST AFRICA
  Boyd, W. The coup
  Boyd, W. Next boat from Douala
  Thomas, M. Come to Africa and save your marriage
WEST INDIAN DIALECT *See* Dialect stories—West Indian
WEST INDIANS
Canada
  Bissoondath, N. Christmas lunch
  Bissoondath, N. Dancing
  Bissoondath, N. Insecurity
  Clarke, A. C. Canadian experience
  Clarke, A. C. Coll. ss. trins. ap. toron.—a fable
  Clarke, A. C. Doing right
  Clarke, A. C. If only: only if . . .
  Clarke, A. C. A short acquaintance
England
  Ferreira, R. Are you stone-cold, Santa Claus?
  King, F. H. I lived for you
  Rhys, J. On not shooting sitting birds
  Rhys, J. The whistling bird
WEST INDIES
  See also Trinidad and Tobago
  Bissoondath, N. Digging up the mountains
  Rhys, J. The day they burned the books
  Rhys, J. Heat
  Rhys, J. The whistling bird
  Shacochis, B. Redemption songs
  Tournier, M. The end of Robinson Crusoe
Politics
  See Politics—West Indies
WEST INDIES REGION *See* Caribbean region
West of October. Bradbury, R.
WEST VIRGINIA
  Pancake, B. D. The salvation of me
  Post, M. D. The sheriff of Gullmore

Farm life
  See Farm life—West Virginia
West wind. Kerrigan, P.
Westall, Robert, 1929-
  The Big Rock Candy Mountain
    Imaginary lands; ed. by R. McKinley
A western. Van Greenaway, P.
WESTERN STATES
  Austin, M. H. The Castro baby
  Austin, M. H. The fakir
  Austin, M. H. The land
  Austin, M. H. The return of Mr. Wills
  Austin, M. H. The Woman at the Eighteen-Mile
  Bausch, R. The man who knew Belle Starr
  Bellow, S. Leaving the yellow house
  Bryant, E. Prairie sun
  Burke, J. L. Hack
  Davis, S. The hermit of Treasure Peaks
  DeMarinis, R. Under the wheat
  Eisenstein, P. In the Western tradition
  Haldeman, J. W. Manifest destiny
  Harte, B. The outcasts of Poker Flat
  Hendrie, L. Armadillo
  Henry, O. The lonesome road
  Hoyt, M. S. Buffalo, sun and strawberries
  Hoyt, M. S. An island of curving stone
  Miller, A. The misfits
  Owens, B. A little piece of room
  Sandberg, P. L. The old bull moose of the woods
Farm life
  See Farm life—Western States
Frontier and pioneer life
  See Frontier and pioneer life—Western States
WESTERN STORIES
  See also Adventure; Cowboys; Frontier and pioneer life—Western States; Ranch life; Western States
  Ahlswede, A. The promise of the fruit
  Atherton, G. F. H. The conquest of Doña Jacoba
  Austin, M. H. The last antelope
  Barker, E. First notch
  Barker, S. O. Outlaw trail
  Bellah, J. W. Big hunt
  Bellah, J. W. Command
  Bixby, J. The draw
  Bonham, F. Chivaree
  Bower, B. M. The lamb of the Flying U
  Bower, B. M. When the cook fell ill
  Brand, M. Cayenne Charlie
  Brand, M. Crazy rhythm
  Brand, M. Dark Rosaleen
  Brand, M. Dust storm
  Brand, M. The fear of Morgan the Fearless
  Brand, M. The golden day
  Brand, M. Half a partner
  Brand, M. The laughter of Slim Malone
  Brand, M. A lucky dog
  Brand, M. Outcast
  Brand, M. Reata's peril trek

WESTERN STORIES—*Continued*

Brand, M. The third bullet
Coover, R. Shootout at Gentry's Junction
Crane, S. A man and some others
Crane, S. Moonlight on the snow
Crider, B. Wolf night
Cunningham, J. M. Yankee gold
Curry, P. S. The brushoff
Curry, P. S. Geranium House
Cushman, D. I.O.U.—one bullet
DeRosso, H. A. Vigilante
Ellison, H. The end of the time of Leinard
Eustis, H. Mister Death and the redheaded woman
Evans, M. One-eyed sky
Farris, J. Fire enough for you
Faust, F. Wine on the desert
Fisher, C. Isley's stranger
Frazee, S. The bounty killers
Frazee, S. The Bretnall feud
Frazee, S. Due process
Frazee, S. The fire killer
Frazee, S. Great medicine
Frazee, S. Learn the hard way
Frazee, S. Luck of Riley
Frazee, S. The man at Gantt's place
Frazee, S. The man who made a beeline
Frazee, S. My brother down there
Frazee, S. The singing sands
Gorman, E. Guild and the Indian woman
Grey, Z. Roping lions in the Grand Canyon
Grey, Z. Tappan's burro
Grey, Z. The wolf tracker
Haycox, E. A day in town
Haycox, E. Stage to Lordsburg
Henry, O. An afternoon miracle
Henry, O. A double-dyed deceiver
Henry, O. The hiding of Black Bill
Henry, O. The lonesome road
Henry, O. Madame Bo-Peep, of the ranches
Henry, O. The princess and the puma
Henry, W. The streets of Laredo
Howard, C. Return to the OK Corral
Johnson, D. M. The hanging tree
Johnson, D. M. A man called Horse
Johnson, W. R. Enough gold
Kelly, C. A season for heroes
Kittredge, W. Phantom Silver
Leonard, E. The captives
Leonard, E. The hard way
Leonard, E. Law of the hunted ones
Mears, S. S. Thirty horses for your daughter
Moore, L. The deep valley
Mulford, C. E. Hopalong sits in
Muller, M. Sweet cactus wine
Oliver, C. One night at Medicine Tail
Olsen, T. V. Vengeance station
Overholser, W. D. Beecher Island
Overholser, W. D. Debt cancelled
Overholser, W. D. The hero

Overholser, W. D. High-grade
Overholser, W. D. Lawyer two-fist
Overholser, W. D. Mean men are big
Overholser, W. D. The O'Keefe luck
Overholser, W. D. Outlaw's wife
Overholser, W. D. Smart
Overholser, W. D. The steadfast
Overholser, W. D. Steel to the west
Overholser, W. D. They hanged Wild Bill Murphy
Overholser, W. D. Winchester wedding
Overholser, W. D. The wooing of Rosy Malone
Patten, L. B. Dobbs Ferry
Patten, L. B. Hell-bent
Patten, L. B. High-carded
Patten, L. B. Massacre at Cottonwood Springs
Patten, L. B. Nester kid
Patten, L. B. Payday
Patten, L. B. The rough string
Patten, L. B. They called him a killer
Patten, L. B. Too good with a gun
Patten, L. B. The winter of his life
Pronzini, B. The hanging man
Raine, W. M. Doan whispers
Rhodes, E. M. Pasó por aquí
Sandoz, M. The girl in the Humbert
Sarrantonio, A. Liberty
Savage, L. Dangerous orders
Schaefer, J. W. Sergeant Houck
Shaw, B. Skirmish on a summer morning
Short, L. Swindle at Piute Sink
Stephenson, M. The pack
Taylor, R. Billy Gashade and glory
Taylor, R. Charley Ford betrayed
Taylor, R. The death of Belle Starr
Taylor, R. Eddy the boy
Taylor, R. Eddy the man
Taylor, R. The fiddler
Taylor, R. Glory
Taylor, R. The history of Frank James
Taylor, R. The James boys ride again
Taylor, R. Jim July Starr
Taylor, R. Jim Reed
Taylor, R. The liberation of the Youngers
Taylor, R. Mrs. Jesse James, mourning
Taylor, R. Pearl Starr alive in Arizona
Taylor, R. Quantrill
Taylor, R. The revealed life of Cole Younger
Taylor, R. Sam Starr
Taylor, R. The tragedy of Bob Ford
Taylor, R. Zerelda James Samuel
Thompson, T. Blood on the sun
Thompson, T. A wollopin' good chew
Tobin, G. The damned
Washburn, L. J. The battle of Reno's Bend
White, S. E. The two-gun man
Williams, J. The debt
Western women are tough. Hughes, L.
Westheimer. Eighner, L.

Westlake, Donald E.
After I'm gone
  Westlake, D. E. Levine
  The Year's best mystery and suspense stories, 1985
The best-friend murder
  Westlake, D. E. Levine
Come back, come back
  Westlake, D. E. Levine
The death of a bum
  Westlake, D. E. Levine
The feel of the trigger
  Westlake, D. E. Levine
Never shake a family tree
  Great detectives; ed. by D. W. McCullough
  Masterpieces of mystery and suspense; ed. by M. H. Greenberg
  Murder and mystery in Boston; ed. by C. L. R. Waugh; F. D. McSherry and M. H. Greenberg
The sound of murder
  Westlake, D. E. Levine

Westlake, Michael, 1942-
Further reading in gastrotopology: a memoir by J. J. Case
  Critical Quarterly 28:45-50 Wint '86
Westland. Baxter, C.
Wet afternoons in Paris. McCandless, H.
Wet behind the ears. Haldeman, J. C.
Wet Stump. Hall, T. T.

Wetering, Janwillem van de *See* Van de Wetering, Janwillem, 1931-

Wetherell, W. D., 1948-
The bass, the river, and Sheila Mant
  Wetherell, W. D. The man who loved Levittown
Calm seas and a prosperous voyage
  A Good deal; ed. by M. Heath and F. M. Robinson
Hundred year war
  The Kenyon Review ns10:65-75 Summ '88
If a woodchuck could chuck wood
  Wetherell, W. D. The man who loved Levittown
The lob
  Wetherell, W. D. The man who loved Levittown
The man who loved Levittown
  Wetherell, W. D. The man who loved Levittown
Narrative of the whale truck essex
  Wetherell, W. D. The man who loved Levittown
Nickel a throw
  Wetherell, W. D. The man who loved Levittown
North of peace
  Wetherell, W. D. The man who loved Levittown

Spitfire autumn
  Wetherell, W. D. The man who loved Levittown
Volpi's farewell
  Wetherell, W. D. The man who loved Levittown
What Peter saw
  TriQuarterly no72:26-40 Spr/Summ '88
Why I love America
  Wetherell, W. D. The man who loved Levittown

Wetjen, Albert Richard
Duty
  Sea captains' tales; ed. by A. Enfield
We've been invited to a party. Aquino, J.

Wexelblatt, Robert
A friend of the family
  The Literary Review (Madison, N.J.) 29:69-85 Fall '85
The punishment of Oscar
  The Literary Review (Madison, N.J.) 27:239-51 Wint '84

Wexler, Jerry, 1950-
Alleywalk
  Wexler, J. The bequest & other stories
Bedclothes
  Wexler, J. The bequest & other stories
The bequest
  Wexler, J. The bequest & other stories
Communes and Sara
  Fatal recurrences; ed. by H. Hugh and P. O'Brien
For Ann
  Fatal recurrences; ed. by H. Hugh and P. O'Brien
Lament for a son
  Wexler, J. The bequest & other stories
Simon goes to London
  Wexler, J. The bequest & other stories
A small crime
  Wexler, J. The bequest & other stories
Two year's absence
  Wexler, J. The bequest & other stories
Women who live in small rooms
  Wexler, J. The bequest & other stories
World of women
  Wexler, J. The bequest & other stories
Your eighteenth birthday was a long time ago
  Wexler, J. The bequest & other stories
The **whale**. Thériault, Y.

Whalen, Tom
The visitation
  Sudden fiction; ed. by R. Shapard and J. Thomas

WHALES
Bullen, F. T. The debt of the whale
Grey, Z. Strange partners of Two-Fold Bay
Hulme, K. One whale, singing
Rodoreda, M. My Christina
Wetherell, W. D. Narrative of the whale truck essex
Whales weep. Boyle, T. C.

WHALING
Brown, G. M. Michael Surfax, whaler
Melville, H. The chase
Wh'appen?. Burt, S.
The **wharf** king. MacDonald, D. R.
Wharton, Edith, 1862-1937
Afterward
The Dark descent; ed. by D. G. Hartwell
The Penguin book of ghost stories
Witches' brew; ed. by M. Muller and B. Pronzini
All Souls'
Yankee witches; ed. by C. G. Waugh; M. H. Greenberg and F. D. McSherry
Bewitched
Mystery in the mainstream; ed. by B. Pronzini; M. H. Greenberg and B. N. Malzberg
Ethan Frome
Wharton, E. Ethan Frome, and other short fiction
The fullness of life
Haunted women; ed. by A. Bendixen
The last asset
Wharton, E. Ethan Frome, and other short fiction
Mr. Jones
The Oxford book of English ghost stories
The other two
Wharton, E. Ethan Frome, and other short fiction
Pomegranate seed
Black water; ed. by A. Manguel
Haunted women; ed. by A. Bendixen
The Norton book of American short stories
Souls belated
Great American love stories; ed. by L. Rosenthal
The touchstone
Wharton, E. Ethan Frome, and other short fiction
The triumph of night
Haunted New England; ed. by C. G. Waugh; M. H. Greenberg and F. D. McSherry
Xingu
Wharton, E. Ethan Frome, and other short fiction
What a boy wants. Macaulay, R.
What a racket. Böll, H.
What a world, said the bicycle rider. Saroyan, W.
What an old woman will wear. Davis, L.
What are friends for? Herrick, A. C.
What are friends for. Yellin, L. N.
What are you frightened of, Johnny? Winters, J.
What became of pampa hash? Ibargüengoitia, J.
What Cindy saw. Shirley, J.

What did the Deazies do? Cowper, R.
What did you do during the revolution, Grandma? Russ, J.
What do people do all day? Cameron, P.
What do you do in San Francisco? Carver, R.
What do you say? Giles, M.
What do you think about three times a day? Brondoli, M.
What do you want to be when you grow up? Winters, J.
What does not kill us, tends to make us stronger. Gustafsson, L.
What doesn't kill me. Glasser, P.
What Ernest says. Miller, S.
What everyone wants. Havazelet, E.
What feels like the world. Bausch, R.
What friends are for. Brunner, J.
What genius. Konas, G.
What good is a glass dagger? Niven, L.
What happened. Thompson, K.
What happened the day of the big meeting? Darwish, A.
What happened to Red Deer. Johnson, W. D.
What have I? Suckow, R.
What his wife knew. Shaw, J. B.
What-ho on the Rialto! Durrell, L.
What I did for Aunt Berthe. Pierce, C.
What I did for love. Schwartz, L. S.
What I learned from Caesar. Vanderhaeghe, G.
What I want. Trow, G. W. S.
What if . . . . Asimov, I.
What is it then between us? Havazelet, E.
What is left to link us. Lish, G.
What is my secret identity? Lurie, M.
What is seized. Moore, L.
What is this movie? Freeman, J.
What is this thing called love? Asimov, I.
What it was like, seeing Chris. Eisenberg, D.
What kind of day did you have? Bellow, S.
What language do bears speak? Carrier, R.
What little girls are made of. Huff, T. S.
What men love for. Phillips, D. R.
What must we look like? Colette
What my mother's father was really the father of. Lish, G.
What Peter saw. Wetherell, W. D.
What shadows we pursue. Kirk, R.
What shall I tell the crow? Rasputin, V. G.
What she really did. Lansky, E.
What Susan saw. Nugent, B.
What the ironwood whispered. Yamanaka, C.
What the twister did. Franzen, B.
What they did for love. Wells, D.
What they had laid out for their vacation. Ade, G.
What time is it? Asimov, I.
What to do about mother. Gerber, M. J.
What to do first. Olmstead, R.

What to do till the postman comes. Steele, M.

What Uncle Tom did. Cullen, E. J.

What use have I got for carnival? Moravia, A.

What was it? O'Brien, F.-J.

What we learned from this morning's newspaper. Silverberg, R.

What we talk about when we talk about love. Carver, R.

What were you wearing when you met? Coplon, J.

What will be. Franco, M.

What would I know? Greenberg, A.

What you hear from 'em? Taylor, P. H.

Whatley, Wallace
  Something to lose
    New stories from the South: the year's best, 1986
    The Southern Review (Baton Rouge, La.) 20:912-18 O '84

What'll we do with Ragland Park? Dick, P. K.

What's a family for? Gerber, M. J.

What's become of your creature? Gold, H.

"**What's** cooking? murder?". Du Lac, L.

What's eating you? Edkins, A.

What's in Alaska. Carver, R.

What's left. Cullen, E. J.

What's on the telly tonight? Braund, M.

What's that in your ear? Hemley, R.

What's the matter with Mary Jane? Garrett, G. P.

What's the purpose of the bayonet? Garrett, G. P.

The **wheat** in the pyramids. Boulanger, D.

Wheatcroft, John, 1925-
  The appeal
    Wheatcroft, J. Slow exposures
  The forfeit
    Wheatcroft, J. Slow exposures
  Hero
    Wheatcroft, J. Slow exposures
  The hitch
    Wheatcroft, J. Slow exposures
  Image of departure
    Wheatcroft, J. Slow exposures
  Kamikaze
    Wheatcroft, J. Slow exposures
  The lapse
    Wheatcroft, J. Slow exposures
  Letter from a stranger
    Wheatcroft, J. Slow exposures
  The shadow of a bear
    Wheatcroft, J. Slow exposures
  Sunday breakfast
    Wheatcroft, J. Slow exposures

Wheatley, Nadia
  The young priestess from the west house
    Room to move; ed. by S. Falkiner

The **wheel**. Wyndham, J.

Wheel-of-fortune. Harrison, B. G.

The **wheelbarrow** boy. Parker, R.

Wheeler, Hugh Callingham, 1912-1987
  All the way to the moon
    The Penguin classic crime omnibus
  The fat cat
    Roger Caras' Treasury of great cat stories
  Little boy lost
    Child's ploy; ed. by M. Muller and B. Pronzini
  Murder in one scene
    Manhattan mysteries; ed. by B. Pronzini; C. L. R. Waugh and M. H. Greenberg
  Puzzle for Poppy
    Hound dunnit; ed. by I. Asimov; M. H. Greenberg and C. L. R. Waugh

Wheeler, Kate
  Judgment
    20 under 30; ed. by D. Spark

Wheeler, Kristi
  Pianola
    Stiller's pond; ed. by J. Agee; R. Blakely and S. Welch

WHEELS
  Wyndham, J. The wheel

Wheels. Dixon, S.

The **wheels** of if. De Camp, L. S.

Whelan, Gloria
  Beneath the fig trees
    Whelan, G. Playing with shadows
  Children in the park
    Whelan, G. Playing with shadows
  The dogs in Renoir's garden
    Whelan, G. Playing with shadows
  A dwelling place for dragons
    Whelan, G. Playing with shadows
  The first city
    Michigan Quarterly Review 25:182-93 Spr '86
  First light
    Whelan, G. Playing with shadows
  Keeping house with Freud
    Whelan, G. Playing with shadows
  Keeping order
    Michigan Quarterly Review 27:48-58 Wint '88
  A lesson in the classics
    Whelan, G. Playing with shadows
  The mummies of Guanajuato
    Whelan, G. Playing with shadows
  Playing with shadows
    Whelan, G. Playing with shadows
  The secret meeting with Mr. Eliot
    Whelan, G. Playing with shadows
  The showing
    Whelan, G. Playing with shadows
  Spies and lovers
    Whelan, G. Playing with shadows
  Sympathy notes
    The Virginia Quarterly Review 60:297-309 Spr '84
    Whelan, G. Playing with shadows
  Two are better than one
    Whelan, G. Playing with shadows

When a felon needs a friend. Hershman, M.
When are you going back? Gilliatt, P.
When Auld's acquaintance is forgot. Ellison, H.
When California was an island. Haas, B.
When can I see you again? Beattie, A.
When Carrie came home. Dagon, J.
When doctors agree. Chesterton, G. K.
When dreams come true. Soman, F. J.
When Dustin "called on". Day, H.
When Etta Reece danced. Sorrells, R. T.
When everyone was pregnant. Updike, J.
When father meets father. Ade, G.
When fortune smiles. Soman, F. J.
When Greek meets Greek. Greene, G.
When I see Hui Lan again. Wong, M. V.
When I was married. Hunnicutt, E.
When I was thirteen. Welch, D.
"When in doubt—wash!". Gallico, P.
When in Rome. Highsmith, P.
When it changed. Russ, J.
When it happens. Atwood, M.
When it's Decoration Day. Burke, J. L.
When it's human instead of when it's dog. Hempel, A.
When life begins! Cooper, J. C.
When man falls, a crowd gathers. Crane, S.
When Mother played Moonshine. Floyd, P. L.
When mountain men make peace. Stuart, J.
When mum died. Davin, D.
When New York hit the fan. Pohl, F.
When our dream world finds us, and these hard times are gone. Abbott, L. K.
When Roger got married. Moffatt, D.
When strangers meet. Soman, F. J.
When the animals leave. Rambach, P.
When the clock strikes. Lee, T.
When the cook fell ill. Bower, B. M.
When the cricket chirrs. Choe, C.-H.
When the kids grow up. Conta, M. M.
When the morning comes. Keith, D. L.
When the pie was opened. Sexson, L.
When the pipes froze. Collins, L.
When the sailor was far away. Sproat, R.
When the sardines came. Plomer, W.
When the timegate failed. Watson, I.
When the train comes. Wicomb, Z.
When the war broke out. Böll, H.
When the war was over. Böll, H.
When the wind is in the south. Rölvaag, O. E.
When things get back to normal. Pierce, C.
When this van is rockin' don't bother knockin'. Abbott, K.
When we are home alone we dance all around the house. Ekström, M.
"When we produce prostitutes and thieves, we shall be a normal people!"— Jabotinsky. Granit, A.
When we went to see the end of the world. Silverberg, R.
When you swing upon a star. Mazel, D.

Where are our M.I.A.'s? Taylor, R.
Where are you going, where have you been? Oates, J. C.
Where dead is best. Murphy, Y.
Where did it go wrong? Keillor, G.
Where do folk sayings come from? Greenberg, A.
Where do you get your ideas? Longyear, B. B.
Where does your music come from? Swados, H.
Where I'd quit. Kauffman, J.
Where I'm calling from. Carver, R.
Where is Garland Steeples now? Abbott, L. K.
Where is the bird of fire? Swann, T. B.
Where is the voice coming from? Wiebe, R. H.
Where men go to cry. Hagy, A. C.
Where Pelham fell. Shacochis, B.
Where she brushed her hair. Steele, M.
Where she was. Cherry, K.
Where Tawe flows. Thomas, D.
Where the action is. Highsmith, P.
Where the apple reddens. Gault, C.
Where the bee sucks . . . . Durrell, L.
Where the buffalo roam. Bloch, R.
Where the cloud breaks. Bates, H. E.
Where the Cluetts are. Finney, J.
Where the heart is. Campbell, R.
Where the magic waits. Hinchman, J.
Where the mountains are. Barich, B.
Where the sea used to be. Bass, R.
Where the summer ends. Wagner, K. E.
Where the tides meet. MacLaverty, B.
Where their fire is not quenched. Sinclair, M.
Where there's a will. Matheson, R. C., and Matheson, R.
Where tomorrow waits. Bates, M.
Where tomorrow waits. Freeman, J. T.
Where we are now. Canin, E.
Where we'll never grow old. De Haven, T.
Where wisdom waits. Katkov, N.
Where you have been, where you are going. Hess, M. S.
Where you'll find me. Beattie, A.
Where's Esther? Goyen, W.
Where's grandma's home? Kelly, C.
Where's Milo. Flora, F.
Which make men remember. London, J.
Which of those two ladies is he married to? See O'Brien, E. Cords
Which way is home? Morrison, M.
A whiff of brimstone. Halligan, M.
While home. Robison, M.
While my guitar gently sings. Hulme, K.
While the heart suffered. Pirandello, L.
While you're up. Ganz, E.
The whimper of whipped dogs. Ellison, H.
The whipping. Bonner, M.
The whirlpool rapids. Atwood, M.

WHIRLPOOLS

Poe, E. A. A descent into the maelström

Whirlwind romance. Ledbetter, E.

WHISKEY

Wilkinson, R. The lean

Whiskey, whiskey, gin, gin, gin. Weaver, G.

Whisnant, Luke

Across from the Motoheads

New stories from the South: the year's best, 1987

Wallwork

New stories from the South: the year's best, 1986

The **whisper** business. Hanson, D.

The **whisperer** in darkness. Lovecraft, H. P.

The **Whisperer** prowls. Rossoff, A.

The **whispering.** Brand, C.

Whispers. Friedman, B. H.

Whistler. Hensley, J. L.

The **whistler.** Rendell, R.

Whistle's complaint. Blaine, E.

Whistling. Ross, V.

The **whistling** bird. Rhys, J.

Whitaker, Malachi, 1895-1975

Accident

Whitaker, M. The Crystal Fountain and other stories

The apprentice

Whitaker, M. The Crystal Fountain and other stories

Blackberry day

Whitaker, M. The Crystal Fountain and other stories

The enchanted morning

Whitaker, M. The Crystal Fountain and other stories

The end of the queue

Whitaker, M. The Crystal Fountain and other stories

Eve

Whitaker, M. The Crystal Fountain and other stories

Five for silver

Whitaker, M. The Crystal Fountain and other stories

Frost in April

Whitaker, M. The Crystal Fountain and other stories

Hannah

Whitaker, M. The Crystal Fountain and other stories

Home to wagonhouses

Whitaker, M. The Crystal Fountain and other stories

Honeymoon

Whitaker, M. The Crystal Fountain and other stories

Landlord of the Crystal Fountain

Whitaker, M. The Crystal Fountain and other stories

The man in black

Whitaker, M. The Crystal Fountain and other stories

The mandoline

Whitaker, M. The Crystal Fountain and other stories

The music-box

Whitaker, M. The Crystal Fountain and other stories

No luggage?

Whitaker, M. The Crystal Fountain and other stories

No stone for Jochebed

Whitaker, M. The Crystal Fountain and other stories

Pin's fee wife

Whitaker, M. The Crystal Fountain and other stories

Spring day at Slater's End

Whitaker, M. The Crystal Fountain and other stories

Strange music

Whitaker, M. The Crystal Fountain and other stories

Sultan Jekker

Whitaker, M. The Crystal Fountain and other stories

Time for chapel

Whitaker, M. The Crystal Fountain and other stories

The wife

Whitaker, M. The Crystal Fountain and other stories

X

Whitaker, M. The Crystal Fountain and other stories

Whitaker, Rodney *See* Trevanian

White, Curtis

Critical theory

White, C. Metaphysics in the Midwest

A disciplined life

White, C. Metaphysics in the Midwest

Howdy Doody is dead

American made; ed. by M. Leyner; C. White and T. Glynn

White, C. Metaphysics in the Midwest

Malice

White, C. Metaphysics in the Midwest

Metaphysics in the Midwest

White, C. Metaphysics in the Midwest

More crimes against the people of Illinois

White, C. Metaphysics in the Midwest

The order of virility

White, C. Metaphysics in the Midwest

The phantom limb

White, C. Metaphysics in the Midwest

You've changed

White, C. Metaphysics in the Midwest

White, E. B. (Elwyn Brooks), 1899-1985

The door

The World of the short story; ed. by C. Fadiman

White, Edmund, 1940-

A man of the world

Shenandoah: an anthology; ed. by J. Boatwright

White, Edmund, 1940-—*Continued*
An oracle
Men on men; ed. by G. Stambolian
White, Edward Lucas, 1866-1934
The house of the nightmare
Young ghosts; ed. by I. Asimov; M. H.
Greenberg and C. G. Waugh
White, Elwyn Brooks *See* White, E. B. (Elwyn Brooks), 1899-1985
White, Lori Ann
Old Mickey Flip had a marvelous ship
L. Ron Hubbard presents Writers of the
future v3
White, Patrick, 1912-
Down at the dump
The Australian short story; ed. by L.
Hergenhan
Five-twenty
The Art of the tale; ed. by D. Halpern
Willy-Wagtails by moonlight
The Treasury of English short stories;
ed. by N. Sullivan
White, Phyllis Dorothy James *See* James, P.
D.
White, Sharon
On voyage
The North American Review 272:15-17
Je '87
White, Stewart Edward, 1873-1946
The two-gun man
The Second reel West; ed. by B. Pronzini and M. H. Greenberg
White, T. H. (Terence Hanbury), 1906-1964
Soft voices at Passenham
The Oxford book of English ghost
stories
The troll
Lost souls; ed. by J. Sullivan
White, Ted, 1926-
Only yesterday
Nightmares in Dixie; ed. by F. McSherry; C. G. Waugh and M. H. Greenberg
White, Terence Hanbury *See* White, T. H.
(Terence Hanbury), 1906-1964
White, William Anthony Parker *See* Boucher,
Anthony, 1911-1968
White, William M.
The anhinga
The Southern Review (Baton Rouge, La.)
23:671-9 Summ '87
The white. Dawson, F.
White and injured. Eskapa, S.
White angel. Cunningham, M.
The white birds. Pilcher, R.
White boy. Goodman, I.
The white cat. Jacobs, W. W.
The white cat. Oates, J. C.
The white cat. Wilson, W. E.
The white cat of Drumgunniol. Le Fanu, J.
S.
White creatures. Benford, G.
The white door. Morazzoni, M.

White dump. Munro, A.
The white eagle. Skrzynecki, P.
The white feather. Aldrich, T. B.
The white flower. Kawabata, Y.
A white geranium petal. Rodoreda, M.
White girl, fine girl. Grau, S. A.
White gold. Faik, S.
White hat. Sladek, J. T.
A white heron. Jewett, S. O.
The white horse. Dumas, H.
The white horse. Kawabata, Y.
The white horse child. Bear, G.
White hyacinths. Norris, H.
The white impala. Thompson, J.
The White Lady. Maupassant, G. de
White lie. Asscher-Pinkhof, C.
White man's milk. Durrell, L.
White mother of shadows. Vandegrift, G.
WHITE MOUNTAINS (N.H. AND ME.)
Hawthorne, N. The ambitious guest
White mountains in the moon. Wilson, B.
White Mud Lake. Brown, J. D.
White night. Anderman, J.
White noise. Soldatow, S.
White on black. Slesinger, T.
White-out. Rummel, M. K.
The white paper beard. Ha, K.-C.
The white people. Machen, A.
The White Pillars murder. Chesterton, G. K.
The white-pinafored black cat. Upward, E.
White places. Flanagan, M.
White powder. See Machen, A. Novel of the
white powder
The white rabbit. Cook, H.
White rabbits. Carrington, L.
The white road. De Lint, C.
The white rooster. Bausch, R.
The white rooster. Goyen, W.
The white silence. London, J.
The white stick. Tuohy, F.
The white umbrella. Jen, G.
The white wand. Hartley, L. P.
White water. Johnson, W. R.
The white wind. Bates, H. E.
White wisdom. Austin, M. H.
The white wolf. Hussey, L. A.
The white wolf. Maupassant, G. de
Whitebear and Graybear: an Indian legend.
Rölvaag, O. E.
Whiteford, Wynne N.
One way to tomorrow
Australian science fiction; ed. by V. Ikin
Whitehead, Henry St. Clair, 1882-1932
The fireplace
Nightmares in Dixie; ed. by F. McSherry; C. G. Waugh and M. H. Greenberg
The trap
Haunted New England; ed. by C. G.
Waugh; M. H. Greenberg and F. D.
McSherry

Whitehead, James
Joiner [excerpt]
Mississippi writers v1: Fiction; ed. by D. Abbott
Whitehouse, Arch
Bataan landing
A Treasury of World War II stories; ed. by B. Pronzini and M. H. Greenberg
Savoias out of Sapporo
A Treasury of World War II stories; ed. by B. Pronzini and M. H. Greenberg
Whitestone & Greenberg. Wilner, H.
Whitfield, Raoul, 1898-1945
The black sampan
The Ethnic detectives; ed. by B. Pronzini and M. H. Greenberg
Sal the Dude
The Black mask boys; ed. by W. F. Nolan
Whitlock, Dean
The million-dollar wound
The Year's best science fiction, fifth annual collection
Whitman, Sylvia
Trial by fire
Redbook 166:78+ Mr '86
Whitman, Walt, 1819-1892
Death in the school-room
Masterpieces of terror and the supernatural; ed. by M. Kaye and S. Kaye
The **Whitman** lesson. Bernard, K.
Whittier, Gayle
Turning out
The Editors' choice: new American stories v2
The Pushcart prize X
Whittier, Gayle Baney
Lost time accident
A Good deal; ed. by M. Heath and F. M. Robinson
Love stories for the time being; ed. by G. D. Chipps and B. Henderson
Whittington, Harry Benjamin, 1915-
Swamp search
The Black Lizard anthology of crime fiction; ed. by E. Gorman
Whittington, Mary K.
Wolfskin
Werewolves; ed. by J. Yolen and M. H. Greenberg
WHITTLING *See* Wood carving
Who am I? Kusenberg, K.
Who are the fools? Cooper, J. C.
Who Big Bob? McKnight, R.
Who dares a Bulbur eat? Dickson, G. R.
Who do you think you are? Munro, A.
Who do you wish was with us? Thomas, D.
Who goes there? Campbell, J. W., Jr.
Who has lived from a child with chickens. Kauffman, J.
Who has seen the wind? Gilbert, M.
Who has seen the wind? McCullers, C.

Who is my love? Schweitzer, G.
Who killed Baker? Crispin, E., and Bush, G.
Who knows? Maupassant, G. de
Who knows how to live? Zhang Jie
Who knows what's up in the attic? Rhys, J.
Who rides with Santa Anna? Hoch, E. D.
Who shall be the judge? Watmough, D.
Who shall escape whipping. Baumbach, J.
Who was Jesse's friend and protector? See Taylor, P. H. A friend and protector
Who was my brother's killer? Vizyēnos, G. M.
Who was Ted? Dawson, F.
'**Who** was that masked man?'. Maniaty, T.
Who we are, what we're doing. Shepard, J.
Who would kill a cat? Fraser, A.
Whodunit. Pronzini, B.
Whoever finds this: I love you. Moskowitz, F.
Whoever was using this bed. Carver, R.
The **whole** idea of Cindy Potts. Jones, L. B.
The **whole** truth. Anthony, P.
The **whole** truth. Geras, A.
The **whole** world is watching. Segal, E.
Whom God hath promised. Flaherty, G.
The **whore.** Doubiago, S.
The **whore** of Babylon. Zeldis, L.
The **whorehouse** picnic. Kranes, D.
Whores in the pulpit. Sullivan, T.
Who's been sitting in my car? Fraser, A.
Who's been sleeping in my bed? Berne, S.
Who's got the lady? Ritchie, J.
Who's innocent? Treat, L.
Who's on first? Biggle, L.
Who's on first? Janowitz, T.
'**Who's** she—the cat's mother?'. Rowe, M.
Who's superstitious? El Hady, W. A.
Who's that knocking? Is it you? Taylor, P. E.
Whose child is this? Keillor, G.
Whose deduction? Škvorecký, J.
Why Abbylonia surrendered. Thanet, O.
Why Agnes left. Rooke, L.
Why can't I kiss daddy good-night? Lewis, G.
Why do straight lines curve for no reason? Sulivan, J.
Why do the heathen rage? O'Connor, F.
Why dolphins don't bite. Sturgeon, T.
Why don't you dance? Carver, R.
Why fade these children of the spring? Gault, C.
Why Heisherik was born. Singer, I. B.
Why, honey? Carver, R.
Why I live at the P.O. Welty, E.
Why I live where I live. Cameron, P.
Why I love America. Wetherell, W. D.
Why I love country music. Tallent, E.
Why I shacked up with Martha. Deaver, P. F.

Why I transformed myself into a nightingale. Hildesheimer, W.

Why I'm here. Hempel, A.

Why Johnny can't speed. Foster, A. D.

Why kill the Countess? Naranjo, C.

Why my walls shake. Hall, T. T.

Why people get cancer. Ferrell, A.

Why the heathens are no more. Rooke, L.

Why the little Frenchman wears his hand in a sling. Poe, E. A.

Why the moon is small and dark when the sun is big and shiny. Stein, J.

Why the sea is salty. Tsui, K.

Why the sky is so far away. Thomas, M.

Wiater, Stanley

  Moist dreams

    Masques II; ed. by J. N. Williamson

Wibberley, Leonard, 1915-1983

  The captive outfielder

    The Saturday Evening Post 257:64-6+ O '85

The **wicked** city. Ahmed, F.

The **wicked** season. Crouch, C.

A **wicked** voice. Lee, V.

The **wicked** world. Gilbert, W. S.

Wickert, Max

  The scythe of Saturn

    Stand one; ed. by M. Blackburn; J. Silkin and L. Tracy

Wickham, John

  The light on the sea

    Américas 38:50-3 My/Je '86

Wickliffe. Conley, R. J.

Wickstrom, Lois

  Vines

    The Clarion awards; ed. by D. Knight

Wicomb, Zoë

  Ash on my sleeve

    Wicomb, Z. You can't get lost in Cape Town

  Behind the Bougainvillea

    Wicomb, Z. You can't get lost in Cape Town

  Bowl like hole

    Wicomb, Z. You can't get lost in Cape Town

  A clearing in the bush

    Wicomb, Z. You can't get lost in Cape Town

  A fair exchange

    Wicomb, Z. You can't get lost in Cape Town

  Home sweet home

    Wicomb, Z. You can't get lost in Cape Town

  Jan Klinkies

    Wicomb, Z. You can't get lost in Cape Town

  A trip to the Gifberge

    Wicomb, Z. You can't get lost in Cape Town

When the train comes

  Somehow tenderness survives; ed. by H. Rochman

  Wicomb, Z. You can't get lost in Cape Town

You can't get lost in Cape Town

  Wicomb, Z. You can't get lost in Cape Town

Wide awake. Gilbert, W. S.

Wide load, where are you? Bonnie, F.

The **wide** net. Welty, E.

Wideman, John Edgar

  Doc's story

    Esquire 106:72-4 Ag '86

  Surfiction

    New American short stories; ed. by G. Norris

    Selected stories from The Southern review, 1965-1985

    The Southern Review (Baton Rouge, La.) 21:633-40 Jl '85

  Tommy [Variant title: Bobby]

    Our roots grow deeper than we know; ed. by L. Gutkind

A **widespread** belief. Rey Rosa, R.

Widmer, Harry

  The corpse laughs

    A Cent a story! Ed. by G. G. Roberts

The **widow.** Gee, M.

The **widow.** Jhabvala, R. P.

The **widow.** Lordan, B.

The **widow.** Zhang Xian

The **widow** and the parrot: a true story. Woolf, V.

The **widow** of Don Juan Manuel. Rey Rosa, R.

WIDOWERS

  Abbott, L. K. Love is the crooked thing

  Aickman, R. The stains

  Barstow, S. Rue

  Bowles, P. Rumor and a ladder

  Broder, G. K. Elena, unfaithful

  Brown, G. M. Darkness and light

  Brown, M. W. The amaryllis

  Colter, C. Girl friend

  Colter, C. Rapport

  Cooper, J. C. The free and the caged

  Dadswell, M. Mr. Macnamee

  Dixon, S. The signing

  Dundas, R. The respecter of persons

  Faulkner, W. Pantaloon in black

  Ferron, J. The grey dog

  Fleming, B. The bookman's tale

  Gustafsson, L. What does not kill us, tends to make us stronger

  Helprin, M. The Schreuderspitze

  Houbein, L. Everything is real

  Kaplan, D. M. In the realm of the herons

  Kotzwinkle, W. Fading tattoo

  La Chapelle, M. Homer

  Leavitt, D. Spouse night

  Leedom-Ackerman, J. The impostor

  Lynn, E. A. The island

WIDOWERS—*Continued*

MacLaverty, B. End of season

Malamud, B. A lost grave

Moravia, A. The woman with the black cloak

Morrison, J. Appointment at Princess Gate

Norris, H. The Christmas wife

Osborn, C. Man Dancing

Petrakis, H. M. The last escapade

Potter, N. A. J. A short vacation

Pritchett, V. S. A story of Don Juan

Robison, J. Rumor

Tallent, E. Favor

Targan, B. Surviving adverse seasons

Trevor, W. On the Zattere

Tsushima, Y. An embrace

Tuohy, F. The license

Vanderhaeghe, G. The expatriates' party

Walton, D. A house divided

Wells, H. G. The presence by the fire

Wetherell, W. D. The man who loved Levittown

Whelan, G. First light

Wolfe, G. Sonya, Crane Wessleman, and Kittee

WIDOWS

Altsheler, J. At the twelfth hour

Auchincloss, L. No friend like a new friend

Auchincloss, L. Suttee

Barthelme, S. Mrs. Sims

Begamudré, V. A promise we shall wake in the pink city after harvest

Benson, E. F. Mrs. Amworth

Blythe, R. Bride Michael

Blythe, R. Everything a man needs

Botwinik, B. A shoemaker for a husband

Brown, M. W. Beyond New Forks

Brown, M. W. The black dog

Brown, M. W. Good-bye, Cliff

Campbell, W. B. Socks

Campion, E. Good morning wardrobe

Campos-De Metro, J. Little mooses

Campos-De Metro, J. Shooting for Jupiter

Capote, T. Miriam

Chopin, K. The story of an hour

Cooke, R. T. A woman

Cooper, J. C. Too hep to be happy!

Covington, V. Magnolia

Cox, E. A sounding brass

Dazai, O. The lady who entertained

Drake, M. Tea break

Drake, R. Mrs. English

Dubus, A. Waiting

East, C. A tribute to the general

Eberhart, M. G. Dangerous widows

Eldridge, M. Solitaire

Evans, E. Desert birds

Farmer, B. Woman in a mirror

Ferron, J. Black cargo ships of war

Ferron, J. Little Red Riding Hood

Ferron, J. Summer Lethe

Flynn, R. Pictures

Fremlin, C. The bonus years

Fremlin, C. The holiday

Furman, L. Eldorado

Gallagher, T. Bad company

Gallant, M. Bonaventure

Gallant, M. Irina

García Márquez, G. Montiel's widow

Gathorne-Hardy, J. The Infant Hercules

Gee, M. The widow

Geras, A. Alice

Gerber, M. J. The mistress of Goldman's Antiques

Gilchrist, E. The young man

Gilliatt, P. As we have learnt from Freud, there are no jokes

Gold, H. A dark Norwegian person

Goyen, W. Ghost and flesh, water and dirt

Grau, S. A. Housekeeper

Grau, S. A. Widow's walk

Graves, Mrs. A. J. Mary and Ellen Grosvenor; or, The two sisters

Hall, D. The smell in Bertha's house

Hall, M. L. The peaceful eye

Hempel, A. Nashville gone to ashes

Hospital, J. T. Mosie

Hospital, J. T. Moving out

Hospital, J. T. Port after port, the same baggage

Hughes, F. 'Dear ghost . . .'

Ibrahim, I. The gap in Kaltouma's fence

Ingalls, R. Third time lucky

Jewett, S. O. All my sad captains

Jewett, S. O. The foreigner

Jhabvala, R. P. The widow

Keeling, N. Big Herb

Kim, Y.-J. The visitor

Kirk, R. Sorworth Place

Kleist, H. von. The Marquise of O—

Komie, L. B. The butterfly

Kono, T. Iron fish

Kumin, M. West

Kundera, M. Let the old dead make room for the young dead

Leavitt, D. Spouse night

Lee, T. La reine blanche

Leffland, E. Last courtesies

Lofts, N. Lord, who is my neighbour?

MacLaverty, B. Words the happy say

Martin, V. The woman who was never satisfied

McKinley, J. Each new springtime, each new summer

Moffatt, D. The lodger

Morand, P. Catalan night

Morris, M. Burning issues

Muller, M. Sweet cactus wine

Murphy, Y. The toys

Nowakowski, M. The washing machine

O'Brien, E. The creature

O'Connor, F. A set of variations on a borrowed theme

O'Kelly, S. Nan Hogan's house

O'Kelly, S. The weaver's grave

WIDOWS—*Continued*
Ozick, C. The pagan rabbi
Paolucci, A. Ciao, mio tesoro
Petrakis, H. M. Chrisoula
Petrakis, H. M. Courtship of the blue widow
Petrakis, H. M. The return of Katerina
Pilcher, R. Tea with the professor
Powell, T. Till death do not us part
Redding, S. Tin of Tube Rose
Rey Rosa, R. The widow of Don Juan Manuel
Rifaat, A. The kite
Rifaat, A. Telephone call
Robison, M. I get by
Roche, S. Structurally sound
Sams, F. Howdy Doody time
Sams, F. The widow's mite
Sanford, W. M. The monument
Schwartz, L. S. Mrs. Saunders writes to the world
Schwartz, L. S. What I did for love
Shaw, J. B. A new life
Singmaster, E. The battleground
Spark, M. Bang-bang you're dead
Stephan, M. The tub
Stern, D. The interpretation of dreams by Sigmund Freud: a story
Taylor, A. Hera
Thompson, J. Yarn
Valle, C. Diary entry #1
Welch, D. Constance, Lady Willet
West, J. The Calla Lily Cleaners & Dyers
Westlake, D. E. Never shake a family tree
Williams, J. Escapes
Williams, T. The coming of something to Widow Holly
Winton, T. Getting ahead
Yourcenar, M. Aphrodissia, the widow
Zhang Xian. The widow
The **widow's** mite. Sams, F.
A **widow's** quilt. Warner, S. T.
Widows' walk. Adisa, O. P.
Widow's walk. Grau, S. A.
Wiebe, Dallas E.
The art of Vietnam
    Wiebe, D. E. Going to the mountain
At the Rotonde
    The North American Review 271:26-8 D '86
    Wiebe, D. E. Going to the mountain
Elegy
    Wiebe, D. E. Going to the mountain
The fairy feller's master stroke
    Wiebe, D. E. Going to the mountain
Going to the mountain
    Wiebe, D. E. Going to the mountain
The green bottle
    Wiebe, D. E. Going to the mountain
My latest sun
    Wiebe, D. E. Going to the mountain
Narodny Rasprava
    Wiebe, D. E. Going to the mountain

Night flight to Miami
    Wiebe, D. E. Going to the mountain
Night flight to Stockholm
    Wiebe, D. E. Going to the mountain
Omega I
    Wiebe, D. E. Going to the mountain
Passage to India
    Wiebe, D. E. Going to the mountain
Wiebe, Rudy Henry, 1934-
The angel of the tar sands
    Alberta bound; ed. by F. Stenson
Where is the voice coming from?
    The Oxford book of Canadian short stories in English
Wier, Allen, 1946-
Bob and the other man
    The Best of the West; ed. by J. Thomas
Campbell Oakley's gospel sun shines on Roy Singing Grass
    Prize stories, Texas Institute of Letters; ed. by M. Terry
WIESEL, ELIE, 1928-
            About
    Mazel, D. Homage
Wiesinger, Steve
Cane Road
    Stories and poems from close to home; ed. by F. Salas
The **wife**. Whitaker, M.
WIFE ABUSE
Allen, P. G. Tough love
Cooper, J. C. He was a man! (But he did himself wrong)
Cooper, J. C. Who are the fools?
Dubus, A. Leslie in California
Gu Hua. The log cabin overgrown with creepers
Hood, M. The goodwife Hawkins
Huggan, I. Sorrows of the flesh
Kauffman, J. Isn't it something?
Kim, Y. I. The snake man
Kincaid, N. Like the old wolf in all those wolf stories
Kye, Y.-M. Adada the idiot
Matsumoto, S. Wait a year and a half
Oates, J. C. Little wife
Petrakis, H. M. The journal of a wife beater
Pronzini, B. Little lamb
Reininger, C. Cache reward
Scofield, S. Trespass
Weldon, F. Alopecia
Wendt, A. Elena's son
WIFE AND HUSBAND *See* Husband and wife
WIFE BEATING *See* Wife abuse
A **wife** for Dino Rossi. Fante, J.
The **Wife** of the Autumn Wind. Kawabata, Y.
WIFE SWAPPING *See* Marriage problems
A **wife's** confession. Maupassant, G. de
The **wife's** new automobile. Cole, D.
The **wife's** search. Kawabata, Y.

A **wife's** story. Mukherjee, B.
The **wife's** tale. Bausch, R.
Wiggen, Henry W. *See* Harris, Mark, 1922-
Wiggins, Marianne
  Herself in love
    The Norton book of American short
      stories
  Kafkas
    Harper's 275:32+ S '87
  Stonewall Jackson's wife
    The Yale Review 73:268-79 Wint '84
Wiggins, P. J.
  In time for the human race
    Critical Quarterly 29:73-8 Wint '87
Wight, James Alfred *See* Herriot, James
Wijenaike, Punyakante
  The visitor
    Short story international 42
Wilbur, Ellen
  A certain view
    Wilbur, E. Wind and birds and human
      voices, and other stories
  Faith
    Love stories for the time being; ed. by
      G. D. Chipps and B. Henderson
    New women and new fiction; ed. by S.
      Cahill
    Wilbur, E. Wind and birds and human
      voices, and other stories
  Home safe
    Redbook 166:81-2+ D '85
  Ned
    Wilbur, E. Wind and birds and human
      voices, and other stories
  Perfection
    Wilbur, E. Wind and birds and human
      voices, and other stories
  Safe
    The Editors' choice v3; ed. by G. E.
      Murphy, Jr.
  Spring baby, early sorrow
    Redbook 163:58+ Ag '84
  A strange elation
    Wilbur, E. Wind and birds and human
      voices, and other stories
  The success and the little failure
    Wilbur, E. Wind and birds and human
      voices, and other stories
  Sundays
    The Pushcart prize X
    Wilbur, E. Wind and birds and human
      voices, and other stories
  Three vignettes
    Wilbur, E. Wind and birds and human
      voices, and other stories
  Wealth
    Wilbur, E. Wind and birds and human
      voices, and other stories
  Wind and birds and human voices
    The Georgia Review 38:37-61 Spr '84
    Wilbur, E. Wind and birds and human
      voices, and other stories

Wilbur Gray falls in love with an idea.
  Deaver, P. F.
Wilcox, Don
  The voyage that lasted 600 years
    Amazing science fiction anthology: The
      war years, 1936-1945; ed. by M. H.
      Greenberg
    Isaac Asimov presents the best science
      fiction firsts
Wilcox, James
  The ivy in the chimney
    The New Yorker 61:28-34 Ja 6 '86
  North Gladiola [excerpt]
    The New writers of the South; ed. by
      C. East
Wild, Margaret
  Tied in knots
    Short story international 61
The **wild** asses of the devil. Wells, H. G.
A **wild** cannon dooms the Claymore. Hugo,
  V.
Wild child. Crapser, W.
WILD CHILDREN
  Carter, A. Peter and the wolf
  Moffett, J. Surviving
Wild clover. Davenport, G.
Wild dog. Nordan, L.
The **wild** dogs. Skrzynecki, P.
Wild Emperor. Clift, C.
Wild flowers. Caldwell, E.
Wild flowers. Lynn, D. H.
Wild garlic. Flanagan, M.
Wild geese. Curley, D.
The **wild** geese. O'Brien, D.
Wild goose chase. Wagoner, D.
Wild horses. Bass, R.
Wild Jack; or, The stolen child. Hentz, C.
  L.
Wild men of Borneo. Dodd, S. M.
Wild mustard. Muller, M.
A **wild** of sand. Nye, N. S.
The **wild** one. Bradley, M. Z.
The **wild** plum tree. Birdsell, S.
Wild rabbits. Little, J.
The **wild** ride of Miss Impala George.
  Metaxas, E.
Wild Talents, Inc. Sheckley, R.
Wild, wild horses. Waldrop, H.
Wildcat. Anderson, P.
The **wildcat.** Boyd, C.
Wildcat. O'Connor, F.
Wildcat John. Crabtree, L. V.
Wilde, Oscar, 1854-1900
  The birthday of the Infanta
    The Treasury of English short stories;
      ed. by N. Sullivan
  The Canterville ghost
    Charles Keeping's Book of classic ghost
      stories
  The fisherman and his soul
    Black water; ed. by A. Manguel
  The selfish giant
    Christian short stories; ed. by M. Booth

Wilde, Oscar, 1854-1900—*Continued*
                    About
   Russ, J. Mr. Wilde's second chance
Wilder, Cherry, 1930-
   Something coming through
      Interzone: the first anthology; ed. by J.
      Clute; C. Greenland and D. Pringle
Wilderness. Winton, T.
WILDERNESS AREAS
   Bukoski, A. Twelve below zero
   Long, D. Clearance
   Woolson, C. F. Castle Nowhere
Wilderness journal. Brady, M.
WILDERNESS SURVIVAL
   Abbey, E. Black sun [excerpt]
   Frazee, S. The man who made a beeline
   Grey, Z. The land of the wild musk-ox
   Quammen, D. Walking out
   St. Pierre, P. H. Dry storm
   Winton, T. Wilderness
Wilding, Michael, 1942-
   I am monarch of all I survey
      Transgressions; ed. by D. Anderson
   Sex in Australia from the man's point of
      view
      The Australian short story; ed. by L.
      Hergenhan
   The words she types
      Australian science fiction; ed. by V. Ikin
Wildlife. Updike, J.
Wilds, Mary Catherine
   Hiram's ghost
      'Teen 31:42+ O '87
      'Teen 31:28+ N '87
Wildtrack. Tremain, R.
Wilful murder. Hornung, E. W.
WILHELM II, GERMAN EMPEROR *See*
      William II, German Emperor, 1859-
      1941
Wilhelm, Kate
   The dragon seed
      Omni (New York, N.Y.) 8:58-60+ D '85
   Forever yours, Anna
      Omni (New York, N.Y.) 9:58-60+ Jl '87
      The Year's best science fiction, fifth an-
      nual collection
   The girl who fell into the sky
      Nebula awards 22
   Isosceles
      Terry's universe; ed. by B. Meacham
   The lookalike
      Redbook 171:60+ O '88
   Never tell anyone
      Redbook 167:46+ Jl '86
   O homo, o femina, o tempora
      Omni (New York, N.Y.) 7:82-4 My '85
   The promise
      Medea: Harlan's world; ed. by H. Ellison
   Some one is watching
      Redbook 167:54+ O '86
   The village
      In the field of fire; ed. by J. Van B.
      Dann and J. Dann

Wilhelm, Peter
   Space invaders
      The Penguin book of Southern African
      stories
Wili Woyi. Conley, R. J.
Wilk, Melvin
   Singing with Skulnick
      Here's the story: fiction with heart; ed.
      by M. Sklar
Wilkerson, Cherie
   The man who watched the glaciers run
      Universe 17
Wilkins, Mary Eleanor *See* Freeman, Mary
      Eleanor Wilkins, 1852-1930
Wilkinson, Alan
   The golden spike
      Critical Quarterly 30:34-8 Wint '88
Wilkinson, Roderick
   The bitch
      Short story international 63
   The ebbing tide
      Short story international 70
   The lean
      Short story international 46
Wilkinson, Sylvia, 1940-
   Chicken Simon
      New stories from the South: the year's
      best, 1986
Will. Evans, E.
The will. Maupassant, G. de
Will and Lou's boy. Tremain, R.
Will as a boy. Dixon, S.
The will of Allah. Owoyele, D.
The will of Stanley Brooke. Campbell, R.
Will the circle be unbroken? Dumas, H.
Willard, Nancy
   How poetry came into the world and why
      God doesn't write it
      The Bread Loaf anthology of contem-
      porary American short stories; ed. by
      R. Pack and J. Parini
   Theo's girl
      A Good deal; ed. by M. Heath and F.
      M. Robinson
Willett, Jincy
   Anticipatory grief
      Willett, J. Jenny and The jaws of life
   The best of Betty
      Willett, J. Jenny and The jaws of life
   Father of invention
      Willett, J. Jenny and The jaws of life
   The haunting of the Lingards
      Willett, J. Jenny and The jaws of life
   The jaws of life
      Willett, J. Jenny and The jaws of life
   Jenny
      Willett, J. Jenny and The jaws of life
   Julie in the funhouse
      Willett, J. Jenny and The jaws of life
   Justine laughs at death
      Willett, J. Jenny and The jaws of life
   Melinda falling
      Willett, J. Jenny and The jaws of life

Willett, Jincy—*Continued*
   Mr. Lazenbee
      Willett, J. Jenny and The jaws of life
      The Yale Review 76:268-84 Wint '87
   My father, at the wheel
      The Massachusetts Review 28:71-80 Spr
      '87
      Willett, J. Jenny and The jaws of life
   Résumé
      Willett, J. Jenny and The jaws of life
   Under the bed
      A Good deal; ed. by M. Heath and F.
      M. Robinson
      Willett, J. Jenny and The jaws of life
Willey, Margaret
   Running from love
      Redbook 163:74+ O '84
Willi. Doctorow, E. L.
**WILLIAM II, GERMAN EMPEROR, 1859-
1941**
                        About
   Doyle, Sir A. C. The death voyage
William Wilson. Poe, E. A.
William Wilson. Rose, G. B.
Williams, Arthur
   Being a murderer myself
      The Penguin classic crime omnibus
Williams, Ben Ames, Jr.
   They grind exceeding small
      The Best Maine stories; ed. by S. Phip-
      pen; C. Waugh and M. Greenberg
Williams, Betty
   The lovers
      Short story international 59
Williams, Charles, 1886-1945
   Et in sempiternum pereant
      Black water; ed. by A. Manguel
      The Oxford book of English ghost
      stories
Williams, David, 1926-
   The bully
      Winter's crimes 16
   Three's a crowd
      Winter's crime 18
Williams, Derek, 1945-
   The good neighbour
      Critical Quarterly 29:27-34 Summ '87
Williams, Diane
   Marriage and the family
      The Ohio Review no42:65-6 '88
Williams, Gordon M., 1934-
   *For works written by this author in
   collaboration with Terry Venables see
   Yuill, P. B.*
Williams, Jay, 1914-1978
   Petronella
      Don't bet on the prince; ed. by J. Zipes
Williams, Jeanne
   The debt
      She won the West; ed. by M. Muller
      and B. Pronzini

Williams, John A., d. 1988
   Captain Blackman [excerpt]
      Mississippi writers v1: Fiction; ed. by D.
      Abbott
Williams, Joy, 1944-
   The blue men
      The Best American short stories, 1987
      Esquire 106:82-5 Ag '86
   Escapes
      New American short stories; ed. by G.
      Norris
      Seventeen 47:138-9+ O '88
   Health
      The Best American short stories, 1986
      The Editors' choice v3; ed. by G. E.
      Murphy, Jr.
      The Graywolf annual 2
   Rot
      Prize stories, 1988
   The skater
      The Best American short stories, 1985
      Esquire 102:46-7+ Ag '84
      The Esquire fiction reader v1
   Taking care
      New women and new fiction; ed. by S.
      Cahill
   The wedding
      American short story masterpieces; ed.
      by R. Carver and T. Jenks
Williams, Oxford
   The angel's gift
      Omni book of science fiction 1
Williams, Robert Moore
   Robot's return
      Machines that think; ed. by I. Asimov;
      P. S. Warrick and M. H. Greenberg
WILLIAMS, ROGER, 1604?-1683
                        About
   Hawthorne, N. Endicott and the Red Cross
Williams, Sherley Anne, 1944-
   The lawd don't like ugly
      Between mothers & daughters; ed. by S.
      Koppelman
   Tell Martha not to moan
      A Good deal; ed. by M. Heath and F.
      M. Robinson
Williams, Susan
   And say good-bye to yourself
      Stiller's pond; ed. by J. Agee; R. Blakely
      and S. Welch
Williams, Tennessee, 1911-1983
   The accent of a coming foot
      Williams, T. Collected stories
   The angel in the alcove
      Williams, T. Collected stories
   Big Black: a Mississippi idyll
      Williams, T. Collected stories
   Chronicle of a demise
      Williams, T. Collected stories
   The coming of something to Widow Holly
      Williams, T. Collected stories
   Completed
      Williams, T. Collected stories

Williams, Tennessee, 1911-1983—*Continued*
The dark room
  Williams, T. Collected stories
Das Wasser ist kalt
  Williams, T. Collected stories
Desire and the black masseur
  Williams, T. Collected stories
Field of blue children
  Mississippi writers v1: Fiction; ed. by D. Abbott
  Williams, T. Collected stories
Gift of an apple
  Williams, T. Collected stories
"Grand"
  Williams, T. Collected stories
Happy August the Tenth
  Williams, T. Collected stories
Hard candy
  Williams, T. Collected stories
The important thing
  Williams, T. Collected stories
In memory of an aristocrat
  Williams, T. Collected stories
The interval
  Williams, T. Collected stories
The inventory at Fontana Bella
  Williams, T. Collected stories
The killer chicken and the closet queen
  Williams, T. Collected stories
The kingdom of earth
  Williams, T. Collected stories
The knightly guest
  Williams, T. Collected stories
A lady's beaded bag
  Williams, T. Collected stories
The malediction
  Williams, T. Collected stories
Mama's old stucco house
  Williams, T. Collected stories
Man bring this up road
  Williams, T. Collected stories
The mattress by the tomato patch
  Williams, T. Collected stories
Miss Coynte of Greene
  Williams, T. Collected stories
Mother yaws
  New directions in prose and poetry 50
  Williams, T. Collected stories
The mysteries of the Joy Rio
  Black water; ed. by A. Manguel
  Williams, T. Collected stories
The night of the Iguana
  Williams, T. Collected stories
One arm
  Williams, T. Collected stories
Oriflamme
  Williams, T. Collected stories
The poet
  Williams, T. Collected stories
Portrait of a girl in glass
  Mississippi writers v1: Fiction; ed. by D. Abbott
  Williams, T. Collected stories

A recluse and his guest
  Williams, T. Collected stories
Resemblance between a violin case and a coffin
  Williams, T. Collected stories
Rubio y Morena
  Williams, T. Collected stories
Sabbatha and solitude
  Williams, T. Collected stories
Sand
  Williams, T. Collected stories
Something about him
  Williams, T. Collected stories
Something by Tolstoi
  Williams, T. Collected stories
Ten minute stop
  Williams, T. Collected stories
Tent worms
  Sudden fiction; ed. by R. Shapard and J. Thomas
  Williams, T. Collected stories
Three players of a summer game
  Williams, T. Collected stories
Twenty-seven wagons full of cotton
  Williams, T. Collected stories
Two on a party
  Williams, T. Collected stories
The vengeance of Nitocris
  Masterpieces of terror and the supernatural; ed. by M. Kaye and S. Kaye
  Williams, T. Collected stories
The vine
  Williams, T. Collected stories
The yellow bird
  Stories of the modern South; ed. by B. Forkner and P. Samway
  Williams, T. Collected stories
Williams, Terry Tempest
The bowl
  The North American Review 273:19-20 D '88
Williams, Thomas Lanier *See* Williams, Tennessee, 1911-1983
Williams, Walter Jon
Dinosaurs
  The Year's best science fiction, fifth annual collection
Sarah runs the weasel
  Omni (New York, N.Y.) 8:44-6+ Mr '86
  Omni (New York, N.Y.) 8:70-72+ Ap '86
Side effects
  The Year's best science fiction, third annual collection
Video star
  A Very large array; ed. by M. M. Snodgrass
  The Year's best science fiction, fourth annual collection
Williams, William Carlos, 1883-1963
Ancient gentility
  Williams, W. C. The doctor stories
Comedy entombed: 1930
  Williams, W. C. The doctor stories

Williams, William Carlos, 1883-1963—*Continued*
Danse pseudomacabre
  Williams, W. C. The doctor stories
A face of stone
  Williams, W. C. The doctor stories
The girl with a pimply face
  Williams, W. C. The doctor stories
The insane
  Williams, W. C. The doctor stories
Jean Beicke
  Williams, W. C. The doctor stories
Mind and body
  Williams, W. C. The doctor stories
A night in June
  Williams, W. C. The doctor stories
Old Doc Rivers
  Williams, W. C. The doctor stories
The paid nurse
  Williams, W. C. The doctor stories
The use of force
  Williams, W. C. The doctor stories
Verbal transcription: 6 A.M.
  Williams, W. C. The doctor stories
Williamson, Barbara
The thing waiting outside
  Ready or not; ed. by J. Kahn
  Sherlock Holmes through time and space
  Young monsters; ed. by I. Asimov; M.
    H. Greenberg and C. G. Waugh
The toy killer
  Handle with care; ed. by J. Kahn
Williamson, Chet
The personal touch
  Sudden fiction; ed. by R. Shapard and
    J. Thomas
Prometheus's ghost
  Afterlives; ed. by P. Sargent and I. Watson
Return of the neon fireball
  Silver scream; ed. by D. J. Schow
Williamson, J. N.
House mothers
  Masques; ed. by J. N. Williamson
They never even see me
  Tales from Ellery Queen's Mystery
    Magazine: short stories for young
    adults
Wordsong
  Masques II; ed. by J. N. Williamson
Williamson, Jack, 1908-
At the human limit
  The Planets; ed. by B. Preiss
Farside station
  Medea: Harlan's world; ed. by H. Ellison
Jamboree
  A Very large array; ed. by M. M. Snodgrass
Wolves of darkness
  The Mammoth book of classic science
    fiction; ed. by I. Asimov; C. G.
    Waugh and M. H. Greenberg
Willie's war. Moffatt, D.

Williford, Lex
Get right or get left
  The Southern Review (Baton Rouge, La.)
    23:709-18 Summ '87
The **Willinger** predicament. Ritchie, J.
Willis, Colby
The plateau
  The Southern Review (Baton Rouge, La.)
    24:202-14 Wint '88
Willis, Connie
All my darling daughters
  Willis, C. Fire watch
And come from miles around
  Willis, C. Fire watch
Blued moon
  Willis, C. Fire watch
  The Year's best science fiction, second
    annual collection
Chance
  The Year's best science fiction, fourth
    annual collection
Daisy, in the sun
  Willis, C. Fire watch
The father of the bride
  Willis, C. Fire watch
Fire watch
  Willis, C. Fire watch
A letter from the Cleary's
  Tales from Isaac Asimov's science fiction
    magazine: short stories for young
    adults
  Willis, C. Fire watch
Lord of hosts
  Omni (New York, N.Y.) 9:110 Je '87
Lost and found
  Willis, C. Fire watch
Mail-order clone
  Willis, C. Fire watch
Samaritan
  Willis, C. Fire watch
Schwarzschild radius
  The Universe; ed. by B. Preiss
Service for the burial of the dead
  Willis, C. Fire watch
The Sidon in the mirror
  Willis, C. Fire watch
  The Year's best science fiction, first annual collection
Substitution trick
  Whispers V
Willis, Ted
The gallows
  Winter's crimes 17
The man from the White Mountains
  The Mammoth book of modern crime
    stories; ed. by G. Hardinge
Willis Carr at Bleak House. Madden, D.
Willow game. Chávez, D.
WILLOW TREES
  Watson, S. Brother Oedipus
The **willows**. Blackwood, A.
Willow's money. Hansen, J.

WILLS
Asimov, I. 1 to 999
Bellow, S. Leaving the yellow house
Blythe, R. The windfall
Bradbury, R. One for his lordship, and one for the road!
Campbell, R. The will of Stanley Brooke
Christie, A. Motive v. opportunity
Colette. Green sealing wax
Faulkner, W. Smoke
Harrington, J. Dispatching Bootsie
Maupassant, G. de. The will
Mortimer, J. C. Rumpole and the dear departed
Pilcher, R. The tree
Spark, M. The executor
Spencer, E. The skater
Vickers, H. Vuidons les tonneaux
Watmough, D. Cousin Petherick and the will
Wells, H. G. The lost inheritance
Woolf, V. The legacy
Woolf, V. The widow and the parrot: a true story
Will's book. Dixon, S.
Willson, Harry
Balloon magic
Willson, H. Duke City tales
A Christmas tale
Willson, H. Duke City tales
Duke City alchemist
Willson, H. Duke City tales
Front seat
Willson, H. Duke City tales
Ground zero
Willson, H. Duke City tales
Half a loaf
Willson, H. Duke City tales
Loyalty erosion
Willson, H. Duke City tales
Moonset near Magdalena
Willson, H. Duke City tales
Tufts and Wink
Willson, H. Duke City tales
Willy. Kercheval, J. L.
Willy-Wagtails by moonlight. White, P.
Wilmot, Jeanne
Dirt angel
The North American Review 270:44-9 Mr '85
Prize stories, 1986
Wilmot, Tony
The finger of suspicion
John Creasey's Crime collection, 1987
The last of the midnight gardeners
John Creasey's Crime collection, 1986
Open and shut case
John Creasey's Crime collection, 1984
Skeleton in the cupboard
John Creasey's Crime collection, 1985

Wilner, Herbert, d. 1977
Air
Wilner, H. The quarterback speaks to his God
Consultations
Wilner, H. The quarterback speaks to his God
Desert couple
Wilner, H. The quarterback speaks to his God
Emergency room bicentennial
Wilner, H. The quarterback speaks to his God
Facial nerve
Wilner, H. The quarterback speaks to his God
In my roommate's room
Wilner, H. The quarterback speaks to his God
Lead
Wilner, H. The quarterback speaks to his God
The quarterback speaks to his god
Wilner, H. The quarterback speaks to his God
Recovery room
Wilner, H. The quarterback speaks to his God
St. Denis
Wilner, H. The quarterback speaks to his God
Ward action
Wilner, H. The quarterback speaks to his God
Whitestone & Greenberg
Wilner, H. The quarterback speaks to his God
Wilson, Sir Angus
More friend than lodger
The Penguin book of modern British short stories
Wilson, Augusta Jane Evans, 1835-1909
The old general and the lost granddaughter
The Art of fiction in the heart of Dixie; ed. by P. D. Beidler
Wilson, Austin
Paul's eyes
Mississippi writers v1: Fiction; ed. by D. Abbott
Wilson, Barbara, 1950-
The back door of America
Wilson, B. Miss Venezuela
Il circo delle donne
Wilson, B. Miss Venezuela
Crater Lake
Wilson, B. Miss Venezuela
Disaster
Wilson, B. Miss Venezuela
Drive-away
Wilson, B. Miss Venezuela
Earthquake baroque
Wilson, B. Miss Venezuela

Wilson, Barbara, 1950-—*Continued*
Emily's arrows
  Wilson, B. Miss Venezuela
Hearings
  Wilson, B. Miss Venezuela
How to fix a roof
  Wilson, B. Miss Venezuela
The Hulk
  Wilson, B. Miss Venezuela
In the archives
  Wilson, B. Miss Venezuela
The investment
  Wilson, B. Miss Venezuela
Looking for the Golden Gate
  Wilson, B. Miss Venezuela
Miss Venezuela
  Wilson, B. Miss Venezuela
Phantom limb pain
  Wilson, B. Miss Venezuela
Pity
  Wilson, B. Miss Venezuela
Sense and sensitivity
  Wilson, B. Miss Venezuela
Stalingrad
  Wilson, B. Miss Venezuela
Starfish
  Wilson, B. Miss Venezuela
Take Louise Nevelson
  Wilson, B. Miss Venezuela
Thin ice
  Wilson, B. Miss Venezuela
Walking on the moon
  Wilson, B. Miss Venezuela
Wilson, Betty
White mountains in the moon
  Alberta bound; ed. by F. Stenson
Wilson, Bill, 1923-
Discoverable laws
  Editor's choice II; ed. by M. Sklar and
  M. Biggs
Wilson, Eric H., 1940-
The axe, the axe, the axe
  A Good deal; ed. by M. Heath and F.
  M. Robinson
  Prize stories, 1985
Wilson, Ethel, 1888-1980
From Flores
  The Oxford book of Canadian short
  stories in English
Wilson, F. Paul (Francis Paul)
Cuts
  Silver scream; ed. by D. J. Schow
The last one mo once golden oldies
  revival
  Whispers V
Wilson, Francis Paul *See* Wilson, F. Paul
  (Francis Paul)
Wilson, Gahan
The substitute
  Masques; ed. by J. N. Williamson
Yesterday's witch
  Great ghost stories; ed. by B. A.
  Schwartz

Wilson, Hayes
Please, no strawberries
  Ready or not; ed. by J. Kahn
Wilson, Karen
Hot as a pistol
  The Womansleuth anthology; ed. by I.
  Zahava
Wilson, Leigh Allison
Country blues for Melissa
  The New writers of the South; ed. by
  C. East
From the bottom up
  The Georgia Review 40:329-38 Spr '86
  Necessary fictions; ed. by S. W. Lind-
  berg and S. Corey
Massé
  The Editors' choice v4; ed. by G. E.
  Murphy, Jr.
  Harper's 272:47-55 Mr '86
  The New generation; ed. by A. Kaufman
Missing persons
  The Kenyon Review ns9:47-57 Spr '87
The raising
  20 under 30; ed. by D. Spark
The snipe hunters
  Homewords: a book of Tennessee
  writers; ed. by D. Paschall
Wilson, Miles
Everything
  The Georgia Review 41:693-705 Wint '87
Outrider
  Southwest Review 73:364-72 Summ '88
Wilson, Paul F.
Soft
  Masques; ed. by J. N. Williamson
Wilson, Richard, 1920-
Farewell party
  100 great fantasy short short stories; ed.
  by I. Asimov; T. Carr and M. H.
  Greenberg
The thing that stared
  100 great fantasy short short stories; ed.
  by I. Asimov; T. Carr and M. H.
  Greenberg
Wilson, Robley, Jr.
Cats
  The New Yorker 60:24-8 Ja 28 '85
Fathers
  The Ploughshares reader: new fiction for
  the eighties
Feature presentations
  The Sewanee Review 96:389-406 Summ
  '88
His cheatin' heart
  Redbook 163:28+ Ag '84
Land fishers
  The Editors' choice: new American
  stories v1
Nam
  The Georgia Review 38:369-75 Summ '84
Payment in kind
  New American short stories; ed. by G.
  Norris

Wilson, Robley, Jr.—*Continued*
   The Sewanee Review 93:20-38 Wint '85
  Petra
   The Sewanee Review 94:45-57 Wint '86
  The States
   Prairie Schooner 61:93-103 Fall '87
  Thief
   Sudden fiction; ed. by R. Shapard and
     J. Thomas
Wilson, Rudy
  Impressions
   The Paris Review 26:14-36 Spr '84
Wilson, William E., 1906-1988
  The white cat
   The North American Review 271:32-3 Mr
    '86
WILTSHIRE (ENGLAND) *See* England—
   Wiltshire
Wily woman. Taylor, S. W.
The **wimp**. Gallagher, T.
Win some, lose some. Ritchie, J.
Wince's story. Taylor, C.
Winchester wedding. Overholser, W. D.
Wind, David
  The sentinel at the edge of the world
   Tales of the Witch World 2
The **wind**. Bradbury, R.
Wind and birds and human voices. Wilbur,
  E.
The **wind** and landscape of Yenang. Yi, P.-J.
The **wind** and the rain. Silverberg, R.
The **wind** beyond the mountains. Ellison, H.
The **wind-child** factor. Gilliatt, P.
The **wind** from the sun. Clarke, A. C.
A **wind** is rising. Sheckley, R.
The **wind** on the plateau. Wang Meng
The **wind** people. Bradley, M. Z.
Wind screams. Lester, D.
The **wind**, the cold wind. Norris, L.
The **wind** wizard. Hoyt, M. S.
The **windcharger**. Bernen, R.
The **windfall**. Blythe, R.
Windfall. Sanford, W. M.
Winding brook way. Feng Jicai
The **windjammer** film. Villiers, A. J.
Window. Leman, B.
Window dressing. Russ, J.
A **window** drunken in the brain. Hulme, K.
A **window** in Mrs X's place. Cowan, P.
The **window** in the forest. Grin, A.
WINDOWS
  Oliphant, M. The library window
  Rendell, R. Hare's house
Windows. Dixon, S.
Windows. Saiki, J.
Windows. Tuohy, F.
The **winds** of change. Asimov, I.
Windsor, Gerard
  Addendum to the first fleet journals
   Windsor, G. Memories of the assassina-
    tion attempt, and other stories

The archbishop; or, The lady
  Windsor, G. Memories of the assassina-
   tion attempt, and other stories
Can these bones live?
  Windsor, G. Memories of the assassina-
   tion attempt, and other stories
Edging around the fat man
  Windsor, G. Memories of the assassina-
   tion attempt, and other stories
Far on the ringing plains
  Windsor, G. Memories of the assassina-
   tion attempt, and other stories
In the house of the dead
  Windsor, G. Memories of the assassina-
   tion attempt, and other stories
The life of a man's man
  Windsor, G. Memories of the assassina-
   tion attempt, and other stories
Memories of the assassination attempt
  Windsor, G. Memories of the assassina-
   tion attempt, and other stories
My father's version of the nurses' story
  Windsor, G. Memories of the assassina-
   tion attempt, and other stories
Press conferences of Ambassador Sweeney
  Windsor, G. Memories of the assassina-
   tion attempt, and other stories
A real little marriage-wrecker
  Home and away; ed. by R. Creswell
  Windsor, G. Memories of the assassina-
   tion attempt, and other stories
Reasons for going into gynaecology
  Transgressions; ed. by D. Anderson
  Windsor, G. Memories of the assassina-
   tion attempt, and other stories
The sad music of men
  Windsor, G. Memories of the assassina-
   tion attempt, and other stories
The Victoria Cross of Timothy O'Hea
  Windsor, G. Memories of the assassina-
   tion attempt, and other stories
Wedding presents for breakfast
  Windsor, G. Memories of the assassina-
   tion attempt, and other stories
Windsor, Patricia, 1938-
  Off track
   Seventeen 47:136-7 Je '88
Windsor. Eighner, L.
WINE AND WINE MAKING
  Archer, J. Honor among thieves
  Bradbury, R. One for his lordship, and
   one for the road!
  Cecil, H. The wanted man
  Chesterton, G. K. The two taverns
  Dahl, R. Taste
  Daudet, A. The elixir
  Ellin, S. The last bottle in the world
  Gilbert, M. The curious conspiracy
  Horsdal, M. An educated taste
  Le Guin, U. K. The trouble with the cot-
   ton people
  Mortimer, J. C. Rumpole and the blind
   tasting

WINE AND WINE MAKING—*Continued*

Perowne, B. Raffles and operation champagne

Poe, E. A. The cask of Amontillado

Pronzini, B. Connoisseur

St. Clair, M. The wines of earth

Ts'ai-hua, T. The feast of "Flower-Pattern" wine

Vickers, H. Vuidons les tonneaux

The **wine-dark** sea. Aickman, R.

Wine of Wyoming. Hemingway, E.

Wine on the desert. Faust, F.

The **wines** of earth. St. Clair, M.

Wing, Betsy

Cotillon

The Southern Review (Baton Rouge, La.)
23:177-84 Ja '87

Possum triptych

The Southern Review (Baton Rouge, La.)
24:605-14 Summ '88

Wings. Yi, S.

Wings. Zinnes, H.

Wings of eucalyptus leaves. Kraski, G.

Wings of the hunter. Barber, D. W.

Wings that will carry us both. Chon, S.-G.

The **winner.** Cartwright, V.

The **winners.** Liben, M.

The **winner's** touch. Tiritilli, P.

The **winning** shot. Doyle, Sir A. C.

The **winnowing.** Asimov, I.

Winslow, Thyra Samter

The best man in town

Arkansas in short fiction; ed. by W. M. Baker and E. C. Simpson

Winston, Clara, 1921-1983

A lovely day

A Good deal; ed. by M. Heath and F. M. Robinson

Winter, Douglas E.

Masks

Midnight; ed. by C. L. Grant

Splatter

Masques II; ed. by J. N. Williamson

Silver scream; ed. by D. J. Schow

The Year's best fantasy, first annual collection

WINTER

Beattie, A. Snow

Conroy, J. Hard winter

Keillor, G. Seeds

Updike, D. Winter

Winter. Frucht, A.

Winter. Thurm, M.

Winter. Updike, D.

Winter cat. O'Brien, D.

Winter count 1973: geese, they flew over in a storm. Lopez, B. H.

Winter courage. Goldreich, G.

Winter dance. O'Hara, J.

Winter dog. MacLeod, A.

Winter ends. Rambach, P.

Winter evenings: spring night. Painter, P.

The **winter** father. Dubus, A.

Winter in Italy. Boyle, K.

Winter in the blood. Welch, J.

Winter is lovely, isn't summer hell. Rooke, L.

Winter journey. Baxter, C.

The **winter** journey. Perec, G.

A **winter** legend. Brown, G. M.

The **winter** market. Gibson, W.

Winter meeting. McCourt, J.

Winter mines. Dilworth, S.

Winter nelis. Jolley, E.

Winter oak. Nagibin, ĬŪ. M.

Winter of '73. Gold, H.

The **winter** of his life. Patten, L. B.

The **winter** of our discontent. Wolfe, T.

Winter rentals. Rossi, A.

Winter run. Hoch, E. D.

Winter term. Meinke, P.

Winterblossom Garden. Low, D.

Wintering. Johnson, G.

Winterkill. Ford, R.

Winters, Arthur Yvor *See* Winters, Yvor, 1900-1968

Winters, Jonathan, 1925-

The artist

Winters, J. Winters' tales

A baby-sitter and why they're weird or turn weird

Winters, J. Winters' tales

The bird that couldn't fly

Winters, J. Winters' tales

The black lunch box

Winters, J. Winters' tales

Black tie

Winters, J. Winters' tales

A blinding snowstorm

Winters, J. Winters' tales

The Blue Hill Massacre

Winters, J. Winters' tales

The campers

Winters, J. Winters' tales

The cardboard man

Winters, J. Winters' tales

The conductor

Winters, J. Winters' tales

The costume

Winters, J. Winters' tales

Did anyone see my doggie?

Winters, J. Winters' tales

Dr. John Wookey to surgery

Winters, J. Winters' tales

The Easter bunny

Winters, J. Winters' tales

The face-lift

Winters, J. Winters' tales

Faces

Winters, J. Winters' tales

The fisherman

Winters, J. Winters' tales

Halloween

Winters, J. Winters' tales

The hijacker

Winters, J. Winters' tales

Winters, Jonathan, 1925— *Continued*
How much money did you make today, little man?
  Winters, J. Winters' tales
I miss dancing with you
  Winters, J. Winters' tales
I stand alone
  Winters, J. Winters' tales
I want to be a soldier
  Winters, J. Winters' tales
I was behind the couch all the time
  Winters, J. Winters' tales
The ivy-covered castle
  Winters, J. Winters' tales
The king who had to be queen too
  Winters, J. Winters' tales
The last day the circus came to town
  Winters, J. Winters' tales
The little bear who didn't know who he was
  Winters, J. Winters' tales
A little boy's Christmas list
  Winters, J. Winters' tales
Lost valley of the gods
  Winters, J. Winters' tales
The marathon runner
  Winters, J. Winters' tales
The mirage
  Winters, J. Winters' tales
The money preacher
  Winters, J. Winters' tales
My bird doesn't sing anymore
  Winters, J. Winters' tales
My hometown is gone—I mean gone
  Winters, J. Winters' tales
My last flight south
  Winters, J. Winters' tales
Niagara Falls
  Winters, J. Winters' tales
Ode to a baby robin
  Winters, J. Winters' tales
Ode to a sea gull
  Winters, J. Winters' tales
An old Indian buries an old friend
  Winters, J. Winters' tales
The postcard
  Winters, J. Winters' tales
The rebels
  Winters, J. Winters' tales
A roll in the hay
  Winters, J. Winters' tales
The snowman
  Winters, J. Winters' tales
Stolen flowers
  Winters, J. Winters' tales
Stung
  Winters, J. Winters' tales
Table for two
  Winters, J. Winters' tales
Thanksgiving
  Winters, J. Winters' tales
The visitor
  Winters, J. Winters' tales

The wedding
  Winters, J. Winters' tales
A well-kept secret
  Winters, J. Winters' tales
What are you frightened of, Johnny?
  Winters, J. Winters' tales
What do you want to be when you grow up?
  Winters, J. Winters' tales
Winters, Yvor, 1900-1968
The brink of darkness
  The Penguin book of horror stories
A **winter's** day. Leskov, N. S.
A **winter's** night. Friesner, E. M.
A **winter's** tale. Brown, C.
Winterson, Jeanette
Orion
  Winter's tales, new ser. v4
Winterton, Paul, 1908-
  For works written by this author under other names see Garve, Andrew, 1908-
Winton, Tim
Bay of Angels
  Winton, T. Minimum of two
Blood and water
  Winton, T. Minimum of two
A blow, a kiss
  Winton, T. Scission
Death belongs to the dead, his father told him, and sadness to the sad
  Winton, T. Minimum of two
Distant lands
  Winton, T. Minimum of two
Forest winter
  Winton, T. Minimum of two
Getting ahead
  Winton, T. Scission
Gravity
  Winton, T. Minimum of two
Heaven in your mind
  Prairie Schooner 62:128-38 Wint '88/'89
Holding
  Winton, T. Minimum of two
Lantern stalk
  Winton, T. Scission
Laps
  Winton, T. Minimum of two
A measure of eloquence
  Winton, T. Scission
Minimum of two
  Winton, T. Minimum of two
More
  Winton, T. Minimum of two
My father's axe
  Winton, T. Scission
Neighbours
  Winton, T. Scission
Nilsam's friend
  Winton, T. Minimum of two
No memory comes
  Winton, T. Minimum of two

Winton, Tim—*Continued*
The oppressed
Winton, T. Scission
Scission
Winton, T. Scission
Secrets
Transgressions; ed. by D. Anderson
Winton, T. Scission
The strong one
Winton, T. Minimum of two
Thomas Awkner floats
Winton, T. Scission
Wake
Winton, T. Scission
The water was dark and it went forever
down
Winton, T. Minimum of two
Wilderness
Winton, T. Scission
The woman at the well
Winton, T. Scission
Wiping the slate clean. Miller, G. W.
The **wire**. Lish, G.
WISCONSIN
19th century
Garland, H. The return of a private
Farm life
See Farm life—Wisconsin
WISDOM
Chesterton, G. K. The end of wisdom
Singer, I. B. Logarithms
A **wise** child. Wainwright, J. W.
The **wise** men: a detail of American life in
Mexico. Crane, S.
Wise men at their end. Bausch, R.
The **wish**. Dahl, R.
Wish. Mason, B. A.
Wish. Sarrantonio, A.
The **wish** house. Kipling, R.
Wish list. Goodman, A.
WISHES
Bradley, M. Z. A dozen of everything
Ellison, H. Gnomebody
Ellison, H. Rain, rain, go away
Gilbert, W. S. Foggerty's fairy
Goldin, S. The world where wishes worked
Hughes, D. B. F. Everybody needs a mink
Jacobs, W. W. The monkey's paw
Kaye, M. Damned funny
Kosztolányi, D. The wondrous visitation
of Krisztina Hrussz
Mazel, D. When you swing upon a star
Norton, A. The toymaker's snuffbox
Sarrantonio, A. Wish
Sheckley, R. Silversmith wishes
Spielberg, P. Prognosis
Stevenson, R. L. The bottle imp
Wishing you and your loved ones every hap-
piness. Morris, W.
WISSAHICKON CREEK (PA.)
Poe, E. A. Morning on the Wissahiccon
WIT *See* Humor
The **witch**. Van Vogt, A. E.

Witch girl. Coatsworth, E. J.
Witch in-grain. Gilchrist, M.
The **witch** of Goingsnake. Conley, R. J.
The **witch** of Park Avenue. Hoch, E. D.
The **witch** sheep. Earle, A. M.
The **witch**, Yazzie, and the nine of clubs.
Hillerman, T.
WITCHCRAFT
See also Demoniac possession; Exor-
cism; Voodooism
Aickman, R. Bind your hair
Aickman, R. The wine-dark sea
Anderson, P. Operation salamander
Barker, C. The madonna
Belden, W. S. Fenneca
Bell, C. The hunting of Lord Etsalian's
daughter
Big Eagle, D. The journey
Bloch, R. Broomstick ride
Bloch, R. Double whammy
Bloch, R. The funnel of God
Bloch, R. Heir apparent
Bloch, R. Sweets to the sweet
Bowles, P. The eye
Bradbury, R. West of October
Brennan, J. P. Canavan's back yard
Byatt, A. S. The dried witch
Campbell, R. Dolls
Campbell, R. The faces at Pine Dunes
Campbell, R. The seductress
Carey, M. The entrance exam
Cirone, P. B. Just another working mom
Coatsworth, E. J. Witch girl
Colette. The rainy moon
Collier, J. The lady on the grey
Collins, M. The green woman
Conley, R. J. Badger
Conley, R. J. Moon Face
Conley, R. J. Wesley's story
Conley, R. J. The witch of Goingsnake
Crispin, A. C. Bloodspell
Dann, J. Bad medicine
Daugherty, S. R. Claws of the white hawk
De Lint, C. The white road
Derleth, A. W. Miss Esperson
Donaldson, S. R. Ser Visal's tale
Doyle, Sir A. C. Lot no 249
Dunn, M. Cat and the Other
Erdrich, L. Fleur
Gilchrist, M. Witch in-grain
Gogol', N. V. The lost letter
Gogol', N. V. A May night; or, The
drowned maiden
Gogol', N. V. A terrible vengeance
Gogol', N. V. Viy
Griffin, P. Oath-bound
Havemann, E. The going home of Ntambo
Hawthorne, N. Feathertop
Hawthorne, N. Young Goodman Brown
Haynes, D. K. Thou shalt not suffer a
witch . . .
Heidbrink, J. R. Of ancient swords and
evil mist

WITCHCRAFT—*Continued*

Howard, V. E. The midnight voyage of the Seagull

Inks, C. Nine words in winter

Jakes, J. The man who wanted to be in the movies

Jakes, J. Storm in a bottle

James, M. R. The ash-tree

Kaplan, D. M. A Mexican tale

Kim, T. Portrait of a shaman

Klein, R. E. Mrs. Rahlo's closet

Kuttner, H. The dark world

Latham, P. Jeannette's hands

Lee, T. Into gold

Lee, T. The pale girl, the dark mage, and the green sea

Lee, T. Prince Amilec

Lee, T. Red as blood

Lee, T. Three days

Lee, T. When the clock strikes

Leinster, M. Devil's henchman

L'Engle, M. Poor little Saturday

Levinson, B. ". . .and he chose a mule"

Linzner, G. The independent fiend

Maitland, S. Let us now praise unknown women and our mothers who begat us

Major, A. R. La Verdad: the magic sword

Malzberg, B. N. Spree

Manners, M. Squeakie's first case

Mayhar, A. Neither rest nor refuge

McKillip, P. A. Baba Yaga and the sorcerer's son

Meiring, J. Bird of my voice

Moikangoa, C. E. Sebolelo comes home

Murphy, P. With four lean hounds

Niven, L. What good is a glass dagger?

Norton, A. One spell wizard

Norton, A. Spider silk

Norton, A. Through the needle's eye

Norton, A. Wizard's world

Ocampo, S. The friends

Pyle, H. The Salem wolf

Quinn, S. Is the Devil a gentleman?

Rey Rosa, R. The sorcerer's son

Rodoreda, M. A letter

Rodoreda, M. The salamander

Russ, J. Existence

Rynas, S. The apprentice sorcerer

Saidi, W. The nightmare

Sayers, D. L. The Cyprian cat

Schmitz, J. H. The witches of Karres

Schwob, M. The embalming-women

Schwob, M. The 'Papier Rouge'

Schwob, M. The sabbat at Mofflaines

Schwob, M. The strigae

Seabrook, W. B. The witch's vengeance

Severance, C. Isle of illusion

Sheckley, R. The accountant

Shwartz, S. M. Rite of failure

Singer, I. B. The Jew from Babylon

Smith, C. A. Necromancy in Naat

Smith, E. E. Teragram

Snodgrass, M. Futures yet unseen

Tall Mountain, M. The sinh of Niguudzagha

Tenn, W. Mistress Sary

Tenn, W. My mother was a witch

Thomas, D. The school for witches

Van Vogt, A. E. The witch

Vinge, J. D., and Vinge, V. The peddler's apprentice

Wellman, M. W. The witch's cat

Wells, H. G. Pollock and the Porroh man

Wilson, G. Yesterday's witch

Wolfe, G. The cat

Wollheim, D. A. The haters

WITCHES *See* Witchcraft

The **witches** of Karres. Schmitz, J. H.

Witch's broom. Hansen, J.

The **witch's** cat. Wellman, M. W.

The **witch's** vengeance. Seabrook, W. B.

With a capital T. Gallant, M.

With a herring in one hand and a bottle of schnapps in the other; oh! how he did dance! Granit, A.

With a little gold pencil. Girion, B.

With a smile for the ending. Block, L.

With delicate mad hands. Tiptree, J.

With Evelyn. Peterson, M.

With four lean hounds. Murphy, P.

With friends. Chekhov, A. P.

With Maya. Shimao, T.

With or without. Dickinson, C.

With the gypsy girls. Eliade, M.

With the original cast. Kress, N.

With this ring . . . Lawrence, K. R.

With Virgil Oddum at the East Pole. Ellison, H.

With voice of joy and praise. Carver, W.

With wings cross water. Pritchard, M.

Witheling End. Hartley, L. P.

The **withered** arm. Hardy, T.

Within. Carter, R.

Within the cloud. Anthony, P.

Within the walls of Tyre. Bishop, M.

Without any ears. Butler, J.

Without love. Cooper, J. C.

Without love. Pasternak, B. L.

Without the option. Wodehouse, P. G.

Without visible means. Coleman, W.

Without wings. Carroll, L. E.

Witness. Blaushild, L.

The **witness**. Garrett, G. P.

The **witness**. Oates, J. C.

The **witness**. Petrakis, H. M.

The **witness**. Russell, E. F.

Witness. Russell, T.

Witness in the dark. Brown, F.

WITNESSES

Crane, S. Adventures of a novelist

Ellison, H. Soft monkey

Ellison, H. The whimper of whipped dogs

Estleman, L. D. The used

Greene, G. The case for the defence

Matsumoto, S. The secret alibi

Oates, J. C. Manslaughter

WITNESSES—*Continued*
Speed, J. Fair's fair
Tripp, M. Form
Witnesses. Gerber, M. J.
Wives in the garden. Dunn, D.
The **wizard** postponed. Manuel, J.
WIZARDS *See* Magicians
Wizard's world. Norton, A.
Wnorowska, Diane
Seven come heaven?
Devils & demons; ed. by M. Kaye and
S. Kaye
The **Wo** family. Clarke, T.
A **wobble** in Wockii futures. Dickson, G. R.
**Wodehouse, P. G. (Pelham Grenville), 1881-
1975**
The artistic career of Corky
Wodehouse, P. G. The world of Jeeves
Aunt Agatha takes the count
Wodehouse, P. G. The world of Jeeves
The aunt and the sluggard
Wodehouse, P. G. The world of Jeeves
The battle of Squashy Hollow
The Saturday Evening Post 257:68-73+
S '85
Bertie changes his mind
Wodehouse, P. G. The world of Jeeves
Bingo and the little woman
Wodehouse, P. G. The world of Jeeves
Clustering round young Bingo
Wodehouse, P. G. The world of Jeeves
Comrade Bingo
Wodehouse, P. G. A Wodehouse bestiary
Wodehouse, P. G. The world of Jeeves
The delayed exit of Claude and Eustace
Wodehouse, P. G. The world of Jeeves
Episode of the dog McIntosh
Wodehouse, P. G. The world of Jeeves
Fixing it for Freddie
Wodehouse, P. G. The world of Jeeves
The go-getter
Wodehouse, P. G. A Wodehouse bestiary
The great sermon handicap
Wodehouse, P. G. The world of Jeeves
Indian summer of an uncle
Wodehouse, P. G. The world of Jeeves
The inferiority complex of old Sippy
Wodehouse, P. G. The world of Jeeves
Jeeves and the Chump Cyril
Wodehouse, P. G. The world of Jeeves
Jeeves and the greasy bird
Wodehouse, P. G. The world of Jeeves
Jeeves and the hard-boiled egg
Wodehouse, P. G. The world of Jeeves
Jeeves and the impending doom
Wodehouse, P. G. A Wodehouse bestiary
Wodehouse, P. G. The world of Jeeves
Jeeves and the kid Clementina
Wodehouse, P. G. The world of Jeeves
Jeeves and the old school chum
Wodehouse, P. G. A Wodehouse bestiary
Wodehouse, P. G. The world of Jeeves

Jeeves and the song of songs
Wodehouse, P. G. The world of Jeeves
Jeeves and the unbidden guest
Wodehouse, P. G. The world of Jeeves
Jeeves and the Yule-tide spirit
Wodehouse, P. G. The world of Jeeves
Jeeves in the springtime
Wodehouse, P. G. The world of Jeeves
Jeeves makes an omelette
Wodehouse, P. G. The world of Jeeves
Jeeves takes charge
Wodehouse, P. G. The world of Jeeves
The love that purifies
Wodehouse, P. G. The world of Jeeves
The Metropolitan touch
Wodehouse, P. G. The world of Jeeves
The mixer
Wodehouse, P. G. A Wodehouse bestiary
Monkey business
Wodehouse, P. G. A Wodehouse bestiary
Open house
Wodehouse, P. G. A Wodehouse bestiary
The ordeal of young Tuppy
Wodehouse, P. G. The world of Jeeves
Pig-hoo-o-o-o-ey!
Wodehouse, P. G. A Wodehouse bestiary
The purity of the turf
Wodehouse, P. G. The world of Jeeves
The rummy affair of old Biffy
Wodehouse, P. G. The world of Jeeves
Scoring off Jeeves
Wodehouse, P. G. The world of Jeeves
Sir Roderick comes to lunch
Wodehouse, P. G. A Wodehouse bestiary
Wodehouse, P. G. The world of Jeeves
Something squishy
Wodehouse, P. G. A Wodehouse bestiary
The spot of art
Wodehouse, P. G. The world of Jeeves
The story of Webster
Roger Caras' Treasury of great cat
stories
Wodehouse, P. G. A Wodehouse bestiary
Ukridge's dog college
Wodehouse, P. G. A Wodehouse bestiary
Uncle Fred flits by
Wodehouse, P. G. A Wodehouse bestiary
Unpleasantness at Bludleigh Court
Wodehouse, P. G. A Wodehouse bestiary
Without the option
Mystery in the mainstream; ed. by B.
Pronzini; M. H. Greenberg and B. N.
Malzberg
Wodehouse, P. G. The world of Jeeves
Wodehouse, Pelham Grenville *See*
Wodehouse, P. G. (Pelham Grenville),
1881-1975
Woden's day. Stafford, J.
Wodhams, Jack
Aunt Agnes
Short story international 46
One clay foot
Australian science fiction; ed. by V. Ikin

Woe to live on. Woodrell, D.

The **woes** of a single woman and her car. Silva, B.

The **woggle**. Mordden, E.

Wohlfeld, Valerie
The phoenix
The North American Review 273:32-3 D '88

Wohmann, Gabriele, 1932-
A party in the country
The Antioch Review 45:354-63 Summ '87
The swan
Voices East and West: German short stories since 1945

Woiwode, Larry
Alpha
The New Yorker 63:34-44+ O 26 '87
Blindness
The Antioch Review 44:276-81 Summ '86
Wanting an orange
The Paris Review 26:88-91 Wint '84

Wojnarowicz, David, 1954-
Self portrait in twenty-three rounds
Between C & D; ed. by J. Rose and C. Texier

WOJTYŁA, KAROL *See* John Paul II, Pope, 1920-

Wolf, Christa
A certain date
Voices East and West: German short stories since 1945

Wolf, Rose
Cat and muse
Magic in Ithkar 4; ed. by A. Norton and R. Adams
Tall dames go walking
Tales of the Witch World 2

Wolf, Stephen
The legacy of Beau Kremel
The Ploughshares reader: new fiction for the eighties

The **wolf**. Baykurt, F.

Wolf from the door. Scarborough, E.

A **wolf** in the heart. Haas, B.

Wolf night. Crider, B.

The **wolf** tracker. Grey, Z.

Wolfe, Gene
Alien stones
Machines that think; ed. by I. Asimov; P. S. Warrick and M. H. Greenberg
All the hues of Hell
The Universe; ed. by B. Preiss
The Year's best science fiction, fifth annual collection
A cabin on the coast
Nebula awards 20
The Year's best science fiction, second annual collection
The cat
Magicats! Ed. by J. Dann and G. Dozois
The Year's best science fiction, first annual collection

Checking out
Afterlives; ed. by P. Sargent and I. Watson

The death of Doctor Island
The Best from Universe

The detective of dreams
Masterpieces of fantasy and enchantment; ed. by D. G. Hartwell

Game in the pope's head
Ripper! Ed. by G. Dozois and S. Casper

In the house of gingerbread
The Architecture of fear; ed. by K. Cramer and P. D. Pautz

Lukora
Terry's universe; ed. by B. Meacham

The map
The Year's best science fiction, second annual collection

The recording
100 great fantasy short short stories; ed. by I. Asimov; T. Carr and M. H. Greenberg

Redbeard
Masques; ed. by J. N. Williamson

Seven American nights
The Dark descent; ed. by D. G. Hartwell

Slaves of silver
Sherlock Holmes through time and space

Sonya, Crane Wessleman, and Kittee
Magicats! Ed. by J. Dann and G. Dozois

War beneath the tree
Omni book of science fiction 3

Wolfe, Linda
Other people's marriages
Ladies' Home Journal 101:91+ Je '84
Think of wives in old China
Ladies' Home Journal 104:84+ Mr '87

Wolfe, Thomas, 1900-1938
The anatomy of loneliness
Wolfe, T. The complete short stories of Thomas Wolfe
An angel on the porch
Wolfe, T. The complete short stories of Thomas Wolfe
April, late April
Wolfe, T. The complete short stories of Thomas Wolfe
Arnold Pentland
Wolfe, T. The complete short stories of Thomas Wolfe
The bell remembered
Wolfe, T. The complete short stories of Thomas Wolfe
The birthday
Wolfe, T. The complete short stories of Thomas Wolfe
Boom town
Wolfe, T. The complete short stories of Thomas Wolfe
The bums at sunset
Wolfe, T. The complete short stories of Thomas Wolfe

Wolfe, Thomas, 1900-1938—*Continued*

Chickamauga
  A Modern Southern reader; ed. by B. Forkner and P. Samway
  A Treasury of Civil War stories; ed. by M. H. Greenberg and B. Pronzini
  Wolfe, T. The complete short stories of Thomas Wolfe

The child by tiger
  Wolfe, T. The complete short stories of Thomas Wolfe

Circus at dawn
  Wolfe, T. The complete short stories of Thomas Wolfe

The Company
  Wolfe, T. The complete short stories of Thomas Wolfe

Dark in the forest, strange as time
  Wolfe, T. The complete short stories of Thomas Wolfe

The dark messiah
  Wolfe, T. The complete short stories of Thomas Wolfe

Death the proud brother
  Wolfe, T. The complete short stories of Thomas Wolfe

'E: a recollection
  Wolfe, T. The complete short stories of Thomas Wolfe

The face of the war
  Wolfe, T. The complete short stories of Thomas Wolfe

Fame and the poet
  Wolfe, T. The complete short stories of Thomas Wolfe

The far and the near
  Wolfe, T. The complete short stories of Thomas Wolfe

For professional appearance
  Wolfe, T. The complete short stories of Thomas Wolfe

The four lost men
  Wolfe, T. The complete short stories of Thomas Wolfe

Gulliver, the story of a tall man
  Wolfe, T. The complete short stories of Thomas Wolfe

His father's earth
  Wolfe, T. The complete short stories of Thomas Wolfe

The hollow men
  Wolfe, T. The complete short stories of Thomas Wolfe

The hollyhock sowers
  Wolfe, T. The complete short stories of Thomas Wolfe

The house of the far and lost
  Wolfe, T. The complete short stories of Thomas Wolfe

In the park
  Wolfe, T. The complete short stories of Thomas Wolfe

Justice is blind
  Wolfe, T. The complete short stories of Thomas Wolfe

Katamoto
  Wolfe, T. The complete short stories of Thomas Wolfe

The lion at morning
  Wolfe, T. The complete short stories of Thomas Wolfe

The lost boy
  Wolfe, T. The complete short stories of Thomas Wolfe

Mr. Malone
  Wolfe, T. The complete short stories of Thomas Wolfe

The names of the nation
  Wolfe, T. The complete short stories of Thomas Wolfe

Nebraska Crane
  Wolfe, T. The complete short stories of Thomas Wolfe

The newspaper [Variant title: Gentlemen of the press]
  Wolfe, T. The complete short stories of Thomas Wolfe

No cure for it
  Wolfe, T. The complete short stories of Thomas Wolfe

No door
  Wolfe, T. The complete short stories of Thomas Wolfe

No more rivers
  Wolfe, T. The complete short stories of Thomas Wolfe

A note on experts: Dexter Vespasian Joyner
  Wolfe, T. The complete short stories of Thomas Wolfe

Oktoberfest
  Wolfe, T. The complete short stories of Thomas Wolfe

Old Catawba [Variant title: Men of Old Catawba]
  Wolfe, T. The complete short stories of Thomas Wolfe

Old Man Rivers
  Wolfe, T. The complete short stories of Thomas Wolfe

On leprechauns
  Wolfe, T. The complete short stories of Thomas Wolfe

One of the girls in our party
  Wolfe, T. The complete short stories of Thomas Wolfe

Only the dead know Brooklyn
  Wolfe, T. The complete short stories of Thomas Wolfe

The plumed knight
  Wolfe, T. The complete short stories of Thomas Wolfe

Polyphemus
  Wolfe, T. The complete short stories of Thomas Wolfe

Wolfe, Thomas, 1900-1938—*Continued*
Portrait of a literary critic
Wolfe, T. The complete short stories of
Thomas Wolfe
A prologue to America
Wolfe, T. The complete short stories of
Thomas Wolfe
The promise of America
Wolfe, T. The complete short stories of
Thomas Wolfe
Return
Wolfe, T. The complete short stories of
Thomas Wolfe
The return of the prodigal
Wolfe, T. The complete short stories of
Thomas Wolfe
So this is man
Wolfe, T. The complete short stories of
Thomas Wolfe
The Spanish letter
Wolfe, T. The complete short stories of
Thomas Wolfe
The sun and the rain
Wolfe, T. The complete short stories of
Thomas Wolfe
Three o'clock
Wolfe, T. The complete short stories of
Thomas Wolfe
The train and the city
Wolfe, T. The complete short stories of
Thomas Wolfe
The winter of our discontent
Wolfe, T. The complete short stories of
Thomas Wolfe
Wolfe, Tom
2020 A.D.
Esquire 103:88-90+ Ja '85
Wolfenstein, Martha
Chayah
The Other woman; ed. by S. Koppelman
Wolfert, Adrienne
The loved one
The North American Review 269:29-32
Je '84
Wolff, Tobias, 1945-
Coming attractions
Wolff, T. Back in the world
Desert breakdown, 1968
The Editors' choice: new American
stories v1
Wolff, T. Back in the world
Hunters in the snow
The Art of the tale; ed. by D. Halpern
Leviathan
The Pushcart prize XI
Wolff, T. Back in the world
The liar
American short story masterpieces; ed.
by R. Carver and T. Jenks
Buying time; ed. by S. Walker
The Substance of things hoped for; ed.
by J. B. Breslin

The missing person
Wolff, T. Back in the world
The other Miller
The Atlantic 257:56-61 Je '86
The Best American short stories, 1987
The Graywolf annual 4
Our story begins
Esquire 102:107-10 Ag '84
The Esquire fiction reader v1
The Graywolf annual [1]
Wolff, T. Back in the world
The poor are always with us
The Atlantic 254:86-90 S '84
Wolff, T. Back in the world
The rich brother
The Best American short stories, 1986
Wolff, T. Back in the world
Say yes
Sudden fiction; ed. by R. Shapard and
J. Thomas
Wolff, T. Back in the world
Sister
Prize stories, 1985
Wolff, T. Back in the world
Smorgasbord
The Best American short stories, 1988
Esquire 108:236-8+ S '87
Soldier's joy
The Editors' choice v3; ed. by G. E.
Murphy, Jr.
Esquire 104:210-12+ O '85
The Esquire fiction reader v2
Soldiers & civilians; ed. by T. Jenks
Wolff, T. Back in the world
Wolfie. Rosenfeld, I.
Wolfland. Lee, T.
The **wolf's** flock. Shwartz, S. M.
Wolfskin. Whittington, M. K.
Wolitzer, Hilma
Mother
The Bread Loaf anthology of contem-
porary American short stories; ed. by
R. Pack and J. Parini
Prairie Schooner 61:97-107 Spr '87
Wollaston, Nicholas
Walkabout
Foreign exchange; ed. by J. Evans
Wollheim, Donald A.
Give her hell
100 great fantasy short short stories; ed.
by I. Asimov; T. Carr and M. H.
Greenberg
The haters
100 great fantasy short short stories; ed.
by I. Asimov; T. Carr and M. H.
Greenberg
Malice aforethought
100 great fantasy short short stories; ed.
by I. Asimov; T. Carr and M. H.
Greenberg

Wollheim, Donald A.—*Continued*
  The rag thing
    100 great fantasy short short stories; ed.
      by I. Asimov; T. Carr and M. H.
      Greenberg
A **wollopin'** good chew. Thompson, T.

Wolverton, Dave

  On my way to paradise
    L. Ron Hubbard presents Writers of the
    future v3

WOLVES
  Baykurt, F. The wolf
  Bird, C. Cave amantem
  Carter, A. Peter and the wolf
  Grey, Z. The wolf tracker
  Matthiessen, P. The wolves of Aguila
  Maupassant, G. de. The white wolf
  Pollard, J. A. Old woman
  Stephenson, M. The pack
  Williamson, J. Wolves of darkness
The **wolves** of Aguila. Matthiessen, P.
The **wolves** of Cernogratz. Saki
Wolves of darkness. Williamson, J.
Wolves of Monte Carlo. Footner, H.
A **woman**. Cooke, R. T.
The **woman** at Otowi Crossing. Waters, F.
The **woman** at Seven Brothers. Steele, W. D.
The **Woman** at the Eighteen-Mile. Austin, M.
  H.
The **woman** at the store. Mansfield, K.
The **woman** at the well. Winton, T.
The **woman** I envied. Baxt, G.
Woman in a lampshade. Jolley, E.
Woman in a mirror. Farmer, B.
The **woman** in love. Corinne, T. A.
A **woman** in my years. Fontane, T.
The **woman** in the bar. Asimov, I.
The **woman** in the bed. Stead, C.
The **woman** in the customs officer's house.
  Moravia, A.
The **woman** in the shadows. Allen, R.
The **woman** in the shadows. Bendel, S. K.
The **woman** in the wardrobe. Barnard, R.
The **woman** in the window. Lowe, R.
A **woman** is missing. Nielsen, H.
A **woman** like Dilsie. Thibault, D.
The **woman** next door. Ferron, J.
A **woman** of Earth. Moore-Bentley, M. A.
A **woman** of her tribe. Robinson, M. A.
A **woman** of properties. Matthews, J.
A **woman** to call mother. Hirabayashi, T.
Woman waiting for train at dusk. Pierce, C.
The **woman** who ate cat food. Bukoski, A.
The **woman** who came at six o'clock. García
  Márquez, G.
The **woman** who couldn't imagine men. Giv-
  ner, J.
The **woman** who fulled clothes. Yi, H.
The **woman** who had everything. Fremlin, C.
The **woman** who hated children. Ronald, J.
The **woman** who loved reindeer. Pierce, M.
  A.

The **woman** who loved the moon. Lynn, E.
  A.
The **woman** who saved Jesse James. Gal-
  lagher, T.
The **woman** who talked to horses. Rooke,
  L.
The **woman** who thought she was beautiful.
  Bernard, K.
The **woman** who took the local paper. Mat-
  sumoto, S.
The **woman** who was never satisfied. Martin,
  V.
The **woman** who would not stay home. Pot-
  ter, N. A. J.
The **woman** with the black cloak. Moravia,
  A.
A **woman's** breast. Landolfi, T.
A **woman's** college from outside. Woolf, V.
The **Woman's** Exchange of Simpkinsville.
  Stuart, R. M.
The **woman's** guide to home companionship.
  Rooke, L.
A **woman's** kingdom. Chekhov, A. P.
A **woman's** life. Wagar, W. W.
The **woman's** rose. Schreiner, O.
A **woman's** vengeance. Barbey d'Aurevilly, J.
Woman's wiles. Maupassant, G. de
Womb ward. Lessing, D. M.
WOMEN
    See also Black women; Jewish wom-
    en; Muslim women; Single women
  Abbott, K. The sea lion
  Abrams, L. Secrets men keep
  Adams, A. Elizabeth
  Adams, A. Mexican dust
  Adams, A. Molly's dog
  Adams, A. My first and only house
  Adams, A. A public pool
  Adams, A. Return trips
  Adams, A. Sintra
  Adams, A. Waiting for Stella
  Adams, A. You are what you own: a
    notebook
  Adams, G. G. Doing yoga
  Alford, E. Half past eight
  Astley, T. The scenery never changes
  Austin, M. H. The basket maker
  Barclay, B. A greenhouse for Maureen
  Barthelme, F. Restraint
  Bartlett, H. Some notes on evolution
  Bates, H. E. A party for the girls
  Beattie, A. Cards
  Bell, M. Helen
  Bell, M. Reba
  Bergland, M. An embarrassment of
    ordinary riches
  Bird, C. Introducing your friends
  Birtha, B. In the deep heart's core
  Bly, C. The last of the gold star mothers
  Borges, J. L. Story of the warrior and the
    captive
  Brady, M. Seneca morning
  Burns, M. Greta

WOMEN—*Continued*

Calisher, H. The library
Caponegro, M. Monday
Carrington, L. Waiting
Chernoff, M. The hills of Andorra
Clark, J. Passage by water
Clark, M. At the exhibition
Codrescu, A. Julie
Colette. Alix's refusal
Colette. One evening
Dadswell, M. An interval of time
Davis, L. What an old woman will wear
Dazai, O. The garden lantern
Diaconú, A. Mamaya
Doubiago, S. Vets
Doubiago, S. Warriors
Doubiago, S. The whore
Drake, R. If she knowed what I knowed, she never would woke
Drake, R. June
Drake, R. Miss Effie, the Peabody, and Father Time
Dubus, A. Waiting
Ekström, M. Death's midwives
Ferron, M. The weaker sex
Filippi, C. L. Pilar, your curls
Flanagan, M. Simple pleasures
Forrest, K. V. Mother was an alien
Freeman, C. The song of Roland
Frucht, A. The anniversary
Frucht, A. How to live alone
Frucht, A. Paradise
Gaitskill, M. Connection
Gaitskill, M. Other factors
Gallagher, T. Girls
García Márquez, G. Eva is inside her cat
Garner, H. The life of art
Gearhart, S. M. The chipko
Gerber, M. J. At the fence
Gilchrist, E. There's a Garden of Eden
Gilliatt, P. The nuisance
Gilliatt, P. Purse
Gilliatt, P. The redhead
Gilliatt, P. Suspense item
Gingher, M. Aurora Island
Givner, J. A climate of extremes
Gordon, M. Now I am married
Hagy, A. C. No kind of name
Hannah, B. Power and light
Hartley, L. P. The shadow on the wall
Hausmann, J. Offices of instruction
Hempel, A. Tonight is a favor to Holly
Henry, O. The princess and the puma
Highsmith, P. Not in this life, maybe the next
Hochstein, R. She should have died hereafter
Ignatow, R. G. Dreams & disappointments
Jolley, E. Winter nelis
Kauffman, J. The Alvordton Spa and Sweat Shop
Kauffman, J. Breaking the news to Doll
Kauffman, J. Harmony

Kauffman, J. Isn't it something?
Keeling, N. Chasing her own tail
Keeling, N. The little axe
Kercheval, J. L. Underground women
Krysl, M. And Judith, daughter of Ester, raised the sword above her head
Krysl, M. Bondage
Krysl, M. The fur of the bear
Krysl, M. Macroscopic phenomena
Krysl, M. Mozart, Westmoreland, and me
La Chapelle, M. Anna in a small town
Listfield, E. Porcupines and other travesties
London, J. The girls love each other
London, J. Sister ships
Lopatin, J. Krystal goes mystical
Lopatin, J. Visitation of the ghost
Lurie, M. Her life: a fragment
Lustig, A. Indecent dreams
Lynn, E. A. The woman who loved the moon
Maitland, S. Let us now praise unknown women and our mothers who begat us
Mansfield, K. Bliss
Mattison, A. Bears
Mattison, A. New Haven
Maupassant, G. de. A fashionable woman
Maupassant, G. de. Joseph
Maupassant, G. de. The signal
McCrory, M. Strangers
McCullers, C. A domestic dilemma
McLaughlin, L. A decent interval
McLaughlin, L. Nancy
McNeal, T. True
Mohr, N. The artist (Inez)
Mohr, N. Aunt Rosana's rocker (Zoraida)
Mohr, N. Brief miracle (Virginia)
Mohr, N. Happy birthday (Lucia)
Mohr, N. A Thanksgiving celebration (Amy)
Mohr, N. A time with a future (Carmela)
Molinaro, U. Bird in ambush
Morand, P. Aurora
Morand, P. Clarissa
Morand, P. Delphine
Moravia, A. Jewellery
Morris, M. The banana fever
Morris, M. The Hall of the Meteorites
Morris, M. Links
Moskowitz, F. Presents
Nevai, L. Red spikes
Norris, H. The quarry
Oates, J. C. Back country
O'Brien, E. Ghosts
Oosthuizen, A. A fine romance
Osborn, C. Dreamer when last seen
Painter, P. Getting to know the weather
Painter, P. Something to do
Paley, G. Listening
Pilcher, R. The before-Christmas present
Prose, F. Other lives
Rambach, P. Winter ends
Rhys, J. The blue bird
Rhys, J. A spiritualist

WOMEN—*Continued*

Rhys, J. Till September Petronella
Riskin, M. Print dresses
Robison, M. Mirror
Rossi, A. Back in the days
Rossi, A. Bums on needles and pins
Ruffolo, L. Candy
Russ, J. Life in a furniture store
Russ, J. Visiting
Russ, J. Visiting day
Samples, H. Home cooking
Sandel, C. Carmen and Maia
Sandel, C. The silken thread
Sandel, C. The women in the bath-house
Sandoz, M. The vine
Schinto, J. Keepsake
Schwartz, L. S. The Thousand Islands
Shacochis, B. Dead reckoning
Sheckley, R. The perfect woman
Smiley, J. Jeffrey, believe me
Smith, C. Canaan [excerpt]
Stark, S. S. The Johnstown Polka
Stein, G. A water-fall and a piano
Strand, M. True loves
Suckow, R. A great Mollie
Telles, L. F. Tigrela
Timperley, R. Hell on both sides of the gate
Tsushima, Y. The silent traders
Valenzuela, L. I'm your horse in the night
Valenzuela, L. Other weapons
Valenzuela, L. Rituals of rejection
Valenzuela, L. The word "killer"
Viramontes, H. M. The Cariboo Cafe
Wegner, H. The stoning of Stanislava
West, J. The condemned librarian
Wilson, L. A. Massé
Wilson, R., Jr. Land fishers
Woolf, V. An unwritten novel

Psychology

Amichai, Y. Nina of Ashkelon
Atwood, M. Loulou; or, The domestic life of the language
Atwood, M. Rape fantasies
Atwood, M. Spring song of the frogs
Austin, M. H. The Coyote-Spirit and the Weaving Woman
Austin, M. H. Frustrate
Bled, R. N. Marielle
Block, S. Leaving Sasha; or, The bed makes the man
Brady, M. The field is full of daisies and I'm afraid to pass
Brondoli, M. Showdown
Broun, H. Rosella, in stages
Caponegro, M. The Star Cafe
Charbonneau-Tissot, C. Compulsion
Chernoff, M. Infinks
De Haven, T. He's all mine
Evans, E. Will
Garro, E. It's the fault of the Tlaxcaltecas
Holt, J. D. "God sent you into that Gomorrah this morning to bring up the truth"

Hood, H. Breaking off
Jolley, E. My father's moon
Kees, W. Gents 50¢/Ladies 25¢
Keillor, G. Darlene makes a move
Lynch, M. Latin lover
Mason, B. A. Shiloh
Nelson, K. Invisible life
O'Brien, E. The doll
Potter, N. A. J. A thin place
Potter, N. A. J. The woman who would not stay home
Rawlings, M. K. Gal young un
Russ, J. Old thoughts, old presences: Daddy's girl
Russ, J. Old thoughts, old presences: The autobiography of my mother
Schwartz, L. S. Life is an adventure, with risks
Schwartz, L. S. So you're going to have a new body!
Shefner, E. The common body
Shefner, E. Royal bones
Summers, H. S. Amaryllis & the telephone
Summers, H. S. Dolly
Thompson, S. Horror show
Varley, J. Manikins
Vreuls, D. The Mary mystery
Walker, A. The abortion
Wilbur, E. A certain view
Willett, J. Father of invention
Willett, J. Jenny
Woolf, V. The lady in the looking-glass: a reflection

Relation to other women

Alden, P. B. Two women
Ashley, M. A. Gracefully afraid
Auchincloss, L. The wedding guest
Austin, M. H. The fakir
Austin, M. H. The Woman at the Eighteen-Mile
Bradley, M. Z. To keep the oath
Brady, M. Novena
Brady, M. The question she put to herself
Brown, R. One of two
Burford, B. Falling
Campbell, W. B. Kisses
Colette. Gribiche
Colette. The kepi
Colette. Mirror games
Colette. Morning glories
Colette. The rivals
Cooper, J. C. Without love
Creswell, R. Epithalamium
Cummings, R. Berrying
Dadswell, M. Swinging round a circle
Dazai, O. The lady who entertained
Dunn, D. The tennis court
Ferron, J. The woman next door
Finger, A. Abortion
Forer, A. U. Thanksgiving with Trudy
Frucht, A. The habit of friendship
Furlong, M. The garden
Gallant, M. Virus X

WOMEN—Relation to other women—*Continued*
Gault, C. The tables
Gilchrist, E. Crazy, crazy, now showing everywhere
Giles, M. Baby pictures
Gomez, J. Don't explain
Hagy, A. C. Nongqause
Hamilton, D. C. Blood, sweat, and fears
Henley, P. Friday night at Silver Star
Henley, P. Moving in
Hospital, J. T. Golden girl
Kercheval, J. L. Willy
King, F. H. Home
Kohler, S. The mountain
Kornblatt, J. R. Lila
Kornblatt, J. R. Susan
Latimer, M. Guardian angel
Lim, C. The ugly one
Martin, H. R. A poet though married
McElroy, J. Daughter of the revolution
Morris, W. Things that matter
Odom, J. Sole owners of the mountain
Paley, G. Friends
Pavese, C. The three girls
Prichard, K. S. Happiness
Rasputin, V. G. The old woman
Roberts, N. Flames
Rooke, L. The woman's guide to home companionship
Rowe, M. 'Who's she—the cat's mother?'
Sanford, W. M. Allie
Sayles, J. The Halfway Diner
Schoemperlen, D. Clues
Schreiner, O. The woman's rose
Shaham, N. The other side of the wall
Sproat, R. Firework night isn't in it
Vogan, S. Sunday's no name band
Wandor, M. Judy's kiss
Wilkinson, R. The bitch
Williams, T. Happy August the Tenth
Woodman, A. Gulf
Woolf, V. A society
Woolf, V. A woman's college from outside
Zhang Jie. The ark
Social conditions
See also Feminism
Atherton, G. F. H. The bell in the fog
Austin, M. H. Kate Bixby's queerness
Austin, M. H. The man who was loved by women
Austin, M. H. The return of Mr. Wills
Brodkey, H. Ceil
Durham, E. M. Deepening dusk
Elgin, S. H. For the sake of Grace
Enchi, F. Blind man's buff
Gilman, C. P. Turned
Gilman, C. P. The yellow wallpaper
Gordon, M. The dancing party
José, F. S. Progress
Kaikō, T. A certain voice
Latimer, M. The family
Le Sueur, M. Sequel to love
Mancuso, C. Mamie

Moore, G. A faithful heart
O'Brien, E. Savages
Paley, G. At that time; or, The history of a joke
Phelps, E. S. The true story of Guenever
Raddall, T. H. The wedding gift
Rinser, L. A handful of white daffodils
Rizkalla, J. The servant of the last hour
Sanford, W. M. Windfall
Silko, L. Private property
Smedley, A. Shan-fei, communist
Tamer, Z. Death of the black hair
Tamer, Z. Sheep
Taylor, P. H. The old forest
Tiptree, J. Your faces, o my sisters! Your faces filled of light!
Tsuboi, S. Umbrella on a moonlit night
Vinge, J. D. Phoenix in the ashes
Wong, S. H. The feminist
Woolf, V. The journal of Mistress Joan Martyn
Woolf, V. Phyllis and Rosamond
China
Chen Rong. At middle age
Grandbois, A. May Blossom
Egypt
Rifaat, A. Another evening at the club
India
Jhabvala, R. P. The housewife
Jhabvala, R. P. Rose petals
Israel
Liphshitz, A. Three women
Pakistan
Rahman, T. The legacy
South Africa
Gordimer, N. Good climate, friendly inhabitants
Wicomb, Z. When the train comes
Sudan
Ibrahim, I. The gap in Kaltouma's fence
WOMEN, BLACK *See* Black women
WOMEN, JEWISH *See* Jewish women
WOMEN, MUSLIM *See* Muslim women
Women. Blinkin, M.
Women and children first. Prose, F.
WOMEN ARTISTS
Atwood, M. The sunrise
Austin, M. H. Blue roses
Ciment, J. Money
Ciment, J. Small claims
Flanagan, M. A parma violet room
Hagy, A. C. Where men go to cry
Hull, H. R. The fire
Latimer, M. The family
Mohr, N. The artist (Inez)
Nevai, L. Resident artist
Thomas, M. Jim Chance
WOMEN ASTRONAUTS
Tiptree, J. With delicate mad hands
WOMEN AUTHORS
Apple, M. Post-modernism
Auchincloss, L. The "fulfillment" of Grace Eliot

WOMEN AUTHORS—*Continued*
Byatt, A. S. On the day that E. M. Forster died
Calisher, H. The passenger
Colette. The kepi
Colette. The rainy moon
Gallant, M. Varieties of exile
Gilchrist, E. Anna, Part 1
Gilliatt, P. Nobody's business
Gilliatt, P. The position of the planets
Gilman, C. P. The yellow wallpaper
Greene, G. The invisible Japanese gentlemen
Ligotti, T. Alice's last adventure
Maugham, W. S. The colonel's lady
Oates, J. C. Détente
Oates, J. C. The man whom women adored
Oates, J. C. My Warszawa: 1980
O'Connor, F. The crop
Rhys, J. The Lotus
Rule, J. Puzzle
Russ, J. Sword blades and poppy seed
WOMEN-HATING *See* Misogyny
WOMEN IN BUSINESS *See* Businesswomen
WOMEN IN POLITICS
Dick, P. K. Novelty act
Guin, W. The delegate from Guapanga
Singer, I. B. The conference
The **women** in the bath-house. Sandel, C.
WOMEN JOURNALISTS
Atwood, M. A travel piece
Colette. Literature
Gilchrist, E. First Manhattans
Gilliatt, P. Broderie anglaise
McGrath, P. The Arnold Crombeck story
WOMEN LAWYERS
Herrick, A. In the air, over our heads
Mortimer, J. C. Rumpole and the female of the species
The **women** men don't see. Tiptree, J.
The **women** on the wall. Stegner, W. E.
WOMEN PAINTERS
Leach, A. R. A captain out of Etruria
Matheson, R. C. Beholder
Welch, D. The fire in the wood
Wilson, B. How to fix a roof
WOMEN PHOTOGRAPHERS
McCormack, E. P. One picture of Trotsky
WOMEN PHYSICIANS
Gilliatt, P. Come back if it doesn't get better
Oates, J. C. Face
West, J. The condemned librarian
WOMEN POETS
Birtha, B. Ice castle
Bumpus, J. Heroes and villains
Singer, I. B. The interview
Thompson, J. The afternoon of the poetess
Wilson, B. In the archives
Zhang Jie. Who knows how to live?

WOMEN PSYCHIATRISTS
Matthiessen, P. Midnight turning gray
WOMEN SCIENTISTS
Eisenberg, L. Dr. Snow Maiden
WOMEN SCULPTORS
Yates, R. Oh, Joseph, I'm so tired
Women who live in small rooms. Wexler, J.
The **women's** baths. al-Idlibi, U.
WOMEN'S CLUBS *See* Clubs
WOMEN'S LIBERATION MOVEMENT *See* Feminism
Women's talk. Asscher-Pinkhof, C.
Womersley, Judith
The year granpa won the Melbourne Cup
Short story international 42
Won by a fall. Hartley, L. P.
The **wonder** horse. Byram, G.
The **wonder** of Jenny. Bates, M.
The **wonder** of Jenny. Ellingson, M.
The **wonderful** day. Arthur, R.
The **wonderful** Tar-Baby story. Harris, J. C.
Wondering who . . . . Ikhlasi, W.
Wonderland. Godshalk, C. S.
The **wondersmith.** O'Brien, F.-J.
The **wondrous** visitation of Krisztina Hrussz. Kosztolányi, D.
Wong, Meng Voon
Doubt
Short story international 62
When I see Hui Lan again
Short story international 42
Wong, Swee Hoon
The feminist
Short story international 66
Won't you walk—. Sturgeon, T.
Wood, Ellen Price *See* Wood, Mrs. Henry, 1814-1887
Wood, Mrs. Henry, 1814-1887
The ghost
Haunting women; ed. by A. Ryan
Wood, Monica
Allison's hair
The North American Review 271:40-1 Je '86
Becoming Elaine
The North American Review 273:36-7 Mr '88
Mom's clean sweep
Redbook 170:42+ Ja '88
Wood. Langford, M. N.
WOOD CARVING
Chavez, A. The angel's new wings
Hawthorne, N. Drowne's wooden image
Inks, C. Mandrake
Norris, H. The cormorant
Phipps, H. J. The saintmaker's wife
Taylor, A. The carving
The **wood** rose. Saiki, J.
Wood you? Anthony, P.
The **Woodcock.** Tournier, M.
WOODCUTTERS
Anthony, P. Wood you?

WOODCUTTERS—*Continued*
Hemingway, E. The doctor and the doctor's wife
Winton, T. My father's axe
The **wooden** box. Hall, T. T.
The **wooden** shoes. Maupassant, G. de
Woodforde, Christopher, 1907-1962
Cushi
The Oxford book of English ghost stories
Woodhead. Eighner, L.
Woodman, Allen
The bear tamers
The North American Review 270:32-3 Je '85
Woodman, A. The shoebox of desire, and other tales
The church of summer sausage
Woodman, A. The shoebox of desire, and other tales
The cruelty of chairs
Woodman, A. The shoebox of desire, and other tales
Fathers
Woodman, A. The shoebox of desire, and other tales
Foreign postcard
Woodman, A. The shoebox of desire, and other tales
Gulf
Woodman, A. The shoebox of desire, and other tales
The lampshade vendor
Woodman, A. The shoebox of desire, and other tales
Life story
Woodman, A. The shoebox of desire, and other tales
The pleasure garden of the root vegetables
Woodman, A. The shoebox of desire, and other tales
The shoebox of desire
Woodman, A. The shoebox of desire, and other tales
Still points
Woodman, A. The shoebox of desire, and other tales
TV guide
Woodman, A. The shoebox of desire, and other tales
Vinyl repair
Woodman, A. The shoebox of desire, and other tales
Waiting for the broken horse
Woodman, A. The shoebox of desire, and other tales
Woodpecker Point. Bird, C.
The **woodpecker** toy fact. Bird, C.
Woodrell, Daniel
Woe to live on
The Editors' choice: new American stories v1

Woodruff, Elvira
Santa knows
Parents 62:129-32+ D '87
Woodruff, Jay
The secret to not getting stuck
The Atlantic 262:82-8 N '88
Woods, Christopher
Acolytes
New England Review and Bread Loaf Quarterly 11:5-7 Aut '88
The quarry
Short story international 54
Two women at nightfall
The Southern Review (Baton Rouge, La.) 24:401-7 Spr '88
Woods, Sara
Every tale condemns me
Winter's crimes 17
The **Woodward** Avenue streetcar. Heise, K.
The **wooing** of Ariadne. Petrakis, H. M.
The **wooing** of Rosy Malone. Overholser, W. D.
The **wool** nightshirt and the horsehair tunic. Ferron, J.
Wooley. Strand, M.
Woolf, Virginia, 1882-1941
Ancestors
Woolf, V. The complete shorter fiction of Virginia Woolf
A dialogue upon Mount Pentelicus
The Times Literary Supplement no4406:979 S 11-17 '87
The Duchess and the jeweller
The Treasury of English short stories; ed. by N. Sullivan
Woolf, V. The complete shorter fiction of Virginia Woolf
The evening party
Woolf, V. The complete shorter fiction of Virginia Woolf
The fascination of the pool
Woolf, V. The complete shorter fiction of Virginia Woolf
Gipsy, the mongrel
Woolf, V. The complete shorter fiction of Virginia Woolf
Happiness
Woolf, V. The complete shorter fiction of Virginia Woolf
A haunted house
Witches' brew; ed. by M. Muller and B. Pronzini
Woolf, V. The complete shorter fiction of Virginia Woolf
In the orchard
Woolf, V. The complete shorter fiction of Virginia Woolf
The introduction
Woolf, V. The complete shorter fiction of Virginia Woolf
The journal of Mistress Joan Martyn
Woolf, V. The complete shorter fiction of Virginia Woolf

Woolf, Virginia, 1882-1941—*Continued*

Kew Gardens
  Woolf, V. The complete shorter fiction of Virginia Woolf

The lady in the looking-glass: a reflection
  Woolf, V. The complete shorter fiction of Virginia Woolf

Lappin and Lapinova
  Woolf, V. The complete shorter fiction of Virginia Woolf

The legacy
  Woolf, V. The complete shorter fiction of Virginia Woolf

The man who loved his kind
  Woolf, V. The complete shorter fiction of Virginia Woolf

The mark on the wall
  Woolf, V. The complete shorter fiction of Virginia Woolf

Memoirs of a novelist
  Woolf, V. The complete shorter fiction of Virginia Woolf

Miss Pryme
  Woolf, V. The complete shorter fiction of Virginia Woolf

Moments of being: 'Slater's pins have no points'
  Woolf, V. The complete shorter fiction of Virginia Woolf

Monday or Tuesday
  Woolf, V. The complete shorter fiction of Virginia Woolf

Mrs. Dalloway in Bond Street
  Woolf, V. The complete shorter fiction of Virginia Woolf

The mysterious case of Miss V.
  Woolf, V. The complete shorter fiction of Virginia Woolf

The new dress
  Woolf, V. The complete shorter fiction of Virginia Woolf

Nurse Lugton's curtain
  Woolf, V. The complete shorter fiction of Virginia Woolf

Phyllis and Rosamond
  Woolf, V. The complete shorter fiction of Virginia Woolf

Portraits
  Woolf, V. The complete shorter fiction of Virginia Woolf

Scenes from the life of a British naval officer
  Woolf, V. The complete shorter fiction of Virginia Woolf

The searchlight
  Woolf, V. The complete shorter fiction of Virginia Woolf

The shooting party
  Woolf, V. The complete shorter fiction of Virginia Woolf

A simple melody
  Woolf, V. The complete shorter fiction of Virginia Woolf

A society
  Woolf, V. The complete shorter fiction of Virginia Woolf

Solid objects
  Woolf, V. The complete shorter fiction of Virginia Woolf

The string quartet
  Woolf, V. The complete shorter fiction of Virginia Woolf

A summing up
  Woolf, V. The complete shorter fiction of Virginia Woolf

The symbol
  Harper's 272:34+ Ja '86
  Woolf, V. The complete shorter fiction of Virginia Woolf

Sympathy
  Woolf, V. The complete shorter fiction of Virginia Woolf

Three pictures
  Woolf, V. The complete shorter fiction of Virginia Woolf

Together and apart
  Woolf, V. The complete shorter fiction of Virginia Woolf

Uncle Vanya
  Woolf, V. The complete shorter fiction of Virginia Woolf

An unwritten novel
  Woolf, V. The complete shorter fiction of Virginia Woolf

The watering place
  Woolf, V. The complete shorter fiction of Virginia Woolf

The widow and the parrot: a true story
  Woolf, V. The complete shorter fiction of Virginia Woolf

A woman's college from outside
  Woolf, V. The complete shorter fiction of Virginia Woolf

Woolrich, Cornell, 1903-1968

  For works written by this author under other names see **Irish, William, 1903-1968**

The body upstairs
  Woolrich, C. Darkness at dawn

The book that squealed
  Women sleuths; ed. by M. H. Greenberg and B. Pronzini

The corpse and the kid [Variant title: Boy with body]
  Woolrich, C. Darkness at dawn

The dancing detective
  Masterpieces of mystery and suspense; ed. by M. H. Greenberg

Dark melody of madness [Variant title: Papa Benjamin]
  Nightmares in Dixie; ed. by F. McSherry; C. G. Waugh and M. H. Greenberg
  Woolrich, C. Darkness at dawn

Dead on her feet
  Woolrich, C. Darkness at dawn

Woolrich, Cornell, 1903-1968—*Continued*
Death at the Burlesque [Variant title: The fatal footlights]
    The Deadly arts; ed. by B. Pronzini and M. Muller
The death of me
    Woolrich, C. Darkness at dawn
Death sits in the dentist's chair [Variant title: Hurting much?]
    Woolrich, C. Darkness at dawn
The detective's dilemma
    Great modern police stories; ed. by B. Pronzini and M. H. Greenberg
Fire escape
    Child's ploy; ed. by M. Muller and B. Pronzini
Hot water
    Woolrich, C. Darkness at dawn
Hurting much? [Variant title: Death sits in the dentist's chair]
    Kill or cure; ed. by M. Muller and B. Pronzini
If the dead could talk
    The Wickedest show on earth; ed. by M. Muller and B. Pronzini
Jane Brown's body
    The Mammoth book of classic science fiction; ed. by I. Asimov; C. G. Waugh and M. H. Greenberg
Kiss of the cobra
    Woolrich, C. Darkness at dawn
Momentum
    Hitchcock in prime time; ed. by F. M. Nevins and M. H. Greenberg
Murder in wax
    Woolrich, C. Darkness at dawn
New York blues
    Manhattan mysteries; ed. by B. Pronzini; C. L. R. Waugh and M. H. Greenberg
The penny-a-worder
    Chapter & hearse; ed. by M. Muller and B. Pronzini
Preview of death
    Woolrich, C. Darkness at dawn
Red liberty
    Woolrich, C. Darkness at dawn
The room with something wrong
    Death locked in; ed. by D. G. Greene and R. C. S. Adey
The showboat murders
    Woolrich, C. Darkness at dawn
Tokyo, 1941
    Baker's dozen: 13 short espionage novels
Walls that hear you
    Woolrich, C. Darkness at dawn
Woolson, Constance Fenimore, 1840-1894
At the château of Corinne
    Woolson, C. F. Women artists, women exiles: "Miss Grief" and other stories
Castle Nowhere
    Woolson, C. F. Women artists, women exiles: "Miss Grief" and other stories

Crowder's Cove: a story of the war
    Civil War women; ed. by F. McSherry; C. G. Waugh and M. Greenberg
Felipa
    Woolson, C. F. Women artists, women exiles: "Miss Grief" and other stories
In the cotton country
    Woolson, C. F. Women artists, women exiles: "Miss Grief" and other stories
The Lady of Little Fishing
    Woolson, C. F. Women artists, women exiles: "Miss Grief" and other stories
Miss Elisabetha
    Woolson, C. F. Women artists, women exiles: "Miss Grief" and other stories
"Miss Grief"
    Woolson, C. F. Women artists, women exiles: "Miss Grief" and other stories
St. Clair Flats
    Woolson, C. F. Women artists, women exiles: "Miss Grief" and other stories
The street of the Hyacinth
    Woolson, C. F. Women artists, women exiles: "Miss Grief" and other stories
Wooton, Carl
Ramblers and spinners
    The Hudson Review 40:561-83 Wint '88
A reconciliation
    The Hudson Review 41:45-70 Spr '88
The tick is full
    The Hudson Review 37:399-420 Aut '84
Worboys' transaction. Griner, P.
WORCESTER (MASS.) *See* Massachusetts—Worcester
The **word** "killer". Valenzuela, L.
Word monkey. Coleman, W.
Word of honor. Bloch, R.
The **word** processor. See King, S. Word processor of the gods
Word processor of the gods. King, S.
Words. Andrić, I.
Words. Erwin, C.
Words. Hemmerchts, K.
Words do not a book make. Pronzini, B.
Words in commotion. Landolfi, T.
Words of love. Maupassant, G. de
Words of love. Ruffolo, L.
Words of power. Yolen, J.
The **words** she types. Wilding, M.
The **words** that count. Campbell, R.
Words the happy say. MacLaverty, B.
Words with Marigold. Tremain, R.
Wordsong. Williamson, J. N.
Work. Crowell, D.
Work. Johnson, D.
Work. MacDonald, D. R.
Work. Parise, G.
Work-horses. Pascoe, B.
Work in progress. Barstow, S.
A **work** of art. Blish, J.
Working, Russell, 1959-
Charis
    Working, R. Resurrectionists

Working, Russell, 1959——_Continued_
  Famous people
    Working, R. Resurrectionists
  Halloween, Via Dolorosa
    The Paris Review 29:83-8 Fall '87
  The monkey
    Working, R. Resurrectionists
  On freedom
    Working, R. Resurrectionists
  Pictures of her snake
    Working, R. Resurrectionists
  Rendering Byzantium
    Working, R. Resurrectionists
  Resurrectionists
    Working, R. Resurrectionists
  Shooting
    Working, R. Resurrectionists
Working. Rossi, A.
Working for a living. Munro, A.
Workouts. Klinkowitz, J.
The **workroom.** Colette
Works of the imagination. Berriault, G.
The **world** according to Hsü. Mukherjee, B.
World after dark. Gardiner, J. R.
". . . the **world**, as we know't.". Waldrop, H.
World champion. Schultz, S. B.
The **world** elsewhere. Verma, N.
The **world** is a bed. Hall, D.
The **world** is a room. Amichai, Y.
The **world** is almost rotten. Abbott, L. K.
The **world** of apples. Abbott, L. K.
The **world** of apples. Cheever, J.
World of dreams, a valediction. Lu Wenfu
The **world** of Rosie Polk. Shockley, A. A.
The **world** of the ceiling. Rosenfeld, I.
World of women. Durban, P.
World of women. Wexler, J.
World of worlds. Anderman, J.
WORLD POLITICS
  See also Treaties
The **world** record holder. Harris, E.
The **world** science fiction convention of 2080. Watson, I.
The **world-timer.** Bloch, R.
The **world** upside down. Altamirano, C. E.
WORLD WAR, 1914-1918
  Davenport, G. The bowmen of Shu
     Aerial operations
  Faulkner, W. Thrift
  Faulkner, W. Turn about
  Kipling, R. Mary Postgate
  Poole, F. F. Airmen
     Casualties
  Hemingway, E. In another country
     Naval operations
  Faulkner, W. Turn about
  'Taffrail'. The luck of the Tavy
  Thomason, J. Mutiny
     Secret service
  Maugham, W. S. The traitor
     England
  Raven, S. The bottle of 1912

     France
  Hill, R. The bull ring
  Sandel, C. One day in November
     Germany
  Barthelme, D. Engineer-private Paul Klee misplaces an aircraft between Milbertshofen and Cambrai, March 1916
  Doyle, Sir A. C. The death voyage
  Willis, C. Schwarzschild radius
     Italy
  Hemingway, E. Now I lay me
  Hemingway, E. A way you'll never be
     United States
  Liben, M. Armistice Day
WORLD WAR, 1939-1945
  Buck, P. S. The enemy
  Durban, P. Notes toward an understanding of my father's novel
  Garrett, G. P. What's the purpose of the bayonet?
  Houbein, L. Magic of this moment
  Kornbluth, C. M. Two dooms
  MacLean, A. Rendezvous
  Martínez-Serros, H. Ricardo's war
  Moore, R. The soldier shows his medal
  Nesvadba, J. The half-wit of Xeenemuende
  Ozick, C. Trust [excerpt]
  Ritchie, J. Chicken Charley
  Shaw, I. Medal from Jerusalem
  Spilman, R. The old man tells his story and gets it wrong
  Yates, R. A compassionate leave
     Aerial operations
  Barrett, W. E. The destroyer
  Gallico, P. Bombardier
  Jameison, L. East from Botwood
  Ritchie, J. Hot air pilot
  Robinson, K. S. The lucky strike
     Atrocities
    See also Holocaust, Jewish (1933-1945)
     Casualties
  Böll, H. Children are civilians too
  Böll, H. Pale Anna
  Böll, H. The ration runners
  Böll, H. Reunion on the avenue
  Böll, H. Reunion with Drüng
  Böll, H. "Stranger, bear word to the Spartans we . . ."
  Clark, M. A footnote to the Kokoda story
  Clark, M. Still hope for God
  Davin, D. Jaundiced
  Kono, T. Iron fish
  Long, D. V-E Day
     Jews
    See also Holocaust, Jewish (1933-1945)
  Federspiel, J. The promised village
  Malaparte, C. The Soroca girls
  Nałkowska, Z. At the railroad track
     Naval operations
  Bradbury, R. Undersea guardians
  Chipulina, E. G. The exiles

WORLD WAR, 1939-1945 — Naval operations—*Continued*
Forester, C. S. Dawn attack
Frazee, S. The crew of the Foraker
MacLean, A. The Arandora Star
MacLean, A. City of Benares
MacLean, A. The Jervis Bay
MacLean, A. Lancastria
MacLean, A. The Meknes
MacLean, A. Rawalpindi
MacLean, A. The sinking of the Bismarck
MacLean, A. They sweep the seas
Marmur, J. The kid in command
Michener, J. A. Coral Sea
Morrill, G. P. Act of honor
Reeman, D. Trouble cargo
Watmough, D. All at sea
Wheatcroft, J. Kamikaze
Naval operations—Submarine
Forester, C. S. Night stalk
Monsarrat, N. "HMS Marlborough will enter harbour"
Monsarrat, N. Night shoot
Yates, T. The living torpedo
Prisoners and prisons
See also Concentration camps
Archer, J. Colonel Bullfrog
Borowski, T. The supper
Fein, Y. Rumkowsky was right
Kohlhaase, W. Invention of a language
Nałkowska, Z. Rock bottom
St. Pierre, P. H. The last day of violence
Underground movements
Haris, P. The third son
Roberts, K. Weihnachtsabend
Australia
Keesing, N. Garden Island people
Austria
Wegner, H. A death in a quiet town
Belgium
Amis, K. My enemy's enemy
Russell, R. Power stories
Canada
Gallant, M. Varieties of exile
China
Murphy, Y. Stories in another language
Crete
Davin, D. Danger's flower
Davin, D. Under the bridge
Czechoslovakia
Lustig, A. The girl with the scar
Lustig, A. Indecent dreams
Egypt
Davin, D. Coming and going
Davin, D. The dog and the dead
Davin, D. Finders and losers
England
Bates, H. E. It's just the way it is
Gallant, M. The colonel's child
Gathorne-Hardy, J. The picnic
Greene, G. Men at work
Jakes, J. Dr. Sweetkill
MacLean, A. The Arandora Star

Martin, D. Amazing powers
Pym, B. Goodbye Balkan capital
Regent, P. Schoolboy war
Rhys, J. I spy a stranger
Rhys, J. A solid house
Sambrot, W. Black night, white night; or, The battle of Dingle on the Dangle
Spark, M. The house of the famous poet
Swift, G. Gabor
Tuohy, F. A war of liberation
Warren, J. Anny's men
Watmough, D. The cross-country run
Welch, D. Memories of a vanished period
Wetherell, W. D. Spitfire autumn
Willis, C. Fire watch
Wyndham, J. Phoney meteor
Europe
Ravin, B. L. Cabin class to Pubjanice
France
Bloch, R. The living dead
Bloch, R. Underground
Böll, H. Vive la France!
Boyle, K. Men
Eisenstein, S. A place of refuge
Gallant, M. A recollection
Glemser, B. The commandos go in
Hemingway, E. Black ass at the cross roads
Muller, R. General Patton did not sleep here
Sagan, F. A country outing
Sandel, C. There's a war on
Germany
Böll, H. And where were you, Adam?
Böll, H. In the darkness
Böll, H. Jak the tout
Böll, H. A soldier's legacy
Böll, H. "Stranger, bear word to the Spartans we . . ."
Böll, H. The train was on time
Böll, H. When the war broke out
Böll, H. When the war was over
Ellis, L. R. Operation wild ass
Matthiessen, P. A replacement
Meckel, C. The fire
Seghers, A. The reed
Wickert, M. The scythe of Saturn
Greece
Davin, D. Below the heavens
Davin, D. The Persian's grave
Haris, P. Before the dawn
Haris, P. A dead city
Haris, P. Four and a half
Haris, P. Lights on the sea
Haris, P. Not a bird in the sky
Haris, P. Of love and darkness
Haris, P. Reinforced concrete
Haris, P. The third son
Haris, P. A young man's dance
Hawaii
Bellah, J. W. Day of terror
Jones, J. The way it is
Saiki, J. Bus stop

WORLD WAR, 1939-1945 — Hawaii — *Continued*
- Saiki, J. My wartime job
- Saiki, J. Suspect alien

Hungary
- Böll, H. Between trains in X
- Dorr, L. The noise was heard afar off
- Dorr, L. A slight momentary affliction

Ireland
- Power, V. No cigarettes, no matches, no lights allowed

Italy
- Bouma, J. L. Final mission
- Brown, H. A walk in the sun
- Calvino, I. Animal woods
- Calvino, I. Fear on the footpath
- Calvino, I. Going to headquarters
- Calvino, I. Hunger at Bévera
- Davin, D. Cassino casualty
- Davin, D. In transit
- Davin, D. Liberation
- Davin, D. North of the Sangro
- Davin, D. Not substantial things
- Davin, D. Psychological warfare at Cassino
- Davin, D. When mum died
- Forester, C. S. Dawn attack
- Horgan, P. To the castle
- King, F. H. Unmaking
- Parise, G. Happiness
- Parise, G. Hotel
- Parise, G. War
- Sambrot, W. The man who hated

Japan
- Endō, S. The war generation
- Ishikawa, J. Moon gems
- Kojima, N. Stars
- Whitehouse, A. Savoias out of Sapporo

Netherlands
- Dundas, R. The uniform

New Caledonia
- Fuller, R. G. Sherman was right

New Zealand
- Haley, R. Looping the loop
- Sligo, J. A new Eden?

Pacific Ocean
- Alter, R. E. The exile
- Evarts, H. G. The trap
- Helprin, M. The Pacific
- Hensley, J. L. Paint doctor
- Lim Beng Hap. Tricked again
- Reed, K. The holdouts
- Styron, W. Love day
- Wheeler, H. C. The fat cat

Palestine
- Davin, D. Unwrung withers

Philippines
- Carunungan, C. A. Hide-out for a hero
- Whitehouse, A. Bataan landing

Poland
- Fink, I. The black beast
- Fink, I. A dog

Romania
- Wellman, M. W. The Devil is not mocked

Soviet Union
- Böll, H. Broommakers
- Böll, H. The casualty
- Böll, H. Cause of death: hooked nose
- Böll, H. That time we were in Odessa
- Böll, H. The unknown soldier
- Okudzhava, B. S. Lots of luck, kid!

Sudan
- Goodis, D. Hawk of the Sudan

United States
- Auchincloss, L. America first
- Barrett, W. E. Dealers in doom
- Fisher, M. F. K. The unswept emptiness
- Freeman, C. Not everyone can be a soldier
- Gilchrist, E. Victory over Japan
- Gold, H. A selfish story
- Swados, H. A story for Teddy

Wales
- Brooks, J. I'll fight you

Yugoslavia
- Aćin-Kosta, M. Arbeit macht Frei

The **world** where wishes worked. Goldin, S.

The **world** with one eye shut. Crace, J.

World without end. Ardizzone, T.

World without end. Bell, M. S.

World without sex. Hamilton, E.

A **world** without toys. Wright, T. M.

The **world's** most amazing prophet, a.k.a. Wallace Mumford Amazon Polleau. Glynn, T.

The **worm** in the apple. Cheever, J.

A **worn** path. Welty, E.

Worrick, Roberta *See* Thomas, Maria, 1941-1989

The **worries** of Laurence Ridley. Haylock, J.

Worrying. Cullen, E. J.

The **worst** crime known to man. Hill, R.

Worton, Michael
  Julia & the damned
    Encounter (London, England) 71:10-16 D '88

Wouk, Herman, 1915-
  The mutiny
    Men at sea; ed. by B. Aymar

The **would-be** father. Baxter, C.

The **wound**. Barthelme, D.

Wounded soldier. Garrett, G. P.

The **wounded** tiger. Lutz, J.

The **wrath-bearing** tree. Schwartz, L. S.

The **wrath** of God. Fante, J.

The **wrath** of Shaykh Muhammad Al-Ajami. Sulayman, N.

The **wrath** of Zeus. Yorke, M.

A **wreath** for Garibaldi. Garrett, G. P.

Wreck. Sanford, W. M.

The **wreck** in the void. Walsh, J. M.

The **wreck** of the Golden Mary. Dickens, C.

The **wreck** of the Visigoth. Kipling, R.

Wrede, Patricia C.
  The improper princess
    The Year's best fantasy, first annual collection

A **wrestler's** tale. Stark, S. S.

WRESTLING
Bedard, B. Sweet Billy
Daniels, C. Mrs. Effie
Stark, S. S. A wrestler's tale
Waldrop, H. Man-Mountain Gentian

Wright, Betty Ren
Coming out Rosy!
Redbook 170:56+ Ap '88
The invisible cat
Alfred Hitchcock's Crimewatch
Morning song
Child's ploy; ed. by M. Muller and B. Pronzini
Sweet remembrance
Alfred Hitchcock's Grave suspicions

Wright, David L.
The hawk
Greening wheat: fifteen Mormon short stories

Wright, Dorothy Winslow
Dinner for two
McCall's 112:20+ Ag '85

Wright, Jack R. *See* Harris, Mark, 1922-

Wright, Richard, 1908-1960
Almos' a man [Variant title: The man who was almost a man]
Look who's talking; ed. by B. Weber
Mississippi writers v1: Fiction; ed. by D. Abbott
Big black good man
The Art of the tale; ed. by D. Halpern
Wright, R. Eight men
Big boy leaves home
Mississippi writers v1: Fiction; ed. by D. Abbott
Man, God ain't like that. . . .
Wright, R. Eight men
Man of all work
Wright, R. Eight men
The man who killed a shadow
Wright, R. Eight men
The man who lived underground
Wright, R. Eight men
The man who saw the flood
Wright, R. Eight men
The man who was almost a man [Variant title: Almos' a man]
A Modern Southern reader; ed. by B. Forkner and P. Samway
Wright, R. Eight men
The man who went to Chicago
Wright, R. Eight men

Wright, T. M., 1947-
A world without toys
The Year's best fantasy, first annual collection
"Write a story with two people in it". Young-Bruehl, E.
The **writer** in the family. Doctorow, E. L.
WRITERS *See* Authors
WRITING
Benford, G. How to sound like an expert

Campos, J. A redhead named Sabina [excerpt]
Carey, P. Report on the shadow industry
Doyle, Sir A. C. The reigate squires
Martínez-Serros, H. "Learn! Learn!"
Murphy, P. Cane toads
Wilding, M. The words she types
Writing it down 1972-1975. Soldatow, S.
A **writing** lesson. Gordon, M.
The **writings** of Althea Swarthmoor. Gilchrist, M.
Written in water. Lee, T.
The **wrong-handed** man. Millman, L.
The **wrong** house. Asimov, I.
The **wrong** house. Hornung, E. W.
Wrong pigeon. Chandler, R.
Wrong play. Brooks, J.
The **wrong** shape. Chesterton, G. K.
Wrong stories. Dillon, M.
Wrongful death. Stodghill, D.
A **wry** sleep of boys. Maiolo, J.
Wryneck, draw me. St. Clair, M.

Wu, Cho-liu
The doctor's mother
The Unbroken chain; ed. by J. S. M. Lau

Wu, William F., 1951-
Hong's bluff
Omni (New York, N.Y.) 7:90-3 Mr '85
Wunderkind. McCullers, C.
WÜRZBURG (GERMANY) *See* Germany—Würzburg

Wyatt, Mary
Sincerely yours
Short story international 45

Wyndham, Francis
The Ground Hostess
Wyndham, F. Mrs. Henderson
The half brother
Wyndham, F. Mrs. Henderson
Mrs. Henderson
Wyndham, F. Mrs. Henderson
Obsessions
Wyndham, F. Mrs. Henderson
Ursula
Wyndham, F. Mrs. Henderson

Wyndham, John, 1903-1969
The lost machine
Machines that think; ed. by I. Asimov; P. S. Warrick and M. H. Greenberg
Phoney meteor
Amazing science fiction anthology: The war years, 1936-1945; ed. by M. H. Greenberg
The wheel
Beyond Armageddon; ed. by W. M. Miller and M. H. Greenberg

Wynne, Anthony
The Cyprian bees
Kill or cure; ed. by M. Muller and B. Pronzini

Wynne, Madelene Yale
The little room
   Haunted women; ed. by A. Bendixen
WYOMING
19th century
Brown, C. A winter's tale
20th century
Hauptman, W. Boom town
Hemingway, E. Wine of Wyoming
Pritchett, M. The barrel racer
Pritchett, M. Close water
Pritchett, M. People
Vogan, S. Angels in the snow
Cheyenne
Overholser, W. D. Steel to the west

X

X. Abbott, L. K.
X. Whitaker, M.
'X-ing a paragrab'. Poe, E. A.
X marks the spot. Dullas, I.
X-ray. Martone, M.
The X Street murders. Commings, J.
Xanthippe. Kessler, J. F.
Xavier speaking. Baxter, C.
Xavier's folly. Evans, M.
Xeethra. Smith, C. A.
Xessex. Forrest, K. V.
XHOSA (AFRICAN PEOPLE)
Becker, J. The stench
Xingu. Wharton, E.
Xmas in the bush. Couani, A.
Xylem and phloem. Pollack, E.

Y

Yac, yac. Stead, C.
YACHT RACING
Clarke, A. C. The wind from the sun
YACHTS AND YACHTING
Adams, J. C. Midshipman, the cat
Rand, P. Baby Boy
Yaffe, James, 1927-
Mom makes a wish
   The Ethnic detectives; ed. by B. Pronzini
      and M. H. Greenberg
Mom sings an aria
   Manhattan mysteries; ed. by B. Pronzini;
      C. L. R. Waugh and M. H. Greenberg
One of the family
   Hitchcock in prime time; ed. by F. M.
      Nevins and M. H. Greenberg
Yahbo the hawk. Novakovich, J.
Yahk fahn, Auntie. Lum, D. H. Y.
Yaikni. Kenny, M.
Yamamoto, Hisaye
Seventeen syllables
   Between mothers & daughters; ed. by S.
      Koppelman

Yamamoto, Michiko, 1936-
Betty-san
   Yamamoto, M. Betty-san
Chair in the rain
   Short story international 55
   Yamamoto, M. Betty-san
Father Goose
   Yamamoto, M. Betty-san
Powers
   Short story international 48
   Yamamoto, M. Betty-san
Yamanaka, Cedric
What the ironwood whispered
   Passages to the dream shore; ed. by F.
      Stewart
Yang, K'uei
Mother Goose gets married
   The Unbroken chain; ed. by J. S. M.
      Lau
Yang Zhenwen
Fu Da regains his wife
   Contemporary Chinese literature; ed. by
      M. S. Duke
Yankee Doodle went to town. Asimov, I.
Yankee gold. Cunningham, J. M.
A Yankee inquisitor. Sanguinetti, E.
Yankel. Botwinik, B.
Yano, Tetsu
The legend of the paper spaceship
   The Penguin world omnibus of science
      fiction
   Tales from the planet Earth
Yanqui Doodle. Tiptree, J.
Yarbro, Chelsea Quinn, 1942-
Cabin 33
   Vampires; ed. by A. Ryan
Disturb not my slumbering fair
   Young monsters; ed. by I. Asimov; M.
      H. Greenberg and C. G. Waugh
Do I dare to eat a peach?
   Shadows 8
Do not forsake me, O my darlin'
   Shadows 7
The end of the carnival
   Masters of darkness; ed. by D. Etchison
Lapses
   Cutting edge; ed. by D. Etchison
The spider glass
   The Best of Shadows; ed. by C. L.
      Grant
Yarbrough, Steve
Between now and then
   The Virginia Quarterly Review 64:37-55
      Wint '88
Family men
   The Southern Review (Baton Rouge, La.)
      20:731-7 Jl '84
The formula
   The Virginia Quarterly Review 63:231-45
      Spr '87
Sara
   The Literary Review (Madison, N.J.)
      31:419-31 Summ '88

The **Yard**. Nolan, W. F.

Yard sale. Theroux, P.

Yarn. Thompson, J.

Yarrow. Oates, J. C.

Yaryura-Tobías, Aníbal
The voyeur
Anthology of contemporary Latin American literature, 1960-1984

Yasuoka, Shōtarō, 1920-
Bad company
The Shōwa anthology 1
Yasuoka, S. A view by the sea
Gloomy pleasures
Yasuoka, S. A view by the sea
The moth
Yasuoka, S. A view by the sea
Rain
Murder in Japan; ed. by J. L. Apostolou and M. H. Greenberg
Yasuoka, S. A view by the sea
Thick the new leaves
Yasuoka, S. A view by the sea
A view by the sea
Yasuoka, S. A view by the sea

Yates, Richard, 1926-
The best of everything
The Art of the tale; ed. by D. Halpern
A compassionate leave
The Ploughshares reader: new fiction for the eighties
Oh, Joseph, I'm so tired
The Pushcart prize IX
The right thing
Esquire 102:53-5+ Ag '84
The Esquire fiction reader v1

Yates, Tom
The living torpedo
A Treasury of World War II stories; ed. by B. Pronzini and M. H. Greenberg

The **Yattering** and Jack. Barker, C.

Yaw, Yvonne
Penny Royal
McCall's 114:63-6 My '87

Ye marvelous legend of Tom Connor's cat. Lover, S.

Ye Yonglie
The Thursday events
Tales from the planet Earth

The **year** granpa won the Melbourne Cup. Womersley, J.

The **year** of getting to know us. Canin, E.

Year of grace. Swados, H.

The **year** of loving dangerously. Spiro, J.

The **year** of the action. Asimov, I.

The **year** of the bulls. Rees, D.

The **year** of the hot jock. Faust, I.

A **year** of their life. Pil'niāk, B.

Years in Kaldar. Kennedy, T. E.

Yellin, Linda Nell
A date with fate
Redbook 168:38+ Ja '87
Even nice women do
Redbook 167:58+ Jl '86

Happily ever after
Redbook 162:58+ Mr '84
Putting out an old flame
Redbook 166:52+ Ja '86
Thinking about babies
Redbook 171:70+ My '88
What are friends for
Redbook 169:74+ S '87

Yellow bird. Silva, B.

The **yellow** bird. Williams, T.

Yellow Bird: an imaginary autobiography. Conley, R. J.

A **yellow** cat. Rey Rosa, R.

The **yellow** deer. Heitkamp, K.

Yellow dust. Peterson, J.

The **yellow** face. Doyle, Sir A. C.

Yellow fever. Borthwick, C.

Yellow flowers. Flores, C. N.

Yellow gal. Lynds, D.

Yellow girl. Caldwell, E.

Yellow Iris. Christie, A.

A **yellow** man and a white. Gates, E.

The **yellow** pill. Phillips, R.

Yellow pride. Pu, S.-L.

Yellow rock. Abbott, K.

Yellow roses. Hillabold, J.

The **yellow** sign. Chambers, R. W.

The **yellow** wallpaper. Gilman, C. P.

Yellow Woman. Silko, L.

YEMEN (PEOPLE'S DEMOCRATIC REPUBLIC)
Taizz
Wali, M. A. A. At a woman's house

YEMEN (SOUTH) See Yemen (People's Democratic Republic)

YENANG (KOREA) See Korea—Yenang

Yermakov, Nicholas
A glint of gold
The Science fictional Olympics; ed. by I. Asimov; M. H. Greenberg and C. G. Waugh

Yerxa, Leroy
Carrion crypt
Haunted New England; ed. by C. G. Waugh; M. H. Greenberg and F. D. McSherry

Yes!. Dawson, F.

Yes, young daddy. Chin, F.

Yesterday house. Leiber, F.

Yesterday I lived! Bradbury, R.

Yesterday's angel. Cardal, M.

Yesterday's witch. Wilson, G.

Yi, Chong-Jun
The dream of a mask
Home-coming, and other Korean short stories
Target
Home-coming, and other Korean short stories

Yi, Ho-Chol
Midnight
Flowers of fire; ed. by P. H. Lee

Yi, Ho-Chol—*Continued*

The sultriness of a cold evening

A Respite, and other Korean short stories

Torn flesh

A Respite, and other Korean short stories

Yi, Hoesŏng

The woman who fulled clothes

Flowers of fire; ed. by P. H. Lee

Yi, Hyosŏk

The buckwheat season

Flowers of fire; ed. by P. H. Lee

The Unenlightened, and other Korean short stories

Yi, Kwang-Su

Halmôm

The Unenlightened, and other Korean short stories

The Unenlightened

The Unenlightened, and other Korean short stories

Yi, Mun-Yol

Early spring, mid-summer

Early spring, mid-summer, and other Korean short stories

Yi, Pŏmsŏn

A stray bullet

Flowers of fire; ed. by P. H. Lee

Yi, Pong-Ju

The wind and landscape of Yenang

The Road to Sampo, and other Korean short stories

Yi, Sang

A discontinued knot

The Unenlightened, and other Korean short stories

Wings

Flowers of fire; ed. by P. H. Lee

The Unenlightened, and other Korean short stories

Yiqh-Yaqh (Ying-Yang, Y'ukq-Y'akq, Y'Shi'Yah). Eakins, P.

Yngve, Rolf

The quail

Sudden fiction; ed. by R. Shapard and J. Thomas

Yoakum: the cruising circuit. Eighner, L.

The yogi. Essop, A.

YOGURT

Apple, M. Business talk

Yoirimba. Prichard, K. S.

YOKOHAMA (JAPAN) *See* Japan—Yokohama

Yolen, Jane

Angelica

100 great fantasy short short stories; ed. by I. Asimov; T. Carr and M. H. Greenberg

Young monsters; ed. by I. Asimov; M. H. Greenberg and C. G. Waugh

Cockfight

Dragons of light; ed. by O. S. Card

Evian Steel

Imaginary lands; ed. by R. McKinley

The foxwife

Moonsinger's friends; ed. by S. Shwartz

Great-grandfather dragon's tale

Dragons and dreams; ed. by J. Yolen; M. H. Greenberg and C. G. Waugh

Green messiah

Werewolves; ed. by J. Yolen and M. H. Greenberg

The lady and the merman

100 great fantasy short short stories; ed. by I. Asimov; T. Carr and M. H. Greenberg

The moon ribbon

Don't bet on the prince; ed. by J. Zipes

Words of power

The Year's best fantasy, first annual collection

Yŏm, Sangsŏp

The last moment

Flowers of fire; ed. by P. H. Lee

YOM KIPPUR

Botwinik, B. The mother's Yom Kippur

Yone, Wendy Law- *See* Law-Yone, Wendy

Yoo, Jae-Yong *See* Yu, Chae-Yong

Yorke, C. B.

Snowbound

Hard-boiled dames; ed. by B. A. Drew

Yorke, Margaret

Gifts from the bridegroom

Winter's crimes 18

The wrath of Zeus

John Creasey's Crime collection, 1986

YORKSHIRE (ENGLAND) *See* England—Yorkshire

Yosef, Yehoshua Bar *See* Bar Yosef, Yehoshua

Yoshiyuki, Junnosuke, 1924-

Are the trees green?

The Shōwa anthology 1

You ain't dead yet. Sutter, B.

You and The Boss. Janowitz, T.

You are here. Ballantyne, S.

You are here. Covino, M.

You are what you own: a notebook. Adams, A.

You by my side. Franco, M.

You can do anything. Rogers, T. N. R.

You can get away with murder. Boeckman, C.

You can go now. Etchison, D.

You can keep your razors & guns but check your loud mouths at the door. Farris, J.

You can never go back. Haldeman, J. W.

You cannot judge a pumpkin's happiness by the smile upon his face. Rule, J.

You can't get lost in Cape Town. Wicomb, Z.

You can't miss it. Abbott, K.

You can't trust a man. Nielsen, H.

You can't win 'em (at) all. Lacy, E.

You could be wrong. Bloch, R.
You could call it blackmail. Block, L.
You could have done better. Gardner, T. S.
You don't know Marta. Tafolla, C.
You don't remember me. Raphael, F.
You don't smell it: you drink it. Fox, W. P.
You drive, dear. Tobey, F. S.
You gave me hyacinths. Hospital, J. T.
You got to have brains. Bloch, R.
You have left your lotus pods on the bus. Bowles, P.
You leave them. Simpson, M.
You live and love. Rasputin, V. G.
You may not be an angel. Bell, D.
You must remember this. Coover, R.
You should have seen the mess. Spark, M.
You taught us good. Koch, C.
You tell me your dreams. Simmie, L.
You told me. Papaellinas, G.
You wouldn't understand. Pacheco, J. E.
You'll lose them before Thanksgiving. Ruffolo, L.
You'll remember me long after. Haas, B.
Young, Al, 1939-
Snakes [excerpt]
Mississippi writers v1: Fiction; ed. by D. Abbott
Young, Carrie
Bank night
The Yale Review 74:96-106 Aut '84
Young, Margaret
Grandpa's growth
The Southern Review (Baton Rouge, La.) 24:671-9 Summ '88
Young, Parris ja
The helldivers
L. Ron Hubbard presents Writers of the future v2
Young, Robert F., 1915-
A drink of darkness
Fantastic stories; ed. by M. H. Greenberg and P. L. Price
Young, Stark, 1881-1963
River house [excerpt]
Mississippi writers v1: Fiction; ed. by D. Abbott
Young-Bruehl, Elisabeth
Cash
Southwest Review 70:10-13 Wint '85
Une éducation sentimentale
Southwest Review 70:22-30 Wint '85
The good soldiers
Southwest Review 70:6-10 Wint '85
The romance
Southwest Review 70:16-22 Wint '85
"Write a story with two people in it"
Southwest Review 70:13-16 Wint '85
A young comrade. Prichard, K. S.
The young couple at home. Brooks, G.
A young girl. Tuohy, F.
Young Goodman Brown. Hawthorne, N.
The young lady of Suruga. Kawabata, Y.

The young man. Gilchrist, E.
Young man, old days. Gold, H.
Young man on a train. Morice, A.
A young man's dance. Haris, P.
The young one. Bixby, J.
Young people. Goodman, A.
The young priestess from the west house. Wheatley, N.
The young wife. Monreal, D. N.
The young zelkova. Kang, S.-J.
YOUNGER, COLE, 1844-1916
About
Taylor, R. The liberation of the Youngers
Taylor, R. The revealed life of Cole Younger
The younger. Asscher-Pinkhof, C.
The younger sister's clothes. Kawabata, Y.
The youngest doll. Ferré, R.
The youngest old lady in the world. Zimmerman, L. H.
Yount, Rena
Pursuit of excellence
The Clarion awards; ed. by D. Knight
The Year's best science fiction, second annual collection
Your appointment is cancelled. Fraser, A.
Your burden is lifted, love returns. DeMarinis, R.
Your eighteenth birthday was a long time ago. Wexler, J.
Your errant mom. Robison, M.
Your faces, o my sisters! Your faces filled of light! Tiptree, J.
Your heart will tell you. Markham, B.
Your left foot is crazy. Kiely, B.
Your obedient servant. Chipulina, E. G.
Your soul comes C.O.D. Reynolds, M.
Your story. DeMarinis, R.
Your tiny hand is frozen. Aickman, R.
Yourcenar, Marguerite
Anna, soror . . .
Yourcenar, M. Two lives and a dream
Aphrodissia, the widow
Yourcenar, M. Oriental tales
The end of Marko Kraljević
Yourcenar, M. Oriental tales
How Wang-Fo was saved
Black water; ed. by A. Manguel
Yourcenar, M. Oriental tales
Kali beheaded
Yourcenar, M. Oriental tales
The last love of Prince Genji
Yourcenar, M. Oriental tales
A lovely morning
Yourcenar, M. Two lives and a dream
The man who loved the Nereids
Yourcenar, M. Oriental tales
Marko's smile
Yourcenar, M. Oriental tales
The milk of death
Yourcenar, M. Oriental tales
An obscure man
Yourcenar, M. Two lives and a dream

Yourcenar, Marguerite—*Continued*
Our-Lady-of-the-Swallows
Yourcenar, M. Oriental tales
The sadness of Cornelius Berg
Yourcenar, M. Oriental tales
You're coughing? Dantin, L.
You're in my story. Oakes, P.
You're it. Liben, M.
You're right, I know you're right. Lipman, E.
Yourgrau, Barry
Oak
Between C & D; ed. by J. Rose and C. Texier
Sand
The Paris Review 27:81-98 Spr '85
Yours. Robison, M.
Yours truly, Jack the Ripper. Bloch, R.
YOUTH
See also Adolescence; Boys; Girls; Students
Adams, G. G. A small hotel
Algren, N. A lot you got to holler
Amado, J. The lights of the carrousel
Boyd, W. Histoire vache
Boyle, K. Peter Foxe
Brady, M. Corsage
Briskin, M. A boy like Astrid's mother
Colette. The advice
Covino, M. The hour of the ungovernable
Covino, M. An intimacy beyond words
Covino, M. Matinee at the Bijou
Covino, M. The return of possibility
Deaver, P. F. Arcola girls
Dubus, A. If they knew Yvonne
Dubus, A. Molly
Dumas, H. Double nigger
Dumas, H. Six days you shall labor
Finger, C. J. Eric
Fink, I. A scrap of time
Flynn, R. Champion of the world
Gallant, M. Between zero and one
Gallant, M. Dédé
Gallant, M. In youth is pleasure
Gare, N. The child
Hannah, B. Testimony of pilot
Henley, P. Picking time
Jones, M. The fugitives
Kay, H. The fifth generation
Kim, Y. I. Gourd Dance Song
Lewis, S. E. Trouble people
MacDonald, J. D. The legend of Joe Lee
Mansfield, K. Taking the veil
McEwan, I. First love, last rites
Monreal, D. N. The weight lifters
Nordan, L. The all-girl football team
O'Hara, J. The moccasins
O'Hara, J. Too young
Petrakis, H. M. The sweet life
Rosenfeld, I. Coney Island revisited
Ross, V. Hunters
Rubin, D. Longing for America
Rule, J. First love/last love

Sanford, W. M. Mary
Silverberg, R. Caught in the organ draft
Sproat, R. Black madonna two-wheel gypsy queen
Storm, T. Immensee
Swados, H. Where does your music come from?
Thomas, D. One warm Saturday
Tournier, M. Death and the maiden
Tuohy, F. The Palace of Culture
Tuohy, F. Thunderbolt
Tuohy, F. A young girl
Updike, D. Out on the marsh
Welch, D. Leaves from a young person's notebook
Wells, H. G. My first aeroplane
White, P. Down at the dump
Wickert, M. The scythe of Saturn
Willard, N. Theo's girl
Williams, T. Field of blue children
Williams, T. The important thing
Zenowich, C. On the roof
Employment
Heller, S. The summer game
Youth. Asimov, I.
Youth. Conrad, J.
Youth. Parise, G.
Youth in Asia. Kalpakian, L.
Youth on Mars. Abbott, L. K.
Youth without youth. Eliade, M.
Youthful folly. Shepard, L.
You've changed. White, C.
You've come a long way, Mickey Mouse. Jafek, B.
Yport. Jespersen, R.
Yu, Chae-Yong
The relationship
Early spring, mid-summer, and other Korean short stories
Short story international 58
Yu, Hyon-Jong
D.M.Z.
Early spring, mid-summer, and other Korean short stories
YUCATAN (MEXICO) See Mexico—Yucatan
Yüeh Chung. Pu, S.-L.
YUGOSLAVIA
Aćin-Kosta, M. The rape
Aćin-Kosta, M. Spring flower
Aćin-Kosta, M. Yugoslavia revisited
Durrell, L. The ghost train
Lurie, M. The day the bottom fell out of Yugoslavia
Strand, M. Zadar
Communism
See Communism—Yugoslavia
Politics
See Politics—Yugoslavia
Bosnia
Andrić, I. Thirst
Yugoslavia revisited. Aćin-Kosta, M.

YUGOSLAVS
New Zealand
Batistich, A. All mixed up
United States
Vreuls, D. The seller of watches
Yuill, P. B.
Hazell and the patriot
The Mammoth book of modern crime stories; ed. by G. Hardinge
The **Yukio** Mishima Cultural Association of Kudzu Valley, Georgia. Bishop, M.
Yukon. Emshwiller, C.
YUKON TERRITORY *See* Canada—Yukon Territory
Yun, Hung-Gil
Group beating
The Road to Sampo, and other Korean short stories
Yunker, Ruth
Santa Claus
The North American Review 272:48-9 D '87
Yunker, Teresa
Margaritas
Hot type; ed. by J. Miller
Yuriko. Kawabata, Y.

Z

Zabel's choice. DeGrazia, E.
Zabriskie, Grace
Games
Erotic interludes; ed. by L. Barbach
Zach. Barthelme, S.
Zacharia, Don
The inheritance
The Kenyon Review ns9:76-86 Wint '87
Zadar. Strand, M.
Zagrowsky tells. Paley, G.
Zahn, Timothy
Cascade point
Zahn, T. Cascade point, and other stories
The Cassandra
Zahn, T. Cascade point, and other stories
The challenge
Zahn, T. Cascade point, and other stories
Dragon pax
Zahn, T. Cascade point, and other stories
The dreamsender
Zahn, T. Cascade point, and other stories
The energy crisis of 2215
Zahn, T. Cascade point, and other stories
The final report on the lifeline experiment
Zahn, T. Cascade point, and other stories

The giftie gie us
Zahn, T. Cascade point, and other stories
Job inaction
Zahn, T. Cascade point, and other stories
Not always to the strong
Zahn, T. Cascade point, and other stories
Return to the fold
Zahn, T. Cascade point, and other stories
The shadows of evening
Zahn, T. Cascade point, and other stories
The talisman
Magic in Ithkar 4; ed. by A. Norton and R. Adams
Teamwork
Zahn, T. Cascade point, and other stories
ZAIRE
Durban, P. All set about with fever trees
Russo, A. The universe of Mama Malkia
Zajdel, Janusz A.
Particularly difficult territory
Tales from the planet Earth
Zalygin, Sergei
The night of the angels
The Barsukov Triangle, The two-toned blond & other stories; ed. by C. R. Proffer & E. Proffer
ZAMBIA
Chishimba, M. Weekend of carousal
Gordimer, N. Abroad
Mulikita, F. M. The tender crop
Farm life
See Farm life—Zambia
Zambreno, Mary Frances
A way out
L. Ron Hubbard presents Writers of the future
Zamour; or, A tale of inheritance. Goyen, W.
Zancanella, Don
Disarmament
Prairie Schooner 59:95-104 Summ '85
Zangwill, Israel, 1864-1926
The big Bow mystery
Great detectives; ed. by D. W. McCullough
Cheating the gallows
Isaac Asimov presents the best crime stories of the 19th century
Zapatos. Salmón, F.
Zapolska, Gabriela
Kitten
Russian and Polish women's fiction; ed. by H. Goscilo
Little frog
Russian and Polish women's fiction; ed. by H. Goscilo

Zapolska, Gabriela—*Continued*
  Virtue (a sketch for a novel)
    Russian and Polish women's fiction; ed.
    by H. Goscilo
Zebrowski, George, 1945-
  The Eichmann variations
    Nebula awards 20
  Gödel's doom
    Mathenauts: tales of mathematical won-
    der; ed. by R. Rucker
  The idea trap
    Universe 16
  Starcrossed
    Machines that think; ed. by I. Asimov;
    P. S. Warrick and M. H. Greenberg
The **Zeigarnik** effect. Kavaler, R.
Zeiss, Todd R.
  At the post office
    Short story international 46
Zelazny, Roger
  And I alone am escaped to tell thee
    [Variant title: And I only am escaped
    to tell thee]
    100 great fantasy short short stories; ed.
    by I. Asimov; T. Carr and M. H.
    Greenberg
  But not the herald
    100 great fantasy short short stories; ed.
    by I. Asimov; T. Carr and M. H.
    Greenberg
  Deadboy Donner and the Filstone Cup
    Terry's universe; ed. by B. Meacham
  Dreadsong
    The Planets; ed. by B. Preiss
  For a breath I tarry
    A Very large array; ed. by M. M. Snod-
    grass
  The George business
    Dragons of light; ed. by O. S. Card
  Home is the hangman
    The Hugo winners v4
  Itself surprised
    Omni (New York, N.Y.) 6:48-51+ Ag '84
  King Solomon's ring
    Fantastic stories; ed. by M. H. Green-
    berg and P. L. Price
  Last of the wild ones
    Omni book of science fiction 3
  Lucifer
    Beyond Armageddon; ed. by W. M. Mil-
    ler and M. H. Greenberg
  Passage to Dilfar
    Robert Adams' Book of soldiers
  Permafrost
    Omni (New York, N.Y.) 8:54-6+ Ap '86
  Quest's end
    Omni (New York, N.Y.) 9:60-1+ Je '87
  Tower of ice
    Baker's dozen: 13 short fantasy novels
  Unicorn variations
    The Hugo winners v5

Zeldis, Leon
  The whore of Babylon
    The Penguin world omnibus of science
    fiction
Zena Dawn. Petrakis, H. M.
Zenith Rand, planet vigilante. Tooker, R.
Zenowich, Christopher
  On the roof
    The Graywolf annual 4
ZEPPELINS *See* Airships
Zerelda James Samuel. Taylor, R.
Zero. O'Hara, J.
Zero db. Bell, M. S.
Zetland: by a character witness. Bellow, S.
Zhang Jie, 1937-
  The ark
    Zhang Jie. Love must not be forgotten
  Emerald
    Zhang Jie. Love must not be forgotten
  Love must not be forgotten
    Roses and thorns; ed. by P. Link
    Zhang Jie. Love must not be forgotten
  The time is not yet ripe
    Short story international 55
    Zhang Jie. Love must not be forgotten
  Under the hawthorn
    Zhang Jie. Love must not be forgotten
  An unfinished record
    Zhang Jie. Love must not be forgotten
  Who knows how to live?
    Zhang Jie. Love must not be forgotten
Zhang Kangkang, and Mei Jin
  The tolling of a distant bell
    Contemporary Chinese literature; ed. by
    M. S. Duke
Zhang Xian
  The widow
    Contemporary Chinese literature; ed. by
    M. S. Duke
Zhang Xianliang, 1936-
  Shorblac: a driver's story
    The Chinese Western; ed. by Zhu Hong
  The story of an old man and a dog
    The Chinese Western; ed. by Zhu Hong
Zhao Zhenkai
  The homecoming stranger
    Contemporary Chinese literature; ed. by
    M. S. Duke
Zheng Wenguang
  The mirror image of the earth
    The Penguin world omnibus of science
    fiction
Zhenia's childhood. See Pasternak, B. L.
    Zhenya Luvers' childhood
Zhenya Luvers' childhood. Pasternak, B. L.
Zhou Peisheng
  (jt. auth) See Wang Hongzhen, and Zhou
  Peisheng
Zhu Lin
  Downpour on a leaky roof
    Contemporary Chinese literature; ed. by
    M. S. Duke

Zhu Xiaoping
Chronicle of Mulberry Tree Village
The Chinese Western; ed. by Zhu Hong
Ziegler, Alan
Ghostly
The New Yorker 62:25 Ag 4 '86
Ziem, Jochen
Before the thunderstorm
Ziem, J. Uprising in East Germany, and
other stories
Clarifications
Ziem, J. Uprising in East Germany, and
other stories
The classy woman
Ziem, J. Uprising in East Germany, and
other stories
Clever
Ziem, J. Uprising in East Germany, and
other stories
His own boss
Ziem, J. Uprising in East Germany, and
other stories
Payday
Ziem, J. Uprising in East Germany, and
other stories
So much happiness
Ziem, J. Uprising in East Germany, and
other stories
Something's missing
Ziem, J. Uprising in East Germany, and
other stories
Statement
Ziem, J. Uprising in East Germany, and
other stories
Uprising in East Germany
Ziem, J. Uprising in East Germany, and
other stories
Zigal, Thomas
Curios
Prize stories, Texas Institute of Letters;
ed. by M. Terry
Ziggy's last dance. Regent, P.
ZIMBABWE
Mungoshi, C. Coming of the dry season
Zimmerman, Lisa Horton
The youngest old lady in the world
Redbook 168:70+ Mr '87
ZIMMERMAN, ROBERT ALLEN *See*
Dylan, Bob, 1941-
Zimpel, Lloyd
Ovenmen
A Good deal; ed. by M. Heath and F.
M. Robinson
Zinberg, Leonard *See* Lacy, Ed, 1911-1968
Zindell, David
Shanidar
L. Ron Hubbard presents Writers of the
future
Zinnes, Harriet
Wings
New directions in prose and poetry 52

Zinsky, Catherine L.
Double feature
'Teen 32:34+ O '88
ZIONISM
Shaham, N. S/S Cairo City
Zipes, Jack David
A fairy tale for our time
Don't bet on the prince; ed. by J. Zipes
The **zipper.** Nizer, L.
The **zippo** stories. Katz, S.
Ziprya. Sadhu, A.
ZoBell, Bonnie
Avenida revolucion
Here's the story: fiction with heart; ed.
by M. Sklar
Zoellner's definition. Bail, M.
Zola, Émile, 1840-1902
Angeline; or, The haunted house
The Penguin book of ghost stories
The death of Olivier Bécaille
The Penguin book of horror stories
ZOMBIES
Burke, T. The hollow man
Parkinson, T. L. The father figure
Zoo. Hoch, E. D.
Zoofield follies. Gibbons, D.
ZOOLOGICAL GARDENS *See* Zoos
ZOOLOGISTS
Chekhov, A. P. The duel
Highsmith, P. The quest for Blank
Claveringi
Warren, J. Erika
ZOOS
Dybek, S. Sunday at the zoo
Hoch, E. D. Zoo
Jennings, J. Tiger hunt
Pronzini, B. Cat's-paw
Rodoreda, M. The elephant
Rosta, H. Belinda's seal
Swift, G. Hoffmeier's Antelope
Zorrilla de Rodríguez, Alicia María
Beyond loneliness
Américas 38:48-50 N/D '86
Zorro. Barthelme, S.
Zugsmith, Leane
Room in the world
Writing red; ed. by C. Nekola and P.
Rabinowitz
Zulfikar Ghose *See* Ghose, Zulfikar, 1935-
ZULUS (AFRICAN PEOPLE)
Gordimer, N. The bridegroom
Haggard, H. R. Black heart and white
heart
Havemann, E. Bloodsong
ZUÑI INDIANS
Austin, M. H. The secret of the holy
places
Zweibel, Alan
Comic dialogue
The Atlantic 253:92-8+ Je '84

Zwicky, Fay, 1933-
 The courts of the lord
  The Australian short story; ed. by L.
   Hergenhan

Hostages
 Echad 4: Jewish writing from down un-
  der: Australia and New Zealand
Only a little of so much
 Room to move; ed. by S. Falkiner

PART II
List of Collections Indexed

20 under 30; best stories by America's new young writers; edited by Debra Spark. Scribner 1986 269p ISBN 0-684-18641-1 LC 86-1769

22 stories. Gilliatt, P.

100 great fantasy short short stories; edited by Isaac Asimov, Terry Carr, and Martin H. Greenberg. Doubleday 1984 311p ISBN 0-385-18165-5 LC 82-45097
Partially analyzed

A

Abbott, Dorothy, 1944-
(ed) Mississippi writers v1: Fiction. *See* Mississippi writers v1: Fiction

Abbott, Keith
The first thing coming; short stories. Coffee House Press 1987 216p ISBN 0-918273-31-5 LC 87-18190
Harum scarum; short stories; with illustrations by Gaylord Schanilec. Coffee House Press 1984 89p il ISBN 0-918273-00-5 LC 84-15003

Abbott, Lee K.
Love is the crooked thing; stories. Algonquin Bks. 1986 182p (Bright leaf short fiction, 3) ISBN 0-912697-30-X LC 85-26823
Strangers in paradise. Putnam 1986 255p ISBN 0-399-13196-5 LC 86-8139

About time. Finney, J.

Abrahams, William
(ed) Prize stories, 1984-1988 *See* Prize stories, 1984-1988

Achebe, Chinua, 1930-
(ed) African short stories. *See* African short stories

Aćin-Kosta, Miloš
Tales of socialist Yugoslavia. Ravnogorski Venac 1984 287 p il LC 84-52846

Ackroyd, Peter
(ed) P.E.N. new fiction I. *See* P.E.N. new fiction I

Acquainted with the night, and other stories. Schwartz, L. S.

The acts of life. Hall, T. T.

Acts of love. McKinley, J.

Adams, Alice, 1926-
Return trips; stories. Knopf 1985 195p ISBN 0-394-53633-9 LC 85-40116

Adams, Gail Galloway
The purchase of order; stories. University of Ga. Press 1988 148p ISBN 0-8203-1040-9 LC 88-4724

Adams, Pamela Crippen
(ed) Robert Adams' Book of soldiers. *See* Robert Adams' Book of soldiers

Adams, Robert
(ed) Magic in Ithkar [1]-2. *See* Magic in Ithkar [1]-2
(ed) Magic in Ithkar 3-4. *See* Magic in Ithkar 3-4

Adams, Robert—Continued
(ed) Robert Adams' Book of soldiers. See Robert Adams' Book of soldiers

Ade, George, 1866-1944
The best of George Ade; with illustrations by John T. McCutcheon; selected and edited by A. L. Lazarus. Indiana Univ. Press 1985 xxii,254p il ISBN 0-253-10609-5 LC 84-43170
Analyzed for short stories only
A Midland Bk.

Adey, Robert C. S.
(ed) Death locked in. See Death locked in

Adisa, Opal Palmer, 1954-
Bake-Face, and other guava stories; introduction by Barbara Christian. Kelsey St. Press 1986 116p ISBN 0-932716-20-2 LC 86-7174

Adler, Bill, 1929-
(comp) Murder in Los Angeles. See Murder in Los Angeles
(comp) Murder in Manhattan. See Murder in Manhattan

The **adventures** of Henry Turnbuckle. Ritchie, J.

The **adventures** of Mike Blair. Searls, H.

The **adventures** of Sherlock Holmes. Doyle, Sir A. C.

Afoot in a field of men. Taylor, P. E.

African short stories; selected and edited by Chinua Achebe & C.L. Innes. Heinemann, W. 1985 159p (African writers series, 270) ISBN 0-435-90270-9 LC 84-218650

African short stories in English; an anthology; [ed. by] J. de Grandsaigne; assistant editor, S. Nnamonu. St. Martin's Press 1985 199p ISBN 0-312-01029-X LC 85-1930

After midnight; edited by Charles L. Grant. Doherty Assocs. 1986 276p ISBN 0-812-51854-3
A TOR Bk

Afterlives; an anthology of stories about life after death; edited by Pamela Sargent & Ian Watson. Vintage Bks. 1986 494p il ISBN 0-394-72986-2 LC 85-40687
Analyzed for short stories only

The **age** of grief. Smiley, J.

Agee, Jonis
(ed) Stiller's pond. See Stiller's pond

Ahern, Tom
Hecatombs of lake; stories. Sun & Moon Press 1984 141p (Sun & Moon Contemporary literature ser) ISBN 0-940650-29-0 LC 83-24251

Aickman, Robert, 1914-1981
The wine-dark sea. Arbor House; Morrow 1988 388p ISBN 1-55710-035-7 LC 88-16823

Airs of Providence. McGarry, J.

Aksenov, Vasilii Pavlovich, 1932-
Surplussed barrelware; [by] Vassily Aksyonov; edited & translated by Joel Wilkinson & Slava Yastremski. Ardis Pubs. 1985 195p ISBN 0-88233-904-4 LC 84-6348

Akutagawa, Ryunosuke, 1892-1927
Hell screen, Cogwheels, A fool's life; with a foreword by Jorge Luis Borges. Eridanos Press 1987 xx, 145p ISBN 0-941419-02-9 LC 87-83298

Alberta bound; thirty stories by Alberta writers; edited by Fred Stenson. NeWest Press 1986 337p ISBN 0-920897-04-5 LC 87-140389

Alcott, Louisa May, 1832-1888
A double life; newly discovered thrillers of Louisa May Alcott. Little, Brown 1988 246p ISBN 0-316-03101-1 LC 87-37827

Alden, Paulette Bates, 1947-
Feeding the eagles; short stories. Graywolf Press 1988 176p (Graywolf short fiction ser) ISBN 1-55597-111-3 LC 88-81022

Alderson, Tom
Michelson in the desert; stories. University of Mo. Press 1987 79p (Breakthrough book, no52) ISBN 0-8262-0621-2 LC 86-16159

Aldiss, Brian Wilson, 1925-
(ed) The Penguin world omnibus of science fiction. *See* The Penguin world omnibus of science fiction
Seasons in flight. Atheneum Pubs. 1986 c1984 157p ISBN 0-689-11538-5 LC 84-24329

Alfred Hitchcock's Crimewatch; edited by Cathleen Jordan. Dial Press 1984 348p ISBN 0-385-27995-7 LC 76-43201

Alfred Hitchcock's Grave suspicions; edited by Cathleen Jordan. Dial Press 1985 c1984 347p ISBN 0-385-19647-4 LC 84-239614

Alfred Hitchcock's Mortal errors; edited by Cathleen Jordan. Dial Press 1984 c1983 348p ISBN 0-385-27994-9 LC 76-43201

Algren, Nelson, 1909-1981
The neon wilderness. Writers & Readers 1986 304p ISBN 0-86316-122-7

Alien cargo. Sturgeon, T.

Aliens, travelers, and other strangers; [by] Boris and Arkady Strugatsky et al.; translated from the Russian by Roger DeGaris. Macmillan 1984 220p ISBN 0-02-615230-4 LC 84-14322

The **all-girl** football team. Nordan, L.
All set about with fever trees, and other stories. Durban, P.
All you can eat. Hemley, R.
The **Alligator** Report. Kinsella, W. P.
The **alternate** Asimovs. Asimov, I.
Alternative histories; eleven stories of the world as it might have been; edited by Charles G. Waugh and Martin H. Greenberg; with an afterword by Gordon B. Chamberlain and a bibliography by Barton C. Hacker and Gordon B. Chamberlain. Garland 1986 363p ISBN 0-8240-8659-7 LC 85-45130

Alurista, 1947-
(ed) Southwest tales. *See* Southwest tales
Amazing science fiction anthology: The war years, 1936-1945; edited by Martin H. Greenberg; introduction by Isaac Asimov; illustrations by George Barr, Hank Jankus, Paul Jaquays. TSR 1987 331p il ISBN 0-88038-440-9 LC 86-51271

Amazing science fiction anthology: The wild years, 1946-1955; edited by Martin H. Greenberg; introduction by Robert Bloch; illustrations by George Barr, Hank Jankus, Paul Jaquays. TSR 1987 318p il ISBN 0-88038-441-7 LC 86-51271

Amazing stories: 60 years of the best science fiction; edited by Isaac Asimov & Martin H. Greenberg. TSR Hobbies [distrib. by Random House] 1985 255p ISBN 0-88038-216-3 LC 85-51055

Amazing stories: visions of other worlds; edited by Martin H. Greenberg. TSR 1986 253p il ISBN 0-88038-302-X LC 86-50724

American made; edited by Mark Leyner, Curtis White, Thomas Glynn; with an introduction by Larry McCaffery. Fiction Collective 1986 214p ISBN 0-914590-98-7 LC 86-4459
At head of title: New fiction from the Fiction Collective

American short story masterpieces; edited by Raymond Carver and Tom Jenks. Delacorte Press 1987 435p ISBN 0-385-29524-3 LC 86-19964

Amichai, Yehuda
The world is a room, and other stories; translated from the Hebrew by Elinor Grumet [et al.]. Jewish Publ. Soc. of Am. 1984 199p ISBN 0-8276-0234-0 LC 83-24881

Amis, Martin
Einstein's monsters. Harmony Bks. 1987 149p ISBN 0-517-56520-X LC 86-25700

The **amoralists** & other tales. Colter, C.

Analog
From mind to mind: tales of communication from Analog. *See* From mind to mind: tales of communication from Analog

[Analog]: Writers' choice v2; edited by Stanley Schmidt. Dial Press; Davis Publs. 1984 285p ISBN 0-385-27996-5 LC 80-69078
Anthology #8

Anaya, Rudolfo A.
(ed) Cuentos Chicanos. *See* Cuentos Chicanos

Ancient voices, and other stories. Mooney, M.

And he tells the little horse the whole story. Barthelme, S.

And Venus is blue. Hood, M.

Anderman, Janusz, 1949-
The edge of the world; preface by Jerzy Pilch; translated by Nina Taylor. Readers Int. 1988 100p ISBN 0-930523-49-0 LC 88-061402

Poland under black light; with the author's new story from Warsaw; introduction by Stanislaw Baranczak; translated by Nina Taylor and Andrew Short. Readers Int. 1985 131p ISBN 0-930523-13-X
Partially analyzed

Anderson, Don, 1939-
(ed) Transgressions. *See* Transgressions

Anderson, Jani, 1949-
(ed) Bringing down the moon. *See* Bringing down the moon

Anderson, Jessica
Stories from the warm zone and Sydney stories. Viking 1987 246p ISBN 0-670-81626-4 LC 87-40022

Anderson, Poul, 1926-
Past times. Doherty Assocs. 1984 288p ISBN 0-812-53081-0 A TOR Bk.

Space wars. *See* Space wars

Andreyev, Leonid, 1871-1919
Visions; stories and photographs; edited and with an introduction by Olga Andreyev Carlisle. Harcourt Brace Jovanovich 1987 325p il ISBN 0-15-193900-4 LC 87-8605
Partially analyzed

Andrina, and other stories. Brown, G. M.

Angry candy. Ellison, H.

The **animal-lover's** book of beastly murder. Highsmith, P.

Another marvelous thing. Colwin, L.

Anthology of contemporary Latin American literature, 1960-1984; edited by Barry J. Luby and Wayne H. Finke. Fairleigh Dickinson Univ. Press; Associated Univ. Presses 1986 319p ISBN 0-8386-3255-6 LC 85-47789

Anthonology. Anthony, P.

Anthony, Piers
Anthonology. Doherty Assocs. 1985 381p ISBN 0-312-93027-5 LC 85-175795
A TOR book

Antrobus complete. Durrell, L.

Apollinaire, Guillaume, 1880-1918
The poet assassinated, and other stories; translated from the French by Ron Padgett. North Point Press 1984 139p ISBN 0-86547-151-7 LC 83-063131

Apostle of immortality. Berdnyk, O.

Apostolou, John L.
(ed) Murder in Japan. *See* Murder in Japan

Apple, Max
Free agents. Harper & Row 1984 197p ISBN 0-06-015282-6 LC 83-48810

Apples and pears, and other stories. Davenport, G.

Apprentice. Gallacher, T.

Arabic short stories; translated by Denys Johnson-Davies. Quartet Bks. 1984 c1983 173p ISBN 0-7043-2367-2

Arcadia, and other stories. Greenwood, R.

Archer, Jeffrey, 1940-
A twist in the tale. Simon & Schuster 1988 240p ISBN 0-671-67148-0 LC 88-23250

The **Architecture** of fear; edited by Kathryn Cramer and Peter D. Pautz. Arbor House 1987 304p ISBN 0-87795-921-8 LC 87-11492

Ardizzone, Tony
The evening news; stories. University of Ga. Press 1986 161p ISBN 0-8203-0860-9 LC 86-1403

Arkansas in short fiction; stories from 1841 to 1984; edited by William M. Baker & Ethel C. Simpson. August House 1986 220p ISBN 0-87483-007-9 LC 86-4506

The **Art** of fiction in the heart of Dixie; an anthology of Alabama writers; edited by Philip D. Beidler. University of Ala. Press 1986 335p ISBN 0-8173-0313-8 LC 86-6919

The **Art** of the tale; an international anthology of short stories, 1945-1985; edited by Daniel Halpern. Viking 1986 816p ISBN 0-670-80592-0 LC 86-5481
An Elisabeth Sifton Bk.

Artists & enemies. Cohen, A.

Ashley, Michael
(ed) The Mammoth book of short horror novels. *See* The Mammoth book of short horror novels

Asimov, Isaac, 1920-
(ed) 100 great fantasy short short stories. *See* 100 great fantasy short short stories

The alternate Asimovs. Doubleday 1986 272p ISBN 0-385-19784-5 LC 85-10295

(ed) Amazing stories: 60 years of the best science fiction. *See* Amazing stories: 60 years of the best science fiction

(ed) Baker's dozen: 13 short fantasy novels. *See* Baker's dozen: 13 short fantasy novels

(ed) Baker's dozen: 13 short science fiction novels. *See* Baker's dozen: 13 short science fiction novels

Banquets of the Black Widowers. Doubleday 1984 212p ISBN 0-385-19541-9 LC 84-1592

The best mysteries of Isaac Asimov. Doubleday 1986 345p ISBN 0-385-19783-7 LC 85-31199

The best science fiction of Isaac Asimov. Doubleday 1986 320p ISBN 0-385-19782-9 LC 85-31200

The edge of tomorrow. Doherty Assocs. 1985 462p ISBN 0-312-93200-6 LC 85-232026
Partially analyzed
A TOR book

(ed) Election Day 2084. *See* Election Day 2084
(ed) Great science fiction. *See* Great science fiction
(ed) Hound dunnit. *See* Hound dunnit
(ed) The Hugo winners v4. *See* The Hugo winners v4
(ed) The Hugo winners v5. *See* The Hugo winners v5
(ed) Intergalactic empires. *See* Intergalactic empires

Asimov, Isaac, 1920--—*Continued*

(ed) Isaac Asimov presents the best crime stories of the 19th century. *See* Isaac Asimov presents the best crime stories of the 19th century

(ed) Isaac Asimov presents the best science fiction firsts. *See* Isaac Asimov presents the best science fiction firsts

(ed) Machines that think. *See* Machines that think

(ed) The Mammoth book of classic science fiction. *See* The Mammoth book of classic science fiction

Other worlds of Isaac Asimov; edited by Martin H. Greenberg. Avenel Bks. [distrib. by Crown] 1987 651p ISBN 0-517-64375-8 LC 87-1153

    Analyzed for short stories only

Robot dreams; illustrated by Ralph McQuarrie; book design by Alex Jay. Berkley Bks. 1986 349p il ISBN 0-425-09345-X LC 86-231210

    A Byron Preiss Visual Publications, Inc. book

(ed) The Science fictional Olympics. *See* The Science fictional Olympics

(ed) Sherlock Holmes through time and space. *See* Sherlock Holmes through time and space

(ed) Witches. *See* Witches

(ed) Wizards. *See* Wizards

(ed) Young extraterrestrials. *See* Young extraterrestrials

(ed) Young ghosts. *See* Young ghosts

(ed) Young monsters. *See* Young monsters

(ed) Young mutants. *See* Young mutants

(ed) Young witches & warlocks. *See* Young witches & warlocks

Asscher-Pinkhof, Clara

Star children; translated by Terese Edelstein and Inez Smidt. Wayne State Univ. Press 1986 255p ISBN 0-8143-1846-0 LC 86-24543

The **assignation**.   Oates, J. C.

Athletes and artists.   Rossi, A.

Atwood, Margaret, 1939-

Bluebeard's egg, and other stories. Houghton Mifflin 1986 281p ISBN 0-395-40424-X LC 86-10336

(ed) The Oxford book of Canadian short stories in English. *See* The Oxford book of Canadian short stories in English

Auchincloss, Louis

Skinny island; more tales of Manhattan. Houghton Mifflin 1987 230p ISBN 0-395-43295-2 LC 86-21100

Aunt Ella stories.   Heise, K.

Austin, Don, 1946-

The portable city. Arsenal Eds. 1983 149p ISBN 0-88978-127-3

    Partially analyzed

Austin, Mary Hunter, 1868-1934

Western trails; a collection of short stories; by Mary Austin; selected and edited by Melody Graulich. University of Nev. Press 1987 309p ISBN 0-87417-127-X LC 87-16501

Australian science fiction; edited and introduced by Van Ikin. Academy Chicago 1984 xl,320p ISBN 0-89733-104-4 LC 84-377

The **Australian** short story; an anthology from the 1890s to the 1980s; edited and introduced by Laurie Hergenhan. University of Qld. Press 1986 xxiv, 329p (Portable Australian authors) ISBN 0-7022-1786-7 LC 85-1016

Avery, Martin, 1956-

The Singing Rabbi; new stories. Oberon Press 1983 104p ISBN 0-88750-490-6 LC 84-114604

Aymar, Brandt

(ed) Men at sea. *See* Men at sea

Azrak, Michel G.
(ed) Modern Syrian short stories. *See* Modern Syrian short stories

B

Back in the world. Wolff, T.
Backbone. Bly, C.
Bad behavior. Gaitskill, M.
Bad girls. Flanagan, M.
Bail, Murray, 1941-
The drover's wife, and other stories. Faber & Faber 1986 144p ISBN 0-571-13860-8 LC 86-11551
Baird-Smith, Robin
(ed) Winter's tales, new ser. v2-4. *See* Winter's tales, new ser. v2-4
Bake-Face, and other guava stories. Adisa, O. P.
Baker, William M. (William McDowell), 1939-
(ed) Arkansas in short fiction. *See* Arkansas in short fiction
Baker's dozen: 13 short espionage novels; edited by Bill Pronzini and Martin H. Greenberg. Bonanza Bks. 1985 515p ISBN 0-517-47647-9 LC 85-12820
Baker's dozen: 13 short fantasy novels; presented by Isaac Asimov; edited by Isaac Asimov, Martin H. Greenberg, and Charles Waugh; with an introduction by Isaac Asimov. Greenwich House 1984 612p ISBN 0-517-44500-X LC 84-6310
Baker's dozen: 13 short science fiction novels; presented by Isaac Asimov; edited by Isaac Asimov, Martin H. Greenberg, and Charles G. Waugh; with an introduction by Isaac Asimov. Bonanza Bks. 1985 574p ISBN 0-517-47646-0 LC 85-3766
Ball, John Dudley, 1911-
(ed) Murder California style. *See* Murder California style
Ballantyne, Sheila
Life on earth; stories. Linden Press/Simon & Schuster 1988 174p ISBN 0-671-60547-X LC 88-1098
Ballard, J. G., 1930-
Memories of the Space Age; art work by Jeffrey K. Potter. Arkham House Pubs. 1988 216p il ISBN 0-87054-157-9 LC 88-15075
Ballard, W. T. (Willis Todhunter)
Hollywood troubleshooter; W.T. Ballard's Bill Lennox stories; edited and introduced by James L. Traylor. Bowling Green Univ. Popular Press 1985 156p il ISBN 0-87972-316-5 LC 84-72510
Balzac's horse, and other stories. Hofmann, G.
Banks, Russell, 1940-
Success stories. Harper & Row 1986 183p ISBN 0-06-015567-1 LC 85-45617
Banquets of the Black Widowers. Asimov, I.
Barasch, Marc
(ed) Writers of the purple sage. *See* Writers of the purple sage
Barbach, Lonnie Garfield, 1946-
(ed) Erotic interludes. *See* Erotic interludes
Barich, Bill
Hard to be good. Farrar, Straus & Giroux 1987 180p ISBN 0-374-16812-1 LC 87-19654
Barker, Clive
The books of blood. Putnam 1988 462p ISBN 0-399-13343-7 LC 88-2404
Previously published as 3 different books: Books of blood, v. 1-3

Barker, Clive—*Continued*
Cabal. Poseidon Press 1988 377p ISBN 0-671-62688-4
LC 88-23308
In the flesh. Poseidon Press 1987 221p ISBN 0-671-62687-6
LC 86-20450
Originally published under title: Books of blood. v. 5
The inhuman condition; tales of terror. Poseidon Press 1986
220p ISBN 0-671-62686-8 LC 86-5086

Barrett, Lynne
The land of go; stories. Carnegie-Mellon Univ. Press 1988
94p ISBN 0-88748-044-6 LC 87-71458

Barstow, Stan, 1928-
The glad eye, and other stories. Joseph, M. 1984 182p ISBN
0-7181-2440-5 LC 84-133573

The **Barsukov** Triangle, The two-toned blond & other stories;
edited by Carl R. Proffer & Ellendea Proffer. Ardis Pubs.
1984 xxxiv, 370p ISBN 0-88233-805-6 LC 84-387

Barthelme, Donald
Forty stories. Putnam 1987 256p il ISBN 0-399-13299-6
LC 87-5999

Barthelme, Frederick
Chroma; stories. Simon & Schuster 1987 173p ISBN
0-671-54255-9 LC 86-31537

Barthelme, Steve
And he tells the little horse the whole story. Johns Hopkins
Univ. Press 1987 147p ISBN 0-8018-3543-7 LC 87-45477
Basic skills. Finger, A.

Bates, H. E. (Herbert Ernest), 1905-1974
A month by the lake & other stories; introduction by Anthony
Burgess. New Directions 1987 209p ISBN 0-8112-1035-9
LC 87-5680
My Uncle Silas; stories; drawings by Edward Ardizzone.
Graywolf Press 1984 189p il ISBN 0-915308-62-2
A party for the girls; six stories. New Directions 1988 243p
ISBN 0-8112-1050-2 LC 87-26874
Battles in the desert & other stories.   Pacheco, J. E.

Baumbach, Jonathan, 1933-
The life and times of Major Fiction; stories. Fiction Collective
1987 c1986 198p ISBN 0-932511-08-2 LC 86-29215

Bausch, Richard, 1945-
Spirits, and other stories. Linden Press/Simon & Schuster 1987
237p ISBN 0-671-63875-0 LC 86-27407

Baxter, Charles
Harmony of the world; stories. University of Mo. Press 1984
149p ISBN 0-8262-0428-7 LC 83-16799
Through the safety net; stories. Viking 1985 216p ISBN
0-670-80477-0 LC 84-48840
Bayou boy, and other stories.   Eighner, L.
Bearded ladies.   Grenville, K.

Beasley, Conger
(ed) Missouri short fiction. *See* Missouri short fiction
Beasts.   Jaffe, H.

Beattie, Ann
(comp) The Best American short stories, 1987. *See* The Best
American short stories, 1987
Where you'll find me, and other stories. Linden Press/Simon
& Schuster 1986 191p ISBN 0-671-62220-X LC 86-7396

Bedard, Brian, 1945-
Hour of the beast, and other stories. Chariton Review Press
1984 109p ISBN 0-933428-04-9 LC 84-12642
The **beggar's** knife.   Rey Rosa, R.

Beidler, Philip D.
(ed) The Art of fiction in the heart of Dixie. *See* The Art of fiction in the heart of Dixie

Believe them. Robison, M.

Bell, Madison Smartt
Zero db, and other stories. Ticknor & Fields 1987 179p ISBN 0-89919-489-3 LC 86-14548

Bell, Martin
Wolf. Ballantine Bks. 1988 182p ISBN 0-345-33773-5 LC 87-47501
Analyzed for short stories only
A Ballantine/Epiphany Bk.

Bellow, Saul
Him with his foot in his mouth, and other stories. Harper & Row 1984 294p ISBN 0-06-015179-X LC 84-48322

Bendixen, Alfred
(ed) Haunted women. *See* Haunted women

Benedict, Pinckney, 1964-
Town smokes; stories. Ontario Review Press 1987 168p ISBN 0-86538-058-9 LC 87-5684

Benford, Gregory, 1941-
(ed) Hitler victorious. *See* Hitler victorious
The **bequest** & other stories. Wexler, J.

Berdnyk, Oles
Apostle of immortality; Ukrainian science fiction; translated from the Ukrainian by Yuri Tkach. Bayda Bks. 1984 129p ISBN 0-908480-12-1

Berger, John, 1926-
Once in Europa. Pantheon Bks. 1987 192p ISBN 0-394-53992-3 LC 86-25287

Bernard, Kenneth
The Maldive chronicles; stories. Performing Arts Journal Publs. 1987 167p ISBN 1-55554-019-8 LC 87-81204

Bernen, Robert
The hills: more tales from the Blue Stacks; stories of Ireland. Scribner 1984 c1983 147p ISBN 0-684-18005-7 LC 83-16424

Berry, R. M.
Plane geometry and other affairs of the heart. Illinois State Univ.; Fiction Collective 1985 189p ISBN 0-914590-88-X LC 84-8172

The **Best** American short stories, 1984; selected from U.S. and Canadian magazines by John Updike with Shannon Ravenel; with an introduction by John Updike. Houghton Mifflin 1984 295p ISSN 0067-6233

The **Best** American short stories, 1985; selected from U.S. and Canadian magazines by Gail Godwin with Shannon Ravenel; with an introduction by Gail Godwin. Houghton Mifflin 1985 300p ISSN 0067-6233

The **Best** American short stories, 1986; selected from U.S. and Canadian magazines by Raymond Carver with Shannon Ravenel; with an introduction by Raymond Carver. Houghton Mifflin 1986 xx,325p ISSN 0067-6233

The **Best** American short stories, 1987; selected from U.S. and Canadian magazines by Ann Beattie with Shannon Ravenel; with an introduction by Ann Beattie. Houghton Mifflin 1987 334p ISSN 0067-6233

The **Best** American short stories, 1988; selected from U.S. and Canadian magazines by Mark Helprin, with Shannon Ravenel; with an introduction by Mark Helprin. Houghton Mifflin 1988 xxxi, 345p ISSN 0067-6233

The **Best** from Universe; edited by Terry Carr. Doubleday 1984 209p ISBN 0-385-17512-4 LC 82-45318

The **Best** horror stories from the Magazine of fantasy and science fiction; edited by Edward L. Ferman and Anne Jordan. St. Martin's Press 1988 403p ISBN 0-312-01894-0 LC 88-1987

The **Best** Maine stories; the marvelous mystery; edited by Sanford Phippen, Charles Waugh & Martin Greenberg. Tapley, L. 1986 314p ISBN 0-912769-07-6 LC 86-5990

The **best** mysteries of Isaac Asimov.   Asimov, I.

The **best** of Ellery Queen.   Queen, E.

The **best** of George Ade.   Ade, G.

The **Best** of Irish wit and wisdom; selected and edited by John McCarthy. Dodd, Mead 1987 324p ISBN 0-396-08998-4 LC 86-24149

The **best** of Margaret St. Clair.   St. Clair, M.

The **best** of Marion Zimmer Bradley.   Bradley, M. Z.

The **Best** of Shadows; edited by Charles L. Grant. Doubleday 1988 219p ISBN 0-385-23894-0 LC 88-14960

The **Best** of the West; new short stories from the wide side of the Missouri; edited by James Thomas with Tom Hazuka, Jonathan Maney, and Denise Thomas. Peregrine Smith Bks. 1988 224p ISBN 0-87905-332-1 LC 88-9932

The **Best** of Winter's crimes. *See* The Mammoth book of modern crime stories

Best science fiction and fantasy of the year #16, Terry Carr's. *See* Terry Carr's Best science fiction and fantasy of the year #16

The **best** science fiction of Isaac Asimov.   Asimov, I.

Best western stories, Max Brand's.   Brand, M.

The **best** western stories of Lewis B. Patten.   Patten, L. B.

The **best** western stories of Steve Frazee.   Frazee, S.

The **best** Western stories of Wayne D. Overholser.   Overholser, W. D.

Best western stories v3, Max Brand's.   Brand, M.

Better mousetraps.   Lutz, J.

Betty-san.   Yamamoto, M.

Between C & D; new writing from the Lower East Side fiction magazine; edited by Joel Rose and Catherine Texier. Penguin Bks. 1988 194p (Contemporary American fiction) ISBN 0-14-010570-0 LC 87-24386

Between mothers & daughters; stories across a generation; edited and with an introduction by Susan Koppelman. Feminist Press 1985 xxxix,293p ISBN 0-935312-26-9 LC 84-13562

Beum, Robert
(ed) Classic European short stories. *See* Classic European short stories

Beyond Armageddon; twenty-one sermons to the dead; edited by Walter M. Miller, Jr. and Martin H. Greenberg. Fine, D.I. 1985 387p ISBN 0-917657-55-1 LC 85-80625

Beyond the dragon's mouth.   Naipaul, S.

Beyond the safe zone.   Silverberg, R.

Beyond this bitter air.   Rossiter, S.

Biggs, Mary
(ed) Editor's choice II. *See* Editor's choice II

Billy Botzweiler's last dance, and other stories.   Choyce, L.

Bird, Carmel, 1940-
Woodpecker Point & other stories. New Directions 1988 153p ISBN 0-8112-1072-3 LC 88-1819

A **bird** in her hair, and other stories.   Bonosky, P.

Birds landing.   Finney, E. J.

The **birth** and death of the miracle man.   Wendt, A.

Birtha, Becky, 1948-
Lovers' choice. Seal Press 1987 152p ISBN 0-931188-56-3 LC 87-17281

Bishop, Michael, 1945-
Close encounters with the deity; stories; foreword by Isaac Asimov. Peachtree Pubs. 1986 306p ISBN 0-931948-96-7 LC 86-61070
One winter in Eden; foreword by Thomas M. Disch; and artwork by Andrew Smith. Arkham House Pubs. 1984 273p il ISBN 0-87054-096-3 LC 83-15842

Bissoondath, Neil, 1955-
Digging up the mountains; stories. Viking 1986 247p ISBN 0-670-81119-X LC 85-40994
Also published by Macmillan of Canada

Bitov, Andreï
Life in windy weather; short stories; edited by Priscilla Meyer. Ardis Pubs. 1986 371p ISBN 0-88233-691-6 LC 85-19931
The **black** & white stories of Erskine Caldwell. Caldwell, E.
The **black** house. Highsmith, P.
The **Black** Lizard anthology of crime fiction; edited with an introduction by Edward Gorman. Black Lizard Bks. 1987 335p ISBN 0-88739-039-0 LC 86-72053
The **Black** mask boys; masters in the hard-boiled school of detective fiction; featuring classic Black mask fiction by: Dashiell Hammett [et al. Edited by] William F. Nolan. Morrow 1985 273p ISBN 0-688-03966-9 LC 84-14778
Black water; the book of fantastic literature; [ed. by] Alberto Manguel. Potter 1983 967p ISBN 0-517-55269-8 LC 83-19091
Partially analyzed

Blackburn, Alex, 1929-
(ed) The Interior country. *See* The Interior country

Blackburn, Michael, 1954-
(ed) Stand one. *See* Stand one
The **blacktop** champion of Ickey Honey, and other stories. Sorrells, R. T.

Blaise, Clark
Resident alien. Penguin Bks. 1986 184p (Penguin short fiction) ISBN 0-14-008234-4

Blakely, Roger
(ed) Stiller's pond. *See* Stiller's pond

Blei, Norbert
The **ghost** of Sandburg's phizzog, and other stories. Ellis Press 1986 196p ISBN 0-944024-01-7 LC 88-140454

Blinkin, Meir, 1879-1915
Stories; translated from the Yiddish by Max Rosenfeld; with an introduction by Ruth R. Wisse. State Univ. of N.Y. Press 1984 166 ilp (SUNY ser. in modern Jewish literature and culture) ISBN 0-87395-818-7 LC 83-15564

Bloch, Robert, 1917-
Lost in time and space with Lefty Feep; eight funny and fanciful fables of the forties, plus one brand-new parable of modern times; edited by John Stanley; cover and sketches by Kenn Davis. Creatures at Large 1987 257p il (Lefty Feep trilogy, v1) ISBN 0-940064-01-4 LC 86-71608
The selected stories of Robert Bloch. Underwood/Miller 1987 3v il ISBN 0-88733-055-X (set) LC 87-34266

Block, Lawrence, 1938-
Like a lamb to slaughter; with an introduction by Joe Gores. Arbor House 1984 265p ISBN 0-87795-526-3 LC 84-9324
Blood and water, and other tales. McGrath, P.
Blood line. Quammen, D.
Bloodsong, and other stories of South Africa. Havemann, E.
The **blue** bedroom, and other stories. Pilcher, R.
The **blue** man, and other stories. Muschg, A.
Bluebeard's egg, and other stories. Atwood, M.

Bly, Carol
   Backbone; short stories. Milkweed Eds. 1985 125p il ISBN
      0-915943-04-2 LC 84-61733

Blythe, Ronald, 1922-
   The visitors; the stories of Ronald Blythe. Harcourt Brace
      Jovanovich 1985 239p ISBN 0-15-193912-8 LC 85-8527
         A Helen & Kurt Wolff Bk.

Boatwright, James, 1933-1988
   (ed) Shenandoah: an anthology. *See* Shenandoah: an anthology
The **Bodega** War, and other stories from western lore.   Lee,
      H.
Bodies of the rich.   Clayton, J. J.
The **bodysurfers.**   Drewe, R.
Bohannon's book.   Hansen, J.

Böll, Heinrich, 1917-1985
   The casualty; translated from the German by Leila Vennewitz.
      Farrar, Straus & Giroux 1987 c1986 189p ISBN 0-374-11967-8
      LC 86-31918
   The stories of Heinrich Böll; translated from the German by
      Leila Vennewitz. Knopf 1986 685p ISBN 0-394-51405-X
      LC 85-40392
A **bolt** of white cloth.   Rooke, L.
The **bones** wizard.   Ryan, A.

Bonner, Marita, 1899-1971
   Frye Street & environs; the collected works of Marita Bonner;
      edited and introduced by Joyce Flynn and Joyce Occomy
      Stricklin. Beacon Press 1987 xxix,286p ISBN 0-8070-6300-2
      LC 87-47450
         Analyzed for short stories only

Bonnie, Fred
   Too hot & other Maine stories. Dog Ear Press 1987 172p
      ISBN 0-937966-21-5 LC 87-5252
   Wide load. Oberon Press 1987 111p ISBN 0-88750-666-6

Bonosky, Phillip, 1916-
   A bird in her hair, and other stories. International Pubs. 1987
      172p ISBN 0-7178-0661-8 LC 87-3432
Book of classic ghost stories, Charles Keeping's. *See* Charles
      Keeping's Book of classic ghost stories
Book of classic science fiction, The Mammoth. *See* The Mammoth
      book of classic science fiction
Book of French-Canadian short stories, The Oxford. *See* The
      Oxford book of French-Canadian short stories
Book of ghost stories, The Penguin. *See* The Penguin book of
      ghost stories
Book of horror stories, The Penguin. *See* The Penguin book
      of horror stories
Book of modern British short stories, The Penguin. *See* The
      Penguin book of modern British short stories
Book of private eye stories, The Mammoth. *See* The Mammoth
      book of private eye stories
The **book** of seeing with one's own eyes.   Doubiago, S.
Book of soldiers, Robert Adams'. *See* Robert Adams' Book of
      soldiers
The **Book** of the dead; thirteen classic tales of the supernatural;
      edited by Alan K. Russell. New Orchard Eds. 1986 382p
      ISBN 1-85079-035-3
The **bookman's** tale, and others.   Fleming, B.
The **books** of blood.   Barker, C.

Booth, Mark
   (ed) Christian short stories. *See* Christian short stories
Bop.   Chernoff, M.

Boswell, Robert, 1953-
 Dancing in the movies. University of Iowa Press 1986 144p
  ISBN 0-87745-134-6 LC 85-13966
Botwinik, Berl, 1885?-1945
 Lead pencil; stories and sketches; translated from the Yiddish
  by Philip J. Klukoff. Wayne State Univ. Press 1984 163p
  il ISBN 0-8143-1745-6 LC 83-19848
Bowering, George, 1935-
 A place to die. Oberon Press 1983 127p ISBN 0-88750-476-0
  LC 83-170335
Bowles, Paul, 1910-
 A distant episode; the selected stories. Ecco Press 1988 352p
  ISBN 0-88001-204-8 LC 88-24553
A **boy** like Astrid's mother. Briskin, M.
Boy with an injured eye. Sheehan, R.
Boyd, William, 1952-
 On the Yankee station; stories. Morrow 1984 217p ISBN
  0-688-03111-0 LC 84-60480
Boylan, James, 1958-
 Remind me to murder you later; short stories. Johns Hopkins
  Univ. Press 1988 131p il ISBN 0-8018-3728-6 LC 88-45417
Boyle, Kay, 1902-
 Life being the best & other stories; edited with an introduction
  by Sandra Whipple Spanier. New Directions 1988 140p ISBN
  0-8112-1052-9 LC 87-32059
  A Revived modern classic
Boyle, T. Coraghessan
 Greasy Lake & other stories. Viking 1985 229p ISBN
  0-670-80542-4 LC 84-23427
The **boys** of Bensonhurst. La Puma, S.
Bradbury, Malcolm, 1932-
 (ed) The Penguin book of modern British short stories. *See*
  The Penguin book of modern British short stories
Bradbury, Ray, 1920-
 A memory of murder. Dell 1984 192p ISBN 0-440-15559-2
 The Toynbee convector; stories. Knopf 1988 275p ISBN
  0-394-54703-9 LC 87-46189
Bradley, Marion Zimmer
 The best of Marion Zimmer Bradley; edited by Martin H.
  Greenberg. Academy Chicago 1985 367p ISBN 0-89733-165-6
  LC 85-18517
Brady, Maureen
 The question she put to herself; stories. Crossing Press 1987
  117p ISBN 0-89594-229-1 LC 87-5307
Brand, Max, 1892-1944
 Max Brand's Best western stories v2; edited with an introduction
  by William F. Nolan. Dodd, Mead 1985 184p ISBN
  0-396-08500-8 LC 81-3204
  Volume 1, entered in 1979-1983 Short story index
 Max Brand's Best western stories v3; edited with an introduction
  by William F. Nolan. Dodd, Mead 1987 237p ISBN
  0-396-08948-8 LC 81-3204
Brandstetter & others. Hansen, J.
The **Bread** Loaf anthology of contemporary American short stories;
  edited by Robert Pack and Jay Parini; published for the
  Bread Loaf Writers' Conference, Middlebury College.
  University Press of New England 1987 331p ISBN
  0-87451-392-8 LC 86-40387
Bread Loaf Writers' Conference of Middlebury College
 The Bread Loaf anthology of contemporary American short
  stories. *See* The Bread Loaf anthology of contemporary
  American short stories
Break it down. Davis, L.

Breaking bread. Kornblatt, J. R.

Breen, Jon L., 1943-

(ed) Murder California style. *See* Murder California style

Brender à Brandis, Madzy

The scent of spruce; illustrated by G. Brender à Brandis. Netherlandic Press 1984 58p il ISBN 0-919417-06-X

Breslin, John B.

(comp) The Substance of things hoped for. *See* The Substance of things hoped for

Brett, Simon, 1945-

Tickled to death, and other stories of crime and suspense. Scribner 1985 231p ISBN 0-684-18486-9 LC 85-14515

Originally published in Great Britain as: A box of tricks

The **bride** of Ambrose, and other stories. Freeman, C.

Bringing down the moon; 15 tales of fantasy and terror; edited by Jani Anderson. Space and Time 1985 251p ISBN 0-917053-03-6 LC 85-10904

Briskin, Mae, 1924-

A boy like Astrid's mother. Norton 1988 222p ISBN 0-393-02603-5 LC 87-33774

Brondoli, Michael

Showdown, and other stories. North Point Press 1984 225p ISBN 0-86547-152-5 LC 83-63129

Brooks, Jeremy

Doing the voices. Viking Salamander 1986 159p ISBN 0-948681-01-2

Broun, Hob

Cardinal numbers. Knopf 1988 150p ISBN 0-394-56261-5 LC 87-40481

Brown, Fredric, 1906-1972

Carnival of crime; the best mystery stories of Fredric Brown; edited by Francis M. Nevins, Jr., and Martin H. Greenberg; introduction by Bill Pronzini. Southern Ill. Univ. Press 1985 314p (Mystery makers) ISBN 0-8093-1192-5 LC 84-10695

Brown, George Mackay

Andrina, and other stories. Chatto & Windus; Hogarth Press 1983 153p ISBN 0-7012-0546-6 LC 82-244358

Brown, Mary Ward

Tongues of flame. Dutton; Lawrence, S. 1986 162p ISBN 0-525-24431-X LC 86-4259

Browning, Robert Marcellus, 1911-

(ed) German romantic novellas. *See* German romantic novellas

Bruccoli, Matthew Joseph, 1931-

(ed) A Matter of crime. *See* A Matter of crime

Budrys, Algis, 1931-

(ed) L. Ron Hubbard presents Writers of the future. *See* L. Ron Hubbard presents Writers of the future

Bukoski, Anthony

Twelve below zero; drawings by Gaylord Schanilec. New Rivers Press 1986 126p il (Minnesota voices project, no24) ISBN 0-89823-072-1 LC 85-62850

Bulychev, K. (Kirill)

Earth and elsewhere. *See* Earth and elsewhere

Bumpus, Jerry

Heroes and villains; stories. Fiction Collective 1986 258p ISBN 0-914590-92-8 LC 84-25945

Burgess, Moira

(ed) Streets of stone. *See* Streets of stone

Burke, James Lee, 1936-

The convict; stories. Louisiana State Univ. Press 1985 145p ISBN 0-8071-1273-9 LC 85-11332

Burnard, Bonnie

(ed) The Old dance. *See* The Old dance

Burns, Mary
  Suburbs of the Arctic Circle. Penumbra Press 1986 158p ISBN 0-920806-79-1 LC 86-141032
Burt, Simon
  Floral Street. Faber & Faber 1986 188p ISBN 0-571-13600-1 LC 85-27383
The **bus** of dreams.   Morris, M.
Busch, Frederick, 1941-
  Too late American boyhood blues; ten stories. Godine 1984 275p ISBN 0-87923-511-X LC 83-48895
Buying time; an anthology celebrating 20 years of the Literature Program of the National Endowment for the Arts; edited by Scott Walker; introduction by Ralph Ellison. Graywolf Press 1985 xxv, 336p ISBN 0-915308-72-X LC 85-80545
  Analyzed for short stories only
Buzzati, Dino, 1906-1972
  The siren; a selection from Dino Buzzati; chosen and translated by Lawrence Venuti. North Point Press 1984 147p il ISBN 0-86547-159-2 LC 84-60682
By land, by sea.   Hoffman, W.
Byatt, A. S. (Antonia Susan), 1936-
  Sugar, and other stories. Scribner 1987 248p ISBN 0-684-18786-8 LC 86-31374
Byte beautiful.   Tiptree, J.

C

Cabal.   Barker, C.
Cahill, Susan Neunzig
  (ed) New women and new fiction. *See* New women and new fiction
Caldwell, Erskine, 1903-1987
  The black & white stories of Erskine Caldwell; selected by Ray McIver; foreword by Erskine Caldwell. Peachtree Pubs. 1984 189p ISBN 0-931948-63-0 LC 84-60921
Calisher, Hortense
  Saratoga, hot. Doubleday 1985 272p ISBN 0-385-19975-9 LC 84-24695
Calvino, Italo
  Difficult loves; translated from the Italian by William Weaver and Archibald Colquhoun and Peggy Wright. Harcourt Brace Jovanovich 1984 290p ISBN 0-15-125610-1 LC 84-685
  A Helen and Kurt Wolff Bk.
Cameron, Peter
  One way or another; stories. Harper & Row 1986 181p ISBN 0-06-015569-8 LC 85-45626
Camoin, François André, 1939-
  Why men are afraid of women; stories. University of Ga. Press 1984 149p ISBN 0-8203-0722-X LC 84-1374
Campbell, Ewing
  Piranesi's dream; stories. Nefertiti Head Press 1986 204p ISBN 0-918722-12-8 LC 86-62523
Campbell, Ramsey, 1946-
  Cold print. Scream/Press 1985 xxi,217p il ISBN 0-910489-13-0
  Scared stiff; tales of sex and death; illustrated by J.K. Potter. Scream/Press 1987 173p il ISBN 0-910489-17-3
Campbell, Wanda Blynn, 1944-
  The promise. Pulp Press 1983 129p ISBN 0-88978-141-9
Campos-De Metro, Joseph
  The slugger heart & other stories. Harcourt Brace Jovanovich 1984 196p ISBN 0-15-183100-9 LC 83-18533
The **canary**, and other tales of martial law.   Nowakowski, M.

The **candles** of your eyes, and thirteen other stories.   Purdy, J.

Canin, Ethan

Emperor of the air; stories. Houghton Mifflin 1988 179p ISBN 0-395-42976-5 LC 87-22540

Caponegro, Mary, 1956-

Tales from the next village; fictions of Mary Caponegro. Lost Roads Pubs. 1985 107p ISBN 0-918786-32-0 LC 85-14888

Captain Maximus.   Hannah, B.

Caras, Roger A.

(comp) Roger Caras' Treasury of great cat stories. *See* Roger Caras' Treasury of great cat stories

(comp) Roger Caras' Treasury of great dog stories. *See* Roger Caras' Treasury of great dog stories

Card, Orson Scott

(ed) Dragons of light. *See* Dragons of light

Cardinal numbers.   Broun, H.

Carlson, Ron

The news of the world; stories. Norton 1987 187p LC 86-5418

Carnival of crime.   Brown, F.

Carr, Terry, 1937-1987

(ed) 100 great fantasy short short stories. *See* 100 great fantasy short short stories

(ed) The Best from Universe. *See* The Best from Universe

(ed) Terry Carr's Best science fiction and fantasy of the year #16. *See* Terry Carr's Best science fiction and fantasy of the year #16

Terry's universe. *See* Terry's universe

(ed) Universe 14-17. *See* Universe 14-17

Carrington, Leonora, 1917-

The house of fear; notes from down below; introduction by Marina Warner; translations by Kathrine Talbot and Marina Warner. Dutton 1988 216p il ISBN 0-525-24648-7 LC 88-3907

Analyzed for short stories only

The seventh horse, and other tales; translations by Kathrine Talbot and Anthony Kerrigan. Dutton 1988 197p il ISBN 0-525-24651-7 LC 88-7072

Analyzed for short stories only

A Dutton Obelisk Bk.

Carter, Angela, 1940-

Saints and strangers. Viking Penguin 1986 126p ISBN 0-670-81139-4 LC 85-41072

Carter, Robert, 1945-

The pleasure within; short stories. Atheneum Pubs. 1988 96p ISBN 0-689-11998-4 LC 88-16626

Carver, Raymond

(ed) American short story masterpieces. *See* American short story masterpieces

(comp) The Best American short stories, 1986. *See* The Best American short stories, 1986

Where I'm calling from; new and selected stories. Atlantic Monthly Press 1988 393p ISBN 0-87113-216-8 LC 87-36778

Cascade point, and other stories.   Zahn, T.

Casper, Susan

(ed) Ripper! *See* Ripper!

The **casualty**.   Böll, H.

The **cat**, and other stories.   Silva, B.

The **Cathay** stories and other fictions.   Harris, M.

A **Cent** a story!; the best from Ten Detective Aces; [comp. by] Garyn G. Roberts. Bowling Green State Univ. Popular Press 1986 179p il ISBN 0-87972-353-X LC 86-070384

The **centre** of the universe is 18 Baedekerstrasse. Gathorne-Hardy, J.

The **ceremony** & other stories. Kees, W.

Chang, Hsin-chang
(comp) Tales of the supernatural. *See* Tales of the supernatural

A **change** for the better. Mathers, P.

Chapter & hearse; suspense stories about the world of books; edited by Marcia Muller and Bill Pronzini. Morrow 1985 372p ISBN 0-688-04184-1 LC 84-16497

Charles Keeping's Book of classic ghost stories. Bedrick Bks. 1986 142p il ISBN 0-87226-096-8 LC 86-10774

Charles Keeping's Classic tales of the macabre. Bedrick Bks. 1987 171p il ISBN 0-87226-168-9

Chasing her own tail. Keeling, N.

Chavez, Angelico
The short stories of Fray Angelico Chavez; edited by Genaro M. Padilla. University of N.M. Press 1987 xx,139p il ISBN 0-8263-0949-6 LC 87-5992

Chavis, Geri Giebel
(ed) Family: stories from the interior. *See* Family: stories from the interior

Chekhov, Anton Pavlovich, 1860-1904
The duel, and other stories; translated with an introduction by Ronald Wilks. Penguin Bks. 1984 245p ISBN 0-14-044415-7 LC 84-211745

The fiancée, and other stories; translated with an introduction by Ronald Wilks. Penguin Bks. 1986 231p ISBN 0-14-044470-X

The party, and other stories; translated with an introduction by Ronald Wilks. Penguin Bks. 1986 233p ISBN 0-14-044452-1

Ch'en, Ying-chen
Exiles at home: short stories; [tr. by] Lucien Miller. University of Mich. Center for Chinese Studies 1986 195p ISBN 0-89264-067-7 LC 85-15148

Chernoff, Maxine, 1952-
Bop; stories. Coffee House Press 1986 126p ISBN 0-918273-19-6 LC 86-4146

Chesterton, G. K. (Gilbert Keith), 1874-1936
Daylight and nightmare; uncollected stories and fables; selected and arranged by Marie Smith. Dodd, Mead 1986 144p ISBN 0-396-08889-9 LC 86-16593

Thirteen detectives; selected and arranged by Marie Smith. Dodd, Mead 1987 256p ISBN 0-396-09211-X LC 87-15469

Child, Lincoln
(ed) Dark banquet. *See* Dark banquet
(ed) Dark company. *See* Dark company

Child's ploy; an anthology of mystery and suspense stories; edited by Marcia Muller and Bill Pronzini. Macmillan 1984 307p (Macmillan midnight lib) ISBN 0-02-599250-3 LC 83-26711

Chin, Frank, 1940-
The Chinaman Pacific & Frisco R.R. Co.; short stories. Coffee House Press 1988 165p ISBN 0-918273-44-7 LC 88-30326

The **Chinaman** Pacific & Frisco R.R. Co. Chin, F.

Chinese story, and other tales. Pil'nĭāk, B.

The **Chinese** Western; short fiction from today's China; translated by Zhu Hong. Ballantine Bks. 1988 224p ISBN 0-345-35140-1 LC 87-91880
An Available Press Bk.

Chipps, Genie
(ed) Love stories for the time being. *See* Love stories for the time being

Choyce, Lesley, 1951-
Billy Botzweiler's last dance, and other stories. blewointmentpress 1984 91p ISBN 0-88971-099-6 LC 85-100622

Christian short stories; an anthology; edited by Mark Booth. Crossroad 1984 200p ISBN 0-8245-0672-1 LC 84-070839

Christie, Agatha, 1891-1976

Hercule Poirot's casebook. Dodd, Mead 1984 860p ISBN 0-396-08417-6 LC 84-13488

Miss Marple; the complete short stories. Dodd, Mead 1985 346p ISBN 0-396-08747-7 LC 85-10220

A **Christmas** carol, and other Christmas stories. Dickens, C.

Christmas ghosts; edited by Kathryn Cramer & David G. Hartwell. Arbor House 1987 284p il ISBN 0-87795-873-4 LC 87-11355

The **Christmas** wife. Norris, H.

Chroma. Barthelme, F.

Chrysanthemums, and other stories. Feng Jicai

Ciment, Jill, 1953-

Small claims. Weidenfeld & Nicolson 1986 197p ISBN 1-55584-000-0 LC 86-5463

Circles of faces. Dadswell, M.

The **city** of refuge. Fisher, R.

Civil to strangers, and other writings. Pym, B.

Civil War women; American women shaped by conflict in stories by Alcott, Chopin, Welty and others; edited by Frank McSherry, Jr., Charles G. Waugh, and Martin Greenberg. August House 1988 175p ISBN 0-87483-061-3 LC 88-6242

Claiborne, Sybil

Loose connections. Academy Chicago 1988 171p ISBN 0-89733-301-2 LC 87-35172

The **Clarion** awards; edited by Damon Knight. Doubleday 1984 177p ISBN 0-385-18383-6 LC 82-46030

Clark, Geoffrey, 1940-

Ruffian on the stair; short stories; jacket design by Marcia Weisbrot. Story Press 1988 96p il ISBN 0-931704-16-2 LC 88-2158

Clark, Manning, 1915-

Collected short stories. Penguin Bks. 1986 160p ISBN 0-14-009294-3

Clarke, Arthur C., 1917-

The sentinel; masterworks of science fiction and fantasy; illustrated by Lebbeus Woods. Berkley Bks. 1983 303p il ISBN 0-425-06183-3 LC 83-234006

A Byron Preiss Visual Publs. Inc. Bk.

Clarke, Austin Chesterfield

Nine men who laughed. Penguin Bks. 1986 225p (Penguin short fiction) ISBN 0-14-008560-2

Clarke, Terence

The day nothing happened. Mercury House 1988 223p ISBN 0-916515-36-2 LC 87-28747

Classic crime omnibus, The Penguin. *See* The Penguin classic crime omnibus

Classic European short stories; edited by Robert Beum. Sugden & Co. 1984 278p ISBN 0-89385-025-X

The **classic** Philip José Farmer, 1952-1964—1964-1973. Farmer, P. J.

Classic tales of the macabre, Charles Keeping's. *See* Charles Keeping's Classic tales of the macabre

Classical illusions. Kessler, J. F.

Clayton, John Jacob

Bodies of the rich; stories. University of Ill. Press 1984 132p (Illinois short fiction) ISBN 0-252-01097-3 LC 83-4873

Clearing in the sky & other stories. Stuart, J.

Clift, Charmian, 1923-1969

Strong-man from Piraeus, and other stories. See Johnston, George, 1912-1970, and Clift, Charmian, 1923-1969

Close encounters with the deity. Bishop, M.

Close-ups. Thompson, S.

Clute, John
 (ed) Interzone: the first anthology. *See* Interzone: the first anthology
 (ed) Interzone: the 2nd anthology. *See* Interzone: the 2nd anthology

Codrescu, Andrei, 1946-
 Monsieur Teste in America & other instances of realism; short stories. Coffee House Press 1987 138p ISBN 0-918273-32-3 LC 87-27731

Cohen, Arthur (Arthur Allen), 1928-1986
 Artists & enemies; three novellas. Godine 1987 274p ISBN 0-87923-650-7 LC 86-45535

Cohen, Matt, 1942-
 (ed) Intimate strangers. *See* Intimate strangers
 Life on this planet, and other stories. Beaufort Bks. 1983 182p ISBN 0-8253-0313-3 LC 85-9059

Cold print. Campbell, R.

Cold tales. Piñera, V.

Colegate, Isabel
 A glimpse of Sion's glory. Viking 1985 153p ISBN 0-670-80897-0 LC 85-40541
  An Elisabeth Sifton Bk.

Coleman, Wanda
 A war of eyes, and other stories. Black Sparrow Press 1988 242p ISBN 0-87685-736-5 LC 88-14714

Colette, 1873-1954
 The collected stories of Colette; edited, and with an introduction, by Robert Phelps; translated by Matthew Ward, Antonia White, Anne-Marie Callimachi, and others. Farrar, Straus & Giroux 1983 605p ISBN 0-374-12629-1 LC 83-16449

Collected short stories. Clark, M.

Collected short stories. Greene, G.

The **collected** short stories. Rhys, J.

The **collected** short stories of Maxim Gorky. Gorky, M.

Collected stories. García Márquez, G.

Collected stories. Gee, M.

Collected stories. McCullers, C.

Collected stories. Petrakis, H. M.

The **collected** stories. Thomas, D.

The **collected** stories. Tuohy, F.

Collected stories. Williams, T.

Collected stories, 1948-1986. Morris, W.

The **collected** stories of Colette. Colette

The **collected** stories of Guy de Maupassant. Maupassant, G. de

Collected stories of Jessamyn West. West, J.

Collected stories of John O'Hara. O'Hara, J.

The **collected** stories of William Humphrey. Humphrey, W.

Collected works. O'Connor, F.

A **Collection** of classic Southern humor; fiction and occasional fact; by some of the South's best storytellers; edited by George William Koon. Peachtree Pubs. 1984 272p ISBN 0-931948-55-X LC 84-60018
  Analyzed for short stories only

Collins, Linda
 Going to see the leaves. Viking 1986 197p ISBN 0-670-80881-4 LC 85-40624

The **Colonel's** daughter, and other stories. Tremain, R.

Colter, Cyrus, 1910-
 The amoralists & other tales; collected stories. Thunder's Mouth Press 1988 283p ISBN 0-938410-67-9 LC 88-9749

Colum, Padraic, 1881-1972
Selected short stories of Padraic Colum; edited by Sanford Sternlicht. Syracuse Univ. Press 1985 xxvi,130p (Irish studies) ISBN 0-8156-2327-5 LC 84-20522

Colwin, Laurie
Another marvelous thing. Knopf 1986 130p ISBN 0-394-55128-1 LC 85-45588

Come to Africa and save your marriage, and other stories. Thomas, M.

Comfort. Kaplan, D. M.

The **coming** triumph of the free world.   DeMarinis, R.

Common body, royal bones.   Shefner, E.

The **complete** short stories of Ernest Hemingway.   Hemingway, E.

The **complete** short stories of H. G. Wells.   Wells, H. G.

The **complete** short stories of L. P. Hartley.   Hartley, L. P.

The **complete** short stories of Raffles—the amateur cracksman. Hornung, E. W.

The **complete** short stories of Thomas Wolfe.   Wolfe, T.

The **complete** shorter fiction of Virginia Woolf.   Woolf, V.

The **complete** tales of Nikolaï Gogol'   Gogol', N. V.

The **conglomeroid** cocktail party.   Silverberg, R.

Conley, Robert J.
The witch of Goingsnake, and other stories; foreword by Wilma P. Mankiller. University of Okla. Press 1988 165p ISBN 0-8061-2148-3 LC 88-4762

The **Connecticut** countess.   Watmough, D.

Connelly, John, 1959-
Man's work; stories. Algonquin Bks. 1987 237p (Bright leaf short fiction, 5) ISBN 0-912697-55-5 LC 86-28671

Conroy, Frank, 1936-
Midair. Dutton; Lawrence, S. 1985 149p ISBN 0-525-24319-4 LC 85-10154

Conroy, Jack, 1899-
The weed king & other stories; edited and with an introduction by Douglas C. Wixson. Hill & Co. 1985 xxxiii,269p ISBN 0-88208-185-3 LC 85-5438

The **consolation** of nature, and other stories.   Martin, V.

Contemporary Chinese literature; an anthology of post-Mao fiction and poetry; edited with introductions by Michael S. Duke for the Bulletin of Concerned Asian Scholars. Sharpe, M.E. 1985 137p il ISBN 0-87332-339-4 LC 85-10866
Analyzed for short stories only
An East Gate Bk.

Continent.   Crace, J.

The **convict.**   Burke, J. L.

Cook, Hugh, 1942-
Cracked wheat, and other stories. Mosaic Press/Valley Eds. [distrib. by Flatiron Bk. Distributors] 1985 122p ISBN 0-88962-266-3 LC 85-154287

Cooper, J. California
Homemade love. St. Martin's Press 1986 175p ISBN 0-312-38895-0 LC 86-3970
A piece of mine. Wild Trees Press 1984 124p ISBN 0-931125-00-6 LC 84-051985
Some soul to keep. St. Martin's Press 1987 211p ISBN 0-312-00684-5 LC 87-4414

Coover, Robert
A night at the movies; or, You must remember this; fictions. Linden Press/Simon & Schuster 1987 187p ISBN 0-671-61796-6 LC 86-20941

Cora Sandel: selected short stories.   Sandel, C.

Corey, Stephen, 1948-
(ed) Necessary fictions. *See* Necessary fictions

Coriolan, John
Dream stud, and other stories. Gay Sunshine Press 1985 157p ISBN 0-917342-04-6

Coskran, Kathleen
The high price of everything; stories. New Rivers Press 1988 133p (Minnesota voices project, no33) ISBN 0-89823-102-7 LC 88-60055

Covino, Michael, 1950-
The off-season; stories. Persea Bks. 1985 197p ISBN 0-89255-099-6 LC 86-131998

Cowan, Peter, 1914-
A window in Mrs X's place; introduced by Bruce Bennett. Penguin Bks. 1986 278p ISBN 0-14-008181-X

Cowper, Richard, 1926-
The custodians, and other stories. Gollancz [distrib. by David & Charles] 1985 c1976 191p ISBN 0-575-02096-2
The Tithonian Factor, and other stories. Gollancz [distrib. by David & Charles] 1984 150p ISBN 0-575-03440-8

Cox, Michael, 1948-
(ed) The Oxford book of English ghost stories. *See* The Oxford book of English ghost stories

Crabtree, Lou V.
Sweet Hollow; stories. Louisiana State Univ. Press 1984 106p ISBN 0-8071-1132-5 LC 83-14934

Crace, Jim
Continent. Harper & Row 1987 c1986 138p ISBN 0-06-015724-0 LC 86-45861

Cracked wheat, and other stories. Cook, H.

Cramer, Kathryn, 1962-
(ed) The Architecture of fear. *See* The Architecture of fear
(ed) Christmas ghosts. *See* Christmas ghosts
(ed) Masterpieces of fantasy and enchantment. *See* Masterpieces of fantasy and enchantment

Crane, Stephen, 1871-1900
Prose and poetry; Maggie: a girl of the streets; The red badge of courage; stories, sketches and journalism, poetry. Library of America 1984 1379p ISBN 0-940450-17-8 LC 83-19908
Analyzed for short stories only

Crapser, William, 1949-
Remains: stories of Vietnam. Sachem Press 1988 175p ISBN 0-937584-13-4 LC 88-6667

The **Crazy** iris, and other stories of the atomic aftermath; edited and with an introduction by Kenzaburō Ōe. Grove Press 1985 204p ISBN 0-394-54944-9 LC 85-71162

Crazy women. Matthews, J.

Creswell, Rosemary
(ed) Home and away. *See* Home and away

Crime collection, 1984-1987, John Creasey's. *See* John Creasey's Crime collection, 1984-1987

The **Crime** of my life; favorite stories by presidents of the Mystery Writers of America; edited by Brian Garfield. Walker & Co. 1984 269p ISBN 0-8027-0761-0 LC 83-40389

Crime Writers' Association
John Creasey's Crime collection, 1984-1987. *See* John Creasey's Crime collection, 1984-1987

Crimes and punishments, Ellery Queen's. *See* Ellery Queen's Crimes and punishments

Crimewatch, Alfred Hitchcock's. *See* Alfred Hitchcock's Crimewatch

Crowley, Aleister, 1875-1947
Golden twigs; edited with an introduction by Martin P. Starr.
Teitan Press 1988 151p ISBN 0-933429-03-7 LC 88-24810
The scrutinies of Simon Iff; edited with an introduction by
Martin P. Starr. Teitan Press 1987 180p ISBN 0-933429-02-9
LC 87-7122

Crown of stars.   Tiptree, J.
The **Crystal** Fountain and other stories.   Whitaker, M.

Cuddon, J. A. (John Anthony), 1928-
(ed) The Penguin book of ghost stories. *See* The Penguin
book of ghost stories
(ed) The Penguin book of horror stories. *See* The Penguin
book of horror stories

Cuentos Chicanos; a short story anthology; edited by Rudolfo
A. Anaya and Antonio Márquez. rev ed. University of N.M.
Press 1984 186p ISBN 0-8263-0771-X LC 84-13066
Partially analyzed

Cullen, E. J.
Our war and how we won it; stories. Viking 1987 238p ISBN
0-670-81526-4 LC 86-24746
An Elisabeth Sifton Bk.

Curley, Daniel
Living with snakes; stories. University of Ga. Press 1985 134p
ISBN 0-8203-0767-X LC 84-22773

Curtiss, Ursula Reilly, 1923-1984
The house on Plymouth Street, and other stories; by Ursula
Curtiss. Dodd, Mead 1985 248p ISBN 0-396-08685-3
LC 85-1597

The **custodians,** and other stories.   Cowper, R.

Cutting edge; edited by Dennis Etchison. Doubleday 1986 290p
ISBN 0-385-23430-9 LC 86-8854

D

Dadswell, Mary, 1943-
Circles of faces; stories. University of Qld. Press 1987 200p
ISBN 0-7022-1969-X LC 86-19

Dance me outside.   Kinsella, W. P.
Dancing in the movies.   Boswell, R.
Dancing with my sister Jane.   Flook, M.

Daniels, Charlie, 1936-
The devil went down to Georgia; stories. Peachtree Pubs. 1985
247p il ISBN 0-931948-85-1 LC 85-62665

Dann, Jack
(ed) In the field of fire. *See* In the field of fire
(ed) Magicats! *See* Magicats!

Dann, Jeanne Van Buren
(ed) In the field of fire. *See* In the field of fire

Dark arrows; great stories of revenge; edited by Alberto Manguel.
Potter 1987 314p ISBN 0-517-56259-6 LC 86-3180

Dark banquet; a feast of twelve great ghost stories; edited by
Lincoln Child. St. Martin's Press 1985 255p ISBN
0-312-18233-3 LC 85-10891

Dark company; the ten greatest ghost stories; edited by Lincoln
Child. St. Martin's Press 1984 334p ISBN 0-312-18231-7
LC 83-13759

The **Dark** descent; edited by David G. Hartwell. Doherty Assocs.
1987 1011p ISBN 0-312-93035-6 LC 87-50476
A TOR Bk.

Dark gods.   Klein, T. E. D.
Dark secrets.   Ross, V.
Darkness.   Mukherjee, B.
Darkness at dawn.   Woolrich, C.

Datlow, Ellen

(ed) Omni book of science fiction 1-3. *See* Omni book of science fiction 1-3

(ed) The Year's best fantasy: first annual collection. *See* The Year's best fantasy: first annual collection

Daughter of Regals, and other tales. Donaldson, S. R.

Davenport, Guy

Apples and pears, and other stories; by Guy Davenport. North Point Press 1984 296p il ISBN 0-86547-162-2 LC 84-60685

The Jules Verne steam balloon; nine stories. North Point Press 1987 150p ISBN 0-86547-295-5 LC 87-06083

Davie, Elspeth

A traveller's room. Hamilton, H. 1985 185p ISBN 0-241-11439-X

Davin, Dan, 1913-

The salamander and the fire; collected war stories. Oxford Univ. Press 1986 212p ISBN 0-19-558147-4

Davis, Dorothy Salisbury, 1916-

Tales for a stormy night; the collected crime stories. Countryman Press 1984 237p ISBN 0-88150-030-5 LC 84-21425

A Foul Play Press Bk.

Davis, Lydia

Break it down; stories. Farrar, Straus & Giroux 1986 177p ISBN 0-374-11653-9 LC 86-7687

Partially analyzed

Davis, Sam, 1850-1918

A miner's Christmas carol, and other frontier tales. Western Tanager Press 1987 86p il ISBN 0-934136-38-6 LC 87-61271

Dawson, Fielding, 1930-

Will she understand?; new short stories; collages by the author. Black Sparrow Press 1988 154p il ISBN 0-87685-730-6 LC 88-2450

Day, Richard Cortez, 1927-

When in Florence. Doubleday 1986 200p ISBN 0-385-23157-1 LC 85-10171

The **day** nothing happened. Clarke, T.

Daylight and nightmare. Chesterton, G. K.

De Haven, Tom

Sunburn Lake. Viking 1988 293p ISBN 0-670-80930-6 LC 87-40456

The **Deadly** arts; edited by Bill Pronzini and Marcia Muller. Arbor House 1985 313p ISBN 0-87795-688-X LC 85-6235

The **dealers'** yard, and other stories. Stark, S. S.

Dealing in futures. Haldeman, J. W.

Death locked in; an anthology of locked room stories; edited by Douglas G. Greene and Robert C.S. Adey. International Polygonics 1987 553p ISBN 0-930330-75-7 LC 87-82449

Partially analyzed

Death of a lover, and other stories. Ebon, W.

The **death** of Methuselah, and other stories. Singer, I. B.

Death's midwives. Ekström, M.

Deaver, Philip F.

Silent retreats; stories. University of Ga. Press 1988 229p ISBN 0-8203-0981-8 LC 87-14313

Decarnin, Camilla

(ed) Worlds apart. *See* Worlds apart

The **decline** of Western Hill. Jackson, G.

DeGrazia, Emilio

Enemy country. New Rivers Press 1984 145p ISBN 0-89823-055-1 LC 84-060334

DeMarinis, Rick, 1934-

The coming triumph of the free world; stories. Viking 1988 177p ISBN 0-670-81982-4 LC 87-40519

DeMarinis, Rick, 1934——*Continued*
Under the wheat. University of Pittsburgh Press 1986 157p
  ISBN 0-8229-3544-9 LC 86-7007

Denneny, Michael
(ed) First love/last love. *See* First love/last love

Dennison, George, 1925-1987
A tale of Pierrot, and other stories. Harper & Row 1987
  287p ISBN 0-06-055079-1 LC 86-46056
The **devil** went down to Georgia. Daniels, C.
Devils & demons; a treasury of fiendish tales old & new; selected
  by Marvin Kaye with Saralee Kaye. Doubleday 1987 587p
  ISBN 0-385-18563-4 LC 87-6772
    Partially analyzed

Dick, Philip K.
I hope I shall arrive soon; edited by Mark Hurst and Paul
  Williams. Doubleday 1985 179p ISBN 0-385-19567-2
  LC 84-28660
Robots, androids, and mechanical oddities; the science fiction
  of Philip K. Dick; edited by Patricia S. Warrick and Martin
  H. Greenberg. Southern Ill. Univ. Press 1984 261p
  (Alternatives) ISBN 0-8093-1159-3 LC 83-19627

Dickens, Charles, 1812-1870
A Christmas carol, and other Christmas stories; illustrations
  by Arthur Rackham, Robert And Barbara Buchanan; afterword
  by A. Edward Newton. Reader's Digest Assn. 1988 287p
  il col il ISBN 0-89577-315-5 LC 88-61574
The signalman & other ghost stories. Academy Chicago 1988
  138p ISBN 0-89733-307-1 LC 87-33490

Dickinson, Charles, 1951-
With or without, and other stories. Knopf 1987 159p ISBN
  0-394-55492-2 LC 86-46151

Dickson, Gordon R.
Mindspan; edited and with introductions by Sandra Miesel.
  Baen Bks. 1986 276p ISBN 0-671-65580-9
Difficult loves. Calvino, I.

Digby, Joan
(ed) Inspired by drink. *See* Inspired by drink

Digby, John, 1938-
(ed.) Inspired by drink. *See* Inspired by drink
Digging up the mountains. Bissoondath, N.

Dilworth, Sharon
The long white. University of Iowa Press 1988 194p (Iowa
  short fiction award) ISBN 0-87745-216-4 LC 88-17307
Dislocations. Hospital, J. T.
Distant danger; the 1988 Mystery Writers of America anthology;
  edited by Janwillem van de Wetering. Wynwood Press 1988
  320p ISBN 0-8007-7201-6 LC 88-10709
A **distant** episode. Bowles, P.
Distant view of a minaret, and other stories. Rifaat, A.
Dividing lines. Sage, V.

Dixon, Stephen, 1936-
The play, and other stories. Coffee House Press 1988 160p
  ISBN 0-918273-45-5 LC 88-30153
Time to go. Johns Hopkins Univ. Press 1984 181p (Johns
  Hopkins: Poetry and fiction) ISBN 0-8018-3234-9
  LC 83-22624
The **doctor** stories. Williams, W. C.

Doctorow, E. L., 1931-
Lives of the poets; six stories and a novella. Random House
  1984 145p ISBN 0-394-52530-2 LC 84-42513

Dodd, Susan M., 1946-
Old wives' tales. University of Iowa Press 1984 181p (Iowa
School of Letters award for short fiction) ISBN 0-87745-132-X
LC 84-8879
The **dogeater.**   Kercheval, J. L.
Doing the voices.   Brooks, J.
Donaldson, Stephen R.
Daughter of Regals, and other tales. Ballantine Bks. 1984 337p
ISBN 0-345-31442-5 LC 83-9244
A Del Rey Bk.
Don't bet on the prince; contemporary feminist fairy tales in
North America and England; [ed. by] Jack Zipes. Methuen
1986 270p il ISBN 0-416-01371-6 LC 85-29794
Analyzed for short stories only
Dorr, Lawrence
A slight momentary affliction; stories. Louisiana State Univ.
Press 1987 136p ISBN 0-8071-1346-8 LC 86-34424
A **dot** on the map.   Faik, S.
Doubiago, Sharon
The book of seeing with one's own eyes; short stories. Graywolf
Press 1988 335p (Graywolf short fiction ser) ISBN
1-55597-101-6 LC 87-81373
A **double** life.   Alcott, L. M.
Douglas Reeman introduces Sea captains' tales. *See* Sea captains'
tales
Doyle, Sir Arthur Conan, 1859-1930
The adventures of Sherlock Holmes; illustrations by Richard
Lebenson; afterword by Fred Strebeigh. Reader's Digest Assn.
1987 270p ISBN 0-89577-277-9 LC 87-62240
The memoirs of Sherlock Holmes; illustrations by Sergio
Martinez; afterword by George Fletcher. Reader's Digest Assn.
1988 256p il ISBN 0-89577-320-1 LC 88-62131
Uncollected stories; the unknown Conan Doyle; compiled and
with an introduction by John Michael Gibson and Richard
Lancelyn Green. Doubleday 1984 c1982 xxiii,456p ISBN
0-385-19028-X
Dozois, Gardner R.
(ed) Magicats! *See* Magicats!
(ed) Ripper! *See* Ripper!
(ed) The Year's best science fiction, first-fifth annual collection.
See The Year's best science fiction, first -fifth annual collection
Dragons and dreams; a collection of new fantasy and science
fiction stories; edited by Jane Yolen, Martin H. Greenberg,
and Charles G. Waugh. Harper & Row 1986 180p ISBN
0-06-026792-5 LC 85-45384
Dragons of light; [ed. by] Orson Scott Card. Bart Bks. 1988
317p il ISBN 1-55785-037-2
Drake, Robert, 1930-
Survivors and others. Mercer Univ. Press 1987 188p ISBN
0-86554-253-8 LC 87-5644
Dream stud, and other stories.   Coriolan, J.
Dreams and swords.   Forrest, K. V.
Dreams of dark and light.   Lee, T.
Drew, Bernard A. (Bernard Alger), 1950-
(ed) Hard-boiled dames. *See* Hard-boiled dames
Drewe, Robert, 1943-
The bodysurfers. Faber & Faber 1984 165p ISBN 0-571-13389-4
LC 84-13528
The **drover's** wife, and other stories.   Bail, M.
Drunk with love.   Gilchrist, E.
Dubus, Andre, 1936-
The last worthless evening; four novellas & two stories. Godine
1986 214p ISBN 0-87923-642-6 LC 86-45530

Dubus, Andre, 1936— *Continued*
Selected stories. Godine 1988 476p ISBN 0-87923-736-8 LC 87-46297
We don't live here anymore; the novellas of Andre Dubus. Crown 1984 279p ISBN 0-517-55362-7 LC 83-26215
The **duel,** and other stories. Chekhov, A. P.
Duke, Michael S.
(ed) Contemporary Chinese literature. *See* Contemporary Chinese literature
Duke City tales. Willson, H.
Dumas, Henry, 1934-1968
Goodbye, sweetwater; new & selected stories; edited and with an introduction by Eugene B. Redmond. Thunder's Mouth Press [distrib. by Consortium Bk. Sales & Distr.] 1988 xx, 347p ISBN 0-938410-59-8 LC 87-29039
Dunlop, Lane
A Late chrysanthemum. *See* A Late chrysanthemum
Dunn, Douglas
Secret villages; stories. Dodd, Mead 1985 218p ISBN 0-396-08606-3 LC 84-21055
The **Dunwich** horror, and others. Lovecraft, H. P.
Durban, Pam
All set about with fever trees, and other stories. Godine 1985 211p ISBN 0-87923-569-1 LC 84-48749
Durrell, Lawrence
Antrobus complete; with drawings by Marc. Faber & Faber 1985 201p il ISBN 0-571-13602-8 LC 85-6995

E

Early sorrow: ten stories of youth; selected by Charlotte Zolotow. Harper & Row 1986 212p ISBN 0-06-026936-7 LC 79-2669
An Ursula Nordstrom Bk.
Early spring, mid-summer, and other Korean short stories; edited by the Korean National Commission for UNESCO. Si-sa-yong-o-sa; Pace Int. Res. 1983 191p (Modern Korean short stories, 10) ISBN 0-89209-211-4
Earth and elsewhere; [by] Kir Bulychev [et al.]; translated from the Russian by Roger DeGaris. Macmillan 1985 315p ISBN 0-02-518240-4 LC 85-18946
Earth power coming; short fiction in native American literature; edited by Simon J. Ortiz. Navajo Community College Press 1983 289p ISBN 0-912586-50-8 LC 83-060959
Partially analyzed
An **earthquake** in my family. Federspiel, J.
East, Charles
(ed) The New writers of the South. *See* The New writers of the South
East is west of here. Thompson, J.
Easy in the islands. Shacochis, B.
Ebon, William
Death of a lover, and other stories. Brunswick 1986 133p ISBN 0-931494-99-0
Echad 2: South African Jewish voices; general editors: Robert & Roberta Kalechofsky. Micah Publs. 1982 269p ISBN 0-916288-10-2 LC 81-83903
Analyzed for short stories only
Echad 4: Jewish writing from down under: Australia and New Zealand; general editors: Robert & Roberta Kalechofsky. Micah Publs. 1984 292p ISBN 0-916288-16-1 LC 84-1098
Analyzed for short stories only
The **edge** of the world. Anderman, J.
The **edge** of tomorrow. Asimov, I.

Editor's choice II; fiction, poetry & art from the U.S. small press; selections from nominations by the editors of independent, noncommercial presses and magazines, of work published by them from 1978 to 1983; edited by Morty Sklar & Mary Biggs. Spirit That Moves Us Press 1987 336p il (Contemporary anthology series, no6) ISBN 0-930370-23-6 LC 86-20352

   Analyzed for short stories only

The **Editors'** choice v1; new American stories; compiled by George E. Murphy, Jr. Bantam Bks. 1985 331p ISBN 0-553-34176-6 LC 84-24157

   A Bantam/Wampeter Press Bk.

The **Editors'** choice v2; new American stories; compiled by George E. Murphy, Jr. Bantam Bks. 1986 c1985 350p ISBN 0-553-34221-5 LC 84-24157

   A Bantam/Wampeter Press Bk.

The **Editors'** choice v3-4; compiled by George E. Murphy, Jr. Bantam Bks. 1986-1987 2v ISBN 0-553-05179-2 (v3); 0-553-34466-8 (v4) LC 84-24157

   A Bantam/Wampeter Press Bk.

Egyptian tales and short stories of the 1970s and 1980s; edited by William M. Hutchins. American Univ. in Cairo Press [distrib. by Columbia Univ. Press] 1987 188p ISBN 977-424-171-1

Eighner, Lars

   Bayou boy, and other stories. Gay Sunshine Press 1985 158p ISBN 0-917342-06-2

Eight men.   Wright, R.

Einstein's monsters.   Amis, M.

Eisen, Jonathan

   (ed) The Nobel reader. *See* The Nobel reader

Eisenberg, Deborah

   Transactions in a foreign currency; stories. Knopf 1986 213p ISBN 0-394-54598-2 LC 85-45591

Eisenstein, Sam

   The inner garden; stories. Sun & Moon Press 1987 248p ISBN 0-940650-71-1

Ekström, Margareta, 1930-

   Death's midwives; stories; translated from the Swedish by Eva Claeson; with a preface by Nadine Gordimer. Ontario Review Press 1985 149p (Ontario Review Press translation series) ISBN 0-86538-046-5 LC 85-18774

Eldridge, Marian, 1936-

   Walking the dog, and other stories. University of Qld. Press 1985 c1984 220p ISBN 0-7022-1784-0 LC 83-12884

Election Day 2084; a science fiction anthology on the politics of the future; edited by Isaac Asimov and Martin H. Greenberg. Prometheus Bks. 1984 301p ISBN 0-87975-258-0 LC 84-42794

Electric city, and other stories.   Grace, P.

The **elephant.**   Mrożek, S.

Eliade, Mircea, 1907-1986

   Youth without youth, and other novellas; edited and with an introduction by Matei Calinescu; translated by Mac Linscott Ricketts. Ohio State Univ. Press 1988 xxxix, 288p ISBN 0-8142-0457-0 LC 87-37576

   A Sandstone Bk.

The **Elizabeth** stories.   Huggan, I.

Ellery Queen's Crimes and punishments; stories collected from issues of Ellery Queen's Mystery Magazine, edited by Ellery Queen; edited by Eleanor Sullivan and Karen A. Prince. Dial Press; Davis Publs. 1984 288p ISBN 0-385-27997-3 LC 84-162319

Ellery Queen's Memorable characters; stories collected from issues of Ellery Queen's Mystery magazine, edited by Ellery Queen; edited by Eleanor Sullivan and Karen A. Prince. Dial Press; Davis Publs. 1984 287p ISBN 0-385-19645-8 LC 84-210462

Ellery Queen's mystery magazine
Tales from Ellery Queen's Mystery Magazine: short stories for young adults. *See* Tales from Ellery Queen's Mystery Magazine: short stories for young adults

Ellery Queen's Prime crimes; edited by Eleanor Sullivan. Dial Press 1984 c1983 287p il ISBN 0-385-27954-X LC 59-13341

Ellery Queen's Prime crimes 2; edited by Eleanor Sullivan and Karen A. Prince. Dial Press 1985 c1984 288p ISBN 0-385-19644-X LC 59-13341

Elliot, Jeffrey M.
(ed) Kindred spirits. *See* Kindred spirits

Ellison, Harlan
Angry candy. Houghton Mifflin 1988 xxiv, 324p il ISBN 0-395-48307-7 LC 88-12712

Ellison wonderland. Bluejay Bks. 1984 195p ISBN 0-312-94133-1 LC 84-12372

(ed) Medea: Harlan's world. *See* Medea: Harlan's world

Ellison wonderland. Ellison, H.

Eminent domain. O'Brien, D.

Emperor of the air. Canin, E.

Endō, Shūsaku, 1923-
Stained glass elegies; stories; translated by Van C. Gessel. Dodd, Mead 1985 165p ISBN 0-396-08643-8 LC 84-24639

Enemy country. DeGrazia, E.

Enfield, Alexander
(comp) Sea captains' tales. *See* Sea captains' tales

Engberg, Susan, 1940-
A stay by the river; stories. Viking 1985 247p ISBN 0-670-80620-X LC 85-5336

Epstein, Leslie
Goldkorn tales. Dutton 1985 244p LC 84-26029

Erotic interludes; tales told by women; edited by Lonnie Barbach. Doubleday 1986 278p ISBN 0-385-23319-1 LC 86-6232

Erotic tales. Moravia, A.

The **Esquire** fiction reader v1; edited by Rust Hills and Tom Jenks. Wampeter Press 1985 206p ISBN 0-931694-36-1 LC 85-50578

The **Esquire** fiction reader v2; edited by Rust Hills and Tom Jenks. Wampeter Press 1986 158p ISBN 0-931694-37-X LC 85-50578

Essop, Ahmed
Hajji Musa and the Hindu fire-walker. Readers Int. 1988 276p ISBN 0-930523-51-2 LC 88-61401

Estleman, Loren D.
General murders. Houghton Mifflin 1988 232p ISBN 0-395-41071-1 LC 88-1869
An Amos Walker Mystery

Etchison, Dennis, 1943-
(ed) Cutting edge. *See* Cutting edge
(ed) Masters of darkness. *See* Masters of darkness

Ethan Frome, and other short fiction. Wharton, E.

The **Ethnic** detectives; masterpieces of mystery fiction; edited by Bill Pronzini and Martin H. Greenberg. Dodd, Mead 1985 360p ISBN 0-396-08545-8 LC 84-24638

Evans, Elizabeth
Locomotion. New Rivers Press 1986 107p (Minnesota voices project, no23) ISBN 0-89823-071-3 LC 85-06849

Evans, Julian, 1955-
(ed) Foreign exchange. *See* Foreign exchange

Evans, Max

Xavier's folly, and other stories. University of N.M. Press 1984 105p ISBN 0-8263-0700-0 LC 83-25907

The **evening** news.   Ardizzone, T.

An **evening** performance.   Garrett, G. P.

Everett, Percival L.

The weather and women treat me fair; stories. August House 1987 115p ISBN 0-87483-013-3 LC 87-11424

Everybody loves you.   Mordden, E.

Everything is real.   Houbein, L.

Exiles at home: short stories.   Ch'en, Y.-C.

Extra(ordinary) people.   Russ, J.

Eye.   Herbert, F.

An **Eye** for justice; the third Private Eye Writers of America anthology; edited by Robert J. Randisi. Mysterious Press 1988 211p ISBN 0-89296-258-5 LC 88-4197

The **Eyes** have it; the first Private Eye Writers of America anthology; edited by Robert J. Randisi. Mysterious Press 1984 327p ISBN 0-89296-083-3 LC 83-63038

Eyestone.   MacDonald, D. R.

F

Fadiman, Clifton, 1904-

(ed) The World of the short story. *See* The World of the short story

Fahy, Christopher

One day in the short happy life of Anna Banana, and other Maine stories; selected by Mary McCarthy. Coastwise Press 1988 62p ISBN 0-9618592-0-2 LC 88-70852

Faik, Sait

A dot on the map; selected stories and poems; edited with an introduction by Talat Sait Halman; editorial assistance by Jayne L. Warner. Indiana Univ. Press 1984 307p il (Indiana University Turkish Studies, 4) LC 83-083161

Analyzed for short stories only

Fair Augusto, and other stories.   Kalpakian, L.

Falkiner, Suzanne, 1952-

(ed) Room to move. *See* Room to move

Family attractions.   Freeman, J.

Family dancing.   Leavitt, D.

Family: stories from the interior; edited by Geri Giebel Chavis. Graywolf Press 1987 328p ISBN 0-915308-93-2 LC 87-80014

A **fanatic** heart.   O'Brien, E.

Fancy goods [and] Open all night.   Morand, P.

Fantastic stories; tales of the weird & wondrous; [ed. by Martin H. Greenberg, Patrick L. Price]; cover artwork, Janet Aulisio; interior artwork, Janet Aulisio [et al.]. TSR 1987 253p il ISBN 0-88038-521-9 LC 87-50406

Fante, John, 1909-1983

The wine of youth; selected stories. Black Sparrow Press 1985 266p ISBN 0-87685-583-4 LC 84-20454

Farmer, Beverley, 1941-

Milk; stories. Gribble; Penguin Bks. 1985 c1983 178p ISBN 0-14-007184-9

Farmer, Philip José

The classic Philip José Farmer, 1952-1964—1964-1973; edited and introduction by Martin H. Greenberg; foreword by Isaac Asimov. Crown 1984 2v (Classics of modern science fiction) ISBN 0-517-55193-4 (1952-1964); 0-517-55545-X (1964-1973)

Fast lanes.   Phillips, J. A.

Fatal recurrences; new fiction in English from Montréal; Hugh Hood, Peter O'Brien, editors. Véhicule Press 1984 134p ISBN 0-919890-65-2

    A Rubicon Ed.

Faust, Irvin, 1924-

The year of the hot jock, and other stories. Dutton 1985 220p ISBN 0-525-24343-7 LC 85-4422

    A William Abrahams Bk.

Federspiel, Jürg, 1931-

An earthquake in my family; stories; translated by Eveline L. Kanes. Dutton 1986 249p ISBN 0-525-24379-8 LC 85-25358

Feeding the eagles. Alden, P. B.

The **Fencepost** chronicles. Kinsella, W. P.

Feng Jicai

Chrysanthemums, and other stories; translated from the Chinese and with an introduction by Susan Wilf Chen. Harcourt Brace Jovanovich 1985 255p ISBN 0-15-117878-X LC 85-925

Ferguson, Patricia

Indefinite nights, and other stories. Deutsch 1987 159p ISBN 0-233-98103-9

Ferguson, William, 1943-

Freedom, and other fictions. Knopf 1984 93p ISBN 0-394-53391-7 LC 83-48852

Ferman, Edward L.

(ed) The Best horror stories from the Magazine of fantasy and science fiction. *See* The Best horror stories from the Magazine of fantasy and science fiction

Ferreira, Ramón

The gravedigger, and other stories. Waterfront Press 1986 xx,215p ISBN 0-943862-29-9

Ferron, Jacques

Selected tales of Jacques Ferron; translated by Betty Bednarski. Anansi 1984 245p ISBN 0-88784-140-6

Fetching the dead. Sanders, S. R.

The **fetishist**. Tournier, M.

The **fiancée**, and other stories. Chekhov, A. P.

The **fields** of memory. Osborn, C.

Fifty years of eternal vigilance, and other stories. Thorman, C.

The **figure** in the carpet, and other stories. James, H.

Filthy the man. Flaherty, G.

Final things. Sligo, J.

Finger, Anne

Basic skills; stories. University of Mo. Press 1988 117p (AWP, 9) ISBN 0-8262-0657-3 LC 87-25520

Fink, Ida

A scrap of time, and other stories; translated from the Polish by Madeline Levine and Francine Prose. Pantheon Bks. 1987 165p ISBN 0-394-55806-5 LC 86-42982

    Analyzed for short stories only

Finke, Wayne

(ed) Anthology of contemporary Latin American literature, 1960-1984. *See* Anthology of contemporary Latin American literature, 1960-1984

Finney, Ernest J.

Birds landing. University of Ill. Press 1986 137p (Illinois short fiction) ISBN 0-252-01311-5 LC 85-31808

Finney, Jack

About time; twelve stories. Simon & Schuster 1986 219p ISBN 0-671-62887-9 LC 86-10077

    A Fireside Bk.

Fire watch. Willis, C.

First fictions: Introduction 9. Faber & Faber 1986 255p ISBN 0-571-13607-9 LC 86-11524
   Previous volumes published with title Introduction; stories by new writers
First love/last love; new fiction from Christopher Street; edited by Michael Denneny, Charles Ortleb, and Thomas Steele. Putnam 1985 288p ISBN 0-399-13082-9 LC 85-9311
The first Rumpole omnibus. Mortimer, J. C.
The first thing coming. Abbott, K.
Fisher, M. F. K. (Mary Frances Kennedy), 1908-
   Sister age. Knopf 1983 243p ISBN 0-394-53066-7 LC 82-48880
Fisher, Rudolph, 1897-1934
   The city of refuge; the collected stories of Rudolph Fisher; edited with an introduction by John McCluskey, Jr. University of Mo. Press 1987 xxxix,196p ISBN 0-8262-0630-1 LC 86-19314
   The short fiction of Rudolph Fisher; edited and introduced by Margaret Perry. Greenwood Press 1987 228p (Contributions in Afro-American and African studies, no107) ISBN 0-313-21348-8 LC 86-29580
Fitzgerald, M. J.
   Rope-dancer. Random House 1987 c1985 158p ISBN 0-394-55921-5 LC 86-26159
Five stories. Watson, S.
Five thousand runaways. Kaikō, T.
Flaherty, Gerald
   Filthy the man; stories. University of Mo. Press 1985 105p (Breakthrough book, no46) ISBN 0-8262-0463-5 LC 84-21893
Flanagan, Mary
   Bad girls. Atheneum Pubs. 1985 237p ISBN 0-689-11593-8 LC 84-24493
Flanagan, Robert
   Naked to naked goes; stories. Scribner 1986 192p ISBN 0-684-18671-3 LC 85-27891
Fleming, Berry, 1899-1989
   The bookman's tale, and others. Cotton Lane Press 1986 221p ISBN 0-9604810-7-9 LC 85-29135
Floating. Thurm, M.
The flood of '64. Long, D.
Flook, Maria
   Dancing with my sister Jane; stories. Ampersand Press 1987 81p ISBN 0-935331-02-6 LC 86-72907
Floral Street. Burt, S.
Flowers of fire; twentieth-century Korean stories; edited by Peter H. Lee. rev ed. University of Hawaii Press 1986 378p ISBN 0-8248-1036-8 LC 85-20968
Floyd, Patty Lou
   The silver DeSoto. Council Oak Bks. [distrib. by Texas Monthly Press] 1987 257p ISBN 0-933031-03-3 LC 86-072491
Flynn, Robert, 1932-
   Seasonal rain, and other stories. Corona 1986 175p ISBN 0-931722-57-8 LC 86-70716
Fools, and other stories. Ndebele, N.
Ford, Richard, 1944-
   Rock Springs; stories. Atlantic Monthly Press 1987 235p ISBN 0-87113-159-5 LC 87-11564
Foreign exchange; edited by Julian Evans. Hamilton, H. 1985 215p ISBN 0-241-11488-8
The foreign legion. Lispector, C.
Forkner, Ben
   (ed) A Modern Southern reader. See A Modern Southern reader
   (ed) Stories of the modern South. See Stories of the modern South

Forrest, Katherine V., 1939-
Dreams and swords. Naiad Press 1987 175p ISBN 0-941483-03-7 LC 87-22447

Forty stories.   Barthelme, D.

Fraknoi, Andrew
(ed) The Universe. *See* The Universe

Franklin, Patrick, 1937-
The uncertainty of strangers, and other stories. Grey Fox Press 1985 141p ISBN 0-912516-91-7 LC 85-7653

Franzen, Bill, 1952-
Hearing from Wayne, and other stories. Knopf 1988 127p ISBN 0-394-55501-5 LC 87-45260

Fraser, Antonia, 1932-
Jemima Shore's first case, and other stories. Norton 1987 c1986 186p ISBN 0-393-02453-9 LC 87-5743

Frazee, Steve, 1909-
The best western stories of Steve Frazee; edited by Bill Pronzini and Martin H. Greenberg; introduction by Bill Pronzini. Southern Ill. Univ. Press 1984 276p (The Western writers ser) ISBN 0-8093-1175-7 LC 83-18052

Free agents.   Apple, M.

Freedom, and other fictions.   Ferguson, W.

Freeman, Castle, 1944-
The bride of Ambrose, and other stories. Soho Press 1987 211p ISBN 0-939149-01-X LC 86-31522

Freeman, Judith, 1946-
Family attractions; stories. Viking 1988 227p ISBN 0-670-82108-X LC 87-40297

Fremlin, Celia
A lovely day to die, and other stories. Doubleday 1984 190p ISBN 0-385-19421-8 LC 84-1651
"Published for the Crime Club"

Friedman, Bruce Jay, 1930-
Let's hear it for a beautiful guy, and other works of short fiction. Fine, D.I. 1984 252p ISBN 0-917657-00-4 LC 84-080787
Analyzed for short stories only

Friedman, Paul, 1937-
Serious trouble. University of Ill. Press 1986 155p (Illinois short fiction) ISBN 0-252-01310-7 LC 85-28843

From mind to mind: tales of communication from Analog; edited by Stanley Schmidt. Davis Publs. 1984 288p ISBN 0-385-19646-6 LC 84-231682
"Anthology 9"

Frucht, Abby
Fruit of the month. University of Iowa Press 1988 167p (Iowa short fiction award) ISBN 0-87745-175-3 LC 87-28405

Fruit of the month.   Frucht, A.

Frye Street & environs.   Bonner, M.

Full measure; modern short stories on aging; edited by Dorothy Sennett; foreword by Carol Bly. Graywolf Press 1988 xxiii, 399p (Graywolf short fiction ser) ISBN 1-55597-105-9 LC 87-83080

The **further** adventures of Slugger McBatt.   Kinsella, W. P.

G

Gabe's fall, and other climbing stories.   Sandberg, P. L.

Gaitskill, Mary, 1954-
Bad behavior. Poseidon Press 1988 203p ISBN 0-671-65871-9 LC 87-38500

Gallacher, Tom
Apprentice. Hamilton, H. [distrib. by David & Charles] 1983 156p ISBN 0-241-10997-3 LC 84-171054

Gallagher, Tess
The lover of horses, and other stories. Harper & Row 1986 184p ISBN 0-06-015627-9 LC 86-45101

Gallant, Mavis
Home truths; sixteen stories. Random House 1985 c1981 330p ISBN 0-394-53198-1 LC 84-45757
Overhead in a balloon; twelve stories of Paris. Random House 1987 c1985 196p ISBN 0-394-54511-7 LC 86-20329

Garber, Eric
(ed) Worlds apart. *See* Worlds apart

García Márquez, Gabriel, 1928-
Collected stories. Harper & Row 1984 311p ISBN 0-06-015364-4 LC 84-47826

The **garden-party.**   Mansfield, K.
The **Garden** State.   Krist, G.

Gardner, Martin, 1914-
The no-sided professor, and other tales of fantasy, humor, mystery, and philosophy. Prometheus Bks. 1987 224p ISBN 0-87975-390-0 LC 86-30487

Garfield, Brian Wynne, 1939-
(ed) The Crime of my life. *See* The Crime of my life

Garfield, Evelyn Picon
(ed.) Women's fiction from Latin America. *See* Women's fiction from Latin America

Garrett, George P., 1929-
An evening performance; [by] George Garrett. Doubleday 1985 518p ISBN 0-385-19094-8 LC 85-1504

Gathorne-Hardy, Jonathan
The centre of the universe is 18 Baedekerstrasse. Hamilton, H. [distrib. by David & Charles] 1985 199p ISBN 0-241-11492-6

Gault, Connie
Some of Eve's daughters. Coteau Bks. 1987 98p ISBN 0-919926-62-2

Gee, Maurice
Collected stories. Penguin Bks. 1986 226p ISBN 0-14-008804-0
General murders.   Estleman, L. D.

Geras, Adèle
Snapshots of paradise. Atheneum Pubs. 1984 168p ISBN 0-689-31045-5 LC 84-2934

Gerber, Merrill Joan
Honeymoon; stories. University of Ill. Press 1985 126p (Illinois short fiction) ISBN 0-252-01205-4 LC 84-28023

German romantic novellas; [by] Heinrich von Kleist and Jean Paul; edited by Frank G. Ryder and Robert M. Browning; foreword by John Simon. Continuum 1985 xxiv,252p (German library, v34) ISBN 0-8264-0294-1 LC 85-5762

German romantic stories; edited by Frank G. Ryder; introduction by Gordon Birrell. Continuum 1988 267p (German library, v35) ISBN 0-8264-0312-3 LC 88-6991

German stories; a bilingual anthology; translated and edited by Harry Steinhauer. University of Calif. Press 1984 451p il ISBN 0-520-05049-5 LC 83-24306
Partially analyzed

Gessel, Van C.
(ed) The Shōwa anthology. *See* The Shōwa anthology
Getting to know the weather.   Painter, P.
The **ghost** of Sandburg's phizzog, and other stories.   Blei, N.
Ghostly populations.   Matthews, J.

Gifkins, Michael

Summer is the Côte d'Azur. Penguin Bks. 1987 151p ISBN 0-14-009732-5

The **gift** of the Magi, and other stories.   Henry, O.

Gilbert, Michael, 1912-

Young Petrella. Harper & Row 1988 222p ISBN 0-06-015934-0

Gilbert, R. A.

(ed) The Oxford book of English ghost stories. *See* The Oxford book of English ghost stories

Gilbert, W. S. (William Schwenck), 1836-1911

The lost stories of W. S. Gilbert; illustrated by 'Bab'; selected and introduced by Peter Haining. Parkwest Publs. 1985 c1982 255p il ISBN 0-88186-725-X LC 83-61272

Gilchrist, Ellen, 1935-

Drunk with love; a book of stories. Little, Brown 1986 239p ISBN 0-316-31311-4 LC 86-10272

Victory over Japan; a book of stories. Little, Brown 1984 277p ISBN 0-316-31303-3 LC 84-11307

Gilchrist, Murray, 1868-1917

The stone dragon, and other tragic romances. Garland 1984 208p ISBN 0-8240-5554-3 LC 82-49096

Giles, Molly

Rough translations; stories. University of Ga. Press 1985 135p ISBN 0-8203-0744-0 LC 84-16363

Gilliatt, Penelope

22 stories. Dodd, Mead 1986 319p ISBN 0-396-08491-5 LC 86-6307

They sleep without dreaming; stories. Dodd, Mead 1985 175p ISBN 0-396-08493-1 LC 85-7078

Analyzed for short stories only

Gingher, Marianne

Teen angel, and other stories of young love. Atheneum Pubs. 1988 209p ISBN 0-689-11967-4 LC 88-1368

Girion, Barbara, 1937-

A very brief season. Scribner 1984 150p ISBN 0-684-18088-X LC 84-1217

The **girl** from Cardigan.   Norris, L.

Girl in a turban.   Morazzoni, M.

The **girl** who would be Russian, and other stories.   Johnson, W.

Givner, Joan, 1936-

Tentacles of unreason; stories. University of Ill. Press 1985 134p (Illinois short fiction) ISBN 0-252-01203-8 LC 84-24154

The **glad** eye, and other stories.   Barstow, S.

Glasser, Perry

Singing on the Titanic; stories. University of Ill. Press 1987 122p (Illinois short fiction) ISBN 0-252-01427-8 LC 87-1654

Glassgold, Peter, 1939-

(ed) New directions in prose and poetry 48-52. *See* New directions in prose and poetry 48-52

A **glimpse** of Sion's glory.   Colegate, I.

Glynn, Thomas, 1935-

(ed) American made. *See* American made

Godwin, Gail

(comp) The Best American short stories, 1985. *See* The Best American short stories, 1985

Gogol', Nikolaï Vasil'evich, 1809-1852

The complete tales of Nikolaï Gogol'; edited, with an introduction and notes, by Leonard J. Kent. The Constance Garnett translation has been revised throughout by the editor. University of Chicago Press 1985 2v ISBN 0-226-30068-4 (v1); 0-226-30069-2 (v2) LC 84-16221

Going to see the leaves.   Collins, L.

Going to the mountain. Wiebe, D. E.

Gold, Herbert, 1924-
Lovers & cohorts; twenty-seven stories. Fine, D.I. 1986 331p
ISBN 0-917657-75-6 LC 85-82496

Golden twigs. Crowley, A.

Goldkorn tales. Epstein, L.

A **Good** deal; selected short stories from the Massachusetts review;
edited by Mary Heath & Fred Miller Robinson. University
of Mass. Press 1988 333p ISBN 0-87023-639-3 LC 88-4734

Good rockin' tonight. Hauptman, W.

Goodbye Harold, good luck. Thomas, A. C.

Goodbye, sweetwater. Dumas, H.

Gordimer, Nadine, 1923-
Six feet of the country. Penguin Bks. 1986 c1983 100p ISBN
0-14-006559-8
Something out there; stories. Viking 1984 203p ISBN
0-670-65660-7 LC 83-40250

Gordon, Mary, 1949-
Temporary shelter; short stories. Random House 1987 213p
ISBN 0-394-55520-1 LC 86-31627

Gorky, Maksim, 1868-1936
The collected short stories of Maxim Gorky; edited by Avrahm
Yarmolinsky and Baroness Moura Budberg. Citadel Press
1988 403p ISBN 0-8065-1075-7

Gorman, Edward
(ed) The Black Lizard anthology of crime fiction. *See* The
Black Lizard anthology of crime fiction
(ed) Westeryear. *See* Westeryear

Goscilo, Helena
(ed) Russian and Polish women's fiction. *See* Russian and
Polish women's fiction

Gotthelf, Jeremias, 1797-1854
Tales of courtship; translated and with an introduction by
Robert Godwin-Jones. Lang, P. 1984 235p (American
university studies, Series I, Germanic languages and literature,
v35) ISBN 0-8204-0177-3 LC 84-48102

The **gourmet,** and other stories of modern China. Lu Wenfu

Goyen, William
Had I a hundred mouths; new & selected stories, 1947-1983;
introduction by Joyce Carol Oates. Potter 1985 275p ISBN
0-517-55764-9 LC 85-493
Analyzed for short stories only

Grace, Patricia, 1937-
Electric city, and other stories. Penguin Bks. 1987 97p ISBN
0-14-010151-9 LC 039741

Grady, Wayne
(ed) Intimate strangers. *See* Intimate strangers

A **Grand** Street reader; edited by Ben Sonnenberg; with an
introduction by Murray Kempton. Summit Bks. 1986 422p
ISBN 0-671-60623-9 LC 86-5687
Analyzed for short stories only

Grandsaigne, Jean de
(ed) African short stories in English. *See* African short stories
in English

Granit, Arthur
I am from Brownsville; illustrated by Gerald Hahn. Philosophical
Lib. 1985 270p il ISBN 0-8022-2456-3 LC 84-1789

Grant, Charles L.
(ed) After midnight. *See* After midnight
(ed) The Best of Shadows. *See* The Best of Shadows
(ed) Midnight. *See* Midnight
(ed) Shadows 7. *See* Shadows 7
(ed) Shadows 8-9. *See* Shadows 8-9

Grau, Shirley Ann, 1929-
  Nine women; short stories. Knopf 1986 c1985 204p ISBN
    0-394-54845-0 LC 85-40340
Grave suspicions, Alfred Hitchcock's. *See* Alfred Hitchcock's Grave
  suspicions
The **gravedigger,** and other stories.   Ferreira, R.
Graveyard plots.   Pronzini, B.
Gray, Alasdair
  Unlikely stories, mostly. Penguin Bks. 1984 c1983 271p il
    ISBN 0-14-006925-9
Gray, Stephen, 1941-
  (ed) The Penguin book of Southern African stories. *See* The
    Penguin book of Southern African stories
The **Graywolf** annual [1]: short stories; edited by Scott Walker.
    Graywolf Press 1985 175p ISSN 0743-7471
The **Graywolf** annual 2: short stories by women; edited by Scott
    Walker. Graywolf Press 1986 176p ISSN 0743-7471
The **Graywolf** annual 4: short stories by men; edited by Scott
    Walker. Graywolf Press 1988 226p ISSN 0743-7471 LC 55-175
Greasy Lake & other stories.   Boyle, T. C.
Great American love stories; selected and with an introduction
    by Lucy Rosenthal. Little, Brown 1988 671p ISBN
    0-316-75734-9 LC 88-586
Great detectives; a century of the best mysteries from England
    and America; edited by David Willis McCullough. Pantheon
    Bks. 1984 728p ISBN 0-394-54065-4 LC 84-42707
      Analyzed for short stories only
Great French detective stories; edited by T.J. Hale. Vanguard
    Press 1984 c1983 284p ISBN 0-8149-0892-6 LC 84-13062
Great ghost stories; selected by Betty Ann Schwartz; illustrated
    by Paul Geiger; cover art by James Warhola. Messner 1985
    177p il ISBN 0-671-60622-0 LC 85-8271
Great modern police stories; edited by Bill Pronzini and Martin
    H. Greenberg. Walker & Co. 1986 223p ISBN 0-8027-0881-1
    LC 85-29605
The **Great** Profundo, and other stories.   MacLaverty, B.
Great science fiction; stories by the world's great scientists; edited
    by Isaac Asimov, Martin H. Greenberg, and Charles G.
    Waugh. Fine, D.I. 1985 400p ISBN 0-917657-26-8
    LC 84-073519
Great wits.   Mattison, A.
The **Greek** generals talk.   Parotti, P.
Greenberg, Alvin
  The man in the cardboard mask; short stories. Coffee House
    Press 1985 114p ISBN 0-918273-02-1 LC 84-15533
Greenberg, Martin Harry
  (ed) 100 great fantasy short short stories. *See* 100 great fantasy
    short short stories
  (ed) Alternative histories. *See* Alternative histories
  (ed) Amazing science fiction anthology: The war years,
    1936-1945. *See* Amazing science fiction anthology: The war
    years, 1936-1945
  (ed) Amazing science fiction anthology: The wild years,
    1946-1955. *See* Amazing science fiction anthology: The wild
    years, 1946-1955
  (ed) Amazing stories: 60 years of the best science fiction.
    See Amazing stories: 60 years of the best science fiction
  (ed) Amazing stories: visions of other worlds. *See* Amazing
    stories: visions of other worlds
  (ed) Baker's dozen: 13 short espionage novels. *See* Baker's
    dozen: 13 short espionage novels
  (ed) Baker's dozen: 13 short fantasy novels. *See* Baker's dozen:
    13 short fantasy novels

Greenberg, Martin Harry—*Continued*

(ed) Baker's dozen: 13 short science fiction novels. *See* Baker's dozen: 13 short science fiction novels

(ed) The Best Maine stories. *See* The Best Maine stories

(ed) Beyond Armageddon. *See* Beyond Armageddon

(ed) Civil War women. *See* Civil War women

(ed) Dragons and dreams. *See* Dragons and dreams

(ed) Election Day 2084. *See* Election Day 2084

(ed) The Ethnic detectives. *See* The Ethnic detectives

(ed) Fantastic stories. *See* Fantastic stories

(ed) Great modern police stories. *See* Great modern police stories

(ed) Great science fiction. *See* Great science fiction

(ed) Haunted New England. *See* Haunted New England

(ed) Hitchcock in prime time. *See* Hitchcock in prime time

(ed) Hitler victorious. *See* Hitler victorious

(ed) Hound dunnit. *See* Hound dunnit

(ed) Intergalactic empires. *See* Intergalactic empires

(ed) Isaac Asimov presents the best crime stories of the 19th century. *See* Isaac Asimov presents the best crime stories of the 19th century

(ed) Isaac Asimov presents the best science fiction firsts. *See* Isaac Asimov presents the best science fiction firsts

(ed) Machines that think. *See* Machines that think

(ed) The Mammoth book of classic science fiction. *See* The Mammoth book of classic science fiction

(ed) The Mammoth book of private eye stories. *See* The Mammoth book of private eye stories

(ed) Manhattan mysteries. *See* Manhattan mysteries

(ed) Masterpieces of mystery and suspense. *See* Masterpieces of mystery and suspense

(ed) Mississippi River tales. *See* Mississippi River tales

(ed) Murder and mystery in Boston. *See* Murder and mystery in Boston

(ed) Murder and mystery in Chicago. *See* Murder and mystery in Chicago

(ed) Murder in Japan. *See* Murder in Japan

(ed) Mystery in the mainstream. *See* Mystery in the mainstream

(ed) The New adventures of Sherlock Holmes. *See* The New adventures of Sherlock Holmes

(ed) Nightmares in Dixie. *See* Nightmares in Dixie

(ed) Robert Adams' Book of soldiers. *See* Robert Adams' Book of soldiers

(ed) Rod Serling's Night gallery reader. *See* Rod Serling's Night gallery reader

(ed) The Science fictional Olympics. *See* The Science fictional Olympics

(ed) The Second reel West. *See* The Second reel West

(ed) Sherlock Holmes through time and space. *See* Sherlock Holmes through time and space

(ed) Space wars. *See* Space wars

(ed) Time wars. *See* Time wars

(ed) A Treasury of Civil War stories. *See* A Treasury of Civil War stories

(ed) A Treasury of World War II stories. *See* A Treasury of World War II stories

(ed) Uncollected crimes. *See* Uncollected crimes

(ed) Werewolves. *See* Werewolves

(ed) The Western hall of fame. *See* The Western hall of fame

(ed) Witches. *See* Witches

(ed) Wizards. *See* Wizards

(ed) Women sleuths. *See* Women sleuths

(ed) Yankee witches. *See* Yankee witches

Greenberg, Martin Harry—*Continued*
(ed) Young extraterrestrials. *See* Young extraterrestrials
(ed) Young ghosts. *See* Young ghosts
(ed) Young monsters. *See* Young monsters
(ed) Young mutants. *See* Young mutants
(ed) Young witches & warlocks. *See* Young witches & warlocks
Greene, Douglas G.
(ed) Death locked in. *See* Death locked in
Greene, Graham, 1904-
Collected short stories. Penguin Bks. 1987 1986 367p ISBN 0-14-008070-8
Greening wheat: fifteen Mormon short stories; edited by Levi S. Peterson. Orion 1983 204p ISBN 0-941214-12-5 LC 84-117138
Greenland, Colin, 1954-
(ed) Interzone: the first anthology. *See* Interzone: the first anthology
Greenwood, Robert
Arcadia, and other stories. Talisman Literary Res. 1985 270p ISBN 0-934614-08-3 LC 85-51263
Grenville, Kate, 1950-
Bearded ladies; stories. University of Qld. Press 1984 168p ISBN 0-7022-1715-8 LC 83-26051
Grey, Zane, 1872-1939
The wolf tracker, and other animal tales; edited by Loren Grey. Santa Barbara Press 1984 164p il ISBN 0-915643-01-4 LC 84-50123
Analyzed for short stories only
Grin, A. (Aleksandr), 1880-1932
Selected short stories; translated by Nicholas Luker. Ardis Pubs. 1987 182p ISBN 0-88233-684-3 LC 85-18706
Grzimek, Martin, 1950-
Heartstop; three stories; translated by Breon Mitchell. New Directions 1984 184p ISBN 0-8112-0921-0 LC 84-11546
Guardian angel, and other stories. Latimer, M.
Gustafsson, Lars, 1936-
Stories of happy people; translated from the Swedish by Yvonne L. Sandstroem and John Weinstock. New Directions 1986 134p ISBN 0-8112-0977-6 LC 85-31052
Gutkind, Lee
(ed) Our roots grow deeper than we know. *See* Our roots grow deeper than we know

H

Haake, Katharine
No reason on earth; a short story collection. Dragon Gate 1986 187p ISBN 0-937872-32-6 LC 86-2004
Haas, Barbara
When California was an island; stories. Story Line Press 1987 142p ISBN 0-934257-11-6
Had I a hundred mouths. Goyen, W.
Hagy, Alyson Carol
Madonna on her back; stories; drawings by Lisa Wilkinson. Wright, S. 1986 118p ISBN 0-913773-19-0 LC 86-50089
Hajji Musa and the Hindu fire-walker. Essop, A.
Haldeman, Joe W.
Dealing in futures; stories. Viking 1985 277p ISBN 0-670-80635-8 LC 85-3359
Analyzed for short stories only
Hale, Hilary
(ed) Winter's crimes 16. *See* Winter's crimes 16
(ed) Winter's crimes 18. *See* Winter's crimes 18

Hale, T. J.
(ed) Great French detective stories. *See* Great French detective stories

Haley, Russell, 1934-
Real illusions; a selection of family lies and biographical fictions in which the ancestral dead also play their part. New Directions 1985 c1984 124p ISBN 0-8112-0928-8 LC 84-14866

Hall, Martha Lacy, 1923-
Music lesson; stories. University of Ill. Press 1984 125p ISBN 0-252-01129-5 LC 83-24151

Hall, Richard Walter
Letter from a great-uncle & other stories. Grey Fox Press 1985 163p ISBN 0-912516-88-7 LC 84-15798

Hall, Tom T.
The acts of life; tales. University of Ark. Press 1986 118p ISBN 0-938626-70-1 LC 86-6998

Halligan, Marion, 1940-
The living hothouse. University of Qld. Press 1988 283p ISBN 0-7022-2140-6 LC 88-17255

Halloween horrors; edited by Alan Ryan. Doubleday 1986 178p ISBN 0-385-19558-3 LC 86-4460

Halpern, Daniel, 1945-
(ed) The Art of the tale. *See* The Art of the tale

Hancock, Geoff
(ed) Invisible fictions. *See* Invisible fictions

Handke, Peter, 1942-
Slow homecoming; translated by Ralph Manheim. Farrar, Straus & Giroux 1985 278p ISBN 0-374-26635-2 LC 84-28597

Handle with care; frightening stories; chosen by Joan Kahn. Greenwillow Bks. 1985 209p ISBN 0-688-04663-0 LC 85-2764

Hankla, Cathryn, 1958-
Learning the mother tongue; stories. University of Mo. Press 1987 84p (Breakthrough book, no53) ISBN 0-8262-0622-0 LC 86-16123

Hannah, Barry
Captain Maximus; stories. Knopf 1985 101p ISBN 0-394-54458-7 LC 84-48738

Hansen, Joseph
Bohannon's book; five mysteries. Countryman Press 1988 221p ISBN 0-88150-103-4 LC 87-32946
A Foul Play Press Bk.

Brandstetter & others; five fictions. Countryman Press 1984 235p ISBN 0-88150-031-3 LC 84-23217
A Foul Play Press Bk.

Hard-boiled dames; stories featuring women detectives, reporters, adventurers, and criminals from the pulp fiction magazines of the 1930s; edited and with an introduction by Bernard A. Drew; preface by Marcia Muller. St. Martin's Press 1986 331p il ISBN 0-312-36188-2 LC 86-3671

Hard to be good. Barich, B.

Hardinge, George, 1921-
(ed) The Mammoth book of modern crime stories. *See* The Mammoth book of modern crime stories
(ed) Winter's crimes 17. *See* Winter's crimes 17

Haris, Petros, 1902-
The longest night; chronicle of a dead city; translated from the original Greek by Theodore Sampson. Nostos Bks. 1985 128p ISBN 0-932963-02-1 LC 85-60641

Harmony of the world. Baxter, C.

Harper, Elizabeth, 1934-
(ed) New directions in prose and poetry 48. *See* New directions in prose and poetry 48

Harper, Elizabeth, 1934——*Continued*
(ed) New directions in prose and poetry 49. *See* New directions in prose and poetry 49

Harris, Herbert
(ed) John Creasey's Crime collection, 1984-1987. *See* John Creasey's Crime collection, 1984-1987

Harris, MacDonald, 1921-
The Cathay stories and other fictions. Story Line Press 1988 189p ISBN 0-934257-14-0 LC 88-60346

Harrison, M. John (Michael John), 1945-
The ice monkey, and other stories. Gollancz 1983 144p ISBN 0-575-03259-6 LC 83-169352

Hartley, L. P. (Leslie Poles), 1895-1972
The complete short stories of L. P. Hartley; with an introduction by Lord David Cecil. Beaufort Bks. 1986 760p ISBN 0-8253-0353-2 LC 86-1019

Hartwell, David G.
(ed) Christmas ghosts. *See* Christmas ghosts
(ed) The Dark descent. *See* The Dark descent
(ed) Masterpieces of fantasy and enchantment. *See* Masterpieces of fantasy and enchantment

Harum scarum. Abbott, K.

Harvor, Elisabeth
If only we could drive like this forever. Penguin Bks. 1988 234p (Penguin short fiction) ISBN 0-14-010383-X

The **hat** of my mother. Steele, M.

Haunted New England; classic tales of the strange and supernatural; edited by Charles G. Waugh, Martin H. Greenberg & Frank D. McSherry, Jr.; foreword by Rick Hautala; illustrated by Peter Farrow. Yankee Bks. 1988 287p il ISBN 0-89909-156-3 LC 88-17097

Haunted women; the best supernatural tales by American women writers; edited by Alfred Bendixen. Ungar 1985 276p ISBN 0-8044-2052-1 LC 84-24018

Haunting women; edited by Alan Ryan. Avon Bks. 1988 210p ISBN 0-380-89881-0 LC 88-91528

Hauptman, William, 1942-
Good rockin' tonight; a collection of short stories. Bantam Bks. 1988 184p ISBN 0-553-34557-5 LC 88-47510

Havazelet, Ehud
What is it then between us?; stories. Scribner 1988 177p ISBN 0-684-18919-4 LC 87-28897

Havemann, Ernst
Bloodsong, and other stories of South Africa. Houghton Mifflin 1987 134p ISBN 0-395-43296-0 LC 86-27342
A Richard Todd Bk.

Hawthorne, Nathaniel, 1804-1864
Nathaniel Hawthorne's tales; authoritative texts, backgrounds, criticism; selected and edited by James McIntosh. Norton 1987 463p ISBN 0-393-02428-8 LC 85-29757

He rau aroha. Taylor, A.

Hear the silence; stories by women of myth, magic & renewal; edited by Irene Zahava. Crossing Press 1986 194p ISBN 0-89594-212-7 LC 86-18901

Hearing from Wayne, and other stories. Franzen, B.

Heart songs, and other stories. Proulx, A.

Heartstop. Grzimek, M.

Heath, Mary, 1931-
(ed) A Good deal. *See* A Good deal

Hecatombs of lake. Ahern, T.

Heinesen, William, 1900-
Laterna magica; translated from the Danish by Tiina Nunnally. Fjord Press 1987 159p (European short stories, no1) ISBN 0-940242-22-2 LC 86-31993

Heise, Kenan
Aunt Ella stories; illustrated by Jeremy Blatchley; introduction by David Mamet. Academy Chicago 1985 191p ISBN 0-89733-140-0

Hell screen, Cogwheels, A fool's life. Akutagawa, R.

Heller, Steve, 1949-
The man who drank a thousand beers; nine short stories. Chariton Review Press 1984 109p ISBN 0-933428-03-0 LC 84-4245

Helprin, Mark
(ed) The Best American short stories, 1988. *See* The Best American short stories, 1988

Hemingway, Ernest, 1899-1961
The complete short stories of Ernest Hemingway; the Finca Vigía edition. Scribner 1987 650p ISBN 0-684-18668-3 LC 87-12888

Hemley, Robin, 1958-
All you can eat; stories. Atlantic Monthly Press 1988 180p ISBN 0-87113-261-3 LC 88-14186

Hempel, Amy
Reasons to live; stories. Knopf 1985 129p ISBN 0-394-53993-1 LC 84-48658

Henderson, Bill, 1941-
(ed) Love stories for the time being. *See* Love stories for the time being
(ed) The Pushcart prize IX-XII: best of the small presses. *See* The Pushcart prize IX-XII: best of the small presses

Henley, Patricia
Friday night at Silver Star; stories; by Patricia Henley. Graywolf Press 1986 127p (The Graywolf short fiction ser) ISBN 0-915308-84-3 LC 85-82574

Henry, DeWitt
(ed) The Ploughshares reader: new fiction for the eighties. *See* The Ploughshares reader: new fiction for the eighties

Henry, O., 1862-1910
The gift of the Magi, and other stories; illustrations by Gordon Grant; afterword by Richard O'Connor. Reader's Digest Assn. 1987 255p il ISBN 0-89577-266-3 LC 87-60922
O. Henry's Texas stories; edited by Marian McClintock and Michael Simms. Still Point Press 1986 xxviii,291p ISBN 0-933841-03-5 LC 85-27951

Henry James' shorter masterpieces. James, H.

Hensley, Joe L., 1926-
Robak's firm. Doubleday 1987 182p ISBN 0-385-23829-0 LC 86-23929
"Published for the Crime Club"

Herbert, Frank
Eye; illustrated by Jim Burns; book design by Alex Jay. Berkley Bks. 1985 328p il (Masterworks of science fiction and fantasy) ISBN 0-425-08398-5 LC 85-237407
"A Byron Preiss Visual Publications, Inc. book"

Hercule Poirot's casebook. Christie, A.

Here's the story: fiction with heart; edited by Morty Sklar. Spirit That Moves Us Press 1985 192p il ISBN 0-930370-19-8 LC 84-23609

Hergenhan, L. T.
(ed) The Australian short story. *See* The Australian short story

Heroes and villains. Bumpus, J.

Hickory cured. Jones, D. C.

The **hidden** side of the moon.   Russ, J.

The **high** price of everything.   Coskran, K.

Highsmith, Patricia, 1921-

The animal-lover's book of beastly murder. Mysterious Press 1986 c1975 229p ISBN 0-89296-171-6 LC 86-91481

A Penzler Bk.

The black house; Patricia Highsmith. Mysterious Press 1988 258p ISBN 0-89296-227-5 LC 87-40395

A Penzler Bk.

Mermaids on the golf course. Mysterious Press 1988 233p ISBN 0-89296-352-2 LC 88-5434

A Penzler Bk.

Hill, Reginald, 1936-

There are no ghosts in the Soviet Union; a novella and five short stories. Countryman Press 1988 230p ISBN 0-88150-119-0 LC 88-16123

A Foul Play Press Bk.

Hills, Rust

(ed) The Esquire fiction reader v1. *See* The Esquire fiction reader v1

(ed) The Esquire fiction reader v2. *See* The Esquire fiction reader v2

The **hills**: more tales from the Blue Stacks.   Bernen, R.

Him with his foot in his mouth, and other stories.   Bellow, S.

Hitchcock in prime time; edited by Francis M. Nevins, Jr. & Martin Harry Greenberg; with an introduction by Henry Slesar. Avon Bks. 1985 356p ISBN 0-380-89673-7 LC 84-45885

Hitler victorious; eleven stories of the German victory in World War II; edited by Gregory Benford and Martin H. Greenberg; with an introduction by Norman Spinrad. Garland 1986 299p ISBN 0-8240-8658-9 LC 85-45131

Hoch, Edward D., 1930-

Leopold's way; detective stories; edited by Francis M. Nevins, Jr., & Martin H. Greenberg; introduction by Francis M. Nevins, Jr. Southern Ill. Univ. Press 1985 339p (Mystery makers) ISBN 0-8093-1233-6 LC 84-27554

The quests of Simon Ark. Mysterious Press 1984 268p ISBN 0-89296-113-9 LC 84-60556

(ed) The Year's best mystery and suspense stories, 1984-1988. *See* The Year's best mystery and suspense stories, 1984-1988

Hoffman, William, 1925-

By land, by sea; stories. Louisiana State Univ. Press 1988 174p ISBN 0-8071-1390-5 LC 87-21381

Hofmann, Gert

Balzac's horse, and other stories; selected and translated by Christopher Middleton. Fromm Int. 1988 200p ISBN 0-88064-074-X LC 87-28923

Hogg, James, 1770-1835

Selected stories and sketches; edited by Douglas S. Mack. Scottish Acad. Press 1984 c1982 211p (Association for Scottish Literary Studies) ISBN 0-7073-0322-2 LC 83-152542

Partially analyzed

Hoke, Helen, 1903-

(comp) Spirits, spooks, and other sinister creatures. *See* Spirits, spooks, and other sinister creatures

(ed) Venomous tales of villainy and vengeance. *See* Venomous tales of villainy and vengeance

Holidays.   Ruffolo, L.

Hollywood troubleshooter.   Ballard, W. T.

Home and away; edited by Rosemary Creswell; published with the assistance of the Literature Board of the Australia Council. Penguin Bks. 1987 213p ISBN 0-14-008075-9

Home-coming, and other Korean short stories; edited by the Korean National Commission for UNESCO. Korea ed. Si-sa-yong-o-sa; Pace Int. Res. 1983 205p (Modern Korean short stories, 8) ISBN 0-89209-209-2 LC 84-141789

Home in your hands.   Lynch, L.

Home truths.   Gallant, M.

Homemade love.   Cooper, J. C.

Homewords: a book of Tennessee writers; Douglas Paschall, editor, Alice Swanson, associate editor. University of Tenn. Press 1986 387p ISBN 0-87049-494-5 LC 85-26394

> Analyzed for short stories only

Honeymoon.   Gerber, M. J.

The **honeymoon.**   Spivack, K.

Hood, Hugh

> (ed) Fatal recurrences. *See* Fatal recurrences

Hood, Mary

> And Venus is blue; stories. Ticknor & Fields 1986 293p ISBN 0-89919-431-1 LC 86-5795

> How far she went; stories. University of Ga. Press 1984 123p ISBN 0-8203-0723-8 LC 84-1375

Hornung, Ernest William, 1866-1921

> The complete short stories of Raffles—the amateur cracksman; with an introductory essay by George Orwell; foreword by Peter Haining. St. Martin's Press 1984 475p ISBN 0-312-15849-1 LC 84-50455

Hospital, Janette Turner, 1942-

> Dislocations; stories. Louisiana State Univ. Press 1988 210p ISBN 0-8071-1508-8 LC 88-9371

Hospital room 205, and other Korean short stories; edited by the Korean National Commission for UNESCO. Korea ed. Si-sa-yong-o-sa; Pace Int. Res. 1983 216p (Modern Korean short stories, 4) ISBN 0-89209-205-X LC 84-141389

Hot type; America's most celebrated writers introduce the next word in contemporary fiction; edited by John Miller, with the editors of Equator magazine [et al.]. Collier Bks. 1988 235p ISBN 0-02-044701-9 LC 88-17585

Hotel Savoy; Fallmerayer the stationmaster [and] The bust of the emperor.   Roth, J.

Houbein, Lolo

> Everything is real. Phoenix Publs. (Qld.) 1984 200p ISBN 0-949780-06-5

Hound dunnit; edited by Isaac Asimov, Martin Harry Greenberg, and Carol-Lynn Rössel Waugh. Carroll & Graf Pubs. 1987 339p ISBN 0-88184-353-9 LC 87-15765

Hour of the beast, and other stories.   Bedard, B.

The **house** of fear.   Carrington, L.

House of heroes, and other stories.   La Chapelle, M.

The **house** on Plymouth Street, and other stories.   Curtiss, U. R.

Houses of ivory.   Wegner, H.

How far she went.   Hood, M.

Howard who?   Waldrop, H.

Hoyt, Myron S.

> Rainbow, river & tree; stories. Green Meadow Bks. 1985 91p ISBN 0-9614817-0-6 LC 85-80095

Hubbard, L. Ron (La Fayette Ron), 1911-1986

> (comp) L. Ron Hubbard presents Writers of the future. *See* L. Ron Hubbard presents Writers of the future

Huggan, Isabel, 1943-

> The Elizabeth stories. Viking 1987 184p ISBN 0-670-81303-6 LC 86-40509

> Also published by Oberon Press

Hughes, David

(ed) Winter's tales, new ser. v1. *See* Winter's tales, new ser. v1

The **Hugo** winners v4; edited by Isaac Asimov. Doubleday 1985 561p ISBN 0-385-18934-6 LC 84-18735

Earlier volumes entered in previous volumes of Short story index

The **Hugo** winners v5; edited by Isaac Asimov. Doubleday 1986 372p ISBN 0-385-18946-X LC 62-14132

Hull, Elizabeth Anne

(comp) Tales from the planet Earth. *See* Tales from the planet Earth

Hull, Helen R.

Last September. Naiad Press 1988 188p il ISBN 0-941483-09-6

Hulme, Keri

Te Kaihau, the windeater. Braziller 1987 239p ISBN 0-8076-1168-9 LC 86-31760

Humphrey, William

The collected stories of William Humphrey. Delacorte Press; Lawrence, S. 1985 371p ISBN 0-385-29400-X LC 84-26046

Hunnicutt, Ellen

In the music library. University of Pittsburgh Press 1987 147p ISBN 0-8229-3567-8 LC 87-40222

Hurston, Zora Neale, 1907-1960

Spunk; the selected stories of Zora Neale Hurston. Turtle Island Foundation 1985 106p ISBN 0-913666-79-3

Hutchins, William M.

(ed) Egyptian tales and short stories of the 1970s and 1980s. *See* Egyptian tales and short stories of the 1970s and 1980s

I

I am from Brownsville. Granit, A.

I am having an adventure. Klass, P.

I hope I shall arrive soon. Dick, P. K.

I see a long journey. Ingalls, R.

The **ice** monkey, and other stories. Harrison, M. J.

If only we could drive like this forever. Harvor, E.

Ignatow, Rose Graubart

Surplus love, and other stories. Copper Beech Press 1985 132p ISBN 0-914278-44-4 LC 85-11012

The **iguana** killer. Ríos, A.

Ikin, Van, 1951-

(ed) Australian science fiction. *See* Australian science fiction

Ikons. Papaellinas, G.

The **image,** and other stories. Singer, I. B.

Imaginary lands; conceived and edited by Robin McKinley. Greenwillow Bks. 1986 246p ISBN 0-688-05213-4 LC 85-21867

Imaginary magnitude. Lem, S.

The **immortal** coil. Van Greenaway, P.

In minor keys. Moore, G.

In the fertile land. Josipovici, G.

In the field of fire; edited by Jeanne Van Buren Dann and Jack Dann. Doherty Assocs. 1987 415p ISBN 0-312-93000-3 LC 86-50955

A TOR Bk.

In the flesh. Barker, C.

In the music library. Hunnicutt, E.

In the penny arcade. Millhauser, S.

Incidental music. Sagan, F.

Indecent dreams. Lustig, A.

Indefinite nights, and other stories. Ferguson, P.

Ingalls, Rachel
  I see a long journey; three novellas. Simon & Schuster 1985 141p ISBN 0-671-62782-1 LC 86-10038
  The pearlkillers; four novellas. Simon & Schuster 1986 215p ISBN 0-671-63340-6 LC 86-31468
  Something to write home about. Harvard Common Press 1988 296p ISBN 0-916782-98-0 LC 88-3029
The **inhuman** condition. Barker, C.
Inland passage. Rule, J.
The **inner** garden. Eisenstein, S.

Innes, Catherine Lynette
  (ed) African short stories. *See* African short stories
Inspecting the vaults. McCormack, E. P.
Inspector Saito's small satori. Van de Wetering, J.
Inspired by drink; an anthology; edited by Joan & John Digby; collages by John Digby. Morrow 1988 xxvii, 461p il ISBN 0-688-06922-3 LC 88-5228
  Partially analyzed
Intergalactic empires; edited by Isaac Asimov, Martin H. Greenberg, and Charles G. Waugh. New Am. Lib. 1983 303p (Isaac Asimov's wonderful worlds of science fiction, no1) ISBN 0-451-12624-6
  A Signet Bk.
The **Interior** country; stories of the modern West; edited by Alexander Blackburn, with Craig Lesley and Jill Landem; with an introduction by Alexander Blackburn. Swallow Press 1987 333p ISBN 0-8040-0887-6 LC 87-1968
An **international** episode, and other stories. James, H.
Interzone: the first anthology; edited by John Clute, Colin Greenland and David Pringle. St. Martin's Press 1986 208p ISBN 0-312-42535-X
Interzone: the 2nd anthology; new science fiction and fantasy writing; edited by John Clute, David Pringle and Simon Ounsley. St. Martin's Press 1987 208p ISBN 0-312-01325-6
Intimate strangers; new stories from Quebec; edited by Matt Cohen and Wayne Grady. Penguin Bks. 1986 203p ISBN 0-14-007958-0
Into love and out again. Lipman, E.
Inventing the Abbotts, and other stories. Miller, S.
The **invention** of flight. Neville, S.
Invisible fictions; contemporary stories from Quebec; edited by Geoff Hancock. Anansi [distrib. by Columbia Univ. Press] 1987 437p il ISBN 0-88784-153-8
Is that what people do? Sheckley, R.
Isaac and the undertaker's daughter. Stern, S.
Isaac Asimov presents the best crime stories of the 19th century; edited by Isaac Asimov, Charles G. Waugh, and Martin H. Greenberg. Dembner Bks. 1988 325p ISBN 0-934878-99-4 LC 87-30581
Isaac Asimov presents the best science fiction firsts; edited by Isaac Asimov, Charles G. Waugh and Martin H. Greenberg. Beaufort Bks. 1984 249p ISBN 0-8253-0184-X LC 83-21405
Isaac Asimov's Tomorrow's voices; collected by the editors of Isaac Asimov's Science Fiction Magazine. Dial Press; Davis Publs. 1984 287p il ISBN 0-385-27998-1 LC 78-60795
Islands. Rees, D.
It came from Schenectady. Longyear, B. B.

J

Jack London's Tales of Hawaii. London, J.
Jack of diamonds, and other stories. Spencer, E.

Jackson, Graham, 1947-
The decline of Western Hill. University of Qld. Press 1984
c1983 164p ISBN 0-7022-1793-X LC 83-5533

Jaffe, Harold
Beasts; fictions. Curbstone Press [distrib. by Talman] 1986
156p ISBN 0-915306-58-1

Jaffery, Sheldon
(ed) Selected tales of grim and grue from the horror pulps.
See Selected tales of grim and grue from the horror pulps
(ed) Sensuous science fiction from the weird and spicy pulps.
See Sensuous science fiction from the weird and spicy pulps
(ed) The Weirds. See The Weirds
The **jaguar** hunter. Shepard, L.

Jahnn, Hans Henny, 1894-1959
Thirteen uncanny stories; translated by Gerda Jordan. Lang,
P. 1984 28, 165, 29-31p (American university studies, Series
I, Germanic languages and literature, v20) ISBN 0-8204-0113-7
LC 84-47544

James, Henry, 1843-1916
The figure in the carpet, and other stories; edited with an
introduction and notes by Frank Kermode. Penguin Bks.
1986 453p ISBN 0-14-043255-8
Henry James' shorter masterpieces; edited with an introduction
and notes by Peter Rawlings. Harvester Press; Barnes &
Noble Bks. 1984 2v ISBN 0-389-20502-8 (v1); 0-389-20503-6
(v2) LC 84-12431
An international episode, and other stories; edited with an
introduction by S. Gorley Putt. Penguin Bks. 1986 238p
ISBN 0-14-043227-2

Janowitz, Tama
Slaves of New York; stories. Crown 1986 278p ISBN
0-517-56107-7 LC 86-8812

Jean Paul, 1763-1825
German romantic novellas. See German romantic novellas
Jemima Shore's first case, and other stories. Fraser, A.

Jenks, Tom
(ed) American short story masterpieces. See American short
story masterpieces
(ed) The Esquire fiction reader v1. See The Esquire fiction
reader v1
(ed) The Esquire fiction reader v2. See The Esquire fiction
reader v2
(ed) Soldiers & civilians. See Soldiers & civilians
Jenny and The jaws of life. Willett, J.

Jeppson, J. O., 1926-
The mysterious cure, and other stories of Pshrinks Anonymous.
Doubleday 1985 180p ISBN 0-385-19085-9 LC 84-21160
Jesus and Fat Tuesday, and other short stories. McElroy, C.
J.
Jewel of the moon. Kotzwinkle, W.

Jhabvala, Ruth Prawer
Out of India; selected stories. Morrow 1986 288p ISBN
0-688-06382-9 LC 85-25961
John Creasey's Crime collection, 1984; an anthology by members
of the Crime Writers' Association; edited by Herbert Harris.
St. Martin's Press 1984 187p ISSN 0890-6173
John Creasey's Crime collection, 1985; an anthology by members
of the Crime Writers' Association; edited by Herbert Harris.
St. Martin's Press 1985 204p ISSN 0890-6173 LC 82-647149
John Creasey's Crime collection, 1986; edited by Herbert Harris.
St. Martin's Press 1986 ISSN 0890-6173

John Creasey's Crime collection, 1987; an anthology by members of the Crime Writers' Association; edited by Herbert Harris. St. Martin's Press 1987 ISSN 0890-6173

Johnson, Charles Richard, 1948-
The sorcerer's apprentice. Atheneum Pubs. 1986 169p ISBN 0-689-11653-5 LC 85-47776

Johnson, Willis, 1938-
The girl who would be Russian, and other stories. Harcourt Brace Jovanovich 1986 180p ISBN 0-15-135691-2 LC 85-24765

Johnson-Davies, Denys
(tr) Arabic short stories. *See* Arabic short stories

Johnston, George, 1912-1970, and Clift, Charmian, 1923-1969
Strong-man from Piraeus, and other stories; [by] George Johnston and Charmian Clift; chosen and introduced by Garry Kinnane; publication assisted by the Literature Board of the Australia Council, the Federal Government's arts funding and advisory body. Penguin Bks. 1986 192p ISBN 0-14-008798-2

Joie d'amour. Villefranche, A.-M.

Jolley, Elizabeth, 1923-
Stories. Viking 1988 312p ISBN 0-670-82113-6 LC 87-40312
Contents: Five acre virgin; The travelling entertainer
Woman in a lampshade; published with the assistance of the Literature Board of the Australia Council. Penguin Bks. 1986 229p ISBN 0-14-008418-5
A King Penguin Bk.

Jones, Douglas C.
Hickory cured; with illustrations by the author. Holt & Co. 1987 224p il ISBN 0-8050-0383-5 LC 86-29405

Jordan, Anne
(ed) The Best horror stories from the Magazine of fantasy and science fiction. *See* The Best horror stories from the Magazine of fantasy and science fiction

Jordan, Cathleen
(ed) Alfred Hitchcock's Crimewatch. *See* Alfred Hitchcock's Crimewatch
(ed) Alfred Hitchcock's Grave suspicions. *See* Alfred Hitchcock's Grave suspicions
(ed) Alfred Hitchcock's Mortal errors. *See* Alfred Hitchcock's Mortal errors

Josipovici, Gabriel, 1940-
In the fertile land. Carcanet Press 1987 212p ISBN 0-85635-716-2
Analyzed for short stories only

The **judge's** chambers, and other stories. Komie, L. B.
The **Jules** Verne steam balloon. Davenport, G.

Jungman, Robert E.
(ed) On being foreign. *See* On being foreign

K

Kahn, Joan
(comp) Handle with care. *See* Handle with care
(comp) Ready or not, here come fourteen frightening stories! *See* Ready or not, here come fourteen frightening stories!

Kaikō, Takeshi, 1930-
Five thousand runaways; stories; translated from the Japanese by Cecilia Segawa Seigle. Dodd, Mead 1987 191p ISBN 0-396-09108-3 LC 87-5427

Kalechofsky, Robert
(ed) Echad 2: South African Jewish voices. *See* Echad 2: South African Jewish voices

Kalechofsky, Robert—*Continued*
   (ed) Echad 4: Jewish writing from down under: Australia and New Zealand. *See* Echad 4: Jewish writing from down under: Australia and New Zealand

Kalechofsky, Roberta, 1931-
   (ed) Echad 2: South African Jewish voices. *See* Echad 2: South African Jewish voices
   (ed) Echad 4: Jewish writing from down under: Australia and New Zealand. *See* Echad 4: Jewish writing from down under: Australia and New Zealand

Kalpakian, Laura
   Fair Augusto, and other stories. Graywolf Press 1986 250p (Graywolf short fiction ser) ISBN 0-915308-90-8 LC 86-81784

Kaplan, David Michael
   Comfort. Viking 1987 204p ISBN 0-670-81399-0 LC 86-40256

Katz, Steve, 1935-
   Stolen stories. Fiction Collective 1984 149p ISBN 0-914590-84-7 LC 83-27410
     Partially analyzed

Kauffman, Janet, 1945-
   Places in the world a woman could walk; stories. Knopf 1984 131p ISBN 0-394-52996-0 LC 83-47672

Kaufman, Alan
   (ed) The New generation. *See* The New generation

Kavaler, Rebecca
   Tigers in the wood. University of Ill. Press 1986 108p (Illinois short fiction) ISBN 0-252-01308-5 LC 85-24648

Kawabata, Yasunari, 1899-1972
   Palm-of-the-hand stories; translated from the Japanese by Lane Dunlop and J. Martin Holman. North Point Press 1988 238p ISBN 0-86547-325-0 LC 87-82590

Kaye, Marvin
   (ed) Devils & demons. *See* Devils & demons
   (ed) Masterpieces of terror and the supernatural. *See* Masterpieces of terror and the supernatural

Kaye, Saralee
   (ed) Devils & demons. *See* Devils & demons
   (ed) Masterpieces of terror and the supernatural. *See* Masterpieces of terror and the supernatural

Kaye Wayfaring in "Avenged". McCourt, J.

Keating, H. R. F. (Henry Reymond Fitzwalter), 1926-
   Mrs. Craggs: crimes cleaned up. St. Martin's Press 1985 220p ISBN 0-312-53506-6 LC 86-13025

Keeling, Nora
   Chasing her own tail. Oberon Press 1985 109p ISBN 0-88750-563-5 LC 85-188599

Keeping, Charles, 1924-
   (comp) Charles Keeping's Book of classic ghost stories. *See* Charles Keeping's Book of classic ghost stories
   (ed) Charles Keeping's Classic tales of the macabre. *See* Charles Keeping's Classic tales of the macabre

Kees, Weldon
   The ceremony & other stories; edited & with an introduction by Dana Gioia. Graywolf Press 1984 147p ISBN 0-915308-45-2 LC 83-83186

Keillor, Garrison
   Leaving home. Viking 1987 xxiii,244p ISBN 0-670-81976-X LC 87-40219

Keller, Gary D.
   Tales of El Huitlacoche. Maize Press 1984 77p ISBN 0-939558-05-X LC 83-062552

Kercheval, Jesse Lee
The dogeater; stories. University of Mo. Press 1987 92p (AWP, 8) ISBN 0-8262-0632-8 LC 86-25066

Kessler, Jascha Frederick, 1929-
Classical illusions; [by] Jascha Kessler. McPherson & Co. 1985 169p ISBN 0-914232-74-6 LC 85-8982

Kiely, Benedict
A letter to Peachtree & nine other stories. Godine 1988 209p ISBN 0-87923-727-9 LC 87-46282

Kilgore, Davida
Last summer; stories. New Rivers Press 1988 87p (Minnesota voices project, no34) ISBN 0-89823-103-5 LC 88-60054

Kill or cure; suspense stories about the world of medicine; edited by Marcia Muller and Bill Pronzini. Macmillan 1985 306p (Macmillan Midnight lib) ISBN 0-02-587880-8 LC 85-15572

Kilworth, Garry
The songbirds of pain; stories from the Inscape. Gollancz 1984 187p ISBN 0-575-03511-0

Kindred spirits; an anthology of gay and lesbian science fiction stories; Jeffrey M. Elliot, editor. Alyson Publs. 1984 262p ISBN 0-932870-42-2

King, Francis Henry, 1923-
One is a wanderer; selected stories; by Francis King. Little, Brown 1985 314p ISBN 0-316-49350-3 LC 85-19705

King, Stephen, 1947-
Skeleton crew. Putnam 1985 512p ISBN 0-399-13039-X LC 84-15947

The **king** in the golden mask, and other writings. Schwob, M.

Kinsella, W. P.
The Alligator Report; stories. Coffee House Press 1985 125p il ISBN 0-918273-10-2 LC 85-17412

Dance me outside; more tales from the Ermineskin Reserve. Godine 1986 c1977 158p ISBN 0-87923-583-7 LC 85-70142

The Fencepost chronicles. Houghton Mifflin 1987 190p ISBN 0-395-44646-5 LC 87-12472

The further adventures of Slugger McBatt; baseball stories. Houghton Mifflin 1988 179p ISBN 0-395-47592-9 LC 87-37824

Kirk, Russell
Watchers at the strait gate; mystical tales; illustrations by Andrew Smith. Arkham House Pubs. 1984 256p il ISBN 0-87054-098-X LC 84-267

Kittredge, William
We are not in this together; stories; edited & with a foreword by Raymond Carver. Graywolf Press 1984 128p (Graywolf short fiction ser) ISBN 0-915308-43-6 LC 83-82866

Klass, Perri, 1958-
I am having an adventure; stories. Putnam 1986 253p ISBN 0-399-13146-9 LC 85-28175

Klein, T. E. D., 1947-
Dark gods; four tales. Viking 1985 259p ISBN 0-670-80590-4 LC 85-3190

Kleist, Heinrich von, 1777-1811
German romantic novellas. *See* German romantic novellas

Klíma, Ivan
My first loves; translated from the Czech by Ewald Osers. Harper & Row 1988 164p ISBN 0-06-015866-2 LC 87-45634

My merry mornings; stories from Prague; translated by George Theiner. Readers Int. 1985 154p il ISBN 0-930523-04-0

Klinkowitz, Jerome
Short season, and other stories; by Jerry Klinkowitz. Johns Hopkins Univ. Press 1988 187p ISBN 0-8018-3614-X LC 87-46311

Knight, Damon Francis, 1922-
(ed) The Clarion awards. *See* The Clarion awards
The **knight** and knave of swords. Leiber, F.

Kōda, Rohan, 1867-1947
Pagoda, skull & samurai; 3 stories; translated by Chieko Irie Mulhern. Tuttle 1985 280p ISBN 0-8048-1499-6 LC 84-052723

Komie, Lowell B.
The judge's chambers, and other stories. Academy Chicago 1987 179p ISBN 0-89733-248-2 LC 86-32271

Koon, George William
(ed) A Collection of classic Southern humor. *See* A Collection of classic Southern humor

Koppelman, Susan
(ed) Between mothers & daughters. *See* Between mothers & daughters
(ed) "May your days be merry and bright" and other Christmas stories by women. *See* "May your days be merry and bright" and other Christmas stories by women
(ed) Old maids. *See* Old maids
(ed) The Other woman. *See* The Other woman

Kornblatt, Joyce Reiser
Breaking bread. Dutton 1987 206p ISBN 0-525-24388-7 LC 86-16674
A William Abrahams Bk.

Kotzwinkle, William
Jewel of the moon; short stories. Putnam 1985 160p ISBN 0-399-13113-2 LC 85-19254

Kress, Nancy
Trinity, and other stories. Bluejay Bks. 1985 279p ISBN 0-312-94438-1 LC 85-6147

Krist, Gary
The Garden State; short stories. Harcourt Brace Jovanovich 1988 178p ISBN 0-15-134292-X LC 88-3349

Krysl, Marilyn, 1942-
Mozart, Westmoreland, and me; stories. Thunder's Mouth Press 1985 124p ISBN 0-938410-30-X LC 85-8043

Kuttner, Henry, 1915-1958
The startling worlds of Henry Kuttner. Warner Bks. 1987 357p ISBN 0-445-20328-5

L

L. Ron Hubbard presents Writers of the future; commentaries by Robert Silverberg [et al.]; edited by Algis Budrys. Bridge Publs. 1985 xx,354p il ISBN 0-88404-170-0 LC 84-73270

L. Ron Hubbard presents Writers of the future v2; commentaries by Frank Herbert [et al.]; edited by Algis Budrys. Bridge Publs. 1986 xxxvi, 391p il ISBN 0-88404-254-5 LC 84-73270

L. Ron Hubbard presents Writers of the future v3; 14 great new tales from the Writers of the future international talent search; plus essays on the art and craft of writing by L. Ron Hubbard [et al.]; edited by Algis Burdrys. Bridge Publs. 1987 429p il ISBN 0-88404-254-6 LC 84-73270

La Chapelle, Mary
House of heroes, and other stories. Crown 1988 243p ISBN 0-517-56782-2 LC 87-21418

La Puma, Salvatore
The boys of Bensonhurst; stories. University of Ga. Press 1987 136p ISBN 0-8203-0891-9 LC 86-7100
Lady Macbeth of Mtsensk, and other stories. Leskov, N. S.
The **land** of go. Barrett, L.

Landem, Jill
(ed) The Interior country. *See* The Interior country

Landolfi, Tommaso, 1908-1979
Words in commotion, and other stories; with an introduction by Italo Calvino; translated and edited by Kathrine Jason. Viking 1986 xxiii,275p ISBN 0-670-80518-1 LC 85-41063
Last days. Oates, J. C.
The **last** laugh, and other stories. Martínez-Serros, H.
Last laughs; the 1986 Mystery Writers of America anthology; edited by Gregory Mcdonald. Mysterious Press 1986 196p ISBN 0-89296-246-1 LC 85-62061
Last September. Hull, H. R.
Last summer. Kilgore, D.
The **last** worthless evening. Dubus, A.
A **Late** chrysanthemum; twenty-one stories from the Japanese; translated by Lane Dunlop; with etchings by Tanaka Ryohei. North Point Press 1986 178p ISBN 0-86547-229-7 LC 85-72979
Later the same day. Paley, G.
Laterna magica. Heinesen, W.

Latimer, Margery, 1899-1932
Guardian angel, and other stories; afterwords by Nancy Loughridge, Meridel Le Sueur, and Louis Kampf. Feminist Press 1984 246p ISBN 0-935312-12-9 LC 84-14175

Lau, Joseph S. M., 1934-
(ed) The Unbroken chain. *See* The Unbroken chain
Laughing Pig, and other stories. Regent, P.

Laughlin, James, 1914-
(ed) New directions in prose and poetry 48-52. *See* New directions in prose and poetry 48-52

Lawson, Henry, 1867-1922
The Penguin Henry Lawson; short stories; edited with an introduction by John Barnes. Penguin Bks. 1987 c1986 229p ISBN 0-14-009215-3

Layman, Richard, 1947-
(ed) A Matter of crime. *See* A Matter of crime
Lazar Malkin enters heaven. Stern, S.
Lead pencil. Botwinik, B.
Learning by heart. Livesey, M.
Learning the mother tongue. Hankla, C.
Learning to swim, and other stories. Swift, G.

Leaton, Anne
Mayakovsky, my love. Countryman Press 1984 205p ISBN 0-88150-015-1 LC 83-23961
Leaving home. Keillor, G.

Leavitt, David, 1961-
Family dancing; stories. Knopf 1984 205p ISBN 0-394-53872-2 LC 84-47679

Lee, Hector, 1908-
The Bodega War, and other stories from western lore; [by] Hector H. Lee. Capra Press 1988 187p il ISBN 0-88496-279-2 LC 87-28814

Lee, Peter H., 1929-
(ed) Flowers of fire. *See* Flowers of fire

Lee, Tanith
Dreams of dark and light; the great short fiction of Tanith Lee; with a foreword by Rosemary Hawley Jarman and interior illustrations by Douglas Smith. Arkham House Pubs. 1986 507p il ISBN 0-87054-153-6 LC 85-28571

Leedom-Ackerman, Joanne, 1948-
No marble angels; short fiction. Texas Center for Writers Press 1985 146p ISBN 0-916092-10-0 LC 86-43043

Legacies. Potter, N. A. J.

Leiber, Fritz, 1910-
The knight and knave of swords. Morrow 1988 303p ISBN 0-688-08530-X LC 88-25192
Analyzed for short stories only

Lem, Stanisław
Imaginary magnitude; translated from the Polish by Marc E. Heine. Harcourt Brace Jovanovich 1984 248p ISBN 0-15-144118-9 LC 83-18624
A Helen and Kurt Wolff Bk.

Leopoldina's dream. Ocampo, S.

Leopold's way. Hoch, E. D.

Leskov, N. S. (Nikolaï Semenovich), 1831-1895
Lady Macbeth of Mtsensk, and other stories; translated with an introduction by David McDuff. Penguin Bks. 1987 424p ISBN 0-14-044491-2
The sealed angel, and other stories; K.A. Lantz, editor and translator. University of Tenn. Press 1984 251p ISBN 0-87049-411-2 LC 83-14547

Lesley, Craig
(ed) The Interior country. *See* The Interior country

Let us know. Vreuls, D.

Let's hear it for a beautiful guy, and other works of short fiction. Friedman, B. J.

Letter from a great-uncle & other stories. Hall, R. W.

Letter from Casablanca. Tabucchi, A.

A letter to Peachtree & nine other stories. Kiely, B.

Levine. Westlake, D. E.

Lewis, Tom J.
(ed) On being foreign. *See* On being foreign

Leyner, Mark
(ed) American made. *See* American made

Liben, Meyer
New York street games and other stories and sketches; foreword by George Dennison. Schocken Bks. 1984 xxix,275p ISBN 0-8052-3849-2 LC 82-10492
Analyzed for short stories only

The life and times of Major Fiction. Baumbach, J.

Life being the best & other stories. Boyle, K.

Life in windy weather. Bitov, A.

Life on earth. Ballantyne, S.

Life on this planet, and other stories. Cohen, M.

The lights of the city: stories from Austin. Taylor, C.

Like a lamb to slaughter. Block, L.

Lindberg, Stanley W.
(ed) Necessary fictions. *See* Necessary fictions

Link, E. Perry (Eugene Perry), 1944-
(ed) Roses and thorns. *See* Roses and thorns

Liphshitz, Arye, 1901-
We built Jerusalem; tales of pioneering days; translated from the Hebrew by Misha Louvish. Cornwall Bks. 1985 175p ISBN 0-8453-4787-X LC 84-45016
A Herzl Press Publ.

Lipman, Elinor
Into love and out again; stories. Viking 1987 194p ISBN
0-670-81193-9 LC 86-40319

Lish, Gordon
Mourner at the door; stories. Viking 1988 162p ISBN
0-670-82061-X LC 87-40324
What I know so far. Holt, Rinehart & Winston 1984 162p
ISBN 0-03-070609-2 LC 83-12980
A William Abrahams Bk.

Lispector, Clarice, 1924-1977
The foreign legion; stories and chronicles; translated with an
afterword by Giovanni Pontiero. Carcanet Press 1986 219p
ISBN 0-85635-627-1
Analyzed for short stories only

Little Face, and other stories. Thompson, J.

Lives of the poets. Doctorow, E. L.

Livesey, Margot
Learning by heart. Penguin Bks. 1986 248p (Penguin short
fiction) ISBN 0-14-008157-7

The **living** hothouse. Halligan, M.

Living with snakes. Curley, D.

A **local** hanging, and other stories. Thompson, K.

Locomotion. Evans, E.

Lofts, Norah, 1904-1983
Saving face, and other stories. Doubleday 1984 c1983 229p
ISBN 0-385-18717-3 LC 82-45872

London, Jack, 1876-1916
Jack London's Tales of Hawaii; introduction by Miriam Rappolt.
Press Pacifica 1984 68p ISBN 0-916630-25-0 LC 81-23492
Young wolf: the early adventure stories of Jack London; edited
by Howard Lachtman. Capra Press 1984 258p ISBN
0-88496-210-5 LC 83-25185

London, Joan, 1948-
Sister ships, and other stories. Penguin Bks. 1988 c1986 118p
ISBN 0-14-010571-9 LC 87-19734

The **lonely** sea. MacLean, A.

Long, David, 1948-
The flood of '64; stories. Ecco Press 1987 213p ISBN
0-88001-127-0 LC 86-19687

The **long** white. Dilworth, S.

The **longest** night. Haris, P.

Longyear, Barry B.
It came from Schenectady. Bluejay Bks. 1984 346p ISBN
0-312-94239-7

Look who's talking; an anthology of voices in the modern American
short story; edited by Bruce Weber. Washington Sq. Press
1986 xxii,362p ISBN 0-671-61739-7

Loose connections. Claiborne, S.

Lopatin, Judy
Modern romances; stories. Fiction Collective 1986 255p ISBN
0-932-51102-3 LC 86-7711

Lost in time and space with Lefty Feep. Bloch, R.

The **lost** salt gift of blood. MacLeod, A.

Lost souls; a collection of English ghost stories; edited by Jack
Sullivan. Ohio Univ. Press 1983 430p ISBN 0-8214-0653-1
LC 82-14420

The **lost** stories of W. S. Gilbert. Gilbert, W. S.

Loukakis, Angelo, 1951-
Vernacular dreams. University of Qld. Press 1986 179p ISBN
0-7022-1897-9 LC 85-14088

Love is the crooked thing. Abbott, L. K.

Love must not be forgotten. Zhang Jie

Love stories for the time being; edited by Genie D. Chipps & Bill Henderson. Pushcart Press 1987 459p ISBN 0-916366-42-1 LC 86-63636

Love, struggle & change; stories by women; edited by Irene Zahava. Crossing Press 1988 183p ISBN 0-89594-264-X LC 87-34916

Analyzed for short stories only

Lovecraft, H. P. (Howard Phillips), 1890-1937

The Dunwich horror, and others; selected by August Derleth; with texts edited by S. T. Joshi; and an introduction by Robert Bloch. Arkham House Pubs. 1985 xxvi, 433p ISBN 0-87054-037-8 LC 84-14478

A **lovely** day to die, and other stories. Fremlin, C.

The **lover** of horses, and other stories. Gallagher, T.

Lovers & cohorts. Gold, H.

Lovers' choice. Birtha, B.

Loving Belle Starr. Taylor, R.

Lu Wenfu, 1928-

The gourmet, and other stories of modern China. Readers Int. 1987 243p ISBN 0-930523-38-5

Luby, Barry J.

(ed) Anthology of contemporary Latin American literature, 1960-1984. *See* Anthology of contemporary Latin American literature, 1960-1984

The **luckiest** man in the world. Silvis, R.

The **lunatics** of Terra. Sladek, J. T.

Lundwall, Sam J.

(ed) The Penguin world omnibus of science fiction. *See* The Penguin world omnibus of science fiction

Lurie, Morris

The night we ate the sparrow; a memoir and fourteen stories. Gribble; Penguin Bks. 1986 c1985 152p ISBN 0-14-008864-4

Analyzed for short stories only

Outrageous behaviour; best stories of Morris Lurie. Penguin Bks. 1984 294p ISBN 0-14-007097-4

Lustig, Arnošt

Indecent dreams. Northwestern Univ. Press 1988 159p ISBN 0-8101-0773-2 LC 88-3202

Lutz, John, 1939-

Better mousetraps; the best mystery stories of John Lutz; edited by Francis M. Nevins, Jr. St. Martin's Press 1988 347p ISBN 0-312-01389-2 LC 87-29930

Lynch, Lee, 1945-

Home in your hands. Naiad Press 1986 222p ISBN 0-930044-80-0 LC 86-12762

Old dyke tales. Naiad Press 1984 205p ISBN 0-930044-51-7 LC 84-3439

M

MacDonald, D. R.

Eyestone; stories. Pushcart Press 1988 206p ISBN 0-916366-48-0 LC 87-083285

Machines that think; the best science fiction stories about robots and computers; edited by Isaac Asimov, Patricia S. Warrick and Martin H. Greenberg. Holt, Rinehart & Winston 1984 c1983 627p ISBN 0-03-061498-8 LC 83-245

MacLaverty, Bernard

The Great Profundo, and other stories. Grove Press 1988 c1987 143p ISBN 0-8021-1048-7 LC 87-34077

Secrets, and other stories. Viking 1984 c1979 130p ISBN 0-670-63077-2 LC 84-40267

MacLean, Alistair, 1922-1987

The lonely sea; collected short stories. Doubleday 1986 222p ISBN 0-385-23596-8 LC 85-31091

MacLeod, Alistair

The lost salt gift of blood; new & selected stories. Ontario Review Press [distrib. by Braziller] 1988 227p ISBN 0-86538-063-5 LC 87-36439

Madness in the family. Saroyan, W.

Madonna on her back. Hagy, A. C.

Magic in Ithkar [1]-2; edited by André Norton and Robert Adams. Doherty Assocs. 1985 2v ISBN 0-812-54740-3 (v1); 0-812-54745-4 (v2)

A TOR book

Magic in Ithkar 3-4; edited by André Norton and Robert Adams. Doherty Assocs. 1986-1987 2v ISBN 0-812-54734-9 (v3); 0-812-54719-5 (v4)

A TOR book

Magicats!; Edited by Jack Dann and Gardner Dozois. Ace Fantasy Bks. 1984 270p ISBN 0-441-51530-4

Maigret at the crossroads. Simenon, G.

Making it new; contemporary Canadian stories; edited by John Metcalf; with photographs by Sam Tata. Methuen 1983 c1982 261p ISBN 0-458-95520-5 LC 82-241675

Analyzed for short stories only

The **Maldive** chronicles. Bernard, K.

Malzberg, Barry N.

(ed) Mystery in the mainstream. *See* Mystery in the mainstream

The **Mammoth** book of classic science fiction; short novels of the 1930s; edited by Isaac Asimov, Charles G. Waugh and Martin H. Greenberg. Carroll & Graf Pubs. 1988 572p ISBN 0-88184-410-1 LC 88-7311

The **Mammoth** book of modern crime stories; edited by George Hardinge. Carroll & Graf Pubs. 1987 512p ISBN 0-88184-356-3 LC 87-15106

Orig. pub. in 2v. as: The Best of Winter's crimes. Macmillan Pubs. 1986

The **Mammoth** book of private eye stories; edited by Bill Pronzini and Martin H. Greenberg. Carroll & Graf Pubs. 1988 592p ISBN 0-88184-430-6 LC 88-20976

The **Mammoth** book of short horror novels; edited by Mike Ashley. Carroll & Graf Pubs. 1988 518p ISBN 0-88184-429-2 LC 88-20975

Man descending. Vanderhaeghe, G.

The **man** in the cardboard mask. Greenberg, A.

The **man** who drank a thousand beers. Heller, S.

The **man** who knew Cary Grant. Schwartz, J.

The **man** who loved Levittown. Wetherell, W. D.

The **man** who sang in his sleep. Skelton, R.

The **man** with a nose, and the other uncollected short stories of H. G. Wells. Wells, H. G.

Manguel, Alberto

(ed) Black water. *See* Black water

(ed) Dark arrows. *See* Dark arrows

(ed) Other fires. *See* Other fires

Manhattan mysteries; edited by Bill Pronzini, Carol-Lynn Rössel Waugh, and Martin H. Greenberg. Avenel Bks. 1987 579p ISBN 0-517-63179-2 LC 86-28720

Man's work. Connelly, J.

Mansfield, Katherine, 1888-1923

The garden-party; Katherine Mansfield's New Zealand stories; illustrated edition. New Amsterdam Bks. 1988 188p il ISBN 0-941533-38-7

Manson, Cynthia
  (ed) Tales from Ellery Queen's Mystery Magazine: short stories for young adults. *See* Tales from Ellery Queen's Mystery Magazine: short stories for young adults
  (ed) Tales from Isaac Asimov's science fiction magazine: short stories for young adults. *See* Tales from Isaac Asimov's science fiction magazine: short stories for young adults

Margaret of the imperfections. Sexson, L.

Markham, Beryl, 1902-1986
  The splendid outcast; Beryl Markham's African stories; compiled and introduced by Mary S. Lovell. North Point Press 1987 139p ISBN 0-86547-301-3 LC 87-060876

Márquez, Antonio, 1940-
  (ed) Cuentos Chicanos. *See* Cuentos Chicanos

Martin, George R. R.
  Nightflyers. Bluejay Bks. 1985 295p ISBN 0-312-94332-6

Martin, Russell
  (ed) Writers of the purple sage. *See* Writers of the purple sage

Martin, Valerie
  The consolation of nature, and other stories. Houghton Mifflin 1988 147p ISBN 0-395-46788-8 LC 87-19735

Martínez-Serros, Hugo, 1930-
  The last laugh, and other stories. Arte Público Press 1988 198p ISBN 0-934770-89-1 LC 88-6359

Martone, Michael
  Safety patrol; short stories. Johns Hopkins Univ. Press 1988 128p ISBN 0-8018-3602-6 LC 87-26868

Martz, Sandra K.
  (ed) When I am an old woman I shall wear purple. *See* When I am an old woman I shall wear purple

Masques; all new works of horror and the supernatural; edited by J. N. Williamson. Maclay & Assocs. 1984 306p ISBN 0-940776-18-9 LC 84-61387
  Analyzed for short stories only

Masques II; all-new stories of horror and the supernatural; edited by J. N. Williamson. Maclay & Assocs. 1987 221p ISBN 0-940776-24-3 LC 87-060415

Masterpieces of fantasy and enchantment; compiled by David G. Hartwell with the assistance of Kathryn Cramer. St. Martin's Press 1988 622p ISBN 0-312-02250-6 LC 88-14752

Masterpieces of mystery and suspense; compiled by Martin H. Greenberg. St. Martin's Press 1988 651p ISBN 0-312-02251-4 LC 88-14753

Masterpieces of terror and the supernatural; a treasury of spellbinding tales old & new; selected by Marvin Kaye with Saralee Kaye. Doubleday 1985 623p ISBN 0-385-18549-9 LC 84-24710
  Analyzed for short stories only

Masters of darkness; edited by Dennis Etchison. Doherty Assocs. 1986 338p ISBN 0-812-51762-8
  A TOR Bk.

Mathenauts: tales of mathematical wonder; edited by Rudy Rucker. Arbor House 1987 300p ISBN 0-87795-891-2 LC 86-32184

Mathers, Peter, 1931-
  A change for the better; short stories. Words & Visions Publs. 1984 178p il ISBN 0-9591186-0-8

Matheson, Richard Christian
  Scars and other distinguishing marks; illustrated by Harry O. Morris; foreword by Stephen King; introduction by Dennis Etchison. Scream/Press 1987 168p il ISBN 0-910489-15-7

Matsumoto, Tomone
  (ed) The Shōwa anthology. *See* The Shōwa anthology

A **Matter** of crime; new stories from the masters of mystery & suspense; edited by Matthew J. Bruccoli & Richard Layman. v1-2. Harcourt Brace Jovanovich 1987 2v ISSN 0892-9416 A Harvest/HBJ Bk.

Matthew, Jean R.
Testimony; stories. University of Mo. Press 1987 72p (Breakthrough book, no54) ISBN 0-8262-0623-9 LC 86-16126

Matthews, Jack
Crazy women; short stories. Johns Hopkins Univ. Press 1985 158p (Johns Hopkins, poetry and fiction) ISBN 0-8018-2633-0 LC 84-25112

Ghostly populations; short stories. Johns Hopkins Univ. Press 1986 171p (Johns Hopkins, poetry and fiction) ISBN 0-8018-3391-4 LC 86-45439

Matthiessen, Peter
Midnight turning gray; short stories. Ampersand Press 1984 94p ISBN 0-9604740-5-6 LC 83-82381

Mattison, Alice
Great wits. Morrow 1988 223p ISBN 0-688-08060-X LC 88-1666

Maupassant, Guy de, 1850-1893
The collected stories of Guy de Maupassant; ten volumes in one. Avenel Bks. 1985 1003p ISBN 0-517-45751-2 LC 84-20316

Max Brand's Best western stories v2.   Brand, M.
Max Brand's Best western stories v3.   Brand, M.
"May your days be merry and bright" and other Christmas stories by women; edited and introduced by Susan Koppelman. Wayne State Univ. Press 1988 260p ISBN 0-8143-2124-0 LC 88-21784

Maya Darpan, and other stories.   Verma, N.
Mayakovsky, my love.   Leaton, A.
The **mayor** of New Orleans.   Shaik, F.

Mazel, David
My heart's world; stories; illustrated by Nyease Somersett. Phunn 1985 143p il ISBN 0-931762-02-2 LC 84-62148

McCarthy, John, 1898-
(ed) The Best of Irish wit and wisdom. *See* The Best of Irish wit and wisdom

McCormack, Eric P.
Inspecting the vaults. Penguin Bks. 1987 234p ISBN 0-14-009636-1

McCourt, James, 1941-
Kaye Wayfaring in "Avenged"; four stories. Knopf 1984 181p ISBN 0-394-52361-X LC 83-49088

McCullers, Carson, 1917-1967
Collected stories; including The member of the wedding and The ballad of the sad café; introduction by Virginia Spencer Carr. Houghton Mifflin 1987 392p ISBN 0-395-44179-X LC 87-3944

McCullough, David W.
(ed) Great detectives. *See* Great detectives

Mcdonald, Gregory, 1937-
(ed) Last laughs. *See* Last laughs

McElroy, Colleen J.
Jesus and Fat Tuesday, and other short stories. Creative Arts 1987 202p ISBN 0-88739-023-4 LC 87-70508

McGarry, Jean
Airs of Providence. Johns Hopkins Univ. Press 1985 130p ISBN 0-8018-2909-7 LC 85-9805

McGrath, Patrick
Blood and water, and other tales. Poseidon Press 1988 192p ISBN 0-671-64405-X LC 87-25667

McGuane, Thomas, 1938-
To skin a cat; stories. Dutton; Lawrence, S. 1986 212p ISBN 0-525-24460-3 LC 86-8916

McKinley, James
Acts of love; short stories. Breitenbush Bks. 1987 152p ISBN 0-932576-47-8 LC 87-708

McKinley, Robin
(ed) Imaginary lands. *See* Imaginary lands

McKnight, Reginald, 1956-
Moustapha's eclipse. University of Pittsburgh Press 1988 129p ISBN 0-8229-3589-9 LC 88-6408

McLaughlin, Lissa, 1952-
Troubled by his complexion. Burning Deck 1988 126p ISBN 0-930901-52-5 LC 87-24988

McLeod, Marion
(comp) Women's work. *See* Women's work

McSherry, Frank D.
(ed) Civil War women. *See* Civil War women
(ed) Haunted New England. *See* Haunted New England
(ed) Mississippi River tales. *See* Mississippi River tales
(ed) Murder and mystery in Boston. *See* Murder and mystery in Boston
(ed) Murder and mystery in Chicago. *See* Murder and mystery in Chicago
(ed) Nightmares in Dixie. *See* Nightmares in Dixie
(ed) Yankee witches. *See* Yankee witches

Meacham, Beth
(ed) Terry's universe. *See* Terry's universe
Mean streets; the second Private Eye Writers of America anthology. Mysterious Press 1986 230p ISBN 0-89296-169-4 LC 86-16303
Medea: Harlan's world; by Jack Williamson [et al.]; illustrations by Kelly Freas; cartography by Diane Duane; [ed. by Harlan Ellison]. Bantam Bks. 1985 532p il ISBN 0-553-34170-7 LC 85-1252
Analyzed for short stories only

Meinke, Peter
The piano tuner; stories. University of Ga. Press 1986 156p ISBN 0-8203-0844-7 LC 85-28864
The **melting** pot, and other subversive stories. Schwartz, L. S.

Melville, Herman, 1819-1891
Pierre; or, The ambiguities, Israel Potter: his fifty years of exile, The piazza tales, The confidence-man: his masquerade, Uncollected prose, Billy Budd, Sailor: (an inside narrative). Library of America 1984 1478p ISBN 0-940450-24-0 LC 84-11249
Analyzed for short stories only
The **memoirs** of Sherlock Holmes. Doyle, Sir A. C.
Memorable characters, Ellery Queen's. *See* Ellery Queen's Memorable characters
Memories of the assassination attempt, and other stories. Windsor, G.
Memories of the Space Age. Ballard, J. G.
A **memory** of murder. Bradbury, R.
Men at sea; the best sea stories of all time from Homer to William F. Buckley, Jr.; edited and with an introduction by Brandt Aymar. Crown 1988 640p il ISBN 0-517-56918-3 LC 87-27408
Analyzed for short stories only
Men, Martians and machines. Russell, E. F.

Men on men; best new gay fiction; edited and with an introduction by George Stambolian. New Am. Lib. 1986 375p ISBN 0-452-25882-0 LC 86-12856

    A Plume Bk.

Men on men 2; best new gay fiction; edited and with an introduction by George Stambolian. New Am. Lib. 1988 371p ISBN 0-453-00635-3 LC 88-12491

    A Plume Bk.

Mercy flights. Peterson, M.

Mermaids on the golf course. Highsmith, P.

Metaphysics in the Midwest. White, C.

Metcalf, John, 1938-

    (ed) Making it new. *See* Making it new

    (ed) The New press anthology #1: best Canadian short fiction. *See* The New press anthology #1: best Canadian short fiction

    (ed) The New press anthology #2: best stories. *See* The New press anthology #2: best stories

Michaelson, L. W., 1920-

    On my being dead, and other stories. Galileo Press 1983 136p il (Ha'penny book series) ISBN 0-913123-02-1 LC 83-81251

Michelson in the desert. Alderson, T.

Midair. Conroy, F.

The **middleman,** and other stories. Mukherjee, B.

Midnight; edited by Charles L. Grant. Doherty Assocs. 1985 284p ISBN 0-812-51850-0

    A TOR Bk.

Midnight turning gray. Matthiessen, P.

Milk. Farmer, B.

Miller, John

    (ed) Hot type. *See* Hot type

Miller, Sue

    Inventing the Abbotts, and other stories. Harper & Row 1987 180p ISBN 0-06-015755-0 LC 86-46089

Miller, Walter M., 1923-

    (ed) Beyond Armageddon. *See* Beyond Armageddon

Millhauser, Steven

    In the penny arcade; stories. Knopf 1986 164p ISBN 0-394-54660-1 LC 85-40122

Millman, Lawrence

    The wrong-handed man; stories. University of Mo. Press 1988 104p (Breakthrough book, no59) ISBN 0-8262-0674-3 LC 87-27200

Mindspan. Dickson, G. R.

A **miner's** Christmas carol, and other frontier tales. Davis, S.

Minimum of two. Winton, T.

Mirrorshades; the cyberpunk anthology; edited by Bruce Sterling. Arbor House 1986 239p ISBN 0-87795-868-8 LC 86-17228

Miss Marple. Christie, A.

Miss Venezuela. Wilson, B.

Mississippi River tales; from the American storytelling tradition; edited by Frank McSherry, Jr., Charles G. Waugh & Martin Harry Greenberg. August House 1988 203p ISBN 0-87483-067-2 LC 88-17554

Mississippi writers v1: Fiction; reflections of childhood and youth; edited by Dorothy Abbott. University Press of Miss. 1985 xli,785p (Center for the Study of Southern Culture series) ISBN 0-87805-231-3 LC 84-5131

Missouri short fiction; 23 stories; edited by Conger Beasley, Jr. BkMk Press 1985 173p ISBN 0-933532-44-X LC 84-72899

Modern romances. Lopatin, J.

A **Modern** Southern reader; major stories, drama, poetry, essays, interviews, and reminiscences from the twentieth-century South; edited by Ben Forkner and Patrick Samway. Peachtree Pubs. 1986 736p ISBN 0-934601-01-1 LC 86-21218
   Analyzed for short stories only

Modern Syrian short stories; translated by Michel G. Azrak; revised by M.J.L. Young. Three Continents Press 1988 131p ISBN 0-89410-440-3 LC 86-51002

Mohr, Nicholasa
   Rituals of survival: a woman's portfolio. Arte Público Press 1985 158p ISBN 0-934770-39-5 LC 84-072300

Monreal, David Nava
   The new neighbor & other stories. Pacific Writers Press 1987 173p ISBN 0-944870-00-7 LC 87-63154

Monsieur Teste in America & other instances of realism. Codrescu, A.

A **month** by the lake & other stories.   Bates, H. E.

Moon mirror.   Norton, A.

Mooney, Michael
   Ancient voices, and other stories. Main Street Press 1987 139p ISBN 0-935399-04-6 LC 87-61544

Moonsinger's friends; an anthology in honor of Andre Norton; edited by Susan Shwartz. Bluejay Bks. 1985 342p ISBN 0-312-94325-3 LC 85-6201

Moore, George, 1852-1933
   In minor keys; the uncollected short stories of George Moore; edited with an introduction by David B. Eakin and Helmut E. Gerber. Syracuse Univ. Press 1985 229p ISBN 0-8156-2338-0

Moore, Lorrie
   Self-help; stories. Knopf 1985 163p ISBN 0-394-53921-4 LC 84-48498

Morality play.   Weaver, G.

Morand, Paul, 1888-1976
   Fancy goods [and] Open all night; stories by Paul Morand; preface by Marcel Proust; translated from the French by Ezra Pound; edited with an introduction by Breon Mitchell. New Directions 1984 xxiv,151p ISBN 0-8112-0888-5 LC 83-23705

Moravia, Alberto, 1907-
   Erotic tales; translated from the Italian by Tim Parks. Farrar, Straus & Giroux 1986 c1983 184p ISBN 0-374-14868-6 LC 85-20411

Morazzoni, Marta, 1950-
   Girl in a turban; translated from the Italian by Patrick Creagh. Knopf 1988 157p ISBN 0-394-56115-5 LC 88-12688

Mordden, Ethan, 1947-
   Everybody loves you; further adventures in gay Manhattan. St. Martin's Press 1988 308p ISBN 0-312-02201-8 LC 88-11545

Morris, Mary, 1947-
   The bus of dreams; stories. Houghton Mifflin 1985 236p ISBN 0-395-36236-9 LC 84-27883

Morris, Wright, 1910-
   Collected stories, 1948-1986. Harper & Row 1986 274p ISBN 0-06-015639-2 LC 86-45334

Morrison, John, 1904-
   This freedom. Penguin Bks. 1986 c1985 200p ISBN 0-14-008633-1

Mortal errors, Alfred Hitchcock's. *See* Alfred Hitchcock's Mortal errors

Mortimer, John Clifford, 1923-
The first Rumpole omnibus. Penguin Bks. 1984 556p ISBN 0-14-006768-X
   Contents: Rumpole of the Bailey; The trials of Rumpole; Rumpole's return
Rumpole for the defence. Penguin Bks. 1984 186p ISBN 0-14-006060-X
The second Rumpole omnibus. Viking 1987 667p ISBN 0-670-81125-4
   Contents: Rumpole for the defence; Rumpole and the golden thread; Rumpole's last case

Moskowitz, Faye
Whoever finds this: I love you. Godine 1988 178p ISBN 0-87923-746-5 LC 87-46372

The **Mother** of dreams, and other short stories; portrayals of women in modern Japanese fiction; edited by Makoto Ueda. Kodansha Int. 1986 279p ISBN 0-87011-775-0 LC 86-45069
The **moths,** and other stories. Viramontes, H. M.
Mourner at the door. Lish, G.
The **mournful** demeanour of Lieutenant Boruvka. Škvorecký, J.
Moustapha's eclipse. McKnight, R.
The **moving** shadow problem. Murphy, P.

Moyer, Kermit, 1943-
Tumbling. University of Ill. Press 1988 128p (Illinois short fiction) ISBN 0-252-01525-8 LC 87-34284

Mozart, Westmoreland, and me. Krysl, M.
Mr. and Mrs. Baby, and other stories. Strand, M.

Mrożek, Sławomir
The elephant; translated from the Polish by Konrad Syrop; illustrated by Daniel Mroz. Grove Press 1984 c1962 176p il ISBN 0-394-62053-4 LC 84-48113

Mrs. Craggs: crimes cleaned up. Keating, H. R. F.
Mrs. Henderson. Wyndham, F.

Mukherjee, Bharati
Darkness. Penguin Bks. 1985 199p (Penguin short fiction) ISBN 0-14-007930-0
The middleman, and other stories. Grove Press 1988 197p ISBN 0-8021-1031-2 LC 87-35048

Muller, Marcia
(ed) Chapter & hearse. *See* Chapter & hearse
(ed) Child's ploy. *See* Child's ploy
(ed) The Deadly arts. *See* The Deadly arts
(ed) Kill or cure. *See* Kill or cure
(ed) She won the West. *See* She won the West
(ed) The Wickedest show on earth. *See* The Wickedest show on earth
(ed) Witches' brew. *See* Witches' brew

Munro, Alice
The progress of love. Knopf 1986 309p ISBN 0-394-55272-5 LC 86-45281

Murder and mystery in Boston; edited by Carol-Lynn Rössel Waugh, Frank D. McSherry, Jr. and Martin H. Greenberg. Dembner Bks. 1987 298p ISBN 0-934878-95-1 LC 87-14361
Murder and mystery in Chicago; edited by Carol-Lynn Rössel Waugh, Frank D. McSherry, Jr., and Martin H. Greenberg. Dembner Bks. 1988 258p ISBN 0-934878-98-6 LC 87-30582
Murder by the tale. Shannon, D.
Murder California style; a collection of short stories; by the Southern California Chapter of Mystery Writers of America; edited by Jon L. Breen and John Ball. St. Martin's Press 1987 291p ISBN 0-312-00620-9 LC 87-4448
   A Thomas Dunne Bk.

Murder in Japan; Japanese stories of crime and detection; edited by John L. Apostolou and Martin H. Greenberg. Dembner Bks. 1987 224p ISBN 0-934878-87-0 LC 86-29121

Murder in Los Angeles; written by Jon L. Breen [et al.]; concept by Bill Adler; introductory note by Thomas Chastain. Morrow 1987 381p ISBN 0-688-06684-4 LC 86-23644

Murder in Manhattan; written by Thomas Chastain [et al.]; concept by Bill Adler. Morrow 1986 307p ISBN 0-688-06475-2 LC 86-5371

Murder round the clock: Pierre Chambrun's crime file. Pentecost, H.

Murphy, George E. (George Edward), 1948-
(comp) The Editors' choice. *See* The Editors' choice

Murphy, Peter, 1945-
The moving shadow problem; stories. University of Qld. Press 1987 c1986 170p ISBN 0-7022-1977-0 LC 85-22726

Murphy, Yannick
Stories in another language. Knopf 1987 143p ISBN 0-394-55707-7 LC 86-46012

Muschg, Adolf, 1934-
The blue man, and other stories; translated from the German by Marlis Zeller Cambon & Michael Hamburger. Braziller 1985 141p ISBN 0-8076-1100-X LC 84-24439

Music lesson. Hall, M. L.

My Christina & other stories. Rodoreda, M.

My first loves. Klíma, I.

My heart's world. Mazel, D.

My merry mornings. Klíma, I.

My mother's sin, and other stories. Vizyēnos, G. M.

My Uncle Silas. Bates, H. E.

The **mysterious** cure, and other stories of Pshrinks Anonymous. Jeppson, J. O.

Mysterious sea stories; compiled and edited by William Pattrick. Salem House 1986 c1985 247p ISBN 0-88162-046-7

Mystery in the mainstream; an anthology of literary crimes; edited by Bill Pronzini, Martin H. Greenberg, and Barry N. Malzberg. Morrow 1986 391p ISBN 0-688-04965-6 LC 86-12410

Mystery Writers of America
The Crime of my life. *See* The Crime of my life
Distant danger. *See* Distant danger

N

Nagibin, Ĭŭriĭ Markovich, 1920-
The peak of success, and other stories; edited by Helena Goscilo. Ardis Pubs. 1986 409p ISBN 0-88233-800-5 LC 85-18696

Naipaul, Shiva, 1945-1985
Beyond the dragon's mouth; stories and pieces. Viking 1985 c1984 424p ISBN 0-670-80392-8 LC 84-40473
Analyzed for short stories only

Naked to naked goes. Flanagan, R.

Narayan, R. K., 1906-
Under the banyan tree, and other stories. Viking 1985 193p ISBN 0-670-80452-5 LC 85-3234
An Elisabeth Sifton Bk.

Nathaniel Hawthorne's tales. Hawthorne, N.

Ndebele, Njabulo
Fools, and other stories. Readers Int. 1986 c1983 280p ISBN 0-930523-19-9

The **Nebula** awards #19; edited by Marta Randall. Arbor House 1984 255p ISBN 0-87795-662-6 LC 83-647399

Nebula awards 20; SFWA'S choices for the best science fiction and fantasy 1984; edited by George Zebrowski. Harcourt Brace Jovanovich 1985 371p ISBN 0-15-164927-8 LC 83-647399

Nebula awards 21; SFWA'S choices for the best science fiction and fantasy, 1985; edited by George Zebrowski. Harcourt Brace Jovanovich 1987 333p ISBN 0-15-164928-6 LC 83-647399

Nebula awards 22; SFWA'S choices for the best science fiction and fantasy, 1986; edited by George Zebrowski. Harcourt Brace Jovanovich 1988 363p ISBN 0-15-164929-4 LC 83-647399

Necessary fictions; selected stories from The Georgia review; edited by Stanley W. Lindberg and Stephen Corey. University of Ga. Press 1986 344p ISBN 0-8203-0882-X LC 86-16079

Nekola, Charlotte
(ed) Writing red. *See* Writing red

The **neon** wilderness. Algren, N.

Nevai, Lucia, 1945-
Star game. University of Iowa Press 1987 152p ISBN 0-87745-174-5 LC 87-16159

Neville, Kris (Kris Ottman), 1925-1980
The science fiction of Kris Neville; edited by Barry N. Malzberg and Martin H. Greenberg. Southern Ill. Univ. Press 1984 241p (Alternatives) ISBN 0-8093-1112-7 LC 83-10514

Neville, Susan
The invention of flight; stories. University of Ga. Press 1984 109p ISBN 0-8203-0706-8 LC 83-24142

Nevins, Francis M., Jr.
(ed) Hitchcock in prime time. *See* Hitchcock in prime time

The **New** adventures of Sherlock Holmes; original stories by eminent mystery writers; edited by Martin Harry Greenberg and Carol-Lynn Rössel Waugh. Carroll & Graf Pubs. 1987 345p il ISBN 0-88184-344-X LC 87-15873
Analyzed for short stories only

New American short stories; the writers select their own favorites; edited by Gloria Norris. New Am. Lib. 1987 c1986 372p ISBN 0-453-00518-7 LC 86-23447

New directions in prose and poetry 48; edited by J. Laughlin with Peter Glassgold and Elizabeth Harper. New Directions 1984 218p ISBN 0-8112-0911-3 LC 37-1751
Analyzed for short stories only

New directions in prose and poetry 49; edited by J. Laughlin with Peter Glassgold and Elizabeth Harper. New Directions 1985 186p ISBN 0-8112-0967-9 LC 37-1751
Analyzed for short stories only

New directions in prose and poetry 50; edited by J. Laughlin with Peter Glassgold and Griselda Ohannessian. New Directions 1986 274p ISBN 0-8112-0993-8 LC 37-1751
Analyzed for short stories only

New directions in prose and poetry 51; edited by J. Laughlin, with Peter Glassgold and Griselda Ohannessian. New Directions 1987 186p ISBN 0-8112-1033-2
Analyzed for short stories only

New directions in prose and poetry 52; edited by J. Laughlin, with Peter Glassgold and Griselda Ohannessian. New Directions 1988 186p ISBN 0-8112-1076-6 LC 37-1751
Analyzed for short stories only

The **New** generation; fiction for our time from America's writing programs; edited by Alan Kaufman; with an introduction by John Knowles. Anchor Press/Doubleday 1987 340p ISBN 0-385-23951-3 LC 87-10034

The **new** girl friend, and other stories of suspense.   Rendell, R.

The **new** neighbor & other stories.   Monreal, D. N.

The **New** press anthology #1: best Canadian short fiction; edited by John Metcalf and Leon Rooke. General 1984 246p (New Press Canadian classics) ISBN 0-7736-7047-5

The **New** press anthology #2: best stories; edited by John Metcalf and Leon Rooke. General 1985 260p (New Press Canadian classics) ISBN 0-7736-7104-8
    Partially analyzed

New stories from the South: the year's best, 1986; edited by Shannon Ravenel. Algonquin Bks. 1986 241p ISBN 0-912867-40-7 LC 86-7971

New stories from the South: the year's best, 1987; edited by Shannon Ravenel. Algonquin Bks. 1987 247p ISBN 0-912697-66-0 LC 87-1356

New stories from the South: the year's best, 1988; edited by Shannon Ravenel. Algonquin Bks. 1988 248p ISBN 0-912697-90-3

New women and new fiction; short stories since the sixties; edited and with an introduction by Susan Cahill. New Am. Lib. 1986 271p ISBN 0-451-62480-7 LC 85-63626
    A Mentor Bk.

The **New** writers of the South; a fiction anthology; edited by Charles East. University of Ga. Press 1987 xxx,287p ISBN 0-8203-0923-0 LC 86-19518

New York street games and other stories and sketches.   Liben, M.

The **news** from Ireland & other stories.   Trevor, W.

The **news** of the world.   Carlson, R.

Night animals.   Pascoe, B.

A **night** at the movies; or, You must remember this.   Coover, R.

Night gallery reader, Rod Serling's. *See* Rod Serling's Night gallery reader

The **night** walk, and other stories.   Upward, E.

The **night** we ate the sparrow.   Lurie, M.

Nightflyers.   Martin, G. R. R.

Nightmares in Dixie; thirteen horror tales from the American South; edited by: Frank D. McSherry, Jr., Charles G. Waugh & Martin Harry Greenberg. August House 1987 260p ISBN 0-87483-034-6 LC 87-1009

Nights in the gardens of Brooklyn.   Swados, H.

Nine men who laughed.   Clarke, A. C.

Nine women.   Grau, S. A.

No marble angels.   Leedom-Ackerman, J.

No reason on earth.   Haake, K.

The **no-sided** professor, and other tales of fantasy, humor, mystery, and philosophy.   Gardner, M.

The **Nobel** reader; short fiction, poetry, and prose by Nobel laureates in literature; edited by Jonathan Eisen and Stuart Troy. Potter 1987 338p ISBN 0-517-56351-7 LC 87-2448
    Analyzed for short stories only

Nolan, William F., 1928-
    (ed) The Black mask boys. *See* The Black mask boys

Nordan, Lewis
    The all-girl football team; stories. Louisiana State Univ. Press 1986 125p ISBN 0-8071-1341-7 LC 86-7440

Norris, Gloria
    (ed) New American short stories. *See* New American short stories

Norris, Helen, 1916-
The Christmas wife; stories. University of Ill. Press 1985 136p (Illinois short fiction) ISBN 0-252-01206-2 LC 84-24080
Water into wine. University of Ill. Press 1988 152p ISBN 0-252-01540-1 LC 87-34289

Norris, Leslie, 1921-
The girl from Cardigan; sixteen stories. Smith, G.M. 1988 164p ISBN 0-87905-296-1 LC 87-31435
A Peregrine Smith Bk.

Norton, Andre, 1912-
(ed) Magic in Ithkar [1]-2. *See* Magic in Ithkar [1]-2
(ed) Magic in Ithkar 3-4. *See* Magic in Ithkar 3-4
Moon mirror. Doherty Assocs. 1988 250p ISBN 0-312-93098-4 LC 88-20136
A TOR Bk.
Moonsinger's friends. *See* Moonsinger's friends
(ed) Tales of the Witch World [1]-2. *See* Tales of the Witch World [1]-2

Norton, Roger C. (Roger Cecil), 1921-
(tr) Voices East and West: German short stories since 1945. *See* Voices East and West: German short stories since 1945
The **Norton** book of American short stories; edited by Peter S. Prescott. Norton 1988 779p ISBN 0-393-02619-1 LC 88-14181

Not a free show. Schulman, H.

Nowakowski, Marek
The canary, and other tales of martial law; translated by Krystyna Bronkowska; with a preface by Leszek Kolakowski. Dial Press 1984 c1983 144p ISBN 0-385-27988-4 LC 83-45562

O

Oates, Joyce Carol, 1938-
The assignation; stories. Ecco Press 1988 192p ISBN 0-88001-200-5 LC 88-3708
Last days; stories. Dutton 1984 241p ISBN 0-525-24248-1 LC 84-1591
Raven's Wing. Dutton 1986 305p ISBN 0-525-24446-8 LC 86-6256
A William Abrahams Bk.

O'Brien, Dan, 1947-
Eminent domain. University of Iowa Press 1987 135p ISBN 0-87745-170-2 LC 86-30846

O'Brien, Edna
A fanatic heart; selected stories of Edna O'Brien. Farrar, Straus & Giroux 1984 461p ISBN 0-374-15342-6 LC 84-13762

O'Brien, Fitz-James, 1828-1862
The supernatural tales of Fitz-James O'Brien v1; edited, with notes and an introduction, by Jessica Amanda Salmonson. Doubleday 1988 xxv, 157p ISBN 0-385-24562-9 LC 87-36525
Volume 1: Macabre tales

O'Brien, Peter
(ed) Fatal recurrences. *See* Fatal recurrences

Ocampo, Silvina, 1889-1952
Leopoldina's dream; translated by Daniel Balderston. Penguin Bks. 1988 205p (Penguin short fiction) ISBN 0-14-010011-3

Ocean of story. Stead, C.

O'Connor, Flannery
Collected works. Library of America 1988 1281p ISBN 0-940450-37-2 LC 87-37829
Partially analyzed

O'Donnell, Peter
Pieces of Modesty. Mysterious Press 1986 c1972 182p ISBN 0-89296-172-4 LC 86-47546

Ōe, Kenzaburō
(ed) The Crazy iris, and other stories of the atomic aftermath. *See* The Crazy iris, and other stories of the atomic aftermath

The **off-season**. Covino, M.

Ohannessian, Griselda
(ed) New directions in prose and poetry 50-52. *See* New directions in prose and poetry 50-52

O'Hara, John, 1905-1970
Collected stories of John O'Hara; selected and with an introduction by Frank MacShane. Random House 1984 414p ISBN 0-394-54083-2 LC 84-42661

O'Kelly, Seumas, 1881-1918
The weaver's grave; Seumas O'Kelly's masterpiece and a selection of his short stories; introduced by Benedict Kiely. Devin-Adair 1984 135p (Classic Irish fiction) ISBN 0-8159-7223-7

The **Old** dance; love stories of one kind or another; edited by Bonnie Burnard. Coteau Bks. 1986 350p ISBN 0-919926-56-8

Old dyke tales. Lynch, L.

The **old** forest, and other stories. Taylor, P. H.

Old maids; short stories by nineteenth century women writers; compiled and with an introduction by Susan Koppelman. Pandora Press 1984 237p ISBN 0-86358-014-9 LC 83-24631

Old wives' tales. Dodd, S. M.

Olmstead, Robert
River dogs; stories. Vintage Bks. 1987 240p ISBN 0-394-74684-8 LC 86-46182

Omni book of science fiction 1-3; edited by Ellen Datlow. Zebra Bks. 1984-1985 3v ISBN 0-8217-1319-1 (v1); 0-8217-1320-5 (v2); 0-8217-1575-5 (v3)

On being foreign; culture shock in short fiction; an international anthology; Tom J. Lewis, Robert E. Jungman, editors. Intercultural Press 1986 xxv,293p ISBN 0-933662-62-9 LC 86-081109

On my being dead, and other stories. Michaelson, L. W.

On the Yankee station. Boyd, W.

Once, a lotus garden, and other stories. Saiki, J.

Once in Europa. Berger, J.

One day in the short happy life of Anna Banana, and other Maine stories. Fahy, C.

One hundred great fantasy short short stories. *See* 100 great fantasy short short stories

One is a wanderer. King, F. H.

One thing leading to another, and other stories. Warner, S. T.

One way, and other Korean short stories; edited by the Korean National Commission for UNESCO. Korea ed. Si-sa-yong-o-sa; Pace Int. Res. 1983 204p (Modern Korean short stories, 5) ISBN 0-89209-206-8 LC 84-150488

One way or another. Cameron, P.

One winter in Eden. Bishop, M.

Oosthuizen, Ann
(ed) Stepping out. *See* Stepping out

Open door. Valenzuela, L.

Oriental tales. Yourcenar, M.

Ortiz, Simon J., 1941-
(ed) Earth power coming. *See* Earth power coming

Ortleb, Charles
(ed) First love/last love. *See* First love/last love

Osborn, Carolyn, 1934-
The fields of memory; short stories. Shearer 1984 276p ISBN 0-940672-23-5 LC 84-72581

Other fires; short fiction by Latin American women; edited by Alberto Manguel. Potter 1986 222p ISBN 0-517-55870-X LC 85-16893

The **other** side of the wall. Shaham, N.

Other weapons. Valenzuela, L.

The **Other** woman; stories of two women and a man; edited and with an introduction by Susan Koppelman. Feminist Press 1984 xxxii, 350p ISBN 0-935312-25-0 LC 84-10099

Other worlds of Isaac Asimov. Asimov, I.

Ounsley, Simon
(ed) Interzone: the 2nd anthology. *See* Interzone: the 2nd anthology

Our roots grow deeper than we know; Pennsylvania writers, Pennsylvania life; Lee Gutkind, editor. University of Pittsburgh Press 1985 290p ISBN 0-8229-3523-6 LC 85-40338
Partially analyzed

Our war and how we won it. Cullen, E. J.

Out of India. Jhabvala, R. P.

Out on the marsh. Updike, D.

Outrageous behaviour. Lurie, M.

Overhead in a balloon. Gallant, M.

Overholser, Wayne D., 1906-
The best Western stories of Wayne D. Overholser; edited by Bill Pronzini and Martin H. Greenberg; introduction by Stephen Overholser. Southern Ill. Univ. Press 1984 xx, 199p ISBN 0-8093-1145-3 LC 83-20111

Oxbridge blues, and other stories. Raphael, F.

The **Oxford** book of Canadian short stories in English; selected by Margaret Atwood & Robert Weaver. Oxford Univ. Press 1986 436p ISBN 0-19-540565-X LC 87-118849

The **Oxford** book of English ghost stories; chosen by Michael Cox and R.A. Gilbert. Oxford Univ. Press 1987 c1986 xvii, 504p ISBN 0-19-214163-5 LC 86-8690

The **Oxford** book of French-Canadian short stories; introduced by Marie-Claire Blais; edited by Richard Teleky. Oxford Univ. Press 1983 268p ISBN 0-19-540298-7

P

P.E.N. new fiction I; edited by Peter Ackroyd. Quartet Bks. 1984 246p ISBN 0-7043-2453-9 LC 84-221000

Pacheco, José Emilio, 1939-
Battles in the desert & other stories; translated by Katherine Silver. New Directions 1987 117p ISBN 0-8112-1019-7 LC 86-28596

Pack, Robert, 1929-
(ed) The Bread Loaf anthology of contemporary American short stories. *See* The Bread Loaf anthology of contemporary American short stories

Pagoda, skull & samurai. Kōda, R.

Painter, Pamela
Getting to know the weather; stories. University of Ill. Press 1985 117p (Illinois short fiction) ISBN 0-252-01195-3 LC 84-24148

Paleo, Lyn
(ed) Worlds apart. *See* Worlds apart

Paley, Grace
Later the same day. Farrar, Straus & Giroux 1985 211p ISBN 0-374-18409-7 LC 84-26072

Palm-of-the-hand stories. Kawabata, Y.

Palma, Clemente, 1872-1944
Malignant tales; translated from the Spanish by Guillermo I. Castillo-Feliú. University Press of Am. 1988 65p ISBN 0-8191-6879-3 LC 87-35997

Paolucci, Anne
Sepia tones; seven short stories; by Anne Attura Paolucci. Rimu 1985 127p il ISBN 0-908703-10-4

Papaellinas, George, 1954-
Ikons; published with the assistance of the Literature Board of the Australia Council. Penguin Bks. 1986 198p ISBN 0-14-008852-0

The **paper** door, and other stories.   Shiga, N.

Parini, Jay
(ed) The Bread Loaf anthology of contemporary American short stories. *See* The Bread Loaf anthology of contemporary American short stories

Parise, Goffredo
Solitudes; introduction by Natalia Ginzburg; translated from the Italian by Isabel Quigly. Vintage Bks. 1985 173p (Adventura: the Vintage Library of contemporary world literature) ISBN 0-394-72994-3 LC 84-40551

Parlour 4, and other stories.   Stewart, J. I. M.

Parotti, Phillip, 1941-
The Greek generals talk; memoirs of the Trojan War. University of Ill. Press 1986 164p maps (Illinois short fiction) ISBN 0-252-01304-2 LC 85-27516

The Trojan generals talk; memoirs of the Greek War. University of Ill. Press 1988 164p maps (Illinois short fiction) ISBN 0-252-01510-X LC 87-34282

The **party**, and other stories.   Chekhov, A. P.

A **party** for the girls.   Bates, H. E.

Paschall, Douglas, 1944-
(ed) Homewords: a book of Tennessee writers. *See* Homewords: a book of Tennessee writers

Pascoe, Bruce, 1947-
Night animals. Penguin Bks. 1986 151p ISBN 0-14-008742-7

Passages to the dream shore; short stories of contemporary Hawaii; edited by Frank Stewart. University of Hawaii Press 1987 222p ISBN 0-8248-1122-4 LC 87-13594
A Kolowalu Bk.

Past times.   Anderson, P.

Pasternak, Boris Leonidovich, 1890-1960
The voice of prose v1; edited by Christopher Barnes. Grove Press 1986 255p ISBN 0-394-55604-6 LC 86-45238
Analyzed for short stories only

Patten, Lewis B.
The best western stories of Lewis B. Patten; edited by Bill Pronzini and Martin H. Greenberg; introduction by Robert E. Briney. Southern Ill. Univ. Press 1987 162p (Western writers series) ISBN 0-8093-1358-8 LC 86-26144

Pattrick, William
(ed) Mysterious sea stories. *See* Mysterious sea stories

Pautz, Peter D.
(ed) The Architecture of fear. *See* The Architecture of fear

Pavese, Cesare
Stories; translated by A. E. Murch. Ecco Press 1987 412p ISBN 0-88001-124-6 LC 86-11505

The **peak** of success, and other stories.   Nagibin, ÍŨ. M.

The **pearlkillers**.   Ingalls, R.

The **Penguin** book of ghost stories; edited by J.A. Cuddon. Penguin Bks. 1984 512p ISBN 0-14-006800-7

The **Penguin** book of horror stories; edited by J.A. Cuddon. Penguin Bks. 1984 607p ISBN 0-14-006799-X

The **Penguin** book of modern British short stories; edited with
an introduction by Malcolm Bradbury. Viking 1987 448p
ISBN 0-670-81926-3

The **Penguin** book of Southern African stories; edited by Stephen
Gray. Penguin Bks. 1986 328p ISBN 0-14-007239-X

The **Penguin** classic crime omnibus; edited by Julian Symons.
Penguin Bks. 1984 378p ISBN 0-14-006739-6

The **Penguin** Henry Lawson. Lawson, H.

The **Penguin** world omnibus of science fiction; an anthology
edited by Brian Aldiss and Sam J. Lundwall. Penguin Bks.
1986 320p ISBN 0-14-008067-8

Pentecost, Hugh, 1903-
Murder round the clock: Pierre Chambrun's crime file. Dodd,
Mead 1985 317p ISBN 0-396-08553-9 LC 84-18784

Peterson, Levi S., 1933-
(ed) Greening wheat: fifteen Mormon short stories. *See* Greening
wheat: fifteen Mormon short stories

Peterson, Mary
Mercy flights; stories. University of Mo. Press 1985 90p
(Breakthrough book, no47) ISBN 0-8262-0464-3 LC 84-19490

Petrakis, Harry Mark
Collected stories. Lake View Press 1987 359p ISBN
0-941702-14-6 LC 86-20859

Pfeil, Fred
Shine on; stories. Lynx House Press [distrib. by Small Press
Distr.] 1987 122p ISBN 0-89924-047-X LC 86-3009

Phillips, Jayne Anne, 1952-
Fast lanes. Dutton; Lawrence, S. 1987 148p ISBN 0-525-24515-4
LC 86-19959

Phippen, Sanford, 1942-
(ed) The Best Maine stories. *See* The Best Maine stories

Phoenix in the ashes. Vinge, J. D.

The **piano** tuner. Meinke, P.

Pictures, moving. Thomas, J.

A **piece** of mine. Cooper, J. C.

Pieces of Modesty. O'Donnell, P.

Piekarski, Vicki
(ed) Westward the women. *See* Westward the women

Pierce, Constance
When things get back to normal, and other stories. Illinois
State Univ.; Fiction Collective 1986 255p ISBN 0-932511-00-7
LC 86-27870

Pierre; or, The ambiguities, Israel Potter: his fifty years of exile,
The piazza tales, The confidence-man: his masquerade,
Uncollected prose, Billy Budd, Sailor: (an inside narrative).
Melville, H.

Pilcher, Rosamunde, 1924-
The blue bedroom, and other stories. St. Martin's Press 1985
257p ISBN 0-312-08527-3 LC 85-1755

Pil'niak, Boris, 1894-1937
Chinese story, and other tales; translated and with an
introduction and notes by Vera T. Reck and Michael Green.
University of Okla. Press 1988 302p ISBN 0-8061-2134-3
LC 88-5757

Piñera, Virgilio
Cold tales; translation by Mark Schafer; revised by Thomas
Christensen; introduction by Guillermo Cabrera-Infante.
Eridanos Press 1988 282p ISBN 0-941419-18-5 LC 88-80807

Pirandello, Luigi, 1867-1936
Tales of suicide; a selection from Luigi Pirandello's Short stories
for a year; translated from the Italian and with an introduction
by Giovanni R. Bussino. Dante Univ. of Am. Press 1988
217p ISBN 0-937832-31-6 LC 87-24549

Piranesi's dream. Campbell, E.

A **place** to die. Bowering, G.

Places in the world a woman could walk. Kauffman, J.

Plane geometry and other affairs of the heart. Berry, R. M.

The **planet** on the table. Robinson, K. S.

The **Planets**; Byron Preiss, editor; Andrew Fraknoi, scientific consultant. Bantam Bks. 1985 336p ISBN 0-553-05109-1 LC 85-47649

    Analyzed for short stories only

The **play,** and other stories. Dixon, S.

Playing with shadows. Whelan, G.

The **pleasure** within. Carter, R.

The **Ploughshares** reader: new fiction for the eighties; edited and with an introduction by DeWitt Henry. Pushcart Press 1985 514p ISBN 0-916366-30-8 LC 84-062095

Poe, Edgar Allan, 1809-1849

Poetry and tales. Library of America 1984 1408p ISBN 0-940450-18-6 LC 83-19931

    Analyzed for short stories only

Tales of suspense; illustrations by Steve Salerno; afterword by James Russell Lowell. Reader's Digest Assn. 1986 271p il ISBN 0-89577-225-6 LC 85-63065

Tales of terror; selected and illustrated by Neil Waldman. Prentice-Hall 1985 186p il ISBN 0-13-884214-0 LC 84-22290

The unabridged Edgar Allan Poe; illustrated by Suzanne Clee. Running Press 1983 1178p il ISBN 0-89471-245-4 LC 83-16023

    Analyzed for short stories only

The **poet** assassinated, and other stories. Apollinaire, G.

Poetry and tales. Poe, E. A.

Pohl, Frederik, 1919-

(comp) Tales from the planet Earth. *See* Tales from the planet Earth

The years of the city. Timescape Bks. 1984 334p ISBN 0-671-49940-8 LC 84-128

Poland under black light. Anderman, J.

Polyphemus. Shea, M.

The **portable** city. Austin, D.

Potter, Nancy A. J.

Legacies. University of Ill. Press 1987 134p (Illinois short fiction) ISBN 0-252-01428-6 LC 86-30851

Power, Victor

The town of Ballymuck. Swallow's Tale Press 1984 162p il ISBN 0-930501-00-4 LC 84-52121

Preiss, Byron

(ed) The Planets. *See* The Planets

(ed) The Universe. *See* The Universe

Prescott, Peter S.

(ed) The Norton book of American short stories. *See* The Norton book of American short stories

Preserving the hunger. Rosenfeld, I.

Price, Patrick L.

(ed) Fantastic stories. *See* Fantastic stories

Prichard, Katharine Susannah, 1884-1969

Tribute; selected stories of Katharine Susannah Prichard; edited by Ric Throssell. University of Qld. Press 1988 xxi, 256p ISBN 0-7022-2166-X

Prime crimes, Ellery Queen's. *See* Ellery Queen's Prime crimes

Prime evil; new stories by the masters of modern horror; edited by Douglas E. Winter. New Am. Lib. 1988 322p ISBN 0-453-00572-1 LC 87-34722

Prime number; 17 stories from Illinois short fiction; edited by Ann Lowry Weir; with an introduction by George Core. University of Ill. Press 1988 xxiv, 326p (Illinois short fiction) ISBN 0-252-01572-X LC 88-10076

Prince, Karen A.
    (ed) Ellery Queen's Crimes and punishments. *See* Ellery Queen's Crimes and punishments
    (ed) Ellery Queen's Memorable characters. *See* Ellery Queen's Memorable characters
    (ed) Ellery Queen's Prime crimes 2. *See* Ellery Queen's Prime crimes 2

Pringle, David
    (ed) Interzone: the first anthology. *See* Interzone: the first anthology
    (ed) Interzone: the 2nd anthology. *See* Interzone: the 2nd anthology

Pritchard, Melissa
    Spirit seizures; stories. University of Ga. Press 1987 182p il ISBN 0-8203-0959-1 LC 87-5932

Pritchett, Michael, 1961-
    The Venus tree. University of Iowa Press 1988 129p (John Simmons short fiction award) ISBN 0-87745-220-2 LC 88-21795

Private—do not open. Soldatow, S.

Private Eye Writers of America
    An Eye for justice. *See* An Eye for justice
    The Eyes have it. *See* The Eyes have it
    Mean streets. *See* Mean streets

The **private** rich. Rand, P.

Prize stories, 1984; The O. Henry Awards; edited and with an introduction by William Abrahams. Doubleday 1984 296p ISBN 0-385-18844-7 LC 21-9372

Prize stories, 1985; The O. Henry Awards; edited and with an introduction by William Abrahams. 65th anniversary ed. Doubleday 1985 319p ISSN 0079-5453 LC 21-9372

Prize stories, 1986; The O. Henry Awards; edited and with an introduction by William Abrahams. Doubleday 1986 274p ISSN 0079-5453 LC 21-9372

Prize stories, 1987; The O. Henry Awards; edited and with an introduction by William Abrahams. Doubleday 1987 320p ISBN 0-385-23594-1 LC 21-9372

Prize stories, 1988; The O. Henry Awards; edited and with an introduction by William Abrahams. Doubleday 1988 366p ISBN 0-385-24183-6 LC 21-9372

Prize stories, Texas Institute of Letters; edited and with an introduction by Marshall Terry. Still Point Press 1986 214p ISBN 0-933841-04-3 LC 85-27953

Proffer, Carl R., 1938-1984
    (ed) The Barsukov Triangle, The two-toned blond & other stories. *See* The Barsukov Triangle, The two-toned blond & other stories

Proffer, Ellendea
    (ed) The Barsukov Triangle, The two-toned blond & other stories. *See* The Barsukov Triangle, The two-toned blond & other stories

The **progress** of love. Munro, A.

The **promise.** Campbell, W. B.

Pronzini, Bill
    (ed) Baker's dozen: 13 short espionage novels. *See* Baker's dozen: 13 short espionage novels
    (ed) Chapter & hearse. *See* Chapter & hearse
    (ed) Child's ploy. *See* Child's ploy
    (ed) The Deadly arts. *See* The Deadly arts

Pronzini, Bill—*Continued*

(ed) The Ethnic detectives. *See* The Ethnic detectives

Graveyard plots; the best short stories of Bill Pronzini. St. Martin's Press 1985 255p ISBN 0-312-34457-0 LC 85-11730

(ed) Great modern police stories. *See* Great modern police stories

(ed) Kill or cure. *See* Kill or cure

(ed) The Mammoth book of private eye stories. *See* The Mammoth book of private eye stories

(ed) Manhattan mysteries. *See* Manhattan mysteries

(ed) Mystery in the mainstream. *See* Mystery in the mainstream

(ed) The Second reel West. *See* The Second reel West

(ed) She won the West. *See* She won the West

Small felonies; fifty mystery short shorts. St. Martin's Press 1988 269p ISBN 0-312-02283-2 LC 88-15856

A Thomas Dunne Bk.

(ed) A Treasury of Civil War stories. *See* A Treasury of Civil War stories

(ed) A Treasury of World War II stories. *See* A Treasury of World War II stories

(ed) Uncollected crimes. *See* Uncollected crimes

(ed) The Western hall of fame. *See* The Western hall of fame

(ed) The Wickedest show on earth. *See* The Wickedest show on earth

(ed) Witches' brew. *See* Witches' brew

(ed) Women sleuths. *See* Women sleuths

Prose, Francine, 1947-

Women and children first; stories. Pantheon Bks. 1988 229p ISBN 0-394-56573-8 LC 87-25827

Prose and poetry. Crane, S.

Proulx, Annie

Heart songs, and other stories. Scribner 1988 151p ISBN 0-684-18717-5 LC 88-11476

Pulaski, Jack

The St. Veronica gig stories. Zephyr Press 1986 170p ISBN 0-939010-10-0 LC 86-50657

The **purchase** of order. Adams, G. G.

Purdy, James, 1923-

The candles of your eyes, and thirteen other stories. Weidenfeld & Nicolson 1987 143p ISBN 1-55584-066-3 LC 86-19087

The **Pushcart** prize IX: best of the small presses; with an index to the first nine volumes; an annual small press reader; edited by Bill Henderson, with the Pushcart Prize editors; introduction by Jayne Anne Phillips. 1984-85 ed. Pushcart Press 1984 588p ISSN 0149-7863 LC 76-58675

Analyzed for short stories only

The **Pushcart** prize X: best of the small presses; with an index to the first ten volumes; an annual small press reader; edited by Bill Henderson, with the Pushcart Prize editors; introduction by George Plimpton; poetry editors: Stanley Plumly, William Stafford. 1985-86 ed. Pushcart Press 1985 xxiv,499p ISSN 0149-7863

Analyzed for short stories only

The **Pushcart** prize XI: best of the small presses; with an index to the first eleven volumes; an annual small press reader; edited by Bill Henderson, with the Pushcart Prize editors; introduction by Cynthia Ozick; poetry editors: Philip Levine, David Wojahn. 1986-87 ed. Pushcart Press 1986 xxvii,459p ISSN 0149-7863 LC 76-58675

Analyzed for short stories only

The **Pushcart** prize XII: best of the small presses; —with an index to the first twelve volumes: an annual small press reader; edited by Bill Henderson, with The Pushcart Prize

editors; introduction by Frank Conroy; poetry editors: Jorie Graham, Robert Hass. Pushcart Press 1987 559p ISSN 0149-7863
  Analyzed for short stories only
Pym, Barbara
  Civil to strangers, and other writings; edited by Hazel Holt. Dutton 1988 388p ISBN 0-525-24593-6 LC 87-30341
  Partially analyzed
Pynchon, Thomas
  Slow learner; early stories. Little, Brown 1984 193p ISBN 0-316-72442-4 LC 84-934

Q

Quammen, David, 1948-
  Blood line; stories of fathers and sons. Graywolf Press 1988 169p ISBN 0-55597-100-8 LC 87-81374
The **quarterback** speaks to his God. Wilner, H.
Queen, Ellery
  The best of Ellery Queen; four decades of stories from the mystery masters; edited by Francis M. Nevins, Jr., and Martin H. Greenberg. Beaufort Bks. 1985 238p ISBN 0-8253-0246-3 LC 84-21572
The **question** she put to herself. Brady, M.
The **quests** of Simon Ark. Hoch, E. D.

R

Rabinowitz, Paula
  (ed) Writing red. See Writing red
Rainbow, river & tree. Hoyt, M. S.
Rambach, Peggy
  When the animals leave; short stories. Ampersand Press 1986 47p ISBN 0-935331-00-X LC 86-70220
Ramírez, Sergio, 1942-
  Stories; translated by Nick Caistor. Readers Int. 1986 118p ISBN 0-930523-28-8
Rand, Peter, 1940-
  The private rich; a family album; stories; photographs edited by Elizabeth Bird. Crown 1984 184p il ISBN 0-517-55449-6 LC 84-14273
Randall, Marta
  (ed) The Nebula awards #19. See The Nebula awards #19
Randisi, Robert J.
  (ed) An Eye for justice. See An Eye for justice
  (ed) The Eyes have it. See The Eyes have it
  (ed) Mean streets. See Mean streets
Raphael, Frederic, 1931-
  Oxbridge blues, and other stories. University of Ark. Press 1984 183p ISBN 0-938626-27-2 LC 83-18268
Rasputin, Valentin Grigor'evich
  You live and love, and other stories; translated by Alan Myers; foreword by Richard Lourie. Vanguard Press 1986 xxii,180p ISBN 0-8149-0916-7 LC 85-26575
Ravenel, Shannon
  (ed) The Best American short stories, 1984-1988. See The Best American short stories, 1984-1988
  (ed) New stories from the South: the year's best, 1986. See New stories from the South: the year's best, 1986
Raven's Wing. Oates, J. C.
Ready or not, here come fourteen frightening stories!; chosen by Joan Kahn. Greenwillow Bks. 1987 159p ISBN 0-688-07167-8 LC 86-31875

Real illusions. Haley, R.

Reasons to live. Hempel, A.

Reclaiming Medusa; short stories by contemporary Puerto Rican women; edited and translated by Diana Vélez. Spinsters/Aunt Lute 1988 161p ISBN 0-933216-41-6 LC 88-11430
   Partially analyzed

Reed, Kit, 1932-
   The revenge of the senior citizens ** plus; a short story collection. Doubleday 1986 189p ISBN 0-385-19315-7 LC 85-22868

Reeman, Douglas
   Sea captains' tales. *See* Sea captains' tales

Rees, David, 1936-
   Islands; a collection of short stories. Knights Press 1984 159p ISBN 0-915175-06-1 LC 84-19408

Regent, Peter
   Laughing Pig, and other stories; with drawings by the author. Clark, R. 1984 183p il ISBN 0-86072-079-9

Remains: stories of Vietnam. Crapser, W.

Remind me to murder you later. Boylan, J.

Rendell, Ruth, 1930-
   The new girl friend, and other stories of suspense. Pantheon Bks. 1986 c1985 172p ISBN 0-394-54813-2 LC 85-43181

A **rendezvous** in Averoigne. Smith, C. A.

Resident alien. Blaise, C.

A **Respite,** and other Korean short stories; edited by the Korean National Commission for UNESCO. Korea ed. Si-sa-yong-o-sa; Pace Int. Res. 1983 169p (Modern Korean short stories, 6) ISBN 0-89209-207-6 LC 84-141663

Resurrectionists. Working, R.

Return trips. Adams, A.

The **revenge** of the senior citizens ** plus. Reed, K.

Rey Rosa, Rodrigo, 1958-
   The beggar's knife; translated by Paul Bowles. City Lights Bks. 1985 95p ISBN 0-87286-166-X LC 85-5742

Rhys, Jean
   The collected short stories; introduction by Diana Athill. Norton 1987 403p ISBN 0-393-02375-3

Rifaat, Alifa
   Distant view of a minaret, and other stories; translated by Denys Johnson-Davies. Quartet Bks. 1984 c1983 116p ISBN 0-7043-2401-6 LC 84-672074

Ríos, Alberto
   The iguana killer; twelve stories of the heart; etchings by Antonio Pazos. Blue Moon-Confluence Press [distrib. by Kampmann & Co.] 1984 119p il ISBN 0-933188-28-5 LC 84-256650

Ripper!; edited by Gardner Dozois and Susan Casper. Doherty Assocs. 1988 xx,427p ISBN 0-812-51700-8 LC 88-50334
   A TOR Horror Bk.

Ritchie, Jack, 1922-1983
   The adventures of Henry Turnbuckle; detective comedies; edited by Francis M. Nevins, Jr. & Martin H. Greenberg; introduction by Francis M. Nevins, Jr. Southern Ill. Univ. Press 1987 374p (Mystery makers) ISBN 0-8093-1397-9 LC 86-31372

Rituals of survival: a woman's portfolio. Mohr, N.

River dogs. Olmstead, R.

The **Road** to Sampo, and other Korean short stories; edited by the Korean National Commission for UNESCO. Si-sa-yong-o-sa; Pace Int. Res. 1983 237p (Modern Korean short stories, 9) ISBN 0-89209-210-6 LC 84-141889

Robak's firm. Hensley, J. L.

Robert Adams' Book of soldiers; edited by Robert Adams, Martin H. Greenberg and Pamela Crippen Adams. New Am. Lib. 1988 348p ISBN 0-451-15559-9

Robert Silverberg's Worlds of wonder; edited and with an introduction by Robert Silverberg. Warner Bks. 1987 352p ISBN 0-446-51369-5 LC 87-21603

Roberts, Garyn G.
(comp) A Cent a story! *See* A Cent a story!

Roberts, Nancy, 1941-
Women and other bodies of water; a short story collection. Dragon Gate 1987 129p ISBN 0-937872-38-5 LC 87-9060

Robinson, Fred Miller, 1942-
(ed) A Good deal. *See* A Good deal

Robinson, Kim Stanley
The planet on the table. Doherty Assocs. 1986 241p ISBN 0-312-93595-1 LC 85-52258
A TOR Bk.

Robison, James
Rumor, and other stories. Summit Bks. 1985 169p ISBN 0-671-52722-3 LC 85-2629

Robison, Mary
Believe them; stories. Knopf 1988 146p ISBN 0-394-53942-7 LC 87-82571

Robot dreams. Asimov, I.

Robots, androids, and mechanical oddities. Dick, P. K.

Rochman, Hazel
(ed) Somehow tenderness survives. *See* Somehow tenderness survives

Rock Springs. Ford, R.

Rod Serling's Night gallery reader; edited by Carol Serling, Charles G. Waugh, & Martin H. Greenberg. Dembner Bks. 1987 326p ISBN 0-934878-93-5 LC 87-14360

Rodoreda, Mercè, 1909-
My Christina & other stories; translated and with an introduction by David H. Rosenthal. Graywolf Press 1984 133p il (Graywolf short fiction ser) ISBN 0-915308-64-9 LC 84-81629

Roger Caras' Treasury of great cat stories. Dutton 1987 495p ISBN 0-525-24398-4 LC 86-2200
A Truman Talley Bk.

Roger Caras' Treasury of great dog stories. Dutton 1987 497p ISBN 0-525-24399-2 LC 86-6264
A Truman Talley Bk.

Rogers, T. N. R.
Too far from home; stories. University of Mo. Press 1988 114p (Breakthrough book, no56) ISBN 0-8262-0671-9 LC 87-25514

Rojas-Urista, Xelina, 1954-
(ed) Southwest tales. *See* Southwest tales

Rölvaag, Ole Edvart, 1876-1931
When the wind is in the south, and other stories; by O. E. Rolvaag; selected and translated by Solveig Zempel. Center for Western Studies 1984 88p il ISBN 0-931170-25-7 LC 84-72484

Rooke, Leon
A bolt of white cloth. Ecco Press 1985 c1984 176p ISBN 0-88001-078-9 LC 84-18868
(ed) The New press anthology #1: best Canadian short fiction. *See* The New press anthology #1: best Canadian short fiction
(ed) The New press anthology #2: best stories. *See* The New press anthology #2: best stories
Sing me no love songs, I'll say you no prayers; selected stories. Ecco Press 1984 290p ISBN 0-88001-036-3 LC 84-4064

Room to move; an anthology of Australian women's short stories; edited by Suzanne Falkiner. Watts 1986 246p ISBN 0-531-15019-4 LC 87-134554

Rope-dancer. Fitzgerald, M. J.

Rose, Daniel Asa

Small family with rooster; stories. St. Martin's Press 1988 227p ISBN 0-312-01826-6 LC 88-1923

Rose, Joel

(ed) Between C & D. *See* Between C & D

Rosenfeld, Isaac, 1918-1956

Preserving the hunger; an Isaac Rosenfeld reader; edited and introduced by Mark Shechner; foreword by Saul Bellow. Wayne State Univ. Press 1988 463p ISBN 0-8143-1879-7 LC 87-27929

Analyzed for short stories only

Rosenthal, Lucy

(ed) Great American love stories. *See* Great American love stories

Roses and thorns; the second blooming of the Hundred Flowers in Chinese fiction, 1979-80; Perry Link, editor. University of Calif. Press 1984 346p ISBN 0-520-04979-9 LC 83-9147

Ross, Veronica

Dark secrets; new stories. Oberon Press 1983 101p ISBN 0-88750-473-6 LC 83-170402

Rossi, Agnes, 1957-

Athletes and artists; stories. New York Univ. Press 1987 81p ISBN 0-8147-7400-8 LC 87-1688

Rossiter, Sarah

Beyond this bitter air. University of Ill. Press 1987 132p (Illinois short fiction) ISBN 0-252-01429-4 LC 87-5031

Roth, Joseph, 1894-1939

Hotel Savoy; Fallmerayer the stationmaster [and] The bust of the emperor; translated from the German by John Hoare. Overlook Press 1986 183p ISBN 0-87951-211-3 LC 86-12507

Rottensteiner, Franz

(ed) The Slaying of the dragon. *See* The Slaying of the dragon

Roubles in words, kopeks in figures, and other stories. Shukshin, V. M.

Rough translations. Giles, M.

Rucker, Rudy von Bitter, 1946-

(ed) Mathenauts: tales of mathematical wonder. *See* Mathenauts: tales of mathematical wonder

Ruffian on the stair. Clark, G.

Ruffolo, Lisa

Holidays; short stories; with artworks by Kathryn Wright. New Rivers Press 1987 107p (Minnesota voices project, no29) ISBN 0-89823-086-1 LC 86-63557

Rule, Jane, 1931-

Inland passage. Naiad Press 1985 273p ISBN 0-930044-58-4 LC 84-20770

Rumor, and other stories. Robison, J.

Rumpole for the defence. Mortimer, J. C.

Rush, Norman

Whites; stories. Knopf 1986 150p ISBN 0-394-54471-4 LC 85-45598

Russ, Joanna, 1937-

Extra(ordinary) people. St. Martin's Press 1984 160p ISBN 0-312-27806-3 LC 83-19156

The hidden side of the moon; stories. St. Martin's Press 1987 229p ISBN 0-312-01105-9 LC 87-16275

Russell, Alan K.

(ed) The Book of the dead. *See* The Book of the dead

Russell, Eric Frank, 1905-
Men, Martians and machines; introduction by George Zebrowski; foreword by Isaac Asimov. Crown 1984 216p (Classics of modern science fiction, v1) ISBN 0-517-55185-3 LC 83-23235

Russian and Polish women's fiction; translated and edited by Helena Goscilo. University of Tenn. Press 1985 343p ISBN 0-87049-456-2 LC 84-20915

Ruta, Suzanne
Stalin in the Bronx, and other stories. Grove Press 1987 154p ISBN 0-8021-0018-X LC 87-8507

A **Ruth** Suckow omnibus.   Suckow, R.

Ryan, Alan, 1943-
The bones wizard. Doubleday 1988 178p ISBN 0-385-24223-9 LC 87-20057
(ed) Halloween horrors. *See* Halloween horrors
(ed) Haunting women. *See* Haunting women
(ed) Vampires. *See* Vampires

Ryder, Frank Glessner, 1916-
(ed) German romantic novellas. *See* German romantic novellas
(ed) German romantic stories. *See* German romantic stories

S

Safety patrol.   Martone, M.

Sagan, Françoise, 1935-
Incidental music; translated by C.J. Richards. Dutton 1984 c1983 154p ISBN 0-525-24213-9 LC 83-20590

Sage, Victor
Dividing lines. Chatto & Windus; Hogarth Press 1985 166p ISBN 0-7011-2811-9

Saiki, Jessica
Once, a lotus garden, and other stories; with drawings by the author. New Rivers Press 1987 130p il (Minnesota voices project, no30) ISBN 0-89823-087-X LC 86-63553

Saints and strangers.   Carter, A.

The **salamander** and the fire.   Davin, D.

Salas, Floyd, 1931-
(ed) Stories and poems from close to home. *See* Stories and poems from close to home

Sams, Ferrol, 1922-
The widow's mite & other stories. Peachtree Pubs. 1987 218p ISBN 0-934601-26-7 LC 87-80971

Samway, Patrick H.
(ed) A Modern Southern reader. *See* A Modern Southern reader
(ed) Stories of the modern South. *See* Stories of the modern South

Sandberg, Peter Lars, 1934-
Gabe's fall, and other climbing stories. Birchfield Bks. 1988 156p il ISBN 0-912871-02-4 LC 87-71862

Sandel, Cora, 1880-1974
Cora Sandel: selected short stories; translated by Barbara Wilson. Seal Press 1985 204p (Women in translation) ISBN 0-931188-31-8 LC 85-22295
The silken thread; stories and sketches; translated from the Norwegian and with an introduction by Elizabeth Rokkan. Ohio Univ. Press 1987 175p ISBN 0-8214-0864-X LC 86-23857

Sanders, Scott R. (Scott Russell), 1945-
Fetching the dead; stories. University of Ill. Press 1984 141p (Illinois short fiction) ISBN 0-252-01115-5 LC 83-17668

Sanford, Winifred M., 1890-
Windfall, and other stories; foreword by Emerett Sanford Miles; afterword by Lou Halsell Rodenberger. Southern Methodist Univ. Press 1988 179p (Southwest life and letters) ISBN 0-87074-267-1 LC 87-43105
Analyzed for short stories only
Sanitary centennial, and selected short stories. Sorrentino, F.
Saratoga, hot. Calisher, H.
Sargent, Pamela
(ed) Afterlives. *See* Afterlives
Saroyan, William, 1908-1981
Madness in the family; edited by Leo Hamalian. New Directions 1988 141p ISBN 0-8112-1064-2 LC 87-28268
Saving face, and other stories. Lofts, N.
Scared stiff. Campbell, R.
Scars and other distinguishing marks. Matheson, R. C.
Scenes from the homefront. Vogan, S.
The **scent** of spruce. Brender à Brandis, M.
Schiff, Stuart David, 1946-
(ed) Whispers V. *See* Whispers V
Schinto, Jeanne, 1951-
Shadow bands; stories. Ontario Review Press [distrib. by Braziller] 1988 164p ISBN 0-86538-065-1 LC 88-19830
Schmidt, Stanley
(ed) [Analog]: Writers' choice v2. *See* [Analog]: Writers' choice v2
(ed) From mind to mind: tales of communication from Analog. *See* From mind to mind: tales of communication from Analog
Schow, David J.
(ed) Silver scream. *See* Silver scream
Schulman, Helen
Not a free show; stories. Knopf 1988 165p ISBN 0-394-56166-X LC 87-40493
Schwartz, Betty Ann
(comp) Great ghost stories. *See* Great ghost stories
Schwartz, Jonathan
The man who knew Cary Grant. Random House 1988 249p ISBN 0-394-56967-9 LC 88-18248
Schwartz, Lynne Sharon
Acquainted with the night, and other stories. Harper & Row 1984 226p ISBN 0-06-015307-5 LC 83-48815
The melting pot, and other subversive stories. Harper & Row 1987 230p ISBN 0-06-015814-X LC 87-45074
Schwartz, Steven, 1950-
To Leningrad in winter; stories. University of Mo. Press 1985 88p (Breakthrough book, no48) ISBN 0-8262-0465-1 LC 84-17387
Schwob, Marcel, 1867-1905
The king in the golden mask, and other writings; selected, translated, and introduced by Iain White. Carcanet New Press 1984 c1982 186p ISBN 0-85635-403-1 LC 82-196577
Partially analyzed
Sciascia, Leonardo
Sicilian uncles; translated from the Italian by N. S. Thompson. Carcanet Press 1986 205p ISBN 0-85635-555-0
The **science** fiction of Kris Neville. Neville, K.
The **science** fiction of Mark Twain. Twain, M.
The **Science** fictional Olympics; edited by Isaac Asimov, Martin H. Greenberg, and Charles G. Waugh. New Am. Lib. 1984 356p (Isaac Asimov's wonderful worlds of science fiction, no2) ISBN 0-451-12976-8
A Signet Bk.
Scission. Winton, T.

A **scrap** of time, and other stories. Fink, I.

The **scrutinies** of Simon Iff. Crowley, A.

Sea captains' tales; compiled by Alexander Enfield. Century [distrib. by David & Charles] 1986 402p ISBN 0-7126-0157-0 LC 86-190042

      At head of title: Douglas Reeman introduces

The **sea-rabbit;** or, The artist of life. Walker, W.

The **sealed** angel, and other stories. Leskov, N. S.

Searls, Hank

  The adventures of Mike Blair. Mysterious Press 1988 214p ISBN 0-89296-918-0 LC 87-33251

    A Dime Detective Bk.

Seasonal rain, and other stories. Flynn, R.

Seasons in flight. Aldiss, B. W.

The **Second** reel West; edited by Bill Pronzini and Martin H. Greenberg. Doubleday 1985 182p ISBN 0-385-23103-2 LC 85-4409

The **second** Rumpole omnibus. Mortimer, J. C.

Secret villages. Dunn, D.

Secrets, and other stories. MacLaverty, B.

Selected short stories. Grin, A.

Selected short stories of Padraic Colum. Colum, P.

Selected stories. Dubus, A.

Selected stories and sketches. Hogg, J.

Selected stories from The Southern review, 1965-1985; edited by Lewis P. Simpson [et al.]. Louisiana State Univ. Press 1988 374p ISBN 0-8071-1443-X LC 87-21383

The **selected** stories of Robert Bloch. Bloch, R.

Selected tales of grim and grue from the horror pulps; edited by Sheldon Jaffery. Bowling Green State Univ. Popular Press 1987 195p il ISBN 0-87972-391-2 LC 86-72859

Selected tales of Jacques Ferron. Ferron, J.

Self-help. Moore, L.

Sennett, Dorothy, 1909-

  (ed) Full measure. *See* Full measure

Sensuous science fiction from the weird and spicy pulps; Sheldon Jaffery, editor. Popular Press 1984 164p il ISBN 0-87972-305-X

The **sentinel.** Clarke, A. C.

Sepia tones. Paolucci, A.

The **sergeant's** cat, and other stories. Van de Wetering, J.

Serious trouble. Friedman, P.

Serling, Carol

  (ed) Rod Serling's Night gallery reader. *See* Rod Serling's Night gallery reader

Serling, Rod, 1924-1975

  Rod Serling's Night gallery reader. *See* Rod Serling's Night gallery reader

The **seventh** horse, and other tales. Carrington, L.

Sexson, Lynda

  Margaret of the imperfections; stories. Persea Bks. 1988 211p ISBN 0-89255-131-3 LC 88-4150

Shacochis, Bob

  Easy in the islands; stories. Crown 1985 213p ISBN 0-517-55549-2 LC 84-15570

Shadow bands. Schinto, J.

Shadows 7; edited by Charles L. Grant. Doubleday 1984 181p ISBN 0-385-18943-5

Shadows 8-9; edited by Charles L. Grant. Doubleday 1985-1986 2v ISBN 0-385-19823-X (v8); 0-385-23486-4 (v9)

Shaham, Nathan

  The other side of the wall; three novellas; translated from the Hebrew by Leonard Gold. Jewish Publ. Soc. of Am. 1983 281p ISBN 0-8276-0223-5 LC 83-65

Shaik, Fatima, 1952-
    The mayor of New Orleans; just talking jazz. Creative Arts
      1987 143p ISBN 0-88739-050-1 LC 87-71147
Shannon, Dell, 1921-
    Murder by the tale. Morrow 1987 226p ISBN 0-688-07538-X
      LC 87-15419
Shapard, Robert, 1942-
    (ed) Sudden fiction. *See* Sudden fiction
Shaw, Janet Beeler, 1937-
    Some of the things I did not do; stories. University of Ill.
      Press 1984 131p (Illinois short fiction) ISBN 0-252-01109-0
      LC 83-18319
She won the West; an anthology of Western & frontier stories
    by women; edited by Marcia Muller & Bill Pronzini. Morrow
    1985 372p ISBN 0-688-04701-7 LC 84-20789
Shea, Michael, 1946-
    Polyphemus; stories; foreword by Algis Budrys; artwork by
      John Stewart. Arkham House Pubs. 1987 245p il ISBN
      0-87054-155-2 LC 87-14411
Sheckley, Robert, 1928-
    Is that what people do?; short stories. Holt, Rinehart & Winston
      1984 402p ISBN 0-03-063707-4 LC 83-12908
Sheehan, Ronan, 1953-
    Boy with an injured eye. Brandon 1983 135p ISBN 0-86322-028-2
      LC 84-110086
Shefner, Evelyn, 1919-
    Common body, royal bones; three stories. Coffee House Press
      1987 119p ISBN 0-918273-33-1 LC 87-27761
Shenandoah: an anthology; James Boatwright, editor. Pushcart
    Press 1985 512p ISBN 0-916366-33-2 LC 85-60719
      Analyzed for short stories only
Shepard, Lucius
    The jaguar hunter; with a foreword by Michael Bishop and
      illustrations by Jeffrey K. Potter. Arkham House Pubs. 1987
      404p il ISBN 0-87054-154-4 LC 86-22282
Sherlock Holmes through time and space; edited by Isaac Asimov,
    Martin Harry Greenberg, and Charles G. Waugh. Bluejay
    Bks. 1984 355p il ISBN 0-312-94400-4 LC 84-18580
Shiga, Naoya, 1883-1971
    The paper door, and other stories; translated by Lane Dunlop.
      North Point Press 1987 173p ISBN 0-86547-260-2
      LC 86-60992
Shine on. Pfeil, F.
The **shoebox** of desire, and other tales. Woodman, A.
Sholem Aleichem, 1859-1916
    Tevye the dairyman and The railroad stories; translated from
      the Yiddish and with an introduction by Hillel Halkin.
      Schocken Bks. 1987 xli, 309p (Library of Yiddish classics)
      ISBN 0-8052-4026-8 LC 86-24835
The **shooting** gallery. Tsushima, Y.
The **short** fiction of Rudolph Fisher. Fisher, R.
Short season, and other stories. Klinkowitz, J.
The **short** stories of Fray Angelico Chavez. Chavez, A.
Short stories of the sea; selected and arranged by George C.
    Solley and Eric Steinbaugh ; with introductions and biographies
    by David O. Tomlinson. Naval Inst. Press 1984 566p ISBN
    0-87021-650-3 LC 84-9823
Short story international 42-47; tales by the world's great
    contemporary writers presented unabridged. International
    Cultural Exchange 1984 6v ISSN 0147-7706
Short story international 48-53; tales by the world's great
    contemporary writers presented unabridged. International
    Cultural Exchange 1985 6v ISSN 0147-7706

Short story international 54-58; tales by the world's great contemporary writers presented unabridged. International Cultural Exchange 1986 5v ISSN 0147-7706

Short story international 59-65; tales by the world's great contemporary writers presented unabridged. International Cultural Exchange 1986-1987 7v ISSN 0147-7706

Short story international 66-71; tales by the world's great contemporary writers presented unabridged. International Cultural Exchange 1988 6v ISSN 0147-7706

Shorter masterpieces, Henry James'. James, H.

The **Shōwa** anthology; modern Japanese short stories; edited by Van C. Gessel, Tomone Matsumoto. Kodansha Int. 1985 2v ISBN 0-87011-739-4 (v1); 0-87011-747-5 (v2) LC 86-175482

Showdown, and other stories. Brondoli, M.

A **Shtetl,** and other Yiddish novellas; edited, with introductions and notes, by Ruth R. Wisse. Wayne State Univ. Press 1986 359p ISBN 0-8143-1848-7 LC 86-15794

Shukshin, Vasilii Makarovich, 1929-1974
Roubles in words, kopeks in figures, and other stories; [by] Vasily Shukshin; translated from the Russian by Natasha Ward and David Iliffe; introduction by Yevgeny Yevtushenko. Boyars, M. 1985 207p ISBN 0-7145-2813-7 LC 84-14675
Analyzed for short stories only

Shwartz, Susan M.
(ed) Moonsinger's friends. *See* Moonsinger's friends

Sicilian uncles. Sciascia, L.

The **signalman** & other ghost stories. Dickens, C.

Silent retreats. Deaver, P. F.

The **silken** thread. Sandel, C.

Silkin, Jon
(ed) Stand one. *See* Stand one

Silva, Beverly
The cat, and other stories. Bilingual Press/Editorial Bilingüe 1986 102p ISBN 0-916950-69-7 LC 86-70702

The **silver** DeSoto. Floyd, P. L.

Silver scream; edited by David J. Schow; introduction by Tobe Hooper; stories by John M. Ford [et al.]; illustrated by Kevin Davies. Dark Harvest 1988 369p il ISBN 0-913165-27-1 LC 130266

Silverberg, Robert
Beyond the safe zone; collected stories. Fine, D.I. 1986 472p ISBN 0-917657-60-8 LC 85-81169

The conglomeroid cocktail party. Arbor House 1984 284p ISBN 0-87795-557-8 LC 84-70410

(ed) Robert Silverberg's Worlds of wonder. *See* Robert Silverberg's Worlds of wonder

Silvis, Randall, 1950-
The luckiest man in the world. University of Pittsburgh Press 1984 212p ISBN 0-8229-3476-0 LC 84-4217

Simenon, Georges, 1903-1989
Maigret at the crossroads; Maigret at the crossroads; Maigret stonewalled; Maigret mystified. Penguin Bks. 1984 317p ISBN 0-14-006652-7

Simpson, Ethel C., 1937-
(ed) Arkansas in short fiction. *See* Arkansas in short fiction

Simpson, Lewis P.
(ed) Selected stories from The Southern review, 1965-1985. *See* Selected stories from The Southern review, 1965-1985

Sing me no love songs, I'll say you no prayers. Rooke, L.

Singer, Isaac Bashevis, 1904-
The death of Methuselah, and other stories. Farrar, Straus & Giroux 1988 244p ISBN 0-374-13563-0 LC 87-21238

Singer, Isaac Bashevis, 1904-—*Continued*
  The image, and other stories. Farrar, Straus & Giroux 1985
    310p ISBN 0-374-17465-2 LC 85-4487
Singing on the Titanic. Glasser, P.
The **Singing** Rabbi. Avery, M.
The **siren**. Buzzati, D.
Sisskind, Mitch
  Visitations; stories. Brightwaters Press 1984 89p ISBN
    0-918305-02-0 LC 84-071460
Sister age. Fisher, M. F. K.
Sister ships, and other stories. London, J.
Six feet of the country. Gordimer, N.
Skeleton crew. King, S.
Skelton, Robin
  The man who sang in his sleep. Porcupine's Quill [distrib.
    by Firefly Bks.] 1984 86p ISBN 0-88984-053-9
Skinny island. Auchincloss, L.
Sklar, Morty, 1935-
  (ed) Editor's choice II. *See* Editor's choice II
  (ed) Here's the story: fiction with heart. *See* Here's the story:
    fiction with heart
Skrzynecki, Peter, 1945-
  The wild dogs; stories. University of Qld. Press 1987 202p
    ISBN 0-7022-2014-0 LC 86-15888
Škvorecký, Josef
  The mournful demeanour of Lieutenant Boruvka; translated
    by Rosemary Kavan, Kaca Polackova and George Theiner.
    Norton 1987 c1973 288p ISBN 0-393-02470-9 LC 87-18504
Sladek, John Thomas
  The lunatics of Terra. Gollancz [distrib. by David & Charles]
    1984 192p ISBN 0-575-03464-5
Slaves of New York. Janowitz, T.
The **Slaying** of the dragon; modern tales of the playful imagination;
    edited and with an introduction by Franz Rottensteiner.
    Harcourt Brace Jovanovich 1984 303p ISBN 0-15-182975-6
    LC 83-26542
A **slight** momentary affliction. Dorr, L.
Sligo, John, 1944-
  Final things. Penguin Bks. 1987 337p ISBN 0-14-009880-1
Slow exposures. Wheatcroft, J.
Slow homecoming. Handke, P.
Slow learner. Pynchon, T.
The **slugger** heart & other stories. Campos-De Metro, J.
Small claims. Ciment, J.
Small family with rooster. Rose, D. A.
Small felonies. Pronzini, B.
Smiley, Jane, 1949-
  The age of grief; a novella and stories. Knopf 1987 213p
    ISBN 0-394-55848-0 LC 87-45120
Smith, Clark Ashton, 1893-1961
  A rendezvous in Averoigne; best fantastic tales of Clark Ashton
    Smith; with an introduction by Ray Bradbury; with
    illustrations by Jeffrey K. Potter. Arkham House Pubs. 1988
    472p il ISBN 0-87054-156-0 LC 87-28990
Smith and other events. St. Pierre, P. H.
Snapshots of paradise. Geras, A.
Snodgrass, Melinda
  (ed) A Very large array. *See* A Very large array
Soldatow, Sasha, 1947-
  Private—do not open. Penguin Bks. 1987 170p ISBN
    0-14-008526-2

Soldiers & civilians; Americans at war and at home; short stories; edited by Tom Jenks. Bantam Bks. 1986 305p ISBN 0-553-05180-6 LC 86-47574

Solitudes. Parise, G.

Solley, George C., 1946-
(ed) Short stories of the sea. *See* Short stories of the sea

Some of Eve's daughters. Gault, C.

Some of the things I did not do. Shaw, J. B.

Some soul to keep. Cooper, J. C.

Somehow tenderness survives; stories of Southern Africa; selected by Hazel Rochman. Harper & Row 1988 147p ISBN 0-06-025022-4 LC 88-916

Something out there. Gordimer, N.

Something to write home about. Ingalls, R.

The **songbirds** of pain. Kilworth, G.

Sonnenberg, Ben
(ed) A Grand Street reader. *See* A Grand Street reader

The **sorcerer's** apprentice. Johnson, C. R.

Sorrells, Robert T., 1932-
The blacktop champion of Ickey Honey, and other stories. University of Ark. Press 1988 231p ISBN 1-55728-045-2; 1-55728-046-0 LC 88-14311

Sorrentino, Fernando
Sanitary centennial, and selected short stories; translated by Thomas C. Meehan. University of Tex. Press 1988 xxvi, 186p (Texas Pan American ser) ISBN 0-292-77608-X LC 88-4972
Analyzed for short stories only

Southwest tales; a contemporary collection in memory of Tomás Rivera; edited by Alurista and Xelina Rojas-Urista. Maize Press 1986 158p ISBN 0-939558-09-2 LC 85-61180
Partially analyzed

Space wars; created by Poul Anderson; edited by Charles Waugh and Martin H. Greenberg. Doherty Assocs. 1988 372p ISBN 0-812-53046-2
A TOR Bk.

Spark, Debra, 1962-
(ed) 20 under 30. *See* 20 under 30

Spark, Muriel
The stories of Muriel Spark. Dutton 1985 314p ISBN 0-525-24330-5 LC 85-10355

Spencer, Elizabeth
Jack of diamonds, and other stories. Viking 1988 184p ISBN 0-670-82261-2 LC 87-40547

Spillane, Mickey, 1918-
Tomorrow I die; introduced and edited by Max Allan Collins. Mysterious Press 1984 234p il ISBN 0-89296-061-2 LC 82-60903
Analyzed for short stories only

Spirit seizures. Pritchard, M.

Spirits, and other stories. Bausch, R.

Spirits, spooks, and other sinister creatures; selected by Helen Hoke. Watts 1984 136p ISBN 0-531-04769-5 LC 83-21603
Analyzed for short stories only

Spivack, Kathleen
The honeymoon; stories. Graywolf Press 1986 123p ISBN 0-915308-85-1 LC 85-82576

The **splendid** outcast. Markham, B.

Sproat, Robert
Stunning the punters. Faber & Faber 1986 190p ISBN 0-571-13823-3 LC 85-29198

Spunk. Hurston, Z. N.

St. Clair, Margaret
    The best of Margaret St. Clair; edited by Martin H. Greenberg. Academy Chicago 1985 271p ISBN 0-89733-163-X LC 85-18599

St. Pierre, Paul H., 1923-
    Smith and other events; stories of the Chilcotin. Beaufort Bks. 1984 318p ISBN 0-8253-0209-9 LC 83-21493

The **St.** Veronica gig stories. Pulaski, J.

Stained glass elegies. Endō, S.

Stalin in the Bronx, and other stories. Ruta, S.

Stambolian, George
    (ed) Men on men. *See* Men on men

Stand one; winners of the Stand Magazine short story competition; edited by Michael Blackburn, Jon Silkin & Lorna Tracy. Gollancz 1984 204p ISBN 0-575-03516-1 LC 85-220460

Standing room. Summers, H. S.

Star children. Asscher-Pinkhof, C.

Star game. Nevai, L.

Stark, Sharon Sheehe
    The dealers' yard, and other stories. Morrow 1985 214p ISBN 0-688-04197-3 LC 84-22811

The **startling** worlds of Henry Kuttner. Kuttner, H.

A **stay** by the river. Engberg, S.

Stead, Christina, 1902-1983
    Ocean of story; the uncollected stories of Christina Stead; edited with an afterword by R. G. Geering. Viking Penguin 1985 552p ISBN 0-670-80996-9
        Analyzed for short stories only

Steele, Max, 1922-
    The hat of my mother; stories. Algonquin Bks. 1988 185p ISBN 0-912697-78-4 LC 87-28995

Steele, Thomas
    (ed) First love/last love. *See* First love/last love

Steinbaugh, Eric
    (ed) Short stories of the sea. *See* Short stories of the sea

Steinhauer, Harry, 1905-
    (ed) German stories. *See* German stories

Stenson, Fred, 1951-
    Alberta bound. *See* Alberta bound

Stepping out; short stories on friendships between women; edited by Ann Oosthuizen. Pandora Press 1986 175p ISBN 0-86358-048-3 LC 85-28298

Sterling, Bruce
    (ed) Mirrorshades. *See* Mirrorshades

Stern, Steve, 1947-
    Isaac and the undertaker's daughter. Lost Roads Pubs. 1983 110p ISBN 0-918786-27-4 LC 83-9894
    Lazar Malkin enters heaven; stories. Viking 1987 249p ISBN 0-670-81379-6 LC 86-40264

Stewart, Frank, 1946-
    (ed) Passages to the dream shore. *See* Passages to the dream shore

Stewart, J. I. M., 1906-
    Parlour 4, and other stories. Norton 1986 184p ISBN 0-393-02292-7 LC 85-21421

Stiller's pond; new fiction from the upper Midwest; edited by Jonis Agee, Roger Blakely, & Susan Welch. New Rivers Press 1988 387p ISBN 0-89823-106-X LC 88-60050

Stolen stories. Katz, S.

The **stone** dragon, and other tragic romances. Gilchrist, M.

Stories. Blinkin, M.

Stories. Pavese, C.

Stories. Ramírez, S.

Stories and poems from close to home; edited by Floyd Salas; assistant editors, Claire Ortalda, Glenn Kraski. Ortalda & Assocs. 1986 509p il ISBN 0-9616101-3-1 LC 85-63696

Analyzed for short stories only

Stories from the warm zone and Sydney stories. Anderson, J.

Stories in another language. Murphy, Y.

The **stories** of Denton Welch. Welch, D.

Stories of happy people. Gustafsson, L.

The **stories** of Heinrich Böll. Böll, H.

The **stories** of Muriel Spark. Spark, M.

Stories of the modern South; edited by Ben Forkner and Patrick Samway. expanded ed. Penguin Bks. 1986 xxvi,530p ISBN 0-14-009695-7 LC 86-9515

Strand, Mark, 1934-

Mr. and Mrs. Baby, and other stories. Knopf 1985 111p ISBN 0-394-51359-2 LC 84-48509

Strangers in paradise. Abbott, L. K.

Streets of stone; an anthology of Glasgow short stories; edited by Moira Burgess and Hamish Whyte. Salamander Press 1985 182p ISBN 0-907540-62-7

Strong-man from Piraeus, and other stories. Johnston, G., and Clift, C.

Strugatskiĭ, Arkadiĭ Natanovich

Aliens, travelers, and other strangers. *See* Aliens, travelers, and other strangers

Strugatskiĭ, Boris Natanovich

Aliens, travelers, and other strangers. *See* Aliens, travelers, and other strangers

Stuart, Jesse, 1907-1984

Clearing in the sky & other stories; with a foreword by Ruel E. Foster; woodcuts by Stanley Rice. University Press of Ky. 1984 262p il ISBN 0-8131-1510-8 LC 83-27404

Stunning the punters. Sproat, R.

Sturgeon, Theodore, 1918-1985

Alien cargo. Bluejay Bks. 1984 284p ISBN 0-312-94008-4 LC 84-12302

The **Substance** of things hoped for; short fiction by modern Catholic authors; selected with an introduction by John B. Breslin. Doubleday 1987 xx,314p ISBN 0-385-23428-7 LC 86-16656

Suburbs of the Arctic Circle. Burns, M.

Success stories. Banks, R.

Suckow, Ruth, 1892-1960

A Ruth Suckow omnibus; with a new introduction by Clarence A. Andrews. University of Iowa Press 1988 310p ISBN 0-87745-207-5 LC 88-15059

A Bur Oak Bk.

Sudden fiction; American short-short stories; edited by Robert Shapard and James Thomas; with a frontistory by Robert Coover; and afterwords, about the short-short story form, by forty of America's finest writers. Smith, G.M. 1986 263p ISBN 0-87905-248-1 LC 86-10039

A Peregrine Smith Bk.

Sugar, and other stories. Byatt, A. S.

Sullivan, Eleanor

(ed) Ellery Queen's Crimes and punishments. *See* Ellery Queen's Crimes and punishments

(ed) Ellery Queen's Memorable characters. *See* Ellery Queen's Memorable characters

(ed) Ellery Queen's Prime crimes. *See* Ellery Queen's Prime crimes

Sullivan, Eleanor—*Continued*
  (ed) Ellery Queen's Prime crimes 2. *See* Ellery Queen's Prime
    crimes 2
  (ed) Tales from Ellery Queen's Mystery Magazine: short stories
    for young adults. *See* Tales from Ellery Queen's Mystery
    Magazine: short stories for young adults
Sullivan, Jack, 1946-
  (ed) Lost souls. *See* Lost souls
Sullivan, Nancy
  (comp) The Treasury of English short stories. *See* The Treasury
    of English short stories
Summer is the Côte d'Azur. Gifkins, M.
Summers, Hollis Spurgeon, 1916-
  Standing room; stories. Louisiana State Univ. Press 1984 104p
    ISBN 0-8071-1191-0 LC 84-10004
The **sun** is not merciful. Walters, A. L.
Sunburn Lake. De Haven, T.
Sunstroke, and other stories. Watson, I.
The **supernatural** tales of Fitz-James O'Brien v1. O'Brien, F.-J.
Surplus love, and other stories. Ignatow, R. G.
Surplussed barrelware. Aksenov, V. P.
Survivors and others. Drake, R.
Swados, Harvey
  Nights in the gardens of Brooklyn; the collected stories of
    Harvey Swados. Viking 1986 381p ISBN 0-670-80974-8
    LC 85-40631
Sweet Hollow. Crabtree, L. V.
Swift, Graham, 1949-
  Learning to swim, and other stories. Poseidon Press 1985 c1982
    189p ISBN 0-671-54613-9 LC 84-25467
Symons, Julian, 1912-
  (ed) The Penguin classic crime omnibus. *See* The Penguin
    classic crime omnibus
Synergy; new science fiction; edited by George Zebrowski. v1.
    Harcourt Brace Jovanovich 1987 243p ISSN 0892-449X
    An Orig. Harvest/HBJ Bk.

T

Tabucchi, Antonio, 1943-
  Letter from Casablanca; stories; translated by Janice M. Thresher.
    New Directions 1986 122p ISBN 0-8112-0985-7 LC 85-28380
A **tale** of Pierrot, and other stories. Dennison, G.
Tales for a stormy night. Davis, D. S.
Tales from Ellery Queen's Mystery Magazine: short stories for
    young adults; selected by Eleanor Sullivan and Cynthia
    Manson; with an introduction by Joan Lowery Nixon.
    Harcourt Brace Jovanovich 1986 250p ISBN 0-15-284205-5
    LC 86-7634
Tales from Isaac Asimov's science fiction magazine: short stories
    for young adults; selected by Sheila Williams and Cynthia
    Manson; with an introduction by Isaac Asimov. Harcourt
    Brace Jovanovich 1986 298p ISBN 0-15-284209-8 LC 86-7591
Tales from the next village. Caponegro, M.
Tales from the planet Earth; created by Frederik Pohl and Elizabeth
    Anne Hull. St. Martin's Press 1986 268p ISBN 0-312-78420-1
    LC 86-13832
Tales of courtship. Gotthelf, J.
Tales of El Huitlacoche. Keller, G. D.
Tales of Hawaii, Jack London's. London, J.
Tales of socialist Yugoslavia. Aćin-Kosta, M.
Tales of suicide. Pirandello, L.
Tales of suspense. Poe, E. A.

Tales of terror. Poe, E. A.

Tales of the supernatural; [comp. by] H.C. Chang. Columbia Univ. Press 1984 169p (Chinese literature, 3) ISBN 0-231-05794-6 LC 81-174030

Tales of the Witch World [1]-2; created by Andre Norton. Doherty Assocs. 1987-1988 2v ISBN 0-312-94475-6 (v1); 0-312-93078-X (v2) LC 87-50473

    A TOR Bk.

Tallent, Elizabeth, 1954-

Time with children; stories. Knopf 1987 157p ISBN 0-394-55783-2 LC 87-45100

Tamer, Zakaria

Tigers on the tenth day, and other stories; translated by Denys Johnson-Davies. Quartet Bks. 1985 123p ISBN 0-7043-2465-2

Taylor, Apirana

He rau aroha; a hundred leaves of love. Penguin Bks. 1986 96p ISBN 0-14-008842-3

Taylor, Chuck

The lights of the city: stories from Austin. Slough Press 1984 128p il ISBN 0-941720-15-2 LC 84-147637

Taylor, Pat Ellis, 1941-

Afoot in a field of men. Atlantic Monthly Press 1988 166p ISBN 0-87113-203-6 LC 87-27707

Taylor, Peter Hillsman, 1917-

The old forest, and other stories. Dial Press 1985 358p ISBN 0-385-27983-3 LC 83-40133

    Analyzed for short stories only

Taylor, Robert, 1941-

Loving Belle Starr; [by] Robert Taylor, Jr. Algonquin Bks. 1984 215p (Bright leaf short fiction, 2) ISBN 0-912697-07-5 LC 83-25669

Te Kaihau, the windeater. Hulme, K.

Teen angel, and other stories of young love. Gingher, M.

Teleky, Richard

(ed) The Oxford book of French-Canadian short stories. *See* The Oxford book of French-Canadian short stories

Temporary shelter. Gordon, M.

Tentacles of unreason. Givner, J.

Terry, Marshall, 1931-

(ed) Prize stories, Texas Institute of Letters. *See* Prize stories, Texas Institute of Letters

Terry Carr's Best science fiction and fantasy of the year #16; edited by Terry Carr. Doherty Assocs. 1987 402p ISBN 0-312-93025-9 LC 87-50472

    A TOR Bk.

Terry's universe; edited by Beth Meacham. Doherty Assocs. 1988 234p ISBN 0-312-93058-5 LC 87-50871

    A TOR Bk.

Testimony. Matthew, J. R.

Texier, Catherine

(ed) Between C & D. *See* Between C & D

There are no ghosts in the Soviet Union. Hill, R.

These things happen. Thurm, M.

They sleep without dreaming. Gilliatt, P.

Thirteen detectives. Chesterton, G. K.

Thirteen uncanny stories. Jahnn, H. H.

This freedom. Morrison, J.

Thomas, Audrey Callahan

Goodbye Harold, good luck. Penguin Bks. 1987 222p ISBN 0-14-008809-1

Thomas, Dylan, 1914-1953

The collected stories. New Directions 1984 362p ISBN 0-8112-0918-0 LC 84-6822

Thomas, James, 1946-
(ed) The Best of the West. *See* The Best of the West
Pictures, moving; a short story collection. Dragon Gate 1985
179p ISBN 0-937872-22-9 LC 85-4334
(ed) Sudden fiction. *See* Sudden fiction

Thomas, Maria, 1941-1989
Come to Africa and save your marriage, and other stories.
Soho Press 1987 235p ISBN 0-939149-06-0 LC 87-9786

Thompson, Jean, 1950-
Little Face, and other stories. Watts 1984 163p ISBN
0-531-09760-9 LC 84-7578

Thompson, Joyce
East is west of here; new & selected short stories. Breitenbush
Bks. 1987 164p ISBN 0-932576-32-X LC 85-5689

Thompson, Kent
A local hanging, and other stories. Fiddlehead Poetry Bks./Goose
Lane Eds. 1984 147p ISBN 0-86492-037-7

Thompson, Sandra
Close-ups; stories. University of Ga. Press 1984 104p ISBN
0-8203-0683-5 LC 83-4981

Thorman, Carolyn
Fifty years of eternal vigilance, and other stories. Peachtree
Pubs. 1988 216p il ISBN 0-934601-62-3 LC 88-61458

Through a glass, darkly; 13 tales of wine and crime; edited
by Barry Woelfel; introduction by Terry Robards. Beaufort
Bks. 1984 223p ISBN 0-8253-0197-1 LC 83-21439

Through other eyes; animal stories by women; edited by Irene
Zahava. Crossing Press 1988 188p ISBN 0-89594-315-8
LC 88-23780
Analyzed for short stories only

Through the eyes of a cat. Virgo, S.
Through the safety net. Baxter, C.

Thurm, Marian
Floating. Viking 1984 210p ISBN 0-670-31952-X LC 83-47995
These things happen. Poseidon Press 1988 173p ISBN
0-671-64924-8 LC 88-15586

Tickled to death, and other stories of crime and suspense.
Brett, S.
Tigers in the wood. Kavaler, R.
Tigers on the tenth day, and other stories. Tamer, Z.
Time to go. Dixon, S.
Time wars; created by Poul Anderson; edited by Charles Waugh
& Martin H. Greenberg. Doherty Assocs. 1986 374p ISBN
0-812-53048-9
A TOR Bk.
Time with children. Tallent, E.

Tiptree, James, 1916-1987
Byte beautiful; eight science fiction stories; [by] James Tiptree,
Jr. Doubleday 1985 177p ISBN 0-385-19653-9 LC 85-10185
Crown of stars. Doherty Assocs. 1988 340p ISBN 0-312-93105-0
LC 88-19234
A TOR Bk.

The **Tithonian** Factor, and other stories. Cowper, R.
To Leningrad in winter. Schwartz, S.
To skin a cat. McGuane, T.
Tomorrow I die. Spillane, M.
Tomorrow's voices, Isaac Asimov's. *See* Isaac Asimov's
Tomorrow's voices
Tongues of flame. Brown, M. W.
Too far from home. Rogers, T. N. R.
Too hot & other Maine stories. Bonnie, F.
Too late American boyhood blues. Busch, F.

Tournier, Michel
  The fetishist; translated from the French by Barbara Wright. Doubleday 1984 c1983 212p ISBN 0-385-15354-6 LC 79-8945
The **town** of Ballymuck. Power, V.
Town smokes. Benedict, P.
The **Toynbee** convector. Bradbury, R.

Tracy, Lorna
  (ed) Stand one. *See* Stand one
Transactions in a foreign currency. Eisenberg, D.
Transgressions; Australian writing now; edited by Don Anderson; published with the assistance of the Literature Board of the Australia Council. Penguin Bks. 1986 245p ISBN 0-14-008393-6
A **traveller's** room. Davie, E.
A **Treasury** of Civil War stories; edited by Martin H. Greenberg and Bill Pronzini. Bonanza Bks. 1985 523p ISBN 0-517-46781-X LC 85-4138
    Analyzed for short stories only
The **Treasury** of English short stories; selected and with an introduction by Nancy Sullivan. Doubleday 1985 xxii,672p ISBN 0-385-18538-3 LC 84-24647
Treasury of great cat stories, Roger Caras'. *See* Roger Caras' Treasury of great cat stories
Treasury of great dog stories, Roger Caras'. *See* Roger Caras' Treasury of great dog stories
A **Treasury** of World War II stories; edited by Bill Pronzini and Martin H. Greenberg. Bonanza Bks. 1985 755p ISBN 0-517-46782-8 LC 85-9723

Tremain, Rose
  The Colonel's daughter, and other stories. Summit Bks. 1984 174p ISBN 0-671-50463-0 LC 83-24316

Trevor, William, 1928-
  The news from Ireland & other stories. Viking 1986 284p ISBN 0-670-81069-X LC 85-40782
    An Elisabeth Sifton Bk.
Tribute. Prichard, K. S.
Trinity, and other stories. Kress, N.
The **Trojan** generals talk. Parotti, P.
Troubled by his complexion. McLaughlin, L.

Troy, Stuart
  (ed) The Nobel reader. *See* The Nobel reader
Trust me. Updike, J.

Tsushima, Yūko
  The shooting gallery; translated and compiled by Geraldine Harcourt. Pantheon Bks. 1988 138p ISBN 0-394-56559-2 LC 87-22171
Tumbling. Moyer, K.

Tuohy, Frank, 1925-
  The collected stories. Holt, Rinehart & Winston 1984 410p ISBN 0-03-057648-2 LC 84-3769
    A William Abrahams Bk.

Twain, Mark, 1835-1910
  The science fiction of Mark Twain; edited with an introduction and notes by David Ketterer. Archon Bks. 1984 xxxiii, 385p ISBN 0-208-02036-5 LC 84-6282
Twelve below zero. Bukoski, A.
Twenty two stories. *See* Gilliatt, P. 22 stories
Twenty under 30. *See* 20 under 30
A **twist** in the tale. Archer, J.
Two lives and a dream. Yourcenar, M.

Two travelers, and other Korean short stories; edited by the Korean National Commission for UNESCO. Si-sa-yong-o-sa; Pace Int. Res. 1983 144p (Modern Korean short stories, 7) ISBN 0-89209-208-4 LC 84-141698

U

Ueda, Makoto
(ed) The Mother of dreams, and other short stories. *See* The Mother of dreams, and other short stories

The **unabridged** Edgar Allan Poe. Poe, E. A.

The **Unbroken** chain; an anthology of Taiwan fiction since 1926; edited by Joseph S.M. Lau. Indiana Univ. Press 1983 279p (Chinese literature in translation) ISBN 0-253-36162-1 LC 83-47904

The **uncertainty** of strangers, and other stories. Franklin, P.

Uncollected crimes; edited by Bill Pronzini and Martin H. Greenberg. Walker & Co. 1987 203p ISBN 0-8027-0967-2 LC 87-2115

Uncollected stories. Doyle, Sir A. C.

Under the banyan tree, and other stories. Narayan, R. K.

Under the wheat. DeMarinis, R.

The **underground** banquet, and other stories. Warren, J.

The **Unenlightened,** and other Korean short stories; edited by the Korean National Commission for UNESCO. Si-sa-yong-o-sa; Pace Int. Res. 1983 234p (Modern Korean short stories, 3) ISBN 0-89209-204-1 LC 100078

The **Universe**; Byron Preiss, editor; Andrew Fraknoi, scientific editor. Bantam Bks. 1987 335p il ISBN 0-553-05227-6 LC 87-47572
> Analyzed for short stories only
> A Byron Preiss Bk.

Universe 14; edited by Terry Carr. Doubleday 1984 182p ISBN 0-385-19134-0 LC 83-20785

Universe 15; edited by Terry Carr. Doubleday 1985 179p ISBN 0-385-19890-6 LC 85-4346

Universe 16; edited by Terry Carr. Doubleday 1986 181p ISBN 0-385-23389-2 LC 86-9000

Universe 17; edited by Terry Carr. Doubleday 1987 180p ISBN 0-385-23853-3 LC 86-29281

Unlikely stories, mostly. Gray, A.

Updike, David
Out on the marsh; stories. Godine 1988 168p ISBN 0-87923-728-7 LC 87-46280

Updike, John
(ed) The Best American short stories, 1984. *See* The Best American short stories, 1984
Trust me; short stories. Knopf 1987 302p ISBN 0-394-55833-2 LC 86-46018

Uprising in East Germany, and other stories. Ziem, J.

Upward, Edward
The night walk, and other stories. Heinemann, W. 1987 178p ISBN 0-434-81173-4
> Partially analyzed

V

Valenzuela, Luisa, 1938-
Open door; stories; translated by Hortense Carpentier [et al.]. North Point Press 1988 201p ISBN 0-86547-310-2 LC 87-82582
Other weapons; translated by Deborah Bonner. Norte 1985 135p ISBN 0-910061-22-X

Vampires; two centuries of great vampire stories; edited by Alan
    Ryan. Doubleday 1987 621p ISBN 0-385-18562-6
    LC 86-24238
Van de Wetering, Janwillem, 1931-
    (ed) Distant danger. *See* Distant danger
    Inspector Saito's small satori. Putnam 1985 189p ISBN
    0-399-13032-2 LC 84-17833
    The sergeant's cat, and other stories. Pantheon Bks. 1987 218p
    ISBN 0-394-54925-2 LC 87-2411
Van Greenaway, Peter, 1929-
    The immortal coil; short stories. Gollancz [distrib. by David
    & Charles] 1985 ISBN 0-575-03577-3
Vanderhaeghe, Guy, 1951-
    Man descending; selected stories. Ticknor & Fields 1985 c1982
    230p ISBN 0-89919-385-4 LC 85-2758
Vélez, Diana Lourdes
    (ed.) Reclaiming Medusa. *See* Reclaiming Medusa
Venomous tales of villainy and vengeance; an anthology; [ed.]
    by Helen Hoke. Dutton 1984 127p ISBN 0-525-67158-7
    LC 84-8065
The **Venus** tree. Pritchett, M.
Verma, Nirmal, 1929-
    Maya Darpan, and other stories. Oxford Univ. Press 1986
    238p ISBN 0-19-561872-6
    The world elsewhere, and other stories. Readers Int. 1988
    238p ISBN 0-930523-46-6
Vernacular dreams. Loukakis, A.
A **very** brief season. Girion, B.
A **Very** large array; New Mexico science fiction and fantasy;
    edited by Melinda M. Snodgrass. University of N.M. Press
    1987 264p ISBN 0-8263-1013-3 LC 87-19173
Victory over Japan. Gilchrist, E.
A **view** by the sea. Yasuoka, S.
Villefranche, Anne-Marie, 1899-1980
    Joie d'amour; an erotic memoir of Paris in the 1920s. Carroll
    & Graf Pubs. 1984 261p ISBN 0-88184-098-X LC 84-12179
Vinge, Joan D., 1948-
    Phoenix in the ashes. Bluejay Bks. 1985 230p il ISBN
    0-312-94364-4
Viramontes, Helena Maria, 1954-
    The moths, and other stories. Arte Público Press 1985 118p
    ISBN 0-934770-40-9 LC 84-072308
Virgo, Seán, 1940-
    Through the eyes of a cat; Irish stories. Sono Nis Press 1983
    65p ISBN 0-919203-07-8 LC 84-107175
Visions. Andreyev, L.
Visitations. Sisskind, M.
The **visitors.** Blythe, R.
Vizyēnos, G. M. (Geōrgios M.), 1849-1896
    My mother's sin, and other stories; translated from the Greek
    by William F. Wyatt, Jr. University Press of New England
    1988 229p ISBN 0-87451-434-7 LC 87-23218
        A Brown Bk.
Vogan, Sara
    Scenes from the homefront. University of Ill. Press 1987 133p
    (Illinois short fiction) ISBN 0-252-01430-8 LC 87-49961
The **voice** of prose v1. Pasternak, B. L.
Voices East and West: German short stories since 1945; translations
    and introduction by Roger C. Norton. Ungar 1984 181p
    ISBN 0-8044-2660-0 LC 84-8899
Vreuls, Diane
    Let us know; stories. Viking 1986 112p ISBN 0-670-80948-9
    LC 85-40633

W

Waldrop, Howard
Howard who?; twelve outstanding stories of speculative fiction. Doubleday 1986 181p ISBN 0-385-19708-X LC 85-31102

Walker, Scott
(ed) Buying time. *See* Buying time
(ed) The Graywolf annual [1]: short stories. *See* The Graywolf annual [1]: short stories
(ed) The Graywolf annual 2: short stories by women. *See* The Graywolf annual 2: short stories by women
(ed) The Graywolf annual 4: short stories by men. *See* The Graywolf annual 4: short stories by men

Walker, Wendy
The sea-rabbit; or, The artist of life; tales. Sun & Moon Press 1988 272p ISBN 1-55713-000-0 LC 87-62613

Walking the dog, and other stories. Eldridge, M.

Walters, Anna Lee, 1946-
The sun is not merciful; short stories. Firebrand Bks. 1985 133p il ISBN 0-932379-11-7 LC 85-16177

A **war** of eyes, and other stories. Coleman, W.

Warner, Sylvia Townsend, 1893-1978
One thing leading to another, and other stories; selected and edited by Susanna Pinney. Viking 1984 199p ISBN 0-670-74990-7 LC 84-40066

Warren, Joyce
The underground banquet, and other stories. Rowan Tree Press 1988 163p ISBN 0-937672-23-8 LC 87-63475

Warrick, Patricia S., 1925-
(ed) Machines that think. *See* Machines that think

Watchers at the strait gate. Kirk, R.

Water into wine. Norris, H.

Watmough, David, 1932-
The Connecticut countess; chronicles of Davey Bryant. Crossing Press 1984 189p ISBN 0-89594-124-4 LC 83-24080

Watson, Ian, 1943-
(ed) Afterlives. *See* Afterlives
Sunstroke, and other stories. Gollancz [distrib. by David & Charles] 1982 190p ISBN 0-575-03138-7 LC 85-217800

Watson, Sheila
Five stories. Coach House Press (Toronto) 1984 76p ISBN 0-88910-298-8 LC 85-127769

Waugh, Carol-Lynn Rössel, 1947-
(ed) Hound dunnit. *See* Hound dunnit
(ed) Manhattan mysteries. *See* Manhattan mysteries
(ed) Murder and mystery in Boston. *See* Murder and mystery in Boston
(ed) Murder and mystery in Chicago. *See* Murder and mystery in Chicago
(ed) The New adventures of Sherlock Holmes. *See* The New adventures of Sherlock Holmes

Waugh, Charles G. (Charles Gordon), 1943-
(ed) Alternative histories. *See* Alternative histories
(ed) Baker's dozen: 13 short fantasy novels. *See* Baker's dozen: 13 short fantasy novels
(ed) Baker's dozen: 13 short science fiction novels. *See* Baker's dozen: 13 short science fiction novels
(ed) The Best Maine stories. *See* The Best Maine stories
(ed) Civil War women. *See* Civil War women
(ed) Dragons and dreams. *See* Dragons and dreams
(ed) Great science fiction. *See* Great science fiction
(ed) Haunted New England. *See* Haunted New England
(ed) Intergalactic empires. *See* Intergalactic empires

Waugh, Charles G. (Charles Gordon), 1943——*Continued*
(ed) Isaac Asimov presents the best crime stories of the 19th century. *See* Isaac Asimov presents the best crime stories of the 19th century
(ed) Isaac Asimov presents the best science fiction firsts. *See* Isaac Asimov presents the best science fiction firsts
(ed) The Mammoth book of classic science fiction. *See* The Mammoth book of classic science fiction
(ed) Mississippi River tales. *See* Mississippi River tales
(ed) Nightmares in Dixie. *See* Nightmares in Dixie
(ed) Rod Serling's Night gallery reader. *See* Rod Serling's Night gallery reader
(ed) The Science fictional Olympics. *See* The Science fictional Olympics
(ed) Sherlock Holmes through time and space. *See* Sherlock Holmes through time and space
(ed) Space wars. *See* Space wars
(ed) Time wars. *See* Time wars
(ed) Witches. *See* Witches
(ed) Wizards. *See* Wizards
(ed) Yankee witches. *See* Yankee witches
(ed) Young extraterrestrials. *See* Young extraterrestrials
(ed) Young ghosts. *See* Young ghosts
(ed) Young monsters. *See* Young monsters
(ed) Young mutants. *See* Young mutants
(ed) Young witches & warlocks. *See* Young witches & warlocks
We are not in this together.   Kittredge, W.
We built Jerusalem.   Liphshitz, A.
We don't live here anymore.   Dubus, A.
The **weather** and women treat me fair.   Everett, P. L.

Weaver, Gordon
Morality play. Chariton Review Press 1985 122p ISBN 0-933428-05-7 LC 85-22408

Weaver, Robert, 1924-
(ed) The Oxford book of Canadian short stories in English. *See* The Oxford book of Canadian short stories in English
The **weaver's** grave.   O'Kelly, S.

Weber, Bruce
(ed) Look who's talking. *See* Look who's talking
The **weed** king & other stories.   Conroy, J.

Wegner, Hart
Houses of ivory; stories. Soho Press 1988 241p ISBN 0-939149-13-3 LC 87-28530

Weir, Ann Lowry, 1946-
(ed) Prime number. *See* Prime number
The **Weirds**; a facsimile selection of fiction from the era of the shudder pulps; compiled and edited by Sheldon Jaffery. Starmont House 1987 173p il ISBN 0-930261-93-3 LC 87-1952

Welch, Denton
The stories of Denton Welch; edited by Robert Phillips. Dutton 1986 c1985 377p ISBN 0-525-24364-X LC 85-25382

Welch, Susan
(ed) Stiller's pond. *See* Stiller's pond

Wells, H. G. (Herbert George), 1866-1946
The complete short stories of H. G. Wells. St. Martin's Press 1987 1038p ISBN 0-312-15855-6 LC 87-27478
The man with a nose, and the other uncollected short stories of H. G. Wells; edited and with an introduction by J. R. Hammond. Athlone Press 1984 212p ISBN 0-485-11247-7 LC 84-14624

Wendt, Albert, 1939-
The birth and death of the miracle man; a collection of short stories. Viking 1986 175p ISBN 0-670-80676-5

Werewolves; a collection of original stories; edited by Jane Yolen and Martin H. Greenberg. Harper & Row 1988 271p ISBN 0-06-026798-4 LC 87-45863

West, Jessamyn, d. 1984
Collected stories of Jessamyn West. Harcourt Brace Jovanovich 1986 480p ISBN 0-15-119010-0 LC 86-12031

The **Western** hall of fame; an anthology of classic western stories; selected by the Western Writers of America; edited by Bill Pronzini and Martin H. Greenberg. Morrow 1984 376p ISBN 0-688-02220-0 LC 83-13049

Western trails. Austin, M. H.

Western Writers of America
The Western hall of fame. *See* The Western hall of fame

Westeryear; stories about the West, past and present; edited by Edward Gorman. Evans & Co. 1988 230p ISBN 0-87131-553-X
Analyzed for short stories only

Westlake, Donald E.
Levine. Mysterious Press 1984 182p ISBN 0-89296-063-9 LC 83-63034

Westward the women; an anthology of western stories by women; edited by Vickie Piekarski. Doubleday 1984 179p ISBN 0-385-19187-1 LC 83-25458

Wetherell, W. D., 1948-
The man who loved Levittown. University of Pittsburgh Press 1985 145p ISBN 0-8229-3520-1 LC 85-1172

Wevers, Lydia
(comp) Women's work. *See* Women's work

Wexler, Jerry, 1950-
The bequest & other stories. Véhicule Press 1984 94p ISBN 0-919890-51-2

Wharton, Edith, 1862-1937
Ethan Frome, and other short fiction; with an introduction by Mary Gordon. Bantam Bks. 1987 237p ISBN 0-553-21255-9

What I know so far. Lish, G.

What is it then between us? Havazelet, E.

Wheatcroft, John, 1925-
Slow exposures. Cornwall Bks. 1986 178p ISBN 0-8453-4735-7 LC 85-47910

Whelan, Gloria
Playing with shadows. University of Ill. Press 1988 147p (Illinois short fiction) ISBN 0-252-01524-X LC 87-35690

When California was an island. Haas, B.

When I am an old woman I shall wear purple; an anthology of short stories and poetry; [editor: Sandra K. Martz]. Papier-Maché Press 1987 177p il ISBN 0-918949-02-5 LC 87-042797
Analyzed for short stories only

When in Florence. Day, R. C.

When the animals leave. Rambach, P.

When the wind is in the south, and other stories. Rölvaag, O. E.

When things get back to normal, and other stories. Pierce, C.

Where I'm calling from. Carver, R.

Where you'll find me, and other stories. Beattie, A.

Whispers V; edited by Stuart David Schiff. Doubleday 1985 208p ISBN 0-385-18944-3 LC 84-13714

Whitaker, Malachi, 1895-1975
The Crystal Fountain and other stories; introduction by Joan Hart. Carcanet Press 1984 179p ISBN 0-85635-517-8 LC 84-164976

White, Curtis
(ed) American made. *See* American made
Metaphysics in the Midwest; stories. Sun & Moon Press 1988 203p ISBN 1-55713-045-0 LC 88-062134

Whites. Rush, N.

Whoever finds this: I love you. Moskowitz, F.

Why men are afraid of women. Camoin, F. A.

Whyte, Hamish
(ed) Streets of stone. *See* Streets of stone
The **Wickedest** show on earth; a carnival of circus suspense; edited by Marcia Muller and Bill Pronzini. Morrow 1985 335p ISBN 0-688-05355-6 LC 85-15229

Wicomb, Zoë
You can't get lost in Cape Town. Pantheon Bks. 1987 185p ISBN 0-394-56030-2 LC 86-42977

Wide load. Bonnie, F.

The **widow's** mite & other stories. Sams, F.

Wiebe, Dallas E.
Going to the mountain. Burning Deck 1988 191p ISBN 0-930901-49-5 LC 87-25627

Wilbur, Ellen
Wind and birds and human voices, and other stories. Wright, S. 1984 113p ISBN 0-913773-11-5 LC 84-50185

The **wild** dogs. Skrzynecki, P.

Wild westerns; stories from the grand old pulps; edited by Bill Pronzini. Walker & Co. 1986 214p ISBN 0-8027-4066-9 LC 86-13220

Will she understand? Dawson, F.

Willett, Jincy
Jenny and The jaws of life; short stories. St. Martin's Press 1987 248p ISBN 0-312-00614-4 LC 87-4373
A Thomas Dunne Bk.

Williams, Sheila
(ed) Tales from Isaac Asimov's science fiction magazine: short stories for young adults. *See* Tales from Isaac Asimov's science fiction magazine: short stories for young adults

Williams, Tennessee, 1911-1983
Collected stories; with an introduction by Gore Vidal. New Directions 1985 xxv,574p ISBN 0-8112-0952-0 LC 85-10642

Williams, William Carlos, 1883-1963
The doctor stories; compiled with an introduction by Robert Coles; afterword by William Eric Williams. New Directions 1984 142p ISBN 0-8112-0925-3 LC 84-8372
Analyzed for short stories only

Williamson, J. N.
(ed) Masques. *See* Masques

Willis, Connie
Fire watch. Bluejay Bks. 1984 274p ISBN 0-312-94162-5

Willson, Harry
Duke City tales. Amador Pubs. 1986 172p ISBN 0-938513-00-1

Wilner, Herbert, d. 1977
The quarterback speaks to his God. Cayuse Press 1987 239p ISBN 0-933529-04-X LC 86-071792

Wilson, Barbara, 1950-
Miss Venezuela. Seal Press 1988 311p ISBN 0-931188-58-X LC 87-35112

Wind and birds and human voices, and other stories. Wilbur, E.

Windfall, and other stories. Sanford, W. M.

Windling, Terri

(ed) The Year's best fantasy: first annual collection. *See* The Year's best fantasy: first annual collection

A **window** in Mrs X's place.　Cowan, P.

Windsor, Gerard

Memories of the assassination attempt, and other stories; published with the assistance of the Literature Board of the Australia Council. Penguin Bks. 1986 c1985 183p ISBN 0-14-008558-0

The **wine-dark** sea.　Aickman, R.

The **wine** of youth.　Fante, J.

Winter, Douglas E.

(ed) Prime evil. *See* Prime evil

Winters, Jonathan, 1925-

Winters' tales; stories and observations for the unusual. Random House 1987 216p ISBN 0-394-56424-3 LC 87-42648

Winter's crimes 16; edited by Hilary Hale. St. Martin's Press 1984 188p ISBN 0-312-88243-2

Winter's crimes 17; edited by George Hardinge. St. Martin's Press 1985 221p ISBN 0-312-88244-0 LC 72-623690

Winter's crimes 18; [edited by Hilary Hale]. St. Martin's Press 1986 189p

Winters' tales.　Winters, J.

Winter's tales, new ser. v1; edited by David Hughes. St. Martin's Press 1985 189p ISSN 0268-2648

Winter's tales, new ser. v2; edited by Robin Baird-Smith. St. Martin's Press 1986 224p ISSN 0268-2648 LC 86-042905

Winter's tales, new ser. v3; edited by Robin Baird-Smith. St. Martin's Press 1987 319p ISSN 0268-2648

Winter's tales, new ser. v4; edited by Robin Baird-Smith. St. Martin's Press 1988 280p ISSN 0268-2648 LC 86-655581

Winton, Tim

Minimum of two; stories. Atheneum Pubs. 1988 c1987 153p ISBN 0-689-11978-X LC 88-3441

Scission. Gribble; Penguin Bks. 1985 155p ISBN 0-14-008060-0

Wisse, Ruth R.

(ed) A Shtetl, and other Yiddish novellas. *See* A Shtetl, and other Yiddish novellas

The **witch** of Goingsnake, and other stories.　Conley, R. J.

Witches; edited by Isaac Asimov, Martin H. Greenberg and Charles G. Waugh. New Am. Lib. 1984 350p (Isaac Asimov's magical worlds of fantasy, no2) ISBN 0-451-12882-6
A Signet Bk.

Witches' brew; horror and supernatural stories by women; edited by Marcia Muller and Bill Pronzini. Macmillan 1984 323p (Macmillan midnight lib) ISBN 0-02-599230-9 LC 84-10026

With or without, and other stories.　Dickinson, C.

Wizards; edited by Isaac Asimov, Martin H. Greenberg and Charles G. Waugh. New Am. Lib. 1983 303p (Isaac Asimov's magical worlds of fantasy, no1) ISBN 0-451-12542-8
A Signet Bk.

Wodehouse, P. G. (Pelham Grenville), 1881-1975

A Wodehouse bestiary; edited and with a preface by D. R. Bensen; foreword by Howard Phipps, Jr. Ticknor & Fields 1985 329p ISBN 0-89919-396-X LC 85-7999

The world of Jeeves. Harper & Row 1988 654p ISBN 0-06-015968-5 LC 88-45072

A **Wodehouse** bestiary.　Wodehouse, P. G.

Woelfel, Barry

(ed) Through a glass, darkly. *See* Through a glass, darkly

Wolf.　Bell, M.

The **wolf** tracker, and other animal tales.　Grey, Z.

Wolfe, Thomas, 1900-1938
The complete short stories of Thomas Wolfe; edited by Francis E. Skipp; foreword by James Dickey. Scribner 1987 xxix, 621p ISBN 0-684-18743-4 LC 86-13782

Wolff, Tobias, 1945-
Back in the world; stories. Houghton Mifflin 1985 221p ISBN 0-395-35416-1 LC 85-10790

Woman in a lampshade. Jolley, E.

The **Womansleuth** anthology: contemporary mystery stories by women; edited by Irene Zahava. Crossing Press 1988 177p ISBN 0-89594-272-0 LC 88-443

Women and children first. Prose, F.

Women and other bodies of water. Roberts, N.

Women artists, women exiles: "Miss Grief" and other stories. Woolson, C. F.

Women sleuths; edited by Martin H. Greenberg & Bill Pronzini. Academy Chicago 1985 221p (Academy mystery novellas, v1) ISBN 0-89733-157-5 LC 85-18558

Women's fiction from Latin America; selections from twelve contemporary authors; edited with translations by Evelyn Picon Garfield. Wayne State Univ. Press 1988 355p il (Latin American literature and culture) ISBN 0-8143-1858-4 LC 88-3670
Partially analyzed

Women's work; contemporary short stories by New Zealand women; chosen by Marion McLeod and Lydia Wevers. Oxford Univ. Press 1986 c1985 267p ISBN 0-19-558136-9

Woodman, Allen
The shoebox of desire, and other tales; illustrated by Ross Zirkle. Swallow's Tale Press 1987 70p il ISBN 0-930501-10-1 LC 86-63358

Woodpecker Point & other stories. Bird, C.

Woolf, Virginia, 1882-1941
The complete shorter fiction of Virginia Woolf; edited by Susan Dick. Harcourt Brace Jovanovich 1985 313p ISBN 0-15-118983-8 LC 85-17719

Woolrich, Cornell, 1903-1968
Darkness at dawn; early suspense classics; edited by Francis M. Nevins, Jr. & Martin H. Greenberg; introduction by Francis M. Nevins, Jr. Southern Ill. Univ. Press 1985 327p (Mystery makers) ISBN 0-8093-1232-8 LC 84-26681

Woolson, Constance Fenimore, 1840-1894
Women artists, women exiles: "Miss Grief" and other stories; edited and with an introduction by Joan Myers Weimer. Rutgers Univ. Press 1988 xlviii, 292p ISBN 0-8135-1347-2 LC 88-6421

Words in commotion, and other stories. Landolfi, T.

Working, Russell, 1959-
Resurrectionists. University of Iowa Press 1987 173p ISBN 0-87745-164-8 LC 86-30754

The **world** elsewhere, and other stories. Verma, N.

The **world** is a room, and other stories. Amichai, Y.

The **world** of Jeeves. Wodehouse, P. G.

The **World** of the short story; a twentieth century collection; selected and edited by Clifton Fadiman. Houghton Mifflin 1986 847p ISBN 0-395-36805-7 LC 85-27292

Worlds apart; an anthology of lesbian and gay science fiction and fantasy; edited by Camilla Decarnin, Eric Garber, and Lyn Paleo. Alyson Publs. 1986 293p ISBN 0-932870-87-2 LC 86-14125

Worlds of wonder, Robert Silverberg's. *See* Robert Silverberg's Worlds of wonder

Wright, Richard, 1908-1960
Eight men; stories; foreword by David Bradley. Thunder's Mouth Press 1987 250p ISBN 0-938410-39-3 LC 87-6430
Writers of the future, L. Ron Hubbard presents. *See* L. Ron Hubbard presents Writers of the future
Writers of the purple sage; an anthology of recent western writing; edited and with an introduction by Russell Martin and Marc Barasch. Viking 1984 xx, 340p ISBN 0-670-50899-3 LC 83-40654
Analyzed for short stories only
Writing red; an anthology of American women writers, 1930-1940; edited by Charlotte Nekola and Paula Rabinowitz; foreword by Toni Morrison. Feminist Press 1987 xiii, 349p ISBN 0-935312-77-3 LC 87-25023
Analyzed for short stories only
The **wrong-handed** man.   Millman, L.
Wyndham, Francis
Mrs. Henderson. Moyer Bell 1985 159p ISBN 0-918825-49-0 LC 86-17377

X

Xavier's folly, and other stories.   Evans, M.

Y

Yamamoto, Michiko, 1936-
Betty-san; stories; translated by Geraldine Harcourt. Kodansha Int./USA 1983 152 p il ISBN 0-87011-565-0 LC 82-48786
Yankee witches; edited by Charles G. Waugh, Martin H. Greenberg & Frank D. McSherry, Jr.; introduction by Frank D. McSherry, Jr.; illustrated by Peter Farrow. Tapley, L. 1988 315p il ISBN 0-912769-32-7 LC 88-2155
Yasuoka, Shōtarō, 1920-
A view by the sea; translated by Kären Wigen Lewis. Columbia Univ. Press 1984 196p (Modern Asian literature ser) ISBN 0-231-05872-1 LC 83-21081
The **year** of the hot jock, and other stories.   Faust, I.
The **Year's** best fantasy: first annual collection; edited by Ellen Datlow and Terri Windling. St. Martin's Press 1988 xxxv, 491p ISBN 0-312-01851-7
Partially analyzed
The **Year's** best mystery and suspense stories, 1984; edited by Edward D. Hoch. Walker & Co. 1984 264p ISBN 0-8027-5597-6 LC 83-646567
The **Year's** best mystery and suspense stories, 1985; edited by Edward D. Hoch. Walker & Co. 1985 200p ISBN 0-8027-5634-4 LC 83-646567
The **Year's** best mystery & suspense stories, 1986; edited by Edward D. Hoch. Walker & Co. 1986 252p ISBN 0-8027-0919-2 LC 83-646567
The **Year's** best mystery and suspense stories, 1987; edited by Edward D. Hoch. Walker & Co. 1987 262p ISBN 0-8027-0945-1
The **Year's** best mystery and suspense stories, 1988; edited by Edward D. Hoch. Walker & Co. 1988 236p ISBN 0-8027-1050-6 LC 83-646567
The **Year's** best science fiction, first annual collection; edited by Gardner Dozois. Bluejay Bks. 1984 575p ISBN 0-312-94482-9 ISSN 0743-1740
The **Year's** best science fiction, second annual collection; edited by Gardner Dozois. Bluejay Bks. 1985 573p ISBN 0-312-94484-5 LC 84-2922

The **Year's** best science fiction, third annual collection; edited by Gardner Dozois. Bluejay Bks. 1986 624p ISBN 0-312-94486-1 LC 84-2922

The **Year's** best science fiction, fourth annual collection; edited by Gardner Dozois. St. Martin's Press 1987 602p ISBN 0-312-00709-4 LC 87-4445

The **Year's** best science fiction, fifth annual collection; edited by Gardner Dozois. St. Martin's Press 1988 xxv, 678p ISBN 0-312-01854-1

The **years** of the city. Pohl, F.

Yolen, Jane
(ed) Dragons and dreams. *See* Dragons and dreams
(ed) Werewolves. *See* Werewolves

You can't get lost in Cape Town. Wicomb, Z.

You live and love, and other stories. Rasputin, V. G.

Young extraterrestrials; edited by Isaac Asimov, Martin H. Greenberg & Charles G. Waugh. Harper & Row 1984 240p ISBN 0-06-020168-1 LC 83-49489

Young ghosts; edited by Isaac Asimov, Martin H. Greenberg, and Charles G. Waugh. Harper & Row 1985 210p ISBN 0-06-020171-1 LC 85-42644

Young monsters; edited by Isaac Asimov, Martin H. Greenberg, and Charles G. Waugh. Harper & Row 1985 213p ISBN 0-06-020170-3 LC 84-48352

Young mutants; edited by Isaac Asimov, Martin Greenberg, and Charles Waugh. Harper & Row 1984 256p ISBN 0-06-020157-6 LC 83-48444

Young Petrella. Gilbert, M.

Young witches & warlocks; edited by Isaac Asimov, Martin H. Greenberg, & Charles G. Waugh. Harper & Row 1987 207p ISBN 0-06-020183-5 LC 85-45849

Young wolf: the early adventure stories of Jack London. London, J.

Yourcenar, Marguerite
Oriental tales; translated from the French by Alberto Manguel, in collaboration with the author. Farrar, Straus & Giroux 1985 147p ISBN 0-374-22728-4 LC 85-12876
Two lives and a dream; translated by Walter Kaiser in collaboration with the author. Farrar, Straus & Giroux 1987 245p ISBN 0-374-28019-3 LC 86-29590

Youth without youth, and other novellas. Eliade, M.

Z

Zahava, Irene
(ed) Hear the silence. *See* Hear the silence
(ed) Love, struggle & change. *See* Love, struggle & change
(ed) Through other eyes. *See* Through other eyes
(ed) The Womansleuth anthology: contemporary mystery stories by women. *See* The Womansleuth anthology: contemporary mystery stories by women

Zahn, Timothy
Cascade point, and other stories. Bluejay Bks. 1986 405p ISBN 0-312-94041-6

Zebrowski, George, 1945-
(ed) Nebula awards 20-22. *See* Nebula awards 20-22
(ed) Synergy. *See* Synergy

Zero db, and other stories. Bell, M. S.

Zhang Jie, 1937-
Love must not be forgotten; introduction by Gladys Yang. China Bks. & Periodicals 1986 207p (New Chinese fiction) ISBN 0-8351-1699-9 LC 86-70557

Ziem, Jochen
Uprising in East Germany, and other stories; translated from the German by Jorn K. Bramann and Jeanette Axelrod. Adler 1985 176p ISBN 0-913623-07-5 LC 84-71439

Zipes, Jack David
(ed) Don't bet on the prince. *See* Don't bet on the prince

Zolotow, Charlotte, 1915-
(comp) Early sorrow: ten stories of youth. *See* Early sorrow: ten stories of youth

PART III

Directory of Publishers and Distributors

Academy Chicago Pubs., 213 W. Institute Pl., Chicago, Ill. 60610 Tel 312-644-1723; 800-248-7323

Ace Fantasy Bks., 200 Madison Ave., New York, N.Y. 10016 Tel 212-686-9820; 800-223-0510

Adler Pub. Co., P.O. Box 9342, Rochester, N.Y. 14604 Tel 716-377-5804

Algonquin Bks.: Algonquin Bks. of Chapel Hill, P.O. Box 2225, Chapel Hill, N.C. 27515-2225

Alyson Publs. Inc., 40 Plympton St., Boston, Mass. 02118 Tel 617-542-5679

Amador Pubs., P.O. Box 12335, Albuquerque, N.M. 87195 Tel 505-877-4395

Ampersand Press Creative Writing Program, Roger Williams College, Bristol, R.I. 02809 Tel 401-253-1040

Anansi, 35 Britain St., Toronto, Ont., Can. M5A 1R7; refer orders to University of Toronto Press, 5201 Dufferin St., Downsview, Ont., Can. M3H 5T8 Tel 416-667-7791

Anchor Press/Doubleday, 245 Park Ave., New York, N.Y. 10167 Tel 212-953-4561; 800-645-6156; refer orders to 501 Franklin Ave., Garden City, N.Y. 11530 Tel 516-294-4400

Arbor House Pub. Co., 105 Madison Ave., New York, N.Y. 10016 Tel 212-481-0350

Archon Bks., 925 Sherman Ave., P.O. Box 4327, Hamden, Conn. 06514 Tel 203-248-6307 or 288-8707

Ardis Pubs., 2901 Heatherway, Ann Arbor, Mich. 48104 Tel 313-971-2367

Arkham House Pubs. Inc., P.O. Box 546, Sauk City, Wis. 53583 Tel 608-643-4500

Arsenal Eds., P.O. Box 3868, Main Post Office, Vancouver, B.C., Can. V6B 3Z3 Tel 604-687-4233

Arte Público Press, University of Houston, 4800 Calhoun, Houston, Tex. 77204 Tel 713-749-4768; refer orders to Bilingual Press, Arizona State Univ., Tempe. Ariz. 85287 Tel 602-965-3867

Associated Univ. Presses, 440 Forsgate Dr., Cranbury, N.J. 08512 Tel 609-655-4770

Atheneum Pubs., c.o. Macmillan Pub. Co., 866 3rd Ave., New York, N.Y. 10022 Tel 212-702-2000; 800-257-5755; refer orders to Front & Brown Sts., Riverside, N.J. 08075 Tel 609-461-6500

Athlone Press Ltd. (The), 1 Park Dr., London WW11 7SG, Eng.

Branch offices
    U.S.: Athlone Press, c.o. Longwood Pub. Group Inc., 27 S. Main St., Wolfeboro, N.H. 03894 Tel 603-569-4576

Atlantic Monthly Press, 19 Union Sq. W., New York, N.Y. 10003 Tel 212-645-4462; refer orders to Little, Brown

August House Inc., P.O. Box 3223, Little Rock, Ark. 72203-3223 Tel 501-663-7300; 1-800-527-0924 (orders only)

Avenel Bks., 225 Park Ave. S., New York, N.Y. 10003 Tel 212-254-1600; 800-526-4264

Avon Bks., 105 Madison Ave., 7th & 8th Floors, New York, N.Y. 10016 Tel 212-481-5600

Baen Bks., 260 5th Ave., New York, N.Y. 10001 Tel 212-532-4111; refer orders to Simon & Schuster

Ballantine Bks., 201 E. 50th St., New York, N.Y. 10022 Tel 212-751-2600; refer orders to 400 Hahn Rd., Westminster, Md. 21157 Tel 800-638-6460

Bantam Bks. Inc., 666 5th Ave., New York, N.Y. 10103 Tel 212-765-6500

Barnes & Noble Bks., 81 Adams Drive, Totowa, N.J. 07512 Tel 201-256-8600

Bart Bks., 155 E. 34th St., New York, N.Y. 10016 Tel 212-696-9141; refer orders to Hearst Corp., International Circulation Div., 250 W. 55th St., 12th Floor, New York, N.Y. 10019 Tel 800-223-0288

Bayda Bks., P.O. Box 4875, Chicago, Ill. 60680

Beacon Press, 25 Beacon St., Boston, Mass. 02108 Tel 617-742-2111; refer orders to Harper & Row

Beaufort Bks. Inc., 226 W. 26th St., New York, N.Y. 10001 Tel 212-727-0190

Bedrick Bks.: Peter Bedrick Bks. Inc., 2112 Broadway, Room 318, New York, N.Y. 10023 Tel 212-496-0751; refer orders except individuals, to Publishers Group West, P.O. Box 8843, Emeryville, Calif. 94662 Tel 800-365-3453

Berkley Bks., 200 Madison Ave., New York, N.Y. 10016 Tel 212-686-9820; 800-223-0510

Bilingual Press/Editorial Bilingüe, Hispanic Res. Center, Ariz. State Univ., Tempe, Ariz. 85287

Birchfield Bks., P.O. Box 1305, N. Conway, N.H. 03860 Tel 603-447-3086

BkMk Press University of Mo.-Kansas City, 5216 Rockhill Rd., Room 204, Kansas City, Mo. 64110-2499 Tel 816-276-2558

Black Lizard Bks., c.o. Creative Arts Bk. Co., 833 Bancroft Way, Berkeley, Calif. 94710 Tel 415-848-4777

Black Sparrow Press, 24 10th St., Santa Rosa, Calif. 95401 Tel 707-579-4011

blewointmentpress, P.O. Box 5432, Postal Station A, Toronto, Ont. Can. M5W 1N6

Blue Moon-Confluence Press, College of Arts & Sciences, Lewis-Clark State College, Lewiston, Idaho 83501 Tel 208-746-2341; refer orders to Kampmann & Co.

Bluejay Bks. Inc., 26 Douglas Rd., Chappequa, N.Y. 10514 Tel 914-238-3491; refer orders to St. Martin's Press

Bonanza Bks., 225 Park Ave. S., New York, N.Y. 10003 Tel 212-254-1600; 800-526-4264

Bowling Green State Univ. Popular Press, Bowling Green State Univ., Bowling Green, Ohio 43403 Tel 419-372-7865

Bowling Green Univ. Popular Press, Bowling Green State Univ., Popular Culture Center, Bowling Green, Ohio 43403 Tel 419-372-7865

Boyars, M.: Marion Boyars Pubs. Ltd. 24 Lacy Rd. London SW15 1NL, Eng. Tel (01) 788-9522
Branch offices
U.S.: Marion Boyars Pubs. Inc., 26 E. 33rd St., New York, N.Y. 10036 Tel 212-213-0167; refer orders to Rizzoli Int. Publs.

Brandon Pub. Co., 601 Jackson Ave., Lexington, Va. 24450

Braziller: George Braziller, Inc., 60 Madison Ave., New York, N.Y. 10010 Tel 212-889-0909

Breitenbush Bks. Inc., P.O. Box 02137, Portland, Or. 97202-0137 Tel 503-230-1900; refer orders to Taylor Pub. Co.

Bridge Publs. Inc., 4751 Fountain Ave., Los Angeles, Calif. 90029 Tel 213-382-0382; 800-843-7389; 800-722-1733 (outside Calif.)

Brightwaters Press Inc., 235 Park Ave. S., New York, N.Y. 10003

Brunswick Pub. Co., Route 1, Box 1A1, Lawrenceville, Va. 23868 Tel 804-848-3865

Burning Deck, 71 Elmgrove Ave., Providence, R.I. 02906; refer orders to Small Press Distr. Inc., 1814 San Pablo Ave., Berkeley, Calif. 94702 Tel 415-549-3336

Capra Press, P.O. Box 2068, Santa Barbara, Calif. 93120 Tel 805-966-4590

Carcanet New Press *See* Carcanet Press

Carcanet Press, 198 6th Ave., New York, N.Y. 10013 Tel 212-334-0988; bookstores & libs. refer orders to Harper & Row Pubs. Inc., Keystone Ind. Park, Scranton, Pa. 18512 Tel 800-242-7737; 800-982-4377 (outside Pa.)

Carnegie-Mellon Univ. Press, P.O. Box 21, Schenley Park, Pittsburgh, Pa. 15213 Tel 412-578-2861; refer orders to Harper & Row

Carroll & Graf Pubs. Inc., 260 5th Ave., New York, N.Y. 10001 Tel 212-889-8772; refer orders to Publishers Group West, P.O. Box 8843, Emeryville, Calif. 94662 Tel 800-365-3453

Cayuse Press, P.O. Box 9086, Berkeley, Calif. 94709 Tel 415-525-8513

Center for Western Studies (The), Augustana College, Sioux Falls, S.D. 57197 Tel 605-336-4007

Chariton Review Press, Northeast Mo. State Univ., Kirksville, Mo. 63501

Chatto & Windus Ltd., 30 Bedford Sq., London WC1B 3SG, Eng. Tel (01) 255 2393; refer orders to Random House
Branch offices
U.S.: Chatto & Windus, 99 Main St., Salem, N.H. 03079

China Bks. & Periodicals Inc., 2929 24th St., San Francisco, Calif. 94110 Tel 415-282-2994

Citadel Press, 120 Enterprise Ave., Secaucus, N.J. 07094 Tel 201-866-4199; 800-572-6657

City Lights Bks., 261 Columbus Ave., San Francisco, Calif. 94133 Tel 415-362-8193; refer orders to The Subterranean Co., P.O. Box 10233, Eugene, Or. 97440 Tel 503-343-6324

Coach House Press (Toronto): The Coach House Press, 401 (rear) Huron St., Toronto, Ont., Can. M5S 2G5 Tel 416-979-7374

Coastwise Press, P.O. Box 194, Thomaston, Me. 04861 Tel 207-354-2210

Coffee House Press, 27 N. 4th St., Suite 400, Minneapolis, Minn. 55401 Tel 612-338-0125; refer orders to Consortium Bk. Sales & Distr., 213 E. 4th St., St. Paul, Minn. 55101 Tel 612-221-9035; 800-283-3572

Collier Bks., c.o. Macmillan Pub. Co., 866 3rd Ave., New York, N.Y. 10022 Tel 212-702-2000; 800-257-5755; refer orders to Front & Brown Sts., Riverside, N.J. 08370 Tel 609-461-6500

Columbia Univ. Press, 136 S. Broadway, Irvington, N.Y. 10533 Tel 914-591-9111

Continuum, 370 Lexington Ave., New York, N.Y. 10017 Tel 212-532-3650; refer orders to Harper & Row

Copper Beech Press, P.O. Box 1852, Brown Univ., Providence, R.I. 02912 Tel 401-863-2393

Cornwall Bks., 440 Forsgate Dr., Cranbury, N.J. 08512 Tel 609-655-4770

Corona Pub. Co., 1037 S. Alamo, San Antonio, Tex. 78210 Tel 512-227-1771; refer orders to Texas Monthly Press, P.O. Box 1569, Austin, Tex. 78767 Tel 512-476-7085; 800-252-4437; 800-288-3288 (outside Tex.)

Coteau Bks., 2337 McIntyre St., Regina, Sask., Can. S4P 2S3 Tel 306-352-5346; refer orders to P.O. Box 239, Sub-Station 1, Moose Jaw, Sask., Can. S6H 5V0 Tel 306-693-5212

Cotton Lane Press, Cotton Lane at 18 8th St., Augusta, Ga. 30902 Tel 404-722-0232

Council Oak Bks., 1428 S. St. Louis, Tulsa, Okla. 74120 Tel 918-587-6454; 800-247-8850; refer orders to Independent Pubs. Group, 814 N. Franklin St., Chicago, Ill. 60610 Tel 312-337-0747

Countryman Press Inc. (The), P.O. Box 175, Woodstock, Vt. 05091 Tel 802-457-1049; 800-635-4901

Creative Arts Bk. Co., 833 Bancroft Way, Berkeley, Calif. 94710 Tel 415-848-4777

Creatures at Large, 1082 Grand Teton Dr., P.O. Box 687, Pacifica, Calif. 94044; refer orders to The Borgo Press, P.O. Box 2845, San Bernardino, Calif. 92406 Tel 714-884-5813

Crossing Press (The), 22D Roache Rd., Freedom, Calif. 95019 Tel 408-722-0711; 800-777-1048; refer orders to P.O. Box 1048, Freedom, Calif. 95019

Crossroad, 370 Lexington Ave., New York, N.Y. 10017 Tel 212-532-3650; refer orders to Harper & Row

Crown Pubs. Inc., 225 Park Ave. S., New York, N.Y. 10003 Tel 212-254-1600; 800-526-4264

Curbstone Press, 321 Jackson St., Willimantic, Conn. 06226 Tel 203-423-9190; refer orders to The Talman Co. Inc., 150 5th Ave., Room 514, New York, N.Y. 10011 Tel 212-620-3182

Dante Univ. of Am. Press (The), 21 Station St., P.O. Box 843, Brookline Village, Mass. 02147; refer orders to Branden Pub. Co., 17 Station St., P.O. Box 843, Brookline Village, Mass. 02147

Dark Harvest, P.O. Box 941, Arlington Heights, Ill. 60006

David & Charles Inc., P.O. Box 257, N Pomfret, Vt. 05053 Tel 802-457-1911; 800-423-4525

Davis Publs. Inc., 380 Lexington Ave., New York, N.Y. 10017 Tel 212-557-9100; refer orders to The Dial Press, 245 Park Ave., New York, N.Y. 10167 Tel 212-605-3000

Delacorte Press, 245 E. 47th St., New York, N.Y. 10017 Tel 212-605-3000; refer orders to Doubleday

Dell Pub. Co. Inc., 666 5th Ave., New York, N.Y. 10103 Tel 212-765-6500

Dembner Bks., 80 8th Ave., New York, N.Y. 10011 Tel 212-924-2525; refer orders to Norton

Devin-Adair Pubs. Inc., 6 N. Water St., Greenwich, Conn. 06830 Tel 203-531-7755

Dial Press (The), 245 Park Ave., New York, N.Y. 10167 Tel 212-605-3000

Dodd, Mead & Co. Inc., 6 Ram Ridge Rd., Spring Valley, N.Y. 10977 Tel 914-352-3900; 800-237-3255; no longer publishing

Dog Ear Press (The), 19 Mason St., Brunswick, Me. 04011 Tel 207-729-7791

Doherty Assocs.: Tom Doherty Assocs. Inc., 49 W. 24th St., New York, N.Y. 10010 Tel 212-741-3100; refer orders to St. Martin's Press

Doubleday & Co. Inc., 666 5th Ave., New York, N.Y. 10103 Tel 212-765-6500; refer orders to 501 Franklin Ave., Garden City, N.Y. 11530 Tel 516-294-4400

Dragon Gate Inc., 6532 Phinney Ave. N., Seattle, Wash. 98103 Tel 206-783-8387

Dutton: E. P. Dutton, 2 Park Ave., New York, N.Y. 10016 Tel 212-725-1818; 800-526-0275; refer orders to P.O. Box 120, Bergenfield, N.J. 07621 Tel 201-387-0600; 800-526-0275

Ecco Press, 26 W. 17th St., New York, N.Y. 10011 Tel 212-645-2214; 800-223-2584; refer orders to Norton

Ellis Press (The), P.O. Box 1443, Peoria, Ill. 61655; refer orders to Bookslinger, 502 N. Prior, St. Paul, Minn. 55104 Tel 612-649-0271

Eridanos Press, 7506 Hygiene Rd., Hygiene, Colo. 80533; refer orders to P.O. Box 211, Hygiene, Colo. 80533 Tel 303-678-8804; refer retail, wholesale & lib. accounts to Rizzoli Int. Publs.

Evans & Co.: M. Evans & Co. Inc., 216 E. 49th St., New York, N.Y. 10017 Tel 212-688-2810; refer orders to Little, Brown

Faber & Faber Ltd., Burnt Mill, Elizabeth Way, Harlow, Essex CM20 2HX, Eng. Branch offices U.S.: Faber & Faber, Inc., 50 Cross St., Winchester, Mass. 01890 Tel 617-721-1427; refer orders to AIDC, 2 Acorn Lane, Sunderland Park, Colchester, Vt. 05446 Tel 800-445-6638

Fairleigh Dickinson Univ. Press, 285 Madison Ave., Madison, N.J. 07940 Tel 201-377-4700; refer orders to Associated Univ. Presses, 440 Forsgate Dr., Cranbury, N.J. 08512 Tel 609-655-4770

Farrar, Straus & Giroux Inc., 19 Union Sq. W., New York, N.Y. 10003 Tel 212-741-6900; refer orders to Harper & Row Pubs. Inc., Keystone Ind. Park, Scranton, Pa. 18512 Tel 800-982-4377; 800-242-7737 (outside Pa.)

Feminist Press (The): Feminist Press at the City Univ. of N.Y., 311 E. 94th St., New York, N.Y. 10128 Tel 212-360-5790; refer orders to The Talman Co. Inc., 150 5th Ave., Room 514, New York, N.Y. 10011 Tel 212-620-3182; 800-537-8894

Fiction Collective Inc., c.o. Brooklyn College, English Dept., Brooklyn, N.Y. 11210 Tel 718-780-5547; refer orders to Sun & Moon Press

Fiddlehead Poetry Bks./Goose Lane Eds., 248 Brunswick St., Fredericton, N.B., Can. E3B 7G9 Tel 506-454-8319

Fine, D.I.: Donald I. Fine, Inc., 19 W. 21st St., New York, N.Y. 10010 Tel 212-727-3270; refer orders to 1205K O'Neill Highway, Dunmore, Pa. 18512 Tel 717-348-9292

Firebrand Bks., 141 The Commons, Ithaca, N.Y. 14850 Tel 607-272-0000

Fjord Press, P.O. Box 16501, Seattle, Wash. 98116; refer orders to Academy Chicago Pubs., 213 W. Institute Pl., Chicago, Ill. 60610 Tel 312-644-1723; 800-248-7323

Fromm Int. Pub. Corp., 560 Lexington Ave., New York, N.Y. 10022 Tel 212-308-4010; refer orders to Kampmann & Co., 226 W. 26th St., New York, N.Y. 10001 Tel 212-727-0190

Galileo Press (The), 15201 Wheeler Lane, Sparks, Md. 21152 Tel 301-771-4544; refer orders to Bookslinger, 502 North Prior, St. Paul, Minn. 55104 Tel 612-649-0271

Garland Pub. Inc., 136 Madison Ave., New York, N.Y. 10016 Tel 212-686-7492; 800-627-6273

Gay Sunshine Press, P.O. Box 40397, San Francisco, Calif. 94140 Tel 415-824-3184; refer orders to Bookpeople, 2929 5th St., Berkeley, Calif. 94710 Tel 415-549-3030

General Pub. Co. Ltd., 30 Lesmill Rd., Don Mills, Ont., Can. M3B 2T6 Tel 416-445-3333

Godine: David R. Godine, Pub., Horticultural Hall, 300 Massachusetts Ave., Boston, Mass. 02115 Tel 617-536-0761; 800-445-6638

Gollancz: Victor Gollancz, Ltd., 14 Henrietta St., London WC2E 8QJ, Eng. Tel (01) 836-2006

Graywolf Press, P.O. Box 75006, St. Paul, Minn. 55175 Tel 612-222-8342; refer orders to Consortium Bk. Sales & Distr., 213 E. 4th St., St. Paul, Minn. 55101 Tel 612-221-9035

Green Meadow Bks., Weld Road Offices, Phillips, Me. 04966

Greenwich House, 225 Park Ave., New York, N.Y. 10003 Tel 212-254-1600; 800-526-4264

Greenwillow Bks., 105 Madison Ave., New York, N.Y. 10016 Tel 212-889-3050

Greenwood Press Inc., 88 Post Road W., Westport, Conn. 06881 Tel 203-226-3571; refer orders to P.O. Box 5007, Westport, Conn. 06881

Grey Fox Press, P.O. Box 31190, San Francisco, Calif. 94131 Tel 415-824-5774; refer orders to The Subterranean Co., P.O. Box 10233, Eugene, Or. 97440 Tel 503-343-6324

Gribble: McPhee Gribble Pubs., 66 Cecil St., Fitzroy, Vic. 3065, Aust.

Griffin House Publs., P.O. Box 81, Whitestone, N.Y. 11357 Tel 718-767-8380

Grove Press Inc., 841 Broadway, New York, N.Y. 10003-4793 Tel 212-529-3600; 800-638-6460; refer orders to Ingram Pubs. Services Inc., P.O. Box 7001, Lavergne, Tenn. 37086-7001 Tel 800-937-5557

Harcourt Brace Jovanovich Pubs., 1250 6th Ave., San Diego, Calif. 92101 Tel 619-231-6616; refer orders to 747 3rd Ave., New York, N.Y. 10164

Harmony Bks., 225 Park Ave. S., New York, N.Y. 10003 Tel 212-254-1600; 800-526-4264

Harper & Row Pubs. Inc., 10 E. 53rd St., New York, N.Y. 10022-5299 Tel 212-207-7000; refer orders to P.O. Box 1531, Hagerstown, Md. 21741 Tel 800-638-3030; or Keystone Ind. Park, Scranton, Pa. 18512 Tel 800-242-7737

Harvard Common Press (The), 535 Albany St., Boston, Mass. 02118 Tel 617-423-5803; refer orders to Kampmann & Co., 226 W. 26th St., New York, N.Y. 10001 Tel 212-727-0190

Harvester Press Ltd. (The), Wolsey House, Wolsey Rd., Hemel Hempstead HP2 4SS, Eng. Tel (0442) 231 900 refer orders to International Bk. Distributors Ltd., 66 Wood Lane End, Hemel Hempstead, Hertfordshire HP2 4RG, Eng. Tel Hemel Hempstead (0442) 231 555

Heinemann, W.: William Heinemann, Ltd., Michelin House, 81 Fulham Rd., London SW3 6RB, Eng. Tel (01) 581-9393 Branch offices
U.S.: William Heinemann, c.o. David & Charles, P.O. Box 257, N. Pomfret, Vt. 05053 Tel 802-457-1911

Hill & Co.: Lawrence Hill & Co. Pubs. Inc., 520 Riverside Ave., Westport, Conn. 06880 Tel 203-226-9392; refer orders to Independent Pubs. Group, 814 N. Franklin St., Chicago, Ill. 60610 Tel 312-337-0747

Hogarth Press Ltd. (The), 30 Bedford Sq., London WC1B 3SG, Eng. Tel (01) 255 2393; refer orders to Random House

Holt & Co.: Henry Holt & Co., 115 W. 18th St., New York, N.Y. 10011 Tel 212-886-9200

Holt, Rinehart & Winston, 301 Commerce St., Suite 3700, Fort Worth, Tex. 76102 Tel 817-334-7500

Houghton Mifflin Co., 2 Park St., Boston, Mass. 02108 Tel 617-725-5000; refer orders to Wayside Rd., Burlington, Mass. 01803 Tel 617-272-1500; 800-225-3362

Illinois State Univ., Normal, Ill. 61761

Indiana Univ. Press, 10th & Morton Sts., Bloomington, Ind. 47404 Tel 812-335-4203

Intercultural Press Inc., P.O. Box 768, Yarmouth, Me. 04096 Tel 207-846-5168

International Cultural Exchange, 6 Sheffield Rd., Great Neck, N.Y. 11021

International Polygonics Ltd., P.O. Box 1563, Madison Sq. Station, New York, N.Y. 10159 Tel 212-683-2914

International Pubs. Co. Inc., 381 Park Ave. S., New York, N.Y. 10016 Tel 212-685-2864

Jewish Publ. Soc. of Am. (The), 1930 Chestnut St., Philadelphia, Pa. 19103-4599 Tel 215-564-5925; 800-234-3151

Johns Hopkins Univ. Press (The), 701 W. 40th St., Suite 275, Baltimore, Md. 21211 Tel 301-338-6990; 800-537-5487 (orders only)

Kelsey St. Press, P.O. Box 9235, Berkeley, Calif. 94709 Tel 415-845-2260

Knights Press, P.O. Box 454, Pound Ridge, N.Y. 10576 Tel 203-322-7381; refer orders to Lyle Stuart Inc., 120 Enterprise Ave., Secaucus, N.J. 07094 Tel 201-866-4199; 800-572-6657

Knopf: Alfred A. Knopf Inc., 201 E. 50th St., New York, N.Y. 10022 Tel 212-751-2600; 800-726-0600; refer orders to Random House

Kodansha Int./USA, 114 5th Ave., New York, N.Y. 10011; refer orders to Harper & Row

Lake View Press, P.O. Box 578279, Chicago, Ill. 60657-8279 Tel 312-935-2694

Lang, P.: Verlag Peter Lang AG, Jupiterstr. 15, Postfach 277, CH-3000 Bern 15, Switzerland Tel (031) 321122
Branch offices
U.S.: Peter Lang Pub. Inc., 62 W. 45th St., New York, N.Y. 10036-4202 Tel 212-302-6740

Lawrence, S.: Seymour Lawrence, Inc., 1 Beacon St., Boston, Mass. 02108 Tel 617-725-5173; 800-225-3362; refer orders to Wayside Rd., Burlington, Mass. 01803 Tel 617-272-1500

Library of America (The), 14 E. 60th St., New York, N.Y. 10022 Tel 212-308-3360; 800-631-3577; refer orders to Viking Order Dept., P.O. Box 120, Bergenfield, N.J. 07621-0120 Tel 201-387-0600

Linden Press/Simon & Schuster Inc., Simon & Schuster Bldg., 1230 Ave. of the Americas, New York, N.Y. 10020 Tel 212-698-7000

Little, Brown & Co. Inc., 34 Beacon St., Boston, Mass. 02108 Tel 617-227-0730; refer orders to 200 West St., Waltham, Mass. 02254 Tel 617-890-0250; 800-343-9204

Lost Roads Pubs., P.O. Box 5848, Weybosset Hill Station, Providence, R.I. 02903 Tel 401-941-4188; refer orders to Small Press Distr. Inc., 1814 San Pablo Ave., Berkeley, Calif. 94702 Tel 415-549-3336

Louisiana State Univ. Press, Baton Rouge, La. 70893 Tel 504-388-6666

Lynx House Press, c.o. 1326 West St., Emporia, Kan. 66801 Tel 316-342-0755

Maclay & Assocs., P.O. Box 16253, Baltimore, Md. 21210 Tel 301-235-7985

Macmillan Pub. Co., 866 3rd Ave., New York, N.Y. 10022 Tel 212-702-2000; 800-257-5755; refer orders to Front & Brown Sts., Riverside, N.J. 08075 Tel 609-461-6500; 800-257-5755

Main Street Press (The), William Case House, Pittstown, N.J. 08867 Tel 201-735-9424

Maize Press, P.O. Box 10, Colorado College, Colorado Springs, Colo. 80903 Tel 303-636-3249

McPherson & Co., P.O. Box 1126, Kingston, N.Y. 12401 Tel 914-331-5807

Mercer Univ. Press, Macon, Ga. 31207 Tel 912-744-2880; 800-342-0841; 800-637-2378 (outside Ga.)

Mercury House Inc., 300 Montgomery St., Suite 700, San Francisco, Calif. 94104 Tel 415-433-7042; refer orders to Consortium Bk. Sales & Distr., 213 E. 4th St., St. Paul, Minn. 55101 Tel 612-221-9035; 800-283-3572 (orders only)

Merrimack Publishers' Circle, 462 Boston St., Topfield, Mass. 01983 Tel 617-887-2440

Messner: Julian Messner, Simon & Schuster Bldg., 1230 Ave. of the Americas, New York, N.Y. 10020 Tel 212-698-7000

Methuen & Co. Ltd., Michelin House, 81 Fulham Rd., London SW3 6RB, Eng. Tel (01) 581-9393
Branch offices
U.S.: Methuen, Inc., 29 W. 35th St., New York, N.Y. 10001 Tel 212-244-3336

Micah Publs., 255 Humphrey St., Marblehead, Mass. 01945 Tel 617-631-7601

Milkweed Eds., P.O. Box 3226, Minneapolis, Minn. 55403 Tel 612-332-3192; refer orders to Consortium Bk. Sales & Distr., 213 E. 4th St., St. Paul, Minn. 55101 Tel 612-221-9035

Morrow: William Morrow & Co. Inc., 105 Madison Ave., New York, N.Y. 10016 Tel 212-889-3050; 800-843-9389

Mosaic Press/Valley Eds., P.O. Box 1032, Oakville, Ont. L6J 5E9, Can.

Moyer Bell Ltd., Colonial Hill, RFD 1, Mt. Kisco, N.Y. 10549 Tel 914-666-0084; 800-759-4100 (charge orders only); refer orders to Consortium Bk. Sales & Distr., 213 E. 4th St., St. Paul, Minn. 55101 Tel 612-221-9035; 800-283-3572 (orders only)

Mysterious Press, 129 W. 56th St., New York, N.Y. 10019 Tel 212-765-0923; refer orders to Ballantine Bks.

Naiad Press Inc. (The), P.O. Box 10543, Tallahassee, Fla. 32302 Tel 904-539-9322

Navajo Community College Press, Navajo Community College, Tsaile, Ariz. 86556

Naval Inst. Press, 2062 Generals Highway, Annapolis, Md. 21401-6780 Tel 301-268-6110; 800-233-8764

Nefertiti Head Press, Drawer J, University Station, Austin, Tex. 78712

Netherlandic Press, 1176 Ouellette Ave., Suite 1004, Windsor, Ont., Can. N9A 6S9

New Am. Lib. Inc. (The), 1633 Broadway, New York, N.Y. 10019 Tel 212-397-8000; refer orders to P.O. Box 120, Bergenfield, N.J. 07621 Tel 201-387-0600; 800-526-0275

New Amsterdam Bks., 171 Madison Ave., New York, N.Y. 10016 Tel 212-685-6159

New Directions Pub. Corp., 80 8th Ave., New York, N.Y. 10011 Tel 212-255-0230; refer orders to W. W. Norton & Co. Inc., 500 5th Ave., New York, N.Y. 10110 Tel 212-354-5500

New Rivers Press, 1602 Selby Ave., St. Paul, Minn. 55104 Tel 612-645-6324; refer orders to Bookslinger, 502 N. Prior, St. Paul, Minn. 55104 Tel 612-649-0271

New York Univ. Press, 70 Washington Sq., New York, N.Y. 10003 Tel 212-998-2575; refer orders to Columbia Univ. Press, 136 S. Broadway, Irvington, N.Y. 10533 Tel 914-591-9111

NeWest Press, 8631 109th St., Suite 204, Edmondton, Alta., Can. T6G 1E8 Tel 403-432-9427

Norte: Ediciones del Norte, P.O. Box A130, Hanover, N.H. 03755

North Point Press, 850 Talbot Ave., Berkeley, Calif. 94706 Tel 415-527-6260; refer orders to Farrar, Straus & Giroux

Northwestern Univ. Press, 625 Colfax, Evanston, Ill. 60201 Tel 312-491-5313

Norton: W. W. Norton & Co. Inc., 500 5th Ave., New York, N.Y. 10110 Tel 212-354-5500; 800-233-4830

Nostos Bks., P.O. Box 19086, Minneapolis, Minn. 55419 Tel 612-825-0387

Oberon Press, 400-350 Sparks St., Ottawa, Ont., Can. K1R 7S8 Tel 613-238-3275

Ohio State Univ. Press, Marketing Dept., 175 Mount Hall, 1050 Carmack Rd., Columbus, Ohio 43210-1002 Tel 614-292-6930

Ohio Univ. Press, Scott Quadrangle, Athens, Ohio 45701-2979 Tel 614-593-1155; 800-242-7737; refer orders to C.U.P. Services, P.O. Box 6525, Ithaca, N.Y. 14851 Tel 800-666-2211 (orders only)

Ontario Review Press, 9 Honey Brook Dr., Princeton, N.J. 08540; refer orders to George Braziller Inc., 60 Madison Ave., New York, N.Y. 10010 Tel 212-889-0909

Orion, 350 South 400 E., Salt Lake City, Utah 84111 Tel 801-531-1483

Ortalda & Assocs., 1202 Delaware St., Berkeley, Calif. 94702

Overlook Press (The), 12 W. 21st St., 12th Floor, New York, N.Y. 10010 Tel 212-675-0585; refer orders to RR1, Box 496, Woodstock, N.Y. 12498 Tel 914-679-6838

Oxford Univ. Press, Walton St., Oxford OX2 6DP, Eng. Tel (0865) 56767

Branch offices

U.S.: Oxford Univ. Press, Inc., 200 Madison Ave., New York, N.Y. 10016 Tel 212-679-7300; 800-458-5833; refer orders to 16-00 Pollitt Dr., Fair Lawn, N.J. 07410 Tel 201-564-6680

Pace Int. Res. Inc., Tide Ave., Falcon Cove, P.O. Box 51, Arch Cape, Or. 97102

Pacific Writers Press, University of Calif., Irvine. Dept. of Spanish & Portuguese, Irvine, Calif. 92717

Pandora Press, 15/17 Broadwick St., London W1V 1FP, Eng. Tel (01) 439 3126; refer orders to Routledge & Kegan Paul, 29 W. 35th St., New York, N.Y. 10001-2291 Tel 212-244-3336

Pantheon Bks. Inc., 201 E. 50th St., New York, N.Y. 10022 Tel 212-751-2600; 800-727-0600; refer orders to Random House Inc., 400 Hahn Rd., Westminster, Md. 21157 Tel 800-492-0782

Papier-Maché Press, 34 Malaga Pl. E., Manhattan Beach, Calif. 90266 Tel 213-545-3812; refer orders to Inland Bk. Co., P.O. Box 261, East Haven, Conn. 06512 Tel 203-467-4257

Parkwest Publs., P.O. Caller Box A-10, Cathedral Station, New York, N.Y. 10025 Tel 212-222-6100

Peachtree Pubs. Ltd., 494 Armour Circle N.E., Atlanta, Ga. 30324 Tel 404-876-8761; 800-282-0225; 800-241-0113 (outside Ga.)

Penguin Bks. Ltd., Bath Rd., Harmondsworth, Middlesex UB7 0DA, Eng. Tel (01) 759 1984/5722

Branch offices

U.S.: Penguin Bks., 40 W. 23rd St., New York, N.Y. 10010 Tel 212-337-5200; 800-631-3577

Penumbra Press, P.O. Box 248, Kapuskasing, Ont., Can. P5N 2Y4 Tel 705-335-2988

Peregrine Smith Bks., 1877 E. Gentile St., Layton, Utah 84041 Tel 801-544-9800; refer orders to P.O. Box 667, Layton, Utah 84041

Performing Arts Journal Publs., 325 Spring St., Room 318, New York, N.Y. 10013 Tel 212-243-3885

Persea Bks. Inc., 225 Lafayette St., New York, N.Y. 10012 Tel 212-431-5270

Philosophical Lib. Inc., 200 W. 57th St., New York, N.Y. 10019 Tel 212-265-6050; refer int. orders to Alpha Bk. Distr., 303 W. 10th St., New York, N.Y. 10014 Tel 212-675-8749; 800-221-8112

Phoenix Publs. (Qld.): Phoenix Publs., P.O. Box 210, Indooroopilly 4068, Queensland, Aust.

Phunn Pubs., P.O. Box 201, Wild Rose, Wis. 54984

Popular Press, Bowling Green State Univ., Bowling Green, Ohio 43403 Tel 419-372-7865

Porcupine's Quill, 68 Main St., Erin, Ont., Can. N0B 1T0 Tel 519-833-9158

Poseidon Press, Simon & Schuster Bldg., 1230 Ave. of the Americas, New York, N.Y. 10020 Tel 212-698-7000; 800-223-4022; refer orders to Simon & Schuster

Potter: Clarkson N. Potter Inc. Pubs., 225 Park Ave. S., New York, N.Y. 10003 Tel 212-254-1600; 800-526-4264; refer orders to Crown

Prentice-Hall Inc., Route 9W, Englewood Cliffs, N.J. 07632 Tel 201-592-2000; refer orders to Prentice Hall Trade, Simon & Schuster Inc., 200 Old Tappan Rd., Old Tappan, N.J. 07675 Tel 800-223-2336 (orders only)

Press Pacifica, P.O. Box 47, Kailua, Hawaii 96734 Tel 808-261-6594

Prometheus Bks., 700 E. Amherst St., Buffalo, N.Y. 14215 Tel 716-837-2475; 800-421-0351 (outside N.Y.)

Pulp Press Bk. Pubs., 100-1062 Homer St., Vancouver, B.C., Can. V6B 2W9 Tel 604-687-4233

Pushcart Press (The), P.O. Box 380, Wainscott, N.Y. 11975 Tel 516-324-9300; refer orders to Norton

Putnam: G. P. Putnam's Sons, 200 Madison Ave., New York, N.Y. 10016 Tel 212-951-8400; 800-631-8571; refer orders to 1 Grosset Dr., Kirkwood, N.Y. 13795 Tel 607-775-1740; 800-847-5515

Quartet Bks. Ltd., 27/29 Goodge St., London W1P 1FD, Eng. Tel (01) 636-3992/4; refer orders to Harper & Row

Random House Inc., 201 E. 50th St., New York, N.Y. 10022 Tel 212-751-2600; 800-726-0600; refer orders to 400 Hahn Rd., Westminster, Md. 21157 Tel 800-733-3000

Ravnogorski Venac, 6221 Walhonding Rd., Washington, D.C. 20816 Tel 301-229-4847

Reader's Digest Assn. Inc. (The), Reader's Digest Rd., Pleasantville, N.Y. 10570 Tel 914-769-7000; 800-431-1726

Readers Int. Inc., 8 Strathvay Gardens, London NW3 4NY, Eng. Tel (011) 435-4363
Branch offices
U.S.: Readers Int. Inc., P.O. Box 959, Columbia, La. 71418-0959 Tel 318-649-7288; refer orders to Consortium Bk. Sales & Distr., 213 E. 4th St., St. Paul, Minn. 55101 Tel 612-221-9035

Rowan Tree Press Ltd., 124 Chestnut St., Boston, Mass. 02108 Tel 617-523-7627; refer orders to Kampmann & Co., 226 W. 26th St., New York, N.Y. 10001 Tel 212-727-0190

Running Press Bk. Pubs., 125 S. 22nd St., Philadelphia, Pa. 19103 Tel 215-567-5080; 800-428-1111

Rutgers Univ. Press, 109 Church St., New Brunswick, N.J. 08901 Tel 201-932-7365; refer orders to R.U.P. Distr. Center, P.O. Box 4869, Baltimore, Md. 21211 Tel 301-338-6947

Sachem Press, P.O. Box 9, Old Chatham, N.Y. 12136 Tel 518-794-8327

Salem House Pubs., 462 Boston St., Topsfield, Mass. 01983 Tel 717-343-4761; refer orders to Harper & Row

Santa Barbara Press, 815 De La Vina St., No. C, Santa Barbara, Calif. 93101-3203; refer orders to Publishers Group West, 4065 Hollis St., Emeryville, Calif. 94608 Tel 415-658-3453; 800-982-8319

Schocken Bks. Inc., 62 Cooper Sq., New York, N.Y. 10003 Tel 212-475-4900; refer orders to Random House Inc, 400 Hahn Rd., Westminster, Md. 21157 Tel 800-492-0782

Scottish Acad. Press Ltd., 33 Montgomery St., Edinburgh EH7 5JX, Scotland Tel (031) 556 2796

Scream/Press, P.O. Box 8531, Santa Cruz, Calif. 95061

Scribner: Charles Scribner's Sons, c.o. Macmillan Pub. Co., 866 3rd Ave., New York, N.Y. 10022 Tel 212-702-2000; 800-257-5755; refer orders to Front & Brown Sts., Riverside, N.J. 08075 Tel 609-461-6500

Seal Press (The), 3131 Western Ave., Suite 410, Seattle, Wash. 98121-1028; Tel 206-283-7844; refer orders to Consortium Bk. Sales & Distr., 213 E. 4th St., St. Paul, Minn. 55101 Tel 612-221-9035

Sharpe, M.E.: M. E. Sharpe, Inc., 80 Business Park Dr., Armonk, N.Y. 10504 Tel 914-273-1800

Shearer Pub., 406 Post Oak Rd., Fredericksburg, Tex. 78624 Tel 512-997-6529

Si-sa-yong-o-sa Inc., 5-3 Kwanchol-dong, Chongno-ku, Seoul 110, S. Korea Tel (02) 2696621
Branch offices
U.S.: Si-sa-yong-o-sa, Inc., 115 W. 29th St., 5th fl., New York, N.Y. 10001

Simon & Schuster Inc. Pubs., Simon & Schuster Bldg., 1230 Ave. of the Americas, New York, N.Y. 10020 Tel 212-698-7000

Slough Press, P.O. Box 1385, Austin, Tex. 78767

Smith, G.M.: Gibbs M. Smith, Inc., 1877 E. Gentile St., Layton, Utah 84041 Tel 801-544-9800; refer orders to P.O. Box 667, Layton, Utah 84041

Soho Press Inc., 1 Union Sq., New York, N.Y. 10003 Tel 212-243-1527; refer orders to Farrar, Straus & Giroux

Sono Nis Press (The), 1745 Blanshard St., Victoria, B.C., Can. V8W 2J8 Tel 604-382-1024

Southern Ill. Univ. Press, P.O. Box 3697, Carbondale, Ill. 62902-3697 Tel 618-453-2281

Southern Methodist Univ. Press, 6410 Airline Dr.; Dallas, Tex. 75205 Tel 214-739-5959; refer orders to Texas A&M Univ. Press

Space and Time, 138 W. 70th St., Apt. 4B, New York, N.Y. 10023-4432 Tel 212-595-0894

Spinsters/Aunt Lute Bk. Co., P.O. Box 410687, San Francisco, Calif. 94141-0687

Spirit That Moves Us Press (The), P.O. Box 1585, Iowa City, Iowa 52244 Tel 319-338-7502

St. Martin's Press Inc., 175 5th Ave., New York, N.Y. 10010 Tel 212-674-5151; 800-221-7945

Starmont House Inc., 3852 E. Mercer Way, Mercer Island, Wash. 98040 Tel 206-232-8484; refer orders to P.O. Box 851, Mercer Island, Wash. 98040

State Univ. of N.Y. Press, State Univ. Plaza, Albany, N.Y. 12246 Tel 518-472-5000; refer orders to P.O. Box 6525, Ithaca, N.Y. 14850 Tel 607-277-2211

Sterling Pub. Co. Inc.: 2 Park Ave., New York, N.Y. 10016 Tel 212-532-7160

Still Point Press, 4222 Willow Grove Rd., Dallas, Tex. 75220 Tel 214-352-8282

Story Line Press, 403 Continential St., Santa Cruz, Calif. 95060 Tel 408-426-5539; refer orders to Bookslinger, 502 N. Prior Ave., St. Paul, Minn. 55104 Tel 612-649-0271

Story Press, P.O. Box 10040, Chicago, Ill. 60610

Sugden & Co.: Sherwood Sugden & Co., 1117 8th St., La Salle, Ill. 61301

Summit Bks., 1230 Ave. of the Americas, New York, N.Y. 10020 Tel 212-698-7000; refer orders to Simon & Schuster Inc., 200 Old Tappan Rd., Old Tappan, N.J. 07675 Tel 800-223-2336

Sun & Moon Press, 6363 Wilshire Blvd., Suite 116, Los Angeles, Calif. 90048; refer orders to P.O. Box 481170, Los Angeles, Calif. 90048 Tel 213-653-6711

Swallow Press, Scott Quadrangle, Athens, Ohio 45701-2979 Tel 614-593-1155; refer orders to C.U.P. Services, P.O. Box 6525, Ithaca, N.Y. 14851 Tel 800-666-2211 (orders only)

Swallow's Tale Press, 736 Greenwillow Run, Wesley Chapel, Fla. 34249

Syracuse Univ. Press, 1600 Jamesville Ave., Syracuse, N.Y. 13244-5160 Tel 315-443-2597

Talisman Literary Res. Inc., P.O. Box 455, Georgetown, Calif. 95634 Tel 916-333-4486

Tapley, L.: Lance Tapley Pub., 86 Winthrop St., P.O. Box 2439, Augusta, Me. 04330 Tel 207-622-1179

Teitan Press (The) Inc., 339 W. Barry Ave., Suite 16B, Chicago, Ill. 60657 Tel 312-929-7892; refer orders to The Distributors, 702 S. Michigan, South Bend, Ind. 46618 Tel 219-232-8500; 800-345-5200

Texas Center for Writers Press Inc., P.O. Box 428, Montrose, Ala. 36559 Tel 205-928-9325

Three Continents Press, 1346 Connecticut Ave. N.W., Suite 224, Washington, D.C. 20036 Tel 202-332-3885

Thunder's Mouth Press, 54 Greene St., Suite 4S, New York, N.Y. 10013 Tel 212-226-0277; refer orders to Bookpeople, 2929 5th St., Berkeley, Calif. 94710 Tel 415-549-3030; 800-624-4466; 800-227-1516 (outside Calif.)

Ticknor & Fields, 52 Vanderbilt Ave., New York, N.Y. 10017 Tel 212-687-8996; 800-225-3362; refer orders to Houghton Mifflin

Timescape Bks., 1230 Avenue of the Americas, New York, N.Y. 10020 Tel 212-245-6400

TSR Inc., P.O. Box 756, Lake Geneva, Wis. 53147 Tel 414-248-3625; 800-372-4667; refer orders to Random House

TSR Hobbies Inc., P.O. Box 756, Lake Geneva, Wis. 53147 Tel 414-248-3625; 800-372-4667; refer orders to Random House

Turtle Island Foundation, 2845 Buena Vista Way, Berkeley, Calif. 94708; refer orders to Subterranean Co.

Tuttle: Charles E. Tuttle Co. Inc., 28 S. Main St., Rutland, Vt. 05701-0410 Tel 802-773-8930; refer orders to P.O. Box 410, Rutland, Vt. 05701-0410

Underwood/Miller, P.O. Box 7930, Beverly Hills, Calif. 90212 Tel 213-659-7530; refer orders to 515 Chestnut St., Columbia, Pa. 17512 Tel 717-684-7335

Ungar Pub. Co., Inc. (The), 370 Lexington Ave., New York, N.Y. 10017 Tel 212-532-3650; refer orders to Harper & Row

University of Ala. Press (The), P.O. Box 2877, Tuscaloosa, Ala. 35487 Tel 205-348-5180

University of Ark. Press, 201 Ozark St., Fayetteville, Ark. 72701 Tel 501-575-3246

University of Calif. Press, 2120 Berkeley Way, Berkeley, Calif. 94720 Tel 415-642-6683; 800-822-6657

University of Chicago Press, 5801 S. Ellis Ave., Chicago, Ill. 60637 Tel 312-702-7700; refer orders to 11030 S. Langley Ave., Chicago, Ill. 60628 Tel 312-568-1550; 800-621-2736

University of Ga. Press (The), Terrell Hall, Athens, Ga. 30602 Tel 404-542-2830

University of Hawaii Press, 2840 Kolowalu St., Honolulu, Hawaii 96822 Tel 808-948-8255

University of Ill. Press, 54 E. Gregory Dr., Champaign, Ill. 61820 Tel 217-333-0950; refer orders to C.U.P. Services, P.O. Box 6525, Ithaca, N.Y. 14851 Tel 607-277-2211; 800-666-2211

University of Iowa Press, 119 West Park Rd., Iowa City, Iowa 52242 Tel 319-335-2000; refer orders to Oakdale Hall, Univ. of Iowa, Iowa City, Iowa 52242 Tel 319-335-4645

University of Mass. Press, P.O. Box 429, Amherst, Mass. 01004 Tel 413-545-2217

University of Mich. Center for Chinese Studies, 104 Lane Hall, Ann Arbor, Mich. 48109 Tel 313-763-7181

University of Mo. Press (The), 200 Lewis Hall, Columbia, Mo. 65211 Tel 314-882-7641; refer orders to Harper & Row

University of N.M. Press, Albuquerque, N.M. 87131 Tel 505-277-2346 or 277-7560

University of Nev. Press, Reno, Nev. 89557-0076 Tel 702-784-6573

University of Okla. Press, 1005 Asp Ave., Norman, Okla. 73019-0445 Tel 405-325-5111; refer individual orders to P.O. Box 1657, Hagerstown, Md. 21741; lib., bookstore, institutional, & wholesale orders: P.O. Box 787, Norman, Okla. 73070-0787

University of Pittsburgh Press, 127 N. Bellefield Ave., Pittsburgh, Pa. 15260 Tel 412-624-4110; 800-638-3030; refer orders to C.U.P. Services, P.O. Box 6525, Ithaca, N.Y. 14850 Tel 800-666-2211

University of Qld. Press, P.O. Box 42, St. Lucia, Qld. 4067, Aust. Tel (07) 377-2440
Branch offices
  U.S.: University of Qld. Press, P.O. Box 1365, New York, N.Y. 10023 Tel 212-799-3854; refer orders to International Specialized Bk. Services Inc., P.O. Box 1632, Beaverton, Or. 97075 Tel 503-292-2606

University of Tenn. Press (The), 293 Communications Bldg., Knoxville, Tenn. 37996-0325 Tel 615-974-3321; refer orders to P.O. Box 6525, Ithaca, N.Y. 14850 Tel 607-277-2211; 800-666-2211(orders only)

University of Tex. Press, P.O. Box 7819, Austin, Tex. 78713-7819 Tel 512-471-4032; 800-252-3200

University Press of Am. Inc., 4720 Boston Way, Lanham, Md. 20706 Tel 301-459-3366

University Press of Ky., 102 Lafferty Hall, Lexington, Ky. 40506-0024 Tel 606-257-2951; refer orders to Harper & Row

University Press of Miss., 3825 Ridgewood Rd., Jackson, Miss. 39211 Tel 601-982-6205

University Press of New England, 17 1/2 Lebanon St., Hanover, N.H. 03755 Tel 603-646-3340; 800-421-1561

Vanguard Press Inc., 424 Madison Ave., New York, N.Y. 10017 Tel 212-753-3906

Véhicule Press, P.O. Box 125, Place du Parc Station, Montreal, Que., Can. H2W 2M9 Tel 514-844-6073; refer orders to Fernwood Bks. Ltd., 67-A Portland St., Toronto, Ont., Can. M5V 2M9 Tel 416-597-1527

Viking *See* Viking Penguin

Viking Penguin Inc., 40 W. 23rd St., New York, N.Y. 10010-5290 Tel 212-337-5200; refer orders to P.O. Box 120, Bergenfield, N.J. 07621-0120 Tel 201-387-0600

Viking Salamander *See* Viking Penguin

Vintage Bks., 201 E. 50th St., New York, N.Y. 10022 Tel 212-751-2600; 800-726-0600; refer orders to Random House Inc., 400 Hahn Rd., Westminster, Md. 21157 Tel 800-492-0782

Walker & Co., 720 5th Ave., New York, N.Y. 10019 Tel 212-265-3632

Wampeter Press, P.O. Box 512, Green Harbor, Mass. 02041

Warner Bks., 666 5th Ave., New York, N.Y. 10103 Tel 212-484-2900; refer orders to Ballantine Bks.

Washington Sq. Press, Simon & Schuster Bldg., 1230 Ave. of the Americas, New York, N.Y. 10020 Tel 212-698-7000

Watts: Franklin Watts, Inc., 387 Park Ave. S., New York, N.Y. 10016 Tel 212-686-7070; 800-843-3749

Wayne State Univ. Press, Leonard N. Simons Bldg., 5959 Woodward Ave., Detroit, Mich. 48202 Tel 313-577-6120

Weidenfeld & Nicolson: George Weidenfeld & Nicolson Ltd., 91 Clapham High St., London SW4 7TA, Eng. Tel (01) 622-9933
Branch offices
  U.S.: Weidenfeld & Nicolson, 841 Broadway, New York, N.Y. 10003-4793 Tel 212-614-7840; refer orders to Ingram Pubs. Services Inc., P.O. Box 7001, Lavergne, Tenn. 37086-7001 Tel 800-937-5557

Western Tanager Press, 1111 Pacific Ave., Santa Cruz, Calif. 95060 Tel 408-425-1111

Wild Trees Press, P.O. Box 378, Navarro, Calif. 95463

Words & Visions Publs., P.O. Box 545, Norwood 5067, S. Aust.

Wright, S.: Stuart Wright Pub./Palaemon Press Ltd., 2100 Faculty Dr., Winston-Salem, N.C. 27106 Tel 919-725-5985; refer orders to P.O. Box 7527, Reynolda Station, Winston-Salem, N.C. 27109

Wynwood Press, 264 5th Ave., 4th Floor, New York, N.Y. 10001 Tel 212-889-4110; 800-544-7955; refer orders to 935 Industrial Park Rd., Iowa Falls, Iowa 50126

Yankee Bks., Depot Sq., Peterborough, N.H. 03458-9986 Tel 603-563-8111; 800-423-2271

Zebra Bks., 475 Park Ave. S., New York, N.Y. 10016 Tel 212-889-2299; 800-221-2647

Zephyr Press, 13 Robinson St., Somerville, Mass. 02145 Tel 617-628-9726; refer orders to Bookslinger, 502 North Prior, St. Paul, Minn. 55104 Tel 612-649-0271

PART IV
Directory of Periodicals

50 Plus. $15. m (ISSN 0163-2027) 50 Plus, 99 Garden St., Marion, OH 43302
>Name changed to New Choices for the Best Years with December 1988

America. $28. w (except first Saturday of the year, and alternate Saturdays in Jl and Ag) (ISSN 0002-7049) America Press Inc., 106 W. 56th St., New York, NY 10019

American Film. $20. m (except bi-m Ja/F, Jl/Ag) (ISSN 0361-4751) Membership Services, American Film, P.O. Box 2046, Marion, OH 43305

The American Scholar. $18. q (ISSN 0003-0937) The American Scholar, Editorial and Circulation Offices, 1811 Q St., N.W., Washington, DC 20009

Américas. $42. bi-m (ISSN 0379-0940) Américas, Journals Div., CUA Press, 303 Administration Bldg., Catholic University of America, Washington, DC 20064

Antaeus. $20 for 4 nos. semi-ann (ISSN 0003-5319) Ecco Press Ltd., 26 W. 17th St., New York, NY 10011

The Antioch Review. $30. q (ISSN 0003-5769) The Antioch Review, P.O. Box 148, Yellow Springs, OH 45387

Artforum. $42. m (except Jl/Ag) (ISSN 0004-3532) Artforum, P.O. Box 3000, Dept. AF, Denville, NJ 07834-9950

The Atlantic. $14.95. m (ISSN 0276-9077) Atlantic Subscription Processing Center, Box 52661, Boulder, CO 80322

Black American Literature Forum. $10. q (ISSN 0148-6179) Black American Literature Forum, Statesman Towers West 1005, Indiana State University, Terre Haute, IN 47809

Blair & Ketchum's Country Journal. $16.95. m (ISSN 0094-0526) Country Journal, P.O. Box 392, Mt. Morris, IL 61054
>Name changed to Country Journal with October 1986

Bread Loaf Quarterly. See New England Review and Bread Loaf Quarterly

Chicago Review. $10. q (ISSN 0009-3696) University of Chicago, Chicago, IL 60637

The Christian Century. $28. w (occasional bi-w issues) (ISSN 0009-5281) Christian Century, Subscription Service Dept., 5615 W. Cermak Rd., Cicero, IL 60650

Christianity Today. $24.95. semi-m (m Ja, My, Je, Jl, Ag, D) (ISSN 0009-5753) Christianity Today Subscription Services, 465 Gundersen Dr., Carol Stream, IL 60188

Coevolution Quarterly. $18. q (ISSN 0095-134X) Point, Box 428, Sausalito, CA 94966
>Merged with: Whole Earth Software Review, to become: Whole Earth Review

Commentary. $39. m (ISSN 0010-2601) American Jewish Committee, 165 E. 56th St., New York, NY 10022

Commonweal. $32. bi-w (m Christmas-New Year's and Jl, Ag) (ISSN 0010-3330) Commonweal Foundation, 15 Dutch St., New York, NY 10038

Country Journal. $16.95. bi-m (ISSN 0094-0526) Country Journal, P.O. Box 392, Mt. Morris, IL 61054

Critical Quarterly. $30. q (ISSN 0011-1562) Manchester University Press, Oxford Rd., Manchester M13 9PL, England

Cross Currents. $12.50. q (ISSN 0011-1953) Cross Currents, Mercy College, Dobbs Ferry, NY 10522

Discover. $27. m (ISSN 0274-7529) Time Inc., P.O. Box 359105, Palm Coast, FL 32035-9105

Encounter (London, England). $39. m (ISSN 0013-7073) Encounter, 44 Great Windmill St., London W1V 7PA, England

Esquire. $15.94. m (ISSN 0194-9535) Esquire Subscriptions, P.O. Box 11362, Des Moines, IA 50350

Essence. $14. m (ISSN 0014-0880) Essence, P.O. Box 53400, Boulder, CO 80322

Gentlemen's Quarterly. $20. m (ISSN 0016-6979) Gentlemen's Quarterly, P.O. Box 2962, Boulder, CO 80322

The Georgia Review. $9. q (ISSN 0016-8386) University of Georgia, Athens, GA 30602

Good Housekeeping. $15.97. m (ISSN 0017-209X) Good Housekeeping, P.O. Box 10055, Des Moines, IA 50350

GQ. See Gentlemen's Quarterly

Grand Street. $24. q (ISSN 0734-5496) Grand Street, 50 Riverside Dr., New York, NY 10024

Harper's. $18. m (ISSN 0017-789X) Harper's Magazine, P.O. Box 1937, Marion, OH 43305

HG. See House & Garden

House & Garden. $24. m (ISSN 0018-6406) House & Garden, Box 5202, Boulder, CO 80322

The Hudson Review. $18. q (ISSN 0018-702X) The Hudson Review, 684 Park Ave., New York, NY 10021

The Kenyon Review. $18. q (ISSN 0163-075X) The Kenyon Review, P.O. Box 1308L, Fort Lee, NJ 07024

Ladies' Home Journal. $19.95. m (ISSN 0023-7124) Ladies' Home Journal, P.O. Box 10895, Des Moines, IA 50336-0895

Latin American Literary Review. $30. semi-ann (ISSN 0047-4134) Dept. of Hispanic Languages and Literatures, University of Pittsburgh, Pittsburgh, PA 15260

Life. $32.50. m (ISSN 0024-3019) Time Inc., Time & Life Building, Rockefeller Center, New York, NY 10020-1393

The Literary Review (Madison, N.J.). $12. q (ISSN 0024-4589) Fairleigh Dickinson University, 285 Madison Ave., Madison, NJ 07940

Mademoiselle. $15. m (ISSN 0024-9394) Mademoiselle, Box 5204, Boulder, CO 80322

The Massachusetts Review. $10. q (ISSN 0025-4878) University of Massachusetts, Memorial Hall, Amherst, MA 01002

McCall's. $13.97. m (ISSN 0024-8908) McCall's Customer Relations Manager, Box 56093, Boulder, CO 80322

Michigan Quarterly Review. $13. q (ISSN 0026-2420) University of Michigan, 3032 Rackham Bldg., Ann Arbor, MI 48109

The Mississippi Quarterly. $10. q (ISSN 0026-637X) Mississippi State University, College of Arts and Sciences, Box 5272, Mississippi State, MS 39762

Money. $33.95. 13 times a yr (ISSN 0149-4953) Money, P.O. Box 2518, Boulder, CO 80323-4420

Mother Jones. $24. 9 times a yr (ISSN 0362-8841) Foundation for National Progress, 1886 Haymarket Sq., Marion, OH 43302

Ms. $16. m (except Jl) (ISSN 0047-8318) Ms. Magazine, P.O. Box 57131, Boulder, CO 80322-7131

National Review. $39. bi-w (48p issue only, pub. in alternate weeks) (ISSN 0028-0038) National Review, Circulation Dept., 150 E. 35th St., New York, NY 10016

NER/BLQ. See New England Review and Bread Loaf Quarterly

New England Review and Bread Loaf Quarterly. $18. q (ISSN 0736-2579) New England Review and Bread Loaf Quarterly, Middlebury College, Middlebury, VT 05753

The New York Review of Books. $37.50. bi-w (m Jl, Ag, S) (ISSN 0028-7504) New York Review, Subscription Service Dept., P.O. Box 940, Farmingdale, NY 11737

The New York Times Book Review. $26. w (ISSN 0028-7806) New York Times Co., Times Sq., New York, NY 10036

The New York Times Magazine. $94 (complete Sunday ed; not sold separately). w New York Times, Times Bldg., 229 W. 43rd St., New York, NY 10036

The New Yorker. $32. w (ISSN 0028-792X) New Yorker Magazine, 25 W. 43rd St., New York, NY 10036

The North American Review. $11. q (ISSN 0029-2397) University of Northern Iowa, 1222 W. 27th St., Cedar Falls, IA 50614

The Ohio Review. $12. 3 times a yr (ISSN 0360-1013) Ohio University, Ellis Hall, Athens, OH 45701-2979

Omni (New York, N.Y.). $24. m (ISSN 0149-8711) Omni Publications International Ltd., 1965 Broadway, New York, NY 10023-5965

Parents. $20. m (ISSN 0195-0967) Parents, P.O. Box 3042, Harlan, IA 51537

The Paris Review. $11. q (ISSN 0031-2037) The Paris Review, 45-39 171 Place, Flushing, NY 11358

Partisan Review. $22. q (ISSN 0031-2525) Boston University, 141 Bay State Rd., Boston, MA 02215

Ploughshares. $18. 4 times a yr (ISSN 0048-4474) Ploughshares, Inc., Box 529, Cambridge, MA 02139

Prairie Schooner. $12. q (ISSN 0032-6682) University of Nebraska, 201 Andrews Hall, Lincoln, NE 68588

Raritan. $20. q (ISSN 0275-1607) Rutgers University, 165 College Ave., New Brunswick, NJ 08903

Reader's Digest. $13.97 (plus .96 for postage) Available in a special Large-Type Edition at $8.95. m (ISSN 0034-0375) Reader's Digest Association, Pleasantville, NY 10570

Redbook. $11.97. m (ISSN 0034-2106) Redbook Consumer Relations Manager, Box 5242, Des Moines, IA 50340

The Review of Contemporary Fiction. $22. 3 times a yr (ISSN 0276-0045) The Review of Contemporary Fiction, 1817 79th Ave., Elmwood Park, IL 60635

Road & Track. $19.94. m (ISSN 0035-7189) Road & Track, P.O. Box 5331, 1255 Portland Pl., Boulder, CO 80321

Rolling Stone. $25.95. bi-w (except combined issues in Jl and at year end) (ISSN 0035-791X) Straight Arrow Publishers, Inc., 745 Fifth Ave., New York, NY 10151

The Saturday Evening Post. $12.97. m (bi-m Ja-F, My-Je, Jl-Ag) (ISSN 0048-9239) Saturday Evening Post Subscription Offices, P.O. Box 10675, Des Moines, IA 50336

Science Digest. $13.97. m (ISSN 0036-8296) Science Digest, P.O. Box 10076, Des Moines, IA 50350
  Ceased publication with September 1986; resumed with March/April 1988

Seventeen. $15.95. m (ISSN 0037-301X) Seventeen Subscription Dept., Radnor, PA 19088

The Sewanee Review. $15. q (ISSN 0037-3052) University of the South, Sewanee, TN 37375

Southern Exposure (Durham, N.C.). $20. q (ISSN 0146-809X) Institute for Southern Studies, P.O. Box 531, Durham, NC 27702

Southern Humanities Review. $12. q (ISSN 0038-4186) Auburn University, 9088 Haley Center, Auburn, AL 36849

The Southern Review (Baton Rouge, La.). $9. q (ISSN 0038-4534) Louisiana State University, Drawer D, University Station, Baton Rouge, LA 70893

Southwest Review. $6. q (ISSN 0038-4712) Southern Methodist University Press, Dallas, TX 75275

Sport (New York, N.Y.). $17.94. m (ISSN 0038-7797) Sport, P.O. Box 5016, Des Moines, IA 50306

Sports Illustrated. $64.26. w (except semi-w issues 3 times a yr and bi-w year end issue) (ISSN 0038-822X) Sports Illustrated, P.O. Box 30602, Tampa, FL 33630-0602

'Teen. $14.95. m (ISSN 0040-2001) Petersen Publishing Co., 8490 Sunset Blvd., Los Angeles, CA 90069

The Times Literary Supplement. $70. w (ISSN 0040-7895) Times Newspapers Ltd., Supplements Subscription Mgr., Oakfield House, 35 Perrymount Rd., Haywards Heath, West Sussex RH16 3DH, England

TLS. See The Times Literary Supplement

TriQuarterly. $26. 3 times a yr (ISSN 0041-3097) TriQuarterly, 2020 Ridge Ave., Evanston, IL 60208

TV Guide. $37.44. w (ISSN 0039-8543) TV Guide, Box 400, Radnor, PA 19088

Twentieth Century Literature. $24. q (ISSN 0041-462X) Twentieth Century Literature, 49 Sheridan Ave., Albany NY 12210

U.S. Catholic. $15. m (ISSN 0041-7548) U.S. Catholic, 205 W. Monroe St., Chicago, IL 60606

The Virginia Quarterly Review. $22. q (ISSN 0042-675X) The University of Virginia, One West Range, Charlottesville, VA 22903

Whole Earth Review. $18. q (ISSN 0749-5056) Point, P.O. Box 15187, Santa Ana, CA 92705-0187
  Merger of: Coevolution Quarterly; and, Whole Earth Software Review

Women's Sports & Fitness. $12.95. 10 times a yr (ISSN 8750-653X) Women's Sports & Fitness, P.O. Box 472, Mt. Morris, IL 61054

The Yale Review. $22. q (ISSN 0044-0124) Yale University Press, 92A Yale Station, New Haven, CT 06520